THIS VOLUME IS DEDICATED TO
SIR PETER MOORES CBE, DL

Oil Paintings in Public Ownership in Lancashire

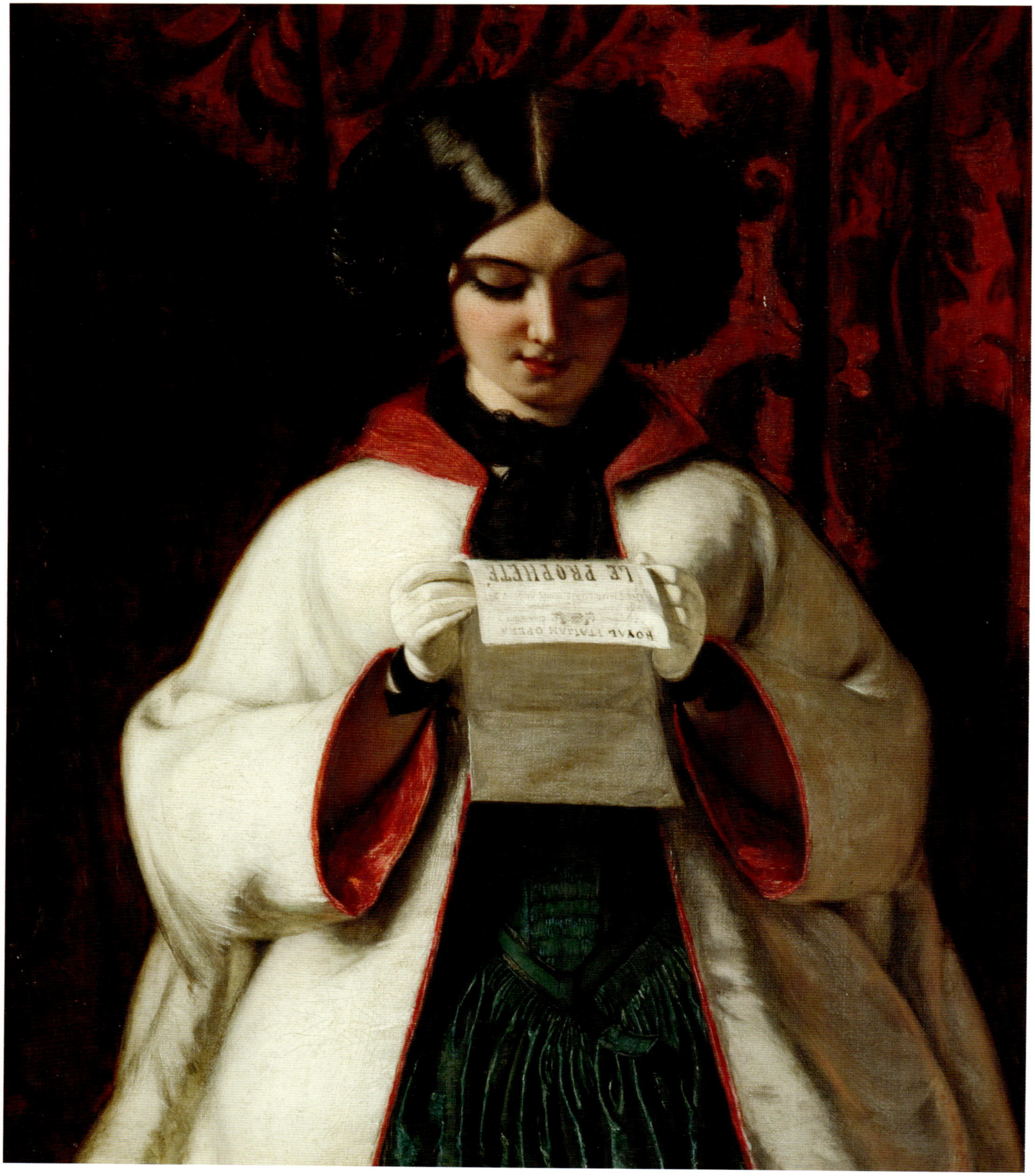
LE PROPHÈTE
ROYAL ITALIAN OPERA

The *Oil Paintings in Public Ownership* series of catalogues is an extraordinary work in progress. Published by The Public Catalogue Foundation, it is the result of the determined efforts of a small team of administrative staff, researchers and photographers spread across the United Kingdom.

Our national collection of oil paintings in public ownership is probably one of the finest anywhere in the world. It is held not just by our museums and galleries but is also to be found in hospitals, universities and other civic buildings throughout the United Kingdom. A large proportion of these paintings are not on display and many have never before been reproduced.

This series of books for the first time allows the public to see an entire photographic record of these works – a collection likely to number some 200,000 in total. In doing so, these volumes provide a unique insight into our nation's artistic and cultural history.

As Patron of The Public Catalogue Foundation, my visits to collections across the country have highlighted to me not only the desire of curators to publicise their paintings, but also the limited resources at their disposal. The Foundation's work goes a long way towards helping to create access to these collections, while at the same time giving the British public the opportunity to see and enjoy *all* the paintings that they own.

I wish The Public Catalogue Foundation every success in its continuing endeavours.

Camilla

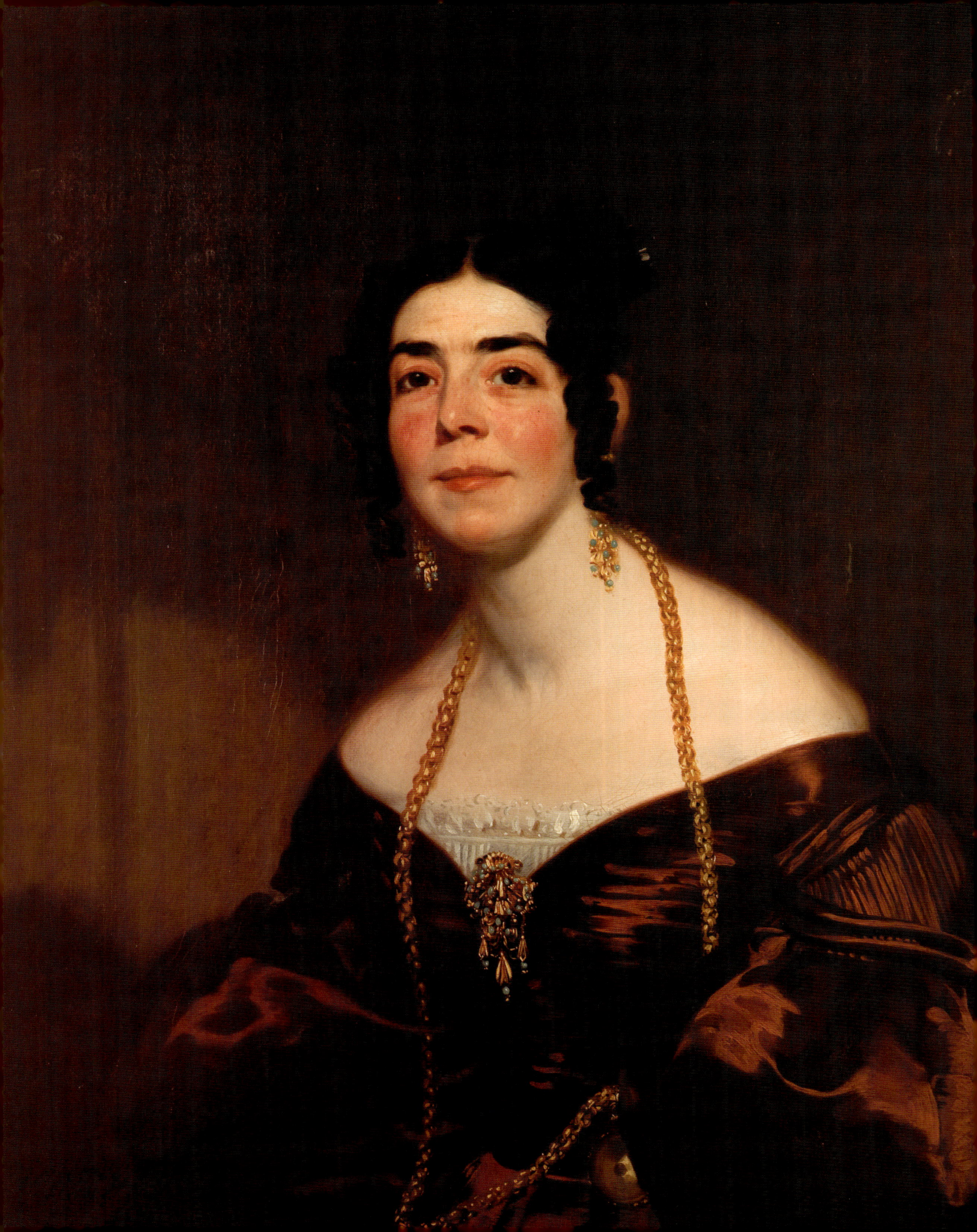

Oil Paintings in Public Ownership
in
Lancashire

Funding Patron
Sir Peter Moores CBE, DL

Coordinator: Adrienne Wallman
Photographer: Walter White

The Public Catalogue Foundation
Patron
HRH The Duchess of Cornwall

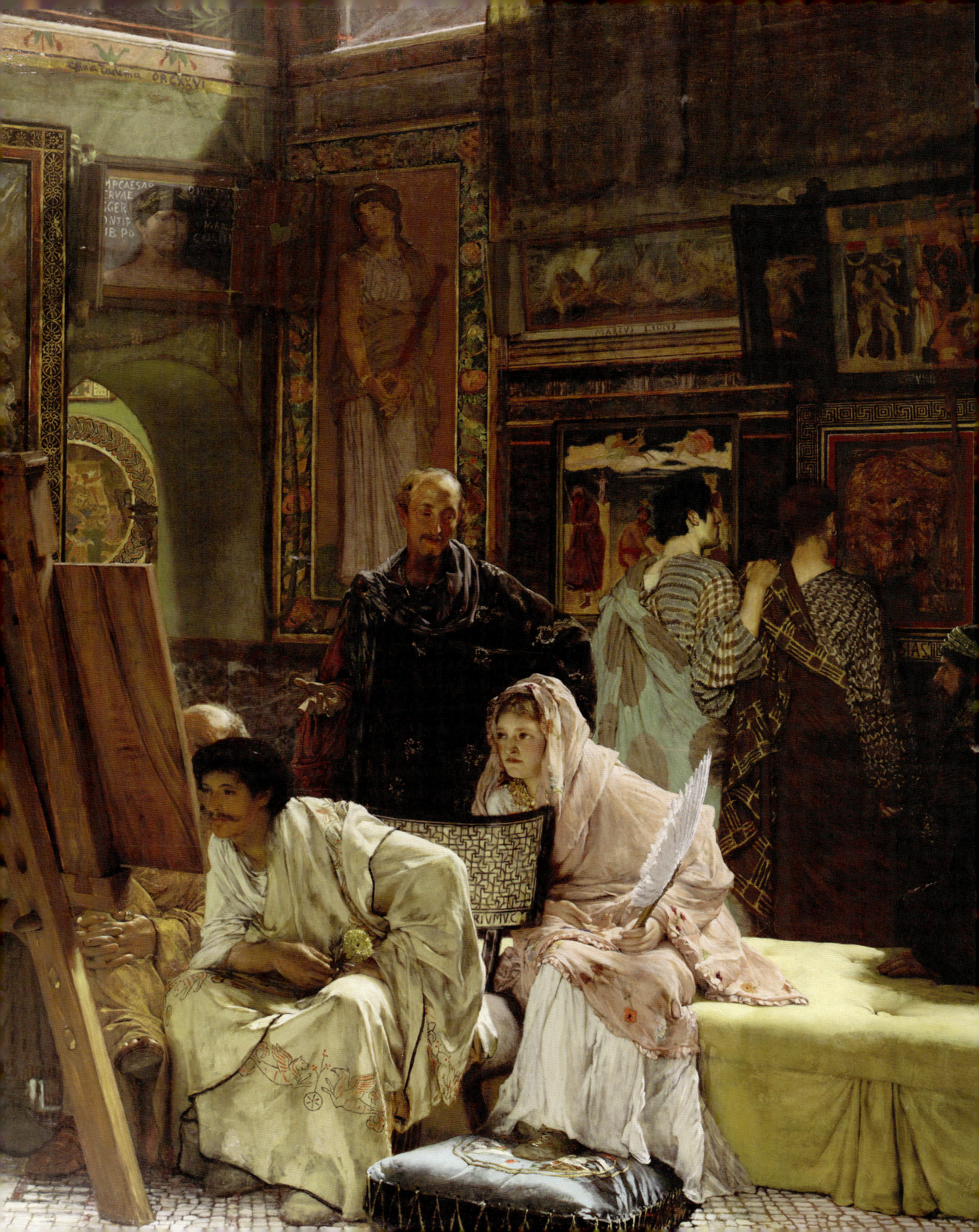

Contents

Facing page: Alma-Tadema, Lawrence, 1836–1912, *The Picture Gallery* (detail), 1874, Towneley Hall Art Gallery & Museum, (p. 125)

Image opposite HRH The Duchess of Cornwall's statement: Egg, Augustus Leopold, 1816–1863, *The Opera Mantle*, 1851, Harris Museum & Art Gallery, (p. 298)
Image opposite title page: Wyatt, Henry, 1794–1840, *Ellen Turner of Helmshore (d.1831)* (detail), 1837, Lancashire County Museum Service, (p. 399)

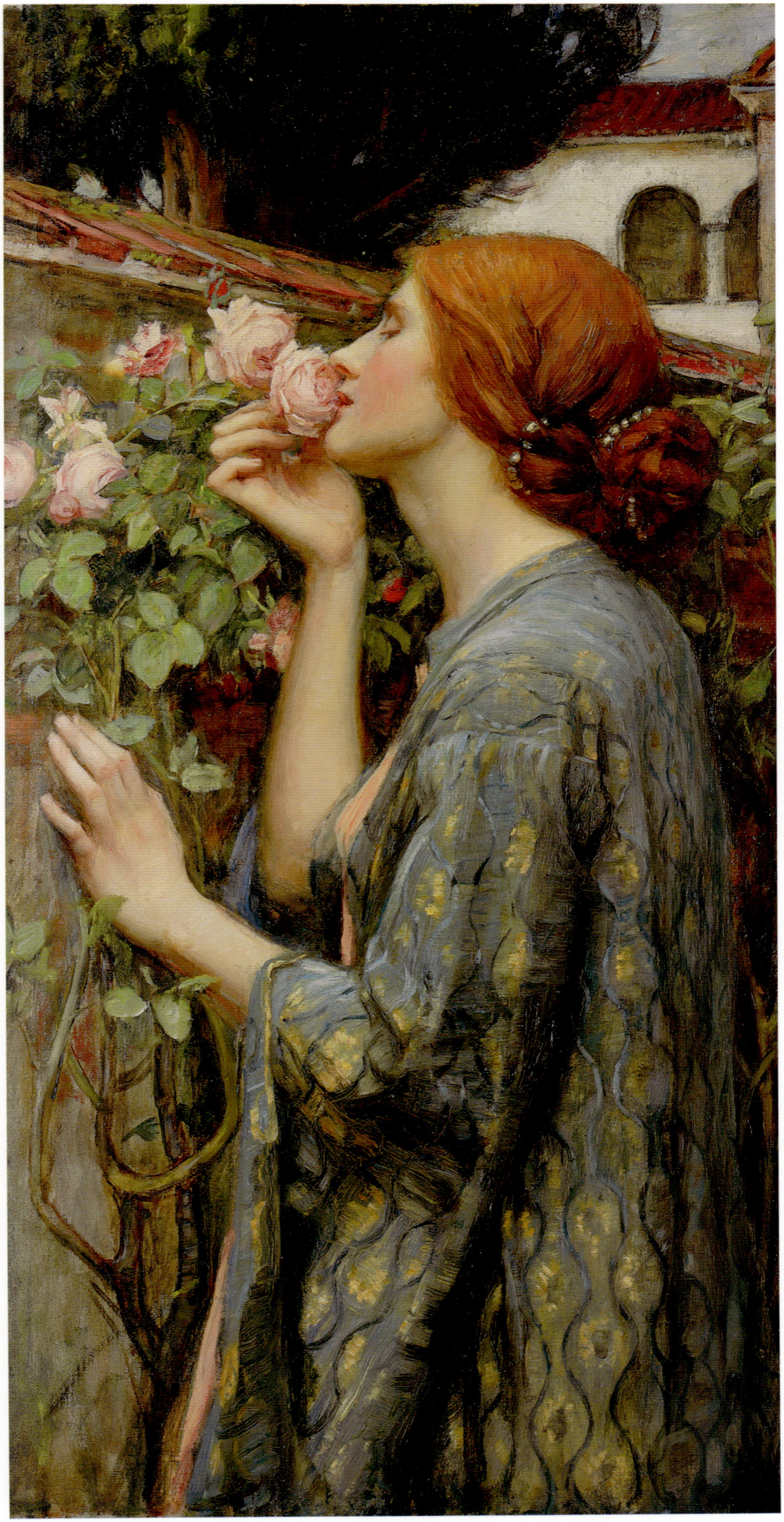

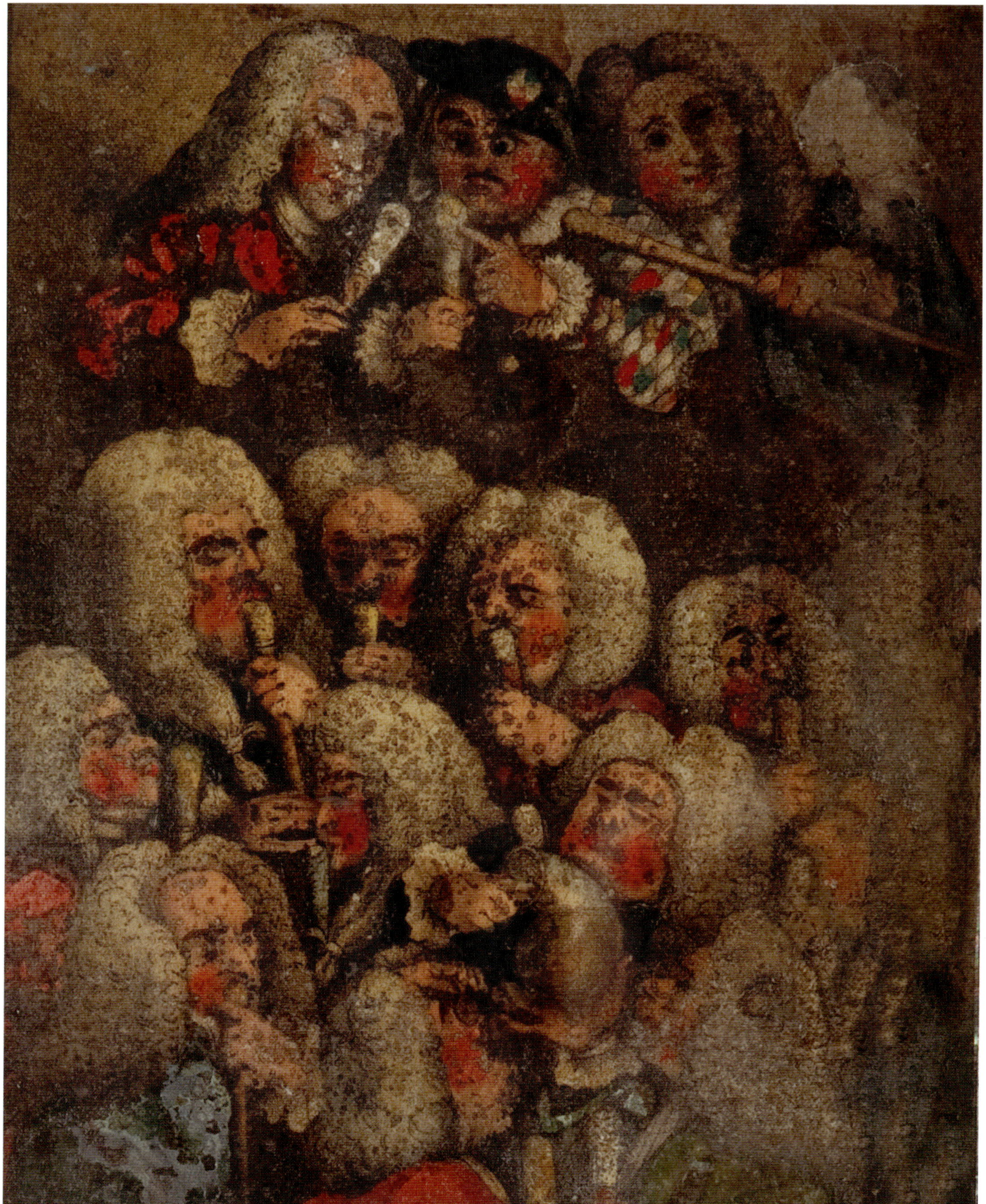

Foreword

The publication of this catalogue has been made possible through the generosity of the Lancastrian philanthropist Sir Peter Moores CBE, DL.

Born in 1932, Sir Peter joined his father's family business, Littlewoods, in 1957. He set up the Peter Moores Foundation in 1964, in order to 'get things done and open doors for people'. In Lancashire, his many charitable initiatives have ranged from land conservation and reclamation to the establishment of the first Transatlantic Slave Trade Gallery in Liverpool in 1994, and from organising a biennial contemporary art exhibition in Liverpool to funding scholarships for promising young singers at the Royal Northern College of Music in Manchester, where he was made an Honorary Fellow in 1985.

Sir Peter was appointed a Deputy Lieutenant of Lancashire in 1992, by HM the Queen. He was awarded a CBE in 1991 and was knighted in 2003 for his services to the arts.

The Public Catalogue Foundation has been the beneficiary of his kindness since the launch of the Warwickshire catalogue in 2009 and we are delighted to be able to recognise his support of this Lancashire volume by naming it after him.

As usual this catalogue would not have come about were it not for the hard work of the team. I need to thank in particular, the co-ordinator, Adrienne Wallman, the photographer, Walter White, Daniel Whibley and the team at Maiden Lane and Sophie Kullmann. Without this team, the work so wonderfully illustrated in this catalogue would never have been achieved. The Foundation is enormously grateful to them.

Fred Hohler, Founder

Facing page: Hogarth, William, 1697–1764, *The Undertakers Company*, Blackburn Museum and Art Gallery (p. 40)

The Public Catalogue Foundation: People Involved

Staff

Andrew Ellis, *Director of the PCF*

Online Division
33 Maiden Lane
Covent Garden
London WC2E 7JS
020 7395 0330

Daniel Whibley, *Head of Editorial and Production*
Katey Goodwin, *Head of Research & Digitisation*
Sarah Hilliam, *Development Manager*
Laura Marriott, *Operations Manager*
Andy Johnson, *Photography Manager (England and Wales)*
Iona Shepherd, *Photography Manager (Scotland and Northern Ireland)*
Dr Joanna Meacock, *Regional Research Manager (Scotland)*
Stella Sharp, *Regional Research Manager (London)*
Dr Camilla Stewart, *Regional Research Manager (Wales, SW England & National Trust)*
Edward Bettella, *Production Manager*
Rachel Collings, *Project Editor*
Jade King, *Project Editor*
Adam Jackman, *Junior Project Editor*
Alice Warley, *Production Editor*
Louis Daly, *Image Assistant*
Sarah Fletcher, *Editorial Assistant*
Alice Payne, *Editorial Assistant*
Rebecca Nicholl, *Production Assistant*
Katherine Vaughan, *Content & Production Assistant*
Katie Carder, *Press & Marketing Officer*
Sonia Roe, *Editorial Consultant*
Mary Rose Rivett-Carnac, *Copyright Officer*
Martina Stender, *Copyright Manager*
Aidan McNeill, *Copyright Assistant*

Printed Catalogue Division
8 Frederick's Place
London EC2R 8AB
020 7600 2920

Dr Fred Hohler
Sophie Kullmann, *Editor*
Ruth Chadwick, *Administrator*

Catalogue Scope and Organisation

Medium and Support
The principal focus of this series is oil paintings. However, tempera and acrylic are also included as well as mixed media, where oil is the predominant constituent. Paintings on all forms of support (e.g. canvas, panel, etc.) are included as long as the support is portable. The principal exclusions are miniatures, hatchments or other purely heraldic paintings and wall paintings *in situ*.

Public Ownership
Public ownership has been taken to mean any paintings that are directly owned by the public purse, made accessible to the public by means of public subsidy or generally perceived to be in public ownership. The term 'public' refers to both central government and local government. Paintings held by national museums, local authority museums, English Heritage and independent museums, where there is at least some form of public subsidy, are included. Paintings held in civic buildings such as local government offices, town halls, guildhalls, public libraries, universities, hospitals, crematoria, fire stations and police stations are also included.

Geographical Boundaries of Catalogues
The geographical boundary of each county is the 'ceremonial county' boundary. This county definition includes all unitary authorities. Counties that have a particularly large number of paintings are divided between two or more catalogues on a geographical basis.

Criteria for Inclusion
As long as paintings meet the requirements above, all paintings are included irrespective of their condition and perceived quality. However, painting reproductions can only be included with the agreement of the participating collections and, where appropriate, the relevant copyright owner. It is rare that a collection forbids the inclusion of its paintings. Where this is the case and it is possible to obtain a list of paintings, this list is given in the Paintings Without Reproductions section. Where copyright consent is refused, the paintings are also listed in the Paintings Without Reproductions section. All paintings in collections' stacks and stores are included, as well as those on display. Paintings which have been lent to other institutions, whether for short-term exhibition or long-term loan, are listed under the owner collection. In addition, paintings on long-term loan are also included under the borrowing institution when they are likely to remain there for at least another five years from the date of publication of this catalogue. Information relating to owners and borrowers is listed in the Further Information section.

Layout
Collections are grouped together under their home town. These locations are listed in alphabetical order. In some cases collections that are spread over a number of locations are included under a single owner collection. A number of collections, principally the larger ones, are preceded by curatorial forewords Within each collection paintings are listed in order of artist surname. Where there is more than one painting by the same artist, the paintings are listed chronologically, according to their execution date.

The few paintings that are not accompanied by photographs are listed in the Paintings Without Reproductions section.

There is additional reference material in the Further Information section at the back of the catalogue. This gives the full names of artists, titles and media if it has not been possible to include these in full in the main section. It also provides acquisition credit lines and information about loans in and out, as well as copyright and photographic credits for each painting. Finally, there is an index of artists' surnames.

Key to Painting Information

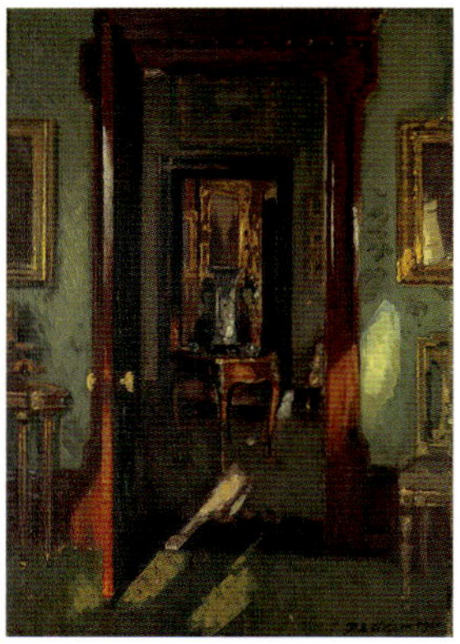

Almost all paintings are reproduced in the catalogue. Where this is not the case they are listed in the Paintings Without Reproductions section. Where paintings are missing or have been stolen, the best possible photograph on record has been reproduced. In some cases this may be black and white. Paintings that have been stolen are highlighted with a red border. Some paintings are shown with conservation tissue attached to parts of the painting surface.

Adam, Patrick William 1854–1929
Interior, Rutland Lodge: Vista through Open Doors 1920
oil on canvas 67.3 × 45.7
LEEAG.PA.1925.0671.LACF ✻

Artist name This is shown with the surname first. Where the artist is listed on the Getty Union List of Artist Names (ULAN), ULAN's preferred presentation of the name is given. In a number of cases the name may not be a firm attribution and this is made clear. Where the artist name is not known, a school may be given instead. Where the school is not known, the painter name is listed as *unknown artist*. If the artist name is too long for the space, as much of the name is given as possible followed by (…). This indicates the full name is given at the rear of the catalogue in the Further Information section.

Painting title A painting title followed by *(?)* indicates that the title is in doubt. Where the alternative title to the painting is considered to be better known than the original, the alternative title is given in parentheses. Where the collection has not given a painting a title, the publisher does so instead and marks this with an asterisk. If the title is too long for the space, as much of the title is given as possible followed by *(…)* and the full title is given in the Further Information section.

Execution date In some cases the precise year of execution may not be known for certain. Instead an approximate date will be given or no date at all.

Artist dates Where known, the years of birth and death of the artist are given. In some cases one or both dates may not be known with certainty, and this is marked. No date indicates that even an approximate date is not known. Where only the period in which the artist was active is known, these dates are given and preceded with the word *active*.

Medium and support Where the precise material used in the support is known, this is given.

Dimensions All measurements refer to the unframed painting and are given in cm with up to one decimal point. In all cases the height is shown before the width. An (E) indicates where a painting has not been measured and its size has been calculated by sight only. If the painting is circular, the single dimension is the diameter. If the painting is oval, the dimensions are height and width.

Collection inventory number In the case of paintings owned by museums, this number will always be the accession number. In all other cases it will be a unique inventory number of the owner institution. (P) indicates that a painting is a private loan. Details can be found in the Further Information section. Accession numbers preceded by 'PCF' indicate that the collection did not have an accession number at the time of catalogue production and therefore the number given has been temporarily allocated by The Public Catalogue Foundation. The ✻ symbol indicates that the reproduction is based on a Bridgeman Art Library transparency (go to www.bridgemanart.com) or that Bridgeman administers the copyright for that artist.

Facing page: Waterhouse, John William, 1849–1917, *Destiny* (detail), 1900, Towneley Hall Art Gallery & Museum, (p. 161)

THE PAINTINGS

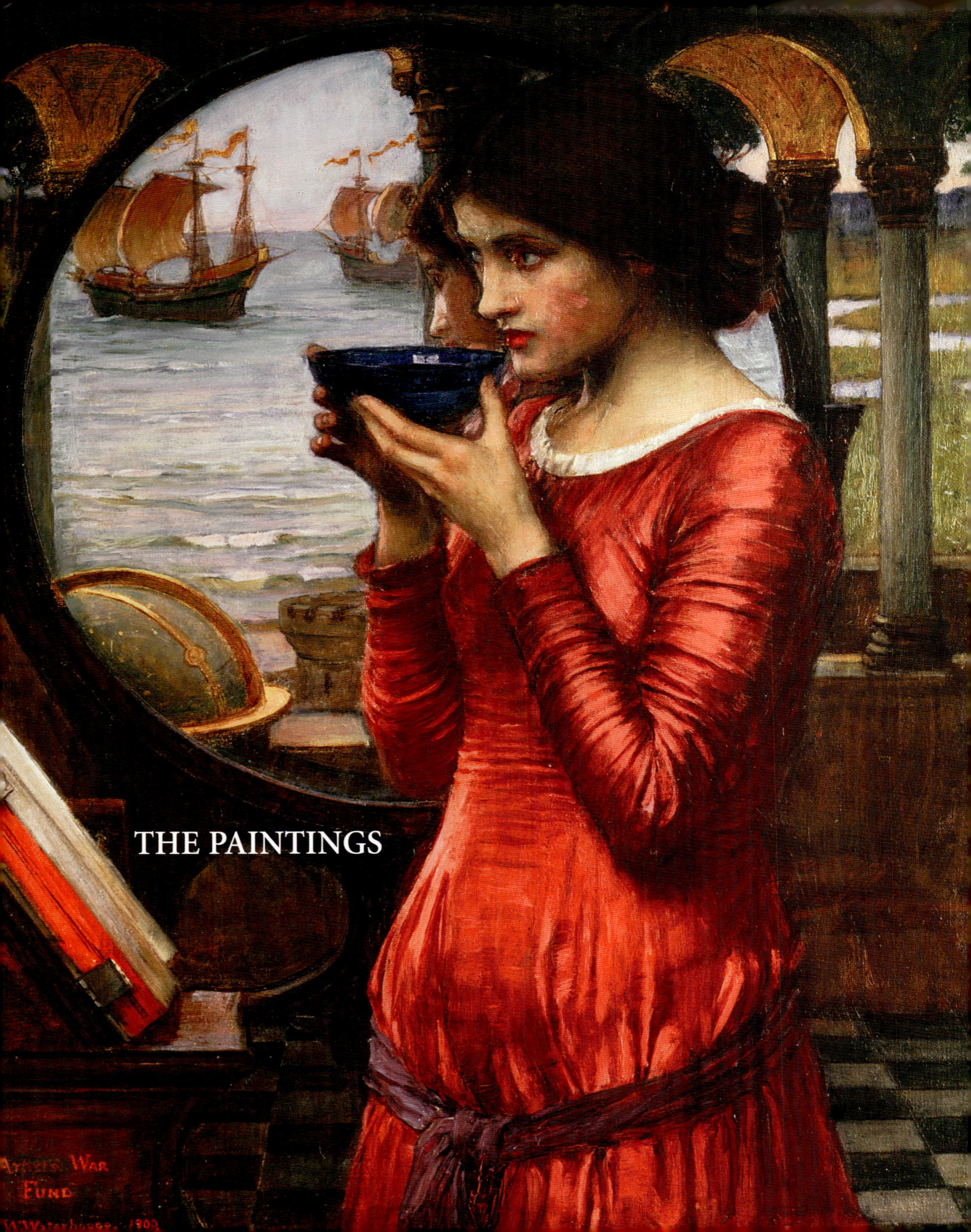

Haworth Art Gallery

It will need no connoisseur of art to appreciate many of the very fine pictures, some by famous artists, which go to form a collection of which Accrington can be proud.

This comment about the display in the newly opened Haworth Art Gallery, was made in the *Observ(er)ations* column of the *Accrington Observer and Times* of 24th September 1921. The pictures available to the first visitors to the Haworth were made up of two distinct groups: those which had been kept and displayed at the Carnegie Public Library in Accrington Town Centre and those bequeathed to the Town by Anne Haworth (1845–1920).

The Carnegie Public Library group consisted of 69 paintings and watercolours which had been collected for the town from 1903 and included one of the finest and rarest of the Haworth Art Gallery's paintings. *The Tempest (Storm off the Coast)* by neo-classical marine painter Claude-Joseph Vernet was given by Alderman Higham in 1908 to mark his year as Mayor of Accrington. Dating from 1754, it describes a shipwreck during a terrifying storm on rocks near the entrance to an imaginary port and is related to the commission Vernet received from Louis XV to paint all of the ports of France. As the painter to the King, Vernet lived in rooms at the Louvre and he died there during the French Revolution of 1789, though the circumstances of his death are not clear.

The Haworth Bequest of July 1920 consisted of 1[illegible]6 items including 20 oils and 30 watercolours, both groups of great quality and merit. The Bequest was made by Anne who was 'simply carrying out her brother's wishes' by giving the collection along with their home Hollins Hill, its outbuildings, stables and grounds, and a sum of £28,000 to the people of Accrington. The pictures were chosen carefully by Anne and her brother, William (1848–1913), who were convinced of the educational merit of bringing great art and ordinary people together and wanted their home, now Haworth Art Gallery, to facilitate this. William and, no doubt, Anne's favourite painting was *My Ladye's Palfrey*, painted in 1849 by John Frederick Herring I. This Charles I costume piece, which hung in William's billiard room, shows the textures of the animals' coats and the characters' clothing in radiant detail. It typifies all the best qualities of the Haworth Bequest pictures and is probably the single most popular painting in the Haworth's collection.

Animal subjects are a theme of the Haworth Bequest and *A Sunlit Barn with Ewes, Lambs and Chickens* by the Belgian painter Eugène Joseph Verboeckhoven is a charming example. William and Anne also liked imagining a simpler past prior to the Industrial Revolution, exemplified by the aforementioned Herring and by William Shayer's *Harvest Time* of 1855, where a family of well-fed labourers is seen resting under the benign gaze of their employer. An empathy with those less fortunate than themselves is another theme of the Bequest and can be seen in paintings like *The Post Office or Hope Deferred Makes the Heart Sick* by Thomas George Webster and *Cottage Hospitality* by William Collins.

The Bequest also contains a group of large paintings representing the varied landscapes of Great Britain: *On the Llygwy, North Wales* by Benjamin Williams Leader, *The Mountains of Moidart* by John MacWhirter, and

Summertime by Edmund Morison Wimperis. The Haworths' favourite annual holiday destination, Scotland, is represented in watercolours by Anthony Vandyke Copley Fielding and Thomas Sidney Cooper, amongst others.

The number of pictures on display at the Haworth increased by 26 with the Nuttall Bequest in 1925. This third grouping repeats and adds to the preferences the Haworths showed for pictures of animals and children, the depiction of a happier past and genre subjects (subjects from everyday life). Mrs Alice Ann Nuttall was the daughter of Alderman Entwistle, JP and Mayor of Accrington in 1886 and 1887. She bequeathed the collection in the name of her husband George Nuttall, the former managing director of Steiner's Calico Printing Works in Church, Accrington. With this gift the Haworth Bequest's two stunning examples of livestock in Kentish landscapes by Thomas Sydney Cooper were doubled to four with a watercolour and a superb outsized oil painting, *Canterbury Meadows, Evening*. Another painting very popular with Haworth visitors also arrived: *The Laundress*, heavily influenced by Vermeer in its composition and quality of light, by the French painter Pierre Edouard Frère.

After a period of closure during the Second World War, a fourth group of 14 oils and 48 watercolour drawings were presented to the people of Accrington. This was from Edwin Hitchon (1874–1966), the son of Alfred Hitchon, who had given over £50,000 to the Accrington Victoria Hospital. Edwin had worked for 20 years as engineering manager of Accrington's textiles machinery firm Howard and Bullough, a firm which his father helped set up and which employed over 5,000 people in its hey-day. In 1946 Edwin Hitchon, who had retired to the Lake District, invited the Haworth Art Gallery Curator, Mr Tom Bent, to select pictures for the Haworth. Bent's selection altered the balance of subject-matter somewhat with his choice of some interesting and unusual landscapes. Amongst the oil paintings were two by artists with links to the French Impressionists through their membership of the St Ives group c.1900: *Incoming Tide* by Albert Julius Olsson and *At Marazion* or *Riverside Farm* by Frederick Milner. From earlier in the nineteenth century, Bent selected two Mediterranean subjects: Giancinto Gianni's 1868 *View of Capri* and *Classical Scene (Ruined Temple)* in the style of the painter Giovanni Paolo Panini. However, his choice of *Venetian Scene*, then ascribed to the famous British landscape and marine painter J. M. W. Turner, turned out to be a twentieth-century pastiche with little merit.

Some other important single gifts of oil paintings had been made by 1946: Miss Mary Wilkinson presented a celebration of childhood innocence, *Early Flowers* by Henry Le Jeune, and Mr J. H. Barnes, Esq., presented two very different idealised female portraits, *Sylvia* by Luke Fildes and *Faith* by Frederic Leighton. These two epitomise the two approaches to oil painting made by high Victorian artists, an expressive and colourful romanticism leading back to Venetian painters like Titian, and to cool and measured neo-classicism, derived originally from the drawing tradition of Florentine artists like Leonardo da Vinci.

The Haworth Art Gallery's modest-sized but high quality paintings collection was brought together around the four main sources described above, largely between the years of 1903 and 1950. Emphasis has subsequently been put not on acquisitions but on producing a lively temporary exhibitions programme and on exploiting the Tiffany glass collection, moved from

Accrington Museum to the Haworth basement for safe-keeping during the Second World War and never returned. This emphasis continues, though in more recent years paintings by some important artists with strong local connections have been added to the collection, nearly all by gift. These include *One Up, One Down* by Robin Bownass, *Self Portrait* and *Portrait of the Artist's Wife* by Gerard de Rose, *Father and Son* and *Coming Home* by Leslie Duxbury and *Accrington from the Coppice* by John Virtue.

Jennifer A. Rennie, Curator and Manager

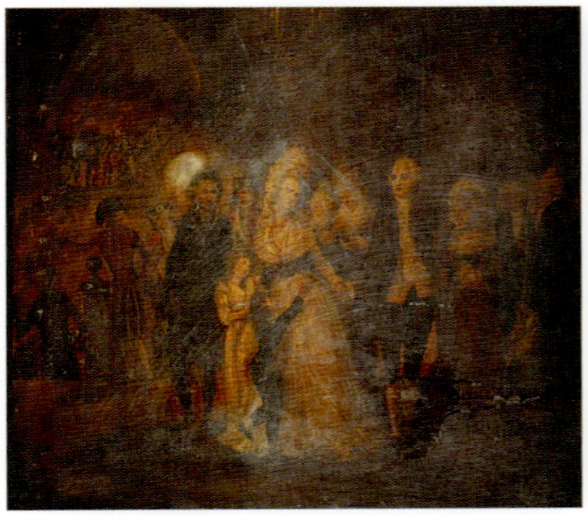

American School
Interior Scene
oil on canvas 65 x 80
HAG545

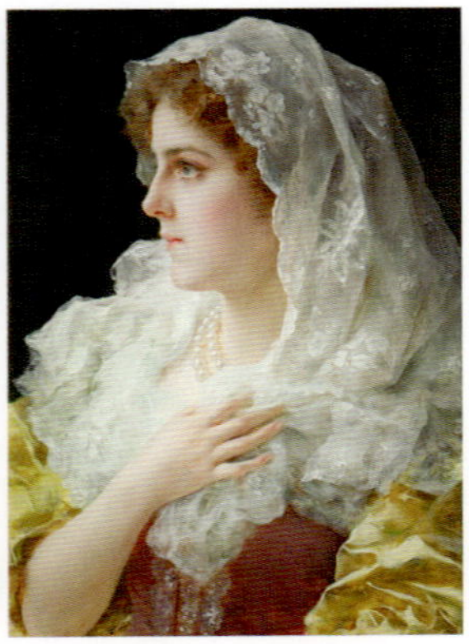

Andreotti, Federico 1847–1930
An English Beauty
oil on canvas 69 x 49
HAG77

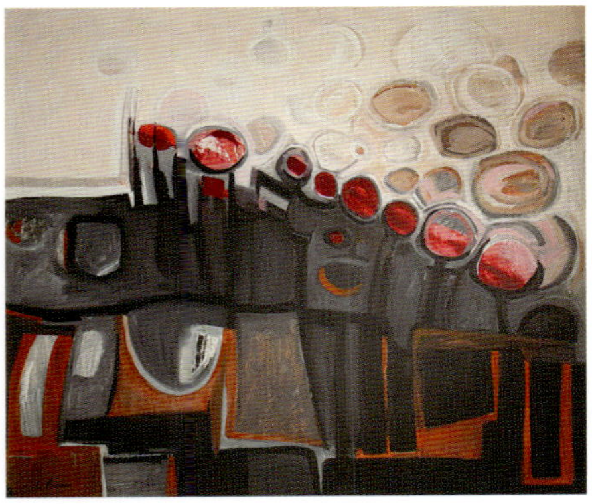

Bonner, A. L. H. active 1964–1966
Poppy Day Forever
oil on canvas 122.5 x 165
HAG594

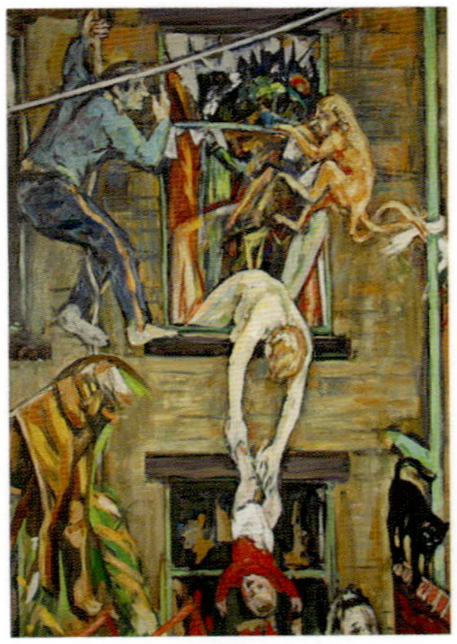

Bownass, Robin Ernest b.1938
One Up, One Down
acrylic (?) on canvas 134 x 110 (E)
HAG641

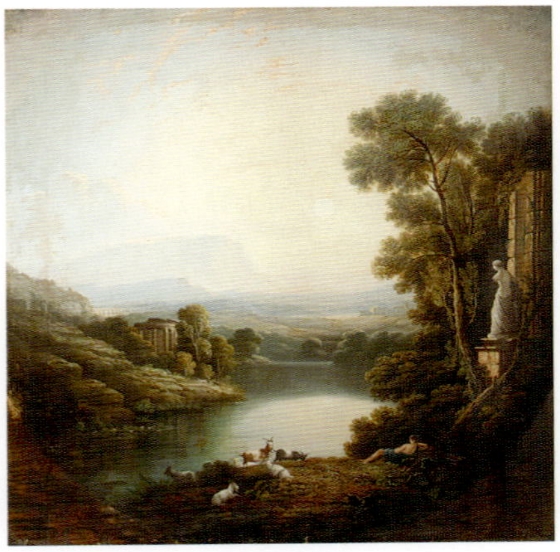

British (English) School
Classical Italian Landscape
oil on canvas 76 x 75
HAG546

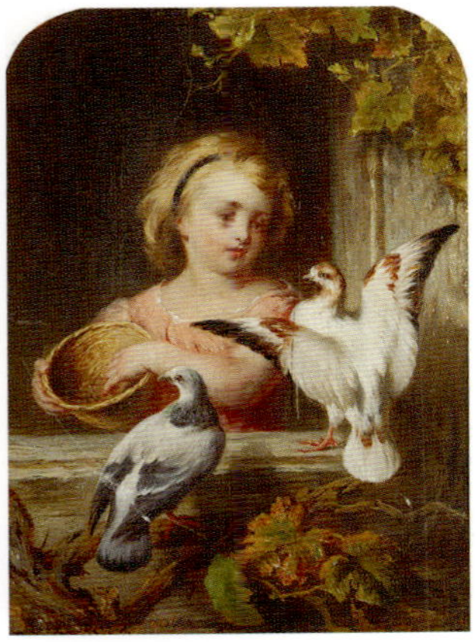

British (English) School
Little Girl and Two Pigeons
oil on canvas 25.5 x 22
HAG179

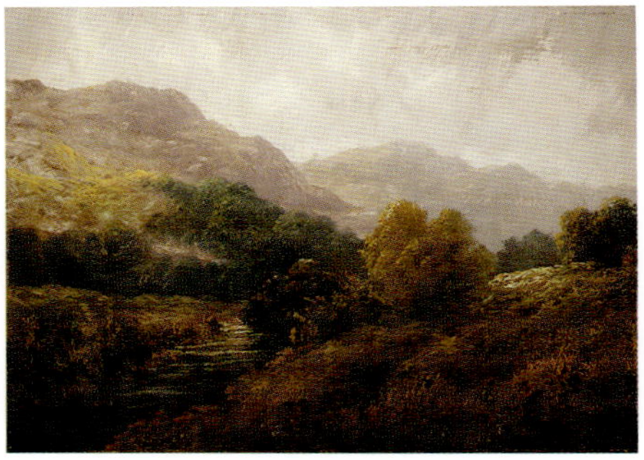

British (English) School
Lowland Landscape
oil on canvas 23 x 36
HAGXXX6

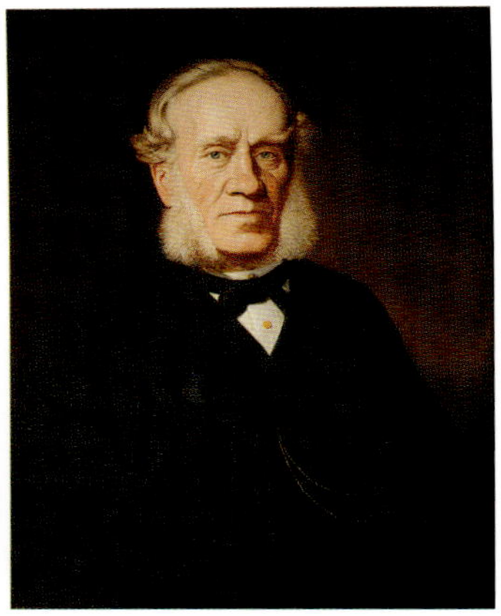

British (English) School
Portrait of a Local Man -2
oil on canvas 77 x 64
HAG559

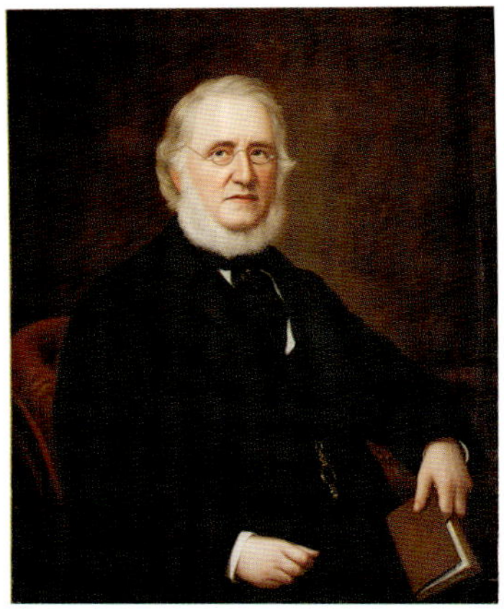

British (English) School
Portrait of a Local Man -3
oil on canvas 92 x 76
HAG561

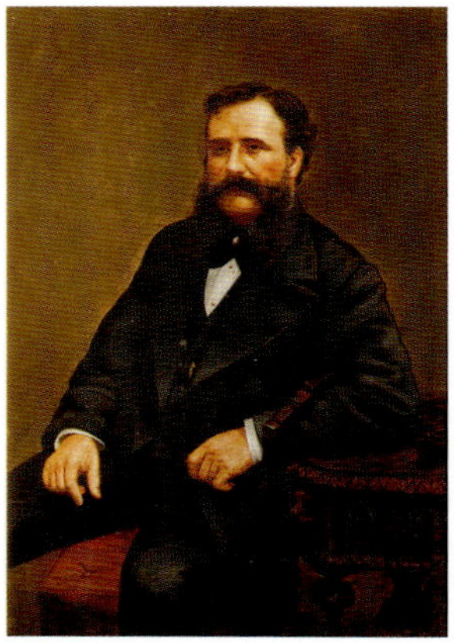

British (English) School
Portrait of a Local Man -4
oil on canvas 59 x 44
HAGXXX7

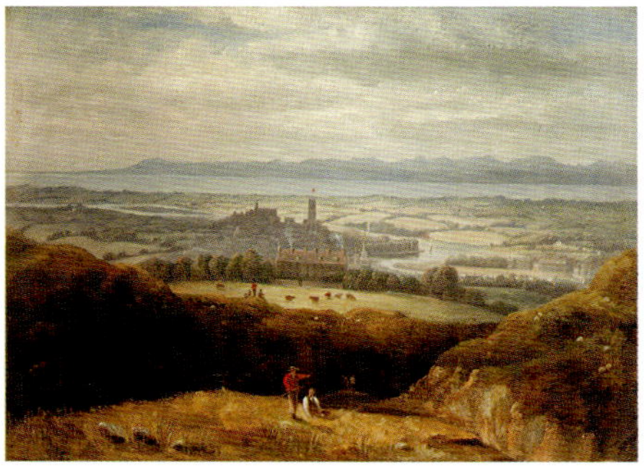

British (English) School
View of Lancaster
oil on canvas 42 x 59
HAG168

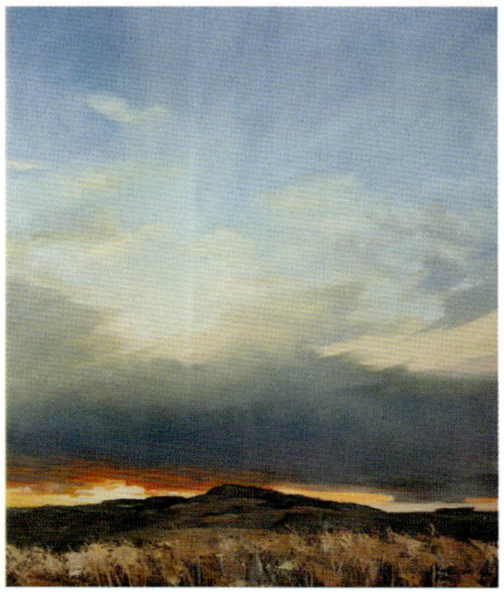

Bushe, Ken b.1954
Sunset over the Moors 1984
oil on canvas 54 x 40
HAG517

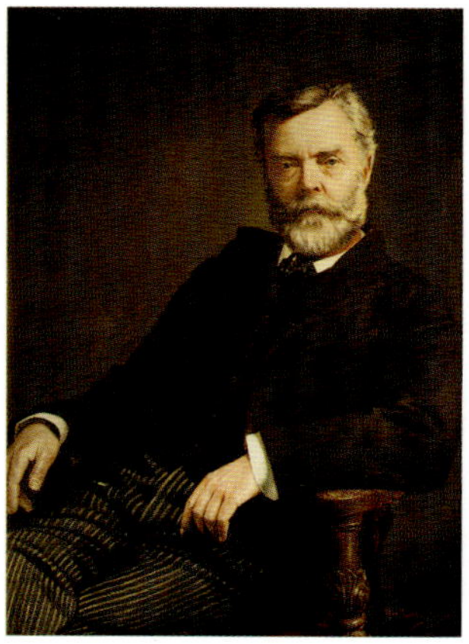

Buttner, Max 1855–1925
Portrait of a Local Man -1
oil on canvas 111 x 81
HAG558

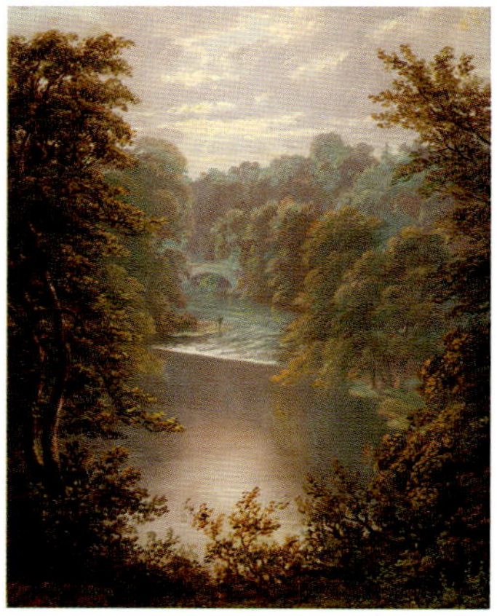

Cauthorne, E. active 1880–1910
The Witches' Pool
oil on canvas 46 x 35.5
HAG554

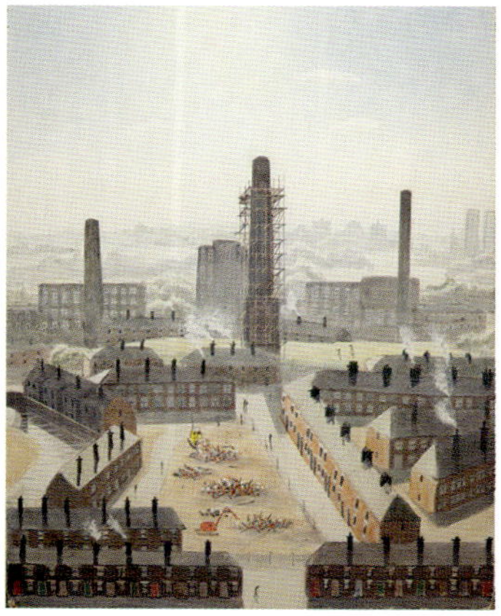

Clapcott, Helen b.1952
Travis Street, Stockport
tempera on board 21 x 15.5
HAG531

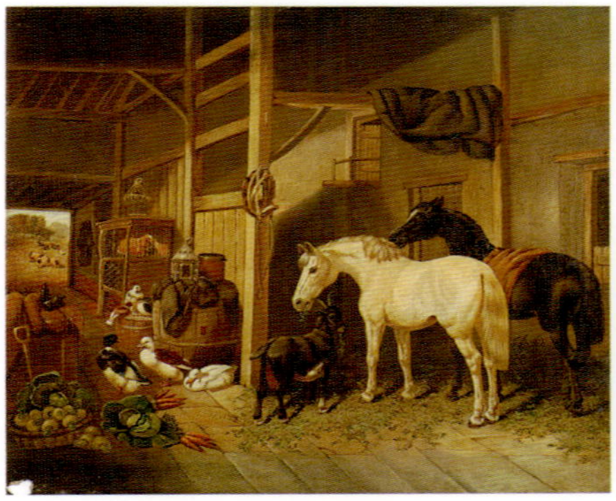

Clark, J.
A Stable Interior
oil on canvas 51 x 61
HAG167

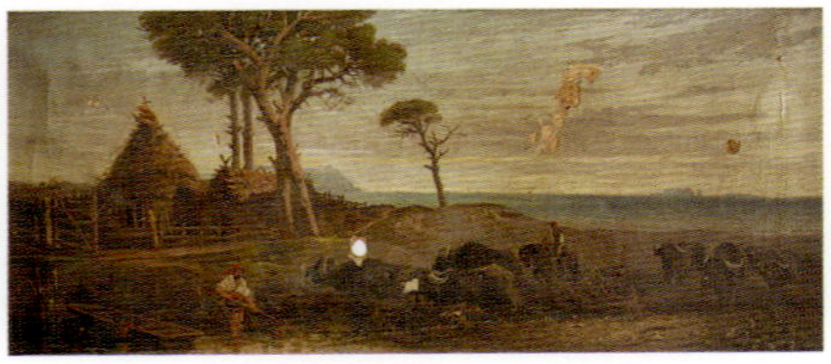

Coleman, Charles 1808–1874
The Ox Driver
oil on canvas 40 x 100
HAG570

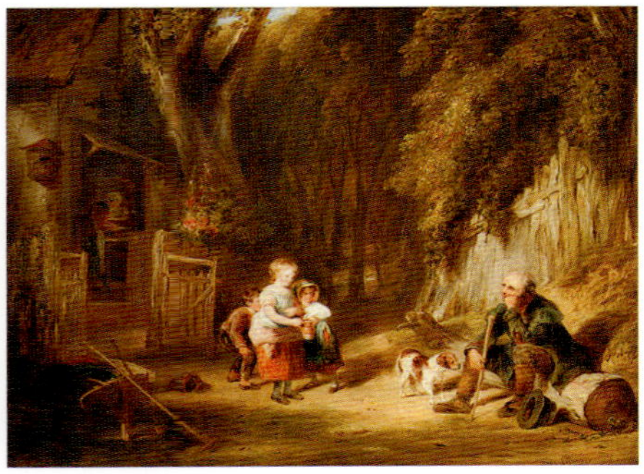

Collins, William 1788–1847
Cottage Hospitality
oil on canvas 79 x 96
HAG11

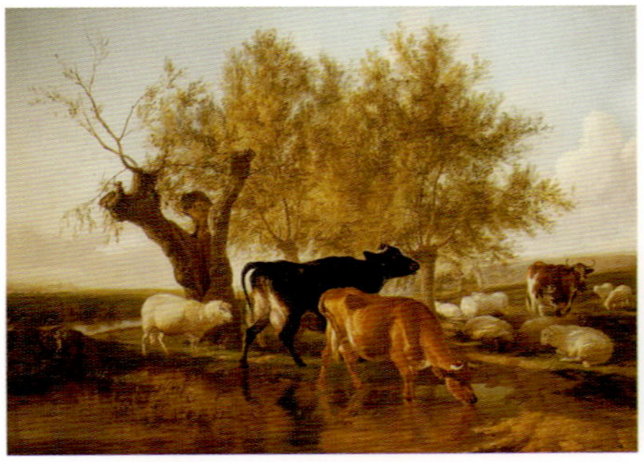

Cooper, Thomas Sidney 1803–1902
Canterbury Meadows, Evening
oil on canvas 97 x 133
HAG173

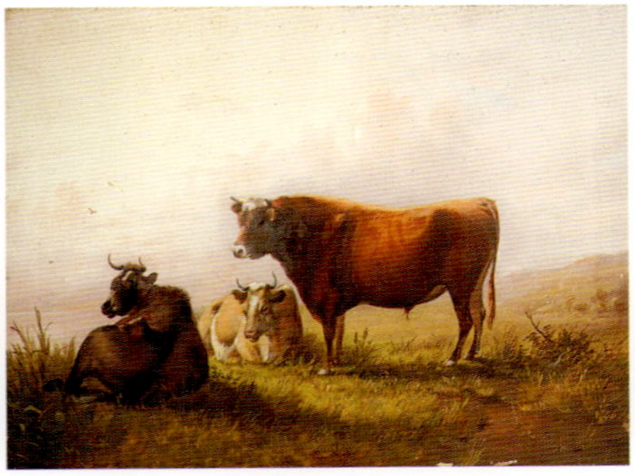

Cooper, Thomas Sidney 1803–1902
Study of Three Cows
oil on canvas 40.5 x 61
HAG578

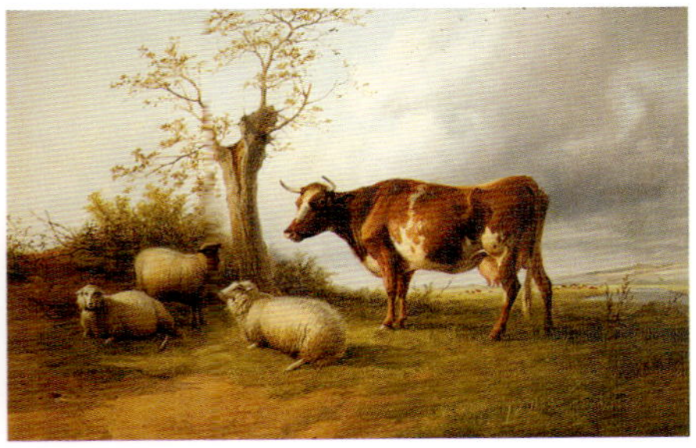

Cooper, Thomas Sidney 1803–1902
View in Stour Valley with Cow
oil on canvas 51.5 x 77
HAG549

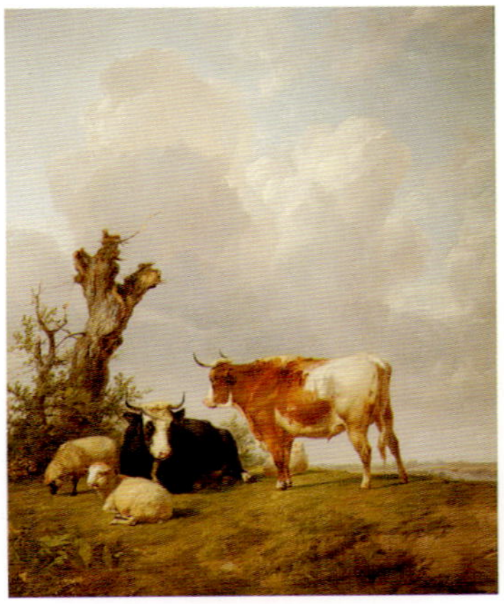

Cooper, Thomas Sidney 1803–1902
View in Stour Valley with Two Cows
oil on canvas 58.5 x 47.5
HAG16

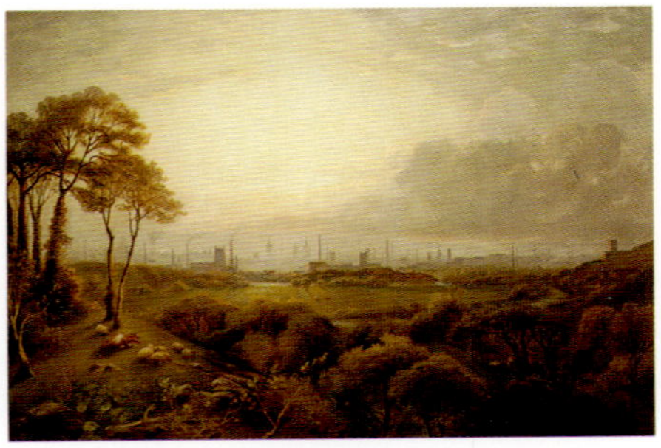

Creswick, Thomas (attributed to) 1811–1869
View of Manchester
oil on canvas 77 x 110
HAG562

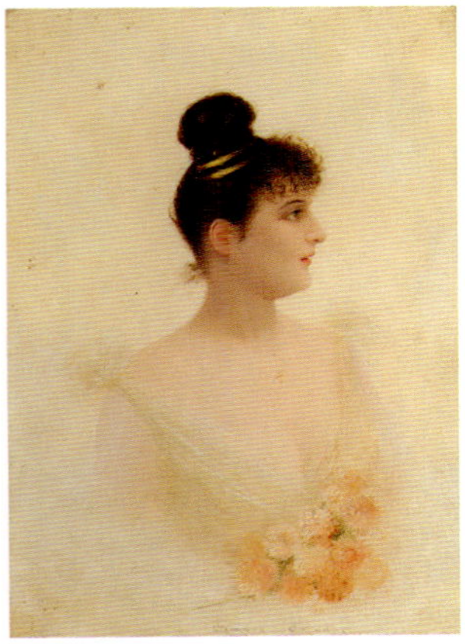

Croegaert, Georges 1848–1923
Bust Portrait of a Woman
oil on canvas 32 x 23
HAG166

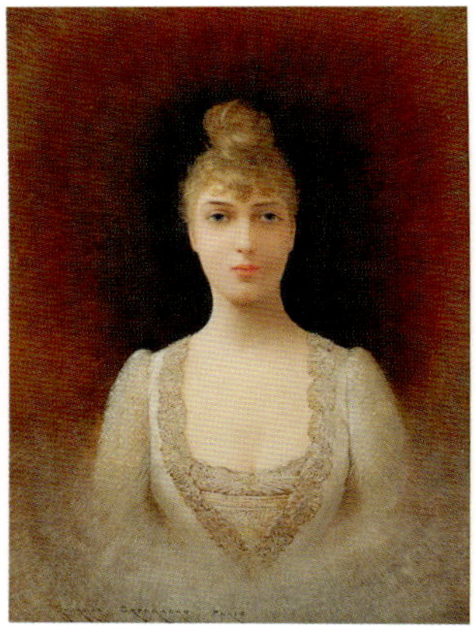

Croegaert, Georges 1848–1923
Portrait of a Flaxen-Haired Woman
oil on canvas 33 x 24
HAG156

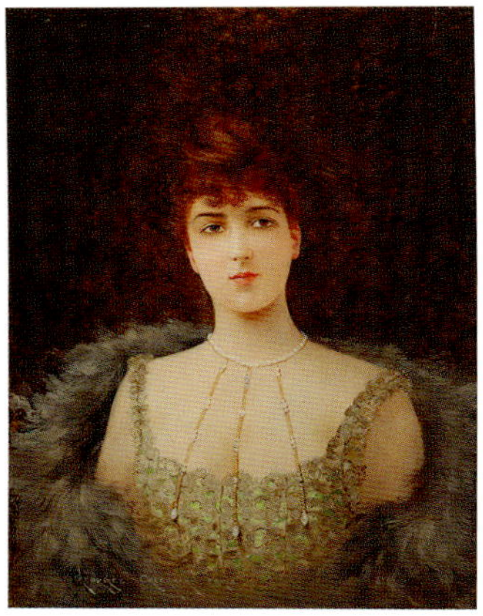

Croegaert, Georges 1848–1923
Portrait of an Auburn-Haired Woman
oil on canvas 32.5 x 24.5
HAG158

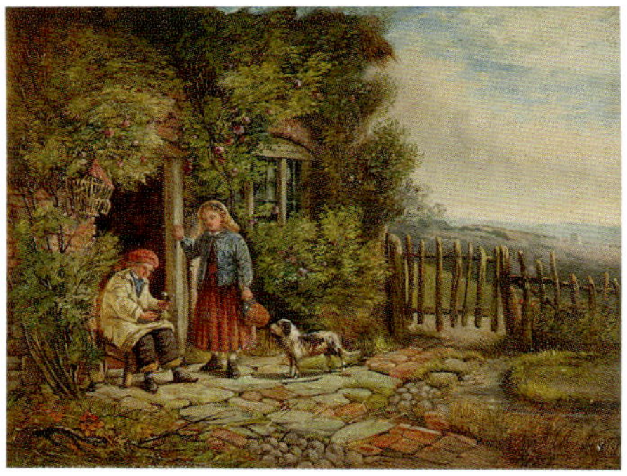

Dell, John Henry (circle of) 1836–1888
Cottagers
oil on canvas 23 x 30.5
HAG638

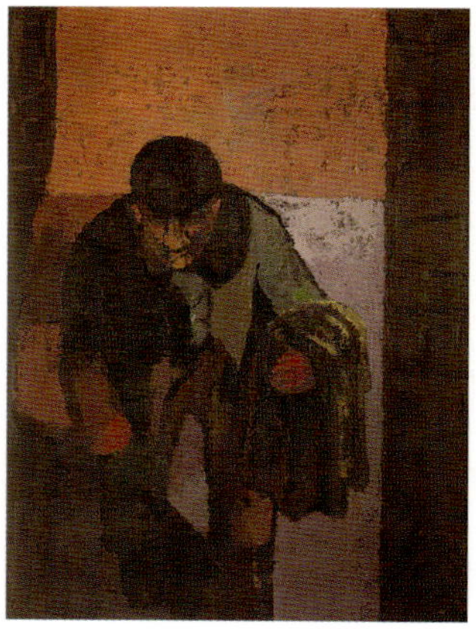

Duxbury, Leslie 1921–2001
Coming Home
acrylic (?) on canvas 149 x 82 (E)
HAG636

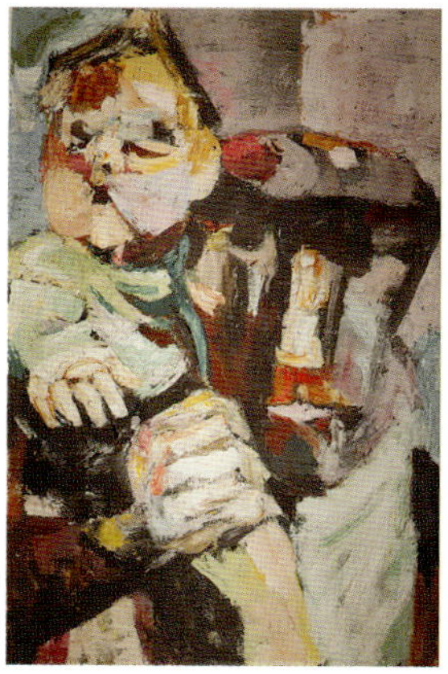

Duxbury, Leslie 1921–2001
Father and Son
acrylic (?) on canvas 77 x 52 (E)
HAG637

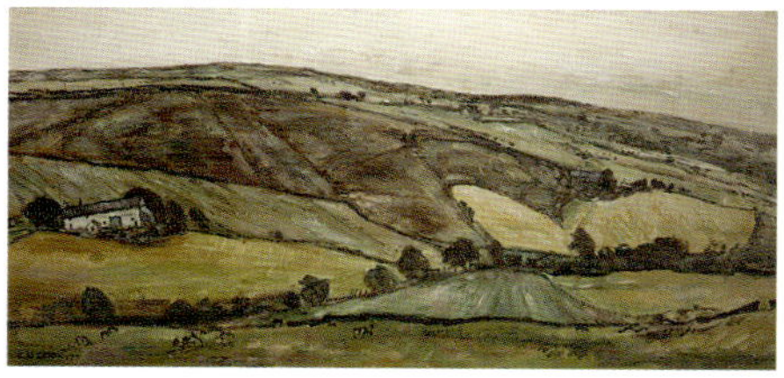

Eaton, Robert
Cocker Lumb, Green Haworth 1977
oil on canvas 31 x 61.5
HAG642

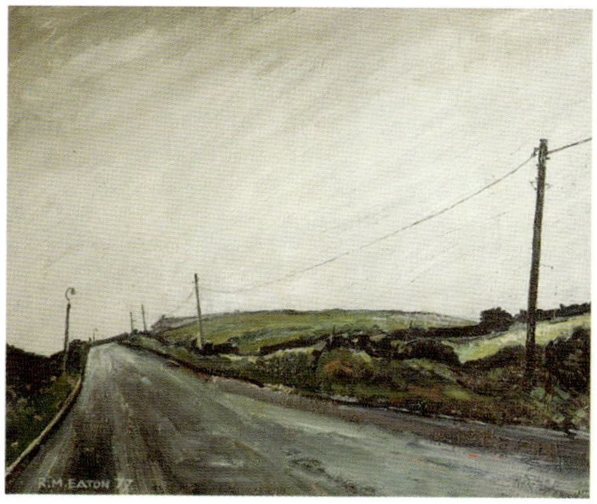

Eaton, Robert
Road to Green Haworth
oil on canvas 25.5 x 30.5
HAG643

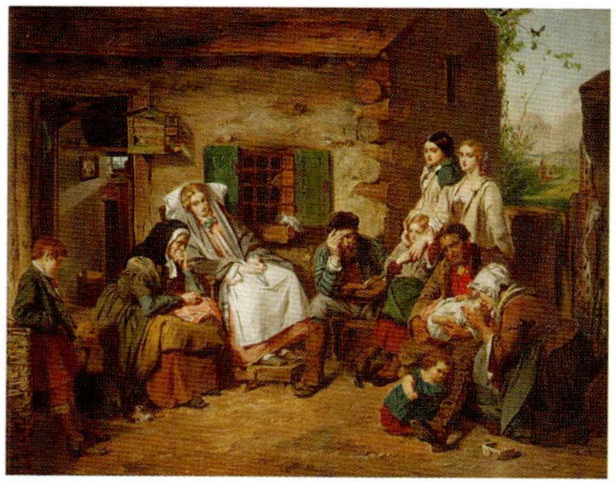

Faed, Thomas 1826–1900
Scottish Settlers in North America
oil on canvas 41 x 50
HAG155

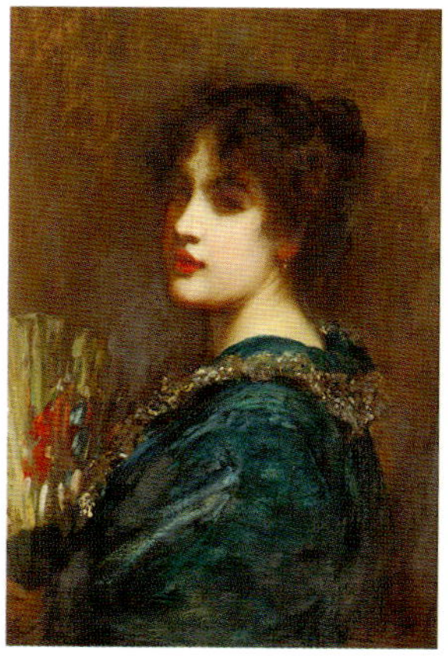

Fildes, Luke 1843–1927
Sylvia
oil on canvas 64 x 47.5
HAG241

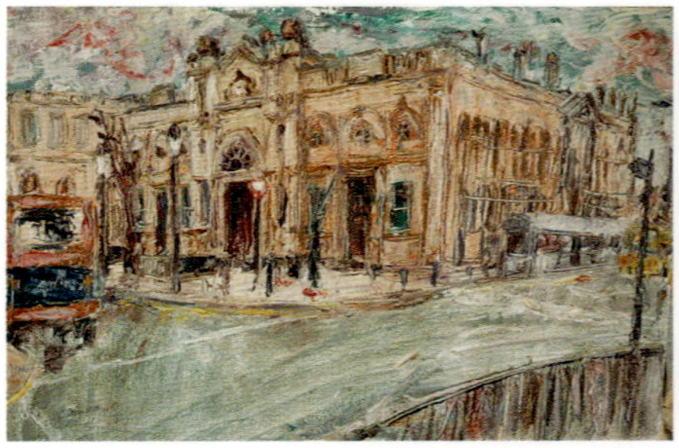

Foster, Richard
Accrington Market Hall, 1860s
oil on paper 53.5 x 77.1
HAG606/12

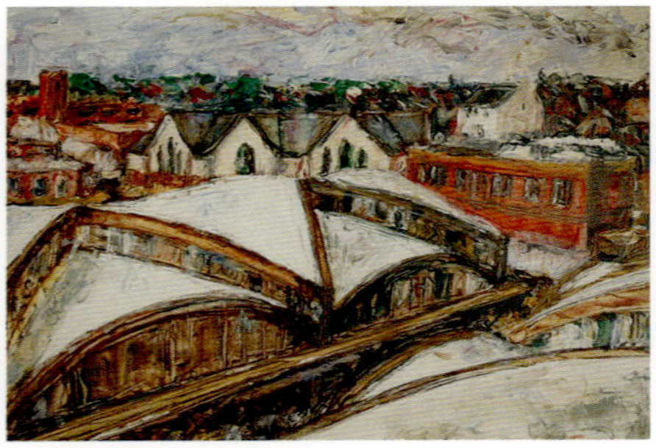

Foster, Richard
Accrington Market Hall, 1960s
oil on paper 55.7 x 76.1
HAG606/2

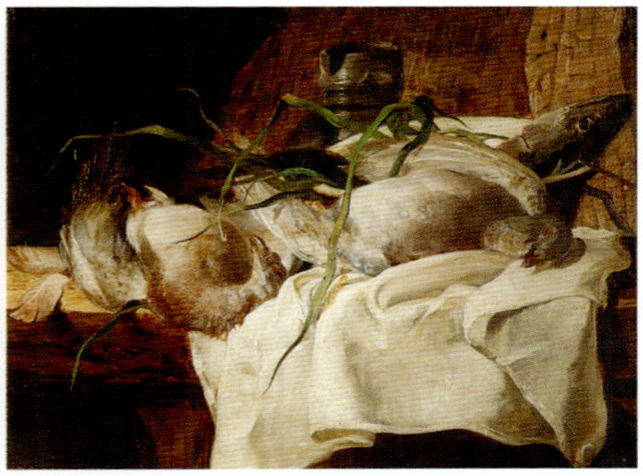

French School
Still Life with Game
oil on canvas 41 x 54
HAG577

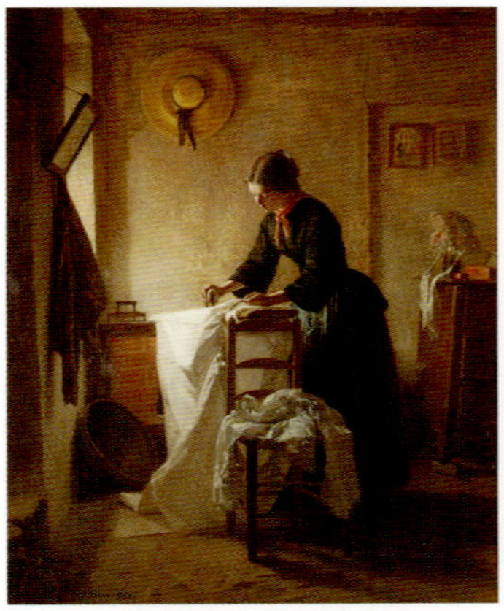

Frère, Pierre Edouard 1819–1886
The Laundress 1858
oil on canvas 50.5 x 42.5
HAG159

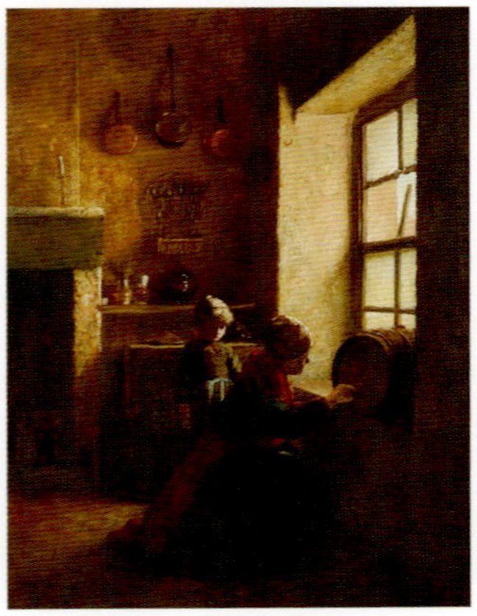

Frère, Pierre Edouard 1819–1886
Tapping the Barrel
oil on canvas 37 x 29
HAG164

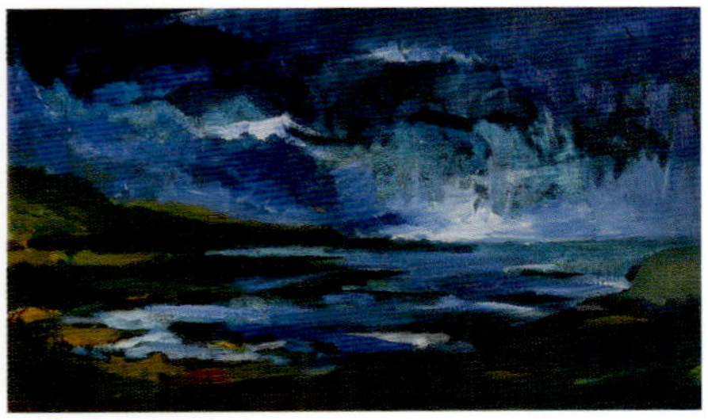

Fryer, Malcolm b.1937
Carling Heugh Bay
oil on canvas 42.7 x 77 (E)
HAG644

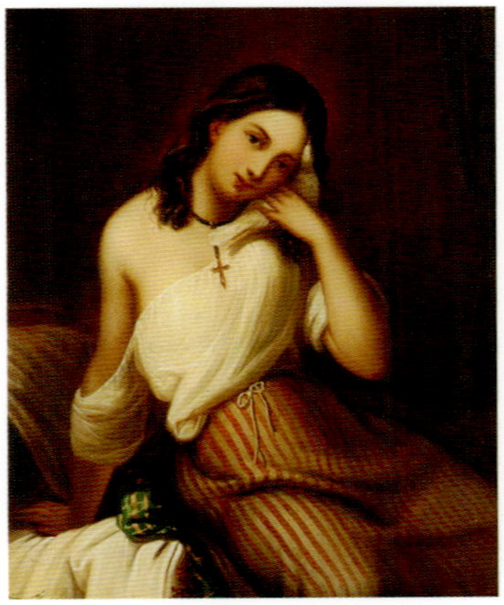

German School
Portrait of a Girl with a Dove
oil on canvas 37 x 33
HAG555

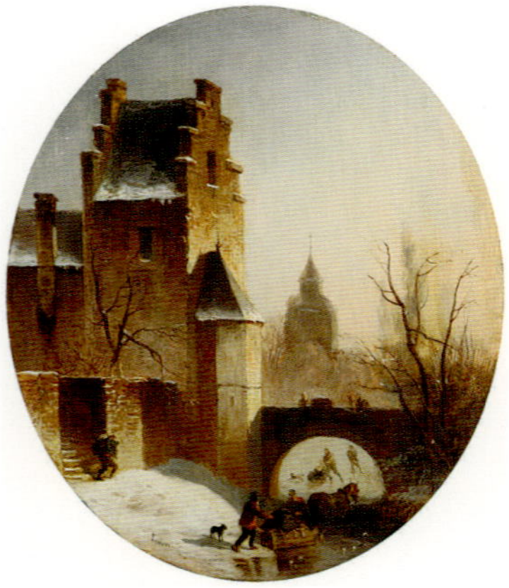

German School
Winter Scene
oil on canvas 30 x 25.5
HAG566

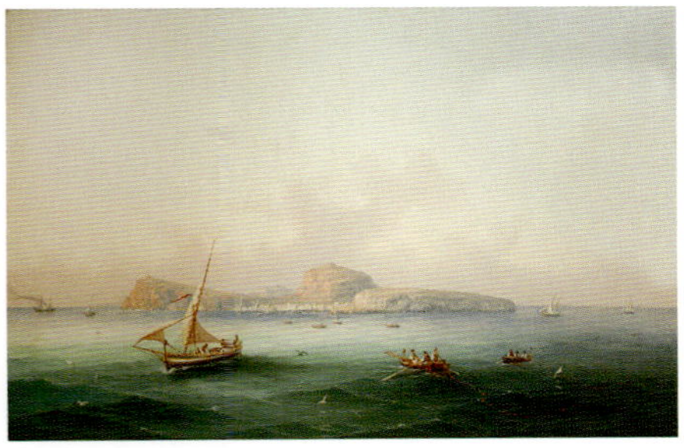

Gianni, Giancinto 1837–1895
View of Capri 1868
oil on canvas 49 x 76.5
HAG174

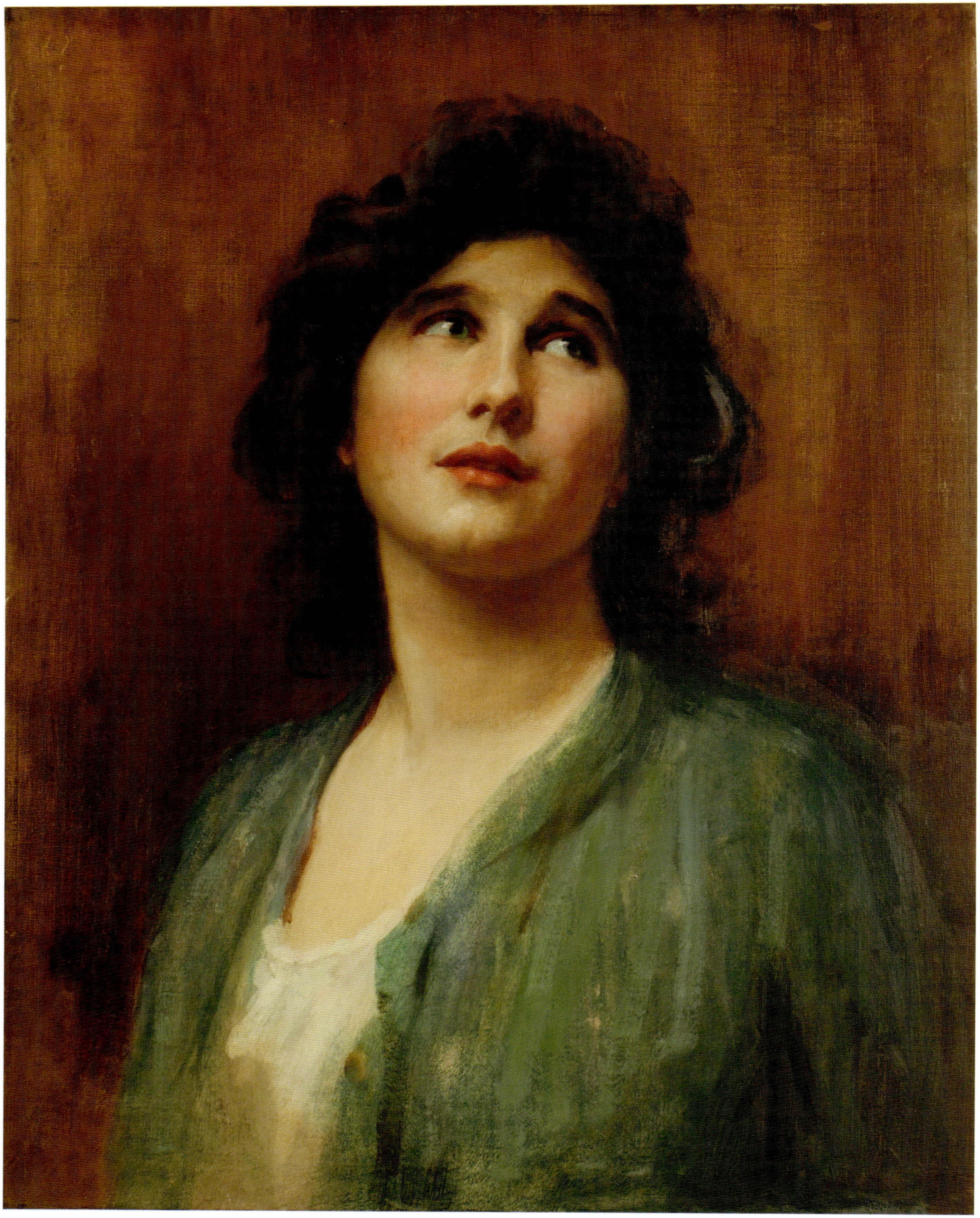

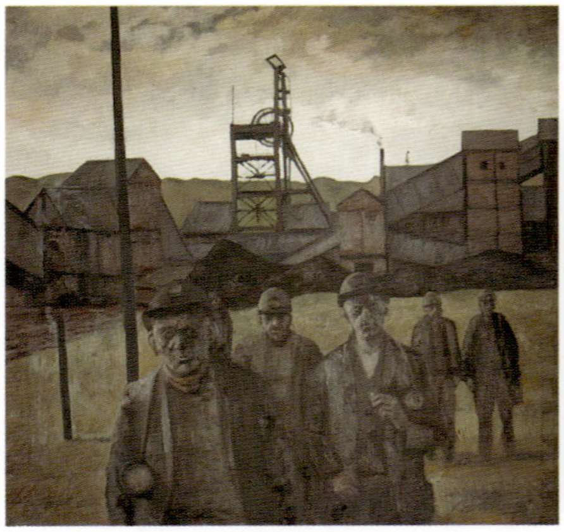

Hampson, Roger 1925–1996
Miners, Hapton Valley
oil on canvas 92 x 92
HAG569

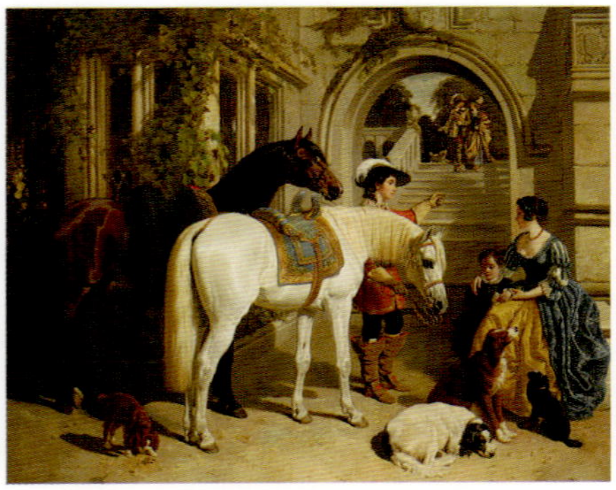

Herring I, John Frederick 1795–1865
My Ladye's Palfrey 1849
oil on canvas 80 x 105.5
HAG1

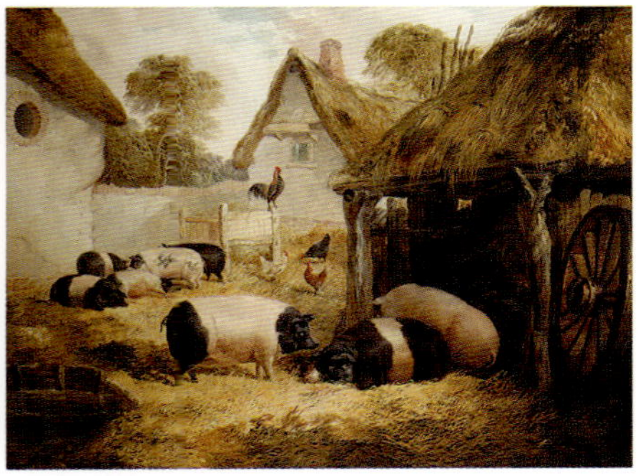

Herring II, John Frederick 1815–1907
Farmyard with Saddlebacks
oil on canvas 56 x 71
HAG560

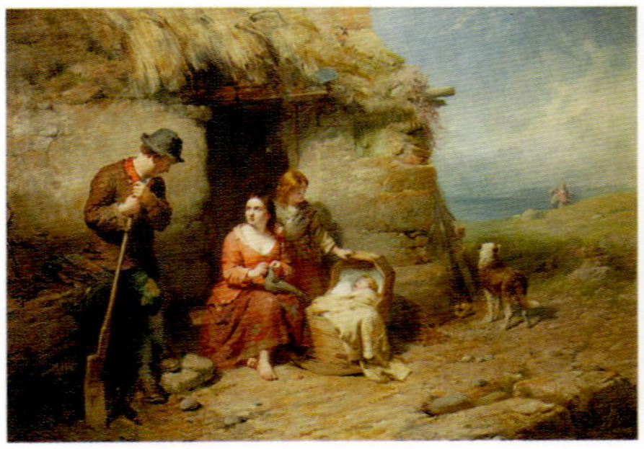

Hill, James John 1811–1882
Exterior of Irish Cabin
oil on canvas 92 x 138
HAG573

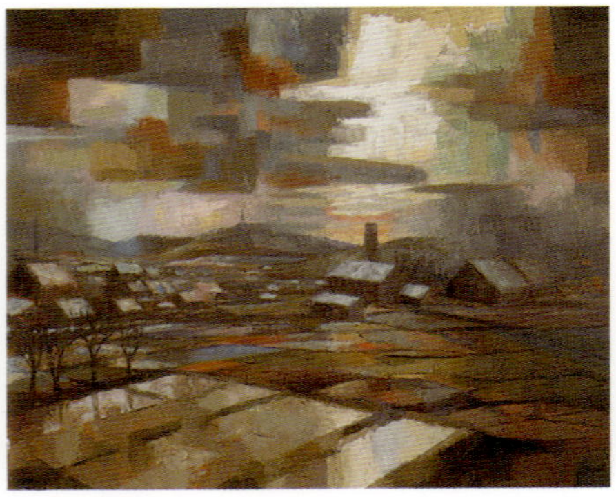

Hough, Jack
Summer, 1962
oil on canvas 50 x 60
HAG567

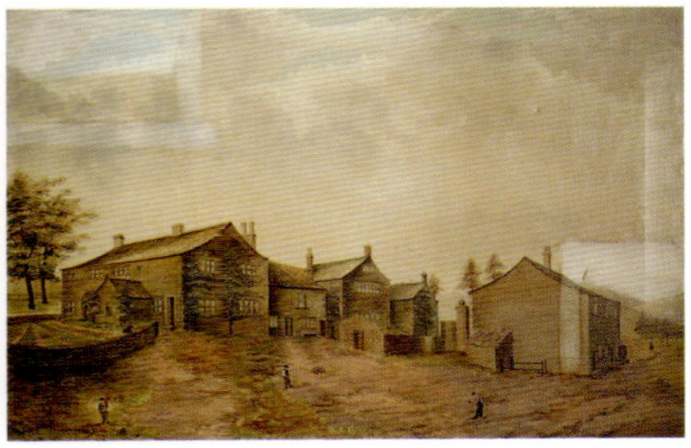

Houlgrave, H.
Old Antley Hall
oil on canvas 60.5 x 91.5
HAGXXX12

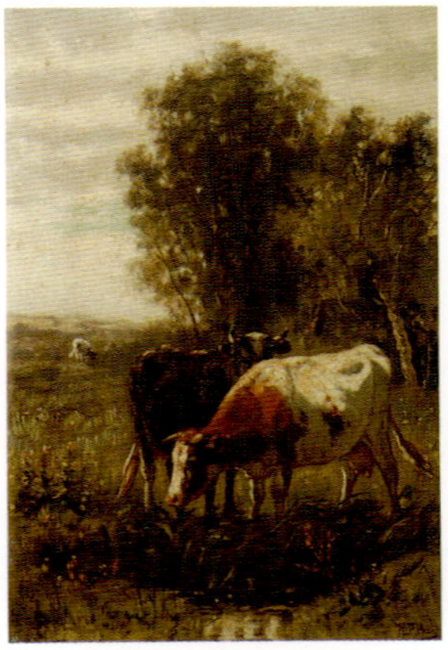

Hulk, William Frederick 1852–1922
Two Cows in a Landscape
oil on canvas 36 x 26
HAG576

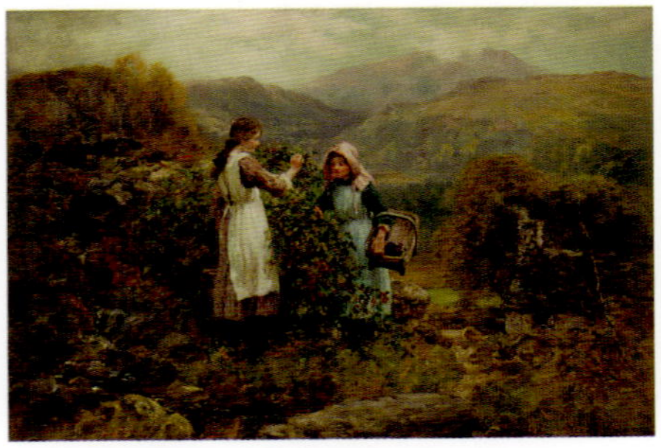

King, Henry John Yeend 1855–1924
Blackberry Gatherers
oil on canvas 55.5 x 81
HAG17

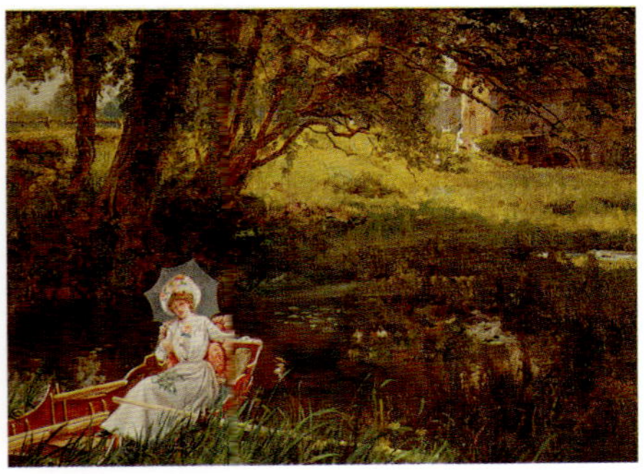

King, Henry John Yeend (circle of) 1855–1924
Lady in a Punt
oil on canvas 51.5 x 76.5
HAG640

Facing page: Fildes, Luke, 1843–1927, *Adoration*, Harris Museum & Art Gallery (p. 300)

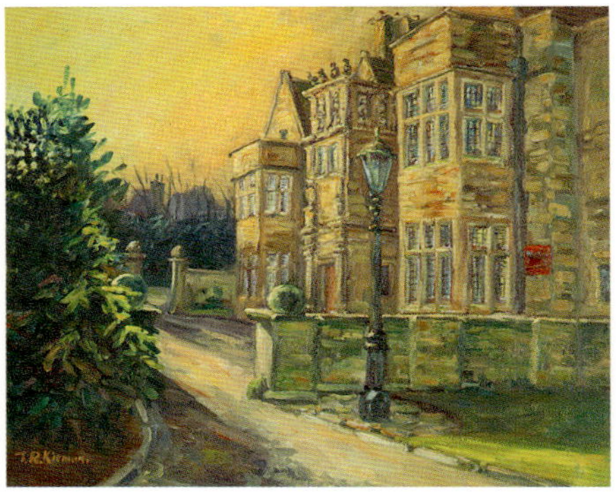

Kirman, Terry 1939–1997
Haworth Art Gallery
oil on canvas 64 x 76
HAG645

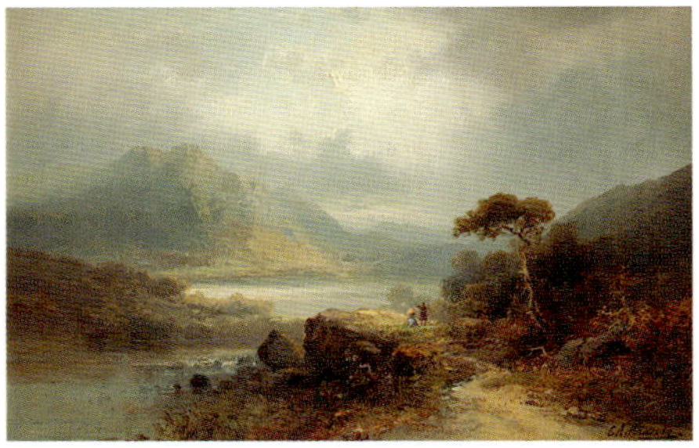

Krause, Emil Albert 1866–1922
Landscape
oil on canvas 30 x 45.5
HAG175

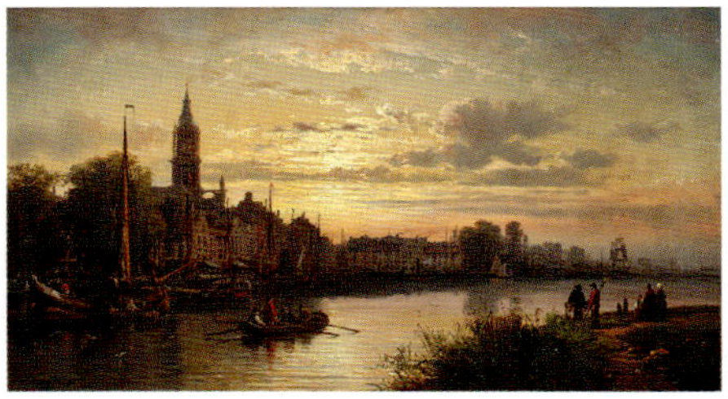

Kuwasseg, Charles Euphrasie 1838–1904
Dutch Sunset Scene
oil on canvas 56 x 100
HAG557

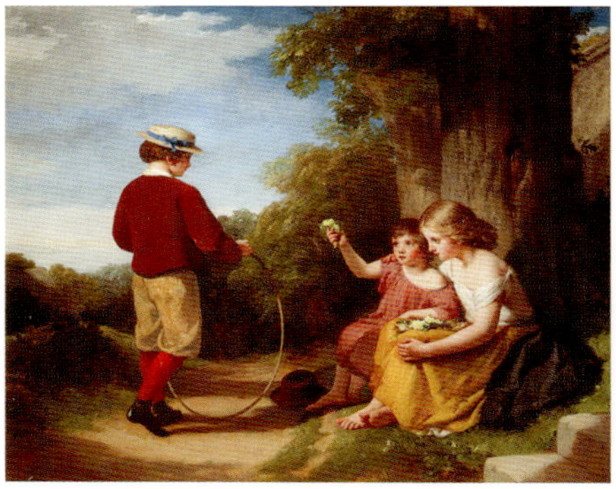

Le Jeune, Henry 1819–1904
Early Flowers
oil on canvas 58.5 x 69
HAG239

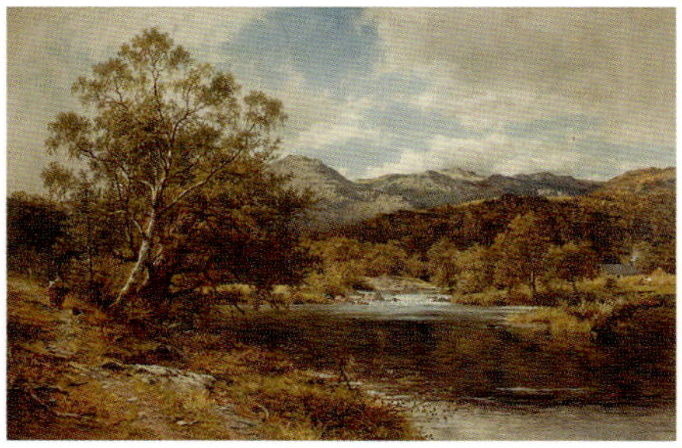

Leader, Benjamin Williams 1831–1923
On the Llygwy, North Wales
oil on canvas 74.5 x 110
HAG5

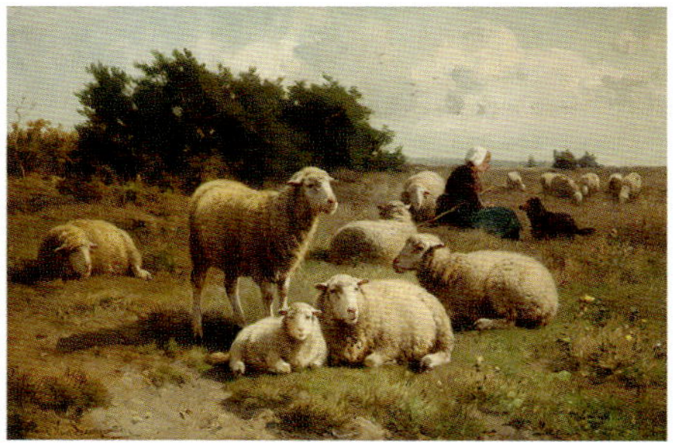

Leemputten, Cornelis van 1841–1902
Dutch Landscape with Shepherdess
oil on canvas 41 x 57
HAG176

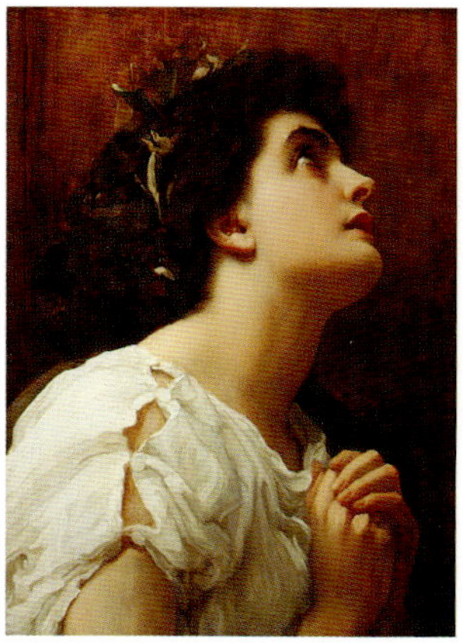

Leighton, Frederic 1830–1896
Faith
oil on canvas 61 x 49.5
HAG240

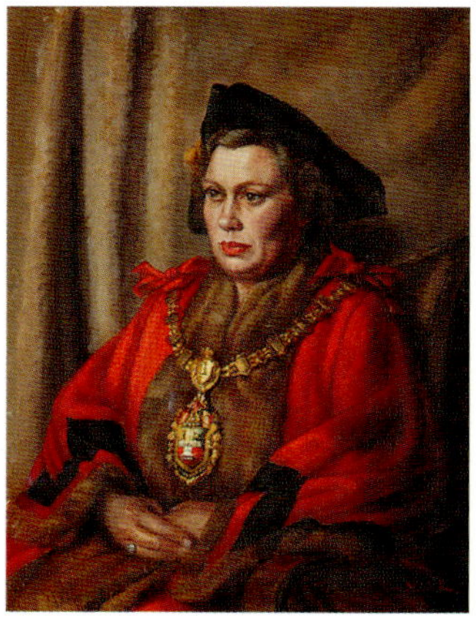

Lindoe, N.
The First Female Mayor of Hyndburn
oil on canvas 77 x 61
HAG635

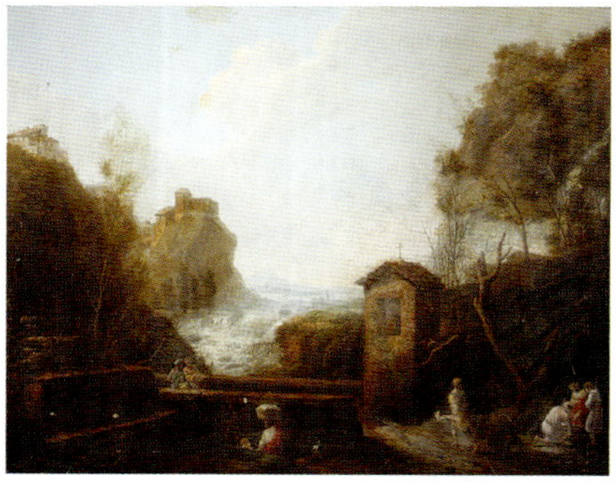

Loo, César van 1743–1821
Classical River Landscape
oil on canvas 81.5 x 105
HAG80

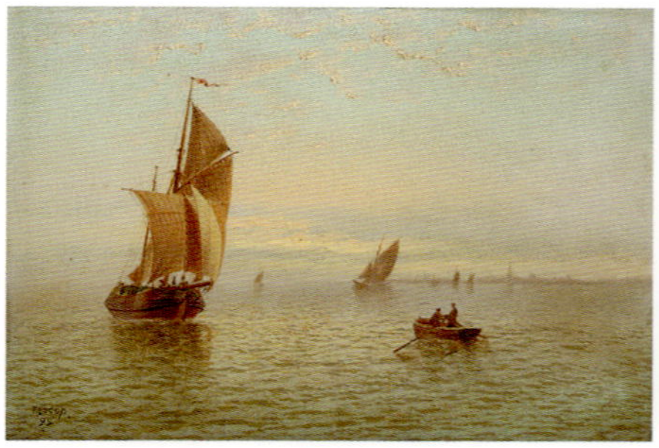

Lucop, Thomas 1834–1911
Evening, Coastal Scene
oil on canvas 20.5 x 30.5
HAG580

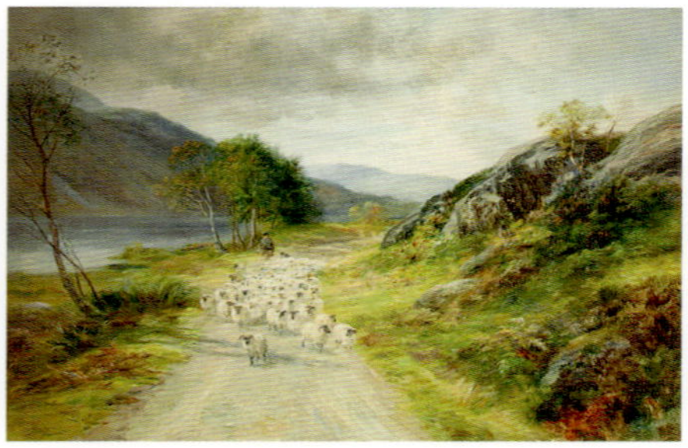

MacWhirter, John 1839–1911
The Mountains of Moidart
oil on canvas 89 x 130
HAG15

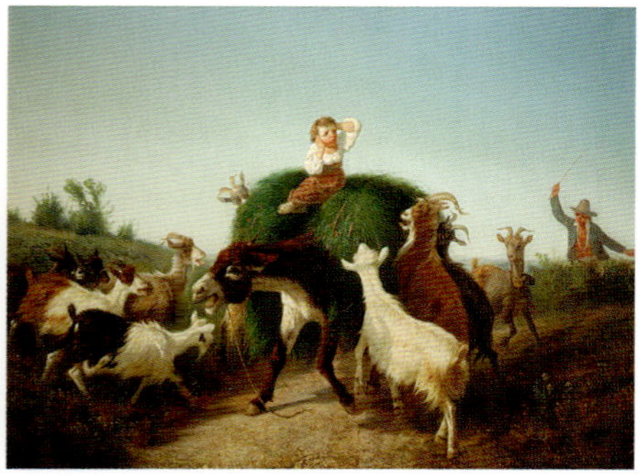

Malone, A.
Italian Child with Donkey and Hay
oil on canvas 51 x 72.5
HAG177

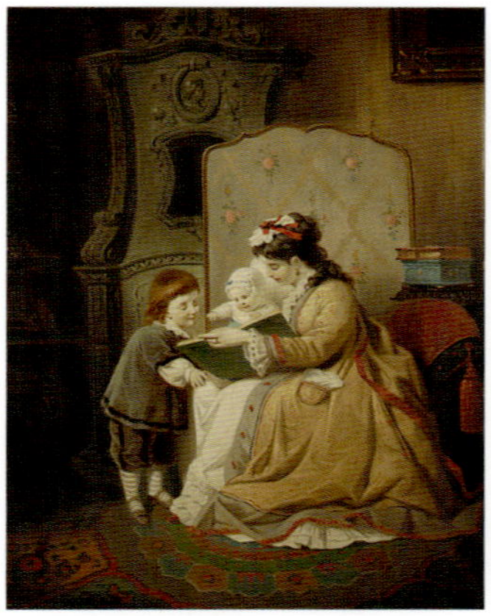

Mazastini
Interior Scene
oil on canvas 79 x 63
HAG543

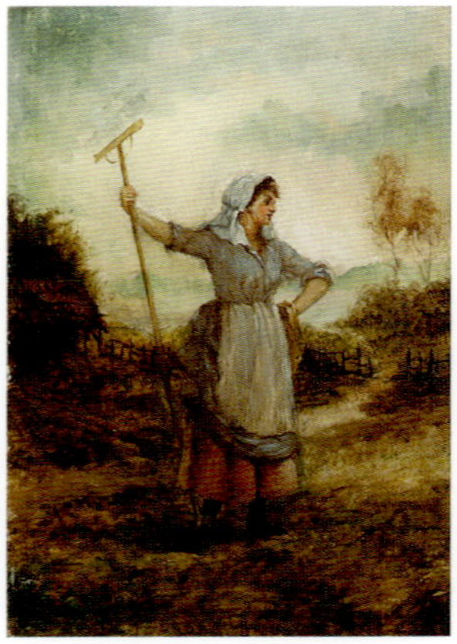

McColvin, John A. 1864–1920
A Harvest Beauty
oil on canvas 30.5 x 20.5
HAG579

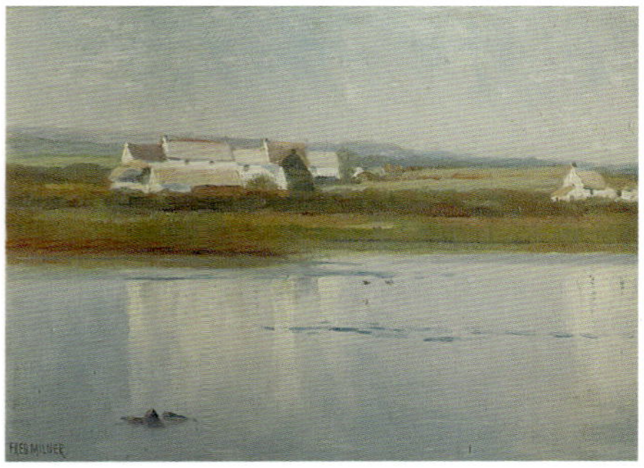

Milner, Frederick 1855–1939
At Marazion (Riverside Farm)
oil on canvas 37 x 47
HAG178

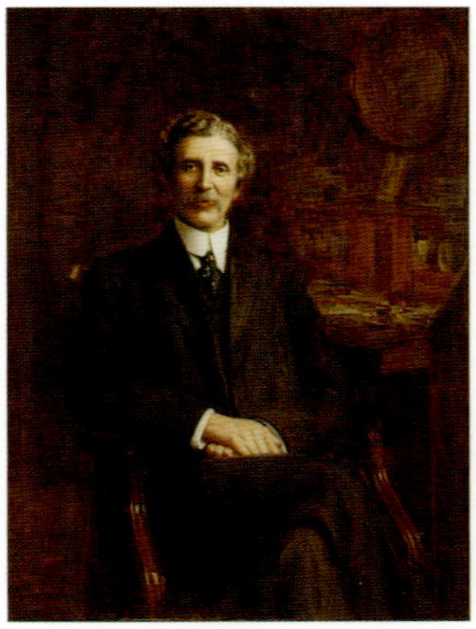

Morrison, Robert Edward 1851–1924
William Haworth, Seated
oil on canvas 126 x 100.5
HAG20

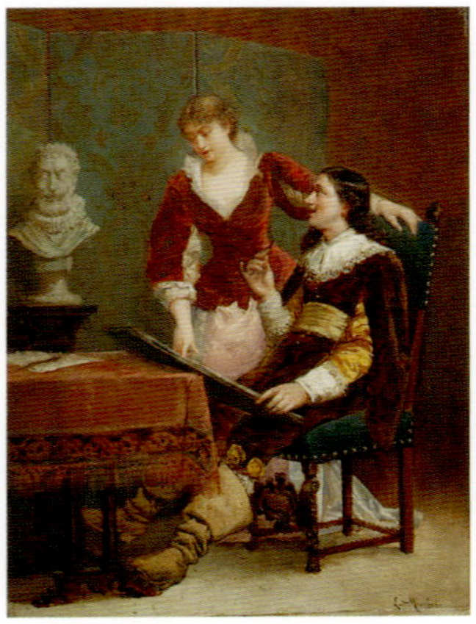

Mouchot, Louis Claude 1830–1891
The Artist's Critic
oil on canvas 40 x 31
HAG18

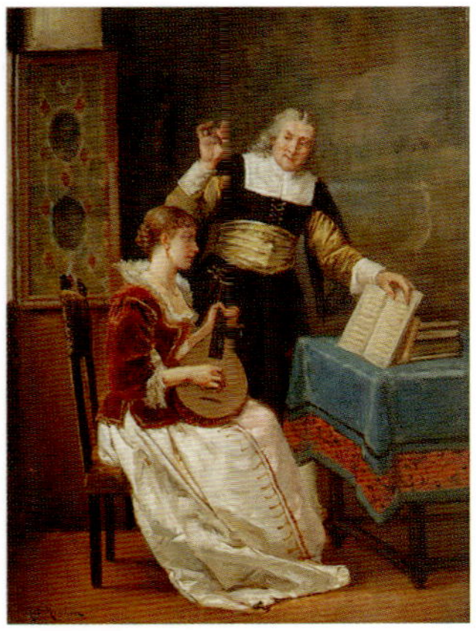

Mouchot, Louis Claude 1830–1891
The Music Master
oil on canvas 40 x 31
HAG19

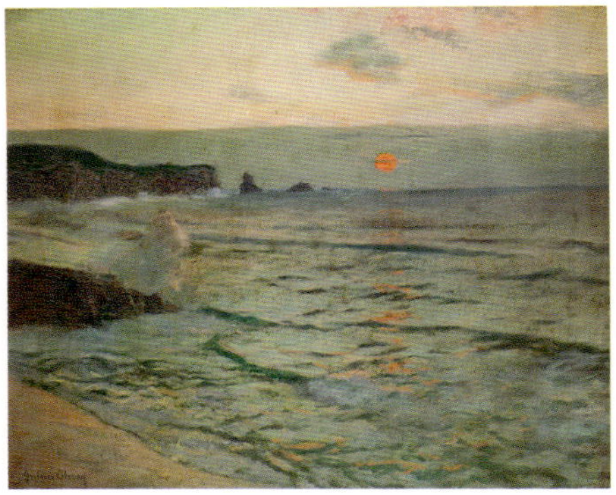

Olsson, Albert Julius 1864–1942
Incoming Tide
oil on canvas 51 x 62
HAG180

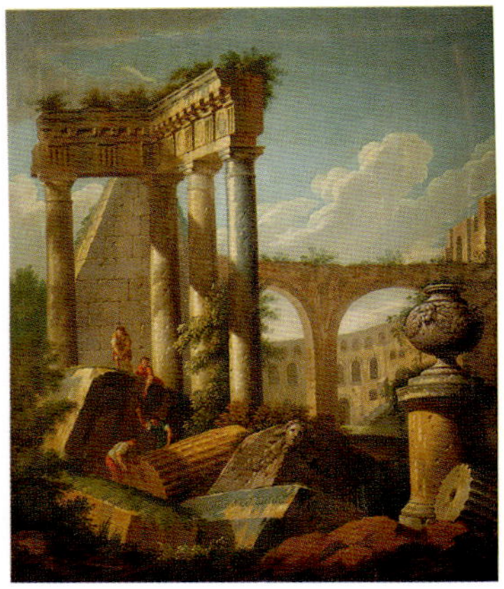

Panini, Giovanni Paolo (style of) 1691–1765
Classical Scene (Ruined Temple) 19th C
oil on canvas 76 x 64
HAG181

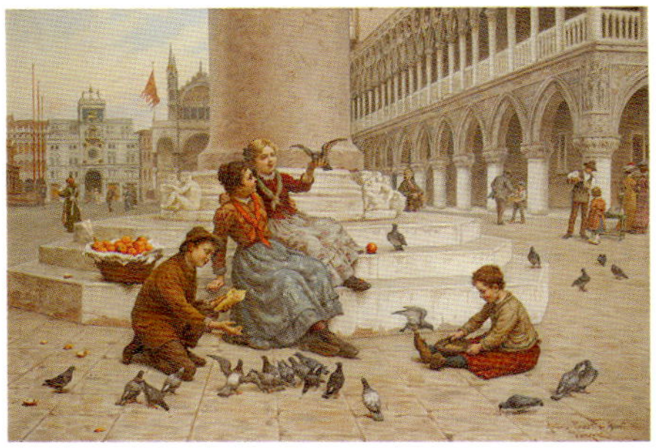

Paoletti, Antonio Ermolao 1834–1912
Pigeons of Venice
oil on canvas 61 x 86
HAG22

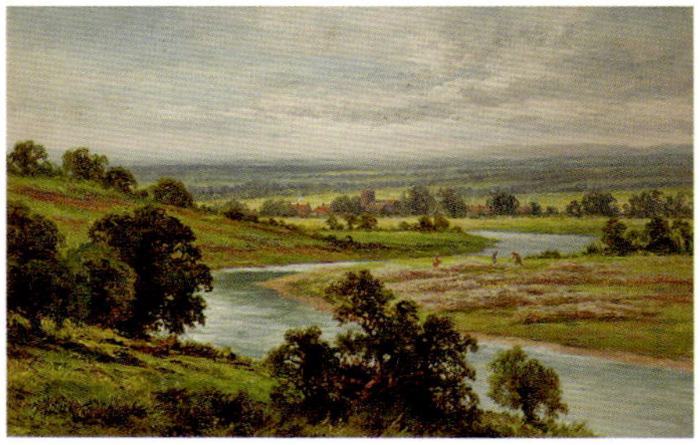

Parker, Henry H. 1858–1930
Ribchester
oil on canvas 31 x 46
HAG550

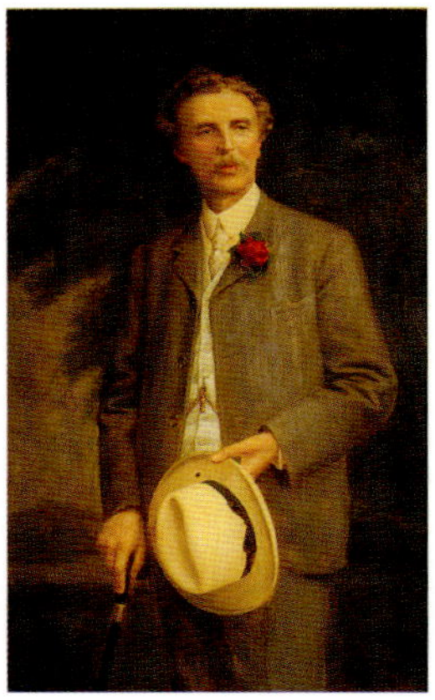

Parker, R. active late 19th C
William Haworth, Standing
oil on canvas 98 x 58.5
HAG553

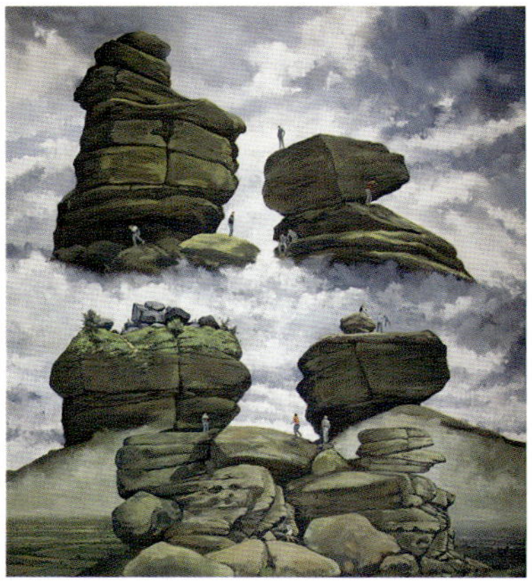

Pearson, J. Alec
Rocks with Figures
oil on canvas 103 x 93
HAG568

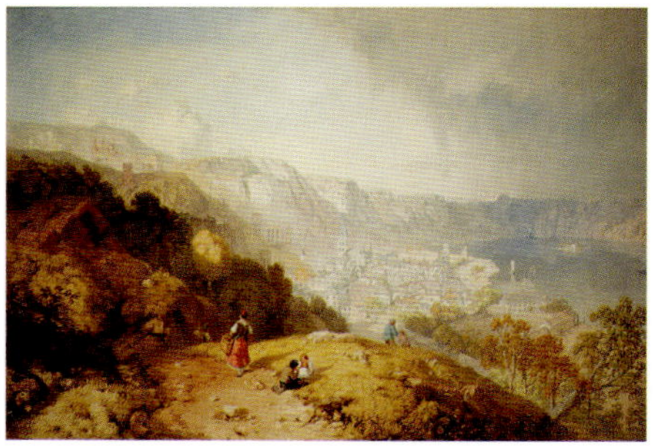

Pyne, James Baker 1800–1870
Bacharach am Rhein
oil on canvas 66 x 92
HAG264

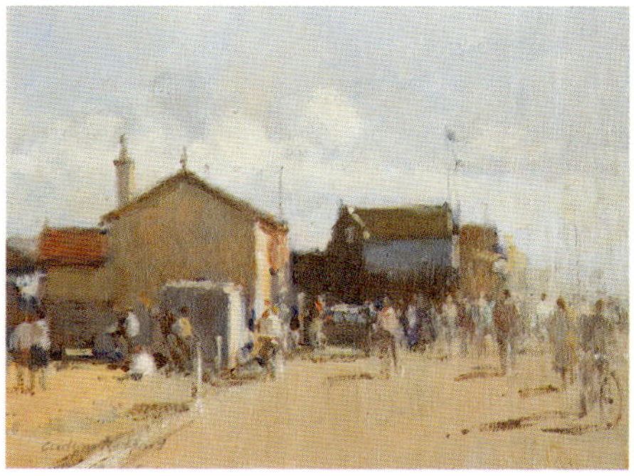

Radford, Gordon b.1936
Fleetwood
oil on canvas 19.5 x 24.5
HAGXXX21

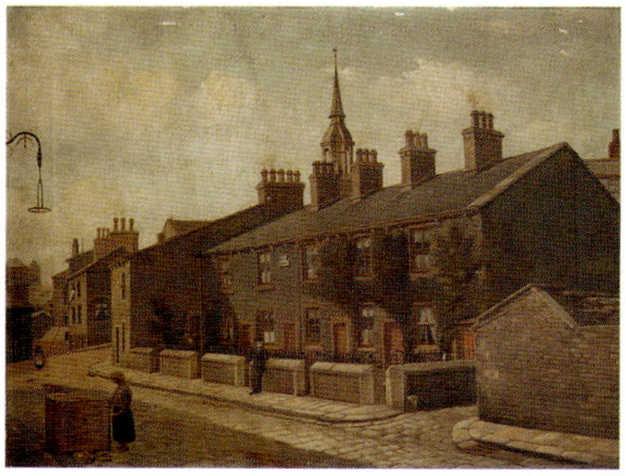

Rawsle, W.
Black Abbey Street
oil on canvas 46 x 61
HAG556

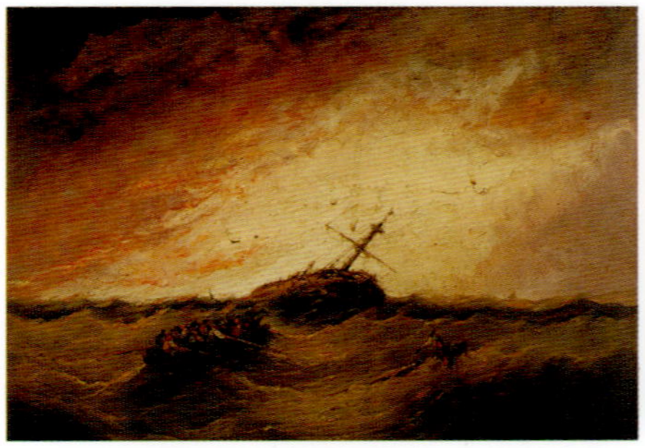

Ready, William James Durant 1823–1873
The Wreck
oil on canvas 34 x 45
HAG182

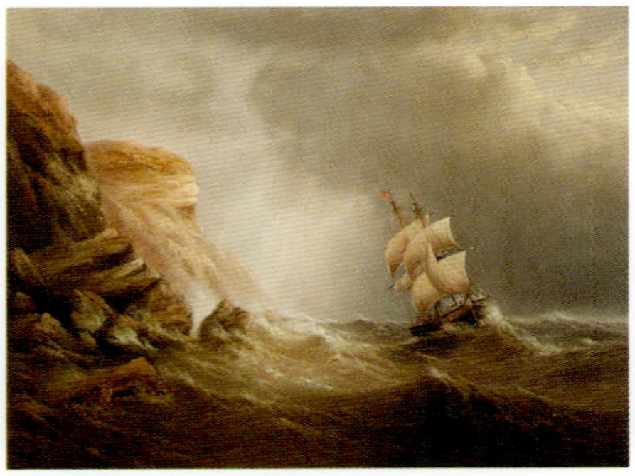

Redmore, Edward King 1860–1941
Rocky Coastal Scene
oil on canvas 64 x 83
HAG544

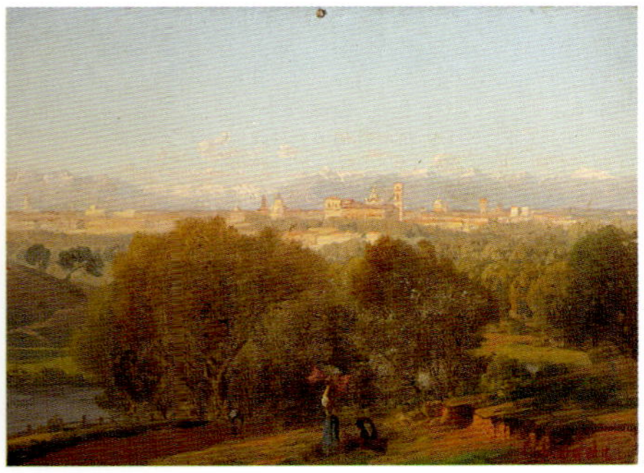

Rodde, Carl Gustav 1830–1906
A View of Rome
oil on canvas 16 x 24
HAG591

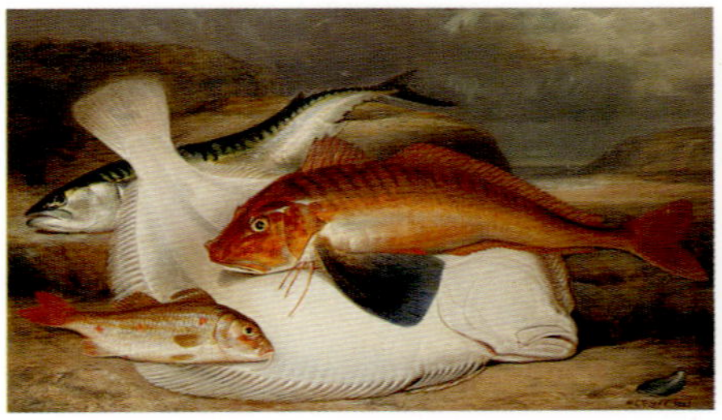

Rolfe, Henry Leonidas 1823–1881
The Catch
oil on canvas 46 x 76
HAG183

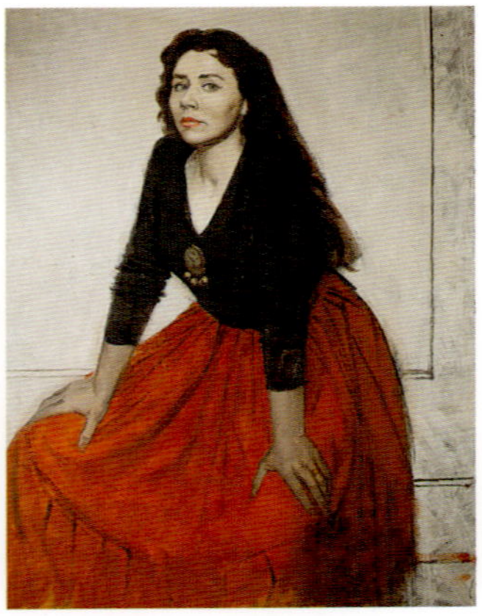

Rose, Gerard de 1918–1987
Portrait of the Artist's Wife
oil on canvas 119 x 91
HAG564

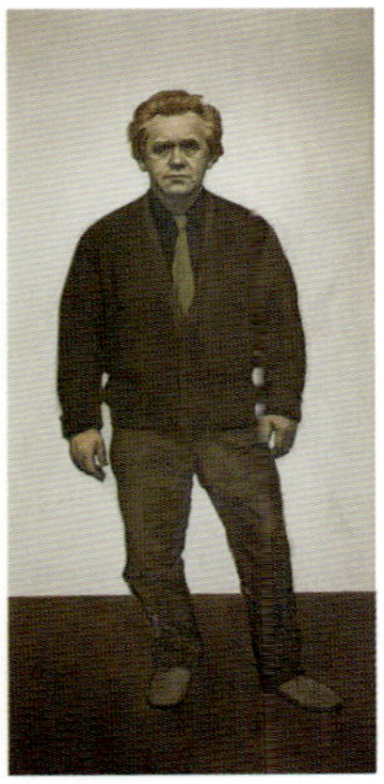

Rose, Gerard de 1918–1987
Self Portrait
oil on canvas 188 x 91.5
HAG565

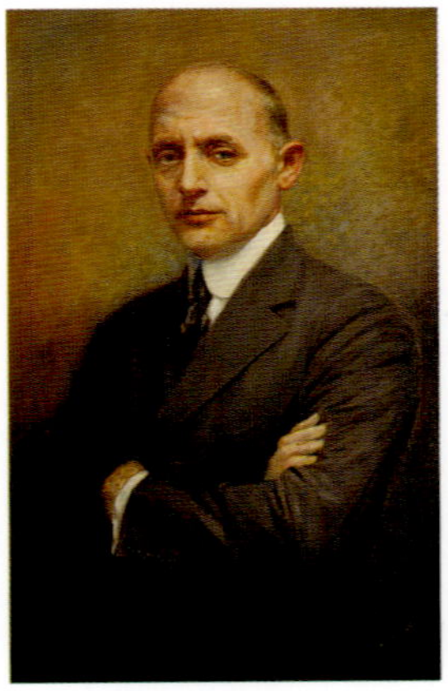

Segall, O.
Joseph Briggs (b.1873) 1924
oil on canvas 89 x 57.5
HAGXXX24

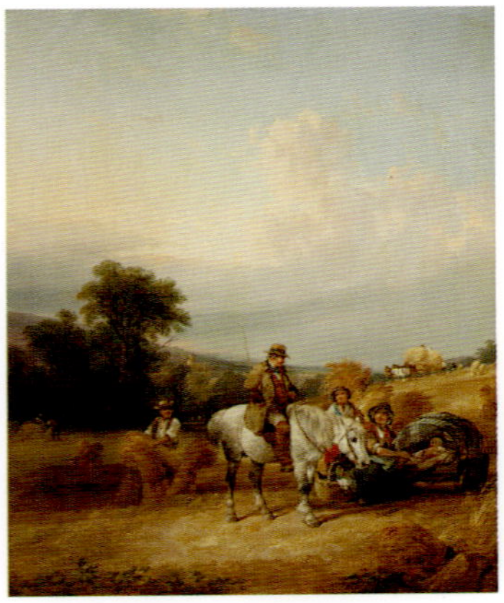

Shayer, William 1788–1879
Harvest Time 1855
oil on canvas 66 x 56
HAG9

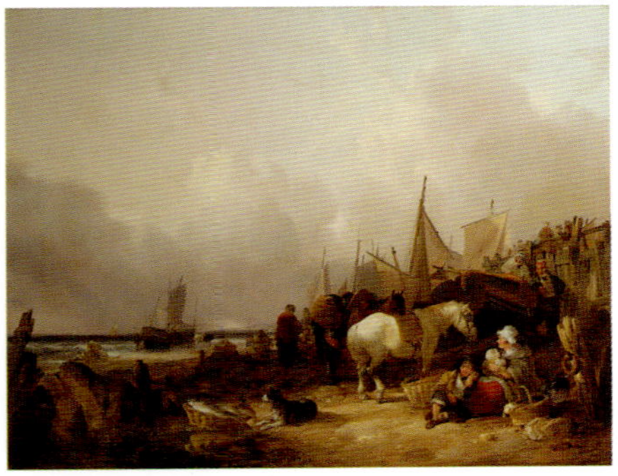

Shayer, William 1788–1879
Coast Scene with Donkey
oil on canvas 84 x 129
HAG75

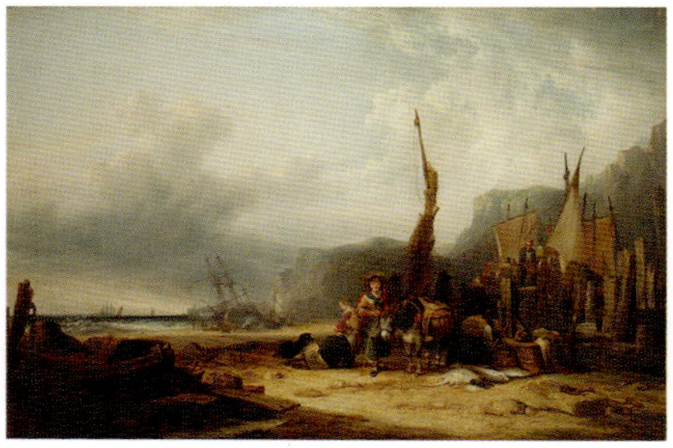

Shayer, William 1788–1879
Coast Scene with Shipping
oil on canvas 84 x 129
HAG3

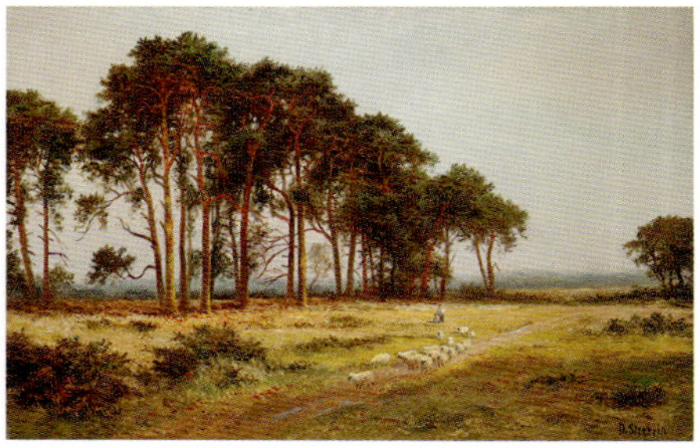

Sherrin, Daniel 1869–1940
Evening at Bletchworth
oil on canvas 50 x 76
HAG551

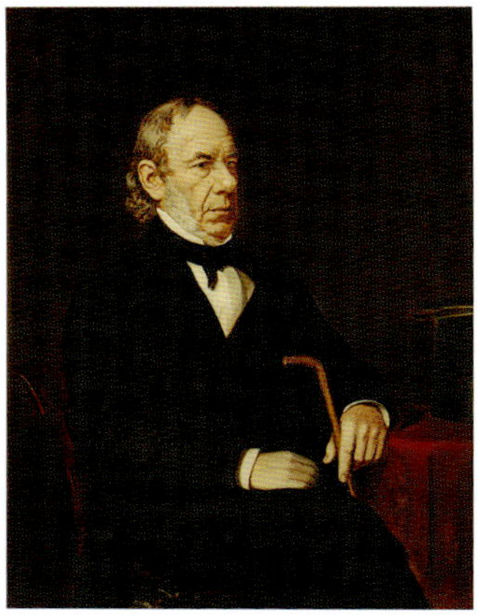

Stanesby, Alexander 1832–1916
John Mercer (1791–1866), FRS, FCS
oil on canvas 63 x 47
HAG122

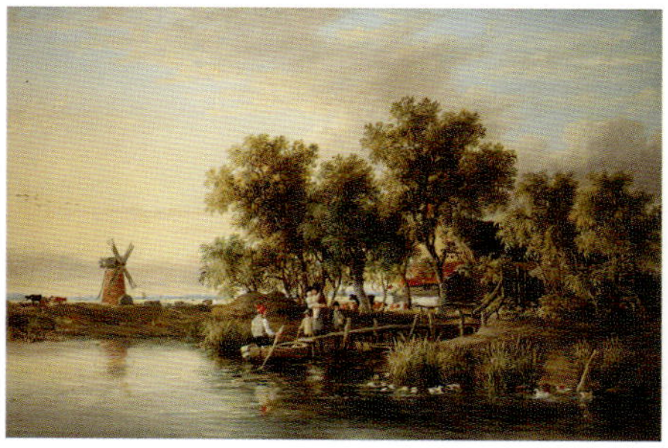

Stark, James 1794–1859
Sunlit Norfolk River Landscape
oil on canvas 37 x 51.5
HAG162

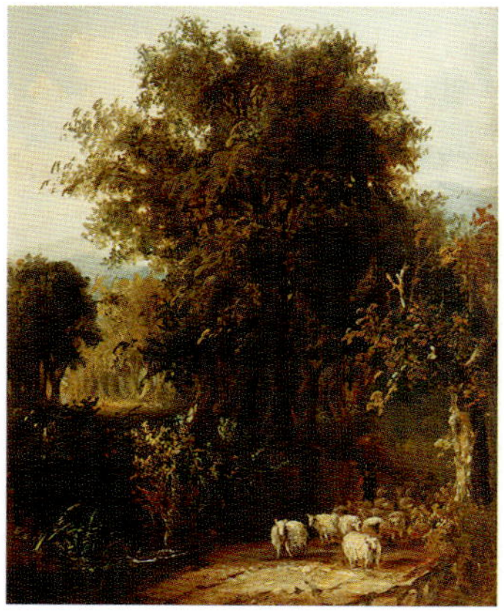

Stark, James (attributed to) 1794–1859
Norfolk Wooded Landscape
oil on canvas 41 x 35
HAG552

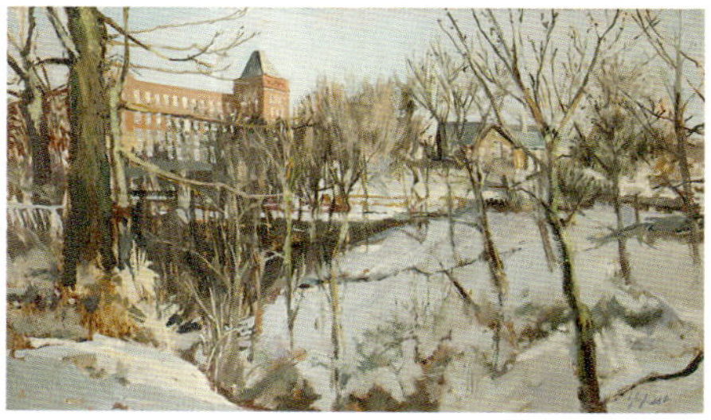

Sykes, George 1863–1933
Springhead, near Oldham
oil on canvas 35.5 x 60
HAGXXX28

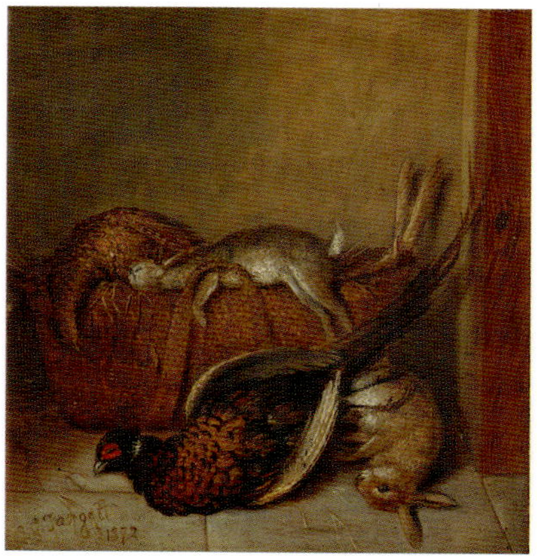

Tarquett, I. G.
Nature morte 1872
oil on canvas 23 x 21.5
HAG574

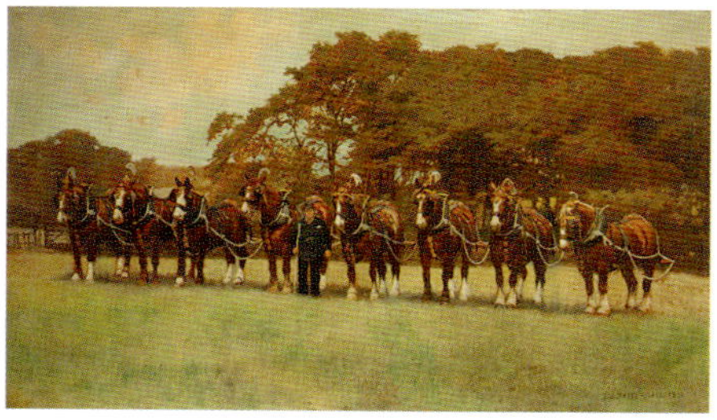

Tattersall, James Weaver 1837–1927
Shire Horses 1896
oil on canvas 76 x 133
HAG563

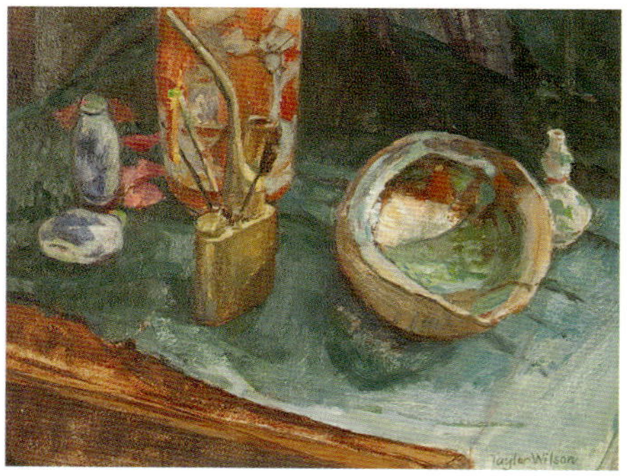

Taylor Wilson, Joanne b.1953
Oriental Still Life 1980
oil on canvas 28.5 x 35.5
HAGXXX30

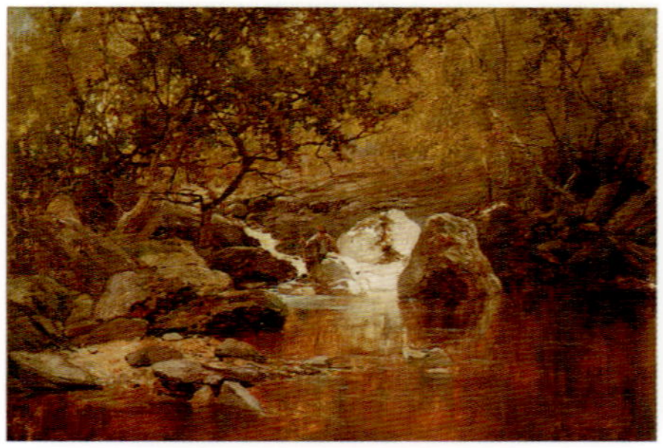

Townshend, James 1879–1949
A Salmon Pool
oil on canvas 50.5 x 76
HAG184

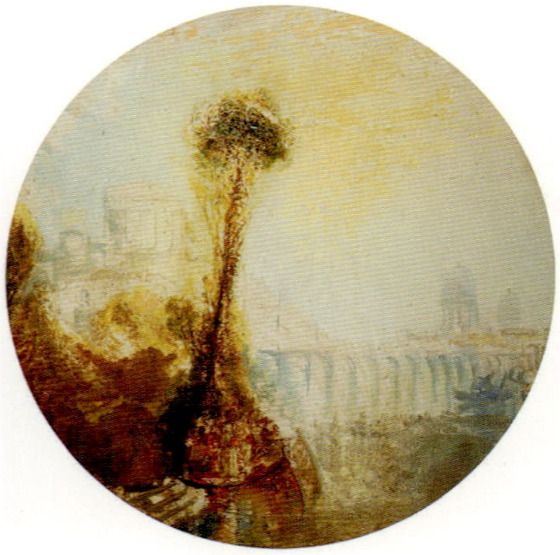

Turner, Joseph Mallord William (after) 1775–1851
Venetian Scene 20th C
oil on canvas 46 x 40
HAG185

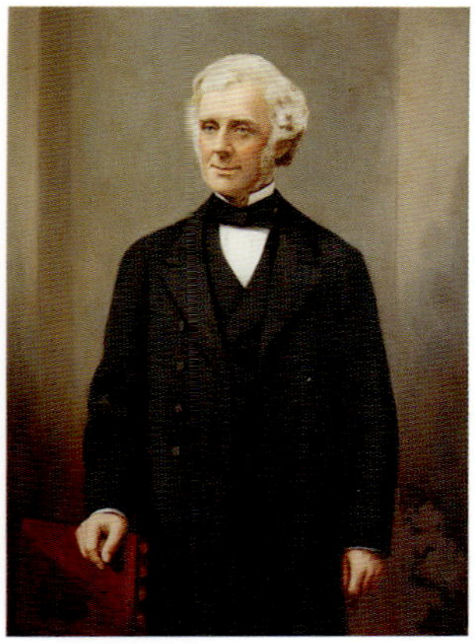

unknown artist
Mr J. Haworth
oil on canvas 64 x 47.5
HAG49A

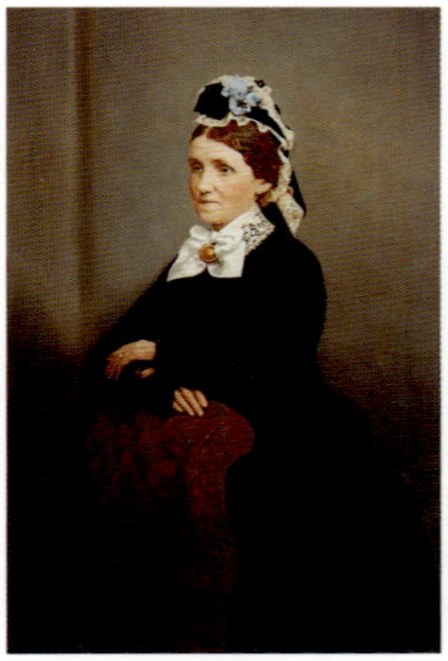

unknown artist
Mrs J. Haworth
oil on canvas 59.5 x 39
HAG49B

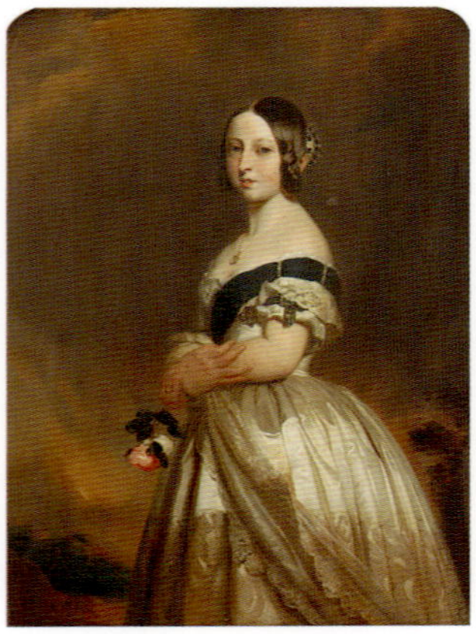

unknown artist
Queen Victoria (1819–1901)
oil on canvas 120 x 90 (E)
HAGXXX1

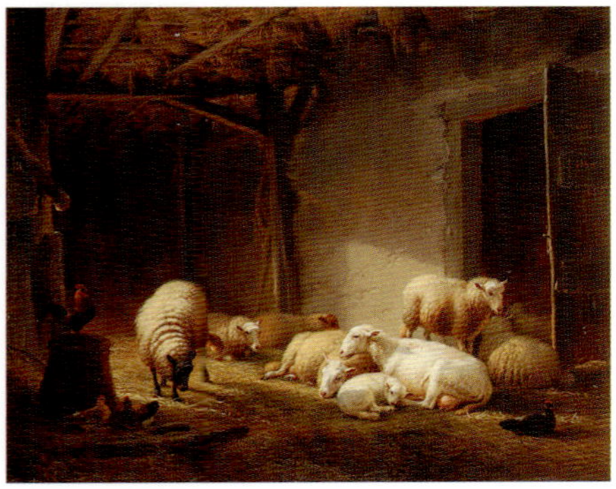

Verboeckhoven, Eugène Joseph 1798–1881
A Sunlit Barn with Ewes, Lambs and Chickens
oil on canvas 27 x 34
HAG10

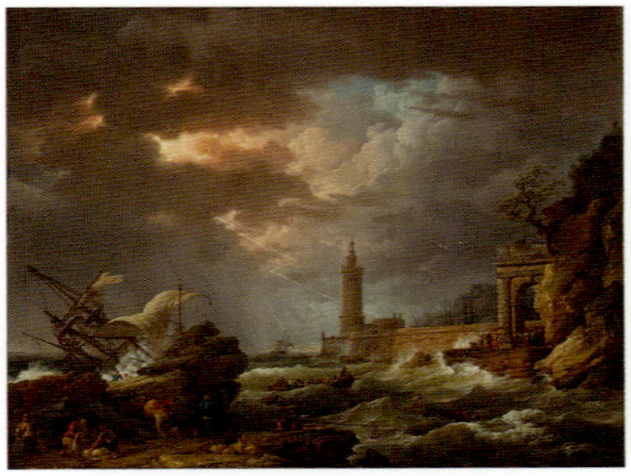

Vernet, Claude-Joseph 1714–1789
The Tempest (Storm off the Coast) 1754
oil on canvas 91.5 x 124.5
HAG81

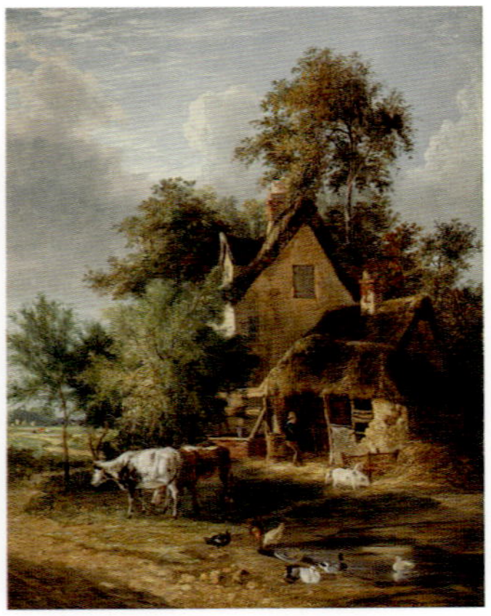

Vincent, George 1796–1831
Farmyard Scene
oil on canvas 56 x 46
HAG157

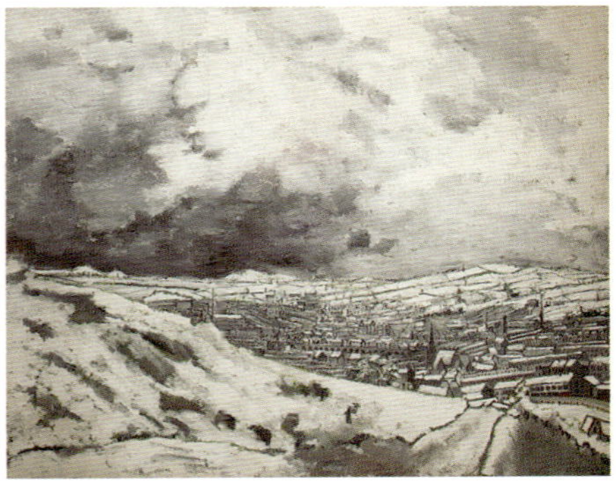

Virtue, John b.1947
Accrington from the Coppice
oil on canvas 122 x 153
HAG572

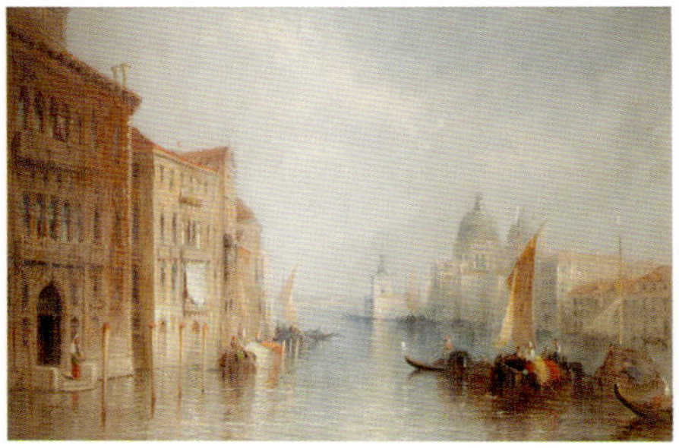

Vivian, Jane active 1861–1877
The Grand Canal, Venice
oil on canvas 51 x 86.5
HAG6

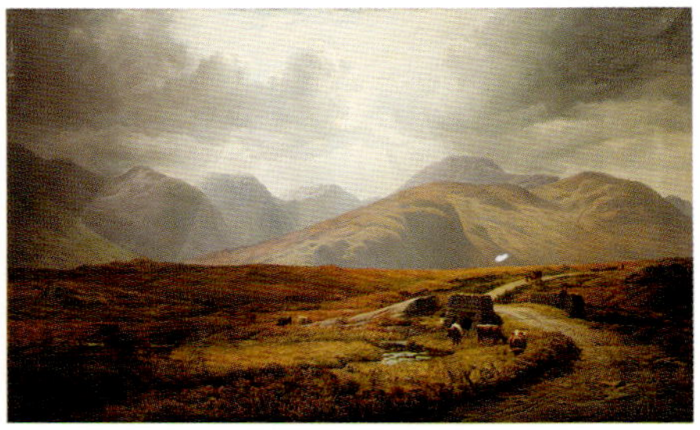

Watkins, Bartholomew Colles 1833–1891
Connemara
oil on canvas 82 x 137
HAGXXX3

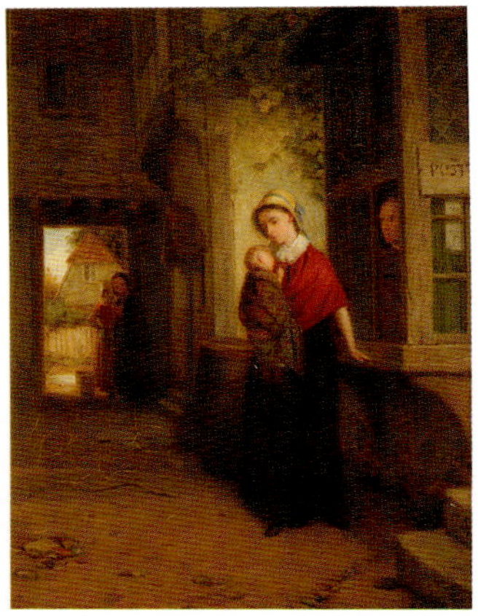

Webster, Thomas George 1800–1886
The Post Office (Hope Deferred Makes the Heart Sick)
oil on canvas 39.9 x 31.5 (E)
HAG12

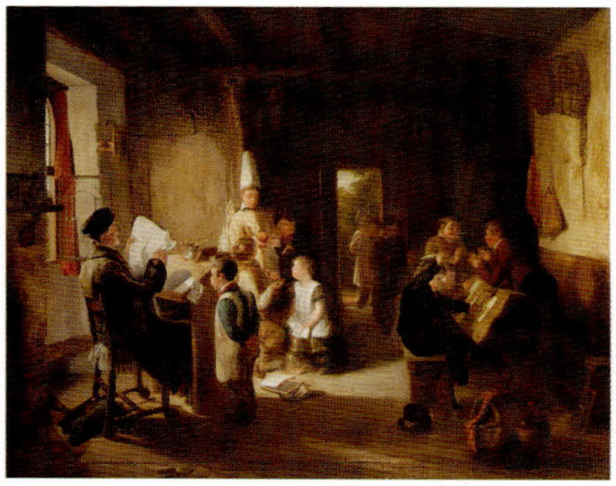

Webster, Thomas George 1800–1886
The School Room
oil on canvas 70.5 x 91.5
HAG2

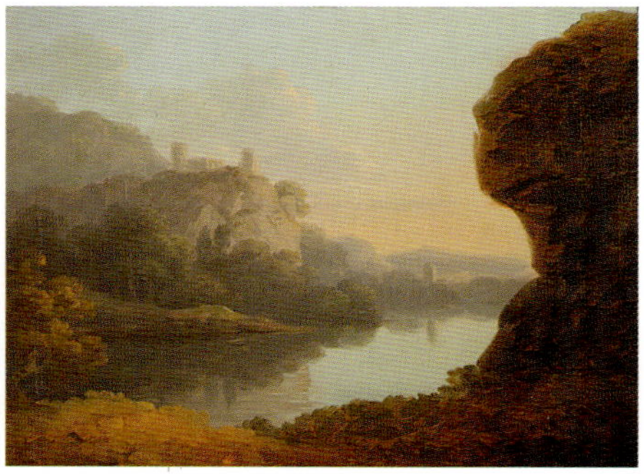

Wilson, Richard (school of) 1712–1782
Castle near Lake
oil on canvas 29.5 x 39.5
HAG186

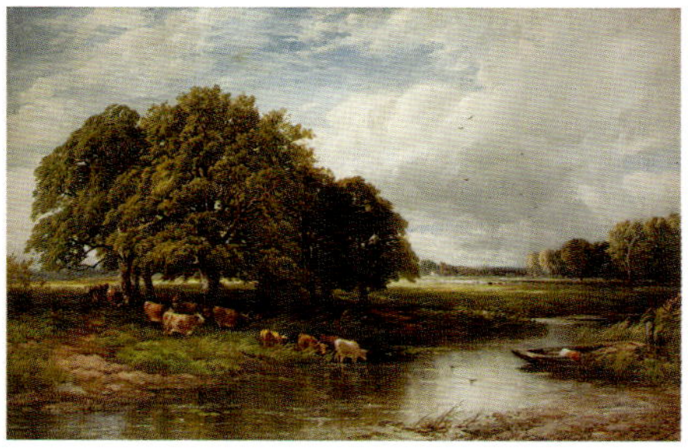

Wimperis, Edmund Morison 1835–1900
Summertime
oil on canvas 82.5 x 133.5
HAG4

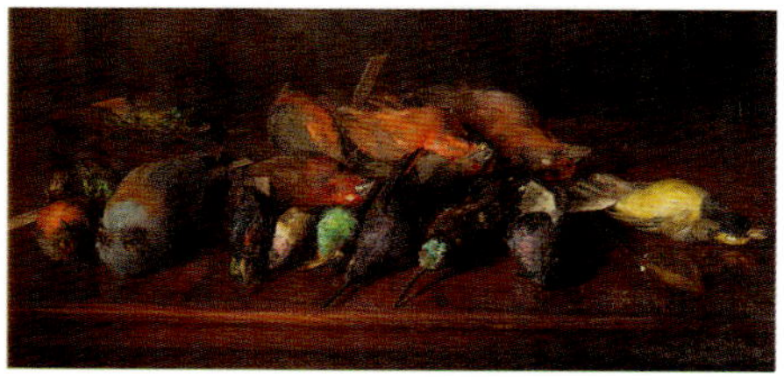

Wood, C. M.
At the Taxidermist
oil on canvas 20.5 x 41
HAG187

Facing page: Gunn, Herbert James, 1893–1964, *Pauline in the Yellow Dress*, 1944, Harris Museum & Art Gallery (p. 306)

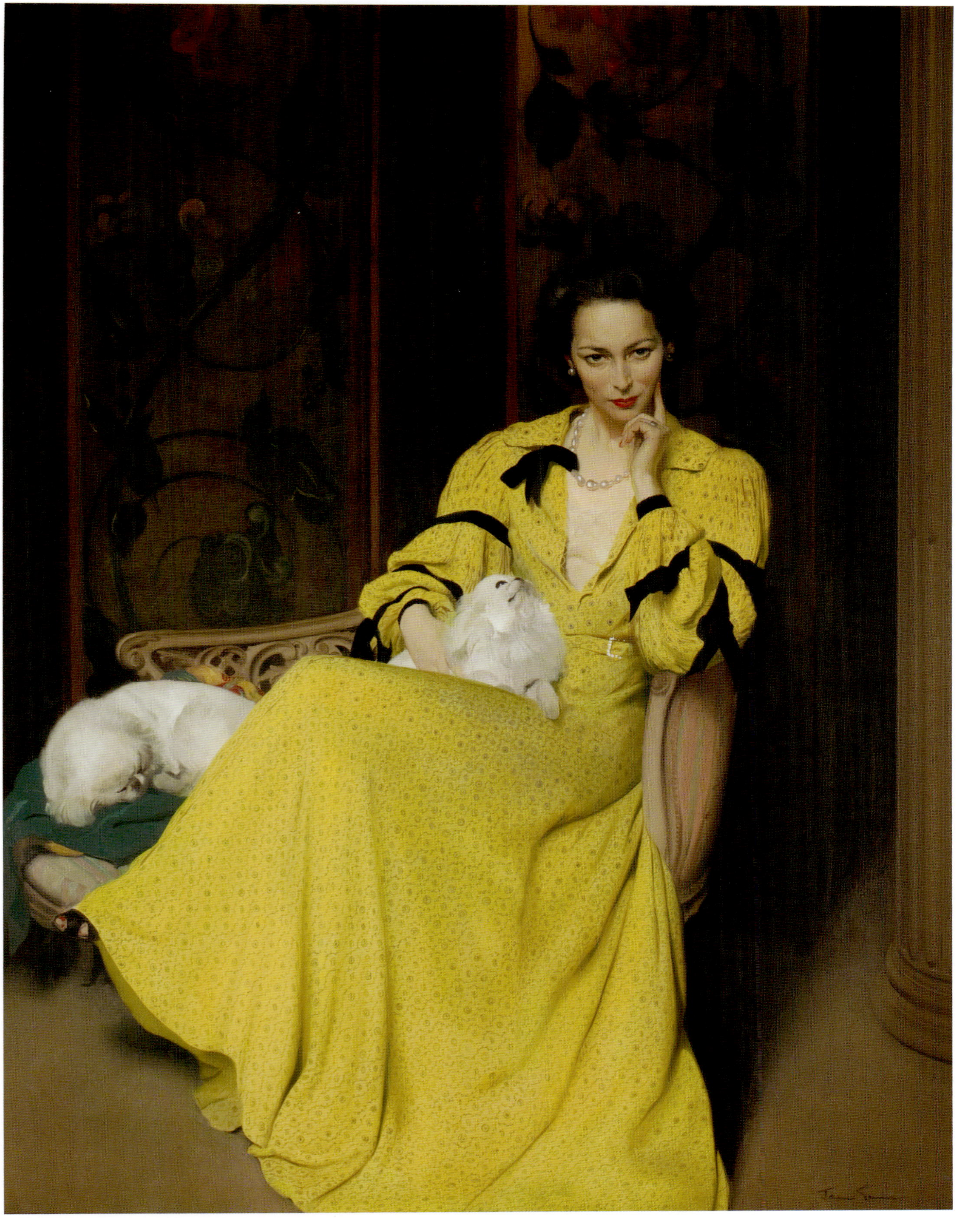

Blackburn Museum and Art Gallery

To outsiders Blackburn might be better known for the adventures of its football team rather than for its place in history as one of the greatest weaving capitals in the world. Weaving transformed what was a small market town into a bustling industrial heartland. The rich collections now housed at Blackburn Museum and Art Gallery were born from the proceeds of this industry and the generosity of its industrialists.

Inspired by the town's motto, 'Arte et Labore' (meaning 'by skill and labour'), the town council and local worthies instigated and funded a museum and library. A competition to design the Museum was won by London architects Woodzell and Colcutt with a Victorian gothic design called 'Knowledge is Power'. Opened in 1874, it was one of the earliest museums amongst Blackburn's industrial neighbours including Preston, Oldham and Bury. Aptly, the Museum's first purchase in 1875 was *Laying the Foundation Stone to the Cotton Exchange, Blackburn* by Russian artist Vladimir Ossipovitch Sherwood.

Wealthy industrial families bequeathed and donated artworks and funds to establish a permanent collection to give back to the town that made them millionaires. The first such bequest was the Dodgson Bequest in 1884 of 59 priceless artworks (in various media) which included works by artists such as J. M. W Turner, David Cox and Myles Birket Foster.

The economic fortunes of the town were undoubtedly reflected in the Museum and in 1894 an extension was added to accommodate more galleries for a loan exhibition, which included works by artists such as Frederic Leighton and John Everett Millais. Of the 315 exhibits, 54 were Blackburn's, indicating that a budding collection was being established.

Perhaps the greatest influence on the quality of art at Blackburn can be credited to Richard Haworth, a reputable local art dealer who also served the neighbouring authorities of Accrington and Burnley. His discerning taste dictated what art was sold to Blackburn's shrewd nouveau riche, some of which later became museum donations or bequests. Haworth was also a key figure in negotiating competitive prices for the Museum, sometimes directly from the artist.

Many of the paintings in the Collection reflect the morals, taste, ideals and religious conviction of the Victorian public. Its strength lies in its representation of British art as a whole, rather than one school or style. The Collection ranges from the Regency, represented by Marcus C. Stone's *Two's Company, Three's None*, to maritime subjects such as Henry Moore's *Rough Weather in the Mediterranean*, to genre paintings by artists such as John and Frederick Morgan. Two of the best moralist paintings are Edwin Long's *Diana or Christ?* depicting an attractive young woman forced by Roman guards to choose certain death if she does not renounce Christianity by offering incense to a statue of Diana, and *Hetty Sorrel* by John Collier. The latter, donated in 1894, was inspired by George Elliot's novel *Adam Bede*; it depicts the vain but weak heroine who runs away from her unwanted baby, which she abandons in a forest.

There are sporting subjects, such as Alfred Munnings's '*Solario*', depicting a locally owned racehorse, and classical and Pre-Raphaelite artworks, represented by Albert Moore and one of his greatest and certainly largest paintings, *The Loves of the Winds and the Seasons.* Moore dedicated his final three years to representing and telling the story of the seasons as a metaphor about love, and their eternal and necessary cycle for life. The painting is a tragic irony as Moore, a lonely reclusive bachelor, died from cancer just days after finishing it.

Perhaps the best known painting at Blackburn is Frederic Leighton's *Mother and Child*, or 'Cherries' as it is more affectionately known, referring to the sweet child feeding her mother ruby red cherries. A lesser-known but exceptionally important and much treasured painting is by James Sharples, a smith turned self-taught artist. His painting *The Forge* is one of the few in art history which depicts the Victorian workplace fuelling the Industrial Revolution and is even rarer for having been painted by a smith. The atmospherically dark canvas is only illuminated by the roaring forge fire which glows orange on the faces of the blacksmiths.

There are also many popular British artists represented in the Collection, such as Richard Ansdell, David Murray, Thomas Faed and Edmund Morison Wimperis. A few nineteenth-century foreign artists are represented including Rosa Bonheur, Eugène Joseph Verboeckhoven and Julien Gustave Gagliardini. The Collection also contains a small number of Old Masters including works by Joshua Reynolds, William Hogarth, Godfrey Kneller and Giovanni Francesco Grimaldi.

Over the course of its history the Museum has built up other substantial and, in some instances, world class collections. There are fine watercolours by local and contemporary artists and by well-known Victorian artists such as Thomas Girtin, Samuel Prout, William Hunt and John Frederick Lewis. Undoubtedly, one of the best collections is the extraordinary Hart Collection of priceless books, manuscripts and numismatics bequeathed in 1946 by Edward Hart. When not overseeing operations at the family business, Lambeth Rope Works, Hart secretly built up a collection of 6,000 rare coins (mainly ancient Greek and Roman) and over 500 exceptional books – Hart's lifetime's work and specialism. Other notable collections include the Thomas Boys Lewis Collection of Japanese woodblock prints (approximately 1,000) and the second largest collection of Eastern European and Russian Icons in the UK (58), many of which were seized by Customs and Excise when they were smuggled into the country from Eastern Europe and, subsequently, they were donated to Blackburn.

After the First World War, Blackburn slipped steadily into industrial decline. The cotton mills which once dominated the landscape have long been demolished, but the rich collections at the Museum serve as a legacy and reminder of the proceeds of weaving cotton and its ancillary industries.

In recent decades, especially with the assistance of the Friends of Blackburn Museum and Art Gallery, both old and new paintings with a local provenance are actively being collected to record and reflect for posterity the changes the Borough has already witnessed.

Vanessa Mitchell, Curator of Art

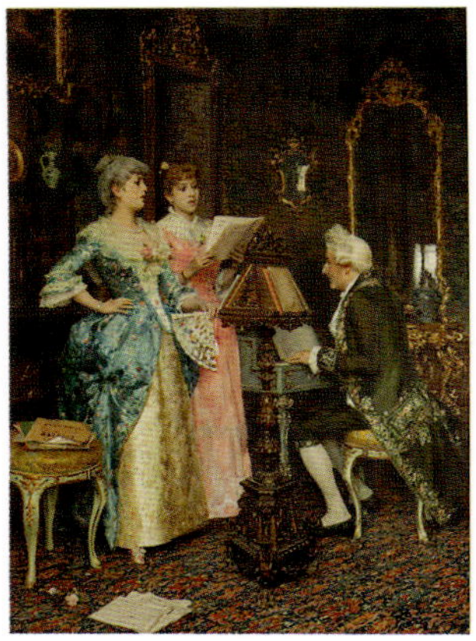

Andreotti, Federico 1847–1930
The Music Lesson late 19th C
oil on canvas 101.6 x 76.2
140

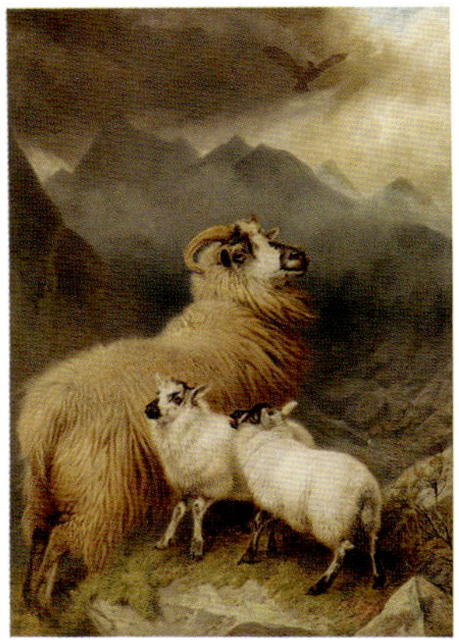

Ansdell, Richard 1815–1885
Spring Passing Clouds, Isle of Skye 1883
oil on canvas 139.7 x 106.7 (E)
239

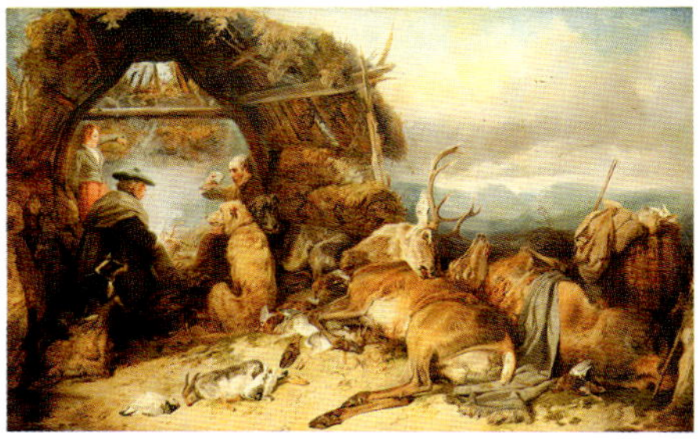

Ansdell, Richard 1815–1885
Highland Bothy c.1883
oil on canvas 107 x 183
237

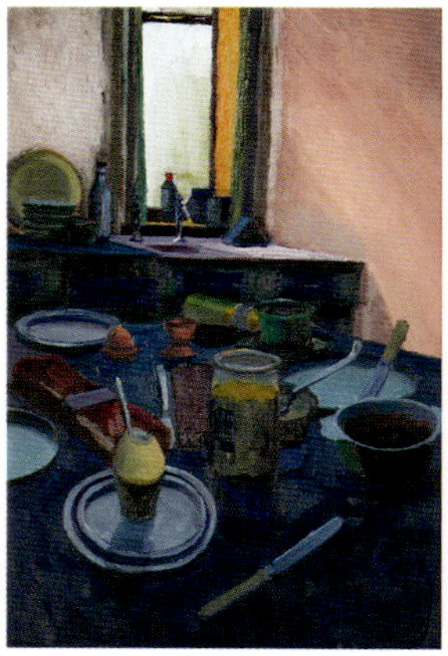

Arkwright, Peter David active 1960s
7 O'Clock
oil on canvas 90 x 60
620

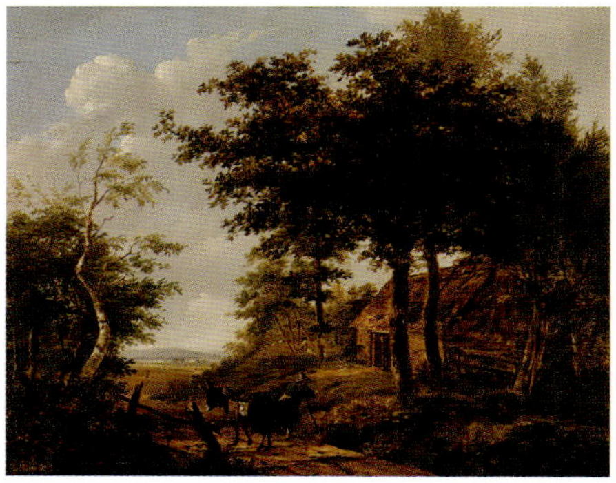

Asch, Pieter Jansz. van (attributed to the circle of) 1603–1678
Landscape
oil on canvas 40 x 50
607

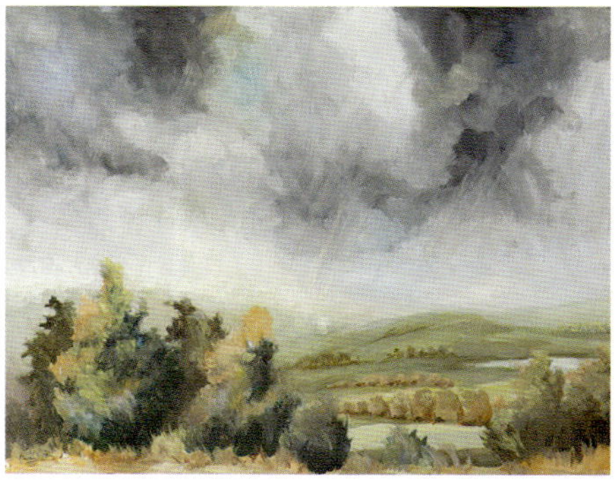

Bahia, Isam active 2000–2008
Stormy Weather, Dean Clough Reservoir 2000
oil on canvas 80 x 99.5
2007.9

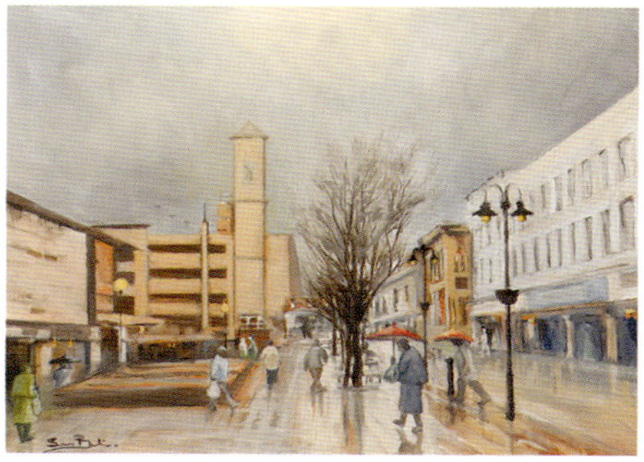

Bahia, Isam active 2000–2008
King William Street, Blackburn 2008
oil on canvas 48 x 68
2008.26

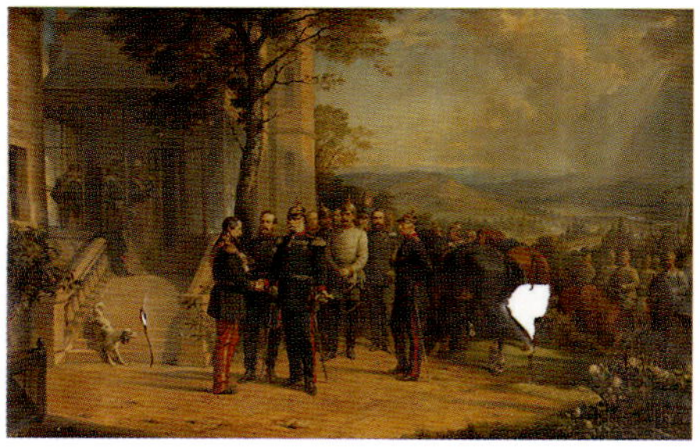

Barker, Thomas Jones 1815–1882
Surrender of Napoleon III at the Battle of Sedan 1870
oil on canvas 169 x 264
2008.54

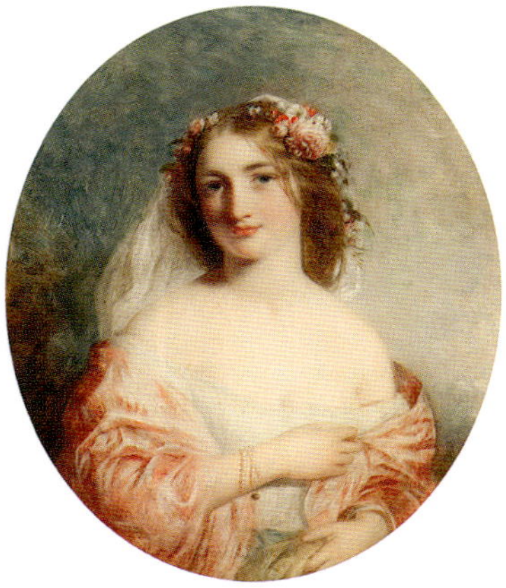

Baxter, Charles 1809–1879
The Blonde
oil on panel 25 x 22
41

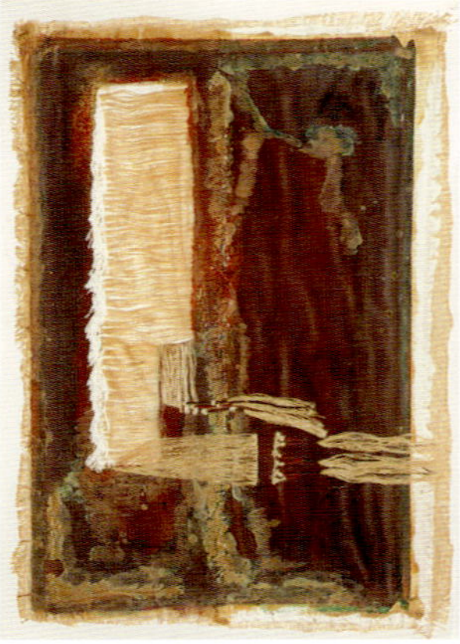

Beattie, Katherine active late 20th C
Unwoven Piece
oil, gum & hemp on canvas (?) 99.6 x 73
1098

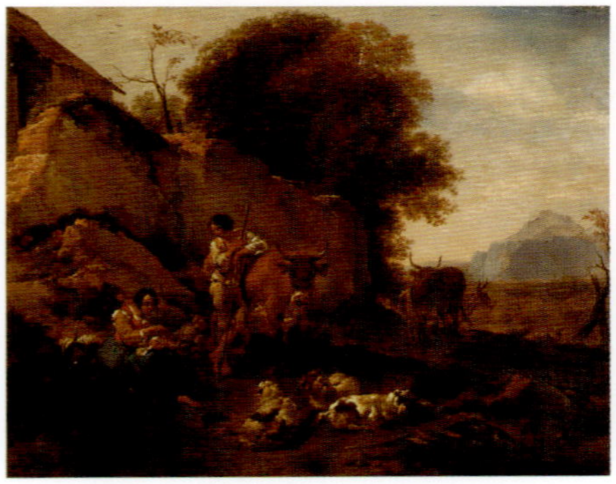

Berchem, Nicolaes 1620–1683
Pastoral Landscape
oil on panel 34.2 x 45.5
592

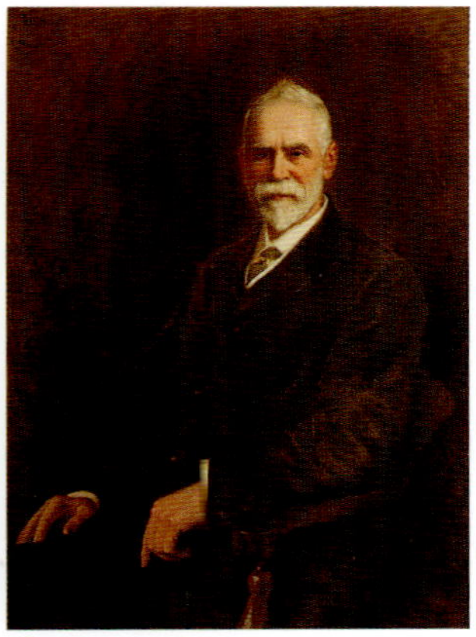

Bertieri, Pilade 1874–1965
Sir Edwin Hamer, Kt, Mayor of Blackburn (1899) early 20th C
oil on canvas 111 x 85
TH. 30

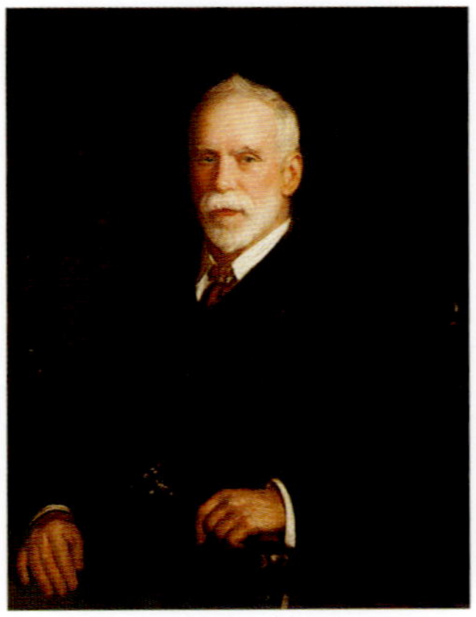

Beulley, J. M. active 1911–1914
Alderman Edwin Hamer, JP (Blackburn) 1911
oil on canvas 90 x 70
TH.13

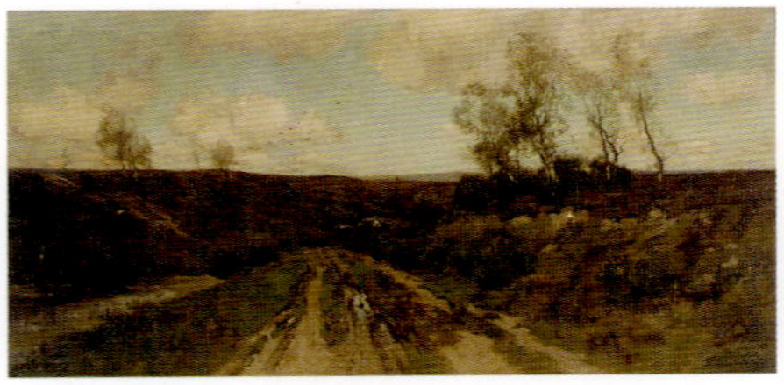

Bock, Théophile de 1851–1904
The Heath 1879
oil on canvas 90 x 193
99

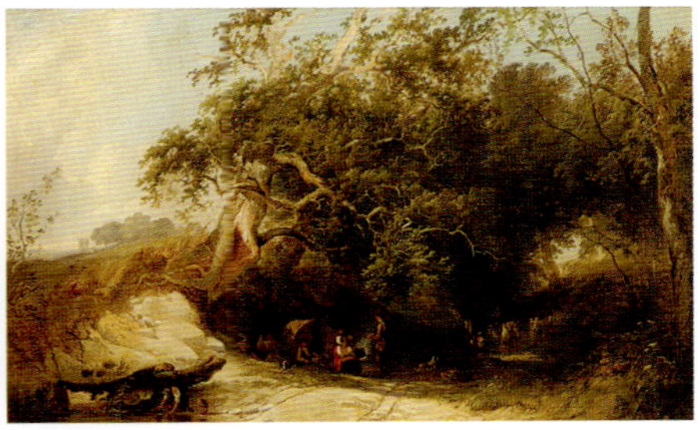

Boddington, Henry John 1811–1865
Gipsy Encampment
oil on canvas 45 x 82
78

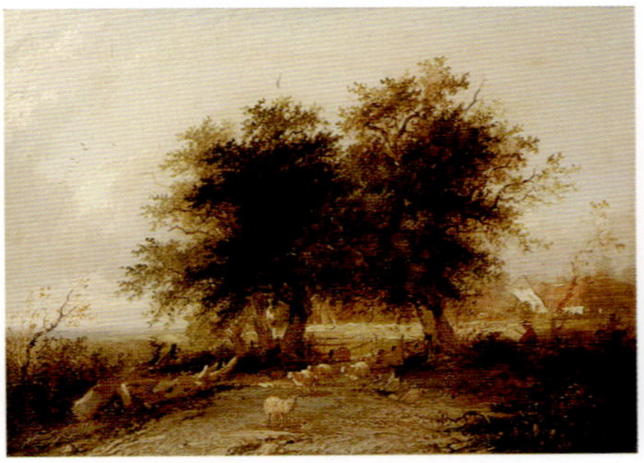

Boddington, Henry John 1811–1865
Landscape
oil on canvas 22.9 x 33
42

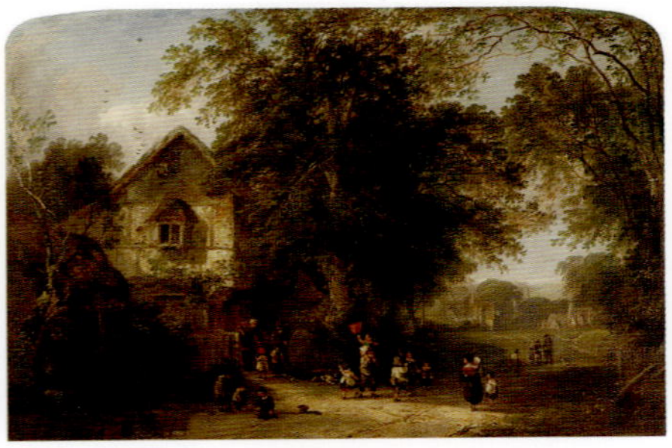

Boddington, Henry John 1811–1865
The Half Holiday
oil on canvas 60 x 88
236

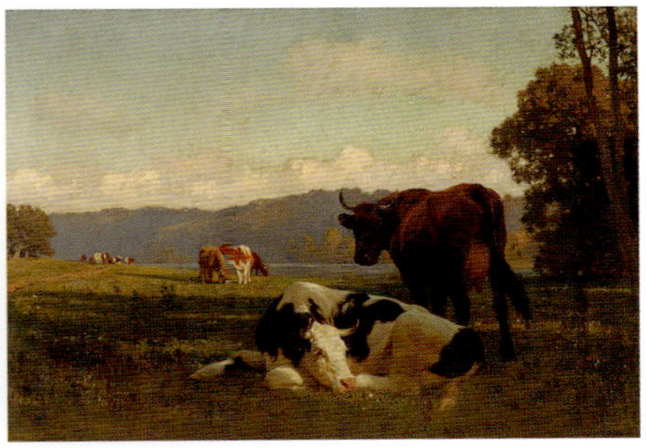

Bonheur, Auguste-François 1824–1884
Cattle on Riverbank in Auvergne late 19th C
oil on canvas 97.8 x 137.2
141

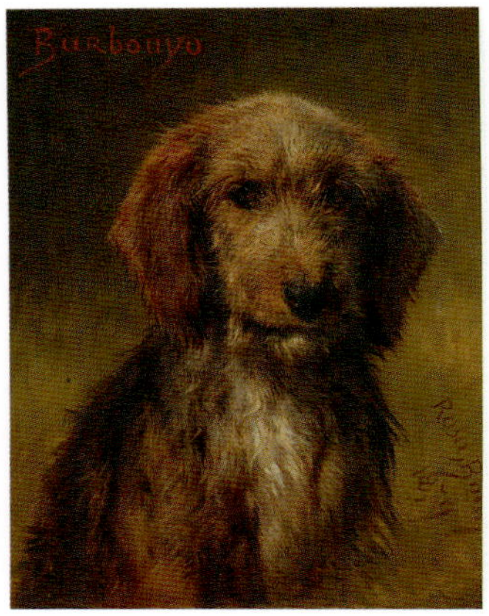

Bonheur, Rosa 1822–1899
'Barbouyo' 1879
oil on canvas 48.8 x 36.9
125

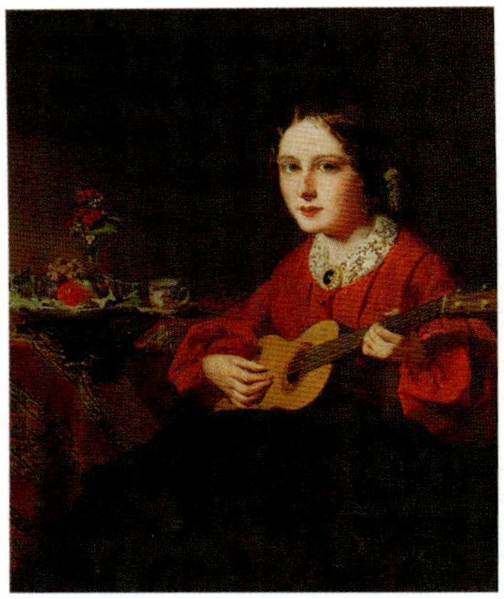

Bostock, John 1808–1872
The Rehearsal
oil on panel 53 x 42
43

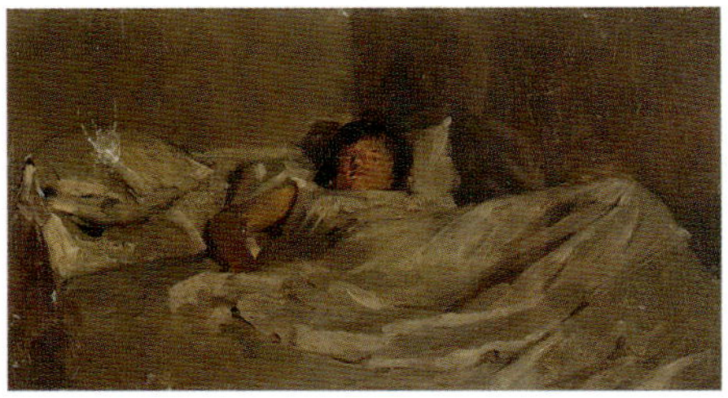

Boutigny, Paul Émile 1854–1929
Study, Female Figure
oil on panel 13.5 x 25.4
333

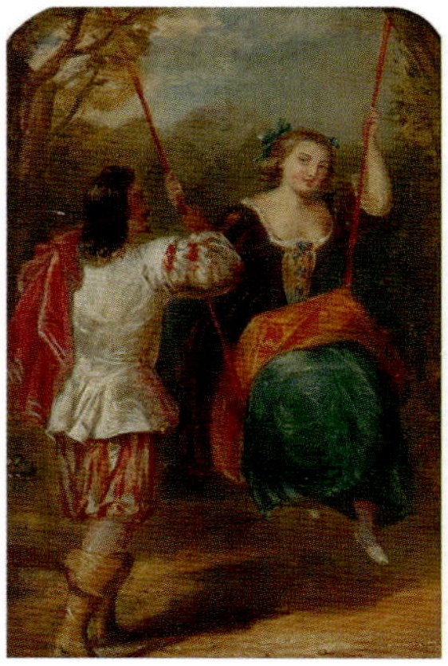

Bouvier, Augustus Jules 1825–1881
The Swing
oil on panel 19 x 14
44

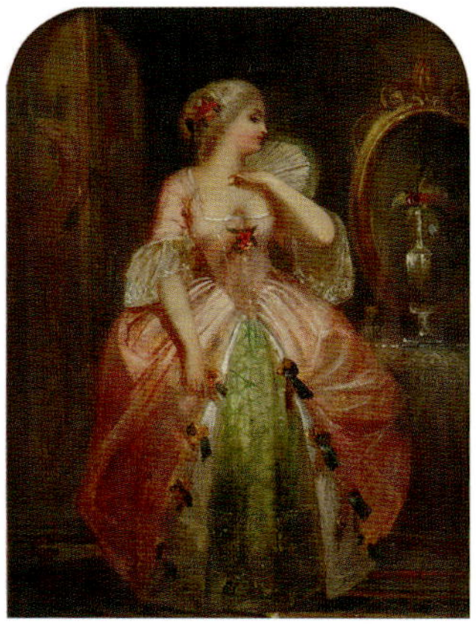

Bouvier, Augustus Jules 1825–1881
The Toilet
oil on canvas 19 x 14
45

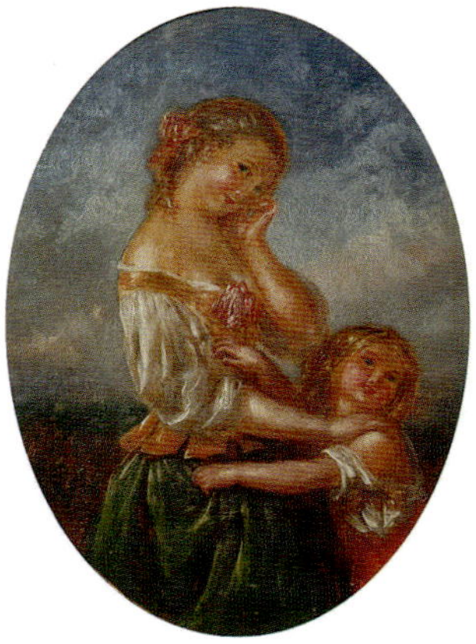

Bouvier, Joseph 1827–1914
Figure Subject (recto)
oil on canvas 19 x 14
47

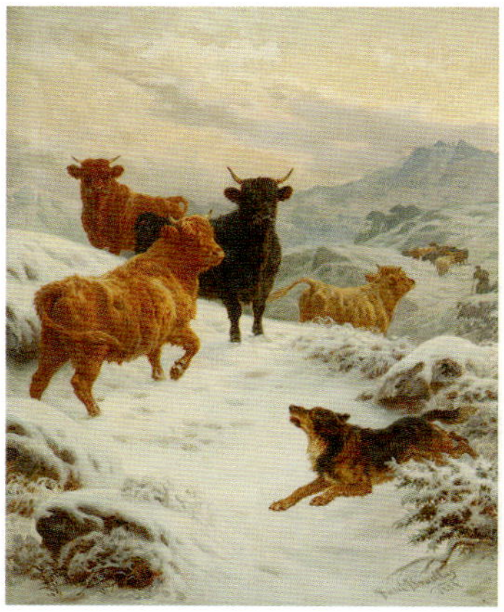

Bradley, Basil 1842–1904
Scotch Rebels 1887
oil on panel 91.4 x 71.2 (E)
69

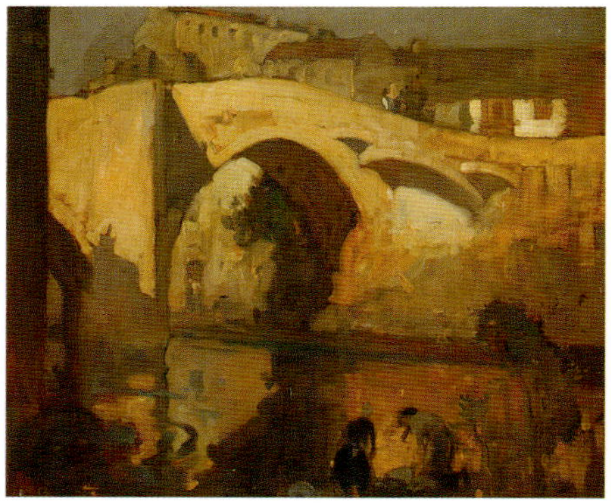

Brangwyn, Frank 1867–1956
Gothic Bridge at Barnard Castle, Yorkshire
oil on canvas 74 x 102
270

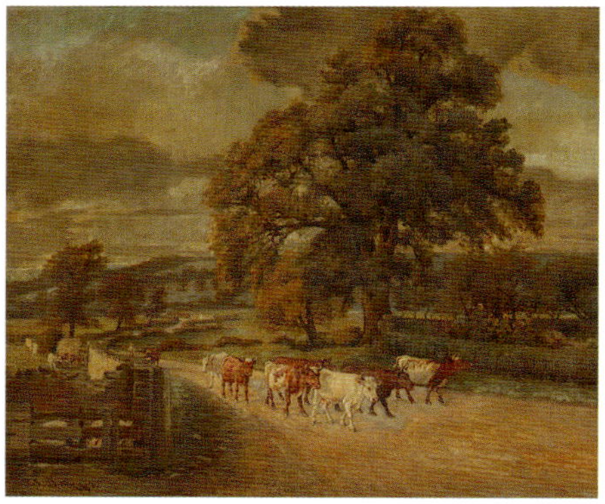

Briggs, S. active 19th C
Cattle on Country Lane
oil on canvas 70 x 90
2011.79

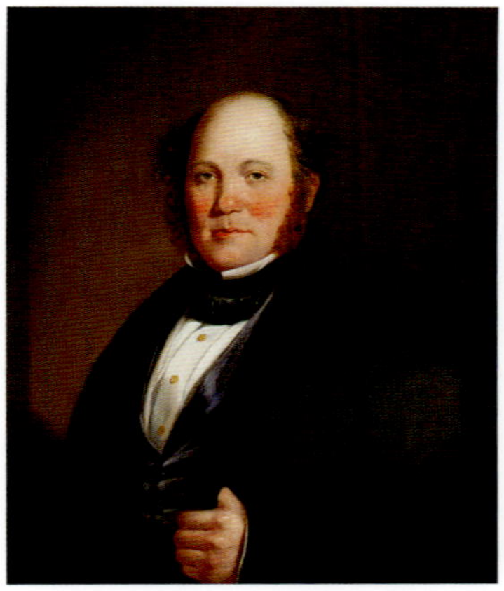

Briggs, William Keighley 1812–1884
James Cunningham (c.1796–1876)
oil on canvas 75 x 62
71

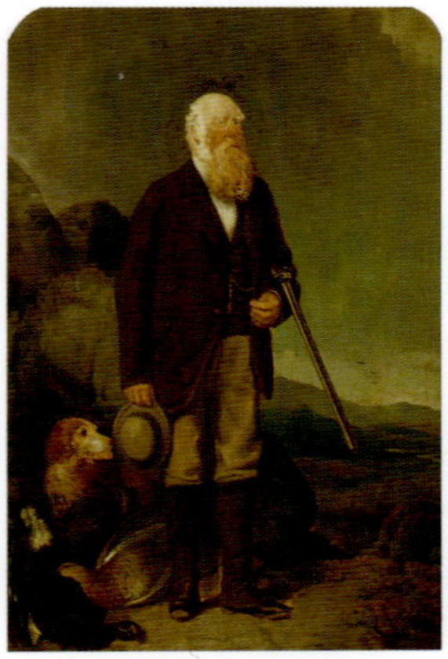

Briggs, William Keighley 1812–1884
James Cunningham
oil on canvas 130 x 90
2011.113

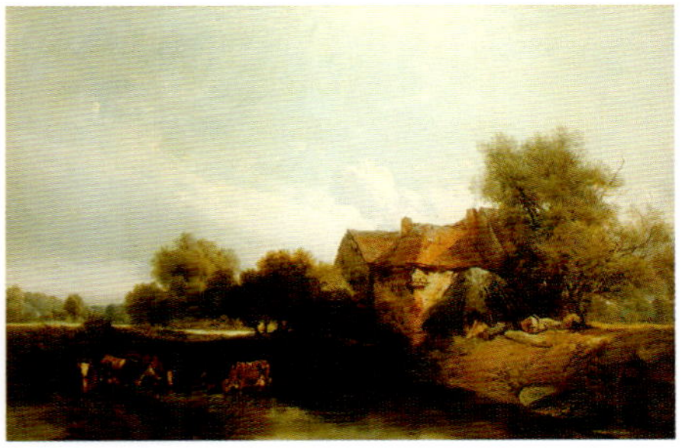

Bright, Henry 1810–1873
Landscape 1853
oil on canvas 76 x 130
2011.73

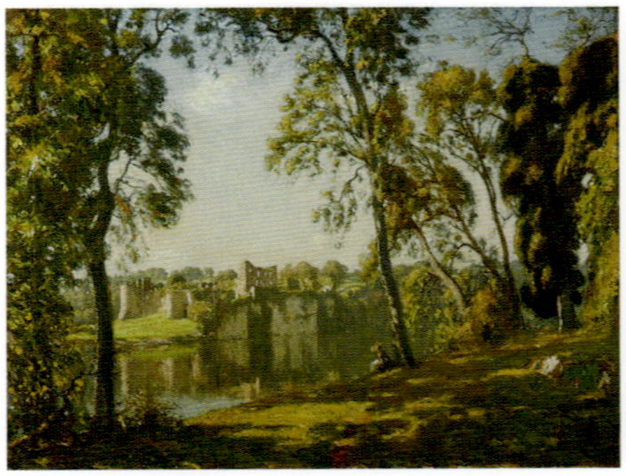

Brown, Frederick 1851–1941
On the Wye, Chepstow
oil on canvas 70 x 90
478

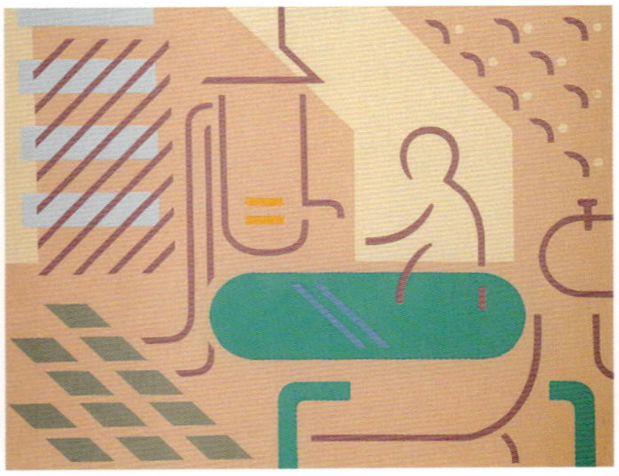

Buhler, Michael 1940–2009
The Pink Bathroom late 20th C
acrylic on canvas 73.9 x 93.9
1096

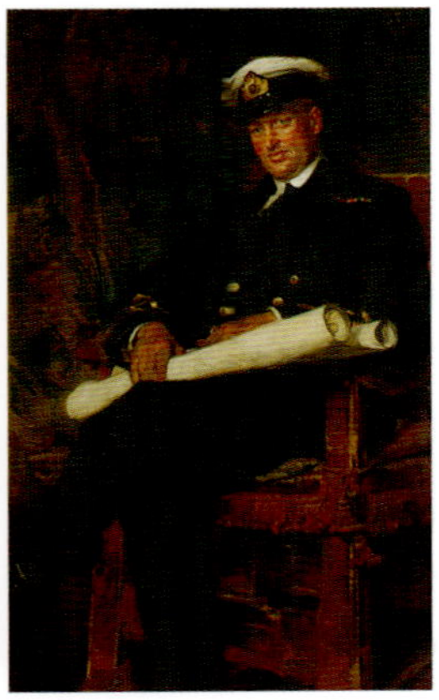

Bundy, Edgar 1862–1922
Lieutenant Commander Percy Thompson Dean (1877–1939), VC c.1918
oil on canvas 150 x 99
297

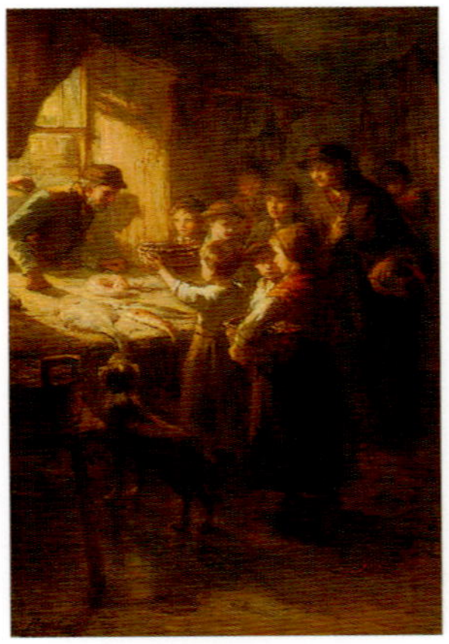

Carter, Hugh 1837–1903
Waiting for the Remnants
oil on canvas 129 x 83
158

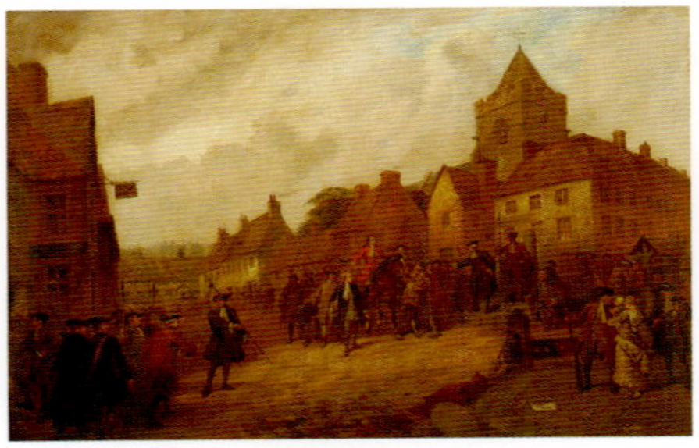

Cattermole, Charles 1832–1900
Old Blackburn
oil on canvas 70 x 105
73

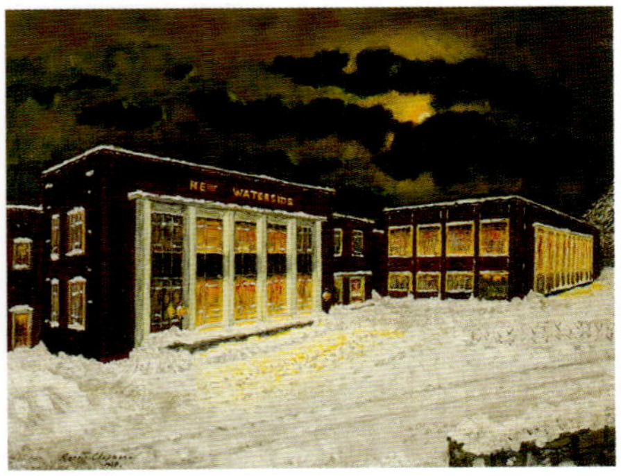

Chapman, Kenric
New Waterside Papermill, Darwen 1968
oil on canvas 39 x 50
2010.20

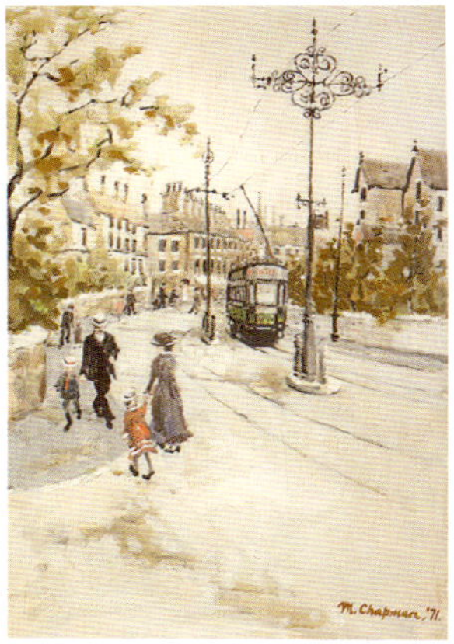

Chapman, Margaret 1940–2000
Sunday Morning, Preston New Road, Blackburn 1971
oil on board 74 x 50
933

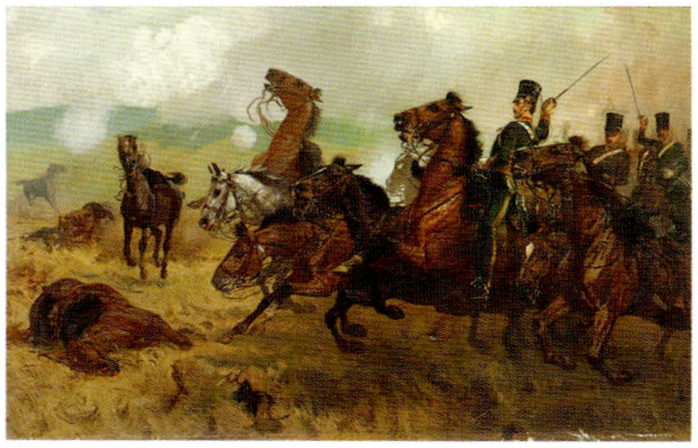

Charlton, John 1849–1917
Balaclava 1889
oil on canvas 161 x 257
87

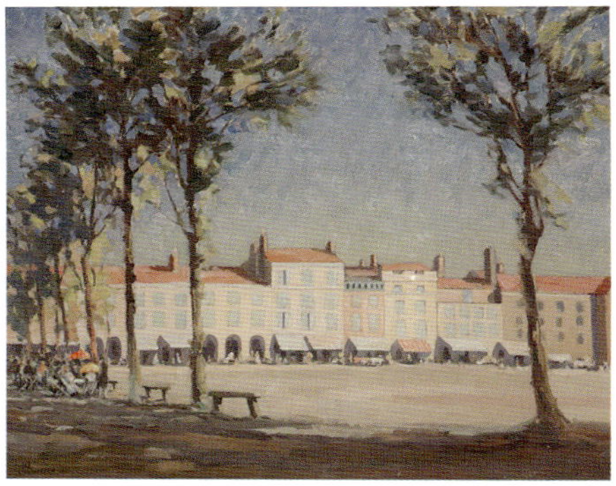

Chettle, James Patchell 1871–1944
Place de Verdun, La Rochelle 1929
oil on canvas 49 x 59
271

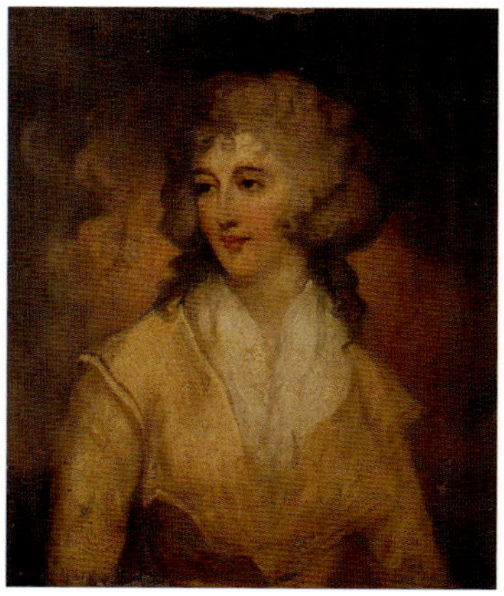

Chinnery, George (attributed to) 1774–1852
Portrait of a Woman 19th C
oil on canvas 65 x 56
2011.76

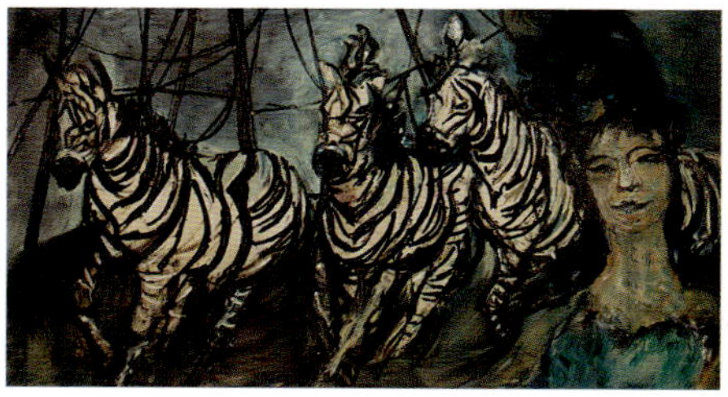

Christopherson, José b.1914
Zebras c.1970
oil on canvas 68 x 129
701

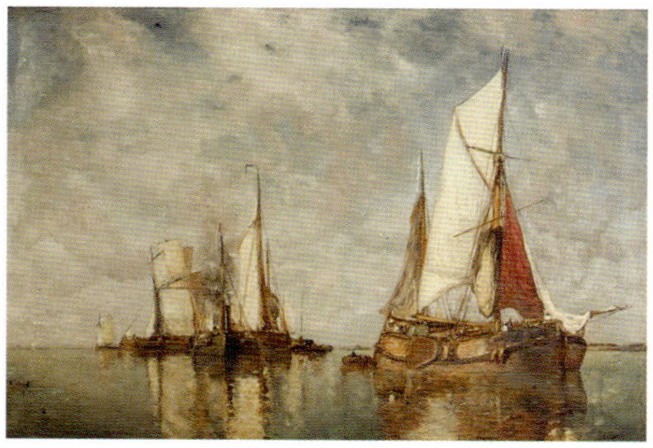

Clays, Paul Jean 1819–1900
A Corner of Dordrecht, Holland 1856
oil on canvas 68 x 97.5
142

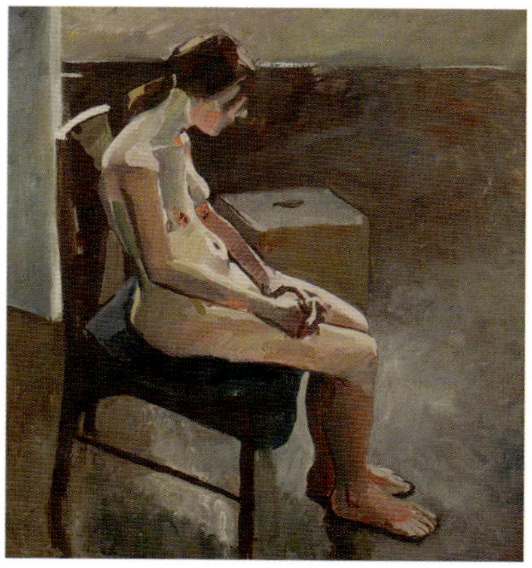

Cochran, Winifred active 1970s
Seated Female Nude c.1970
oil on canvas 74 x 68
837

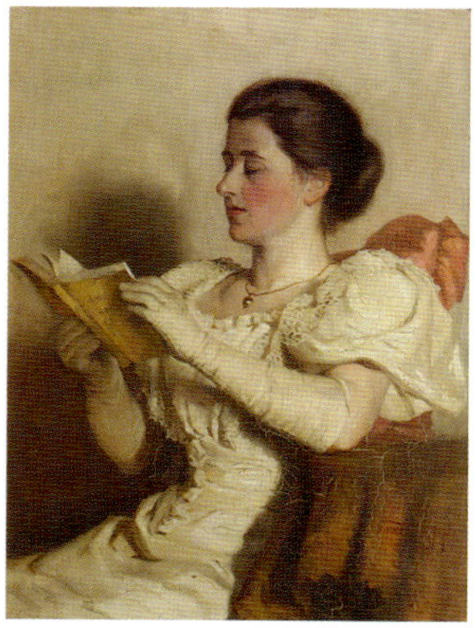

Coddington Lewis, Hillary 1871–1936
Self Portrait 1899
oil on canvas 79 x 68
649

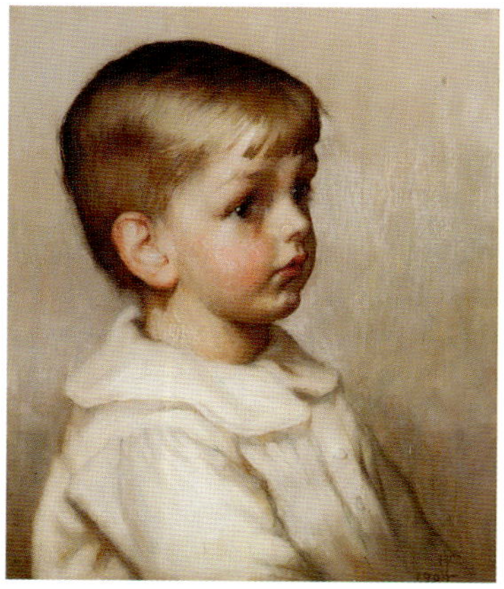

Coddington Lewis, Hillary 1871–1936
Richard Boys Lewis (b.1900) 1903
oil on canvas 44.5 x 37
1154

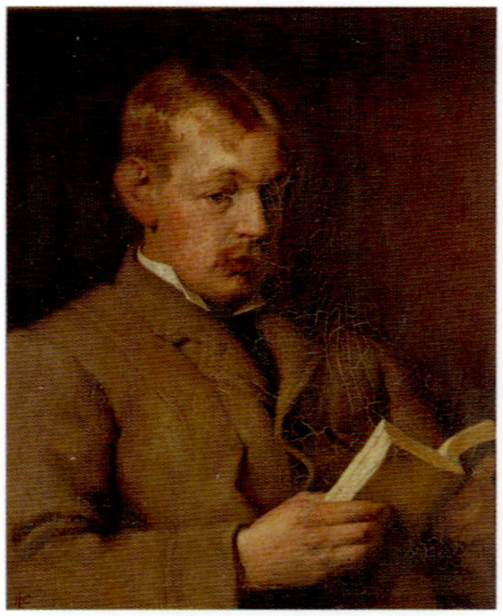

Coddington Lewis, Hillary 1871–1936
Thomas Boys Lewis (1869–1942) 1904
oil on canvas 59.5 x 49.5
648

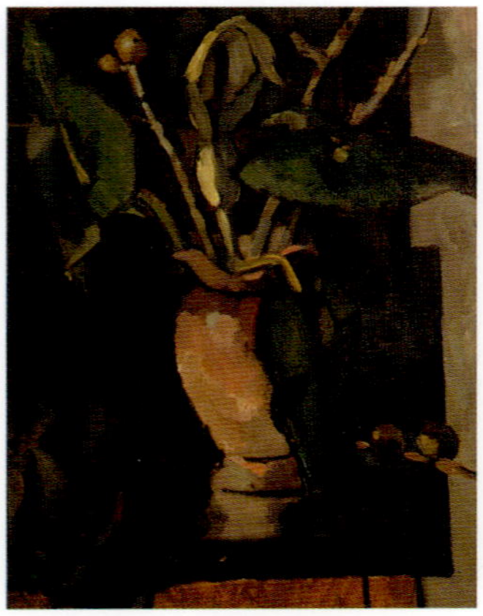

Coldstream, William Menzies 1908–1987
Lords and Ladies mid-20th C
oil on canvas 45 x 35
591

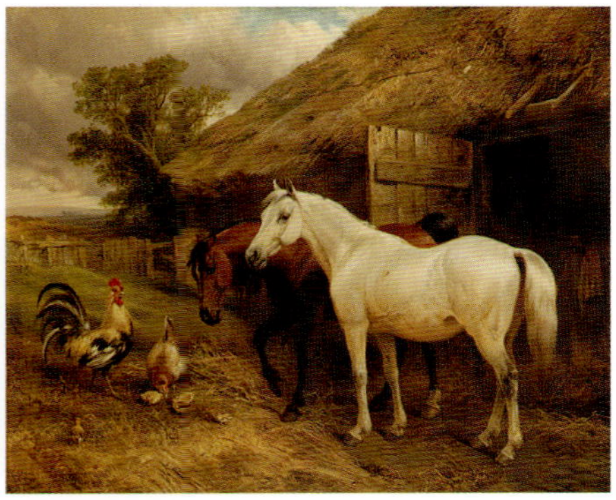

Cole, George 1810–1883
Horses
oil on canvas 55.9 x 76.2 (E)
211

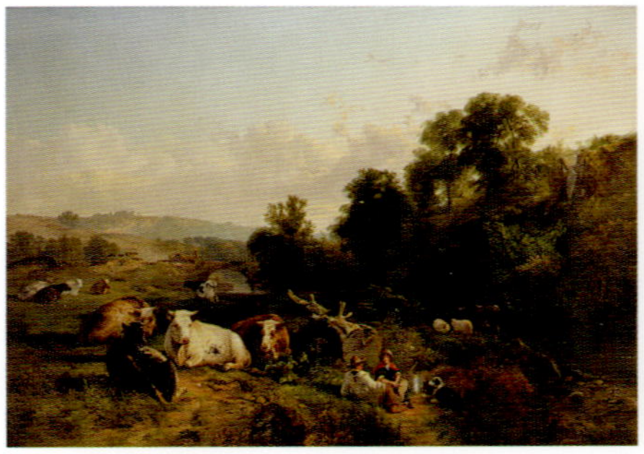

Cole, George Vicat 1833–1893
Midday Rest 1857
oil on canvas 121.9 x 182
321

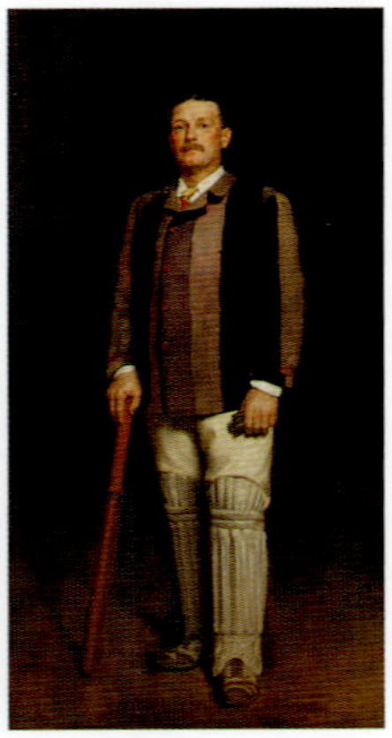

Collier, John 1850–1934
A. N. Hornby (1847–1925) 1893
oil on canvas 212 x 105
82

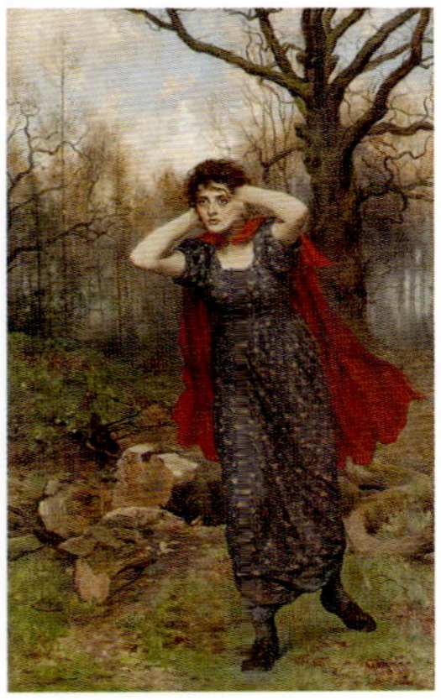

Collier, John 1850–1934
Hetty Sorrel
oil on canvas 140 x 85
85

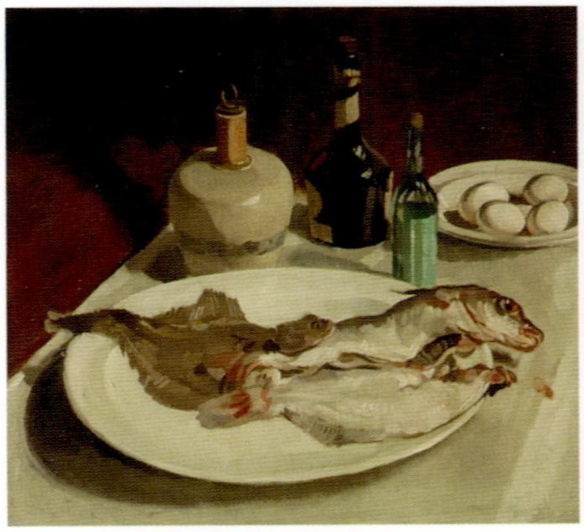

Connard, Philip 1875–1958
Still Life early 20th C
oil on canvas 49 x 59
267

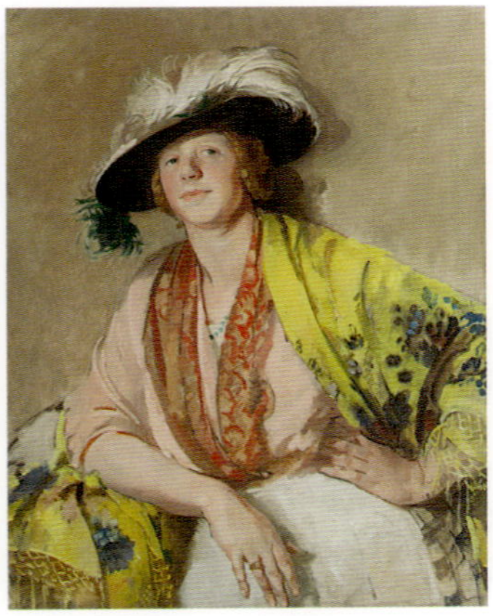

Connard, Philip 1875–1958
Hardy of Chelsea Green
oil on canvas 89.5 x 69.5
268

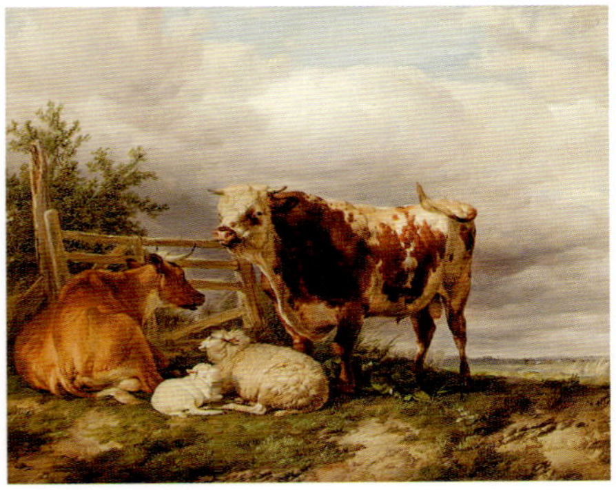

Cooper, Thomas Sidney 1803–1902
Cattle 1837
oil on panel 42.5 x 53.5
472

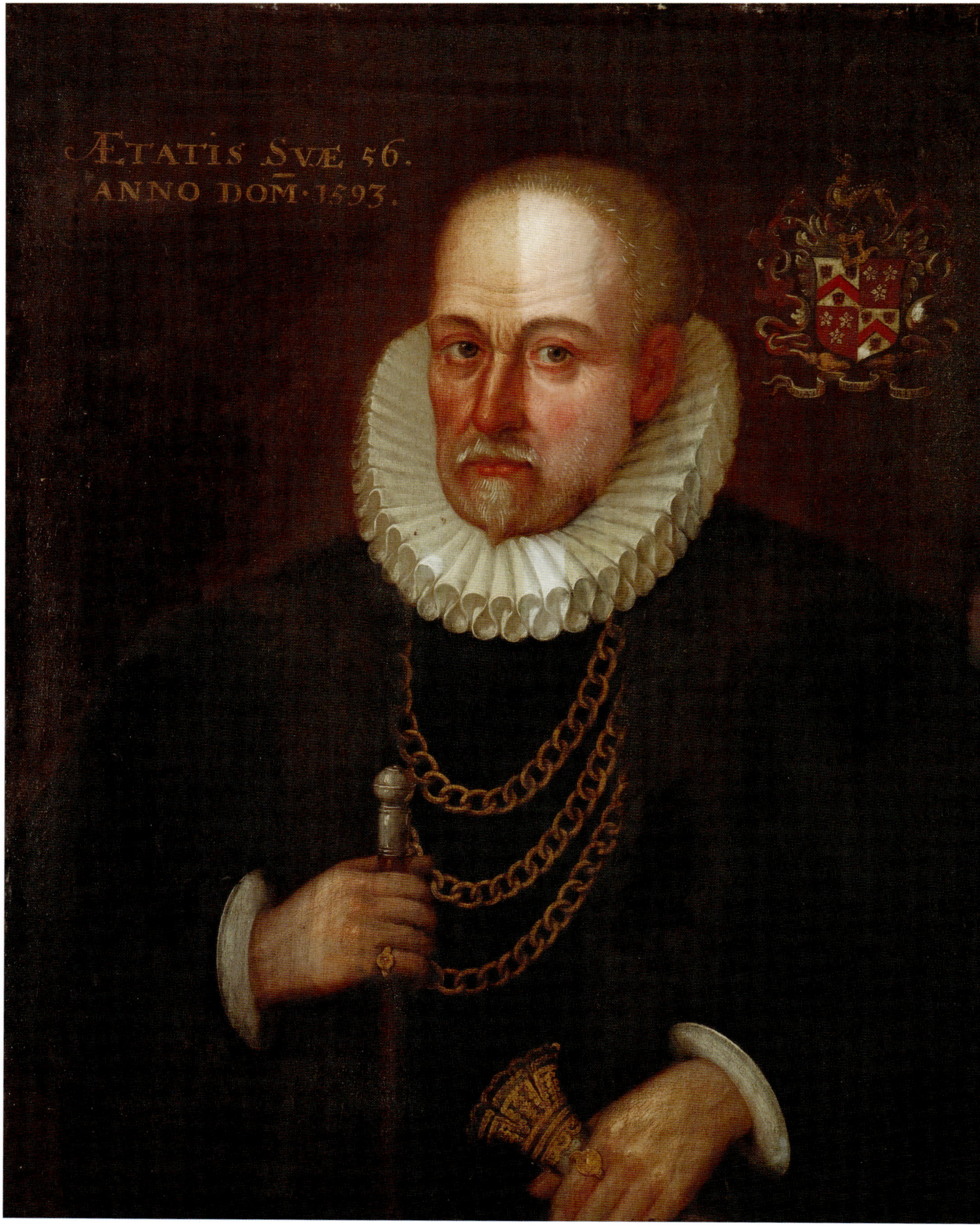
ÆTATIS SVÆ 56.
ANNO DOM· 1593.

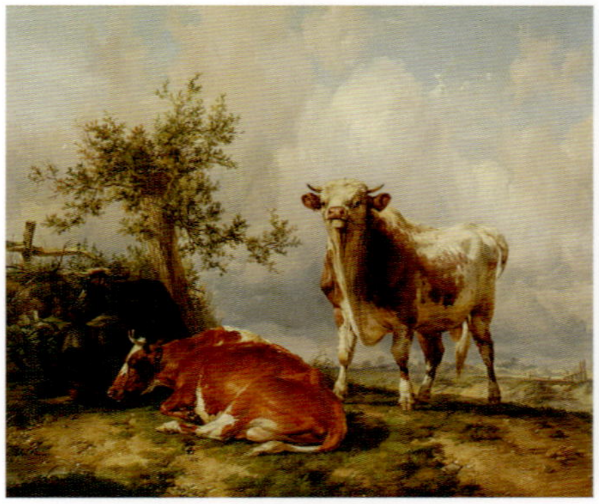

Cooper, Thomas Sidney 1803–1902
Cattle and Sheep c.1837
oil on panel 42.5 x 53.5
473

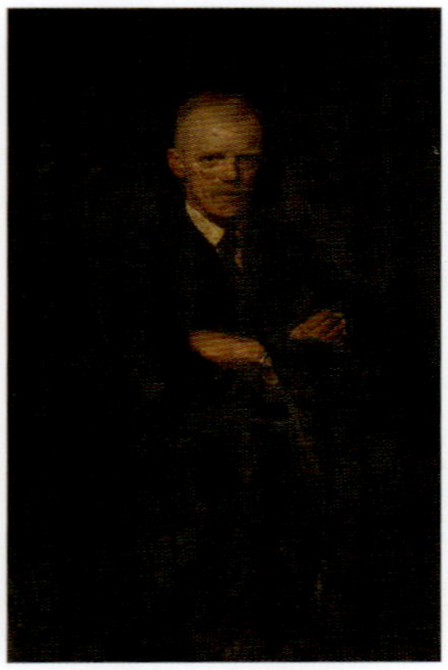

Copnall, Frank Thomas 1870–1949
George Holden, Mayor of Darwen (1907–1908) c.1907
oil on canvas 141 x 84
TH. 17

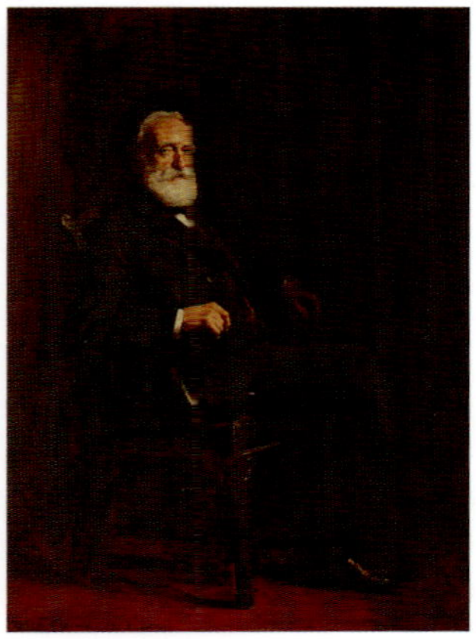

Copnall, Frank Thomas 1870–1949
Alderman William Thompson, Mayor of Blackburn (1914–1915) 1913
oil on canvas 180 x 135 (E)
TH. 21

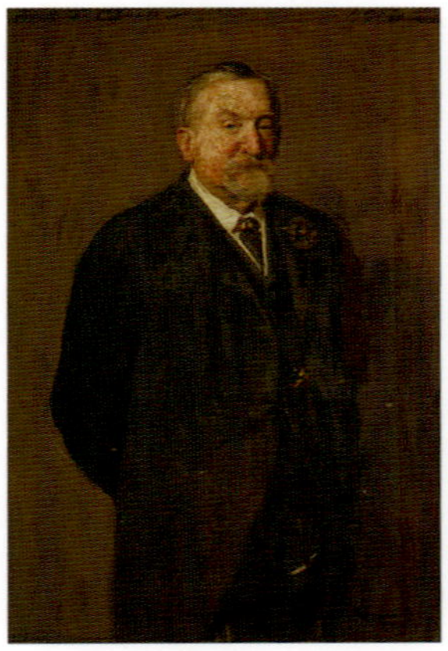

Copnall, Frank Thomas 1870–1949
Joshua Hacking, President of the Blackburn Chamber of Commerce (1917–1925) 1913
oil on canvas 122 x 82
1987.62.2

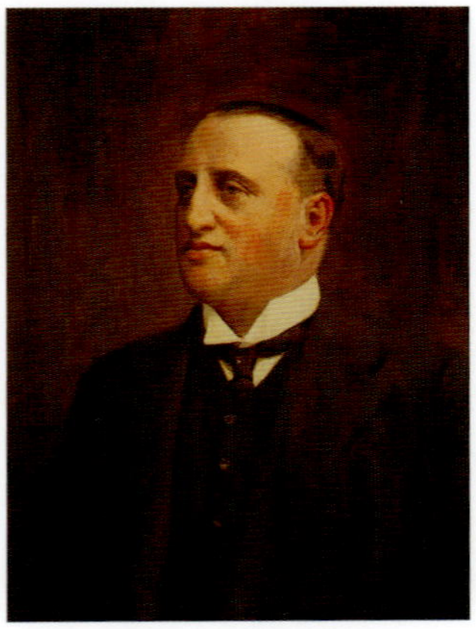

Copnall, Frank Thomas 1870–1949
Alfred Nuttall, Mayor of Blackburn (1915–1917) c.1917
oil on canvas 75 x 60
TH.5

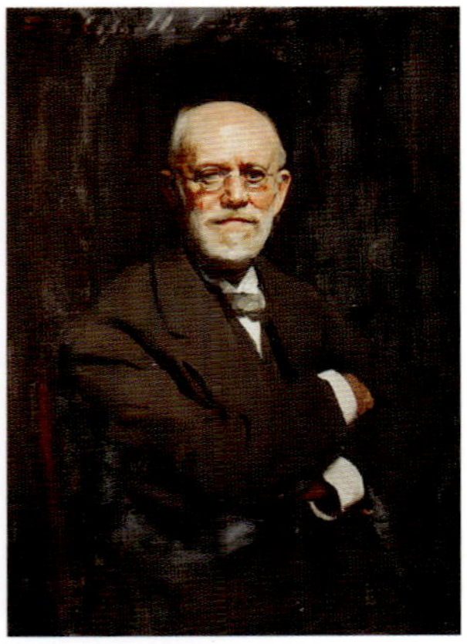

Copnall, Frank Thomas 1870–1949
Thomas Purvis Ritzema (1853–1938) 1931
oil on canvas 91 x 70
610

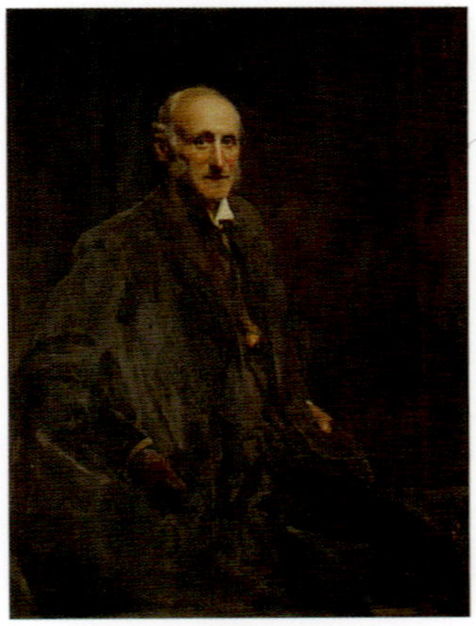

Copnall, Frank Thomas 1870–1949
Portrait of a Man (probably an Alderman of Darwen) 20th C
oil on canvas 126 x 100
TH.19

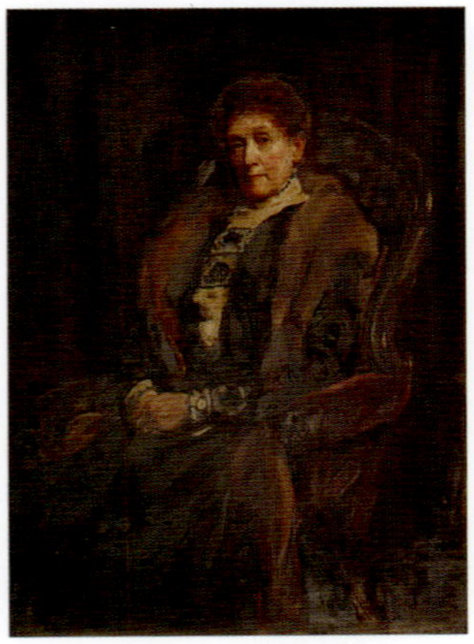

Copnall, Frank Thomas 1870–1949
Mrs Charles Costekin or Costello (?) early 20th C
oil on canvas 126 x 100
TH.15

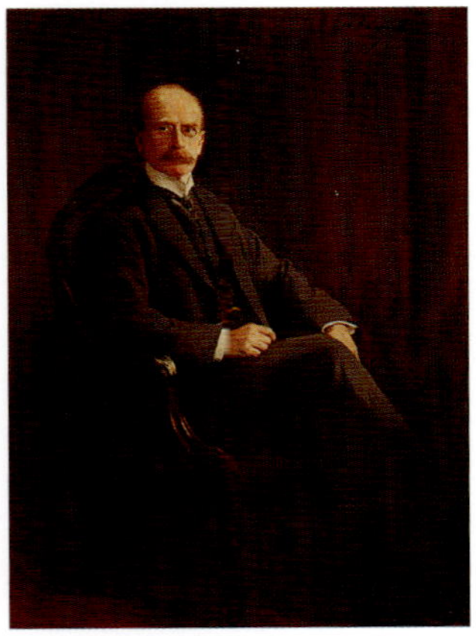

Copnall, Frank Thomas 1870–1949
Samuel Crossley JP, Mayor of Blackburn (1911) early 20th C
oil on canvas 170 x 130
TH. 27

Facing page: Gheeraerts the younger, Marcus, 1561/1562–1635/1636, *Sir William ffaryngton of Worden Hall (1537–1610), Leyland, Lancashire*, 1593, Lancashire County Museum Service (p. 381)

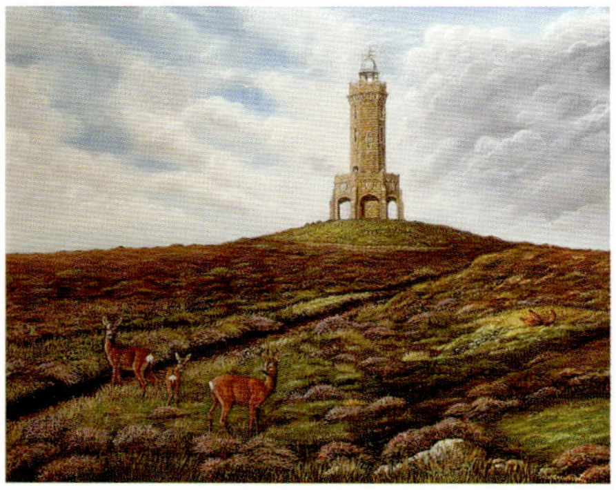

Crewdson, Jack
Jubilee Tower, Darwen c.2009
oil on canvas 60.9 x 76.2 (E)
2010.21

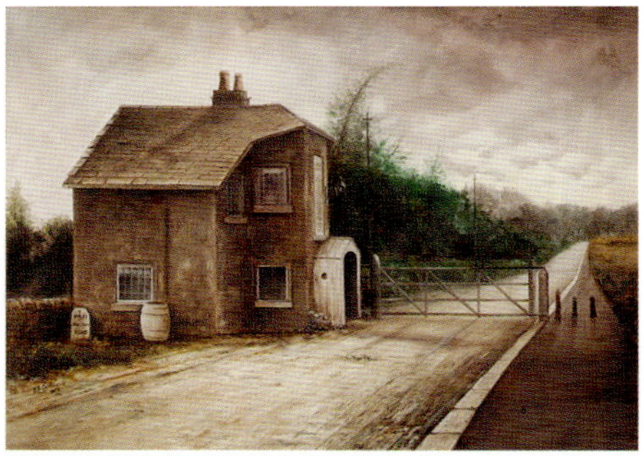

Crossland, Henry Symons 1859–1943
Shackerley Toll Bar, Mellor, Preston New Road 1877
oil on canvas 57.7 x 88.9
816

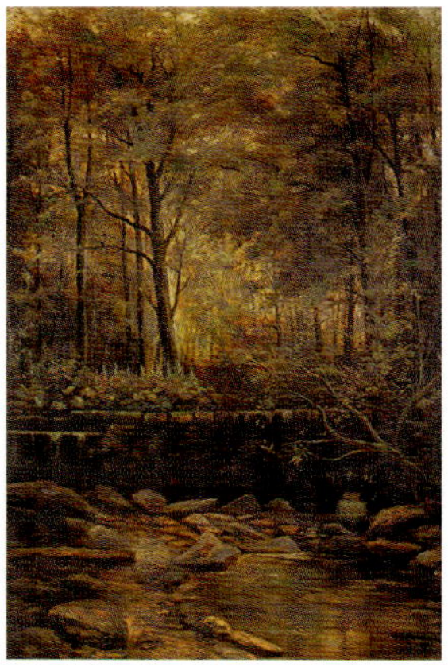

Crossland, James Henry 1852–1939
Alum Scar 1901
oil on canvas 90 x 59
306

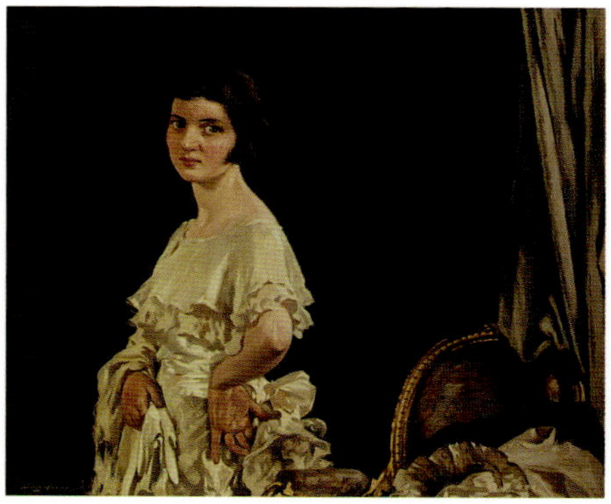

Cursiter, Stanley 1887–1976
Roberta
oil on canvas 84.5 x 100
249

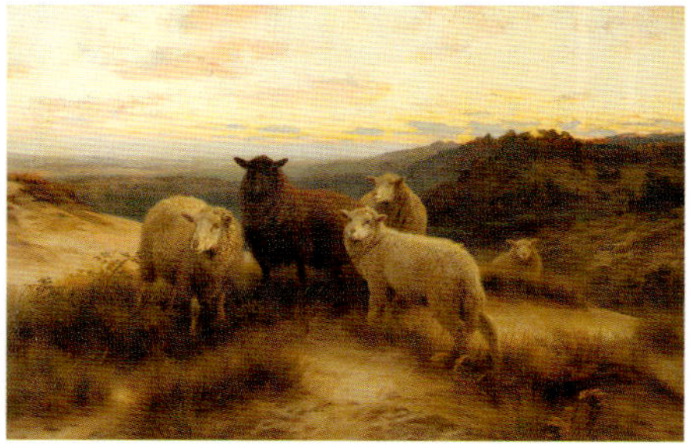

Davis, Henry William Banks 1833–1914
Close of Day 1885
oil on canvas 50.8 x 73.2
123A

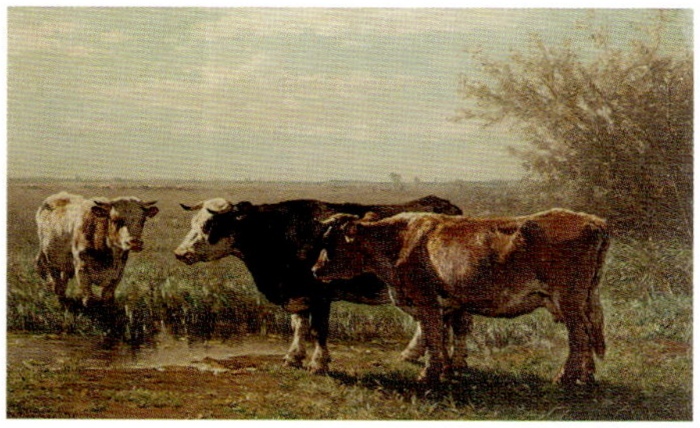

de Haas, Johannes Hubertus Leonardus 1832–1908
Cattle and Landscape 1879
oil on canvas 67.5 x 99
130

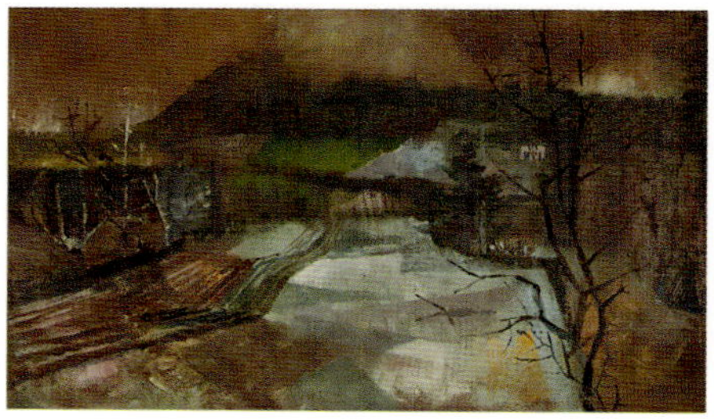

Derbyshire, Paul 1936–2007
Pendle Hill in Winter late 20th C
oil on board 40 x 67
2011.28

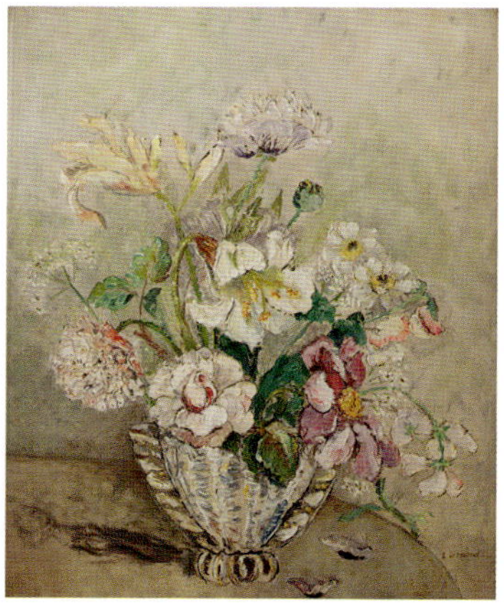

Dimond, Louise 1878–1943
Floral Decoration c.1940
oil on canvas 48 x 39
384

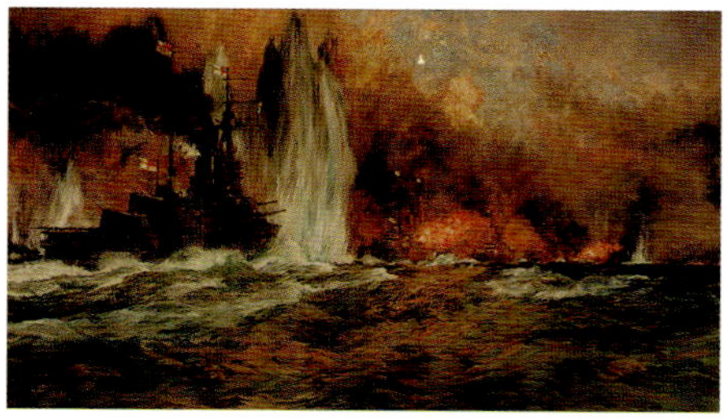

Dixon, Charles 1872–1934
The Battle of Jutland 1916
oil on canvas 105 x 181.5
243

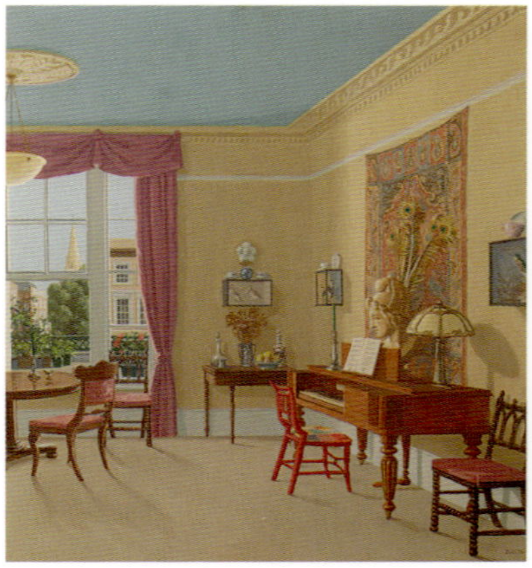

Dodd, Alan b.1942
Interior, London N1 1976
oil on board 85.4 x 78.1
1095

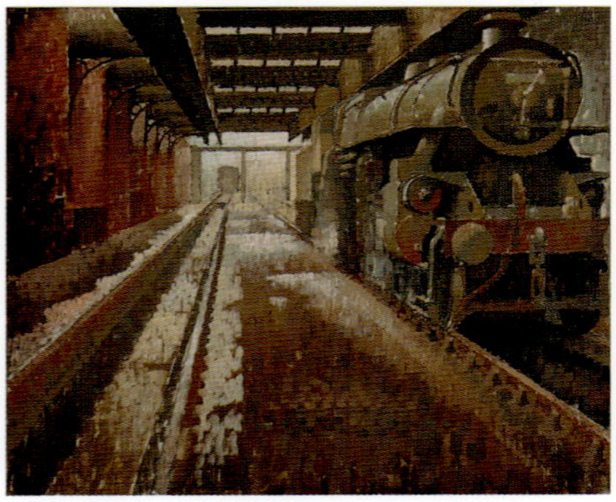

Dolby, James 1909–1975
Engine Shed c.1966
oil on canvas 50 x 59
702

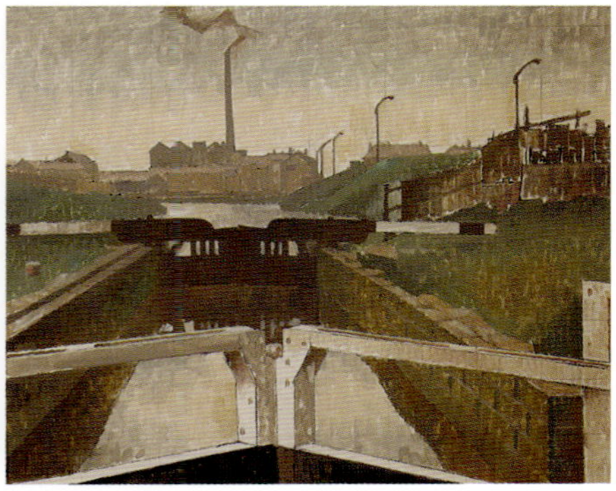

Dolby, James 1909–1975
Blackburn Bottom Lock
oil on canvas 49 x 59
703

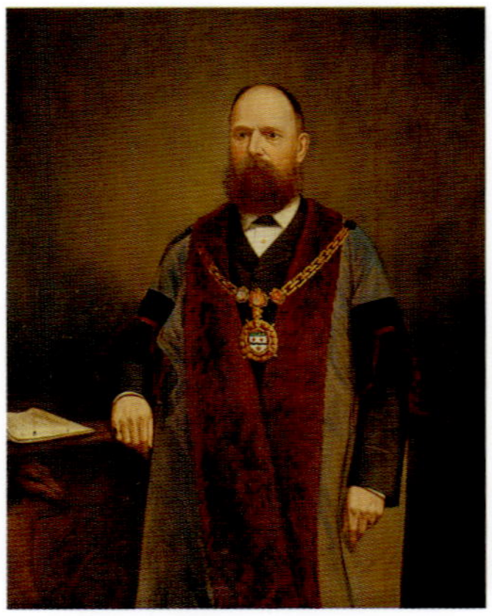

Du Val active late 19th C
Alderman T. Farrar Baynes
oil on canvas 124 x 99
TH. 26

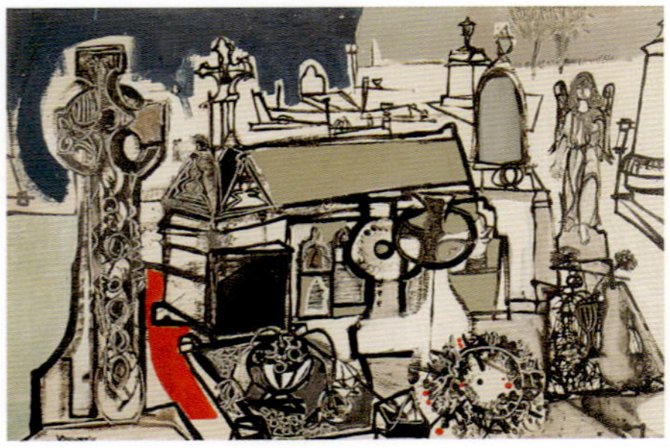

Duckworth, Valerie
Graveyard I 1965
oil on board 60 x 90
2011.82

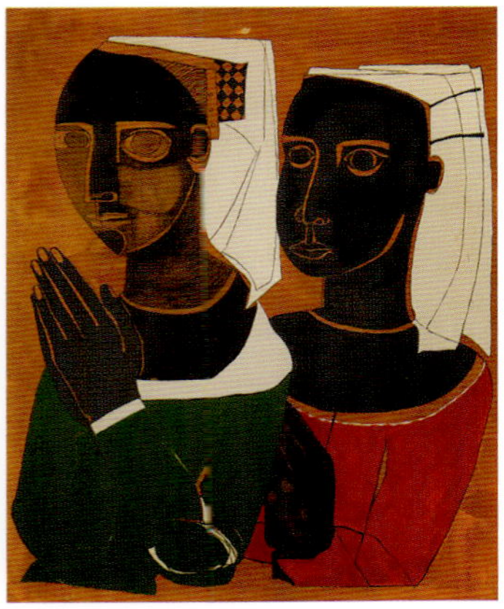

Duckworth, Valerie
Two Sisters
oil on panel 70 x 59.5
2011.97

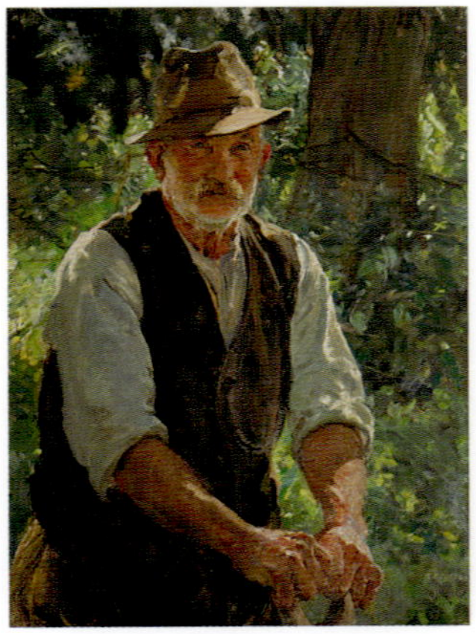

Dugdale, Thomas Cantrell 1880–1952
Mr Kersey, Suffolk early 20th C
oil on canvas 90 x 70
494

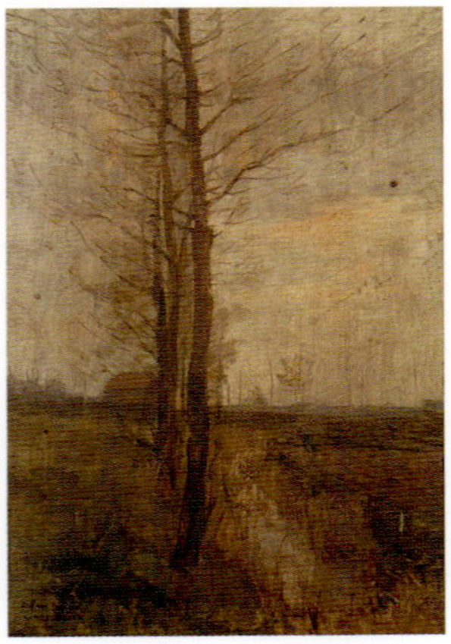

Duhem, Henri Aimé 1860–1941
River Scene late 19th C
oil on panel 33 x 23
332

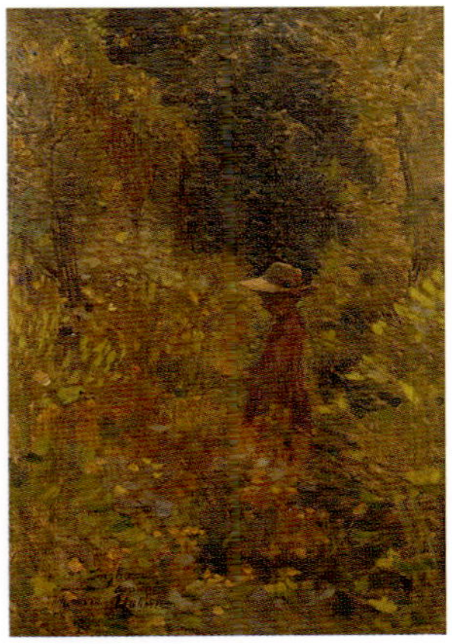

Duhem, Marie Geneviève 1871–1918
A Woodland Scene
oil on panel 32.5 x 21.2
341

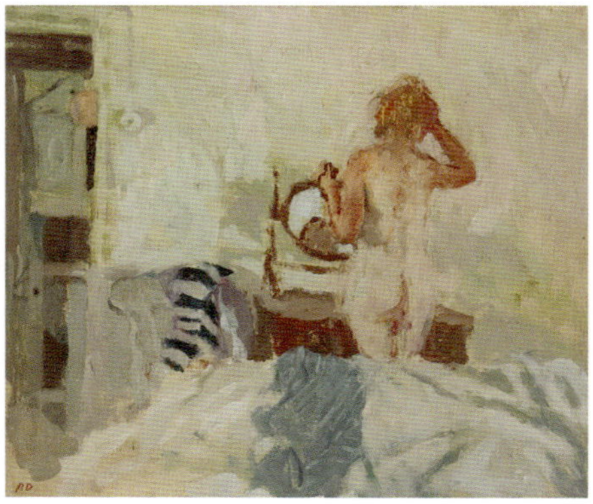

Dunstan, Bernard b.1920
Brushing Hair; Summer Morning
oil on canvas 25 x 30
2002.704

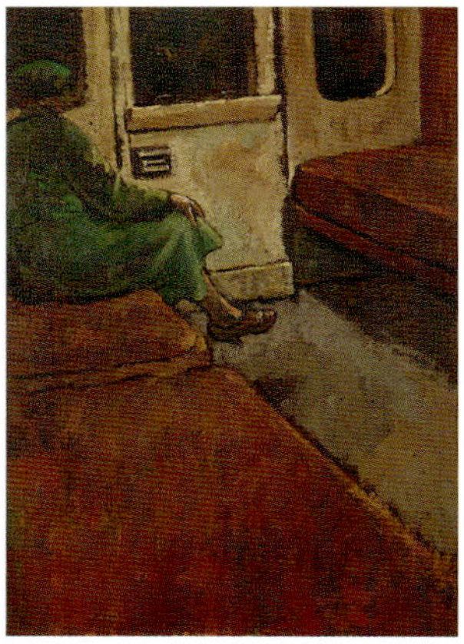

Dyson, A. M.
Last Train from Waterloo Station c.1962
oil on canvas 79 x 55
618

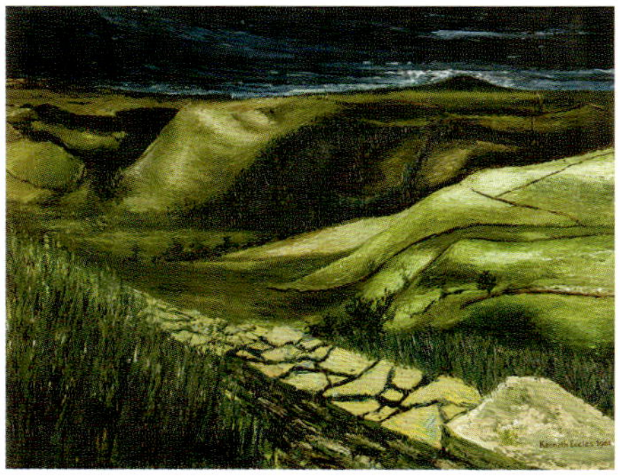

Eccles, Kenneth
Grane Moorscape 1961
oil on board 60 x 90
621

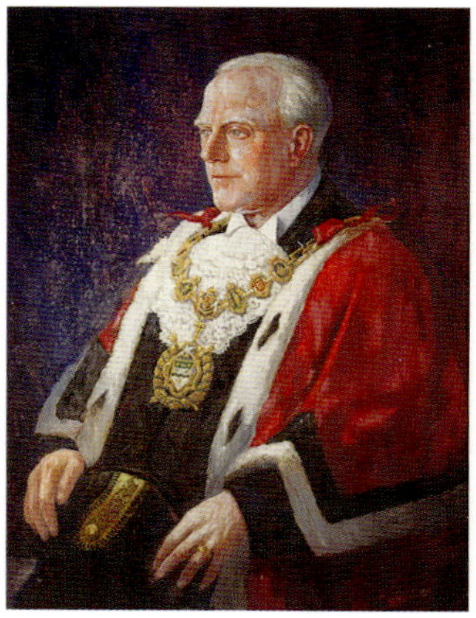

Edwards, Garth Stuart 1924–2008
W. A. Henshall, Mayor of Blackburn (1956)
1958
oil on canvas 100 x 75
TH.3

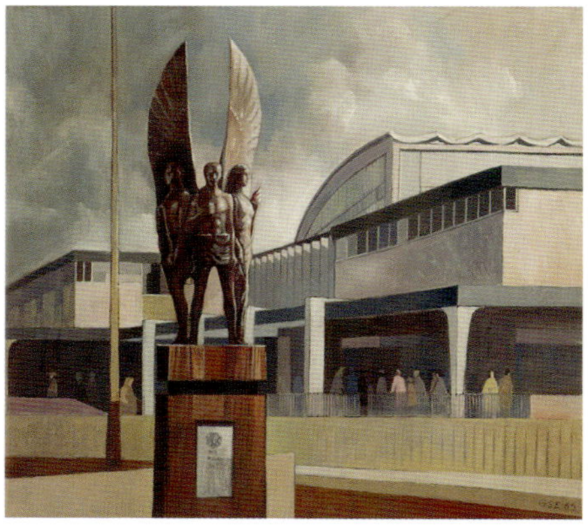

Edwards, Garth Stuart 1924–2008
New Market Construction, Blackburn 1965
oil on canvas 50 x 60
2011.114

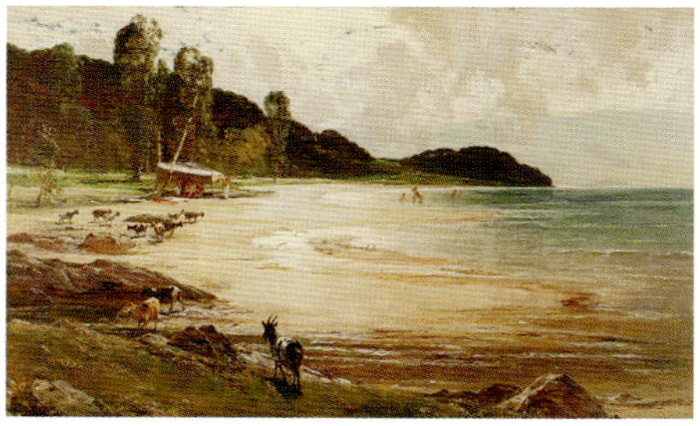

Ellis, Edwin 1842–1895
Welsh Coast
oil on canvas 112 x 181
118

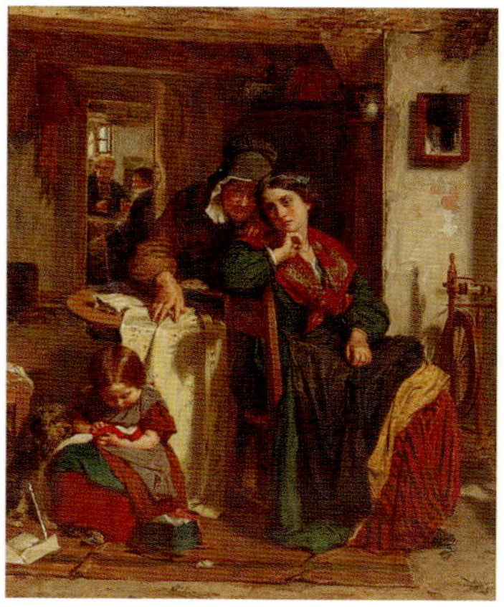

Faed, Thomas 1826–1900
The Silken Gown 1862
oil on canvas 49 x 38.5
80

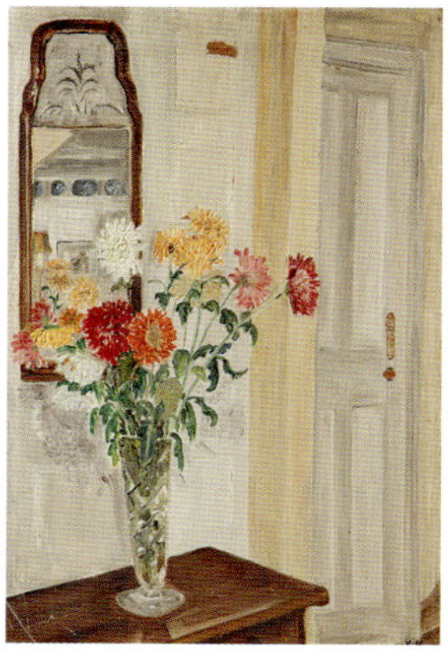

Ferrier, Kathleen 1912–1953
Interior c.1940
oil on canvas 49 x 40
KF.2009.1

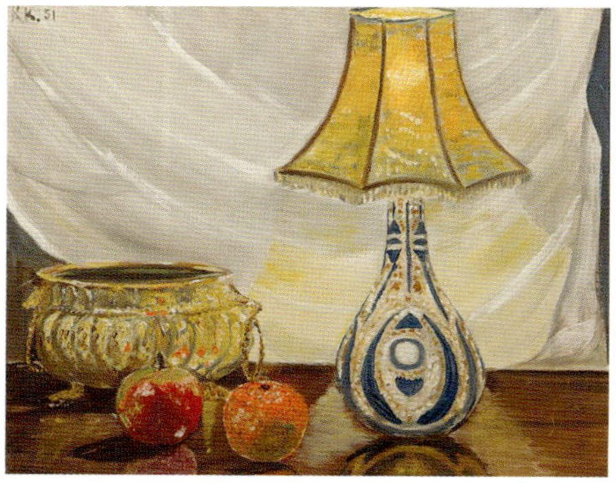

Ferrier, Kathleen 1912–1953
Still Life (Glass Vase on Sideboard) 1951
oil on canvas 40 x 50
KF.2009.2.1

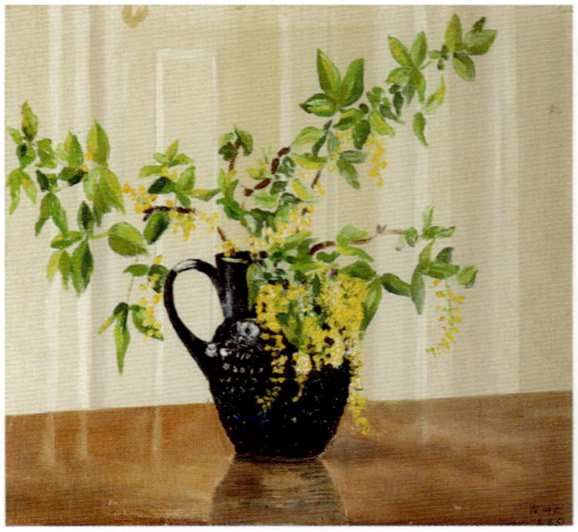

Ferrier, Winifred 1904–1995
Still Life (Blue Jug with Yellow Flowers) 1951
oil on canvas 40 x 50
KF.2009.2.2

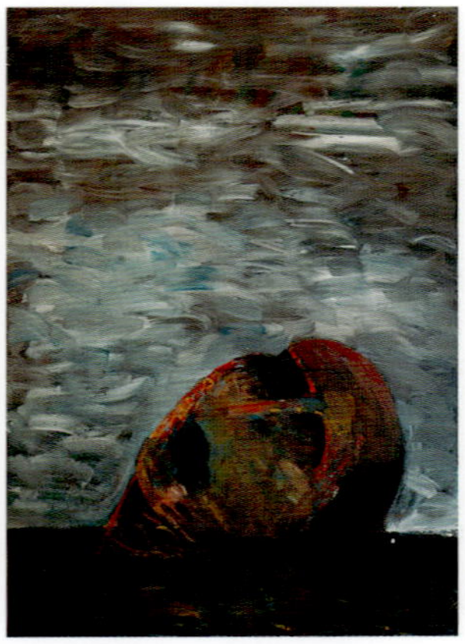

Fisher, Howard active c.1976–1996
Ophelia c.1976
oil on board 167 x 120
1150

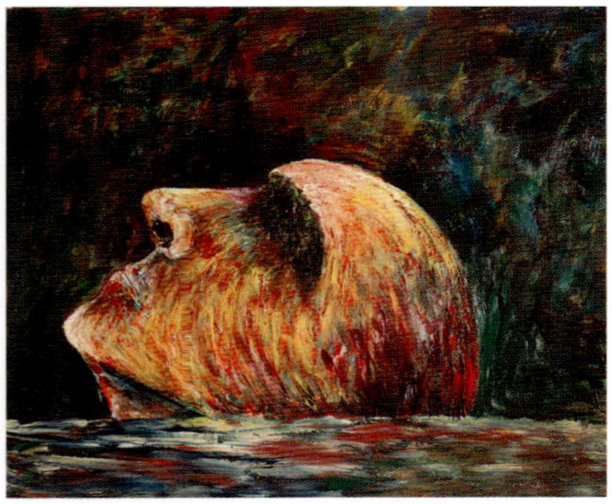

Fisher, Howard active c.1976–1996
Sanctuary 1985
acrylic on canvas 140 x 168
1151

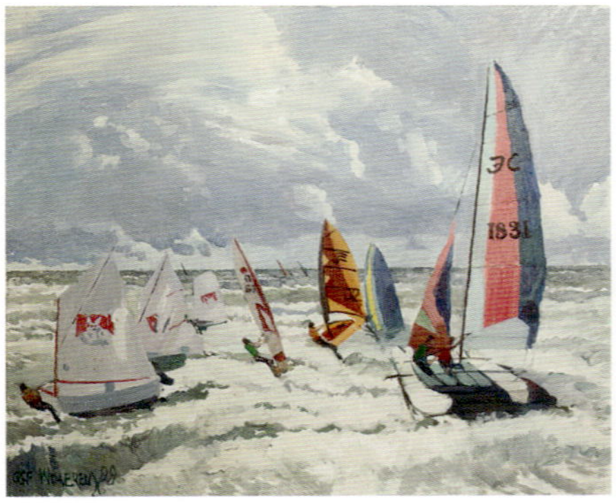

Fletcher, Geoffrey Scowcroft 1923–2004
Wimereux 1999
oil on canvas 51 x 66
2008.63

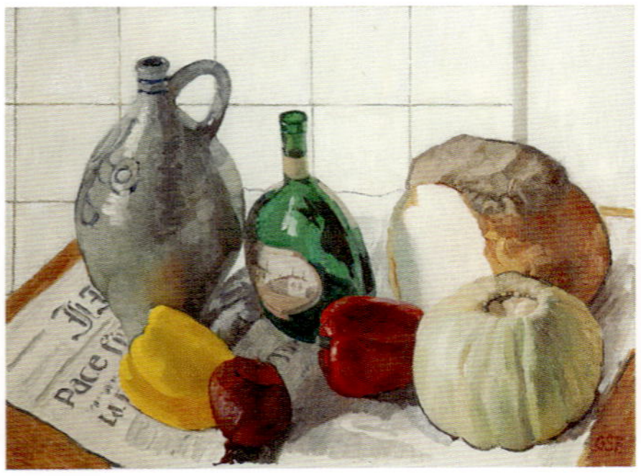

Fletcher, Geoffrey Scowcroft 1923–2004
Still Life Study 2000
oil on canvas 54 x 64
2008.62

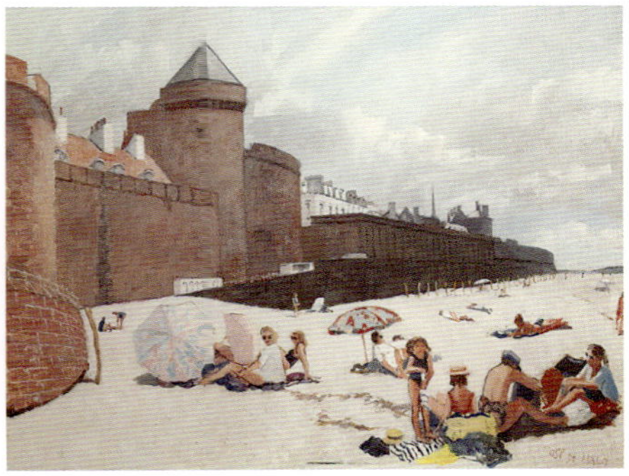

Fletcher, Geoffrey Scowcroft 1923–2004
St Malo c.2000
oil on canvas 56 x 71
2008.64

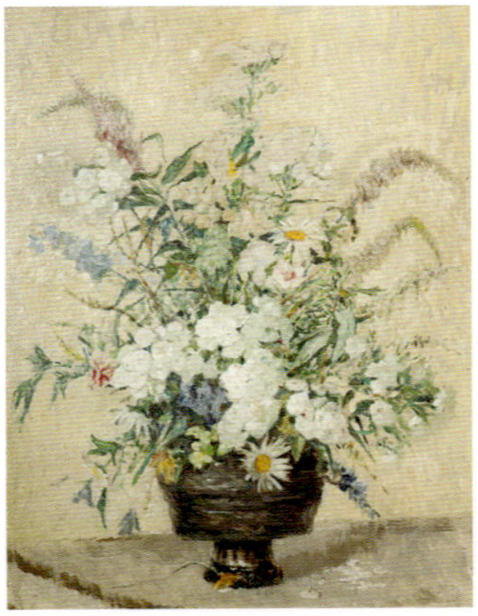

Fordham, Ethel 1915–1999
Floral Symphony
oil on canvas 70 x 55
393

Foster, Barry
Sky Scene 1969
oil on canvas 151 x 121
769

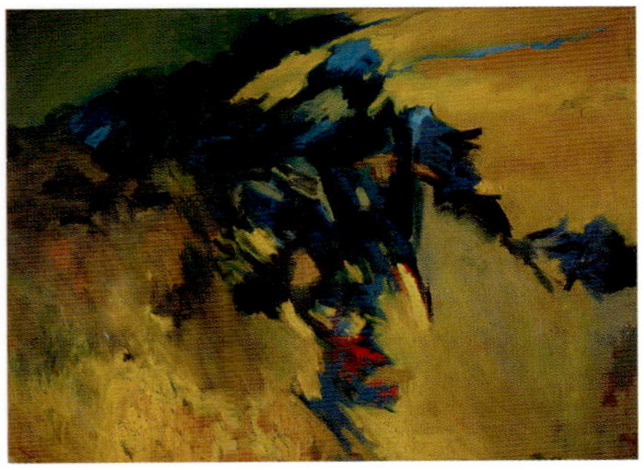

Fryer, Malcolm b.1937
Landscape Edge 1965
oil on canvas 91 x 122
676

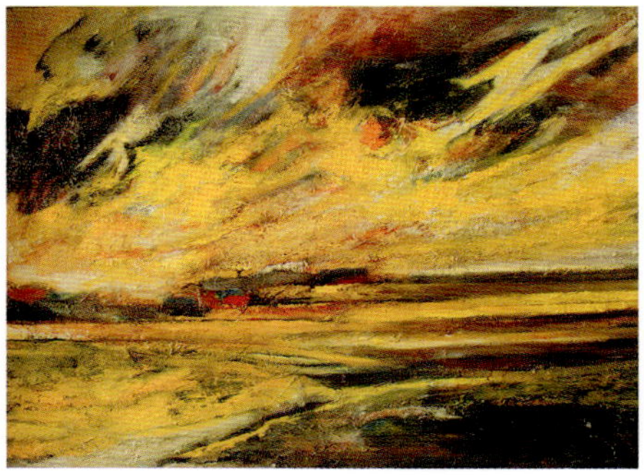

Fryer, Malcolm b.1937
Angus Landscape mid-20th C
oil on canvas 91 x 121
2011.83

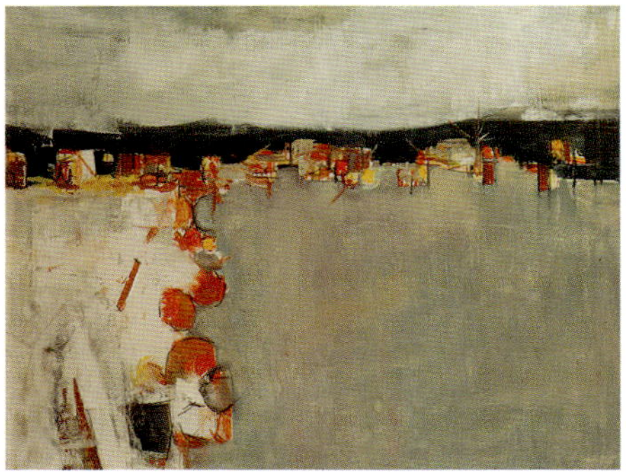

Fryer, Malcolm b.1937
Continental Landscape mid-20th C
oil on canvas 46 x 66
640

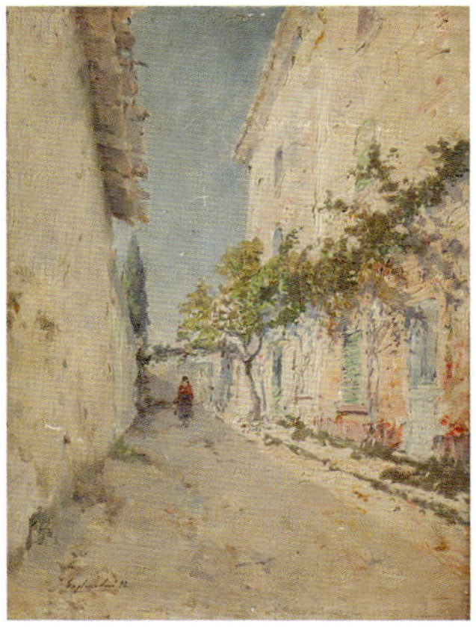

Gagliardini, Julien Gustave 1846–1927
A Road at Midday 1876
oil on board 46 x 37
330

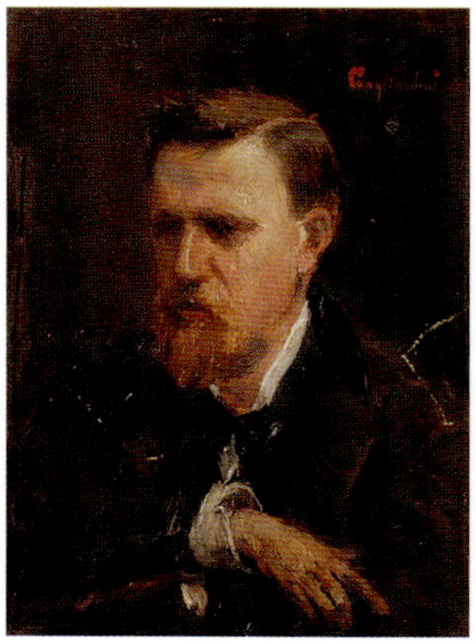

Gagliardini, Julien Gustave 1846–1927
Thomas Ingham (d.c.1936) late 19th C
oil on panel 20.4 x 15.3
327

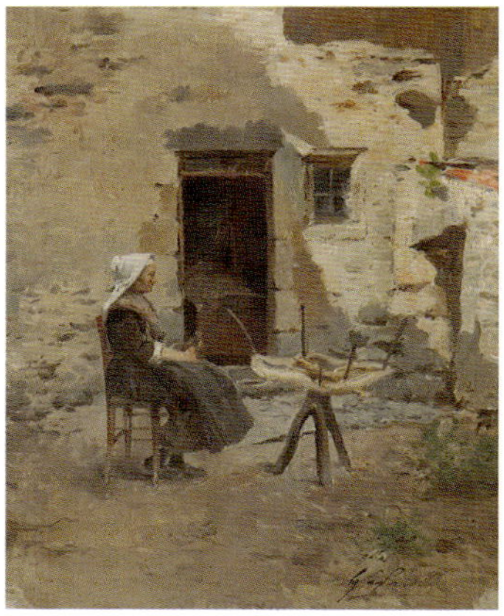

Gagliardini, Julien Gustave 1846–1927
Woman at Spinning Wheel late 19th C
oil on canvas 45 x 36.8
331

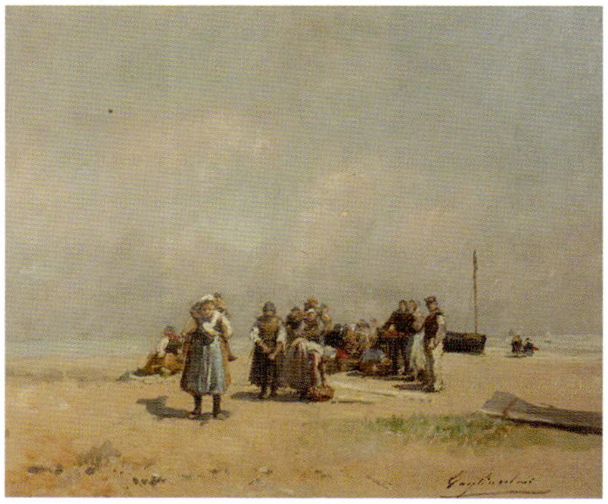

Gagliardini, Julien Gustave 1846–1927
Fish Market
oil on canvas 36 x 44
325

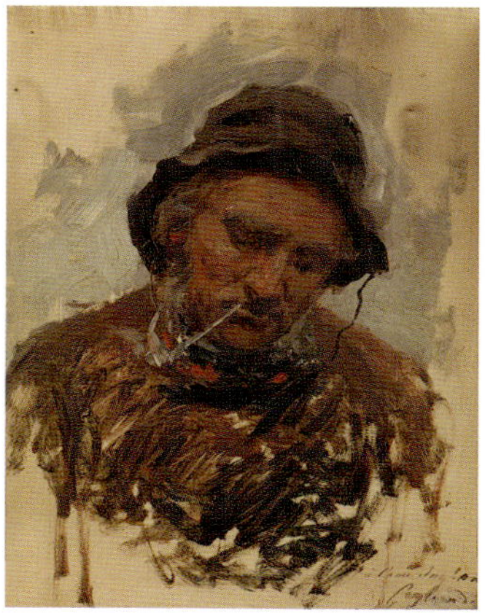

Gagliardini, Julien Gustave 1846–1927
French Fisherman
oil on canvas 34 x 26
329

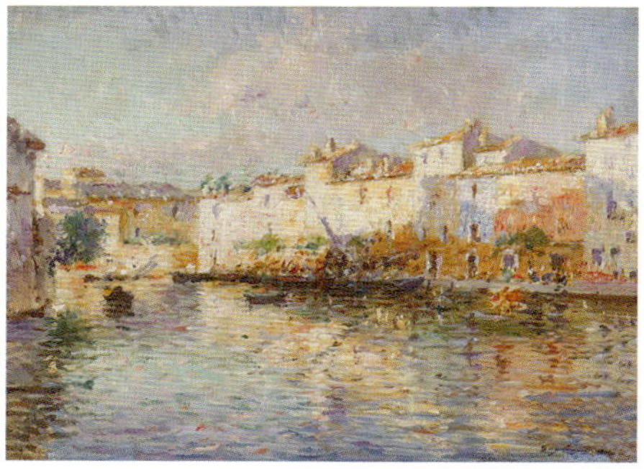

Gagliardini, Julien Gustave 1846–1927
The Quay
oil on canvas 48 x 63
326

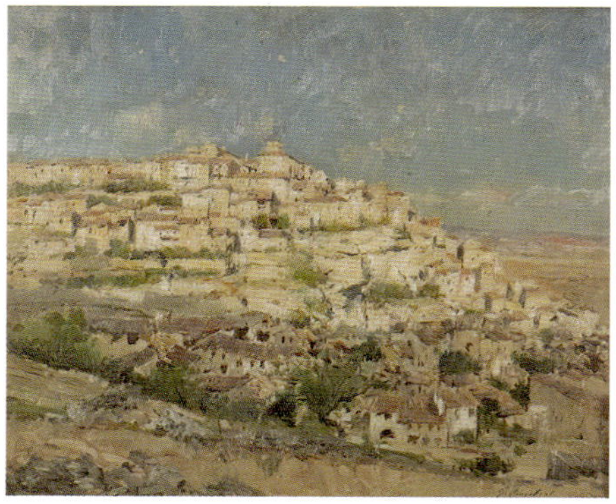

Gagliardini, Julien Gustave 1846–1927
The Town of Gordes
oil on canvas 35 x 43
328

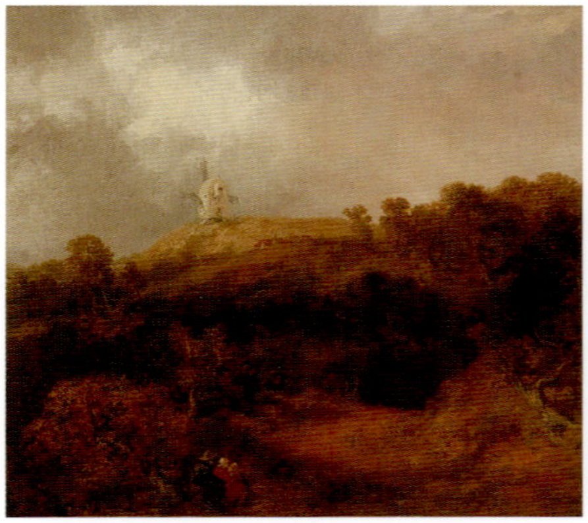

Gilbert, John 1817–1897
Keston Common, Kent 1856
oil on canvas 42 x 47
89

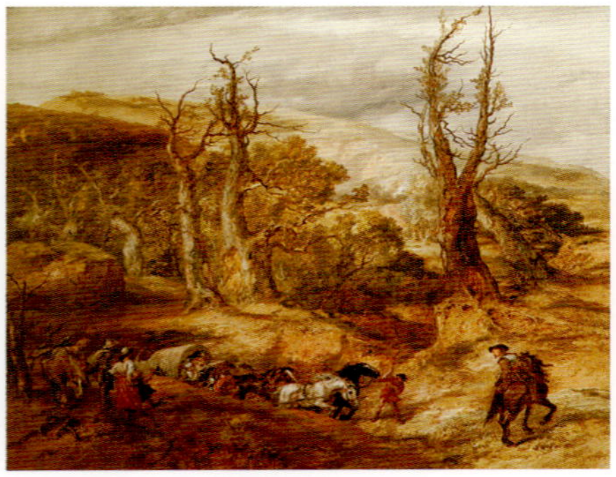

Gilbert, John 1817–1897
Baggage Wagon 1886
oil on canvas 101 x 126
88

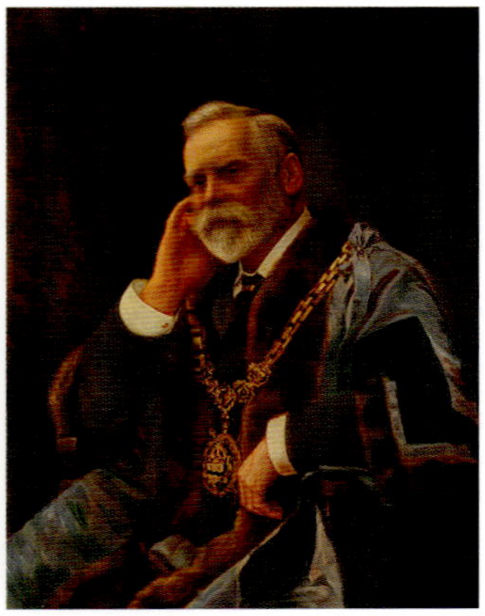

Gittleson, Albert Abram b.1887
Portrait of an Unidentified Mayor of Blackburn 1908
oil on canvas 90 x 70
TH. 6

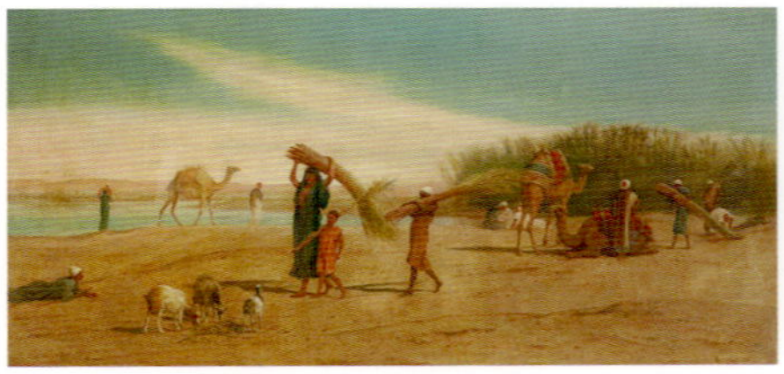

Goodall, Frederick 1822–1904
Scene on the Nile 1879
oil on canvas 59 x 125
356

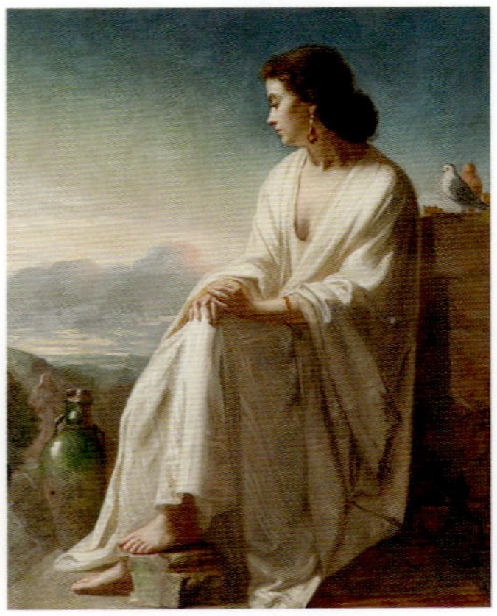

Goodall, Frederick 1822–1904
Rebecca at the Well late 19th C
oil on canvas 72.5 x 60
212

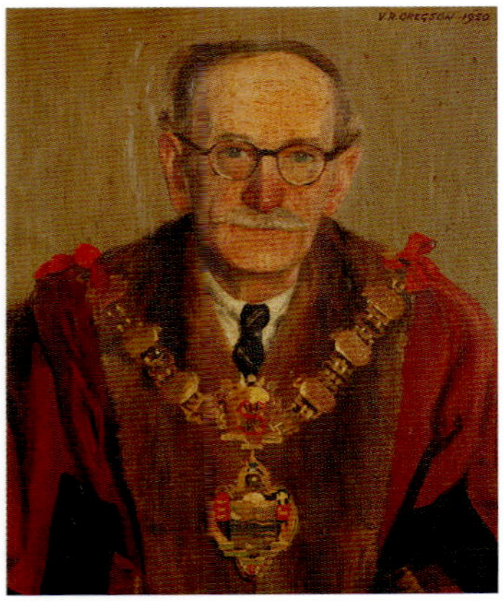

Gregson, V. R. active 1928–1950
Councillor Fred Taylor, Mayor of Darwen (1949–1950) 1950
oil on canvas 55 x 44
TH.7

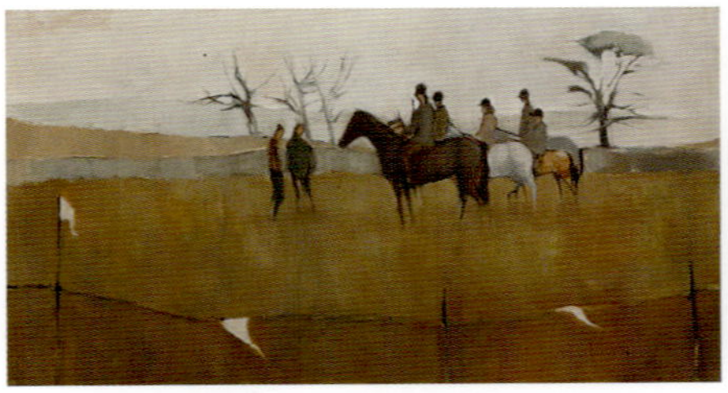

Griffiths, Patricia active 1950–1960s
Gymkhana c.1962
oil on canvas 30 x 55
616

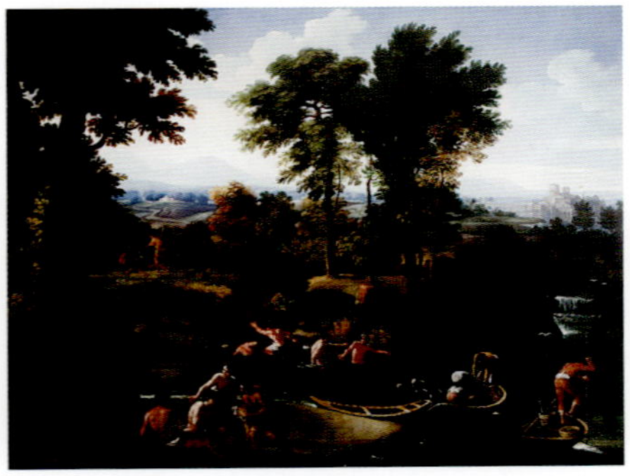

Grimaldi, Giovanni Francesco 1606–1680
Classical Italian Landscape c.1675–1680
oil on canvas 123 x 170.5
444

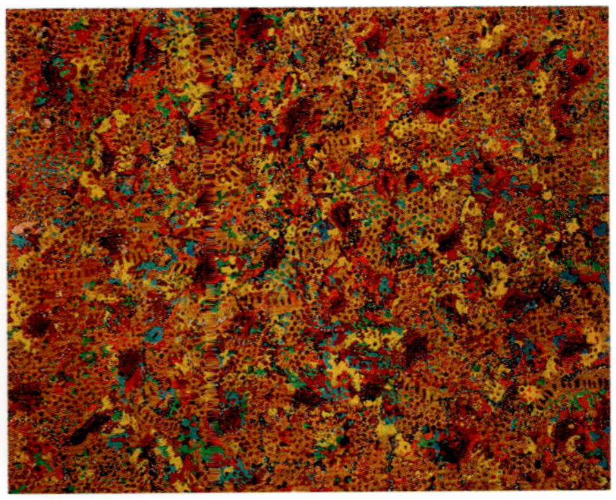

Grimbleby, David b.1949
Drifting Ground
oil on canvas 80 x 101
2011.8

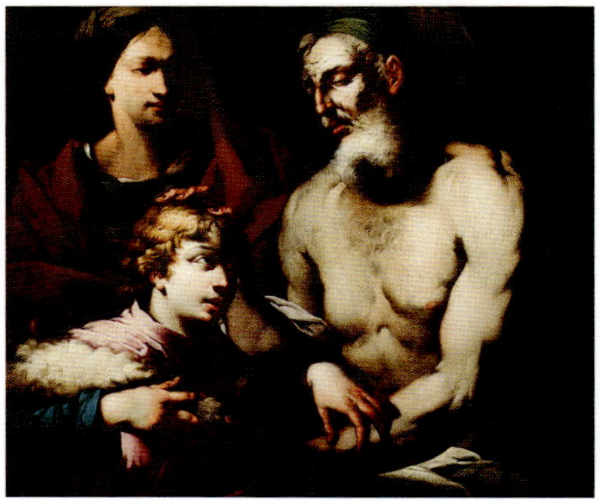

Guarino, Francesco (circle of) 1611–1654
Isaac Blessing Jacob
oil on canvas 94 x 117.5
613

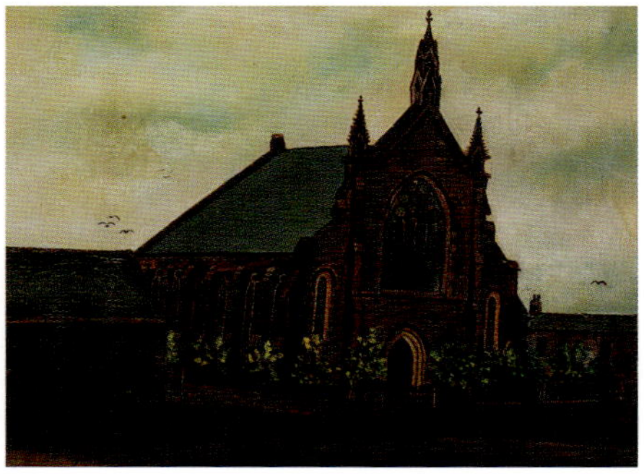

H., J.
Church 1927
oil on board 39 x 52
2011.95

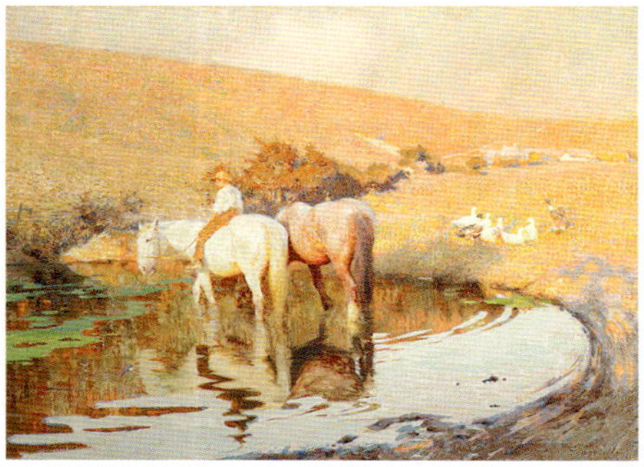

Hall, Frederick 1860–1948
Golden Evening 1899
oil on canvas 104.1 x 134.6 (E)
102

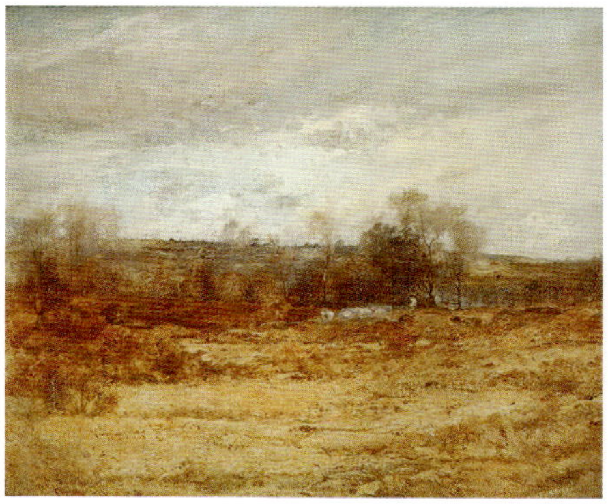

Hall, Oliver 1869–1957
Landscape 20th C
oil on canvas 66 x 81
477

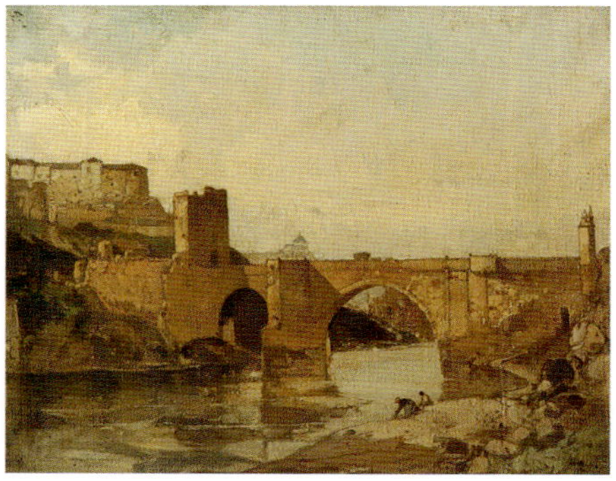

Hall, Oliver 1869–1957
Bridge at Toldeo, Spain
oil on canvas 54 x 67.5
248

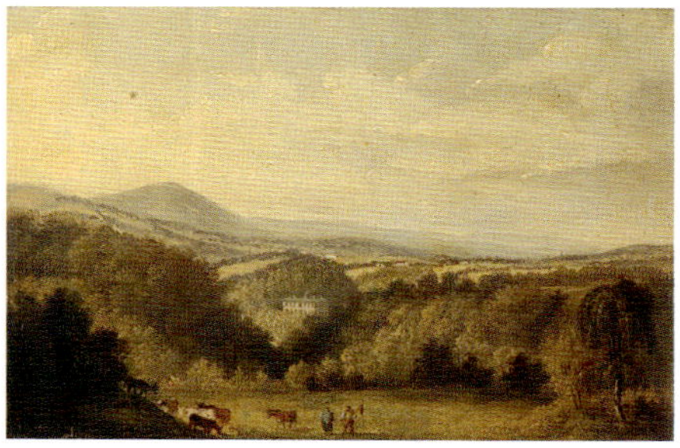

Hamilton, Mary active 19th C
Witton House in Feniscowles
oil on panel 15 x 22
600

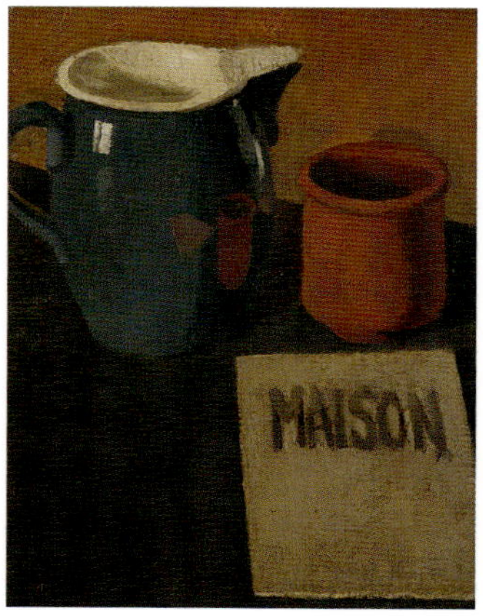

Hamnett, Nina 1890–1956
Still Life 1918
oil on canvas 44 x 34
653

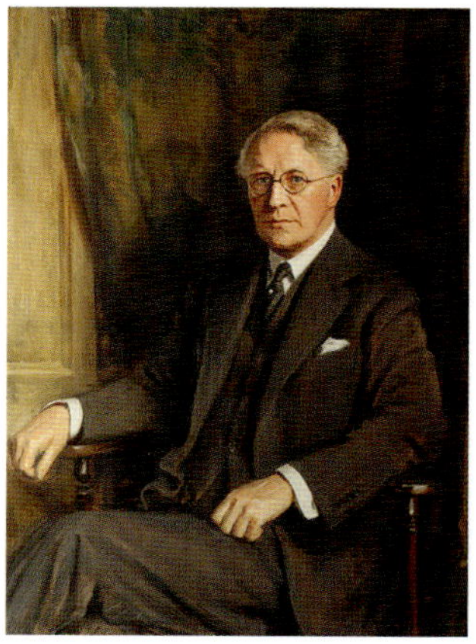

Harcourt, George 1868–1947
John Taylor 1937
oil on canvas 101 x 84
TH. 32

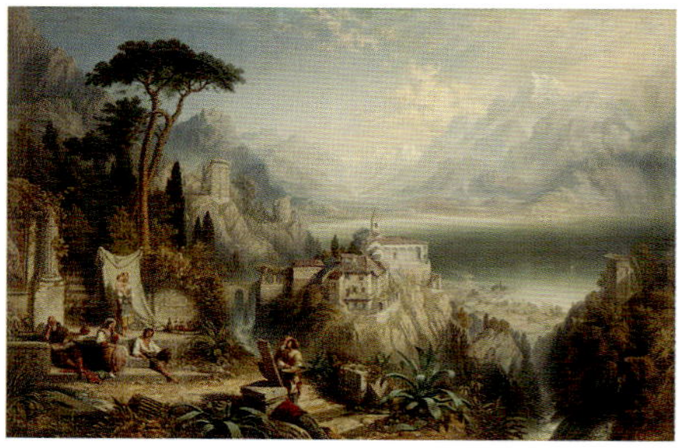

Harding, James Duffield 1798–1863
Locarno, Switzerland
oil on canvas 117 x 178.5
144

Facing page: Hampson, Roger, 1925–1996, *Miners, Hapton Valley*, Haworth Art Gallery (p. 11)

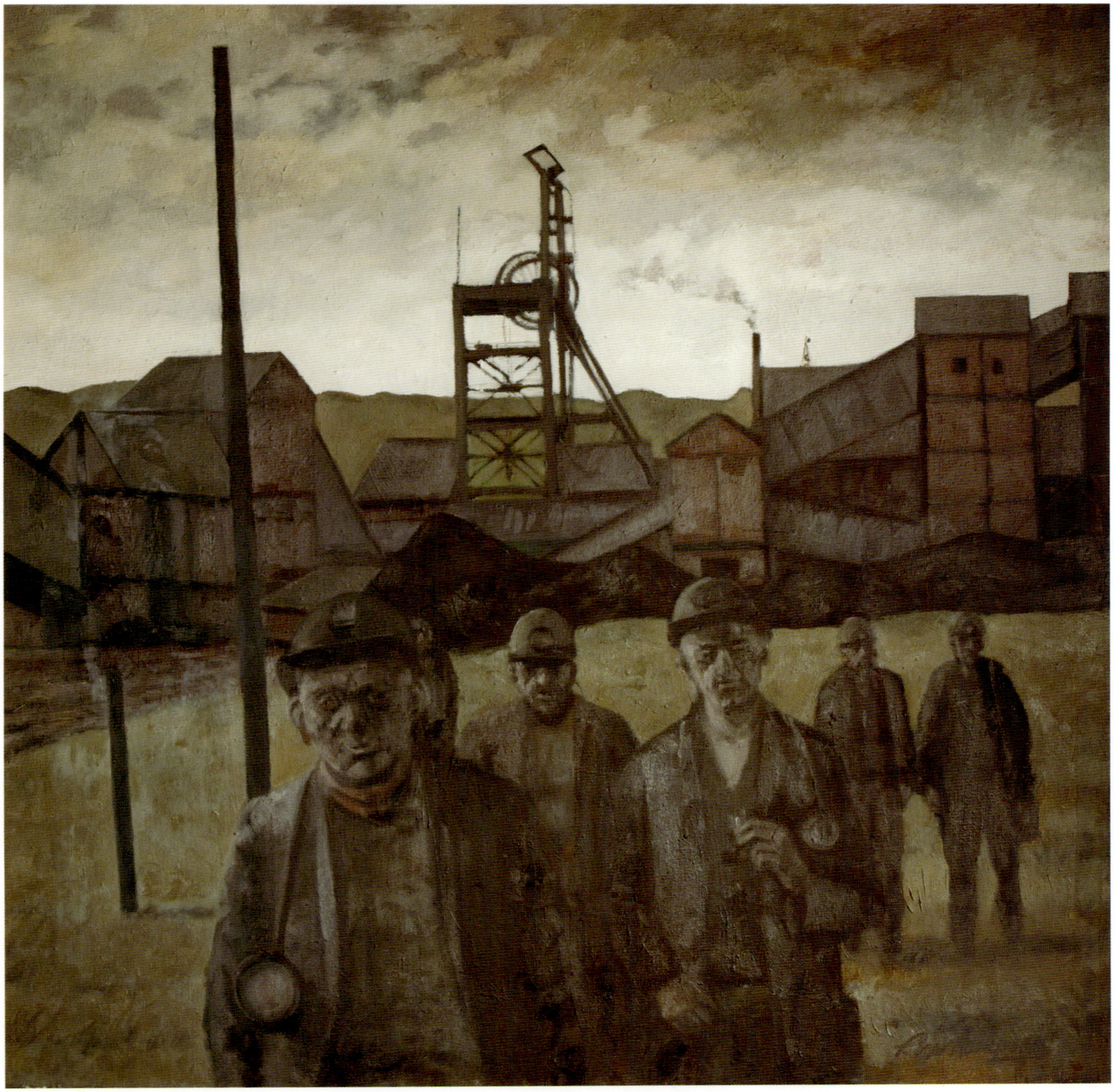

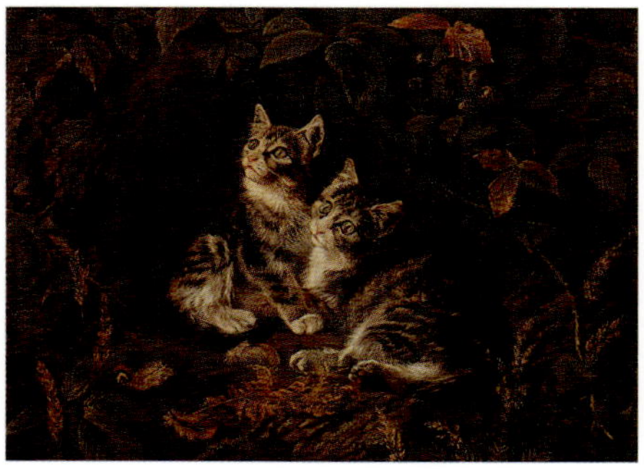

Harrison, George L. 1855–1925
Innocents Abroad 1883
oil on canvas 44 x 59
92

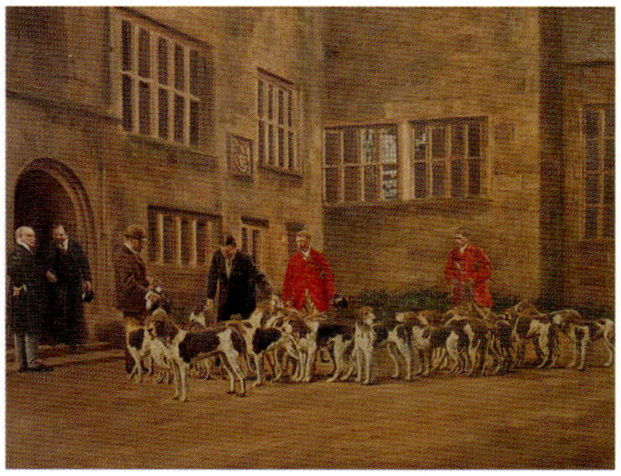

Harrison, J. F.
King George V Inspecting the Holcombe Hounds at Houghton Tower 1925
oil on canvas 70 x 90
931

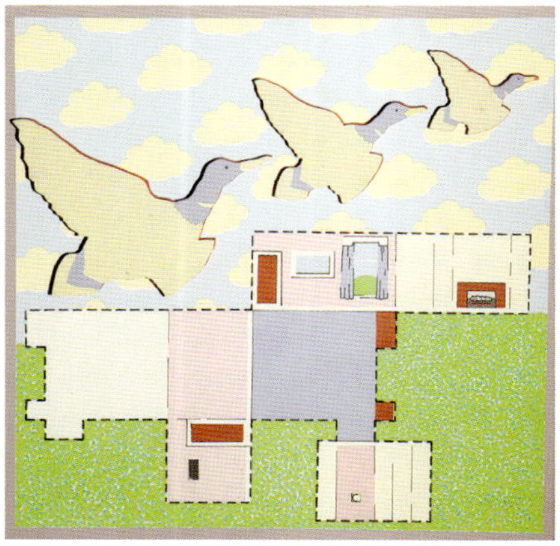

Harwood, Frank b.1955
Open House
acrylic & wood on board 80.9 x 80.9
1094

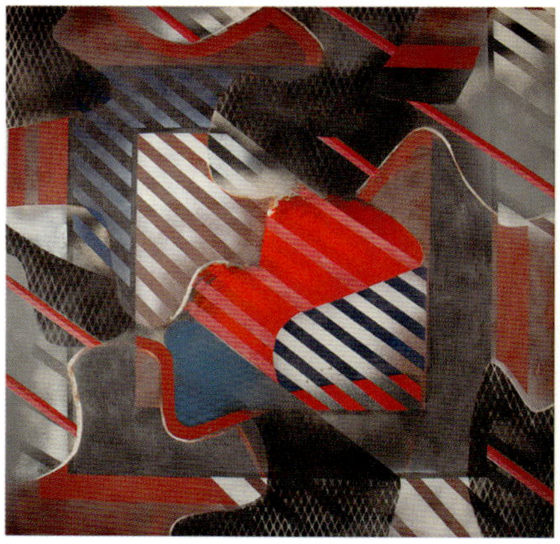

Haslam, Raymond active 1967
Square Shift
oil on board 122 x 122
714

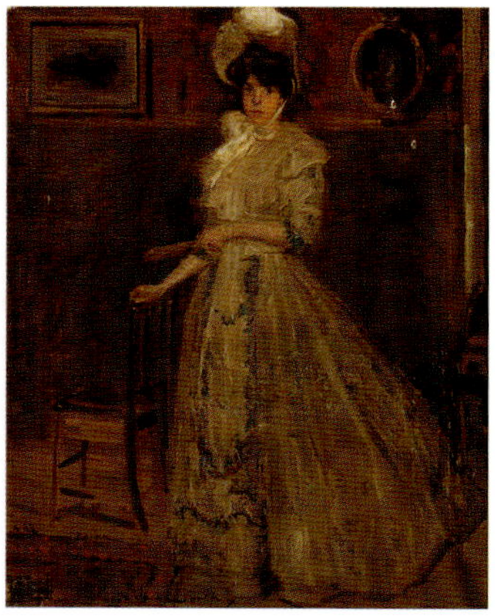

Haworth, Charles Singleton 1884–1917
La Debutante 1910
oil on canvas 59 x 49
810

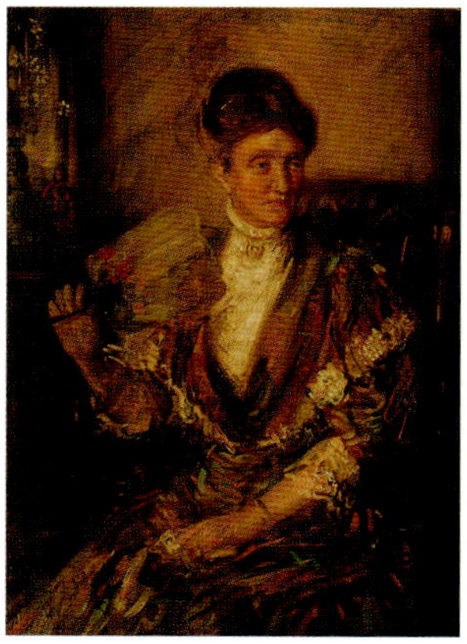

Haworth, Charles Singleton 1884–1917
Margaret Haworth 1912
oil on canvas 90 x 70
812

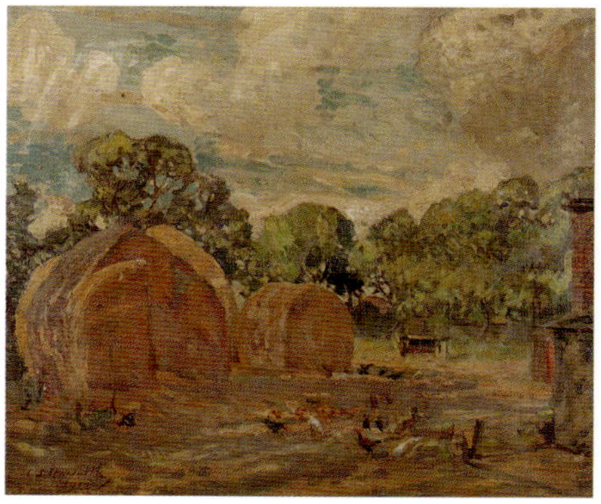

Haworth, Charles Singleton 1884–1917
The Stack Yard, Sydney's Far, Freshfields, near Southport 1912
oil on canvas 60 x 75
811

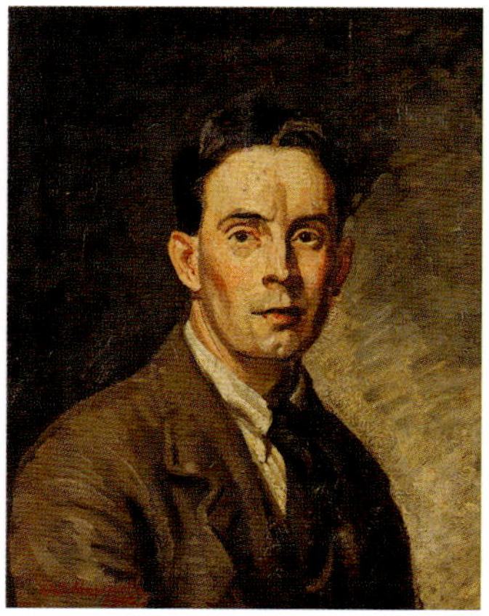

Haworth, Charles Singleton 1884–1917
Self Portrait 1916
oil on canvas 50 x 39
809

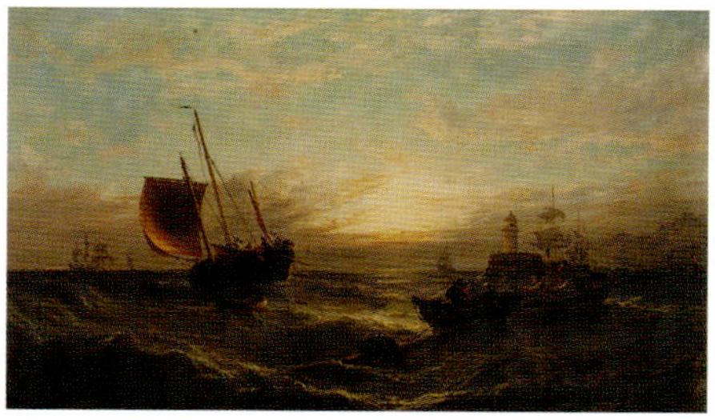

Hayes, Edwin 1819–1904
Off Ramsgate late 19th C
oil on canvas 69 x 120
584

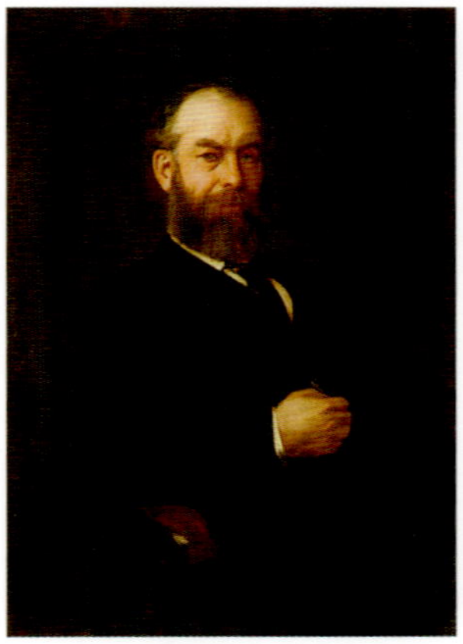

Hayes, William active 1850–1882
James Dickinson (1830–1887) 1882
oil on canvas 90 x 67
273

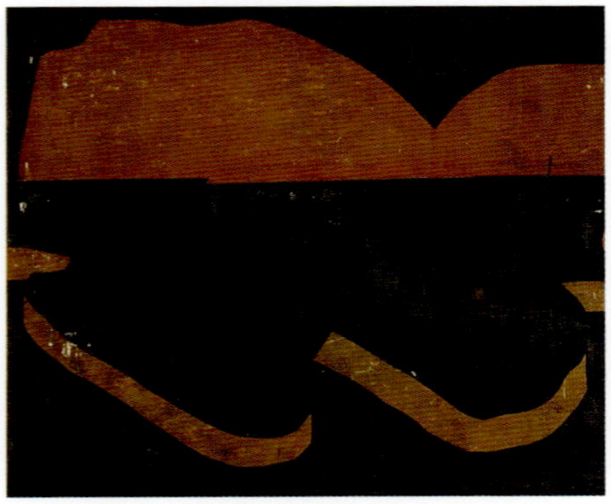

Hellawell, Harry 1921–2004
Landscape Form c.1969
oil on board 56 x 64
772

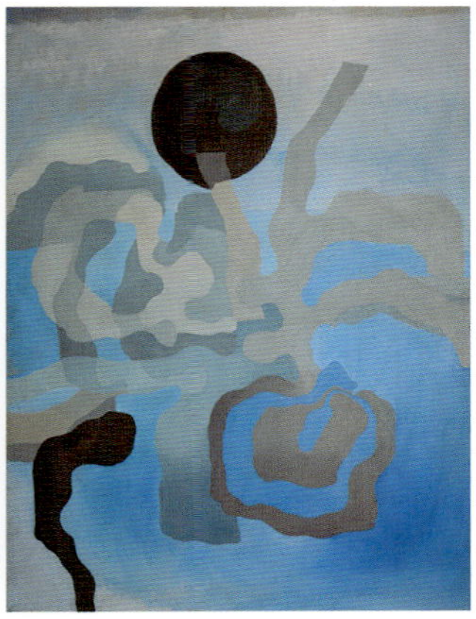

Hellawell, Harry 1921–2004
Release c.1969
oil on canvas 153 x 122
770

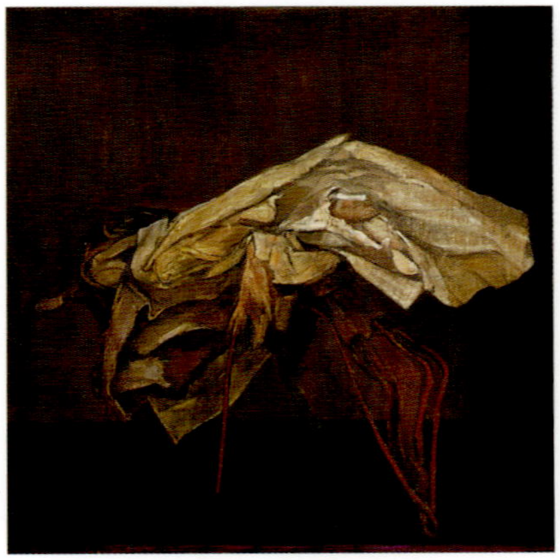

Hellawell, Harry 1921–2004
Pram Cover
oil on canvas 120 x 121
771

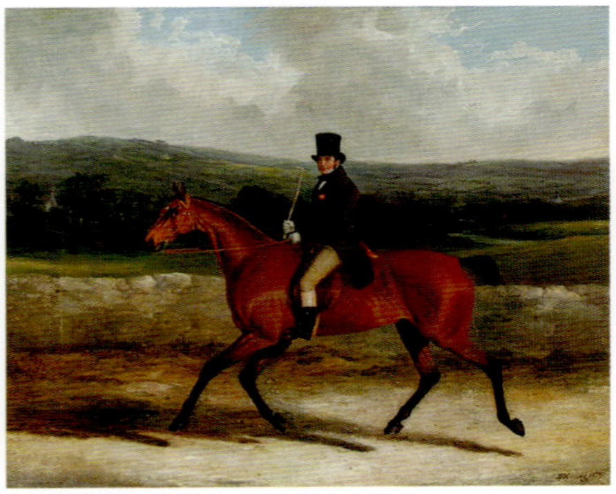

Herring I, John Frederick 1795–1865
William Ward on Horseback 1839
oil on canvas 75 x 82.5
424

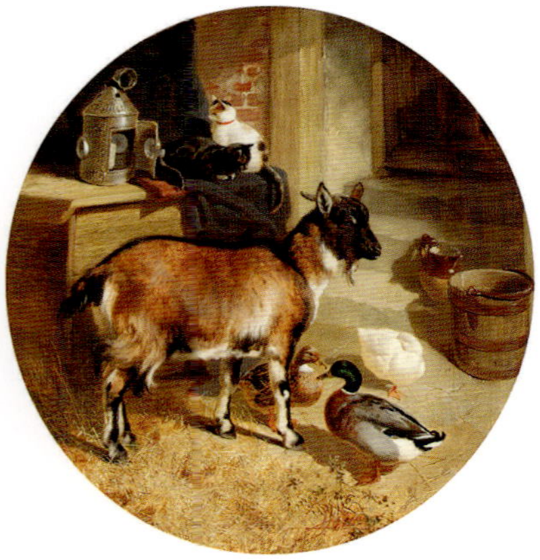

Herring I, John Frederick 1795–1865
Nanny 1848
oil on canvas 54.6 x 54.6
72

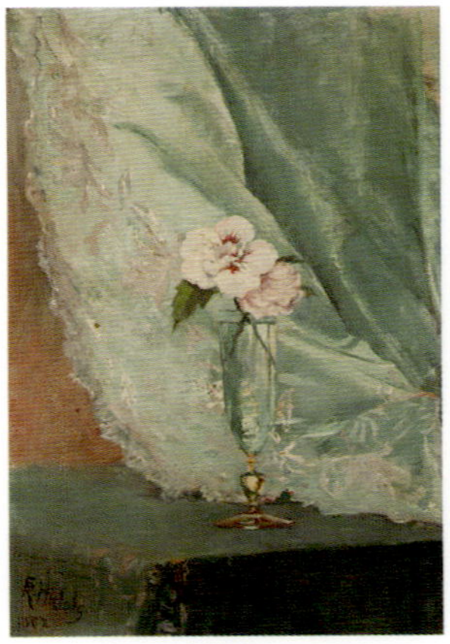

Hidalgo y Padilla, Félix Resurreccion 1857–1915
Still Life (Flowers in a Vase) 1882
oil on canvas 53 x 36
335

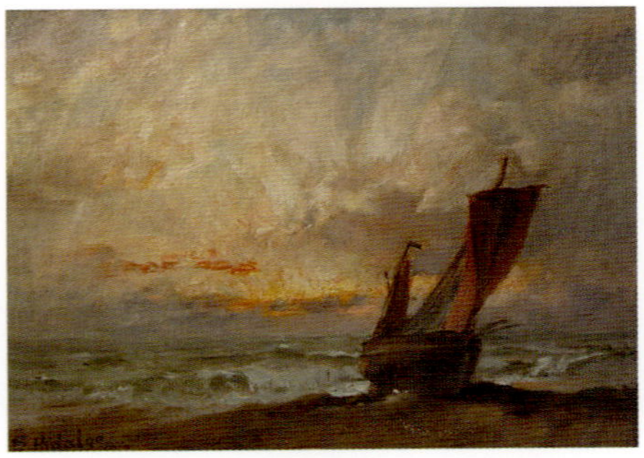

Hidalgo y Padilla, Félix Resurreccion 1857–1915
Seascape c.1910
oil on canvas 22 x 32
334

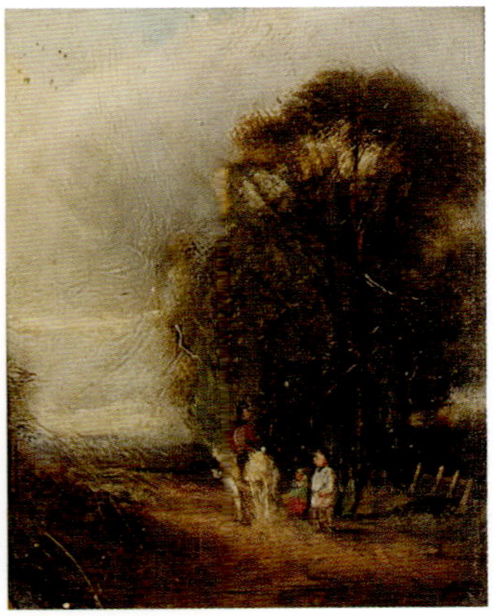

Hindle, William 1811–1890
Landscape
oil on panel 12 x 10
638

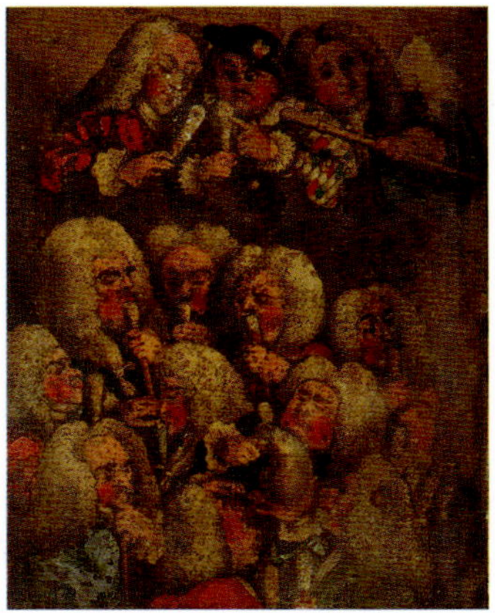

Hogarth, William 1697–1764
The Undertakers Company
oil on paper 13 x 11
971

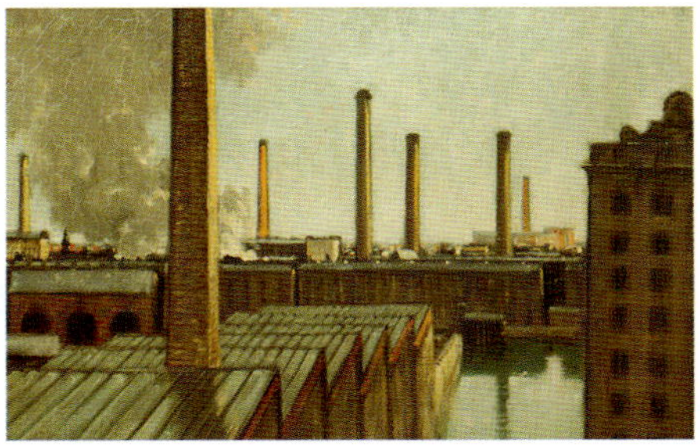

Holmes, Charles John 1868–1936
Seven Chimneys early 20th C
oil on canvas 43 x 78
647

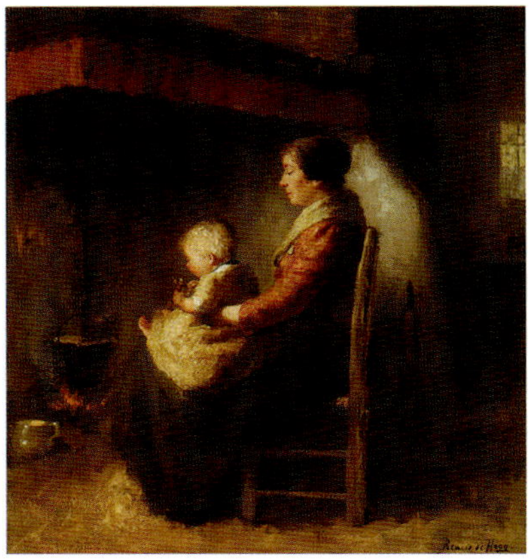

Hoog, Bernard de 1867–1943
Dutch Interior
oil on canvas 59.8 x 53.4
121

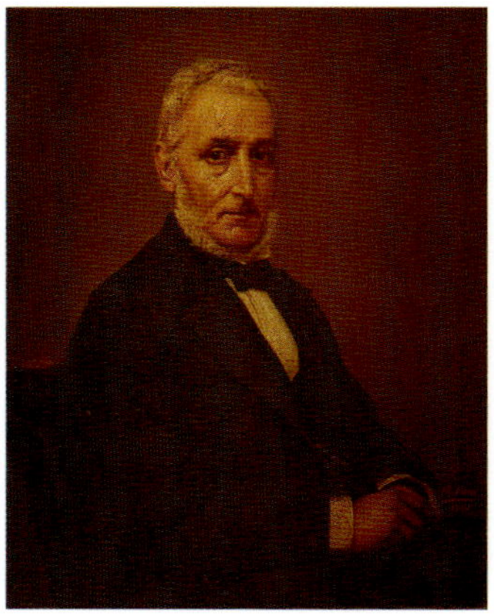

Hora, H. active 1860–1881
Thomas Ainsworth (1801–1890), Clerk to the County Magistrates 1881
oil on canvas 39 x 32
112

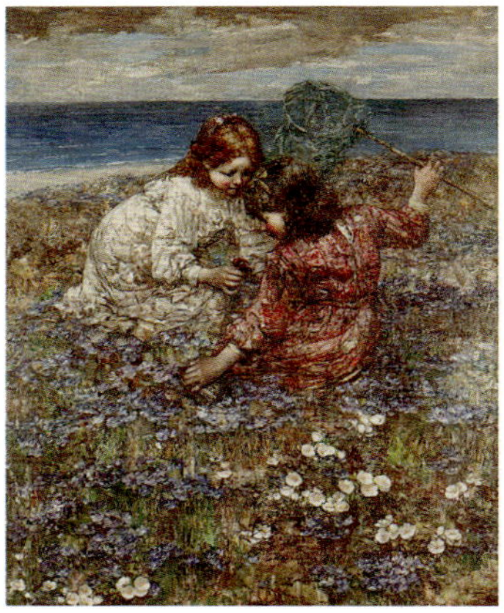

Hornel, Edward Atkinson 1864–1933
End of the Butterfly Chase 1911
oil on canvas 150 x 120
135

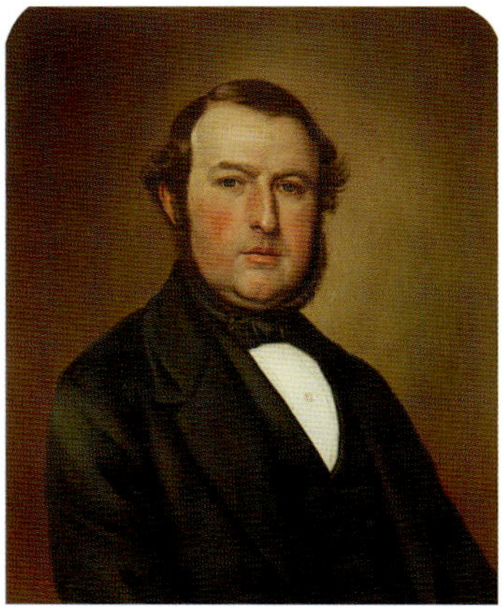

Hoyoll, Philipp 1818–1876
Alderman Robert Duckworth, JP 1859
oil on canvas 59 x 50
TH.2

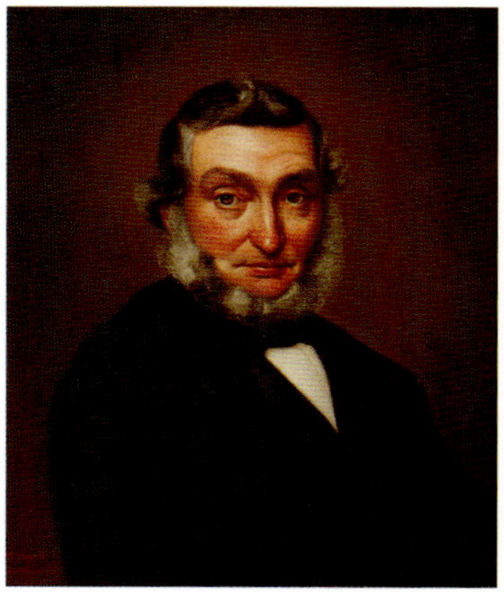

Hoyoll, Philipp 1818–1876
Thomas Butterfield 1859
oil on canvas 32 x 27.5
104

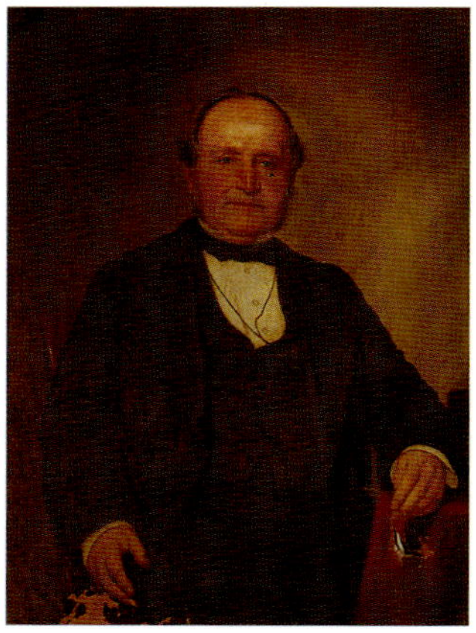

Hoyoll, Philipp 1818–1876
Thomas Hart (1799–1859), JP 1859
oil on canvas 89 x 68
2011.89

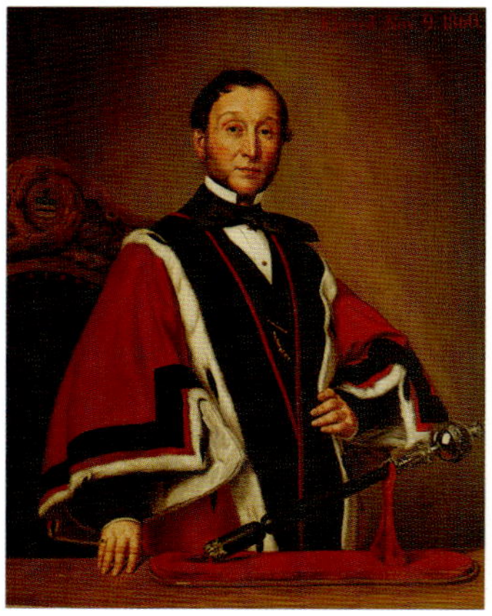

Hoyoll, Philipp 1818–1876
Thomas Thwaites 1861
oil on canvas 109 x 85
TH. 31

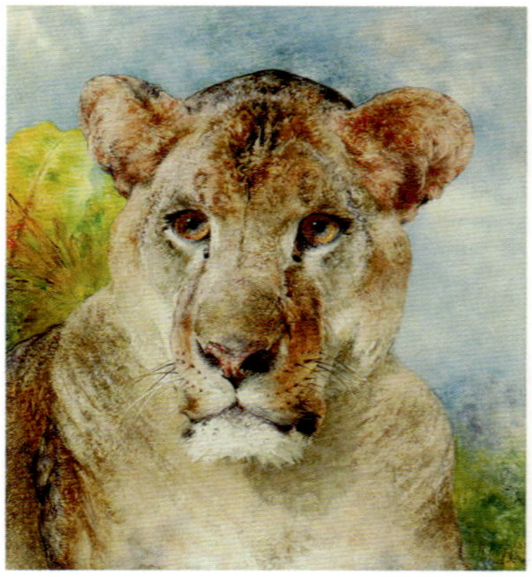

Huggins, William 1820–1884
Head of a Lioness 1878
oil on canvas 55.3 x 45.7 (E)
97

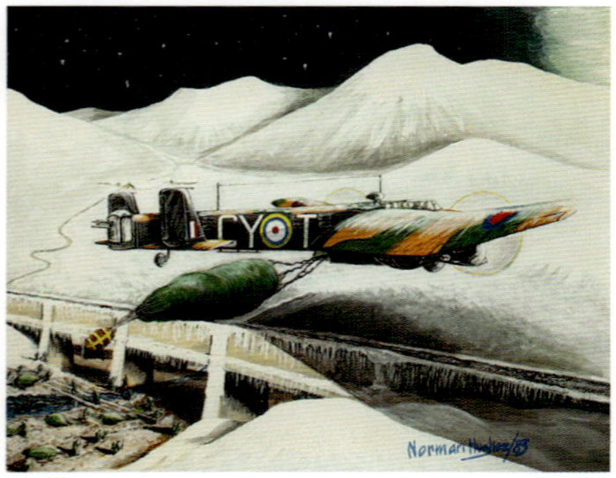

Hughes, Norman
Operation Colossus 1983
oil on canvas 90 x 120
2011.85

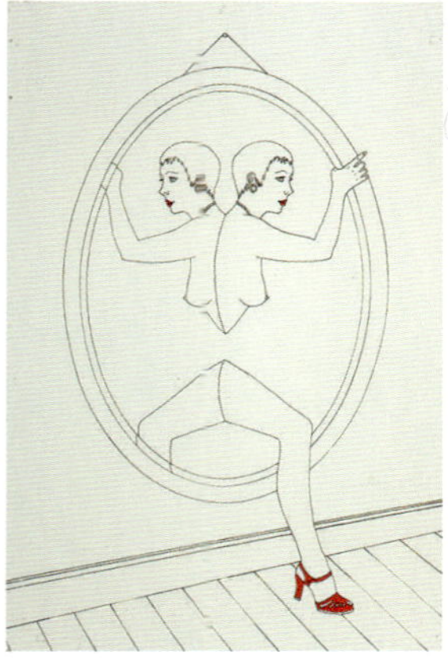

Hughes, Patrick b.1939
Out into the Interior late 20th C
gloss & enamel on board 91.4 x 60.9
1089

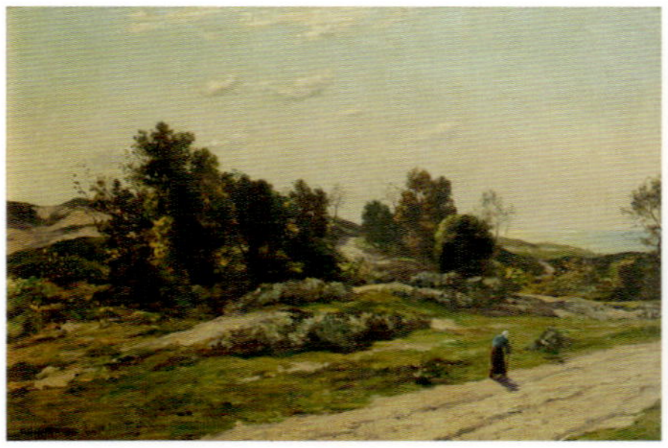

Hughes-Stanton, Herbert Edwin Pelham 1870–1937
Sunlight across the Sea 1912
oil on canvas 72 x 103
139

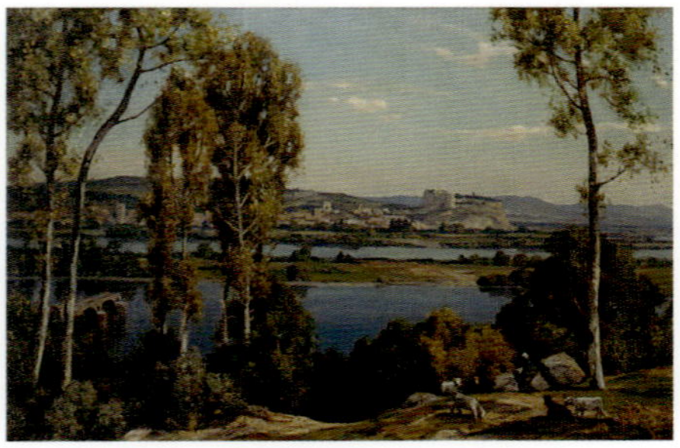

Hughes-Stanton, Herbert Edwin Pelham 1870–1937
Villeneuve les Avignon 1921
oil on canvas 59 x 89
241

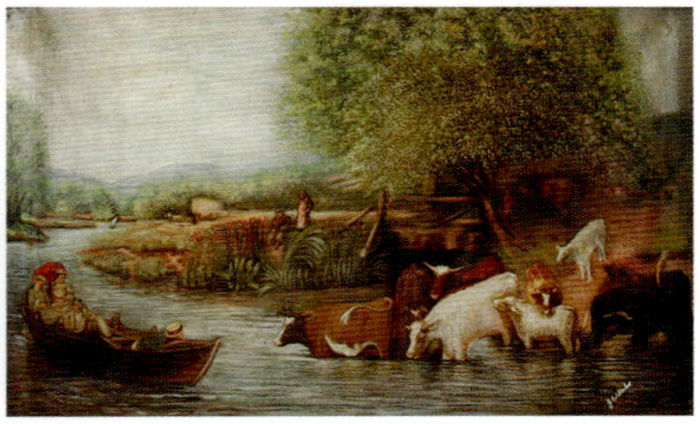

Hulse, J. W. active late 19th C–early 20th C
Landscape
oil on canvas 81 x 135
2011.74

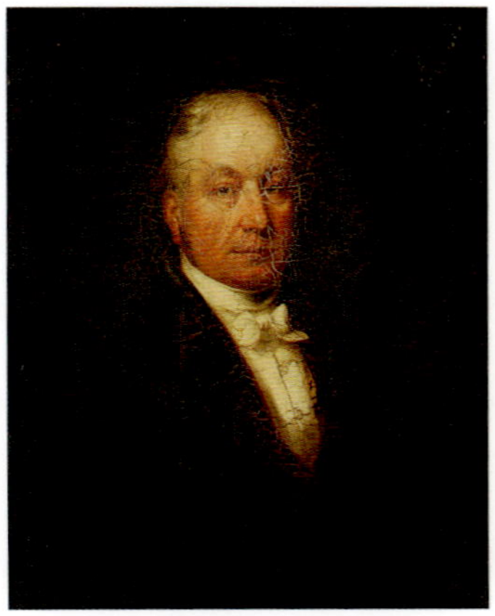

Illidge, Thomas Henry 1799–1851
James Pickup
oil on canvas 74 x 62
49

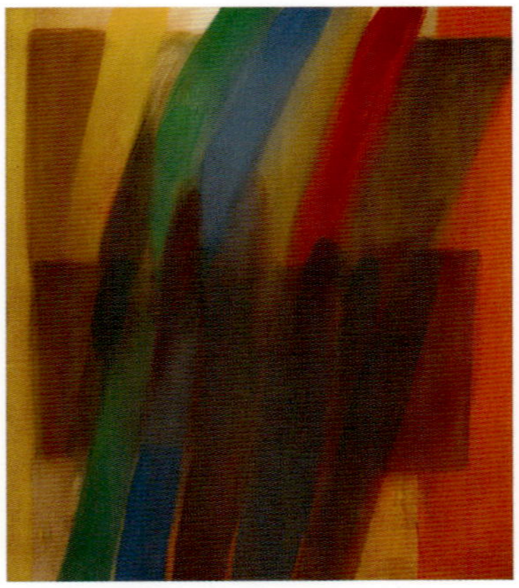

Irvin, Albert b.1922
Rider 1969
oil on canvas 203 x 178
2011.70

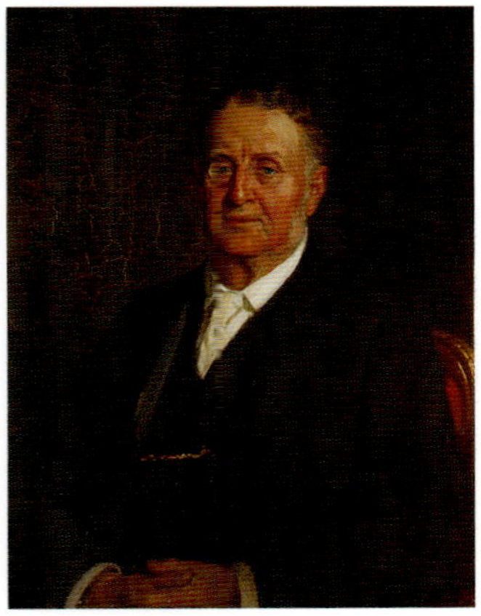

Jacomb-Hood, George Percy 1857–1929
Sir William Hornby (1841–1928), MP 1918
oil on canvas 75 x 62
TH. 28

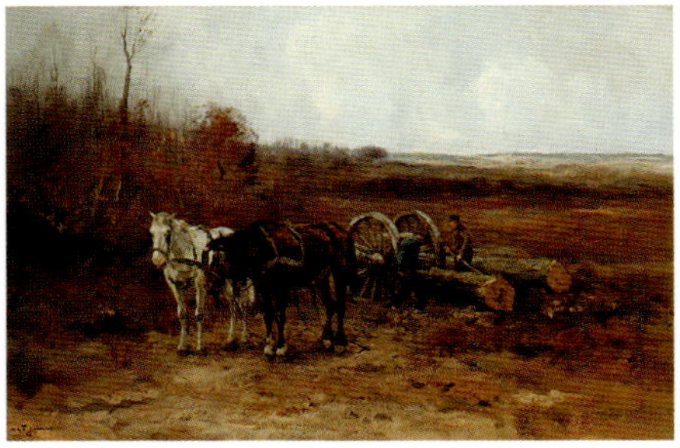

Jansen, Willem Georg Frederik 1871–1949
Hauling Timber
oil on canvas 92.5 x 137
266

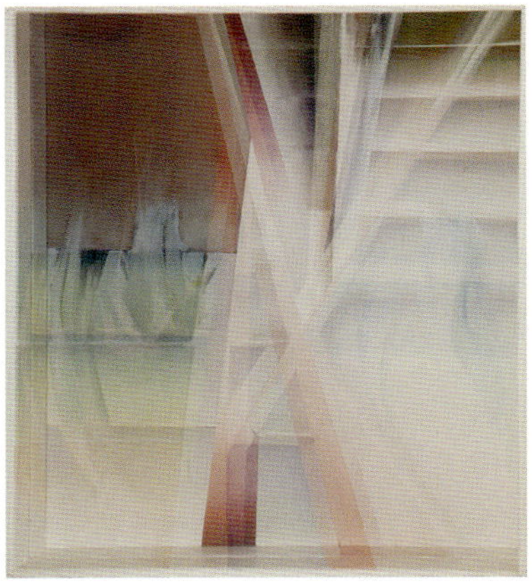

Johnson, Llima active late 20th C
Movement on Staircase
oil & nylon mesh in perspex box on canvas 94.6 x 94.6
1100

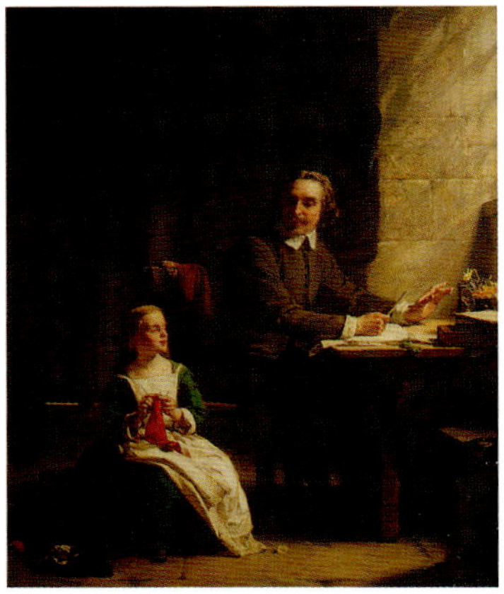

Johnston, Alexander 1815–1891
John Bunyan in Bedford Prison late 19th C
oil on canvas 108 x 88
824

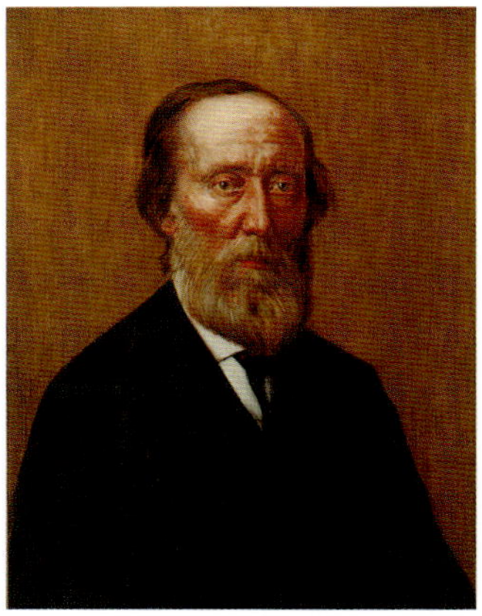

Johnston, William Herbert 1848–1897
William Billington (1825–1884), Blackburn Poet and Author
oil on canvas 97 x 60
114

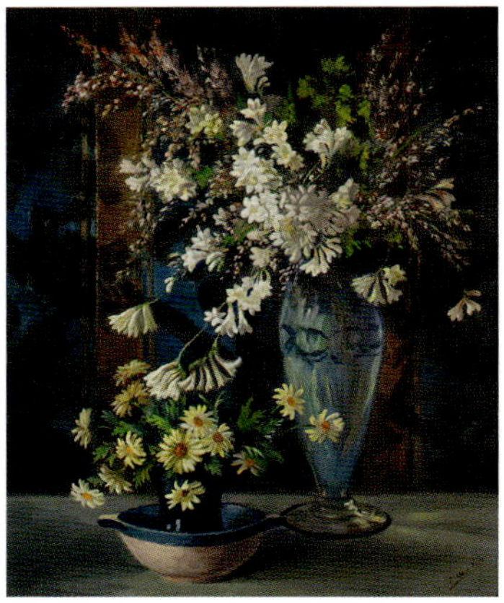

Kerr, Esther Barbara Nicloux 1861–1950
Freesias
oil on board 75 x 62
307

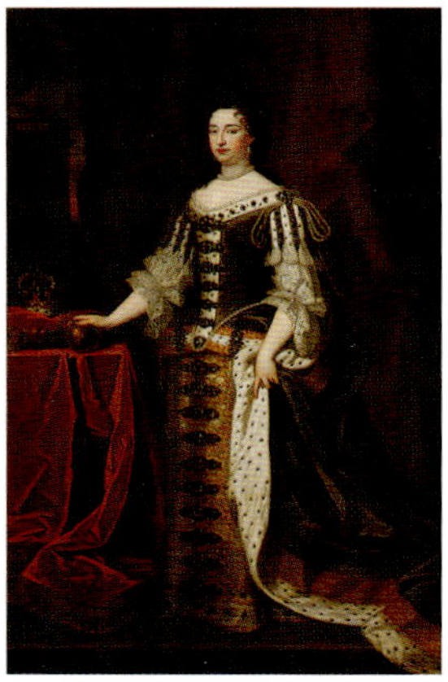

Kneller, Godfrey 1646–1723
Mary II (1662–1694)
oil on canvas 233.3 x 142.2
250

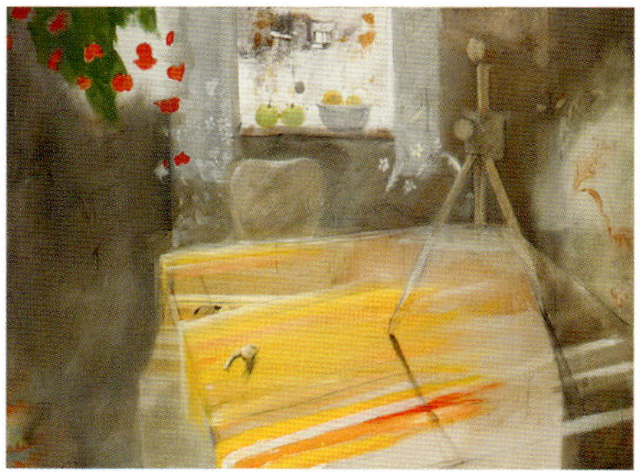

Knight, Frances active late 20th C
Untitled
oil & collage on canvas 60.9 x 91.4
1092

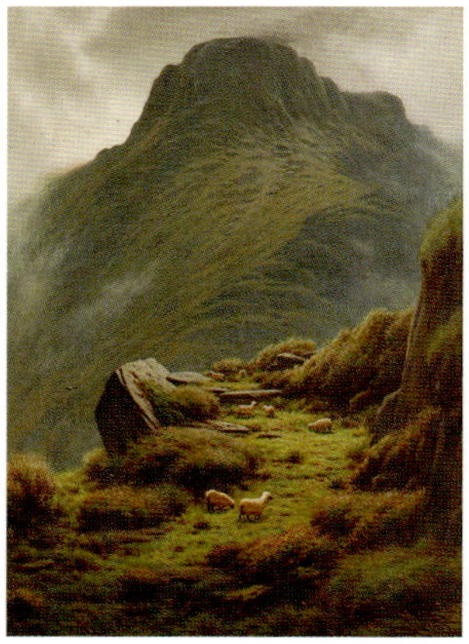

Knight, Joseph 1837–1909
Y Garn Mountains 1891
oil on canvas 121.92 x 86.36
86

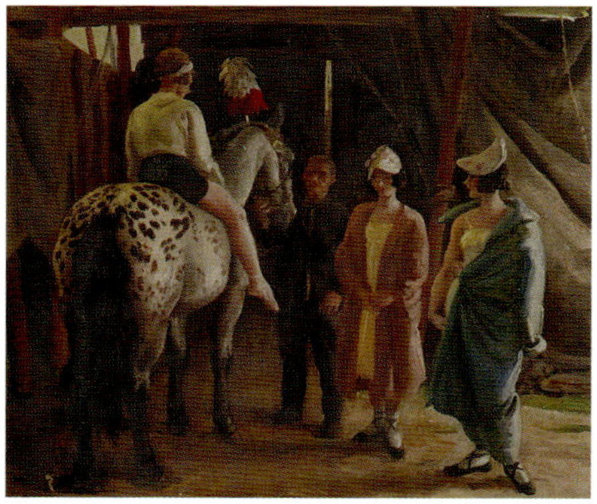

Knight, Laura 1877–1970
Ready to Show
oil on canvas 44 x 49
361

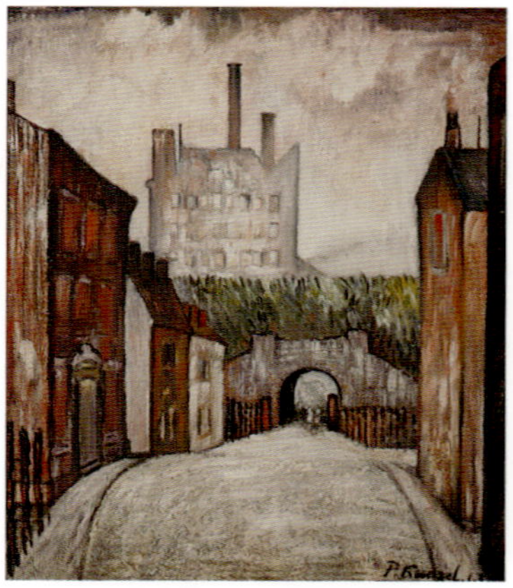

Kunzel, Prudence 1921–1989
Railway Bridge 1963
oil on board 47 x 40
2011.8

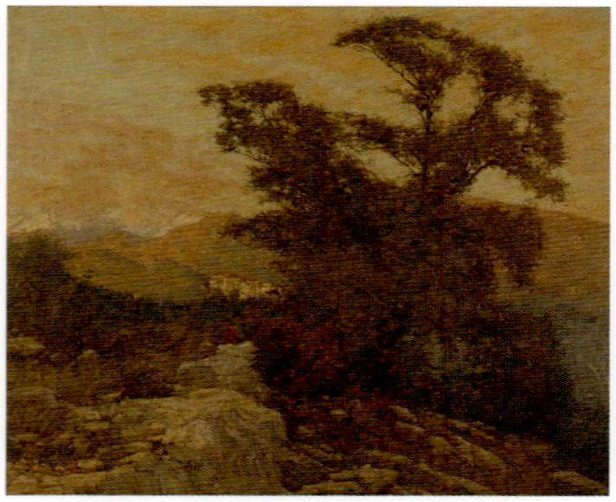

La Thangue, Henry Herbert 1859–1929
A Mountain Frontier c.1910
oil on canvas 71 x 81.5
390

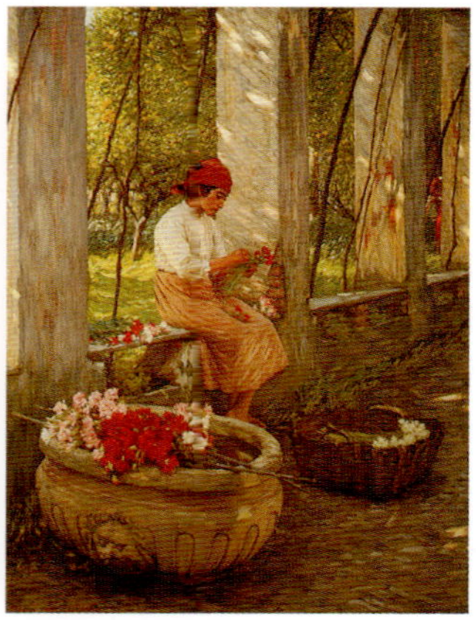

La Thangue, Henry Herbert 1859–1929
A Ligurian Flower Girl
oil on canvas 104 x 88
259

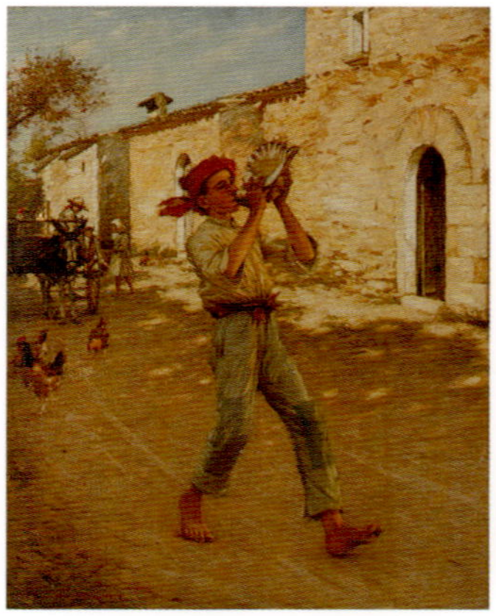

La Thangue, Henry Herbert 1859–1929
Crying Fish in Spain
oil on canvas 84 x 69
389

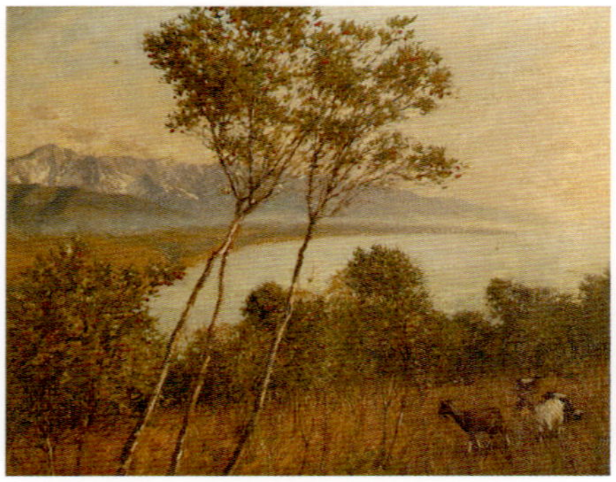

La Thangue, Henry Herbert 1859–1929
Ligurian Artrobus
oil on canvas 58 x 72.5
392

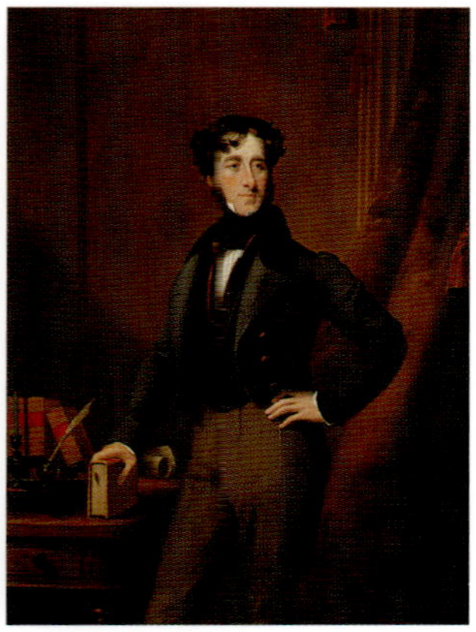

Lawrence, Thomas (circle of) 1769–1830
John Fowden Hindle
oil on canvas 141 x 111
107

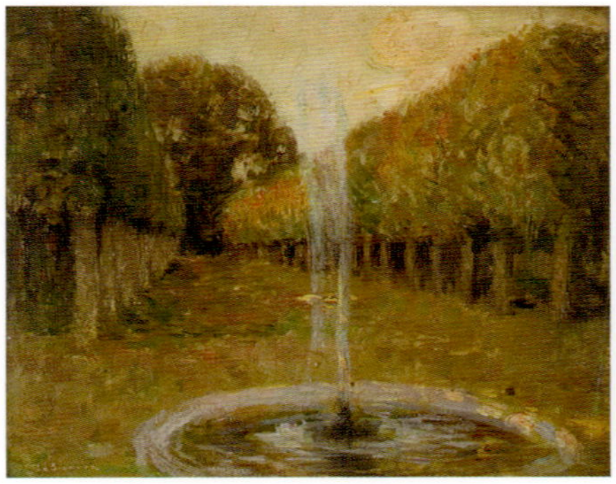

Le Sidaner, Henri Eugène 1862–1939
Corner of Versailles Park
oil on panel 16 x 20
336

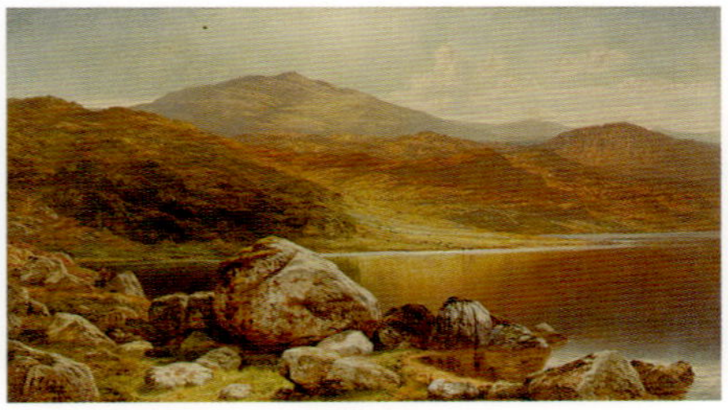

Leader, Benjamin Williams 1831–1923
A Fine Autumn Day, North Wales 1866
oil on canvas 73.5 x 130
83

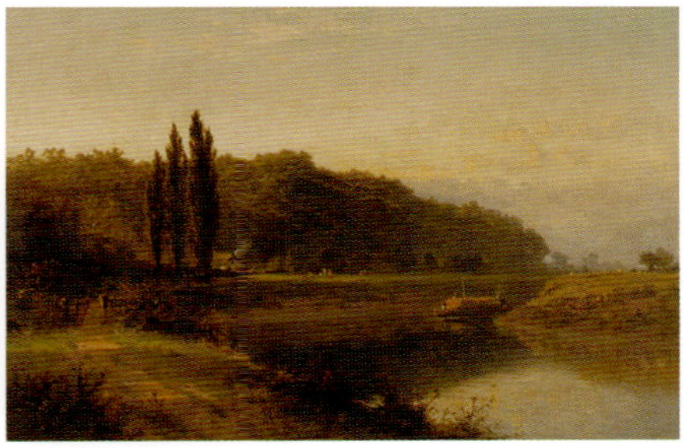

Leader, Benjamin Williams 1831–1923
On the Severn below Worcester 1889
oil on canvas 66 x 100
143

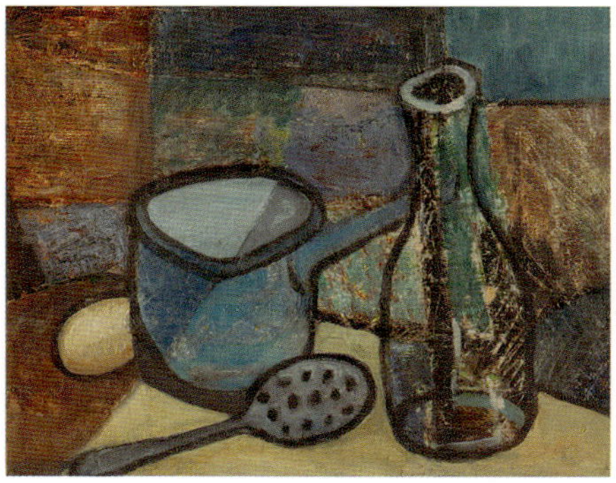

Learoyd, Barbara active 1963–c.1965
Still Life with Egg
oil on canvas 29 x 39
670

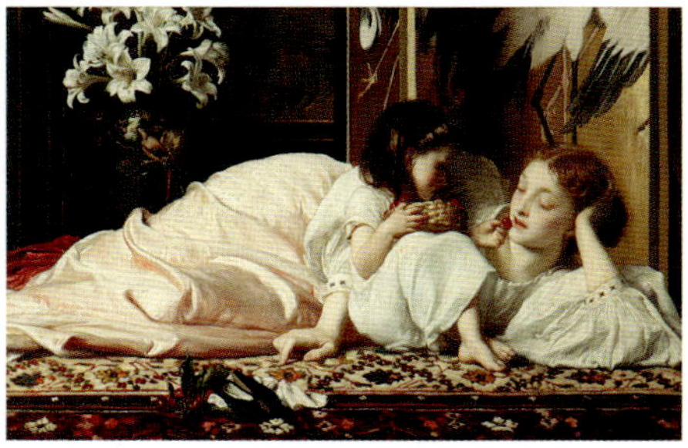

Leighton, Frederic 1830–1896
Mother and Child 1865
oil on canvas 48 x 82
127

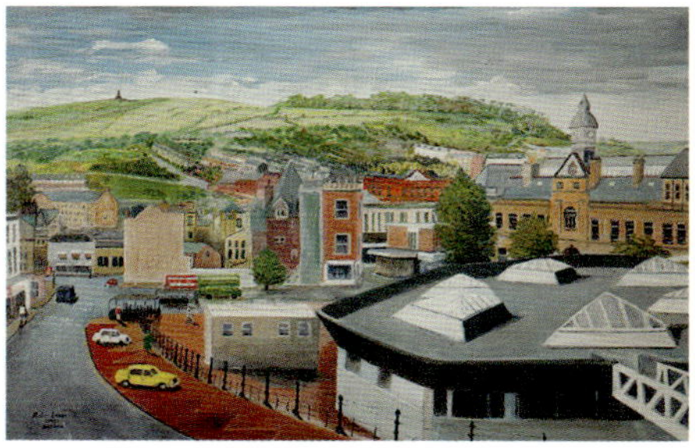

Lever, Ruby b.1912
Darwen 1992
oil on board 46 x 71
2009.140

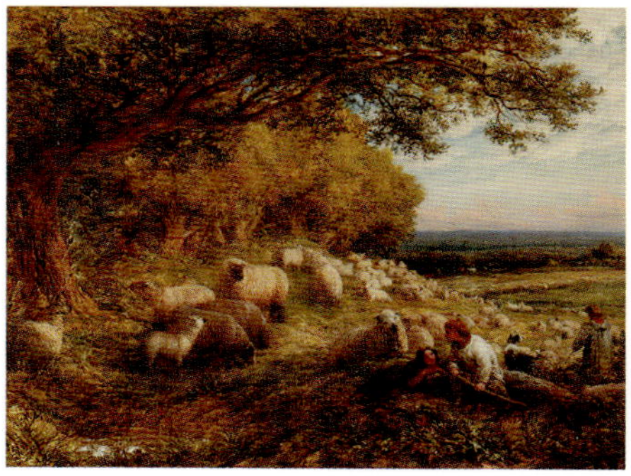

Linnell, John 1792–1882
Sheep 1867
oil on canvas 68 x 93
437

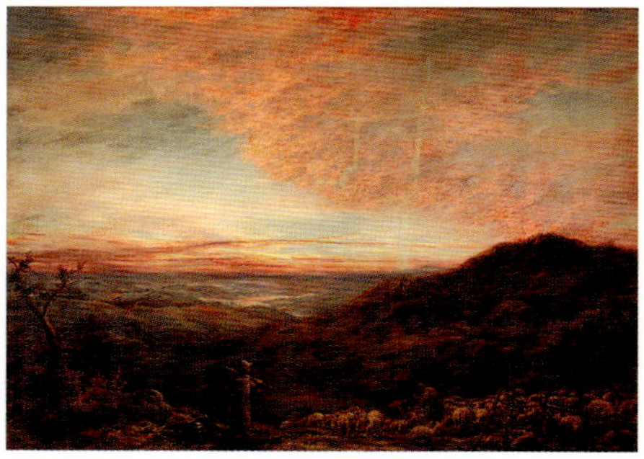

Linnell, William 1826–1906
Hesperus 1876
oil on canvas 135 x 182
110

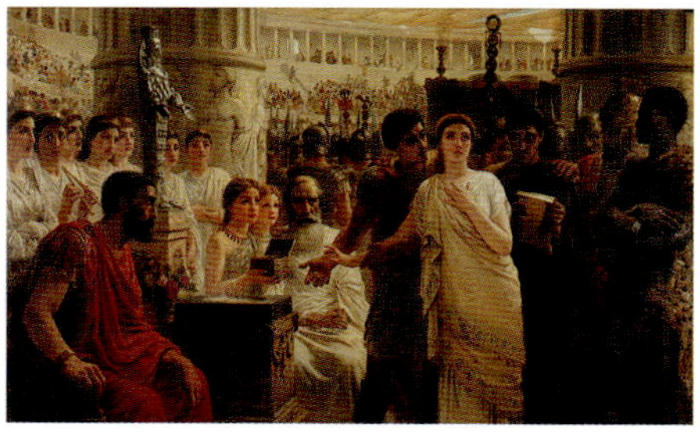

Long, Edwin 1829–1891
Diana or Christ? 1881
oil on canvas 121 x 211
146

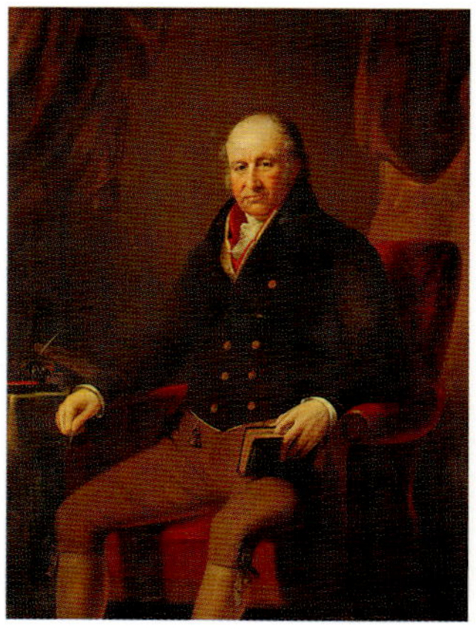

Lonsdale, James 1777–1839
John Hornby (1763–1841) 1839
oil on canvas 125 x 100
2006.7

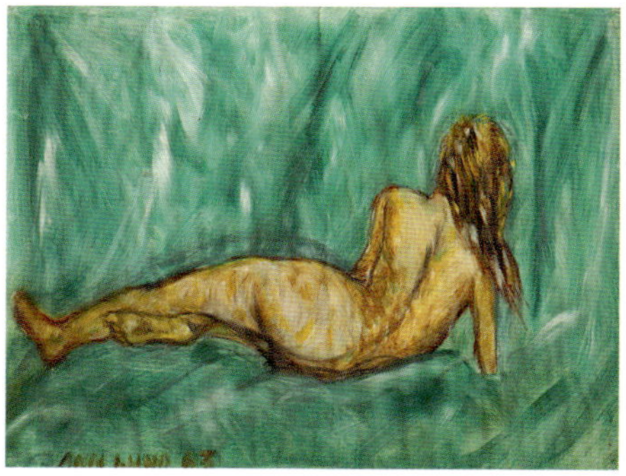

Lund, Ann
The Bronze Figure 1963
acrylic on paper 50 x 75
1194

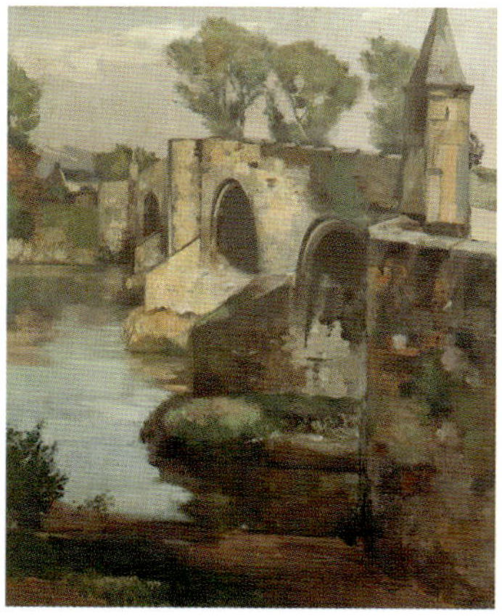

MacGregor, William York 1855–1923
Stirling Bridge 1906
oil on canvas 91 x 80
684

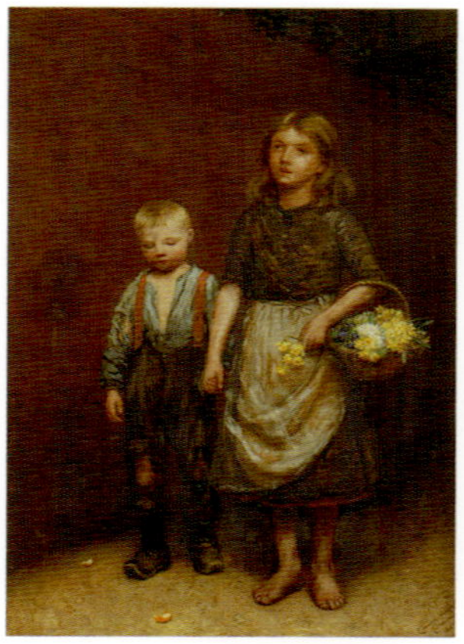

Magnus, Emma 1856–1936
Won't You Buy My Pretty Flowers
oil on canvas 90.2 x 61
70

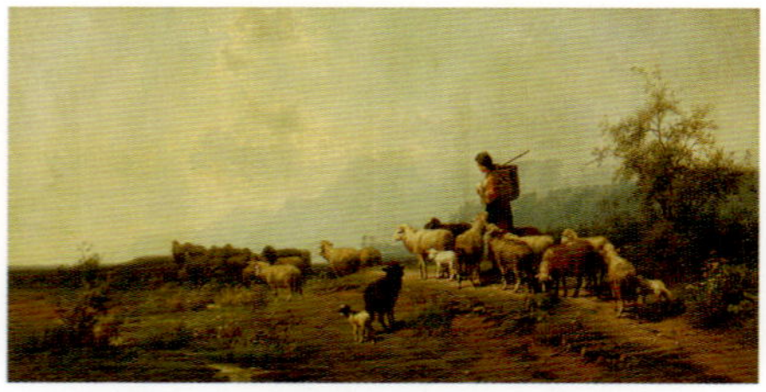

Mali, Christian Friedrich 1832–1906
The Shepherd's Return 1871
oil on canvas 48.3 x 94
213

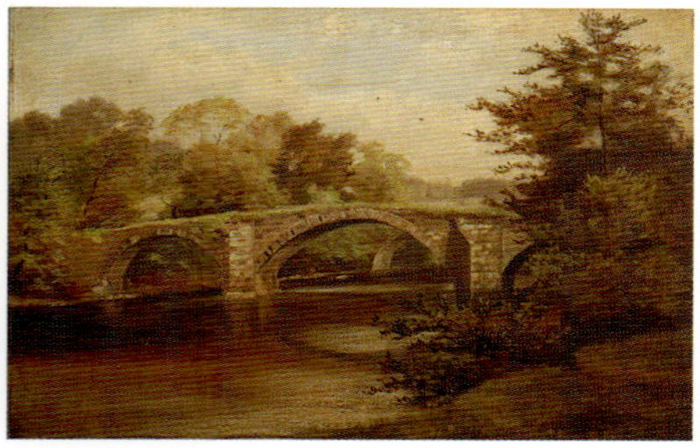

Masson, A. active late 19th C
Lower Hodder Bridge
oil on canvas 30 x 45
597

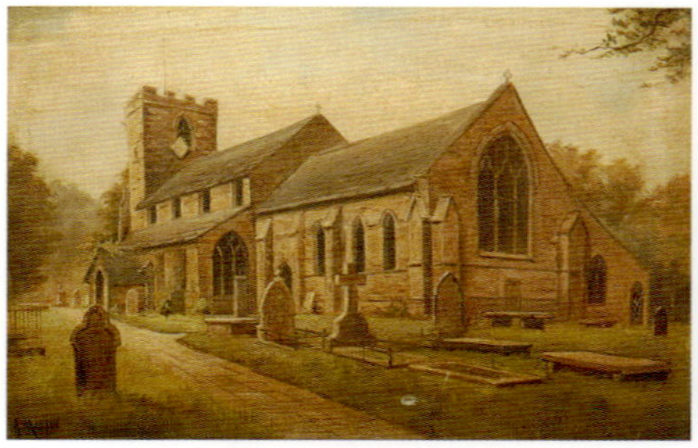

Masson, A. active late 19th C
Whalley Church
oil on canvas 30 x 45
598

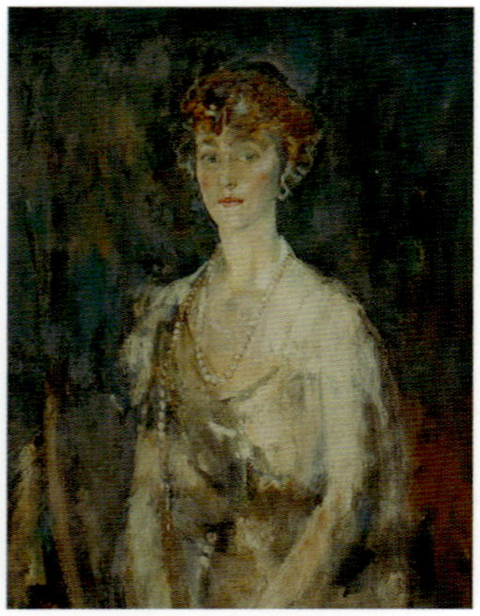

McEvoy, Ambrose 1878–1927
Countess of Granard
oil on canvas 92 x 72
323

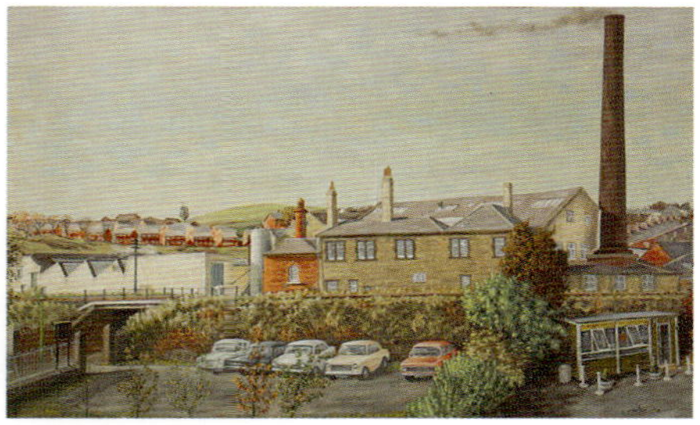

Miller, George E. 1913–1983
Lumb Bank Farm 1973
oil on canvas 59 x 95
942

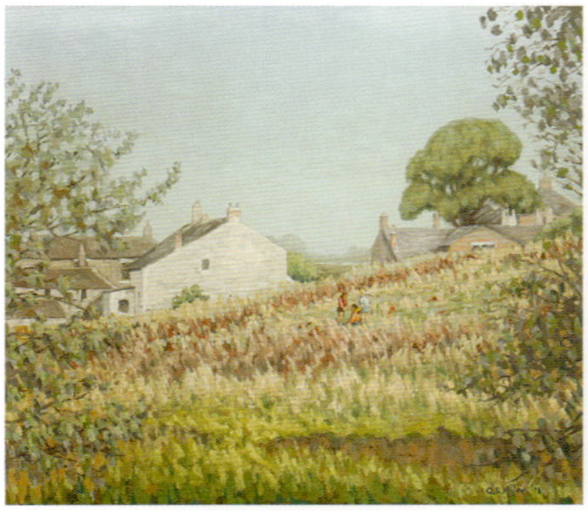

Miller, George E. 1913–1983
Pleckgate Fold 1973
oil on board 59 x 75
2008.57

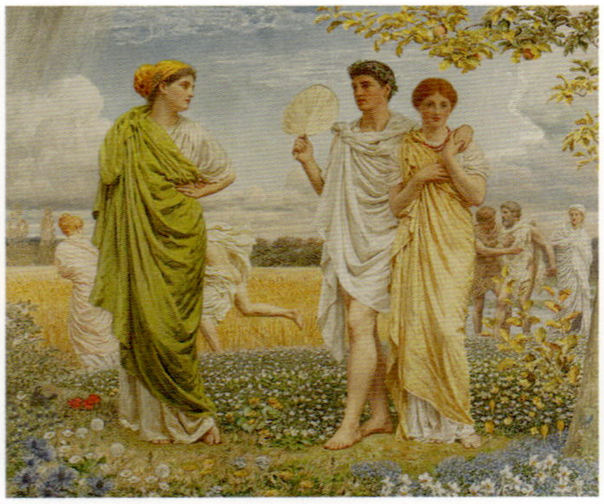

Moore, Albert Joseph 1841–1893
The Loves of the Winds and the Seasons 1893
oil on canvas 180 x 214.5
136

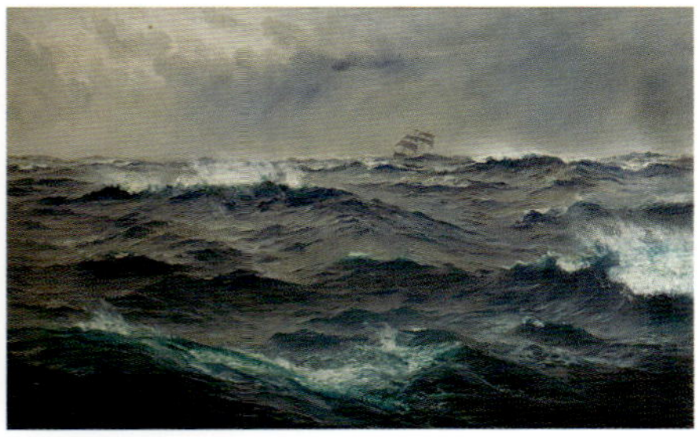

Moore, Henry 1831–1895
Rough Weather in the Mediterranean 1874
oil on canvas 99 x 155
115

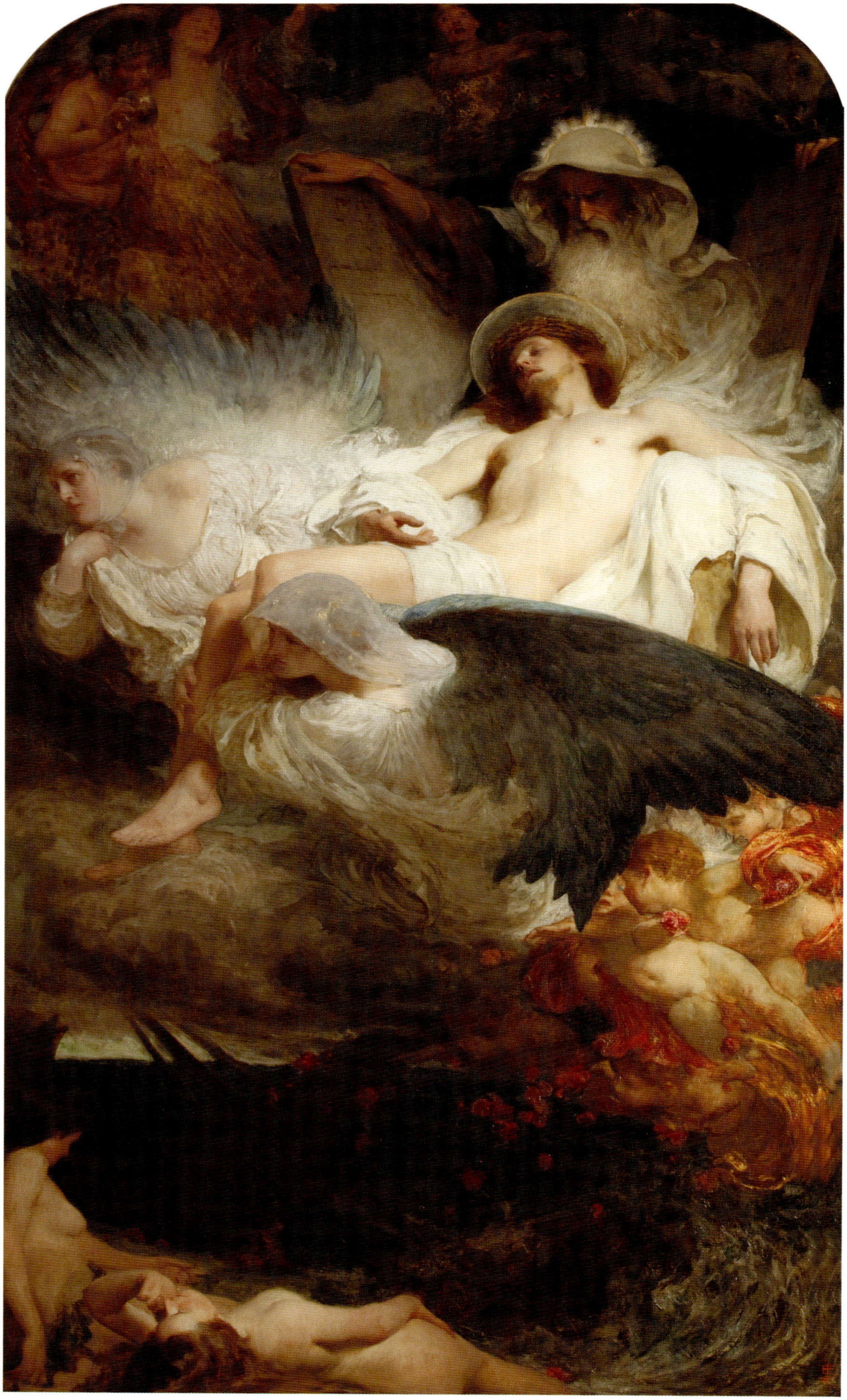

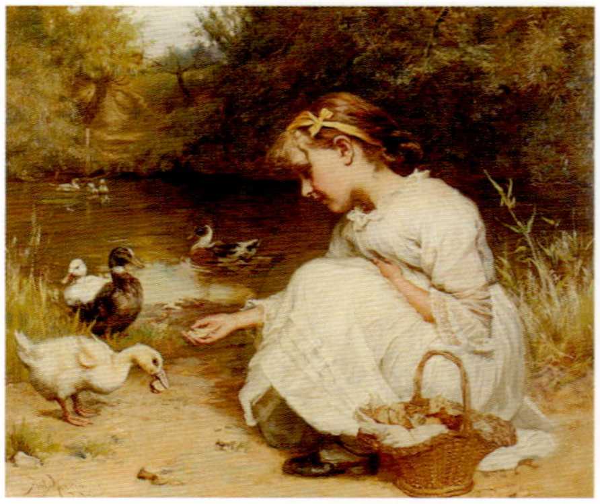

Morgan, Frederick 1856–1927
Making Friends 1885
oil on canvas 63 x 73
230

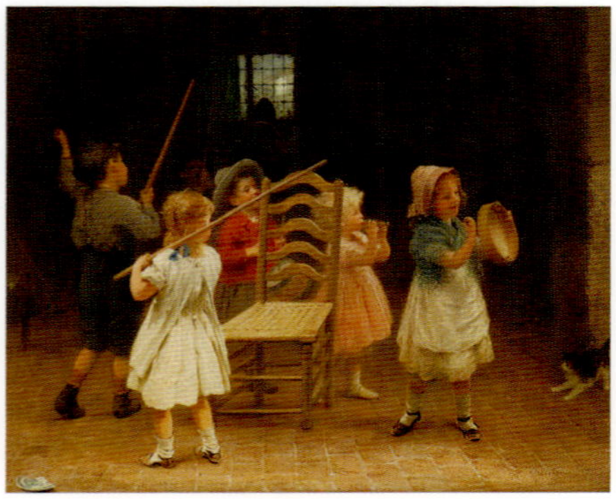

Morgan, John 1823–1886
Playing at Soldiers
oil on canvas 70 x 90
299

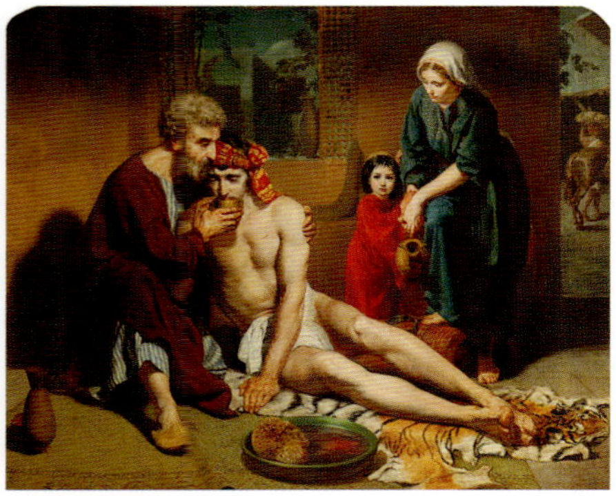

Morris, Philip Richard 1836–1902
The Good Samaritan 1857
oil on canvas 99 x 126
105

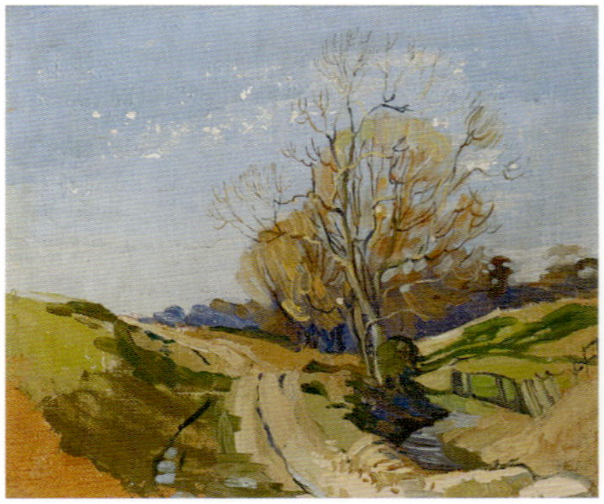

Morton, James Hargreaves 1881–1918
Landscape with Bare Trees early 20th C
oil on board 32 x 40
885

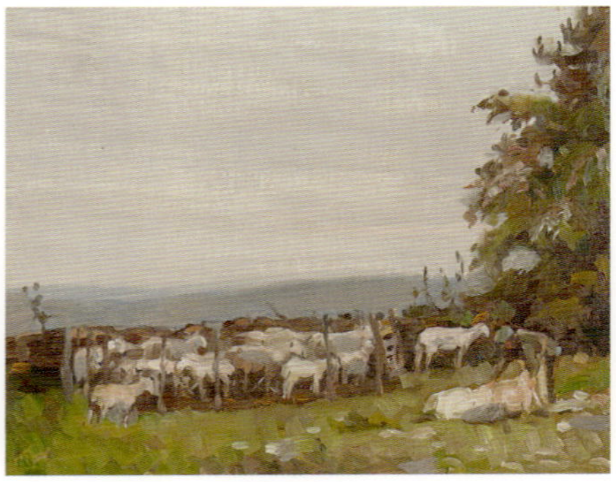

Morton, James Hargreaves 1881–1918
Sheep Shearing early 20th C
oil on board 38 x 48
880

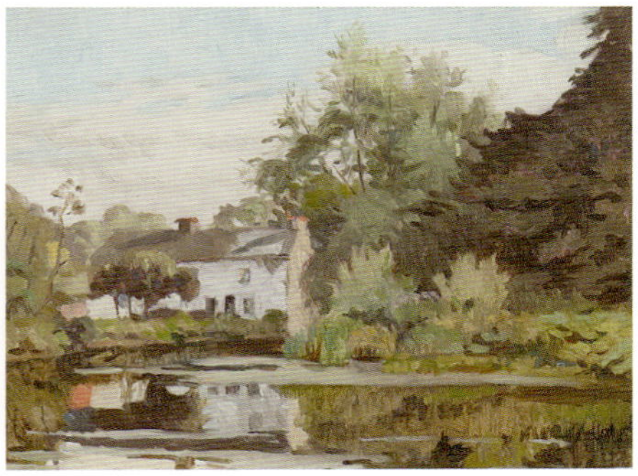

Morton, James Hargreaves 1881–1918
Washing early 20th C
oil on board 30 x 39
886

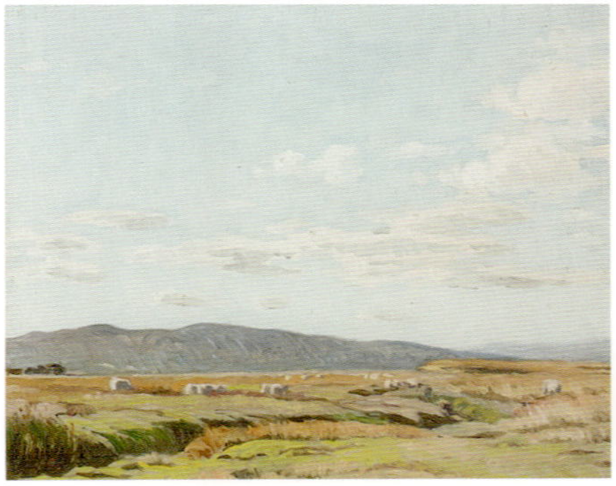

Morton, James Hargreaves 1881–1918
Blue Hills
oil on board 30 x 38
881

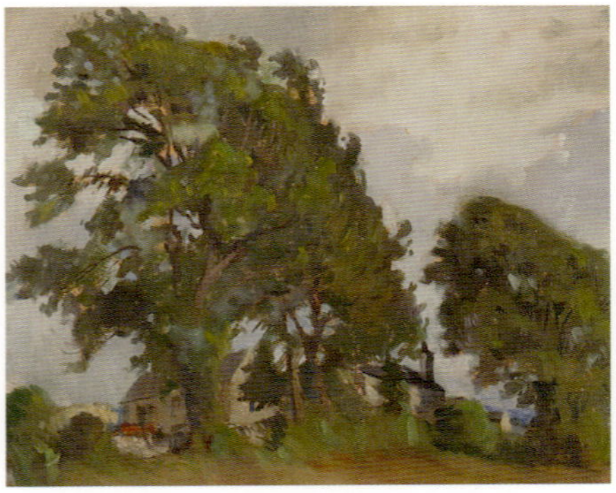

Morton, James Hargreaves 1881–1918
Windswept Trees
oil on board 30 x 38
884

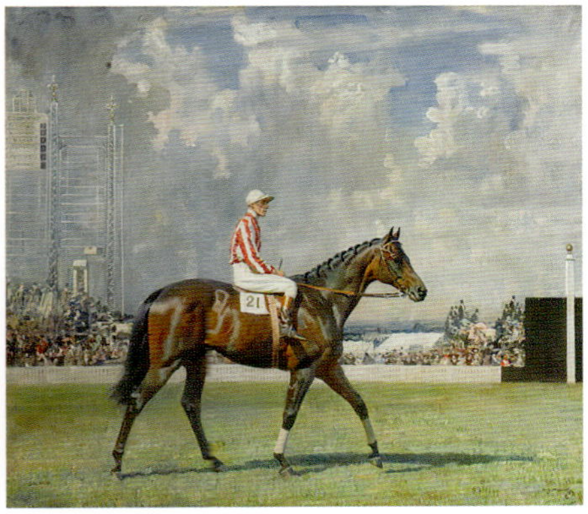

Munnings, Alfred James 1878–1959
'Solario' c.1926
oil on canvas 94 x 101.5
277

Facing page: Solomon, Solomon Joseph, 1860–1927, *An Allegory*, 1904, Harris Museum & Art Gallery (p. 342)

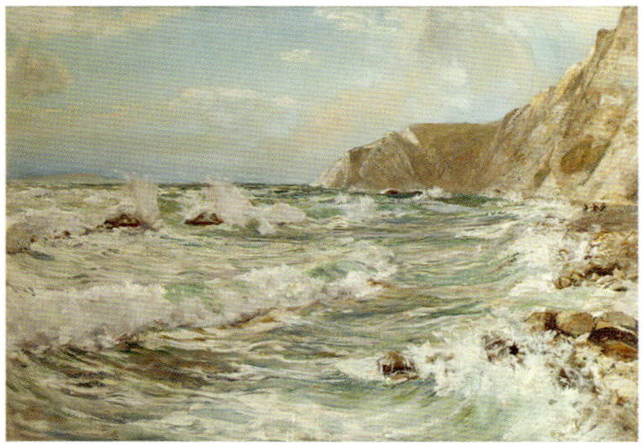

Murray, David 1849–1933
St Oswald's Bay, Lulworth
oil on canvas 119 x 181
367

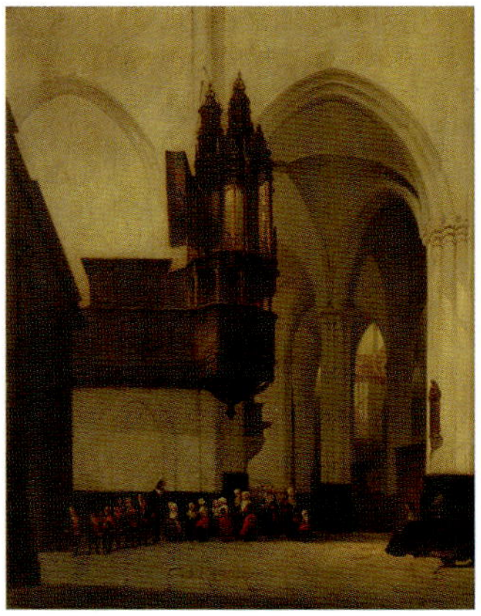

Neyt, Bernard 1825–1880
Church Interior, Amsterdam 1862
oil on canvas 85 x 69
214

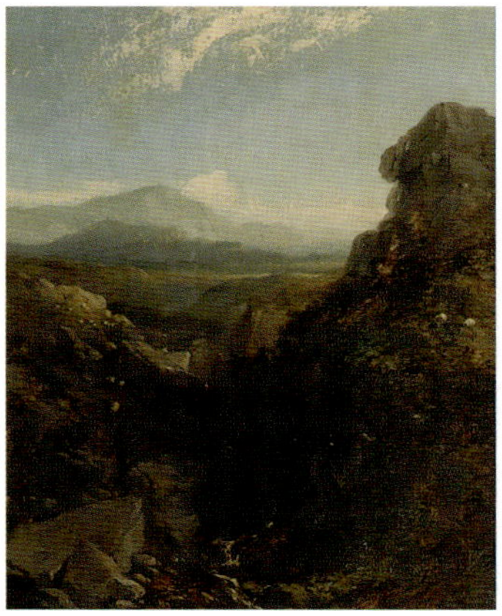

Niemann, Edmund John 1813–1876
Rocky Landscape
oil on canvas 49 x 38
55

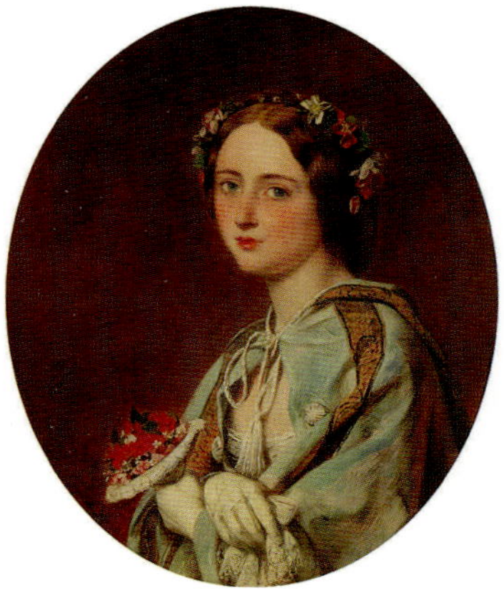

O'Neil, Henry Nelson 1817–1880
The Opera Box 1859
oil on canvas 27 x 22.86
56

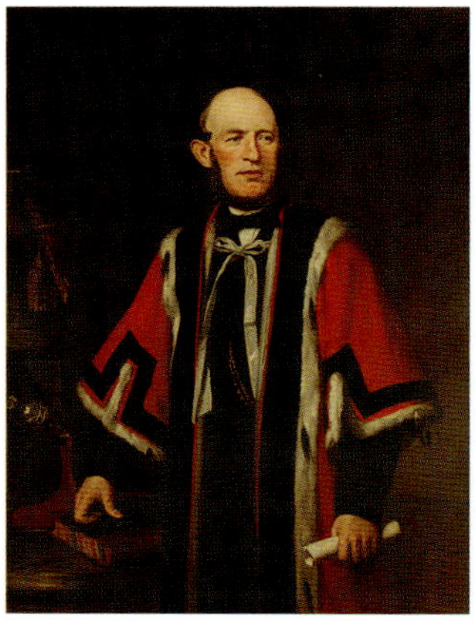

Occonomo active mid-19th C
Alderman James Thompson, JP, Mayor of Blackburn (1865–1866)
oil on canvas 120 x 93
TH. 24

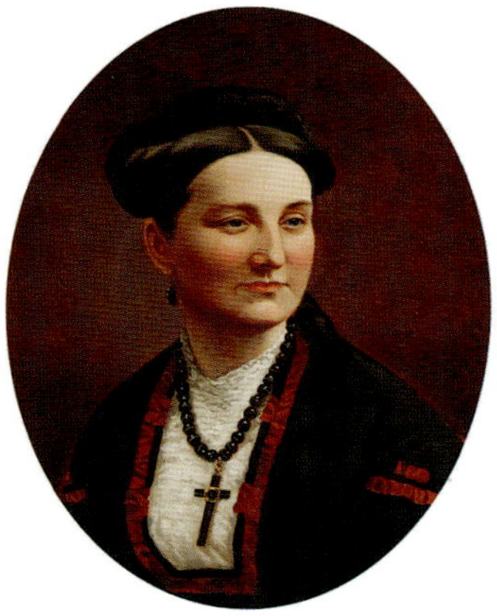

Ogg, Charles Herbert 1819–1889
Mrs Richard Barton Dodgson (d.c.1884)
c.1831
oil on canvas 52 x 41
59

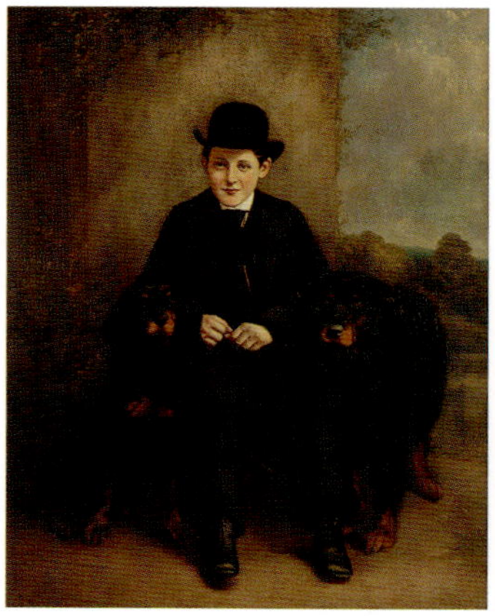

Ogg, Charles Herbert 1819–1889
Richard James Pickup Dodgson 1876
oil on canvas 89 x 70
51

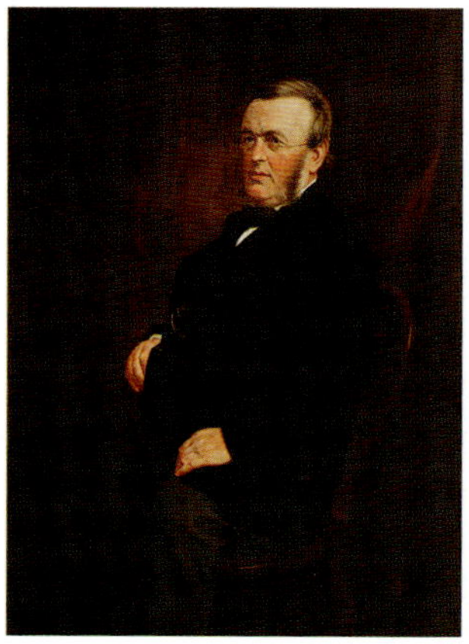

Ogg, Charles Herbert 1819–1889
James Boyle
oil on canvas 123 x 98
TH. 22

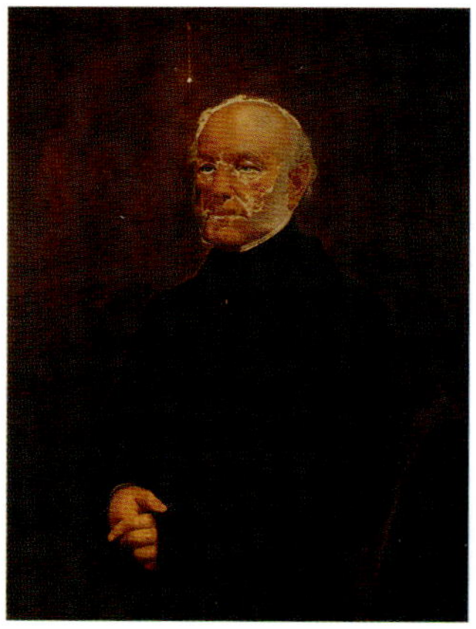

Ogg, Charles Herbert 1819–1889
Mr Cross
oil on canvas 89 x 69
50

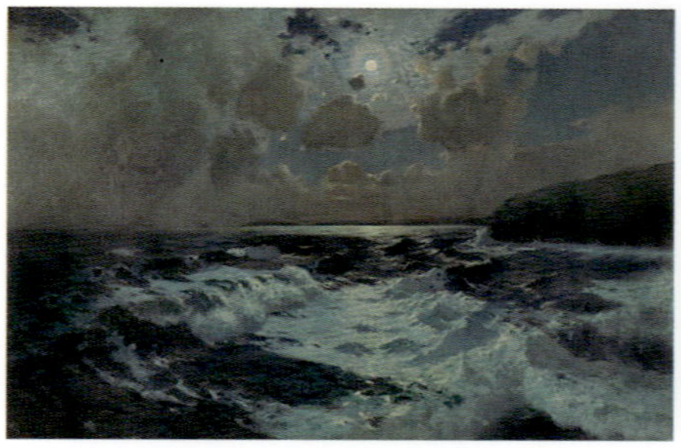

Olsson, Albert Julius 1864–1942
The Reef, St Ives Bay, Cornwall
oil on canvas 120 x 181
129

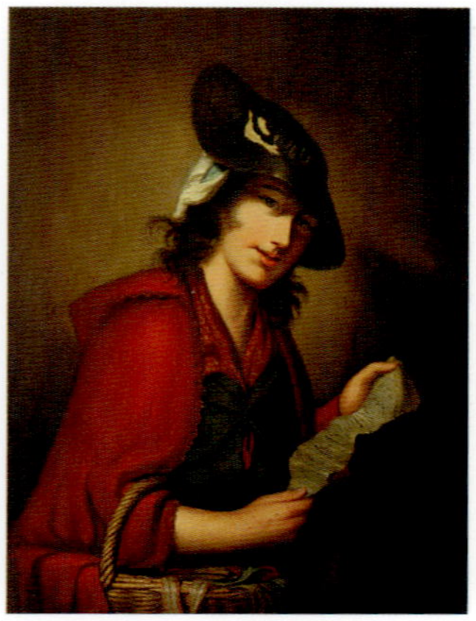

Opie, John 1761–1807
Figure Study
oil on canvas 72 x 58
652

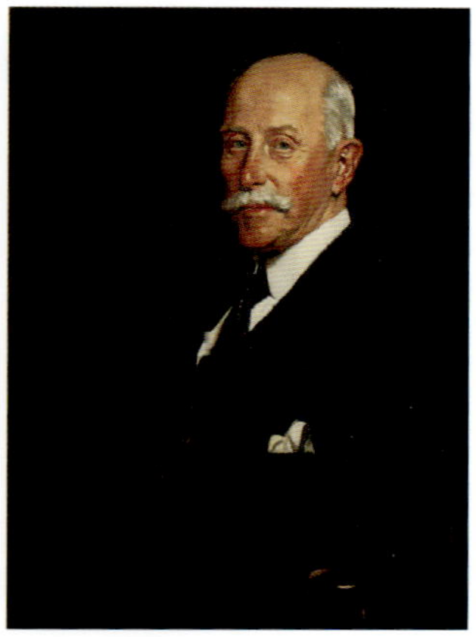

Orpen, William 1878–1931
Sir John Rutherford (1854–1932)
oil on canvas 75 x 62
493

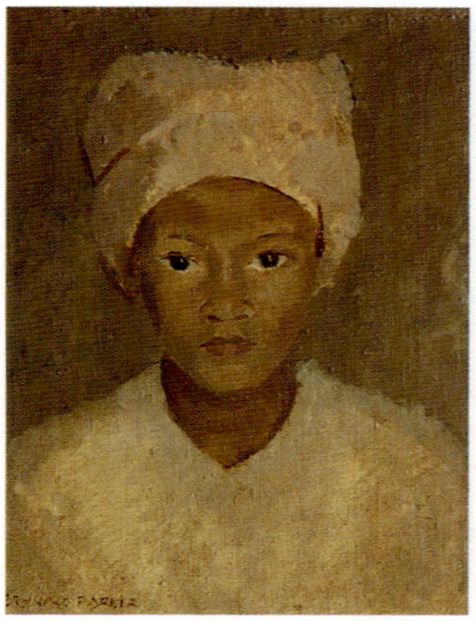

Parker, Brynhild 1907–1987
Portrait
oil on canvas 39 x 30
595

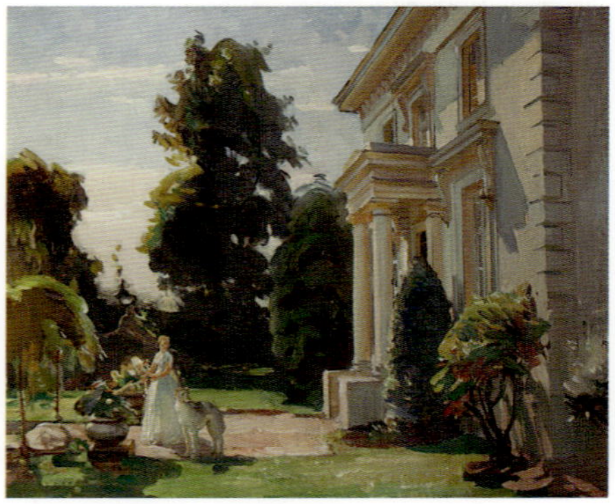

Penn, William Charles 1877–1968
The Victorian Home 1929
oil on canvas 51 x 64
261

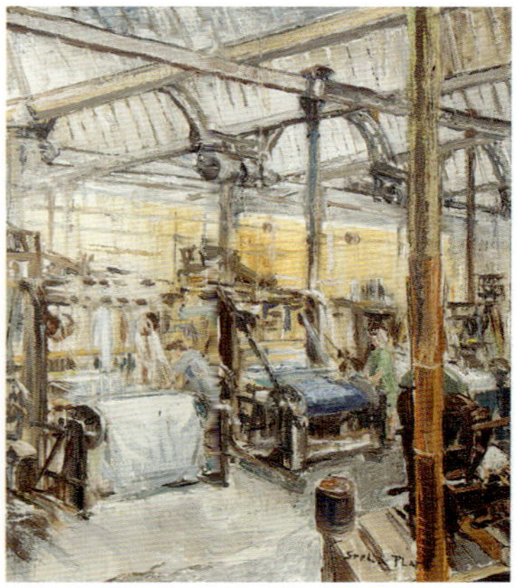

Peppercorn, Arthur Douglas 1847–1926
Landscape
oil on canvas 80 x 45
685

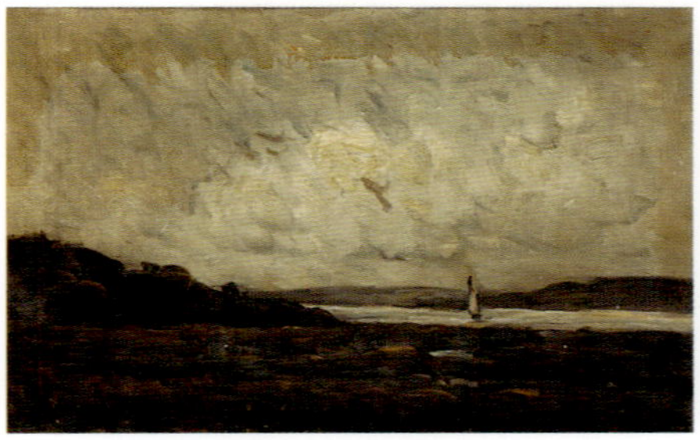

Platt, Stella 1913–2011
Queen's Mill, Longridge c.1966
oil on canvas 62 x 75
686

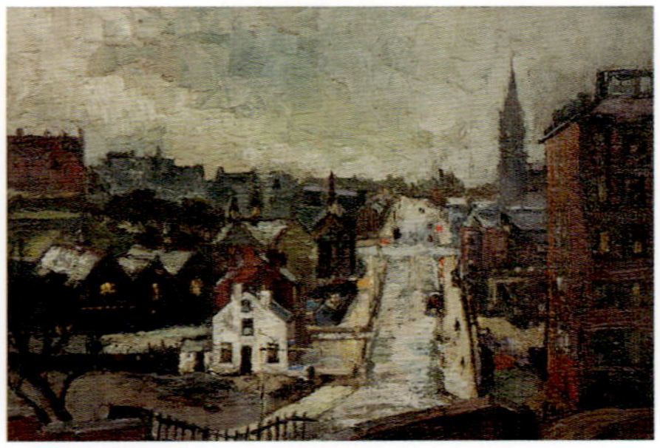

Platt, Stella 1913–2011
Rochdale (recto) c.1971
oil on canvas 40 x 68
877

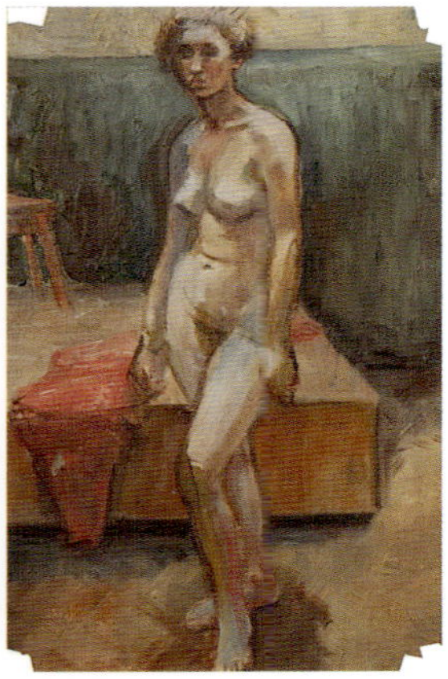

Platt, Stella 1913–2011
Nude (verso) c.1971
oil on canvas 68 x 40
877R

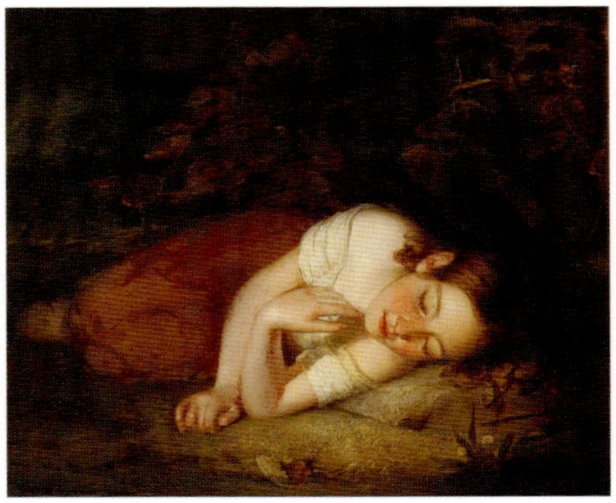

Pollitt, J. G.
Sleeping Beauty
oil on canvas 62 x 76
113

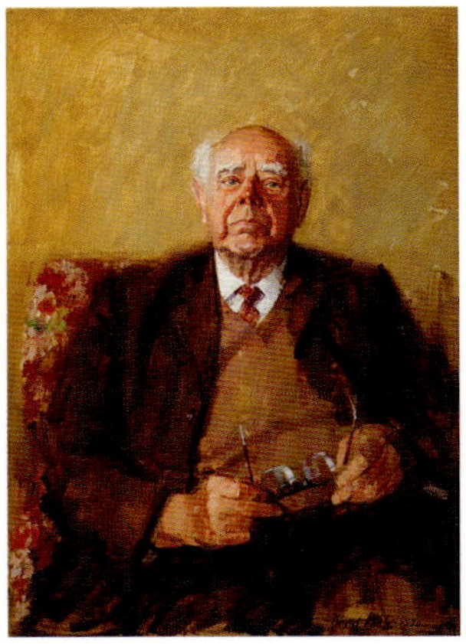

Poole, David b.1931
Sir George Eddie, Leader of Blackburn Council
c.1974
oil on canvas 89 x 69
TH.20

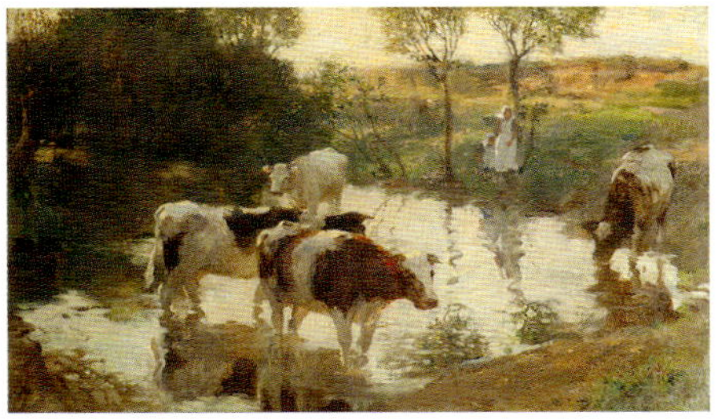

Priestman, Bertram 1868–1951
The Watering Place, Evening 1898
oil on canvas 63.5 x 99
138

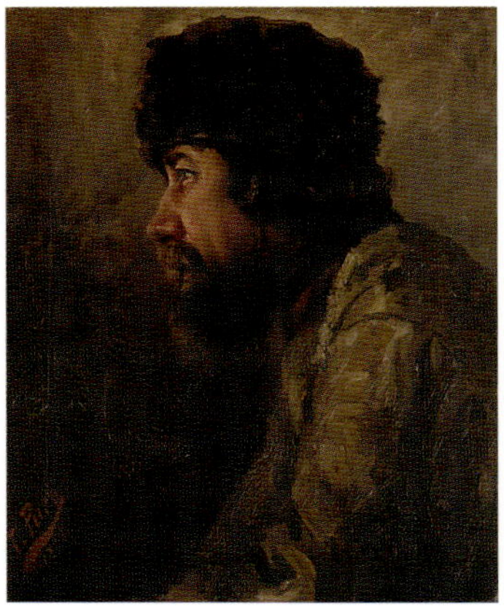

Pucz, T.
Russian Moujik 1890s
oil on canvas 51 x 42
377

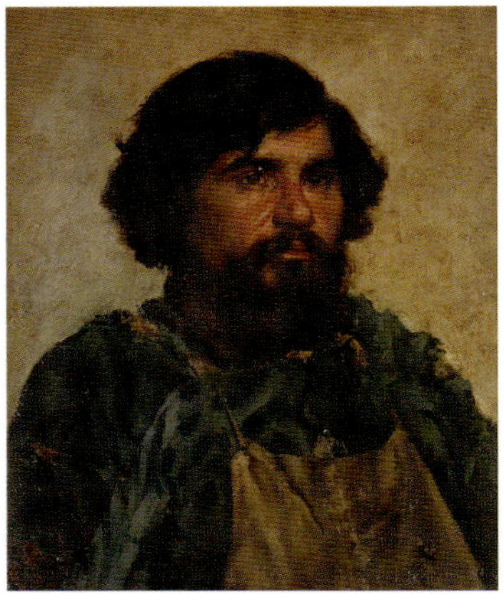

Pucz, T.
Russian Workman
oil on canvas 51 x 41
376

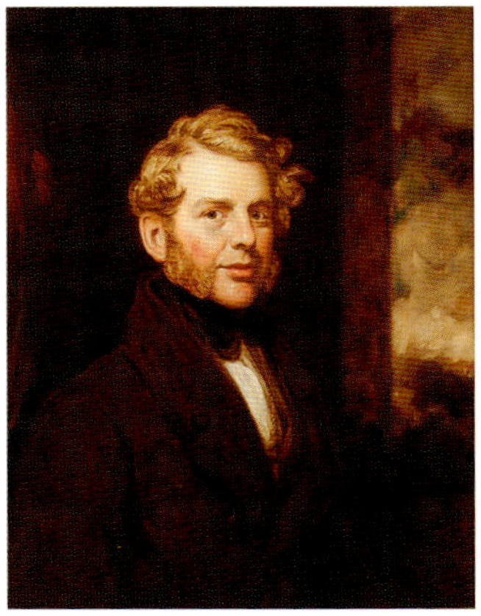

Puzier, Robert
Samuel Brooks (1792–1864) 1885
oil on canvas 75 x 62
2011.69

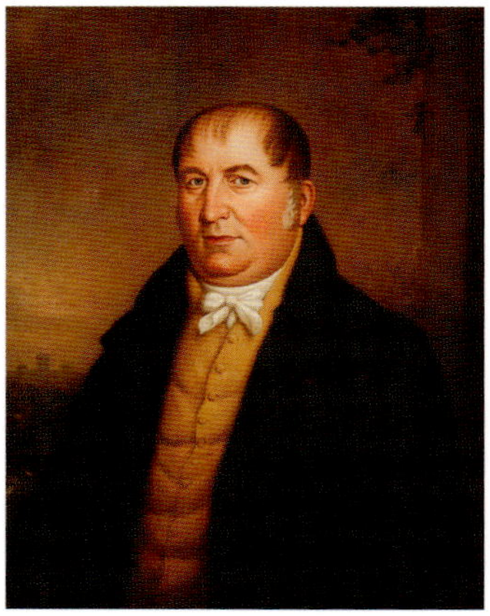

Puzier, Robert
William Brooks (1762–1846) 1885
oil on canvas 75 x 62
2011.68

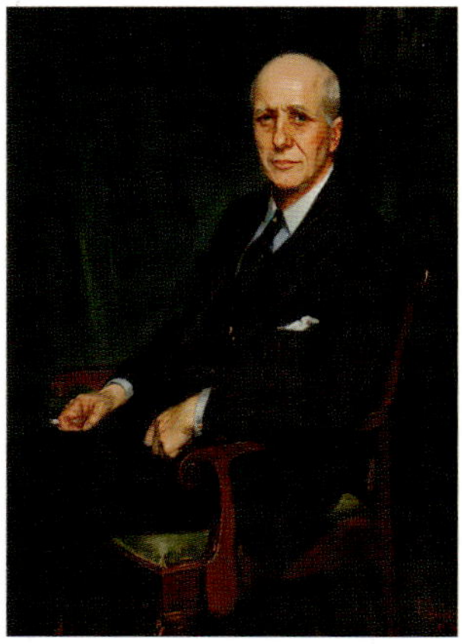

Quinn, James Peter 1869–1951
Dr Robert Aitken (1869–1951) 1932
oil on canvas 105 x 80
2009.139.1

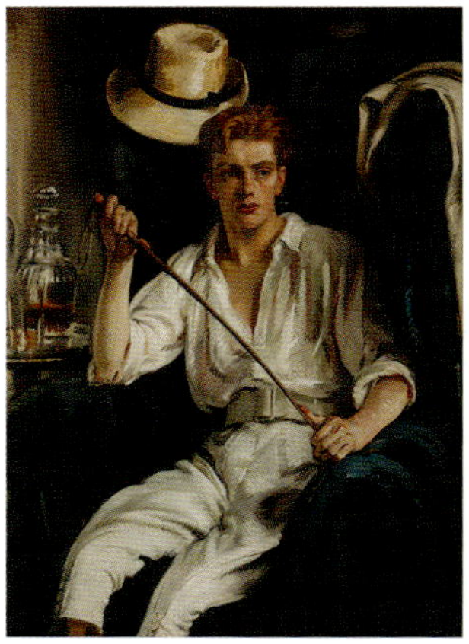

Ranken, William Bruce Ellis 1881–1941
The Young Polo Player 1920
oil on canvas 128 x 101
435

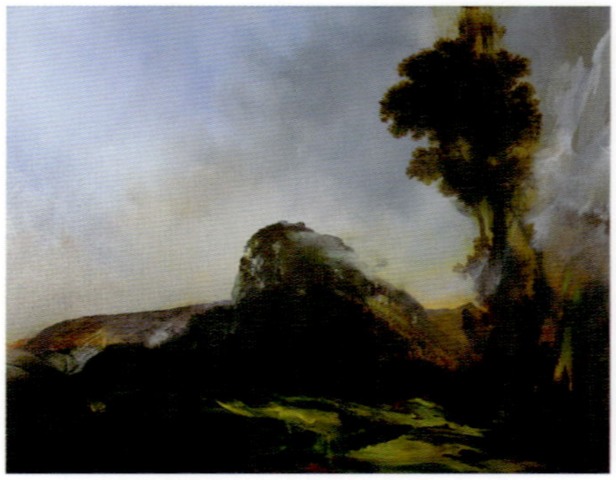

Rankle, Alan b.1952
Study for 'Montsegur' 2007
oil on canvas 80 x 97
2009.141

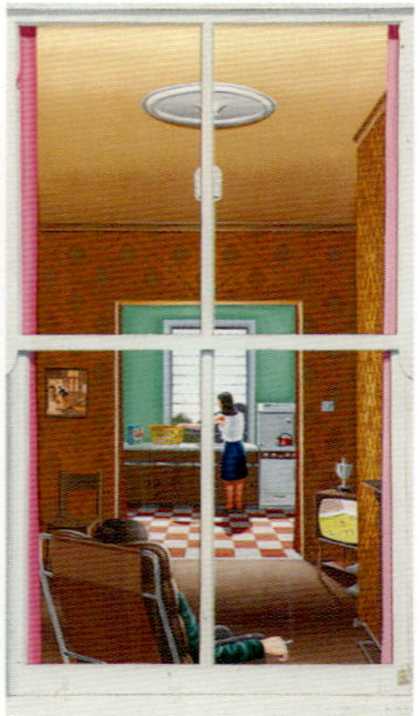

Redfern, David b.1947
Look through Any Window 1976
oil on perspex 74.9 x 40.3
1090

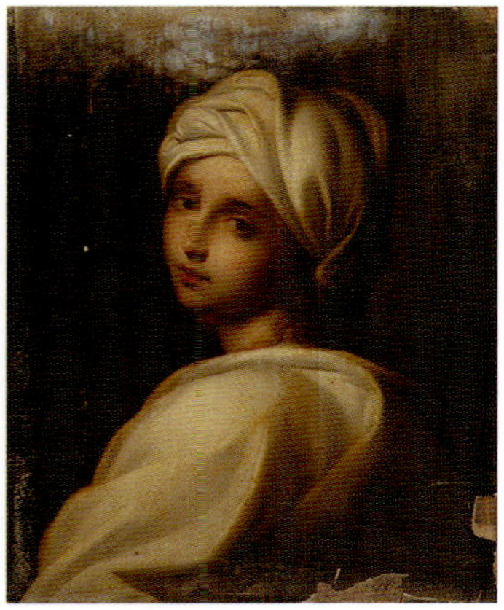

Reni, Guido (copy after) 1575–1642
Beatrice Cenci (1577–1599)
oil on canvas 51 x 48
2011.101

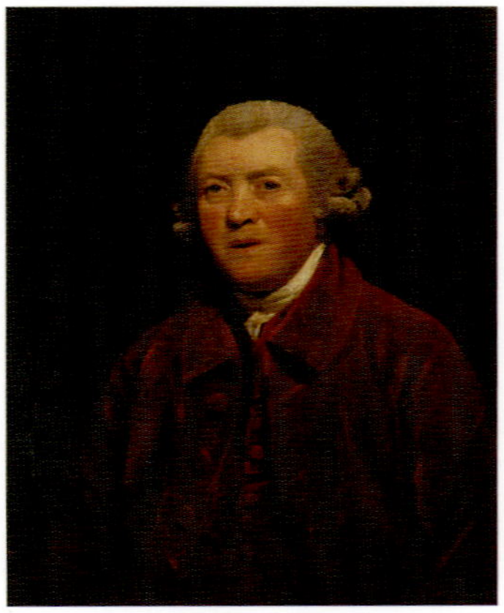

Reynolds, Joshua 1723–1792
William Fowden 1781
oil on canvas 73 x 58.5
106

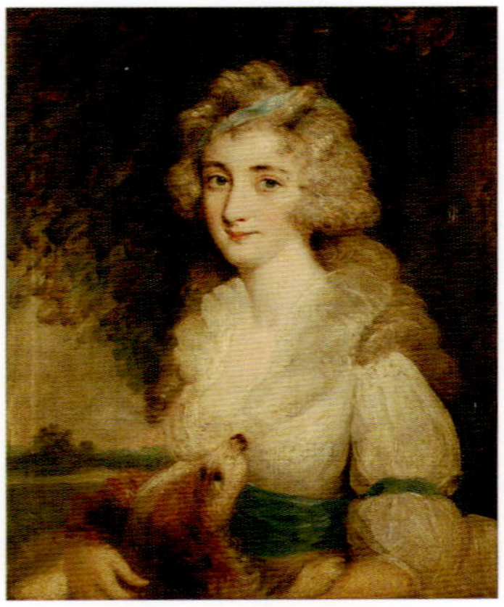

Reynolds, Joshua (attributed to) 1723–1792
Jane Barton
oil on canvas 73 x 62
52

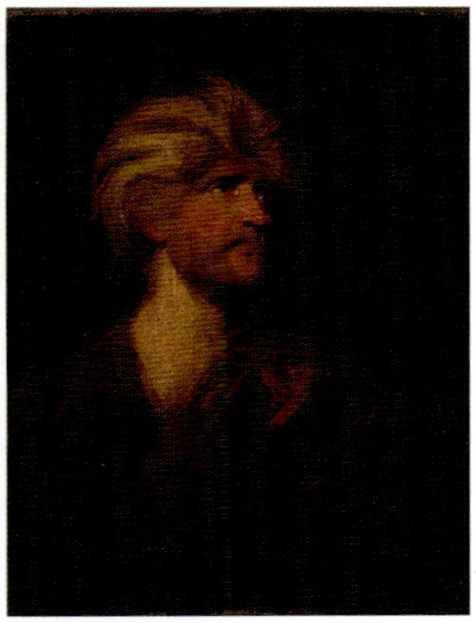

Reynolds, Joshua (style of) 1723–1792
Study for 'Beggar Man (George White)' late 18th C
oil on canvas 30.5 x 24.5
2011.93

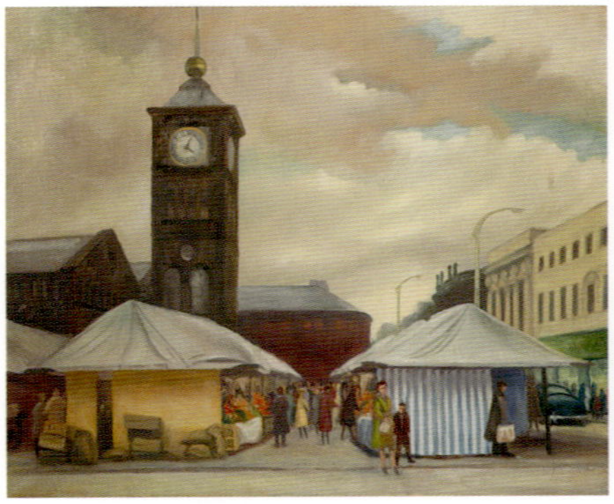

Riley, Eric C. active 1960s
Blackburn Market c.1963
oil on canvas 50 x 62
641

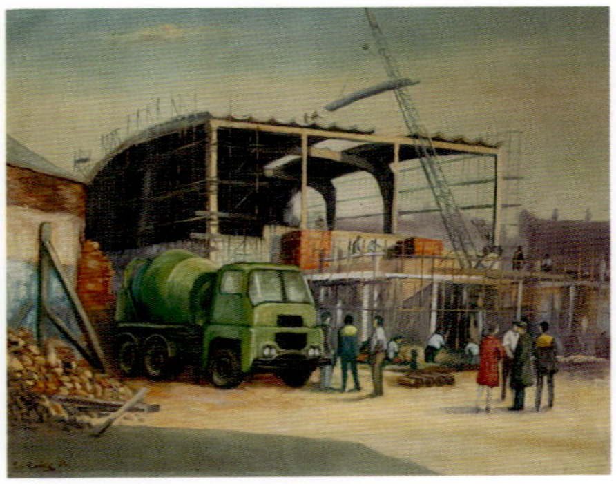

Riley, Eric C. active 1960s
New Market Construction 1964
oil on canvas 49 x 63
668

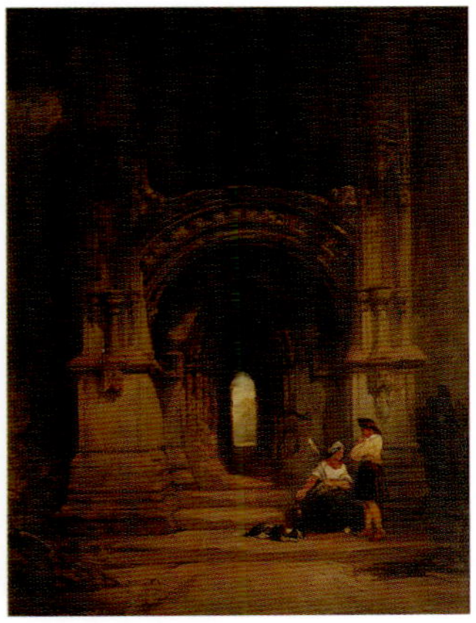

Roberts, David 1796–1864
Porch to Roslyn Chapel 1859
oil on canvas 58 5 x 43.5
126

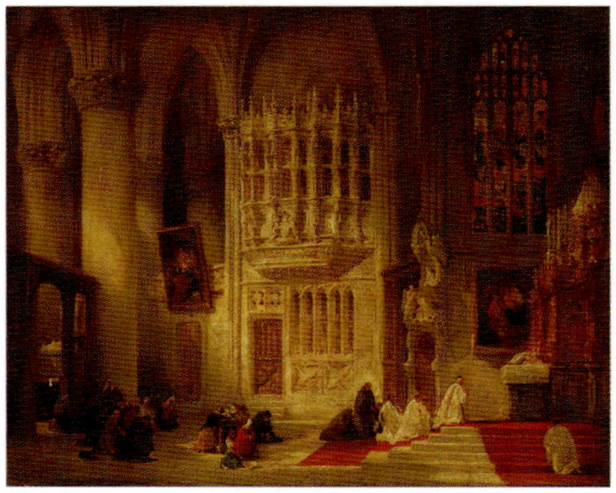

Roberts, David 1796–1864
Toledo Cathedral
oil on canvas 65 x 93
650

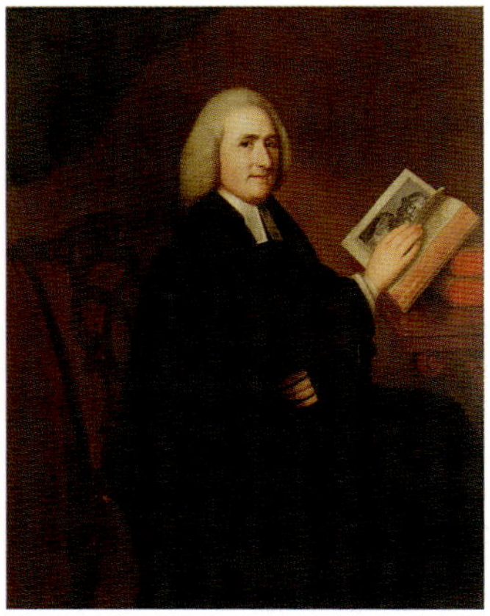

Romney, George 1734–1802
Dr Scales late 18th C
oil on canvas 116 x 94
54

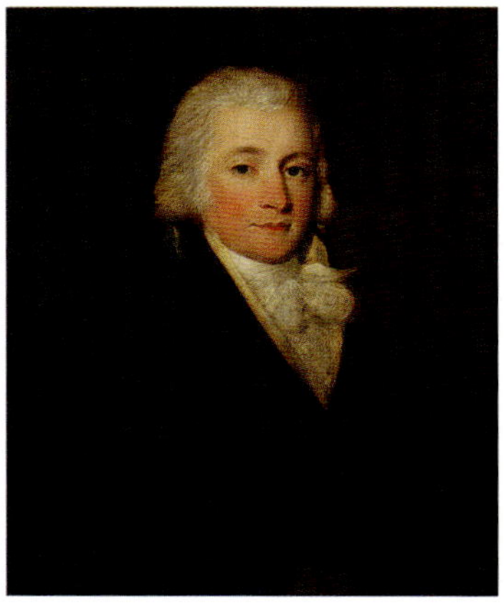

Romney, George (attributed to) 1734–1802
Mr Barton
oil on canvas 73 x 60
53

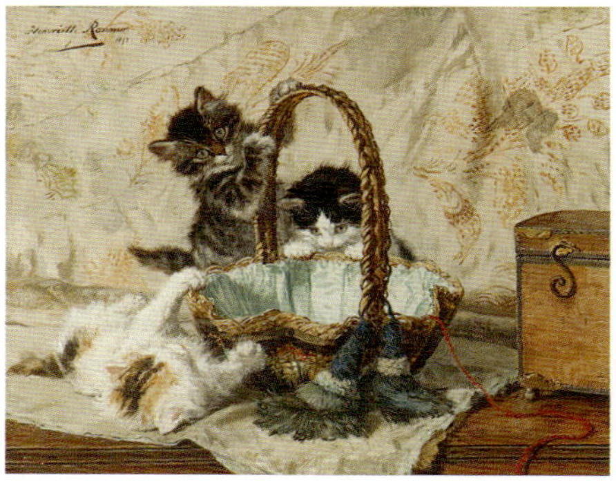

Ronner, Henriette 1821–1909
A Merry Party 1892
oil on panel 43.3 x 54
91

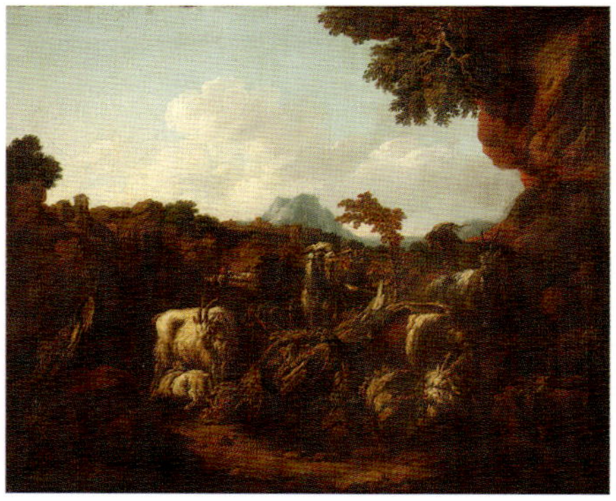

Roos, Philipp Peter 1657–1706
Pastoral Landscape
oil on canvas 99 x 123
736

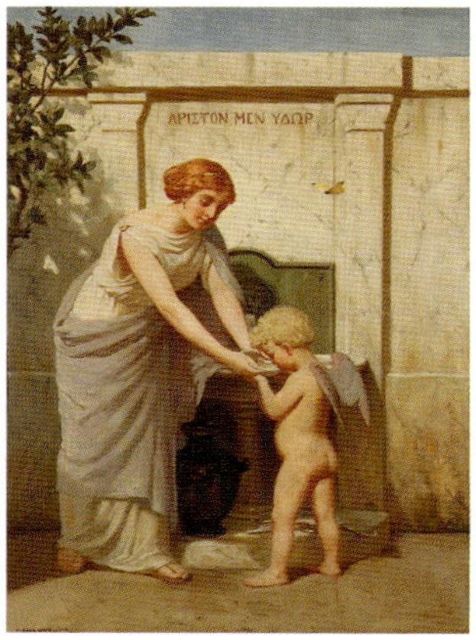

Ruith, Horace van 1839–1923
Water Is Best c.1915
oil on canvas 92.5 x 65.5
2009.113

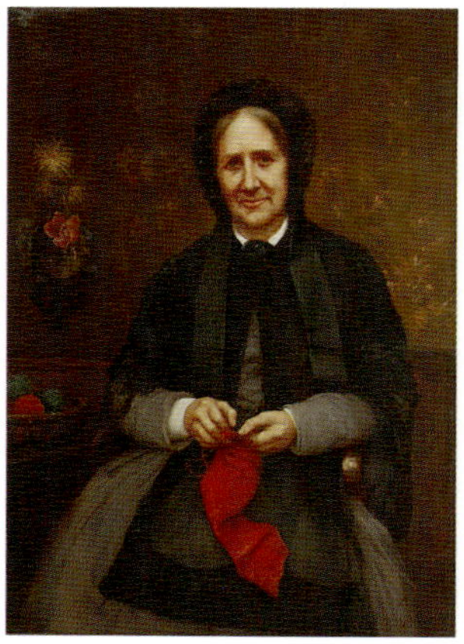

Russell, Edwin Wensley 1830–1915
Nancy Hargreaves c.1894
oil on canvas 110 x 85
90A

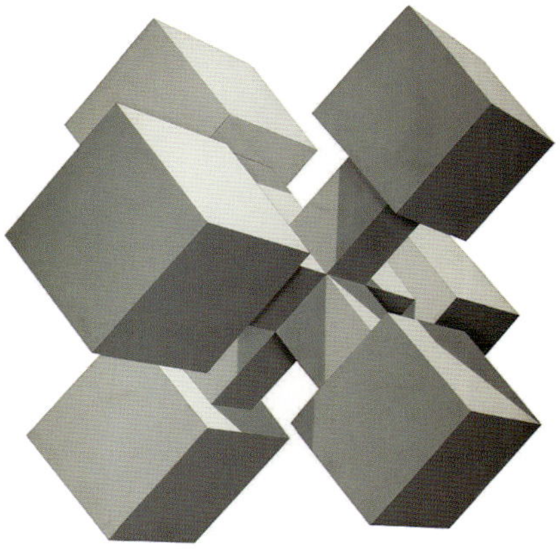

Sartin, Stephen
Martial Cubes
oil on wood 173 x 176
817

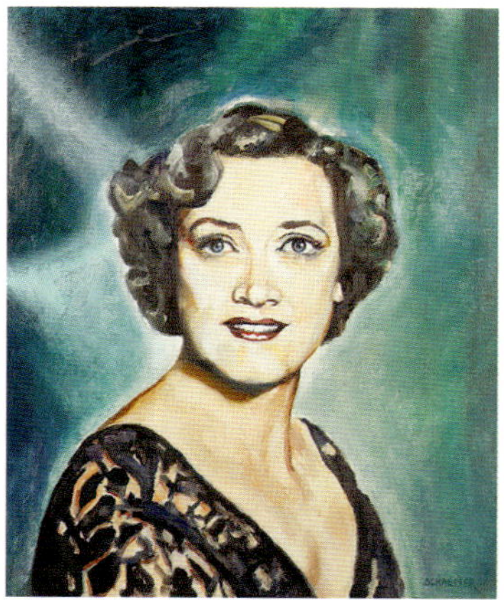

Schaeffer, Johannes Bartholomeus 1927–2000
Kathleen Ferrier (1912–1953) c.1940
oil on canvas 60 x 49
KF.2010.12

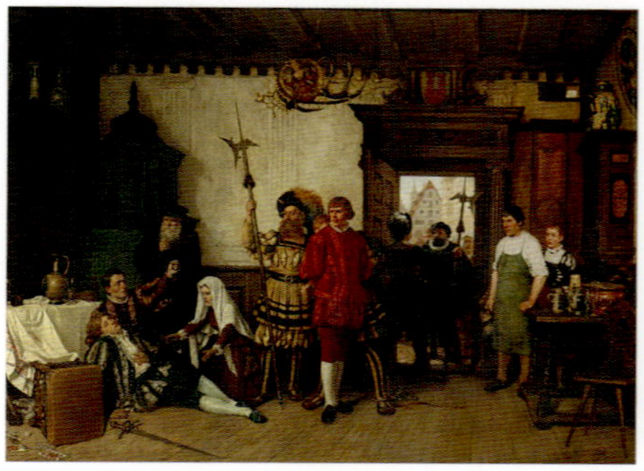

Schuch, H. active 1900
The Quarrel
oil on canvas 99 x 144.8
366

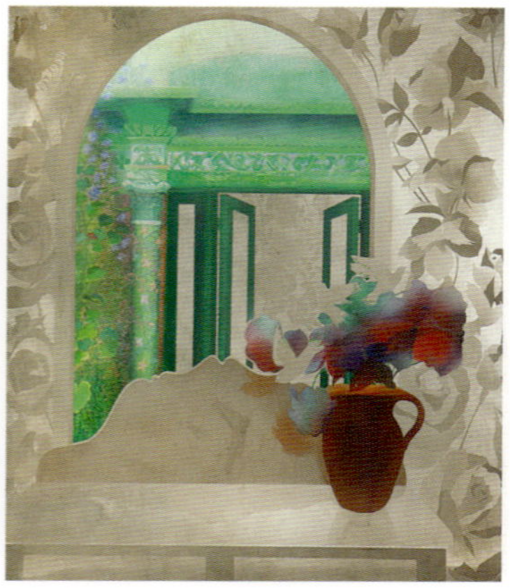

Scott active late 20th C
Inside Out
oil on polished aluminium 96 x 96
1099

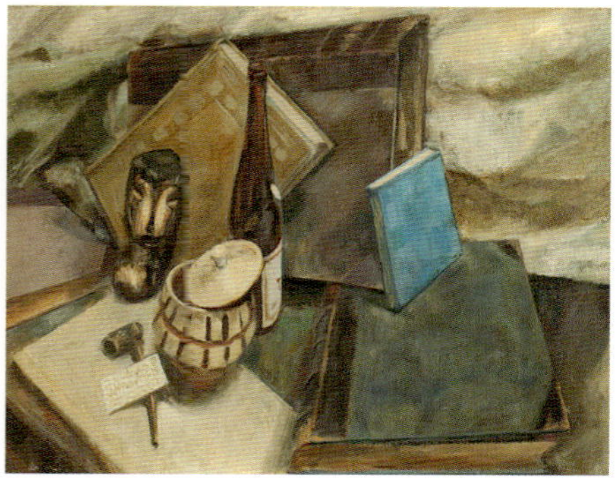

Scott, Bernard 1918–1990
Still Life
oil on canvas 69 x 90
619

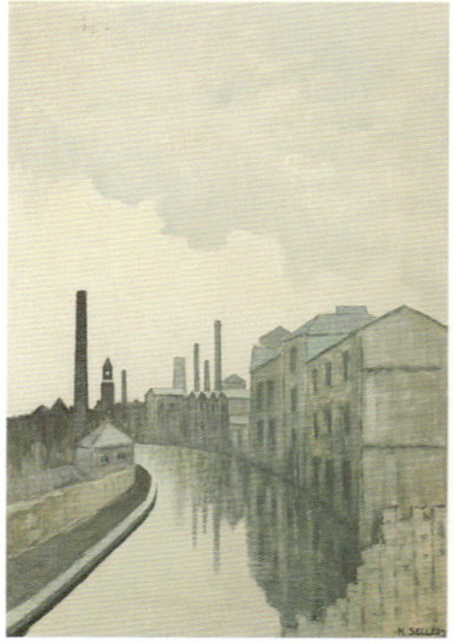

Sellers, M.
Canal Scene c.1970
oil on board 89 x 62
870

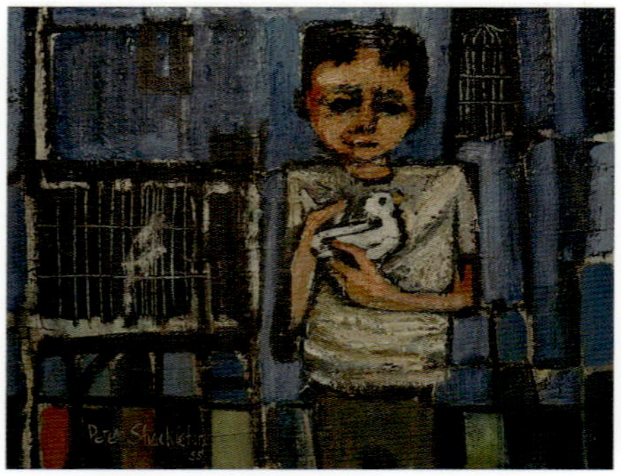

Shackleton, Peter b.1933
Boy with White Bird 1955
oil on canvas 39 x 49
611

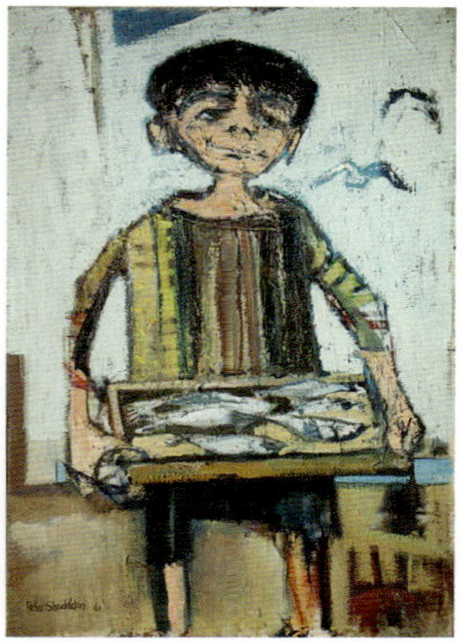

Shackleton, Peter b.1933
Fish Boy 1961
oil on canvas 95 x 66
875

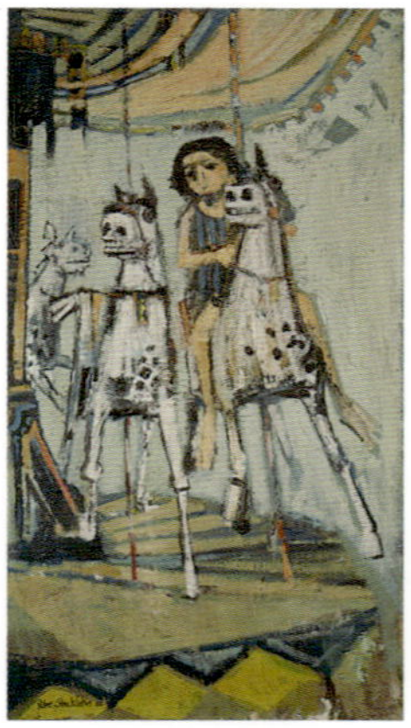

Shackleton, Peter b.1933
Merry Go Round 1962
oil on board 102 x 57 (E)
820

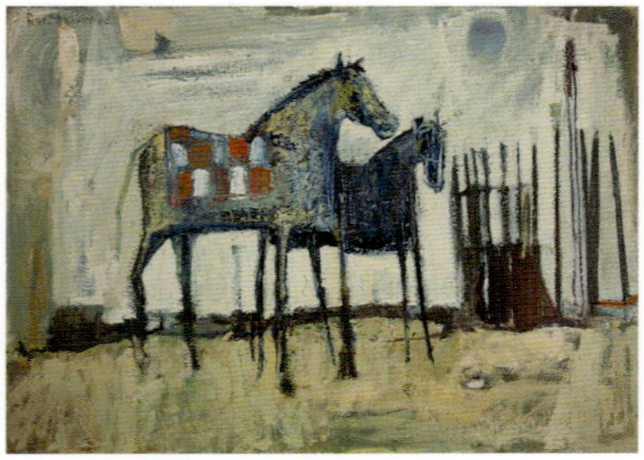

Shackleton, Peter b.1933
Circus Horses 1963
oil on board 66 x 91
1188

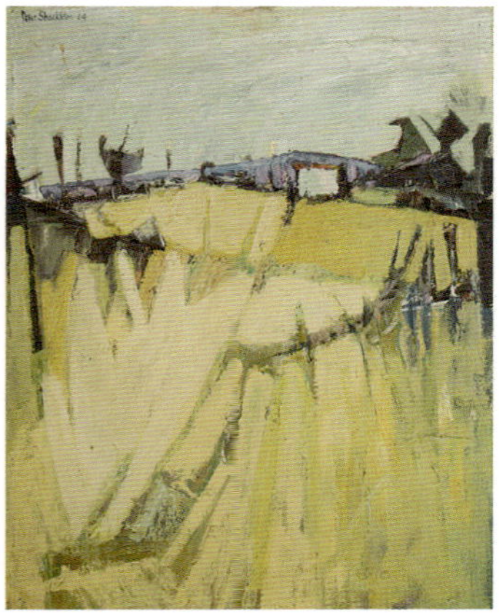

Shackleton, Peter b.1933
Summer Landscape 1964
oil on board 92 x 71
876

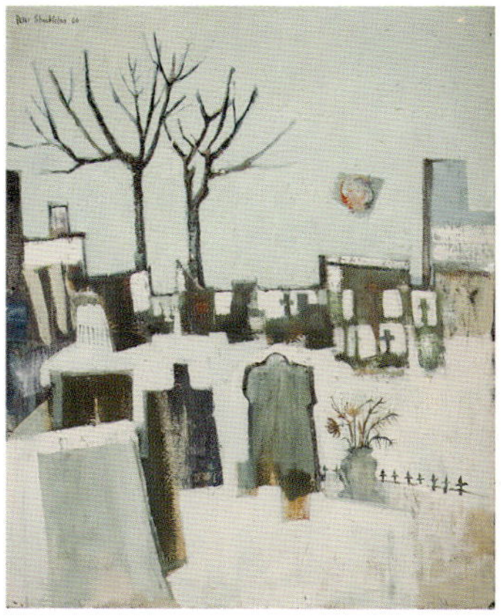

Shackleton, Peter b.1933
Winter Stones 1966
oil on board 122 x 86
821

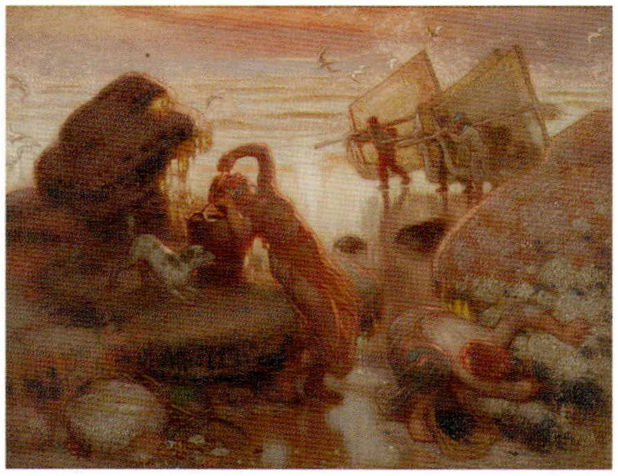

Shackleton, William 1872–1933
Mussel Gatherers 1911
oil on canvas 53 x 67
359

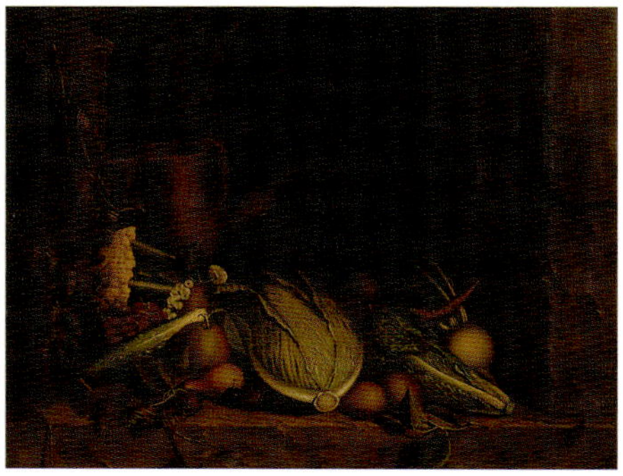

Sharples, James 1825–1893
Fruit and Vegetable Still Life 1844
oil on canvas 51 x 66.5
2011.111

Sharples, James 1825–1893
The Forge 1847
oil on canvas 89 x 129
601 (P)

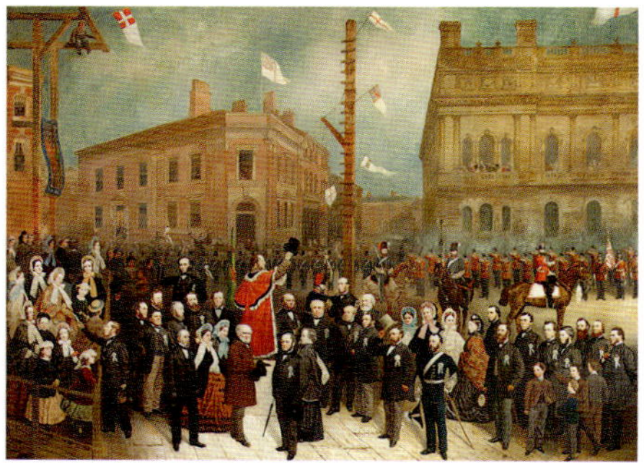

Sherwood, Vladimir Ossipovitch 1832–1897
Laying the Foundation Stone to the Cotton Exchange, Blackburn c.1863
oil on canvas 175 x 241
2008.24

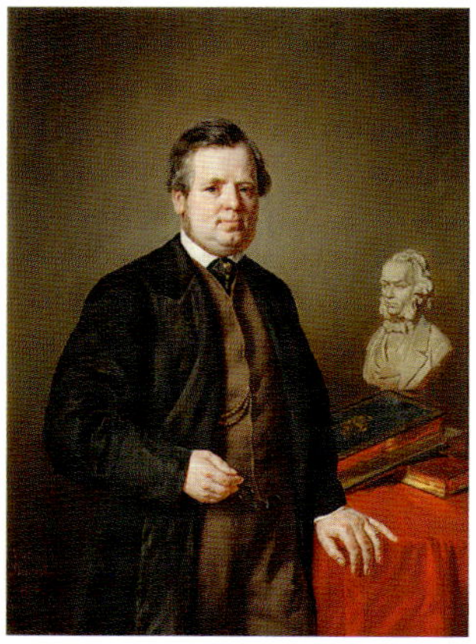

Sherwood, Vladimir Ossipovitch 1832–1897
Mr Healey 1866
oil on canvas 90 x 70
797

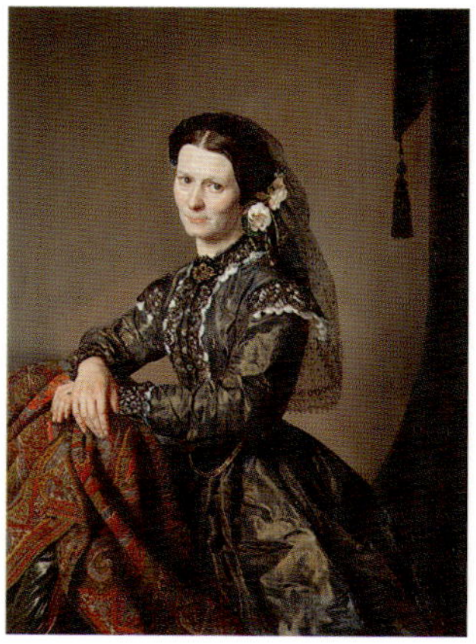

Sherwood, Vladimir Ossipovitch 1832–1897
Mrs Healey late 19th C
oil on canvas 90 x 70
798

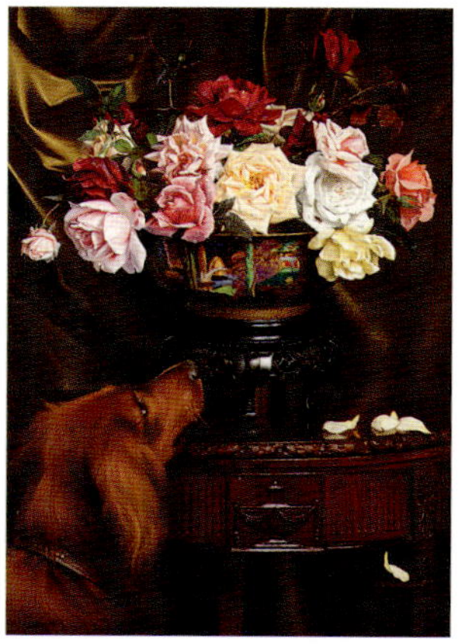

Spencelayh, Charles 1865–1958
The Scent
oil on canvas 73.6 x 50.8
357

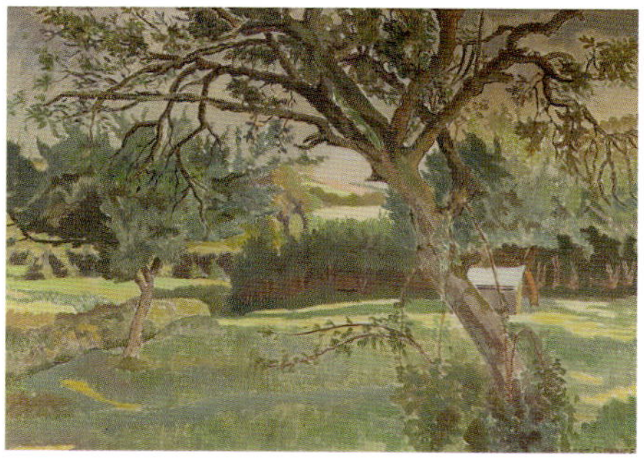

Spencer, Gilbert 1892–1979
Wooded Landscape
oil on canvas 44 x 59
990

Facing page: Romney, George, 1734–1802, *Serena Reading*, c.1780–1785, Harris Museum & Art Gallery (p. 336)

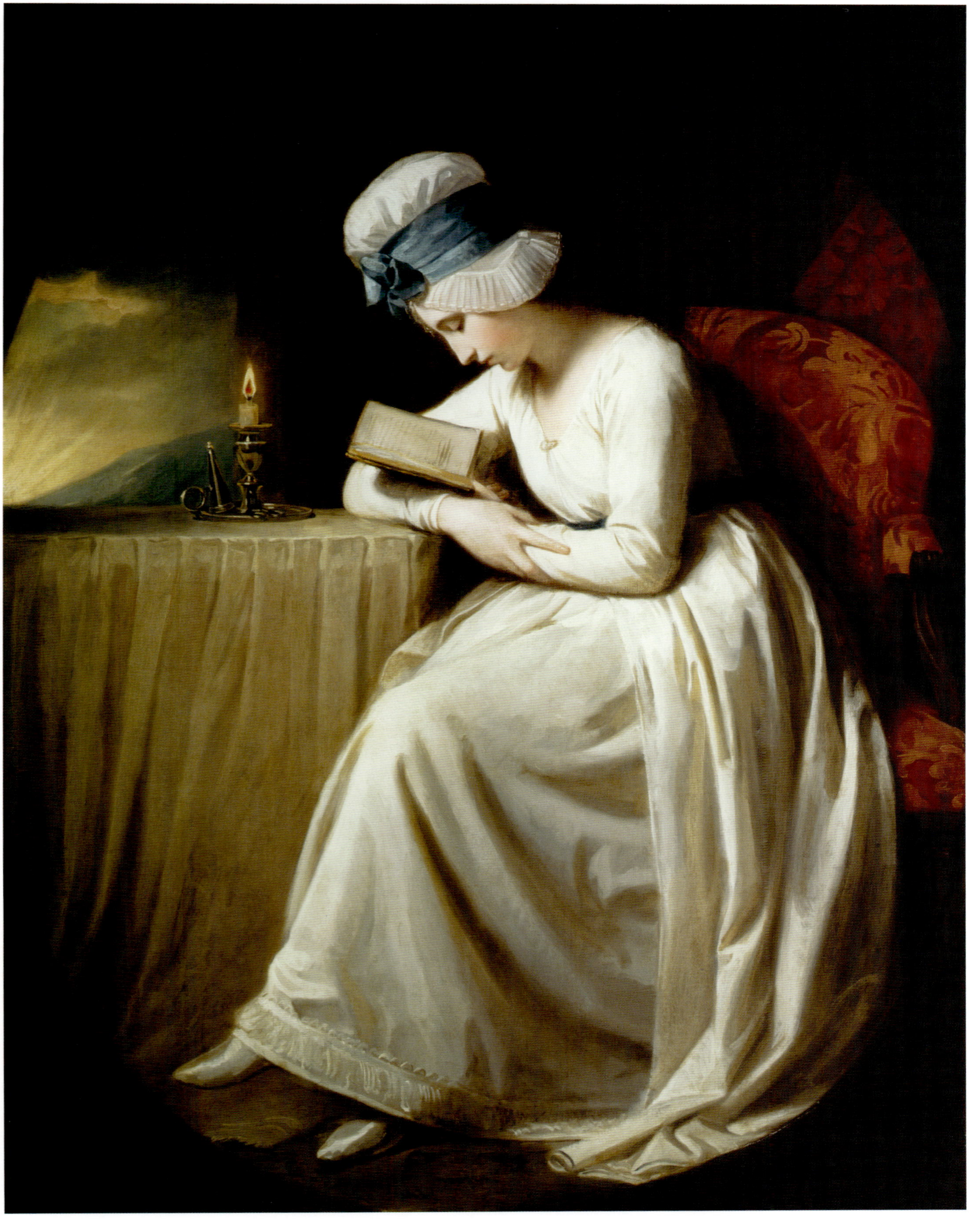

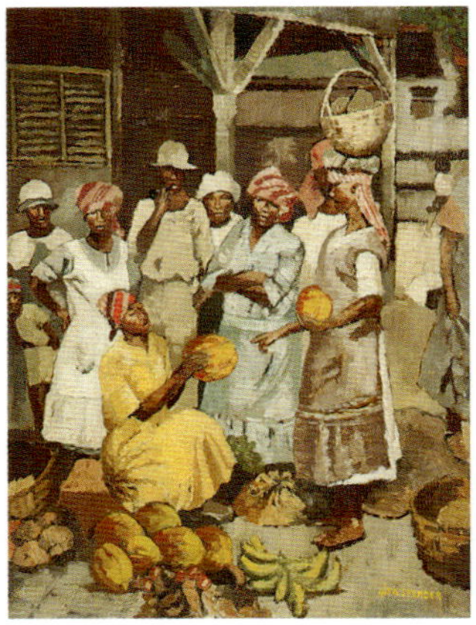

Spencer, Rita active 1965
Market in Antigua
oil on canvas 59 x 49
667

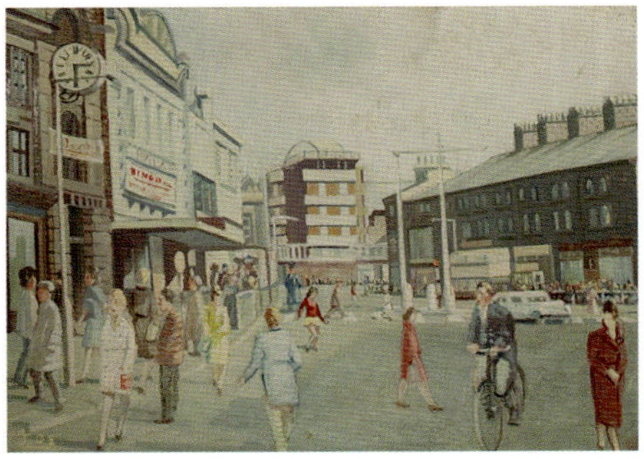

Spencer, Terrance G. active 20th C
St James' Street, Burnley
oil on board 52 x 68
2011.81

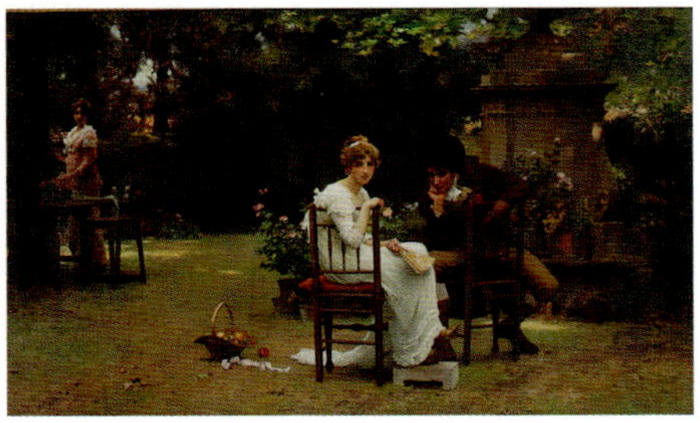

Stone, Marcus C. 1840–1921
Two's Company, Three's None 1892
oil on canvas 91 x 152
84

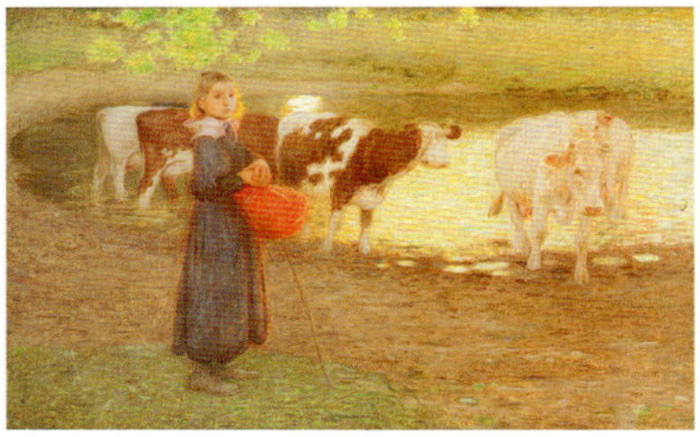

Stott, Edward William 1859–1918
The Watering Place
oil on canvas 61 x 85
137

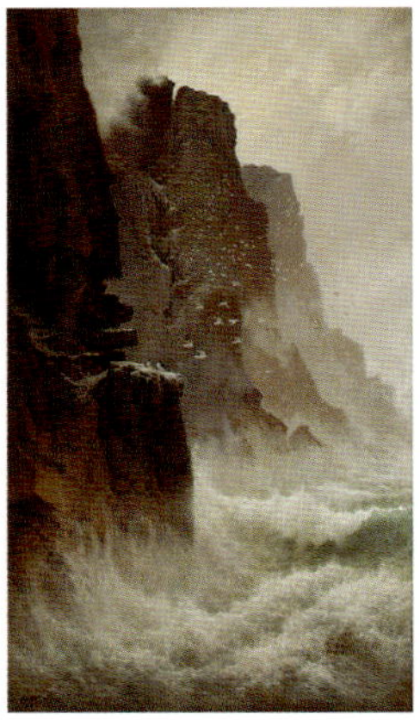

Suker, Arthur 1857–1902
After the Storm, North Cornwall late 19th C
oil on canvas 127 x 63.5 (E)
2011.72

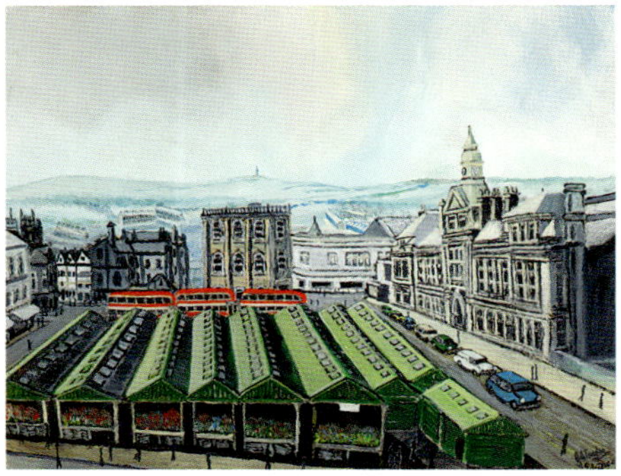

Taylor, J. A.
Darwen Market 2000
oil on canvas 45 x 60
2011.108

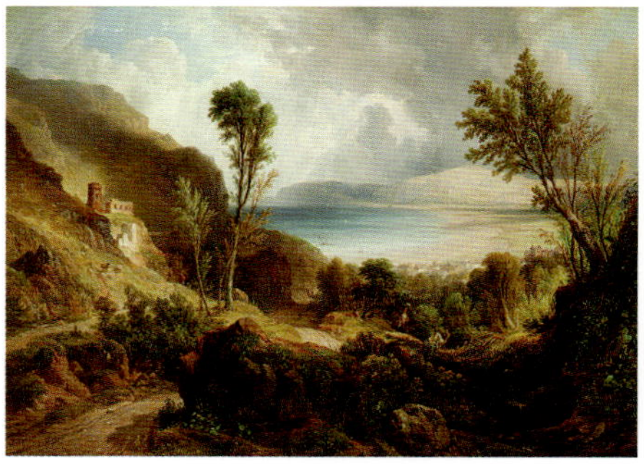

Tennant, John F. 1796–1872
View of Old Llandudno 1860
oil on canvas 64 x 104
489

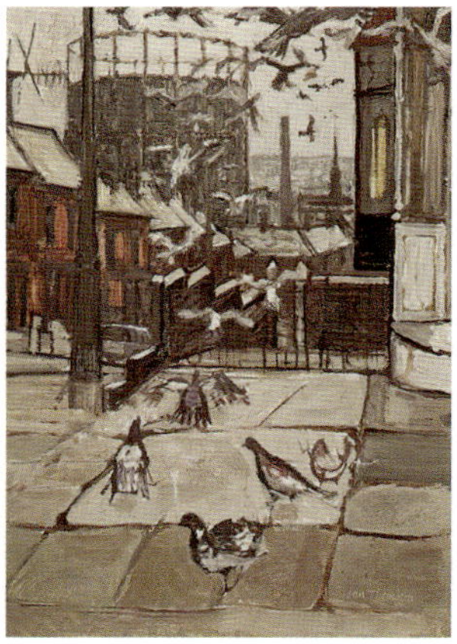

Thompson, Ian active 1960s
Junction of Saunders Road and Downham Street, Blackburn 1960s
oil on board 46 x 32
699

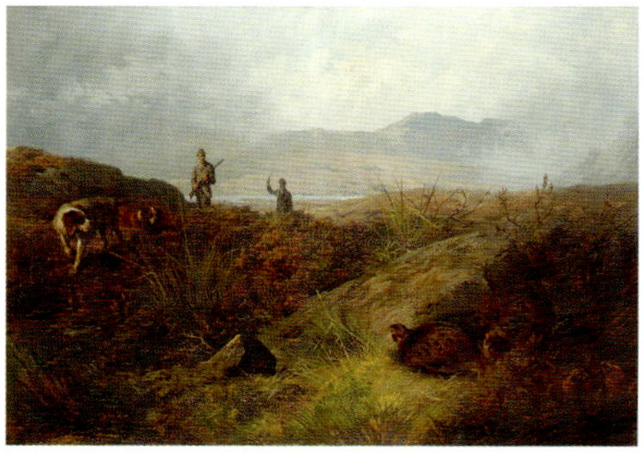

Thorburn, Archibald 1860–1935
Suspense 1894
oil on canvas 69 x 113
90

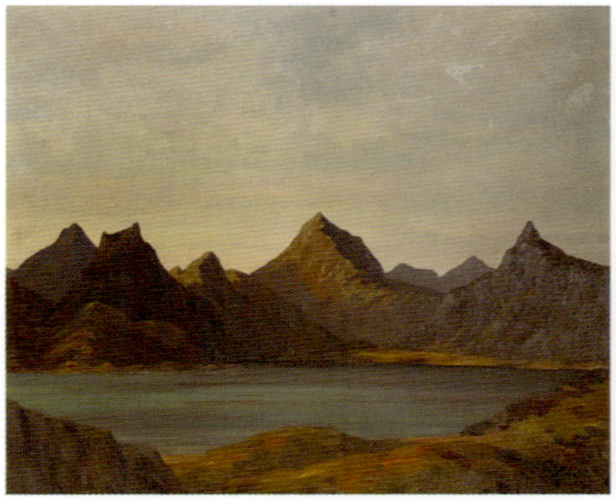

Tinker, F. E.
Lock Scavaig, Skye c.1970
oil on canvas 41 x 52
2011.98

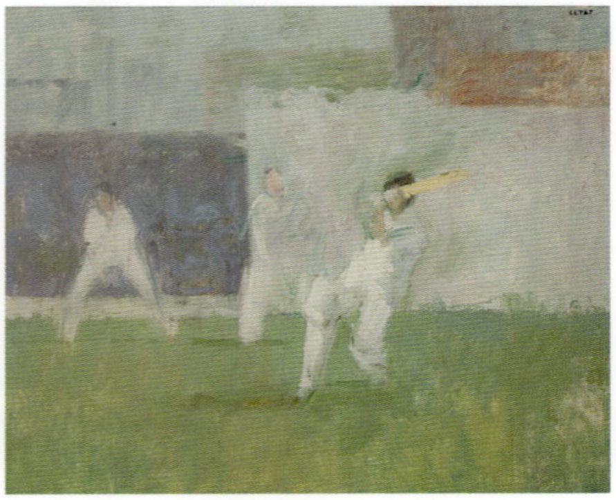

Toynbee, Lawrence 1922–2002
Square Cut 1967
oil on board 49 x 59
747

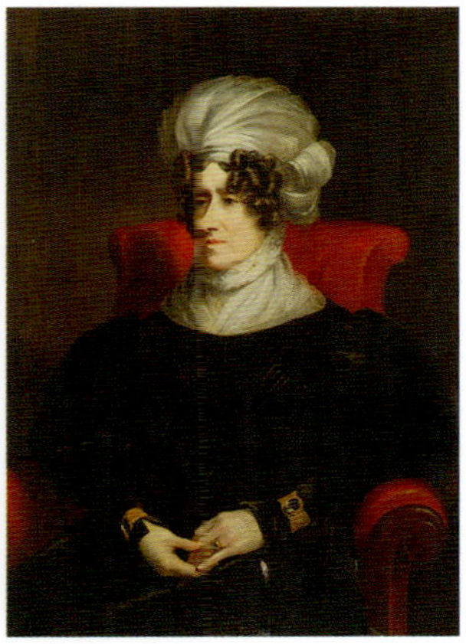

unknown artist
Mrs Fowden Hindle c.1800
oil on canvas 90 x 69
109

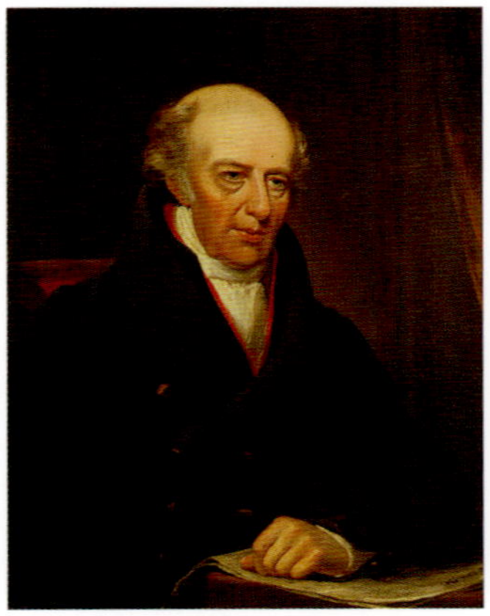

unknown artist
William Fowden Hindle c.1800
oil on canvas 75 x 62
108

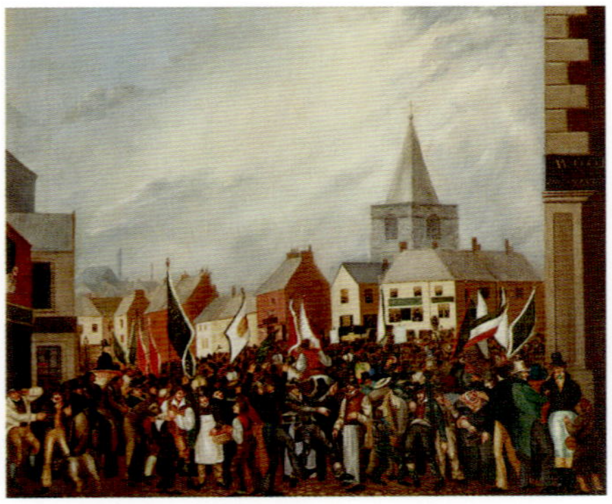

unknown artist
The 1832 Blackburn Election c.1832
oil on canvas 54 x 62
918 (P)

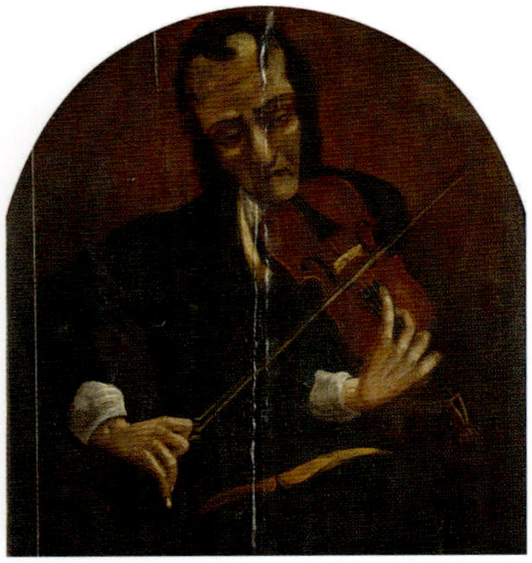

unknown artist
Inn Sign with Portrait of Niccolò Paganini
c.1833
oil on canvas 82 x 75
2003.1807

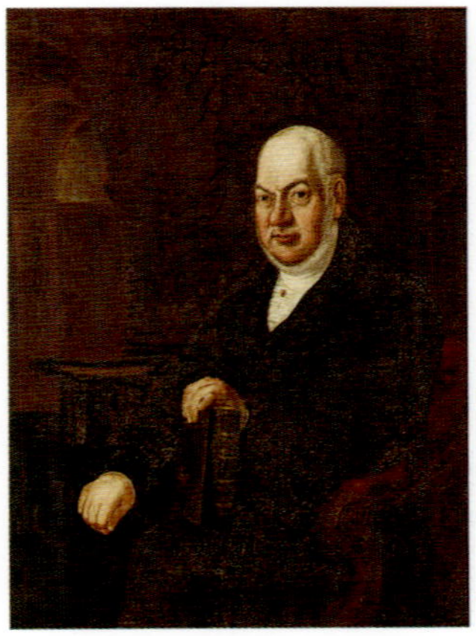

unknown artist
Alderman Richard Martland, MD c.1860
oil on canvas 111 x 89
TH. 29

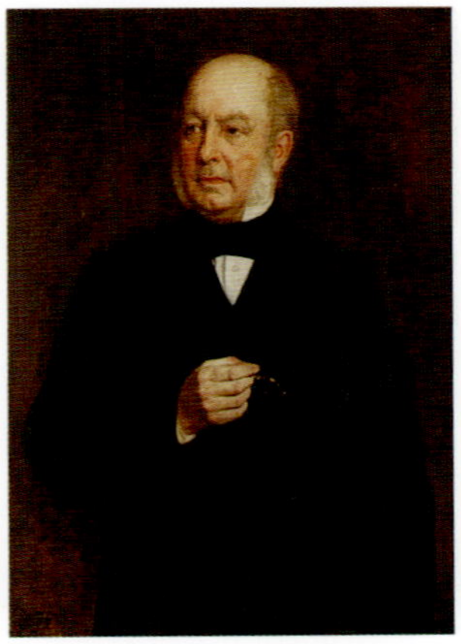

unknown artist
Joseph Harrison (1805–1880) 1874
oil on canvas 90 x 70
2011.75

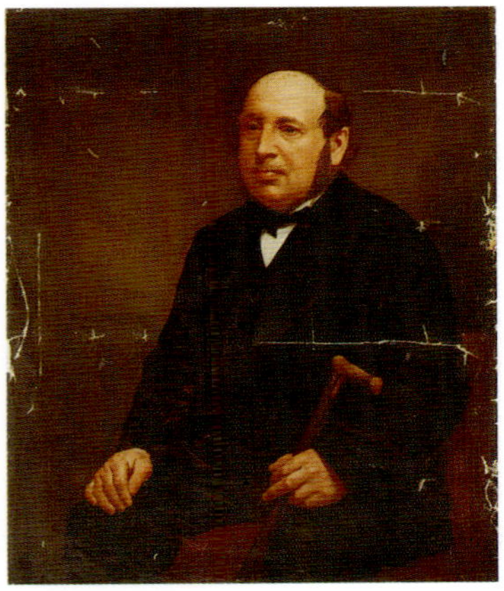

unknown artist
William Rostron, Founder of Scoltabrook (?) Paper Mill, Darwen 1877
oil on canvas 60 x 50
2011.107

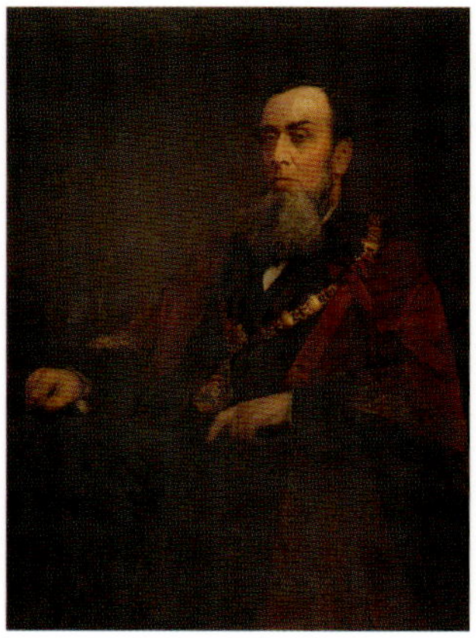

unknown artist
Alderman William Snape, 1st Mayor of Darwen (1878) c.1878
oil on canvas 109 x 87
TH.16

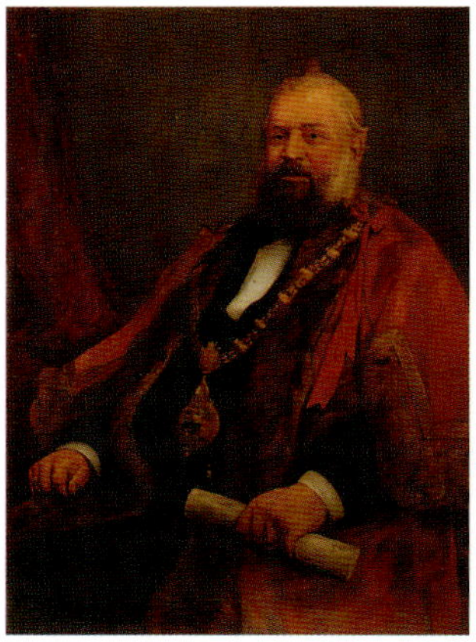

unknown artist
Alderman William Entwistle, Mayor of Darwen (1883) c.1883
oil on canvas 110 x 85
TH. 18

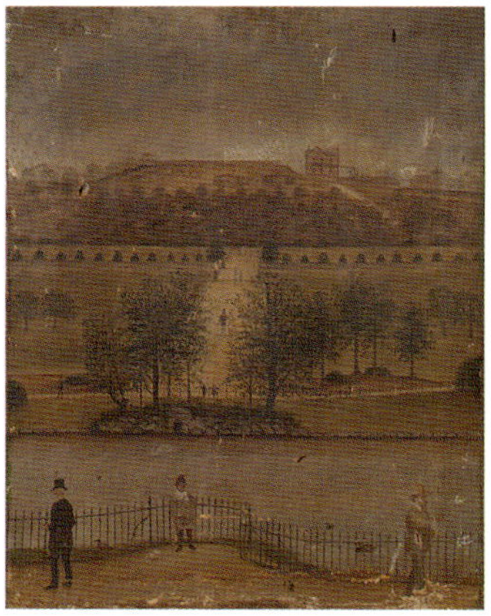

unknown artist
Corporation Park, Blackburn 1889
oil on canvas 77 x 55.5
2009.102

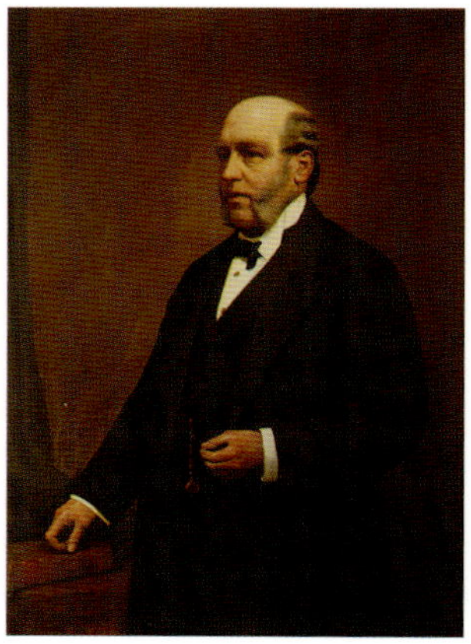

unknown artist
Councillor James Beads, JP 1889
oil on canvas 120 x 90
TH.1

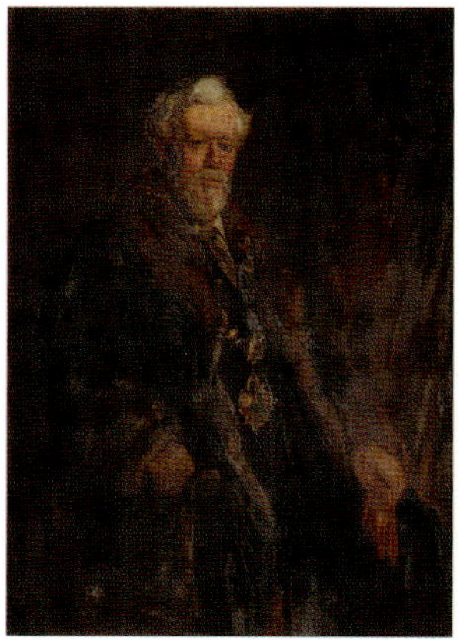

unknown artist
Charles Philip Huntington (1833–1906), Mayor of Darwen (1897) c.1897
oil on canvas 125 x 100
TH.14

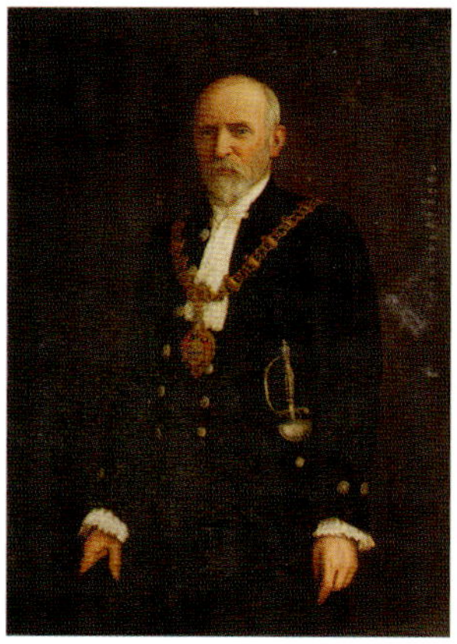

unknown artist
Councillor Dr James T. Ballantyne, Mayor of Darwen (1898) 1898–1899
oil on canvas 130 x 94
TH.9

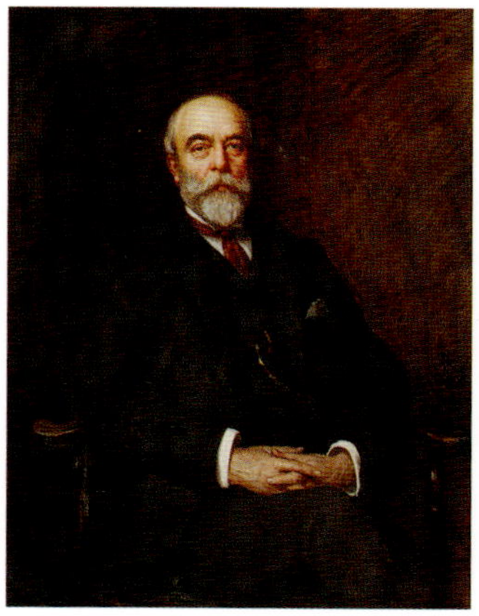

unknown artist
Henry Harrison (1834–1914), President of the Blackburn Chamber of Commerce (1887–1914) 1899
oil on canvas 120 x 97
1987.64.1

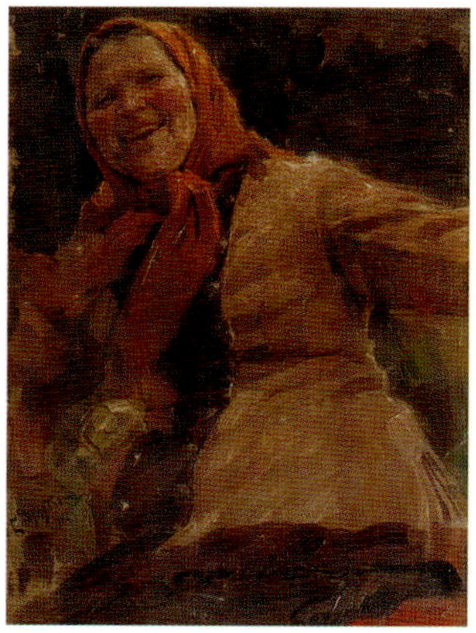

unknown artist
Russian Woman 1911
oil on canvas 49.5 x 40
378

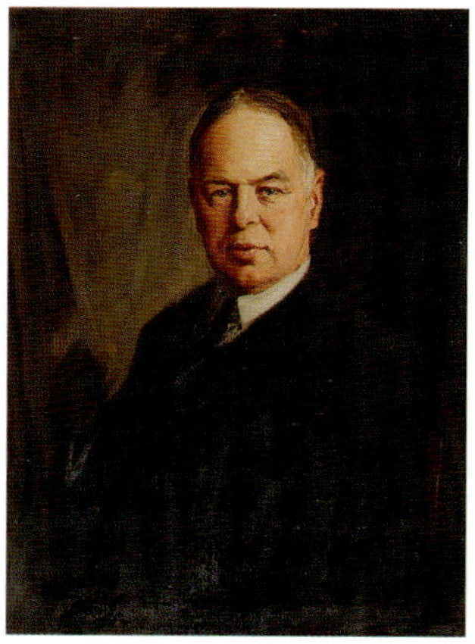

unknown artist
Alderman Edwin Hamer, JP (Blackburn) c.1940
oil on canvas 76 x 63
TH.11

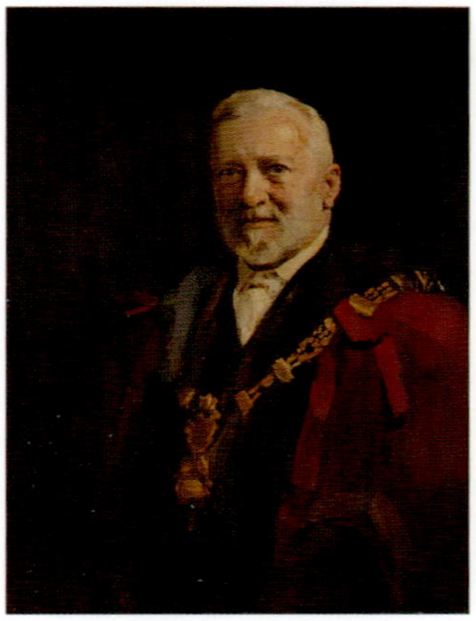

unknown artist
Alderman Timothy Lightbrown, Mayor of Blackburn (1884–1886)
oil on canvas 90 x 69
TH. 4

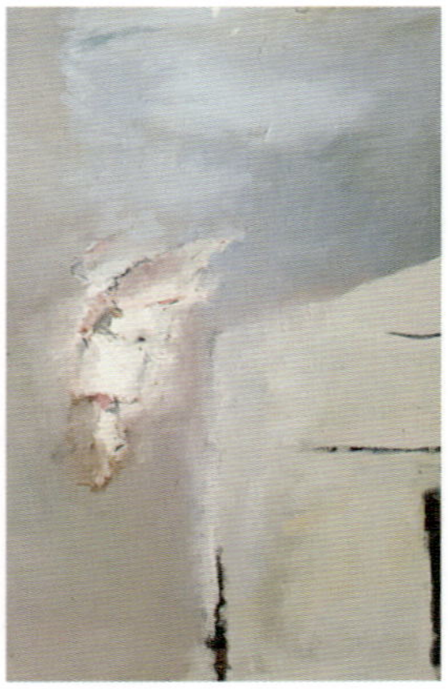

unknown artist
Blue Abstract with White Horse
oil on canvas 142 x 92
2011.87

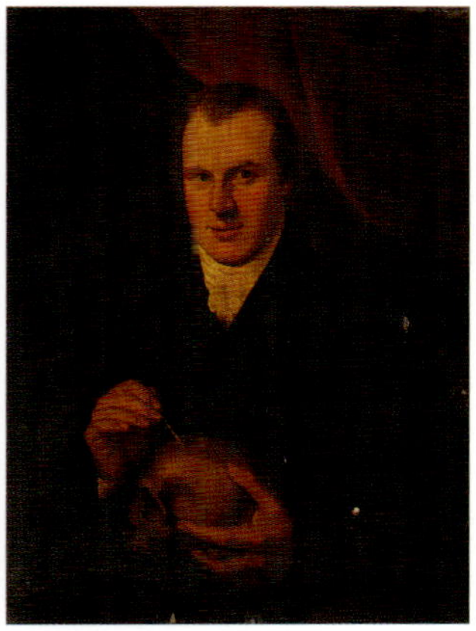

unknown artist
Dr Barlow
oil on canvas 76 x 60
68A

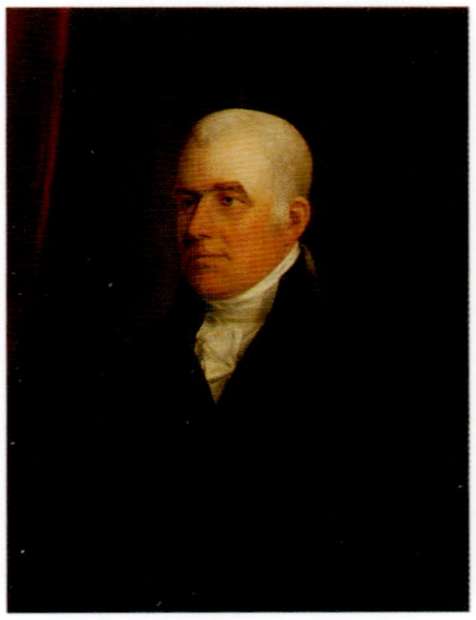

unknown artist
Dr Barlow
oil on canvas 75 x 61
952

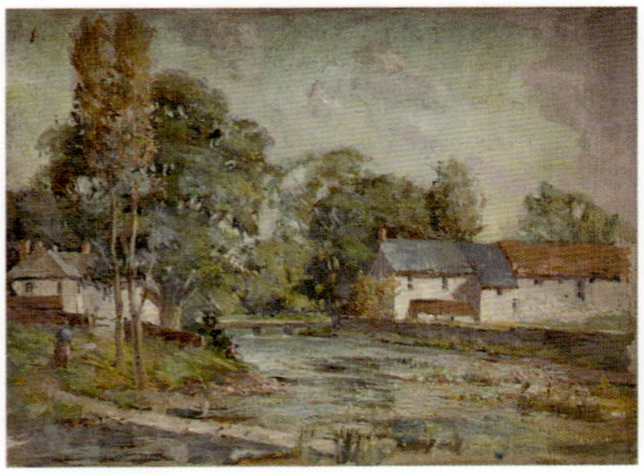

unknown artist
Cottages by River, Malham
oil on board 25 x 35
2011.104

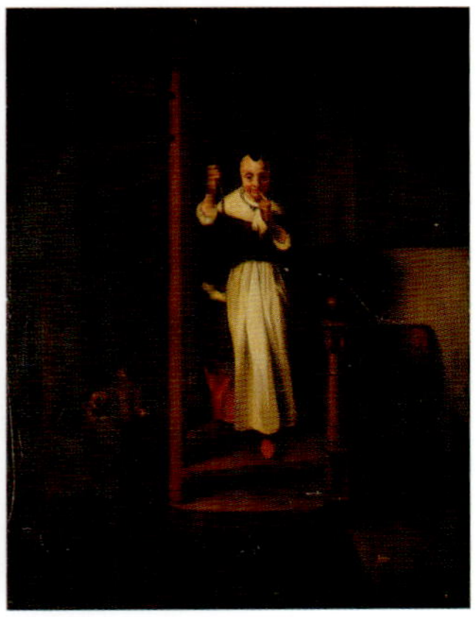

unknown artist
Girl Walking down Stairs
oil on panel 74 x 55
2011.94

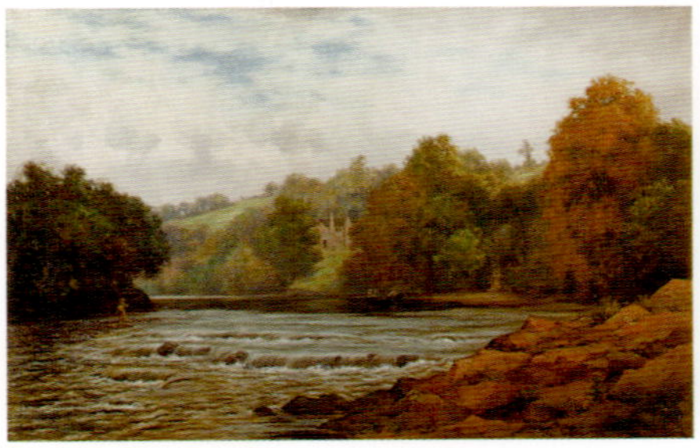

unknown artist
Hacking Hall
oil on canvas 80 x 100 (E)
2011.112

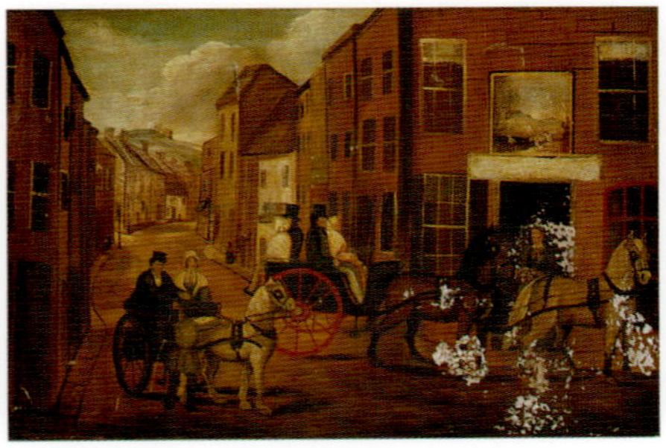

unknown artist
High Street outside a Public House
oil on canvas 63 x 99
2011.78

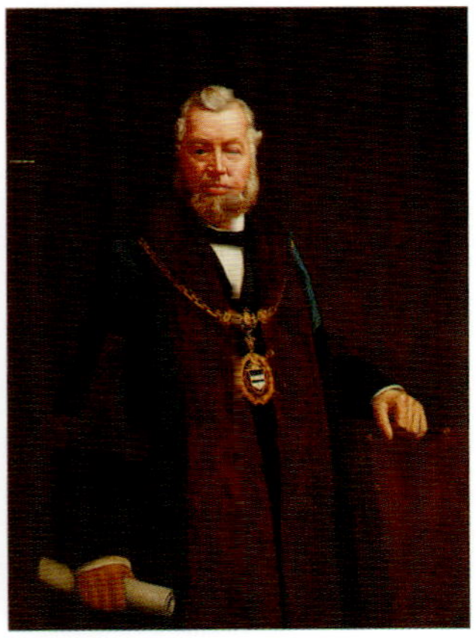

unknown artist
James Hoyle, Mayor of Blackburn (1882–1884)
oil on canvas 90 x 70
TH. 25

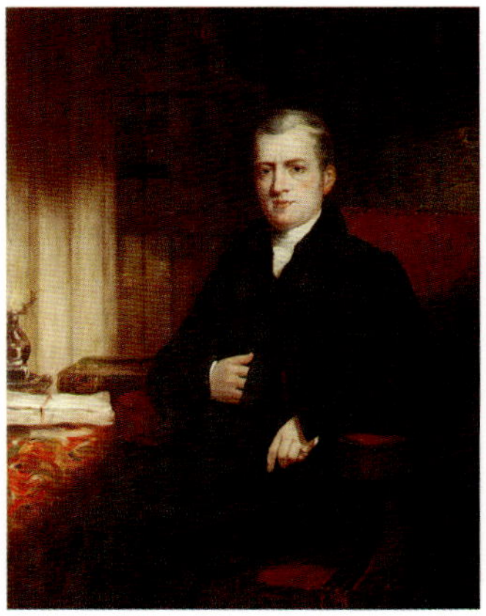

unknown artist
John Hargreaves, MP
oil on canvas 126 x 100
TH. 23

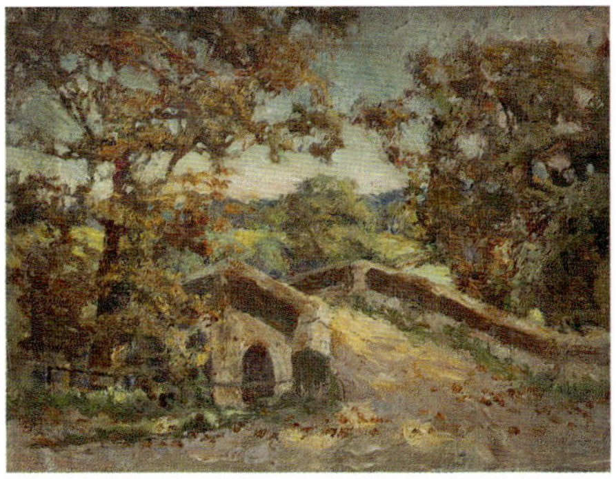

unknown artist
Landscape with Bridge
oil on board 22.5 x 30
2011.103

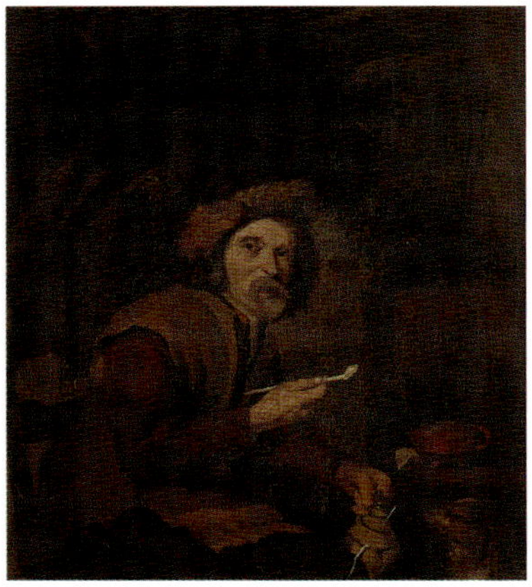

unknown artist
Man with Clay Pipe (believed to be Jan Stein)
oil on canvas 31 x 28
2011.92

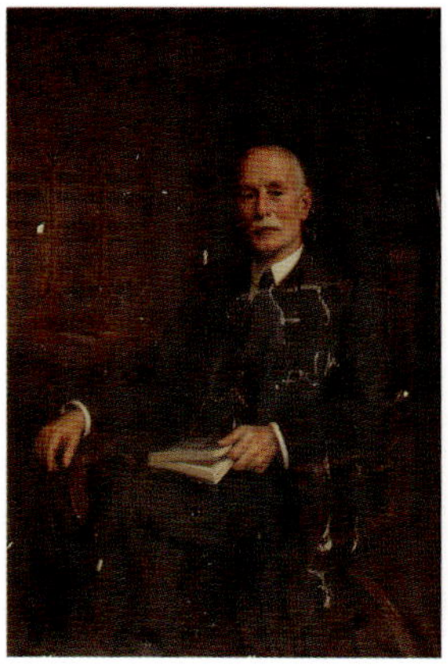

unknown artist
Portrait of a Man
oil on canvas 135 x 101
2011.77

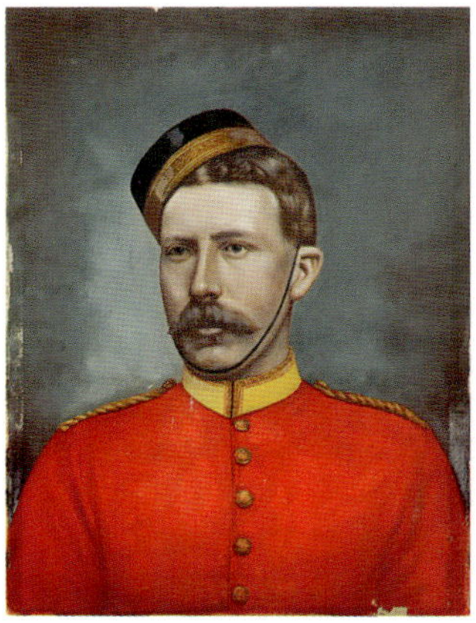

unknown artist
Portrait of a Man in Uniform
oil on board 62 x 49
2011.102

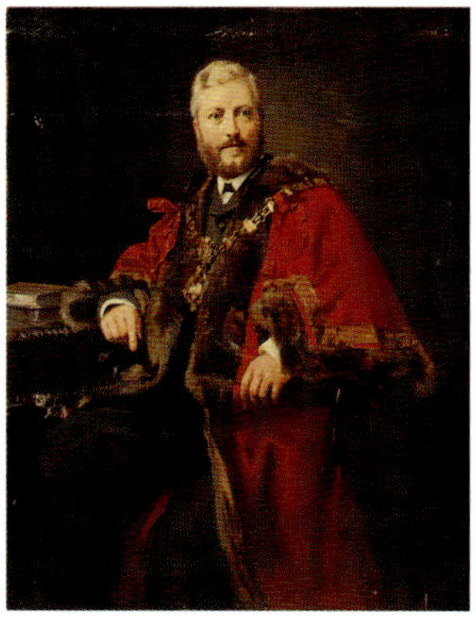

unknown artist
Portrait of an Unidentified Mayor (Blackburn or Darwen)
oil on canvas 140 x 112
TH.10

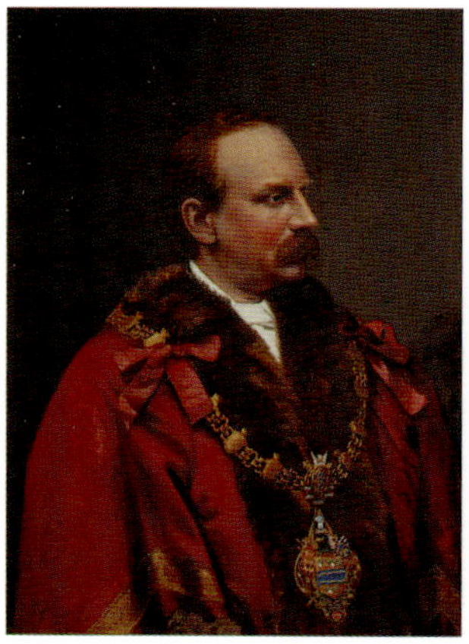

unknown artist
Portrait of an Unidentified Mayor of Darwen
oil on canvas 90 x 70
TH.8

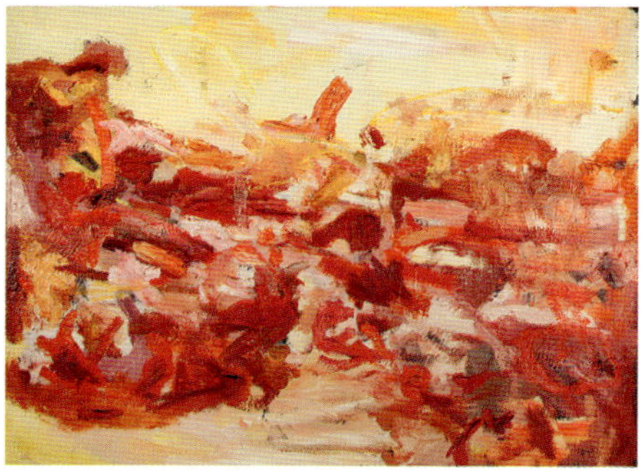

unknown artist
Red Abstract
oil on canvas 92 x 122
2011.99

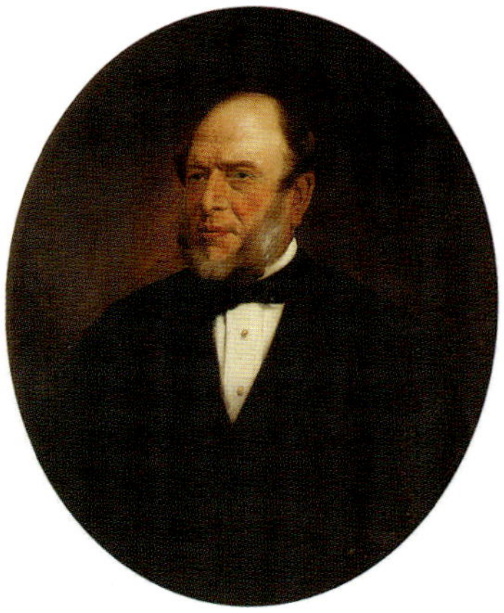

unknown artist
Robert Raynford Jackson
oil on canvas 76 x 62
1940.2.1

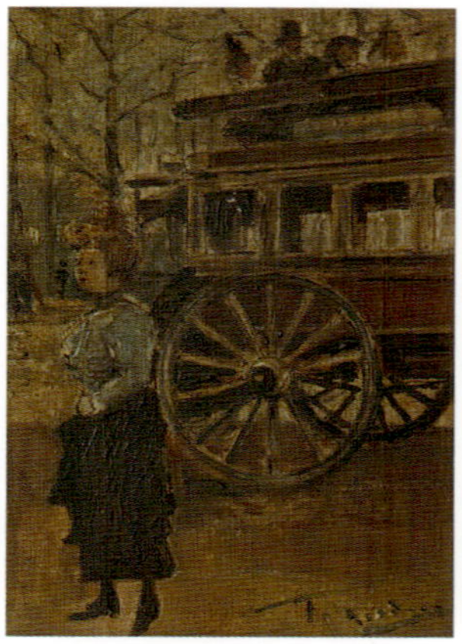

unknown artist
Street Scene, Paris
oil on board 18 x 12
342

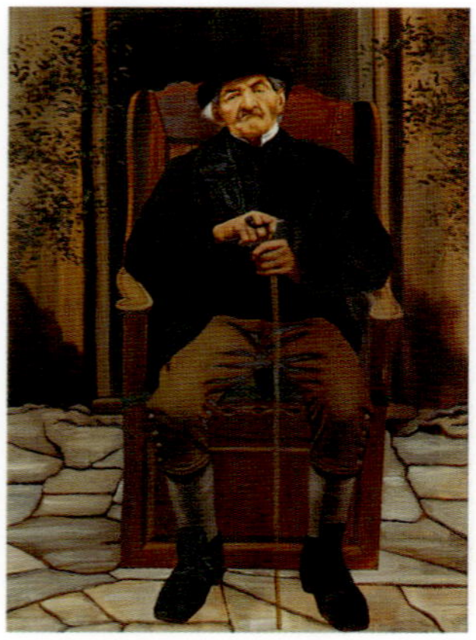

unknown artist
The Salesbury Centenarian, William Hayhurst
oil on canvas 59 x 44
2011.109

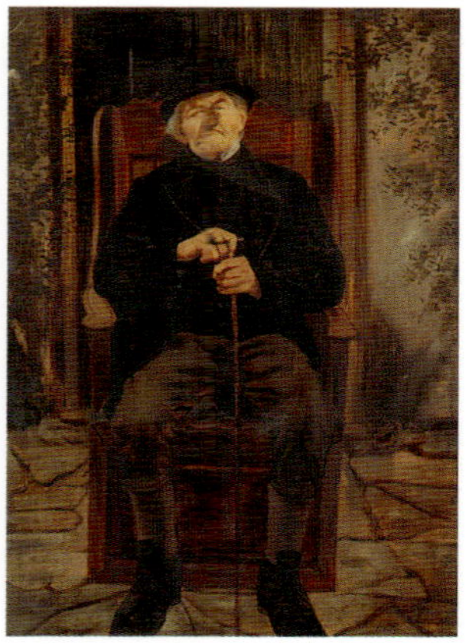

unknown artist
The Salesbury Centenarian, William Hayhurst
oil on canvas 59 x 44
2011.11

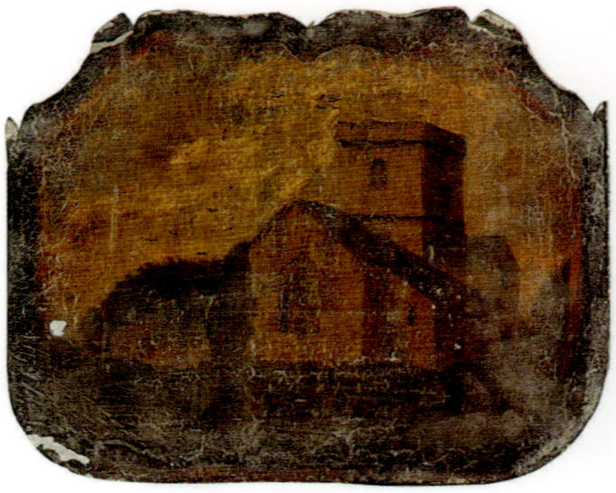

unknown artist
View of an Unidentified Church
oil on metal 20 x 25
2011.1

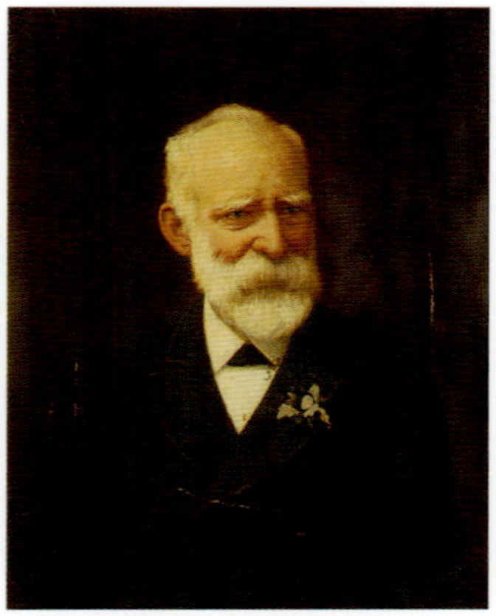

unknown artist
William Gregson (1820–1890)
oil on canvas 75 x 59
TH.12

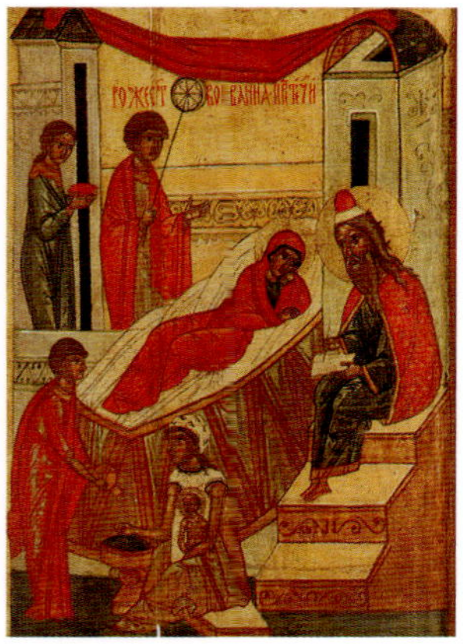

unknown artist
Birth of Saint John the Baptist c.1500
tempera on panel 48 x 36.4
856 (P)

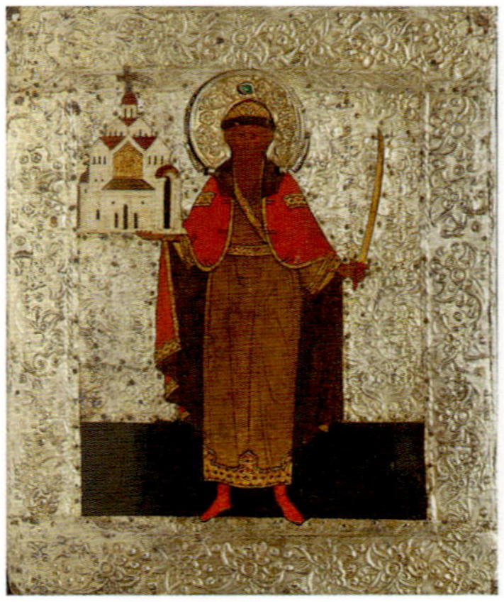

unknown artist
Saint Vsevolod, Grand Prince and Wonder Worker c.1575
tempera on panel 13 x 10.2
1231

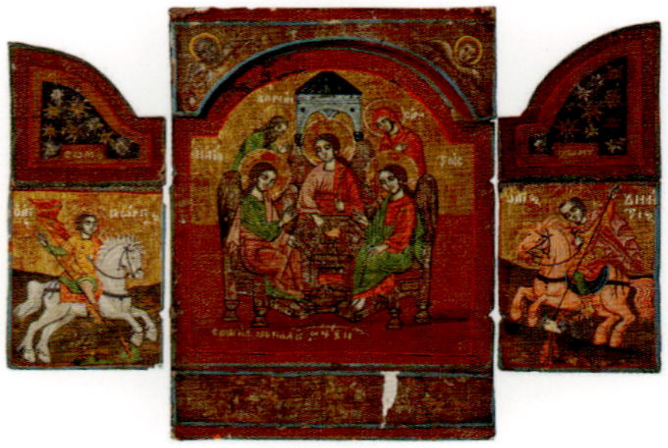

unknown artist
Old Testament Trinity (triptych) c.1768
tempera on panel 32.2 x 22.6
861

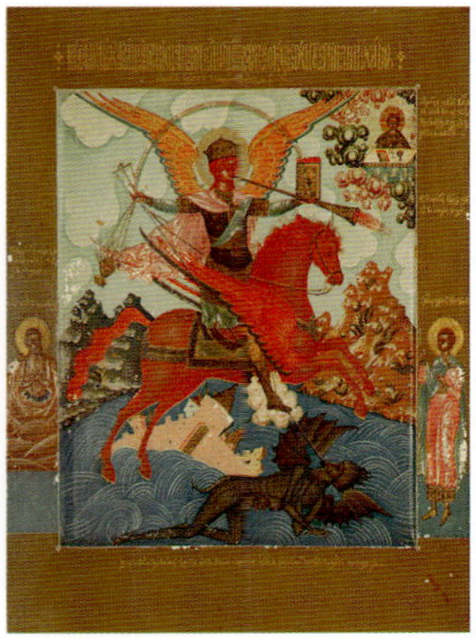

unknown artist
Archangel Michael c.1800
tempera on panel 44.5 x 37.2
855 (P)

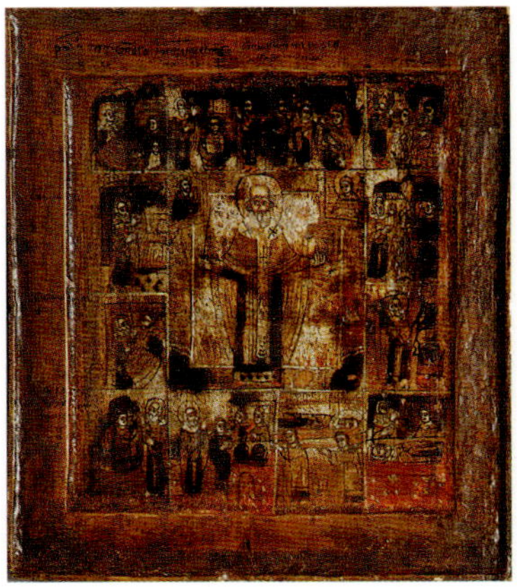

unknown artist
Scenes from the Life of Saint Nicholas c.1800
tempera on panel 31.3 x 27.7
1085

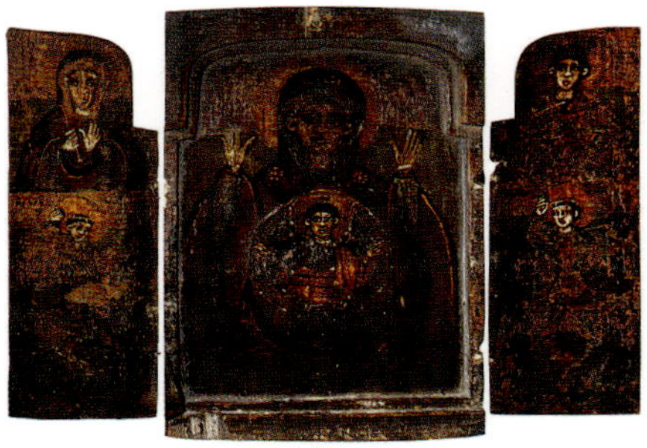

unknown artist
The Virgin of God the Sign (triptych) c.1800
tempera on panel 28.6 x 34.3
1082

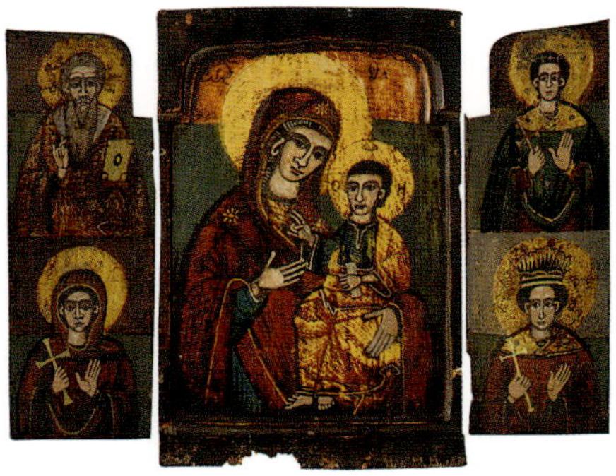

unknown artist
Virgin and Child (triptych) c.1800
tempera on panel 29.2 x 36
864

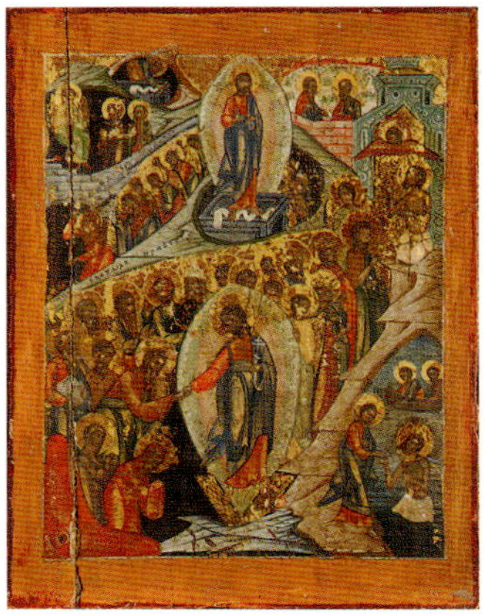

unknown artist
Anastasis
tempera on panel 30 x 23
1223

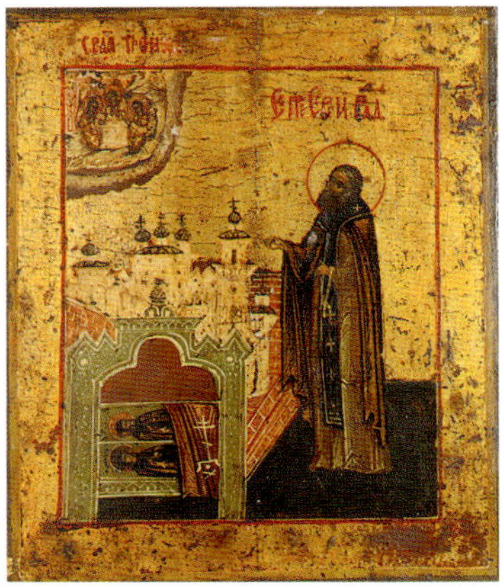

unknown artist
Apparition of the Holy Trinity to Saint Sergei
tempera on panel 31 x 25.8
1217

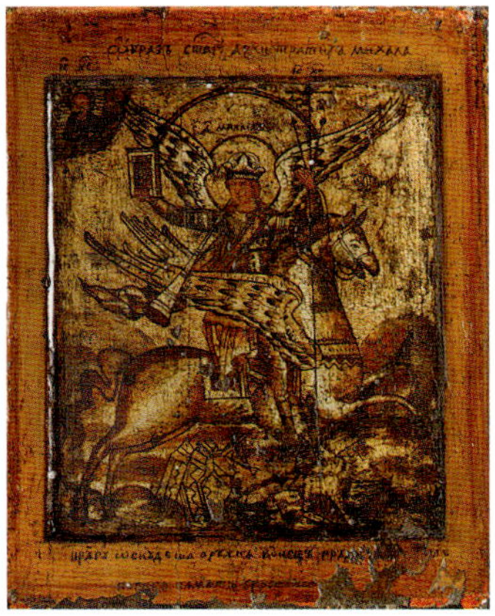

unknown artist
Archangel Michael
tempera on panel 30 x 25.7
1083

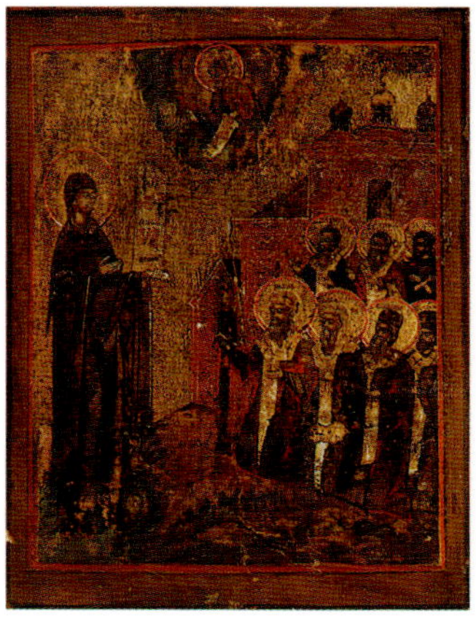

unknown artist
Bogolubskaya 'The Loved by God'
tempera on panel 28.7 x 23
1080

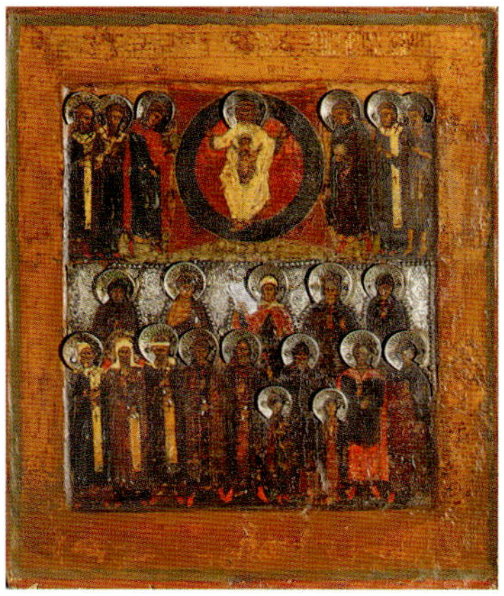

unknown artist
Christ in Majesty
tempera on panel 31.1 x 26.9
1069

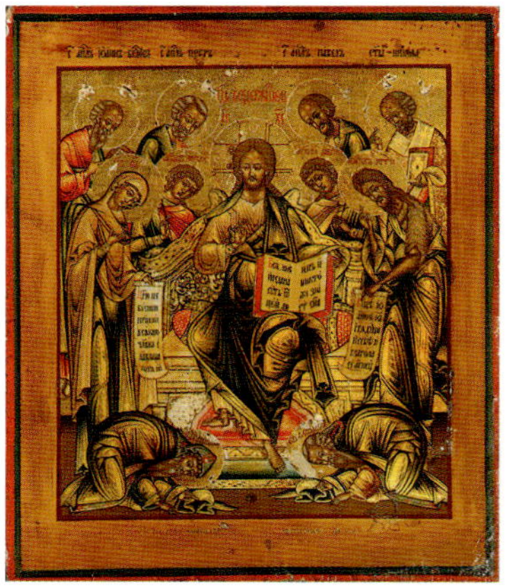

unknown artist
Christ Pantocrator
tempera on panel 27.1 x 23
1073

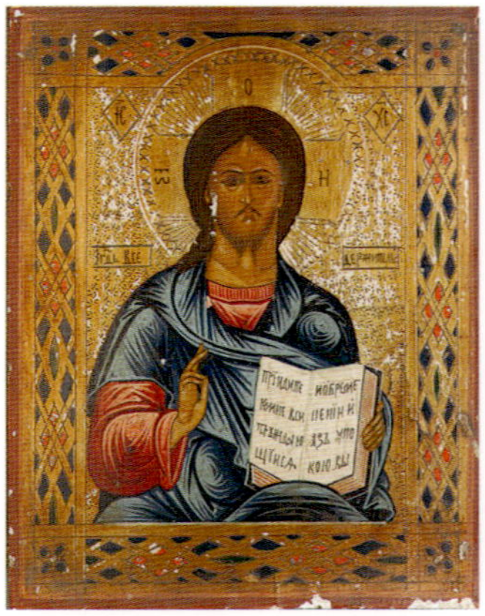

unknown artist
Christ Vsederzhitel
tempera on panel 22.2 x 17.5
1201

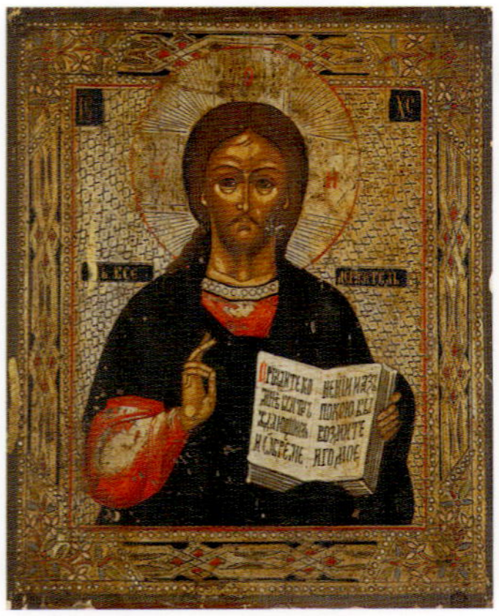

unknown artist
Christ Vsederzhitel
tempera on panel 31 x 26.5
1209

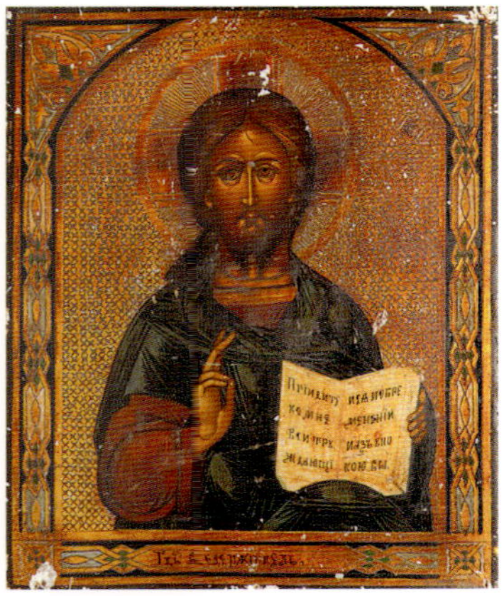

unknown artist
Christ Vsederzhitel
tempera on panel 35 x 30.3
1221

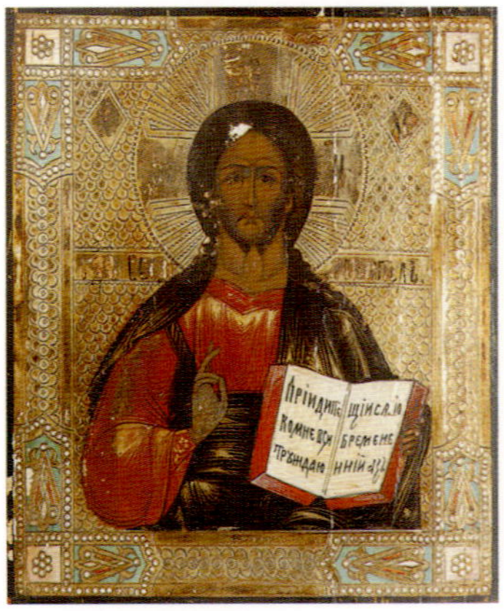

unknown artist
Christ Vsederzhitel
tempera on panel 30.5 x 27
1224

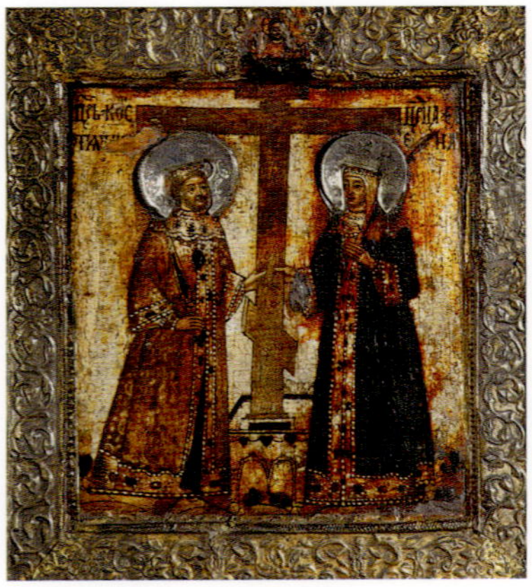

unknown artist
Constantine and Helen
tempera on panel 31.1 x 26.9
1074

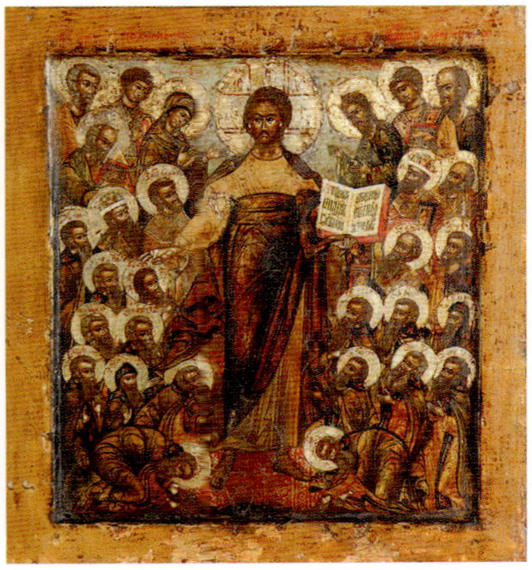

unknown artist
Deesis with Saints
tempera on panel 35.2 x 30.2
1071

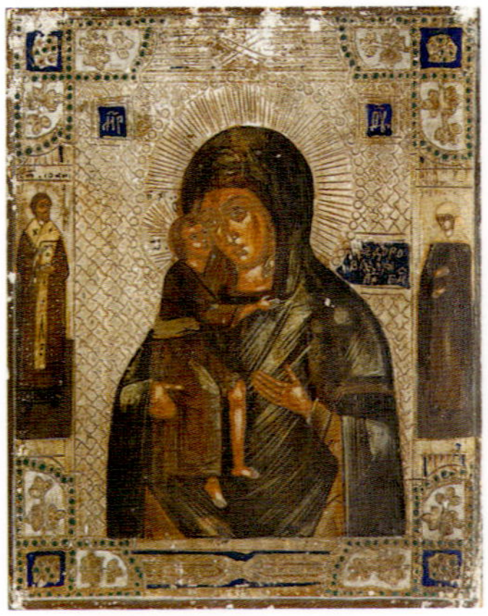

unknown artist
Fedorovskaya, Mother of God
tempera on panel 22 x 17.8
1202

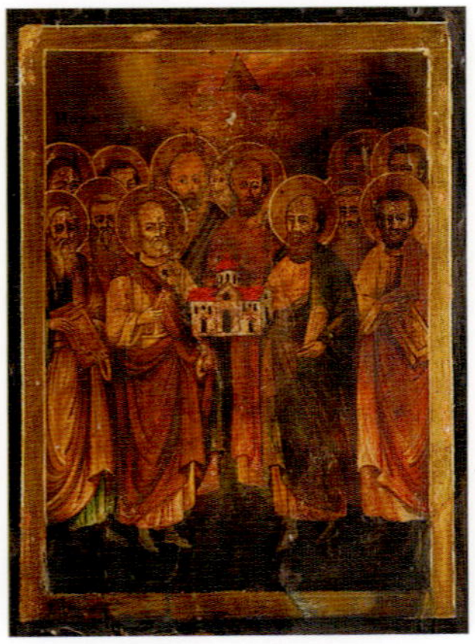

unknown artist
God the All Seeing
tempera on panel 37.2 x 30.1
1075

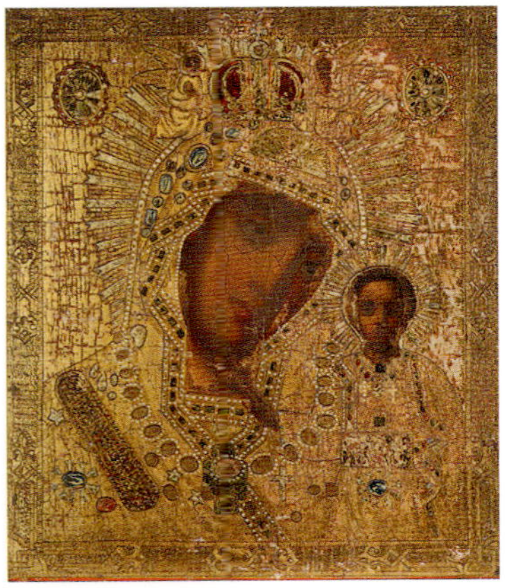

unknown artist
Kazanskaya Mother of God
tempera on panel 31 x 26.5
1215

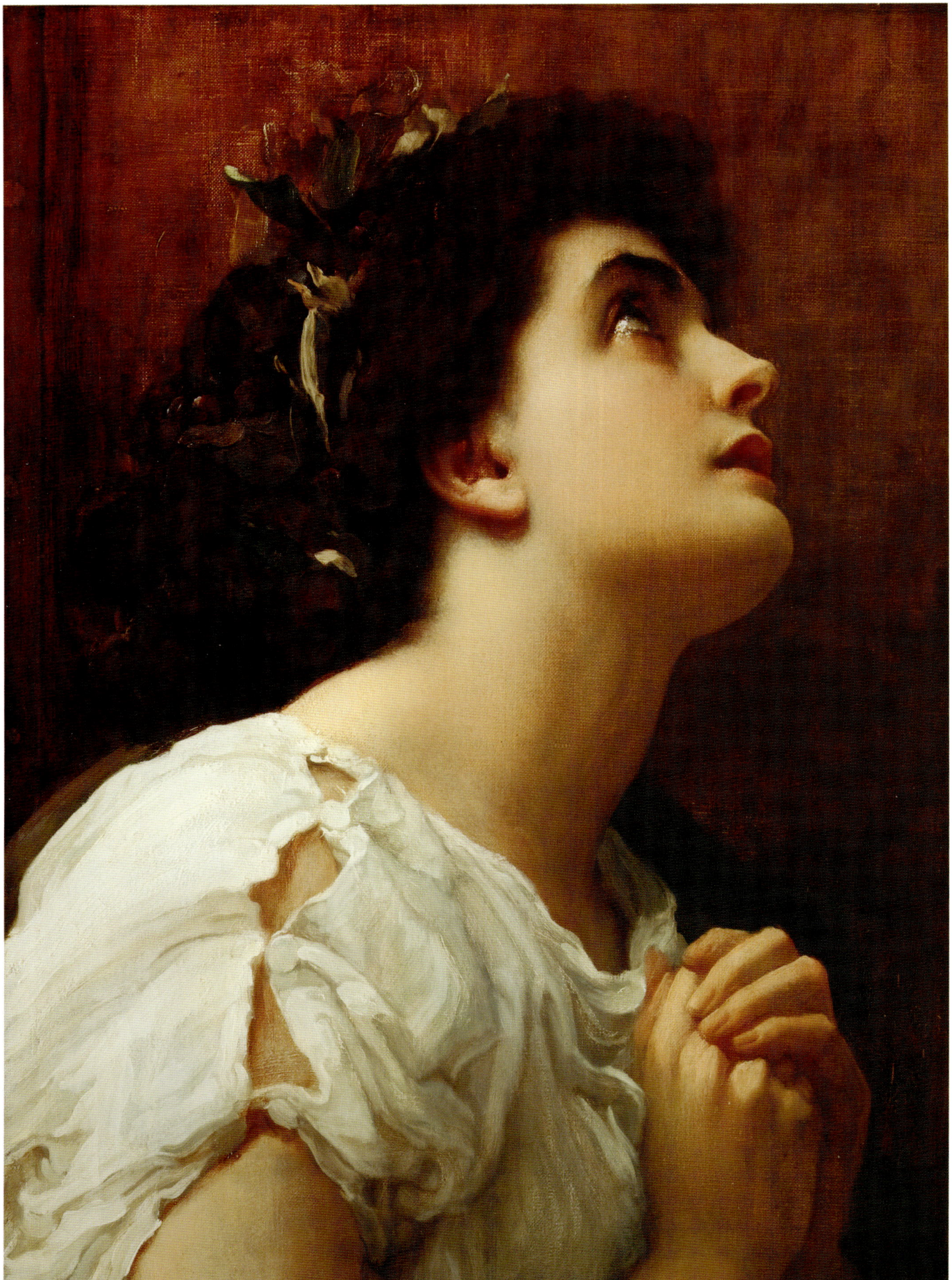

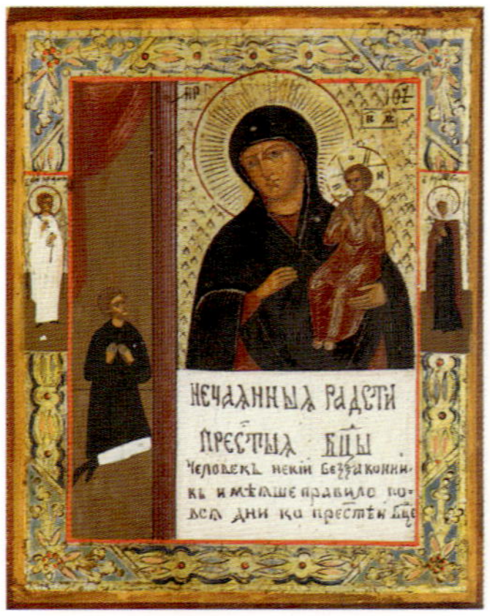

unknown artist
Mother of God of Unexpected Joy
tempera on panel 22.5 x 17.5
1204

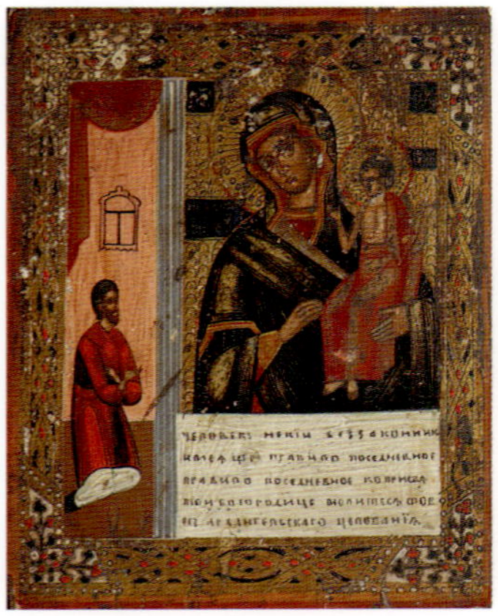

unknown artist
Mother of God of Unexpected Joy
tempera on panel 26.5 x 22.5
1226

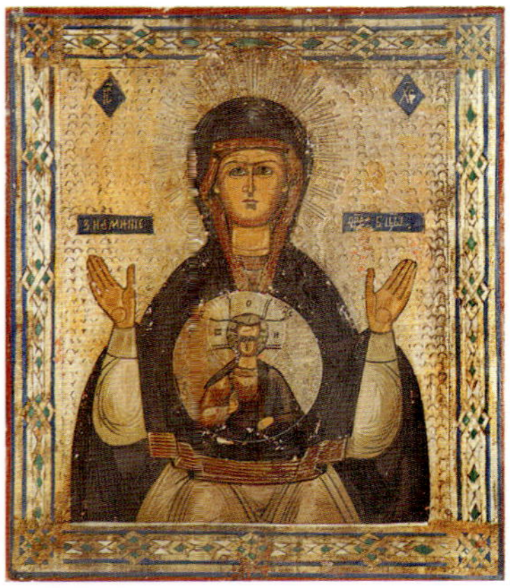

unknown artist
Mother of God the Sign
tempera on panel 35.3 x 30.8
1212

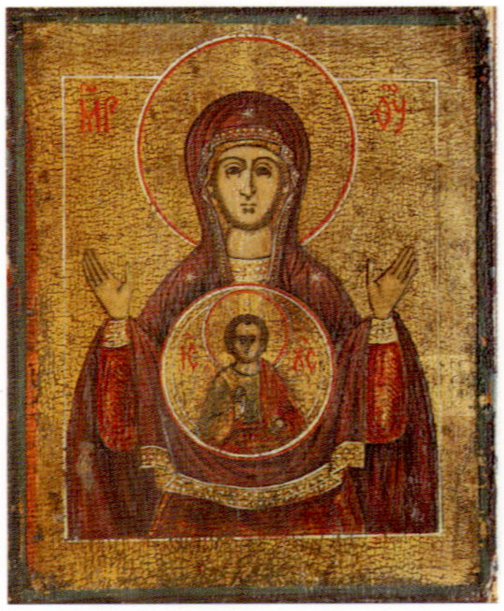

unknown artist
Mother of God the Sign (Orans)
tempera on panel 17.7 x 14.5
1205

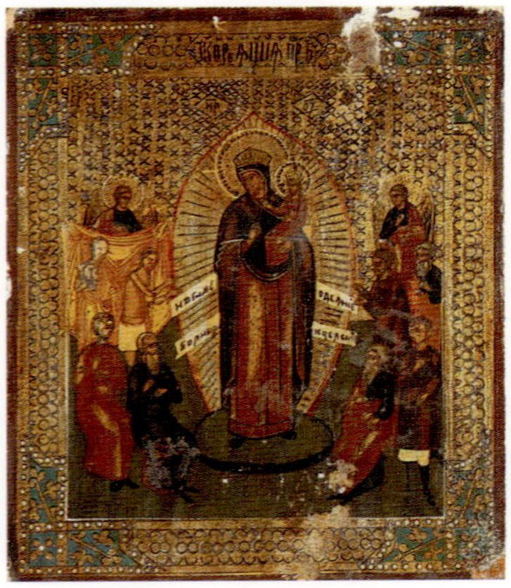

unknown artist
Mother of God to Those Who Grieve
tempera on panel 26.2 x 21.8
1208

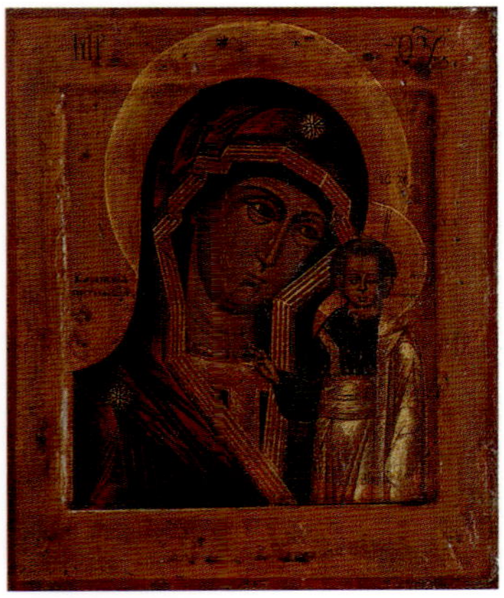

unknown artist
Our Lady of Kazan
tempera on panel 31.5 x 27
1084

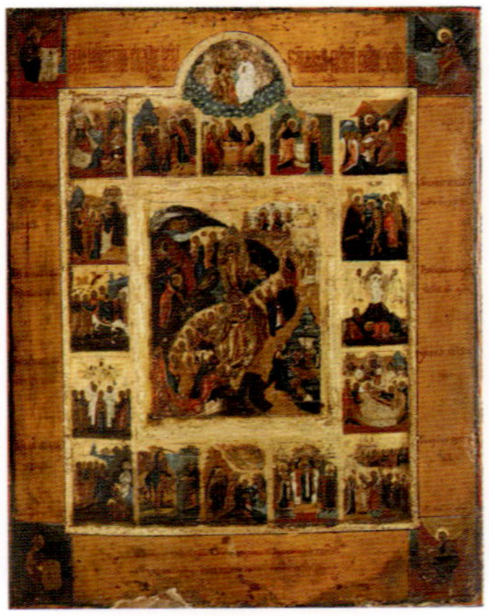

unknown artist
Resurrection and Descent into Hell
tempera on panel 35.2 x 30.5
1068

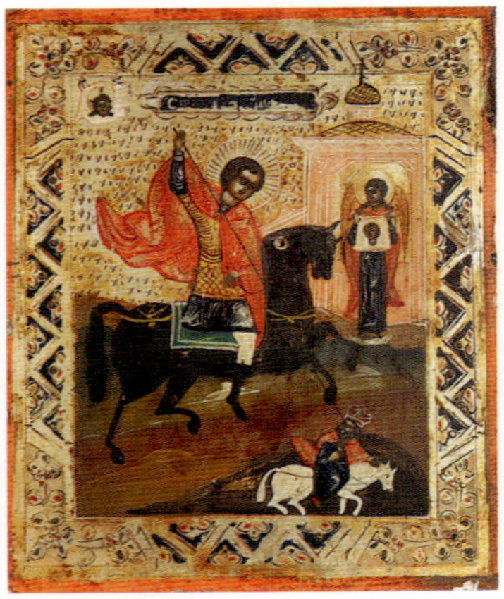

unknown artist
Saint Demetrius Vanquishing a Pagan Saint
tempera on panel 26.4 x 21.7
1225

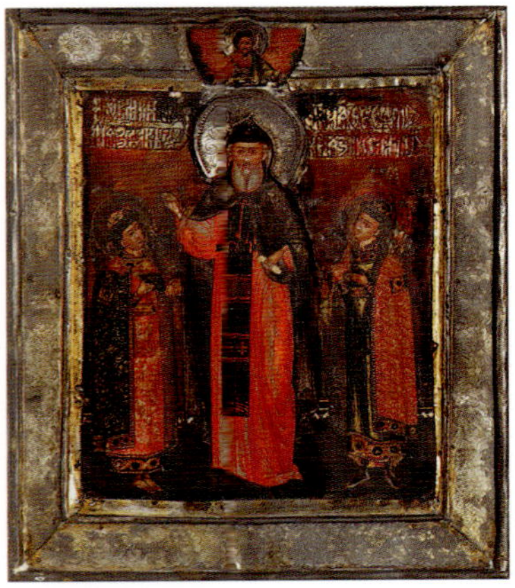

unknown artist
Saint Feodor
tempera on panel 31.5 x 27.2
1077

Facing page: Leighton, Frederic, 1830–1896, *Faith*, Haworth Art Gallery (p. 12)

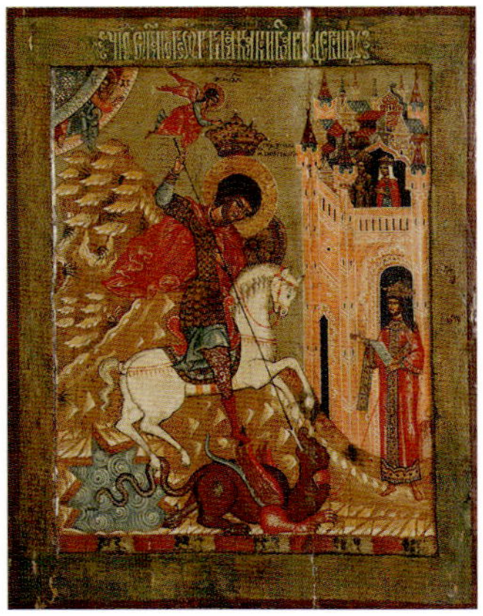

unknown artist
Saint George and the Dragon
tempera on panel 74 x 60
854 (P)

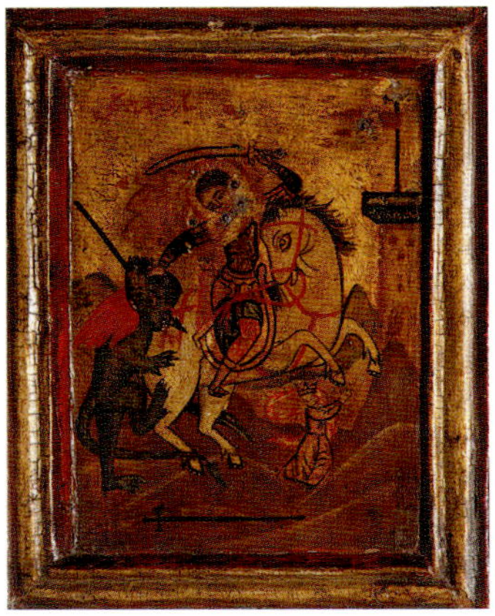

unknown artist
Saint George and the Dragon
tempera on panel 24.5 x 20.3
857

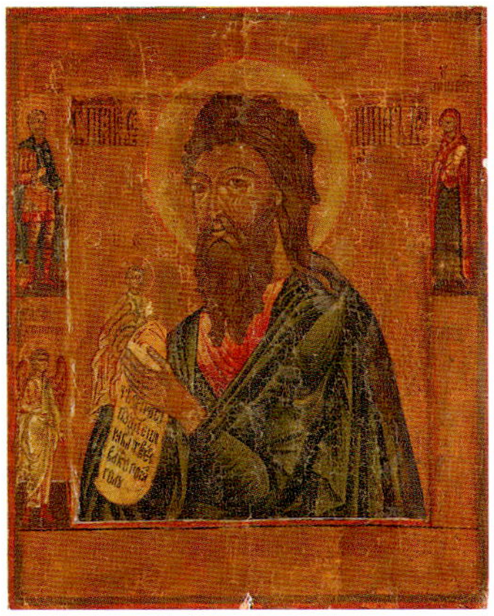

unknown artist
Saint John the Baptist
tempera on panel 31.1 x 26.5
1211

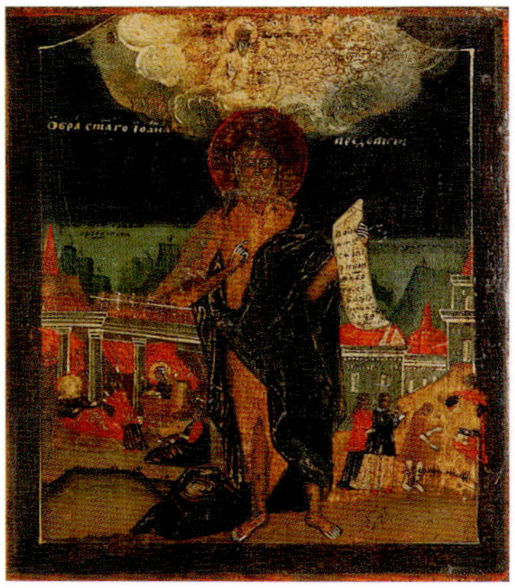

unknown artist
Saint John the Baptist the Foreteller
tempera on panel 33.3 x 26.9
1079

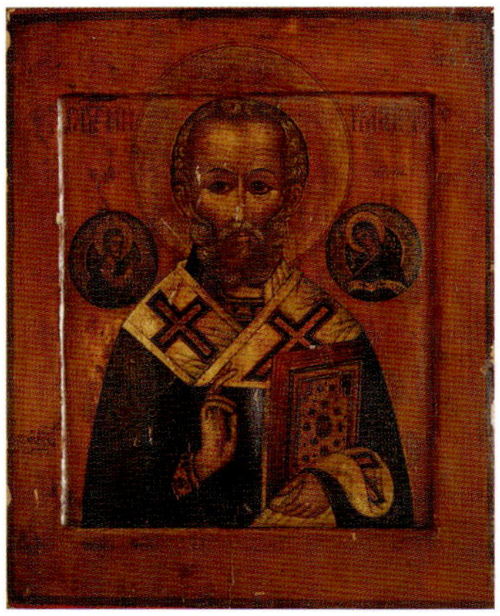

unknown artist
Saint Nicholas
tempera on panel 31.1 x 26.9
1072

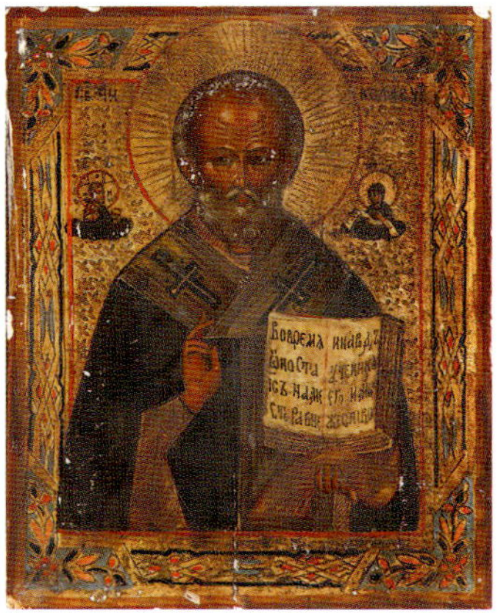

unknown artist
Saint Nicholas
tempera on panel 22.5 x 17.5
1203

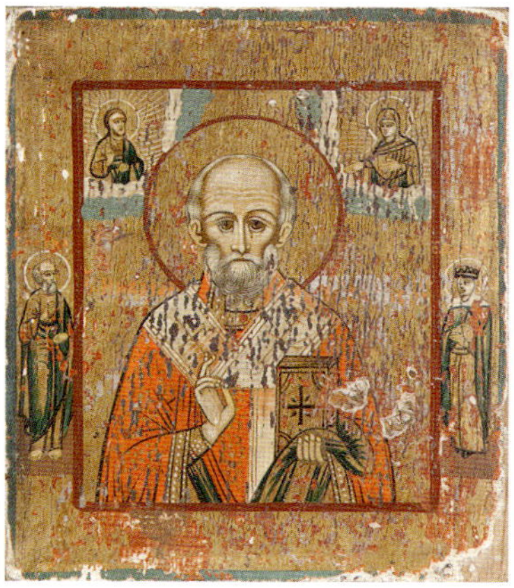

unknown artist
Saint Nicholas
tempera on panel 13.5 x 11.5
1206

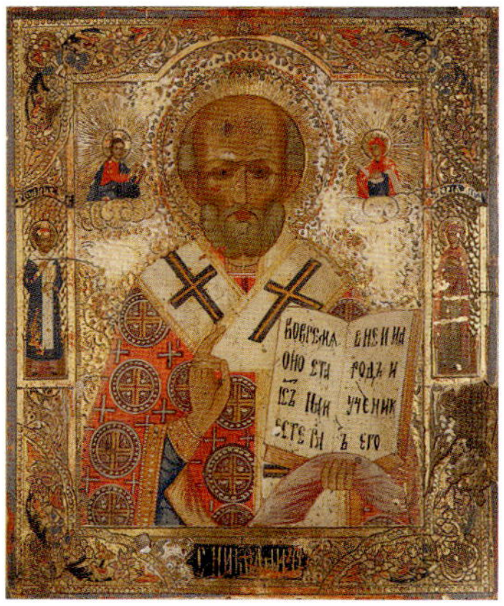

unknown artist
Saint Nicholas
tempera on panel 31.1 x 26.7
1210

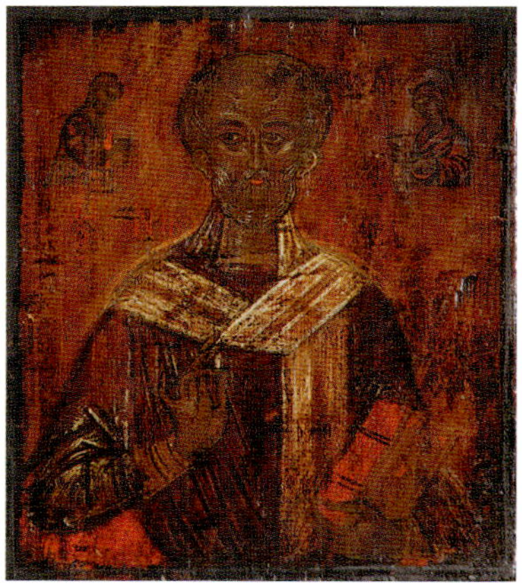

unknown artist
Saint Nicholas of Mira
tempera on panel 19.6 x 17.1
859

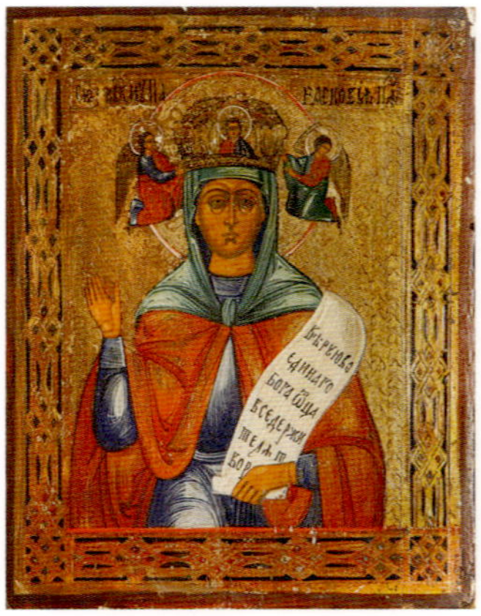

unknown artist
Saint Paraskeva
tempera on panel 26.3 x 21
1207

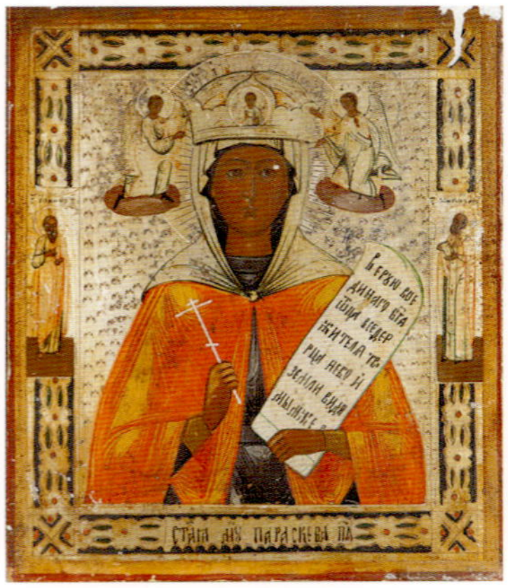

unknown artist
Saint Paraskeva
tempera on panel 31 x 26.2
1222

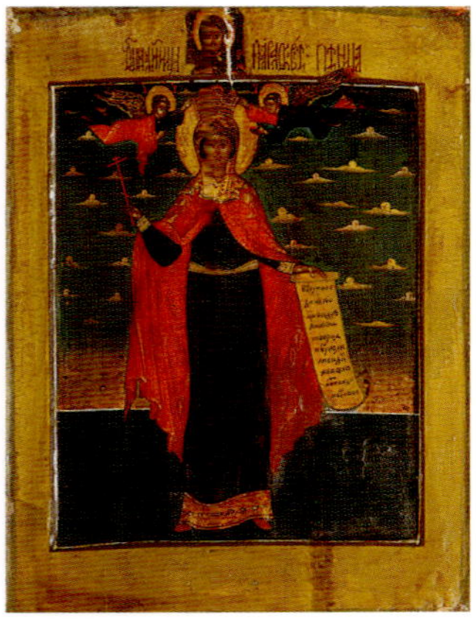

unknown artist
Saint Paraskeva Paranitsa
tempera on panel 31.8 x 27.1
1081

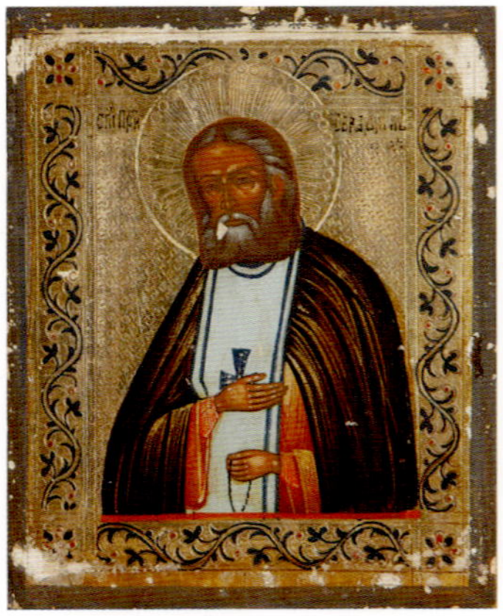

unknown artist
Saint Serafim of Sarov
tempera on panel 17.6 x 14.4
1200

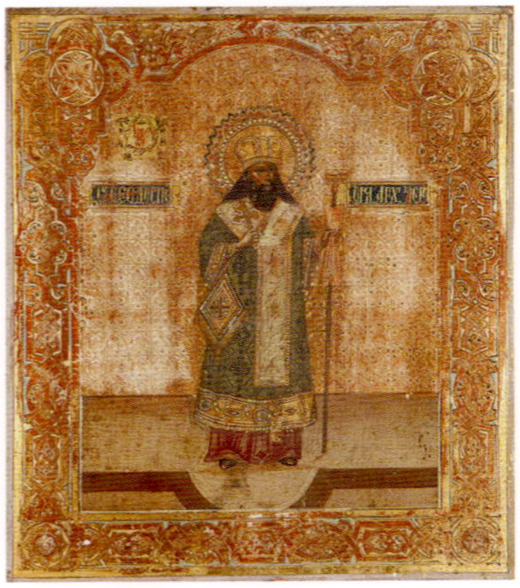

unknown artist
Saint Theodosi
tempera on panel 31 x 27
1214

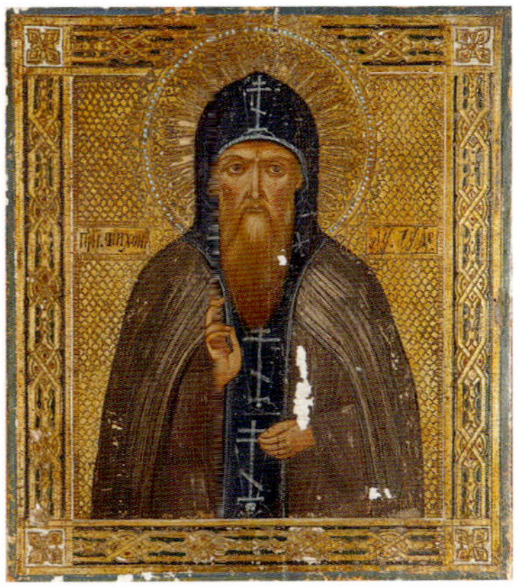

unknown artist
Saint Tikhon Zadonsky
tempera on panel 31 x 26.7
1213

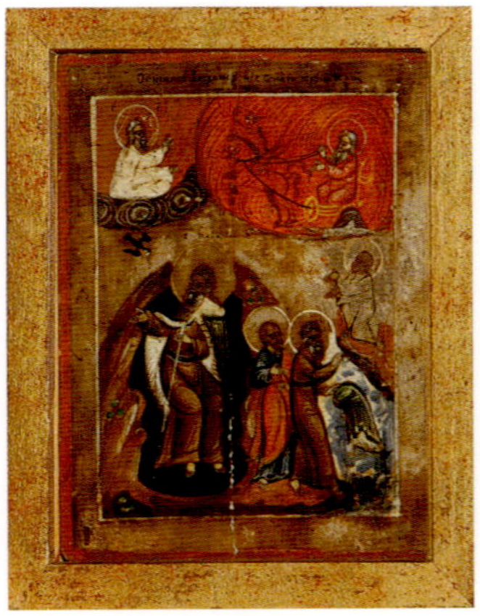

unknown artist
Scenes from the Life of Prophet Elijah
tempera on panel 13 x 10.2
869

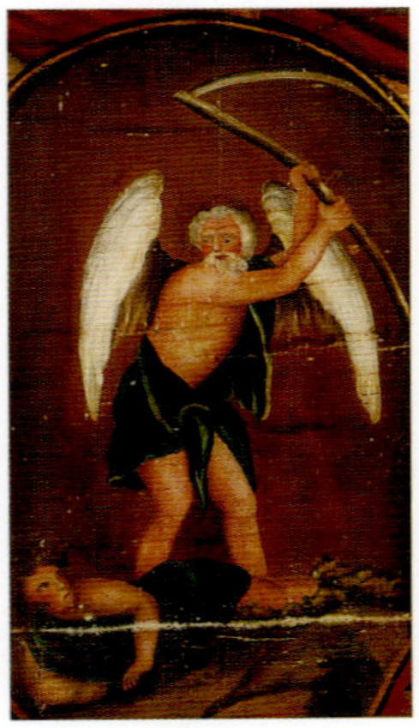

unknown artist
Slaying Angel
oil on canvas 82 x 45
2011.9

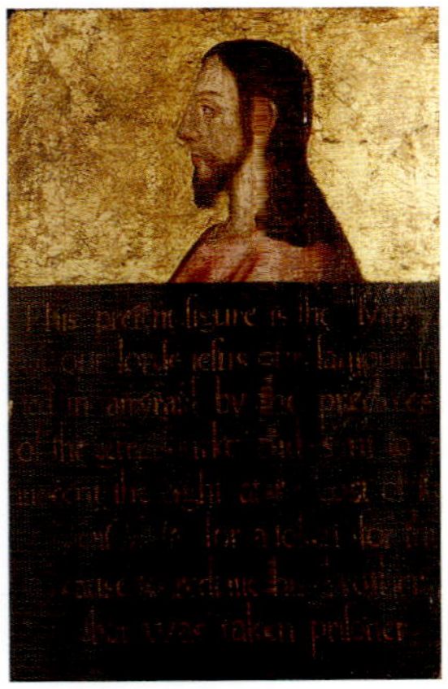

unknown artist
The Amaryld Vernicle
tempera on panel 16.5 x 8.5
858

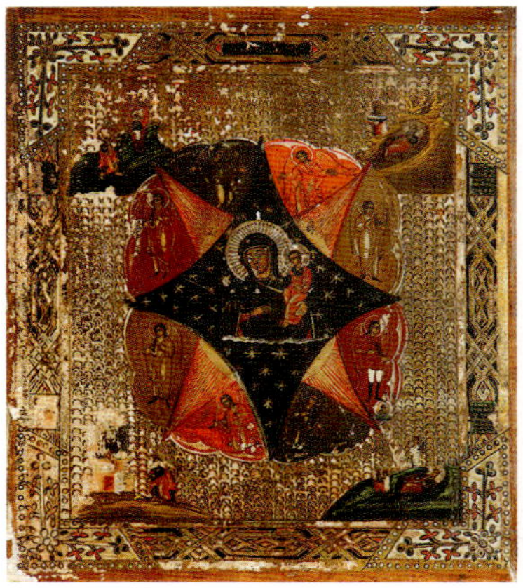

unknown artist
The Burning Bush
tempera on panel 35.5 x 31
1220

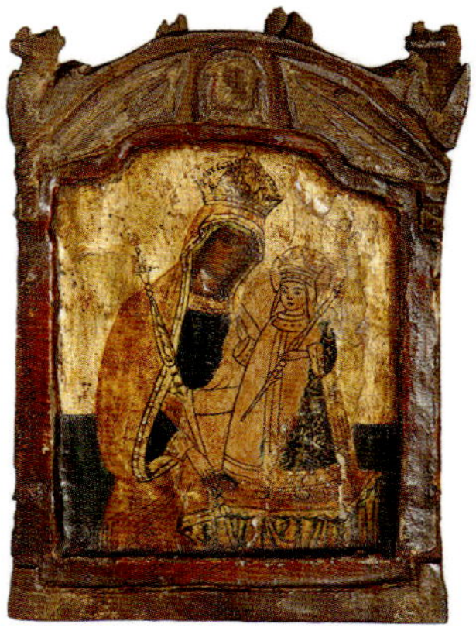

unknown artist
The Crowned Virgin and Infant
tempera on panel 19.7 x 15.2
862

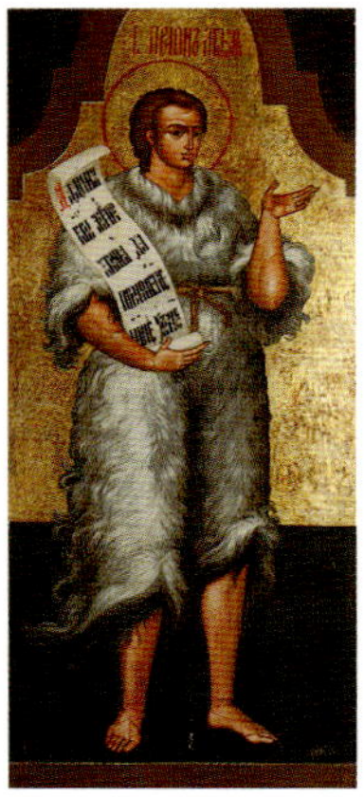

unknown artist
The Forefather Abel
tempera on panel 104.4 x 41.8
1171

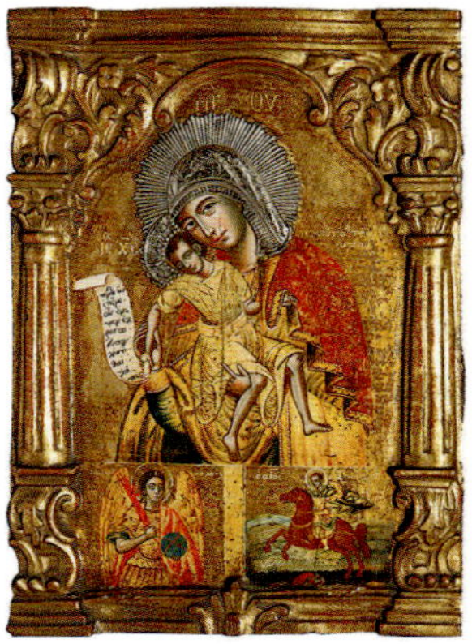

unknown artist
The Kykko Mother of God or Eleousa
tempera on panel 16.5 x 8.5
867

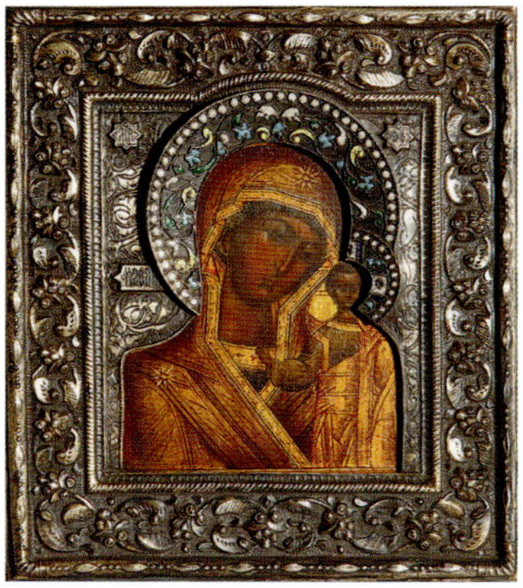

unknown artist
The Virgin of Kazan
tempera on panel 13.1 x 10.4
868

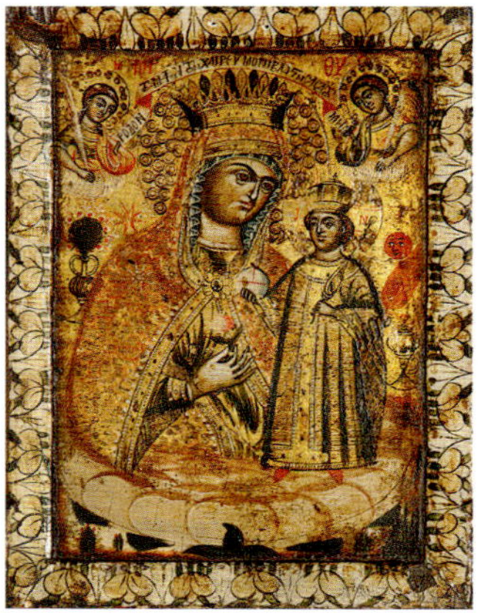

unknown artist
The Virgin of the Unfading Rose
tempera on panel 22.6 x 17
865

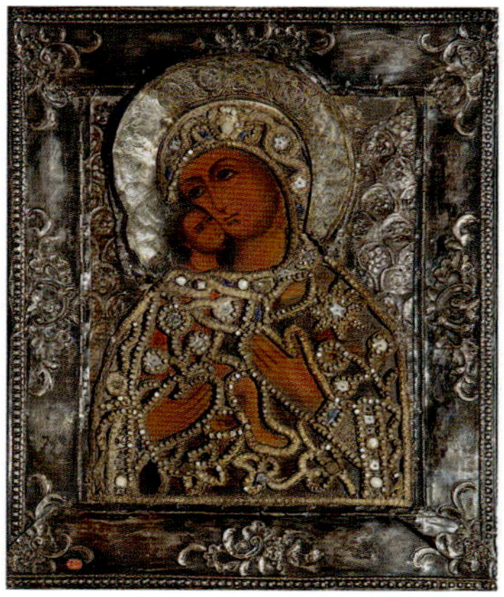

unknown artist
The Vladimir Mother of God
tempera on panel 32 x 25.5
1070

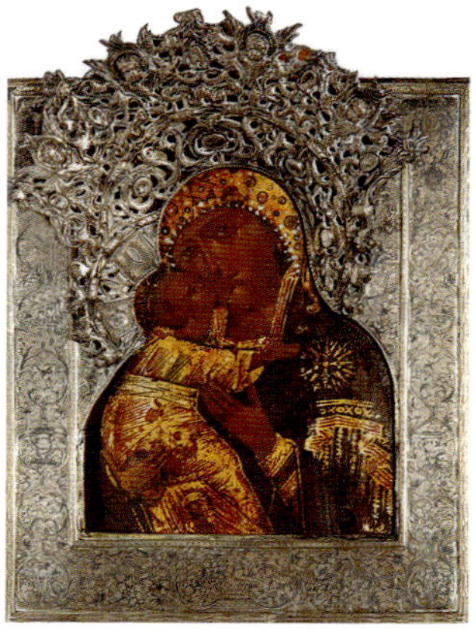

unknown artist
The Vladimir Mother of God
tempera on panel 22.9 x 19
1078

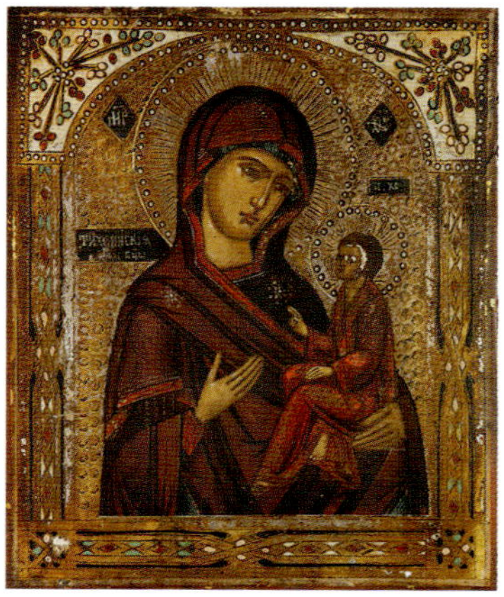

unknown artist
Tikhvin Mother of God
tempera on panel 30 x 25
1218

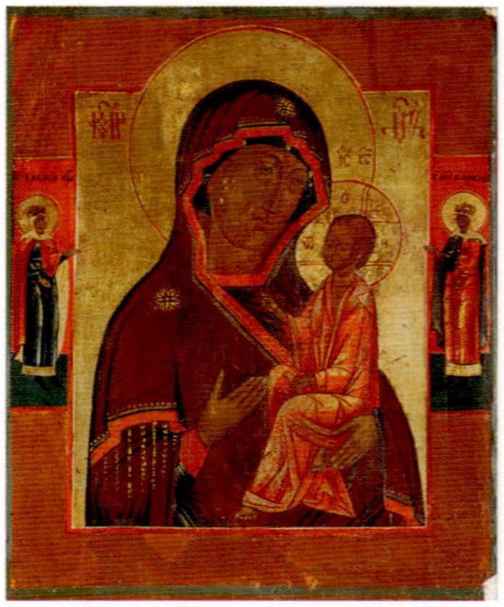

unknown artist
Tikhvin Mother of God
tempera on panel 30 x 25
1219

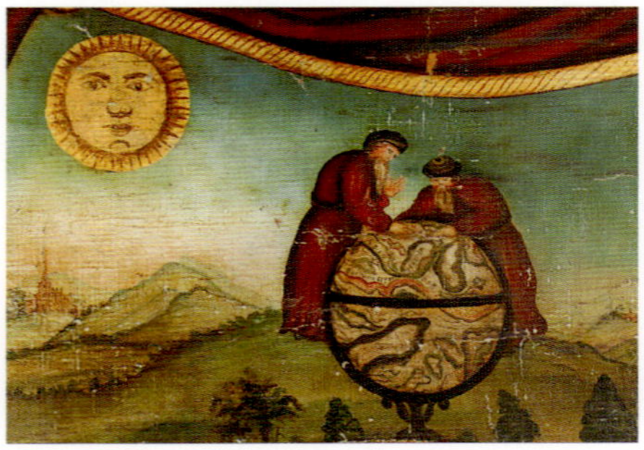

unknown artist
Two Men with Globe
oil on canvas 54 x 75
2011.86

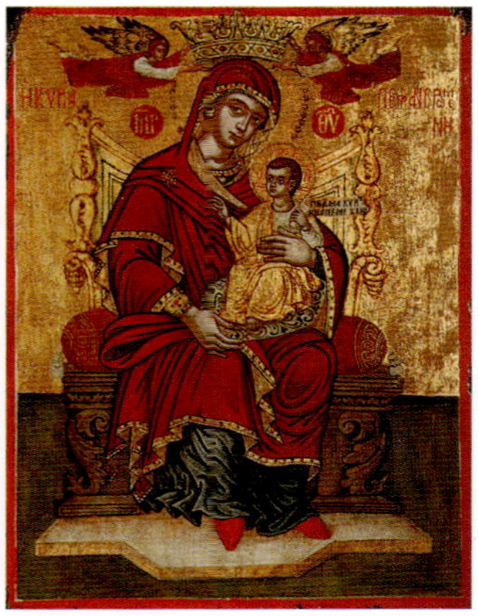

unknown artist
Virgin and Child Enthroned
tempera on panel 47.3 x 36.8
866

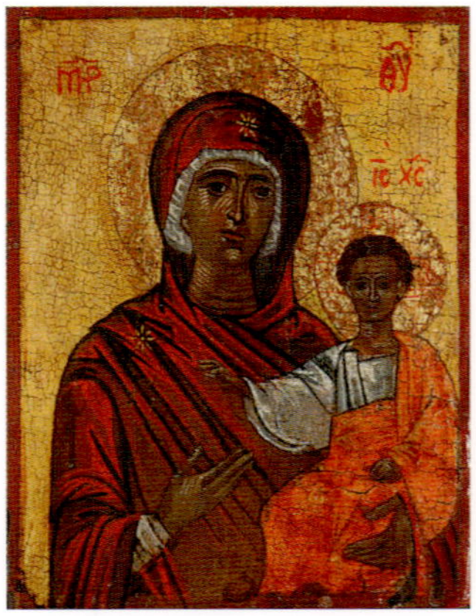

unknown artist
Virgin Hodegetria
tempera & gesso on panel 19.1 x 15.6
860

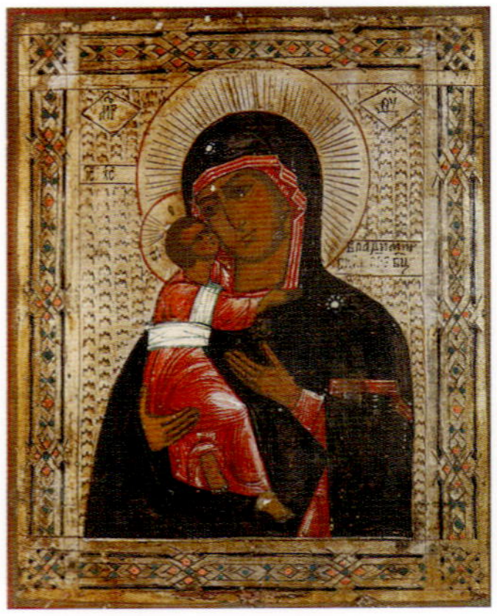

unknown artist
Vladimir Mother of God
tempera on panel 22.5 x 17.5
1216

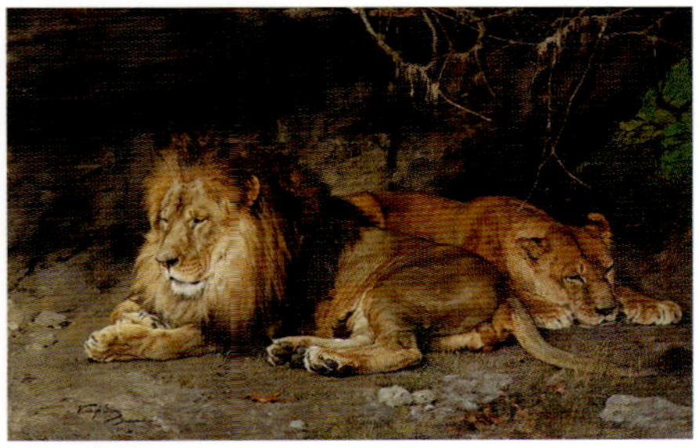

Vastagh, Géza 1866–1919
A Siesta late 19th C
oil on canvas 92.8 x 152.5
206

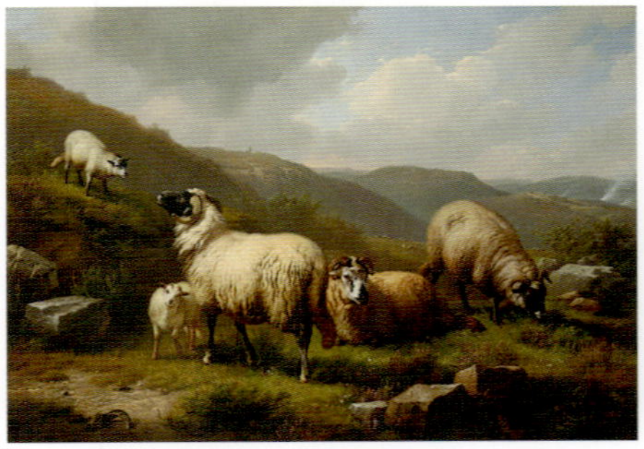

Verboeckhoven, Eugène Joseph 1798–1881
Landscape with Sheep c.1862
oil on panel 58.5 x 85
646

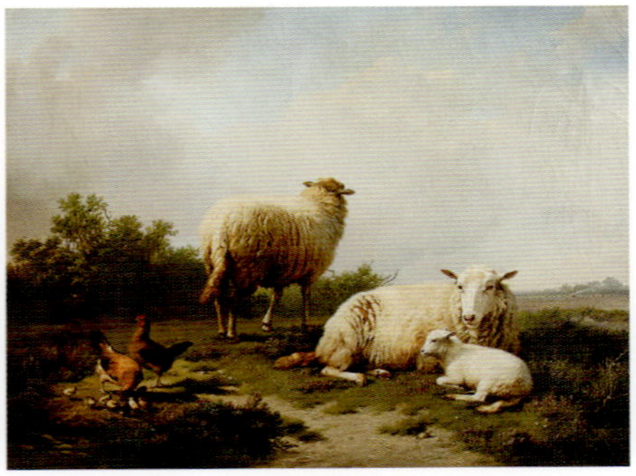

Verboeckhoven, Eugène Joseph 1798–1881
Landscape with Sheep 1867
oil on canvas 68 x 86
2011.71

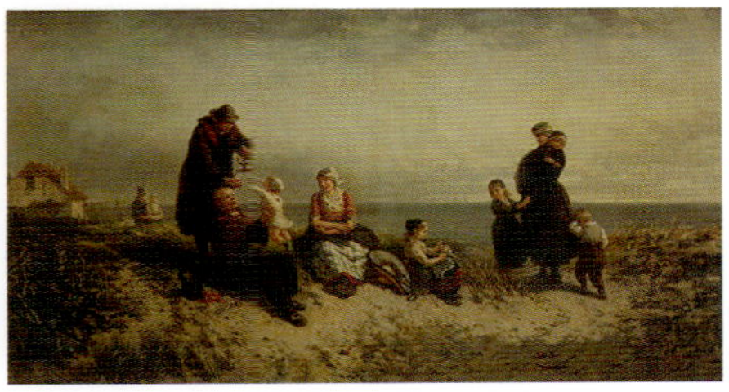

Verveer, Elchanon Leonardus 1826–1900
Sand Dunes at Scheveningen 1886
oil on canvas 53.5 x 112.5
215

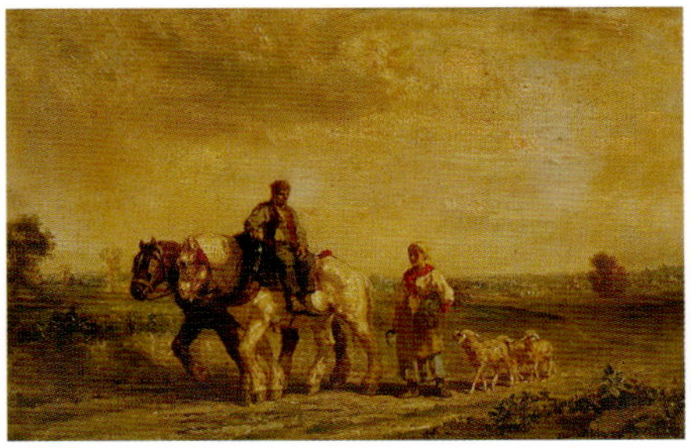

Veyrassat, Jules Jacques 1828–1893
Return from Labour c.1869
oil on canvas 21.5 x 34.4
216

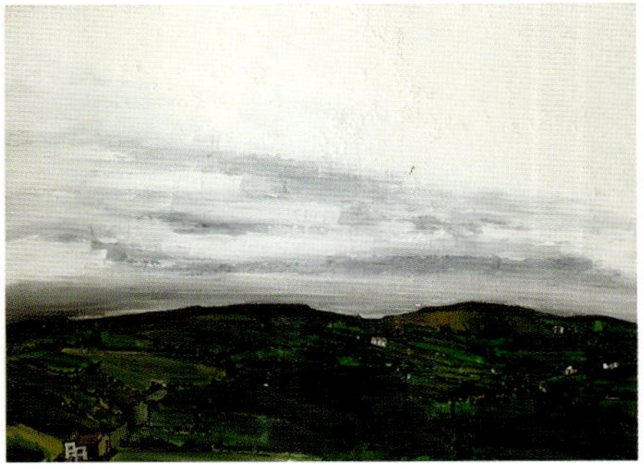

Virtue, John b.1947
View of Oswaldtwistle 1972
oil on board 122 x 184
2011.96

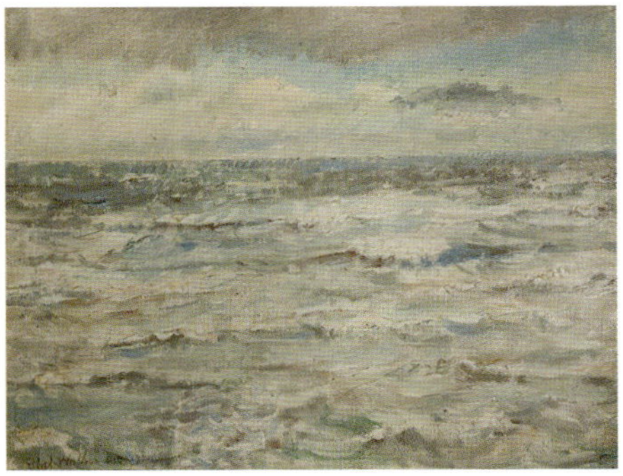

Walker, Ethel 1861–1951
Seascape 20th C
oil on canvas 48 x 64
471

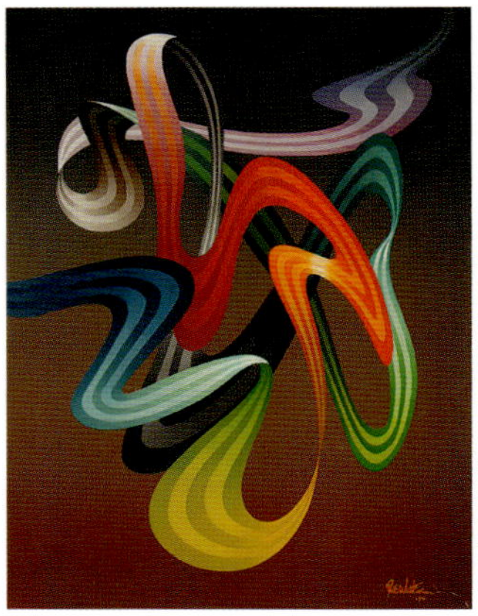

Watkinson, Bob 1914–1992
Untitled Abstract 1971
oil on canvas 91 x 70
893

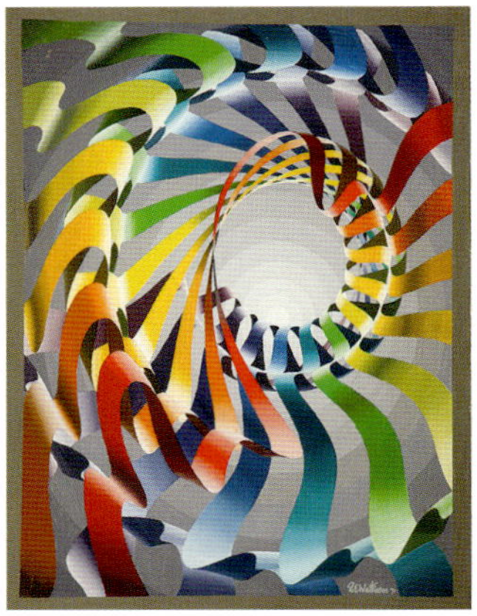

Watkinson, Bob 1914–1992
Untitled Abstract late 20th C
oil on canvas 76 x 63
892

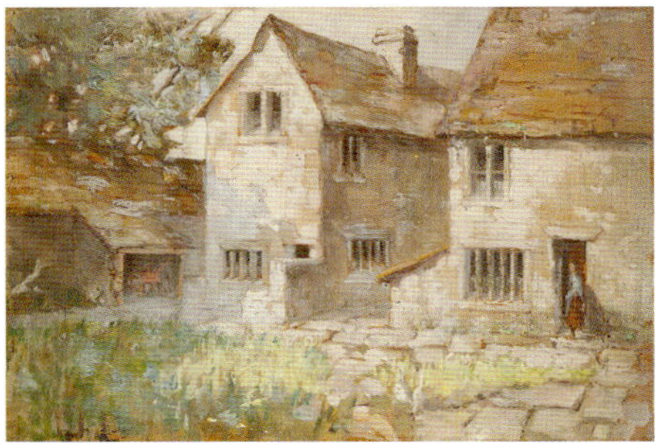

Weaver, G. R. active 20th C
Cottages
oil on wood 24 x 39
2011.105

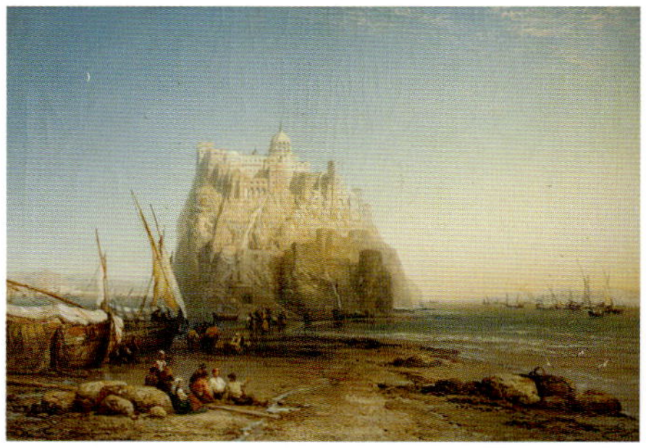

Webb, James 1825–1895
Ischia 1875
oil on canvas 64 x 105
231

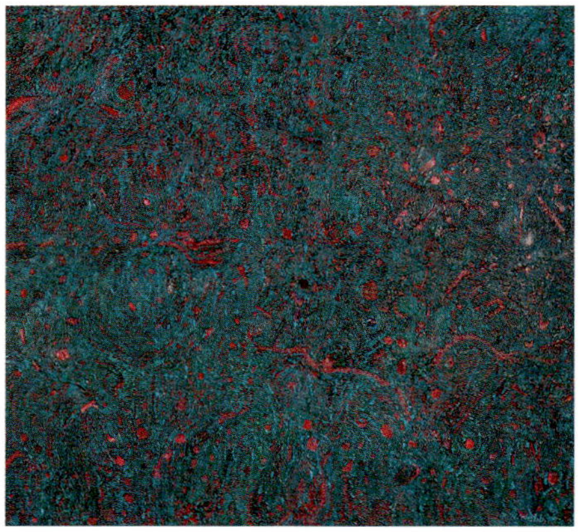

Webb, Ronald William b.1945
Alto Rhapsody c.2008
oil on canvas 90 x 90
2008.81

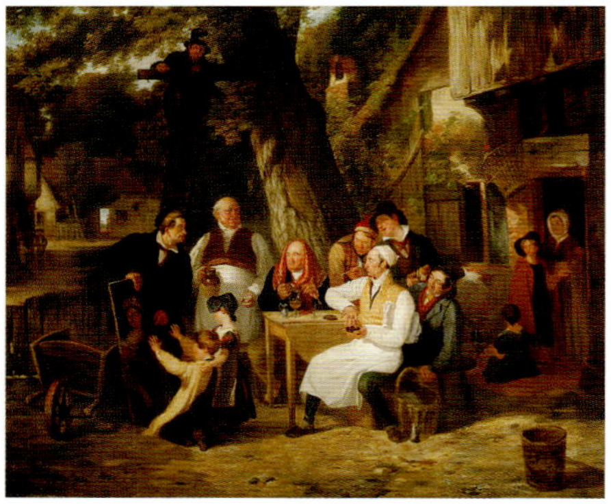

Webster, Thomas George 1800–1886
The New Sign
oil on canvas 70 x 90
436

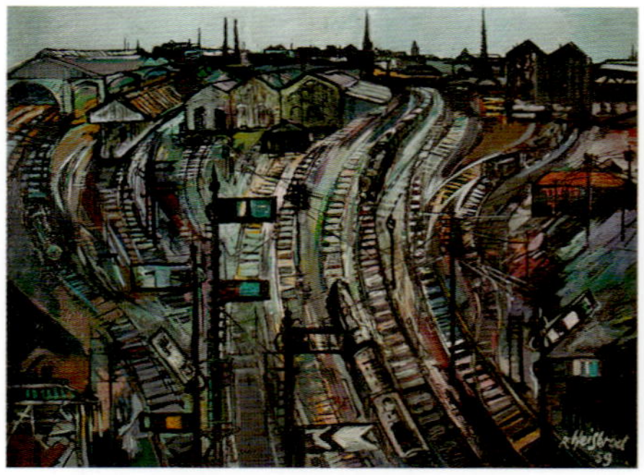

Weisbrod, Richard 1906–1991
Preston Station 1959
oil on board 97 x 158
655

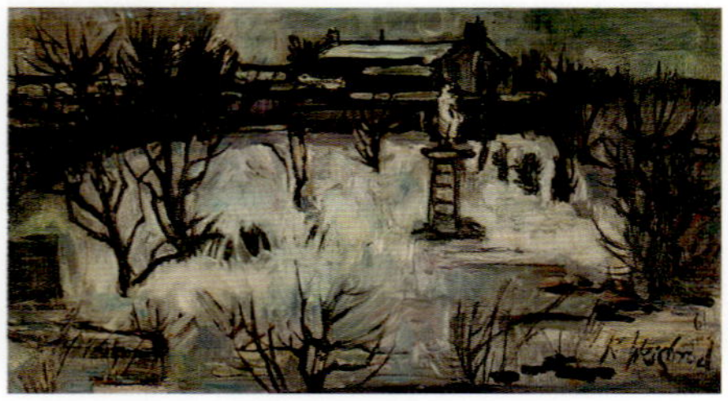

Weisbrod, Richard 1906–1991
Lancashire Snow Scene 1961
oil on board 44 x 84
2011.84

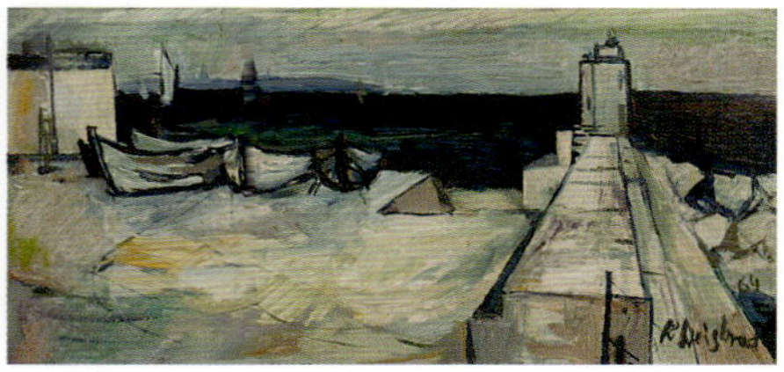

Weisbrod, Richard 1906–1991
At Carro
oil on board 32 x 72
656

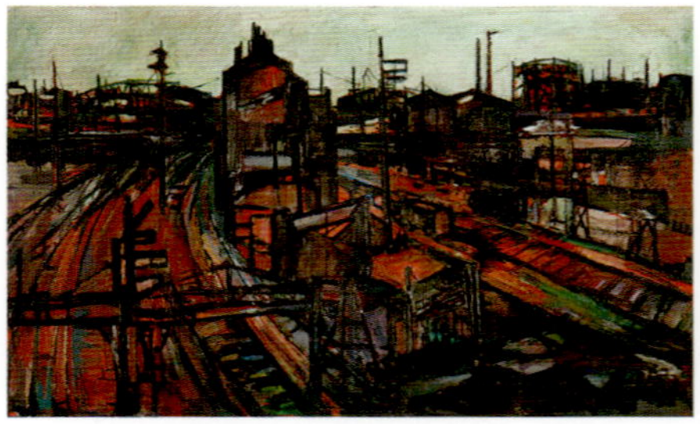

Weisbrod, Richard 1906–1991
Railway Yard
oil on board 60 x 122
657

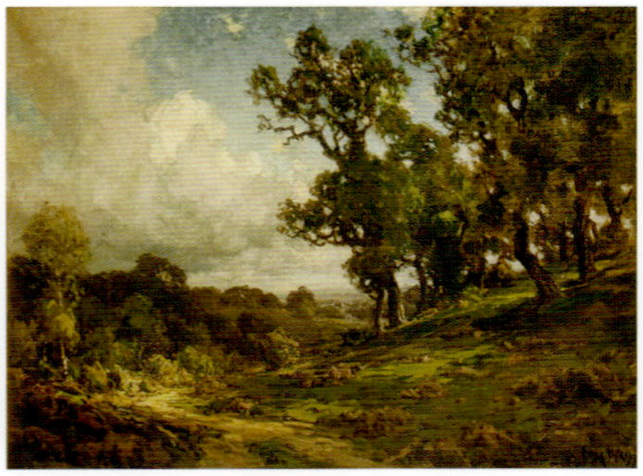

Weiss, José 1859–1919
Arundel Park
oil on canvas 79 x 120
210

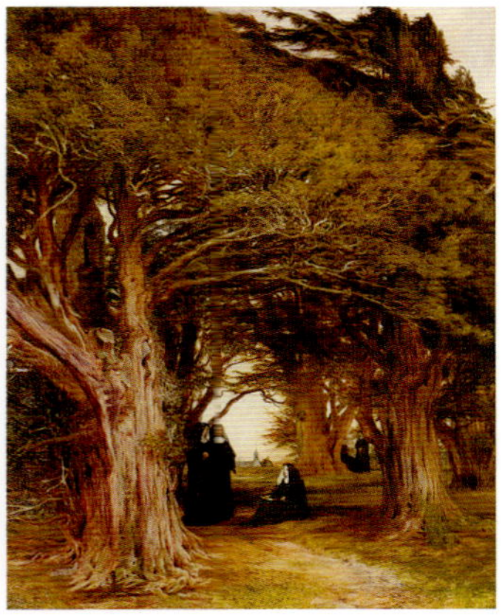

Whaite, Henry Clarence 1828–1912
The Convent Garden 1864
oil on canvas 126 x 100
96

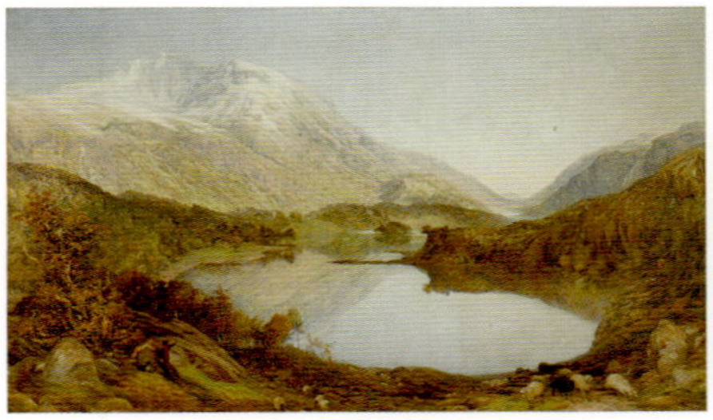

Whaite, Henry Clarence 1828–1912
Thirlmere 1873
oil on canvas 100.3 x 181.6 (E)
111

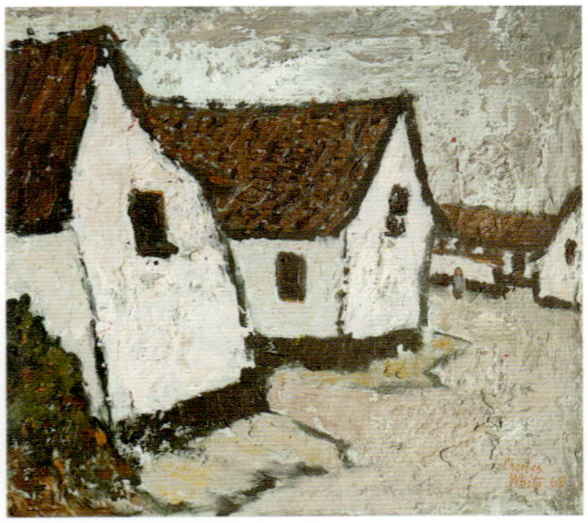

White, Charles F. 1905–1975
French Village 1968
oil on board 40 x 42
819

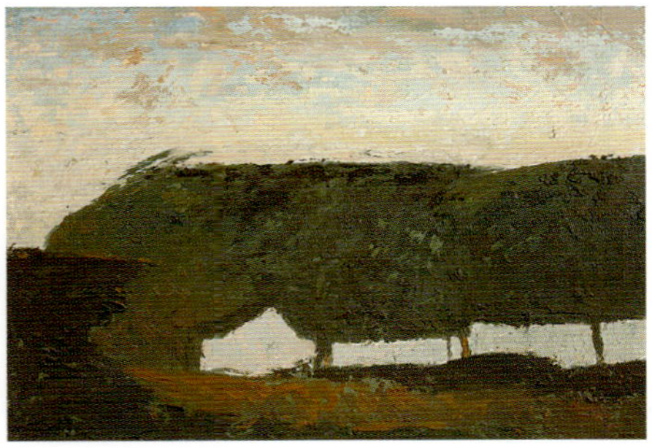

White, Charles F. 1905–1975
Farm in the Wood 1969
oil on board 38 x 55
818

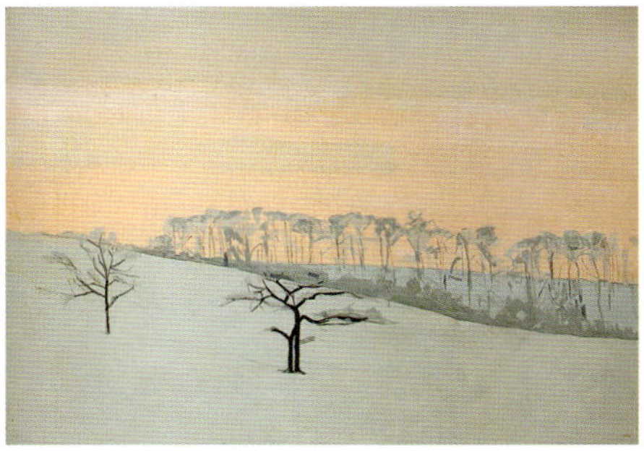

Wild, David b.1931
Winter Landscape, Cliviger c.1963
oil on canvas 120 x 182
710

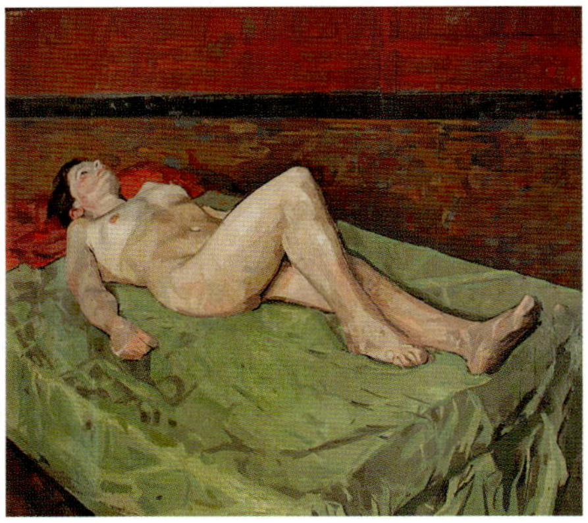

Wild, David b.1931
Nude 1964
oil on board 118 x 149
709

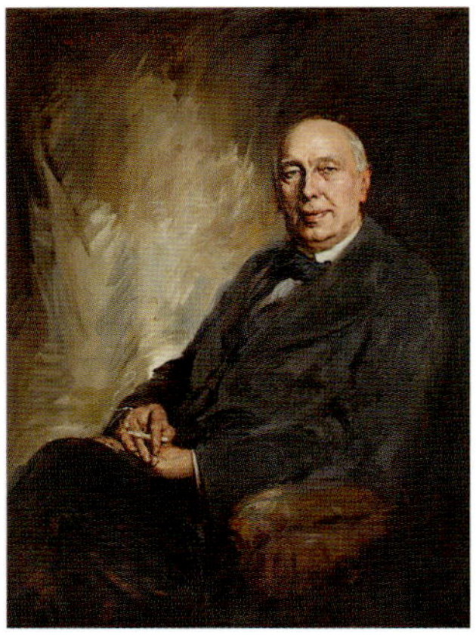

Wilkinson, Herbert active 1931–1979
Alderman Francis John Greeves (d.1945) 1935
oil on canvas 110 x 84
312

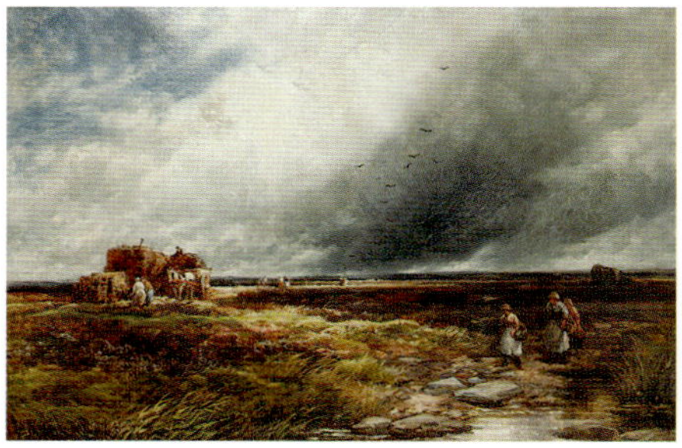

Wimperis, Edmund Morison 1835–1900
A Yorkshire Moor 1898
oil on canvas 80 x 120
100

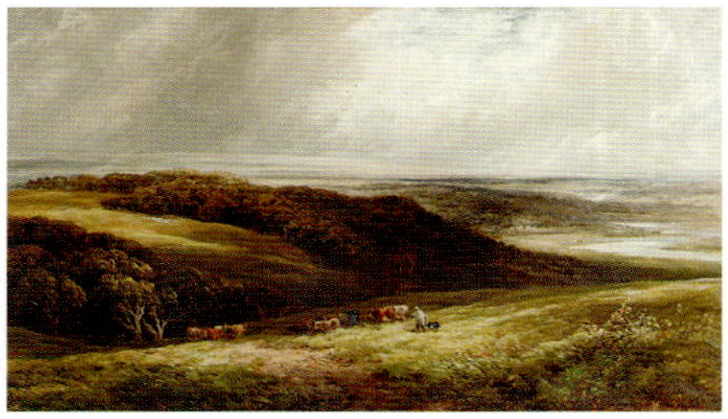

Wimperis, Edmund Morison 1835–1900
In Wensleydale 1898
oil on canvas 80 x 120 (E)
430

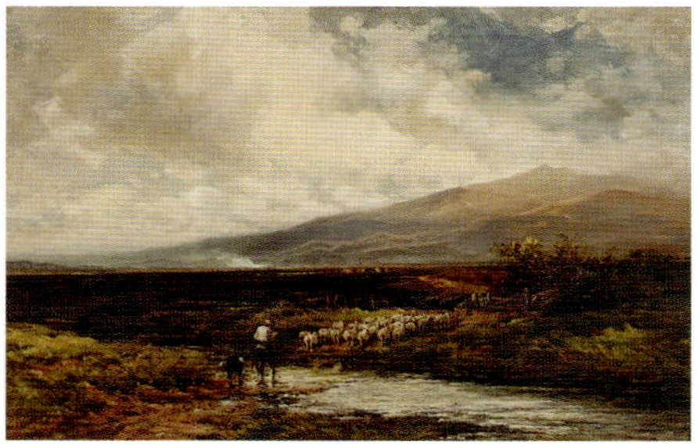

Wimperis, Edmund Morison 1835–1900
On a Yorkshire Moor c.1899
oil on canvas 58 x 88
639

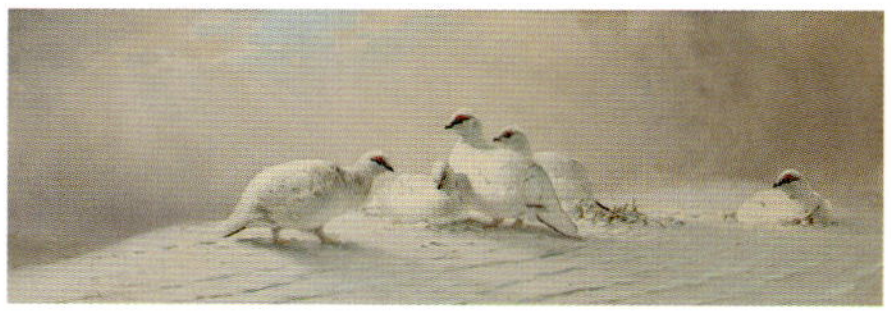

Wolf, Joseph 1820–1899
Ptarmigan 1861
oil on canvas 53 x 151
209

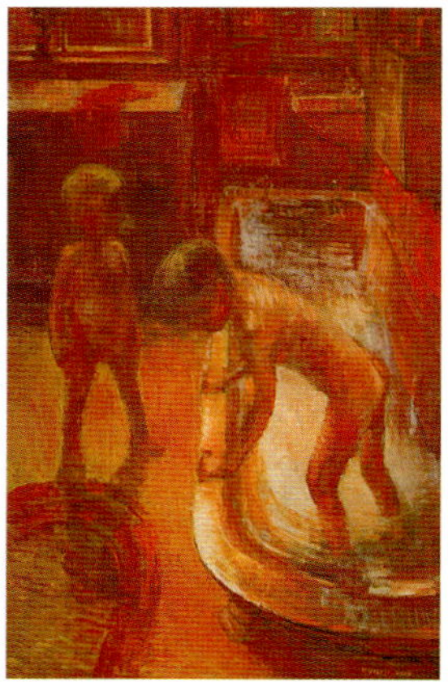

Wood, Elizabeth b.1930
The Bath 1964
oil on board 185 x 122
674

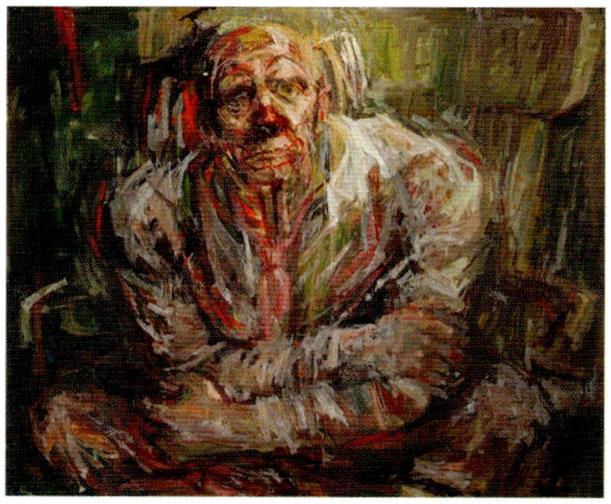

Wood, Elizabeth b.1930
Clown
oil on canvas 105 x 136
673

Facing page: Moore, Albert Joseph, 1841–1893, *The Loves of the Winds and the Seasons,* 1893, Blackburn Museum and Art Gallery (p. 45)

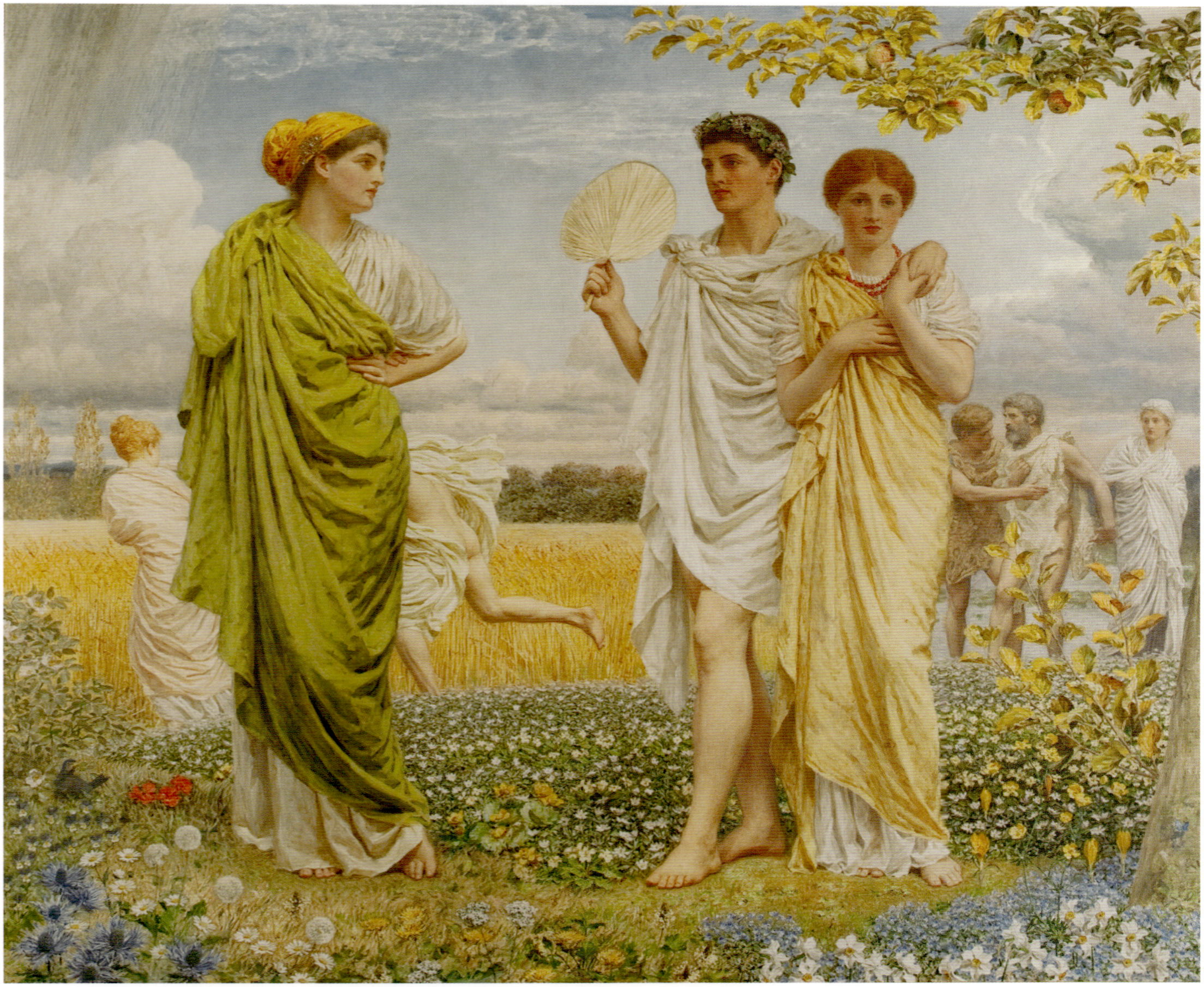

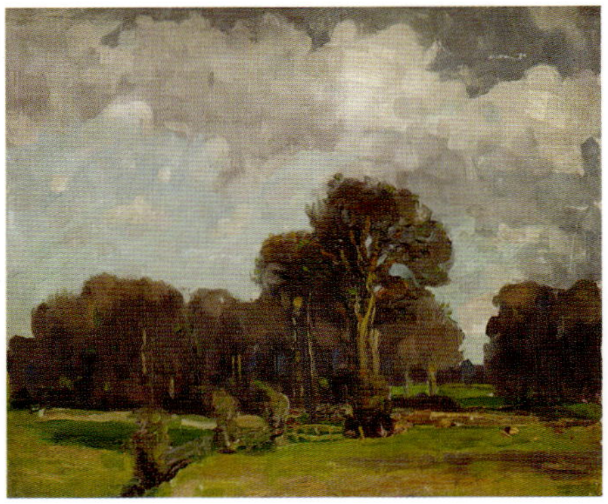

Yates, John 1885–1969
Arley Brook
oil on board 32.5 x 40.5
2011.106

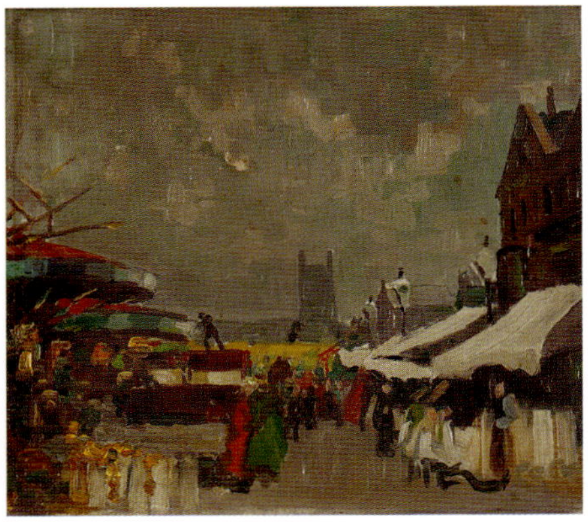

Yates, John 1885–1969
Blackburn Fair
oil on board 35.5 x 40
791

East Lancashire Hospitals NHS Trust

East Lancashire Hospitals NHS Trust was formed on 1st April 2003, following the merger of Blackburn, Hyndburn and Ribble Valley Health Care NHS Trust and Burnley Health Care NHS Trust.

The Trust owns a small collection of paintings which hang on the walls of Blackburn, Burnley and Pendle hospitals. Many of them, such as the three triptychs *Flying Geese, Swans and Seagulls* by D. A. Wilkinson, on the stairwells in Blackburn, are brightly coloured and fun and make the hospital environment less forbidding. There are also more complex paintings such as *The Phoenix*, which hangs outside the Trust headquarters in Blackburn, *Montage with Faces* in the urology corridor at the Royal Blackburn Hospital, and *Tool Cupboard* by Margaret Jackson, on the wall of one of the main corridors at the Royal Blackburn Hospital and commissioned by Blackburn, Hyndburn and Ribble Valley Health Care NHS Trust.

There is just one painting in Burnley General Hospital, a portrait by Tom Comley Vivian of *Caleb Thornber*. Thornber was a cotton-spinning manufacturer, Mayor of Burnley and a local benefactor. As well as being a supporter of the hospital in its early days he had bequeathed money for the erection of a War Memorial in Towneley Park and he gave a substantial bequest to Towneley Hall Art Gallery and Museums which enabled it to buy *The Picture Gallery* by Lawrence Alma-Tadema in 1925.

Adrienne Wallman, Lancashire Coordinator

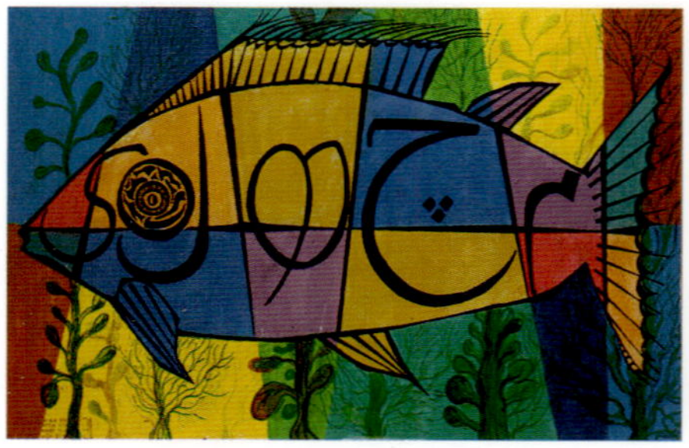

Akhtar, Tahira, Khan, Samia
Fish with Abstract Symbols 1991
oil on canvas 60 x 100, 60 x 100
ELHT_PEN_4

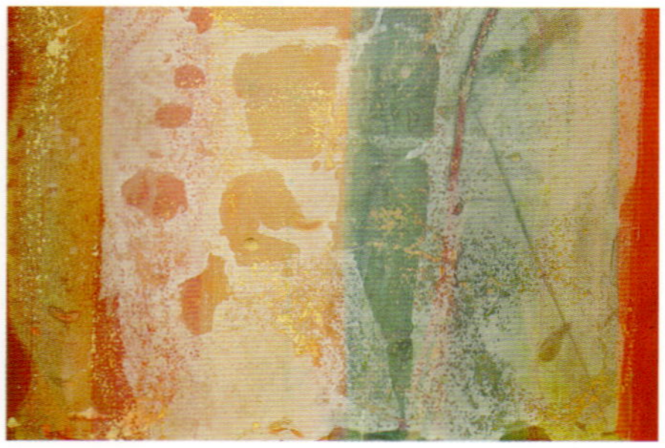

Bruch, Matthew
It's All about Angles
oil & mixed media on paper (?) 78 x 110.5
ELHT_BLA_10

Collins, Nicola
Travelling Inwards
oil & mixed media on canvas 120 x 89
ELHT_BLA_6

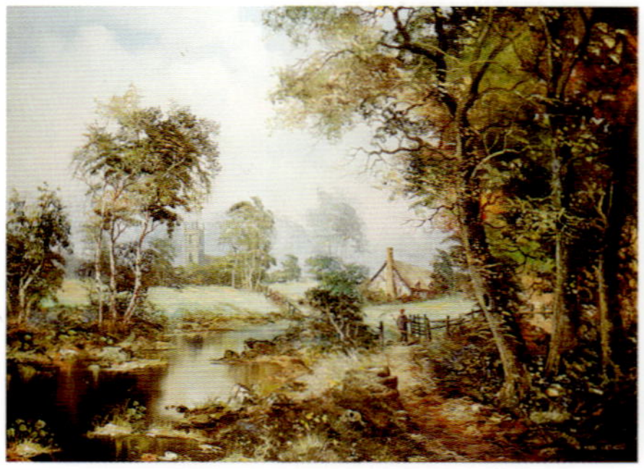

Corcoran, John b.1940
Landscape with a Church
oil on canvas 49 x 74.5
ELHT_PEN_9

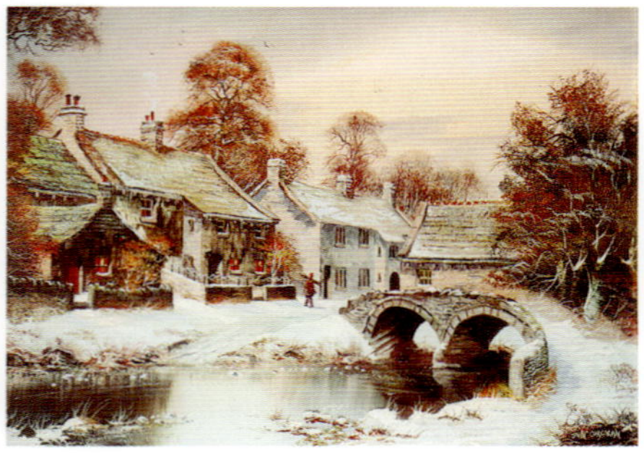

Corcoran, John b.1940
Snowy Scene with a River and a Bridge
oil on canvas 49 x 74
ELHT_PEN_2

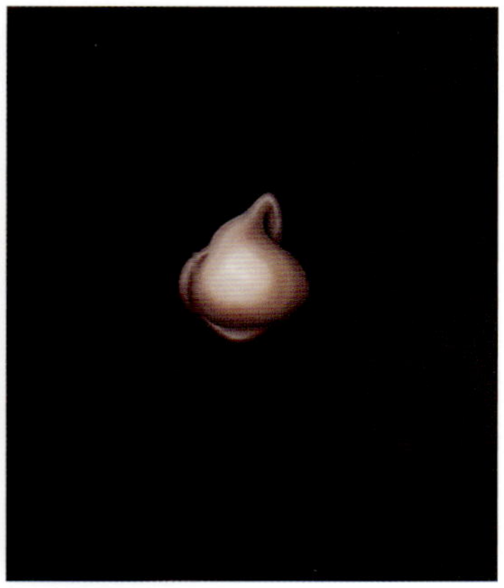

Gallagher, Paula
Untitled 1
acrylic on canvas 91.5 x 91
ELHT_BLA_28

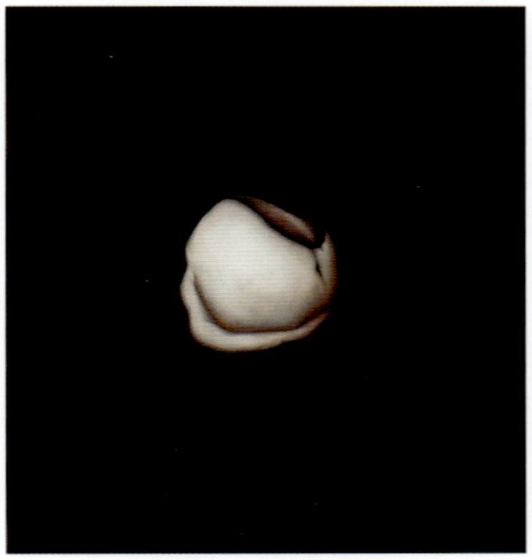

Gallagher, Paula
Untitled 2
acrylic on canvas 91.5 x 91
ELHT_BLA_27

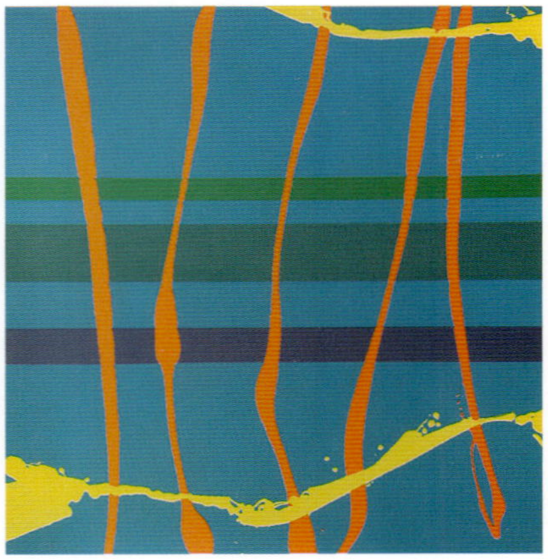

Heath, Eleanor
Painting for the Burger Man (panel 1 of 3)
oil on canvas 119 x 118.5
ELHT_BLA_7

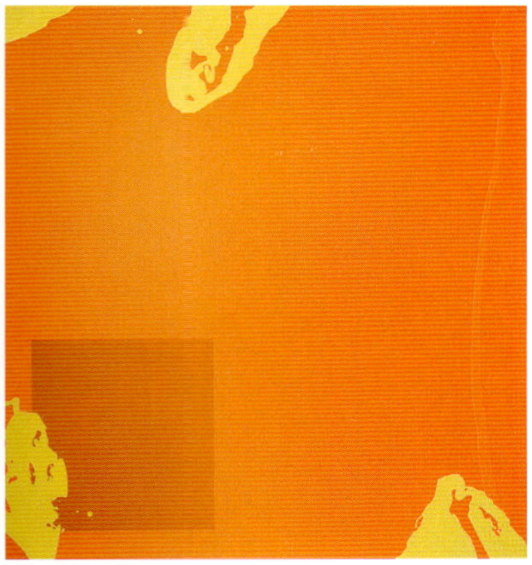

Heath, Eleanor
Painting for the Burger Man (panel 2 of 3)
oil on canvas 119 x 118.5
ELHT_BLA_8

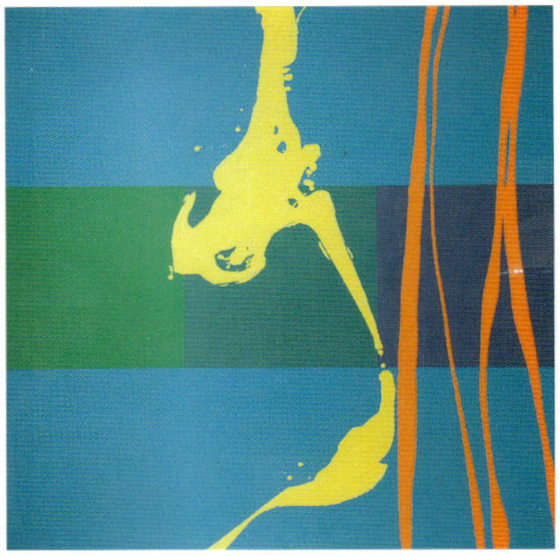

Heath, Eleanor
Painting for the Burger Man (panel 3 of 3)
oil on canvas 119 x 118.3
ELHT_BLA_9

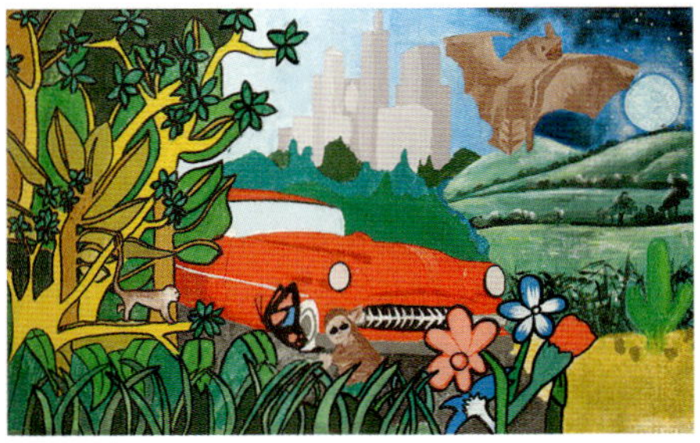

Hughes, Sarah
Red Car in a Jungle with Skyscrapers 1991
oil on canvas 59.5 x 100
ELHT-PEN_5

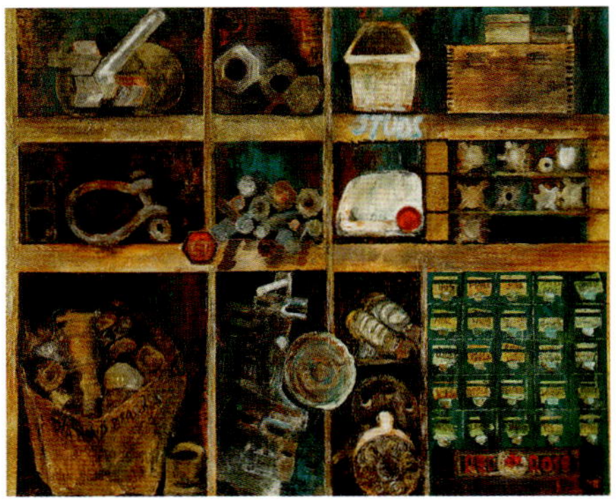

Jackson, Margaret
Tool Cupboard
oil on board 95 x 124.5
ELHT_BLA_14

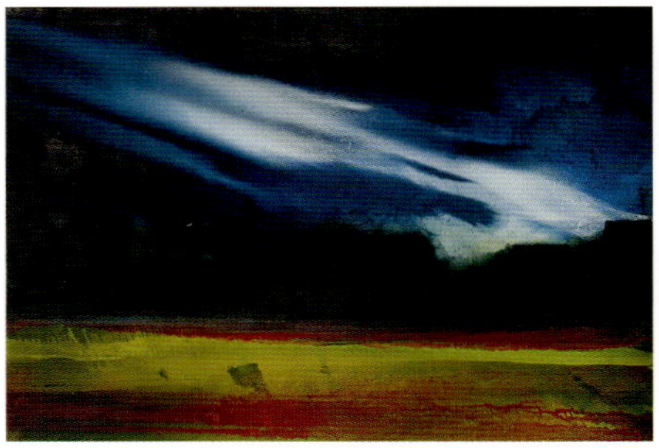

Maggs, James
Luna Ascendant
oil on paper (?) 133 x 225.5
ELHT_BLA_11

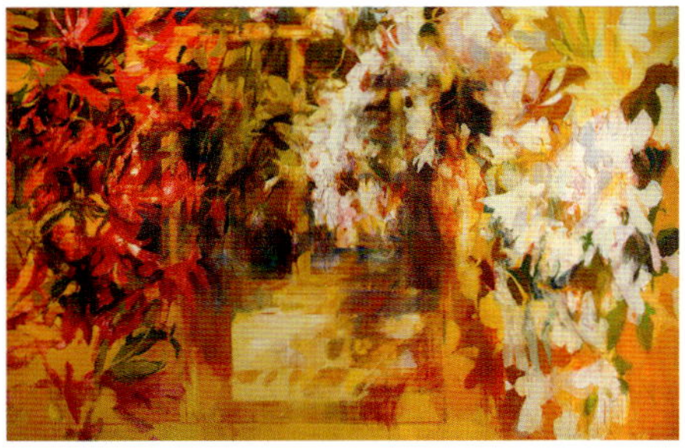

Martyn, Channing (possibly)
Floral Window 1977
oil on canvas 119 x 211
ELHT_BLA_16

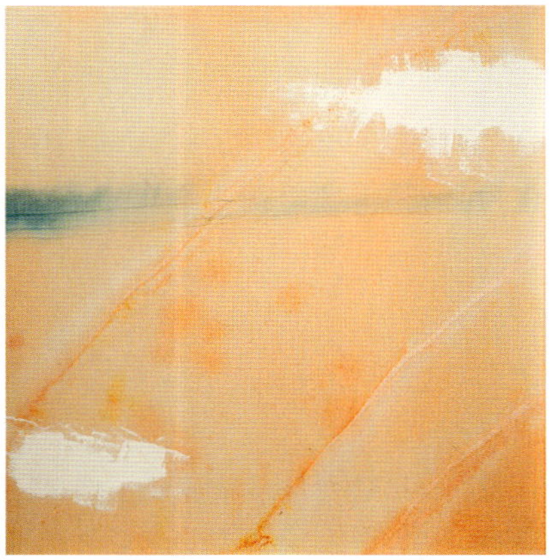

Millea, Joanne
Amber Lines
acrylic on canvas 60 x 59.5
ELHT_BLA_4

Millea, Joanne
Aquamarine Lines
acrylic on canvas 60 x 59.5
ELHT_BLA_1

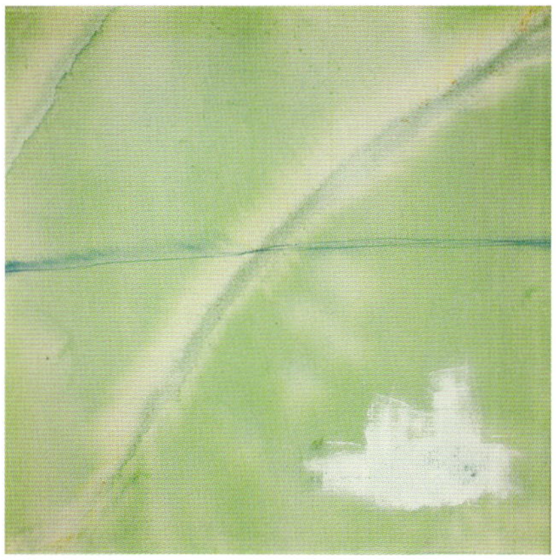

Millea, Joanne
Jade Lines
acrylic on canvas 60 x 60
ELHT_BLA_5

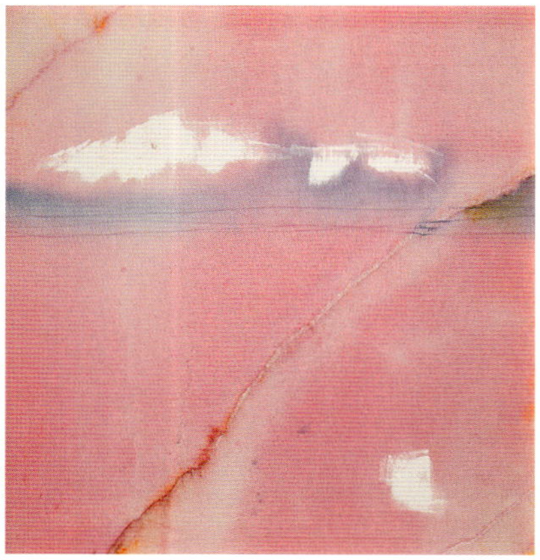

Millea, Joanne
Magenta Lines
acrylic on canvas 59.5 x 60
ELHT_BLA_3

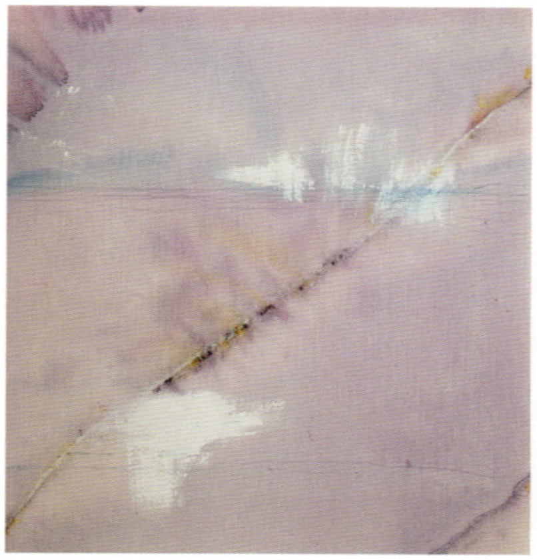

Millea, Joanne
Rose Lines
acrylic on canvas 58 x 58
ELHT_BLA_2

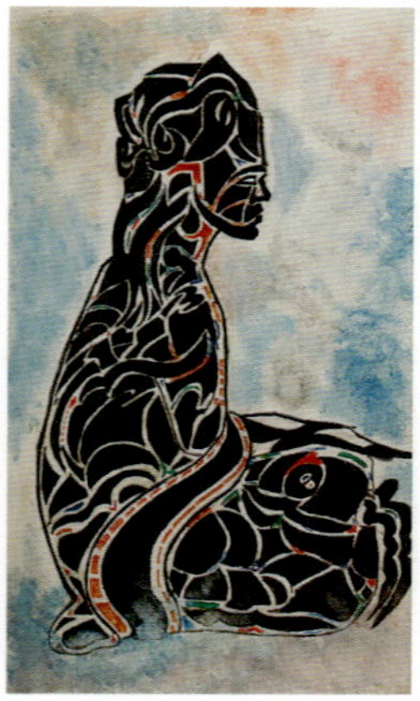

unknown artist
Abstract Black Figure
oil on canvas 98 x 60
ELHT_PEN_11

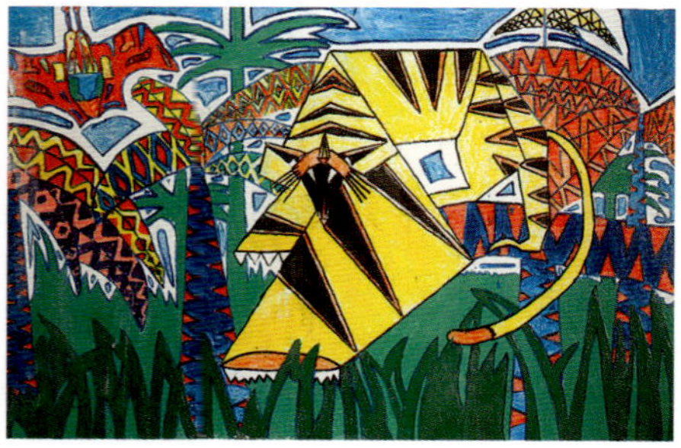

unknown artist
Abstract Tiger
oil on canvas 60 x 100
ELHT_PEN_1

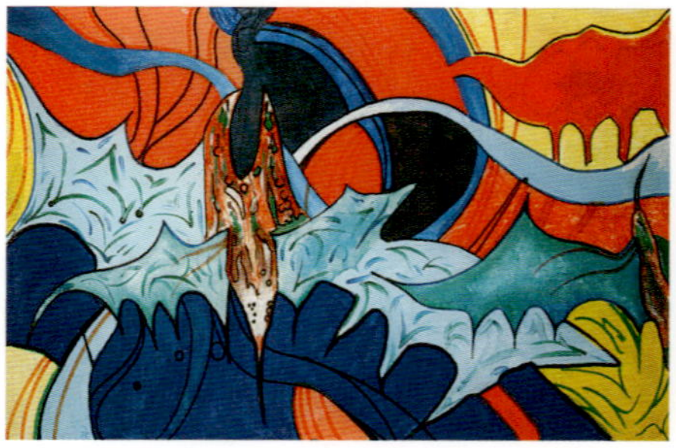

unknown artist
Bat
oil on canvas 60.5 x 100
ELHT_PEN_10

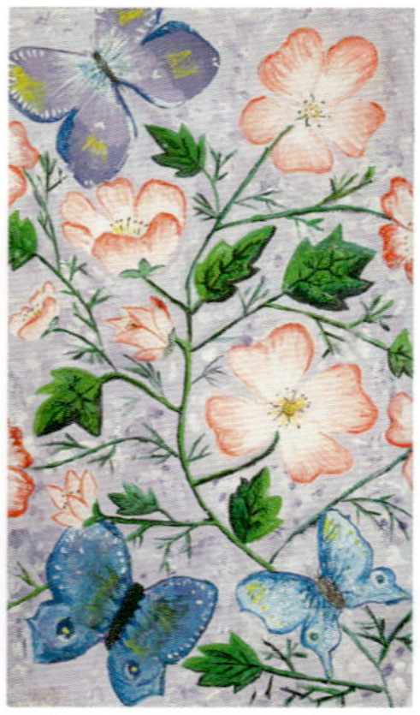

unknown artist
Flowers and Butterflies
oil on canvas 100.5 x 60
ELHT_PEN_6

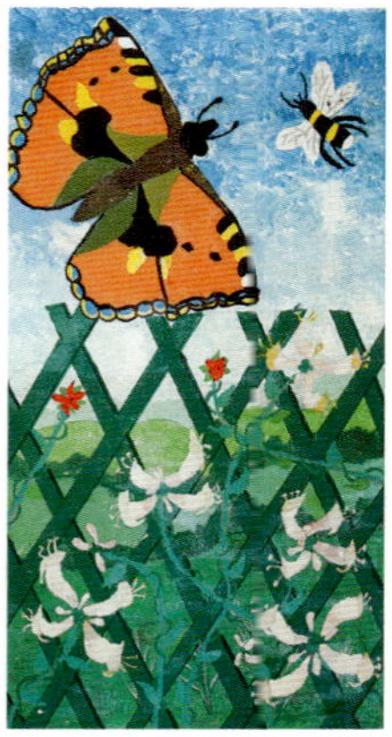

unknown artist
Green Fence with a Butterfly and a Wasp
oil on canvas 100 x 59.5
ELHT_PEN_8

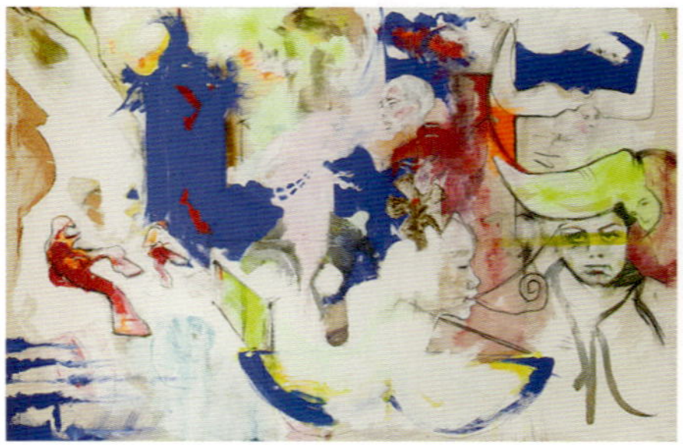

unknown artist
Montage with Faces
oil on canvas 121 x 182.5
ELHT_BLA_17

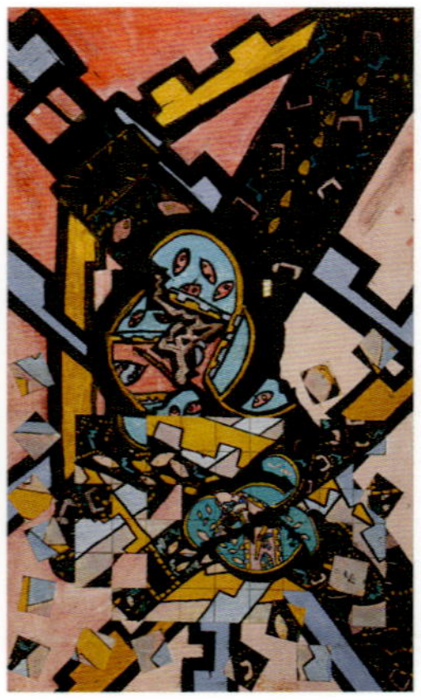

unknown artist
Pink and Blue Abstract
oil on canvas 98 x 60
ELHT_PEN_12

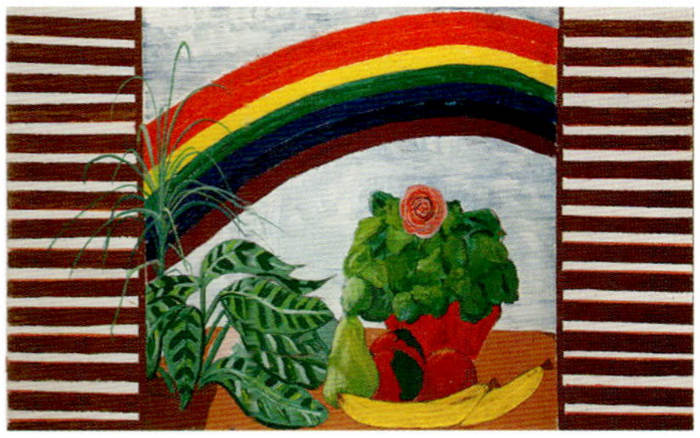

unknown artist
Rainbow with a Plant
oil on canvas 60 x 100
ELHT_PEN_3

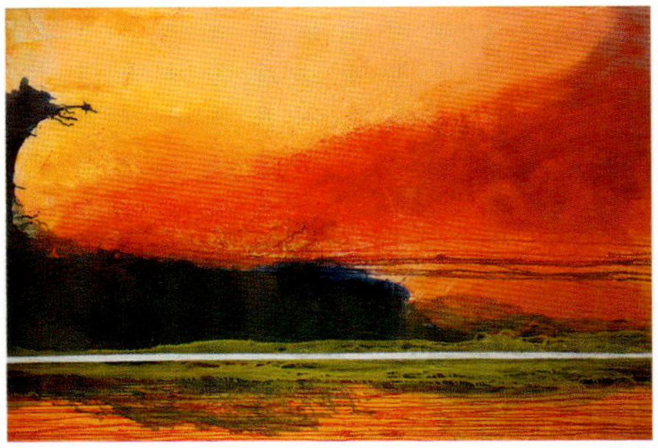

unknown artist
Red Sunset
oil on paper 126.5 x 222
ELHT_BLA_12

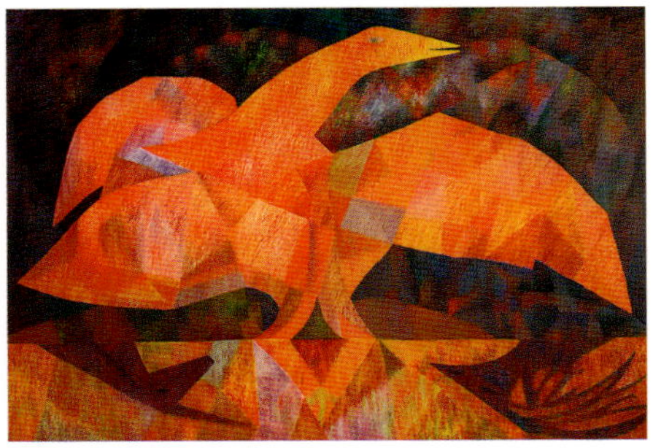

unknown artist
The Phoenix
acrylic (?) on canvas 181 x 237.5
ELHT_BLA_15

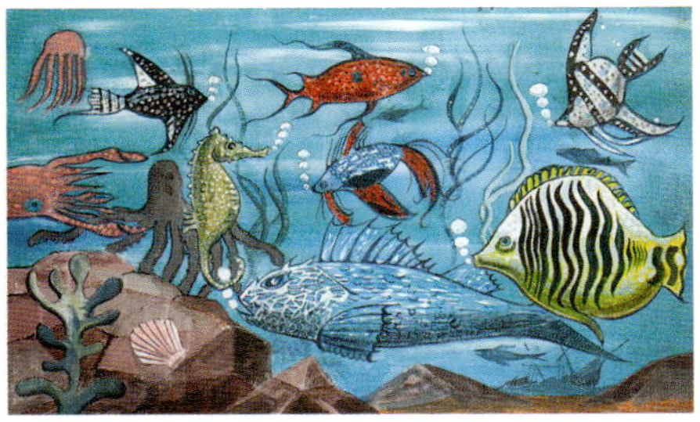

unknown artist
Underwater Scene with Octopus, Fish and Sea Horses
oil on canvas 60 x 97.5
ELHT_PEN_7

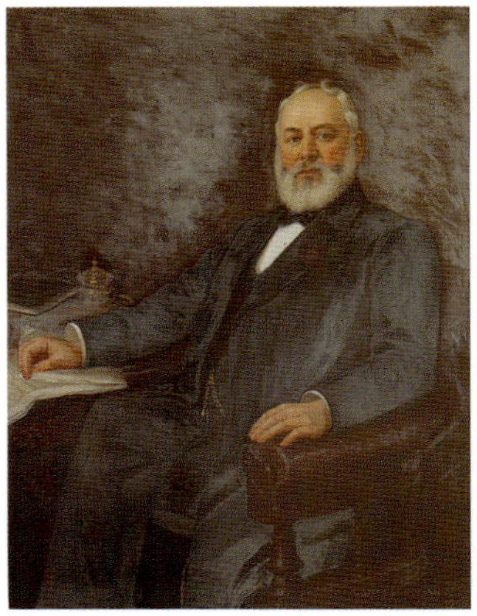

Vivian, Tom Comley 1847–1908
Caleb Thornber 1905
oil on canvas 90 x 70 (E)
ELHT_BURN_1

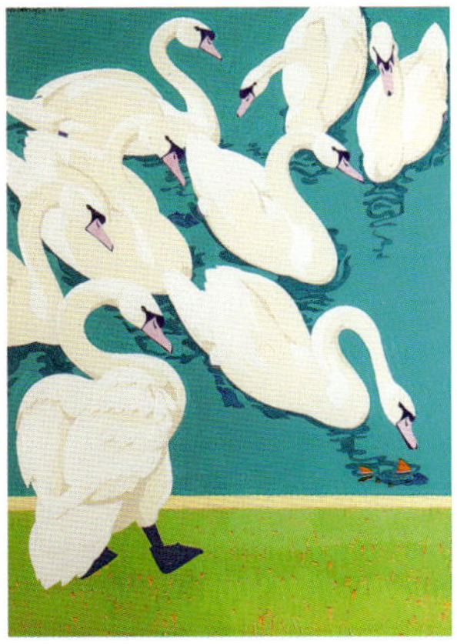

Wilkinson, D. A.
Swans (panel 1 of 3) 1994
acrylic on canvas 118 x 89
ELHT_BLA_18

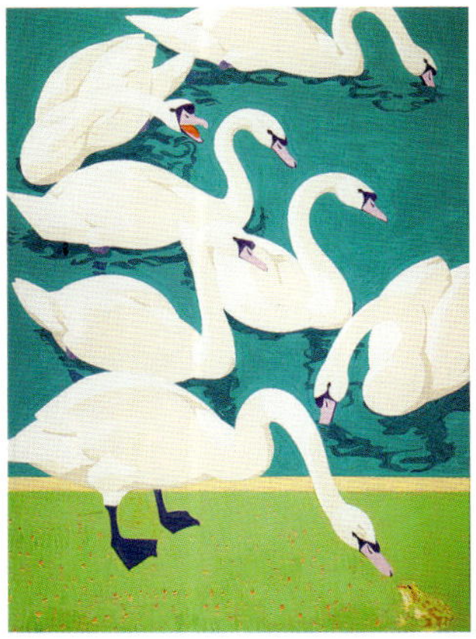

Wilkinson, D. A.
Swans (panel 2 of 3) 1994
acrylic on canvas 118 x 89
ELHT_BLA_19

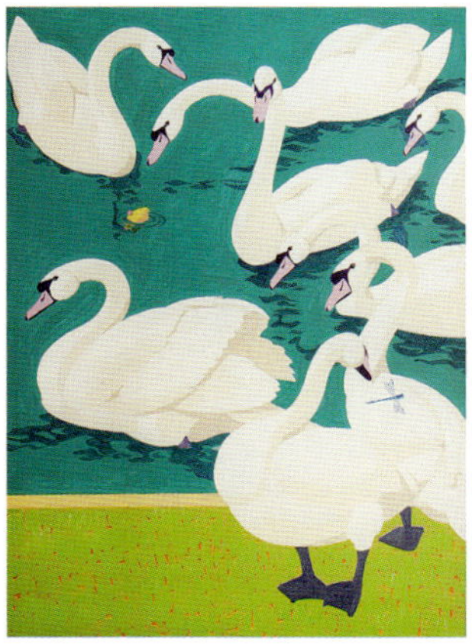

Wilkinson, D. A.
Swans (panel 3 of 3) 1994
acrylic on canvas 118 x 89
ELHT_BLA_20

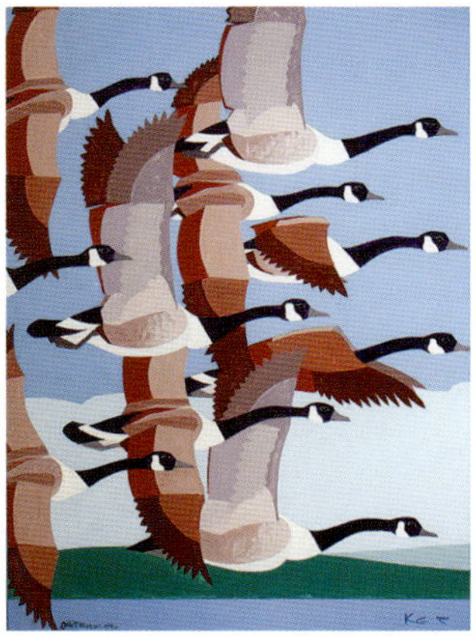

Wilkinson, D. A.
Flying Geese (panel 1 of 3)
acrylic on canvas 118 x 89
ELHT_BLA_21

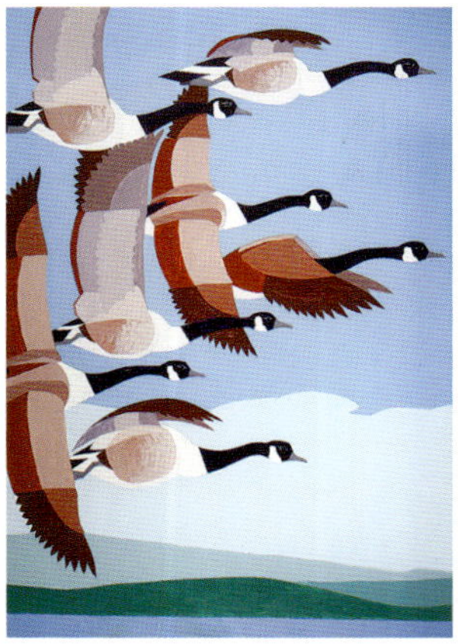

Wilkinson, D. A.
Flying Geese (panel 2 of 3)
acrylic on canvas 118 x 89
ELHT_BLA_22

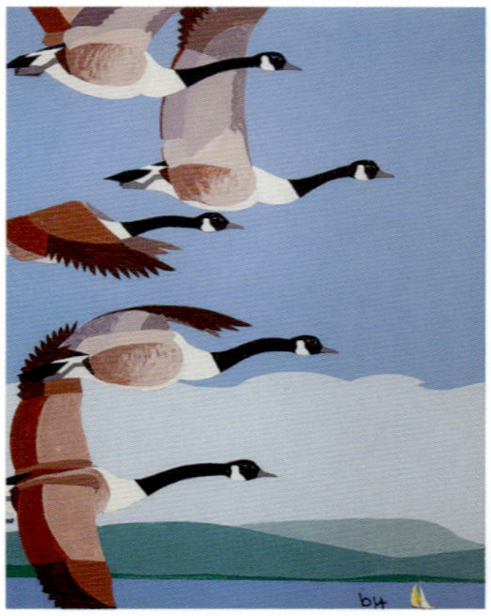

Wilkinson, D. A.
Flying Geese (panel 3 of 3)
acrylic on canvas 118 x 89
ELHT_BLA_23

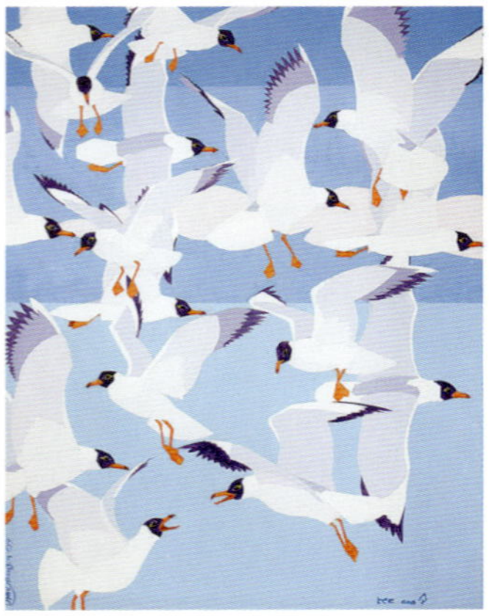

Wilkinson, D. A.
Seagulls (panel 1 of 3)
acrylic on canvas 118 x 89
ELHT_BLA_24

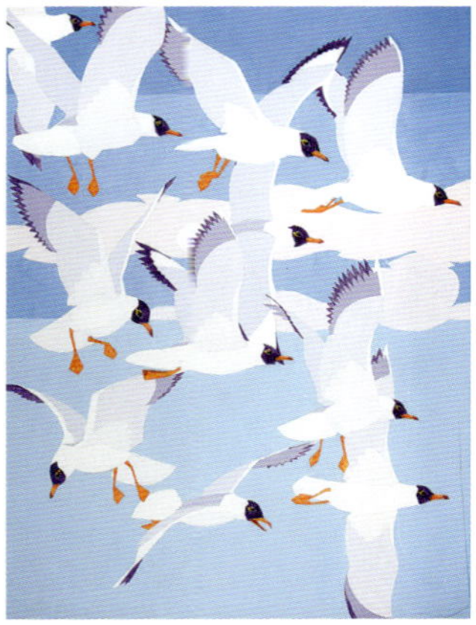

Wilkinson, D. A.
Seagulls (panel 2 of 3)
acrylic on canvas 118 x 89
ELHT_BLA_25

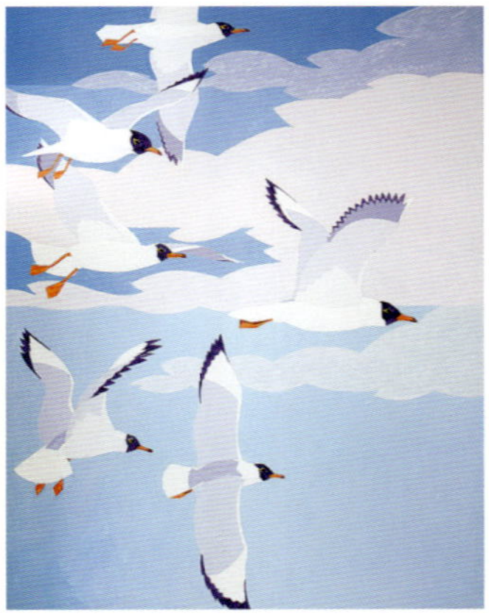

Wilkinson, D. A.
Seagulls (panel 3 of 3)
acrylic on canvas 118 x 89
ELHT_BLA_26

Blackpool Town Hall

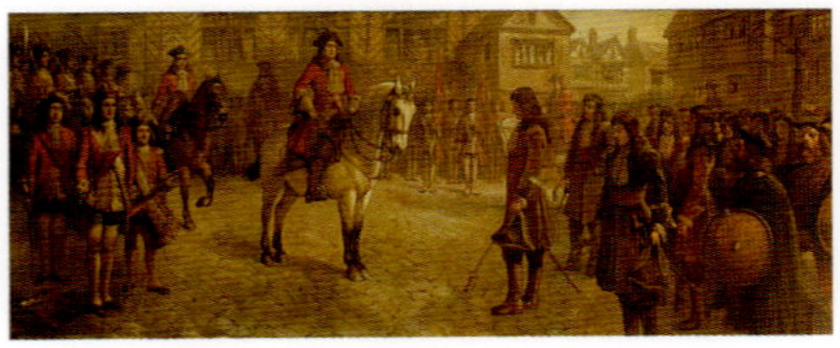

Brown, J. R.
Surrender of the Rebel Stuart Forces at Preston in 1715 1901
oil on canvas 130 x 300 (E)
2

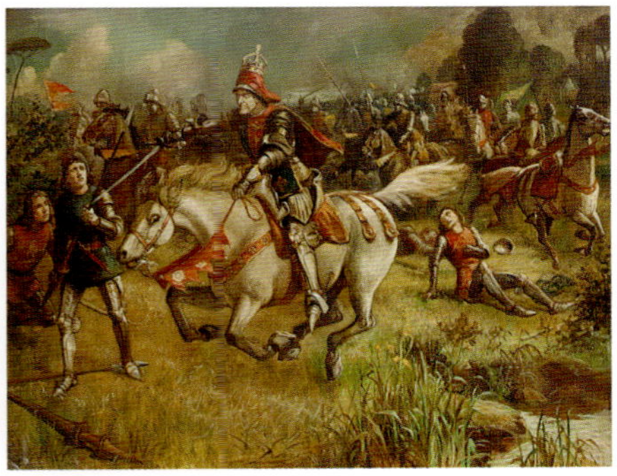

Brown, J. R.
Final Horse Charge of Richard III at Bosworth Field c.1901
oil on canvas 130 x 150 (E)
3

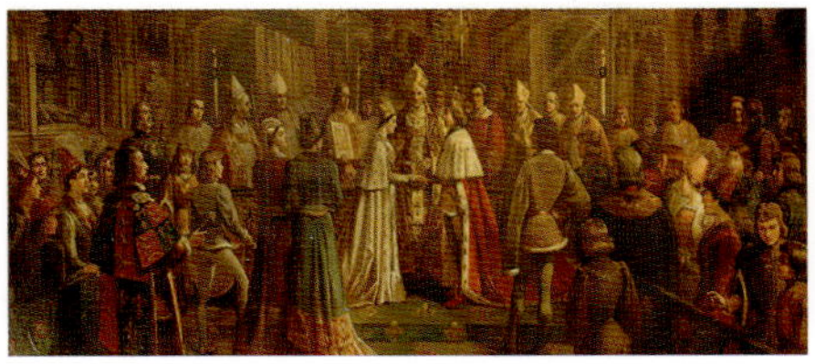

Brown, J. R.
Joining of the Houses of Lancaster and York in 1436 c.1901
oil on canvas 150 x 300 (E)
1

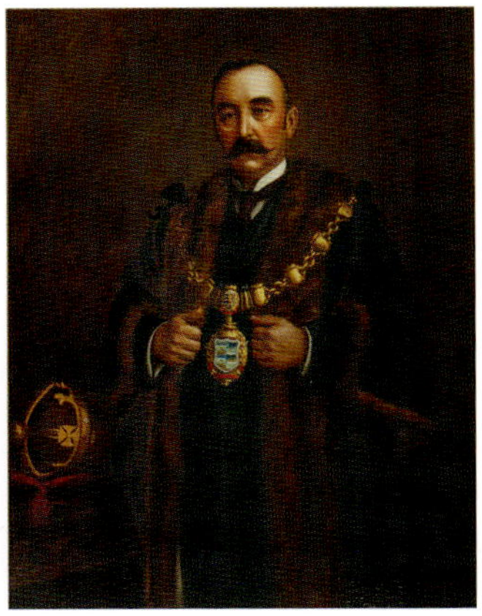

Marton, W.
Alderman R. B. Mather, JP
oil on canvas 124 x 100
7

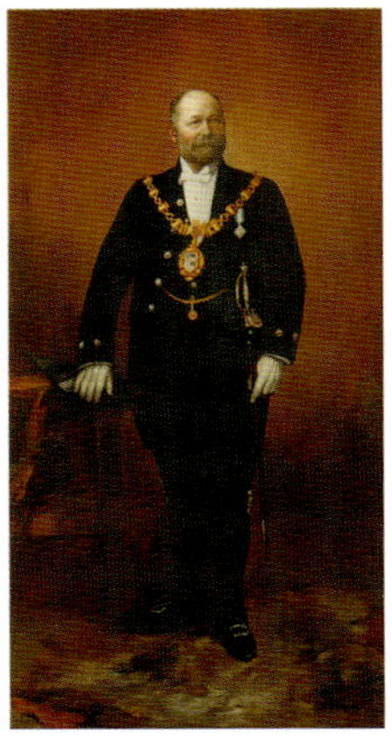

Parrinson, K.
Alderman James Ward 1914
oil on canvas 210 x 116
6

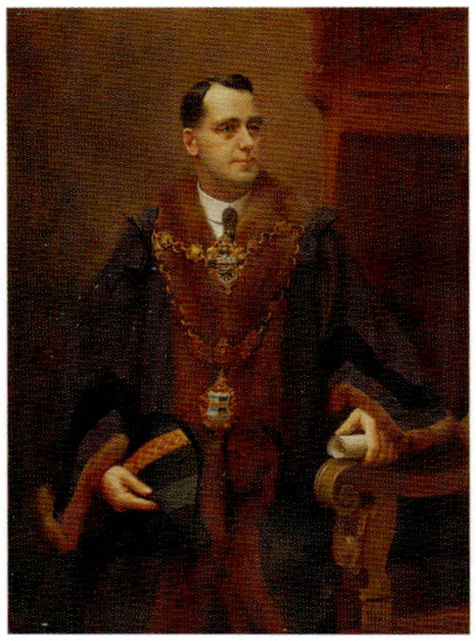

Townsend, Ernest 1885–1944
Alderman A. Lindsay Parkinson 1918
oil on canvas 123.5 x 98
10

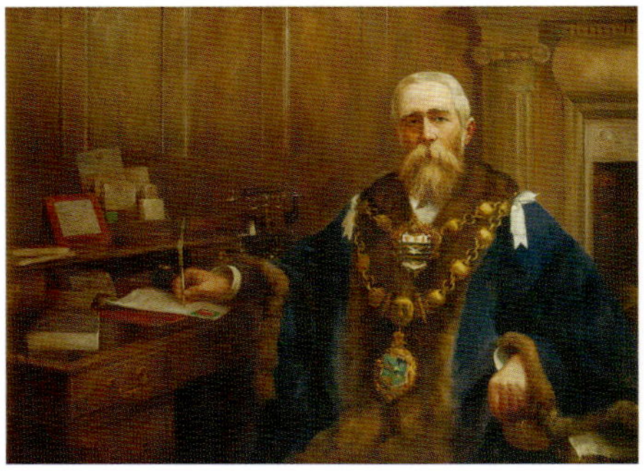

unknown artist
Alderman James Heyes 1904
oil on canvas 118 x 148
5

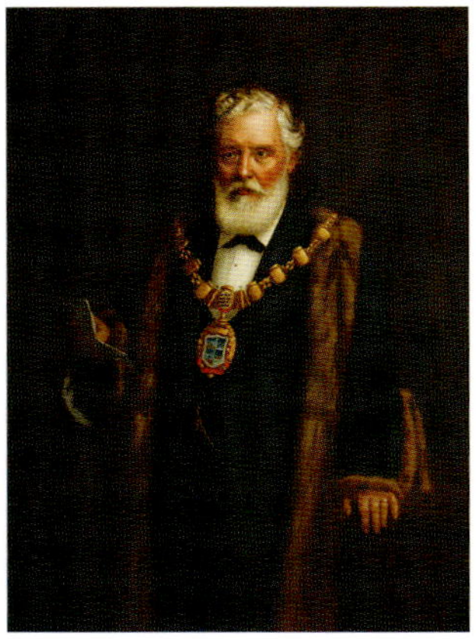

unknown artist
Alderman James Fish, JP
oil on canvas 123 x 99
4

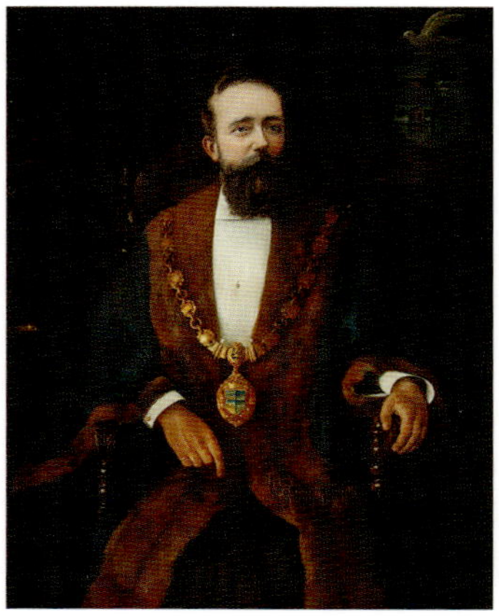

unknown artist
Alderman John Bickerstaffe
oil on canvas 123.5 x 98
9

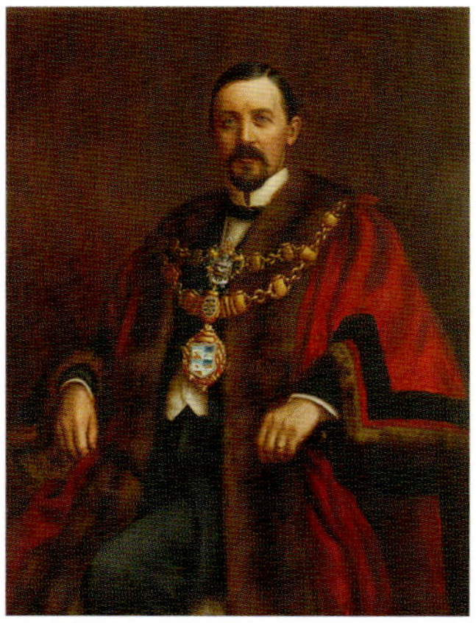

unknown artist
Alderman Joseph Heap
oil on canvas 125 x 98
8

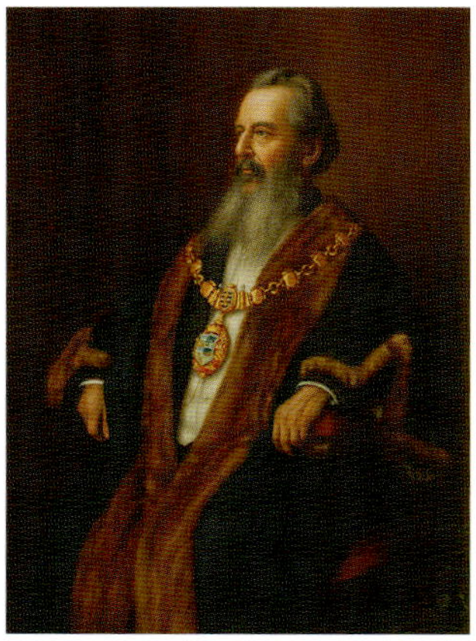

unknown artist
Alderman W. H. Cocker
oil on canvas 124 x 98
11

Grundy Art Gallery

Grundy Art Gallery first opened to the public in 1911. The building was commissioned by Blackpool Council in 1908 following a bequest of over 20 paintings and a financial gift from brothers John and Sir Cuthbert Grundy, both of whom were artists. Cuthbert was described at the time as 'a leader of the artistic, literary and scientific life of the town.' Sir Cuthbert Grundy in particular was influential in other arts organisations across the UK: he was President for 21 years of the Royal Cambrian Academy, Honorary Vice President of the Royal British Colonial Society of Artists, an exhibitor at the Manchester Academy, the South Wales Art Society, and the Imperial Arts League, and an invited exhibitor with the Lake Artists' Society. He was also President for 17 years of the Bury Society of Fine Arts which his brother John established.

The Grundy Art Gallery's Collection, which is currently displayed as part of the temporary exhibitions programme and is not on permanent display, includes Victorian oils and watercolours, modern British paintings, oriental ivories, ceramics, photographs and souvenirs of Blackpool, and contemporary prints, jewellery, sculpture and video.

The original Grundy Bequest consisted solely of oil paintings, many of which had been created by the brothers. Upon the opening of the Gallery, Blackpool Council created an acquisitions fund that was administered by Council members who formed the Library and Art Gallery Committee. By 1927 purchases from the Royal Academy's Summer Exhibition had become the main source of acquisition, and by the mid-1930s the Collection and the Committee's ambition had outgrown the original building and two additional exhibition spaces were built. The Collection has been strengthened by gifts and bequests. The works acquired during this period can be roughly categorised thematically: enlightenment, romantic, toil, landscape and seascape.

Funding and ambition for the Gallery dwindled post-Second World War while acquisitions from the local art society increased. While a proportion of the painting collection could be described as being acquired through passive collecting, even after the introduction of a formal acquisitions policy, such works offer the Collection a richness of style and taste if not historically important work.

There are a number of significant British artists represented in the painting collection, including Anna Airy, Craigie Aitchison, Samuel John Lamorna Birch, Stephen Bone, Reginald Grange Brundrit, Jeffrey Camp, Thomas Sidney Cooper, Charles Ernest Cundall, Frederick William Elwell, Richard Ernst Eurich, Stanhope Alexander Forbes, Patrick Hughes, Augustus Edwin John, Laura Knight, Moffat Peter Lindner, John Linnell, Charles S. Ricketts, David Roberts, Charles Spencelayh, Henry Scott Tuke, and Lucy Kemp Welsh.

The most popular and requested painting in the Collection is Charles Spencelayh's *The Laughing Parson*. Spencelayh was a founder member of the Royal Society of Miniature Painters and painted a postage-stamp-sized portrait of George V for Queen Mary's celebrated Doll House. *The Laughing Parson* is one of two works by Spencelayh in the Grundy Collection, and is a fine example of the meticulous rendering of detail he achieved in his work –

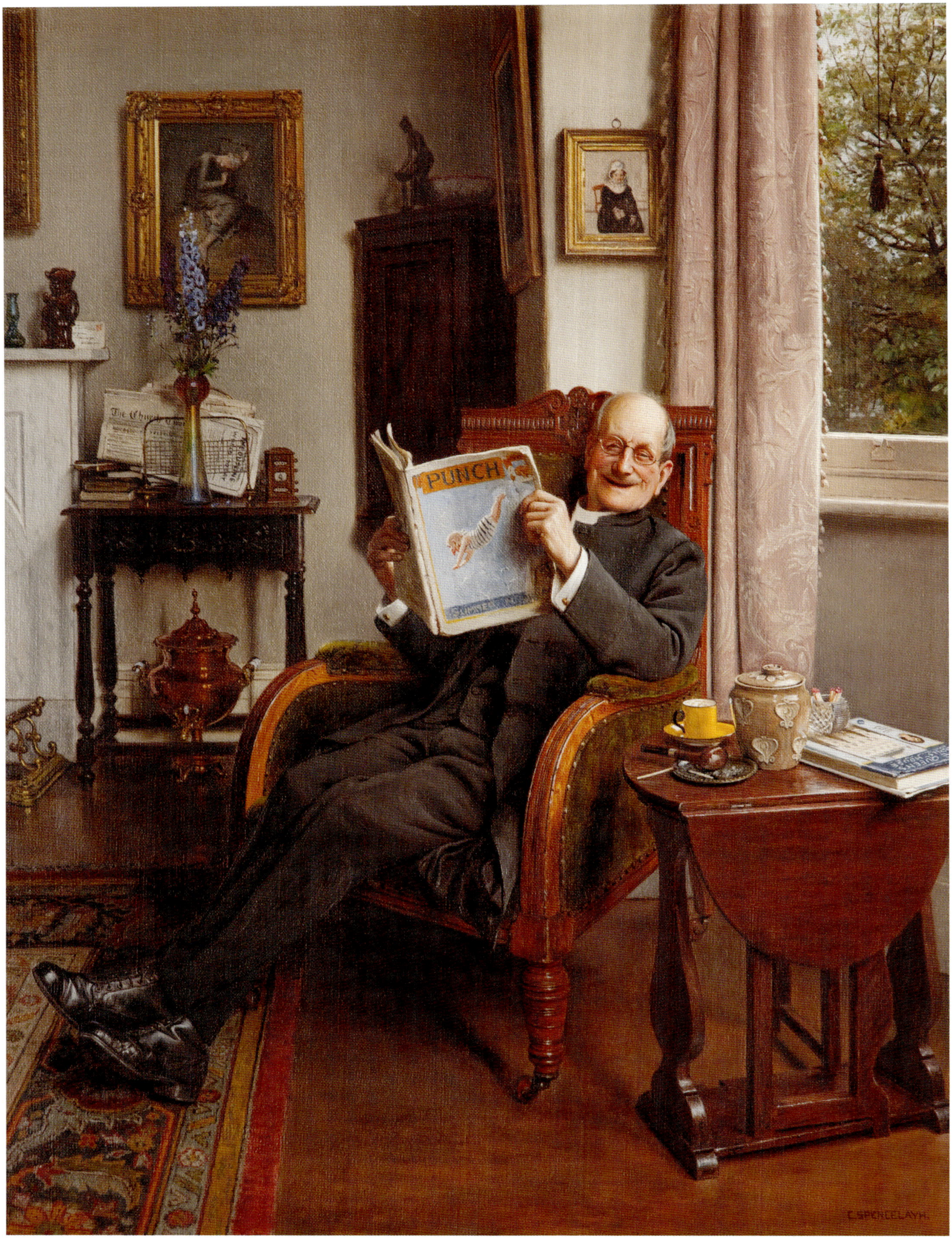
PUNCH

an old man of the clergy leans back in his armchair situated within a scene of domesticity while laughing and gazing up from the copy of *Punch* magazine he is reading to look at the viewer. The painting was included in the Tate Britain exhibition 'Rude Britannia' in 2010.

More unorthodox interest lies in two other paintings in the Collection. When first accessioned, Alexander Johnston's *The Pillar Box* was believed to be by John Everett Millais. Presented to the Gallery as a gift in 1933, it was only when examined by Sotheby's that the work was acknowledged to be by Johnston. They wrote 'this painting [*The Pillar Box*] is not by Sir John Everett Millais and the monogram on the painting, which is an imitation of his own signature, is typical of a most common faker of Millais. In all probability, when that monogram was added the faker would have covered up the genuine signature now showing at the bottom left of the painting either because the painting has been recently cleaned or simply that the cover paint has sunk into the canvas.'

The Pass of Leney by Alfred de Breanski has an addition of a different kind. The painting depicts a mountainous landscape with a hunter aiming his rifle across the valley. When comparing the painting to a photograph, presumed to have been produced at the time the work was acquired as a gift, a stag has appeared standing on a grassy ledge in the centre of the painting, and a flock of birds who had commanded the rifleman's attention have disappeared. The stag has clearly been painted by a hand other than that of the artist as it lacks the finesse of the overall painting. It is known that a past member of gallery staff, who also jobbed as a magician, was keen to exercise his ability in frame and painting restoration and has been authored with the sleight of hand that has created the remarkable intervention here.

The Grundy Art Gallery is a longstanding member of the Contemporary Art Society and the majority of its important modern works have been acquired through this association. The Gallery has not acquired a painting into its Collection for the past eight years and its focus is now drawn more towards sculpture, print, video and installation, having implemented a policy of acquiring works as gifts from artists who have exhibited through the Gallery's temporary exhibitions programme.

Stuart Tulloch, Curator

Facing page: Spencelayh, Charles, 1865–1958, *The Laughing Parson,* 1935, Grundy Art Gallery (p. 112)

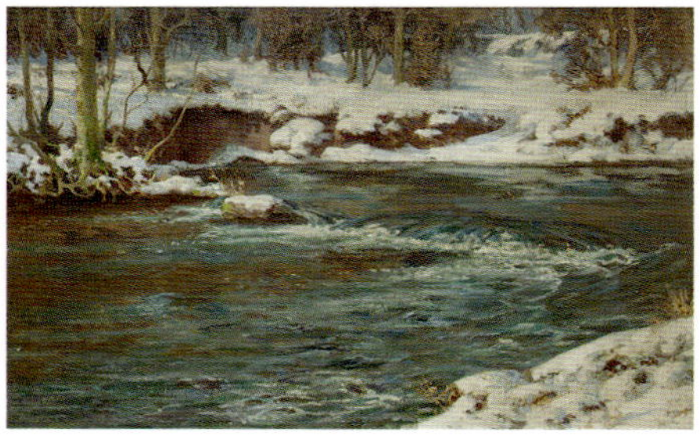

Adams, Harry William 1868–1947
Hunt of the Grayling 1925
oil on canvas 74 x 112.5
G2

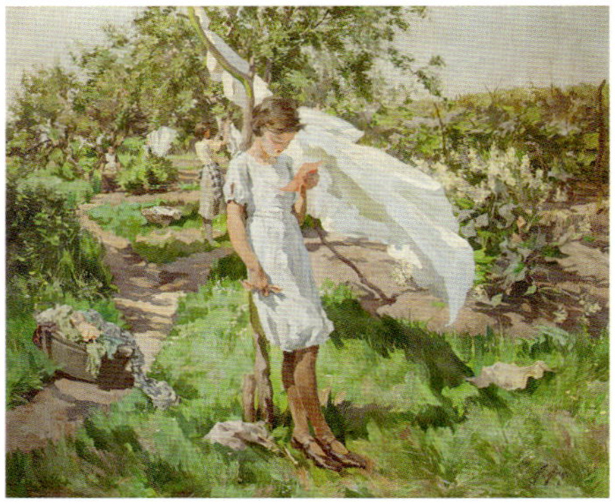

Airy, Anna 1882–1964
Message of May 1937
oil on canvas 151 x 183
G3

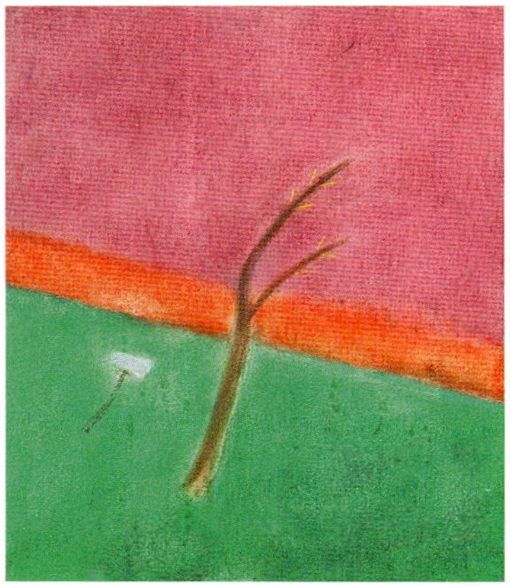

Aitchison, Craigie Ronald John 1926–2009
Tree 1978
oil on canvas 36 x 31
G524

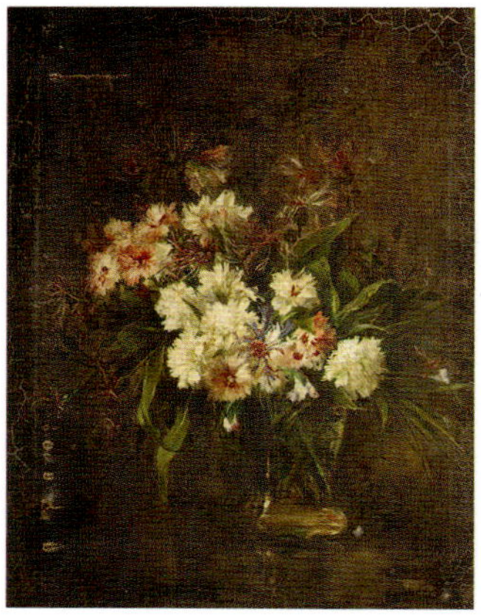

Algie, Jessie 1859–1927
Pinks
oil on canvas 51.5 x 41
G322

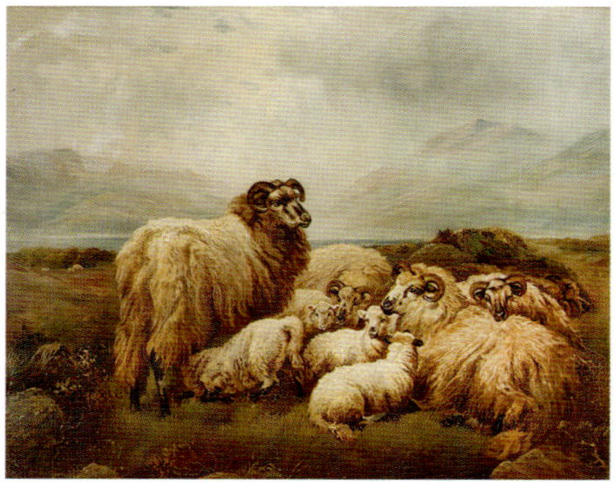

Ansdell, Richard 1815–1885
Sheep 1869
oil on canvas 43.5 x 59
G4

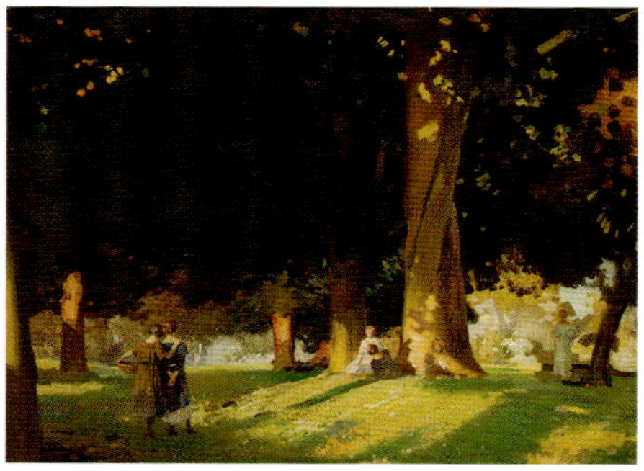

Appleyard, Frederick 1874–1963
The Nightingale 1921
oil on canvas 69 x 93.5
G6

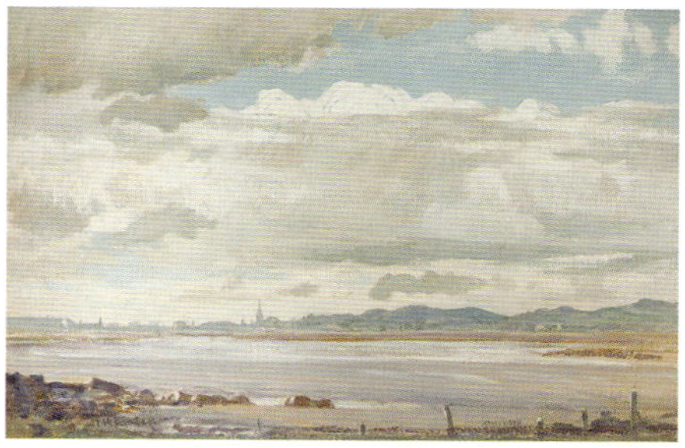

Atherton, John Smith 1877–1943
Foxfield Estuary
oil on board 38 x 54
G364

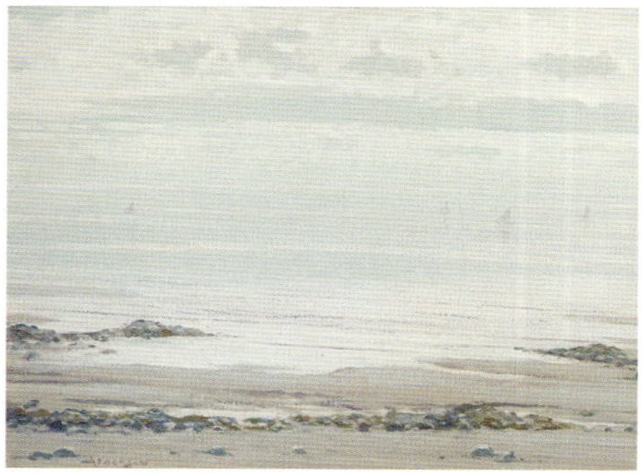

Atherton, John Smith 1877–1943
Near Bardsea
oil on board 47 x 54.5
G366

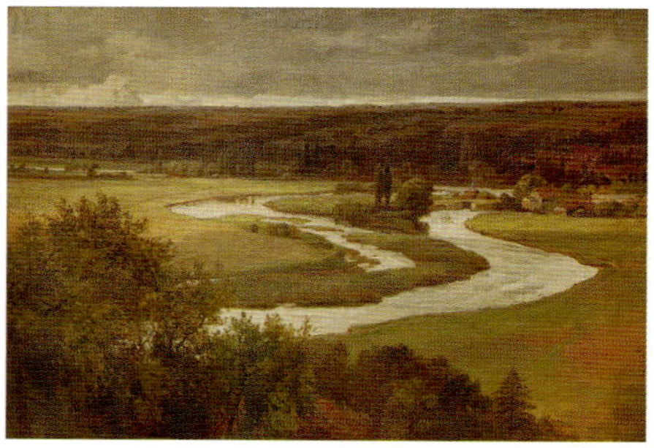

Aumonier, James 1832–1911
The Thames at Great Marlowe 1876
oil on canvas 66 x 96
G10

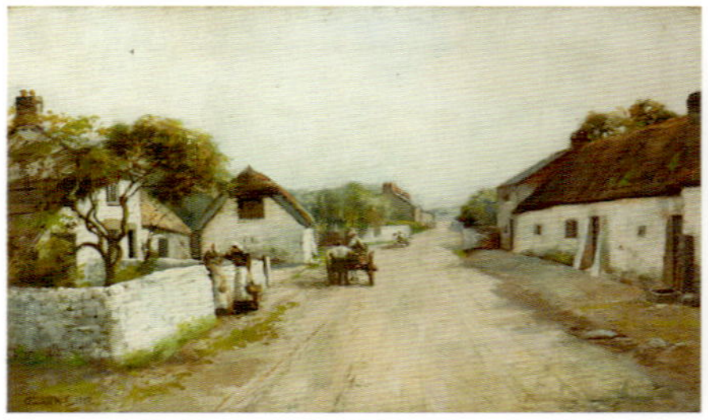

Auty, Charles 1858–1936
Bispham Village in 1880 1880s
oil on canvas 50 x 82
G11

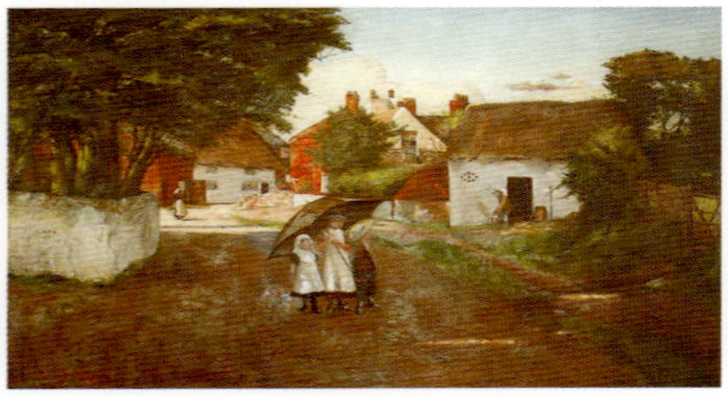

Auty, Charles 1858–1936
Bispham Village Scene
oil on canvas 111 x 183
G363

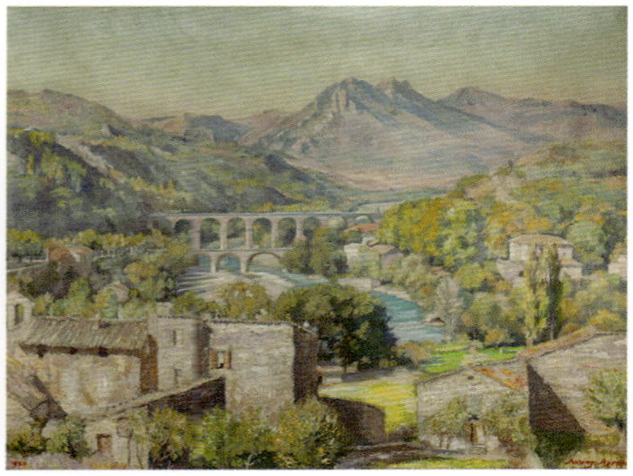

Ayrton, Anthony
Alpine Landscape 1939
oil on canvas 50 x 75
G14

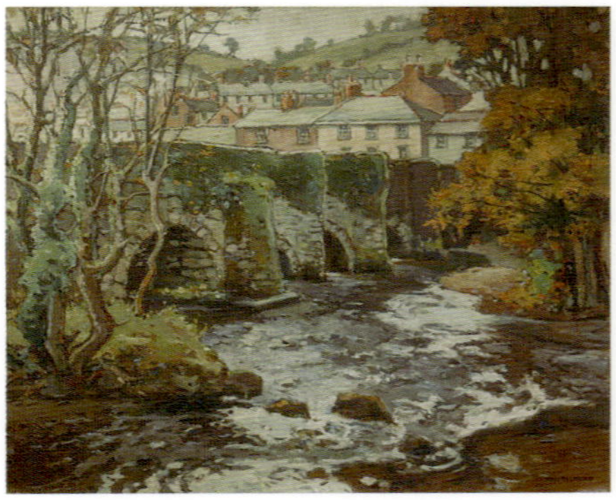

Balmford, Hurst 1871–1950
Lostwithiel, Cornwall c.1930
oil on canvas 63 x 75
G15

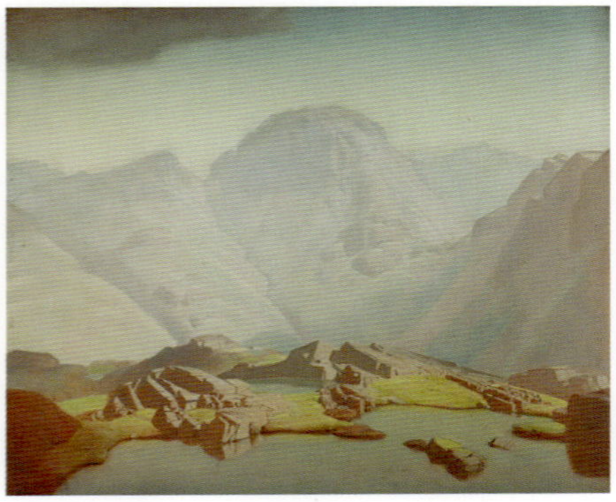

Banner, Delmar Harmood 1896–1983
Great Gable 1944
oil on canvas 64.5 x 76.5
G241

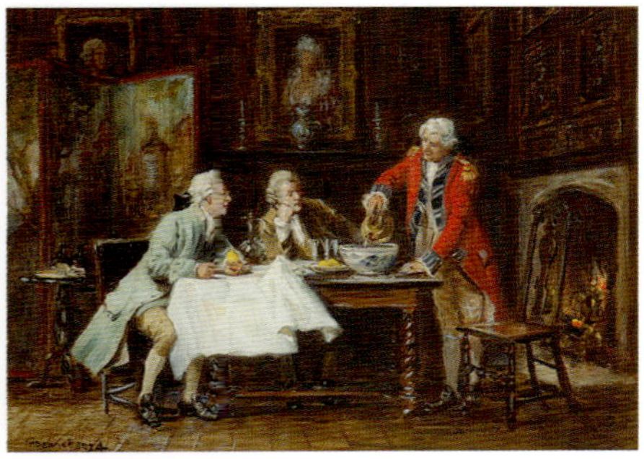

Bennett, Frank Moss 1874–1952
Hot Punch 1924
oil on canvas 32.5 x 48.5
G505

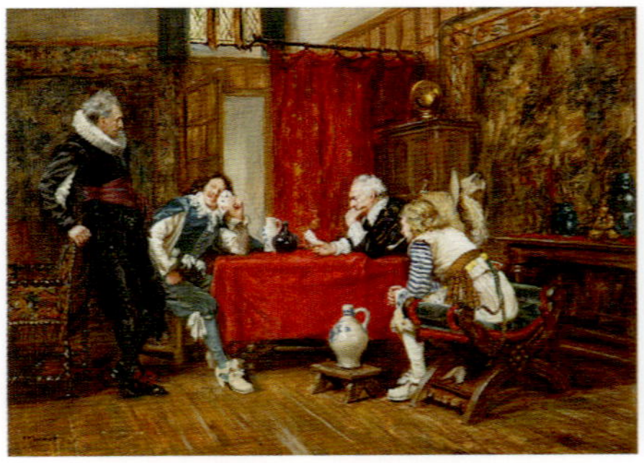

Bennett, Frank Moss 1874–1952
A Good Hand 1928
oil on canvas 34 x 49.5
G506

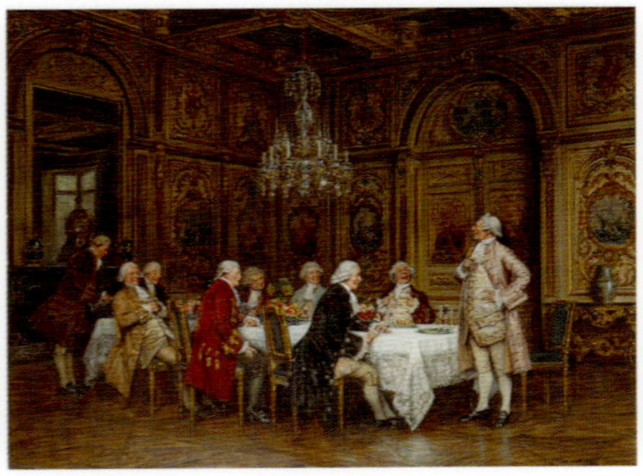

Bennett, Frank Moss 1874–1952
Un bon mot 1938
oil on canvas 70.5 x 90
G17

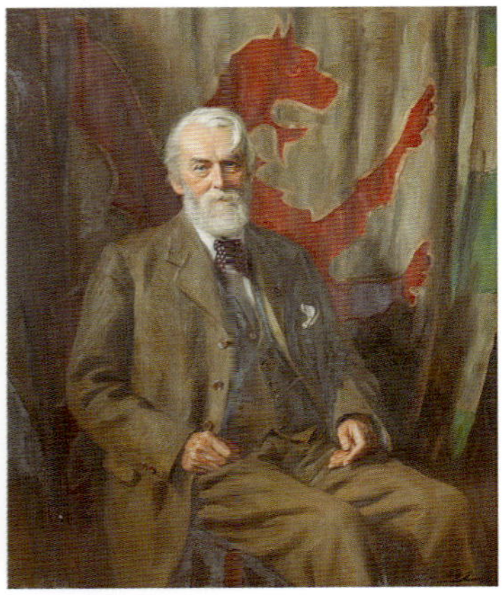

Berrie, John Archibald Alexander 1887–1962
Cuthbert Grundy (1846–1946)
oil on canvas 126 x 100
G613

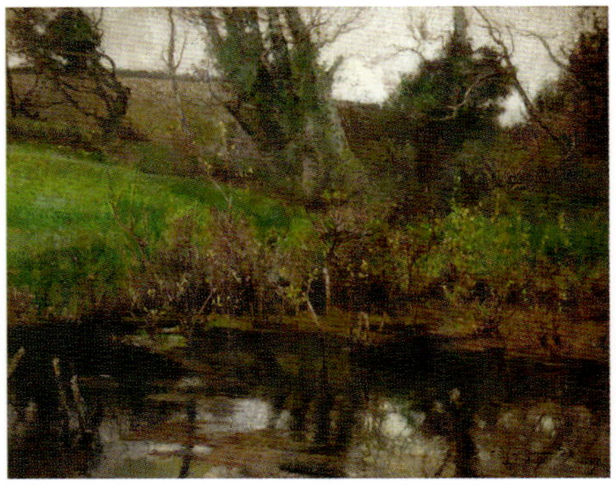

Birch, Samuel John Lamorna 1869–1955
The Lonely Pool 1897
oil on canvas 90.5 x 106
G19

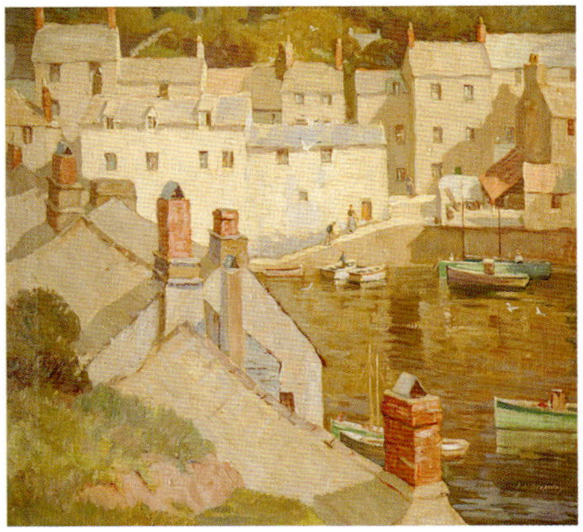

Blakeley, John Harold b.1867
Polperro, Cornwall
oil on canvas 50 x 60
G444

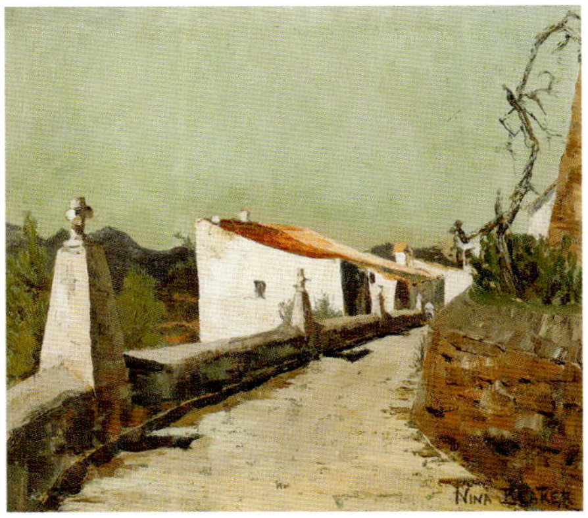

Blaker, Nina
Santa Eulalia, Ibiza
oil on canvas 44.5 x 54.5
G383

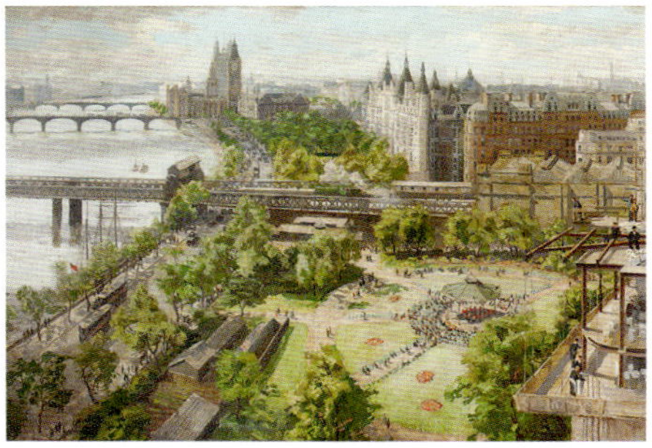

Bone, Stephen 1904–1958
Westminster 1939
oil on canvas 141 x 201
G22

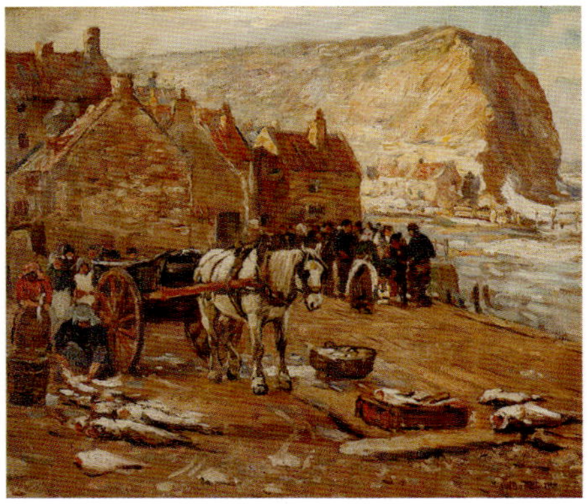

Booth, James William 1867–1953
Fish Sales, Staithes 1900
oil on canvas 49 x 59.5
G24

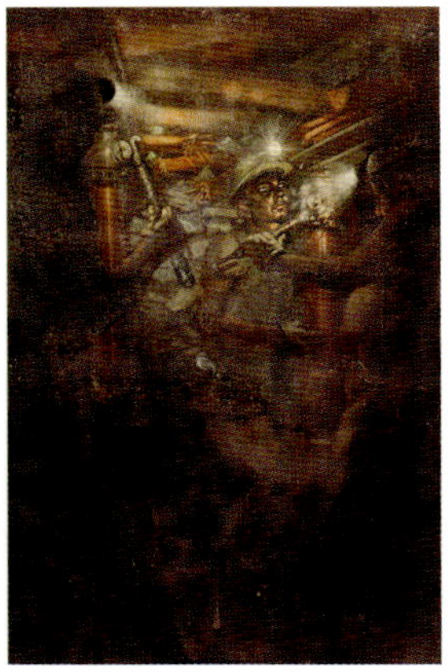

Boulton, Margaret
Moving Dowty Props
oil on canvas 138 x 91
G443

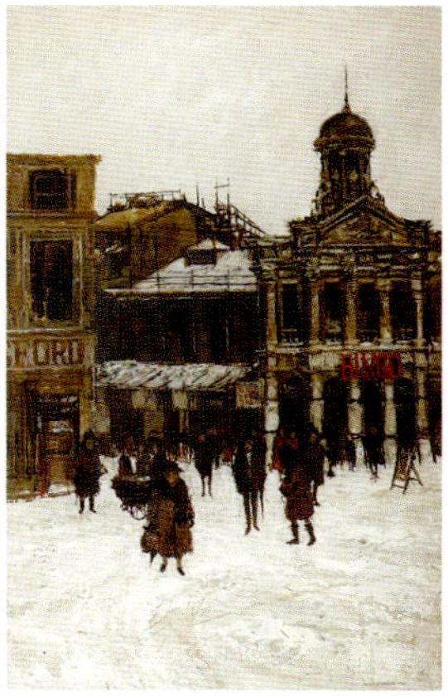

Brannan, Peter 1926–1994
The Old Theatre
oil on board 75 x 45
G381

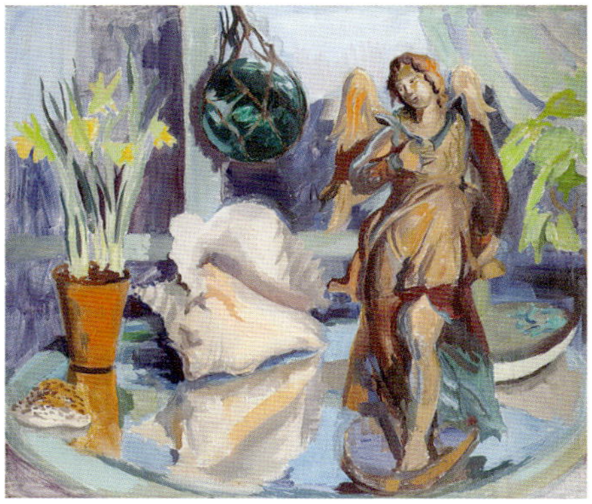

Bray, Phyllis 1911–1991
Still Life
oil on canvas 64 x 77
G288

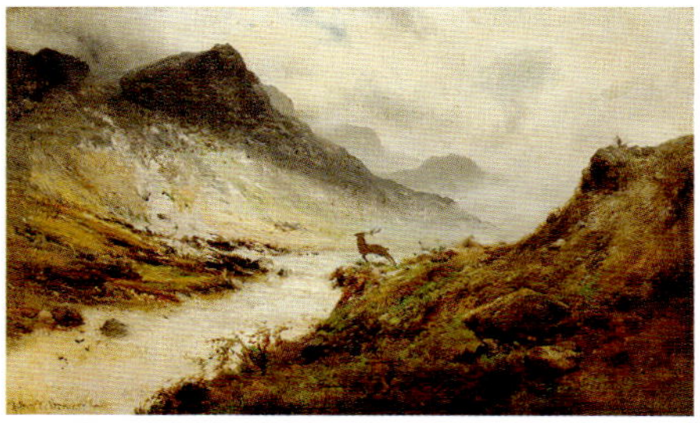

Breanski, Alfred de 1852–1928
The Pass of Leney
oil on canvas 61 x 91.5
G28

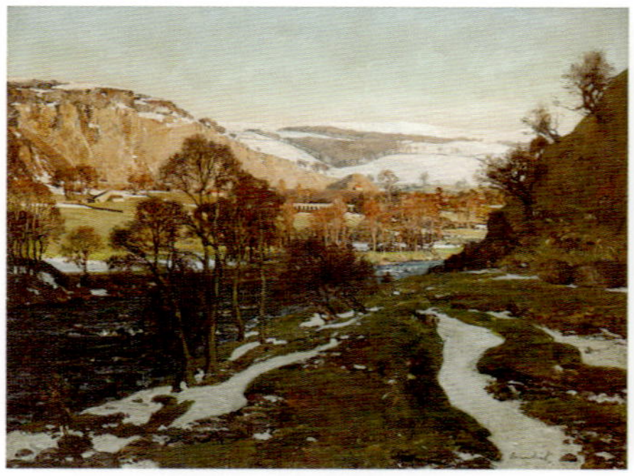

Brundrit, Reginald Grange 1883–1960
Ribblesdale 1929
oil on canvas 105 x 126
G30

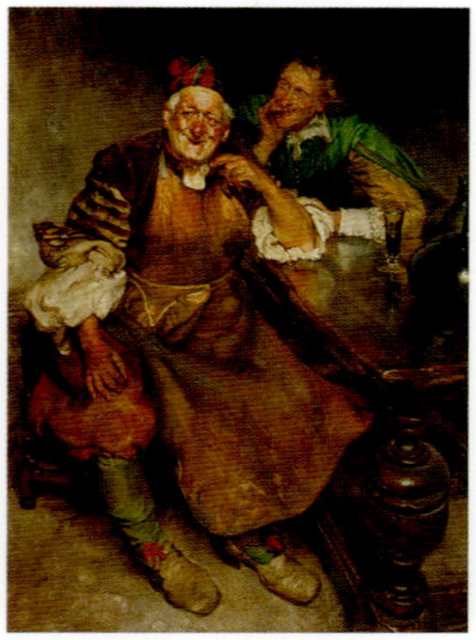

Bundy, Edgar 1862–1922
Scandal 1917
oil on canvas 128 x 95
G32

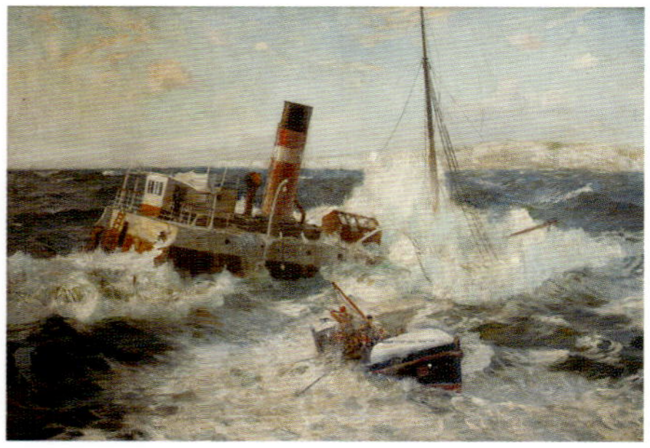

Burgess, Arthur James Wetherall 1879–1957
Abandoned 1909
oil on canvas 123 x 184.5
G33

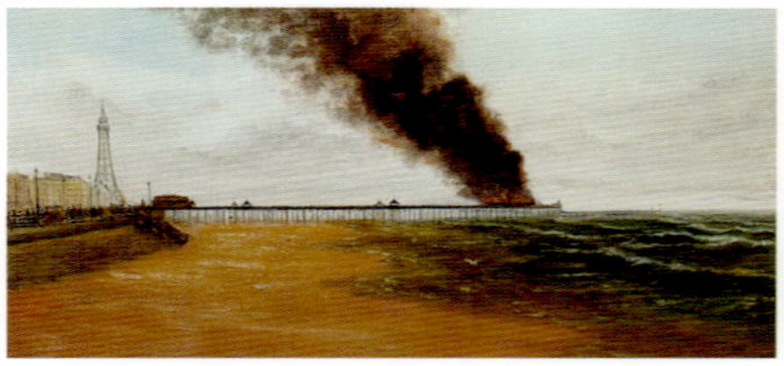

Burrell, H.
Pavilion Fire, North Pier, 1921 1921
oil on board 39 x 76.5
G221 M131

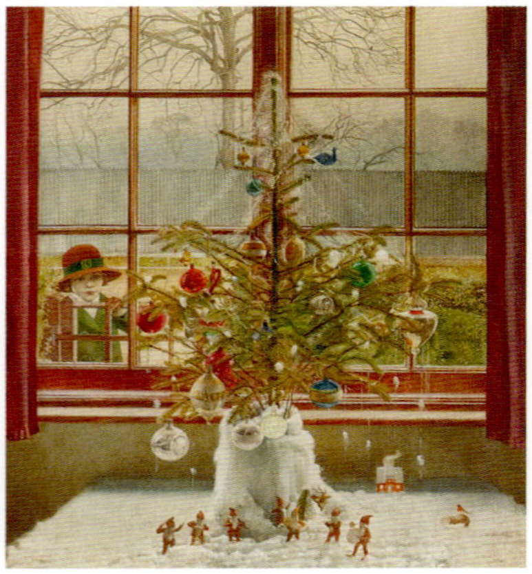

Bush, Harry 1883–1957
The Christmas Tree 1933
oil on canvas 105 x 95
G36

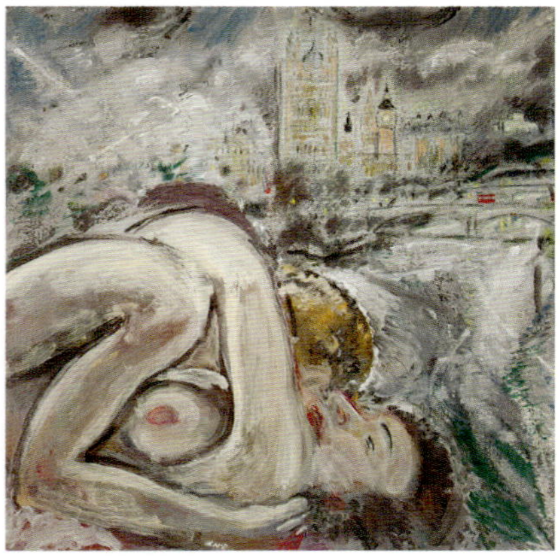

Camp, Jeffery b.1923
Millbank
oil on canvas 88 x 88
G614

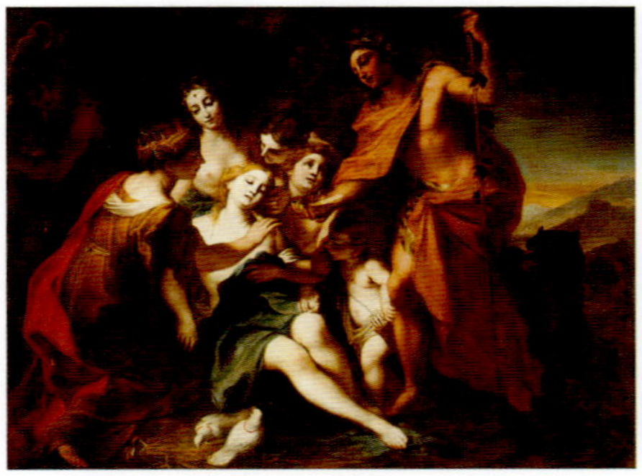

Casali, Andrea 1705–1784
Bacchus and Ariadne c.1750
oil on canvas 171 x 230
G39

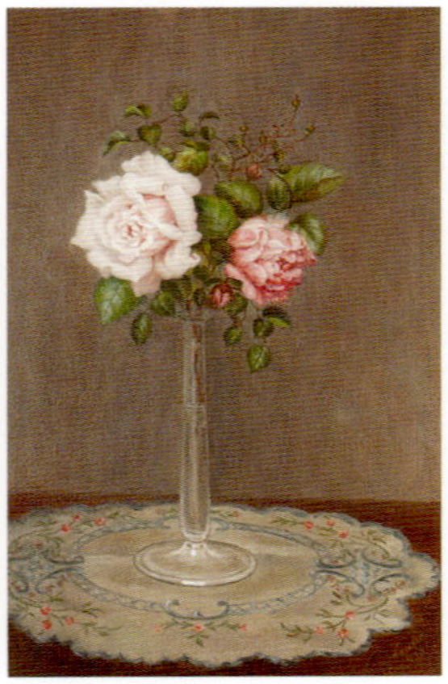

Cave, Vera
Roses
oil on board 55 x 35
G40

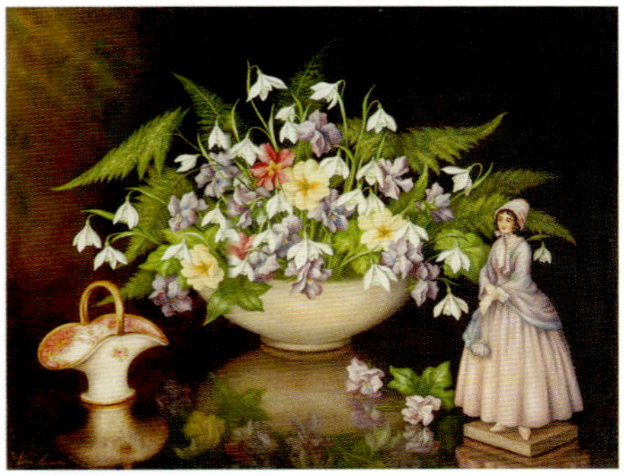

Cave, Vera
Spring Flowers
oil on board 38 x 47.5
G41

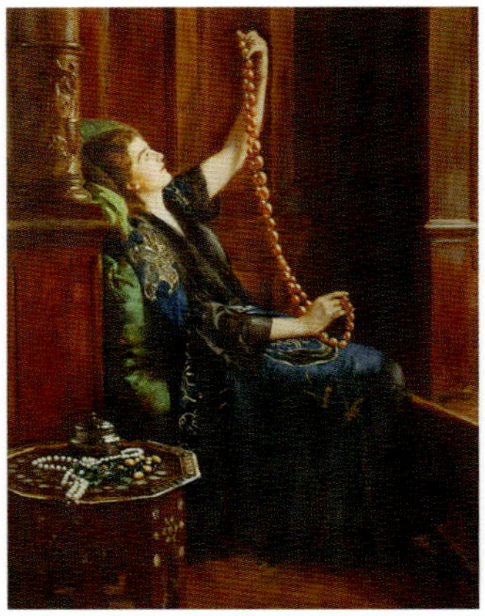

Collier, John 1850–1934
The Amber Necklace 1930
oil on canvas 90 x 70
G46

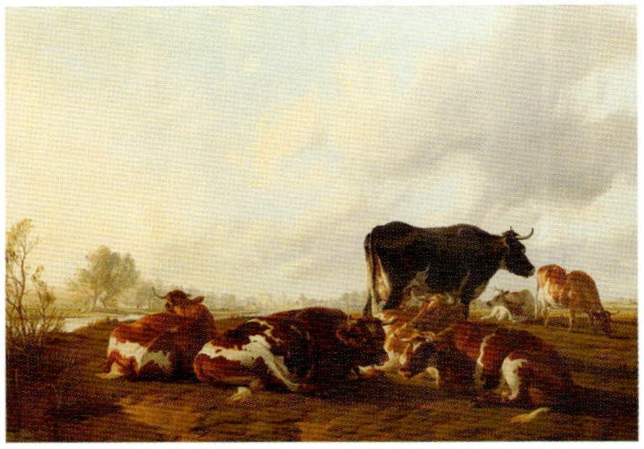

Cooper, Thomas Sidney 1803–1902
Cattle Grazing 1870
oil on canvas 74 x 103
G49

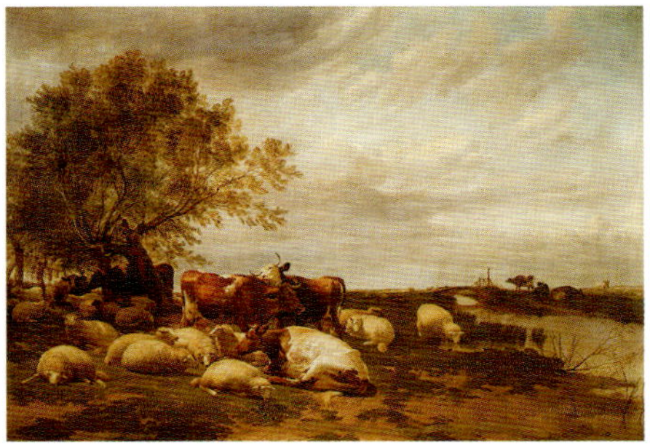

Cooper, Thomas Sidney 1803–1902
Canterbury Meadows
oil on canvas 135 x 189.5
G48

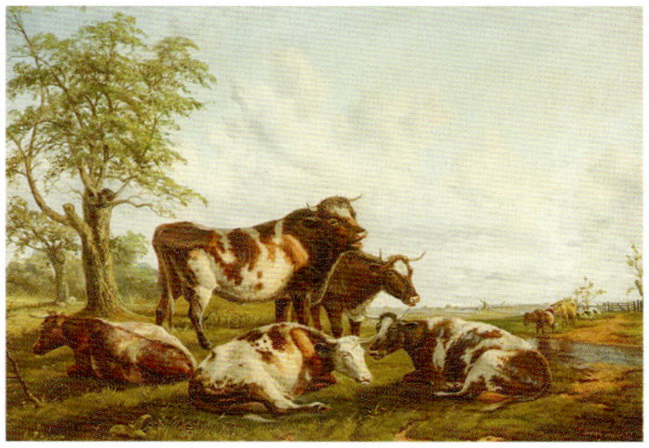

Cooper, Thomas Sidney 1803–1902
Landscape
oil on canvas 63.5 x 76.5
G287

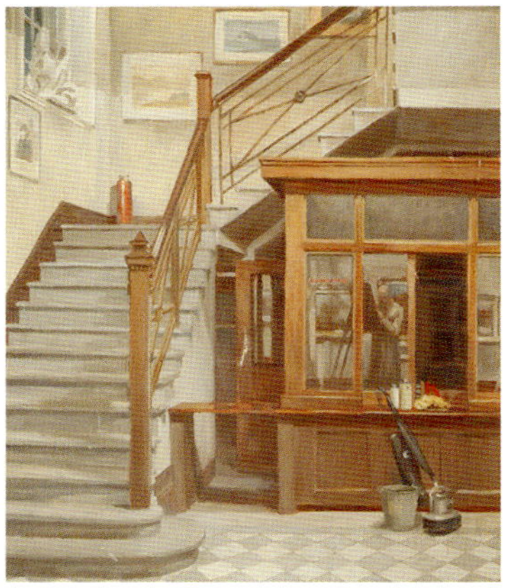

Crabtree, Jack b.1938
Portrait of the Artist
oil on canvas 63 x 55
G294

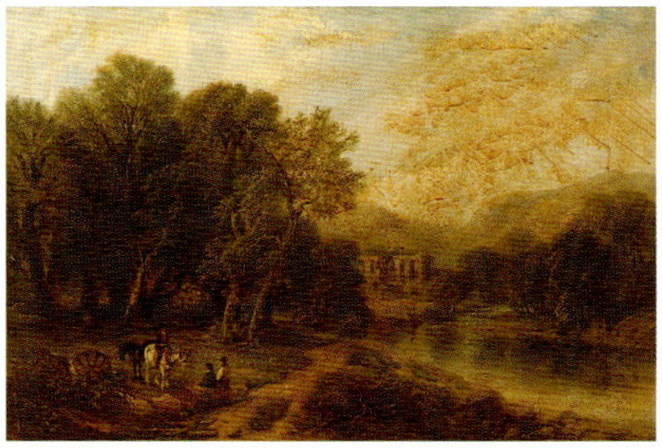

Creswick, Thomas 1811–1869
Bolton Abbey 1840
oil on canvas 50 x 74
G376

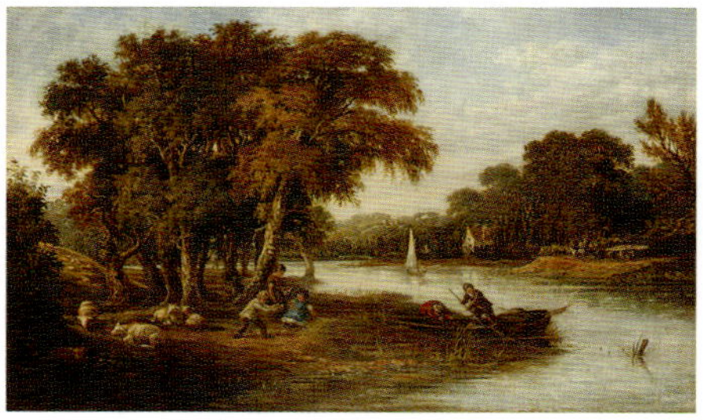

Crome, John 1768–1821
River Wensum
oil on canvas 39 x 59.5
G50

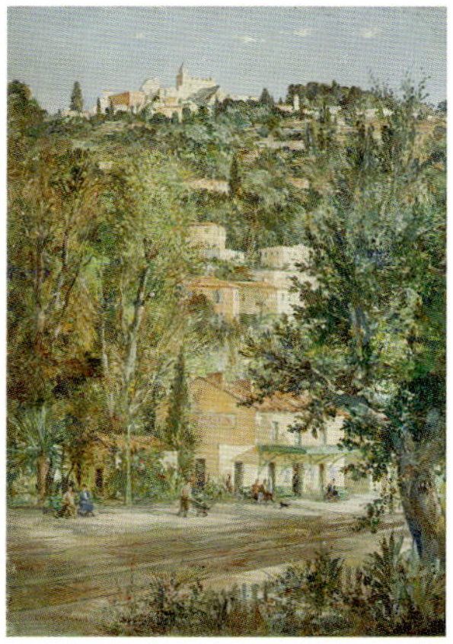

Cundall, Charles Ernest 1890–1971
Rocquebrune-Cap-Martin Station
oil on canvas 75 x 54.5
G342

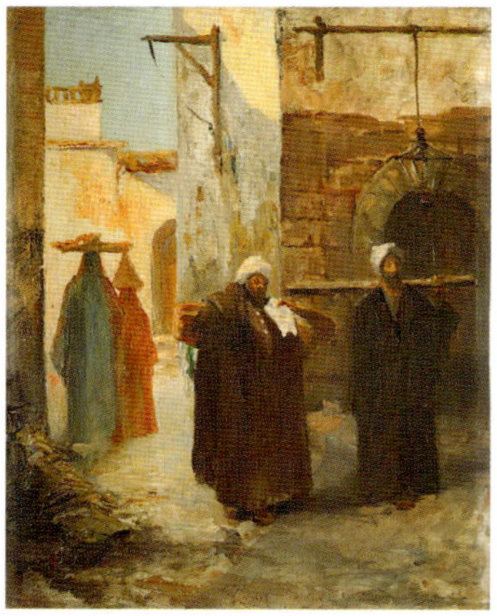

d'Erlanger, Rodolphe 1872–1932
Returning from Market 1924
oil on canvas 72 x 58.5
G54

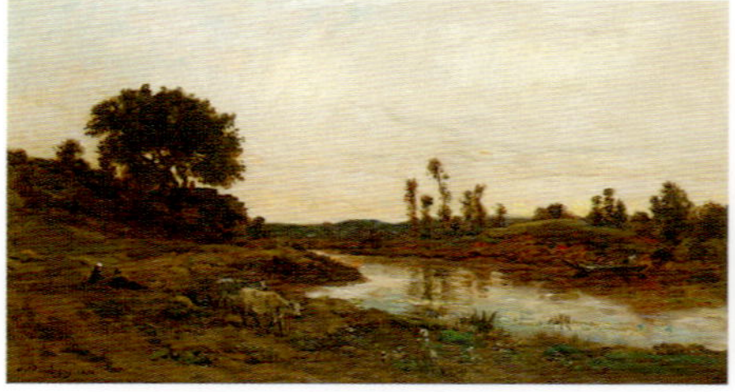

Daubigny, Charles-François 1817–1878
Cattle and Figures by a River at Dusk 1874
oil on canvas 38 x 66.5
G622

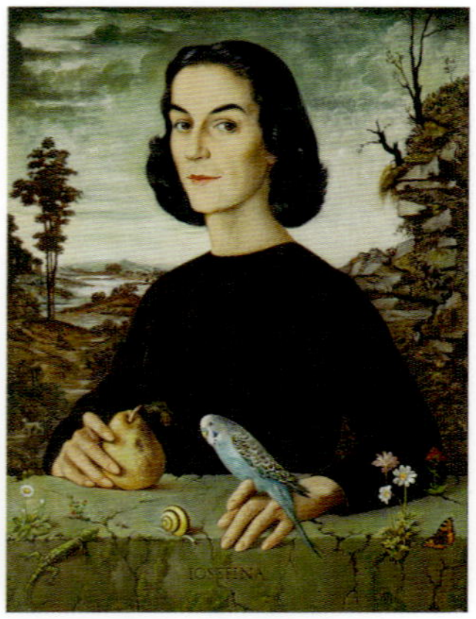

de Montfort, Lisa b.1906
Josefina
oil on canvas 65 x 50
G260

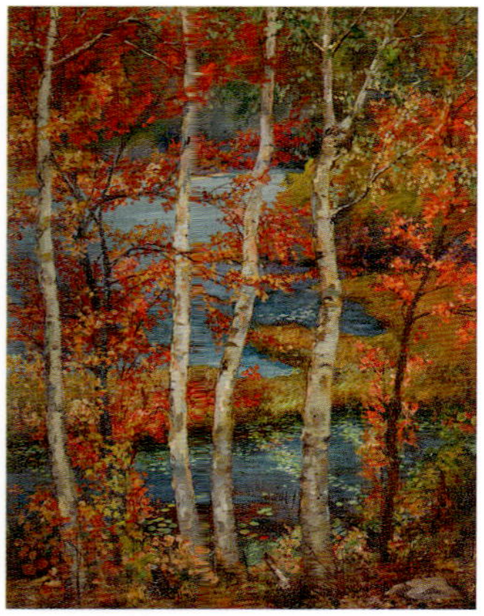

Dignam, Mary Ella Williams 1857–1938
By the Lake
oil on canvas 77 x 64
G56

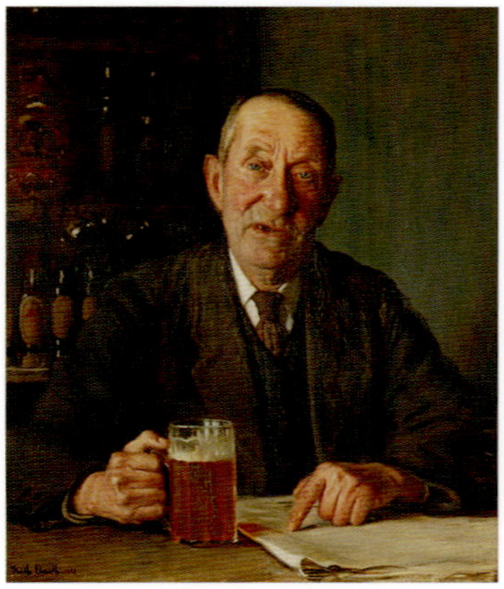

Elwell, Frederick William 1870–1958
Man with a Pint 1932
oil on canvas 75.5 x 63
G64

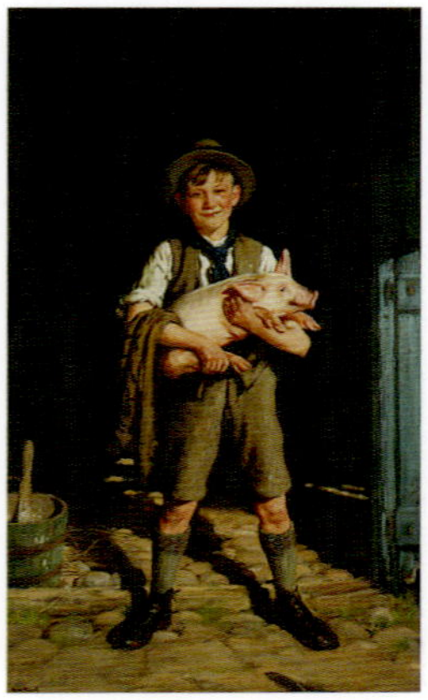

Elwell, Frederick William 1870–1958
A Boy with a Pig 1934
oil on canvas 151 x 90.5
G63

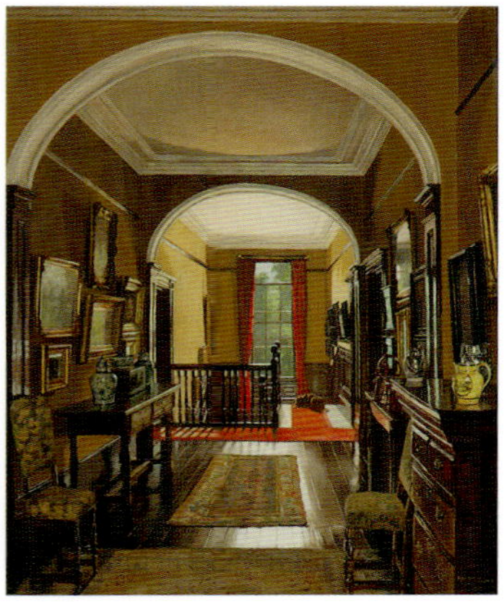

Elwell, Mary Dawson 1874–1952
The Landing in Summer 1930
oil on canvas 73 x 65
G65

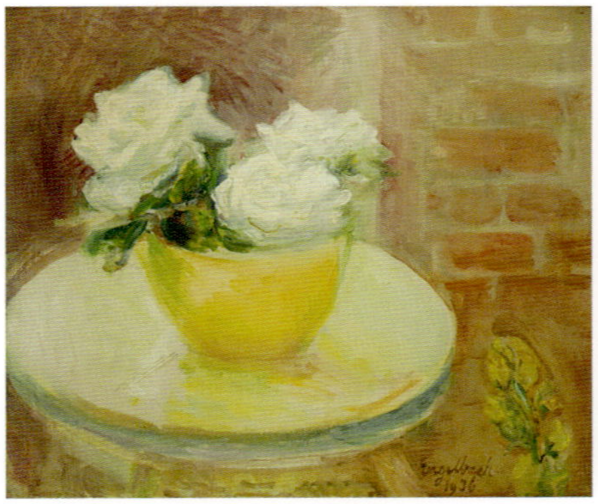

Engelbach, Florence 1872–1951
White Roses in a Yellow Bowl c.1936
oil on board 40 x 50.5
G68

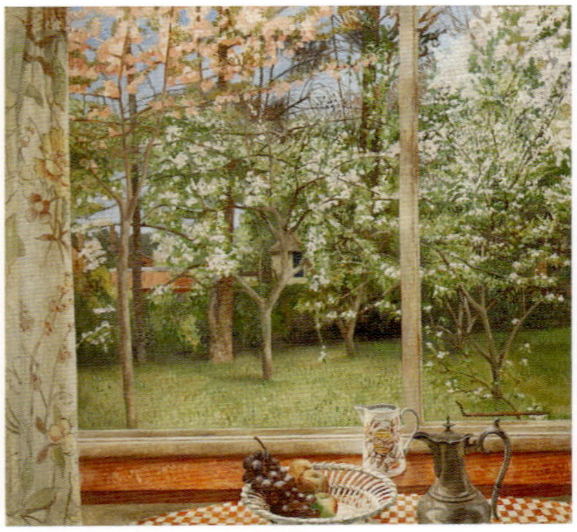

Eurich, Richard Ernst 1903–1992
The Window
oil on canvas 63 x 76.5
G307

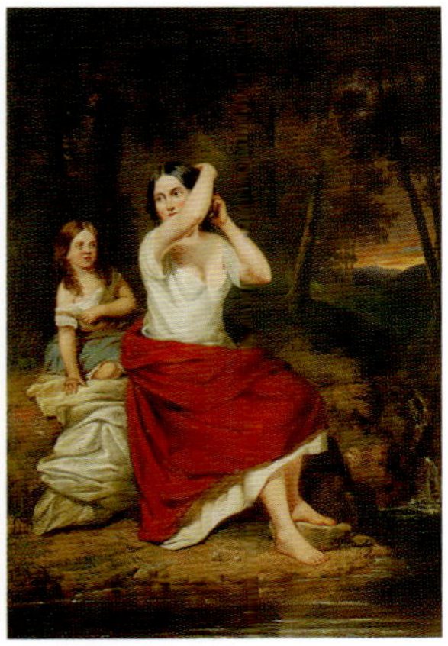

Faed, Thomas 1826–1900
Molly's Toilet 1855
oil on canvas 60 x 45.5
G69

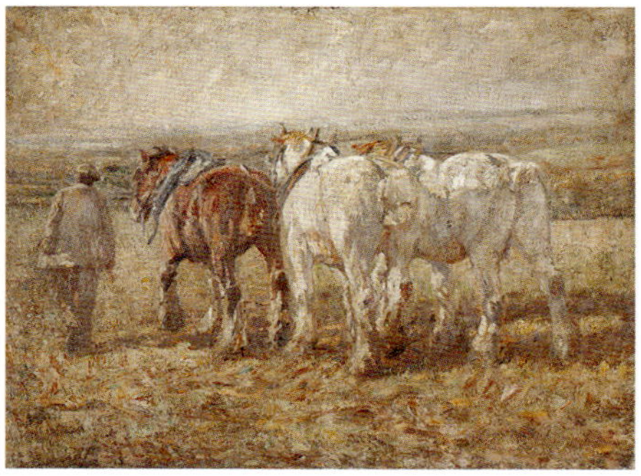

Fidler, Harry 1856–1935
Going Home 1919
oil on canvas 154 x 172
G71

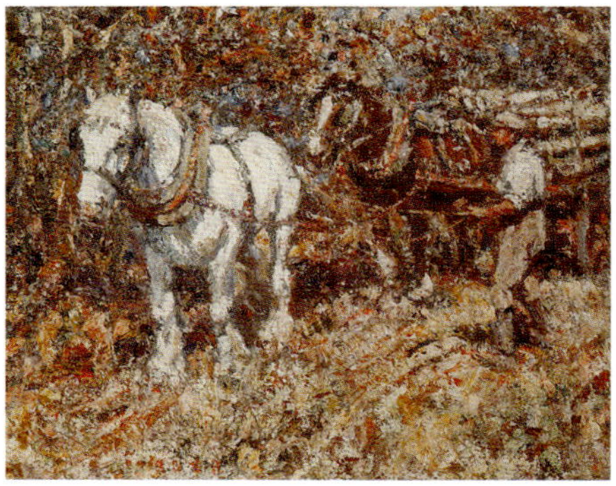

Fidler, Harry 1856–1935
Timber Wagon c.1930
oil on canvas 39.5 x 49
G72

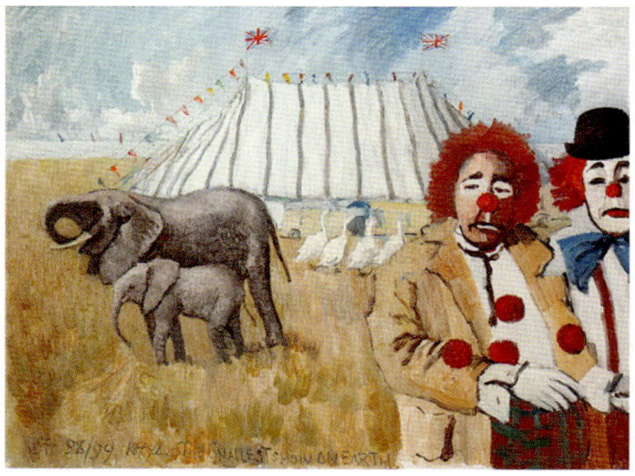

Fletcher, Geoffrey Scowcroft 1923–2004
The Smallest Show on Earth 1998
oil on canvas 61 x 75
G662

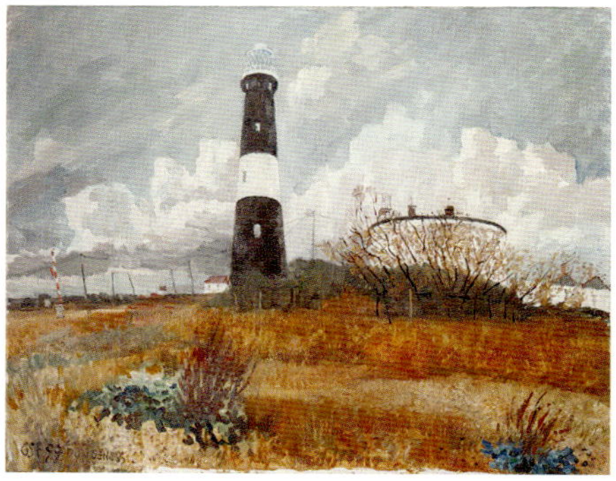

Fletcher, Geoffrey Scowcroft 1923–2004
Dungeness 1999
oil on canvas 56 x 71
G664

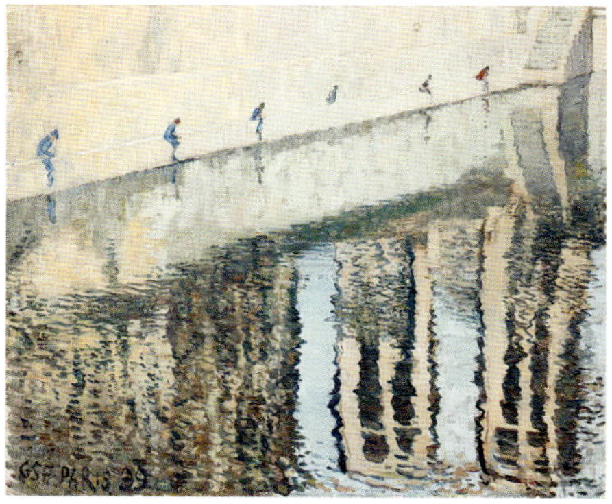

Fletcher, Geoffrey Scowcroft 1923–2004
Notre Dame, Reflections 1999
oil on canvas 50 x 61
G665

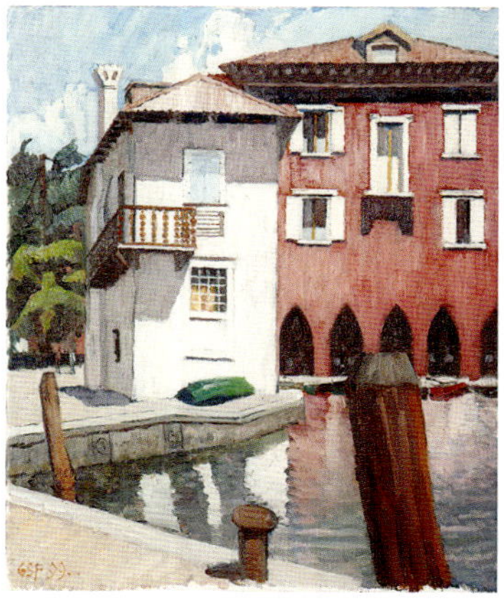

Fletcher, Geoffrey Scowcroft 1923–2004
Tarbole 1999
oil on canvas 61 x 51
G663

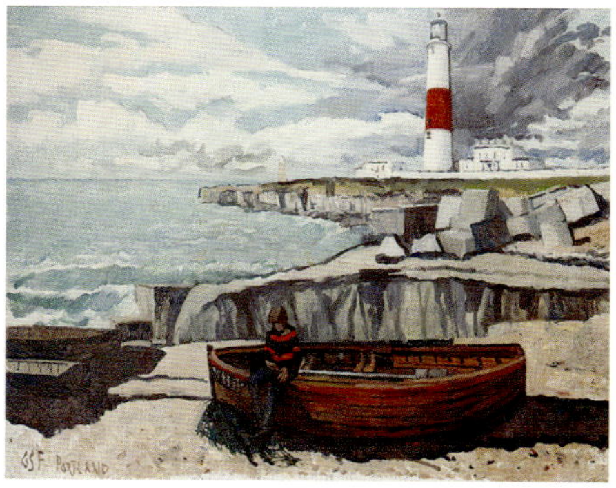

Fletcher, Geoffrey Scowcroft 1923–2004
Portland 2000
oil on canvas 51 x 66
G667

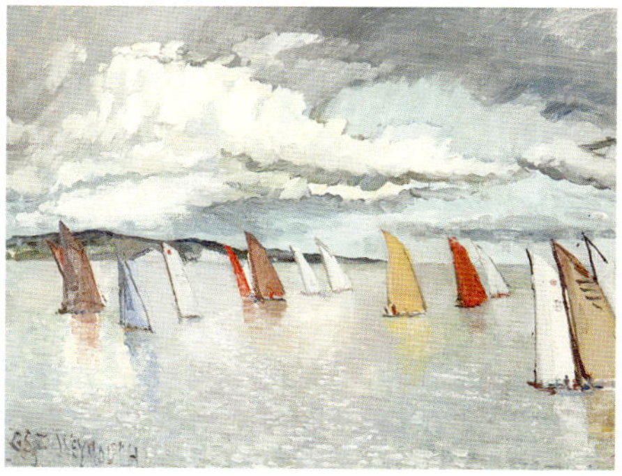

Fletcher, Geoffrey Scowcroft 1923–2004
Weymouth, June 2000 2000
oil on canvas 39 x 49
G668

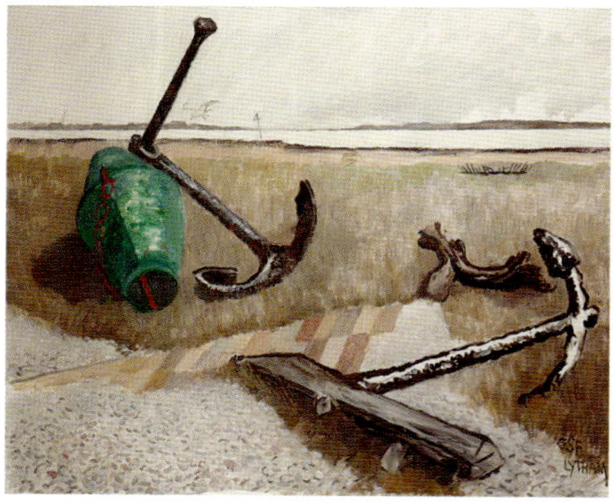

Fletcher, Geoffrey Scowcroft 1923–2004
Lytham 2001
oil on canvas 56 x 71.5
G670

Facing page: Melville, Arthur, 1855–1904, *The White Piano*, 1897, Harris Museum & Art Gallery (p. 324)

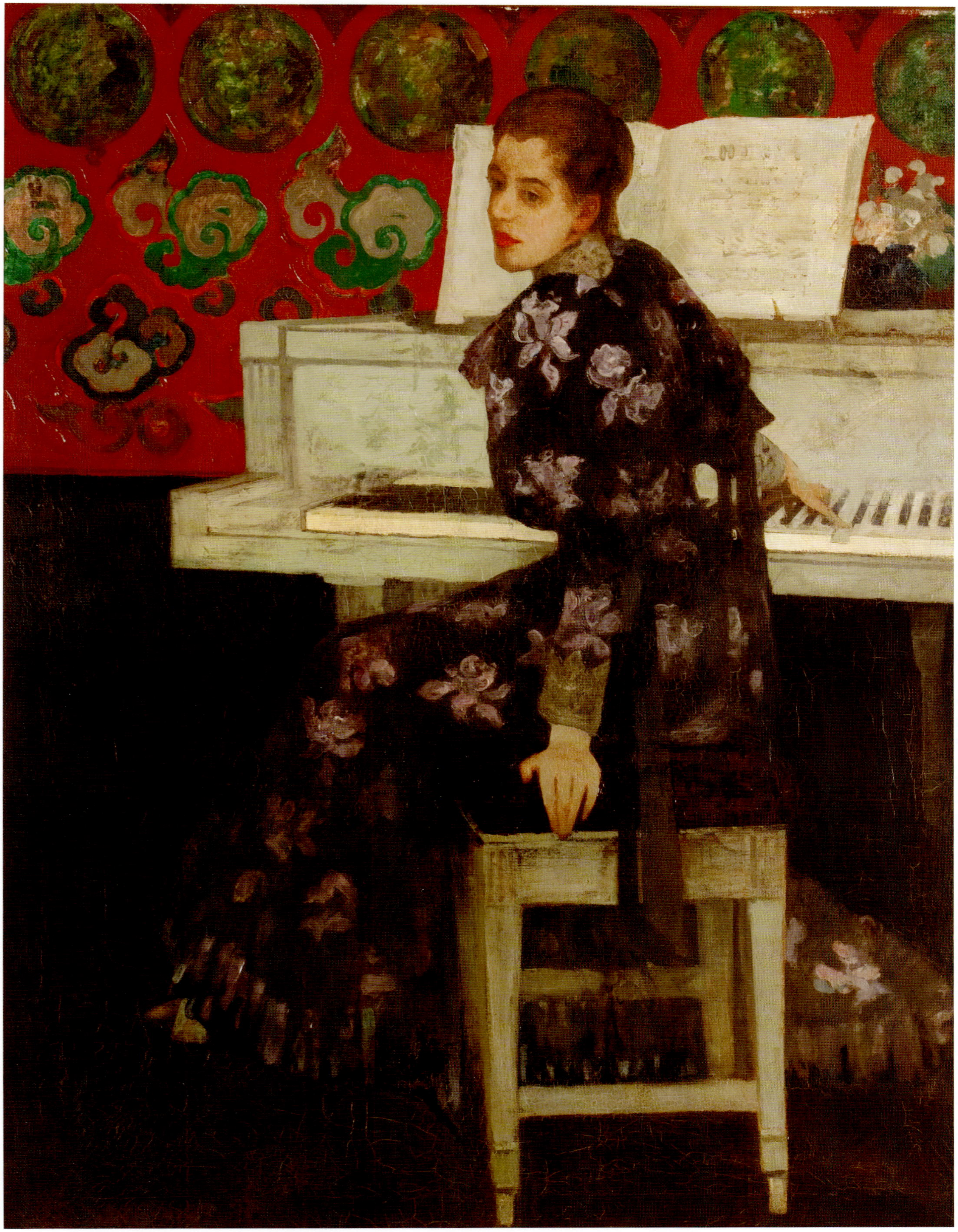

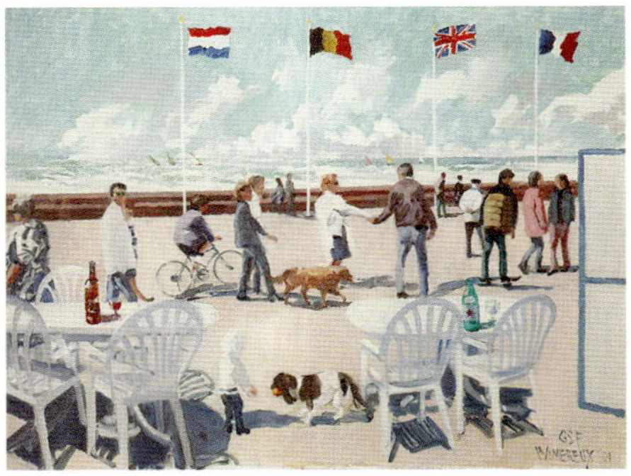

Fletcher, Geoffrey Scowcroft 1923–2004
Wimereux 2001
oil on canvas 78 x 100
G683

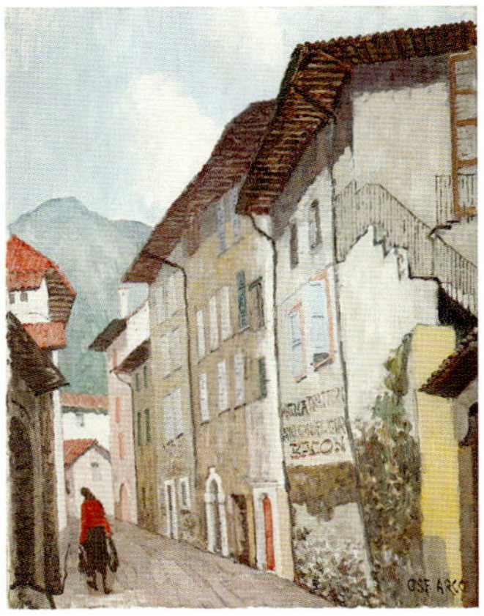

Fletcher, Geoffrey Scowcroft 1923–2004
Arco, Lake Garda 2002
oil on canvas 101 x 81
G681

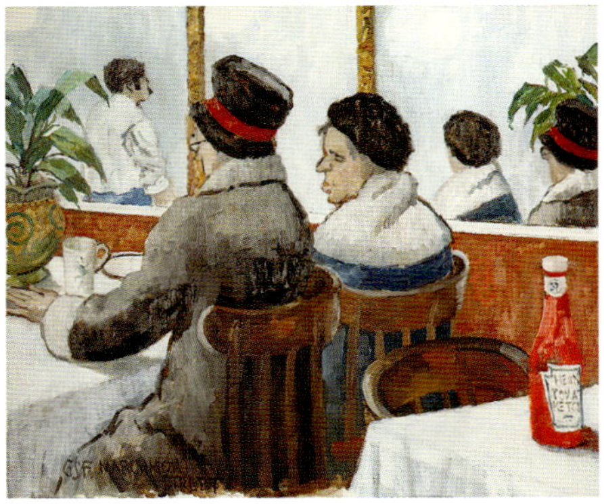

Fletcher, Geoffrey Scowcroft 1923–2004
Café Society 2002
oil on canvas 50.5 x 61
G676

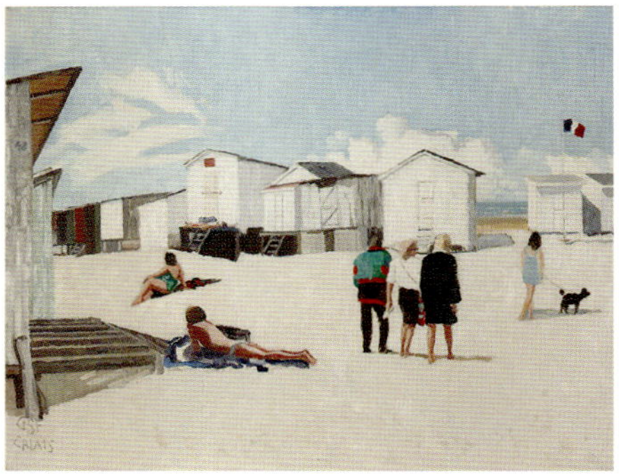

Fletcher, Geoffrey Scowcroft 1923–2004
Calais, 2002 2002
oil on canvas 53.5 x 61
G682

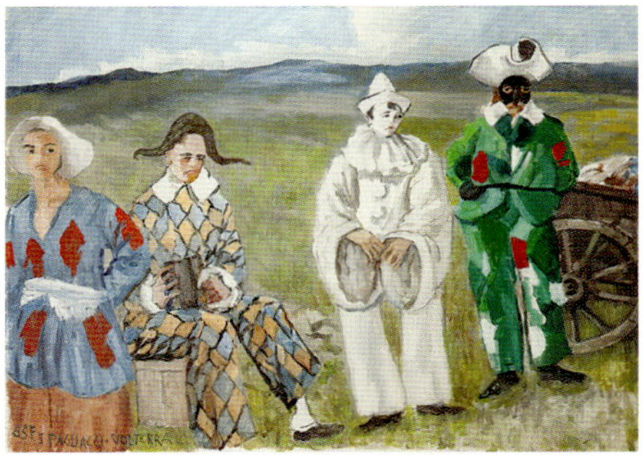

Fletcher, Geoffrey Scowcroft 1923–2004
I paglacci Volterra 2002
oil on canvas 99 x 176
G679

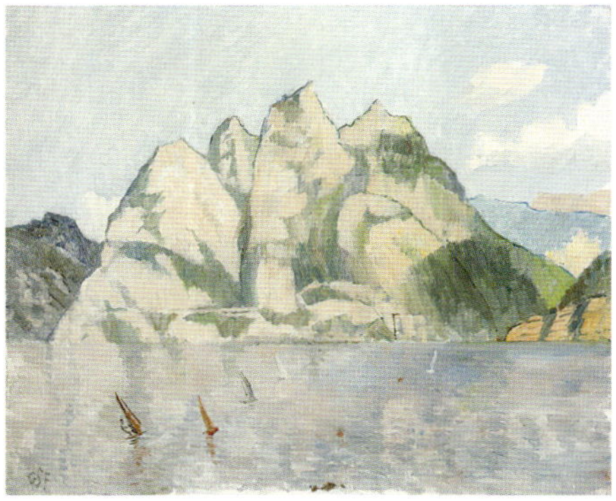

Fletcher, Geoffrey Scowcroft 1923–2004
Lake Garda 2002
oil on canvas 41 x 55.5
G680

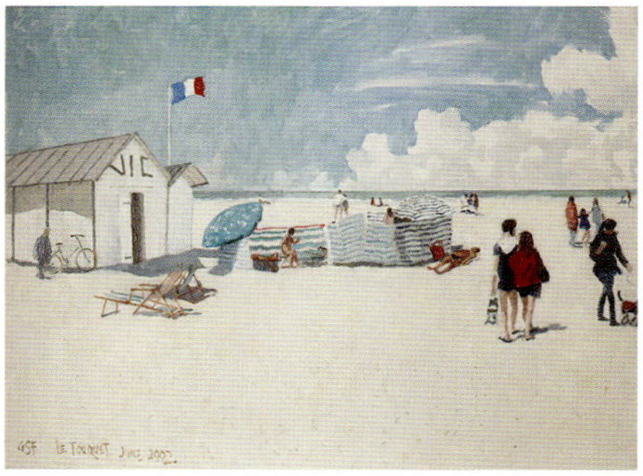

Fletcher, Geoffrey Scowcroft 1923–2004
Le Touquet 2002
oil on canvas 56 x 71.5
G686

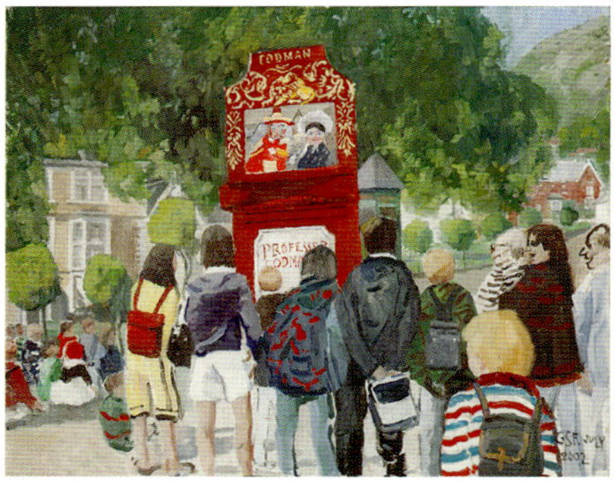

Fletcher, Geoffrey Scowcroft 1923–2004
Llandudno, Punch and Judy 2002
oil on canvas 54.5 x 76
G687

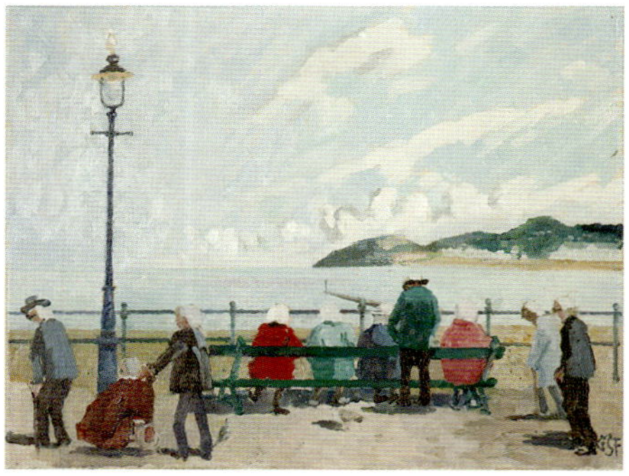

Fletcher, Geoffrey Scowcroft 1923–2004
Old Timers on Prom 2002
oil on canvas 69.5 x 105
G688

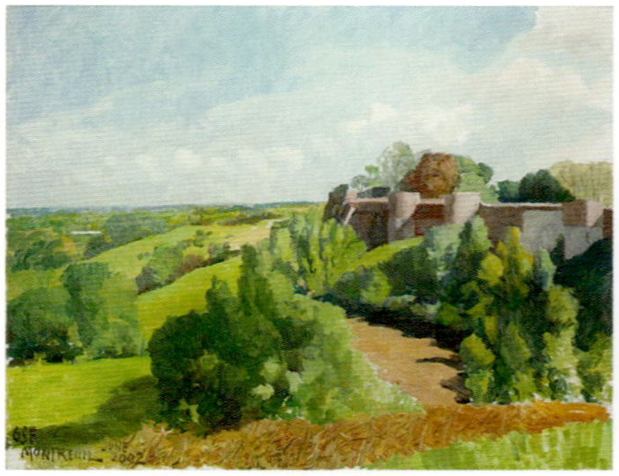

Fletcher, Geoffrey Scowcroft 1923–2004
Ramparts, Montreuil 2002
oil on canvas 69.5 x 89
G684

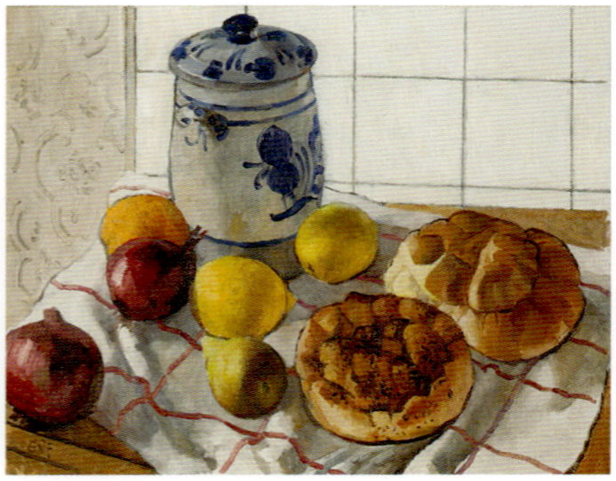

Fletcher, Geoffrey Scowcroft 1923–2004
Still Life – Bread, Fruit and Jar 2002
oil on canvas 62 x 75
G690

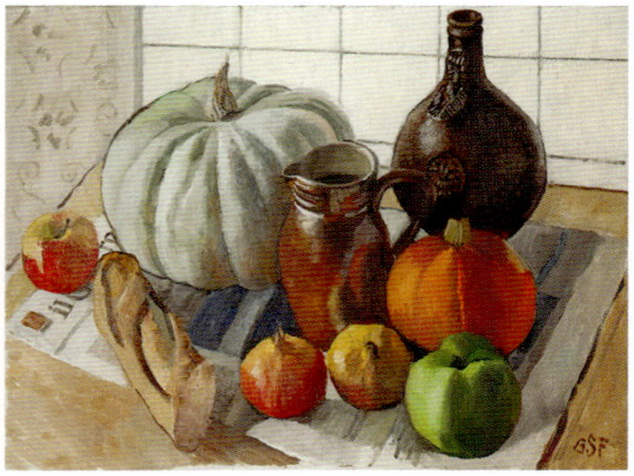

Fletcher, Geoffrey Scowcroft 1923–2004
Still Life – Fruit 2002
oil on canvas 80.5 x 126.5
G685

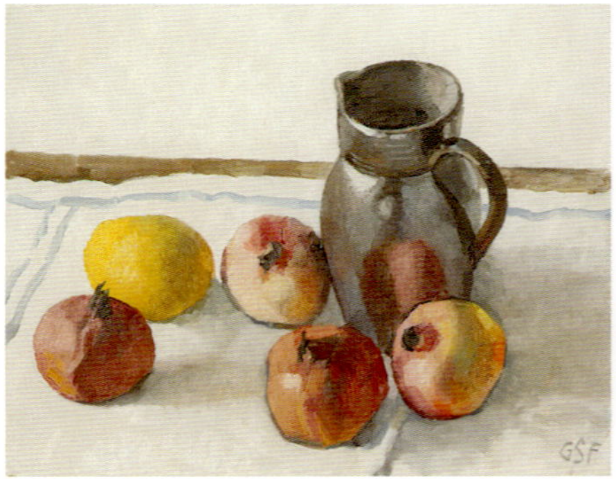

Fletcher, Geoffrey Scowcroft 1923–2004
Still Life – Fruit 2002
oil on canvas 70 x 106
G689

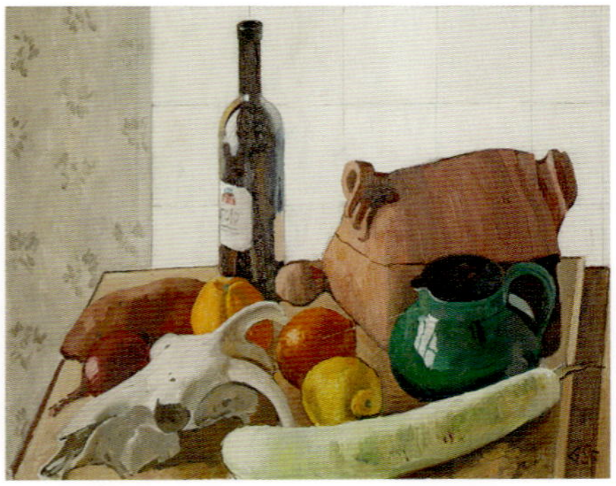

Fletcher, Geoffrey Scowcroft 1923–2004
Still Life with Sheep Skull 2002
oil on canvas 29.5 x 39
G669

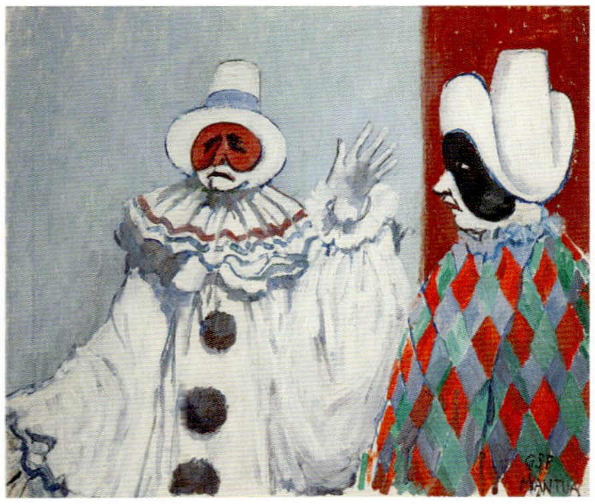

Fletcher, Geoffrey Scowcroft 1923–2004
Harlequins
oil on canvas 51 x 62
G666

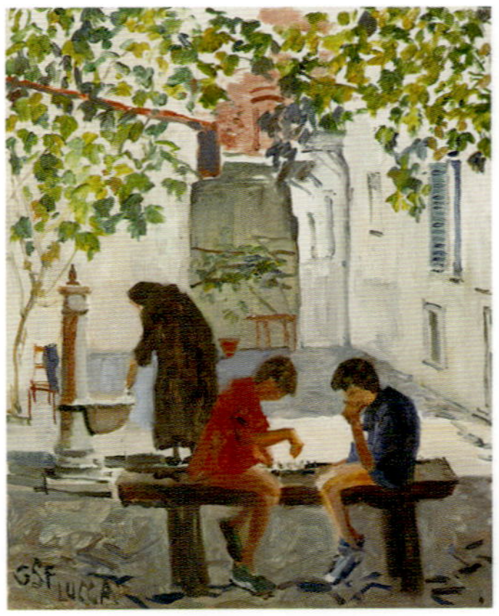

Fletcher, Geoffrey Scowcroft 1923–2004
Lucca
oil on canvas 41 x 33.5
G678

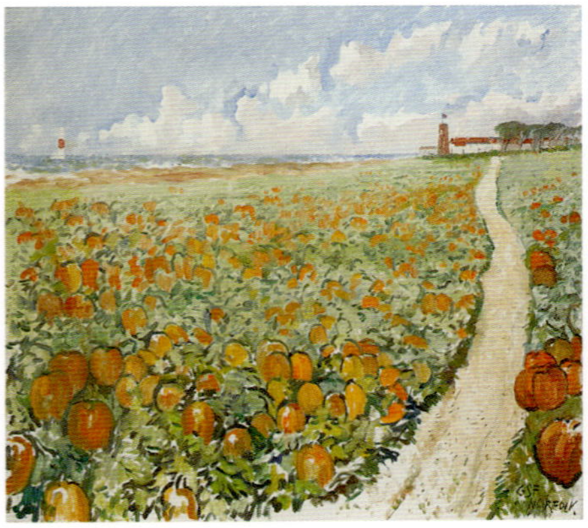

Fletcher, Geoffrey Scowcroft 1923–2004
Pumpkin Field
oil on canvas 58 x 83 (E)
G675

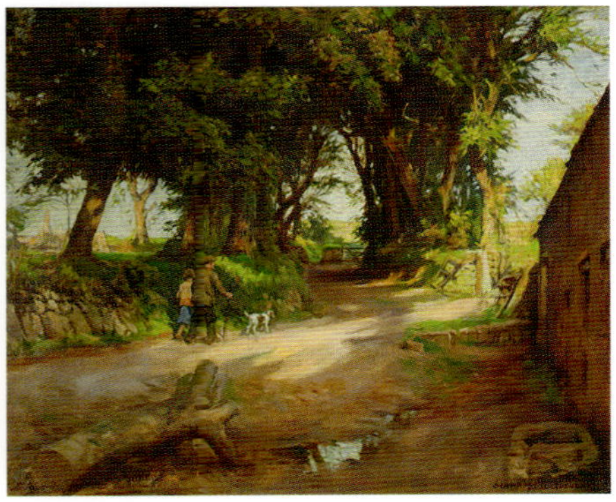

Forbes, Stanhope Alexander 1857–1947
Fading Leaf and Fallen Tree 1937
oil on canvas 60 x 74
G74

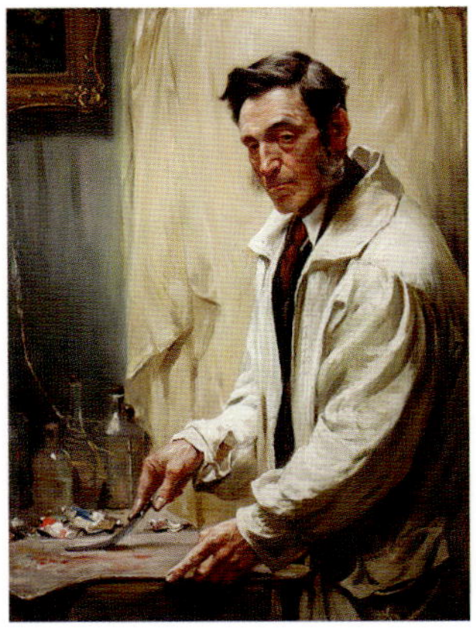

Fowler, Robert 1853–1926
Clean Palette c.1918
oil on canvas 100 x 78
G77

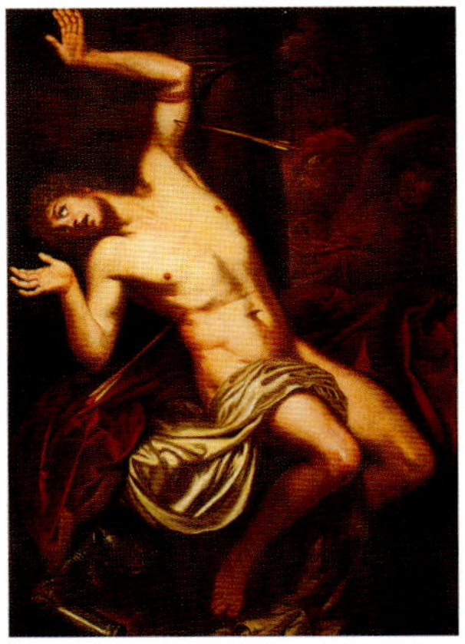

Furini, Francesco 1603–1646
The Martyrdom of Saint Sebastian
oil on canvas 184 x 125.5
G311

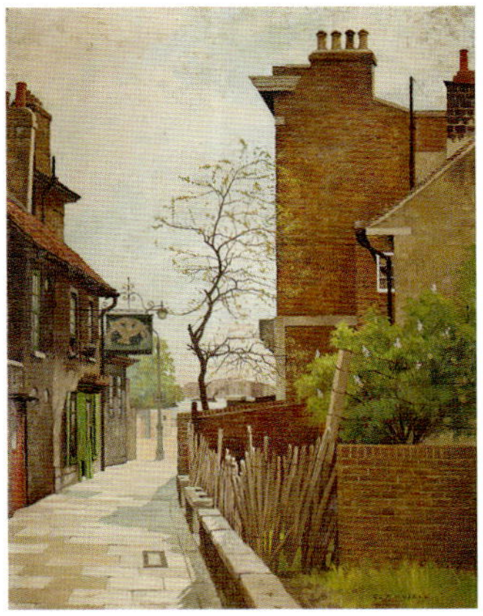

Glanville, Roy 1911–1965
The Little Tree
oil on board 98 x 76
G304

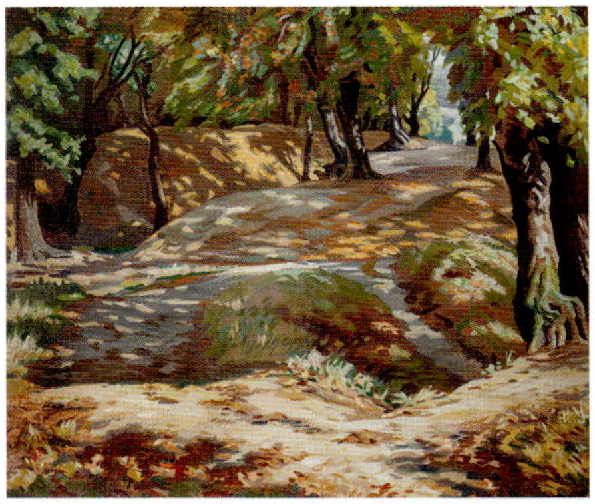

Glasbury, F. H.
Sunshine and Shadow in Epping Forest
oil on canvas 62 x 75
G78

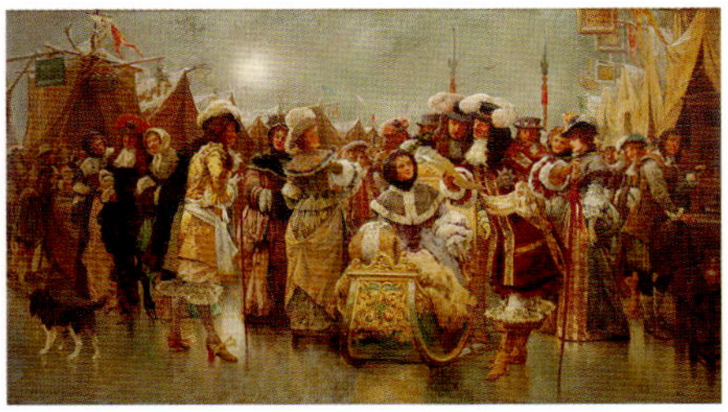

Glindoni, Henry Gillard 1852–1913
Frost Fair, 1684 1900
oil on canvas 99 x 176
G79

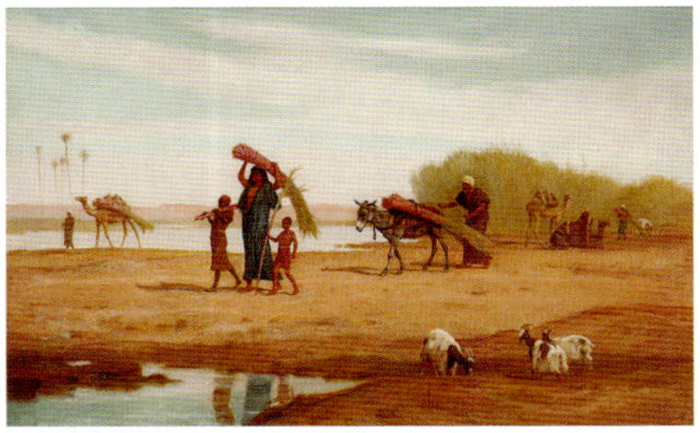

Goodall, Frederick 1822–1904
Getting in the Sugar Cane, River Nile c.1875
oil on canvas 80.5 x 126.5
G80

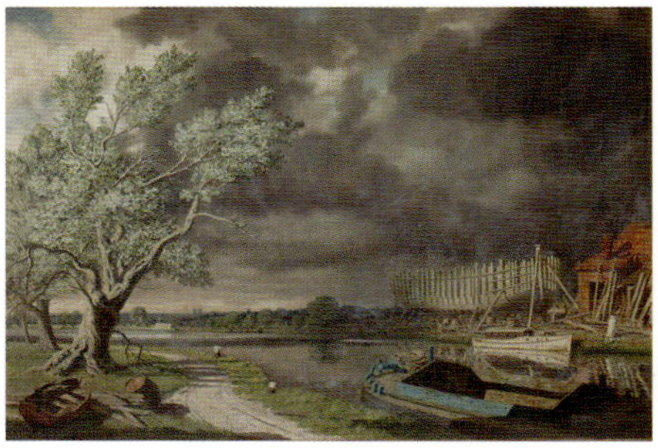

Goodin, Walter 1907–1992
The River Beverley 1938
oil on board 81 x 101
G81

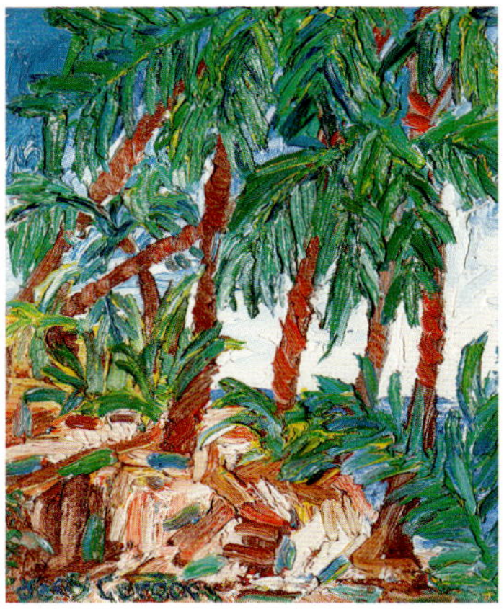

Gordon, Jerry b.1955
Batista Beach, Trinidad, 1996 c.2000
acrylic on canvas 65 x 54
G652

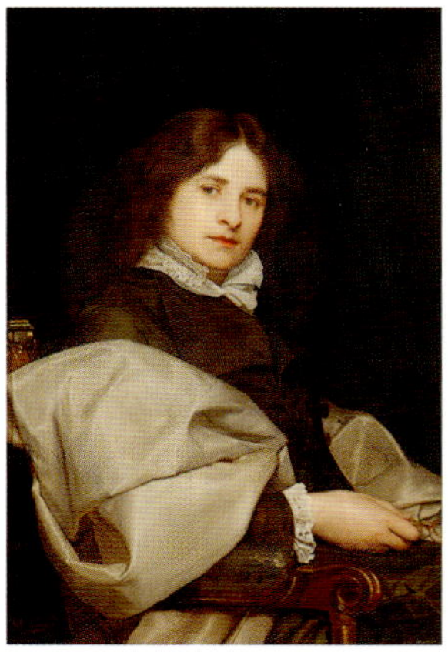

Goupil, Jules Adolphe 1839–1883
Portrait of a Lady c.1880
oil on canvas 83 x 58
G82

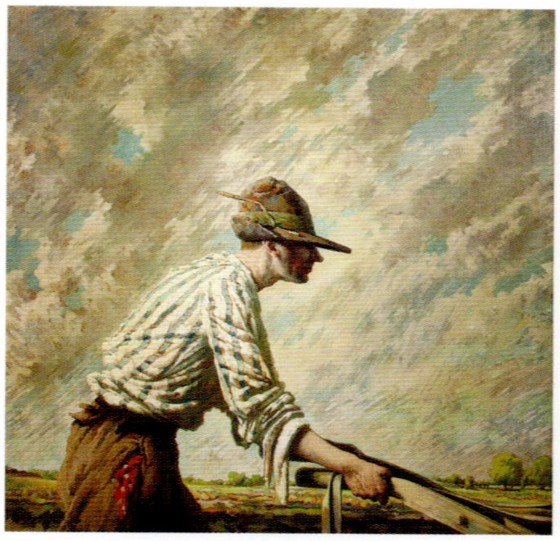

Greenwood, Orlando 1892–1989
The Ploughman 1922
oil on canvas 125.5 x 125.5
G84

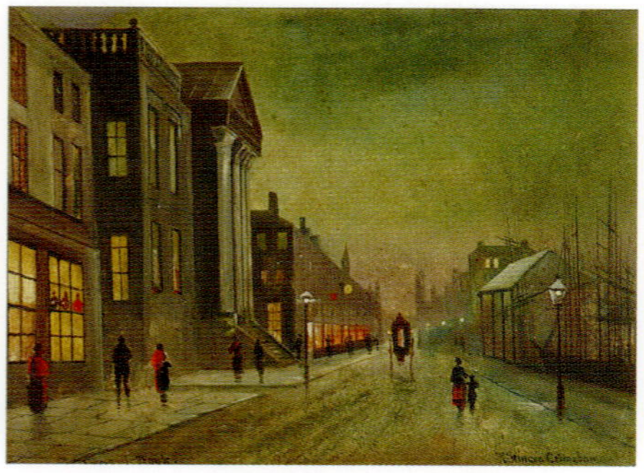

Grimshaw, John Atkinson (attributed to) 1836–1893
Liverpool Docks (panel 1 of 5)
oil on panel 22.5 x 28
G325

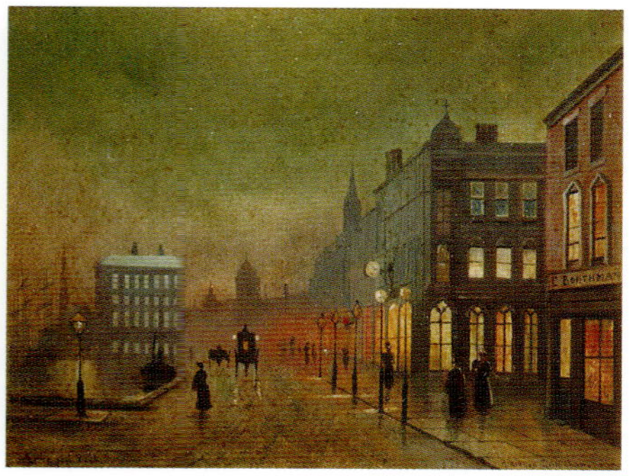

Grimshaw, John Atkinson (attributed to) 1836–1893
Liverpool Docks (panel 2 of 5)
oil on panel 21.5 x 29
G325

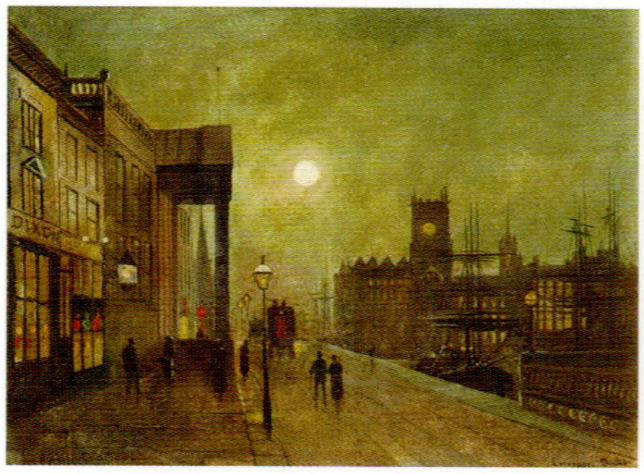

Grimshaw, John Atkinson (attributed to) 1836–1893
Liverpool Docks (panel 3 of 5)
oil on panel 21.5 x 29
G325

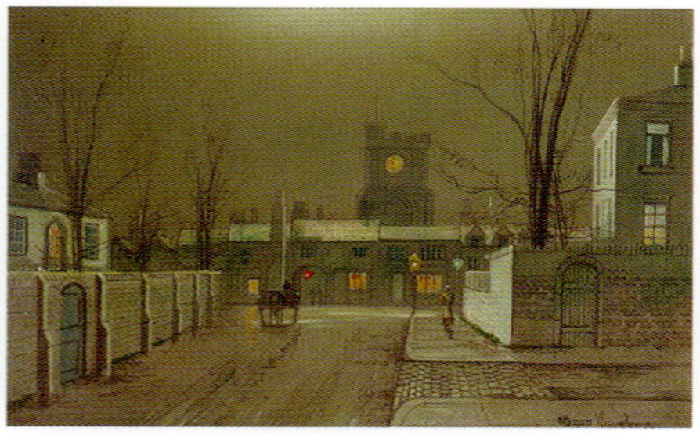

Grimshaw, John Atkinson (attributed to) 1836–1893
Liverpool Docks (panel 4 of 5)
oil on panel 21.5 x 29
G325

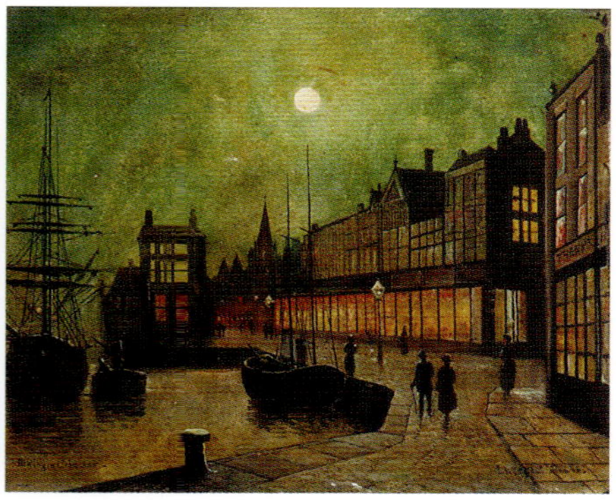

Grimshaw, John Atkinson (attributed to) 1836–1893
Liverpool Docks (panel 5 of 5)
oil on panel 22 x 37
G325

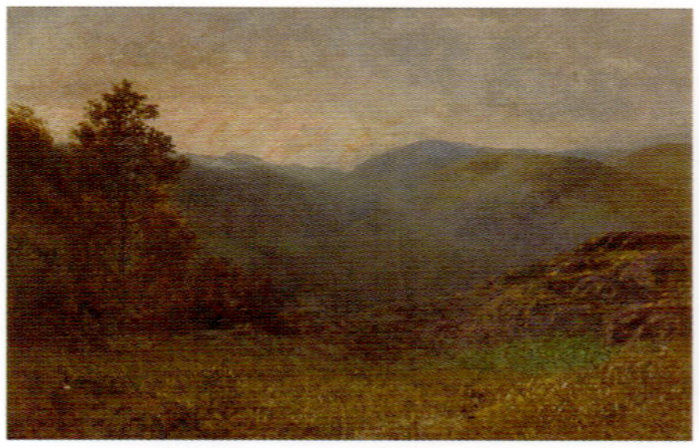

Grundy, Cuthbert Cartwright 1846–1946
Dawn 1900
oil on canvas 69.5 x 105
G85

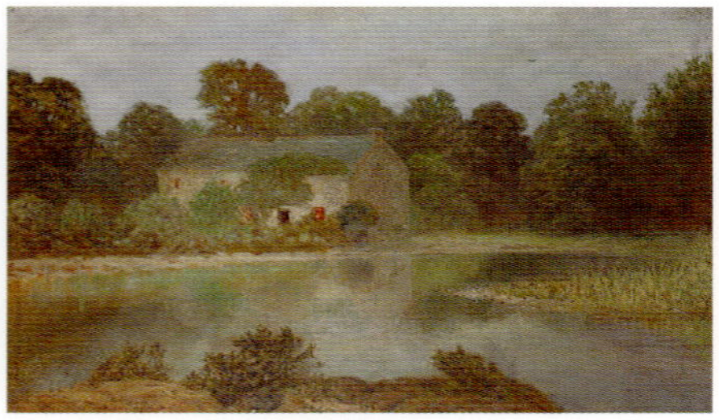

Grundy, Cuthbert Cartwright 1846–1946
The Old Millhouse, Milnthorpe c.1900
oil on canvas 70 x 106
G86

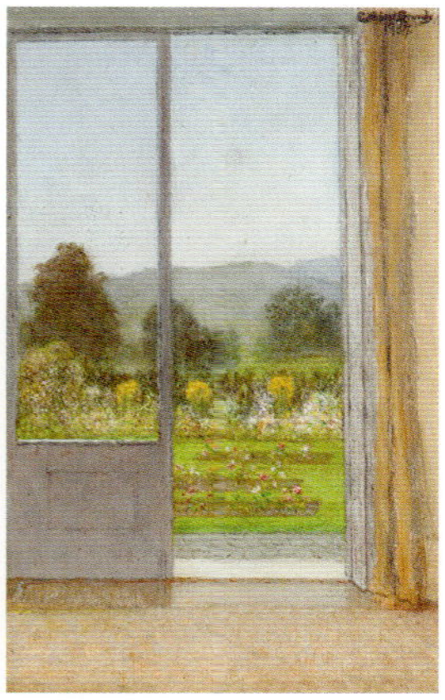

Grundy, Cuthbert Cartwright 1846–1946
View from My Window 1937
oil on board 28 x 19
G434

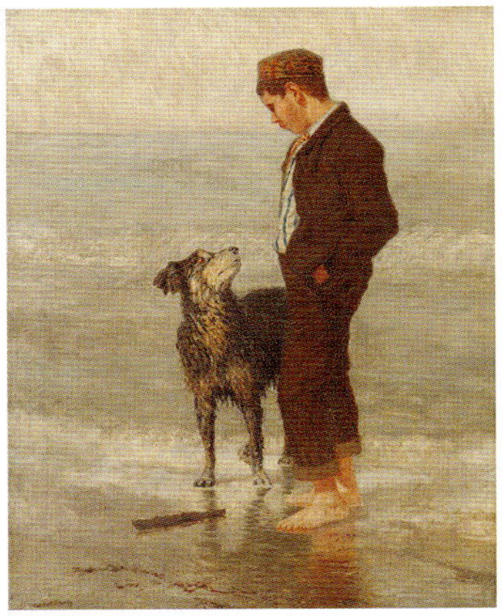

Grundy, Cuthbert Cartwright 1846–1946
Throw It Again (Companions)
oil on canvas 90.5 x 70
G410

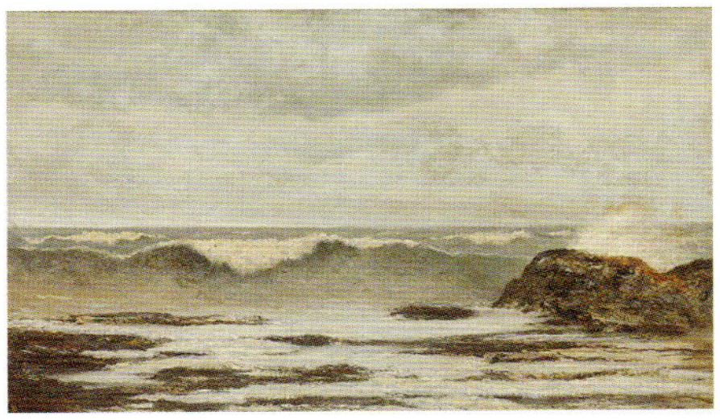

Grundy, John Relph Greenhow 1841–1915
Breakers c.1890
oil on canvas 80 x 135
G87

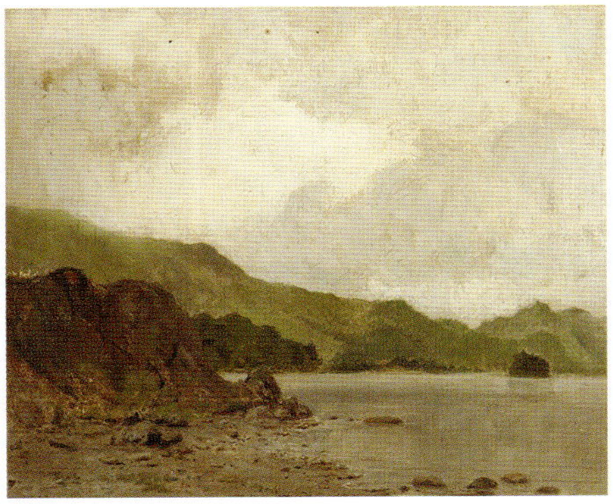

Grundy, John Relph Greenhow 1841–1915
Derwentwater c.1890
oil on canvas 29.5 x 39
G88

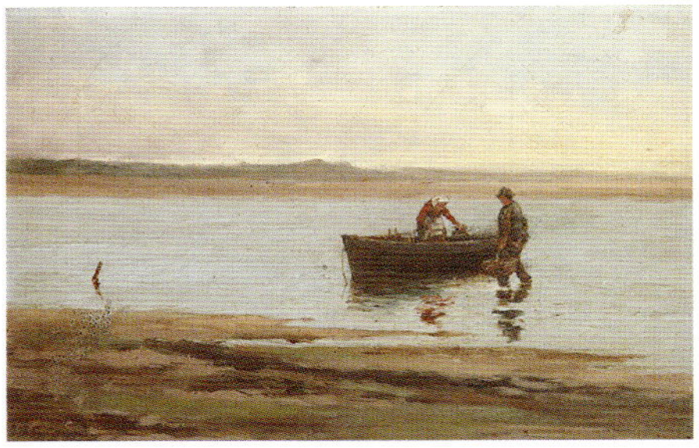

Grundy, John Relph Greenhow 1841–1915
Coastal Scene with Figures
oil on panel 15.4 x 24.1
G435

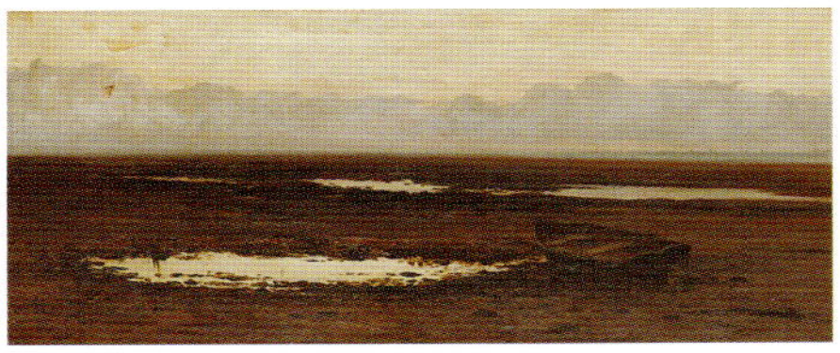

Grundy, John Relph Greenhow 1841–1915
Twilight – Morecambe Bay
oil on canvas 43.5 x 92
G274

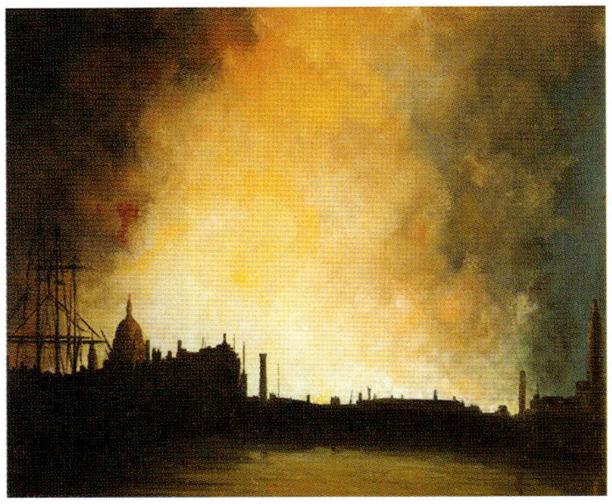

Haines, Wilfred Stanley 1905–1944
Seventh September 1940 1940
oil on board 41 x 55.5
G89

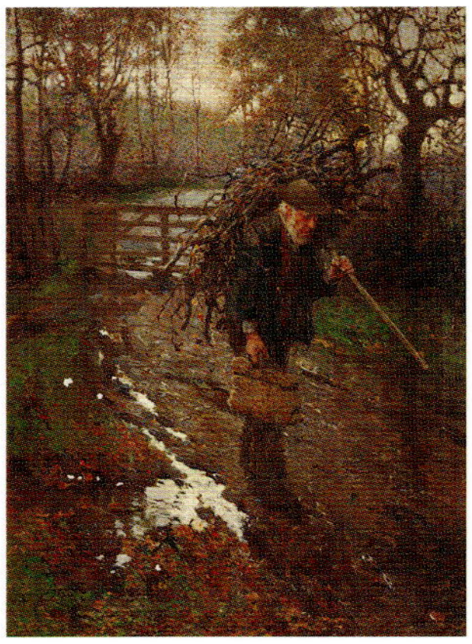

Hall, Frederick 1860–1948
Homeward 1913
oil on canvas 89 x 69.5
G90

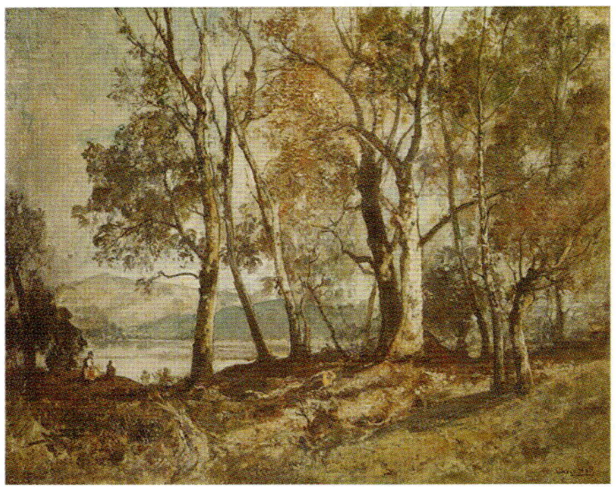

Hall, Oliver 1869–1957
Forest Trees 1942
oil on canvas 54.5 x 76
G91

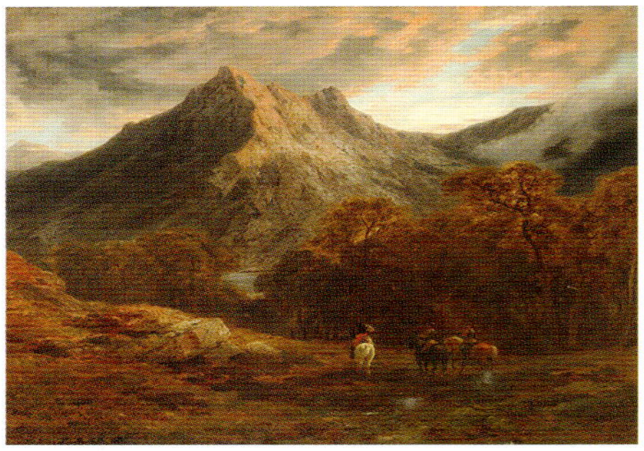

Hargitt, Edward 1835–1895
Marauders c.1860
oil on canvas 61 x 75
G93

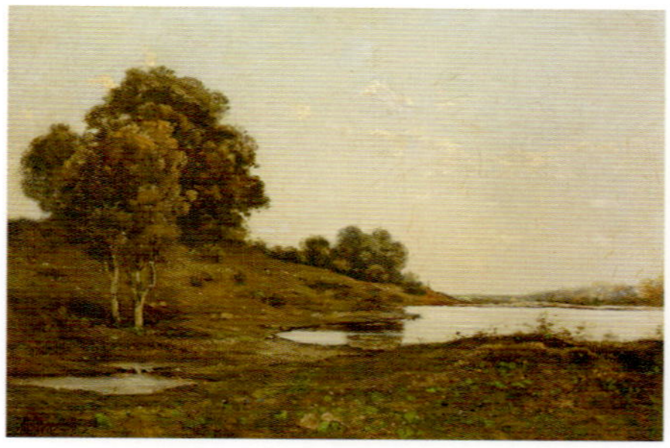

Harpignies, Henri-Joseph 1819–1916
Rural Landscape 1873
oil on canvas 38.5 x 55
G623

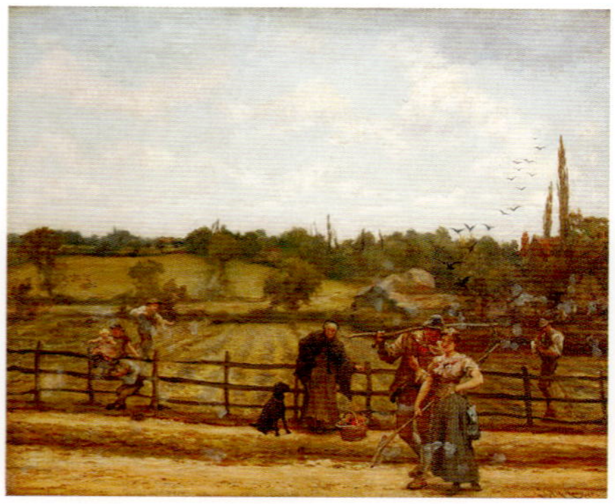

Herkomer, Hubert von 1849–1914
Haymaking and Lovemaking
oil on canvas 71 x 92
G99

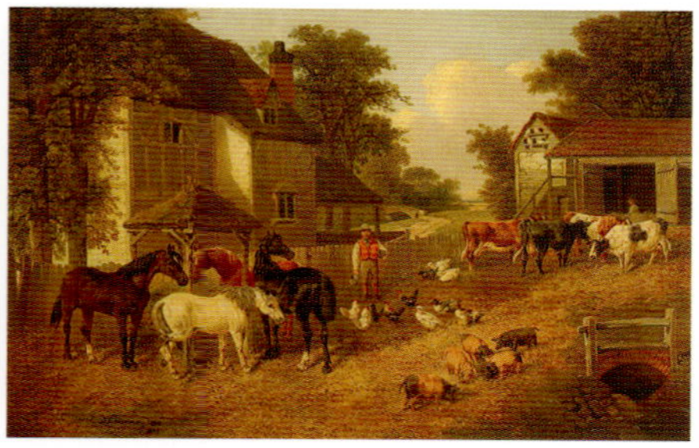

Herring II, John Frederick 1815–1907
Summer 1845
oil on canvas 56 x 82
G100

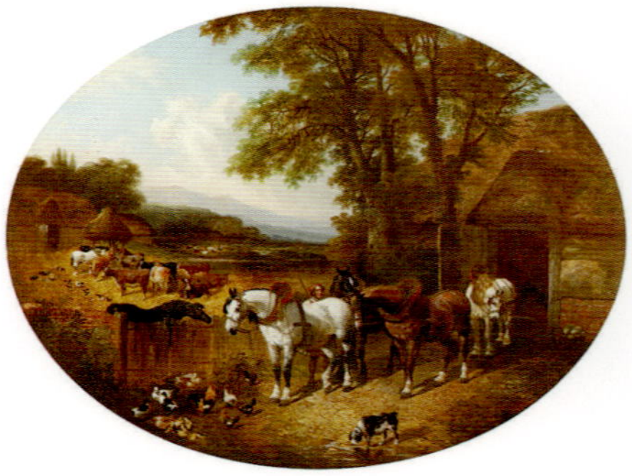

Herring II, John Frederick 1815–1907
Landscape with Horses 1857
oil on canvas 80 x 105
G285

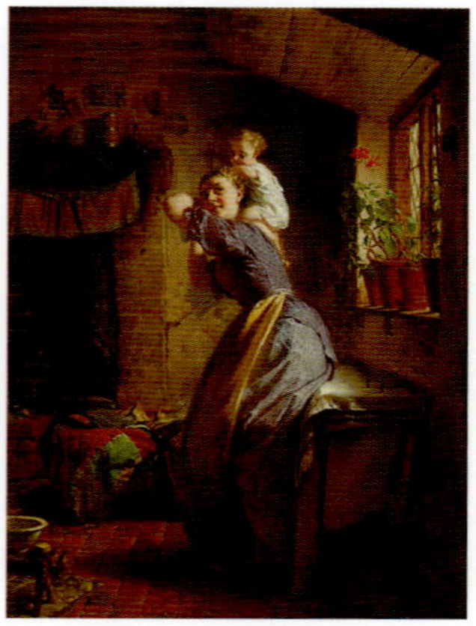

Hicks, George Elgar 1824–1914
The Happy Mother 1866
oil on canvas 90.5 x 75
G102

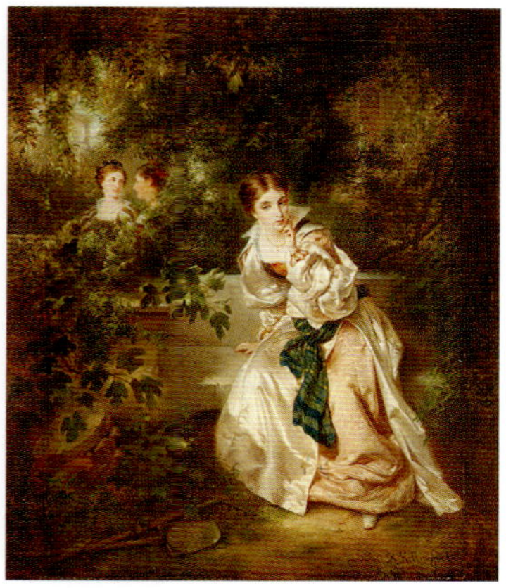

Hillingford, Robert Alexander 1825–1904
Much Ado About Nothing
oil on board 57 x 50.5
G263

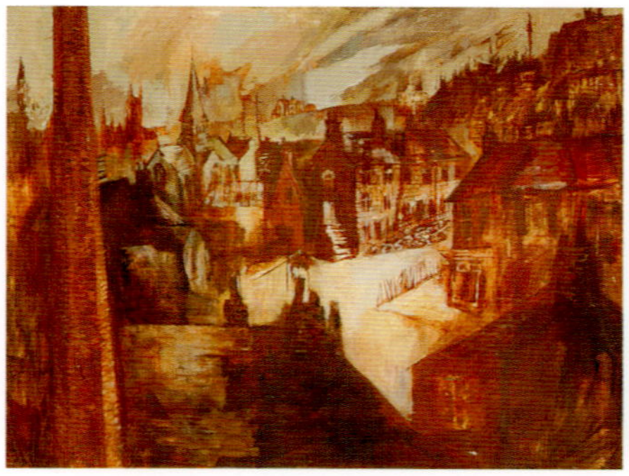

Hipkins, W. M.
Victoriana
oil on canvas 70 x 90
G397

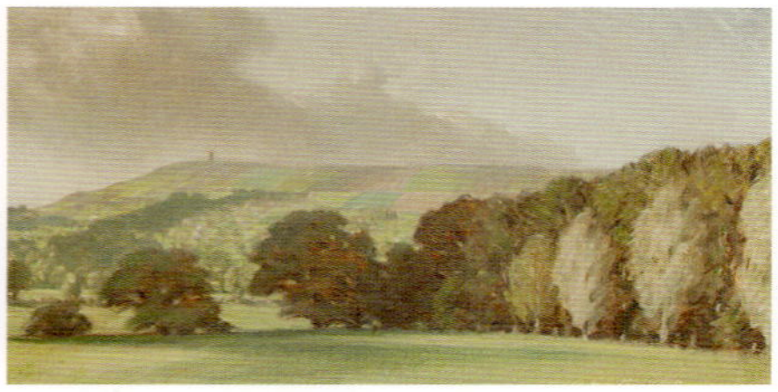

Holmes, Charles John 1868–1936
Penrith Beacon
oil on canvas 44.5 x 80
G250

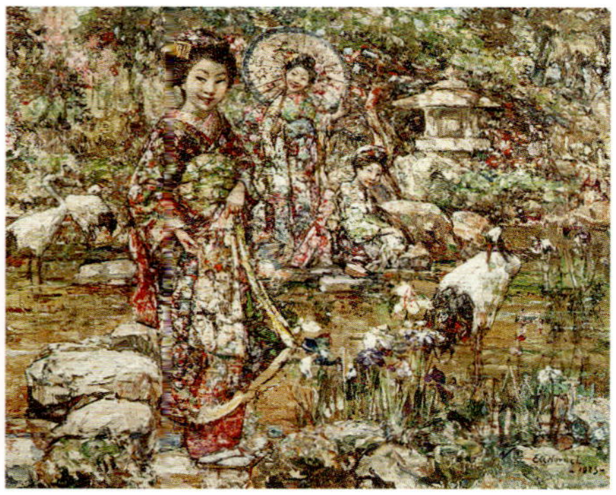

Hornel, Edward Atkinson 1864–1933
The Iris Pool c.1920
oil on canvas 64 x 76.5
G104

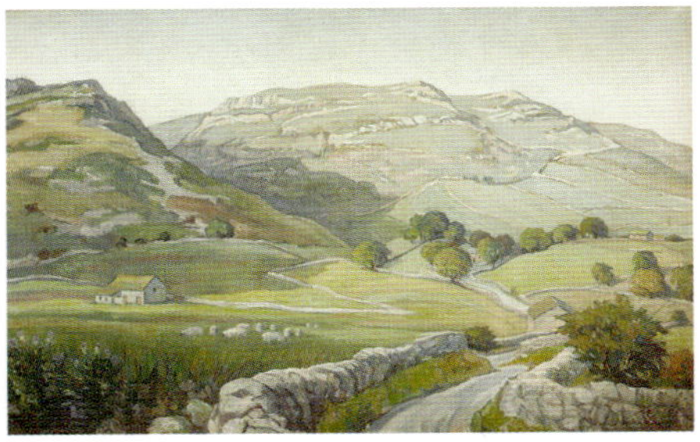

Horsnell, Walter Cecil 1911–1997
Gordale Scar c.1940
oil on board 52.5 x 74
G105

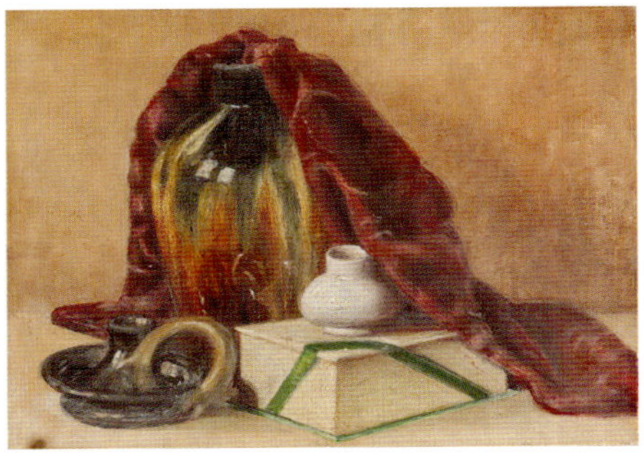

Hossack, G.
Still Life
oil on canvas 25.5 x 35.5
G278

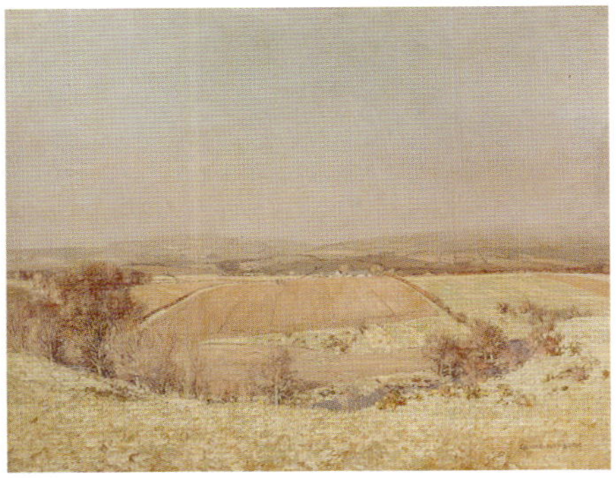

Houston, George 1869–1947
April in Ayrshire c.1905
oil on canvas 71 x 90.5
G106

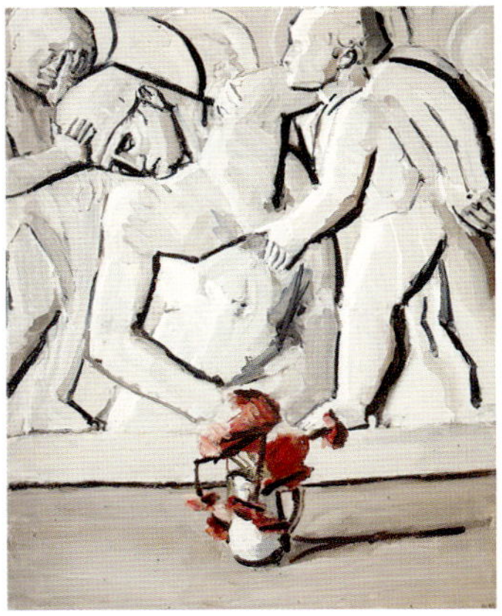

Hoyland, Francis b.1930
Requiem 1988
oil on canvas 93.5 x 71
G615

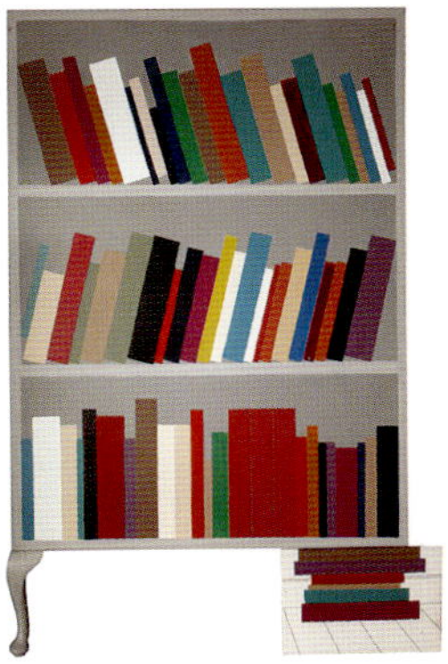

Hughes, Patrick b.1939
Learning
acrylic on canvas 151 x 91.5
G626

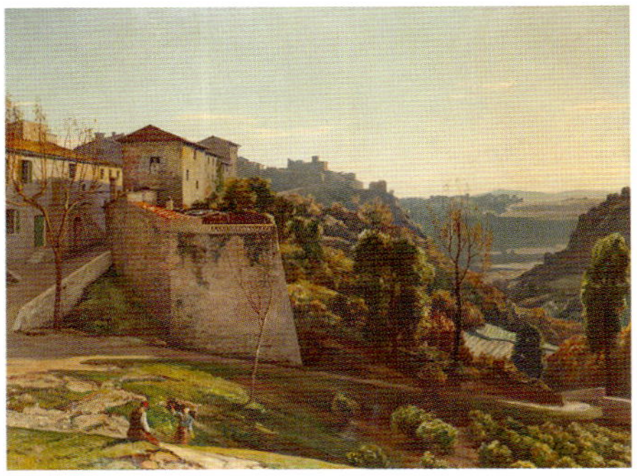

Hughes-Stanton, Herbert Edwin Pelham 1870–1937
Cagnes 1930
oil on canvas 93.5 x 107
G178

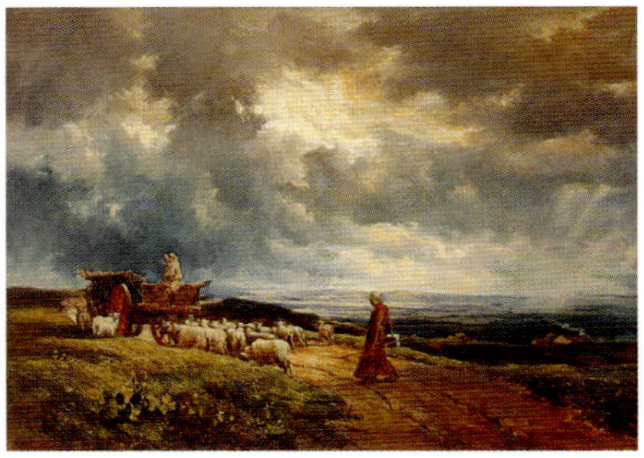

Hughes-Stanton, Herbert Edwin Pelham 1870–1937
Struggling Light
oil on canvas 87 x 106.5
G308

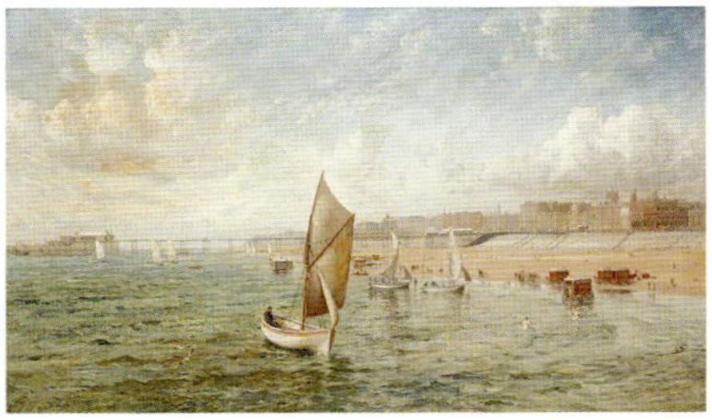

Huson, Thomas 1844–1920
View of North Pier, Blackpool, from the South West c.1900
oil on canvas 76.5 x 126.5
G619

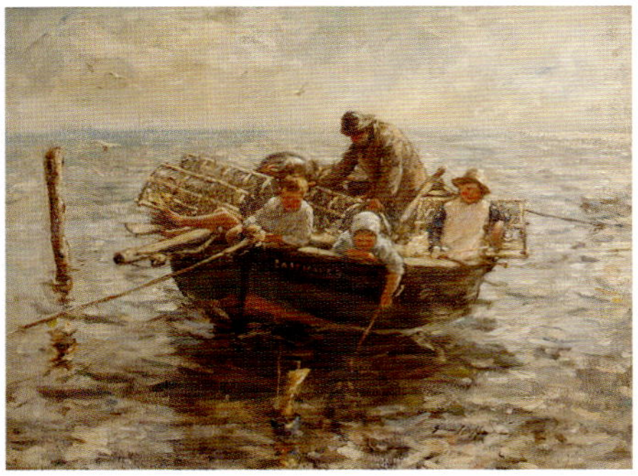

Hutchinson, Robert Gemmell 1855–1936
Skipper and His Crew c.1915
oil on canvas 69.5 x 90
G109

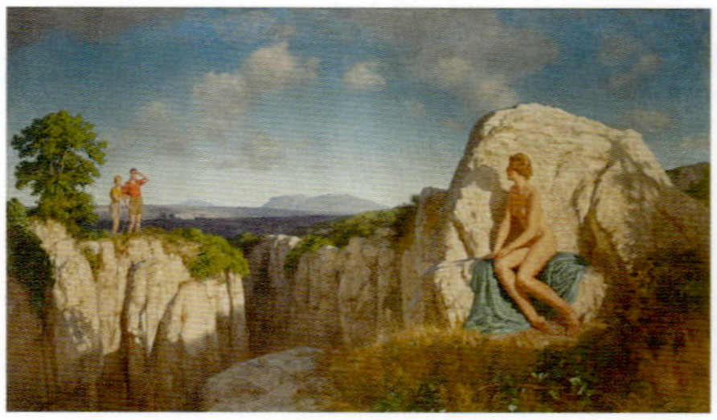

Hutton, Walter Charles Stritch b.1871
They See an Oread
oil on canvas 110 x 202.5
G108

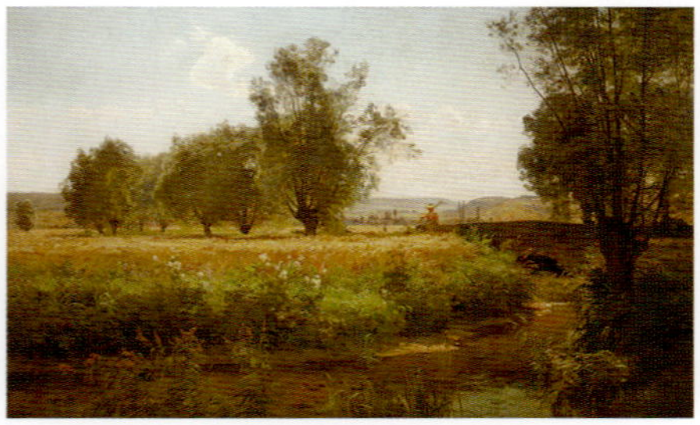

Isenbart, Marie Victor Émile 1846–1921
L'été c.1880
oil on canvas 121 x 191
G110

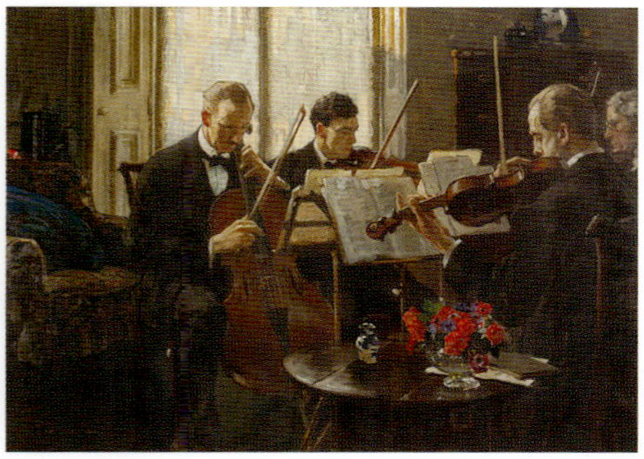

Jack, Richard 1866–1952
The Quartette 1910
oil on canvas 129 x 182
G111

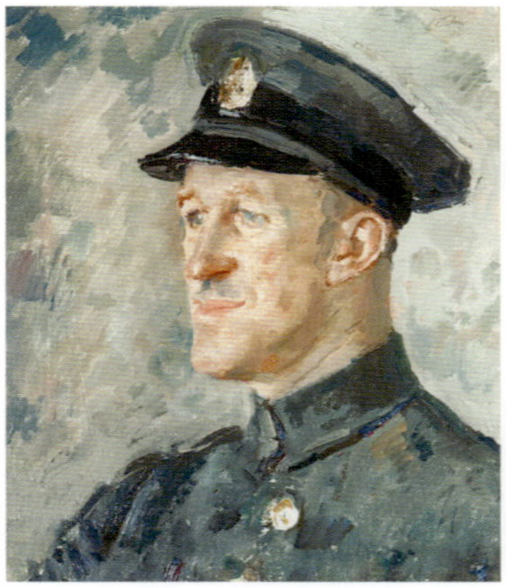

John, Augustus Edwin 1878–1961
Air Mechanic Shaw (Colonel T. E. Lawrence of Arabia, 1888–1935) 1935
oil on canvas 50 x 39
G112

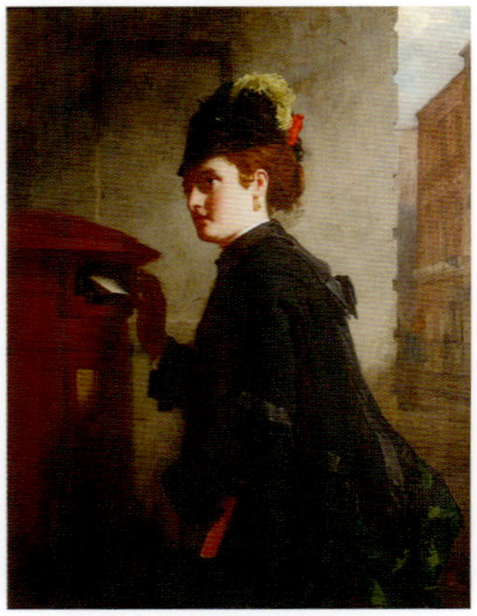

Johnston, Alexander 1815–1891
The Pillar Box 1876
oil on canvas 108 x 84
G133

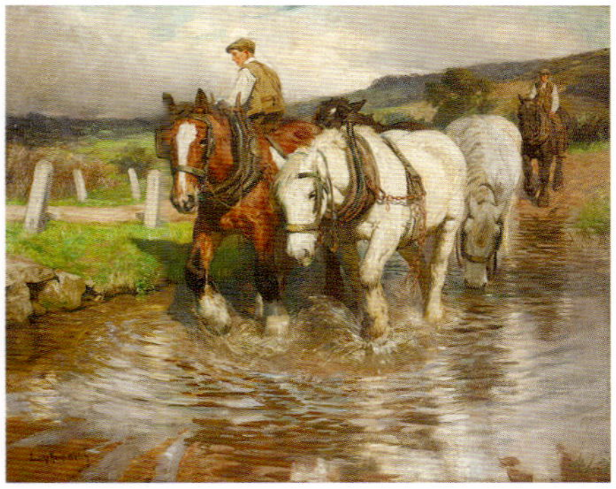

Kemp-Welch, Lucy 1869–1958
The Waterway c.1914
oil on canvas 181 x 228.5
G197

King, Margaret b.1932
Beach Scene, St Annes 1978
oil on canvas 50 x 70.5
G447

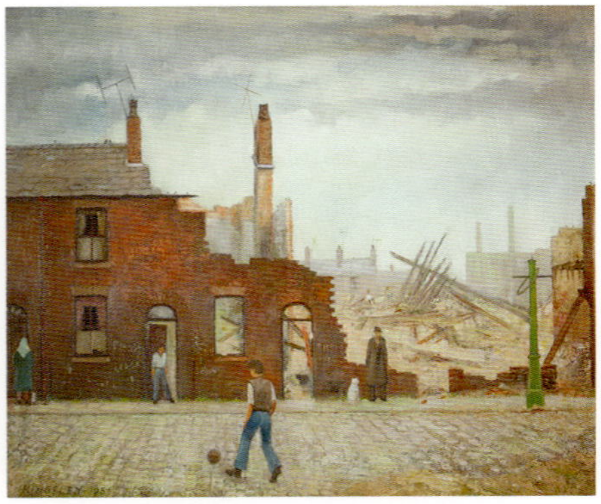

Kingsley, Harry 1914–1998
Beswick, Manchester 1957
oil on board 49 x 59.5
G516

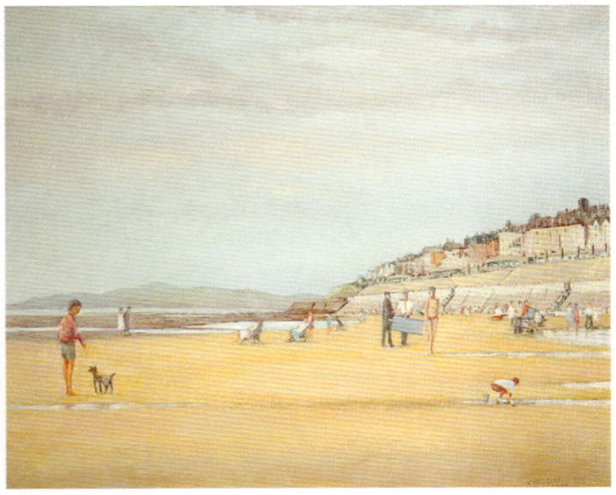

Kingsley, Harry 1914–1998
Blackpool Weekend 1959
oil on board 38 x 47
G487

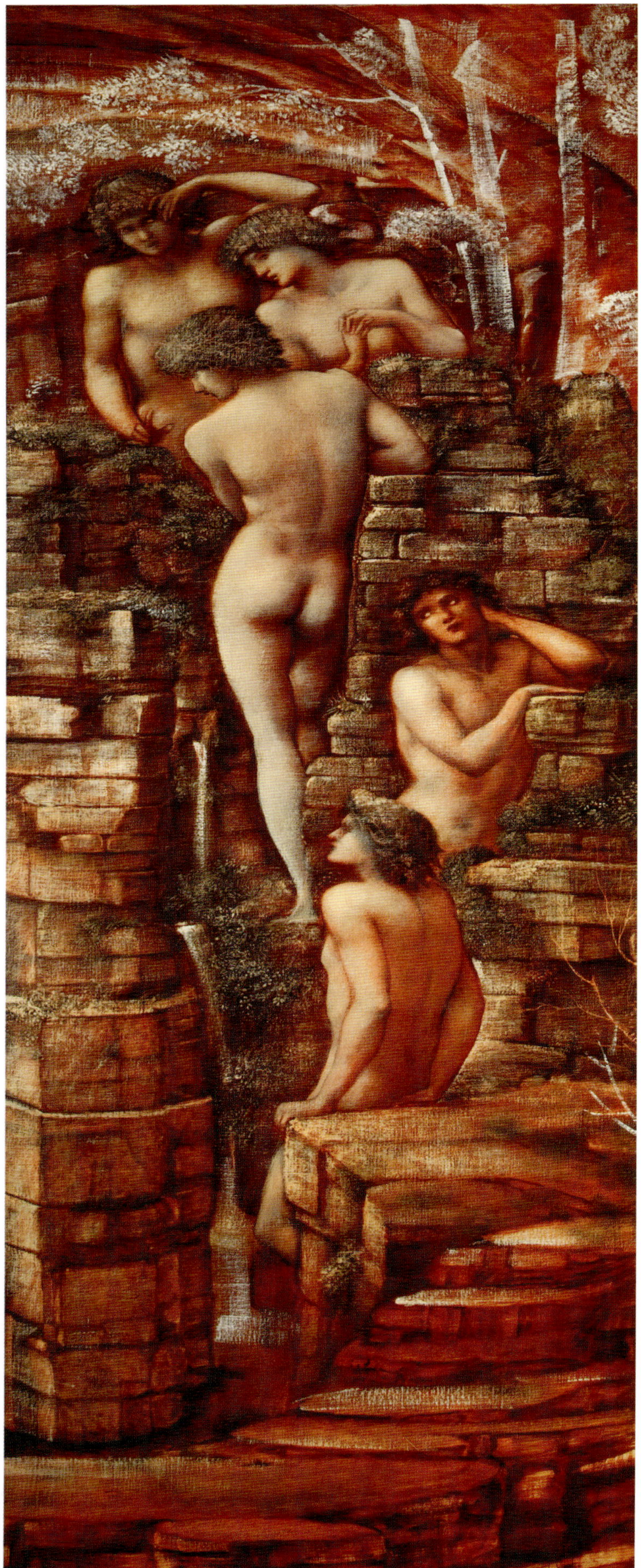

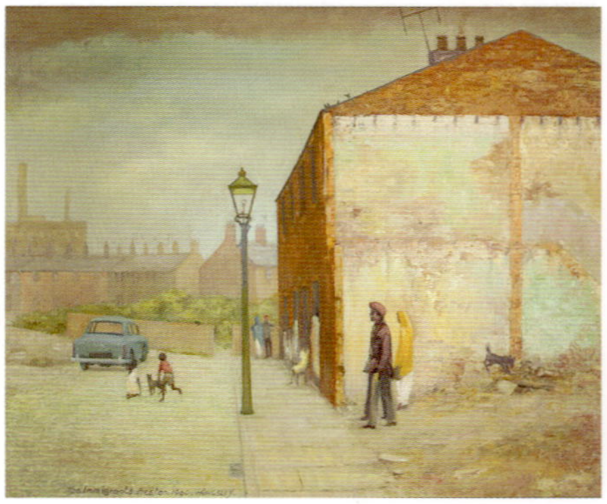

Kingsley, Harry 1914–1998
The Immigrants, Preston, 1960 1960
oil on board 45 x 55
G399

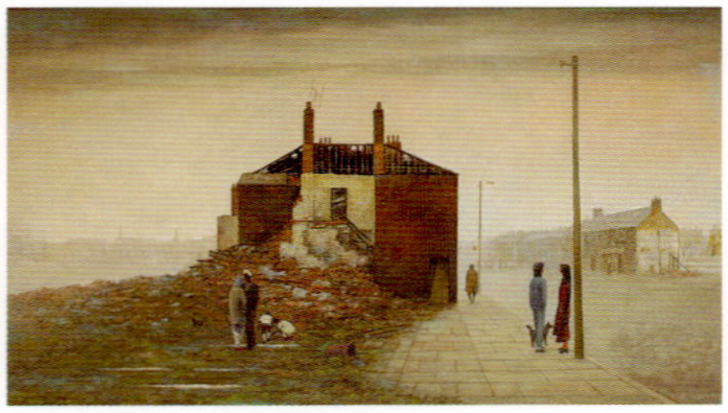

Kingsley, Harry 1914–1998
Christmas Day, Manchester, 1971 1971
oil on board 75 x 120
G398

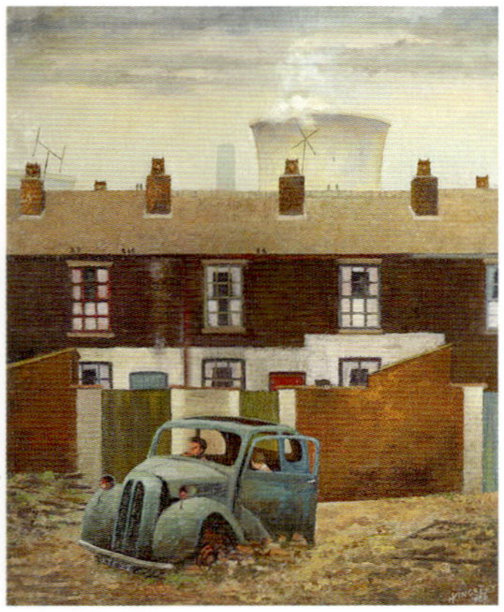

Kingsley, Harry 1914–1998
Playmates, Bradford
oil on board 61 x 50
G403

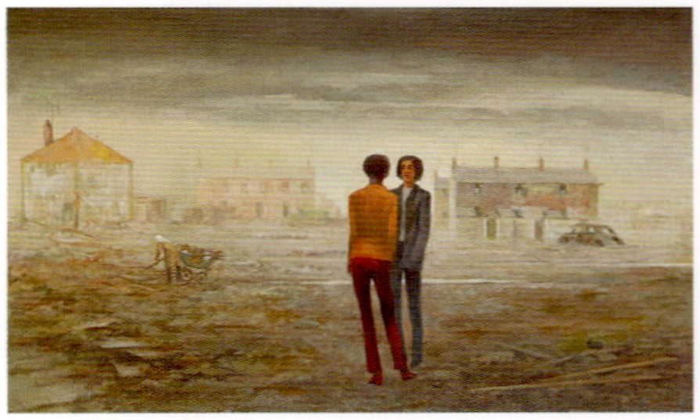

Kingsley, Harry 1914–1998
The Meeting
oil on board 49 x 74
G404

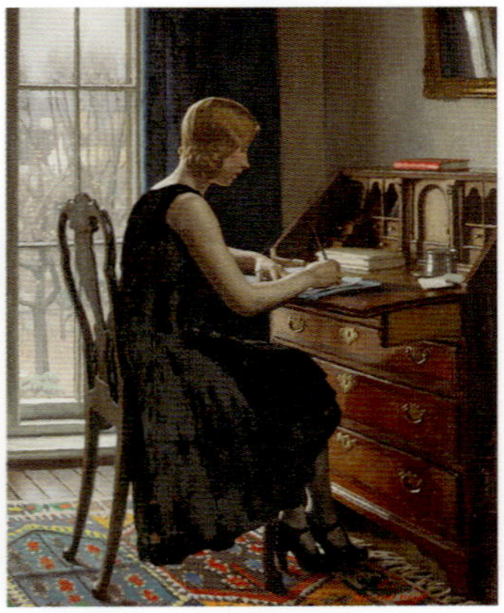

Knight, Harold 1874–1961
Girl Writing 1931
oil on canvas 52 x 42
G117

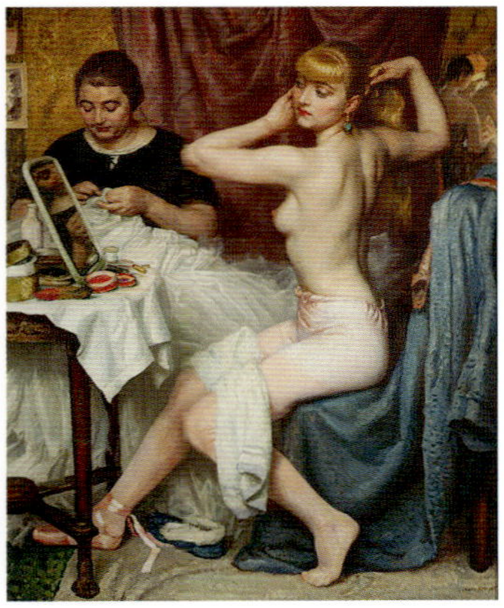

Knight, Laura 1877–1970
No.1 Dressing Room 1947
oil on canvas 151 x 126
G116

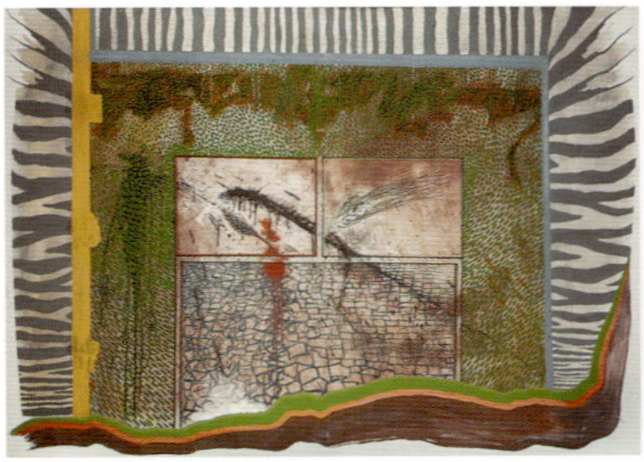

Kowalski, Nicholas b.1956
Modern Civilisation 1976
acrylic on canvas 168 x 228.5
G518

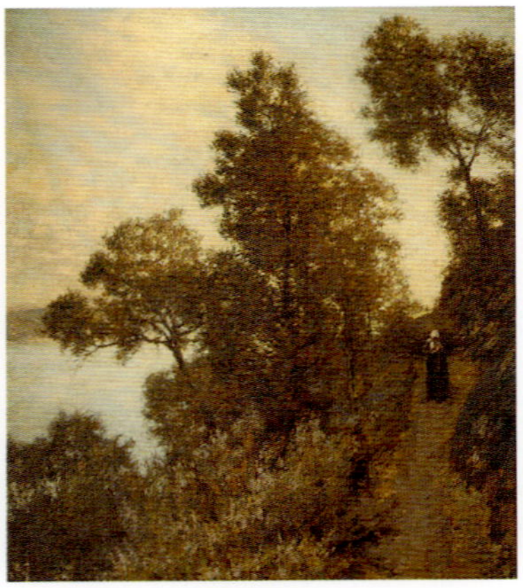

La Thangue, Henry Herbert 1859–1929
Ligurian Bridle Path c.1920
oil on canvas 90 x 81
G122

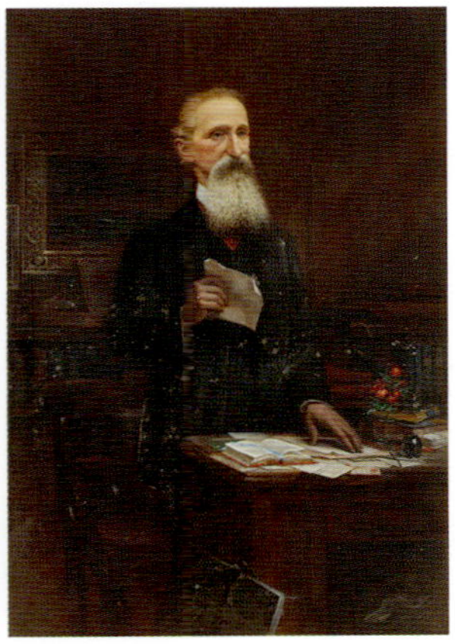

Lacok
Samuel Lawson Booth
oil on canvas
G33/214

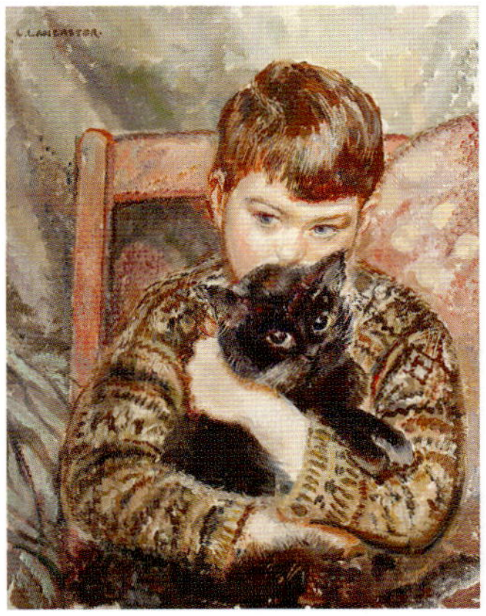

Lancaster, Lilian Gardiner 1887–1973
The Boy and the Cat 1933
oil on canvas 57 x 46.5
G120

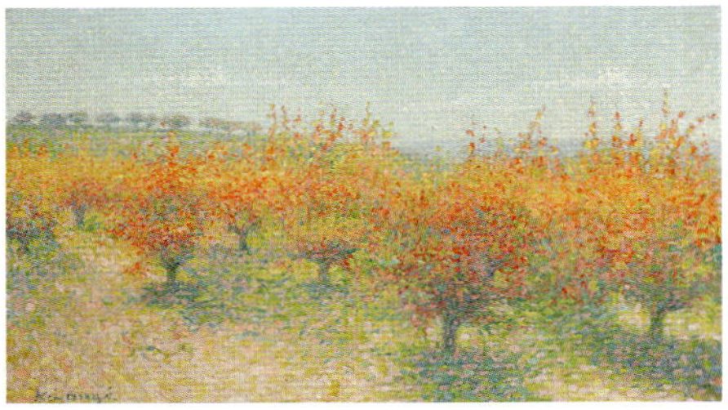

Laugé, Achille 1861–1944
Vignes en automne
oil on canvas 43.5 x 72
G621

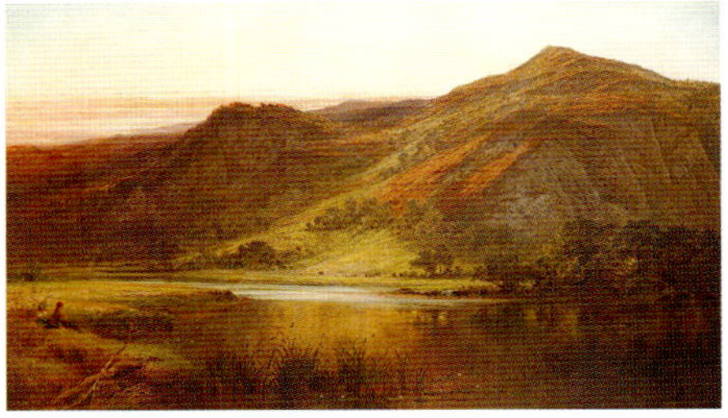

Leader, Benjamin Williams 1831–1923
A Summer Evening, Derwentwater 1869–1910
oil on canvas 89.5 x 151
G123

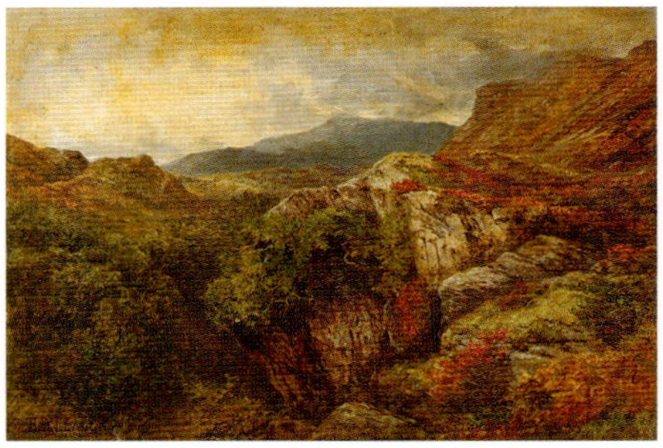

Leader, Benjamin Williams 1831–1923
View near Llanberis, North Wales c.1915
oil on canvas 47.5 x 67.5
G124

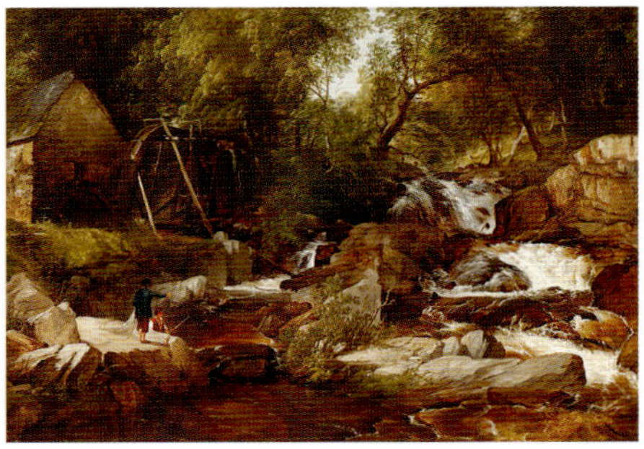

Lee, Frederick Richard 1798–1879
A Highland Stream
oil on canvas 10.5 x 14.1
G126

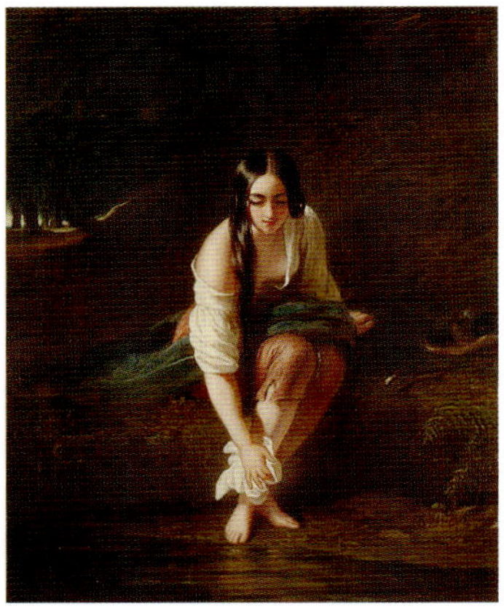

Leslie, Charles Robert 1794–1859
At the Pool 1840
oil on canvas 32 x 25.5
G127

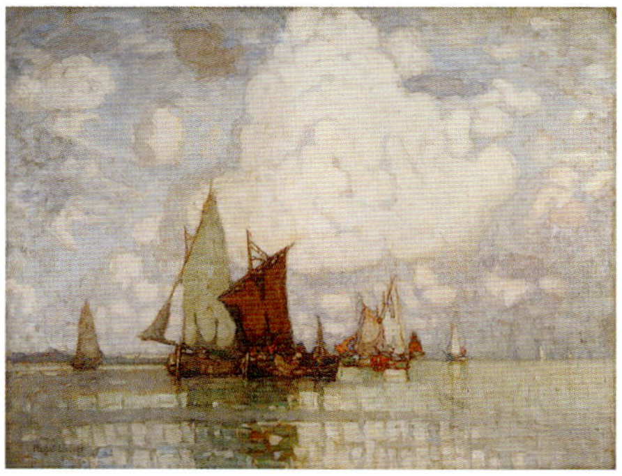

Lindner, Moffat Peter 1852–1949
A Storm Cloud, Etaples c.1900
oil on canvas 77 x 102
G128

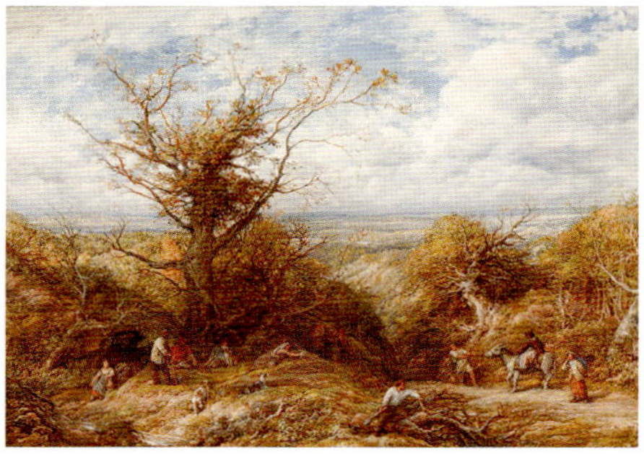

Linnell, John 1792–1882
Woods and Forests c.1875
oil on canvas 102 x 144
G292

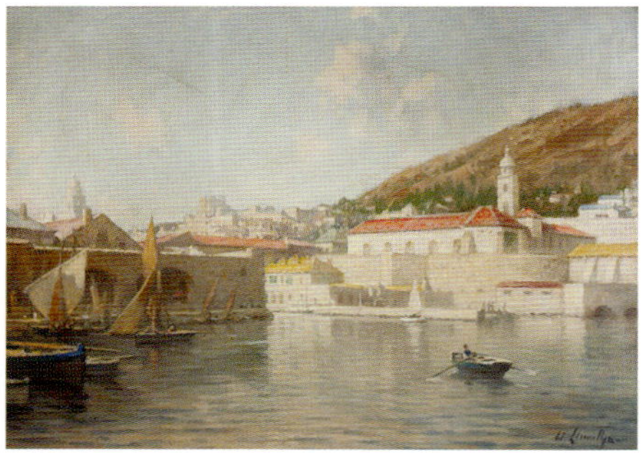

Llewellyn, Samuel Henry William 1858–1941
Dubrovnik (Ragusa) Harbour 1938
oil on canvas 67.5 x 86
G129

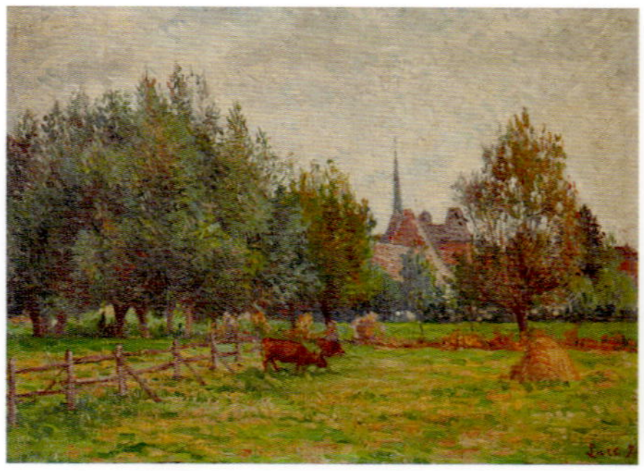

Luce, Maximilien 1858–1941
Prairie à Eragny 1895
oil on canvas 35 x 47.5
G624

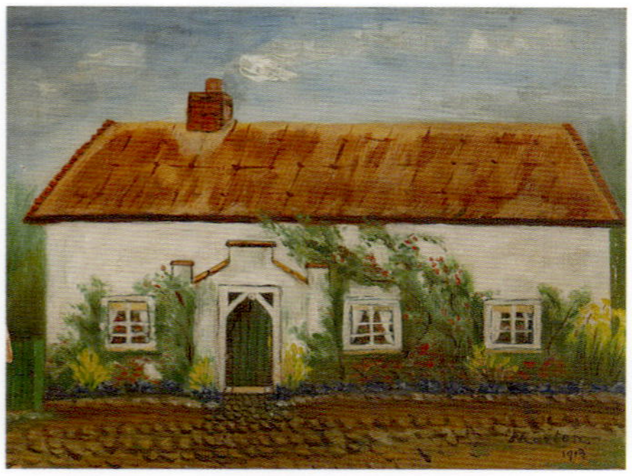

Lumb, Levi active 1913–1942
Cottage at Marton 1913
oil on board 22 x 28
G221 M104

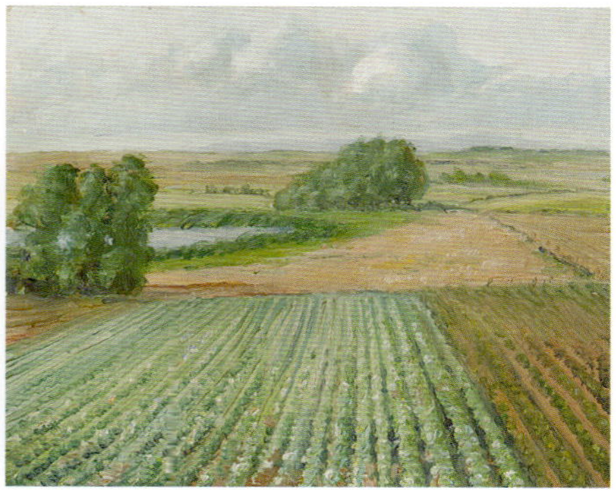

Lumb, Levi active 1913–1942
Marton Mere 1942
oil on panel 21 x 27
G441

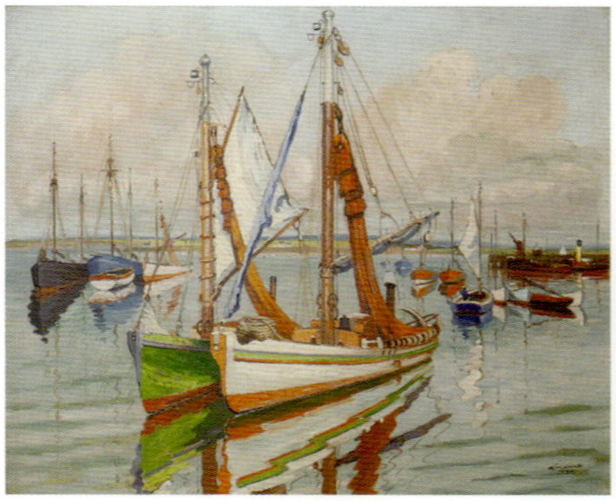

Lumb, Levi active 1913–1942
Fishing Boats
oil on canvas 61 x 74
G368

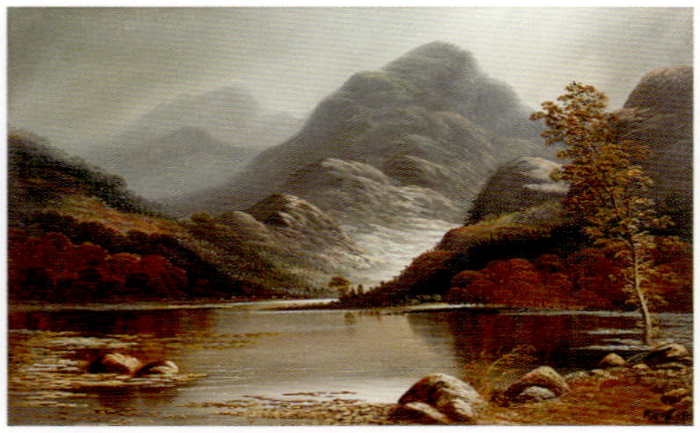

Marshall, George 1815–1860
Lakeland Scene
oil on canvas 60 x 90.5
G507

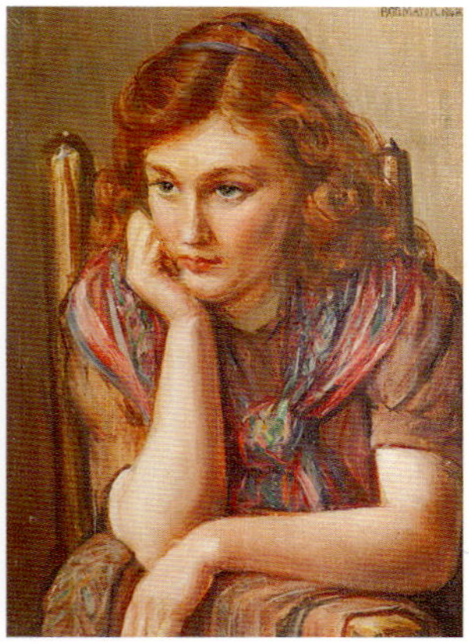

Mayor, Patti 1872–1962
Pienso 1944
oil on board 45 x 35.5
G453

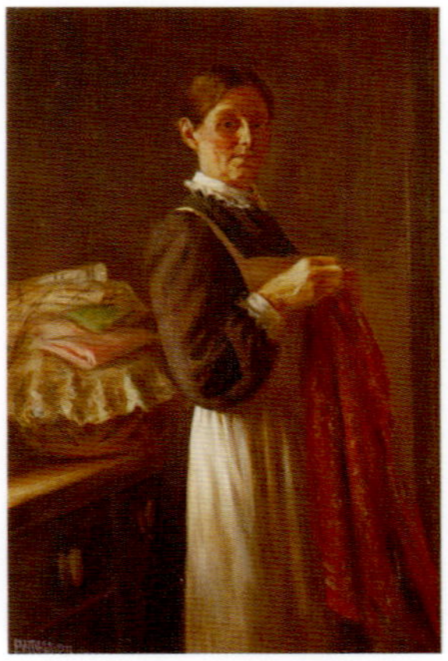

Mayor, Patti 1872–1962
Aunt Sally
oil on canvas 75 x 50
G722

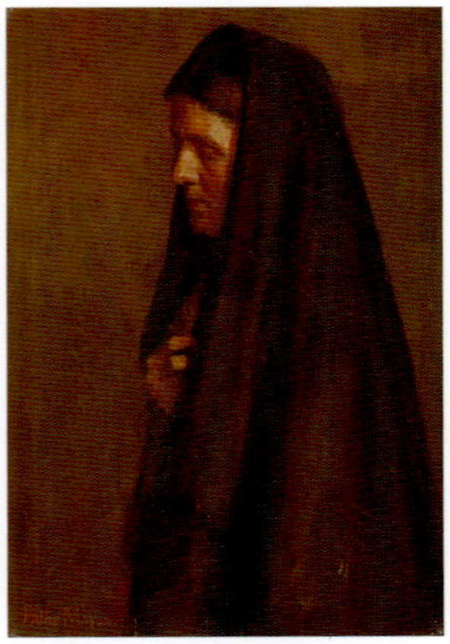

Mayor, Patti 1872–1962
Black Shawl
oil on canvas 61.5 x 45
G337

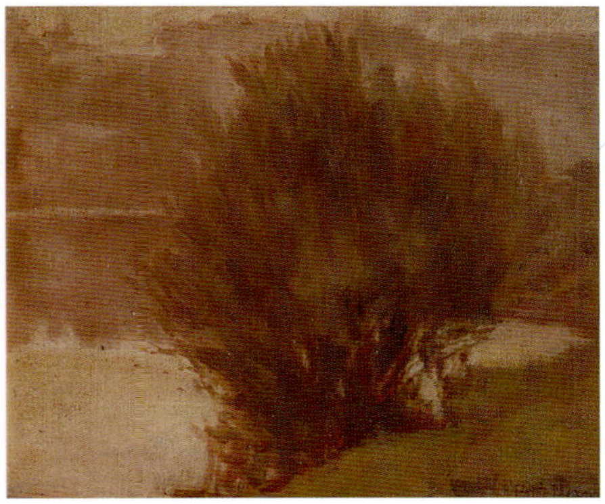

Mayor, Patti 1872–1962
Bush by a River
oil on canvas 25.5 x 35
G719

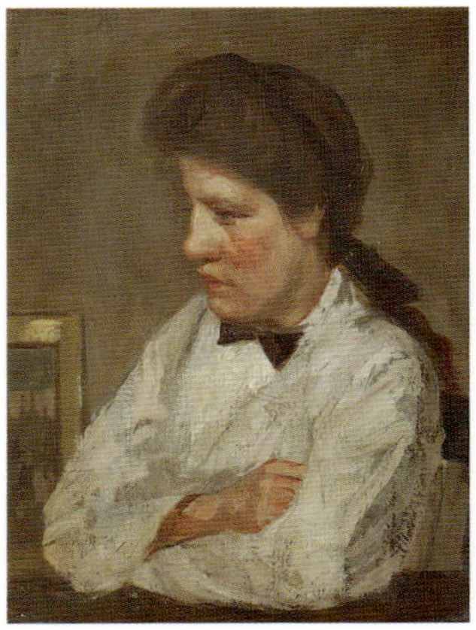

Mayor, Patti 1872–1962
Florrie in a White Blouse
oil on canvas 50 x 39
G718

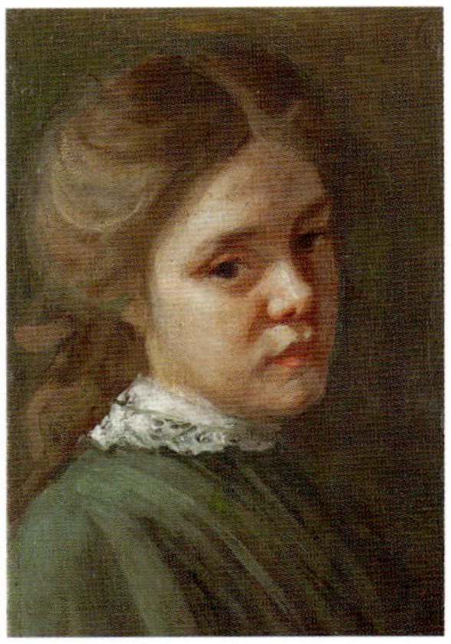

Mayor, Patti 1872–1962
Girl in a Green Dress
oil on canvas 34 x 26.5
G721

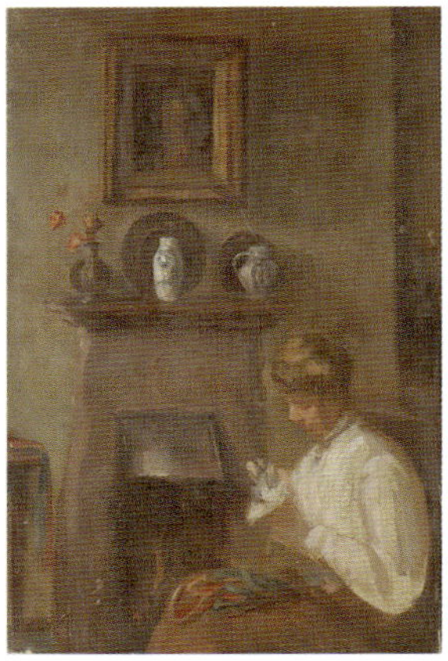

Mayor, Patti 1872–1962
Girl Sewing by a Fireside
oil on board 47 x 21.5
G546

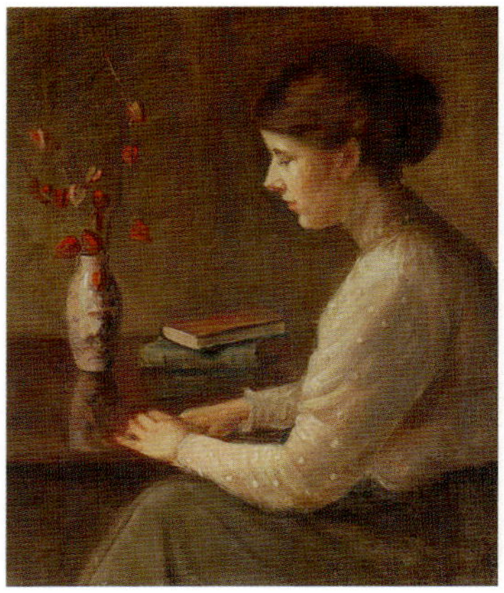

Mayor, Patti 1872–1962
Girl Thinking
oil on board 45 x 39.5
G452

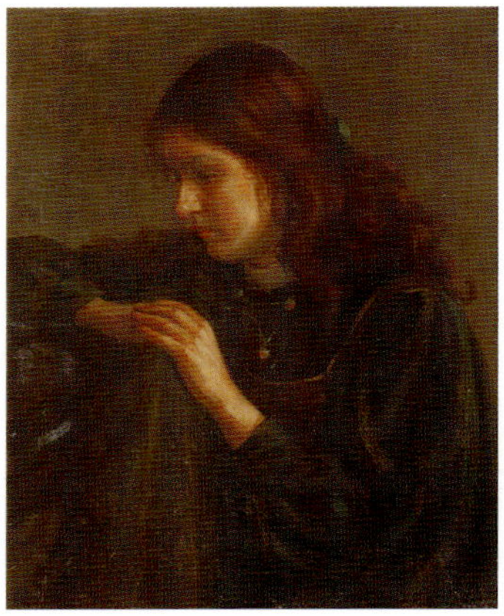

Mayor, Patti 1872–1962
Girl Thinking
oil on canvas 61.5 x 50
G723

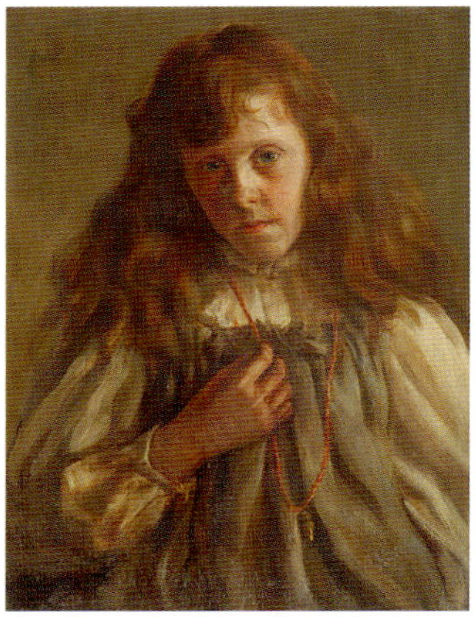

Mayor, Patti 1872–1962
Girl with a Necklace
oil on canvas 47 x 36
G548

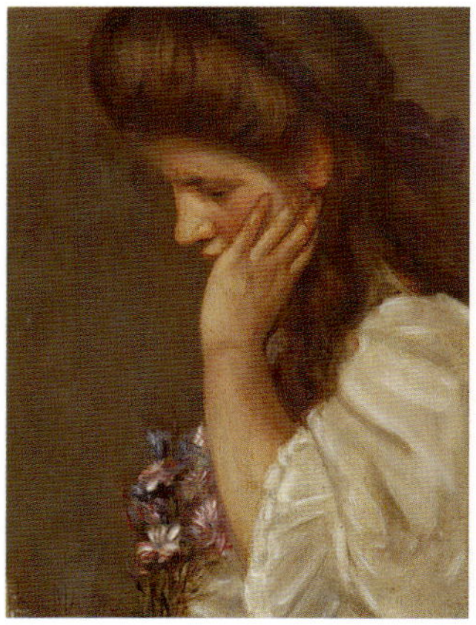

Mayor, Patti 1872–1962
Girl with a Posy
oil on canvas 44.5 x 34
G563

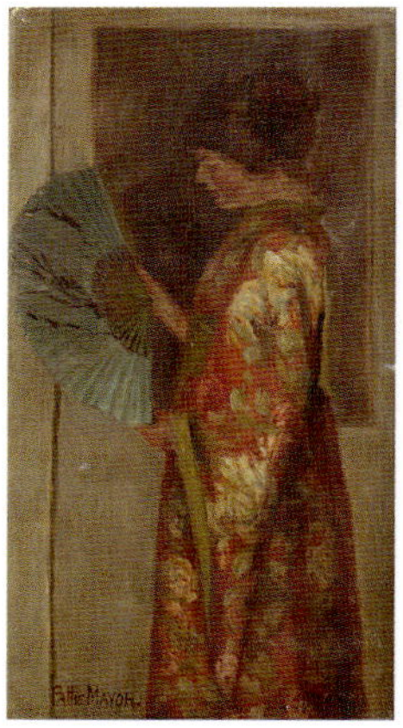

Mayor, Patti 1872–1962
Japanese Lady with a Fan
oil on board 31 x 15
G547

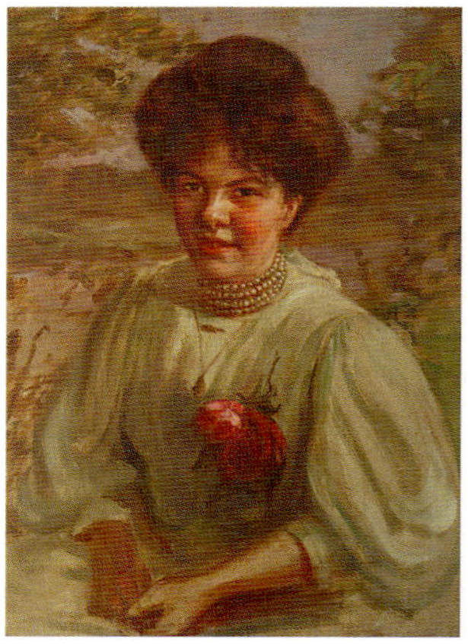

Mayor, Patti 1872–1962
Miss Kitty Ferguson
oil on canvas 76.5 x 53.5
G567

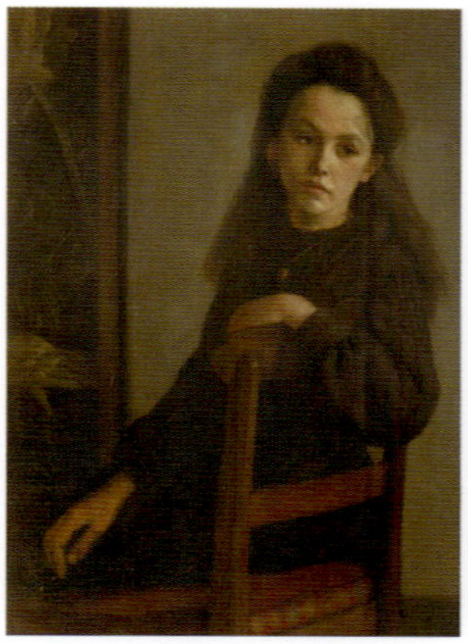

Mayor, Patti 1872–1962
Norah
oil on canvas 59 x 46.5
G315

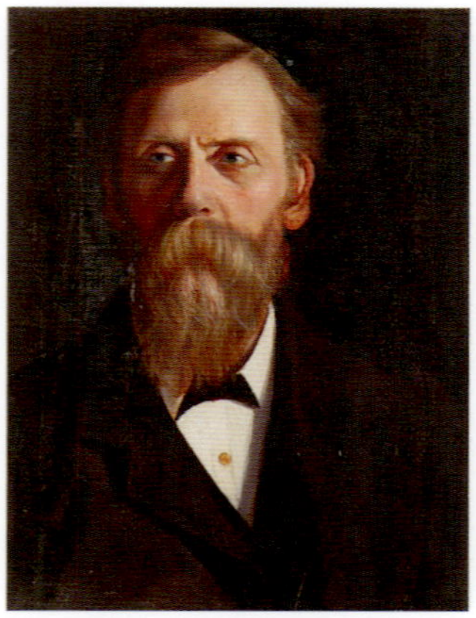

Mayor, Patti 1872–1962
Portrait of a Gentleman with a Beard
oil on canvas 46 x 35.5
G562

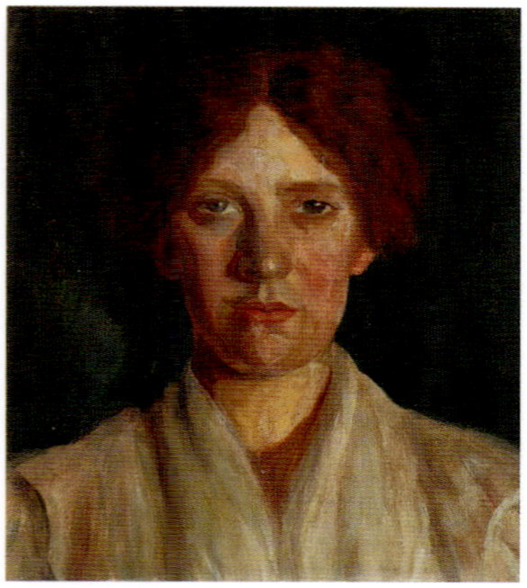

Mayor, Patti 1872–1962
Portrait of a Girl
oil on canvas 34.5 x 30
G545

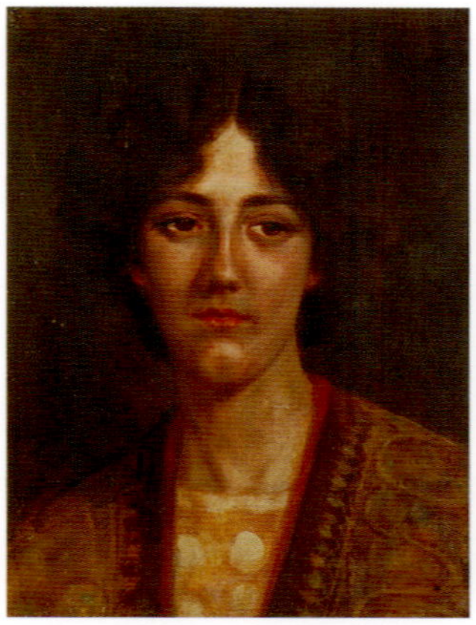

Mayor, Patti 1872–1962
Portrait of a Woman
oil on canvas 44 x 34.5
G716

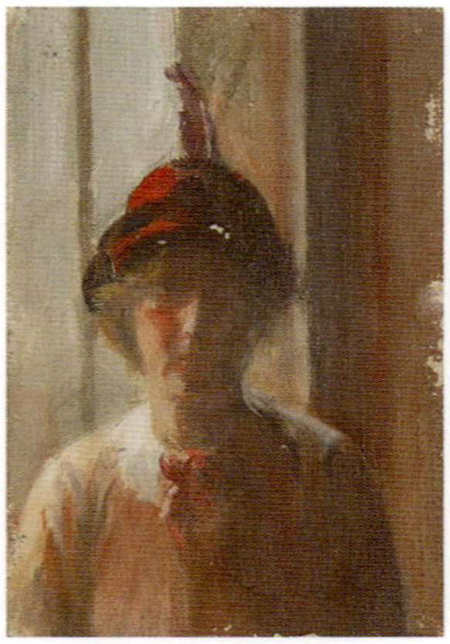

Mayor, Patti 1872–1962
Portrait of an Unknown Woman
oil on card 16.5 x 11.5
G900

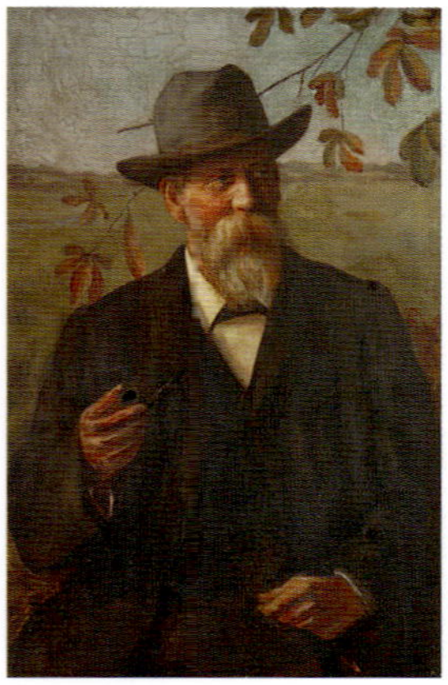

Mayor, Patti 1872–1962
Portrait of Father
oil on canvas 76 x 54
G544

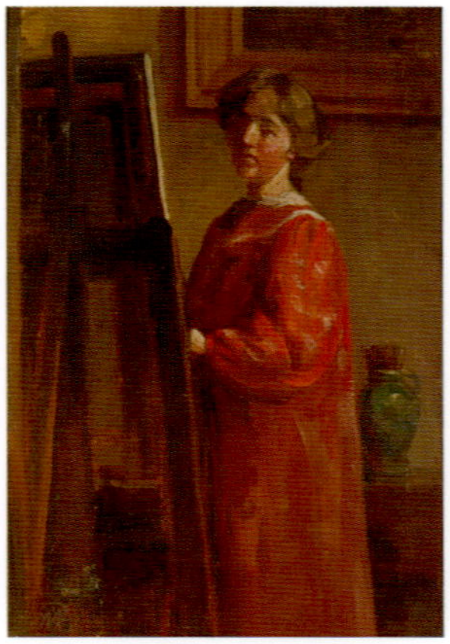

Mayor, Patti 1872–1962
Self Portrait
oil on canvas 56.5 x 41
G560

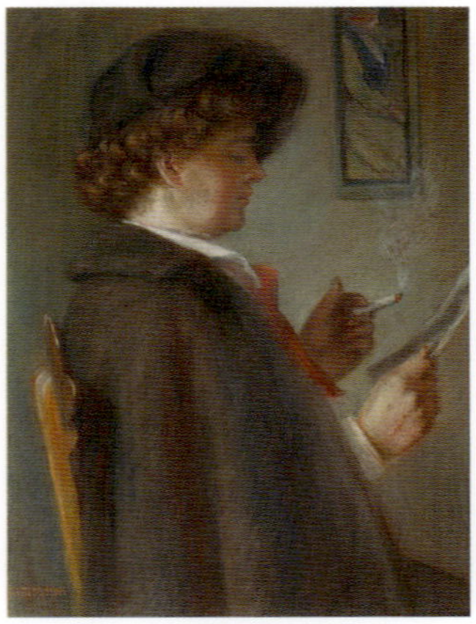

Mayor, Patti 1872–1962
Self Portrait
oil on board 59 x 46
G564

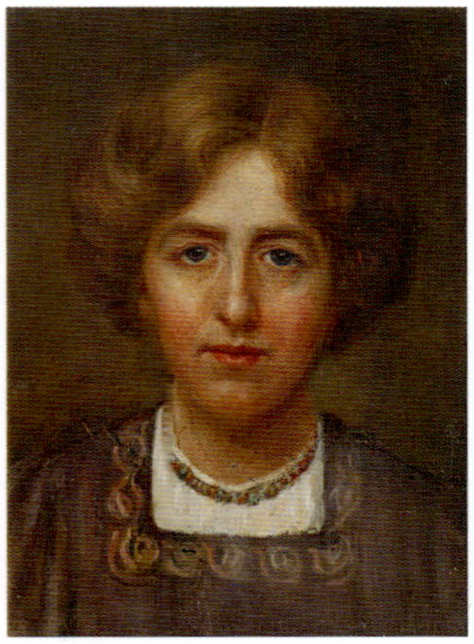

Mayor, Patti 1872–1962
Self Portrait
oil on canvas 39 x 31.5
G720

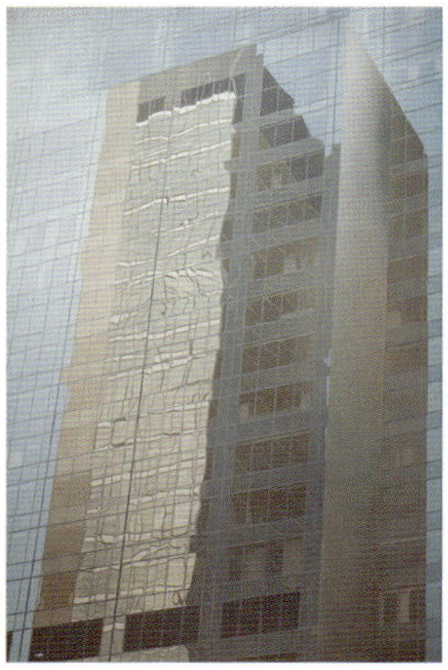

Neiland, Brendan b.1941
Building Projection 1977
acrylic on canvas 207 x 139
G605

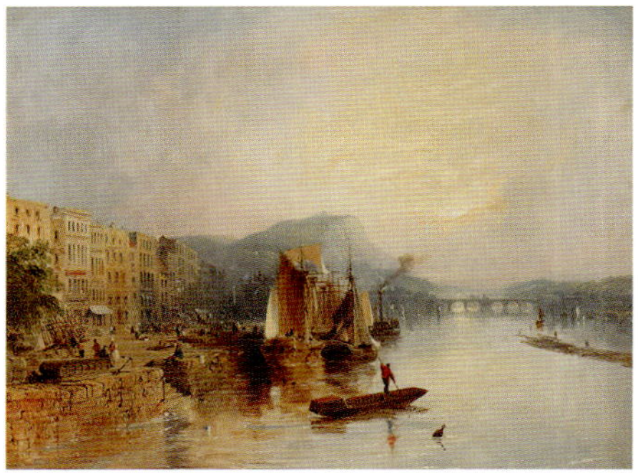

Niemann, W.
Boats at a Quayside 1845
oil on board 33 x 43
G283

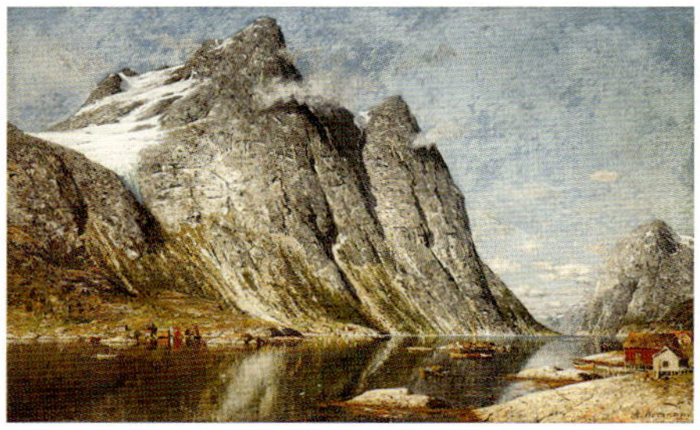

Normann, Adelsteen 1848–1918
Geiranger Fjord, Norway c.1890
oil on canvas 99.5 x 158.5
G146

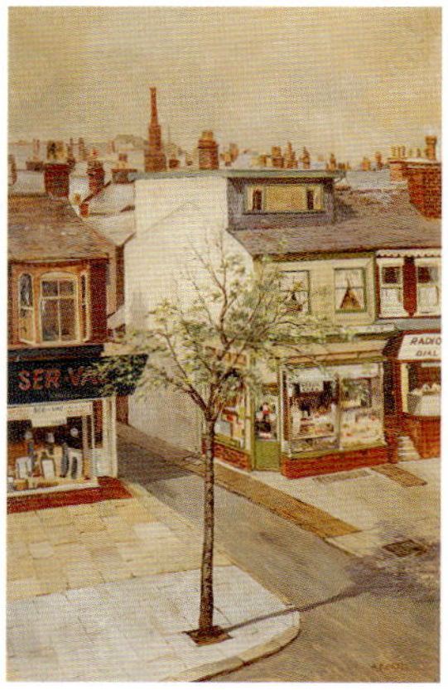

Okell, A. C.
Shops on Church Street
oil on board 68 x 45
G138

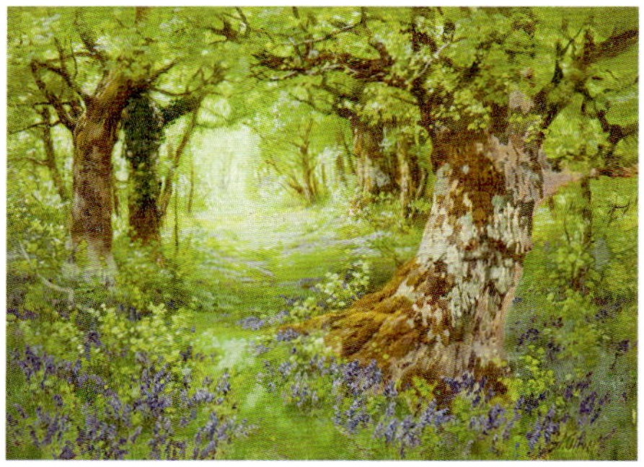

Oliver, Alfred 1871–1947
Fairy Dell, Capel Curig c.1920
oil on board 24 x 34.5
G316

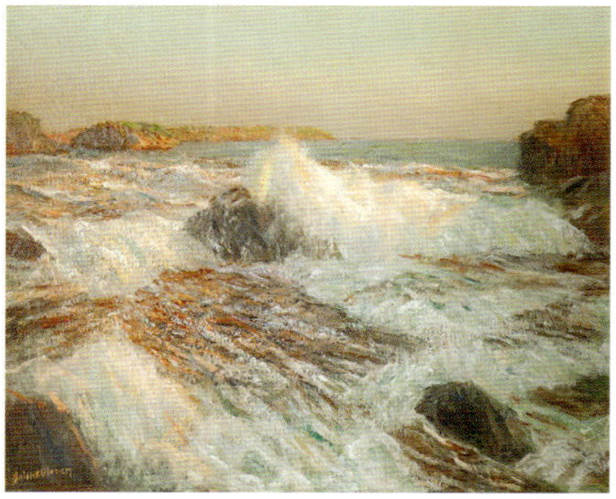

Olsson, Albert Julius 1864–1942
Waterfall in Sweden c.1940
oil on board 44.5 x 59.5
G150

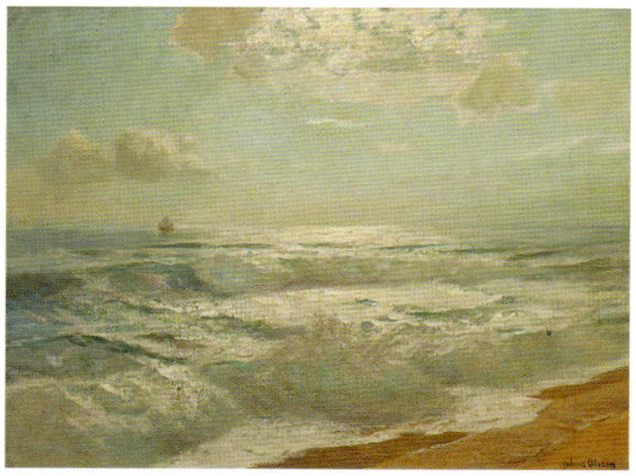

Olsson, Albert Julius 1864–1942
Silver Sea
oil on canvas 59.5 x 74
G149

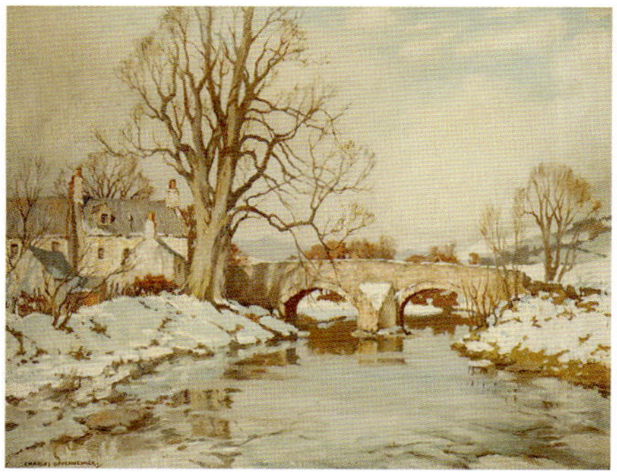

Oppenheimer, Charles 1875–1961
Winter Landscape in Galloway
oil on canvas 45 x 60
G261

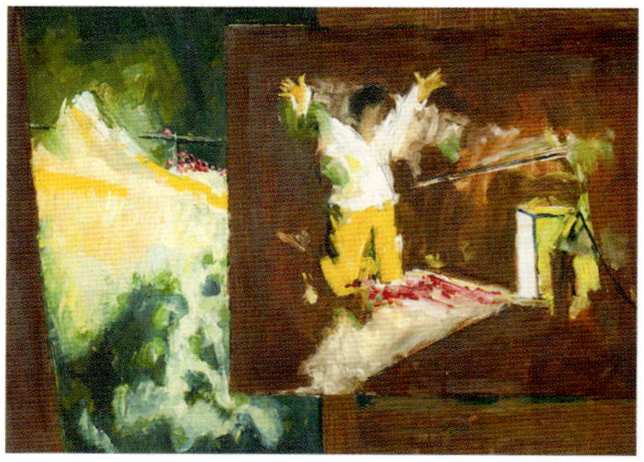

Palmer, Frederick
Variation on Goya's 'Third of May' with Garden Shadow
oil on board 52 x 76
G459

Facing page: Grimshaw, John Atkinson, 1836–1893, *In the Golden Olden Times*, c.1870, Harris Museum & Art Gallery (p. 305)

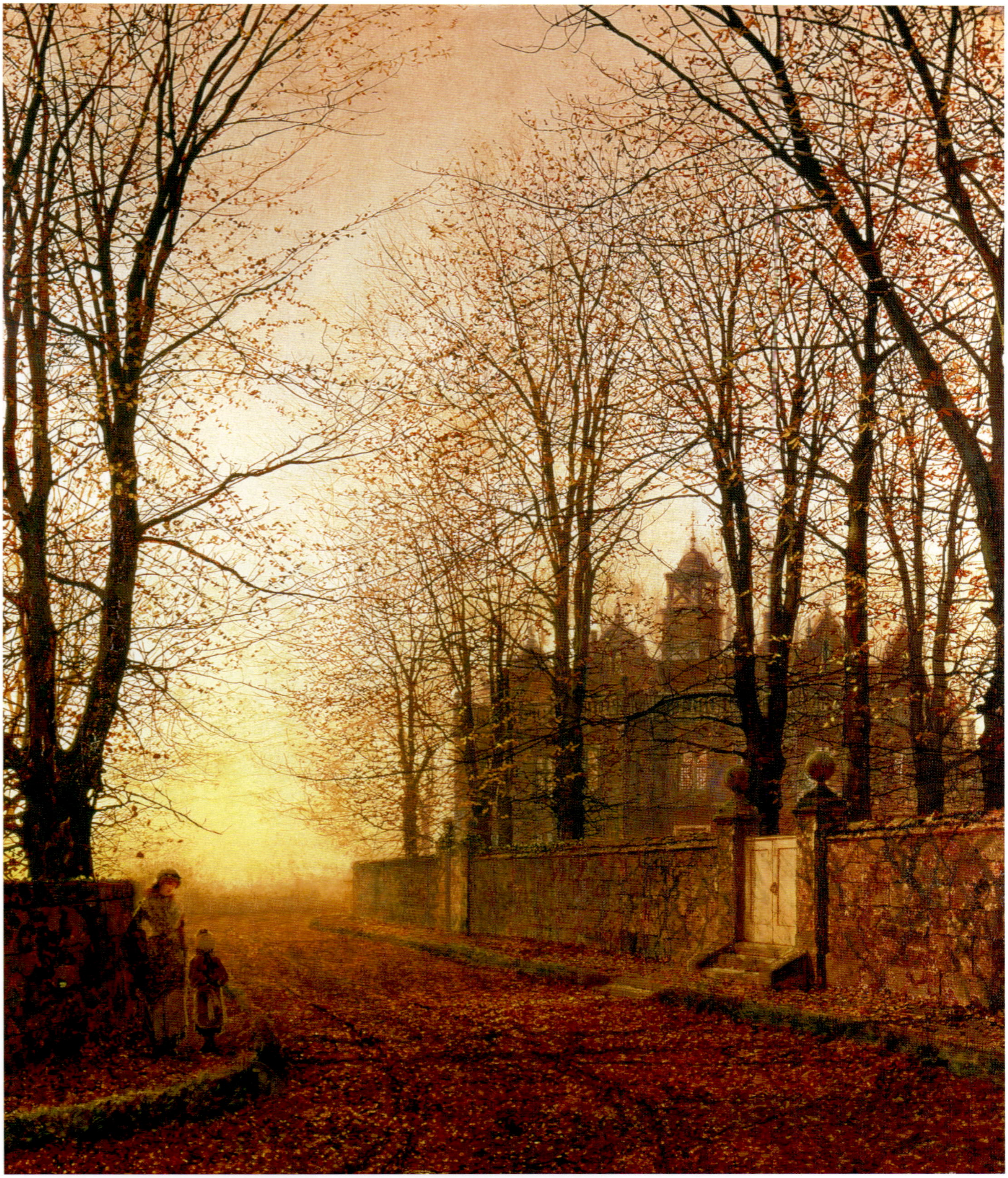

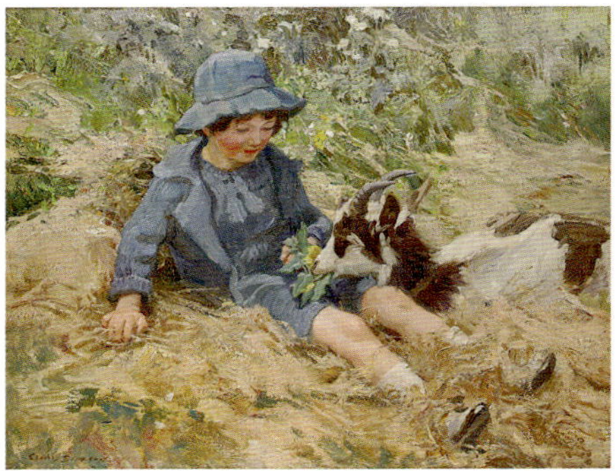

Simpson, Charles Walter 1885–1971
The Pet Goat c.1920
oil on canvas 76 x 100
G171

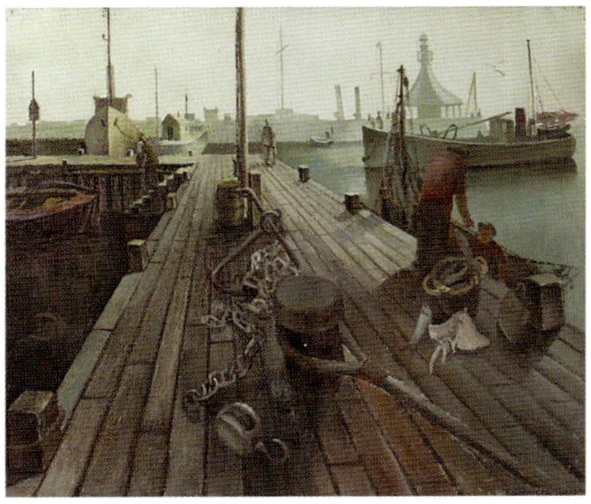

Smith, David T. b.1920
The Harbour Entrance
oil on canvas 63 x 75.5
G172

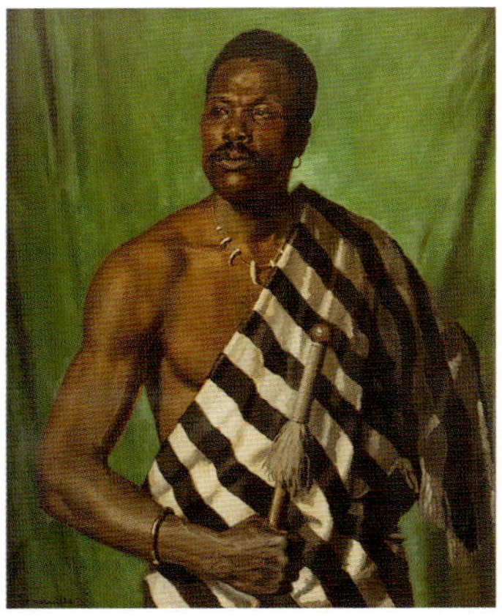

Somerville, Howard 1873–1952
Nigel, a Zulu c.1930
oil on canvas 91 x 76
G272

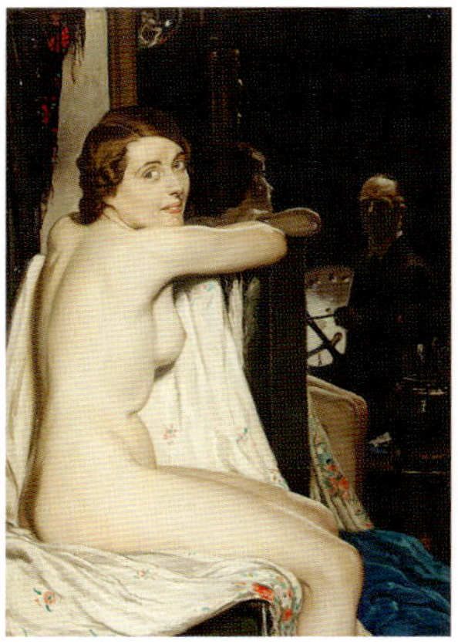

Somerville, Howard 1873–1952
Laurita
oil on canvas 100 x 75
G271

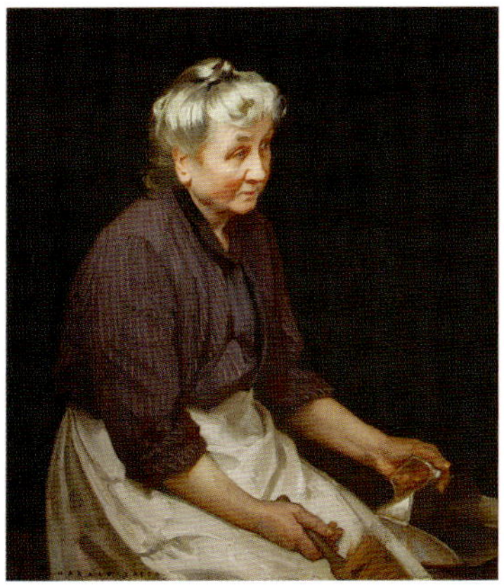

Speed, Harold 1872–1957
The Labourer's Wife 1937
oil on canvas 98.5 x 89.5
G174

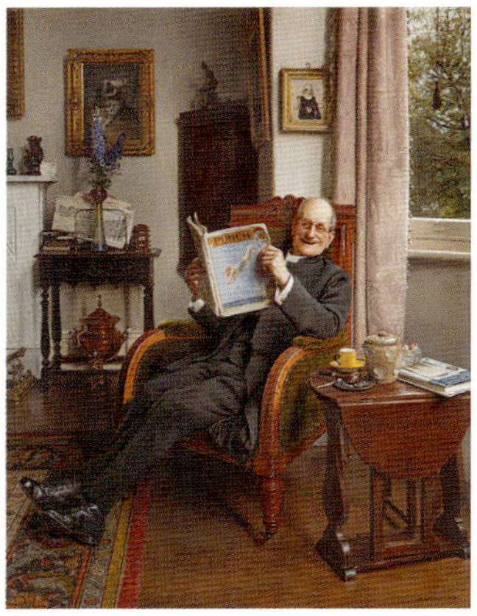

Spencelayh, Charles 1865–1958
The Laughing Parson 1935
oil on canvas 49.5 x 39
G176

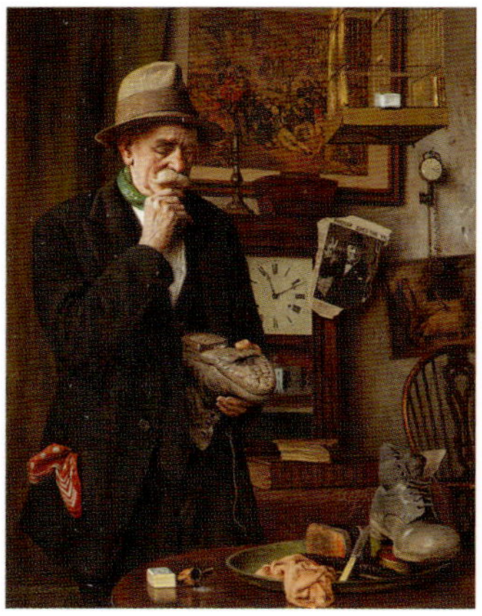

Spencelayh, Charles 1865–1958
It's War 1942
oil on canvas 59.5 x 48.5
G175

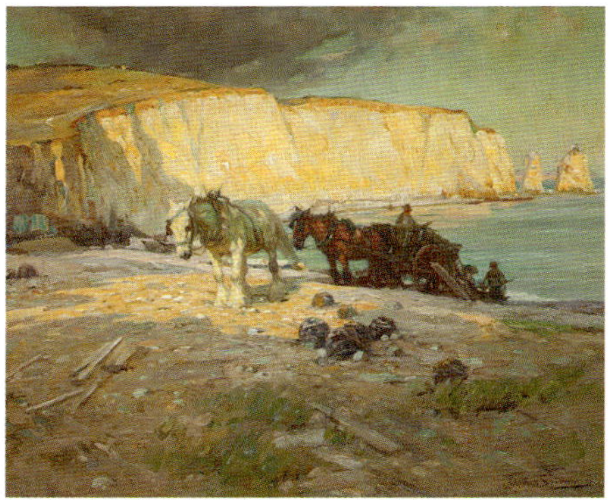

Spooner, Arthur 1873–1962
Freshwater Bay
oil on canvas 68.5 x 81.5
G177

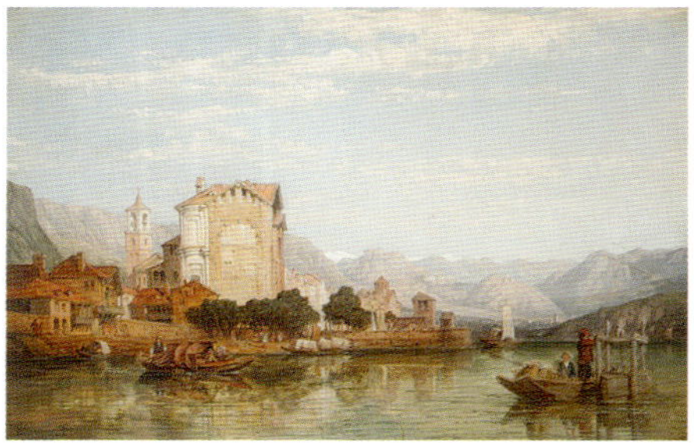

Stanfield, George Clarkson 1828–1878
Anglers on Lake Maggiore
oil on canvas 29 x 45
G293

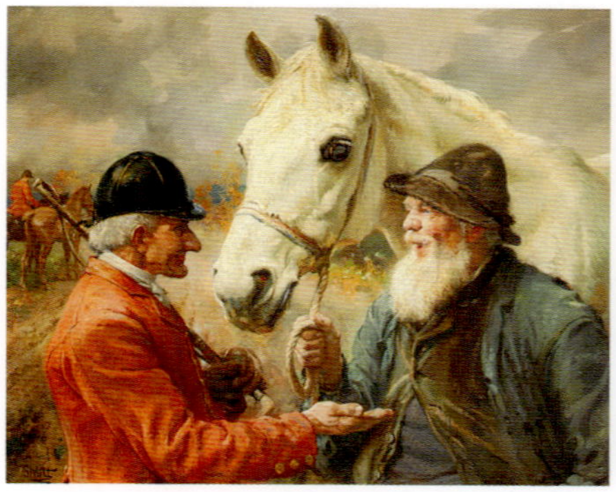

Strutt, Alfred William 1856–1924
A Sporting Offer c.1910
oil on canvas 90 x 115
G179

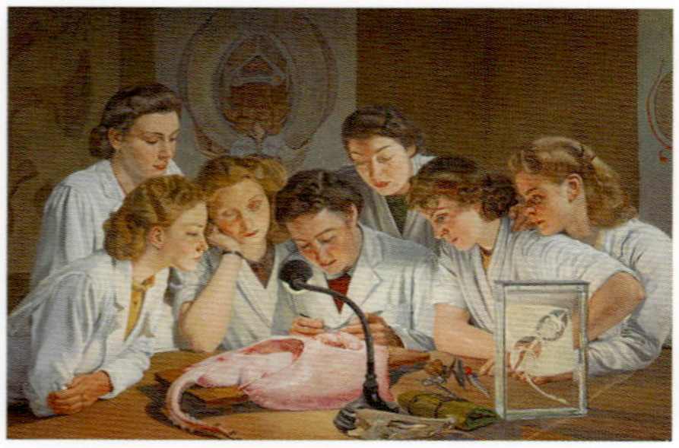

Tafani, Emilio C. L. 1885–1963
Demonstration in Dissection 1945
oil on canvas 70 x 98
G180

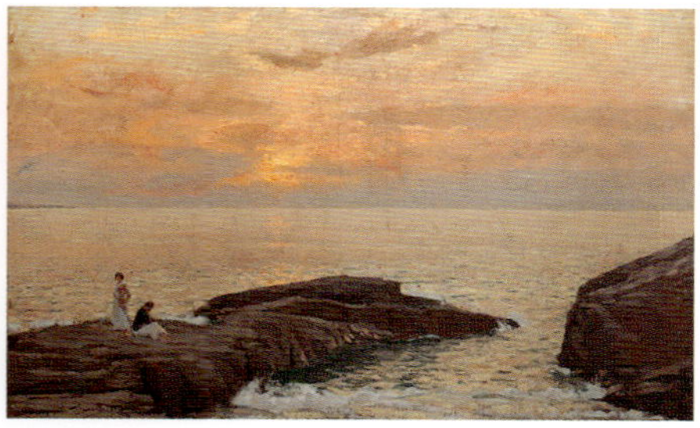

Talmage, Algernon 1871–1939
The Western Sky 1926
oil on canvas 72 x 106.5
G181

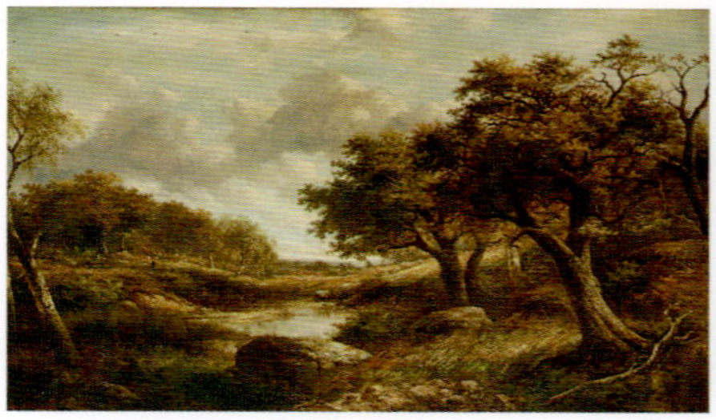

Thors, Joseph 1835–1920
The Forest of Fontainbleu
oil on canvas 86 x 124
G372

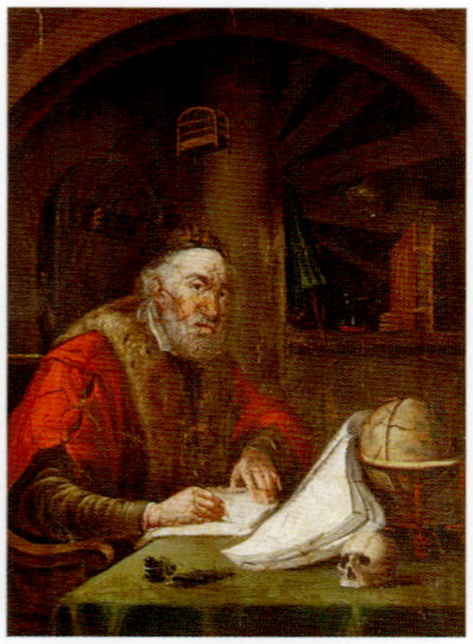

Tol, Dominicus van 1635–1676
A Philosopher
oil on panel 33 x 25
G185

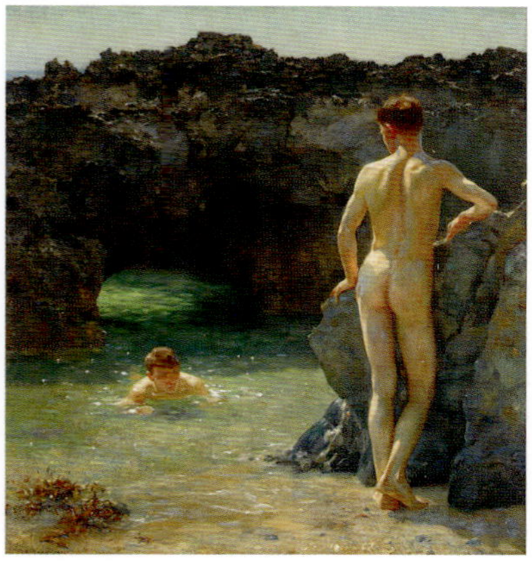

Tuke, Henry Scott 1858–1929
The Green Waterways 1926
oil on canvas 122 x 112
G183

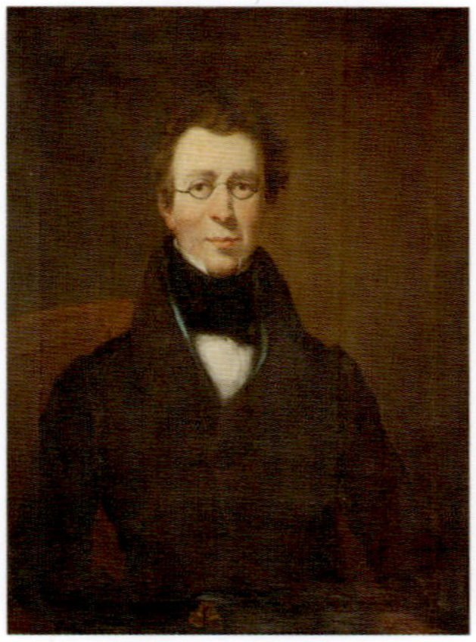

unknown artist
Richard Rossall c.1830
oil on canvas 74.5 x 62
G534

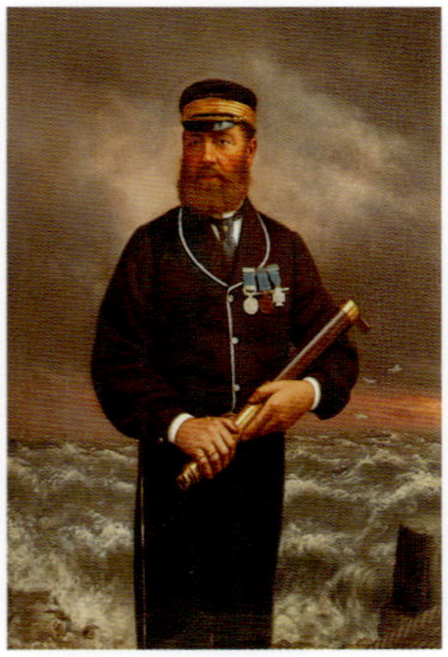

unknown artist
Coxswain R. Bickerstaffe
oil on canvas 90 x 70
G221 M218

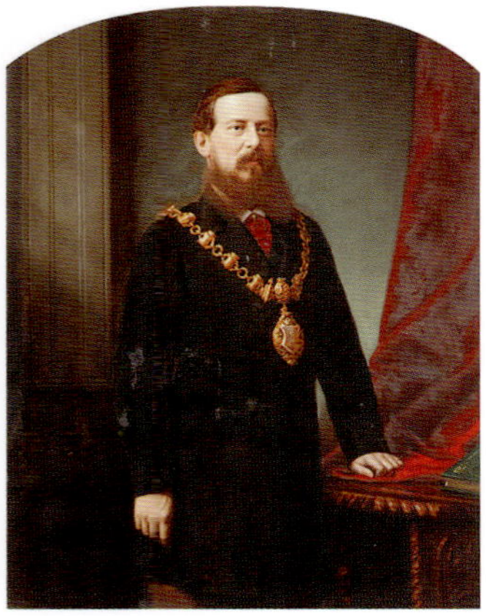

unknown artist
Dr Cocker
oil on board 58 x 47
G215

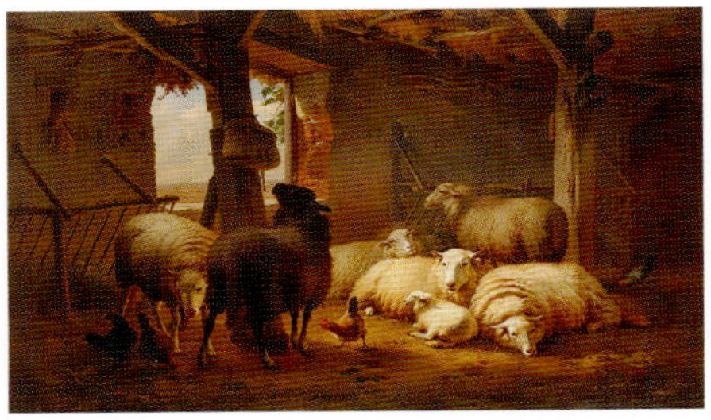

Verboeckhoven, Eugène Joseph 1798–1881
Sheep c.1840
oil on canvas 72.5 x 111.5
G186

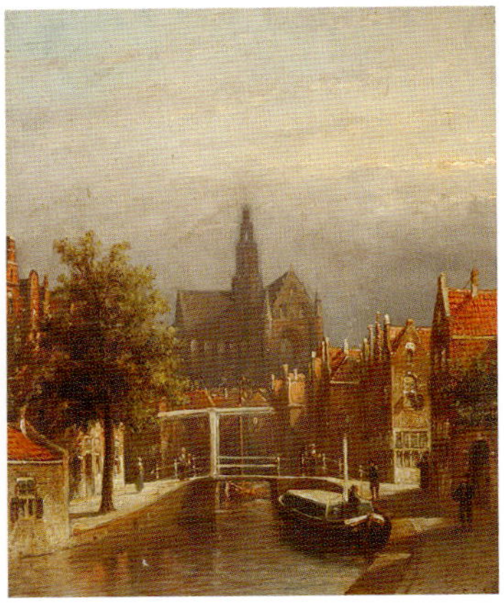

Vertin, Petrus Gerardus 1819–1893
Haarlem, Holland
oil on panel 34.5 x 29
G324

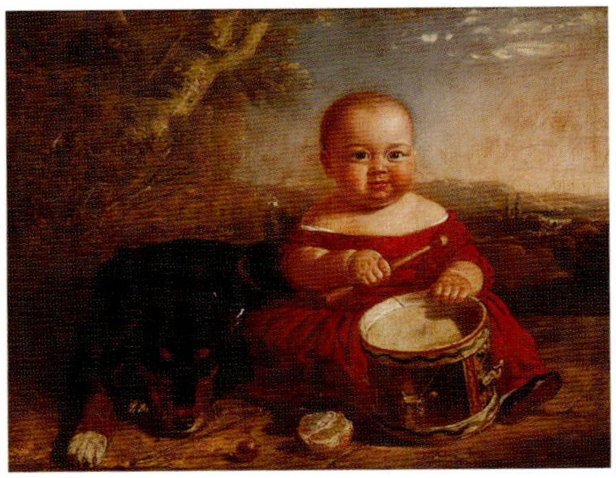

Wadham, Benjamin Brassett 1816–1904
Child with a Drum
oil on canvas 62 x 75
G574

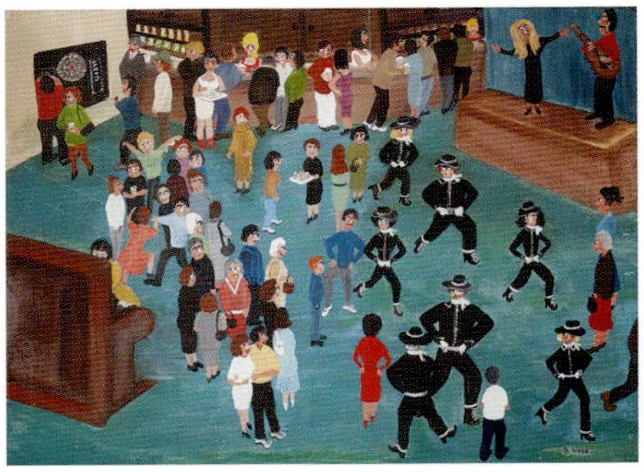

Ward, Beryl
Bootskooters
acrylic on canvas 60 x 80.5
G650

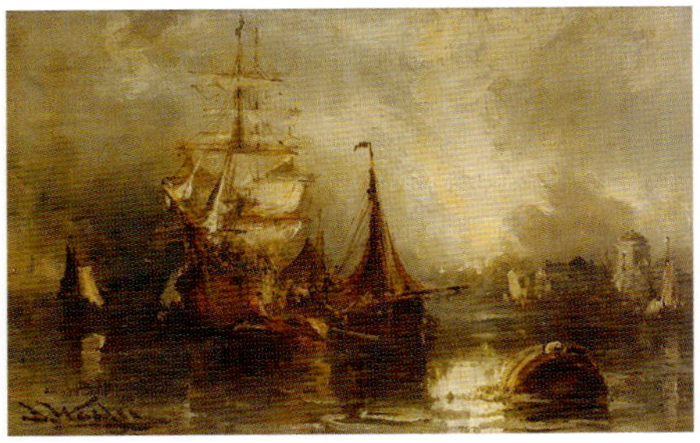

Wasley, Frank 1848–1934
Near the Port c.1890
oil on canvas 59.5 x 105
G191

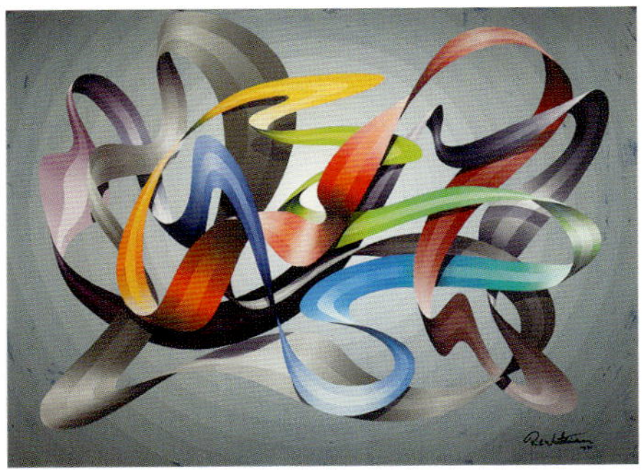

Watkinson, Bob 1914–1992
Ribbon Development
oil on board 79 x 103
G391

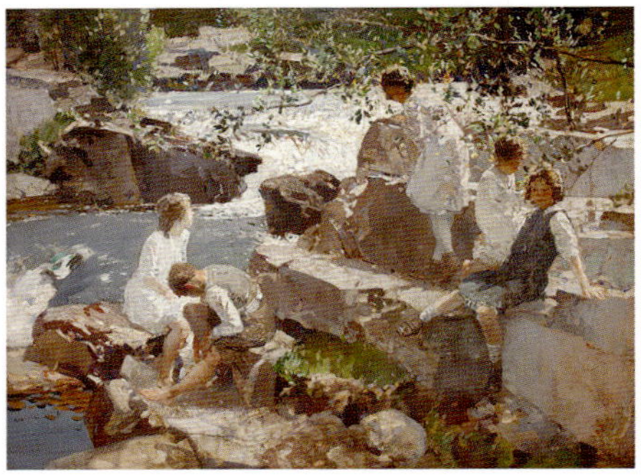

Watson, Harry 1871–1936
Saturday c.1921
oil on canvas 105 x 136
G192

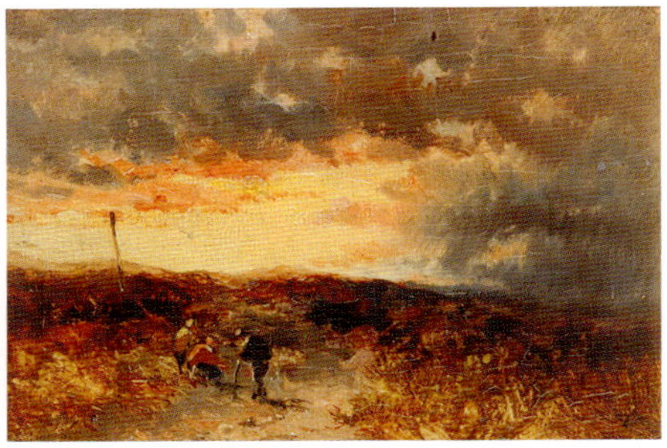

Webb, James 1825–1895
Moorland Scene
oil on board 12 x 19
G193

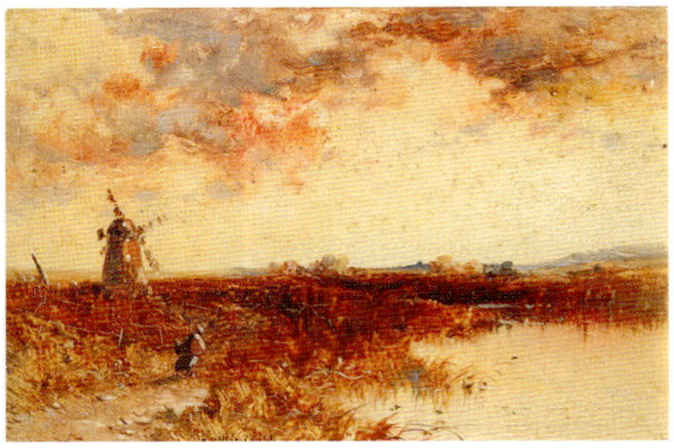

Webb, James 1825–1895
Scene with a Windmill
oil on board 12 x 19
G194

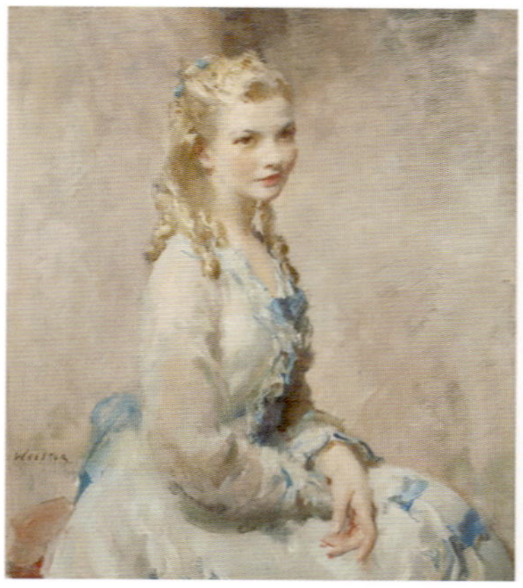

Webster, Walter Ernest 1877–1959
The Golden Age c.1939
oil on canvas 75 x 62
G195

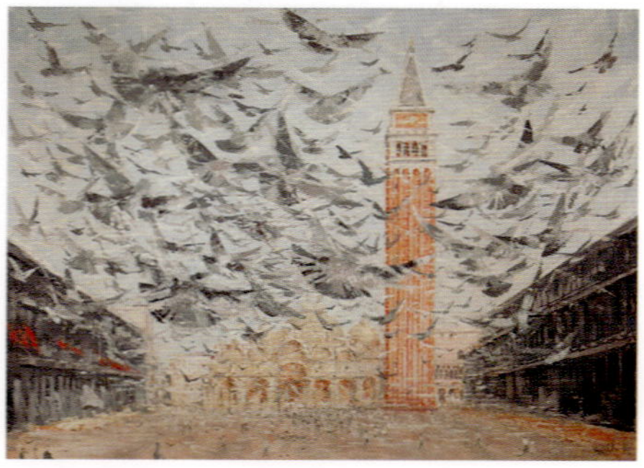

Welsh, John
Piazza San Marco c.1963
oil on canvas 77 x 102
G336

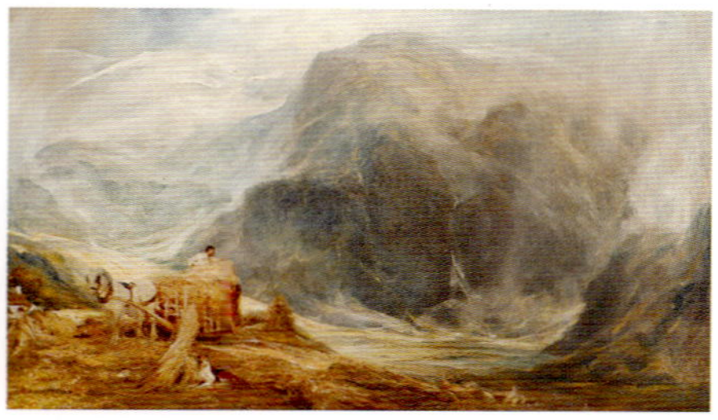

Whaite, Henry Clarence 1828–1912
Harvest, North Wales c.1905
oil on canvas 78 x 133.5
G198

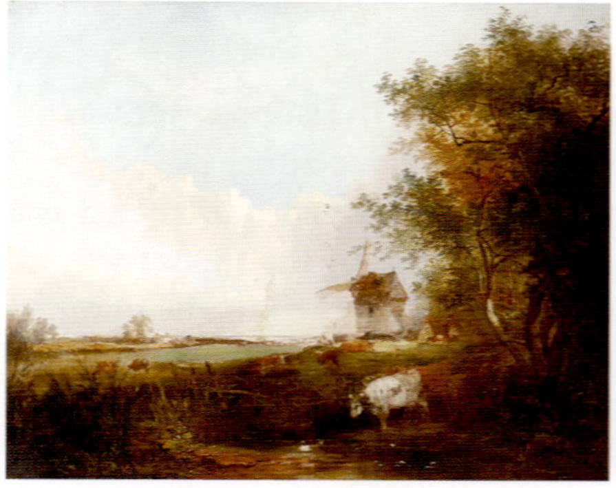

William (senior), Edward Charles 1807–1881
A View of Norfolk
oil on canvas 63 x 76.5
G204

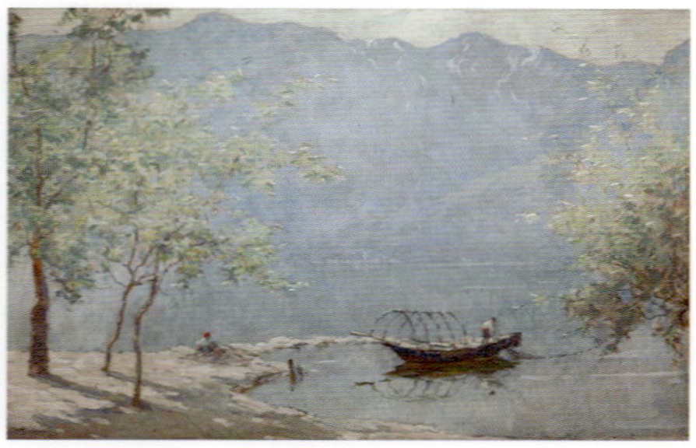

Williams, Terrick John 1860–1936
Morning, Locarno
oil on canvas 73.5 x 98
G205

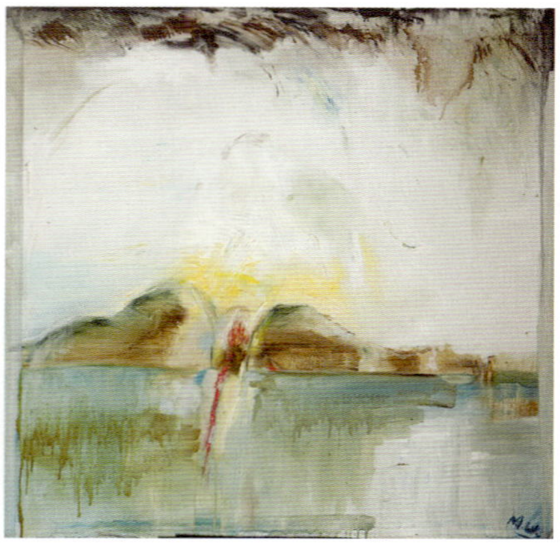

Wishart, John Michael 1928–1996
Lac d'Annecy
oil on canvas 74 x 74
G321

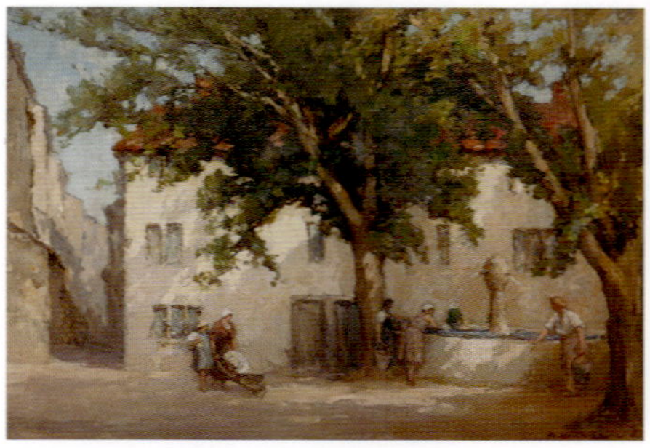

Withers, Alfred 1856–1932
Old Market Place, Vaison
oil on canvas 52 x 69.5
G208

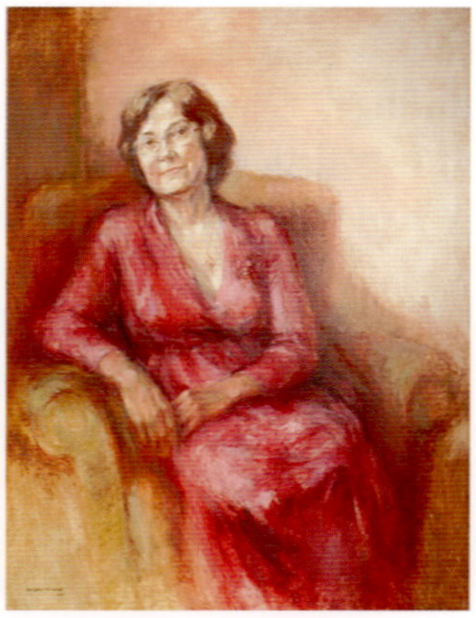

Wood, Elizabeth b.1930
Patrica Seed (d.1978), MBE 1978
oil on canvas 151 x 120
G466

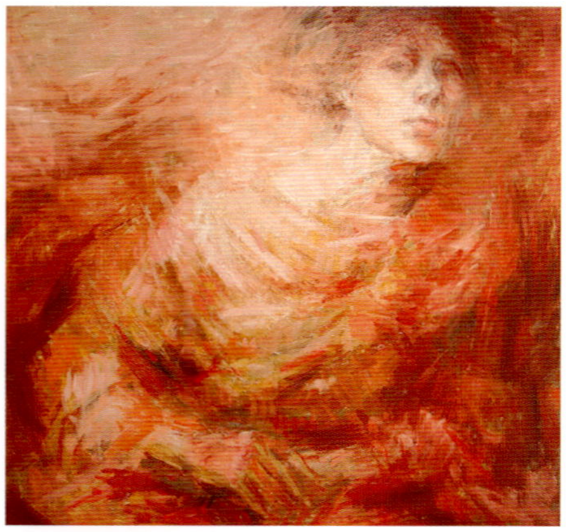

Wood, Elizabeth b.1930
Portrait Study
oil on board 105 x 121
G350

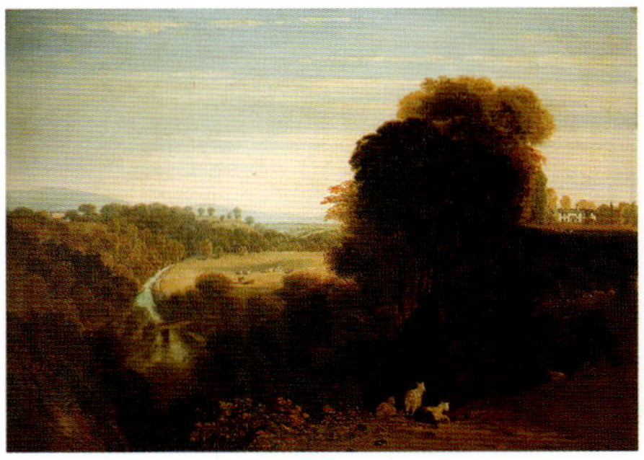

Linton, William 1791–1876
The Eagley Valley and Birtenshaw Hall
oil on canvas 64.3 x 89.5
PCF13

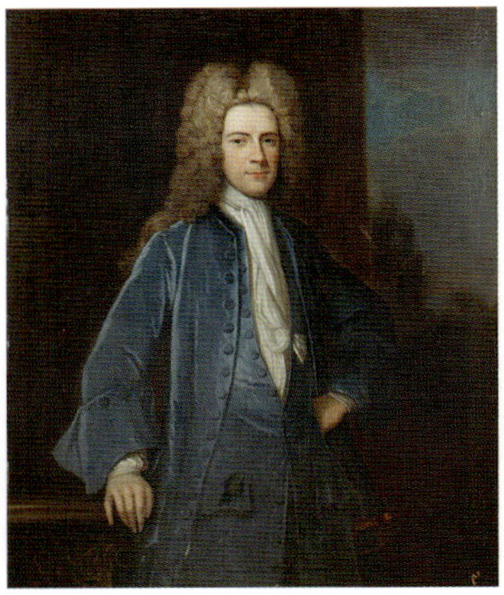

Richardson the elder, Jonathan 1664–1745
Portrait of a Gentleman (traditionally identified as Samuel Chetham)
oil on canvas
2009.133.2 & LANMS.2007.3.1

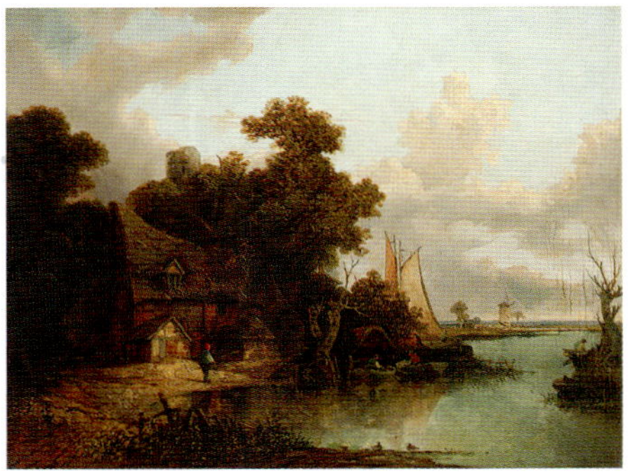

Stark, James 1794–1859
A View from Norwich
oil on canvas 70.4 x 90
paoil148

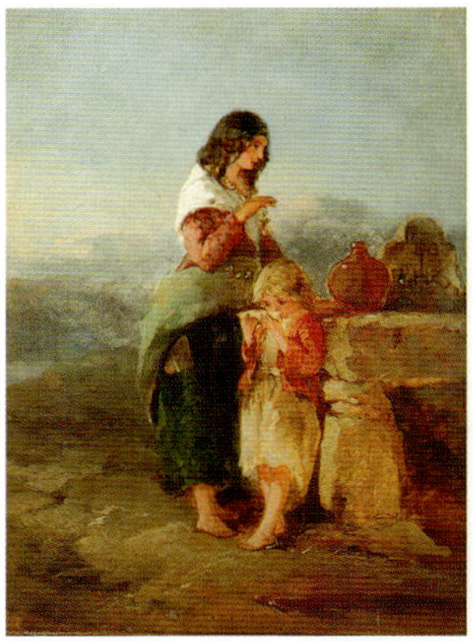

Topham, Francis Williams 1808–1877
At the Well
oil on canvas 35 x 26.7
BMAG.57

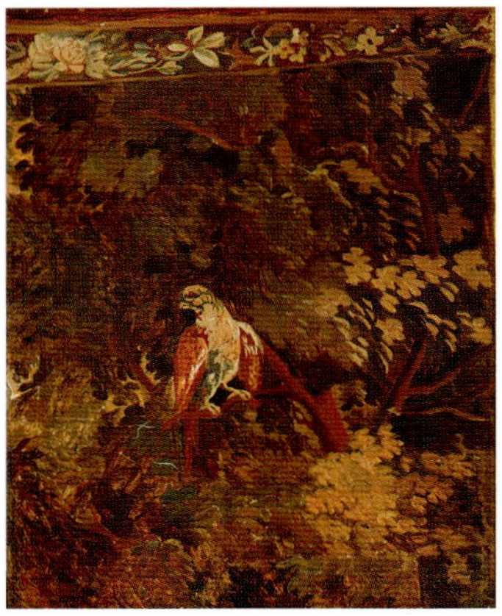

unknown artist
A Bird in a Tree
oil on canvas 45 x 36.5
PCF21

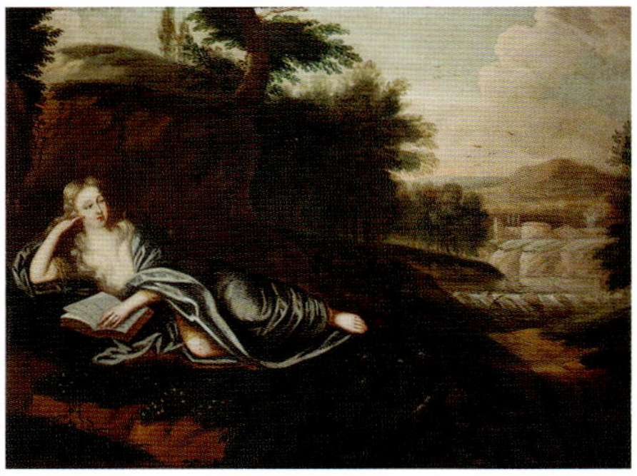

unknown artist
A Female Relaxing under a Tree
oil on canvas 93.3 x 122.8 (E)
PCF11

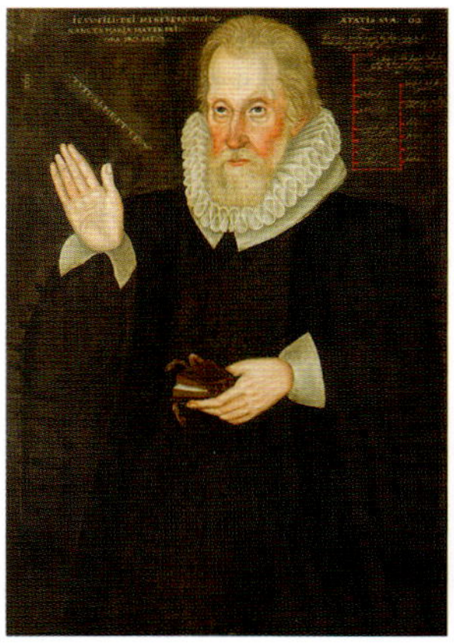

unknown artist
Alexander Barlow
oil on panel (?) 104 x 70.8 (E)
BMAG.951

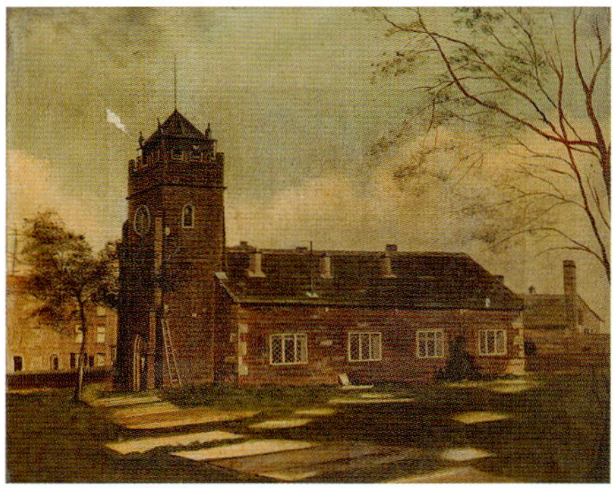

unknown artist
Bradshaw Chapel
oil on canvas 27.3 x 32.3
P.73

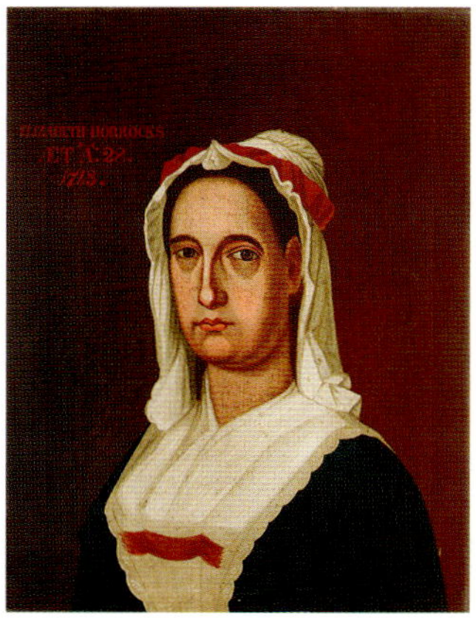

unknown artist
Elizabeth Horrocks
oil on panel (?) 60 x 49.9
P.42

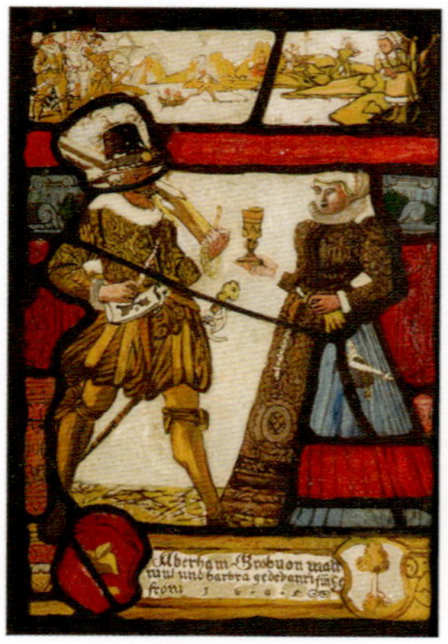

unknown artist
Figures in Sixteenth-Century Costume
oil on stained glass
PCF23

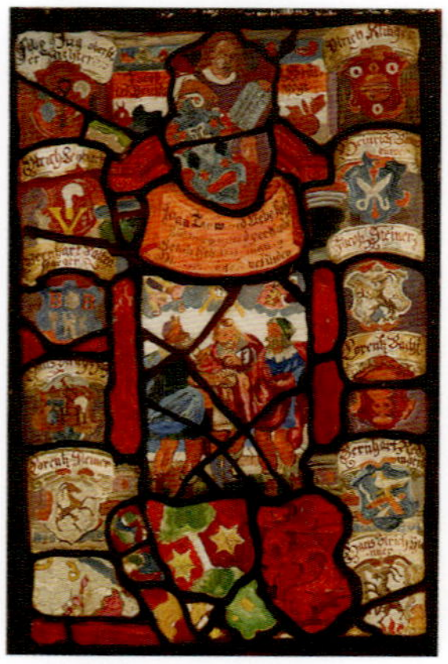

unknown artist
German Heraldic Piece with Three Figures
oil on stained glass 37 x 25
PCF18

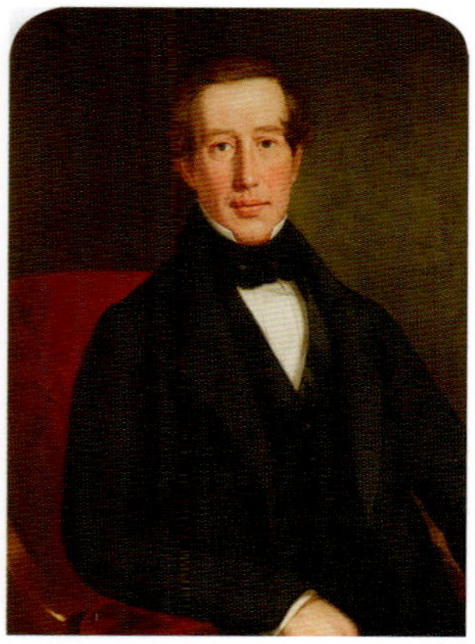

unknown artist
James Knowles
oil on canvas 74.9 x 61.6
P.20

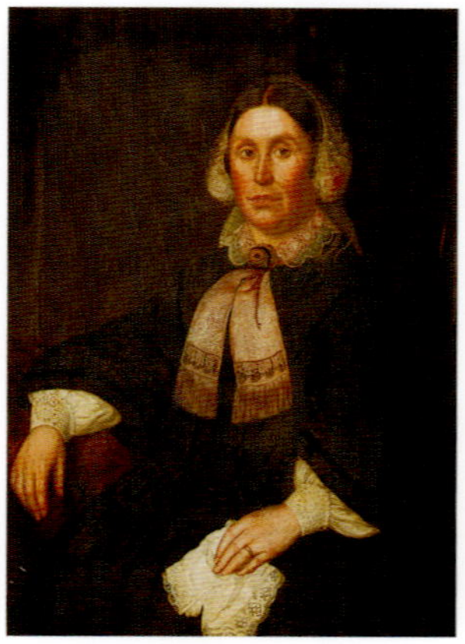

unknown artist
Jane Kay
oil on canvas 89.3 x 71
P.36

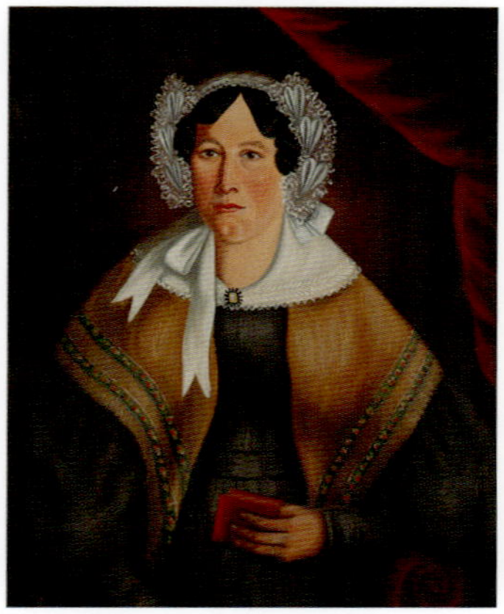

unknown artist
Lady Holding a Small Red Book
oil on canvas 74 x 62 (E)
PCF3

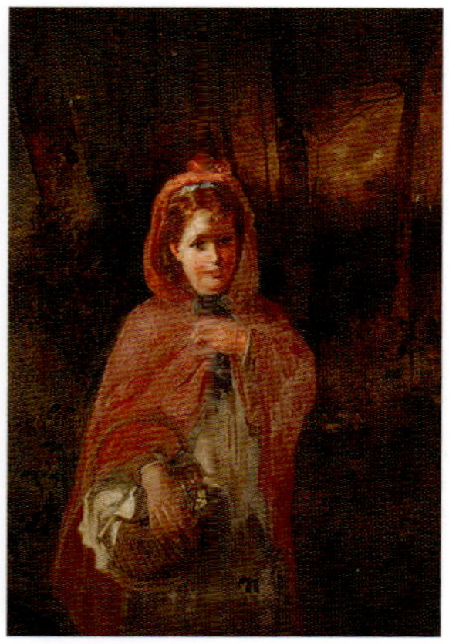

unknown artist
Little Red Riding Hood
oil on canvas 90 x 79
PCF5

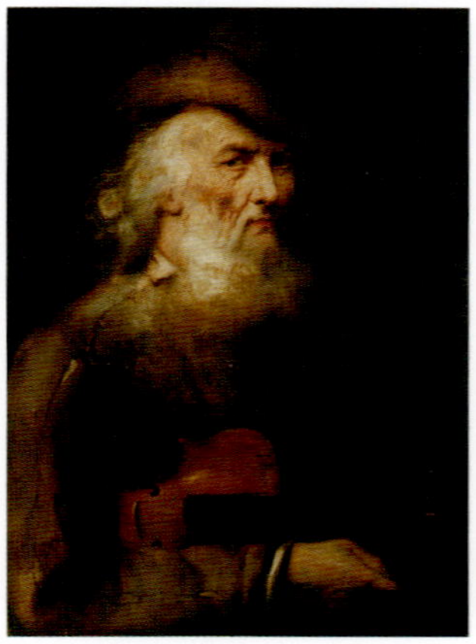

unknown artist
Man with a Violin
oil on canvas 50 x 39.5
PCF7

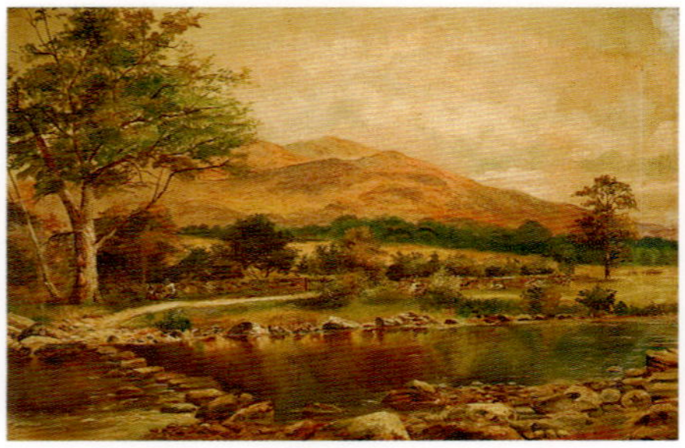

unknown artist
Mountain and Lake with Two Figures
oil on canvas 52 x 74.9
PCF14

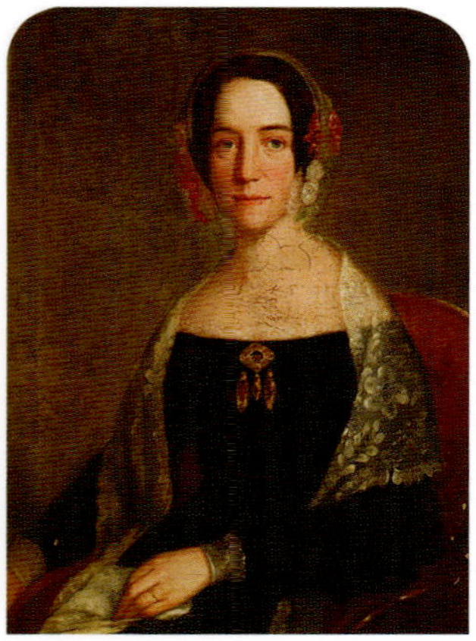

unknown artist
Mrs Knowles
oil on canvas 74.9 x 61.6 (E)
P.21

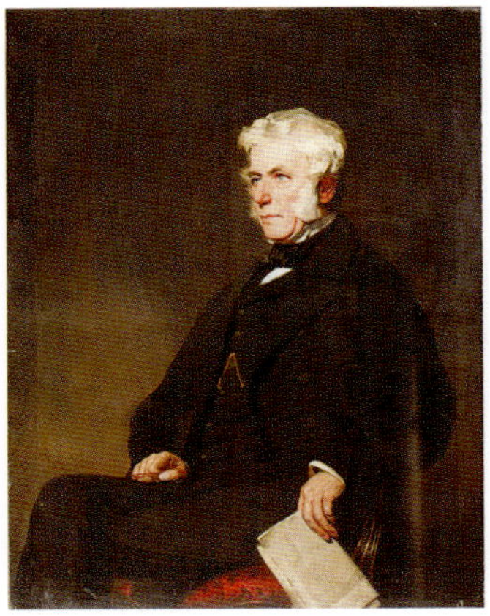

unknown artist
Portrait of a Gentleman (thought to be either Edmund Ashworth or James Barlow)
oil on canvas 127.3 x 101.9
P.2

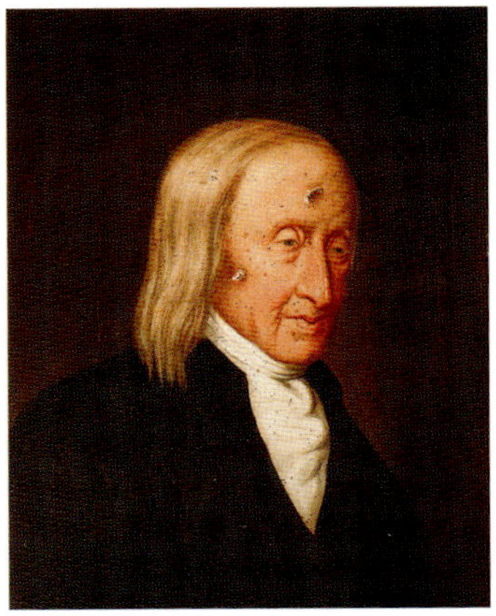

unknown artist
Portrait of a Gentleman (possibly Samuel Crompton (1753–1827) as an Old Man)
oil on canvas 60 x 49.7
PCF17

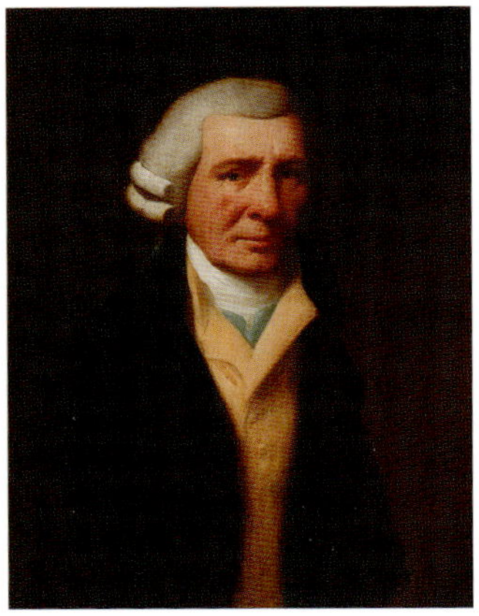

unknown artist
Portrait of a Gentleman with a Wig
oil on canvas 74 x 62 (E)
PCF1

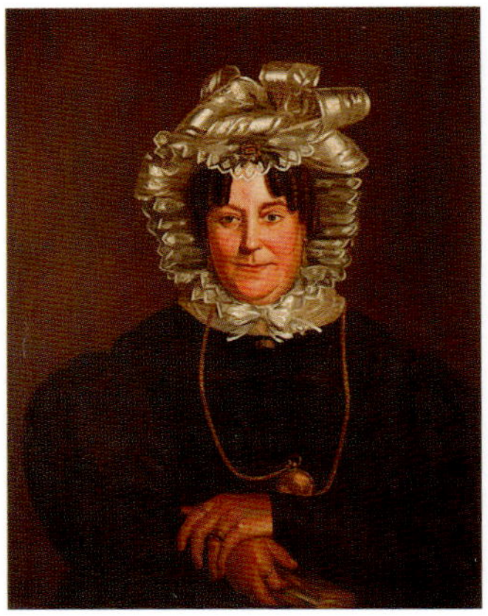

unknown artist
Portrait of a Lady with a Fancy Bonnet (possibly Mrs A. Trimble)
oil on canvas 74 x 62
PCF2

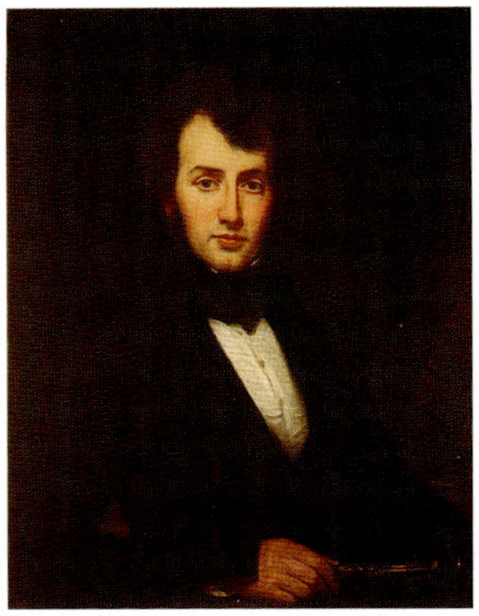

unknown artist
Stephen Blair
oil on canvas 75.8 x 62
P.22

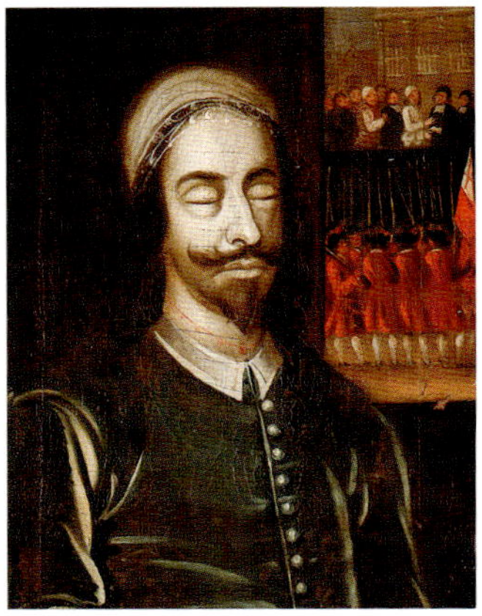

unknown artist
The Death Mask of Charles I
oil on canvas 38.8 x 30
PCF4

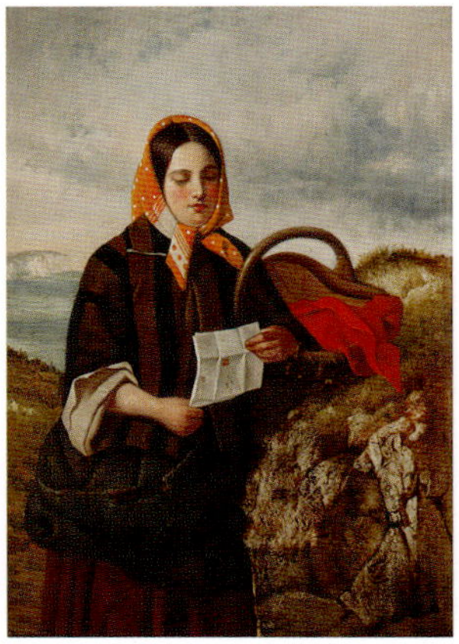

unknown artist
The Letter
oil on canvas 30 x 24.3
BMAG.VMT.68

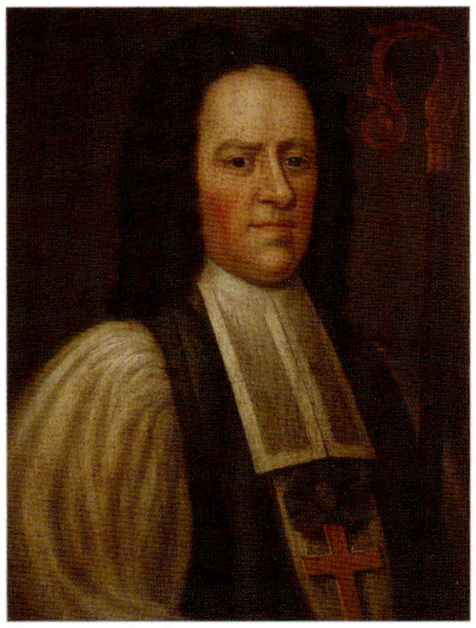

unknown artist
Thomas Deacon
oil on canvas 51.2 x 41.2
PCF10

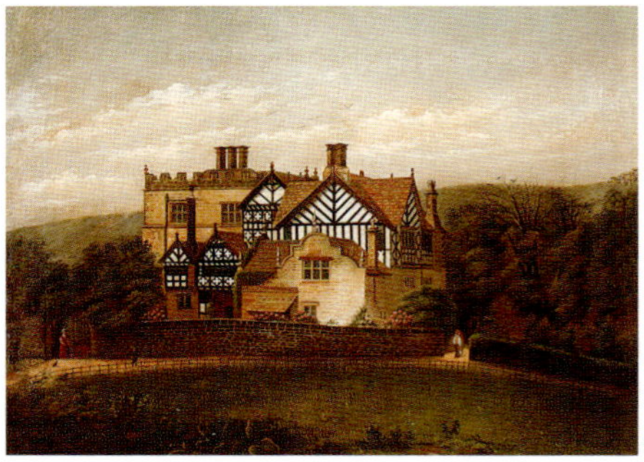

unknown artist
View of Turton Tower from the East
oil on canvas 47.4 x 65.7
PCF9

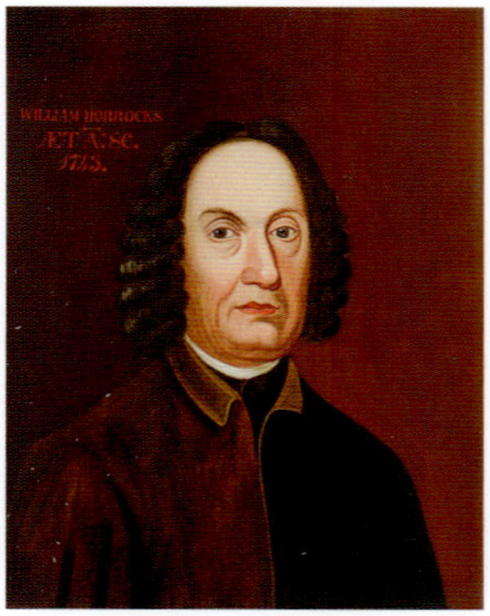

unknown artist
William Horrocks
oil on panel (?) 57.5 x 47.5
P.43

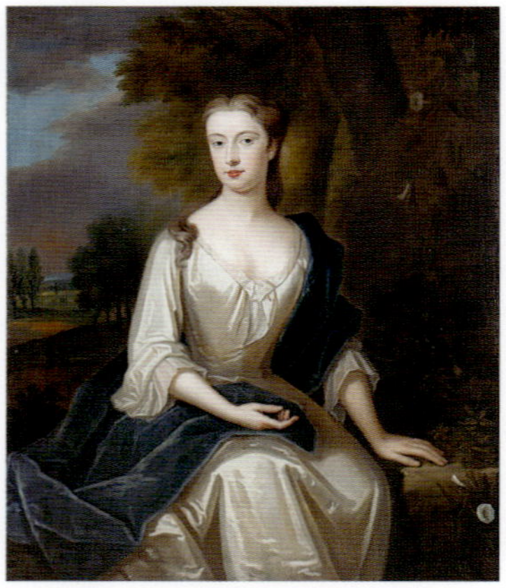

Verelst, Maria 1680–1744
Portrait of a Lady (traditionally identified as Mary Chetham)
oil on canvas
2009.133.1 & LANMS.2007.3.2

Towneley Hall Art Gallery & Museum

Towneley Hall was the home of the Towneley Family for over 500 years but in 1901 it was sold to Burnley Corporation and today is the town's Art Gallery and Museum, run and owned by Burnley Borough Council. The family left in March 1902 leaving behind a building almost completely empty except for a couple of tables and a few pictures in the chapel. The gardens were opened as a public park in June 1902 and in May 1903 the entrance hall and the south wing of the house were opened for a loan exhibition of paintings.

The Collection of oil paintings was built up first through gifts and purchases using money from the rates. In 1921, an annual income was made available from the bequest of a local brewer, Edward Stocks Massey (1850–1909), to be used 'for the advancement of art at Towneley Hall'. Today there are over 300 oil paintings in the Collection, the acquisitions being evenly divided between gifts and purchases plus around 20 paintings transferred from Burnley Central Library and Padiham Museum in the 1970s.

The early purchase policy, implemented by a committee of the town council together with co-opted volunteers, was to build up a collection of works by established British artists within a limited budget. The long-term aim was to be no longer reliant on loan exhibitions. The most successful of the early acquisitions was *Destiny* by John William Waterhouse. In 1908, a purpose built art gallery was established on the top floor of the north wing, removing the old bedrooms and installing new and higher roofs with glazing to provide top light for viewing the paintings beneath. By 1912, the committee was itself able to loan out paintings for exhibition elsewhere.

The annual grant from the Massey Bequest Fund allowed the Collection to grow more quickly, with an average of two or three oil paintings bought each year for the next 40 years. The Bequest Fund also helped to furnish the place as a country house, with ceramics and furniture to complement the fine art collections. Money from the Massey Bequest allowed the Whalley Abbey vestments to be purchased at auction in 1922. These High Mass vestments, made for Whalley Abbey c.1425, were brought to Towneley for safekeeping by

Sir John Towneley (1473–1540) c.1537 and remained there for over 360 years until 1902.

A further family auction in 1939 allowed the return of Towneley's most famous painting *Charles Townley and Friends in His Library at Park Street, Westminster* by Johann Zoffany, purchased with the assistance of the National Art Collections Fund. In the nineteenth century there were over 130 family portraits on display at Towneley and today around a dozen have returned including *John and Mary Towneley and Family* painted by an unknown artist in 1601.

In the first 30 years most acquisitions, both gifts and purchases, were products of the second half of the nineteenth century. The main subjects were landscapes and history paintings. The committee was as careful in the acceptance of gifts as in selecting purchases and those accepted, such as the popular *The Sun Had Closed the Winter's Day* by Joseph Farquharson, were often accepted on loan for several years before being acquired permanently. In 1923, the remaining bedrooms on the top floor of the north wing were replaced by a watercolour gallery. This was opened by Lord Leverhulme, who also made a gift of *Wood Nymphs* by Edward Burne-Jones.

One important purchase, in 1925, arose from a bequest of £1,000 from a local man, Caleb Thornber. Up to this point, no single purchase by the Art Gallery committee had cost more than £500. They decided to use this bequest to buy one outstanding painting and Richard Haworth's of Blackburn satisfied this desire by offering *The Picture Gallery* by Lawrence Alma-Tadema. In 1933, purchases were made at the Royal Academy's Summer Exhibition and then, in response to a visitor's suggestion, *Smile* and *His Favourite* by Charles Spencelayh were purchased from the artist. Later that same decade, the committee went on to collect work from the first half of the nineteenth century by artists such as David Cox the elder, Philip Reinagle and James Ward.

Richard Haworth's of Blackburn helped to improve the quality of the Collection between 1948 and 1953, offering each year a range of important genre and history paintings including *Life in the Hop Garden* by Phoebus Levin, *St Mark's, Venice* by Adolf Echtler, *Harmony* by Frank Dicksee, and *On the Temple Steps* by Edward John Poynter. They also provided something completely different in 1950 with a late sixteenth-century continental work *The Building of the Tower of Babel*, by Marten van Valckenborch I. The 40-year pursuit of a balanced collection of oil paintings concluded with the purchase of portraits by Peter Lely, Thomas Hudson and William Beechey. These portraits were selected more to furnish the house than to enhance the Art Gallery. Today, about half the oil paintings are on public display in most of the rooms around the house.

From the 1970s onwards the purchase policy has been to collect works by professional artists from the local region, works of local topography, or works with Towneley family connections. Towneley Hall still receives money each year from the Massey Bequest, although in relative terms this cannot buy as much as in earlier years due to the great increase in the price of objects at auction. Now in the twenty-first century, the main concern is the conservation of those objects acquired in the twentieth century.

Tony Kitto, Museum Volunteer

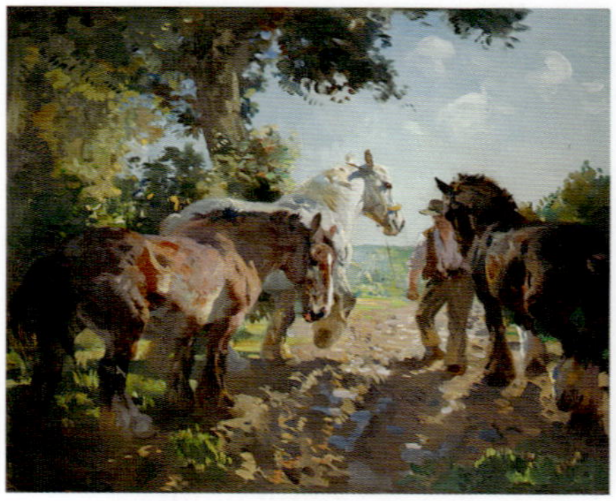

Adamson, Dorothy 1894–1934
Going to Pasture c.1933
oil on canvas 95.9 x 109
BURGM:paoil89

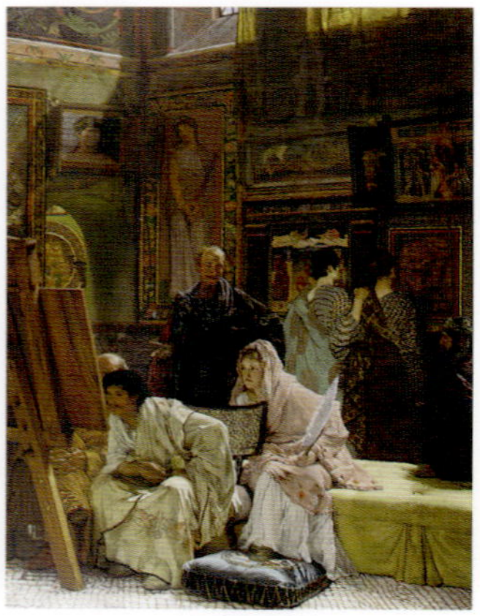

Alma-Tadema, Lawrence 1836–1912
The Picture Gallery 1874
oil on canvas 218 x 166
BURGM:paoil58

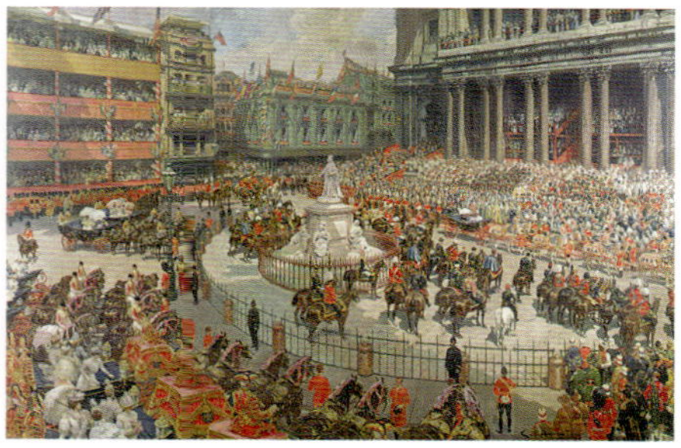

Amato, Gennaro d' 1857–1947
Queen Victoria's Diamond Jubilee 1897–1899
oil on canvas 142 x 218
BURGM:paoil13

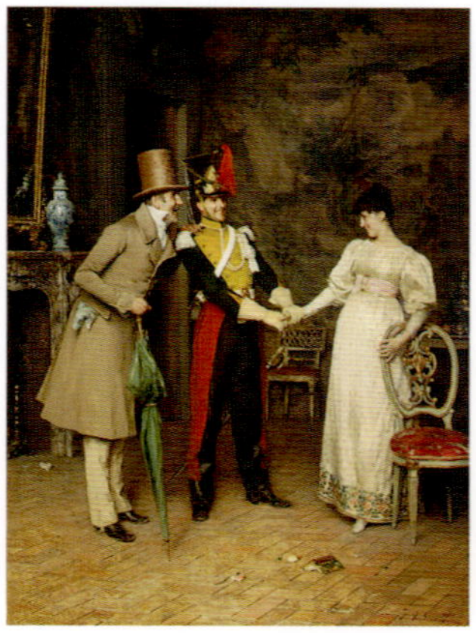

Andreotti, Federico 1847–1930
The Introduction
oil on canvas 102 x 75.6
BURGM:paoil151

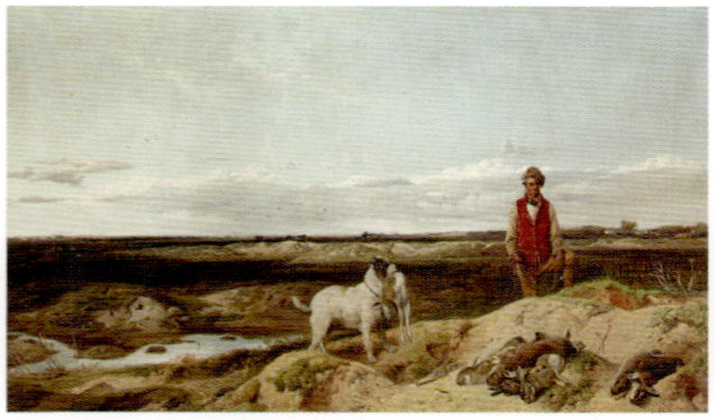

Ansdell, Richard 1815–1885
Ferreting 1863
oil on canvas 43.2 x 96.5
BURGM:paoil193

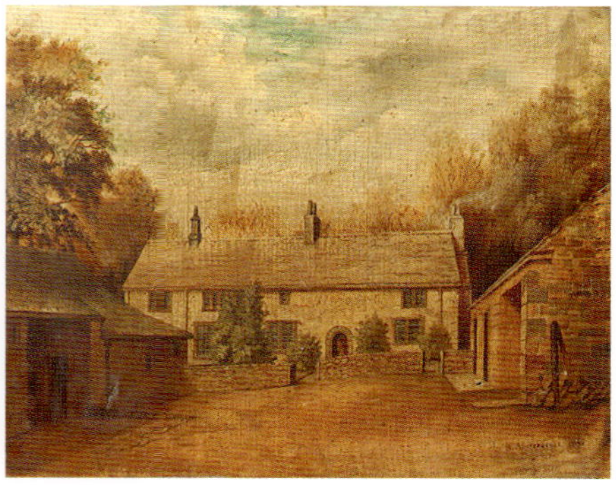

Austerberry, Stocks 1842–1899
Tattersall's Dwellings 1899
oil on canvas 40.6 x 55.9
BURGM:paoil261

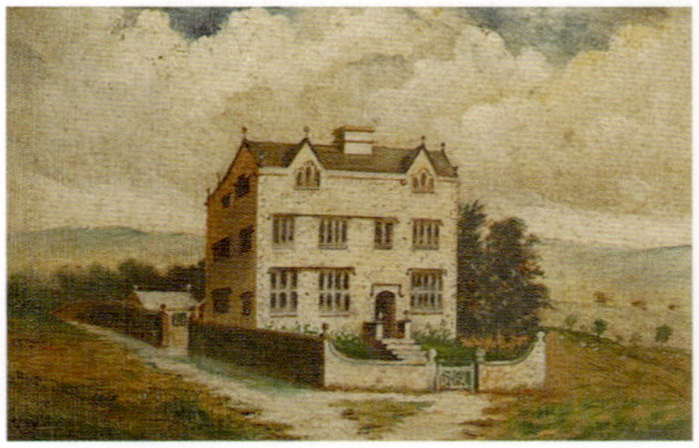

Austerberry, Stocks 1842–1899
Extwistle Hall
oil on canvas 19.1 x 28.6
BURGM:paoil335

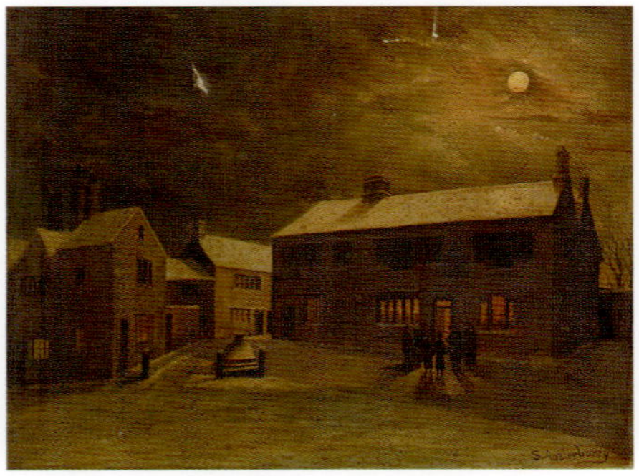

Austerberry, Stocks 1842–1899
Market Cross and Old Sparrow Hawk, Burnley
oil on canvas 48.9 x 67.9
BURGM:paoil262

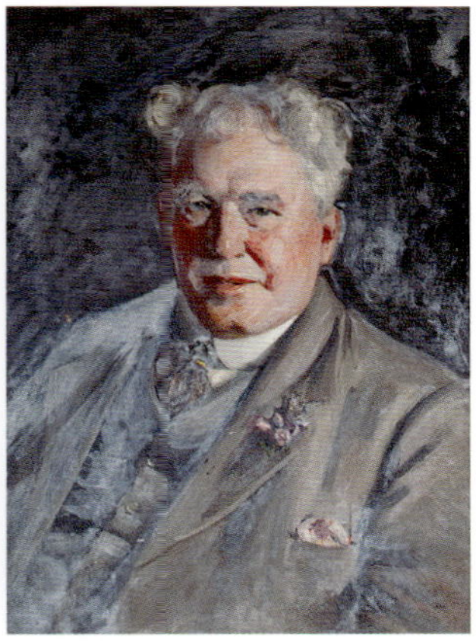

Balshaw, Fred 1860–1936
James Holmes c.1923
oil on canvas 66 x 48.3
BURGM:paoil241

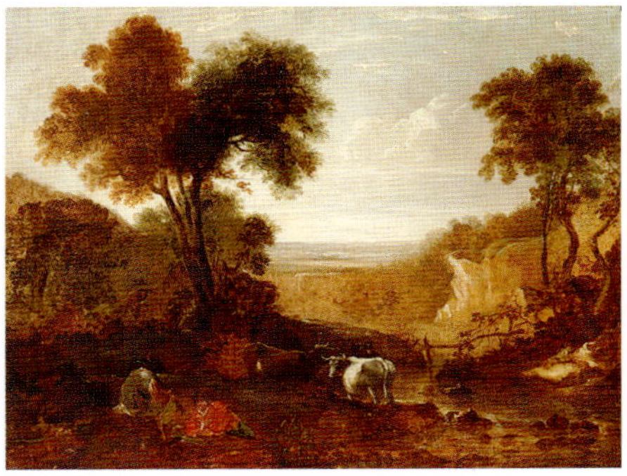

Barker, Thomas 1769–1847
Landscape with Figures and Cattle 1830
oil on canvas 44.5 x 59.7
BURGM:paoil187

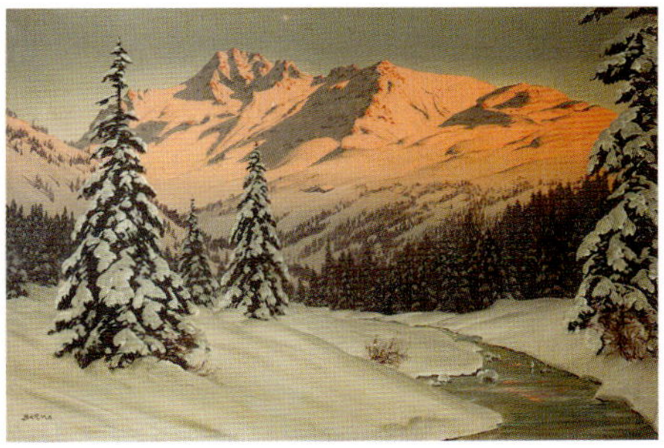

Barma, Hans Smatlak 1903–1978
The Dolomites Sunset
oil on canvas 62.2 x 91.4
BURGM:paoil177

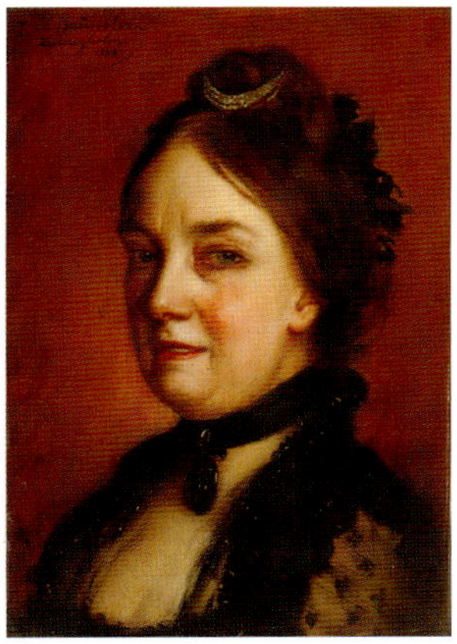

Barmelov, A de.
Lucy Ellen Towneley (c.1818–1900) 1888
oil on canvas 33.7 x 24.1
BURGM:paoil197

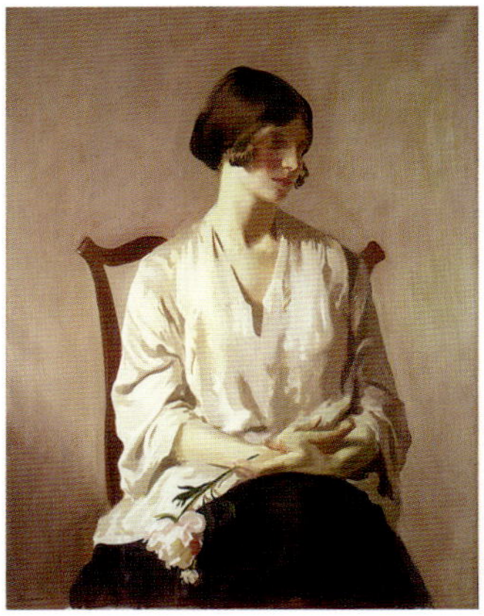

Barnes, Archibald George 1887–1972
Portrait of a Young Lady c.1920
oil on canvas 100 x 72.4
BURGM:paoil242

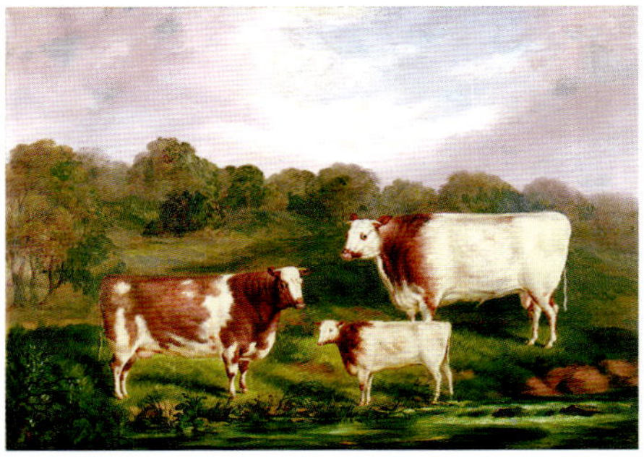

Barraud, Henry 1811–1874
Towneley Pedigrees 1858–1861
oil on canvas 81.3 x 112
BURGM:paoil292

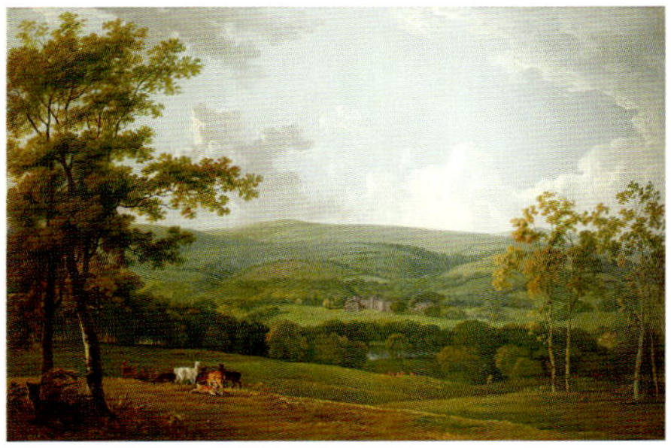

Barret the elder, George 1728–1784
A Distant View of Towneley Hall c.1777
oil on canvas 113 x 163
BURGM:paoil119

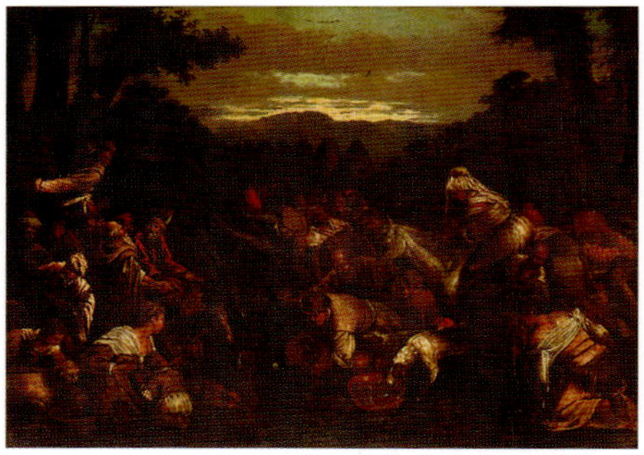

Bassano family active 16th C–17th C
Moses Striking the Rock 1570–1620
oil on canvas 102 x 140
BURGM:paoil282

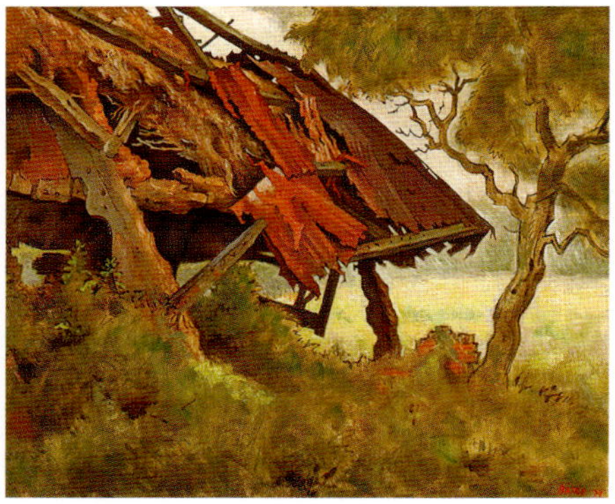

Bates, David F.
Old Cruck Building c.1974
oil on canvas 43.2 x 59.7
BURGM:paoil243

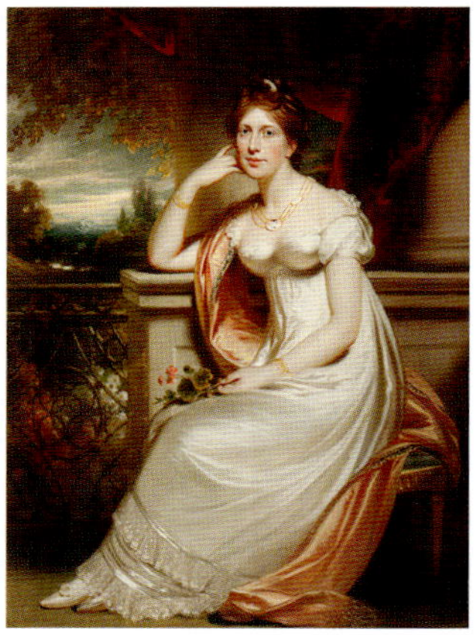

Beechey, William 1753–1839
The Honourable Mrs W. Noel 1818
oil on canvas 138 x 109
BURGM:paoil202

Facing page: Hitchens, Ivon, 1893–1979, *The Red Curtain*, c.1940, Lancaster City Museums (p. 207)

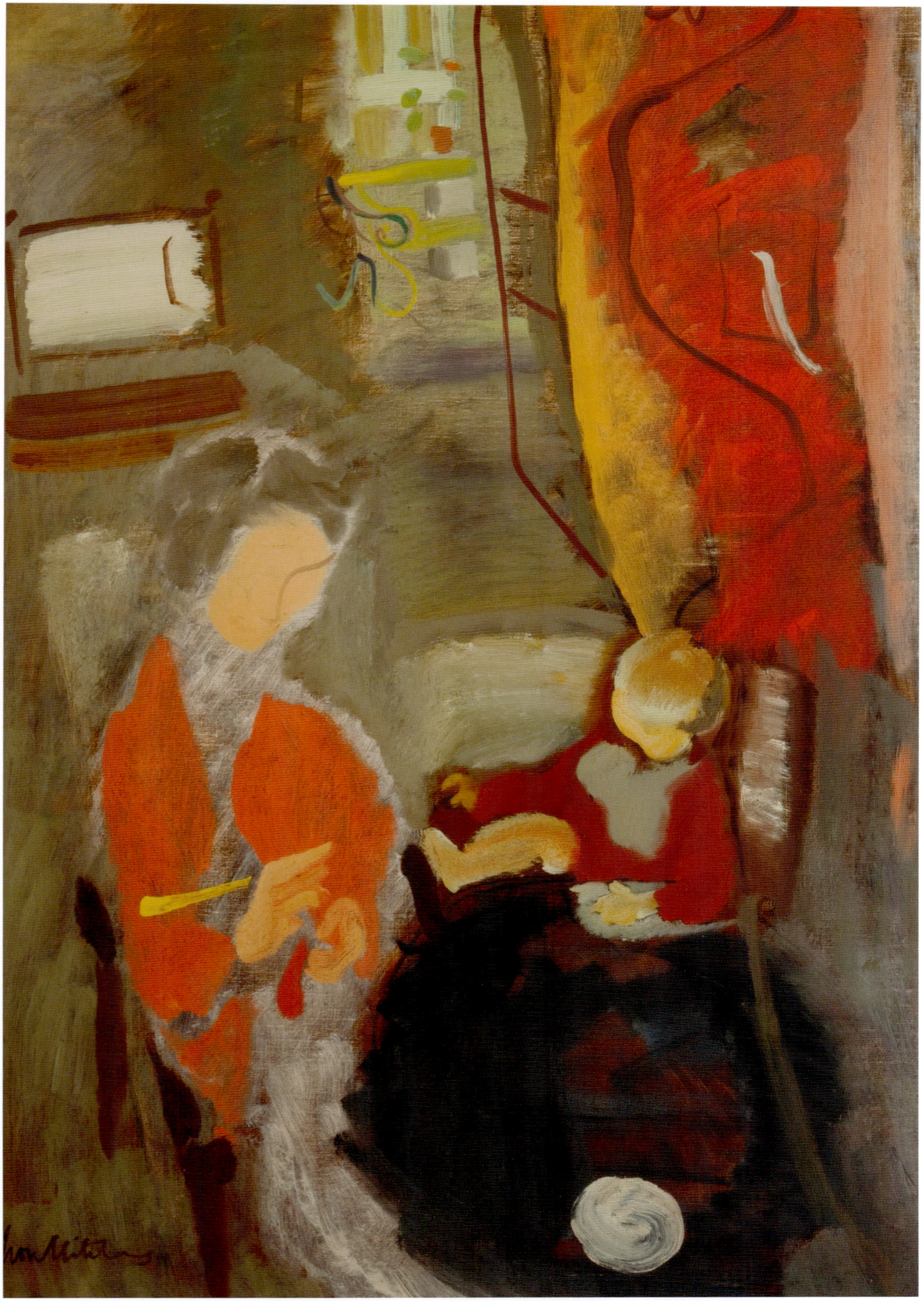

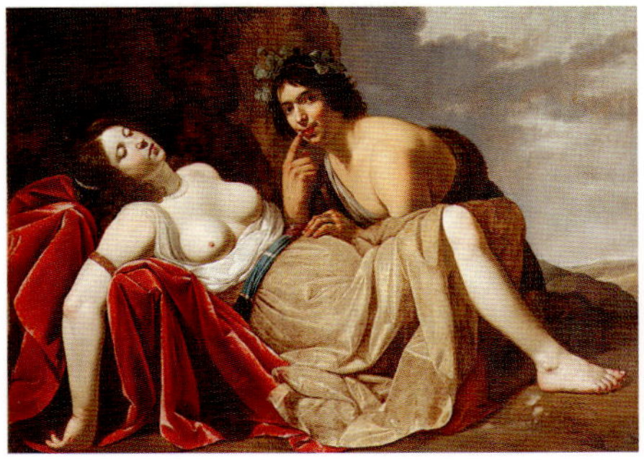

Bijlert, Jan van 1597–1671
Shepherd and Sleeping Girl 1623–1630
oil on canvas 96.5 x 137
BURGM:paoil283

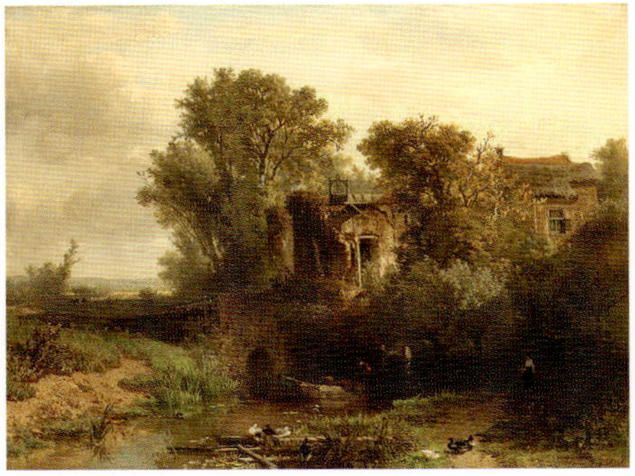

Bilders, Johannes Wernardus 1811–1890
A Dutch Landscape
oil on canvas 69.9 x 92.7
BURGM:paoil24

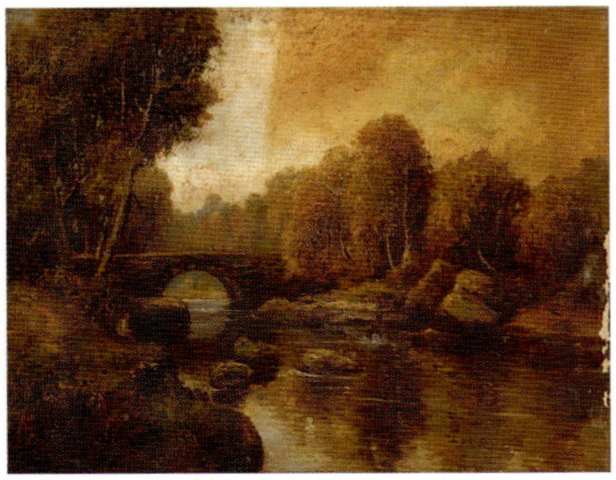

Bird, Archibald 1885–1975
River Scene 1910
oil on canvas 61.0 x 91.4
BURGM:paoil335a

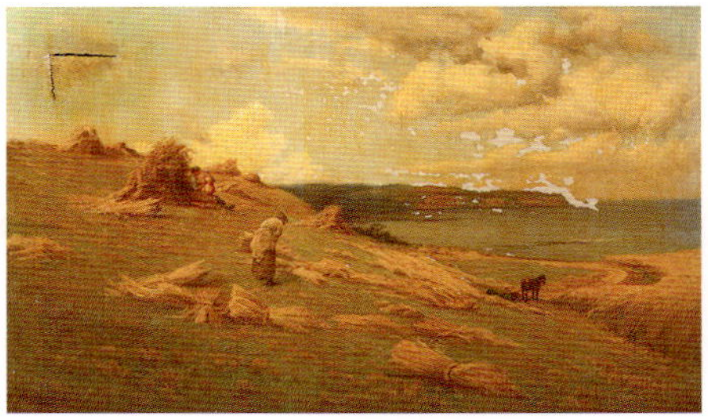

Blackburn, Arthur 1853–1925
Haymaking Scene
oil on canvas 74.9 x 124
BURGM:paoil278

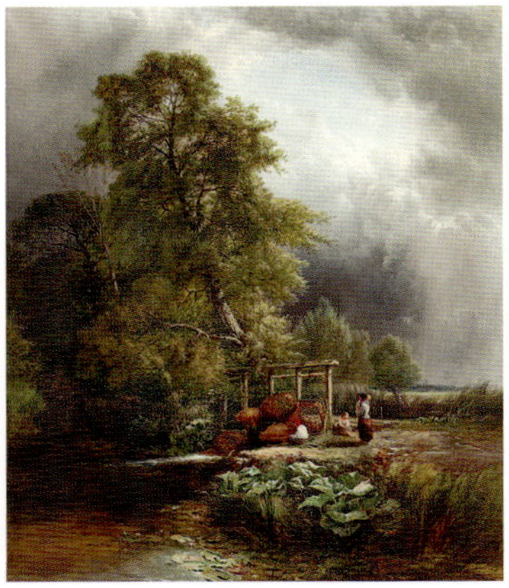

Boddington, Henry John 1811–1865
The Calm before the Storm
oil on canvas 108 x 91.4
BURGM:paoil213

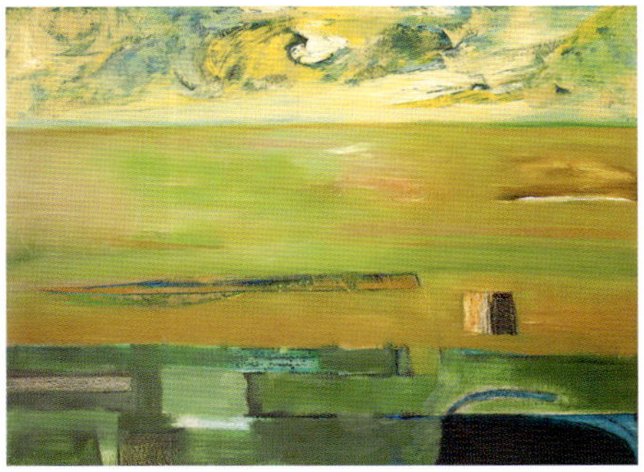

Bonner, Lonsdale b.1926
Pilling Marshes c.1974
oil on board 121 x 151
BURGM:paoil244

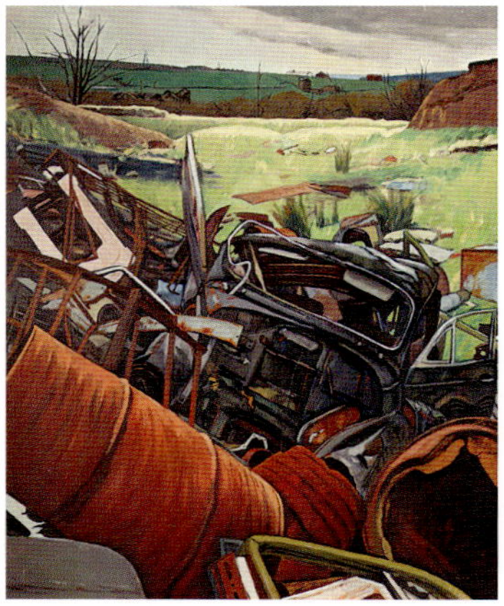

Bownass, Robin Ernest b.1938
Scrap at the Base of Slag Heap c.1974
oil on canvas over board 159 x 130
BURGM:paoil245

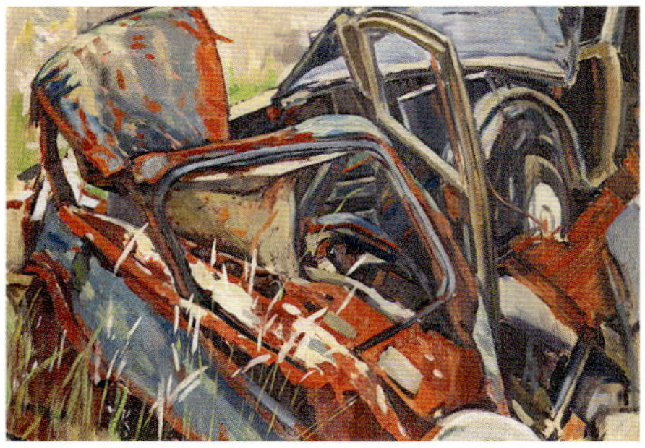

Bownass, Robin Ernest b.1938
Scrap at the Base of Slag Heap c.1974
oil on canvas over board 55.9 x 78.7
BURGM:paoil248

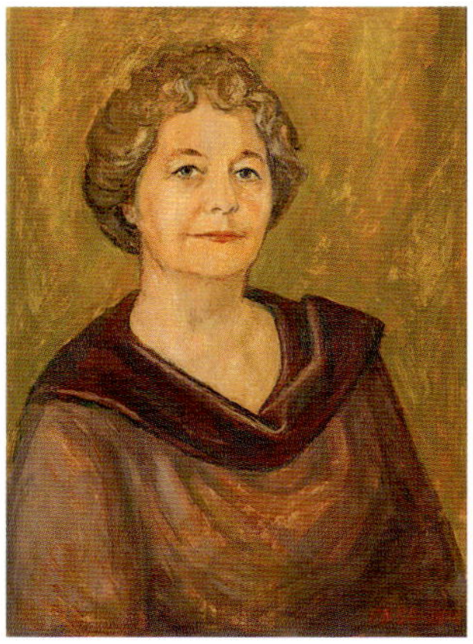

Brannan, Peter 1926–1994
Edna Ascroft (d.c.1988) c.1980
oil on board 40 x 29.2
BURGM:paoil300

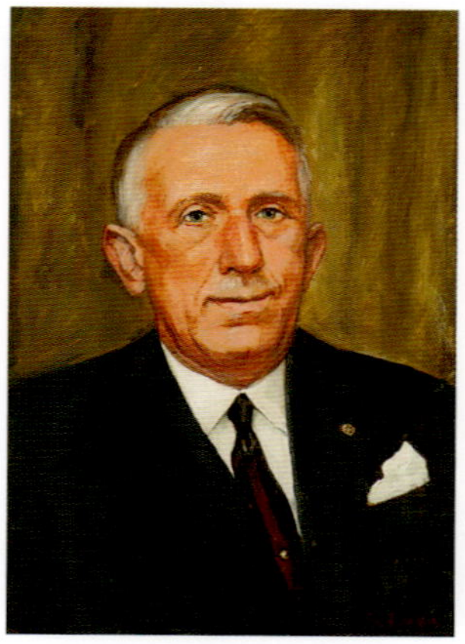

Brannan, Peter 1926–1994
Frank Ascroft c.1980
oil on board 38.7 x 28.6
BURGM:paoil301

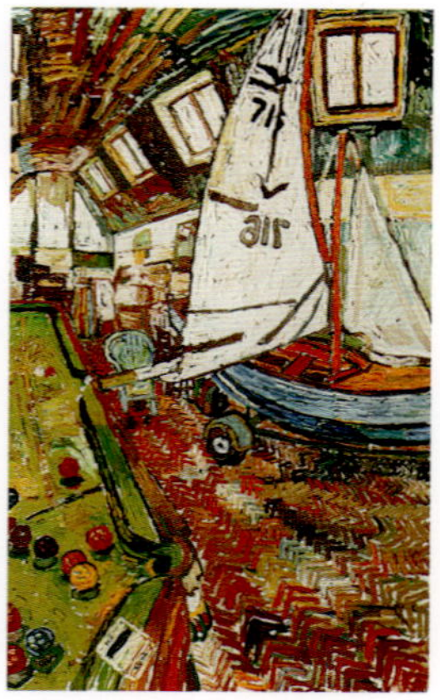

Bratby, John Randall 1928–1992
Sailboat in the Artist's Studio
oil on canvas 142 x 81.3
BURGM:paoil231

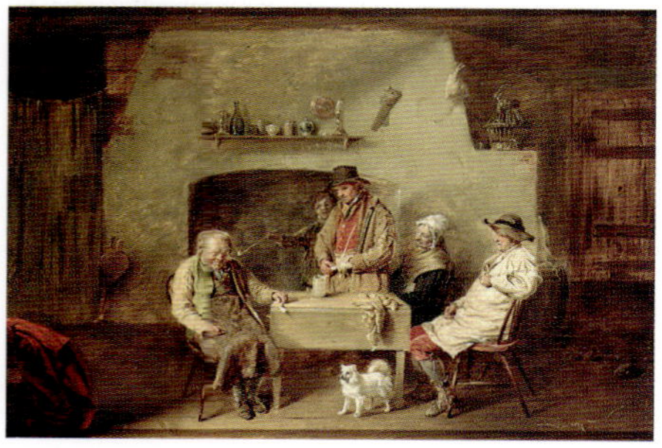

Bristow, Edmund 1787–1876
The End of the Chapter 1822
oil on panel 21.6 x 31.8
BURGM:paoil143

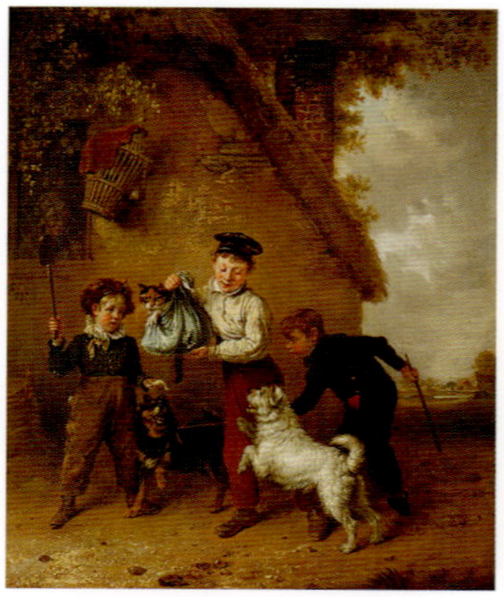

Bristow, Edmund 1787–1876
Mischief
oil on panel 35.6 x 30.5
BURGM:paoil107

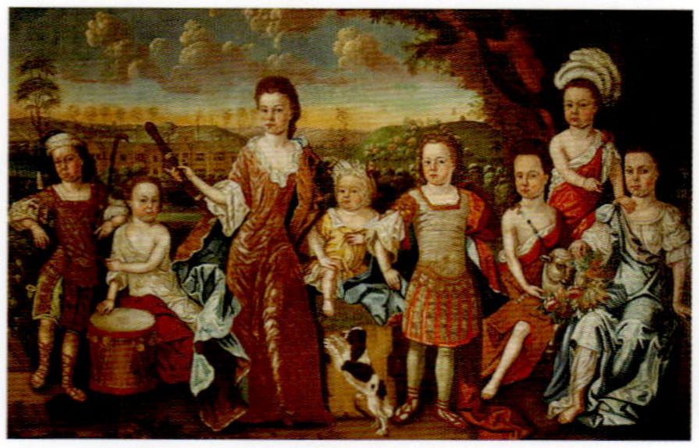

British (English) School
The Strachey Family c.1710
oil on canvas 150 x 242
LOAN2002 (P)

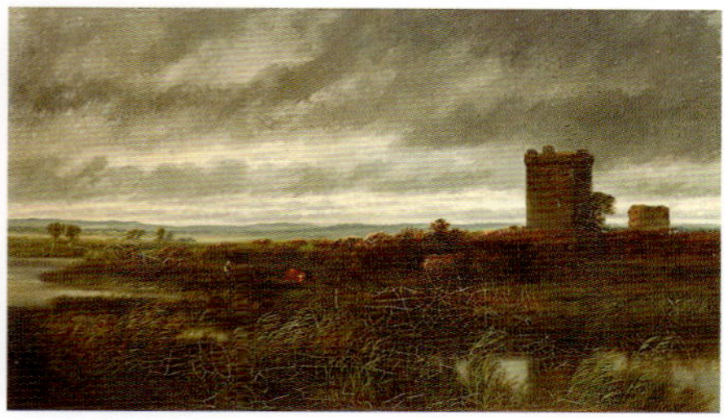

Brown, William Beattie 1831–1909
Landscape with Castle
oil on canvas 66 x 114
BURGM:paoil277

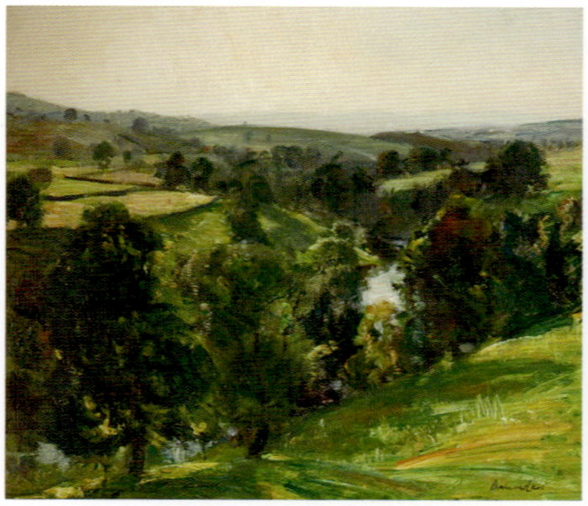

Brundrit, Reginald Grange 1883–1960
The Wooded Vale 1933
oil on canvas 49.5 x 59.7
BURGM:paoil87

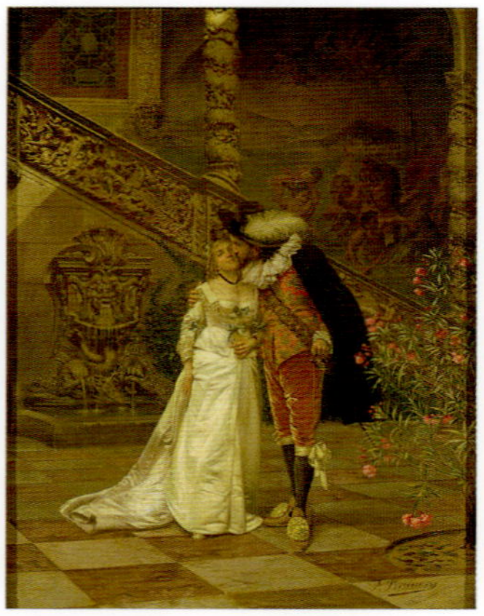

Brunery, Francesco 1845–1926
I Will
oil on canvas 59.7 x 44.5
BURGM:paoil189

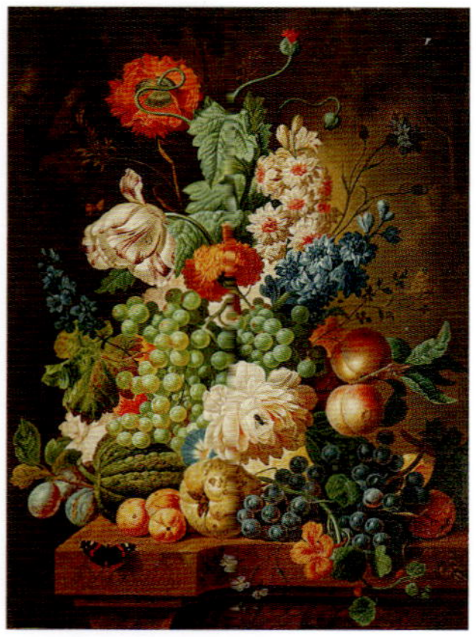

Brussel, Paul Theodor van 1754–1795
Fruit and Flowers on a Marble Table 1794
oil on panel 77.5 x 57.8
BURGM:paoil115

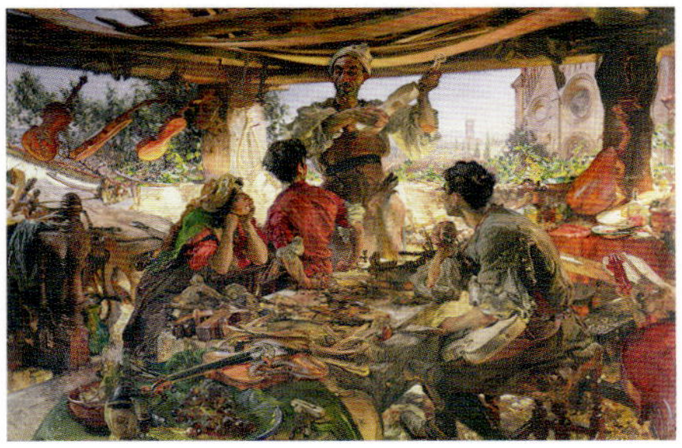

Bundy, Edgar 1862–1922
Stradivarius in His Workshop at Cremona
1913
oil on canvas 100 x 151
BURGM:paoil54

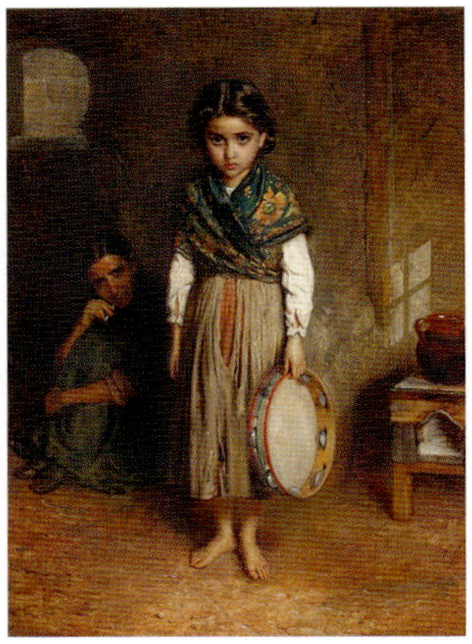

Burgess, John Bagnold 1829–1897
A Little Spanish Gipsy c.1868
oil on canvas 72.4 x 56.5
BURGM:paoil198

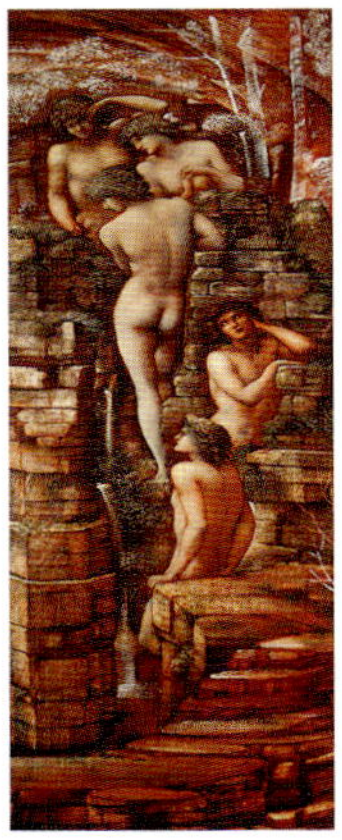

Burne-Jones, Edward 1833–1898
Wood Nymphs 1881–1885
oil on canvas 183 x 59.7
BURGM:paoil52

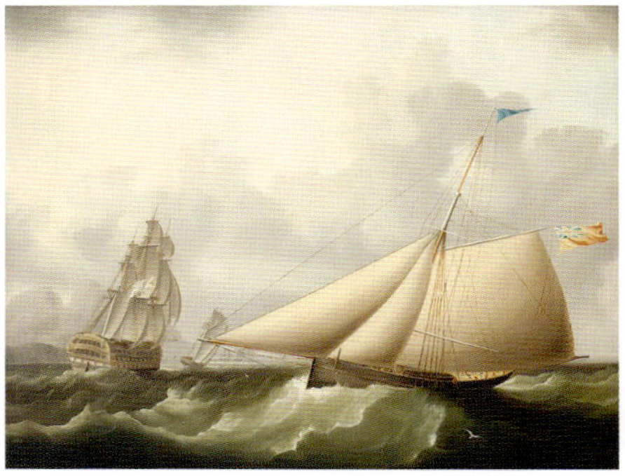

Buttersworth, James Edward 1817–1894
Seascape
oil on canvas 69.9 x 89.5
BURGM:paoil111

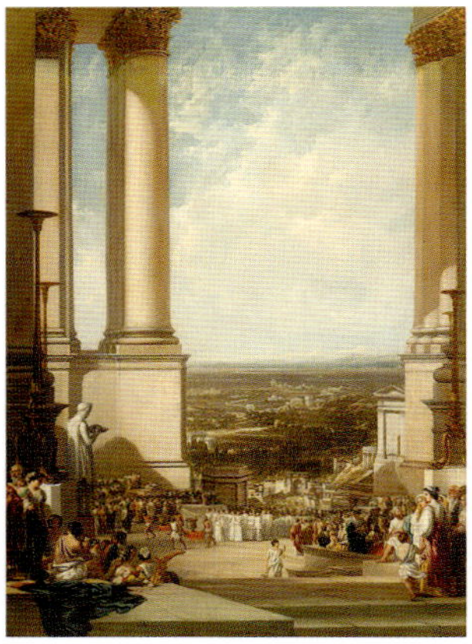

Callcott, Augustus Wall 1779–1844
The Temple of Aesculapius 1837
oil on canvas 114 x 77.5
BURGM:paoil21

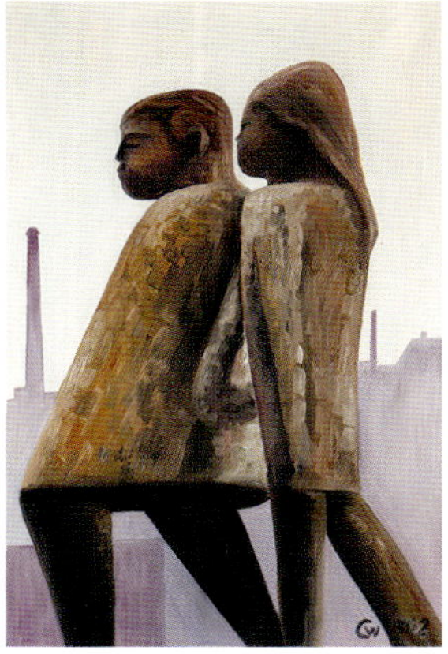

Carney, W. D.
Centenary Statue, Burnley 1962
oil on canvas 90.2 x 59.7
BURGM:paoil239

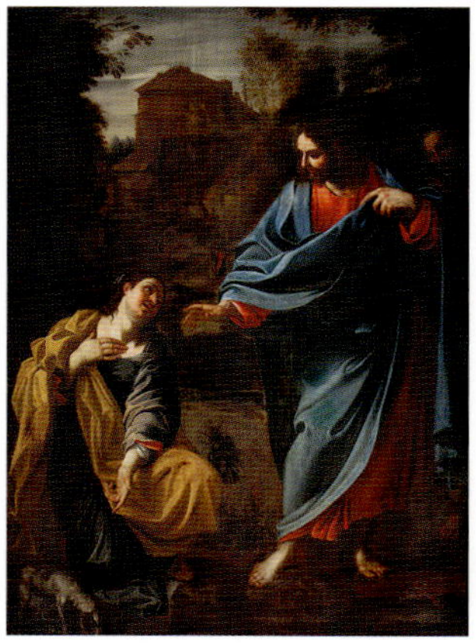

Carracci, Ludovico (after) 1555–1619
Christ and the Woman of Canaan 1595–1620
oil on canvas 249 x 193
BURGM:paoil8

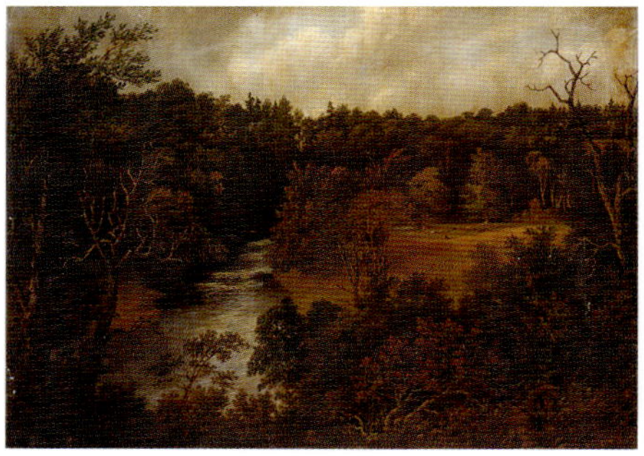

Cawthorne, E. active late 19th C
Autumn on the Ribble
oil on canvas 96.5 x 140
BURGM:paoil269

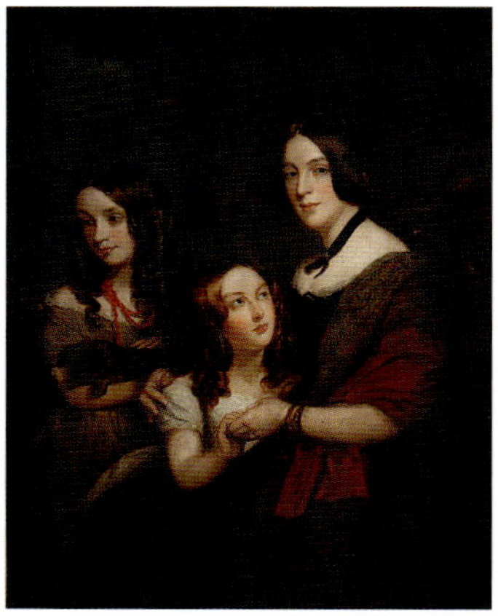

Clarke, George Frederick 1823–1906
Lady Caroline Towneley with Two of Her Daughters, Caroline and Emily (copy after Francis Grant) 1860
oil on canvas 124 x 99.1
BURGM:paoil103

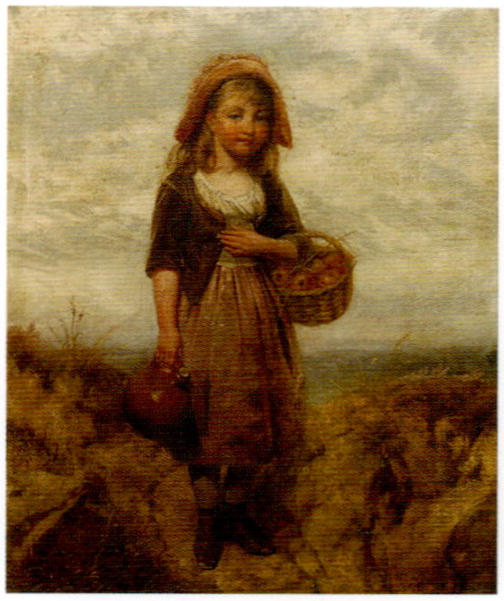

Cobbett, Edward John 1815–1899
Girl with a Basket of Apples
oil on canvas 74.9 x 62.2
BURGM:paoil159

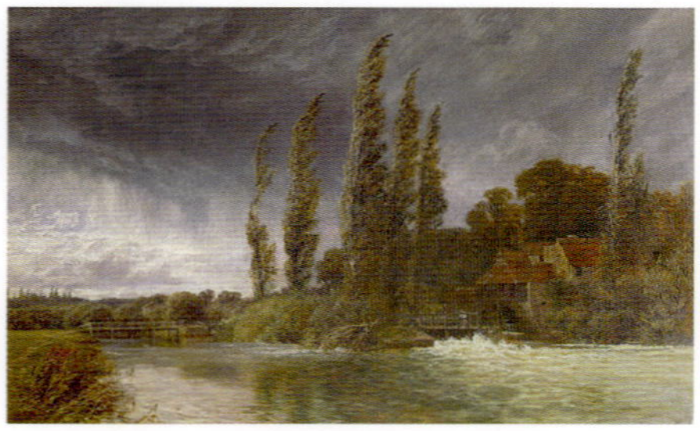

Cole, George Vicat 1833–1893
Iffley Mill 1884
oil on canvas 88.9 x 144
BURGM:paoil76

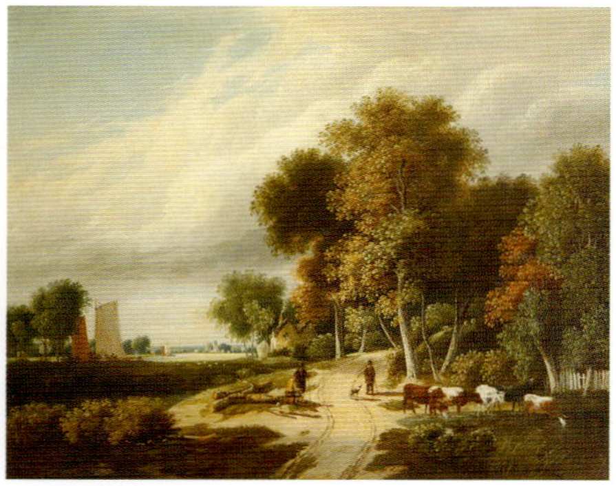

Colkett, Samuel David 1806–1863
A Scene in Norfolk
oil on canvas 63.5 x 76.2
BURGM:paoil97

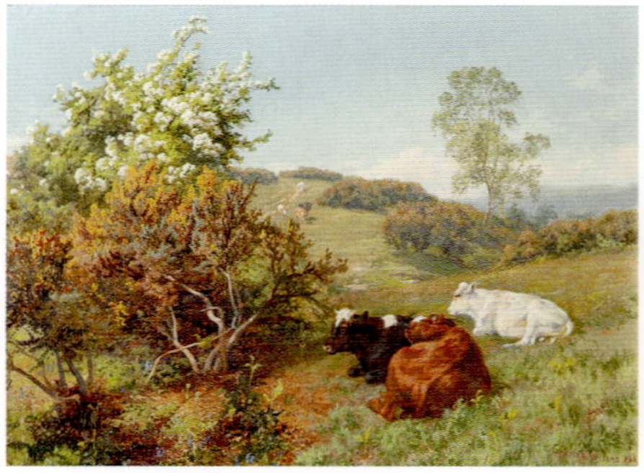

Collins II, Charles 1851–1921
In the Nower, Dorking
oil on canvas 29.2 x 37.5
BURGM:paoil142

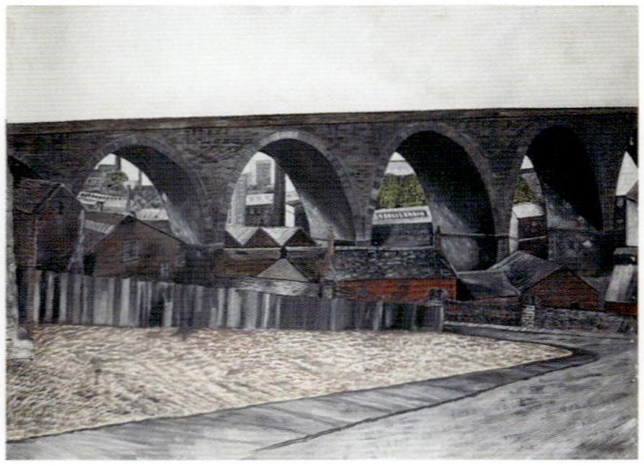

Collinson, Brian
Old Railway Arches, Burnley c.1970
oil on canvas 76.2 x 107
BURGM:paoil226

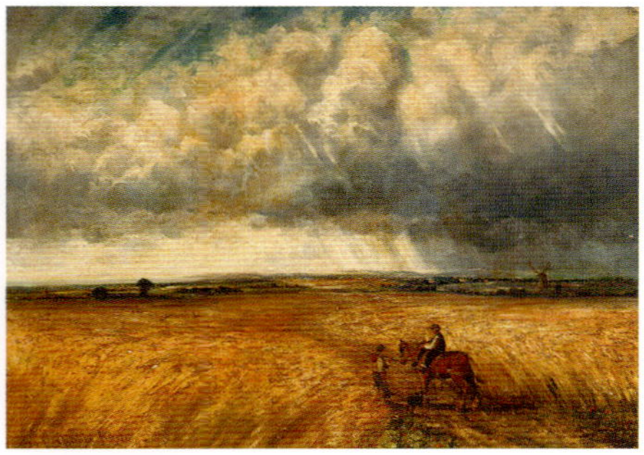

Constable, John (style of) 1776–1837
The Gathering Storm 1819
oil on canvas 91.4 x 124
BURGM:paoil179

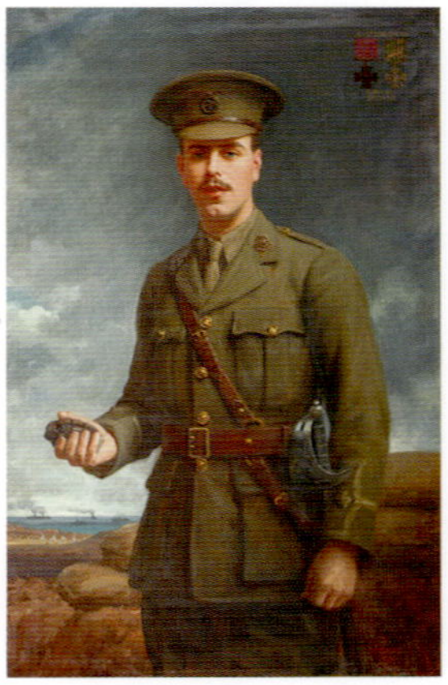

Cooke, Isaac 1846–1922
2nd Lieutenant Alfred Victor Smith (1891–1915), VC 1916
oil on canvas 131 x 85.1
BURGM:paoil40

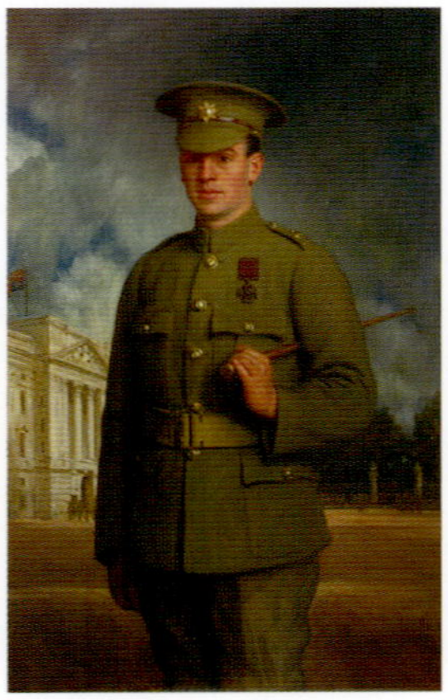

Cooke, Isaac 1846–1922
Private Thomas Whitham (1888–1924), VC 1918
oil on canvas 131 x 85.1
BURGM:paoil41

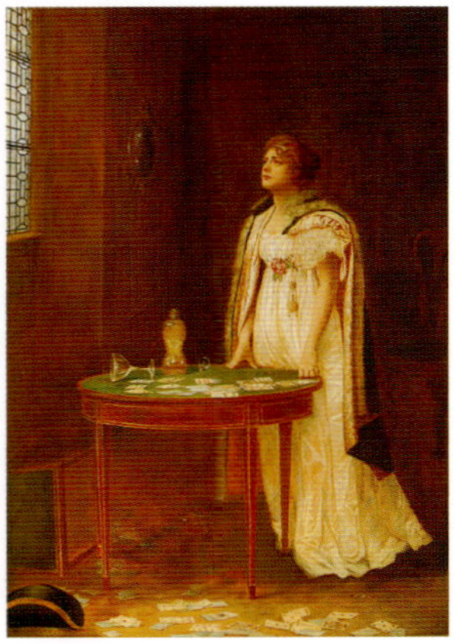

Cookesley, Margaret Deborah 1844–1927
The Gambler's Wife 1897
oil on canvas 150 x 105
BURGM:paoil14

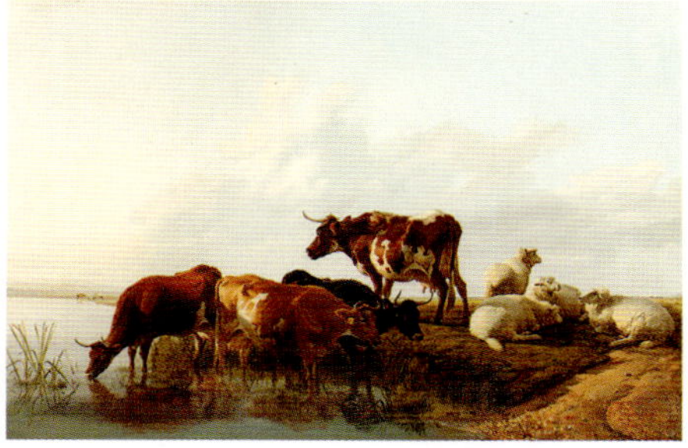

Cooper, Thomas Sidney 1803–1902
A Summer Afternoon 1861
oil on canvas 74.9 x 110
BURGM:paoil23

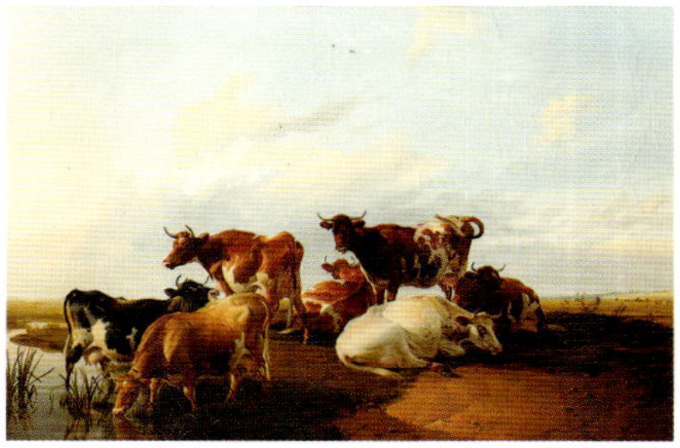

Cooper, Thomas Sidney 1803–1902
Evening in the Meadows 1871
oil on canvas 74.9 x 110
BURGM:paoil227

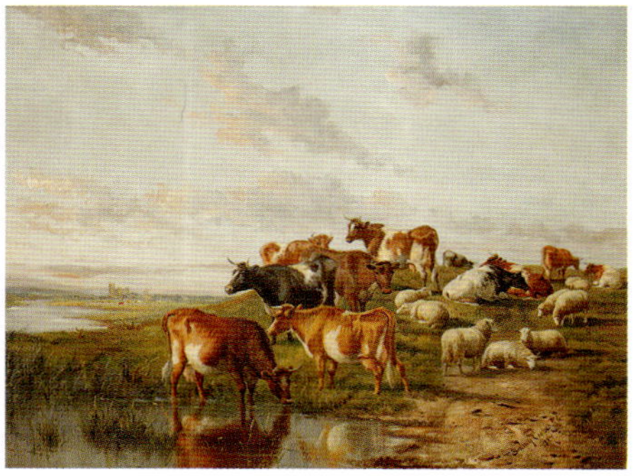

Cooper, Thomas Sidney 1803–1902
The Watering Place 1887
oil on canvas 66 x 86.4
BURGM:paoil144

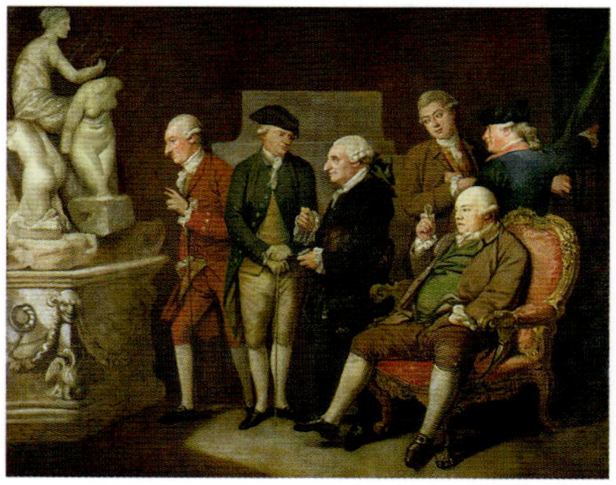

Cosway, Richard 1742–1821
Group of Connoisseurs 1775
oil on canvas 83.8 x 105
BURGM:paoil195

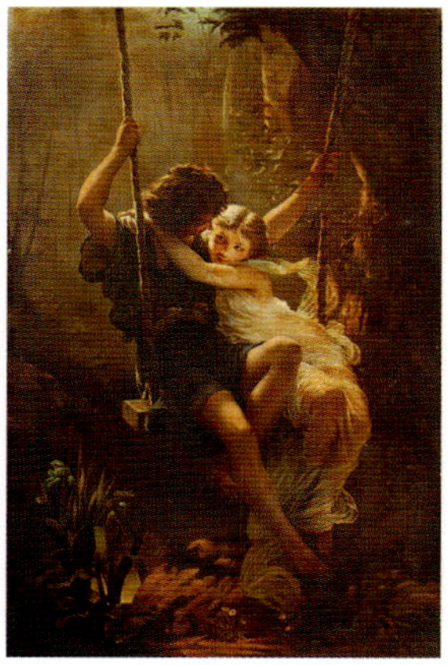

Cot, Pierre Auguste (after) 1837–1883
Le printemps
oil on canvas 168 x 109
BURGM:paoil286

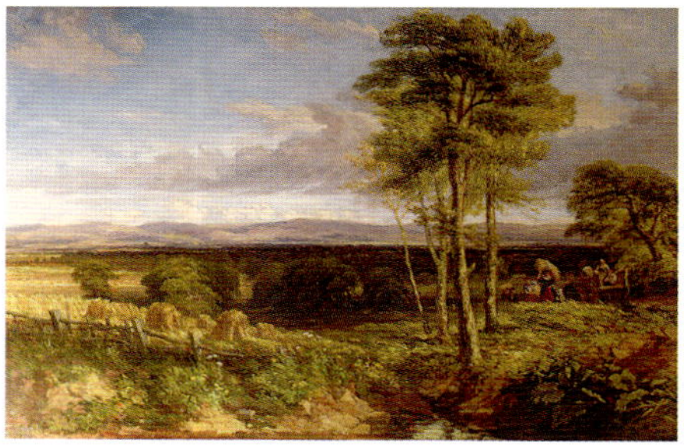

Cox the elder, David 1783–1859
The Vale of Clwyd 1846
oil on canvas 91.4 x 138
BURGM:paoil94

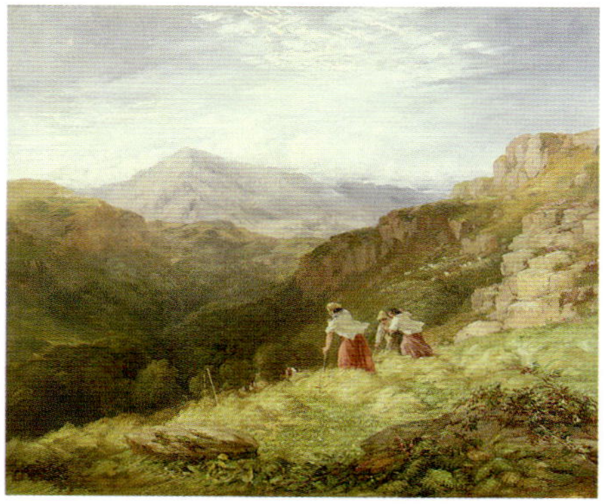

Cox the elder, David 1783–1859
Haymaking on Snowdon 1847
oil on canvas 61 x 72.4
BURGM:paoil122

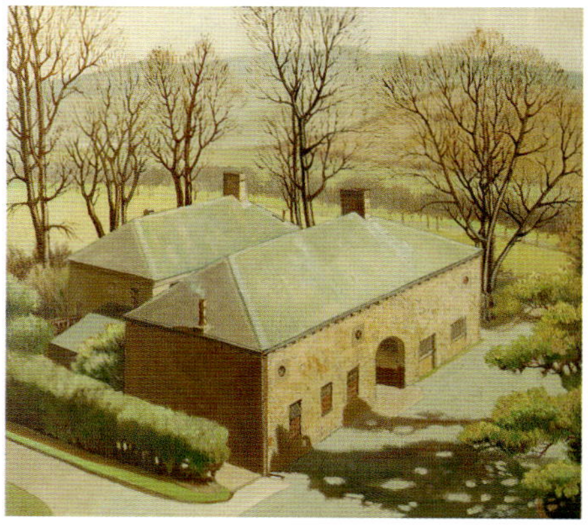

Crabtree, Joseph active 1941–1950
A View of Towneley Stables
oil on canvas 49.5 x 54
BURGM:paoil158

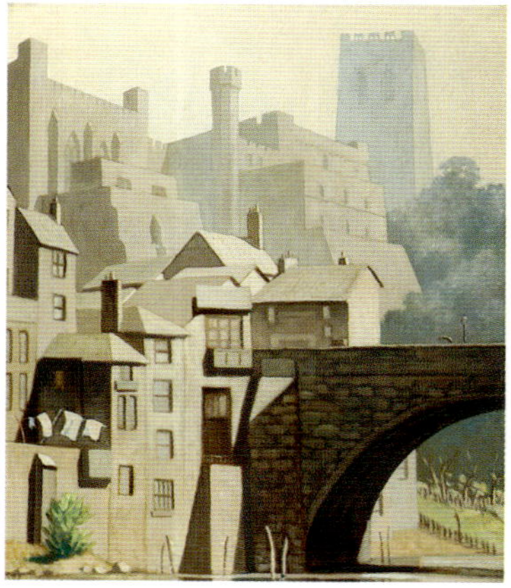

Crabtree, Joseph active 1941–1950
Durham
oil on canvas 64.8 x 55.9
BURGM:paoil156

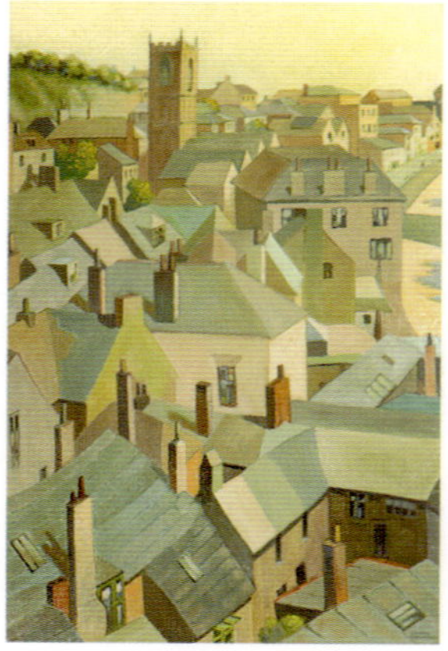

Crabtree, Joseph active 1941–1950
St Ives
oil on canvas 62.2 x 49.5
BURGM:paoil157

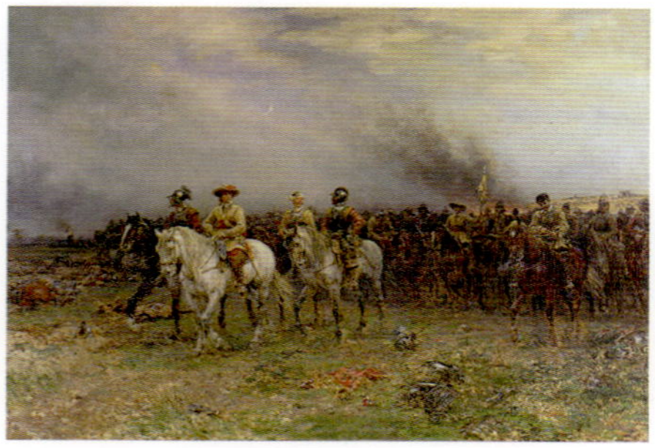

Crofts, Ernest 1847–1911
Cromwell after the Battle of Marston Moor
1909
oil on canvas 100 x 145
BURGM:paoil29

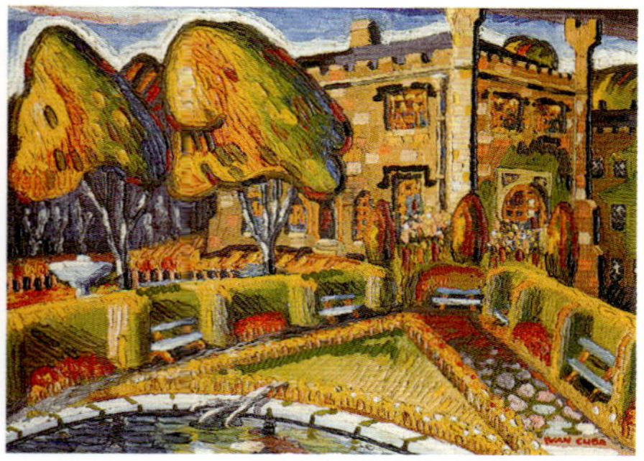

Cuba, Ivan 1920–2007
Towneley Hall c.1955
oil on board 48.3 x 66
BURGM:paoil219

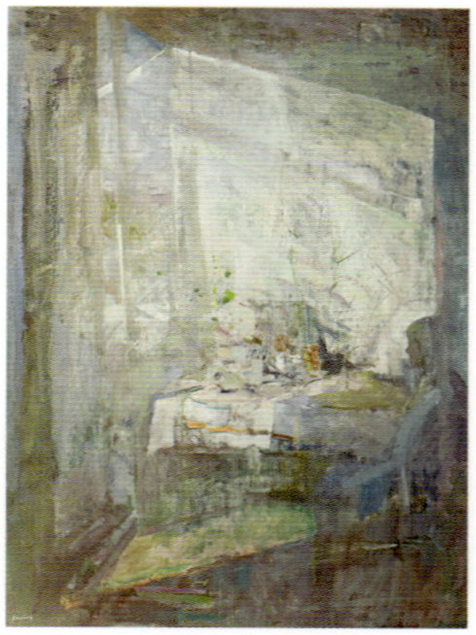

Cuming, Frederick b.1930
The Studio
oil on board 119 x 88.9
BURGM:paoil291

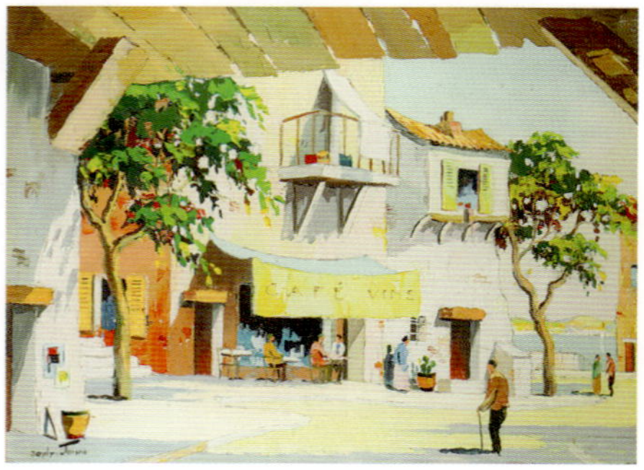

D'Oyly-John, Cecil Rochfort 1906–1993
Café Vins, South of France
oil on canvas 40.6 x 55.9
BURGM:paoil176

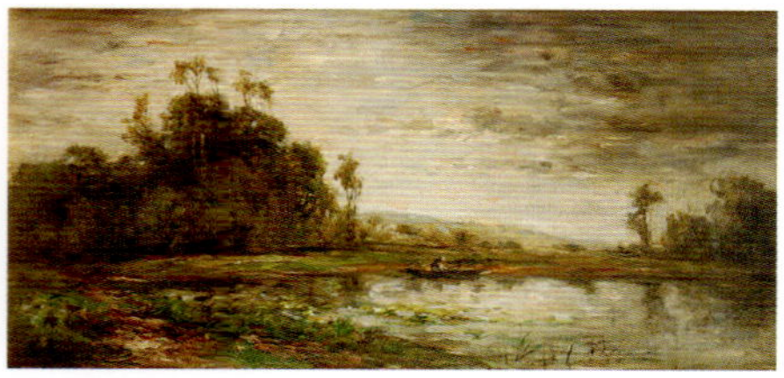

Daubigny, Charles-François 1817–1878
River Scene at Sunset 1875
oil on canvas 37.5 x 76.2
BURGM:paoil136

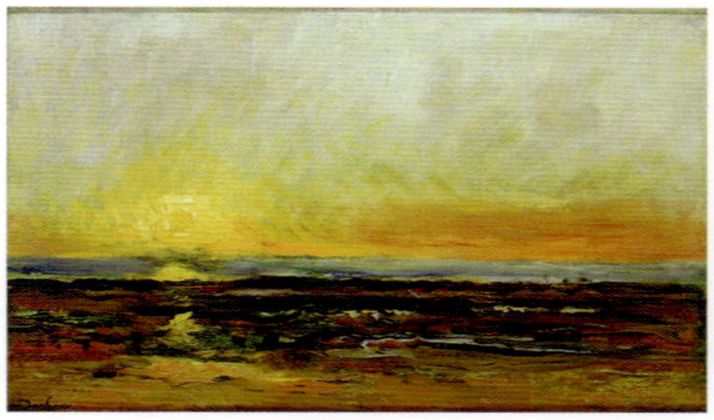

Daubigny, Charles-François 1817–1878
Sunset on the Sea Coast
oil on panel 24.1 x 40
BURGM:paoil131

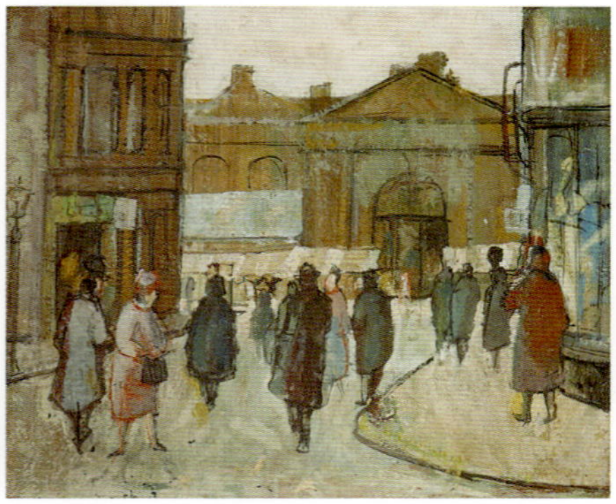

Dawson, Ida b.1931
Market Hall, Burnley c.1960
oil on canvas 43.8 x 52.1
BURGM:paoil324

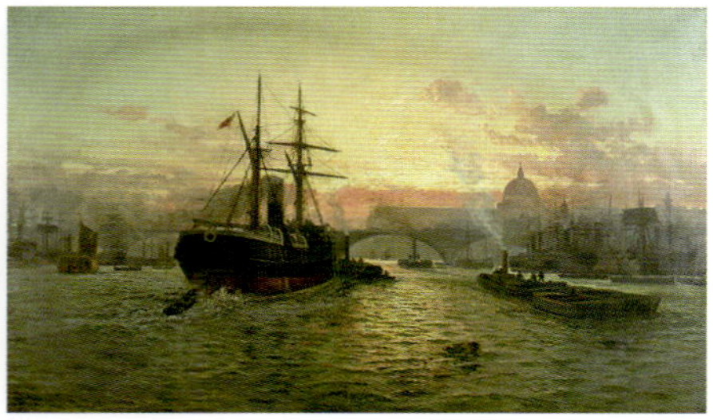

De Lacy, Charles John 1856–1936
London Bridge 1884
oil on canvas 73.7 x 124
BURGM:paoil238

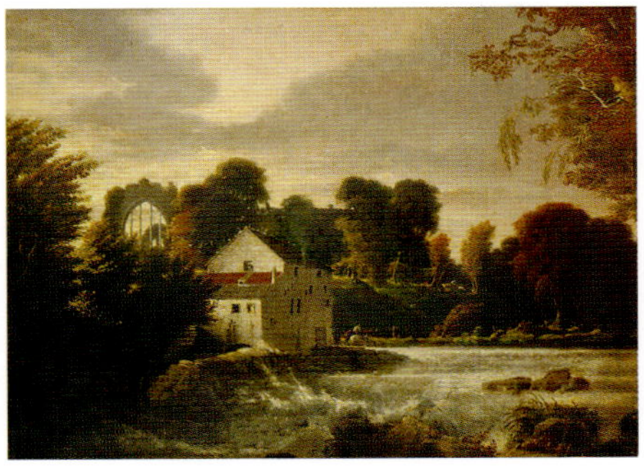

De Wint, Peter 1784–1849
A Watermill near Egglestone Abbey, Durham c.1814
oil on canvas 57.2 x 76.2
BURGM:paoil102

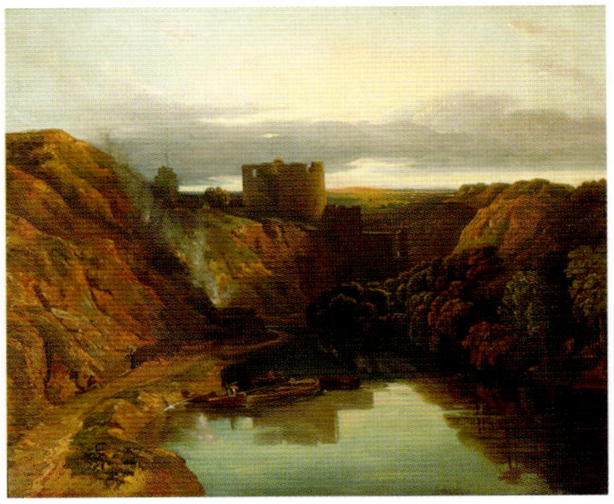

De Wint, Peter 1784–1849
Cilgerran Castle
oil on canvas 55.9 x 69.9
BURGM:paoil109

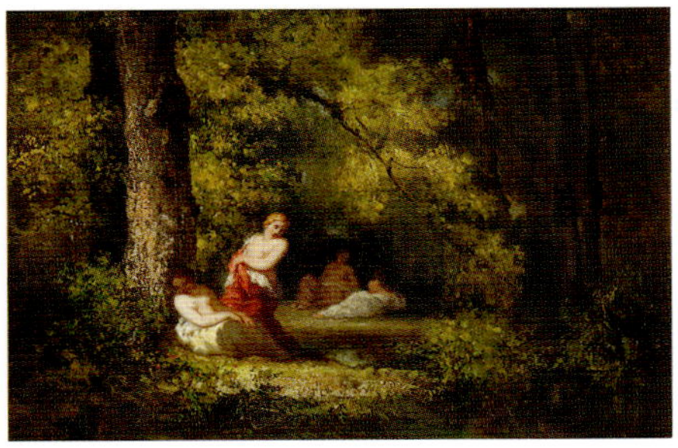

Diaz de la Peña, Narcisse Virgile 1807–1876
Four Nymphs in a Wood
oil on canvas 25.4 x 38.1
BURGM:paoil138

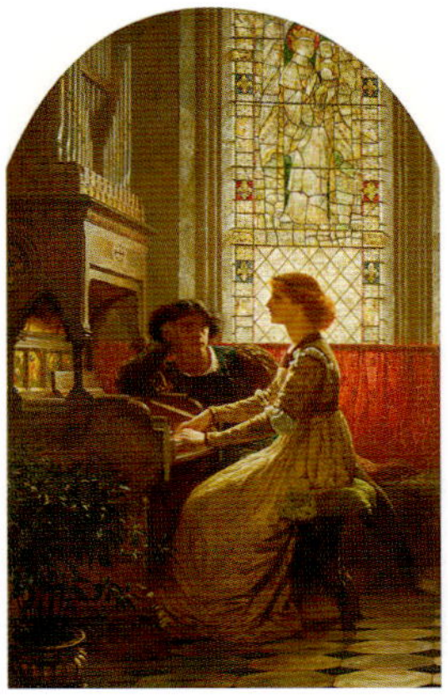

Dicksee, Frank 1853–1928
Harmony 1879
oil on canvas 117 x 69.2
BURGM:paoil150

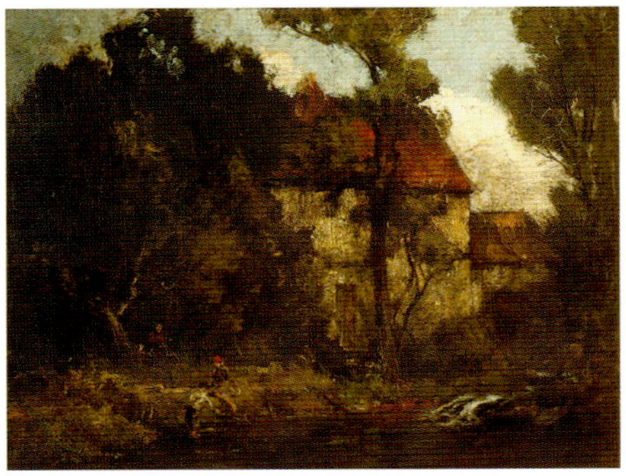

Dods-Withers, Isobelle Ann 1876–1939
The White House
oil on canvas 73.7 x 99.1
BURGM:paoil60

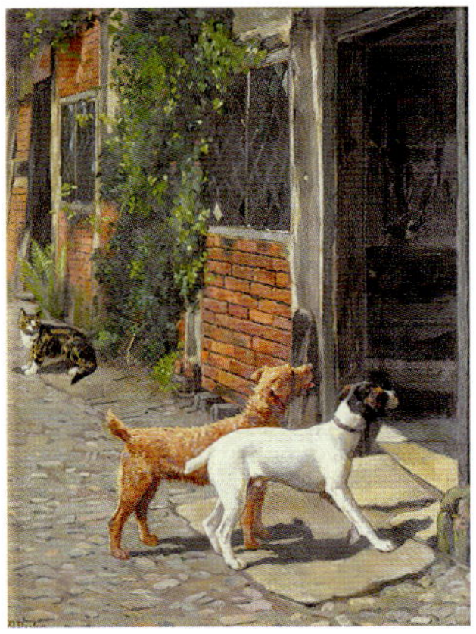

Duke, Alfred 1836–1915
Hesitation c.1900
oil on canvas 36.8 x 27.9
BURGM:paoil249

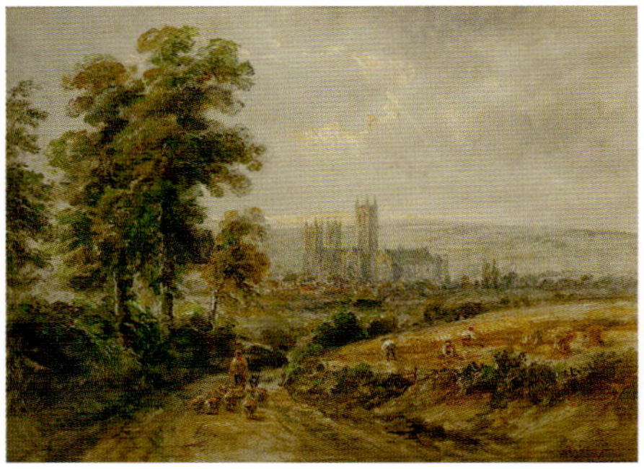

Earp, Henry 1831–1914
Canterbury Cathedral
oil on canvas 24.8 x 34.7
BURGM:paoil332

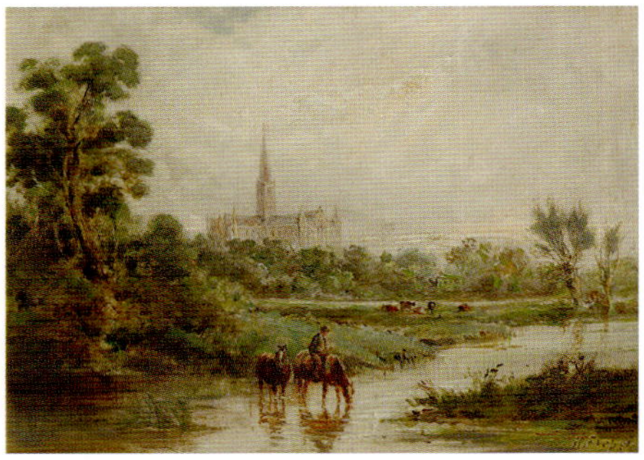

Earp, Henry 1831–1914
Salisbury Cathedral
oil on canvas 24.8 x 34.7
BURGM:paoil333

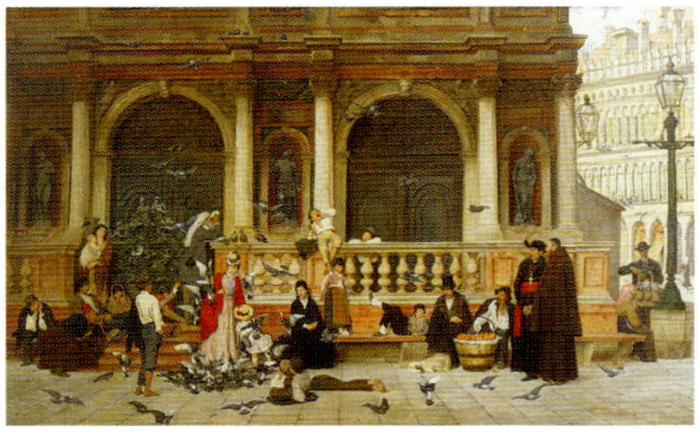

Echtler, Adolf 1843–1914
St Mark's, Venice
oil on canvas 102 x 163
BURGM:paoil153

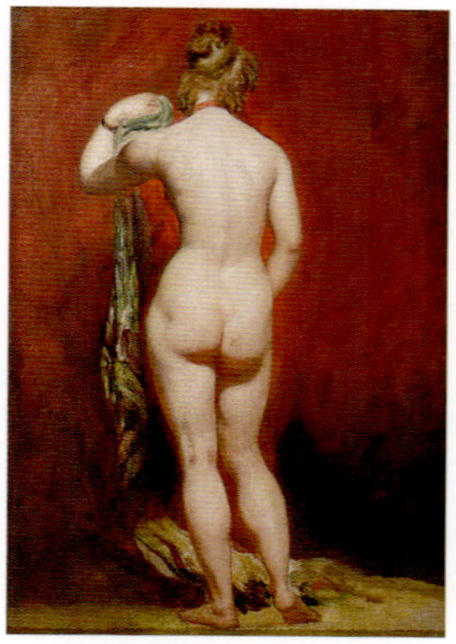

Etty, William 1787–1849
Standing Female Nude
oil on canvas 64.8 x 44.5
BURGM:paoil140

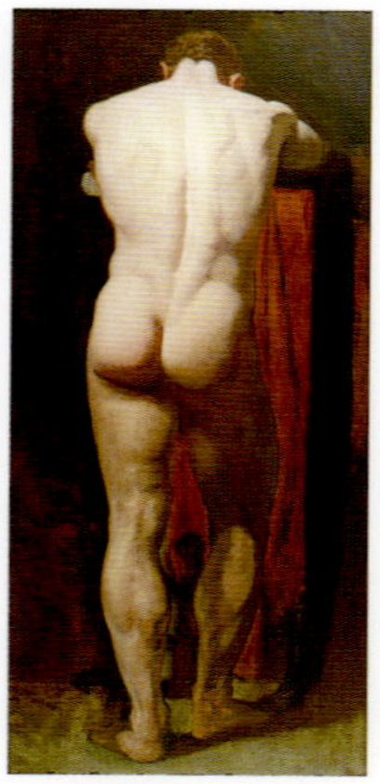

Etty, William 1787–1849
Standing Male Nude
oil on canvas 196 x 88.9
BURGM:paoil188

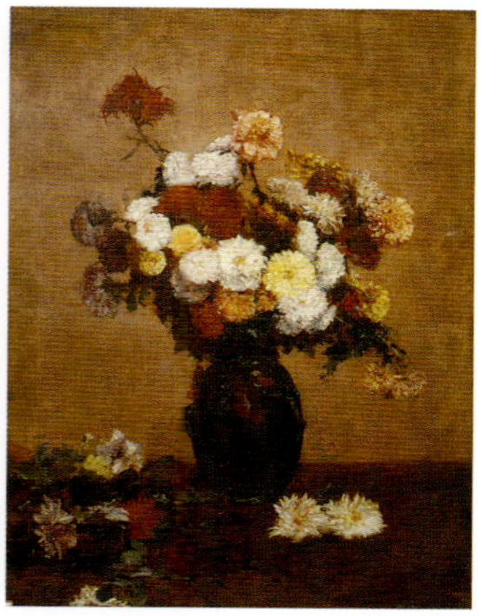

Fantin-Latour, Henri (style of) 1836–1904
Flowers in a Vase 1872
oil on canvas 88.9 x 68.6
BURGM:paoil135

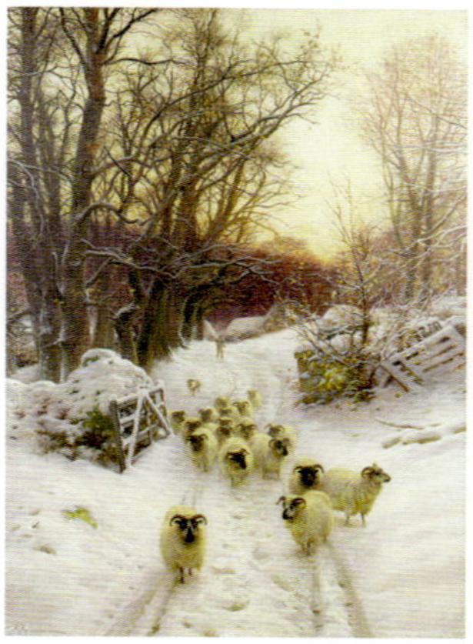

Farquharson, Joseph 1846–1935
The Sun Had Closed the Winter's Day c.1904
oil on canvas 169 x 121
BURGM:paoil61

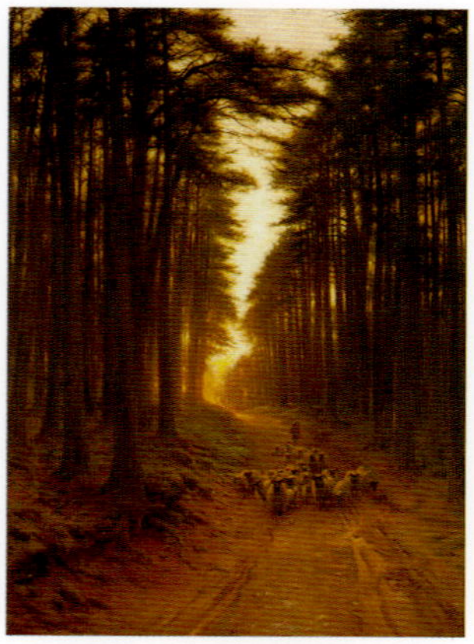

Farquharson, Joseph 1846–1935
Now Came Still Evening On c.1905
oil on canvas 165 x 121
BURGM:paoil116

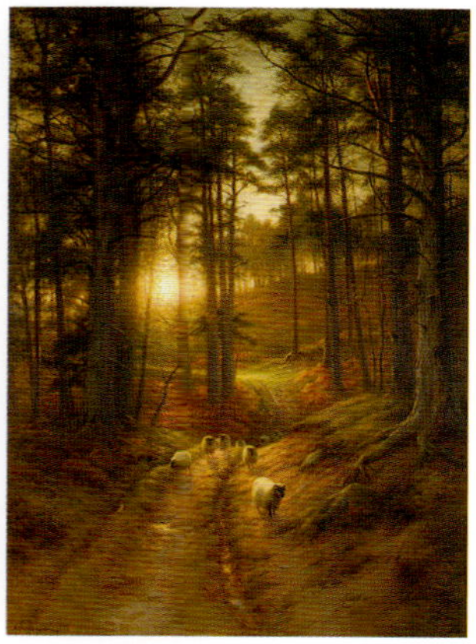

Farquharson, Joseph 1846–1935
The Sun Fast Sinks in the West
oil on canvas 137 x 100
BURGM:paoil45

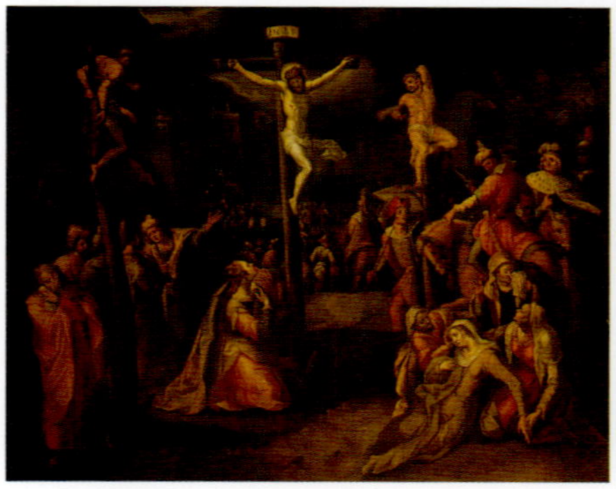

Flemish School
The Crucifixion 1550–1700
oil on canvas 94 x 124
BURGM:paoil65

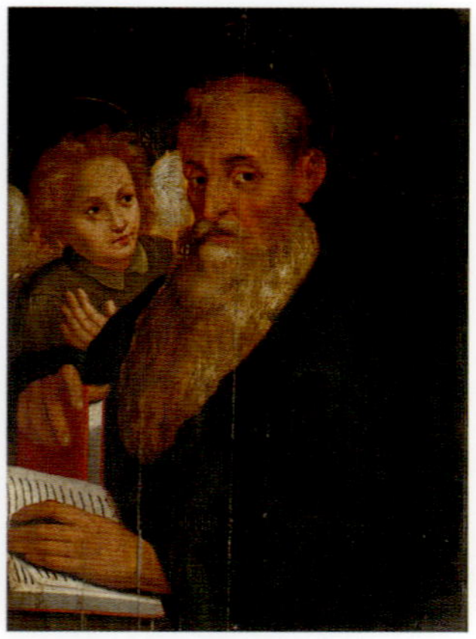

Flemish School
Saint Matthew, One of the Four Evangelists
19th C
oil on panel 63.5 x 48.3
BURGM:paoil1

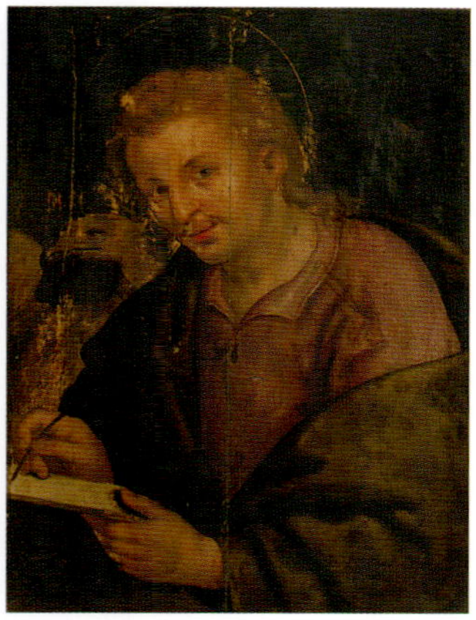

Flemish School
Saint John, One of the Four Evangelists
oil on panel 63.5 x 48.3
BURGM:paoil14

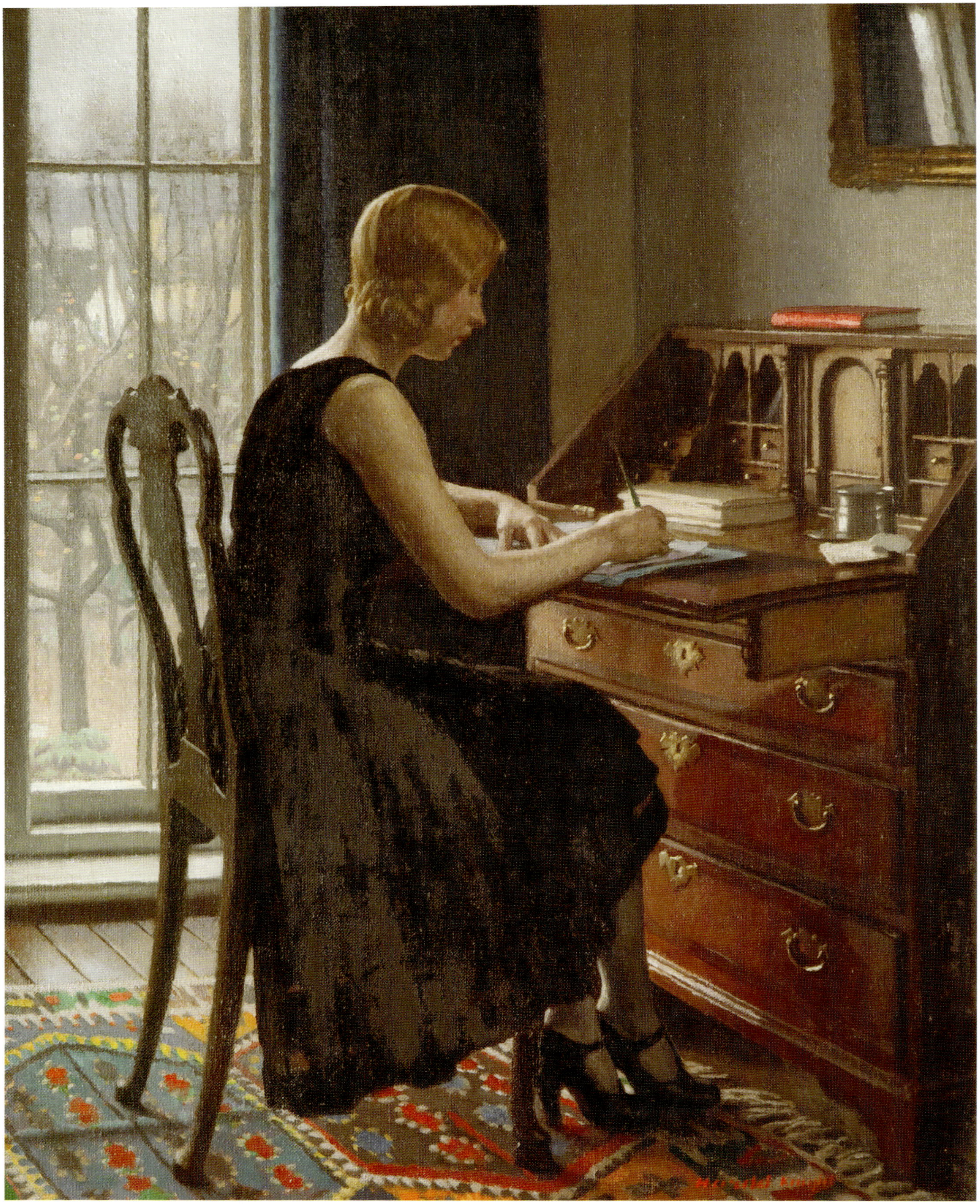

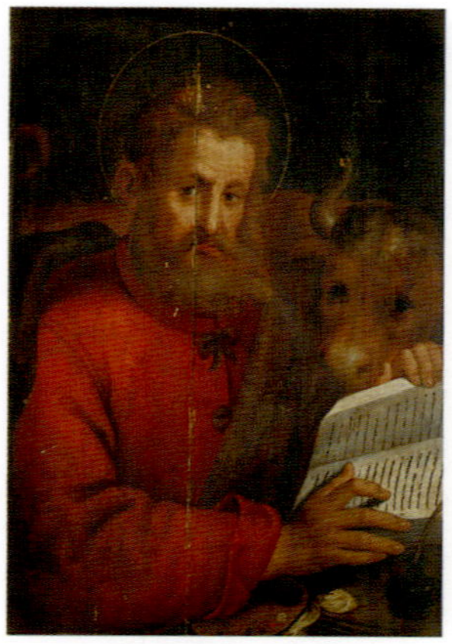

Flemish School
Saint Luke, One of the Four Evangelists
oil on panel 63.5 x 48.3
BURGM:paoil3

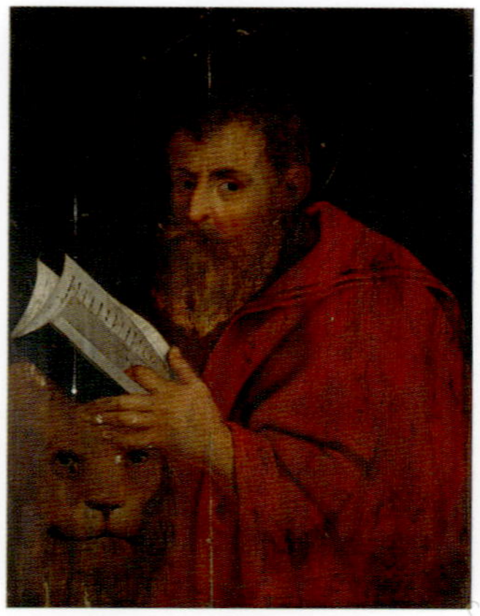

Flemish School
Saint Mark, One of the Four Evangelists
oil on panel 63.5 x 48.3
BURGM:paoil2

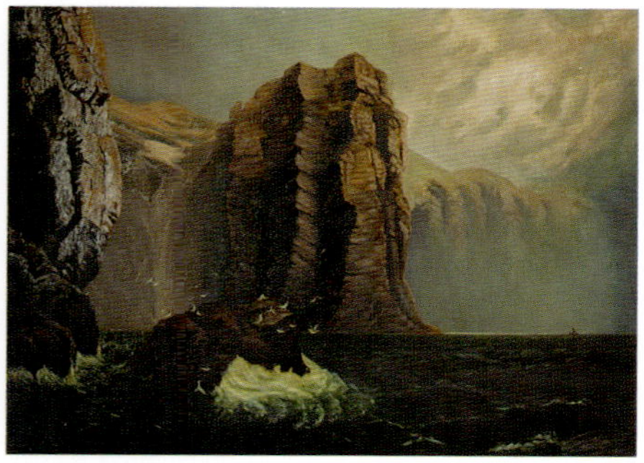

Fryer, William active 19th C
Seascape
oil on canvas 68.6 x 107
BURGM:paoil235

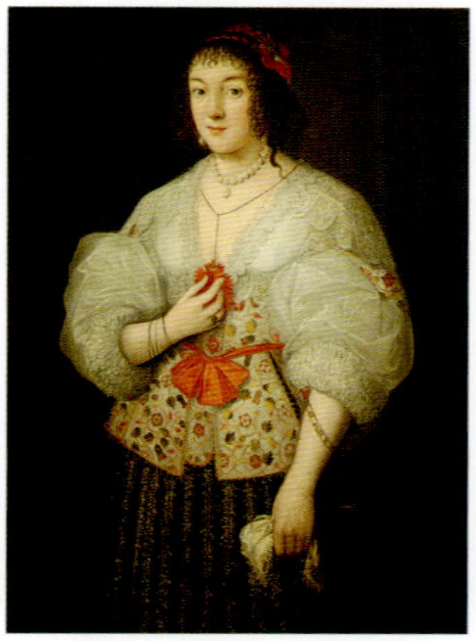

Gheeraerts the younger, Marcus (style of) 1561–1636
Portrait of a Lady 1610–1630
oil on canvas 104 x 81.3
BURGM:paoil185

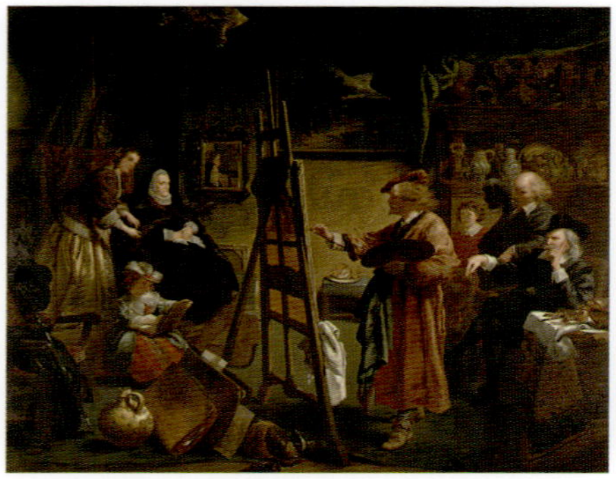

Gilbert, John 1817–1897
Rembrandt in His Studio
oil on canvas 119 x 150
BURGM:paoil99

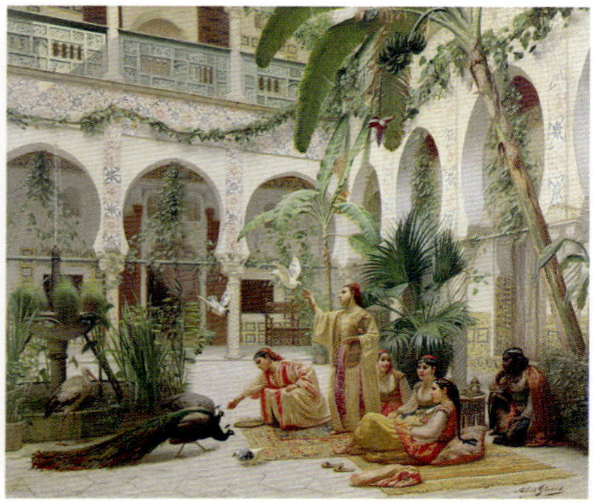

Girard, Paul-Albert 1839–1920
Moorish Courtyard
oil on canvas 61 x 71.1
BURGM:paoil186

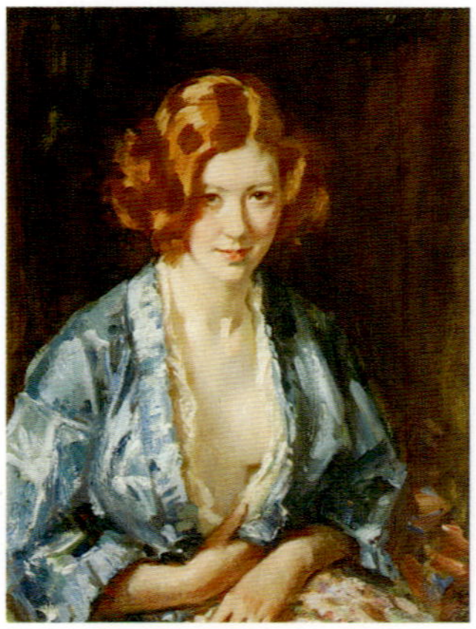

Glehn, Wilfrid Gabriel de 1870–1951
Clare c.1933
oil on canvas 69.9 x 54.6
BURGM:paoil86

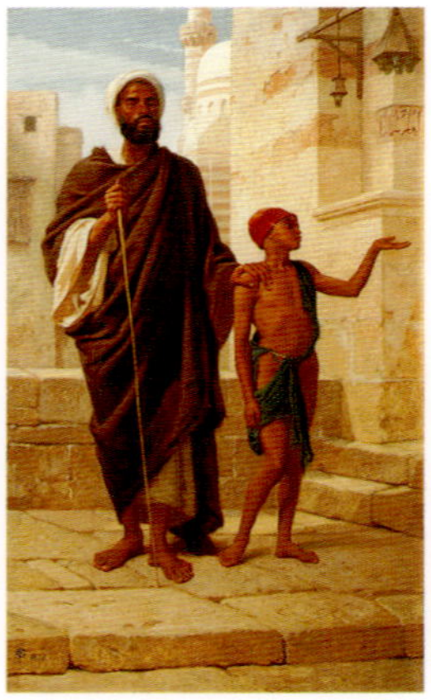

Goodall, Frederick 1822–1904
The Blind Beggar 1872
oil on canvas 91.4 x 53.3
BURGM:paoil12

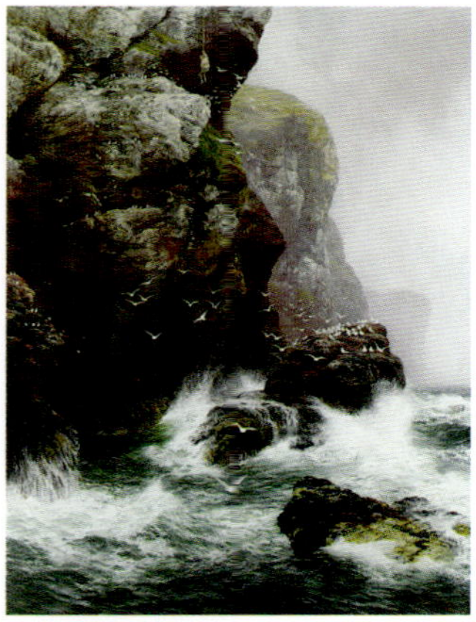

Graham, Peter 1836–1921
The Fowlers Crag 1887
oil on canvas 163 x 122
BURGM:paoil46

Facing page: Knight, Harold, 1874–1961, *Girl Writing*, 1931, Grundy Art Gallery (p. 101)

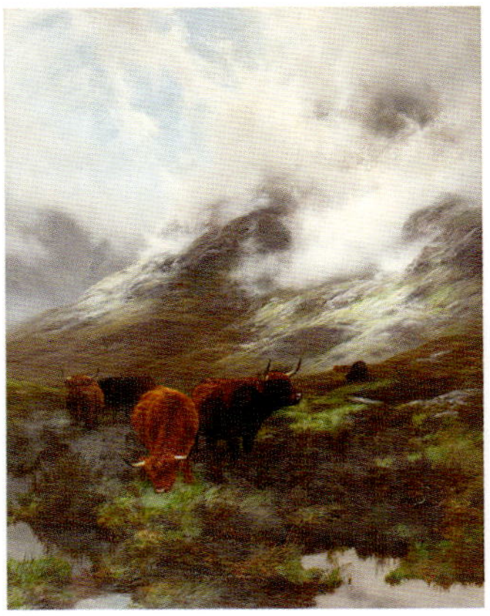

Graham, Peter 1836–1921
The Head of the Glen 1894
oil on canvas 161 x 121
BURGM:paoil27

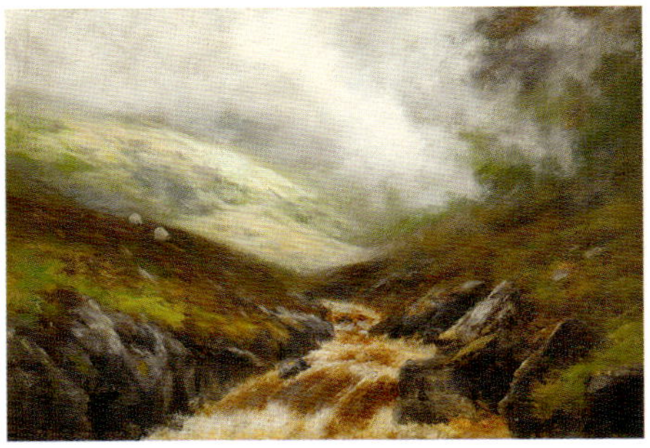

Graham, Peter 1836–1921
A Mountain Burn 1910
oil on canvas 43.2 x 63.5
BURGM:paoil257

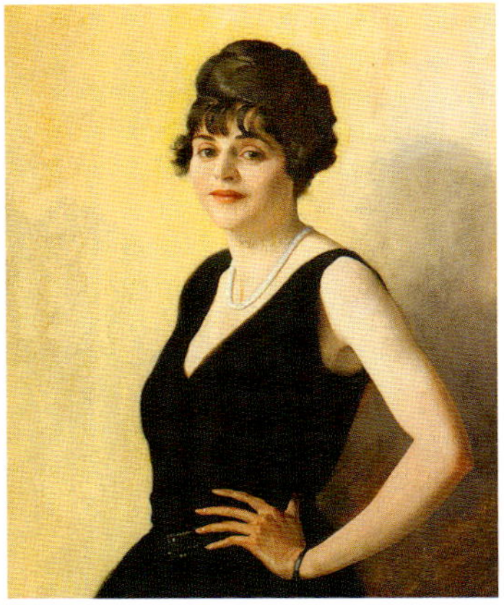

Greenwood, Orlando 1892–1989
The Lady in Black c.1945
oil on canvas 74.3 x 62.2
BURGM:paoil139

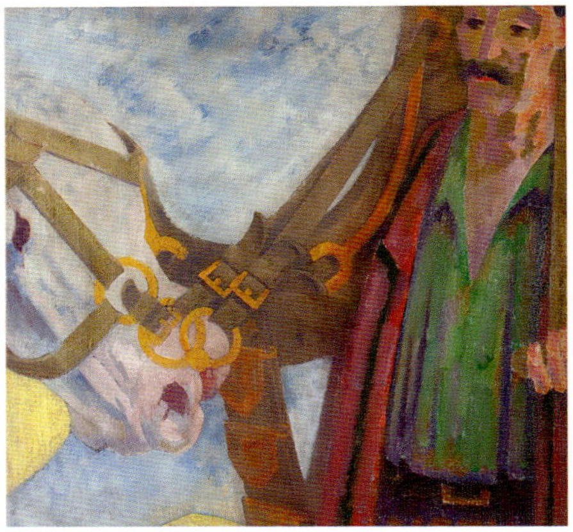

Greenwood, Orlando 1892–1989
April: Farmer with Bull
oil on canvas 61 x 66
BURGM:paoil331

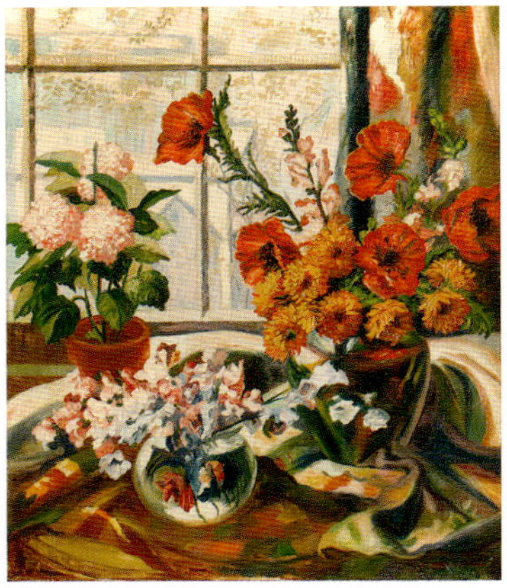

Greenwood, Orlando 1892–1989
Flowers on a Windowsill
oil on canvas 71.1 x 61
BURGM:paoil317

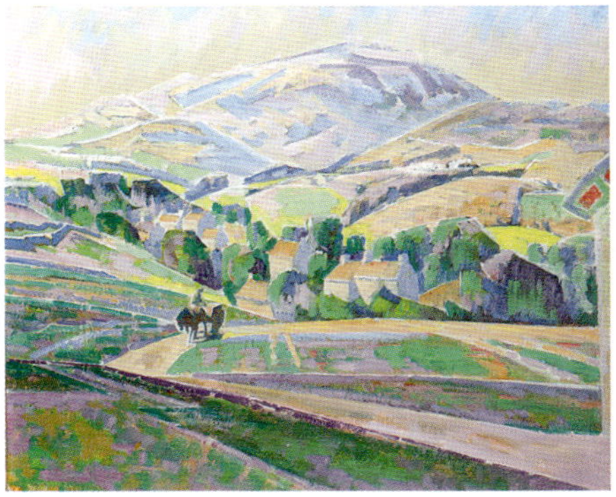

Greenwood, Orlando 1892–1989
Pendle
oil on canvas 55.9 x 66
BURGM:paoil306

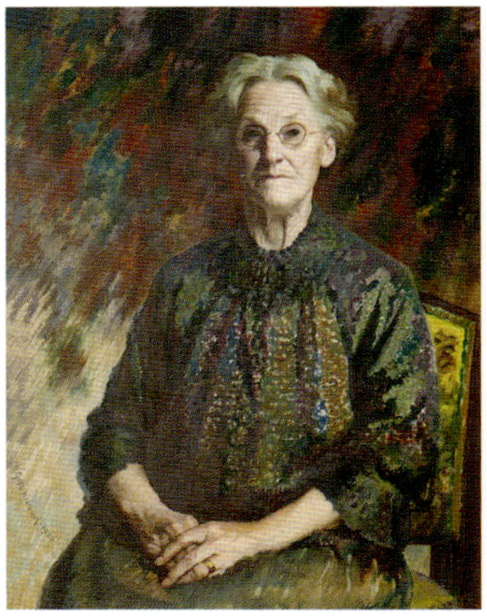

Greenwood, Orlando 1892–1989
Portrait of the Artist's Mother
oil on canvas 91.4 x 73.7
BURGM:paoil330

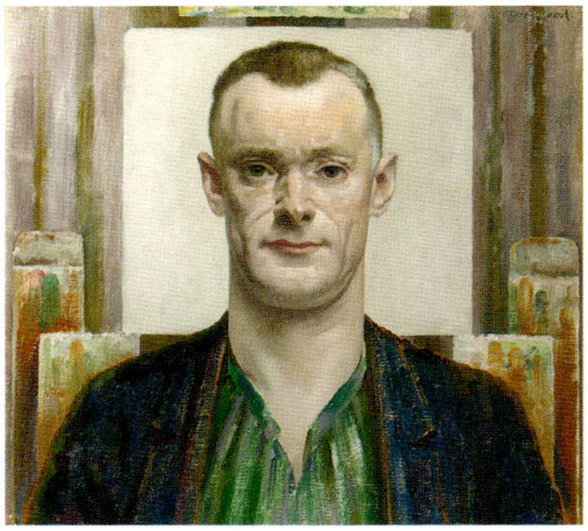

Greenwood, Orlando 1892–1989
Self Portrait
oil on canvas 47 x 50.8
BURGM:paoil307

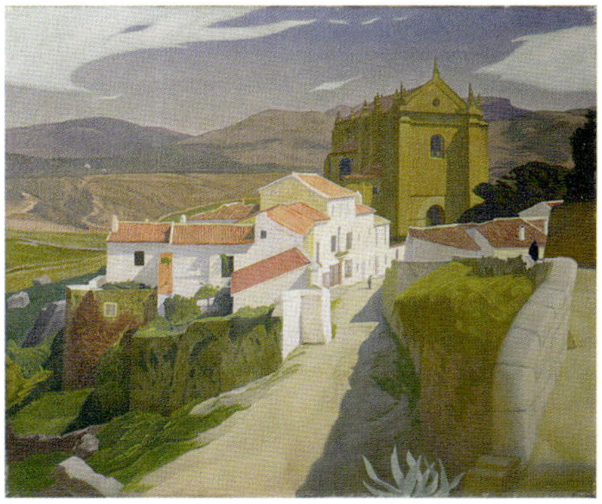

Gresty, Hugh 1899–1958
Andalusian Village 1937
oil on canvas 48.3 x 58.4
BURGM:paoil297

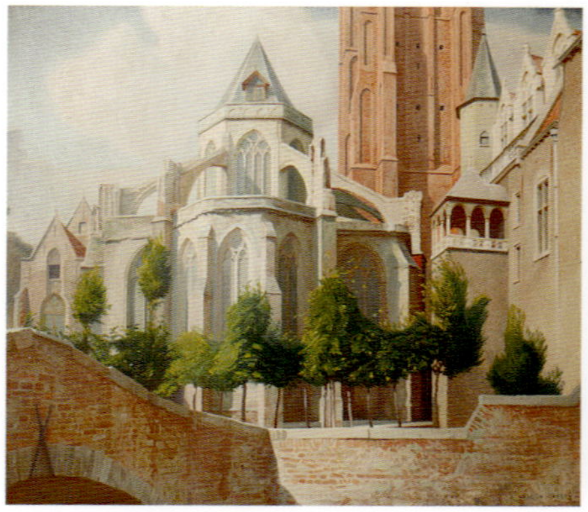

Gresty, Hugh 1899–1958
Gothic Suite, Bruges
oil on canvas 94 x 105
BURGM:paoil209

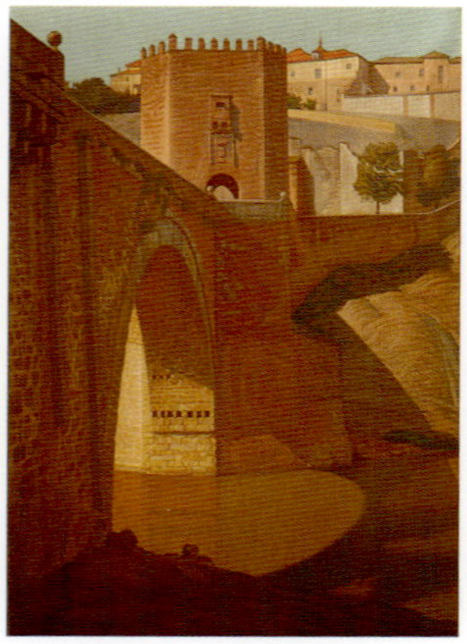

Gresty, Hugh 1899–1958
The Alcántara, Toledo
oil on canvas 104 x 74.3
BURGM:paoil208

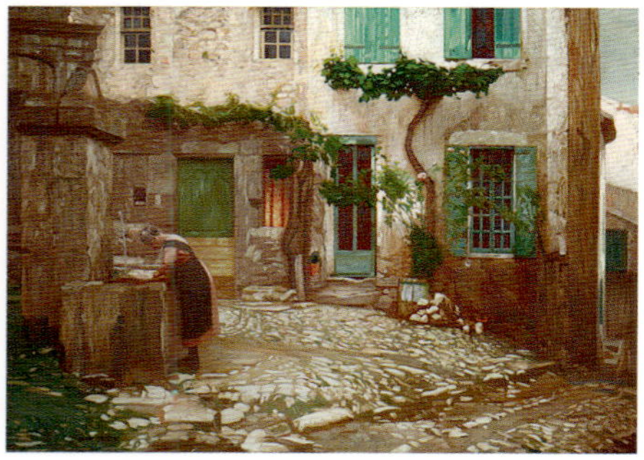

Gresty, Hugh 1899–1958
Woman at a Well
oil on panel 58.4 x 86.4
BURGM:paoil207

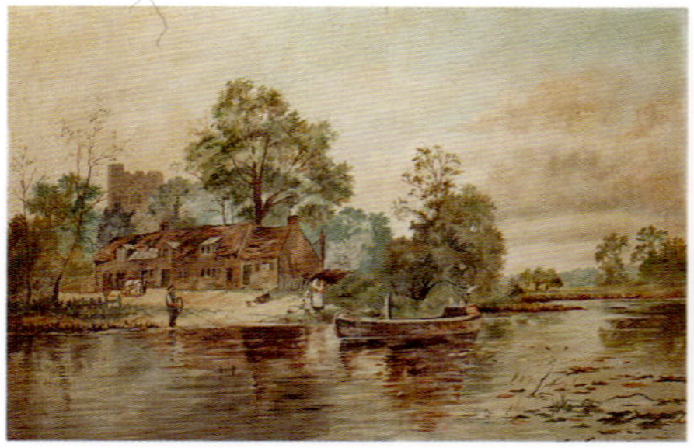

Grimshaw, Thomas active 1920–1930
A River Scene
oil on canvas 61 x 88.9
BURGM:paoil274

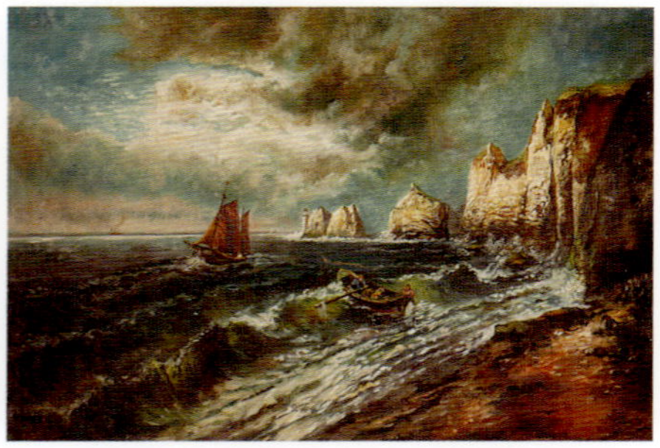

Grimshaw, Thomas active 1920–1930
The Needles, Isle of Wight
oil on canvas 61 x 88.9
BURGM:paoil273

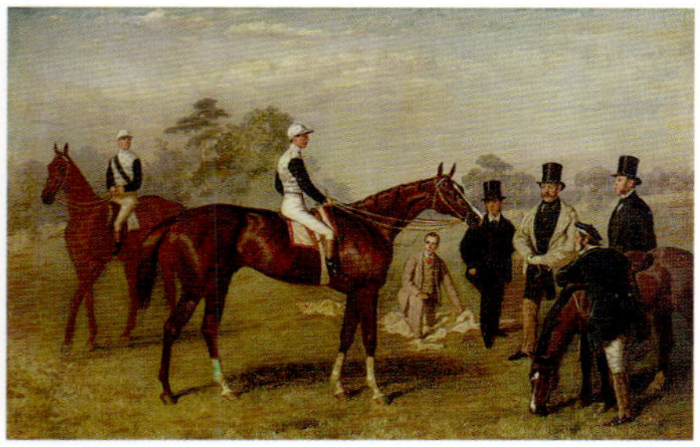

Hall, Harry 1814–1896
'Kettledrum' 1861–1862
oil on canvas 86.4 x 132
BURGM:paoil38

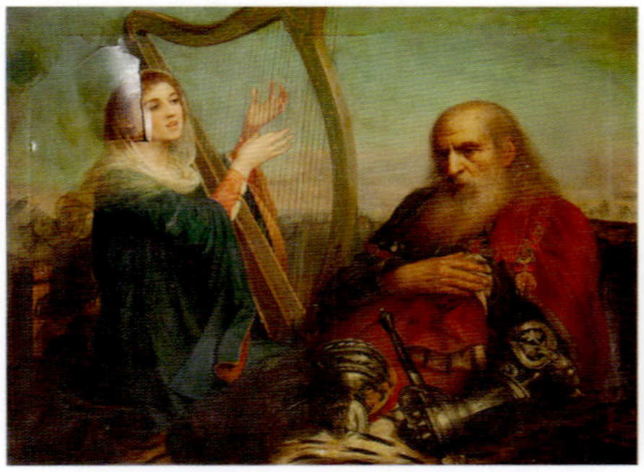

Hallé, Charles Edward 1846–1919
'Sic transit gloria mundi'
oil on canvas 112 x 152
BURGM:paoil149

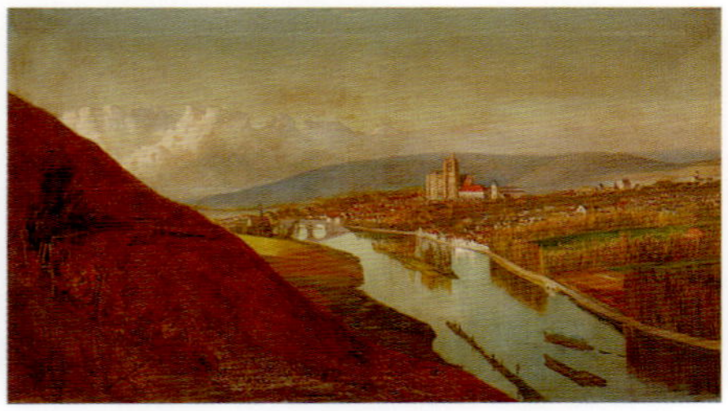

Hamerton, Philip Gilbert 1834–1894
Sens from the Vineyards 1863
oil on canvas 91.4 x 152
BURGM:paoil11

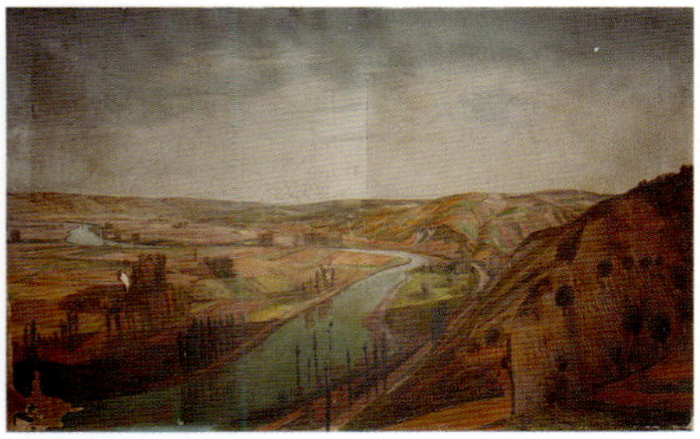

Hamerton, Philip Gilbert 1834–1894
The River Yonne 1863
oil on canvas 91.4 x 152
BURGM:paoil10

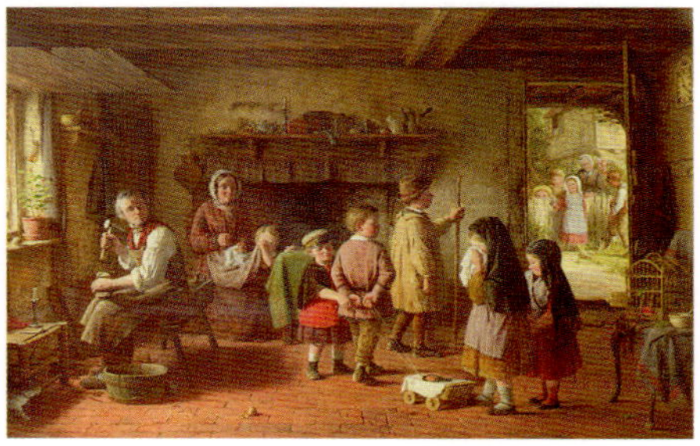

Hardy, Frederick Daniel 1827–1911
Early Sorrow 1861
oil on canvas 21.6 x 34.3
BURGM:paoil124

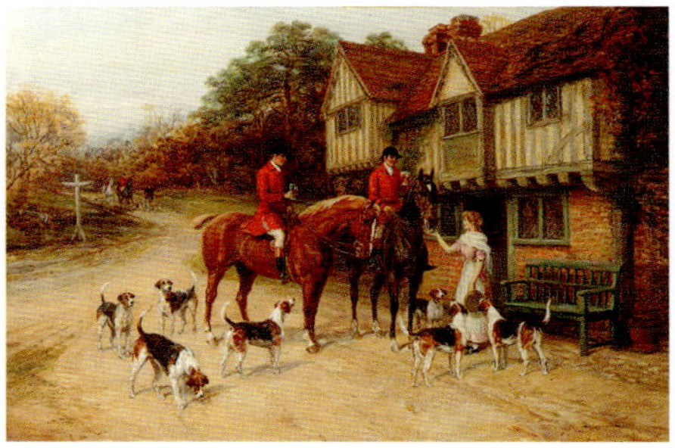

Hardy, Heywood 1842–1933
A Refresher at the 'Dragon'
oil on canvas 43.2 x 66
BURGM:paoil230

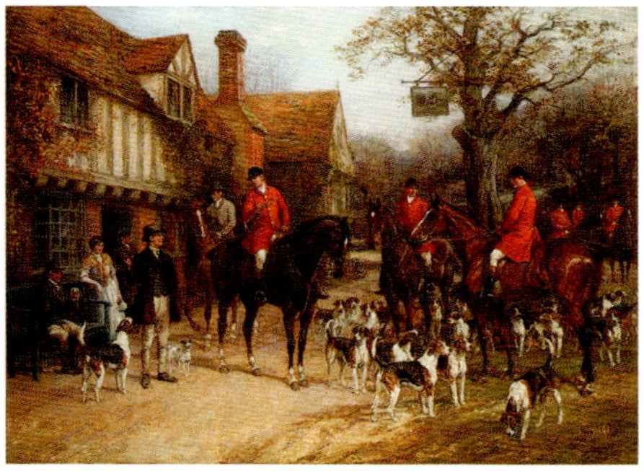

Hardy, Heywood 1842–1933
The Meet, 'Ye Olde Wayside Inn'
oil on canvas 68.6 x 100
BURGM:paoil228

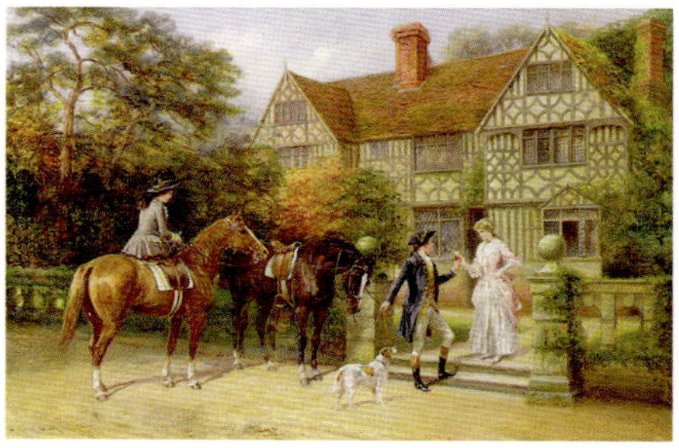

Hardy, Heywood 1842–1933
The Two Roses
oil on canvas 43.2 x 66
BURGM:paoil229

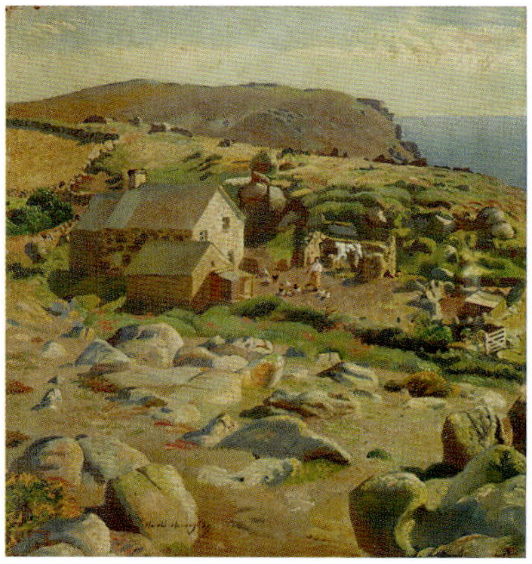

Harvey, Harold C. 1874–1941
The Little Farm 1929
oil on canvas 61 x 55.9
BURGM:paoil263

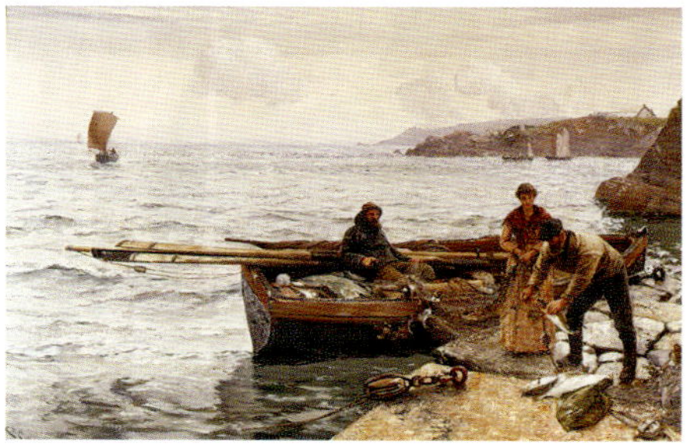

Hemy, Charles Napier 1841–1917
Crabbers Bait 1891
oil on canvas 80 x 121
BURGM:paoil33

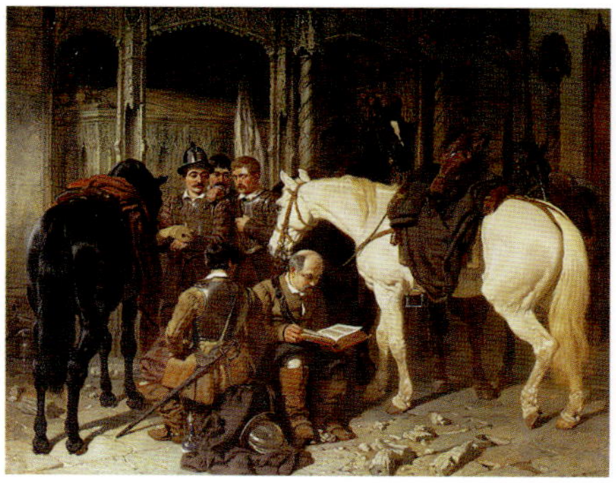

Herring I, John Frederick 1795–1865
Roundheads at an Arundel Church 1847–1851
oil on canvas 100 x 126
BURGM:paoil214

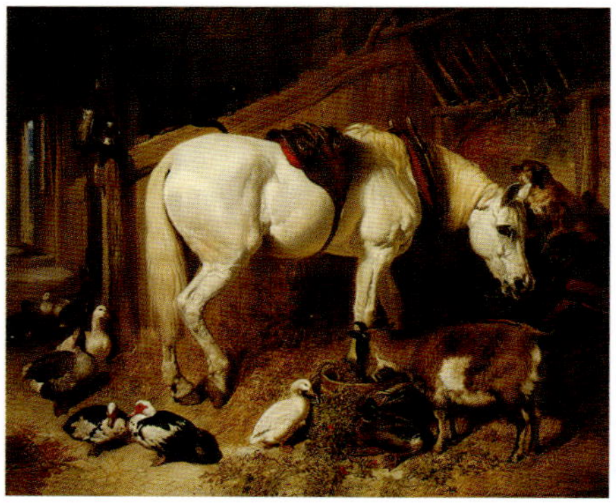

Herring I, John Frederick 1795–1865
The Midday Meal 1850
oil on canvas 99.1 x 126
BURGM:paoil78

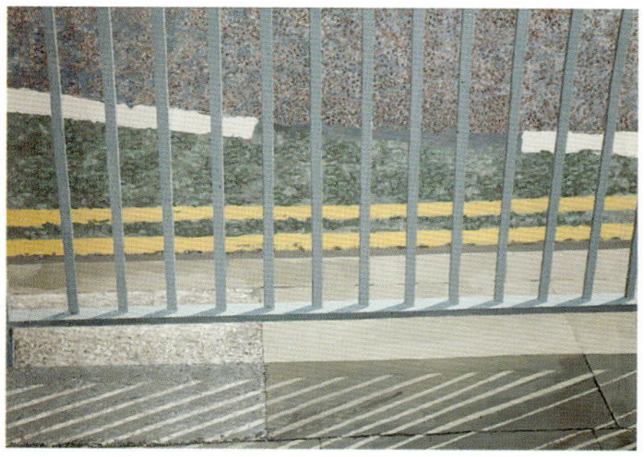

Hickson, Charles C. b.1957
Urban Intersection (Blue) c.1977
acrylic on canvas 76.2 x 110
BURGM:paoil305

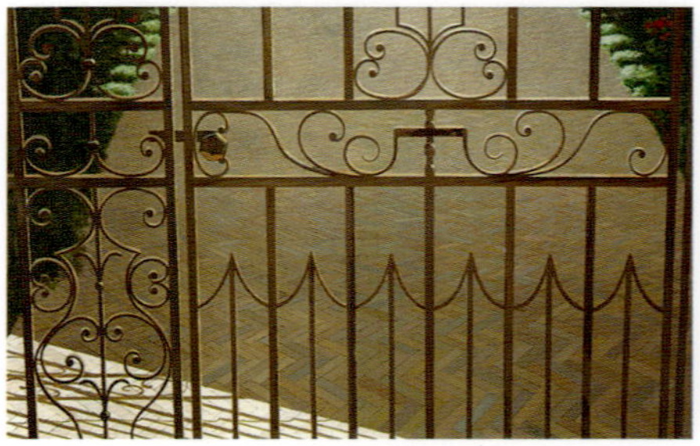

Hickson, Charles C. b.1957
Private Pathway 1980
oil on canvas 90.8 x 152
BURGM:paoil304

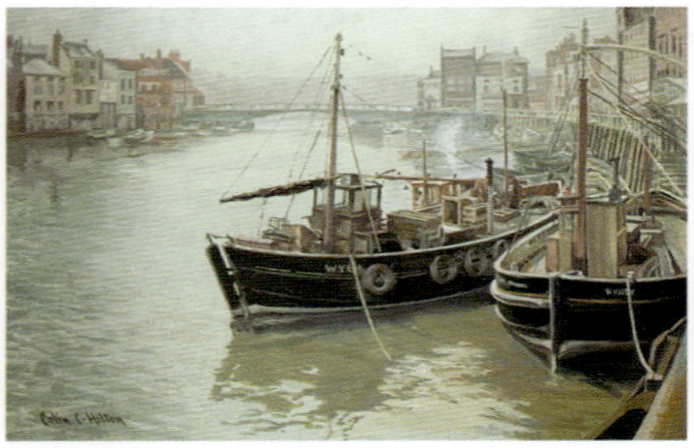

Hilton, Colin Clough 1902–1984
Whitby Harbour
oil on canvas 59.7 x 89.5
BURGM:paoil205

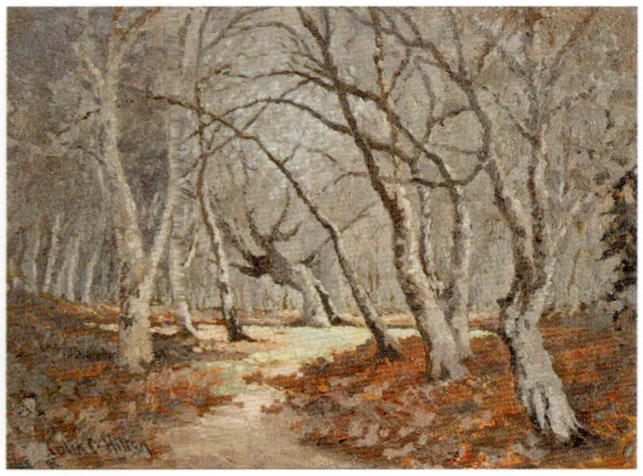

Hilton, Colin Clough 1902–1984
Woodland Scene, Burnham Beeches
oil on canvas 39.4 x 59.7
BURGM:paoil205

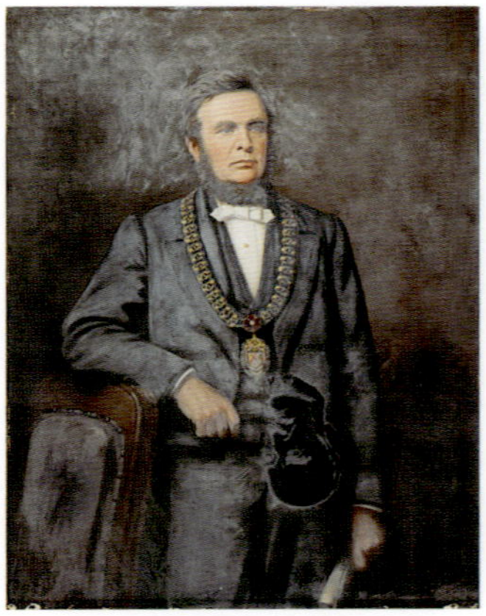

Hodges, J. Sidney Willis 1829–1900
William Thompson in Mayoral Chain 1877
oil on canvas 127 x 103
BURGM:paoil251

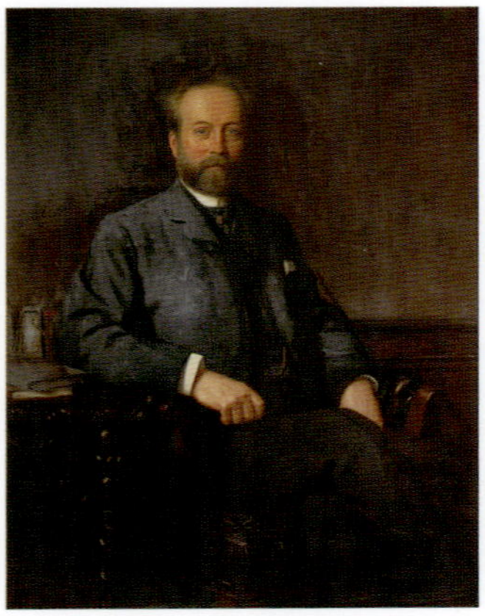

Hodges, J. Sidney Willis 1829–1900
Cornelius M. Foden 1893
oil on canvas 127 x 99.1
BURGM:paoil240

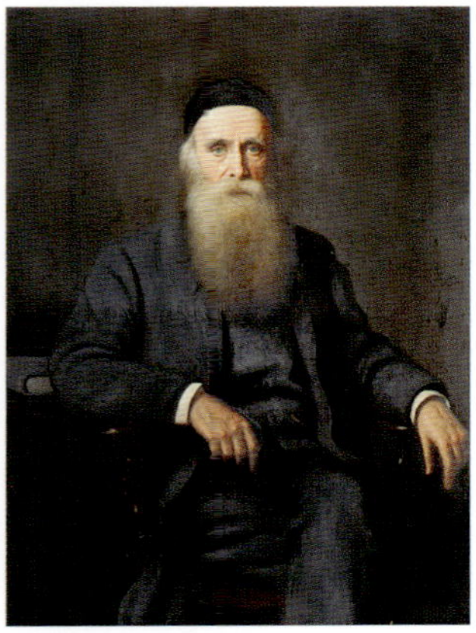

Hodges, J. Sidney Willis 1829–1900
Henry Houlding 1895–1900
oil on canvas 109 x 83.8
BURGM:paoil9

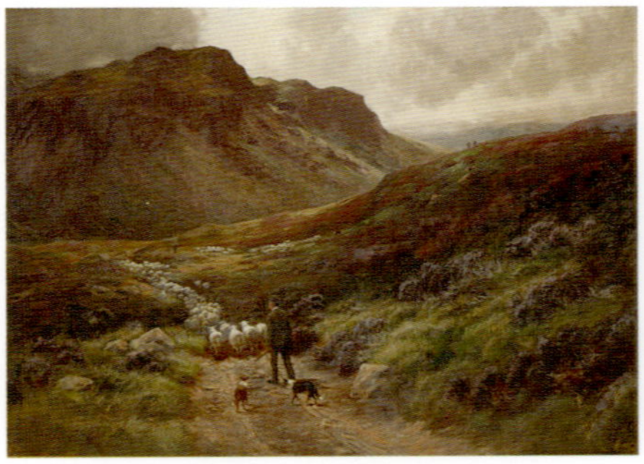

Hogley, Stephen Enoch 1842–1927
Landscape
oil on canvas 58.4 x 88.9
BURGM:paoil84

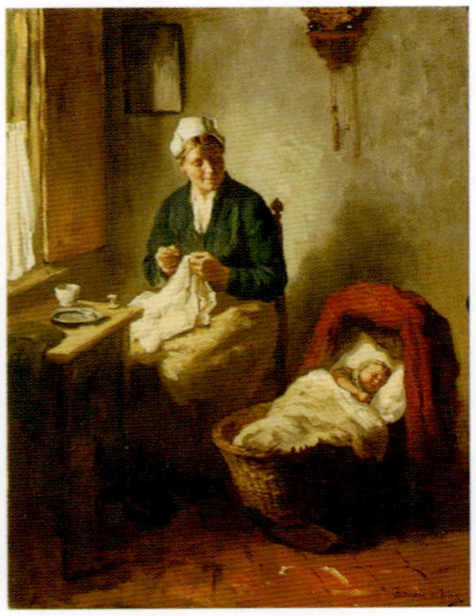

Hoog, Bernard de 1867–1943
A Dutch Interior
oil on canvas 72.4 x 58.4
BURGM:paoil70

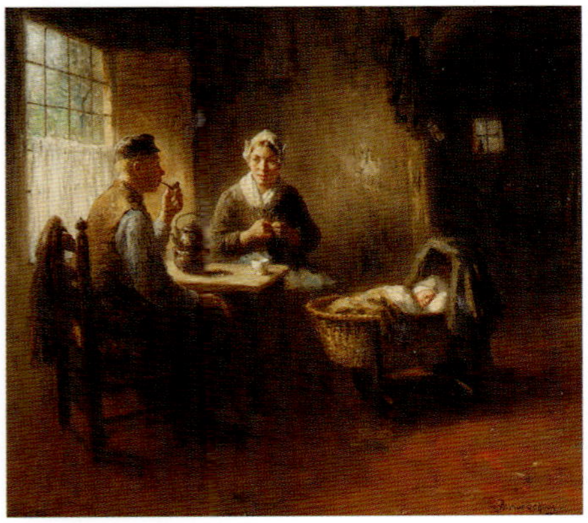

Hoog, Bernard de 1867–1943
Morning
oil on canvas 83.8 x 94
BURGM:paoil31

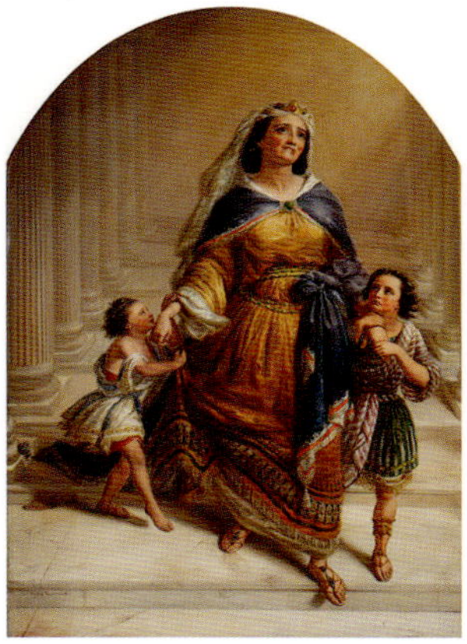

Hopley, Edward William John 1816–1869
Mariamne, Wife of King Herod, and Her Children going to Their Execution 1868
oil on canvas 131 x 90.2
BURGM:paoil74

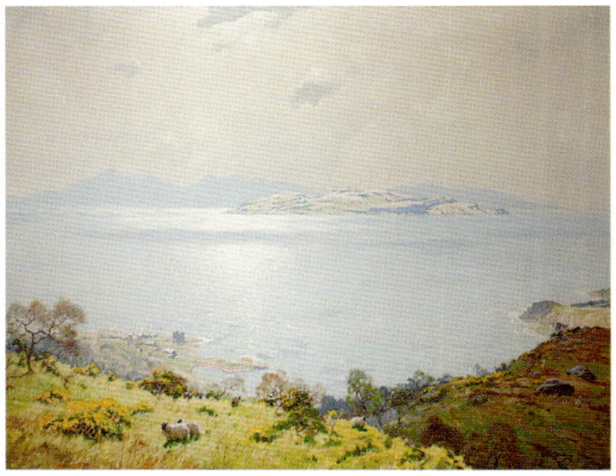

Houston, Robert 1891–1940
The Shores of the Clyde c.1933
oil on canvas 99.7 x 125
BURGM:paoil88

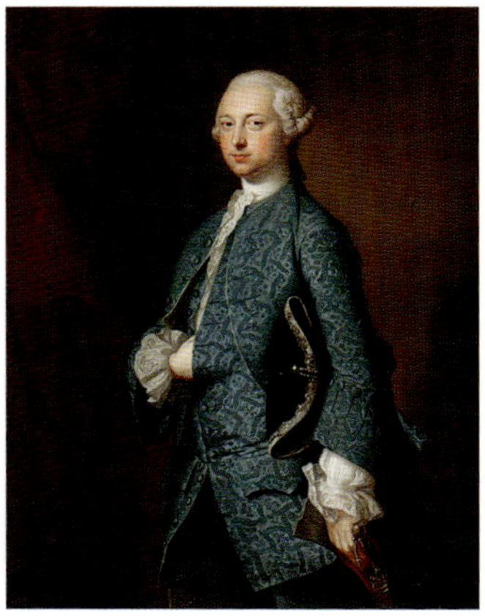

Hudson, Thomas 1701–1779
Sir Henry Oxenden (1721–1804) c.1755
oil on canvas 124 x 99.1
BURGM:paoil183

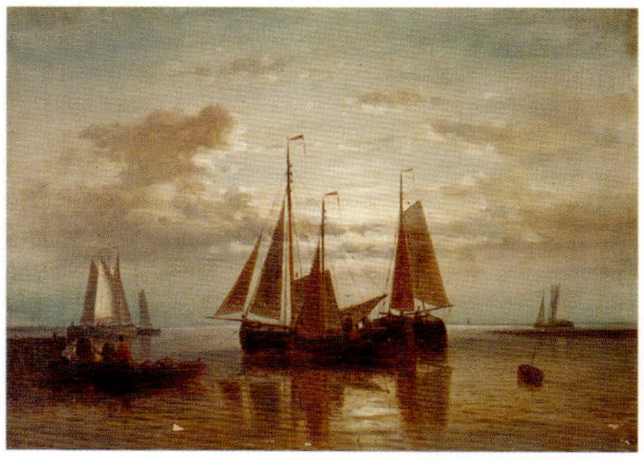

Hulk I, Abraham 1813–1897
Shipping Becalmed
oil on canvas 39.4 x 58.4
BURGM:paoil170

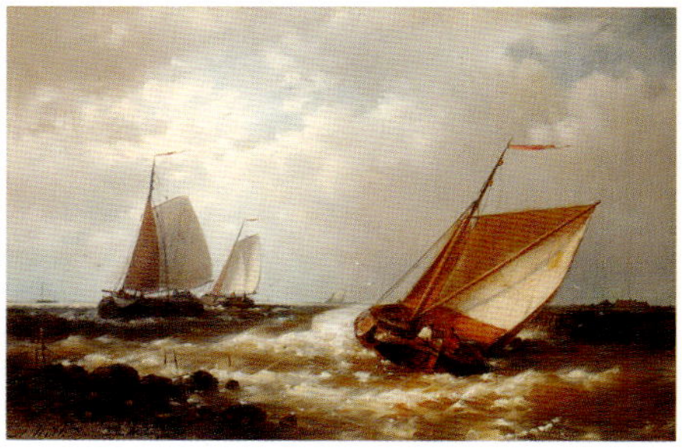

Hulk I, Abraham 1813–1897
Shipping in a Breeze
oil on canvas 39.4 x 59.7
BURGM:paoil169

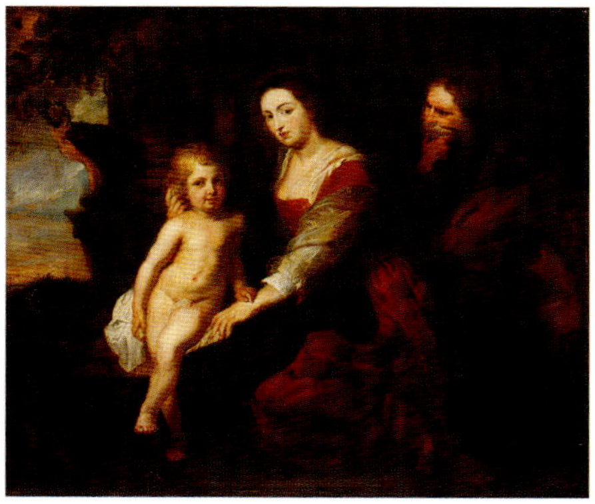

Husník, Jakub 1837–1916
The Holy Family (after Peter Paul Rubens) 19th C
oil on canvas 163 x 193
BURGM:paoil225

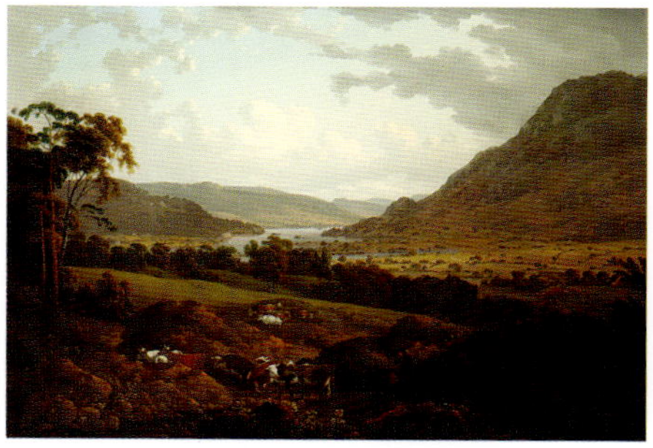

Ibbetson, Julius Caesar 1759–1817
A Scene in the Lake District
oil on canvas 58.4 x 90.2
BURGM:paoil112

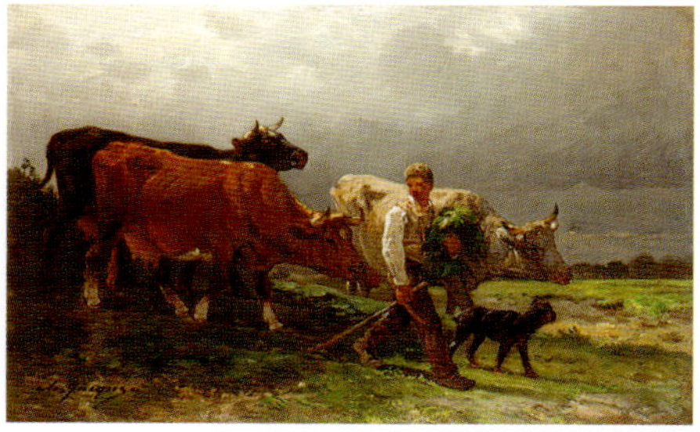

Jacque, Charles Émile 1813–1894
Breton Lad with Cattle
oil on canvas 40.6 x 67.3
BURGM:paoil137

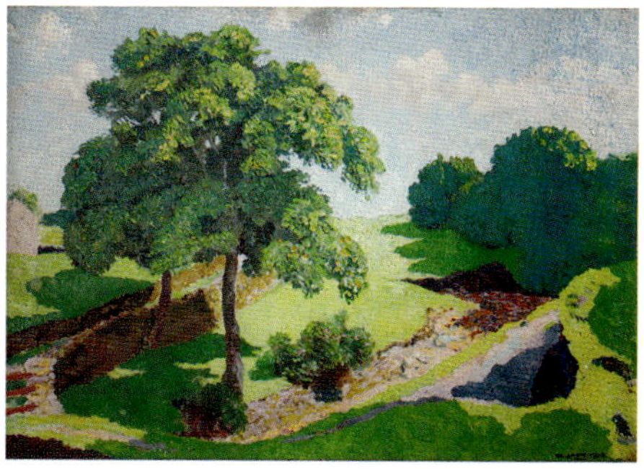

Japp, Darsie 1883–1973
In Dentdale
oil on canvas 53.3 x 74.9
BURGM:paoil55

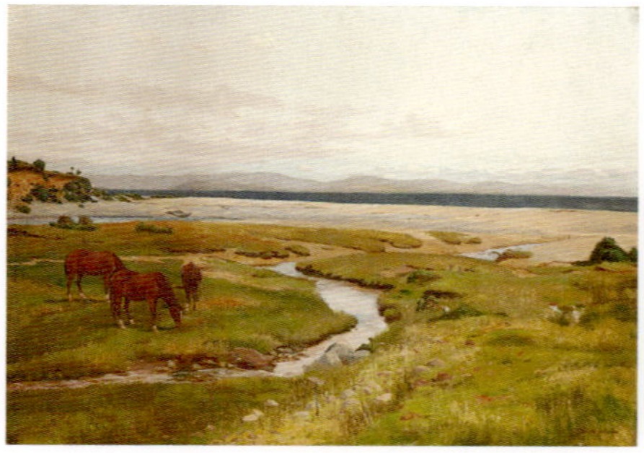

Johnson, George Frederick Waldo 1862–1917
Shore Scene with Horses
oil on canvas 55.9 x 90.2
BURGM:paoil279

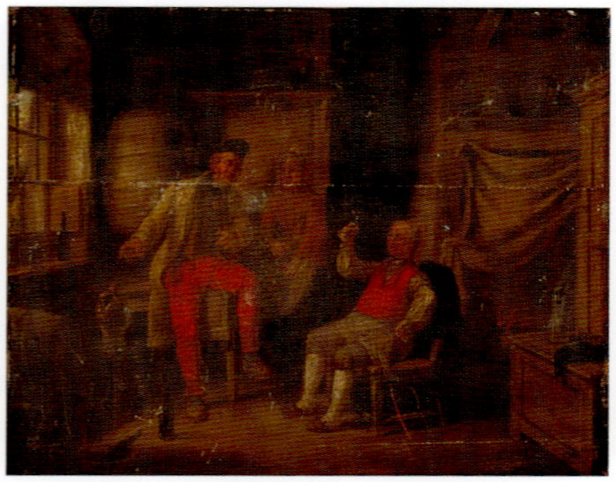

Johnston, Alexander 1815–1891
Scottish Interior
oil on panel 38.1 x 48.3
BURGM:paoil288

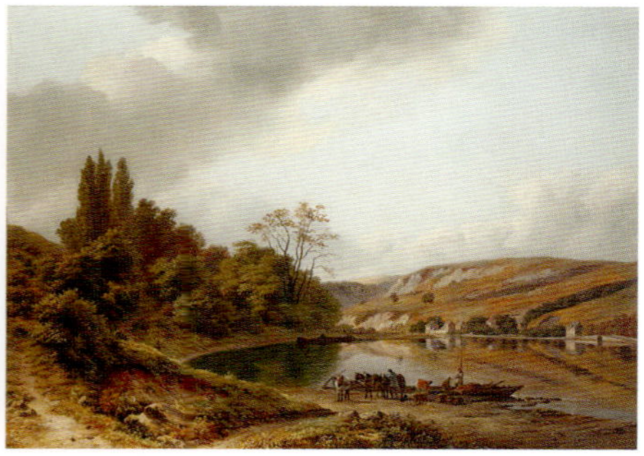

Jonghe, Jan Baptiste de 1785–1844
The Ferry
oil on panel 51.4 x 71.8
BURGM:paoil16[illegible]

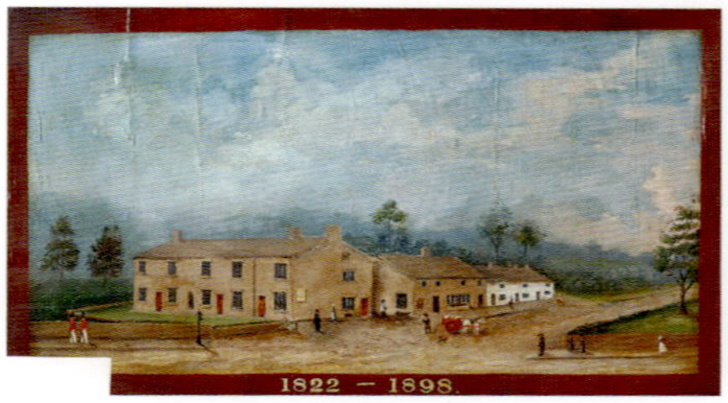

Kay, James active 19th C
Ebenezer Chapel, Colne Road, c.1840
oil on board 24.1 x 48.3
BURGM:paoil222

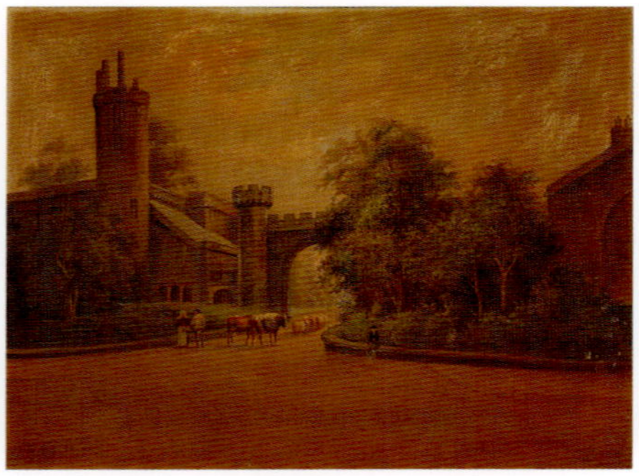

Kernik, W. active 1904
Entrance to Towneley Holmes, with Cattle
oil on canvas 50.8 x 76.2
BURGM:paoil264

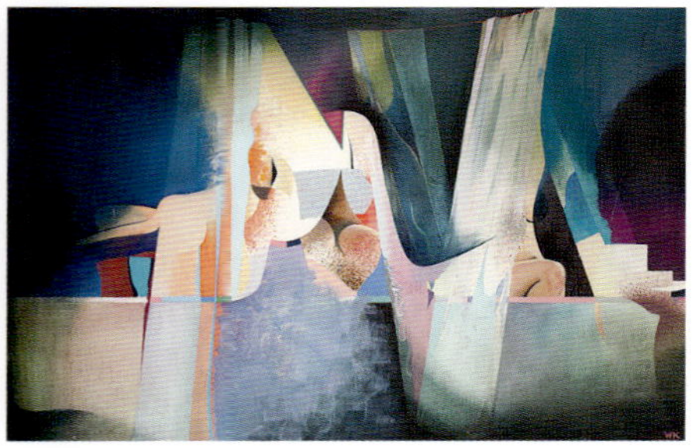

Kershaw, Walter b.1940
Nude in a Polythene Interior
oil on board 6[illegible] x 91.4
BURGM:paoil253

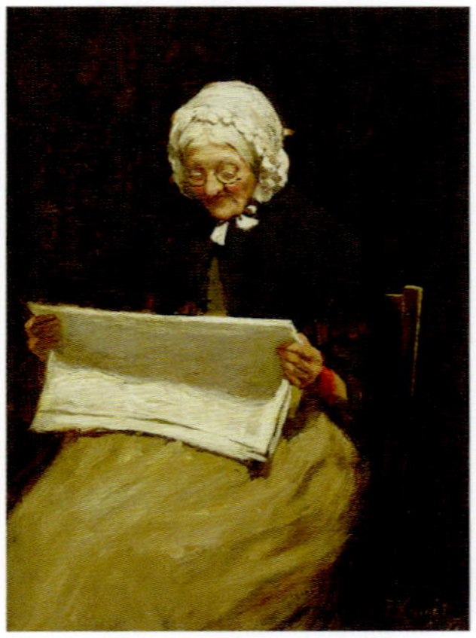

Knight, Paul active 1883–1904
Grandmother 1895
oil on canvas 39.4 x 29.2
BURGM:paoil165

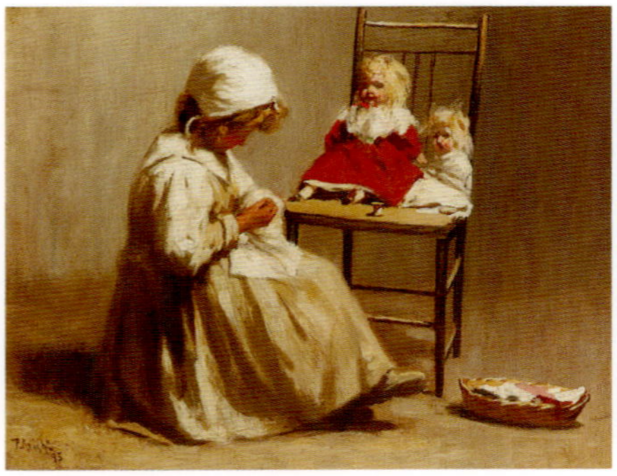

Knight, Paul active 1883–1904
The Sewing Girl 1895
oil on canvas 28.6 x 38.7
BURGM:paoil164

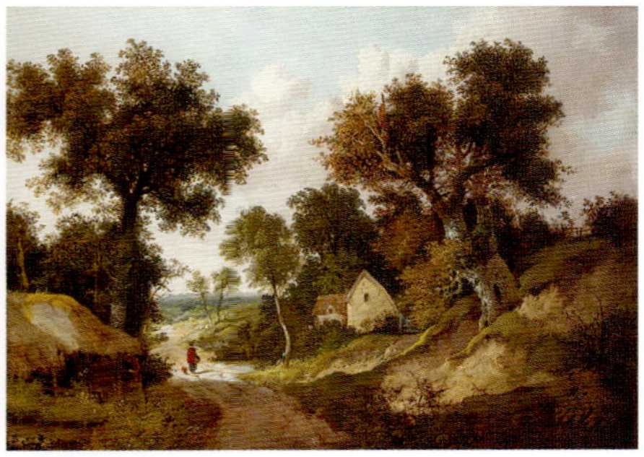

Ladbrooke, John Berney 1803–1879
A Country Lane in Norfolk 1878
oil on canvas 49.5 x 74.9
BURGM:paoil101

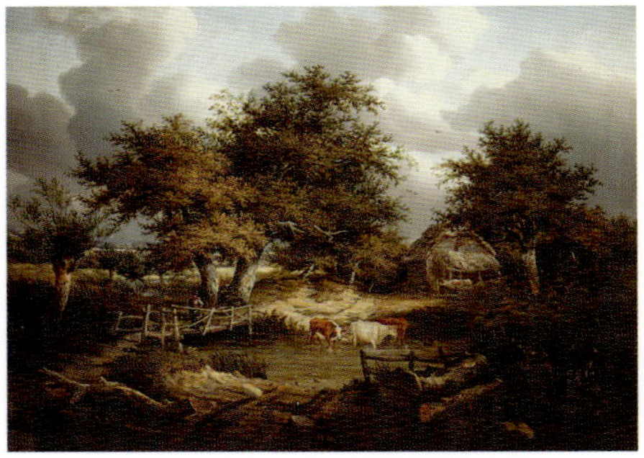

Ladbrooke, Robert 1770–1842
The Old Farmstead
oil on canvas 74.9 x 99.7
BURGM:paoil100

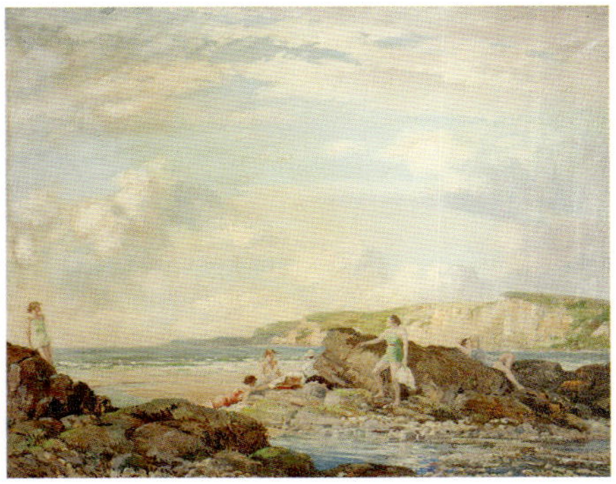

Lancaster, Percy 1878–1951
The Seashore
oil on canvas 61 x 73.7
BURGM:paoil181

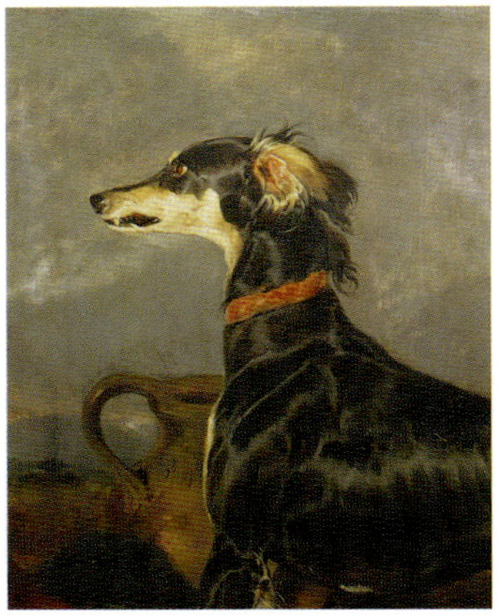

Landseer, Edwin Henry 1802–1873
A Saluki Dog 1840–1844
oil on canvas 73.7 x 57.8
BURGM:paoil72

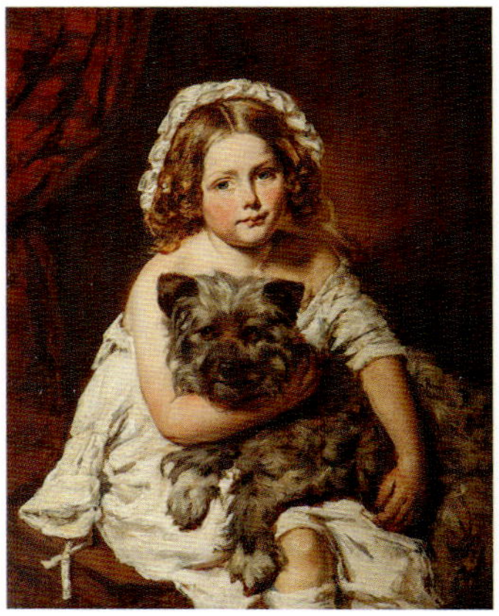

Landseer, Edwin Henry (style of) 1802–1873
Young Girl with a Dog
oil on canvas 74.3 x 61.6
BURGM:paoil161

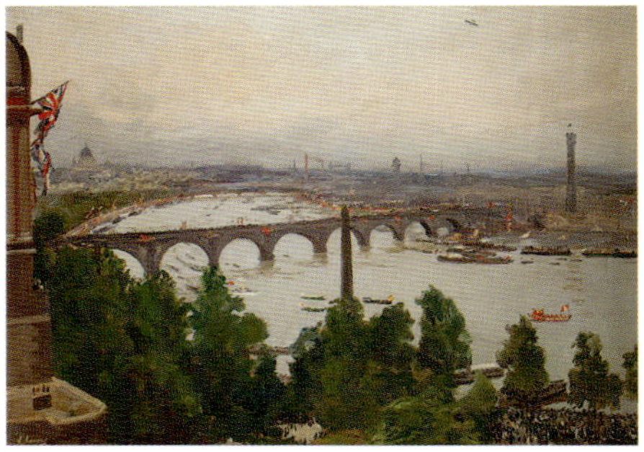

Lavery, John 1856–1941
The River Pageant, as Seen from the Home of Sir James Barries, Adelphi Terrace, London, 4 August 1919 1919
oil on canvas 68.6 x 104
BURGM:paoil171

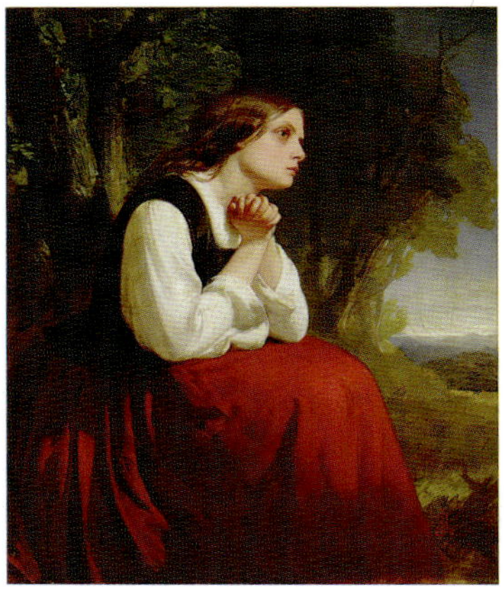

Le Jeune, Henry 1819–1904
Evangeline
oil on canvas 59.1 x 49.5
BURGM:paoil215

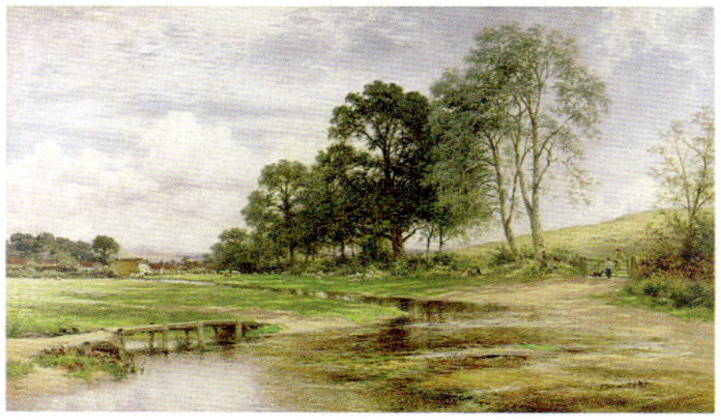

Leader, Benjamin Williams 1831–1923
By Mead and Stream 1893
oil on canvas 133 x 225
BURGM:paoil26

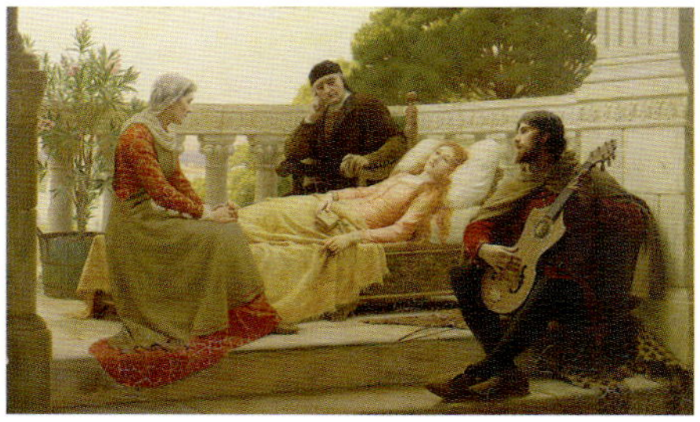

Leighton, Edmund Blair 1852–1922
How Liza Loved the King 1890
oil on canvas 99.1 x 163
BURGM:paoil47

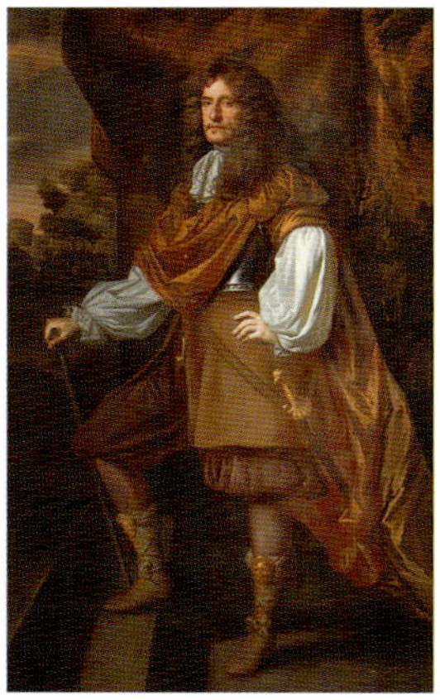

Lely, Peter 1618–1680
Sir William Ashburnham 1643–1670
oil on canvas 218 x 135
BURGM:paoil196

Facing page: Connard, Philip, 1875–1958, *Hardy of Chelsea Green*, Blackburn Museum and Art Gallery (p. 27)

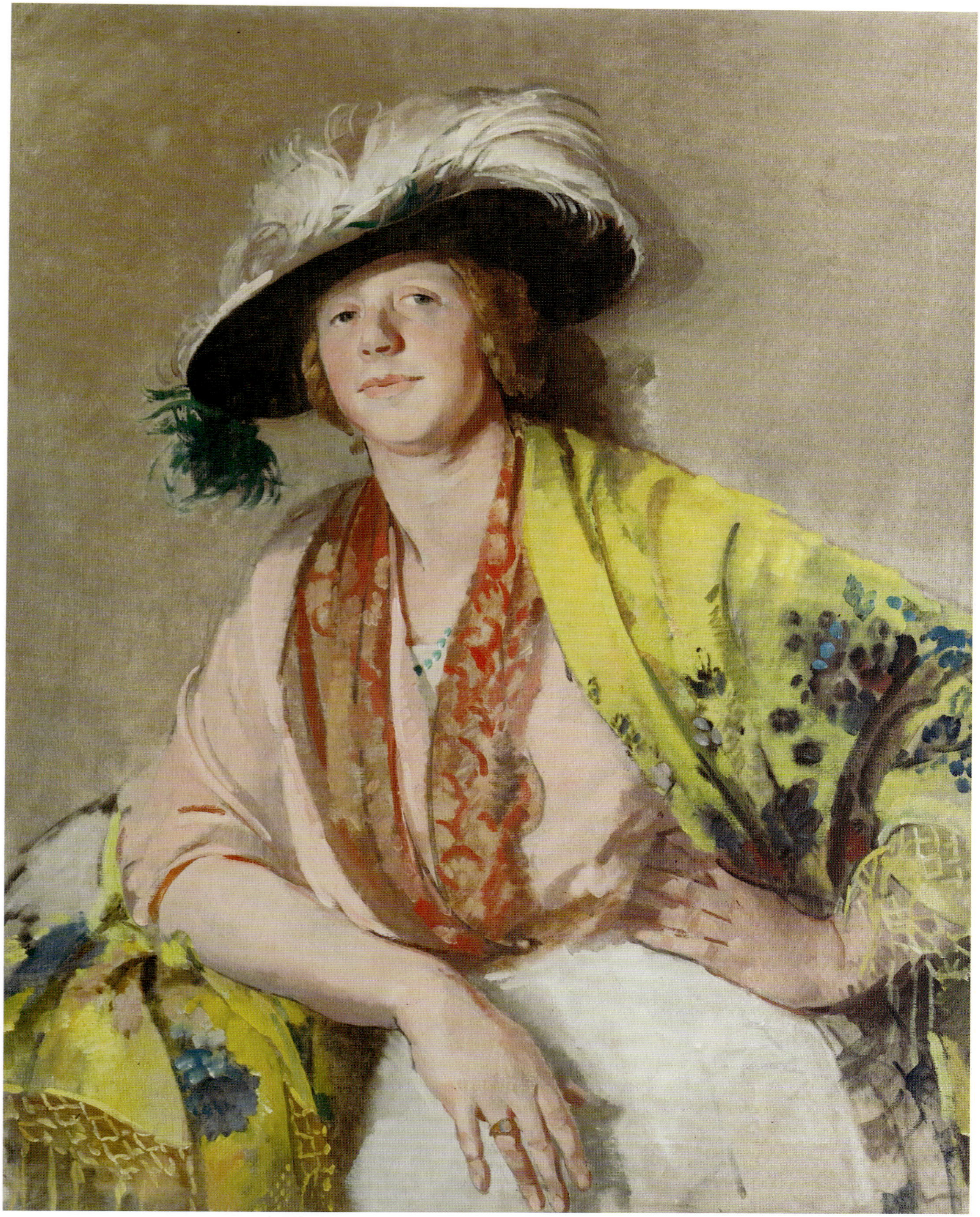

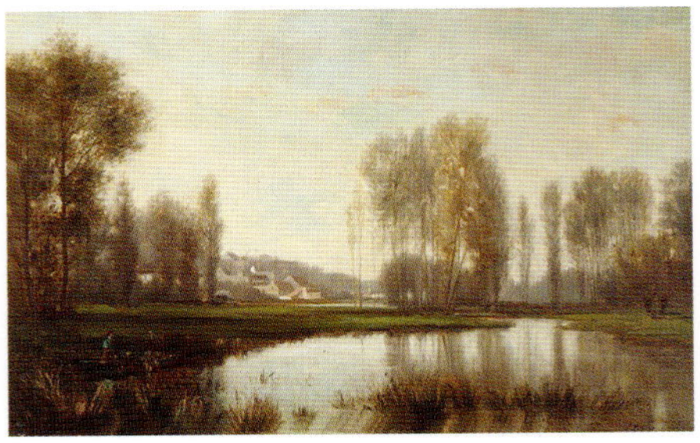

Lépine, Stanislas 1835–1892
River Scene
oil on panel 23.5 x 38.7
BURGM:paoil130

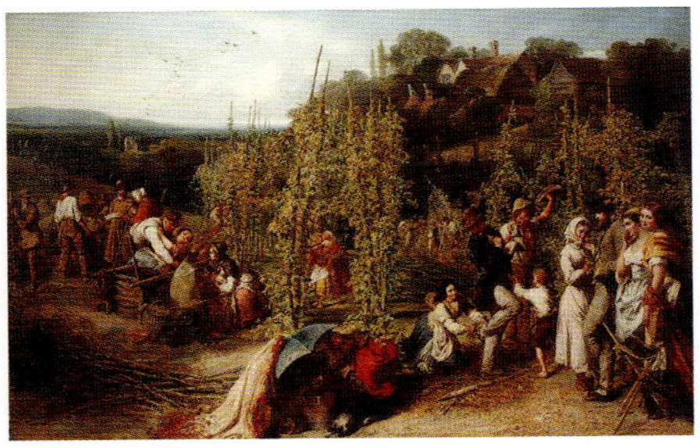

Levin, Phoebus 1836–1908
Life in the Hop Garden 1859
oil on canvas 64.8 x 112
BURGM:paoil163

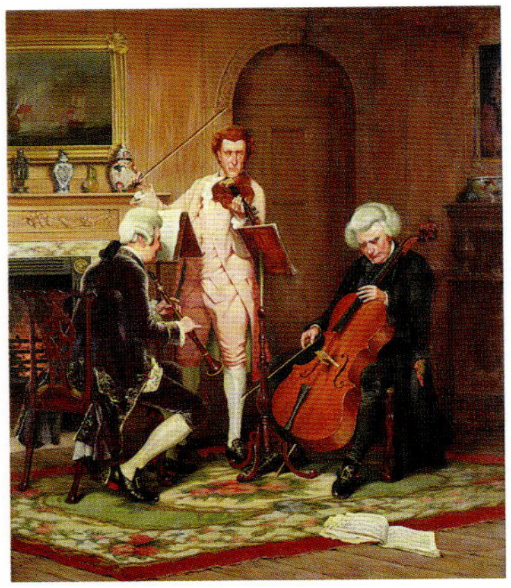

Lewin, Stephen Samuel 1848–1909
The Lost Chord 1892
oil on canvas 80 x 66
BURGM:paoil252

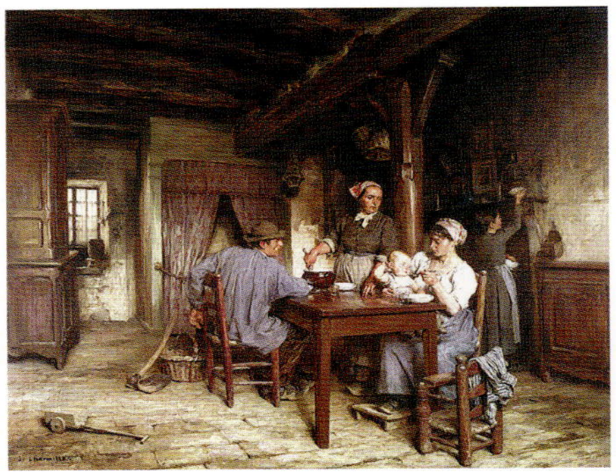

Lhermitte, Léon-Augustin 1844–1925
The Midday Meal 1875–1880
oil on canvas 71.1 x 94
BURGM:paoil192

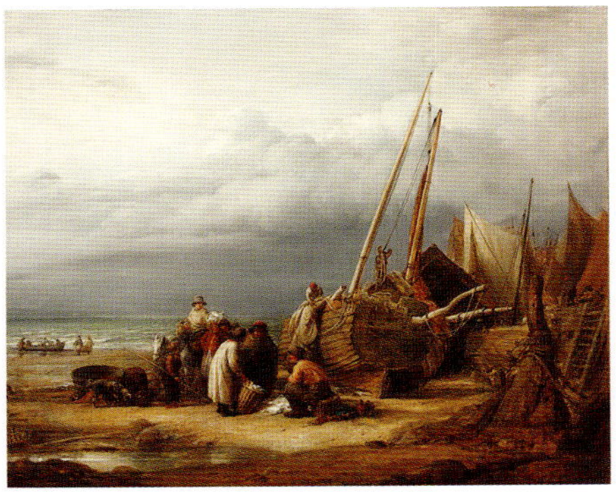

Linnell, John 1792–1882
The Hastings Coast 1832
oil on panel 54.6 x 68.6
BURGM:paoil147

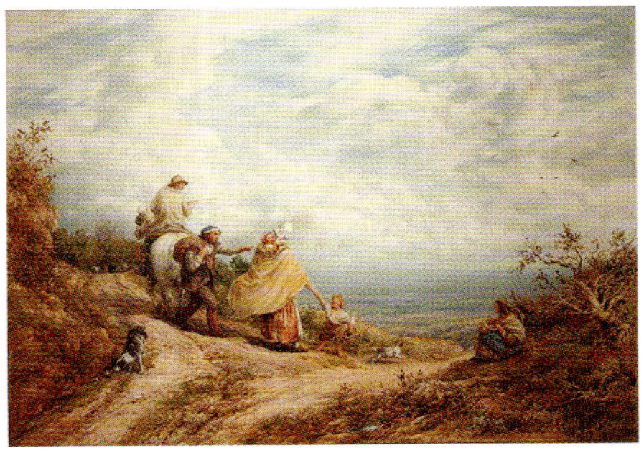

Linnell, John 1792–1882
Pointing Out the Way 1874
oil on canvas 76.2 x 108
BURGM:paoil49

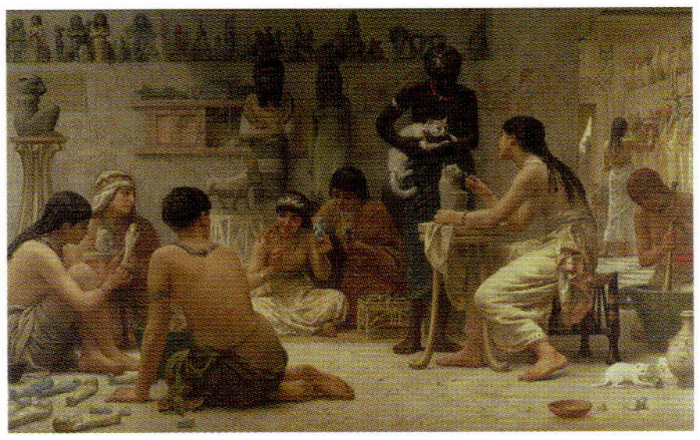

Long, Edwin 1829–1891
The Gods and Their Makers 1878
oil on canvas 142 x 224
BURGM:paoil174

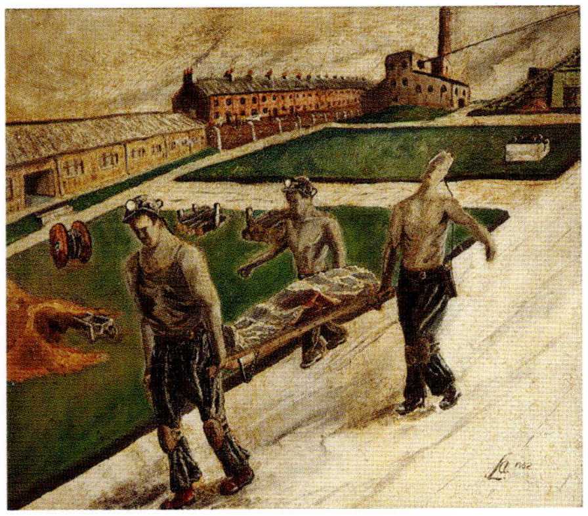

Lord, Albert 1938–2000
Bank Hall Colliery, 1962 1962
oil on canvas 27.5 x 32.5
BURGM:paoil334

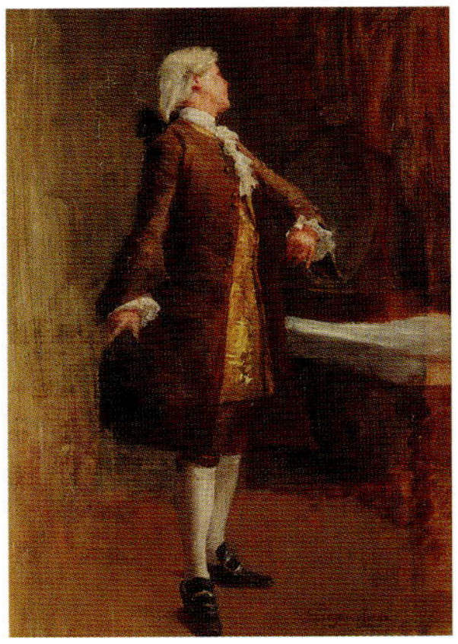

Lucas, John Seymour 1849–1923
Vanity
oil on canvas 33.7 x 24.1
BURGM:paoil167

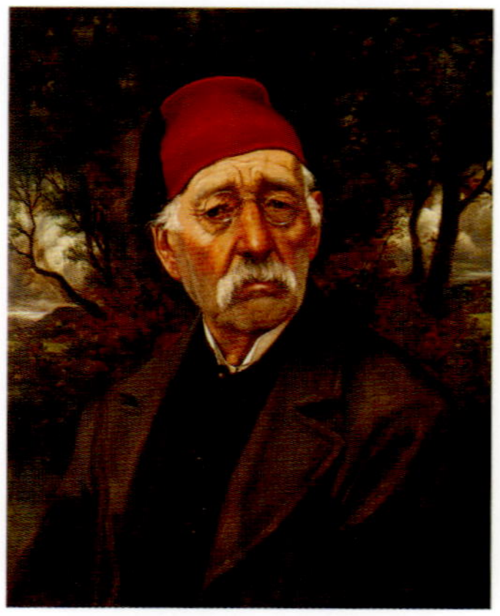

Lynch, Francis 1866–1932
Tattersall Wilkinson 1915
oil on canvas 61 x 49.5
BURGM:paoil294

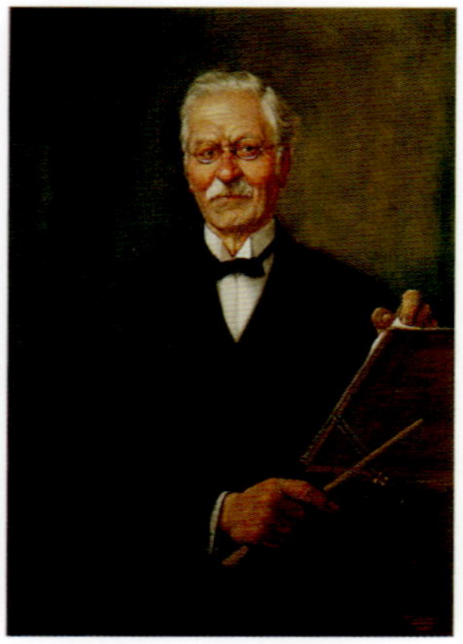

Lynch, Francis 1866–1932
Fred Myers 1929
oil on canvas 53.3 x 35.6
BURGM:paoil75

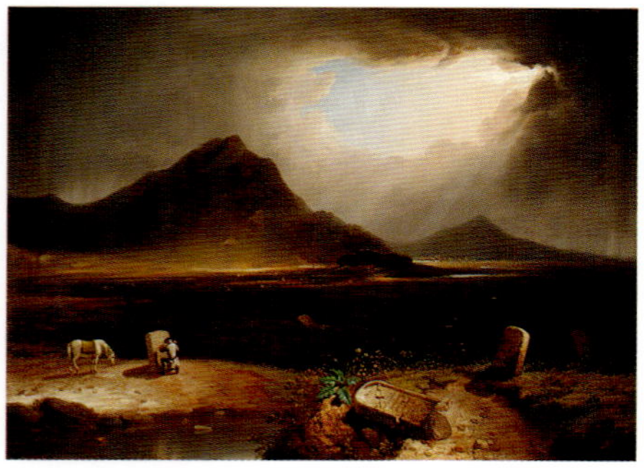

Mackenzie, Daniel N. active late 19th C
Extensive Landscape with Stonemason
oil on canvas 61 x 92.7
BURGM:paoil270

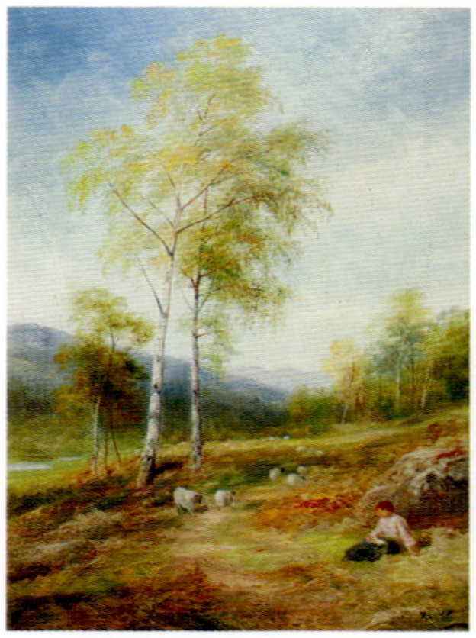

MacWhirter, John 1839–1911
Autumn, Strathglass, Invernesshire
oil on canvas 73.7 x 48.9
BURGM:paoil141

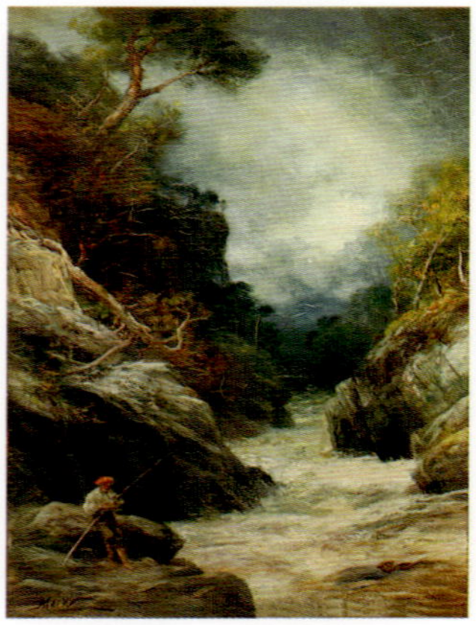

MacWhirter, John 1839–1911
The Waters of Glen Affric
oil on canvas 105 x 72.4
BURGM:paoil20

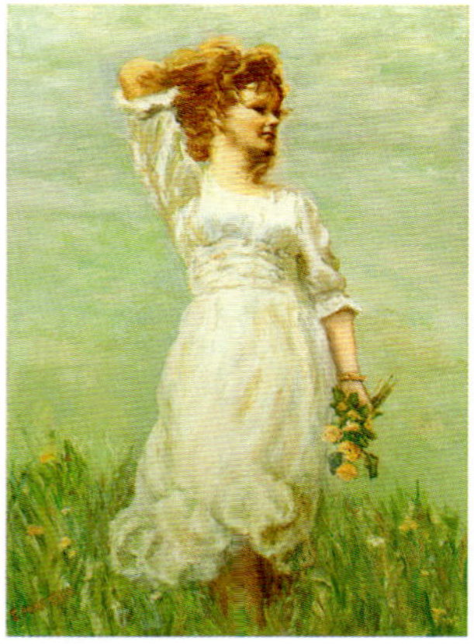

Marston, Edith Floyd 1904–1988
Vanessa Henderson c.1960
oil on canvas 73.7 x 49.5
BURGM:paoil299

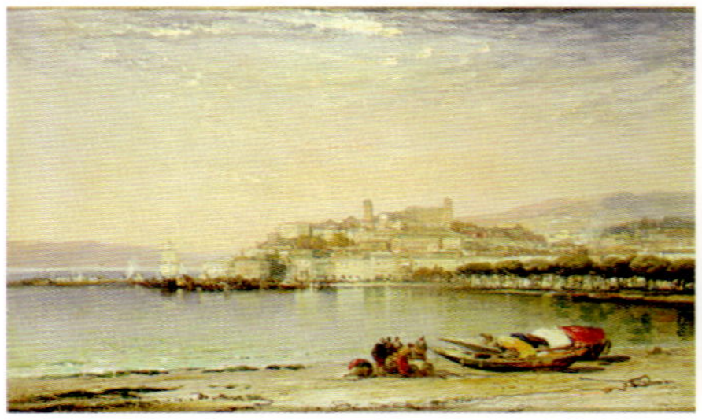

Meadows, Arthur Joseph 1843–1907
Cannes 1897
oil on canvas 29.2 x 48.9
BURGM:paoil71

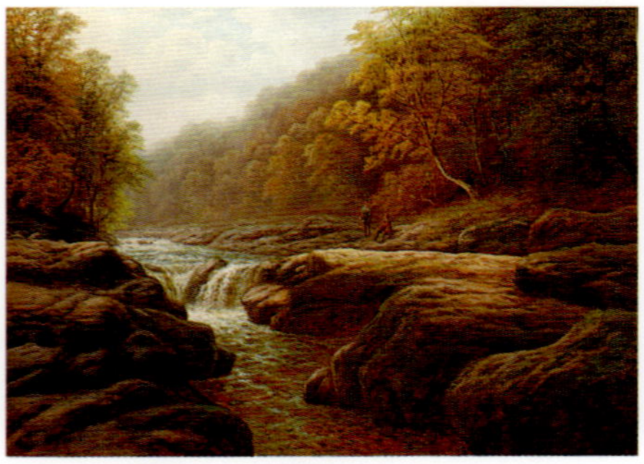

Mellor, William 1851–1931
A River Scene with Anglers
oil on canvas 61 x 91.4
BURGM:paoil152

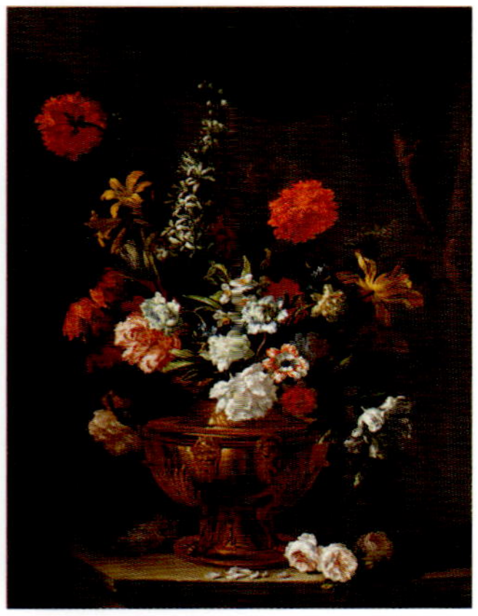

Monnoyer, Jean-Baptiste 1636–1699
Flowers in a Sculptured Vase 1670–1699
oil on canvas 149 x 109
BURGM:paoil118

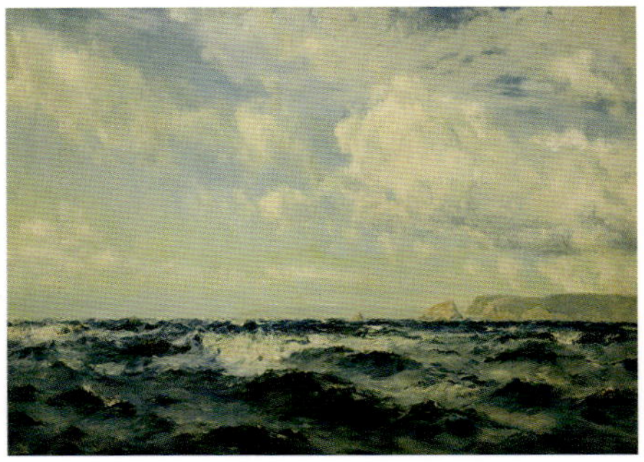

Moore, Henry 1831–1895
A Breezy Day off the Isle of Wight 1890
oil on canvas 88.9 x 156
BURGM:paoil35

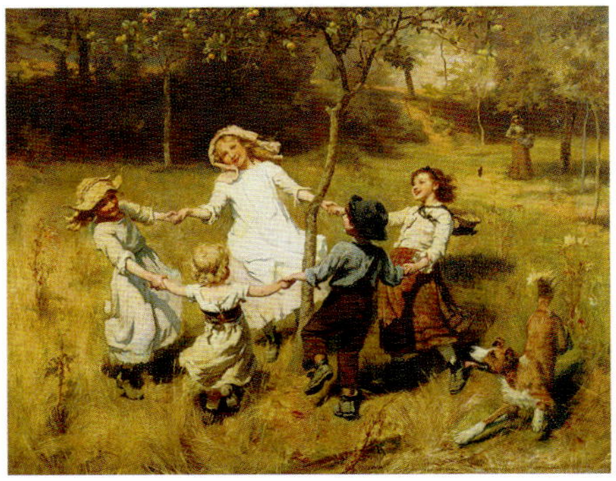

Morgan, Frederick 1856–1927
Ring-a-Ring-a-Roses-Oh c.1885
oil on canvas 81.3 x 104
BURGM:paoil36

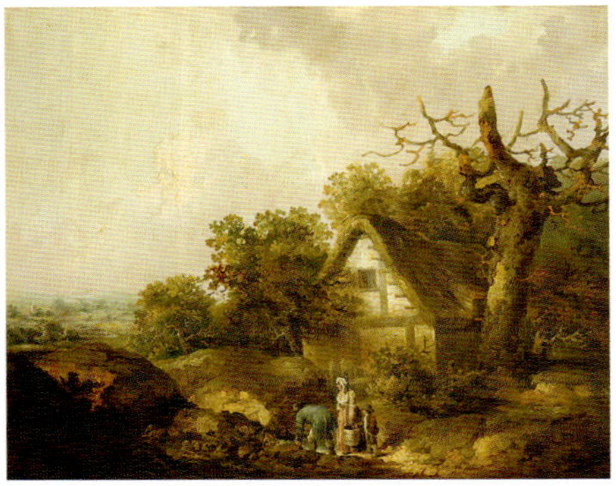

Morland, George 1763–1804
A Rustic Cottage
oil on canvas 69.9 x 88.3
BURGM:paoil125

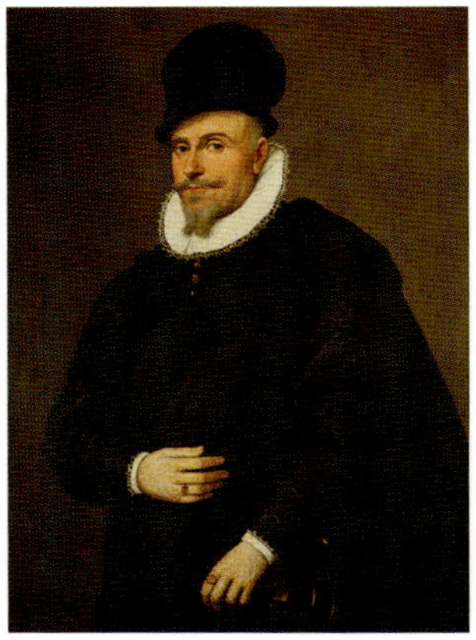

Moroni, Giovanni Battista (after) 1525–1578
Locollo Souardi 1560–1578
oil on canvas 112 x 81.9
BURGM:paoil175

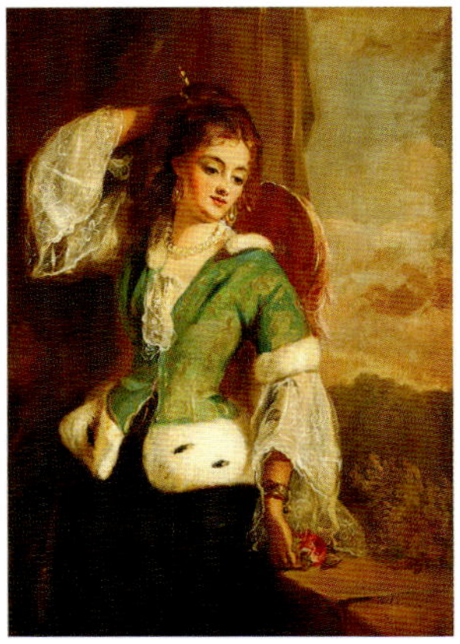

Morris, Philip Richard 1836–1902
Portrait of a Lady in a Green Jacket 1890
oil on canvas 86.4 x 68.6
BURGM:paoil73

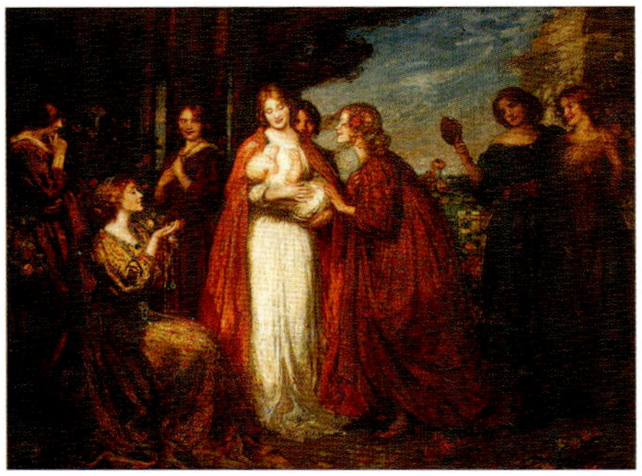

Mostyn, Thomas Edwin 1864–1930
Garden of Love
oil on canvas 201 x 274
BURGM:paoil67

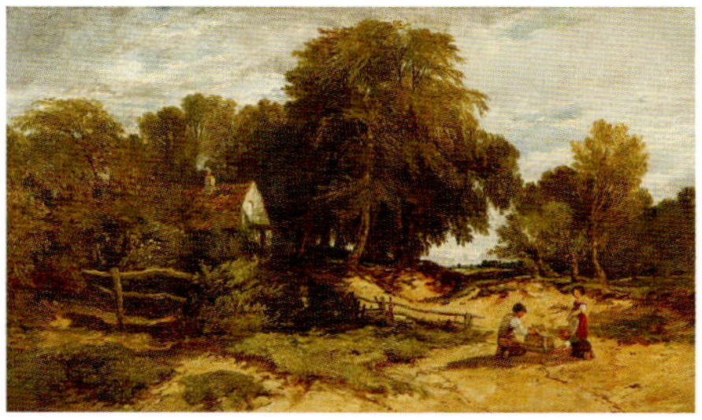

Muller, William James 1812–1845
Wooded Landscape with Children 1845
oil on canvas 68.6 x 88.9
BURGM:paoil134

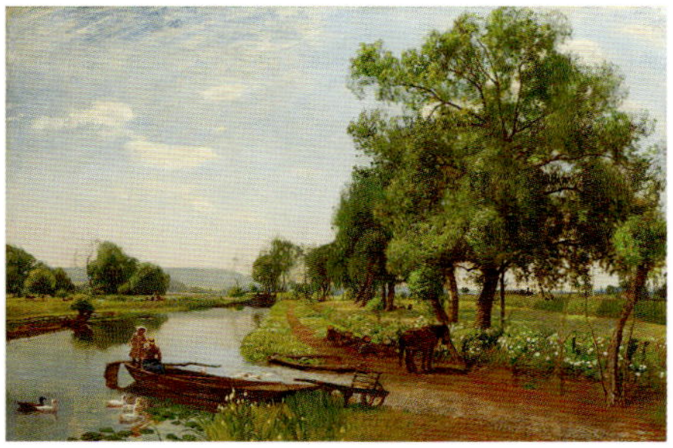

Murray, David 1849–1933
River and Rail 1896
oil on canvas 119 x 180
BURGM:paoil121

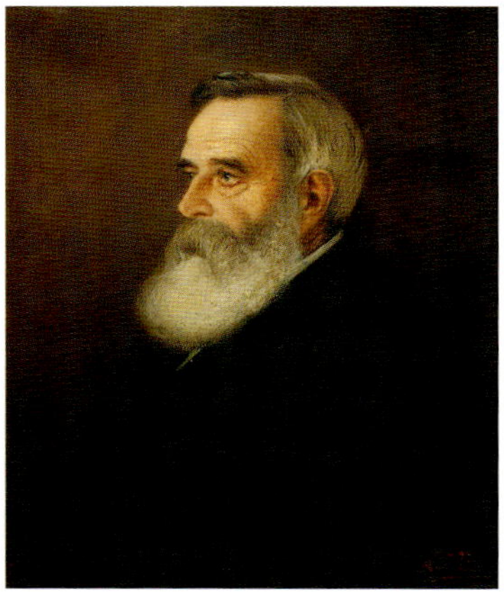

Naudé, Pieter Hugo 1869–1941
Dr Brown
oil on canvas 73.7 x 58.4
BURGM:paoil59

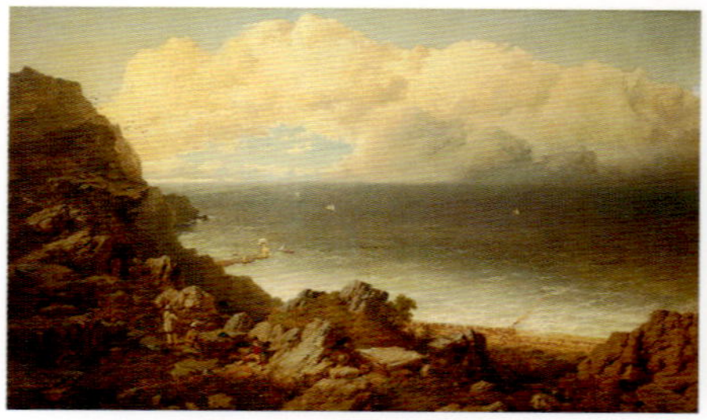

Niemann, Edmund John 1813–1876
Penmaenmawr 1872
oil on canvas 61.6 x 112
BURGM:paoil18

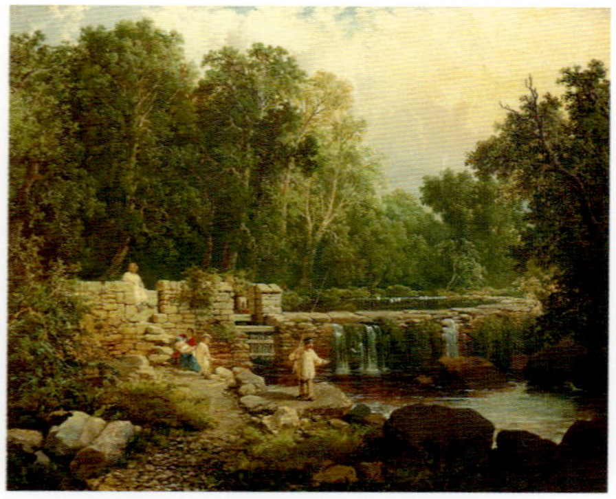

Niemann, Edmund John 1813–1876
Stapleton
oil on canvas 68.6 x 94
BURGM:paoil19

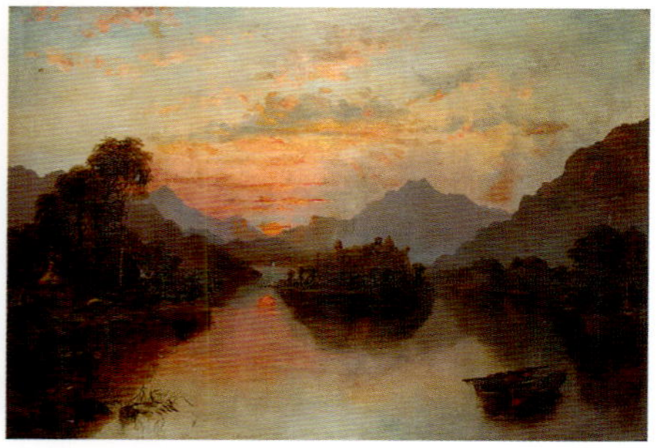

Nisbet, Herkis Hume 1849–1923
Highland Loch with Ruined Castle 1884
oil on canvas 86.4 x 127
BURGM:paoil254

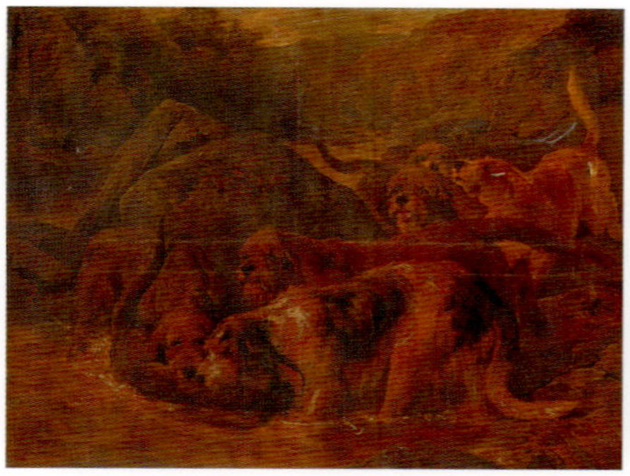

Noble, John Sargeant 1848–1896
Death of the Otter
oil on canvas 91.4 x 127
BURGM:paoil284

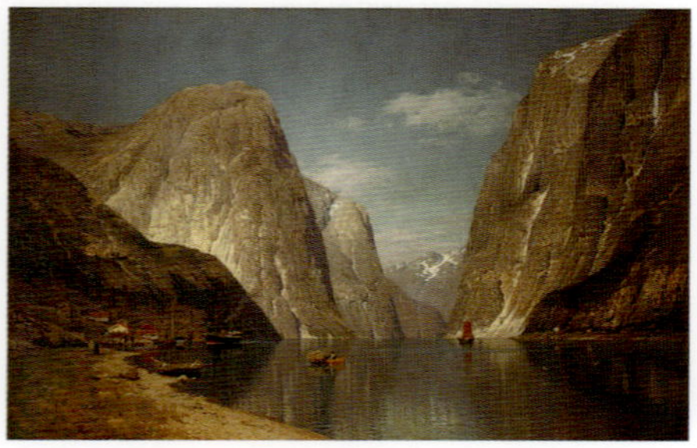

Normann, Adelsteen 1848–1918
Near Gudvangen on the Sogne Fjord 1876
oil on canvas 117 x 183
BURGM:paoil57

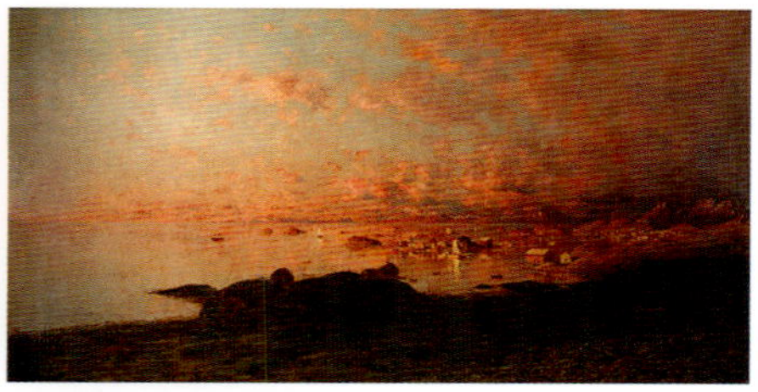

Normann, Adelsteen 1848–1918
Midsummer Night, Lofoten, Norway
oil on canvas 164 x 291
BURGM:paoil56

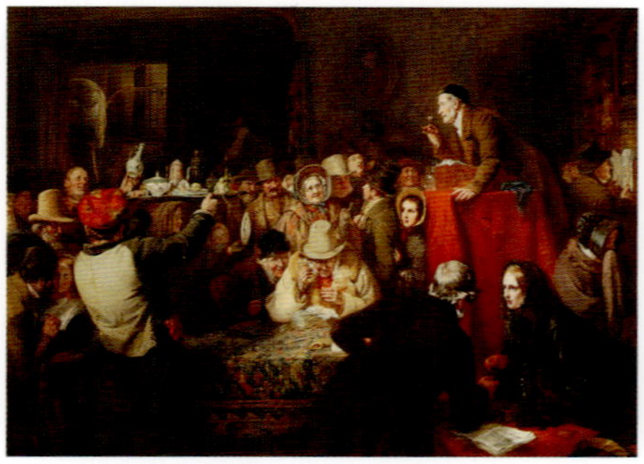

O'Neill, George Bernard 1828–1917
The Last Day of the Sale 1857
oil on canvas 73.7 x 113
BURGM:paoil48

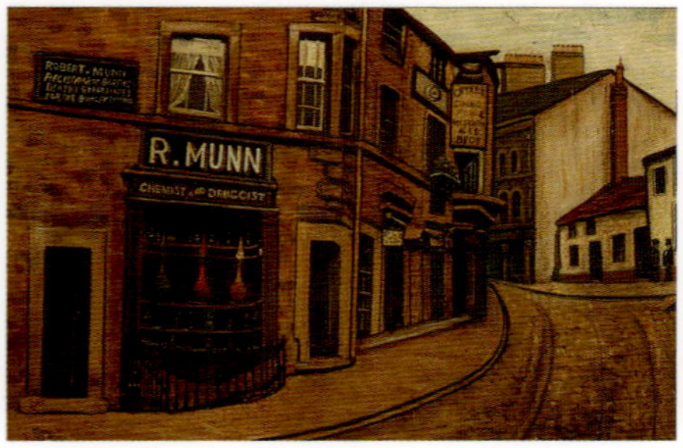

O'Shea
Munn's Corner, 1890
oil on canvas 35.6 x 55.9
BURGM:paoil184

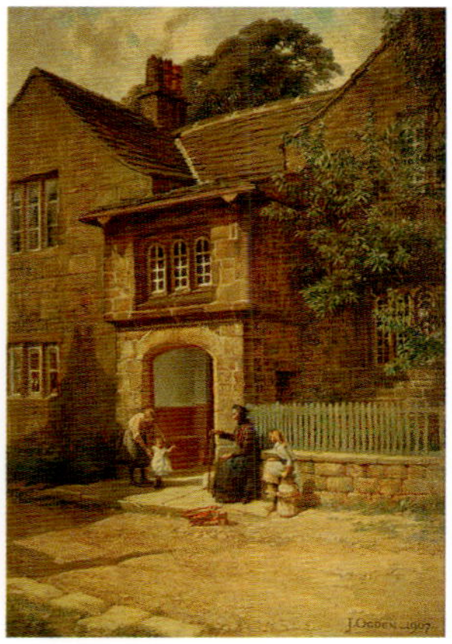

Ogden, Joseph 1862–1925
The Porch, Spenser's Cottage, Hurstwood 1907
oil on canvas 74.9 x 54.6
BURGM:paoil62

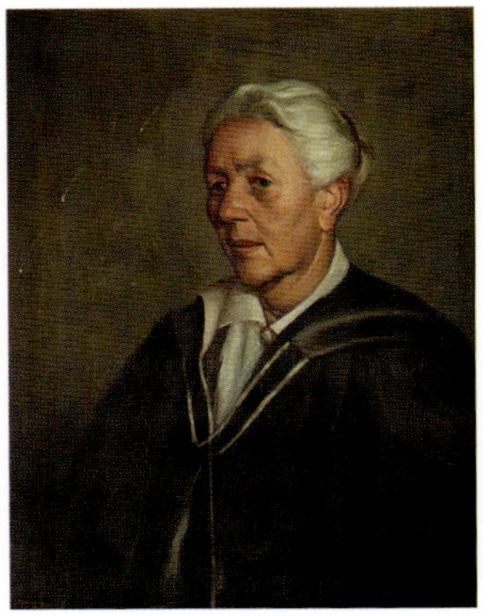

Oliver, Charles William 1911–2004
Miss Dorothy Howard 1959
oil on canvas 76.2 x 61
BURGM:paoil296

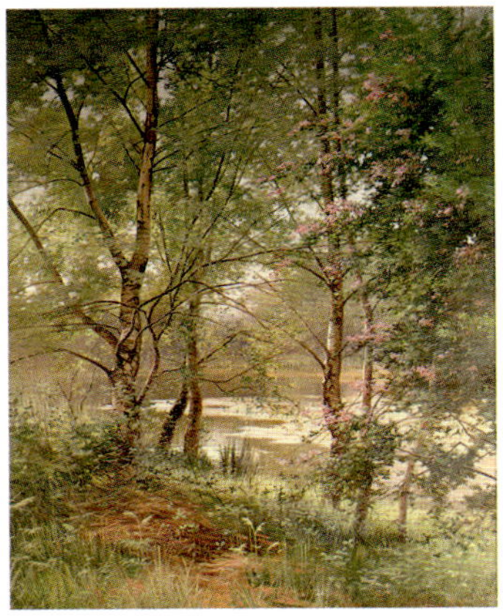

Parton, Ernest 1845–1933
In a Fairy Woodland
oil on canvas 137 x 107
BURGM:paoil145

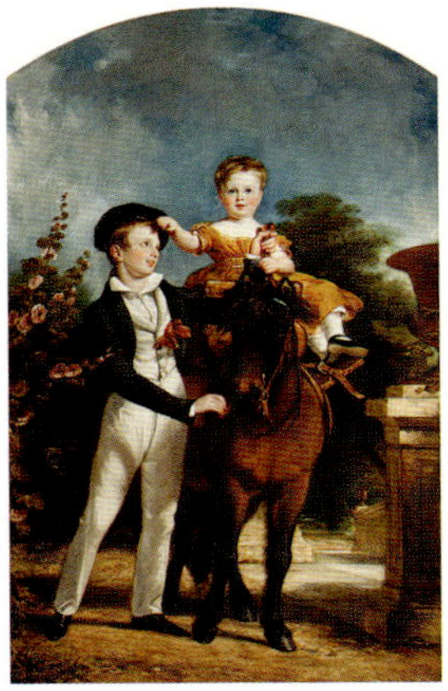

Partridge, John 1789–1872
George Glynn and Oswald Petre, Sons of Henry William Petre of Dunkenhalgh 1836
oil on canvas 231 x 147
LOAN15420 (P)

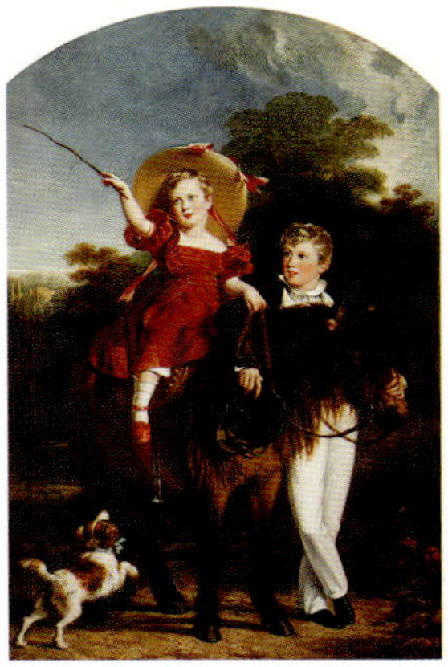

Partridge, John 1789–1872
Henry Petre, Eldest Son, and Edward Petre, 3rd Son, of Henry William Petre of Dunkenhalgh 1836
oil on canvas 231 x 147
LOAN15419 (P)

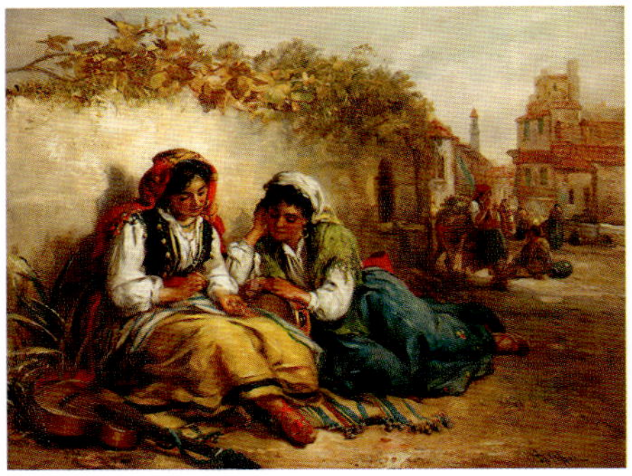

Pelham, Thomas Kent 1831–1907
The Gypsies
oil on canvas 69.9 x 90.2
BURGM:paoil37

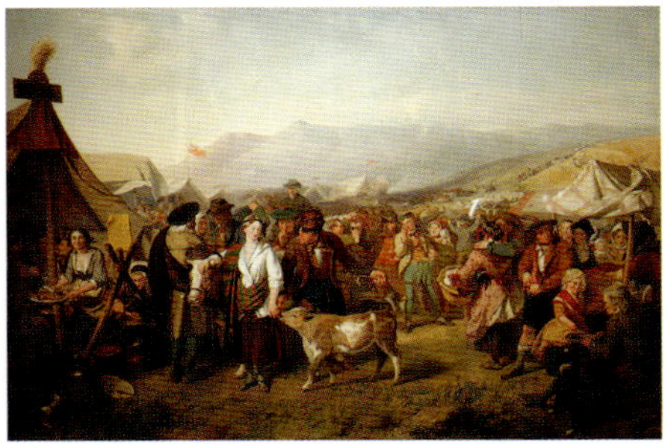

Phillip, John 1817–1867
A Scottish Fair 1851
oil on canvas 88.9 x 135
BURGM:paoil92

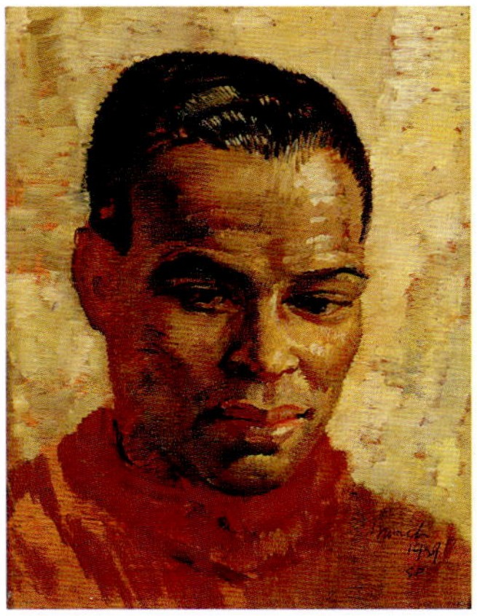

Philpot, Glyn Warren 1884–1937
Portrait of a Man (possibly Henry Thomas) 1929
oil on panel 38.7 x 31.1
BURGM:paoil160

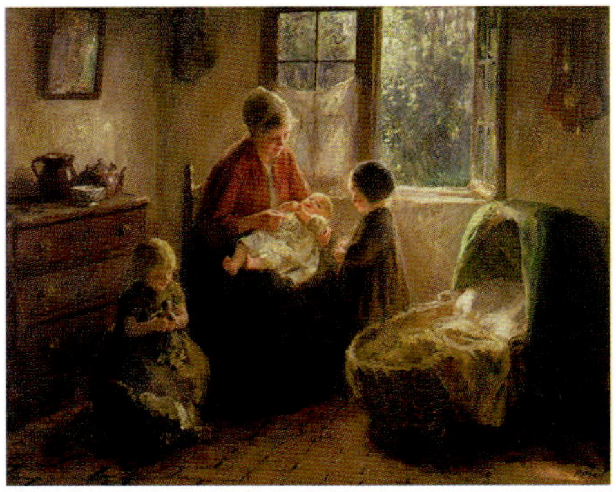

Pothast, Bernard Jean Corneille 1882–1966
Dutch Interior with Mother and Children
oil on canvas 95.3 x 119
BURGM:paoil44

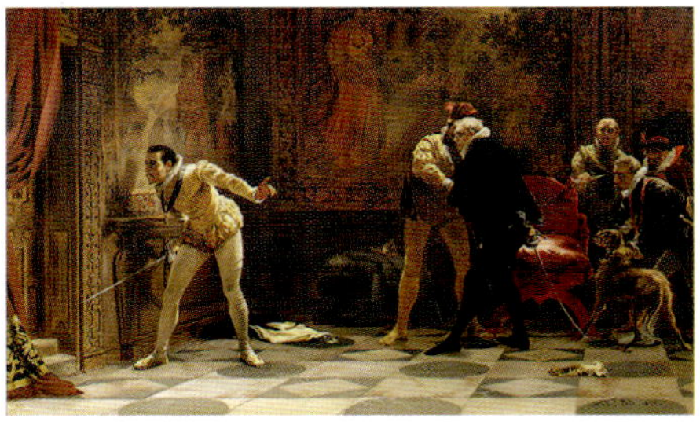

Pott, Laslett John 1837–1898
Waiting for the King's Favourite 1877
oil on canvas 54.6 x 89.5
BURGM:paoil80

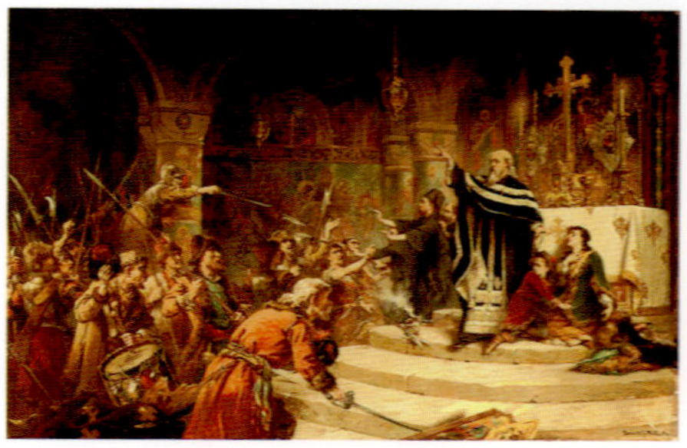

Pott, Laslett John 1837–1898
A Refugee in a Church 1894
oil on canvas 122 x 183
BURGM:paoil28

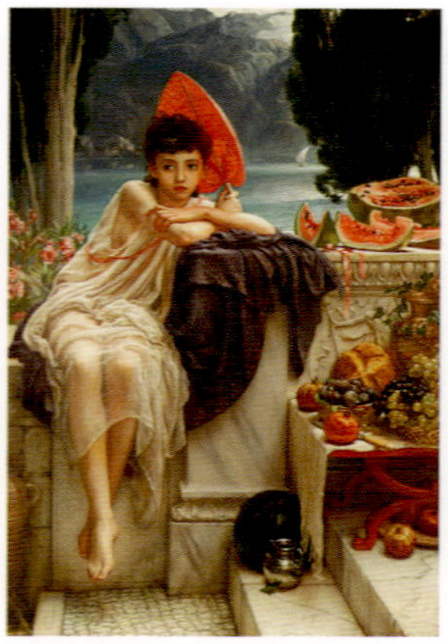

Poynter, Edward John 1836–1919
On the Temple Steps 1889
oil on canvas 77.5 x 52.1
BURGM:paoil173

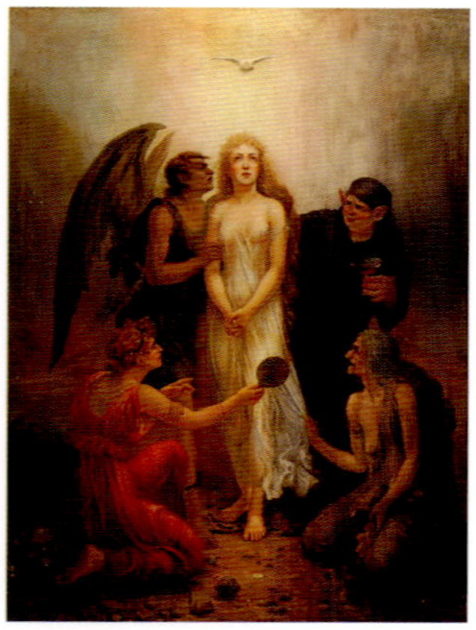

Preston, Nonnie
Beauty and Temptation 1894
oil on canvas 124 x 102
BURGM:paoil255

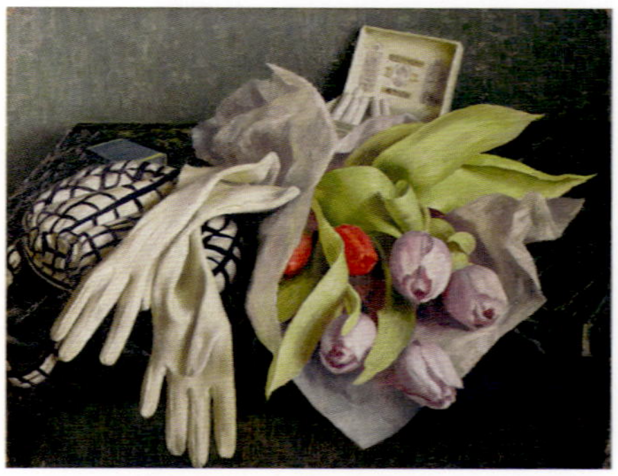

Procter, Dod 1892–1972
The Hall Table
oil on canvas 38.1 x 49.5
BURGM:paoil211

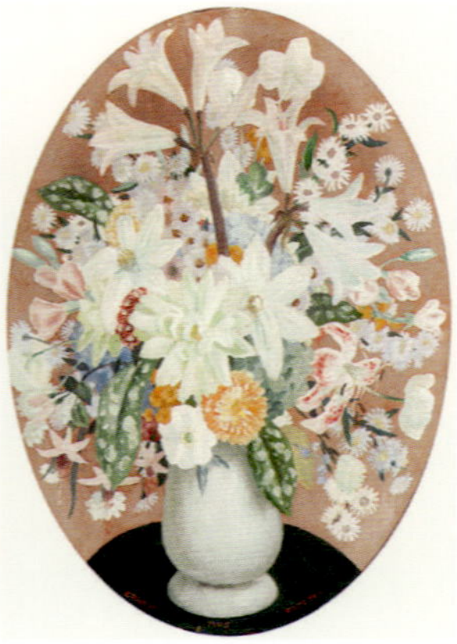

Procter, Ernest 1886–1935
Flower Study 1927
oil on canvas 58.4 x 43.2
BURGM:paoil210

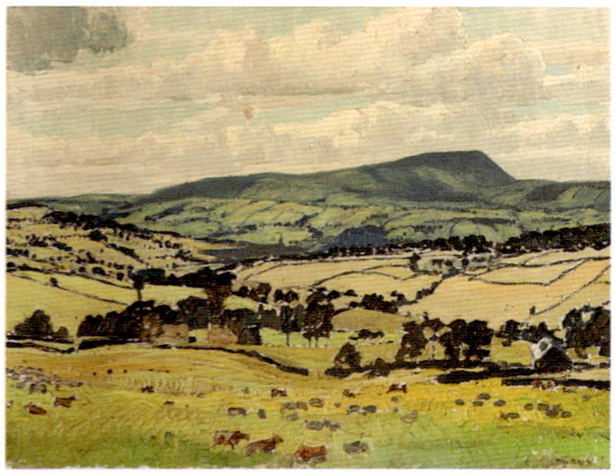

Purdy, James 1900–1972
Pendle from Boulsworth
oil on canvas 71.1 x 91.4
BURGM:paoil275

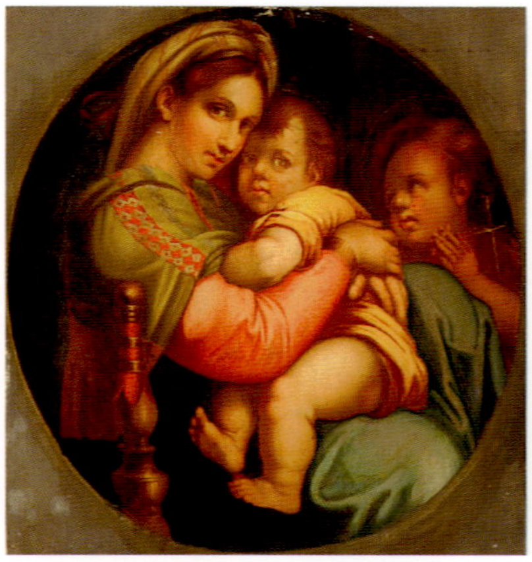

Raphael (after) 1483–1520
La Madonna della Sedia 19th C
oil on canvas 40.6 x 40.6
BURGM:paoil168

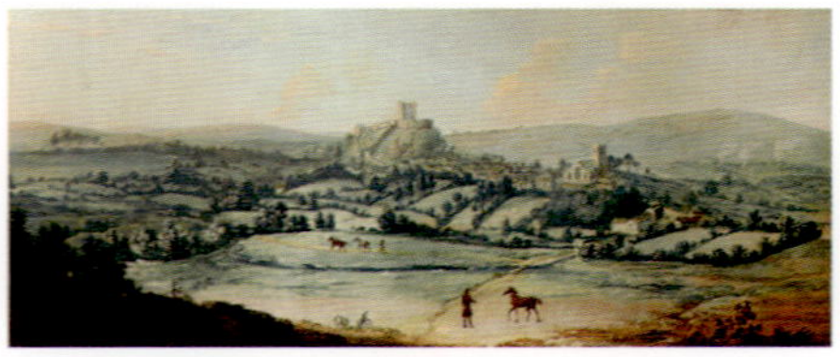

Read, Matthias 1669–1747
Distant View of Clitheroe c.1730
oil on canvas board 46.4 x 113
BURGM:paoil302

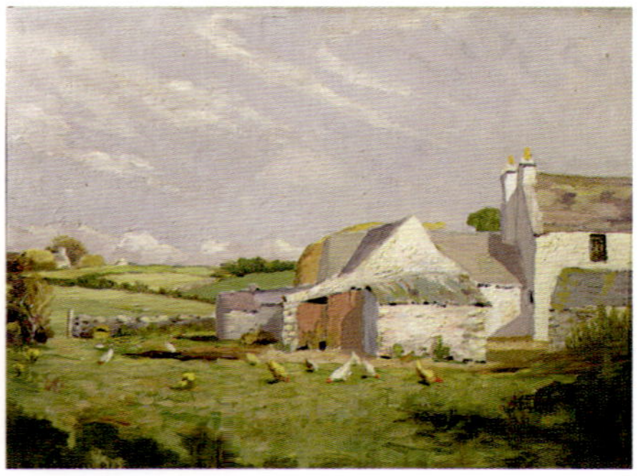

Reekie, William Maxwell 1869–1948
An Anglesey Cottage c.1925
oil on panel 28.5 x 38.7
BURGM:paoil66

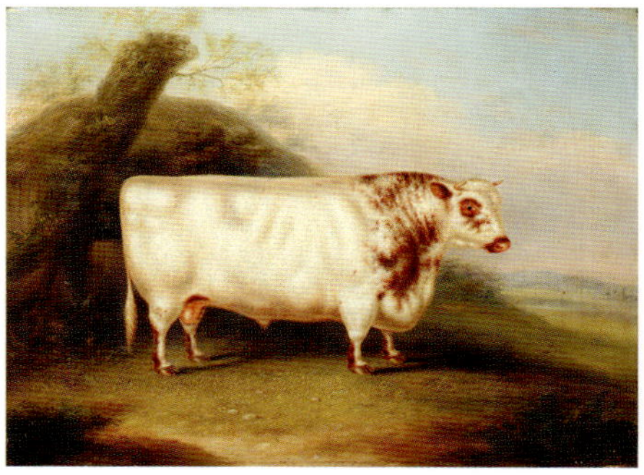

Stafford, Henry 1830–1873
'Harlsonia' (Shorthorn Bull) c.1855
oil on canvas 53.3 x 71.1
BURGM:paoil234.1

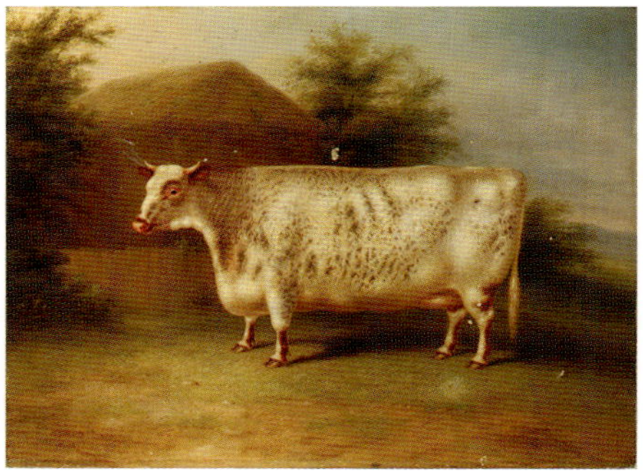

Stafford, Henry 1830–1873
A Shorthorn Cow c.1855
oil on canvas 53.3 x 71.1
BURGM:paoil234.2

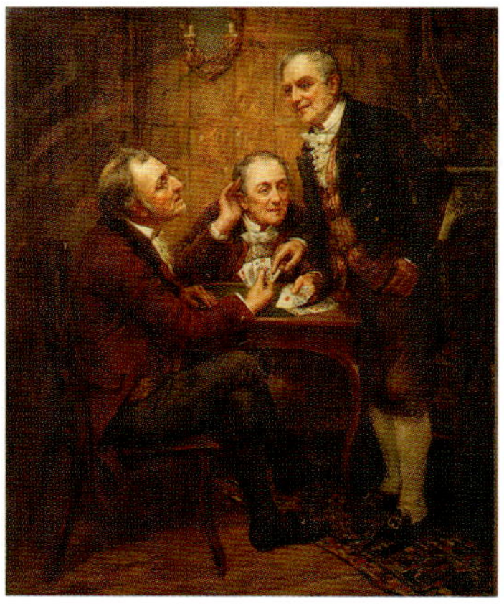

Steadman, Joseph Thomas 1850–1938
The Disputed Deal 1894
oil on canvas 73.7 x 59.7
BURGM:paoil250

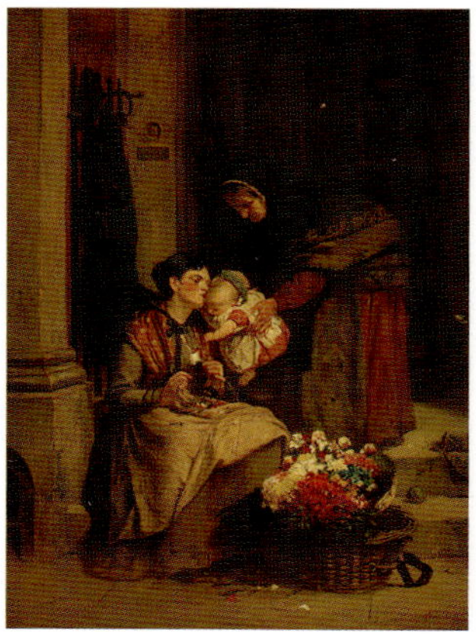

Stocks, Arthur 1846–1889
Her Sweetest Flower 1880
oil on canvas 150 x 110
BURGM:paoil15

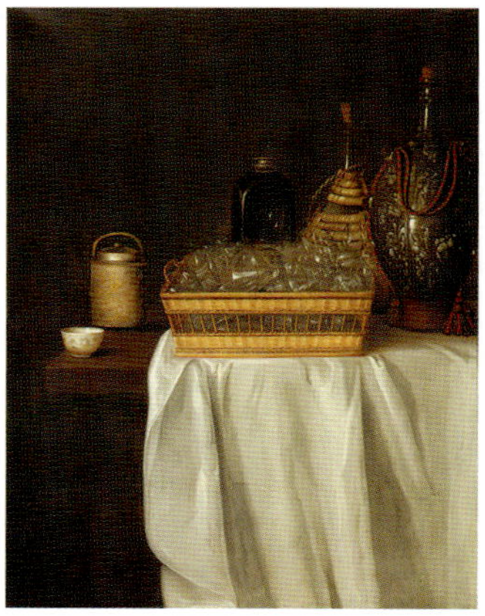

Stoskopf, Sebastian 1597–1657
A Still Life of Wine Glasses and Flagons
1620–1640
oil on canvas 118 x 99.1
BURGM:paoil220

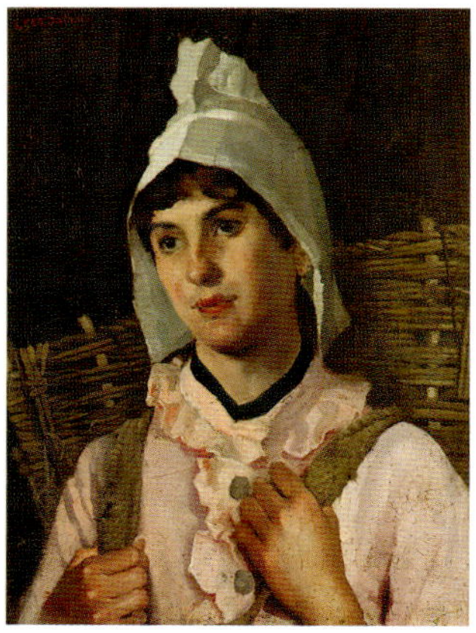

Suthers, Leghe 1856–1924
Breton Girl
oil on canvas 57.2 x 44.5
BURGM:paoil180

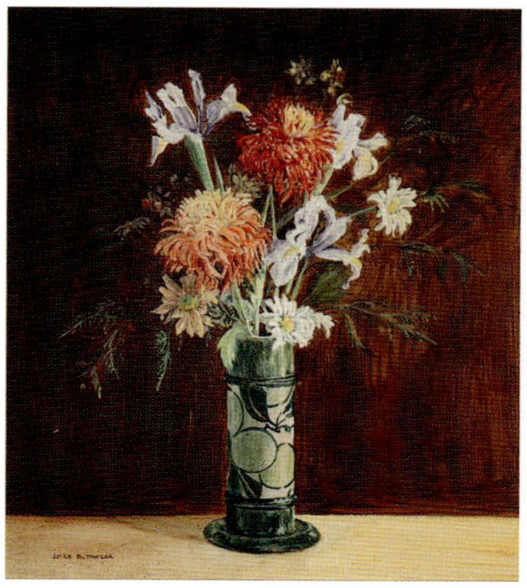

Taylor, Joyce B. 1921–2007
Chrysanths in a Doulton Vase
oil on board 35.6 x 31.8
BURGM:paoil327

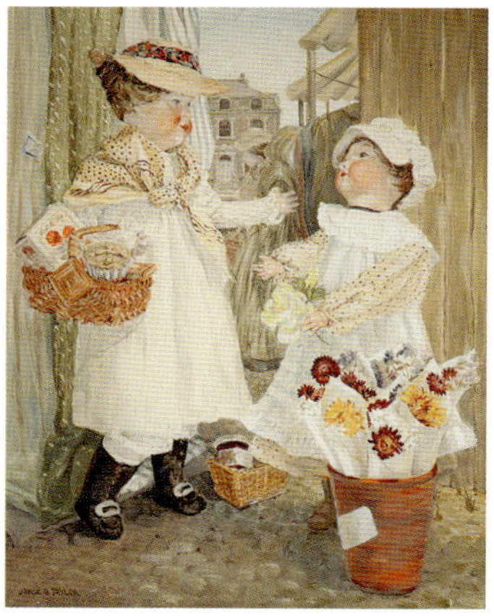

Taylor, Joyce B. 1921–2007
In the Market
oil on board 44.5 x 34.3
BURGM:paoil328

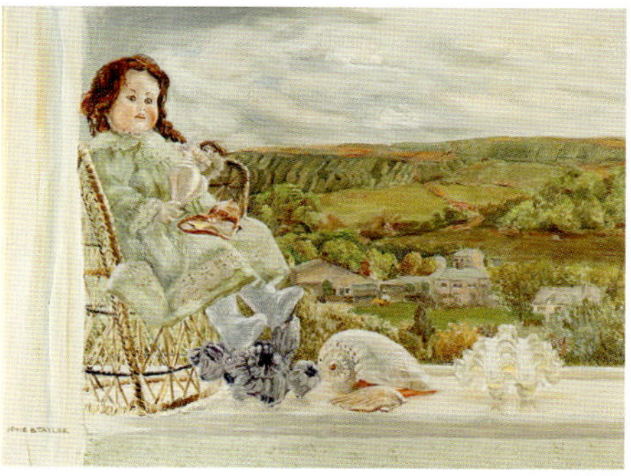

Taylor, Joyce B. 1921–2007
The Shell Collector at Home
oil on board 29.8 x 39.4
BURGM:paoil326

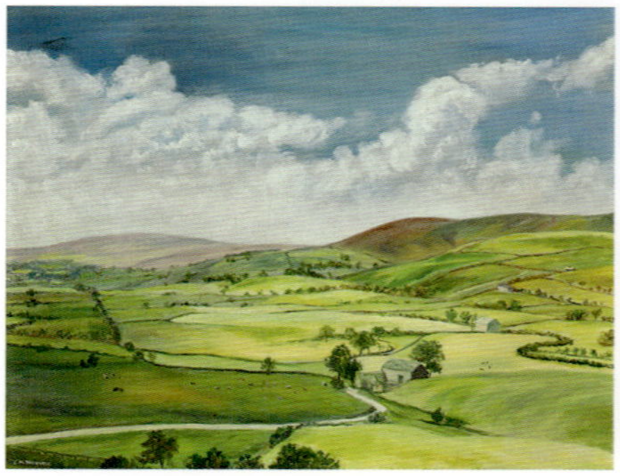

Thornber, Clara M.
The Valley of Sabden c.1960
oil on board 39.4 x 48.3
BURGM:paoil203

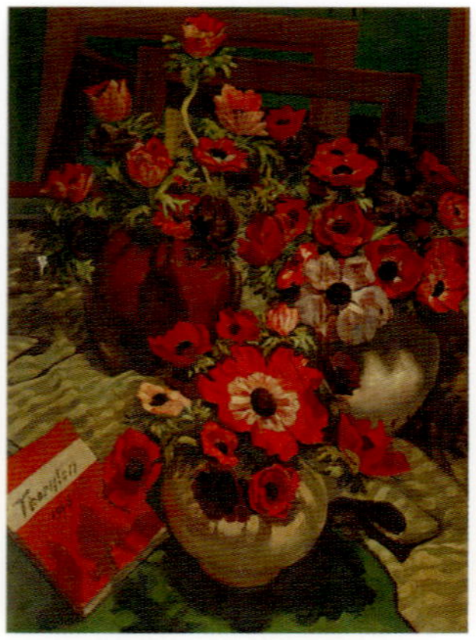

Thornton, Harold 1907–1975
Anemones 1948
oil on canvas 71.1 x 53.3
BURGM:paoil200

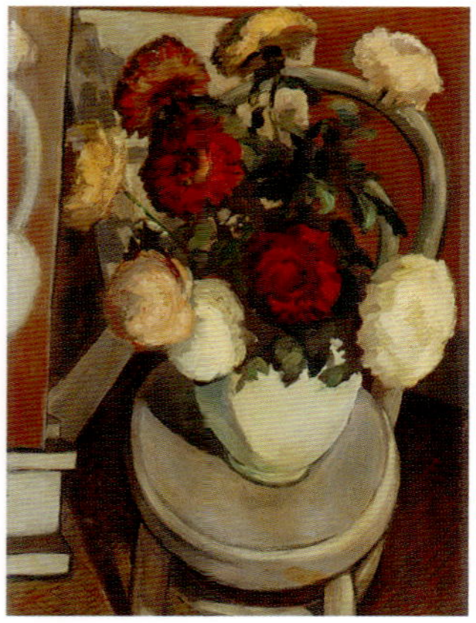

Thornton, Harold 1907–1975
Chrysanthemums 1948
oil on cavas 71.1 x 52.1
BURGM:paoil289

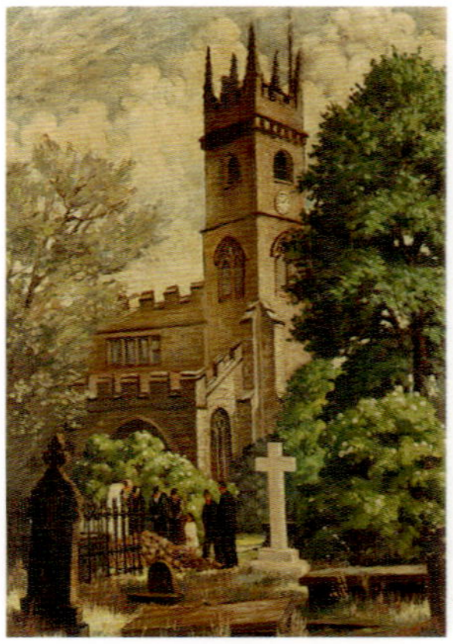

Thornton, Harold 1907–1975
St Peter's Church, Burnley
oil on canvas 59.1 x 48.9
BURGM:paoil199

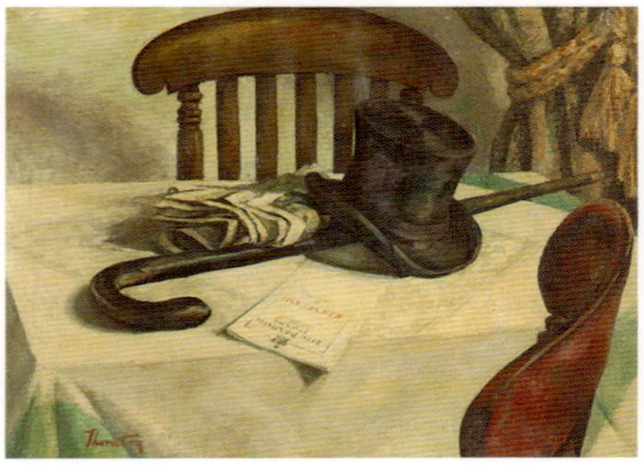

Thornton, Harold 1907–1975
Still Life
oil on canvas 52.1 x 72.4
BURGM:paoil201

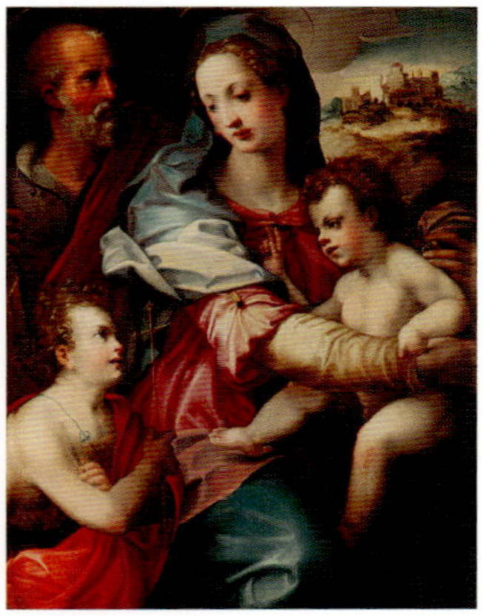

Tosini, Michele (after) 1503–1577
The Holy Family with the Infant Saint John the Baptist 16th C
oil on panel 86 4 x 71.1
BURGM:paoil182

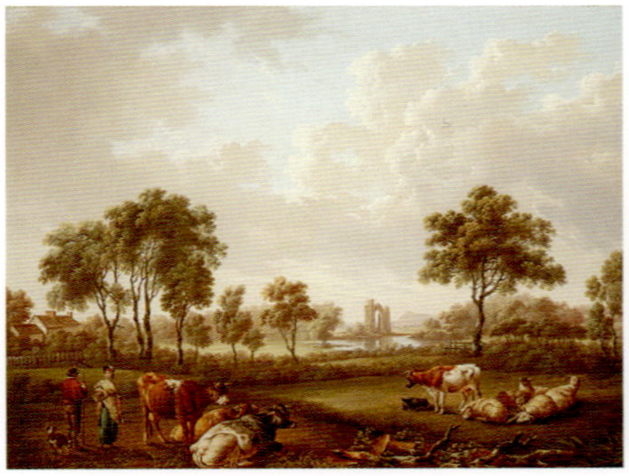

Towne, Charles 1781–1854
A Classical Landscape with Figures and Cattle 1812
oil on panel 39.4 x 50.8
BURGM:paoil108

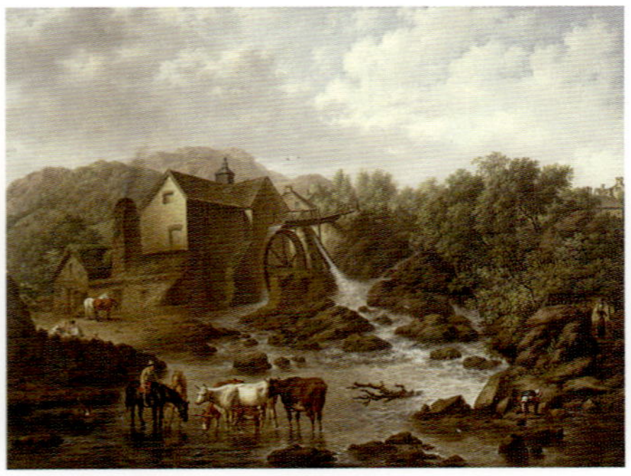

Towne, Charles 1781–1854
The Old Watermill 1833
oil on canvas 55.9 x 73.7
BURGM:paoil172

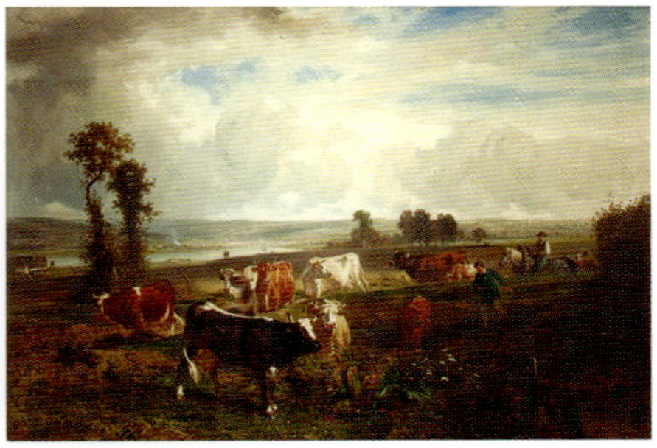

Troyon, Constant 1810–1865
Landscape, les hauteurs de Suresnes 1856
oil on canvas 86 4 x 130
BURGM:paoil132

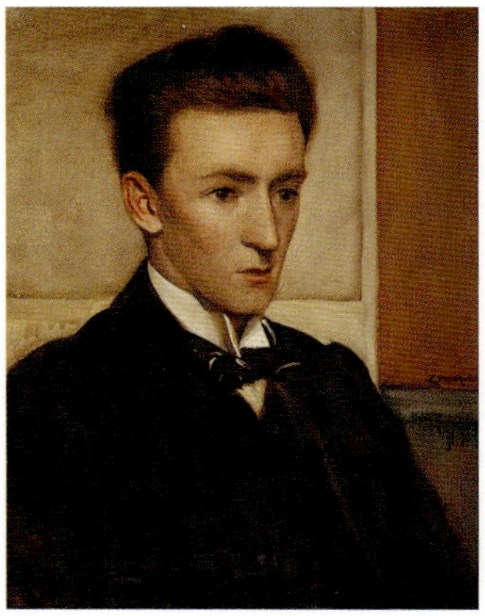

Underwood, Leon 1890–1975
Noel Harry Leaver (1889–1951) 1911
oil on canvas 61 x 50.8
BURGM:paoil329

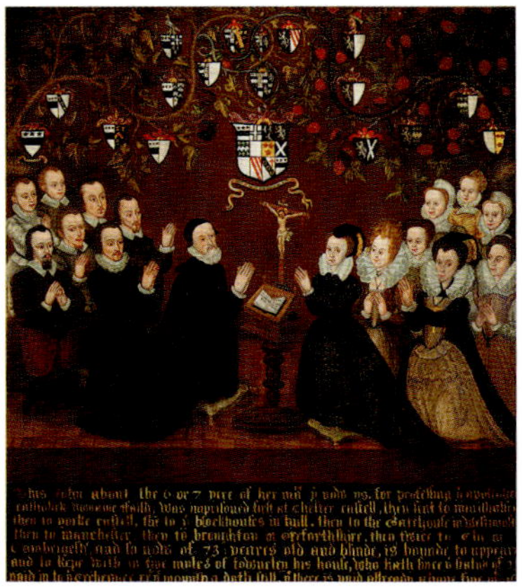

unknown artist
John and Mary Towneley and Family 1601
oil on panel 103 x 90.2
BURGM:paoil117

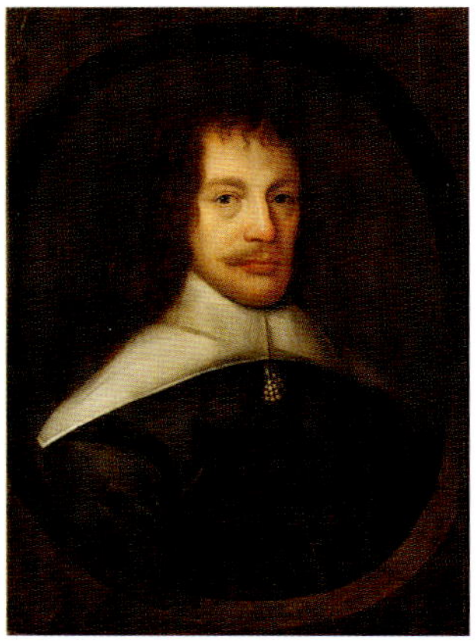

unknown artist
Christopher Towneley (1604–1674) c.1630
oil on canvas 73 x 54
BURGM:paoil314

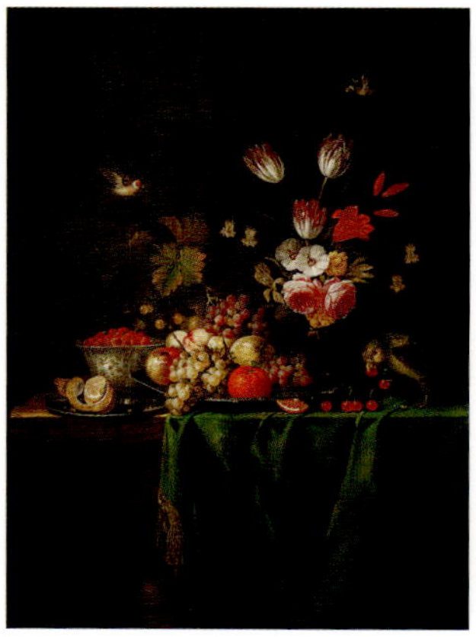

unknown artist
Still Life c.1660
oil on canvas 127 x 91.4
BURGM:paoil93

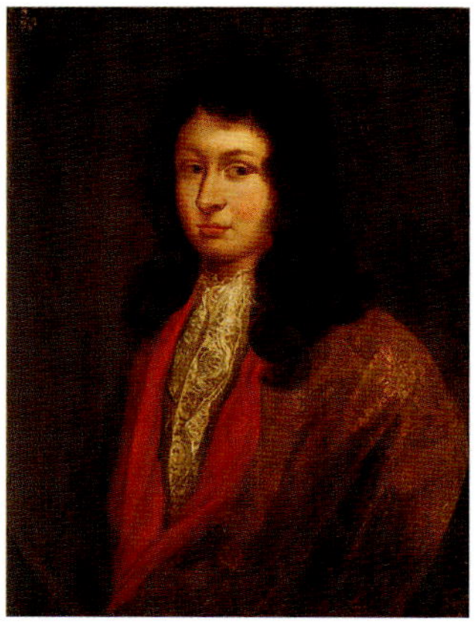

unknown artist
Cuthbert Kennet of Coxhoe (1652–1689) c.1680
oil on canvas 69.2 x 54
BURGM:paoil312

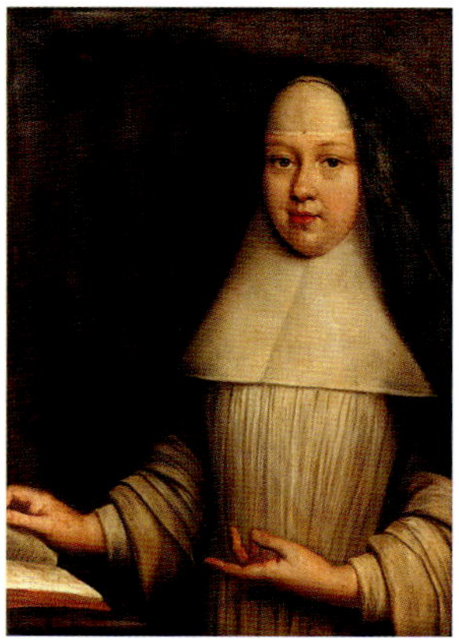

unknown artist
Margaret Towneley (1667–1731), Augustinian Canoness of Paris c.1680
oil on canvas 73 x 54
BURGM:paoil313

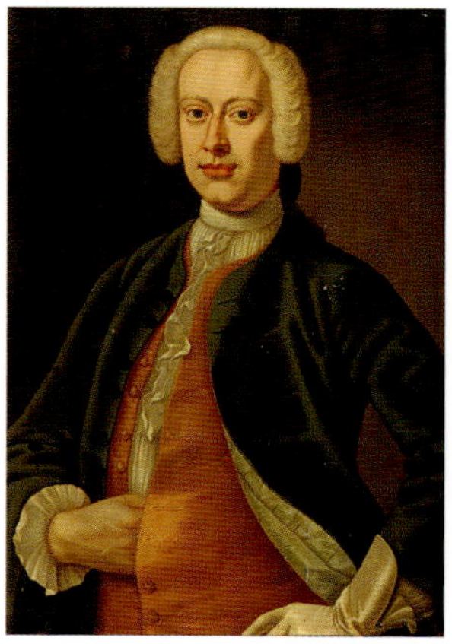

unknown artist
William Towneley of Towneley (1714–1741) c.1735
oil on canvas 73 x 54
BURGM:paoil311

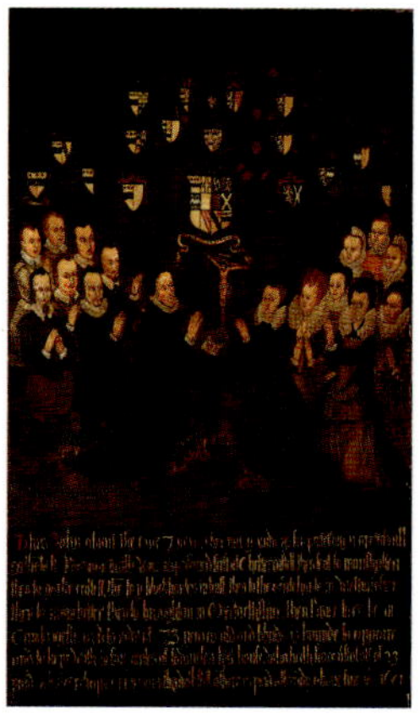

unknown artist
The Towneley Family at Prayer c.1800
oil on canvas 91.4 x 61
BURGM:paoil39

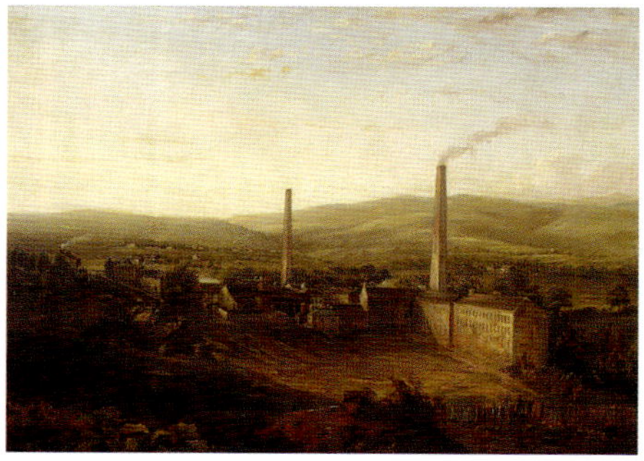

unknown artist
Lowerhouse Printworks, Burnley c.1830
oil on canvas 66 x 91.4
BURGM:paoil309

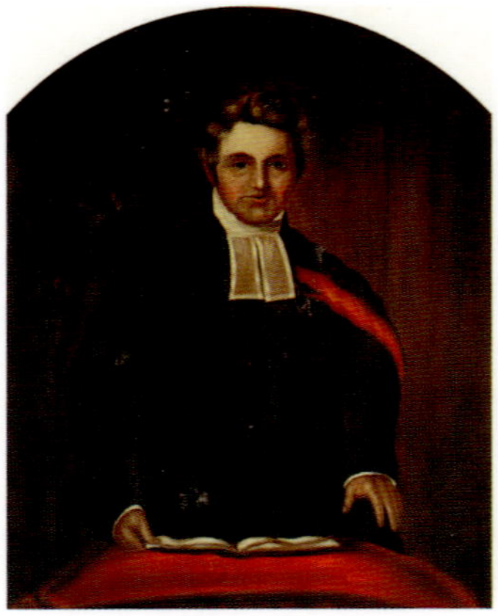

unknown artist
Archdeacon Master c.1850
oil on board 45.7 x 35.6
BURGM:paoil258

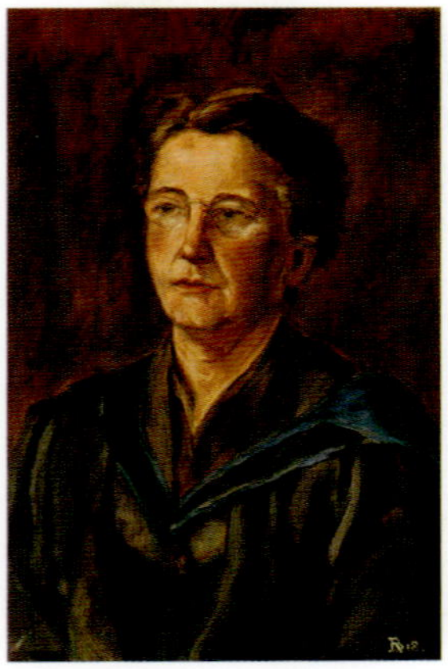

unknown artist
Miss L. J. Wood, MBA, MA 1918
oil on canvas 56.5 x 41
BURGM:paoil295

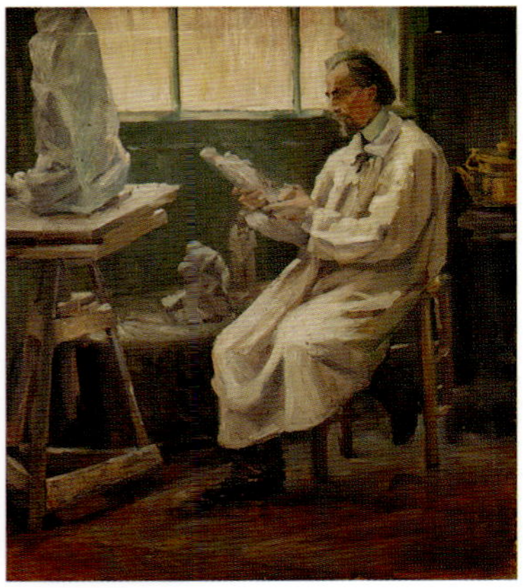

unknown artist
A Sculptor in His Studio
oil on canvas 100 x 81.3
BURGM:paoil260

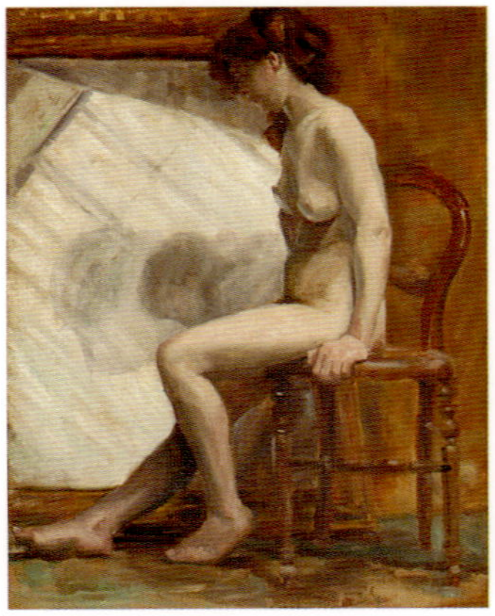

unknown artist
A Seated Female Nude
oil on canvas 81.3 x 63.5
BURGM:paoil266

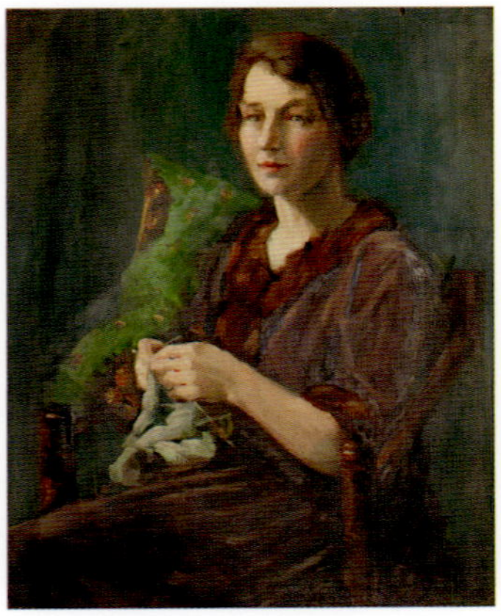

unknown artist
A Woman Knitting
oil on canvas 81.3 x 64.8
BURGM:paoil267

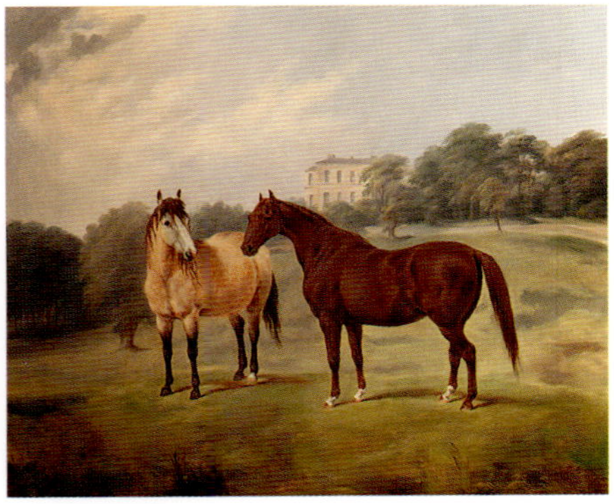

unknown artist
Bank Hall
oil on canvas 81.3 x 96.5
BURGM:paoil32

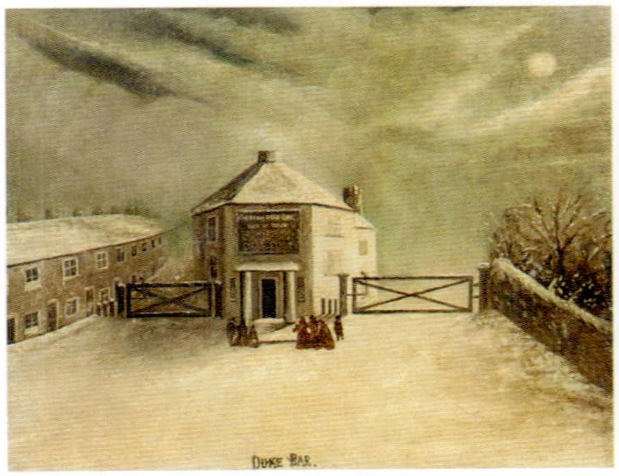

unknown artist
Duke Bar, Burnley, around 1850
oil on canvas 38.1 x 48.3
BURGM:paoil233

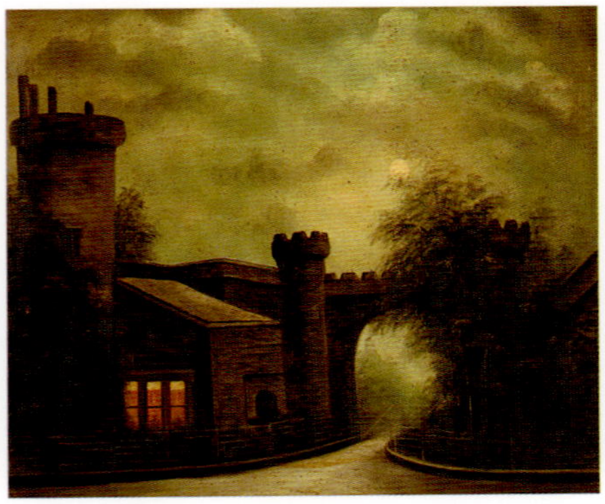

unknown artist
Entrance to Towneley Park, by Moonlight
oil on board 50.8 x 76.2
BURGM:paoil265

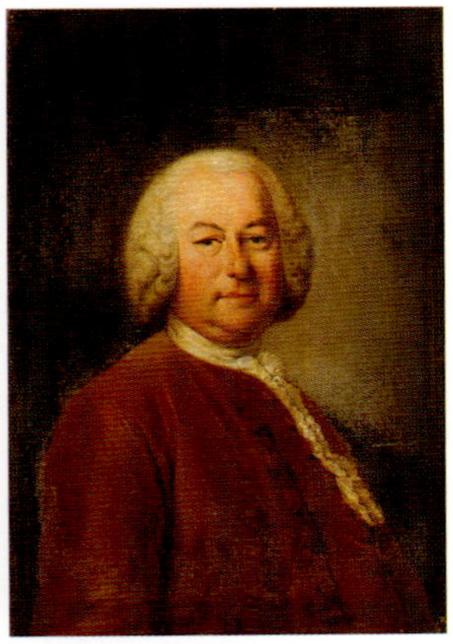

unknown artist
George Towneley of Leighton (1706–1786)
oil on canvas 73 x 54
BURGM:paoil315

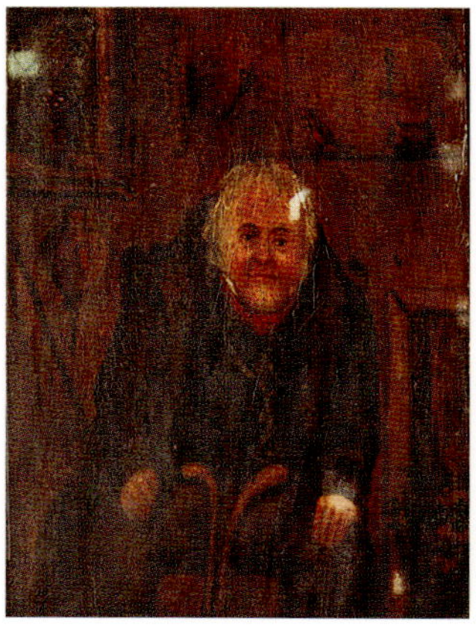

unknown artist
Henry or William Hargreaves
oil on card 27.9 x 24.1
BURGM:paoil298

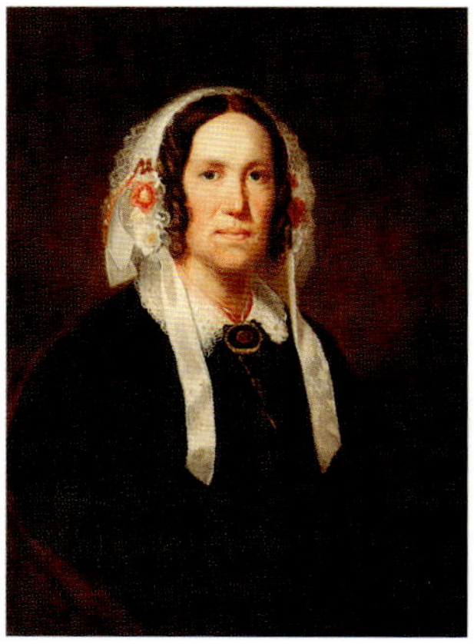

unknown artist
Janet Hunter
oil on cavas 74.9 x 61
BURGM:paoil290

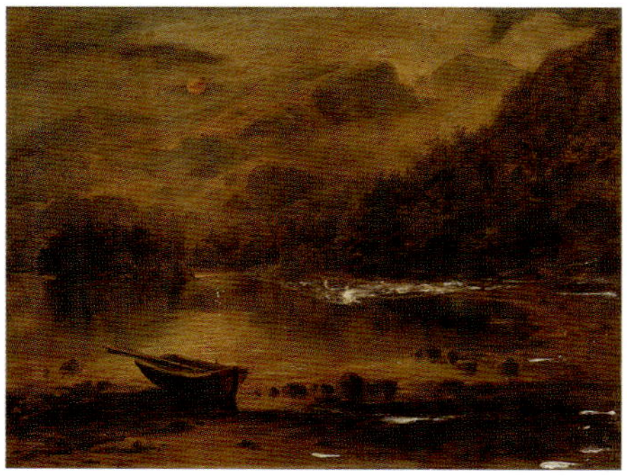

unknown artist
Landscape
oil on canvas 53 x 71
BURGM:paoil237

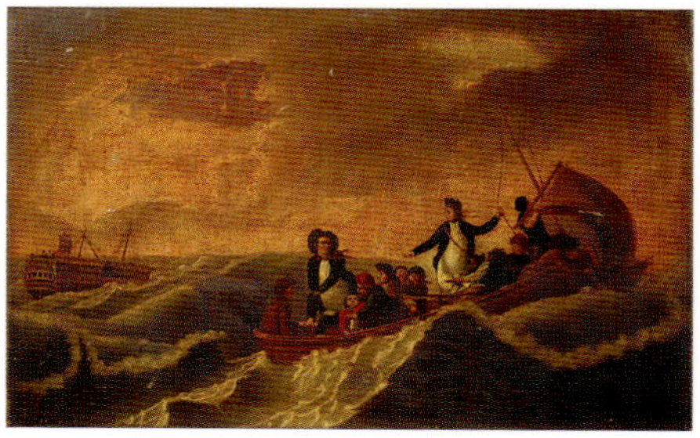

unknown artist
Survivors from a Shipwreck
oil on canvas 72.4 x 113
BURGM:paoil268

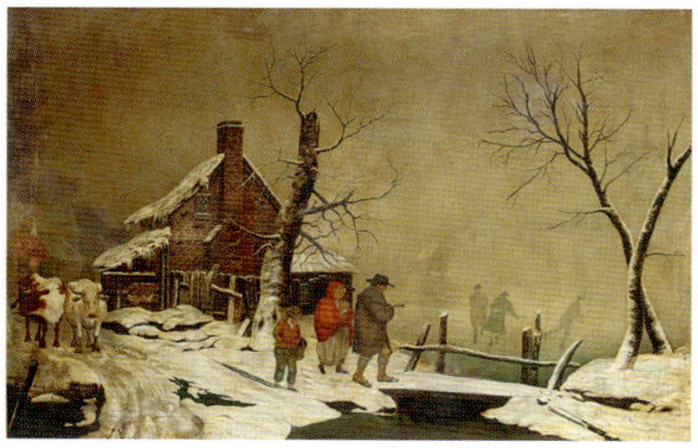

unknown artist
The Skaters
oil on canvas 83.8 x 124
BURGM:paoil236

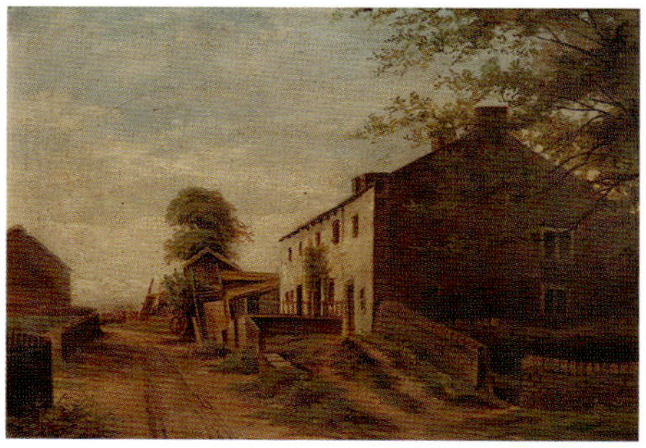

unknown artist
Whins Lane, Simonstone
oil on board 21.6 x 31.8
BURGM:paoil287

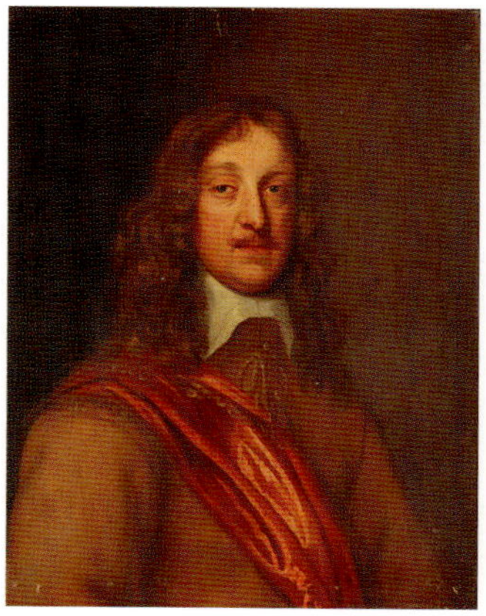

unknown artist
William (c.1631–1676), 2nd Lord Widdrington
oil on canvas 73 x 60.3
BURGM:paoil316

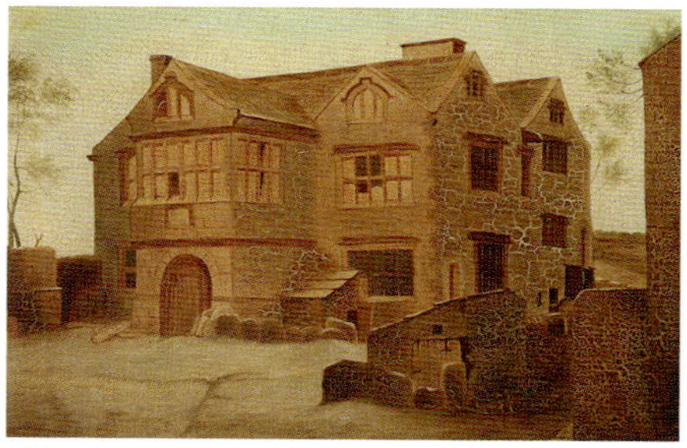

unknown artist
Worsthorne Old Hall
oil on canvas 29.8 x 45.7
BURGM:paoil259

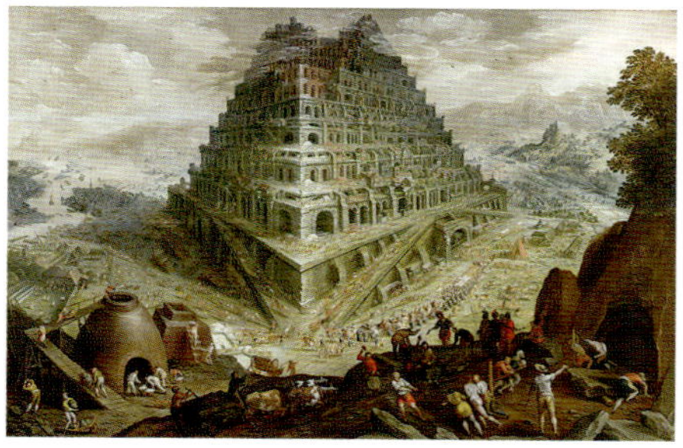

Valckenborch I, Marten van 1534–1612
The Building of the Tower of Babel c.1600
oil on panel 102 x 152
BURGM:paoil155

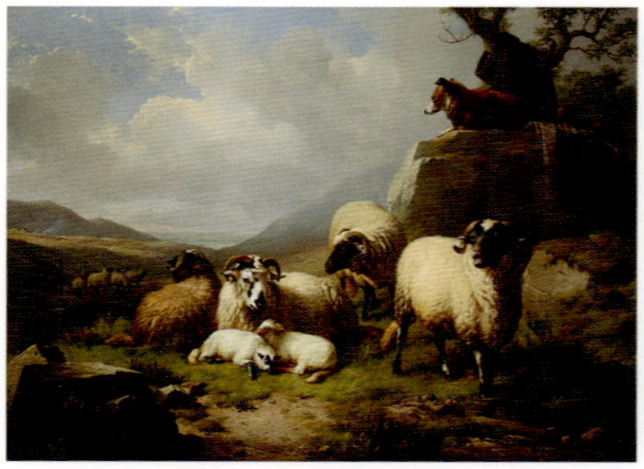

Verboeckhoven, Eugène Joseph 1798–1881
Group of Sheep 1863
oil on panel 69.9 x 97.8
BURGM:paoil79

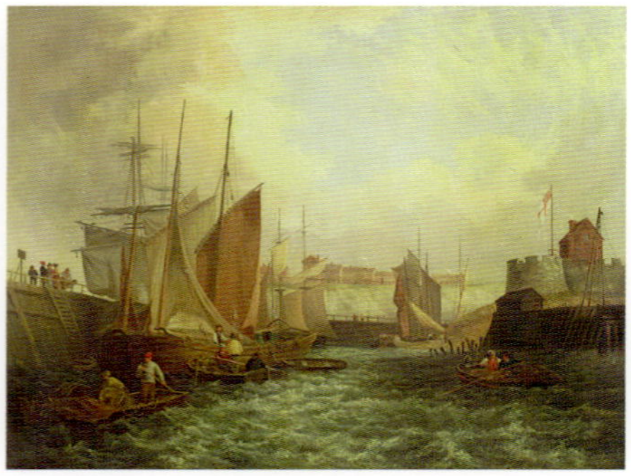

Vincent, George 1796–1831
Mouth of the Yare 1821
oil on canvas 71.1 x 91.4
BURGM:paoil96

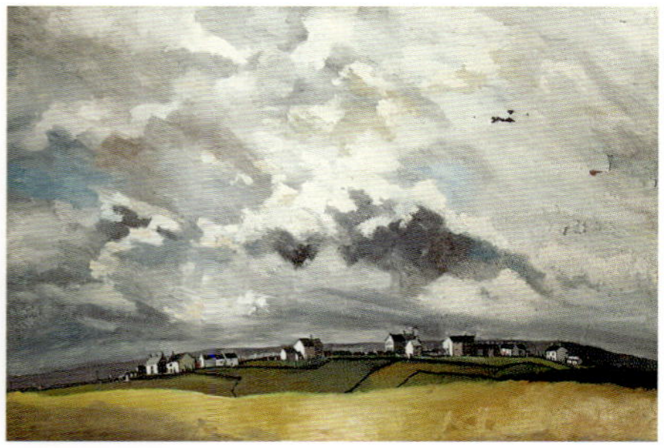

Virtue, John b.1947
View of Green Haworth from the North c.1974
oil on board 122 x 182
BURGM:paoil246

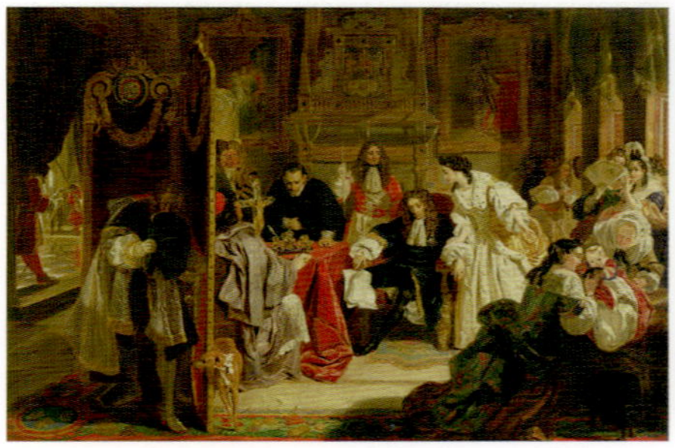

Ward, Edward Matthew 1816–1879
King James Receiving News of the Landing of William of Orange 1851
oil on canvas 50.8 x 75.6
BURGM:paoil16

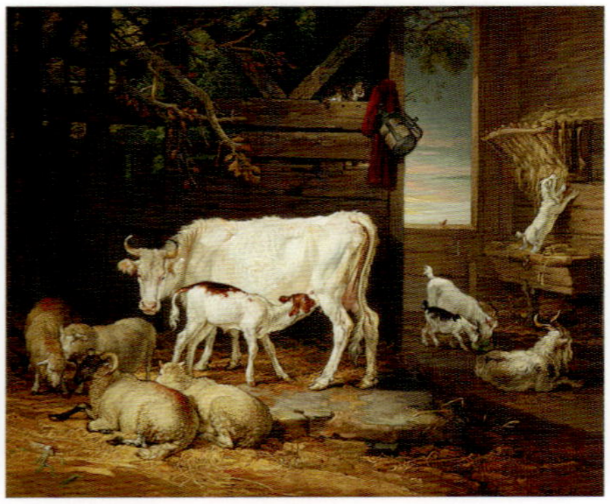

Ward, James 1769–1859
Interior of a Stable 1810
oil on canvas 68.6 x 88.9
BURGM:paoil98

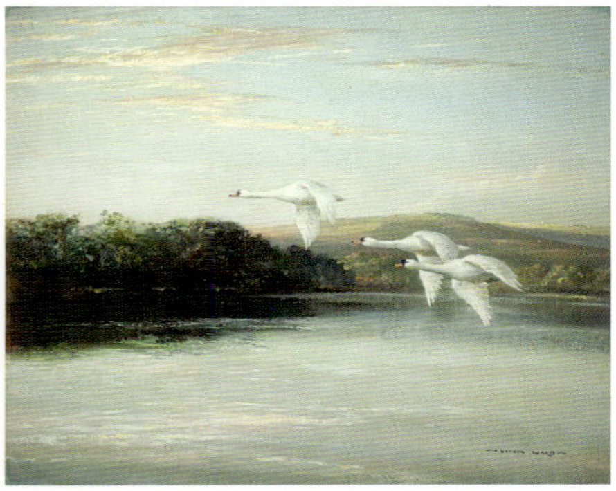

Ward, Vernon 1905–1985
Wild Geese
oil on canvas 39.4 x 49.5
BURGM:paoil133

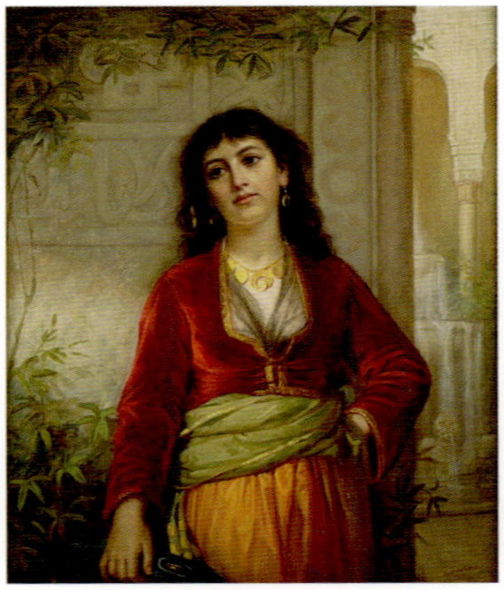

Waterhouse, John William 1849–1917
The Unwelcome Companion c.1872
oil on canvas 59.1 x 49.5
BURGM:paoil166

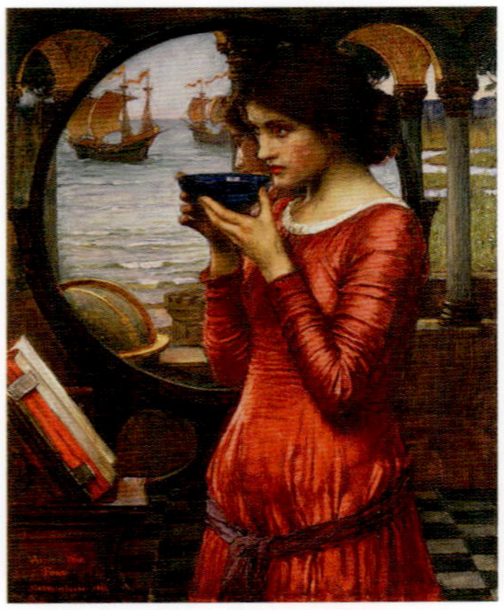

Waterhouse, John William 1849–1917
Destiny 1900
oil on canvas 68.6 x 54.6
BURGM:paoil17

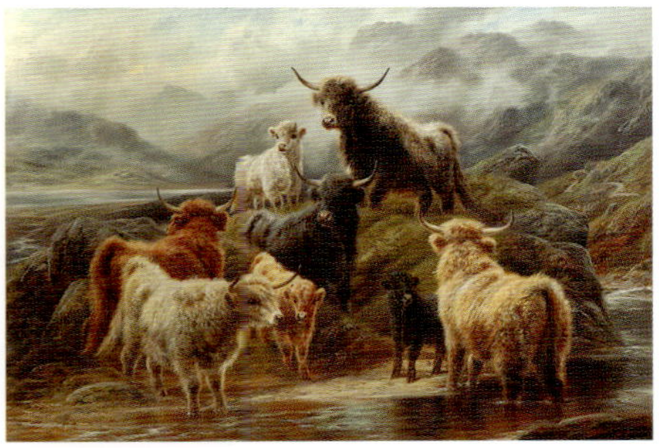

Watson, Robert 1865–1916
Highland Cattle 1894
oil on canvas 61 x 88.9
BURGM:paoil271

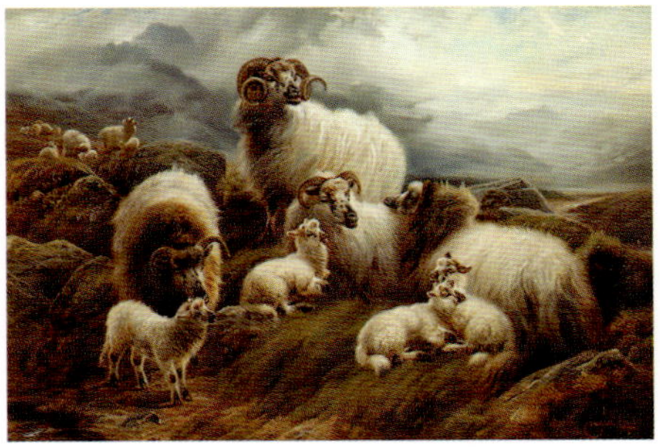

Watson, Robert 1865–1916
Sheep in a Landscape 1894
oil on canvas 61 x 88.9
BURGM:paoil272

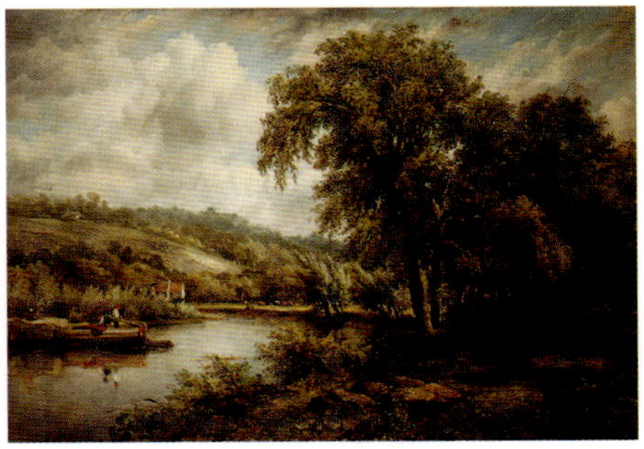

Watts, Frederick Waters 1800–1870
On the Thames
oil on canvas 91.4 x 130
BURGM:paoil105

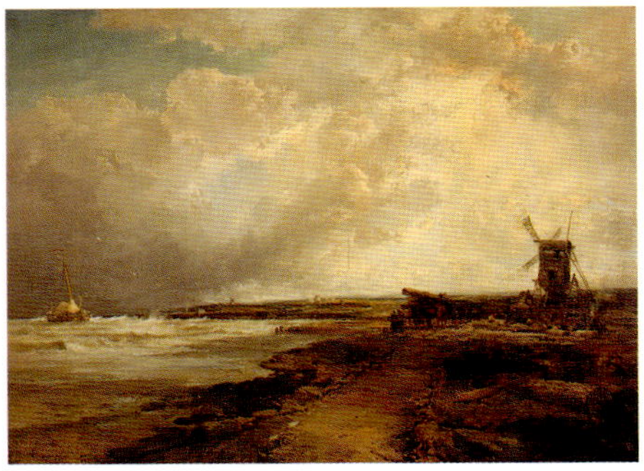

Webb, James 1825–1895
After a Thunderstorm on the Sussex Coast 1882–1883
oil on canvas 91.4 x 138
BURGM:paoil22

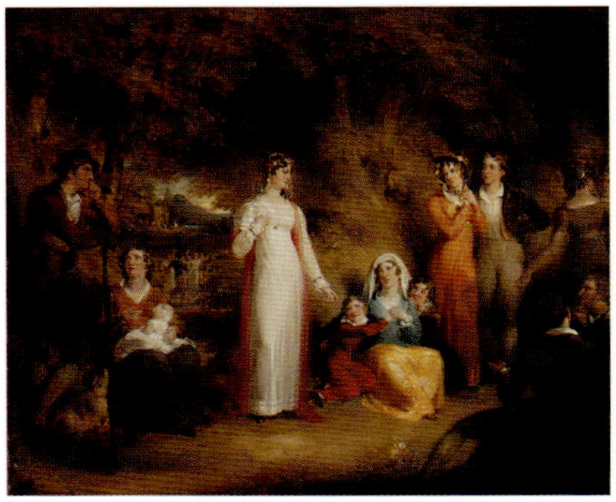

Westall, Richard 1765–1836
The Village Bride
oil on canvas 62.2 x 74.3
BURGM:paoil104

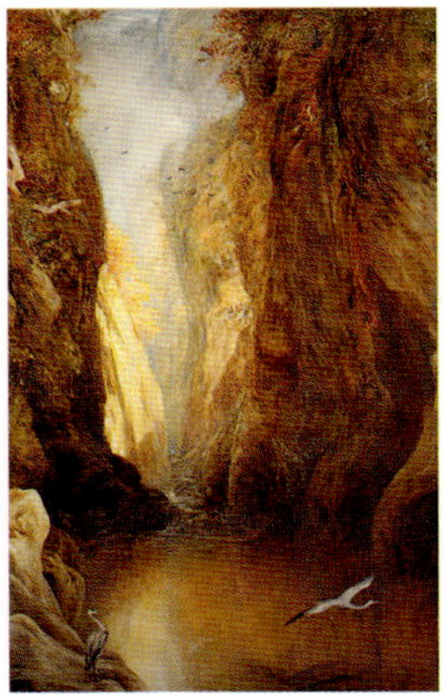

Whaite, Henry Clarence 1828–1912
The Fairy Glen, Bettws-y-Coed
oil on canvas 185 x 104
BURGM:paoil77

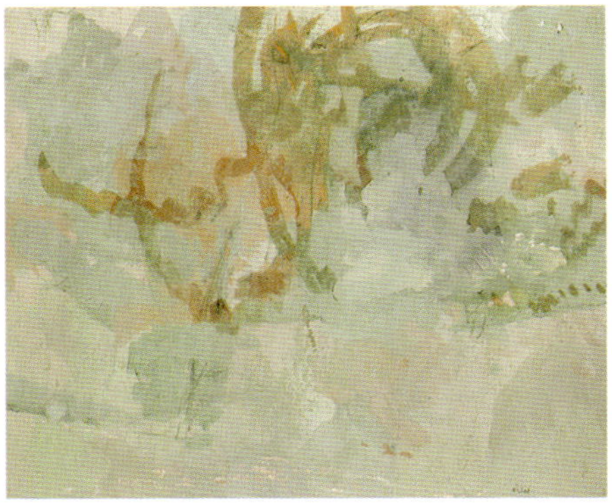

Wild, David b.1931
Fruhlingstraum, Dream of Spring c.1974
acrylic on board 30.5 x 39.4
BURGM:paoil247

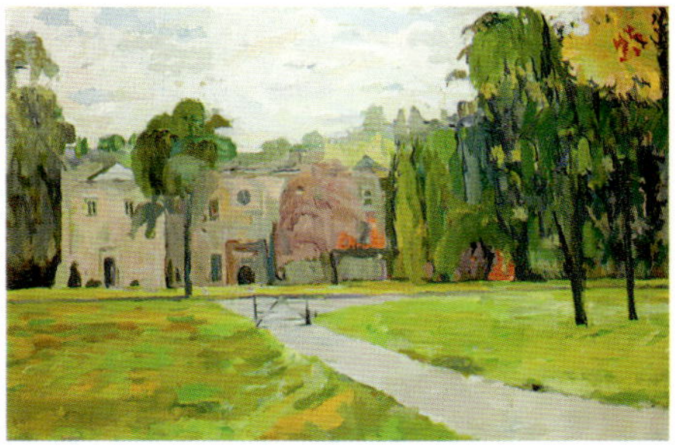

Wild, David b.1931
Towneley Hall 1993
oil on board 71 x 122
BURGM:paoil310

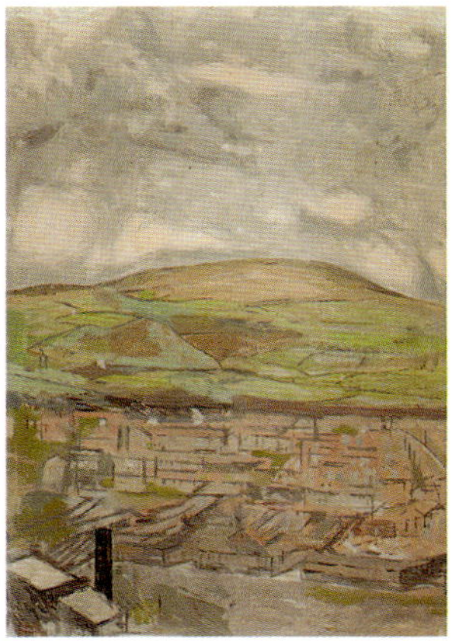

Wild, David b.1931
Bouldsworth Hill
oil on board 64.1 x 45.1
BURGM:paoil303

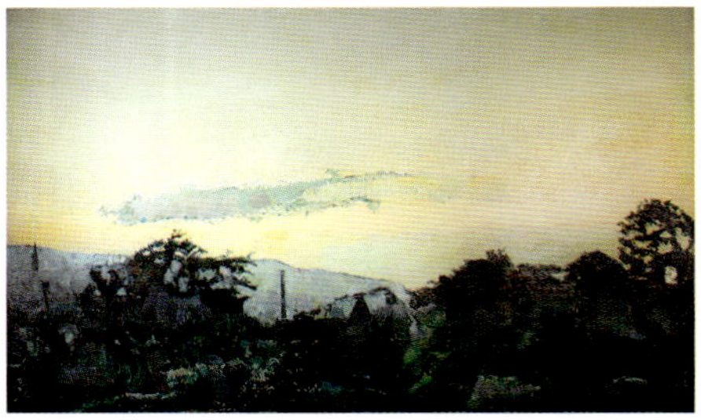

Wild, David b.1931
Hambledon Viewed from the Roof of Burnley College, Twilight
oil on board 178 x 302
BURGM:paoil325

Facing page: Duckworth, Valerie, *Two Sisters*, Blackburn Museum and Art Gallery (p. 31)

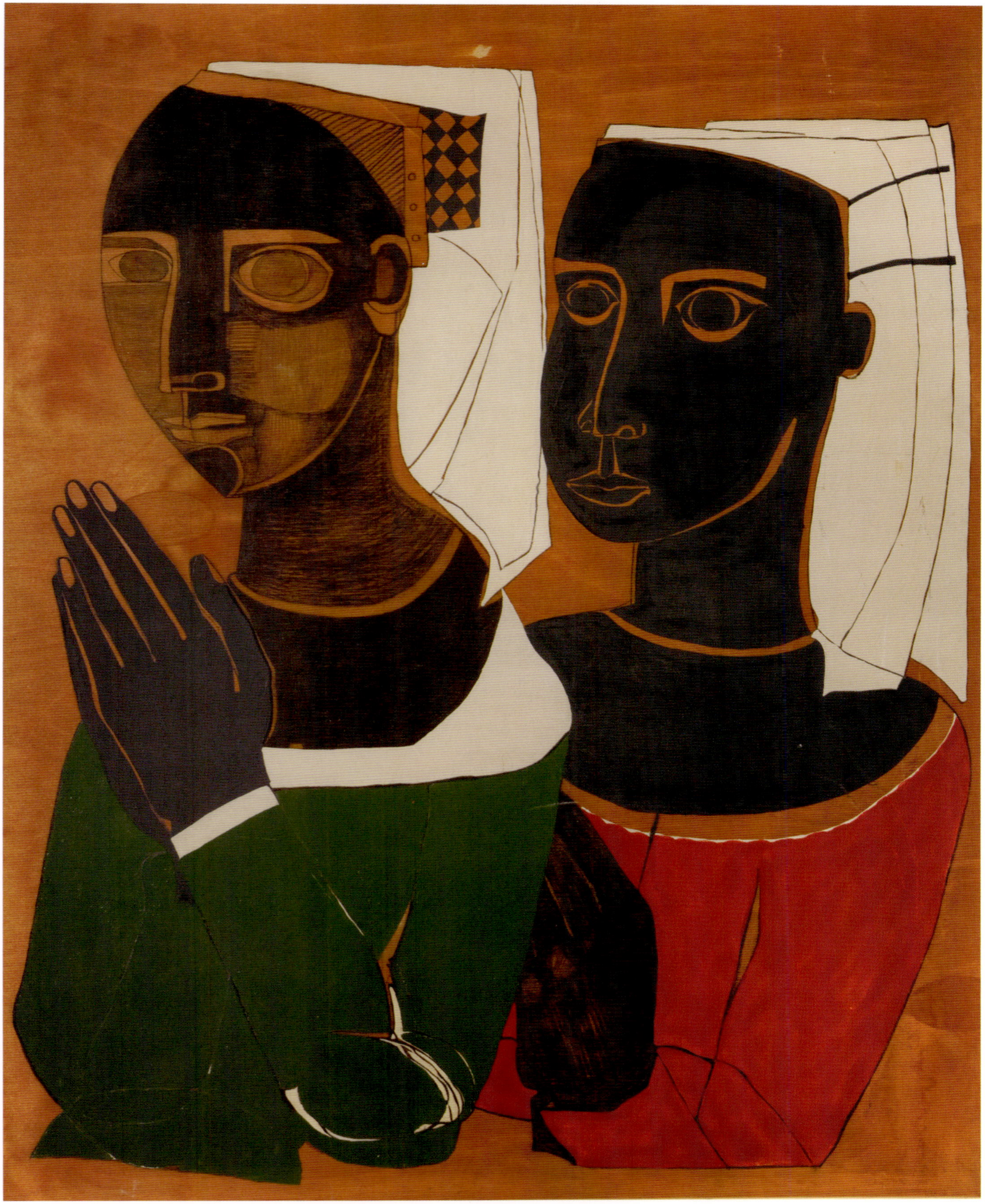

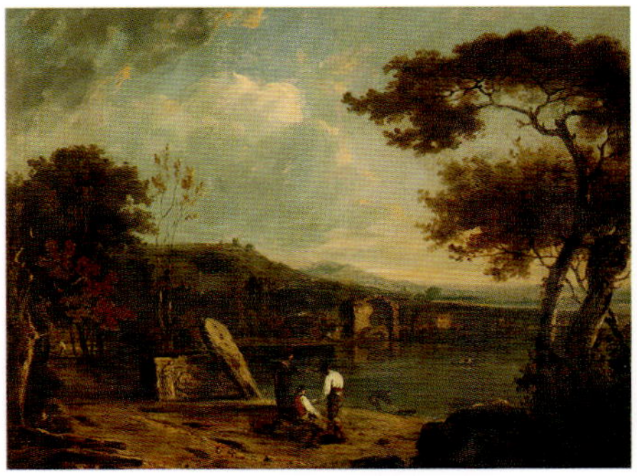

Wilson, Richard (after) 1712–1782
Italian Landscape (Lake Avernus) with Figures 18th C
oil on canvas 68.6 x 87
BURGM:paoil126

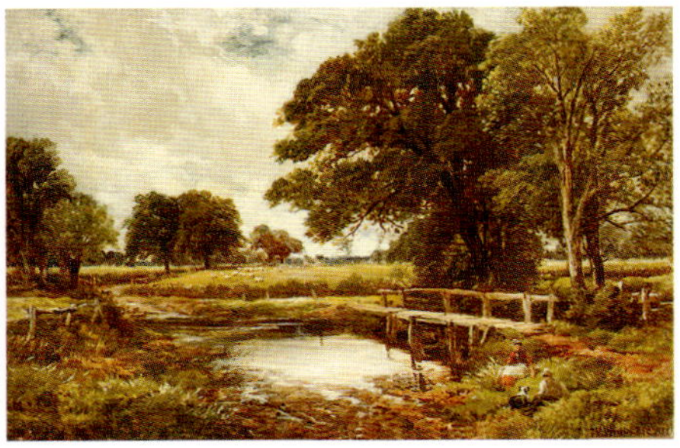

Wimperis, Edmund Morison 1835–1900
A Hampshire Ford 1891
oil on canvas 36.8 x 57.2
BURGM:paoil69

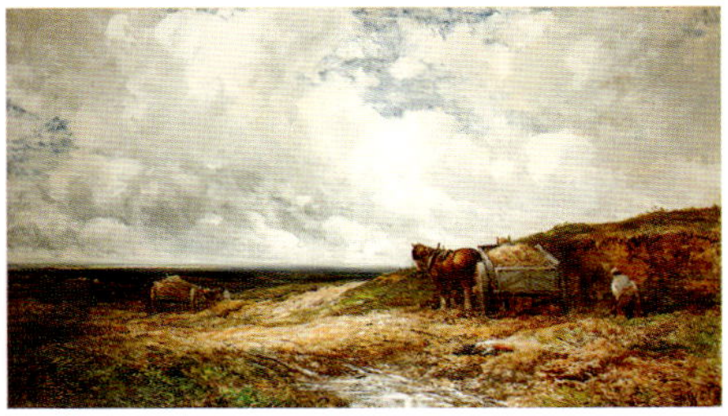

Wimperis, Edmund Morison 1835–1900
Carting Gravel
oil on canvas 74.9 x 126
BURGM:paoil50

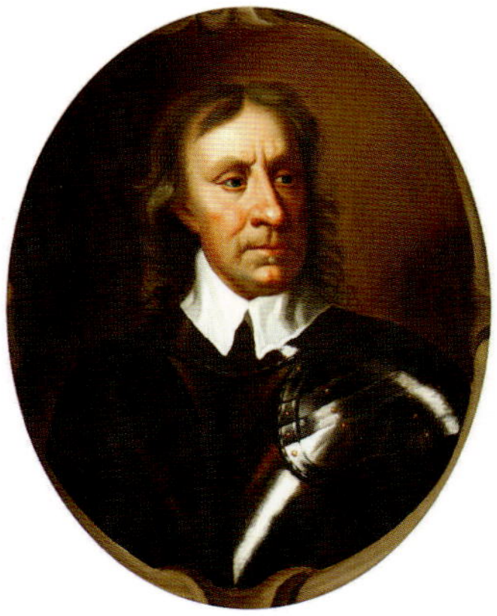

Wissing, Willem (after) 1656–1687
Oliver Cromwell (1599–1658) 17th C
oil on canvas 71.1 x 59.7
BURGM:paoil216

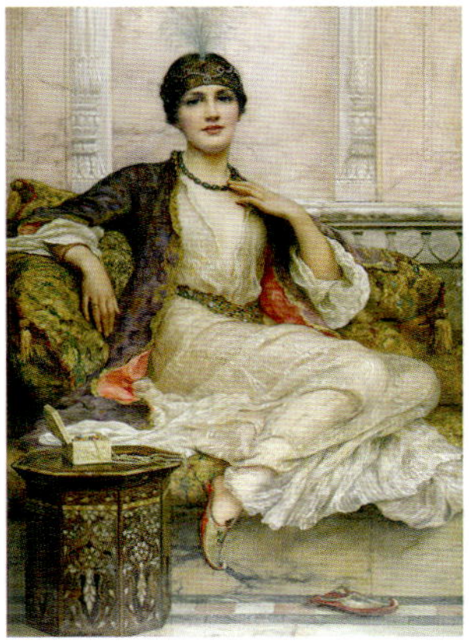

Wontner, William Clarke 1857–1930
Jade Necklace for an Eastern Princess 1908
oil on canvas 152 x 104
BURGM:paoil53

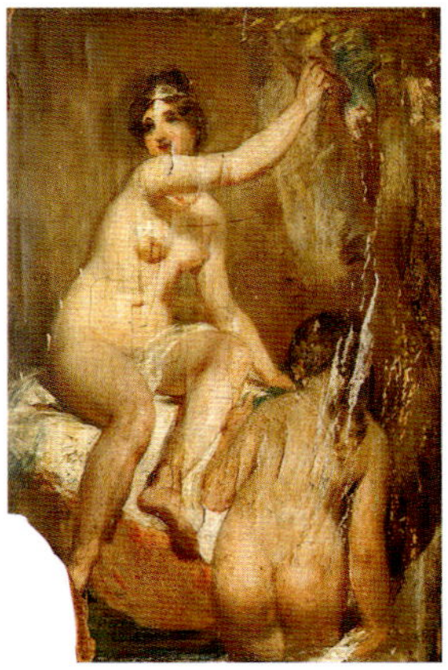

Wood, John 1801–1870
Two Female Nudes
oil on wood panel 25.4 x 16.5
BURGM:paoil293

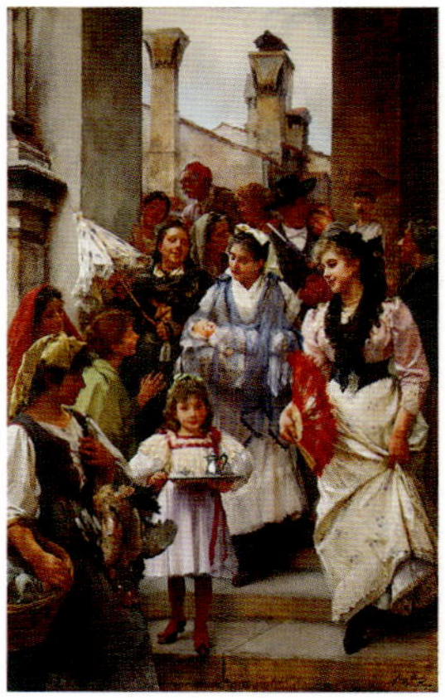

Woods, Henry 1846–1921
A Venetian Christening Party 1896
oil on canvas 163 x 105
BURGM:paoil34

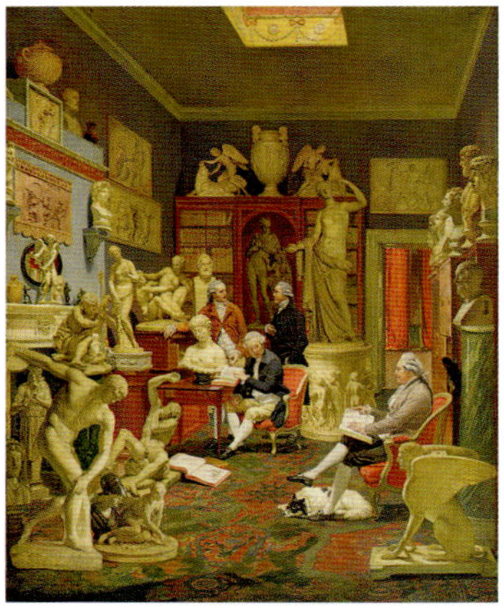

Zoffany, Johann 1733–1810
Charles Townley and Friends in His Library at Park Street, Westminster 1781–1790 & 1798
oil on canvas 127 x 99.1
BURGM:paoil120

Astley Hall Museum and Art Gallery

Astley Hall is a Grade I listed historic house built in 1578 by the Charnock family. Since then it has been the residence of a number of prominent Lancashire families, namely the Brookes, Townley-Parkers and Tattons. Reginald Arthur Tatton gave the Hall and its contents to Chorley Borough Council in 1922 and it opened to the public in 1924. Tatton left a range of items 'sufficient in fact to keep up the character of the place as an example of a dwelling house of a century or more ago'.

Astley Hall houses a diverse collection of fine art, decorative art, furniture, ceramics and tapestries; these continue to be the collecting "themes". As well as watercolours, engravings and sketches, Astley Hall has a fine collection of oil paintings. Many of these depict the families who owned the Hall, although some are of more national acclaim such as *Highland Cattle* by Richard Ansdell and *A Breezy Day on the Normandy Coast* by William Clarkson Stanfield.

The original Tatton donation forms the core of the collection, included in which are around 36 oil paintings. Many of them illustrate family members, including the British (English) School painting *Captain Robert 'One-Eye' Charnock, Chief Justice* who lost his eye when fighting in the civil war at the Battle of Preston. There is also a portrait of Oliver Cromwell in armour by Robert Walker; Cromwell is rumoured to have stayed at Astley Hall after fighting in the same battle. In addition to the oil portraits, the painted panels in the Great Hall depict a variety of notable personalities from the fifteenth to the seventeenth centuries including well known figures such as Queen Elizabeth I and Sir Francis Drake alongside more unusual choices such as Skanderbeg and Ferdinand Magellan.

A donation of oil paintings by Violet Caroline Townley-Parker in the 1970s makes up another large part of the collection. Violet was the granddaughter of Robert Townley-Parker, who was responsible for the east wing extension of the early 1800s. Again, this collection of oil paintings mainly consists of family portraits. They are on permanent display in the Great Hall and Dining Room.

The rest of the oil paintings in the Hall's possession have been gifted or bequeathed by a variety of different people. Although these acquisitions have been recorded, Astley Hall did not have a curator until the 1990s, which means that some are of uncertain origin. William Clarkson Stanfield's impressive painting *A Breezy Day on the Normandy Coast* is one of these untraced finds.

Like many other museums, we have limited space to display the collection of paintings and therefore concentrate on displaying portraits relating to the families or depictions of Astley Hall itself. This allows for a more coherent interpretation of the Hall for visitors. With this in mind, the current acquisitions policy dictates that we collect pieces specifically related to the families or the local area.

We have two temporary exhibition spaces where we display in-house collections alongside touring exhibitions. The Hall is planning on re-interpreting some of the collections that are currently on display; this may mean that space will become available for the display of some of the oil paintings we currently hold in store.

We are pleased that we have been able to take part in the Public Catalogue Foundation project and feel that the improved accessibility of our oil paintings will be immensely rewarding.

Emily Cooke, Museum Assistant, and Amy Grundy, Museum Assistant

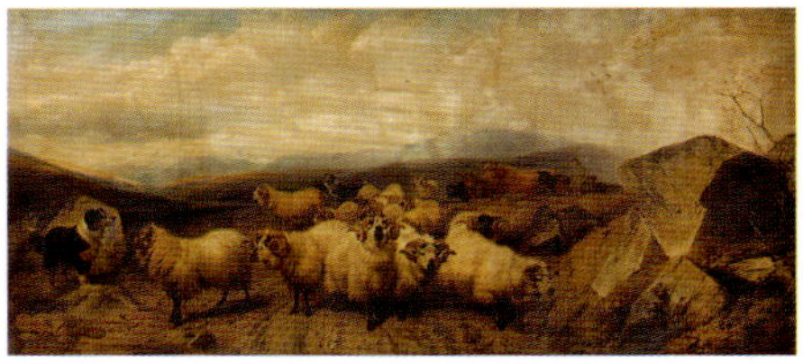

Ansdell, Richard 1815–1885
Highland Cattle 1872
oil on canvas 91.5 x 190.5
1930:1

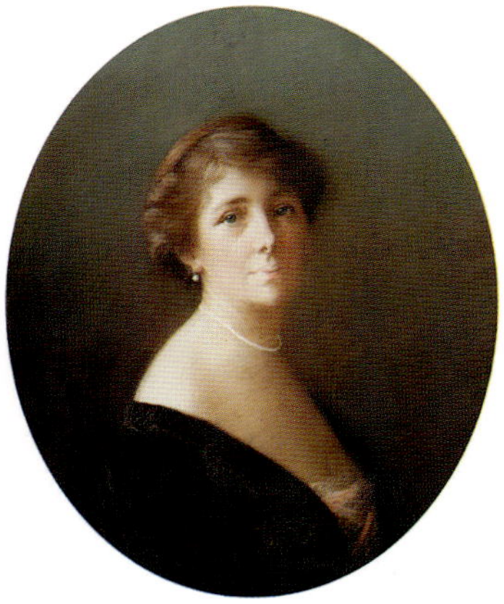

Banton, T. E.
Amy Hewlett
oil on canvas 66 x 58
1991.8.1

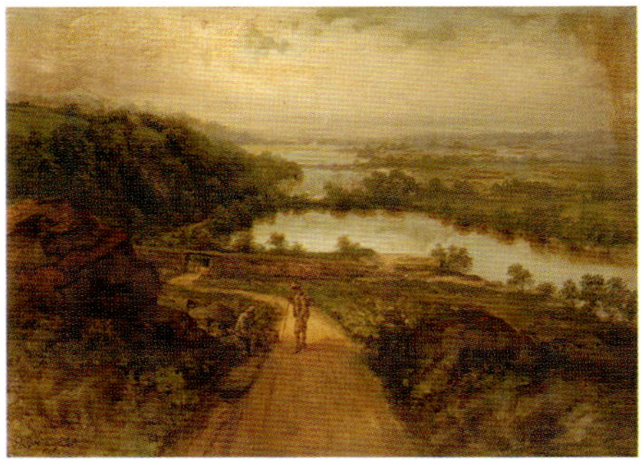

Booth, Samuel Lawson 1836–1928
Rivington Lakes 1907
oil on canvas 39 x 60
1984:24

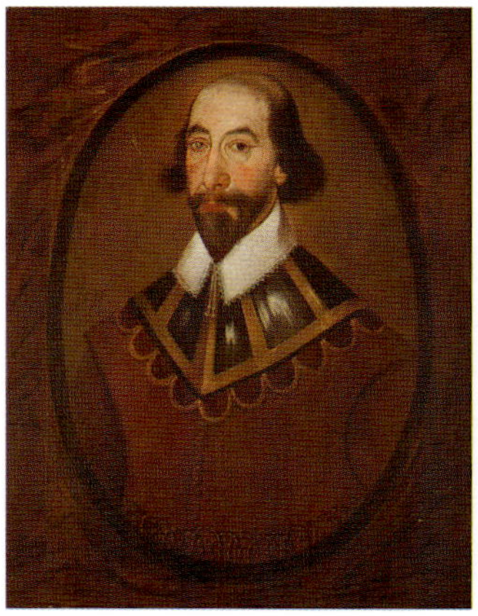

British (English) School
Captain Robert 'One-Eye' Charnock, Chief Justice c.1650
oil on canvas 76 x 63.5
1922:18

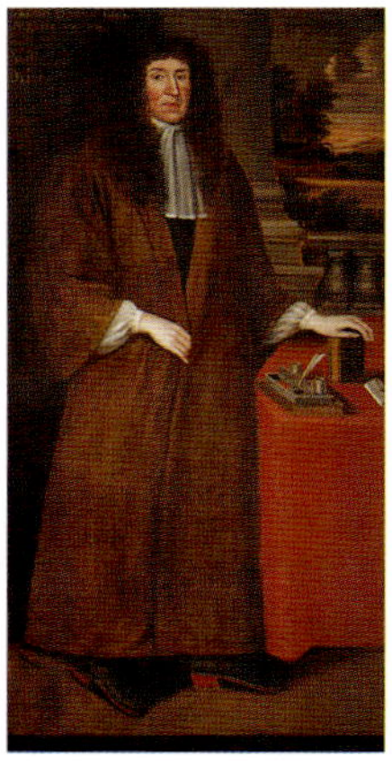

British (English) School
A Gentleman in Clerical Robes 1682
oil on canvas 224 x 102
1922:14

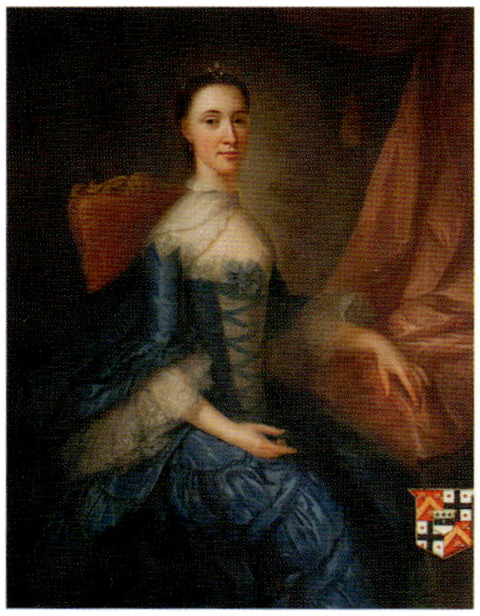

British (English) School
Anne Townley c.1750
oil on canvas 127 x 102
1976:6

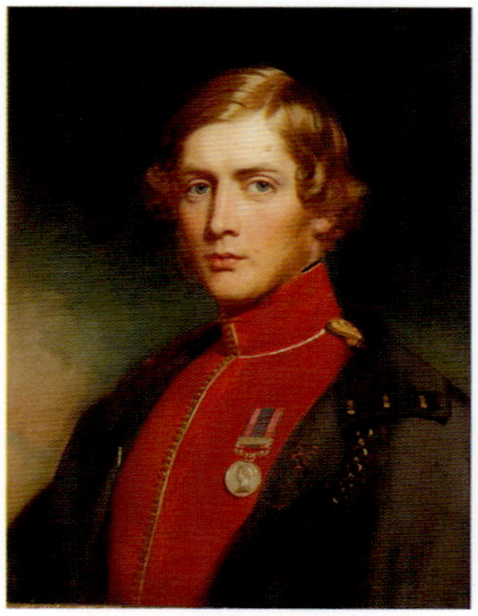

British (English) School
Robert Townley-Parker as Captain of the 53rd Regiment of Foot 1850
oil on canvas 59 x 48
1979:109

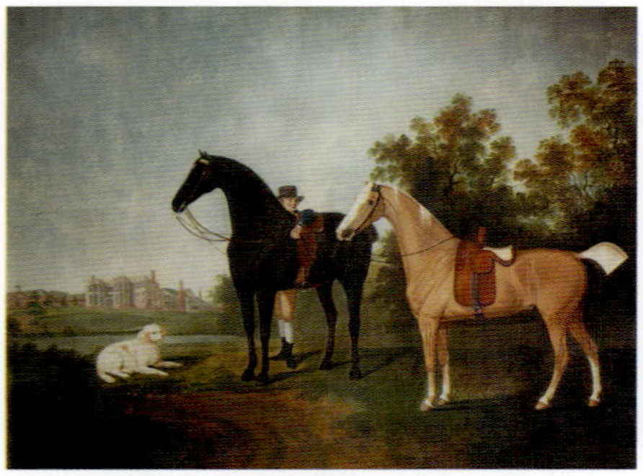

British (English) School
A Groom with a Chestnut and Palomino Horse in the Grounds of Astley Hall
oil on canvas 88 x 120
1922:53

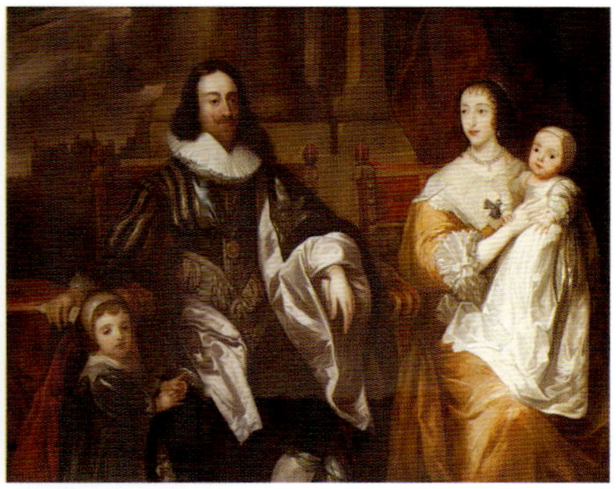

British (English) School
Charles I (1600–1649) and His Family (after Anthony van Dyck)
oil on canvas 152.5 x 203
1922:15

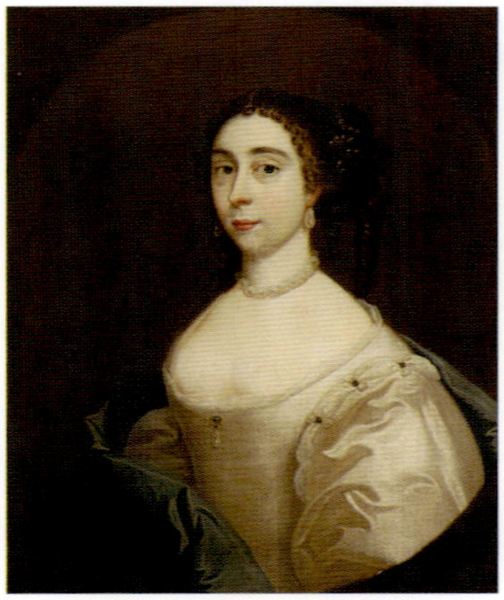

British (English) School
Jane Brooke
oil on canvas 75 x 66
1922:26

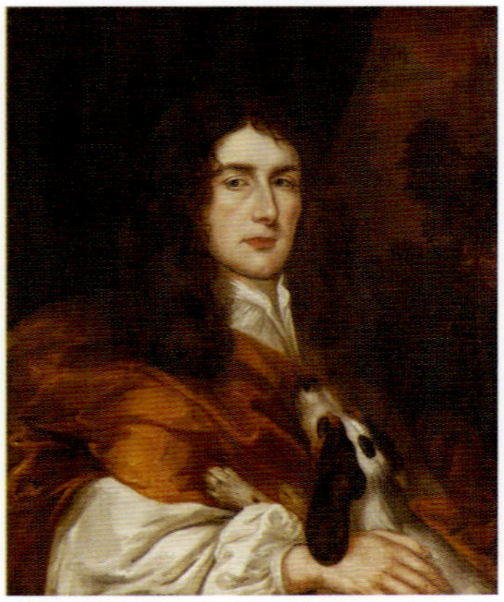

British (English) School
Richard Brooke (1640–1715)
oil on canvas 76 x 63.5
1922:25

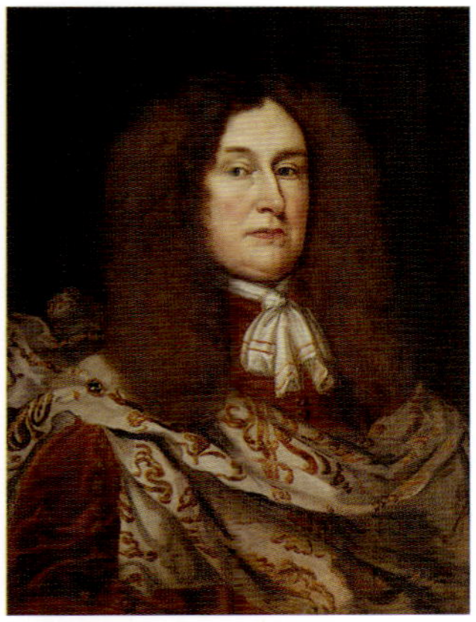

British (English) School
Sir Peter Brooke of Mere
oil on canvas 76 x 63.5
1922:23

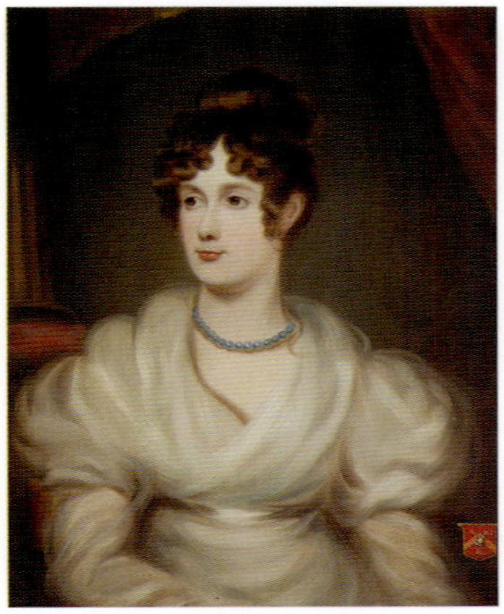

British (English) School
Susannah Townley-Parker, née Brooke (1762–1852)
oil on canvas 76.2 x 63.5
1922:51

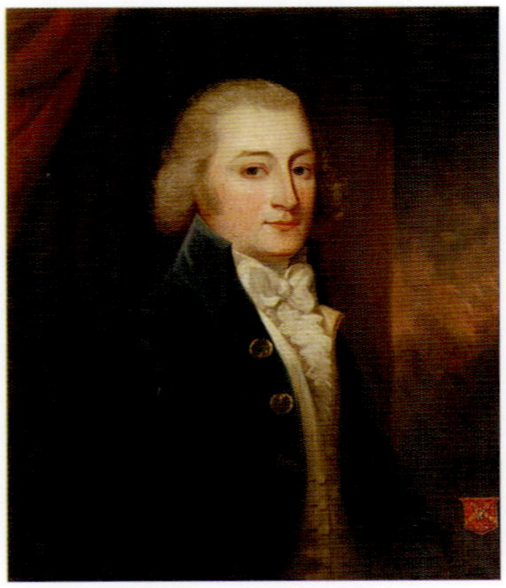

British (English) School
Thomas Townley-Parker (1822–1906)
oil on canvas 76.2 x 63.5
1922:49

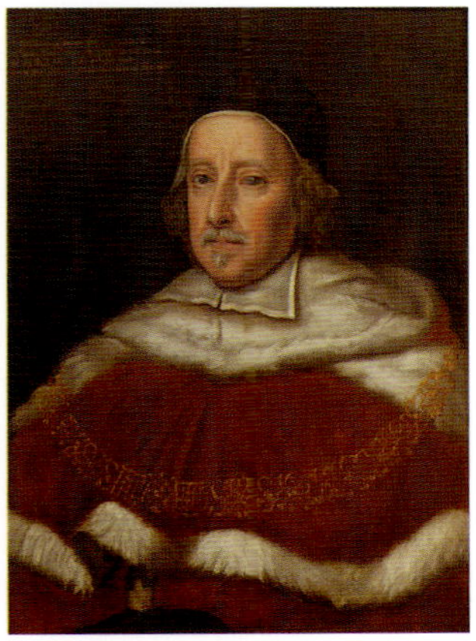

British School
Sir Matthew Hale (1609–1676) c.1690
oil on canvas 79 x 64
1922:19

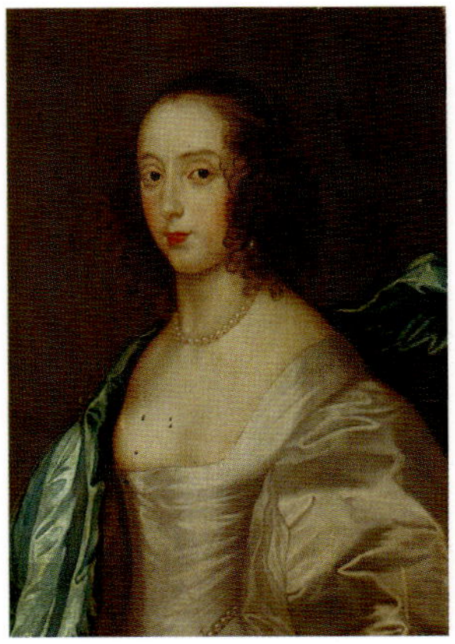

British School
Elizabeth Brooke c.1700
oil on canvas 69.5 x 51
1922:22

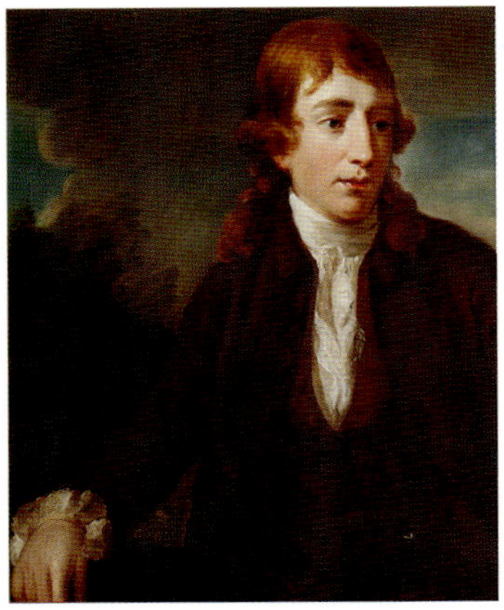

British School
Peter Brooke c.1820
oil on canvas 76 x 61
1922:55

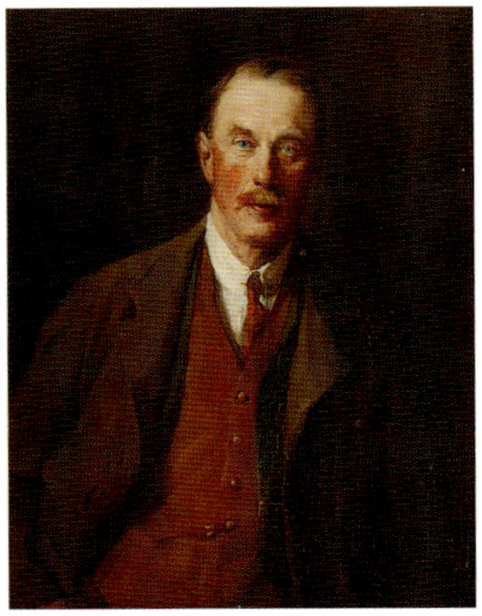

British School
Reginald Arthur Tatton (1857–1926) c.1920
oil on canvas 74 x 61
1984:16

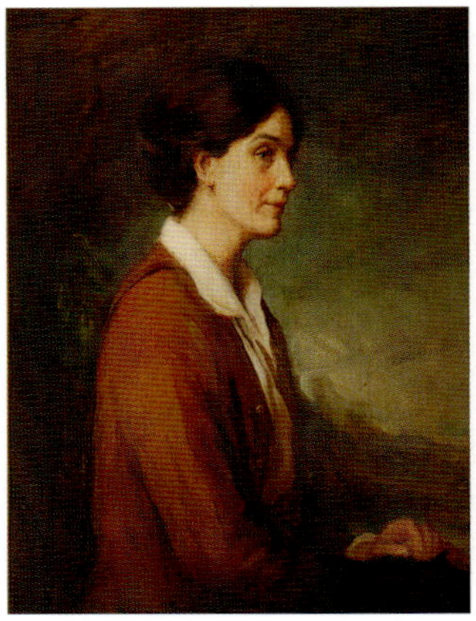

British School
Winifred Eva Tatton (c.1867–1939) c.1920
oil on canvas 74 x 61
1984:17

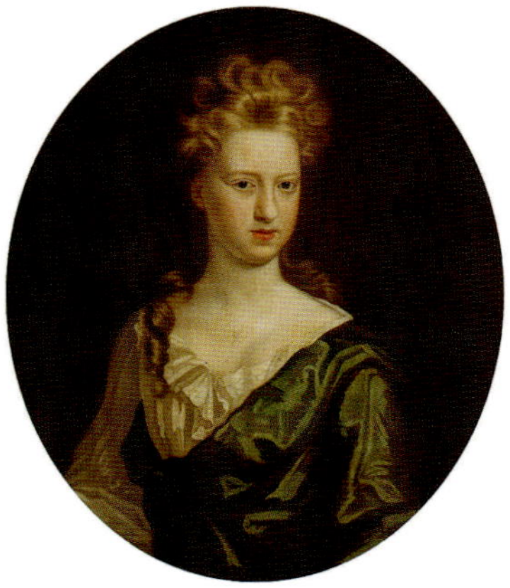

British School
A Lady Wearing a Blue Bodice (Peter Brooke's Wife)
oil on canvas 76 x 63.5
1922:16

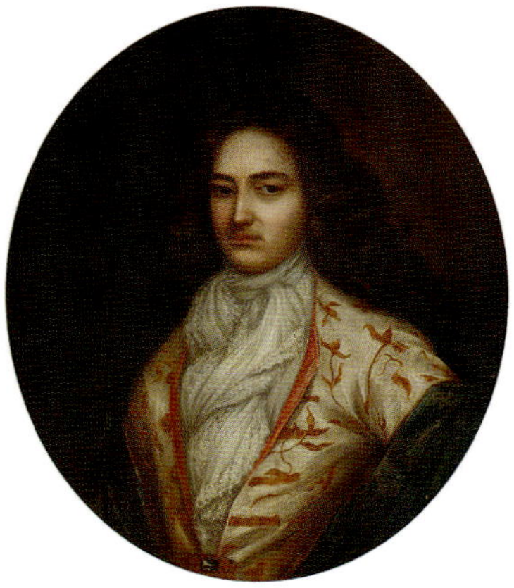

British School
Peter Brooke
oil on canvas 76 x 63.5
1922:17

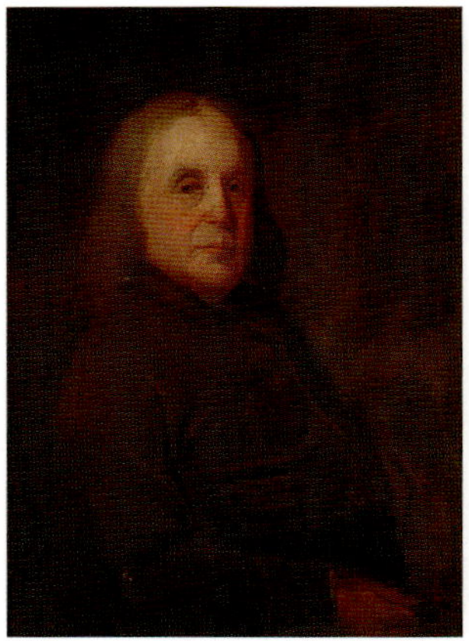

British School
Portrait of an Unknown Gentleman
oil on canvas 76 x 64
PCF 1

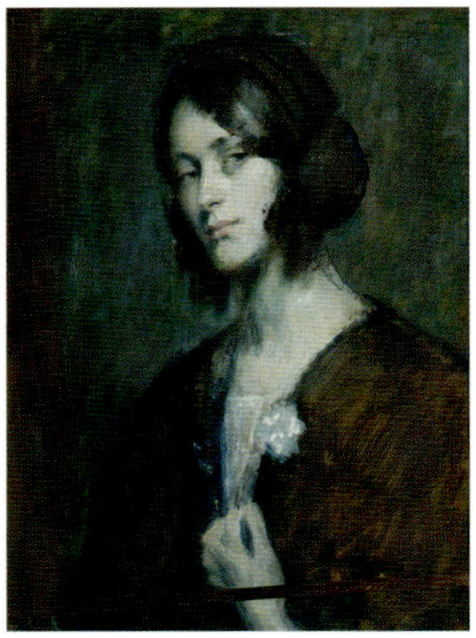

Brockhurst, Gerald Leslie (attributed to) 1890–1978
Twilight
oil on canvas 59 x 39
1934:2

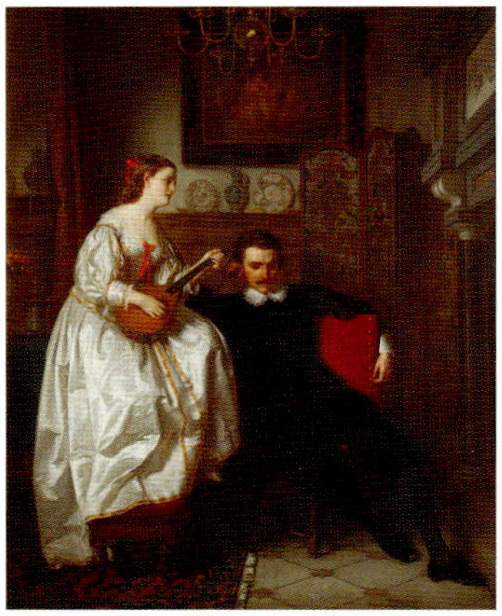

Bure, Paul
Memories 1874
oil on canvas 74 x 86
1922:369

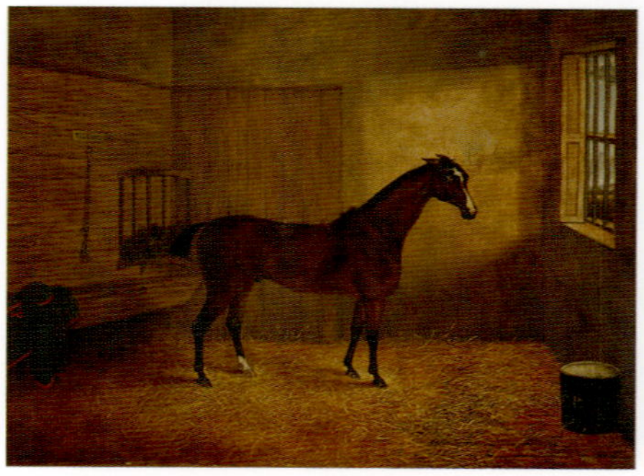

Clarke, Frederick
Family Horse in Stables 1885
oil on canvas 71 x 91
1979:113

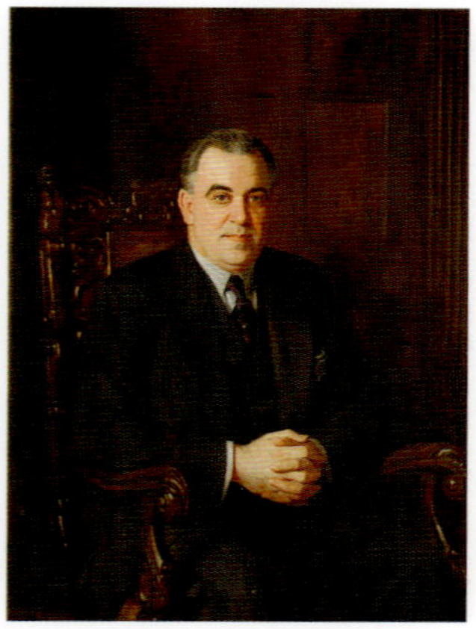

Collings, Albert Henry 1858–1947
Portrait of a Gentleman
oil on canvas 110 x 84
1984:194

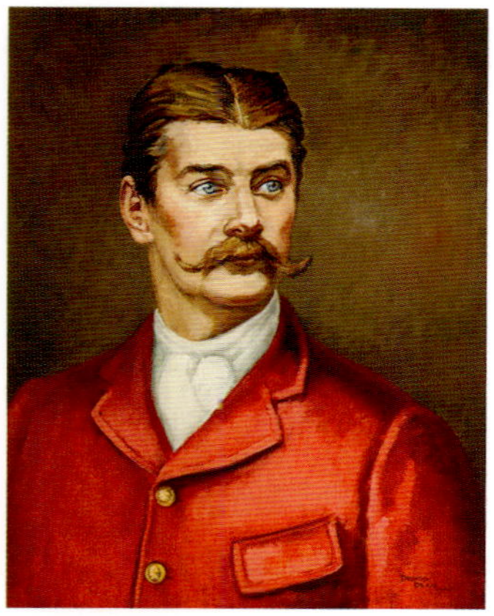

Dean, Dorothy
Gerald Townley-Parker (1858–1892)
oil on canvas 61 x 51
1979:110

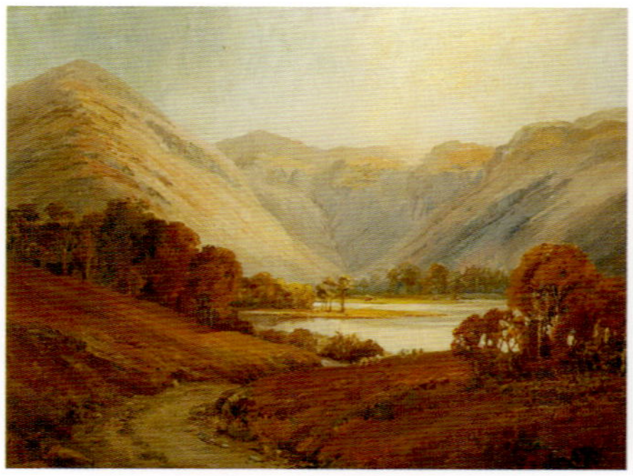

Eastwood, Walter 1867–1943
Golden Autumn – Buttermere
oil on canvas 56 x 81
1984:31

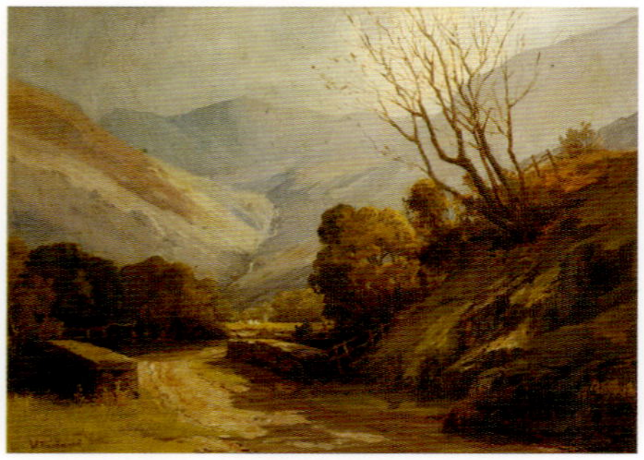

Eastwood, Walter 1867–1943
Little Langdale
oil on canvas 56 x 81
1984:30

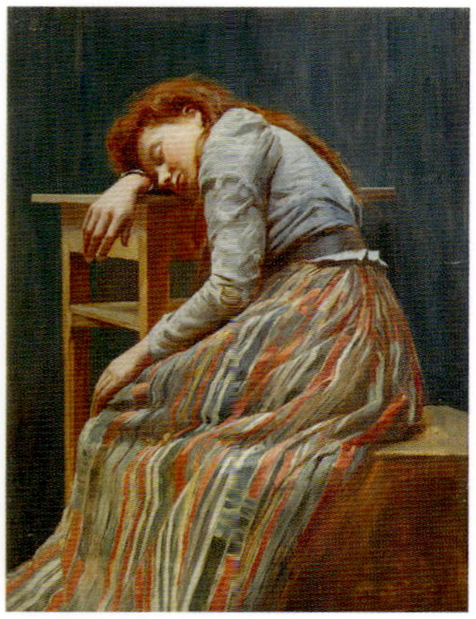

Fisher, Ben active 1890–1908
Young Girl Asleep
oil on canvas 75 x 60.5
1934:1

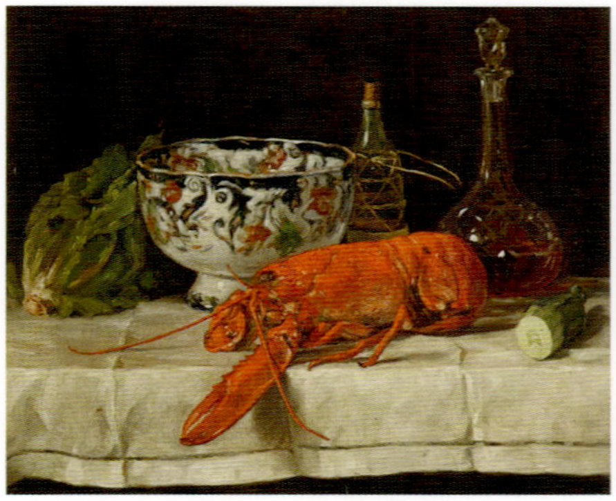

Fisher, Ralph active 1908–1912
A Salad 1908
oil on canvas 45 x 59
1934:4

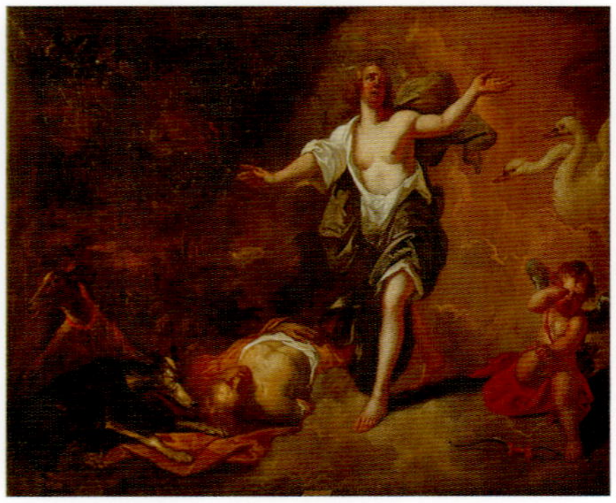

Flemish School
Venus and Adonis
oil on canvas 80 x 110
1922:269

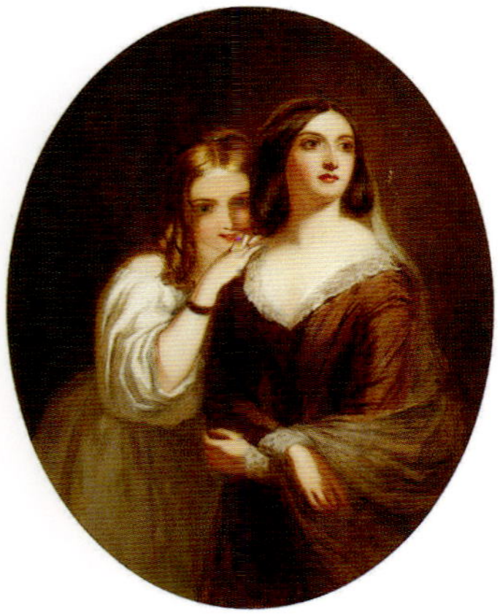

Frith, William Powell 1819–1909
Portrait of Two Girls
oil on canvas 27.5 x 23
1984:35

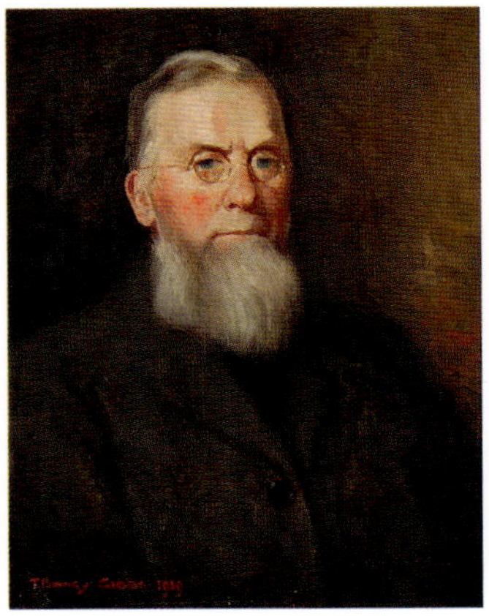

Gibbs, Thomas Binney 1870–1947
W. W. Burwell, JP, Chairman of Chorley Council 1919
oil on canvas 65 x 50
1984:34

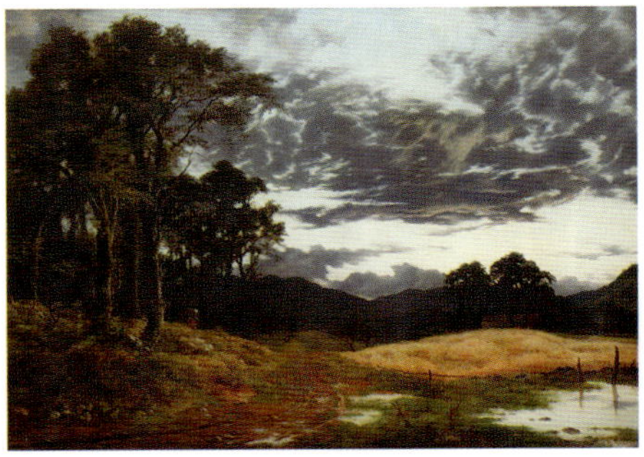

Graham, Peter 1836–1921
Twilight after Rain 1864
oil on canvas 89 x 138
1926:3 (P)

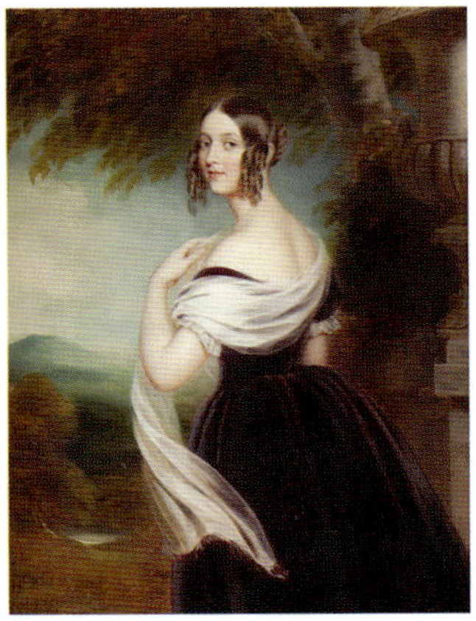

Grant, Francis (circle of) 1803–1878
Catherine Blackburn
oil on canvas 127 x 102
1976:4

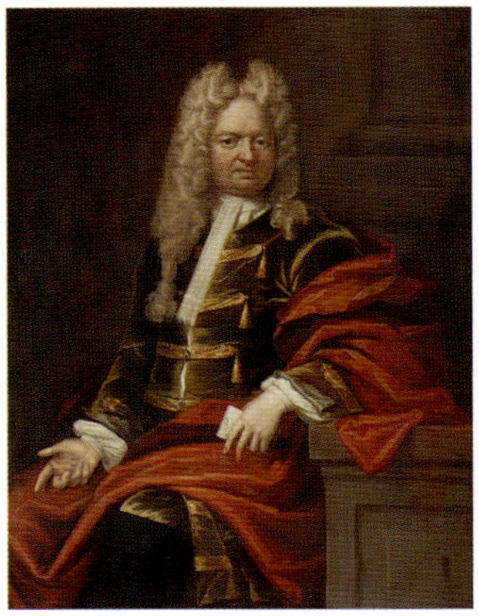

Kerseboom, Johann (circle of) 1638–1708
Thomas Brooke (1684–1734)
oil on canvas 127 x 102
1922:21

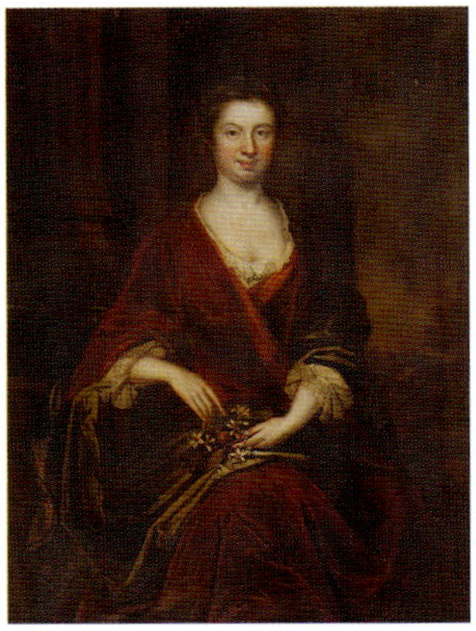

Kneller, Godfrey (circle of) 1646–1723
Margaret Wharton
oil on canvas 127 x 102
1922:20

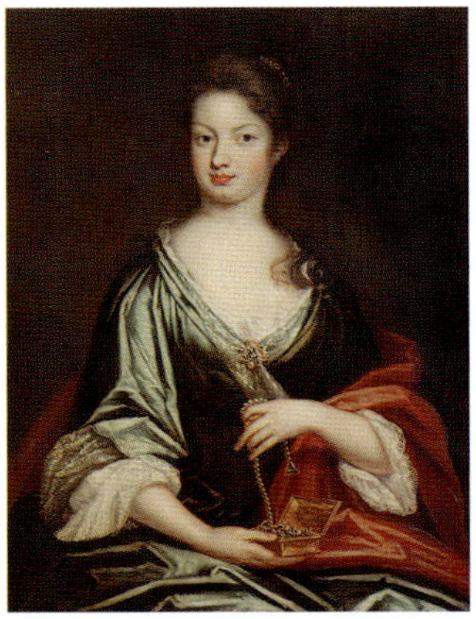

Kneller, Godfrey (circle of) 1646–1723
Margert Wharton
oil on canvas 91 x 71
1922:24

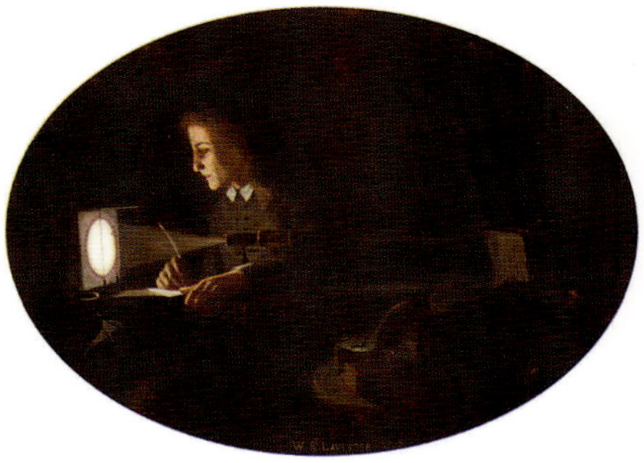

Lavender, William Richard 1877–1915
Jeremiah Horrocks (1618–1641) 1903
oil on canvas 61 x 91.5
1962:2

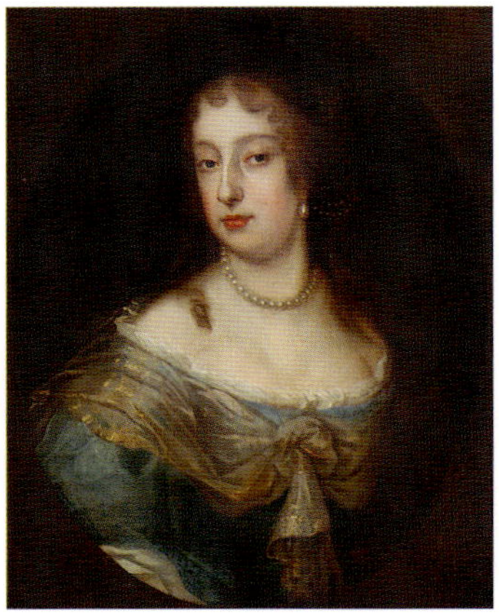

Lely, Peter (circle of) 1618–1680
Portrait of an Unknown Lady in a Blue and White Dress Wearing a Pearl Necklace
oil on canvas 64 x 53
1984:37

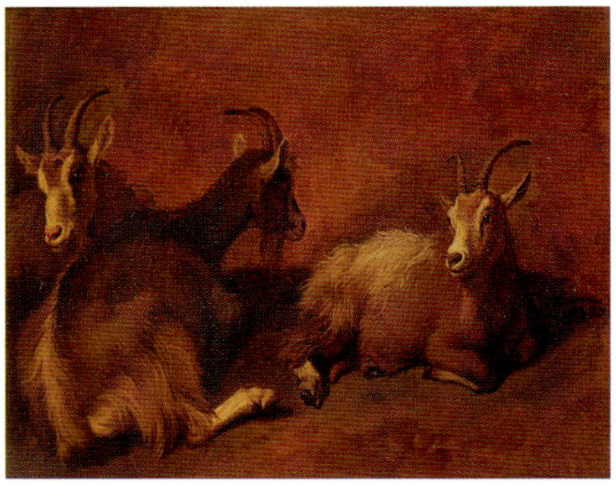

Londonio, Francesco (attributed to) 1723–1783
Goats
oil on canvas 29 x 43
1979:116.1-1

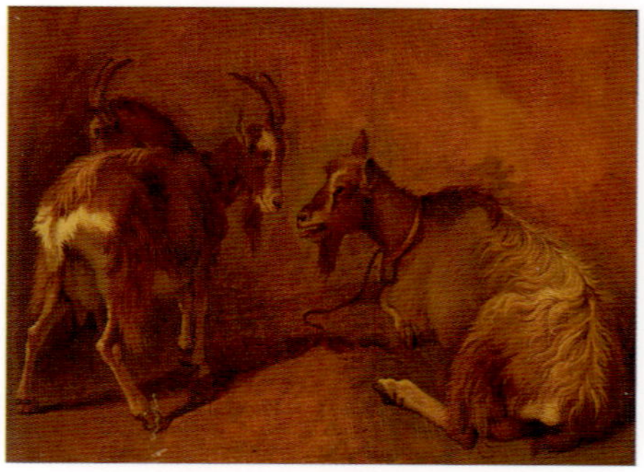

Londonio, Francesco (attributed to) 1723–1783
Goats
oil on canvas 29 x 43
1979:116.1-2

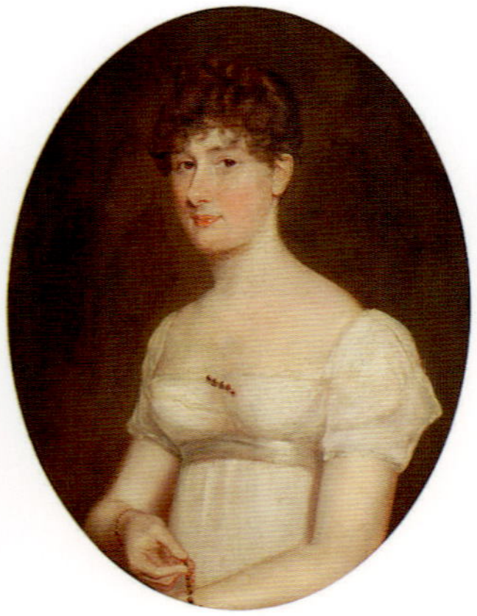

Lonsdale, James 1777–1839
Anne Townley-Parker 1808–1809
oil on canvas 76 x 63.5
1922:47

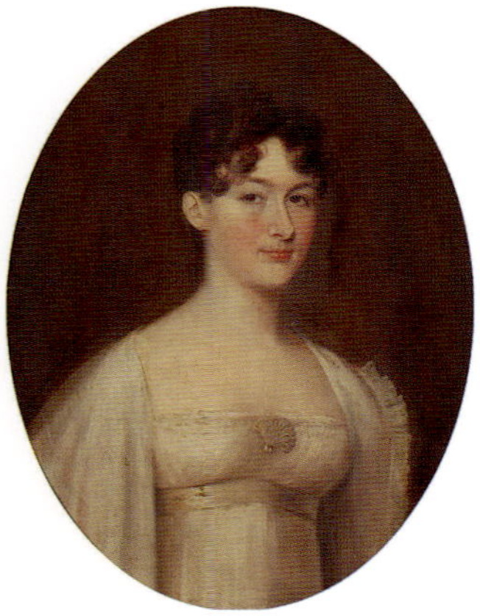

Lonsdale, James 1777–1839
Susan, Daughter of Thomas Townley-Parker 1808–1809
oil on canvas 68.6 x 56
1922:46

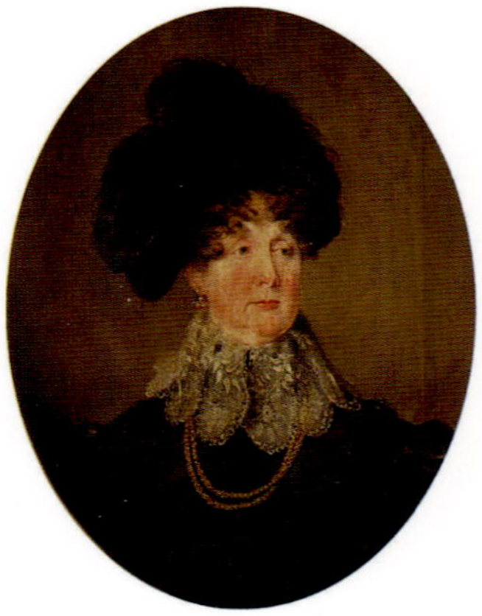

Lonsdale, James (attributed to) 1777–1839
Lady Susannah Hoghton
oil on canvas 76 x 64
1922:48

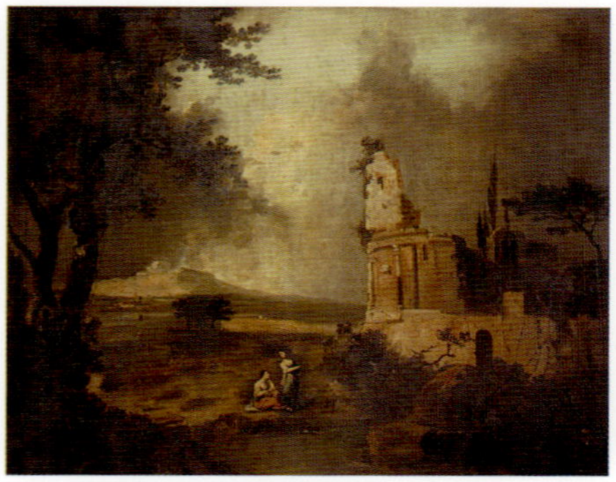

Lorrain, Claude (attributed to) 1604–1682
Figures Conversing in the Foreground; In the Distance, Bethlehem
oil on canvas 81 x 107
1984:47

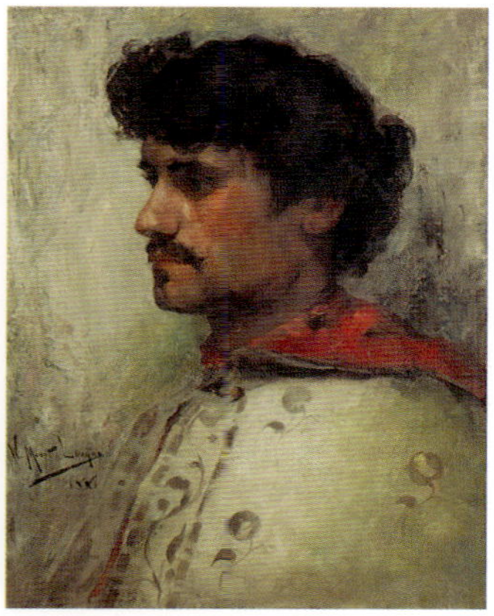

Loudan, William Mouat 1868–1925
Roman Noble 1881
oil on canvas 53 x 42
1935:1

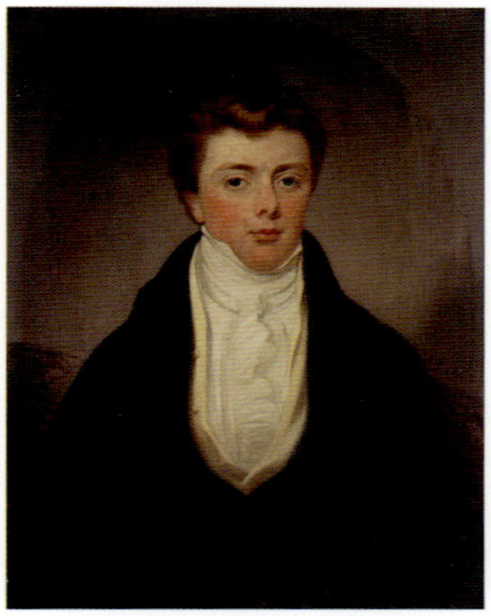

Lucas, William 1840–1895
Robert Townley-Parker (1793–1879) 1875
oil on canvas 76.2 x 63.5
1922:50

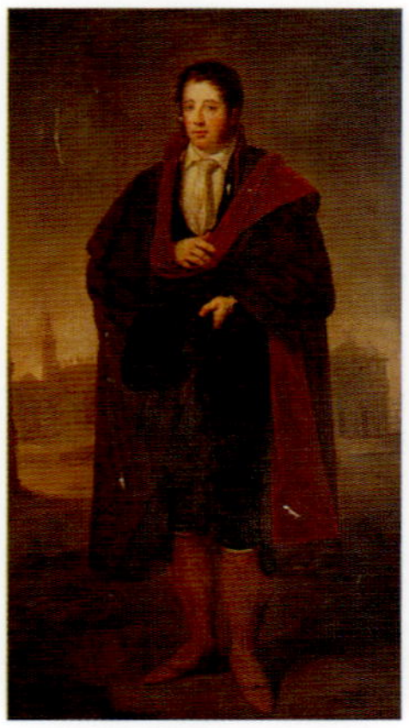

Mauzaisse, Jean-Baptiste 1784–1844
Frank Hall Standish of Duxbury (1799–1840) (after Gulhierez)
oil on canvas 216 x 118
1984:27

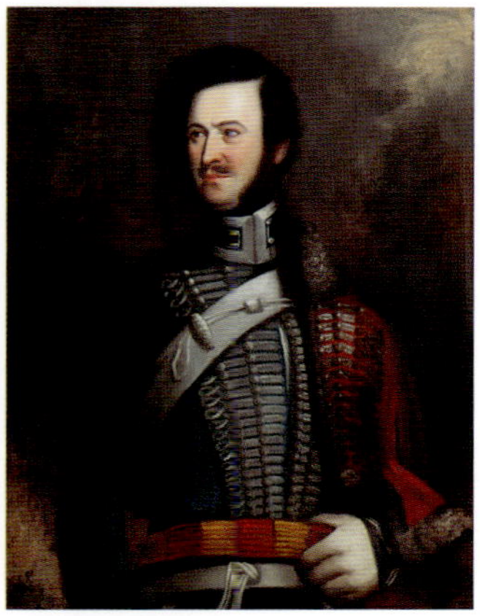

Millais, John Everett (attributed to) 1829–1896
William Carr Standish
oil on canvas 86 x 71
1960:3

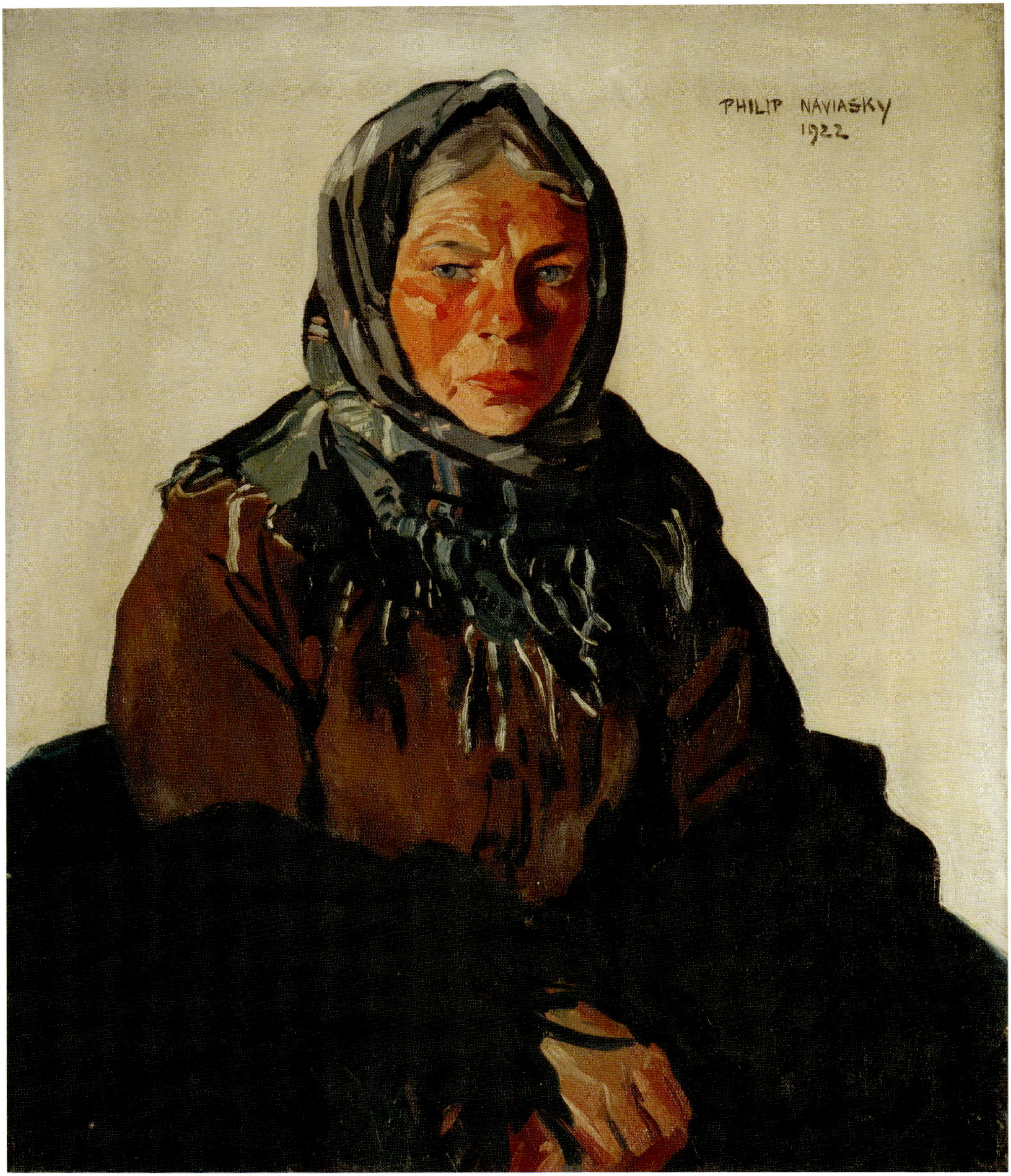
PHILIP NAVIASKY
1922

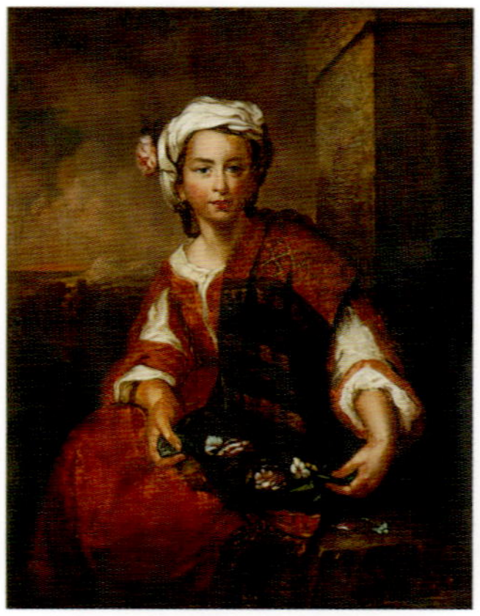

Murillo, Bartolomé Esteban (after) 1617–1682
The Flower Vendor 19th C
oil on canvas 85 x 71
1984:22

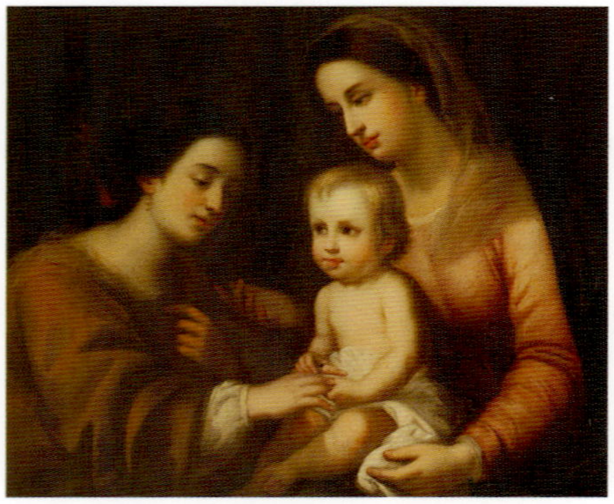

Murillo, Bartolomé Esteban (after) 1617–1682
The Mystical Marriage of Saint Catherine early 19th C
oil on canvas 74 x 86
1988:12

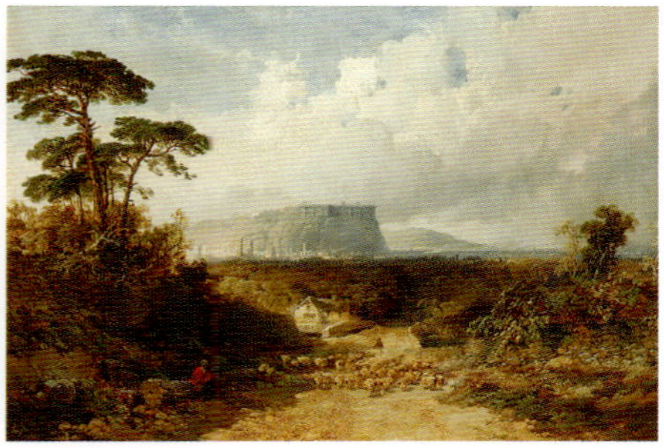

Niemann, Edmund John 1813–1876
Nottingham Castle 1857
oil on canvas 31 x 48
1922:370

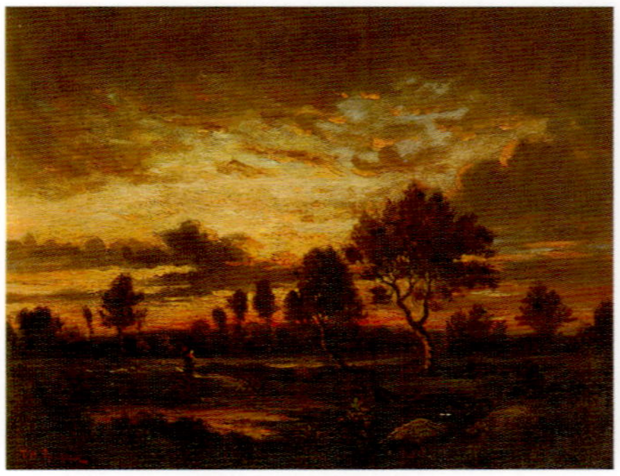

Rousseau, Théodore 1812–1867
Paysage au soleil couchant
oil on panel 23.5 x 33
1991:8.2

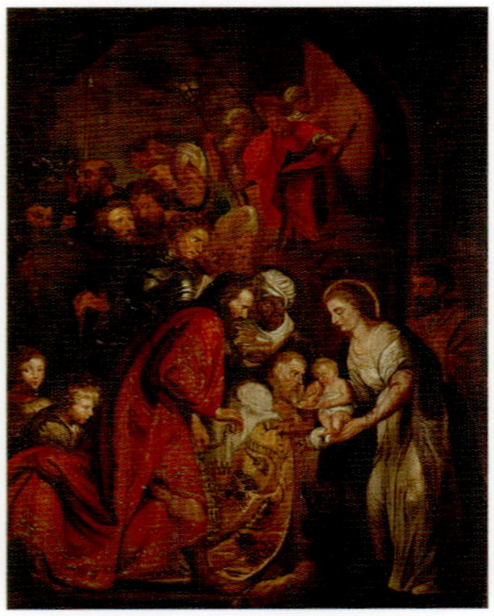

Rubens, Peter Paul (after) 1577–1640
The Adoration of the Magi c.1700
oil on panel 57 x 42
1979:112

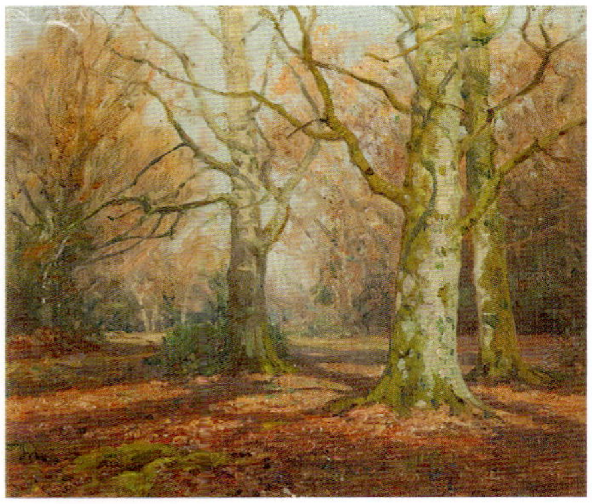

Short, Frederick Golden 1863–1936
New Forest
oil on mill board 24 x 29
1979:120.1

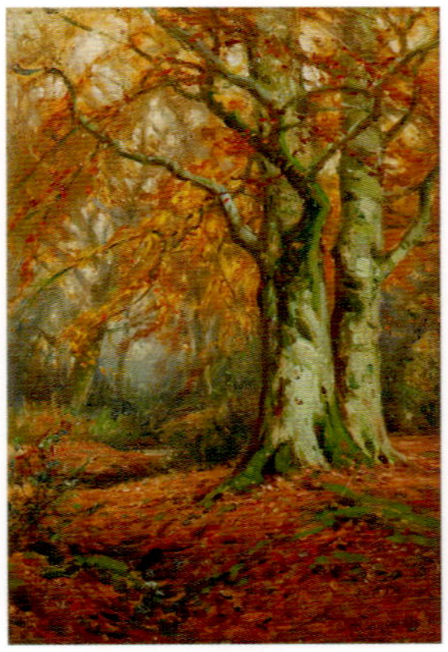

Short, Frederick Golden 1863–1936
New Forest
oil on mill board 29 x 22
1979:120.3

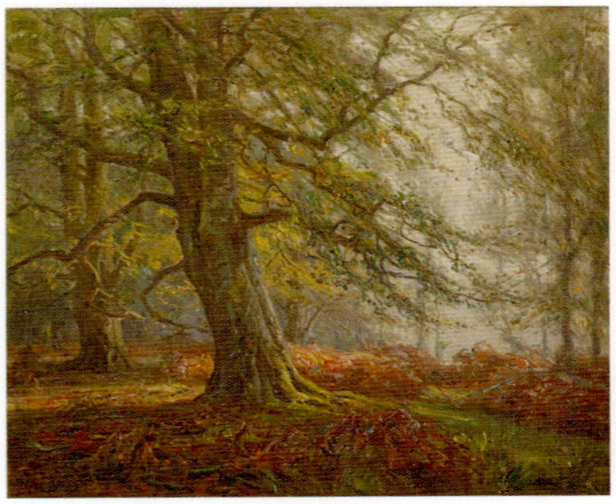

Short, Frederick Golden 1863–1936
New Forest
oil on mill board 27 x 37
1979:120.6

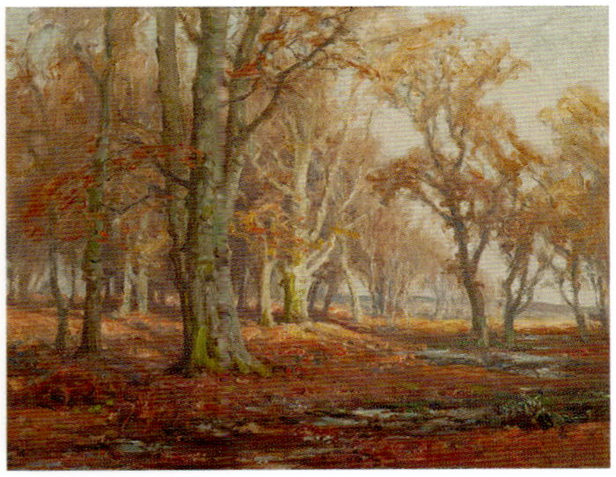

Short, Frederick Golden 1863–1936
New Forest
oil on mill board 25 x 29
1979:120.7

Facing page: Naviasky, Philip, 1894–1982, *Connemara,* 1922, Harris Museum & Art Gallery (p. 328)

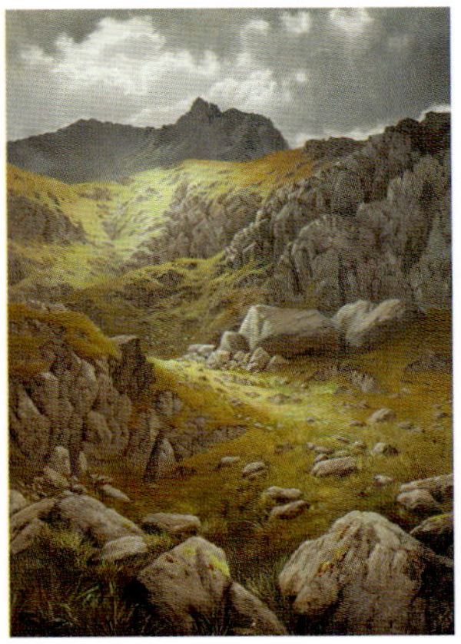

Smith, Reginald
Mountain Scene
oil on canvas 80 x 60
1955:2

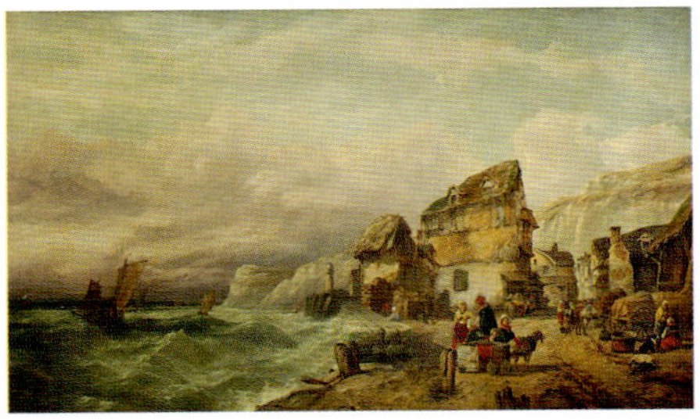

Stanfield, William Clarkson 1793–1867
A Breezy Day on the Normandy Coast 1853
oil on canvas 91.5 x 168
1984:28

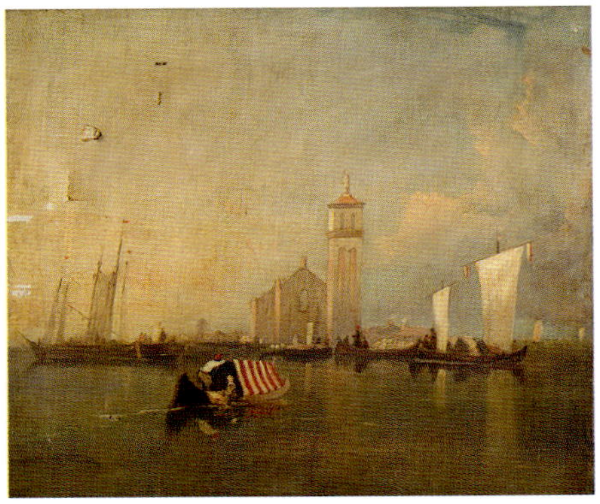

Stanfield, William Clarkson (attributed to) 1793–1867
North Italian Coastal Scene
oil on canvas 46 x 57
1984:29

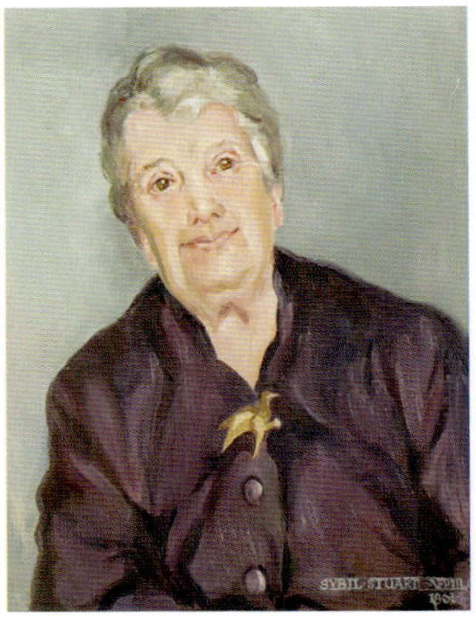

Stuart, Sybil
Florence Bennet of Chorley 1961
oil on canvas 58 x 49
1984:46

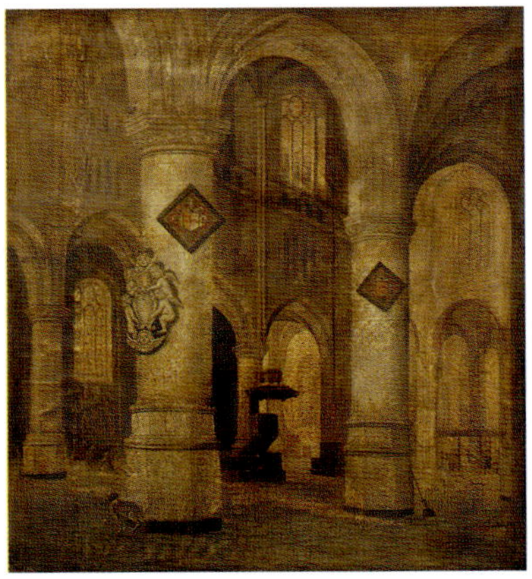

Thomas, C. N.
Church Interior
oil on canvas 49 x 39
1922:11

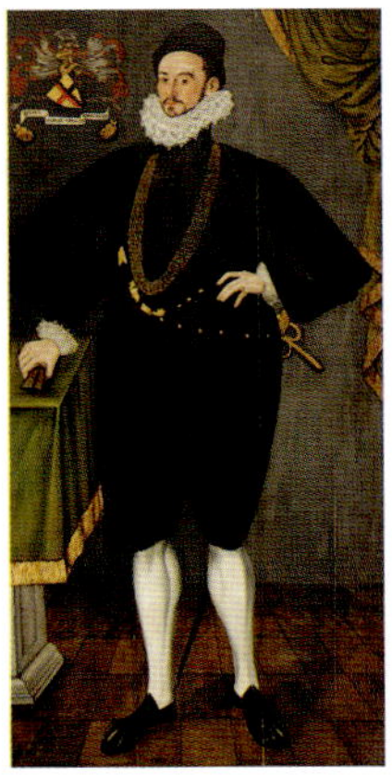

unknown artist
Thomas Brooke of Houghton 1580
oil on canvas 183 x 91
1922:39

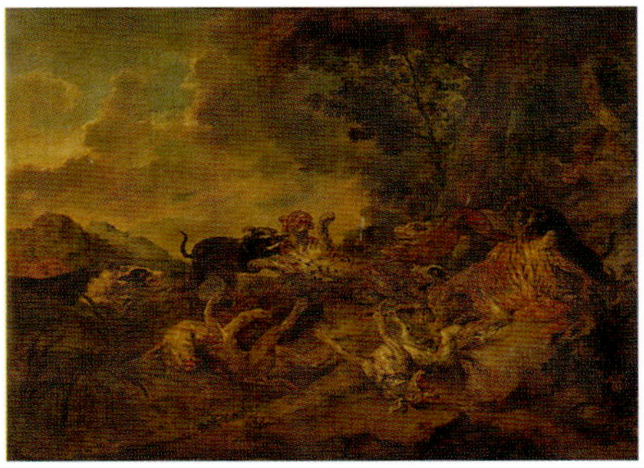

unknown artist
A Tiger Hunt
oil on canvas 65.5 x 80
1922:56

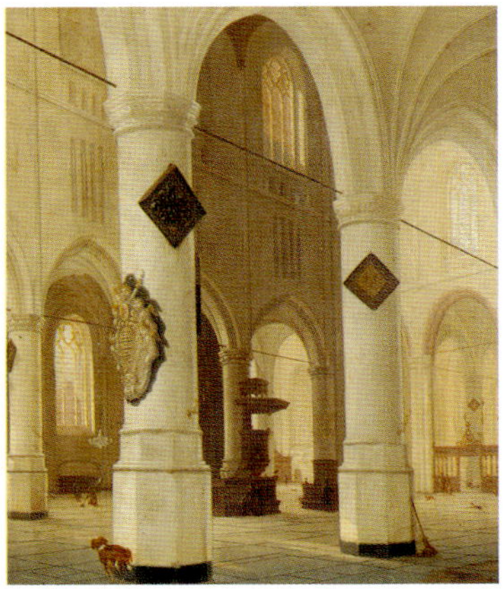

unknown artist
Church Interior
oil on canvas 28 x 23
1922:12

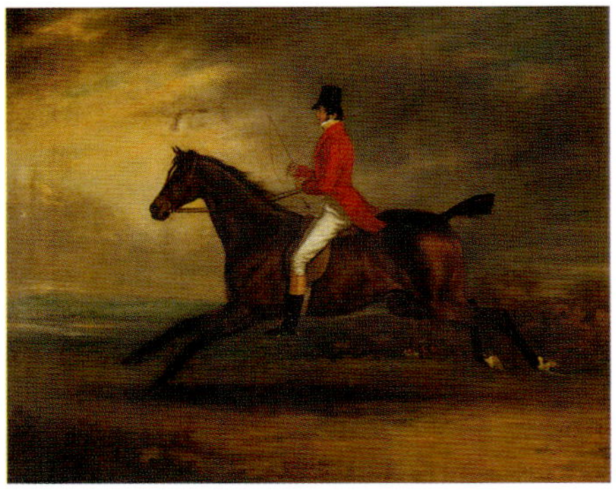

unknown artist
Count D'Orsey in a Red Jacket on Horseback
oil on canvas 46 x 56
1979:115

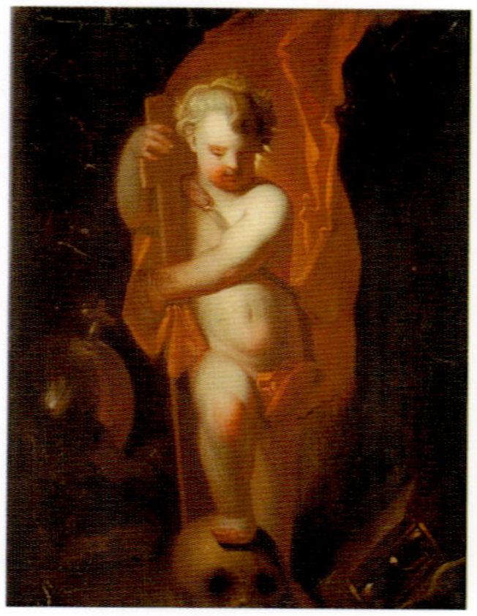

unknown artist
Cupid
oil on canvas 71.5 x 61
1922:267

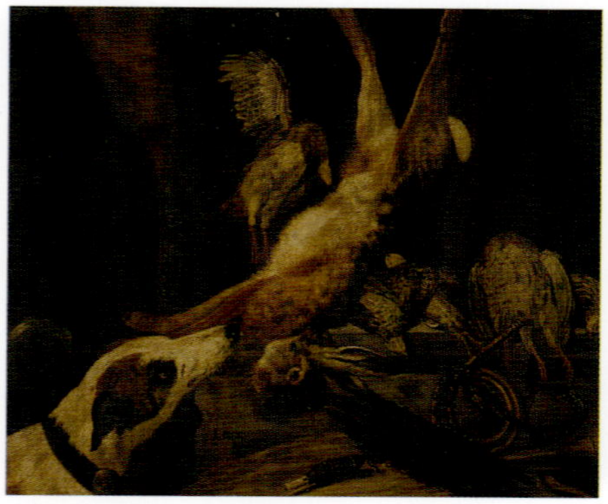

unknown artist
Dead Game and Deerhound
oil on canvas 66 x 85
1922:54

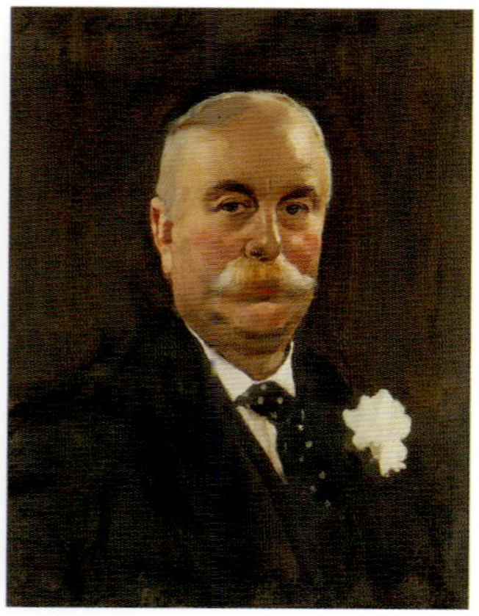

unknown artist
Henry Flemming Hibbert (1850–1927), 1st Bt
oil on canvas 59 x 50
1984:195

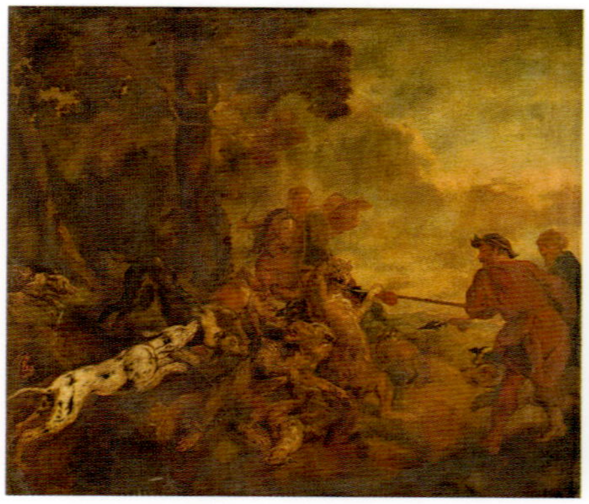

unknown artist
Hunting Scene with Hounds and Tigers
oil on canvas 65 x 79.5
1922: 58

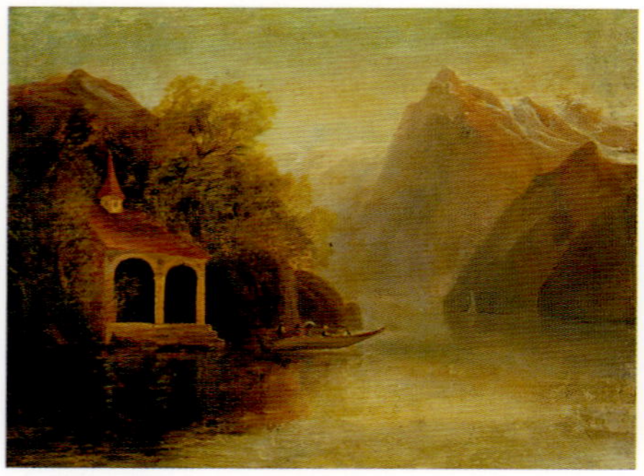

unknown artist
Italian Lake View
oil on canvas 41.5 x 54.5
1978:4

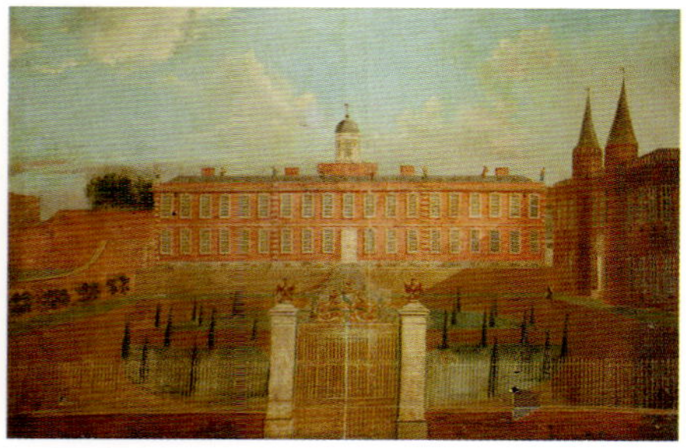

unknown artist
Knowsley Hall
oil on canvas 127 x 208
1922:10

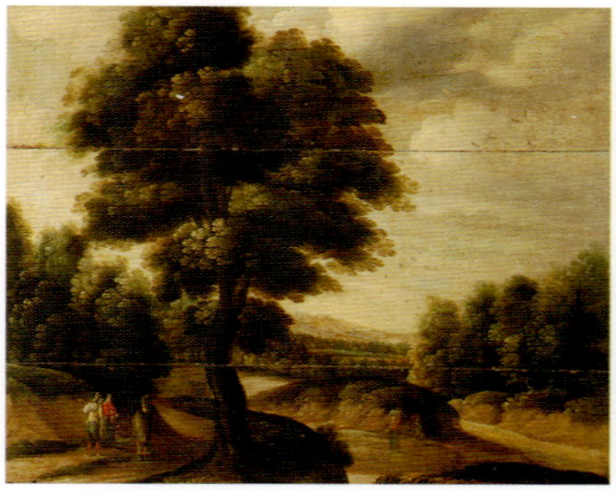

unknown artist
Landscape and Figures
oil on panel 43 x 60
1922:266

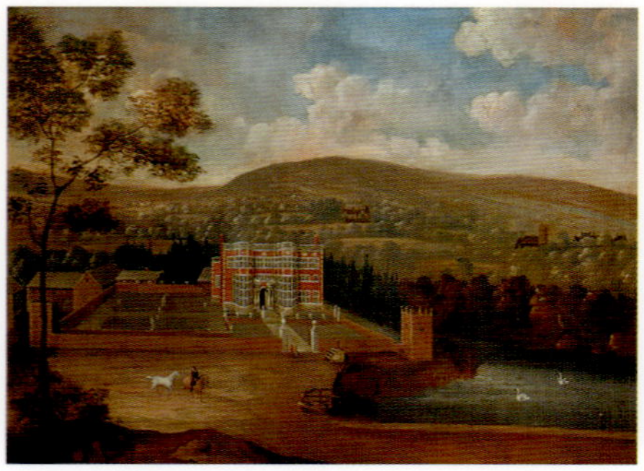

unknown artist
Landscape with Astley Hall
oil on canvas 91 x 130
1922:52

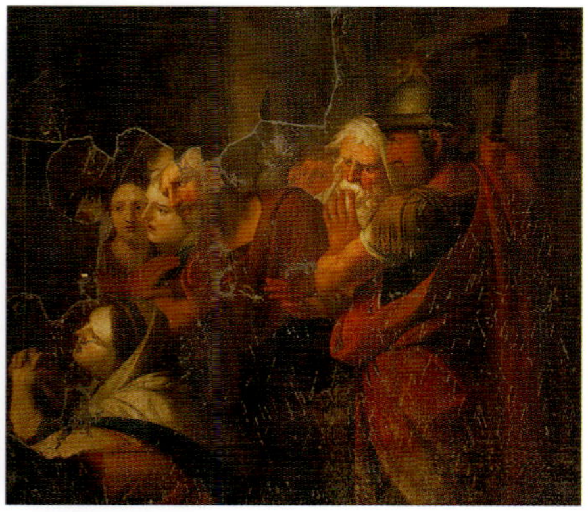

unknown artist
The Judgement of Solomon (The Adoration)
oil on canvas 101.6 x 152.4
1922:368

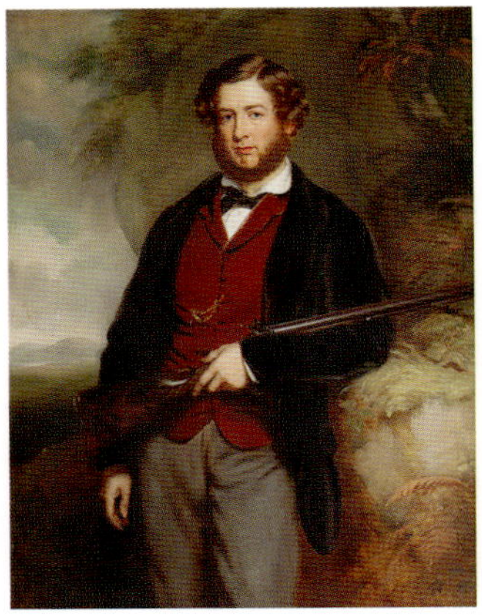

unknown artist
Thomas Townley-Parker (1822–1906)
oil on canvas 127 x 101.6
1976:3

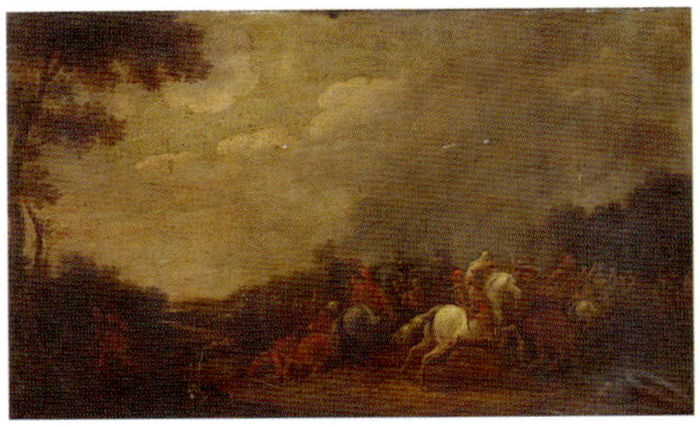

Verschuring, Hendrik (follower of) 1627–1690
Battle Scene
oil on canvas 49 x 83.5
1922:65

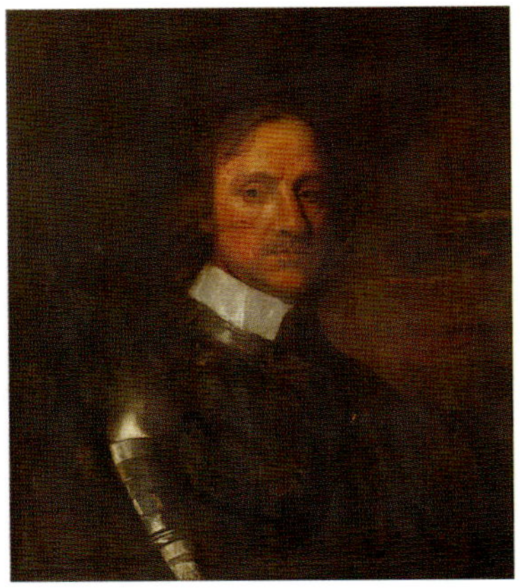

Walker, Robert (after) 1599–1658
Oliver Cromwell (1599–1658) 18th C
oil on canvas 76 x 64
1922:13

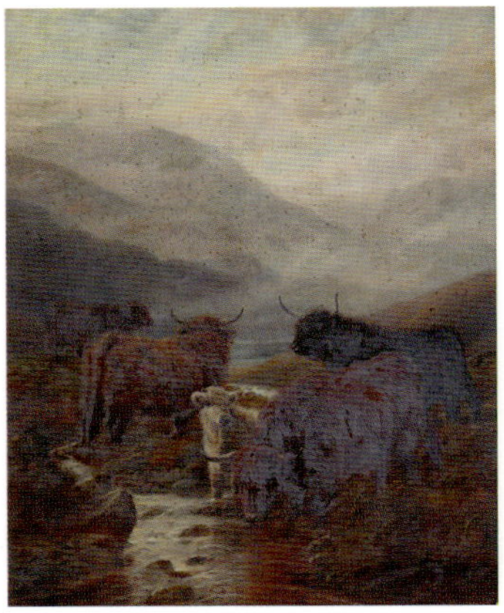

Watson, Robert
Highland Cattle 1848
oil on canvas 89 x 69
1946:2.1

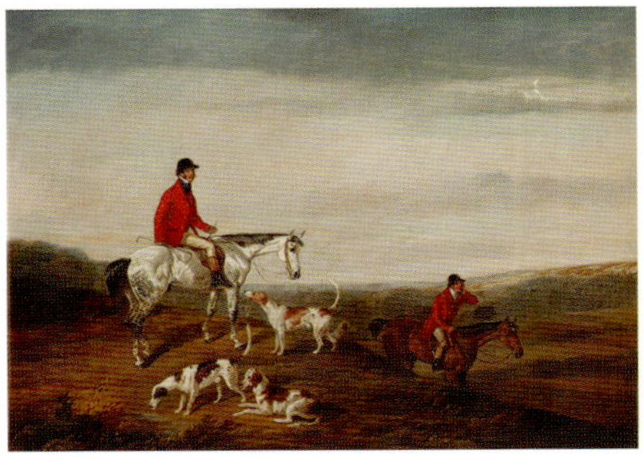

Webb, Bryon
M. T. H. in a Red Jacket on a Grey Horse with Three Hounds (after John Nost Sartorious)
oil on canvas 43 x 48.5
1979:111

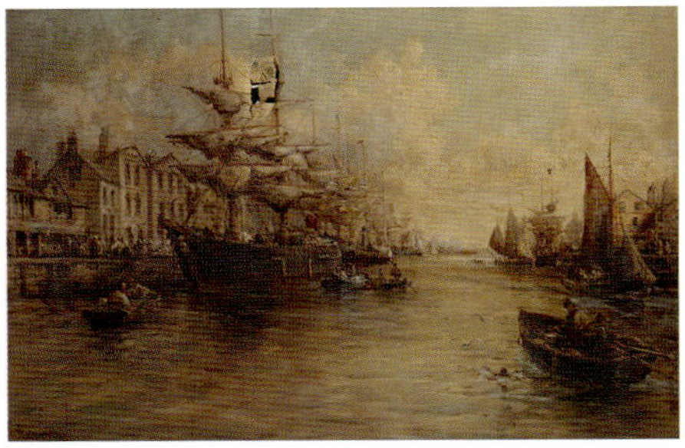

Webb, William Edward 1862–1903
Ship and Boats 1893
oil on canvas 76 x 127
1984:196

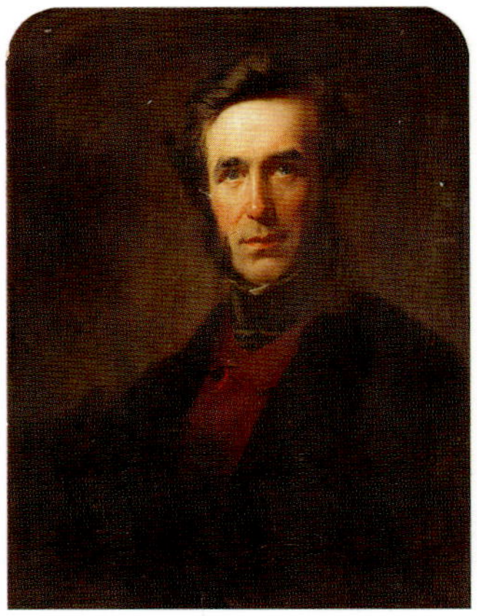

Westcott, Philip 1815–1878
Sir Robert Rawlinson (1810–1898)
oil on canvas 76 x 63.5
1984:33

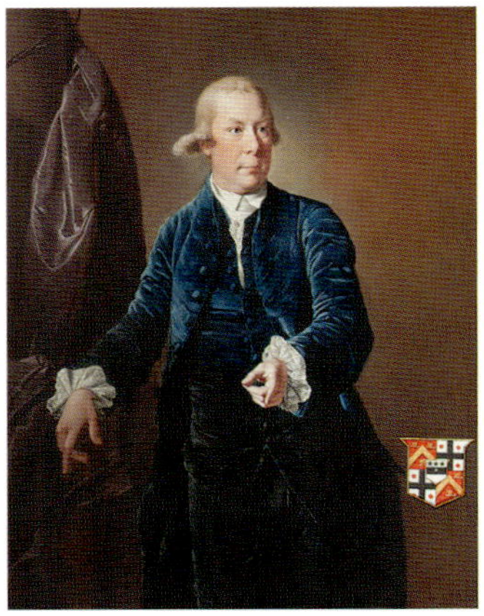

Wright of Derby, Joseph 1734–1797
Robert Parker of Cuerden Hall
oil on canvas 127 x 102
1976:5

Clitheroe Castle Museum

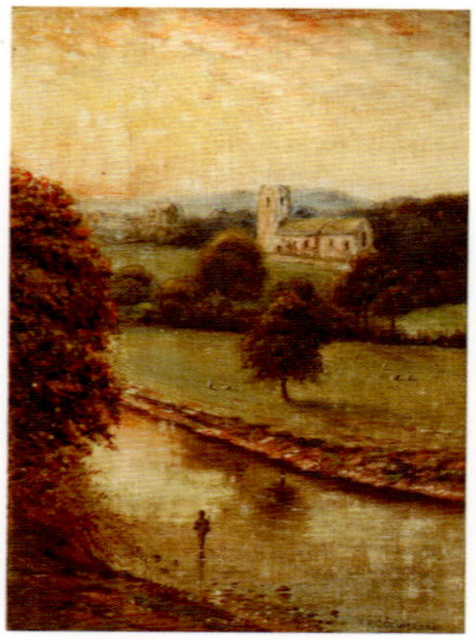

Cawthorne
Mytton Flatt and River
oil on canvas 48 x 36 (E)
CL 1003

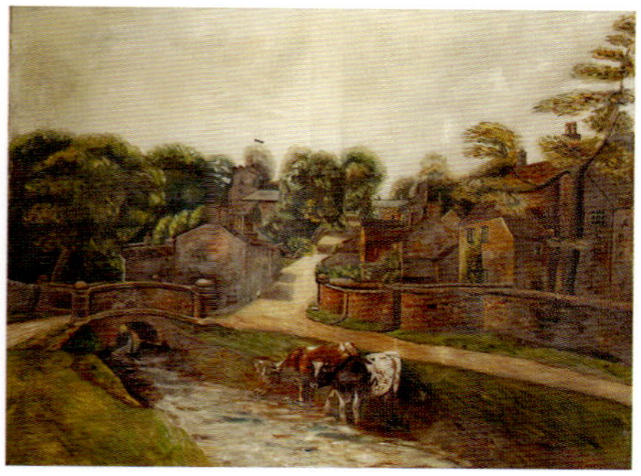

Jones, Lily
View of Downham 1906
oil on canvas 76 x 97
CL1098

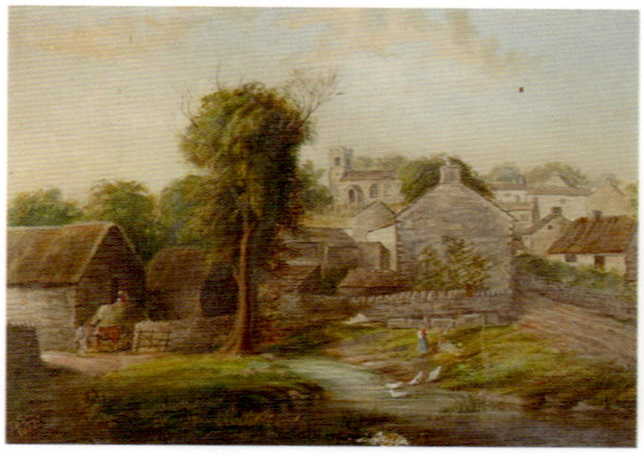

Satterthwaite, Benjamin 1848–1923
Downham 1879
oil on board 39 x 60 (E)
LANCL.912

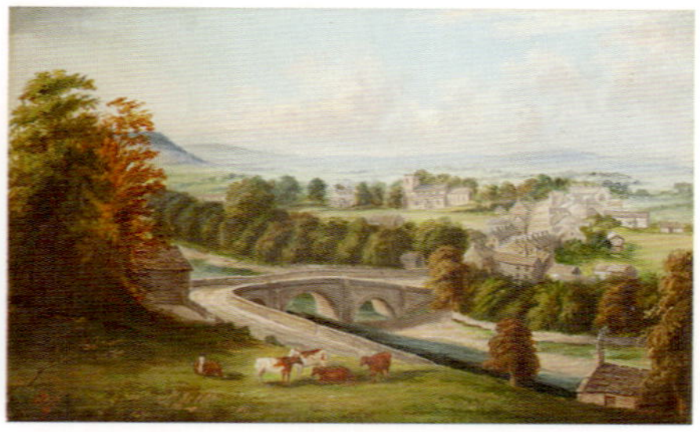

Satterthwaite, Benjamin 1848–1923
Whalley Abbey from Whalley Nab 1879
oil on board 50 x 60 (E)
LANCL.912.1

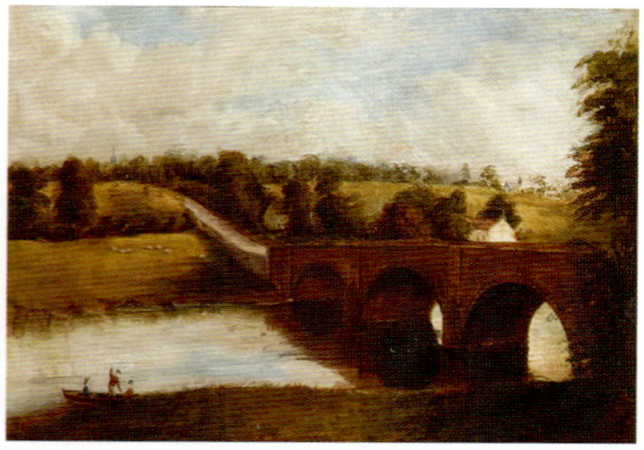

Satterthwaite, Benjamin 1848–1923
Boating at Brungerley
oil on canvas 50 x 60 (E)
CL 1299

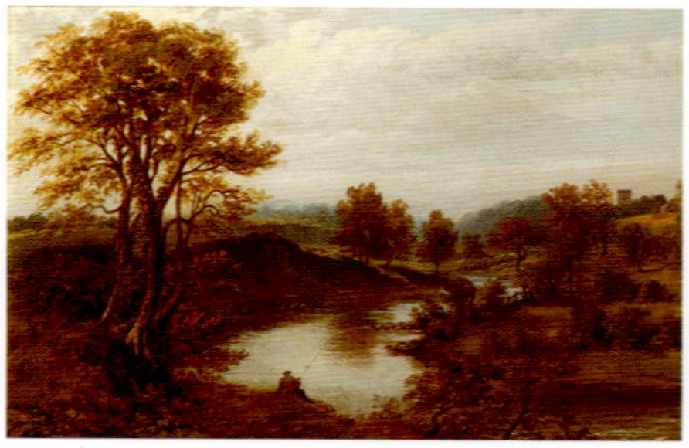

unknown artist
A Man Fishing on a River
oil on canvas 39 x 60 (E)
PCF1

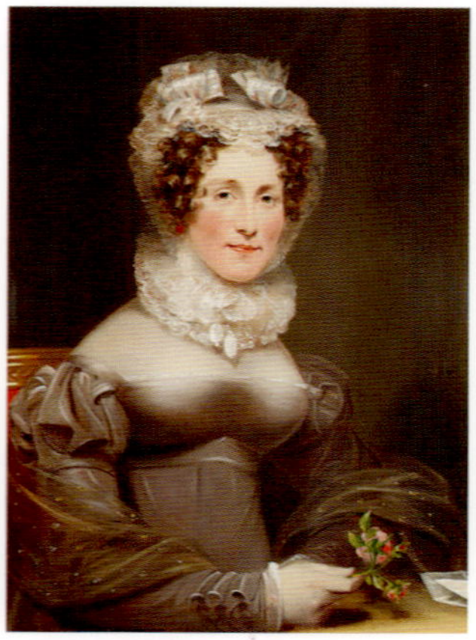

unknown artist
Cecilia Thomson
oil on canvas 60 x 50 (E)
CL 924/2

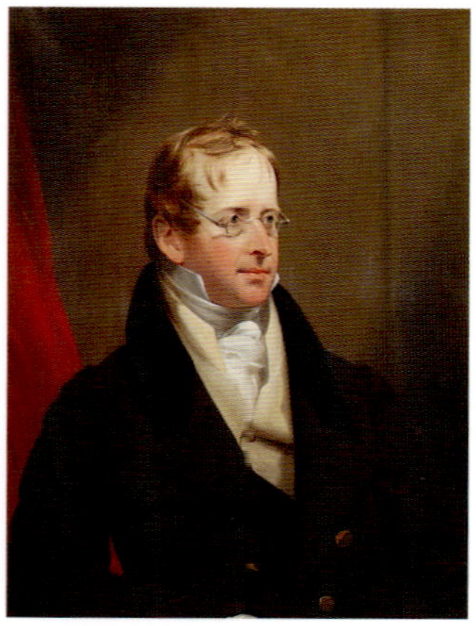

unknown artist
James Thomson
oil on canvas 60 x 50 (E)
CL 924/1

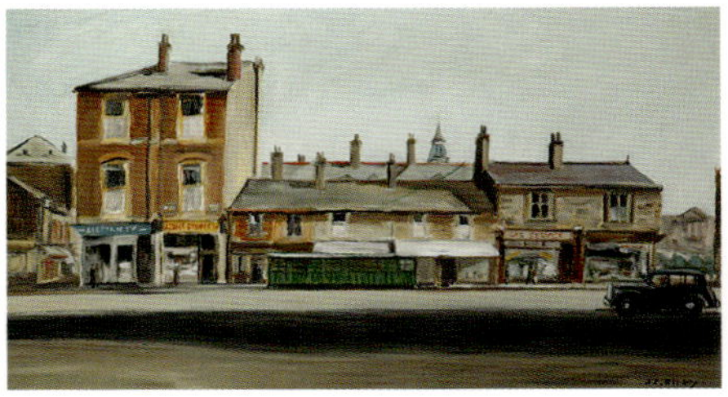

Riley, James Lewis b.1925
Market Street, Darwen c.1979–1991
oil on canvas 41 x 74
DARL5

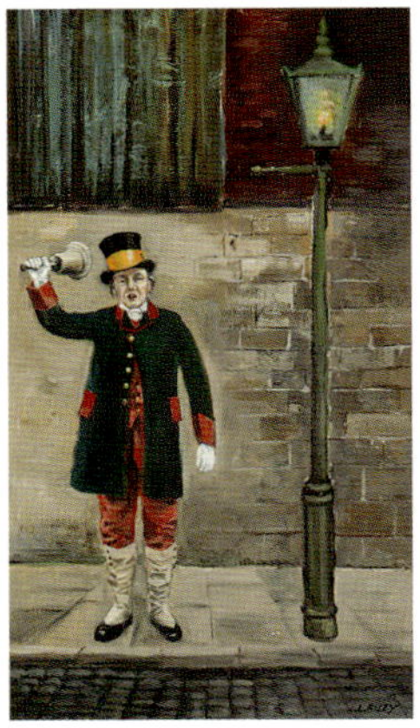

Riley, James Lewis b.1925
Self Portrait in a Bellman's Outfit c.1979–1991
oil on canvas 61 x 35
DARL3

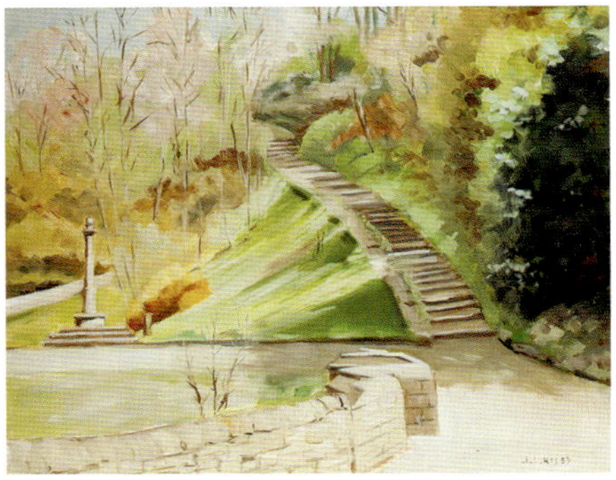

Riley, James Lewis b.1925
Sunnyhurst Wood, Darwen c.1979–1991
oil on canvas 44 x 58
DARL1

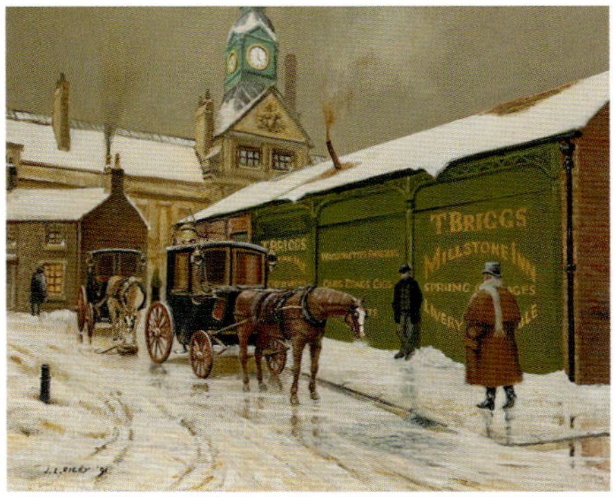

Riley, James Lewis b.1925
Brigg's Stables, Market, Darwen 1991
oil on canvas 48 x 61
DARL2

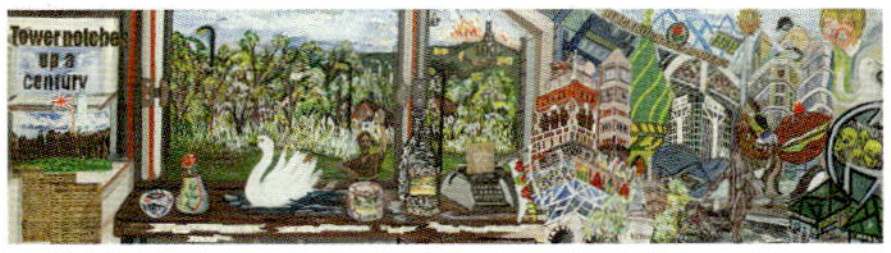

unknown artist
Tower Notches up a Century 1995
oil (?) on canvas 30 x 95 (E)
DARTH1

King's Own Royal Regiment Museum

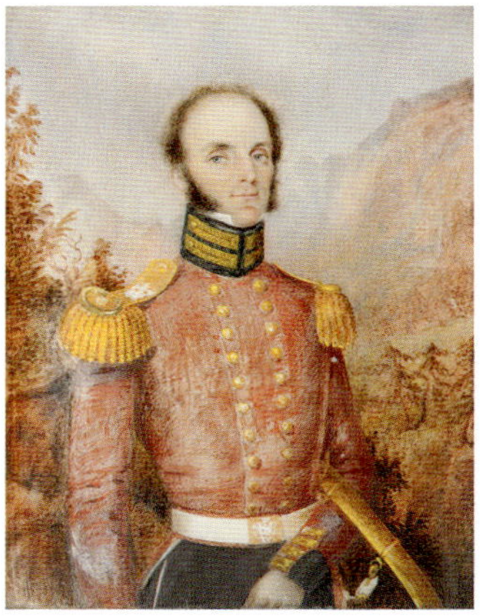

Barnard, Philip Augustus 1812–1897
Colonel Henry William Breton, 4th Regiment of Foot c.1830
oil on canvas 11.8 x 9.3
ko1391/01

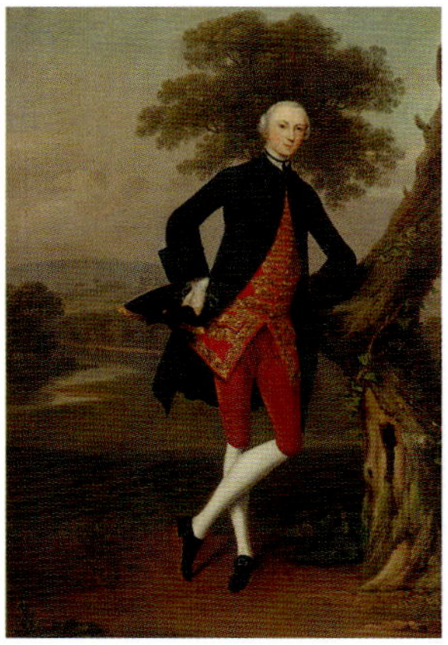

Devis, Arthur 1712–1787
Colonel Sir Robert Rich 1756
oil on canvas 58 x 39
ko0566/01

Facing page: Wright of Derby, Joseph, 1734–1797, *Richard Arkwright (1732–1792)*, 1783–1785, Harris Museum & Art Gallery (p. 369)

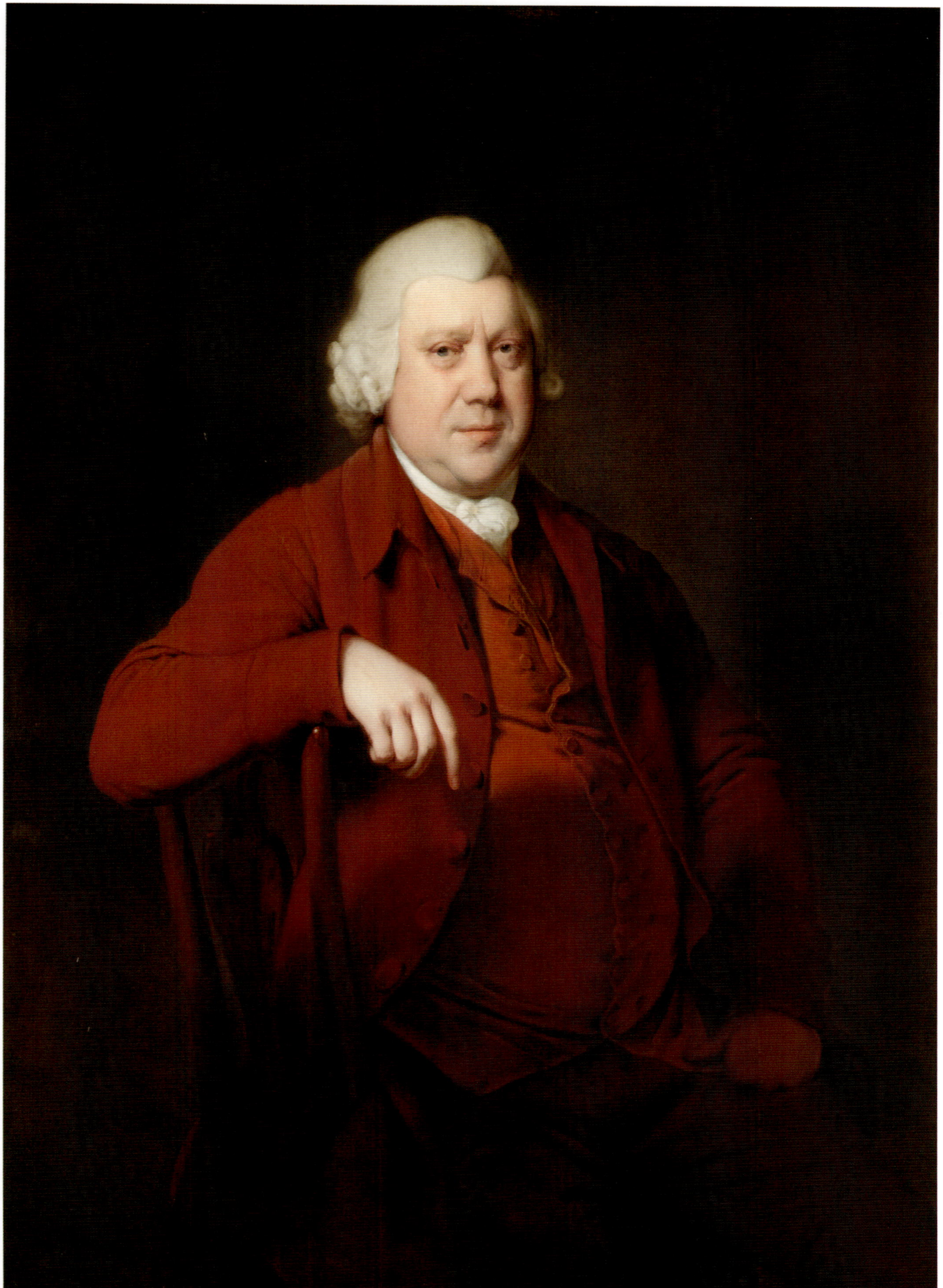

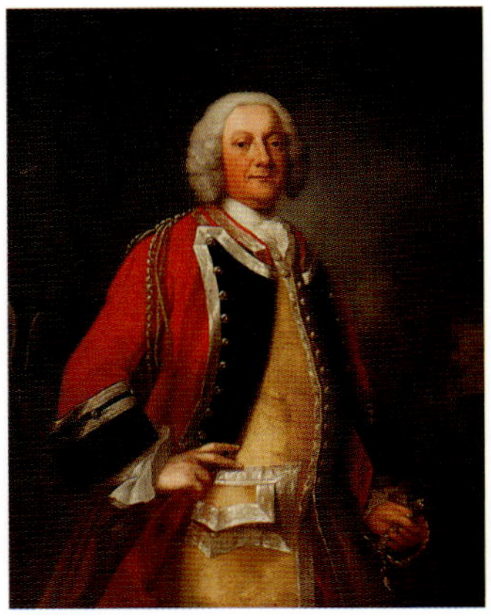

Frye, Thomas 1710–1762
Lieutenant Colonel George Walsh 1750
oil on canvas 128.3 x 100.4
ko1450/01

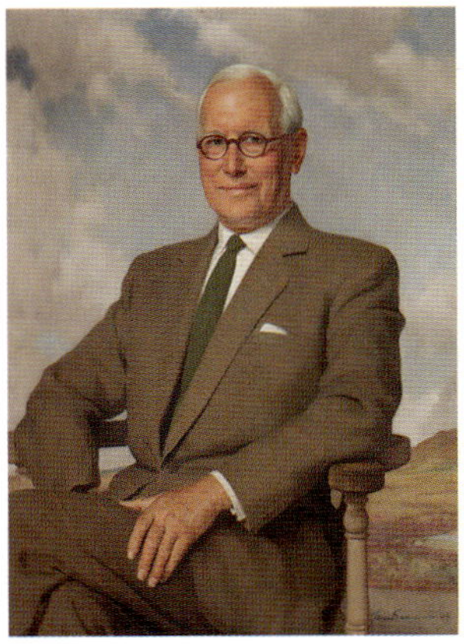

Gunn, Herbert James 1893–1964
Richard Leslie Brown, GC 1964
oil on canvas 99 x 73.8
ko2568/01

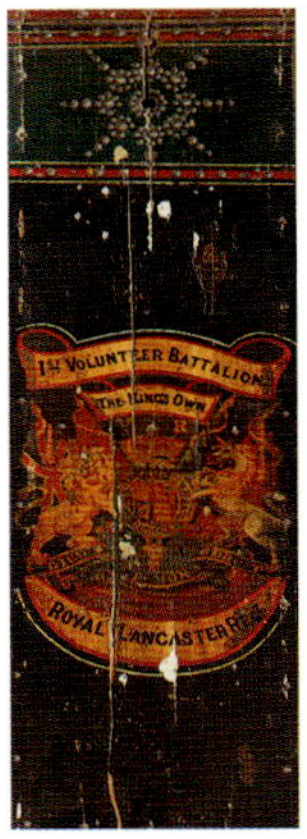

Henry Potter & Son
Drum Shell, 1st Volunteer Battalion, King's Own Royal Lancaster Regiment (1883–1901) c.1883
oil on wood 122 x 35.2
ko0122/01

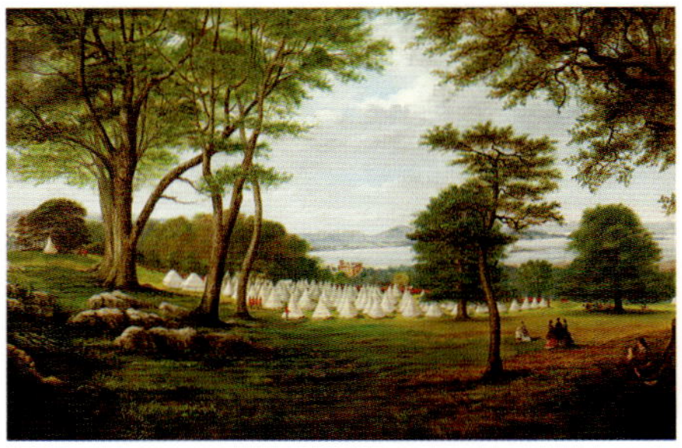

Howe, R.
10th Lancashire Rifle Volunteers at Camp, Bardsea, 1875 1875
oil on canvas 54.2 x 88.5
ko1791/01

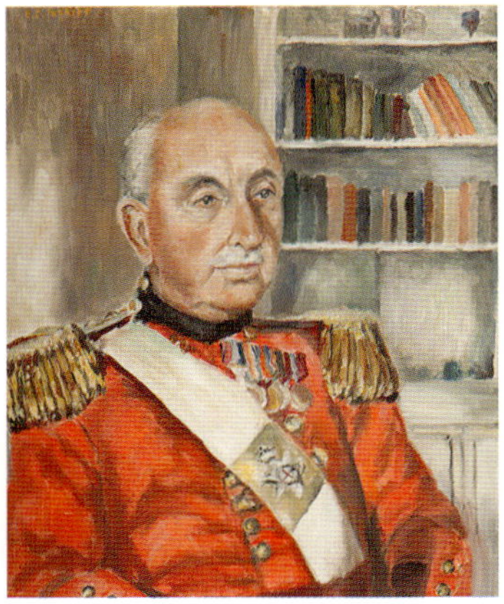

Inskipp, E. C. active 1927–1930s
Lieutenant Colonel Christopher Lefroy Hodgson, King's Own Royal Lancaster Regiment (1901–1927)
oil on board 58.9 x 49.4
ko0968/01

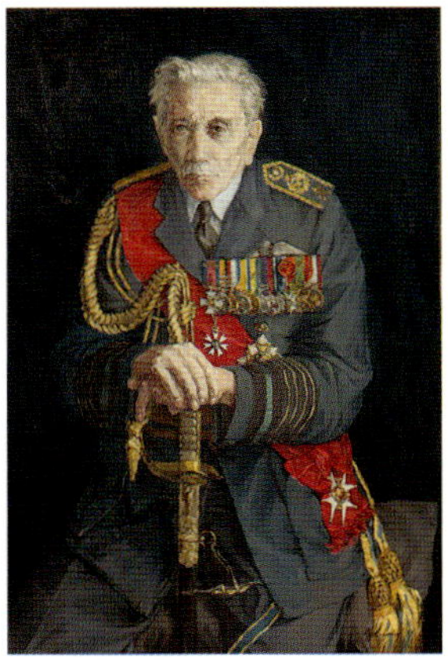

Kearsley, Roy active 1957–1975
Sir John Salmond (1881–1968), GCB, CMG, CVO, DSO, DCL, LLD, The King's Own Royal Lancaster Regiment (1901–1912) (...) 1957
oil on canvas 75.5 x 50
ko0924/01

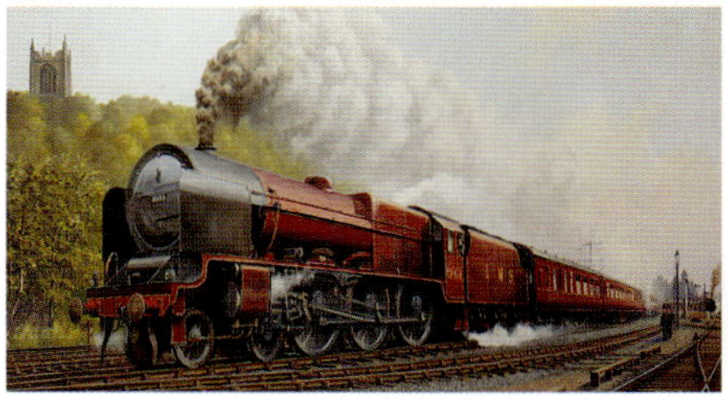

Owens, Trevor R. b.1935
London Midland and Scottish Railway Locomotive Number 6161 'King's Own' 1991
oil on canvas 56.5 x 118.5
ko1905/01

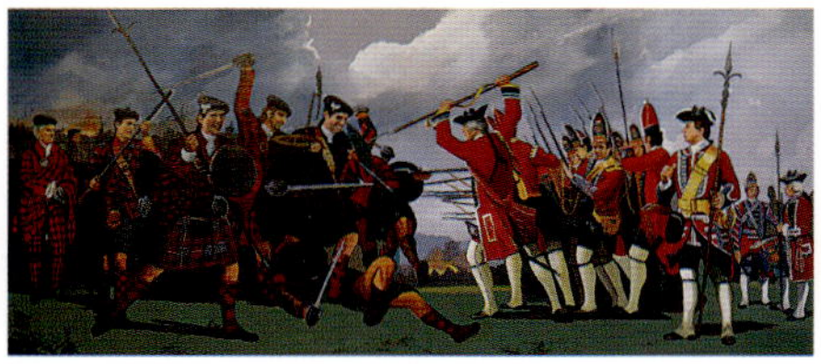

Perkins, Frank
The Battle of Culloden, April 1746 (after David Morier) 1997
oil on aluminium 168 x 398
ko_PCF1

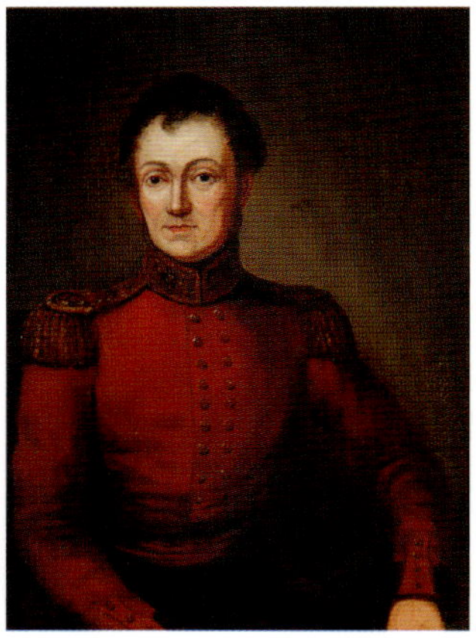

unknown artist
Colonel John Plumbe-Tempest, 1st Royal Lancashire Militia (1819–1852) c.1830
oil on canvas 39 x 28.7
ko0281

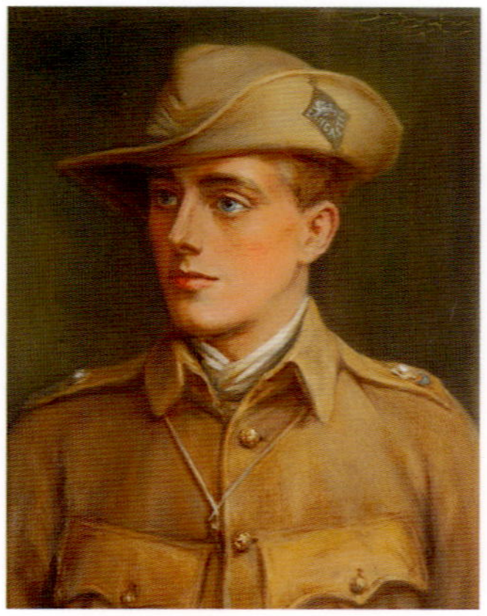

unknown artist
2nd Lieutenant James Mackay, 4th Militia Battalion, King's Own Royal Lancaster Regiment, Killed in Action, (...) c.1899
oil on canvas 30.5 x 24
ko1378/01

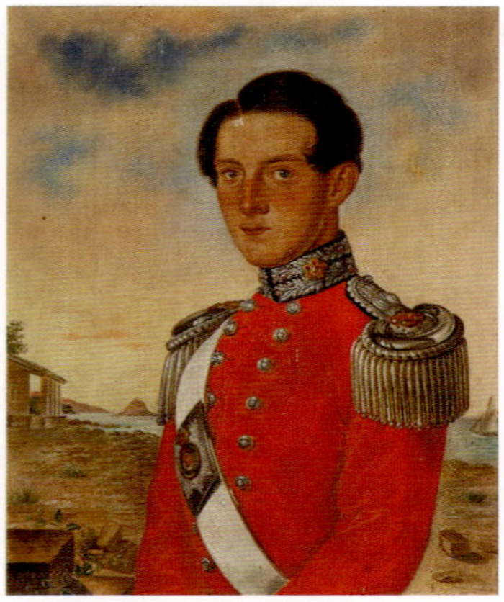

unknown artist
Captain Thomas Hinde Thompson, 1st Royal Lancashire Militia, 1855 1855
oil on canvas 26 x 21
ko1660/01

Lancaster City Council

Lancaster City Council holds paintings at Lancaster Town Hall, Morecambe Town Hall and the Ashton Memorial in Williamson Park. These are in addition to its collections housed at Lancaster City Museums.

Lancaster Town Hall was officially opened on the 27th December 1909, by Lord Ashton – the local industrialist, James Williamson, Junior. It replaced the existing Town Hall, now the City Museum in Market Square, as the then Lancaster Corporation had outgrown its building. The new town hall complex – including a police station, fire station and large public hall – was another civic gift from the local multi-millionaire businessman. The family's wealth was centred on oil cloth and linoleum production.

Most of the works in the Town Hall are portraits of local politicians, industrialists and other well-known public figures. They include a portrait of the donor's father; *James Williamson, Senior (Alderman Williamson)* – founder of the family business – painted by an unknown artist after a formal cabinet photograph (probably posthumously). At the top of the main stairs is a portrait of *James Williamson (1842–1930), Lord Ashton, DL* himself, by Scottish artist Howard Somerville. It was, again, painted posthumously as Lord Ashton would not allow representations of himself inside the building, other than his heraldic coat of arms. It is modelled on a satirical sketch from *Vanity Fair* showing James Williamson giving a speech in Parliament under the title *Philanthropy*. Lady Ashton presented it to Lancaster in 1932.

Above the fireplace in the Mayor's Parlour is a portrait of *Lady Ashton, CBE,* also by Howard Somerville. A prominent public figure, after her husband's death Lady Ashton became the first female Freeman of the Borough in 1932. There is also a striking portrait of *James Mansergh, FRS,* a Freeman of the Borough and renowned engineer responsible for the Lancaster Waterworks, painted by his son-in-law William Mainwaring Palin.

The collection includes five paintings by Lancaster-born artist James Lonsdale. Lonsdale first worked as a pattern designer at Margerison and Glover's print-works in Catterall. In 1799 he moved to London where he is reputed to have been, briefly, the pupil of the portrait artist George Romney.

Lonsdale became portrait painter extraordinary to Queen Caroline. He exhibited 138 works at the Royal Academy and 87 at the Society of British Artists (where he was a founder member) between 1802 and 1838. Subjects represented at the Town Hall include a posthumous portrait of the national hero, *Admiral Lord Nelson*, presented to the town by the artist in 1806. The gift may have proved useful to the artist as the Corporation promptly commissioned a further portrait from him. In 1807 it received a companion portrait of *The Right Honourable William Pitt the Younger (1759–1806)*, the country's youngest Prime Minister. It must also be seen as a memorial painting as the respected politician had died just months before Lonsdale's commission.

One of Lancaster's most famous sons is the naturalist Sir Richard Owen (1804–1892). He was born a stone's throw from the Town Hall, although the building was demolished around 1950. The Town Hall houses a portrait of Owen by the Irish artist Henry Jones Thaddeus (1859–1929). It shows the man who gave dinosaurs their name, the first Director of the Natural History Museum in London – and bitter opponent of Charles Darwin and his evolutionist theories – in thoughtful old age.

Four miles away, overlooking the sea stands Morecambe Town Hall. This Grade II listed building was opened in June 1931. The paintings housed there reflect the distinctiveness of Morecambe as a seaside town and Heysham as a harbour town. Works include *'Brier' Coming into Harbour* by local artist Arthur Knowles and *Coastal Scene* by the nineteenth-century artist Luke Gorst. Gorst is the only artist known to have painted a portrait of James Williamson/Lord Ashton in the sitter's lifetime. The 1890 portrait bust is held within the City Museum collections and can only be described as not unduly flattering. Perhaps this is why the local industrialist and philanthropist shunned both photography and formal portraiture!

The Ashton Memorial is perched on the highest point of Williamson Park. Its distinctive dome is visible throughout the city and for all travelling north or south, past the city. It was commissioned by Lord Ashton in memory of members of his close family (his two wives and his daughter) and was completed in 1909. Described by Sir Nikolaus Pevsner as 'the grandest monument', it marked the culmination of Lord Ashton's second phase of redevelopment of this park, that had largely been begun by his father, James Williamson, and that had transformed rough moorland and quarries into stunning parkland.

At the top of the building is a gallery which hosts exhibitions by local artists. Many of them have donated works which hang permanently on the walls of the curved staircase. These include a series of images of *Williamson Park Lake* in bold blocks of colour by R. Danks, and an impressionistic depiction of the *Millennium Bridge* by Graeme Atkinson.

Susan Ashworth, Collections Manager and Adrienne Wallman, Lancashire Coordinator, Public Catalogue Foundation

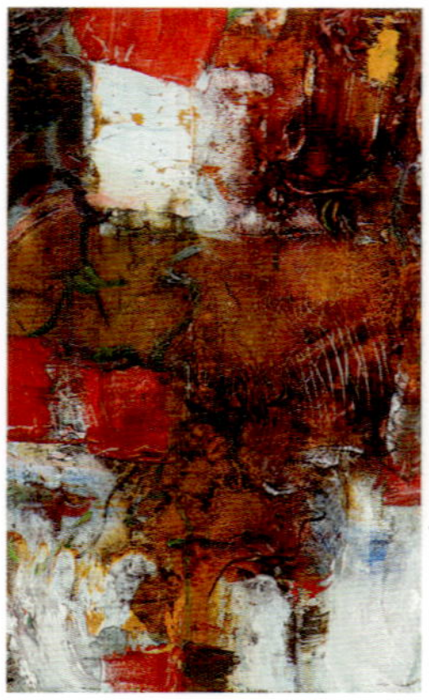

Amriding, Chris 1935–2005
Abstract Red Brown
oil on canvas 38.5 x 29
38

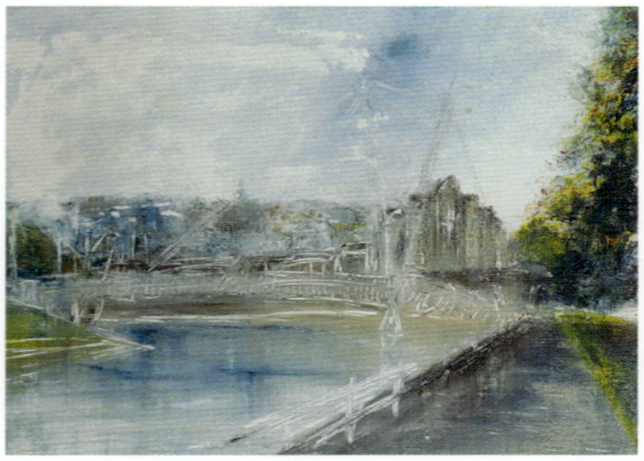

Atkinson, Graeme b.1972
Millennium Bridge
oil on paper 49 x 69
39

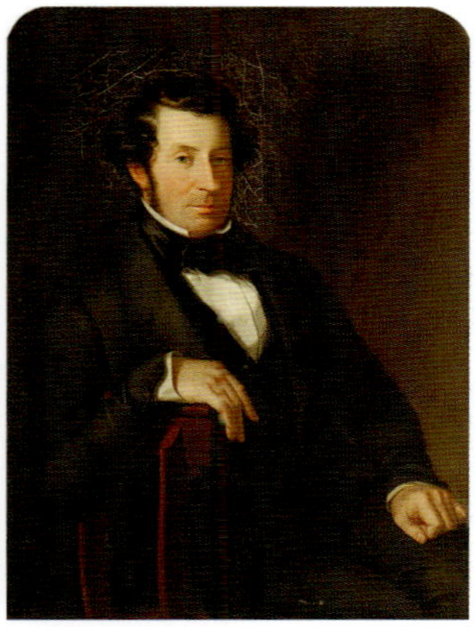

Barker, J. active 1800–1850
James Giles, Esq., MA (Oxon)
oil on canvas 75.5 x 50 (E)
LTH010

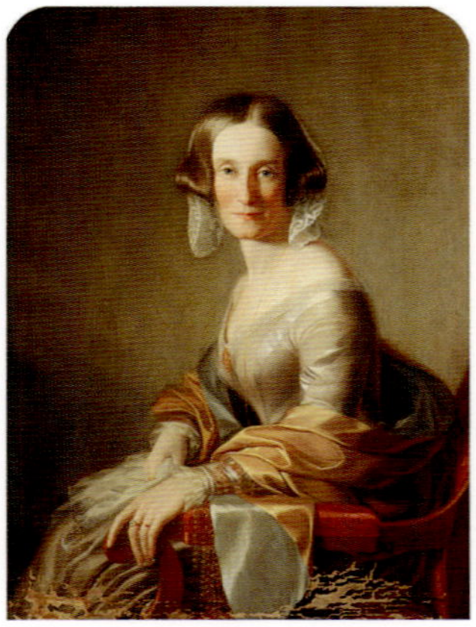

Barker, J. active 1800–1850
Mrs Elizabeth Giles
oil on canvas 75.5 x 50 (E)
LTH011

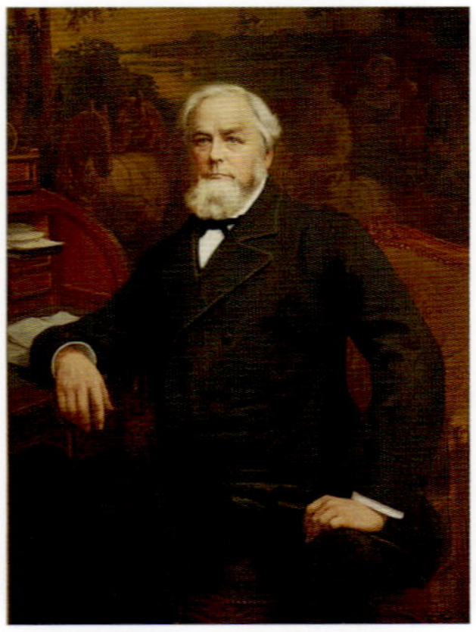

Bulfield, Joseph M. active 1894–1912
Alderman Thomas Preston (d.1894), JP
oil on canvas 143 x 110
LTH003

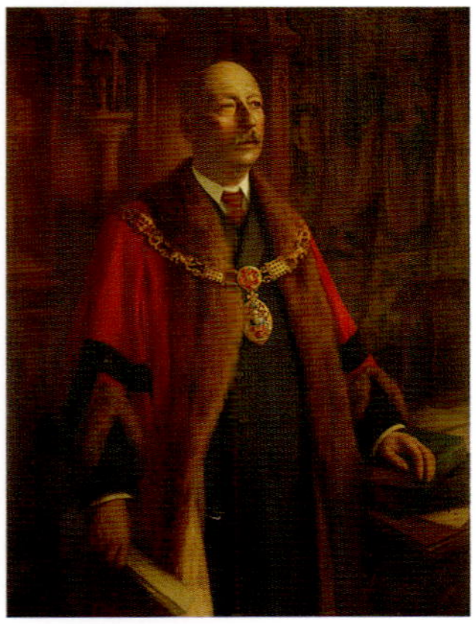

Bulfield, Joseph M. active 1894–1912
Alderman William Bell
oil on canvas 138 x 104
LTH007

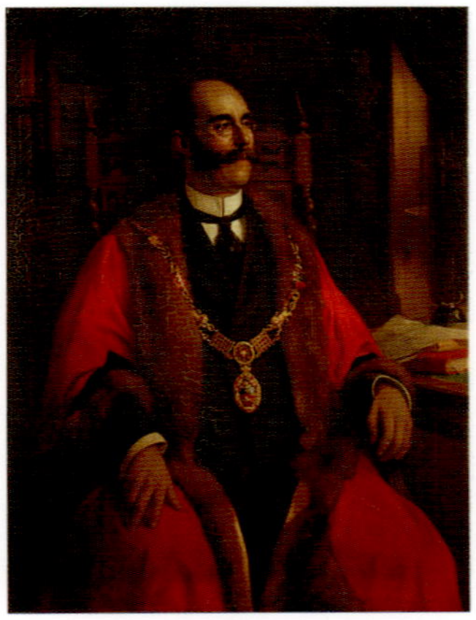

Bulfield, Joseph M. active 1894–1912
Alderman William Smith
oil on canvas 141 x 105
LTH008

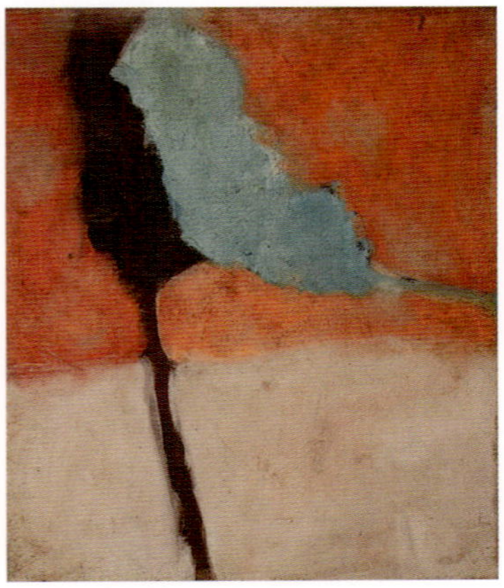

Bulley, Emma b.1961
Flower
oil on canvas 36 x 30.5
27

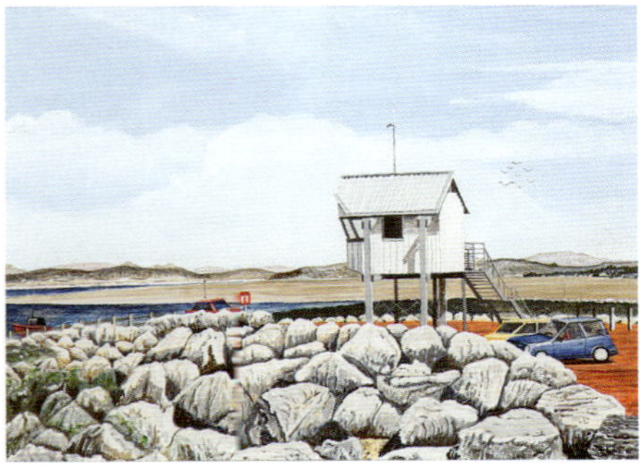

Cumpsty, David b.1939
Lookout over Morecambe Bay
oil on canvas 25 x 32.5
14

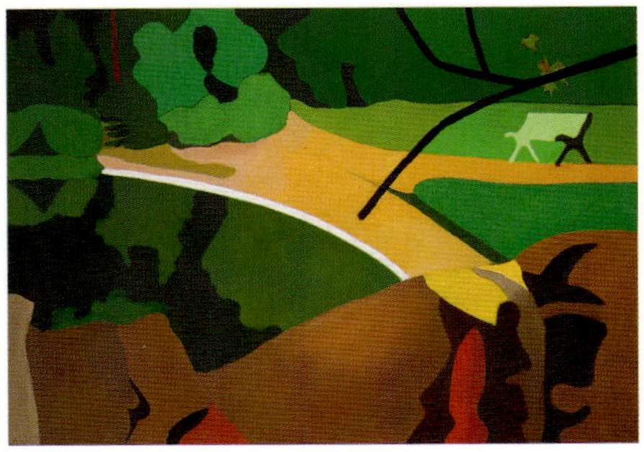

Danks, R.
Williamson Park Lake
oil on canvas 40.5 x 61
16

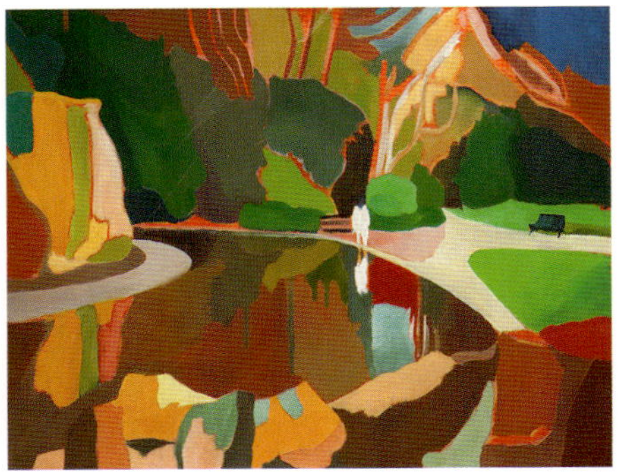

Danks, R.
Williamson Park Lake
oil on canvas 40.5 x 61
17

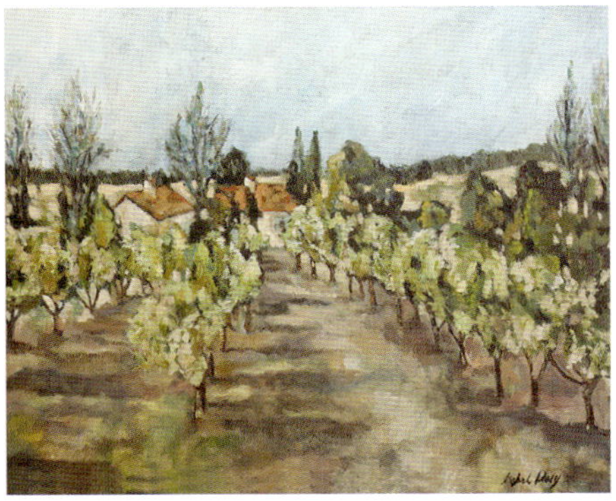

Davy, Isabel
Trees and Cottages
oil on canvas 49 x 59
48

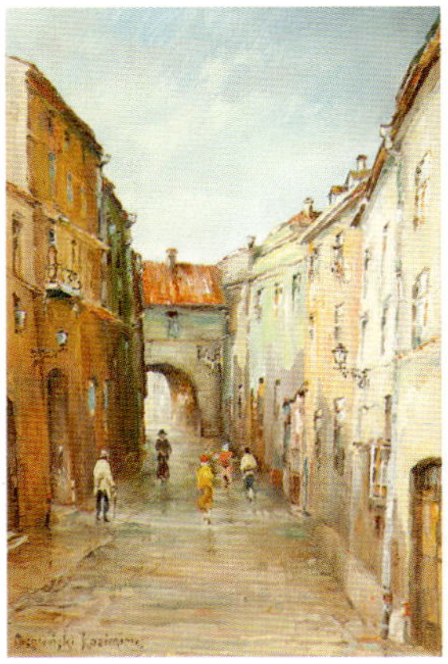

Drzewinski, Kazimierz
Street Scene
oil on canvas 54 x 39
LTH031

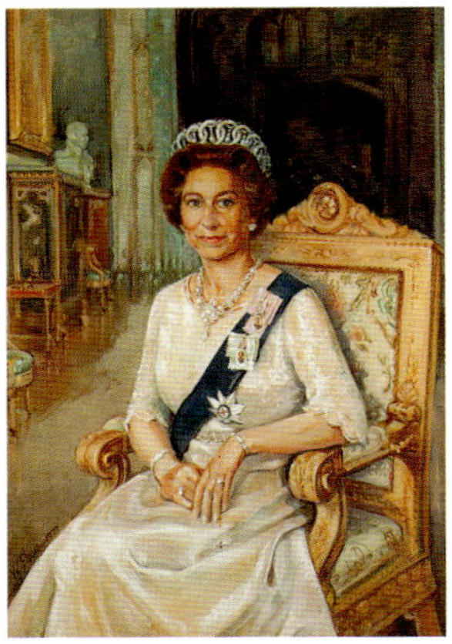

Elsom, V.
Elizabeth II (b.1926) 1977
oil on canvas 141 x 97
LTH029

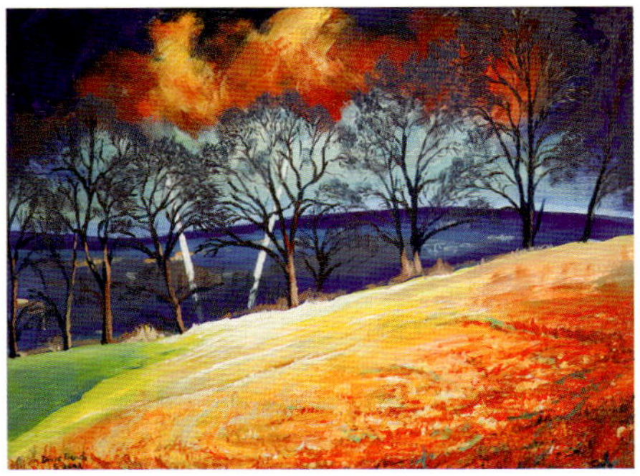

French, David Jonathan b.1963
Red Blue Landscape with Red Clouds 2002
acrylic on paper 34.5 x 49.5
50

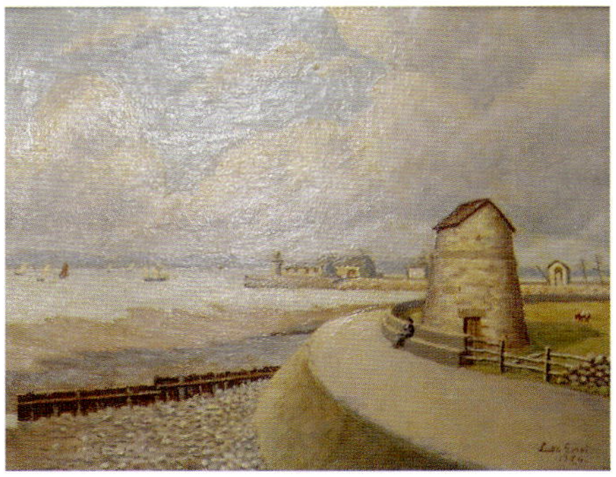

Gorst, Luke 1849–1929
Coastal Scene 1884
oil on canvas
MTH004

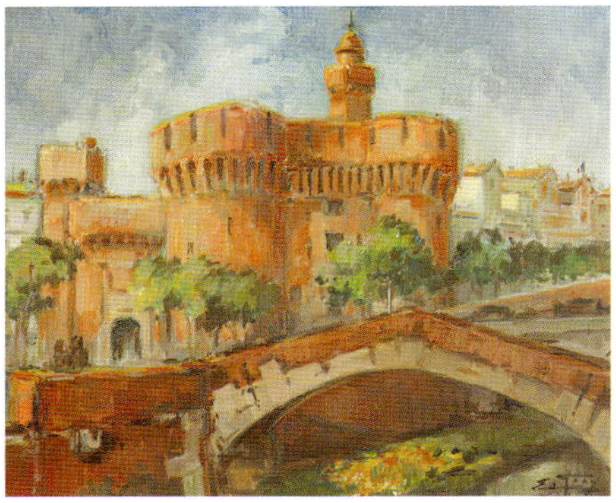

Gray, E.
Castle and Bridge
oil on canvas 32 x 39.5
LTH032

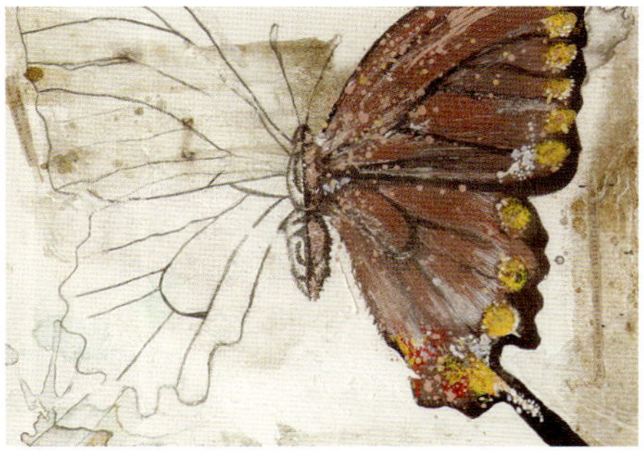

Grieg, N.
Butterfly
poster paint (?) on paper 24 x 34
17

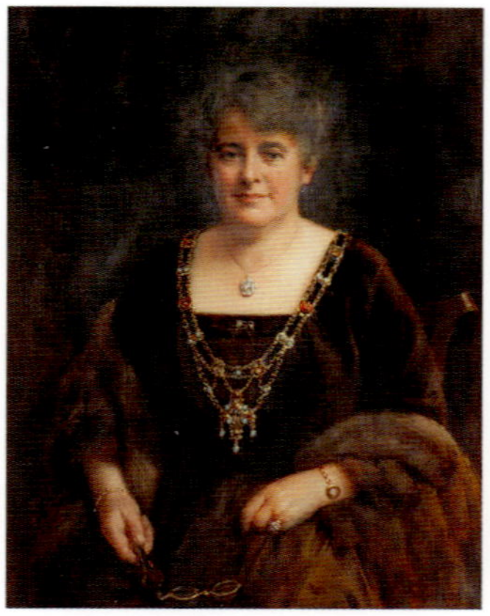

Harrison, R. E.
Mrs Briggs
oil on canvas 90 x 68
LTH014

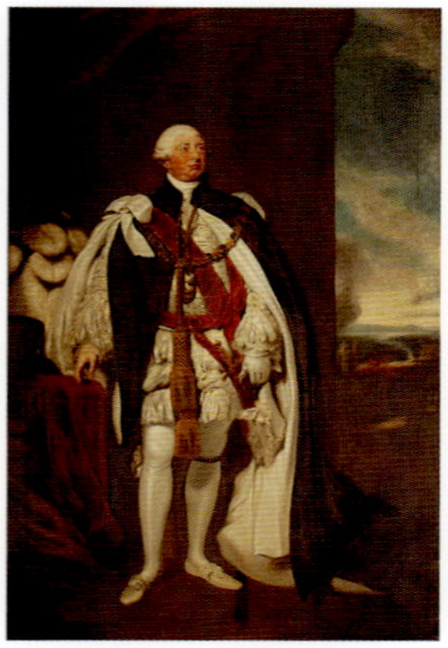

Henderson, Cornelius 1799–1852
George III (1738–1820) (copy of Thomas Lawrence)
oil on canvas 290 x 200 (E)
LTH025

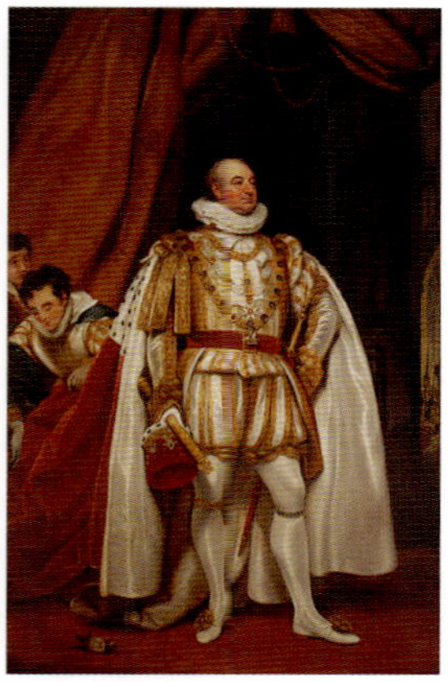

Henderson, Cornelius 1799–1852
His Royal Highness the Duke of York (1763–1827) (copy of Thomas Phillips)
oil on canvas 260 x 180
LTH026

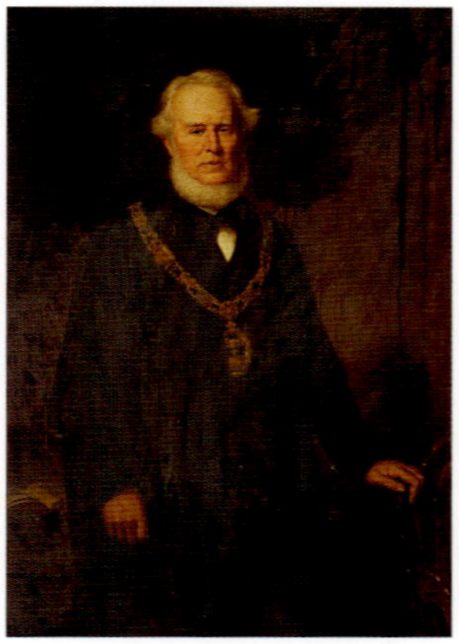

Hodges, J. Sidney Willis 1829–1900
Alderman Charles Blades, JP
oil on canvas 143 x 109 (E)
LTH004

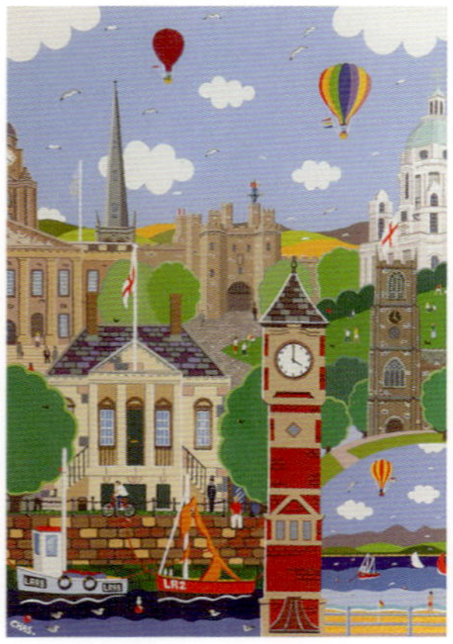

Jacobs, Chas b.1957
Lancaster Montage
oil on canvas 34 x 24.5
19

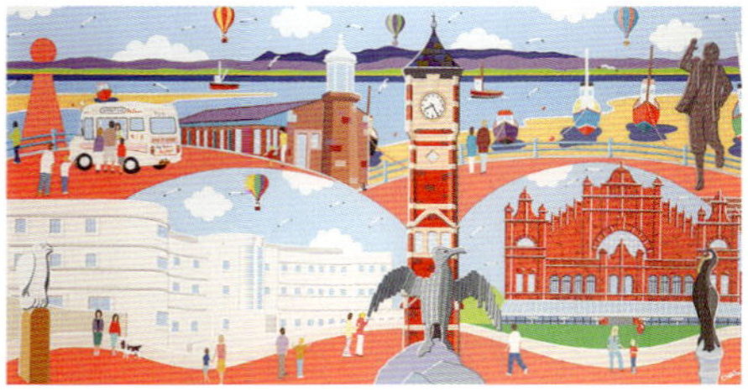

Jacobs, Chas b.1957
Morecambe Sea Front
acrylic on canvas 31 x 61
MTH006

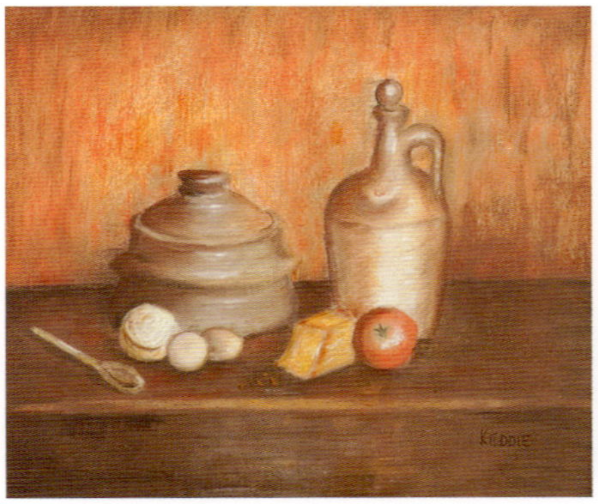

Keddie, John
Still Life
oil on canvas (?) 22 x 26.25
20

King, Margaret b.1932
Sea
oil on canvas 26 x 29
21

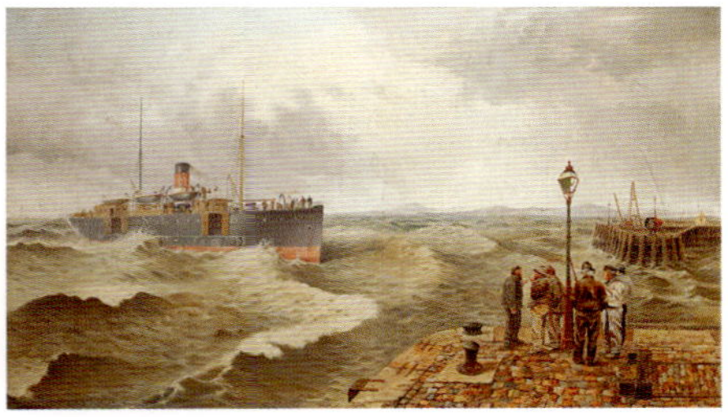

Knowles, Arthur 1870–1955
'Brier' Coming into Harbour
oil on canvas 60 x 106
MTH002

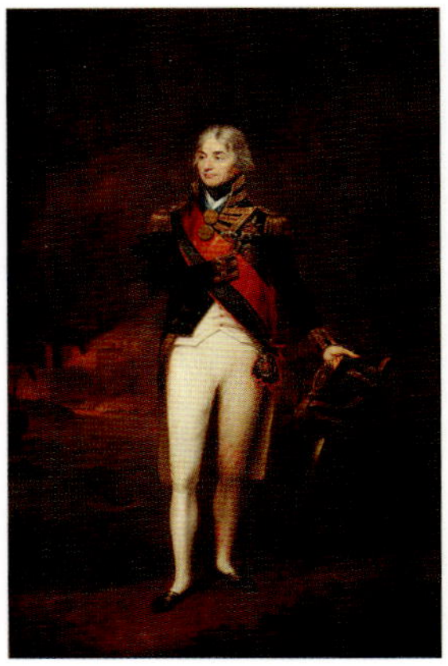

Lonsdale, James 1777–1839
Admiral Lord Nelson (1758–1805) 1806
oil on canvas 290 x 144 (E)
LTH027

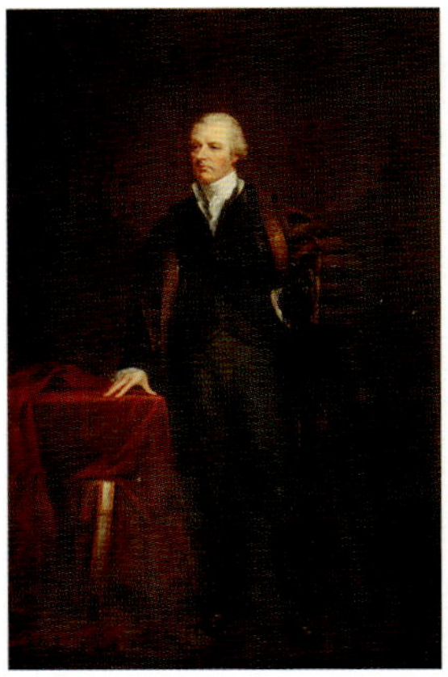

Lonsdale, James 1777–1839
The Right Honourable William Pitt the Younger (1759–1806) 1806
oil on canvas 290 x 144 (E)
LTH021

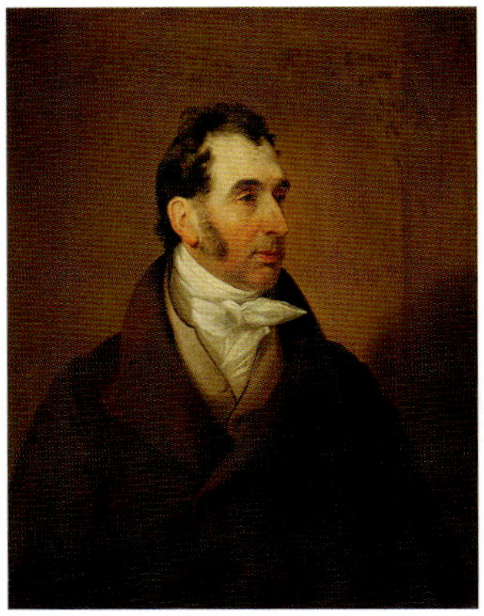

Lonsdale, James 1777–1839
Alderman Thomas Giles
oil on canvas 76 x 61
LTH009

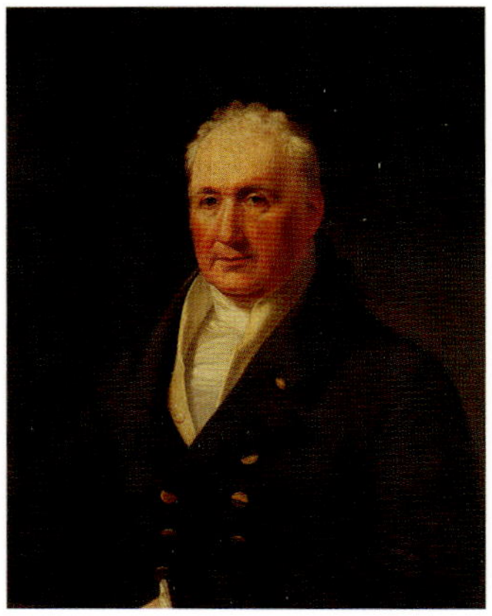

Lonsdale, James 1777–1839
Samuel Gregson
oil on canvas 75.5 x 61.5
LTH006

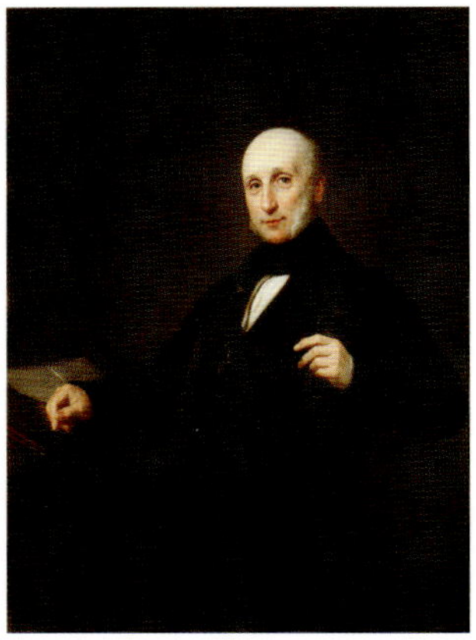

Lonsdale, James 1777–1839
Samuel Gregson
oil on canvas 124.5 x 99
LTH024

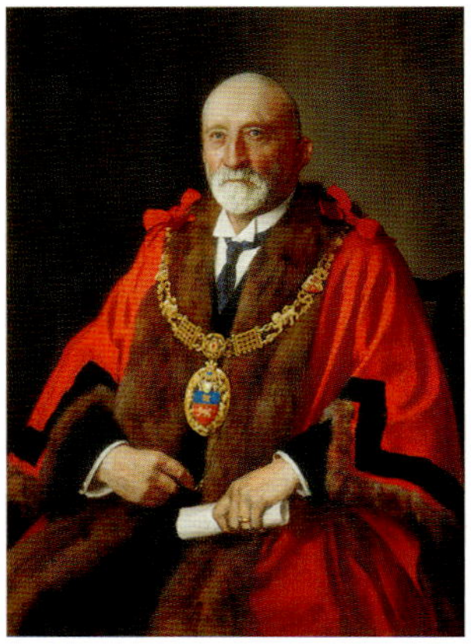

Neale, George Hall 1863–1940
Alderman George Jackson
oil on canvas 112 x 80 (E)
LTH019

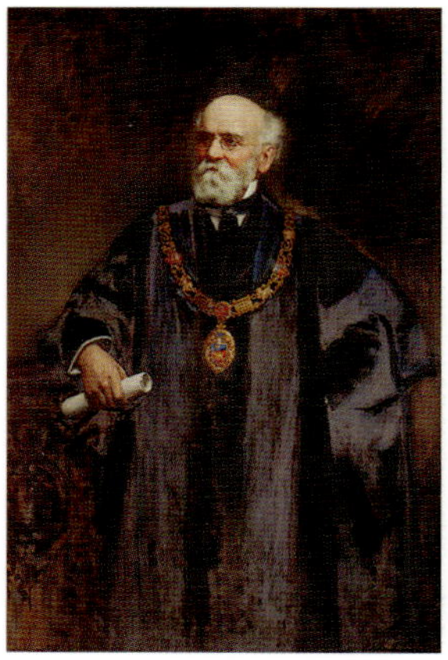

Neale, George Hall 1863–1940
Sir Thomas Storey, KT
oil on canvas 142 x 90.5 (E)
LTH020

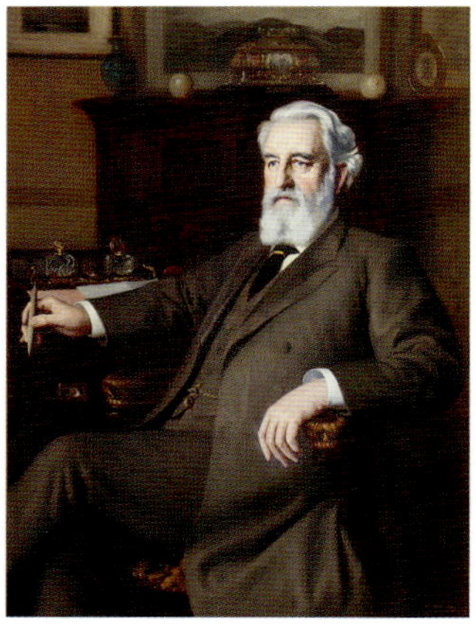

Palin, William Mainwaring 1862–1947
James Mansergh (1834–1905), FRS 1903
oil on canvas 130 x 90.5 (E)
LTH018

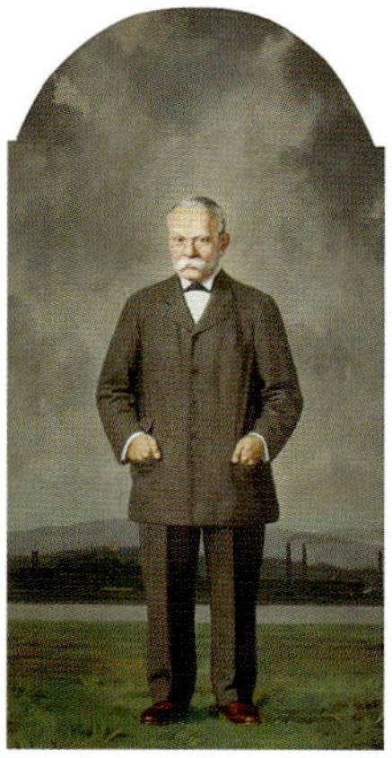

Somerville, Howard 1873–1952
James Williamson (1842–1930), Lord Ashton, DL 1900
oil on canvas 200 x 131 (E)
LTH028

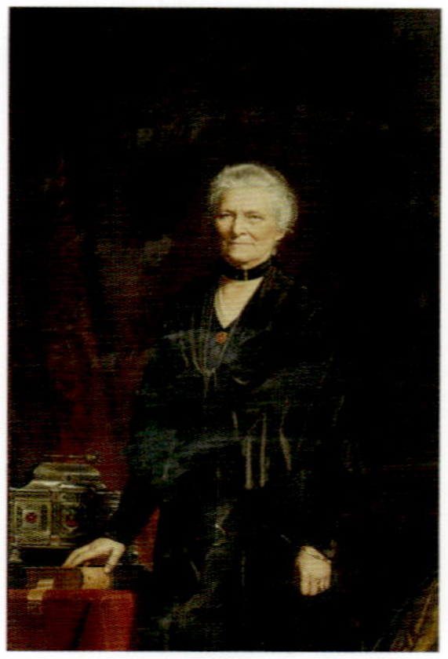

Somerville, Howard 1873–1952
Lady Ashton (d.1944), CBE
oil on canvas 160 x 105
LTH016

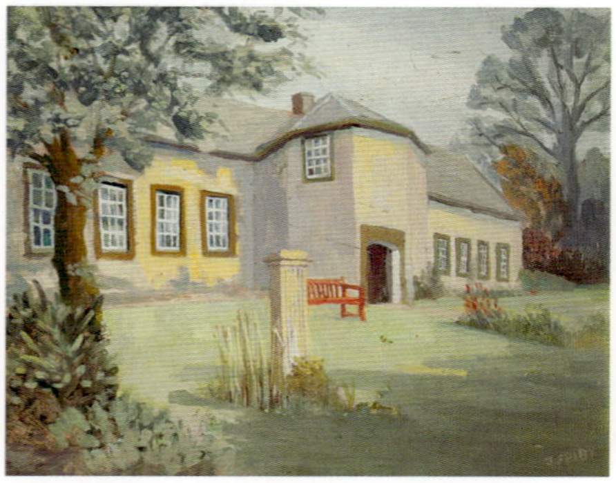

Spiby, J.
Quaker Meeting House, Lancaster
oil on canvas 34.5 x 49
AM28

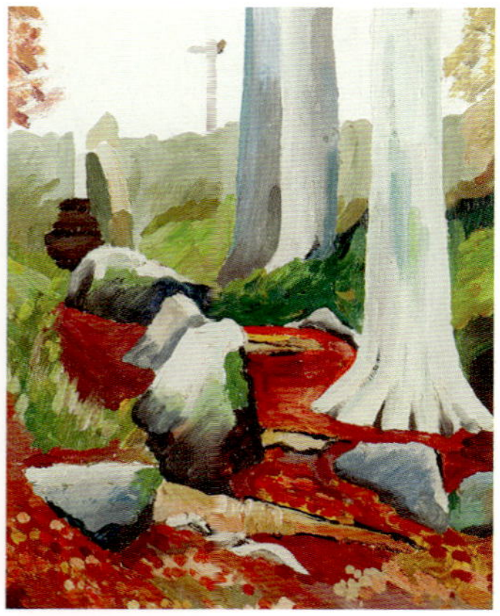

Stafford, Andrew b.1944
Trees in a Rocky Wood
oil on paper 37.5 x 31.3
57.1

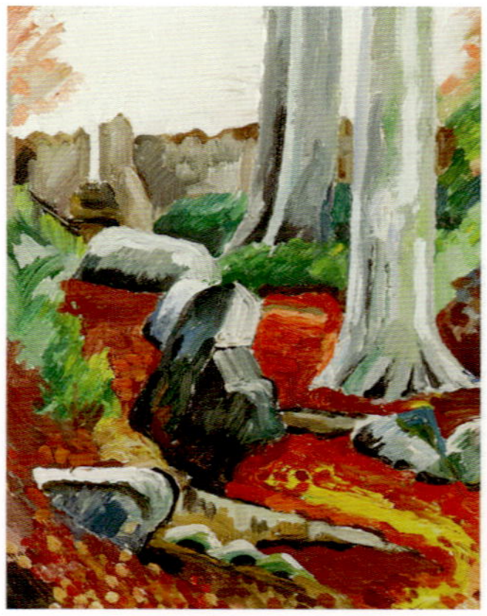

Stafford, Andrew b.1944
Trees in a Rocky Wood
oil on paper 37.5 x 31.3
57.2

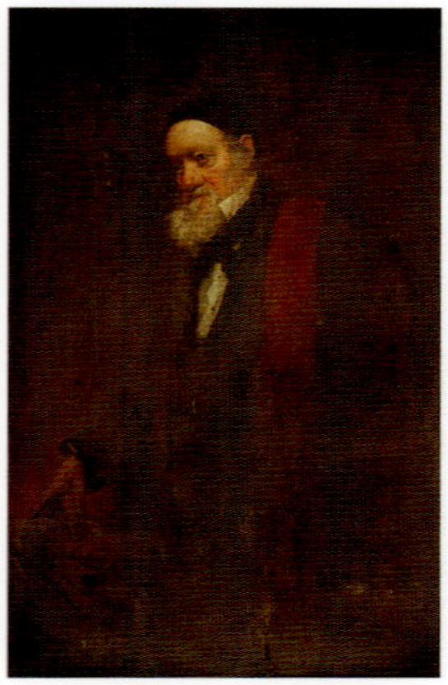

Thaddeus, Henry Jones 1859–1929
Sir Richard Owen (1804–1892), FRS, KGB
oil on canvas 166 x 111
LTH022

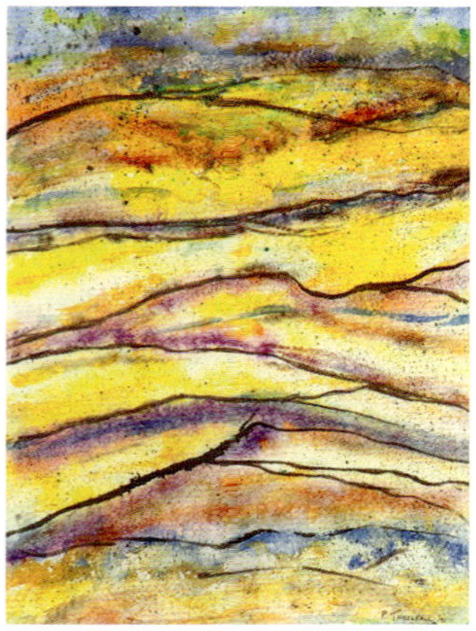

Threlfall, P.
Abstract Landscape 1991
oil on canvas (?) 35.5 x 26.5
33

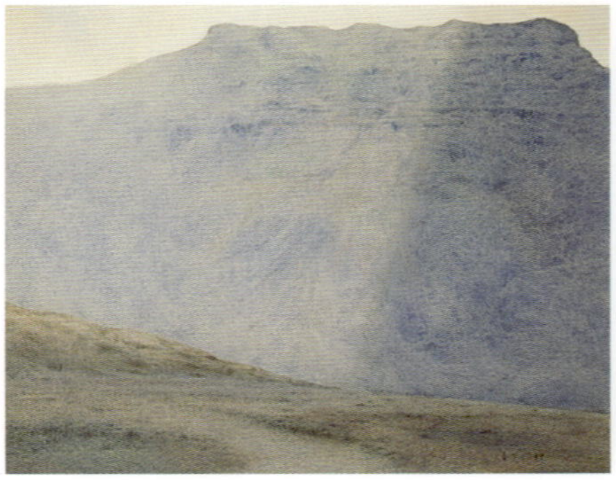

unknown artist
Misty Blue Hillside 1999
oil on paper (?) 24 x 33
44

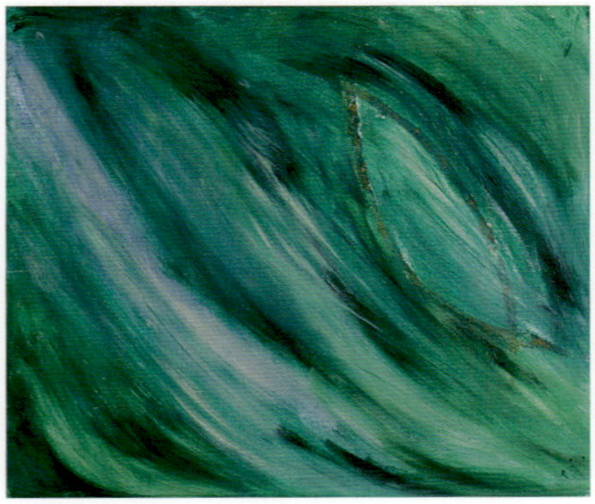

unknown artist
Abstract Green Blue
oil on canvas 41 x 51
11

unknown artist
Abstract Red Black
acrylic (?) on canvas 60 x 30 (E)
68

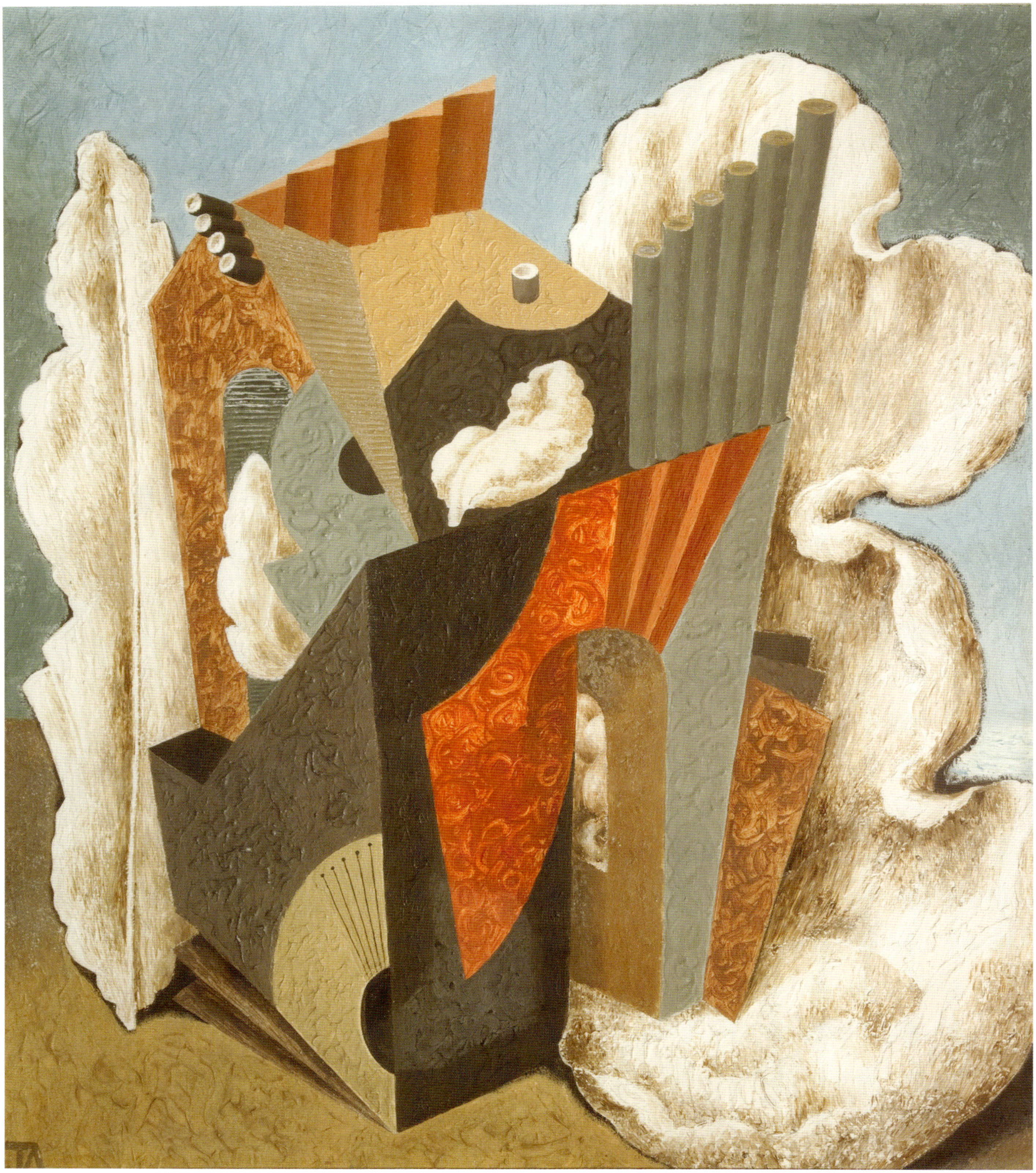

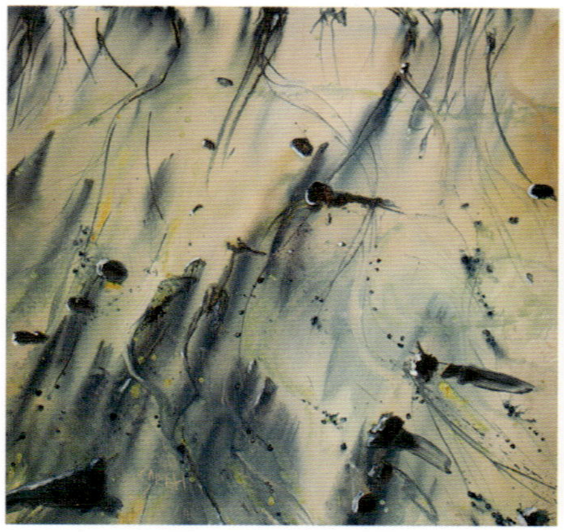

unknown artist
Abstract Underwater Blue Swirl
oil on canvas 121.5 x 106.5
6

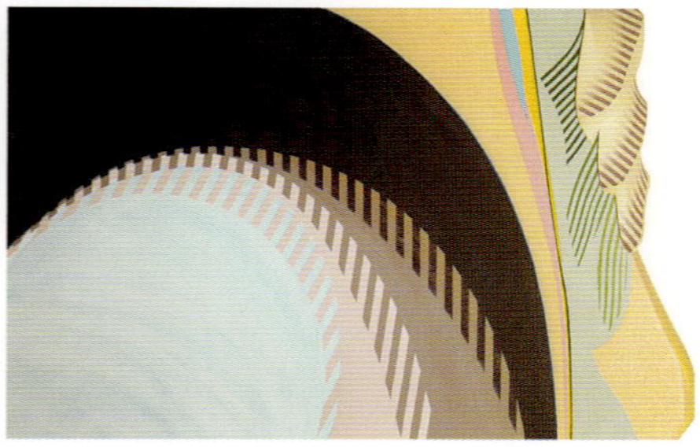

unknown artist
Abstract with Fluted Side
acrylic (?) on canvas 61.5 x 101
4

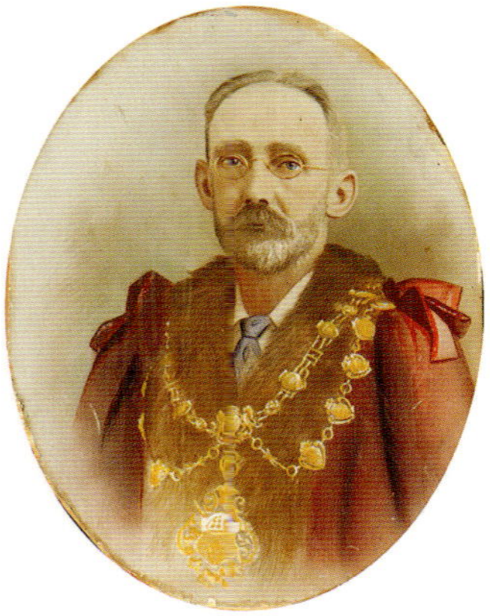

unknown artist
Alcunius Coulthard
oil on card 50 x 40.5
MTH005

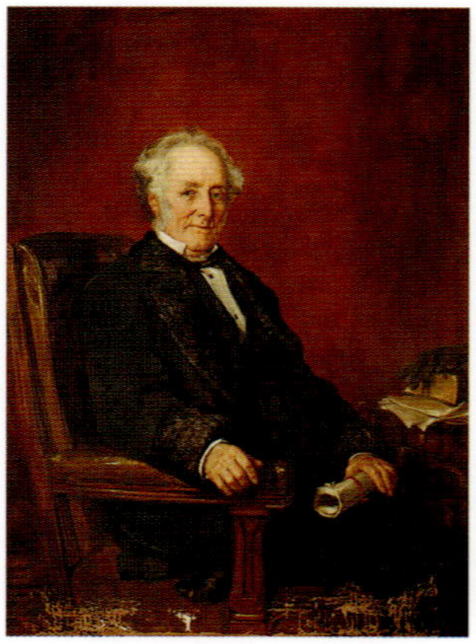

unknown artist
Alderman Greg
oil on canvas 150 x 107 (E)
LTH013

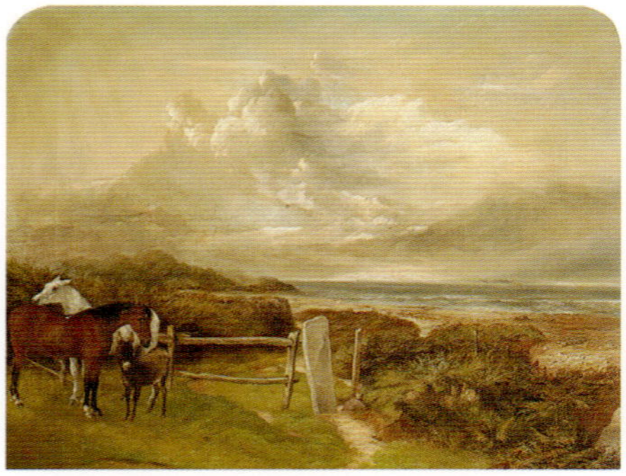

unknown artist
Footpath to Heysham
oil on canvas 43 x 60
MTH003

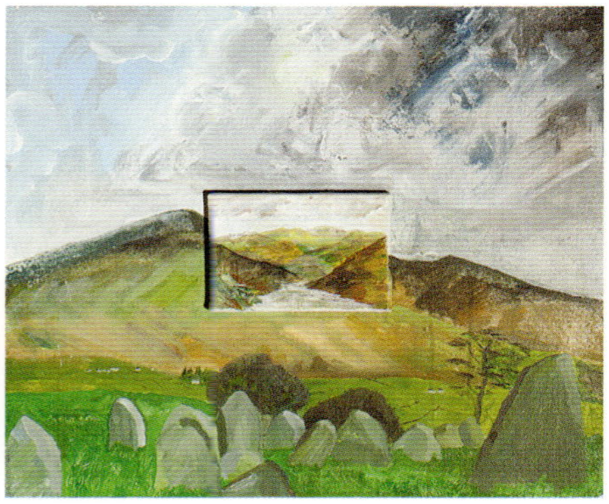

unknown artist
Graveyard with Hills
oil on canvas 35 x 40 (E)
67

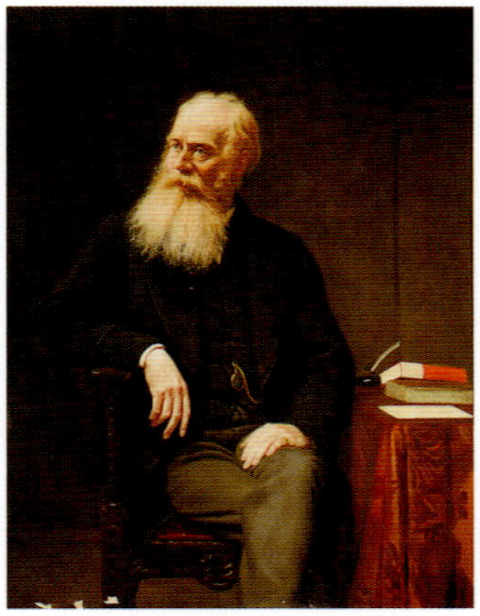

unknown artist
James Williamson, Senior (Alderman Williamson)
oil on canvas 150 x 140 (E)
LTH012

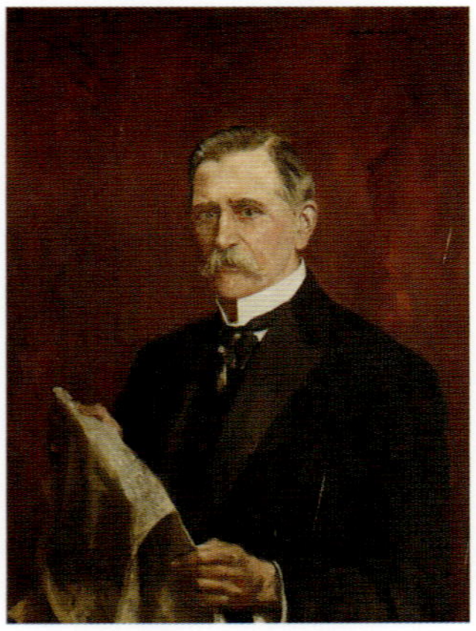

unknown artist
Sir Norval Watson Helme (1849–1932), KT
oil on canvas 90 x 68 (E)
LTH017

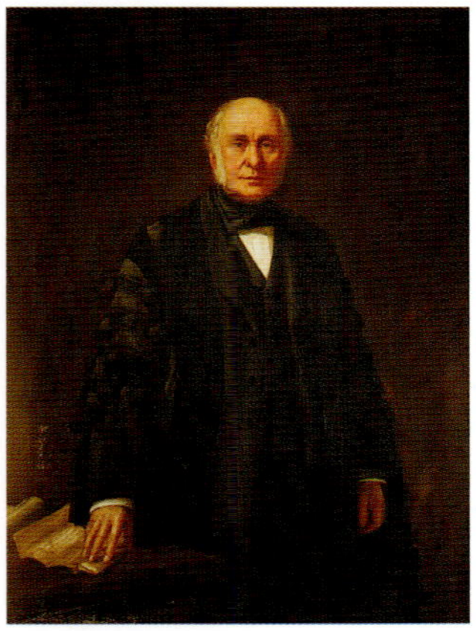

unknown artist
Thomas Swainson
oil on canvas 143 x 110 (E)
LTH002

Facing page: Armstrong, John, 1893–1973, *Abstract*, 1950–1969, Harris Museum & Art Gallery (p. 275)

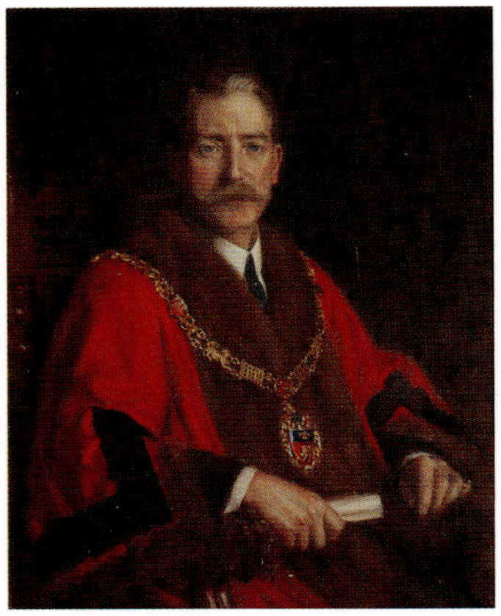

unknown artist
William Briggs
oil on canvas 90 x 68
LTH015

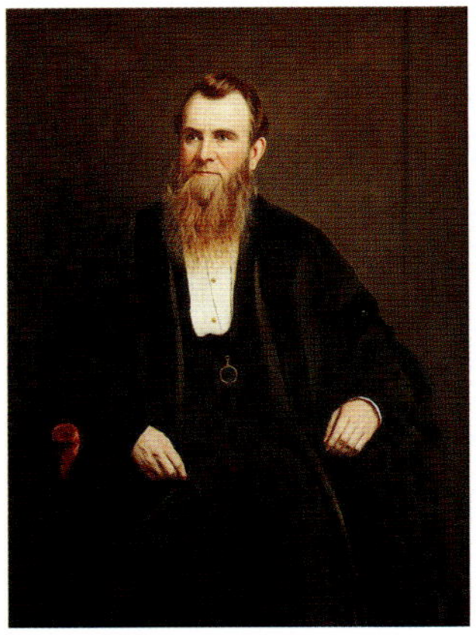

unknown artist
William Storey, JP
oil on canvas 143 x 109
LTH001

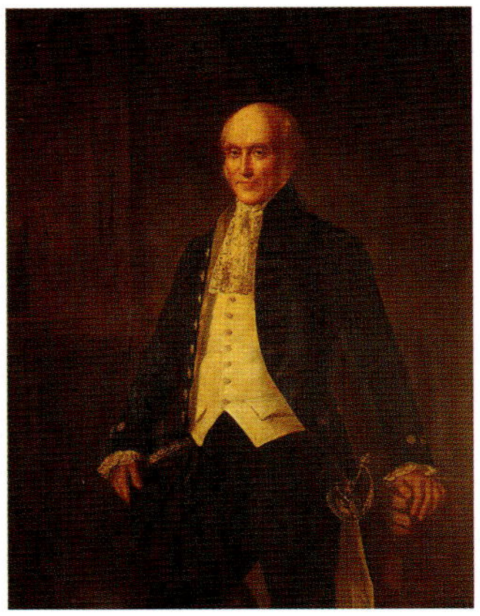

Walker, John Hanson 1844–1933
Thomas Greene
oil on canvas 143 x 109 (E)
LTH005

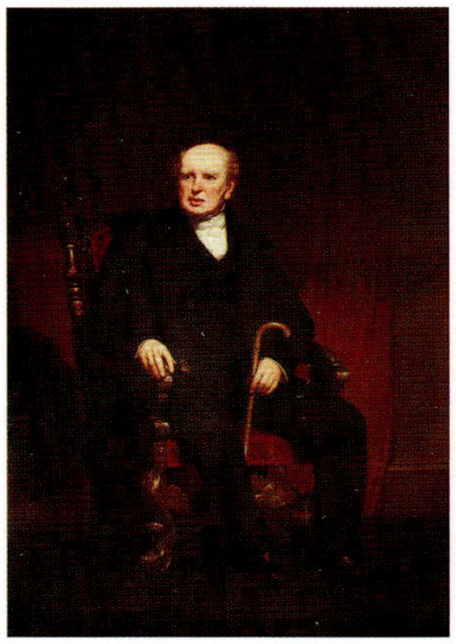

Westcott, Philip 1815–1878
Alderman Leonard Redmayne 1860
oil on canvas 290 x 145 (E)
LTH023

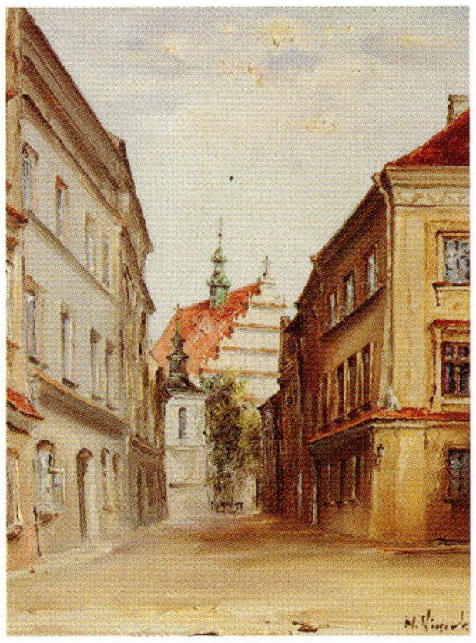

Wiacek, M.
Lublin Street Scene
oil on canvas 30 x 23
LTH030

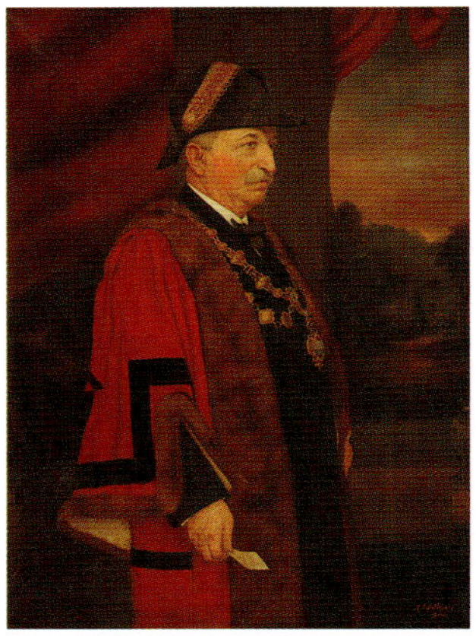

Willman, J.
Ephraim Barnsbee 1903
oil on canvas 123 x 89.5
MTH001

Lancaster City Museums

Lancaster City Museum was established in 1923 in the vacated Georgian Town Hall. In 1985 the Maritime Museum opened in the town's former Custom House, on St George's Quay, designed by Richard Gillow in 1764. The City Museums' collection spans both sites. It has its foundations firmly in the Victorian period. Like most civic collections it owes much to the philanthropy of local industrialists. In Lancaster this fell largely to the energies of Sir Thomas Storey and his family's various businesses. Messrs Storey Brothers were oilcloth and table baize manufacturers with supporting cotton mills. There was also a chemical works and even a fine art print works (Rembrandt Intaglio Printing Company).

In 1887, to mark Queen Victoria's Golden Jubilee, Sir Thomas Storey rebuilt Lancaster's Mechanics' Institute. It was renamed the Storey Institute and opened in 1891, greatly expanded, with a Science and Technology School, an Art Gallery, Library and School for Art. Storey's intension was to provide the local community with high quality education resources enabling them to build better futures.

The opening exhibition included paintings from South Kensington Museum (now the Victoria & Albert Museum) and loans from local collectors; some donated paintings to launch a permanent collection. Amongst these a Lancaster furniture dealer gave the Italian Baroque *The Sacrifice of Isaac*, originally attributed to the seventeenth-century Neapolitan artist Guercino. The painting has been re-assessed by experts at the National Gallery as by a follower of Guercino.

The Storey family were important patrons and collectors of art, donating works purchased at the Royal Academy in London and directly from artists. They supported talented artists and students from Lancashire. The landscape painter, William Hoggatt, found patronage from H. L. Storey, JP, DL to continue his studies in Paris from 1901–1903 before finally settling on the Isle of Man. Samuel John Lamorna Birch came from Liverpool to work in Lancaster and exhibited paintings at the Storey Institute before leaving to study in Paris in 1895. He later moved to Cornwall to join other artists around the coastal village of Lamorna.

In the 1960s the Storey Institute became part of Preston Polytechnic and the collection transferred to the City Museum. The Storey collection covered local, British and European paintings from the eighteenth to the early twentieth century. There are landscape, architectural and narrative subjects such as the North European Reformation scene of *The Conference* (c.1880) by Max Gaisser; the mythological painting of *Penelope* (1891) by Francis Sydney Muschamp; the Aesthetic portrait of *Charlotte Elizabeth Fuller-Maitland of Borwick Hall* (c.1886) by W. Blake Richmond and a notable European example is the 1589 portrait of a *Spanish Noble Woman aged 12*, from the Court of Philip II, by Pantoja de la Cruz.

There are several genre paintings in the collection including *The Water Carriers* by Richard Ansdell; *The Cockler's Return* by local artist John Crane; and *The Reaper and the Flowers* (1876–1878) by Philip Morris with symbolism linked to the Plague Years. *The Picture Book* (1887) by Kate Gray, a domestic and maternal image, is among several works by women artists of the nineteenth and twentieth centuries. Gray was married to the artist Philip Thomson Gilchrist, RBA who lived at Sunderland Point and donated a classical history painting of *Xerxes Burning Athens: Flight of the Athenians* in 1951.

The collection holds portraits by both unidentified and significant artists, dating from the seventeenth century onwards. These include George Romney's *Reverend Oliver Marton, Vicar of Lancaster* and James Lonsdale's series of Dalton family portraits – Catholic landowners with estates in Lancaster and at Thurnham Hall. There are portraits of local Quaker families like the early nineteenth-century portrait of the wife of Robert Lawson Ford of Leeds, *Hannah Benson-Pease (or Mrs Robert Lawson Ford) as a Child* and of Richard Owen – Lancaster-born natural scientist and first Director of the Natural History Museum in London – including one in old age by the Head of the Storey Institute School of Art, W. H. Gilbert.

Landscapes are well represented, particularly eighteenth- and nineteenth-century views of Lancaster and the River Lune, with works by the Lake District painter Julius Caesar Ibbetson; John Henderson of Lancaster; Joseph Farington; Robert W. Salmon; Samuel John Lamorna Birch; William Linton and a view of Heysham by Alfred Waterhouse. More distant landscapes include *The Port of Amsterdam* by Clara Montalba and *The Tower of London* (1897) by Albert Goodwin.

The collection was reinvigorated by the enthusiasm and dedication of Edith Tyson, Curator of Lancaster City Museum from 1965 to1983. She added good examples of modern and contemporary artists. Amongst those she helped acquire are works by Cumbrian artist Sheila Fell *Gathering Sticks in the Snow* (1957); an early figurative work by the Keeper and Professor of Painting at the Royal Academy (1986–2000) Norman Adams, *The Preacher on the Mount* (1961); a painting by the modernist painter Ivon Hitchens *The Red Curtain* (c.1940); and the locally based neo-romantic portrait painter Claude Harrison *Island of Comedians* (1971).

Mrs Tyson also acquired a number of works by contemporary naïve painters; a series of the local silk mill at Galgate by former mill worker Albert Bond; two paintings by Frances Bond including *The Wedding* (1971); and *The Sitting Room* (1983) by Jerzy Marek (aka George Murray). She was also responsible for the acquisition of the first work from Lancaster's twin towns, a painting from 1966 by the French abstract painter, Serge Bonacase, from Perpignan.

Lancaster City Museum continues to build its collections through occasional purchases, donations and bequests. All acquisitions are now made within a formally adopted Acquisitions and Disposals Policy. In the past, however, they varied widely. One of the collection's few religious history paintings, for example, *Joseph Interpreting the Dream of the Chief Baker* (c.1820) by George Hayter was acquired as a gift from the local Mitchell's Brewery in 1946. More recently, a significant collection of works by the Morecambe artist William Woodhouse – a painter of animals, game birds and local landscapes – was bequeathed by the artist's daughter in 1996.

Deborah Keaveney, Temporary Documentation Assistant and Susan Ashworth, Museums' Collections Manager

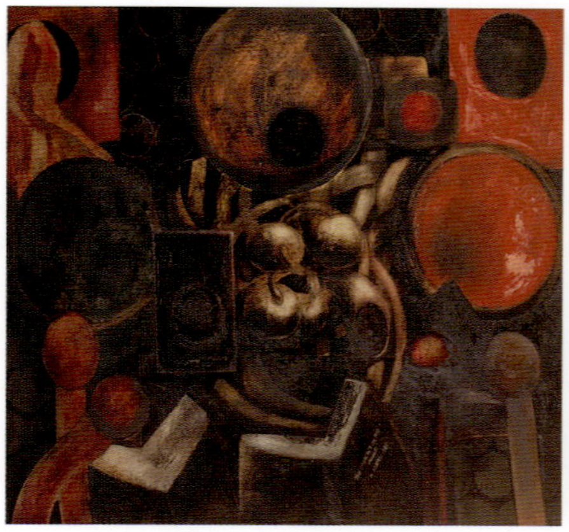

Adams, Norman 1927–2005
The Preacher on the Mount 1961
oil on canvas 87 x 104
LANLM.1973.31.1

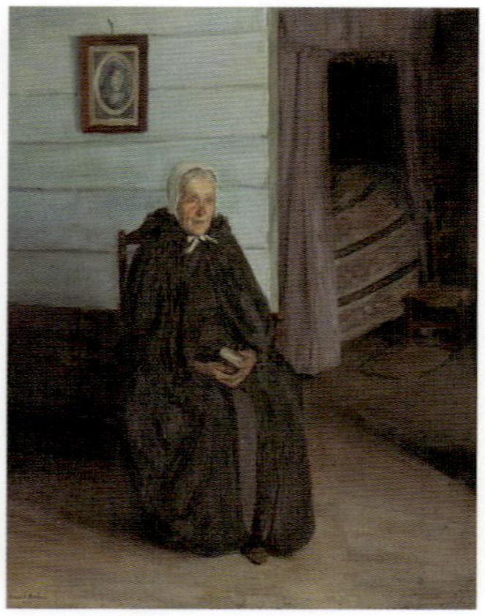

Andre, David
Old Woman 1905
oil on canvas 63.5 x 52
LMA 121

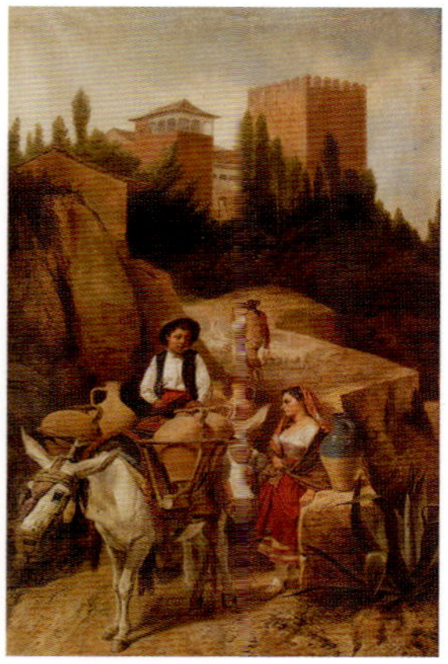

Ansdell, Richard 1815–1885
The Water Carriers 1866
oil on canvas 153 x 97 (E)
LANLM.1911.3

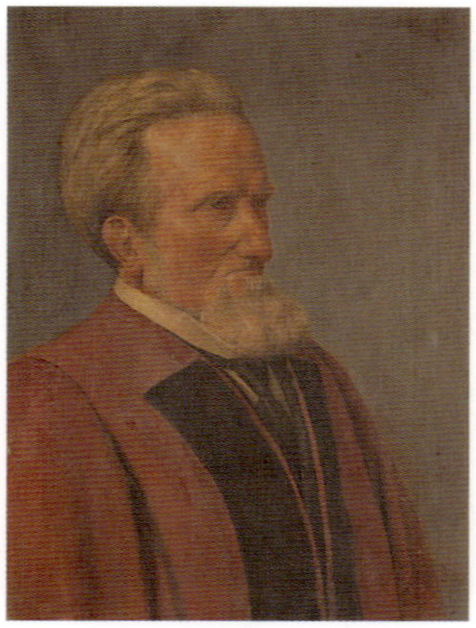

Ashford, G. (attributed to) 1855–1945
Alderman George Bowness 1905
oil on canvas 61 x 46 (E)
LANLM.1974.26.39

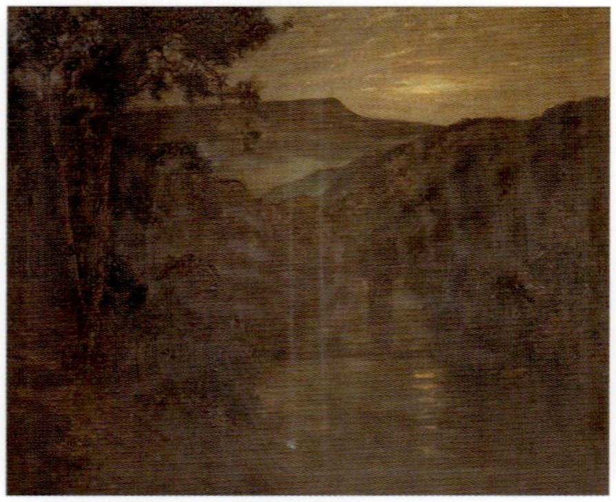

Aspinwall, Reginald 1858–1921
A Dream of the Crook O'Lune c.1880
oil on canvas 100 x 123
LMA 116

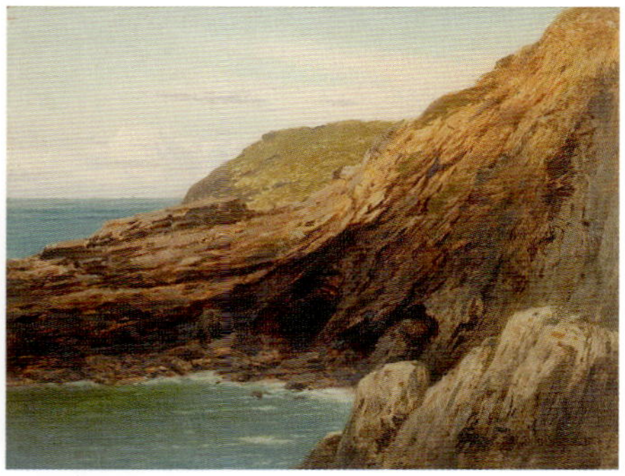

Aspinwall, Reginald 1858–1921
Caves at Tintagel on the Coast of Cornwall c.1880
oil on canvas 23 x 30
LANLM.1951.13

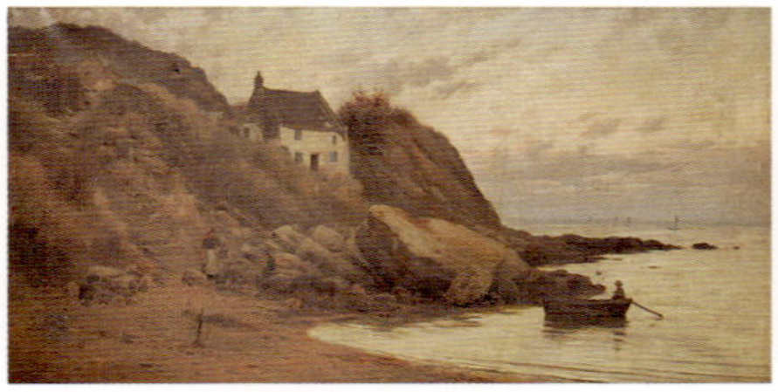

Aspinwall, Reginald 1858–1921
Cottage by the Sea c.1880
oil on canvas 73 x 152
LMA 144

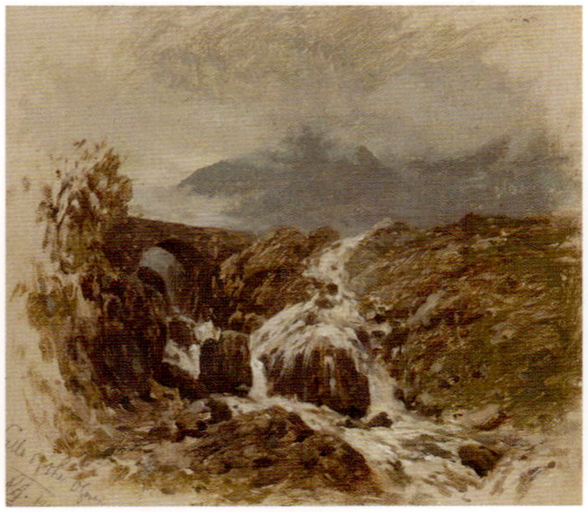

Aspinwall, Reginald 1858–1921
Falls of Ogwen, Nant Ffrancon c.1881
oil on canvas 35 x 37.7
LANLM.1939.2.1

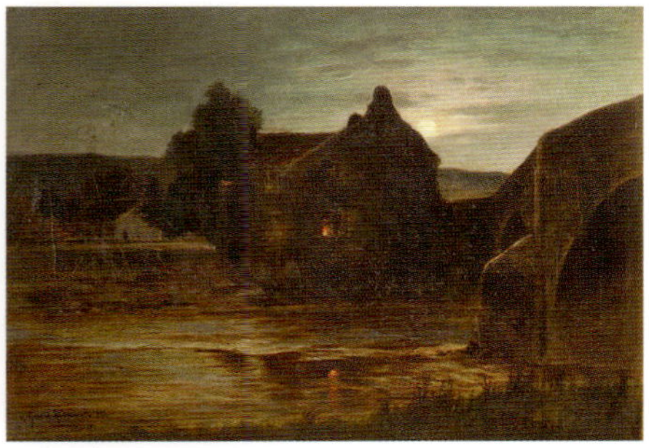

Aspinwall, Reginald 1858–1921
House by a River and a Bridge by Night 1886
oil on canvas (?)
LANLM.1931.6

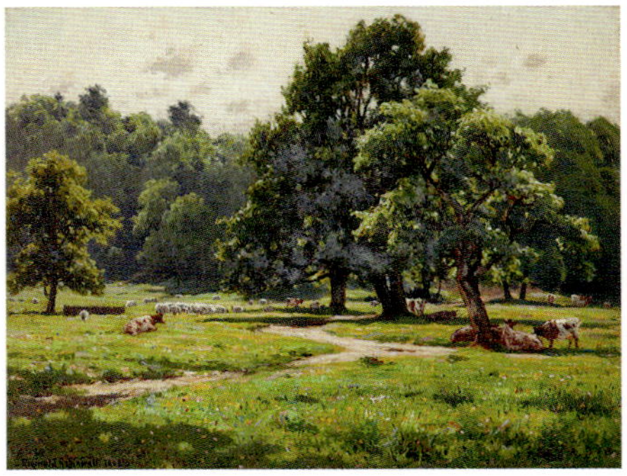

Aspinwall, Reginald 1858–1921
Grassyard Park, Caton 1908
oil on canvas 29.5 x 44.5
LANLM.1939.2.3

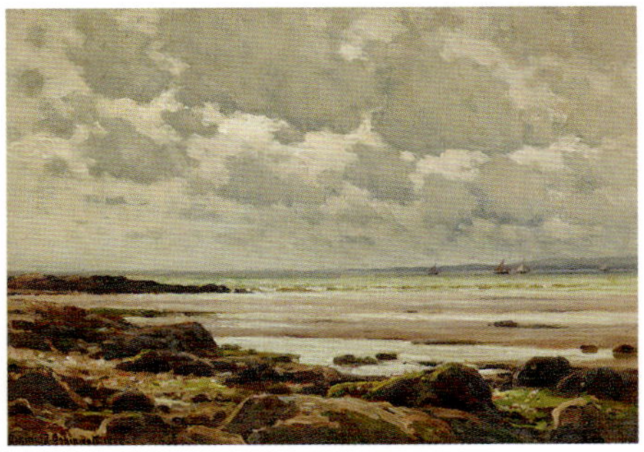

Aspinwall, Reginald 1858–1921
Heysham Shore 1908
oil on canvas 24 x 35 (E)
LANLM.1939.2.2

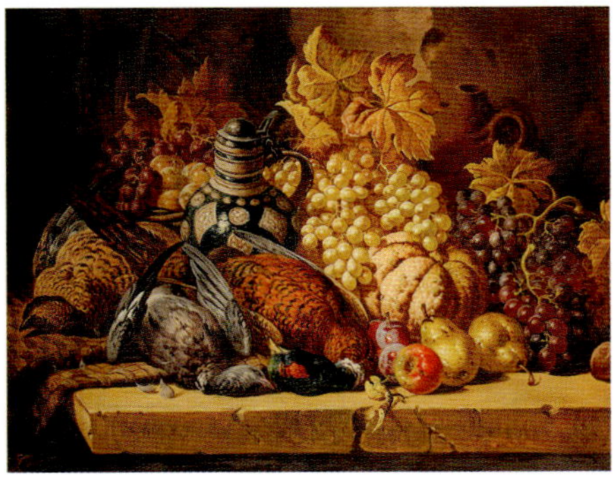

Bale, Charles Thomas 1849–1925
Fruit and Game 1888
oil on canvas 69 x 88
LANLM.1946.16.2

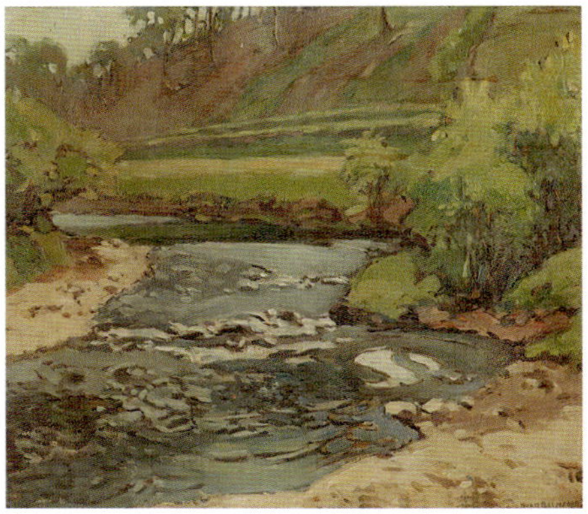

Balmford, Hurst 1871–1950
Near Wray c.1930
oil on canvas 38 x 45
LANLM.1991.2.1

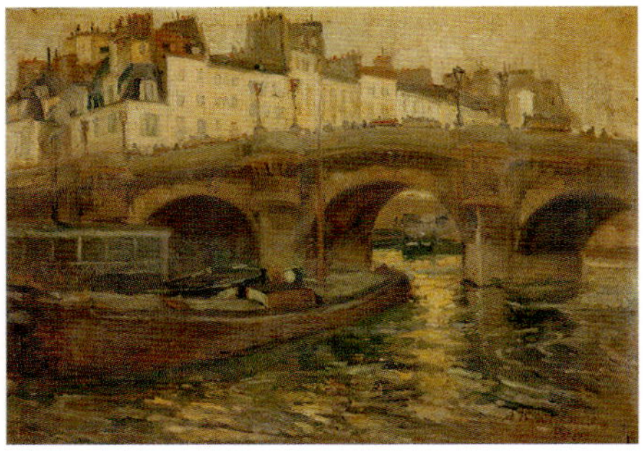

Beaumont, A. active 1860–1900
Paris
oil on canvas 37 x 53
LMA 19

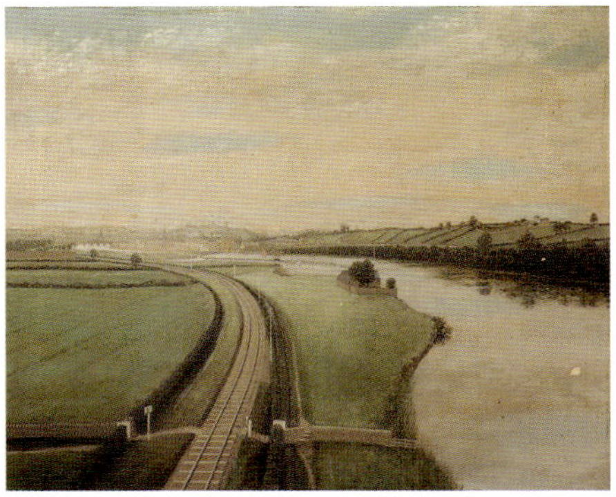

Bell, James 1845–1915
Lancaster from the Aqueduct Bridge c.1880
oil on canvas 46 x 60.5 (E)
LANLM.1948.31.2

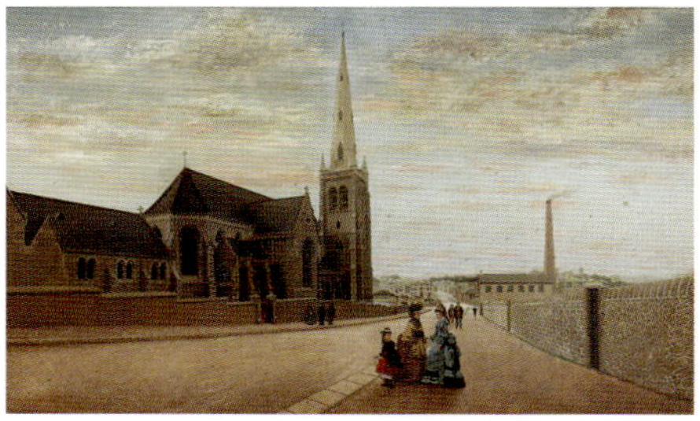

Bell, James 1845–1915
St Peter's Cathedral, East Road, Lancaster c.1880
oil on canvas 84 x 126.4
LANLM.1948.31.3

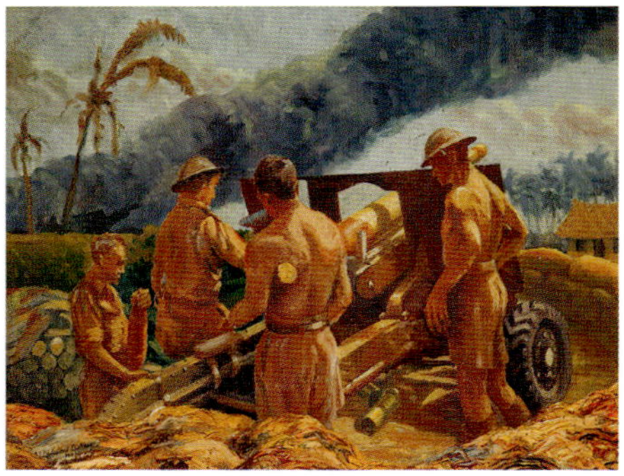

Bettany, Desmond b.1919
The Last Gun Position at Singapore in 1942 (recto) 1946
oil on panel 53 x 74
LANLM.1980.8

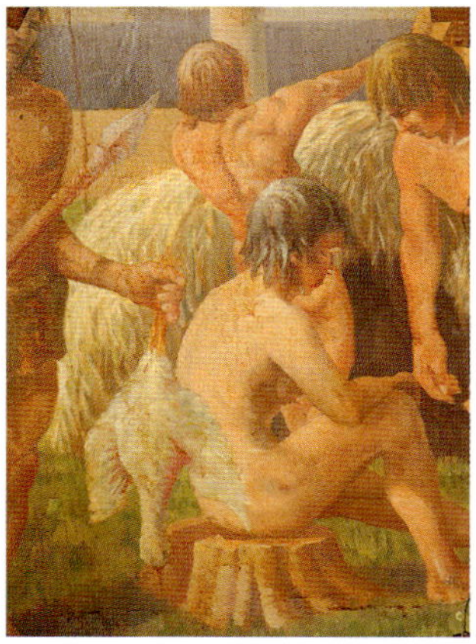

Bettany, Desmond b.1919
Figures with Spear and Goose (verso)
oil on panel 74 x 53
LANLM.1980.8.1

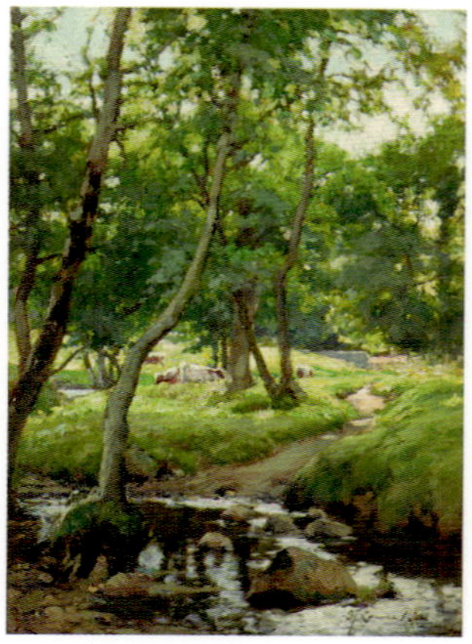

Birch, Samuel John Lamorna 1869–1955
Caton 1895
oil on board 35.5 x 25.5 (E)
LANLM.1975.36.5

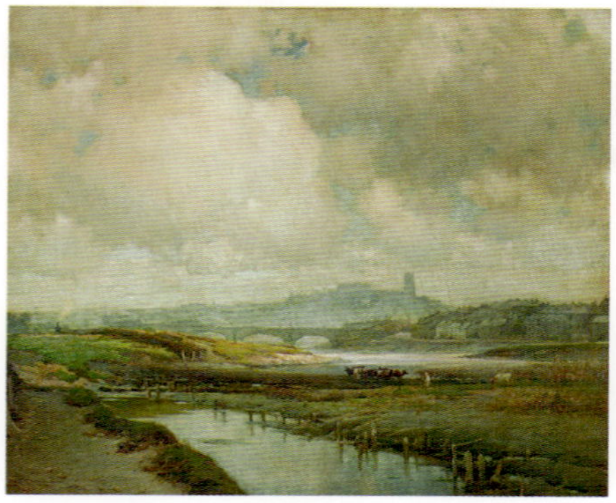

Birch, Samuel John Lamorna 1869–1955
Lancaster 1903
oil on canvas 119 x 150
LANLM.1907.4.1

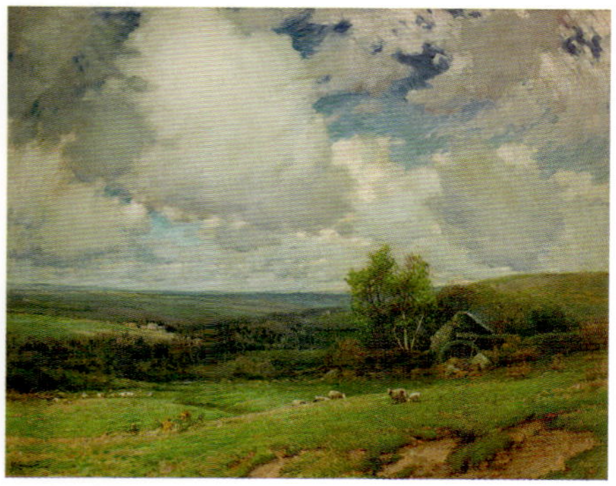

Birch, Samuel John Lamorna 1869–1955
Spring in the Lune Valley 1904
oil on canvas 86 x 119
LANLM.1914.1

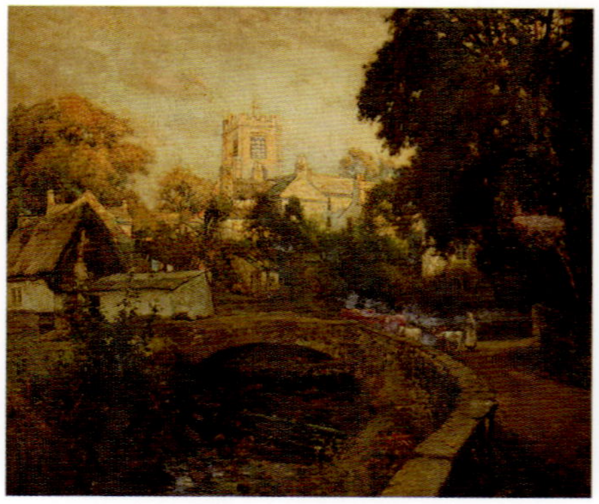

Birch, Samuel John Lamorna 1869–1955
Brookhouse 1906
oil on canvas 90.5 x 122.5
LANLM.1953.491.3

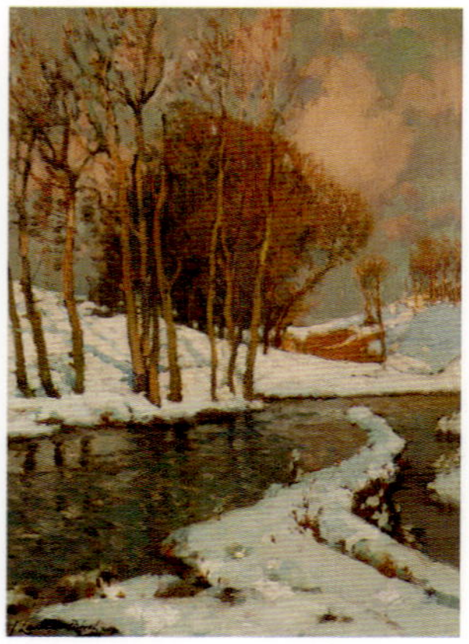

Birch, Samuel John Lamorna 1869–1955
Trees in the Snow by a River 1906
oil on board 44.4 x 33.7 (E)
LANLM.1975.36.3

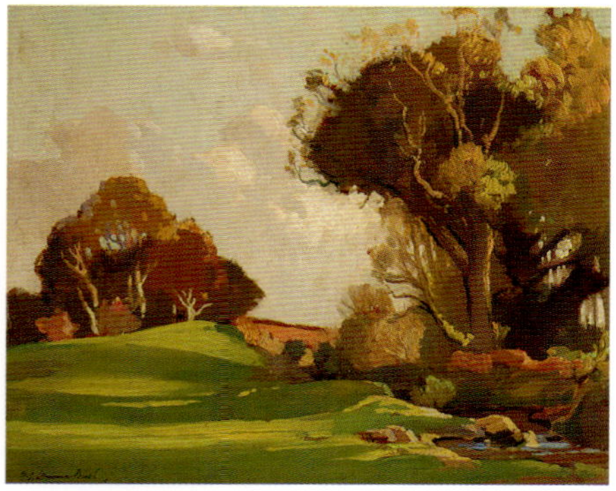

Birch, Samuel John Lamorna 1869–1955
Landscape with Trees c.1906
oil on board 29 x 38.5 (E)
LANLM.1975.36.7

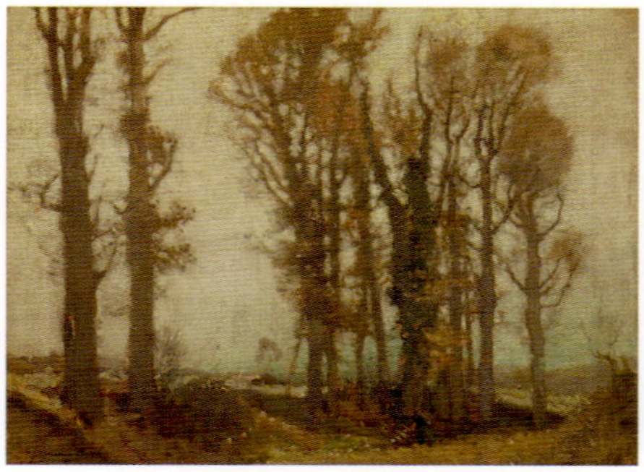

Birch, Samuel John Lamorna 1869–1955
Trees, Sombre Tones c.1906
oil on canvas 37 x 50 (E)
LANLM.1975.36.4

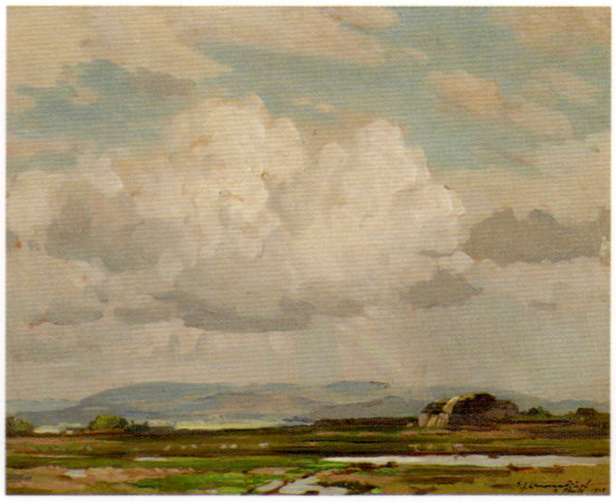

Birch, Samuel John Lamorna 1869–1955
Moorland, Distant Hills 1928
oil on board 31.5 x 39.3 (E)
LANLM.1975.36.6

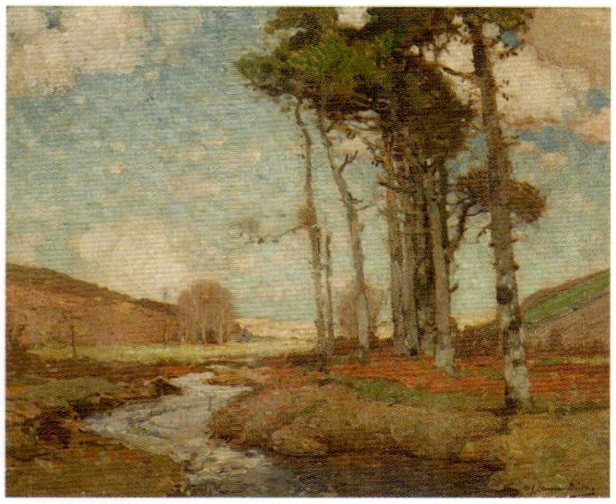

Birch, Samuel John Lamorna 1869–1955
Trees by a Moorland stream c.1928
oil on canvas 46.2 x 61.6 (E)
LANLM.1975.36.1

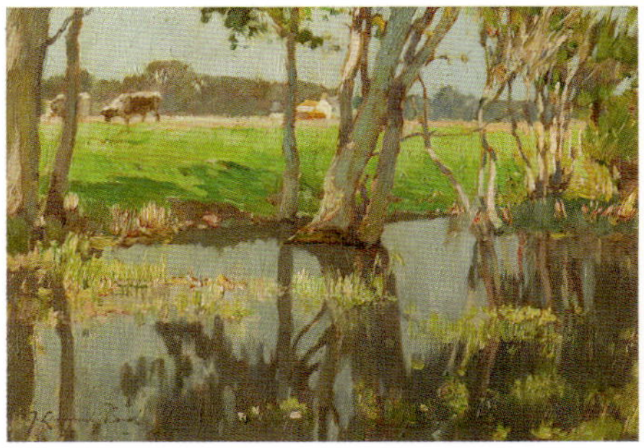

Birch, Samuel John Lamorna 1869–1955
Stream, Trees, Pastureland c.1930
oil on canvas 14.7 x 22 (E)
LANLM.1975.36.8

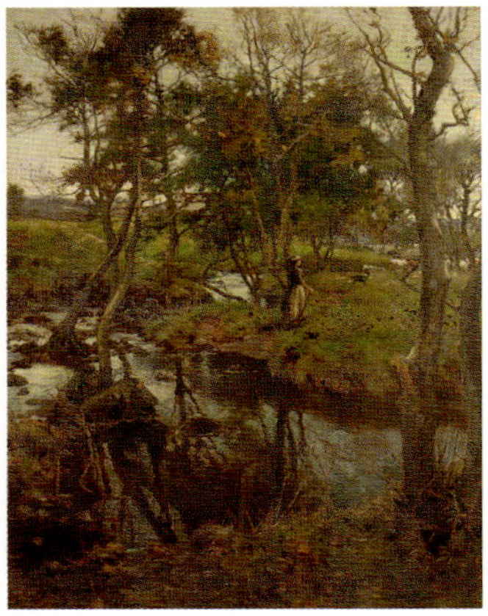

Birch, Samuel John Lamorna 1869–1955
Evensong: the Brook at Halton Green
oil on canvas 117 x 88.5 (E)
LMA 20

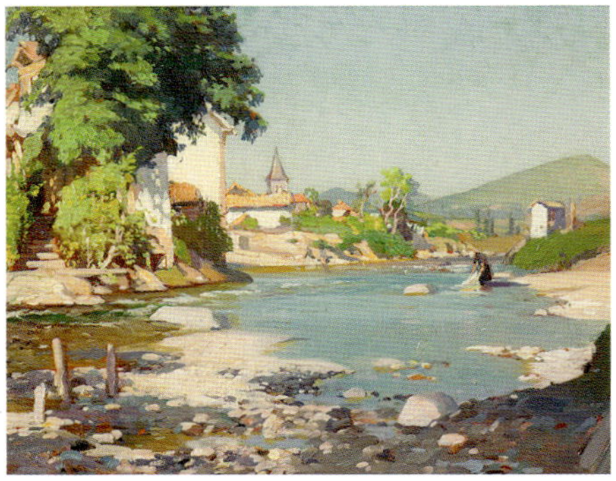

Birch, Samuel John Lamorna 1869–1955
St Jean Pied de Port, Basse Pyrenees
oil on board
LANLM.1975.36.2

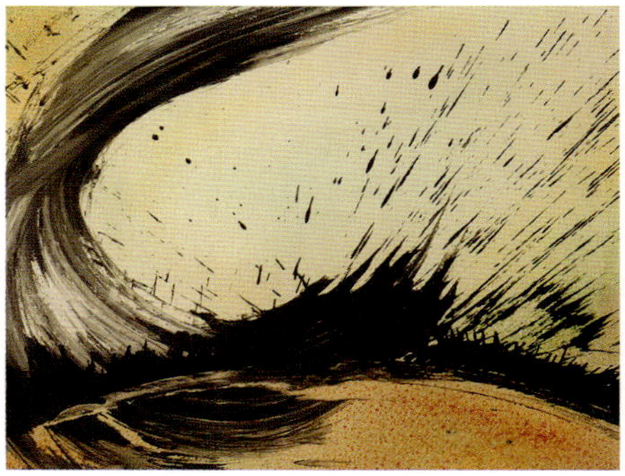

Bonacase, Serge b.1924
Rythme de la vie, No.18 1966
oil on canvas 50 x 61 (E)
LANLM.1983.47

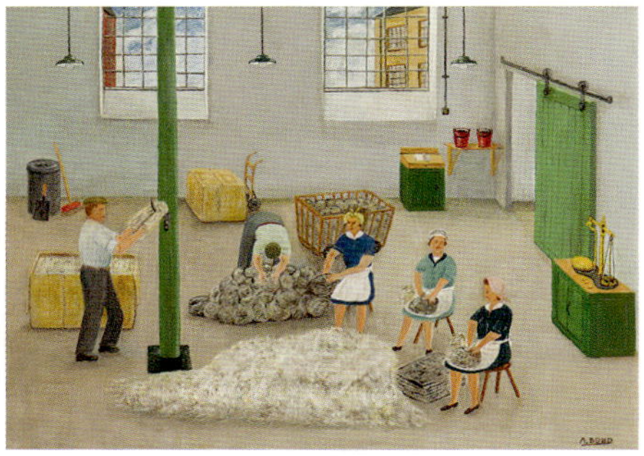

Bond, Albert 1905–1998
Opening and Bagging of Raw Silk Waste at Galgate Silk Mill 1972
acrylic on board 30.5 x 41.3 (E)
LANLM.1983.42.1

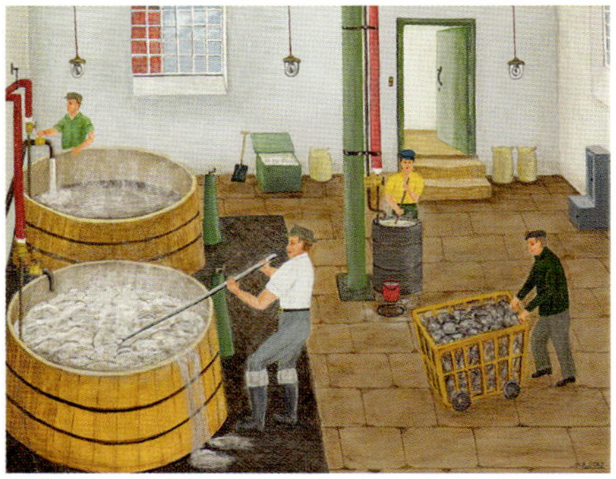

Bond, Albert 1905–1998
De-Gumming Raw Silk Waste at Galgate Silk Mill 1973
acrylic on board 30 x 40 (E)
LANLM.1983.42.2

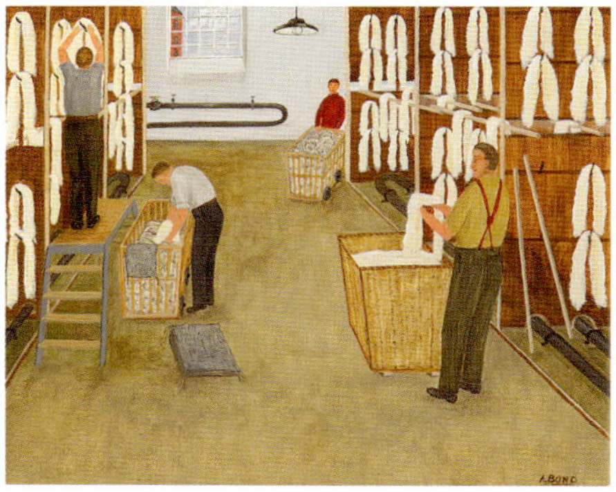

Bond, Albert 1905–1998
The Drying Loft at Galgate Silk Mill 1973
acrylic on board 30 x 40 (E)
LANLM.1983.42.3

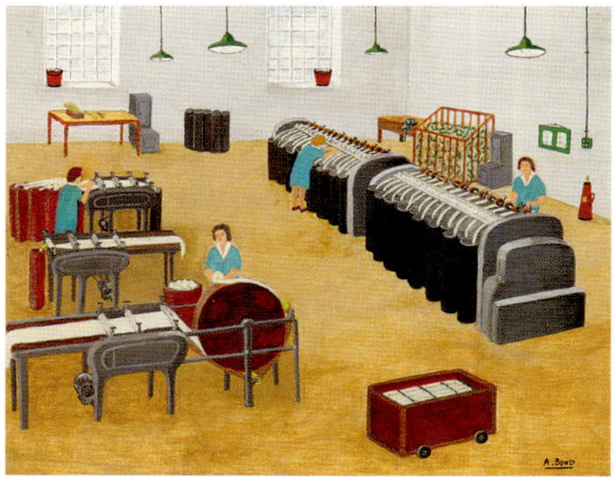

Bond, Albert 1905–1998
Drawing and Gillroving at Galgate Silk Mill 1975
acrylic on board 30 x 40 (E)
LANLM.1983.42.5

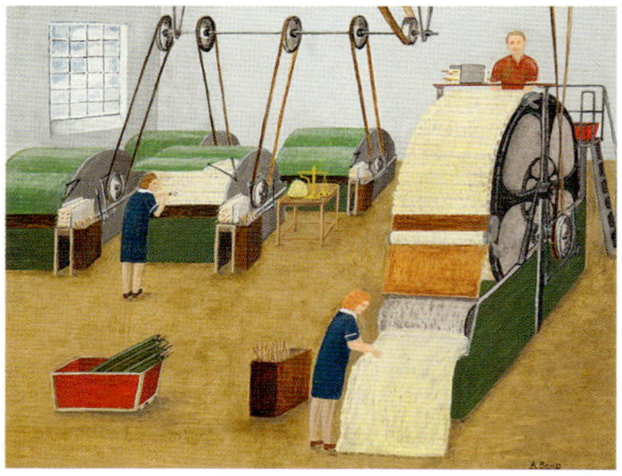

Bond, Albert 1905–1998
Silk Dressing at Galgate Mill 1976
acrylic on board 30 x 40 (E)
LANLM.1983.42.4

Facing page: Knight, Laura, 1877–1970, *A Musical Clown,* 1930, Harris Museum & Art Gallery (p. 316)

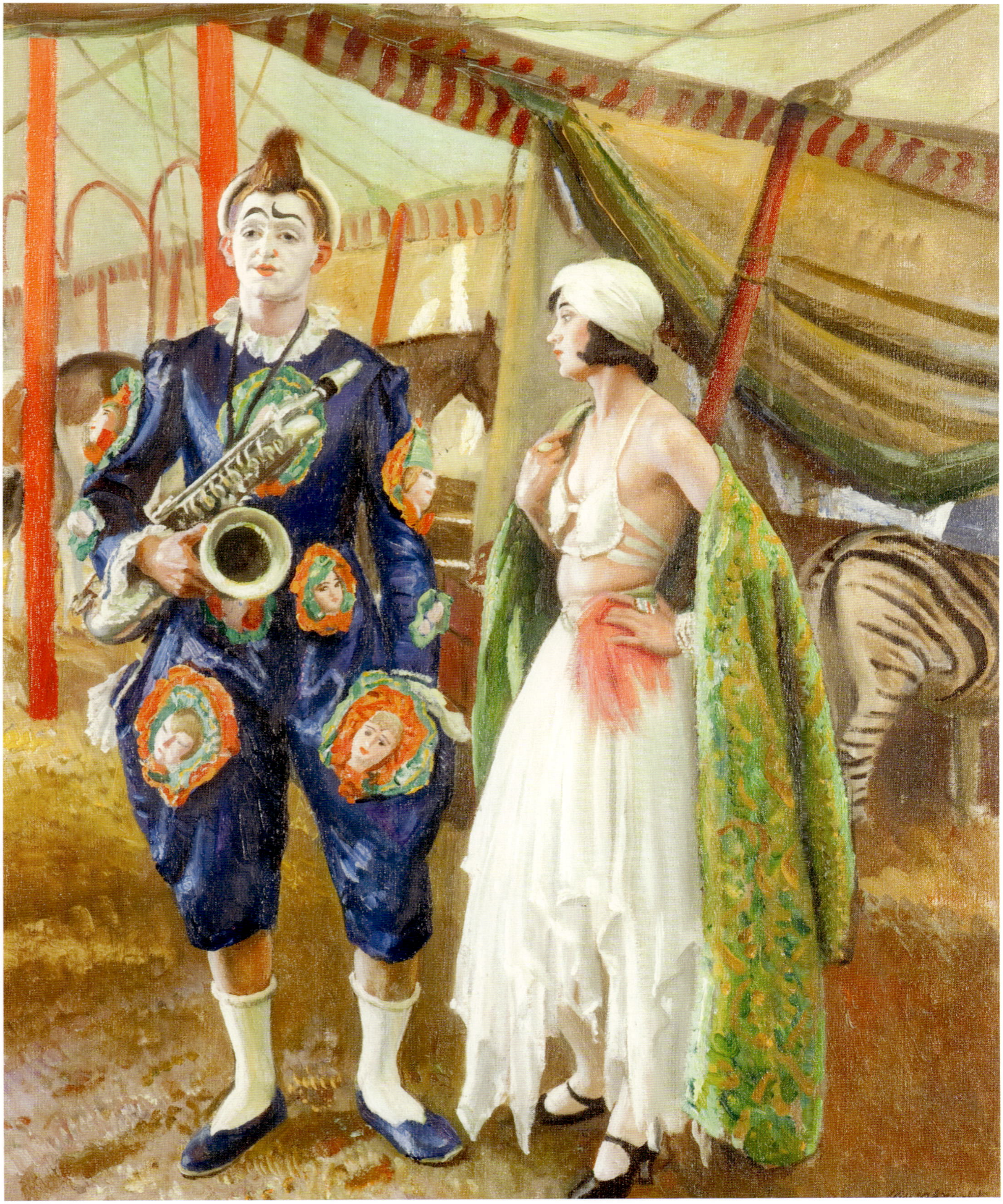

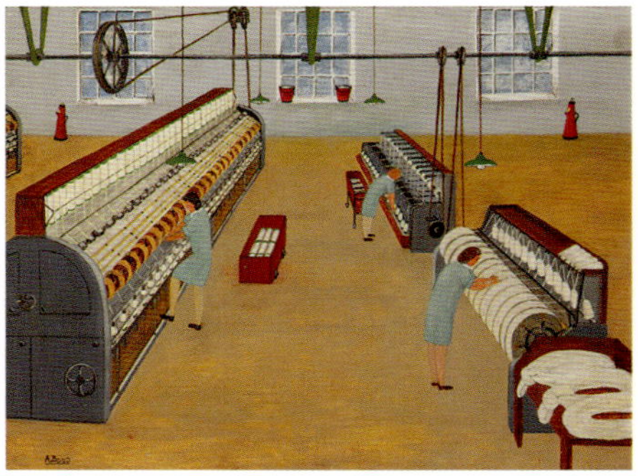

Bond, Albert 1905–1998
Spinning, Assembly Winding and Reeling, Galgate Silk Mill 1976
acrylic on board 30 x 40 (E)
LANLM.1983.42.6

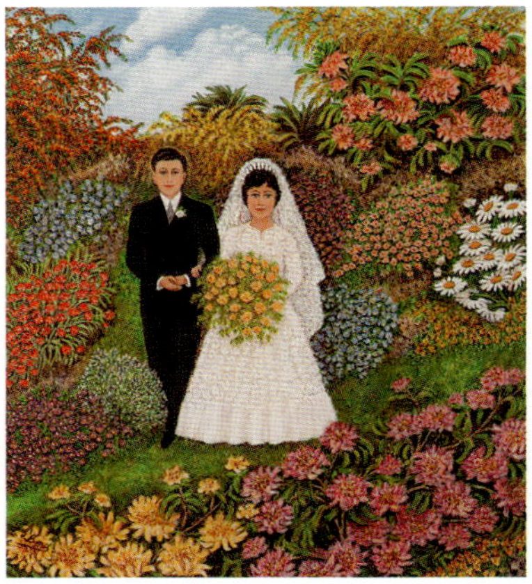

Bond, Frances 1905–1978
The Wedding 1971
acrylic on board 41.5 x 38 (E)
LANLM.1983.42.7

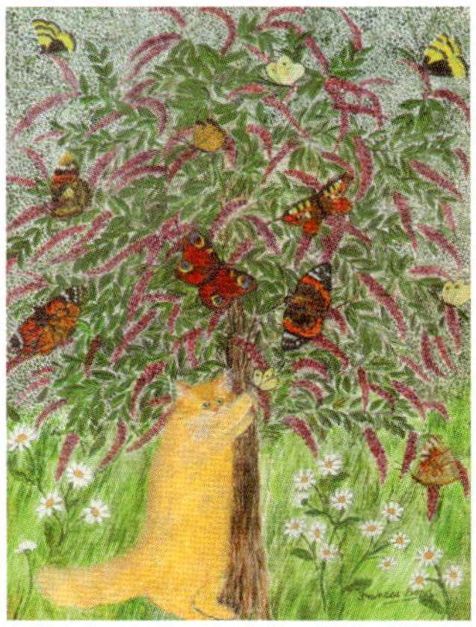

Bond, Frances 1905–1978
The Butterfly Tree 1977
acrylic on board 40.7 x 30.3 (E)
LANLM.1981.3.1

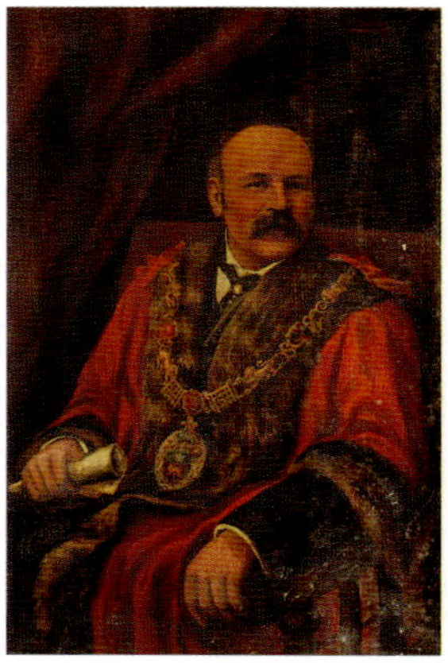

Bradshaw, E. 1871–1955
William Huntington, Esq. 1901
oil 91.5 x 61 (E)
LANLM.1948.19

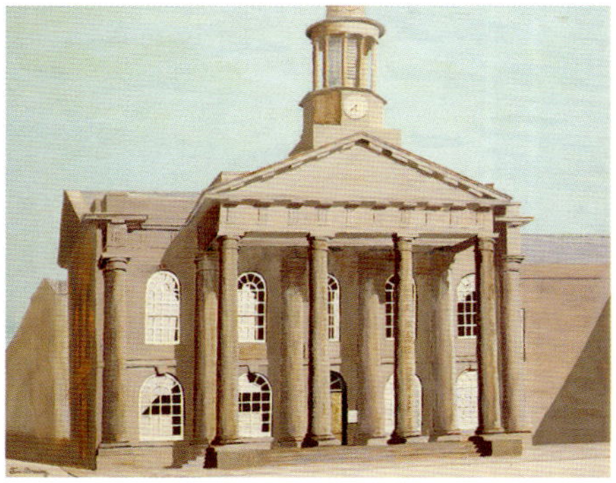

Brealey, John
The Old Town Hall, Lancaster c.1890
oil on board 45.5 x 61 (E)
LANLM.1986.167

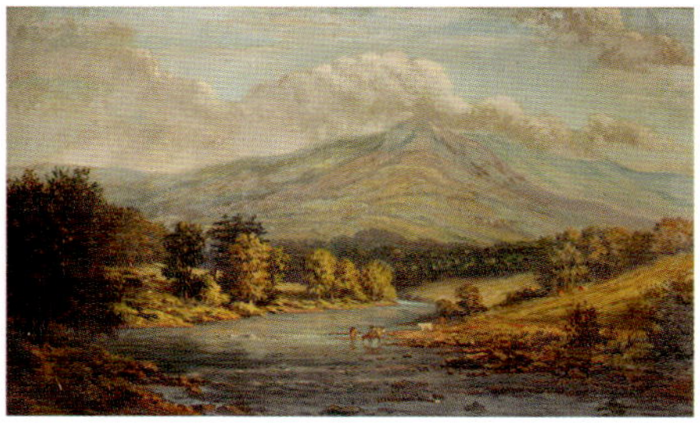

Brighton, T.
Near Lowgill 1901
oil on canvas 74 x 124 (E)
LANLM.1947.36

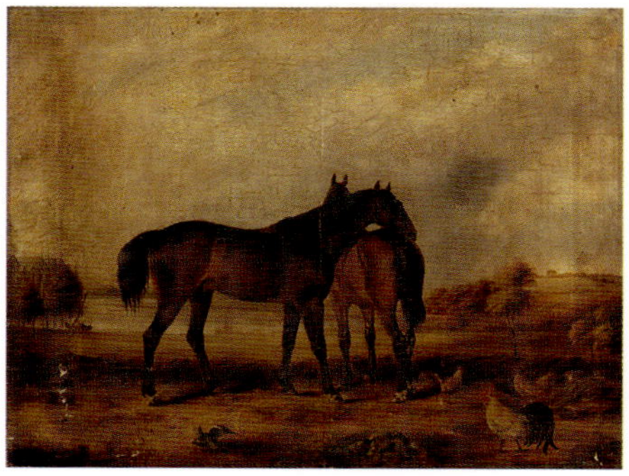

Brown, R. G. 1815–1905
Two Horses Belonging to John Armstrong 1845
oil on canvas 45.8 x 60.8
LANLM.1935.29.2

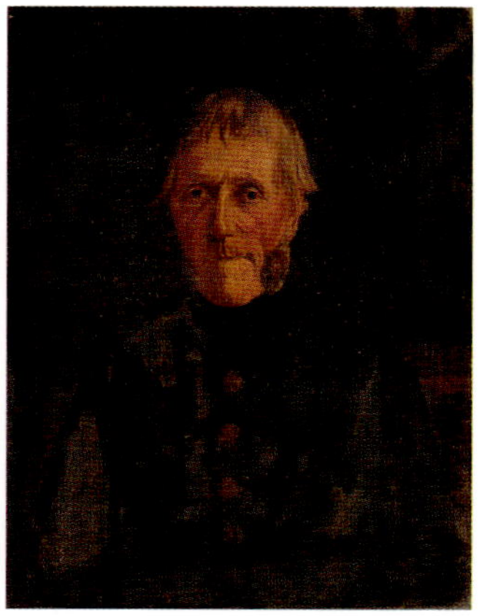

Brown, R. G. 1815–1905
Self Portrait 1855
oil on canvas 58.5 x 48.5 (E)
LANLM.1952.3

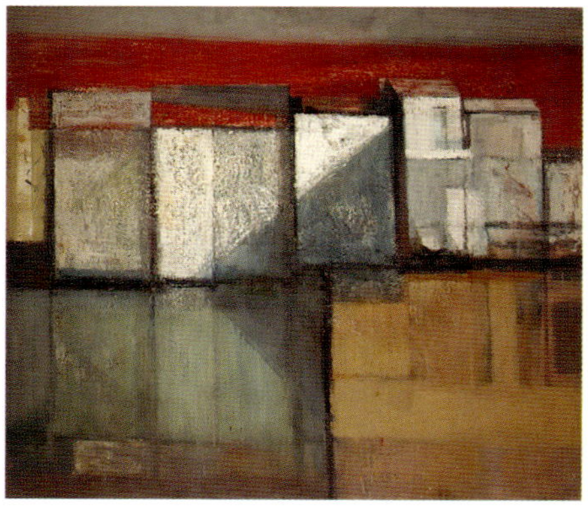

Bull, Michael b.1925
Ancient Buildings 1962
oil on board 91 x 122 (E)
LANLM.1986.38

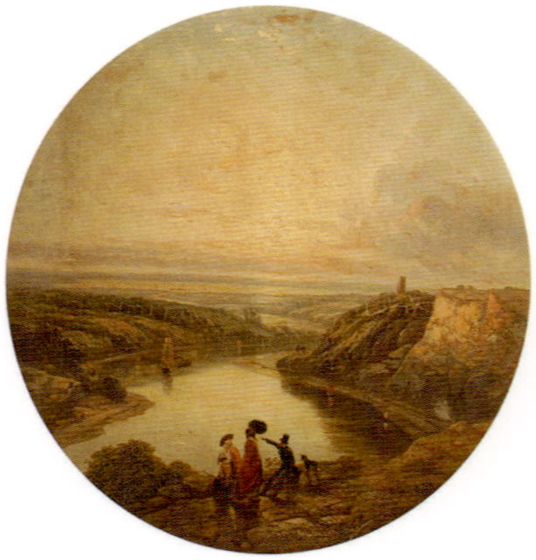

Carter, William 1863–1939
The Avon, Severn and Welsh Hills c.1893
oil on canvas 91 x 91
LANLM.1935.43

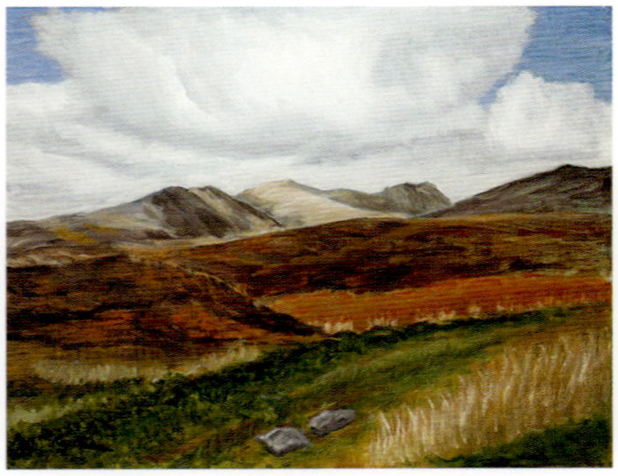

Chesterman, Ross 1909–1999
Towards Scafell, Cumbria c.1987
oil on board 44 x 58.5
LANLM.1999.85

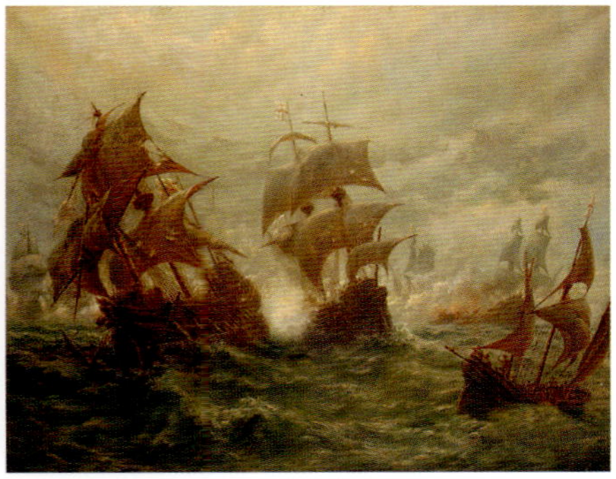

Clarke Marshall, J.
Entertaining the Dons, 1588 1893
oil on canvas 64 x 88.5
LANLM.1893.3

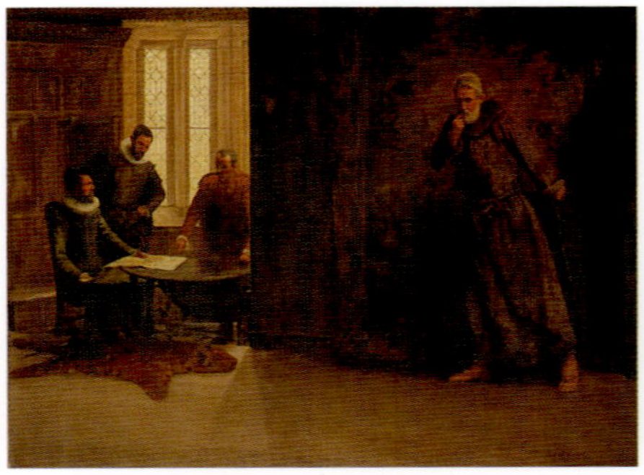

Craft, Percy Robert 1856–1934
Walls Have Ears 1880–1934
oil on canvas 72.7 x 103.8 (E)
LANLM.1936.23

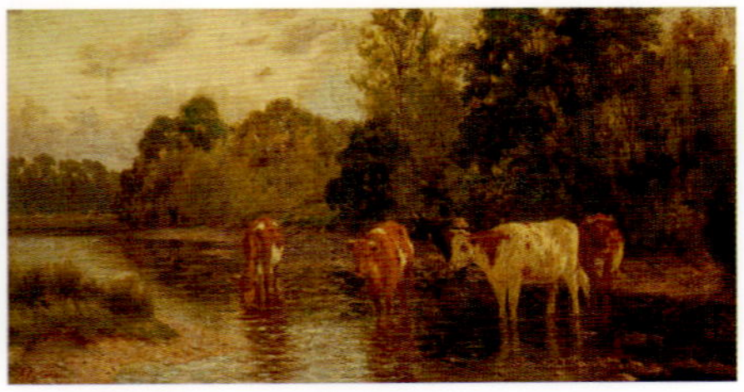

Crane, John 1850–1915
Cattle in a Shallow Stream c.1880
oil on canvas 30 x 57
LANLM.1982.33

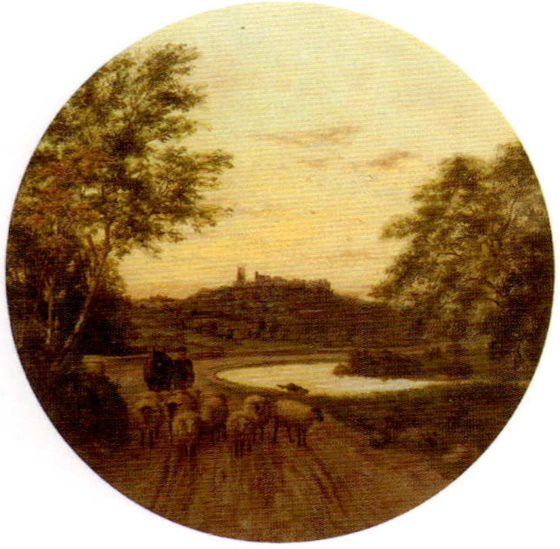

Crane, John 1850–1915
Lancaster from the Canal 1882
oil on panel 47.3 x 47.4 (E)
LANLM.1965.36.1

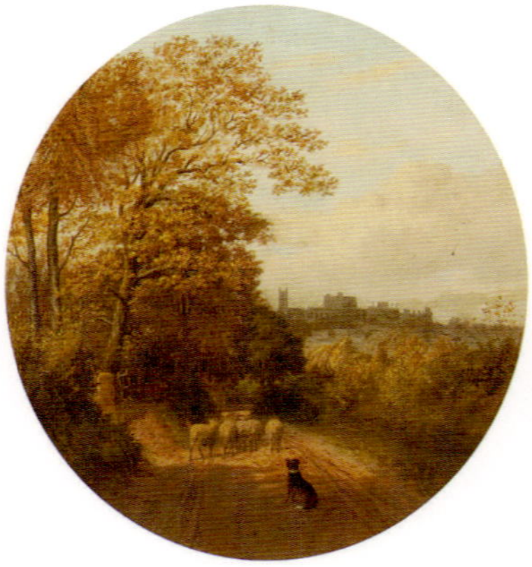

Crane, John 1850–1915
Lancaster from the North West 1882
oil on panel 47.3 x 47.4
LANLM.1965.36.2

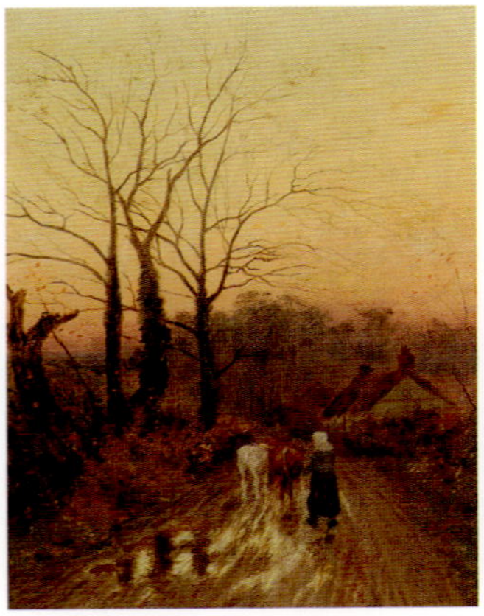

Crane, John 1850–1915
Driving Cattle at Dusk c.1890
oil on board 47.1 x 37.6 (E)
LANLM.1991.11.3

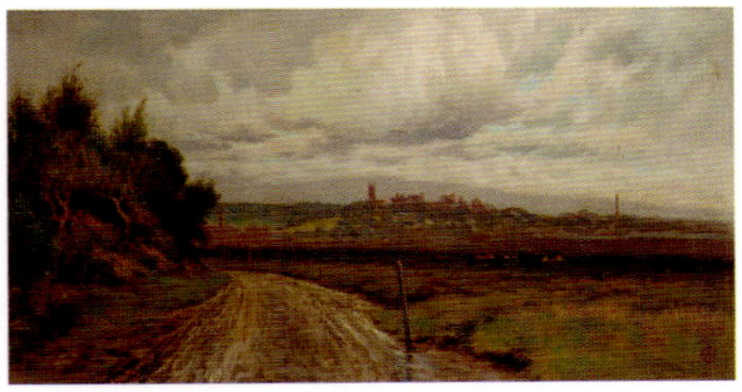

Crane, John 1850–1915
Lancaster from Scratchems c.1890
oil on board 31.2 x 50.2 (E)
LANLM.1988.11

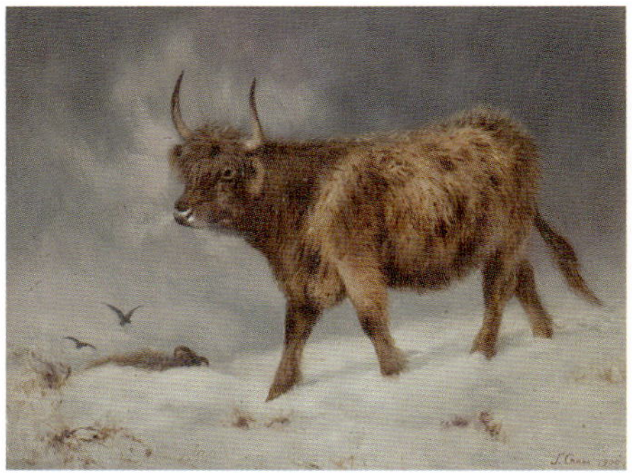

Crane, John 1850–1915
Highland Cow in the Snow 1900
oil on canvas 25 x 33
LANLM.1991.11.4

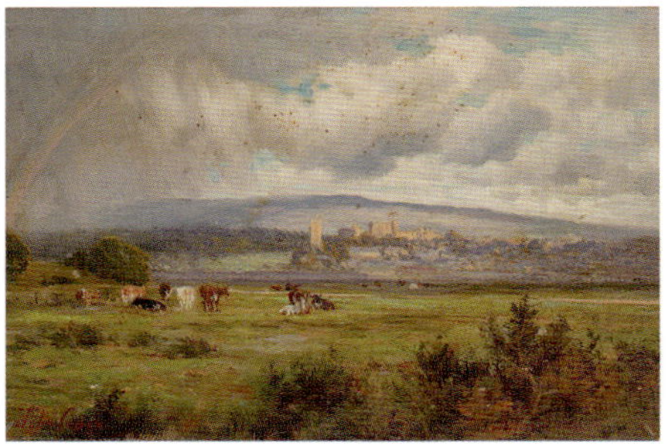

Crane, John 1850–1915
Distant View of Lancaster from the West c.1900
oil on board 16 x 21
LANLM.1975.36.27

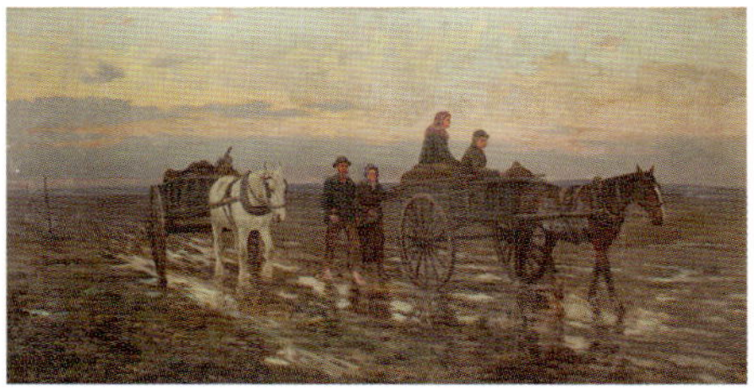

Crane, John 1850–1915
The Cockler's Return
oil on canvas 76 x 150
LANLM.1917.5

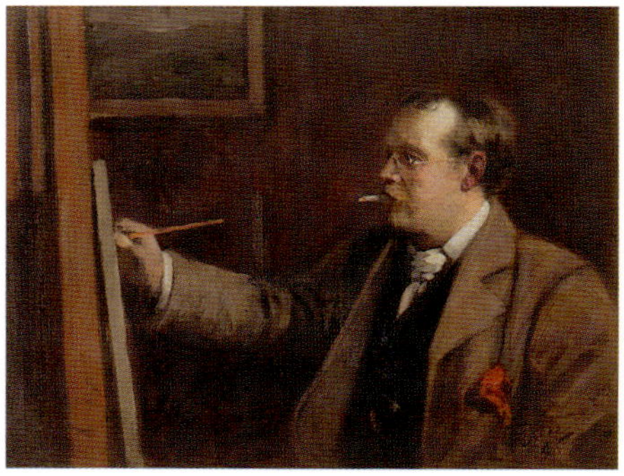

Cross, Joseph 1851–1897
Reginald Aspinwall (1858–1921) 1895
oil on canvas
LANLM.1956.20

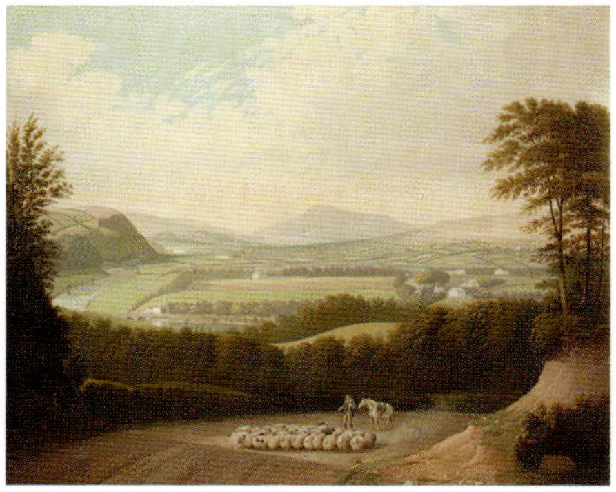

Cuitt the younger, George 1779–1854
Vale of Lonsdale
oil on canvas 56 x 72
LANLM.1989.9

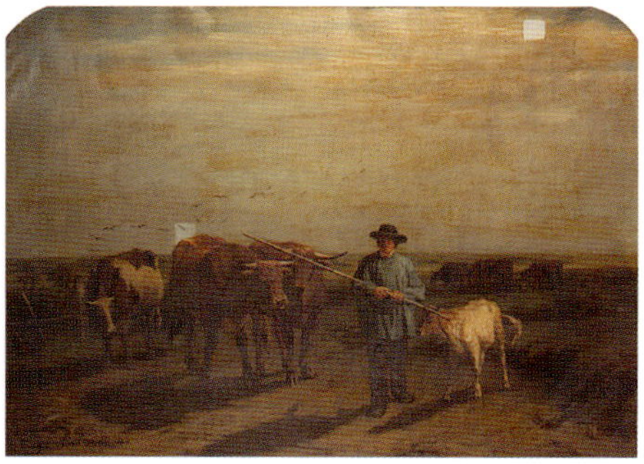

de Pratere, Edmond Joseph 1826–1888
Cattle and Drover 1860
oil on canvas 83.5 x 118
LANLM.1899.2

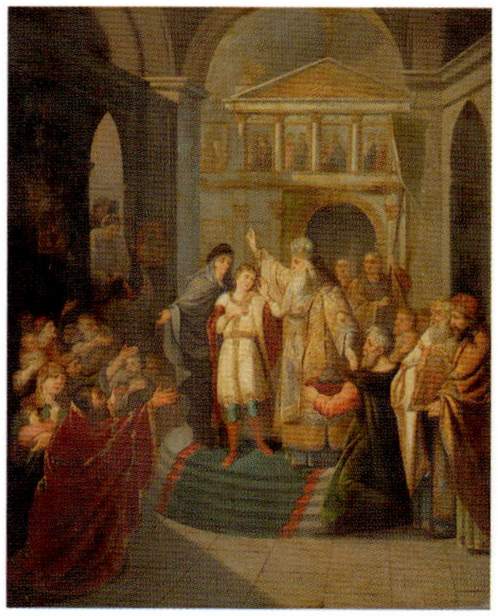

de Vorkavitch, Paul
Coronation of Ivan the Terrible 1896
oil on canvas 99 x 80
LANLM.1931.34

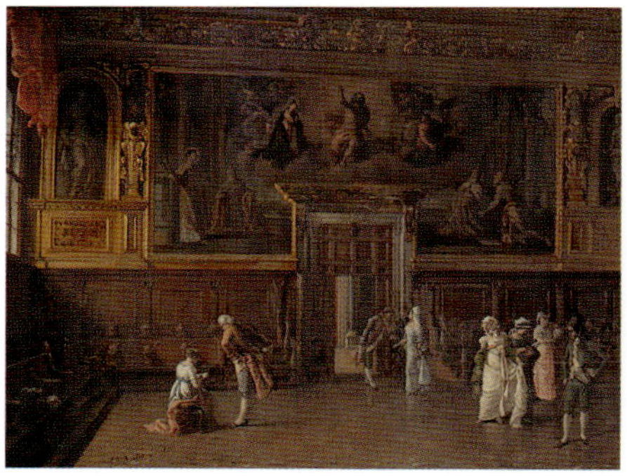

Dulla, S. active 1750–1800
Court Interior
oil on canvas 76.5 x 90.1
LANLM.1950.2

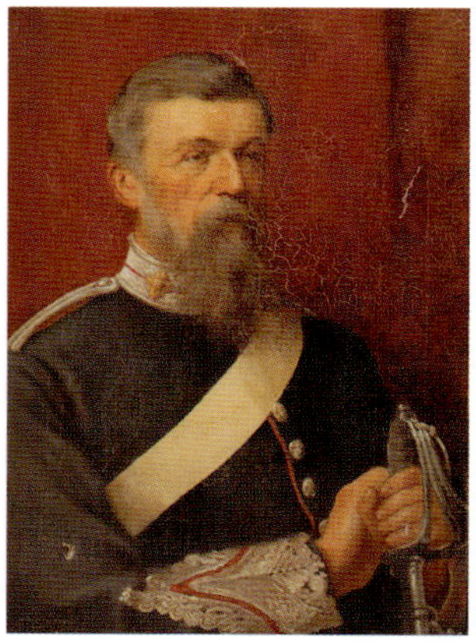

Eaton, Ernest 1859–1898
Richard Coupland 1860–1900
oil on canvas 79.8 x 64.5 (E)
LANLM.2004.7.1

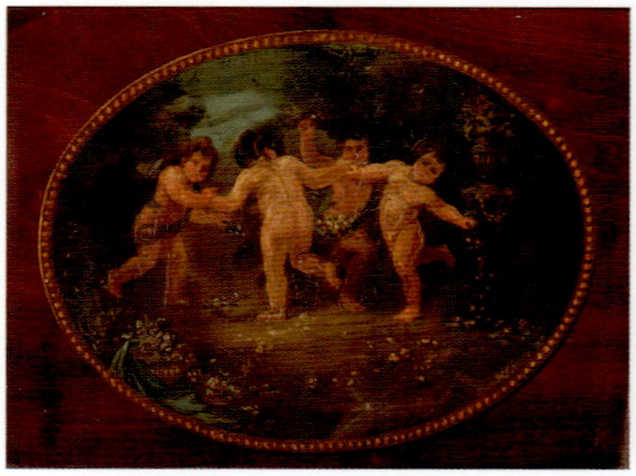

Eccles, W. 1875–1955
Putti Dancing c.1915
oil on panel 17 x 23.5
LANLM.1990.13.1

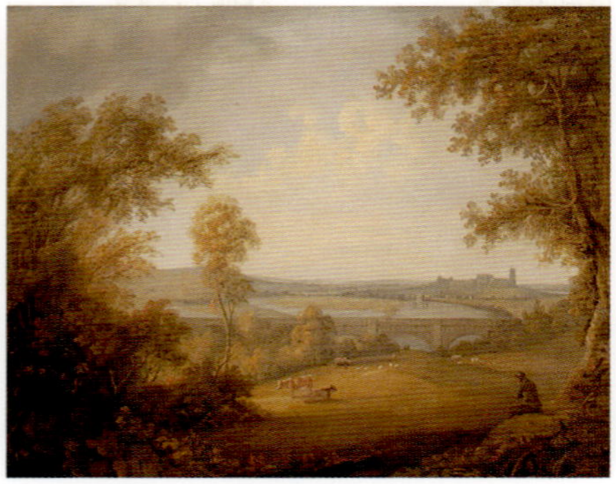

Farington, Joseph 1747–1821
Lancaster from above the Aqueduct Bridge c.1790
oil on canvas 46 x 61
LANLM.1997.14

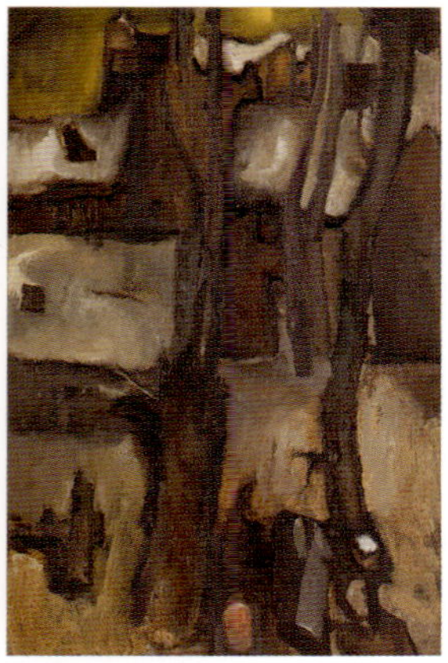

Fell, Sheila Mary 1931–1979
Gathering Sticks in the Snow 1957
oil on canvas 100 x 74
LANLM.1973.31.2

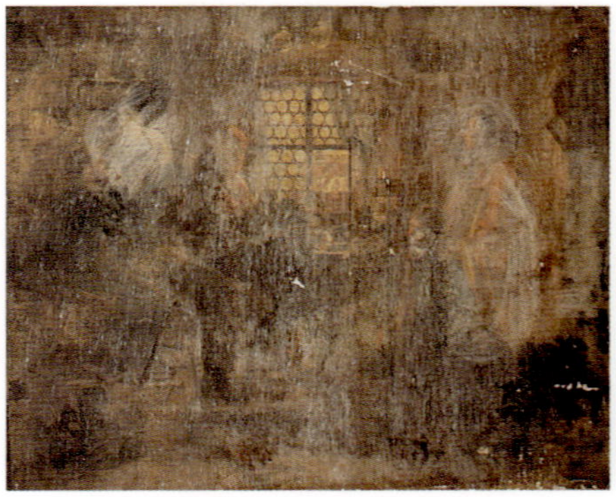

Fildes, Luke 1843–1927
The Truant Apprentice 1860–1927
oil on canvas 92.5 x 118
LANLM.1952.34.1

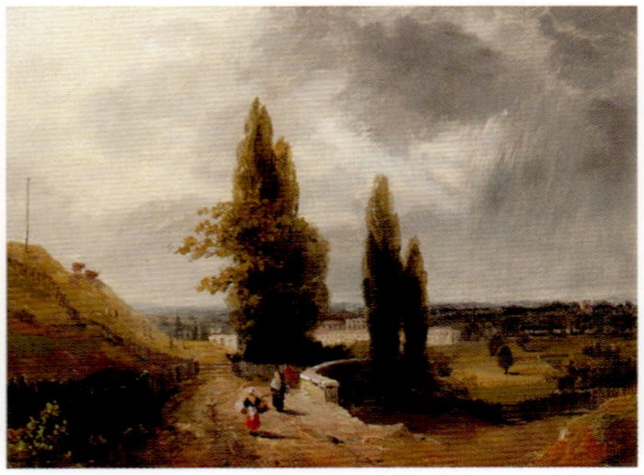

Fraser, A.
Heaton Mersey 1831
oil on canvas 22.5 x 32.5
LMA 40

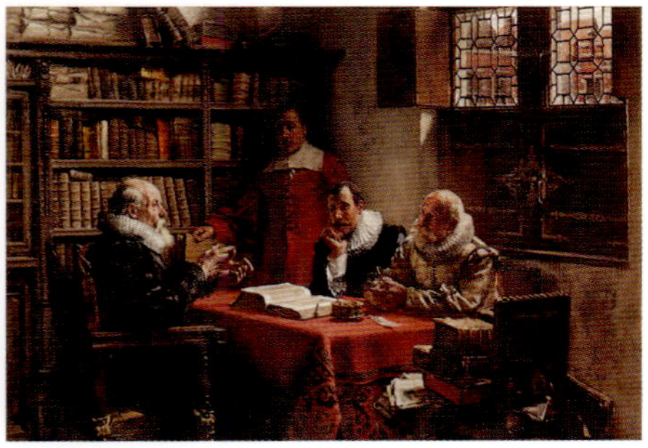

Gaisser, Max 1857–1922
The Conference c.1880
oil on canvas 69.5 x 99.5 (E)
LMA 139

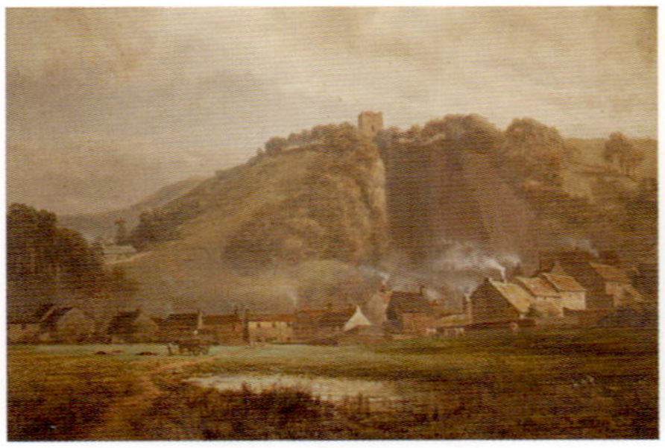

Gallon, Robert 1845–1925
Peak Cavern, Derbyshire 1864
oil on canvas 60 x 100
LMA 41.1

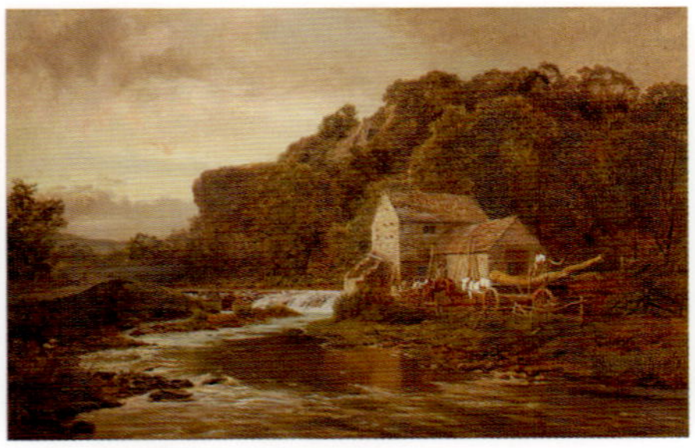

Gallon, Robert 1845–1925
The Sawmill 1884
oil on canvas 60 x 100
LMA 41.2

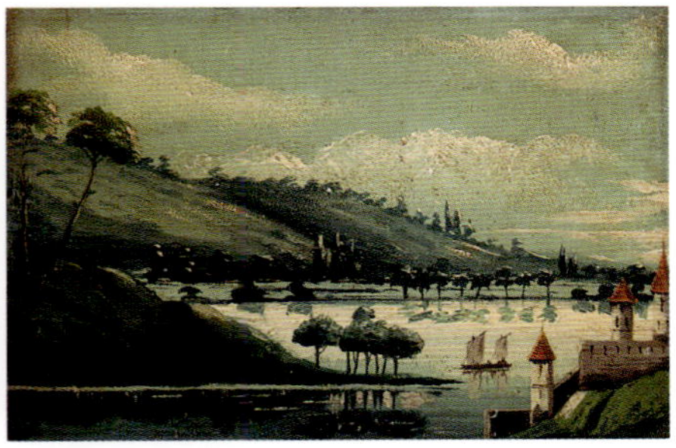

Gervaise, Charles Arthur 1821–1891
Castle and Lake 1873–1874
oil on board 15 x 22.5
LANLM.1936.41.1

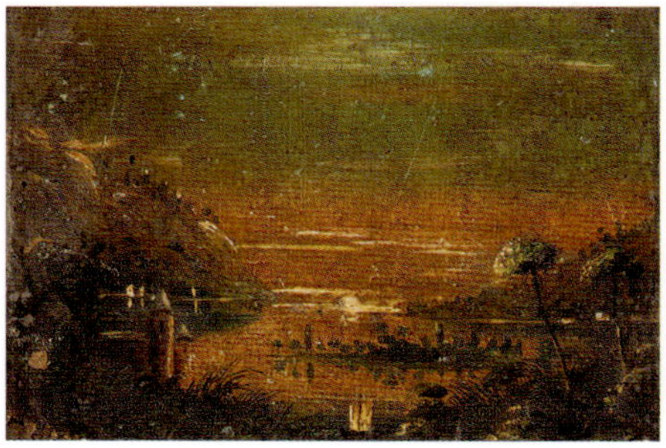

Gervaise, Charles Arthur 1821–1891
Castle and Lake 1873–1874
oil on board 15 x 22.5
LANLM.1936.41.4

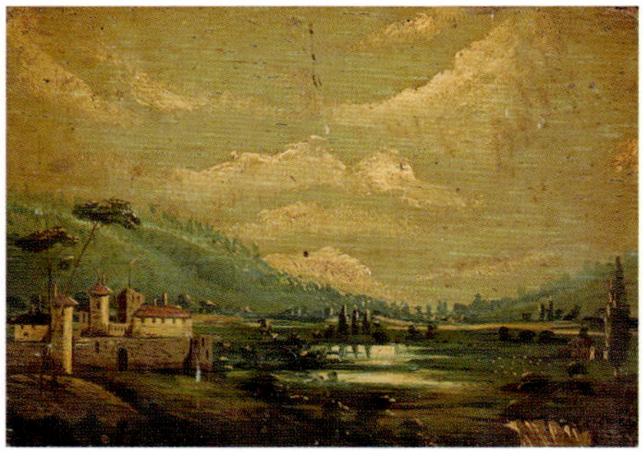

Gervaise, Charles Arthur 1821–1891
Castle in Valley 1873–1874
oil on board 20 x 30
LANLM.1936.41.6

Gervaise, Charles Arthur 1821–1891
Cottages on Cliffs 1873–1874
oil on board 15 x 23
LANLM.1936.41.5

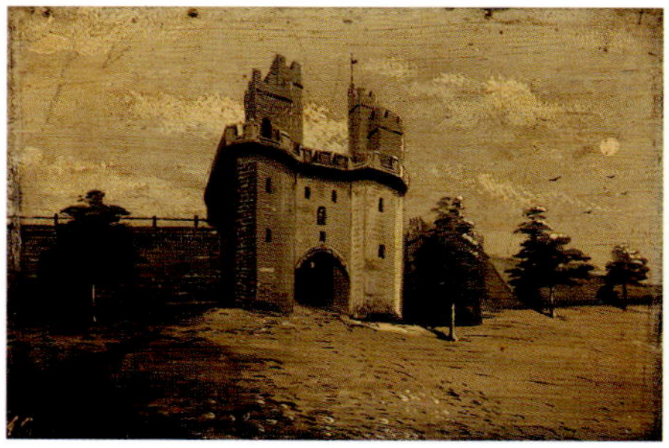

Gervaise, Charles Arthur 1821–1891
Lancaster Castle Gateway 1873–1874
oil on board 15 x 23
LANLM.1936.41.2

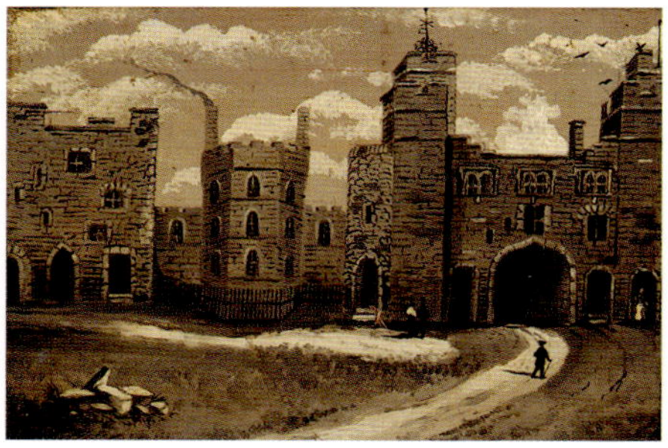

Gervaise, Charles Arthur 1821–1891
Lancaster Castle Interior 1873–1874
oil on board 15 x 22.5
LANLM.1936.41.3

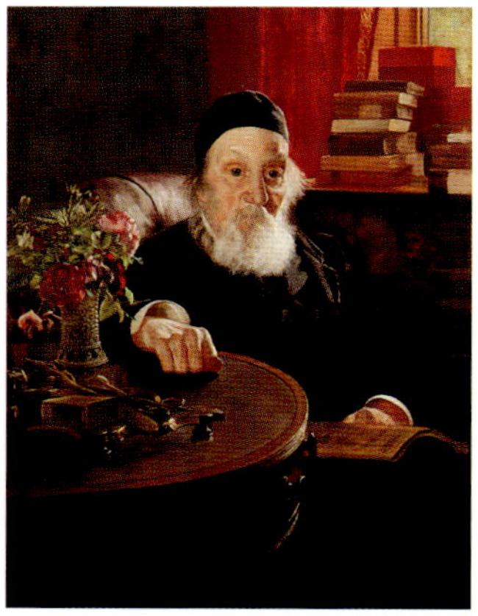

Gilbert, William 1832–1896
Sir Richard Owen (1804–1892) c.1890
oil on canvas 75 x 62 (E)
LMA 43

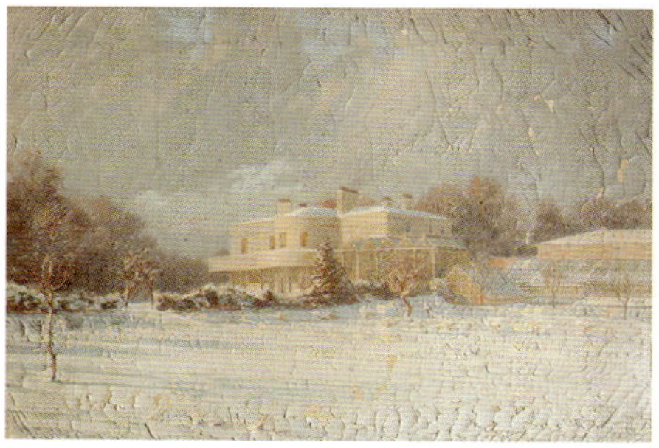

Gilchrist, Philip Thomson 1865–1956
Bella Villa
oil on canvas 35 x 40 (E)
LANLM.2008.17

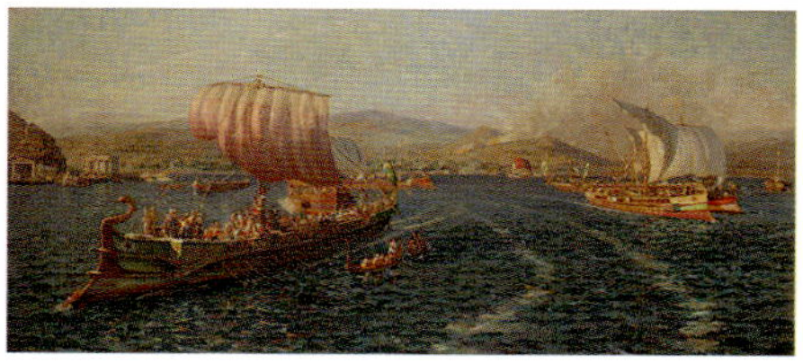

Gilchrist, Philip Thomson 1865–1956
Xerxes Burning Athens: Flight of the Athenians
oil on canvas 61 x 137.5 (E)
LANLM.1951.21

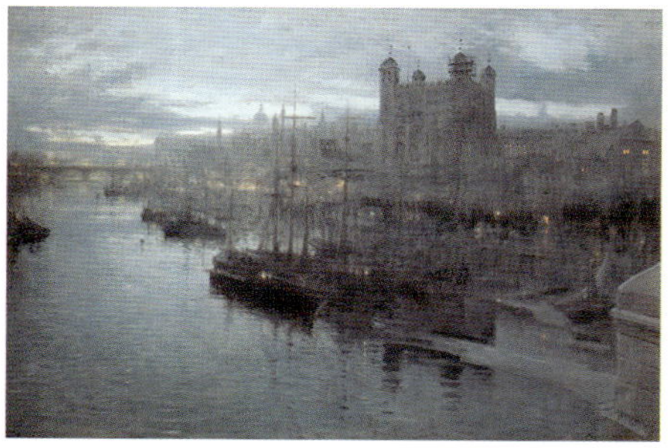

Goodwin, Albert 1845–1932
The Tower of London 1897
oil on canvas 94 x 140
LMA 44

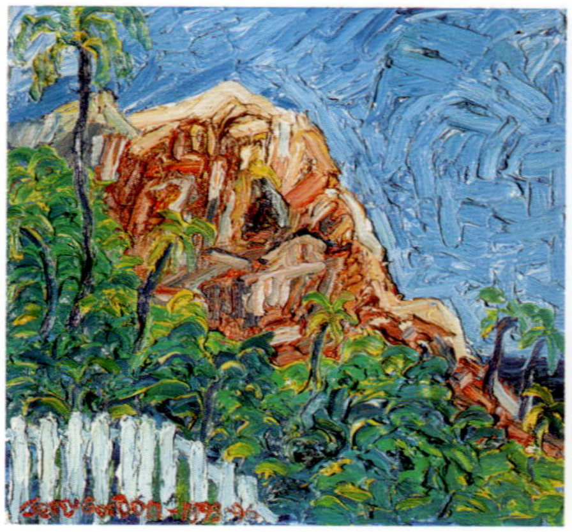

Gordon, Jerry b.1955
Fletcher Christian's Cave on Pitcairn Island
1994
oil on canvas 56 x 61
LANLM.2000.17

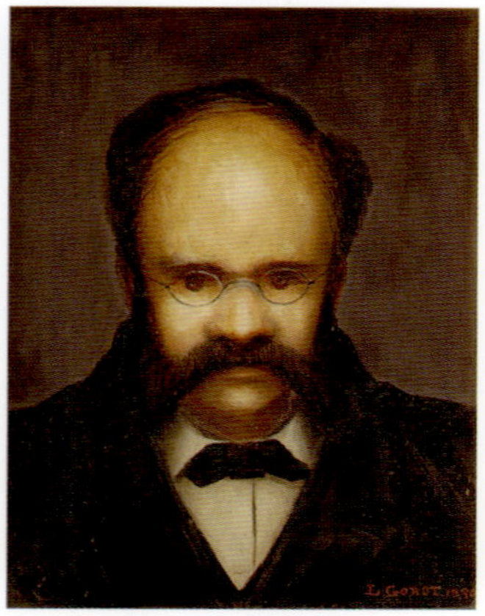

Gorst, Luke 1849–1929
James Williamson II, Baron (Lord) Ashton
1890
oil on canvas 46.5 x 41 (E)
LANLM.1939.24

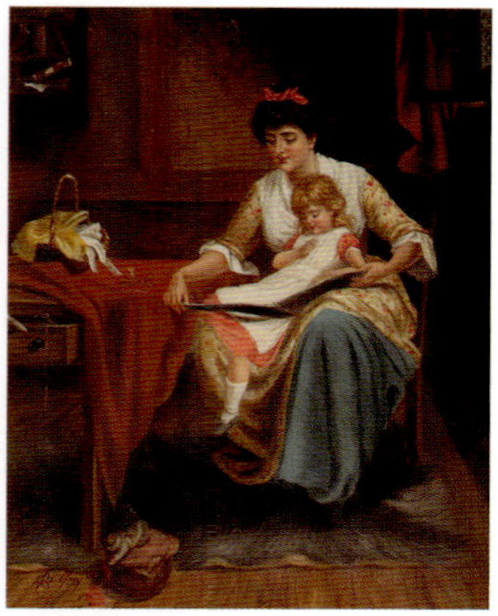

Gray, Kate active 1864–1931
The Picture Book 1887
oil on canvas 67.5 x 59
LANLM.1946.16.5

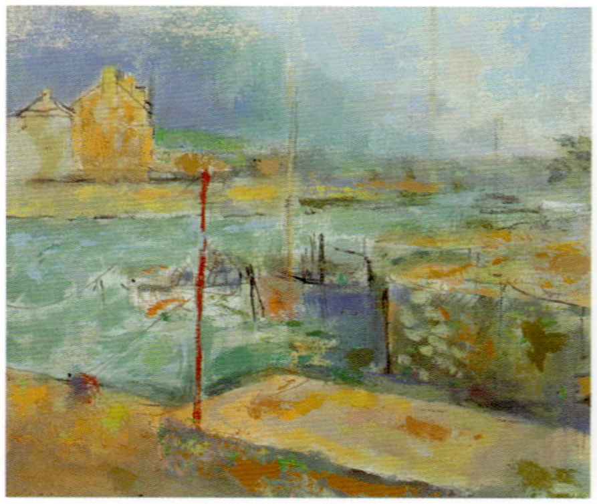

Griffith, Frank 1889–1979
Rain, Glasson Dock c.1962
oil on board 30 x 41
LANLM.1971.73

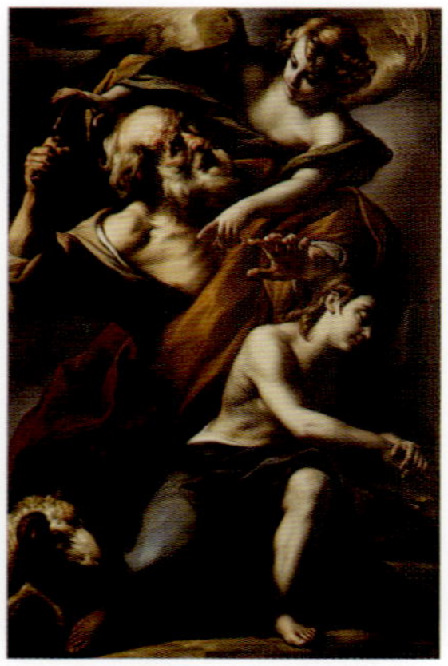

Guercino (follower of) 1591–1666
The Sacrifice of Isaac c.1660
oil on canvas 171 x 120
LANLM.1892.4

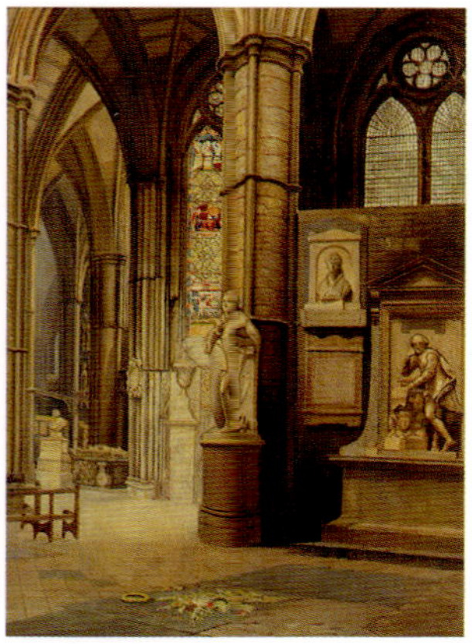

Hackworth, T.
Poets' Corner, Westminster Abbey
oil on canvas 64.5 x 44
LANLM.1946.16.4

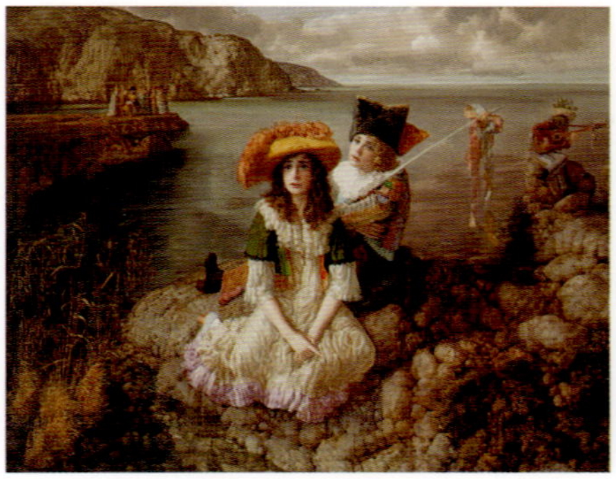

Harrison, Claude 1922–2009
Island of Comedians 1971
oil & acrylic on board 43.1 x 73.8 (E)
LANLM.1971.13

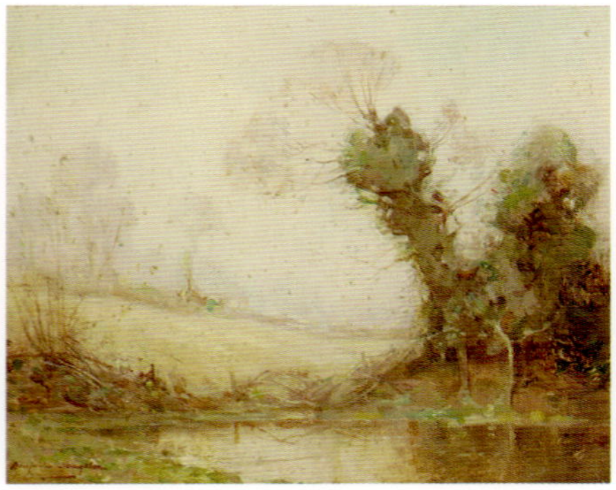

Haughton, Benjamin 1865–1924
The Pool, East Downs 1880–1924
oil on board 21 x 28
LANLM.1937.7

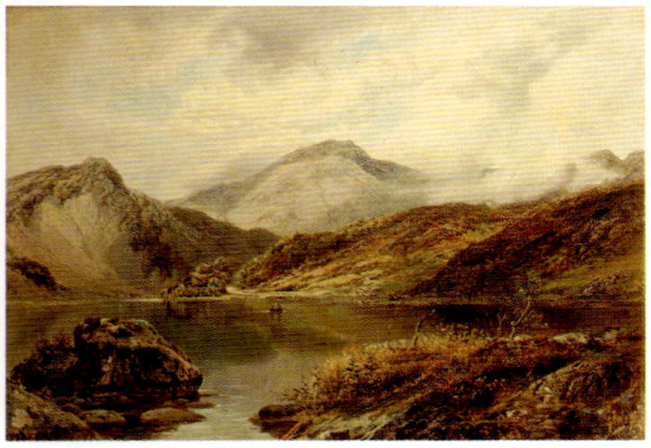

Hayes, E. R.
Llyn Dinas, Beddgelert 1850–1900
oil on canvas 48 x 75
LANLM.1946.16.3

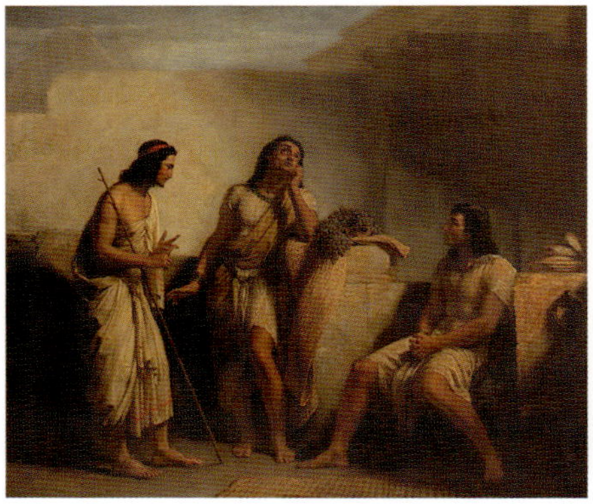

Hayter, George 1792–1871
Joseph Interpreting the Dream of the Chief Baker c.1820
oil on canvas 132 x 152
LANLM.1946.6

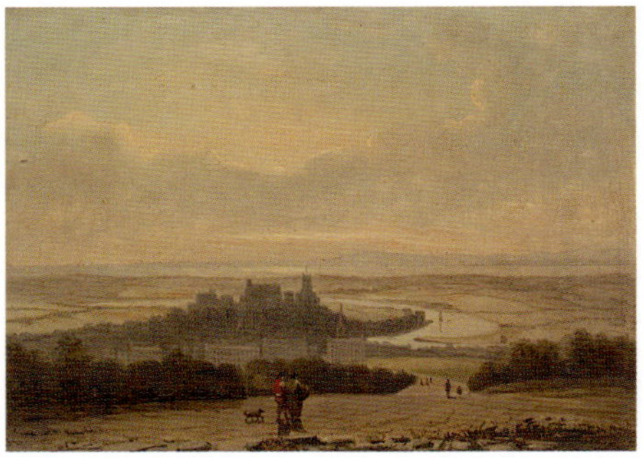

Henderson, John 1765–1853
Lancaster from the East c.1800
oil on panel 32.4 x 40.3 (E)
LANLM.1931.12.11

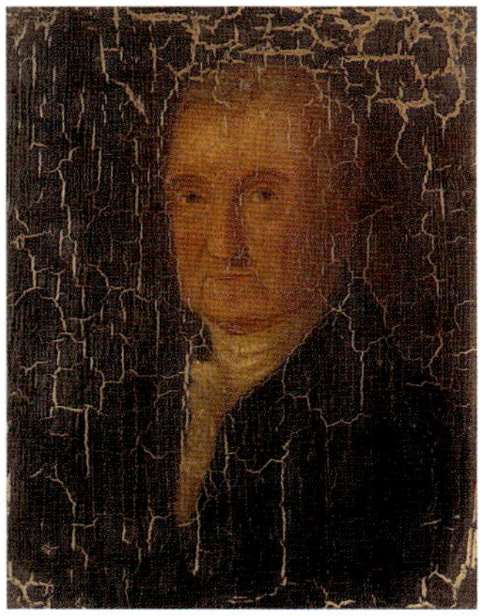

Henderson, John 1765–1853
Parson Thomas c.1800
oil on board 28 x 23.5 (E)
LANLM.1974.90.7

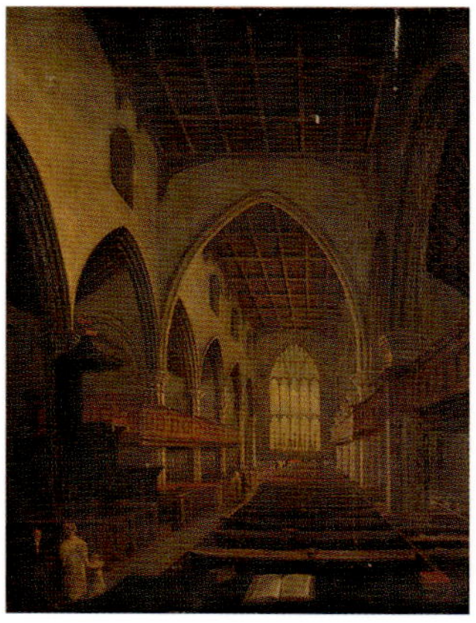

Henderson, John 1765–1853
St Mary's Church, Lancaster c.1805
oil on canvas 76 x 63.5 (E)
LM 91

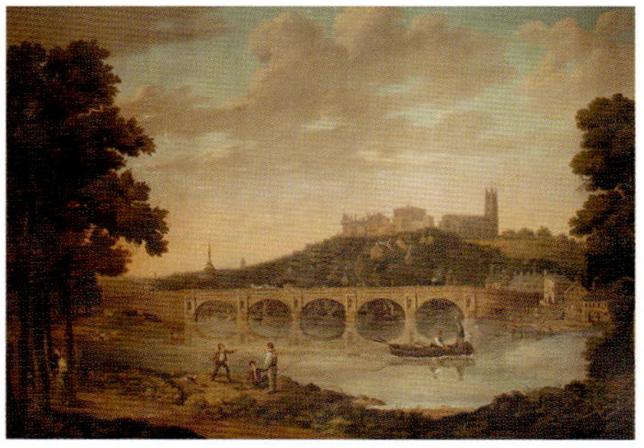

Henderson, John 1765–1853
Lancaster from Ladies' Walk c.1825
oil on canvas 119 x 178 (E)
LANLM.1912.1

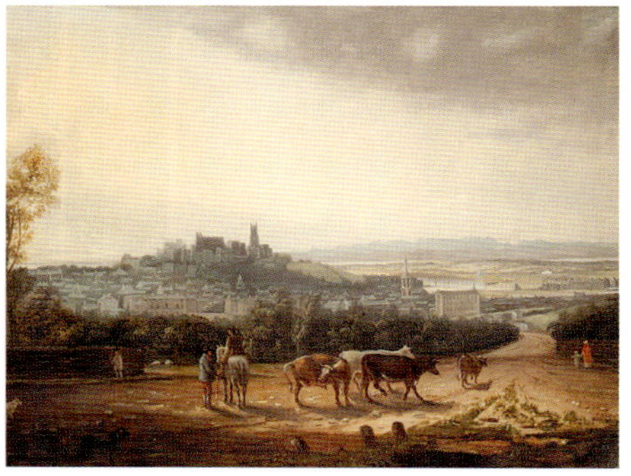

Henderson, John 1765–1853
Lancaster from the East c.1830
oil on canvas 51.3 x 64.5 (E)
LANLM.2001.8

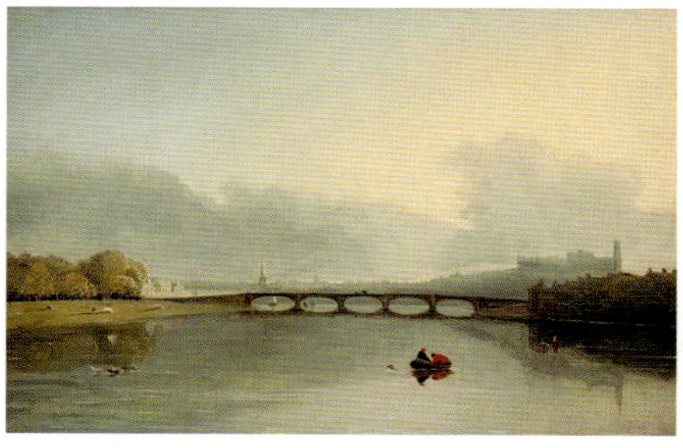

Henderson, John 1765–1853
Lancaster from the River with Skerton Bridge 1819
oil on panel 33.1 x 48.9 (E)
LANLM.1995.8

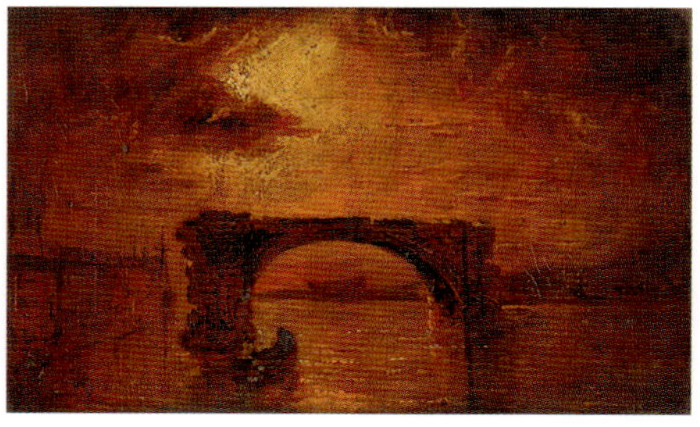

Henderson, John 1765–1853
Lancaster Old Bridge with Skerton Shipyard Beyond
oil on canvas 16.5 x 31.7 (E)
LANLM.1928.10

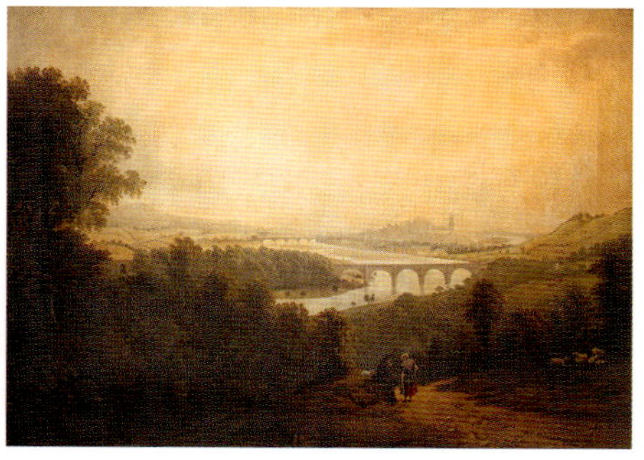

Henderson, John 1765–1853
Lancaster with the Aqueduct Bridge
oil on canvas 72 x 99
AP.2011.1

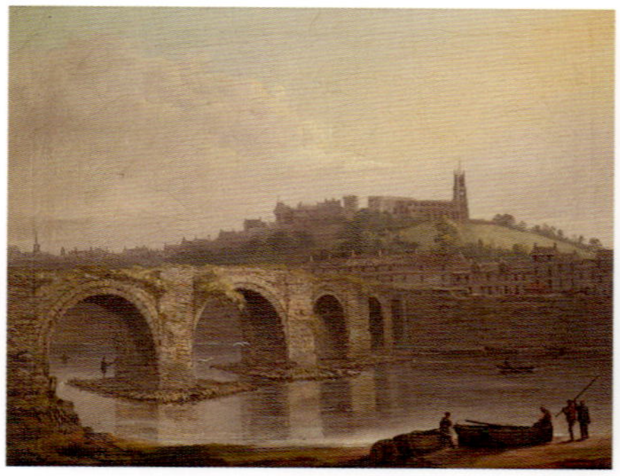

Henderson, John (attributed to) 1765–1853
Lancaster Old Bridge
oil on canvas 49 x 74 (E)
LM 2

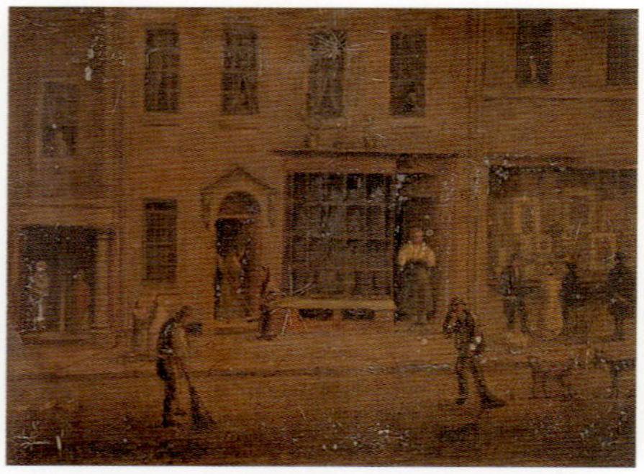

Henderson, John (attributed to) 1765–1853
Market Street
oil on canvas 29 x 44 (E)
LANLM.1950.21.2

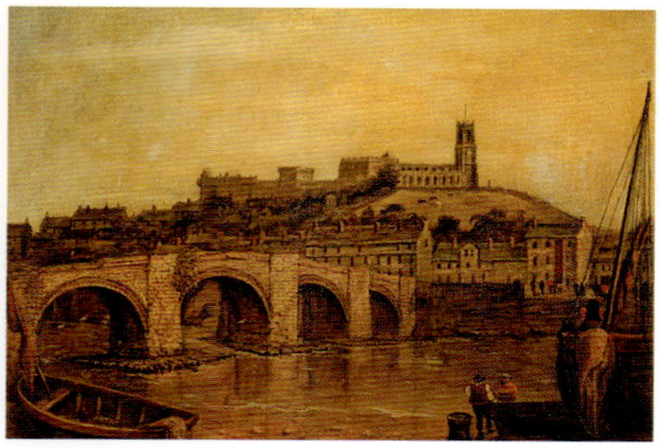

Henderson, John (attributed to) 1765–1853
Old Loyne Bridge
oil on canvas 48 x 73 (E)
LANLM.1936.26.2

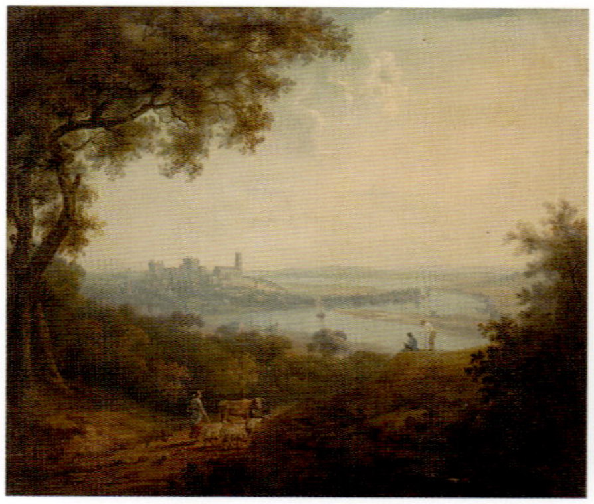

Henderson, John (attributed to) 1765–1853
Lancaster from the Ridge c.1820
oil on canvas 53 x 66
LANLM.1936.26.1

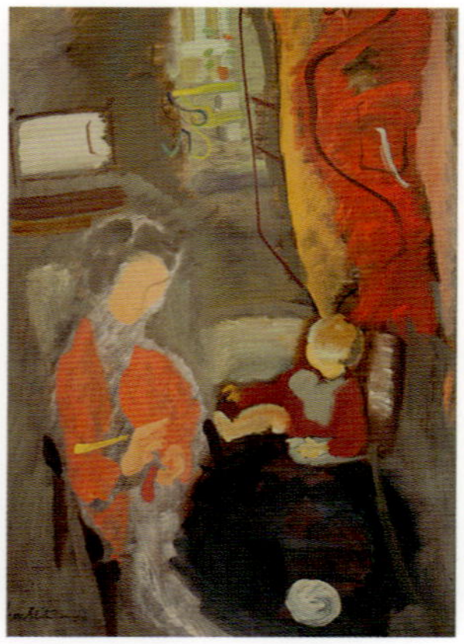

Hitchens, Ivon 1893–1979
The Red Curtain c.1940
oil on canvas 89 x 67
LANLM.1969.16

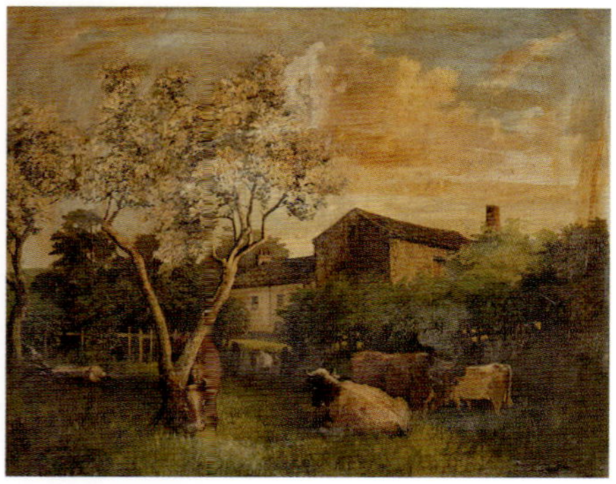

Hodgson, Harold 1865–1955
The Old Mill, Scotforth 1921
oil on canvas 43 x 62.5
LANLM.1963.1

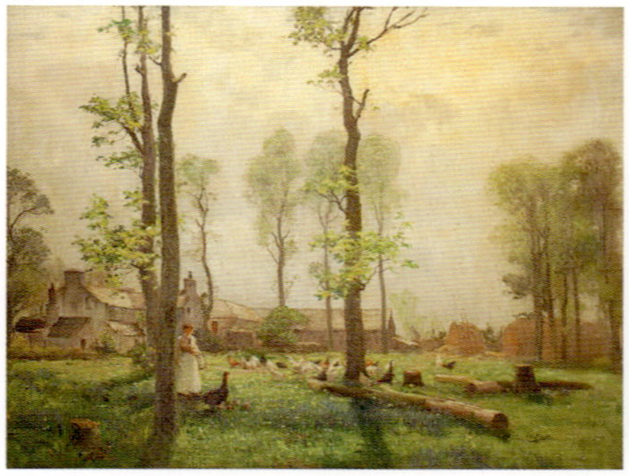

Hoggatt, William 1879–1961
Early Spring 1900–1918
oil on canvas 120 x 150
LANLM.1918.3.1

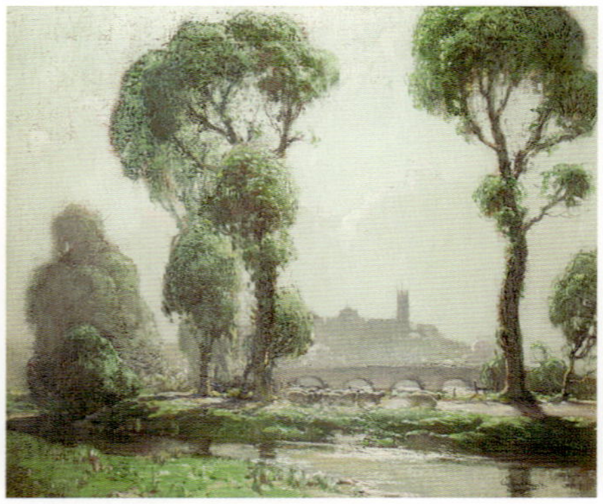

Hoggatt, William 1879–1961
Lancaster from Ladies' Walk c. 1900
oil on canvas 69 x 89 (E)
LANLM.1915.6

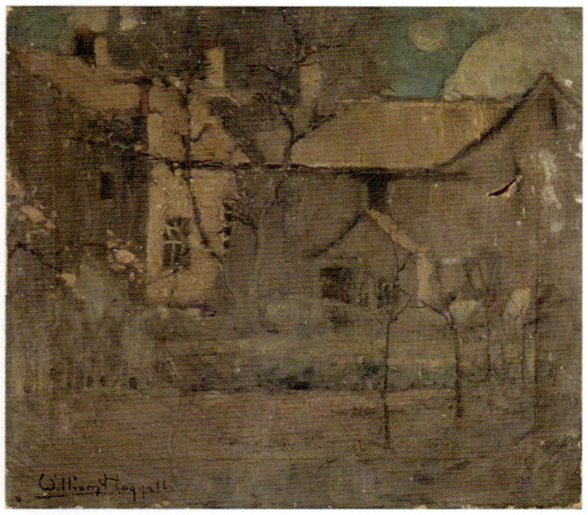

Hoggatt, William 1879–1961
The Back Garden at Brookhouse c.1900
oil on canvas 30.5 x 35.5 (E)
LANLM.1979.44.1

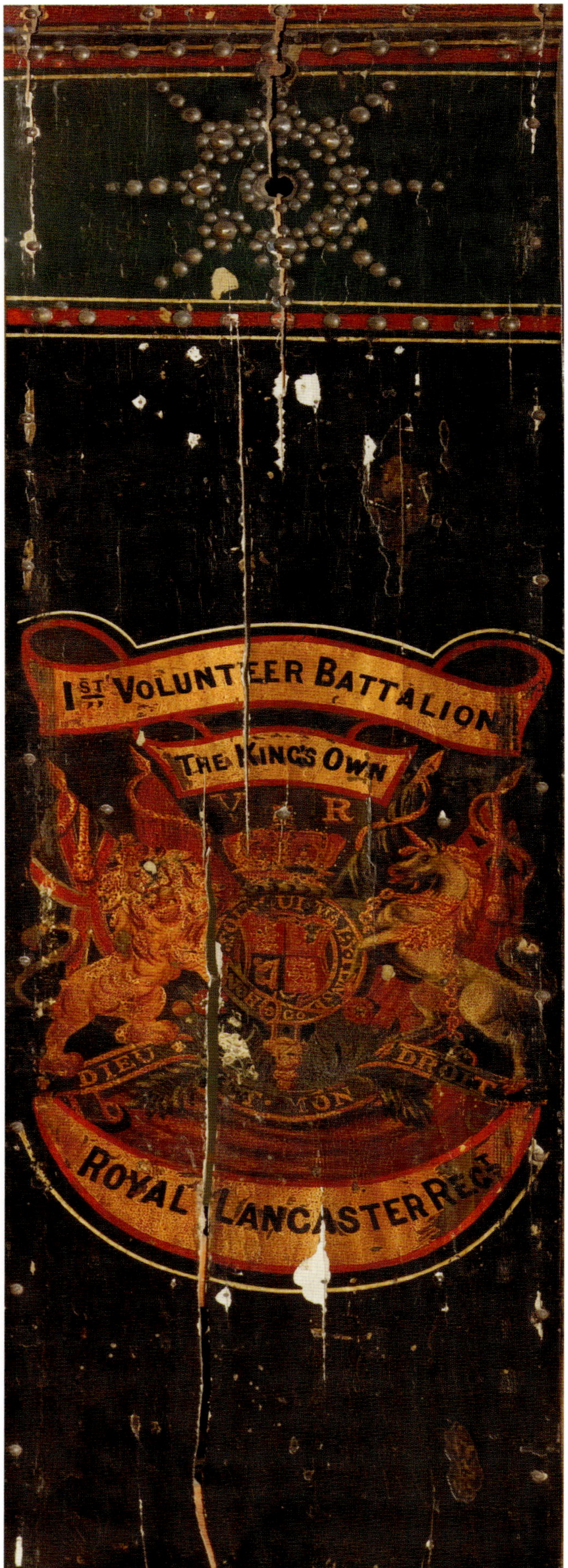
1ST VOLUNTEER BATTALION
THE KING'S OWN
V R
DIEU ET MON DROIT
ROYAL LANCASTER REGT

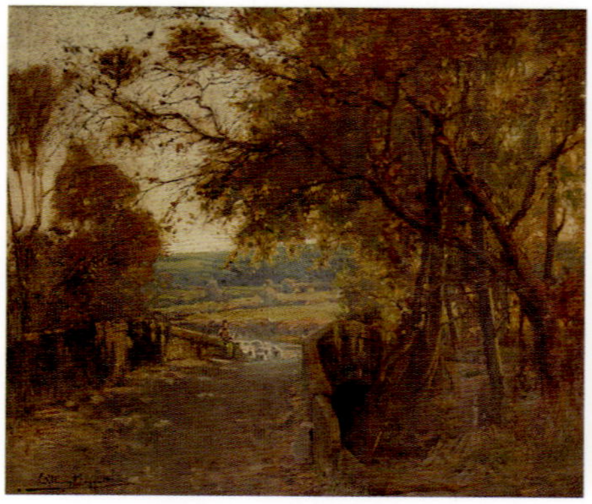

Hoggatt, William 1879–1961
Morning Sunlight, Brookhouse c.1904
oil on canvas 59.5 x 75.5 (E)
LANLM.1936.1

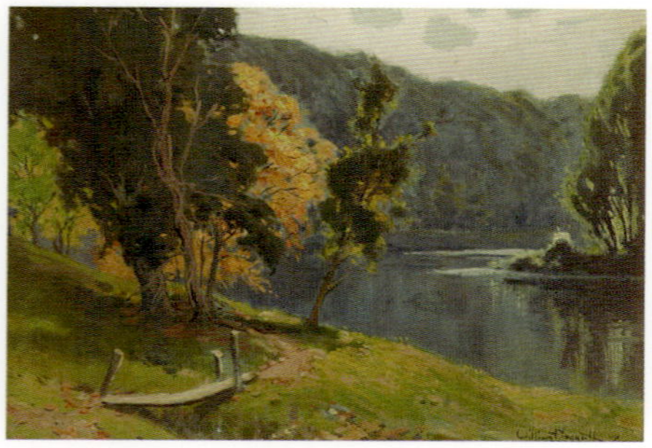

Hoggatt, William 1879–1961
Crook O'Lune 1905
oil on canvas 29 x 44 (E)
LANLM.1965.20

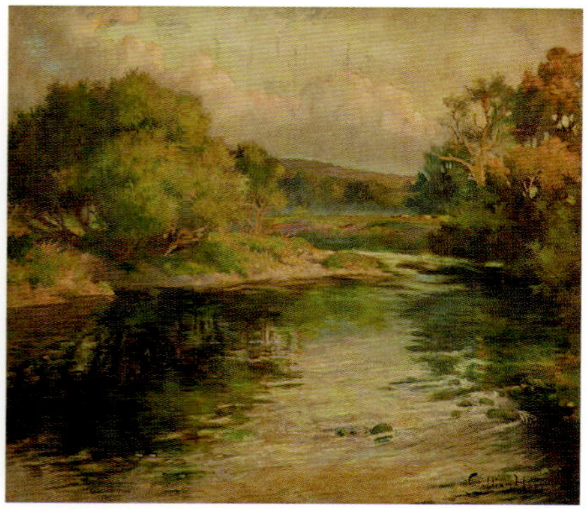

Hoggatt, William 1879–1961
From Green to Gold, the Lune above Caton
c.1905
oil on canvas 67.5 x 83 (E)
LANLM.1936.1.2

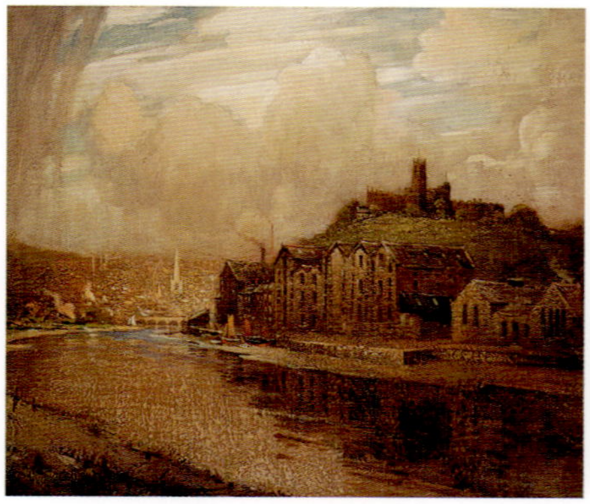

Hoggatt, William 1879–1961
St George's Quay, Lancaster c.1910
oil on canvas 60 x 74
LANLM.1956.12

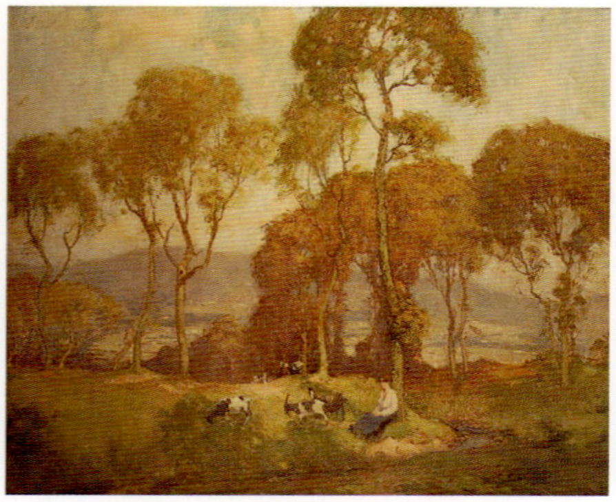

Hoggatt, William 1879–1961
Autumn in a Manx Glen c.1915
oil on canvas 123 x 152.5 (E)
LANLM.1918.3.2

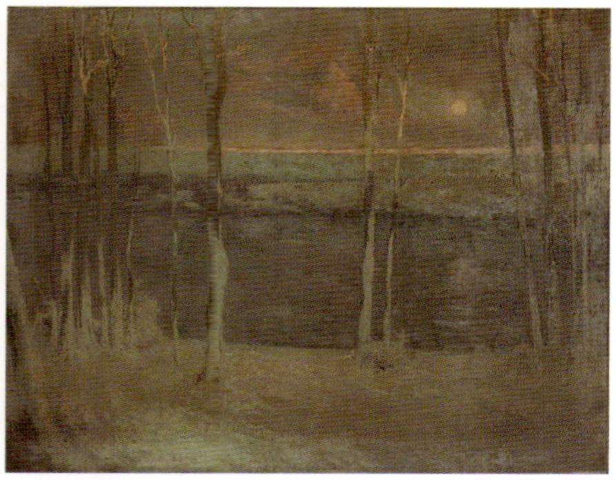

Hoggatt, William 1879–1961
Solitude c.1915
oil on canvas 88 x 113 (E)
LANLM.1918.5.2

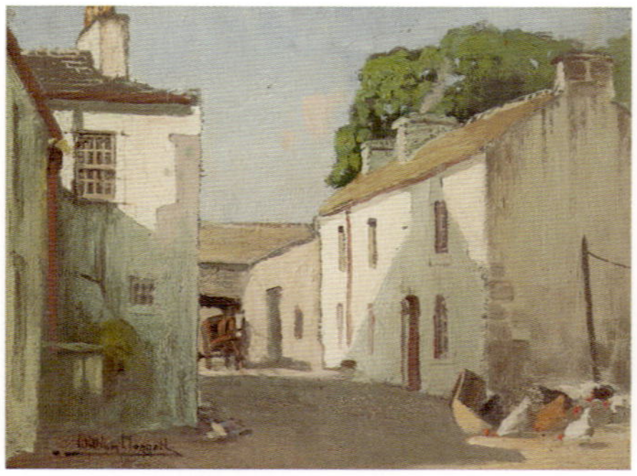

Hoggatt, William 1879–1961
The Deemster's Farm, Ballacurry, Port Erin, Isle of Man c.1920
oil on canvas 29.5 x 39.5 (E)
LANLM.1936.27.2

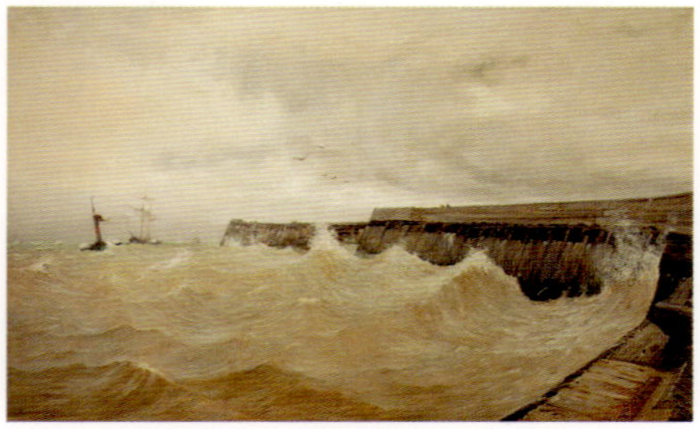

Holloway, Charles Edward 1838–1897
Deal Harbour 1881
oil on canvas 90 x 150
LANLM.1950.6.1

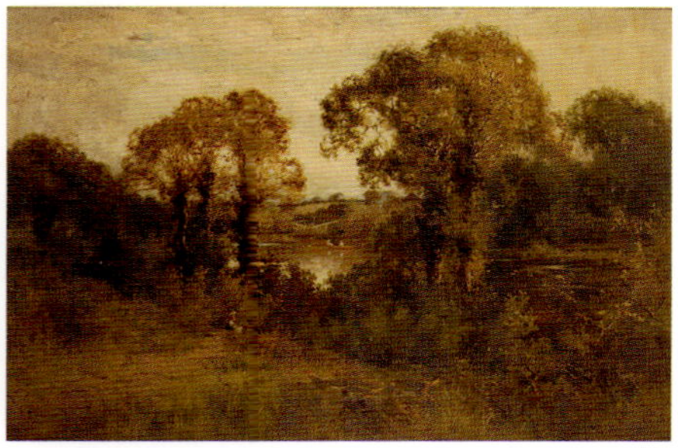

Hooper, John Horace 1837–1912
Shiplake from Wargrave Hill 1870–1891
oil on canvas 93.9 x 124.2 (E)
LANLM.1899.3

Facing page: Henry Potter & Son, *Drum Shell, 1st Volunteer Battalion, King's Own Royal Lancaster Regiment (1883–1901)*, c.1883, King's Own Royal Regiment Museum (p. 182)

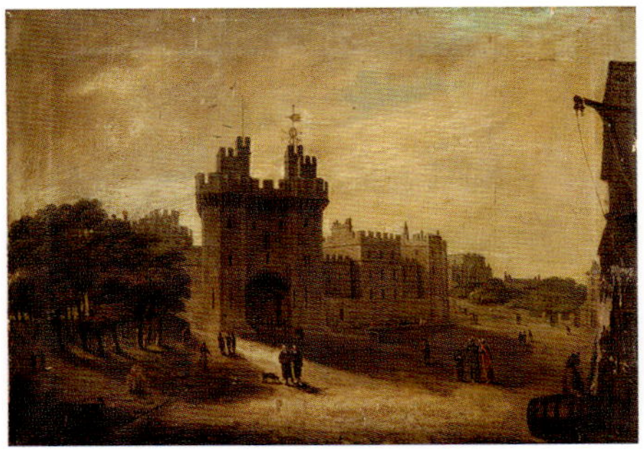

Hume of Lancaster 1780–1850
Lancaster Castle Gateway c.1820
oil on canvas 35.2 x 52.1 (E)
LANLM.1916.3

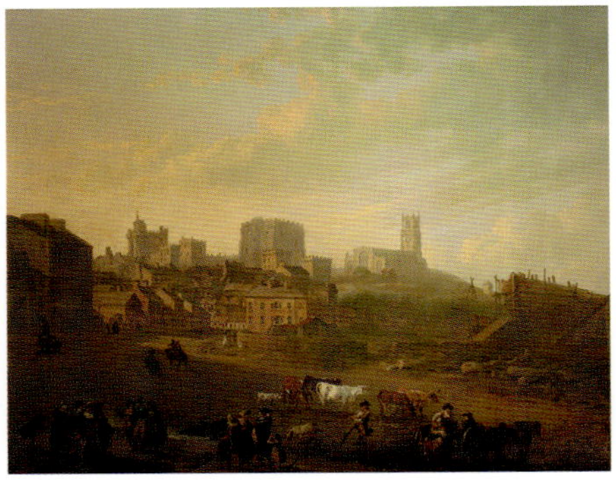

Ibbetson, Julius Caesar 1759–1817
Lancaster from Cable Street 1798
oil on canvas 70 x 88
LANLM.1930.2

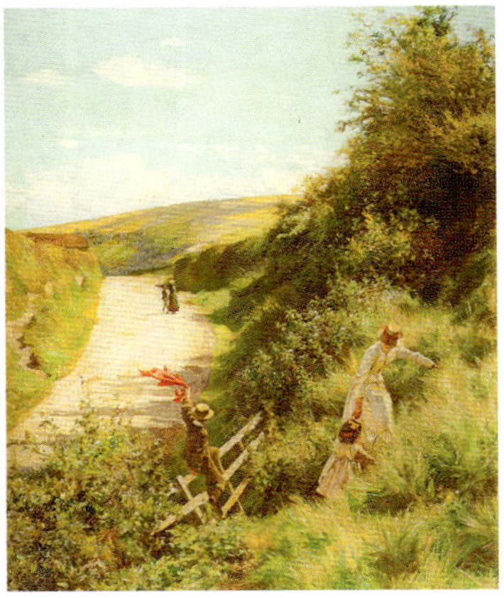

King, Gunning 1859–1940
A Sunny Day c.1920
oil on canvas 74 x 62
LMA 141

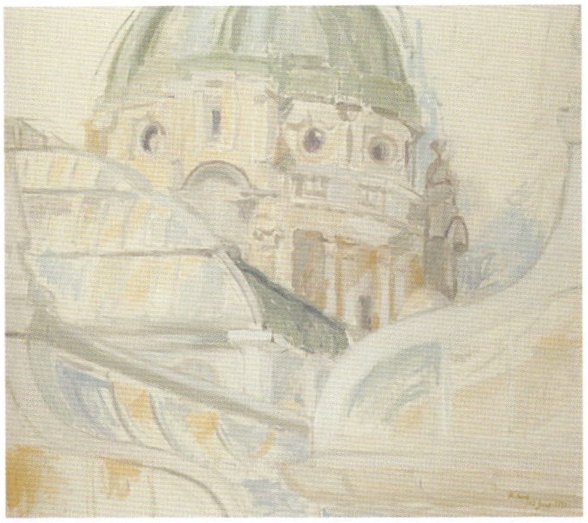

King, Margaret b.1932
The Ashton Memorial, Lancaster 1991
oil on canvas 81 x 96.5 (E)
LANLM.1992.35.1

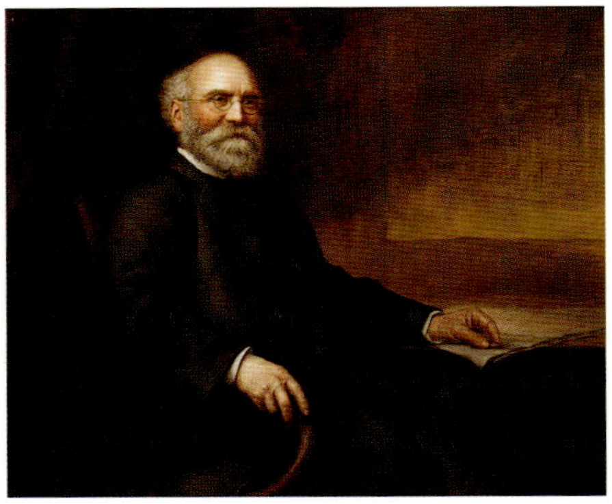

Klíc, Karel 1841–1926
Sir Thomas Storey (1825–1898) 1892
oil on canvas 99 x 123
LANLM.1892.7

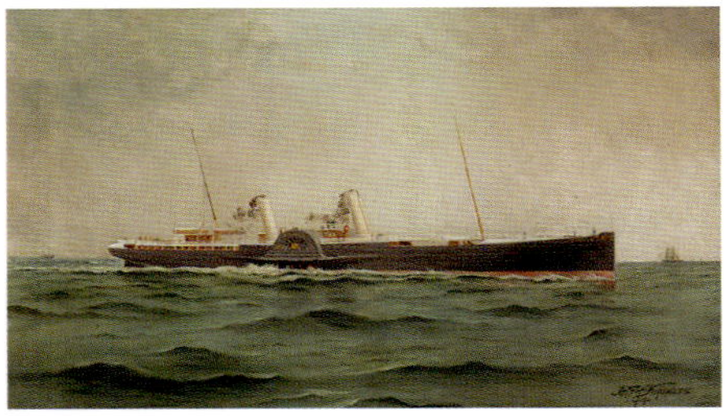

Knowles, Arthur 1870–1955
PS 'Manx Queen' 1894
oil on canvas 33 x 60
LANLM.1995.67

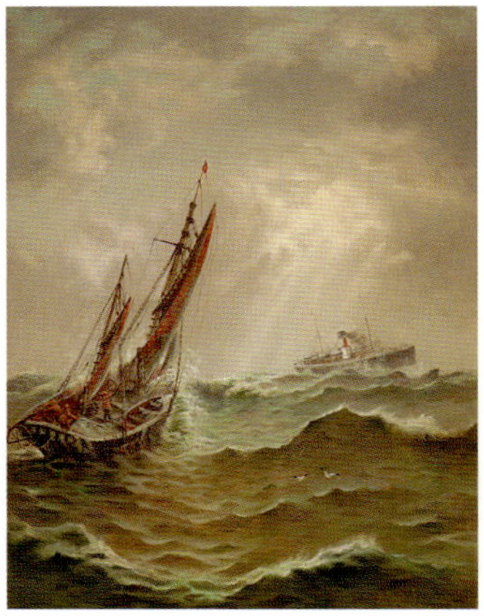

Knowles, Arthur 1870–1955
SS 'Brier' and Deep Sea Fishing Boat in a Gale c.1900
oil on canvas 60 x 48
LANLM.1991.83.2

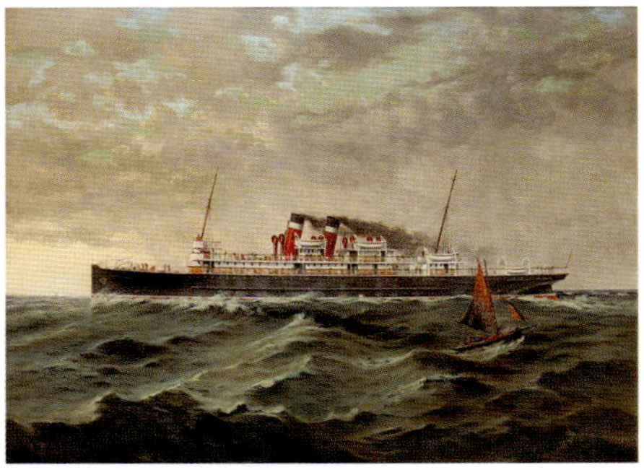

Knowles, Arthur 1870–1955
SS 'Manxman' c.1920
oil on canvas 39 x 60
LANLM.1991.83.1

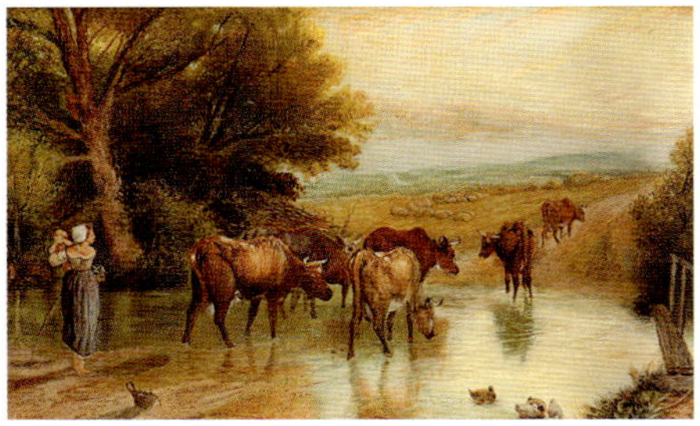

Knowles, Arthur 1870–1955
Highland Cattle c.1930
oil on canvas 35 x 60
LANLM.1993.7

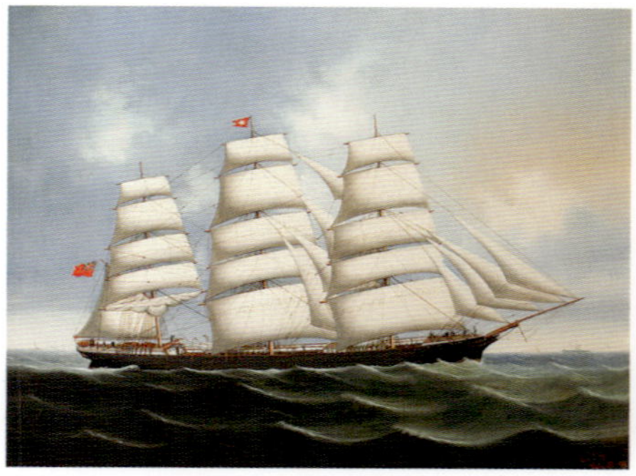

Lai Fong active c.1870–c.1905
'Dawpool' 1888
oil on canvas 62 x 85
LANLM.1931.11

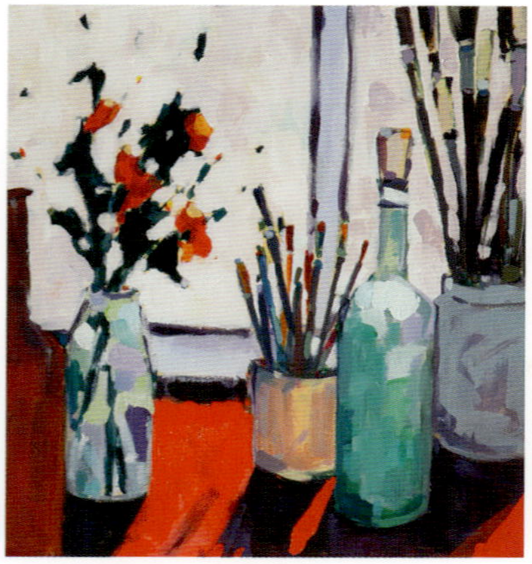

Lamb, Arthur d..2008
Studio Windowsill c.1999
acrylic on canvas 64 x 64
LANLM.2000.23

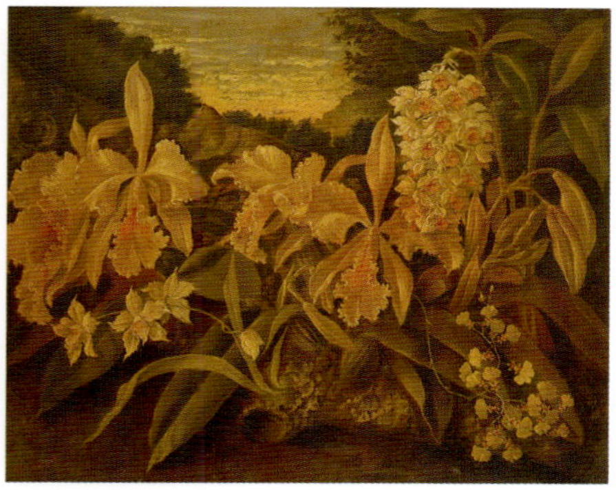

Lambert, W. 1835–1925
Orchids c.1870
oil on board 45 x 60 (E)
LANLM.1968.52.1

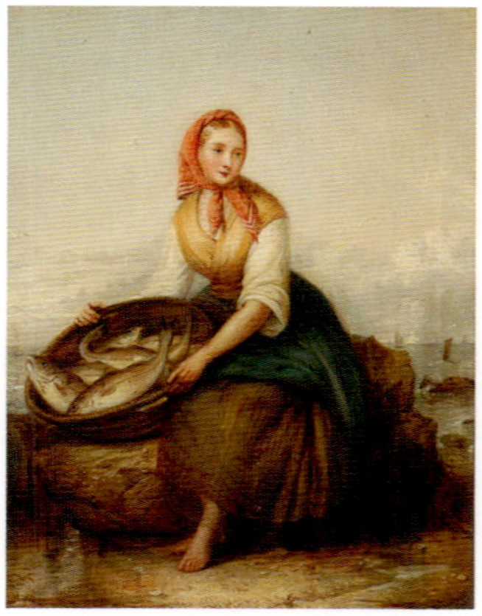

Leggat, James (attributed to) 1865–1955
Fishergirl c.1910
oil on canvas 60 x 50
LANLM.1965.1

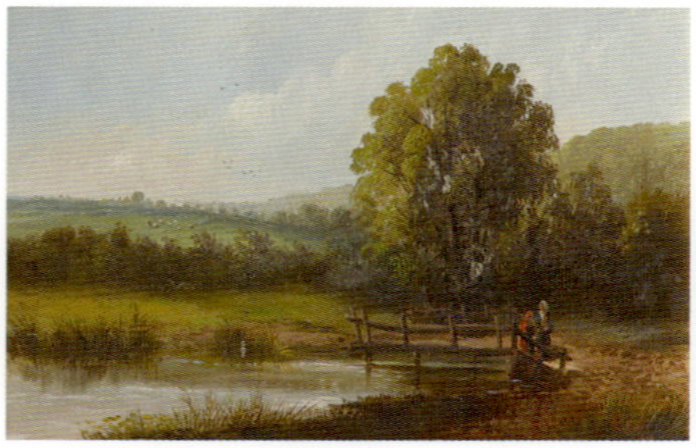

Lewis, L. 1775–1845
Landscape with Figures and Footbridge 1829
oil on canvas 24 x 38
LANLM.1945.6.5

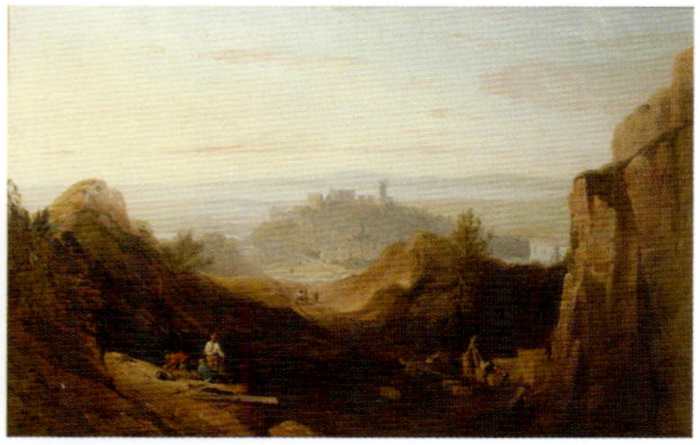

Linton, William 1791–1876
Lancaster from the Stone Quarries c.1852
oil on canvas 91.5 x 126.5 (E)
LANLM.1998.17

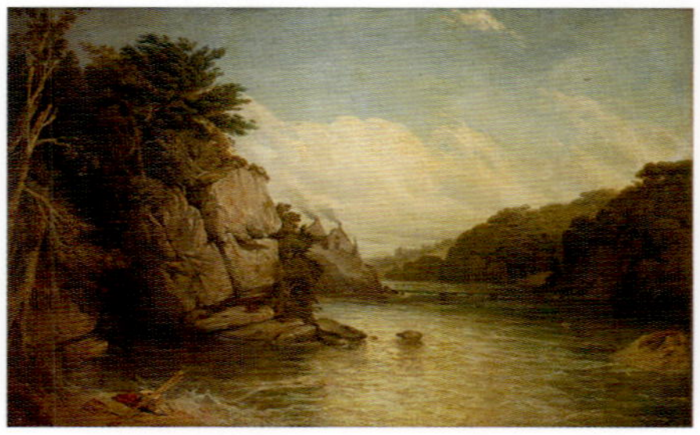

Linton, William 1791–1876
Halton Forge on the Lune c.1855
oil on canvas 95 x 166
LANLM.1951.1

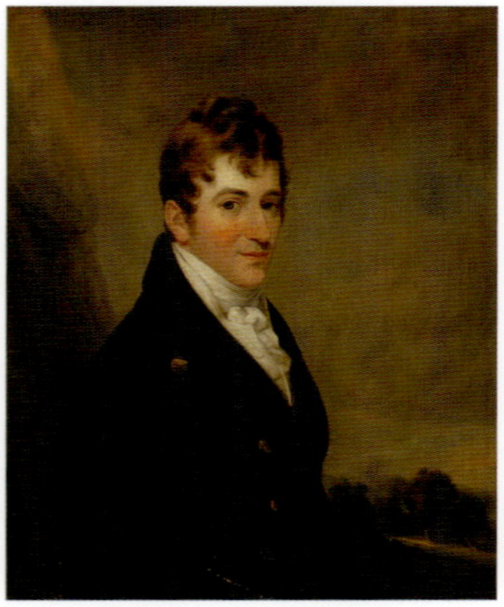

Lonsdale, James 1777–1839
John Dalton, Junior, Son of John and Mary Dalton c.1800
oil on canvas 98.5 x 85.7 (E)
LANLM.1983.43.14

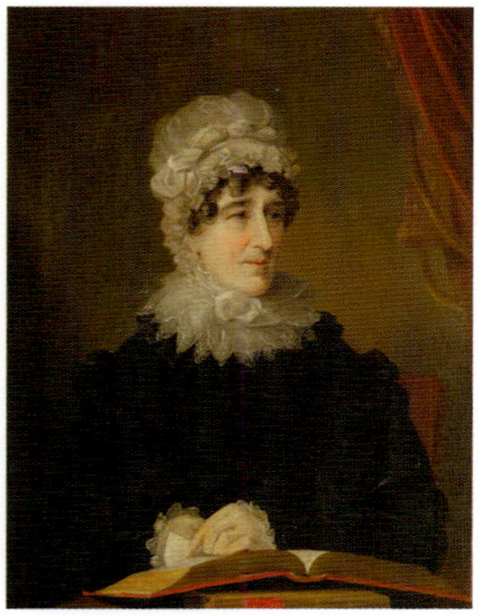

Lonsdale, James 1777–1839
Mary Dalton, née Gage c.1800
oil on canvas 98.5 x 86 (E)
LANLM.1983.43.12

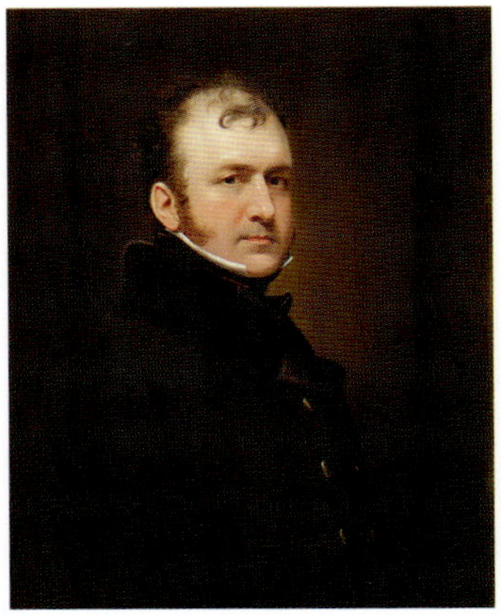

Lonsdale, James 1777–1839
Self Portrait c.1810
oil on canvas 74 x 61.5 (E)
LANLM.1957.1

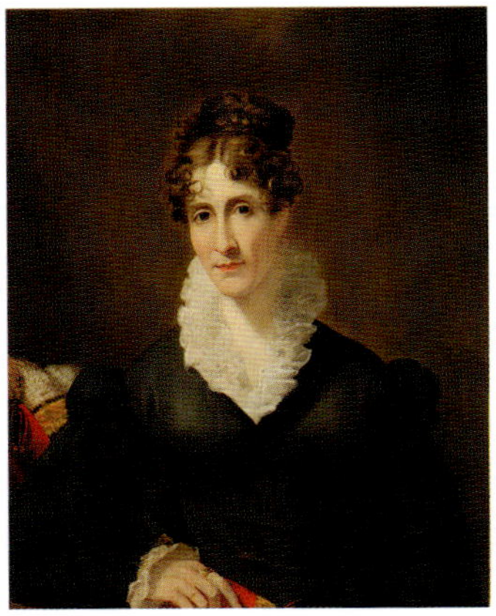

Lonsdale, James 1777–1839
Bridget Dalton 1819
oil on canvas 98.7 x 86 (E)
LANLM.1983.43.15

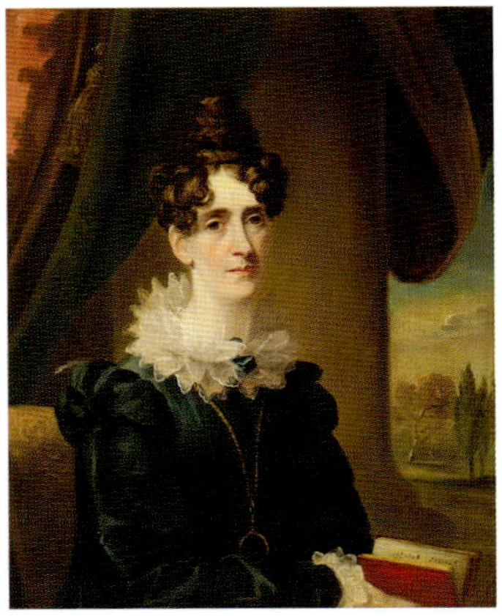

Lonsdale, James 1777–1839
Elizabeth Dalton 1819
oil on canvas 100 x 87 (E)
LANLM.1983.43.9

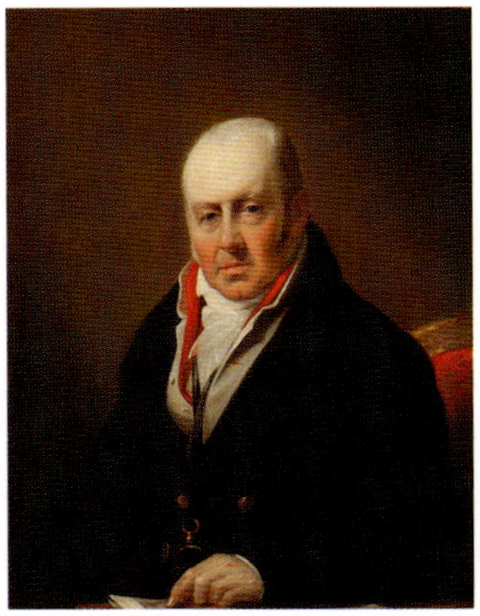

Lonsdale, James 1777–1839
John Dalton of Thurnham 1819
oil on canvas 98.5 x 85.5 (E)
LANLM.1983.43.11

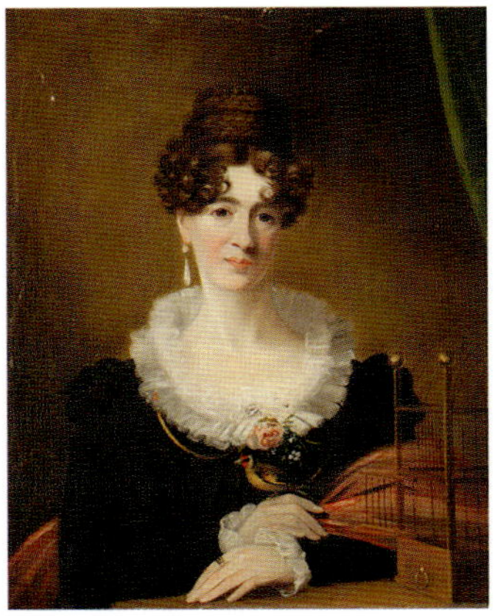

Lonsdale, James 1777–1839
Mary Dalton, Daughter of John Dalton and Mary Dalton, née Gage c.1819
oil on canvas 99.5 x 86.7 (E)
LANLM.1983.43.10

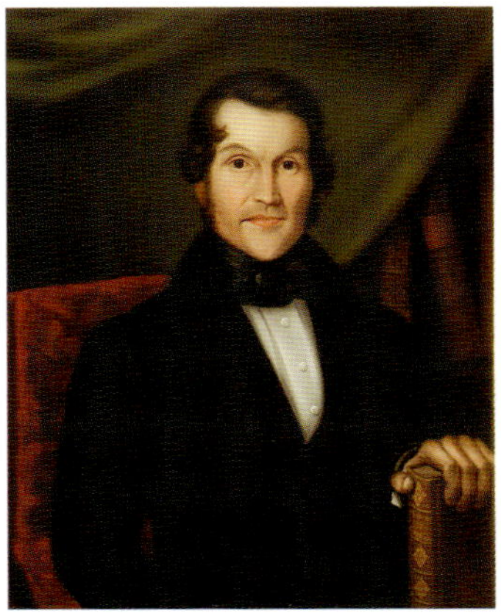

Lonsdale, Richard T. active c.1836–c.1850
James John Lonsdale c.1850
oil on canvas 78.3 x 66.1 (E)
LANLM.1986.118

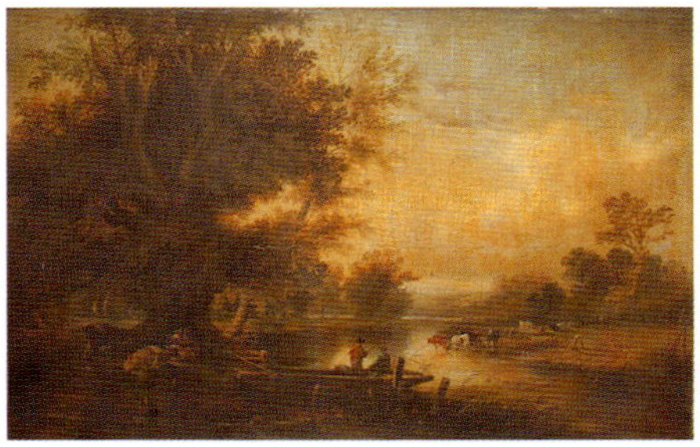

Maartens, Wontern
River Scene with Cattle and Two Men in a Boat c.1870
oil on canvas 55 x 90
LANLM.1899.4

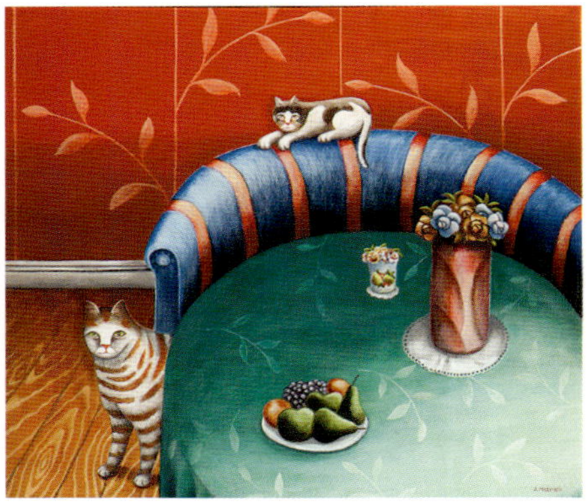

Marek, Jerzy b.1925
The Sitting Room 1983
acrylic on board 38.5 x 48
LANLM.1983.42.8

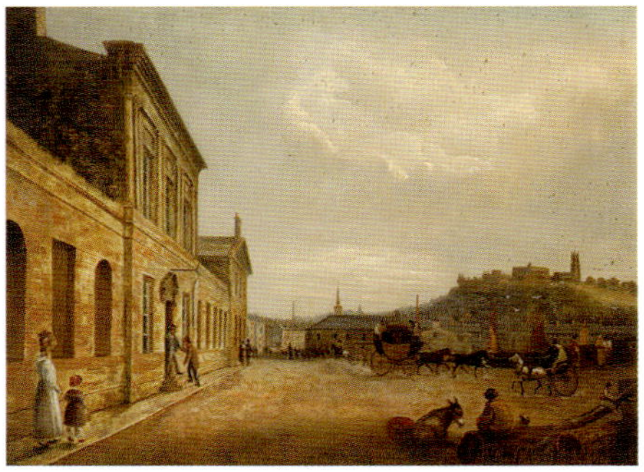

Marlow, William (attributed to) 1740–1813
Bridge End, Lancaster c.1790
oil on canvas 50.5 x 75.7 (E)
LANLM.1935.35

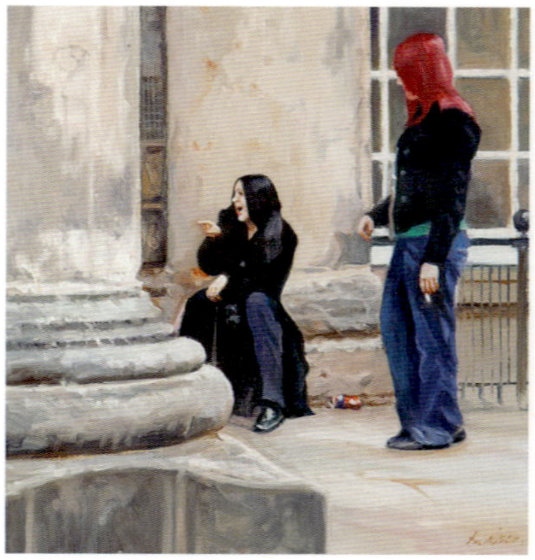

Mitchell, Sue b.1942
Chit Chat by the Museum, Lancaster 2007
oil on canvas 40.1 x 40.5 (E)
LANLM.2010.13

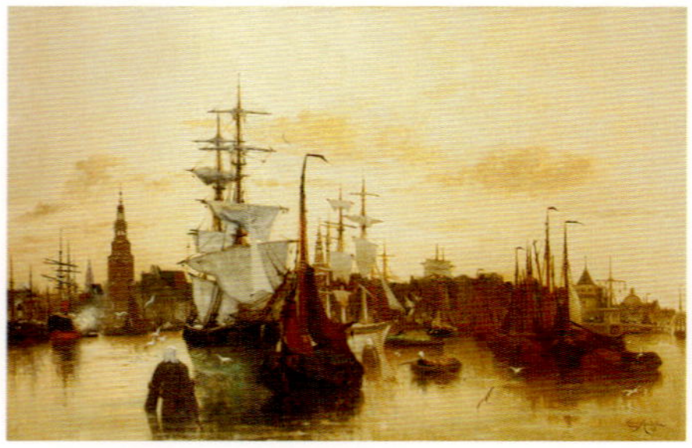

Montalba, Clara 1842–1929
The Port of Amsterdam 1886
oil on canvas 89.5 x 169
LANLM.1892.3.1

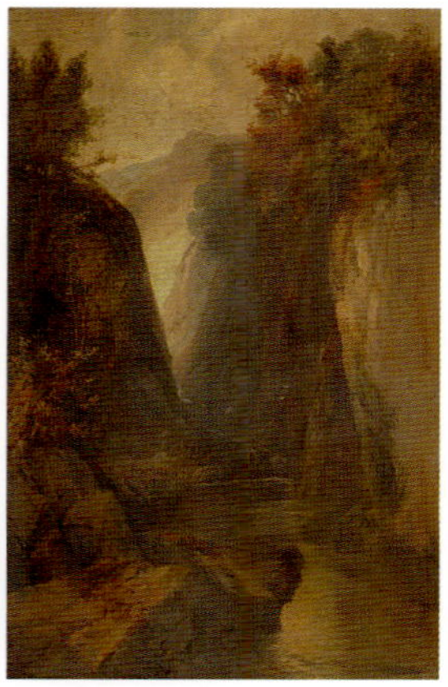

Morris, J. D.
Fairy Glen
oil on canvas 101.5 x 76
LANLM.1932.12.1

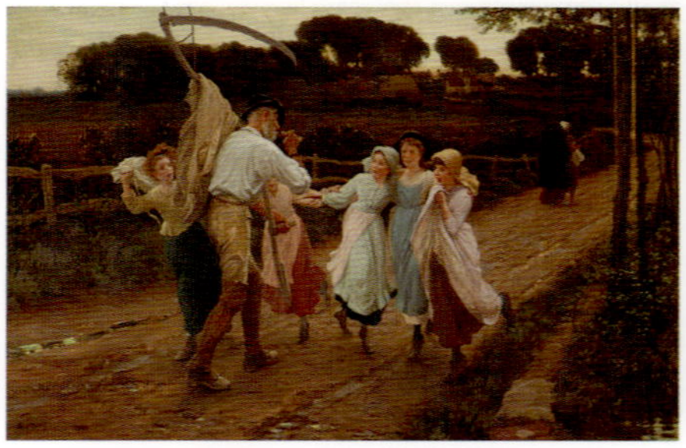

Morris, Philip Richard 1836–1902
The Reaper and the Flowers 1876–1878
oil on canvas 86 x 100
LANLM.1930.18.6

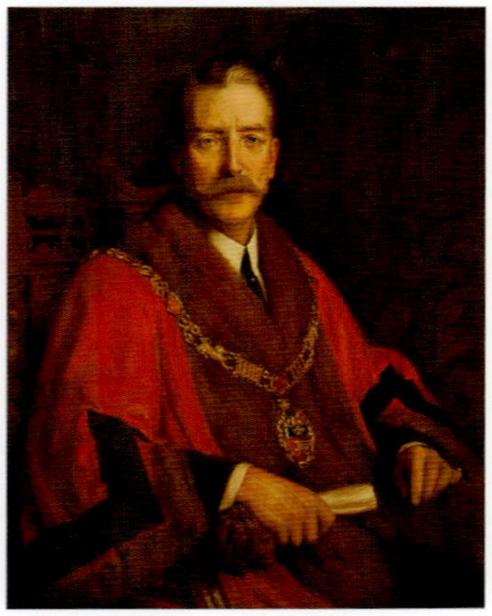

Morrison, Robert Edward 1851–1924
Alderman W. N. Briggs, JP, DL 1919
oil on canvas 90 x 70 (E)
LANLM.1975.83.2

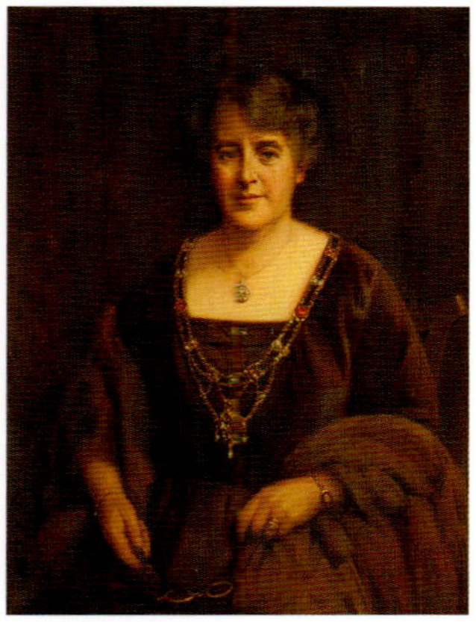

Morrison, Robert Edward 1851–1924
Mrs Briggs, Mayoress 1919
oil on canvas 90 x 70 (E)
LANLM.1975.83.3

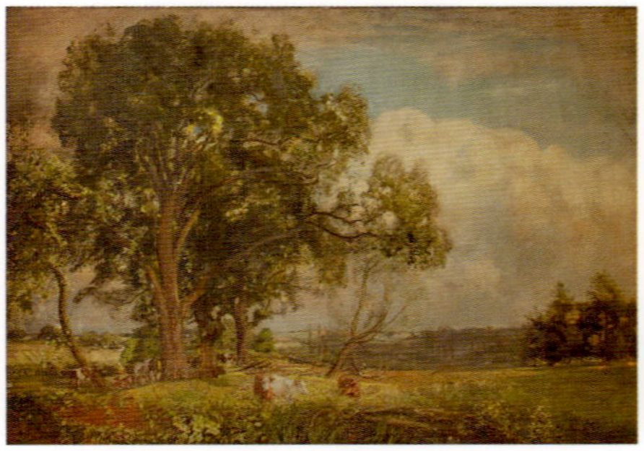

Murray, David 1849–1933
Valley of the Stour, East Bergholt, Suffolk 1870–1933
oil on canvas 121.5 x 183
LANLM.1939.22

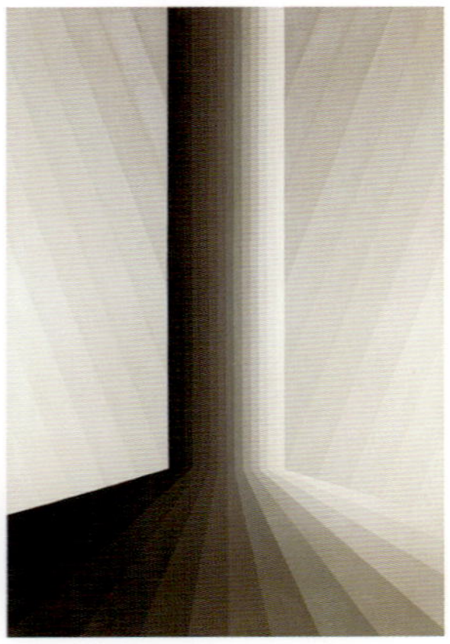

Murray, George b.1930
Aspiring Column (artist also known as Jerzy Marek) 1967
acrylic on canvas 152 x 101
LANLM.1983.42.11

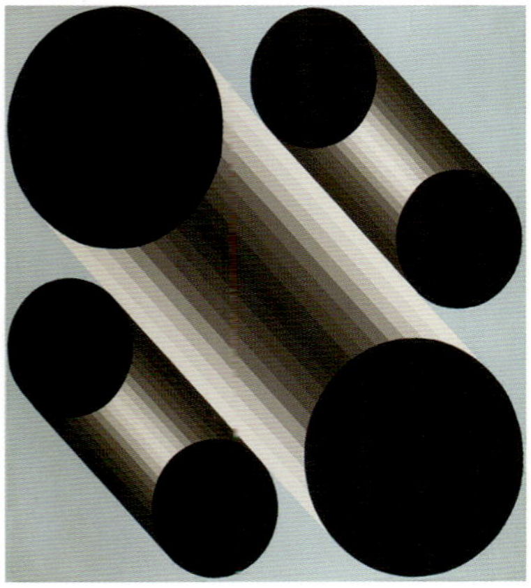

Murray, George b.1930
Pilot Fish (artist also known as Jerzy Marek) 1967
acrylic on canvas 91.5 x 91.5
LANLM.1983.42.9

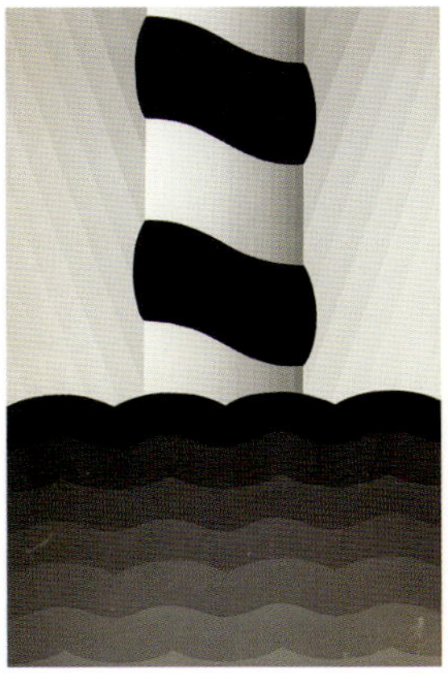

Murray, George b.1930
Sea Column (artist also known as Jerzy Marek) 1967
acrylic on canvas 154 x 103
LANLM.1983.42.10

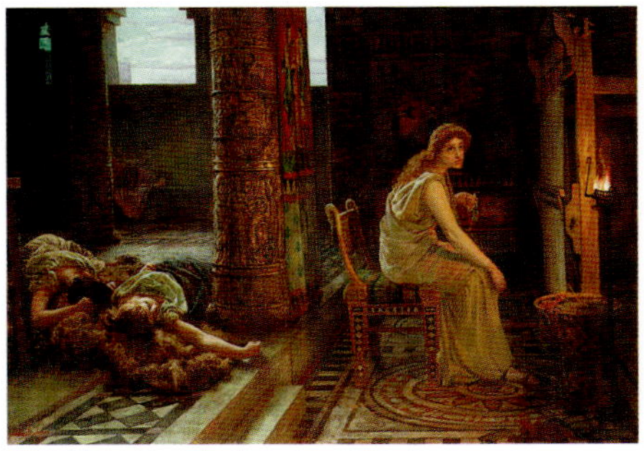

Muschamp, Francis Sydney 1851–1929
Penelope 1891
oil on canvas 70 x 115
LMA 52

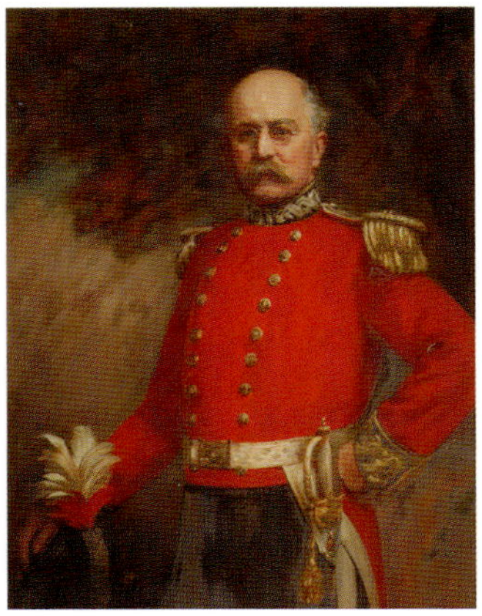

Neale, George Hall 1863–1940
Herbert Lushington Storey, JP, DL 1934
oil on canvas 105 x 85 (E)
LANLM.1930.12

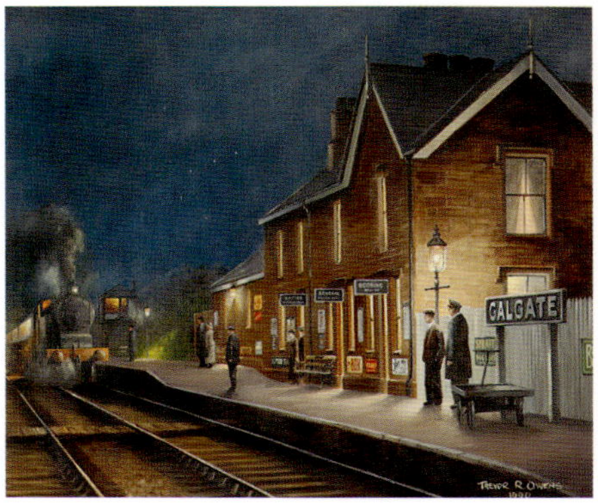

Owens, Trevor R. b.1935
Galgate Station by Night 1990
oil on canvas 59 x 68.9 (E)
LANLM.1990.14.1

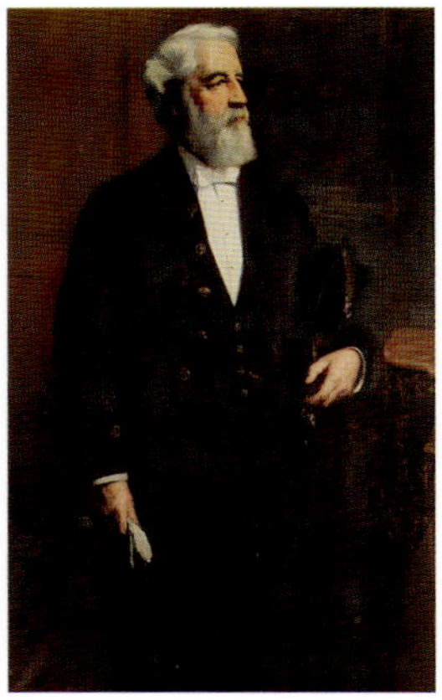

Palin, William Mainwaring 1862–1947
James Mansergh (1834–1905), Freeman of the Borough
oil on canvas 140 x 100
LANLM.1903.5

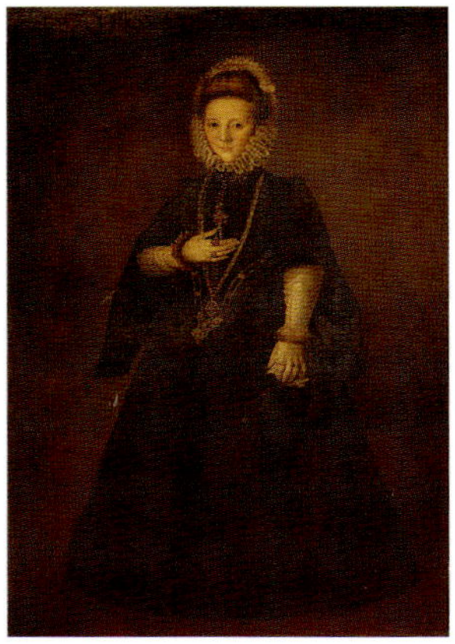

Pantoja de la Cruz, Juan 1553–1608
Spanish Noble Woman (from the Court of Philip II) 1598
oil on canvas 170.5 x 100 (E)
LMA 37

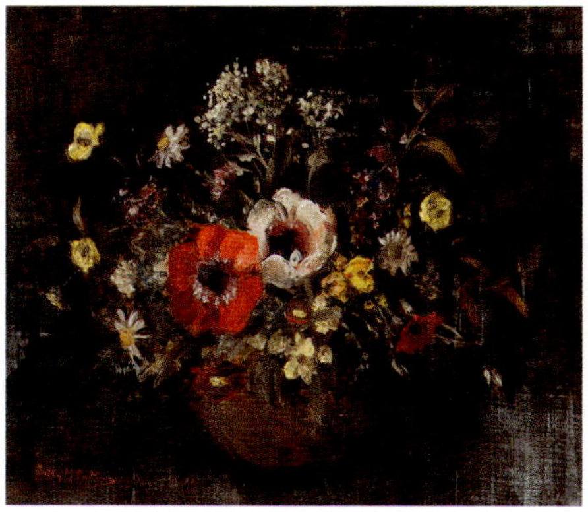

Paterson, Emily Murray 1855–1934
Anemones and Wild Flowers c.1910
oil on board 25.5 x 33
LANLM.1935.24.1

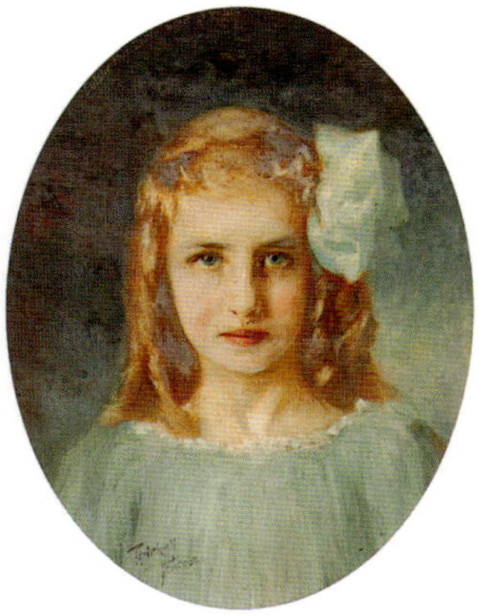

Pearce, Thirkell 1885–1955
Eulalie More Dalton c.1930
oil on canvas 61 x 48 (E)
LANLM.1983.43.22

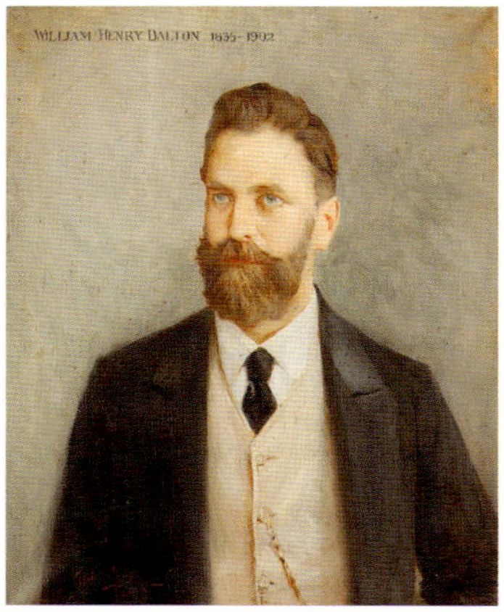

Pearce, Thirkell 1885–1955
William Henry Dalton (1832–1902) c.1930
oil on canvas
LANLM.1983.43.34

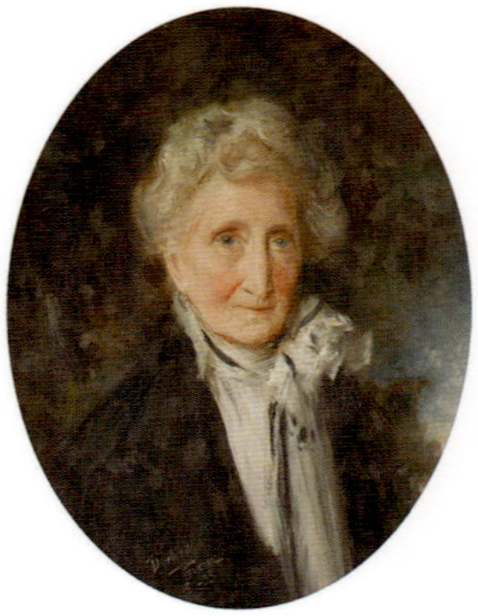

Pearce, Thirkell 1885–1955
Mrs Dalton 1933
oil on canvas 66 x 53 (E)
LANLM.1983.43.23

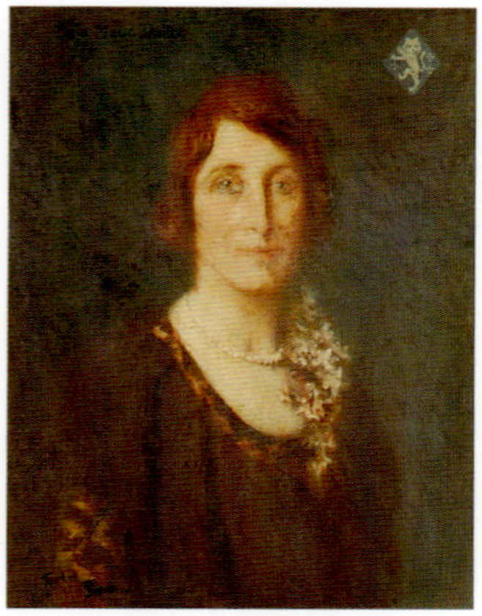

Pearce, Thirkell 1885–1955
Lola Maud Dalton c.1933
oil on canvas 60 x 49.5 (E)
LANLM.1983.43.25

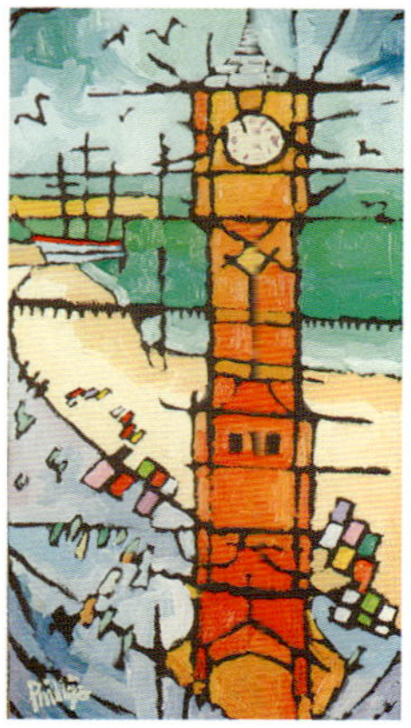

Phillips, Brian b.1939
Clock Tower, Morecambe c.1971
oil on board 85 x 46 (E)
LANLM.1984.31

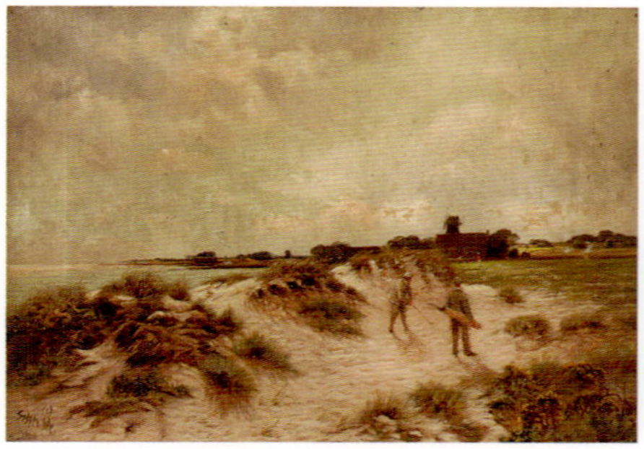

Pike, Sidney 1846–1907
The Golf Links 1900
oil on canvas 30.5 x 46
LANLM.1963.44.21

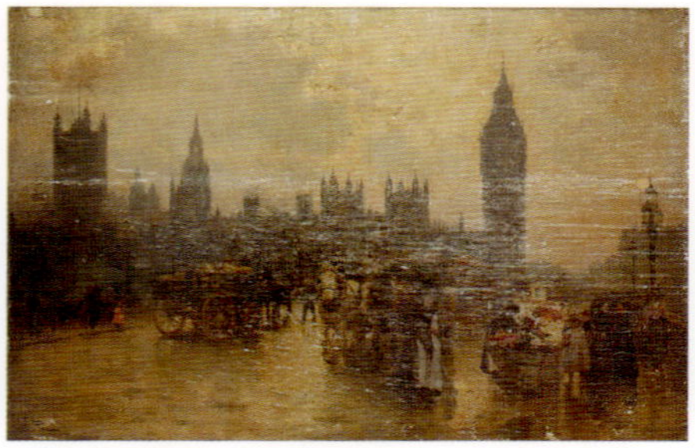

Pisa, Alberto 1864–1931
Westminster Bridge 1890–1899
oil on canvas 69 x 105
LMA 220

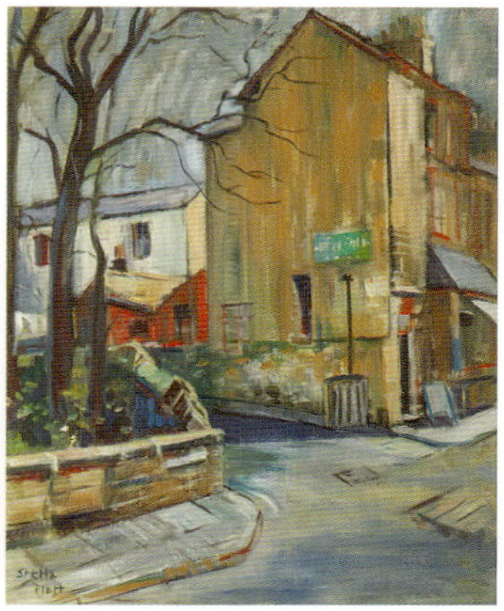

Platt, Stella 1913–2011
Road to Bath Mill 1967
oil on canvas 73 x 62.7 (E)
LANLM.1967.18

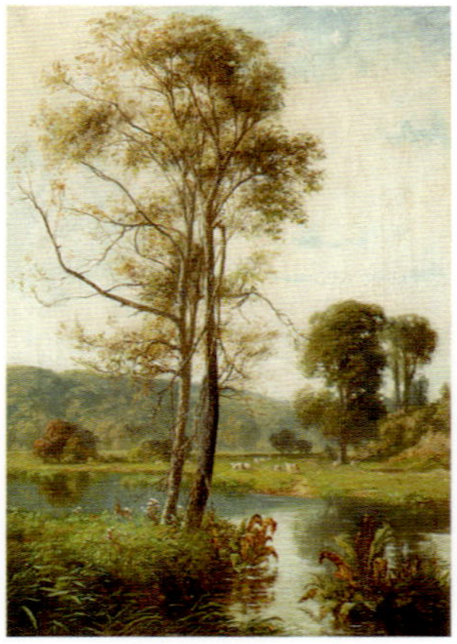

Pyne, Thomas 1843–1935
Trees and River c.1895
oil on canvas 63 x 45
LANLM.1943.12

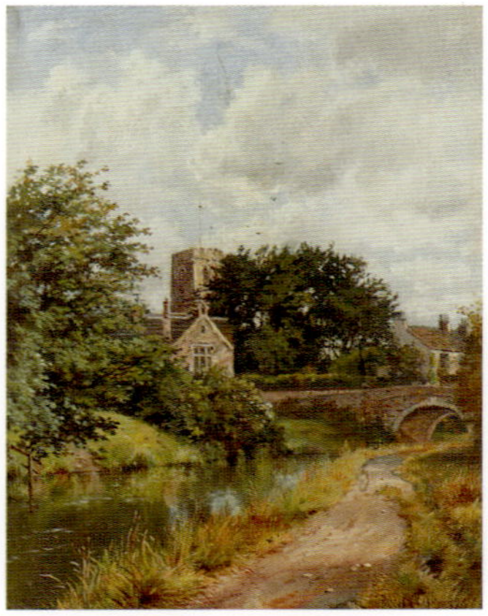

Rampling, Robert 1835–1909
Bolton-le-Sands from the Canal 1880
oil on canvas 31 x 24 (E)
LANLM.1950.21.1

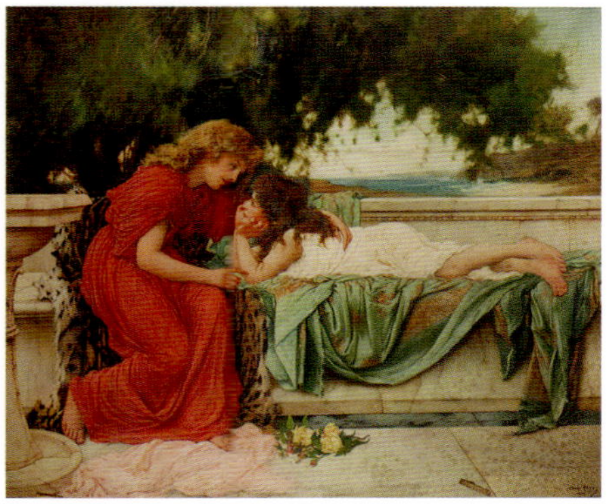

Rhys, Oliver 1853–1928
Rebecca 1895
oil on canvas 102 x 126
LANLM.1952.34.2

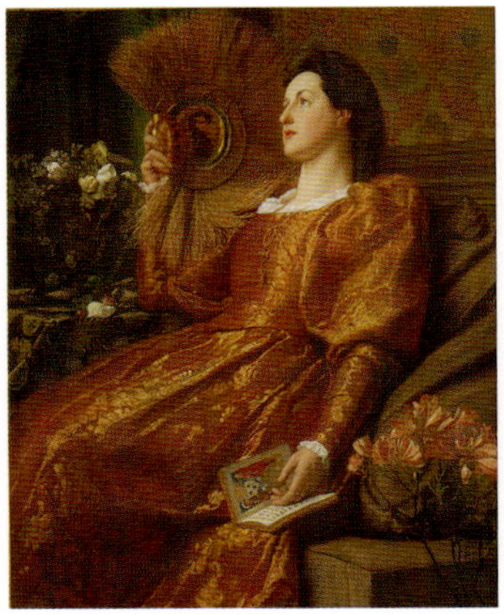

Richmond, William Blake 1842–1921
Charlotte Elizabeth Fuller-Maitland of Borwick Hall c.1886
oil on canvas 123 x 107
LMA 67

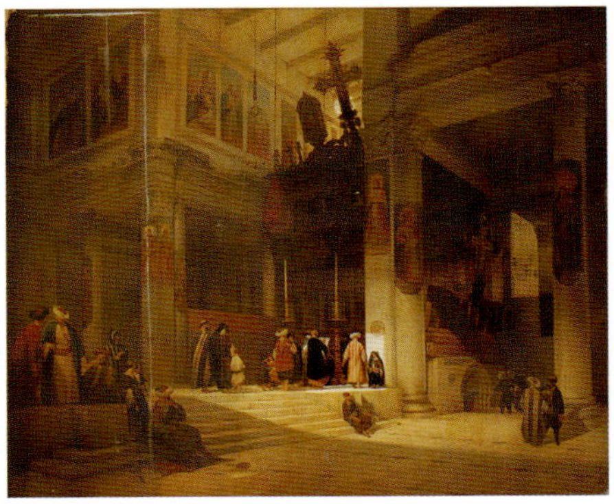

Roberts, David (attributed to) 1796–1864
Moorish Church Interior (Eastern Church) 1832
oil on canvas
LANLM.1915.4

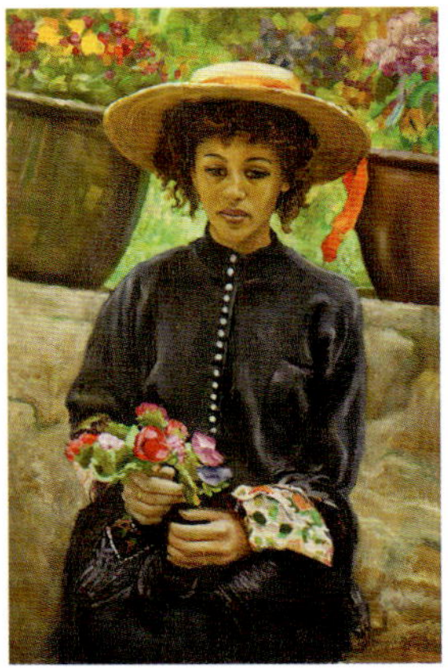

Robinson, Christopher b.1945
Clare Weze c.1994
oil on canvas 109.2 x 78.9 (E)
LANLM.1995.3.1

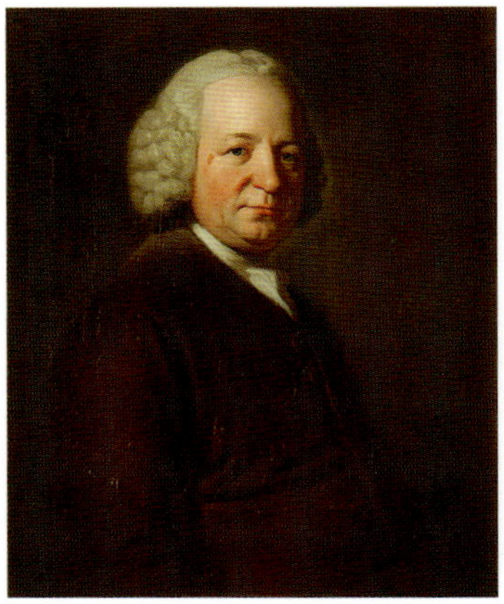

Romney, George 1734–1802
Thomas Hutton Rawlinson (1712–1769) c.1760
oil on canvas 75 x 62.5 (E)
LANLM.1934.45.9

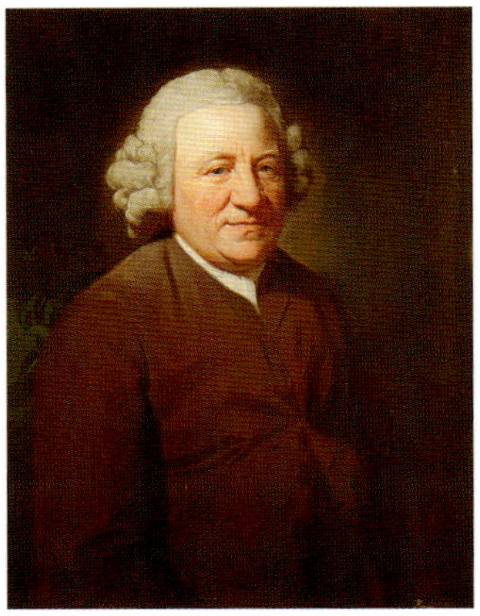

Romney, George 1734–1802
Abraham Rawlinson (1709–1780) 1772
oil on canvas 76 x 63.5 (E)
LANLM.2009.12.1

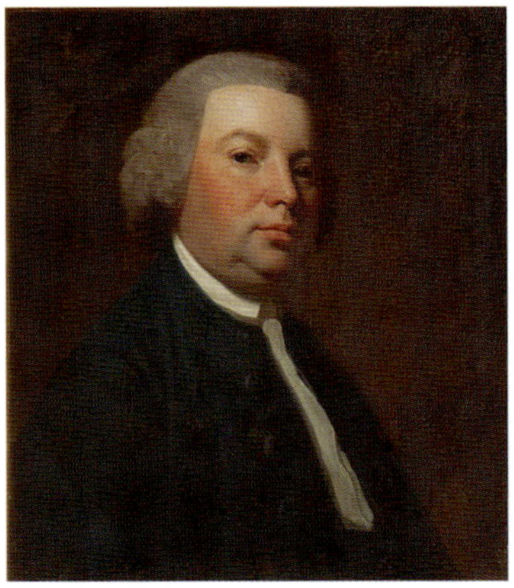

Romney, George 1734–1802
Reverend Oliver Marton, Vicar of Lancaster (1767–1794) c.1790
oil on canvas 67.7 x 63 (E)
LANLM.1980.79

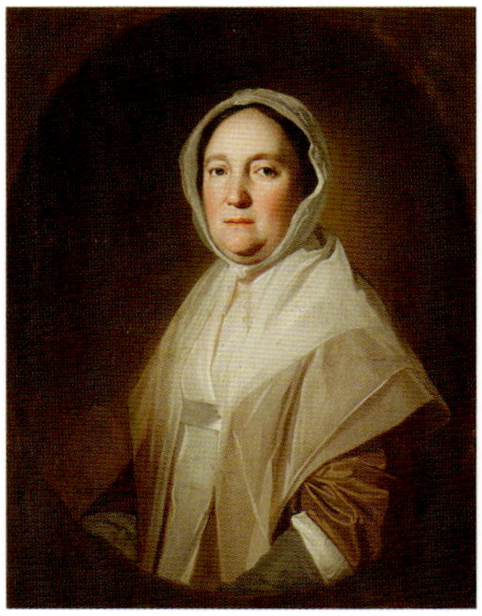

Romney, George (attributed to) 1734–1802
Mary Rawlinson 1740–1760
oil on canvas 75.5 x 62.5 (E)
LANLM.1934.45.8

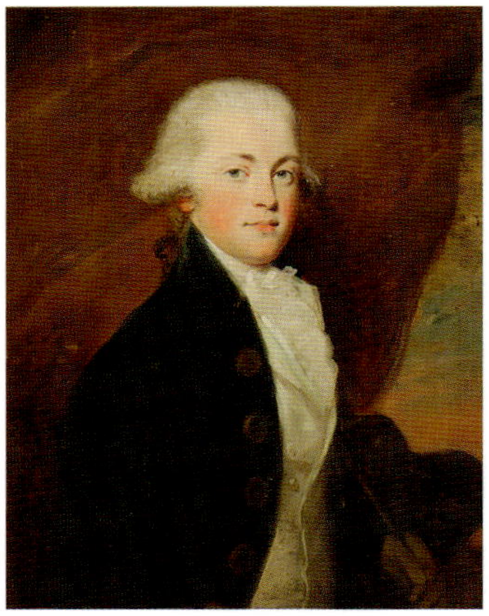

Romney, George (attributed to) 1734–1802
Thomas Hutton Rawlinson (1712–1769) c.1750
oil on canvas 75 x 62 (E)
LANLM.1932.13

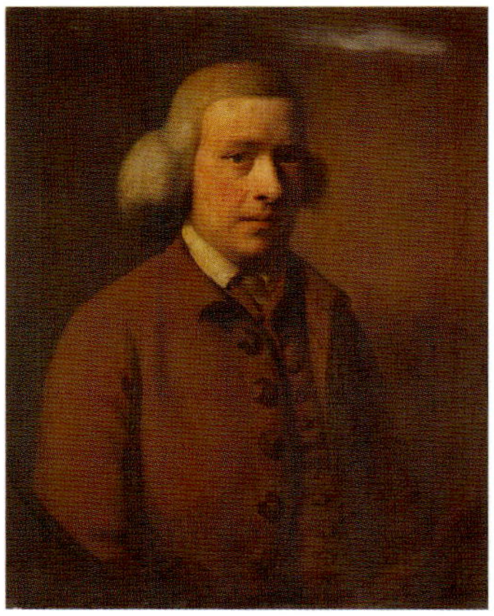

Romney, George (attributed to) 1734–1802
Isaac Ford 1759–1765
oil on canvas 76 x 63.5 (E)
LANLM.1934.45.7

Facing page: Devis, Arthur William, 1762–1822, *John Addison,* 1784–1795, Harris Museum & Art Gallery (p. 296)

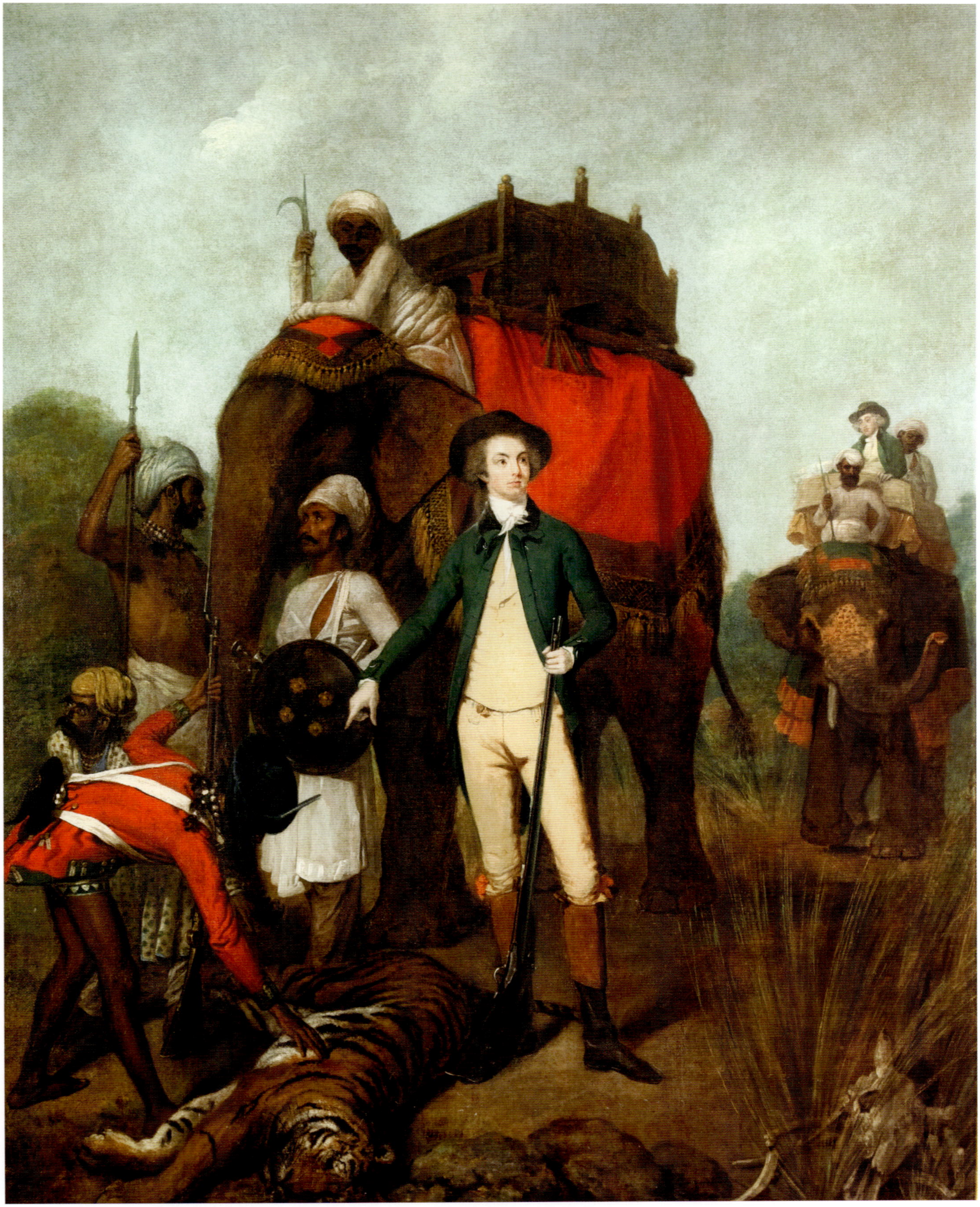

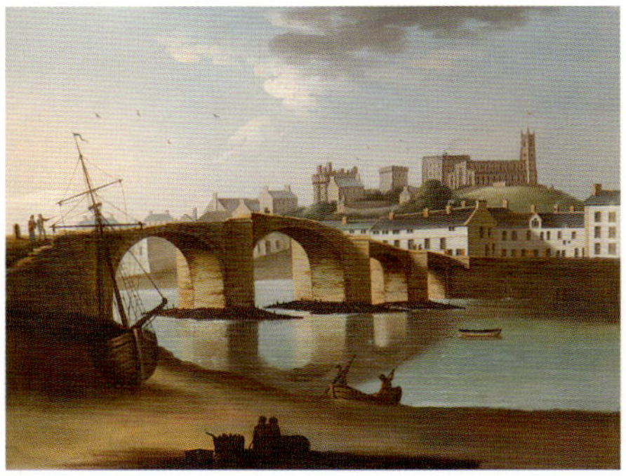

Salmon, Robert W. (attributed to) 1775–1851
Lancaster Castle from the River Lune c.1790
oil on copper plate 27 x 39
LANLM.1998.16

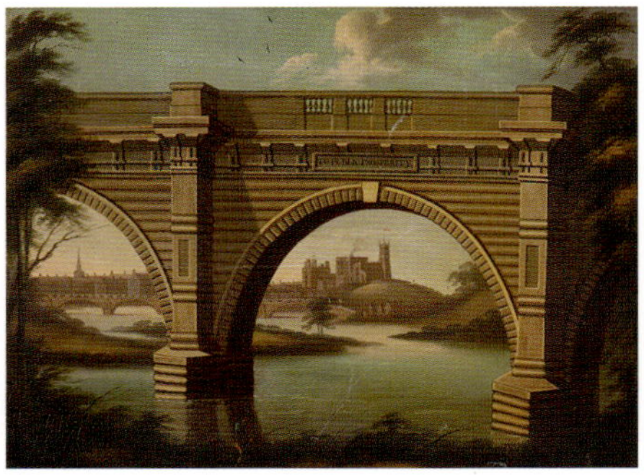

Salmon, Robert W. (attributed to) 1775–1851
View of Lancaster and the Lune Aqueduct c.1790s
oil on copper plate 27 x 40
LANLM.2010.4.2

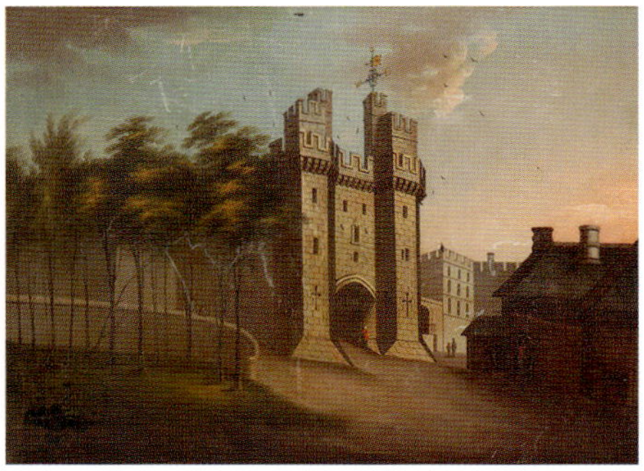

Salmon, Robert W. (attributed to) 1775–1851
View of the John O'Gaunt Gateway, Lancaster Castle c.1790s
oil on copper plate 27 x 41
LANLM.2010.4.1

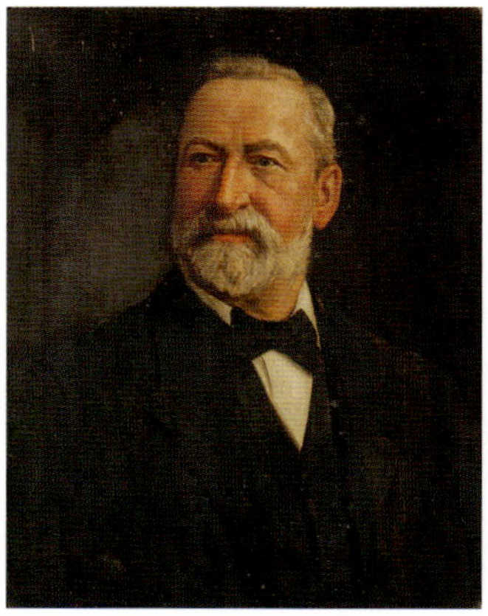

Salomon, Harry Herman 1860–1936
Portrait of a Man with an Imperial Beard c.1900
oil on canvas
LMA 68

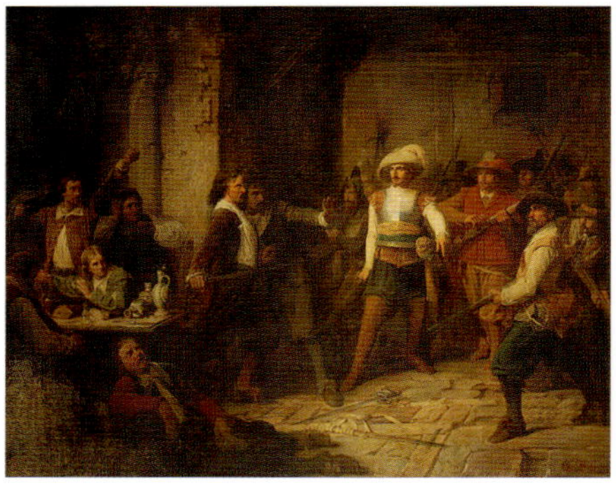

Sell, Christian 1831–1883
German Soldiers Surprised in an Inn by the Swedes c.1869
oil on canvas 96 x 130
LANLM.1892.3.2

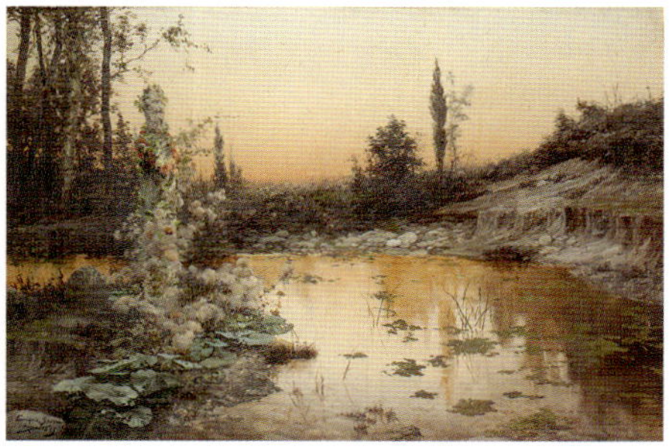

Serra, Enrique 1859–1918
Antique Effigy 1885
oil on canvas 69 x 114
LMA 70

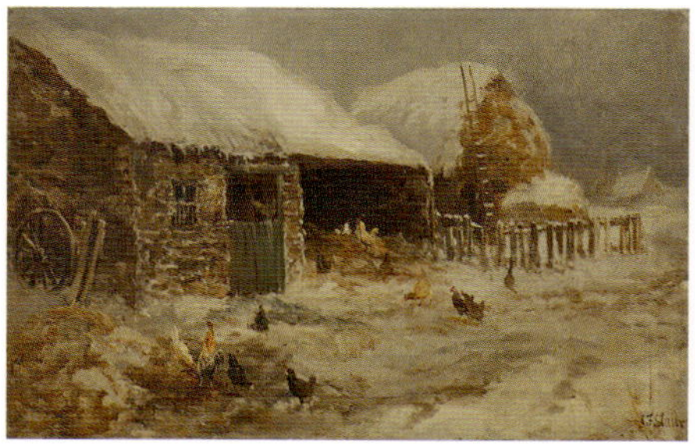

Slater, G. F.
Winter Weather
oil on canvas 45 x 75
LANLM.1940.7.11

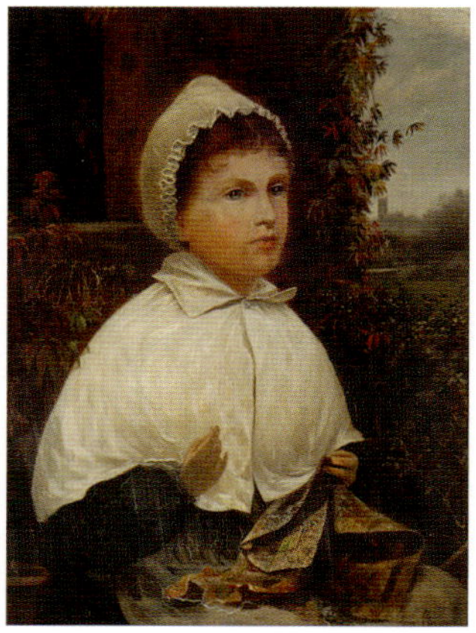

Slinger, Ann 1855–1935
The Bluecoat Girl c.1890
oil on canvas 47.5 x 38 (E)
LANLM.1908.4

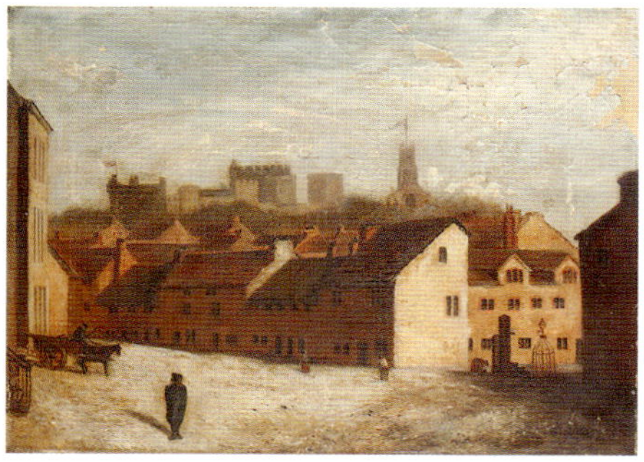

Slinger, Ann 1855–1935
Stonewell and Pumps c.1900
oil on canvas 27 x 34.5
LANLM.1945.6.1

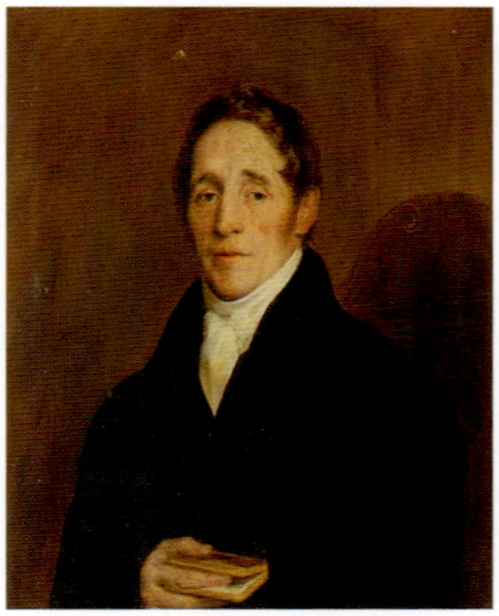

Spindler, Louis Pierre 1800–1889
Jeremiah Wane (1787–1852) 1841
oil on canvas 74 x 62 (E)
LANLM.1970.3.2

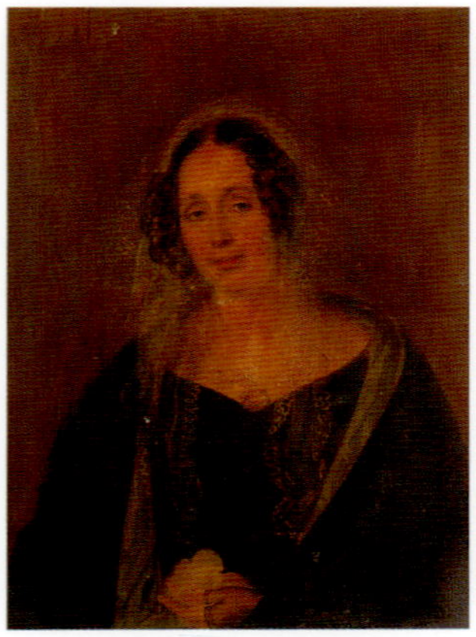

Spindler, Louis Pierre 1800–1889
Mrs Ann Rawsthorne 1841
oil on canvas 77 x 63.5 (E)
LANLM.1969.20.1

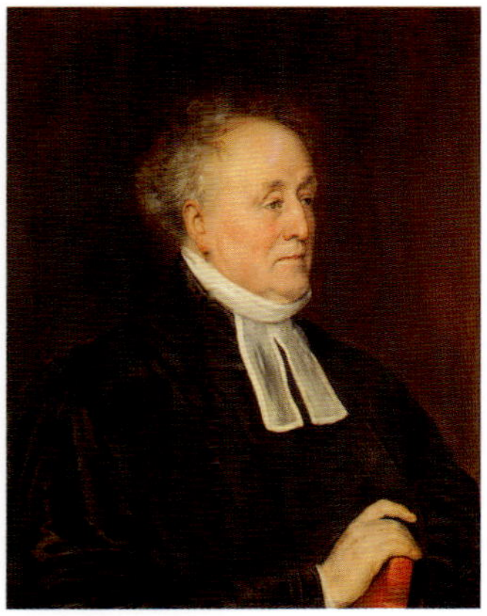

Spindler, Louis Pierre 1800–1889
Reverend John Manby of Lancaster (1806–1844) 1841
oil on canvas 76 x 63
LANLM.1937.12

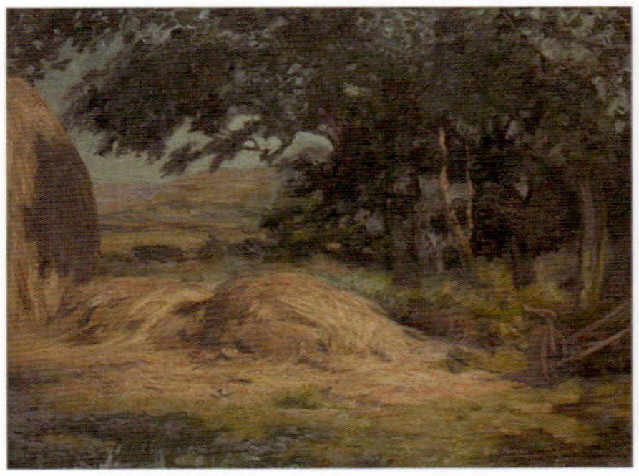

Stephenson, G.
Countryside with Hayricks (Morecambe)
c.1950
oil on canvas 49 x 70
LANLM.1960.1

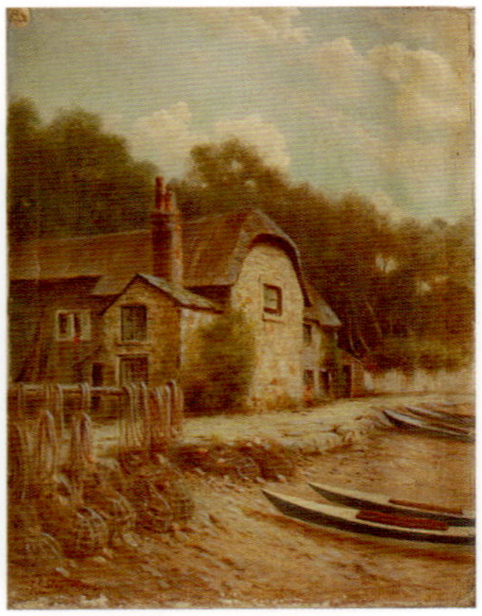

Stephenson, T. 1865–1945
Cottage and Boats along the Lune Coast
(possibly Sunderland Point) 1883
oil on board 53 x 42
LANLM.1960.7.1

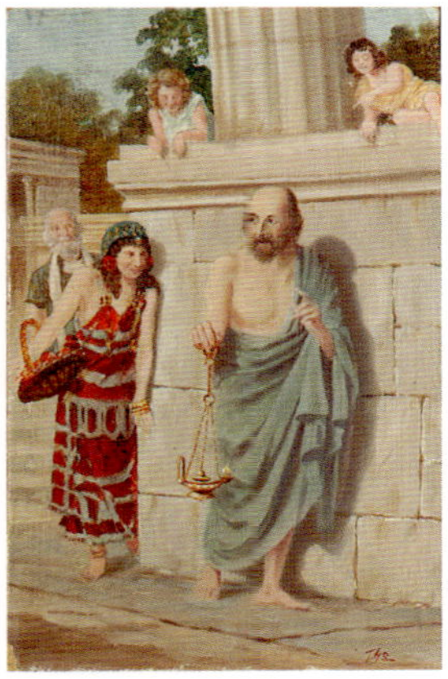

Stephenson, T. 1865–1945
Classical Scene c.1900
oil on board 32.5 x 20.5
LANLM.1960.7.27

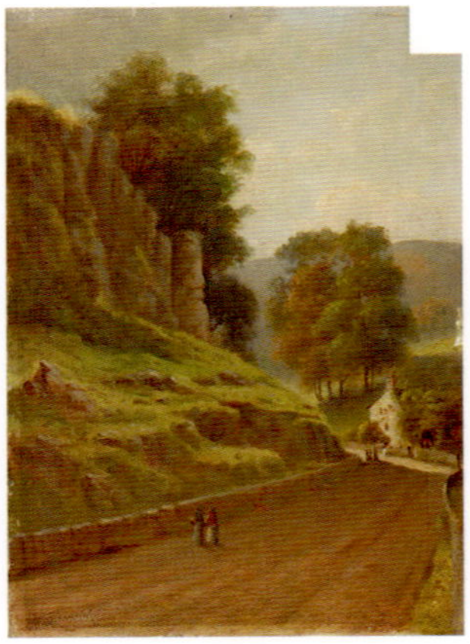

Stephenson, T. 1865–1945
Lakeland Landscape with Country Road
c.1900
oil on canvas 38 x 28.5
LANLM.1960.7.18

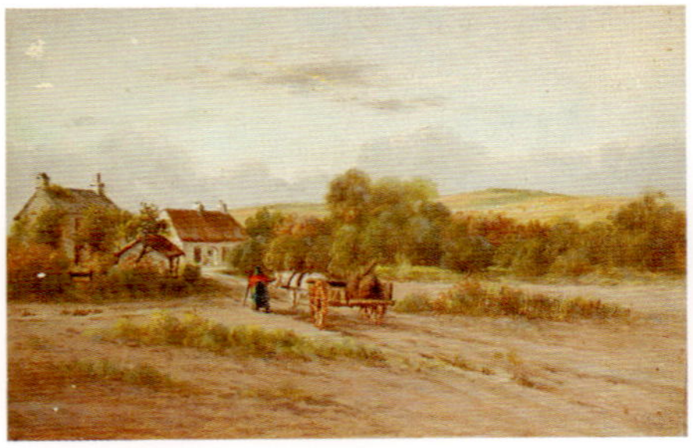

Stephenson, T. 1865–1945
Reed Huwe, near Gleaston, Morecambe Bay
c.1900
oil on canvas 25 x 38
LANLM.1960.7.17

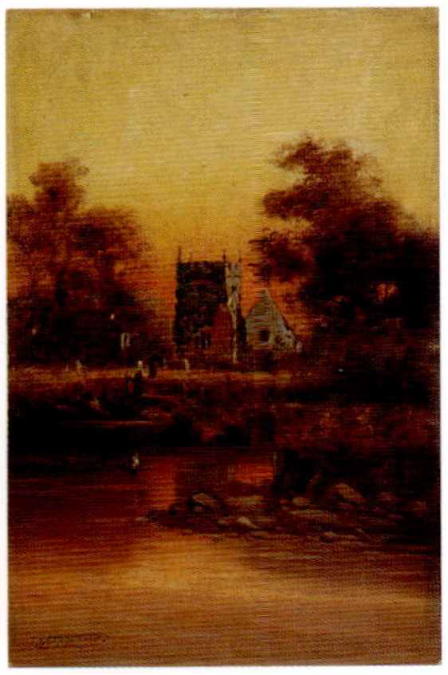

Stephenson, T. 1865–1945
River Bank with Church Tower and Figures
c.1910
oil on board 45 x 31
LANLM.1960.7.19

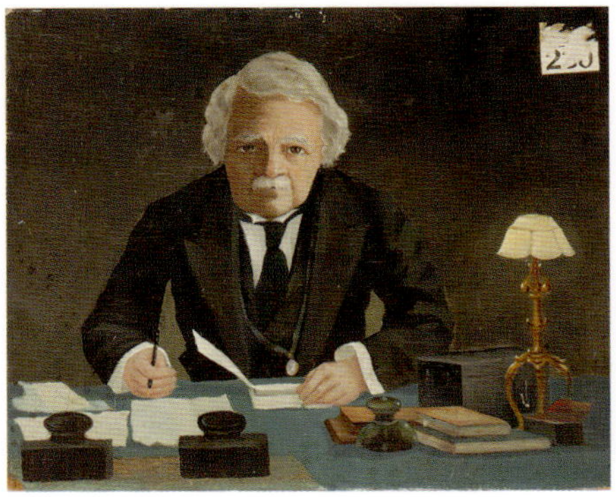

Stephenson, T. 1865–1945
Lloyd George (1863–1945) c.1920
oil on board 26 x 33.5
LANLM.1960.7.21

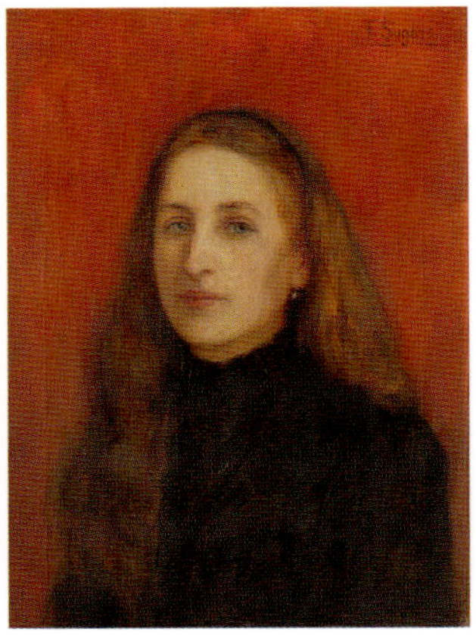

Sugars, Fanny 1856–1933
Miss Dalton c.1904
oil on canvas 51 x 38 (E)
LANLM.1983.43.24

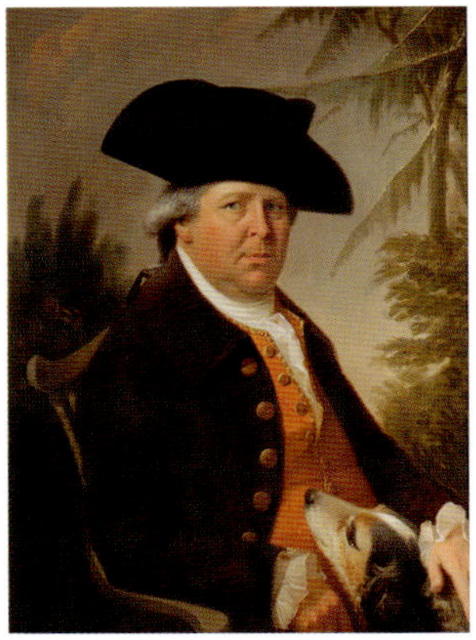

Tate, William (attributed to) 1747–1806
Mr Dodshon Foster of Lancaster (1730–1793) 1770–1793
oil on canvas 89 x 71
LANLM.1992.64

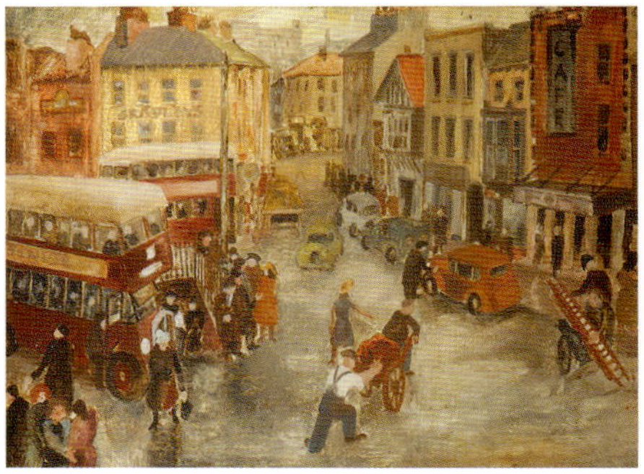

Tobin, John b.1924
Market Square, Lancaster 1950s
oil on canvas 54.2 x 71 (E)
LANLM.1967.9

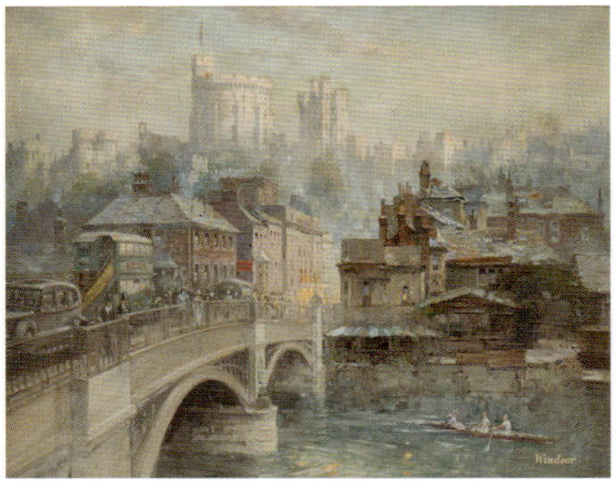

Turner, Charles E. 1883–1965
Windsor Castle c.1938
oil on canvas 50 x 74
LANLM.1953.15

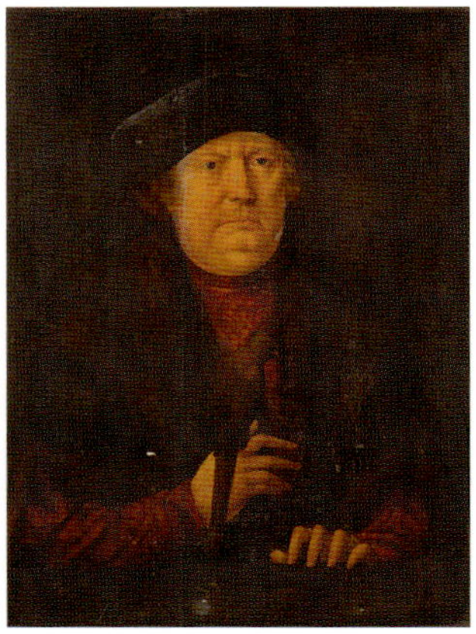

unknown artist
Tudor Gentleman c.1550
oil on panel 80 x 65 (E)
LMA 91

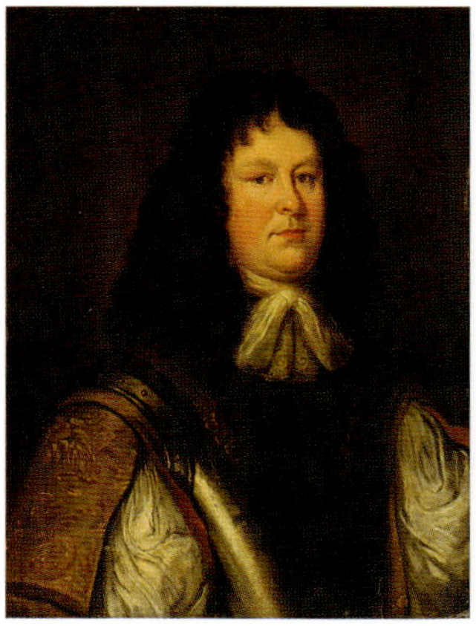

unknown artist
Thomas Dalton of Thurnham Hall c.1640
oil on canvas 71 x 61
LANLM.1983.43.5

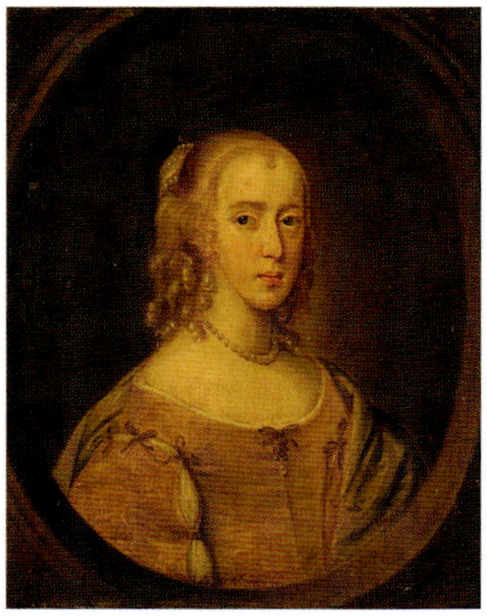

unknown artist
A Young Lady of the Dalton family c.1660
oil on canvas 70 x 59.5 (E)
LANLM.1983.43.1

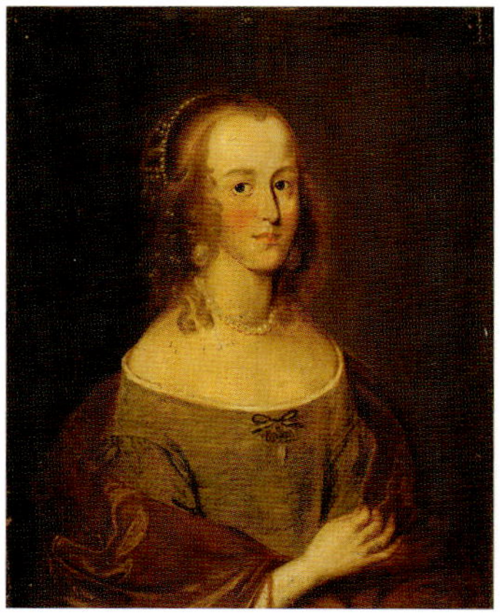

unknown artist
An Unidentified Young Lady of the Dalton Family c.1660
oil on canvas 71 x 61 (E)
LANLM.1983.43.4

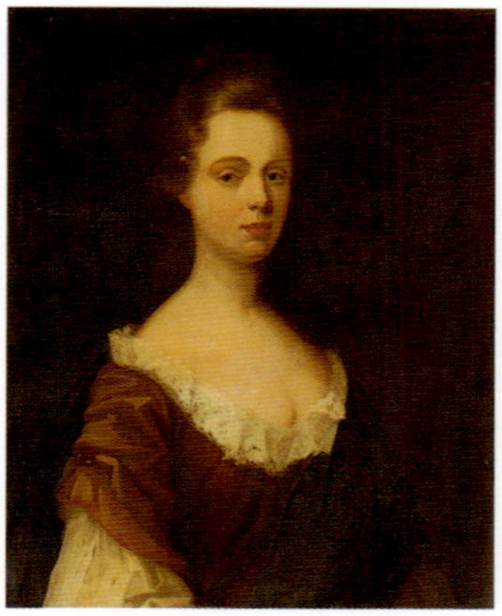

unknown artist
Elizabeth Dalton, First Wife of Robert Dalton of Thurnham c.1660
oil on canvas 72 x 61 (E)
LANLM.1983.43.19

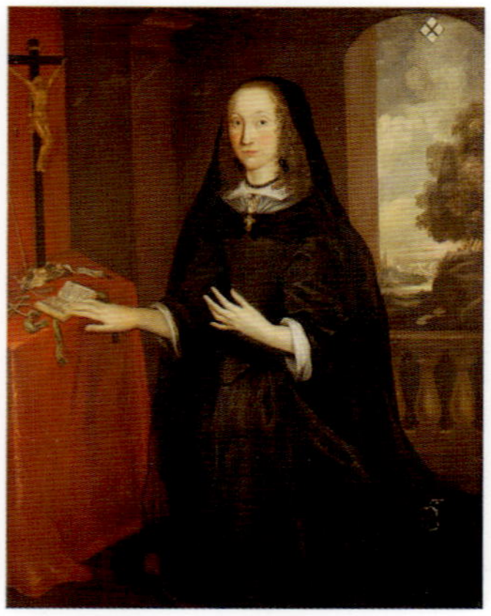

unknown artist
Elizabeth Dalton, née Middleton of Leighton c.1670
oil on canvas 150 x 125 (E)
LANLM.1983.43.6

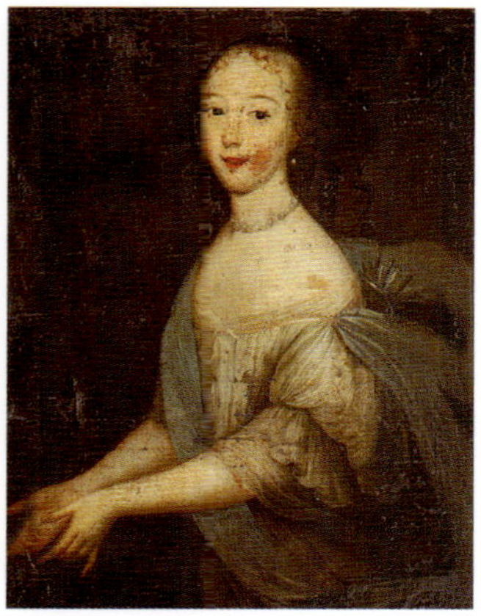

unknown artist
Portrait of a Young Lady c.1670
oil on canvas 72 x 61.5 (E)
LANLM.1983.43.7

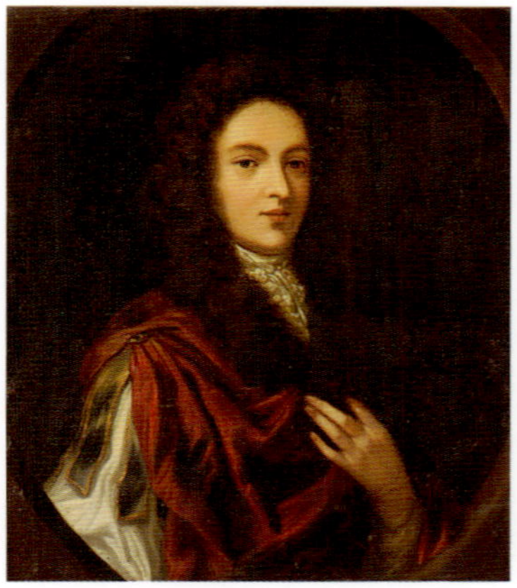

unknown artist
A Young Gentleman of the Dalton Family of Thurnham c.1680
oil on canvas 70 x 59.5 (E)
LANLM.1983.43.18

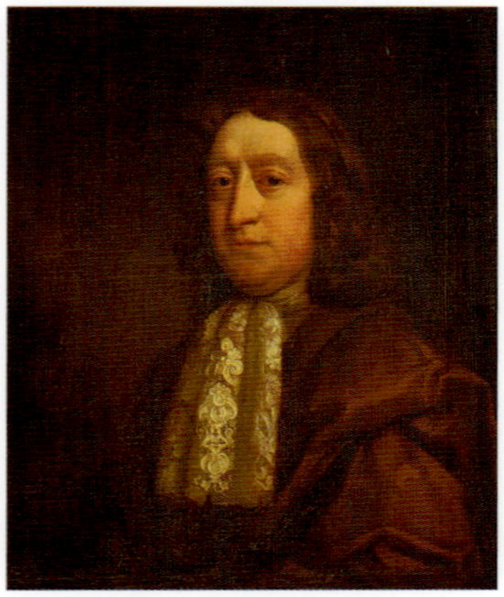

unknown artist
An Unidentified Gentleman of the Dalton Family (possibly Robert Dalton) c.1680
oil on canvas 71.8 x 61.2 (E)
LANLM.1983.43.17

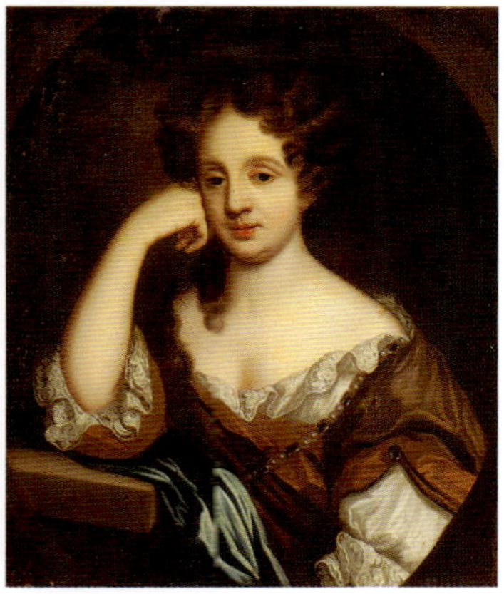

unknown artist
Mary Dalton, née Biddulph c.1680
oil on canvas 70 x 61 (E)
LANLM.1983.43.13

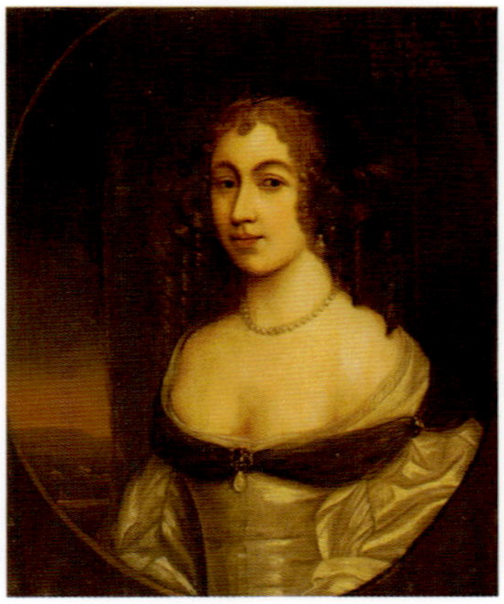

unknown artist
Elizabeth Dalton, née Selby c.1688
oil on canvas 70 x 61
LANLM.1983.43.16

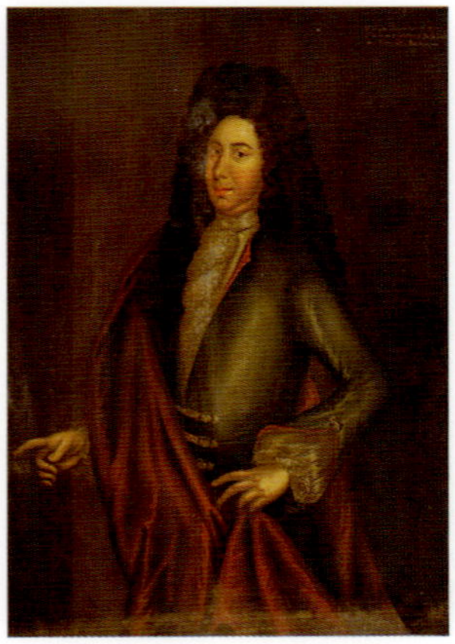

unknown artist
William Hoghton c.1710
oil on canvas 125 x 94 (E)
LANLM.1983.43.2

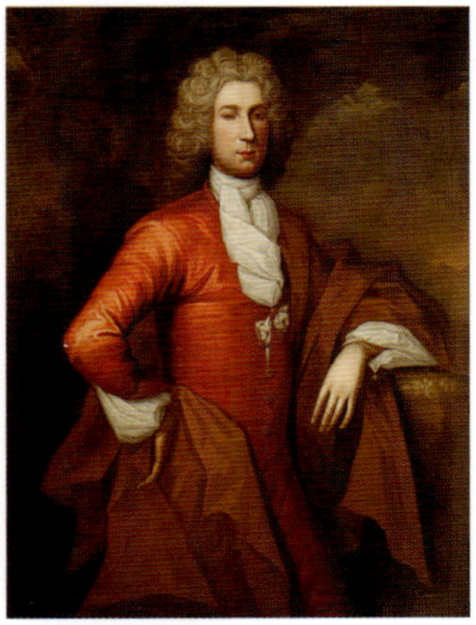

unknown artist
A Gentleman of the Belasyse Family c.1725
oil on canvas 124 x 99.5 (E)
LANLM.1948.6.5

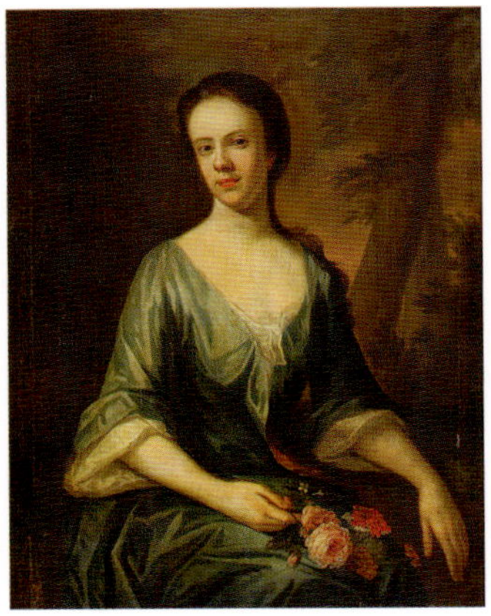

unknown artist
Frances Hoghton Dalton c.1750
oil on canvas 103.5 x 84.5 (E)
LANLM.1983.43.3

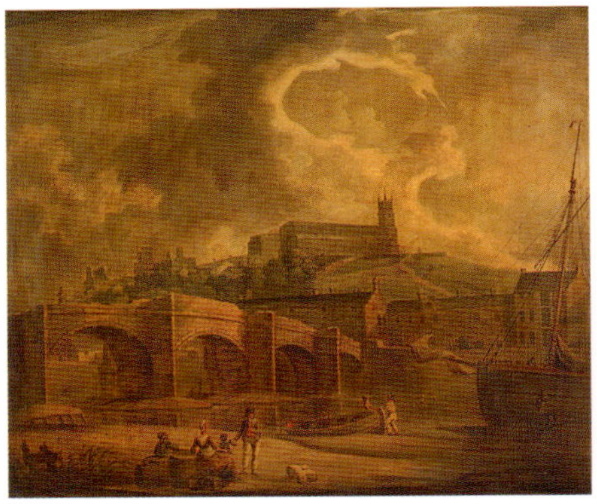

unknown artist
Lancaster Old Bridge c.1750
oil on canvas 62 x 73.5 (E)
LANLM.1925.10

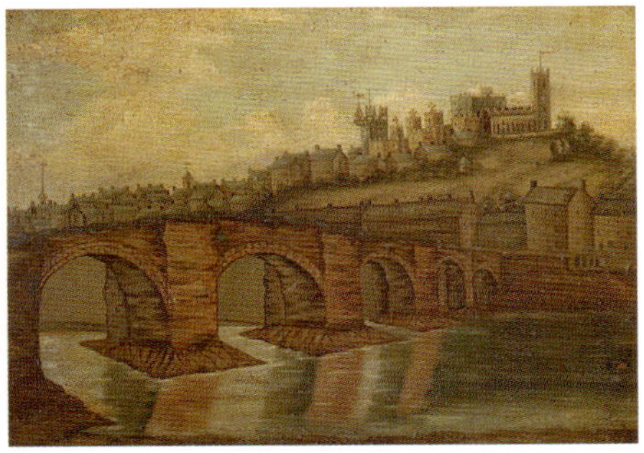

unknown artist
Loyne Bridge, Castle, Parish Church, Old Town Hall and St John's Church c.1750
oil on canvas 45 x 62 (E)
LANLM.1937.15

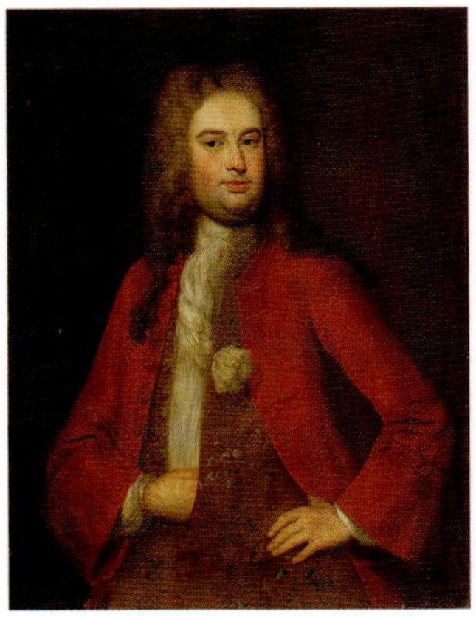

unknown artist
Mr John Hoghton Dalton c.1750
oil on canvas 104.5 x 84.5 (E)
LANLM.1983.43.8

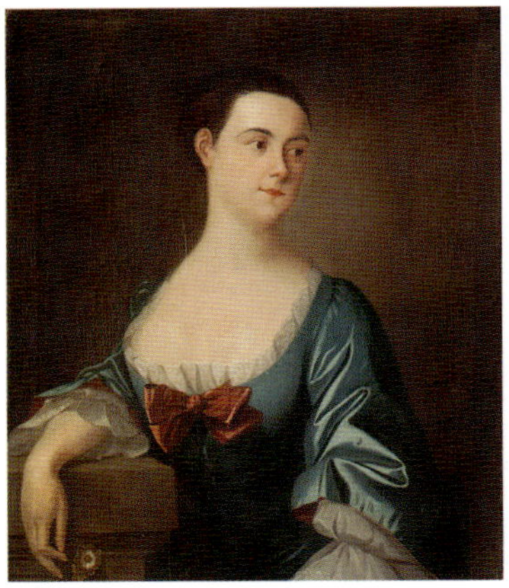

unknown artist
A Lady of the Dalton Family c.1752
oil on canvas 75 x 62.5
LANLM.1983.43.20

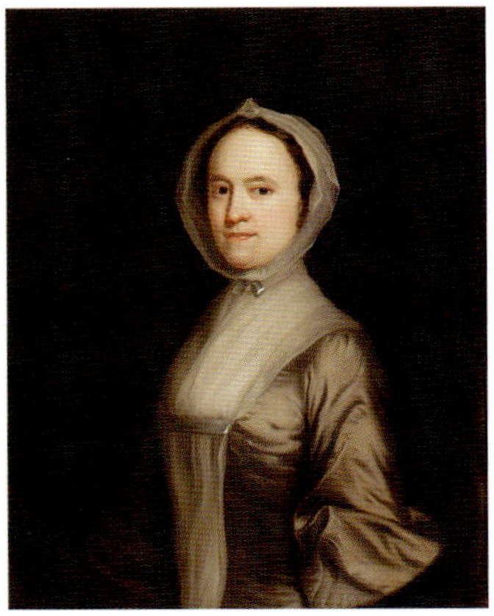

unknown artist
Ellenor Godsalve Rawlinson (1716–1766) c.1772
oil on canvas 74 x 60
LANLM.2009.12.2

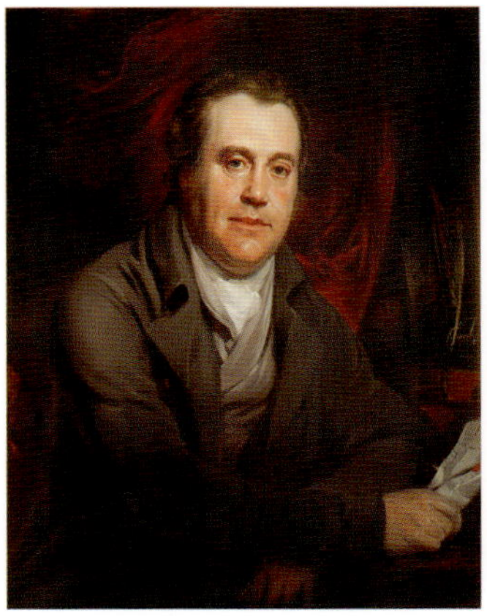

unknown artist
James Booth, Collector of HM Customs, Port of Lancaster c.1780
oil on canvas 75 x 61
LANLM.1930.1

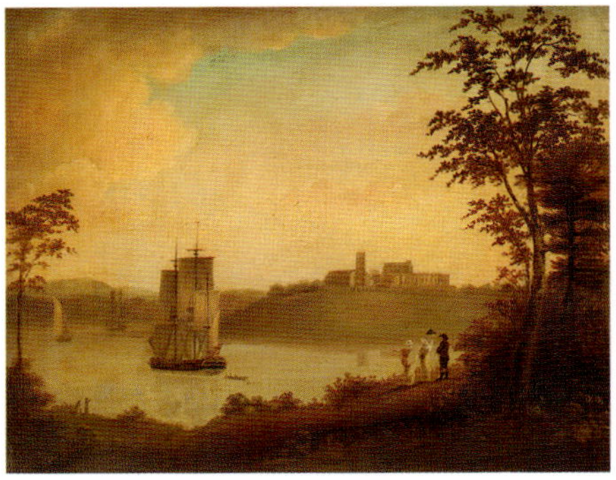

unknown artist
Lancaster from Skerton with a Sailing Ship c.1780
oil on canvas 48 x 63 (E)
LANLM.1928.14.2.a

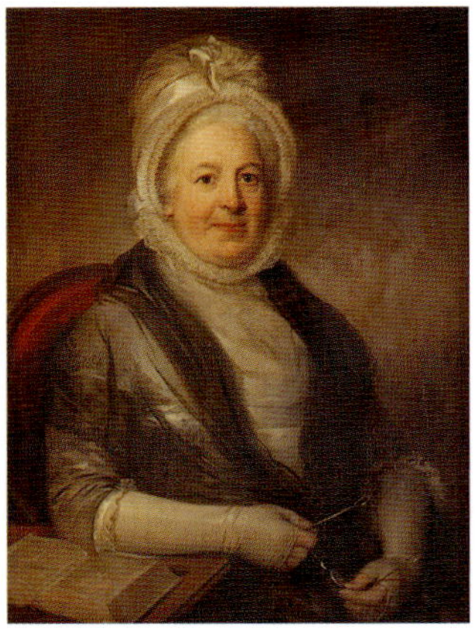

unknown artist
Mrs Alice Worswick, née Gillow c.1780
oil on canvas 120 x 95 (E)
LANLM.1926.10.2

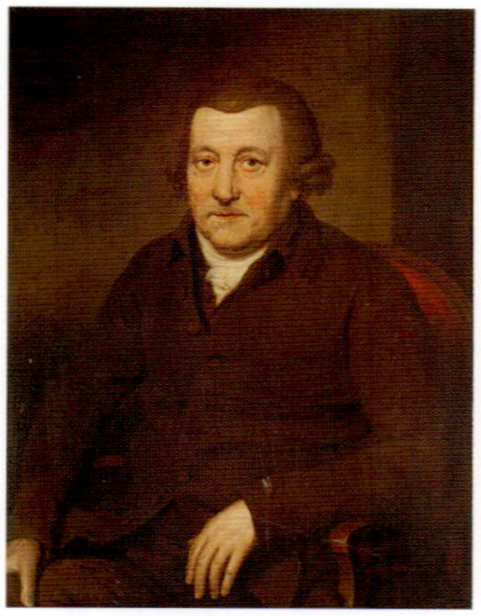

unknown artist
Thomas Worswick of Lancaster c.1780
oil on canvas 120 x 95 (E)
LANLM.1926.10.1

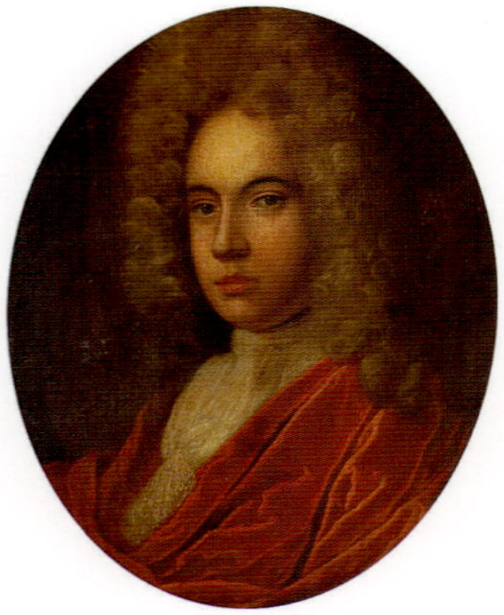

unknown artist
A Young Gentleman of the Dalton Family c.1790
oil on canvas 60 x 50 (E)
LANLM.1983.43.21

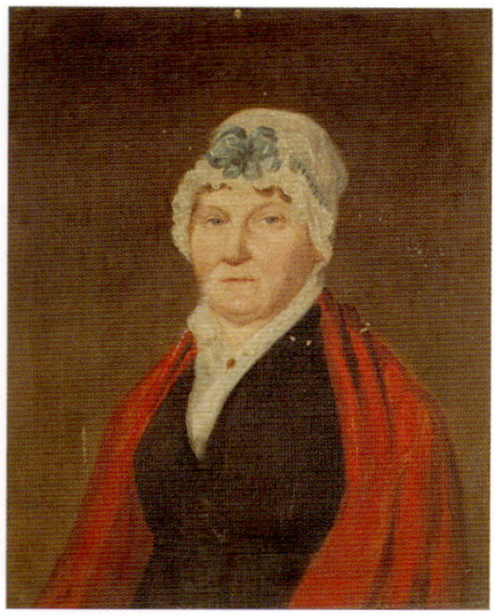

unknown artist
Mrs J. Redmayne c.1790
oil on canvas 35 x 28 (E)
LANLM.1948.6.8

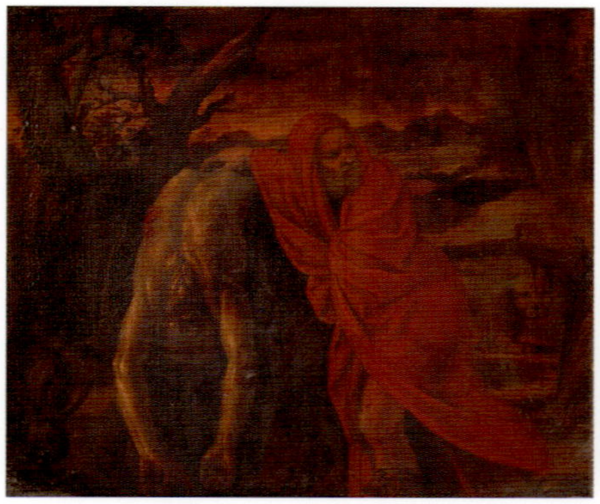

unknown artist
The Good Samaritan 1800–1850
oil on canvas 52 x 65 (E)
LANLM.1948.2

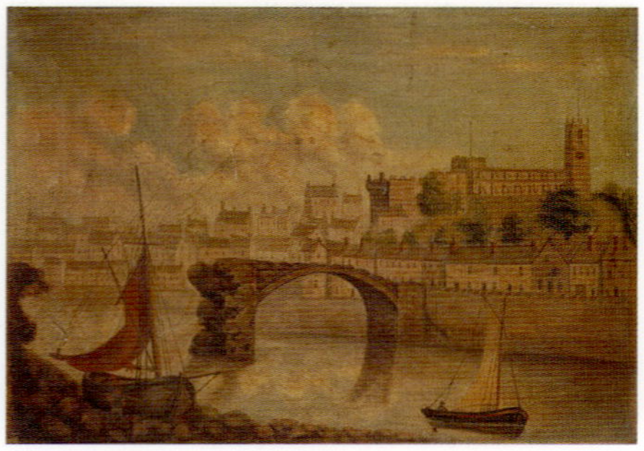

unknown artist
Lancaster Castle, Church and Old Bridge c.1800
oil on canvas 29 x 41 (E)
LANLM.1950.9

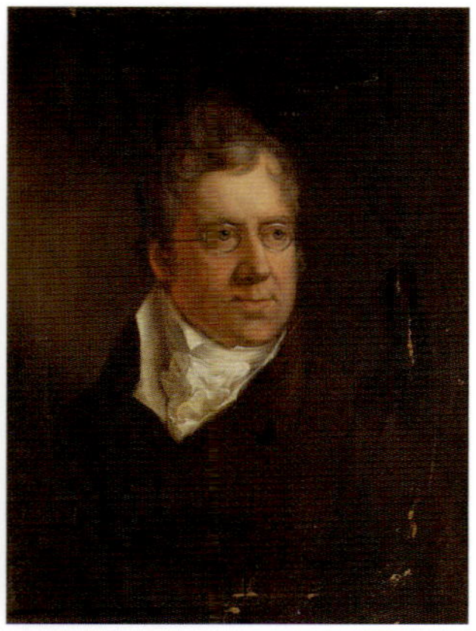

unknown artist
John Ford c.1810
oil on canvas 41.5 x 33 (E)
LANLM.1946.3.1

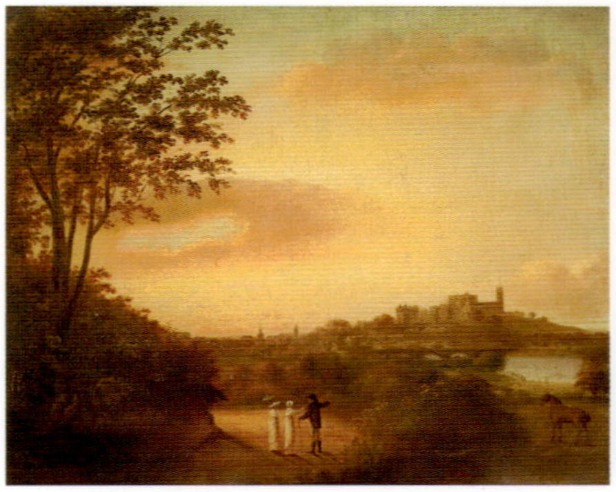

unknown artist
Lancaster from the Ridge c.1810
oil on canvas 45 x 70 (E)
LANLM.1928.14.3

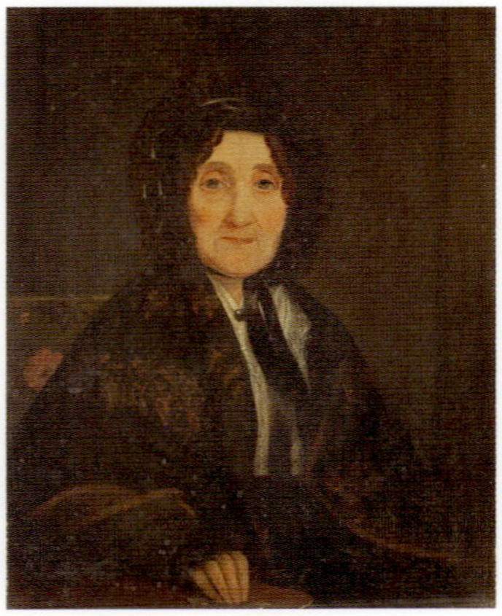

unknown artist
Mrs Jane Rawsthorne, née Stout c.1810
oil on canvas 35 x 27.7 (E)
LANLM.1969.20.2

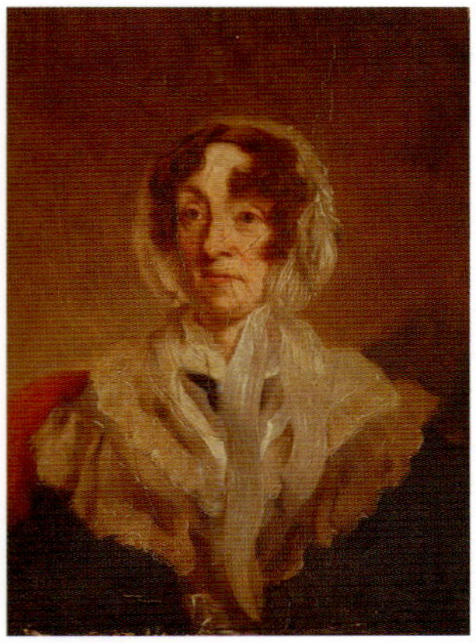

unknown artist
Mrs Mary Ford c.1810
oil on canvas 47 x 36.5 (E)
LANLM.1946.3.2

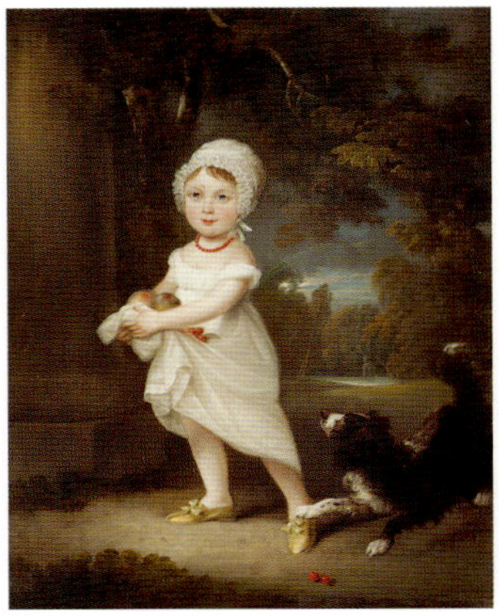

unknown artist
Hannah Benson-Pease (or Mrs Robert Lawson Ford) as a Child c.1815
oil on canvas 116 x 90
LANLM.1934.45.2

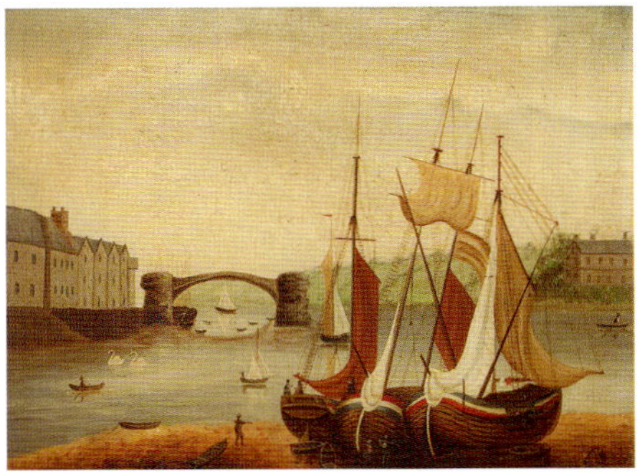

unknown artist
Last Arch of the Old Loyne Bridge from the North East c.1817
oil on canvas 38 x 51
LANLM.1892.20

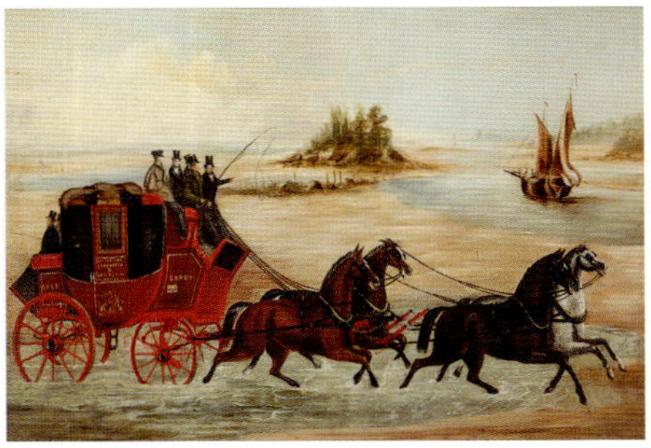

unknown artist
Coach Crossing Lancaster Sands c.1820
oil on panel 43.5 x 71
LANLM.1961.17

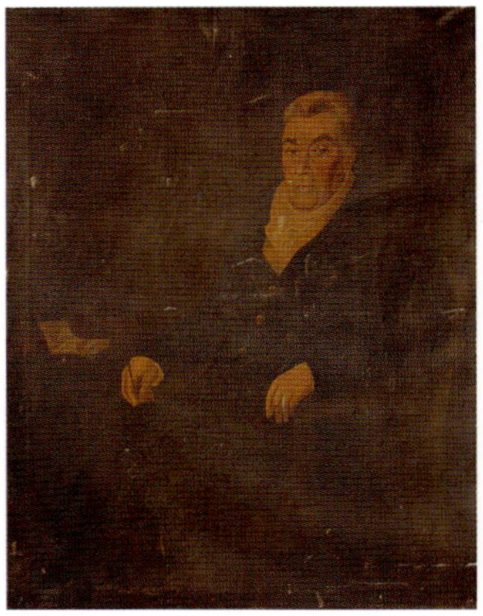

unknown artist
Dr David Campbell (1749–1832), MD c.1820
oil on canvas 132 x 102
LANLM.1967.37

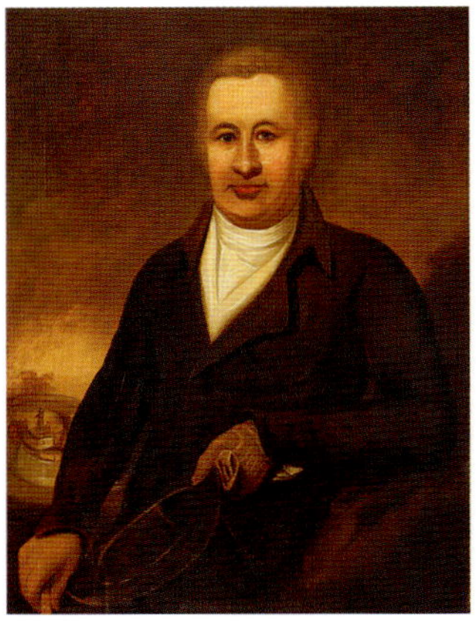

unknown artist
John Armstrong c.1820
oil on canvas 92.5 x 73.4 (E)
LANLM.1971.67.1

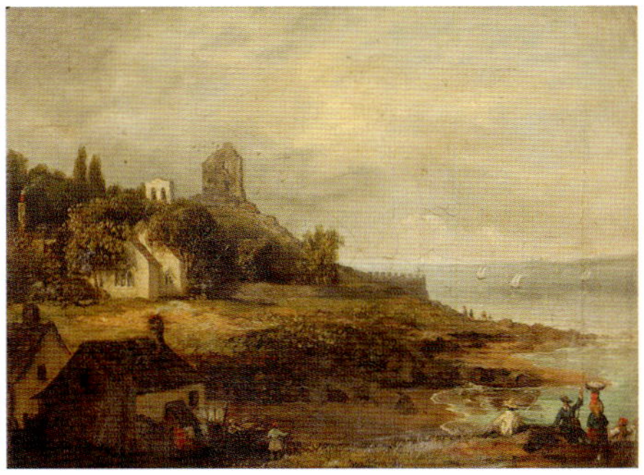

unknown artist
Heysham Village 1820–1830
oil on canvas 40.5 x 50.5 (E)
LANLM.2004.12.2

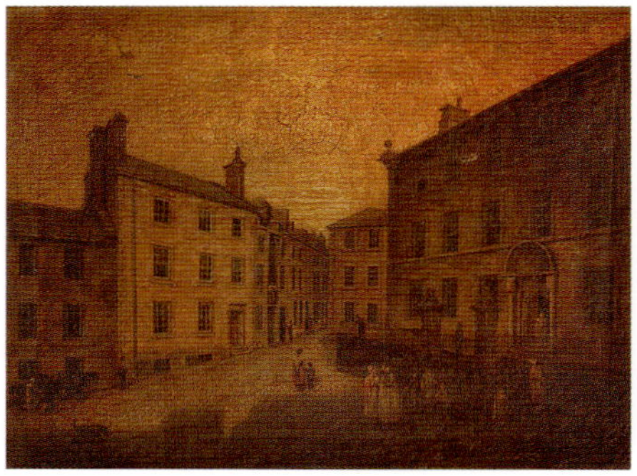

unknown artist
The Judges' Lodgings c.1820
oil on canvas
LANLM.1956.7.42

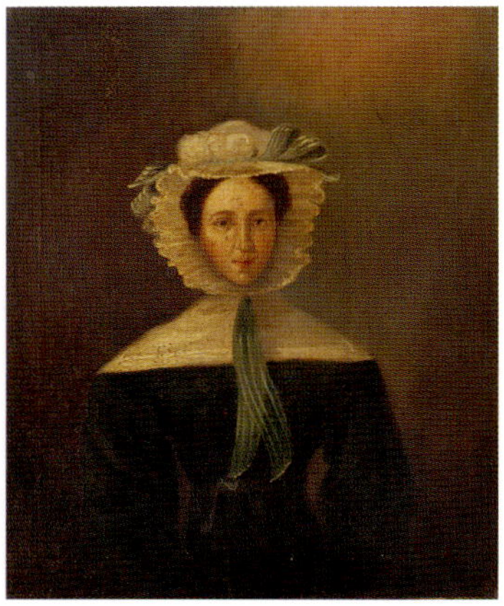

unknown artist
Agnes Boyer c.1830
oil on canvas 32 x 28 (E)
LANLM.1937.2

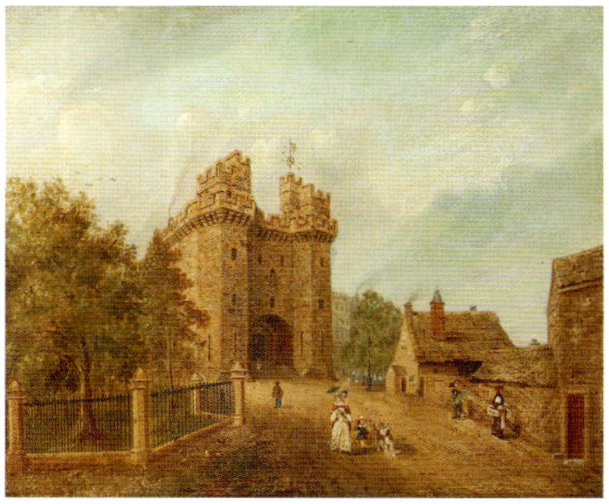

unknown artist
Castle Gateway c.1830
oil on panel 39 x 52.5 (E)
LANLM.1915.2.1

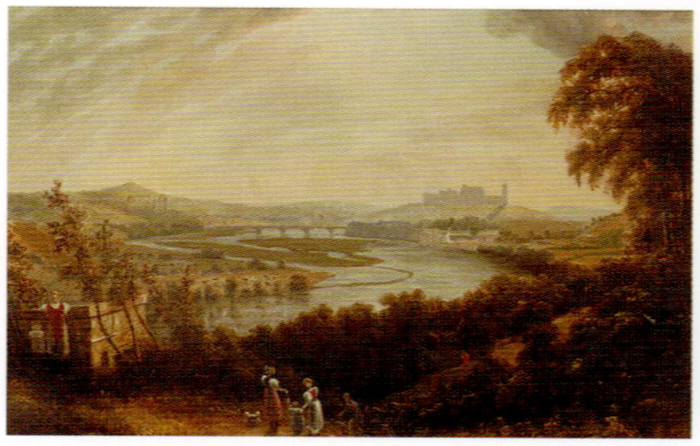

unknown artist
Lancaster from the North East c.1830
oil on canvas 48.5 x 73.5
LANLM.1949.1

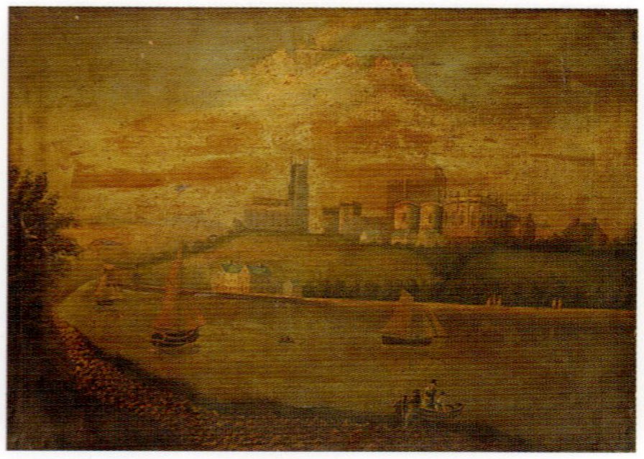

unknown artist
Lancaster with the River, Castle and Church Seen from the North West c.1830
oil on canvas 60 x 86 (E)
LANLM.1934.29

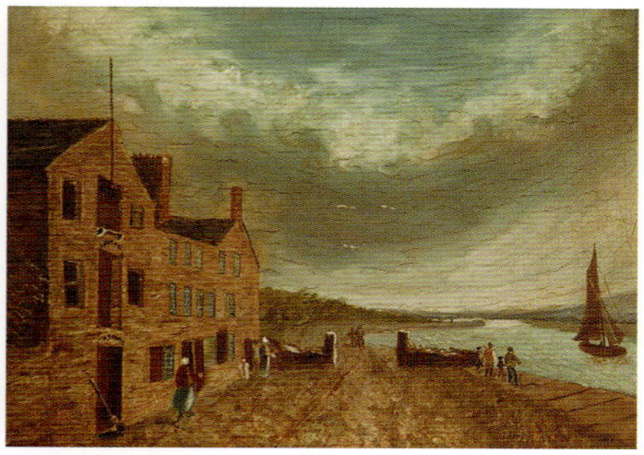

unknown artist
St George's Quay - Last Warehouse and Cottages c.1830
oil on panel 24 x 30
LANLM.1983.57

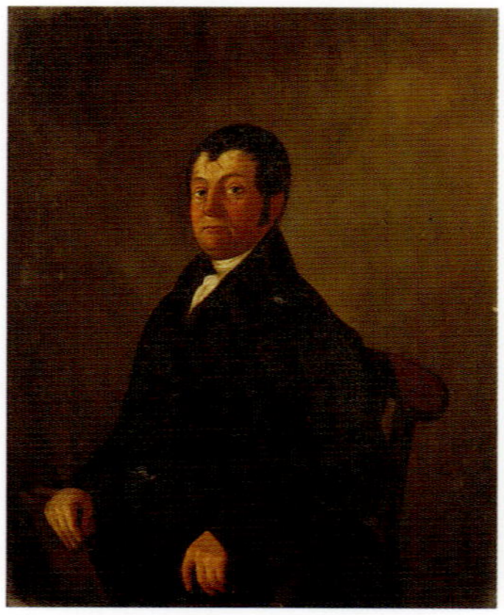

unknown artist
Thomas Boyer c.1830
oil 32 x 28 (E)
LANLM.1937.19

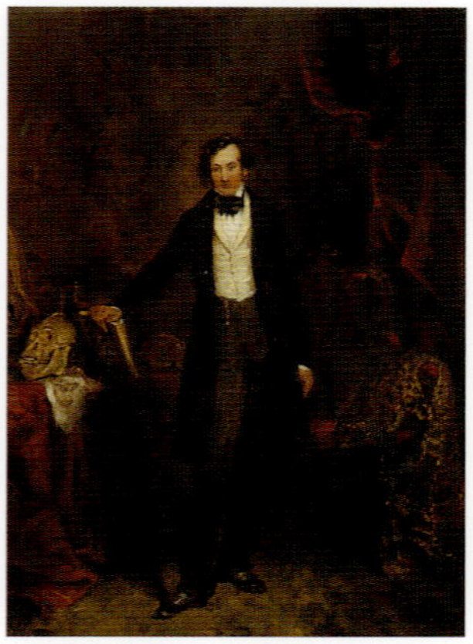

unknown artist
Sir Richard Owen as a Young Man c.1836
oil on canvas 59 x 48 (E)
LANLM.1888.1

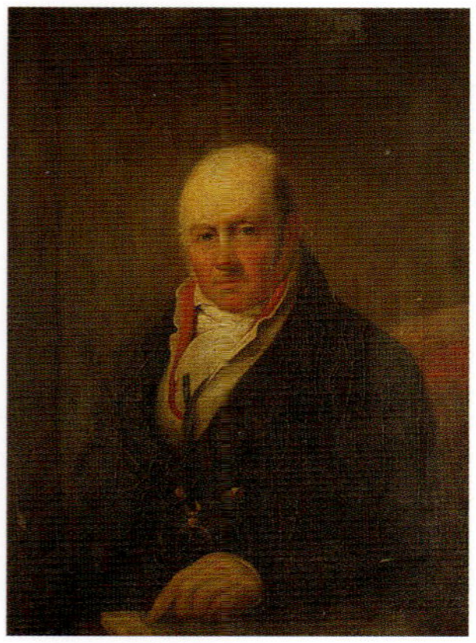

unknown artist
John Dalton c.1837
oil on canvas 44.5 x 34 (E)
LANLM.1983.43.26

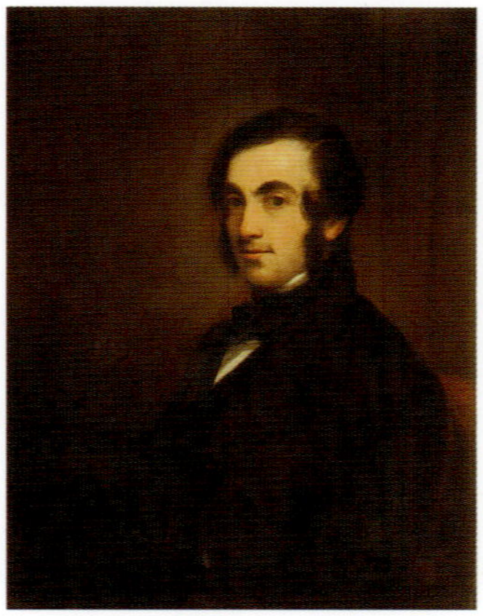

unknown artist
William Constantine 1840
oil on canvas 74.5 x 62 (E)
LANLM.1933.33

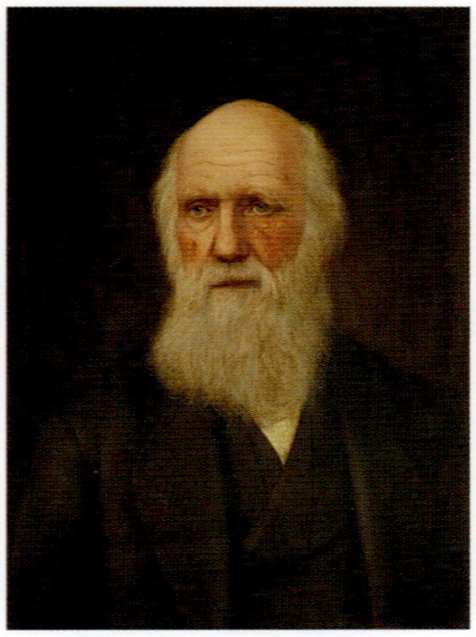

unknown artist
Dr William Whewhell (1794–1866), DD c.1850
oil on canvas 60 x 50 (E)
LANLM.1925.3.1

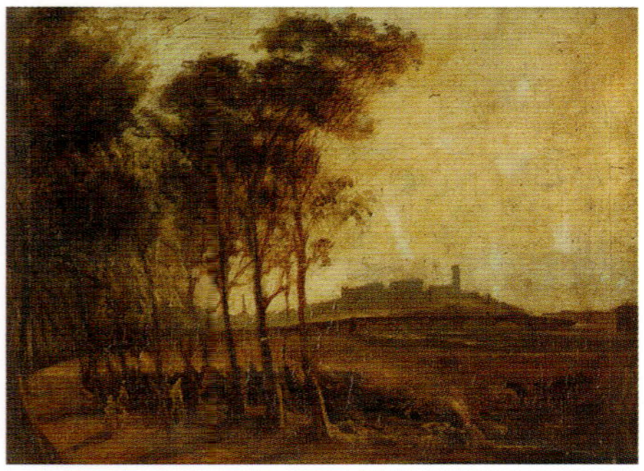

unknown artist
Lancaster from Ladies' Walk c.1850
oil on canvas 47 x 73.5
LANLM.1930.30

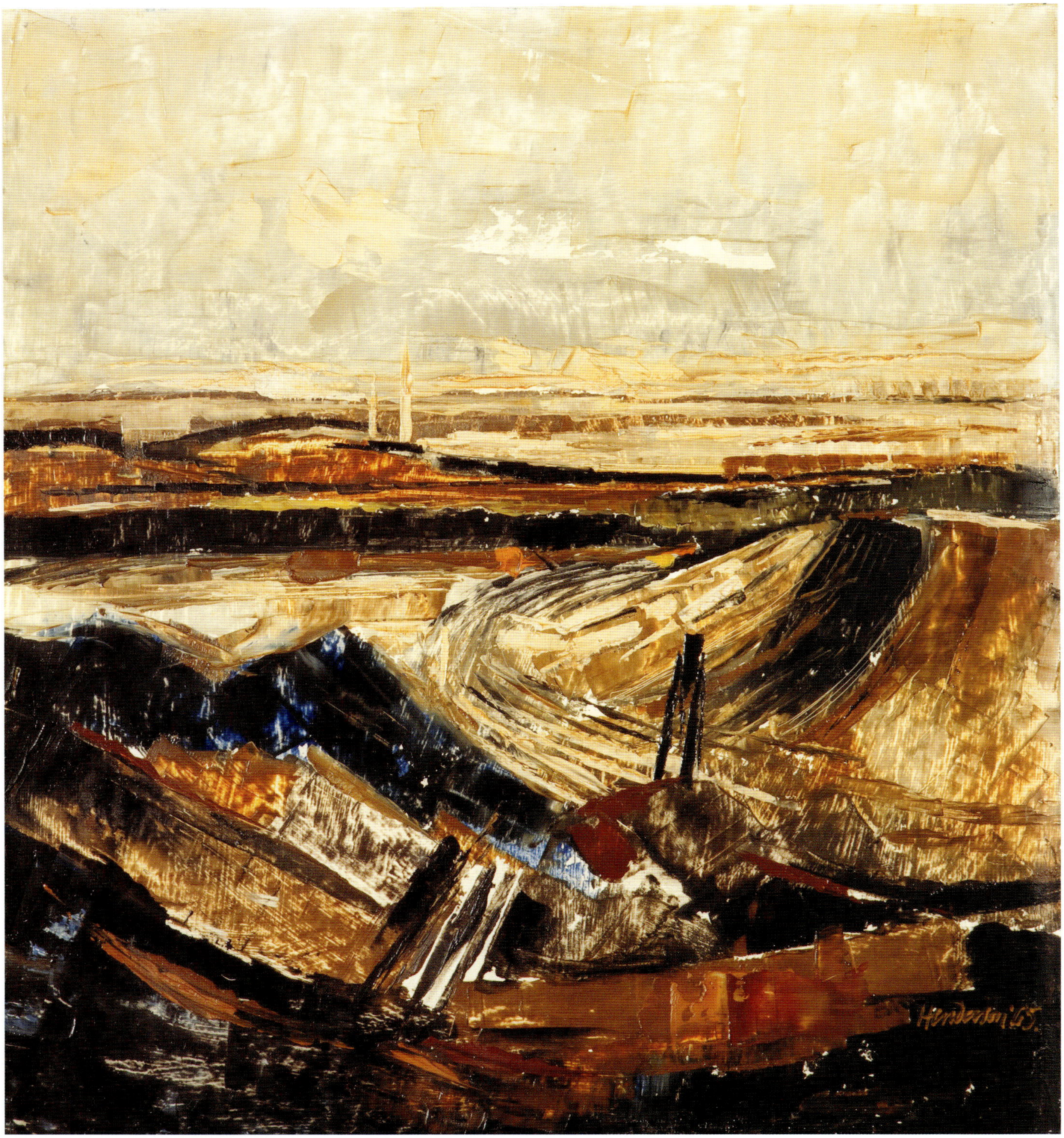
Henderson '55

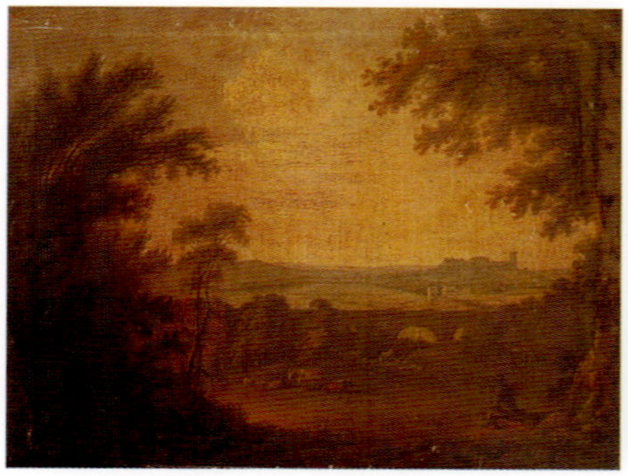

unknown artist
Lancaster from the East c.1850
oil on canvas 46 x 63.5 (E)
LANLM.1928.14.1

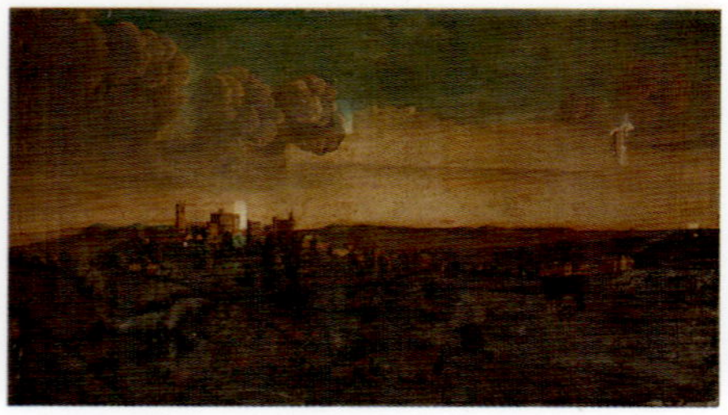

unknown artist
Lancaster from the South West c.1850
oil on canvas 76 x 143
LANLM.1923.4

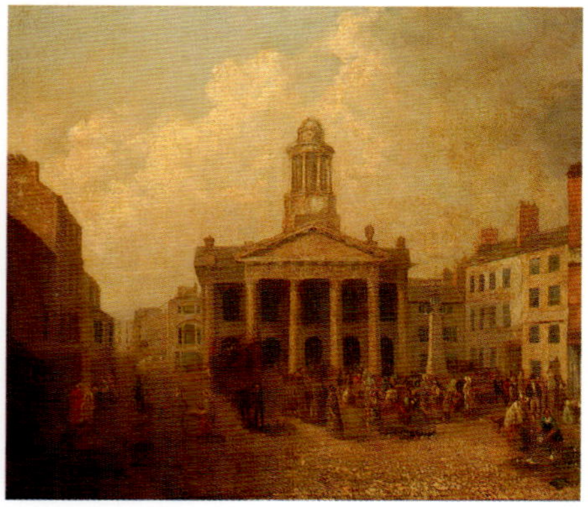

unknown artist
Lancaster Old Town Hall c.1850
oil on canvas 61.5 x 73 (E)
LANLM.1942.6

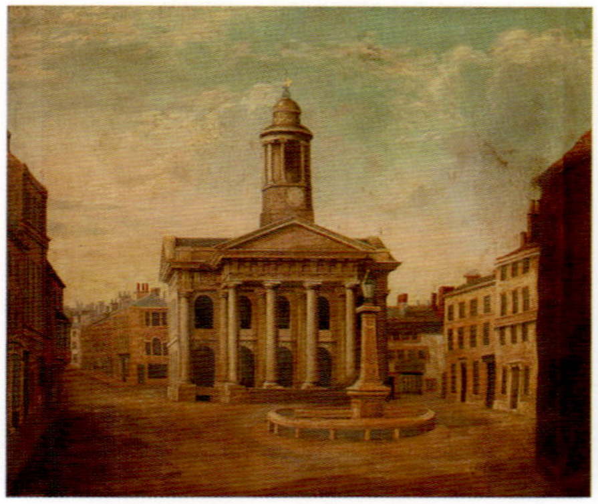

unknown artist
Lancaster Old Town Hall c.1850
oil on canvas 64 x 80 (E)
LMA 93.1

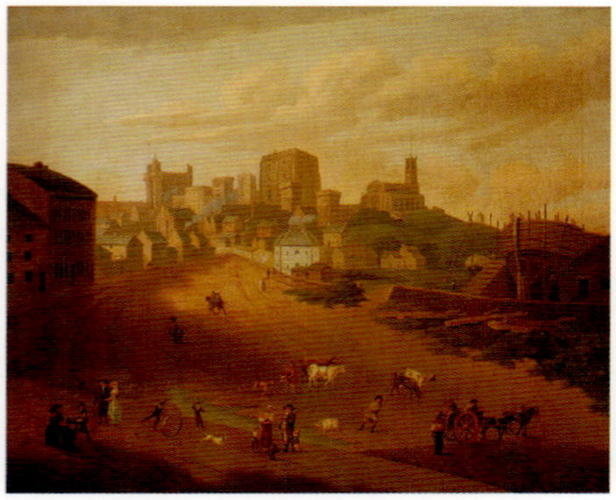

unknown artist
Lancaster from Cable Street c.1860
oil on canvas 80 x 100 (E)
LMA 50

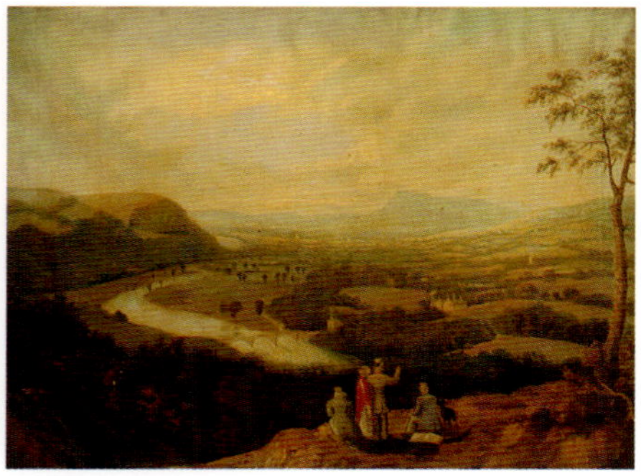

unknown artist
Ingleborough and the Lune Valley c.1880
oil on canvas 65 x 90
LMA 221

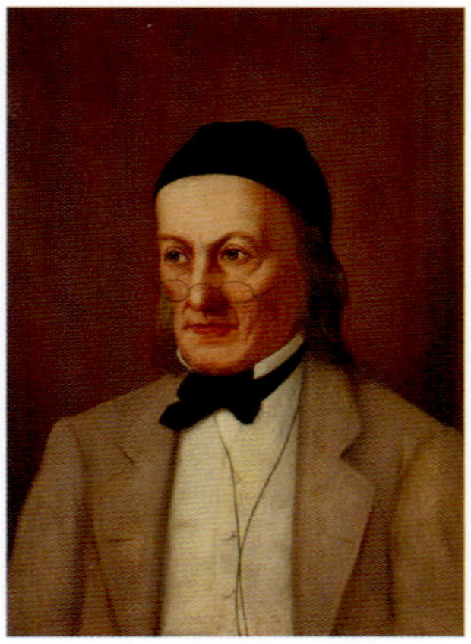

unknown artist
Sir Richard Owen (1804–1892) c.1880
oil on canvas 75 x 62 (E)
LANLM.1925.3.2

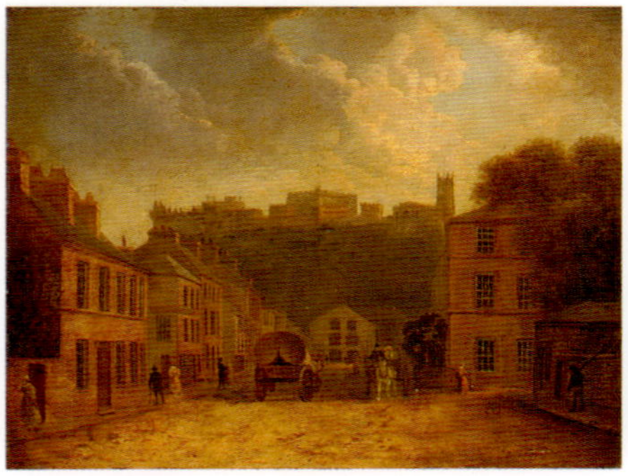

unknown artist
Lancaster Castle from Cable Street c.1890
oil on board 34.5 x 42
LANLM.1915.2.2

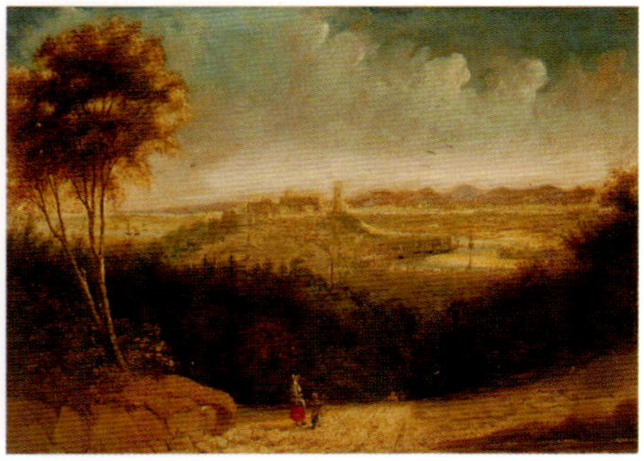

unknown artist
Lancaster from the Moor c.1890
oil on canvas 48 x 72
LANLM.1923.2

Facing page: Henderson, Ian, b.1939, *Digmore Area from Back Lane, Showing Earth-Moving and Beginning of Pimbo Industrial Area*, 1965, Lancashire County Museum Service (p. 382)

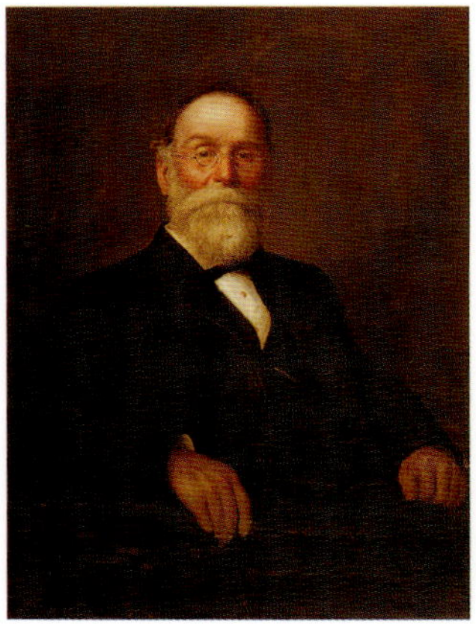

unknown artist
Edward Storey, Esq. (1820–1913), JP c.1900
oil on canvas 97 x 76.5 (E)
LANLM.1953.1.1

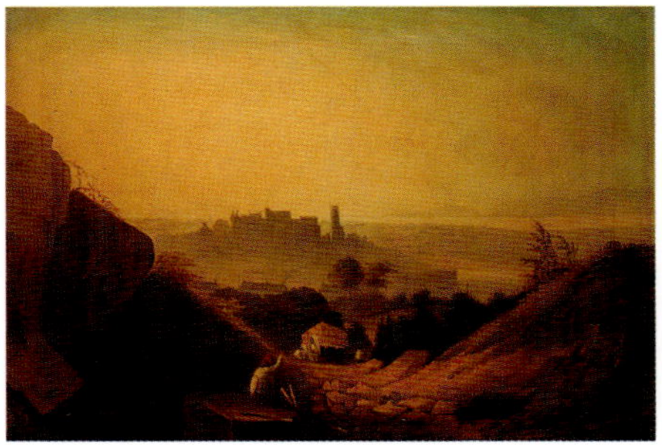

unknown artist
Lancaster from the Old Stone Quarry c.1905
oil on canvas 80 x 121.5 (E)
LANLM.1907.6

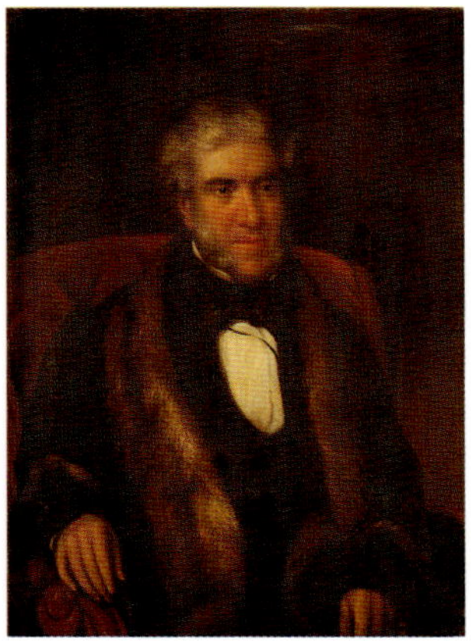

unknown artist
Portrait of an Alderman c.1910
oil on canvas 95 x 74 (E)
LMA 92

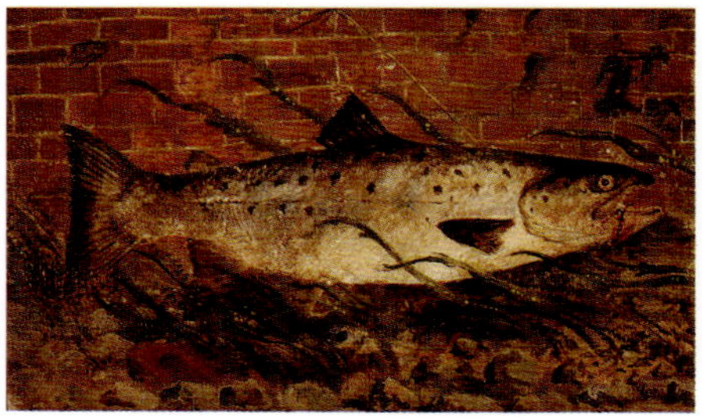

unknown artist
Sucking on a Black Doctor c.1985
oil on canvas 41 x 60 (E)
LANLM.1991.63

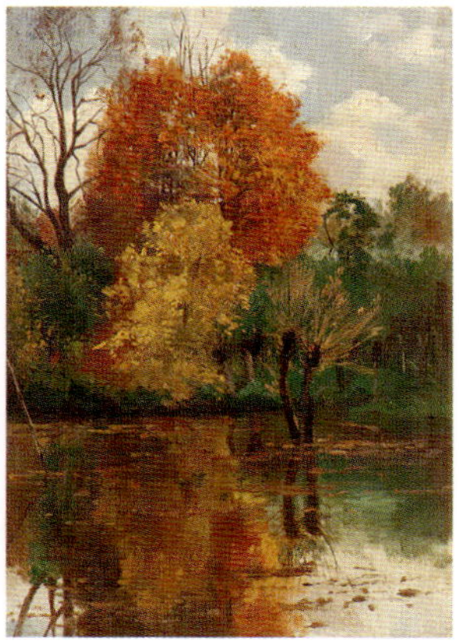

unknown artist
Autumn Trees by a River
oil on canvas 38 x 27
LANLM.1963.44.20

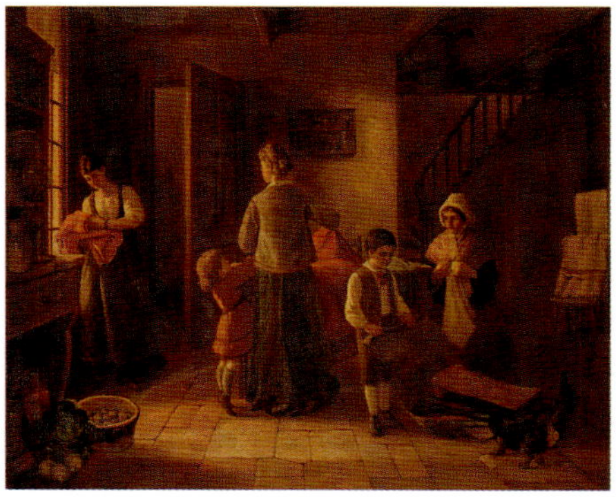

unknown artist
Cottage Interior
oil on canvas 70 x 90
LANLM.1960.6

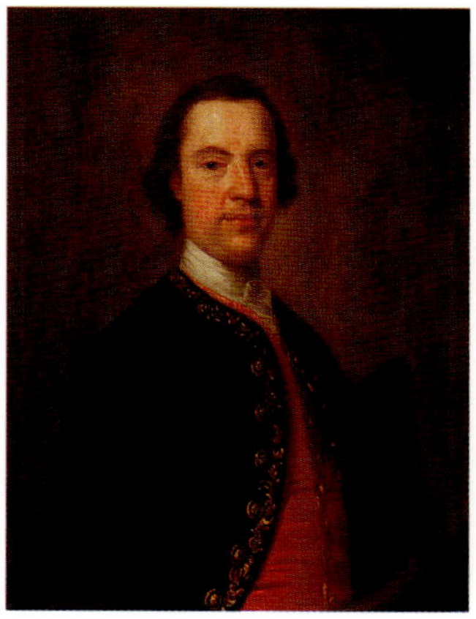

unknown artist
Edward Marton
oil on canvas 74 x 61 (E)
LANLM.1946.10

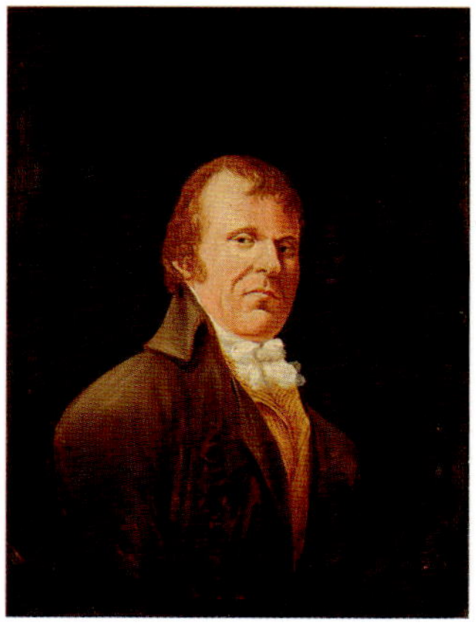

unknown artist
Joseph Redmayne
oil on canvas 35 x 27.5 (E)
LANLM.1948.6.6

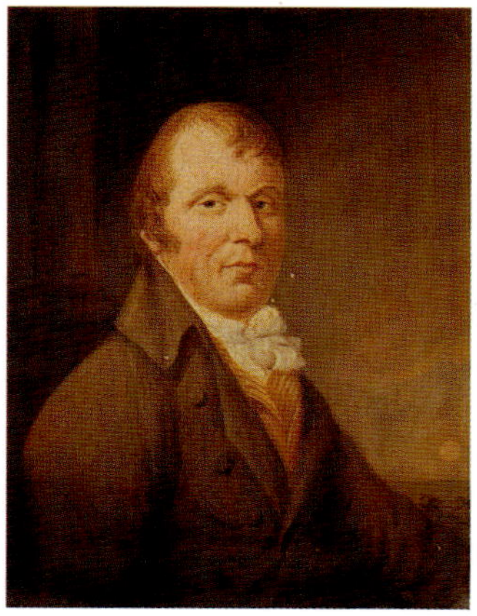

unknown artist
Joseph Redmayne
oil on canvas 35 x 27.5
LANLM.1948.6.6.1

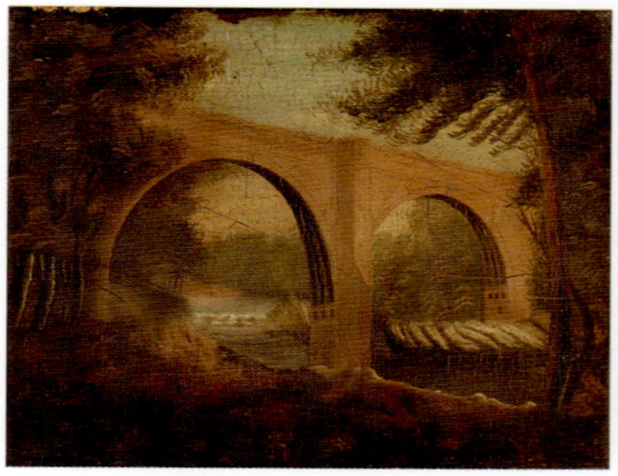

unknown artist
Kirkby Bridge
oil on panel 39.5 x 50
LANLM.1986.115

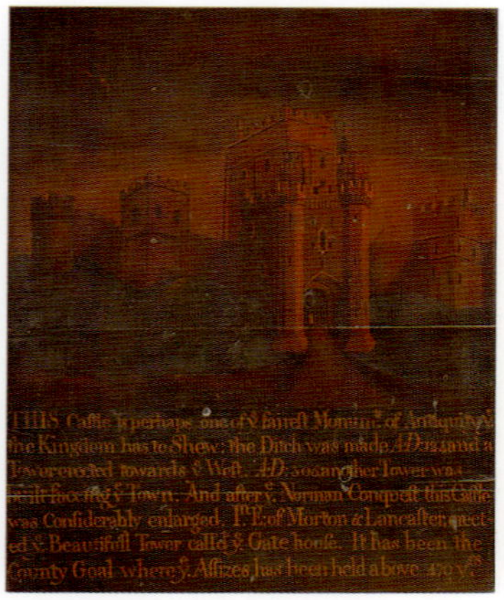

unknown artist
Lancaster Castle Gateway
oil on board 96.5 x 91
LANLM.1929.2

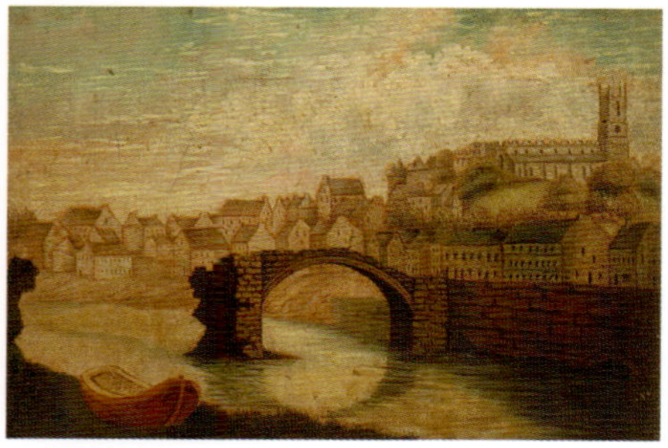

unknown artist
Lancaster: Last Arch of the Old Bridge from the North West
oil on canvas 33 x 51.5 (E)
LANLM.1931.3

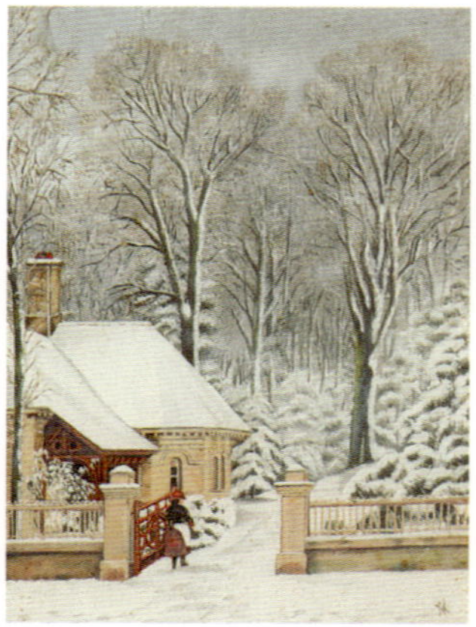

unknown artist
Park Field Lodge in Winter
oil on board 42.5 x 35
LANLM.1948.4.1

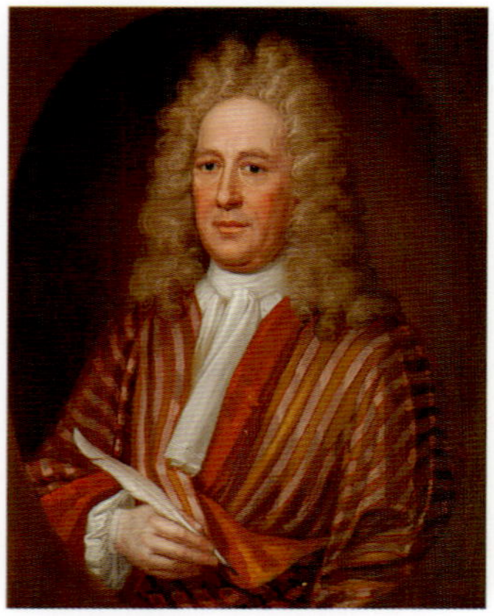

unknown artist
Portrait of a Gentleman in a Wig and Striped Robe
oil on canvas 72.5 x 61 (E)
LMA 219.1

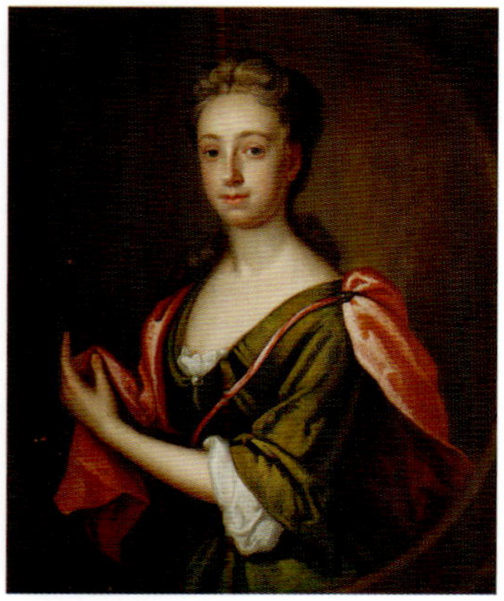

unknown artist
Portrait of a Lady Holding Drapery in Her Left Hand
oil on canvas 73.5 x 61 (E)
LMA 219.3

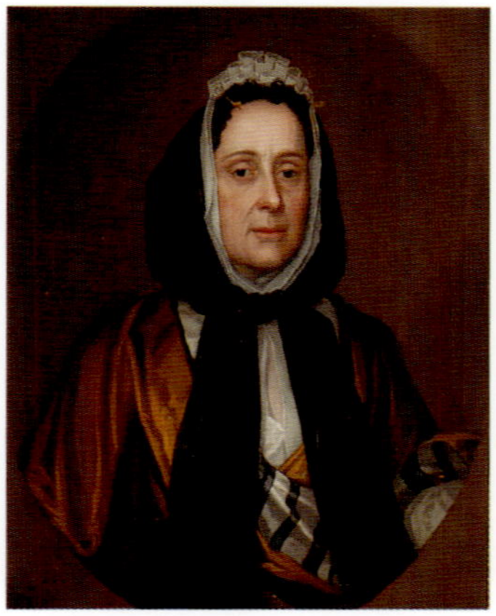

unknown artist
Portrait of a Lady in a Frilled Cap and Hood
oil on canvas 72 x 61
LMA 219.4

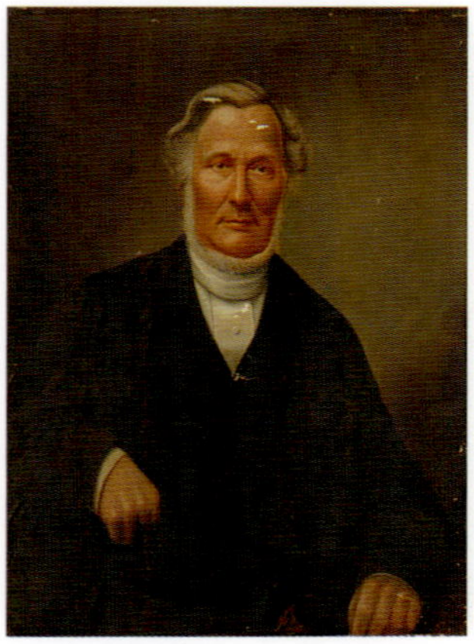

unknown artist
Portrait of a Man with Mutton Chops
oil on canvas
LMA 90

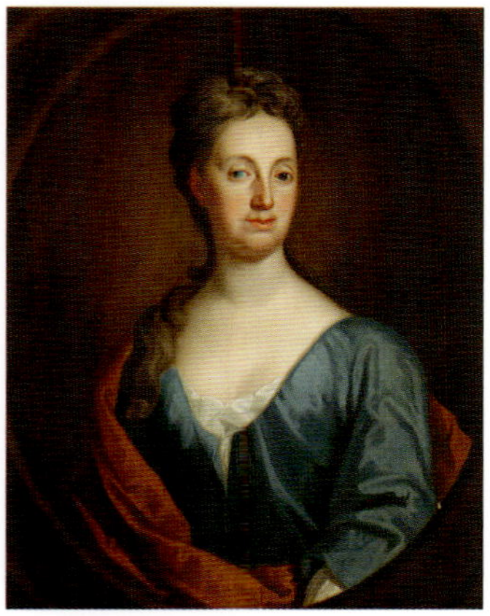

unknown artist
Portrait of an Unknown Woman
oil on canvas 73 x 60.5 (E)
LMA 219.2

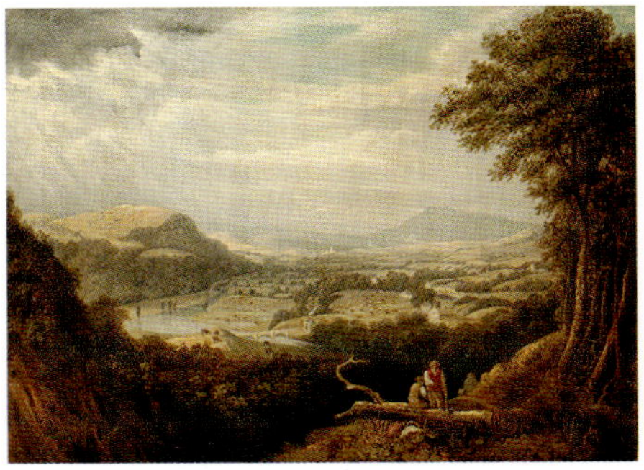

unknown artist
Vale of Lonsdale
oil on canvas
LANLM.1919.1

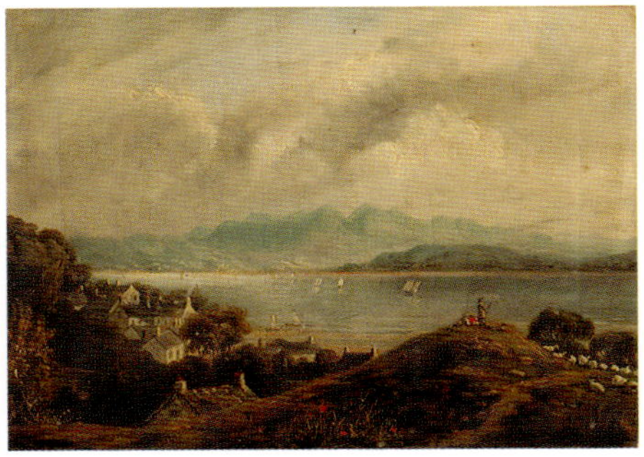

unknown artist
View of the Cumberland Hills
oil on canvas 40.5 x 50.5 (E)
LANLM.2004.12.1

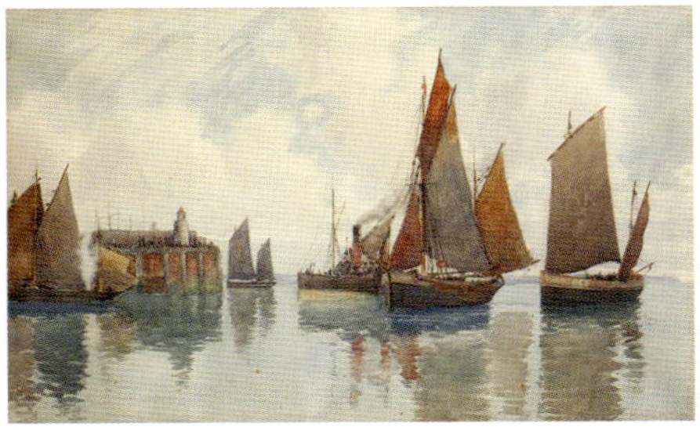

Wane, Harold 1879–1900
Fishing Boats, Isle of Man
oil on canvas 65 x 90.3
LANLM.1947.7.14

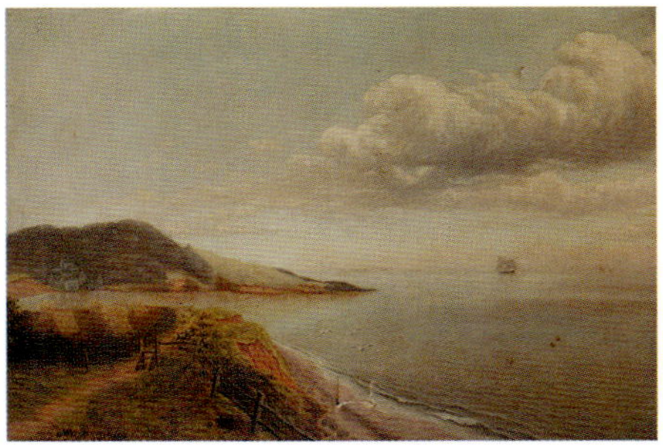

Waterhouse, Alfred 1830–1905
View of Heysham 1889
oil on canvas 49.5 x 75
LANLM.1950.21.32

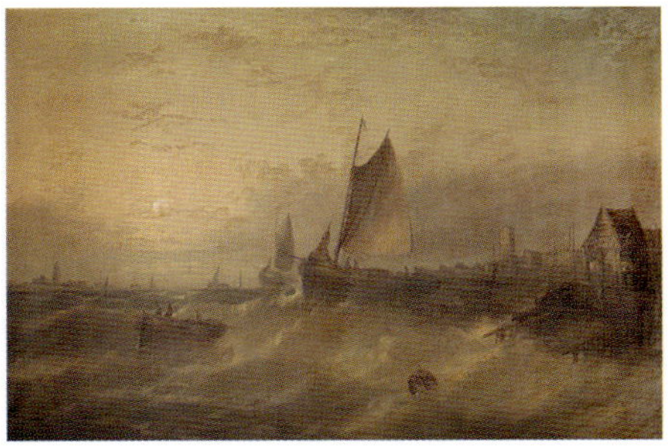

Williamson, William Henry 1820–1883
Fishing Craft off Dover 1850–1875
oil on canvas 75 x 125
LMA 222

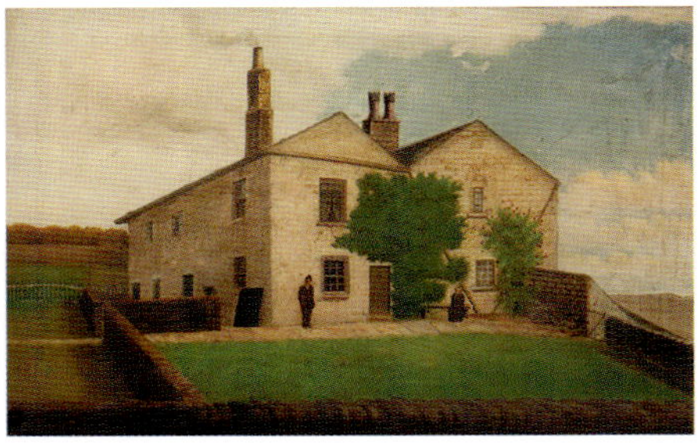

Willman, J.
Moor Place Farm, Golgotha 1903
oil on canvas 40.5 x 66 (E)
LANLM.1965.42

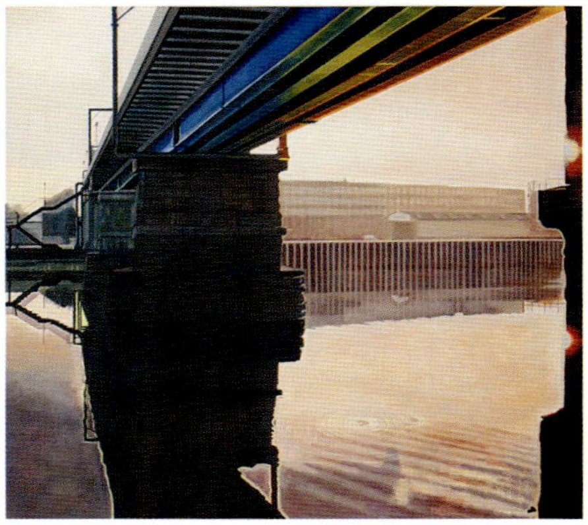

Woodhead, Geoffrey 1941–2007
Carlisle Bridge, Lancaster 1999
acrylic on canvas 79.4 x 89
LANLM.2008.14

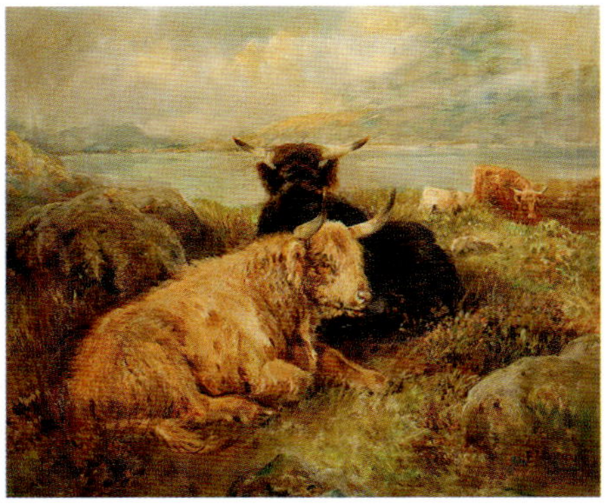

Woodhouse, E. active 1880–1940
Highland Cattle 1880–1940
oil on canvas 44 x 54
LANLM.1996.50.24

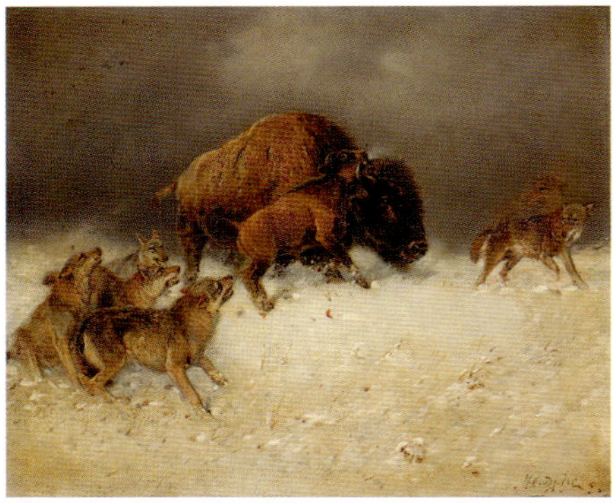

Woodhouse, William 1857–1939
Bison and Wolves 1880–1939
oil on canvas 45 x 59.5
LANLM.1996.50.27

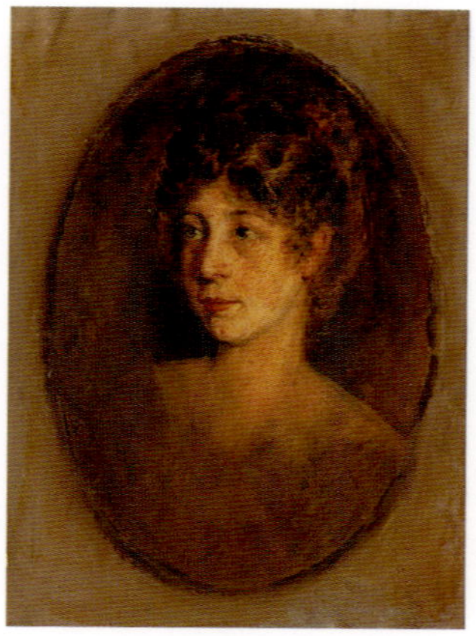

Woodhouse, William 1857–1939
Edith Emsley 1880–1939
oil on canvas 35.5 x 28
LANLM.1996.50.21

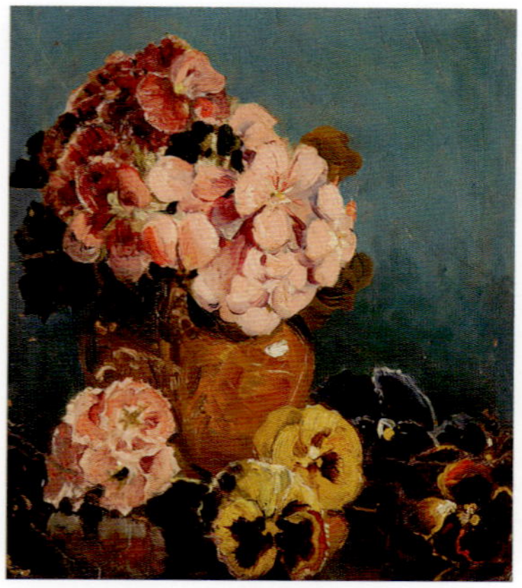

Woodhouse, William 1857–1939
Geraniums 1880–1939
oil on board 27 x 26
LANLM.1996.50.28

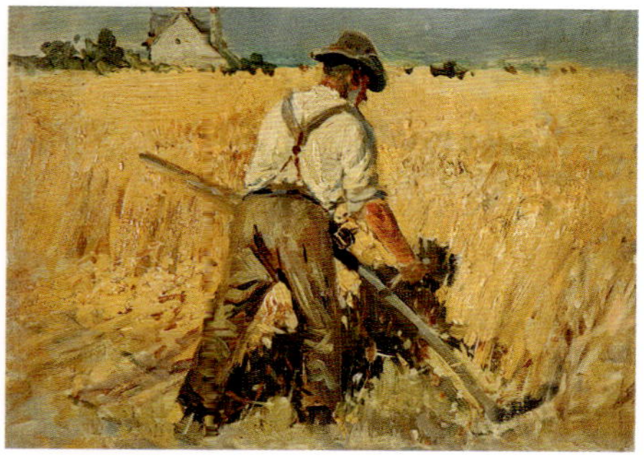

Woodhouse, William 1857–1939
Harvesting Balmoral Road, near Kenilcote (the Artist's Home) 1880–1939
oil on board 20.1 x 28.6 (E)
LANLM.1996.50.29

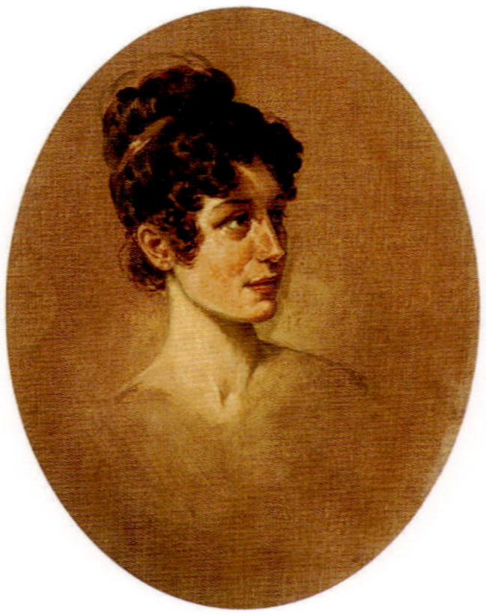

Woodhouse, William 1857–1939
Maria Elizabeth 1880–1939
oil on canvas 27 x 20
LANLM.1996.50.22

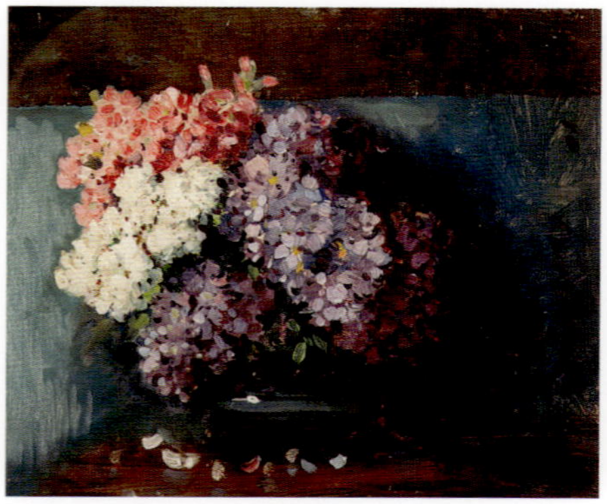

Woodhouse, William 1857–1939
Stocks 1880–1939
oil on board 29 x 38.3
LANLM.1996.50.25

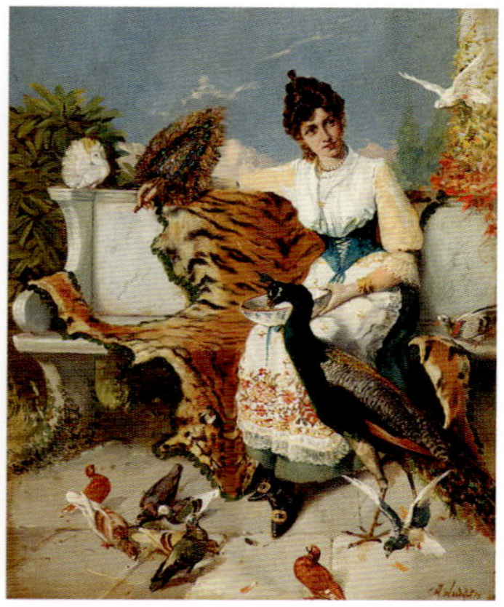

Woodhouse, William 1857–1939
Marie Elizabeth, the Artist's Wife 1885–1925
oil on canvas 60 x 50
LANLM.1996.50.19

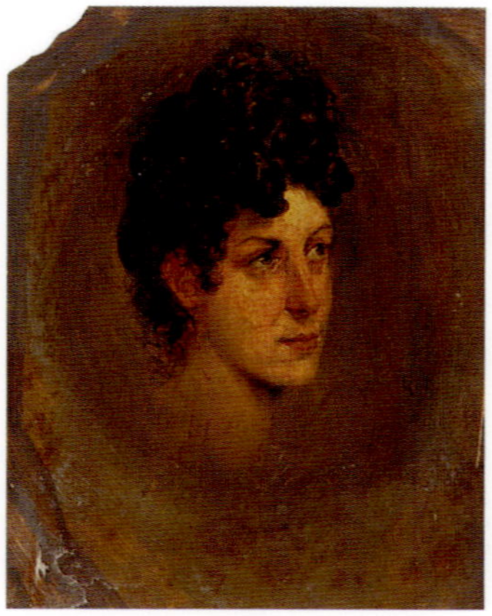

Woodhouse, William 1857–1939
The Artist's Wife, Maria Elizabeth 1885–1925
oil on board 18.5 x 16.5
LANLM.1996.50.13

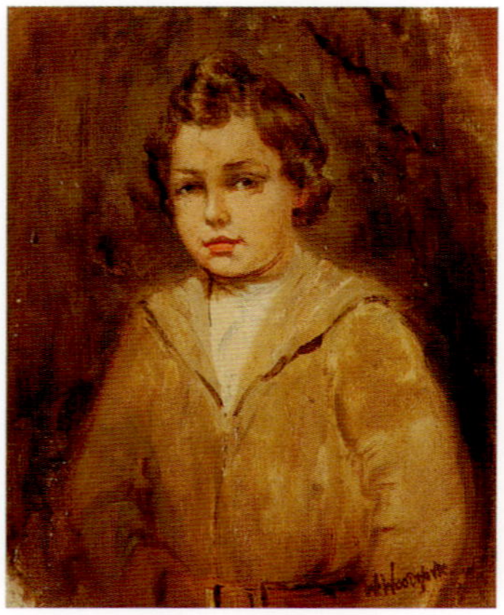

Woodhouse, William 1857–1939
Roy Woodhouse c.1890
oil on canvas 27 x 23
LANLM.2004.3.2

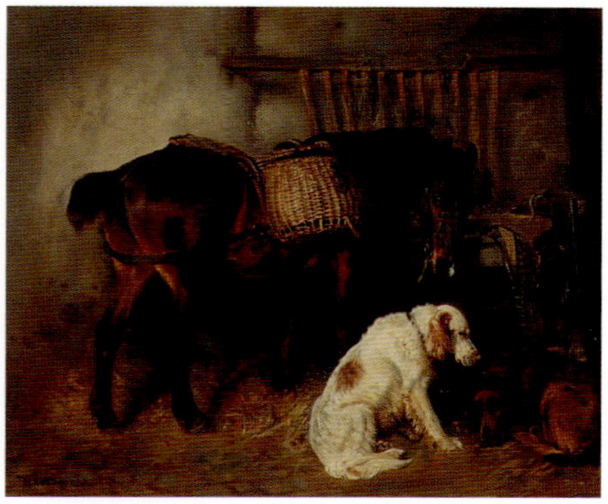

Woodhouse, William 1857–1939
Stable Companions c.1900
oil on canvas 50 x 59
LMA 75/1

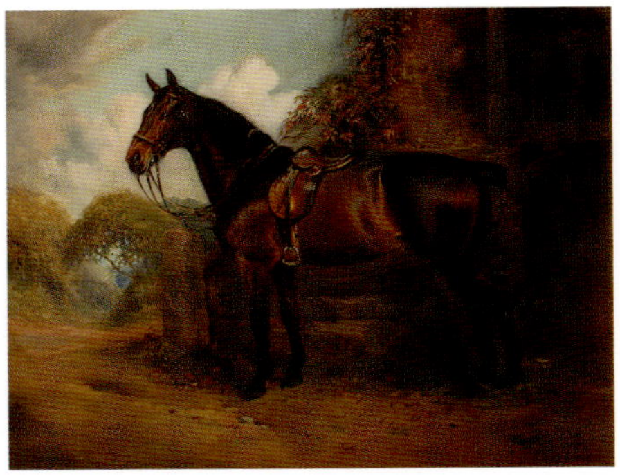

Woodhouse, William 1857–1939
'Majestic' 1909
oil on canvas 69 x 91
LANLM.1954.23

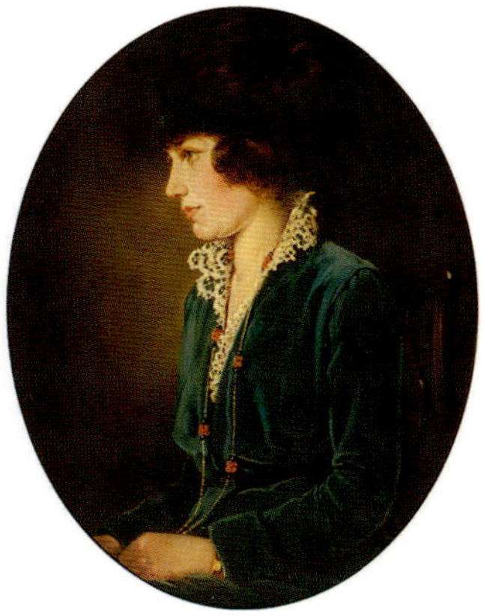

Woodhouse, William 1857–1939
Marie Winifred (Winnie) 1912
oil on canvas 54 x 44.5
LANLM.1996.50.10

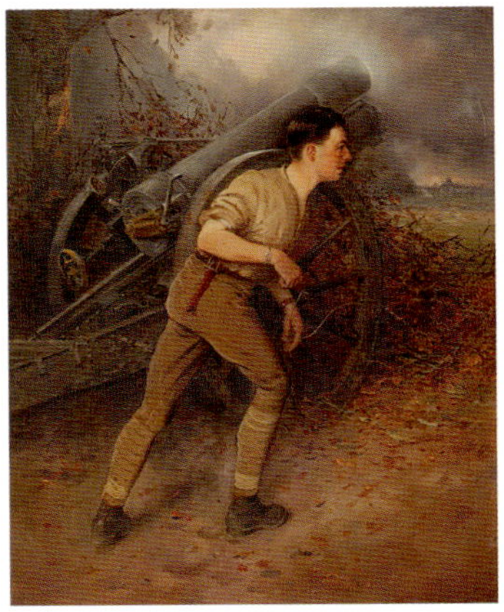

Woodhouse, William 1857–1939
Roy Woodhouse 1918
oil on canvas 72.3 x 62.2 (E)
LANLM.1987.164

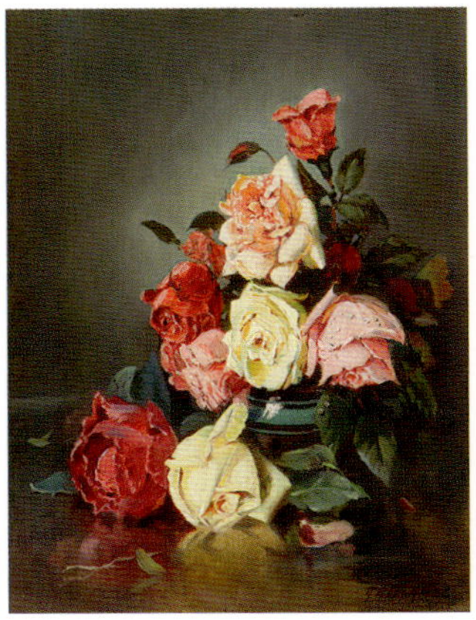

Woodhouse, William 1857–1939
Still Life, Zetland Ville Roses c.1920
oil on board 29 x 23
LANLM.1994.115

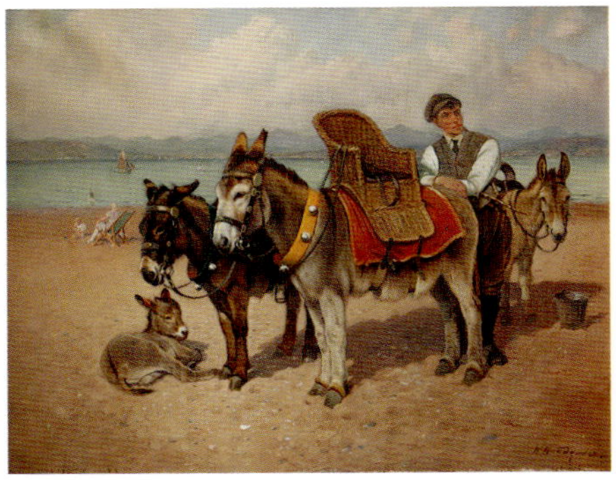

Woodhouse, William 1857–1939
The Donkey Boy c.1925
oil on canvas 70 x 90
LANLM.1932.1

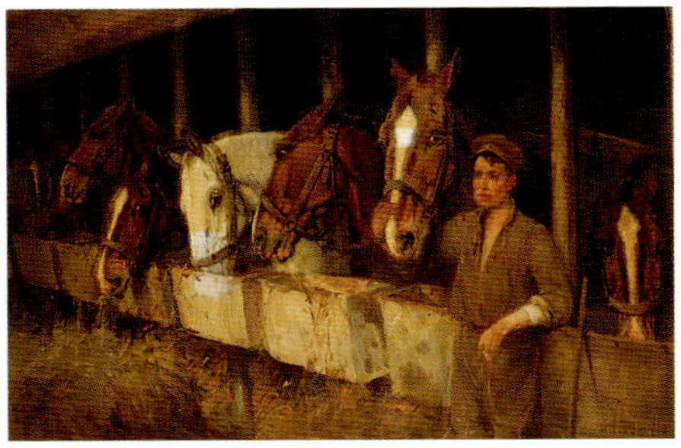

Woodhouse, William 1857–1939
Army Horses in Stables
oil on canvas 37 x 61
LANLM.1996.50.11

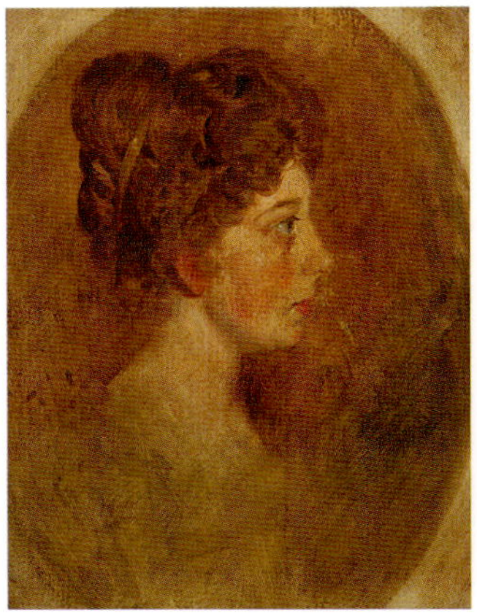

Woodhouse, William 1857–1939
Edith Emsley
oil on board 24 x 21.5
LANLM.1996.50.12

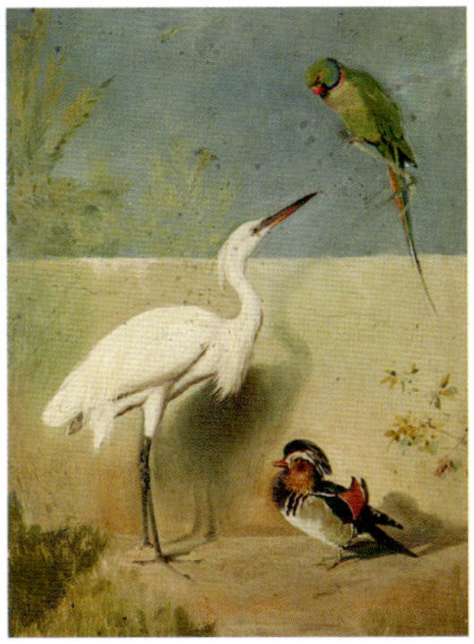

Woodhouse, William 1857–1939
Egret, Parakeet and Mandarin Duck
oil on board 36 x 27
LANLM.1996.50.16

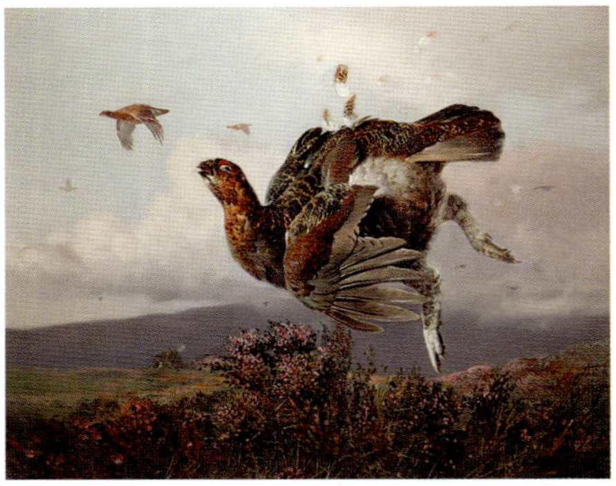

Woodhouse, William 1857–1939
Grouse Shot in Flight
oil on canvas 50 x 60 (E)
LMA 75/2

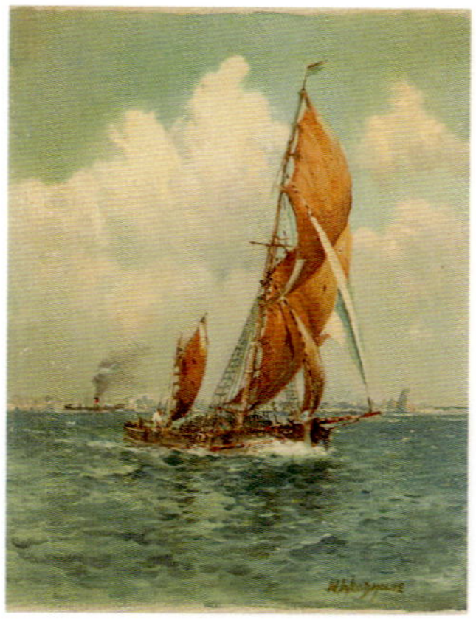

Woodhouse, William 1857–1939
Sailing Ships and Steamer
oil on canvas 35.8 x 27.1 (E)
LANLM.1996.50.4

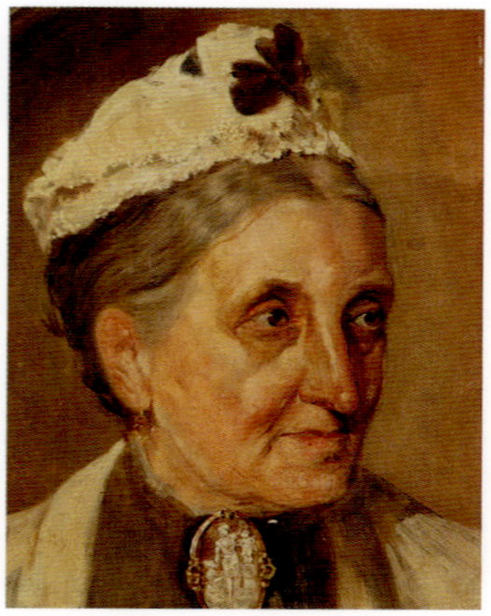

Woodhouse, William 1857–1939
Sarah Elmsley
oil on canvas 37.5 x 31 (E)
LANLM.2004.3.1

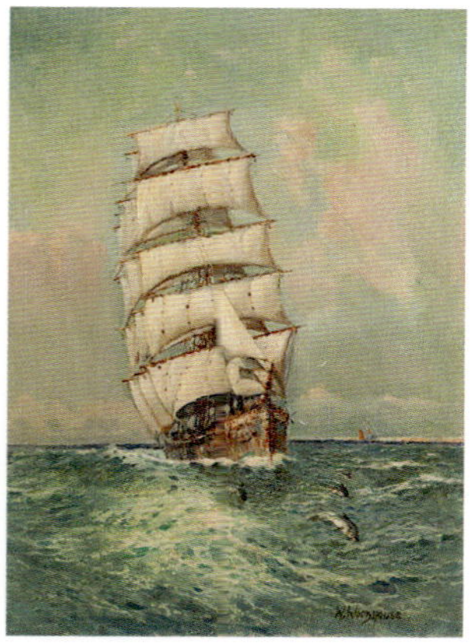

Woodhouse, William 1857–1939
Ship in Full Sail
oil on canvas 35.8 x 27.5 (E)
LANLM.1996.50.3

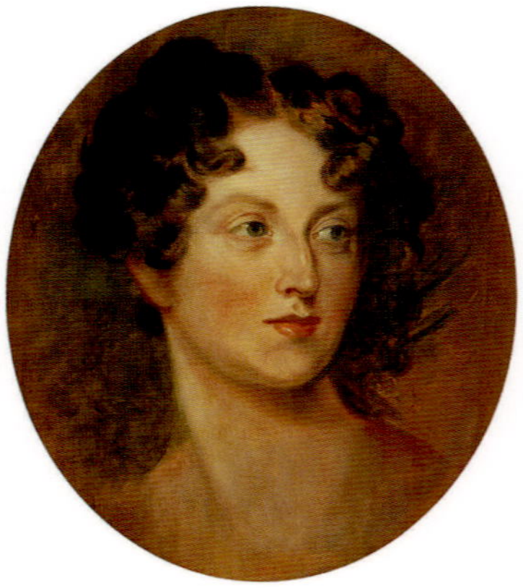

Woodhouse, William 1857–1939
Study of a Head
oil on canvas 58 x 54 (E)
LANLM.1996.50.2

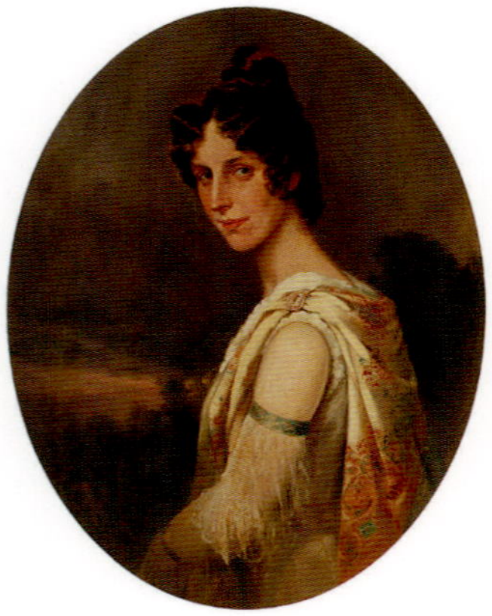

Woodhouse, William 1857–1939
The Artist's Wife, Maria Elizabeth
oil on canvas 86 x 72 (E)
LANLM.1981.58

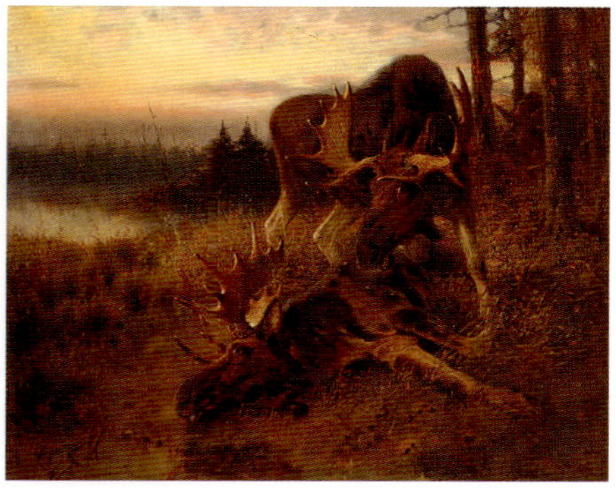

Woodhouse, William 1857–1939
Vanquished
oil on canvas 62.5 x 77.7 (E)
LANLM.1996.50.6

Lancaster University Management School

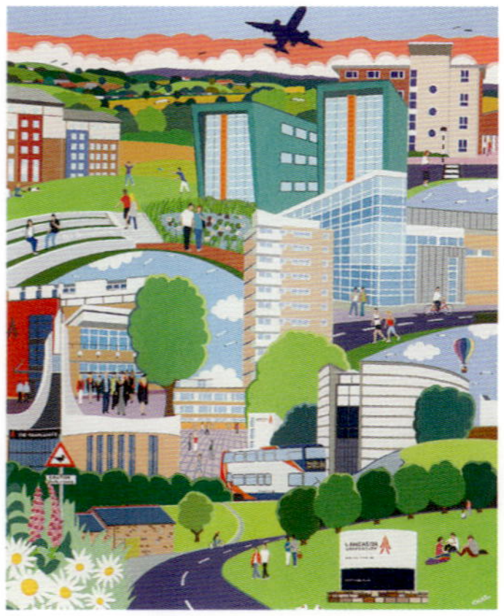

Jacobs, Chas 1957
Lancaster University Campus 2009
acrylic on canvas 60 x 50
LUMS.1

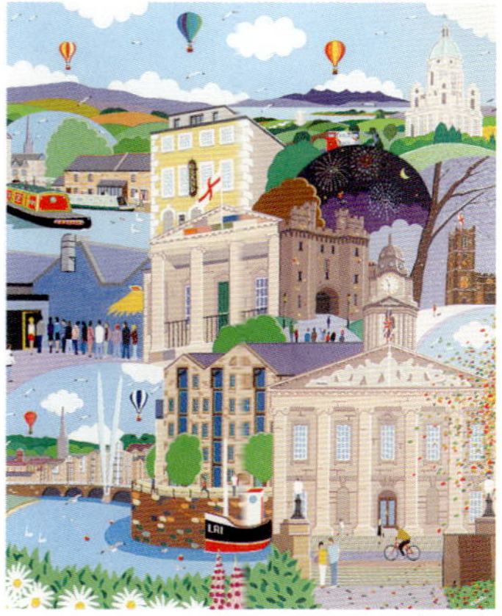

Jacobs, Chas 1957
Lancaster University City 2010
acrylic on canvas 60 x 50.5
LUMS.2

Peter Scott Gallery

The Peter Scott Gallery is a key element of the combined arts organisation Live at LICA (Lancaster Institute for the Contemporary Arts) and plays a major role in providing a distinctive cultural opportunity to the students and staff of Lancaster University, as well as public visitors, through its collections and temporary programme. The programme reflects new developments in the field and the Gallery meets sector standards in its work; this enables the Gallery to deliver exciting visual arts practice to the general visitor whilst engaging with and remaining relevant to the University's teaching and research activity.

The Gallery has stood in its current location at Lancaster University since 1988, following the relocation of the previous campus based gallery which was established in 1974. The Gallery houses a collection that has been built since the late 1960s and is named after Peter F. Scott, CBE, in memorial of his benevolence to Lancaster University.

The Peter Scott Gallery Collection has resulted from acquisitions made by Lancaster University, the Peter Scott Gallery Charitable Trust, two major bequests and other gifts and donations. It broadly comprises of twentieth-century prints and paintings, Pilkington's ceramics and related archival material, Chinese and Japanese paintings and prints, and a small number of antiquities. Acquisitions for the painting collection have largely focused on British artists, including a group of works by Norman Adams, paintings by leading twentieth-century women artists Wilhelmina Barns-Graham and Winifred Nicholson, and four works by Terry Frost. However, a host of international artists are represented thanks to the Irene Manton Bequest. Professor Irene Manton, FRS, (1904–1988) was an eminent international scientist, Professor of Botany at Leeds University and Honorary Fellow in Electron Microscopy at Lancaster University. For 30 years Professor Manton was also a collector of art and in 1988 loaned selected works from her collection to form the opening exhibition in the Peter Scott Gallery. The exhibition, entitled 'Another Way of Looking' ran from 25th April until 3rd June; the featured paintings and prints were subsequently bequeathed to Lancaster University. The remainder of Professor Manton's collection was gifted to the Peter Scott Gallery by Leeds University in 1995 to keep it intact.

The Peter Scott Gallery Collection continues to grow and recent acquisitions include the work of contemporary artists. The Collection is not on permanent display, but does feature in the temporary programme.

Richard Smith, Exhibitions & Events Officer

Facing page: Frost, Terry, 1915–2003, *Blue Black Sun*, 1986, Peter Scott Gallery (p. 238)

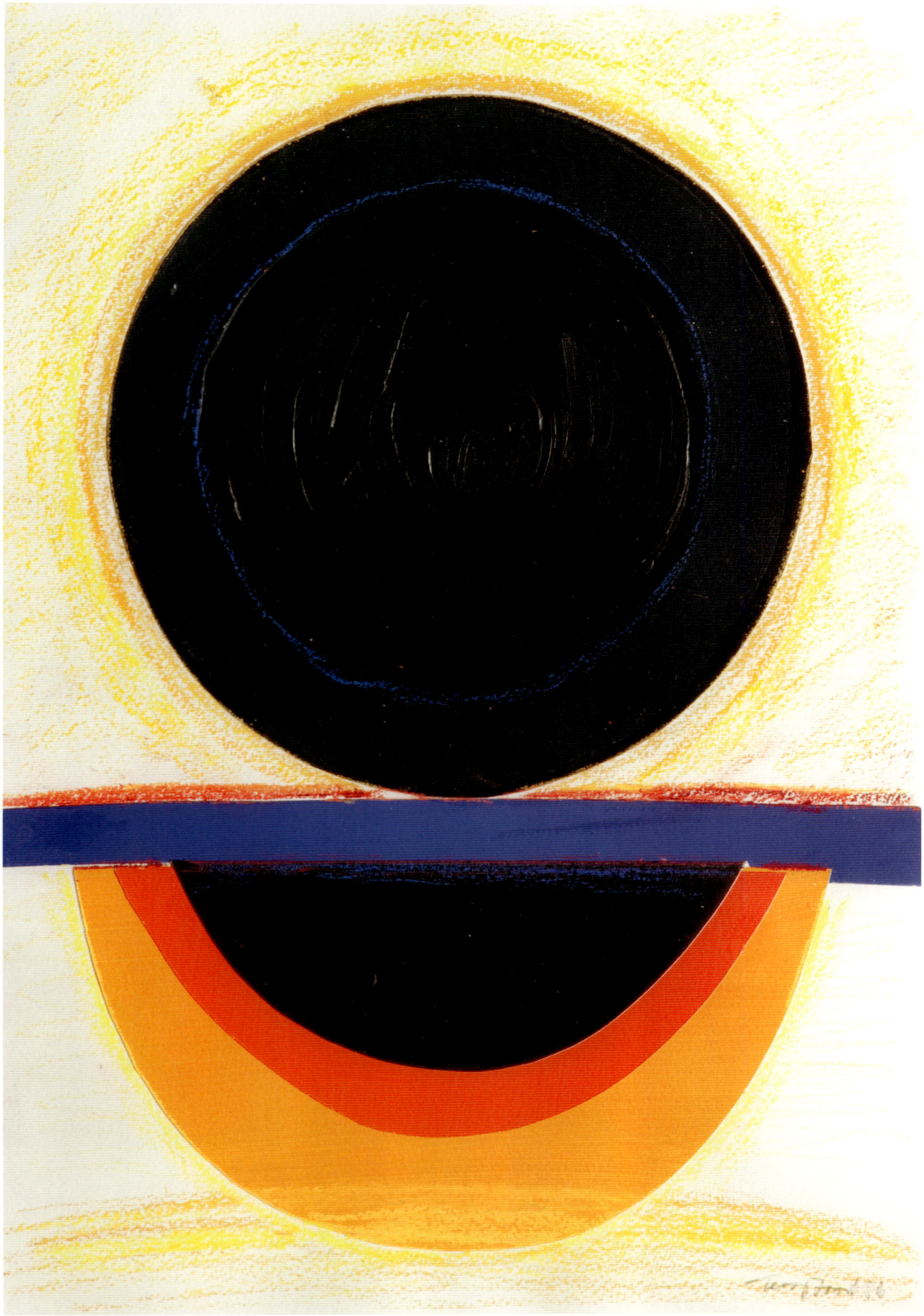

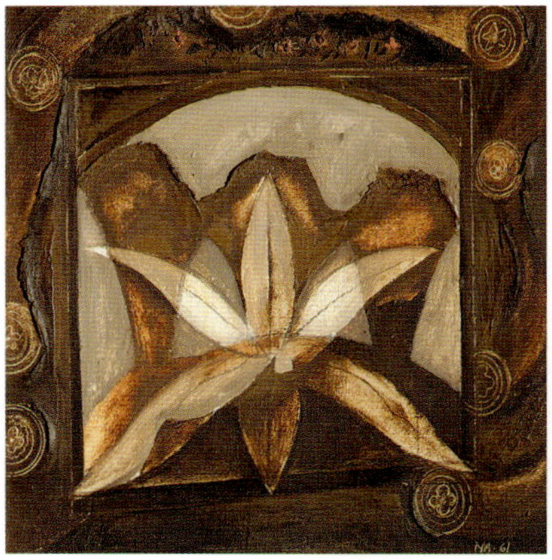

Adams, Norman 1927–2005
Golgotha 1 1961
oil on canvas 44.5 x 40
LANPS.ZF21

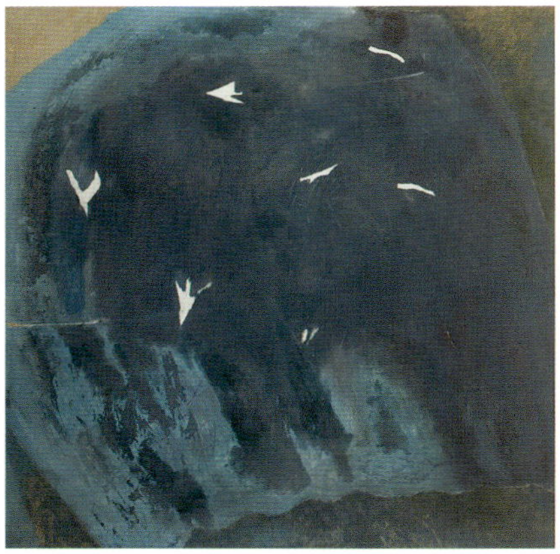

Adams, Norman 1927–2005
Seabirds Scarp 1969
oil on canvas 124 x 127
LANPS.OW204

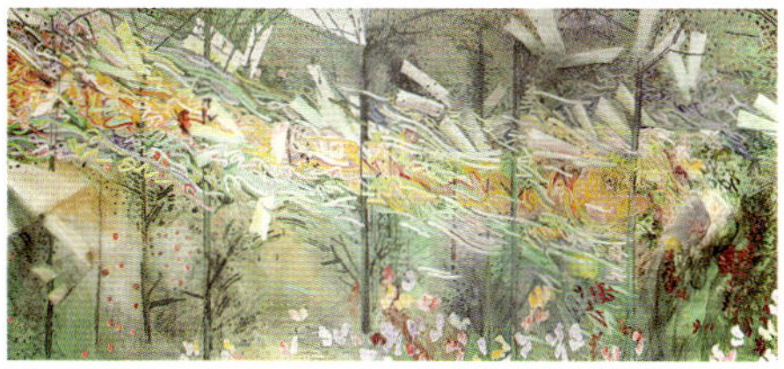

Adams, Norman 1927–2005
Expulsion from the Garden of Eden 1974
oil on canvas 151 x 363 (E)
LANPS.OW205

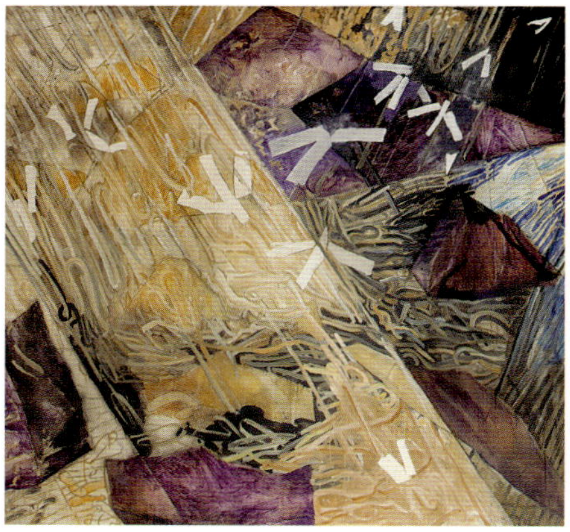

Adams, Norman 1927–2005
Sea, Light, Rocks, Birds 1974
oil on canvas 200 x 213
PCF1

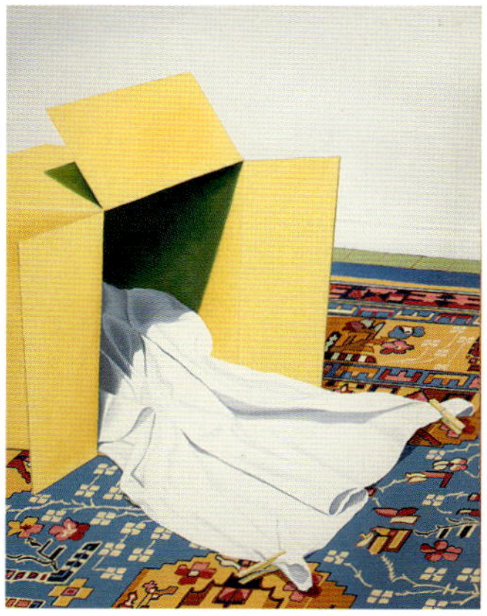

Avrett, Marty b.1945
Sleeping Cloth Fabric 1974
acrylic on canvas 121 x 93
LANPS.OW184

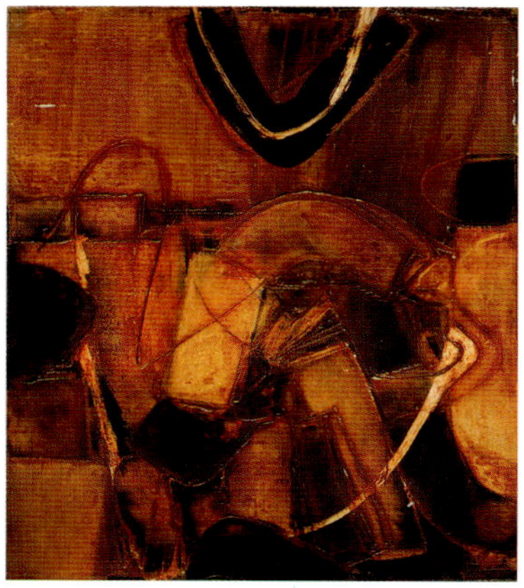

Bailey, John b.1926
Apotheosis 1967
oil on hardboard 76 x 61
LANPS.OW194

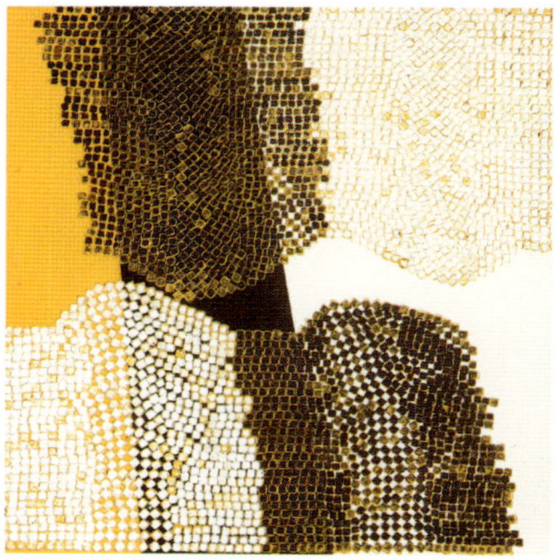

Barns-Graham, Wilhelmina 1912–2004
Contact (Bridge Series) 1968
oil & acrylic on hardboard 30.5 x 30.5
PSGCT.OW384

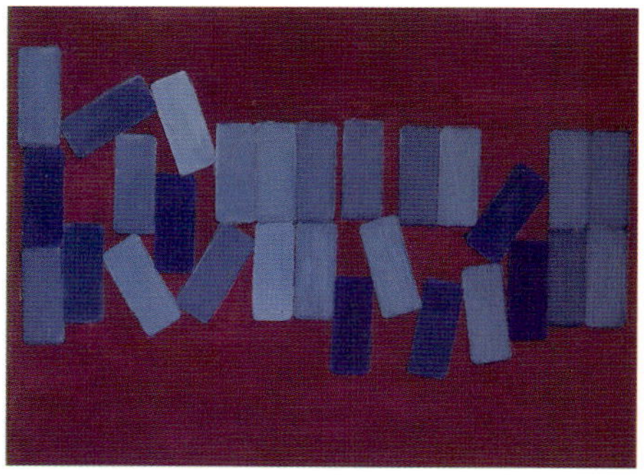

Barns-Graham, Wilhelmina 1912–2004
Oblongs Cobalt Blue on Violet 1969
oil on panel 18 x 26
PSGCT.OW295

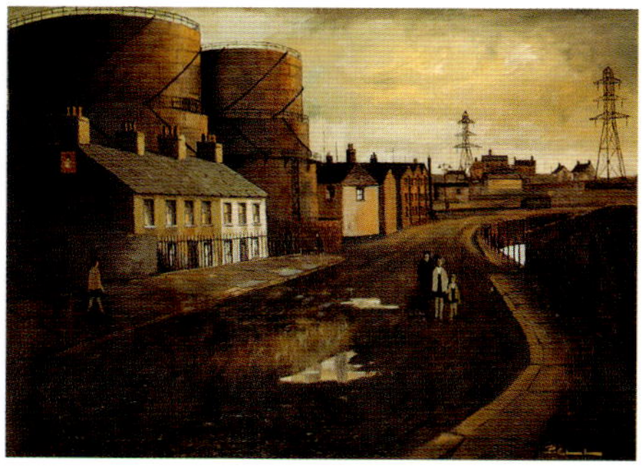

Bell, W. G.
The Queen's Head, Workington
oil on board 69 x 104
LANPS.OW236

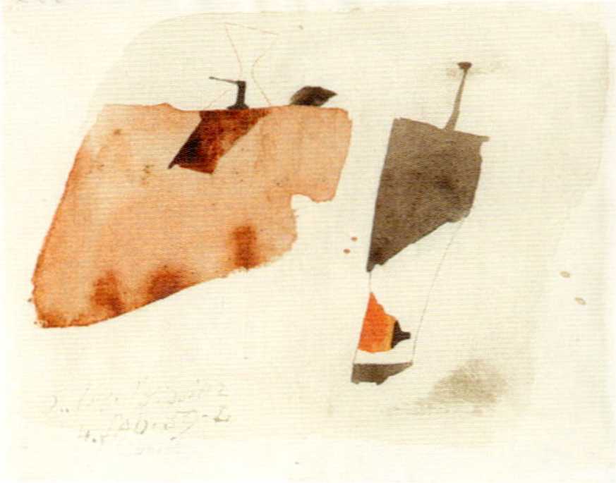

Bissier, Julius Heinrich 1893–1965
4 February 1959, Lake Zurich 1959
oil & tempera on textile 18 x 23.5
PSGCT.OW296

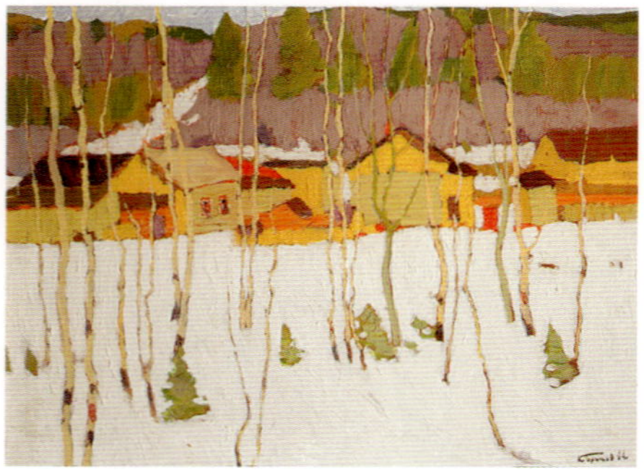

Britov, Kim Nikolaevich 1925–1996
Winter Landscape 1964
oil on board 42.5 x 60
PSGCT.OW385

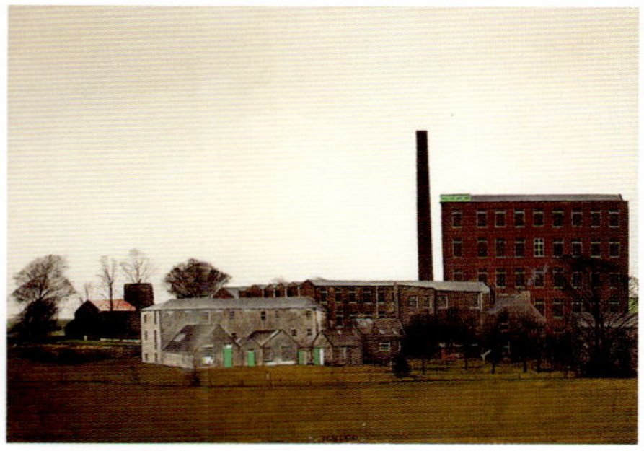

Brook, Peter 1927–2009
Galgate Mill
oil on canvas 102 x 152
LANPS.OW225

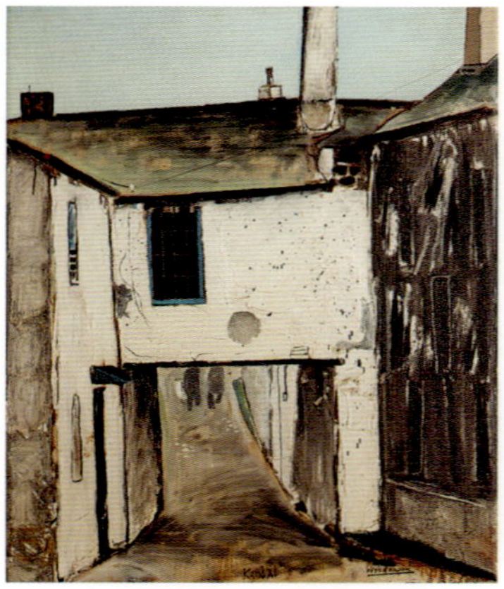

Brook, Peter 1927–2009
Kendal
oil on canvas 61 x 51
LANPS.OW226

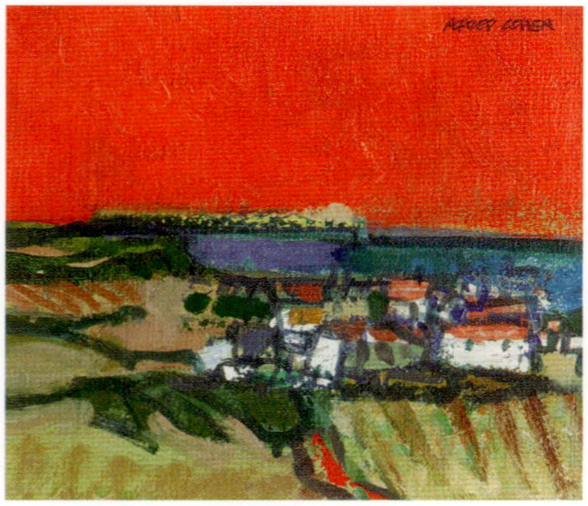

Cohen, Alfred 1920–2001
Fairlight No.1 1975
oil on board 24 x 29
PSGCT.OW299

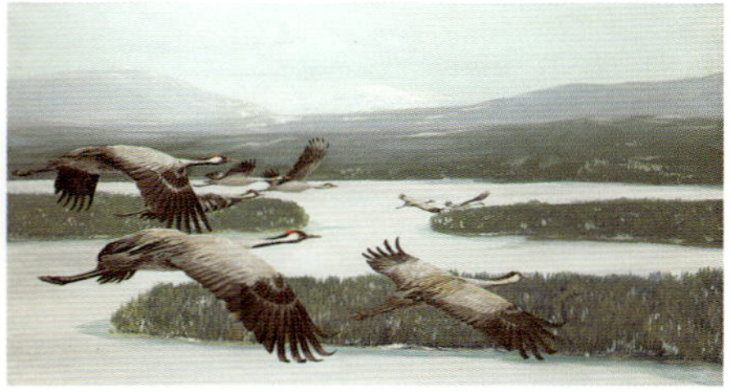

Coombs, Charles John Franklin 1908–1989
Common Cranes in Swedish Lapland
oil on canvas 90 x 180 (E)
LANPS.OW208

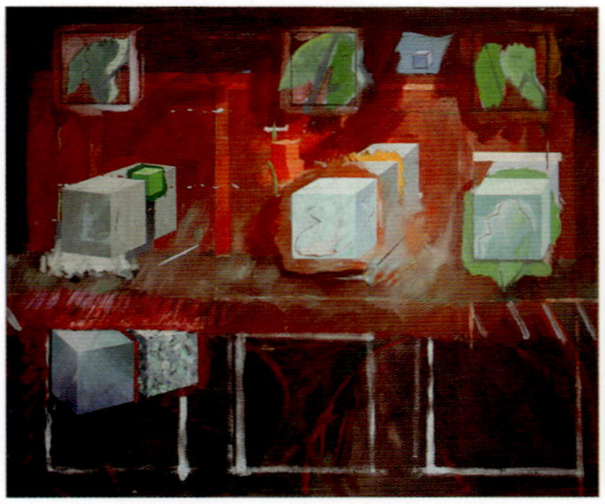

Cooper, Julian b.1947
Untitled
oil on canvas 101 x 122
LANPS.OW216

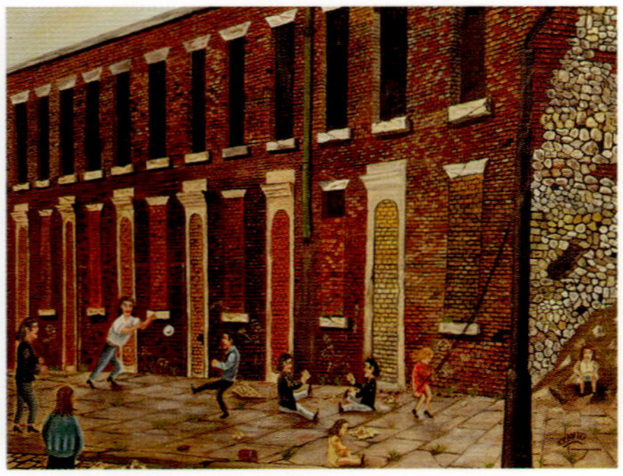

Dafter, William Robert 1901–1994
Play Centre 1970
oil on board 39 x 59
LANPS.OW186

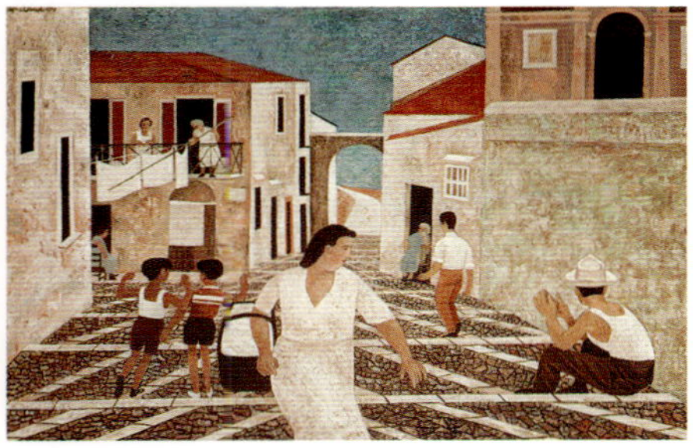

Daniels, Alfred b.1924
Monreale 1956
oil on hardboard 66 x 91
LANPS.OW180

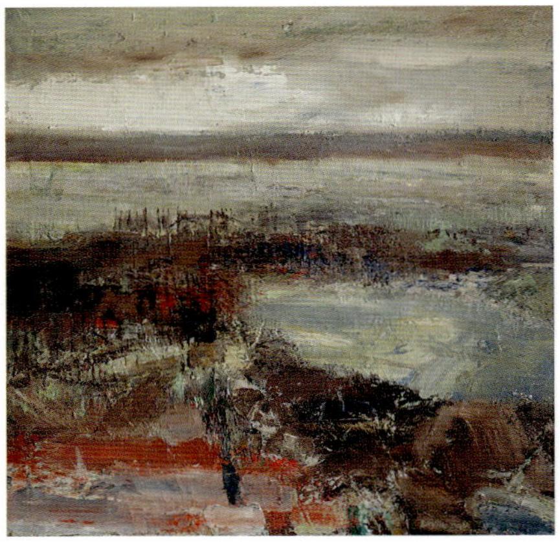

Day, Bryan
Salmon Nets 1968
oil on canvas 76 x 81
LANPS.OW207

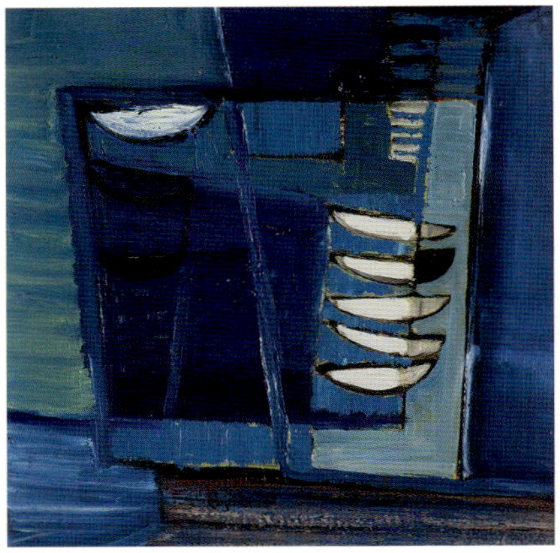

Frost, Terry 1915–2003
Walking down the Quays, St Ives 1954
oil on board 35 x 37
PSGCT.OW303

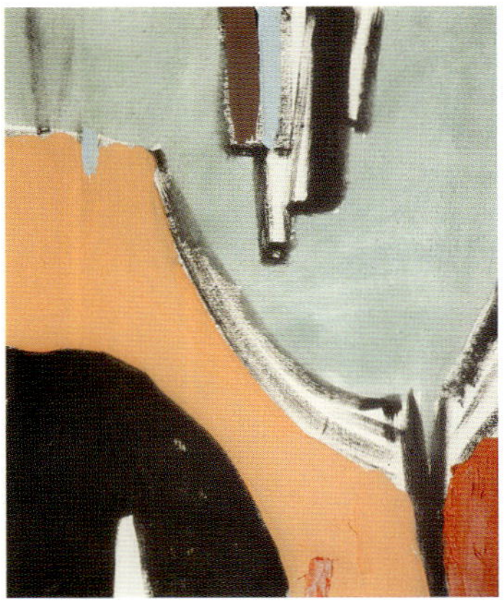

Frost, Terry 1915–2003
Green and Pink (Border) 1958
oil on canvas 59.5 x 49.5
PSGCT.OW386

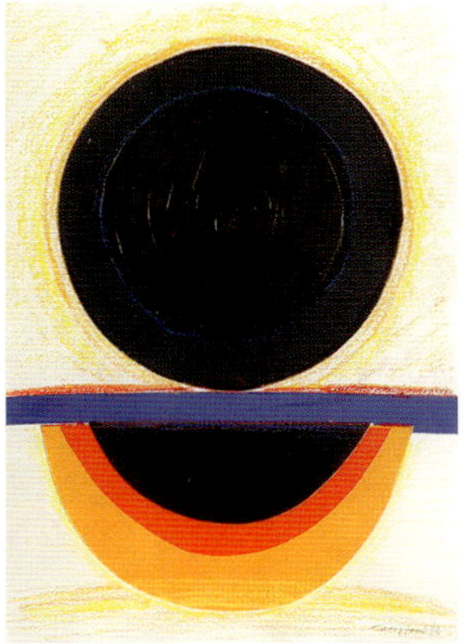

Frost, Terry 1915–2003
Blue Black Sun 1986
acrylic, oil & oil crayon collage on paper 41.5 x 29
PSGCT.OW305

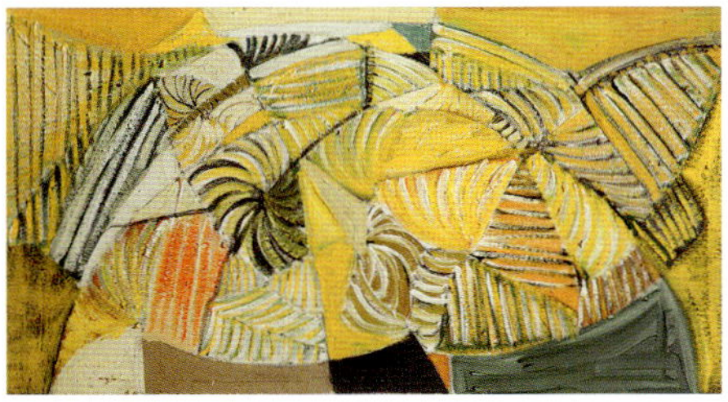

Frost, Terry 1915–2003
Yellow
oil on board 42 x 77
PSGCT.OW304

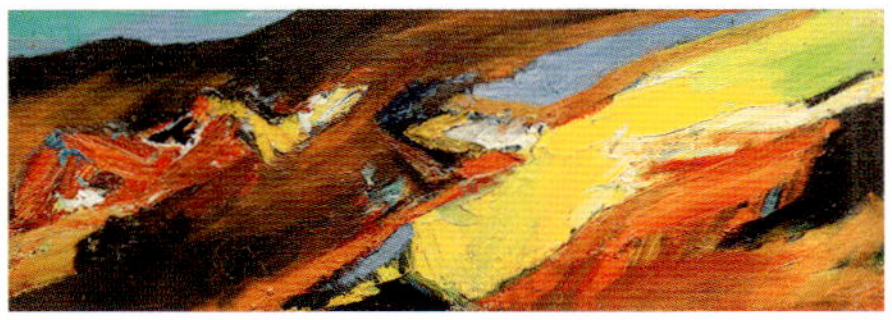

Fryer, Malcolm b.1937
Abstracted Landscape II
oil on board 30 x 92
LANPS.OW234

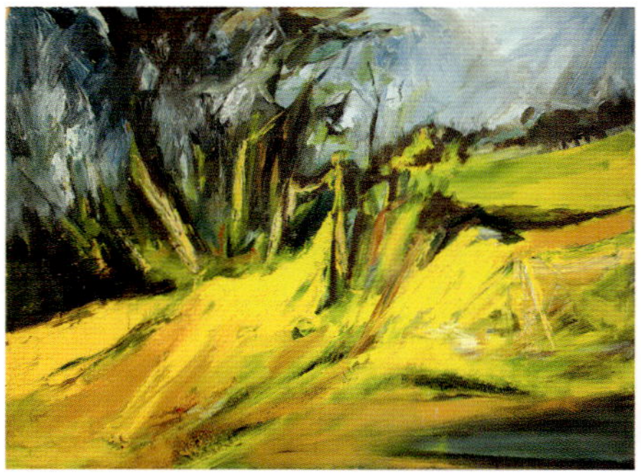

Fryer, Malcolm b.1937
Copse
oil on board 93 x 123
LANPS.OW233

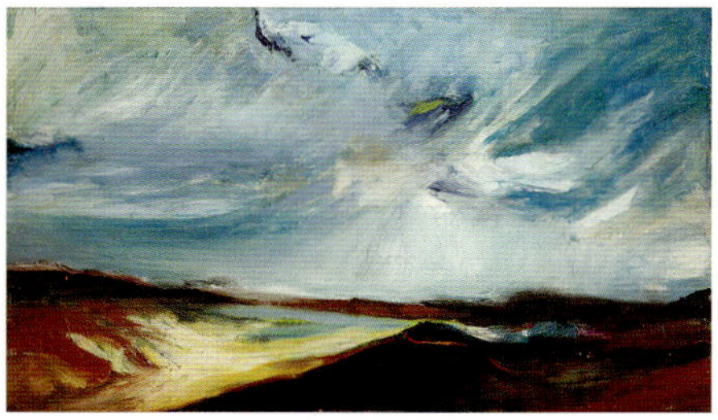

Fryer, Malcolm b.1937
Glenurquhart
oil on board 43 x 81
LANPS.OW232

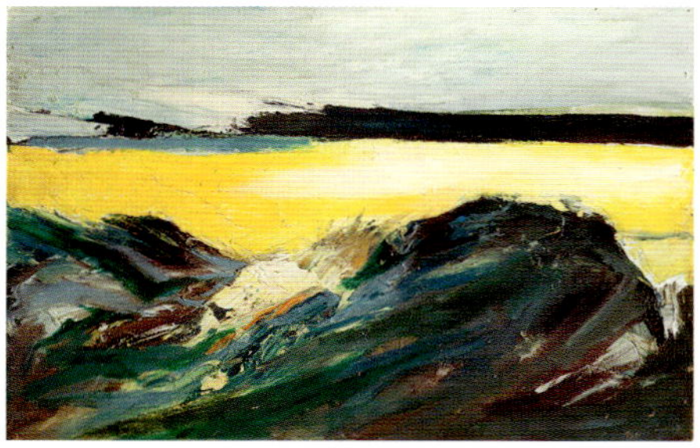

Fryer, Malcolm b.1937
Silverdale
oil on board 47 x 75
LANPS.OW379

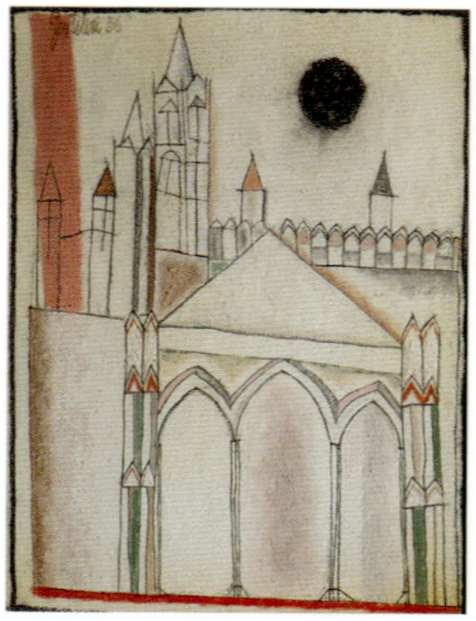

Gentilini, Franco 1909–1981
Church in Italy 1956
oil on board 65 x 45.5
PSGCT.OW387

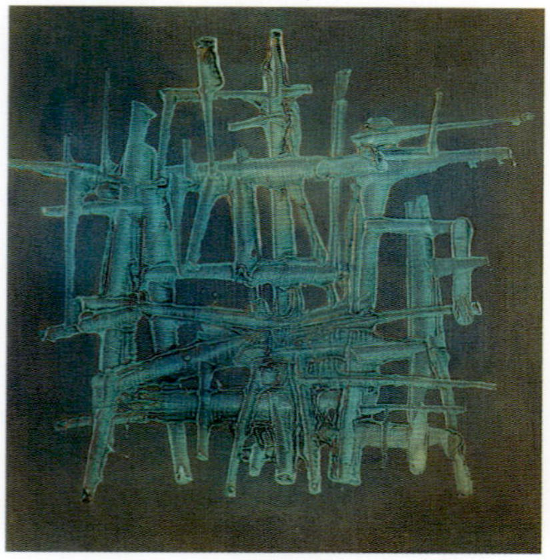

Giovannetti, Luigi Pericle 1916–2001
Grated Jadegate 1962
oil on canvas 33 x 33 (E)
PSGCT.OW390

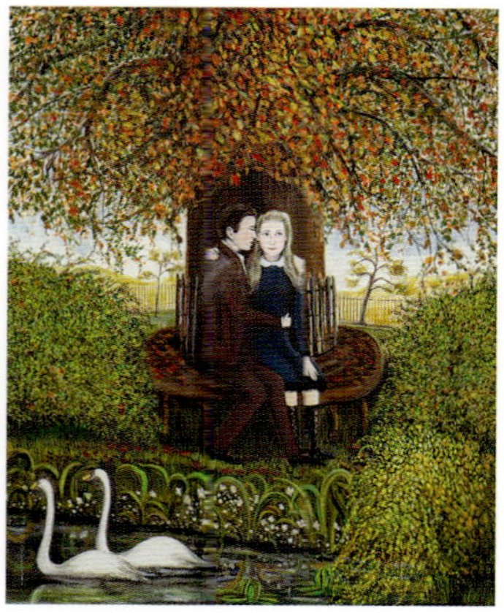

Goulding, Arthur 1921–2011
Whispering 1970
oil on canvas 58 x 48
LANPS.OW215

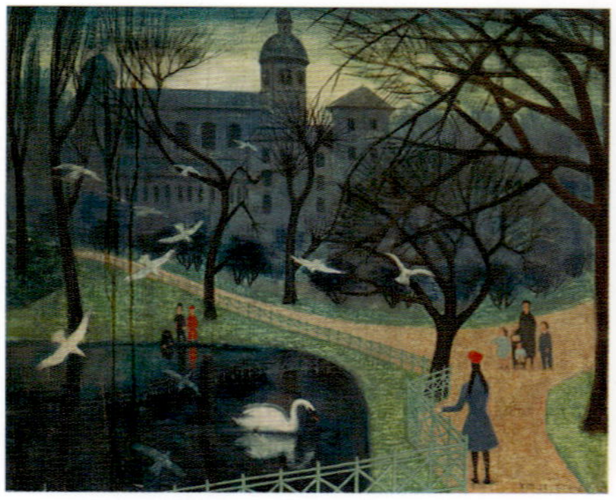

Guthrie, Kathleen 1905–1981
Waterlow Park 1972
oil on canvas 45.5 x 55.5
LANPS.OW193

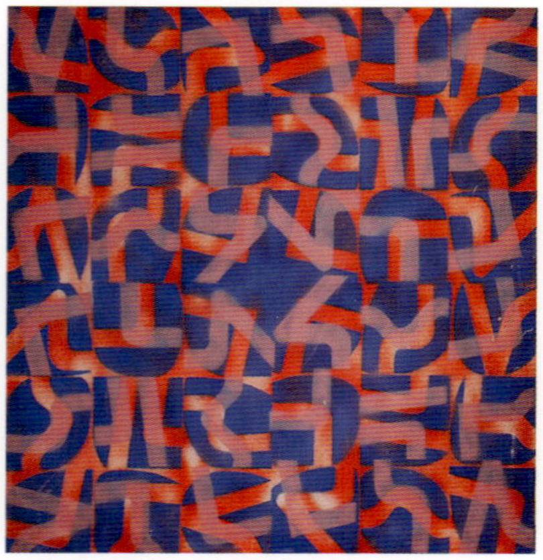

Haslam, Raymond active 1967
Spinner
acrylic on canvas 91 x 91
LANPS.OW199

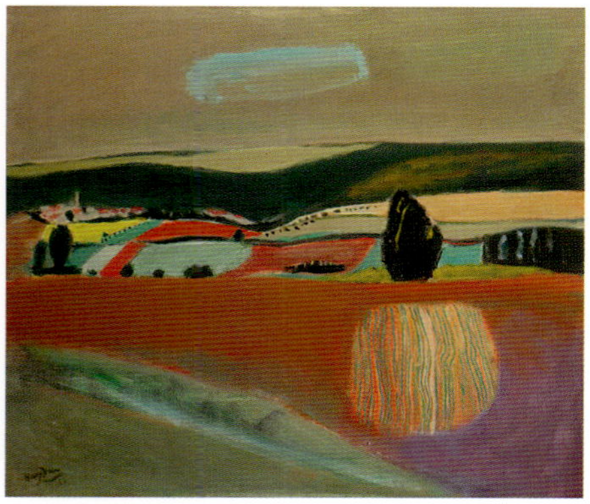

Hayden, Henri 1883–1970
Extensive Hilly Landscape 1962
oil on canvas 48 x 64
PSGCT.OW307

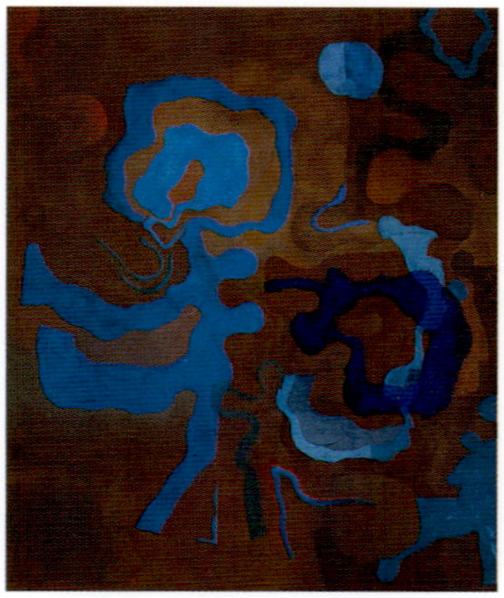

Hellawell, Harry 1921–2004
The Long Night 1967
oil on canvas 162 x 127
LANPS.OW213

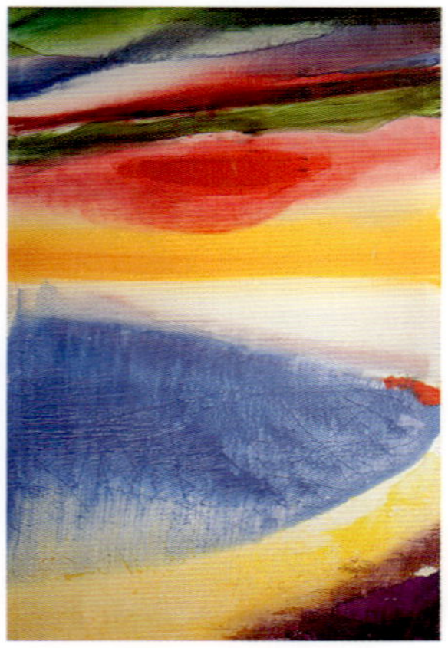

Hoare, Jeff b.1923
Open Space 1971
oil on canvas 244 x 183
LANPS.OW197.1

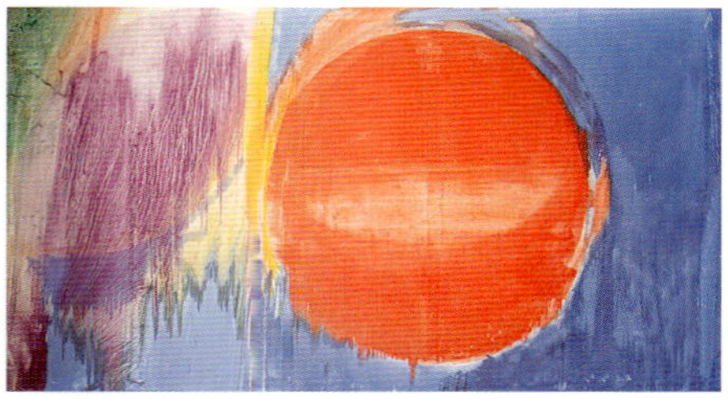

Hoare, Jeff b.1923
Open Space 1971
oil on canvas 183 x 366
LANPS.OW197.2

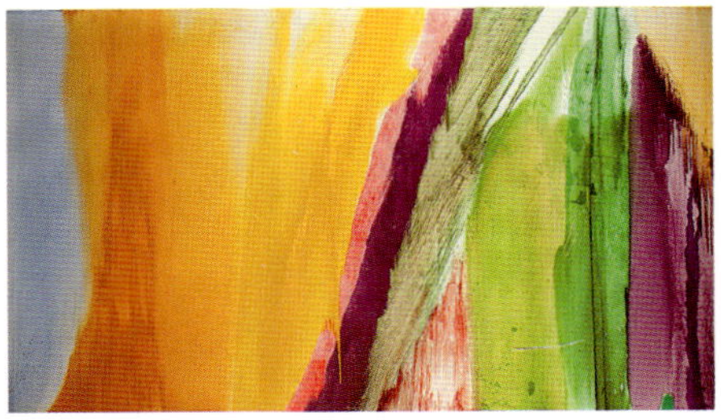

Hoare, Jeff b.1923
Open Space 1971
oil on canvas 183 x 366
LANPS.OW197.3

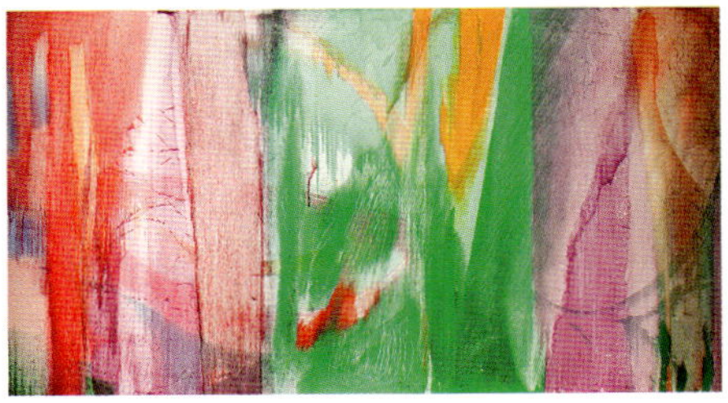

Hoare, Jeff b.1923
Open Space 1971
oil on canvas 183 x 366
LANPS.OW197.4

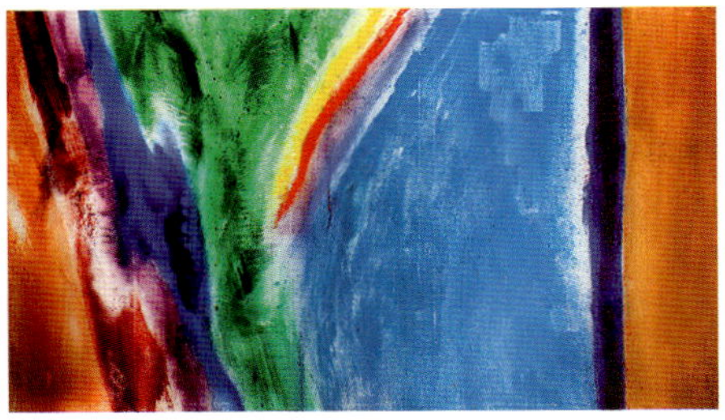

Hoare, Jeff b.1923
Open Space 1971
oil on canvas 183 x 366
LANPS.OW197.5

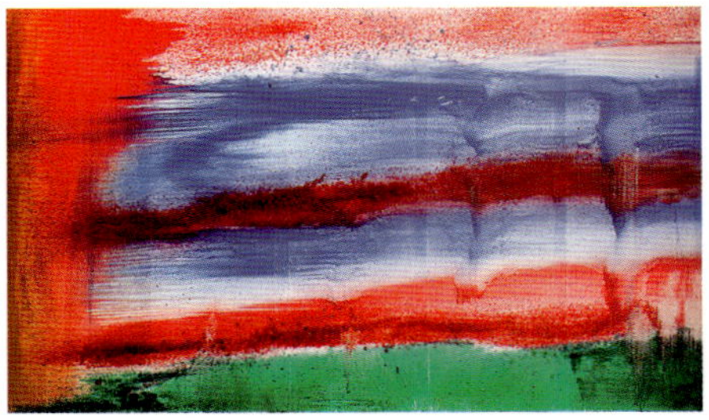

Hoare, Jeff b.1923
Open Space 1971
oil on canvas 183 x 366
LANPS.OW197.6

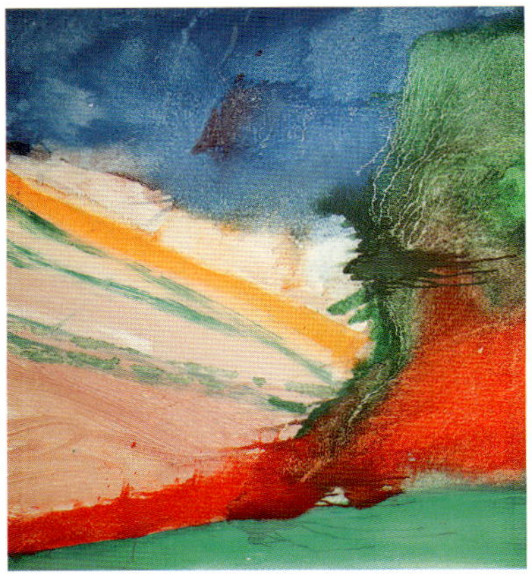

Hoare, Jeff b.1923
Ullswater
oil on canvas 128 x 111
LANPS.OW378

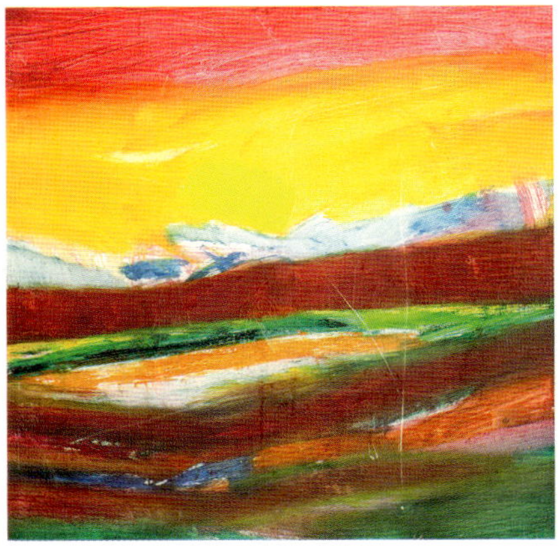

Hoare, Jeff b.1923
Untitled
oil on canvas 114.5 x 101.5
LANPS.OW198

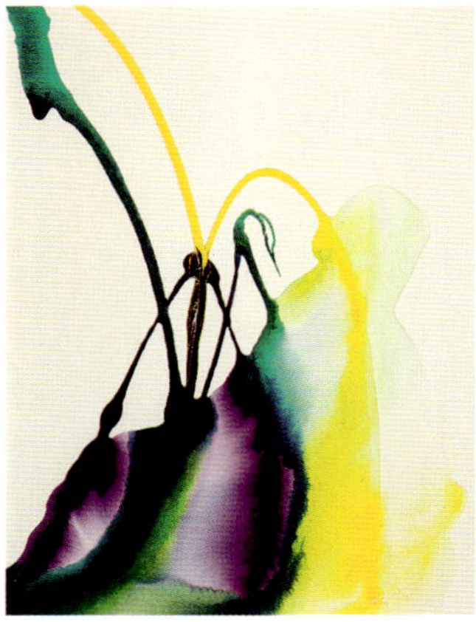

Jenkins, Paul b.1923
Philomena Violet Talks 1965
oil on canvas 50.5 x 40.5
PSGCT.OW308

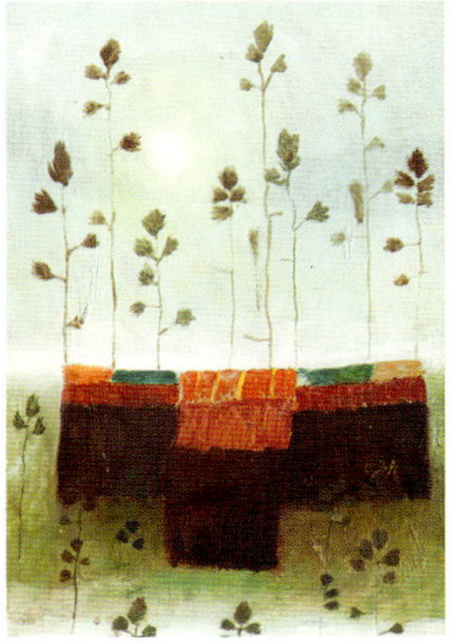

Newcomb, Mary 1922–2008
Barn and Grasses 1975
oil on board 37 x 26.5
PSGCT.OW388

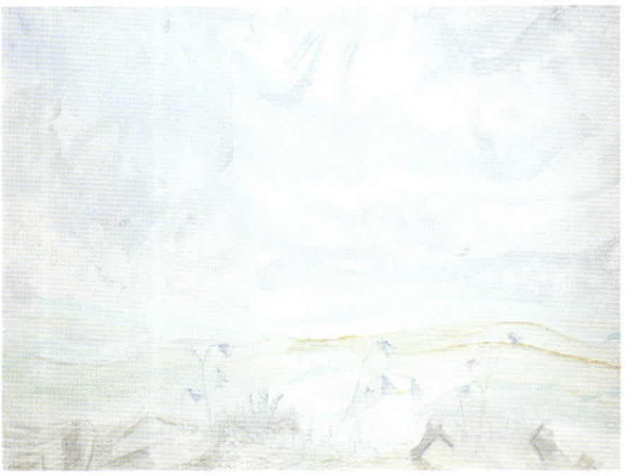

Nicholson, Winifred 1893–1981
Harebells near Housesteads Camp 1969
oil on board 50 x 75
LANPS.OW188

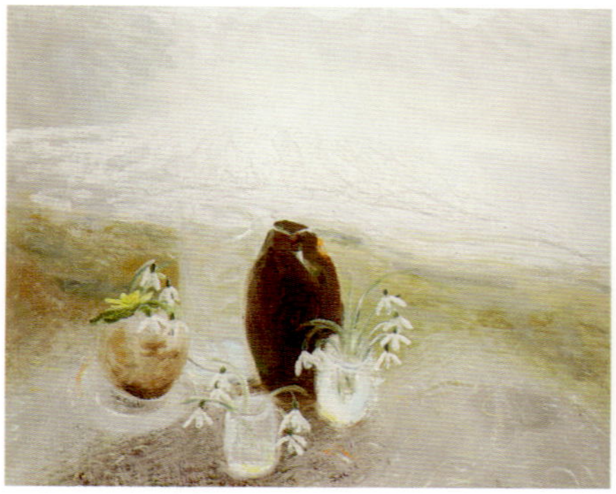

Nicholson, Winifred 1893–1981
Snowdrops in Winter, Bankshead 1969
oil on canvas 59.5 x 79
LANPS.OW187

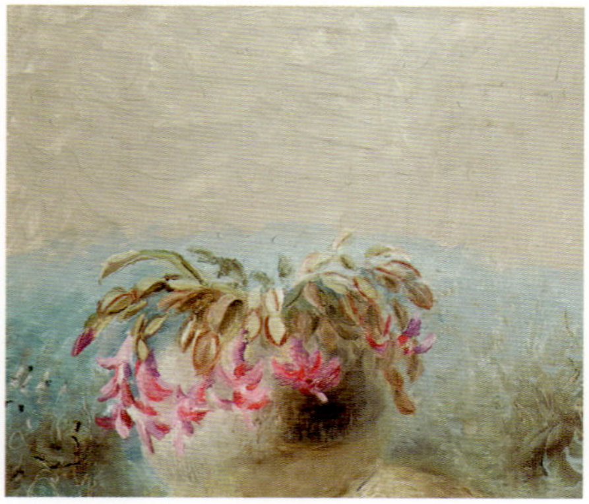

Nicholson, Winifred 1893–1981
Christmas Cacti 1979
oil on board 46 x 56
PSGCT.OW310

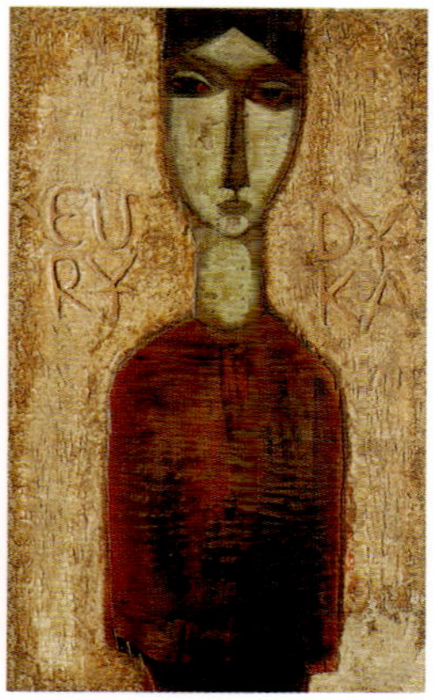

Niemczyc, Adam b.1914
Woman 1962
oil on board 73 x 48.5
PSGCT.OW389

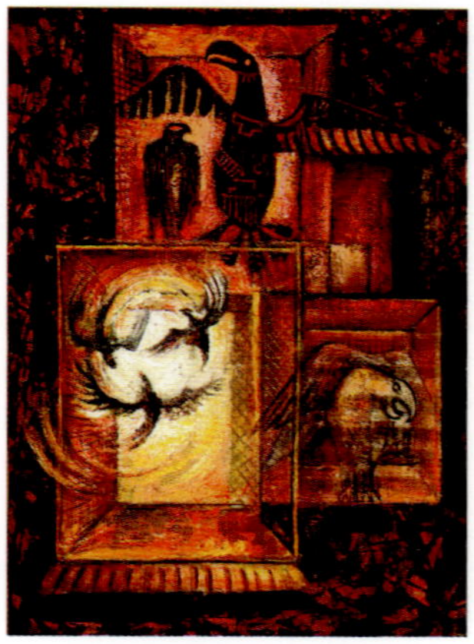

Nisbet, Scott 1910–2002
Phoenix Rising 1965
oil on board 122 x 92
LANPS.OW227

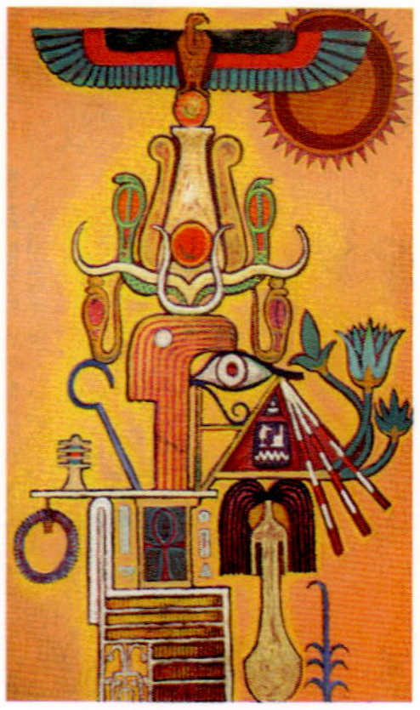

Nisbet, Scott 1910–2002
Egyptian Fantasy
oil on board 178 x 120
LANPS.OW229 (P)

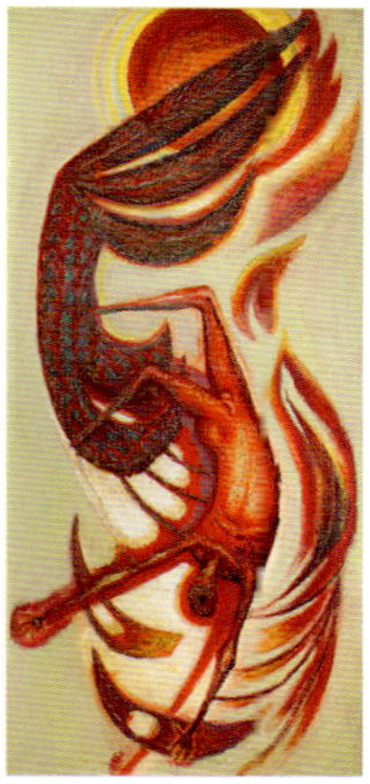

Nisbet, Scott 1910–2002
Icarus
oil on board 274.5 x 122
LANPS.OW230 (P)

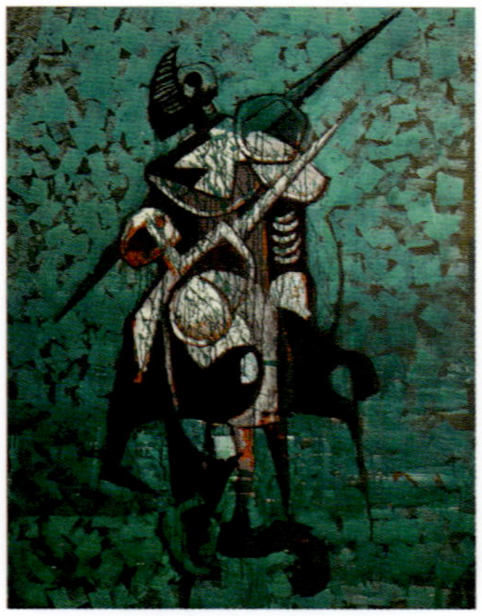

Nisbet, Scott 1910–2002
The Searches
oil on board 122 x 92
LANPS.OW228

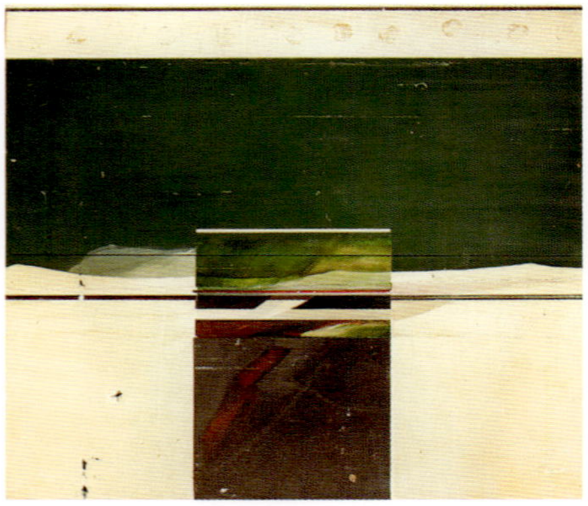

Plummer, Brian b.1934
Wast Green, Lake District
acrylic co-polymer on board 137 x 137
LANPS.OW231

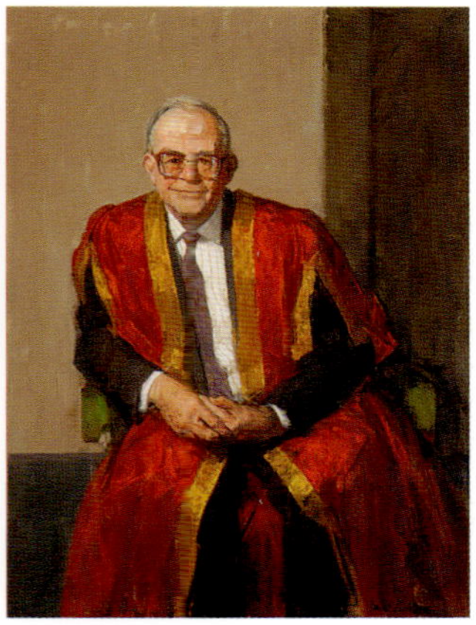

Poole, David b.1931
Professor Harry Hanham 1995
oil on canvas 100 x 75
LANPS.OW1120

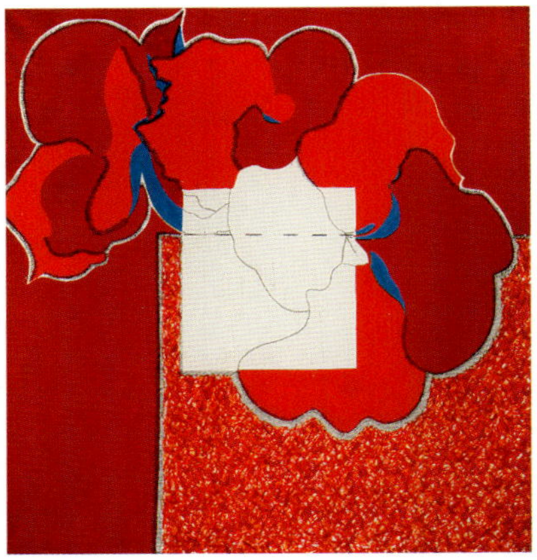

Roeves, A. T.
Untitled
oil on canvas 92 x 91
LANPS.OW181

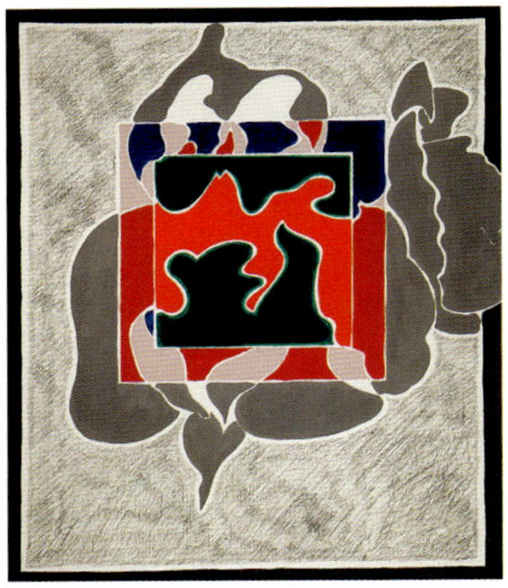

Roeves, A. T.
Untitled
oil on canvas 91 x 76
LANPS.OW182

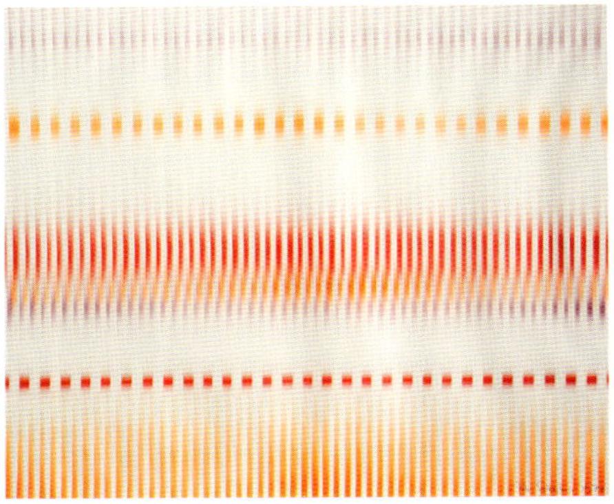

Sedgley, Peter b.1930
Counterpoint 1977
acrylic on paper 51 x 61
PSGCT.PD533

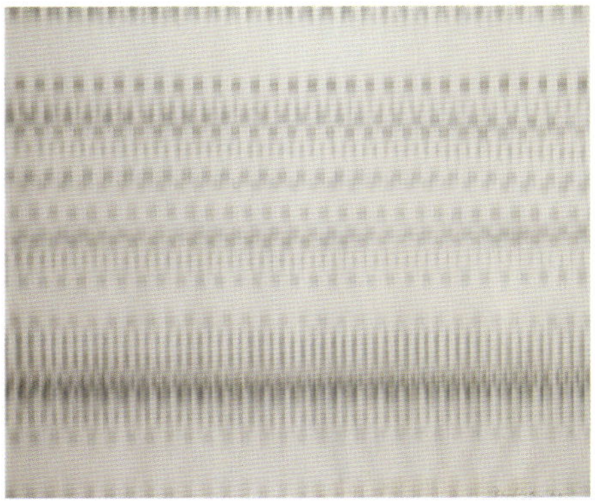

Sedgley, Peter b.1930
Untitled 1977
acrylic on paper 51 x 61
PSGCT.PD526

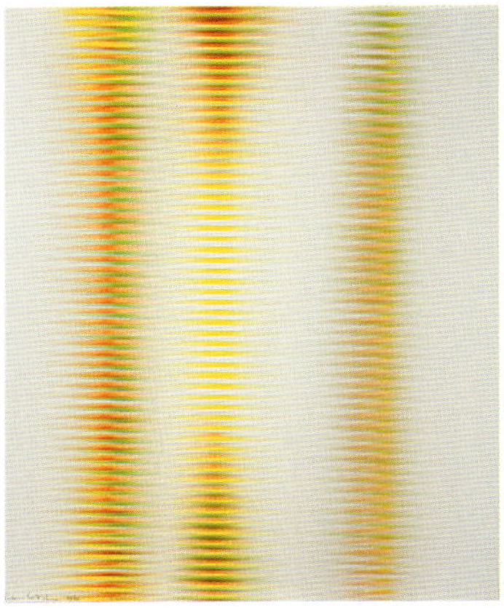

Sedgley, Peter b.1930
Untitled 1977
acrylic on paper 61 x 51
PSGCT.PD527

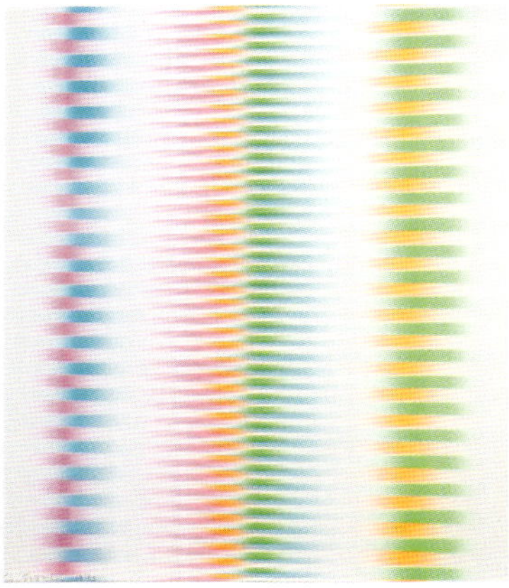

Sedgley, Peter b.1930
Untitled 1977
acrylic on paper 44 x 39
PSGCT.PD528

Sedgley, Peter b.1930
Untitled 1977
acrylic on paper 37 x 44
PSGCT.PD529

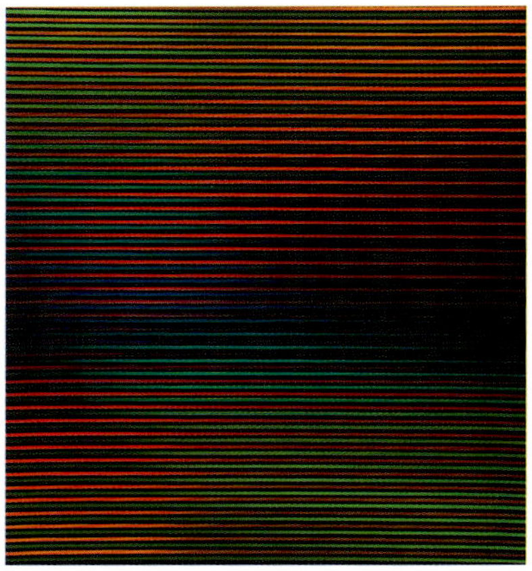

Sedgley, Peter b.1930
Black Pincer Movement I 1980
acrylic on card 52 x 51
PSGCT.OW311

Sedgley, Peter b.1930
Oranges and Lemons I 1980
acrylic on card 35.5 x 35.5
PSGCT.OW380

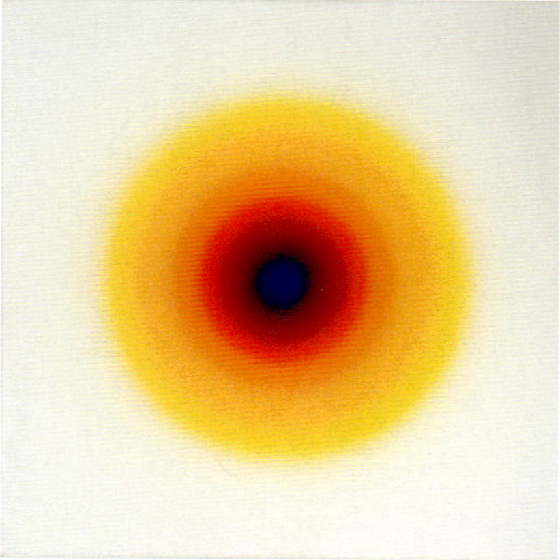

Sedgley, Peter b.1930
Glow
spray paint on canvas 50 x 50
PSGCT.OW312

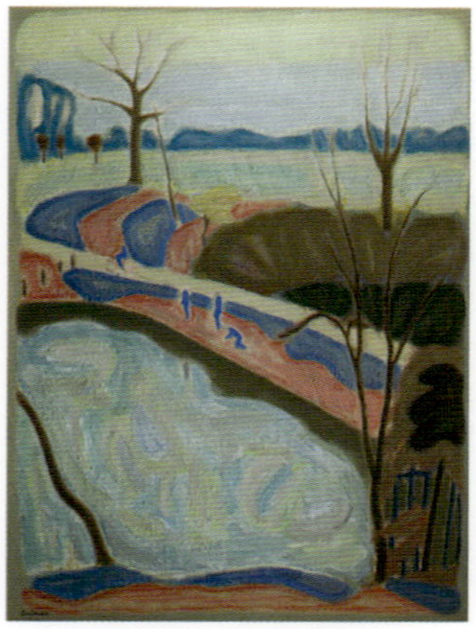

Senior, Bryan b.1935
Pond with Blue Figures 1964
oil on canvas 78 x 63
PSGCT.OW391

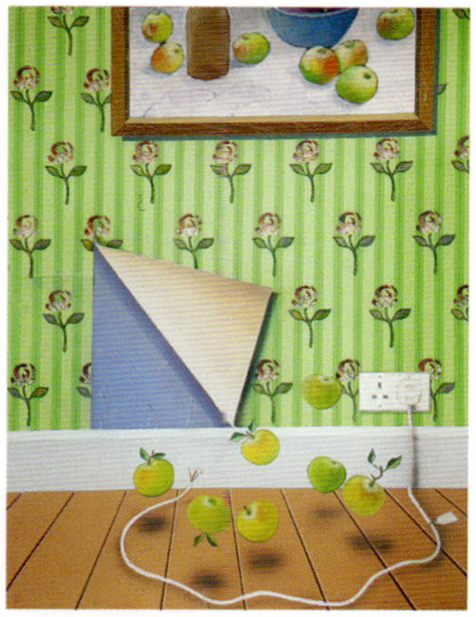

Skelton, Mike
Apples
acrylic on canvas 121 x 93
LANPS.OW183

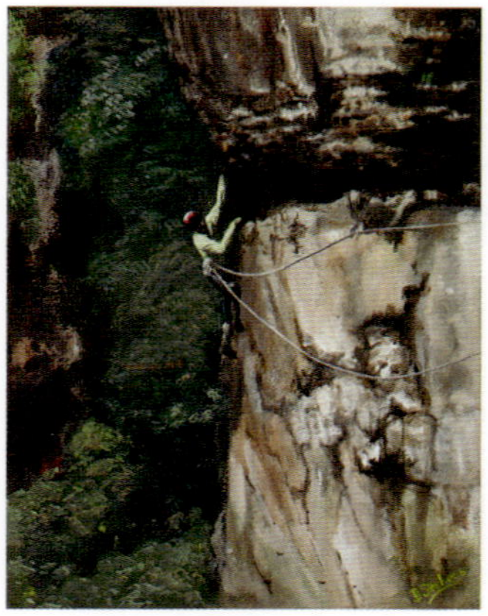

Stephens, Bev b.1935
The Climber early 1970s
oil on board 76 x 59
LANPS.OW218

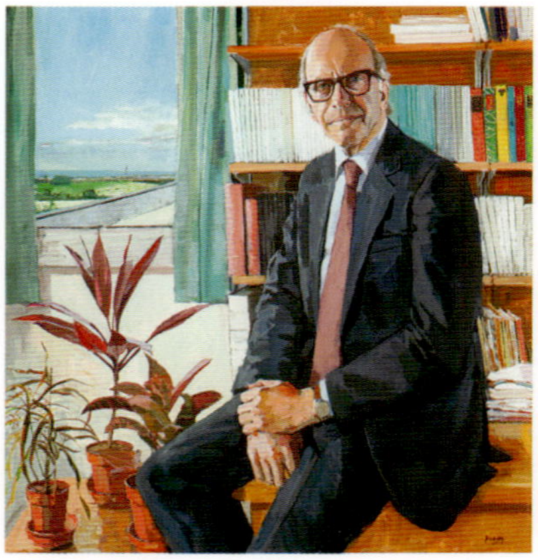

Stubley, Trevor 1932–2010
Professor Reynolds
oil on canvas 89 x 89
LANPS.OW222

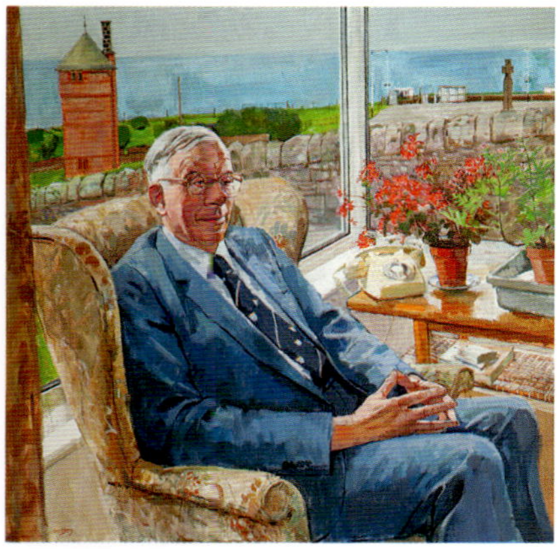

Stubley, Trevor 1932–2010
Sir Charles Carter (1919–2002)
oil on canvas 89 x 89
LANPS.OW223

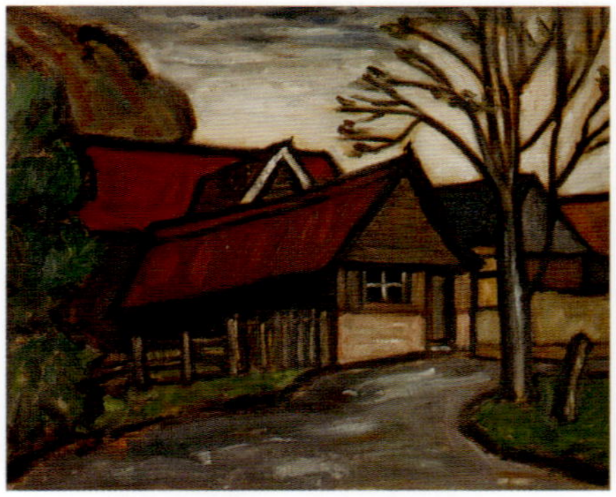

White, Kathleen active 1967–1968
Suffolk Farm
oil on board 60 x 75
LANPS.OW195

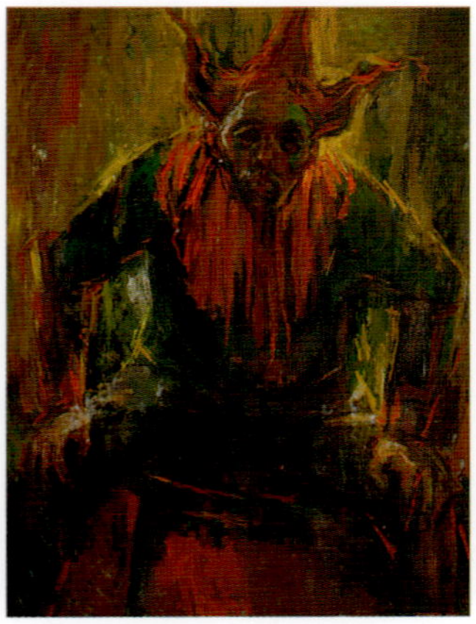

Wood, Elizabeth b.1930
The Jester 1969
oil on hardboard 152.5 x 122
LANPS.OW214

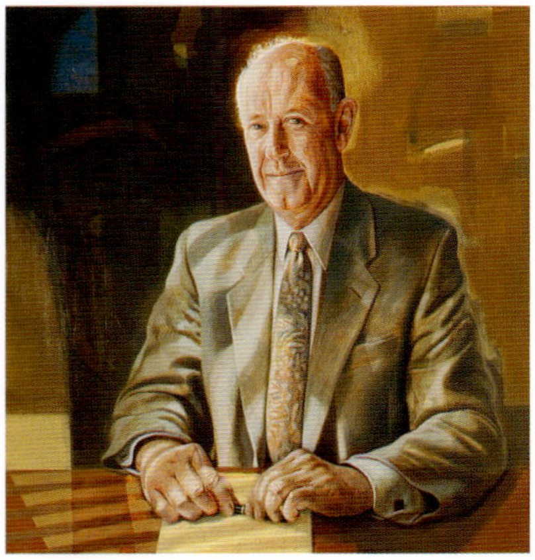

Wood, Tom b.1955
Professor William Ritchie
oil on board 88 x 83
LANPS.Z49

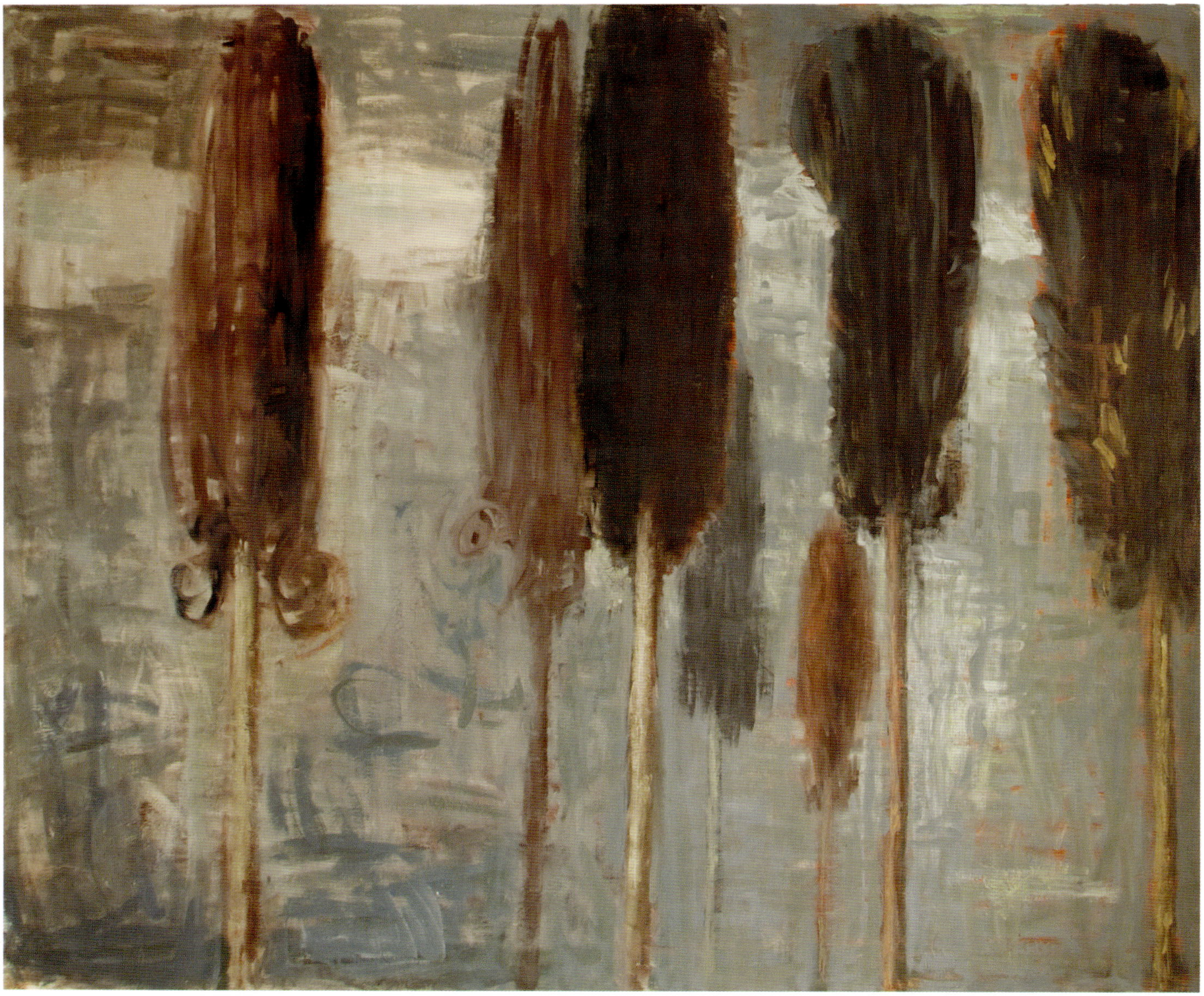

Ruskin Library, Lancaster University

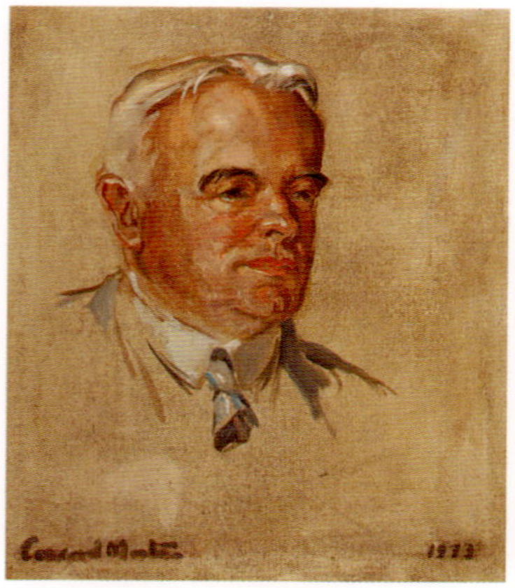

Morton, Concord 1911–1979
John Howard Whitehouse (1873–1955) 1933
oil on canvas 61 x 51
1996P0372

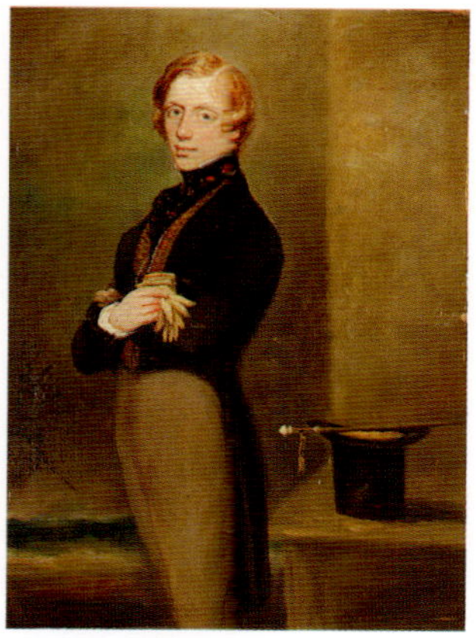

Richmond II, Thomas 1802–1874
John Ruskin (1819–1900) c.1841
oil on canvas 33.5 x 26
1996P0421

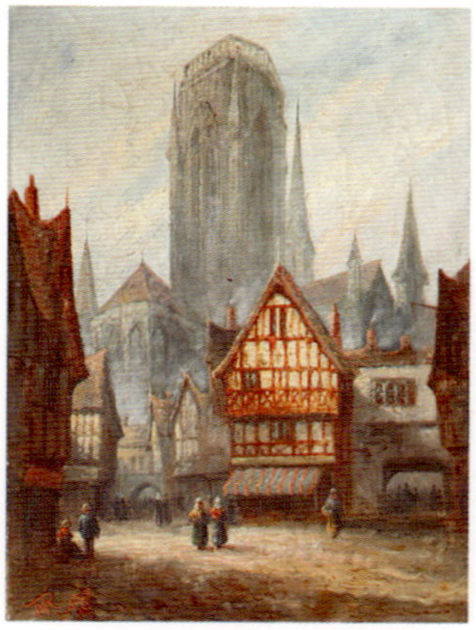

Rooke, Thomas Matthews 1842–1942
Coutances 1895
oil on canvas 40.5 x 30.5
1996P0772

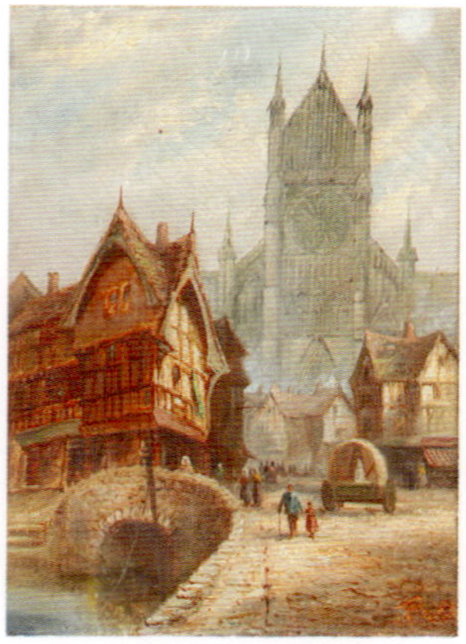

Rooke, Thomas Matthews 1842–1942
Rouen 1895
oil on canvas 40.5 x 30.5
1996P0774

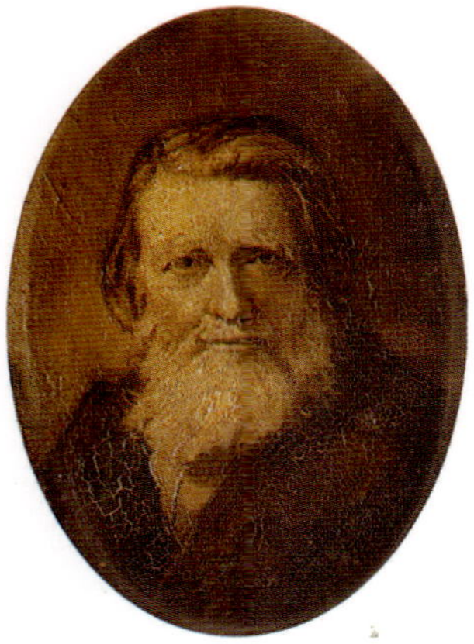

Sands, Henry H. active 1886–1906
John Ruskin (1819–1900) (copy after a photograph of 1882 by H. R. Barraud)
oil on board 23 x 15.3
1996P3078

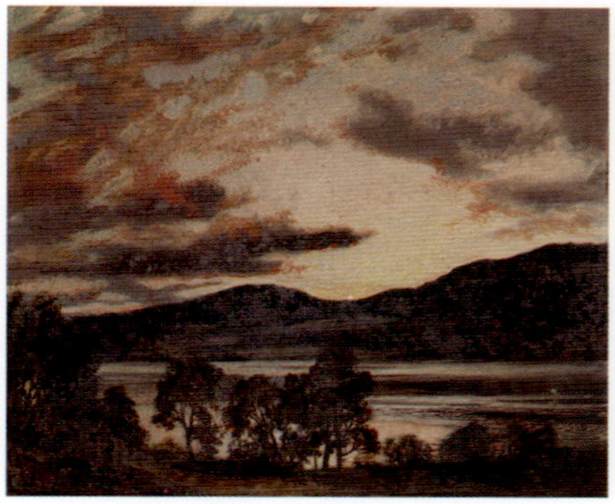

Severn, Arthur 1842–1931
Evening View over Coniston Lake
oil on board 25 x 31.3
1996P0790

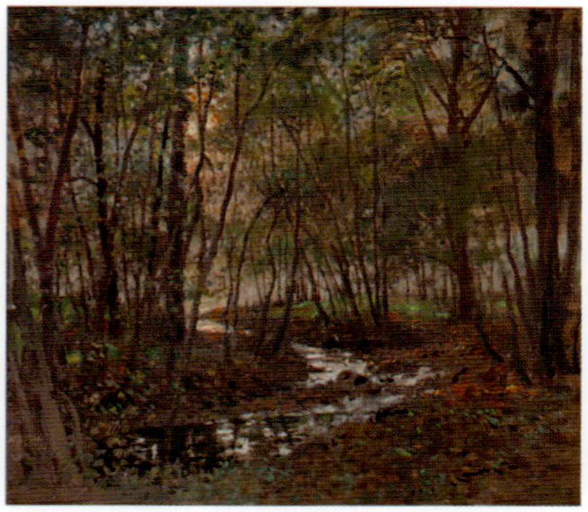

Severn, Arthur (attributed to) 1842–1931
Brantwood Estate: Beck Leven Running into the Lake
oil on canvas 51 x 61
1996P0498

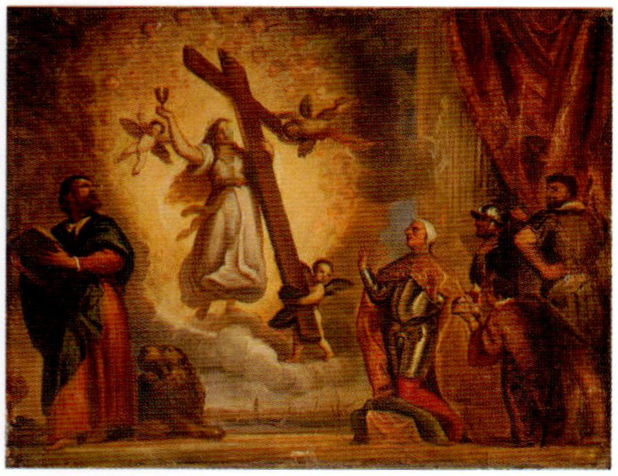

Severn, Joseph 1793–1879
Doge Antonio Grimani Kneeling before Faith (after Titian)
oil on canvas 45.5 x 58.5
1996P0552

Facing page: Le Brun, Christopher, b.1951, *Grove,* 1987, Harris Museum & Art Gallery (p. 317)

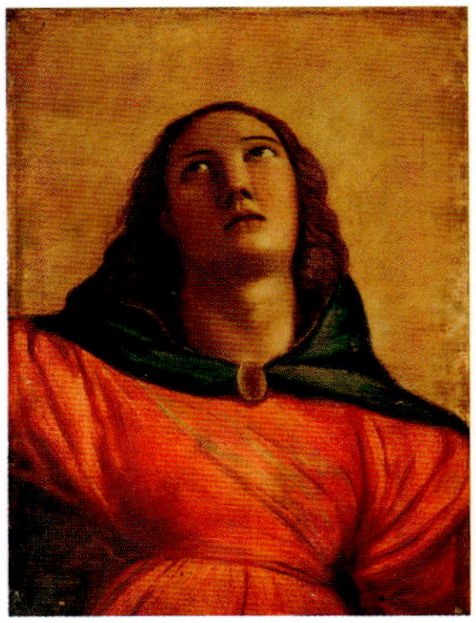

Severn, Joseph 1793–1879
Head of the Virgin (after Titian)
oil on canvas 58.5 x 45
1996P0553

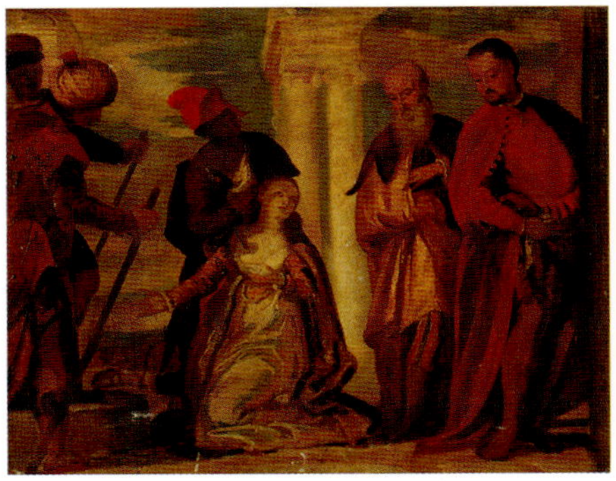

Severn, Joseph 1793–1879
Saint Agata Martyr (after Paolo Veronese)
oil on canvas 45 x 56
1996P0554

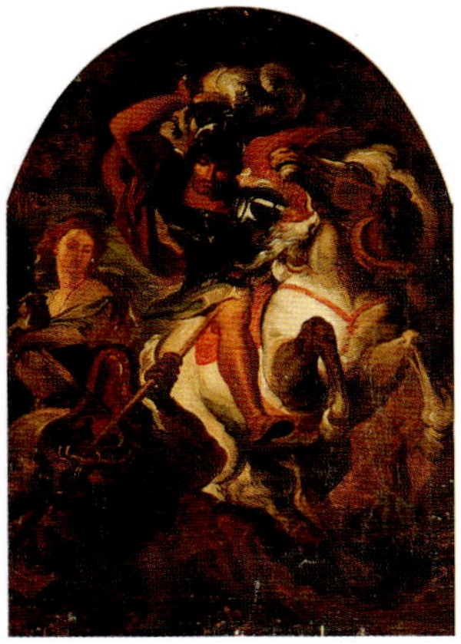

Severn, Joseph 1793–1879
Saint George and the Dragon (after Peter Paul Rubens)
oil on canvas 61 x 44.5
1996P0777

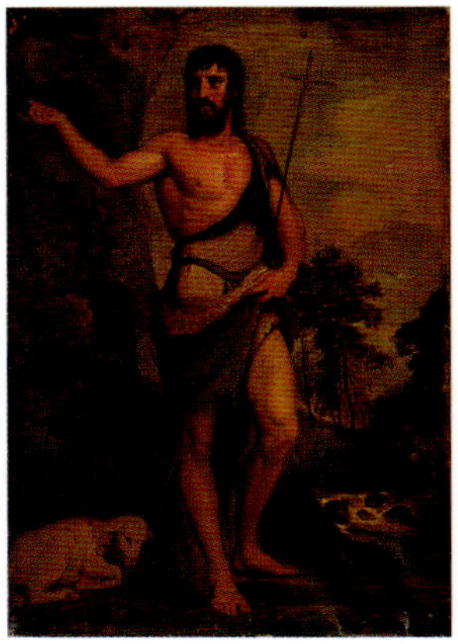

Severn, Joseph 1793–1879
Saint John the Baptist (after Titian)
oil on canvas 58 x 42
1996P0778

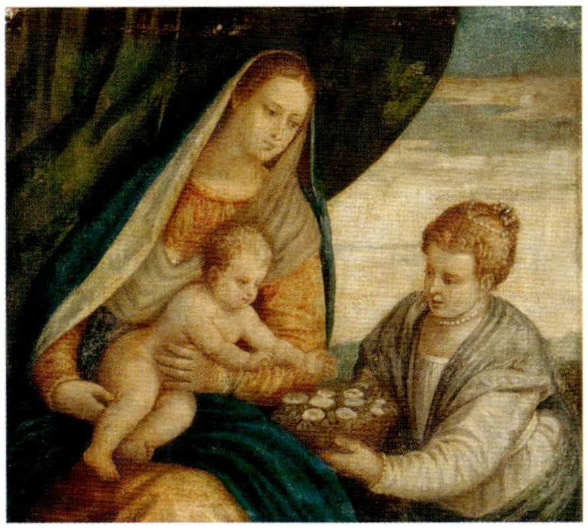

Severn, Joseph 1793–1879
The Mystic Marriage of Saint Catherine (after Jacopo Tintoretto)
oil on canvas 71 x 86.5
1996P0551

The Shire Hall, Lancaster Castle

Lancaster Castle has been associated with law and order for over 800 years, and today still houses a working Crown Court; indeed, it should be mentioned that when the Crown Court is in session, visitors to the building are only able to see the three paintings on display in the Shire Hall courtroom – all other rooms being off-limits to all but court personnel. Amongst the more famous, and infamous, trials associated with the building are those of the Lancashire Martyrs (1584–1646), the Lancashire Witches (1612), George Fox (a number of times, but perhaps most notably in 1664), the Birmingham Six (1975) and the Case of the Handless Corpse (1981). Between 1800 and 1910 over 260 people were sentenced to death in what became known as the 'Hanging Court', and were subsequently executed either at 'Hanging Corner' (until 1865), or behind the Castle walls. Not surprisingly, therefore, the vast majority of artwork on display in the building is concerned with people who were associated in some way with the legal process. Of course, there are exceptions and the Castle itself has on many occasions inspired artists to produce works of exceptional quality in a wide variety of media; at present, however, very few of these are on display at the Shire Hall.

Given the continued working nature of the building, and the subject matter of much of the artwork, it is not surprising that the collection housed at the Shire Hall has been accumulated in a rather *ad hoc* fashion. Therefore, the various Chairmen of the Quarter Sessions from the later nineteenth to the early twentieth centuries (P. J. Hibbert, Matthew Talbot Baines, Richard Assheton Cross, Edward Bousfield Dawson, John Fell, William Hulton, and Henry Fletcher Rigge) were, each in turn, honoured by having their portraits painted and displayed in the Grand Jury Room. A notable exception is that of Patrick McCall, painted in 1974, who had the distinction of being the last Clerk of the Peace of the County Palatine – behind him one can see a portrait of Roger Kenyon who was the first holder of the same post. Similarly a few local MPs (Lord Winmarleigh, who also served for a time as Constable of Lancaster Castle, John Blackburne, who also served as High Sheriff of Lancashire, and Thomas Stanley) were honoured with portraits in the Shire Hall.

Occasionally, as one would perhaps expect, 'spectacular' court cases sometimes drew the attention of artists, and in 1826 it was that of Edward Gibbon Wakefield, a prominent diplomat, which inspired Dawson Watson, a solicitor from Sedbergh, to put paint to canvas. Wakefield was put on trial for the abduction of 15 year old heiress Ellen Turner – he was found guilty and sentenced to serve three years in Newgate Prison.

One final work to mention is the very large equestrian portrait of George III, painted by James Northcote in 1806, for which he was paid 150 guineas. It is a spectacular image: George is seated on a white horse (a symbol of the Hanoverians), with the Castle in the background. The relationship of King and Castle is visually left in no doubt; as monarch, George III was also the Duke of Lancaster, and by this Right owned the Castle (as is still the case today with Her Majesty Queen Elizabeth II). As a result, Northcote placed one of the front hooves of George's horse above the Castle symbolising ownership. Interestingly, George III never actually sat for the portrait; instead, Northcote painted everything but the face, which he later filled in using a previous portrait of the King which he had borrowed for the purpose. This painting was not available to be photographed due to conservation work being carried out at the time.

Colin Penny, Museum Manager

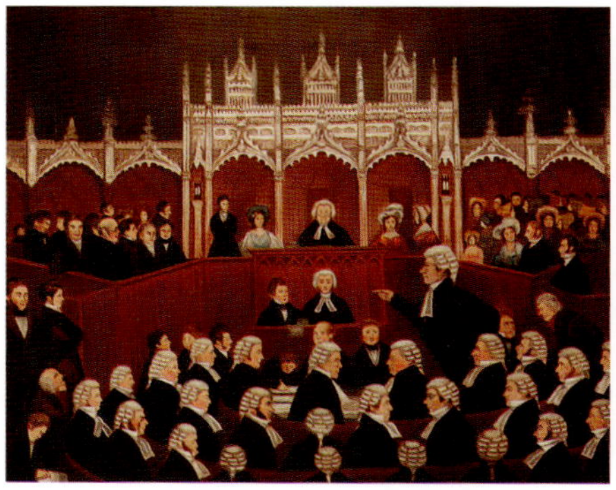

Dawson Watson
A Sketch in the Shire Hall (Trial of Edward Gibbon Wakefield, 1826) c.1827–1828
oil on canvas 34.3 x 44.4
LC40

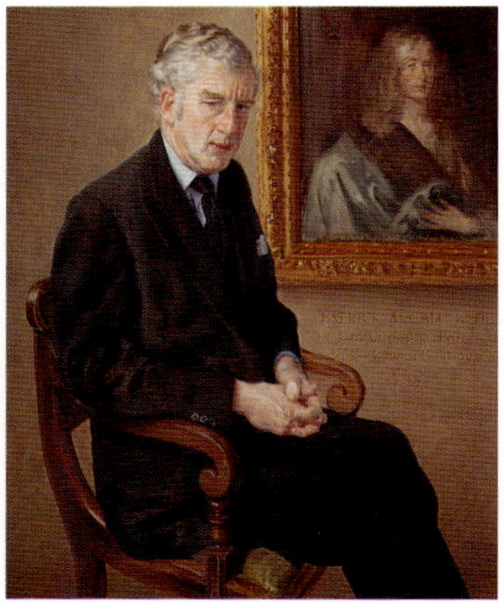

Harrison, Claude 1922–2009
Patrick McCall 1974
oil on canvas 76.2 x 63.5
LC71

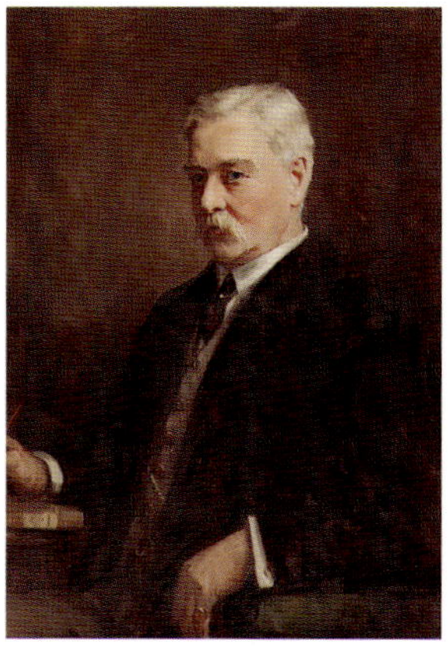

Hayward, Alfred Robert 1875–1971
P. J. Hibbert 1927
oil on canvas 91.4 x 71.1
LC66

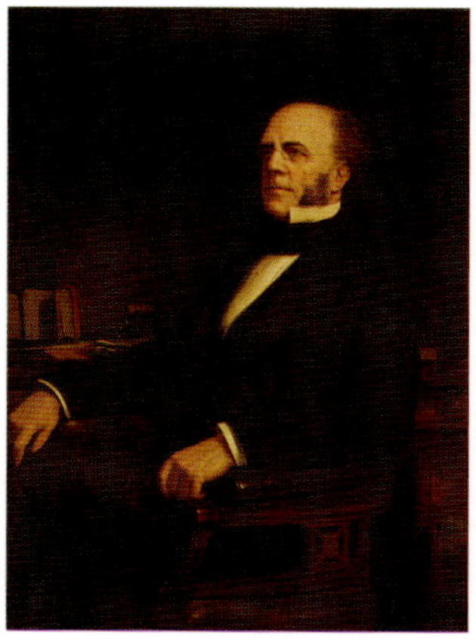

Hodges, J. Sidney Willis 1829–1900
Right Honourable Matthew Talbot Baines, QC, MP 1891
oil on canvas 127 x 101.6
LC57

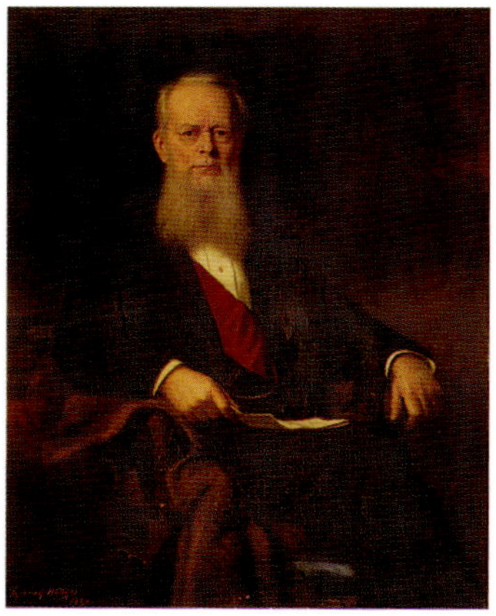

Hodges, J. Sidney Willis 1829–1900
Right Honourable Richard Assheton Cross (1823–1914) 1891
oil on canvas 127 x 101.6
LC60

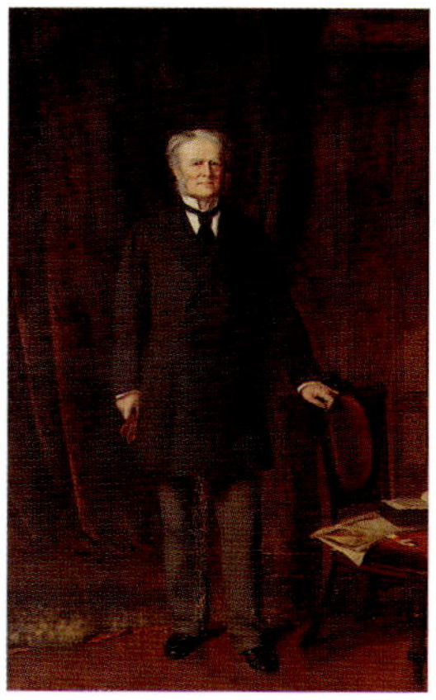

Hodges, J. Sidney Willis 1829–1900
Lord Winmarleigh (1802–1892)
oil on canvas 120 x 85 (E)
LC74

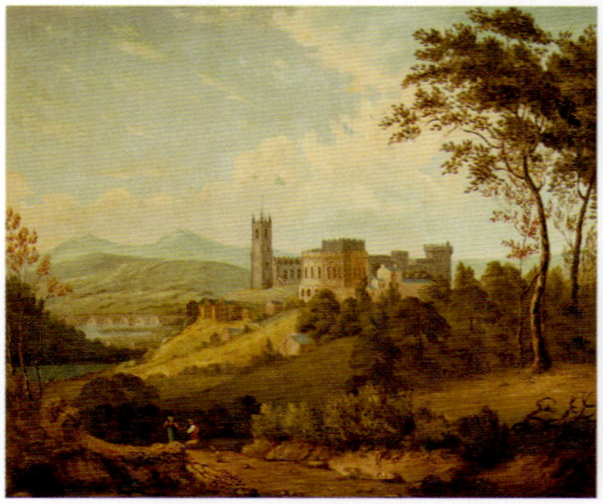

Letherbarrow junior, John
View of Lancaster Castle 1822
oil on canvas 69.2 x 91.4
LC38

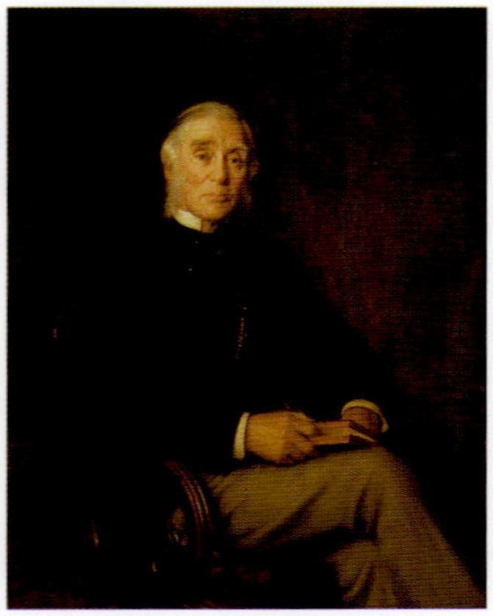

Morrison, Robert Edward 1851–1924
John Fell, JP, DL 1903
oil on canvas 127 x 101.6
LC62

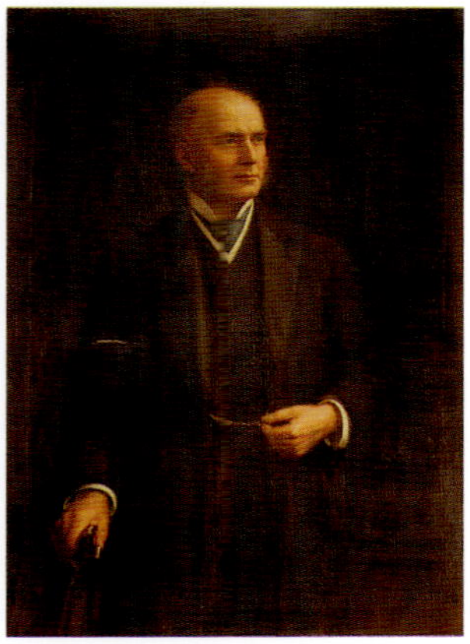

Morrison, Robert Edward 1851–1924
William Hulton 1908
oil on canvas 132.1 x 96.5
LC70

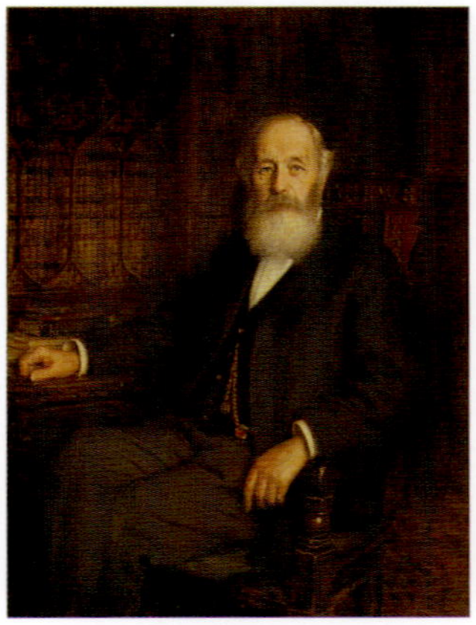

Morrison, Robert Edward 1851–1924
Edward Bousfield Dawson (d.1916) 1914
oil on canvas 127 x 101.6
LC61

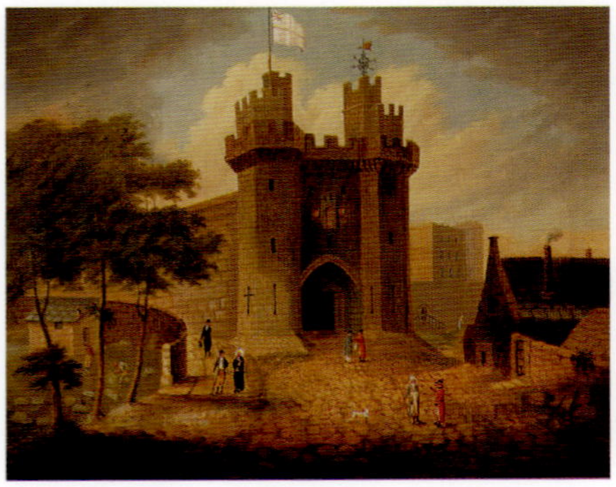

unknown artist
Gateway to Castle c.1770s
oil on canvas 69.9 x 89
LC39

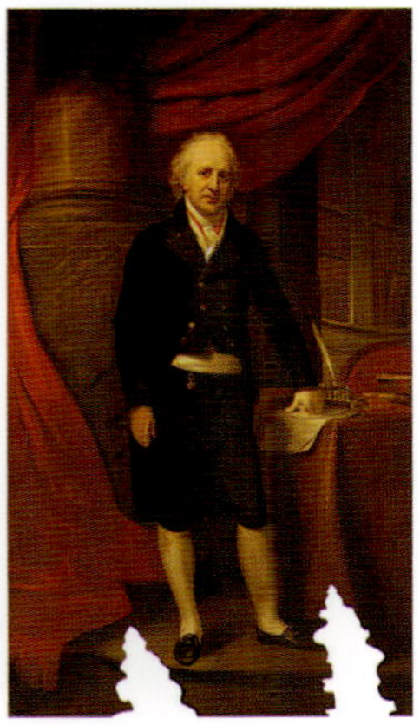

unknown artist
John Blackburne of Orton Hall (1754–1833) c.1781
oil on canvas 120 x 85 (E)
LC58

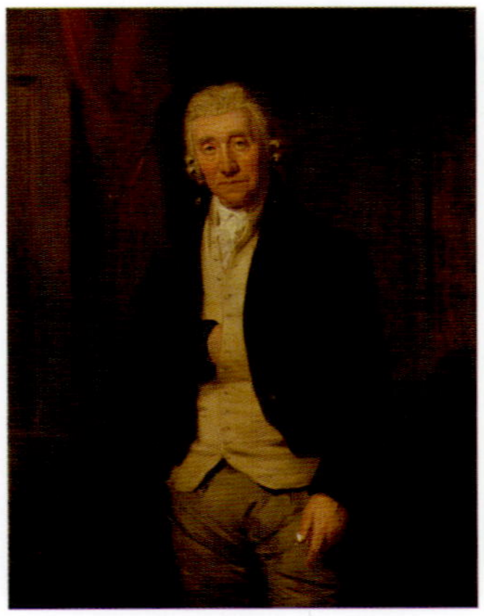

unknown artist
Alexander Butler of Kirkland, High Sheriff (1767) c.1803–1811
oil on canvas 127 x 101.6
LC59

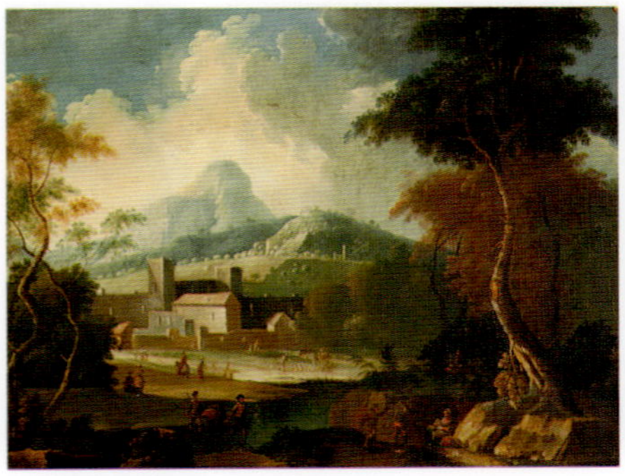

unknown artist
Hunting Party
oil on canvas 64 x 88
PCFLC.15

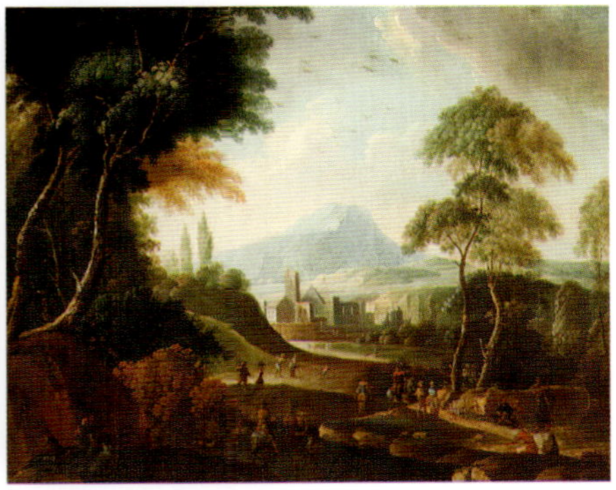

unknown artist
Landscape with Church and Mountain
oil on canvas 45 x 75 (E)
PCFLC.13

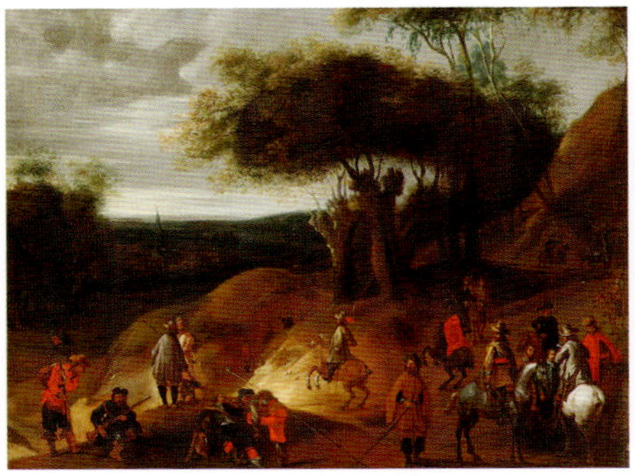

unknown artist
Landscape with House and Church
oil on canvas 75 x 125 (E)
PCFLC.14

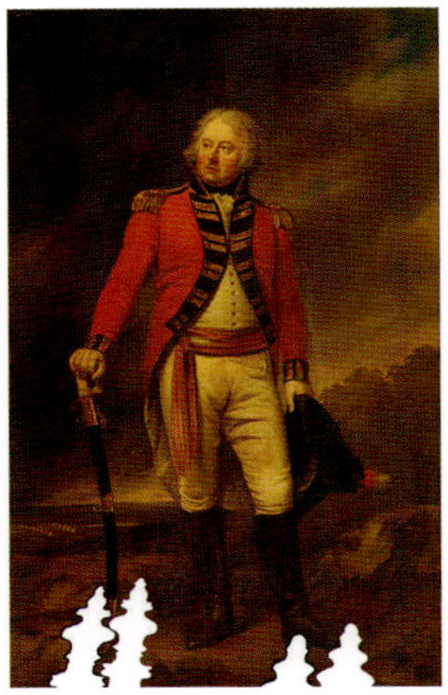

unknown artist
Thomas Stanley
oil on canvas 120 x 85 (E)
LC73

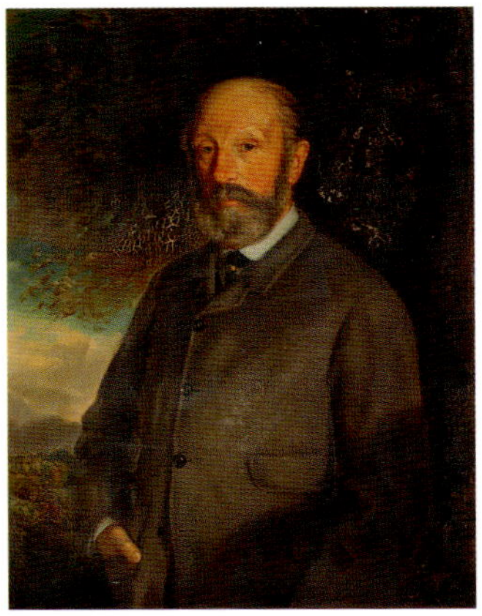

Walker, Charles John active 1864–1875
Henry Fletcher Rigge 1875
oil on canvas 91.4 x 71.1
LC72

British Commercial Vehicle Museum

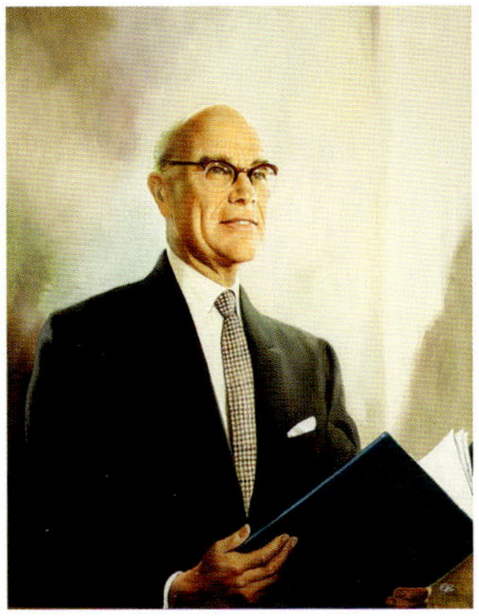

G., R.
Lord Stokes of Leyland (1914–2008)
oil on canvas 74 x 62
VM2009

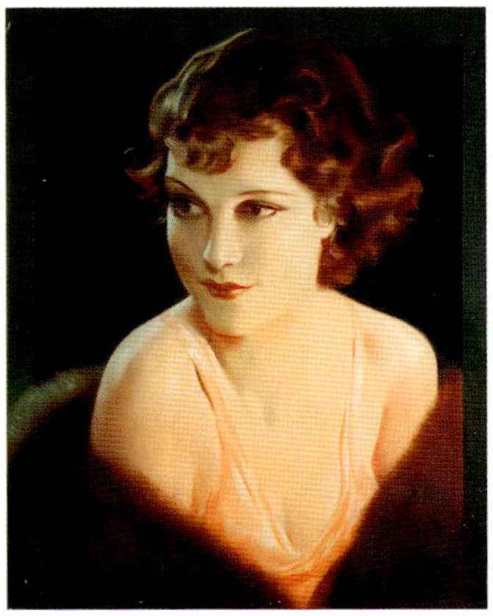

Lambert, Walter
She's a Leyland Lady, 1938
oil on canvas 74 x 57
A0006

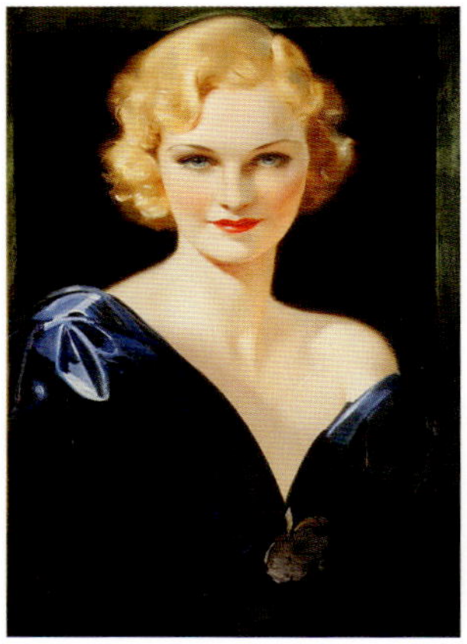

Lambert, Walter
She's a Leyland Lady, 1939
oil on canvas 74 x 50
A0007

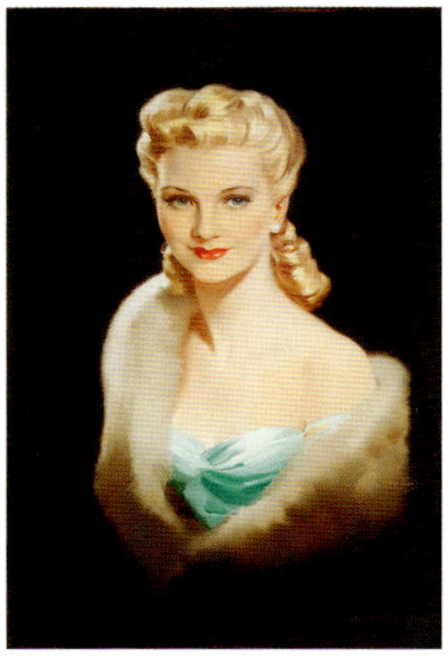

Lambert, Walter
She's a Leyland Lady, 1947
oil on canvas 74 x 48
A0011

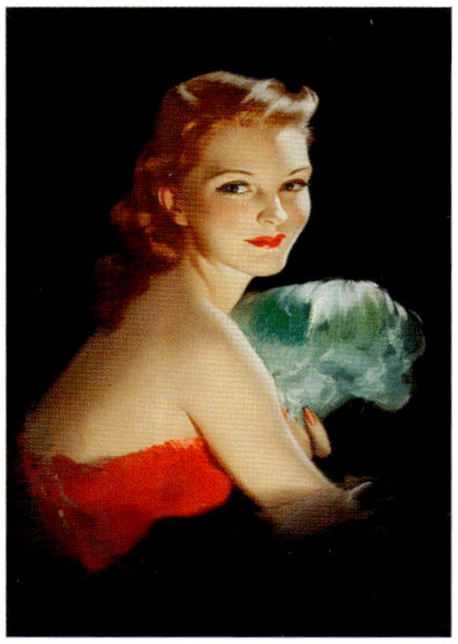

Lambert, Walter
She's a Leyland Lady, 1948
oil on canvas 74 x 50
A0012

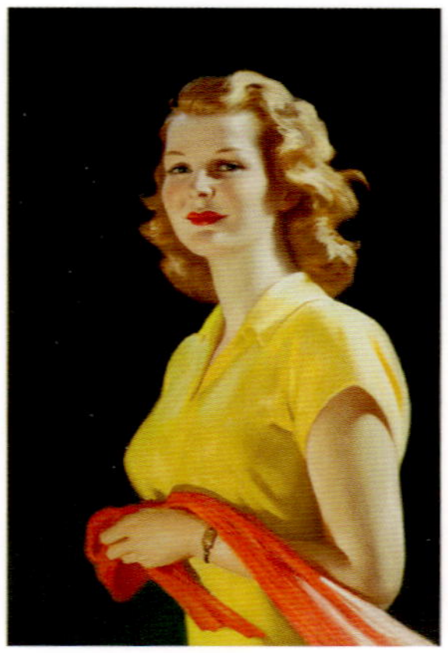

Lambert, Walter
She's a Leyland Lady, 1950
oil on canvas 74 x 50
A0013

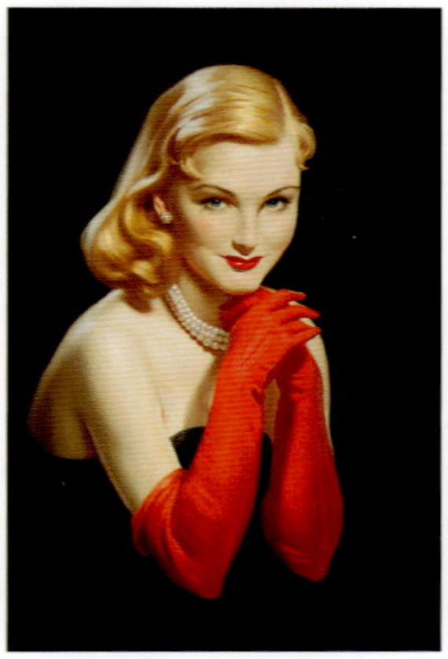

Lambert, Walter
She's a Leyland Lady, 1951
oil on canvas 74 x 48
A0014

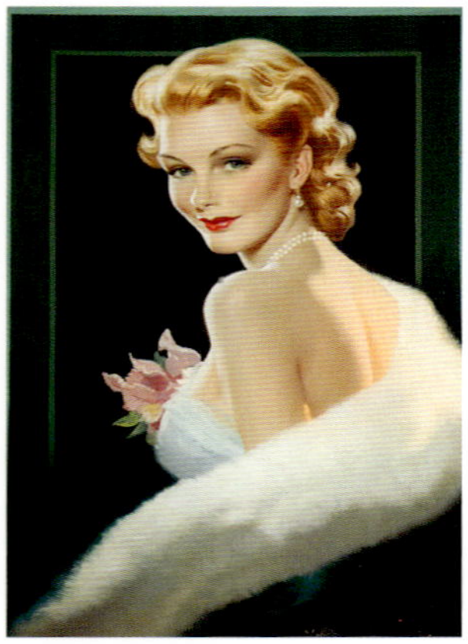

Lambert, Walter
She's a Leyland Lady, 1953
oil on canvas 80 x 57
A0016

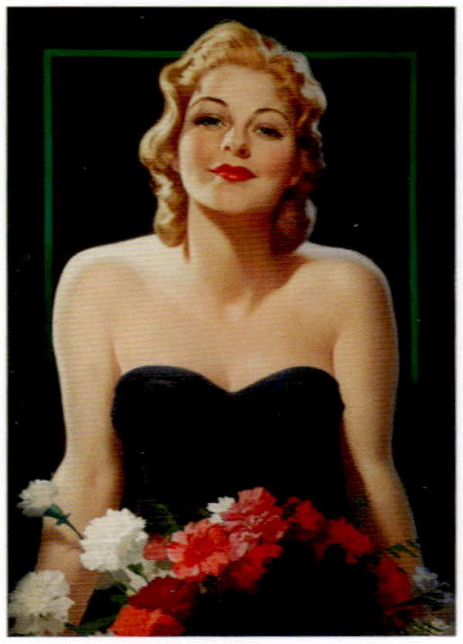

Lambert, Walter
She's a Leyland Lady, 1954
oil on board 80 x 57
A0017

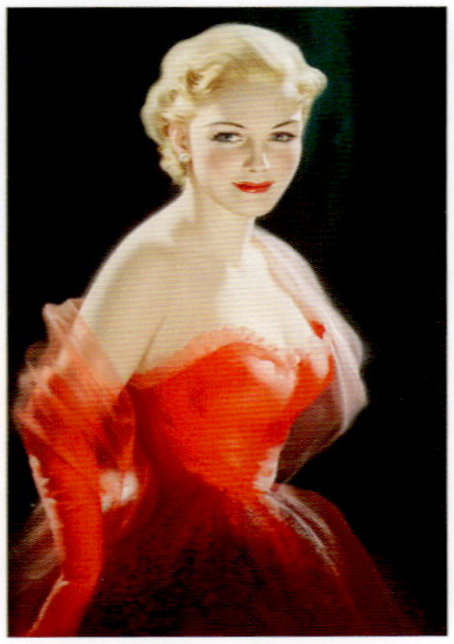

Lambert, Walter
She's a Leyland Lady, 1955
oil on canvas 86 x 57
A0018

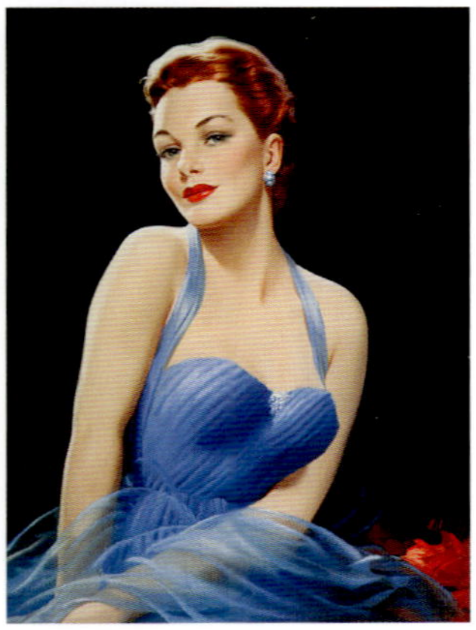

Lambert, Walter
She's a Leyland Lady, 1956
oil on canvas 74 x 57
A0019

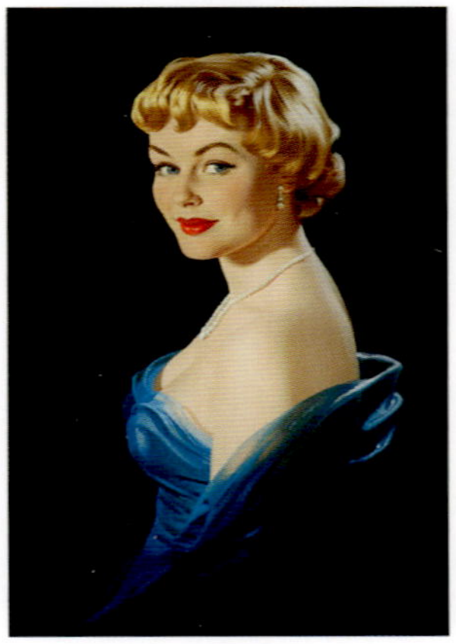

Lambert, Walter
She's a Leyland Lady, 1959
oil on canvas 63 x 42
A0020

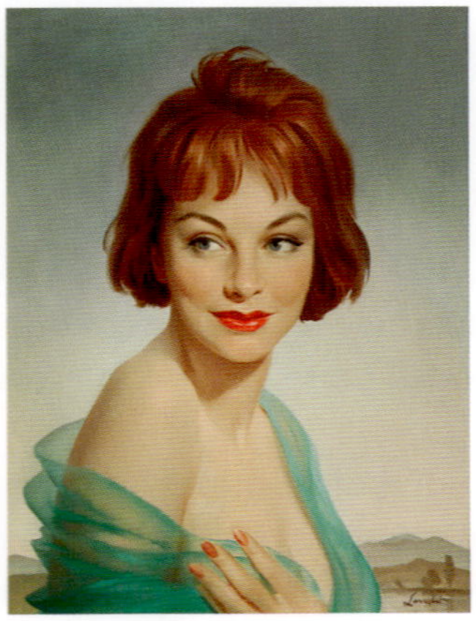

Lambert, Walter
She's a Leyland Lady, 1965
oil on canvas 49.8 x 39.8
A0023

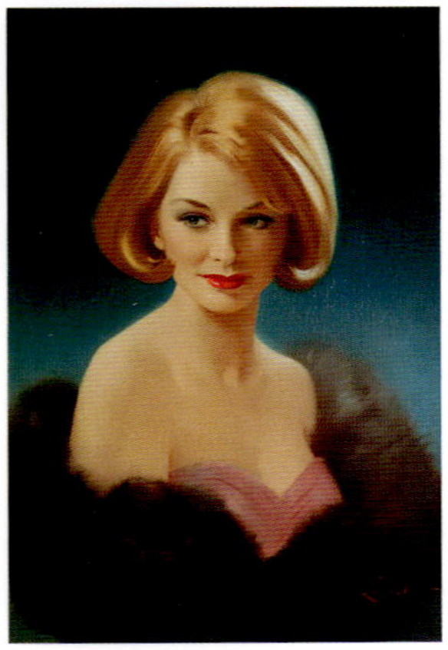

Lambert, Walter
She's a Leyland Lady, 1966
oil on canvas 74 x 48.5
A0024

The portraits of *Agnes Critchley* and her son-in-law *John Walton* are part of a set discovered during the restoration of the local alms houses. As portraits of prime movers in the establishment of the local hand weaving trade they are of great interest. Quite interesting things do sometimes come in small packages after all.

David Hunt, Museum Curator

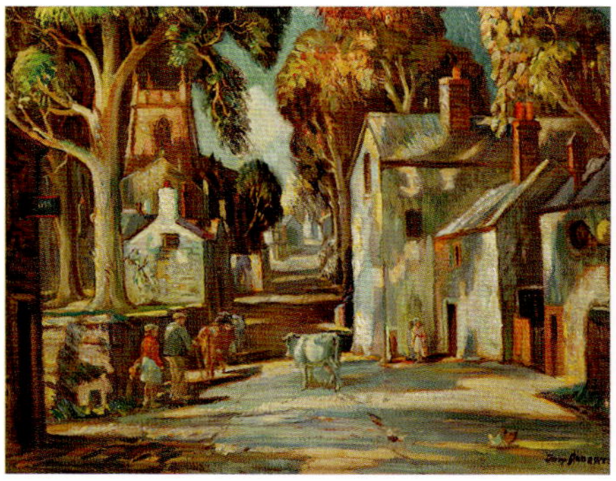

Anderton, Tom 1894–1956
Brindle Village: Evening c.1950
oil on board 46 x 61
2002/797/3

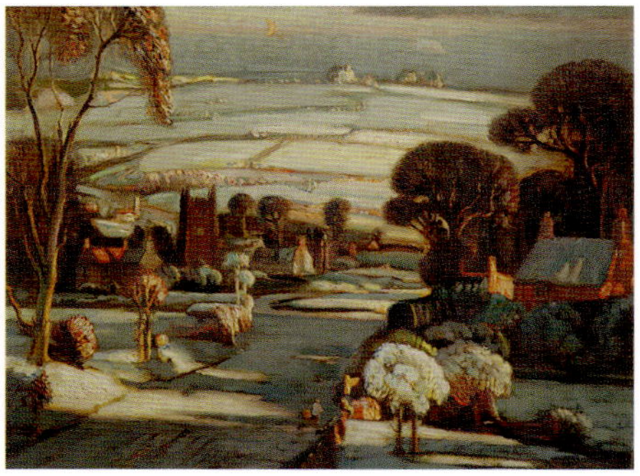

Anderton, Tom 1894–1956
Brindle Village: Winter c.1950
oil on board 42 x 55
2002/797/4

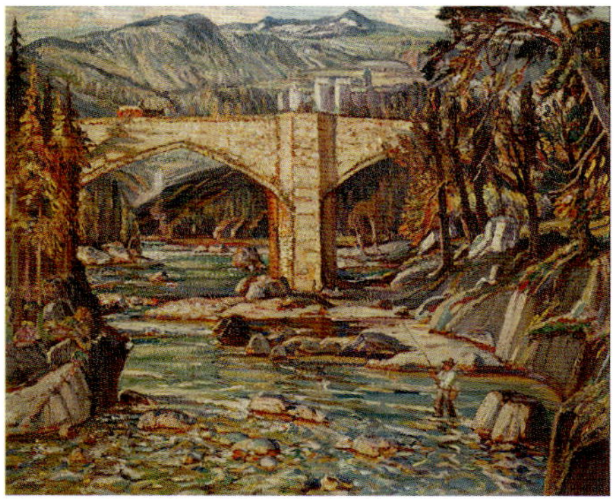

Anderton, Tom 1894–1956
Fisherman, Upland Landscape with Bridge (1) c.1950
oil on canvas 64 x 77
2002/797/6

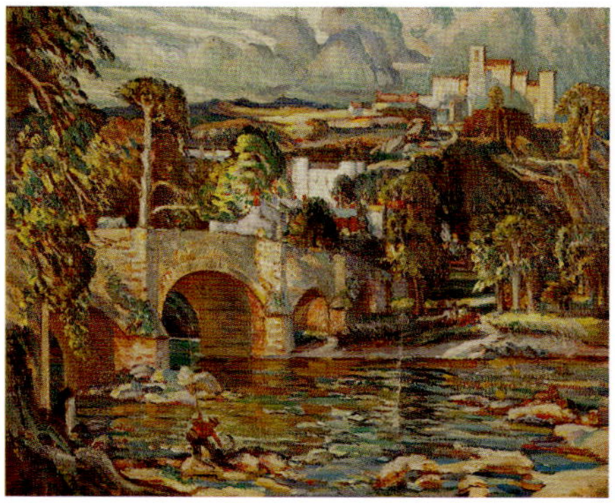

Anderton, Tom 1894–1956
Fisherman, Upland Landscape with Bridge (2) c.1950
oil on canvas 64 x 77
2002/797/7

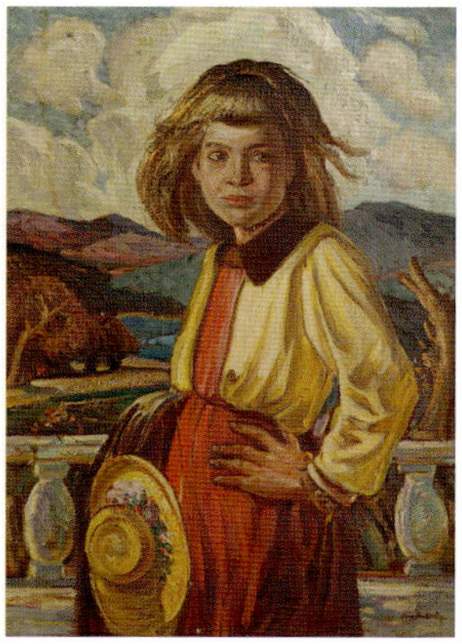

Anderton, Tom 1894–1956
Girl on a Veranda c.1950
oil on canvas 61 x 46
2002/797/2

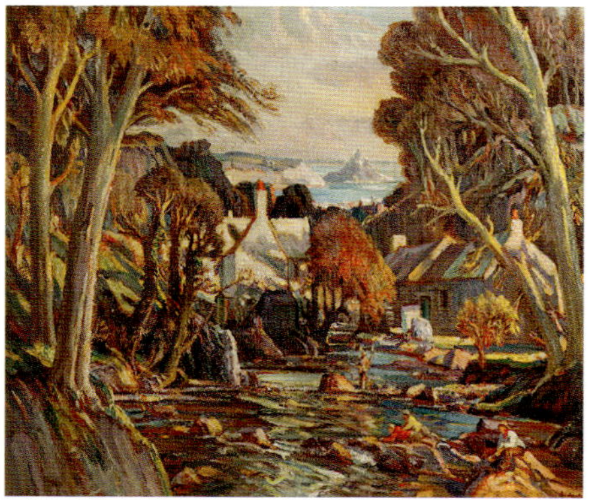

Anderton, Tom 1894–1956
Saint Michael's Mount, Cornwall c.1950
oil on canvas 64 x 77
2002/797/5

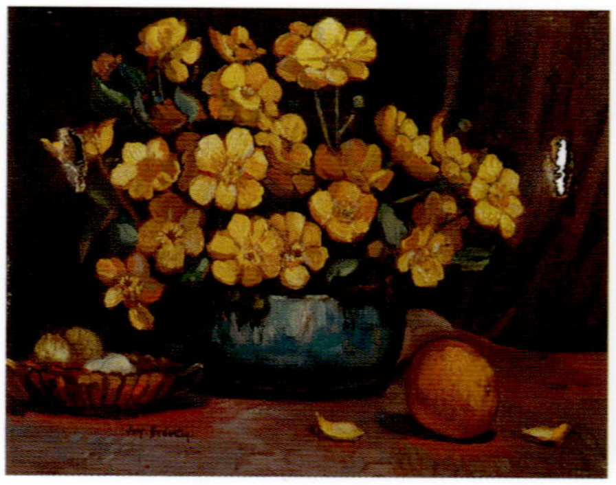

Anderton, Tom 1894–1956
Still Life c.1950
oil on canvas 26 x 36
2002/797/1

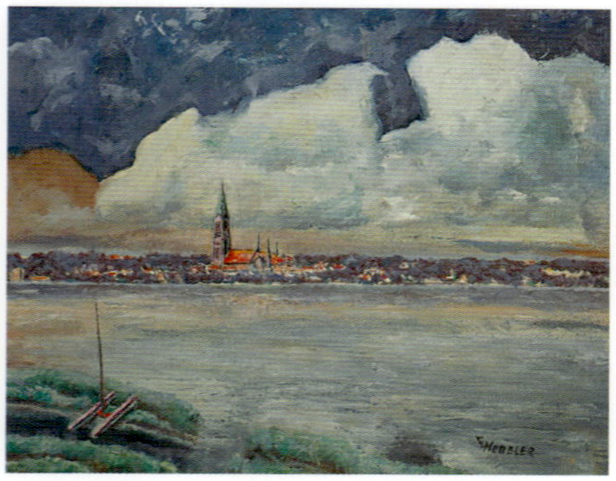

Hebeler, F.
Schleswig c.1980
oil on canvas 60 x 76
PCF1

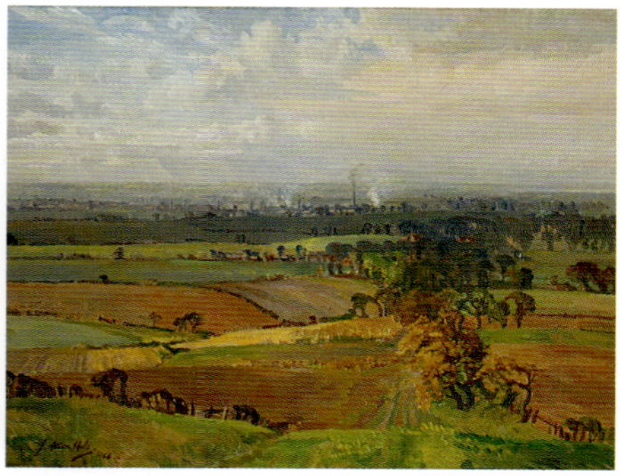

Hill, James Allen 1903–1985
Panoramic View of Leyland and Farington 1955
oil on board 73 x 91
2005/852

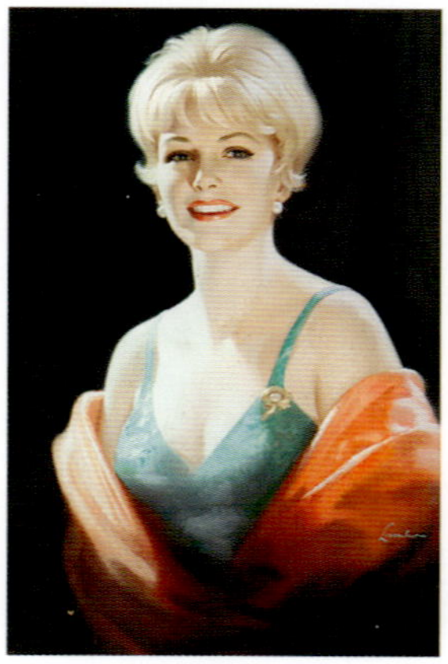

Lambert, Walter
She's a Leyland Lady, 1968 1968
oil on canvas 80 x 50
1995/638

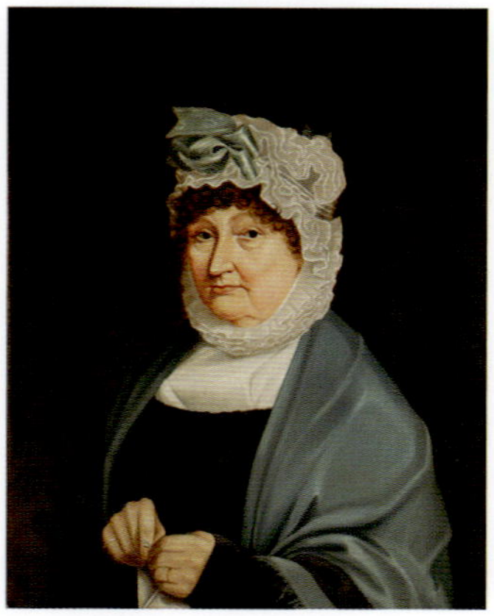

unknown artist
Agnes Critchley (1748–1828) c.1810
oil on canvas 77 x 63
1988/57/1

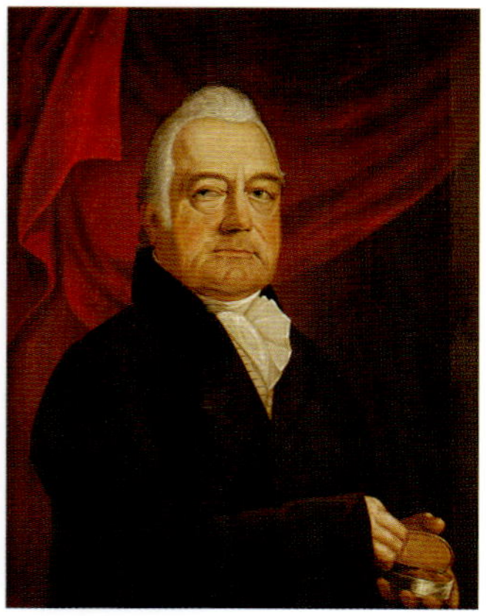

unknown artist
John Walton c.1810
oil on canvas 77 x 63
1988/57/2

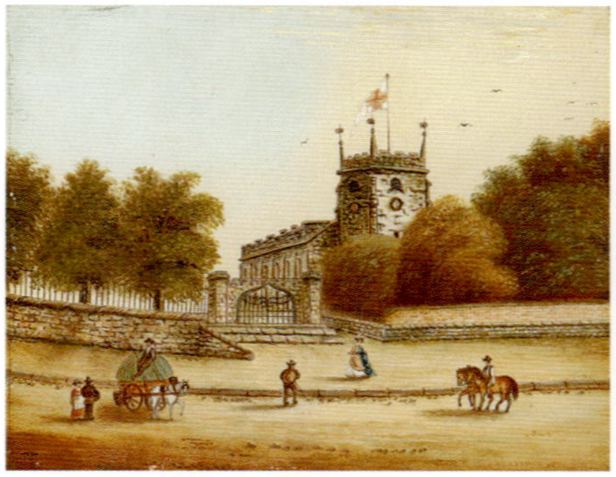

unknown artist
Leyland Parish Church 1874
oil on card 22 x 30
2000/841

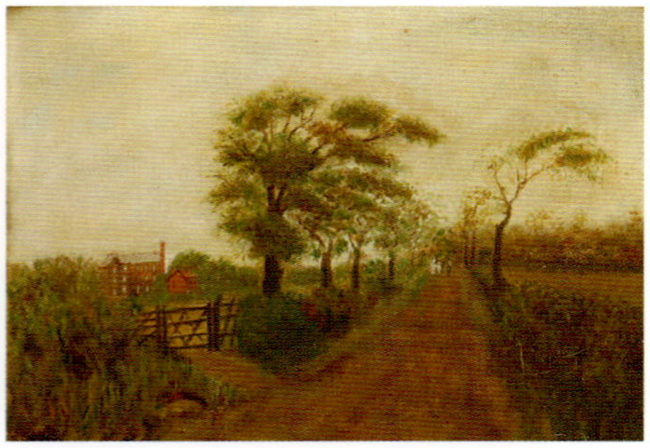

unknown artist
Farington Corn Mill before 1900
oil on canvas 25 x 40
1995/642

Lytham Art Collection of Fylde Borough Council

The Lytham Art Collection is among the finest town hall collections in the country. In the 1700s, along with many seaside towns, Lytham gained a reputation as a health resort. In the 1840s the railways arrived, thus expanding the area's connections to the industrial cities of the North West. Lytham St Annes became a prosperous area of the Fylde, with a high percentage of residents being businessmen and merchants from Manchester and Liverpool.

There were a number of local parish and district councils in the area but on 1st May 1922 Lytham and St Annes joined as a single district council. In 1925 the council purchased the Southdown Hydro hotel as its new town hall. Centred on the new Town Hall was a desire to promote the cultural importance of the town and the idea of an art collection, donated by local individuals for the public benefit, was developed. The most important artist who has a connection with the area was the Victorian artist Richard Ansdell RA (1815–1885). An area of Lytham St Annes, Ansdell, is named after the artist.

Appropriately, the first painting to be presented (on 29th June 1925) was *The Herd Lassie* by Ansdell which was donated by John Booth (1856–1941), son of E. H. Booth who founded the famous grocery business which still operates across the north-west. In 1926 the grandchildren of Richard Ansdell donated *Lytham Sandhills* (1860). Altogether there are 26 major works in the collection by Ansdell.

The collection concentrates on Victorian Art of a very high quality, and major historical scenes include *The Deathbed of Robert, King of Naples* by Alfred Elmore (1815–1881) and *A Classical Lake Scene (Carthage)* by George Sheffield Junior (1839–1892). The collection's core is genre scenes including *In Disgrace* by Charles Burton Barber (1845–1894) and *Boys Playing* by John Morgan (1823–1886).

In 1930 the collection received its most iconic painting, *The Vision of Catherine of Aragon* by the Neoclassical German artist Henry Fuseli (1741–1825), which was purchased by Mrs Tiller and donated to the museum by Alderman Dawson in 1950.

In 1941 Mrs Percy Bibby donated *The Italian Flower Girl* by Eugen de Blaas (1843–1931). This image was used to market the family's animal feed and soap manufacture business and appeared in the famous 'Bibby Annual' as one of the Christmas prints.

Some of the paintings remain on display in the town hall, which now houses the administrative offices for Fylde Borough Council. Although the collection does not have a permanent gallery, in 2007, in partnership with one of its original donor's families, Booths, a gallery was built within the Booths grocery store in Lytham St Annes. This gallery is used to display a selection of the paintings in a series of themed exhibitions.

It is striking is that this high quality collection has been amassed purely through public donation, for example Alderman Dawson donated 28 paintings between 1931 and 1955, and this trend continues today.

Heather C. Davis, Conservation Manager, Lancashire County Museum Service

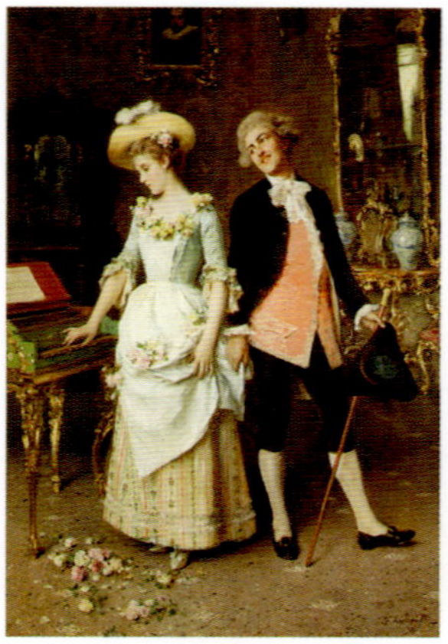

Andreotti, Federico 1847–1930
The Proposal
oil on canvas 101.6 x 74.9
206

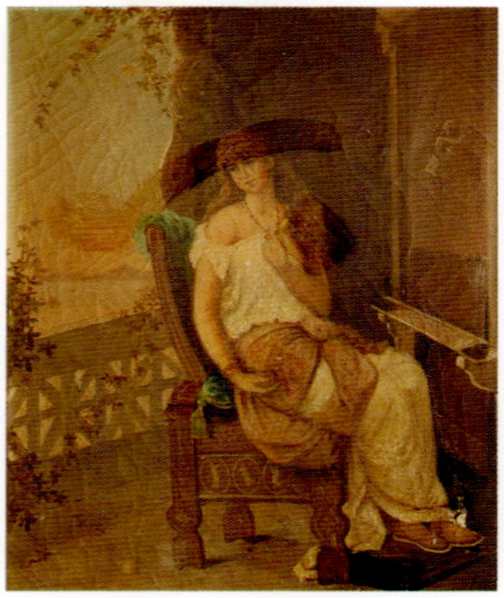

Andrieux, Alfred Louis 1879–1945
A Lady Seated on a Balcony
oil on canvas 69.2 x 55.2
188

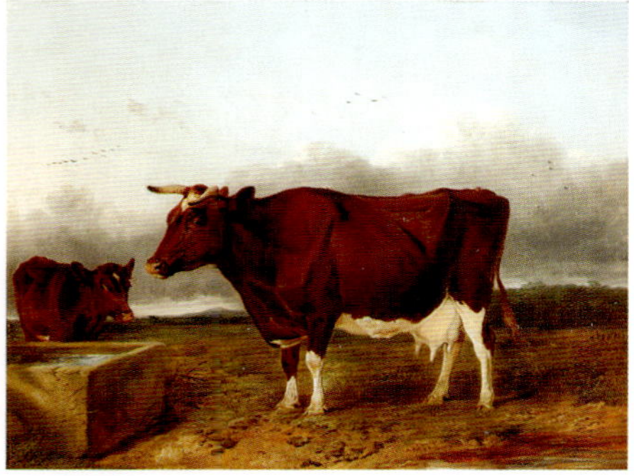

Ansdell, Richard 1815–1885
The Red Cow c.1860
oil on canvas 60.9 x 76.2
54

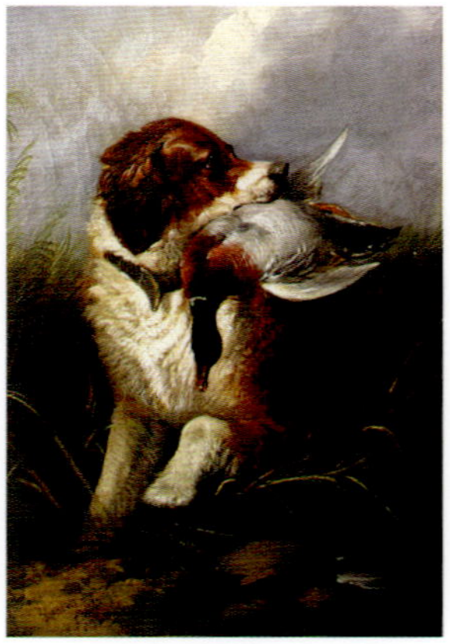

Ansdell, Richard 1815–1885
Dog and Mallard: Waiting for Good Bag 1865
oil on canvas 35.5 x 31.1
58

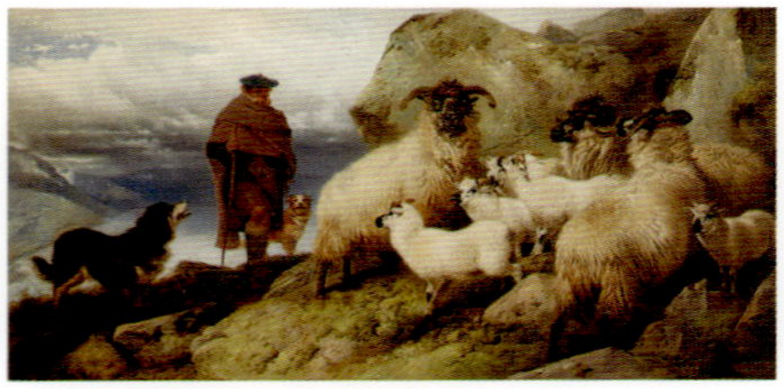

Ansdell, Richard 1815–1885
In the Highlands 1865
oil on canvas 76.8 x 153
80

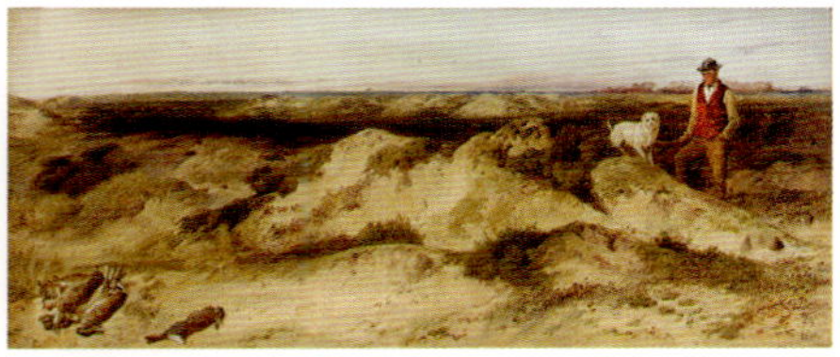

Ansdell, Richard 1815–1885
Lytham Sandhills 1866
oil on canvas 53.3 x 149.9
76

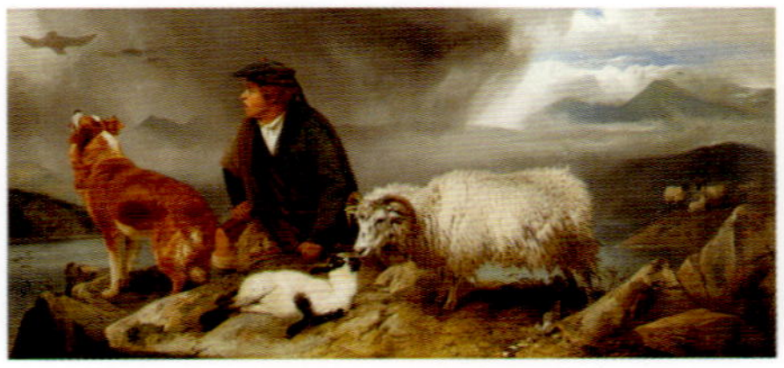

Ansdell, Richard 1815–1885
The Rescue 1866
oil on canvas 68.5 x 148.6
72

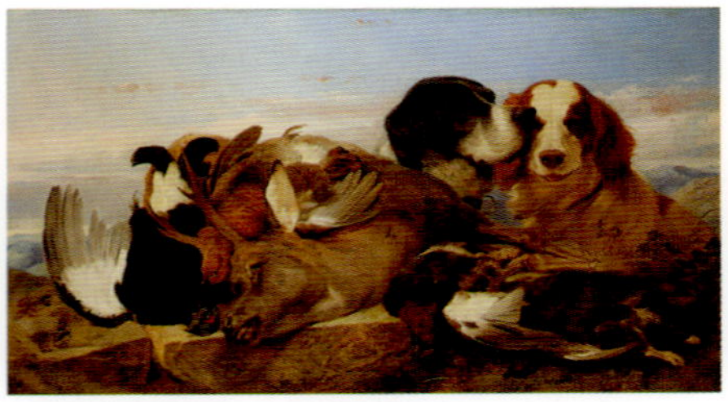

Ansdell, Richard 1815–1885
A Day's Sport 1867
oil on canvas 43.2 x 73.6
18

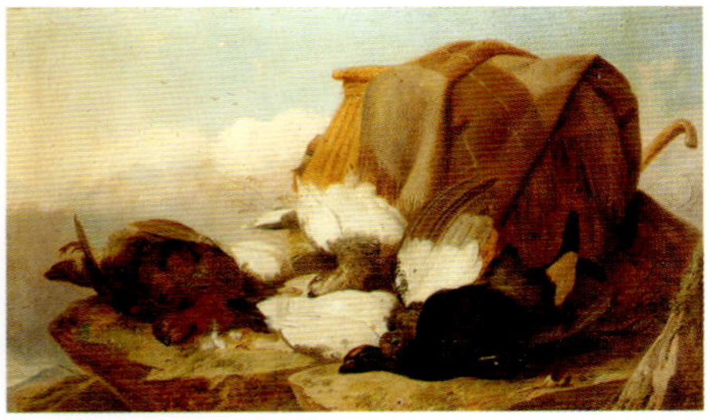

Ansdell, Richard 1815–1885
Dead Game, Pannier and Plaid 1867
oil on canvas 73.5 x 132.1
91

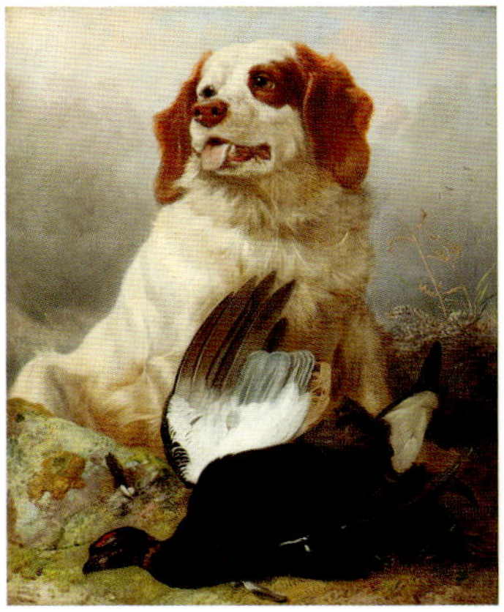

Ansdell, Richard 1815–1885
Waiting for Master 1867
oil on canvas 74.9 x 62.2
40

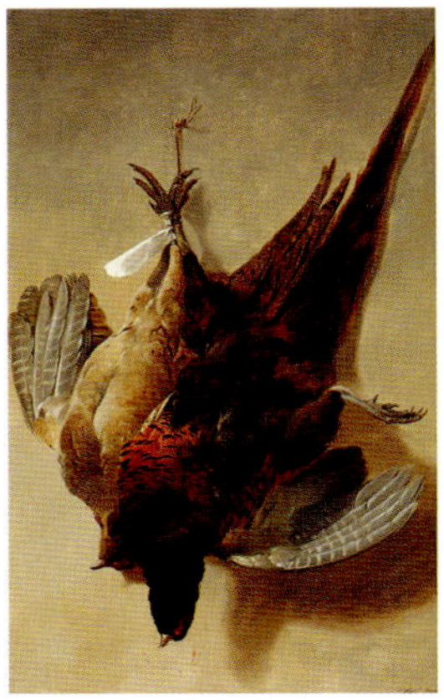

Ansdell, Richard 1815–1885
A Brace of Pheasants 1868
oil on canvas 92.7 x 57.2
16

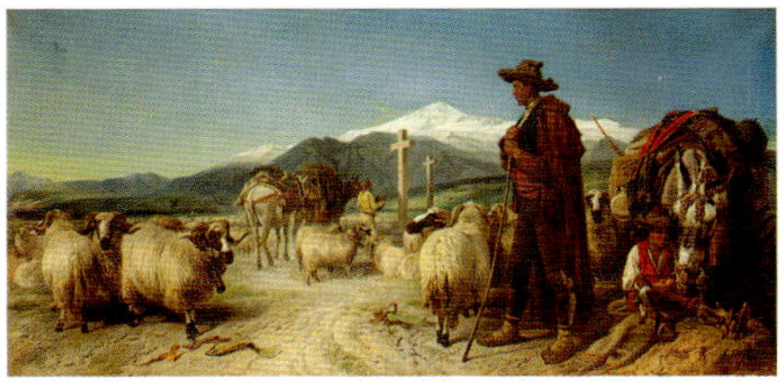

Ansdell, Richard 1815–1885
On the Road to Seville 1868
oil on canvas 91.4 x 195.6
81

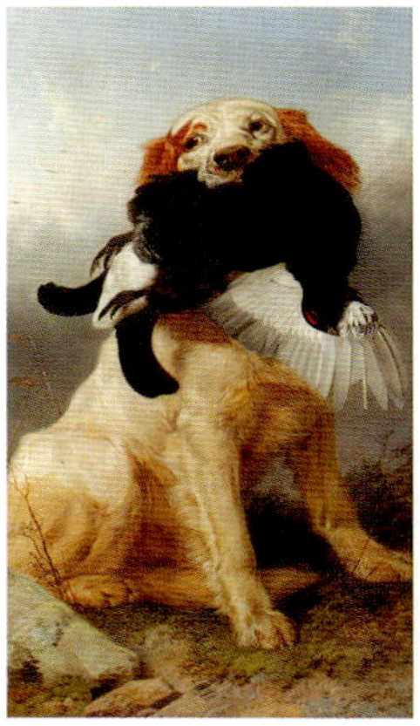

Ansdell, Richard 1815–1885
Retriever with Black Capercaillie 1868
oil on canvas 114.3 x 61
175

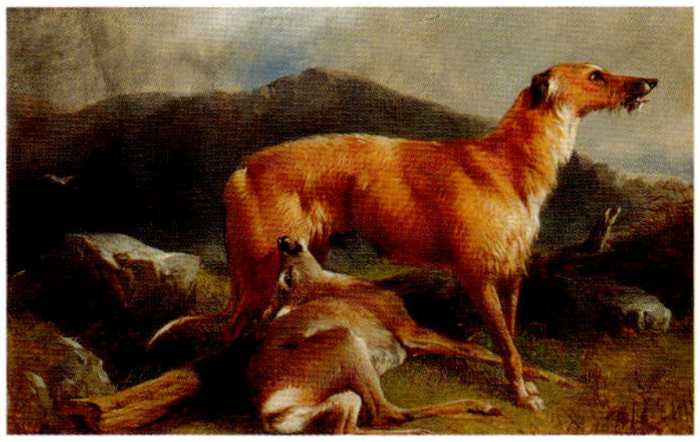

Ansdell, Richard 1815–1885
Staghound and Hind 1868
oil on canvas 27.9 x 43.2
7

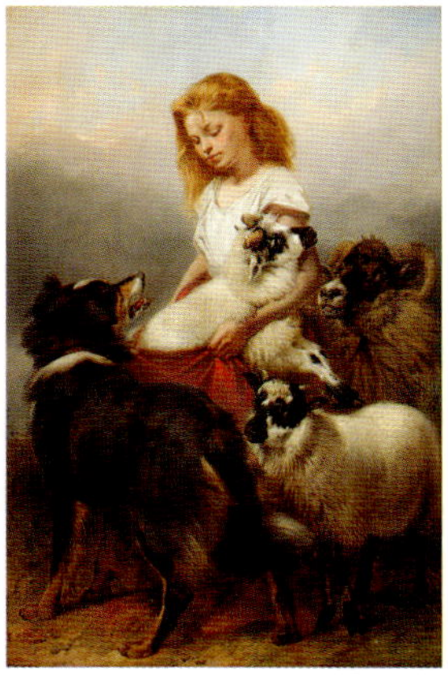

Ansdell, Richard 1815–1885
The Herd Lassie 1876
oil on canvas 149.8 x 104.1
87

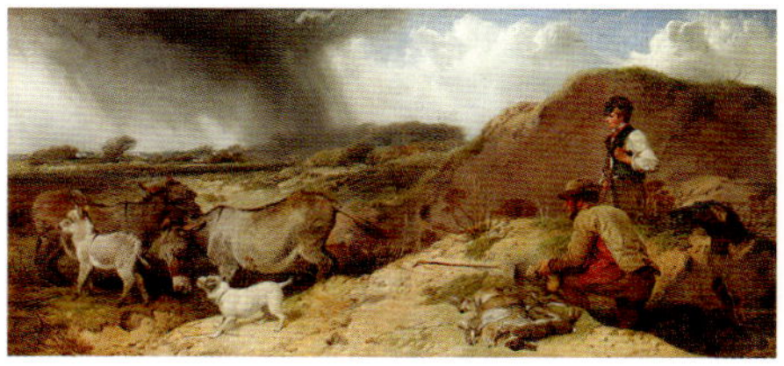

Ansdell, Richard 1815–1885
Rabbiting on Lytham Sandhills 1878
oil on canvas 71.1 x 152.4
78

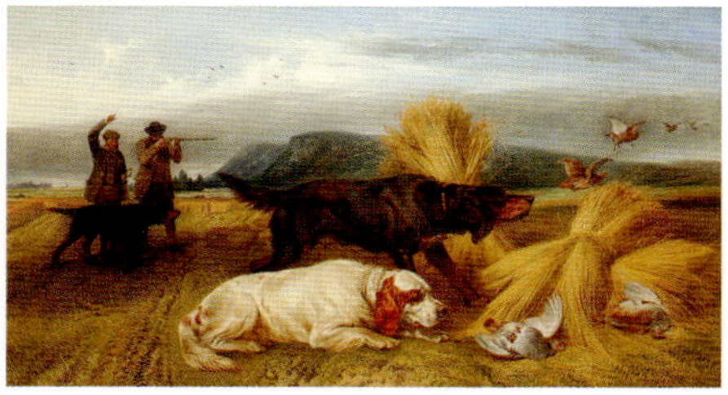

Ansdell, Richard 1815–1885
Partridge Shooting 1879
oil on canvas 73.6 x 134.6
20

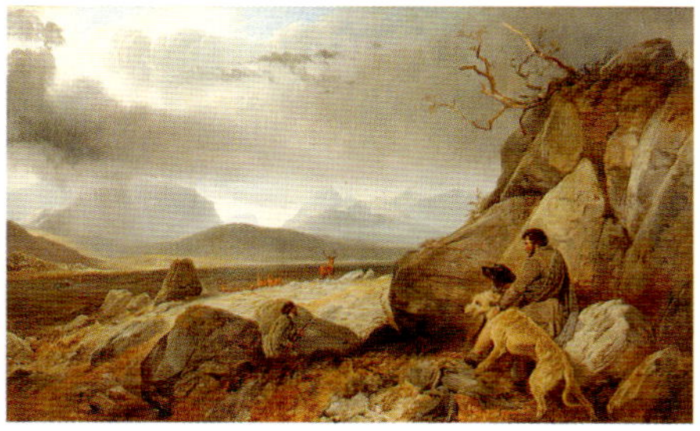

Ansdell, Richard 1815–1885
A Scottish Landscape with Stalkers
oil on canvas 53.3 x 88.9
21

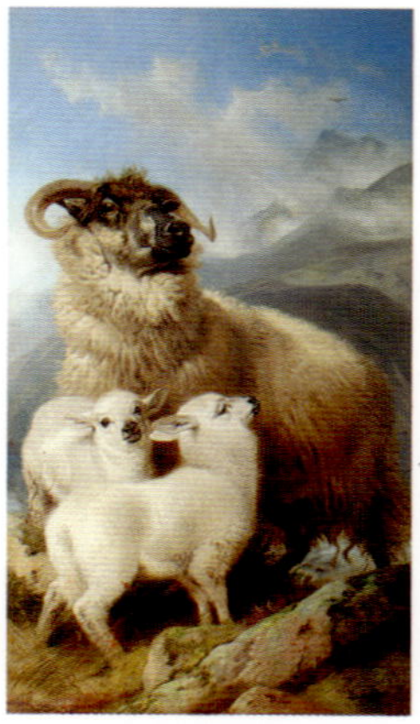

Ansdell, Richard 1815–1885
A Startled Ewe
oil on canvas 163.1 x 77.5
176

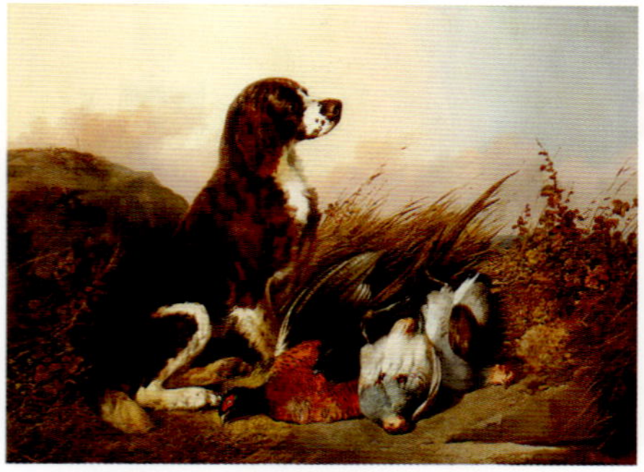

Ansdell, Richard 1815–1885
Dog and Game
oil on canvas 91.4 x 121.9
6

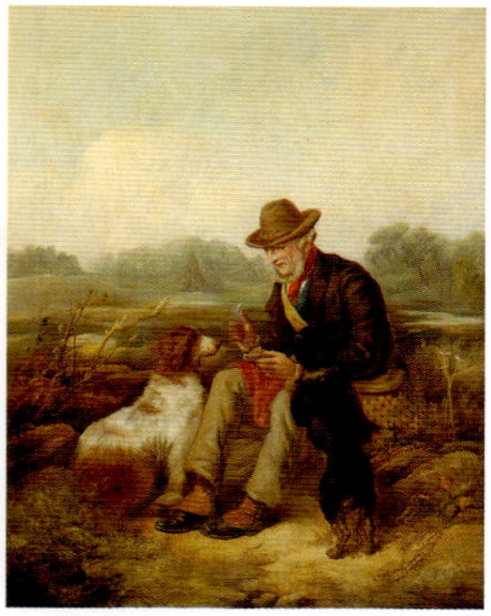

Ansdell, Richard 1815–1885
Gamekeeper with Spaniels
oil on canvas 73.6 x 61.0
43

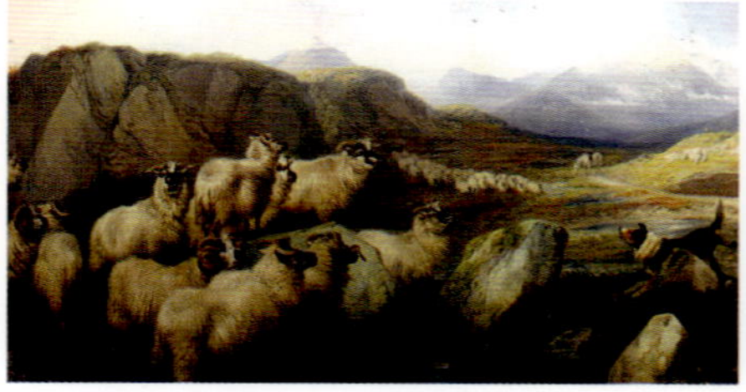

Ansdell, Richard 1815–1885
Gathering Flocks on the Grampian Hills
oil on canvas 91.4 x 195.6
79

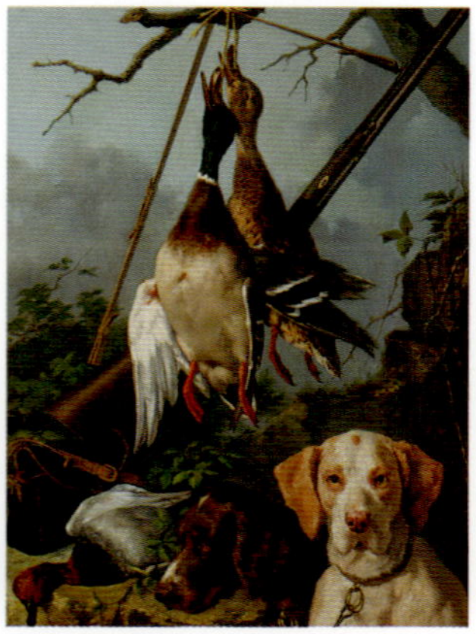

Ansdell, Richard 1815–1885
Gundogs and Game
oil on canvas 106.6 x 78.7
55

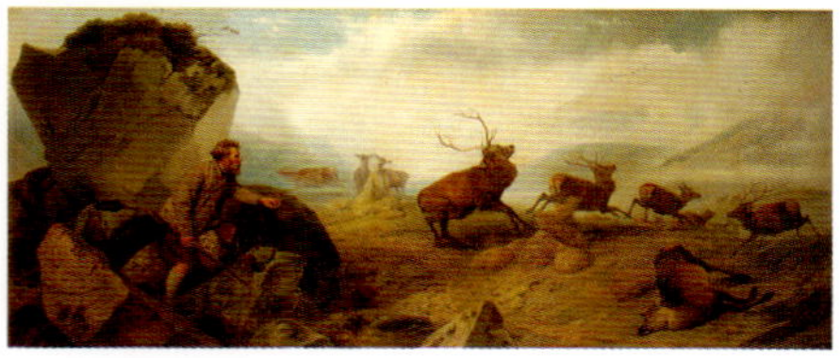

Ansdell, Richard 1815–1885
Hunter and Deer in a Highland Landscape
oil on canvas 73.6 x 180.3
64

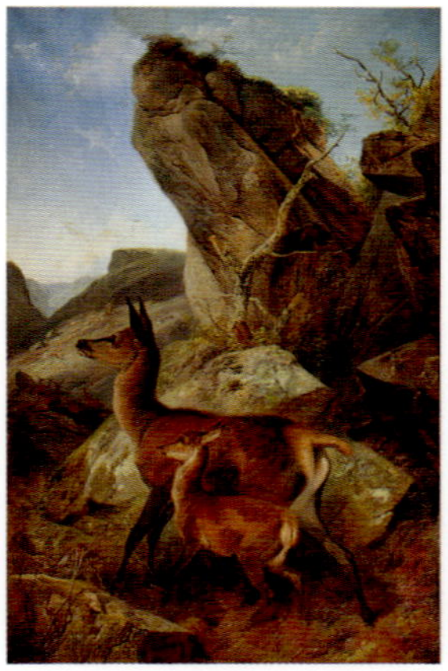

Ansdell, Richard 1815–1885
Startled Deer
oil on canvas 180.3 x 121.9
75

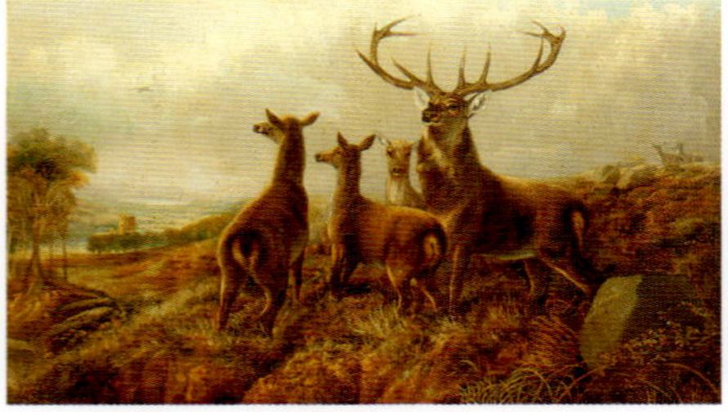

Ansdell, Richard 1815–1885
Startled Deer in a Landscape
oil on canvas 91.4 x 149.9
77

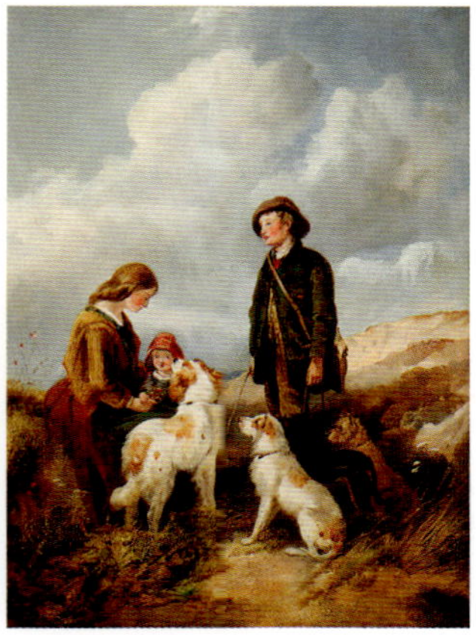

Ansdell, Richard 1815–1885 & **Frith, William Powell** 1819–1909
A Boy and a Girl with Hounds 1860
oil on canvas 91.4 x 68.6, 91.4 x 68.6
94

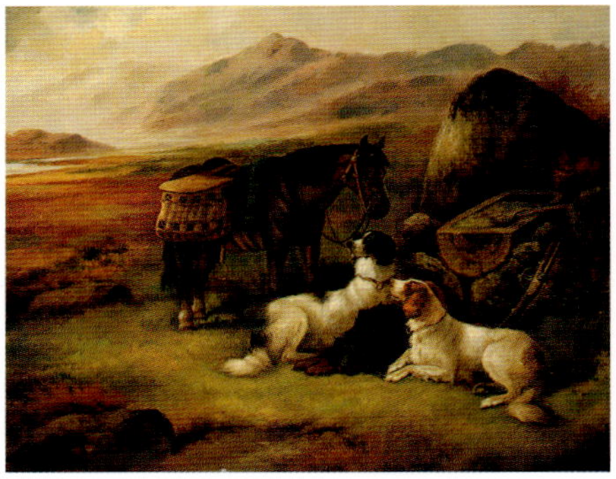

Ansdell, Richard 1815–1885 & **Morris, John Charles** active 1851–1889
Waiting for Master 1865
oil on canvas 99 x 121.9, 99 x 121.9
42

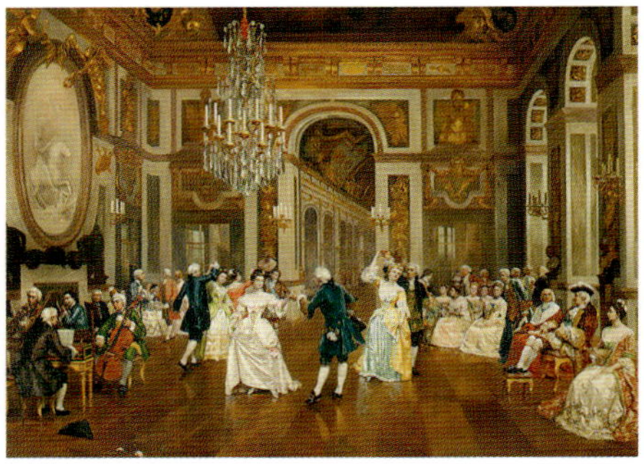

Baratti, Filippo active 1868–1901
The Minuet
oil on canvas 93.9 x 134.6
69

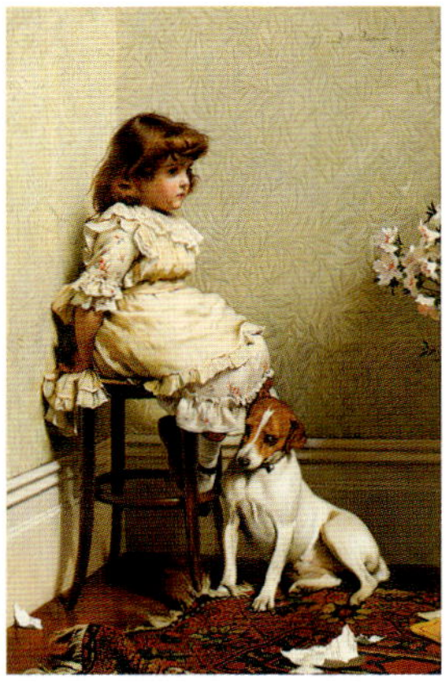

Barber, Charles Burton 1845–1894
In Disgrace 1886
oil on canvas 104.1 x 71.1
203

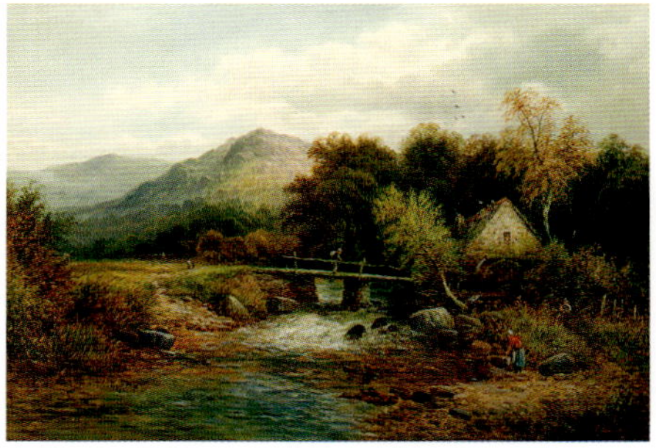

Bennet, E.
Easedale, Westmorland
oil on canvas 61 x 91.4
30

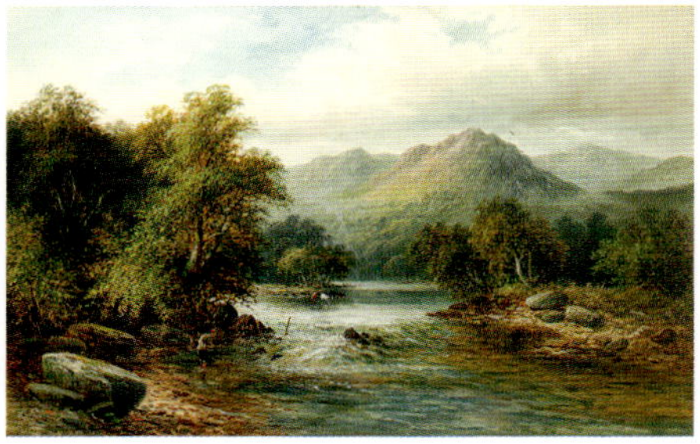

Bennet, E.
On the River Dee, North Wales
oil on canvas 60.9 x 91.4
29

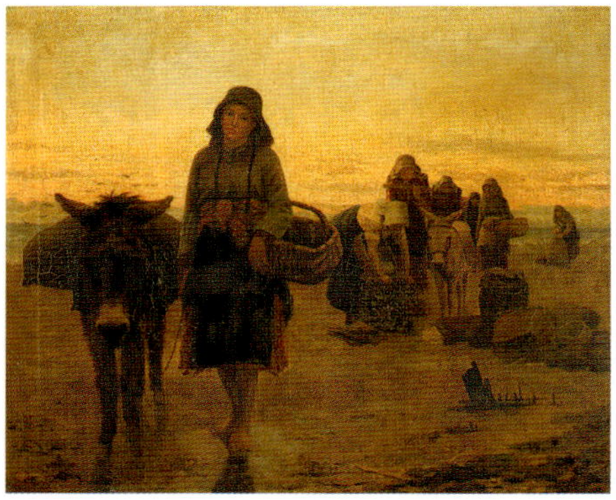

Bennett, Alfred 1861–1916
Landing the Catch
oil on canvas 101.6 x 127
35

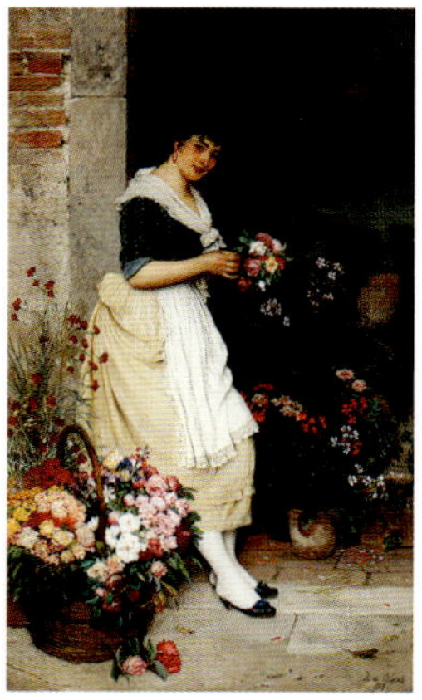

Blaas, Eugen von 1843–1931
The Italian Flower Girl 1887
oil on canvas 180.3 x 109.2
37

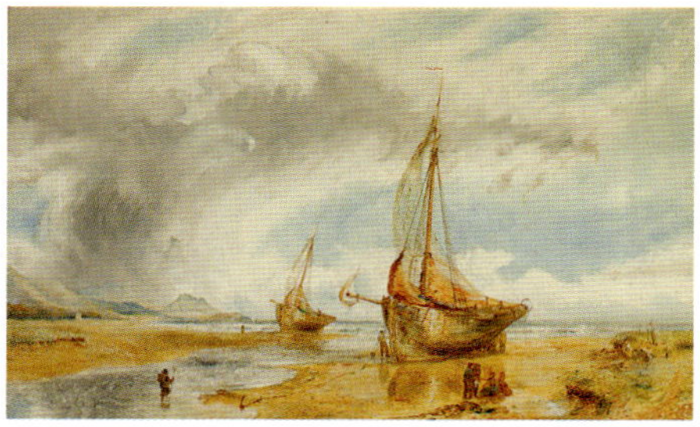

Bond, William Joseph Julius Caesar 1833–1926
Shore Scene with Trawlers 1893
oil on canvas 55.9 x 85.1
164

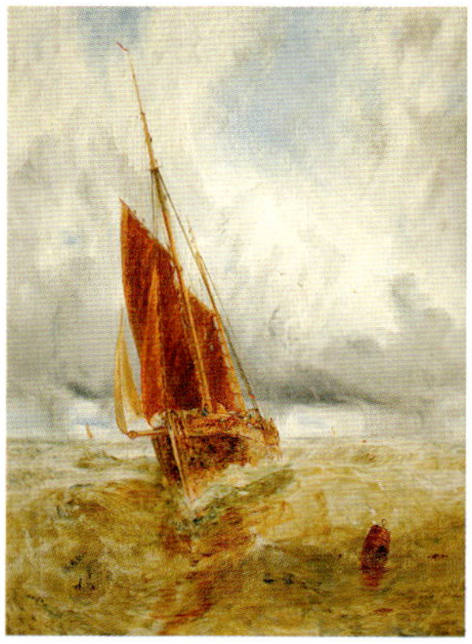

Bond, William Joseph Julius Caesar 1833–1926
Returning Home from the Fishing Grounds 1899
oil on canvas 91.4 x 71.1
104

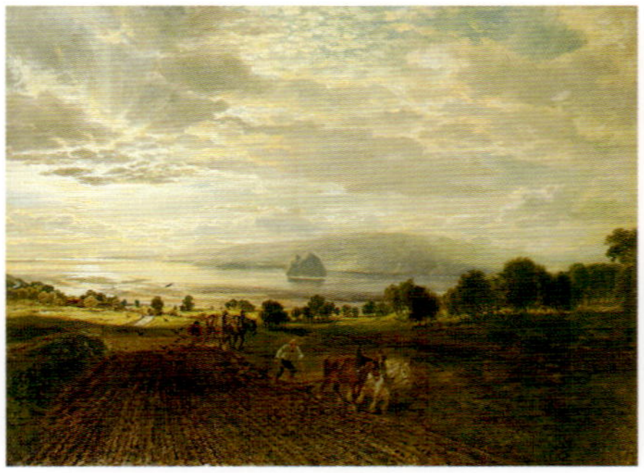

Bough, Samuel 1822–1878
Bass Rock, Dumbarton
oil on canvas 93.9 x 132.1
66

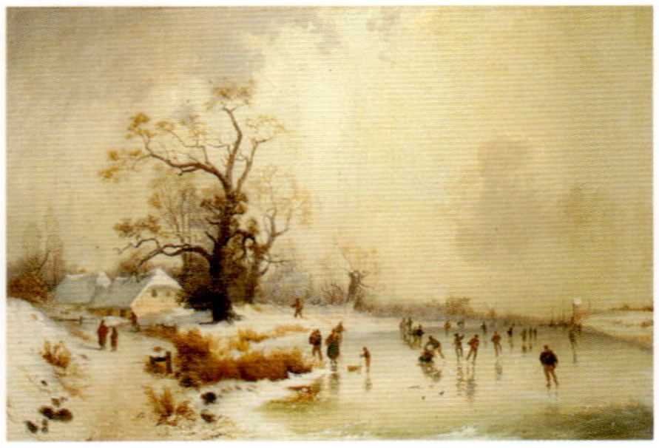

Boyer
Winter in Holland
oil on canvas 67.9 x 105.4
3

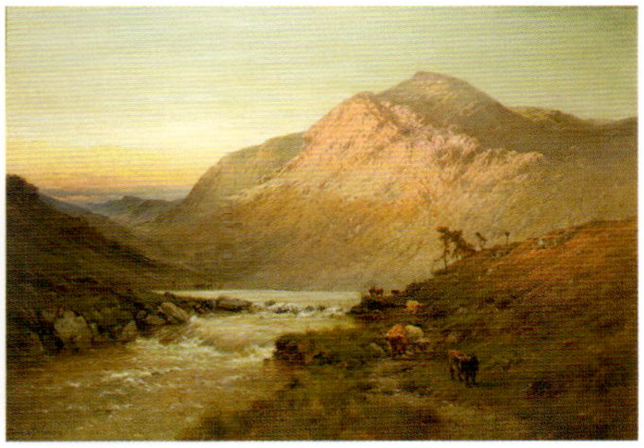

Breanski, Alfred de 1852–1928
Loch Nagar 1869
oil on canvas 67.9 x 105.4
5

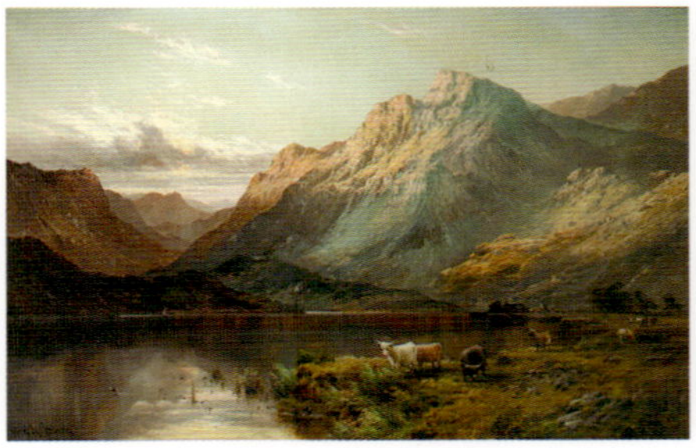

Breanski, Alfred de 1852–1928
Loch Nagar
oil on canvas 76.2 x 121.9
73

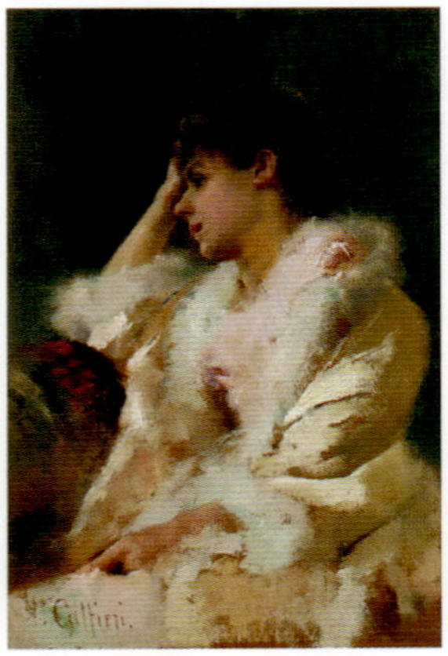

Caffieri, Hector 1847–1932
Portrait of a Lady
oil on canvas 30.4 x 20.3
60

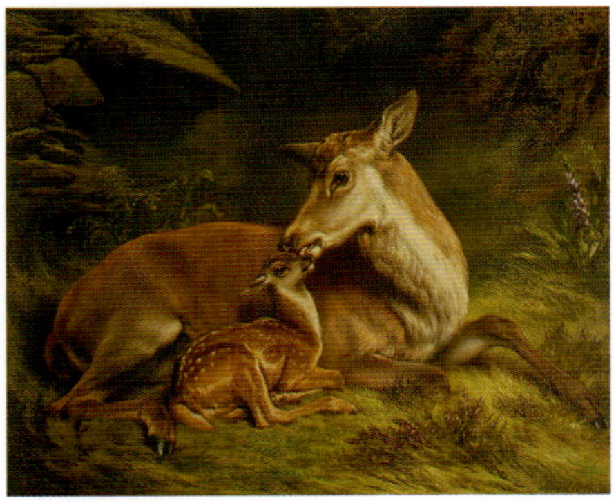

Carter, Samuel John 1835–1892
Fallow Deer with Fawn 1885
oil on canvas 101.6 x 127
71

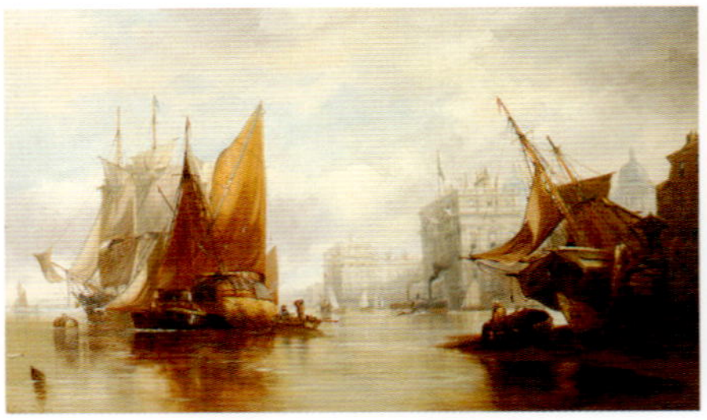

Chambers I, George (attributed to) 1803–1840
On the Thames at Greenwich
oil on canvas 76.2 x 124.5
47

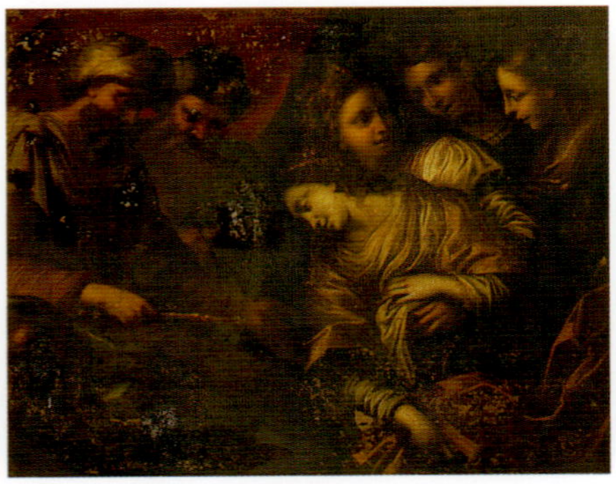

Cignani, Carlo (attributed to) 1628–1719
Esther and Ahasuerus
oil on canvas 119.3 x 147.3
88

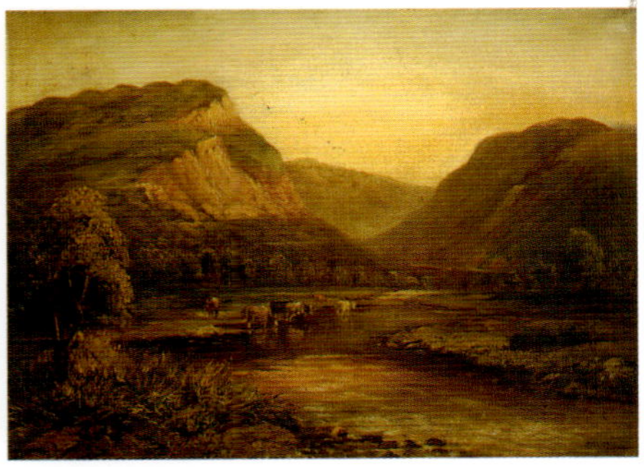

Clause, M.
Sulby Glen, Isle of Man
oil on canvas
19

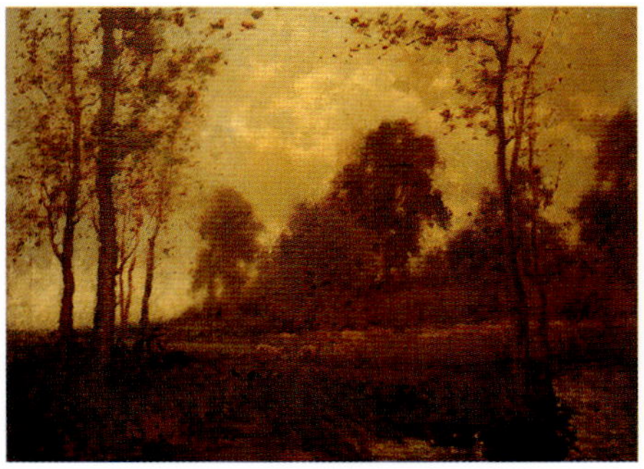

Clausen, George (attributed to) 1852–1944
Shepherd Boy in Wooded Glade
oil on canvas 50.8 x 91.4
27

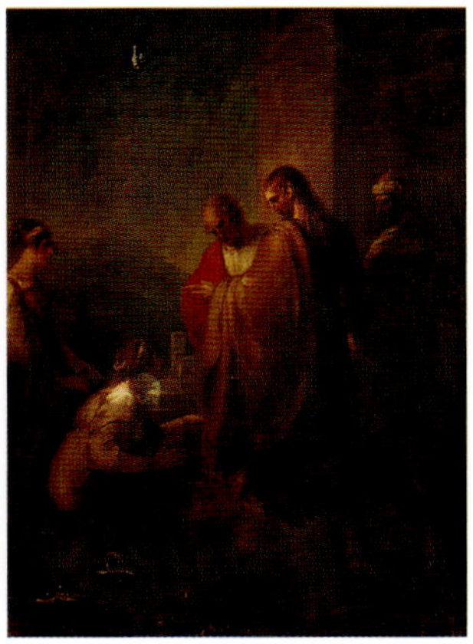

Constantine, George Hamilton 1875–1968
Christ and Mary Magdalene
oil on canvas 124.4 x 99.1
178

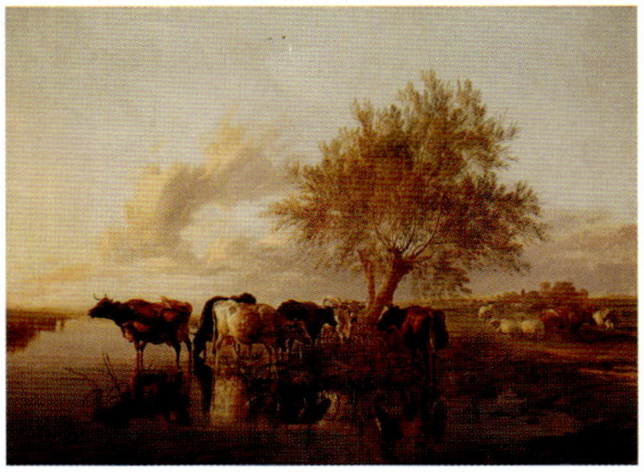

Cooper, Thomas Sidney 1803–1902
Canterbury Meadows 1865
oil on canvas 91.4 x 124.5
207

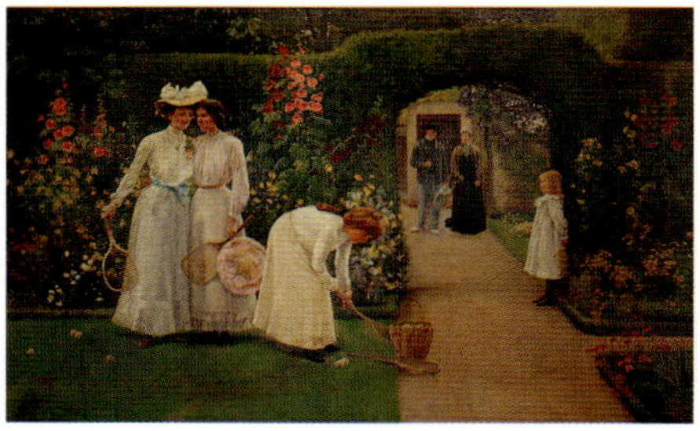

Craft, Percy Robert 1856–1934
The New Curate
oil on canvas 81.2 x 132.1
174

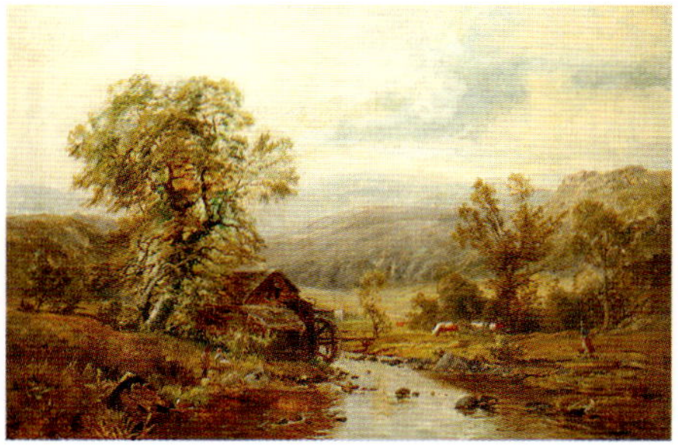

Creswick, Thomas 1811–1869
The Old Water Mill at Bettws-y-Coed 1857
oil on canvas 50.8 x 76.8
12

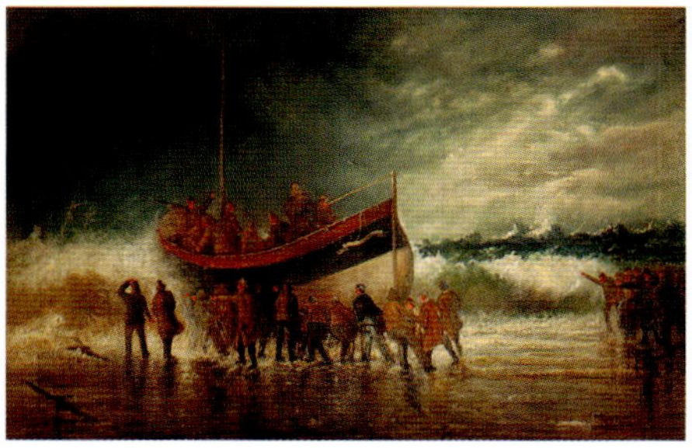

Crossley, W. active 1898–1903
Launching the Lifeboat on the Yorkshire Coast 1903
oil on canvas 73.6 x 127
92

Dyck, Anthony van (copy after) 1599–1641
Henry Percy, 9th Earl of Northumberland, Wearing the Chancellor's Robes and the Garter Ribbon
oil on canvas 91.4 x 73.7
63

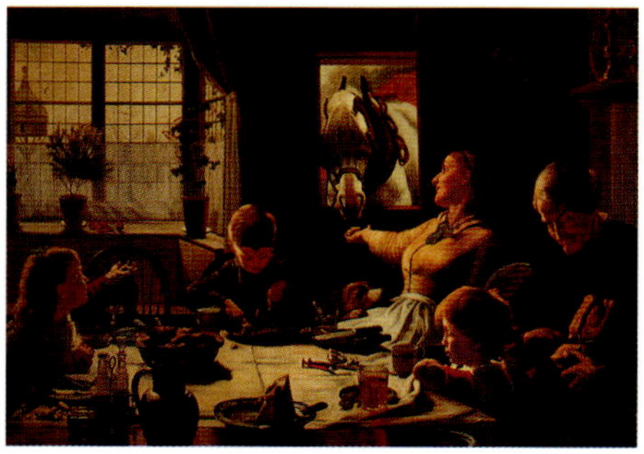

Dyson, Louise H. 1892–1942
One of the Family (copy after Frederick George Cotman) 1911–1912
oil on canvas 83.8 x 132.1
44

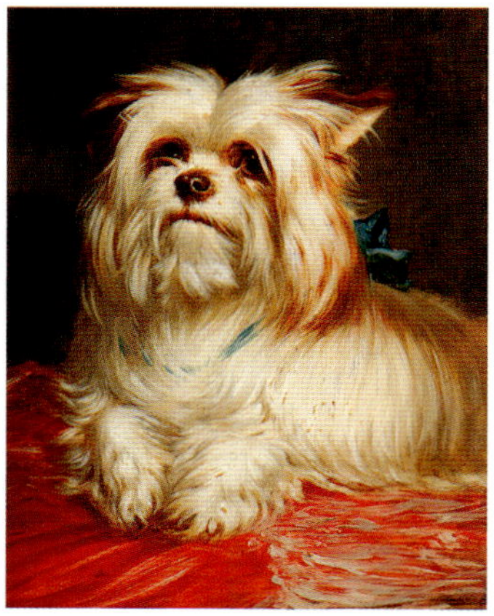

Earl, Maud 1863–1943
A Yorkshire Terrier
oil on canvas 20.3 x 14
8

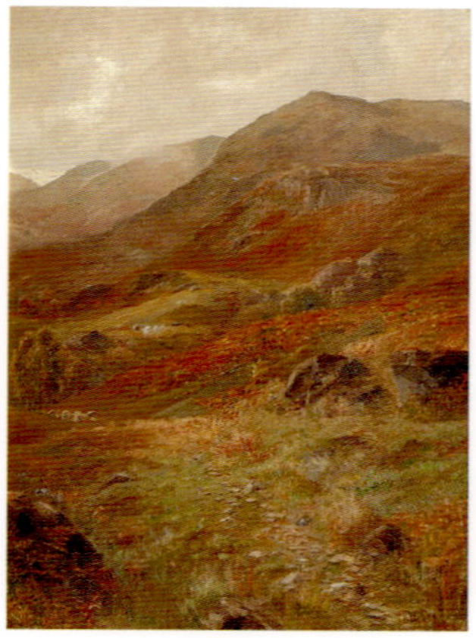

Eastwood, Walter 1867–1943
The Fell Side, Haweswater
oil on canvas 58.4 x 43.2
17

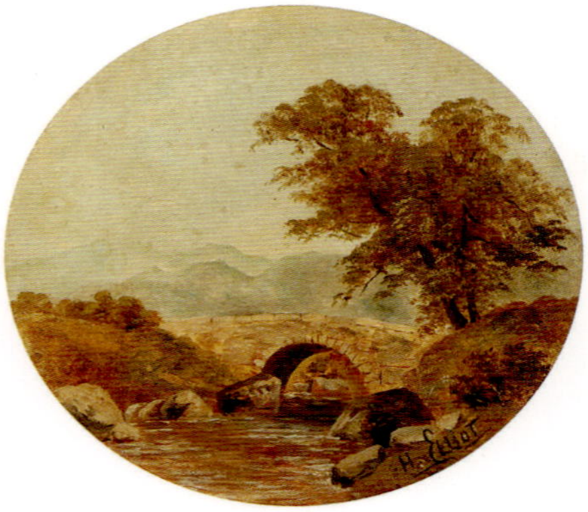

Elliott, John 1858–1925
A Bridge near Llangollen
oil on canvas 22.8 x 27.9
162

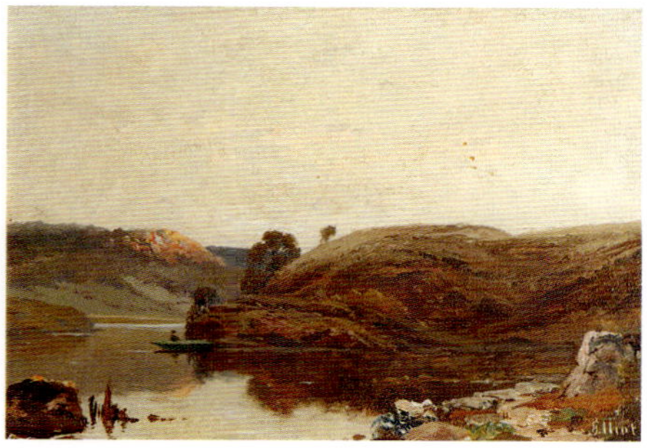

Elliott, John 1858–1925
Highland Loch
oil on canvas 18.5 x 28
135

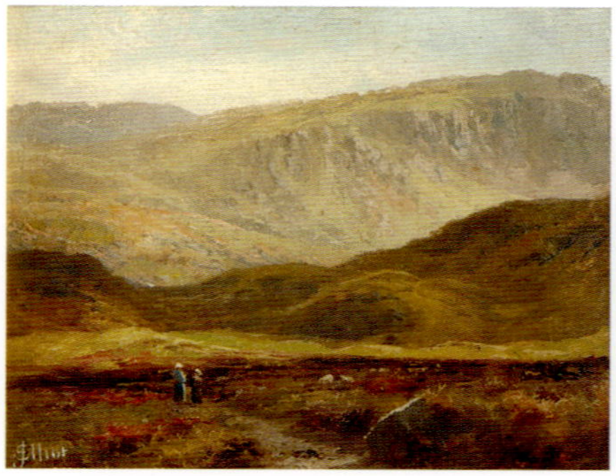

Elliott, John 1858–1925
Mountainous Landscape
oil on card 21.5 x 27.3
153

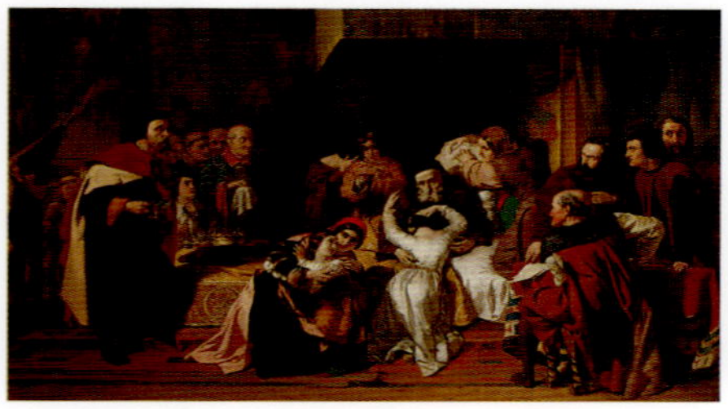

Elmore, Alfred 1815–1881
The Deathbed of Robert, King of Naples 1848
oil on canvas 97.7 x 162.6
53

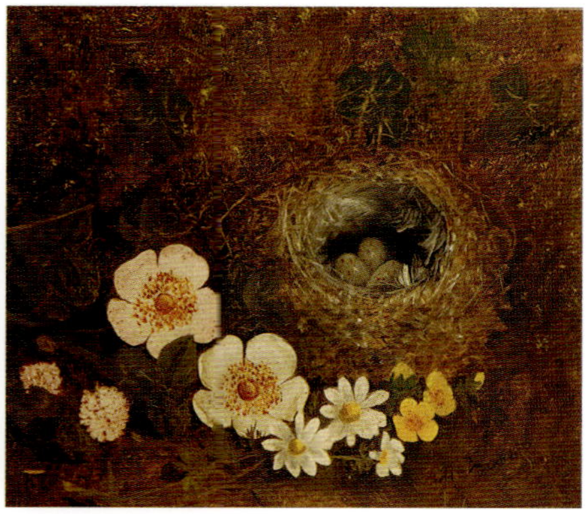

Ensor, Mary Annie 1837–1886
Bird's Nest and Flowers
oil on canvas 22.8 x 27.9
148

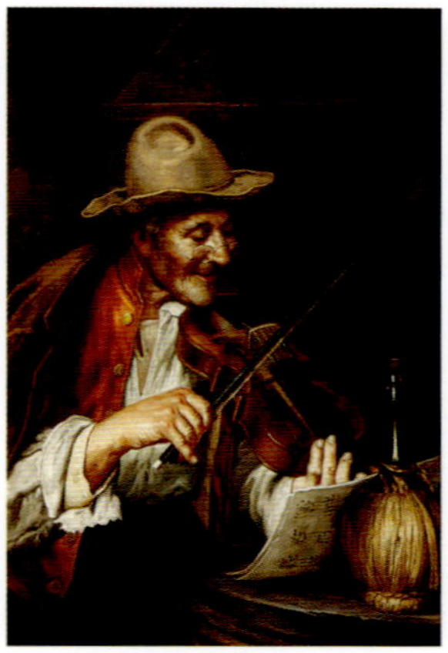

Farnetti, Stefano 1855–1926
An Italian Fiddler c.1896
oil on canvas 86.3 x 61
67

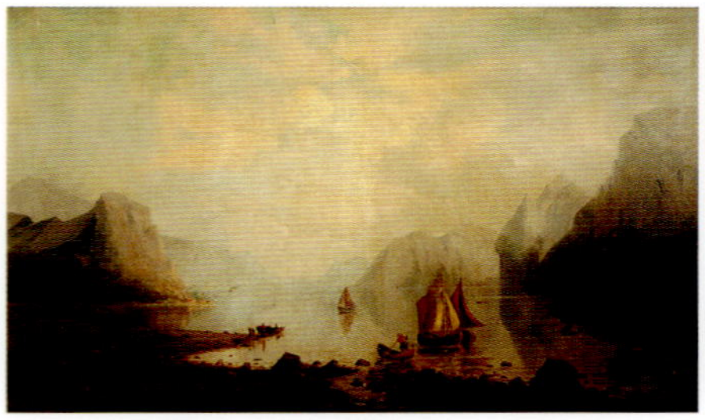

Fuchs, Theodor
Lake Geneva 1885
oil on canvas 93.9 x 142.2
41

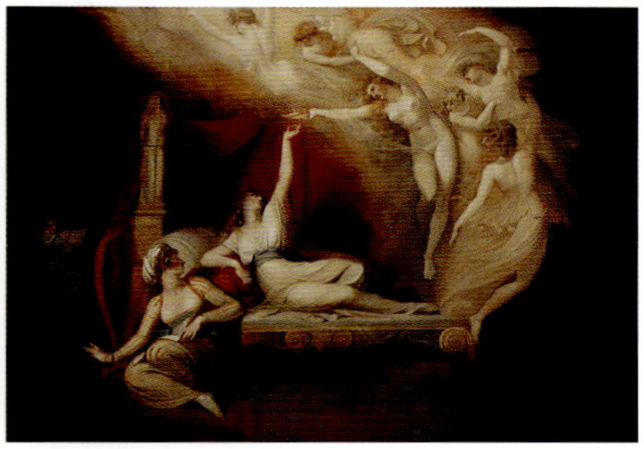

Fuseli, Henry 1741–1825
The Vision of Catherine of Aragon
oil on canvas 147.3 x 210.8
52

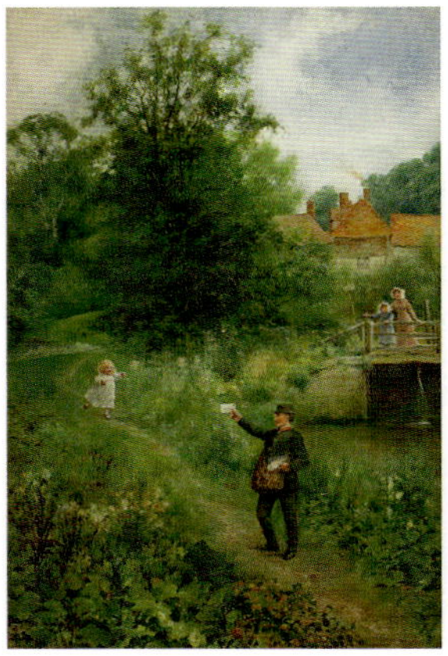

Glendening, Alfred Augustus 1840–1921
The Village Postman
oil on canvas 76.2 x 50.8
158

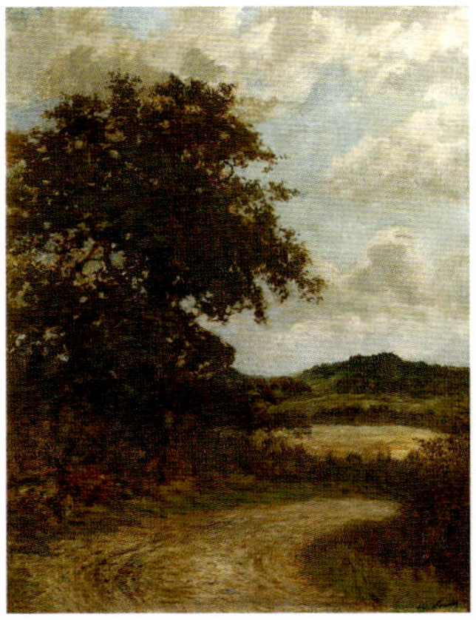

Grundy, Cuthbert Cartwright 1846–1946
Coming Rain
oil on canvas 55.8 x 40.6
49

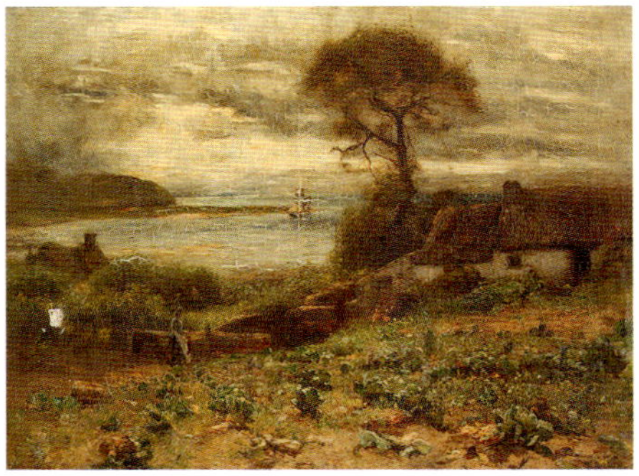

Hague, Joshua Anderson 1850–1916
The Fisherman's Cottage, Deganwy
oil on canvas 71.7 x 101.6
187

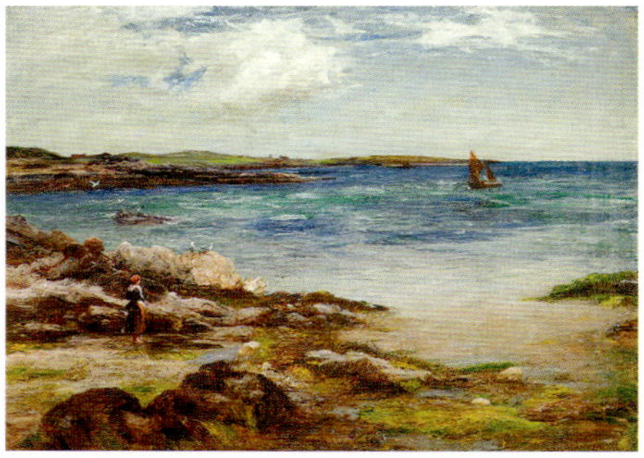

Hague, Joshua Anderson 1850–1916
The Young Fishwife
oil on canvas 71.1 x 101.6
90

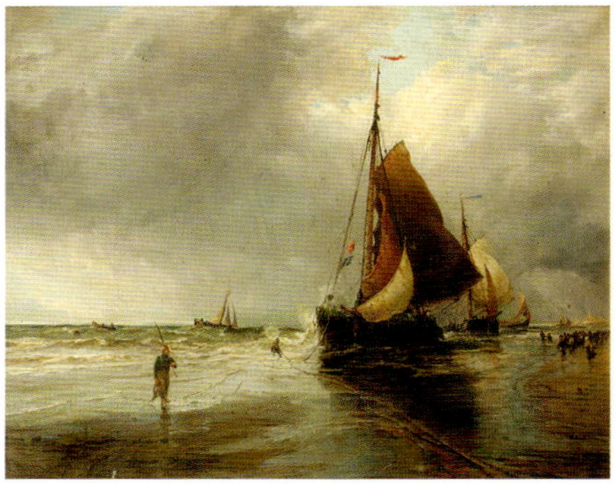

Hayes, Edwin 1819–1904
Dutch Pinks Returning from the Sea, Katwyke, Holland
oil on canvas 101.6 x 134.6
39

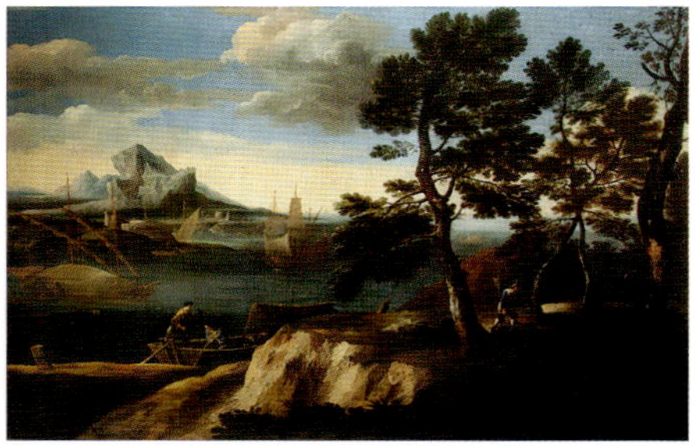

Heusch, Jacob de 1657–1701
River Landscape with Figures in a Boat 1693
oil on canvas 111.7 x 162.6
177

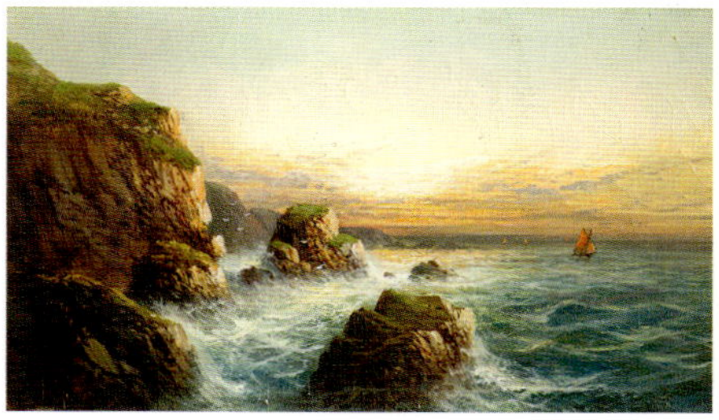

Hider, Frank 1861–1933
Rocky Coast Scene at Sunset, Devon
oil on canvas 27.9 x 50.8
150

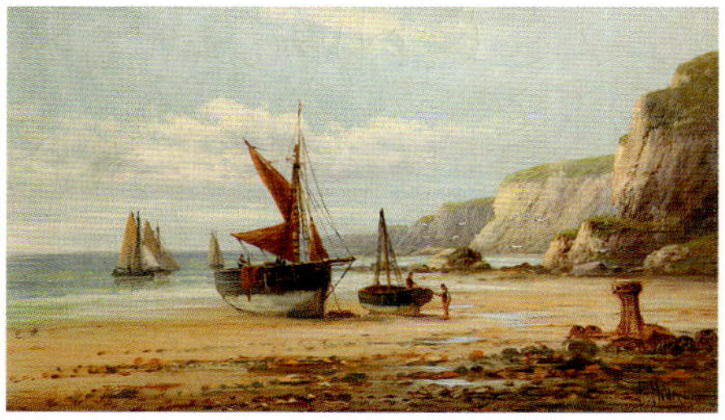

Hider, Frank 1861–1933
Shore Scene with Boats in Cornwall
oil on canvas 29.2 x 49.5
163

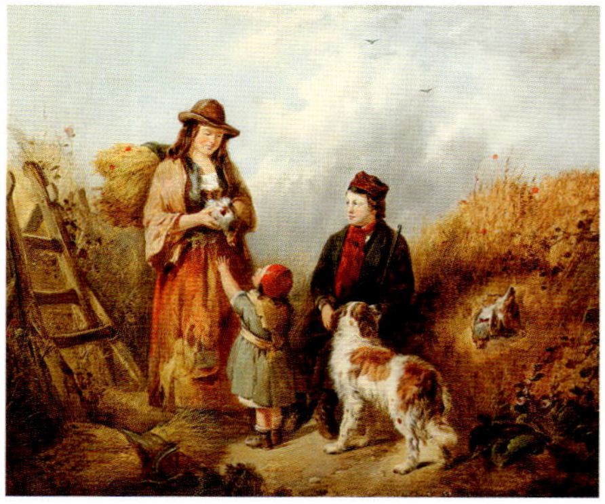

Hoog, Bernard de 1867–1943
After a Day's Sport
oil on canvas 55.8 x 73.7
101

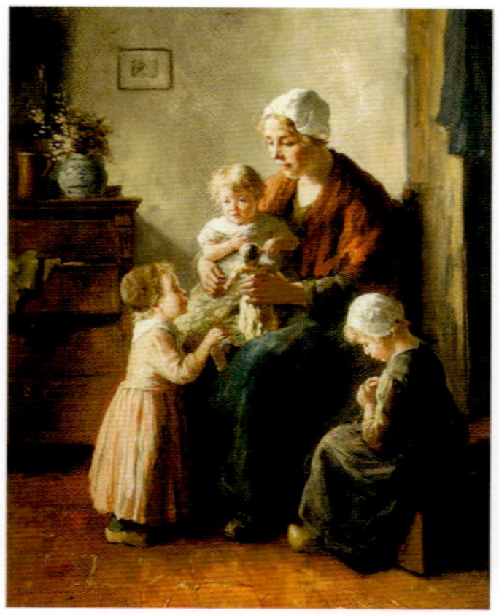

Hoog, Bernard de 1867–1943
Mother and Child (Children) 1925
oil on canvas 73.6 x 58.4
50

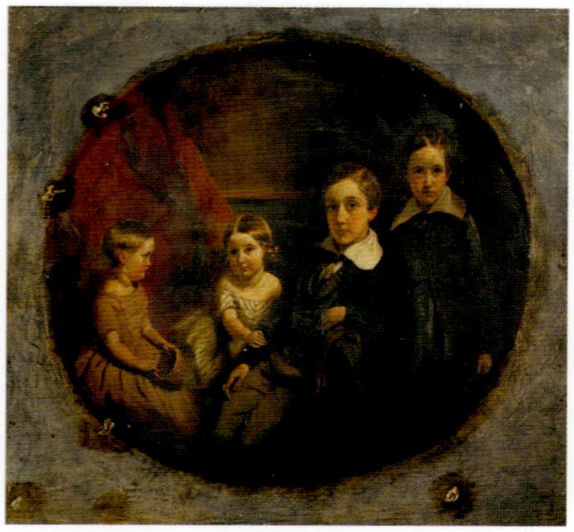

Huggins, William 1820–1884
Children of the Jorden Family 1845
oil on canvas 63.5 x 76.2
100

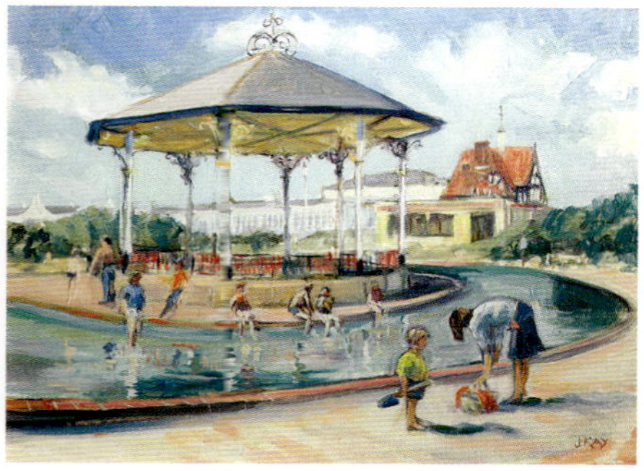

Kay-Hilton, Jacqueline b.1941
Happy Days
oil on canvas 30.5 x 38.1 (E)
243

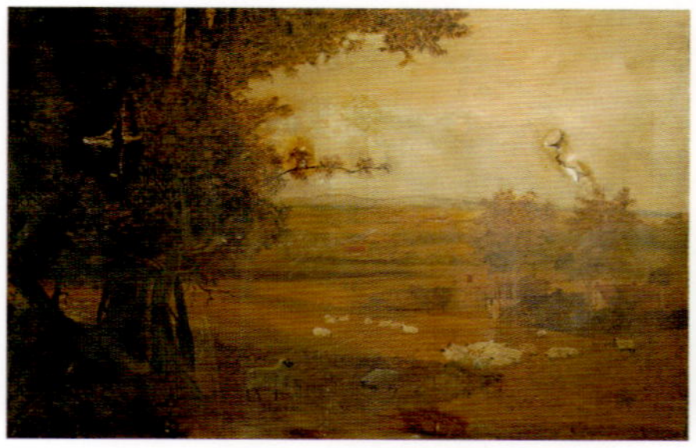

Lamputtier, Com van (attributed to)
Pastoral Scene
oil on canvas
195

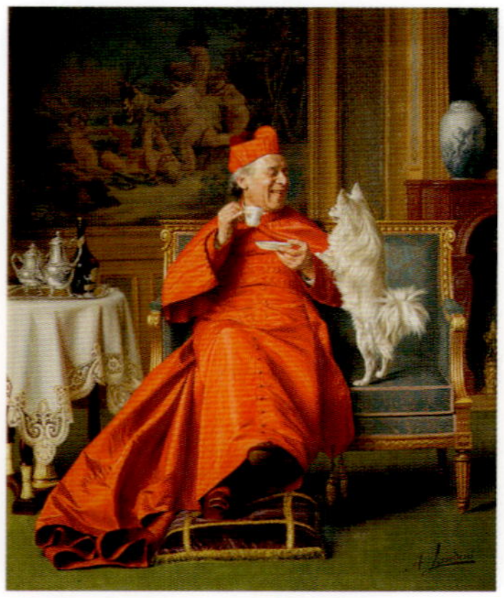

Landini, Andrea 1847–1912
L'impatier
oil on canvas 44.4 x 36.8
204

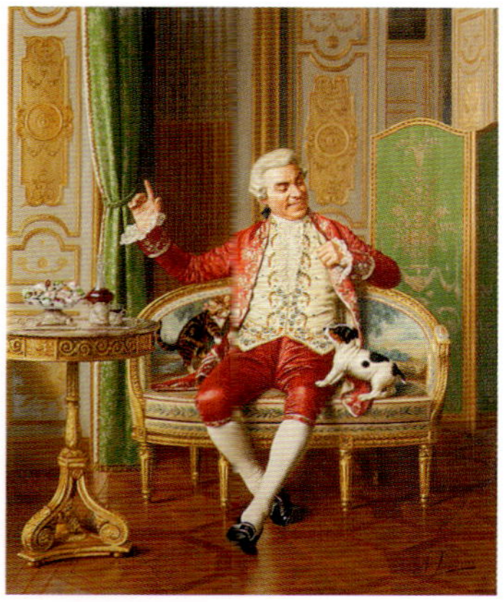

Landini, Andrea 1847–1912
Mes deux petits amis
oil on canvas 44.4 x 36.8
205

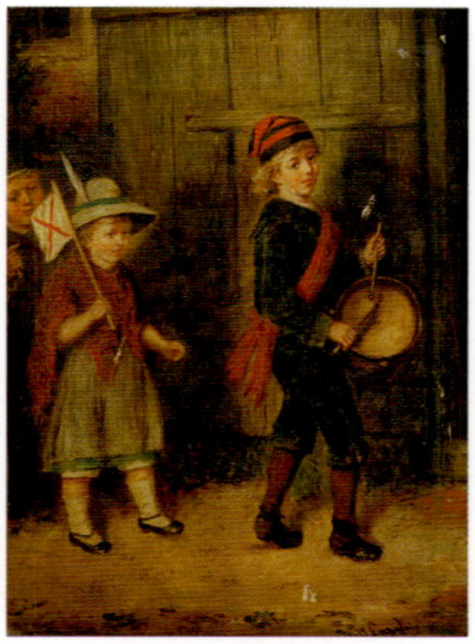

Langlois, Mark William 1848–1924
The Drummer Boy
oil on canvas 48.2 x 38.1
15

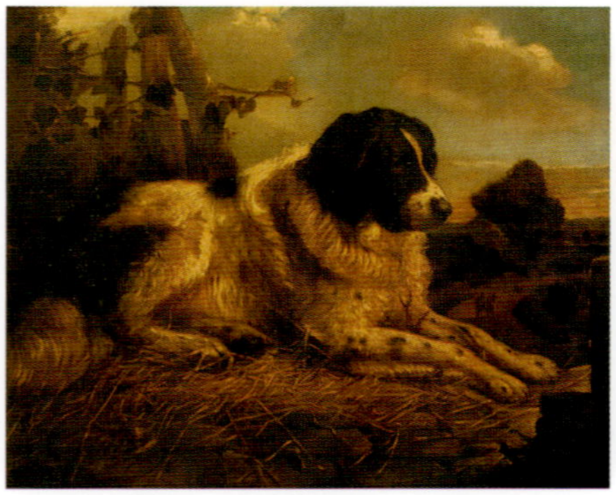

Llangl, H. active late 19th C
A Saint Bernard Dog
oil on canvas 99 x 124.5
36

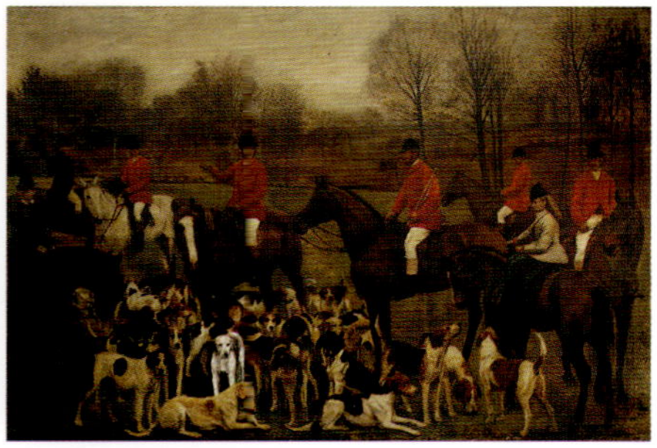

Lutyens, Charles Augustus Henry 1829–1915
The Burnley Meet 1875
oil on canvas 200.6 x 304.8
59

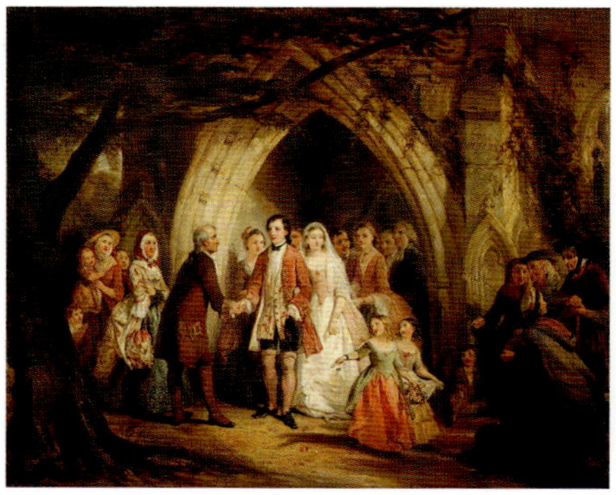

Marshall, Thomas Falcon 1818–1878
The Village Wedding
oil on canvas 69.8 x 90.2
2

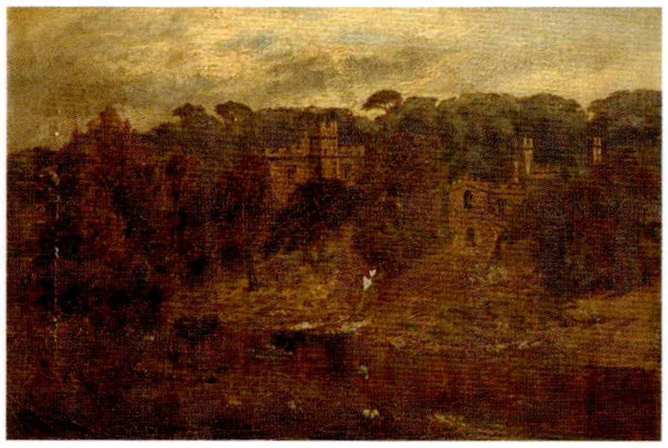

Mennie, J.
Haddon Hall, Derbyshire
oil on canvas 35.5 x 53.3
24

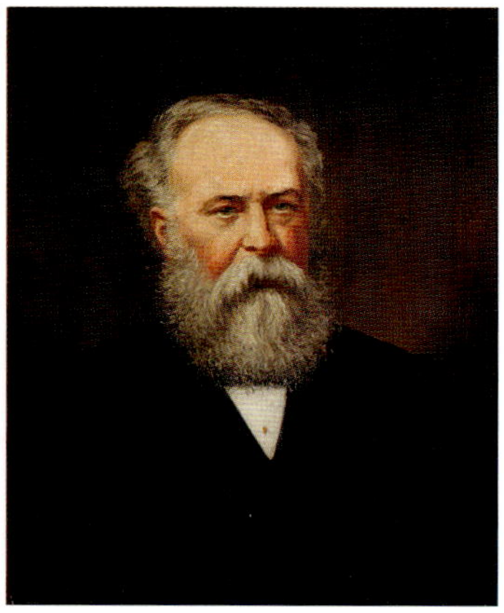

Millington, C. A. active 1882–11913
W. S. Porritt, the Lifeboat Coxswain
oil on canvas 76.2 x 50.8
146

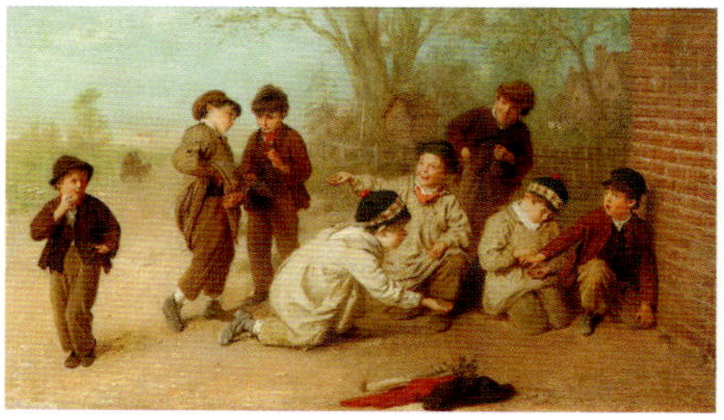

Morgan, John 1823–1886
Boys Playing
oil on canvas 60.9 x 104.1
208

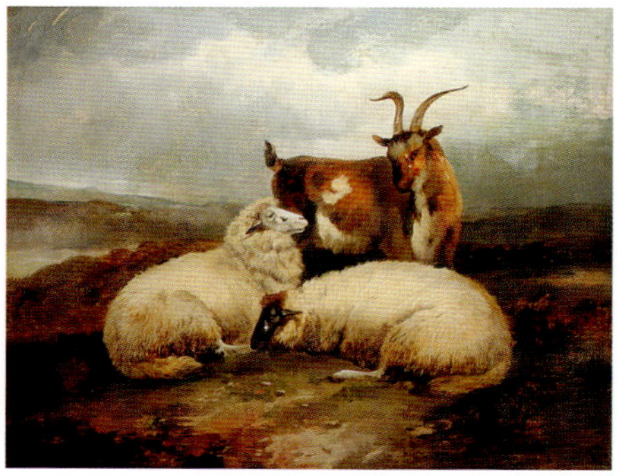

Morris, Alfred active 1853–1896
Sheep and Goat 1860
oil on canvas 60.9 x 73.7
4

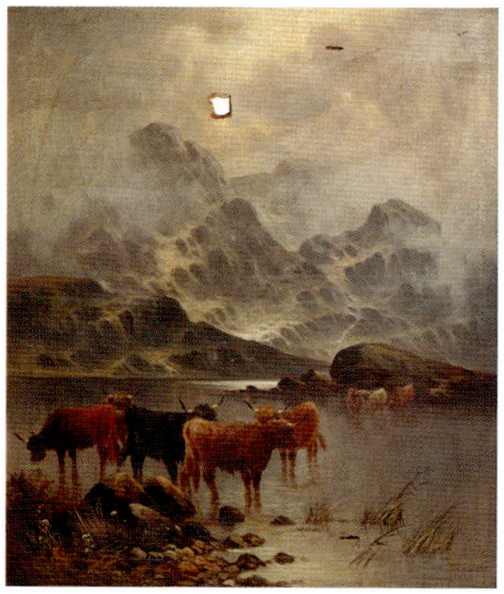

Oswald, Charles W. b.1850
Cattle at Lakeside, Drinking
oil on canvas 60.9 x 49.5
191

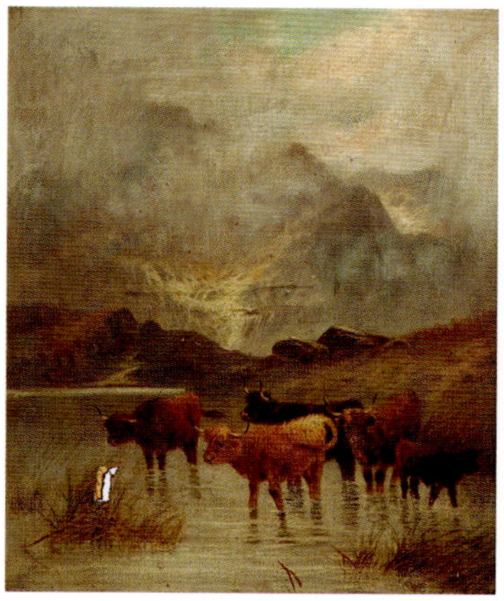

Oswald, Charles W. b.1850
Cattle Wading in a Lake
oil on canvas 60.9 x 49.5
192

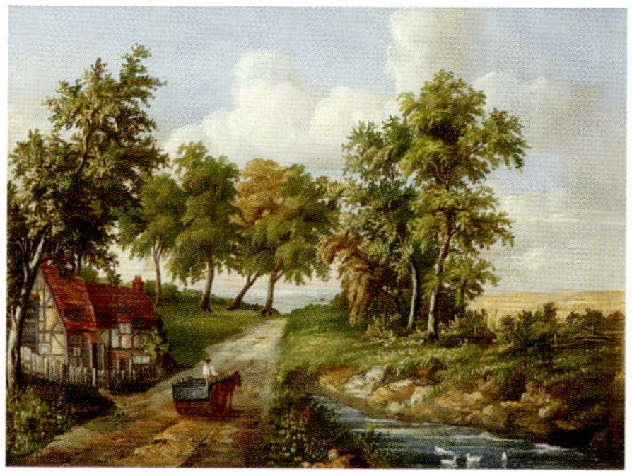

Parger
Landscape with Horseman
oil on canvas 22.8 x 29.2
119

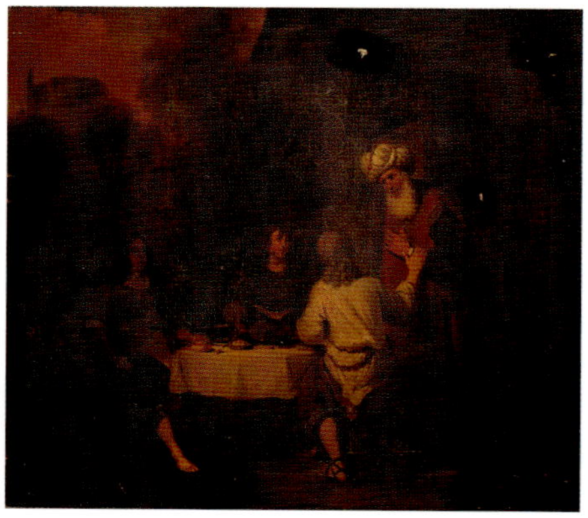

Rembrandt van Rijn (after) 1606–1669
A Scene from the Old Testament
oil on canvas 63.5 x 76.2
189

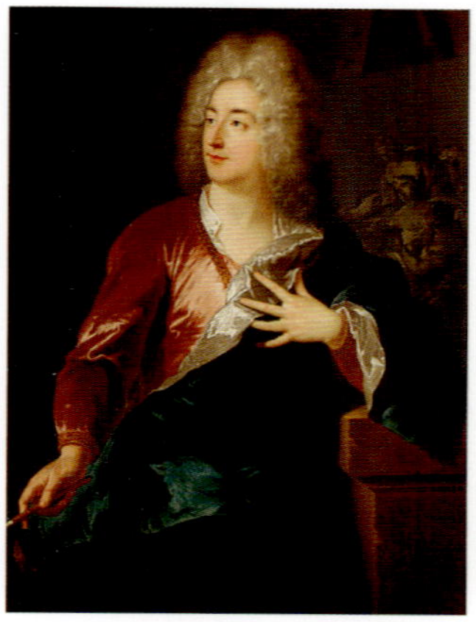

Rigaud, Hyacinthe (attributed to) 1659–1743
Portrait of an Artist
oil on canvas 113.1 x 87.1
56

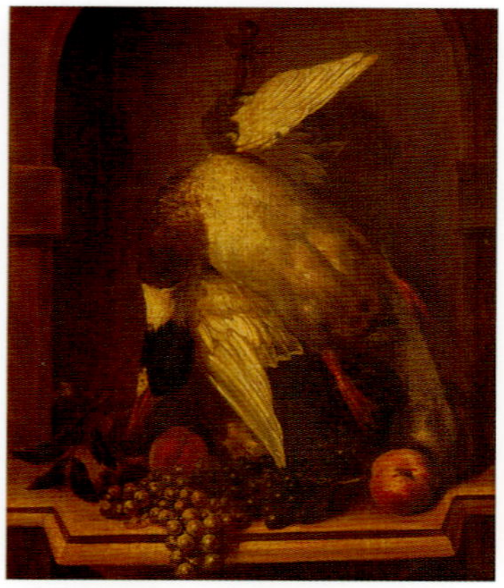

Schneider, N. N. active 1753
Still Life with Dead Game and Fruit
oil on canvas 76.2 x 63.5
28

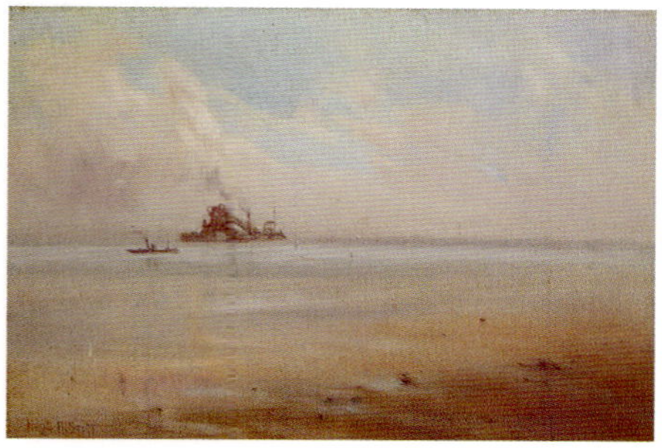

Scott, Hugh Berry 1854–1924
Dredging on the Ribble
oil on board 29.2 x 41.9
62

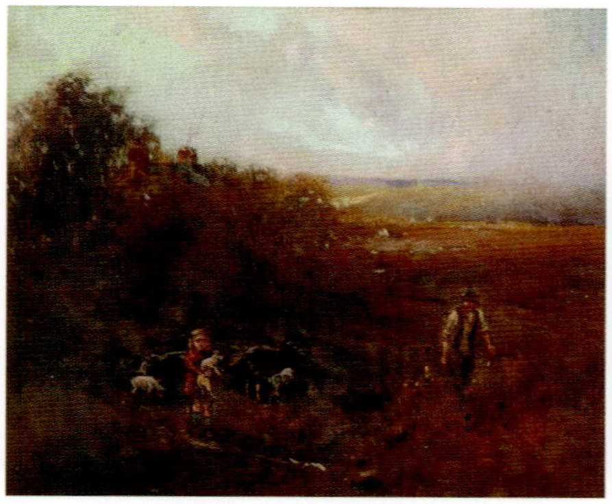

Scott, Hugh Berry 1854–1924
The Herdsman
oil on canvas 27.9 x 35.6
11

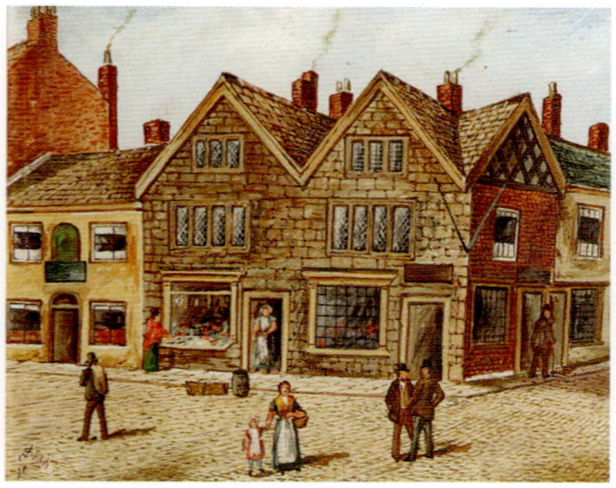

Shaw, John active 1889–1900
Town View
oil on board 21.5 x 28.5
109

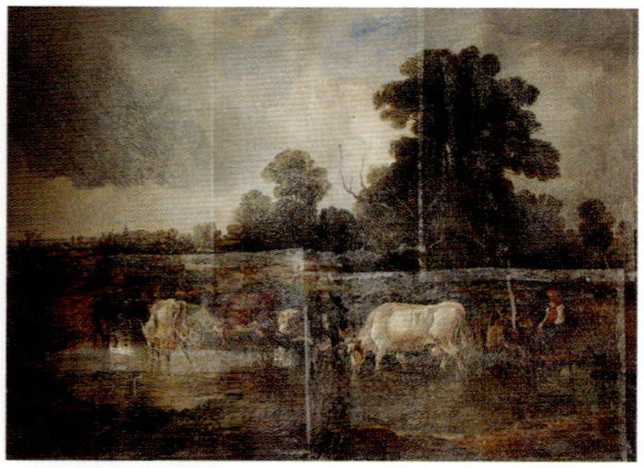

Shayer, William 1788–1879
The Watering Place
oil on canvas 111.7 x 149.9
22

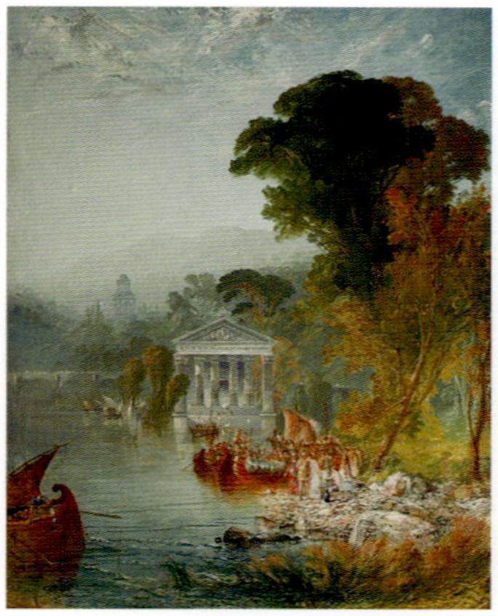

Sheffield Junior, George 1839–1892
A Classical Lake Scene (Carthage) 1866
oil on canvas 182.8 x 144.8
51

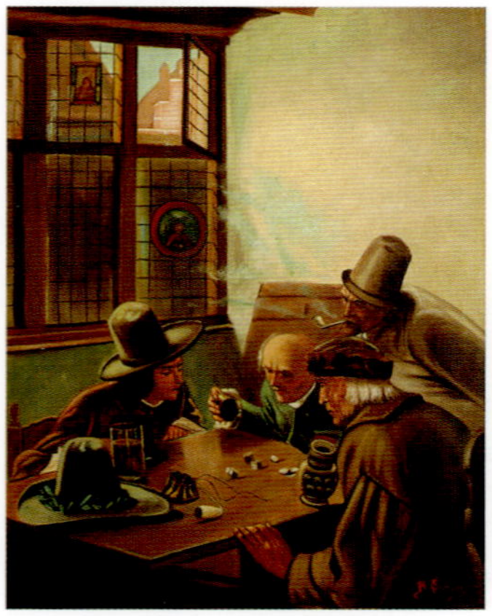

Sonn, Albert H. 1867–1936
The Dice Throwers
oil on canvas 66 x 53.3
13

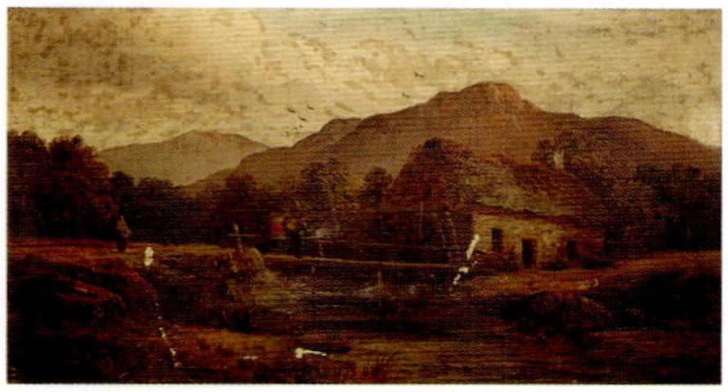

Thompson
Pandy Mill, Dolgelly, North Wales
oil on canvas 23 x 32 (E)
186

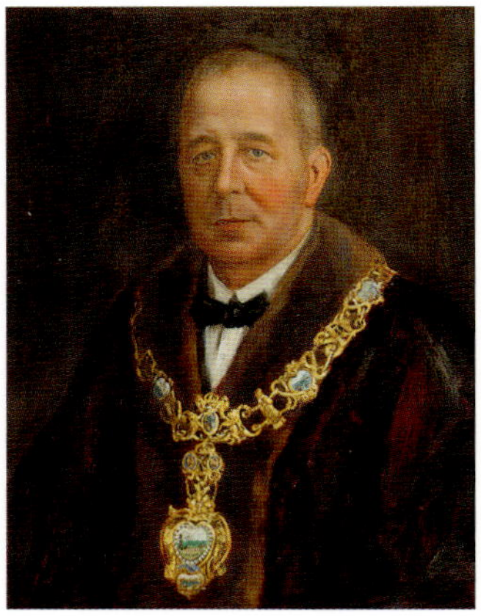

unknown artist
Alderman C. F. Critchley
oil on canvas 55 x 40 (E)
229

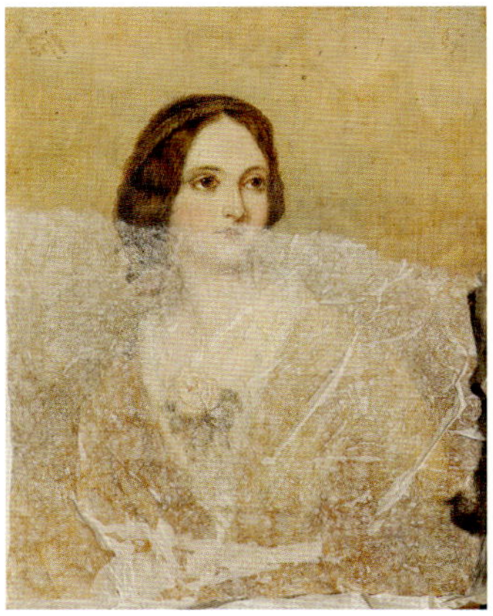

unknown artist
Portrait of a Lady
oil on canvas 25.4 x 20.3
23

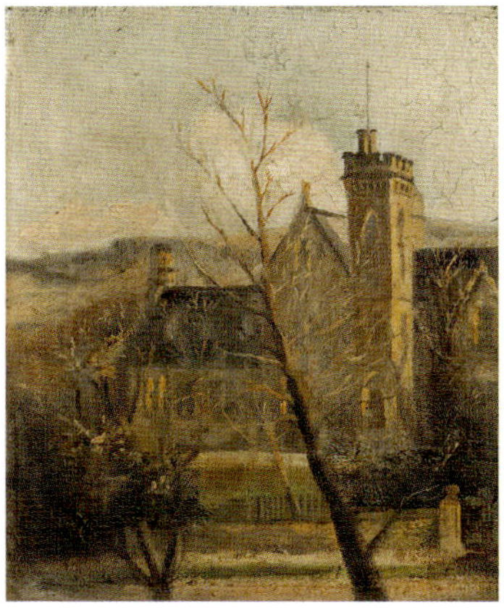

unknown artist
View of a Church
oil on canvas 40 x 25 (E)
194

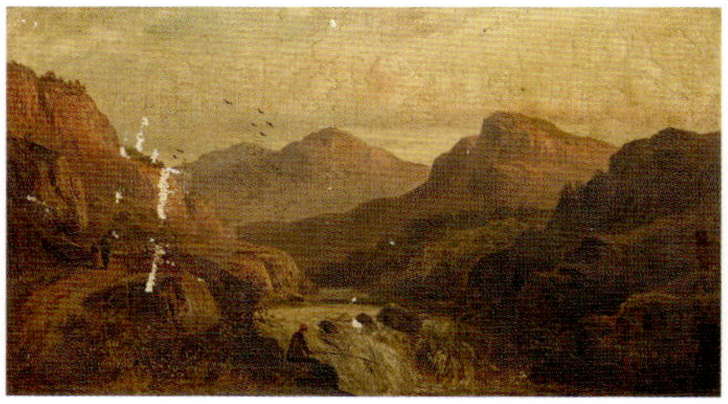

unknown artist
View of Glencoe
oil on canvas
185

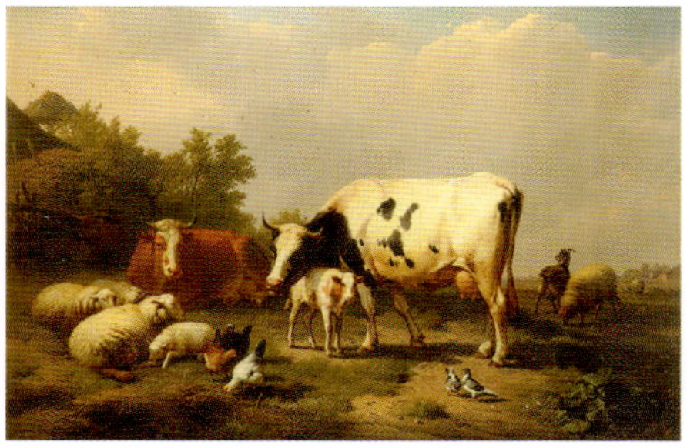

Verboeckhoven, Eugène Joseph 1798–1881
Cattle and Sheep in a Landscape 1874
oil on canvas 71.1 x 109.2
1

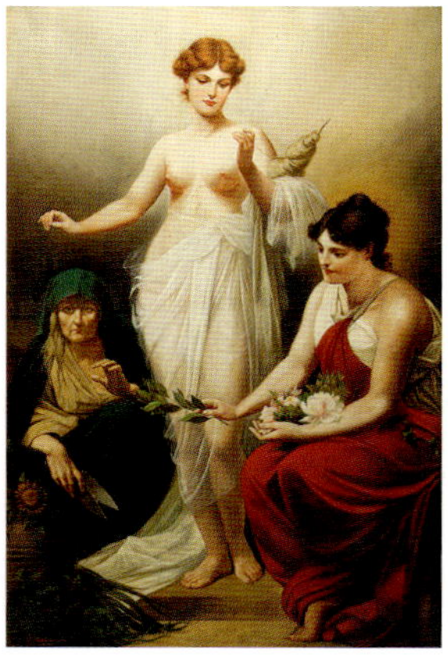

Wardleworth, Jack Leigh 1863–1925
The Thread of Life 1889
oil on canvas 124.4 x 83.8
74

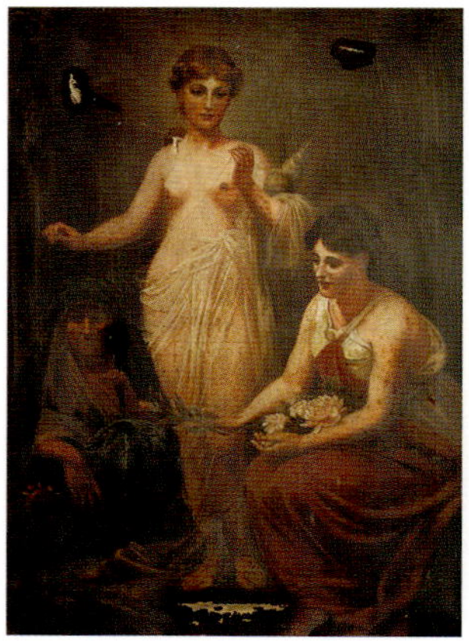

Wardleworth, Jack Leigh 1863–1925
The Thread of Life
oil on canvas 139.7 x 114.3
193

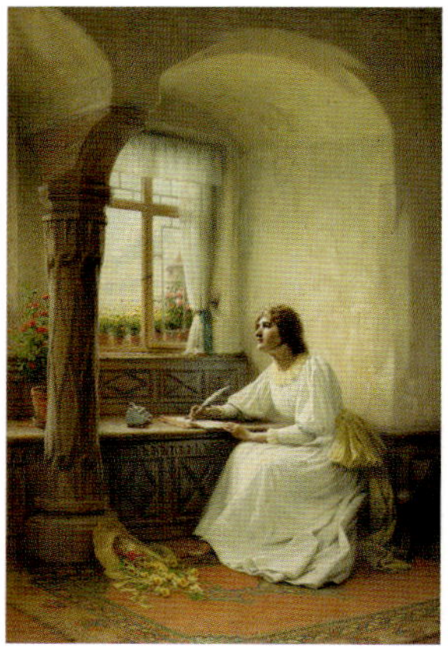

Wasse, Arthur 1854–1930
Goodbye 1892
oil on canvas 121.9 x 86.4
48

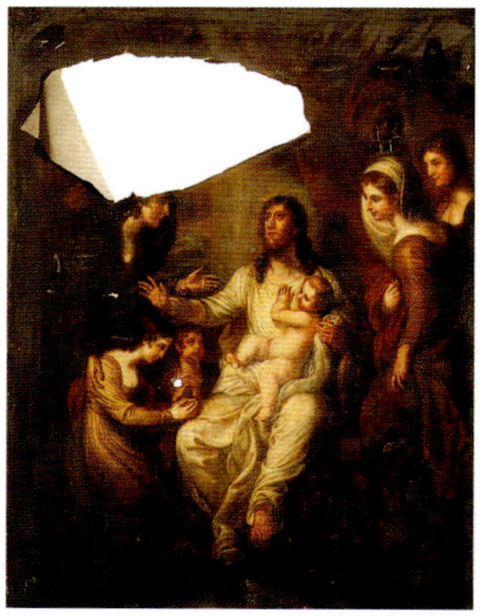

West, William (attributed to) 1801–1861
Christ Blessing the Children
oil on canvas 119.3 x 99.1
179

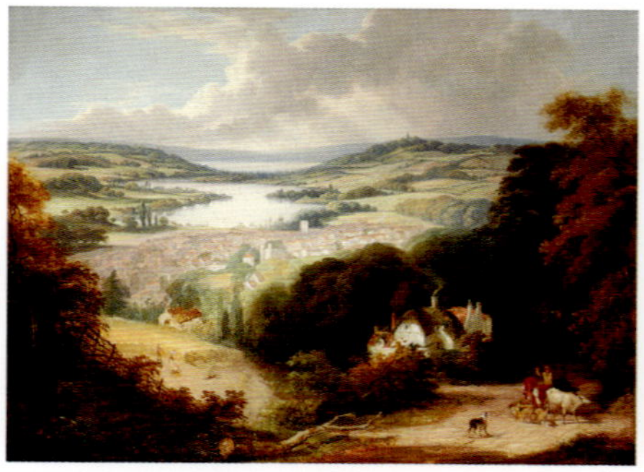

Williams, Harry (John Henry) (attributed to) 1807–1877
Village Overlooking an Estuary
oil on canvas 83.8 x 111.8
14

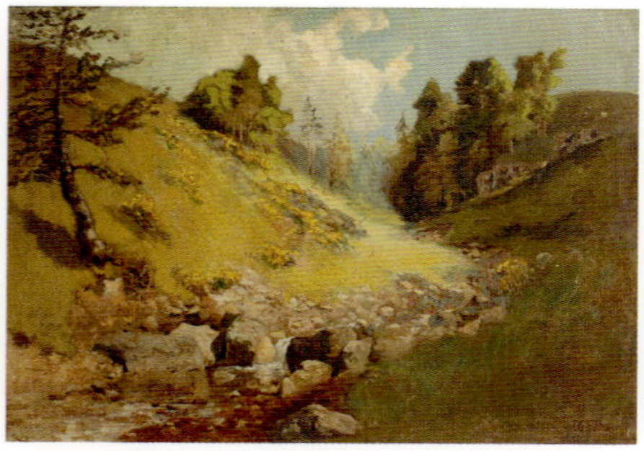

Woodhead, Walter 1861–1946
A Yorkshire Dale
oil on canvas 63.5 x 88.9
117

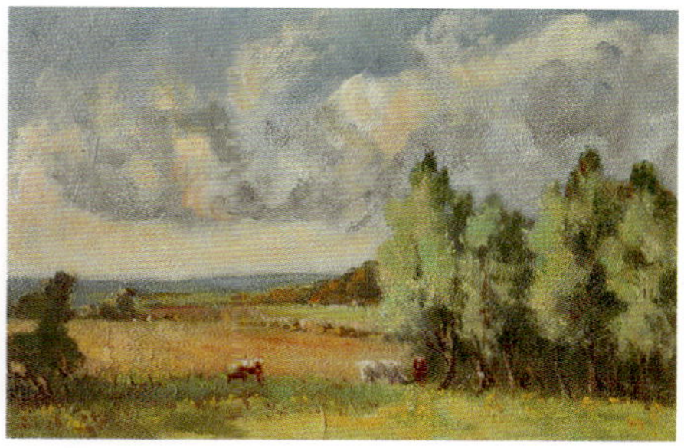

Woodhead, Walter 1861–1946
Fylde Landscape
oil on canvas 20.7 x 31.1
96

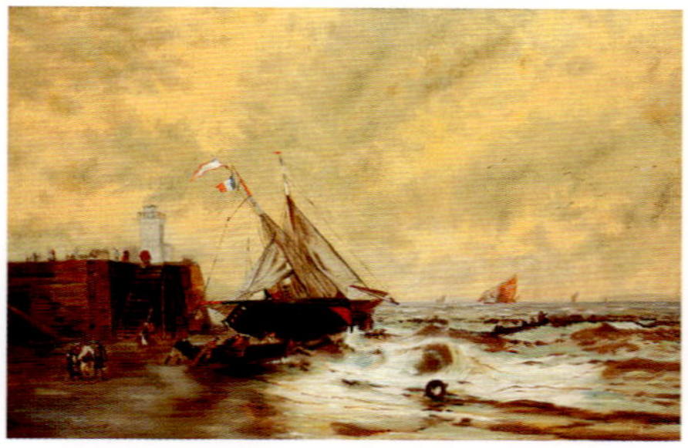

Woodhouse, Susan 1866–1948
Shore Scene with Beached Boat in Rough Water
oil on canvas 50.8 x 76.2
97

Duke of Lancaster's Own Yeomanry Museum

The Duke of Lancaster's Own Yeomanry (DLOY) was created as successor to older units of yeomanry in the county of Lancashire, and brought together existing troops based in Furness, Bolton and Wigan. The new name was given at an audience granted by William IV to Major Thomas Braddyll in September 1834. The DLOY had continuous existence under this same title until as recently as 1992 when it was reduced in scale to a squadron. The name is now retained by 'D' Squadron (The Duke of Lancaster's Own Yeomanry) as a part of the Royal Mercian and Lancastrian Yeomanry. The unit is thus part of the modern Territorials, but also has a history that encompasses service in the Boer War and World Wars.

The Regimental Collection is an accredited museum with its own trustee body, co-located with the Museum of Lancashire at Stanley Street, Preston. The collaboration with Lancashire County Council Museums Service commenced in the 1980s. The Collection includes a small number of paintings and a full range of artefacts telling the history of the Regiment.

Stephen Bull, Curator Military History, Lancashire Museums

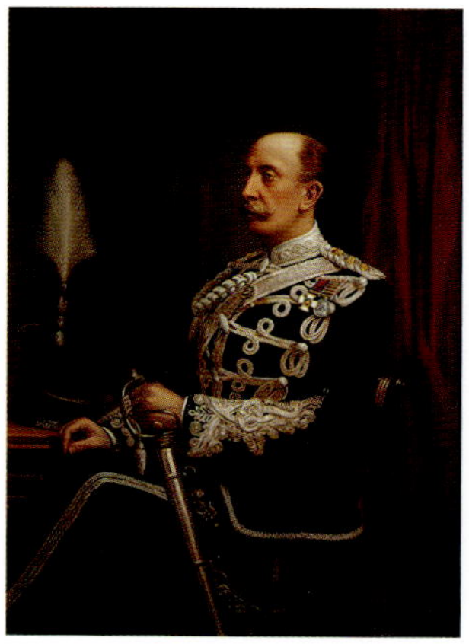

Booth, Samuel Lawson 1836–1928
Colonel W. C. Gerard c.1903
oil on canvas 65 x 45 (E)
LANOY 572

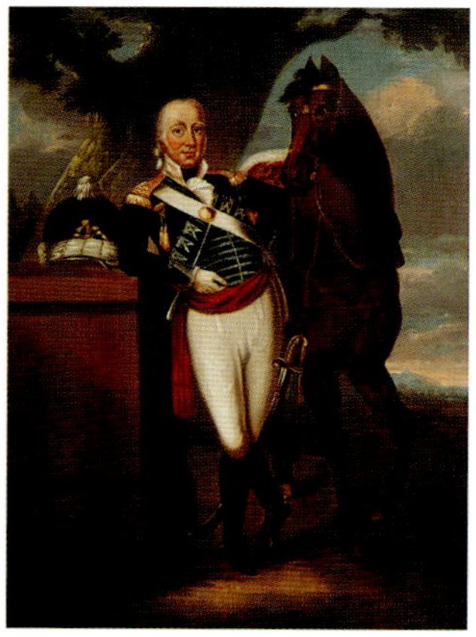

Craik
T. P. Legh of Lyme Park c.1795
oil on canvas 60 x 46
LANOY.453

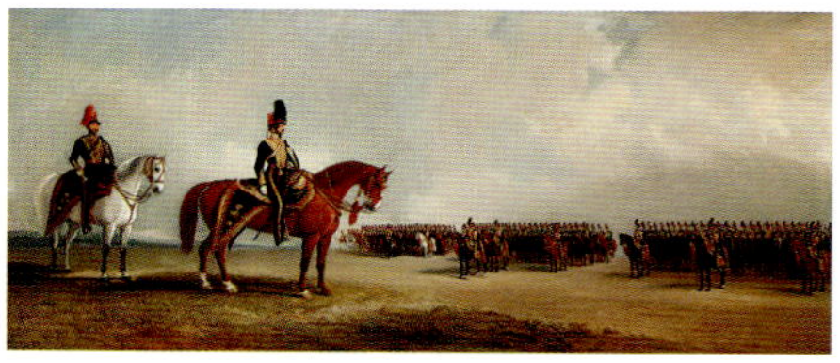

Ferneley I, John E. 1782–1860
Lieutenant Colonel Sir Robert Tolver Gerard, Bt, and His Regiment, the Lancashire Hussars, on Parade 1851
oil on canvas 73.5 x 151
LANOY.448

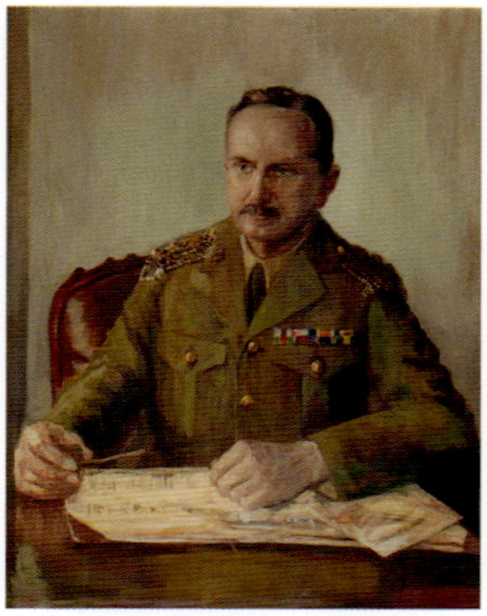

unknown artist
Lieutenant Colonel D. H. Bates, MC, TC, Commanding Officer Duke of Lancaster's Own Yeomanry (1930–1934)
oil on canvas 75.5 x 59
LANOY.576

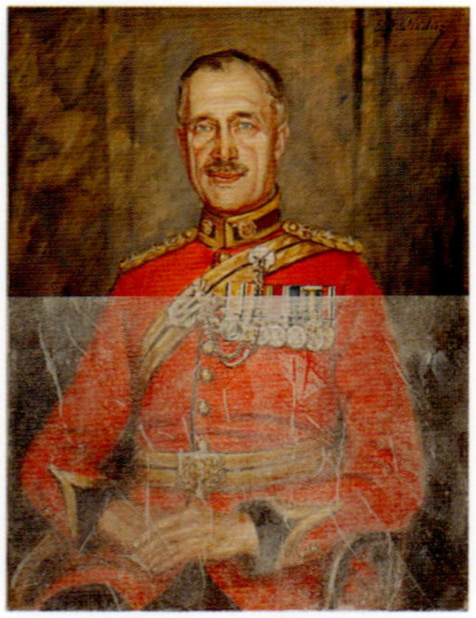

Widdas, Ernest Alfred 1879–1960
Colonel J. Heaton, TD c.1938
oil on canvas 60 x 50 (E)
LANOY.455

Harris Museum & Art Gallery

The Harris' extensive art collection mostly comprises British paintings, drawings, prints and sculpture from the eighteenth century to the present day. It is complemented by excellent collections of British decorative arts including pottery and porcelain, glass, costume and textiles. One highlight is the Mrs French Collection of almost 3,000 scent bottles. There is a wide-ranging history collection, and a collection of photography from the mid-nineteenth to the twentieth century, which helps to tell the story of Preston life, its people and industry.

The Harris itself is a very fine Grade I listed, neo-classical building in the heart of Preston's city centre. Its construction was funded through a bequest in 1877 made by local solicitor Edmund Harris in memory of his father, the Reverend Robert Harris, who had been vicar of a local church for 64 years. The building was officially opened in 1893.

Knowing a suitable museum and gallery was being developed, another local solicitor, Richard Newsham, bequeathed his substantial art collection to Preston in 1883. Newsham befriended, and bought directly from, some of the most esteemed artists of his time including William Powell Frith and David Roberts. He regularly made purchases from Royal Academy exhibitions and in this way acquired some famous oil paintings of the day such as *The Royal Family of France in the Prison of the Temple* by Edward Matthew Ward and *In the Bey's Garden* by John Frederick Lewis. Untypical of Newsham's usual taste, and his only purchase from a Pre-Raphaelite artist, is a striking watercolour by William Holman Hunt, *The Sphinx, Gizeh*. In total, the Newsham Bequest brought 107 quality artworks to the Harris and founded its art collection.

A later but equally important bequest was the Reverend John Haslam's collection of watercolours in 1949. This significantly increased the Harris' holdings in the English landscape tradition and added important works by Samuel Palmer and J. M. W. Turner, including the latter's spectacular *Kidwelly Castle, Carmarthenshire*.

Aside from paintings, the collection is particularly rich in bronzes of the New Sculpture movement c.1880–1930, featuring work by William Reynolds Stephens, Gilbert Bayes, Alfred Gilbert, Alfred Drury and William Hamo Thornycroft.

During the first half of the twentieth century, the Harris continued the collecting policy of founding benefactor Richard Newsham with regular purchases from the Royal Academy. A significant collection of paintings by the leading academic artists of the day was built up in this way, including two of our visitors' favourite works: Charles Spencelayh's *Why War?* and Herbert James Gunn's elegant *Pauline in the Yellow Dress*.

A taste for the academic was complemented by the occasional purchase of more Modernist works such as Stanley Spencer's *Resurrection: The Hill of Zion* and the Jacob Epstein bronze bust, *Portrait of the Artist in a Storm Cap*. The Harris collection has been greatly broadened by the Contemporary Art Society which has gifted numerous works since 1924, including Walter Richard Sickert's *Two Women* and Lucian Freud's remarkable *Still Life with Squid and Sea Urchin* plus works by Matthew Arnold Bracey Smith, Graham Sutherland (watercolour works) and David Bomberg. The CAS and the Arts Council helped support a renewed period of acquisitions from 1985 until 1997, during which about 60 new works of contemporary art were added to the collection by artists including Bridget Riley (works in gouache), Ian McKeever, Bruce McLean, Thérèse Oulton and Andy Goldsworthy

Artists with a local connection typically feature in the art collection. Most eminent is the Devis family of painters, an artistic dynasty which originated in Preston. Arthur Devis (1712–1787) specialised in informal group portraits, a style known as the 'conversation piece', which were popular during the 1740s and 1750s. In contrast, his half-brother, Anthony (1729–1816), was a succesful painter of landscapes; about 150 ink and watercolour works are held by the Harris. Two of Arthur Devis's sons, Thomas Anthony (1757–1810) and Arthur William (1762–1822) practised as portrait painters. The latter had a particularly colourful career and, after surviving a shipwreck, worked in India before returning to England where he specialised in portraits and historical scenes.

Preston-based Edwin Beattie is represented by almost 100 watercolours and ink drawings in the collection. His quaint images of bygone times still resonate with local visitors.

The Harris retains the ambition of its founders and still seeks to add works of international quality to its collection. Through the generosity of the Art Fund, Heritage Lottery Fund, Victoria and Albert Museum Purchase Grant Fund, Friends of the Harris and other supporters, the Harris has acquired some stunning works in recent years. George Romney's *Serena Reading* and Joseph Wright of Derby's portrait of local industrialist *Richard Arkwright* (co-owned with the National Portrait Gallery) add to the notable collection of eighteenth-century portraiture. In 2011 we added *Puck*, by that most notorious Victorian fairy painter Richard Dadd, to our nineteenth century collection. As well as strengthening the historic collection, the Harris is also building a collection of contemporary art with a focus on digital media.

Amanda Draper, Keeper of Fine Art

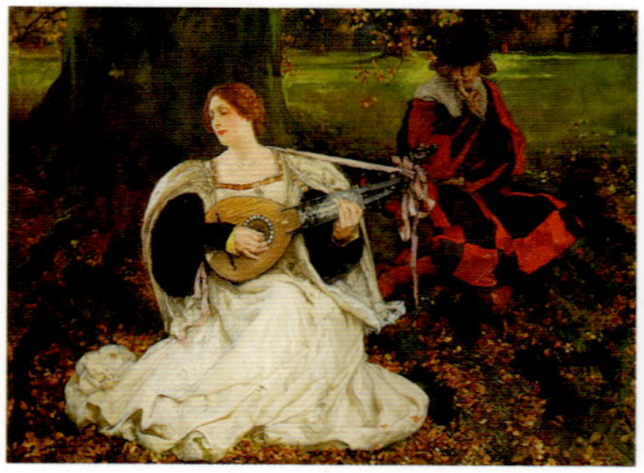

Abbey, Edwin Austin 1852–1911
Fair Is My Love c.1900
oil on canvas 62.4 x 91.7
PRSMG : P1

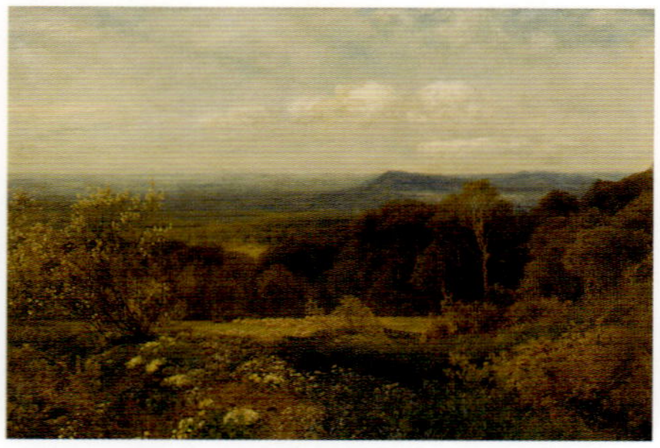

Adams, John Clayton 1840–1906
Surrey Flowers 1897
oil on canvas 104.5 x 150
PRSMG : P2

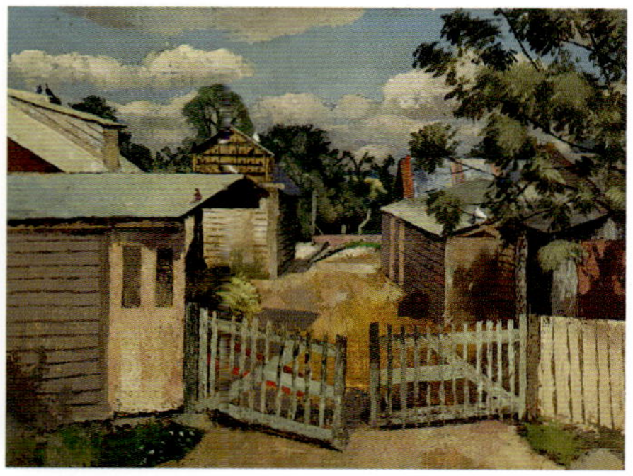

Aldridge, John Arthur Malcolm 1905–1983
The Dovecote before 1950
oil on panel 45.8 x 60.9
PRSMG : P928

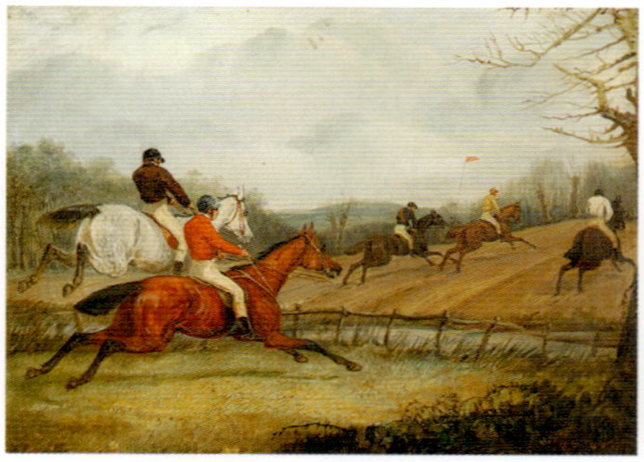

Alken, Henry Thomas 1785–1851
Five Steeplechasers, with a River in the Middle Distance and a Red Flag on the Horizon
oil on canvas 24.5 x 34.8
PRSMG : P1425.2

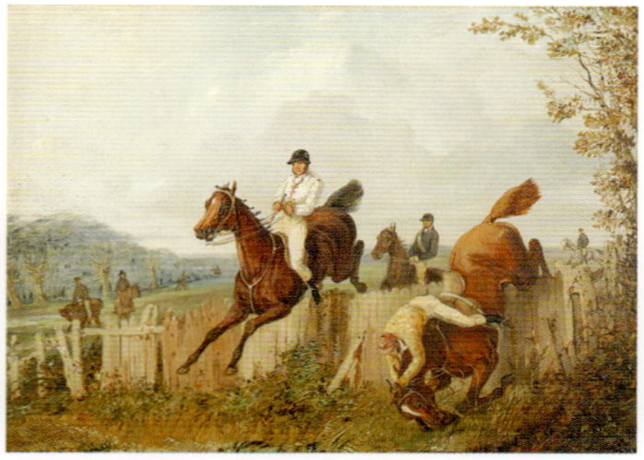

Alken, Henry Thomas 1785–1851
Steeplechasers Jumping a Fence
oil on canvas 24.5 x 34.8
PRSMG : P1425.3

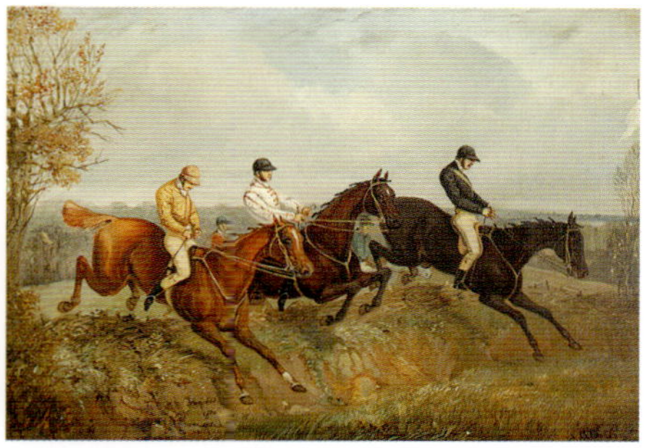

Alken, Henry Thomas 1785–1851
Three Steeplechasers Clearing a Ditch
oil on canvas 24.5 x 34.8
PRSMG : P1425.1

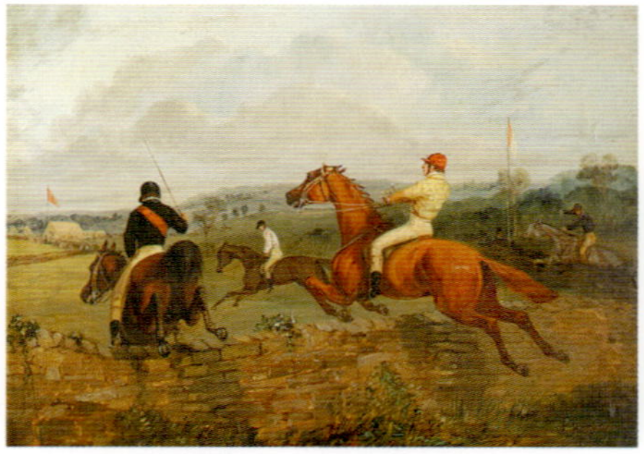

Alken, Henry Thomas 1785–1851
Two Steeplechasers Clearing a Wall, with Two Steeplechasers in the Middle Distance
oil on canvas 24.5 x 34.8
PRSMG : P1425.4

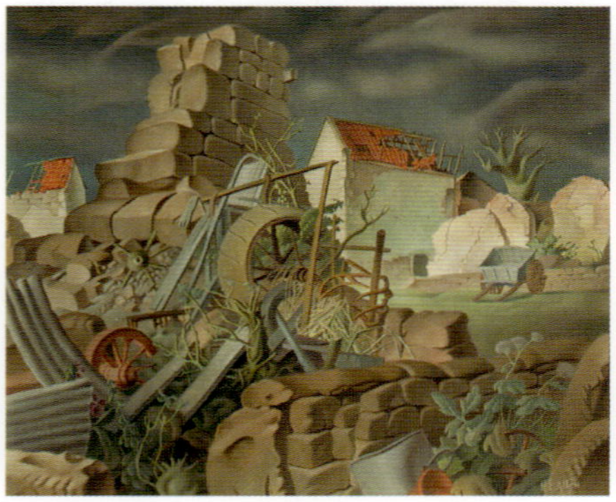

Allen, Harry Epworth 1894–1958
The Derelict Farm 1949
tempera on board 48.3 x 59.7
PRSMG : P1285

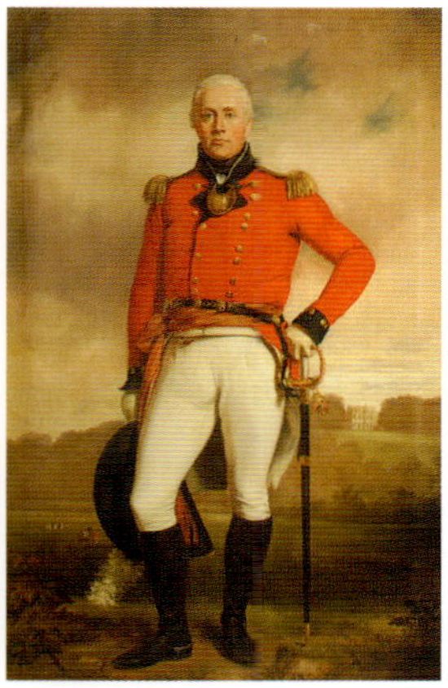

Allen, Joseph 1769–1839
Nicholas Grimshaw 1801
oil on canvas 233.5 x 147.3
PRSMG : P3

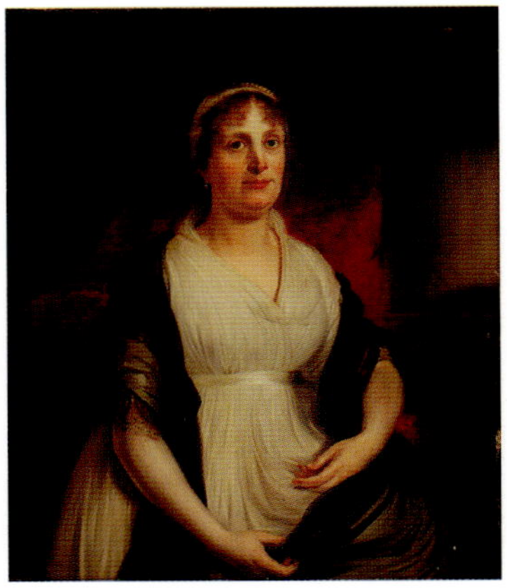

Allen, Joseph 1769–1839
Mrs Esther Mary Grimshaw
oil on canvas 106.6 x 91.5
PRSMG : P4

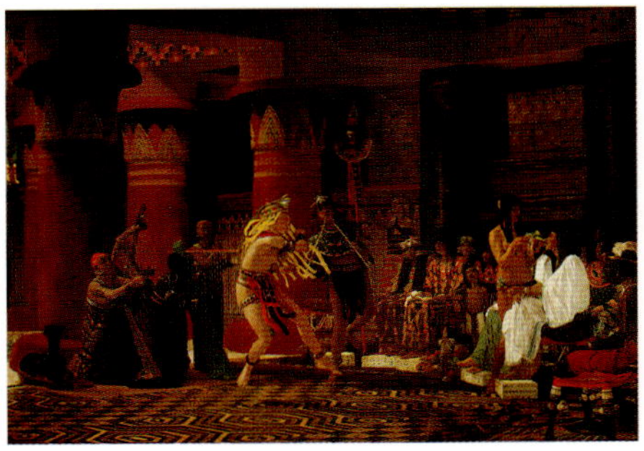

Alma-Tadema, Lawrence 1836–1912
Pastime in Ancient Egypt Three Thousand Years Ago 1863
oil on canvas 99.5 x 135.7
PRSMG : P8

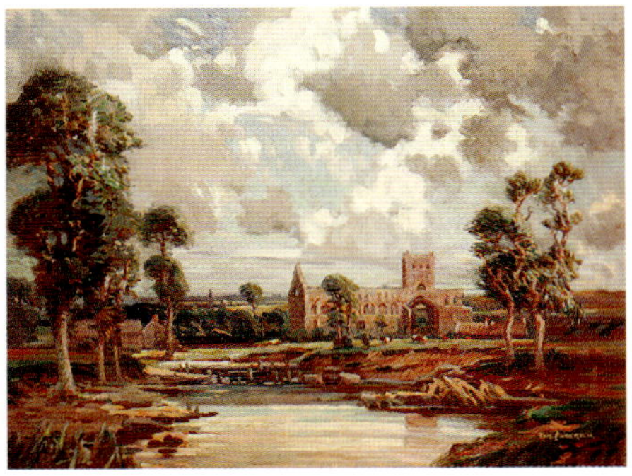

Anderton, Tom 1894–1956
Jedburgh Abbey
oil on canvas 71 x 91.5
PRSMG : P926

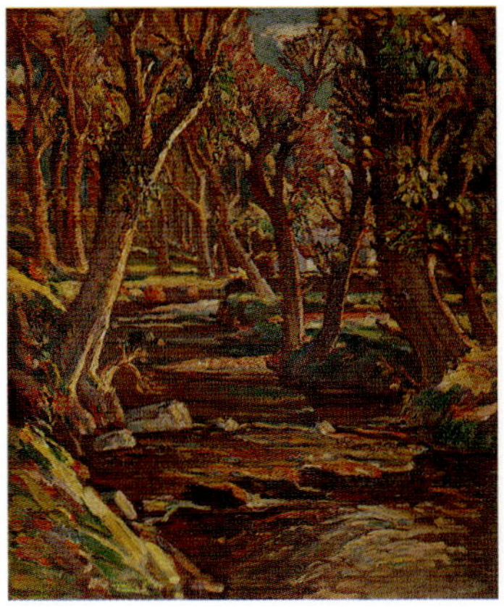

Anderton, Tom 1894–1956
Woodland Scene
oil on canvas 50 x 40
PRSMG : 2008.50

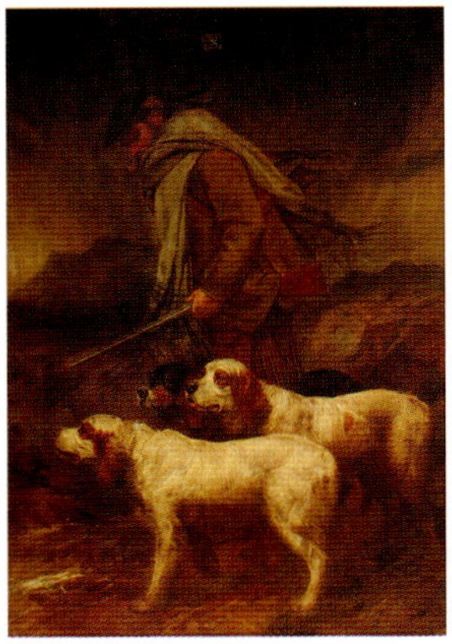

Ansdell, Richard 1815–1885
Dull Day, Shooter Returning with Dogs
1840–1870
oil on canvas 137.2 x 98
PRSMG : P15

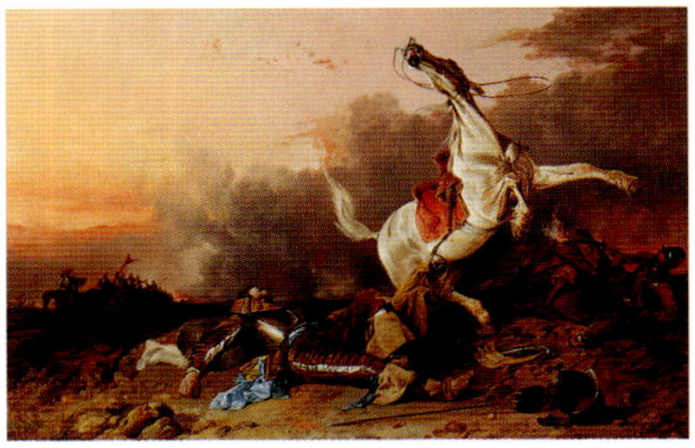

Ansdell, Richard 1815–1885
The Death of Sir William Lambton at the Battle of Marston Moor 1842
oil on canvas 145 x 237.5
PRSMG : P11

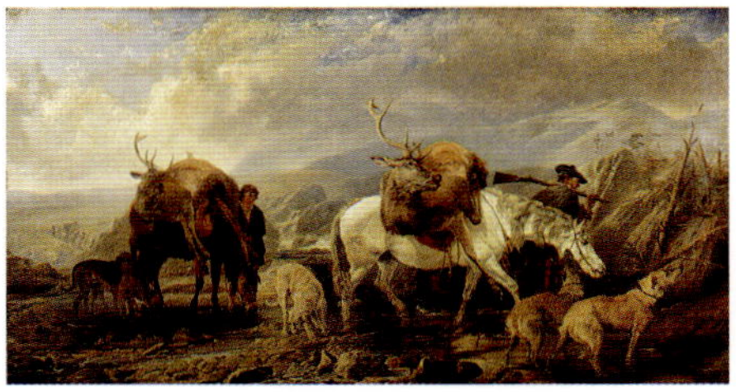

Ansdell, Richard 1815–1885
The Deer Stalker's Return 1846
oil on canvas 96.5 x 183
PRSMG : P13

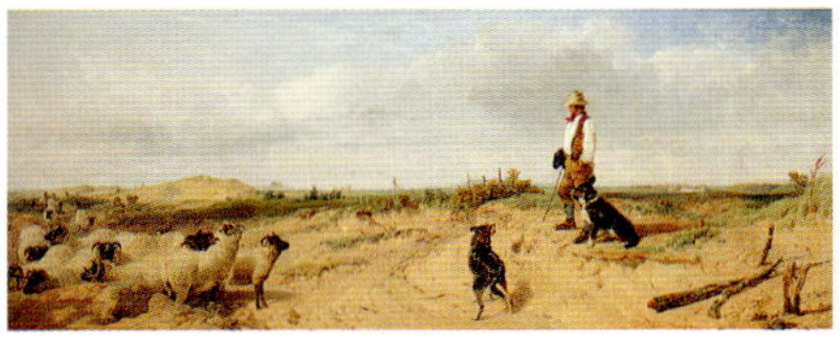

Ansdell, Richard 1815–1885
Lytham Sand Hills 1864
oil on canvas 36.7 x 99.5
PRSMG : P10

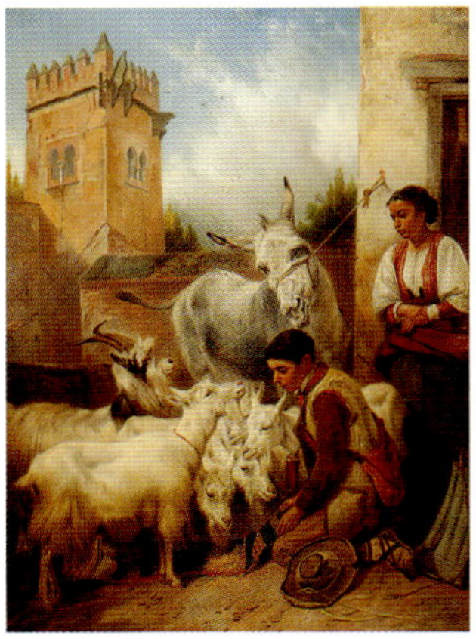

Ansdell, Richard 1815–1885
Feeding Goats in the Alhambra 1871
oil on canvas 110.5 x 86.5
PRSMG : P12

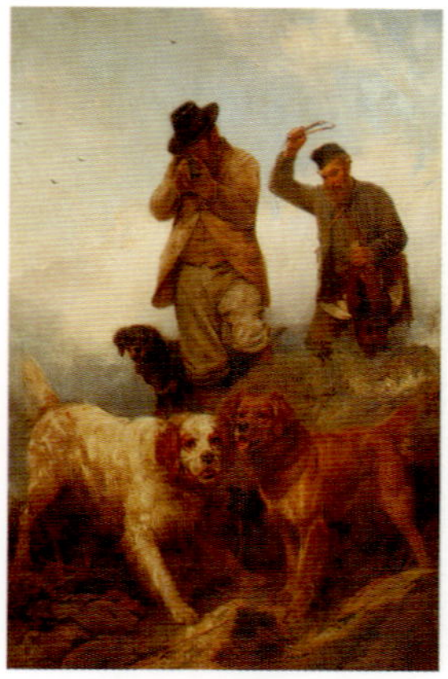

Ansdell, Richard 1815–1885
A Clear Day, Shooter and Dogs
oil on canvas (?) 137.2 x 98
PRSMG : P14

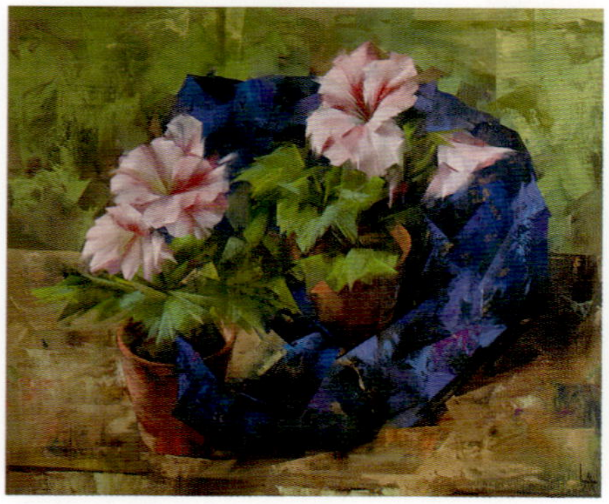

Appelbee, Leonard 1914–2000
Flower Piece 1958
oil on canvas 50.9 x 60.3
PRSMG : P1606

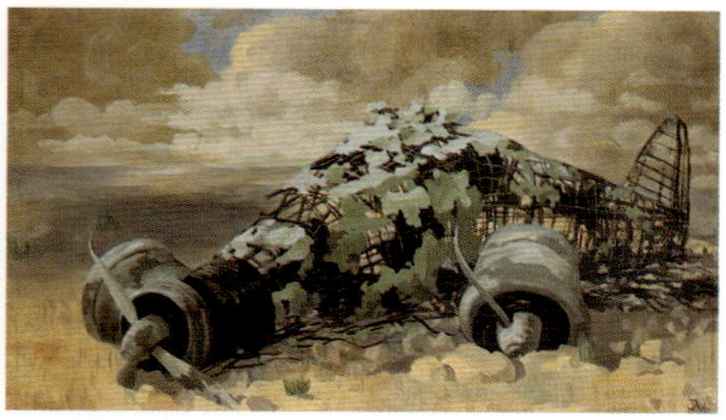

Armstrong, John 1893–1973
Burnt Out Aeroplane 1941
oil on canvas 27.5 x 46.5 (E)
PRSMG : P1111

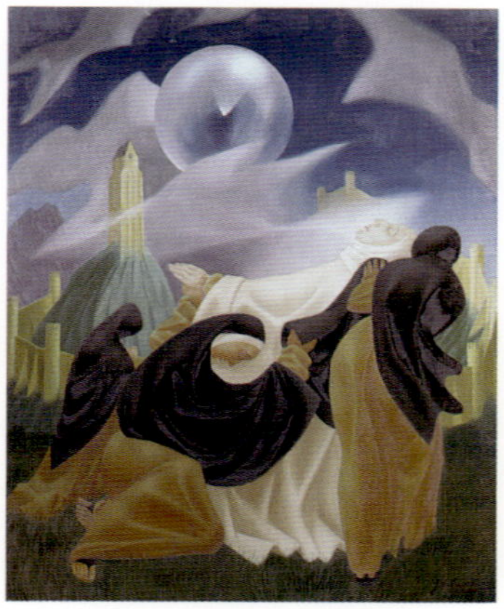

Armstrong, John 1893–1973
A Vision of Saint Teresa 1950–1953
oil on canvas 91.5 x 76
PRSMG : P1456

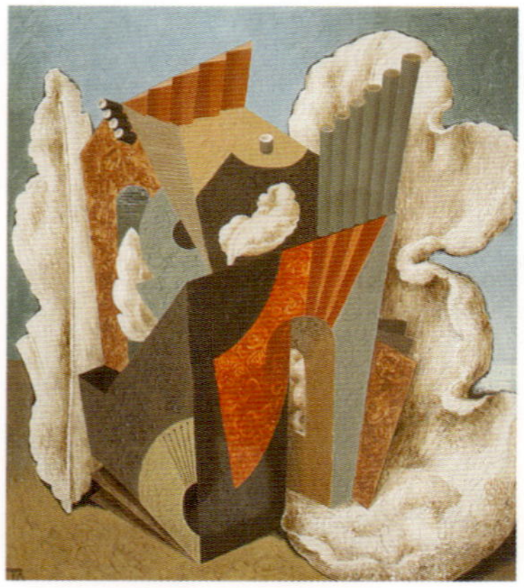

Armstrong, John 1893–1973
Abstract 1950–1969
tempera on board 61 x 51
PRSMG : P1751

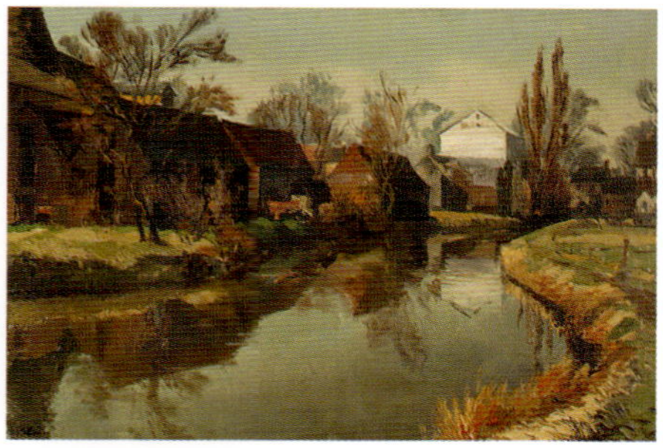

Askew, Victor 1909–1974
The Lea, Sawbridgeworth, Hertfordshire 1949
oil on canvas 66 x 96.5
PRSMG : P1284

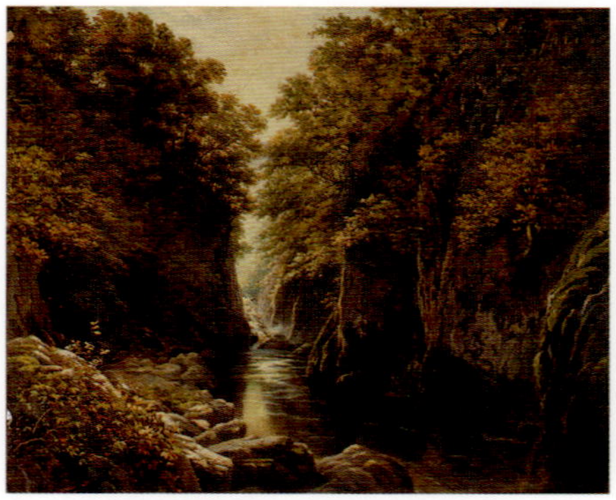

Aspinwall, Reginald 1858–1921
Fairy Glen, Betws-y-Coed 1876
oil on canvas 50.5 x 68.5
PRSMG : P17

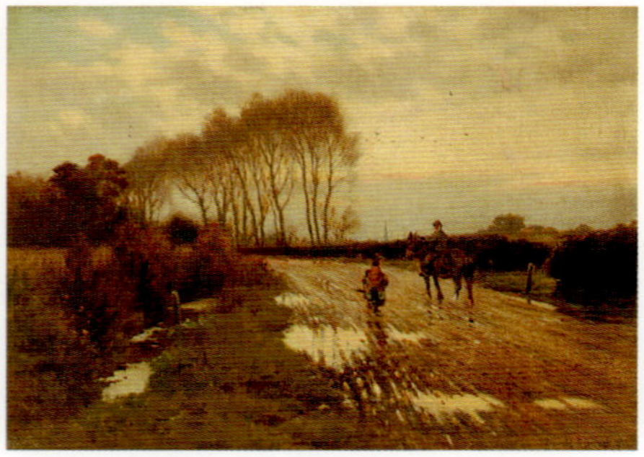

Aspinwall, Reginald 1858–1921
November Eve, Chichester 1891
oil on canvas 30.5 x 45.5
PRSMG : P47

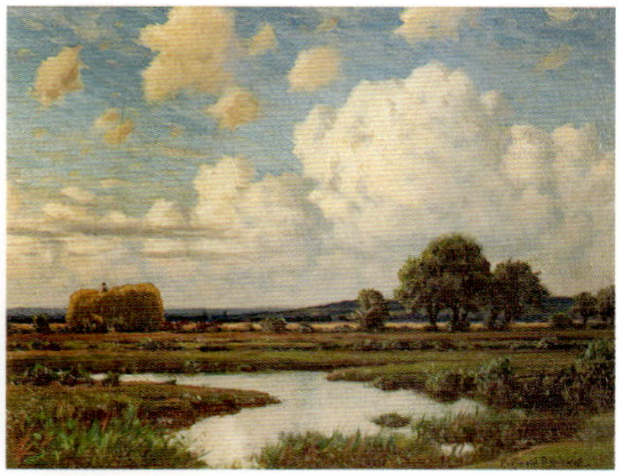

Aspinwall, Reginald 1858–1921
Cumulus Clouds: Haymaking 1906
oil on canvas 21.5 x 29
PRSMG : P29

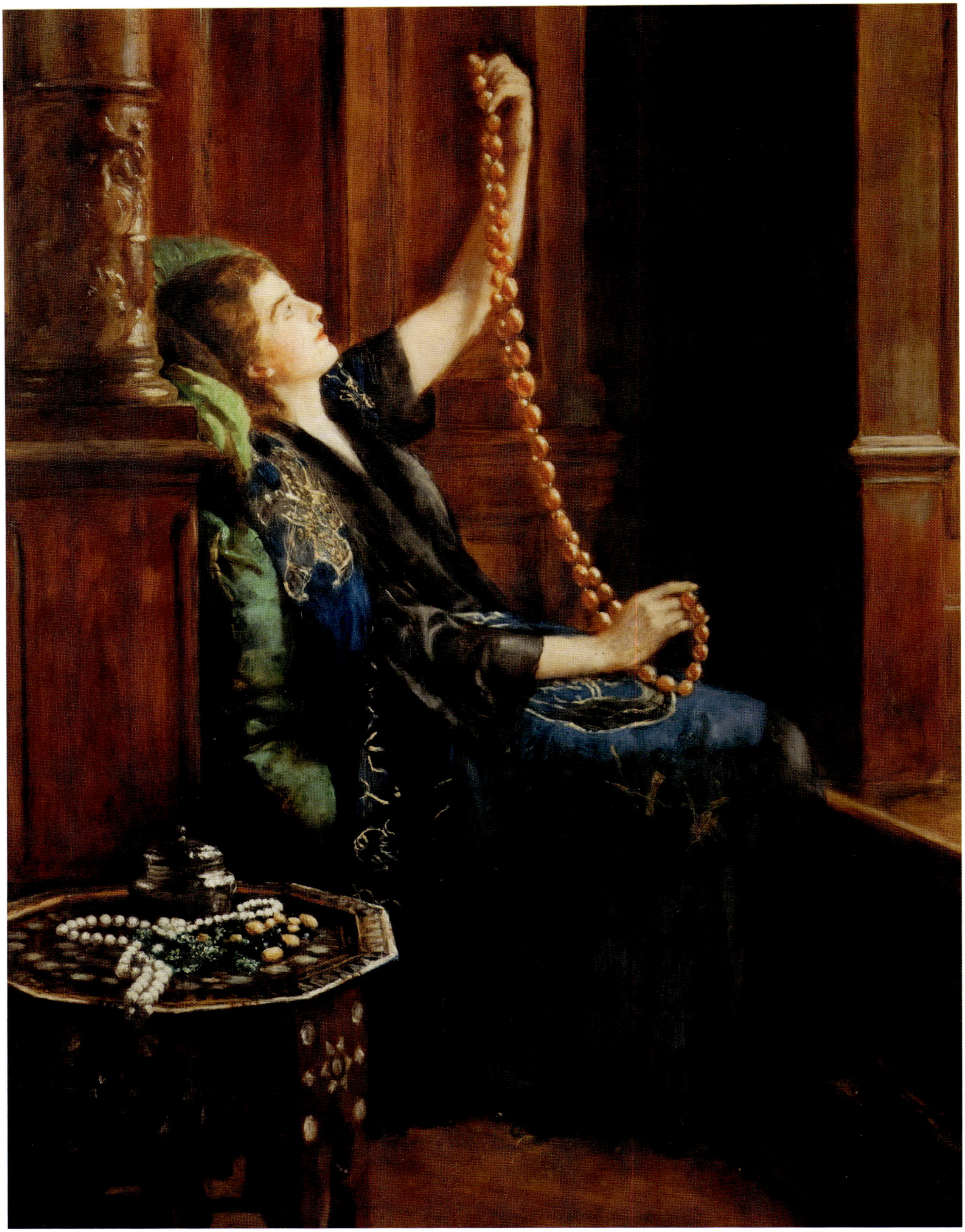

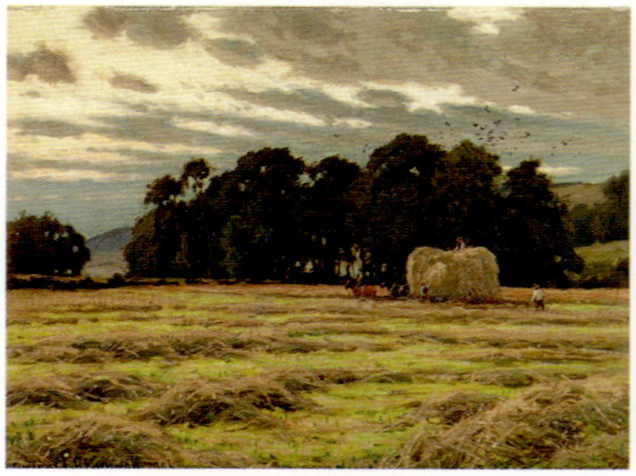

Aspinwall, Reginald 1858–1921
Haymaking, Twilight, Caton 1906
oil on canvas 24 x 34.3
PRSMG : P18

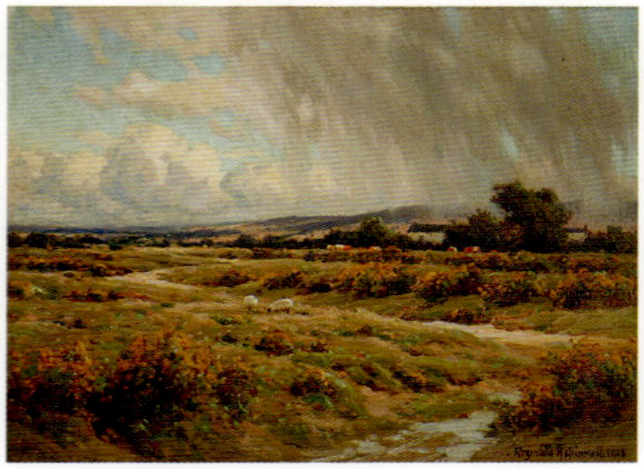

Aspinwall, Reginald 1858–1921
Landscape – Rain O'er the Common 1906
oil on canvas 29.8 x 39.5
PRSMG : P28

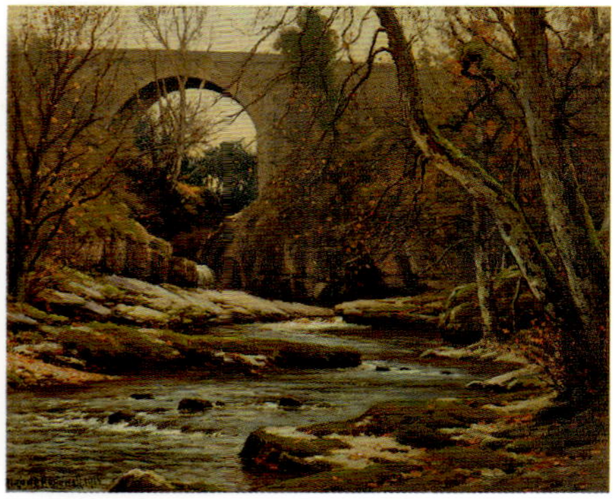

Aspinwall, Reginald 1858–1921
Landscape with Bridge 1906
oil on canvas 30.5 x 38
PRSMG : P31

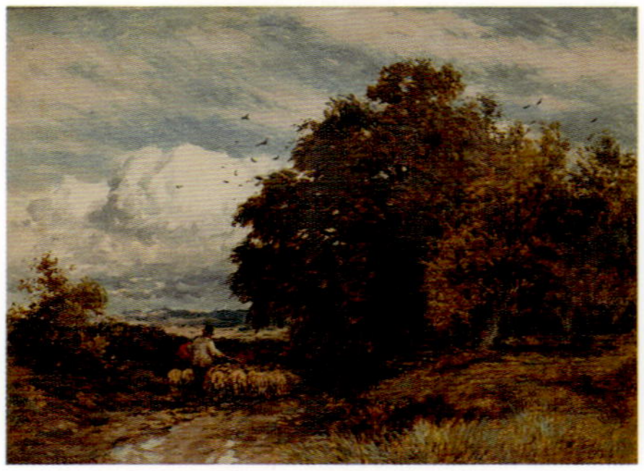

Aspinwall, Reginald 1858–1921
Landscape with Sheep 1906
oil on canvas 24 x 31.5
PRSMG : P25

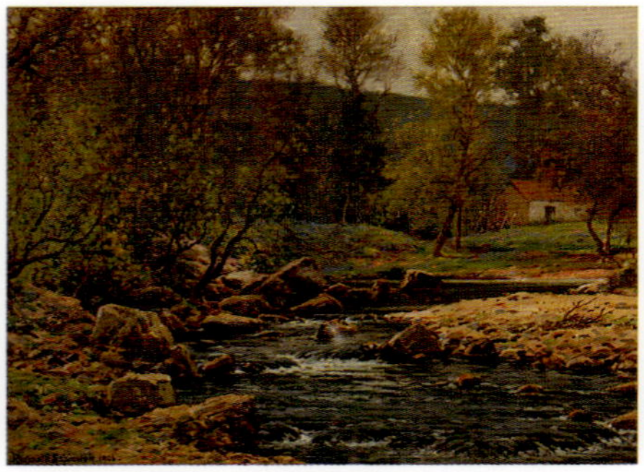

Aspinwall, Reginald 1858–1921
Springtime on the Wyre, Dolphinholme 1906
oil on canvas 30.5 x 40.5
PRSMG : P30

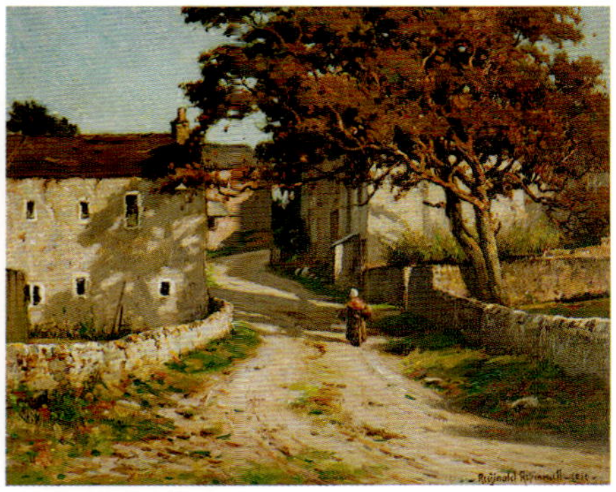

Aspinwall, Reginald 1858–1921
The Light of an October Evening, Bolton-le-Sands 1910
oil on canvas 29 x 36.8
PRSMG : P19

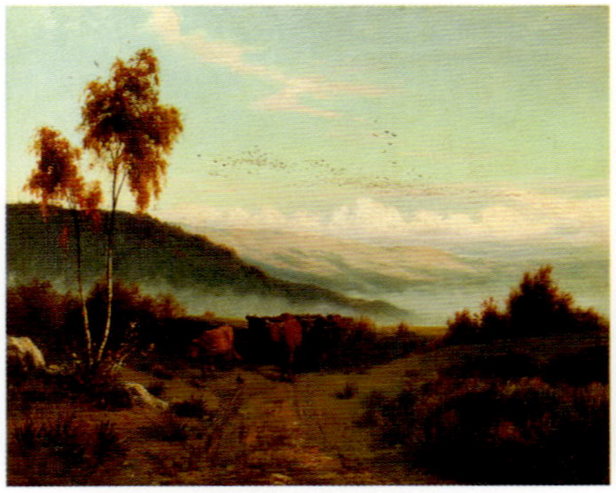

Aspinwall, Reginald 1858–1921
Eventide
oil on canvas 29.1 x 41.2
PRSMG : P1859

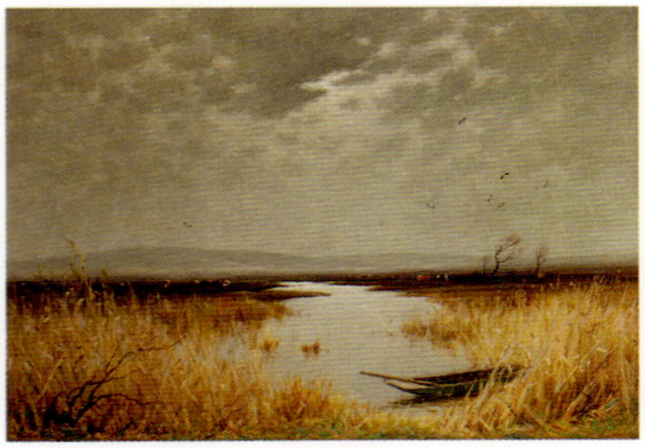

Aspinwall, Reginald 1858–1921
Marshland
oil on canvas 45 x 60.5
PRSMG : P1860

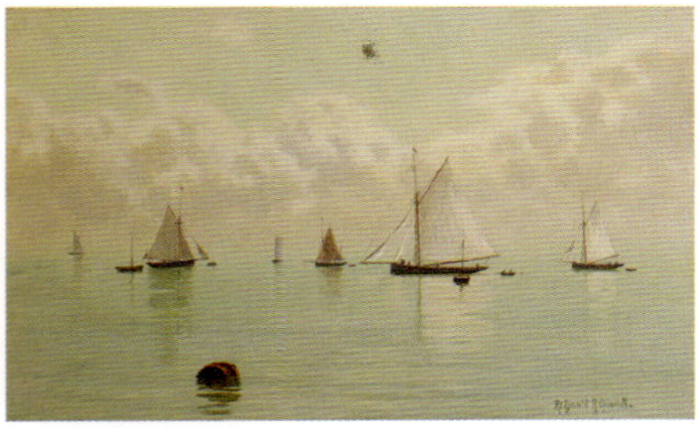

Aspinwall, Reginald 1858–1921
Morecambe Bay
oil on canvas 25.5 x 45
PRSMG : P1499

Facing page: Collier, John, 1850–1934, *The Amber Necklace*, 1930, Grundy Art Gallery (p. 88)

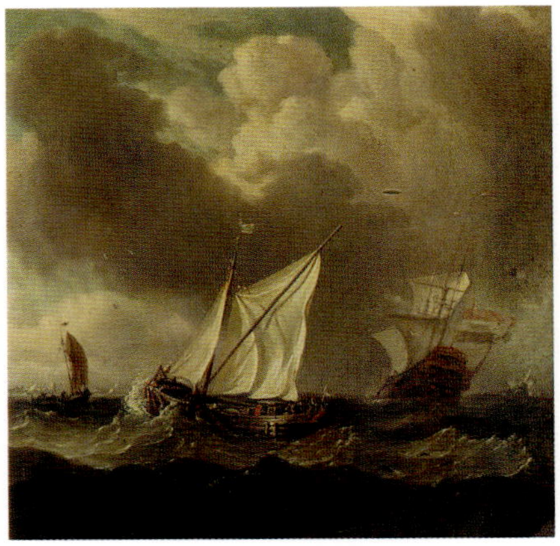

Backhuysen I, Ludolf 1630–1708
Seascape
oil on canvas 26.5 x 26.5 (E)
PRSMG : P36

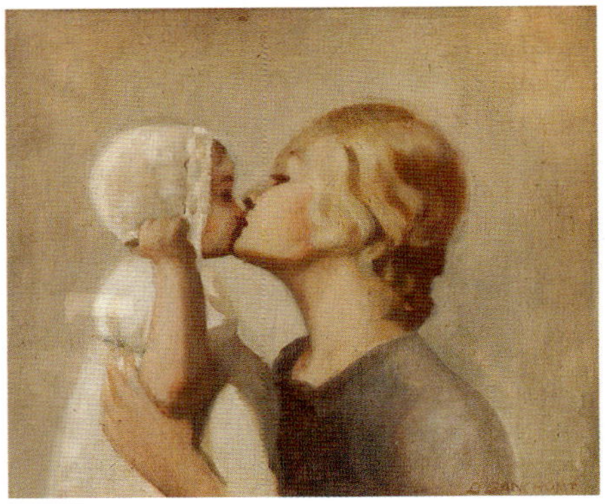

Bancroft, David F. active 1900–1950
Two Good Friends
oil on board 30.2 x 34.8
PRSMG : P1861

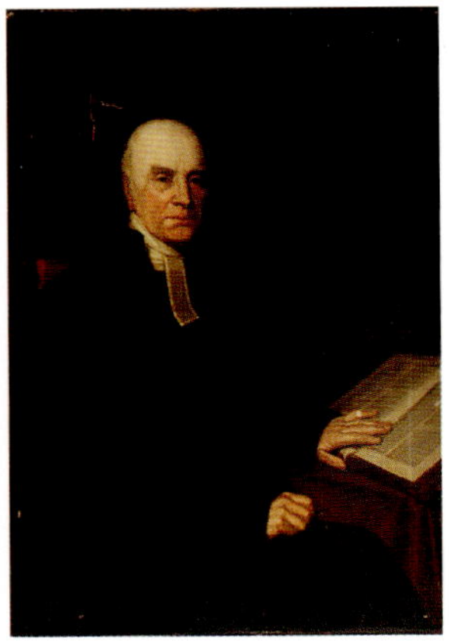

Barker, J. active 1800–1850
Reverend Robert Harris (1764–1862)
oil on canvas 111.8 x 86.4
PRSMG : P618

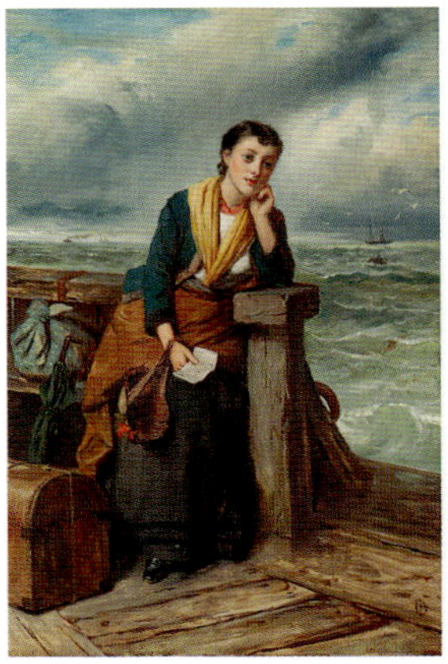

Barnes, Edward Charles 1830–1890
The Emigrant
oil on canvas 76.2 x 51
PRSMG : P1543

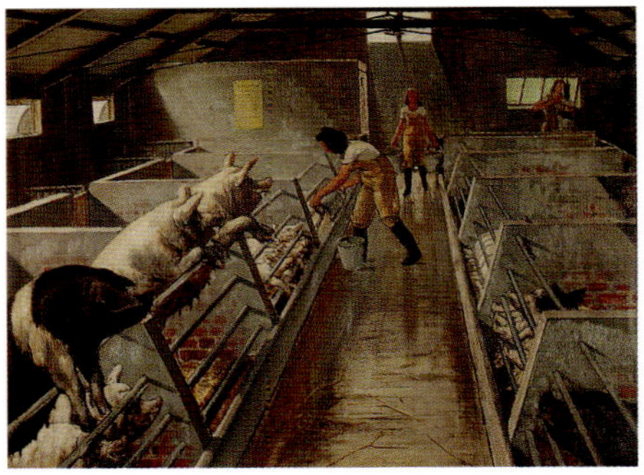

Bateman, James 1893–1959
Women's Land Army at Work 1940
oil on canvas 45.7 x 61
PRSMG : P1113

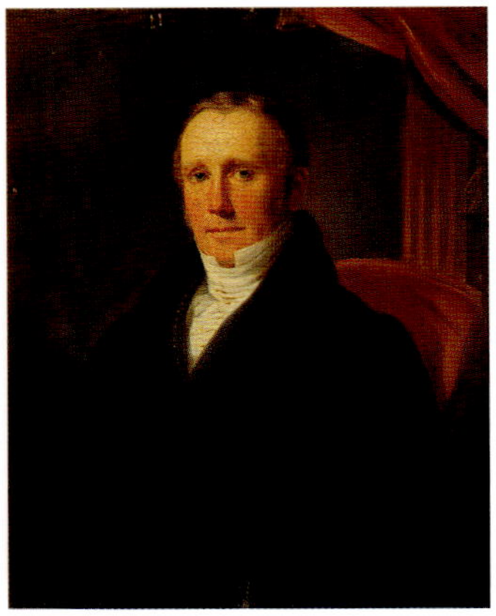

Beattie, Robert 1810–1874
John Horrocks 1835
oil on canvas 76.2 x 63.1
PRSMG : P497

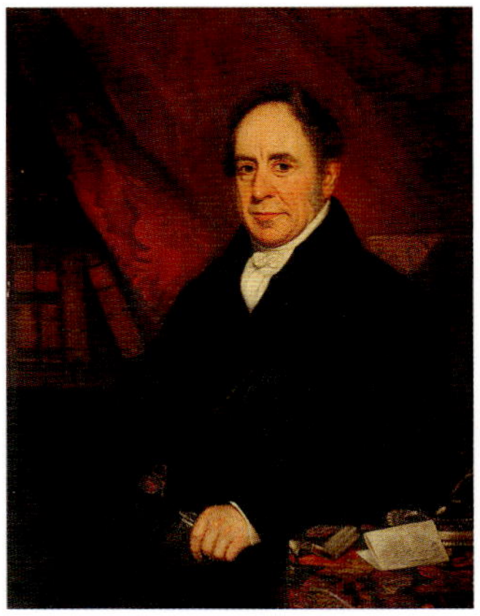

Beattie, Robert 1810–1874
Richard Palmer
oil on canvas 91.5 x 72.5
PRSMG : P1863

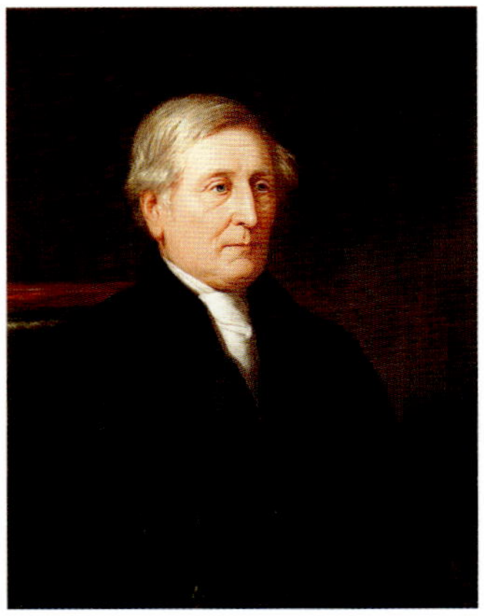

Bedhest
Satterthwaite (?)
oil on canvas 88 x 65 (E)
PRSMG : 1997.95.2

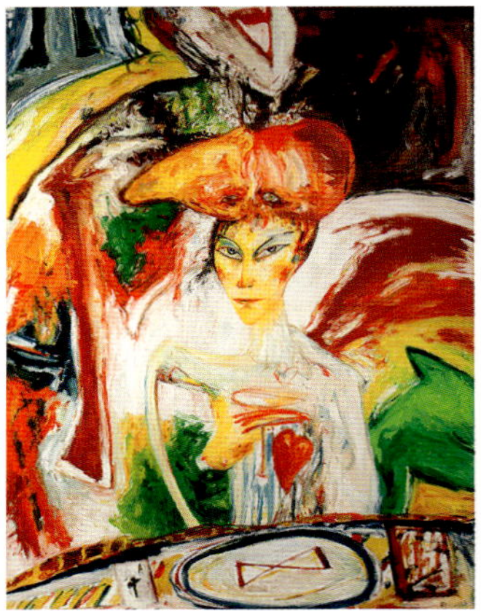

Bellany, John b.1942
Untitled c.1988
oil on canvas 155 x 122
PRSMG : 2005.187

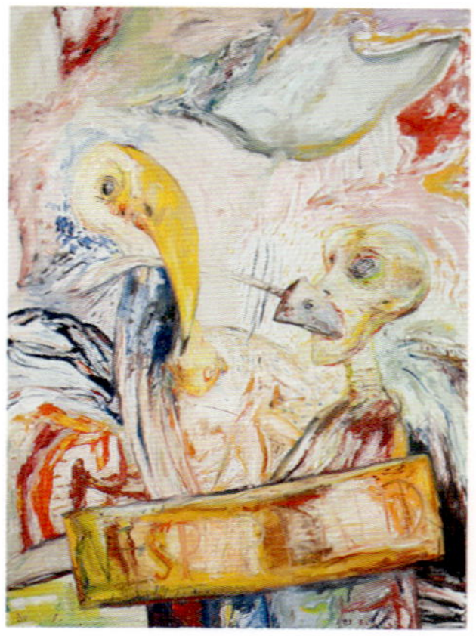

Bellany, John b.1942
Vesperland c.1988
oil on canvas 122 x 92
PRSMG : 2005.188

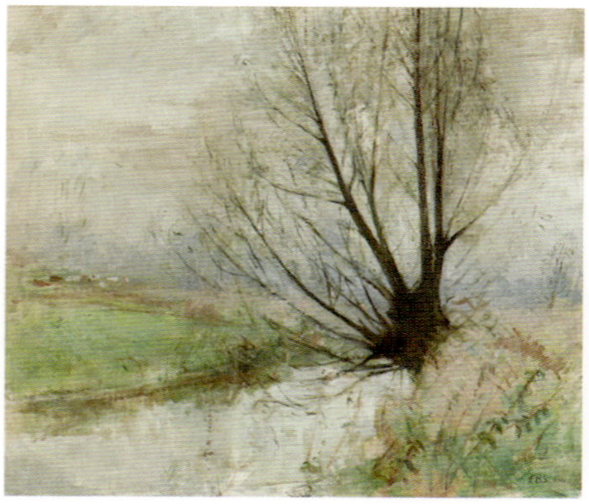

Bellingham-Smith, Elinor 1906–1988
The Willow Tree 1930–1960
oil on canvas 50.7 x 61
PRSMG : P1630

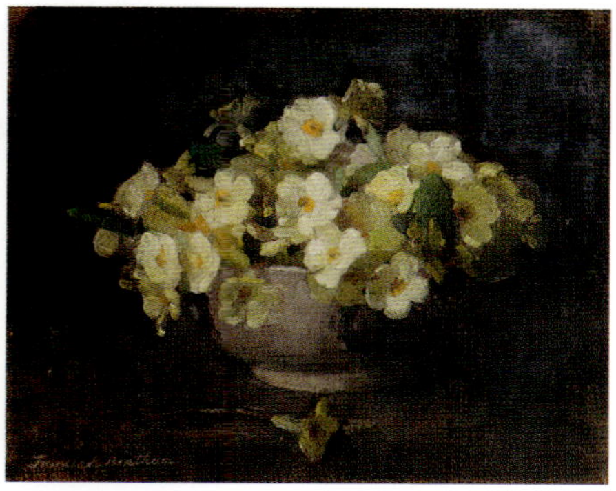

Bentham, Frances Mary 1871–1941
Primroses 1924
oil on board 20.3 x 26
PRSMG : P39

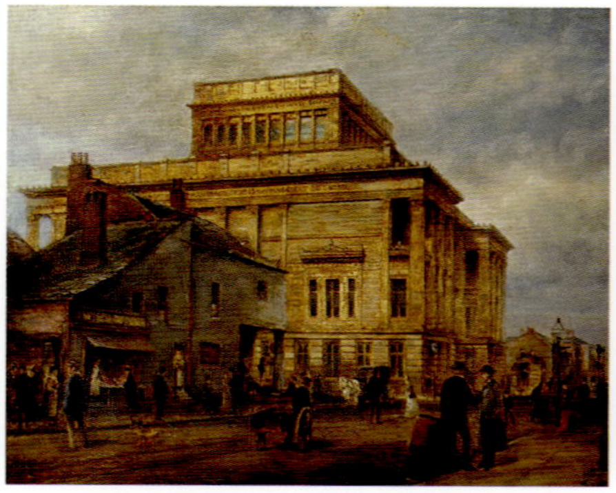

Bentham, Robert H. active 1850–1900
Lancaster Road, Preston
oil on card 41.5 x 53
PRSMG : P762

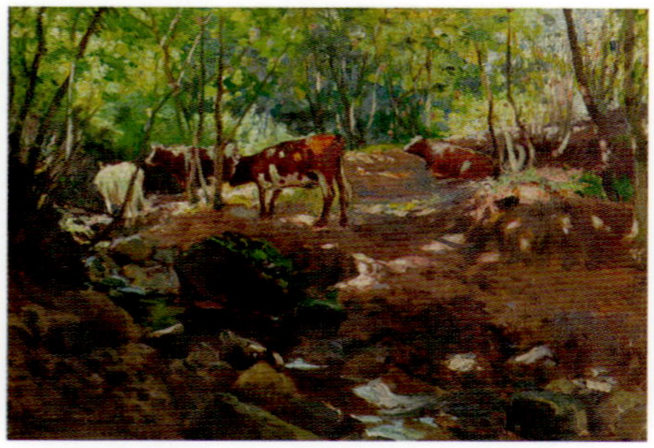

Birch, Samuel John Lamorna 1869–1955
Cattle by a Stream 1898
oil on panel 23.5 x 38
PRSMG : P1763

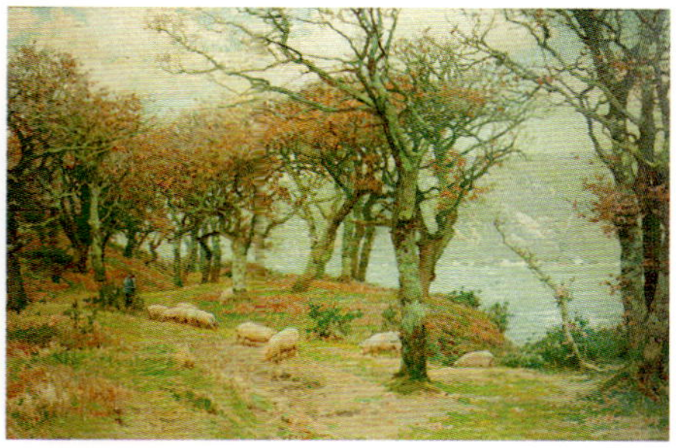

Birch, Samuel John Lamorna 1869–1955
Fallen Acorns 1904
oil on canvas 85 x 122
PRSMG : P43

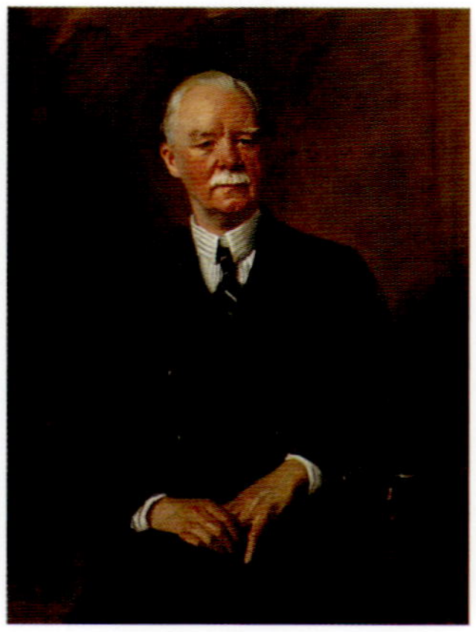

Birley, Oswald Hornby Joseph 1880–1952
Alderman H. Astley-Bell 1936
oil on canvas 106 x 85.3
PRSMG : P736

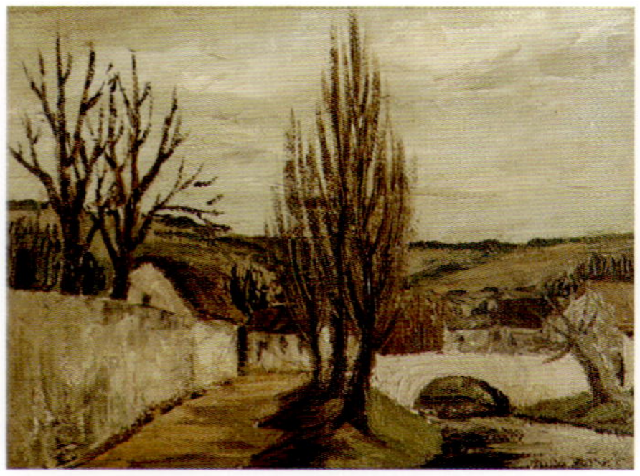

Bissill, George William 1896–1973
Shalbourne
oil on canvas 25.5 x 35.5
PRSMG : P924

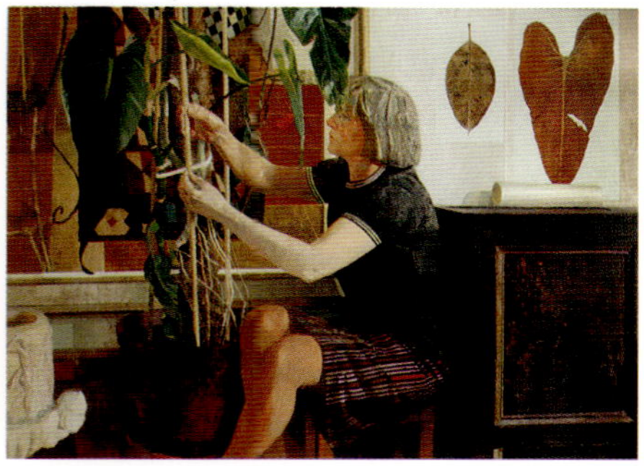

Blamey, Norman Charles 1914–2000
The New Shoot 1970
oil on canvas 114.3 x 165
PRSMG : P1773

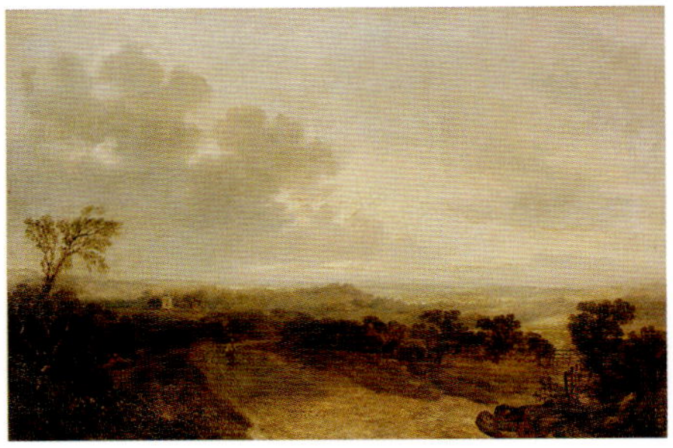

Boddington, Henry John 1811–1865
The Gypsy Encampment
oil on canvas 50.8 x 76.5
PRSMG : P1428

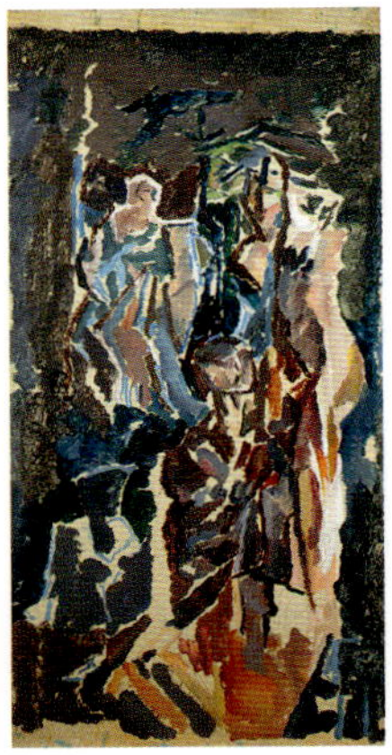

Bomberg, David 1890–1957
Composition 1919
oil on paper 88 x 37.5
PRSMG : P1853

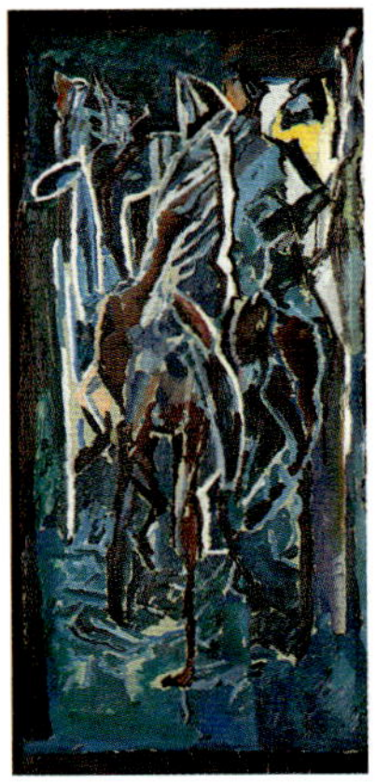

Bomberg, David 1890–1957
Composition: Stable Interior – Horses with Riders 1919
oil on paper 88 x 37.5
PRSMG : P1852

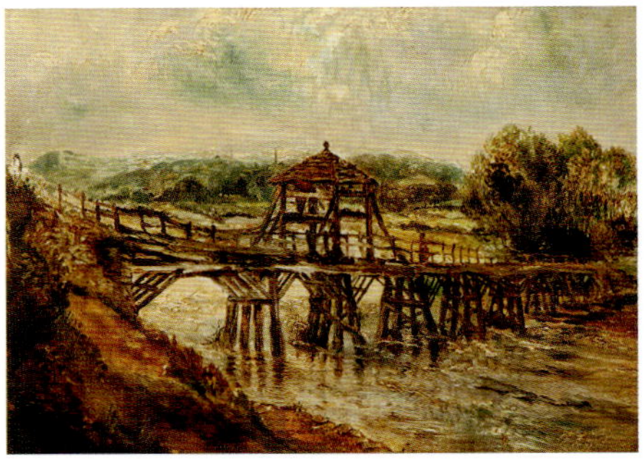

Bond, William Joseph Julius Caesar 1833–1926
Avenham Bridge, Preston, 1857
oil on canvas (?) 19 x 33
PRSMG : 2011.99

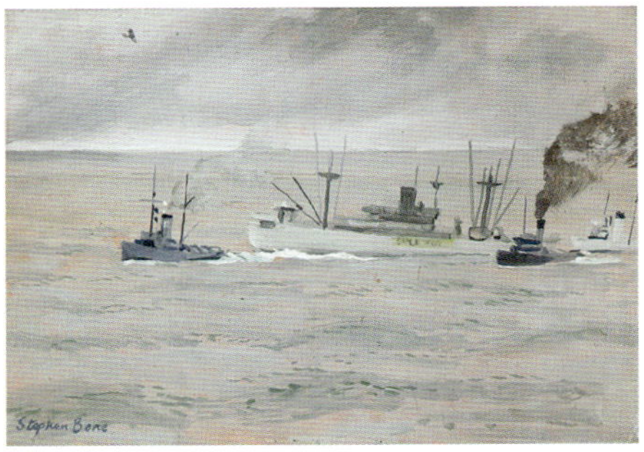

Bone, Stephen 1904–1958
Bringing in a Casualty 1944
oil on board 22.8 x 34.5
PRSMG : P1354

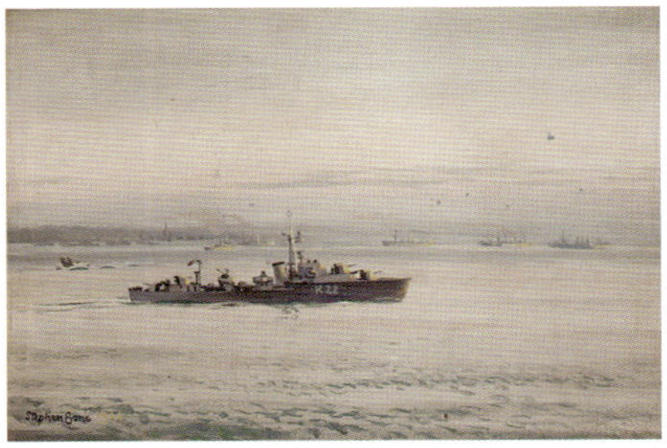

Bone, Stephen 1904–1958
Destroyer off the Normandy Beaches 1944
oil on board 35.5 x 50.8
PRSMG : P1109

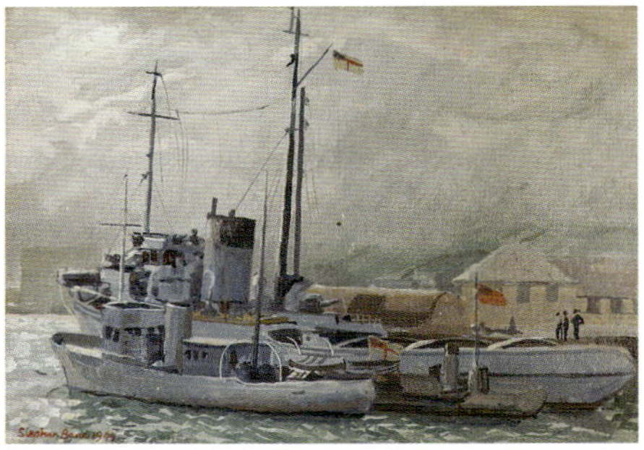

Bone, Stephen 1904–1958
HM Rescue Tug 'Samsonia', with Water-Boat and HM Yacht 'Martinetta' 1944
oil on board 25.5 x 35.5
PRSMG : P1355

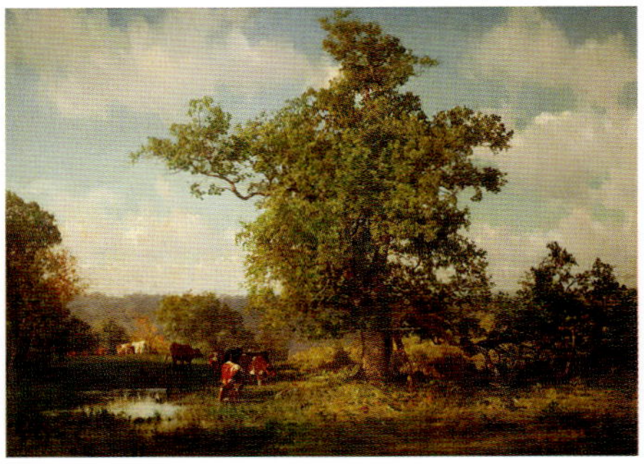

Bonheur, Auguste-François 1824–1884
Oak Tree and Sylvan Glade 1860–1884
oil on canvas 71 x 102.1
PRSMG : P48

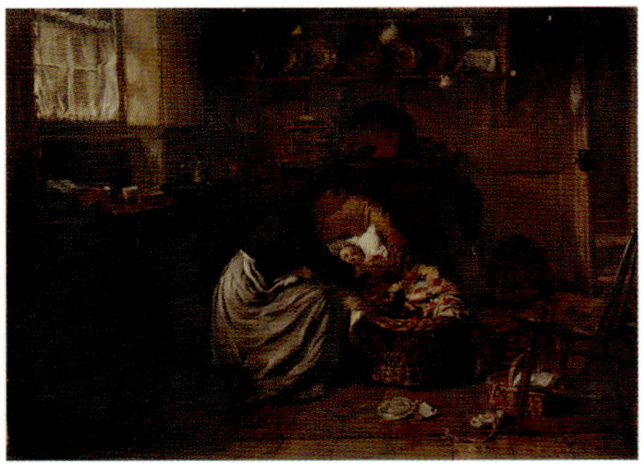

Booker, H. active 1850–1900
Come to Me
oil on canvas 45.8 x 61
PRSMG : P49

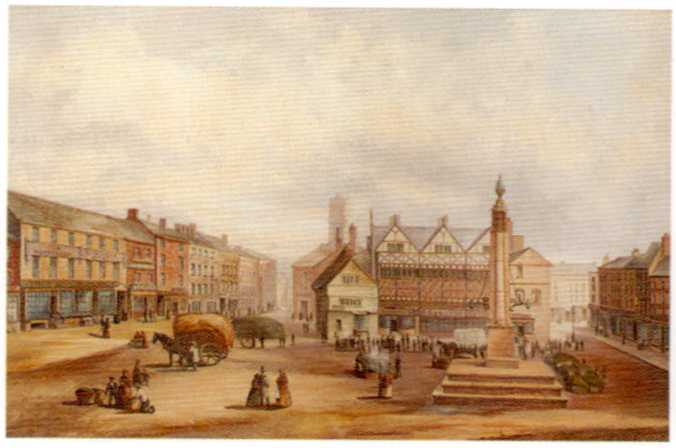

Booth, H. C.
Market Square, Preston 1851
oil on canvas 51 x 76.2
PRSMG : P1423

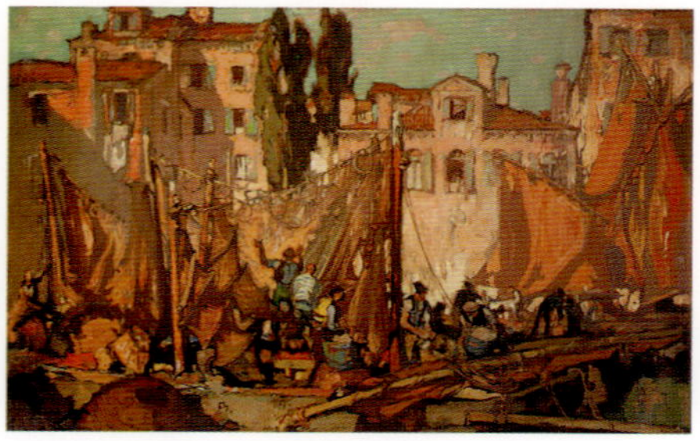

Brangwyn, Frank 1867–1956
Fishermen's Quarters, Venice 1890–1940
oil on canvas 62 x 97.5
PRSMG : P50

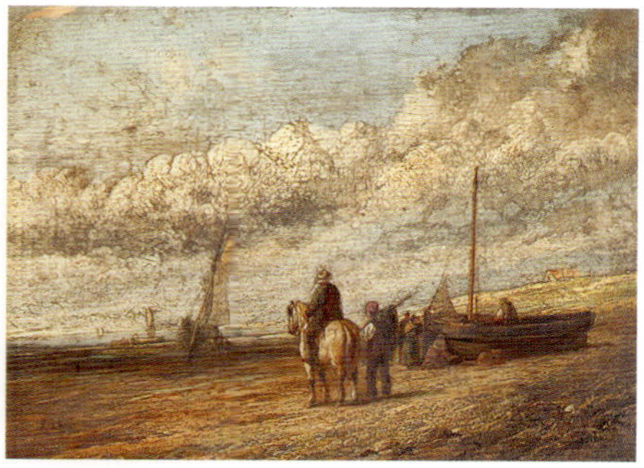

Bridgehouse, Robert 1818–1881
Waiting for the Tide
oil on canvas (?) 25.5 x 35.7
PRSMG : P1865

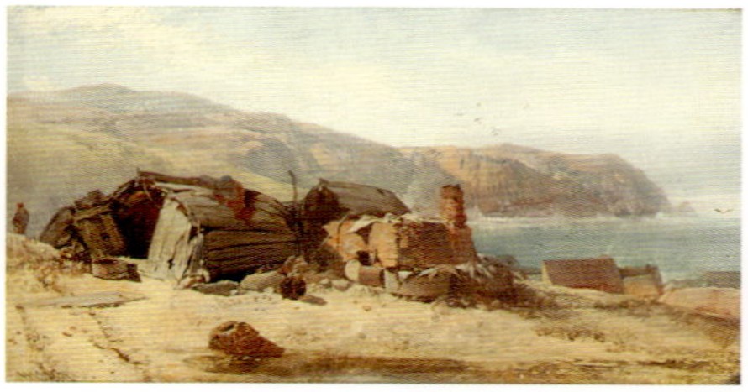

Bright, Henry 1810–1873
Coast Scene
oil on canvas 16.5 x 31.8
PRSMG : P51

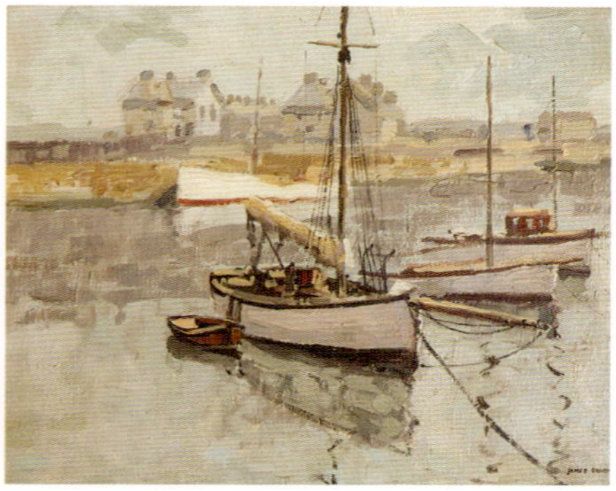

Brindle, James active 1850–1900
Glasson Dock, Lancaster
oil on board 24.8 x 31.7
PRSMG : P1544

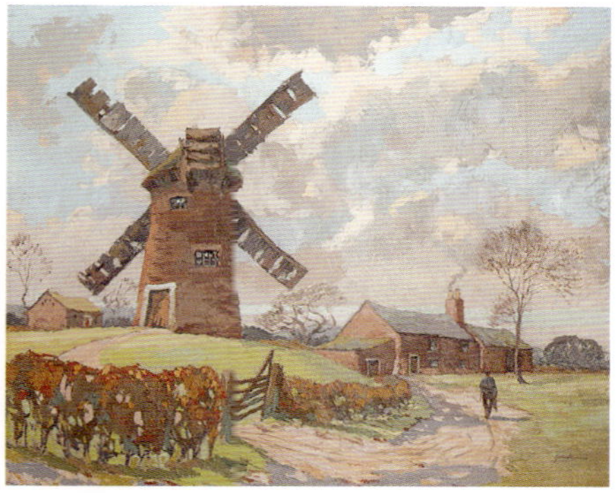

Brindle, James active 1850–1900
The Mill in the Fylde (Treale Mill)
oil on canvas 50.3 x 61
PRSMG : P1657

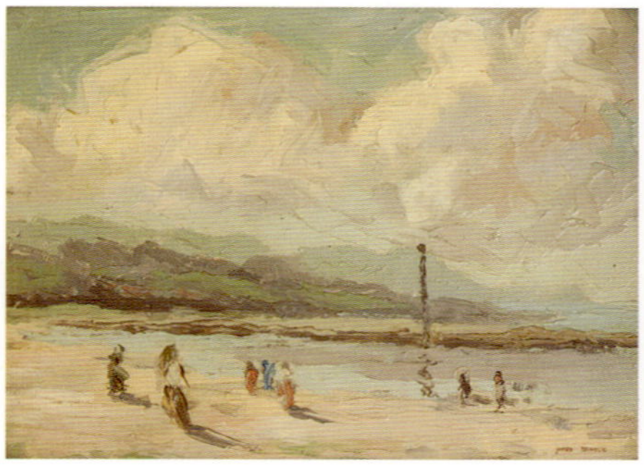

Brindle, James active 1850–1900
Welsh Coast
oil on board 22.9 x 31.7
PRSMG : P1545

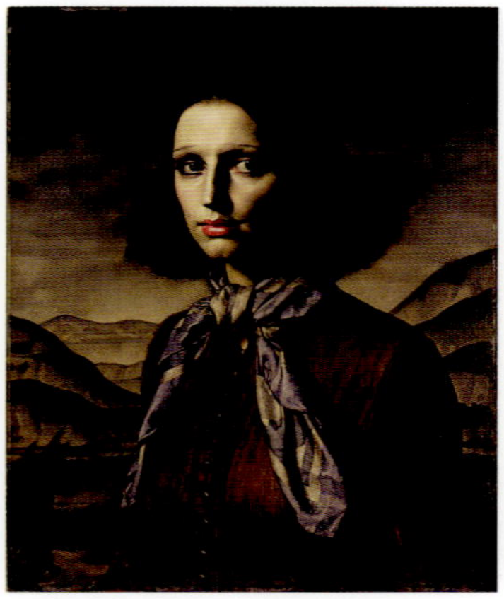

Brockhurst, Gerald Leslie 1890–1978
Dorette 1933
oil on panel 61 x 49.5
PRSMG : P56

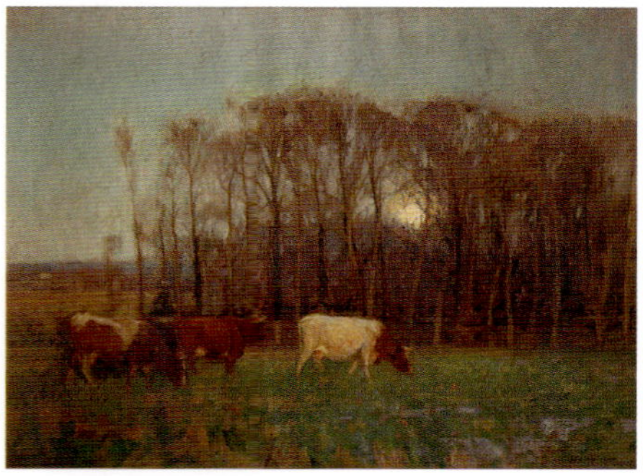

Brown, John Alfred Arnesby 1866–1955
Fading Day 1890–1910
oil on canvas 62 x 93
PRSMG : P60

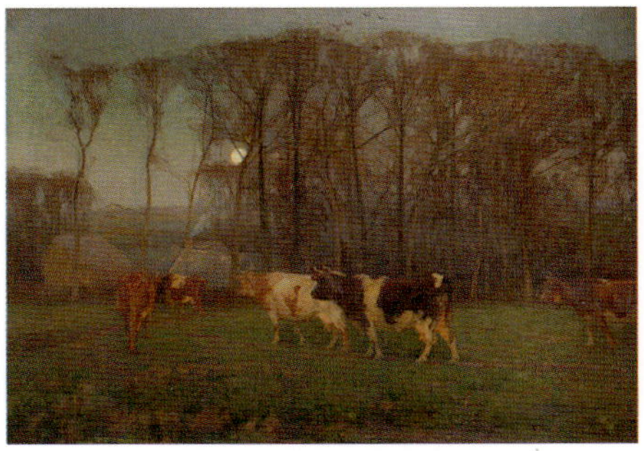

Brown, John Alfred Arnesby 1866–1955
Homeward 1896
oil on canvas 122.9 x 172
PRSMG : P58

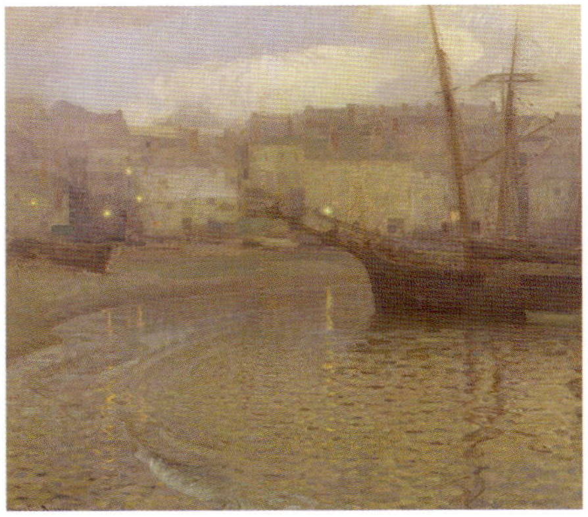

Brown, John Alfred Arnesby 1866–1955
The Harbour 1905
oil on canvas 92.5 x 105.5
PRSMG : P59

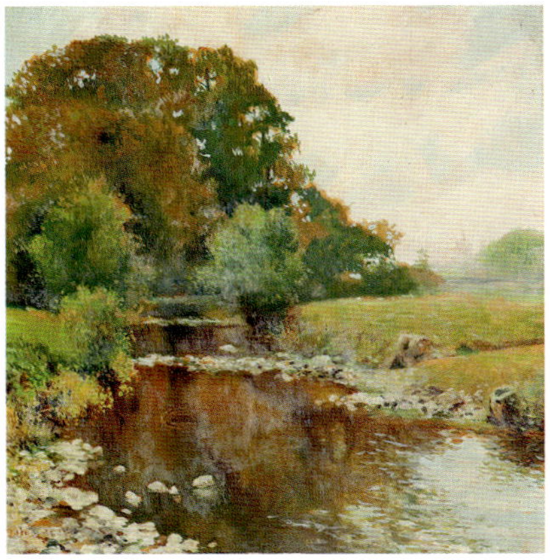

Burgess, William
Brock 1929
oil on panel 35.5 x 35.5
PRSMG : P62

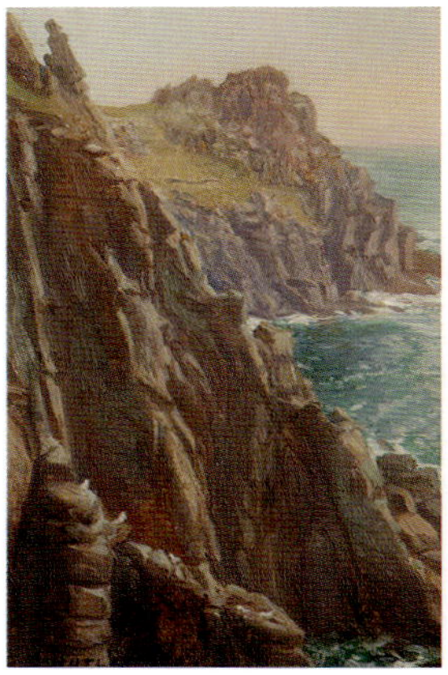

Butler, Charles Ernest 1864–1933
Rocks at Land's End 1890–1918
oil on card 19.8 x 11.9
PRSMG : P1866

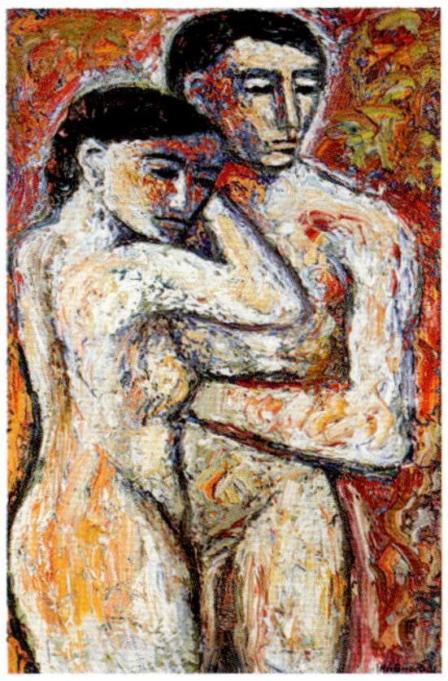

Byars, Hugh Gerard b.1957
Untitled and Adam and Eve 1991
oil on canvas 130 x 78.5
PRSMG : 2005.191

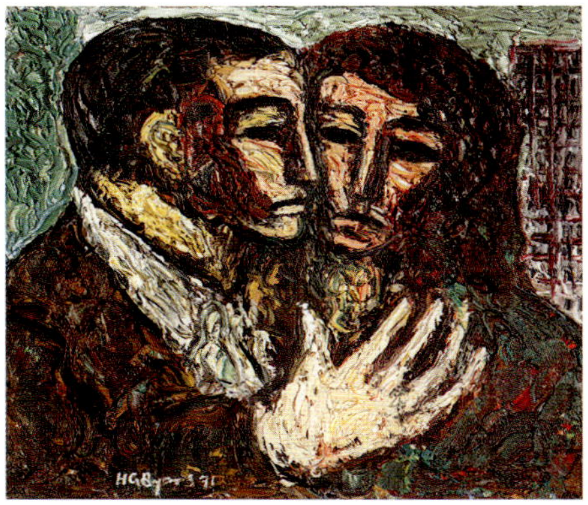

Byars, Hugh Gerard b.1957
Untitled and Embrace 1991
oil on canvas 62 x 72
PRSMG : 2005.192

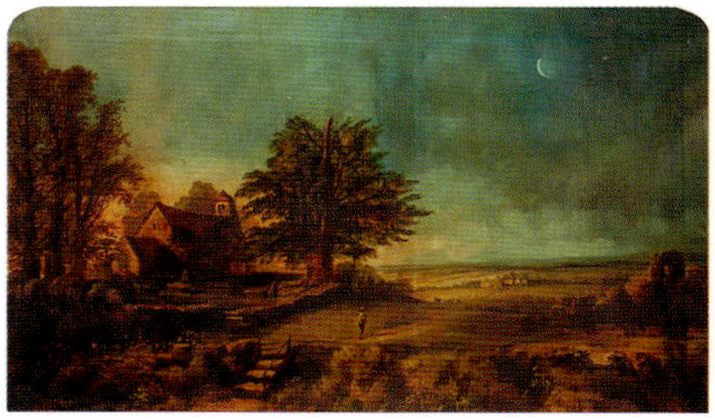

C., W. H.
Landscape, with Crescent Moon, Church and Graveyard 1878
oil on canvas 82.5 x 140
PRSMG : P1967

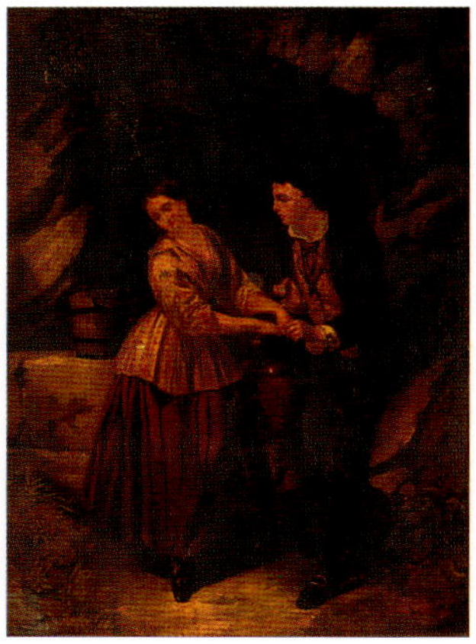

Calland, G. D.
A Man and a Woman by a Well 1848
oil on canvas 61 x 47.5
PRSMG : P1867

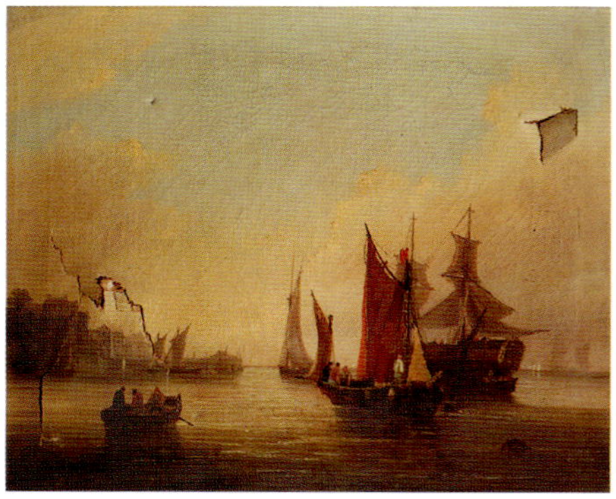

Calvert, Frederick 1785–1845
Sea View
oil on canvas 45.5 x 61.3
PRSMG : P65

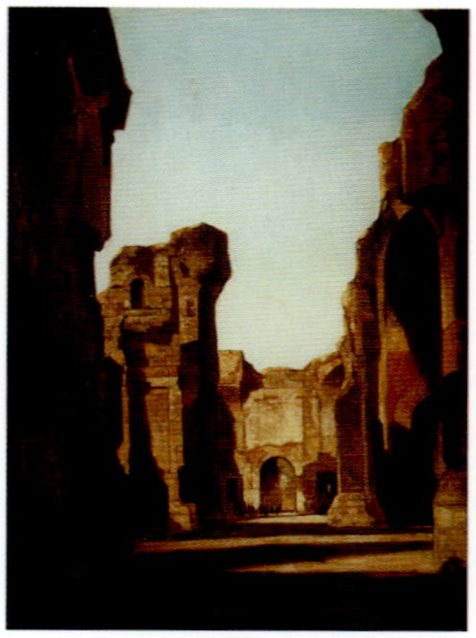

Cameron, David Young 1865–1945
The Baths of Caracalla 1924
oil on canvas 105.5 x 90.2
PRSMG : P66

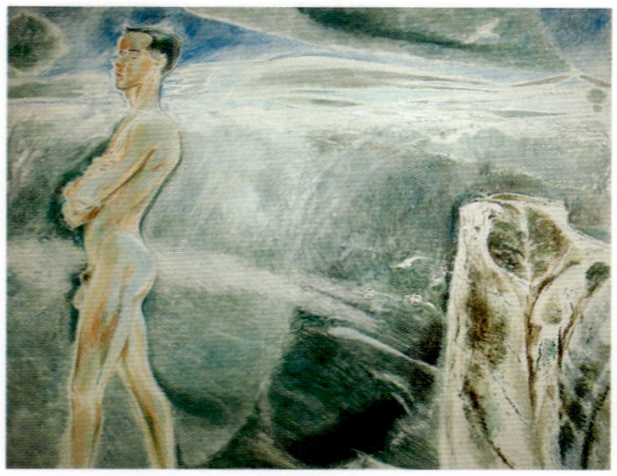

Camp, Jeffery b.1923
South Coast Walking 1985
oil on canvas 200 x 260
PRSMG : P1857

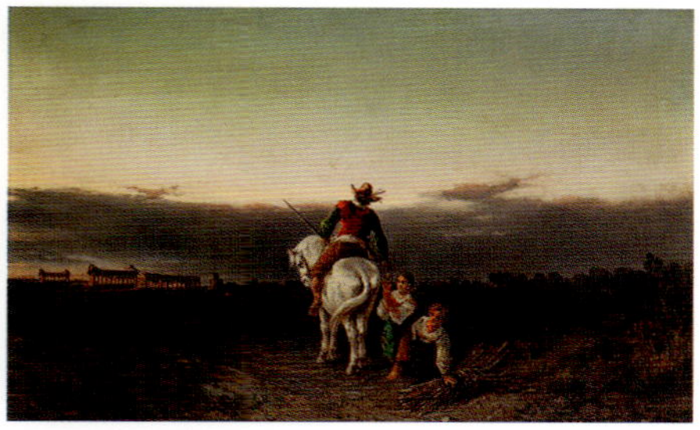

Carelli, Consalvo 1818–1900
Landscape with Figures and Classical Ruins 1850–1900
oil on canvas 40.5 x 67.3
PRSMG : P1550

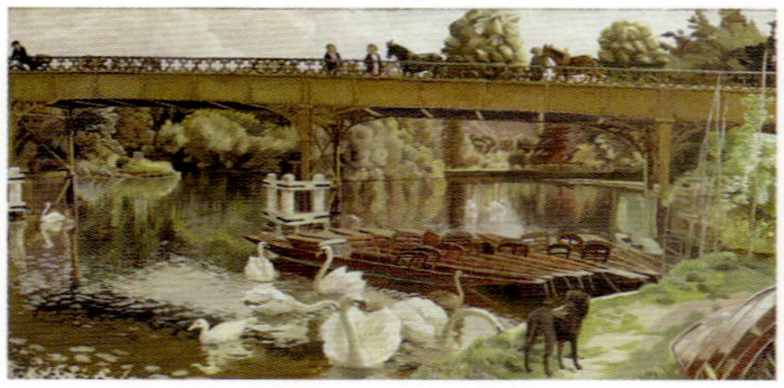

Carline, Hilda Anne 1889–1950
Swans, Cookham Bridge 1935
oil on canvas 38 x 76.6
PRSMG : P69

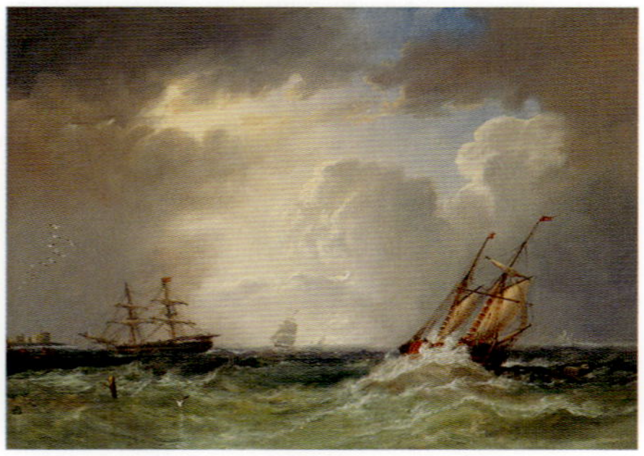

Carmichael, John Wilson 1799–1868
Seascape – Boats in Sail 1847
oil on panel 25 x 35.5
PRSMG : P1426

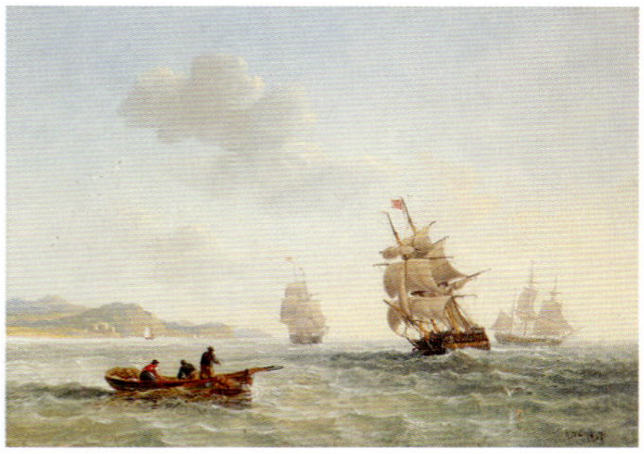

Carmichael, John Wilson 1799–1868
Seascape with Boats and Fishermen 1847
oil on panel 25.5 x 35.5
PRSMG : P1427

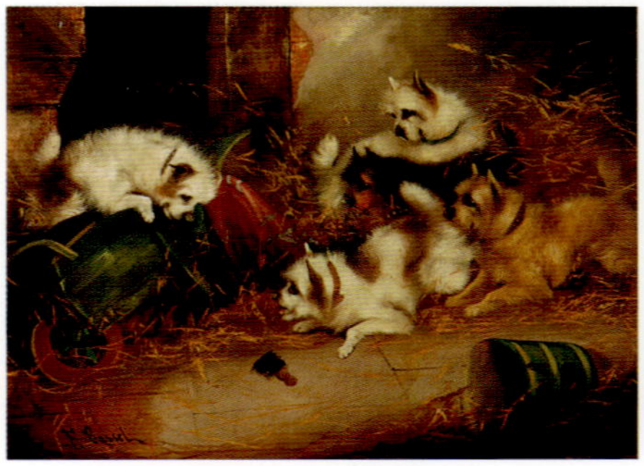

Cassel, F. active 1830–1880
Playful Dogs
oil on canvas 30.5 x 40.8
PRSMG : P1540

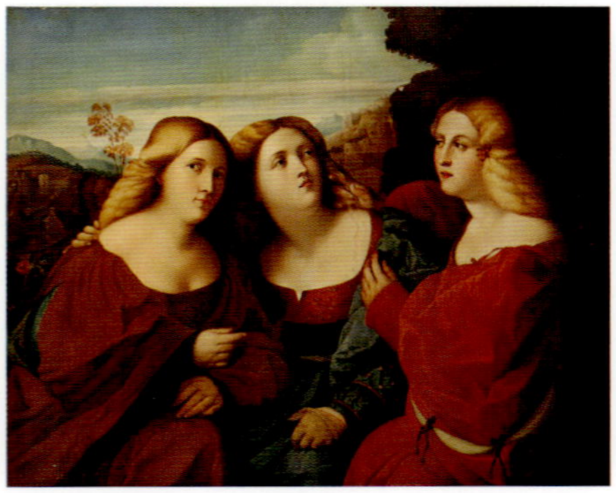

Castelli active 19th C
The Three Sisters
oil on canvas 86.5 x 122
PRSMG : P626

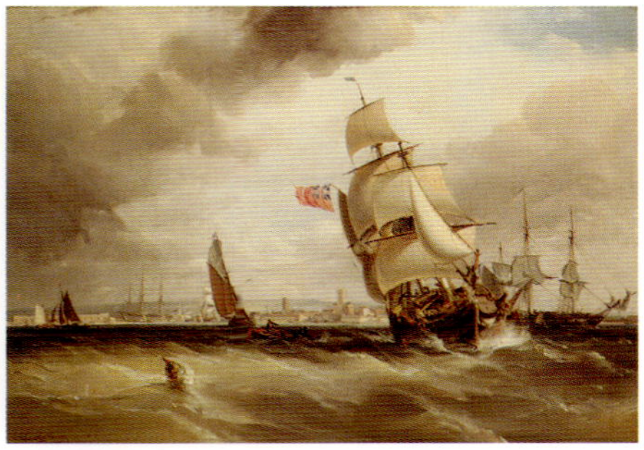

Chambers I, George 1803–1840
Off Portsmouth, in the Distance Nelson's Flagship, the 'Victory' 1839
oil on canvas 44.5 x 68.5
PRSMG : P72

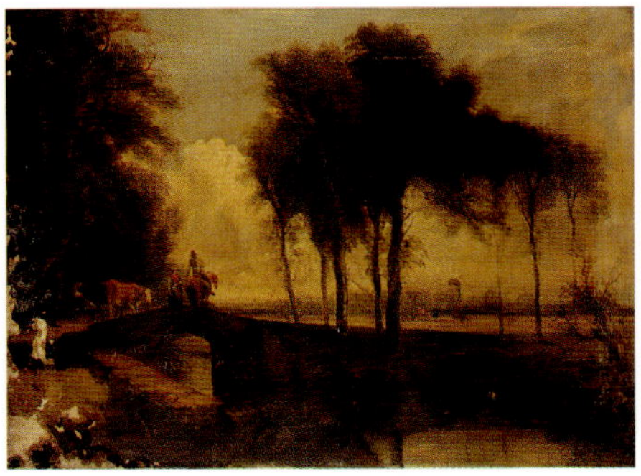

Charles, E. J. active 1870–1906
Landscape – Bridge with Cattle
oil on canvas 72.5 x 107
PRSMG : P1868

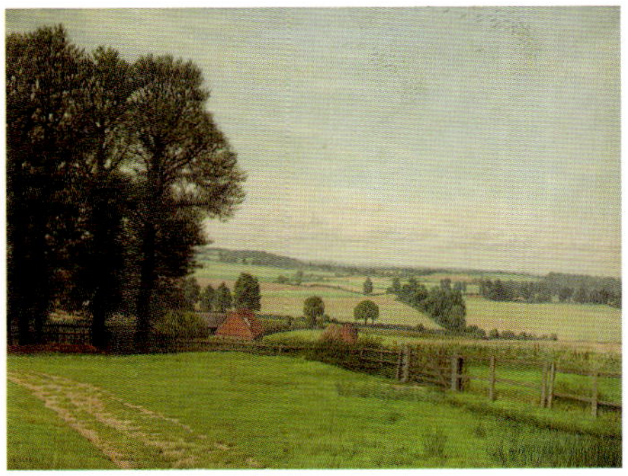

Chubb, Ralph Nicholas 1892–1960
A Berkshire Valley 1920
oil on canvas 71.5 x 92
PRSMG : P1608

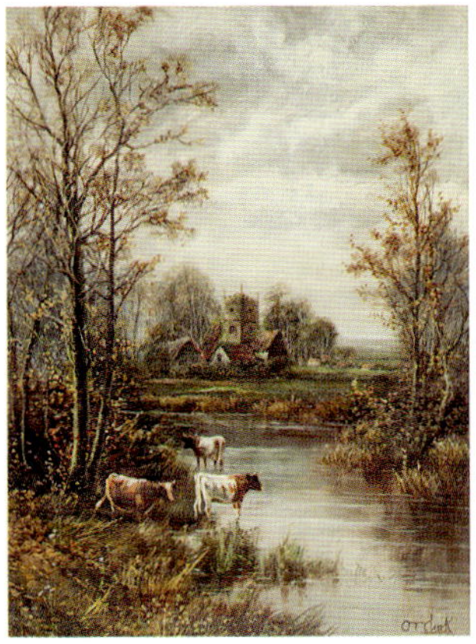

Clark, Octavius T. 1850–1921
Landscape with Cows 1870–1900
oil on canvas 35.5 x 25.5
PRSMG : P1878.1

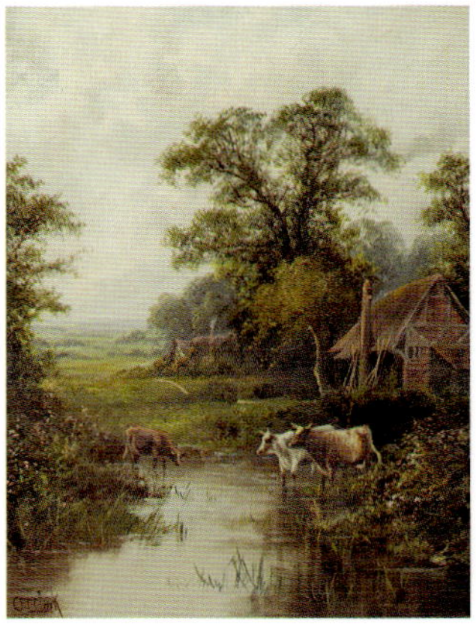

Clark, Octavius T. 1850–1921
Landscape with Cows 1870–1900
oil on canvas 35.5 x 25.5
PRSMG : P1878.2

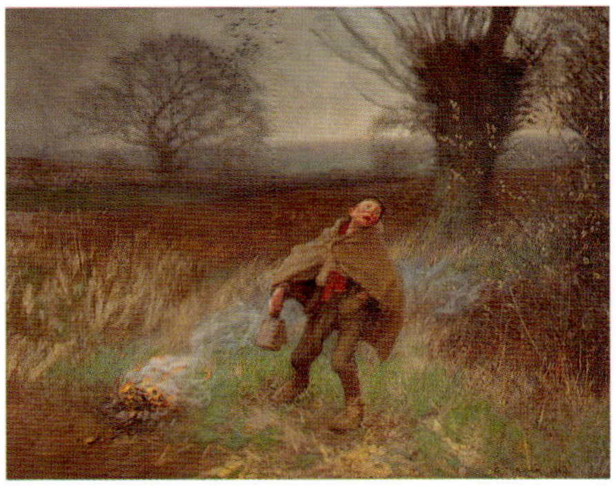

Clausen, George 1852–1944
Bird Scaring – March 1896
oil on canvas 127 x 151
PRSMG : P74

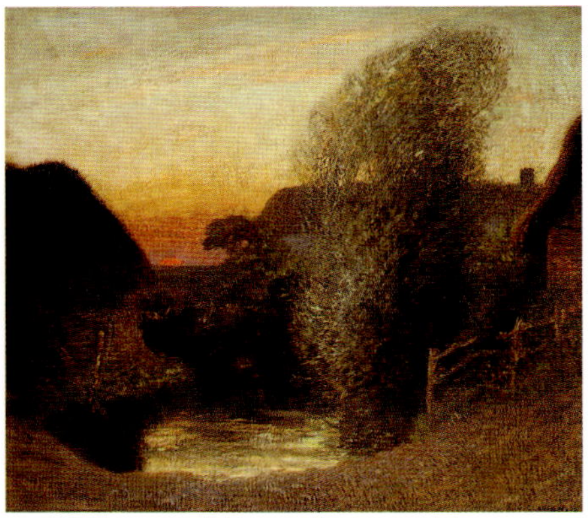

Clausen, George 1852–1944
Sunset 1907
oil on canvas 54 x 61.8
PRSMG : P75

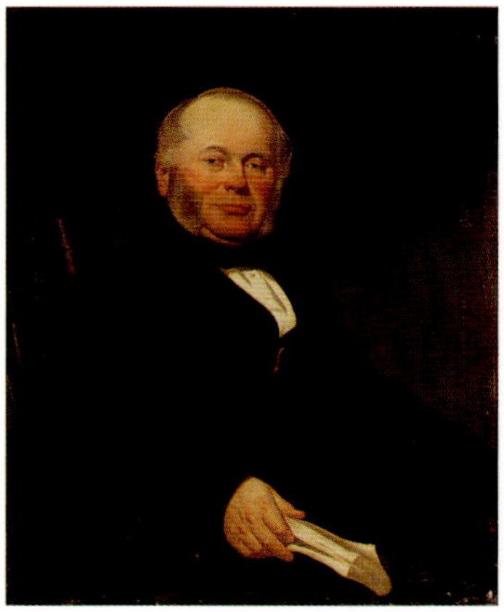

Clay, Alfred Barron 1831–1868
Phillip Park 1856
oil on canvas 91.5 x 71
PRSMG : P611

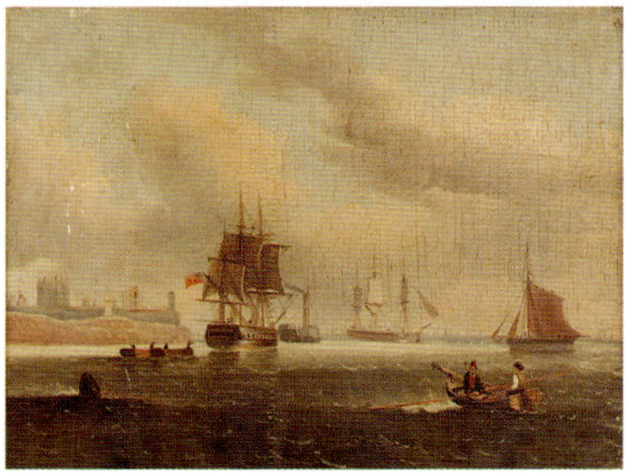

Clayton, John active 1800–1850
Harbour Scene
oil on canvas 30.5 x 40.5
PRSMG : P1965

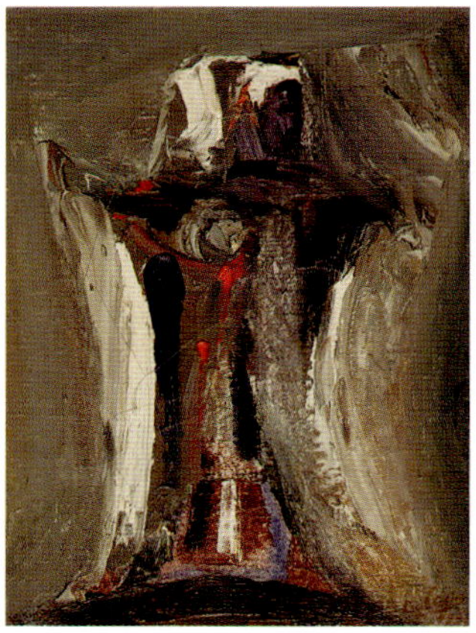

Collins, Cecil 1908–1989
The Priestess 1958
oil on canvas 25.5 x 18
PRSMG : P2337

Facing page: Hoyland, Francis, b.1930, *Requiem,* 1988, Grundy Art Gallery (p. 98)

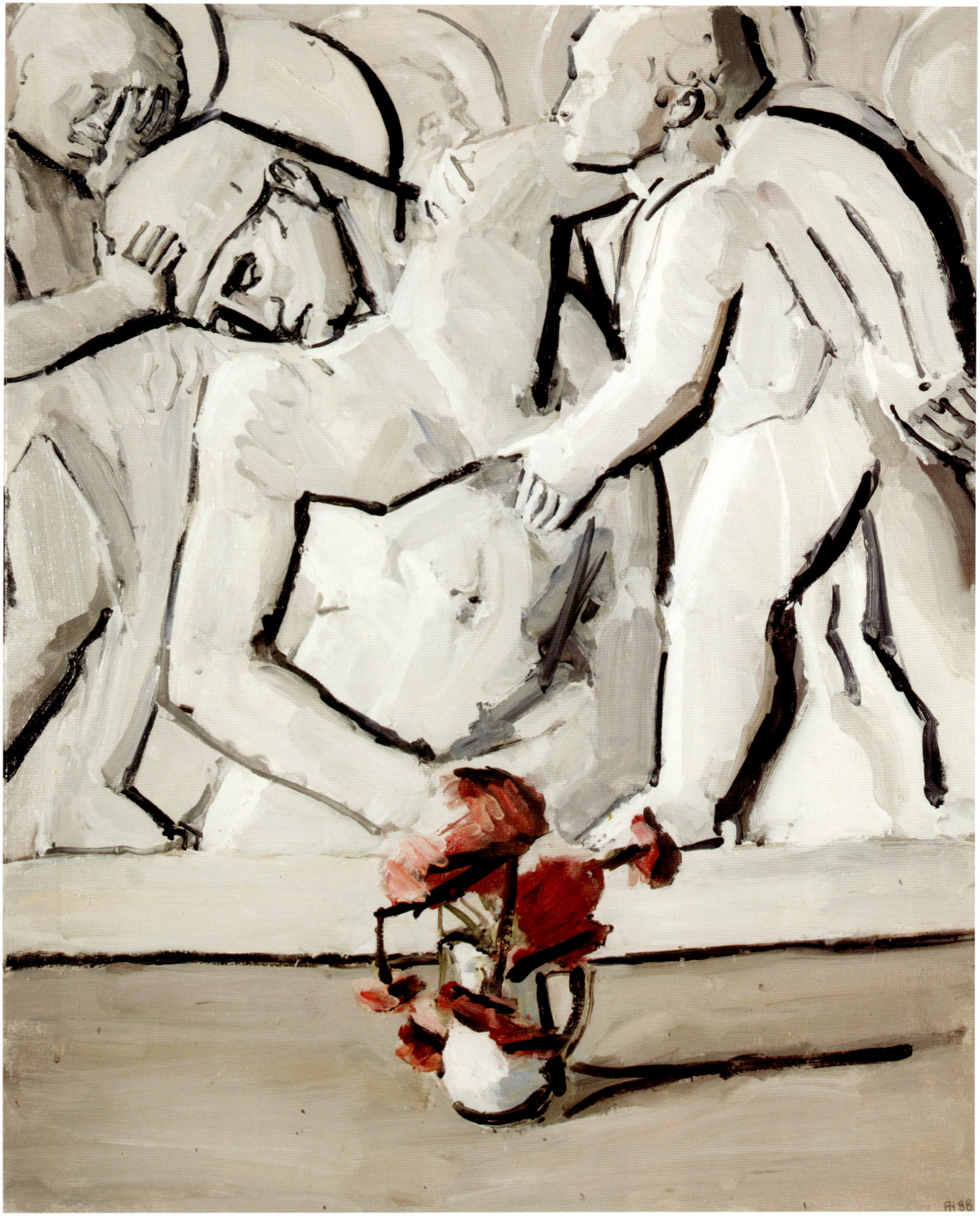

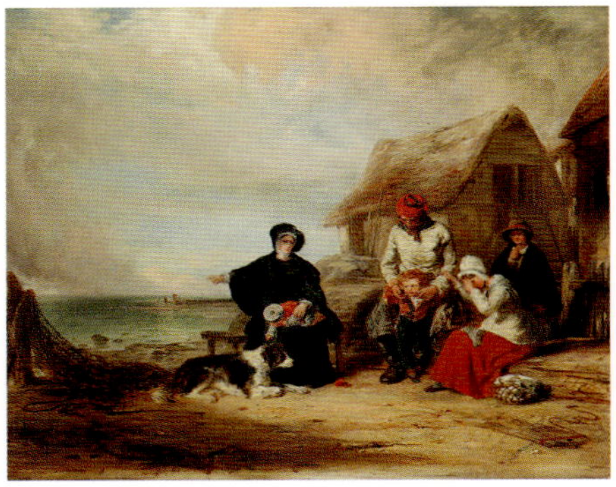

Collins, William 1788–1847
The Mariner's Widow 1835
oil on panel 61 x 76.3
PRSMG : P79

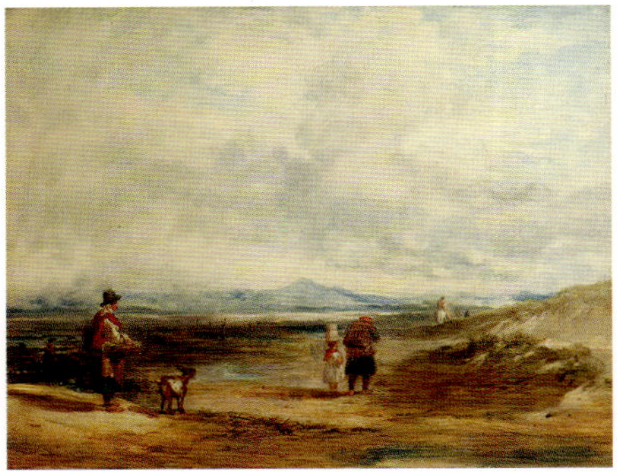

Collins, William 1788–1847
Welsh Peasants Returning from Market; Scene near Barmouth 1843
oil on panel 30.5 x 40.5
PRSMG : P80

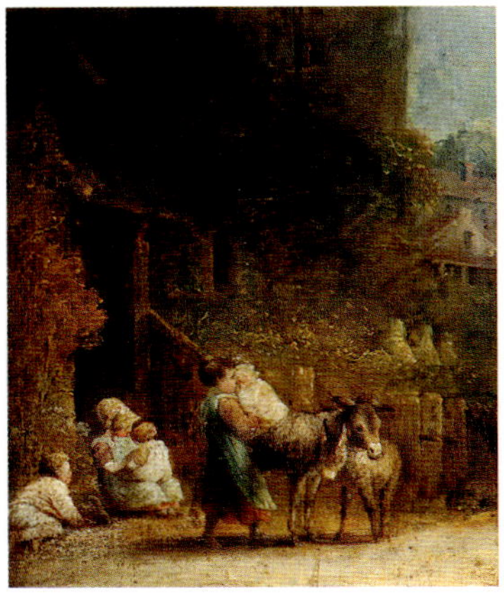

Collins, William 1788–1847
My Favourite Cottage
oil on panel 29.2 x 22.8
PRSMG : P1546

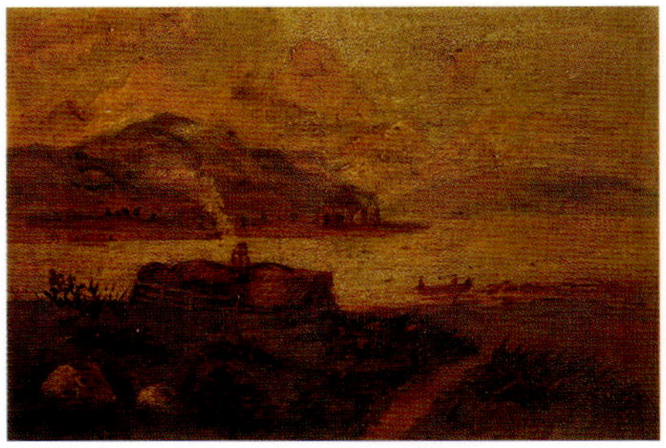

Cook, E. active 1850–1900
Landscape – Lake Scene, Croft with Smoking Chimney 1896
oil on panel 17.5 x 25.5
PRSMG : P1869

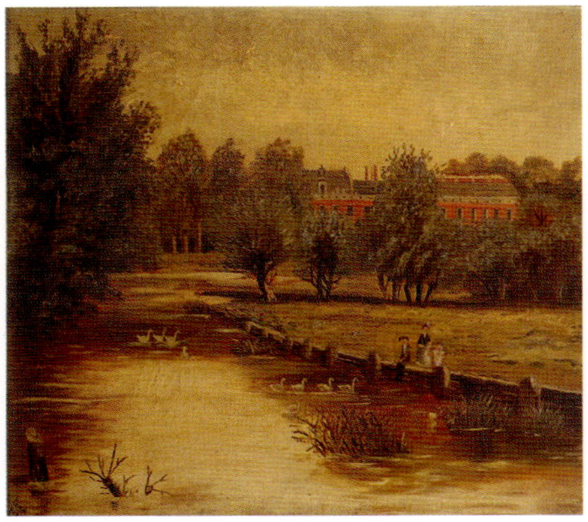

Cook, E. active 1850–1900
Landscape – Three Figures by a Riverside 1899
oil on canvas 41 x 50.7
PRSMG : P1872

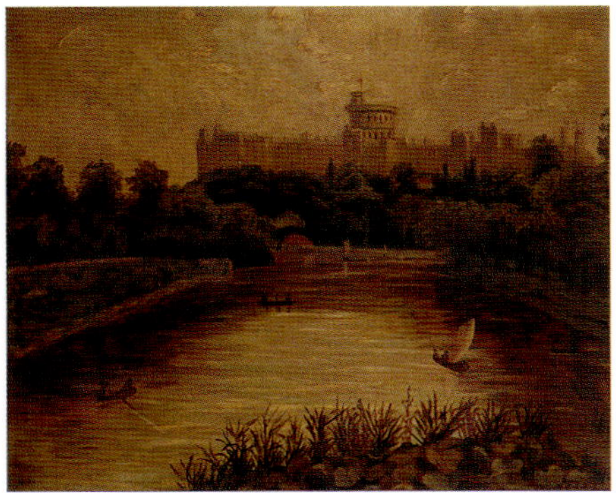

Cook, E. active 1850–1900
Windsor Castle 1899
oil on canvas 42.5 x 50.6
PRSMG : P1976

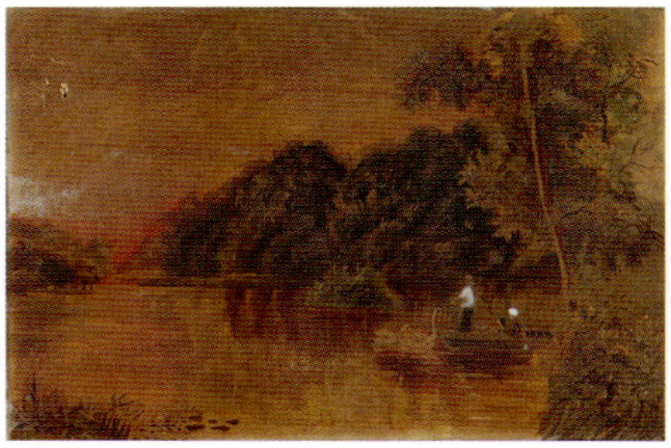

Cook, E. active 1850–1900
Landscape – Figures in a Boat
oil on canvas 25.5 x 40.7
PRSMG : P1870

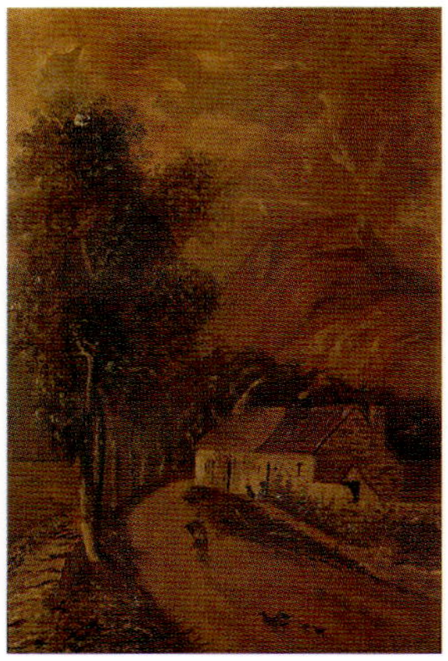

Cook, E. active 1850–1900
Landscape – Lane Scene
oil on canvas 53.4 x 35.6
PRSMG : P1871

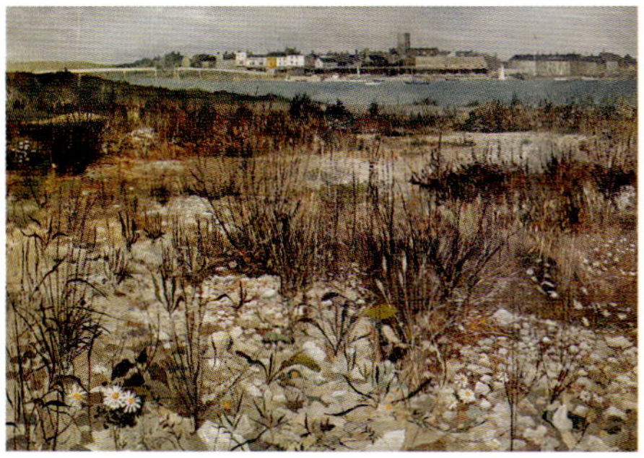

Cooke, Anthony R. b.1933
Shoreham Beach No.18 1967
oil on hardboard 91.5 x 122
PRSMG : P1744

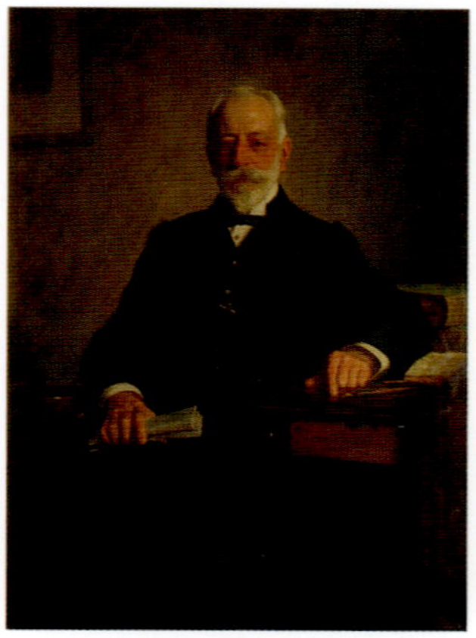

Cooke, John Percy 1870–1940
Sir F. W. Tomlinson 1906
oil on canvas 127 x 101.5
PRSMG : P81

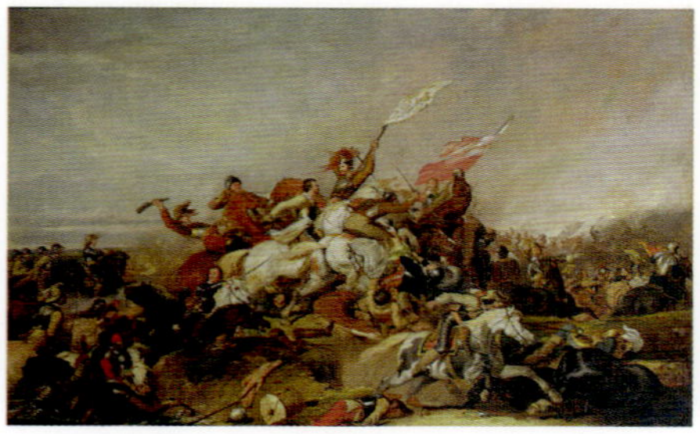

Cooper, Abraham 1787–1868
Marston Moor 1819
oil on panel 67.8 x 103.2
PRSMG : P909

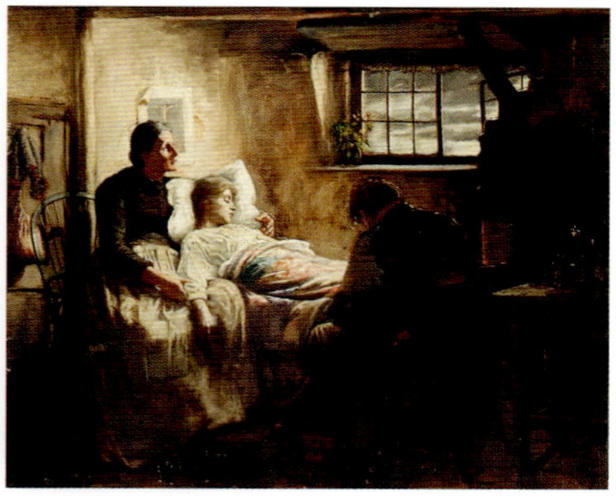

Cooper, Florence M. active 1886–1935
Dawn 1889
oil on canvas 71 x 91.5
PRSMG : P82

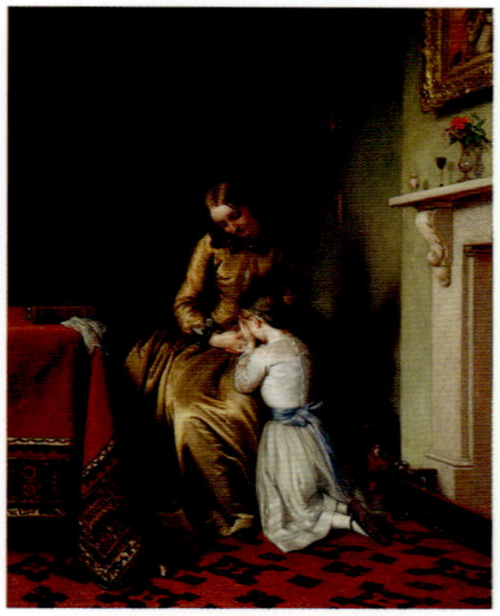

Cope, Charles West 1811–1890
Prayer Time – Mrs Cope and Her Daughter Florence 1854
oil on canvas 71 x 55.3
PRSMG : P84

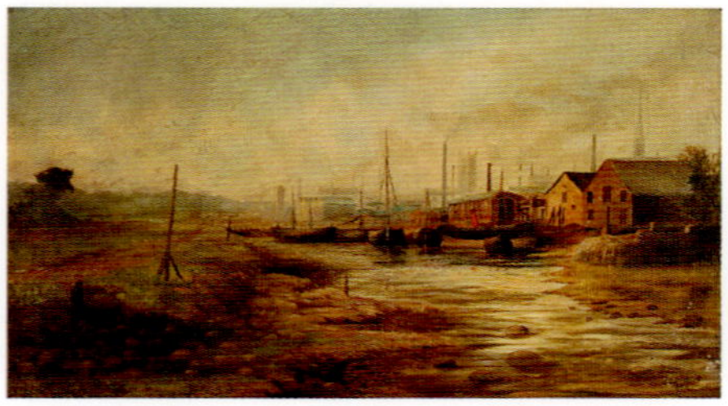

Copland
Evening – Old Quay, Preston on Ribble 1884
oil on canvas 51 x 92
PRSMG : P1874

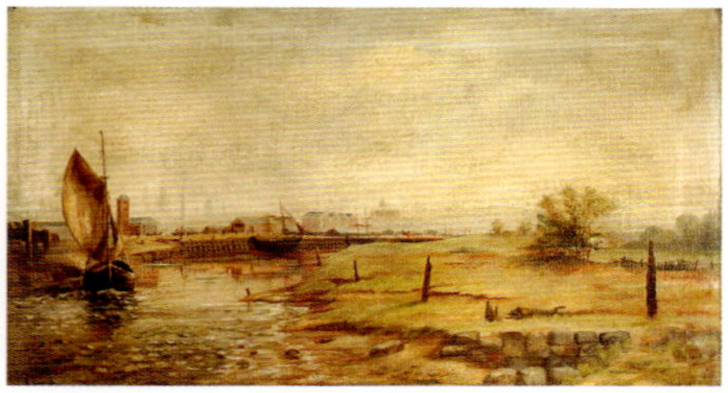

Copland
Morning – Old Quay, Preston on Ribble 1884
oil on canvas 51 x 92
PRSMG : P1873

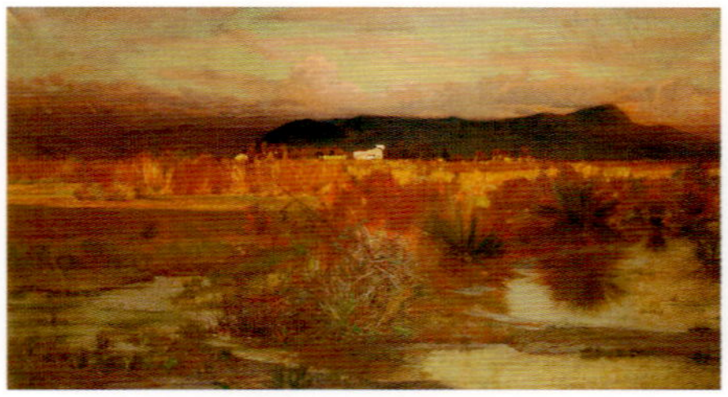

Corbet, Matthew Ridley 1850–1902
Afterglow in Italy – Evening
oil on canvas 114.3 x 212
PRSMG : P86

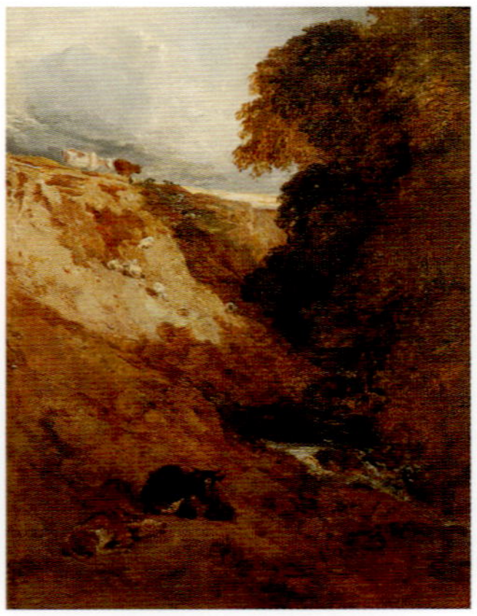

Cotman, John Sell 1782–1842
Pastoral Landscape 1812
oil on panel 45.5 x 32.2
PRSMG : P598

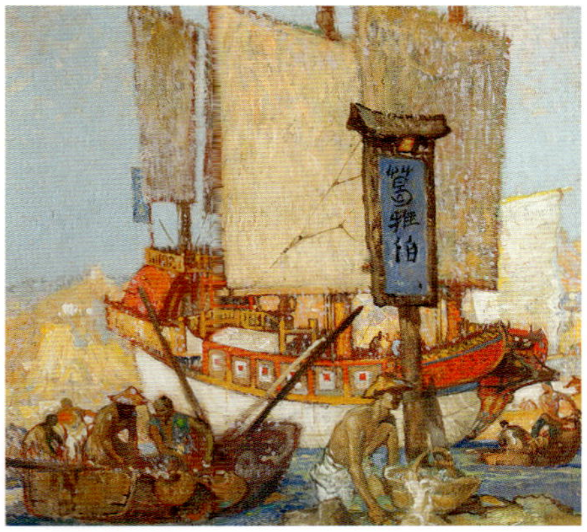

Cox, Elijah Albert 1876–1955
In the Land Where Time Moves Slowly
tempera on board 56.9 x 62
PRSMG : P1246

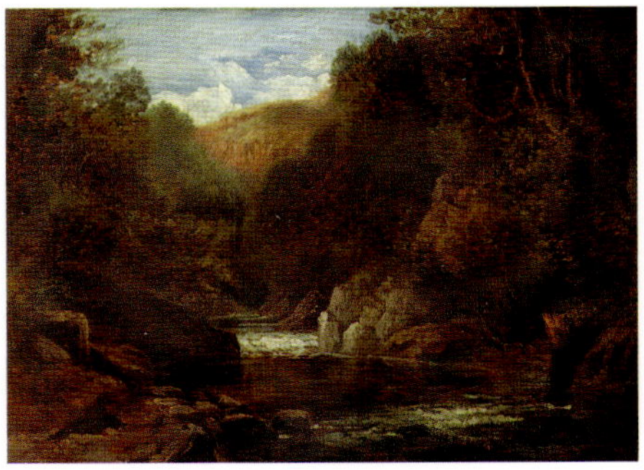

Cox the elder, David 1783–1859
Dell Scene near Betws-y-Coed
oil on canvas 30.5 x 44.5
PRSMG : P92

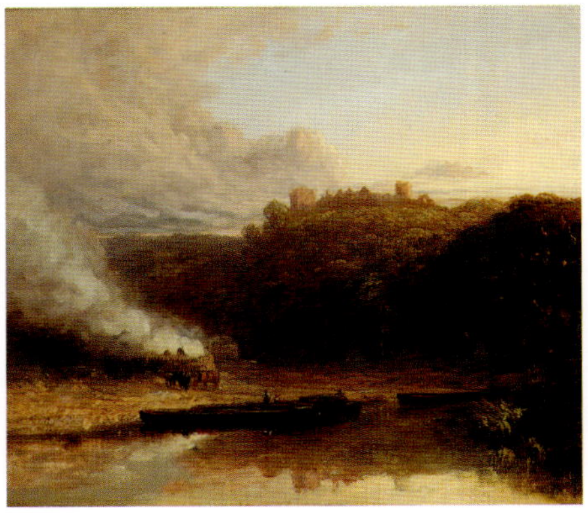

Cox the elder, David 1783–1859
Dudley Castle
oil on canvas 41.9 x 50.3
PRSMG : P94

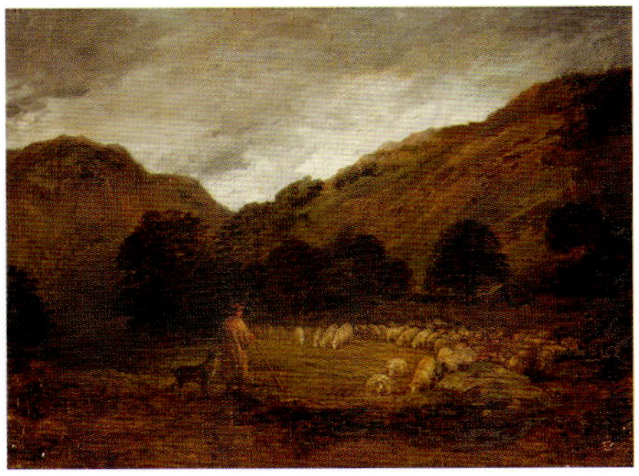

Cox the elder, David 1783–1859
Hilly Landscape, North Wales
oil on canvas 47.2 x 65.2
PRSMG : P91

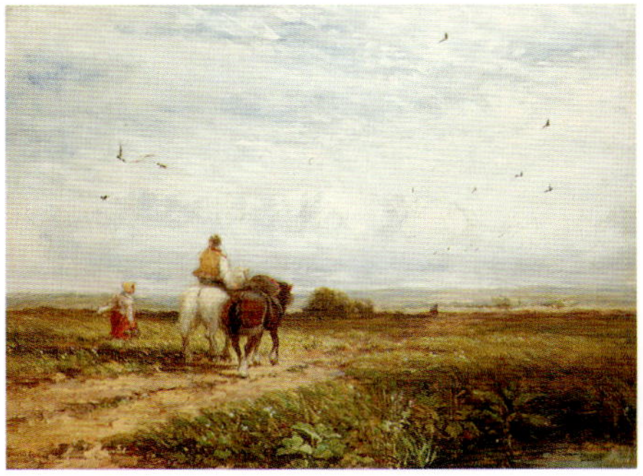

Cox the elder, David 1783–1859
The Way to the Hayfield
oil on canvas 33.3 x 44.5
PRSMG : P93

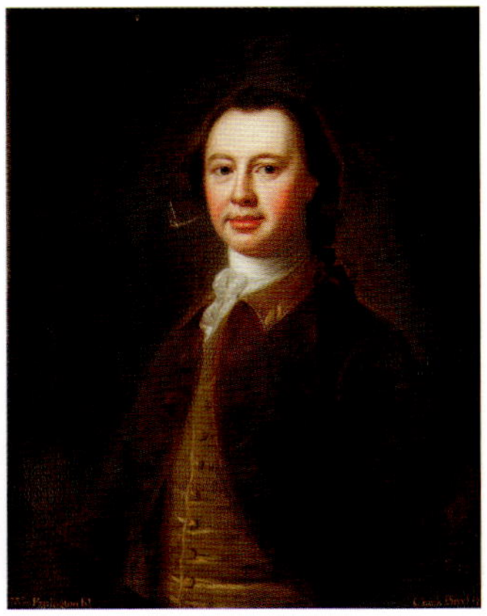

Cranke, William active 1730–1780
William Farington 1749
oil on canvas 75.5 x 64
PRSMG : LOAN7 (P)

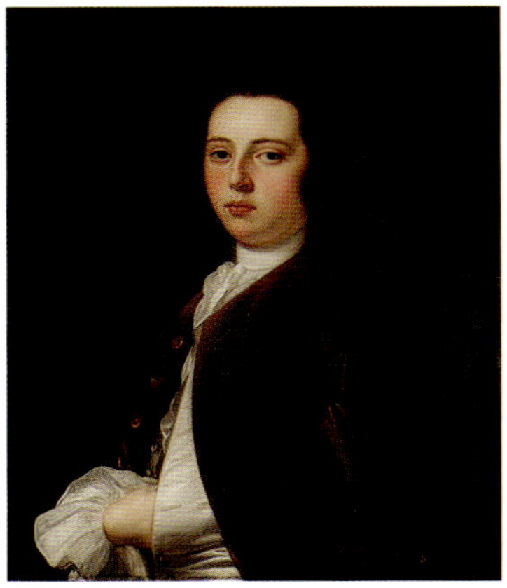

Cranke, William active 1730–1780
Henry Farington
oil on canvas 76.3 x 63.2
PRSMG : P1403

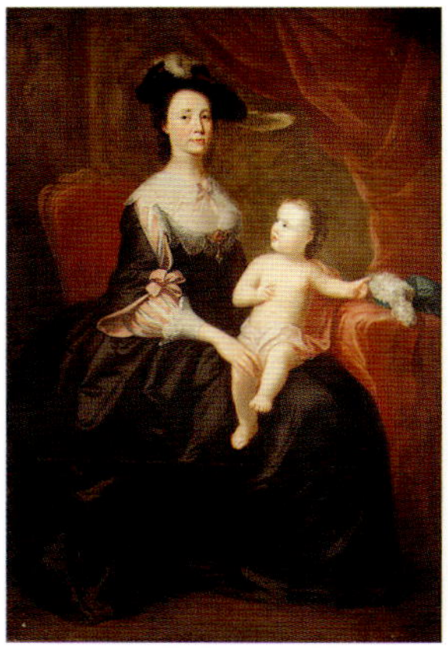

Cranke the elder, James 1707–1780
Mrs Winkley and Child
oil on canvas 165 x 114.5
PRSMG : P911

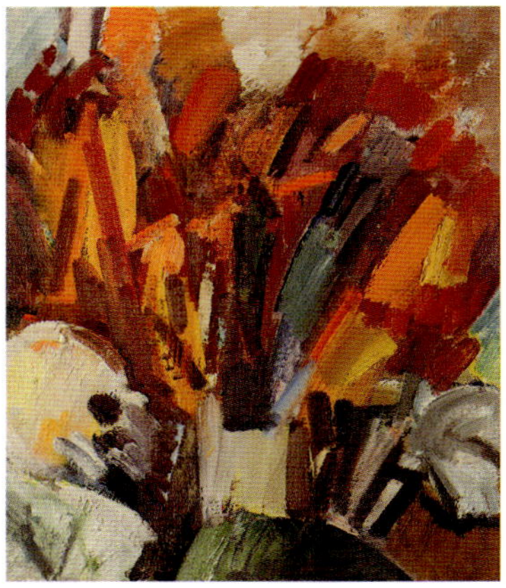

Creffield, Dennis b.1931
Flowers with Skull 1976
oil on canvas 92 x 77
PRSMG : 2009.251

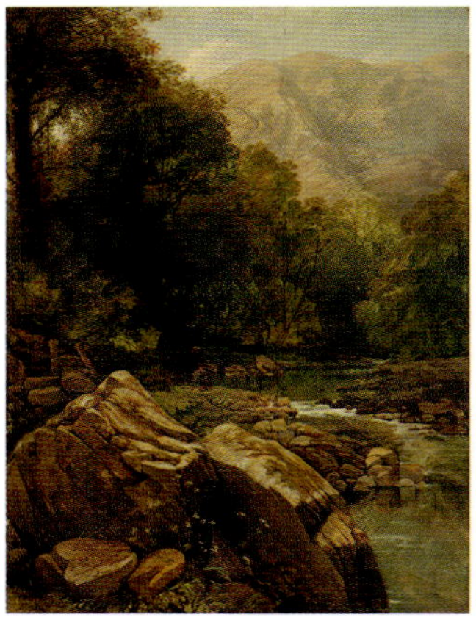

Creswick, Thomas 1811–1869
Summertime, Scene on the Llugwy, North Wales 1847
oil on panel 49.5 x 39.3
PRSMG : P106

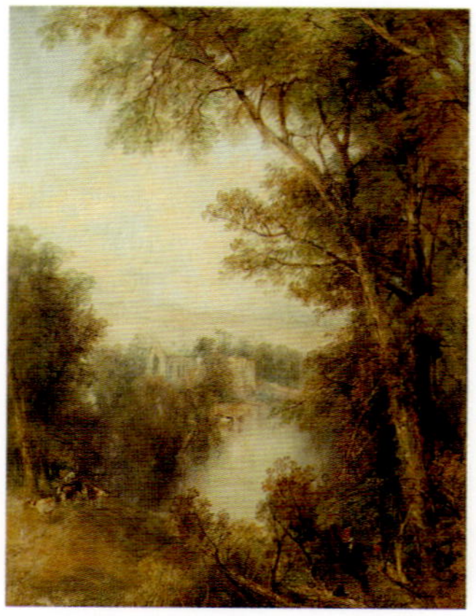

Creswick, Thomas 1811–1869
Bolton Abbey
oil on canvas 76.8 x 63.7
PRSMG : P108

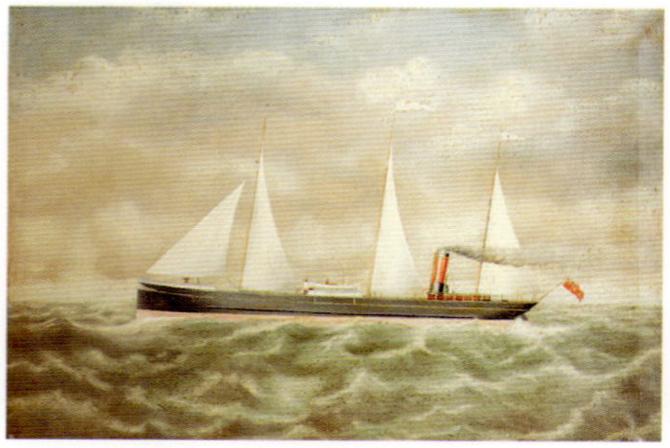

Crewdson, J. active 1900–1950
The 'Lady Alice Kenlis'
oil on canvas 67.3 x 98
PRSMG : P1364

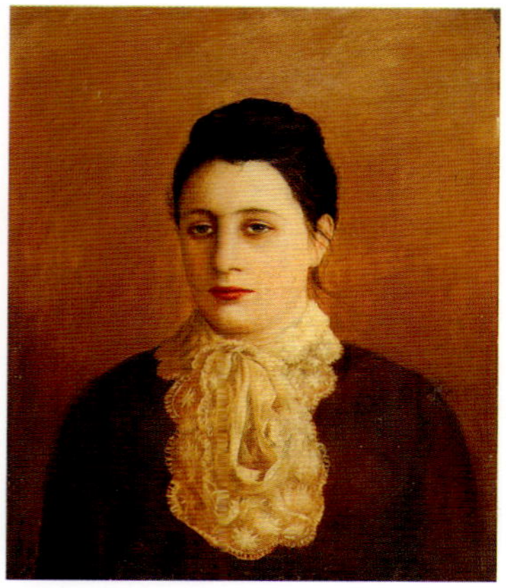

Crooke, Reginald Hoghton 1864–1929
Ida 1886–1887
oil on canvas 50.8 x 40.5
PRSMG : P109

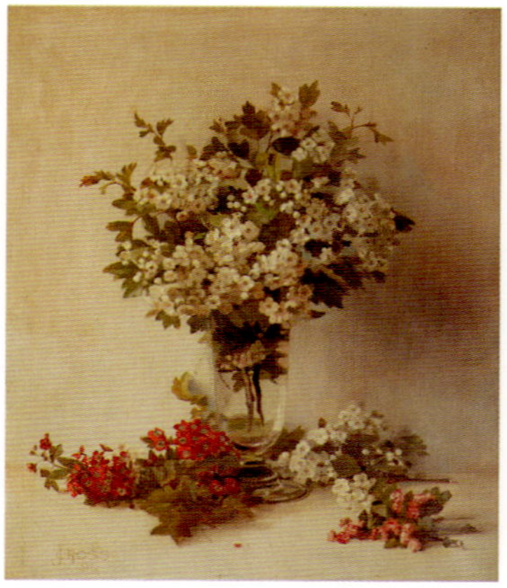

Cross, Joseph 1851–1897
Flower Piece 1894
oil on canvas 53.3 x 37.5
PRSMG : P1769

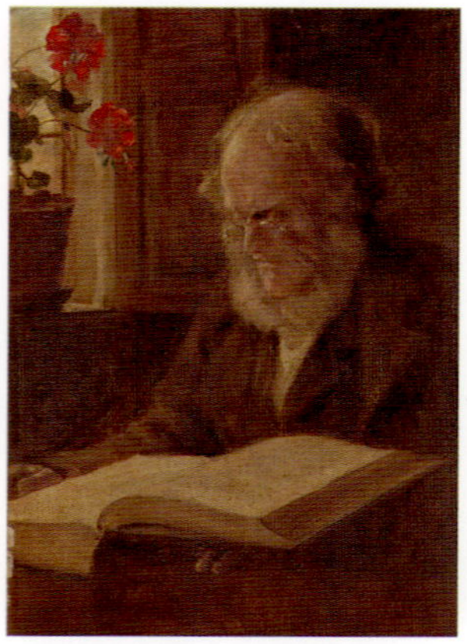

Cross, Joseph 1851–1897
Portrait of an Old Man 1896
oil on panel 35.5 x 25.5
PRSMG : P1768

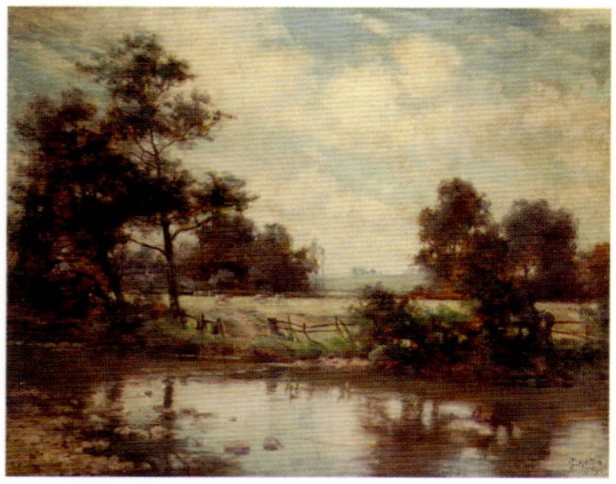

Cross, Joseph 1851–1897
The Stream, Brock 1897
oil on canvas 70 x 90.2
PRSMG : P112

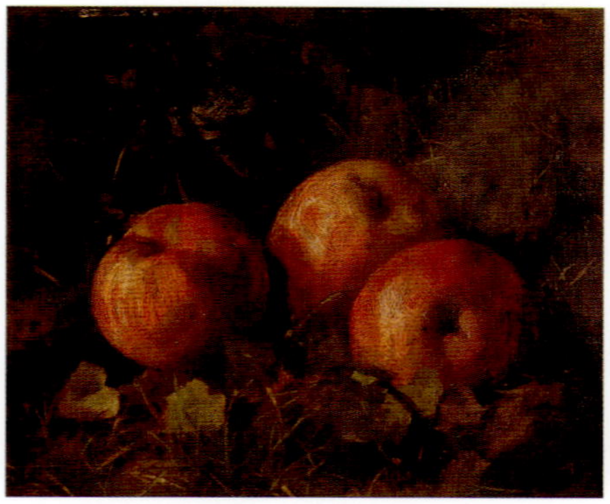

Cross, Joseph 1851–1897
Study of Apples
oil on canvas 21.4 x 26.1
PRSMG : P113

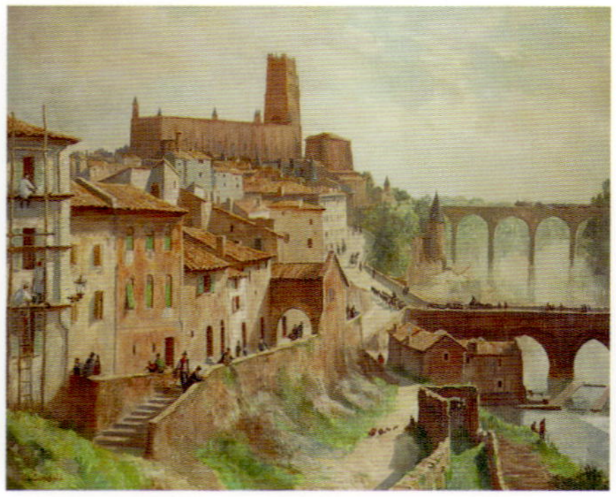

Cundall, Charles Ernest 1890–1971
Albi 1930
oil on canvas 59.8 x 76.2
PRSMG : P115

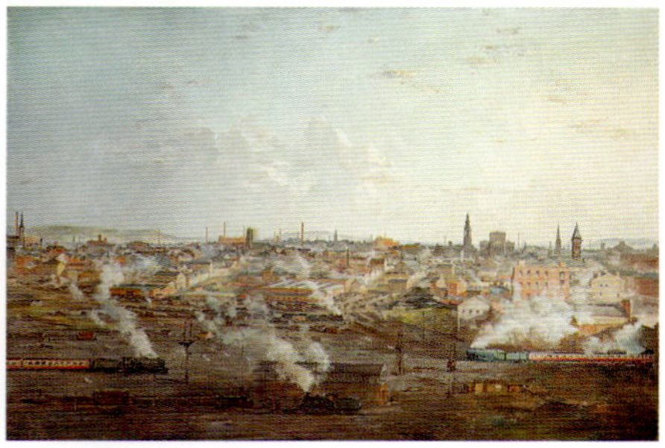

Cundall, Charles Ernest 1890–1971
Preston 1952
oil on canvas 85 x 148.5
PRSMG : P1404

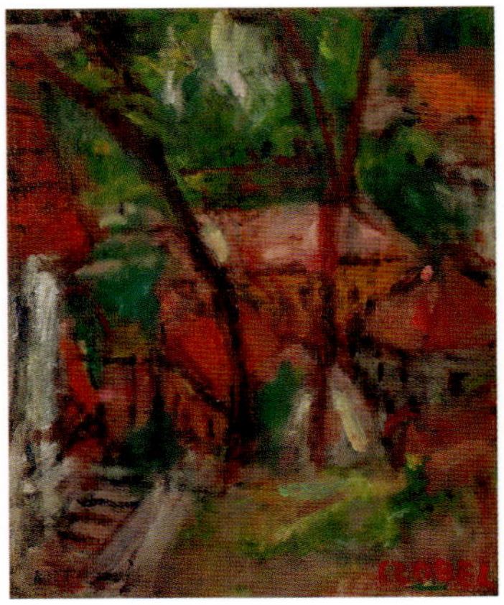

Czóbel, Béla Adalbert 1883–1976
Szentendre 1963
oil on canvas 65 x 54
PRSMG : P2348

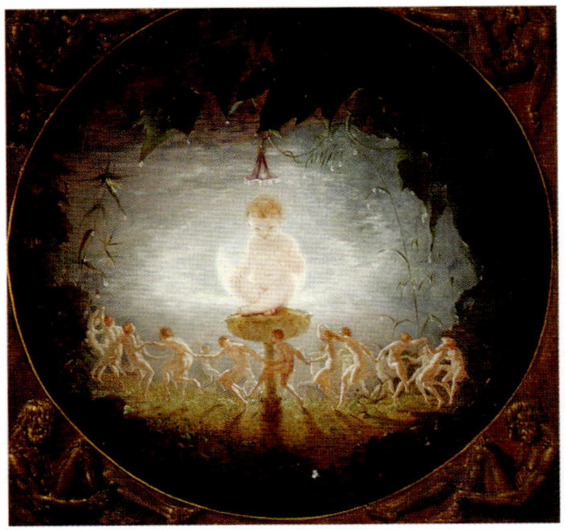

Dadd, Richard 1817–1886
Puck
oil on canvas (?) 52.9 x 52.9
PRSMG : 2011.88

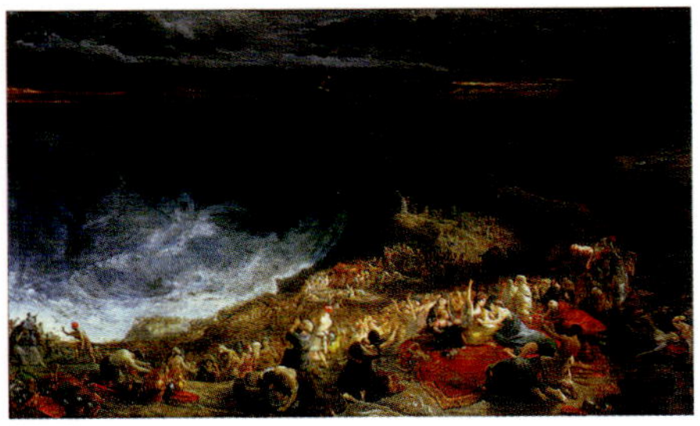

Danby, Francis 1793–1861
The Delivery of Israel out of Egypt 1855
oil on canvas 149.5 x 240
PRSMG : P116

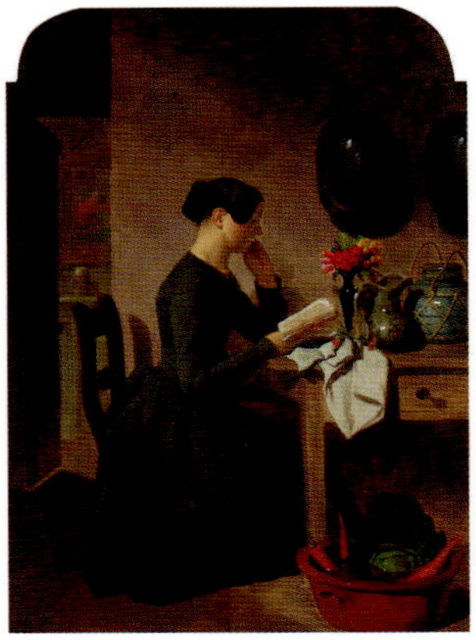

Davies, J. 1828–1891
The Housekeeper c.1888
oil on canvas 54 x 38
PRSMG : P856

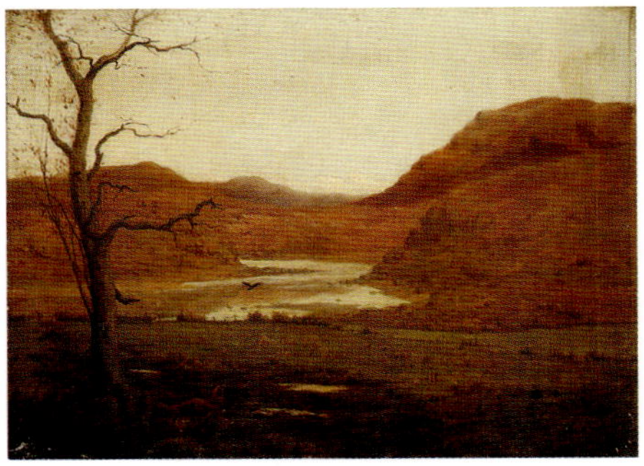

Davies, James H. 1828–1958
Landscape 1889
oil on canvas 76 x 51
PRSMG : P117

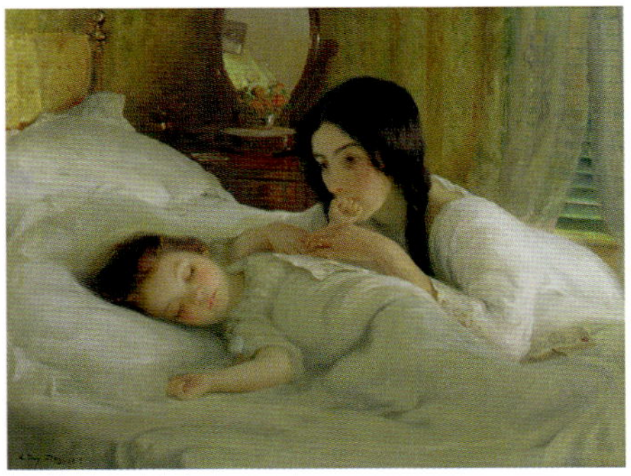

Day, Walter Percy 1878–1965
The Eleventh Hour, the Eleventh Day of the Eleventh Month, 1918 1919
oil on canvas 72 x 92
PRSMG : P122

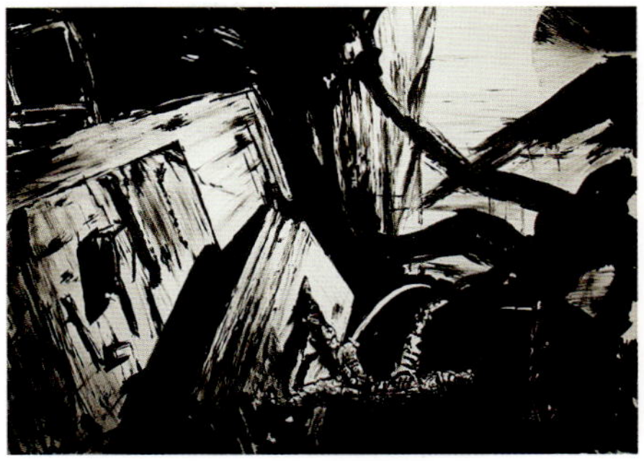

de Thame, Gerard b.1958
Edge of the Night 1984
acrylic on paper on canvas 182.9 x 254
PRSMG : P1841

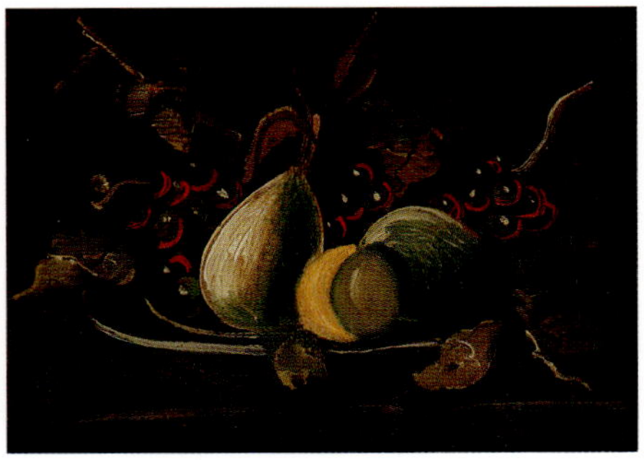

Derain, André 1880–1954
Still Life with Fruit c.1935–1940
oil on canvas 23.5 x 34
PRSMG : P2343

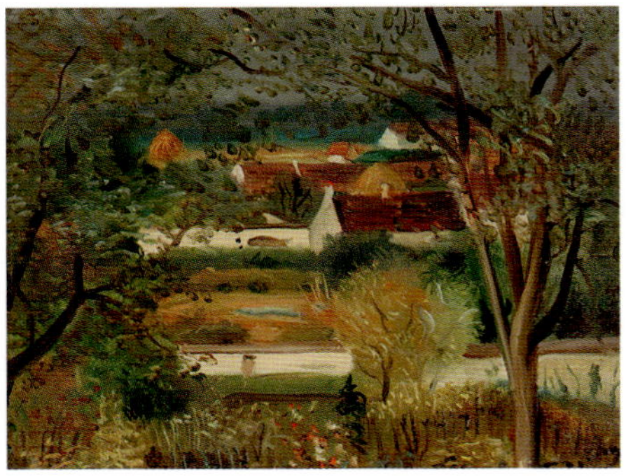

Derain, André 1880–1954
Jardins a Donnemarie en Montois c.1940–1945
oil on canvas on board 26.5 x 34
PRSMG : P2344

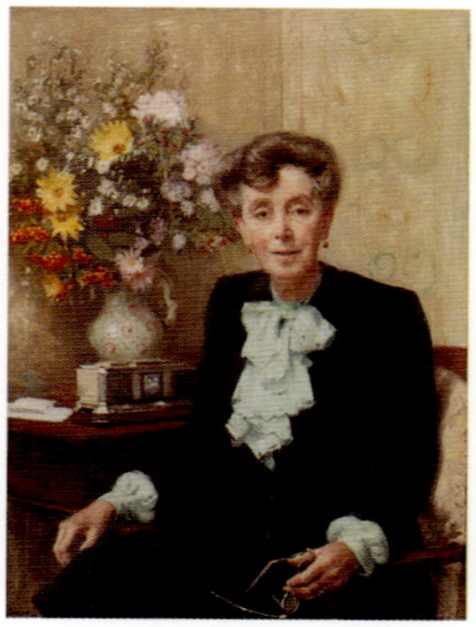

Devas, Anthony 1911–1958
Mrs Avice Margaret Pimblett (1880–1963)
1949
oil on canvas 101 x 76
PRSMG : P1281

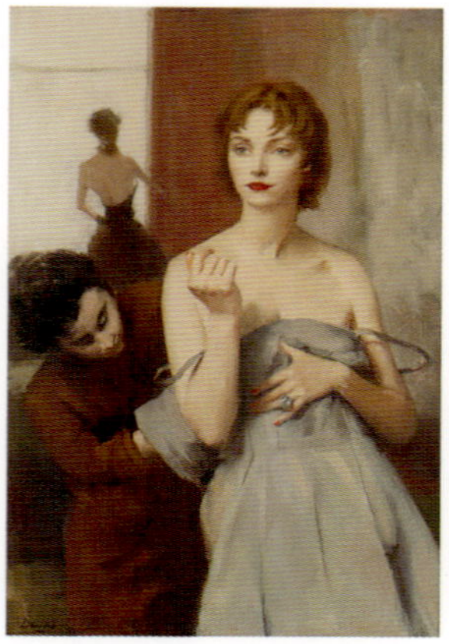

Devas, Anthony 1911–1958
At the Couturier 1955
oil on canvas 91.7 x 61.3
PRSMG : P1473

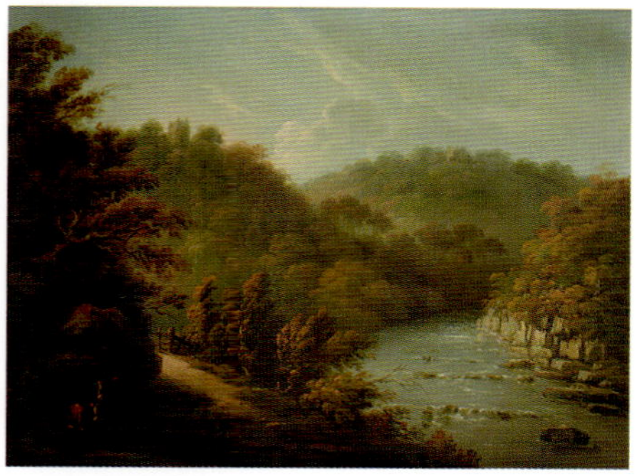

Devis, Anthony 1729–1816
The River Ure at Hackfall, near Ripon, West Riding of Yorkshire c.1770
oil on canvas 62 x 83.8
PRSMG : P1828

Devis, Anthony 1729–1816
The Weeping Rock – A Waterfall at Hackfall near Ripon, West Riding of Yorkshire c.1770
oil on canvas 61 x 84.5
PRSMG : P1827

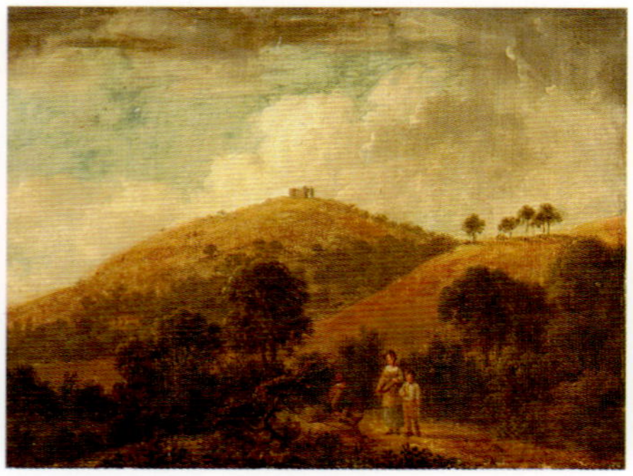

Devis, Anthony 1729–1816
Landscape with the Ruins of St Martha's Chapel Beyond 1780–1816
oil on wood 17.7 x 25.3
PRSMG : P1206

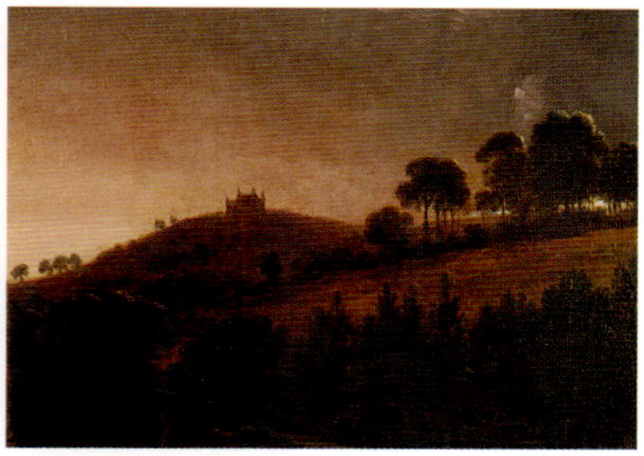

Devis, Anthony 1729–1816
St Martha's from Mr Devis's House at Albury, Surrey 1780–1816
oil on panel 30 x 47
PRSMG : P1207

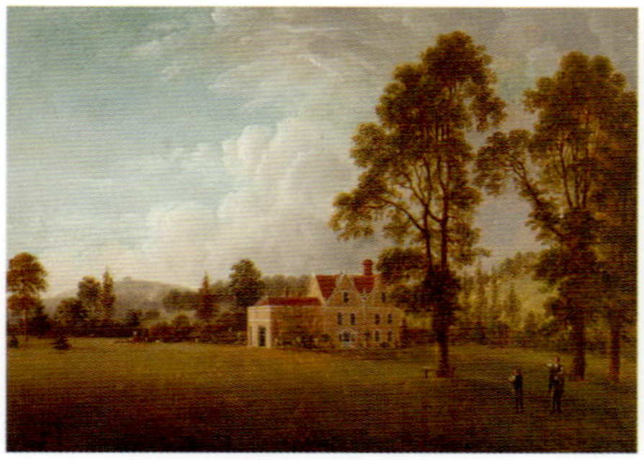

Devis, Anthony 1729–1816
Albury House, Surrey 1792
oil on panel 30.1 x 45.4
PRSMG : P140

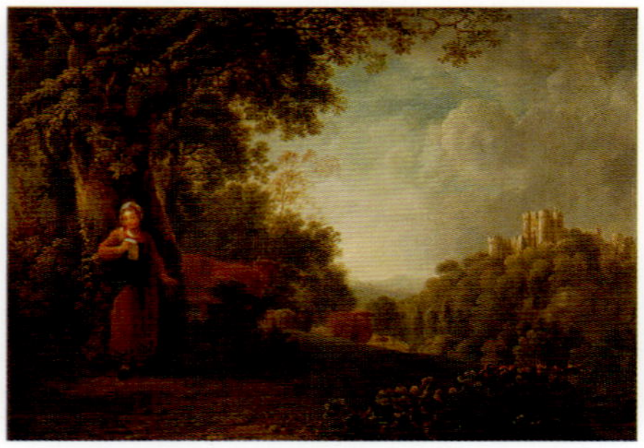

Devis, Anthony 1729–1816
Romantic Landscape with Cattle and a Milkmaid 1793
oil on panel 31.2 x 42.8
PRSMG : P1607

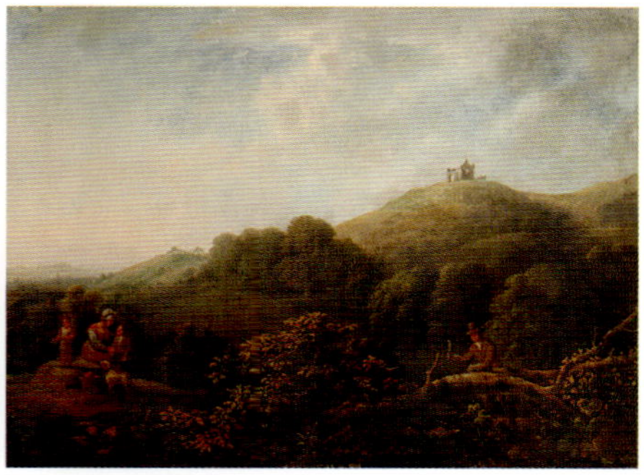

Devis, Anthony 1729–1816
Landscape with St Martha's Chapel c.1814
oil on panel 39.8 x 61
PRSMG : P1204

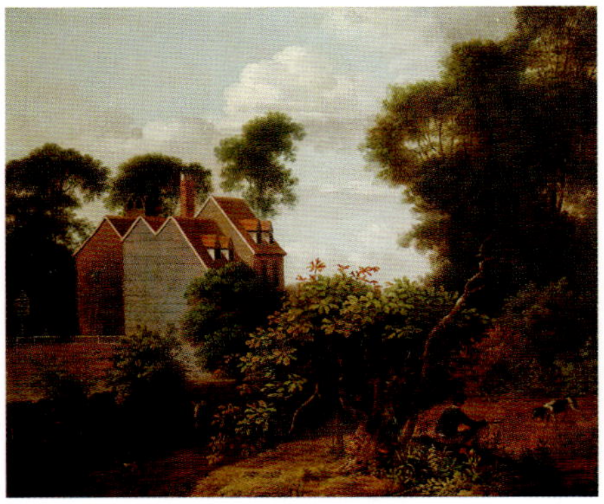

Devis, Anthony 1729–1816
Landscape with House on the Edge of a Wood
c.1815
oil on canvas 61 x 79
PRSMG : P1815

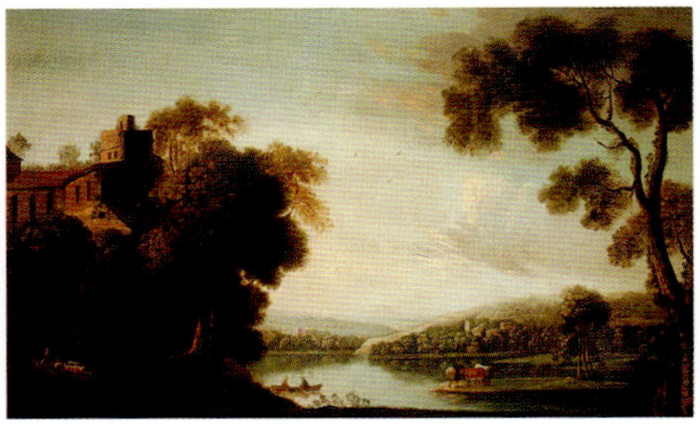

Devis, Anthony 1729–1816
A River Scene with a Mansion Amongst Trees
oil on canvas 87 x 160
PRSMG : P139

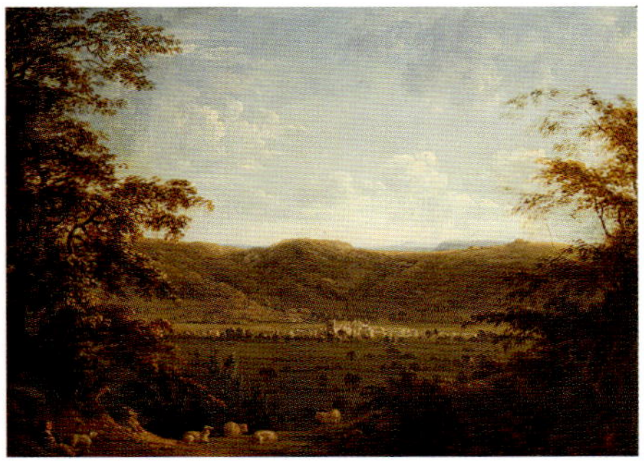

Devis, Anthony 1729–1816
Dursley, Gloucestershire
oil on panel 32 x 43
PRSMG : P1236

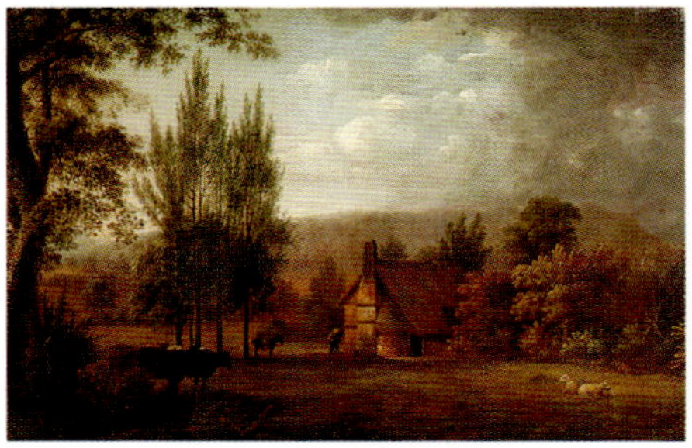

Devis, Anthony 1729–1816
Landscape – Cottages and Cattle
oil on panel 35.1 x 65.1
PRSMG : P142

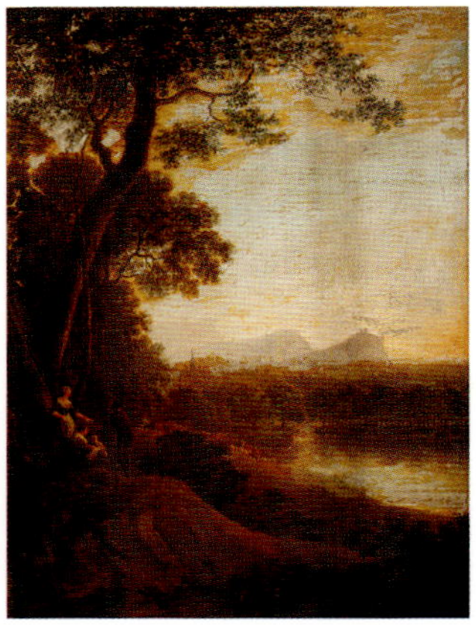

Devis, Anthony 1729–1816
Landscape – View of Stirling Castle
oil on canvas (?) 127 x 102
PRSMG : P2234

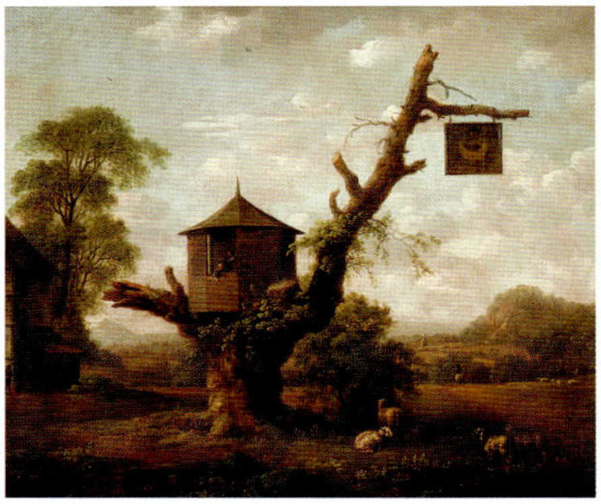

Devis, Anthony 1729–1816
Landscape with a Hut in an Oak Tree and the 'Man in the Moon' Inn
oil on canvas 63.2 x 76
PRSMG : P1405

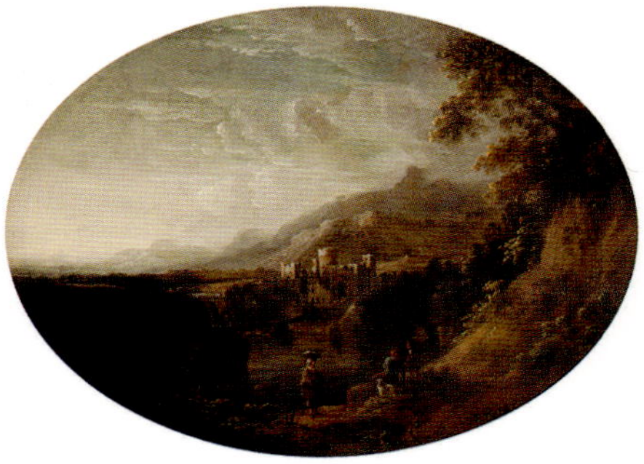

Devis, Anthony 1729–1816
Landscape with Castle
oil on panel 41 x 54.8
PRSMG : P1203

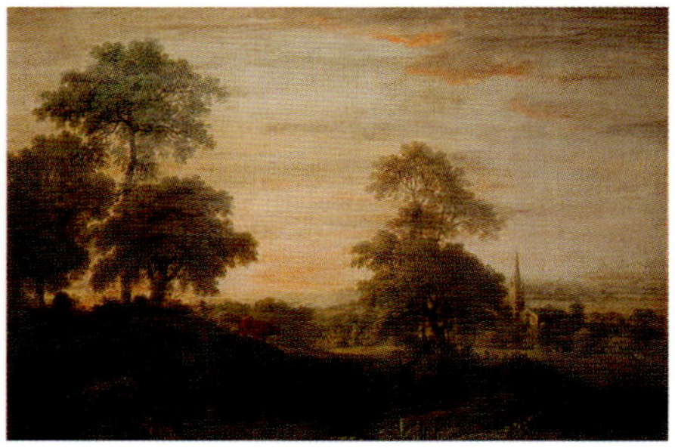

Devis, Anthony 1729–1816
Landscape, Church and Village
oil on canvas 42.2 x 63.8
PRSMG : P141

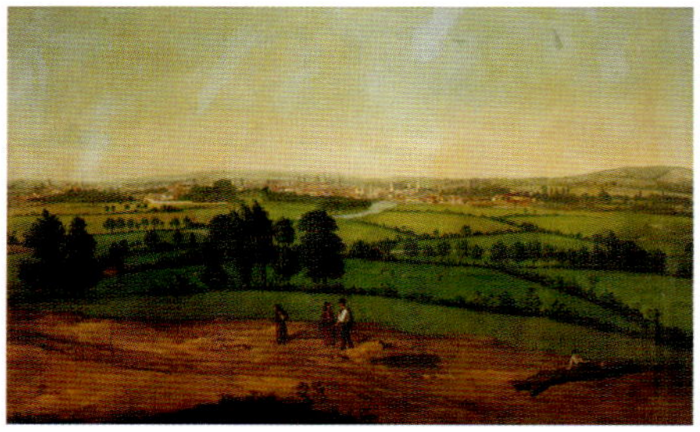

Devis, Anthony 1729–1816
Oxford
oil on canvas 60.9 x 101.5
PRSMG : P143

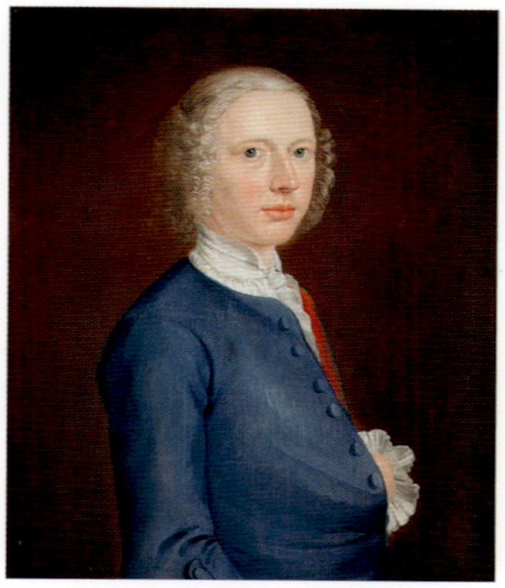

Devis, Arthur 1712–1787
Portrait of the Artist c.1737
oil on canvas 70.5 x 58
PRSMG : P1349

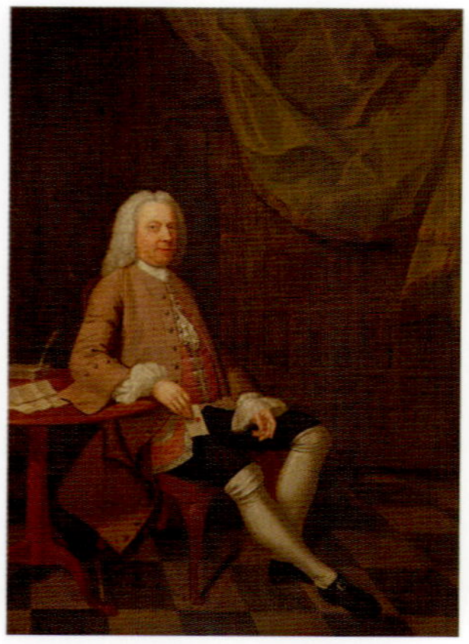

Devis, Arthur 1712–1787
John Orlebar c.1740
oil on canvas 51 x 35.5
PRSMG : P135

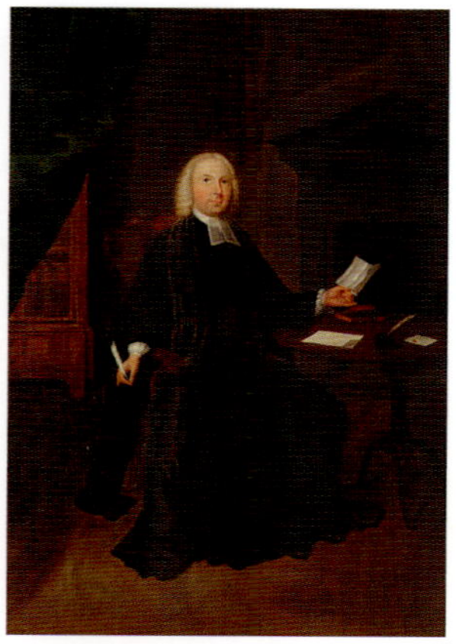

Devis, Arthur 1712–1787
The Reverend William Farington c.1741–1742
oil on canvas (?) 50.7 x 35
PRSMG : P2237

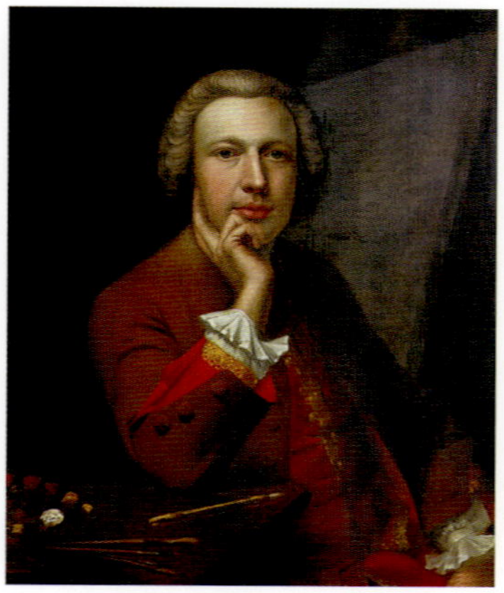

Devis, Arthur 1712–1787
Portrait of the Artist 1742
oil on canvas 77 x 65
PRSMG : P137

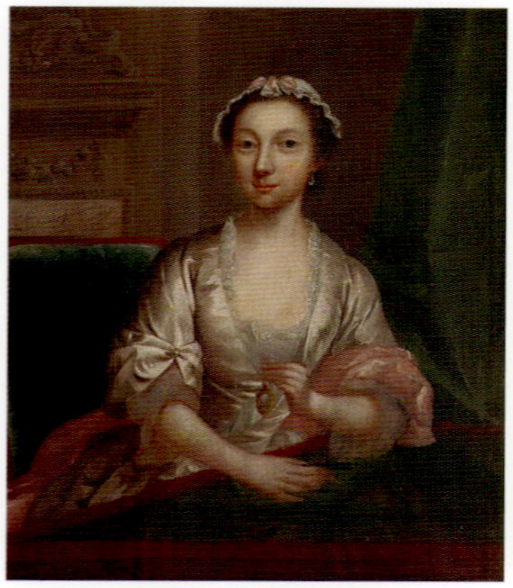

Devis, Arthur 1712–1787
Elizabeth Faulkner, Wife of Arthur Devis
c.1742
oil on panel 19 x 16.5
PRSMG : P1810

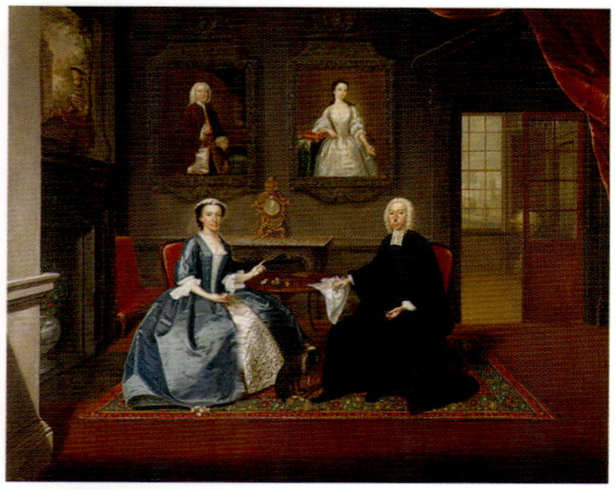

Devis, Arthur 1712–1787
The Reverend Streynsham Master and His Wife, Margaret of Croston, Lancashire
1743–1744
oil on canvas 103 x 121
PRSMG : P2355

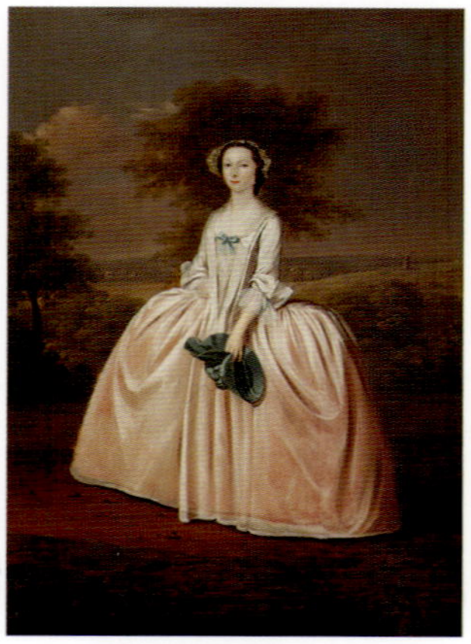

Devis, Arthur 1712–1787
Mary du Cane, née Norris 1747–1749
oil on canvas 74 x 53
PRSMG : P2350

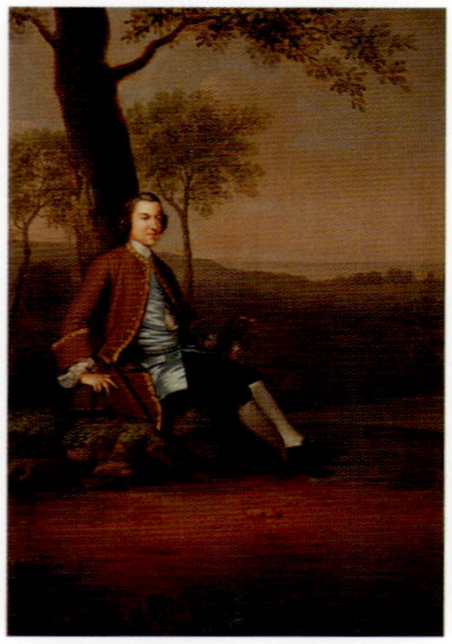

Devis, Arthur 1712–1787
Mr Peter du Cane (1713–1803) 1747–1749
oil on canvas 74 x 53
PRSMG : P2350

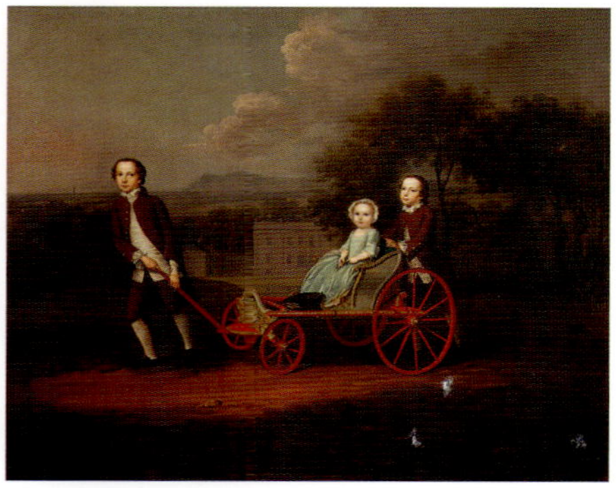

Devis, Arthur 1712–1787
Richard, Mary and Peter – The Children of Peter and Mary du Cane 1747–1749
oil on canvas 83 x 94
PRSMG : P2350

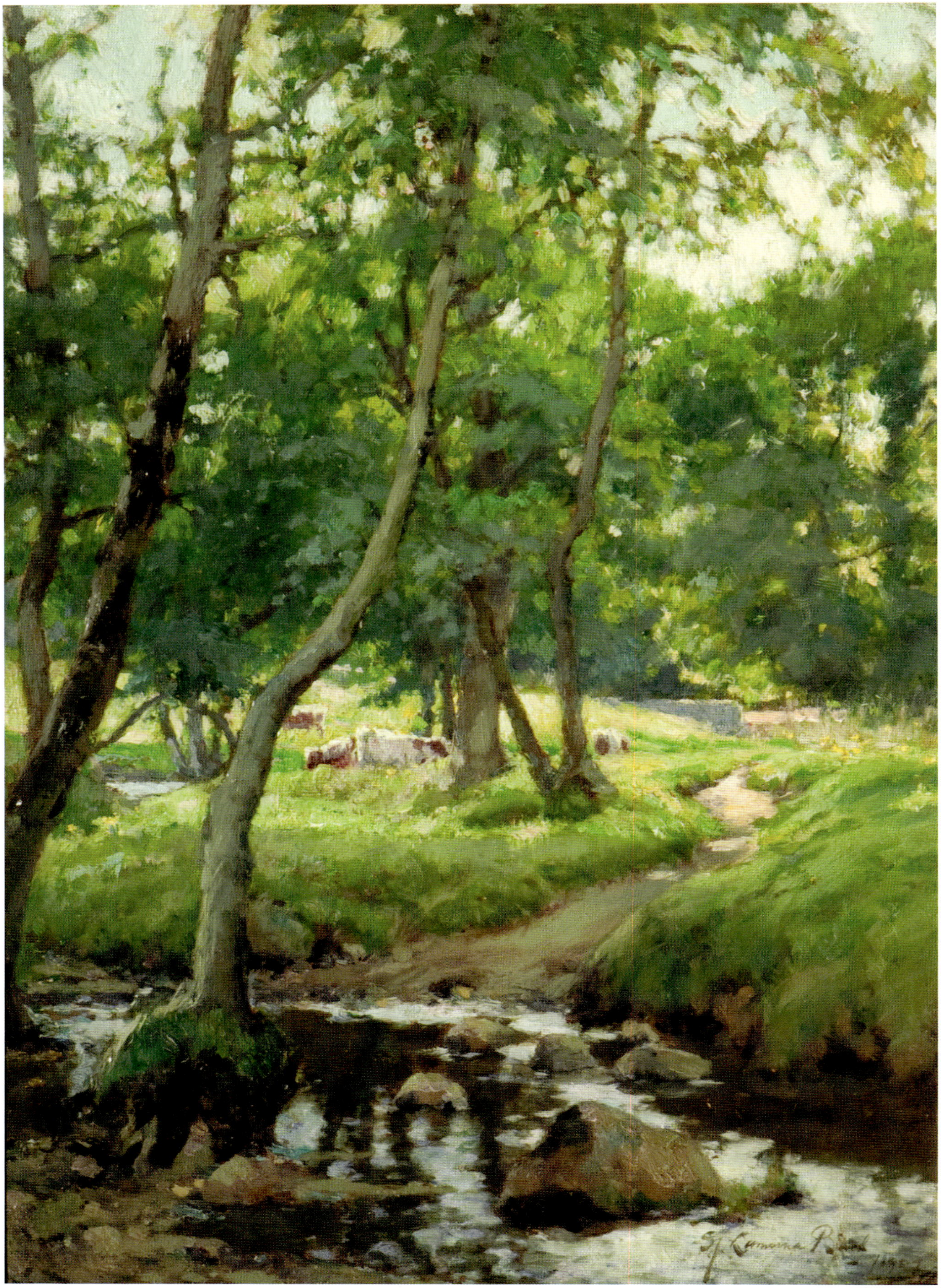

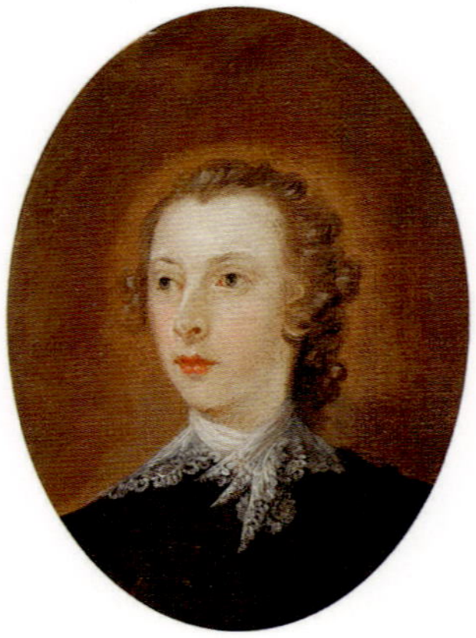

Devis, Arthur 1712–1787
Anthony Devis (1729–1816) c.1747
oil on canvas on panel 19.9 x 12.7
PRSMG : P2362

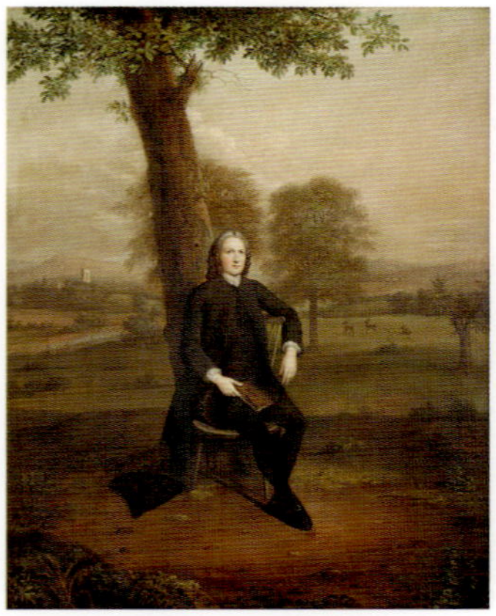

Devis, Arthur 1712–1787
Thomas Starkie 1749
oil on canvas 237 x 146.5
PRSMG : P136

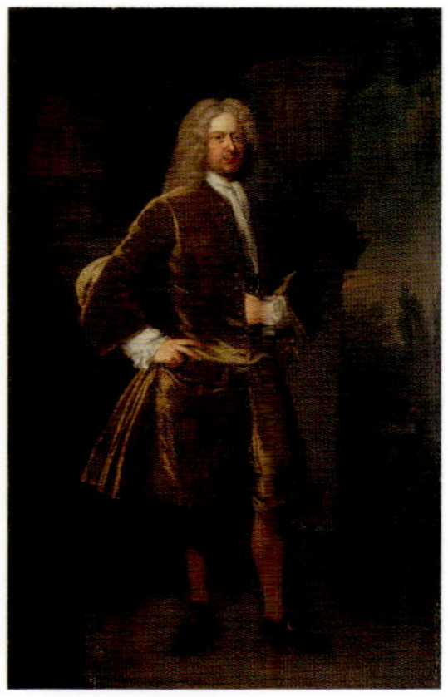

Devis, Arthur 1712–1787
The Right Honourable Daniel Pulteney c.1750
oil on canvas 241.5 x 147.8
PRSMG : P133

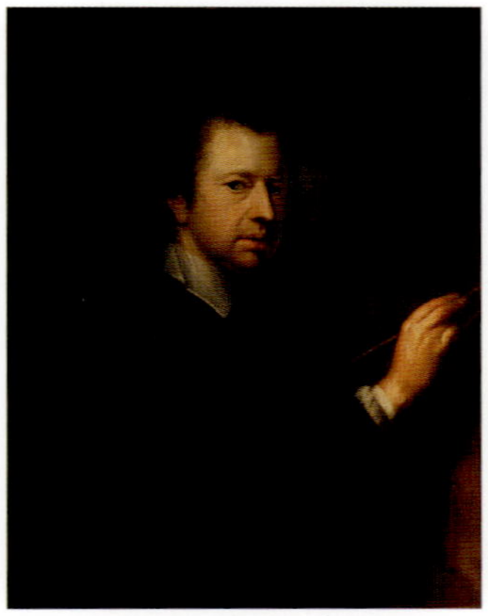

Devis, Arthur 1712–1787
Portrait of the Artist c.1754
oil on canvas 76.5 x 62.5
PRSMG : P811

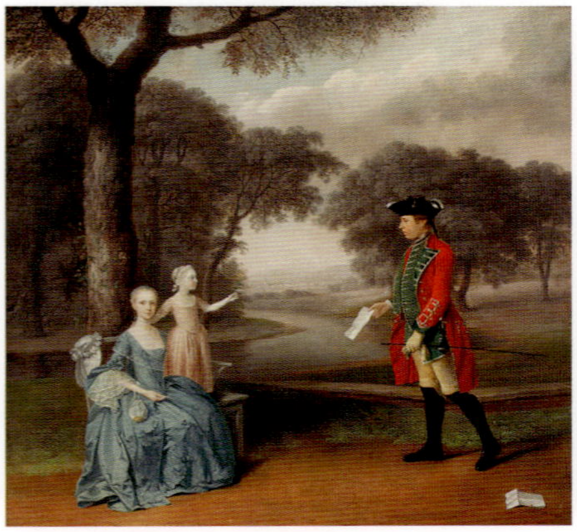

Devis, Arthur 1712–1787
Francis Vincent of Weddington Hall, Warwickshire, with His Wife Mercy and Daughter Ann 1763
oil on canvas 120 x 115
PRSMG : P1562

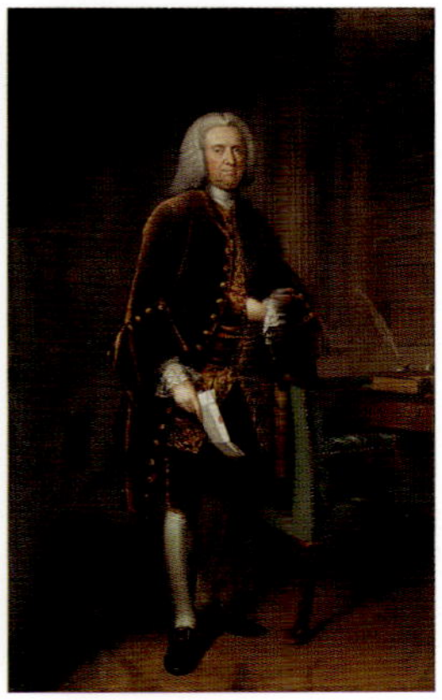

Devis, Arthur 1712–1787
Nicholas Fazakerley (d.1767) 1763
oil on canvas 234 x 147.5
PRSMG : P132

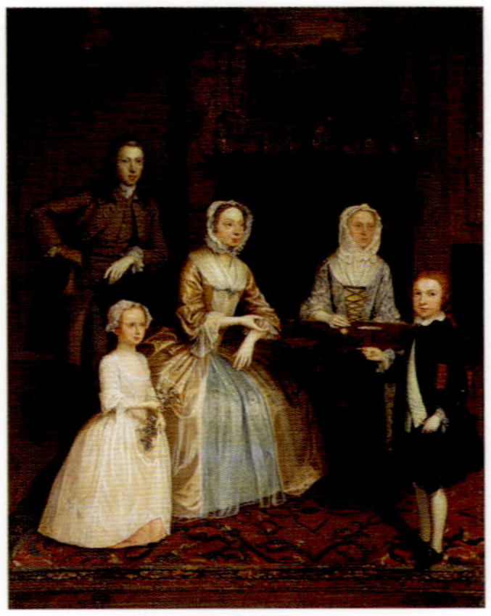

Devis, Arthur 1712–1787
Mr and Mrs Richard Bull and Family
oil on canvas 67 x 54
PRSMG : P746

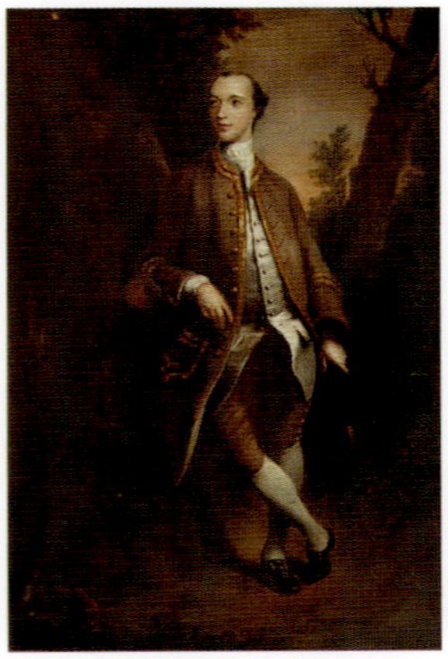

Devis, Arthur 1712–1787
Portrait of a Man
oil on canvas 66 x 38.7
PRSMG : P134

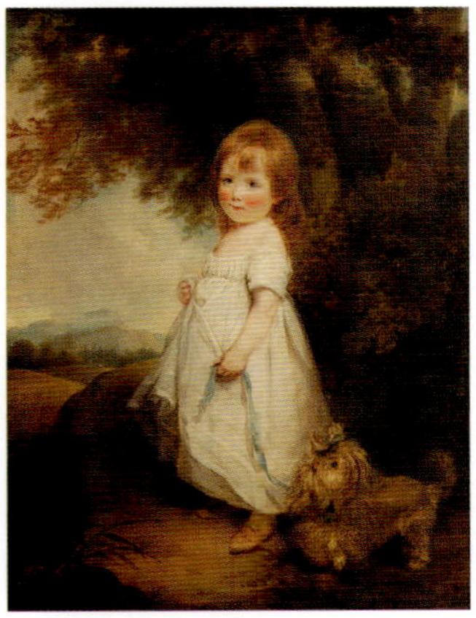

Devis, Arthur William 1762–1822
Miss Anderson with Her Dog 1780–1822
oil on canvas 127 x 101.5
PRSMG : P907

Facing page: Birch, Samuel John Lamorna, 1869–1955, *Caton,* 1895, Lancaster City Museums (p. 197)

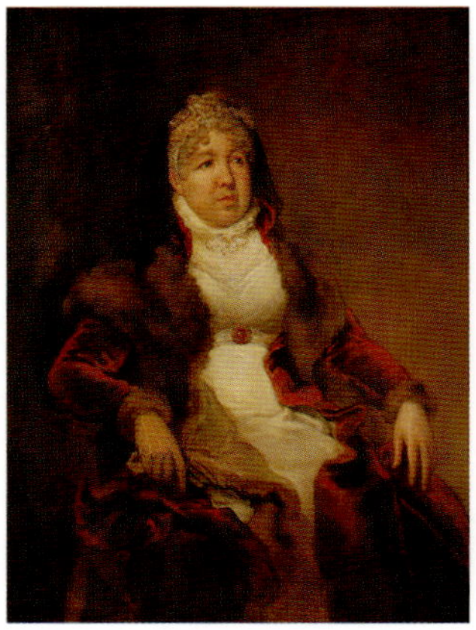

Devis, Arthur William 1762–1822
Miss Ellen Devis 1780–1822
oil on canvas 106.9 x 92
PRSMG : P138

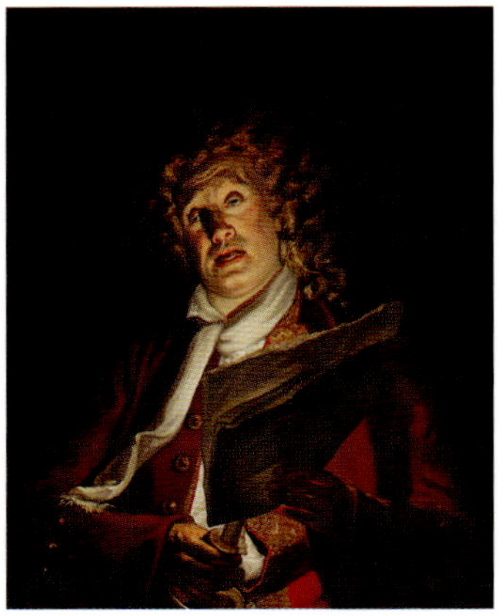

Devis, Arthur William 1762–1822
Portrait of an Actor (possibly Charles Dibdin) 1780–1822
oil on canvas 86.5 x 75.5
PRSMG : P1415

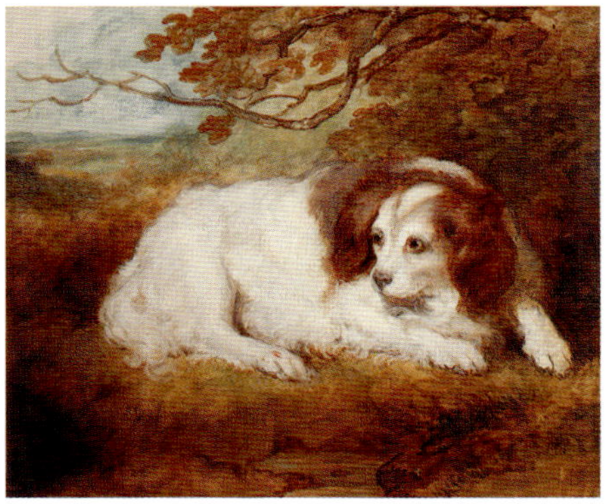

Devis, Arthur William 1762–1822
The Dog Dido 1780–1822
oil on canvas 64.3 x 77.1
PRSMG : P1369

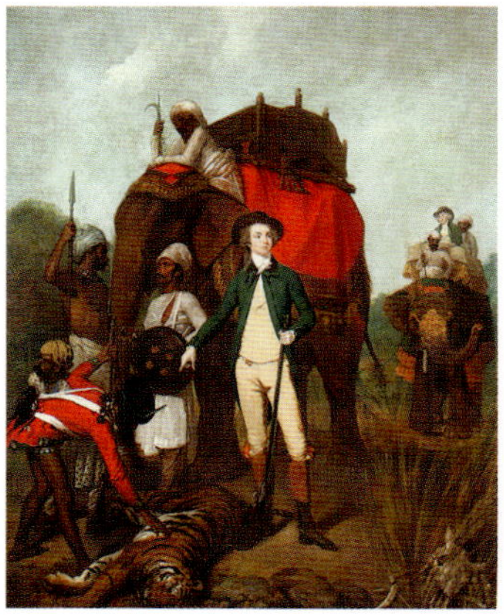

Devis, Arthur William 1762–1822
John Addison 1784–1795
oil on canvas 127 x 103.5
PRSMG : P1330

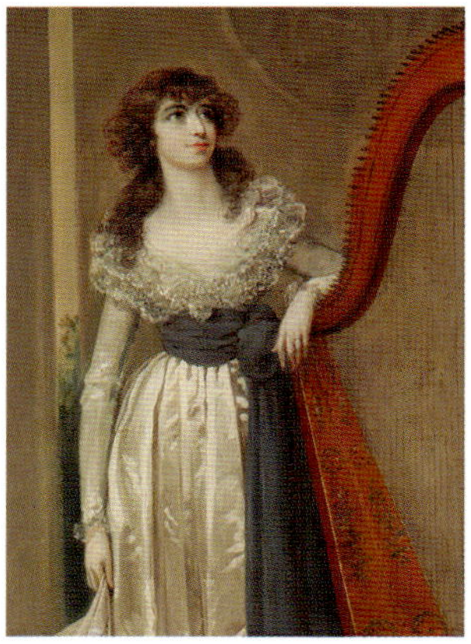

Devis, Arthur William 1762–1822
Ann Debonnaire 1786
oil on canvas 48.5 x 36.7
PRSMG : P1406

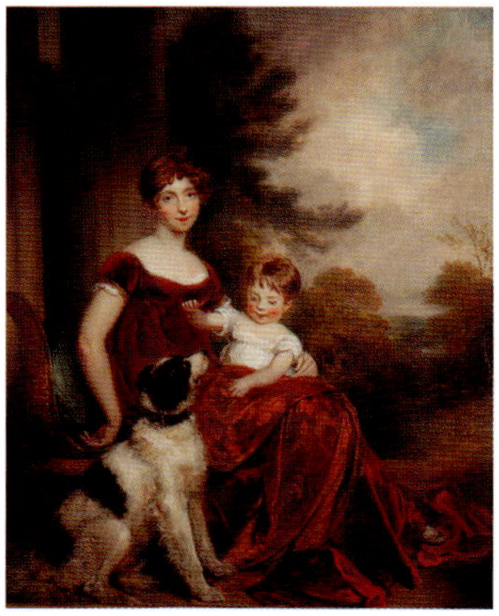

Devis, Arthur William 1762–1822
Mrs Anderson and Her Son William c.1800
oil on canvas 76.4 x 64
PRSMG : P906

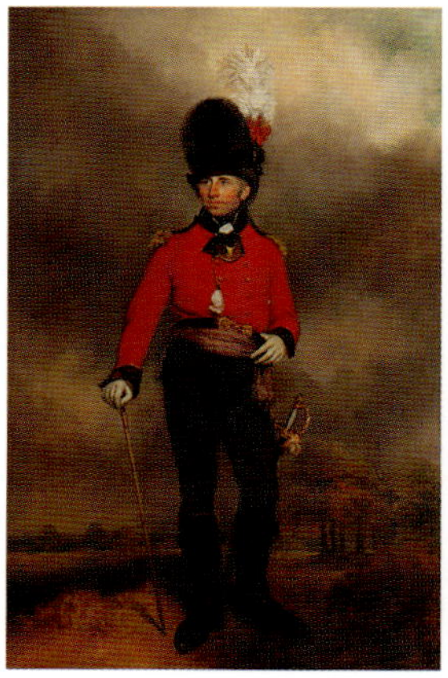

Devis, Arthur William 1762–1822
William Pitt Amherst (1773–1857), 1st Earl Amherst of Arracan, Viscount Holmesdale and Baron Amherst of Montreal 1803
oil on canvas 224 x 138 (E)
PRSMG : P2327

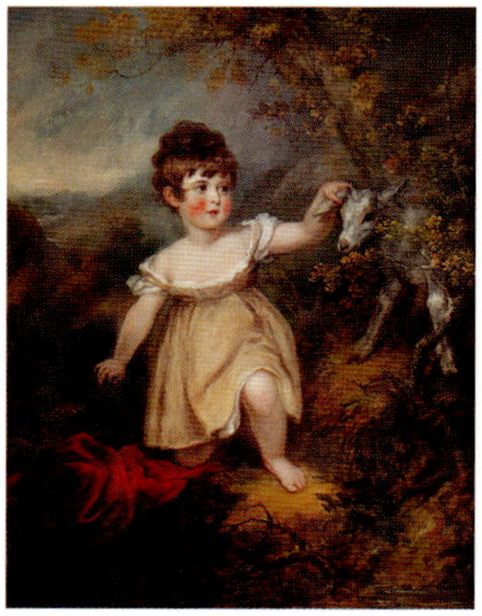

Devis, Arthur William 1762–1822
Marianna Augusta Cockburn 1808
oil on canvas 125.5 x 100.5
PRSMG : P1471

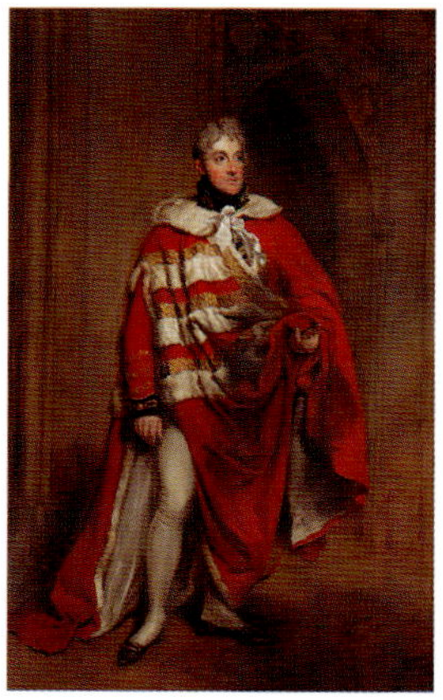

Devis, Arthur William 1762–1822
William Henry Vane (1766–1842), 3rd Earl of Darlington, Later 1st Duke of Cleveland 1810
oil on canvas 238 x 147
PRSMG : P1636

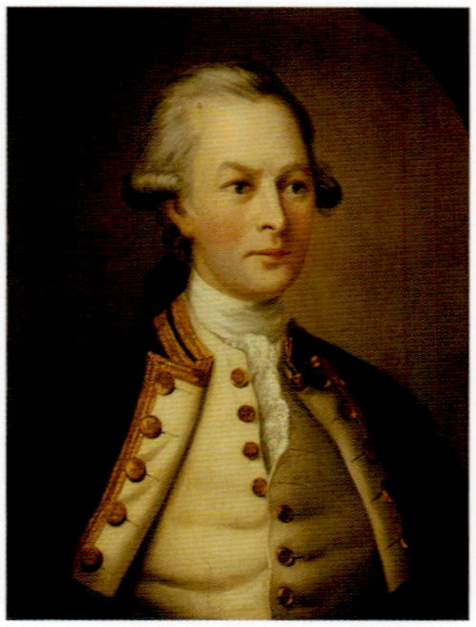

Devis, Thomas Anthony 1757–1810
Admiral Michael Clements 1778
oil on canvas 61.3 x 51.2
PRSMG : P1556

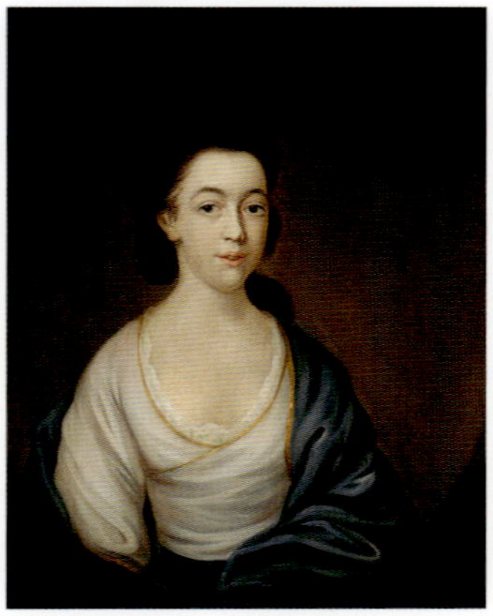

Devis, Thomas Anthony 1757–1810
Portrait of a Lady 1780
oil on canvas 75.2 x 62.8
PRSMG : P844

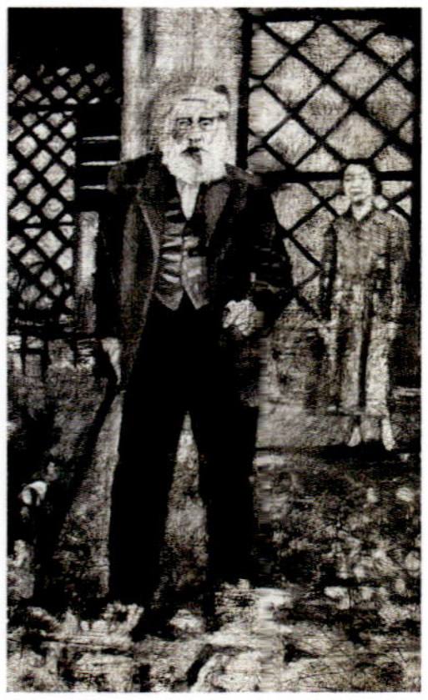

Di Stefano, Arturo b.1955
Thérèse Lessore Sickert 1990
oil on linen 170 x 99
PRSMG : P2303

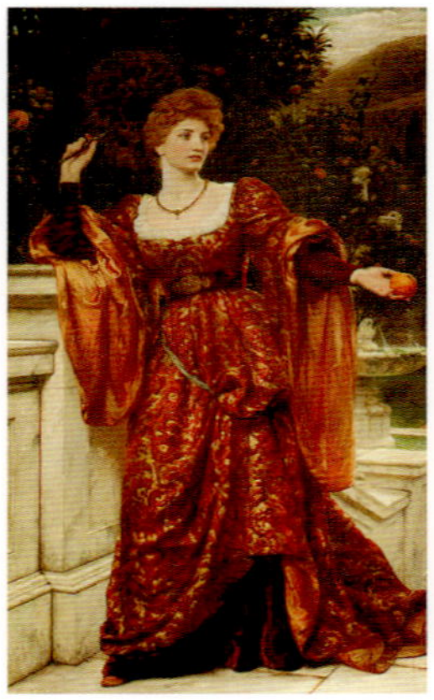

Dicksee, Frank 1853–1928
Hesperia 1887
oil on canvas 250 x 156
PRSMG : P819

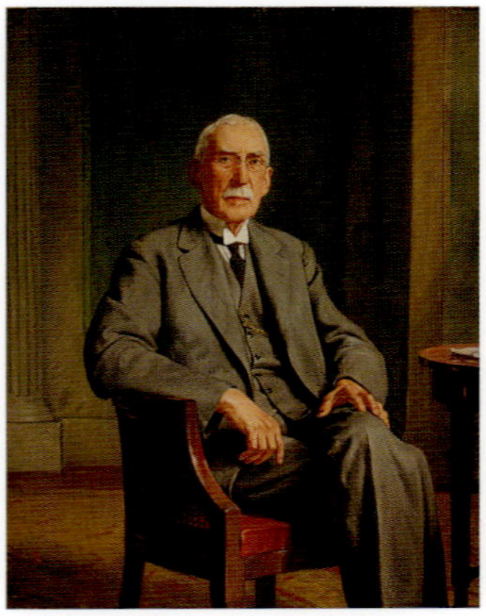

Dodd, Francis 1874–1949
Alderman Frederick W. F. Matthew 1938
oil on canvas 128.8 x 102.4
PRSMG : P744

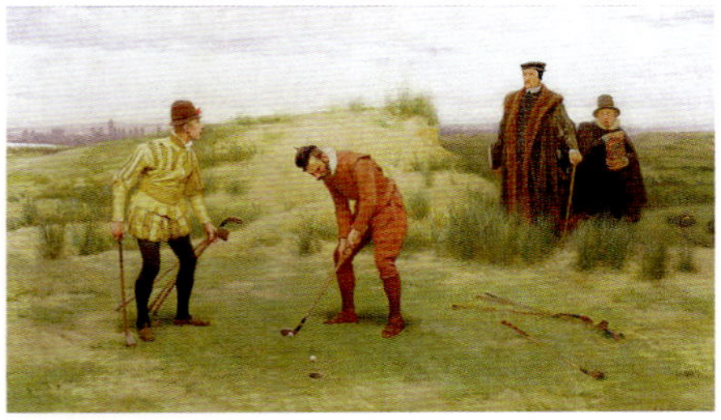

Dollman, John Charles 1851–1934
During the Time of the Sermonses 1896
oil on canvas 86.7 x 142.5
PRSMG : P201

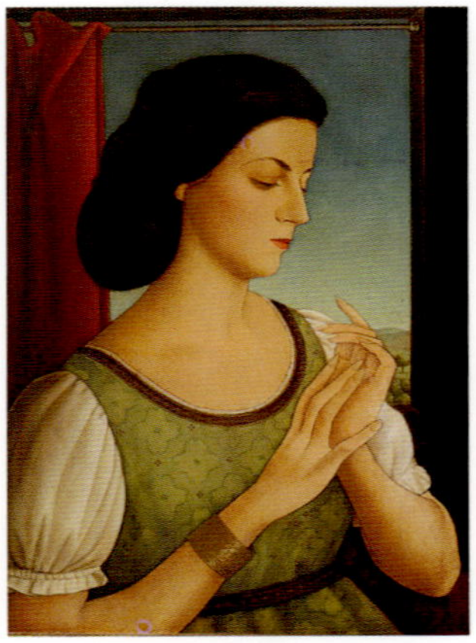

Downton, John 1906–1991
Woman at the Window c.1934
tempera on mahogany 49.8 x 34
PRSMG : P2319

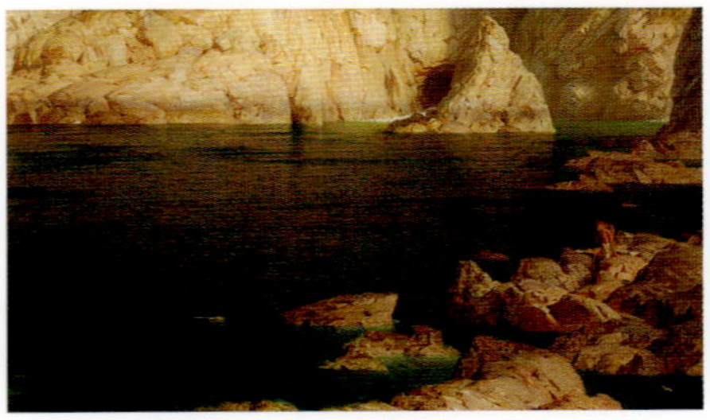

Draper, Herbert James 1864–1920
The Ebb 1900
oil on canvas 67.5 x 95.5
PRSMG : P202

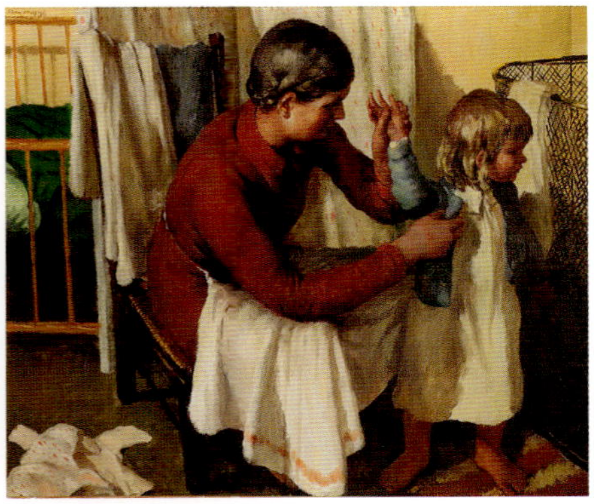

Dring, William D. 1904–1990
Going to Bed 1946
oil on canvas 63.4 x 76.3
PRSMG : P940

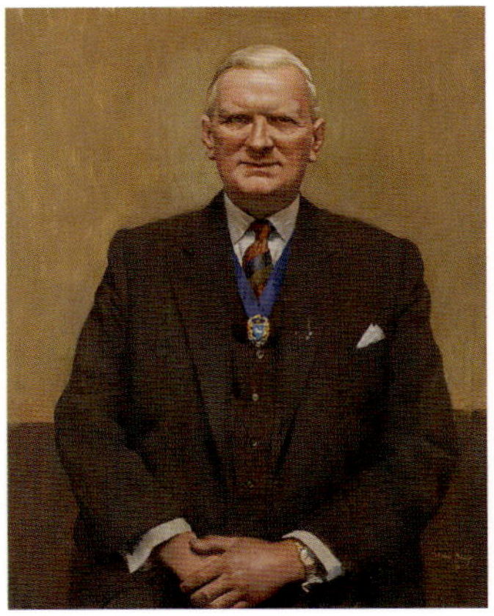

Dring, William D. 1904–1990
Alderman W. Beckett 1964
oil on canvas 91.5 x 71.1
PRSMG : P1684

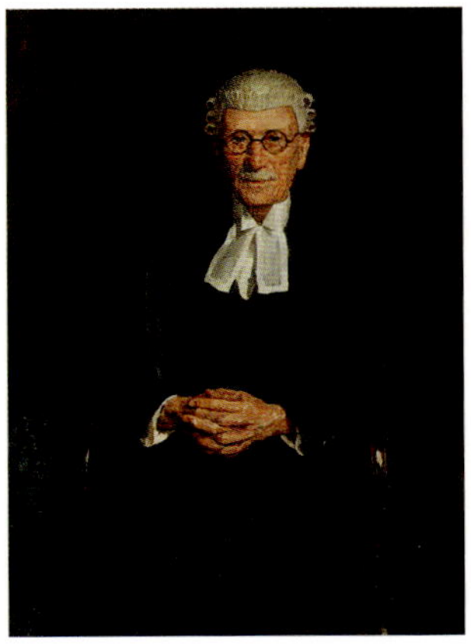

Dugdale, Thomas Cantrell 1880–1952
Sir Alfred Howarth, JP, Town Clerk of Preston (1907–1933) 1936
oil on canvas 120 x 90.5
PRSMG : P735

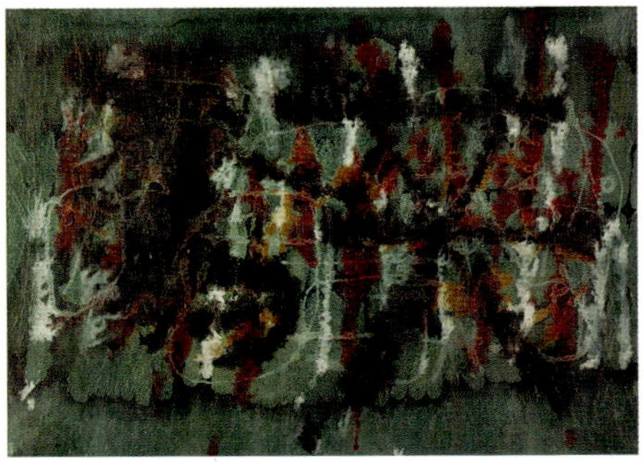

Duncan, Joseph b.1920
Abstract (J'écoute) 1958
oil on canvas 95.5 x 109
PRSMG : P1647

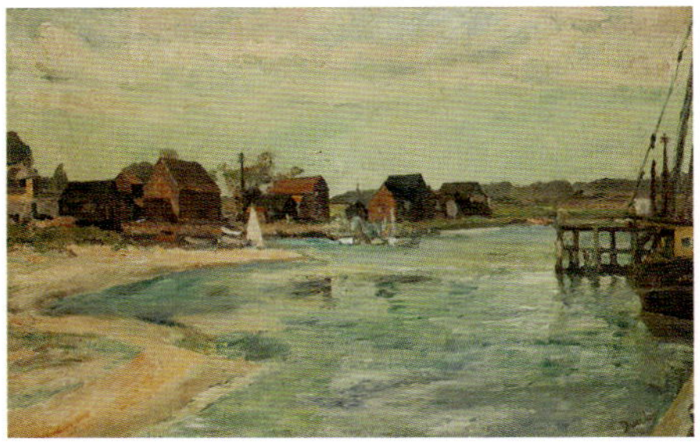

Dunlop, Ronald Ossory 1894–1973
Walberswick 1934
oil on canvas 77.5 x 127
PRSMG : P204

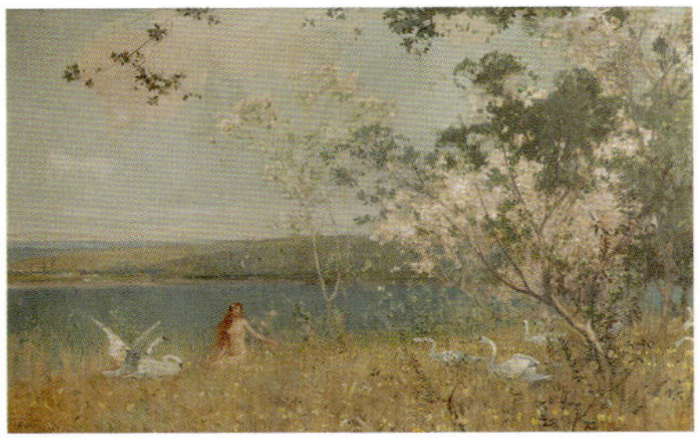

East, Alfred 1844–1913
An Idyll of Spring 1897
oil on canvas 146 x 233.5
PRSMG : P207

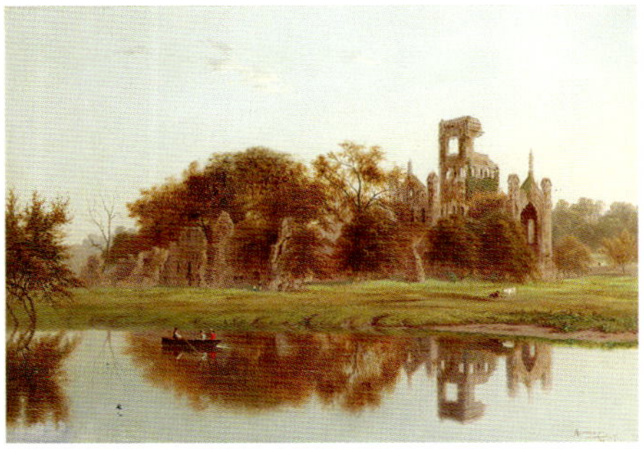

East, Alfred 1844–1913
Kirkstall Abbey
oil on canvas 44.5 x 69.2
PRSMG : P1494

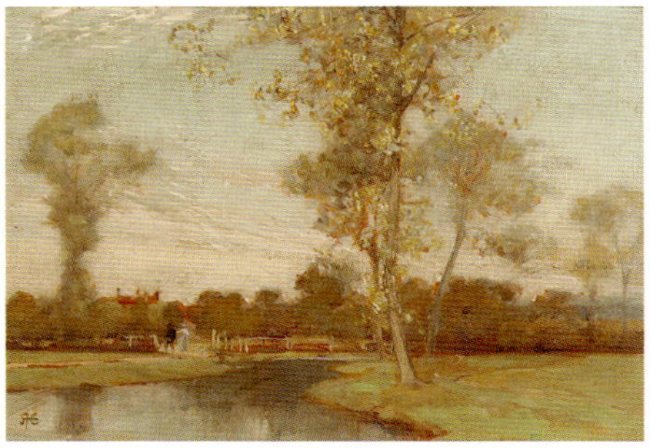

East, Alfred 1844–1913
On the Cole near Gardley Woods
oil on panel 16.5 x 24
PRSMG : P1351

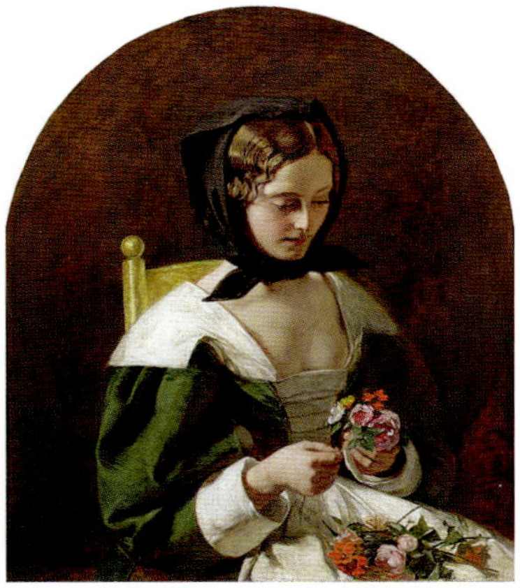

Egg, Augustus Leopold 1816–1863
Girl Making a Bouquet of Flowers 1849
oil on canvas 34.3 x 29.2
PRSMG : P215

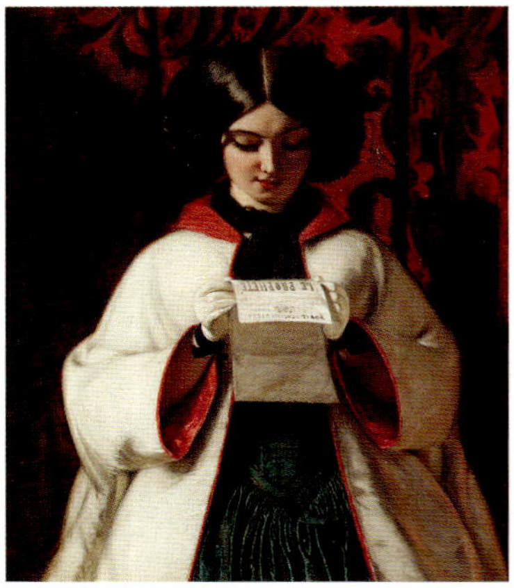

Egg, Augustus Leopold 1816–1863
The Opera Mantle 1851
oil on canvas 34.3 x 33
PRSMG : P214

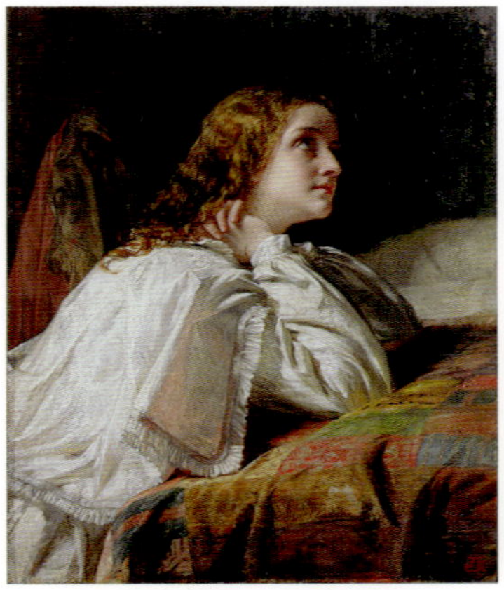

Elmore, Alfred 1815–1881
Supplication 1840–1860
oil on panel 42.5 x 35
PRSMG : P216

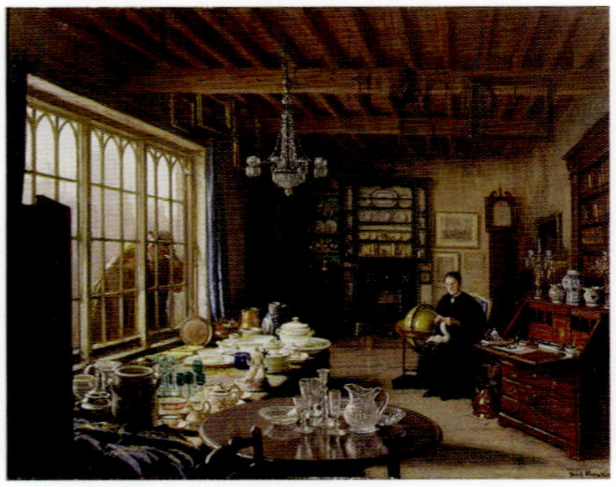

Elwell, Frederick William 1870–1958
The Curiosity Shop 1929
oil on canvas 102.5 x 128
PRSMG : P217

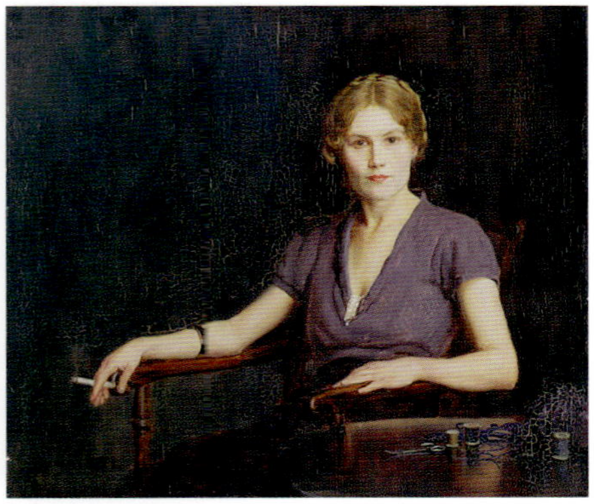

Elwell, Frederick William 1870–1958
Girl with a Cigarette 1942
oil on panel 49.8 x 56
PRSMG : P899

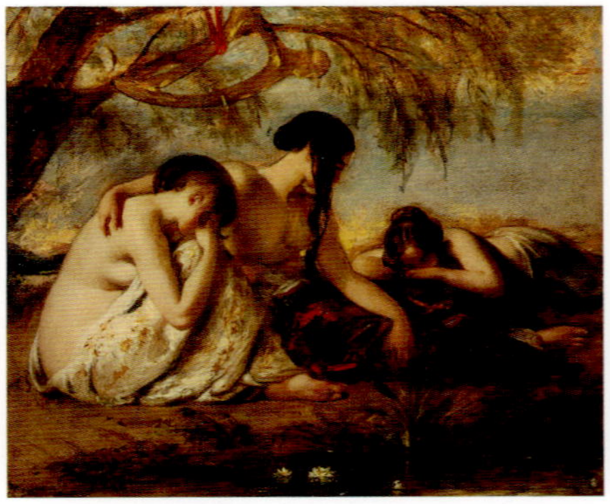

Etty, William 1787–1849
'By the waters of Babylon we sat down and wept' 1832
oil on millboard on panel 58.5 x 67.3
PRSMG : P218

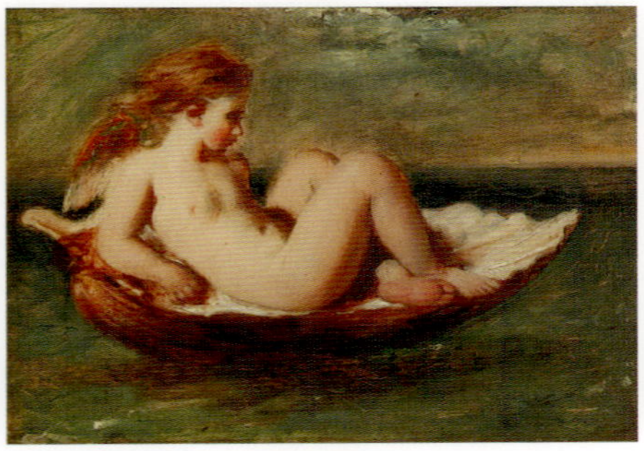

Etty, William 1787–1849
Cupid in a Shell
oil on panel 22.8 x 33
PRSMG : P219

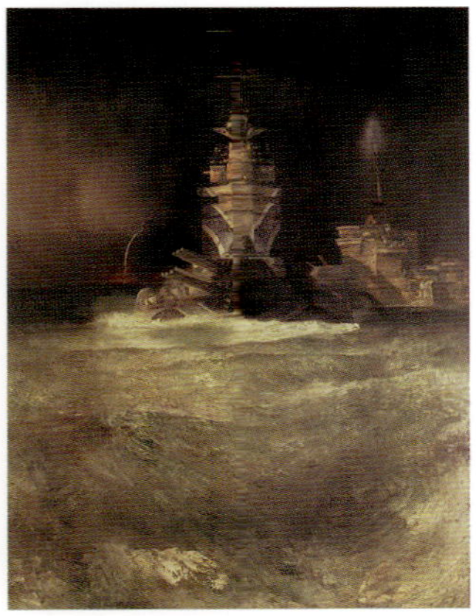

Eurich, Richard Ernst 1903–1992
D-Day, Reconstruction (Battleships at Sea) 1944
oil on panel 102 x 77
PRSMG : P1115

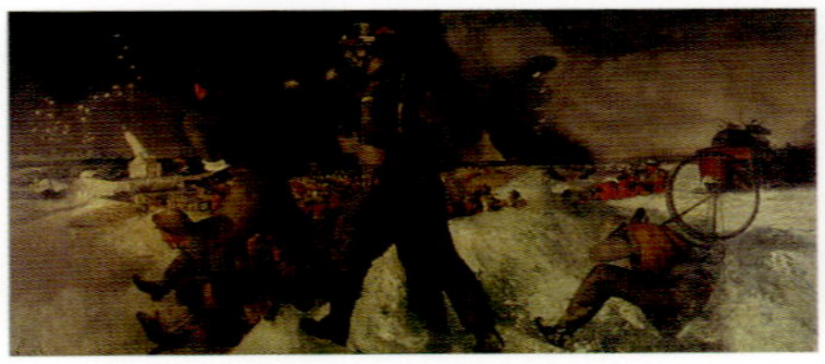

Eurich, Richard Ernst 1903–1992
D-Day, Reconstruction (Beach Landing) 1944
oil on panel 102 x 228.5
PRSMG : P1115

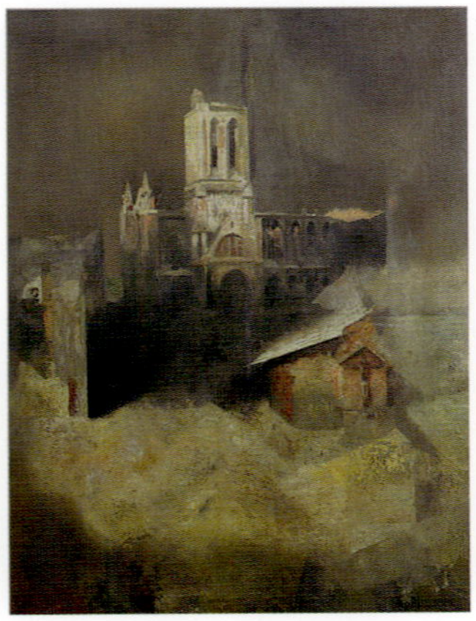

Eurich, Richard Ernst 1903–1992
D-Day, Reconstruction (Bombed Cathedral) 1944
oil on panel 102 x 77
PRSMG : P1115

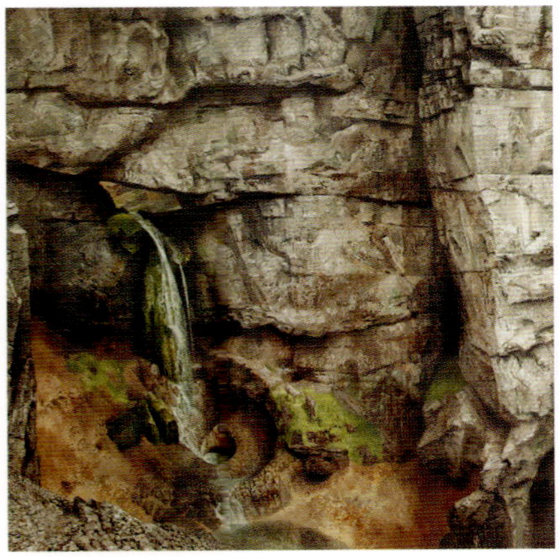

Eurich, Richard Ernst 1903–1992
The Watercourse, Gordale 1949
oil on canvas 102.6 x 102.3
PRSMG : P1368

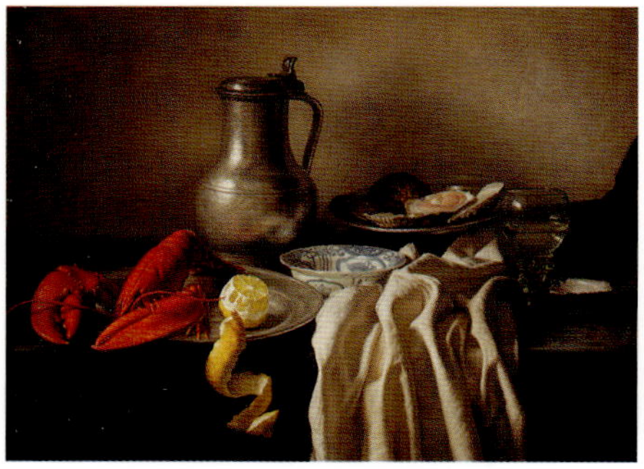

Eversen, Johannes Hendrik 1906–1995
Seafood 1958
oil on canvas 50.8 x 70.2
PRSMG : P1605

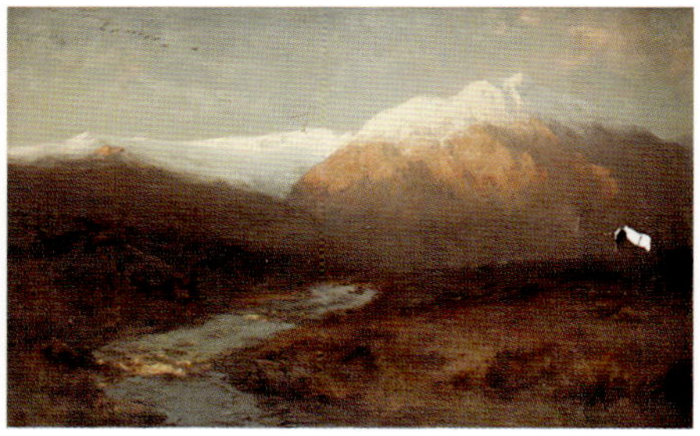

Farquharson, David 1839–1907
Sunrise
oil on canvas 75 x 131
PRSMG : P223

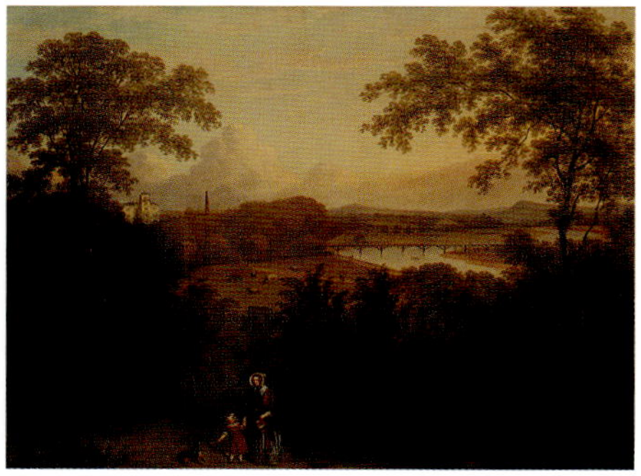

Ferguson, James active 1830–1860
Avenham Park 1852
oil on canvas 71.6 x 91.4
PRSMG : P225

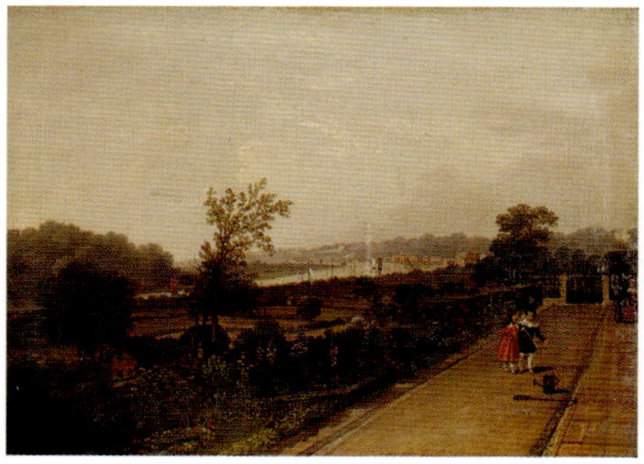

Ferguson, James active 1830–1860
The Ribble from Stanley Terrace
oil on canvas 44.5 x 62.2
PRSMG : P224

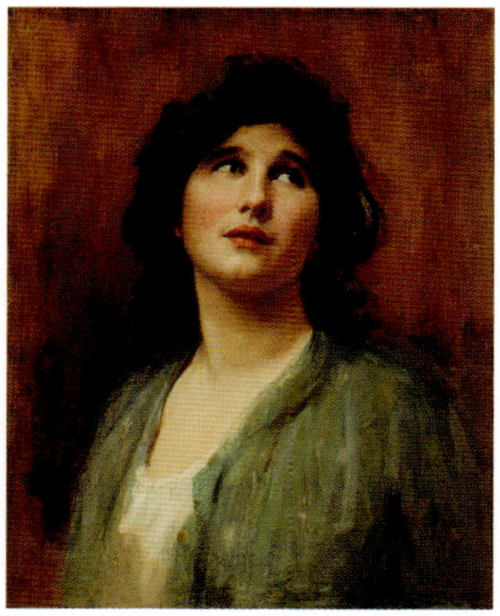

Fildes, Luke 1843–1927
Adoration
oil on canvas 61 x 44.5
PRSMG : P228

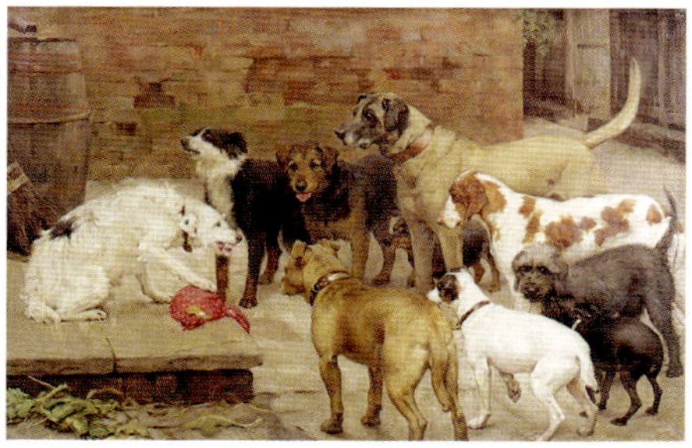

Fisher, Percy Harland 1867–1944
Dog With His Master's Dinner - La Fontaine's Fables 1892
oil on canvas 101.5 x 152.5
PRSMG : P229

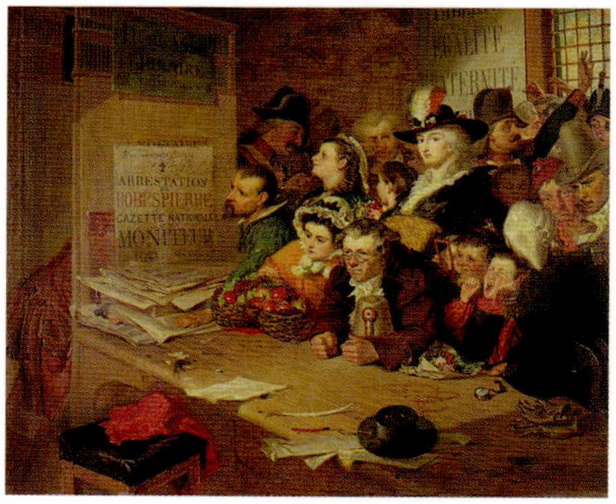

Fisk, William Henry 1827–1884
Awaiting Publication of 'Le Moniteur' for News of the Arrest of Robespierre
oil on canvas 63.6 x 76.5
PRSMG : P1558

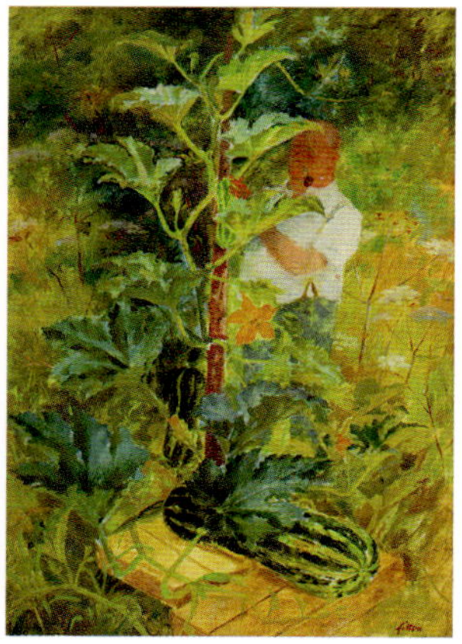

Fitton, James 1899–1982
The Long Green 1946
oil on canvas 78.4 x 51
PRSMG : P1030

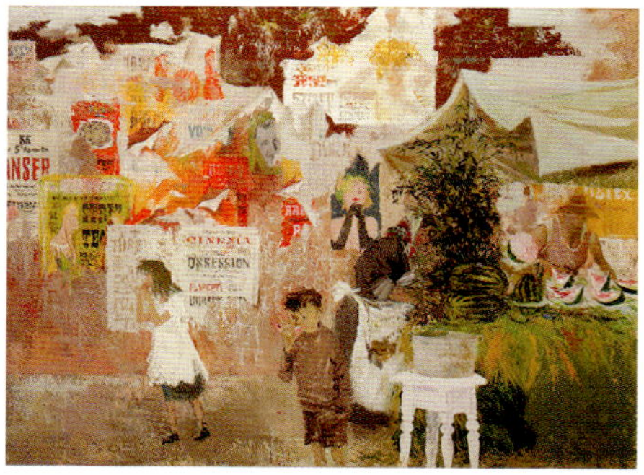

Fitton, James 1899–1982
Fresco 1961
oil on canvas 76.4 x 101
PRSMG : P1639

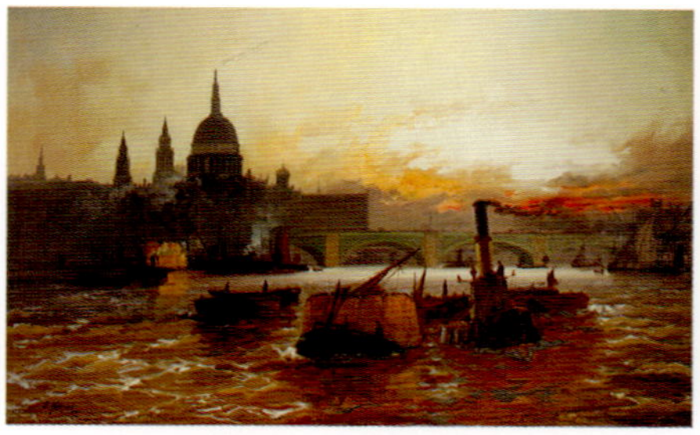

Fletcher, Edwin Henry Eugene 1857–1945
The Pool of London 1900–1945
oil on canvas 51.3 x 91.7
PRSMG : P1411

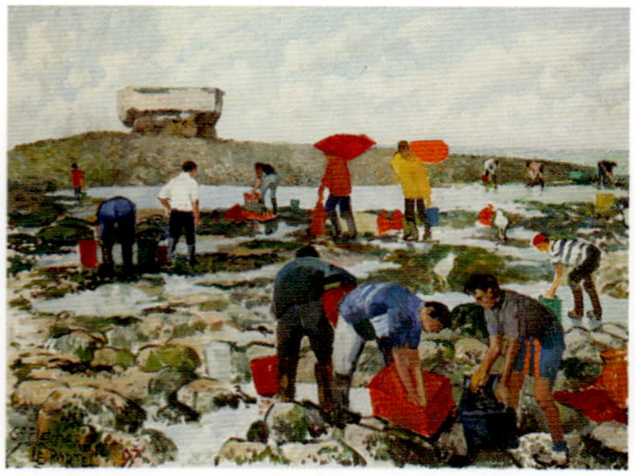

Fletcher, Geoffrey Scowcroft 1923–2004
Le Portel 1998
acrylic on canvas 50 x 68 (E)
PRSMG : P2331

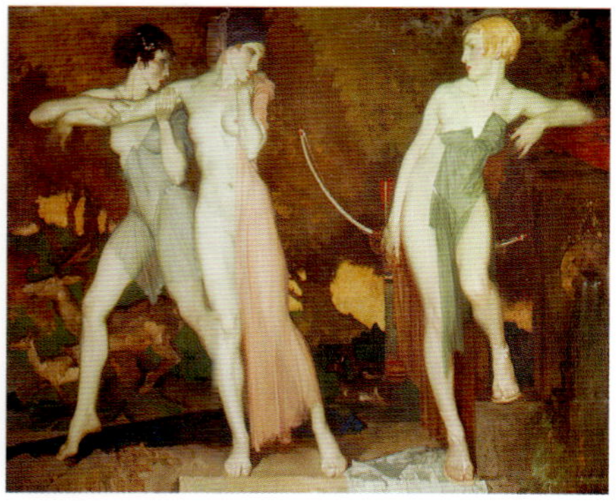

Flint, William Russell 1880–1969
Artemis and Chione 1931
oil on canvas 106.5 x 147.5
PRSMG : P231

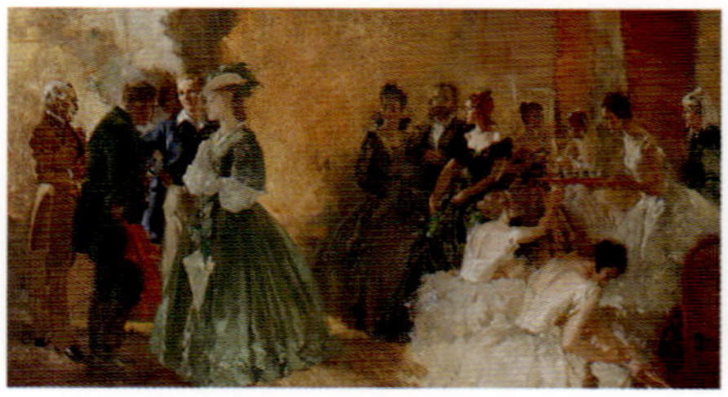

Flint, William Russell 1880–1969
Matinee entr'acte – An Essay in Portraiture 1947
oil on canvas 43 x 76
PRSMG : P1118

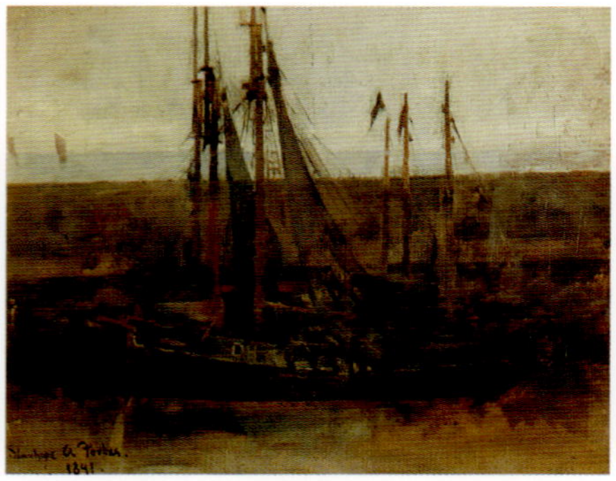

Forbes, Stanhope Alexander 1857–1947
Fishing Boats – Sketch 1891
oil on canvas 35.5 x 50.7
PRSMG : P1539

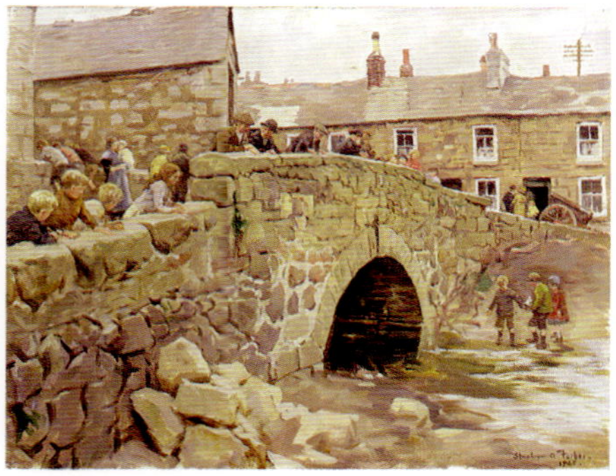

Forbes, Stanhope Alexander 1857–1947
On the Bridge 1925
oil on canvas 61 x 76
PRSMG : P233

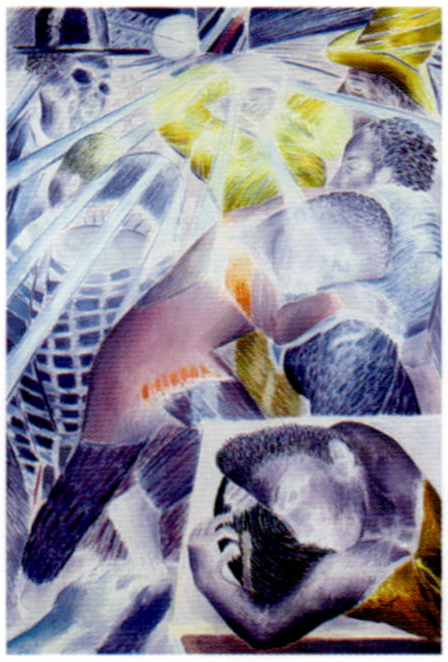

Forrester, Denzil b.1956
Dub Scratchers 1990
oil on canvas 183 x 122
PRSMG : P2258

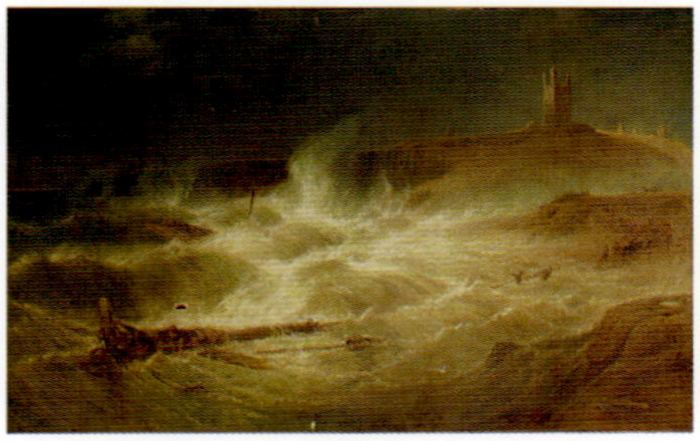

Foster, Myles Birket 1825–1899
The Wreck, Morning after the Storm, Scene at Dunstanbora 1870
oil on canvas 99.5 x 153
PRSMG : P235

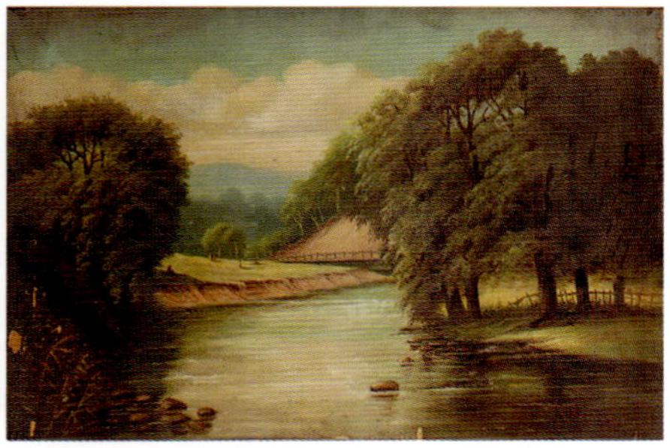

Fowler, F.
River Landscape 1932
oil on canvas 33.4 x 51.2
PRSMG : P1876

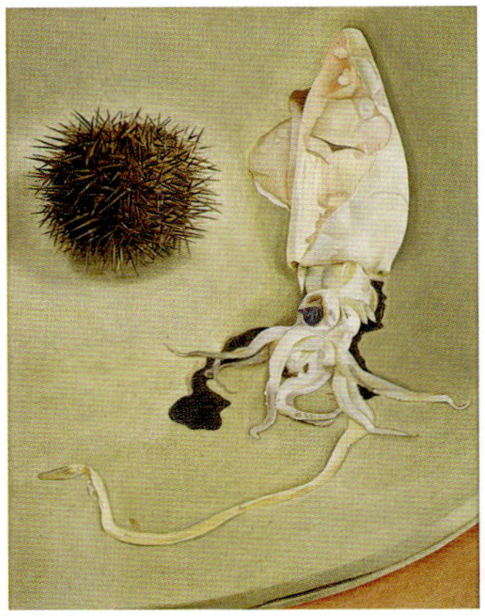

Freud, Lucian 1922–2011
Still Life with Squid and Sea Urchin 1949
oil on copper 38 x 30
PRSMG : P1402

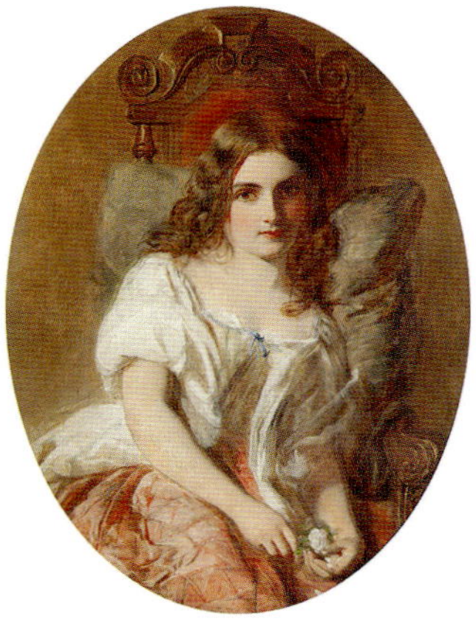

Frith, William Powell 1819–1909
Nora Creina 1845
oil on canvas 30.7 x 24
PRSMG : P241

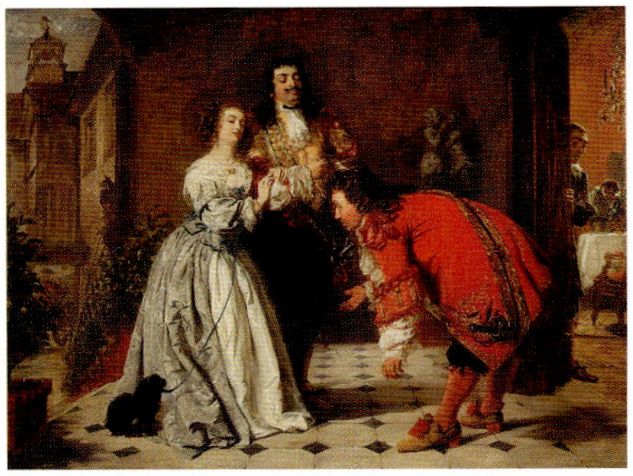

Frith, William Powell 1819–1909
A Scene from 'Le Bourgeois Gentilhomme' 1848
oil on canvas 72 x 92.8
PRSMG : P242

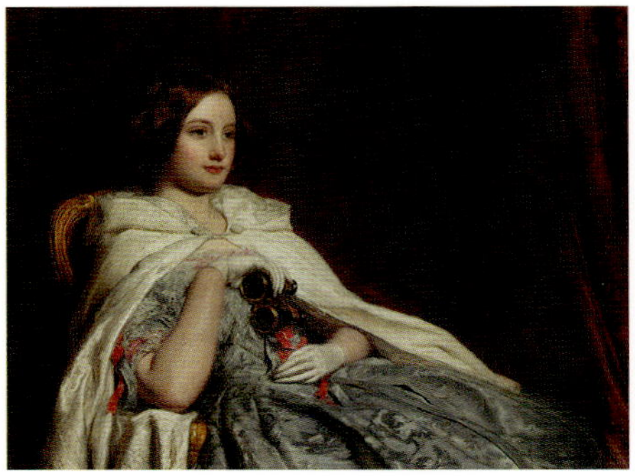

Frith, William Powell 1819–1909
At the Opera 1855
oil on canvas 34.9 x 45
PRSMG : P240

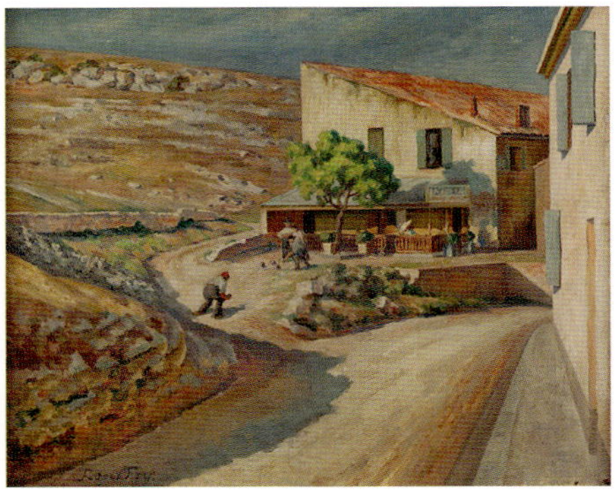

Fry, Roger Eliot 1866–1934
A Game of Bowls 1920–1931
oil on canvas 65.8 x 81.7
PRSMG : P244

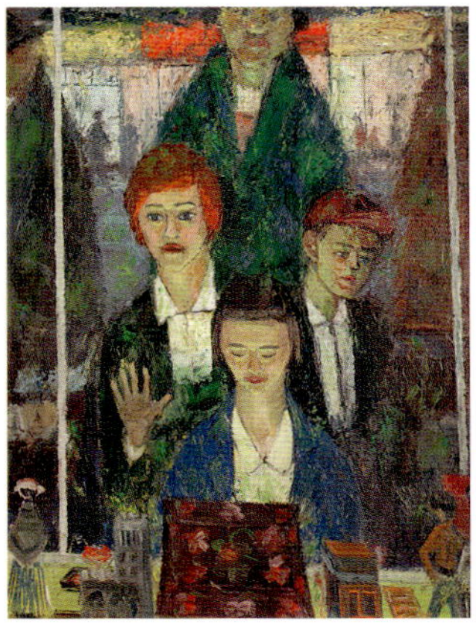

Gabrysch, Leonard 1921–1993
Window Gazers 1958
oil on canvas 63.5 x 53.8
PRSMG : P1596

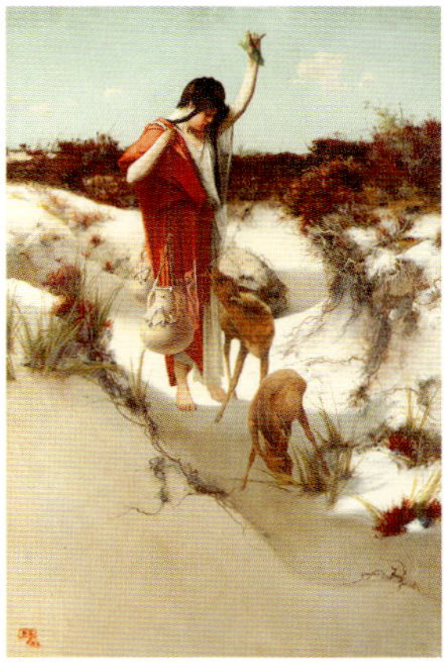

Gandy, Herbert 1857–1934
Companions
oil on canvas 66 x 45.8
PRSMG : P1566

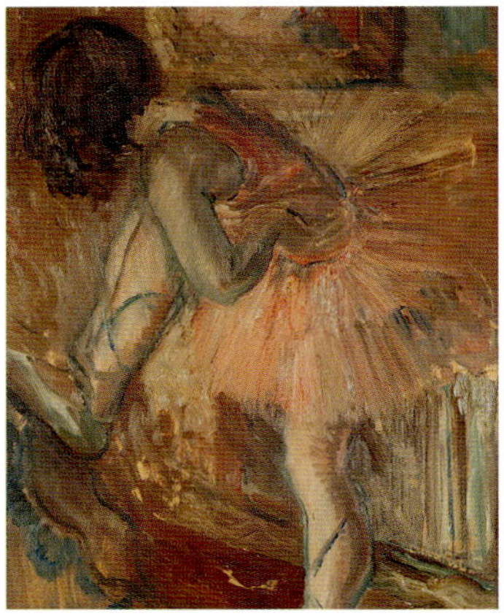

Gerrard, Charles 1892–1964
The Young Dancer 1935
oil on panel 54.5 x 45.7
PRSMG : P249

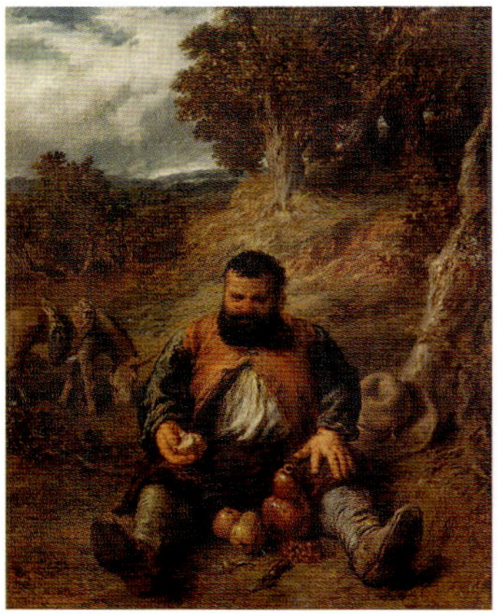

Gilbert, John 1817–1897
Sancho Panza 1859
oil on canvas 77 x 64
PRSMG : P1201

Facing page: Lawrence, Thomas, 1769–1830, *Joseph Farington (1747–1821), RA,* 1794–1796, Lancashire County Museum Service (p. 385)

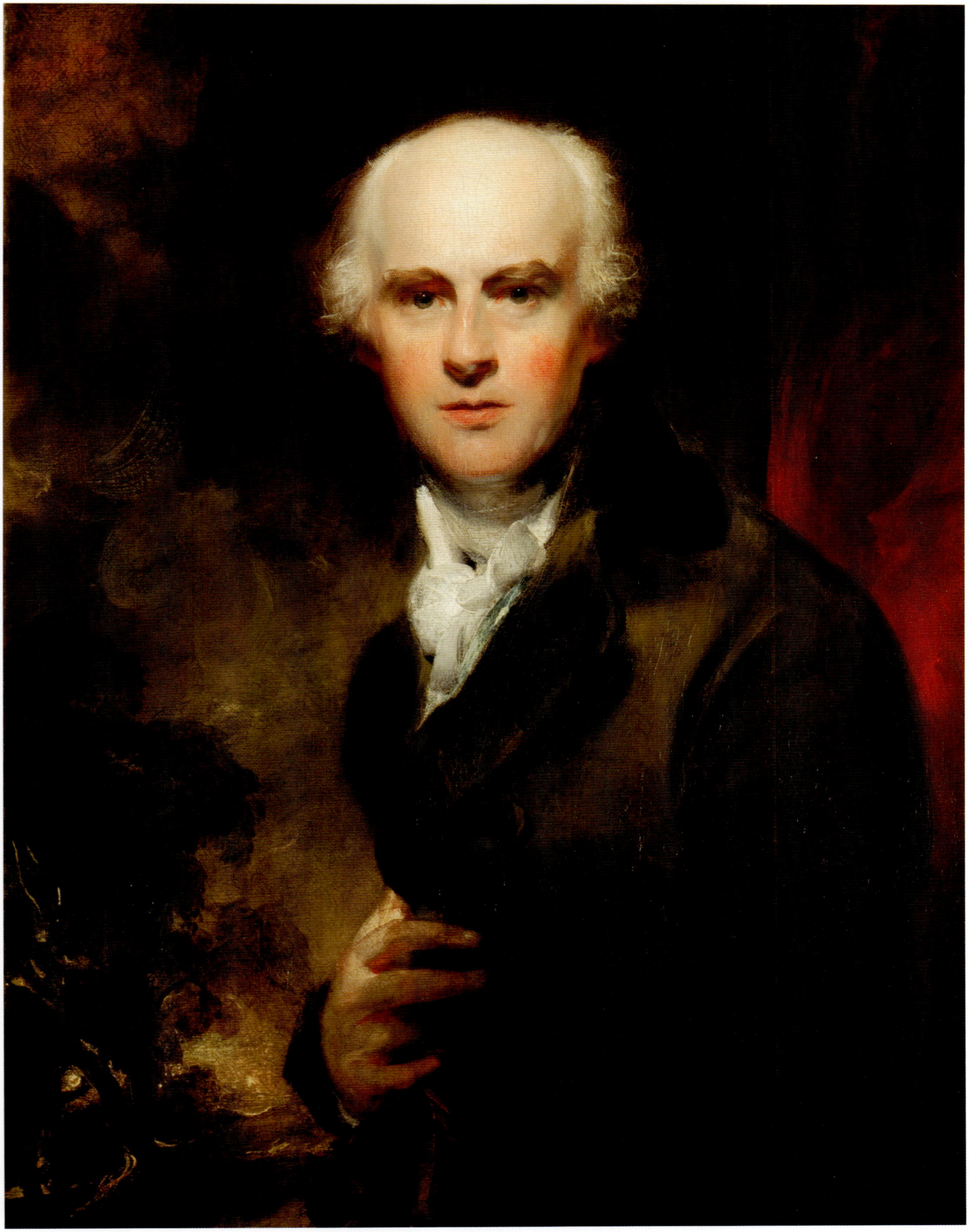

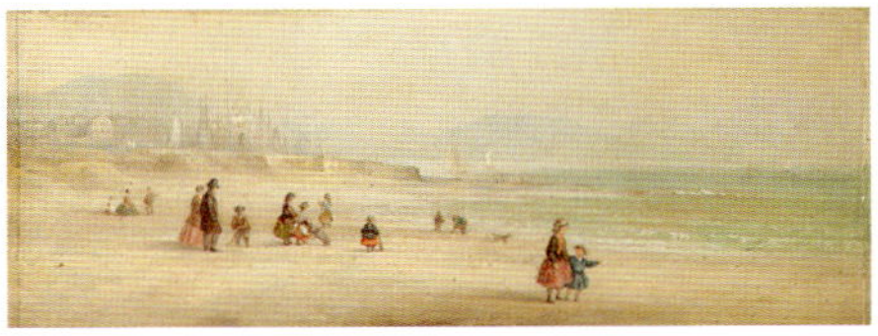

Gill, William Ward 1823–1894
Swansea Bay
oil on panel 16 x 41.5
PRSMG : P1880

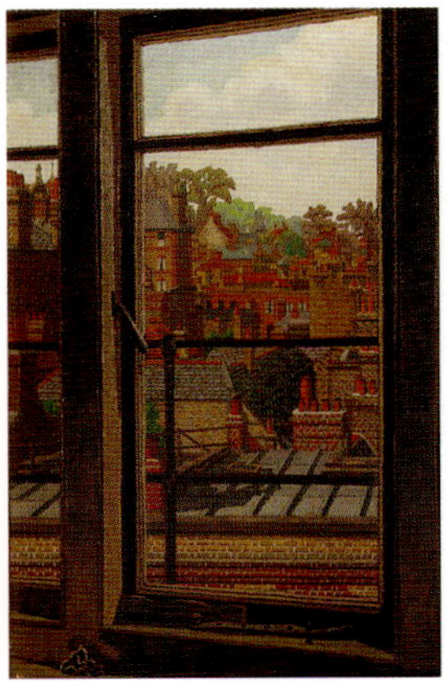

Ginner, Charles 1878–1952
Rooftops 1900–1935
oil on canvas 92 x 61.9
PRSMG : P252

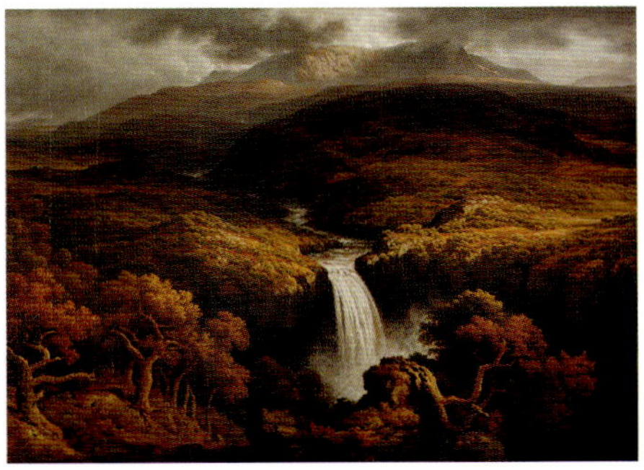

Glover, John 1767–1849
Landscape
oil on canvas 114.2 x 159
PRSMG : P254

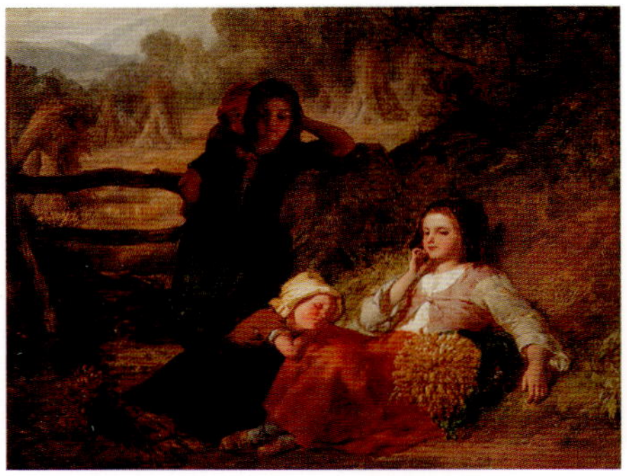

Goodall, Frederick 1822–1904
The Tired Gleaners c.1855
oil on panel 42.5 x 52.7
PRSMG : P256

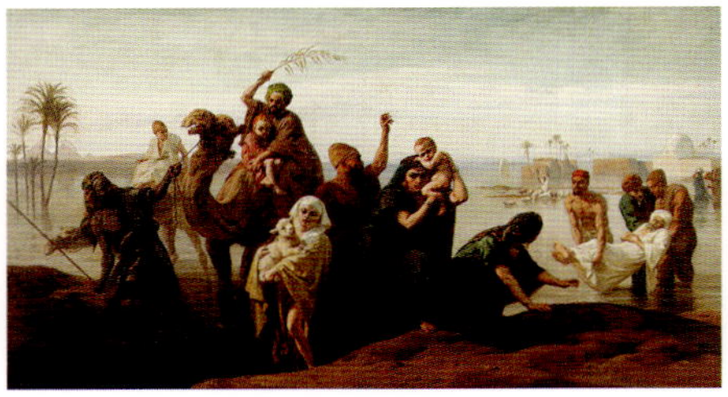

Goodall, Frederick 1822–1904
The Sudden Rising of the Nile 1865
oil on canvas 147 x 270.5
PRSMG : P257

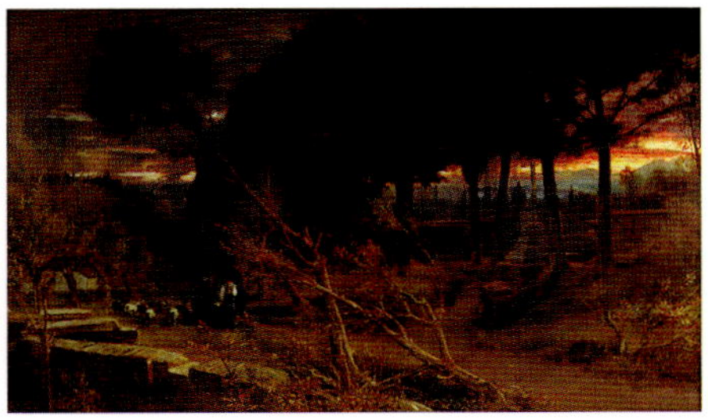

Goodwin, Albert 1845–1932
Florence, Evening 1896
oil on canvas 122 x 203
PRSMG : P258

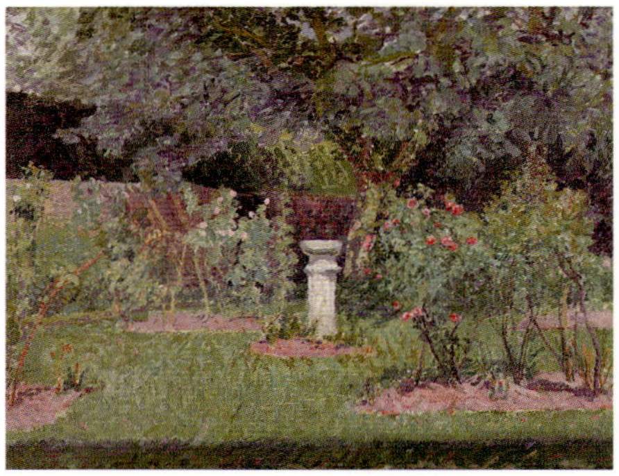

Gore, Spencer 1878–1914
Garden at Hertingfordbury c.1908
oil on canvas 40.5 x 50.8
PRSMG : P927

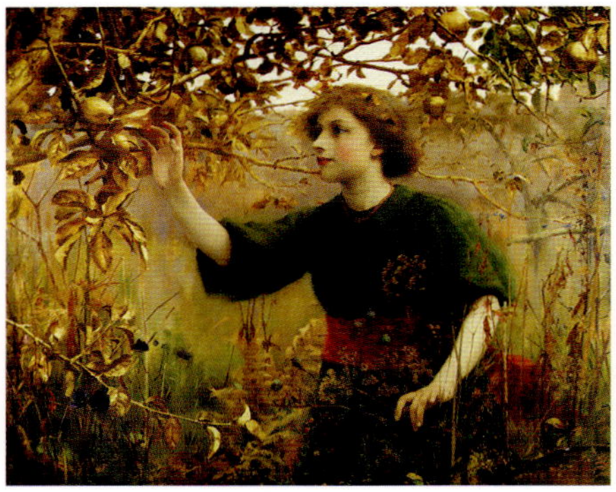

Gotch, Thomas Cooper 1854–1931
A Golden Dream 1893
oil on canvas 128 x 147
PRSMG : P259

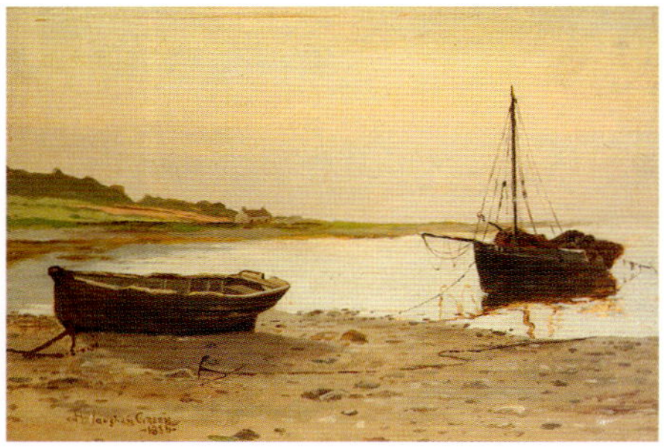

Green, H. Vaughan active 1880–1900
A Sunny Evening, Lochranza 1886
oil on canvas 22.8 x 33
PRSMG : P1352

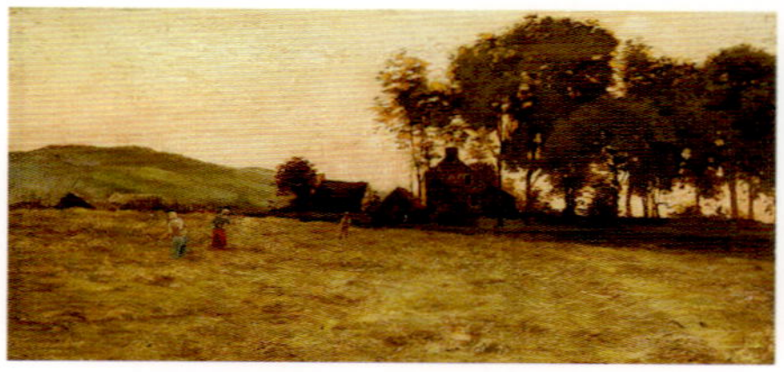

Green, H. Vaughan active 1880–1900
Landscape
oil on canvas 21.5 x 44.5
PRSMG : P260

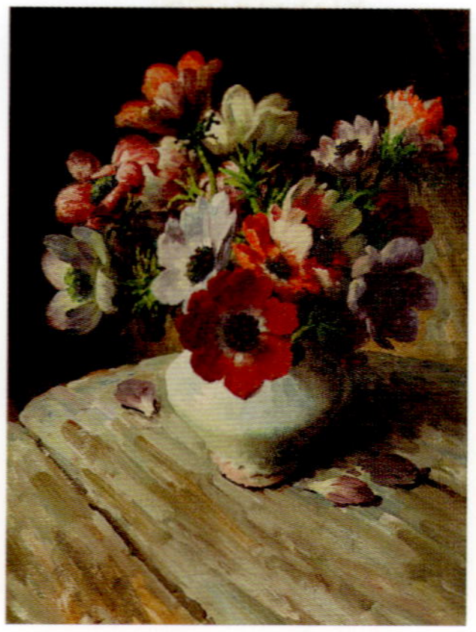

Greenwood, Orlando 1892–1989
Anemones 1932
oil on canvas 55.2 x 45.3
PRSMG : P262

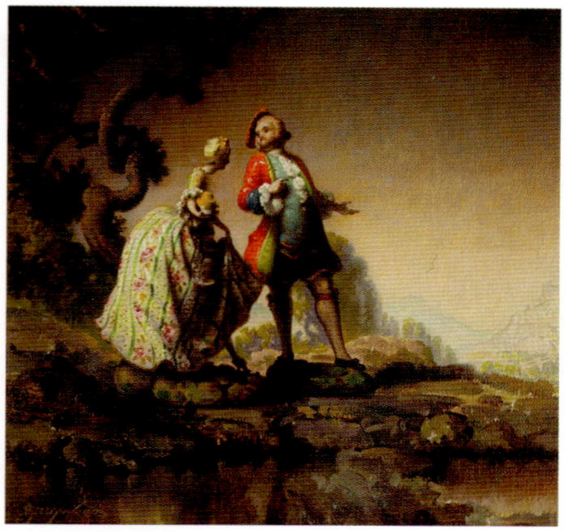

Greenwood, Orlando 1892–1989
I Will Give You a Castle 1934
oil on canvas 46 x 59
PRSMG : P263

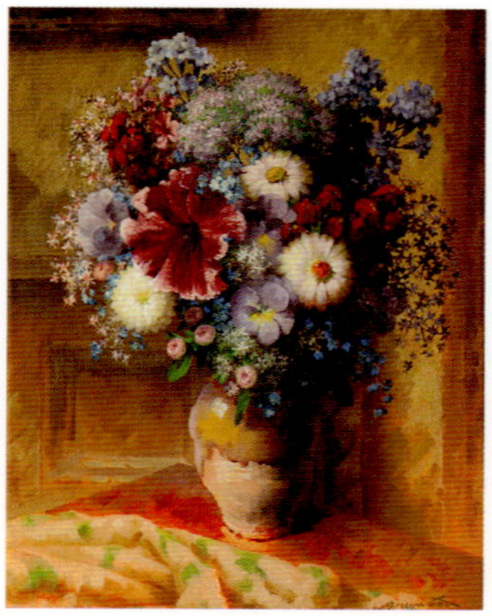

Greenwood, Orlando 1892–1989
June 1935
oil on canvas 53 x 45.5
PRSMG : P264

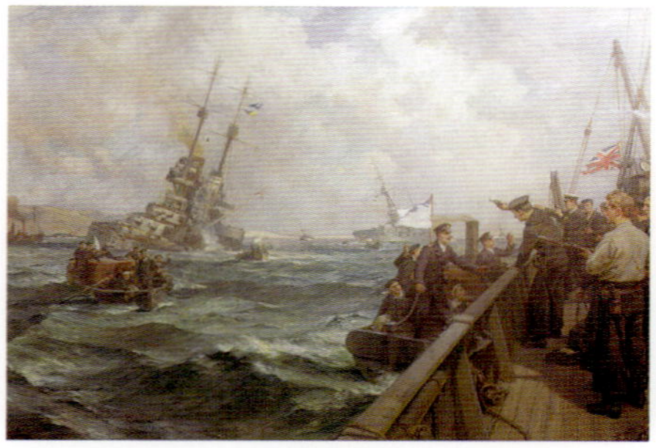

Gribble, Bernard Finnigan 1872–1962
Scapa Flow, 21 June 1919 1920
oil on canvas 125.7 x 181.5
PRSMG : P266

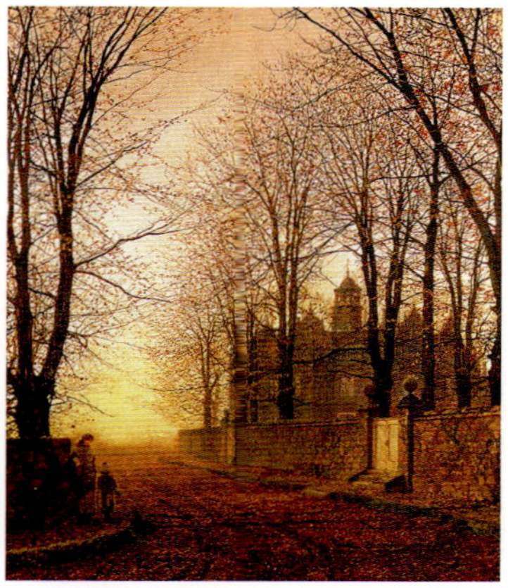

Grimshaw, John Atkinson 1836–1893
In the Golden Olden Times c.1870
oil on canvas 151 x 127
PRSMG : P268

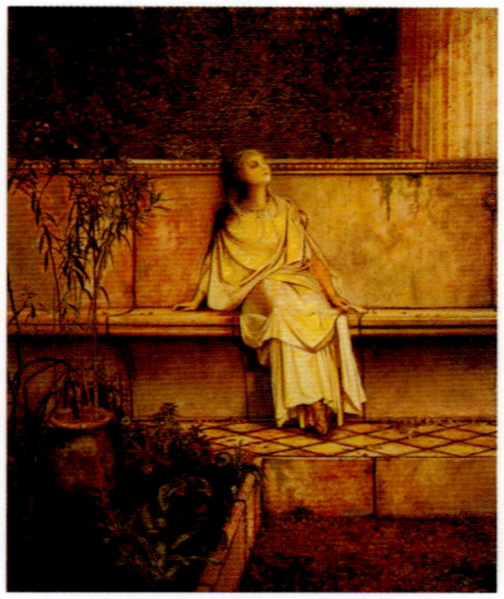

Grimshaw, John Atkinson 1836–1893
Golden Visions 1870
oil on canvas 76.6 x 63.8
PRSMG : P269

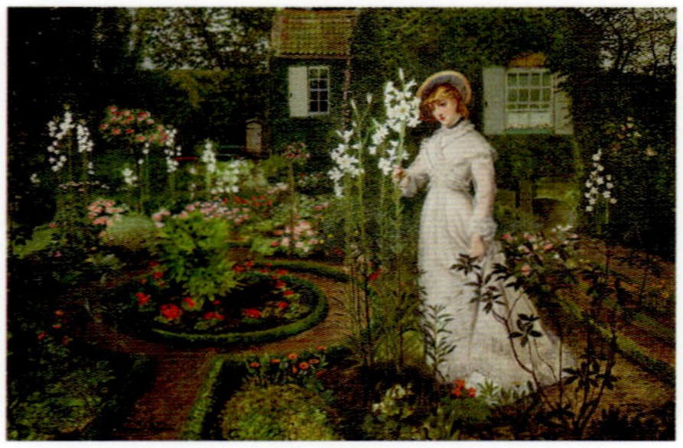

Grimshaw, John Atkinson 1836–1893
The Rector's Garden, Queen of the Lilies 1877
oil on canvas 105 x 143
PRSMG : P267

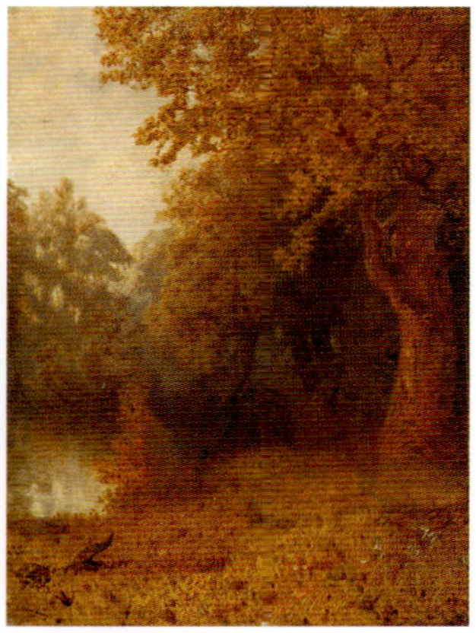

Grundy, Cuthbert Cartwright 1846–1946
Autumn 1900–1919
oil on canvas 111 x 86
PRSMG : P271

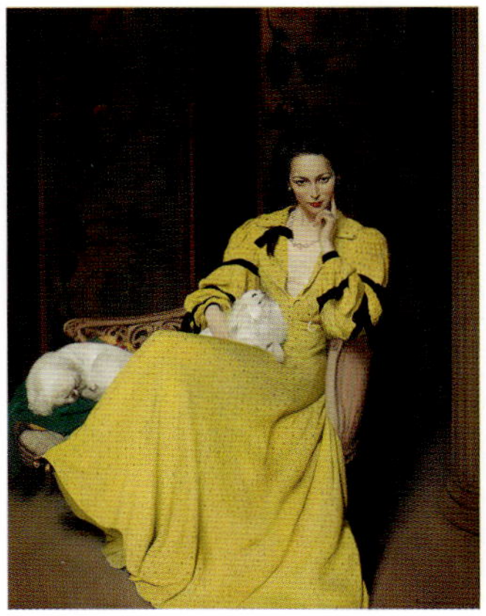

Gunn, Herbert James 1893–1964
Pauline in the Yellow Dress 1944
oil on canvas 150 x 120
PRSMG : P919

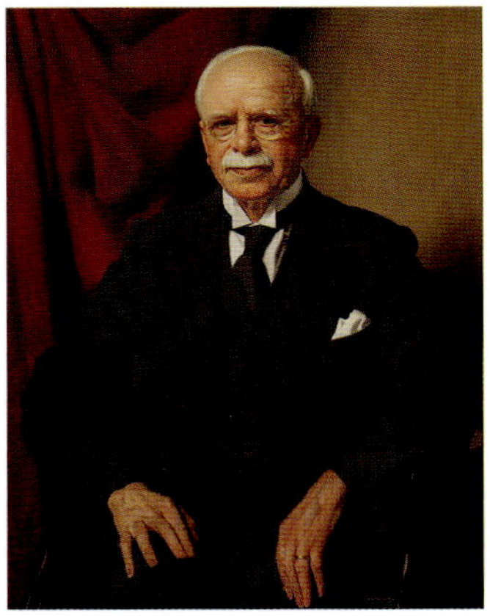

Gunn, Herbert James 1893–1964
James Harrison 1950
oil on canvas 89 x 69.5
PRSMG : P1793

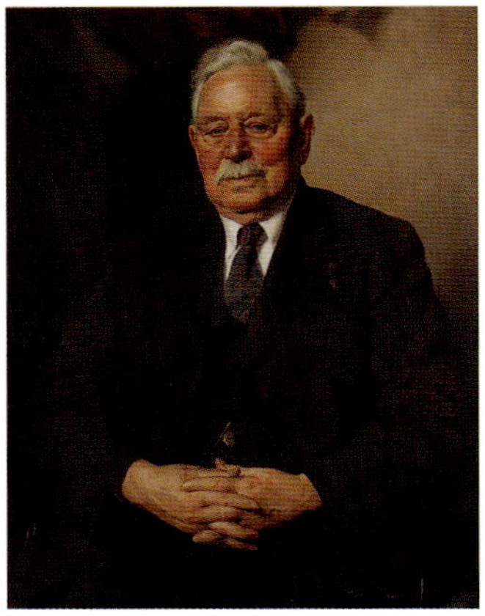

Gunn, Herbert James 1893–1964
Richard Durham 1950
oil on canvas 91.7 x 71.3
PRSMG : P1282

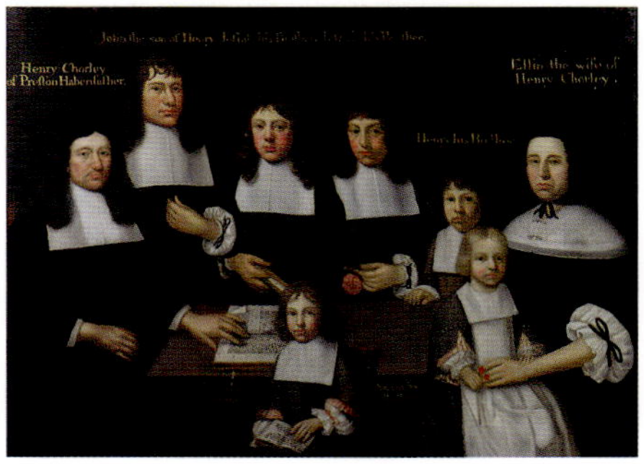

H., J.
The Chorley Family of Preston 1665–1670
oil on canvas 149 x 196
PRSMG : P2297

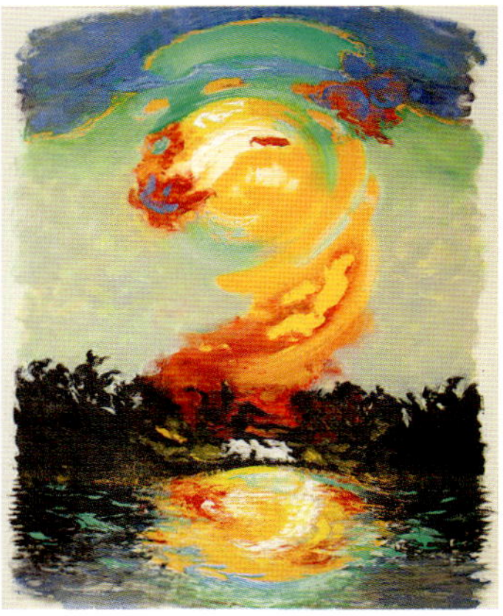

Hambling, Maggi b.1945
July Sunrise, Orwell Estuary, No.2 1985
oil on canvas 160 x 122
PRSMG : P2243

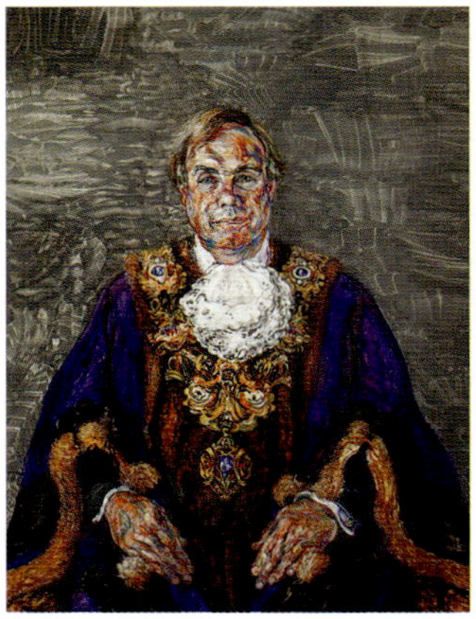

Hambling, Maggi b.1945
Harold Parker, Preston's Guild Mayor (1992)
1993
oil on canvas 106.7 x 91.5
PRSMG : P2306

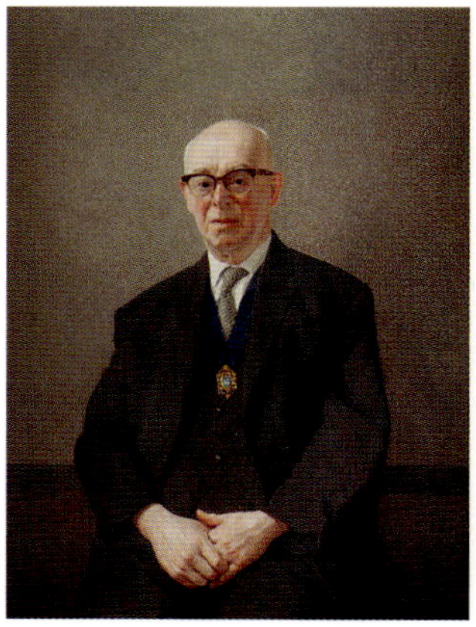

Harrison, Claude 1922–2009
Frank Jamieson 1964
oil on canvas 94.9 x 74.4
PRSMG : P1685

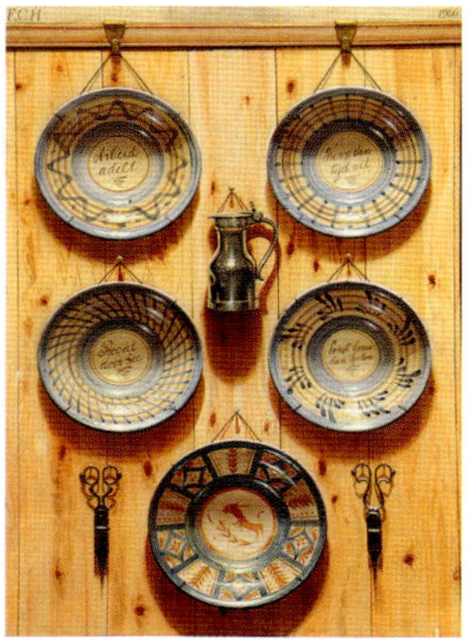

Harrison, Frederick Clifford 1901–1984
Still Life – Plates 1967
oil on hardboard 99.5 x 78.1
PRSMG : P1745

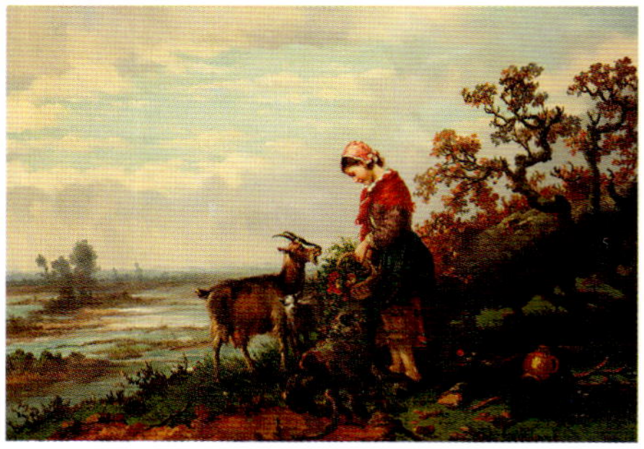

Harvey, James
Girl Feeding a Goat 1862
oil on canvas 63 x 92
PRSMG : P1966

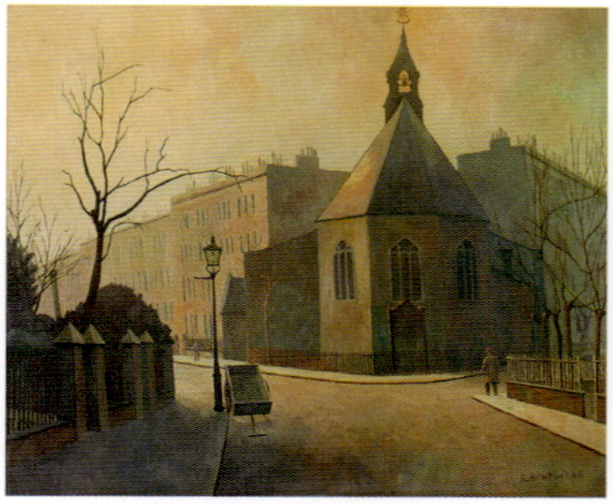

Hawthorne, Elwin 1905–1954
Street Scene 1934
oil on canvas 53.5 x 63.6
PRSMG : P1489

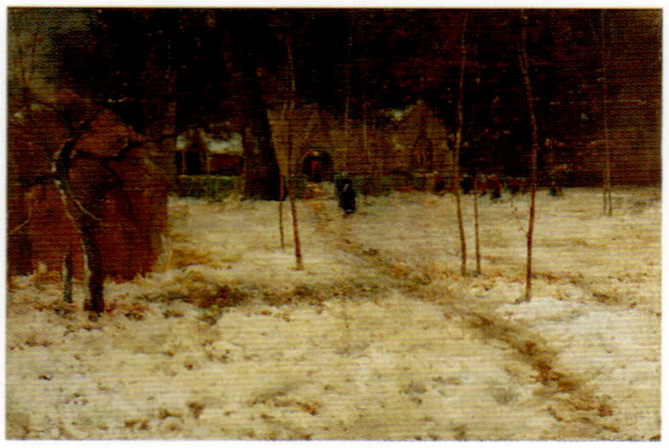

Hayes, Claude 1852–1922
Evensong 1903
oil on canvas 50.7 x 71
PRSMG : P278

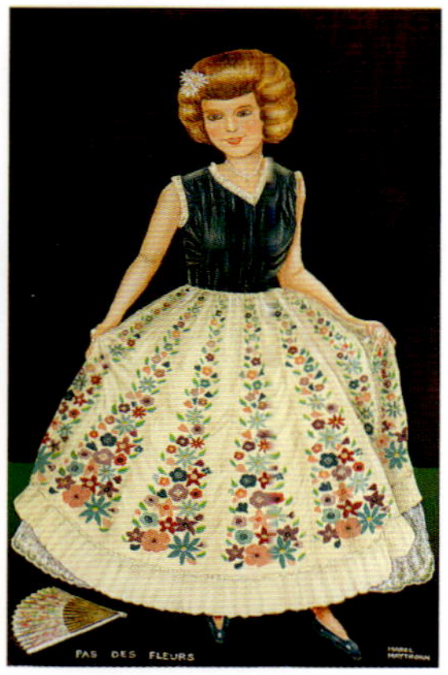

Haythorn, Mabel active 1900–1950
Pas des fleurs
oil on panel 60 x 37
PRSMG : P1881

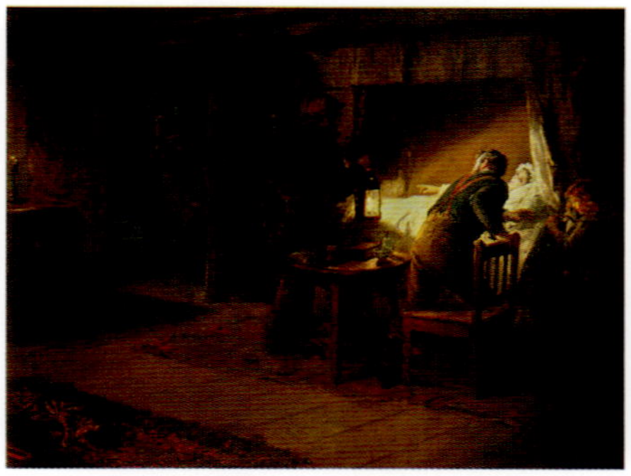

Hedley, Ralph 1848–1913
'Go, and God's will be done!' 1891
oil on canvas 138 x 181
PRSMG : P1921

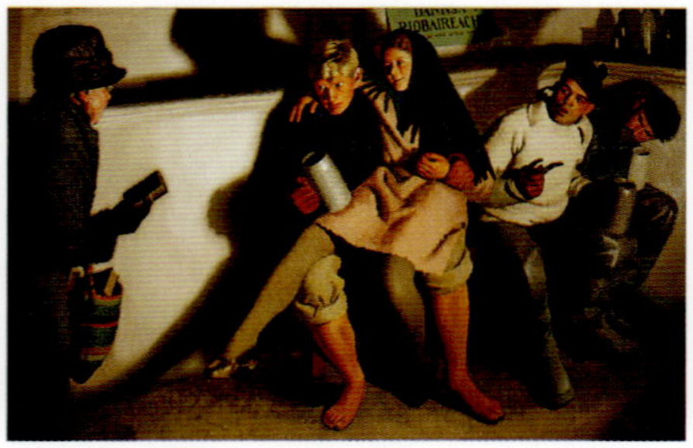

Henderson, Keith 1883–1982
The Word 1931
oil on canvas 96.5 x 157.5
PRSMG : P279

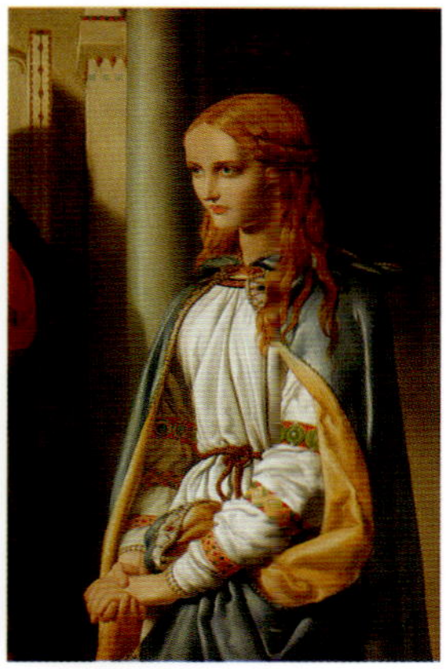

Herbert, John Rogers 1810–1890
Cordelia Disinherited 1850
oil on canvas 100.5 x 61
PRSMG : P283

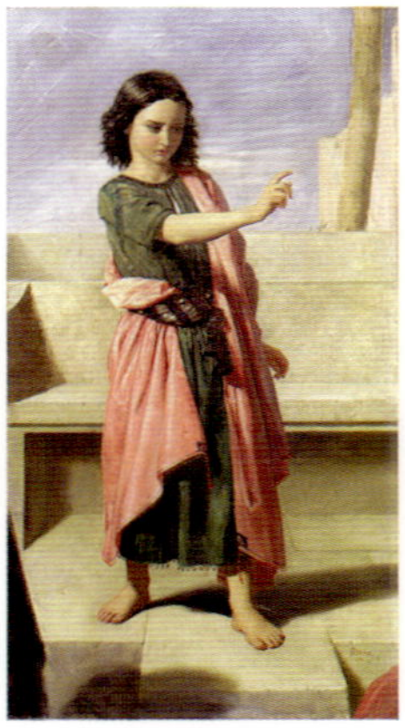

Herbert, John Rogers 1810–1890
The Judgement of Daniel 1851
oil on canvas 120 x 64.2
PRSMG : P282

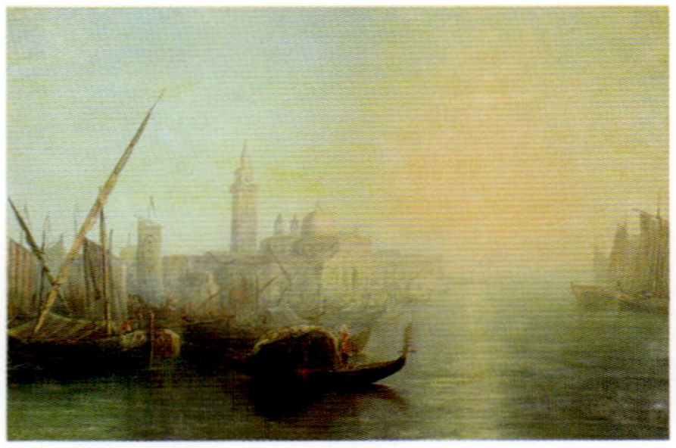

Herbert, Sydney 1854–1914
San Giorgio Maggiore, Venice 1876
oil on canvas 61 x 91
PRSMG : P1882

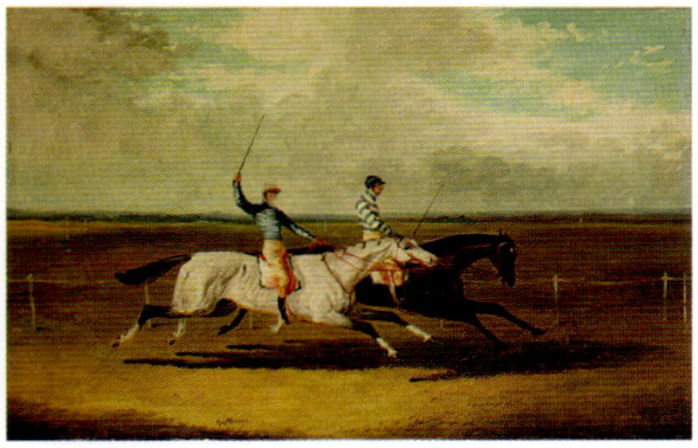

Herring I, John Frederick (school of) 1795–1865
Two Racehorses – Grey Momus' and 'Caravan' – Racing 1830–1850
oil on canvas 30.5 x 45.7
PRSMG : P1824

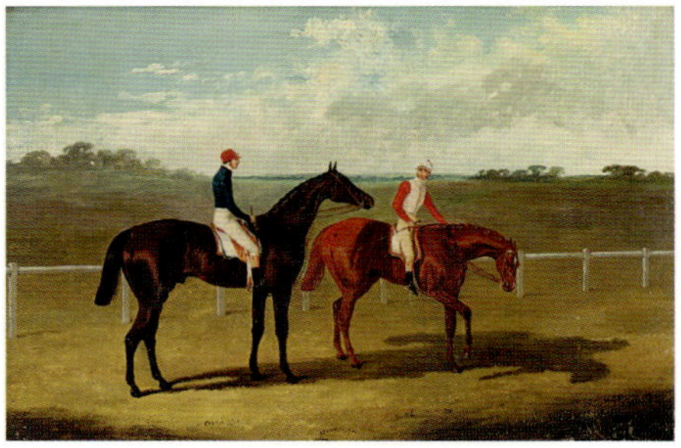

Herring I, John Frederick (school of) 1795–1865
Two Racehorses – 'Charles XII' and 'Buella' – with Jockeys 1840
oil on panel 30.5 x 45.7
PRSMG : P1823

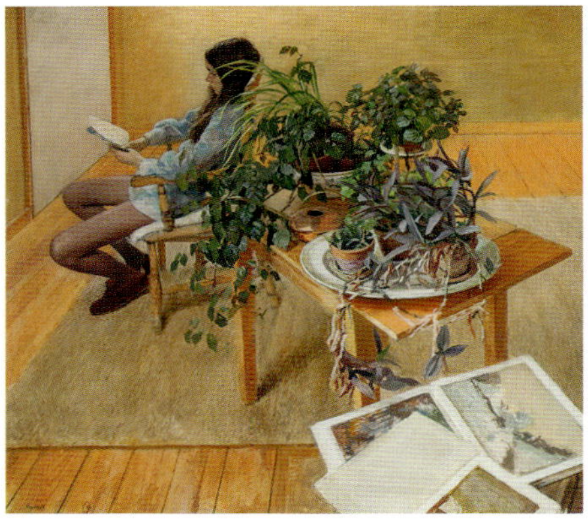

Heyworth, Alfred 1926–1976
Ann with Indoor Plants 1971
oil on canvas 122 x 134 (E)
PRSMG : P1783

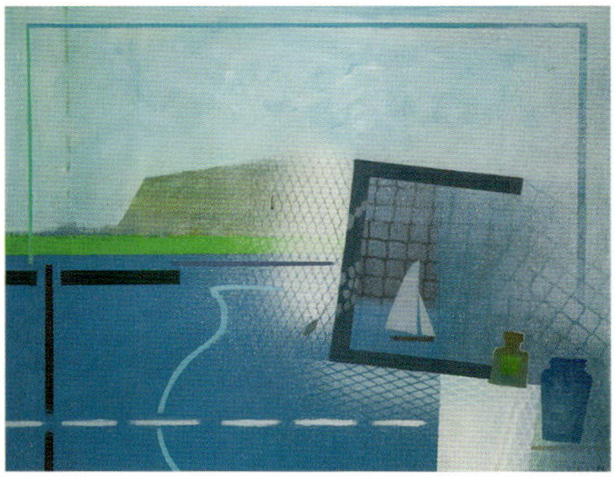

Hicks, Philip b.1928
Mirror on the Balcony Overlooking the Bay 1978
acrylic on canvas 50.8 x 61
PRSMG : P2279

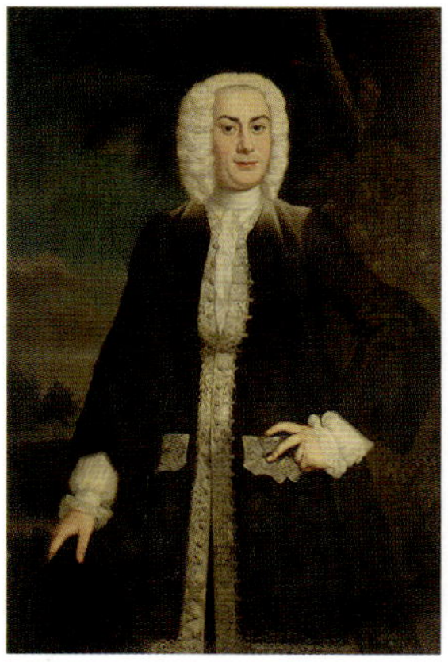

Highmore, Joseph 1692–1780
Portrait of a Gentleman 1730–1780
oil on canvas 124.5 x 100
PRSMG : P604

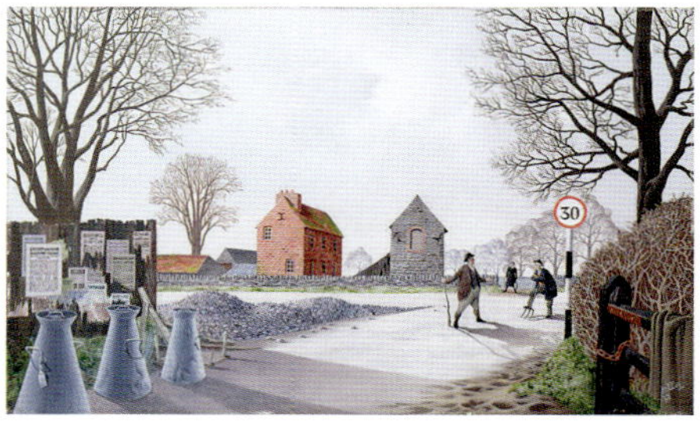

Hillier, Tristram Paul 1905–1983
The Argument 1943
oil on panel 26.7 x 40.6
PRSMG : P929

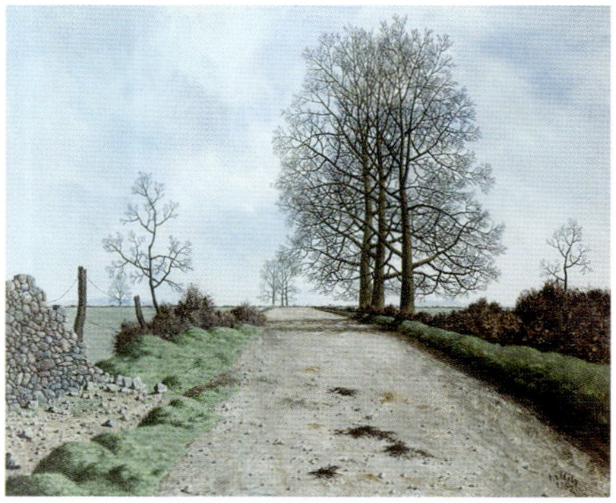

Hillier, Tristram Paul 1905–1983
January Landscape, Somerset 1962
oil on canvas 50.8 x 61
PRSMG : P1653

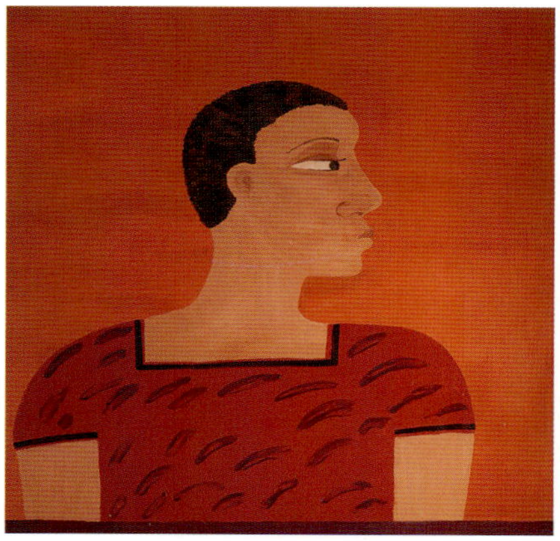

Himid, Lubaina b.1954
Hannibal's Sister 1989
acrylic on canvas 183 x 183
PRSMG : P2328

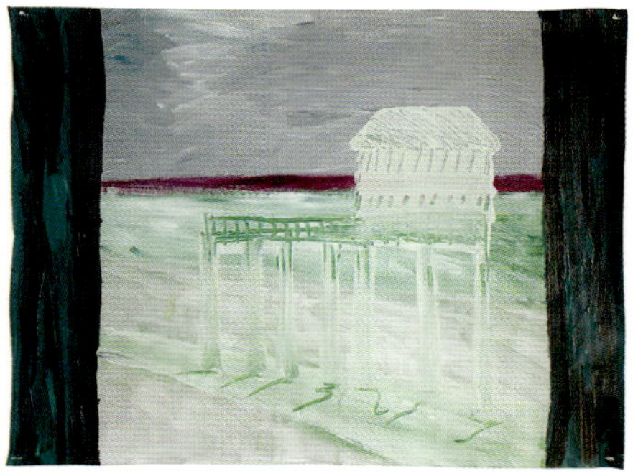

Himid, Lubaina b.1954
Tuesday 1994
acrylic on paper 60 x 84
PRSMG : P2329

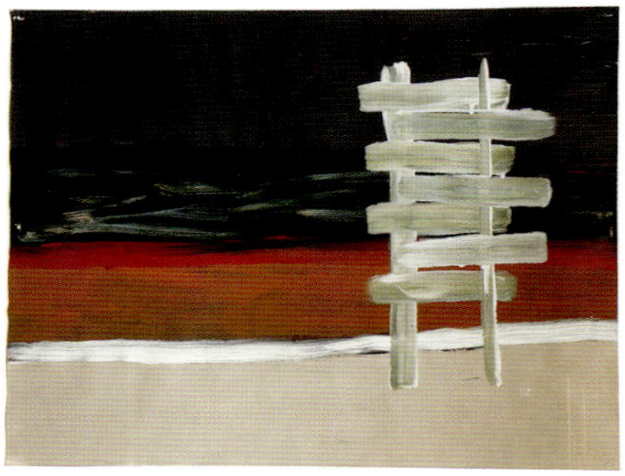

Himid, Lubaina b.1954
Weave 1994
acrylic on paper 60 x 84
PRSMG : P2330

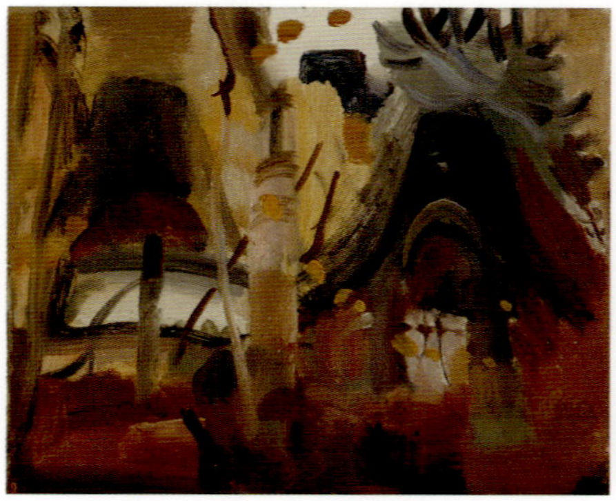

Hitchens, Ivon 1893–1979
Two Ways through a Wood c.1945
oil on canvas 30.5 x 43
PRSMG : P2352

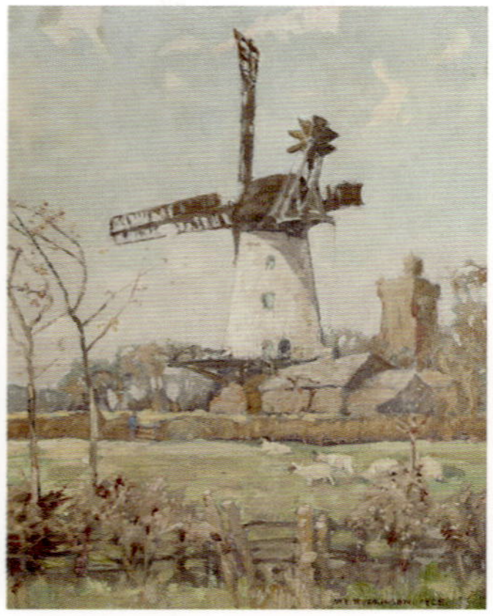

Hodkinson, W. E.
Clifton Windmill 1928
oil on canvas 39.2 x 30.5
PRSMG : P287

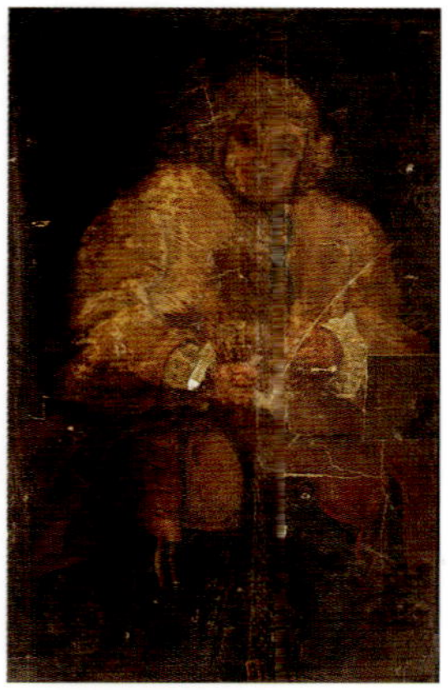

Hogarth, William 1697–1764
Lord Lovat late 18th C
oil on canvas 154 x 106
PRSMG : P1940

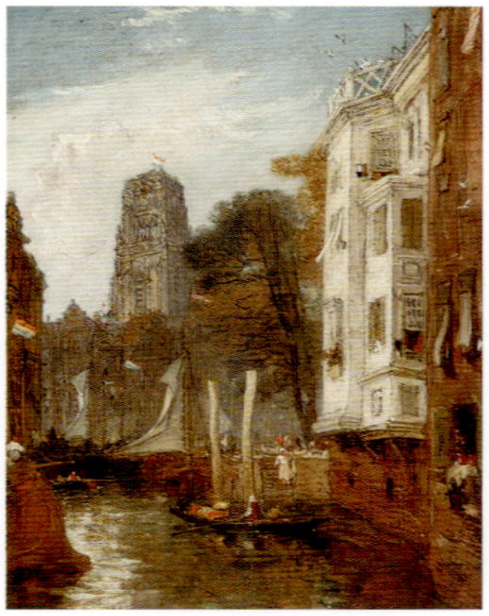

Holland, James 1799–1870
Rotterdam 1853
oil on panel 35.5 x 28
PRSMG : P289

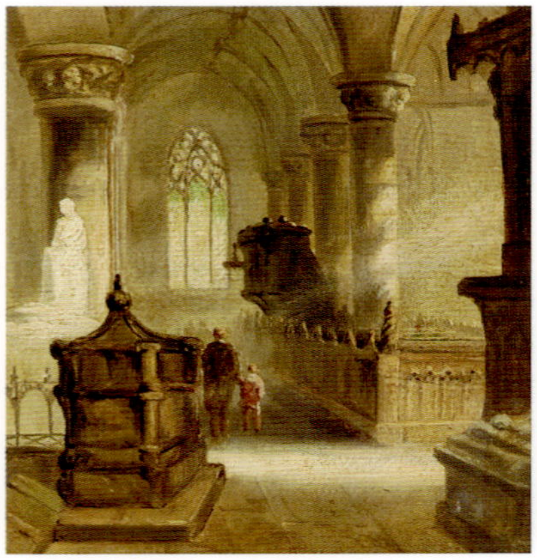

Holland, James 1799–1870
The Chancel
oil on board 25.5 x 24.7
PRSMG : P1501

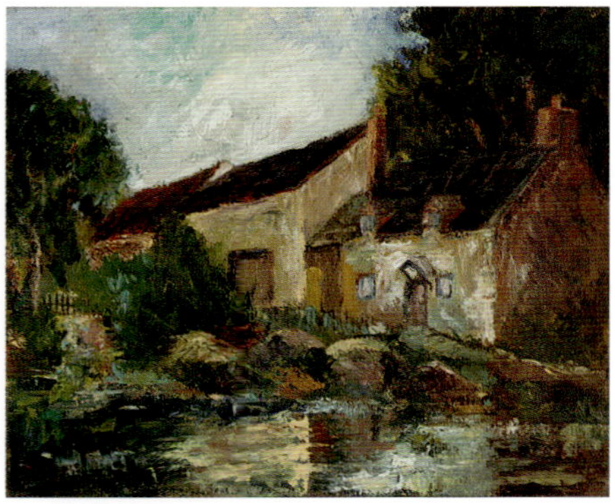

Hollis, Gerald b. 1908
A Welsh Cottage 1950
oil on canvas 40.6 x 50.8
PRSMG : P1362

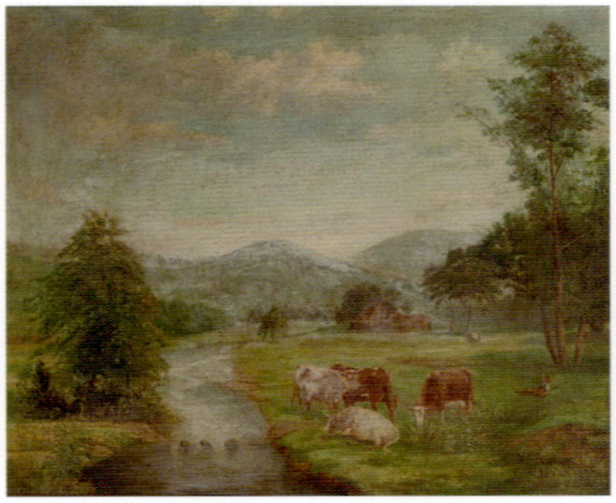

Holman, W. H.
Landscape with Cattle 1921
oil on canvas 43.5 x 53.7
PRSMG : P1883

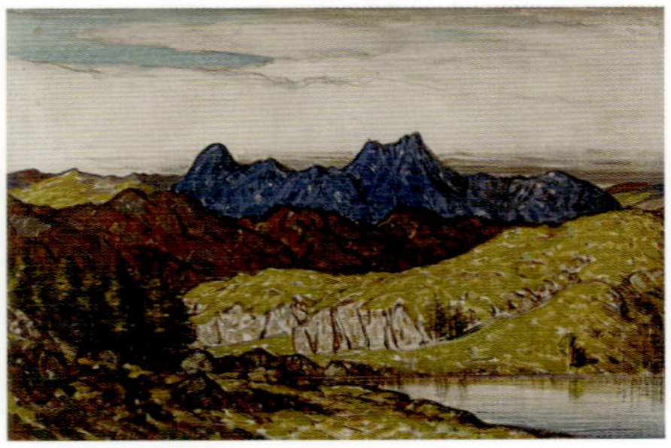

Holmes, Charles John 1868–1936
Langdale Pikes 1917
oil on canvas 50.5 x 76.5
PRSMG : P294

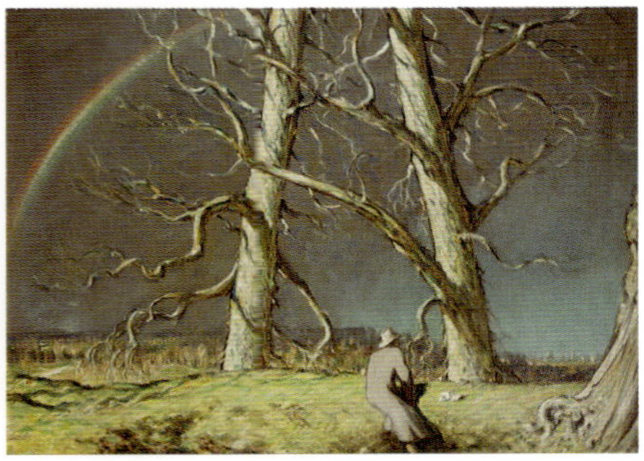

Holmes, Charles John 1868–1936
Scholar Gipsy 1917
oil on canvas 51 x 76.5
PRSMG : P295

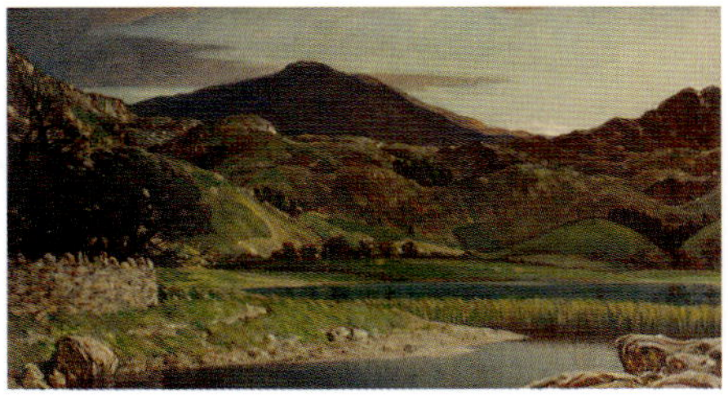

Holmes, Charles John 1868–1936
Watendlath Tarn, near Keswick 1919
oil on canvas 46.5 x 82
PRSMG : P293

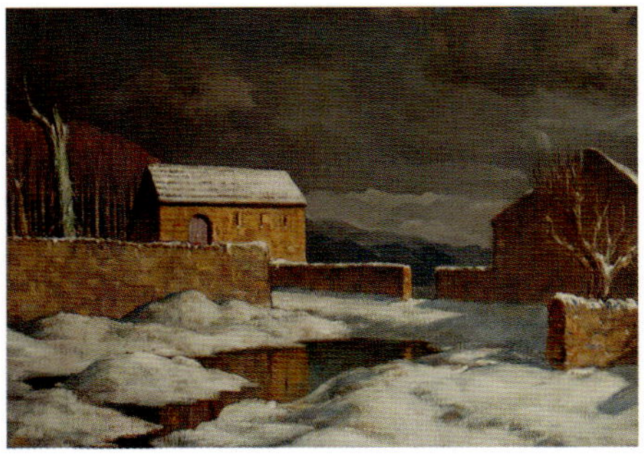

Holmes, Charles John 1868–1936
Farmyard, Winter 1921
oil on canvas 46.5 x 86.7
PRSMG : P810

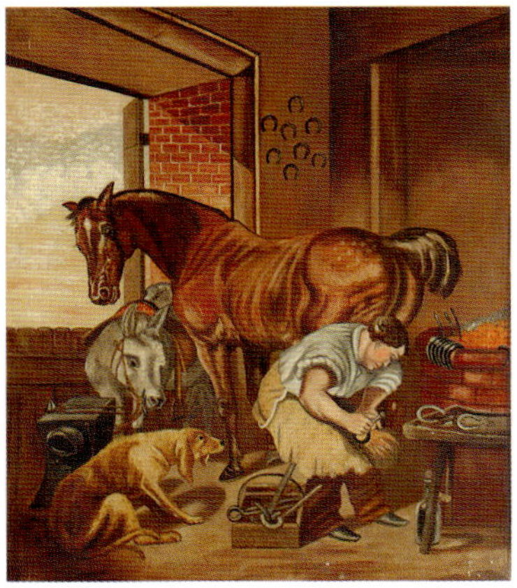

Holmes, Richard 1868–1938
Blacksmith at Work 1882
oil on canvas 76 x 65.8
PRSMG : P1884

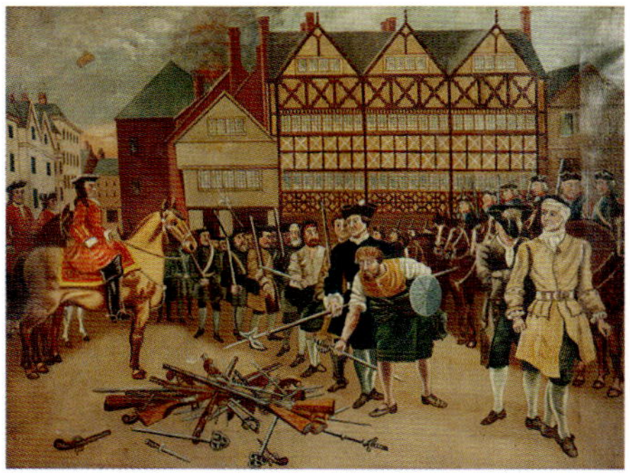

Holmes, Richard 1868–1938
Jacobite Troops Surrendering Their Arms to General Wills in Preston Market Place, 1715
oil on canvas 54.5 x 70
PRSMG : P763

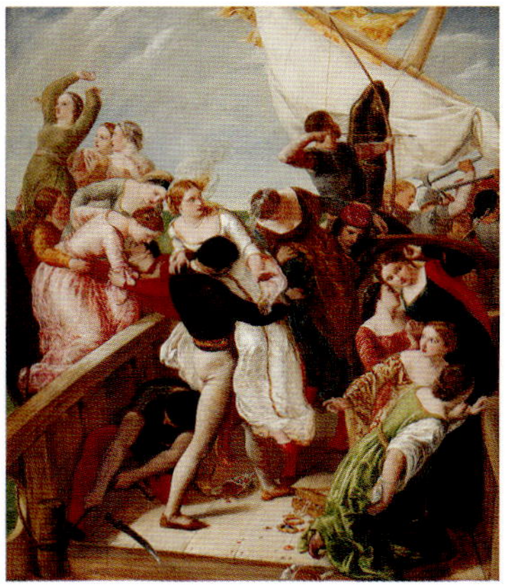

Hook, James Clarke 1819–1907
The Rescue of the Brides of Venice 1851
oil on canvas 129.5 x 108
PRSMG : P299

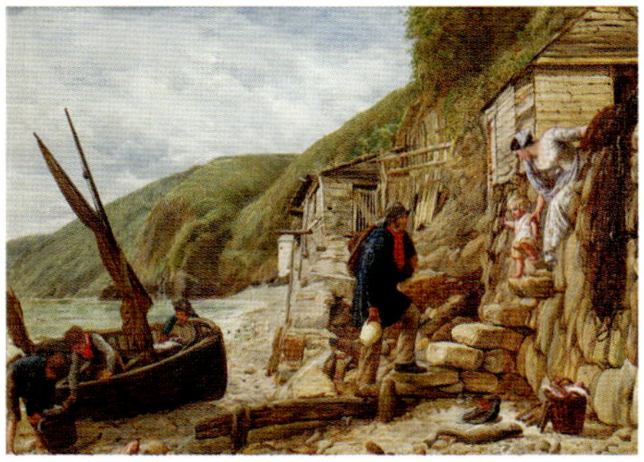

Hook, James Clarke 1819–1907
Welcome, Bonny Boat! The Fisherman's Return (Scene at Clovelly, North Devon) 1856
oil on canvas 63 x 94.7
PRSMG : P298

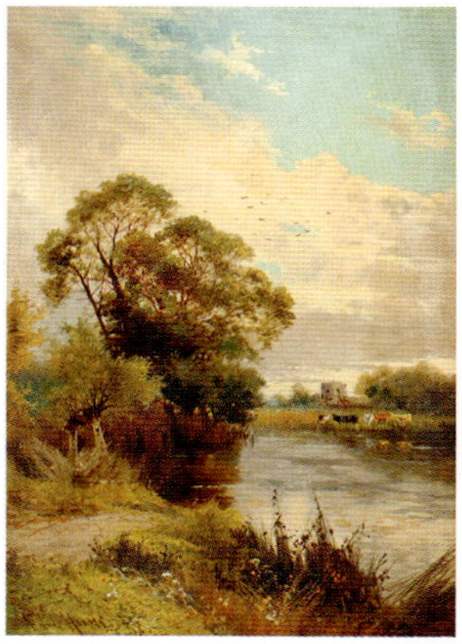

Hooper, John Horace 1852–1906
Cookham on Thames
oil on canvas 76.5 x 51.2
PRSMG : P1493

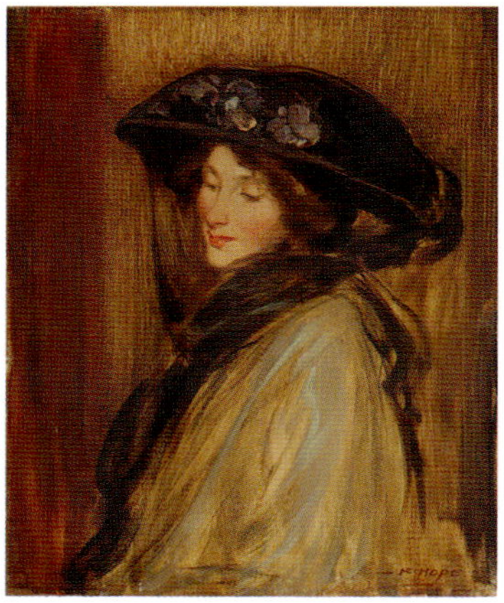

Hope, Robert 1869–1936
Portrait of a Lady with a Motoring Veil
1910–1915
oil on canvas 60.5 x 50.8
PRSMG : P1443

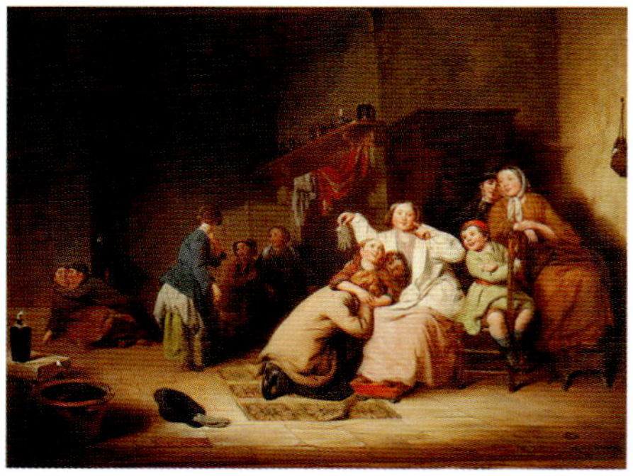

Horsley, John Callcott 1817–1903
Forfeits 1887
oil on panel 40.7 x 52
PRSMG : P1583

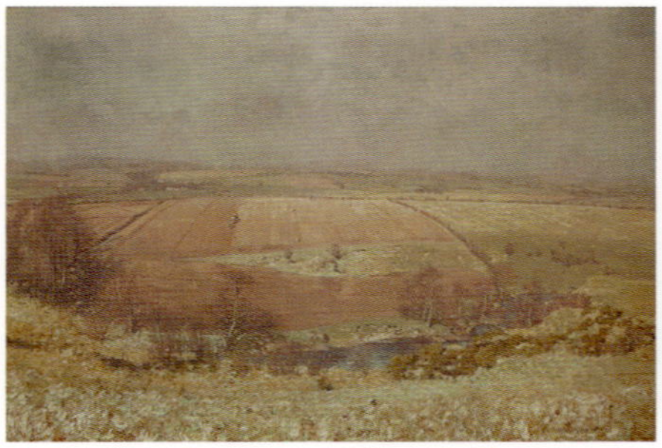

Houston, George 1869–1947
Seed Time in Ayrshire 1908
oil on canvas 102.2 x 152.8
PRSMG : P303

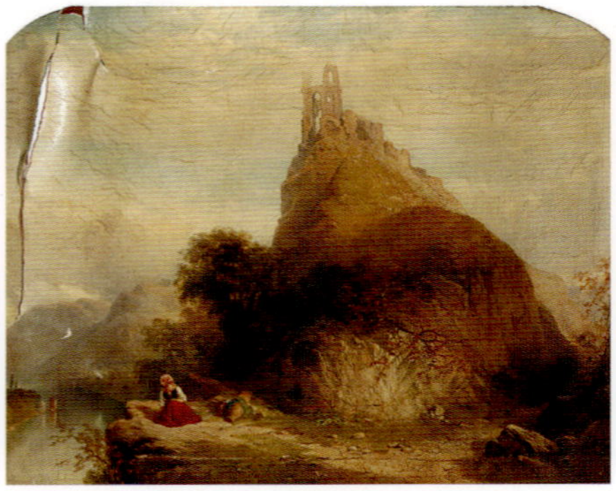

Houston, John Adam 1812–1884
View near Trarbach on the Moselle 1850–1884
oil on canvas 85 x 110.5
PRSMG : P305

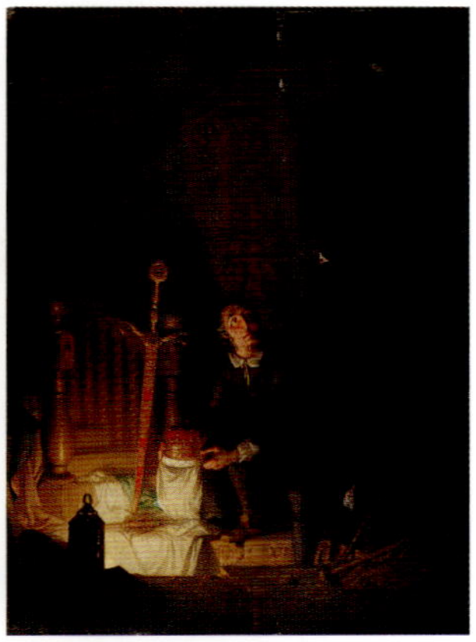

Houston, John Adam 1812–1884
The Secreting of the Regalia of Scotland in Kineff Church, 1652
oil on canvas 111.8 x 88
PRSMG : P304

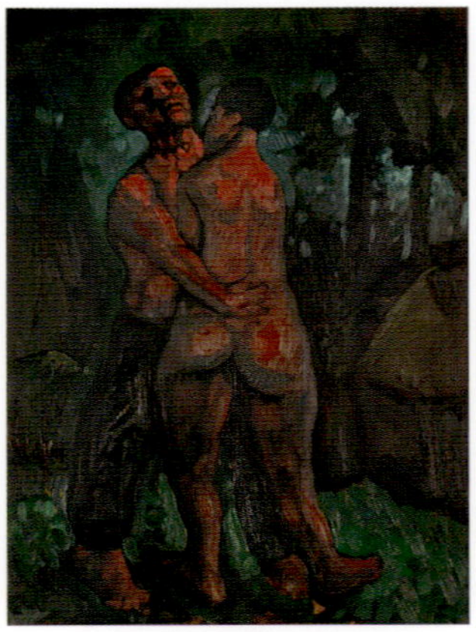

Howson, Peter b.1958
Untitled and Two Figures in a Wood
oil on canvas 30 x 24
PRSMG : 2005.195

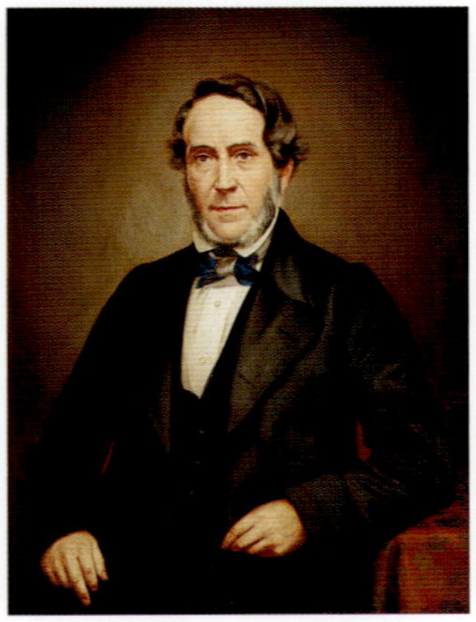

Hoyoll, Philipp 1818–1876
Isaac Simpson c.1860
oil on canvas 87 x 71.5
PRSMG : P2284

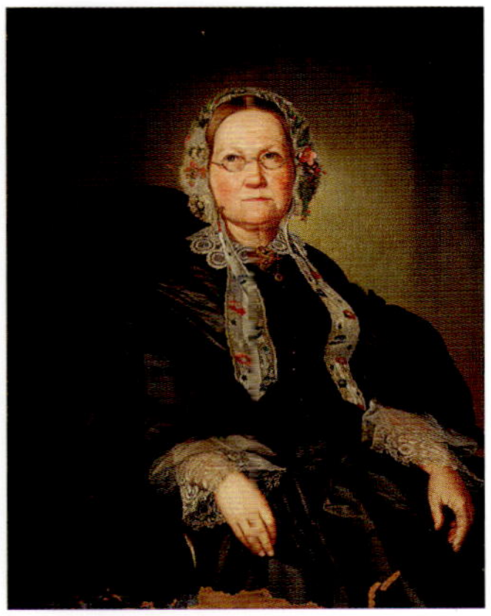

Hoyoll, Philipp 1818–1876
Mary Simpson c.1860
oil on canvas 92 x 71.5
PRSMG : P2285

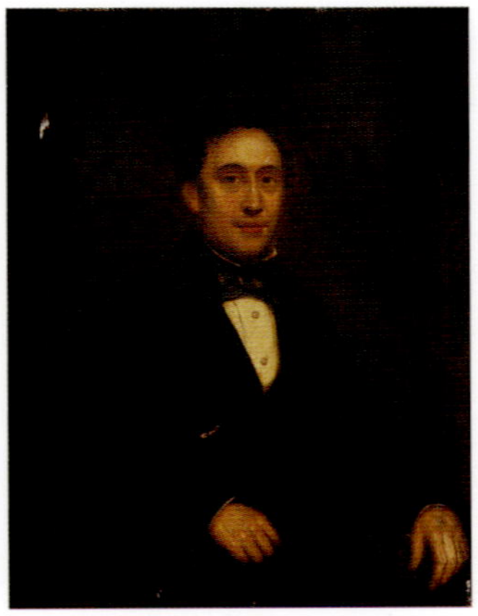

Hoyoll, Philipp 1818–1876
Stephen Simpson c.1860
oil on canvas 92 x 71.5
PRSMG : P2286

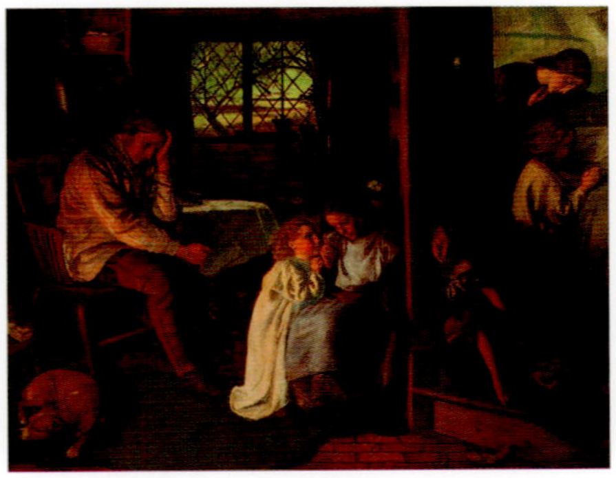

Hughes, Arthur 1832–1915
Bedtime 1862
oil on canvas 130 x 160.5
PRSMG : P1486

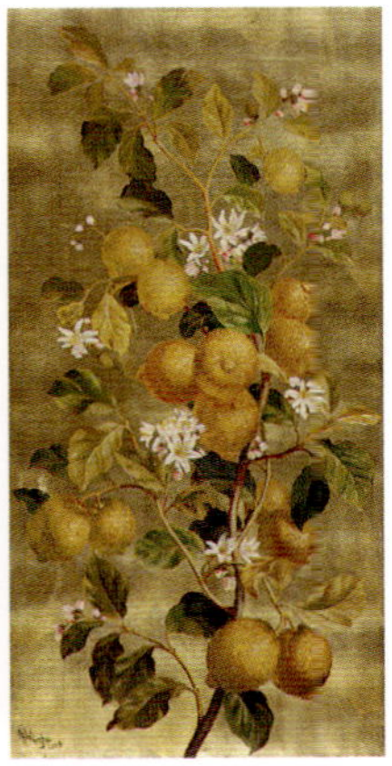

Hughes, William 1842–1901
Lemons and Flowers
oil on canvas 83.8 x 40.5
PRSMG : P308

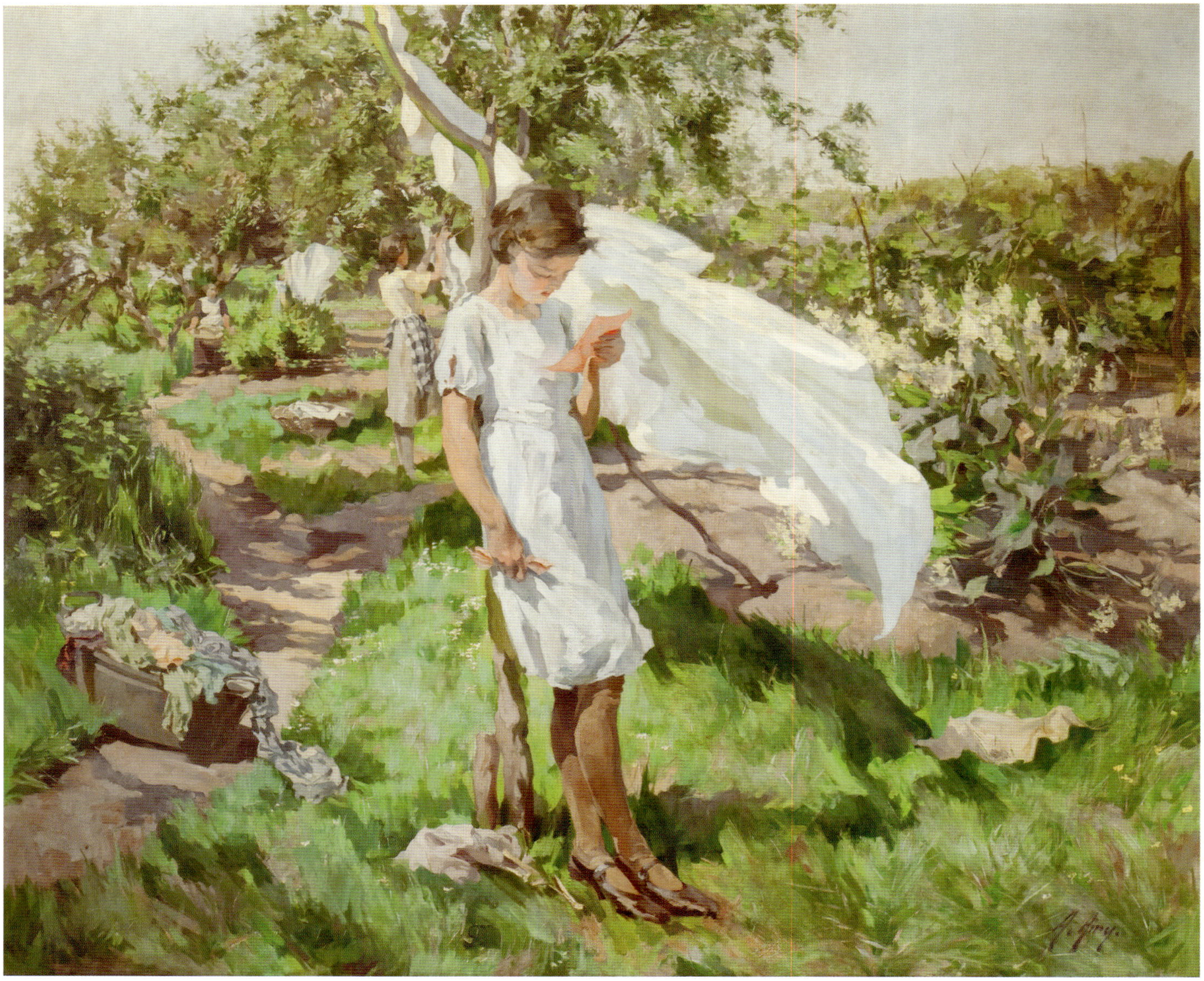

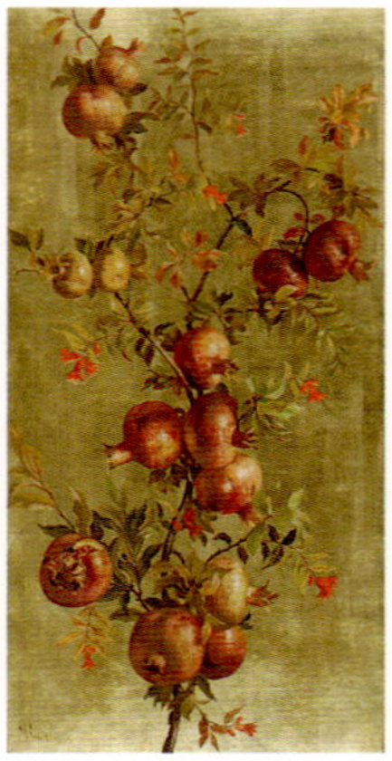

Hughes, William 1842–1901
Pomegranates and Flowers
oil on canvas 84 x 40.5
PRSMG : P309

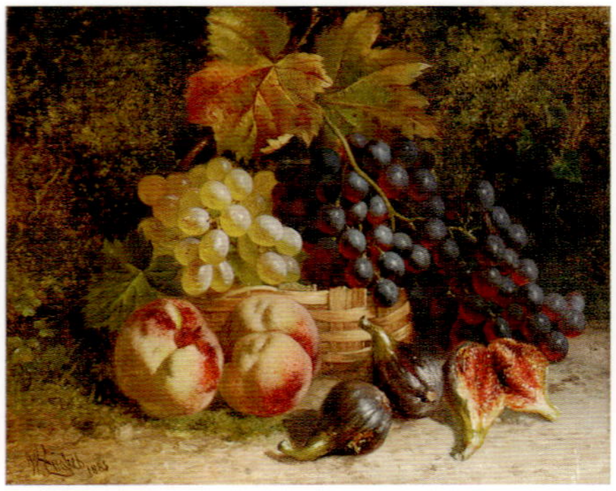

Hughes, William 1842–1901
Still Life – Fruit
oil on canvas 34.2 x 44.5
PRSMG : P307

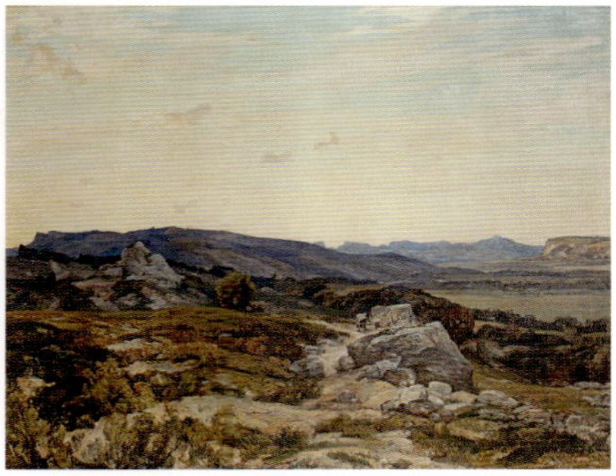

Hughes-Stanton, Herbert Edwin Pelham 1870–1937
Early Morning – Les beaux Provence 1923
oil on canvas 101.5 x 127
PRSMG : P310

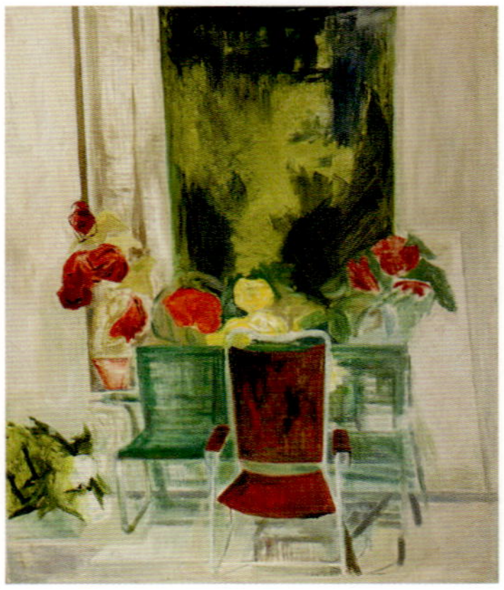

Hulbert, Thelma 1913–1995
Window on the Terrace 1958
oil on canvas 99.2 x 87.9
PRSMG : P1615

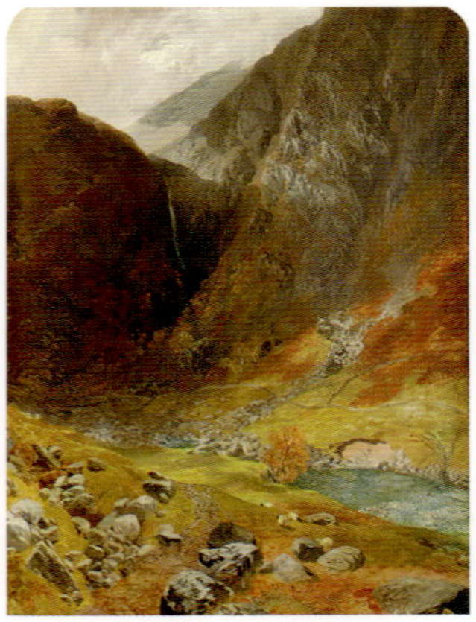

Hunt, Alfred William 1830–1896
Styhead Pass, Borrowdale
oil on canvas 91.4 x 71.2
PRSMG : P1202

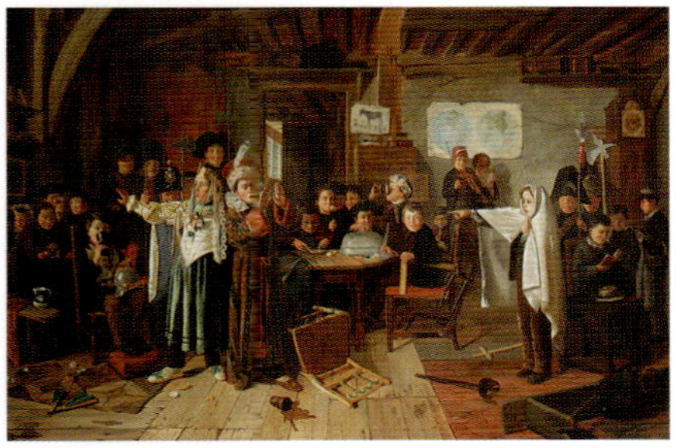

Hunt, Charles 1803–1877
The Masquerade 1860–1870
oil on canvas 61 x 91.5
PRSMG : P1392

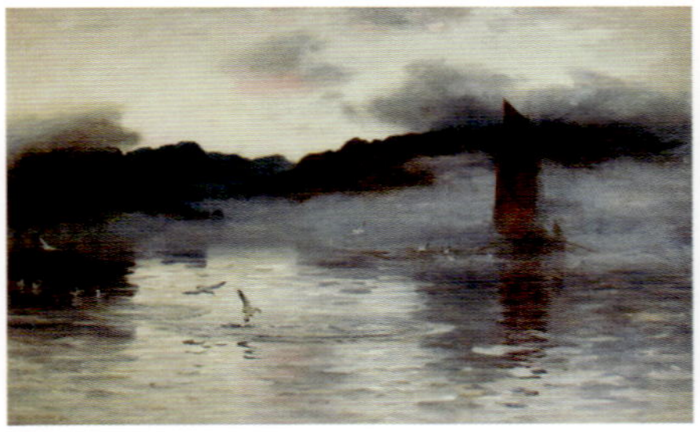

Hunter, Colin 1841–1904
Signs of Herring 1899
oil on canvas 101.5 x 183
PRSMG : P334

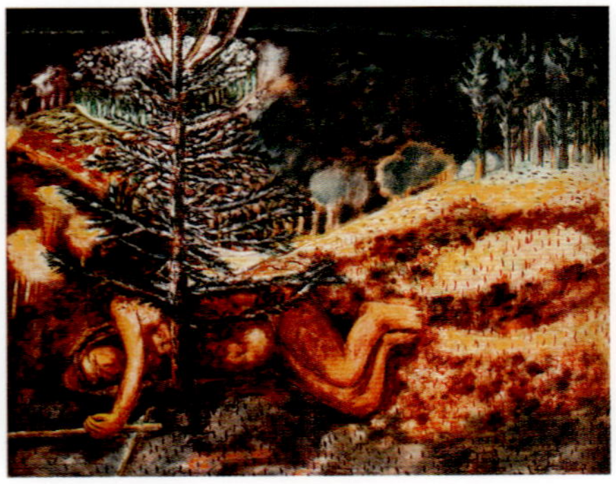

Jackowski, Andrzej b.1947
The Fir Tree 1983
oil on canvas 152.5 x 182.5
PRSMG : P2283

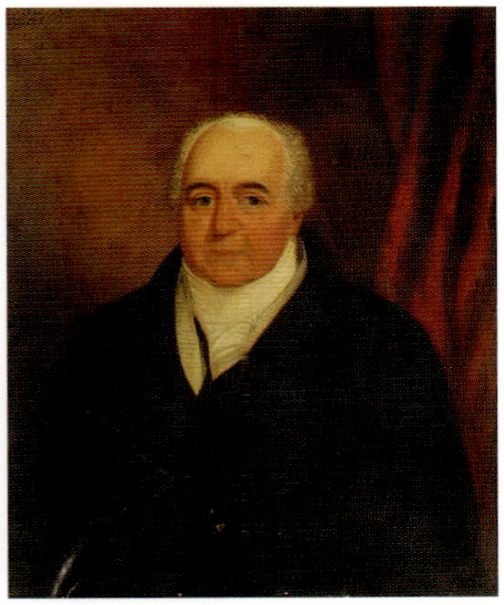

Jackson, G. active 1798–1816
Edward Robert Travers
oil on canvas 76.2 x 63.5
PRSMG : P336

Facing page: Airy, Anna, 1882–1964, *Message of May,* 1937, Grundy Art Gallery (p. 84)

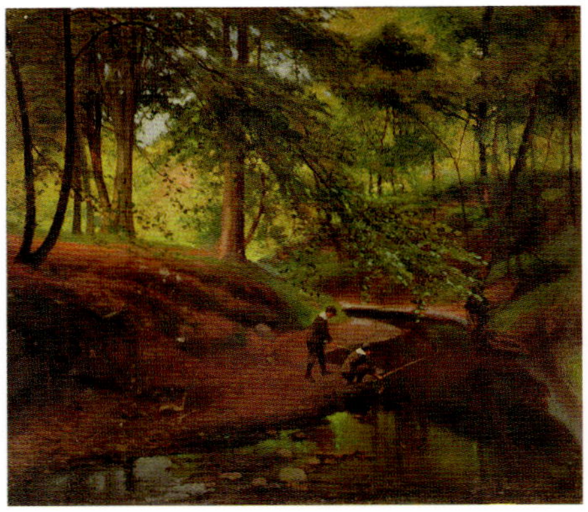

Jackson, Joseph 1858–1922
Anderton's Wood, near Preston
oil on canvas 48.2 x 58
PRSMG : P338

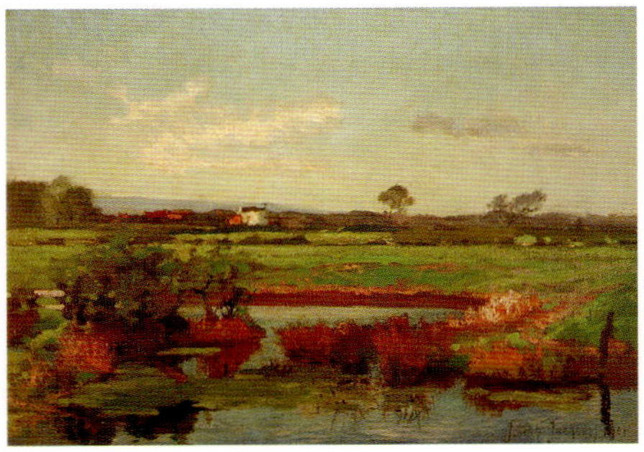

Jackson, Joseph 1858–1922
In Summer Time
oil on canvas 50.8 x 76.2
PRSMG : P337

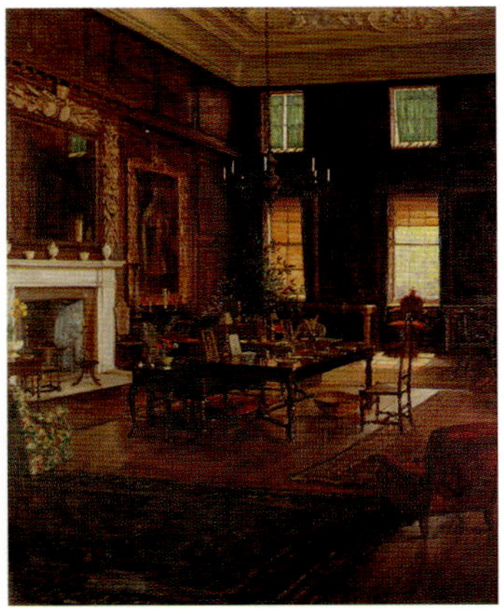

Jacomb-Hood, George Percy 1857–1929
State Room, Governor's House, Royal Hospital, Chelsea 1922
oil on canvas 91.5 x 76.2
PRSMG : P340

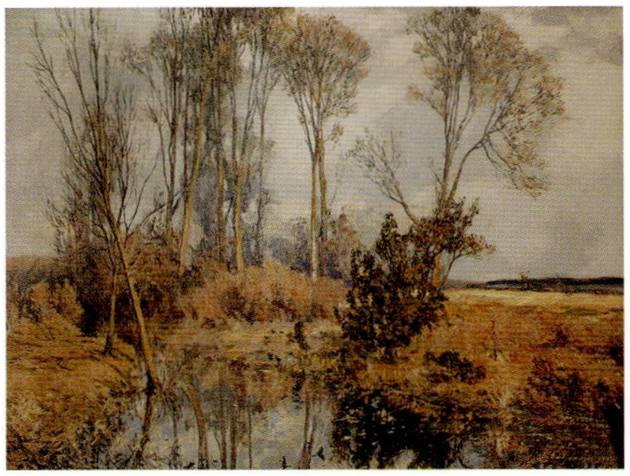

Jamieson, Alexander 1873–1937
The Old Moat, Weston Turville 1930
oil on canvas 86.5 x 111.7
PRSMG : P341

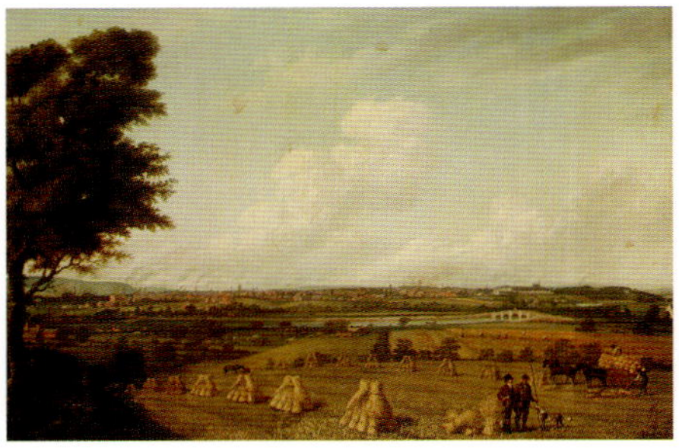

Jenkinson, John P. active 1790–1821
View of Preston from Penwortham Hill 1821
oil on canvas 107 x 151.5
PRSMG : P1618

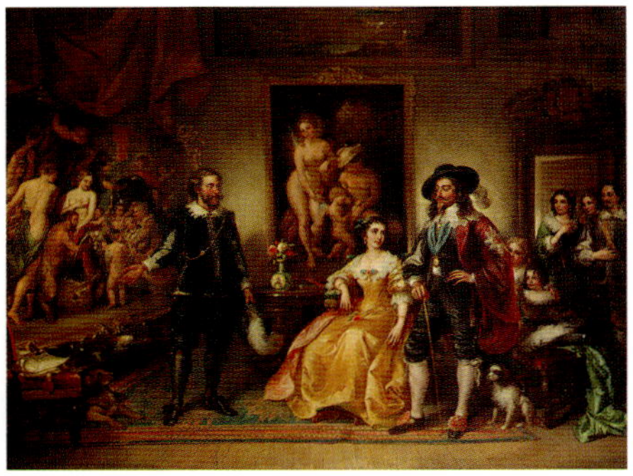

Jérôme, Ambrosini 1810–1883
Rubens Presenting His Picture 'Peace and War' to Charles I 1858–1871
oil on canvas 110 x 140.3
PRSMG : P342

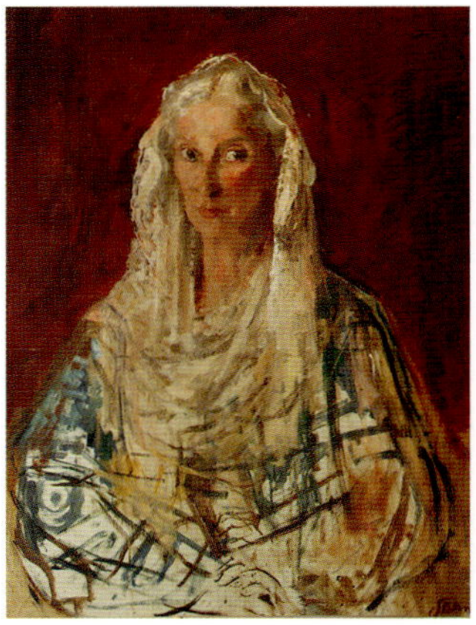

John, Augustus Edwin 1878–1961
Dorelia 1959
oil on canvas 91.5 x 71
PRSMG : P1616

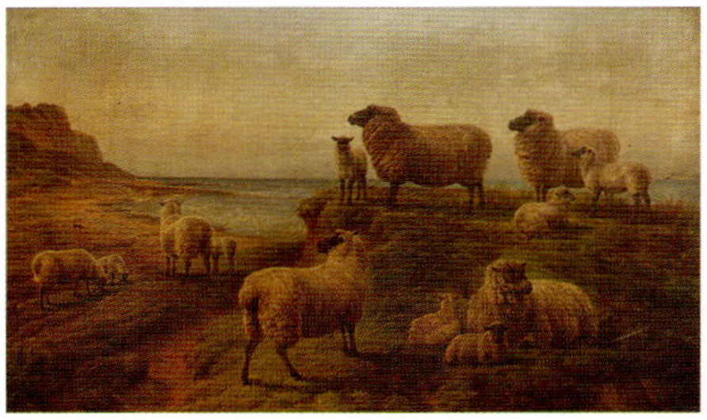

Jones, Charles 1836–1902
Seaside Landscape with Sheep
oil on canvas 87.5 x 128.5
PRSMG : P344

Image unavailable due to copyright restrictions

Jonzen, Basil 1913–1967
Coast at Puerto de la Cruz 1937
oil on canvas 50.8 x 61
PRSMG : P852

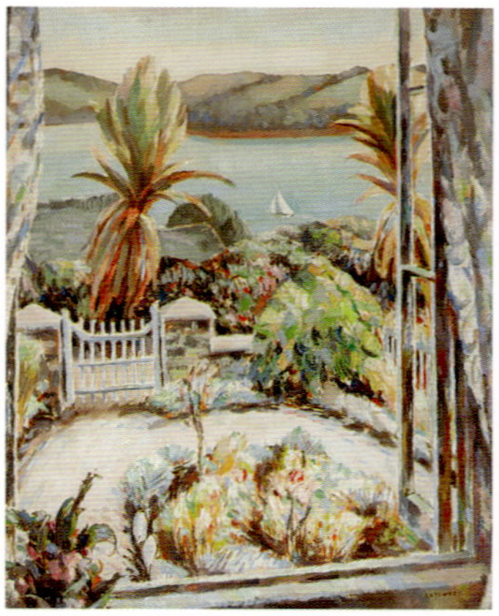

Jowett, Percy Hague 1882–1955
Window in Cornwall 1942
oil on canvas 63 x 51.3
PRSMG : P897

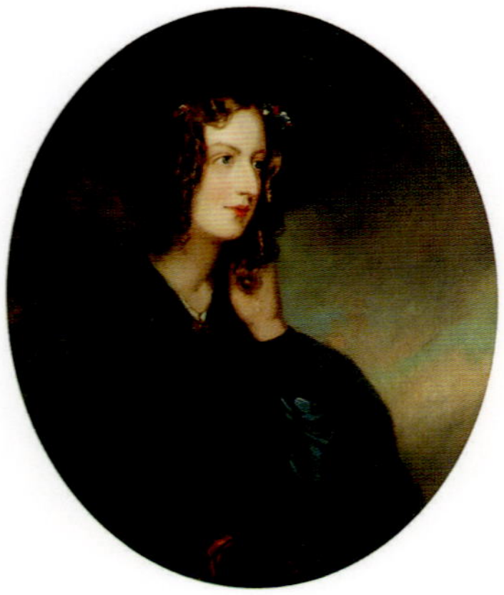

Joy, Thomas Musgrave 1812–1866
Fredrica Horne 1830–1850
oil on canvas 73.6 x 63.7
PRSMG : P1688

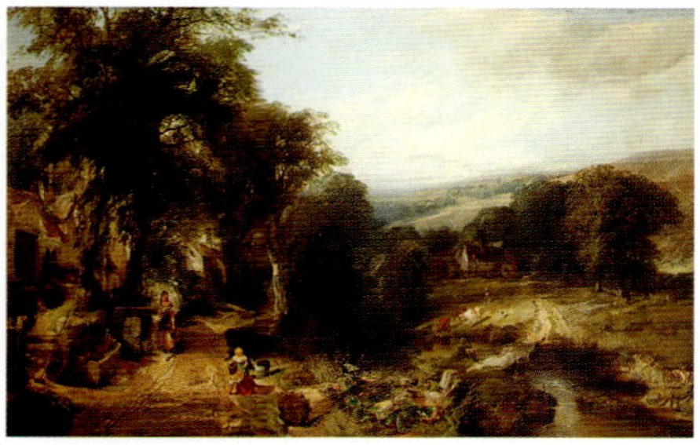

Jutsum, Henry 1816–1869
Landscape 1866
oil on canvas 76.2 x 122
PRSMG : P345

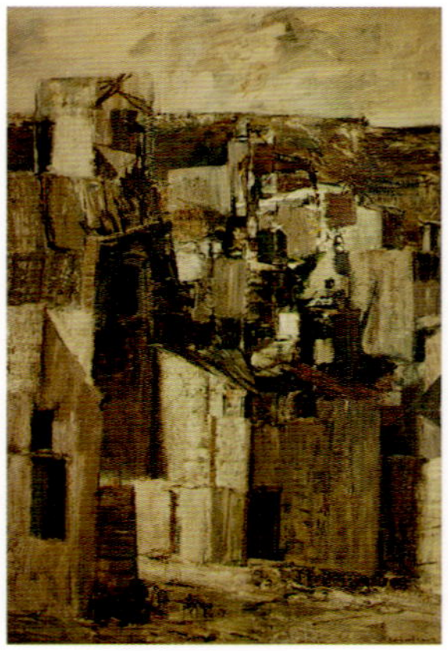

Kay, Bernard b.1927
Deserted Hill Village 1957
oil on canvas 172.3 x 122.5
PRSMG : P1594

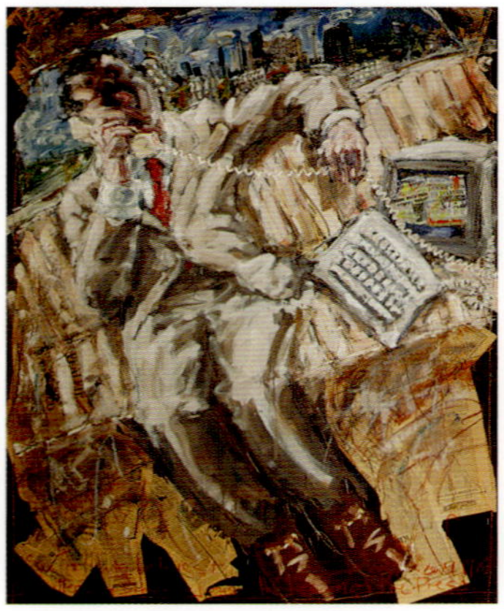

Keane, John b.1954
Controlling Interest 1987
oil on canvas 167.5 x 124.7
PRSMG : P2241

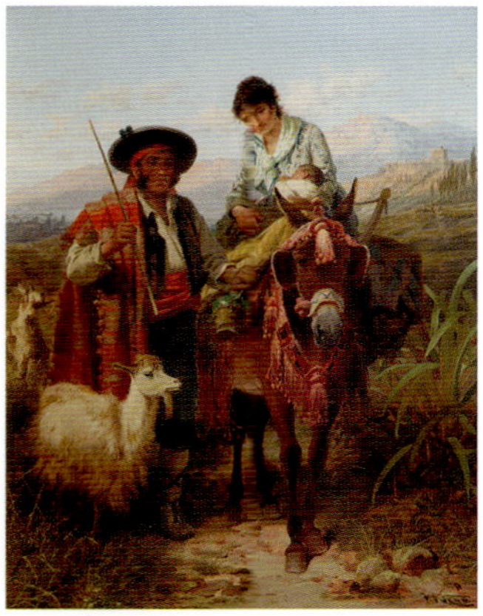

Kemm, Robert 1830–1895
A Muleteer of Granada c.1880
oil on canvas 45 x 35
PRSMG : P1565

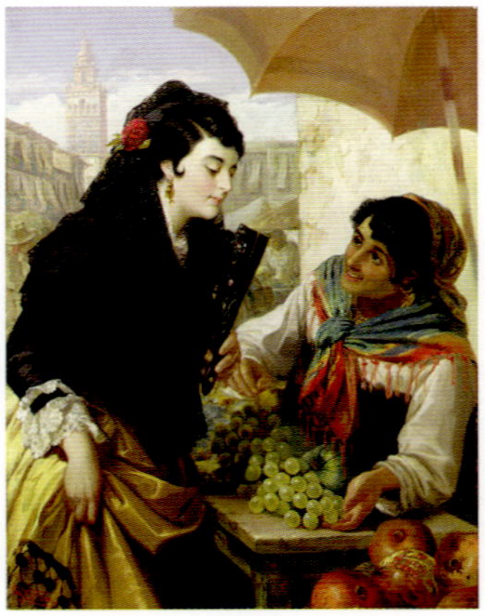

Kemm, Robert 1830–1895
The Spanish Fruit Seller
oil on canvas 92.4 x 71.9
PRSMG : P823

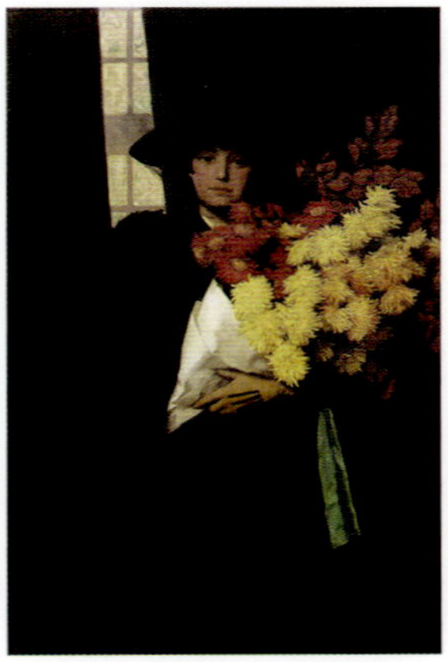

Kerr, Charles Henry Malcolm 1858–1907
Chrysanthemums
oil on canvas 137 x 91.5
PRSMG : P350

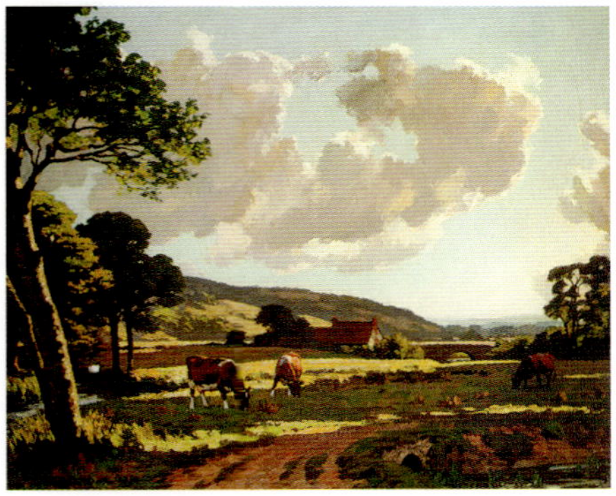

King, Gunning 1859–1940
Hampshire Meads 1931
oil on canvas 64.5 x 77.5
PRSMG : P352

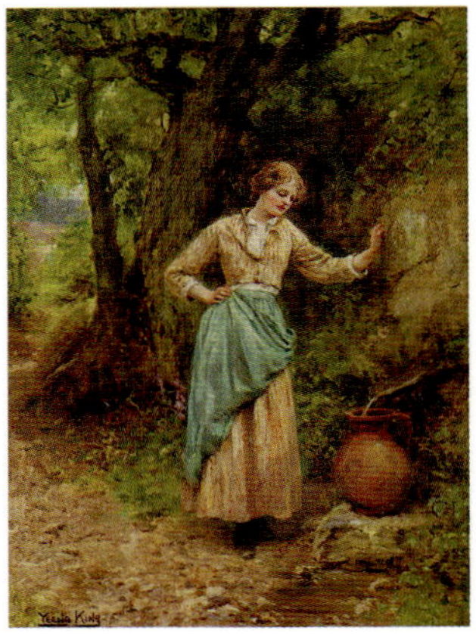

King, Henry John Yeend 1855–1924
Girl at a Well
oil on canvas 61.2 x 46.2
PRSMG : P353

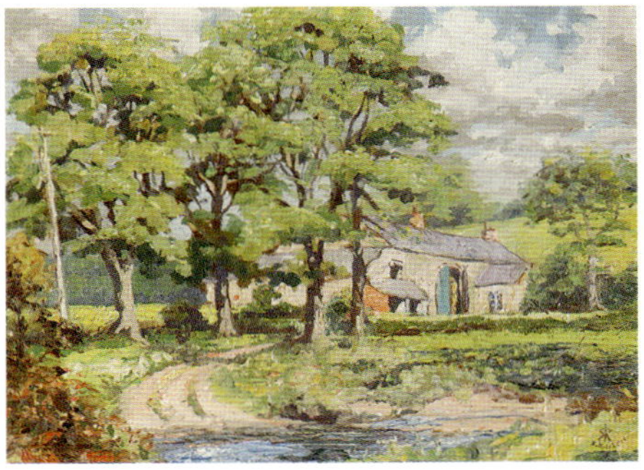

Kitchen, R.
Hoghton Bottoms, near Preston 1973
oil on board 30.8 x 41
PRSMG : P1887

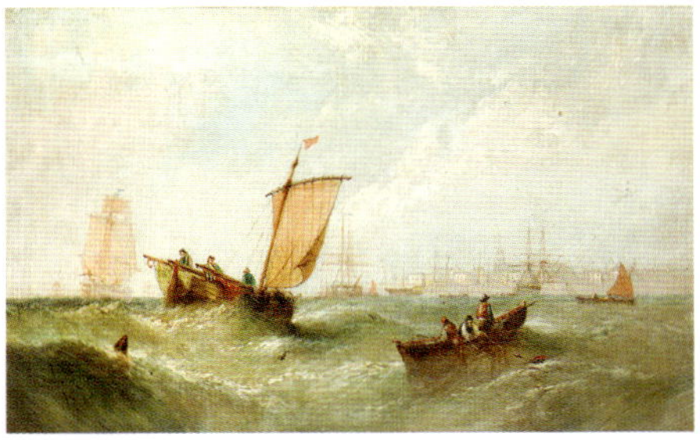

Knell, William Calcott 1830–1880
Fishing Boats off Harwich 1873
oil on canvas 30.5 x 50.8
PRSMG : P1502

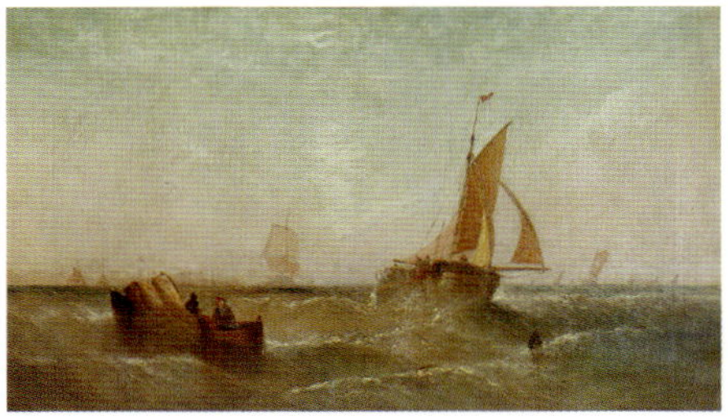

Knell, William Calcott 1830–1880
Summer Morning off Yarmouth 1873
oil on canvas 30.5 x 50.8
PRSMG : P1552

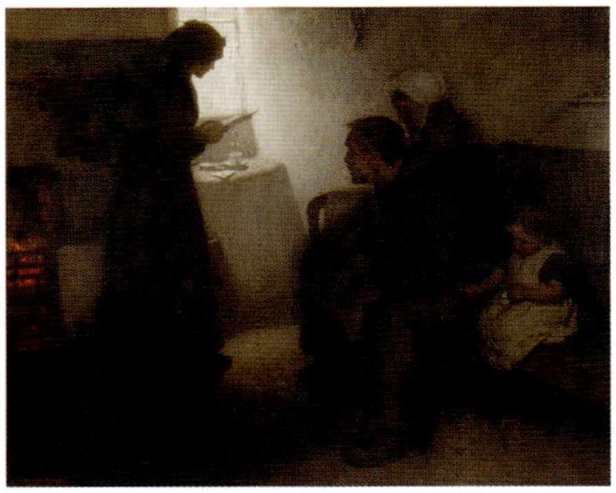

Knight, Harold 1874–1961
The Girl and the Letter 1906
oil on canvas 101.5 x 127
PRSMG : P354

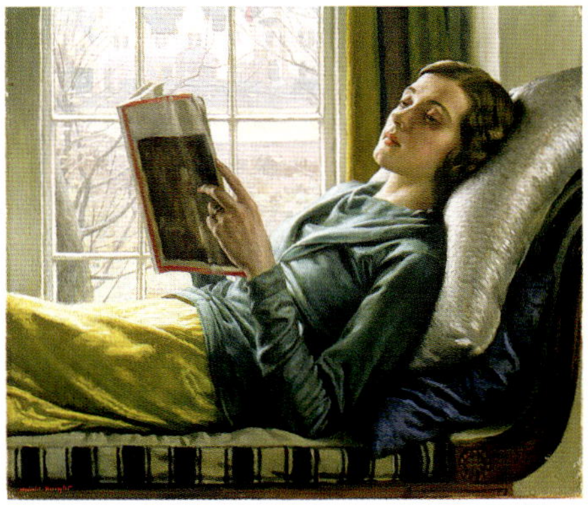

Knight, Harold 1874–1961
Girl Reading 1932
oil on canvas 46.2 x 50.5
PRSMG : P355

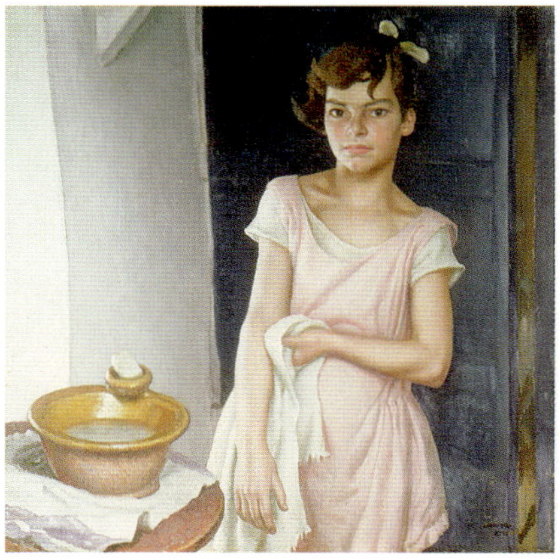

Knight, Laura 1877–1970
Susie and the Wash Basin 1929
oil on canvas 61 x 61
PRSMG : P356

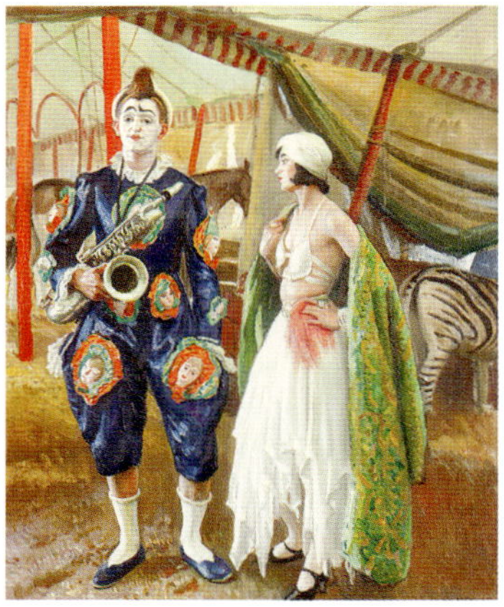

Knight, Laura 1877–1970
A Musical Clown 1930
oil on canvas 76.2 x 63.5
PRSMG : P357

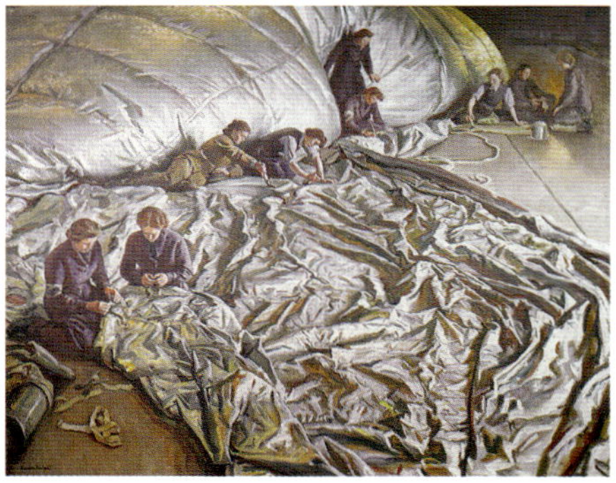

Knight, Laura 1877–1970
In for Repairs 1942
oil on canvas 101.5 x 127
PRSMG : P1116

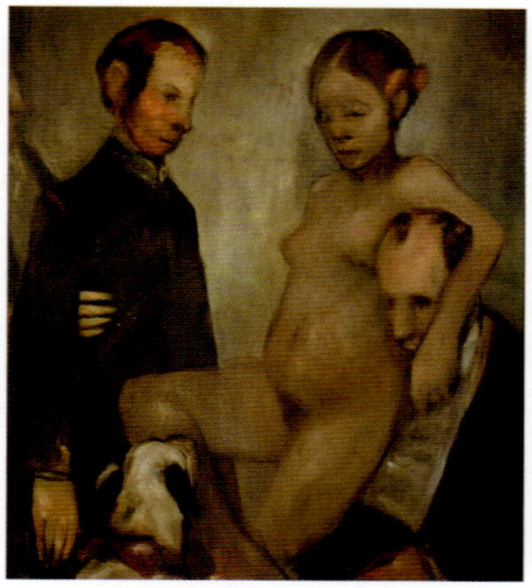

Krut, Ansel b.1959
The Ventriloquist's Convention 1988
oil on canvas 100 x 90
PRSMG : P2282

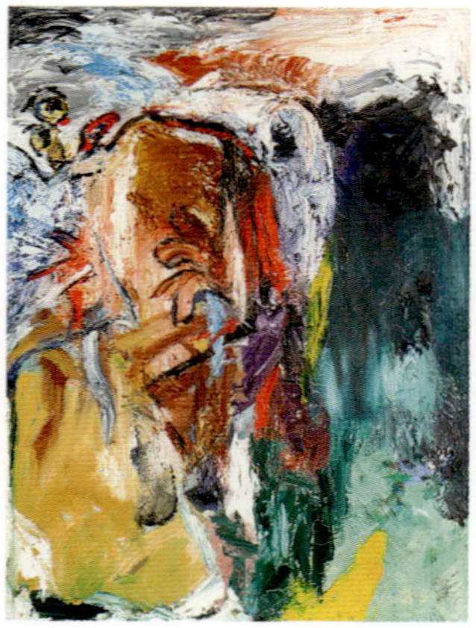

Lai Ming-Hoi, Victor b.1961
After Talking with Michael c.1990
oil on canvas 122.5 x 91.5
PRSMG : 2005.190

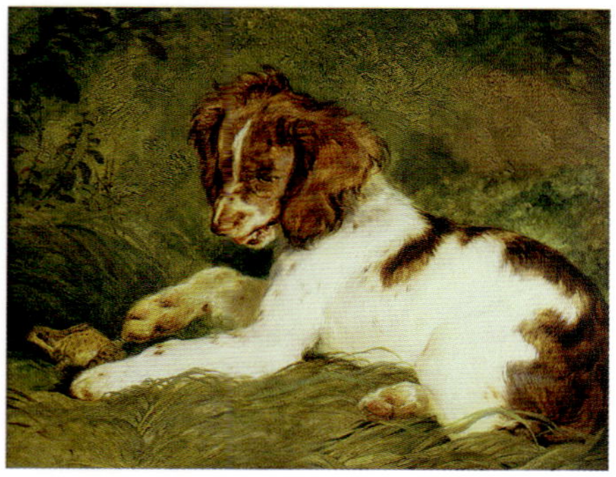

Landseer, Edwin Henry 1802–1873
A Puppy Teasing a Frog 1824
oil on panel 35.5 x 44.5
PRSMG : P362

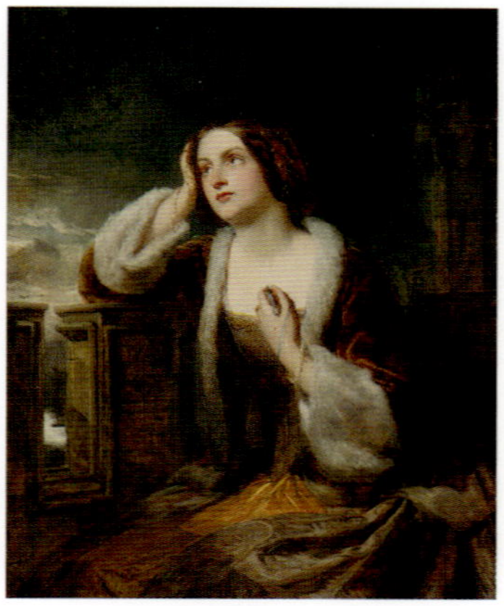

Landseer, Edwin Henry (attributed to) 1802–1873
Catherine Seyton Looking from the Battlements at Loch Leven Castle
oil on canvas 40.5 x 34.2
PRSMG : P243

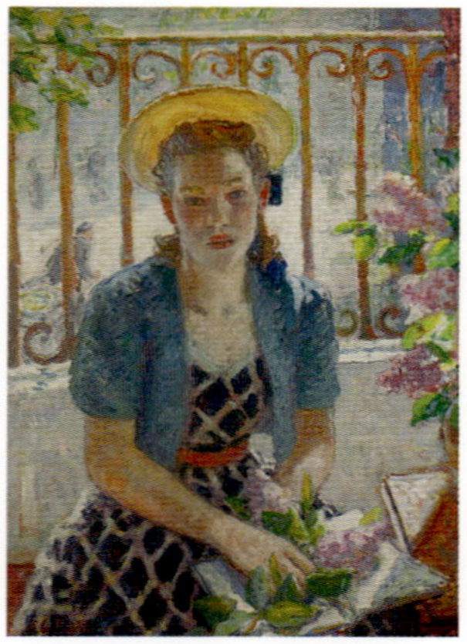

Le Bas, Edward 1904–1966
By the Window 1943
oil on canvas 90 x 62.5
PRSMG : P931

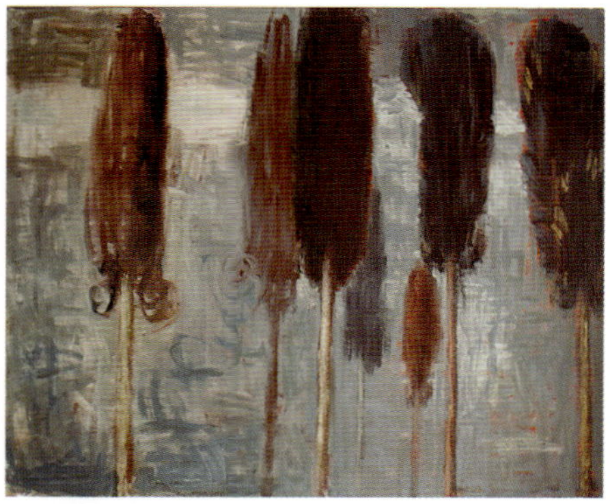

Le Brun, Christopher b.1951
Grove 1987
oil on canvas 219 x 267
PRSMG : P2239

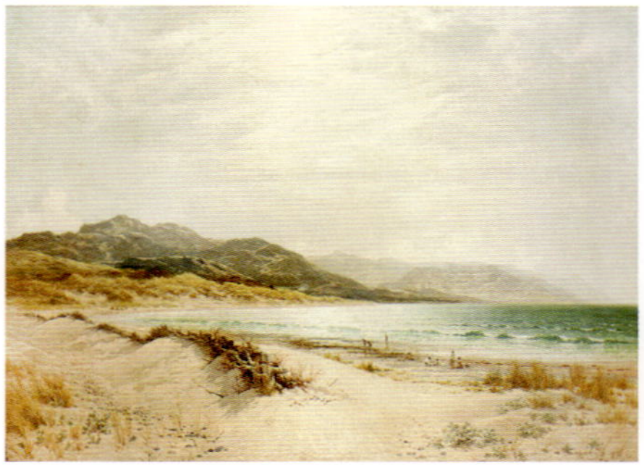

Leader, Benjamin Williams 1831–1923
Cambria's Coast 1889
oil on canvas 102.6 x 187
PRSMG : P363

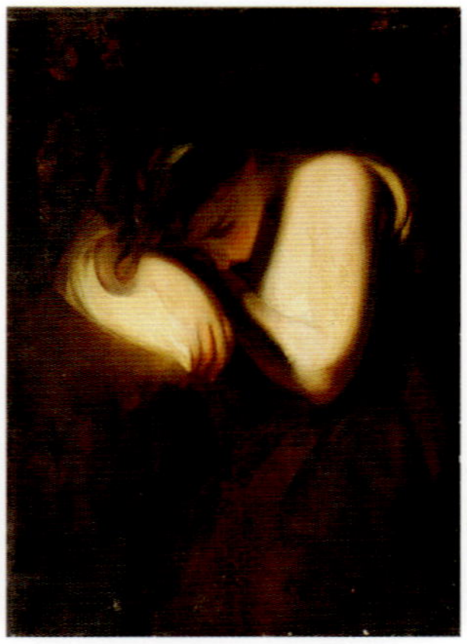

Lee, Frederick Richard 1798–1879
Study of a Woman
oil on canvas 76.2 x 63.5
PRSMG : P2236

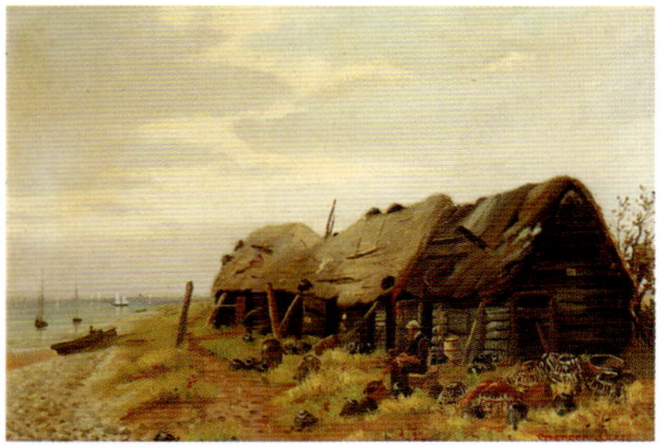

Leese, Spencer 1843–1894
Lancashire Coast Scene c.1892
oil on canvas 33.3 x 52
PRSMG : P365

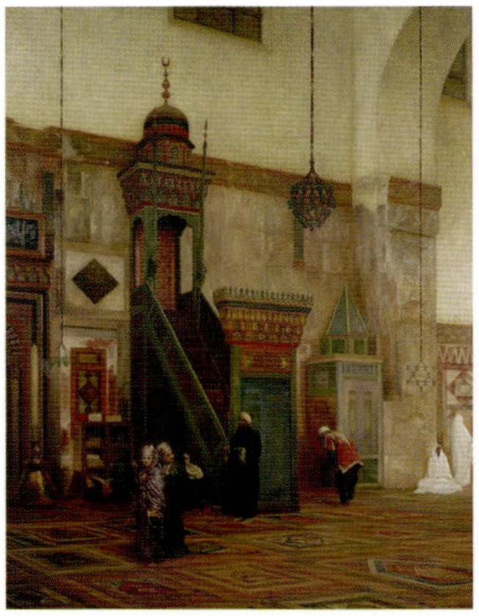

Leighton, Frederic 1830–1896
Interior of the Grand Mosque, Damascus 1870–1896
oil on canvas 158.1 x 122
PRSMG : P366

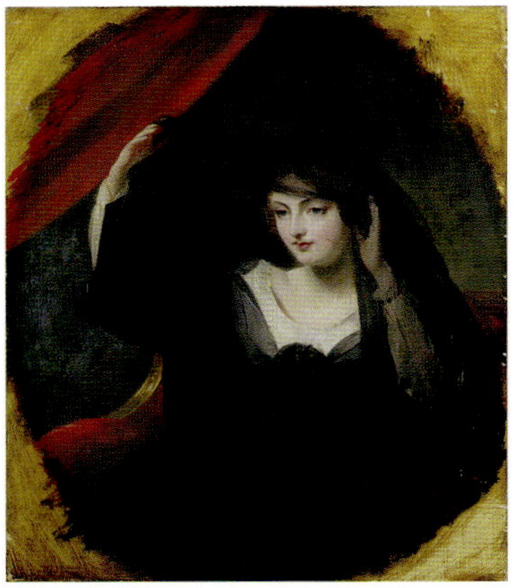

Leslie, Charles Robert 1794–1859
Olivia Raising her Veil 1845
oil on panel 49.7 x 42
PRSMG : P369

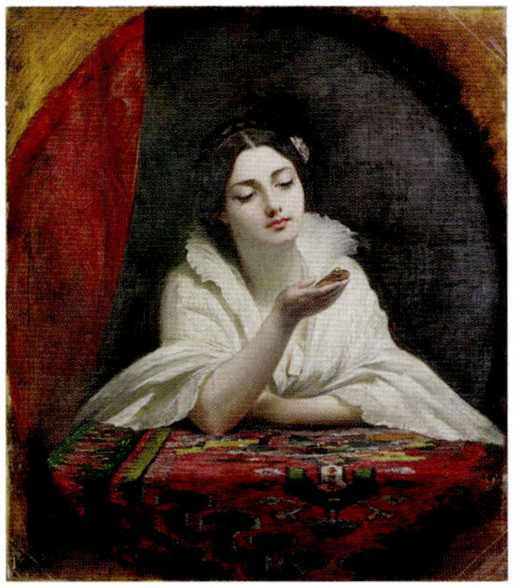

Leslie, Charles Robert 1794–1859
The Present 1845
oil on panel 49 x 42
PRSMG : P368

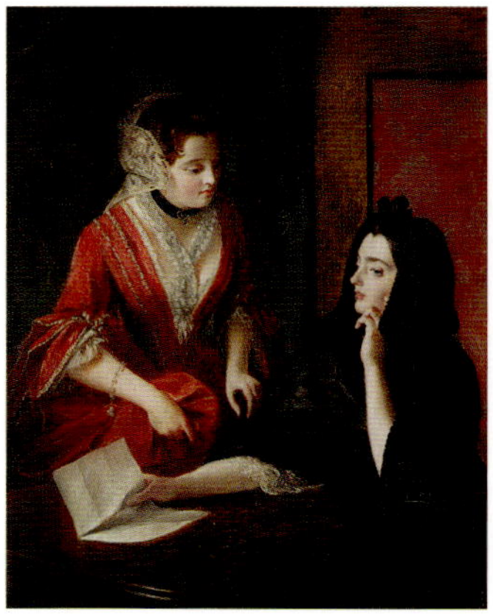

Leslie, Charles Robert 1794–1859
Consultation 1852
oil on canvas 43 x 33 (E)
PRSMG : P370

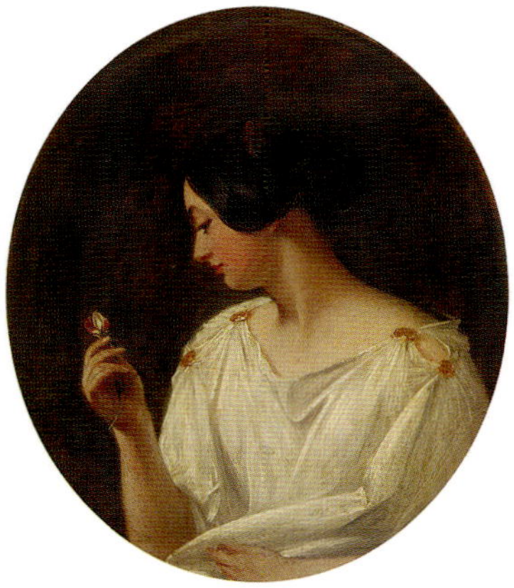

Leslie, Charles Robert 1794–1859
Perdita
oil on canvas 29 x 22.8
PRSMG : P367

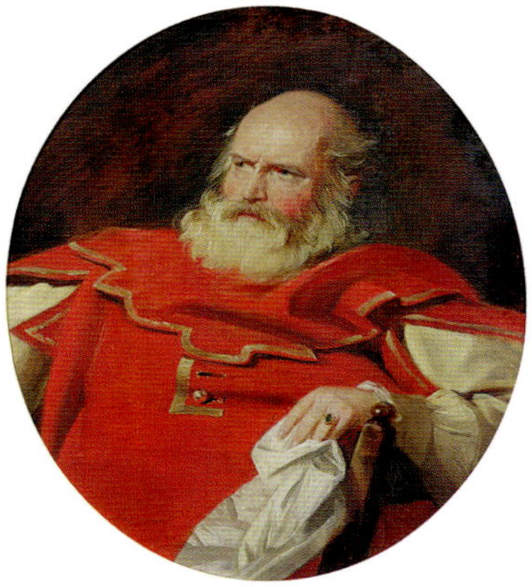

Leslie, Charles Robert 1794–1859
Sir John Falstaff
oil on canvas 38 x 33
PRSMG : P371

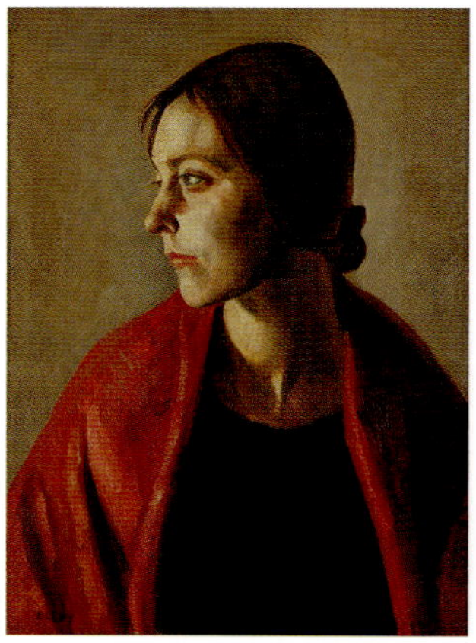

Levy, Emmanuel 1900–1986
The Red Shawl 1929
oil on canvas 50 x 40.5
PRSMG : P372

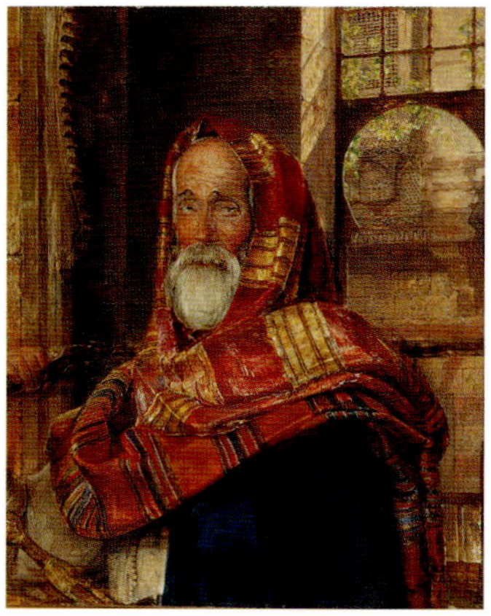

Lewis, John Frederick 1804–1876
A Bashi-Bazouk 1854
oil on panel 29.8 x 24.7
PRSMG : P374

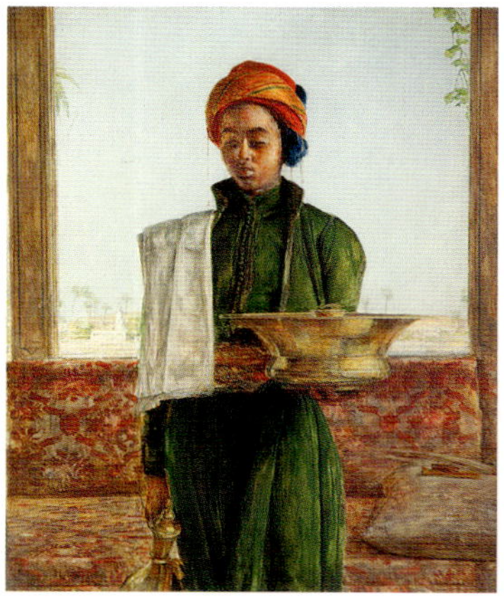

Lewis, John Frederick 1804–1876
The Attendant on the Bath 1854
oil on panel 30 x 24.7
PRSMG : P373

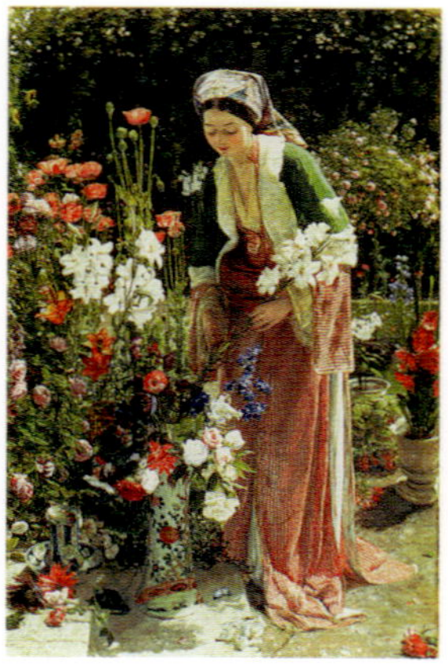

Lewis, John Frederick 1804–1876
In the Bey's Garden 1865
oil on panel 143 x 105
PRSMG : P375

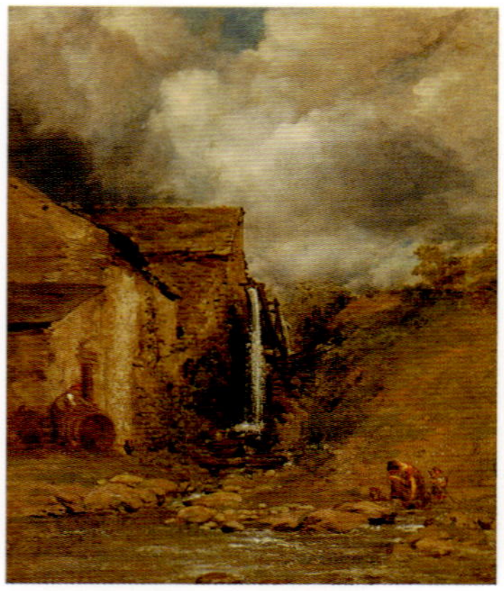

Linnell, John 1792–1882
An Overshot Mill 1830–1880
oil on canvas 42 x 34.2
PRSMG : P387

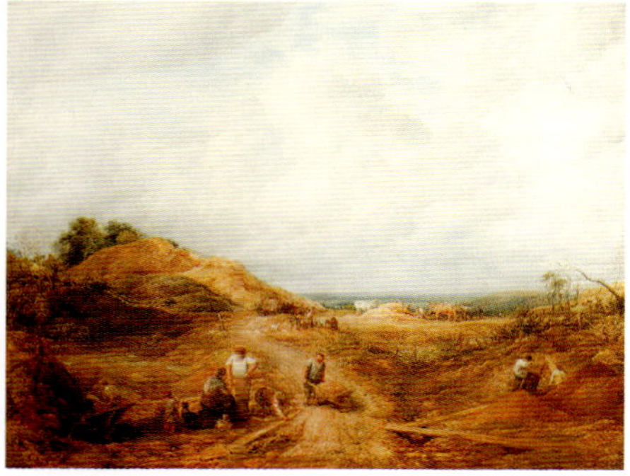

Linnell, John 1792–1882
Kensington Gravel Pits 1849
oil on canvas 68.5 x 89
PRSMG : P386

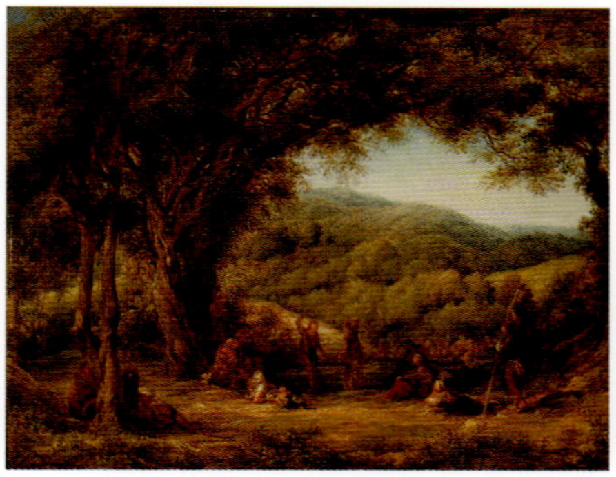

Linnell, John 1792–1882
L'allegro, 'Many a youth and many a maid, dancing in the chequered shade' 1849
oil on canvas 45.6 x 61
PRSMG : P379

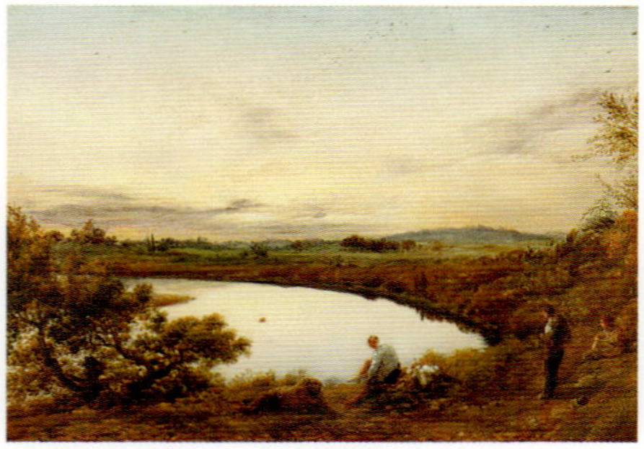

Linnell, John 1792–1882
Summer Evening, Boys Bathing 1849
oil on canvas 36.8 x 58.5
PRSMG : P382

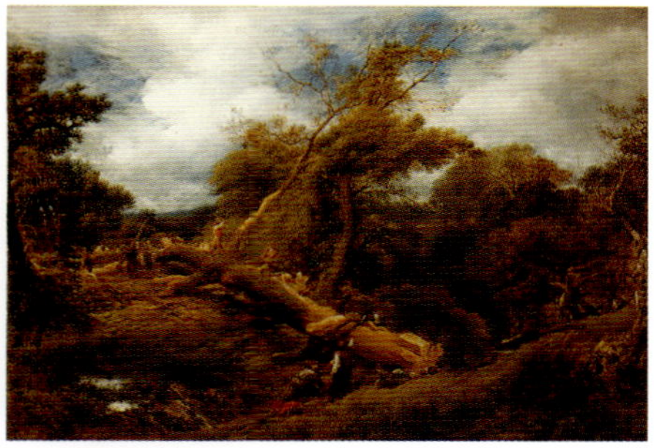

Linnell, John 1792–1882
The Fallen Monarch of the Forest 1850–1880
oil on canvas 68 x 101
PRSMG : P381

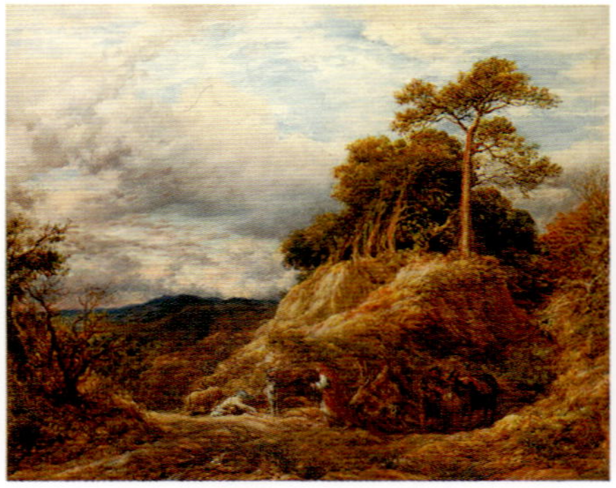

Linnell, John 1792–1882
The Disobedient Prophet (1 Kings, Chapter 13) 1859
oil on canvas 52 x 67.5
PRSMG : P384

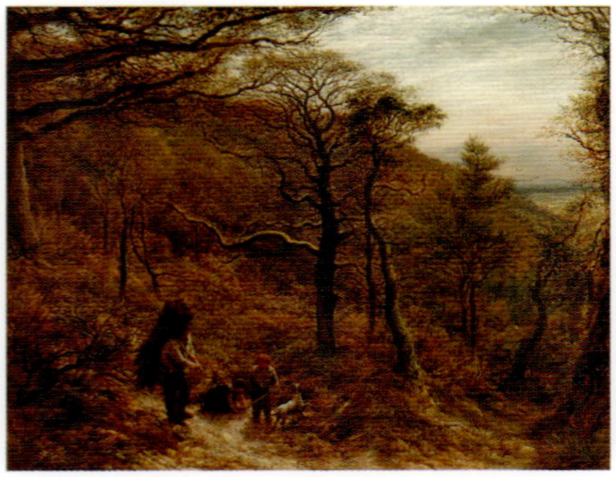

Linnell, John 1792–1882
The Woodcutter's Return 1859
oil on canvas 68.5 x 89
PRSMG : P378

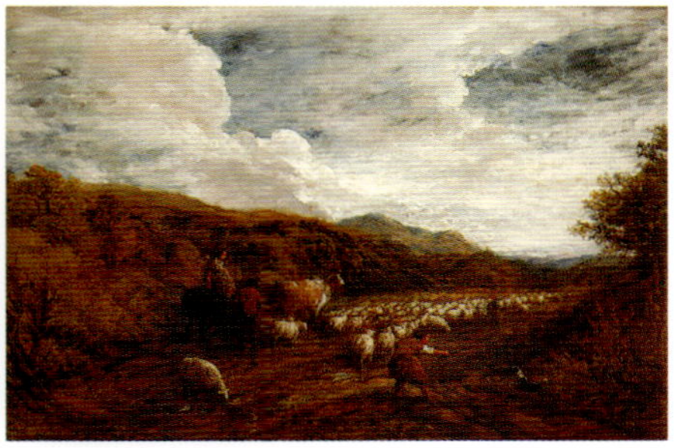

Linnell, John 1792–1882
The Vale of Dolwyddelan, as it was in 1814 1868
oil on canvas 35.5 x 57.8
PRSMG : P383

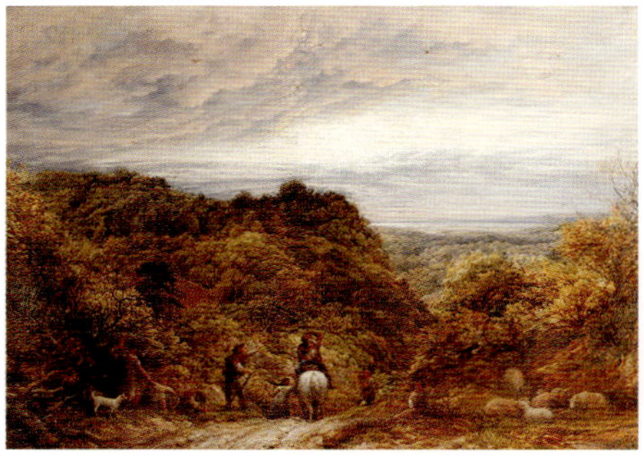

Linell, John 1792–1882
The Traveller's Rest 1869
oil on canvas 73.5 x 101
PRSMG : P380

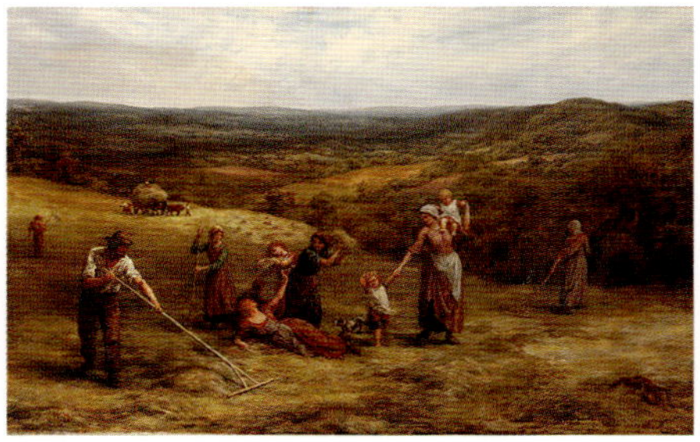

Linnell, John 1792–1882
Haying and Playing 1872
oil on canvas 101.5 x 160
PRSMG : P388

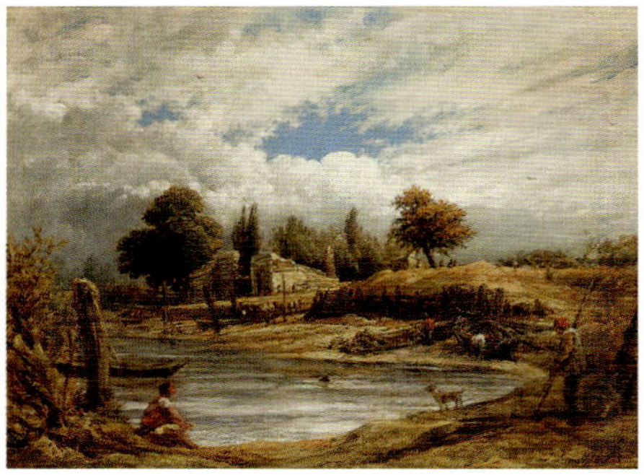

Linnell, John 1792–1882
Scene on the Thames with Boats 1873–1875
oil on canvas 30.5 x 44
PRSMG : P385

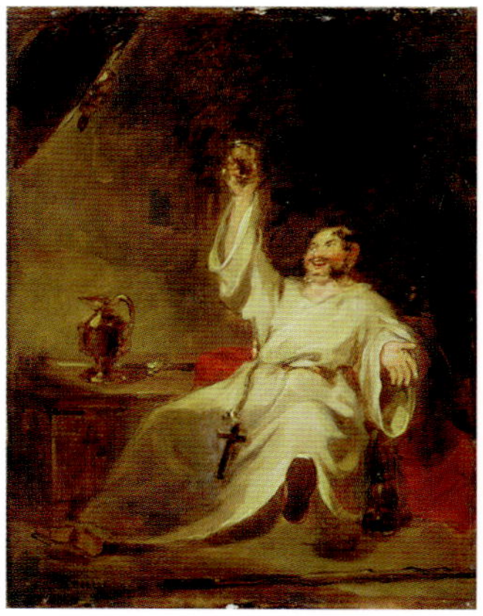

Liverseege, Henry 1803–1832
Friar Tuck
oil on canvas 34.8 x 25
PRSMG : P1431

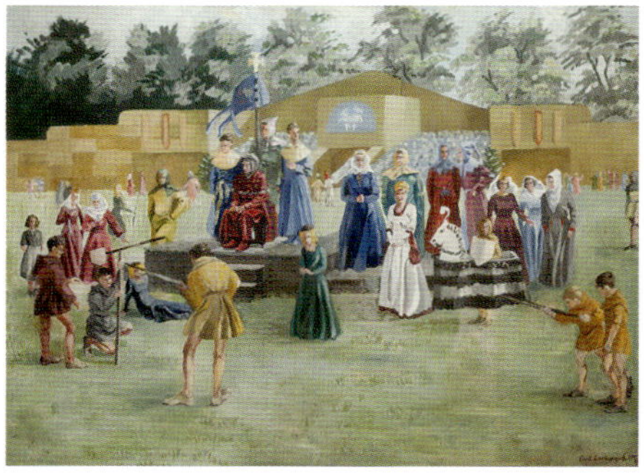

Lockwood, Enid
The Guild, 1328
oil on canvas (?) 60 x 91
PRSMG : T10

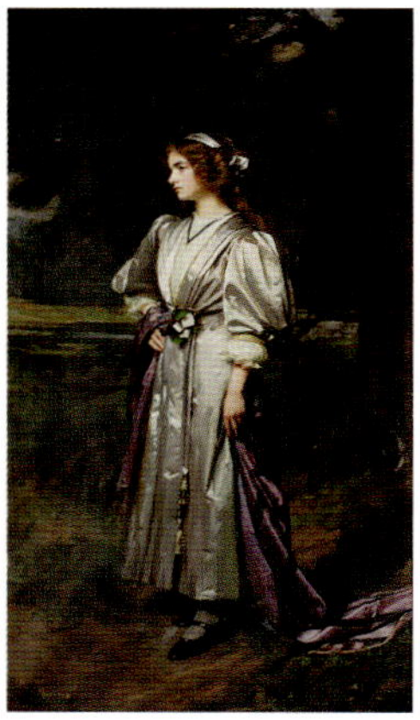

Logsdail, William 1859–1944
Mary Logsdail 1910
oil on canvas 209.5 x 104
PRSMG : P390

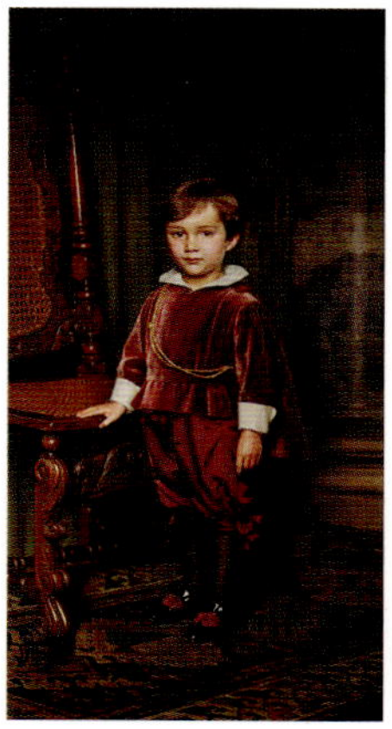

Logsdail, William 1859–1944
Master Coleridge Hills 1910
oil on canvas 160 x 93.5
PRSMG : LOAN2 (P)

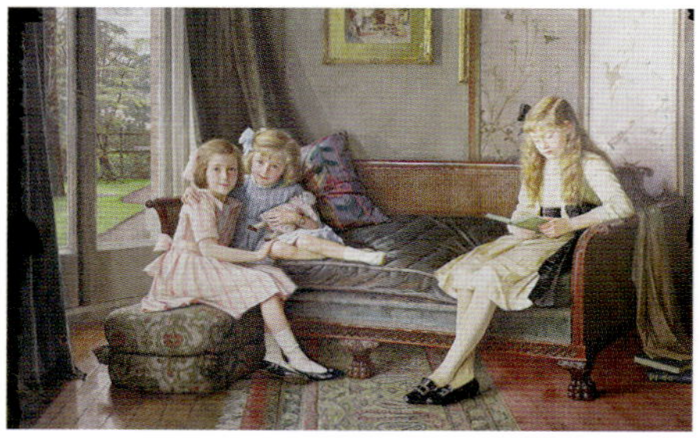

Logsdail, William 1859–1944
The Children of James Todd 1920
oil on canvas 146.5 x 240
PRSMG : P1609

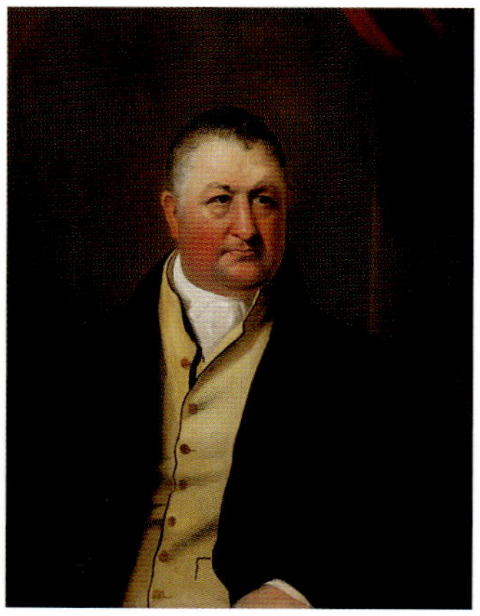

Lonsdale, James 1777–1839
Samuel Horrocks (1767–1842) c.1820
oil on canvas 76.2 x 63.5
PRSMG : P859

Facing page: Beechey, William, 1753–1839, *The Honourable Mrs W. Noel*, 1818, Towneley Hall Art Gallery & Museum (p. 126)

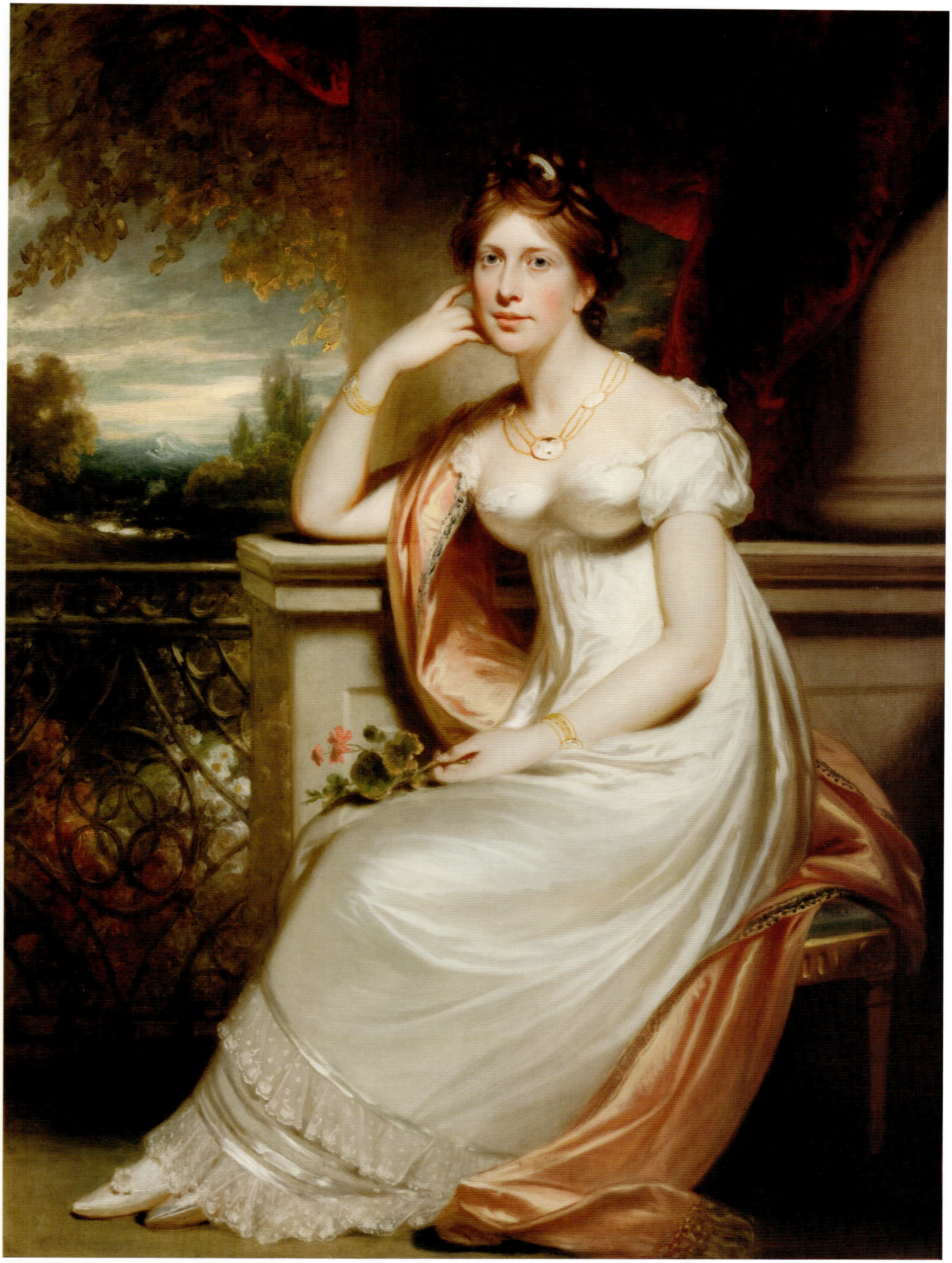

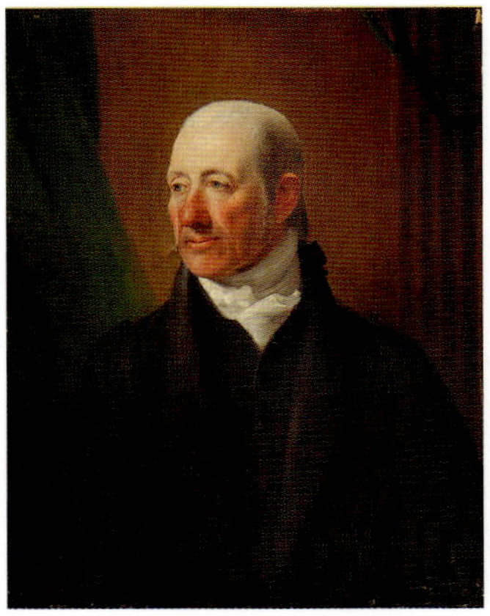

Lonsdale, James 1777–1839
Dr William St Clair
oil on canvas 76.2 x 63.5
PRSMG : P858

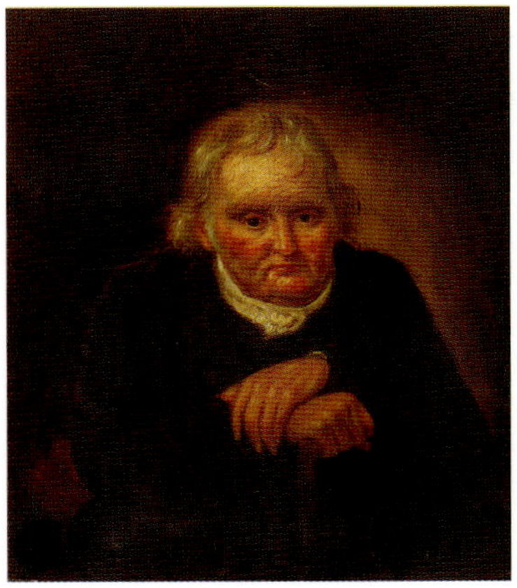

Lonsdale, James 1777–1839
Robert Holden
oil on canvas 33 x 28
PRSMG : P391

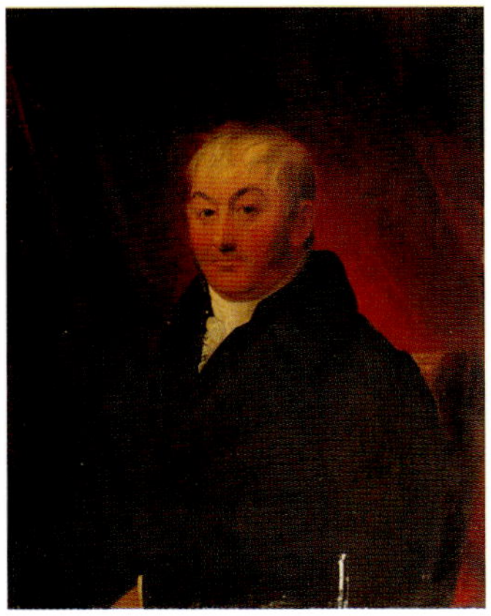

Lonsdale, James 1777–1839
William Farington of Shawe Hall
oil on canvas 77 x 64.2
PRSMG : P1888

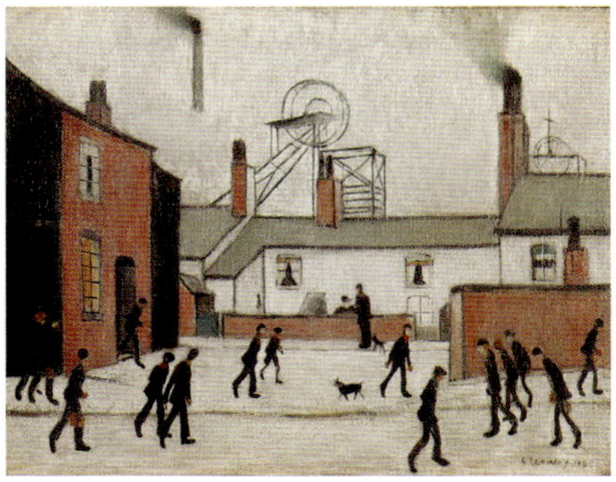

Lowry, Laurence Stephen 1887–1976
Millworkers 1948
oil on canvas 62 x 70
PRSMG : P2301

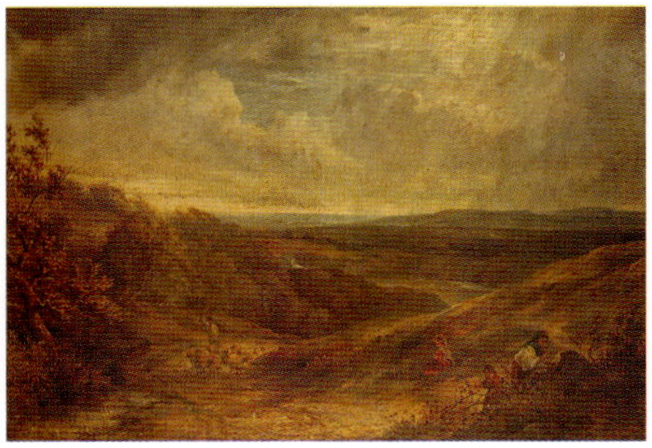

Lucas, George 1840–1912
Landscape
oil on canvas 89 x 145
PRSMG : P1889

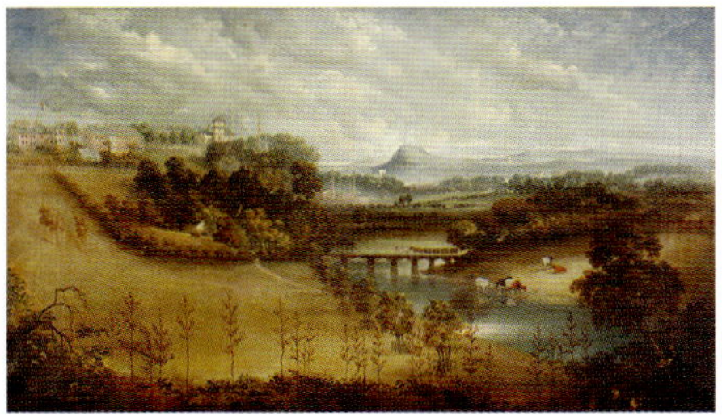

Lynch, Thomas active 1830–1880
View of Avenham Park with Tram Bridge 1862
oil on canvas 56 x 94
PRSMG : P1747

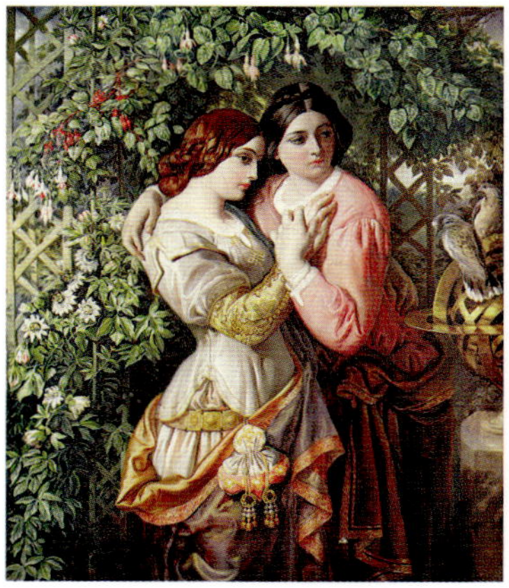

Maclise, Daniel 1806–1870
Rosalind and Celia
oil on canvas 76.2 x 63.5
PRSMG : P401

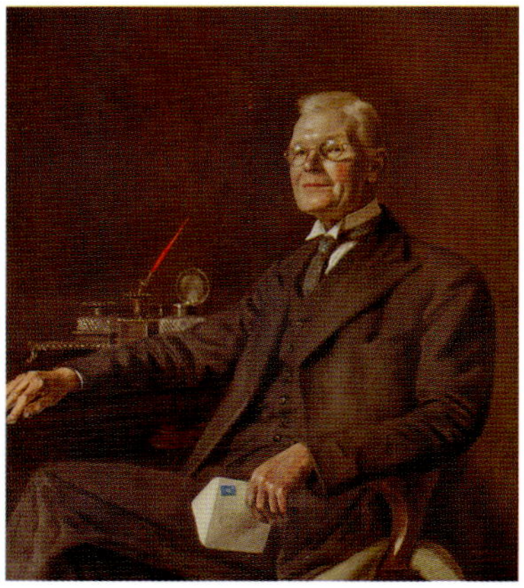

Markiewicz, Herbert Otto b.1900
Alderman R. C. Pye 1949
oil on canvas 106.6 x 91.2
PRSMG : P1283

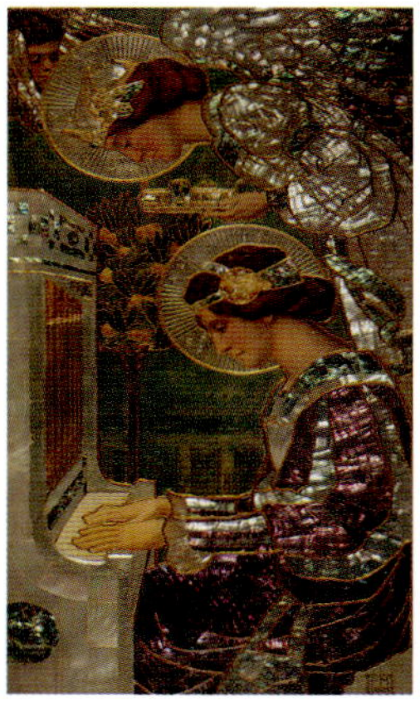

Marriott, Frederick 1860–1941
Saint Cecilia 1903
oil on wood 62.5 x 31
PRSMG : P2263

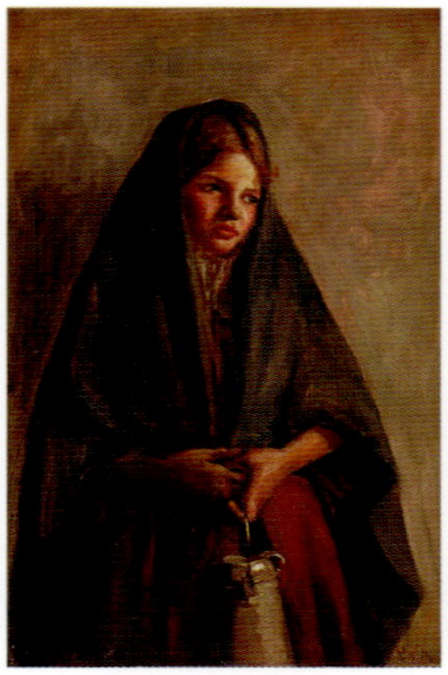

Mayor, Patti 1872–1962
The Half-Timer 1906–1908
oil on canvas 88 x 62
PRSMG : P2361

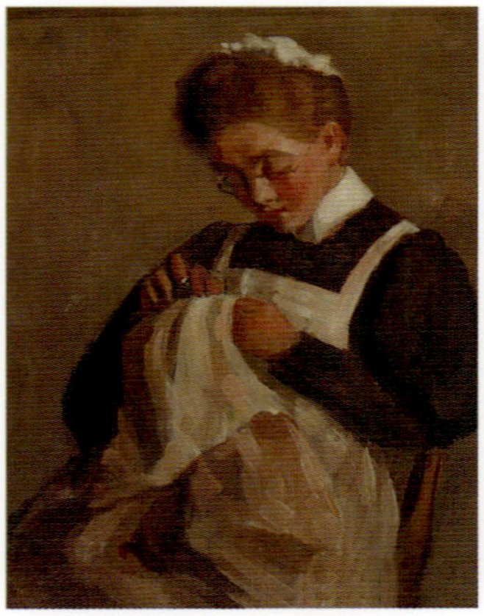

Mayor, Patti 1872–1962
The Sewing Maid 1910–1930
oil on panel 38.5 x 28.5
PRSMG : P1416

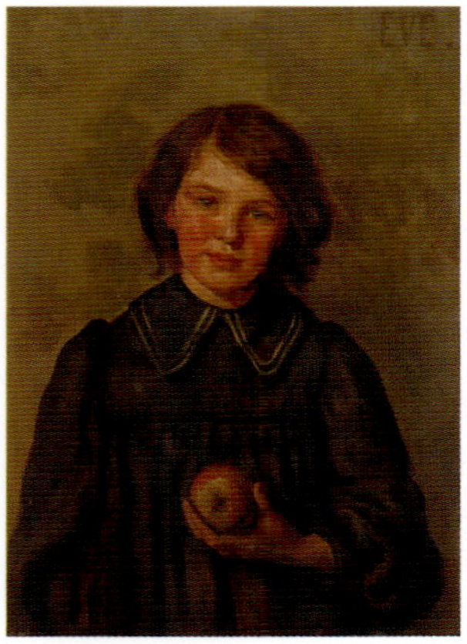

Mayor, Patti 1872–1962
Portrait of a Girl with an Apple 1920–1940
oil on canvas 70 x 50.8
PRSMG : P1417

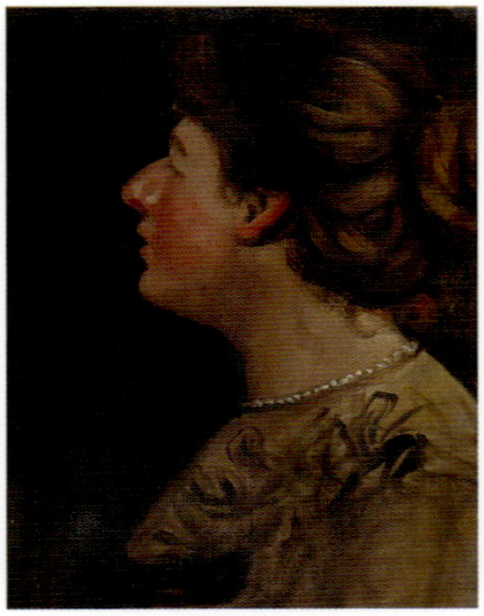

Mayor, Patti 1872–1962
Self Portrait 1920–1960
oil on canvas 39 x 25.7
PRSMG : P1779

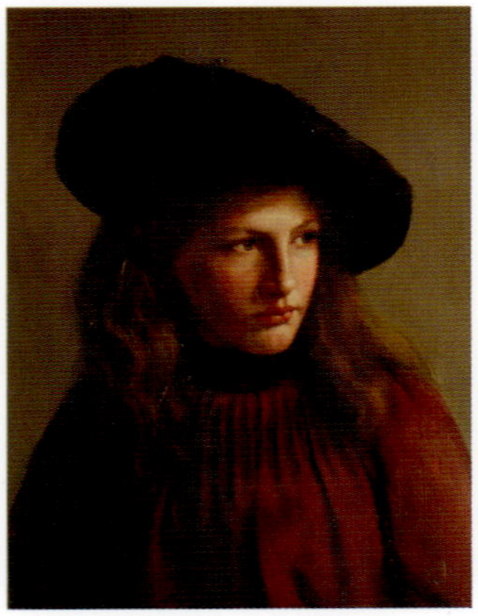

Mayor, Patti 1872–1962
Portrait of a Girl in a Cap 1924
oil on canvas 50.8 x 42.6
PRSMG : P398

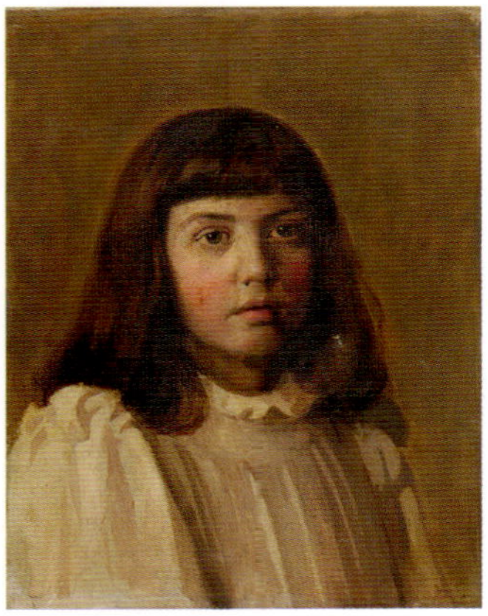

Mayor, Patti 1872–1962
Portrait of a Young Girl c.1930
oil on canvas 40.7 x 30.5
PRSMG : P2311

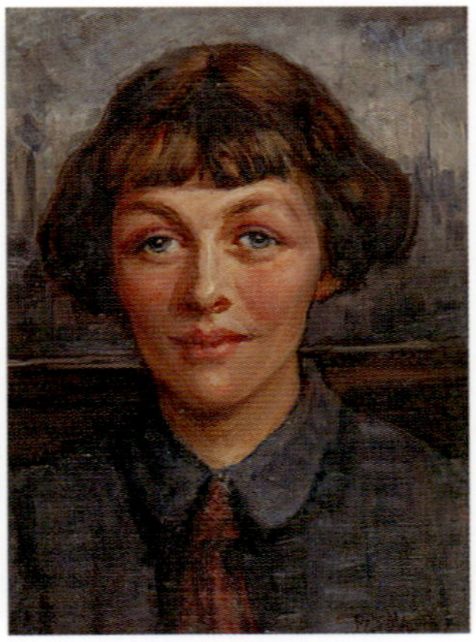

Mayor, Patti 1872–1962
Miss Mary Martin 1937
oil on canvas 40 x 30
PRSMG : P2307

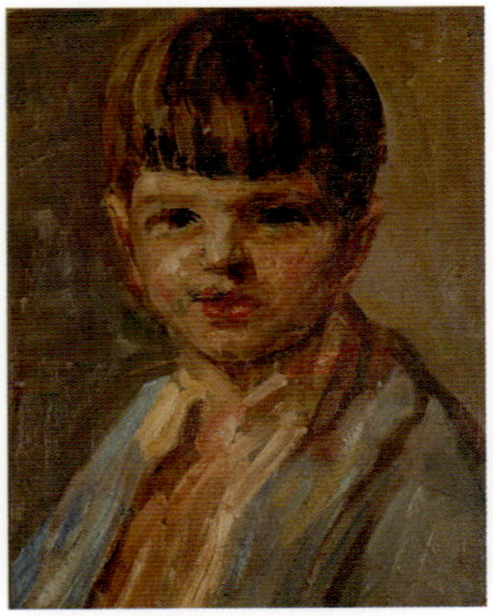

Mayor, Patti 1872–1962
Head of a Boy c.1940
oil on card 30.5 x 24.5
PRSMG : P2312

Mayor, Patti 1872–1962
A Bowl Filled with Red Flowers
oil on card 23.5 x 26.5
PRSMG : P1890

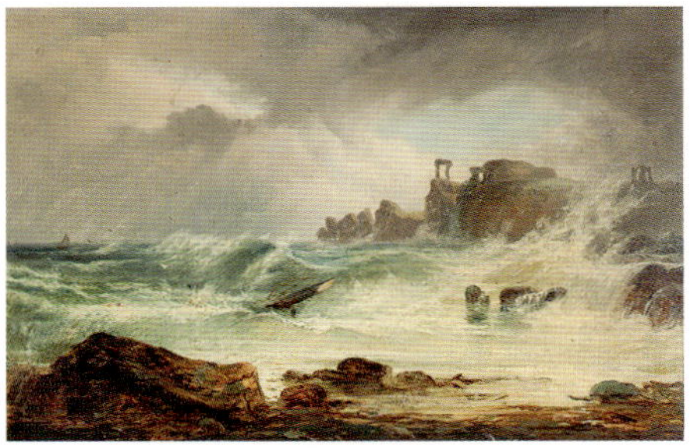

McCulloch, Horatio 1805–1867
Dunbar Castle
oil on canvas 38 x 56
PRSMG : P1554

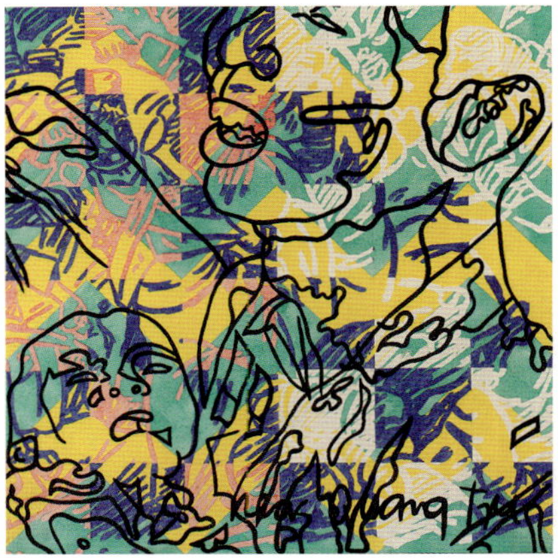

McCulloch, Ian b.1935
Near Quang Tri, Vietnam 1973
acrylic on canvas 61 x 61
PRSMG : P1814

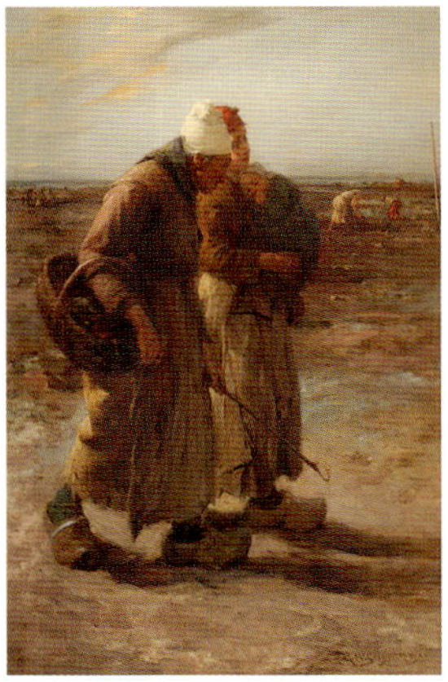

McGregor, Robert 1847–1922
Three Generations 1909
oil on canvas 143.3 x 97
PRSMG : P402

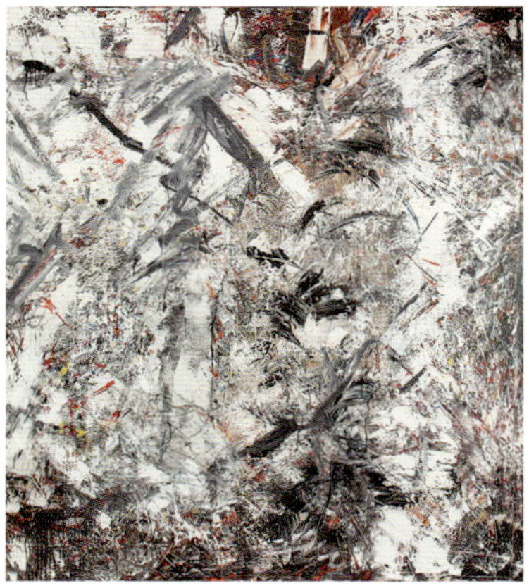

McKeever, Ian b.1946
Traditional Landscape: Beside the Brambled Ditch 1983
oil on canvas 230 x 208
PRSMG : P1838

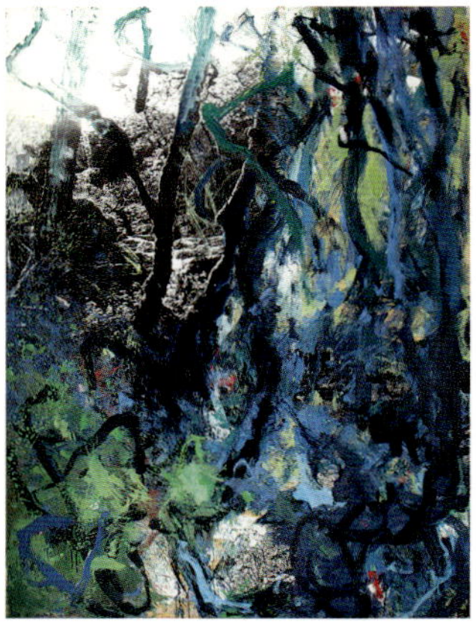

McKeever, Ian b.1946
Old Trees – Blue 1985
oil on canvas 220 x 170
PRSMG : P1830

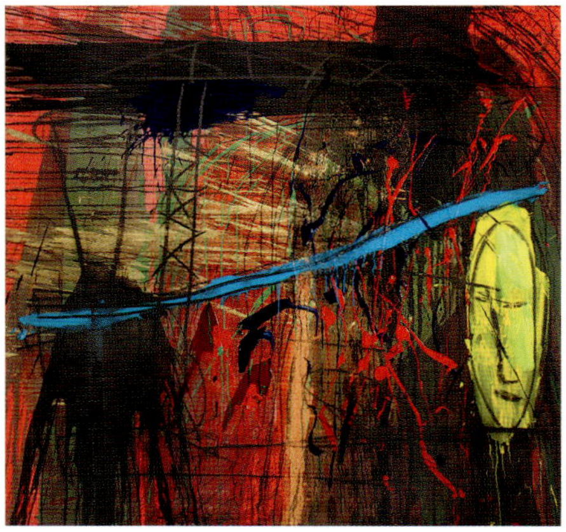

McLean, Bruce b.1944
Untitled 1988
acrylic on canvas 239 x 237 (E)
PRSMG : P2244

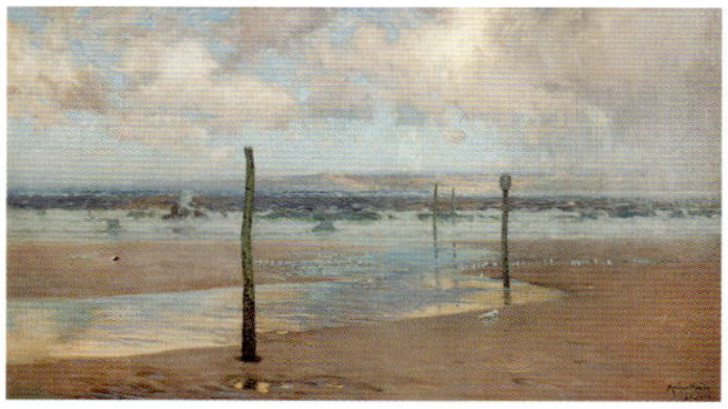

Meade, Arthur 1863–1948
A Wind-Swept Shore 1903
oil on canvas 81.2 x 152.5
PRSMG : P403

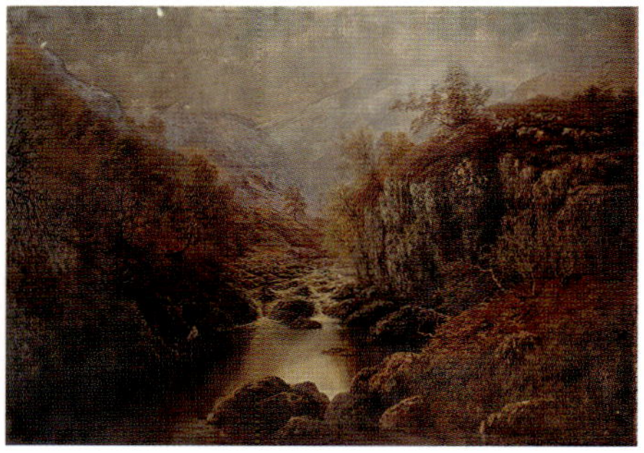

Mellor, William 1851–1931
On the Lledr, North Wales 1870–1900
oil on canvas 76 x 107
PRSMG : P1891

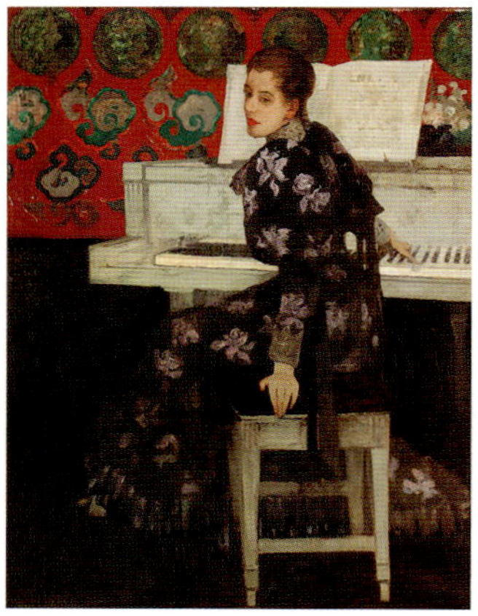

Melville, Arthur 1855–1904
The White Piano 1897
oil on canvas 202 x 170
PRSMG : P404

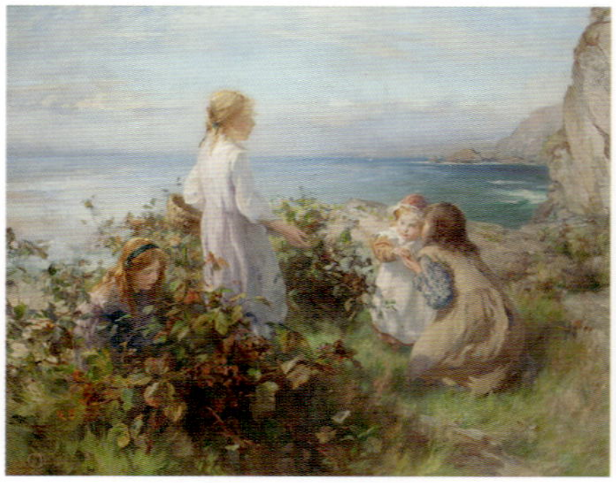

Menzies, John active 1871–1939
September Morning in the Hebrides 1918
oil on canvas 101.5 x 127
PRSMG : P405

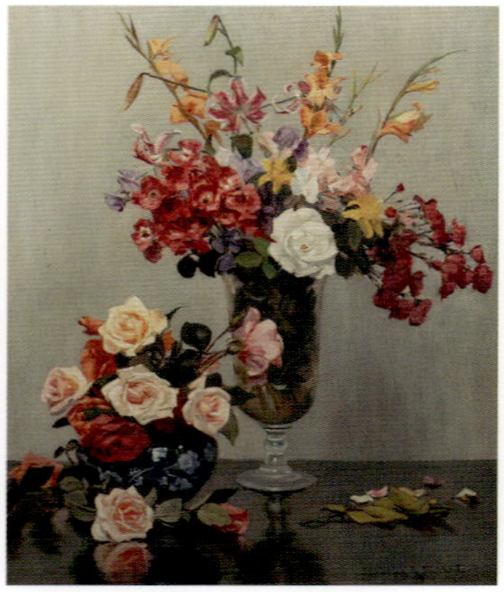

Merchant, Henry active 1883–1940
Glories of Summer 1930
oil on canvas 73 x 60
PRSMG : P406

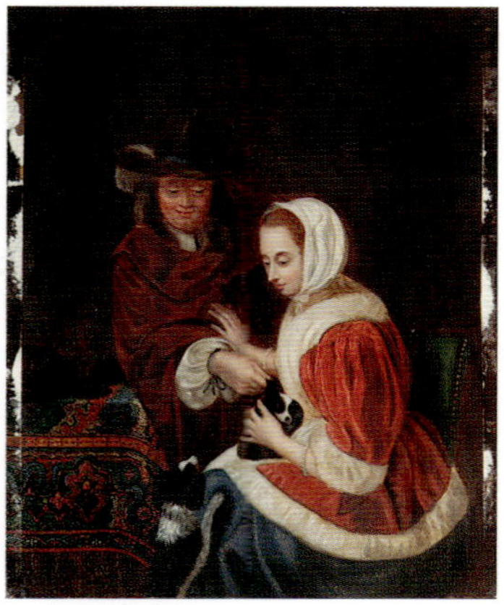

Mieris the younger, Frans van (attributed to) 1689–1763
Interior with Two Figures
oil on panel 25.5 x 20.4
PRSMG : P407

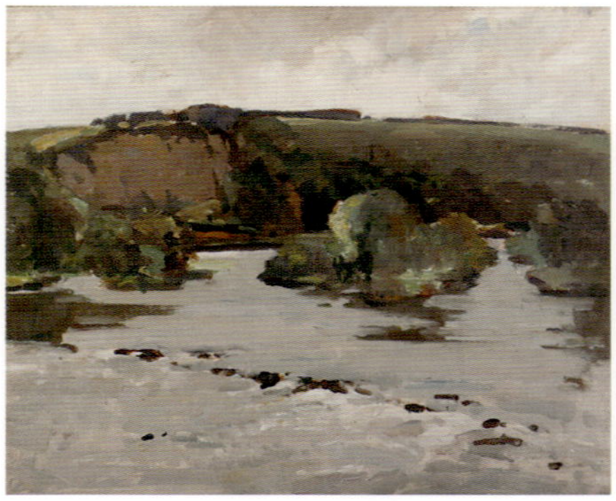

Milner, Frederick 1855–1939
Near Ludlow 1900–1939
oil on panel 38 x 45.7
PRSMG : P860

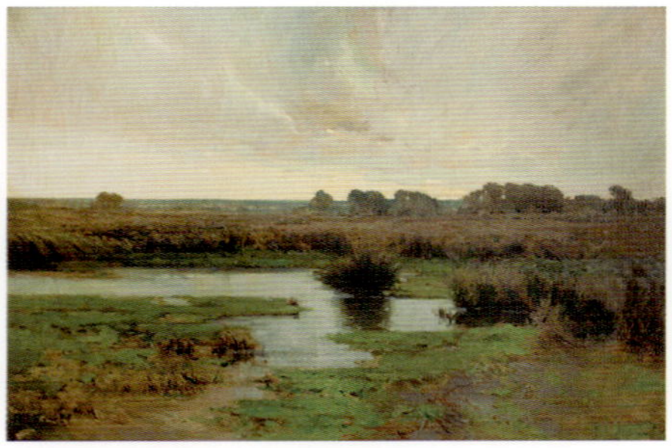

Milner, Frederick 1855–1939
Marshland 1903
oil on canvas 121 x 193
PRSMG : P411

Mohalyi, Yolanda 1909–1978
Painting No.7 1960–1965
oil on canvas 154 x 131
PRSMG : P1752

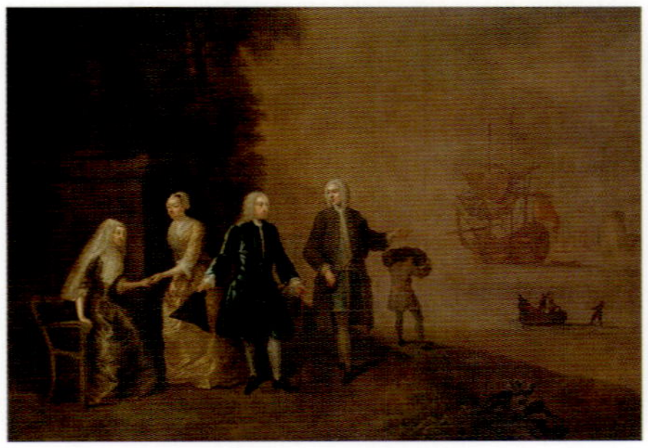

Monamy, Peter 1681–1749
A Gentleman Taking Leave of His Family
oil on canvas 87.7 x 126
PRSMG : P1826

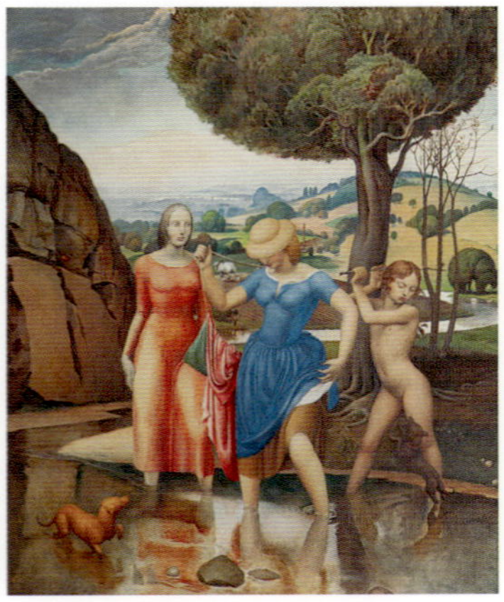

Moody, Victor Hume 1896–1990
Crossing the Brook 1934
oil on panel 49.5 x 42
PRSMG : P413

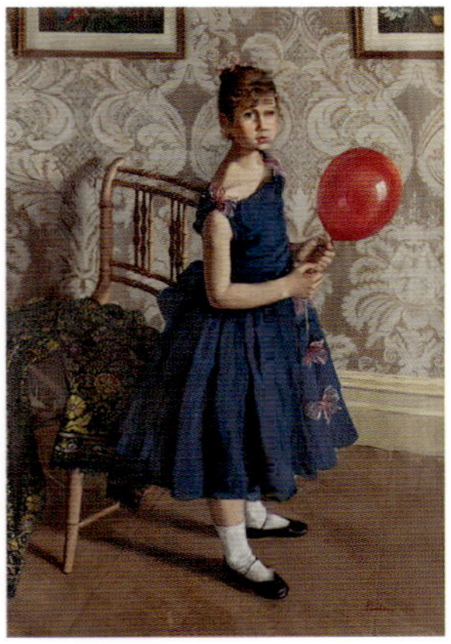

Moore, Pandora active 1954–1958
Chloe 1954
oil on canvas 152.5 x 111.8
PRSMG : P1469

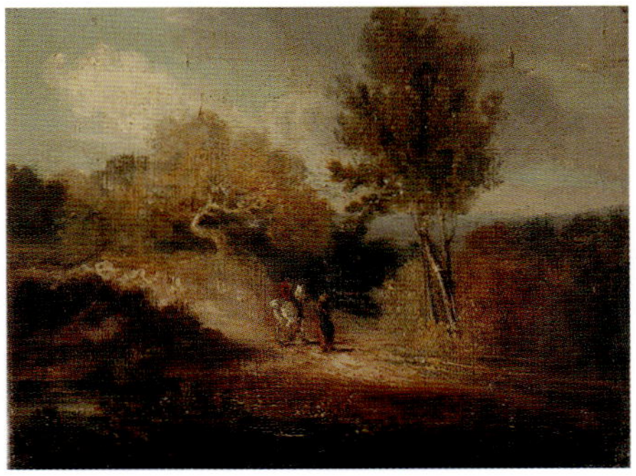

Morland, George 1763–1804
Huntsman Asking the Way
oil on canvas 14 x 17.8
PRSMG : P1549

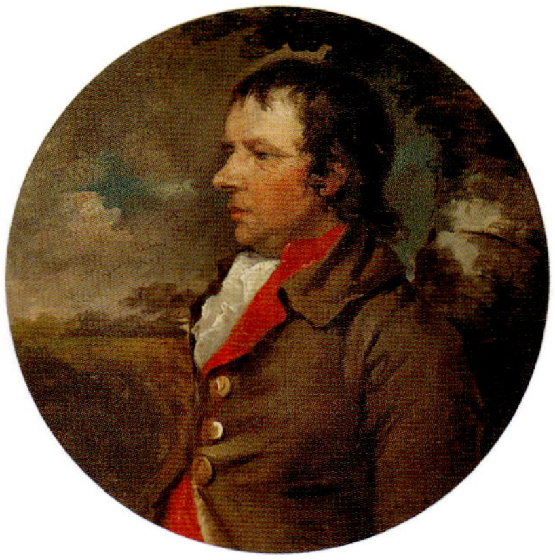

Morland, George 1763–1804
Portrait of a Man
oil on canvas 33 x 34.3
PRSMG : P831

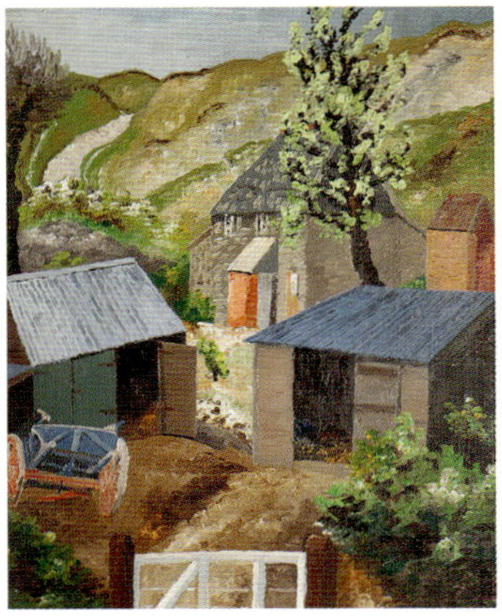

Morris, Cedric Lockwood 1889–1982
The Farmyard, Dorset 1928
oil on canvas 62.2 x 52.7
PRSMG : P414

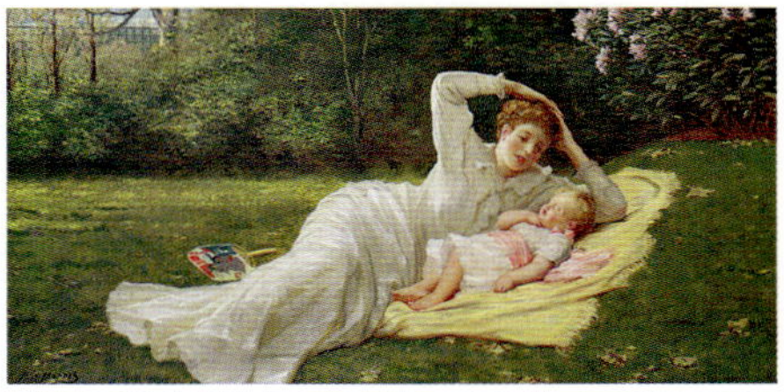

Morris, Philip Richard 1836–1902
The First Born
oil on canvas 77 x 145
PRSMG : P415

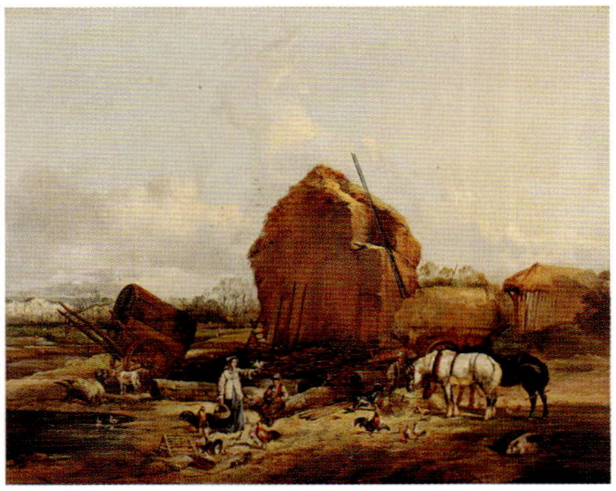

Morris, William 1834–1896
Landscape
oil on canvas 50.8 x 61
PRSMG : P917

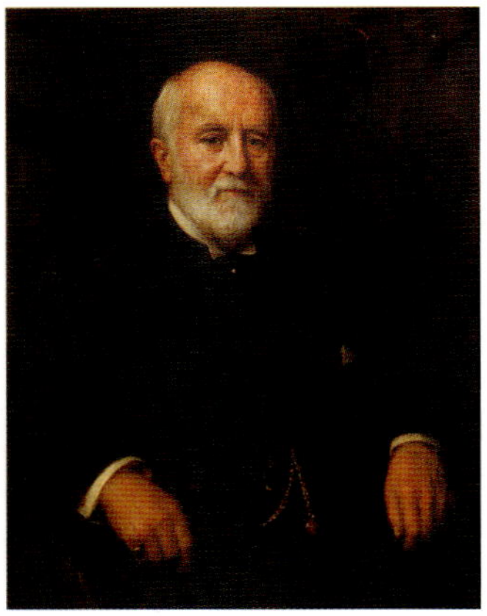

Morrison, Robert Edward 1851–1924
Sir William Ascroft
oil on canvas 91.7 x 72.1
PRSMG : P812

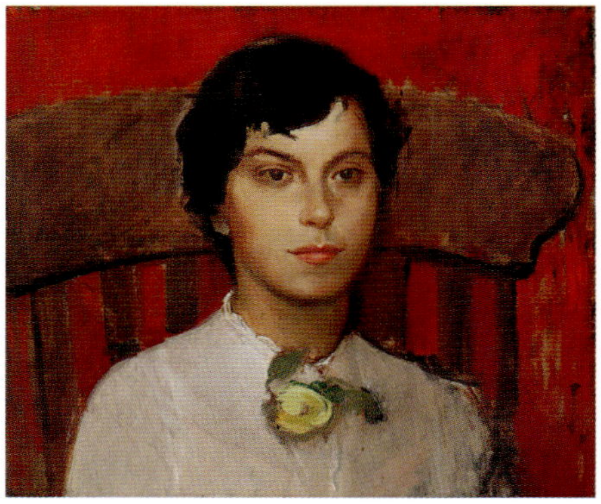

Moynihan, Rodrigo 1910–1990
Gabriele Annan 1951
oil on canvas 45.8 x 58.5
PRSMG : P1390

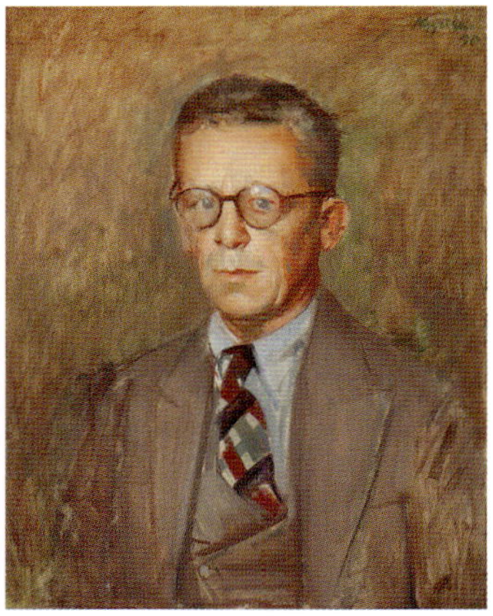

Moynihan, Rodrigo 1910–1990
Dennis Carlton Walmsley 1952
oil on canvas 61 x 50.8
PRSMG : P1631

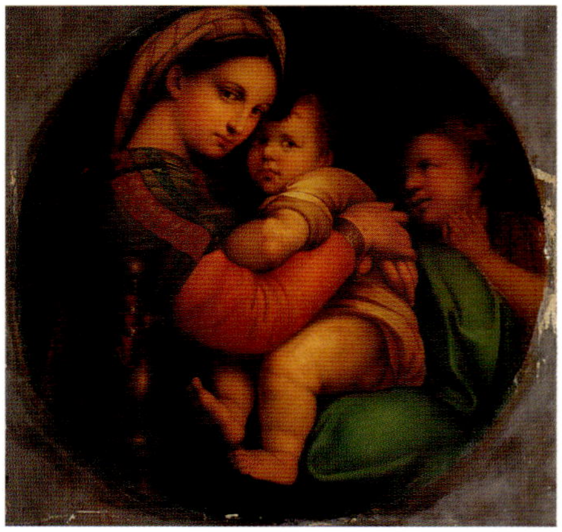

Muller, F. 1812–1882
Madonna and Child (copy of Raphael)
oil on canvas 71 x 71
PRSMG : P416

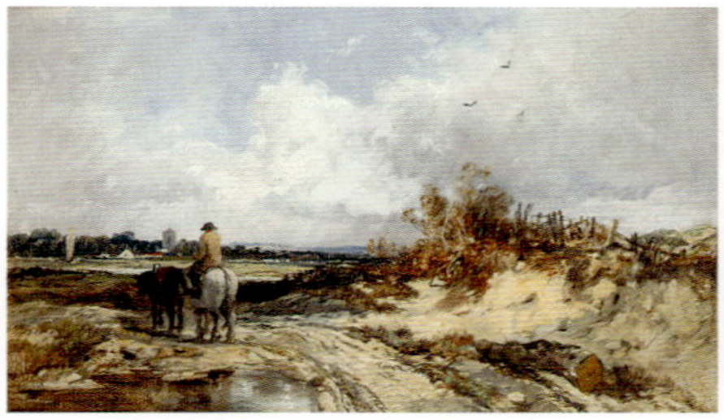

Muller, William James 1812–1845
Scene near Whitchurch c.1842
oil on canvas 35.3 x 60
PRSMG : P418

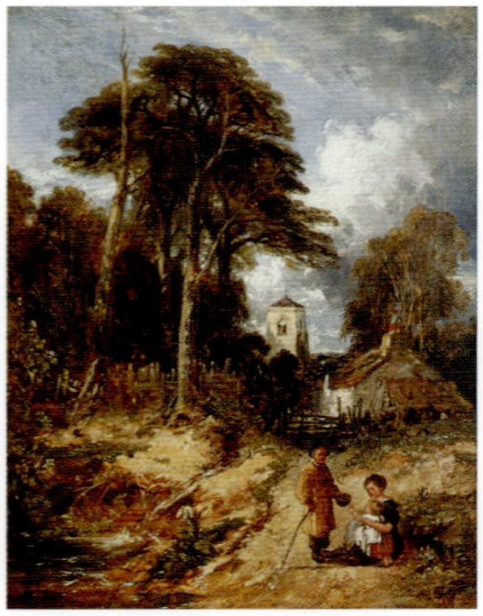

Muller, William James 1812–1845
Whitchurch 1843
oil on canvas 78.5 x 66
PRSMG : P419

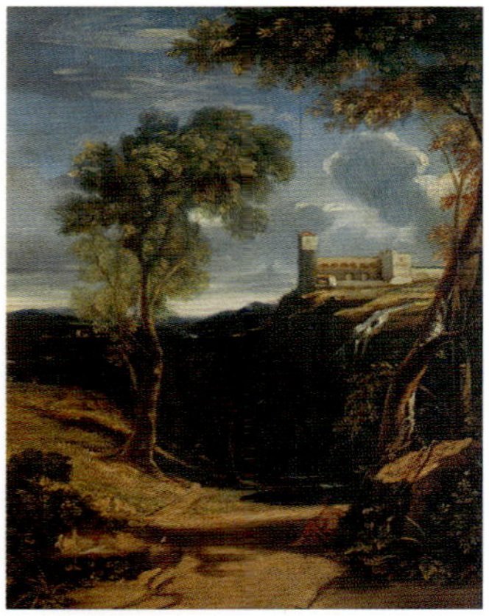

Muller, William James 1812–1845
Classical Landscape
oil on canvas 35.5 x 25.5
PRSMG : P1498

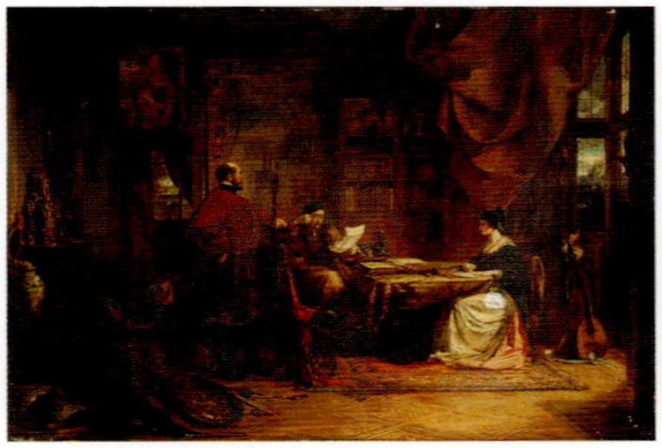

Muller, William James 1812–1845
Elizabethan Interior: The Court Messenger
oil on canvas 93.1 x 141.2
PRSMG : P417

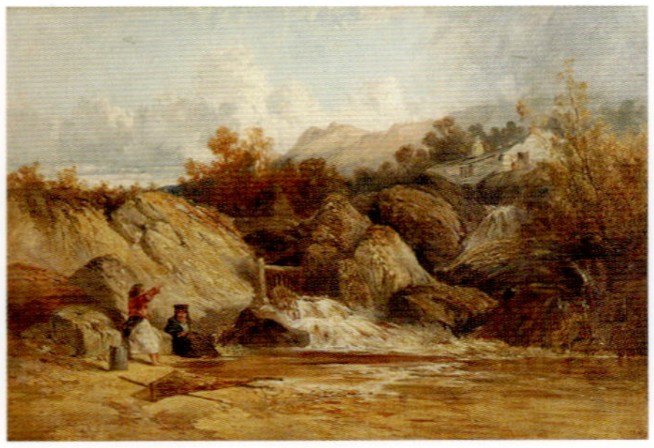

Muller, William James 1812–1845
Salmon Trap, near Pont-y-Pridd, South Wales
oil on canvas 49.4 x 67
PRSMG : P421

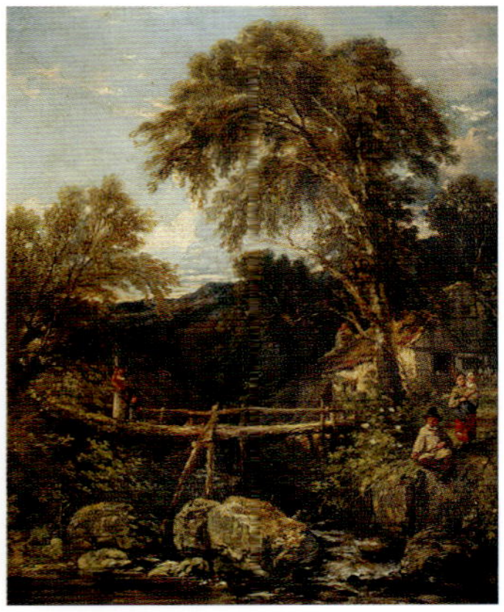

Muller, William James 1812–1845
Scene in Wales
oil on canvas 76.3 x 64
PRSMG : P420

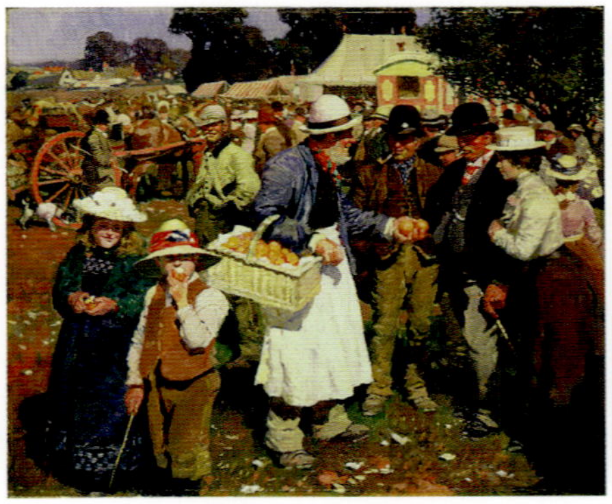

Munnings, Alfred James 1878–1959
Whitsuntide – A Gala Day 1902
oil on canvas 83 x 92
PRSMG : P425

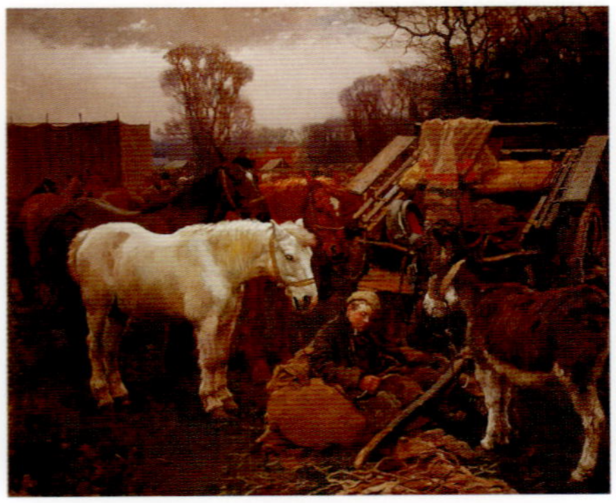

Munnings, Alfred James 1878–1959
The Last of the Fair 1903
oil on canvas 94 x 114.5
PRSMG : P424

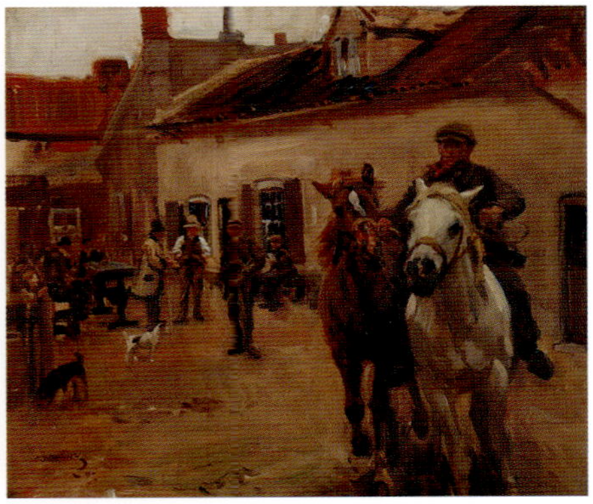

Munnings, Alfred James 1878–1959
The Inn Yard 1910
oil on canvas 50.8 x 61
PRSMG : P426

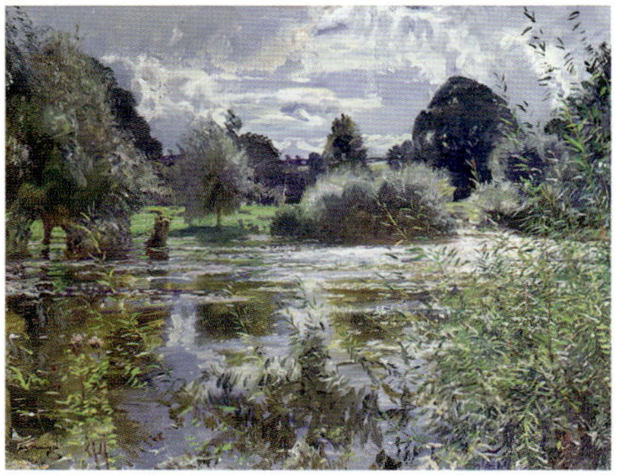

Munnings, Alfred James 1878–1959
The Full River 1932
oil on canvas 58 x 73.5
PRSMG : P427

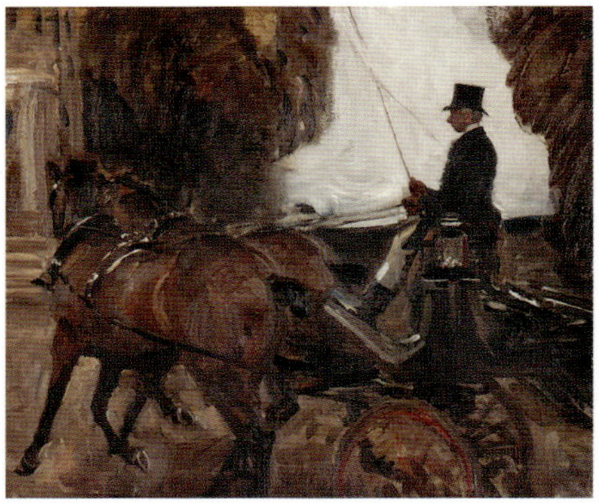

Munnings, Alfred James 1878–1959
Old John, the Coachman
oil on canvas 63.6 x 76.4
PRSMG : P1756

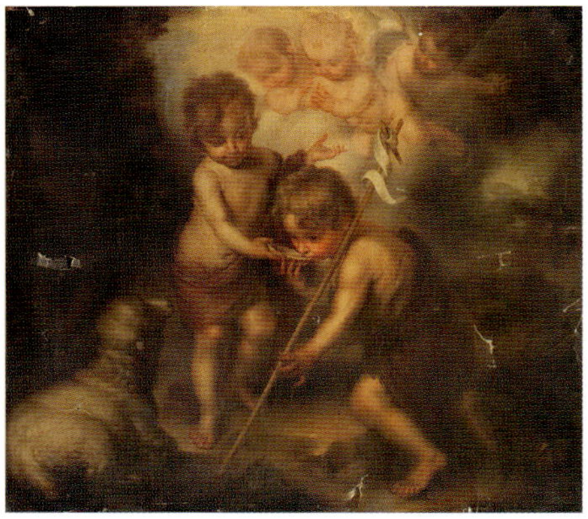

Murillo, Bartolomé Esteban (after) 1617–1682
The Children of the Shell
oil on canvas 105 x 125
PRSMG : P428

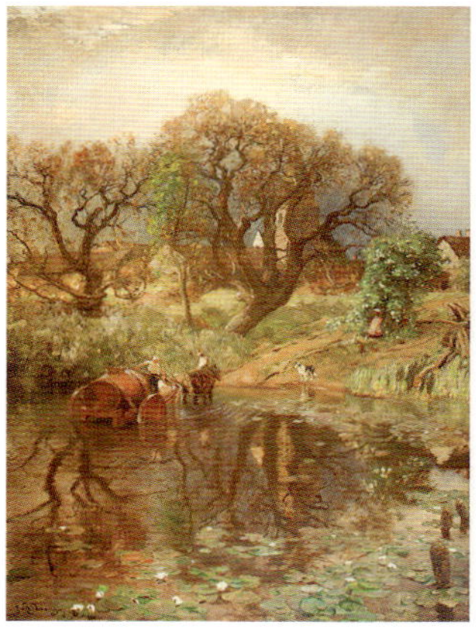

Murray, David 1849–1933
The Water Cart 1880–1930
oil on canvas 183 x 122
PRSMG : P839

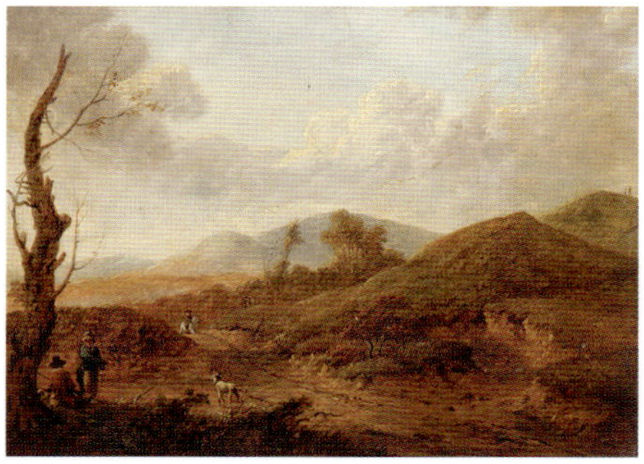

Nasmyth, Patrick 1787–1831
Landscape with Sportsmen
oil on panel 22.8 x 30.5
PRSMG : P1538

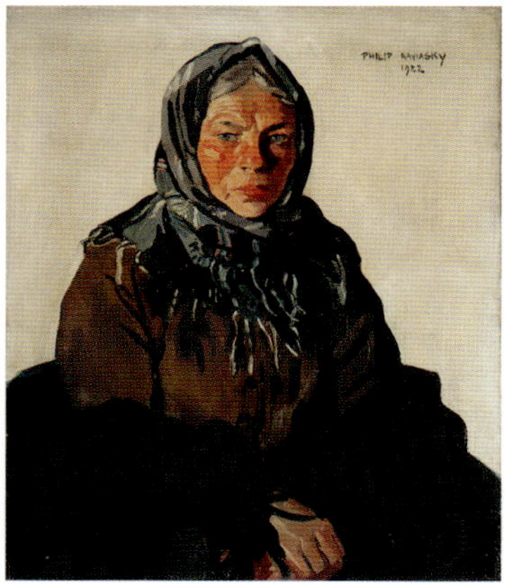

Naviasky, Philip 1894–1982
Connemara 1922
oil on canvas 75 x 61
PRSMG : P434

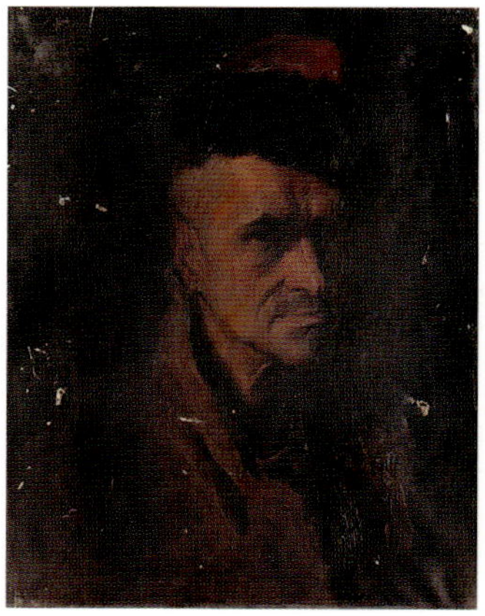

Naziere, David active 19th C
Hungarian Gipsy
oil on canvas 54 x 43.3
PRSMG : P1892

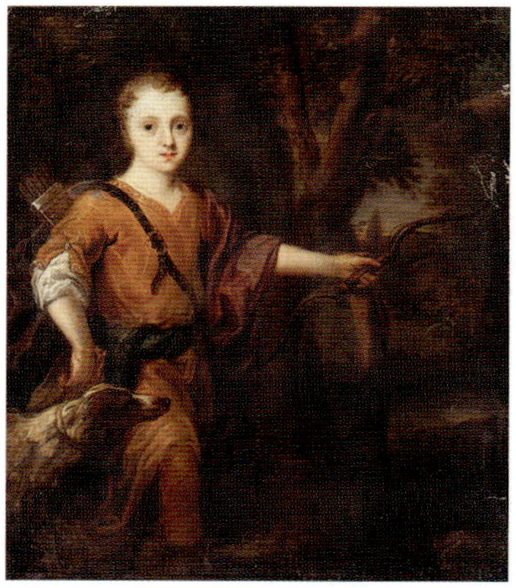

Netscher, Caspar 1639–1684
Diana
oil on canvas 57 x 49.5
PRSMG : P830

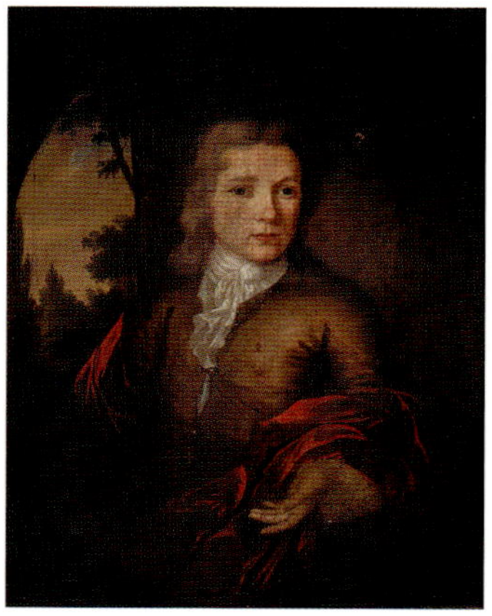

Netscher, Caspar 1639–1684
Isaac Newton (1642–1727)
oil on canvas 45.7 x 35.5
PRSMG : P827

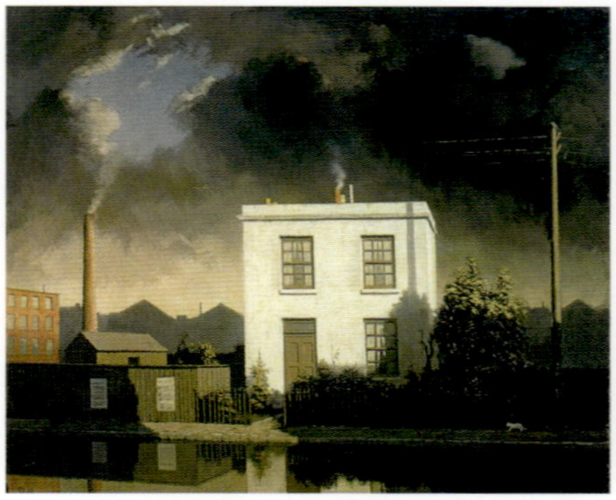

Newton, Algernon Cecil 1880–1968
The House by the Canal 1945
oil on canvas 50.8 x 61
PRSMG : P939

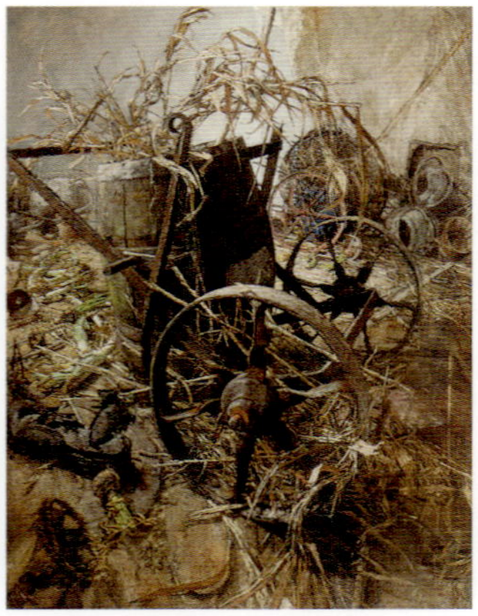

Newton, Kenneth 1933–1984
Water Barrel and Carrier 1964
oil on canvas 91.5 x 76.8
PRSMG : P1681

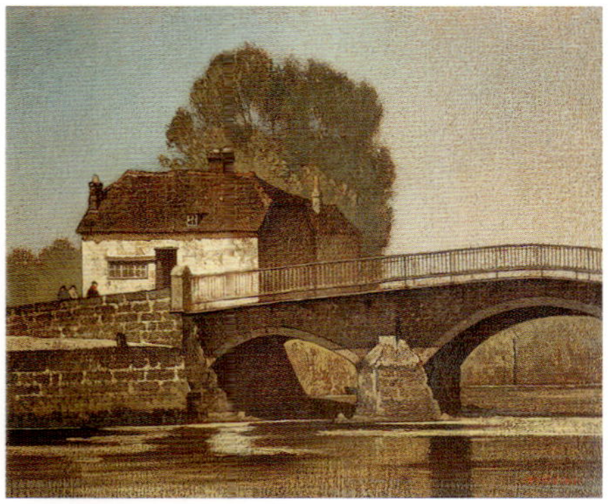

Nicholls, Bertram 1883–1974
By a Sussex Stream 1926
oil on canvas 35.7 x 45.8
PRSMG : P435

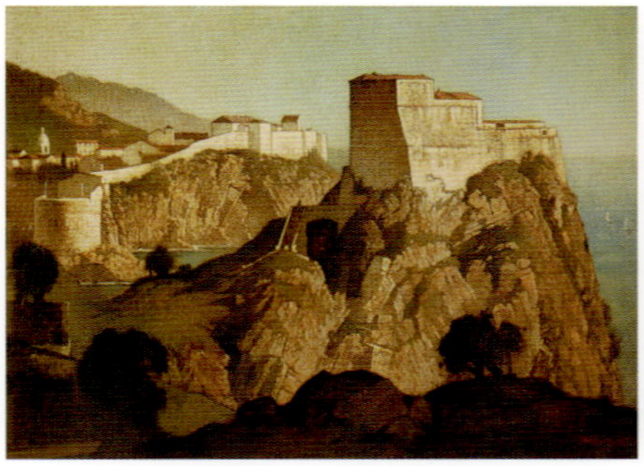

Nicholls, Bertram 1883–1974
Ragusa 1930
oil on canvas 50.8 x 76.2
PRSMG : P436

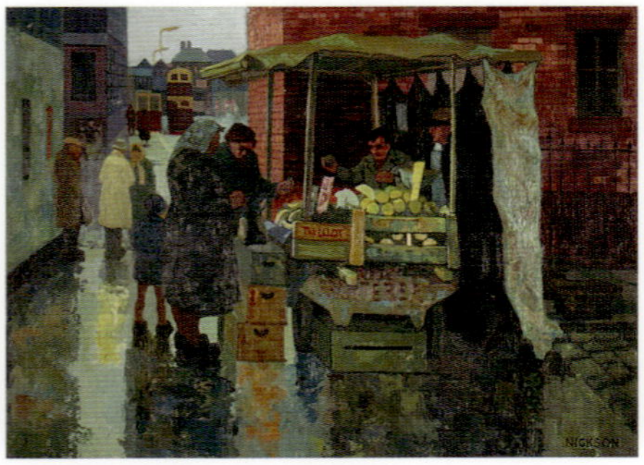

Nickson, Robert Peter
Study for 'Ward's End' 1958
oil on canvas 52.5 x 76
PRSMG : P1597

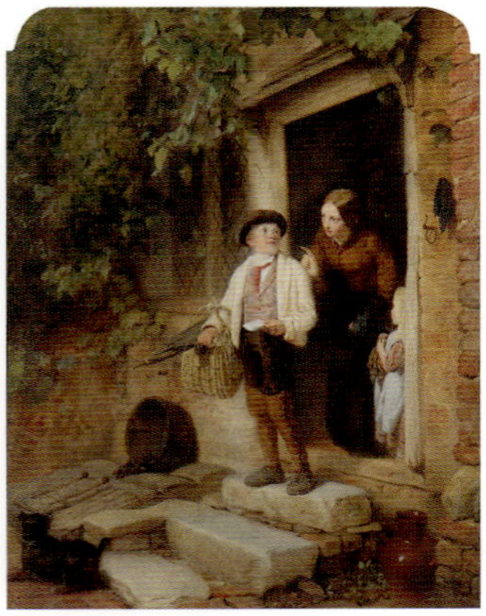

O'Neill, George Bernard 1828–1917
The Message 1857
oil on panel 45.8 x 35
PRSMG : P449

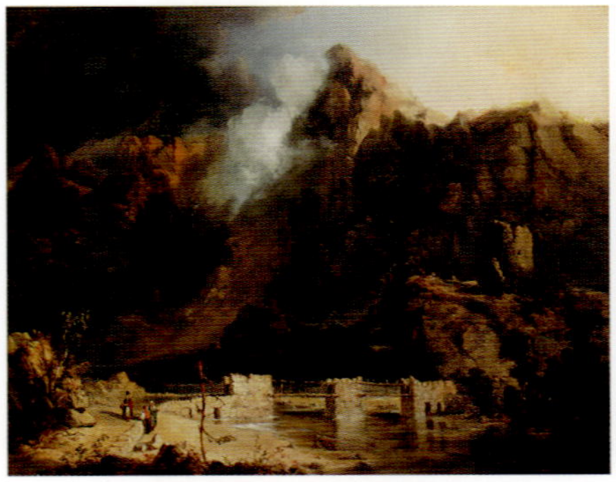

Oakes, John Wright 1820–1887
Slate Quarries, Llanberis 1840–1847
oil on canvas 51.5 x 66
PRSMG : P1429

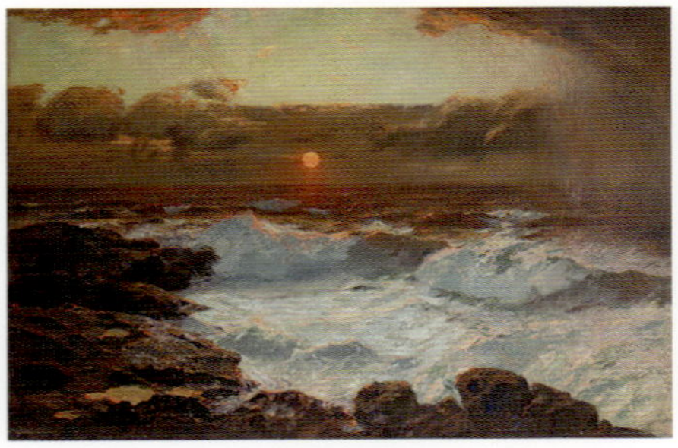

Olsson, Albert Julius 1864–1942
Sunset at Land's End 1910
oil on canvas 117 x 161.5
PRSMG : P448

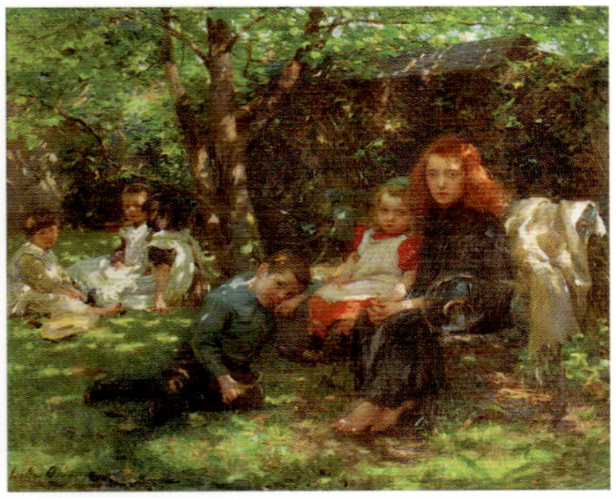

Osborne, Walter Frederick 1859–1903
Summertime 190[illegible]
oil on canvas 106.5 x 122
PRSMG : P450

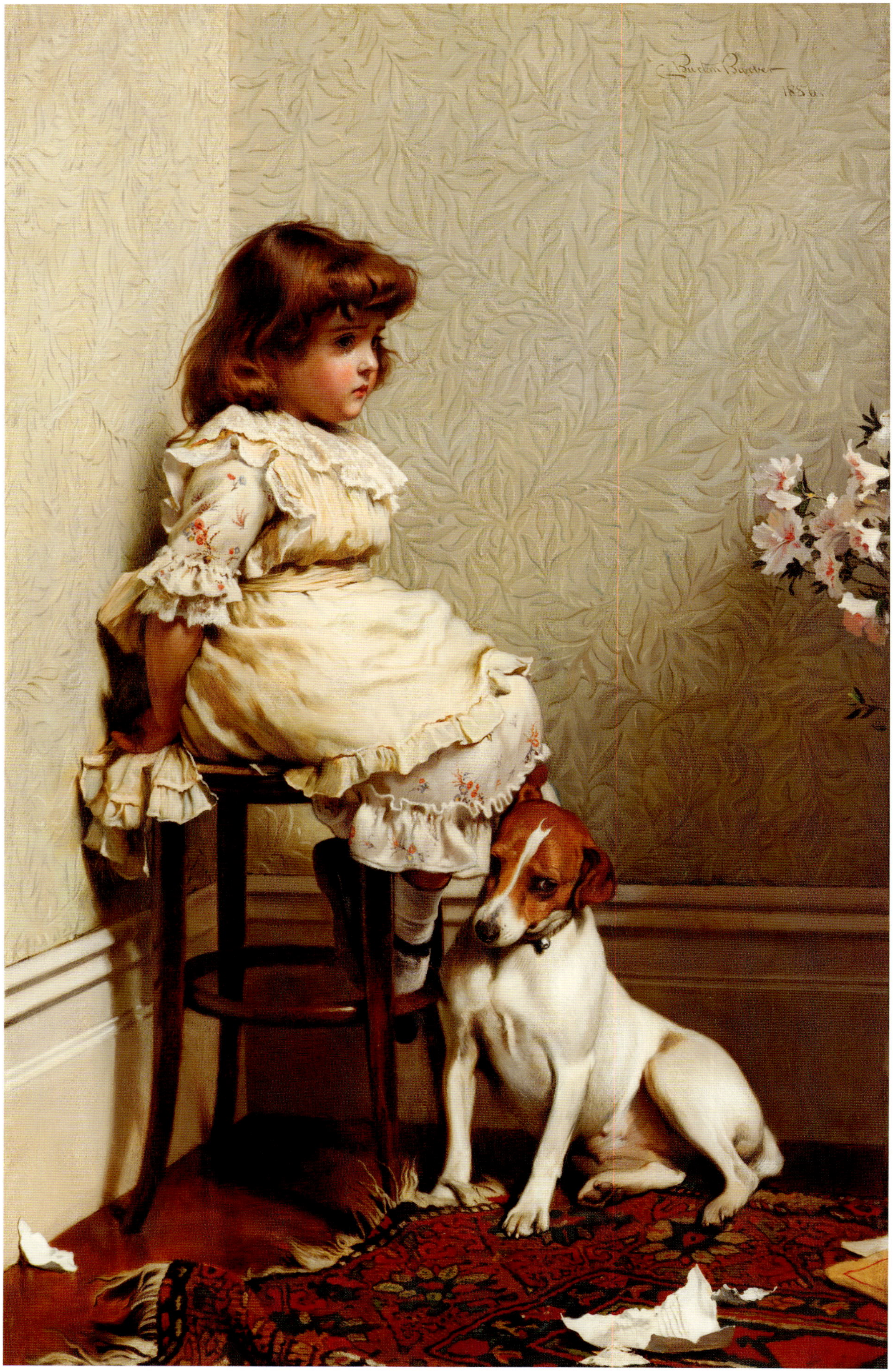
C. Burton Barber

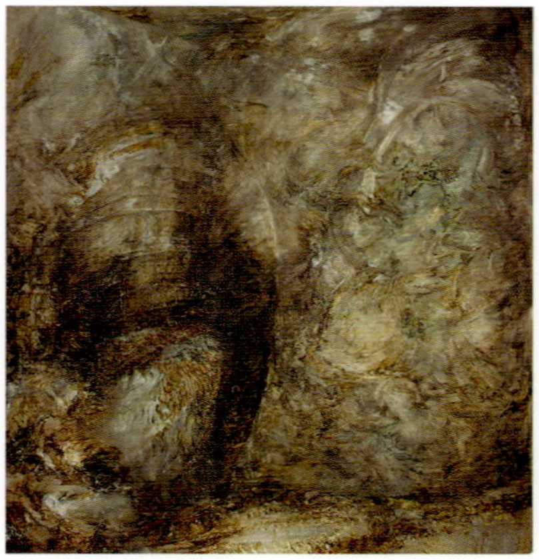

Oulton, Thérèse b.1953
Spoils 1985
oil on canvas 239 x 208
PRSMG : P1835

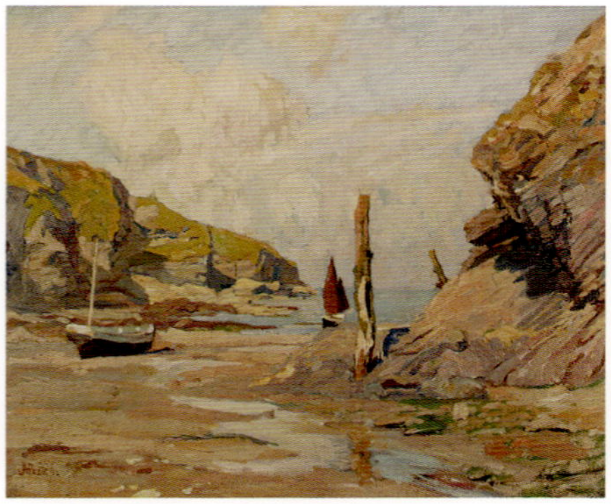

Park, John Anthony 1880–1962
Port Gavern at Low Tide 1914
oil on canvas 49.5 x 59.5
PRSMG : P451

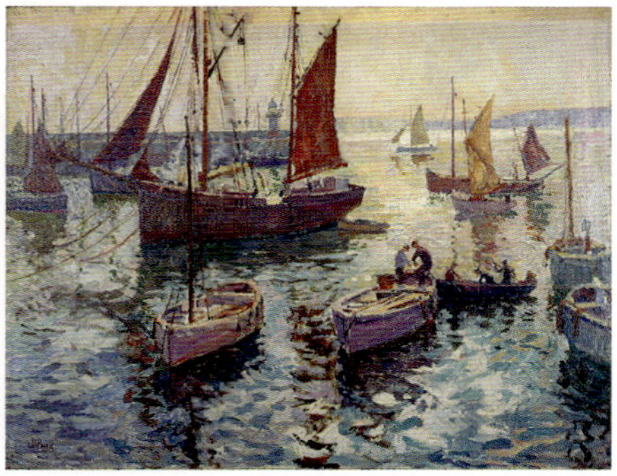

Park, John Anthony 1880–1962
Morning Tide 1922
oil on canvas 66 x 91.5
PRSMG : P452

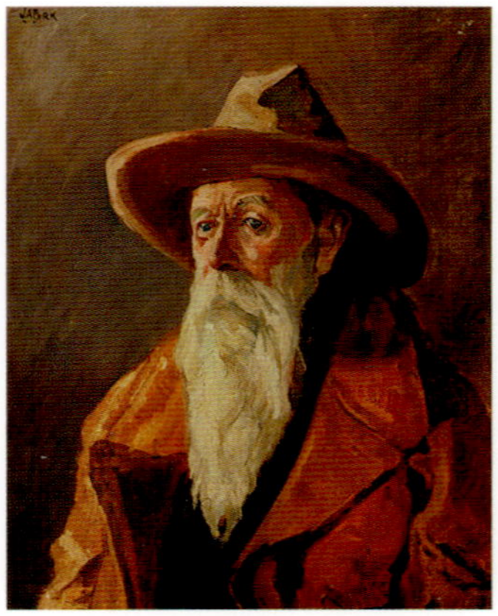

Park, John Anthony 1880–1962
Aloysius Smith (Trader Horn) 1931
oil on canvas 67 x 57
PRSMG : P453

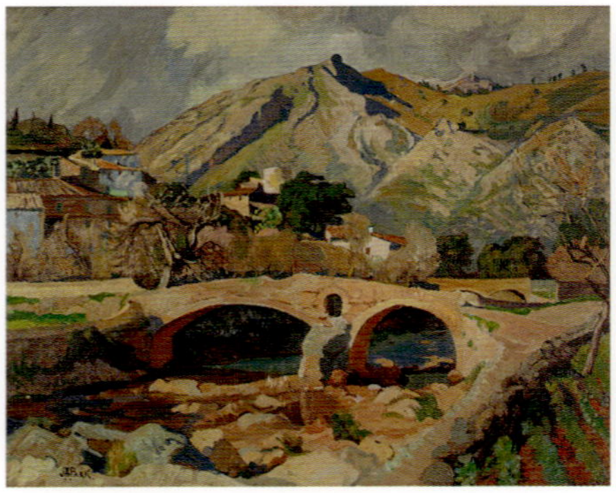

Park, John Anthony 1880–1962
Roman Bridge, Pollensa, Mallorca 1934
oil on canvas 61.5 x 76.2
PRSMG : P455

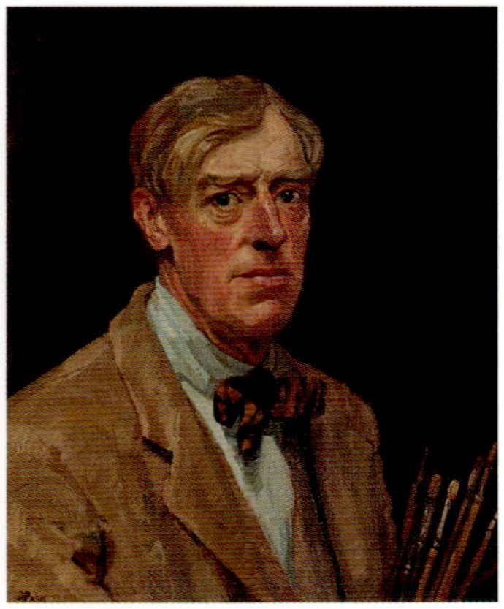

Park, John Anthony 1880–1962
Portrait of the Artist 1935
oil on canvas 61 x 51
PRSMG : P454

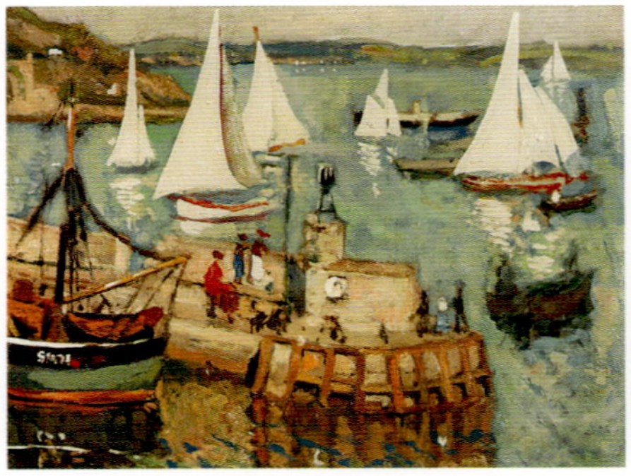

Park, John Anthony 1880–1962
Harbour Scene with Yachts
oil on canvas 29 x 33.5
PRSMG : P2364

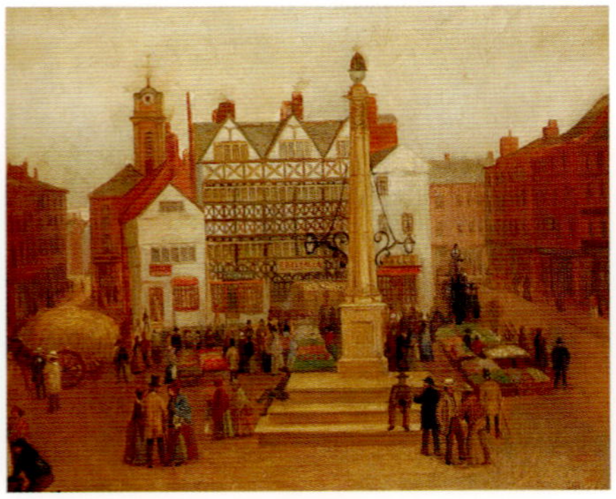

Park, John Anthony 1880–1962
Preston Market in the Olden Days
oil on canvas 43 x 56
PRSMG : P1412

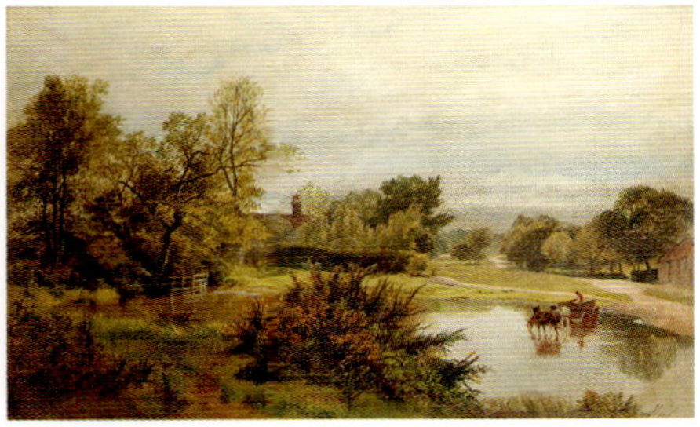

Peel, James 1811–1906
Totteridge, near Hampstead 1850–1900
oil on canvas 40.6 x 66
PRSMG : P1492

Facing page: Barber, Charles Burton, 1845–1894, *In Disgrace,* 1886, Lytham Art Collection of Fylde Borough Council (p. 260)

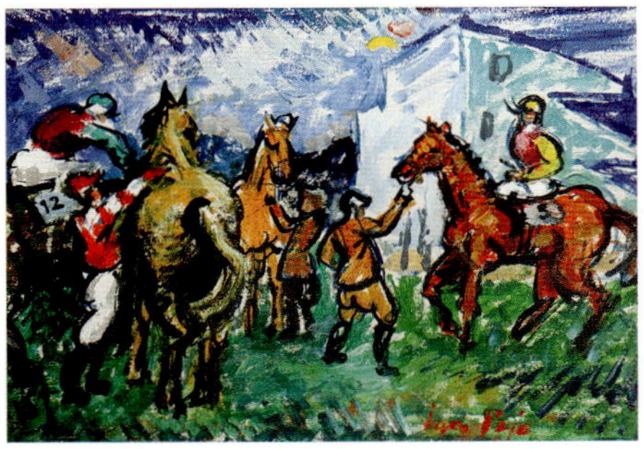

Pejo, John active 1900–1950
Horses and Jockeys
oil on canvas 38.5 x 53
PRSMG : P1239

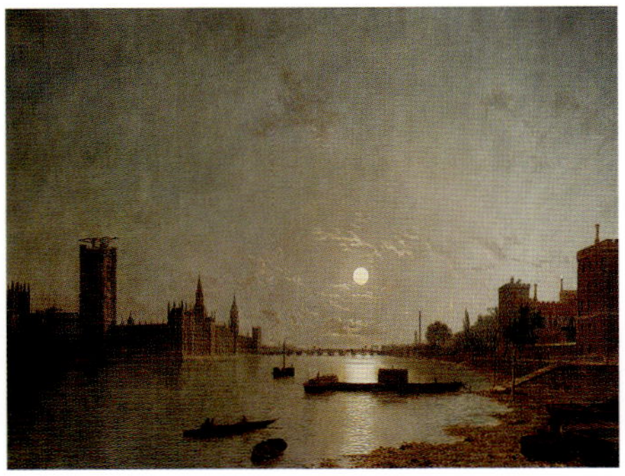

Pether, Henry 1801–1880
Westminster in the Moonlight 1845–1862
oil on canvas 62.2 x 91.5
PRSMG : P915

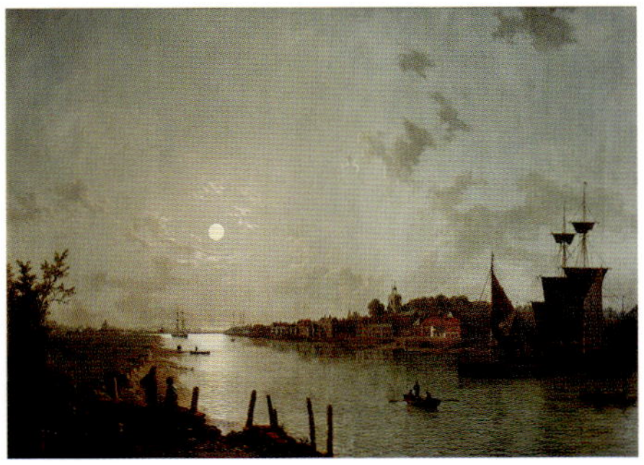

Pether, Henry 1801–1880
Scene on the Thames
oil on canvas 61.5 x 92
PRSMG : P916

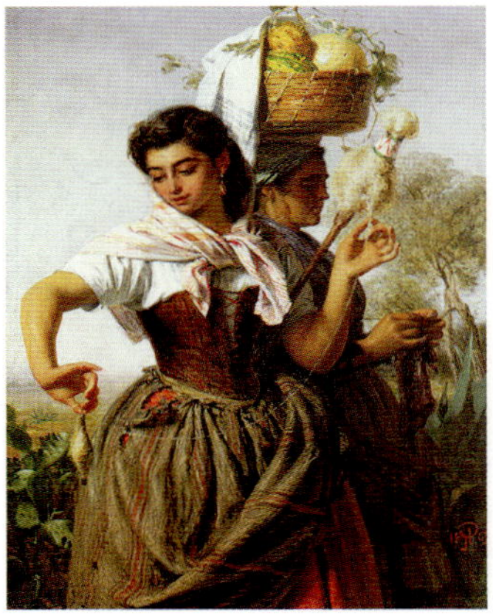

Phillip, John 1817–1867
Spanish Industry 1863
oil on canvas 66 x 50.7
PRSMG : P460

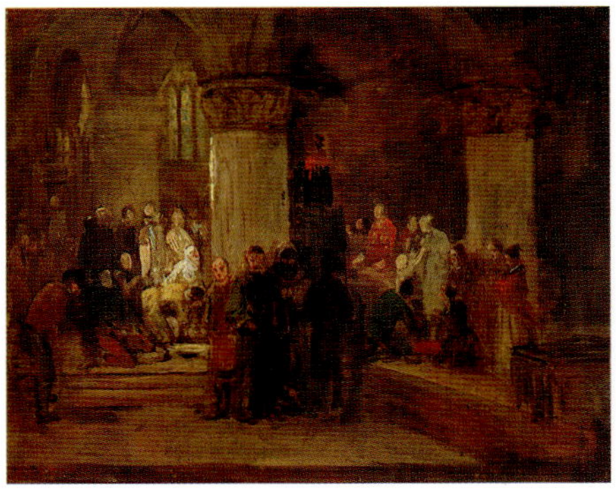

Phillip, John 1817–1867
Church Interior with Figures
oil on panel 17.7 x 21.5
PRSMG : P1542

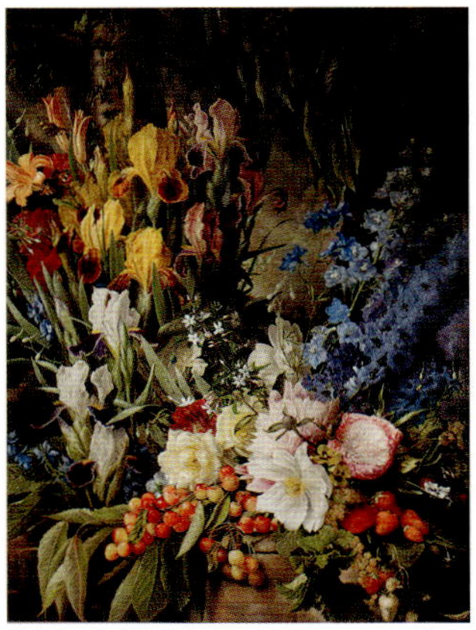

Philpot, Leonard Daniel 1877–1973
June's Largesse 1930
oil on canvas 91.5 x 71
PRSMG : P461

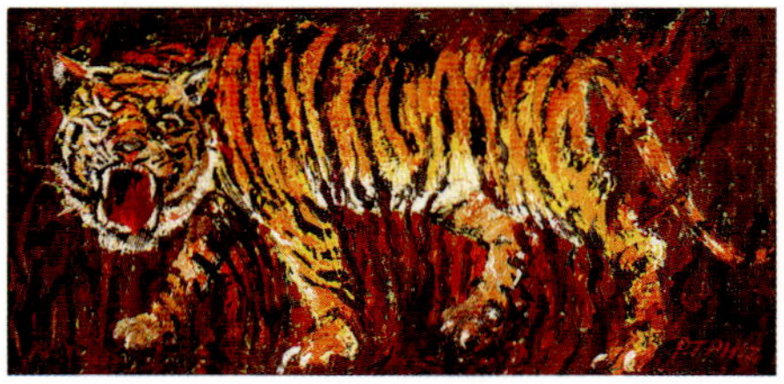

Phizackerley, Patrick Terence 1931–2002
Tiger 1971
oil on hardboard 36 x 72.6 (E)
PRSMG : P1777

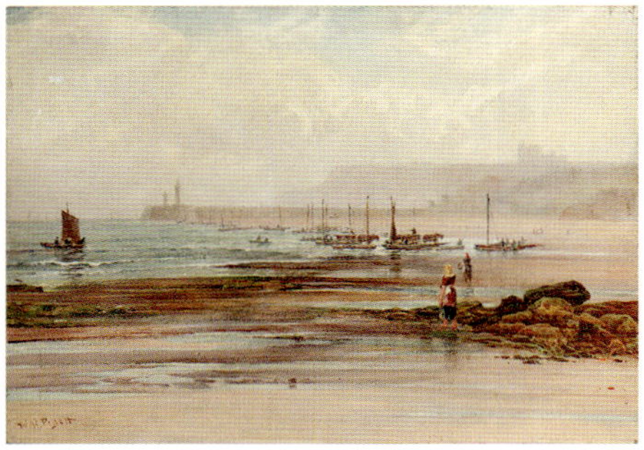

Pigott, William Henry 1810–1901
Yorkshire Coast 1850–1900
oil on canvas 44.5 x 60.5
PRSMG : P1495

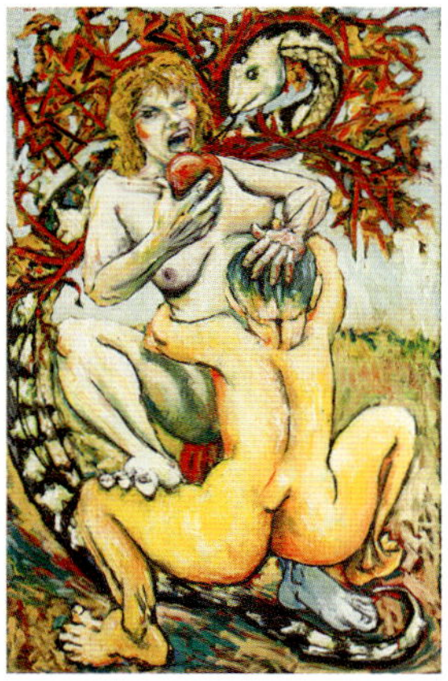

Pilbro, Anthony b.1954
Adam and Eve 1986
oil on canvas 59 x 39
PRSMG : 2005.193

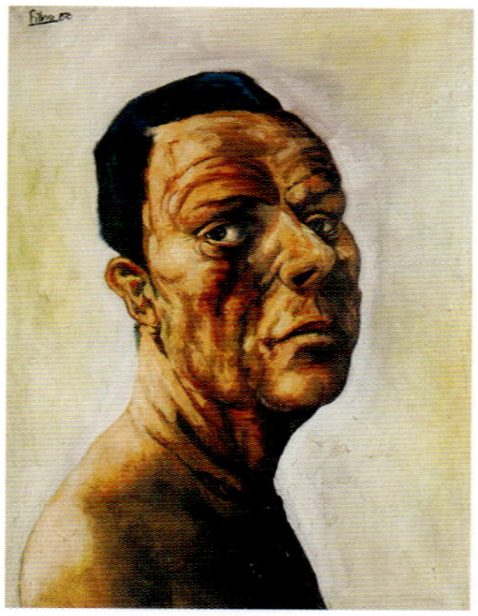

Pilbro, Anthony b.1954
A Portrait 2000
oil on canvas 121 x 91
PRSMG : 2005.194

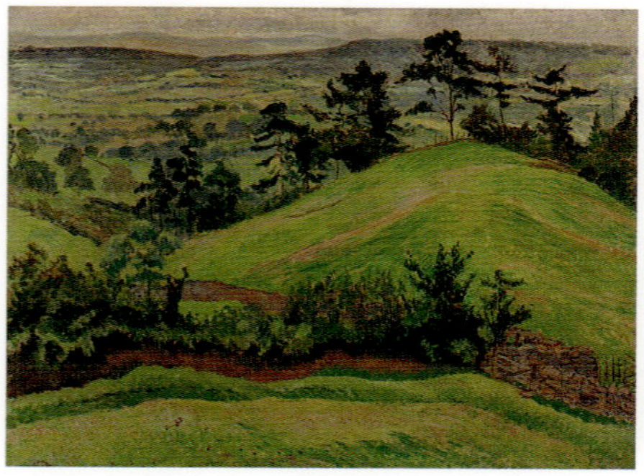

Pissarro, Lucien 1863–1944
Eden Valley 1914
oil on canvas 53.2 x 64.5
PRSMG : P463

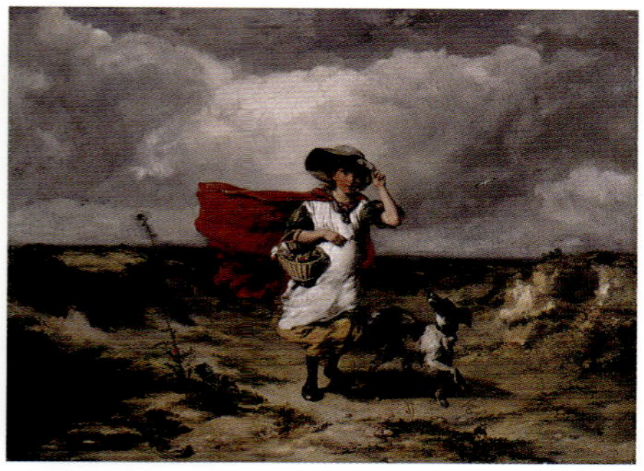

Poole, Paul Falconer 1807–1879
Crossing the Heath, Windy Day 1836
oil on canvas 52 x 70
PRSMG : P464

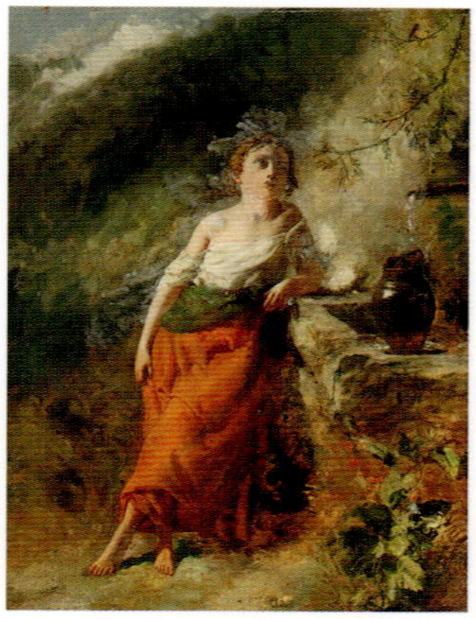

Poole, Paul Falconer 1807–1879
Autumn: Welsh Girl at a Mountain Stream 1848
oil on canvas 54.5 x 44.5
PRSMG : P466

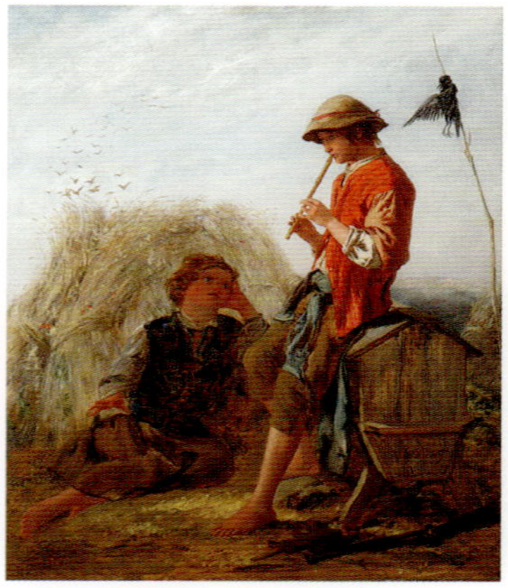

Poole, Paul Falconer 1807–1879
Shepherd Boys and the Scarecrow 1849
oil on panel 56 x 45.7
PRSMG : P465

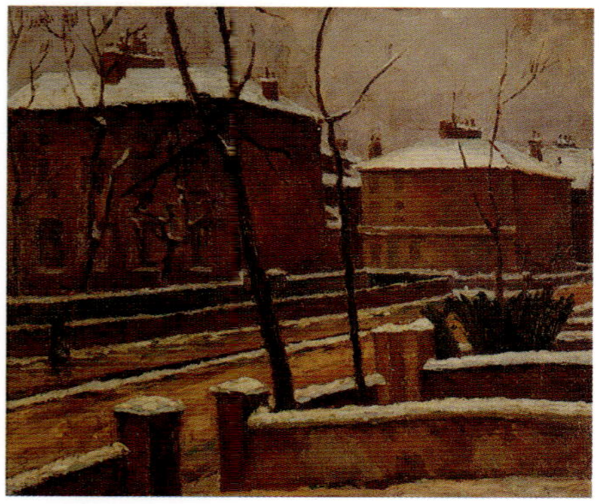

Porter, Frederick James 1883–1944
Hanover Square
oil on canvas 53.2 x 64.8
PRSMG : P467

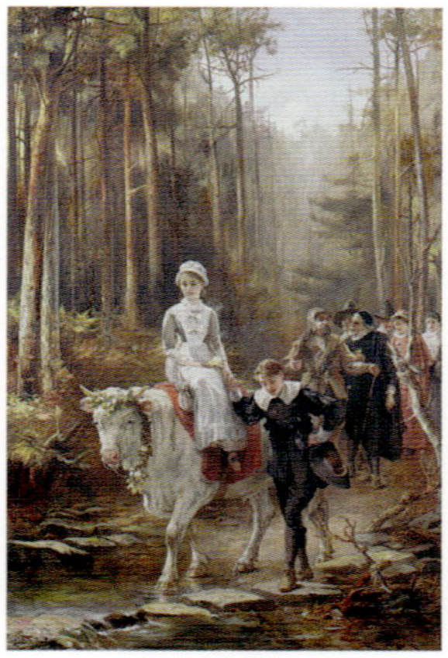

Pott, Laslett John 1837–1898
Priscilla, the Courtship of Miles Standish 1885
oil on canvas 152.5 x 101.5
PRSMG : P468

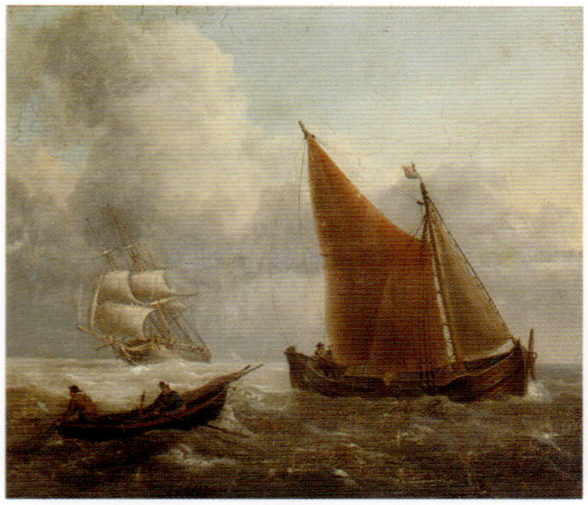

Powell, Charles Martin 1775–1824
Seascape
oil on panel 26.7 x 31.8
PRSMG : P1551

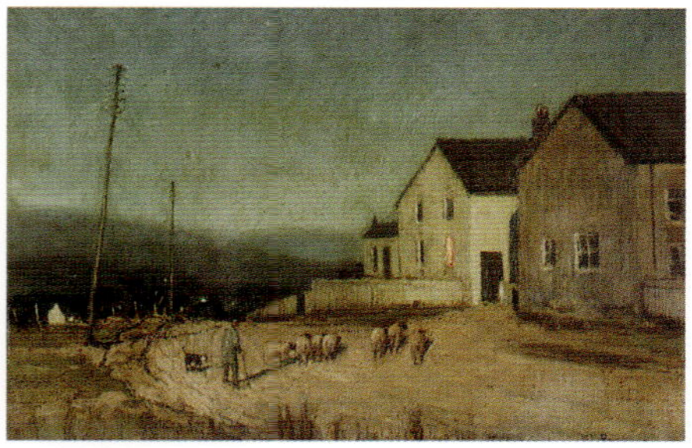

Pritt, William 1870–1944
August Moonlight 1920
oil on canvas 30.5 x 45.7
PRSMG : P1008

Pritt, William 1870–1944
Impression of the 1922 Guild 1922
oil on canvas 51 x 41
PRSMG : P1894

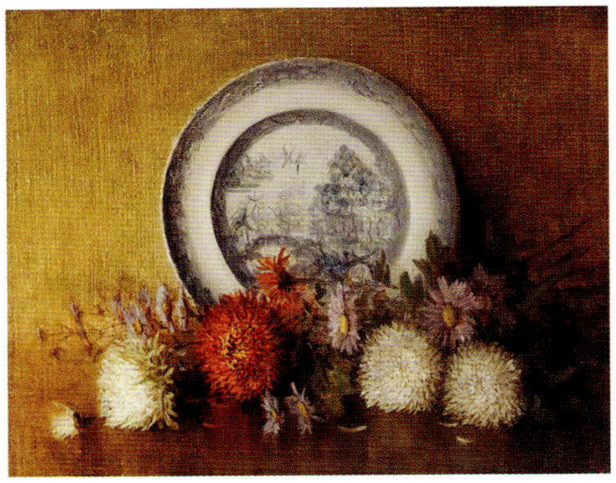

Pritt, William 1870–1944
Michaelmas Flowers 1932
oil on canvas 33.5 x 44.5
PRSMG : P469

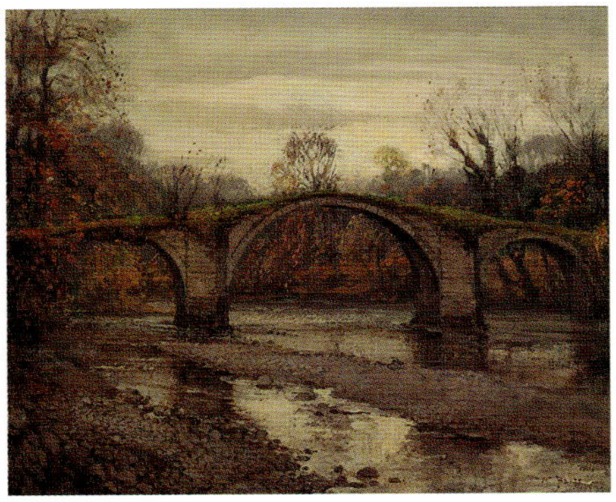

Pritt, William 1870–1944
Hodder Bridge
oil on canvas 30.5 x 40.5
PRSMG : P1646

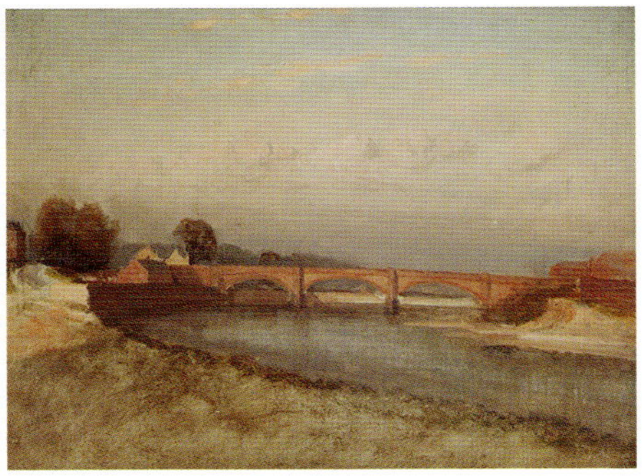

Pritt, William 1870–1944
Old Walton Bridge
oil on canvas 33 x 43.2
PRSMG : P1893

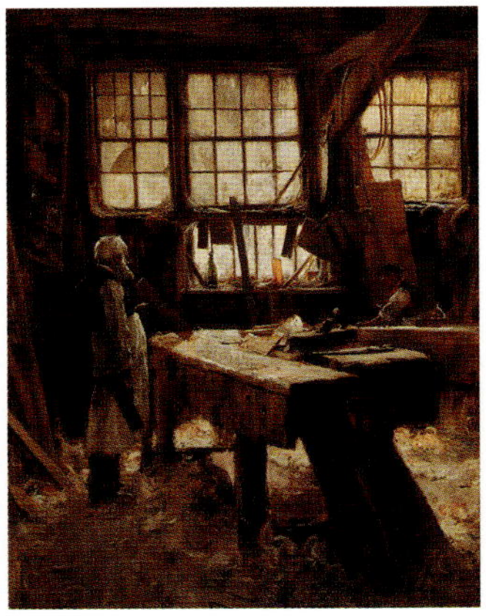

Proctor, Adam Edwin 1864–1913
The Carpenter's Shop 1892
oil on canvas 75 x 50.8
PRSMG : P470

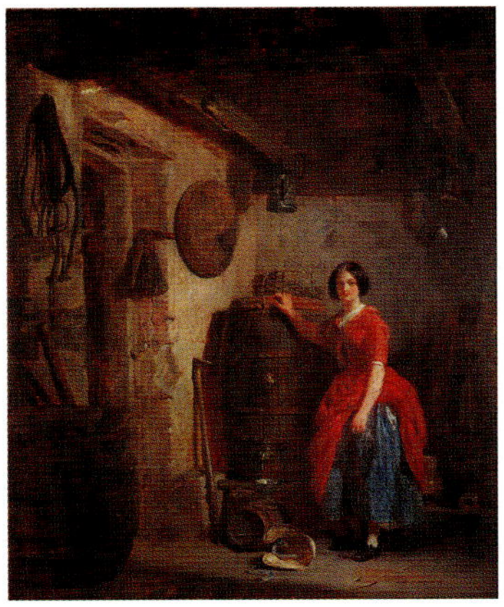

Provis, Alfred 1818–1890
Harvest Ale 1849
oil on canvas 65 x 60
PRSMG : P842

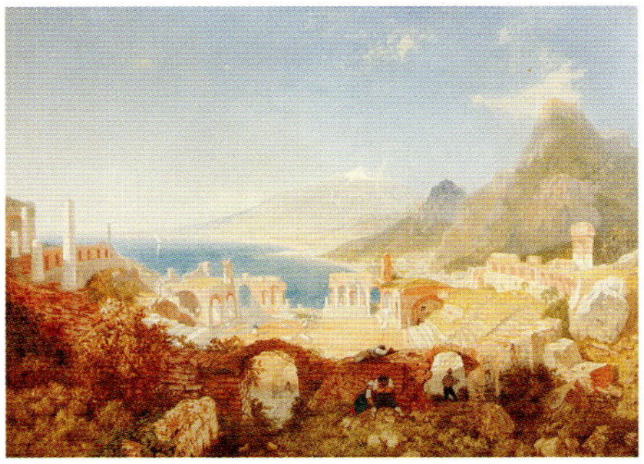

Pyne, James Baker 1800–1870
Mount Etna from the Theatre, Taormina
oil on canvas 66 x 91.5
PRSMG : P474

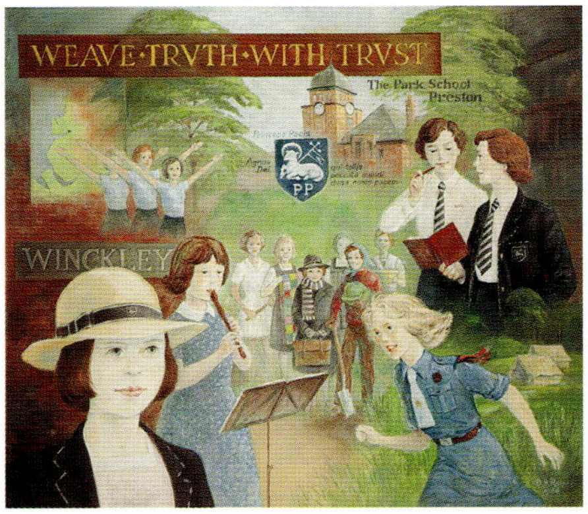

Ralphs, D.
Park School, Preston c.1984
oil on canvas 46.5 x 52.5
PRSMG : P2335

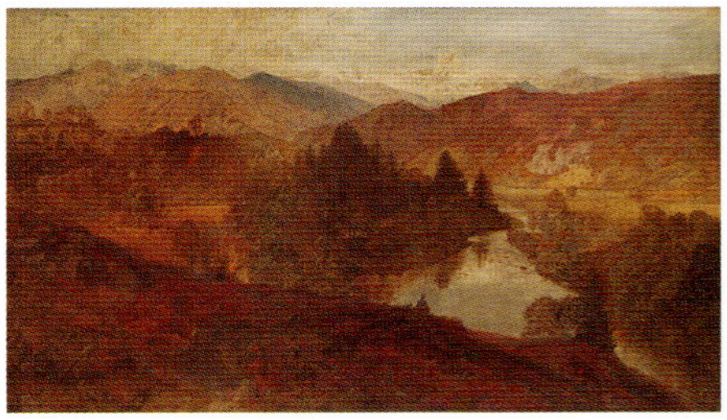

Raven, John Samuel 1829–1877
'Let the hills be joyful together' 1874
oil on canvas 52.3 x 97
PRSMG : P481

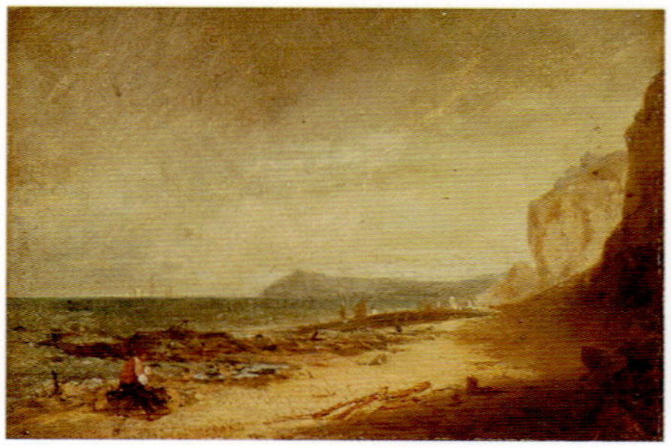

Raven, John Samuel 1829–1877
Seascape: Hastings Coast Scene
oil on panel 14 x 21
PRSMG : P480

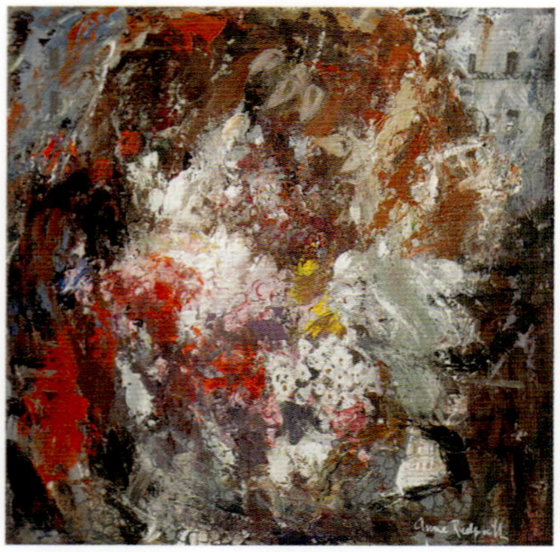

Redpath, Anne 1895–1965
Flower Stall at Lisbon 1962
oil on canvas 77.1 x 77.1
PRSMG : P1652

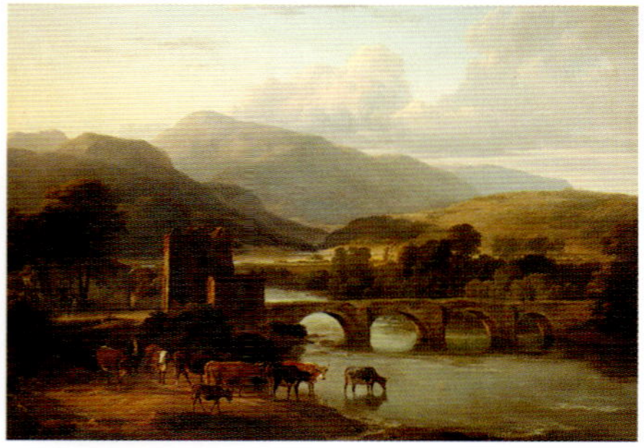

Reinagle, Ramsay Richard 1775–1862
Landscape 1809
oil on canvas (?) 53.5 x 94
PRSMG : P912

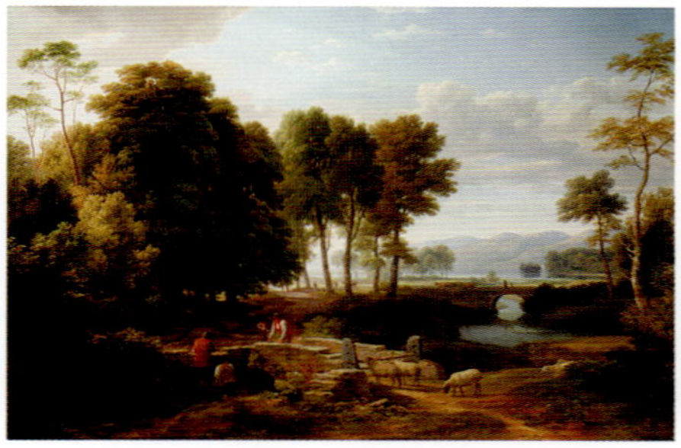

Reinagle, Ramsay Richard 1775–1862
Windermere 1809
oil on canvas 63.5 x 94
PRSMG : P913

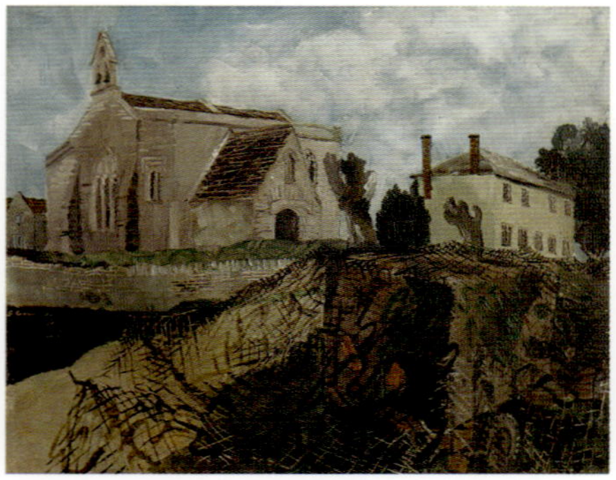

Richards, Albert 1919–1945
Inglesham Church and Rectory
oil on canvas (?) 24 x 31
PRSMG : P2007.118.2

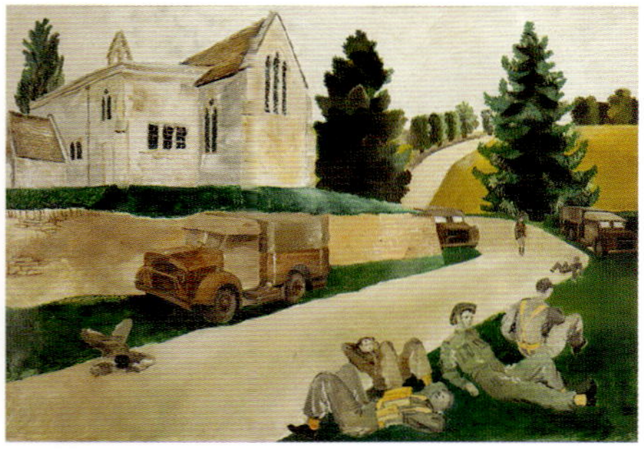

Richards, Albert 1919–1945
The Minute Halt
oil on canvas (?) 49 x 74
PRSMG : P2007.118.1

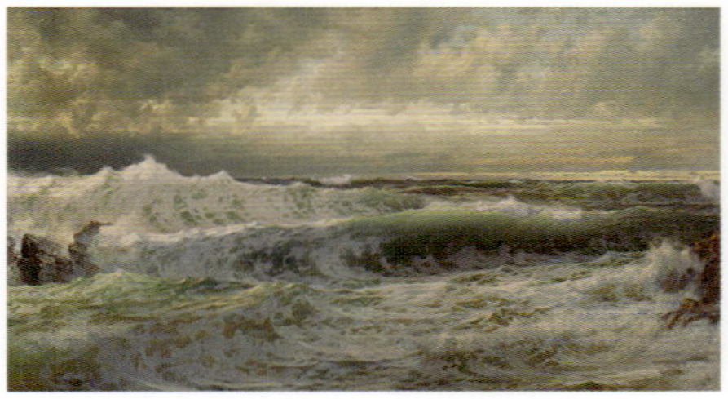

Richards, William Trost 1833–1905
After a Gale 1903
oil on canvas 101.5 x 183
PRSMG : P484

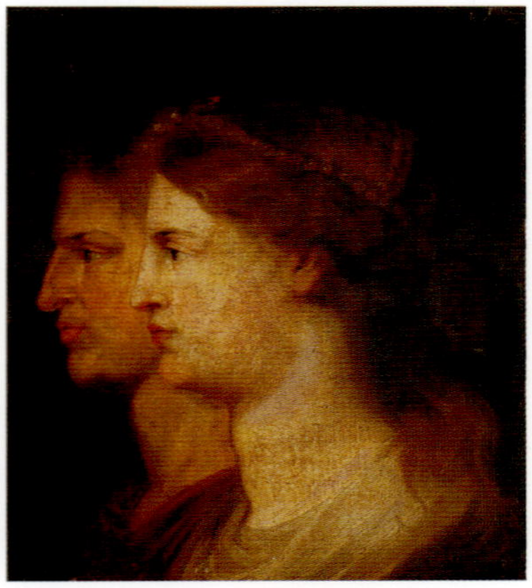

Richmond, W. active 19th C
Profiles of Two Heads
oil on canvas 54.5 x 47.5
PRSMG : P1896

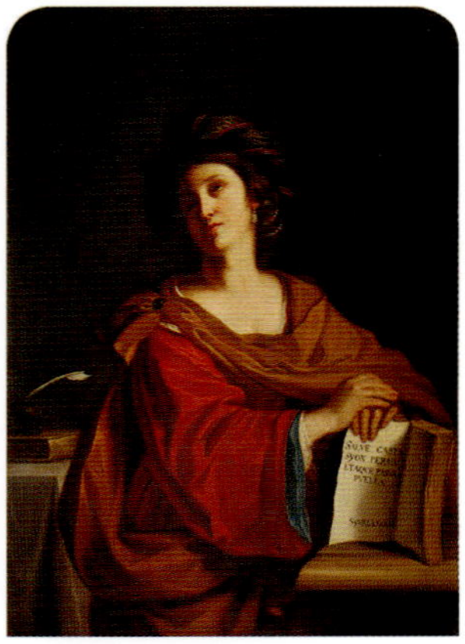

Richmond, William Blake 1842–1921
A Sibyl
oil on canvas 117 x 95.5
PRSMG : P1895

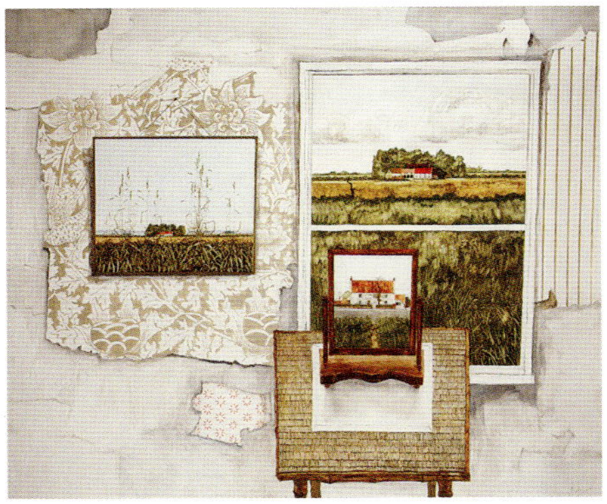

Ridgewell, John 1937–2004
Reflections
oil on canvas 101.5 x 127
PRSMG : P1749

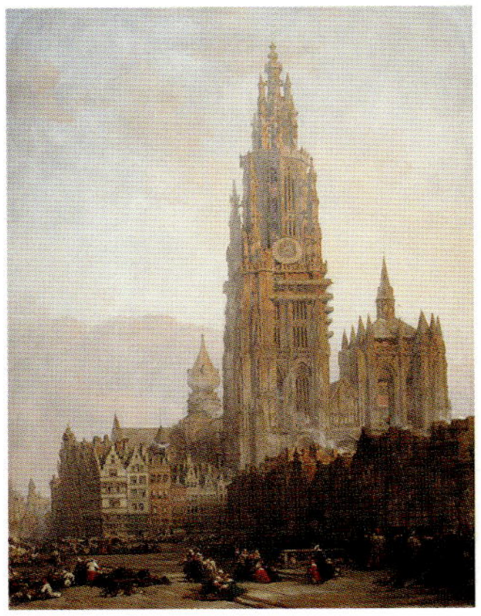

Roberts, David 1796–1864
Antwerp Cathedral 1847
oil on canvas 141 x 100.5
PRSMG : P490

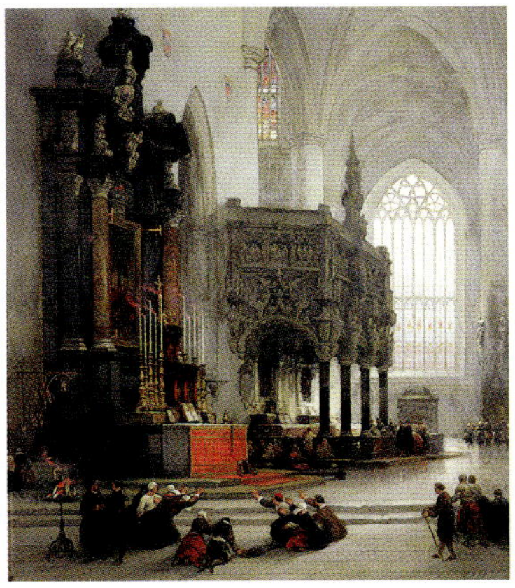

Roberts, David 1796–1864
Shrine of Saint Gomar at Lierre, Belgium 1849
oil on canvas 81.3 x 68.5
PRSMG : P489

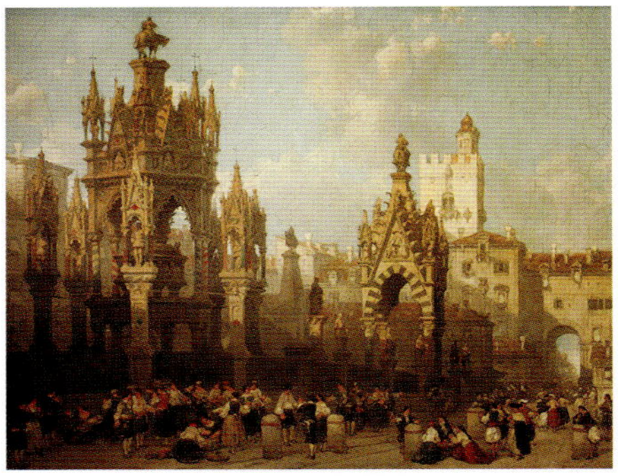

Roberts, David 1796–1864
The Tombs of the Scaligeri at Verona 1856
oil on canvas 76 x 102.3
PRSMG : P491

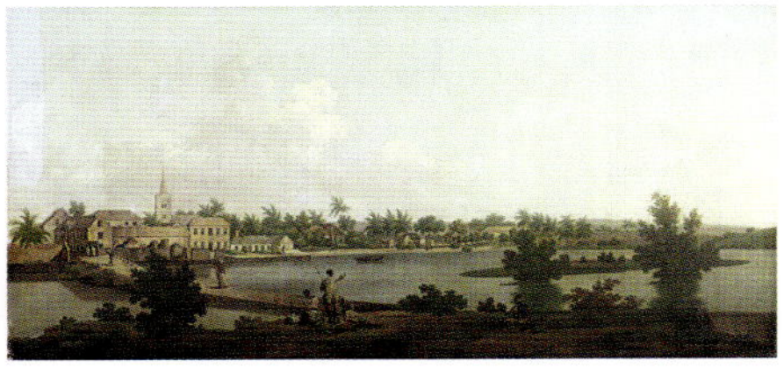

Robertson, George 1724–1788
Jamaican Landscape
oil on canvas 59.5 x 123
PRSMG : P826

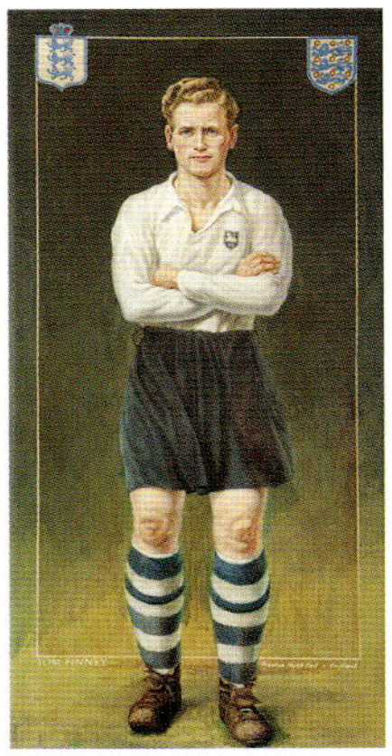

Robinson, Edward 1896–1975
Tom Finney (b.1922) 1951
oil on canvas 122.2 x 61.1
PRSMG : P2309

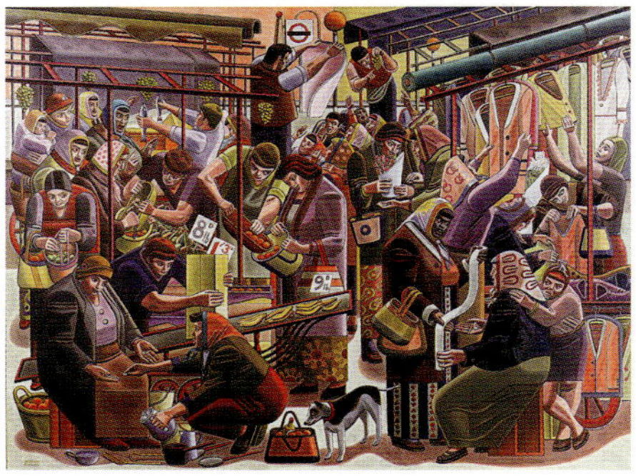

Roberts, William Patrick 1895–1980
The Common Market 1963
oil on canvas 168 x 214
PRSMG : P1673

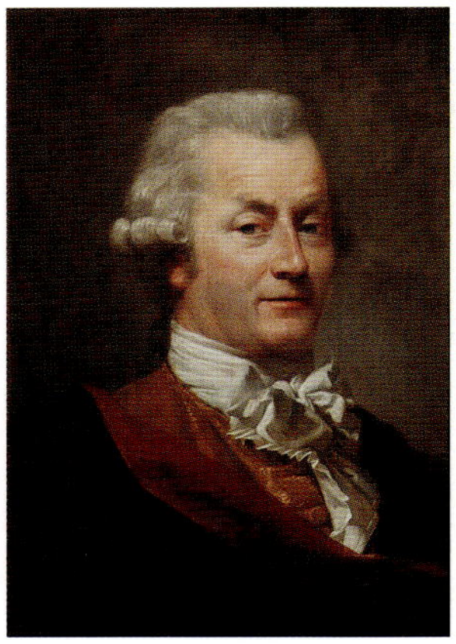

Robin, Jean Baptiste Claude 1734–1818
Portrait of a Man
oil on canvas 60 x 48.6
PRSMG : P829

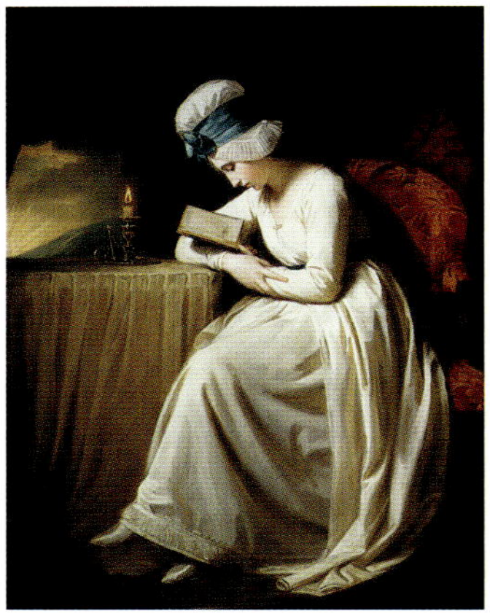

Romney, George 1734–1802
Serena Reading c.1780–1785
oil on canvas 180 x 145
PRSMG : P2365

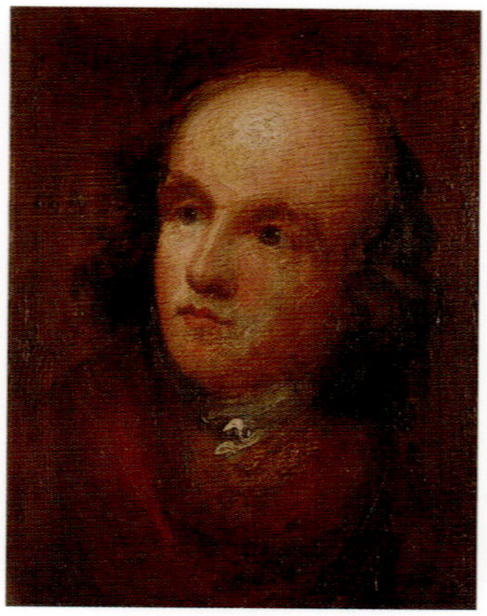

Romney, George (attributed to) 1734–1802
John Flaxman (1755–1826)
oil on panel 18.5 x 14.5
PRSMG : P494

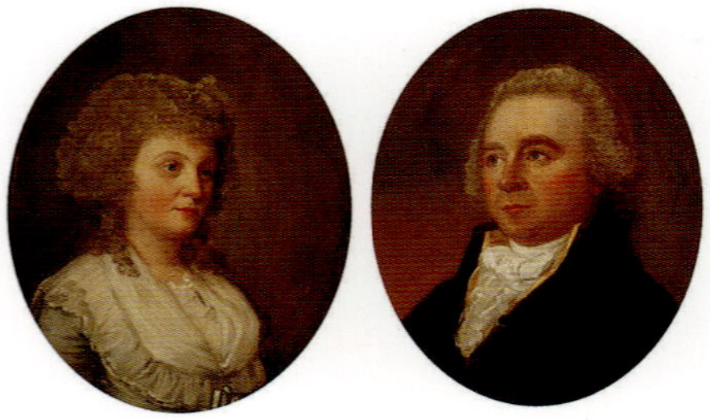

Romney, George (attributed to) 1734–1802
Mr Threlfall and Mrs Ann Threlfall
oil on canvas 28 x 22.8
PRSMG : P495

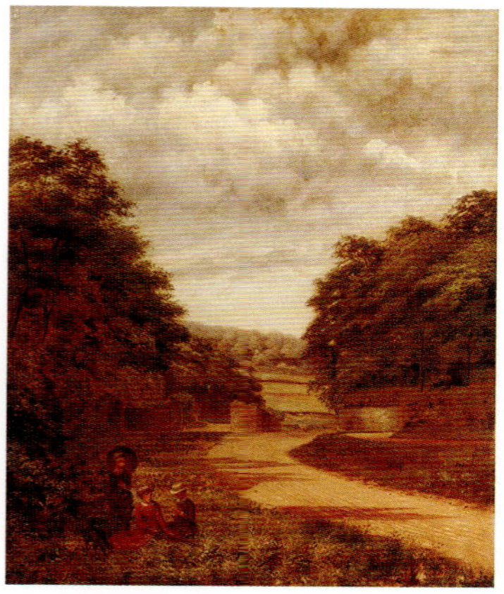

Roscoe, Frederick William 1838–1902
Entrance to the Willows, Ashton-on-Ribble
1889
oil on canvas 76.5 x 63.5
PRSMG : P1897

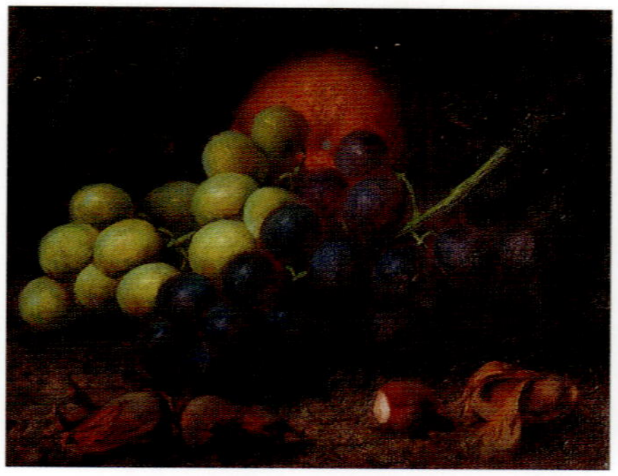

Roscoe, Frederick William 1838–1902
Still Life – Grapes, Orange and Hazelnuts
oil on canvas 20 x 25
PRSMG : P1802

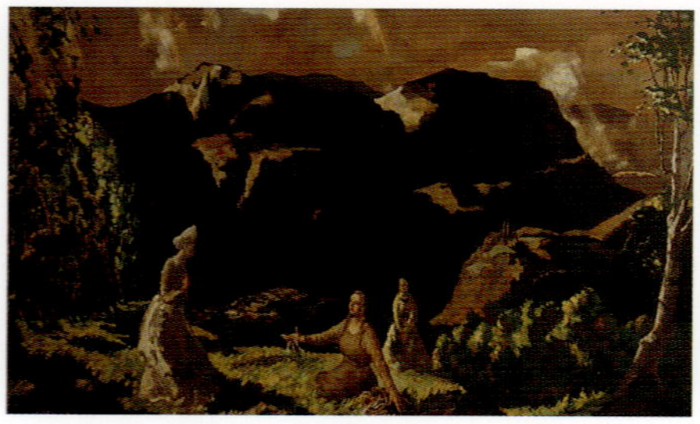

Rosenvinge, Olaf 1913–2004
Bavarian Idyll 1934
oil on panel 59.8 x 102.4
PRSMG : P498

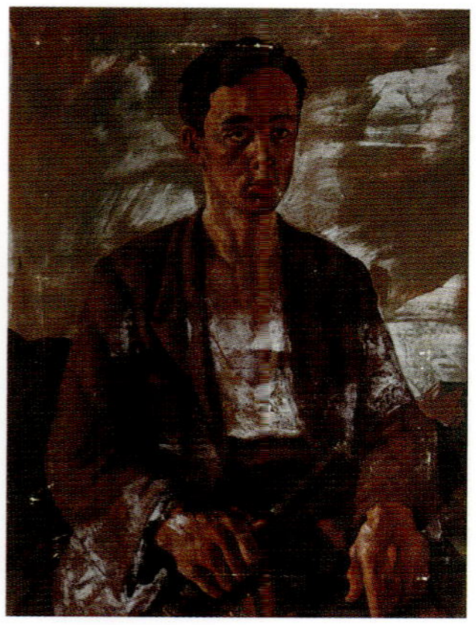

Rosenvinge, Olaf 1913–2004
Portrait of a Boy
oil on panel 73 x 57.7
PRSMG : P1898

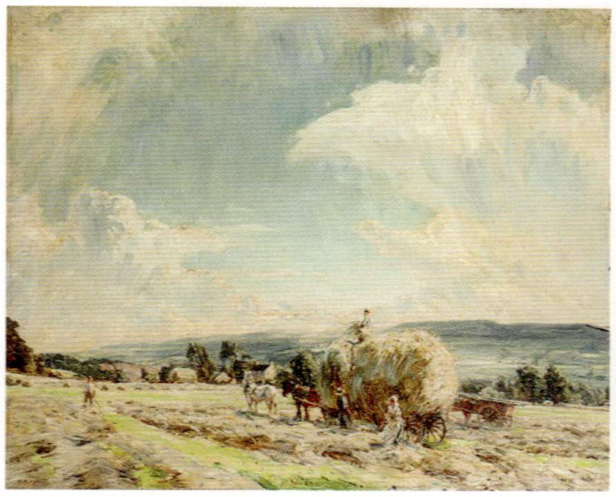

Royle, Herbert F. 1870–1958
Morning in the Hay Meadows 1935
oil on canvas 62.2 x 75
PRSMG : P514

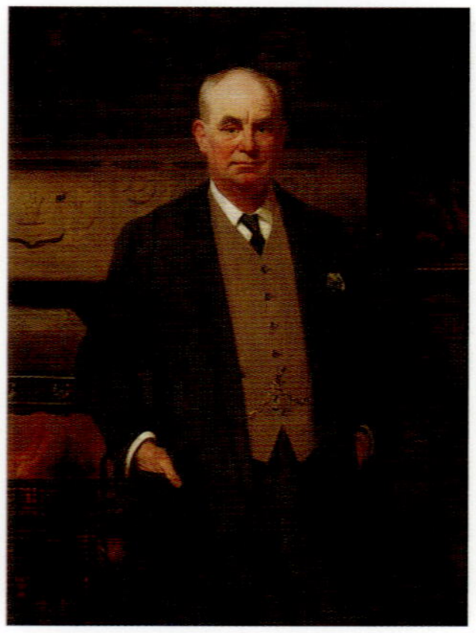

Salisbury, Frank O. 1874–1962
Sir Frank Hollins
oil on canvas 137 x 101.5
PRSMG : P750

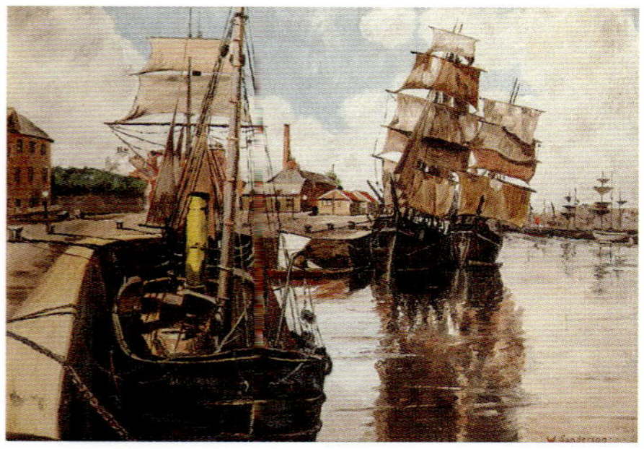

Sanderson, William
The Ayr Harbour 1930
oil on panel 23.5 x 34.2
PRSMG : P525

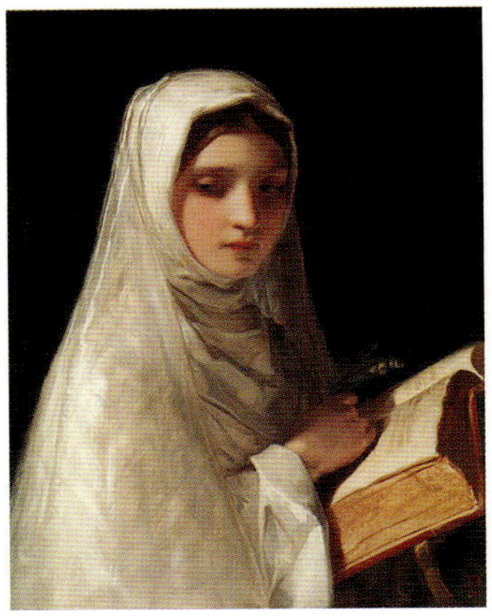

Sant, James 1820–1916
The Novice 1856
oil on canvas 61 x 50.8
PRSMG : P526

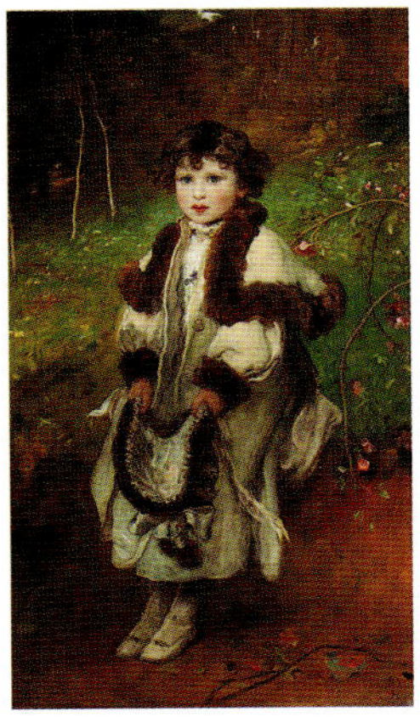

Sant, James 1820–1916
Julie, Daughter of Spencer H. Gollan, Esq. 1898
oil on canvas 134.5 x 77.5
PRSMG : P1483

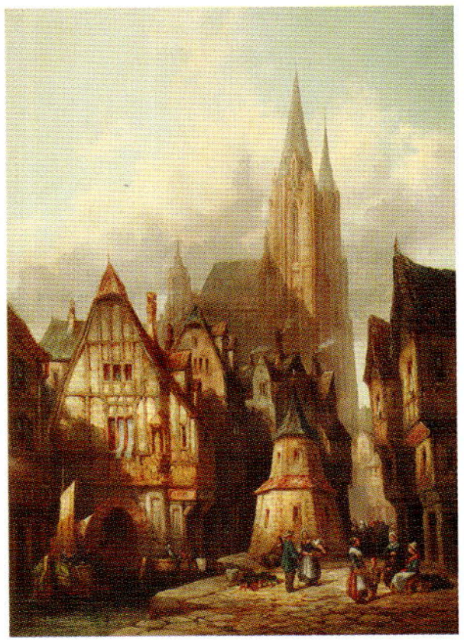

Schafer, Henry Thomas 1854–1915
Ratisbon, Bavaria 1884
oil on canvas 76.2 x 50.8
PRSMG : P1553

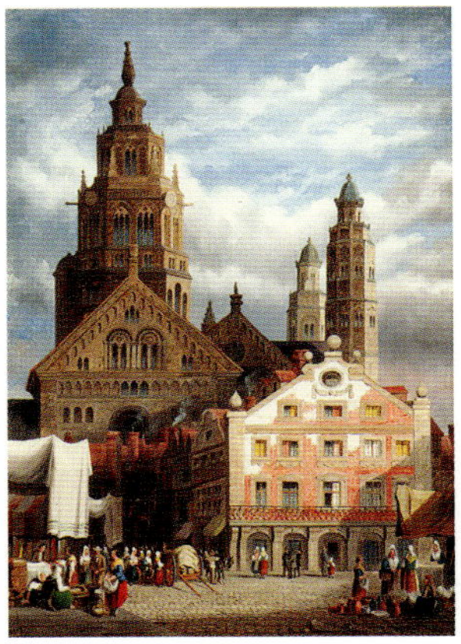

Schafer, Henry Thomas 1854–1915
Mayence
oil on canvas 66 x 49.5
PRSMG : P527

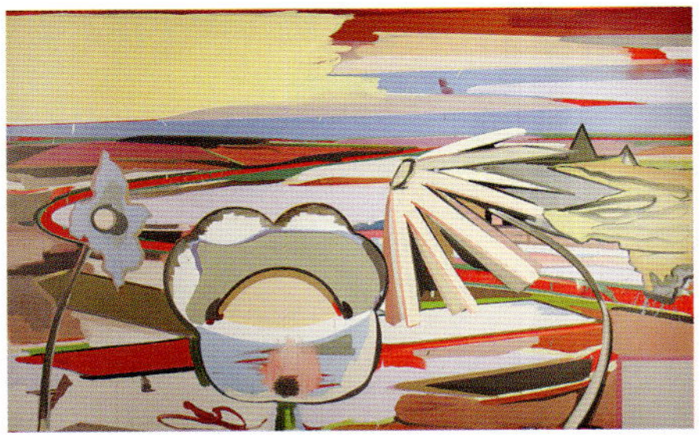

Scheibitz, Thomas b.1968
Low Sweetie 1999
oil on canvas 170 x 270
PRSMG : P2336

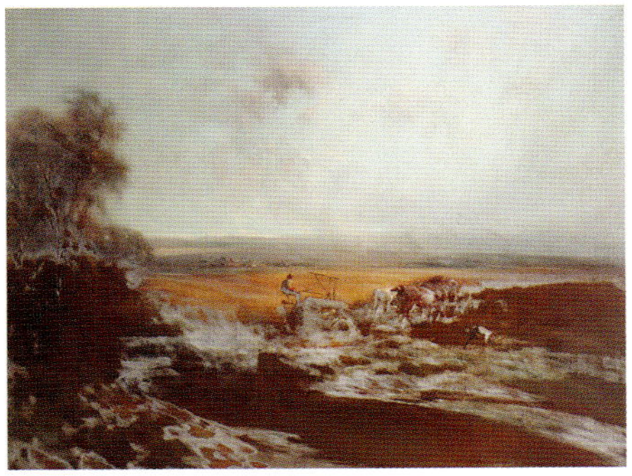

Scott, Hugh Berry 1854–1924
Harvesting, a Field of Yellow Plenty 1929
oil on canvas 71.2 x 91.5
PRSMG : P531

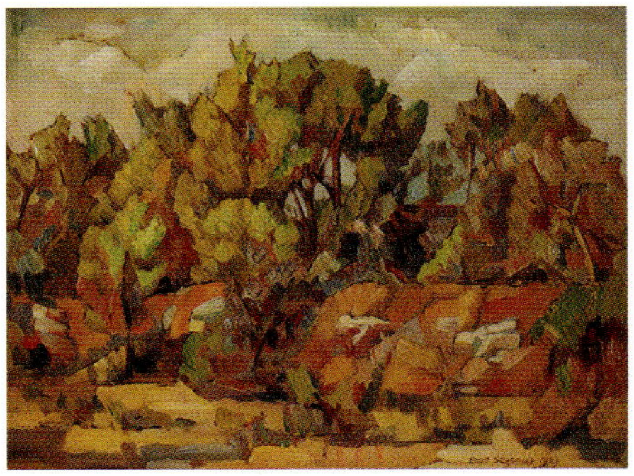

Seabrooke, Elliott 1886–1950
Bank of Trees 1929
oil on panel 44.7 x 62.5
PRSMG : P532

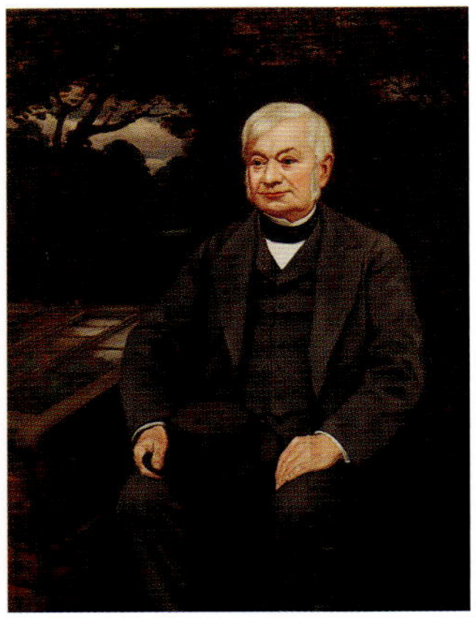

Seabrooke, Elliott 1886–1950
Joseph Livesey
oil on canvas 127 x 101.5
PRSMG : P534

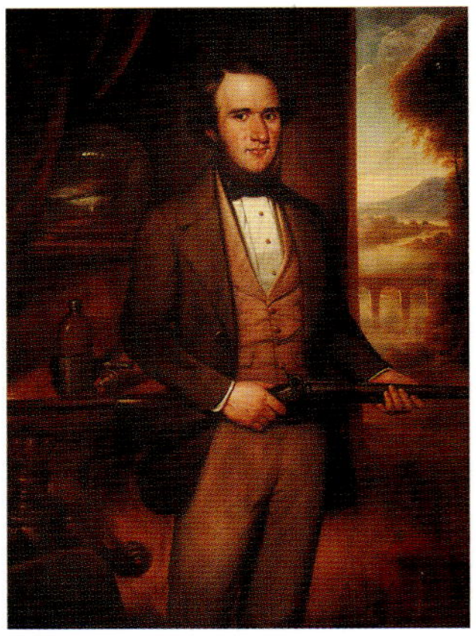

Seed, T. active 1838–1850
Portrait of an Unknown Man with a Gun
oil on canvas 146 x 118.2
PRSMG : P1942

Facing page: Somerville, Howard, 1873–1952, *Lady Ashton (d.1944), CBE*, Lancaster City Council (p. 189)

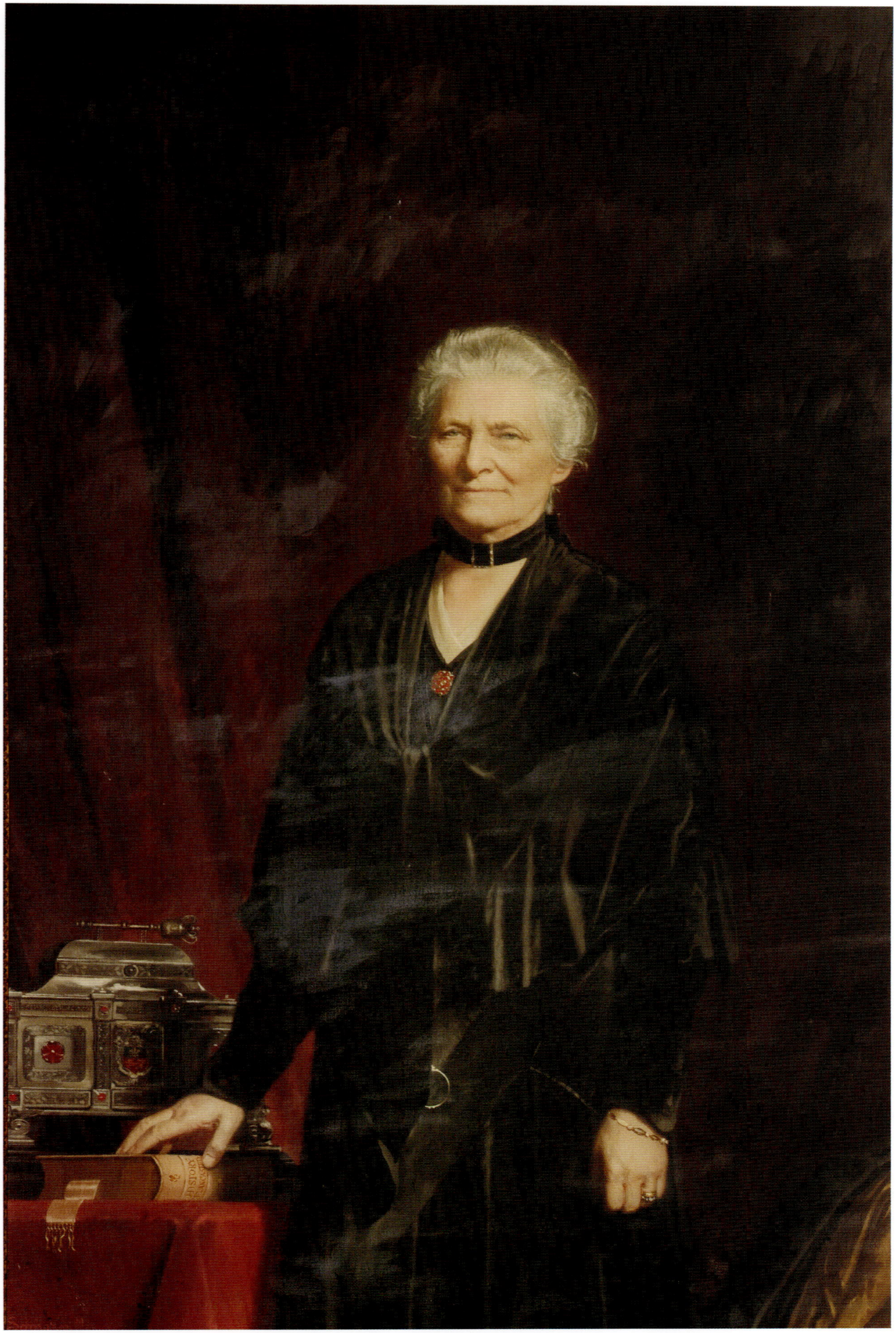

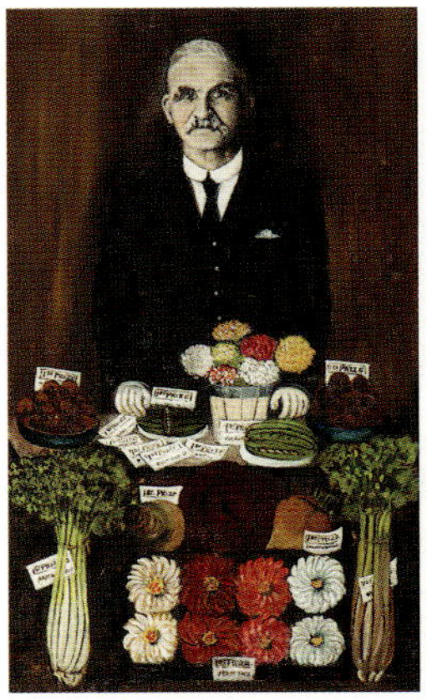

Sewell, Robert
The Prizewinner c.1937
oil on canvas 50.9 x 30.5
PRSMG : P2310

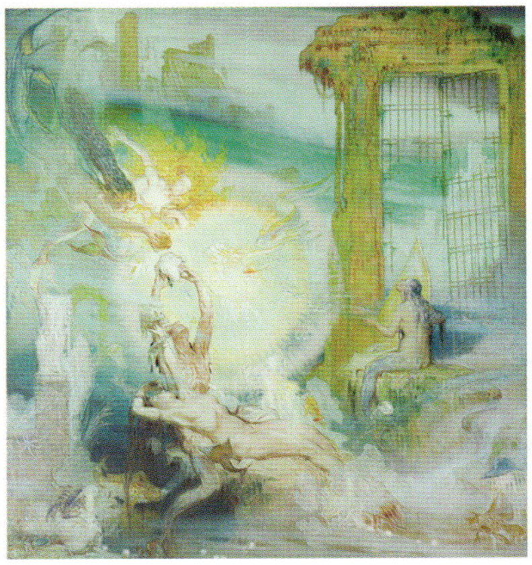

Shackleton, William 1872–1933
The City of the Golden Gates 1919–1922
oil on canvas 127 x 120
PRSMG : P820

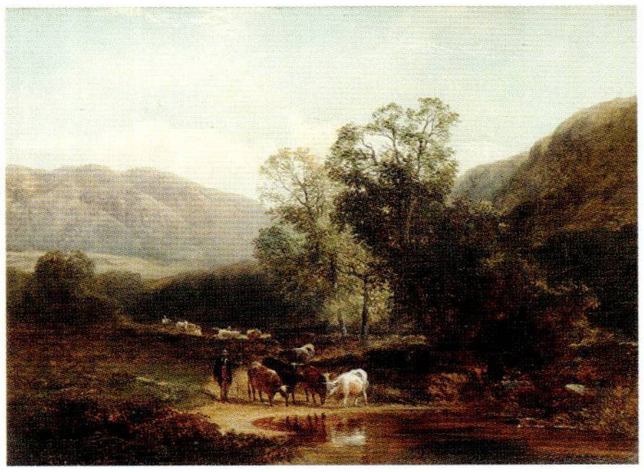

Shalders, George 1826–1873
Scene in Wales 1857
oil on canvas 25.5 x 35.5
PRSMG : P1564

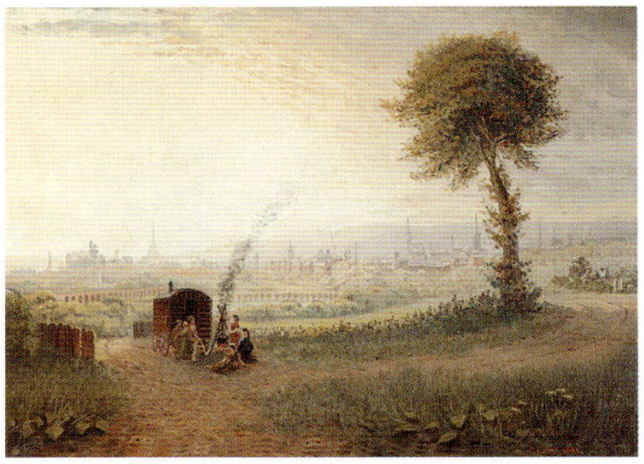

Shaw, Charles Edward 1870–1959
General View of Preston
oil on canvas 15.2 x 30.2
PRSMG : P1396

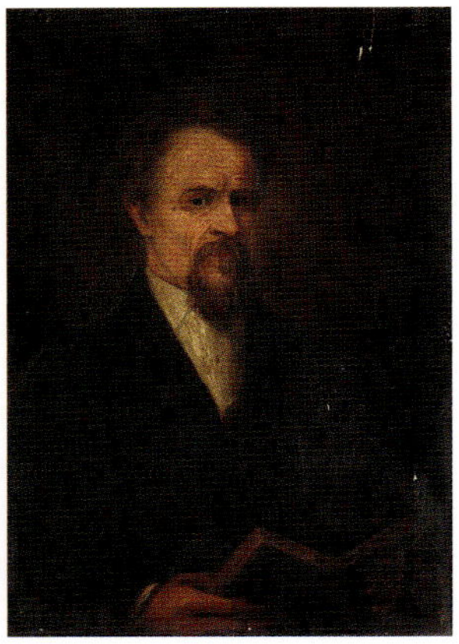

Shaw, Charles Edward 1870–1959
Portrait of a Gentleman
oil on canvas 63.5 x 51.8
PRSMG : P1683

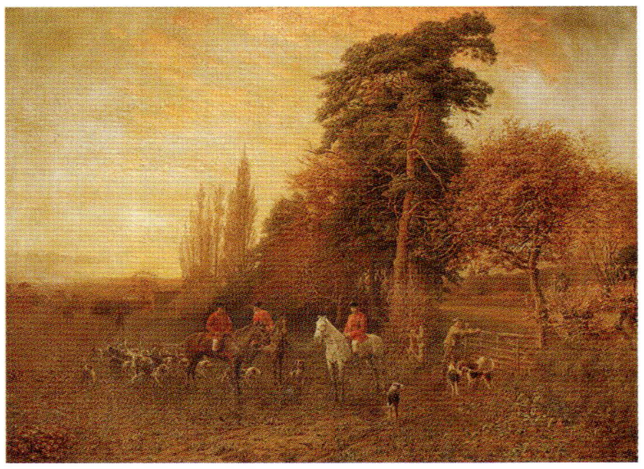

Shaw, Charles Edward 1870–1959
Sporting
oil on canvas 86 x 113
PRSMG : P720

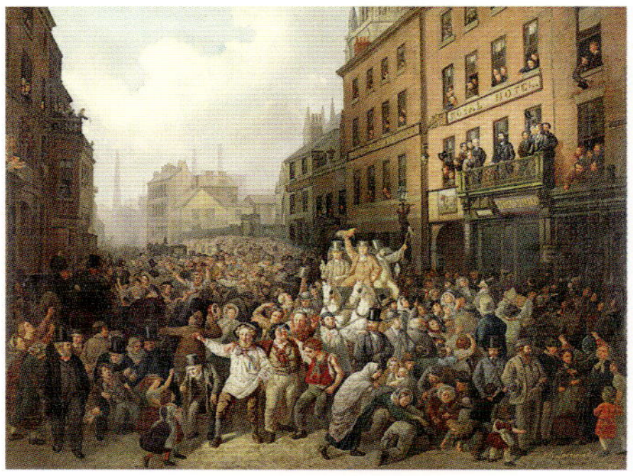

Sherwood, Vladimir Ossipovitch 1832–1897
The Preston By-Election of 1862 1862
oil on canvas 91.5 x 118
PRSMG : P1690

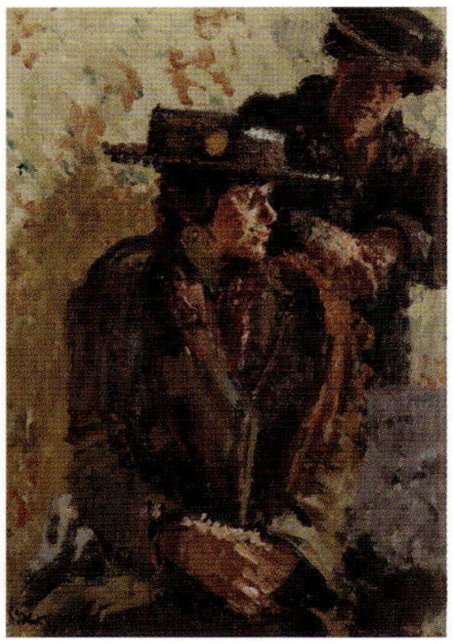

Sickert, Walter Richard 1860–1942
Two Women 1911
oil on canvas 52 x 41.6
PRSMG : P2278

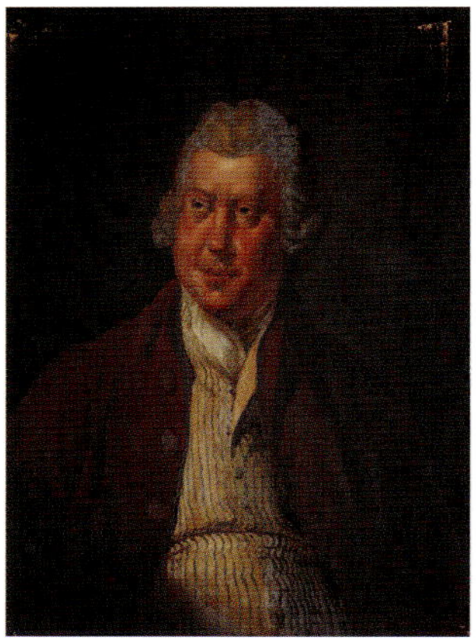

Simm, William Norris 1885–1948
Sir Richard Arkwright (1732–1792) 1929
oil on canvas 81.2 x 66
PRSMG : P537

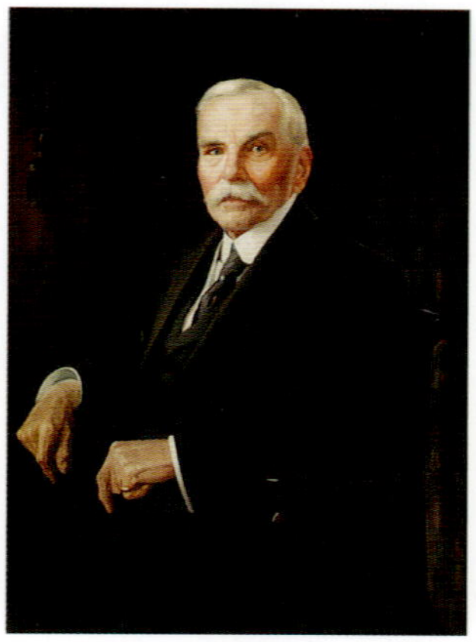

Simm, William Norris 1885–1948
Alderman John Crook Hamilton 1936
oil on canvas 101.5 x 76.2
PRSMG : P540

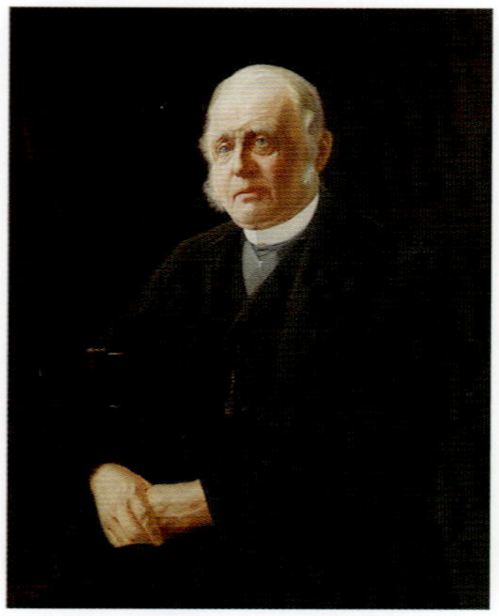

Simm, William Norris 1885–1948
Dr Sir Charles Brown 1936
oil on canvas 97.7 x 76.3
PRSMG : P538

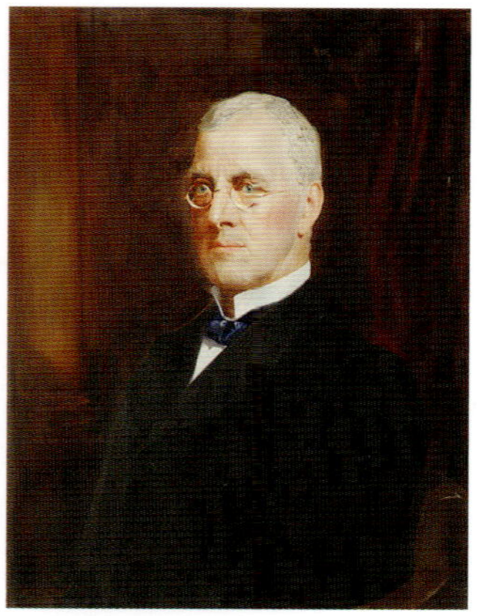

Simm, William Norris 1885–1948
John Forshaw 1936
oil on canvas 76.2 x 63.5
PRSMG : P539

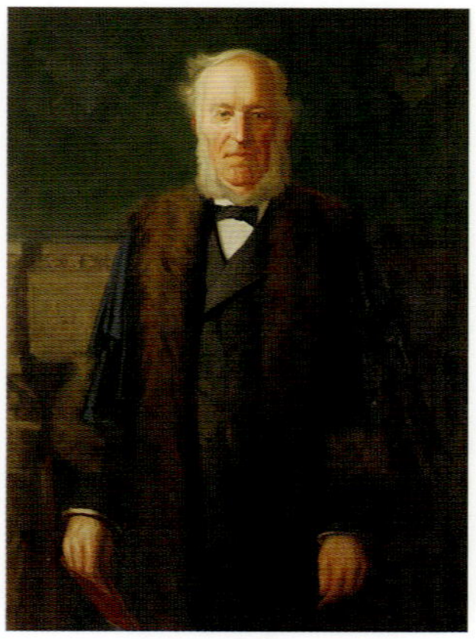

Simm, William Norris 1885–1948
Alderman Edmund Birley 1937
oil on canvas 104.5 x 78.9
PRSMG : P734

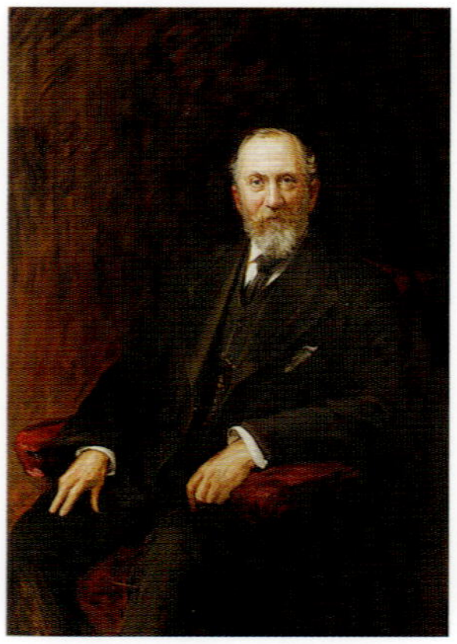

Simm, William Norris 1885–1948
Frederick Stanley (1841–1908), 16th Earl of Derby, Guild Mayor (1902) 1937
oil on canvas 140 x 115.8
PRSMG : P541

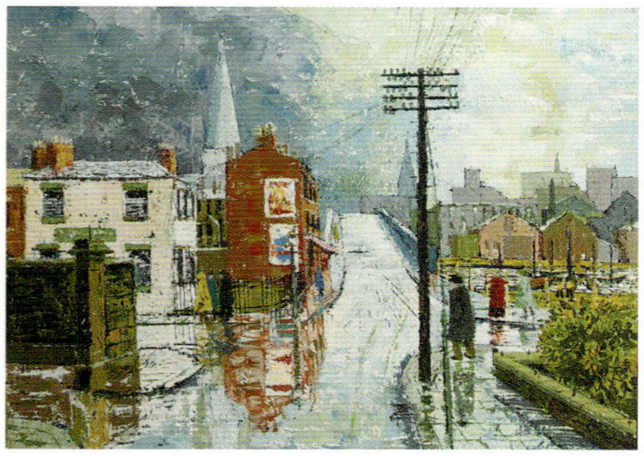

Singleton, Rosemary L. active 1958–1959
Typical 1959
oil on canvas 70.1 x 90
PRSMG : P1612

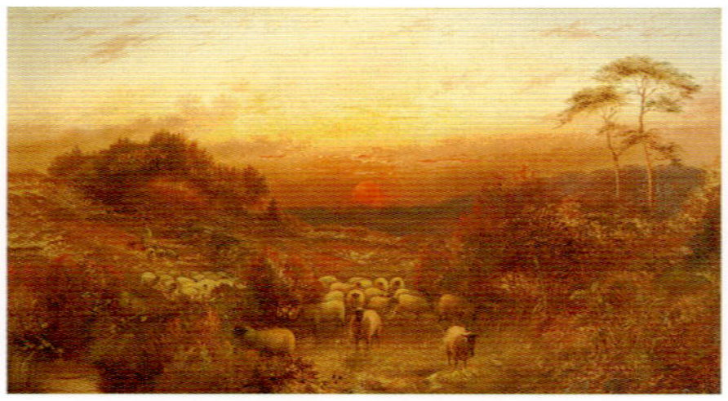

Smith, Charles active 1857–1908
Dartford Heath, Kent
oil on canvas 20.3 x 38
PRSMG : P1503

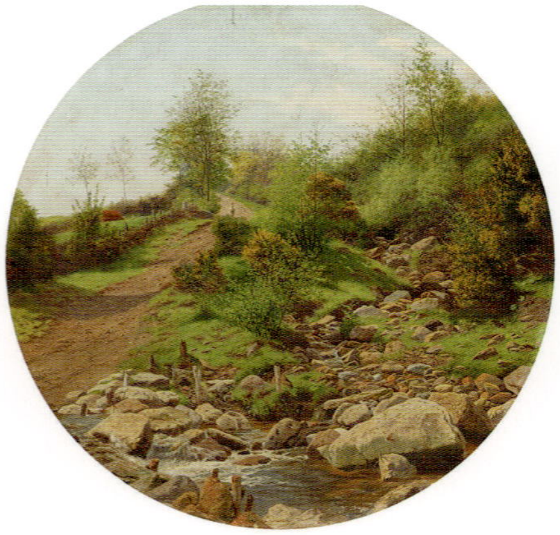

Smith, James Burrell 1822–1897
Landscape 1865
oil on canvas laid on board 52 x 52
PRSMG : P1900

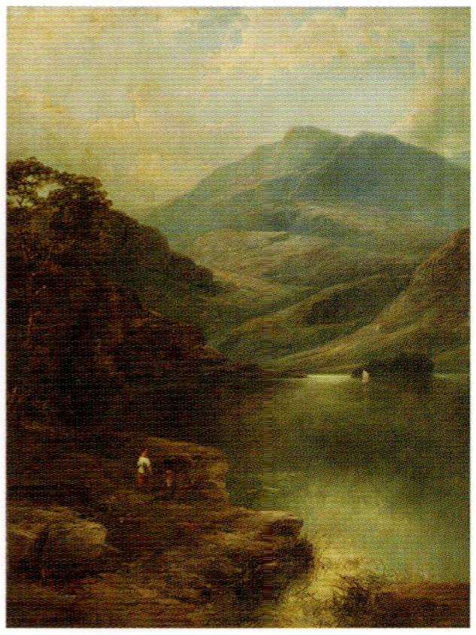

Smith, John Brandon 1848–1884
Killarney 1872
oil on canvas 91.5 x 71.2
PRSMG : P544

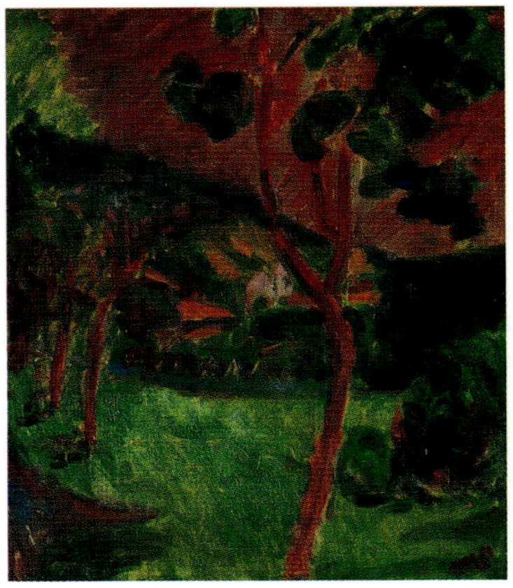

Smith, Matthew Arnold Bracy 1879–1959
Pont Aven Landscape c.1921
oil on canvas 45 x 36
PRSMG : P2342

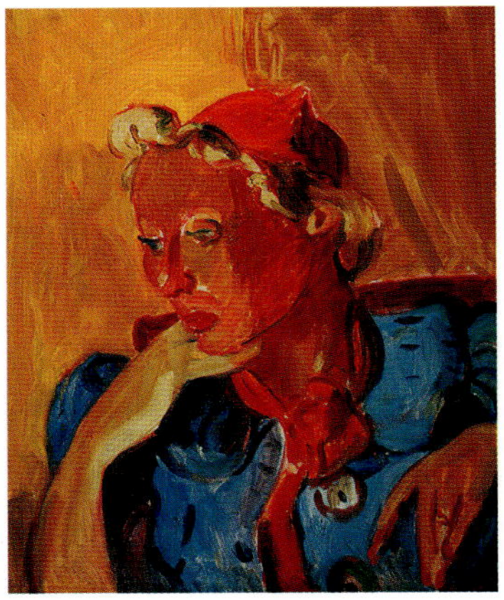

Smith, Matthew Arnold Bracy 1879–1959
Reflections 1938
oil on canvas 64.8 x 54.5
PRSMG : P1256

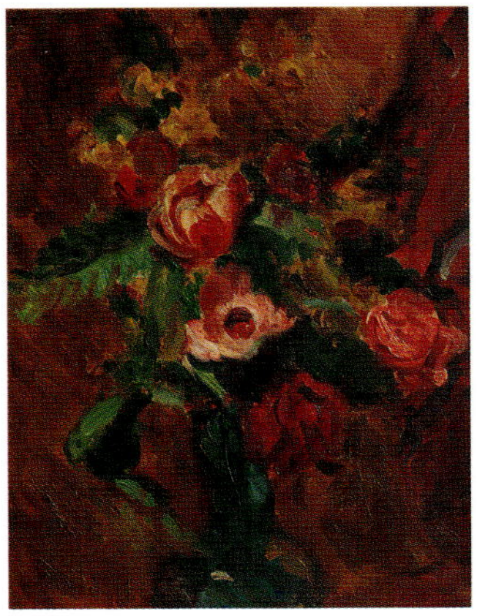

Smith, Matthew Arnold Bracy 1879–1959
Roses in a Vase
oil on canvas 46 x 37.5
PRSMG : P2341

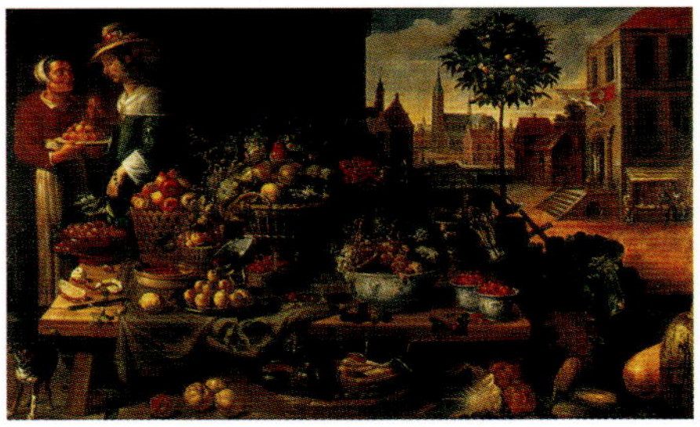

Snyders, Frans (studio of) 1579–1657
The Fruit Stall c.1640
oil on canvas 200 x 275
PRSMG : P1598

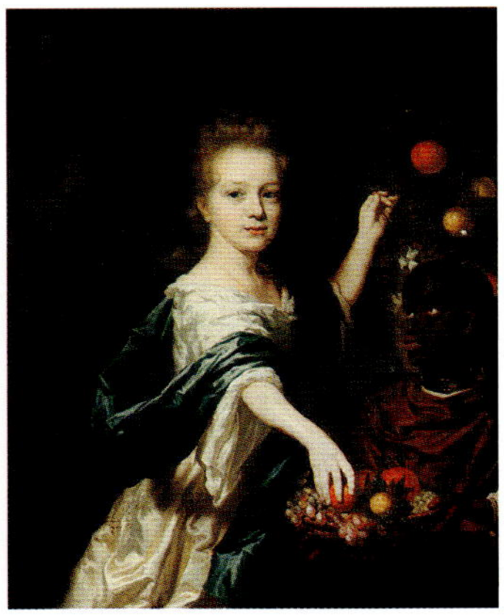

Soest, Gerard 1600–1681
Lady and Attendant with Fruit
oil on canvas 59.5 x 49.5
PRSMG : P546

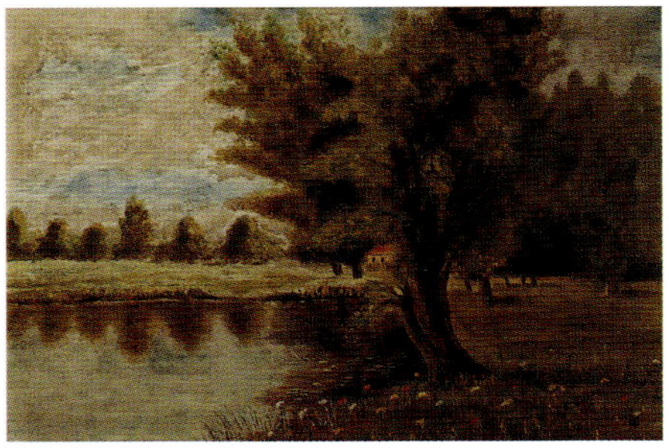

Solbach, K.
Landscape with a Pond 1948
oil on wood 30.5 x 44.5
PRSMG : P2369

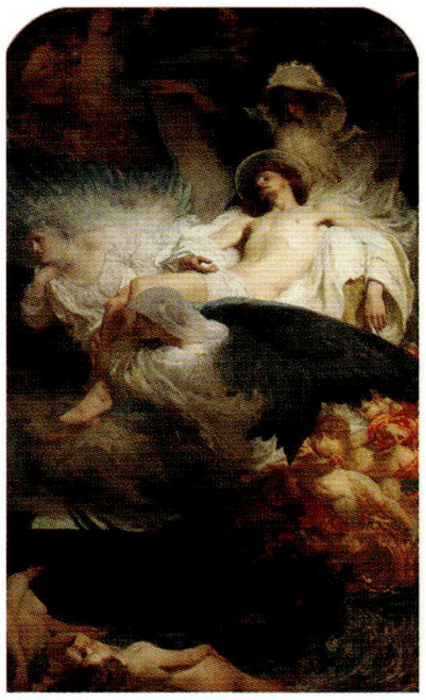

Solomon, Solomon Joseph 1860–1927
An Allegory 1904
oil on canvas 269 x 150
PRSMG : P547

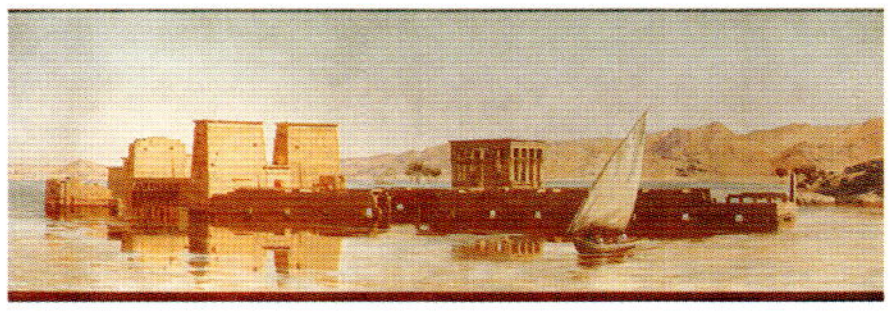

Somerscales, John 1846–1945
The Temple of Isis at Philae 1909
oil on canvas 174 x 520
PRSMG : EB3

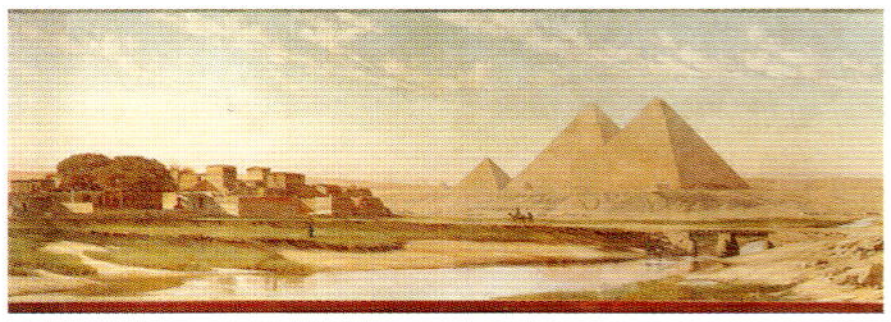

Somerscales, John 1846–1945
Pyramids at Giza 1910
oil on canvas 174 x 520
PRSMG : EB1

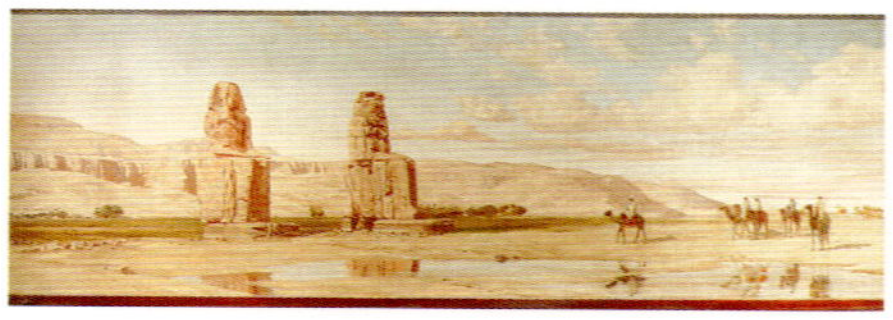

Somerscales, John 1846–1945
The Colossi of Memnon at Thebes 1911
oil on canvas 174 x 520
PRSMG : EB5

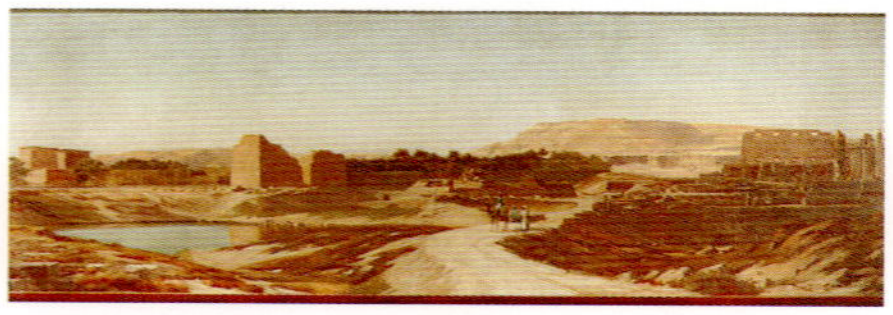

Somerscales, John 1846–1945
The Great Temple of Amun-Ra at Karnak
1911
oil on canvas 174 x 520
PRSMG : EB2

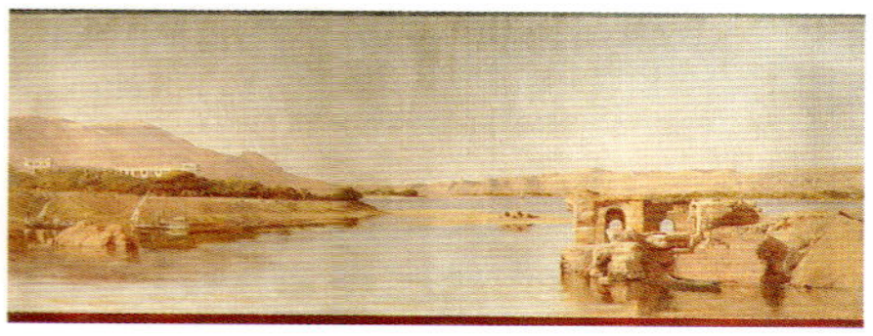

Somerscales, John 1846–1945
The Nile at Aswan 1912
oil on canvas 174 x 520
PRSMG : EB8

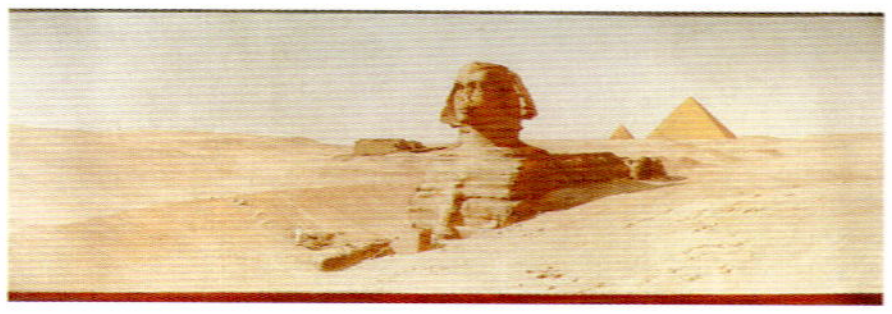

Somerscales, John 1846–1945
The Sphinx, Gizeh 1912
oil on canvas 174 x 520
PRSMG : EB6

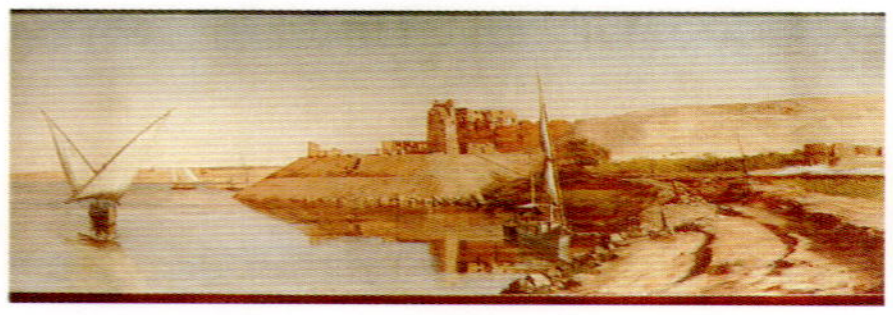

Somerscales, John 1846–1945
The Temple of Kom Ombo 1912
oil on canvas 174 x 520
PRSMG : EB7

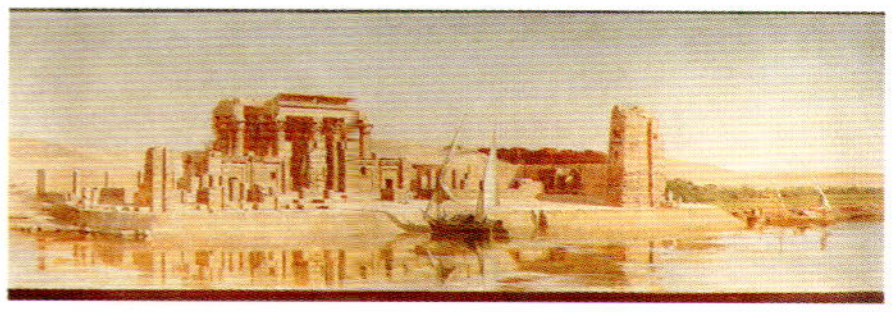

Somerscales, John 1846–1945
The Temple of Kom Ombo
oil on canvas 174 x 520
PRSMG : EB4

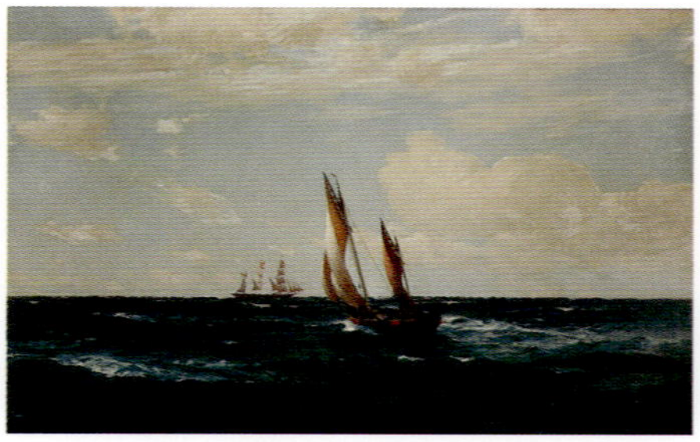

Somerscales, Thomas Jacques 1842–1927
Hove to for a Pilot 1896
oil on canvas 122 x 183
PRSMG : P556

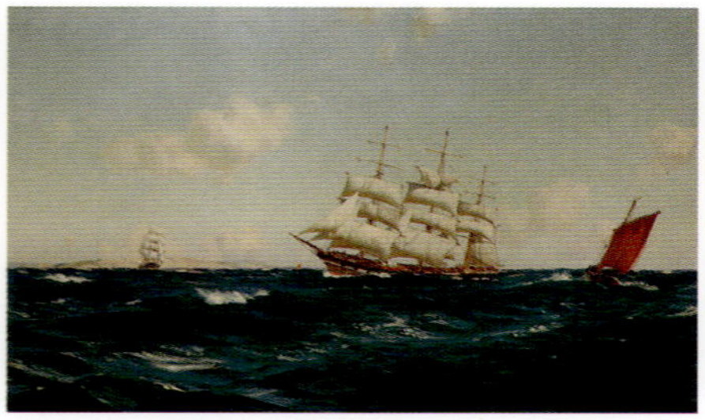

Somerscales, Thomas Jacques 1842–1927
A Strong Breeze in the Channel 1903
oil on canvas 51.8 x 92
PRSMG : P557

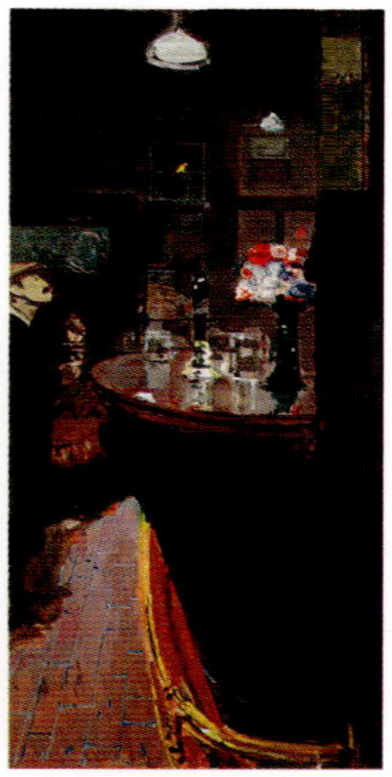

Spear, Ruskin 1911–1990
Alf and the Canary 1963
oil on canvas 132 x 61
PRSMG : P1671

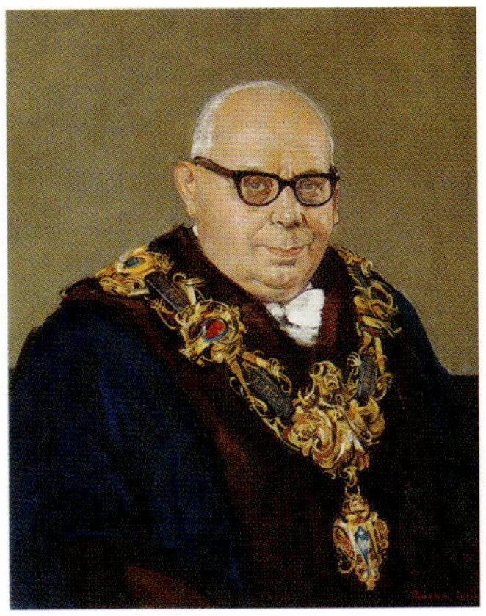

Spear, Ruskin 1911–1990
Alderman Gray 1972
oil on canvas 76 x 59.5
PRSMG : P1968

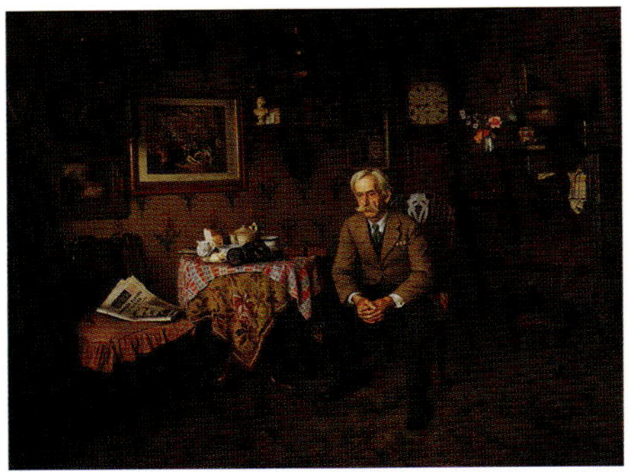

Spencelayh, Charles 1865–1958
Why War? 1938
oil on canvas 94 x 115
PRSMG : P845

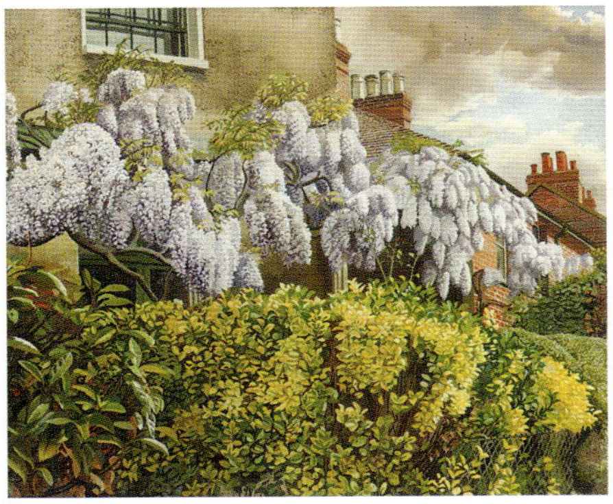

Spencer, Stanley 1891–1959
Wisteria c.1940
oil on canvas 81 x 92
PRSMG : P898

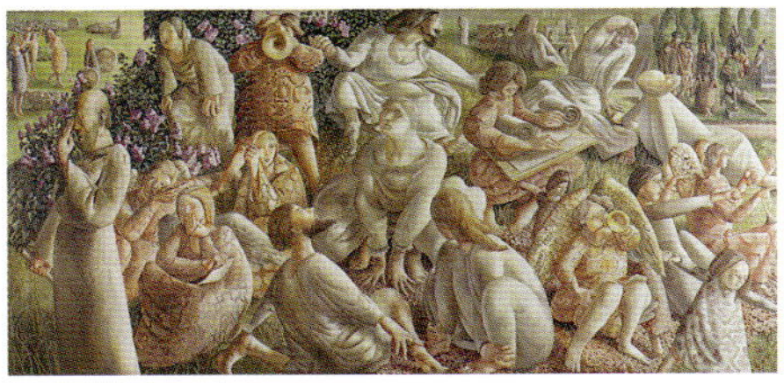

Spencer, Stanley 1891–1959
Resurrection: The Hill of Zion 1946
oil on canvas 110 x 205
PRSMG : P1367

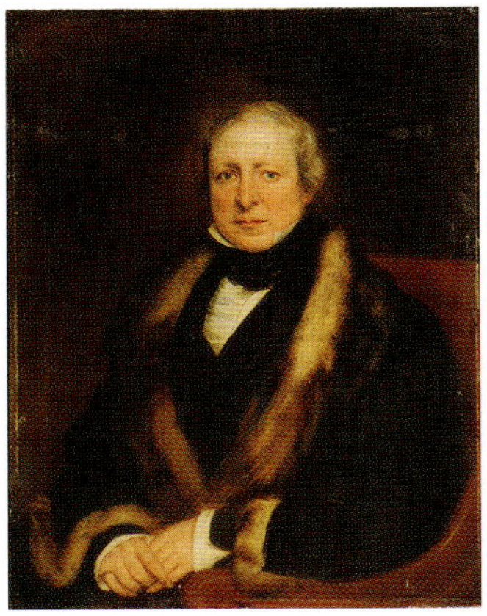

Spender active 19th C
Peter Haydock
oil on canvas 91.5 x 76.2
PRSMG : P571

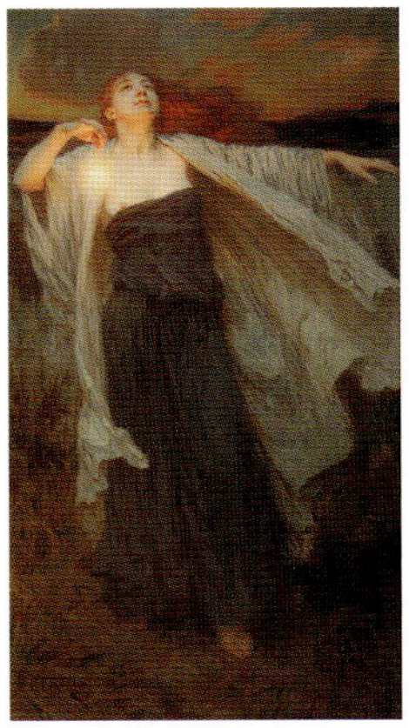

Stead, Frederick 1863–1940
Will-o'-the-wisp 1903
oil on canvas 129.3 x 69.8
PRSMG : P574

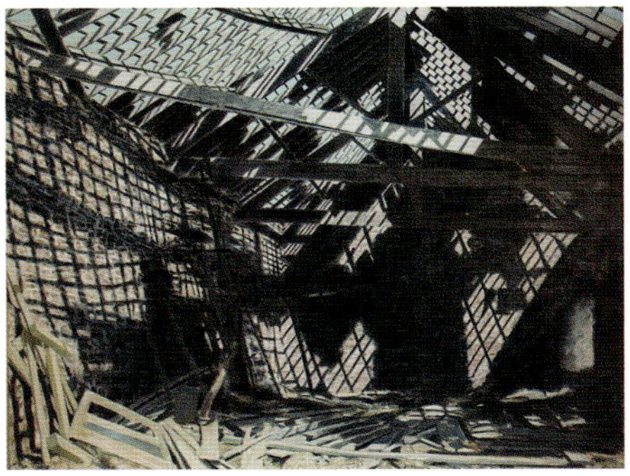

Stevens, Norman 1937–1988
Barn 1981–1982
oil on canvas 152.5 x 213.5
PRSMG : P1834

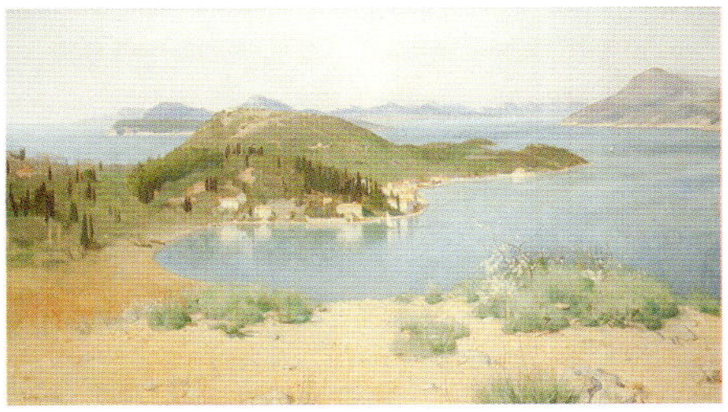

Stokes, Adrian Scott 1854–1935
Islands of the Adriatic 1906
oil on canvas 91.5 x 155
PRSMG : P575

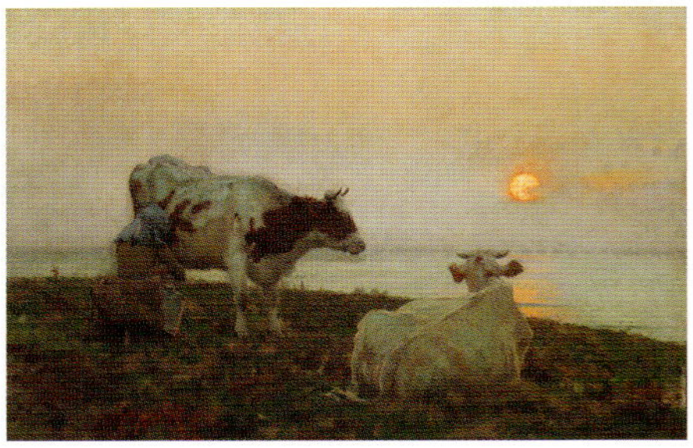

Stokes, Adrian Scott 1854–1935
The Setting Sun 1909
oil on canvas 116.7 x 183
PRSMG : P576

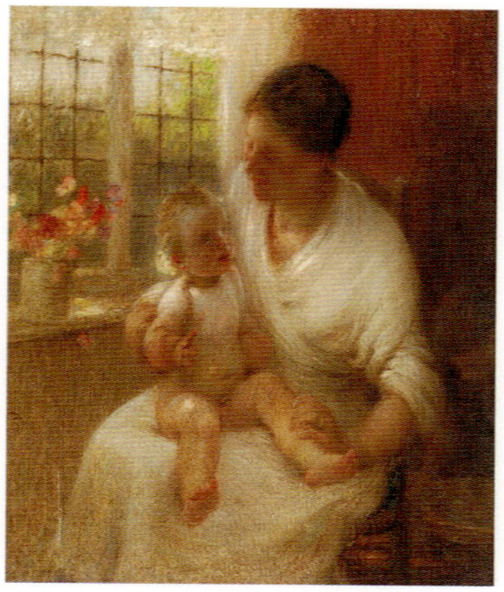

Stott, Edward William 1859–1918
A Cottage Madonna 1907
oil on canvas 74 x 61 (E)
PRSMG : P577

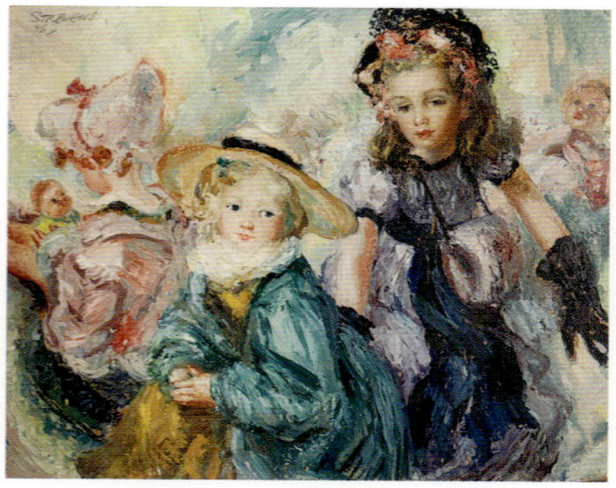

Strevens, John Lloyd 1902–1990
Dressing Up 1947
oil on panel 64.6 x 79.5
PRSMG : P1117

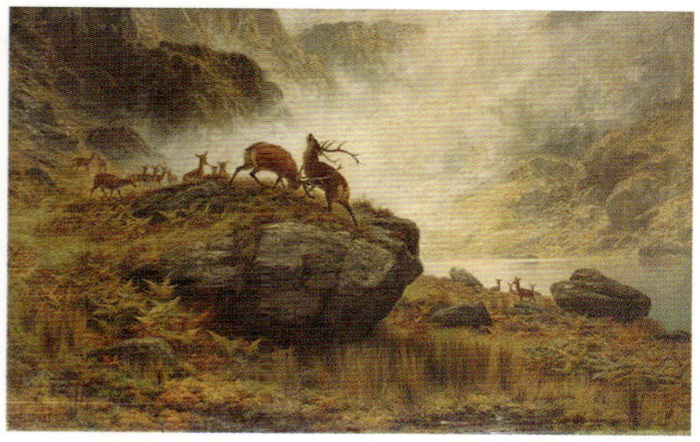

Stuart, Charles active 1854–1904
Disputed Rights 1894–1895
oil on canvas 132 x 178
PRSMG : P578

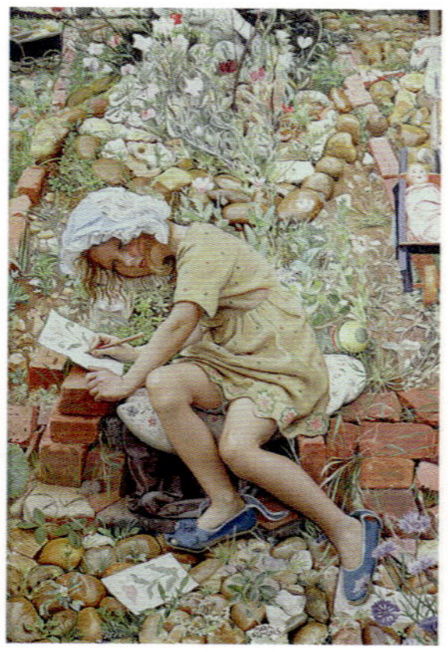

Symons, Mark Lancelot 1887–1935
Molly in the Garden 1930
oil on panel 54.5 x 36.9
PRSMG : P579

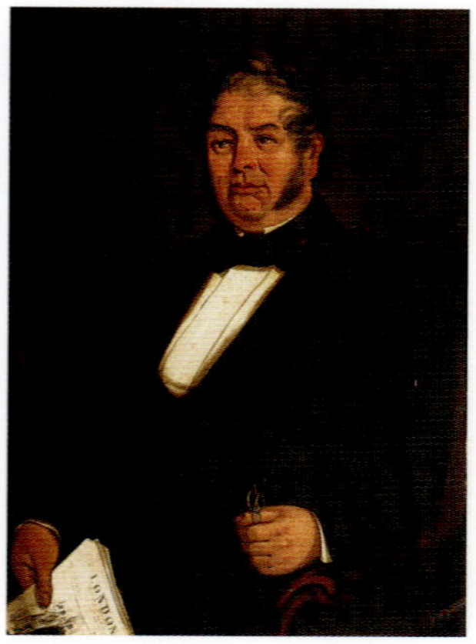

T., E.
John Best 1853
oil on canvas 93 x 71
PRSMG : P1875

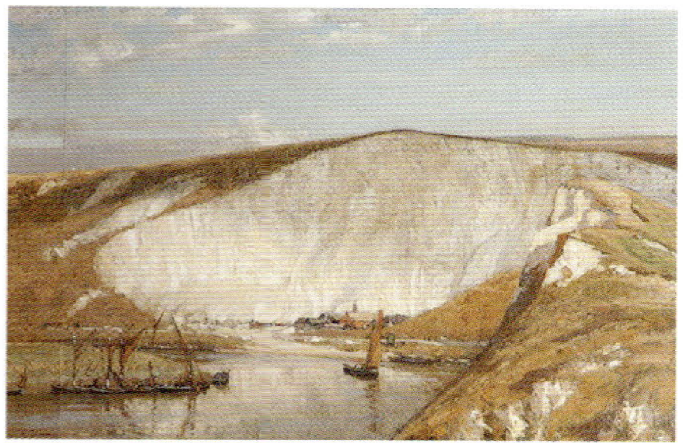

Talmage, Algernon 1871–1939
The Chalk Pit 19[illegible]1
oil on canvas 122 x 178
PRSMG : P581

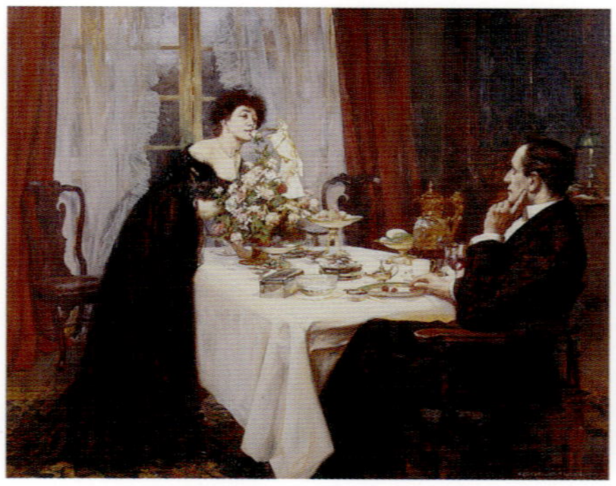

Tayler, Albert Chevallier 1862–1925
The Anniversary 1909
oil on canvas 102 x 127.8
PRSMG : P584

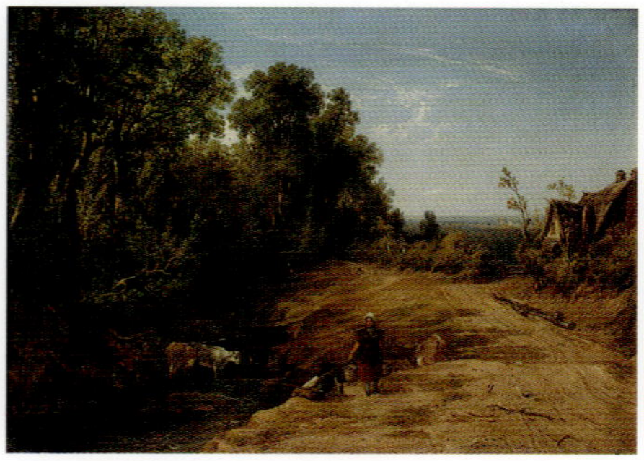

Tennant, John F. 1796–1872
Landscape with Figures, near St Omer 1836
oil on canvas 50.8 x 68.5
PRSMG : P585

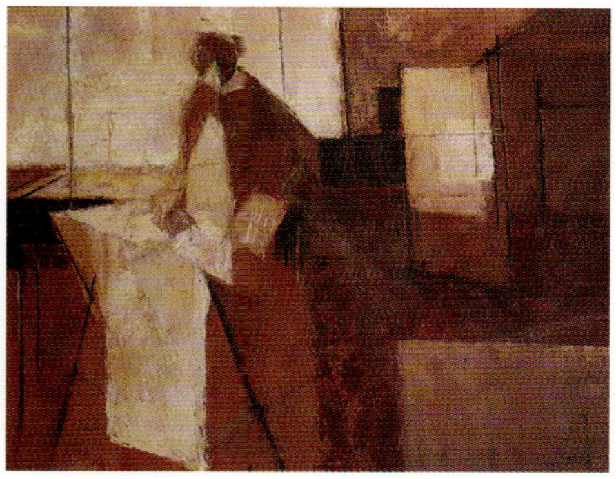

Thomas, Glynne
Kitchen Study 1962
oil on hardboard 71.2 x 91.5
PRSMG : P1644

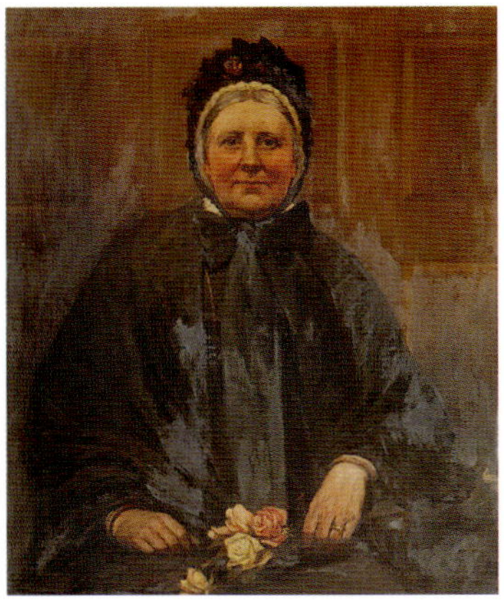

Thompson, Charles Herbert 1870–1946
Portrait of a Woman Holding Roses
oil on canvas 76 x 61
PRSMG : P1973

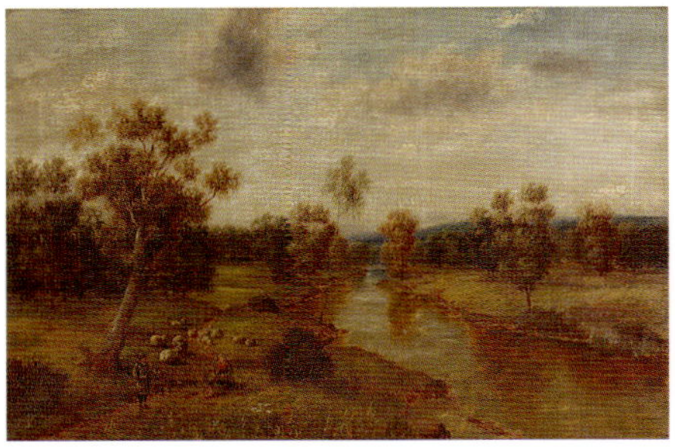

Thompson, G. active 19th C
Landscape
oil on canvas 40.7 x 61
PRSMG : P1978

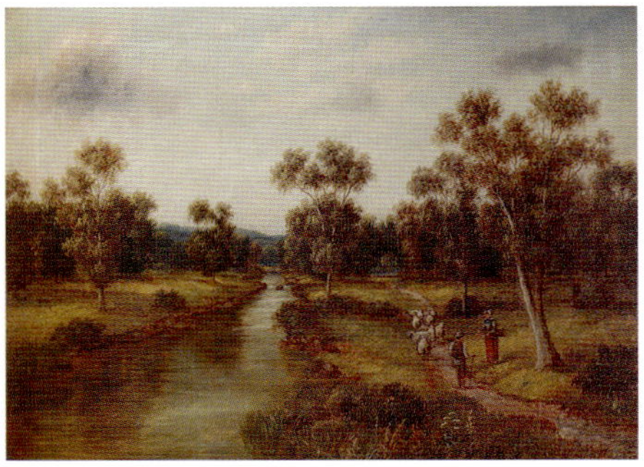

Thompson, G. active 19th C
Landscape
oil on canvas 40.7 x 61
PRSMG : P1979

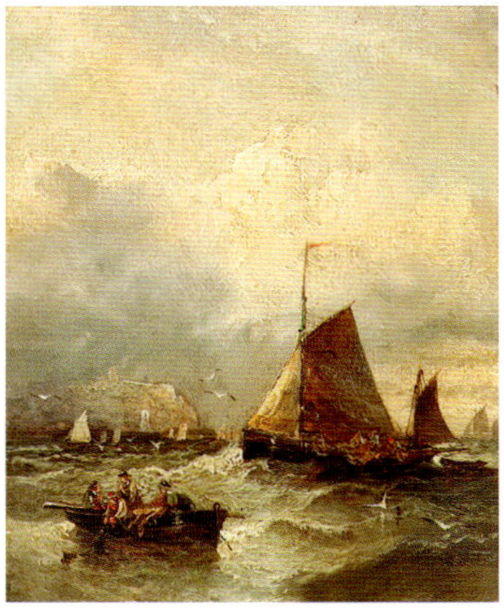

Thornley, Georges William 1857–1935
Seascape – Fishing Boats 1886
oil on panel 25.3 x 20.3
PRSMG : P1497

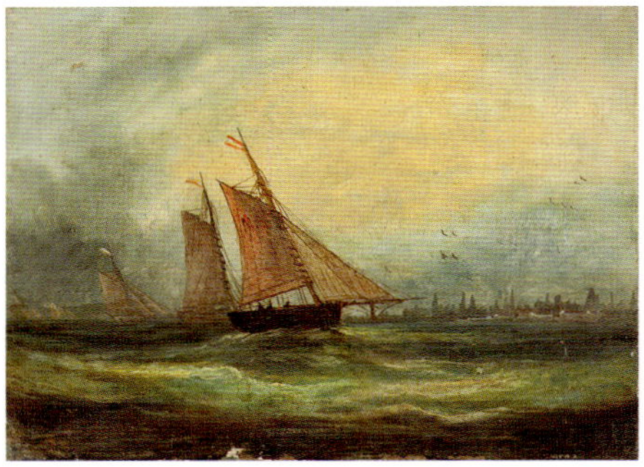

Thornley, Georges William 1857–1935
Racing Yachts
oil on canvas 38 x 50.6
PRSMG : P1974

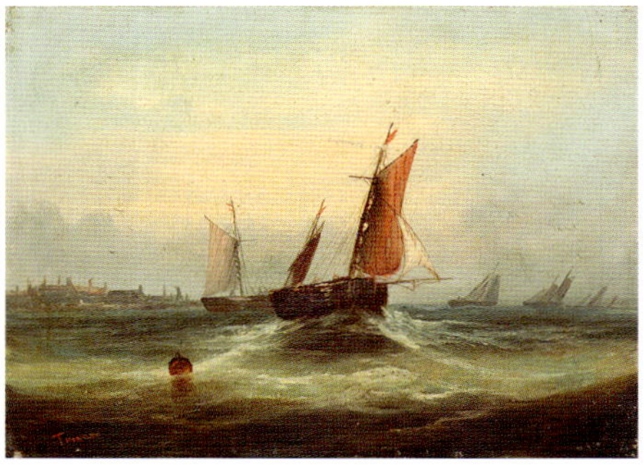

Thornley, Georges William 1857–1935
Racing Yachts in Rough Seas
oil on canvas 37.9 x 50.6
PRSMG : P1975

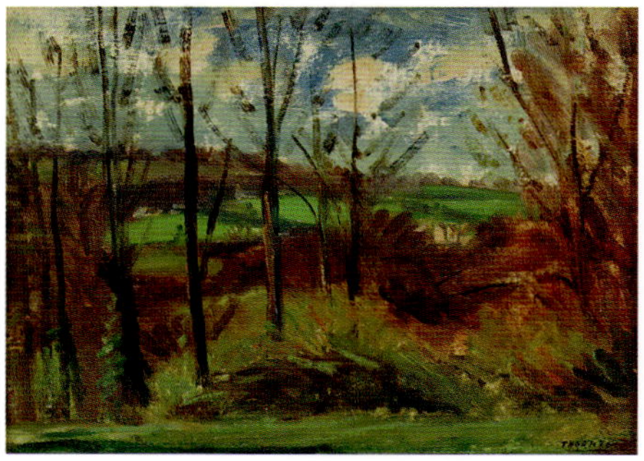

Thornton, Alfred Henry Robinson 1863–1939
November 1928
oil on panel 24 x 31.7
PRSMG : P853

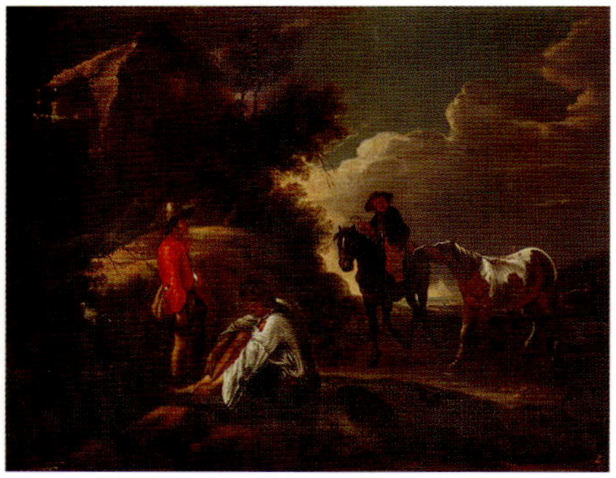

Tillemans, Peter (attributed to) 1684–1734
Figures in a Landscape
oil on canvas 50.8 x 67.5
PRSMG : P1541

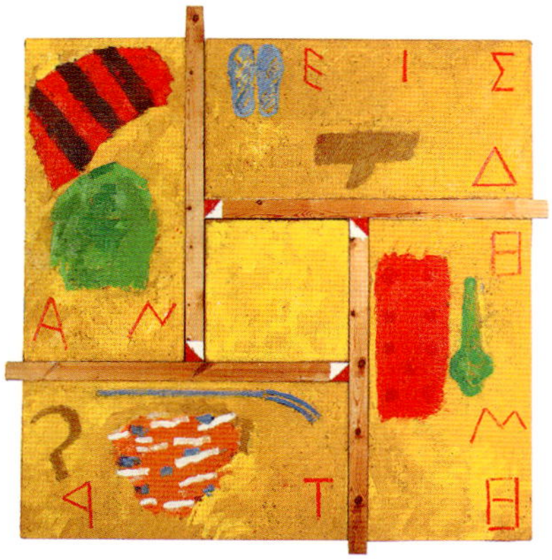

Tilson, Joe b.1928
Road to Eleusis 2 1987
oil on canvas 200 x 206
PRSMG : P2242

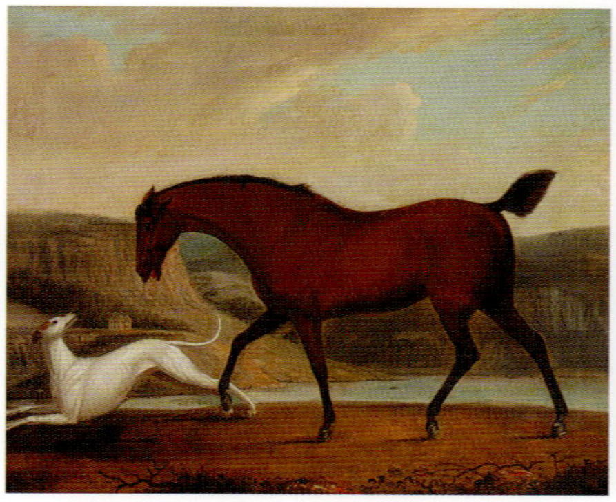

Tomson, Clifton circle of 1775–1828
Horse and Greyhound
oil on canvas 51 x 61.6
PRSMG : P910

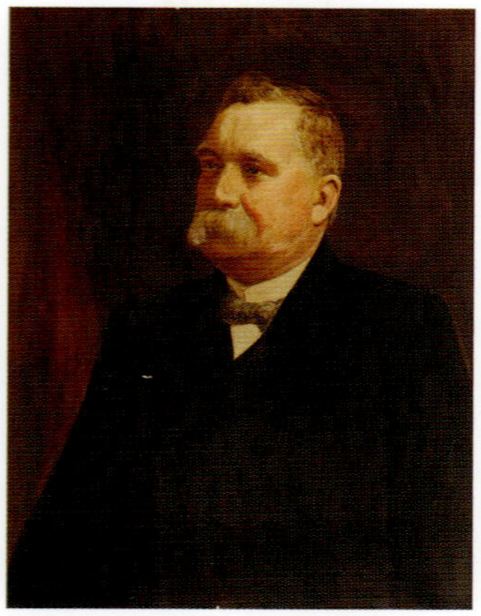

Turner
Joseph Swarbrick
oil on canvas (?) 75.5 x 62
PRSMG : P2010.169

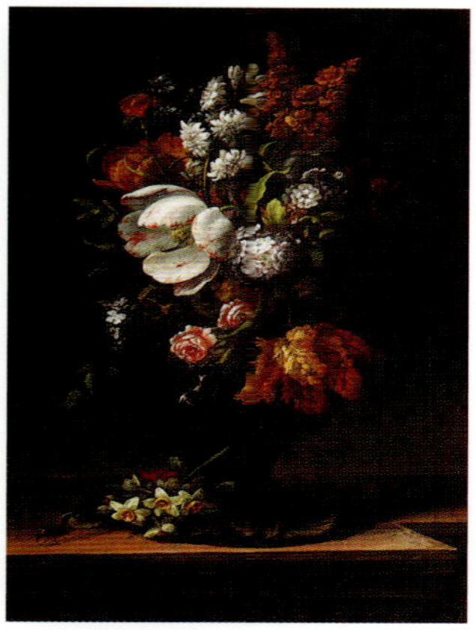

unknown artist
Summer Flowers 1693
oil on canvas 65.5 x 43.2
PRSMG : P828

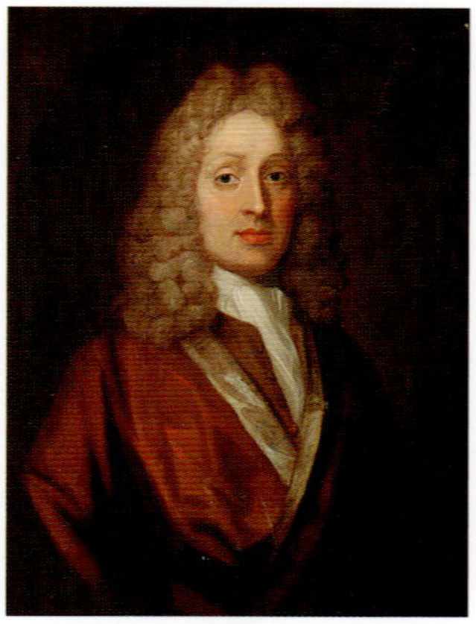

unknown artist
John Atherton c.1700
oil on canvas 75 x 63
PRSMG : 1997.98.5

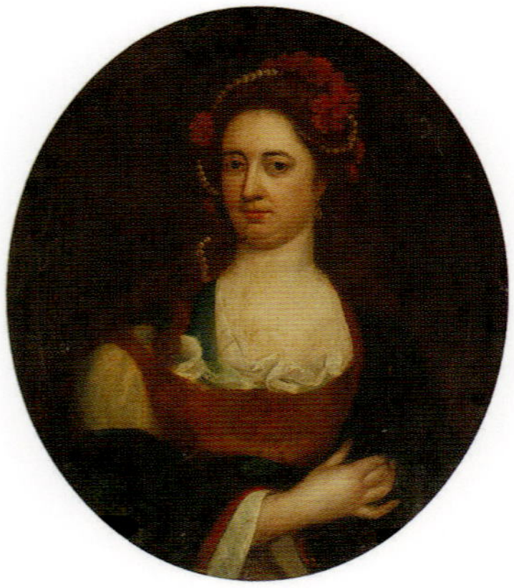

unknown artist
Portrait of a Lady in Blue and White Dress
c.1710–1720
oil on canvas 73.7 x 63.5
PRSMG : P606

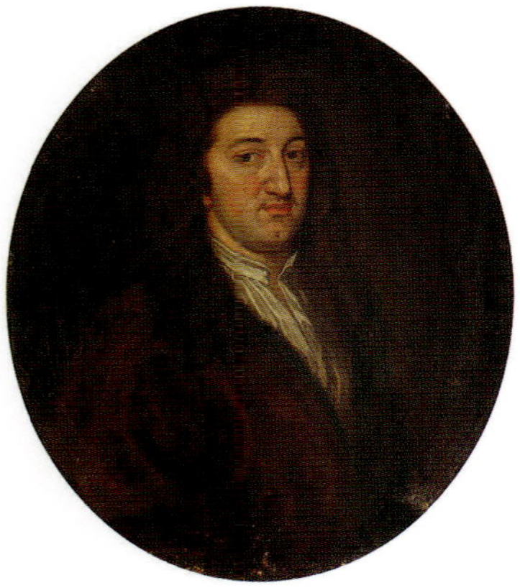

unknown artist
Portrait of a Man c.1710–1720
oil on canvas 73.7 x 63.5
PRSMG : P605

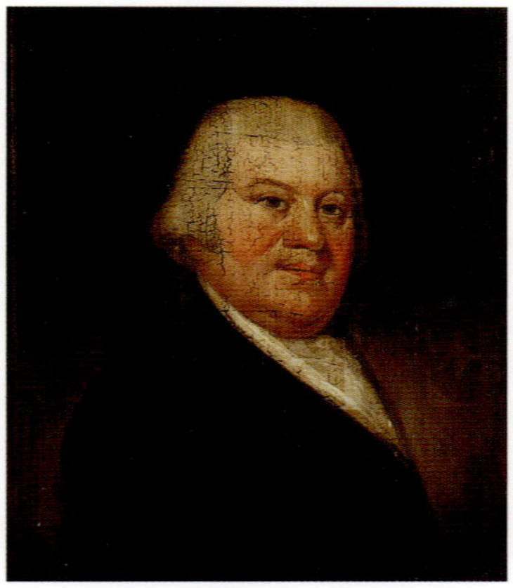

unknown artist
William Cross of Red Scar (1771–1827)
1810–1827
oil on panel 24 x 18.8
PRSMG : P602

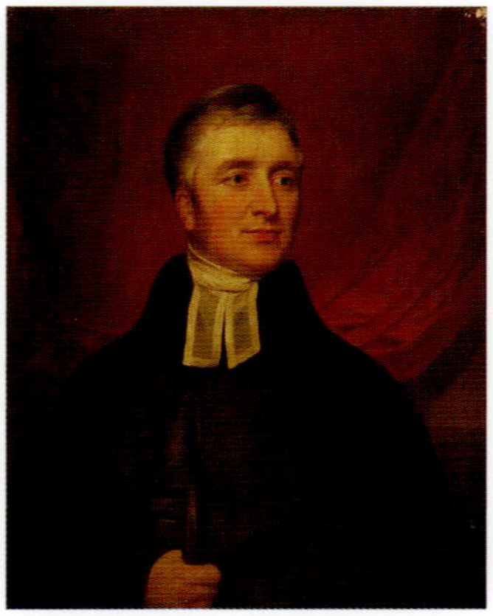

unknown artist
The Reverend Roger Carus Wilson 1817–1839
oil on canvas 76.2 x 63.5
PRSMG : P612

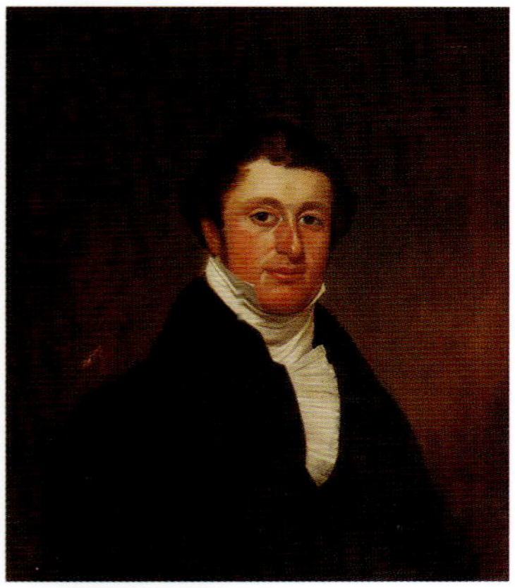

unknown artist
Samuel Horrocks, Guild Mayor (1842)
1820–1846
oil on canvas 74.2 x 62.6
PRSMG : P857

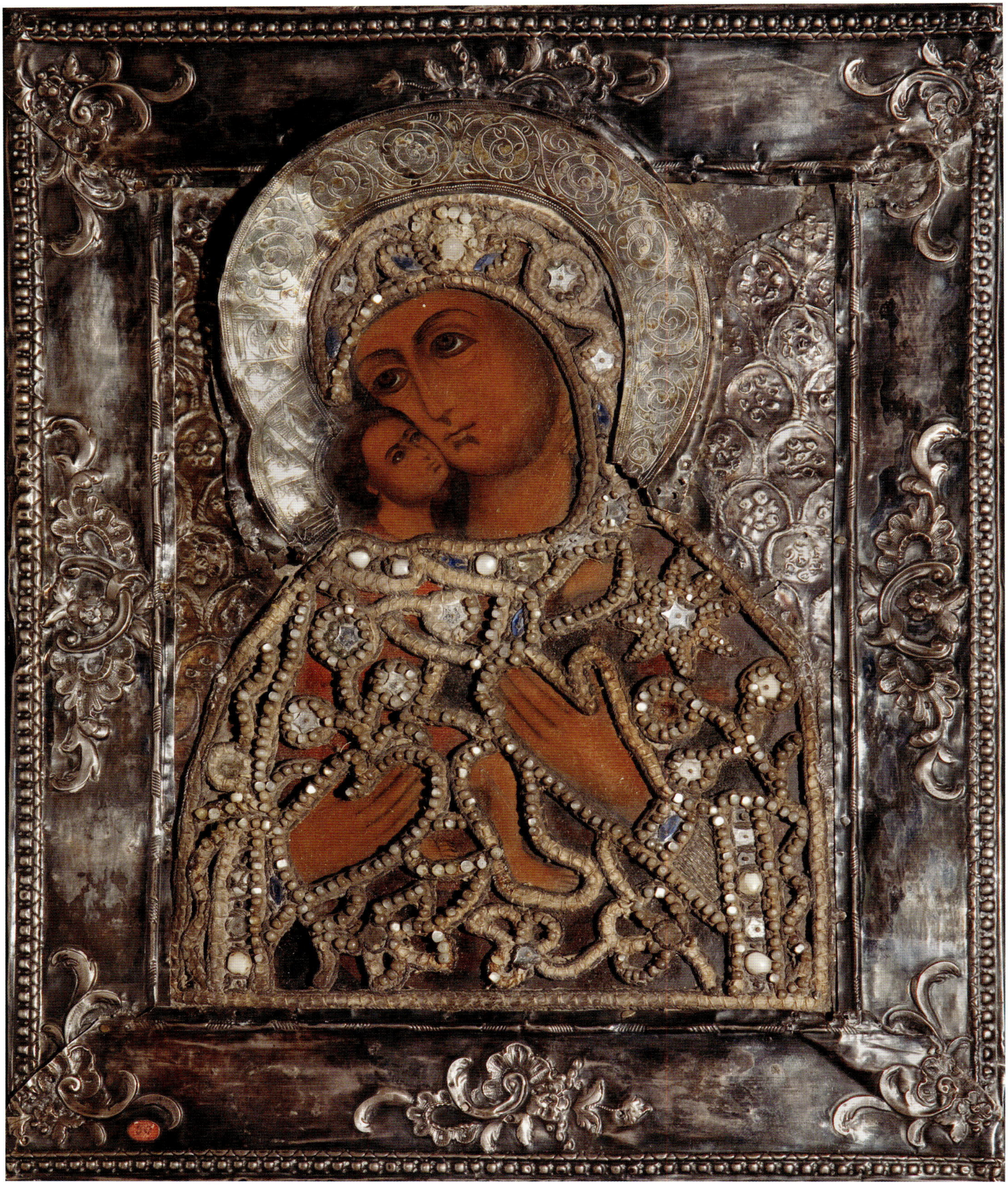

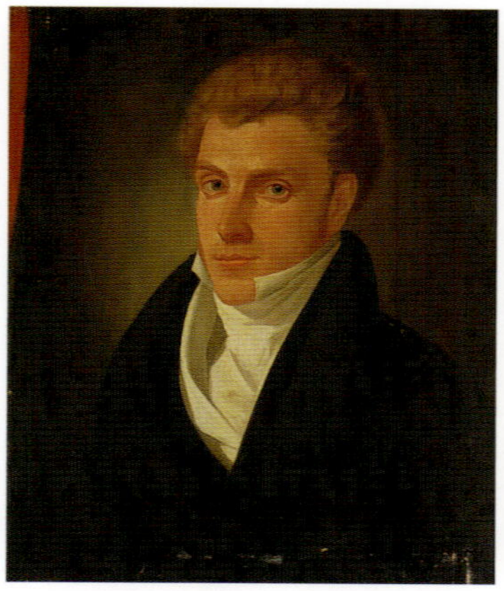

unknown artist
Hugh Foster 1820–1860
oil on canvas 61 x 50.8
PRSMG : P754

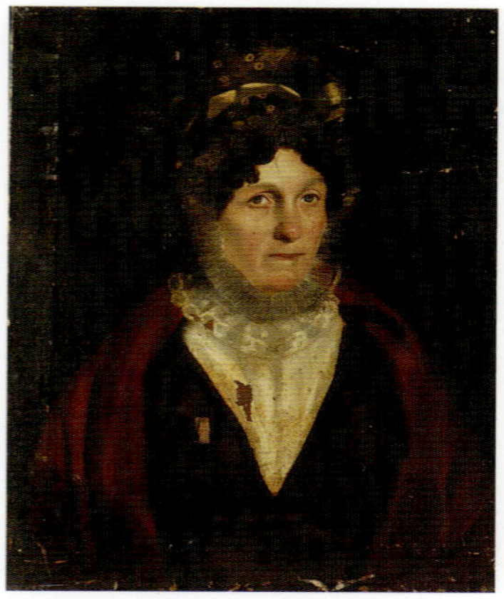

unknown artist
Mrs Buxton of Royal Lodge, Preston 1821
oil on canvas 75.4 x 62.1
PRSMG : P1938

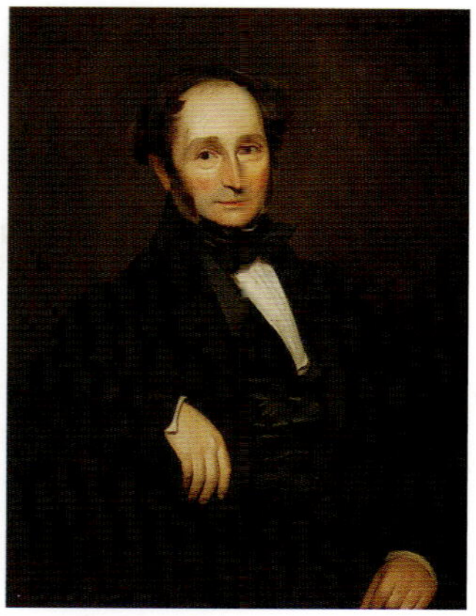

unknown artist
George Jacson, JP c.1825
oil on canvas 92.2 x 70.8
PRSMG : P758

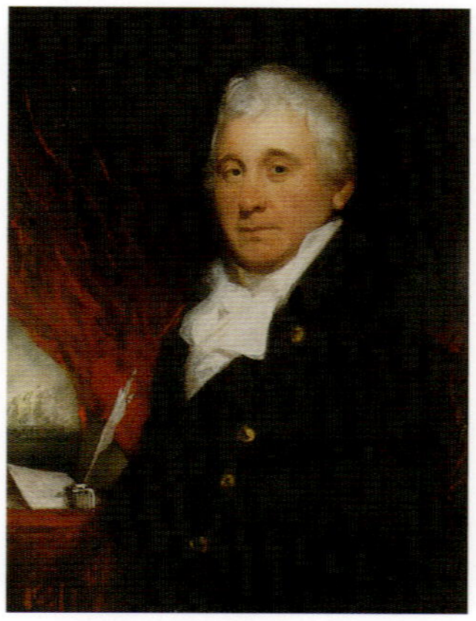

unknown artist
John Horrocks 1830–1850
oil on canvas 76 x 64.5
PRSMG : P757

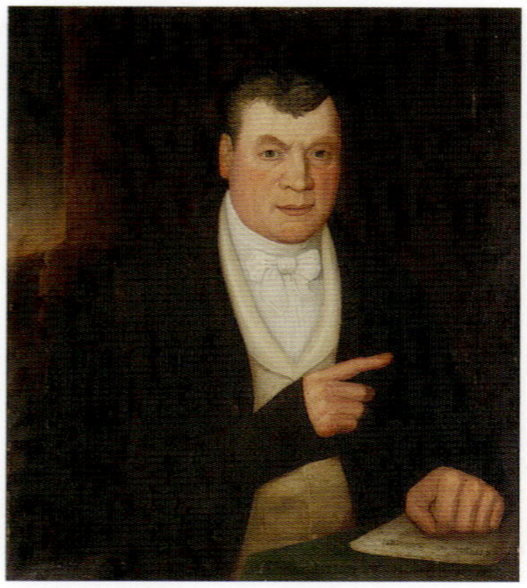

unknown artist
Mr Thomas Swindlehurst 1830–1850
oil on canvas 73.7 x 63.5
PRSMG : P817

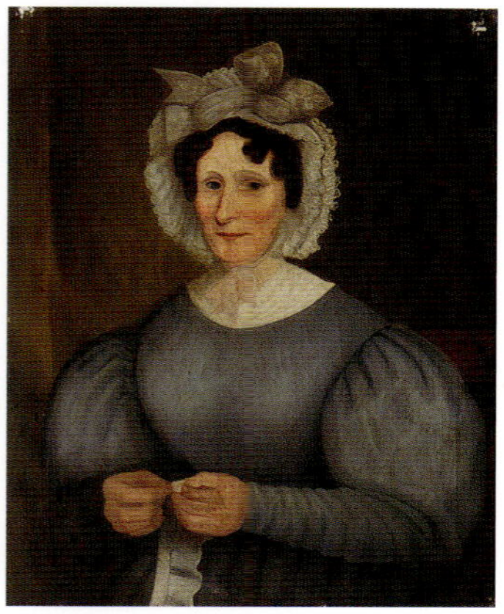

unknown artist
Mrs Thomas Swindlehurst 1830–1850
oil on canvas 76 x 63.5
PRSMG : P816

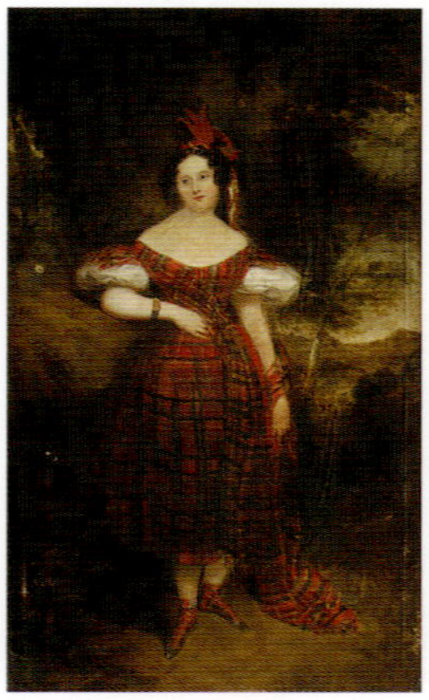

unknown artist
Portrait of a Lady in Highland Costume
1830–1850
oil on canvas 234 x 145.5
PRSMG : P1941

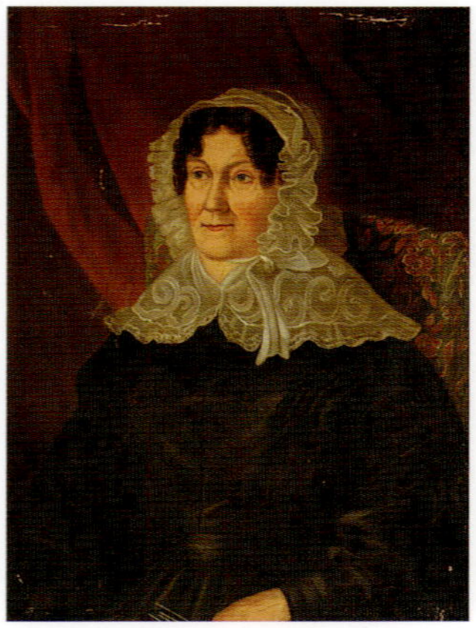

unknown artist
Grace Ascroft c.1835
oil on canvas 77 x 62.5
PRSMG : P2315

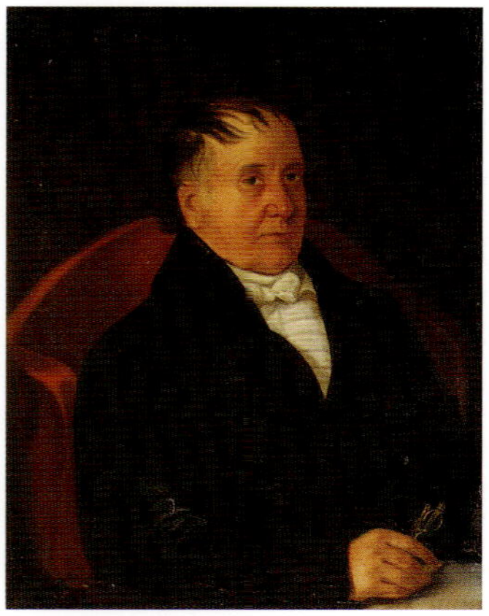

unknown artist
William Ascroft c.1835
oil on canvas 77 x 62.5
PRSMG : P2314

Facing page: unknown artist, *The Vladimir Mother of God,* Blackburn Museum and Art Gallery (p. 68)

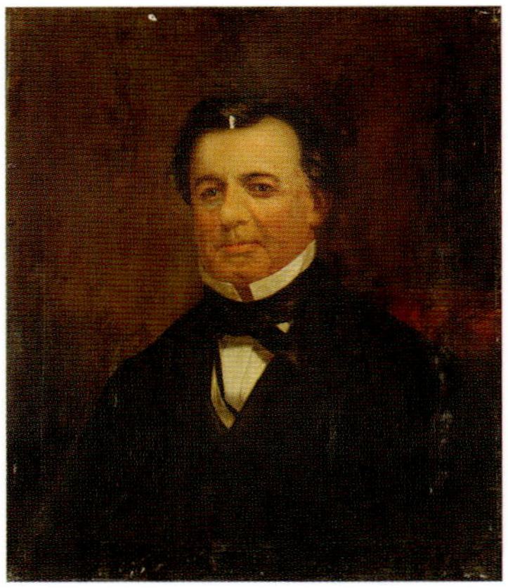

unknown artist
Alderman John Goodier, Mayor of Preston (1860–1861) 1850–1861
oil on canvas 76.3 x 63.5
PRSMG : P613

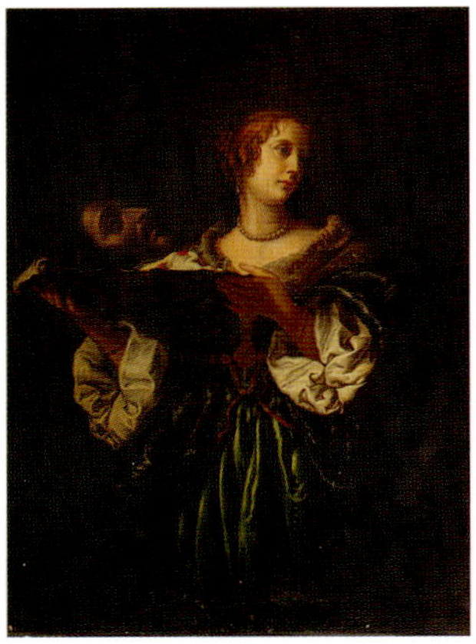

unknown artist
Salome with the Head of John the Baptist 1870
oil on canvas 91 x 70.5
PRSMG : P1926

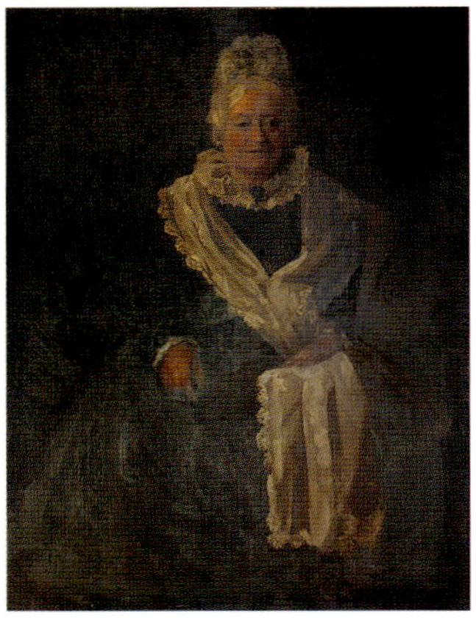

unknown artist
Margaret Pedder 1870–1897
oil on canvas 102 x 86.5
PRSMG : P1939

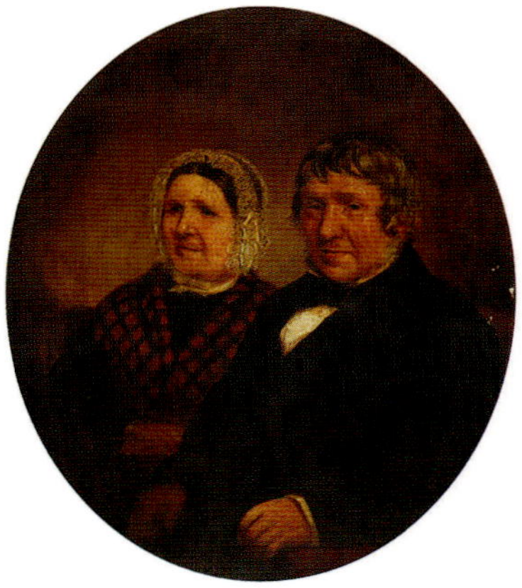

unknown artist
Portrait of an Elderly Couple 1889
oil on canvas 50.7 x 42
PRSMG : P1962

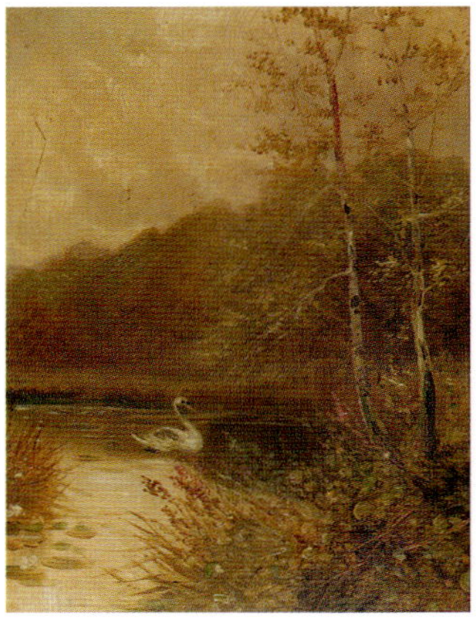

unknown artist
Landscape with a Swan on a Lake 1905
oil on canvas 30.7 x 23
PRSMG : P1914

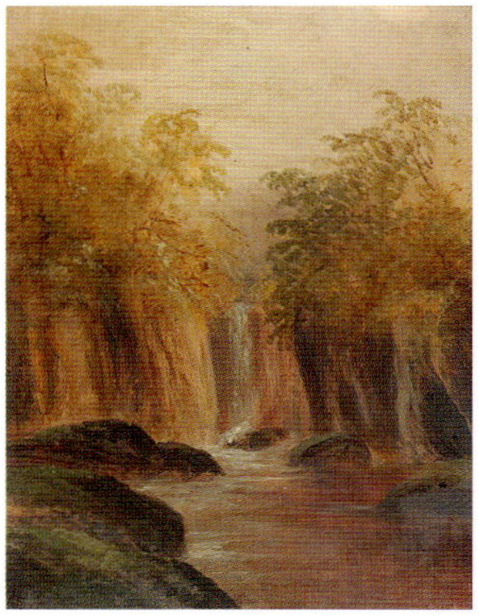

unknown artist
Landscape with a Waterfall 1905
oil on canvas 30.6 x 22.9
PRSMG : P1917

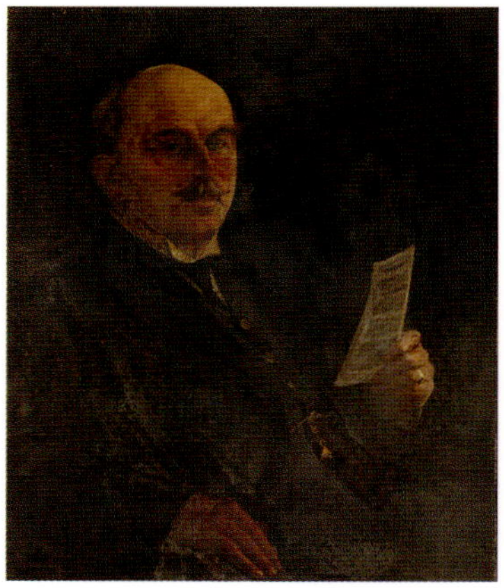

unknown artist
Portrait of a Man Reading a Letter 1908
oil on canvas 30 x 25
PRSMG : P1947

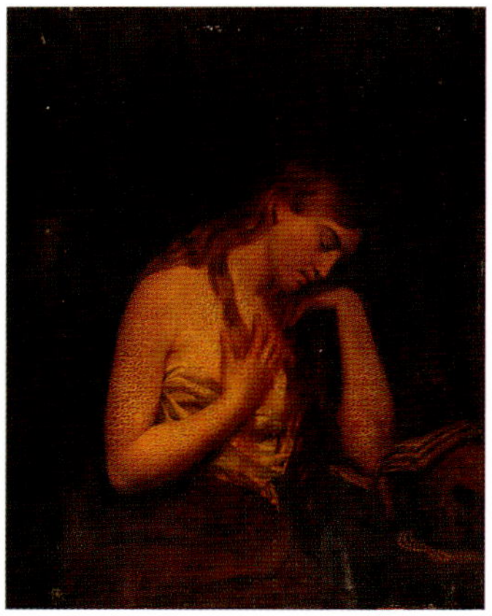

unknown artist
A Magdalene
oil on canvas 90.5 x 81.5
PRSMG : P1935

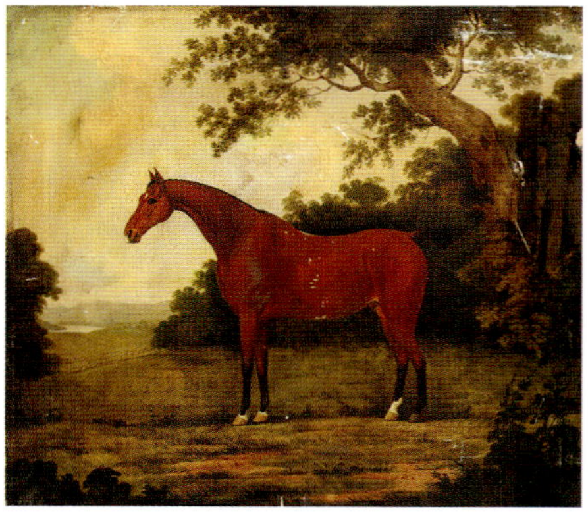

unknown artist
Bay Horse
oil on canvas (?) 62 x 77
PRSMG : 2011.98

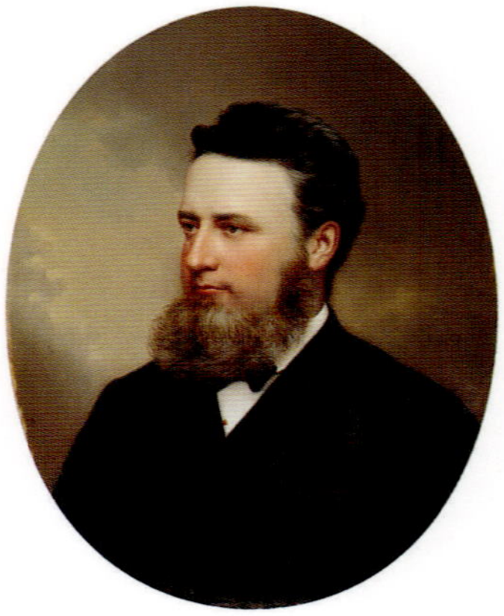

unknown artist
Benjamin Sykes
oil on canvas 66.2 x 53.1
PRSMG : P1602

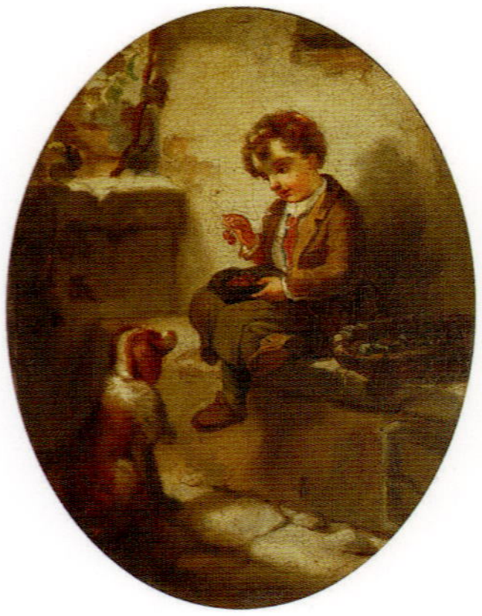

unknown artist
Boy on a Stone Bench with a Capful of Cherries
oil on panel 28 x 24
PRSMG : P1929.2

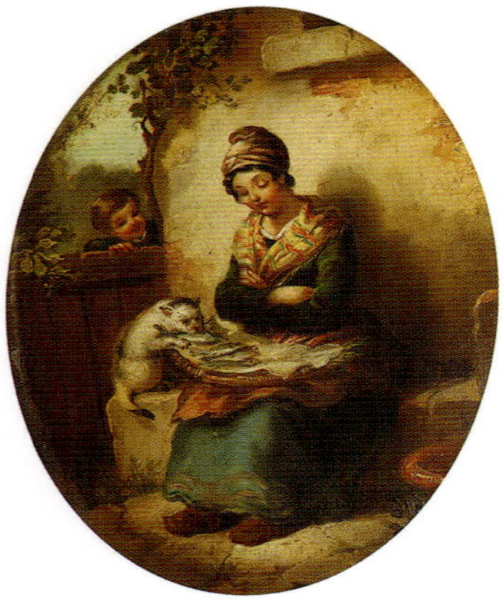

unknown artist
Boy Watching a Cat Steal Fish
oil on panel 28 x 24
PRSMG : P1929.1

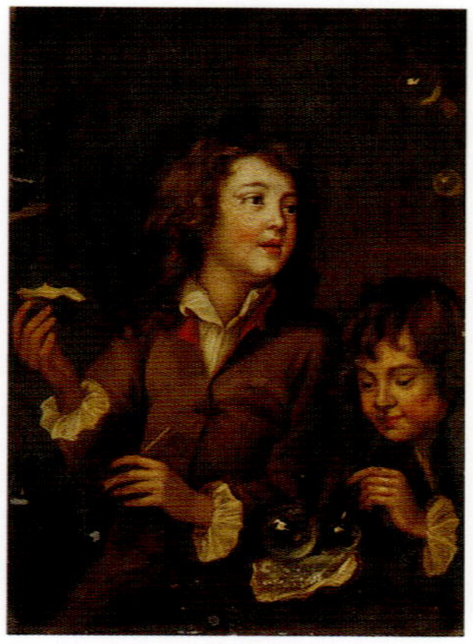

unknown artist
Boys Blowing Bubbles
oil on copper 25.6 x 19.4
PRSMG : P1936

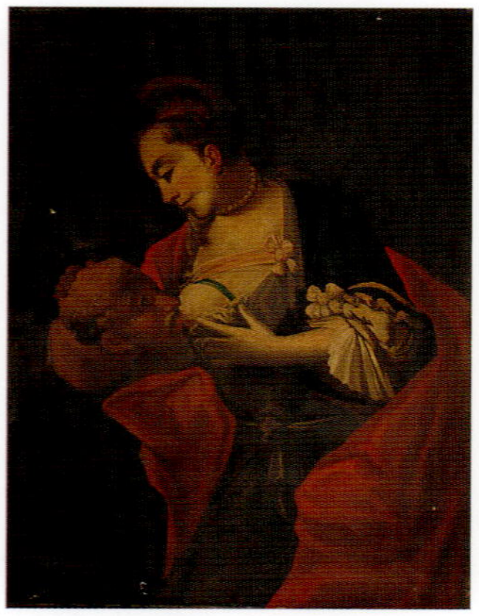

unknown artist
Caritas
oil on canvas 107 x 81
PRSMG : P1934

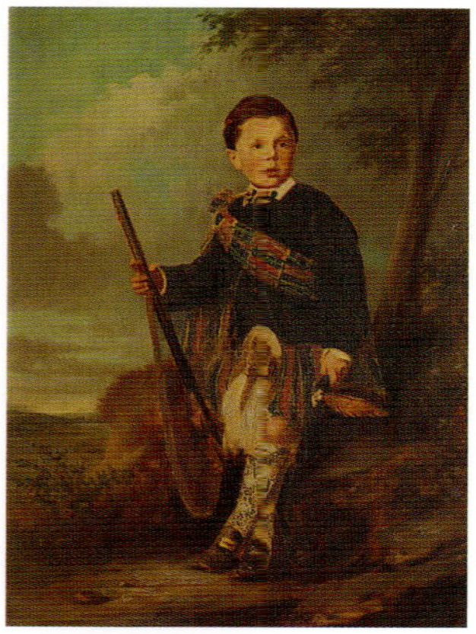

unknown artist
Charles Robert Brown
oil on canvas 62 x 51
PRSMG : P1621

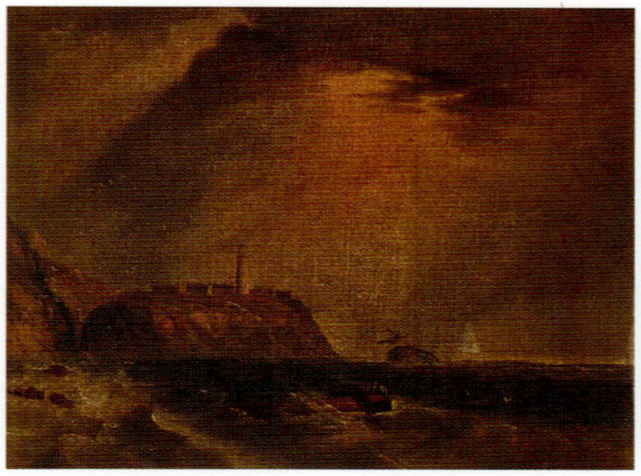

unknown artist
Coastal Scene
oil on canvas 30.5 x 40
PRSMG : P1912

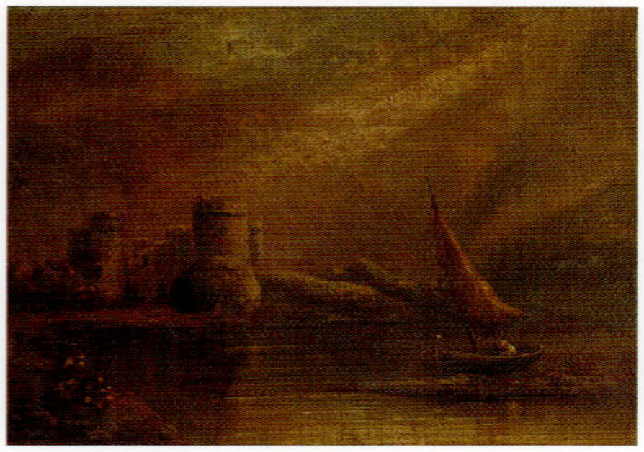

unknown artist
Coastal Scene with Castle
oil on panel 19 x 29
PRSMG : P1920

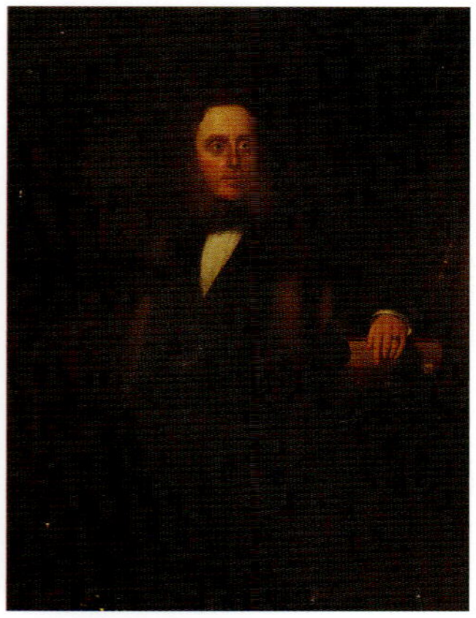

unknown artist
Colonel T. Birchall of Ribbleton
oil on canvas 142.3 x 111.8
PRSMG : P752

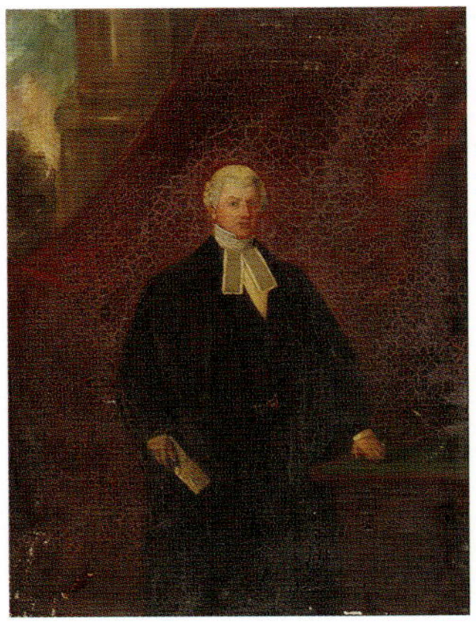

unknown artist
Edmund Grimshaw
oil on canvas (?) 61 x 46
PRSMG : 2011.100

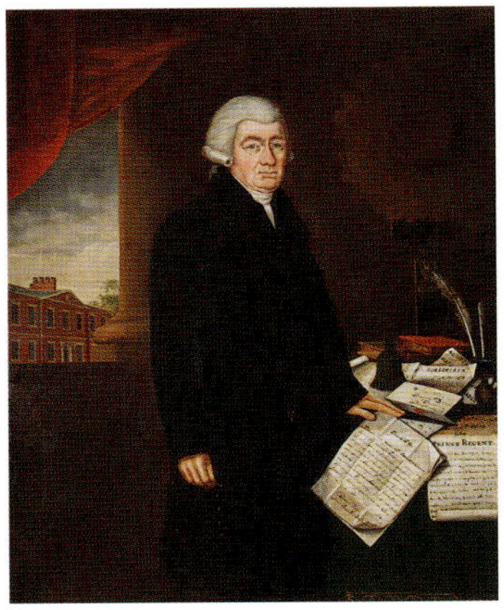

unknown artist
Father Joseph Dunn
oil on canvas (?) 182 x 133
PRSMG : LOAN123

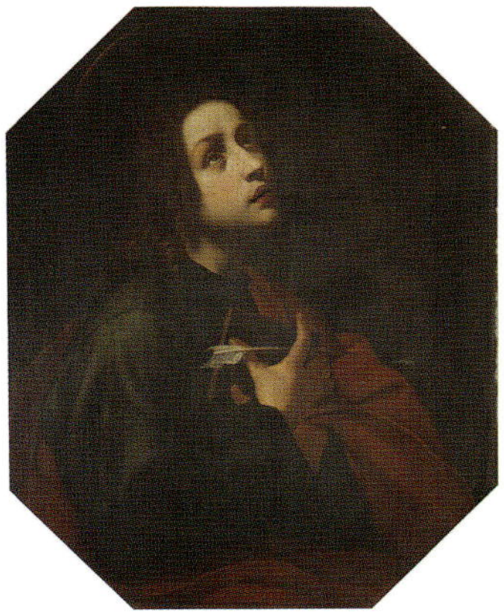

unknown artist
Figure with a Book and a Quill Pen
oil on canvas 80 x 65
PRSMG : P1899

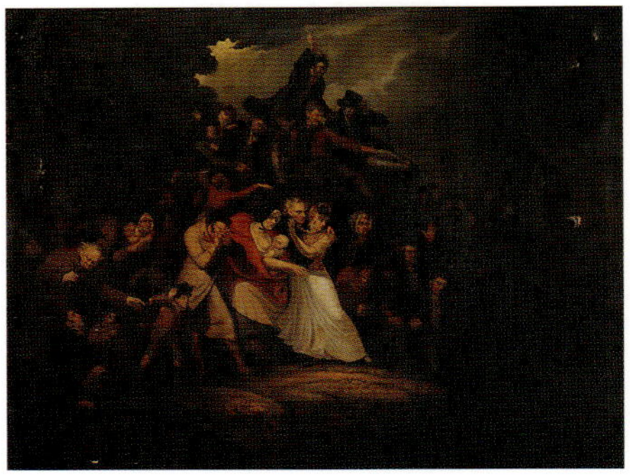

unknown artist
Frightened People on a Hillside
oil on canvas 107.5 x 138.5
PRSMG : P1922

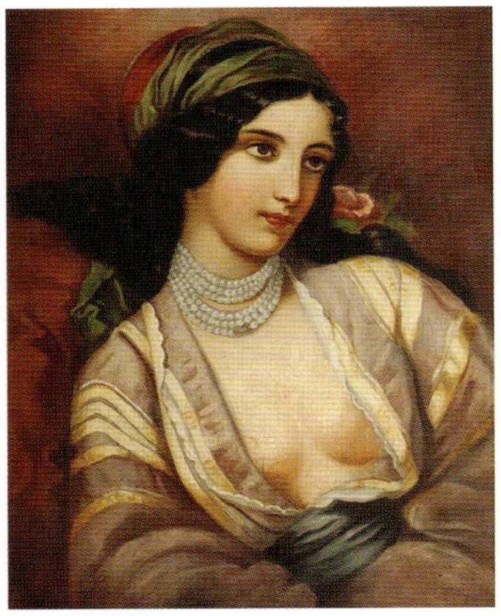

unknown artist
Gipsy Girl
oil on canvas 61 x 50.8
PRSMG : P1923

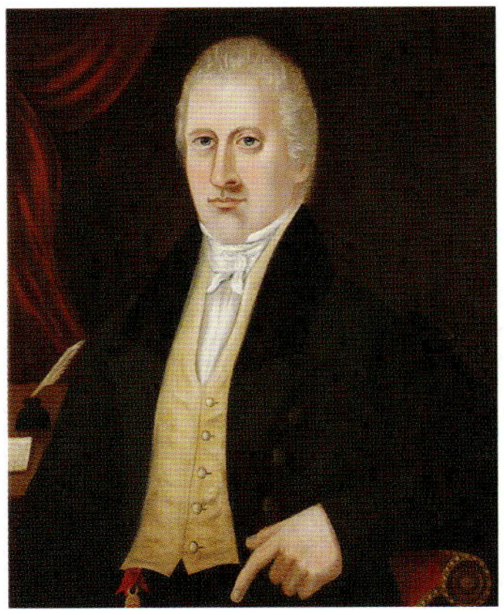

unknown artist
Henry Hunt, MP for Preston
oil on canvas 82 x 69.3
PRSMG : P755

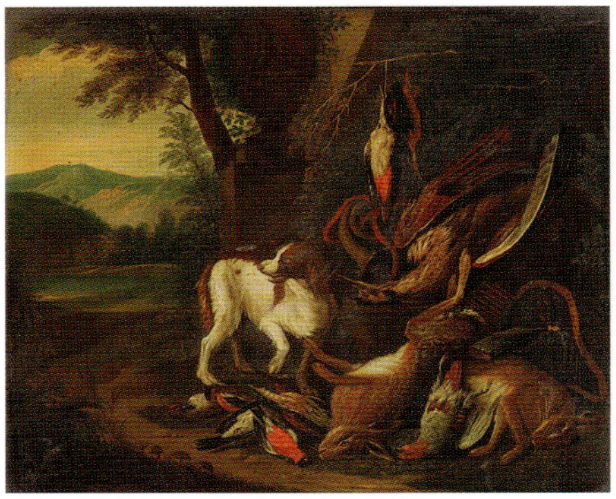

unknown artist
Hunting Scene: Dog with Game
oil on panel 24.6 x 33.5
PRSMG : P1930

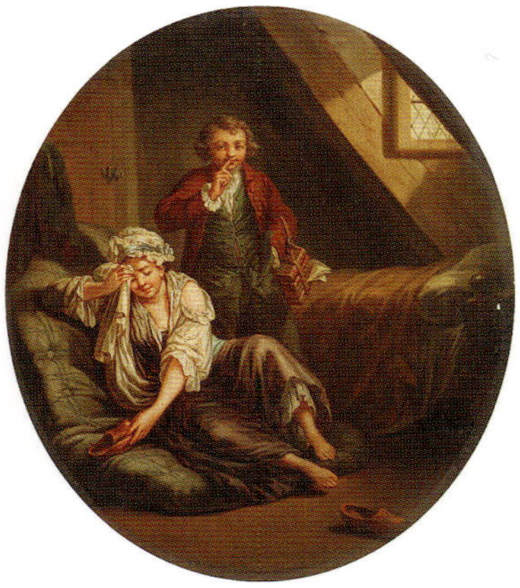

unknown artist
Interior – Chambermaid and Man with Books
oil on canvas 46 x 38
PRSMG : P1933

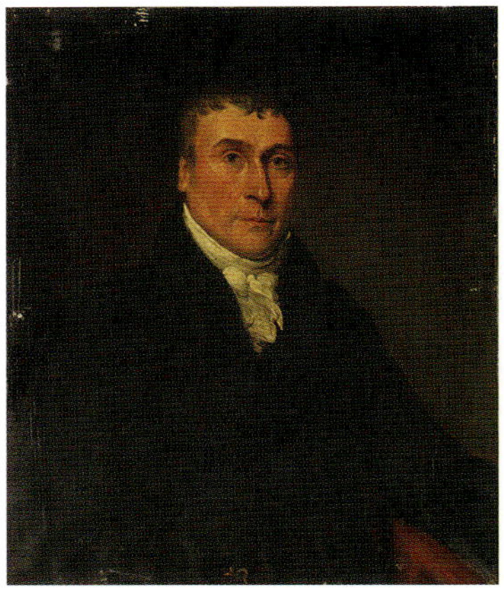

unknown artist
J. Arrowsmith, DD
oil on canvas 76.5 x 63.5
PRSMG : P1937

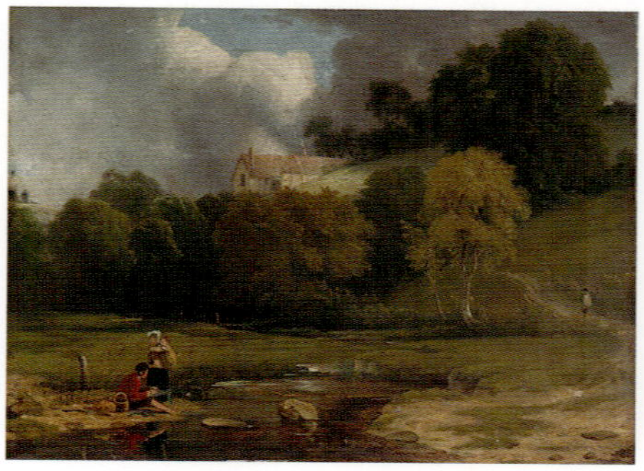

unknown artist
Landscape
oil on canvas 25.5 x 35.5
PRSMG : P1909

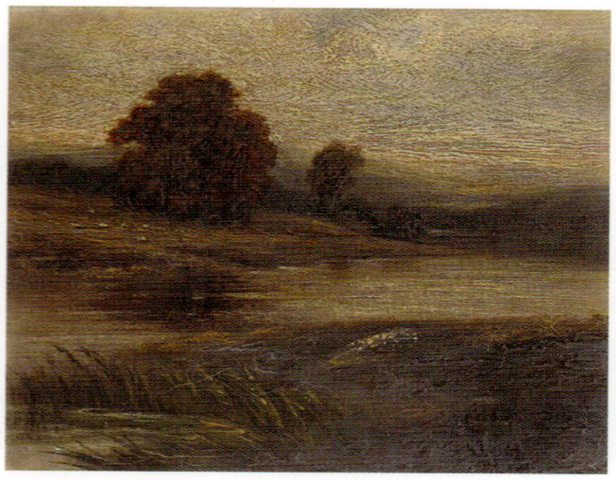

unknown artist
Landscape
oil on canvas 23 x 30.8
PRSMG : P1911

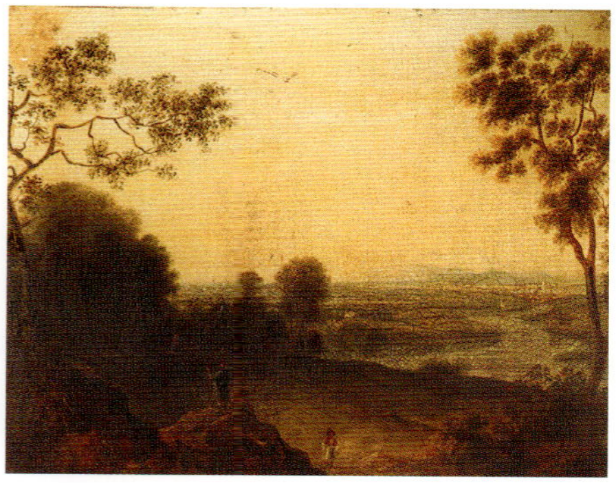

unknown artist
Landscape
oil on canvas 35.5 x 44.7
PRSMG : P1913

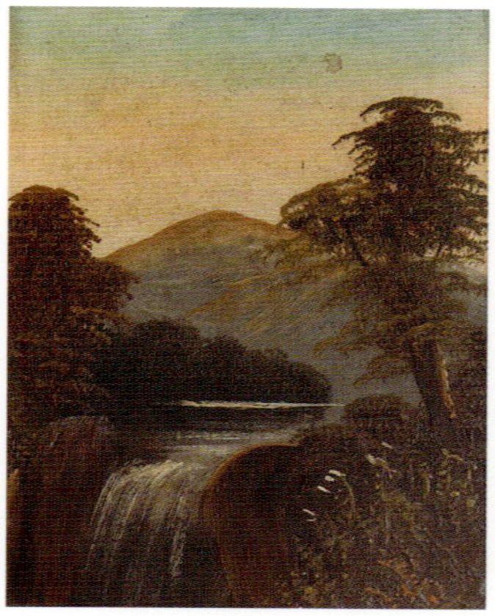

unknown artist
Landscape
oil on card 22.5 x 18
PRSMG : P1915

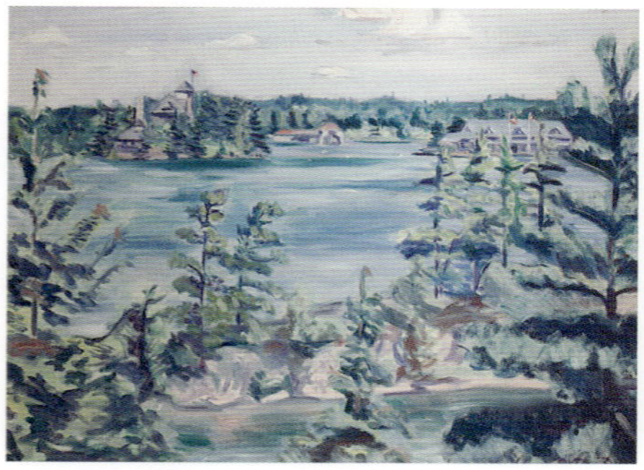

unknown artist
Landscape
oil on canvas 43 x 59
PRSMG : P1918

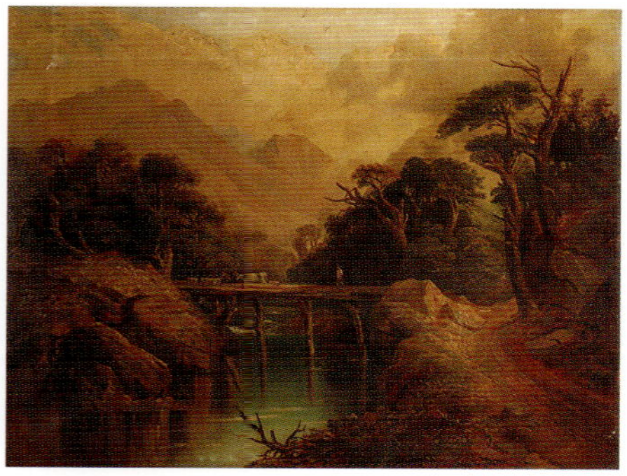

unknown artist
Landscape – Man Driving Cattle and Sheep
oil on canvas 71.8 x 91.5
PRSMG : P1977

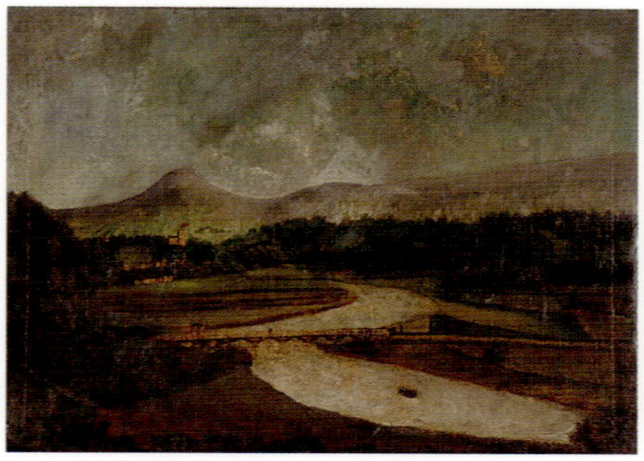

unknown artist
Landscape – Panoramic View of a River Valley
oil on canvas 63 x 88
PRSMG : P1905

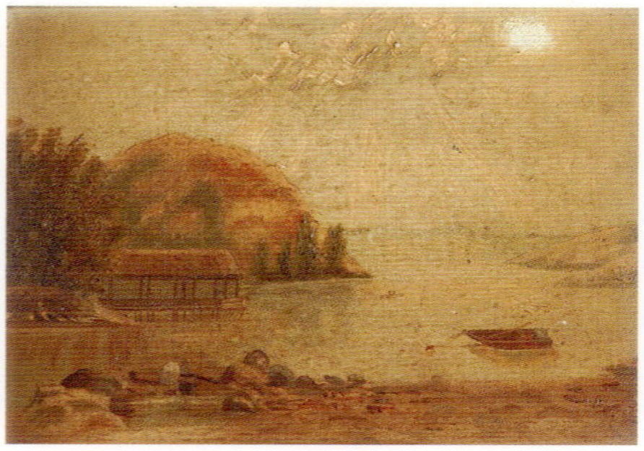

unknown artist
Landscape with a Lake in the Foreground and Mountains in the Middle Distance
oil on panel 15.5 x 22.5
PRSMG : P1904

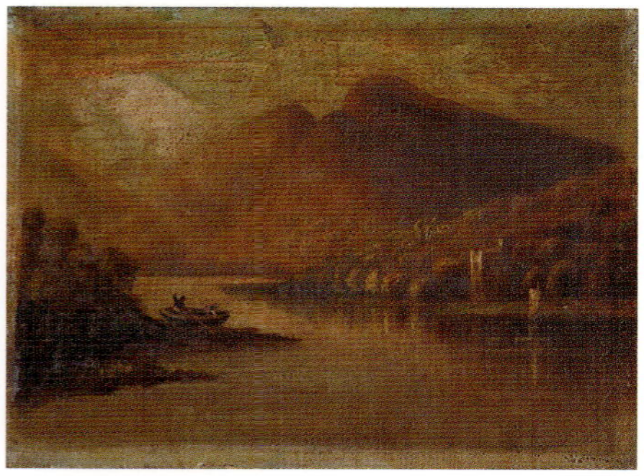

unknown artist
Landscape with a Mountain Lake, a Small Castle and Fishermen
oil on board 19.5 x 26
PRSMG : P1907

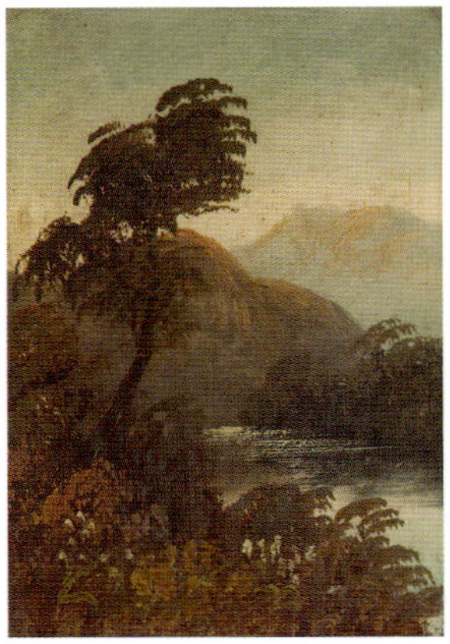

unknown artist
Landscape with a Tree, Water and Hills
oil on canvas 26 x 17.5 (E)
PRSMG : P1916

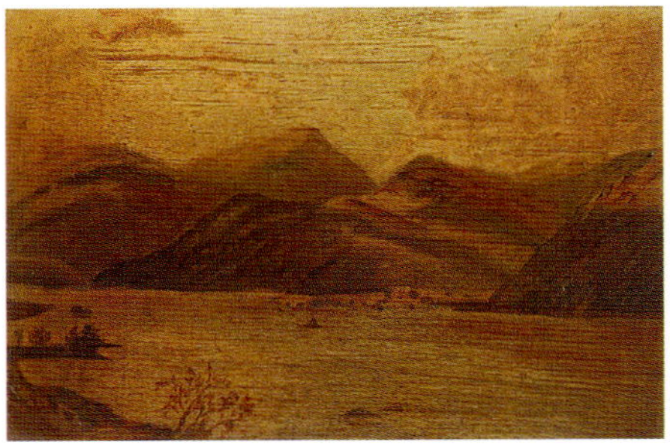

unknown artist
Landscape with Mountains
oil on canvas (?) 14 x 22
PRSMG : 2011.105

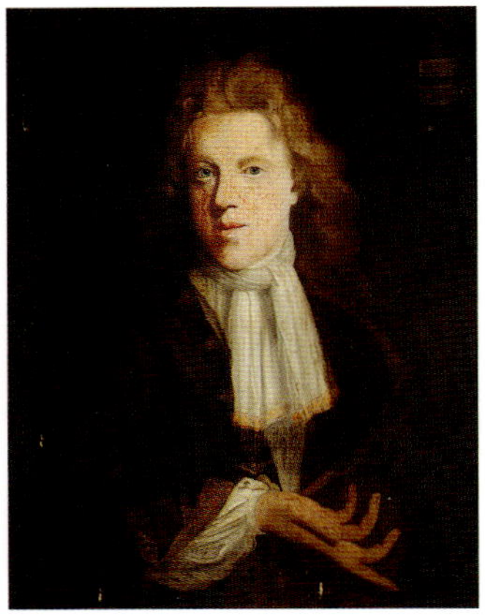

unknown artist
Lord Ribblesdale
oil on canvas (?) 76 x 63.5
PRSMG : 2011.97

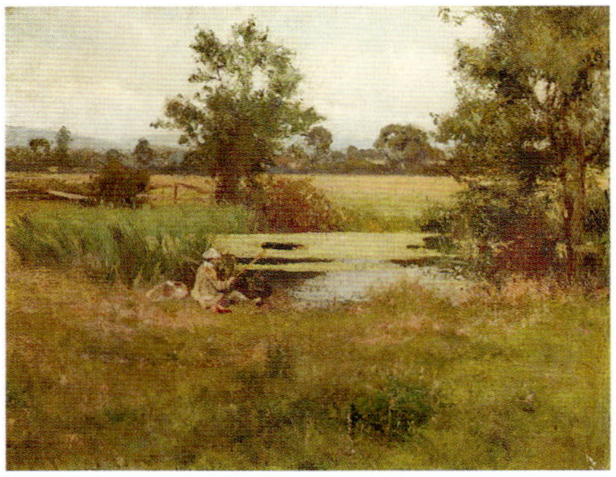

unknown artist
Man Fishing
oil on canvas (?) 51 x 77
PRSMG : 2011.103

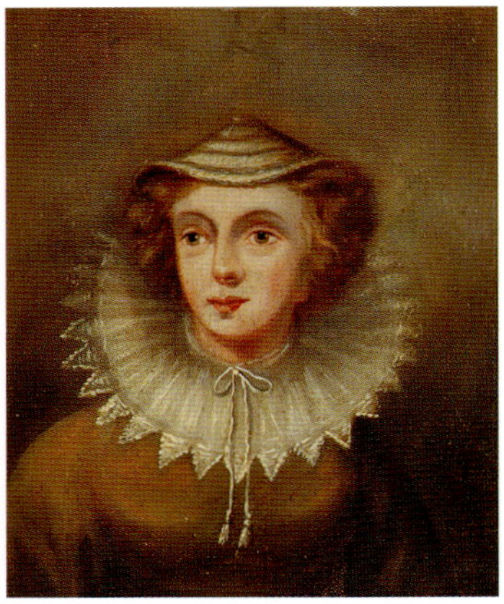

unknown artist
Mary, Queen of Scots (1542–1587)
oil on copper 16.5 x 13.7
PRSMG : P1504

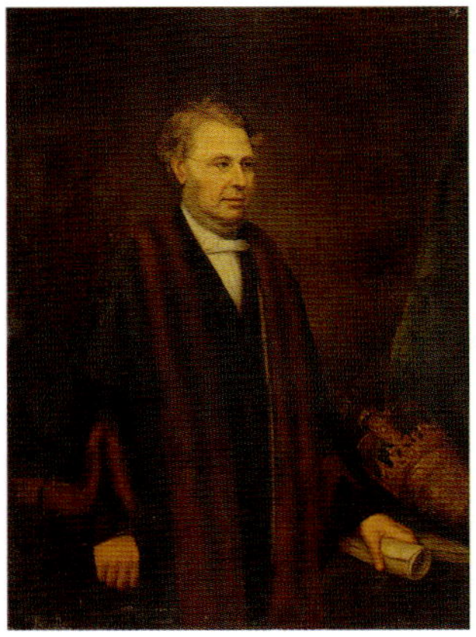

unknown artist
Miles Myres
oil on canvas 111.8 x 86.3
PRSMG : P608

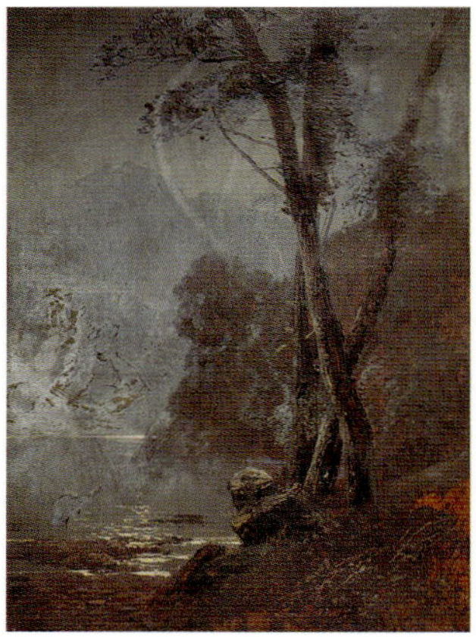

unknown artist
Moonlight
oil on canvas 50.6 x 40.5
PRSMG : P1910

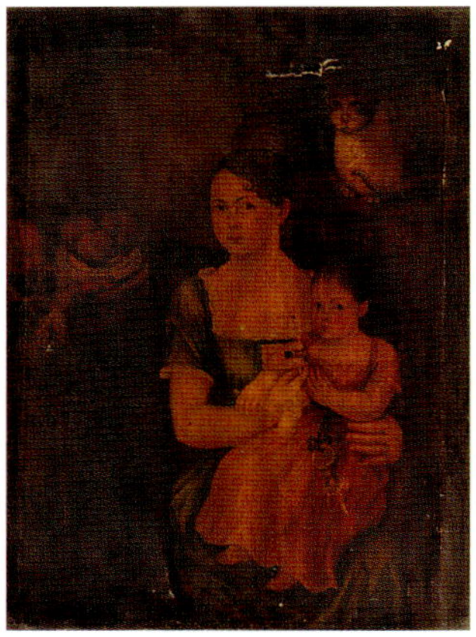

unknown artist
Mother and Child
oil on canvas 67.3 x 58.8
PRSMG : P1924

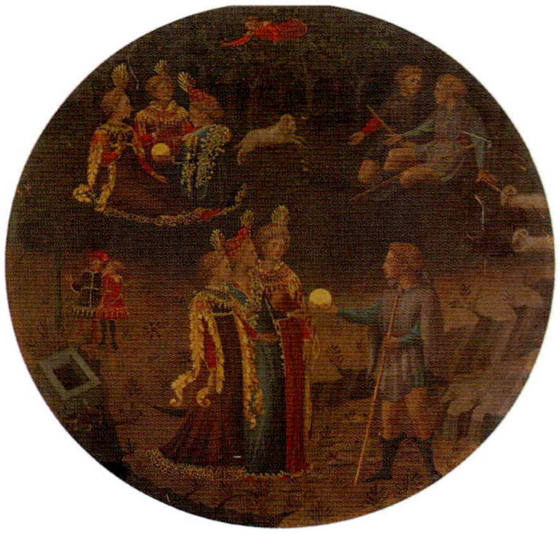

unknown artist
Mythological Scenes (possibly 'The Judgment of Paris')
oil on panel 58.8 x 58.8
PRSMG : P1927

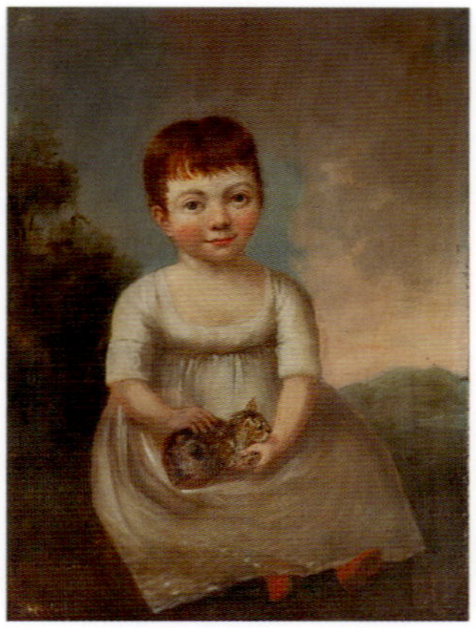

unknown artist
Portrait of a Girl Holding a Cat
oil on panel 31 x 22.5
PRSMG : P1945.3

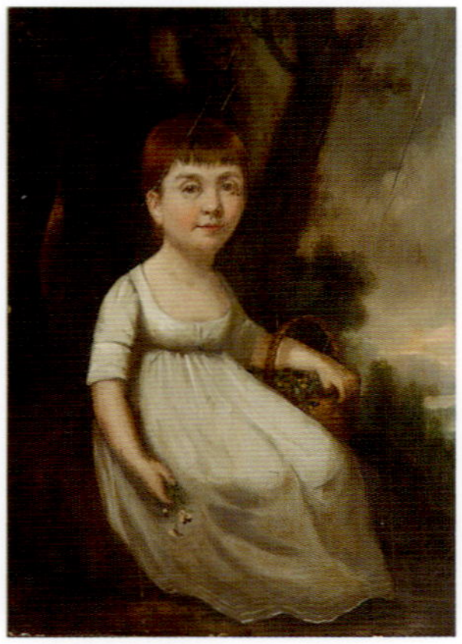

unknown artist
Portrait of a Girl Holding Flowers
oil on panel 31 x 22.5
PRSMG : P1945.4

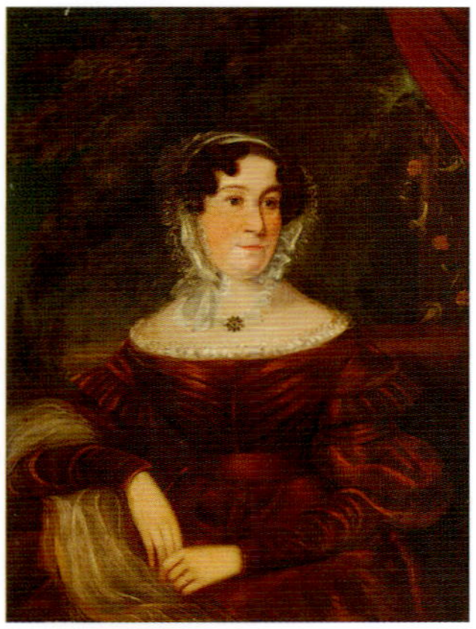

unknown artist
Portrait of a Lady
oil on canvas 92 x 72
PRSMG : P1960

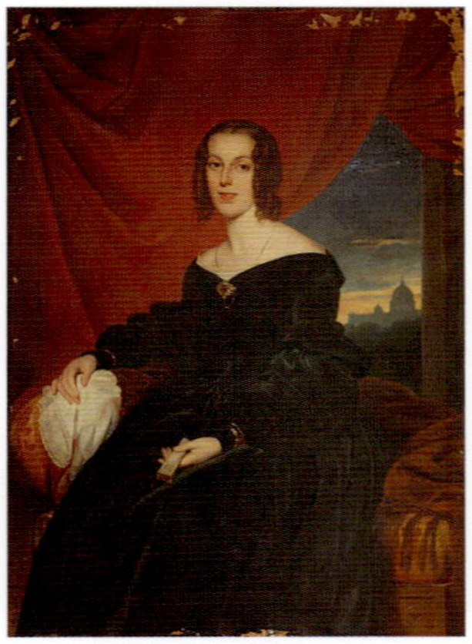

unknown artist
Portrait of a Lady with a Black Dress and Brooch
oil on canvas (?) 128 x 95
PRSMG : 2010.168

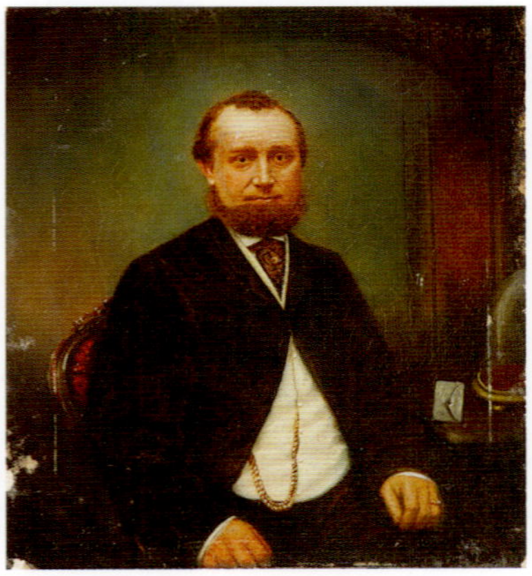

unknown artist
Portrait of a Man
oil on panel 25 x 21
PRSMG : P1943

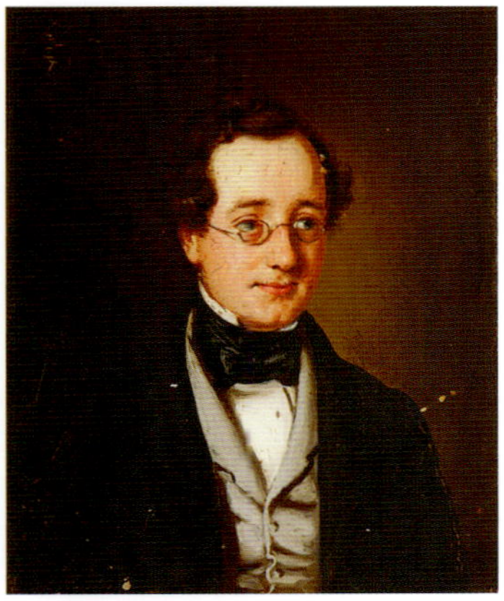

unknown artist
Portrait of a Man
oil on panel 17.3 x 14.6
PRSMG : P1944

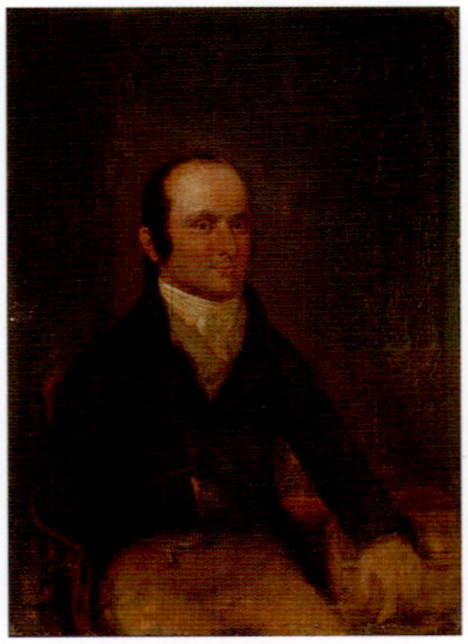

unknown artist
Portrait of a Man
oil on panel 31 x 22.5
PRSMG : P1945.1

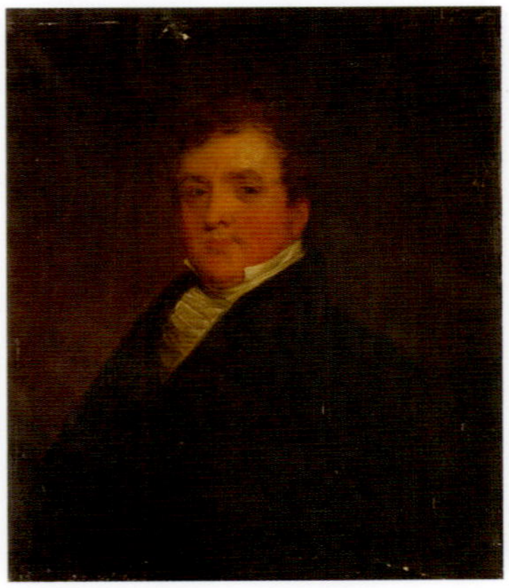

unknown artist
Portrait of a Man
oil on canvas 76 x 63.5
PRSMG : P1946

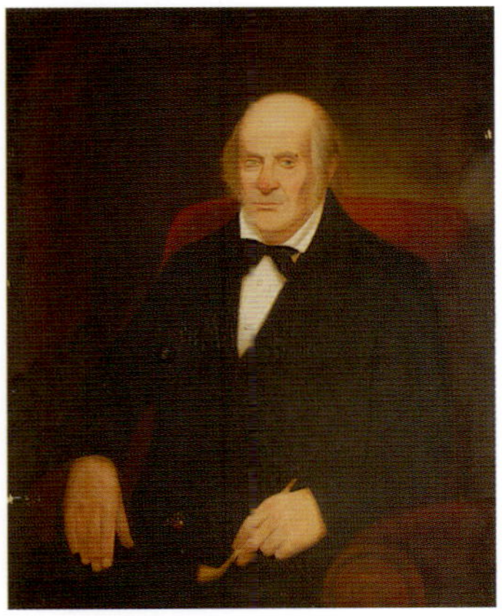

unknown artist
Portrait of a Man
oil on canvas 89.5 x 71
PRSMG : P1949

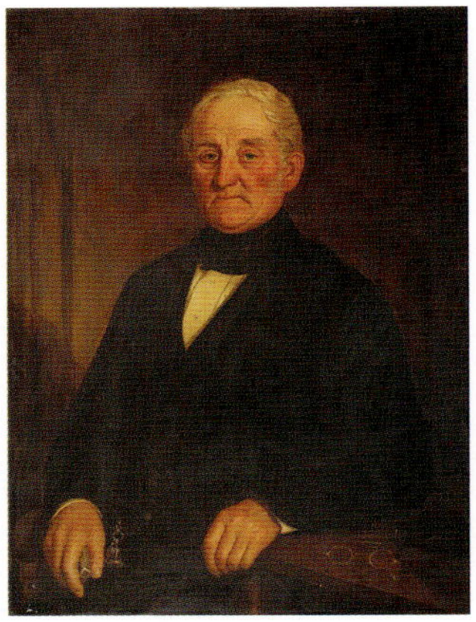

unknown artist
Portrait of a Man
oil on canvas 91 x 71
PRSMG : P1950

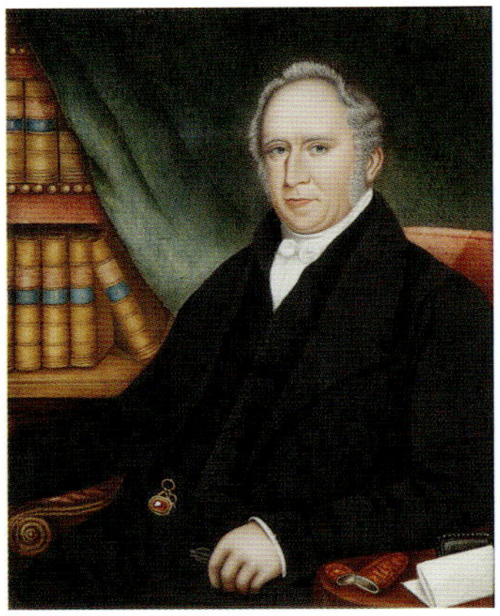

unknown artist
Portrait of a Man
oil on porcelain 21.5 x 16.5
PRSMG : P1951

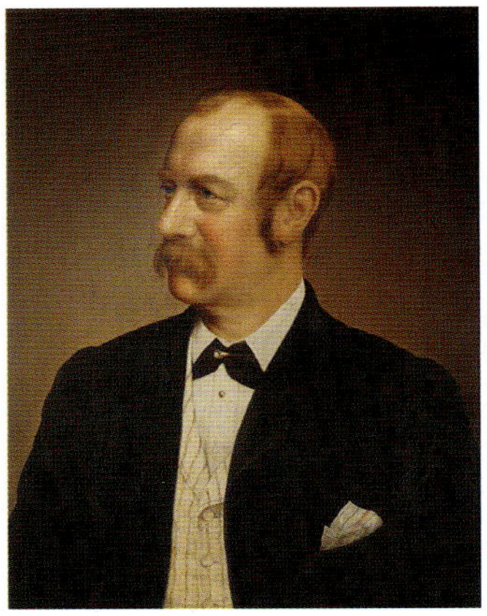

unknown artist
Portrait of a Man
oil on canvas 90 x 55.5
PRSMG : P1952

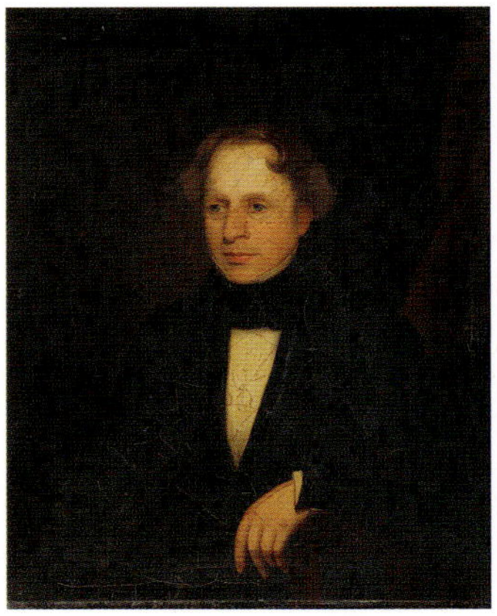

unknown artist
Portrait of a Man
oil on canvas 91.5 x 70
PRSMG : P1953

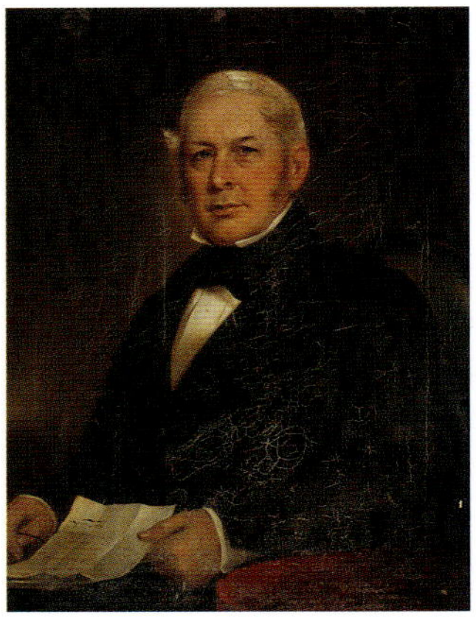

unknown artist
Portrait of a Man
oil on canvas 91 x 70
PRSMG : P1957

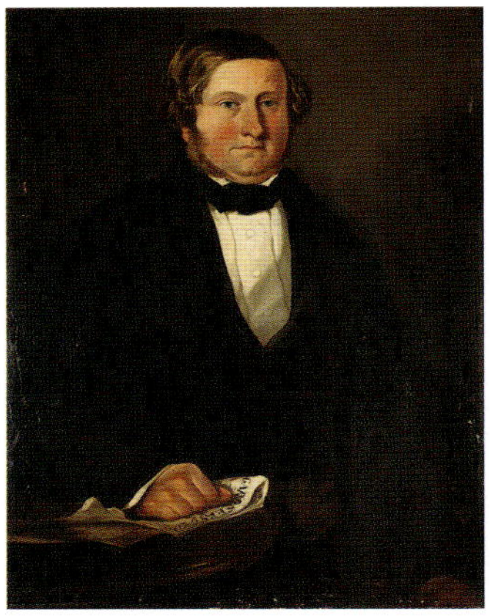

unknown artist
Portrait of a Man Holding a Gardening Magazine
oil on canvas 76.2 x 63.5
PRSMG : P1954

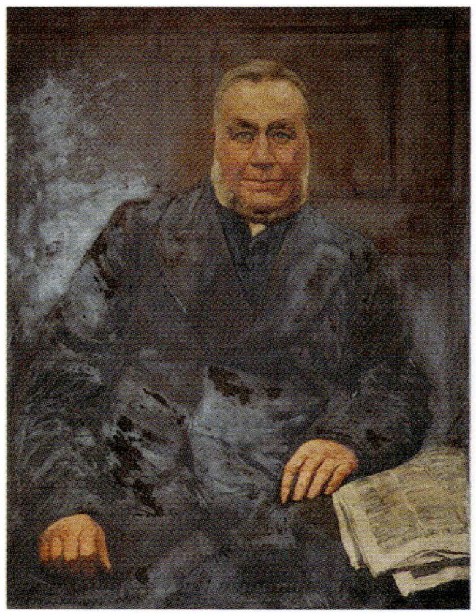

unknown artist
Portrait of a Man in Black with Sidewhiskers and a Newspaper
oil on canvas 76.5 x 61.1
PRSMG : P1948

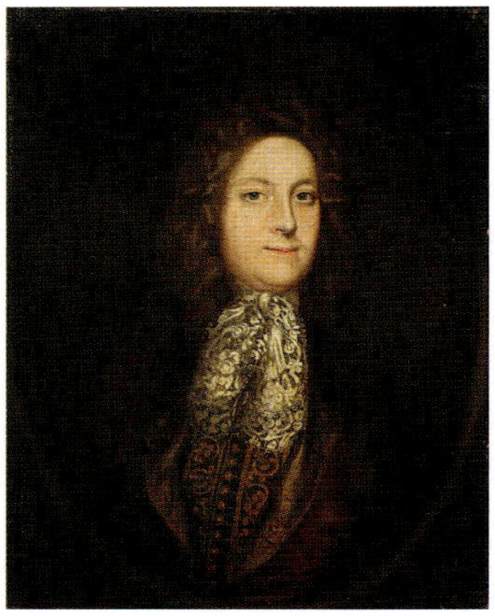

unknown artist
Portrait of a Man with a Gold Embroidered Lace Cravatte
oil on canvas 76.2 x 63.5
PRSMG : P1955

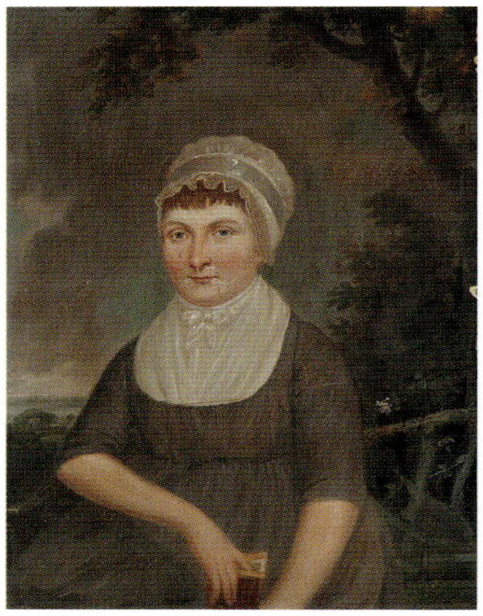

unknown artist
Portrait of a Woman
oil on panel 31 x 22.5
PRSMG : P1945.2

Facing page: Philpot, Glyn Warren, 1884–1937, *Portrait of a Man*, 1929, Towneley Hall Art Gallery & Museum (p. 150)

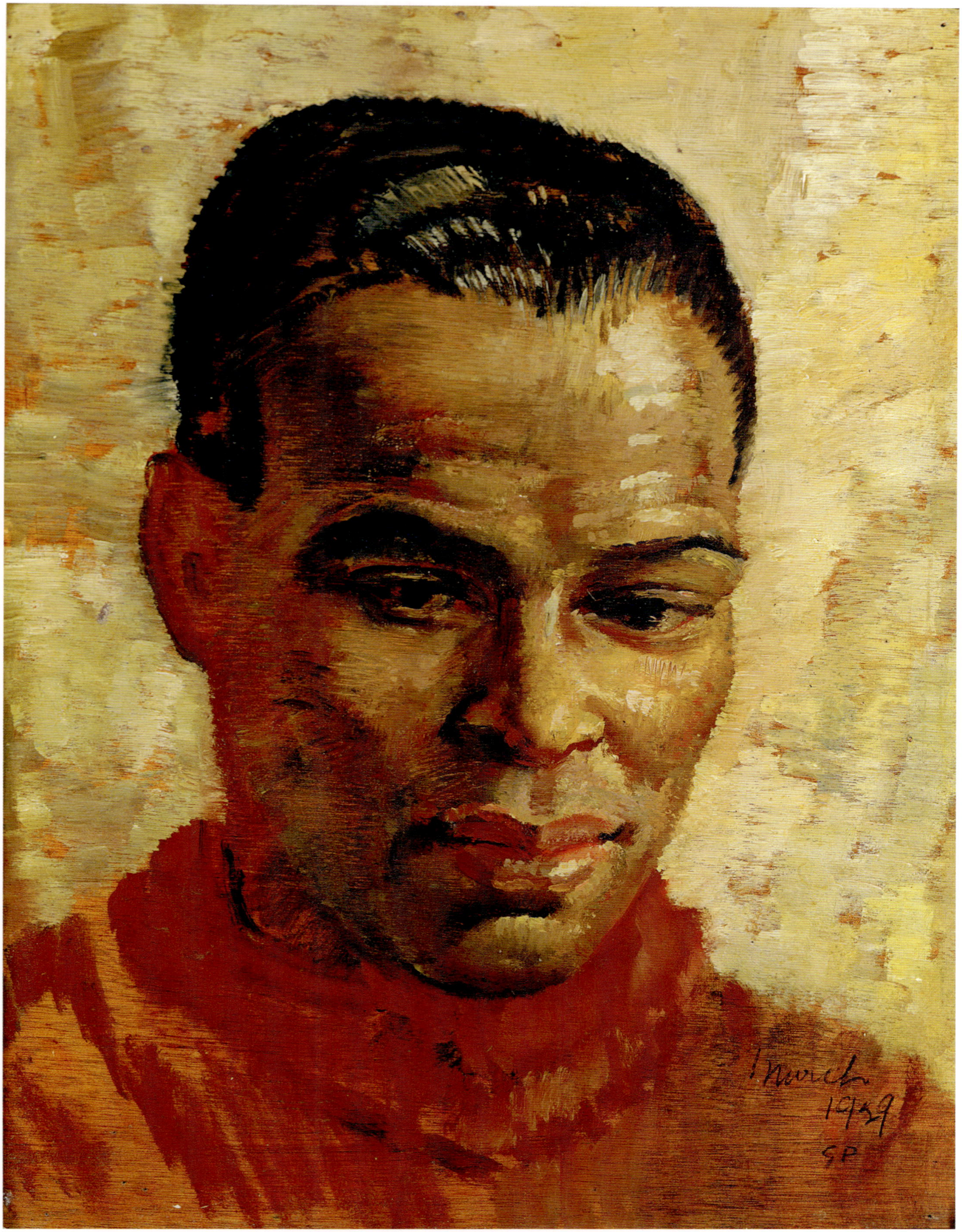
1 March
1929
GP

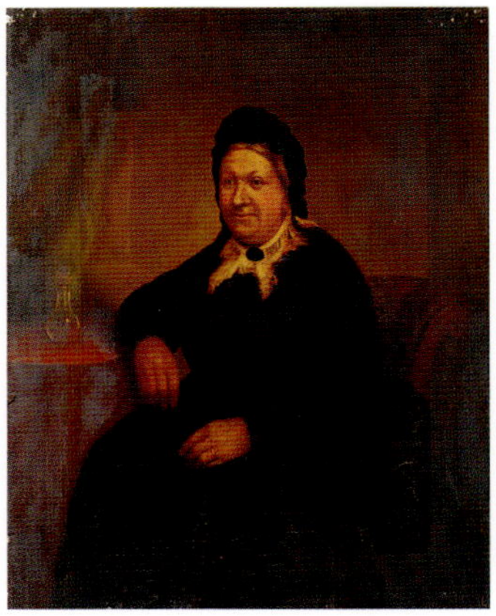

unknown artist
Portrait of a Woman
oil on canvas 76.2 x 63.5
PRSMG : P1961

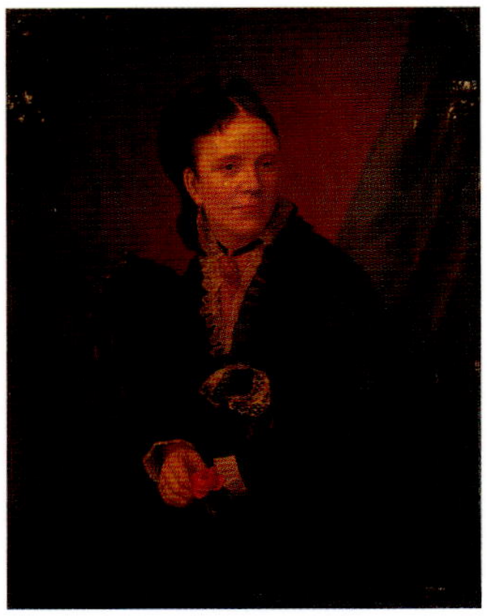

unknown artist
Portrait of a Woman Holding a Rose
oil on canvas 91.5 x 71
PRSMG : P1959

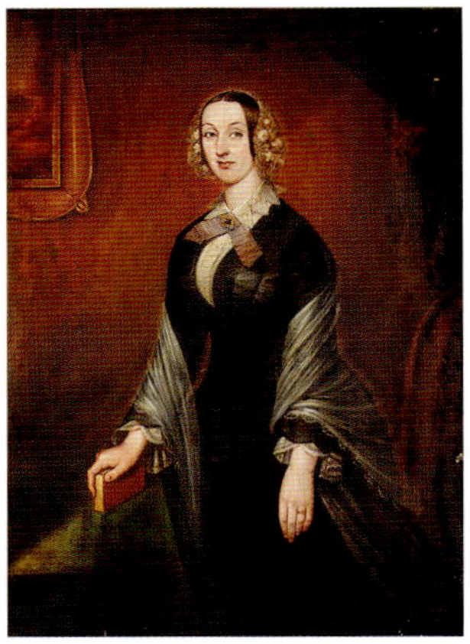

unknown artist
Portrait of a Woman in a Flowered Bonnet
oil on canvas (?) 142 x 112
PRSMG : 2010.167

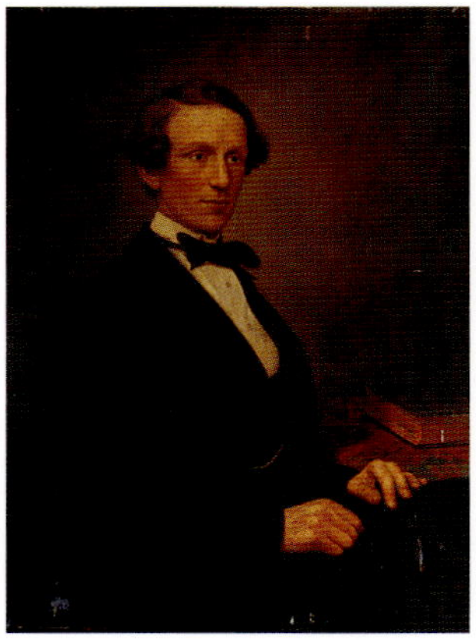

unknown artist
Portrait of a Young Man
oil on canvas 91.5 x 71
PRSMG : P1956

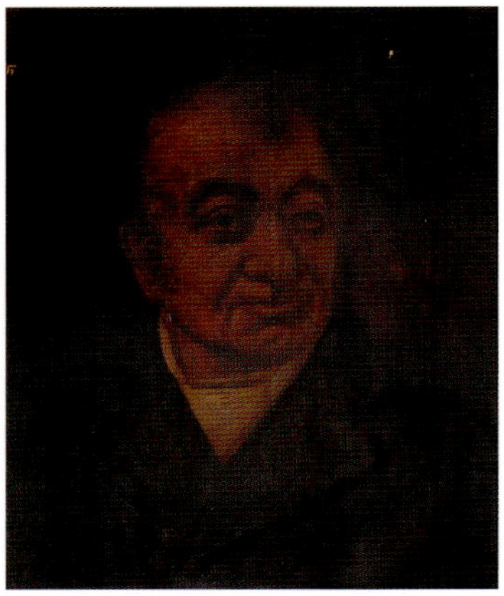

unknown artist
Portrait of an Elderly Man (possibly Joseph Livesey)
oil on canvas 61.5 x 50.5
PRSMG : P1958

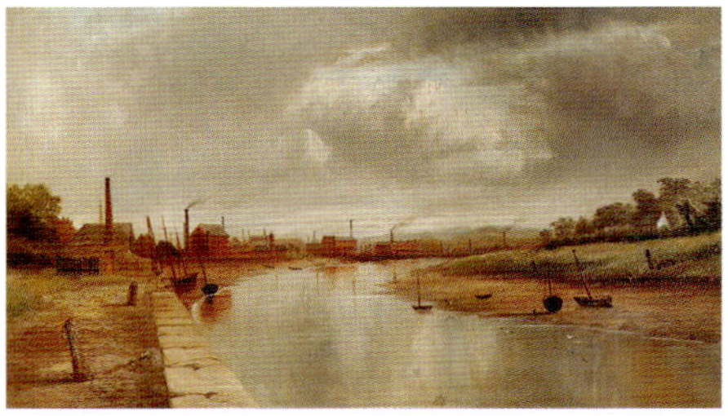

unknown artist
Preston from the Old Quay
oil on canvas 36.5 x 67
PRSMG : P1906

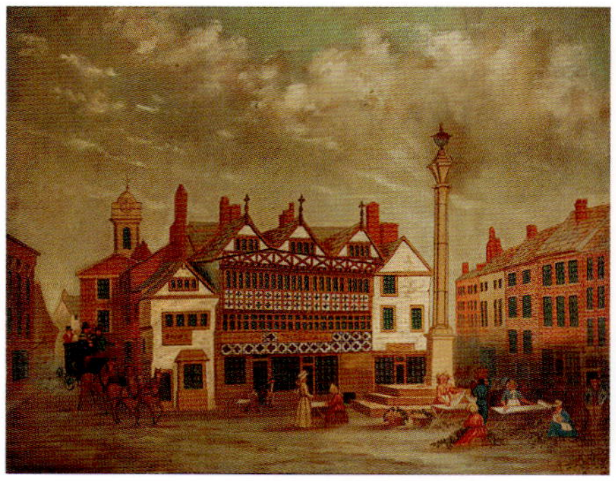

unknown artist
Preston Market Place, 1820
oil on canvas 70 x 92
PRSMG : P1925

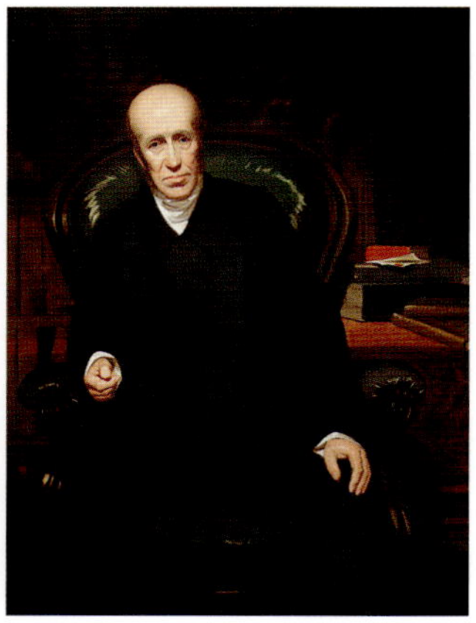

unknown artist
Reverend John Clay
oil on canvas 127 x 101.5
PRSMG : P617

unknown artist
River Landscape
oil on canvas 56.2 x 76.4
PRSMG : P1908

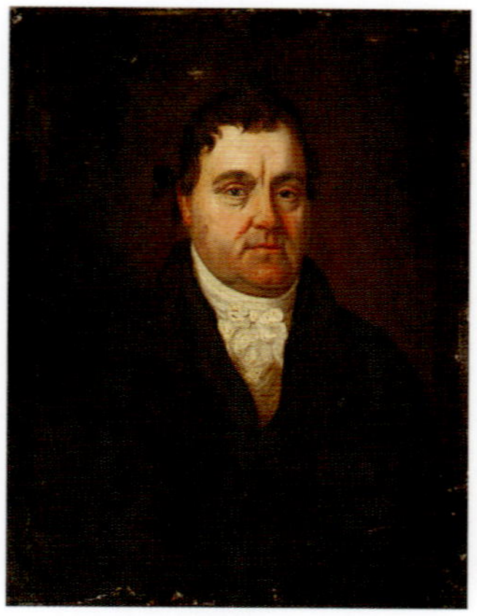

unknown artist
Samuel G. Crane
oil on canvas 76.2 x 63.5
PRSMG : P753

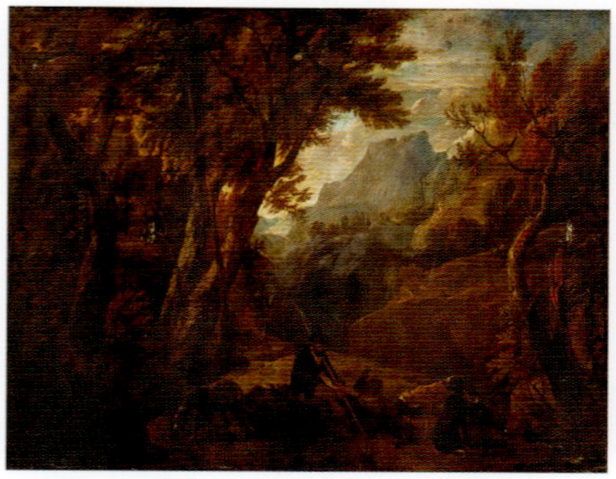

unknown artist
Seated Figure with Three Dogs
oil on canvas 134 x 199.5
PRSMG : P1903

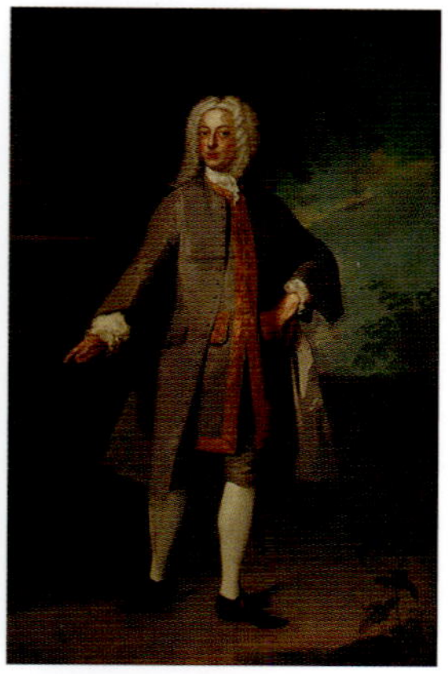

unknown artist
Sir Edward Stanley, Mayor of Preston (1731–1732)
oil on canvas 233.5 x 152.2
PRSMG : P607

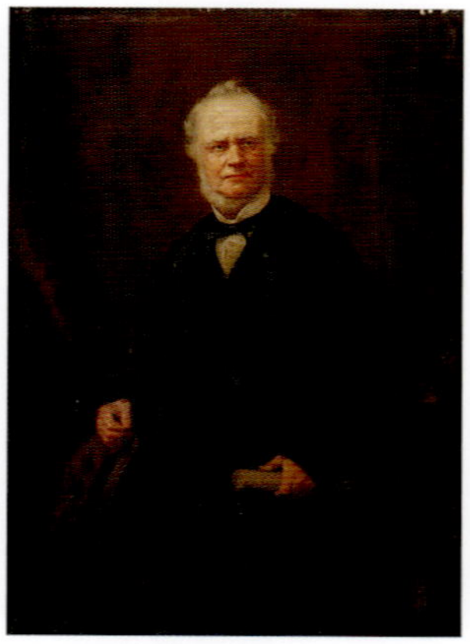

unknown artist
Sir Robert Ascroft
oil on canvas 91.5 x 71
PRSMG : P615

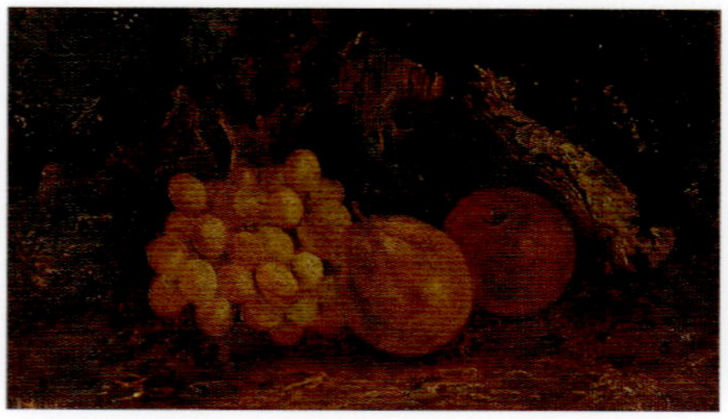

unknown artist
Still Life – Grapes, Apple and Pear
oil on panel 25.5 x 43.3
PRSMG : P1928

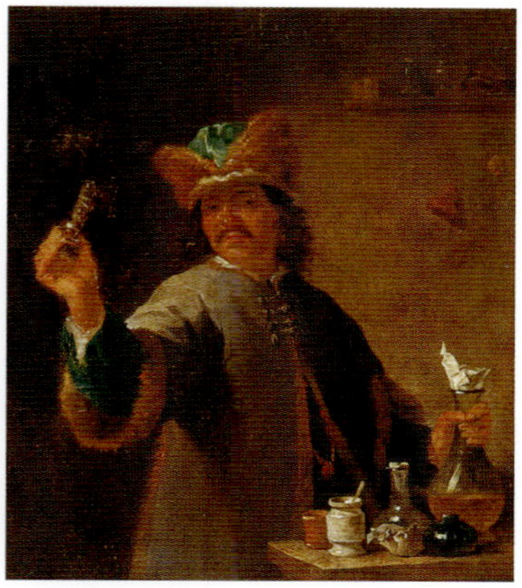

unknown artist
The Alchemist
oil on panel 25.5 x 22.3
PRSMG : P601

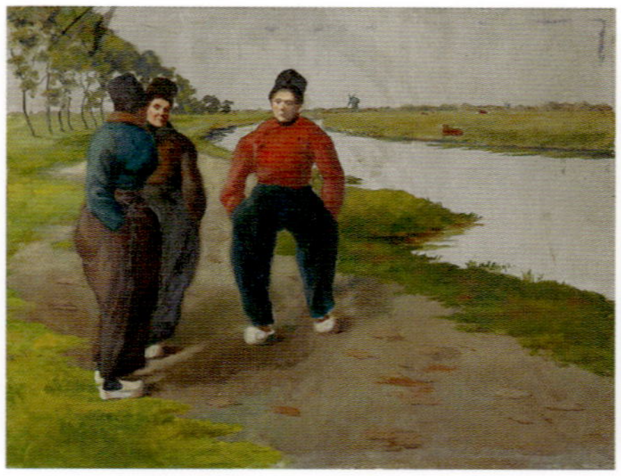

unknown artist
Three Dutch People in National Costume
oil on canvas 34.7 x 44.5
PRSMG : P1932

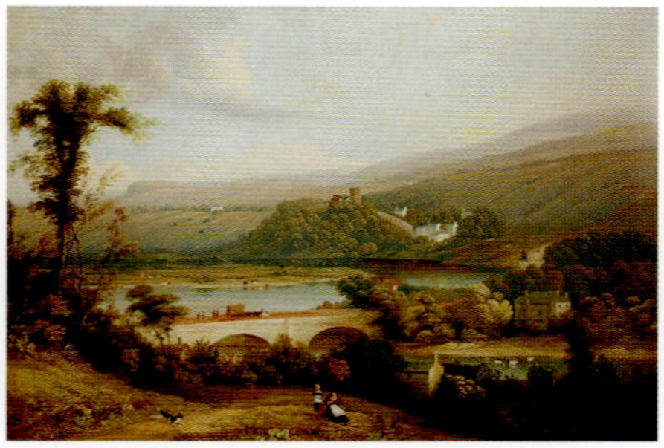

unknown artist
Walton le Dale from Frenchwood
oil on canvas 112 x 134
PRSMG : P1791

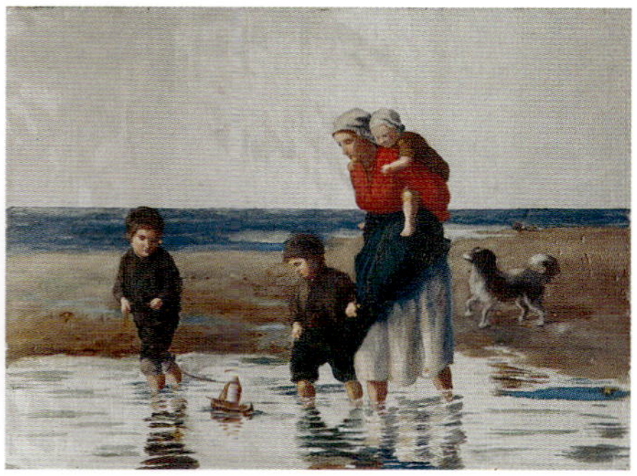

unknown artist
Woman with Three Children and a Dog
oil on silk laid on board 34.7 x 44.5
PRSMG : P1931

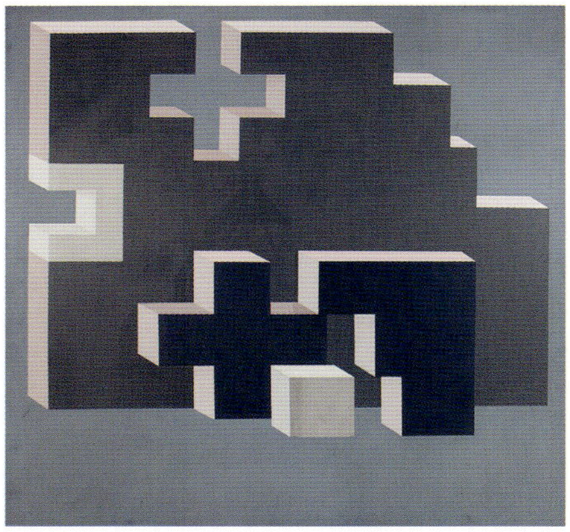

Vaughan, Michael b.1938
Blue Cross and Grey Block 1971
oil on canvas 183 x 183.3
PRSMG : P1785

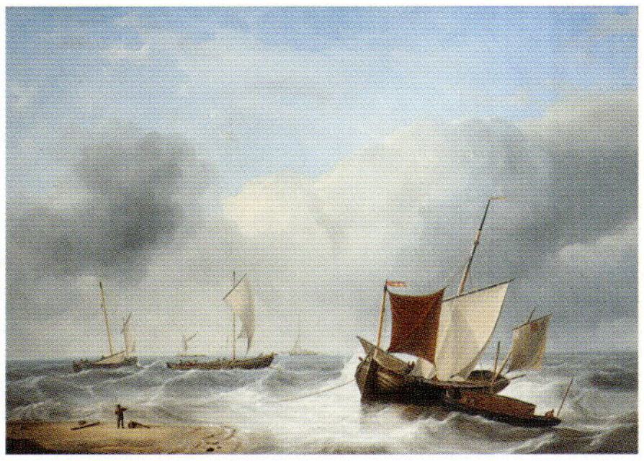

Verboeckhoven, Charles Louis 1802–1889
Coast Scene
oil on canvas 40 x 54.5
PRSMG : P1667

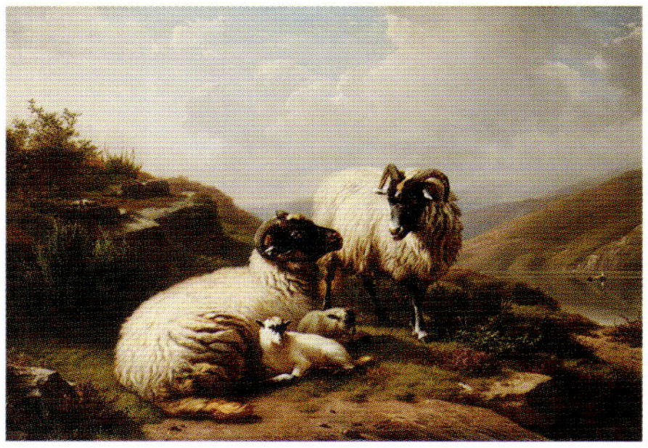

Verboeckhoven, Eugène Joseph 1798–1881
Sheep 1859
oil on canvas 59.4 x 82.2
PRSMG : P1680

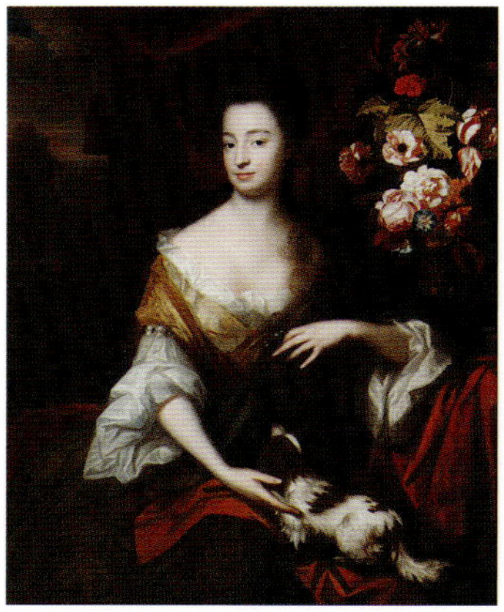

Verelst, Herman 1642–1702
Portrait of a Lady with a Dog 1689
oil on canvas 124.5 x 101.5
PRSMG : P1821

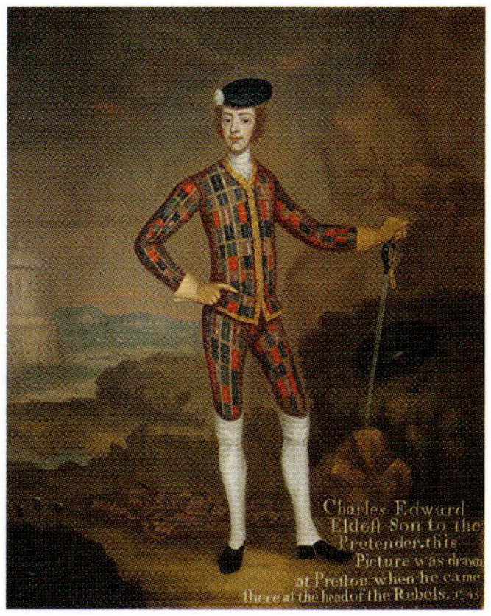

Verelst, Willem (attributed to) 1700–1756
Prince Charles Edward Stuart (1720–1788), Son of the Old Pretender 1745
oil on canvas 76.2 x 61
PRSMG : P1820

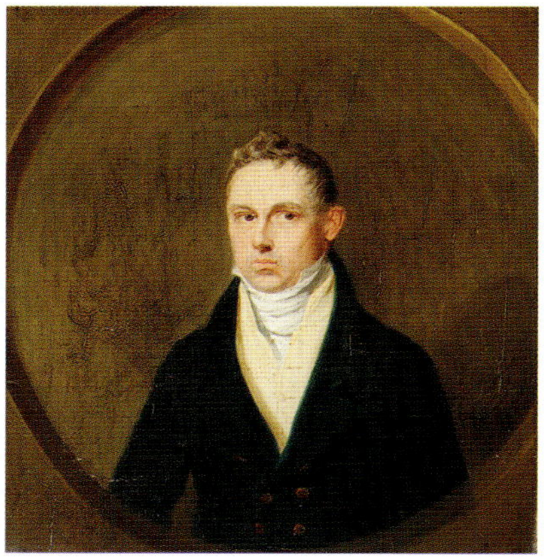

W., T.
Edmund Robert Harris (c.1804–1877)
1825–1835
oil on board 23.3 x 21
PRSMG : LOAN4

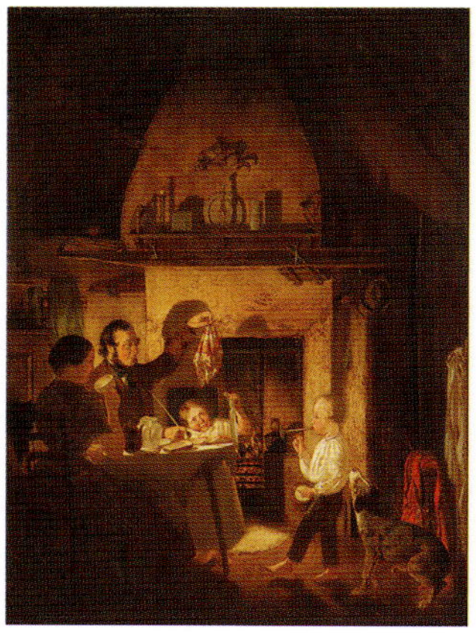

Wade, Thomas 1828–1891
'Come whoam to thi childer an' me' 1850–1857
oil on canvas 63 x 53.3
PRSMG : P633

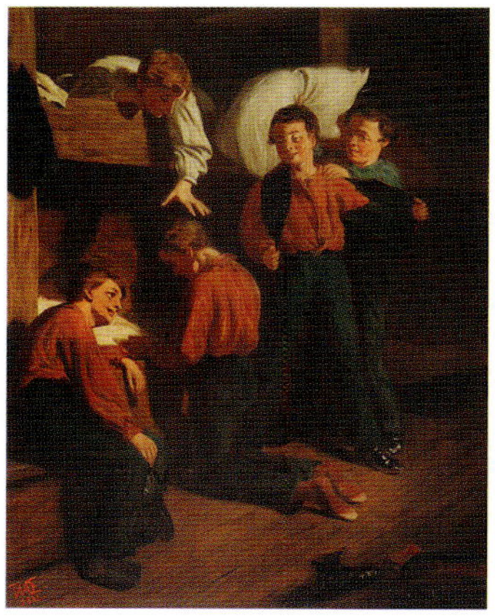

Wade, Thomas 1828–1891
The First Night at Sea 1861
oil on canvas 45.8 x 35.5
PRSMG : P1832

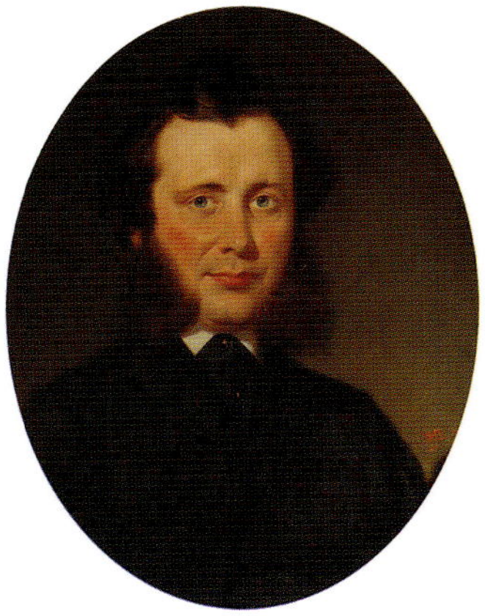

Wade, Thomas 1828–1891
William Edmondson Fell 1861
oil on canvas 61.3 x 51
PRSMG : P1831

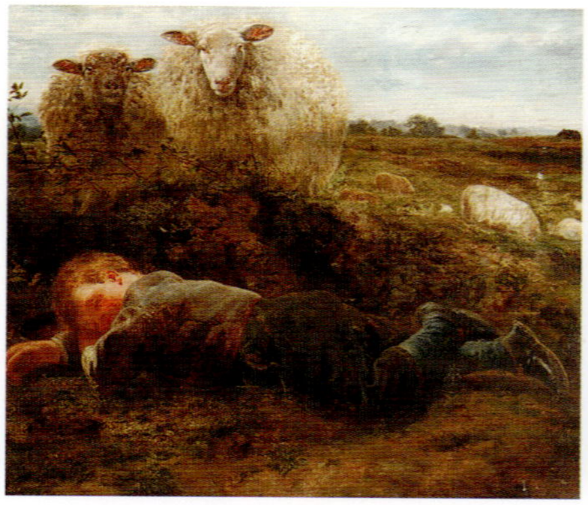

Wade, Thomas 1828–1891
'Where's the boy that minds the sheep?' 1866
oil on canvas 30.5 x 35.5
PRSMG : P642

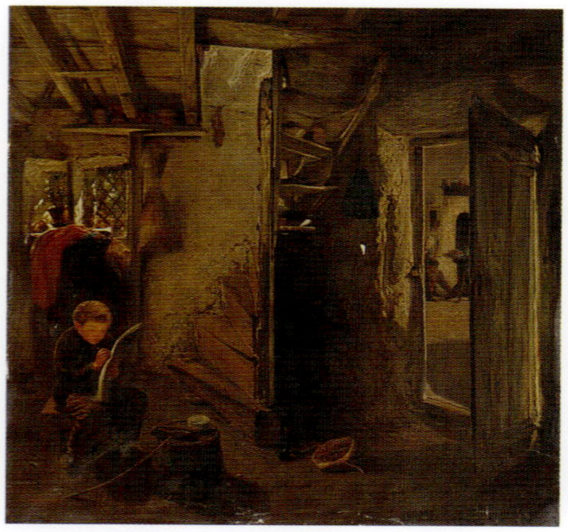

Wade, Thomas 1828–1891
Interior with a Boy Drawing 1866
oil on canvas 52 x 51
PRSMG : P651

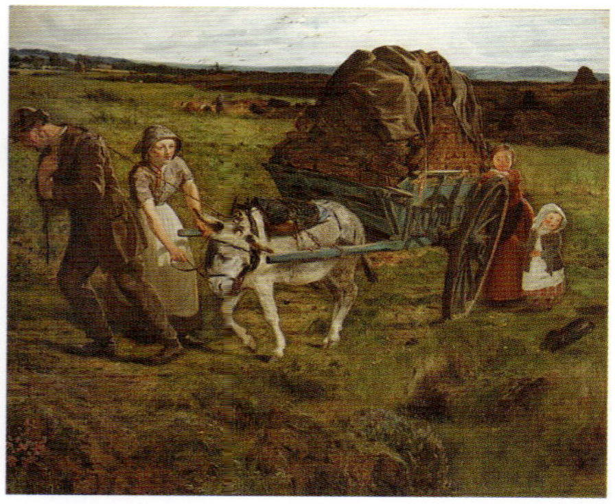

Wade, Thomas 1828–1891
Carting Turf from Farington Moss 1866–1868
oil on canvas 76 5 x 91
PRSMG : P656

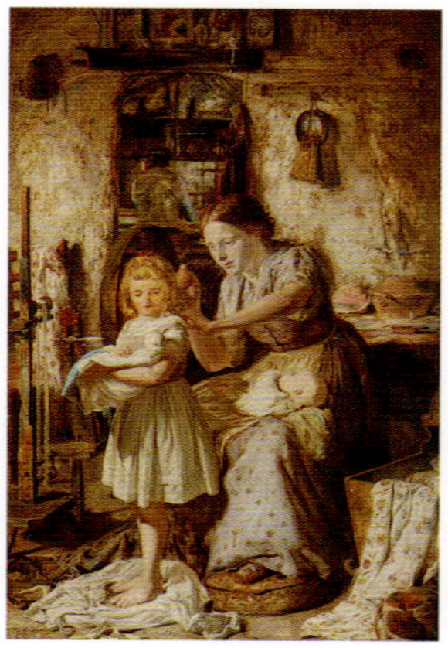

Wade, Thomas 1828–1891
A Stitch in Time 1868
oil on panel 53.3 x 35.5
PRSMG : P813

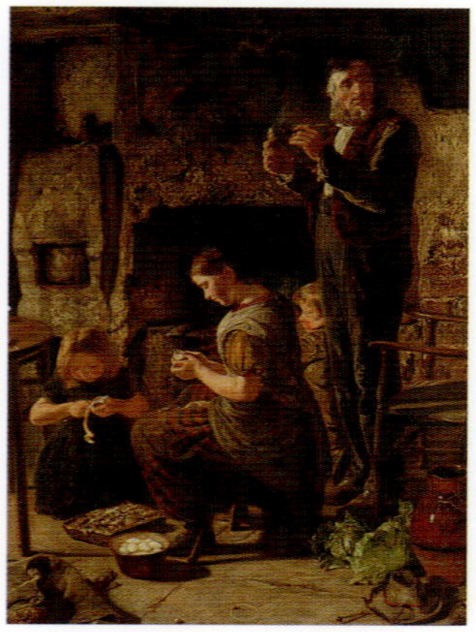

Wade, Thomas 1828–1891
The Poacher's Home 1868
oil on canvas 42.8 x 33.5
PRSMG : P854

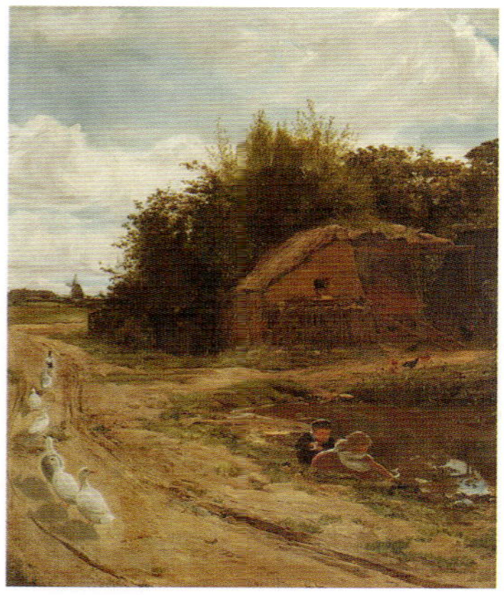

Wade, Thomas 1828–1891
Sailing Feathers 1870
oil on canvas 79.3 x 65
PRSMG : P771

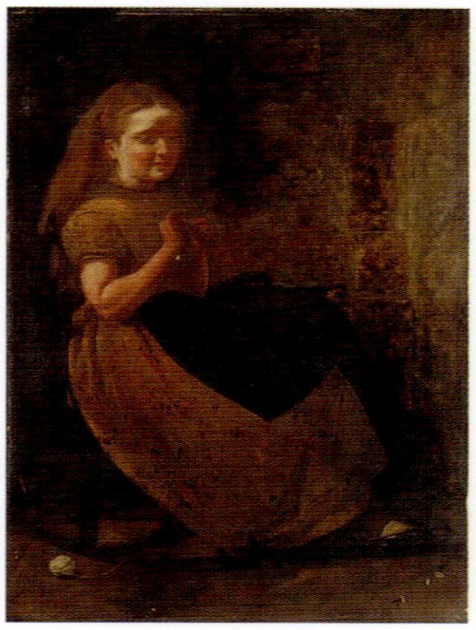

Wade, Thomas 1828–1891
A Girl Knitting 1872
oil on canvas 35.5 x 25.5
PRSMG : P639

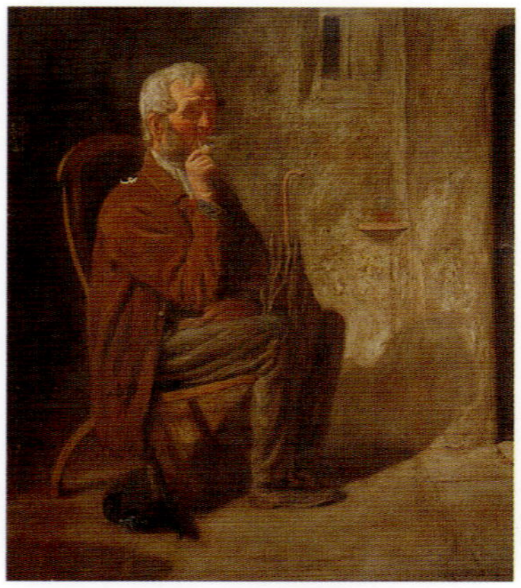

Wade, Thomas 1828–1891
Waiting 1881
oil on canvas 35.5 x 30.5
PRSMG : P636

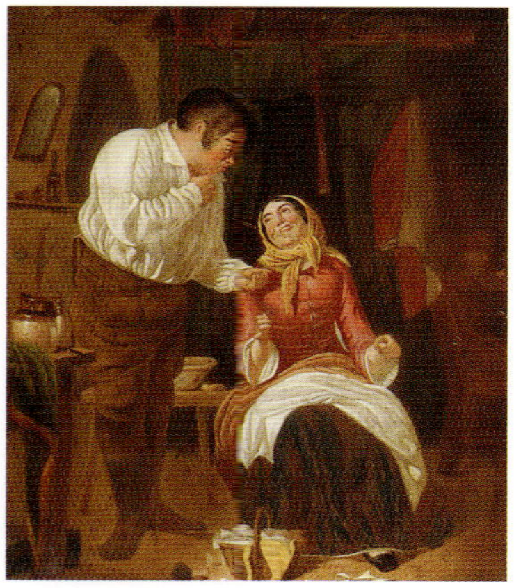

Wade, Thomas 1828–1891
'Can you see any green in my eye?'
oil on canvas 35.5 x 29.7
PRSMG : P855

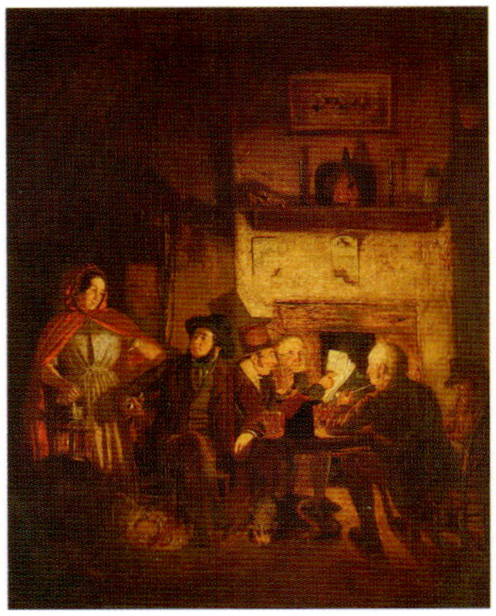

Wade, Thomas 1828–1891
'Come whoam to thi childer an' me'
oil on canvas 67.3 x 55.7
PRSMG : P634

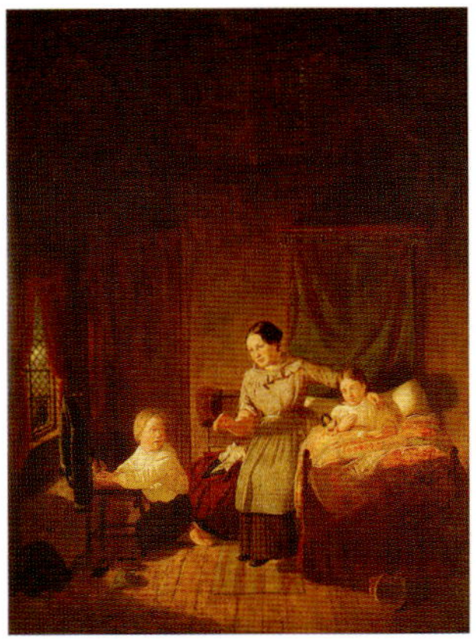

Wade, Thomas 1828–1891
'Come whoam to thi childer an' me'
oil on canvas 64 x 53.3
PRSMG : P635

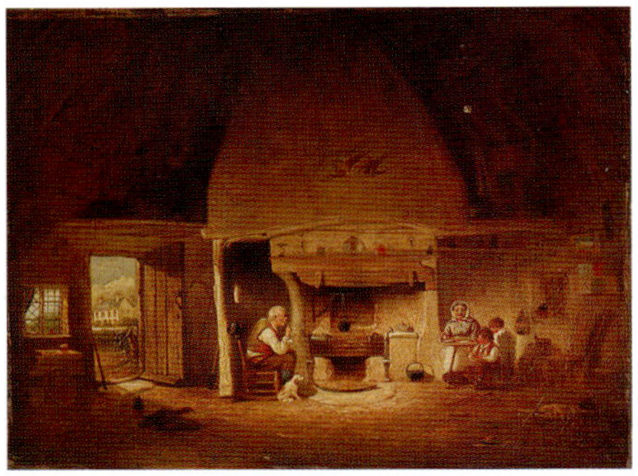

Wade, Thomas 1828–1891
Cottage Interior
oil on canvas 38 x 48.2
PRSMG : P643

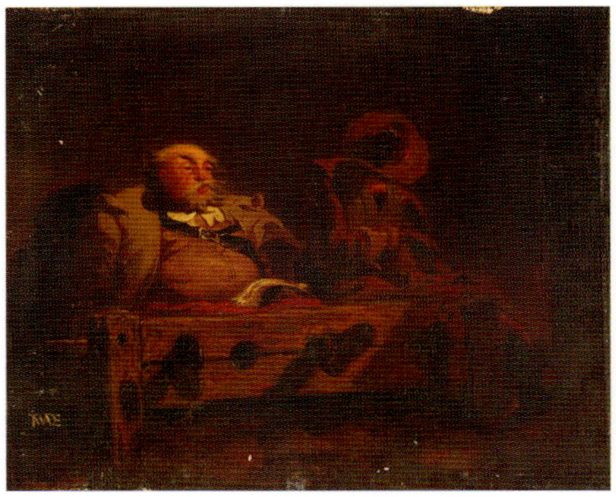

Wade, Thomas 1828–1891
Falstaff
oil on canvas 30.4 x 37.7
PRSMG : P1963

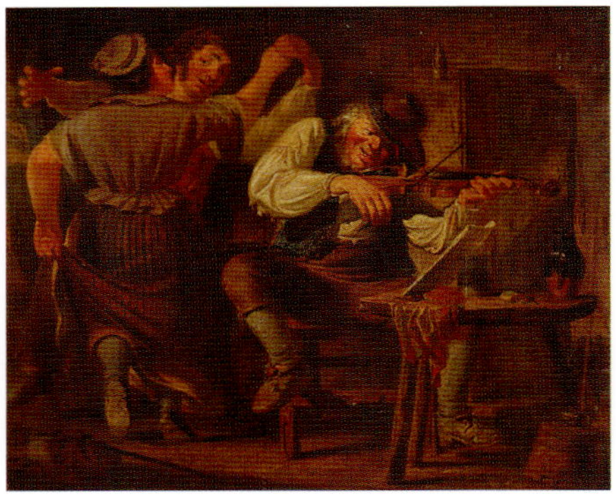

Wade, Thomas 1828–1891
Fiddler and Dancing Peasants
oil on panel 30 x 35.5
PRSMG : P1591

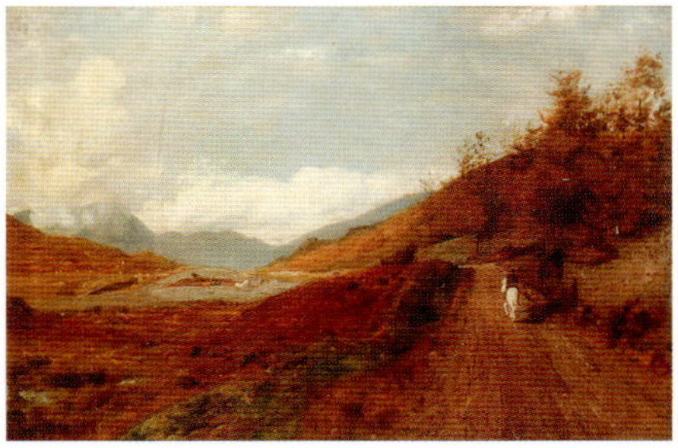

Wade, Thomas 1828–1891
Man on a White Horse in Mountain Scenery
oil on canvas 47.5 x 80.8
PRSMG : P655

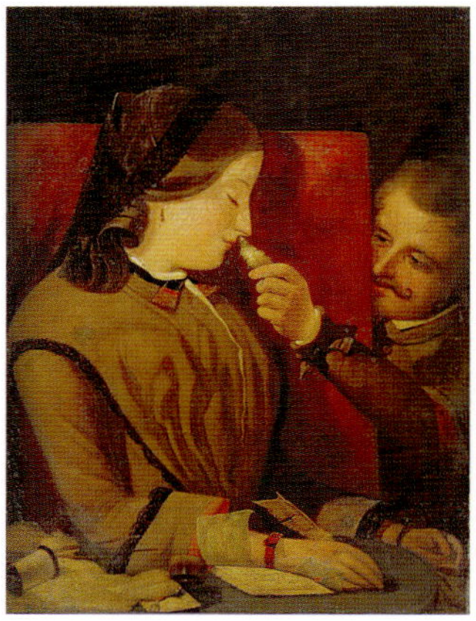

Wade, Thomas 1828–1891
Man Tickling a Woman's Nose with a Feather
oil on canvas 45 x 34
PRSMG : P1964

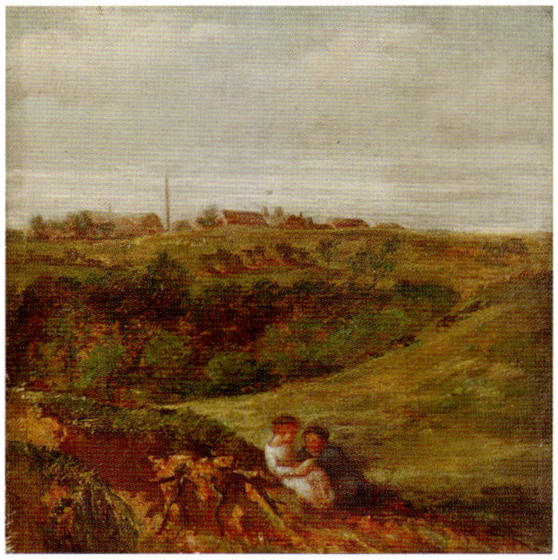

Wade, Thomas 1828–1891
Rustic Lovers on the Outskirts of a Town
oil on canvas 22.8 x 21.5
PRSMG : P644

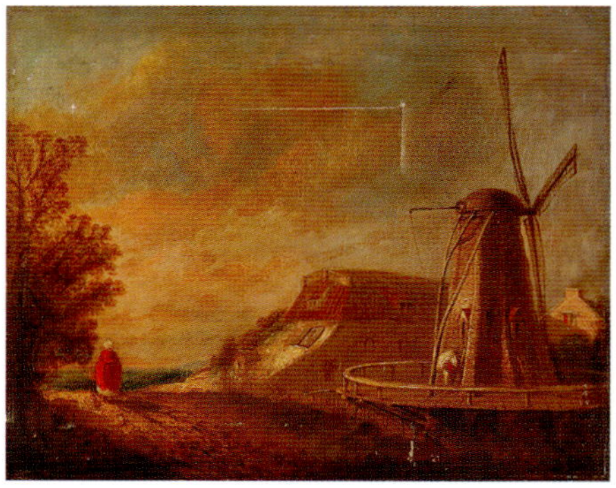

Wade, Thomas 1828–1891
The Old Mill, Kirkham
oil on canvas 33 x 43
PRSMG : P638

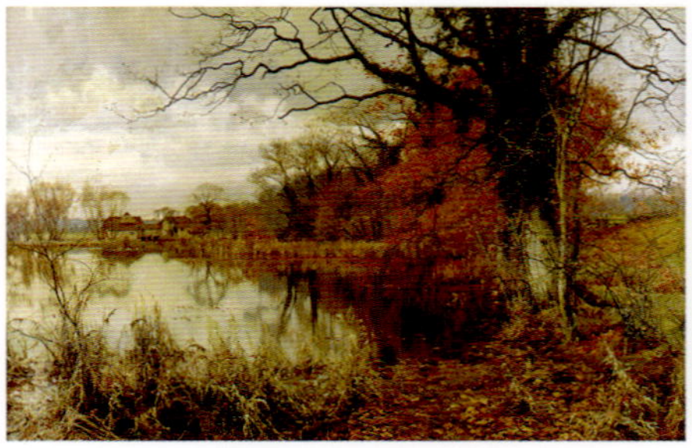

Waite, Edward Wilkins 1854–1924
'The mellow year is hastening to its close' 1896
oil on canvas 122 x 183
PRSMG : P662

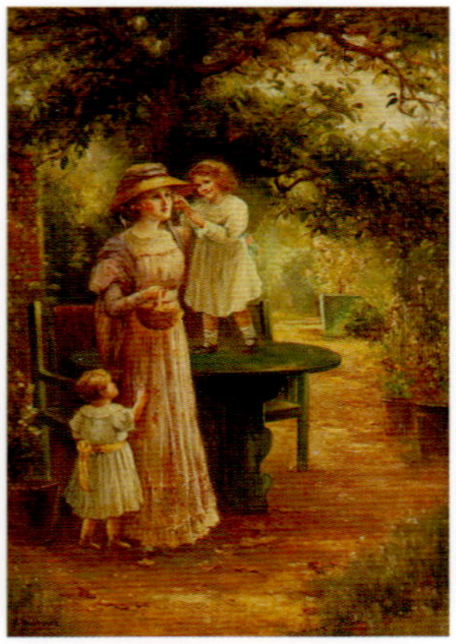

Walbourne, Ernest 1872–1927
Children's Delight
oil on canvas 76.2 x 50.6
PRSMG : P837

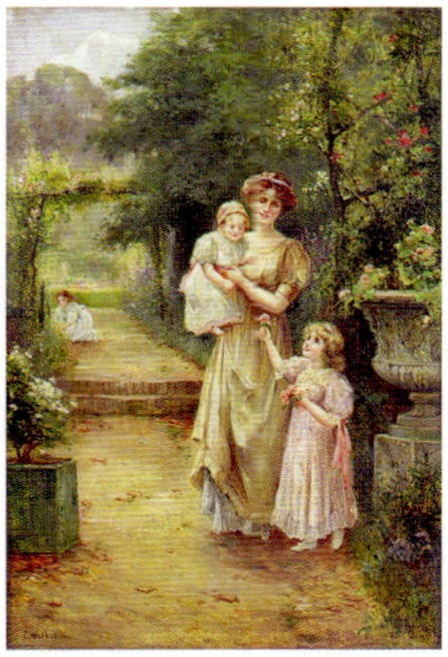

Walbourne, Ernest 1872–1927
One for Baby
oil on canvas 76.2 x 50.6
PRSMG : P838

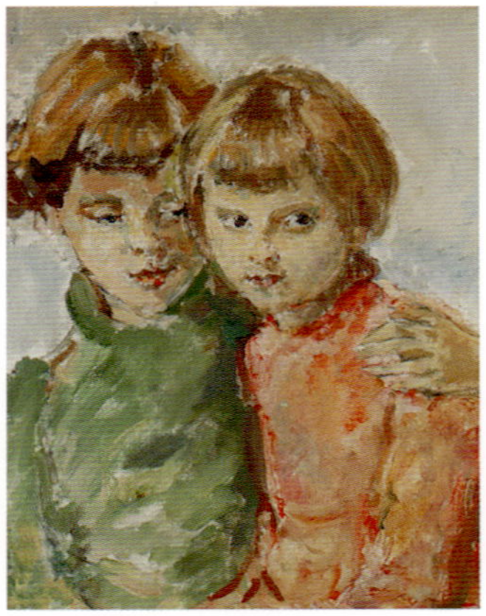

Walker, Ethel 1861–1951
Iris and Kathleen 1900–1950
oil on canvas 51.6 x 40.9
PRSMG : P1470

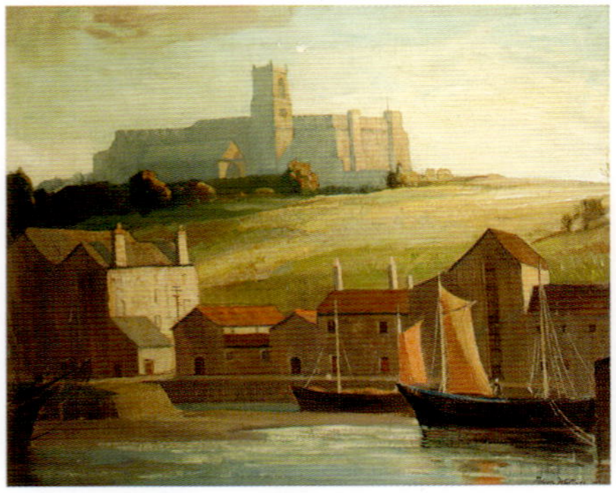

Wallace, Robin 1879–1952
Lancaster Quay 1930
oil on canvas 51.3 x 61
PRSMG : P815

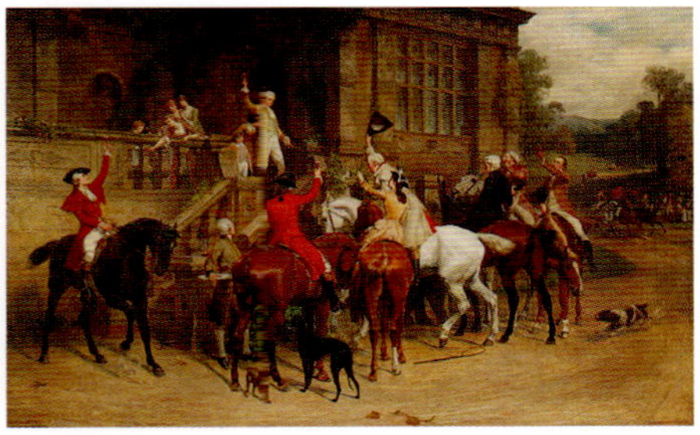

Waller, Samuel Edmund 1850–1903
One and Twenty 1891
oil on canvas 162.5 x 259
PRSMG : P739

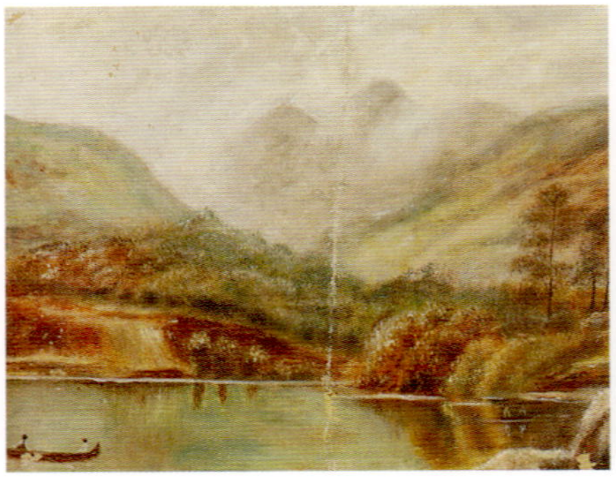

Ward
Lake with Canoists
oil on canvas (?) 18 x 23 (E)
PRSMG : P2261.2

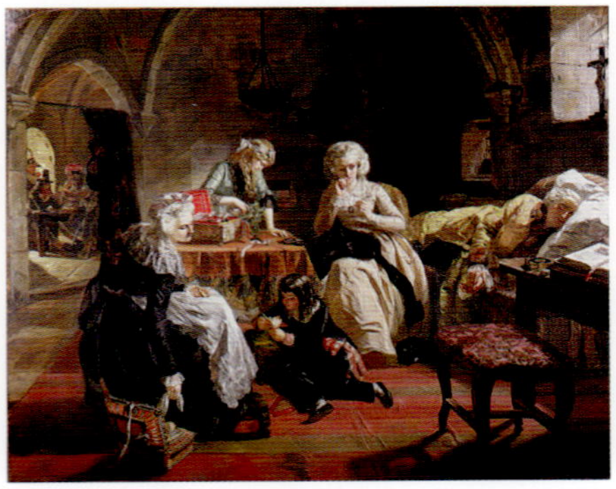

Ward, Edward Matthew 1816–1879
The Royal Family of France in the Prison of the Temple 1851
oil on canvas 103.2 x 128
PRSMG : P667

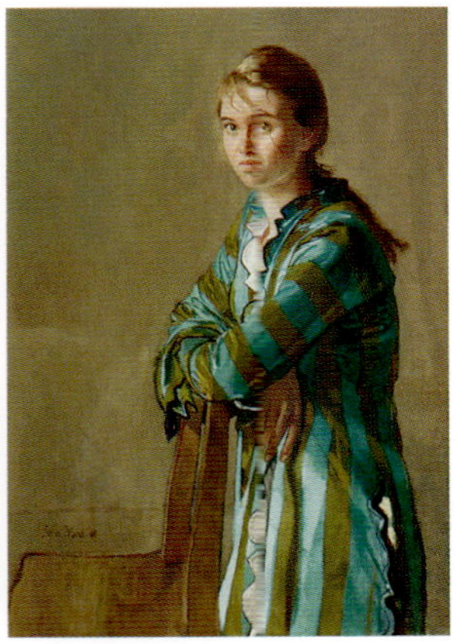

Ward, John Stanton 1917–2007
Linda 1968
oil on canvas 91.5 x 71.3
PRSMG : P1748

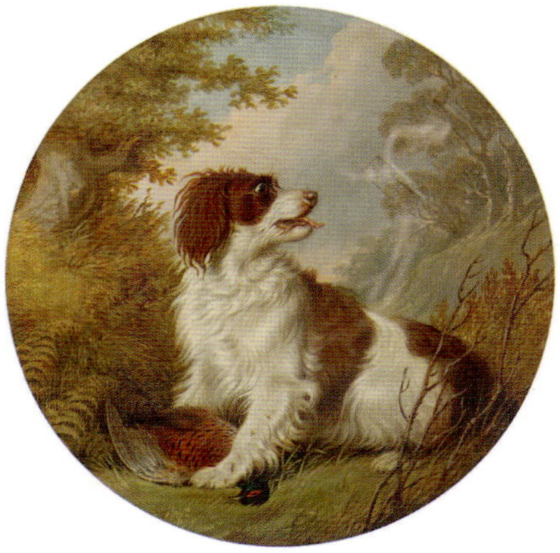

Ward, Martin Theodore 1799–1874
Dog and Game Bird
oil on canvas 26.5 x 26.5
PRSMG : P1536

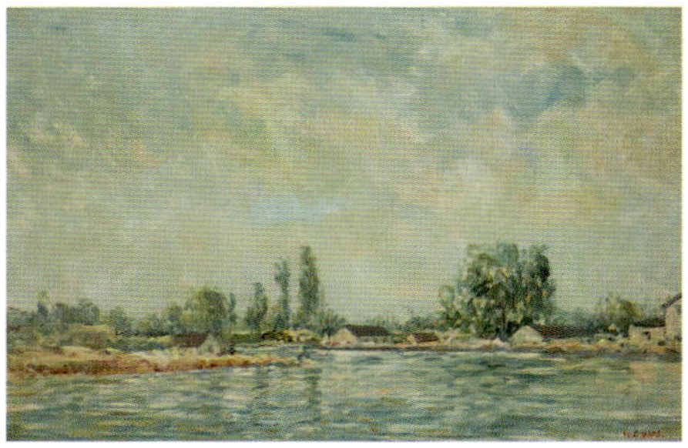

Ware, William 1915–1997
Landscape on the Loire
oil on canvas 50.8 x 76.3
PRSMG : P1238

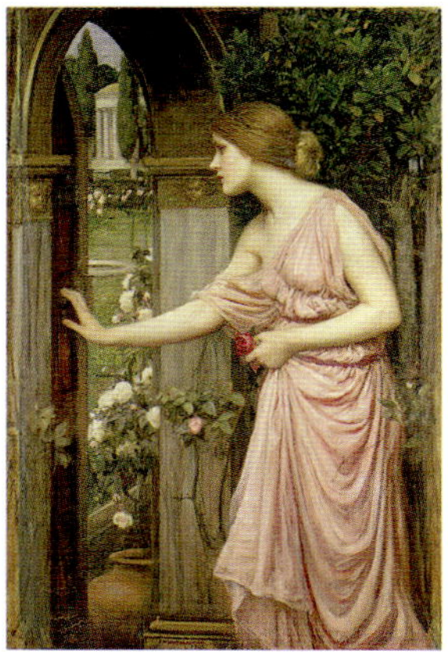

Waterhouse, John William 1849–1917
Psyche Entering Cupid's Garden 1903
oil on canvas 143 x 105
PRSMG : P773

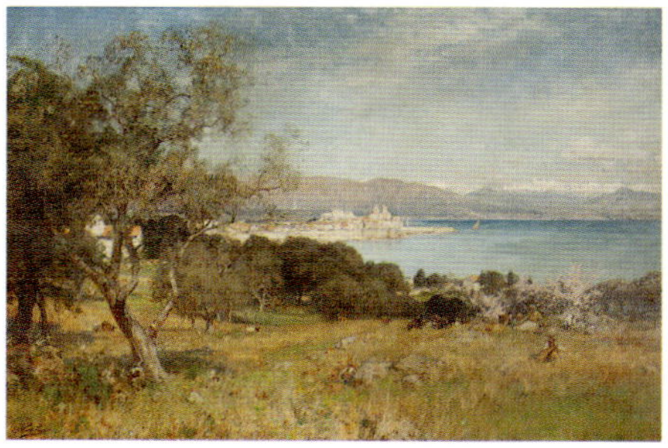

Waterlow, Ernest Albert 1850–1919
La Cote d'Azur 1899
oil on canvas 122 x 183
PRSMG : P772

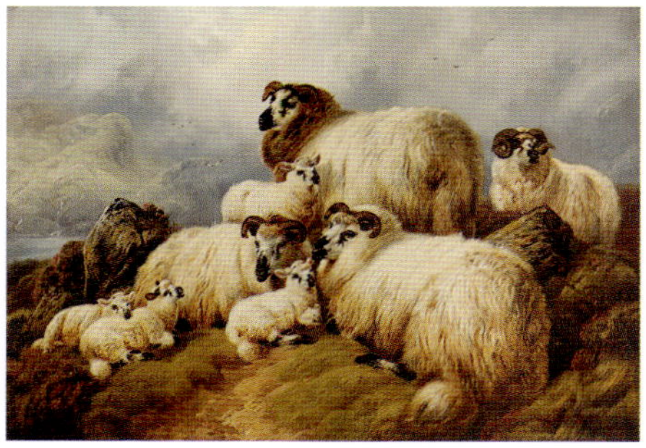

Watson, Charles John 1846–1927
Sheep 1884
oil on canvas 61 x 91.5
PRSMG : P1016

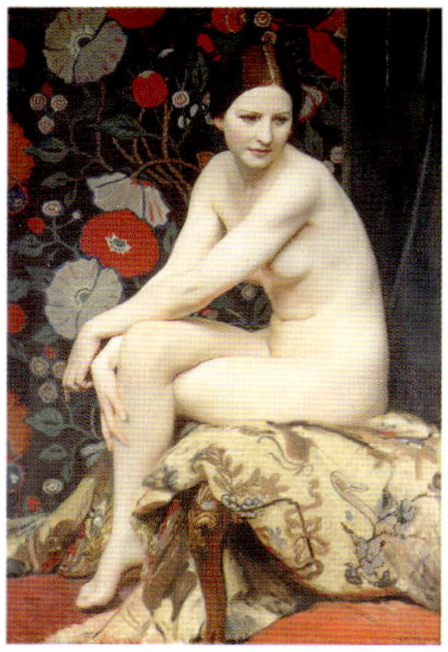

Watson, George Spencer 1869–1934
Nude 1927
oil on canvas 117 x 81.5
PRSMG : P670

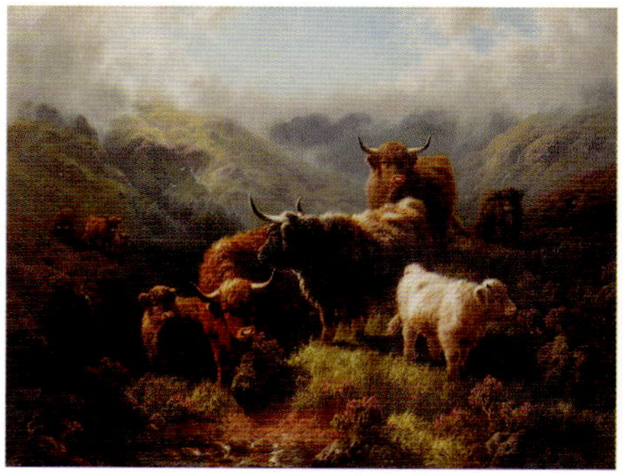

Watson, Sydney Robert 1892–1971
Highland Cattle – Loch Long, Argyllshire 1909
oil on canvas 35.7 x 48.8
PRSMG : P1413

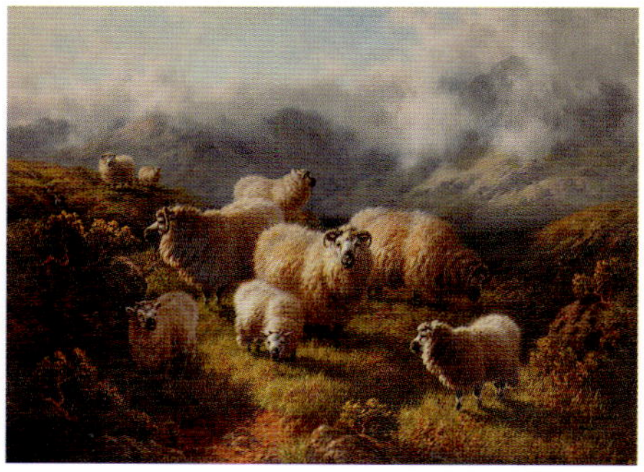

Watson, Sydney Robert 1892–1971
Highland Sheep 1909
oil on canvas 35.7 x 48.5
PRSMG : P1414

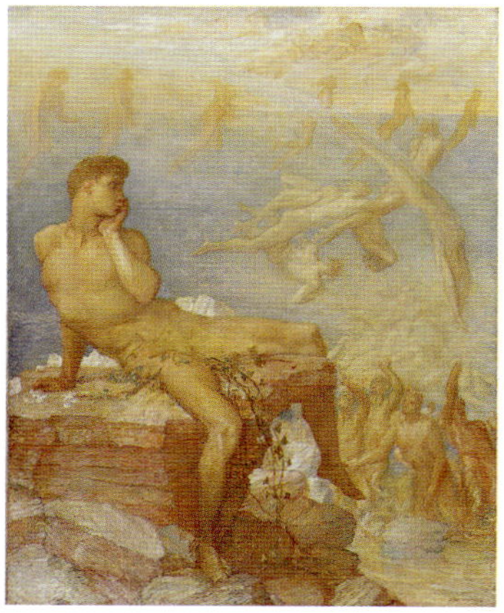

Watts, George Frederick 1817–1904
The Genius of Greek Poetry 1850–1900
oil on canvas 66 x 53.3
PRSMG : P671

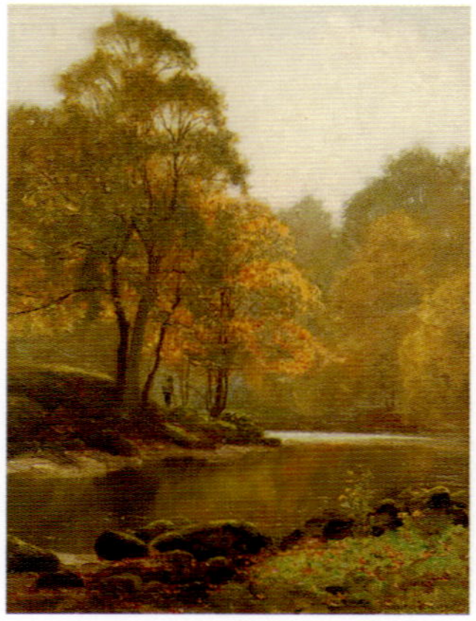

Watts, James Thomas 1853–1930
Autumn Evening on the Wharfe
oil on canvas 30.5 x 23
PRSMG : P1500

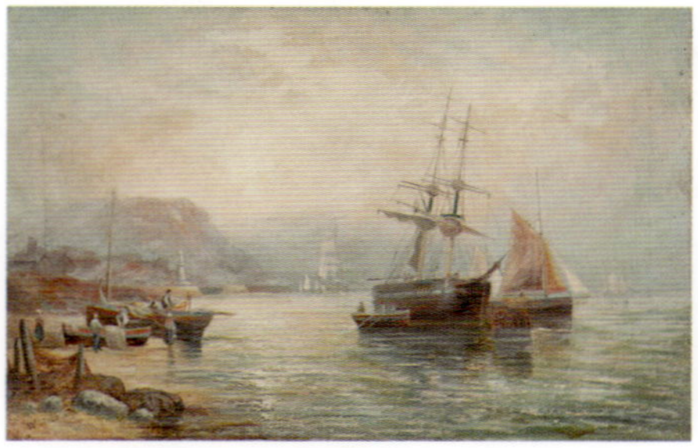

Webb, William Edward 1862–1903
The Jetty at Deal
oil on canvas 40.5 x 61
PRSMG : P2235

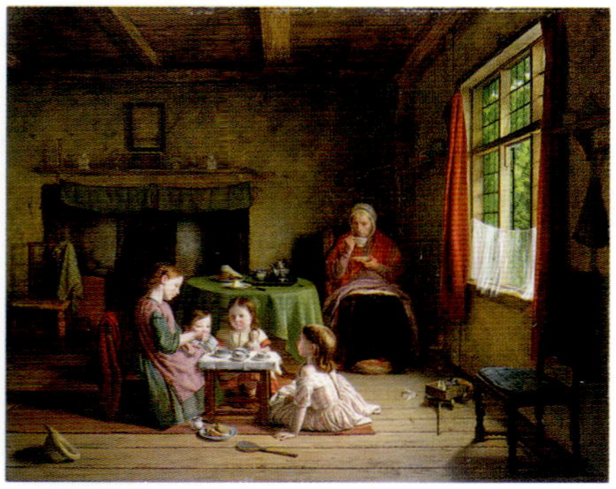

Webster, Thomas George 1800–1886
A Tea Party 1862
oil on panel 50.8 x 61
PRSMG : P672

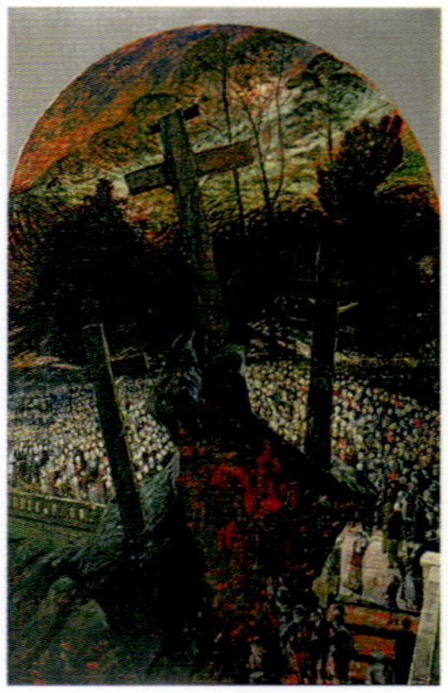

Weight, Carel Victor Morlais 1908–1997
Crucifixion 1959
oil on hardboard 244 x 152.5
PRSMG : P1617

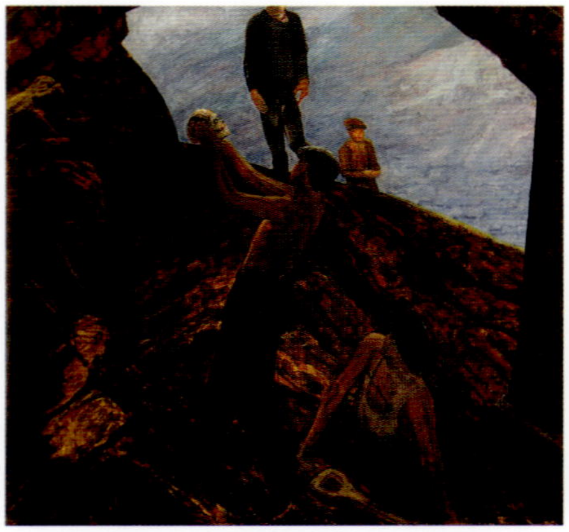

Weight, Carel Victor Morlais 1908–1997
Hamlet 1962
oil on canvas 210 x 200
PRSMG : P2287

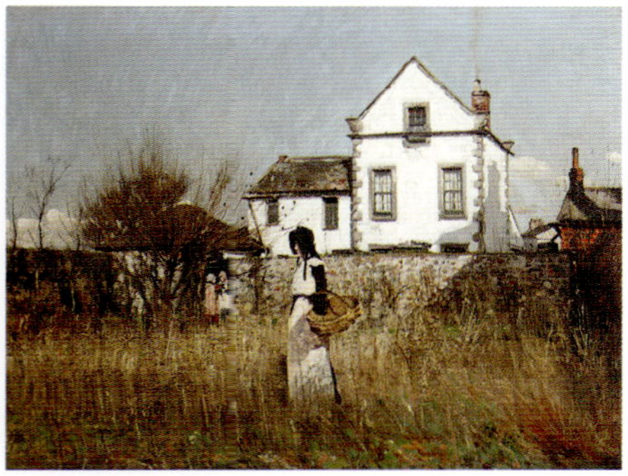

Wells, William Page Atkinson 1872–1923
Landscape with a White House c.1900
oil on canvas 61 x 91.5
PRSMG : P675

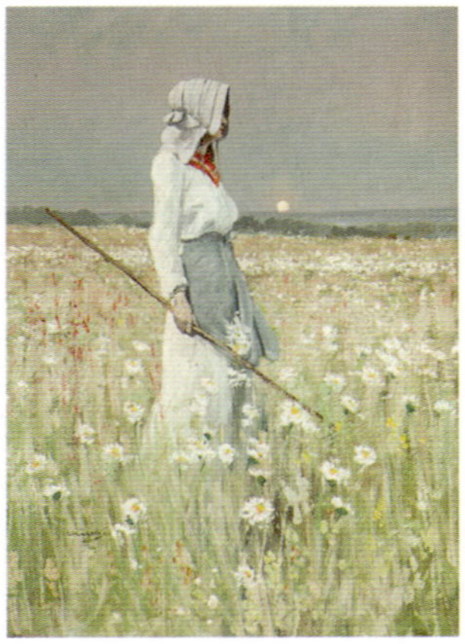

Wells, William Page Atkinson 1872–1923
Landscape – Girl in a Meadow 1905
oil on canvas 61 x 45.7
PRSMG : P1463

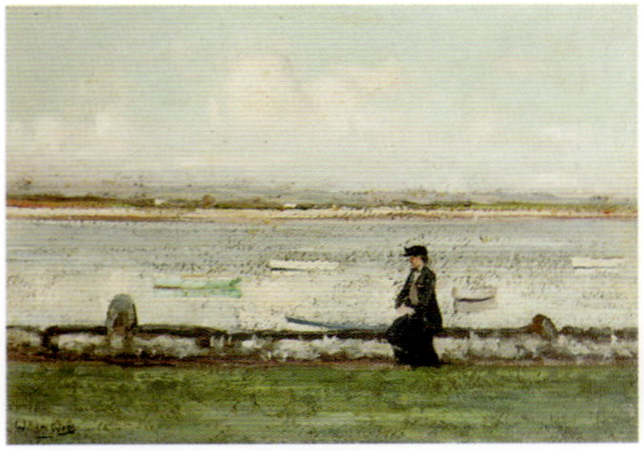

Wells, William Page Atkinson 1872–1923
The Lune at Sunderland Point c.1910
oil on panel 25.5 x 35.5
PRSMG : P1127

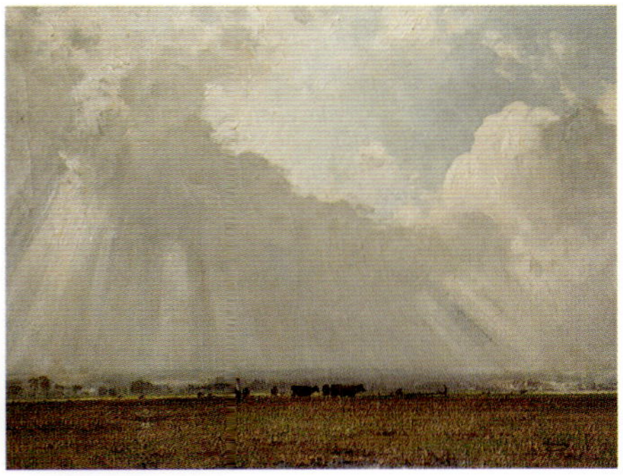

Wells, William Page Atkinson 1872–1923
Beneath the Haldon Hills, Devon 1923
oil on canvas 80 x 100.5
PRSMG : P674

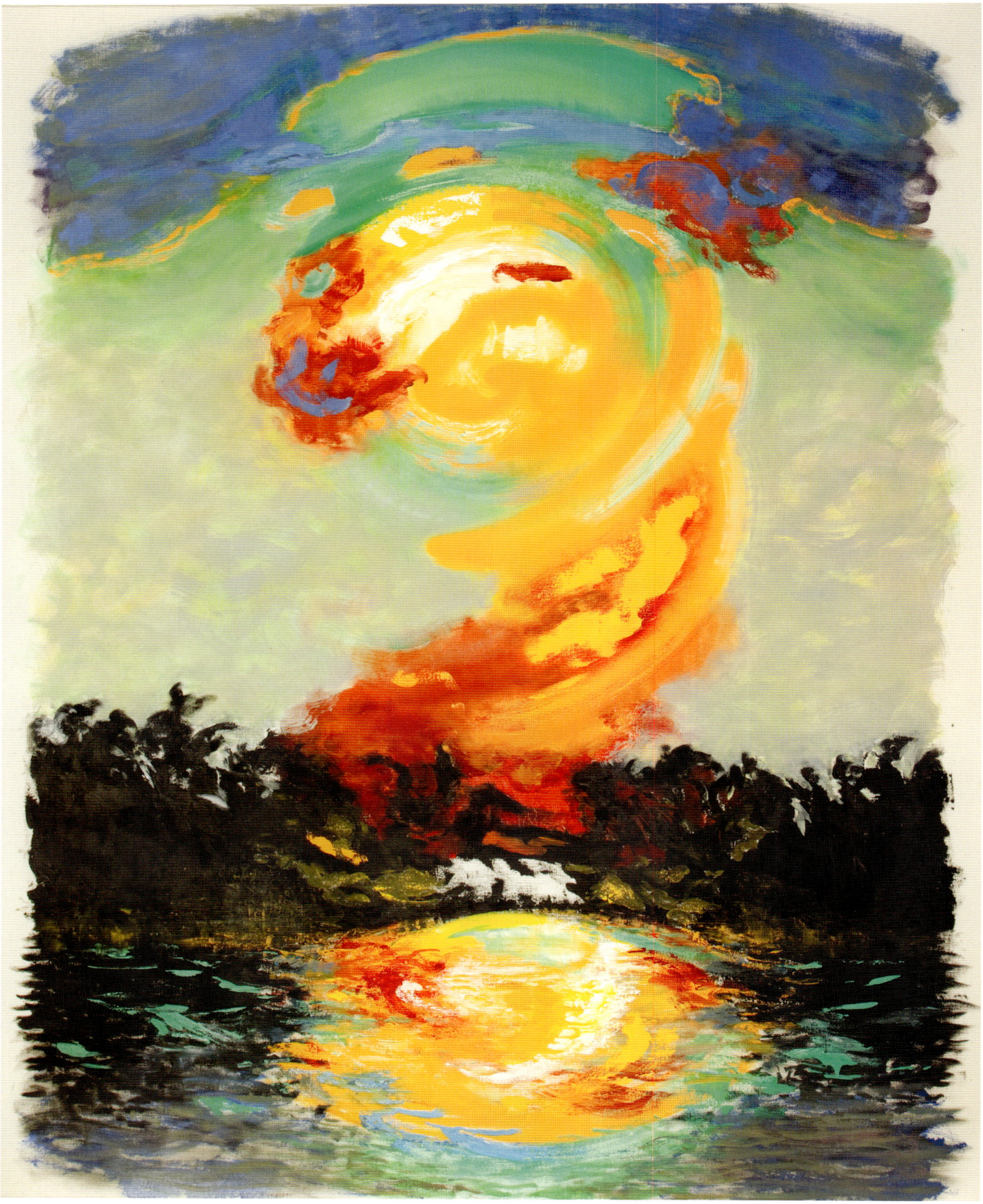

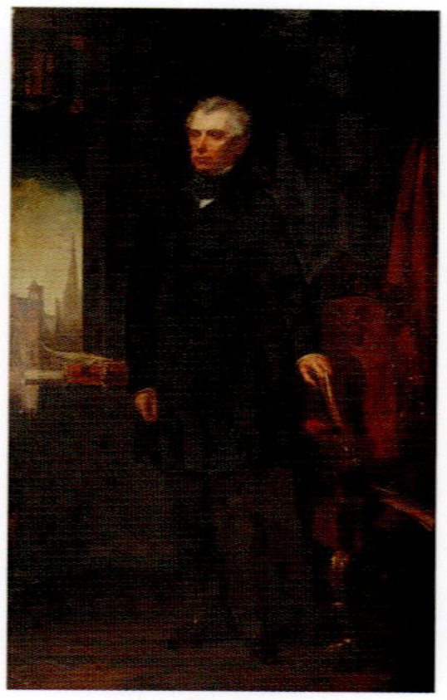

Westcott, Philip 1815–1878
Robert Towneley Parker (1793–1879), MP for Preston 1857
oil on canvas 238.4 x 147.6
PRSMG : P747

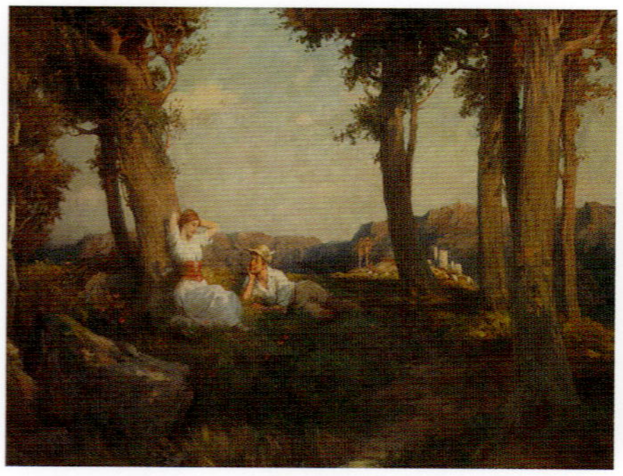

Wetherbee, George Faulkner 1851–1920
'Forever wilt thou love and she be fair' 1907
oil on canvas 80 x 126
PRSMG : P678

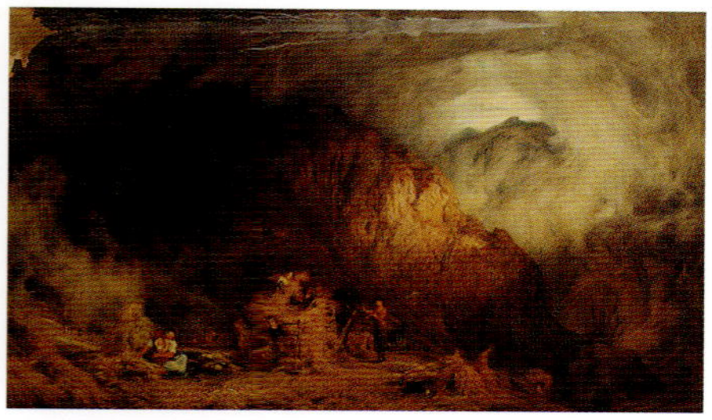

Whaite, Henry Clarence 1828–1912
The Coming Storm
oil on canvas 101 x 187
PRSMG : P679

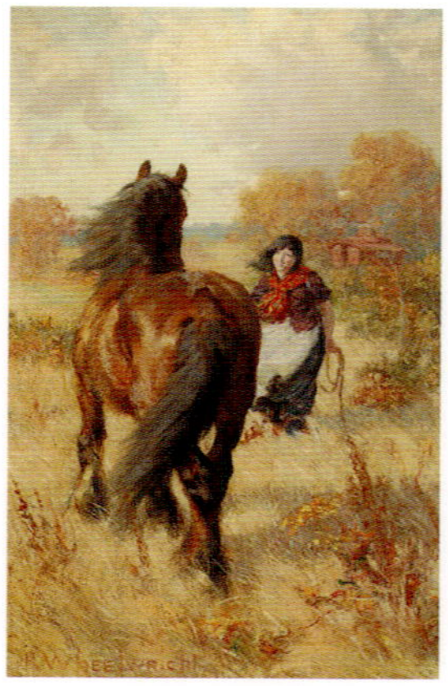

Wheelwright, Rowland 1870–1955
'Trust her not, she is fooling thee' 1898
oil on canvas 127 x 76.2
PRSMG : P680

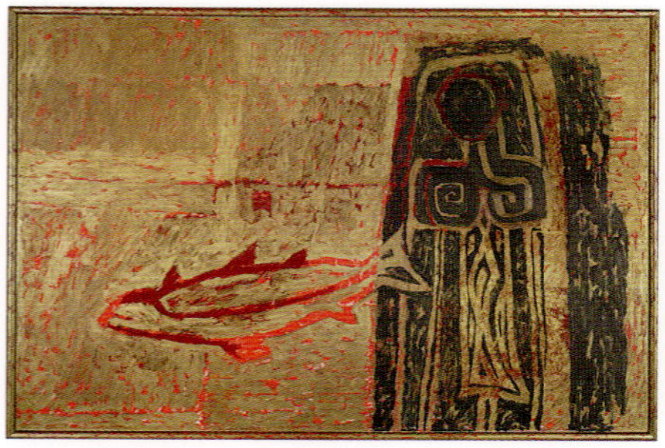

Whiteford, Kate b.1952
Lustra 1984
oil on canvas 200 x 300
PRSMG : P1850

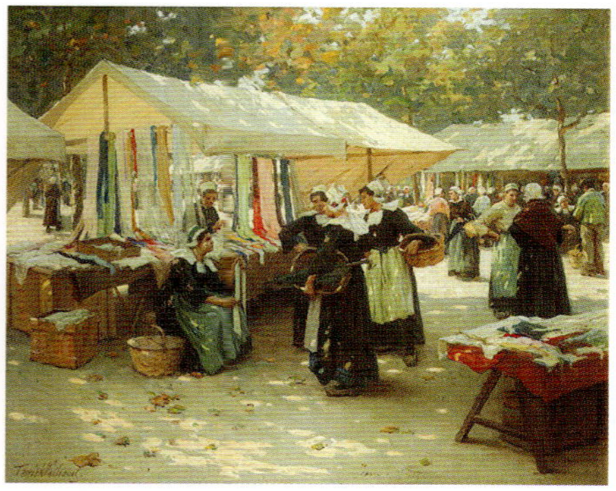

Williams, Terrick John 1860–1936
Ribbons and Laces 1907
oil on canvas 87.3 x 113.5
PRSMG : P686

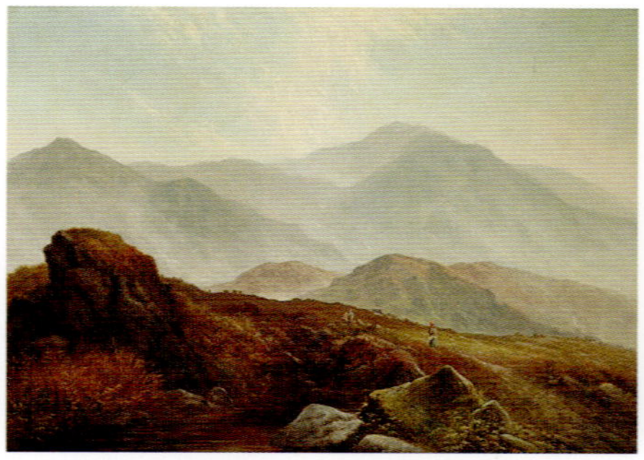

Williams, Walter Heath 1835–1906
The Pass of Llanberis
oil on canvas 60 x 91
PRSMG : P1358

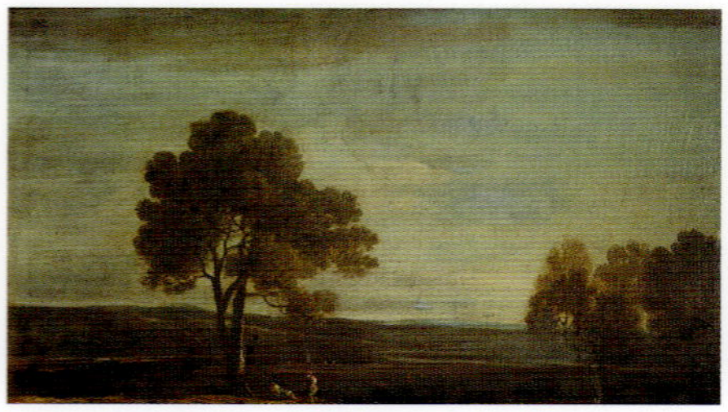

Wilson, Richard 1712–1782
Landscape
oil on canvas 36.8 x 62.2
PRSMG : P1472

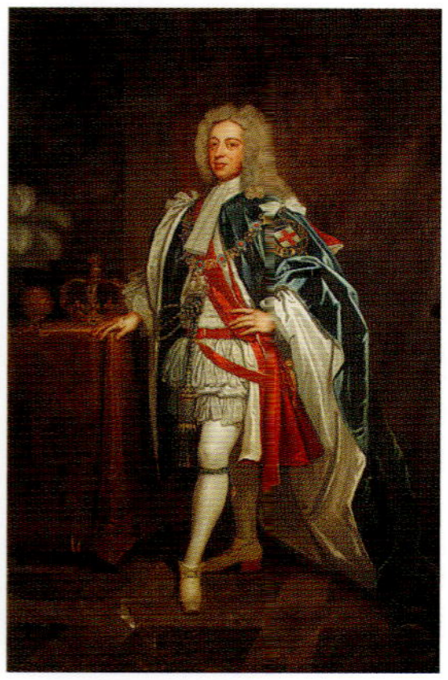

Winstanley, Hamlet 1694–1756
George II (1683–1760)
oil on canvas 242 x 147
PRSMG : P609

Facing page: Hambling, Maggi, b.1945, *July Sunrise, Orwell Estuary, No.2,* 1985, Harris Museum & Art Gallery (p. 306)

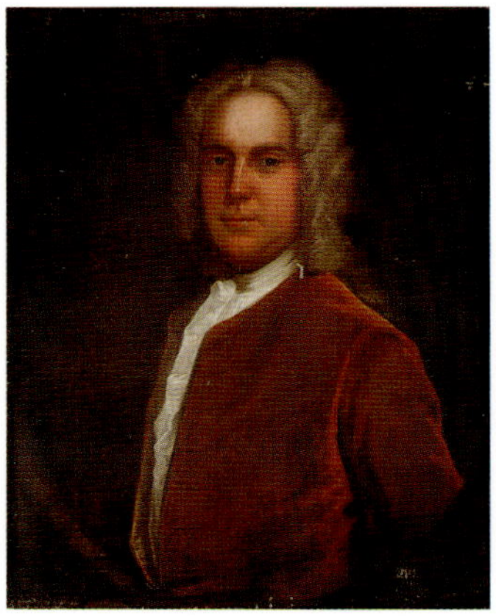

Winstanley, Hamlet 1694–1756
Richard Shepherd
oil on canvas 76 x 63.5
PRSMG : P614

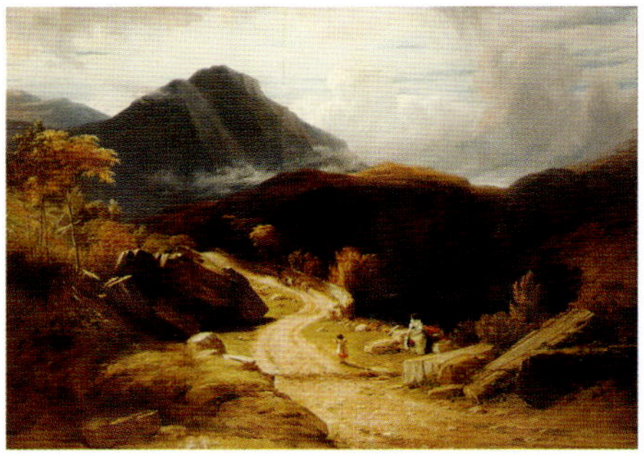

Witherington, William Frederick 1785–1865
Llanberis Pass 1830
oil on canvas 84.5 x 113.5
PRSMG : P1442

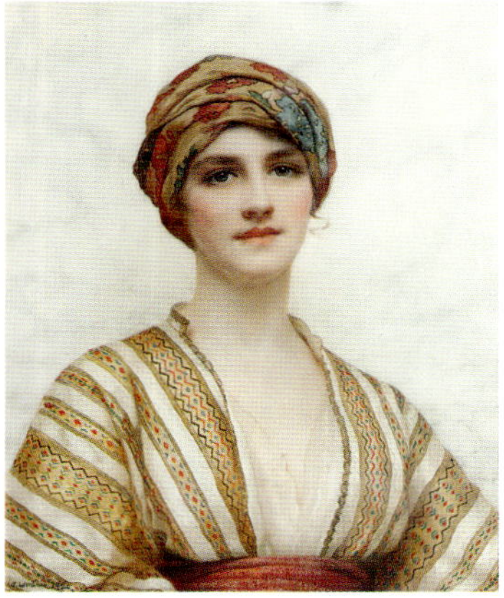

Wontner, William Clarke 1857–1930
Portrait of a Young Woman 1920
oil on canvas 69.9 x 59.7
PRSMG : P1460

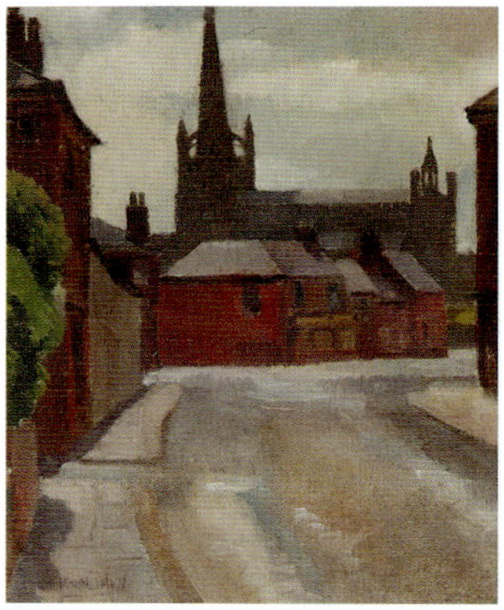

Wood, Harold b.1918
St Peter's Church, Preston, from Fylde Road 1947
oil on canvas 25 x 20.2
PRSMG : P2261

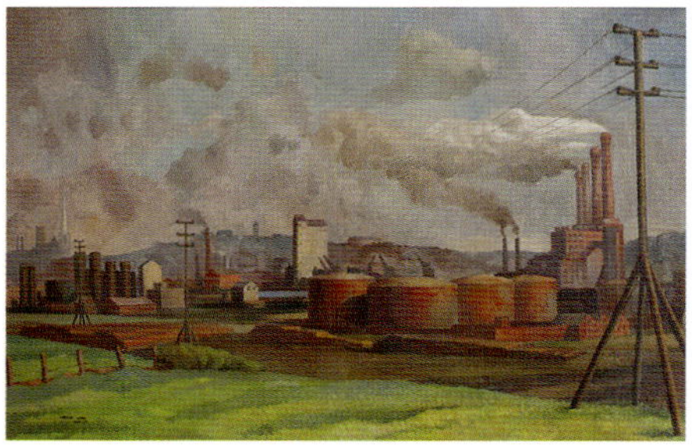

Wood, Harold b.1918
A View of Preston
oil on canvas 61.1 x 91.6
PRSMG : P1245

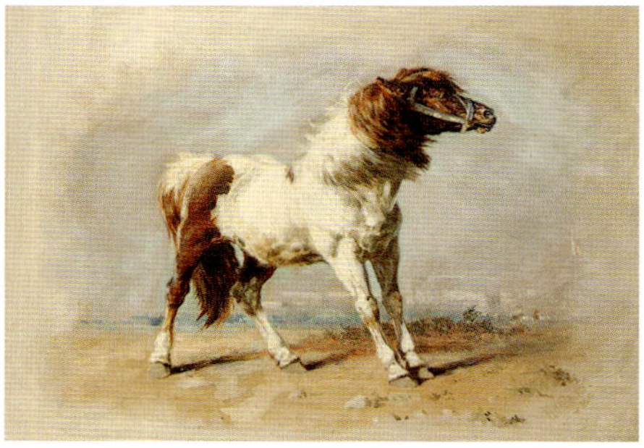

Woodhouse, William 1857–1939
Pit Pony
oil on canvas 41.8 x 56.5
PRSMG : P938

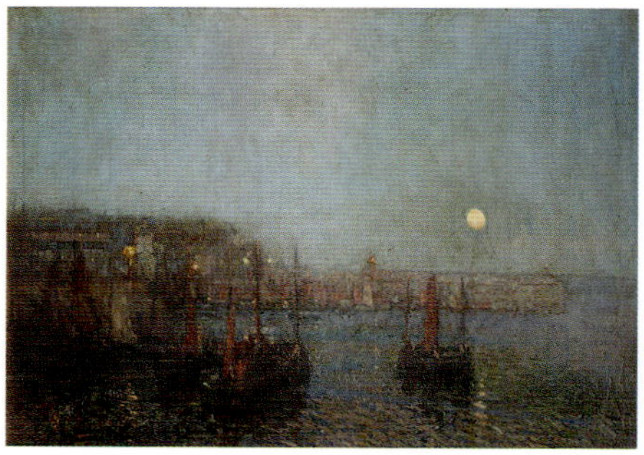

Woods, Albert 1871–1944
Twilight, St Ives Harbour 1900–1910
oil on canvas 61.2 x 92
PRSMG : P694

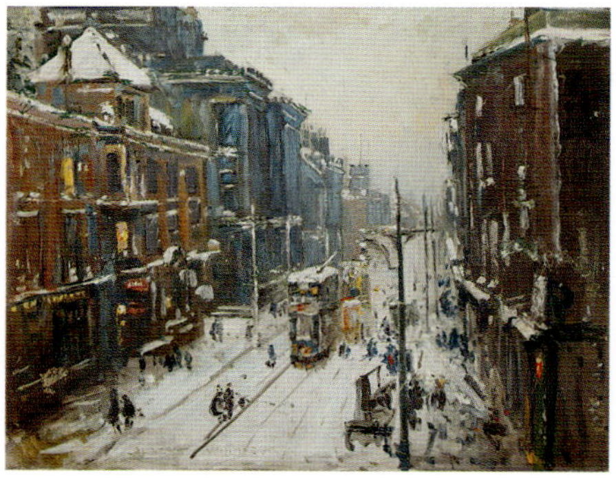

Woods, Albert 1871–1944
Lancaster Road in Snowy Weather 1900–1926
oil on canvas 61.2 x 76.7
PRSMG : P695

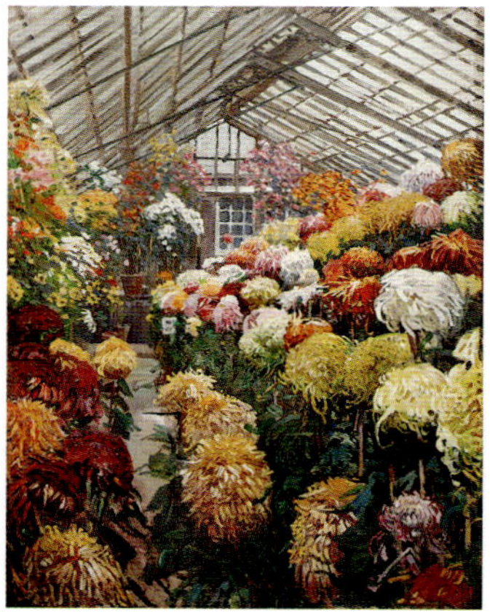

Woods, Albert 1871–1944
Preston Corporation Chrysanthemum House 1921
oil on canvas 85 x 61
PRSMG : P696

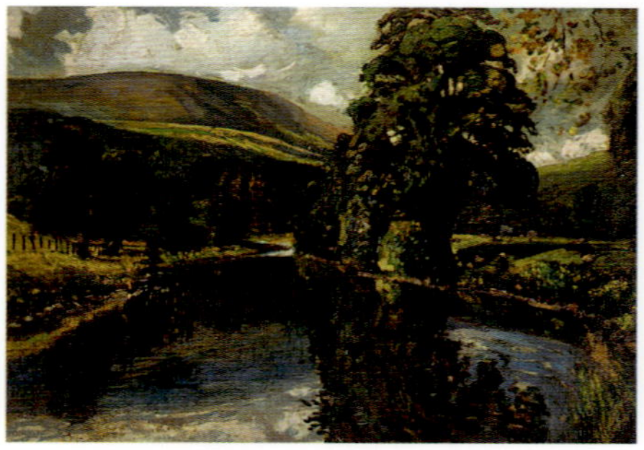

Woods, Albert 1871–1944
A Peaceful Valley, Whitewell
oil on canvas 60.7 x 89.8
PRSMG : P1491

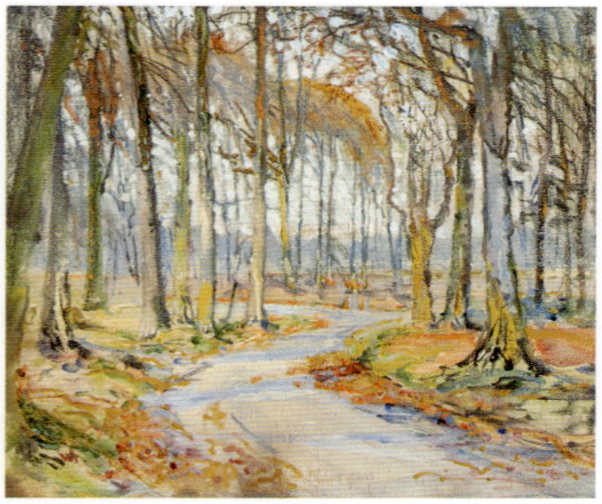

Woods, Albert 1871–1944
Autumn in the Woods
oil on canvas (?) 51 x 60 (E)
PRSMG : T9

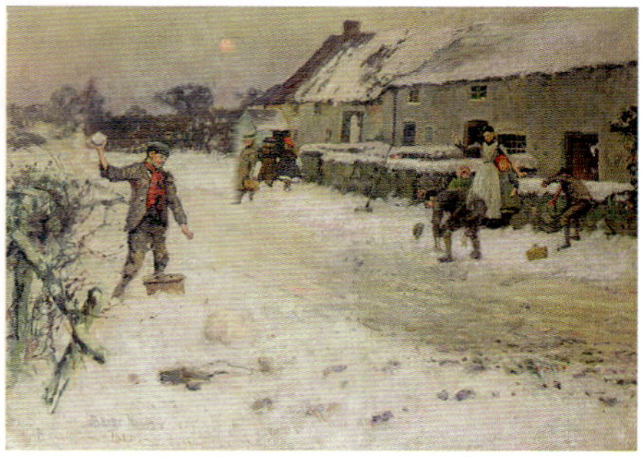

Woods, Albert 1871–1944
Snowballing
oil on canvas 72 x 97.5
PRSMG : P1629

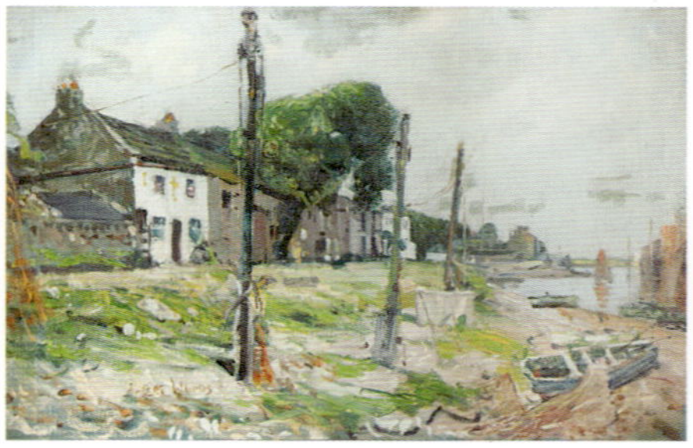

Woods, Albert 1871–1944
Sunderland Point
oil on canvas 50.7 x 80
PRSMG : P697

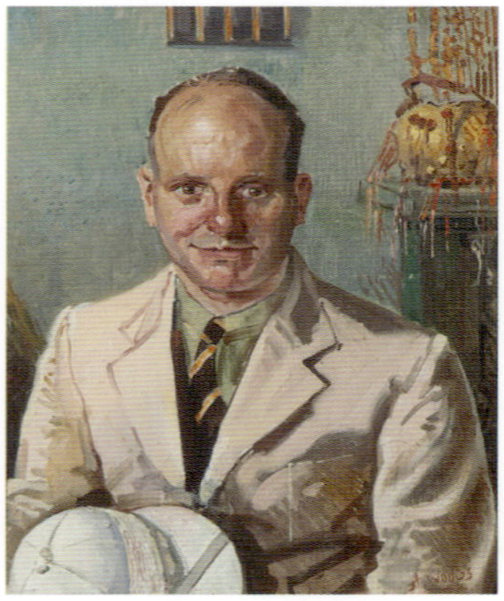

Woods, Albert 1871–1944
William Allan Lambert
oil on panel 61.2 x 50
PRSMG : P1627

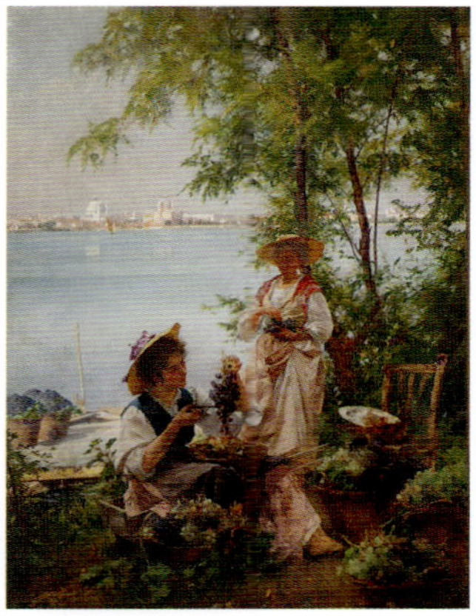

Woods, Henry 1846–1921
A Venetian Vintage 1905
oil on canvas 106.2 x 74
PRSMG : P727

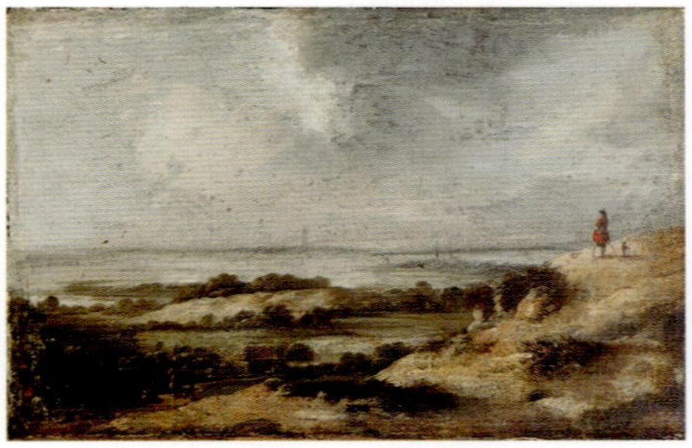

Wouwerman, Philips 1619–1668
Landscape 1640–1668
oil on canvas 19 x 28
PRSMG : P728

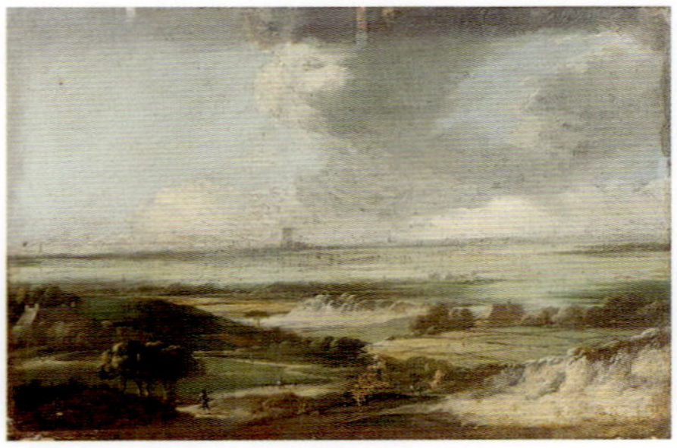

Wouwerman, Philips 1619–1668
Landscape 1640–1668
oil on canvas 19 x 28
PRSMG : P729

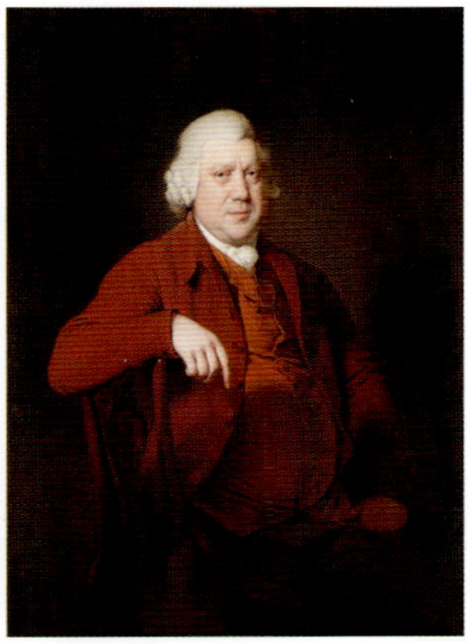

Wright of Derby, Joseph 1734–1797
Richard Arkwright (1732–1792) 1783–1785
oil on canvas 126 x 102
PRSMG : 2009.2

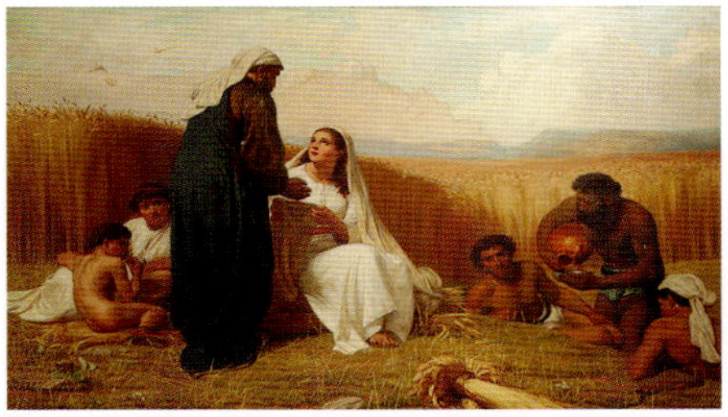

Wynfield, David Wilkie 1837–1887
Ruth and Boaz 1879
oil on canvas 101.5 x 162.5
PRSMG : P733

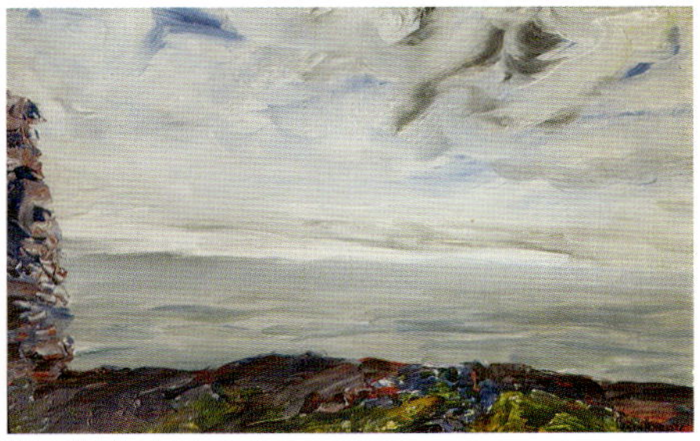

Yeats, Jack Butler 1871–1957
The Coast of Clare from Dun Aengus 1925
oil on board 22.5 x 35.5
PRSMG : P2345

Her Majesty's Court Service, Preston Crown Court

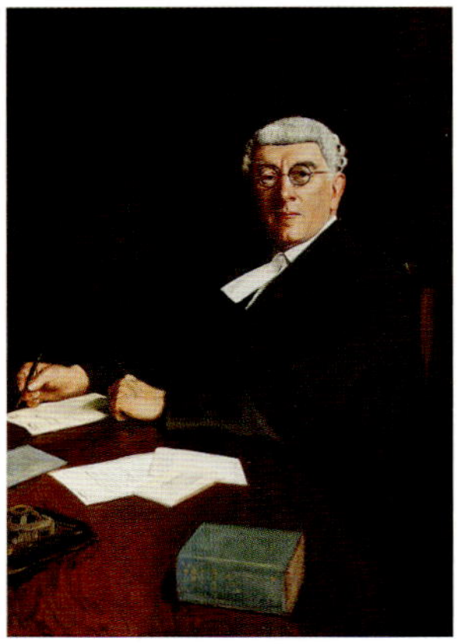

Berrie, John Archibald Alexander 1887–1962
Sir James Openshaw c.1935
oil on canvas 150 x 90 (E)
1099

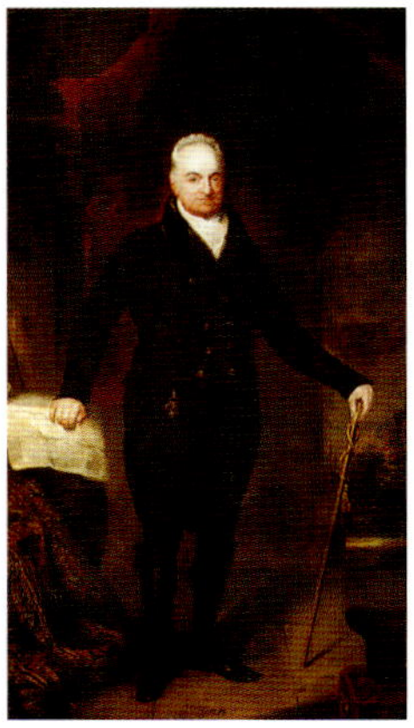

British School
Thomas Clayton, Esq. (1777–1854), High Sheriff c.1808
oil on canvas 160 x 85 (E)
1101

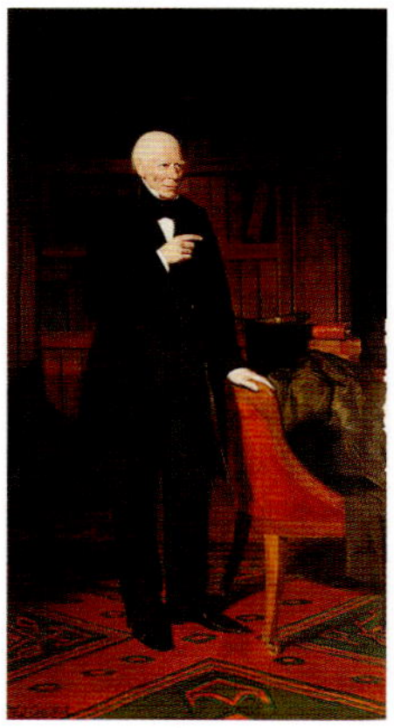

British School
Thomas Batty Addison, Esq. (1788–1874) c.1862
oil on canvas 240 x 120 (E)
1102

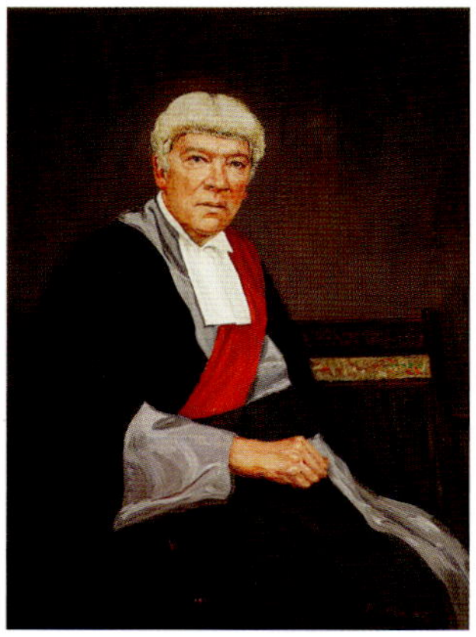

British School
His Honour Judge Openshaw
oil on canvas 130 x 90 (E)
1100

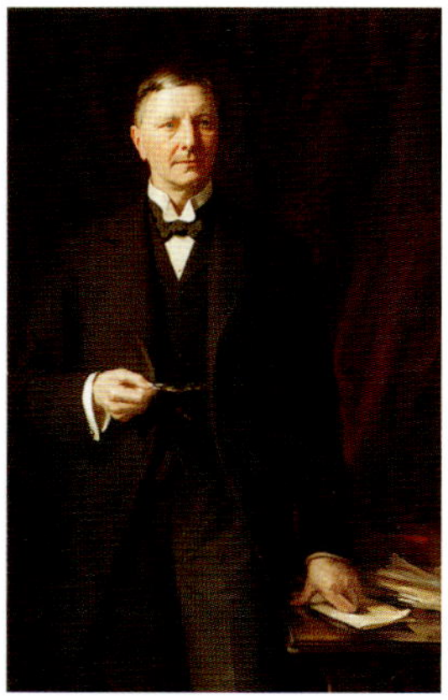

Llewellyn, Samuel Henry William 1858–1941
Sir Harcourt Everard Clare (1854–1922) c.1916
oil on canvas 150 x 90 (E)
1097

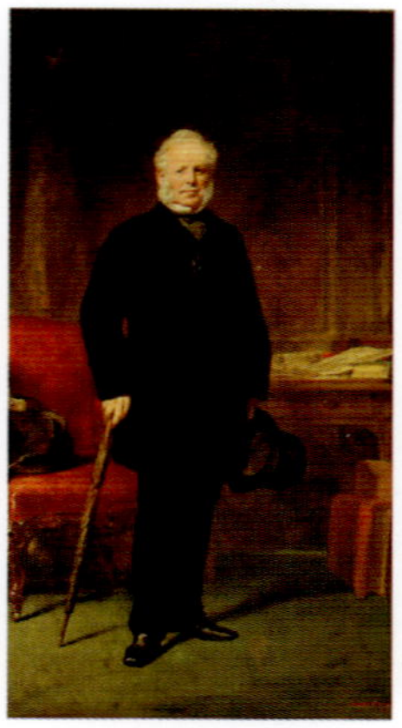

Macnee, Daniel 1806–1882
Reverend John Shepherd Birley (1805–1883)
oil on canvas 240 x 120 (E)
1096

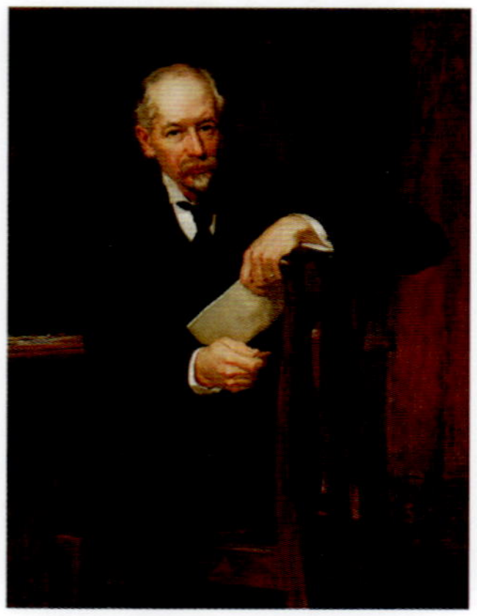

Riviere, Hugh Goldwin 1869–1956
Henry Wilson Worsley-Taylor c.1904
oil on canvas 155 x 90 (E)
1098

14th/20th King's Hussars Museum

The 14th Light Dragoons were formed as early as 1715, being raised by Lieutenant General James Dormer in answer to the threat of war. They fought their first battle against the army of the 'Old Pretender' at Preston in November that year, helping to bring to a close the First Jacobite Rebellion. They served in various wars of the eighteenth century, and most famously in the Peninsular, under the Duke of Wellington. The eagle cap badge was granted in honour of Princess Frederica of Prussia, Royal Patroness of the Regiment and Duchess of York.

The 14th were brought together with the 20th Hussars to create the 14th/20th King's Hussars in 1922. More recently, the merger of 1992 also brought together the old 10thand 11th Royal Hussars in the modern King's Royal Hussars. So it is that the new Regiment boasts a history that combines the story of the Napoleonic Wars, South Africa, both World Wars and most conflicts of recent times.

Fittingly, recruits are still found from the Lancashire area, and the accredited museum relating to the 14th and 20th is housed with the Duke of Lancaster's Own Yeomanry and the Museum of Lancashire on the site of the 1715 battle. The Collection includes a wide range of artefacts and a small number of paintings of regimental significance.

Stephen Bull, Curator Military History, Lancashire Museums

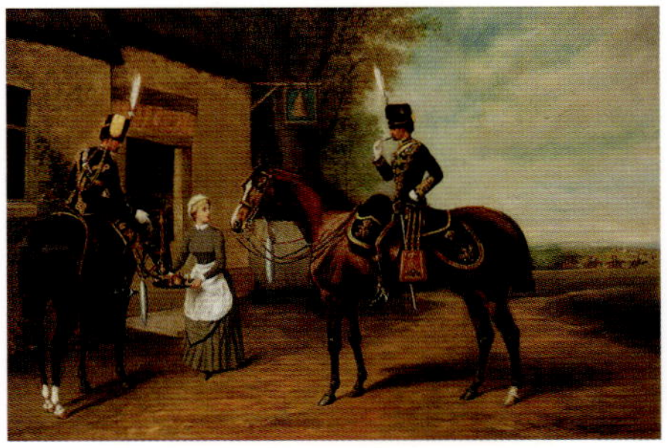

Matthews, J.
Officers of the 14th King's Hussars 1889
oil on canvas 60 x 90
LANKH.797

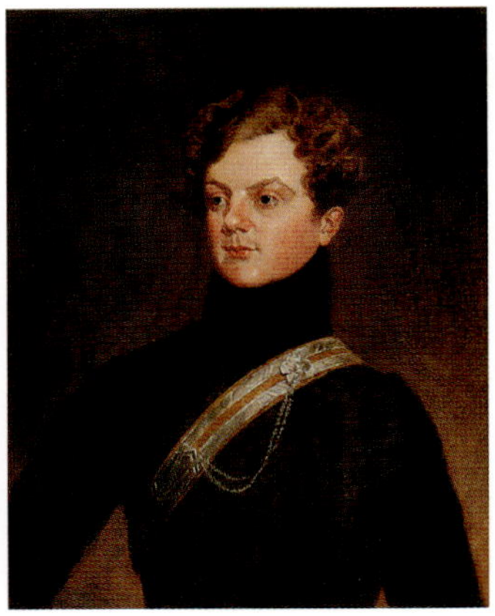

unknown artist
Major John Woolmer Smith, 14th Light Dragoons c.1826
oil on canvas 29.6 x 24.6 (E)
LANKH.260

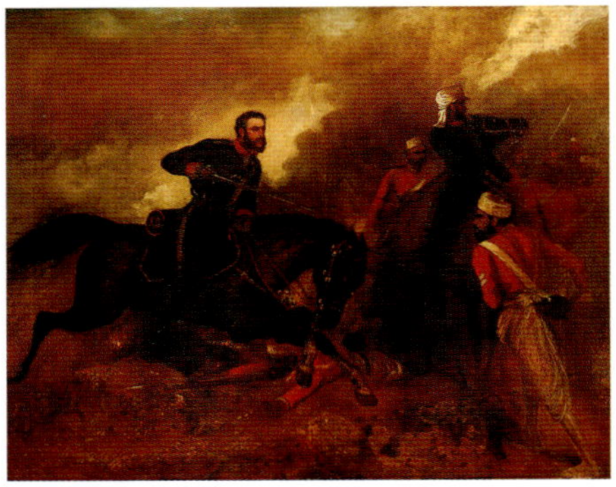

unknown artist
Major James Leith Winning the Victoria Cross 1858
oil on canvas 86 x 110
LANKH.592

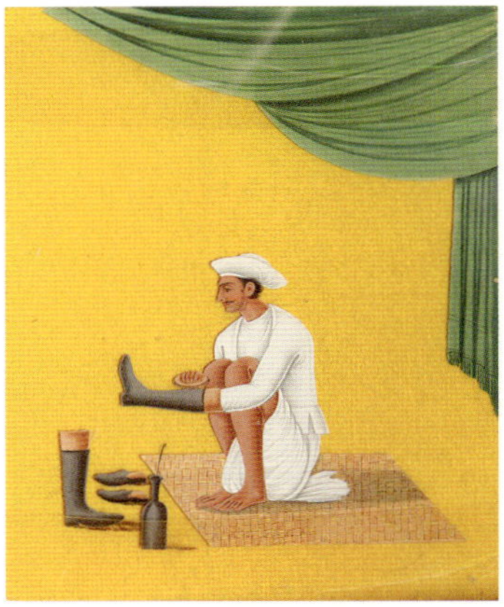

unknown artist
Indian Servant with Boots
oil on mica 14.5 x 10.5
LANKH.200.2

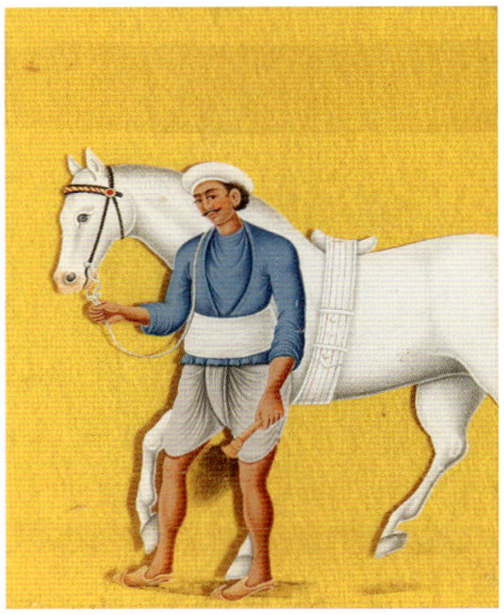

unknown artist
Indian Servant with Horse
oil on mica 14.5 x 10.5
LANKH.200.1

Lancashire County Council

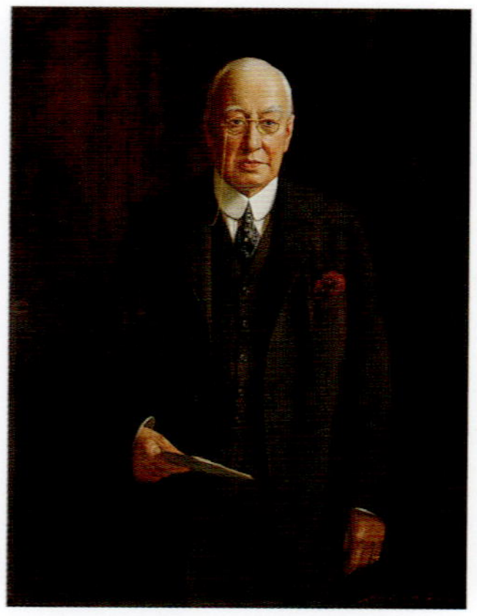

Berrie, John Archibald Alexander 1887–1962
Sir James Travis-Clegg (1874–1942)
oil on canvas 120 x 96
PCF5

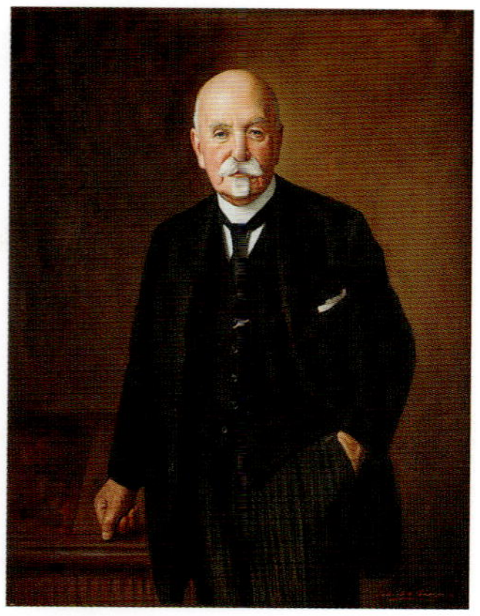

Berrie, John Archibald Alexander 1887–1962
Sir William Hodgson
oil on canvas 120 x 95
PCF6

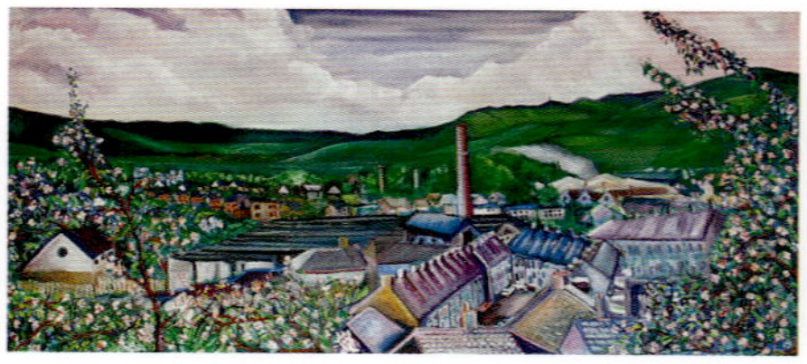

Holt, John
May Grane 1997
oil on canvas 130 x 252
LLHAS.1

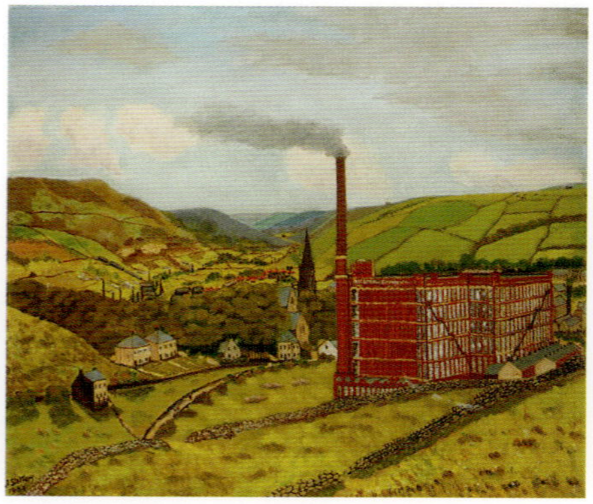

Slattery, Edward 1892–1974
Ross Mill
oil on canvas 66 x 79
LLBAC.1

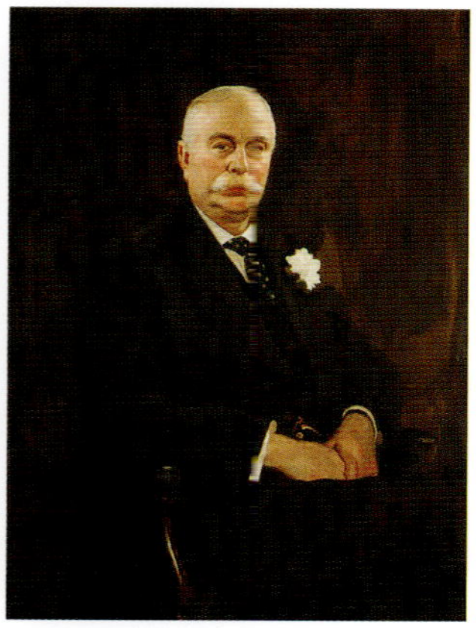

unknown artist
Sir Henry Hibbert (1850–1927), Bt
oil on canvas 120 x 95
PCF3

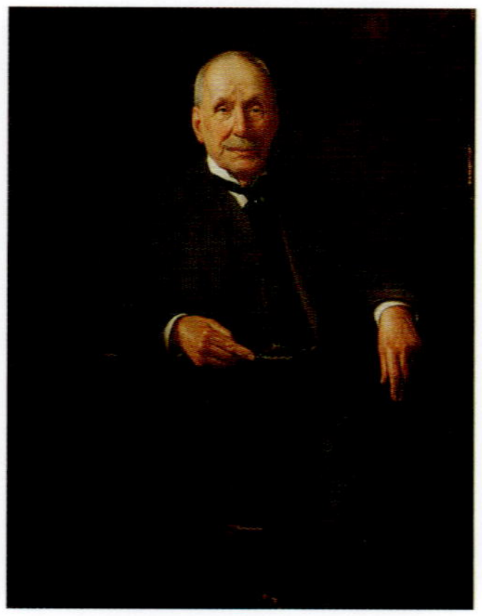

unknown artist
Sir Henry Wade Deacon
oil on canvas 120 x 96
PCF4

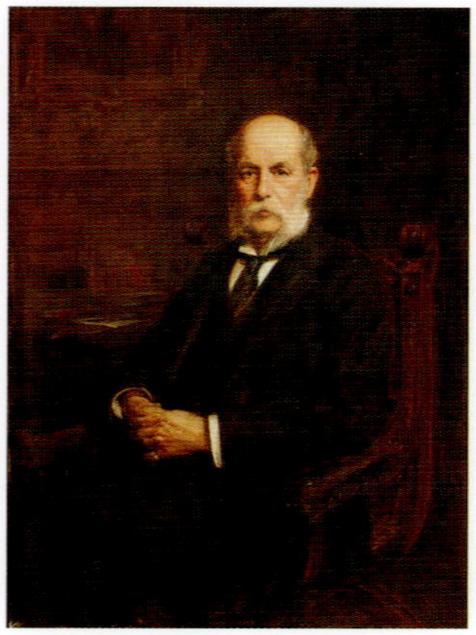

unknown artist
Sir William Scott Barrett, Kt
oil on canvas 120 x 95
PCF2

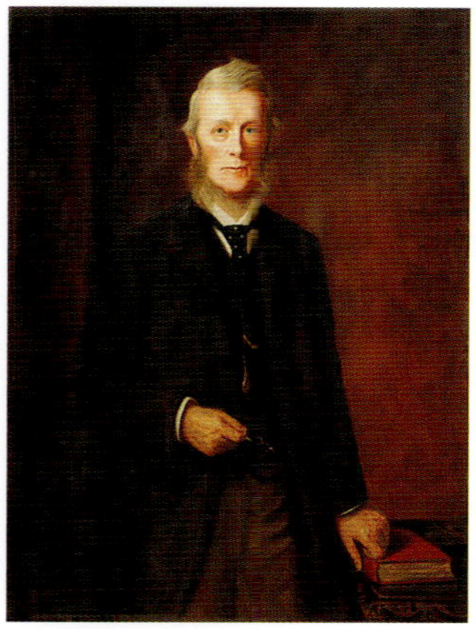

unknown artist
The Right Honorable Sir John Hibbert
oil on canvas 120 x 95
PCF1

Lancashire County Museum Service

Lancashire County Museum Service, administered by Lancashire County Council, was established in 1972 as part of the reorganisation of the County of Lancashire. Working from a small office in North Road, Preston, its newly appointed Director, John Blundell, brought together a team whose aim was to collect material specifically relating to all aspects of the history of Lancashire. From those early beginnings, the Museum Service now administers several museums housing nationally important collections across the county. These include Fleetwood Museum (founded 1974), which occupies the Old Custom House, and has a fine collection relating to the deep sea and inshore fishing industry; the Judges' Lodgings, Lancaster (founded 1975), an historic town house, with period rooms and an extremely fine collection of furniture made by the famous cabinet-making firm of Gillows of Lancaster; the Museum of Lancashire (founded 1978), based in the former County Court House, with important collections relating to the social and administrative history of Lancashire; Helmshore Mills Textile Museum (managed as a county museum from 1975, and enlarged in 1982), comprising Higher Mill, an eighteenth-century water-powered fulling mill, and Whittaker's Mill, a nineteenth-century cotton-spinning manufactory with working machinery, both of which house nationally important collections relating to the cotton industry, and Queen Street Mill Textile Museum, Burnley (managed as a county museum from 1992), a working nineteenth-century steam-powered weaving mill, with an important collection of textile machinery.

Much of the time and expenditure in the early years was taken up in acquiring the historic collections of original material, which, in the case of the rapidly declining textile and fishing industries, was imminently in danger of being destroyed. In addition, the historic buildings acquired to house and display the collections were in urgent need of restoration after years of neglect, and required sensitive conversion to their new roles as museums. Since the appointment of a Curator of Art in 1986, nationally important works of fine art have been acquired for the museums of the Service, with the generous assistance of the Art Fund, the Victoria and Albert Museum Purchase Grant Fund and the Heritage Lottery Fund.

The Museum of Lancashire, Preston, is based at the headquarters of Lancashire County Museum Service. It has a modest general collection of works of fine art, some of which, mostly portraits, have been acquired from sources within Lancashire County Council, and other portraits and topographical works. Particularly fine is the poetic portrait *John Braddyll of Portfield and Whalley*, c.1590, by Robert Peake. Interestingly, although Braddyll held high ministerial office in Elizabethan England, his family had strong Roman Catholic ties. It can surely be no coincidence that the artist has included a solitary magpie in the clearing near where Braddyll is standing in the portrait. Also notable is *Sir William ffaryngton of Worden Hall (1537–1610), Leyland, Lancashire*, 1593, by Marcus Gheeraerts the younger.

Fleetwood Museum is fortunate in having an active Friends of Fleetwood Museum which has encouraged local artists to record all aspects of the fishing industry, the port, its trawlers, and local topographical landmarks for its

Facing page: Peake, Robert, c.1551–1619, *John Braddyll of Portfield and Whalley,* c.1590, Lancashire County Museum Service (p. 387)

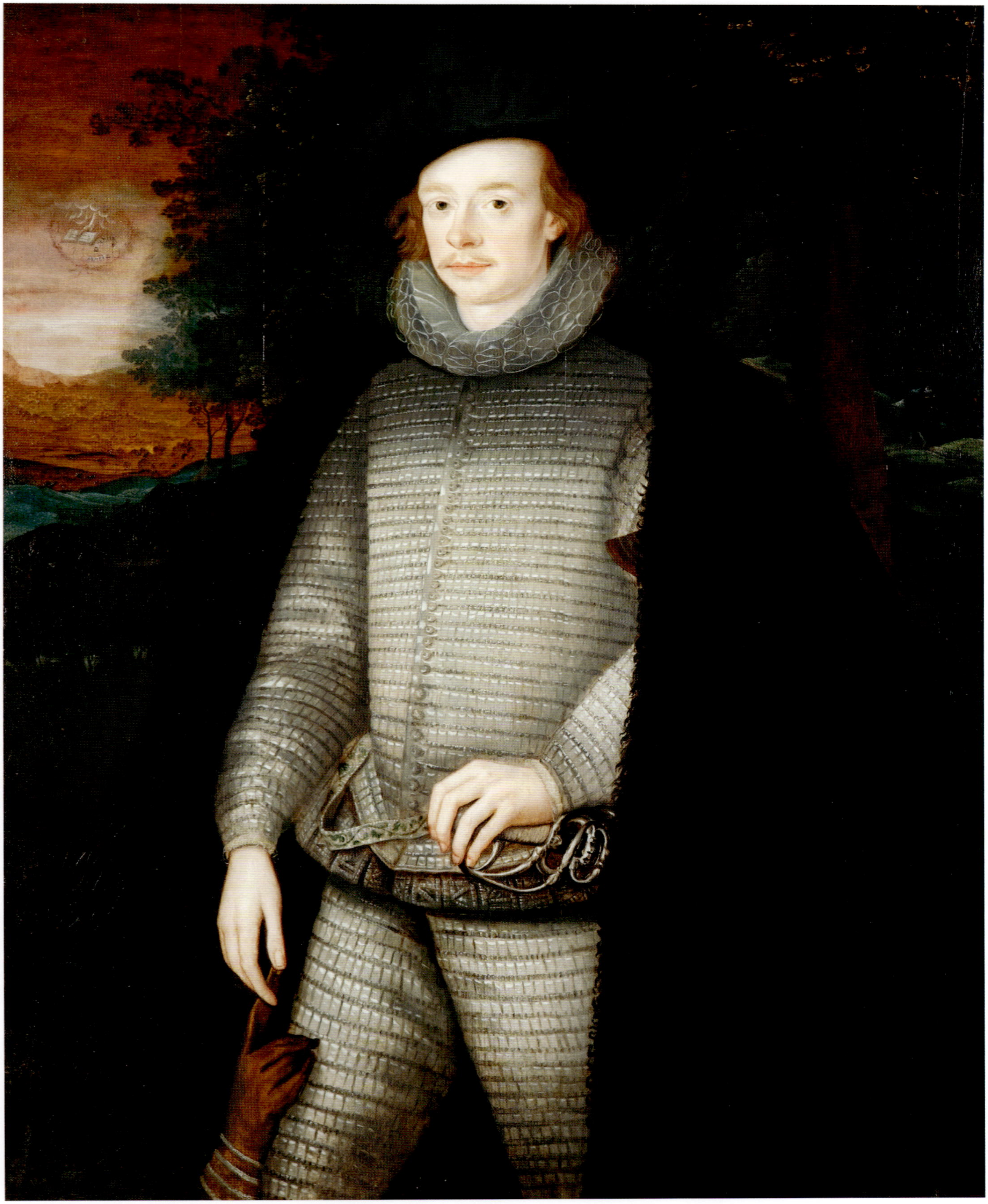

collections. These include a fine series of paintings by Tom Roskell, a former skipper, of work on board the vessels and in port. Of particular importance in the Collection is the painting *The Mussel Gatherers at Sunderland Point, Lancashire*, c.1908, by William Page Atkinson Wells, which depicts the traditional local occupation of mussel gathering on the Lancashire coast. Also significant is *View of Fleetwood*,1842, by Francis English, an artist working for Decimus Burton, architect of Fleetwood, showing the sea front as it was going to look when completed.

The Judges' Lodgings, Lancaster, holds a very fine collection of works of fine art, some of which are from private sources, including the Holt and Hewlett collections, all of which were donated by the Art Fund to furnish the period rooms of the house. Of particular importance is a group of five Impressionist works from the Hewlett Bequest, two of which *La Creuse a Genetin*, c.1880, and *Les Dunes de la Covarde, Ile de Re*, 1893, are by Armand Guillaumin, and others by Maxime Maufra, Adrien Jacques Sauzay, and Hippolyte-Camille Delpy. Other notable portraits include *Joseph Farington (1747–1821), RA, 1794–1796*, by Thomas Lawrence; *Mrs James Hardman of Rochdale and Allerton Hall*, 1769, by Joseph Wright of Derby; and *Abraham Rawlinson (1738–1803), MP, of Ellel Hall, near Lancaster*, c.1765–1767, by George Romney. In addition, the Collection includes two paintings by Arthur Devis, a very early landscape, *Hornby Hall and Castle*, c.1736, and a very late work, *Squire ffrance of Rawcliffe Hall*, c.1768–1772, of a type by the artist described by Horace Walpole as 'a new species of painting behind glass'.

Helmshore Mills Textile Museum and Queen Street Mill Textile Museum hold few works of fine art, but those they have are important in the context of the history of the textile industry. At Helmshore Museum there is a particularly fine portrait of Sir Richard Arkwright, 1790, inventor of the 'Water-Frame', the first practicable spinning machine, painted by Joseph Wright of Derby. The portrait represents one of the most inspiring icons of the early Industrial Revolution: Thomas Carlisle's description of Arkwright as 'a plain, almost gross, bag-cheeked, pot-bellied Lancashire man, with an air of painful reflection, yet also of copious free digestion,' was based not on personal knowledge of the man, but on this picture. The portrait fittingly hangs next to the last surviving complete water-frame from Cromford Mill, which is also at Helmshore Museum. Also worthy of mention are two views of Industrial Revolution premises concerned with printing and dyeing of textiles, *Broad Oak Printworks, near Accrington*, c.1827, (at Queen Street Mill Textile Museum), and *Bury from Blackford Bridge*, 1833, (at Helmshore Mills Textile Museum), both painted by William Linton, who was himself an authority on the chemistry of pigments used in printing and dyeing cloth.

Stephen Sartin, Associate Curator of Art

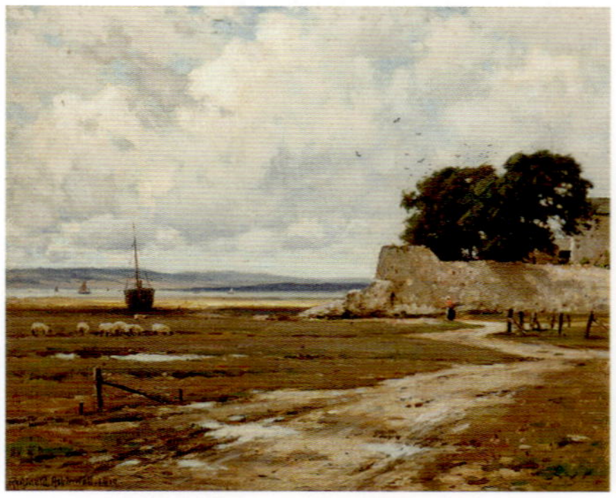

Aspinwall, Reginald 1858–1921
Sunderland Point 1910
oil on canvas 50 x 58 (E)
LANMS.1996.72

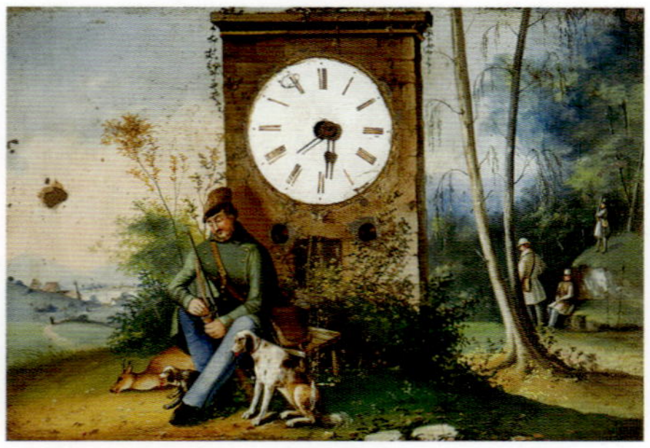

Austrian School (possibly)
Picture Clock c.1835
oil on iron 22 x 32
JLTEMP.1

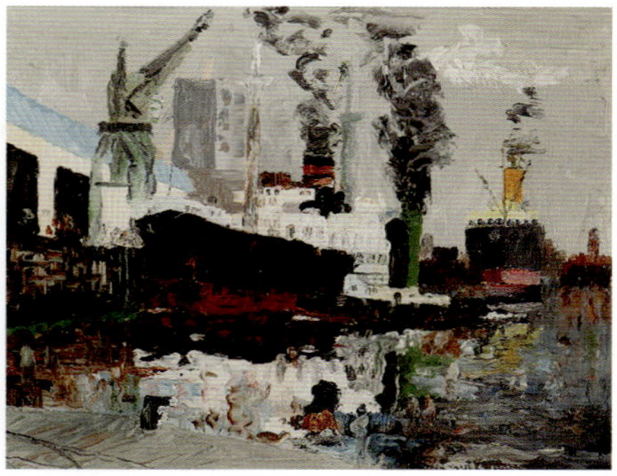

Baxter, Ron
Liners at Quayside 1970
acrylic on hardboard 40.5 x 54
LANMS.1974.149.117

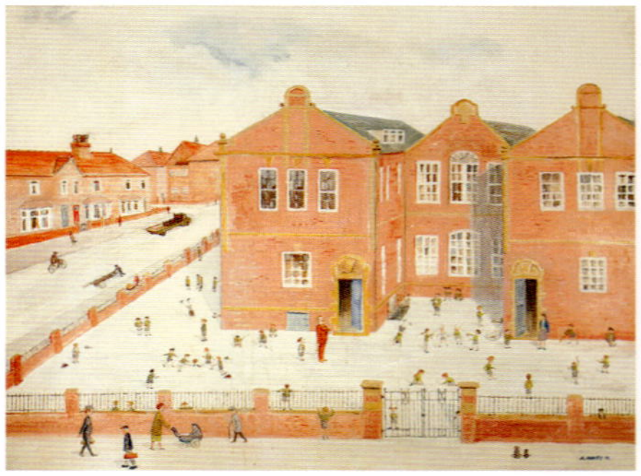

Berry, R.
Milton Street Primary School, Fleetwood 1998
oil on MDF 106.5 x 121.5
N3886

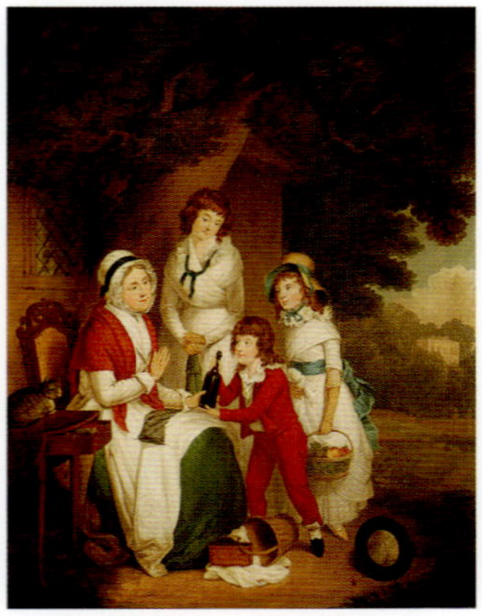

Bigg, William Redmore 1755–1828
A Bottle of Wine c.1815
oil on canvas 55.6 x 45.3
LANMS.1991.406.5

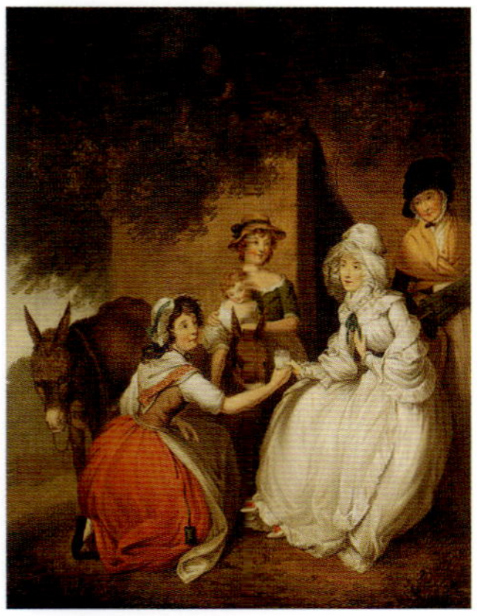

Bigg, William Redmore 1755–1828
A Glass of Milk c.1815
oil on canvas 56 x 45.5
LANMS.1991.406.4

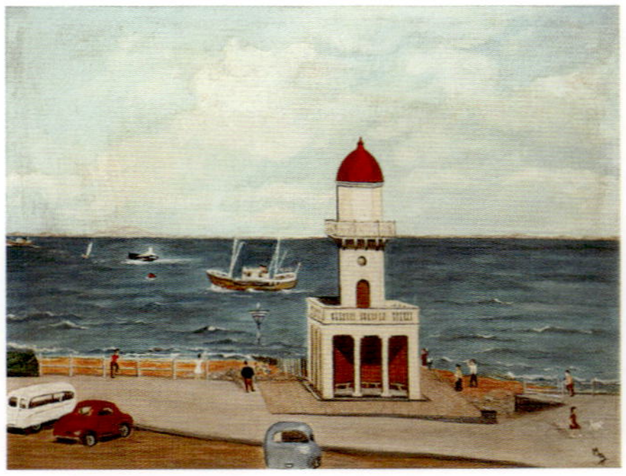

Birkett, Mary
Fleetwood Lower Lighthouse
oil on hardboard 34.5 x 49.5
LANMS.2011.31

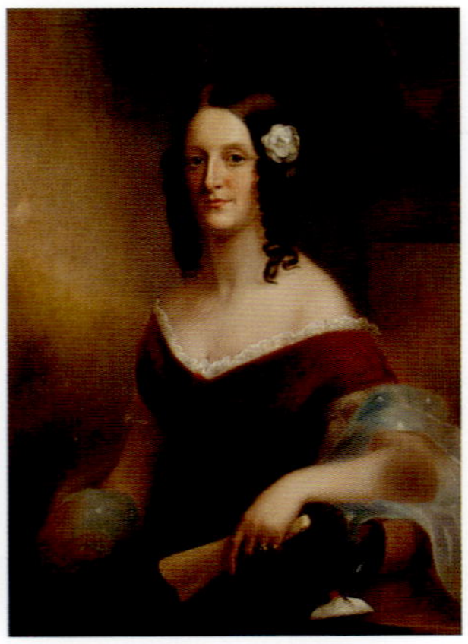

British (English) School
Georgiana Hulton, Wife of William Ford 1839
oil on canvas 90 x 70 (E)
LOAN.1999.2 (P)

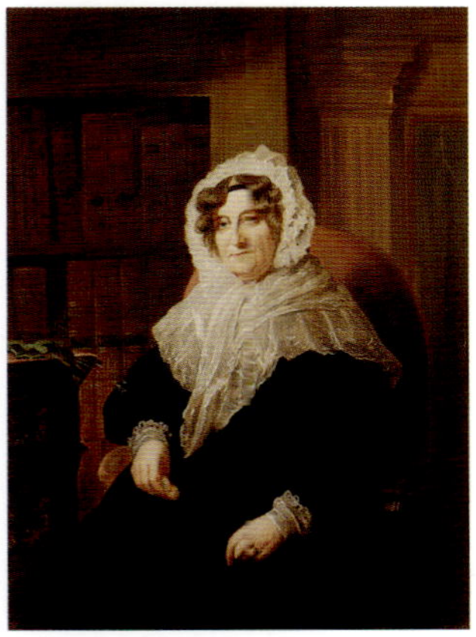

British (English) School
Sally (Sarah) Chorley (1774–1852) c.1845
oil on canvas 56 x 30 (E)
LANMS.2006.2.6

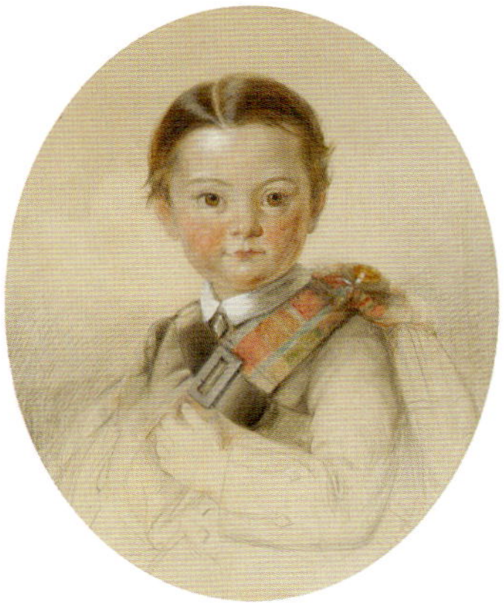

Brodie, John Lamont active c.1834–1881
Portrait of a Boy in Highland Dress 1862
oil on canvas 54 x 45
LANMS.1977.83.1

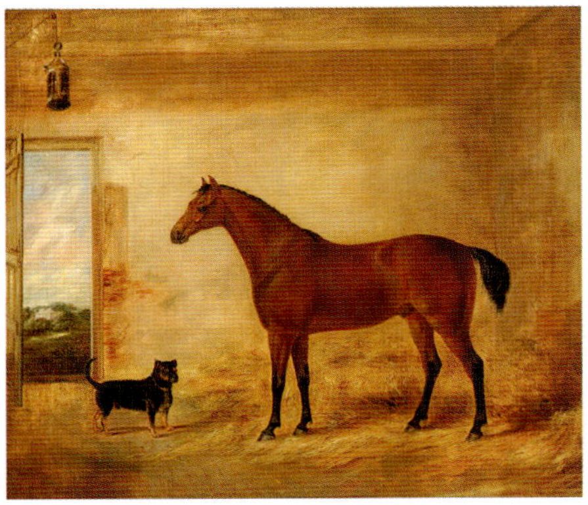

Brown, R. G. 1815–1905
Horse and Dog in Stable 1843
oil on canvas 50 x 56.5 (E)
LANMS.1985.294.338

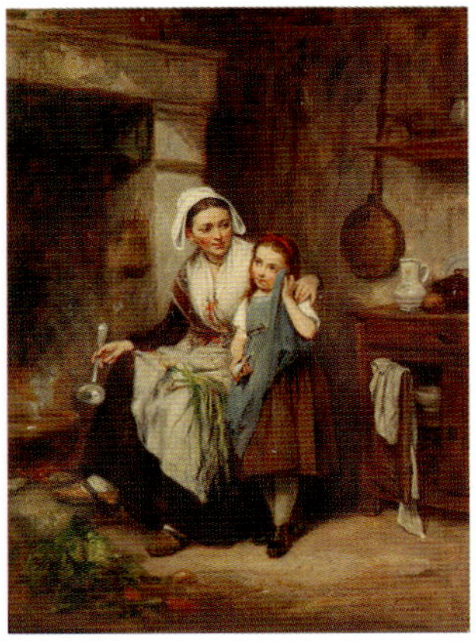

Caille, Léon Émile 1836–1907
Mother and Daughter in Domestic Interior 1871
oil on panel 37 x 23 (E)
LANMS.2002.11.4

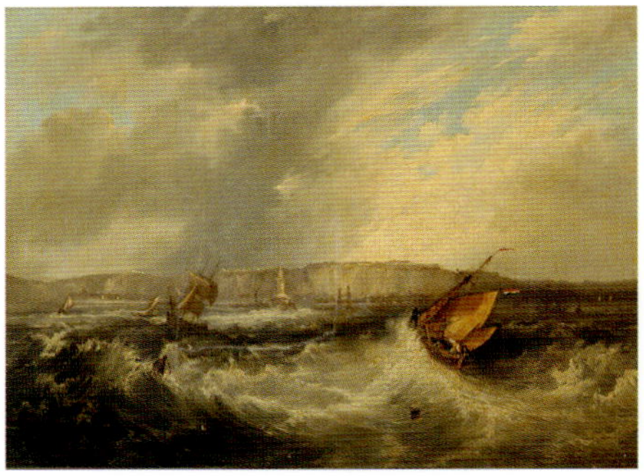

Calvert, Frederick 1785–1845
Shipping Scene with Lighthouse
oil on canvas 43 x 58
LANMS.2002.11.3

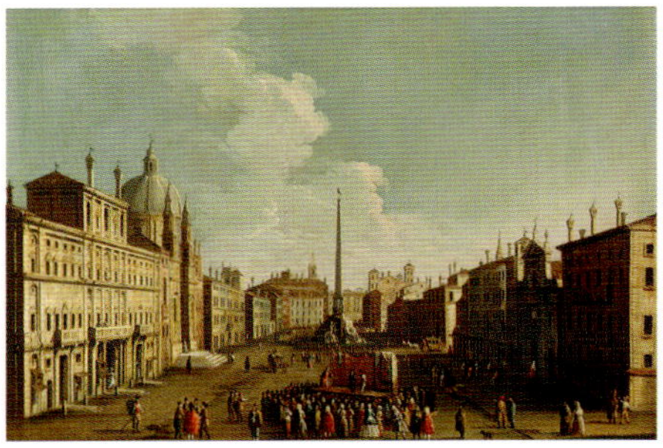

Canaletto (school of) 1697–1768
Piazza Navona, Rome
oil on canvas 50.8 x 70.5 (E)
LANMS.1991.406.1

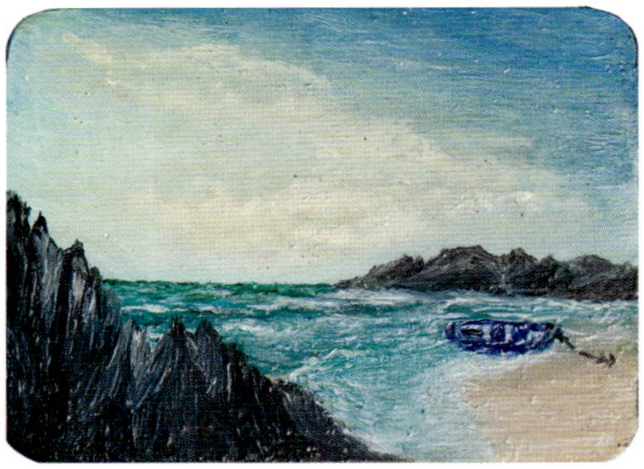

Cartmell, John Thomas 1905–1975
Beach with Blue Boat and Rocks
oil on tin 7 x 10
LANMS.2011.45.4.1

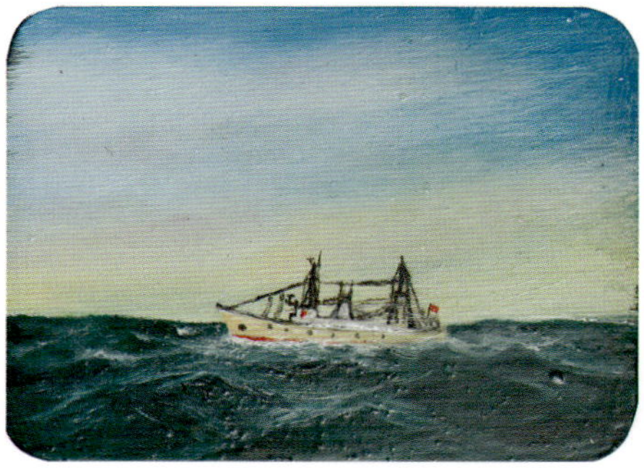

Cartmell, John Thomas 1905–1975
Boat with Portholes
oil on tin 7 x 10
LANMS.2011.45.5.1

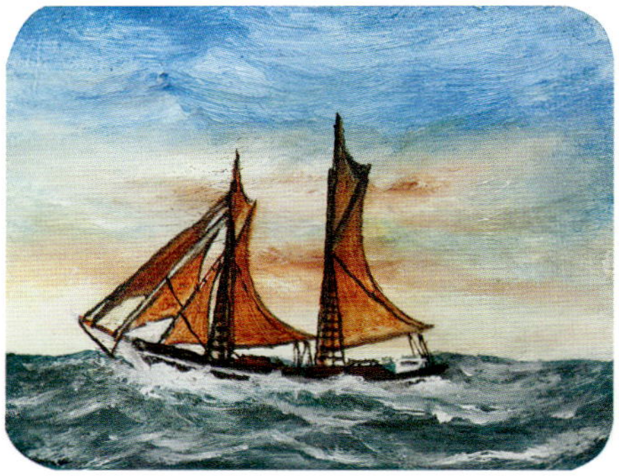

Cartmell, John Thomas 1905–1975
Sailing Ship with Light Brown Sails
oil on tin 7 x 10
LANMS.2011.45.2.2

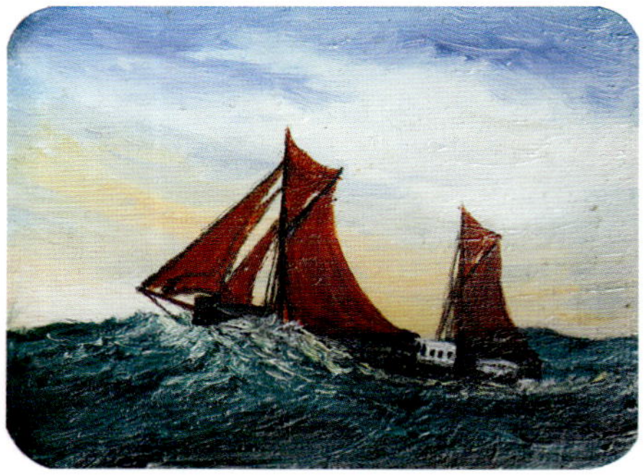

Cartmell, John Thomas 1905–1975
Ship with Red Sails by Black Rocks
oil on tin 7 x 10
LANMS.2011.45.2.1

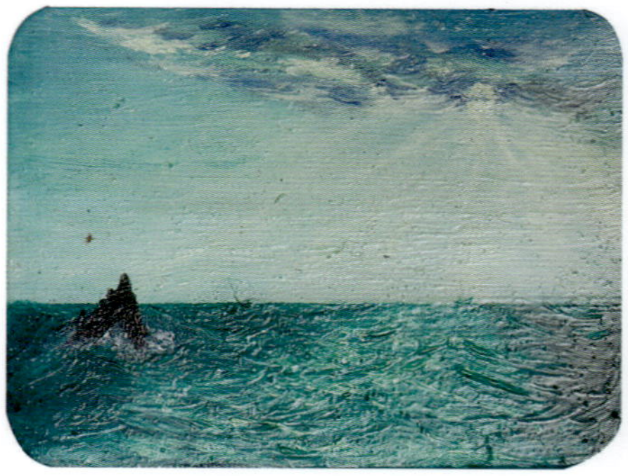

Cartmell, John Thomas 1905–1975
Shipping Scene
oil on tin 7 x 10
LANMS.2011.45.1.1

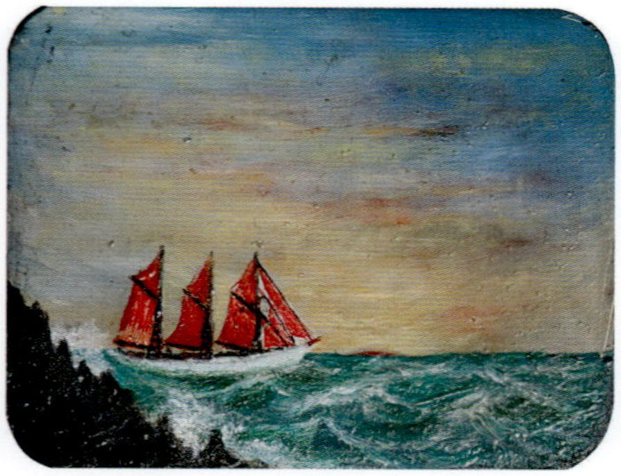

Cartmell, John Thomas 1905–1975
Shipping Scene
oil on tin 7 x 10
LANMS.2011.45.1.2

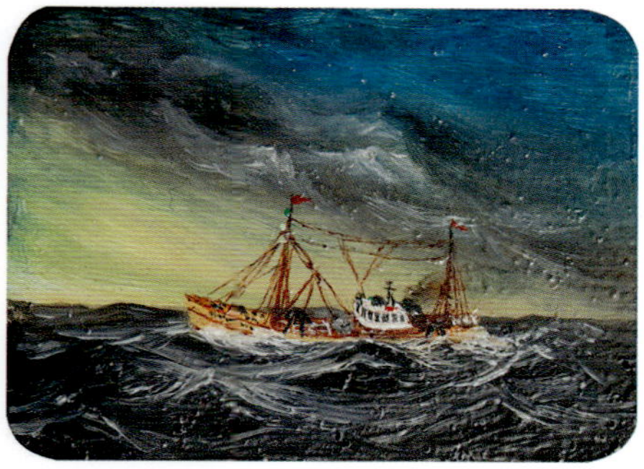

Cartmell, John Thomas 1905–1975
Shipping Scene
oil on tin 7 x 10
LANMS.2011.45.3.1

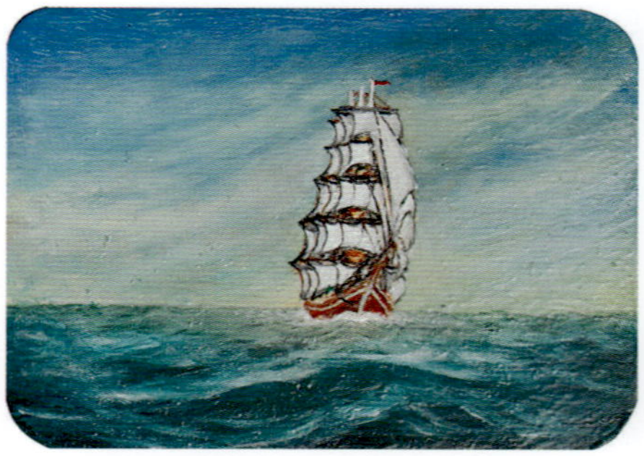

Cartmell, John Thomas 1905–1975
Tall Ship in Full Sail
oil on tin 7 x 10
LANMS.2011.45.4.2

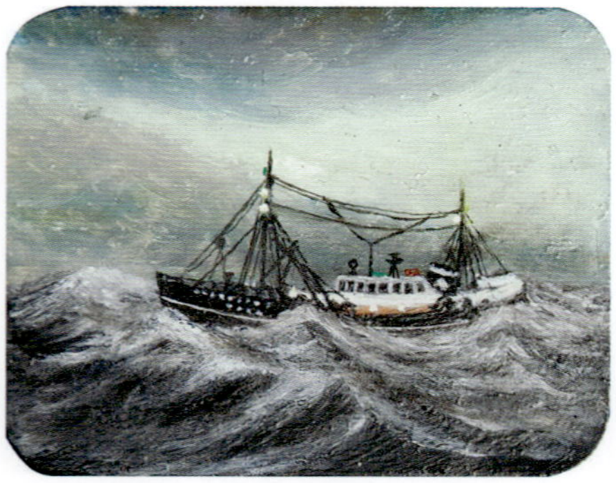

Cartmell, John Thomas 1905–1975
Trawler on Rough Grey Sea
oil on tin 7 x 10
LANMS.2011.45.3.2

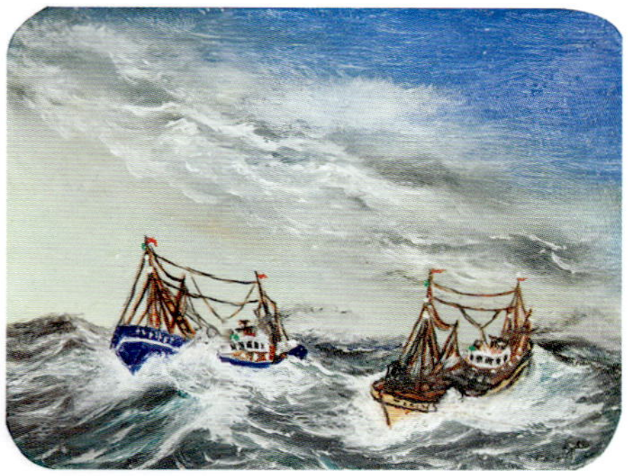

Cartmell, John Thomas 1905–1975
Two Boats
oil on tin 7 x 10
LANMS.2011.45.6.2

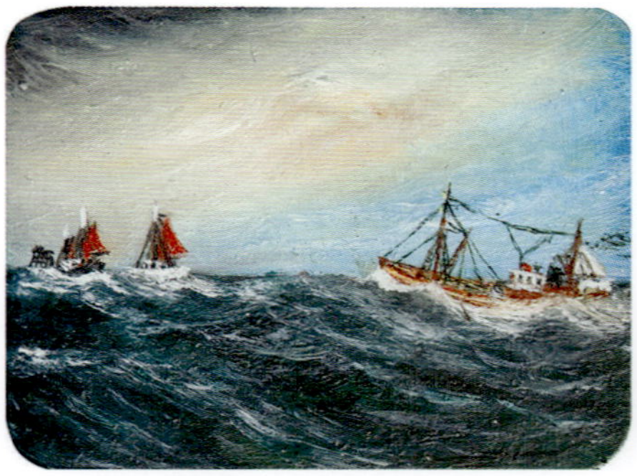

Cartmell, John Thomas 1905–1975
Two Boats with Red Sails
oil on tin 7 x 10
LANMS.2011.45.6.1

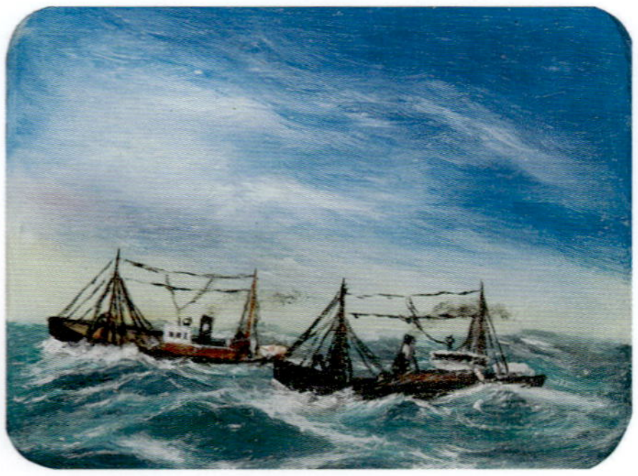

Cartmell, John Thomas 1905–1975
Two Trawlers
oil on tin 7 x 10
LANMS.2011.45.5.2

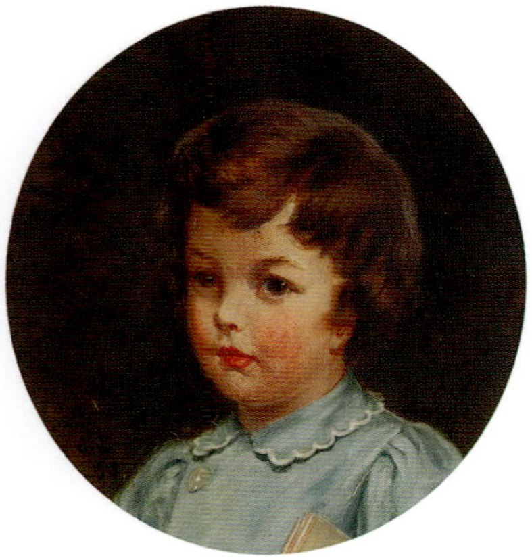

Charlton, John 1849–1917
George P. Holt 1913
oil on canvas 34.4 x 34.4 (E)
LANMS.1991.406.7

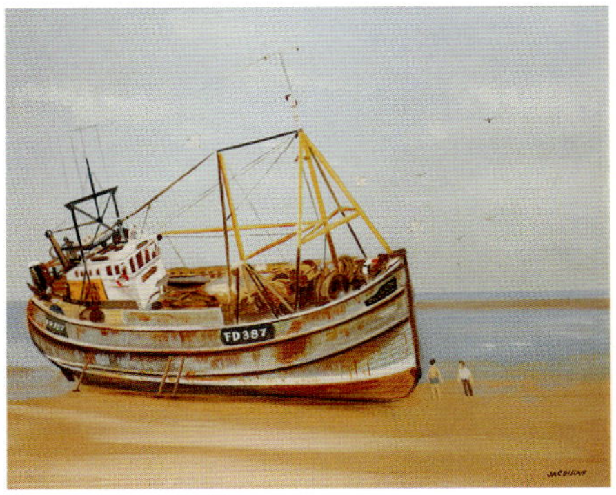

Collins, J. A. active 1994–2002
Beached Trawler 1994
oil on hardboard 39 x 48
LANMS.2011.56

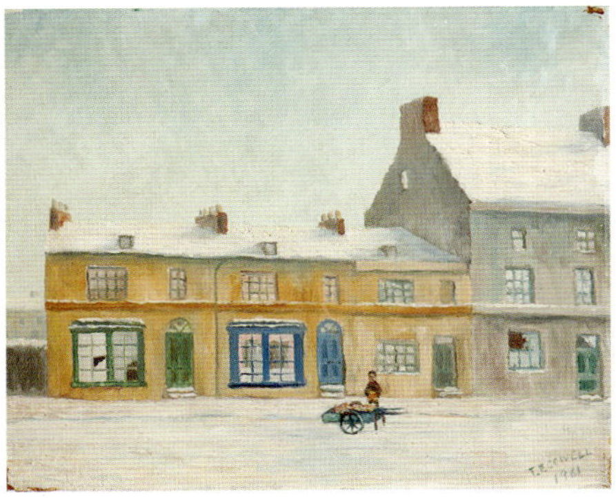

Cowell, T. F.
Old Cottages and Old House in Warren Street 1961
oil on hardboard 31.4 x 39.1
LANMS.1974.149.105

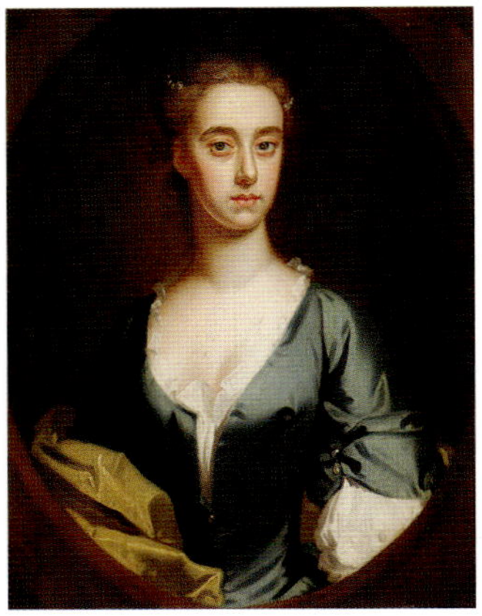

Dahl I, Michael (follower of) 1656–1743
Beatrix Hulton (1722–1774), Wife of Thomas Lister of Gisburne Park c.1748
oil on canvas 75 x 61 (E)
LOAN.1999.2 (P)

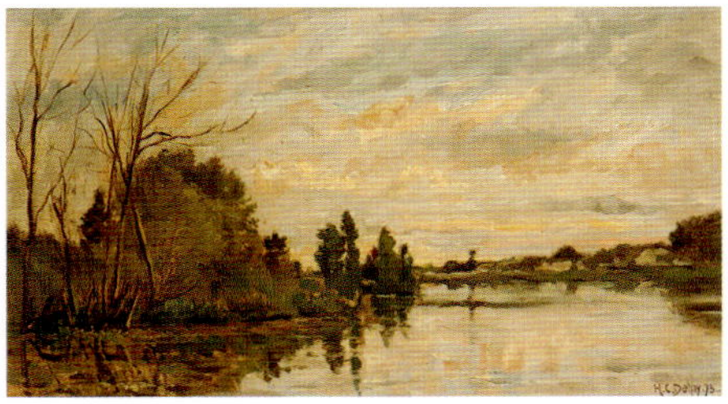

Delpy, Hippolyte-Camille 1842–1910
A River at Dusk 1893
oil on panel 24 x 45 (E)
LANMS.1995.29.3

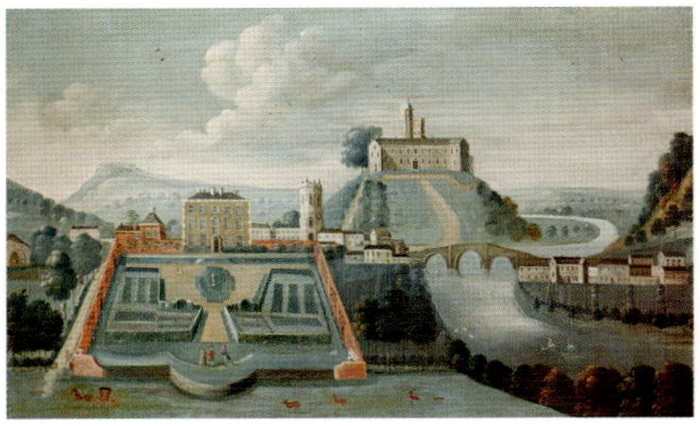

Devis, Arthur 1712–1787
Hornby Hall and Castle c.1736
oil on canvas 67 x 113.4 (E)
LANMS.1991.118

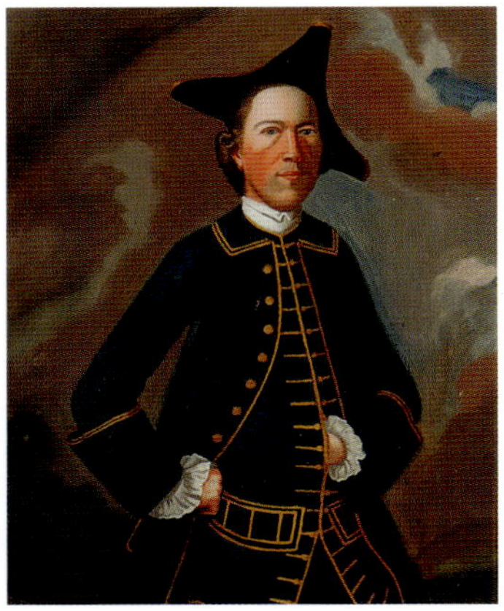

Devis, Arthur 1712–1787
Squire John ffrance (1727–1817) of Rawcliffe Hall, Lancashire c.1768–1772
oil on glass 23 x 18 (E)
LANMS.1991.408

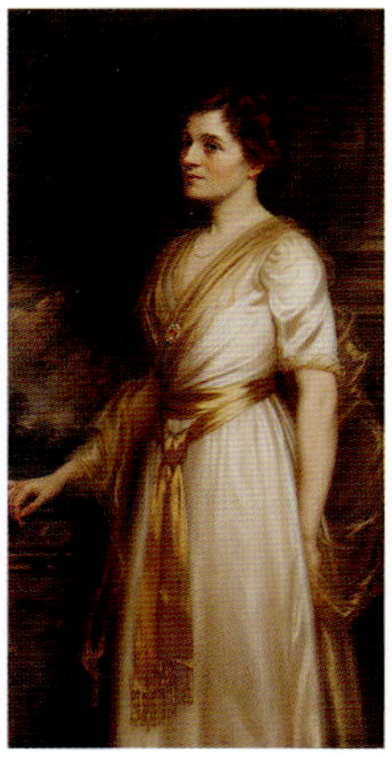

Draper, Herbert James 1864–1920
The Mother of George P. Holt c.1910
oil on canvas 148 x 71 (E)
LANMS.1991.406.6

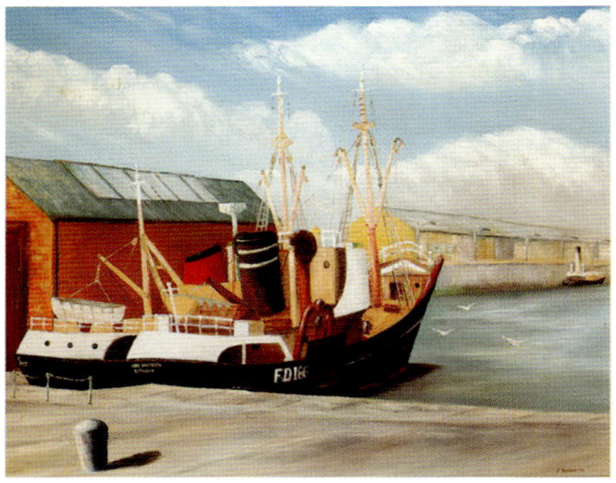

Duckett, J.
The 'Wyre Victory' in Fleetwood Dock
oil on hardboard 47 x 64.5
LANMS.1990.501.2

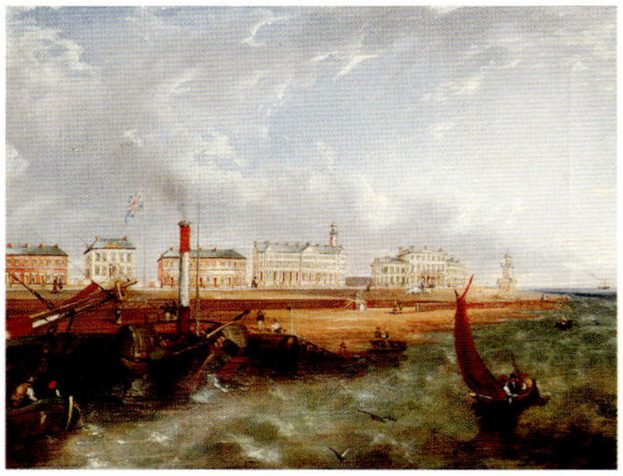

English, Francis
View of Fleetwood 1842
oil on canvas 33 x 45
LANMS.1996.69

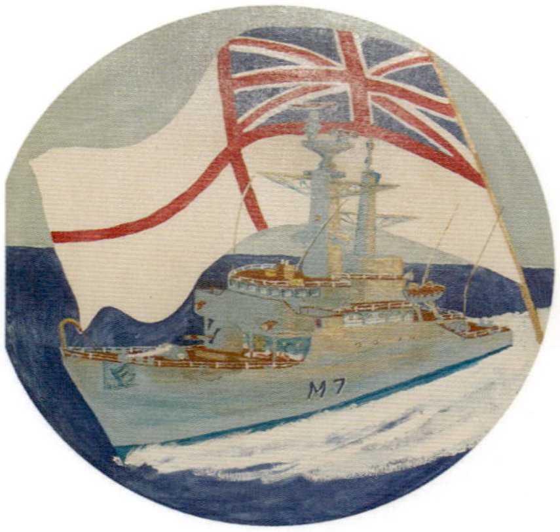

English, J. W.
M7 in the Centre of a Life Buoy
oil on canvas 45 x 66
LANMS.2011.40

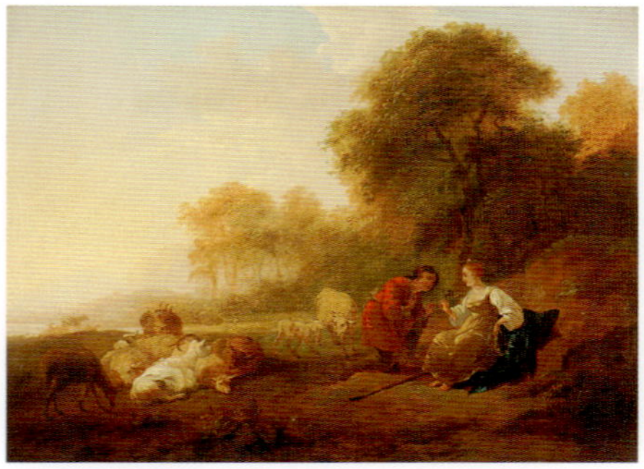

French School
Figures in a Landscape c.1810
oil on panel 27 x 41
LANMS.2002.11.5

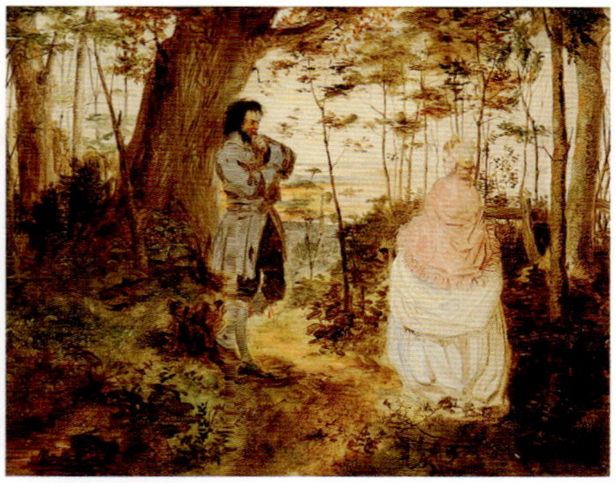

Frith, William Powell 1819–1909
Hugh and Dolly Varden (from the novel 'Barnaby Rudge' by Charles Dickens) c.1863
oil on panel 29 x 38 (E)
LANMS.1991.406.3

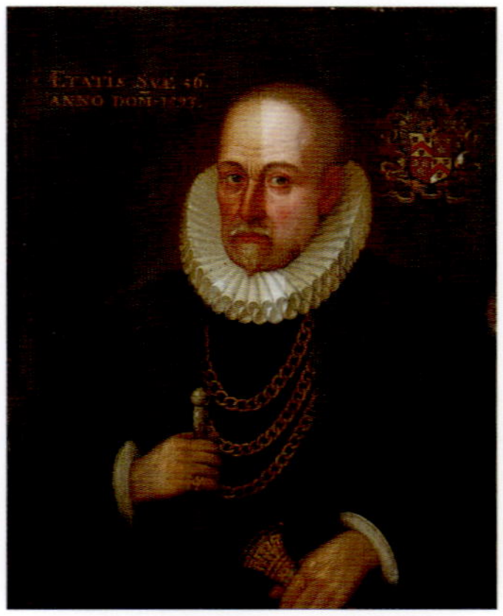

Gheeraerts the younger, Marcus 1561–1636
Sir William ffaryngton of Worden Hall (1537–1610), Leyland, Lancashire 1593
oil on canvas 62.6 x 59 (E)
LANMS.1994.131

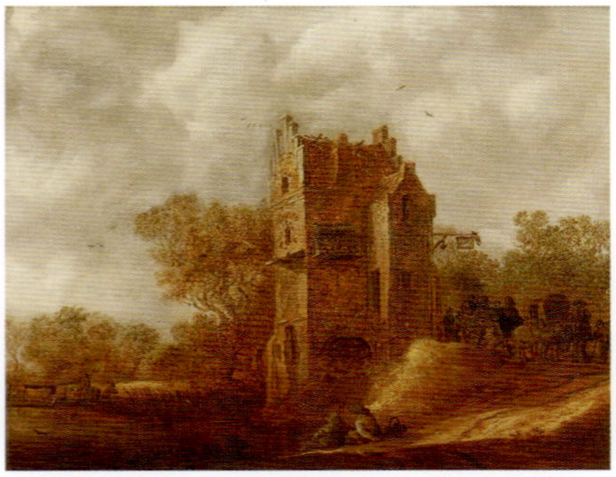

Goyen, Jan van (attributed to) 1596–1656
Landscape with Travellers outside an Inn 1635
oil on canvas 38 x 43.5 (E)
LANMS.2002.11.1

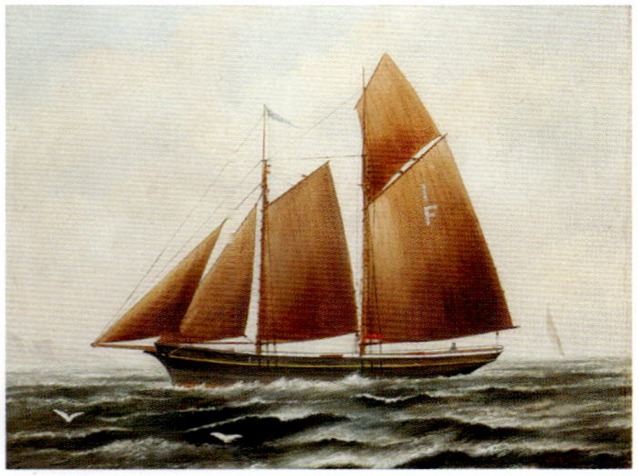

Green, J. W.
The 'Falcon' 1897
oil on canvas 34.3 x 44
LANMS.1974.149.63

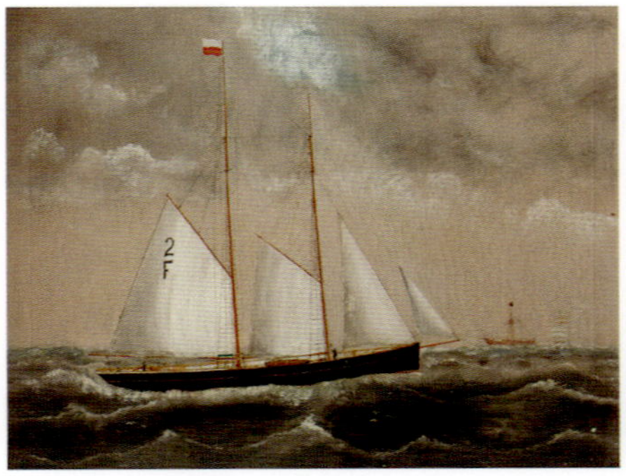

Green, J. W.
Pilot Cutter 'Leader F2' in Full Sail
oil & gouache on canvas 36.5 x 48
LANMS.1974.149.57

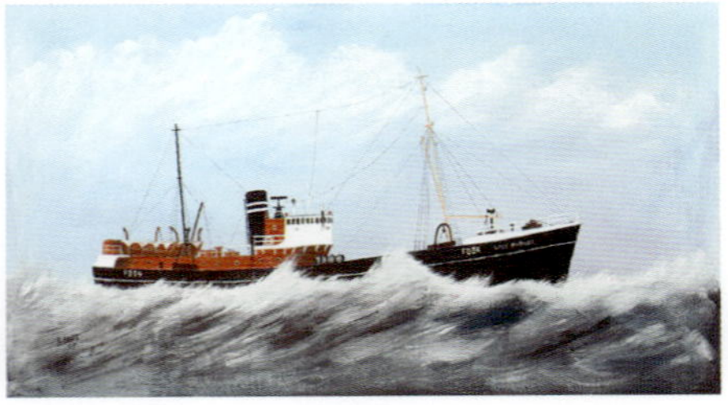

Griff, B.
'Wyre Mariner' 1995
oil on canvas 36.5 x 48
LANMS.2011.48

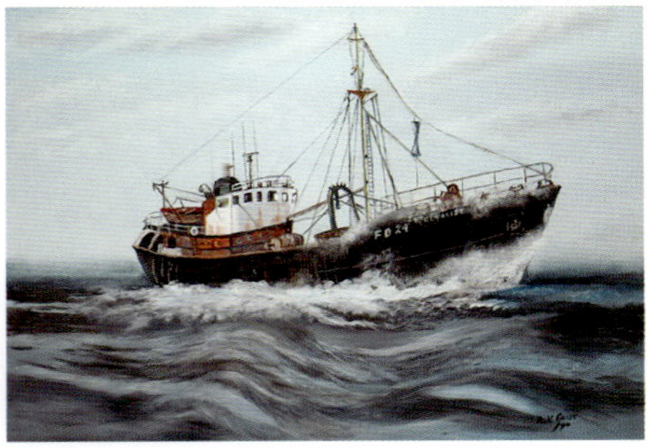

Guest, A. Vera
'Royalist FD24' 1990
oil on hardboard 49.5 x 75
LANMS.2011.38

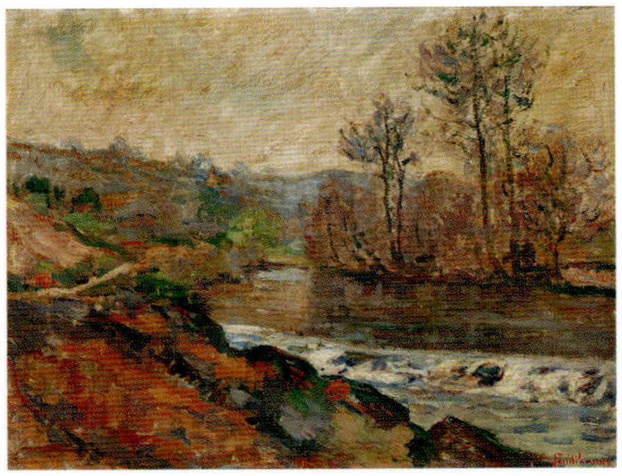

Guillaumin, Armand 1841–1927
La Creuse a Genetin c.1880
oil on canvas 37 x 53.5
LANMS.1995.29.1

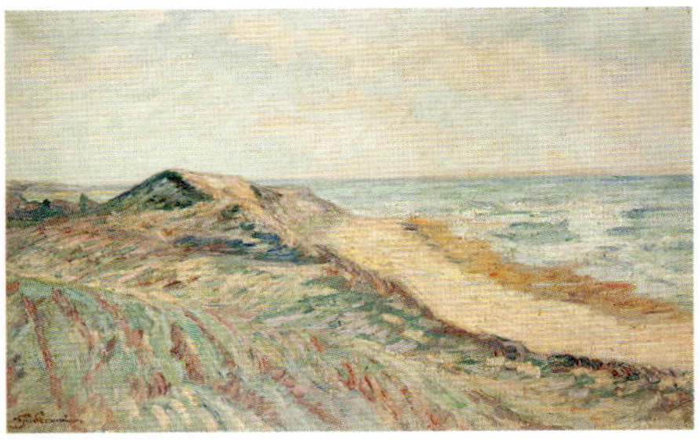

Guillaumin, Armand 1841–1927
Les Dunes de la Covarde, Ile de Re 1893
oil on canvas 38 x 64
LANMS.1995.29.2

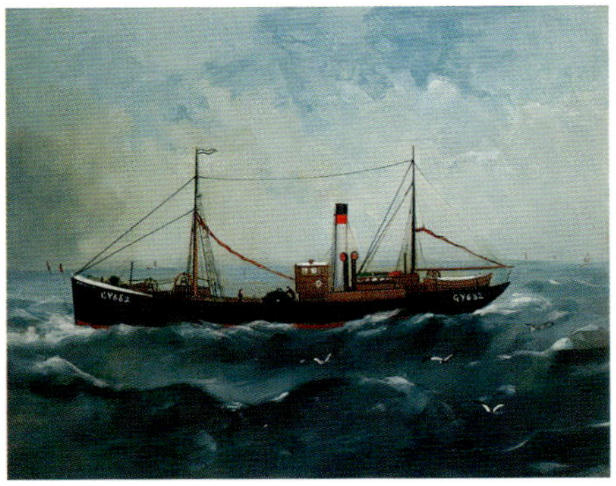

H., M. E.
'Majestic GY682'
oil on canvas 38 x 49
LANMS.2011.30

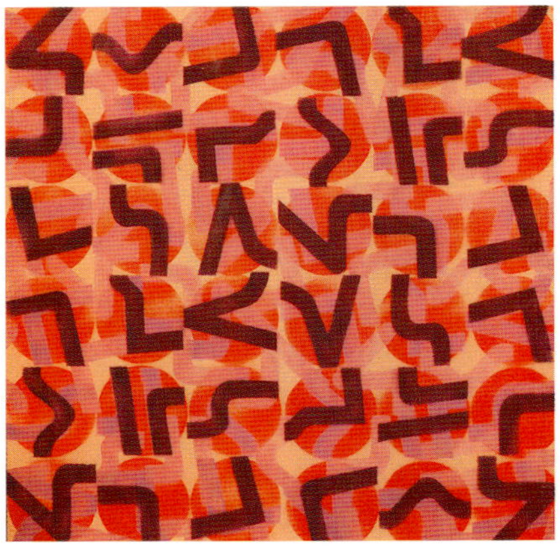

Haslam, Raymond active 1967
Cleanway
oil on canvas 91.5 x 91
LANMS.1974.30.2

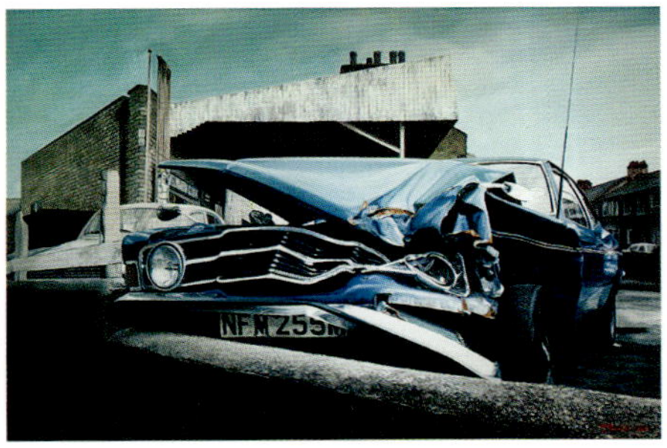

Haslam, Raymond active 1967
Crashed Cortina
acrylic on canvas 101 x 148
LANMS.1993.315

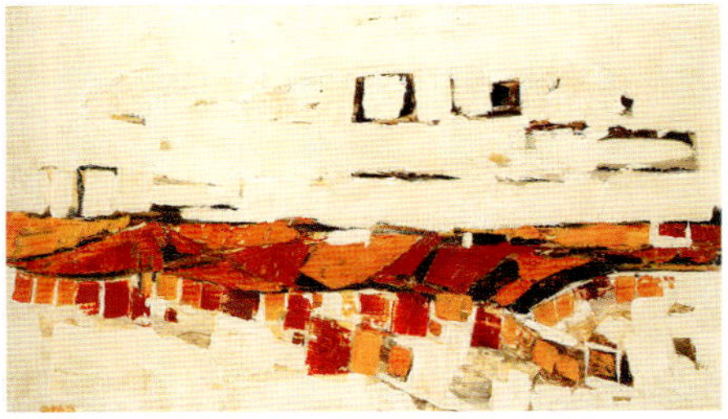

Henderson, Ian b.1939
Contemporary Treatment of Windswept Skelmersdale Landscape 1965
oil on board 61.5 x 122
LANMS.1991.218.8

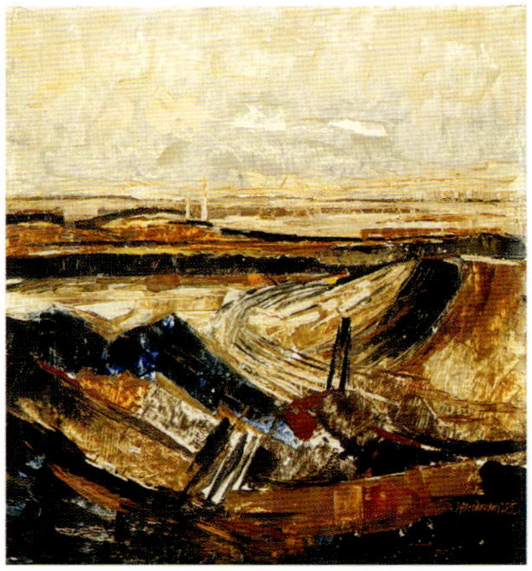

Henderson, Ian b.1939
Digmore Area from Back Lane, Showing Earth-Moving and Beginning of Pimbo Industrial Area 1965
oil & acrylic on board 62 x 62
LANMS.1991.218.3

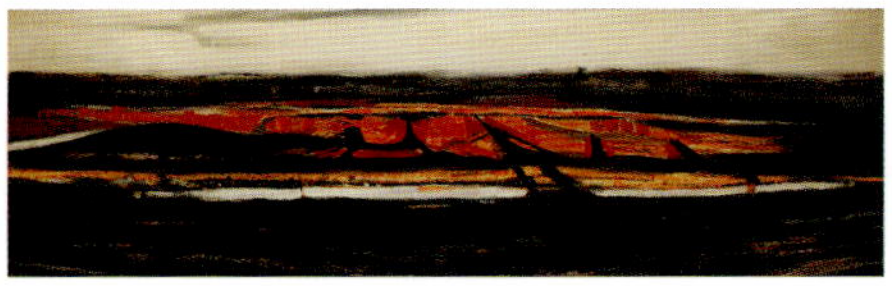

Henderson, Ian b.1939
Future View from Ashursts Ridge Looking Out over the Designated Area 1965
oil & acrylic on board 69 x 252
LANMS.1991.218.11

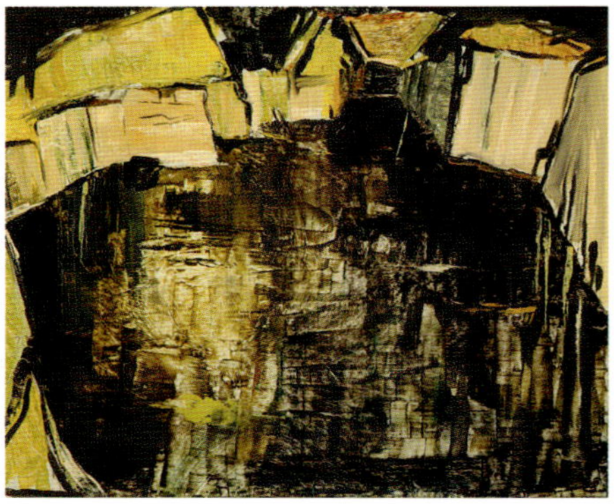

Henderson, Ian b.1939
Landscape in Green, Beige and Black 1965
oil & acrylic on board 64 x 84
LANMS.1991.218.5

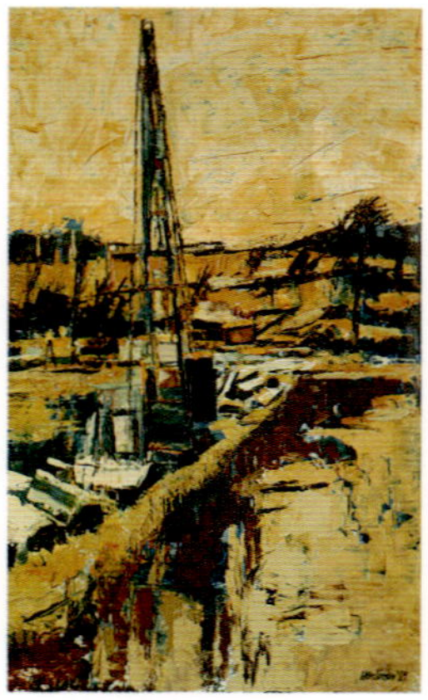

Henderson, Ian b.1939
Laying Sewage Pipe Sections at Tawd Bridge
1965
oil & acrylic on board 94 x 64
LANMS.1991.218.6

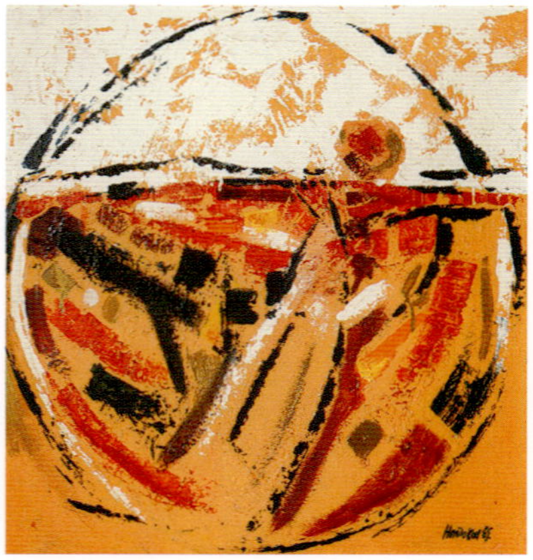

Henderson, Ian b.1939
Skelmersdale New Town 1965
oil & acrylic on board 69.5 x 68.5
LANMS.1991.218.4

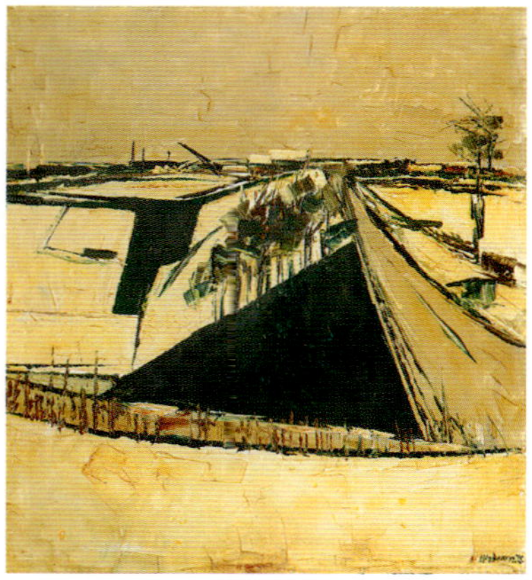

Henderson, Ian b.1939
Snowscape from Spencer's Lane Looking towards Gillibrands and New Church Farm along Wigan Road 1965
oil & acrylic on board 61.5 x 60.5
LANMS.1991.218.1

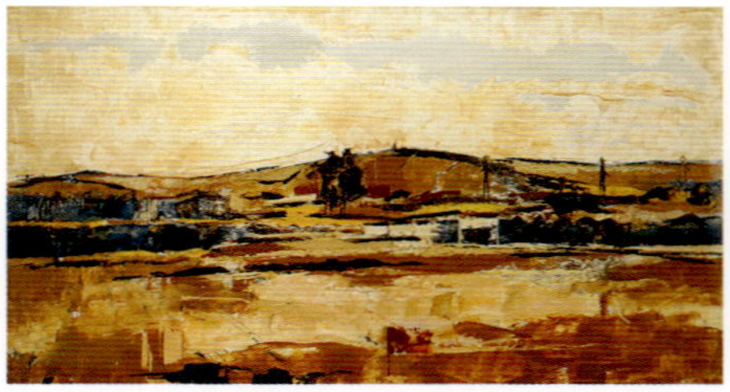

Henderson, Ian b.1939
View of Beacon and Designated Area from Ormskirk Approach 1965
oil on board 61 x 122
LANMS.1991.218.9

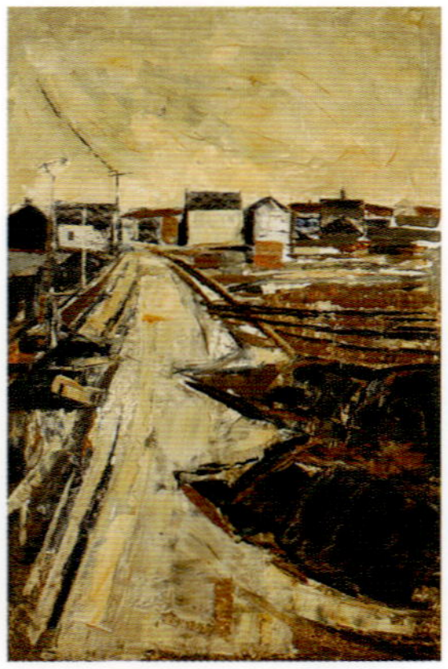

Henderson, Ian b.1939
View of Digmore Redevelopment Area 1965
oil & acrylic on board 96 x 64
LANMS.1991.218.7

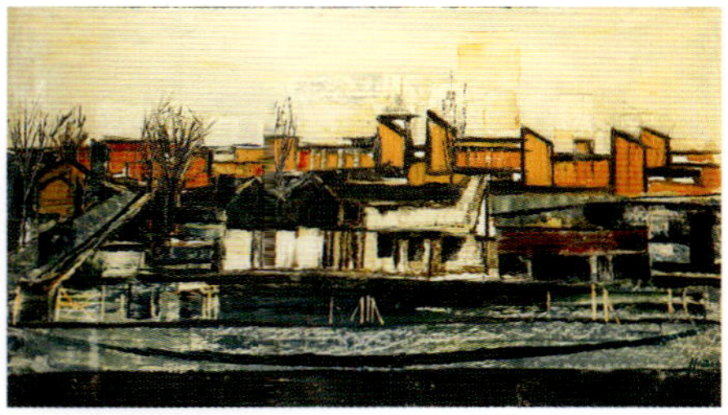

Henderson, Ian b.1939
View of New Church Farm from Gillibrands Industrial Area 1965
oil on board 61.5 x 122
LANMS.1991.218.10

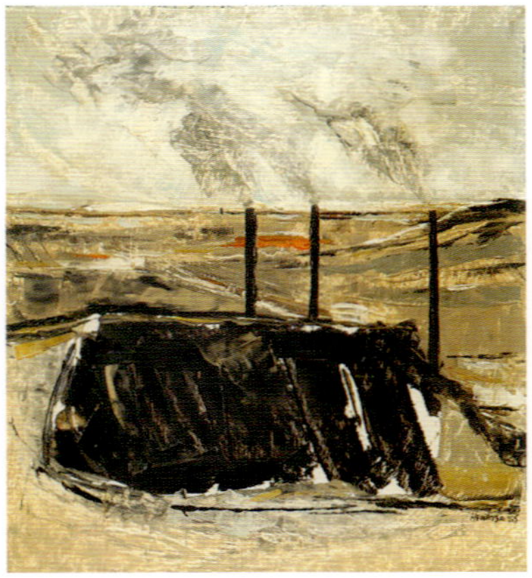

Henderson, Ian b.1939
View of Skelmersdale New Town Designated Area from behind Ravenhead Brick Works
1965
oil & acrylic on board 61 x 60.5
LANMS.1991.218.2

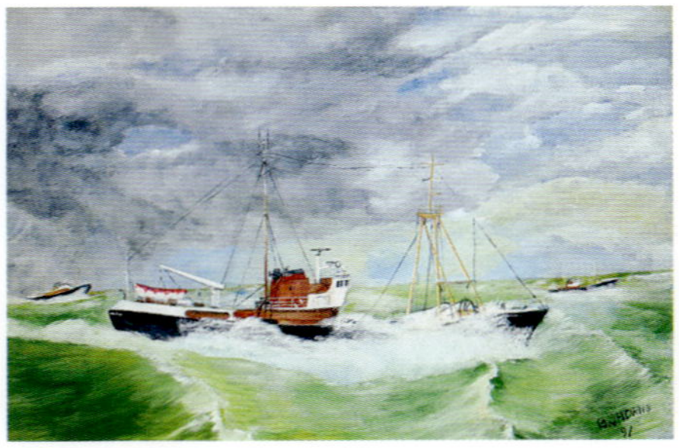

Horne, B. J.
'Boston Phantom' 1991
acrylic on hardboard 48 x 74
LANMS.2011.53

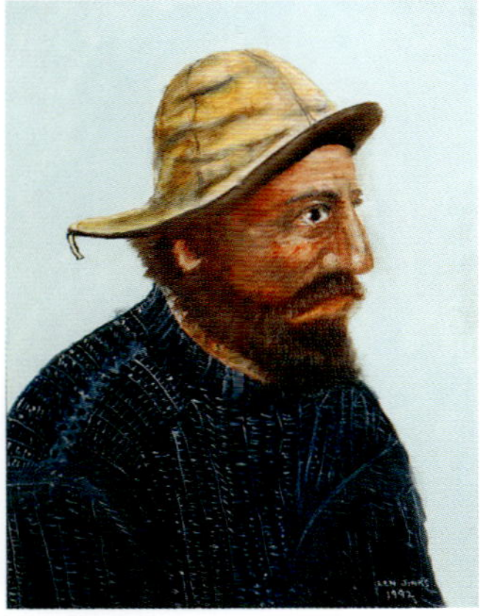

Jinks, Len
The Fisherman 1992
oil on canvas (?) 45 x 34.5
LANMS.2011.57

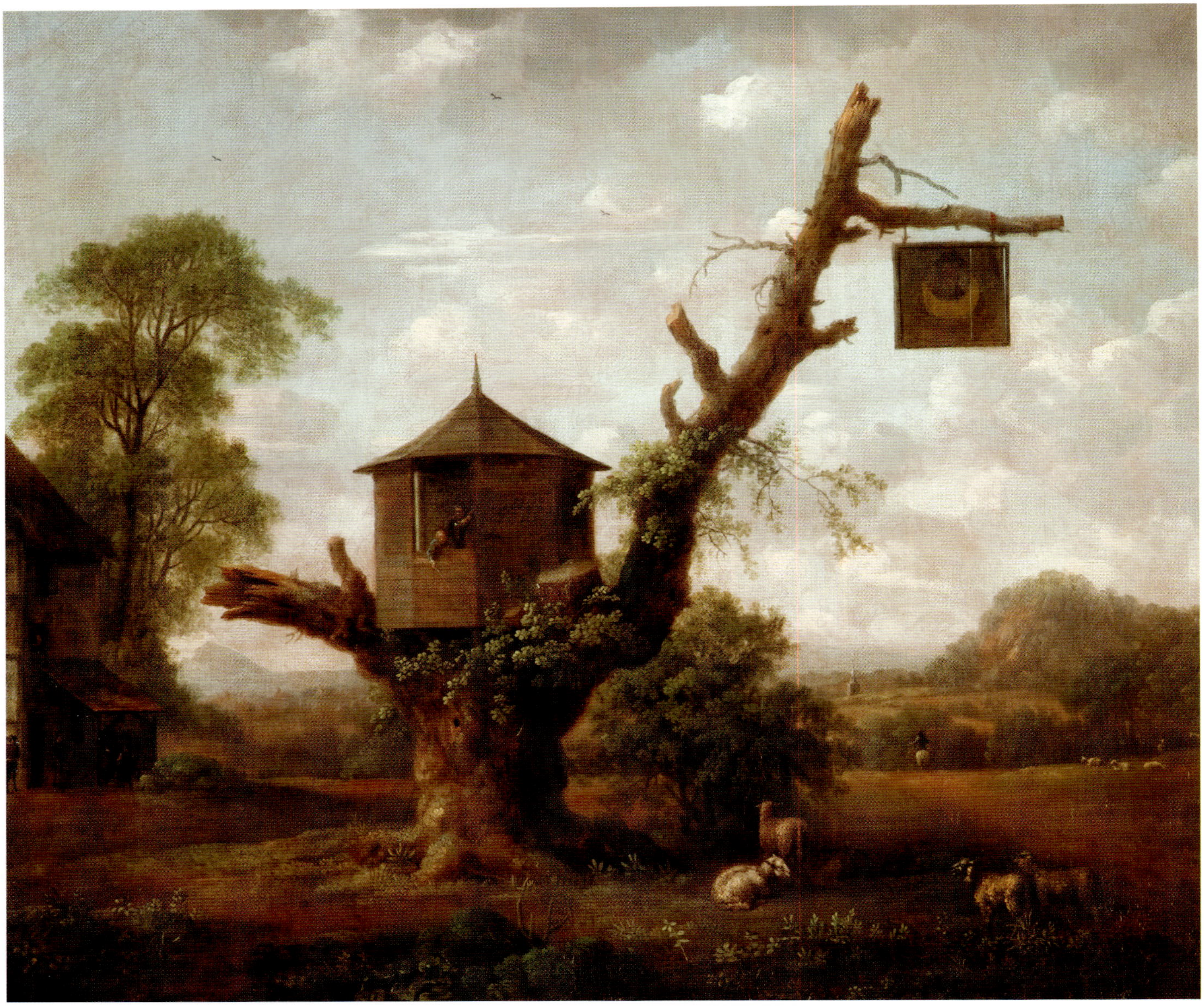

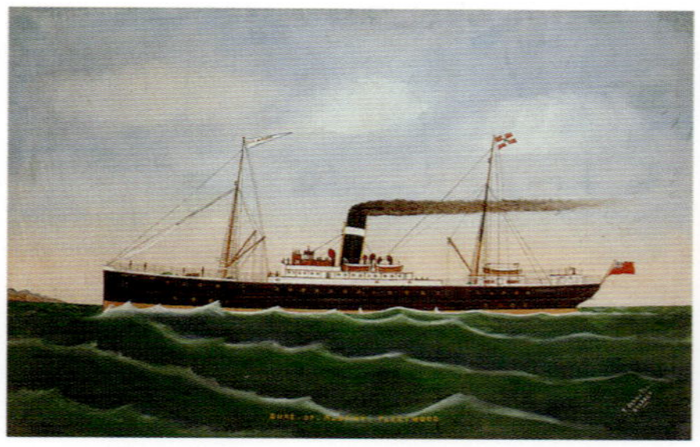

Johnston, T.
'Duke of Albany'
oil on canvas 39 x 66
LANMS.1974.149.169

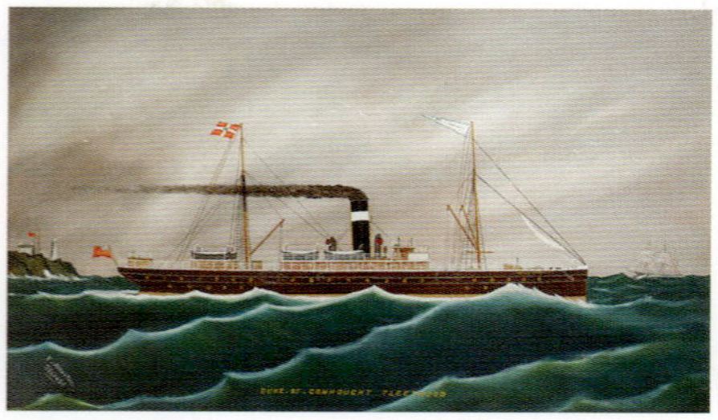

Johnston, T.
'Duke of Connaught'
oil on canvas 36 x 66
LANMS.1974.149.184

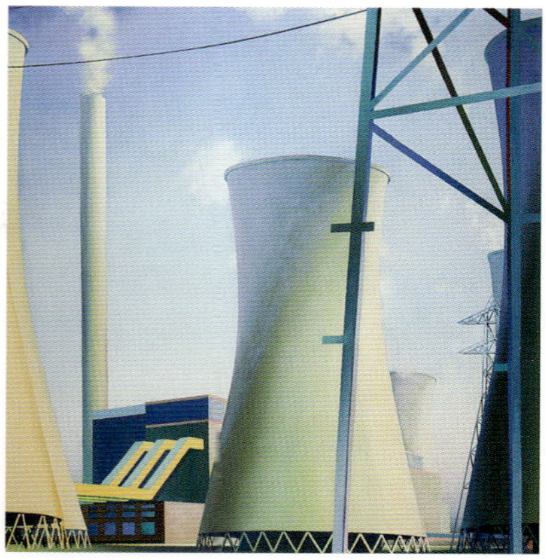

Kershaw, Walter b.1940
Fiddlers Ferry 1974
oil on canvas 115 x 115
LANMS.1974.63.2

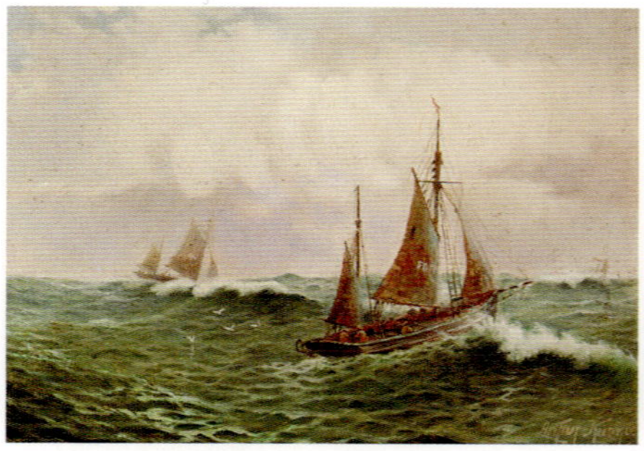

Knowles, Arthur 1870–1955
Fleetwood Deep Sea Trawlers Hove To in a Gale of Wind in the Channel
oil on hardboard 22 x 32
LANMS.2011.47

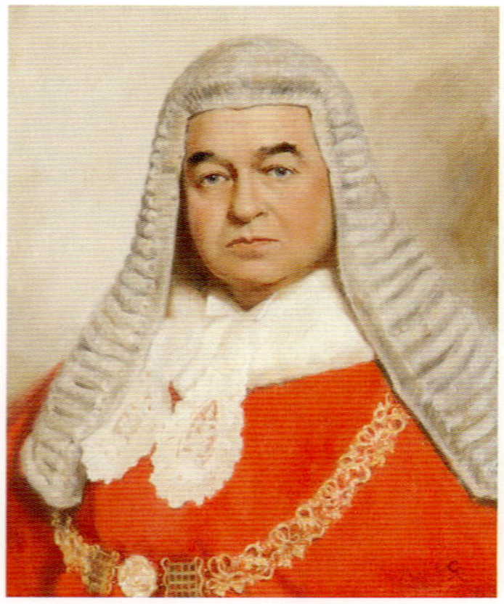

Lander, John Saint-Helier (after) 1869–1944
Baron Hewart of Bury (1840–1943) 1933
oil on canvas 57.5 x 49
LANMS.2001.7.1

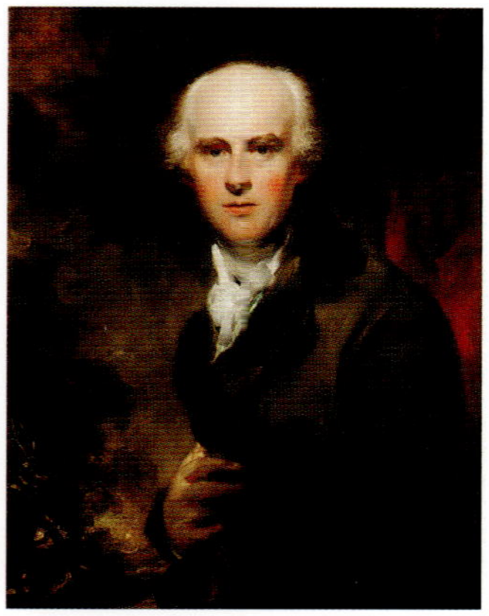

Lawrence, Thomas 1769–1830
Joseph Farington (1747–1821), RA 1794–1796
oil on canvas 73.8 x 65
LANMS.1991.407

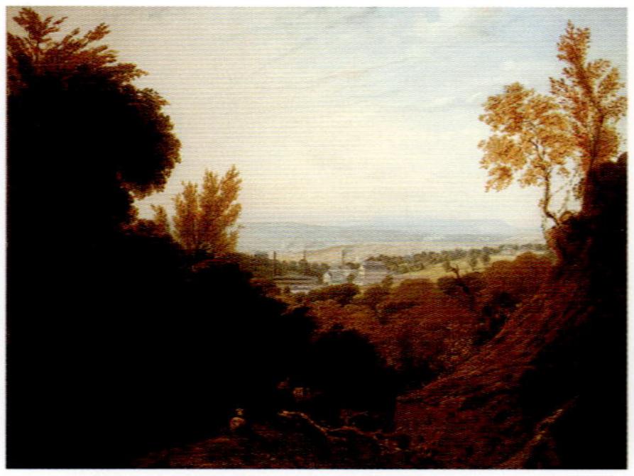

Linton, William 1791–1876
Broad Oak Printworks, near Accrington c.1827
oil on canvas 84 x 110
LANMS.2003.10

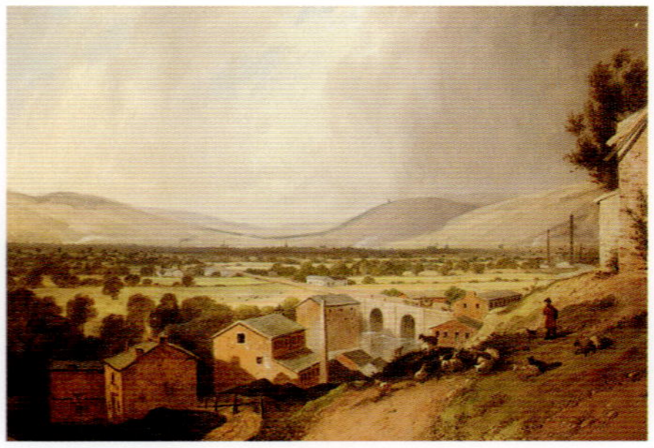

Linton, William 1791–1876
Bury from Blackford Bridge 1833
oil on canvas 83 x 123.5
LANMS.2002.3

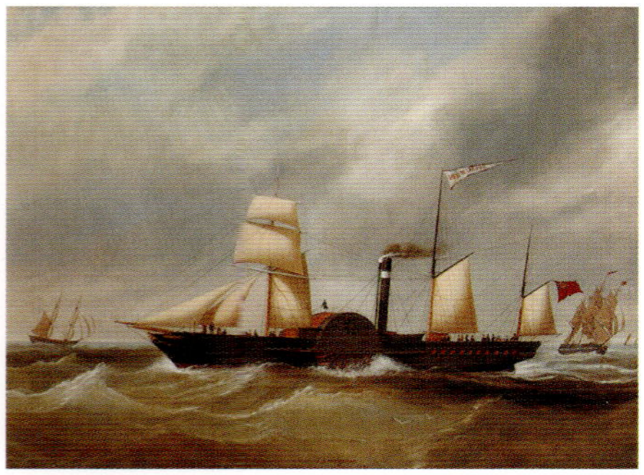

Livingstone, John active 1840–1846
'Her Majesty' Paddle Steamer 1846
oil on canvas 36.5 x 48
LANMS.1974.149.62

Facing page: Devis, Anthony, 1729–1816, *Landscape with a Hut in an Oak Tree and the 'Man in the Moon' Inn*, Harris Museum & Art Gallery (p. 292)

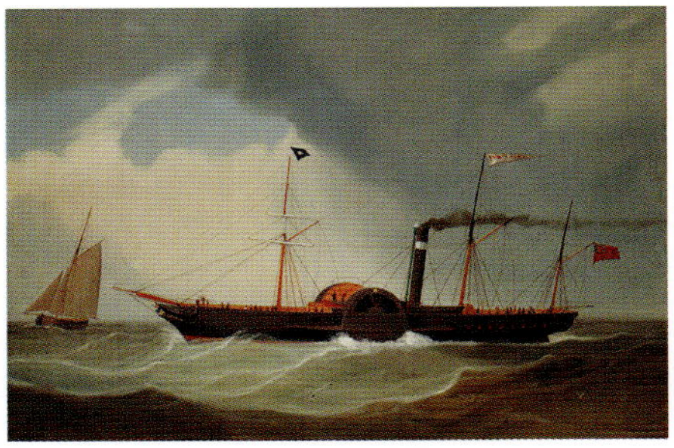

Livingstone, John (possibly) active 1840–1846
'Prince of Wales'
oil on canvas 65 x 98
LANMS.AL.1974.160

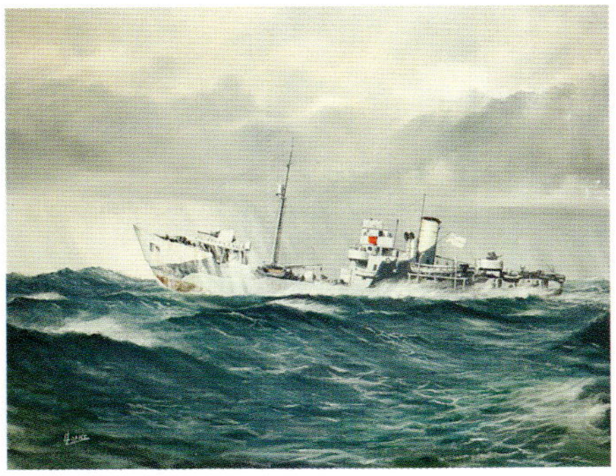

Long, E.
HMT 'Northern Sun'
oil on canvas 44.4 x 59.5
LANMS.2011.37.6

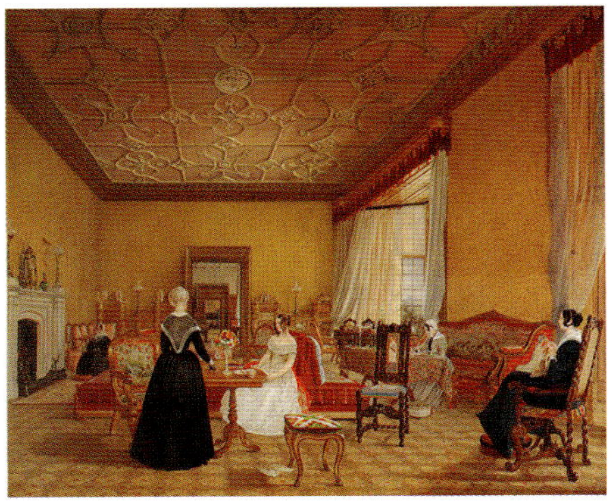

Lonsdale, Richard T. active c.1836–c.1850
The Drawing Room at Whittington Hall
1843–1844
oil on canvas 71 x 92
LANMS.1998.18

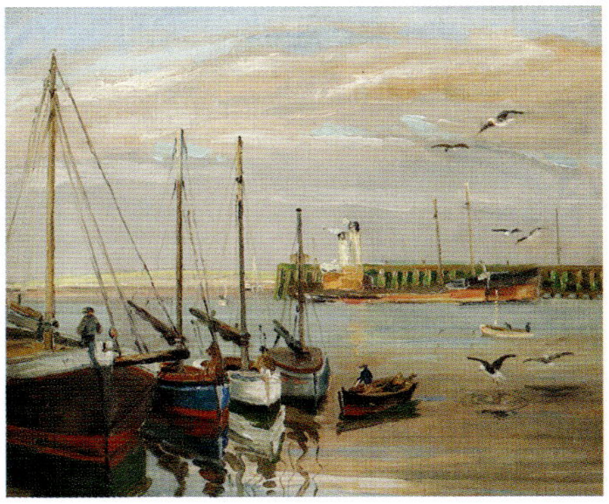

Lumb, Levi active 1913–1942
Docked Trawlers, Fleetwood 1930s
oil on board 39.5 x 49
LANMS.2010.75.2

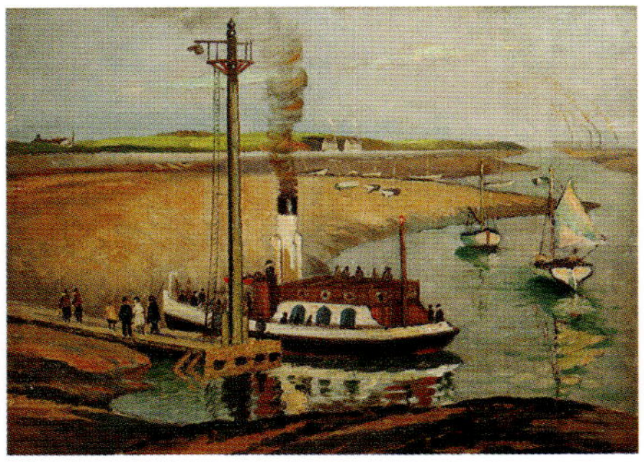

Lumb, Levi active 1913–1942
Ferry at Knott End 1930s
oil on board 39.4 x 49.2
LANMS.2010.75.1

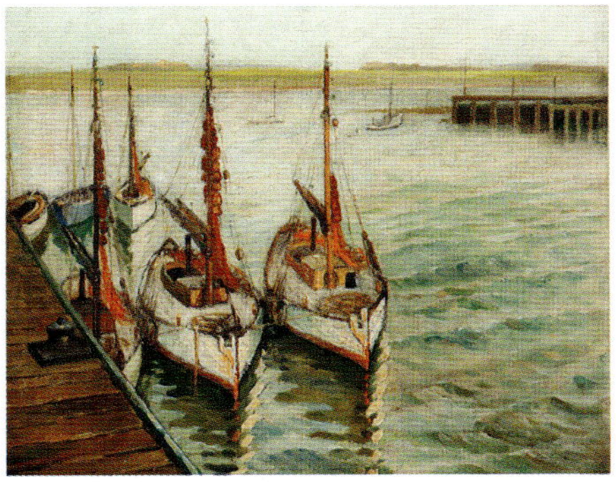

Lumb, Levi active 1913–1942
Trawlers, Fleetwood Dock 1930s
oil on board 39.2 x 49
LANMS.2010.75.3

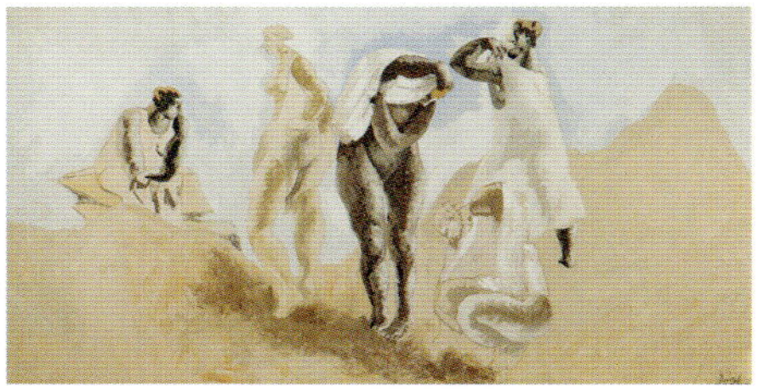

Lurçat, Jean 1892–1966
Baigneuses c.1925
oil on canvas 39.5 x 68 (E)
LANMS.1991.406.62

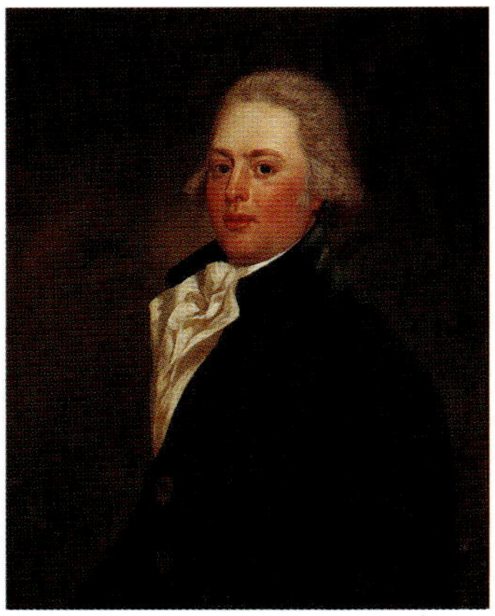

Martin, Daniel (follower of)
William Hulton of Hulton Park (1739–1773)
c.1760
oil on canvas 75 x 61
LOAN.1999.2 (P)

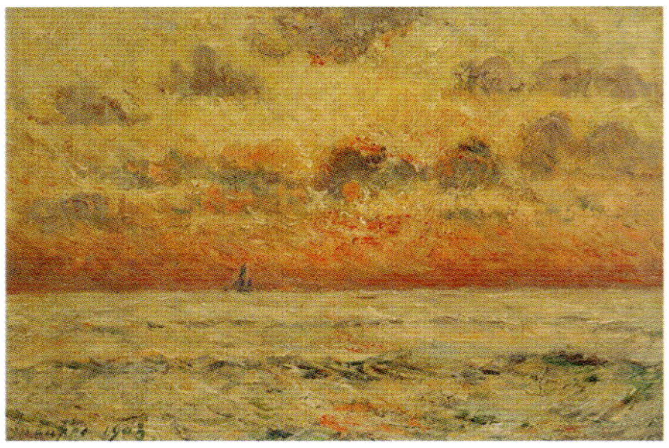

Maufra, Maxime 1861–1918
Soleil Couchant en Mer, Quiberon 1903
oil on canvas 31.5 x 53.5
LANMS.1995.29.5

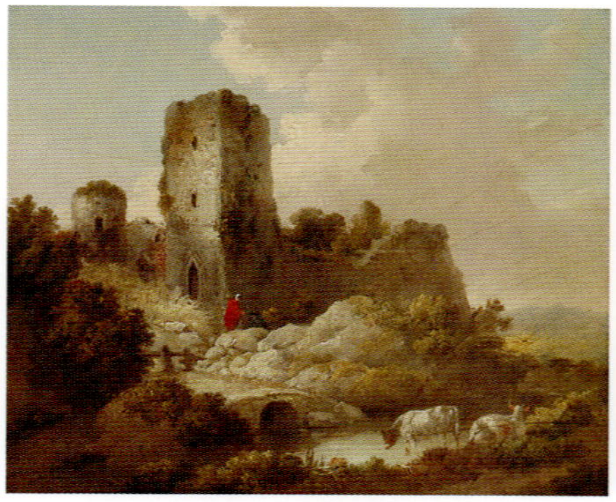

Morland, George 1763–1804
Landscape with Ruined Castle
oil on panel 24.5 x 29.5 (E)
LANMS.1995.29.8

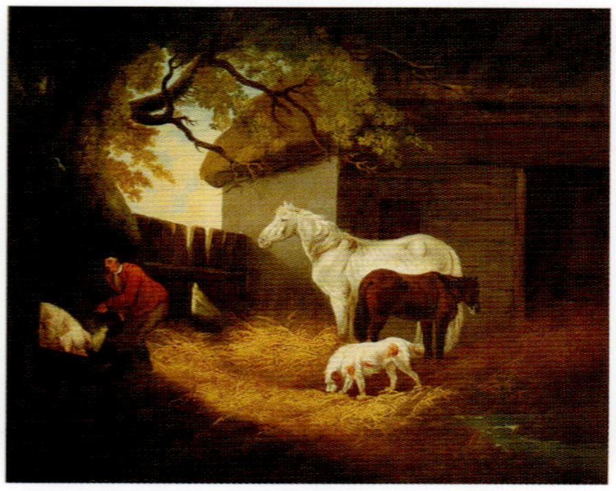

Morland, George (after) 1763–1804
Feeding Time in the Farmyard 1793
oil on canvas 68 x 87
LANMS.1995.29.7

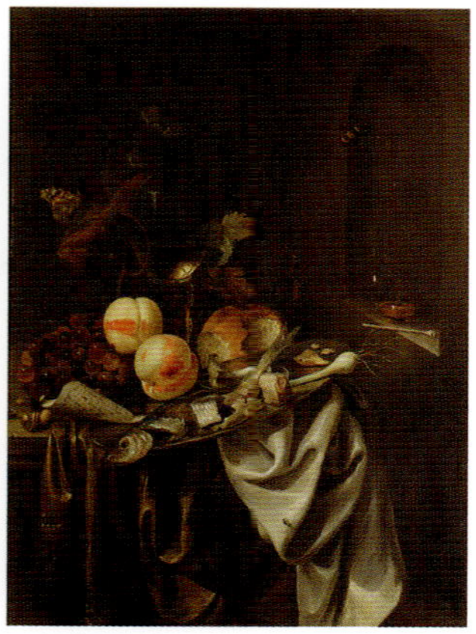

Mortel, Jan 1650–1719
Still Life with Fish, Bread and Fruit 1683
oil on oak panel 64.5 x 46 (E)
LANMS.2002.11.2

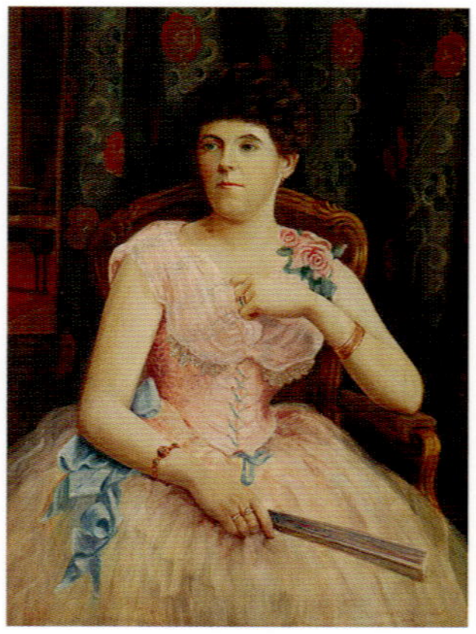

North Sergeant, M.
Portrait of a Lady in a Pink Dress c.1939
oil on canvas 87 x 66
DB.1985.1092

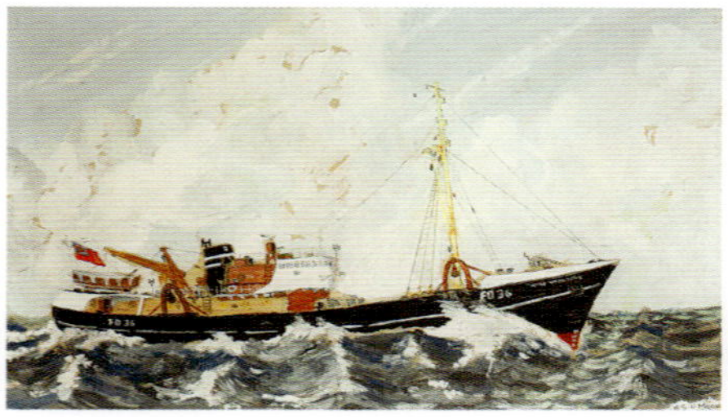

O'Moore, A. S.
'Wyre Vanguard'
oil on card 31 x 50
LANMS.2011.52

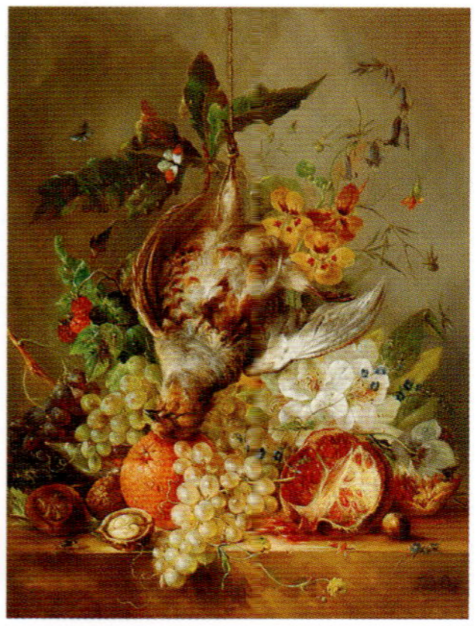

Os, Jan van 1744–1808
Still Life with Dead Bird, Fruit and Flowers
c.1780
oil on canvas 62.5 x 52 (E)
LANMS.1991.406.2

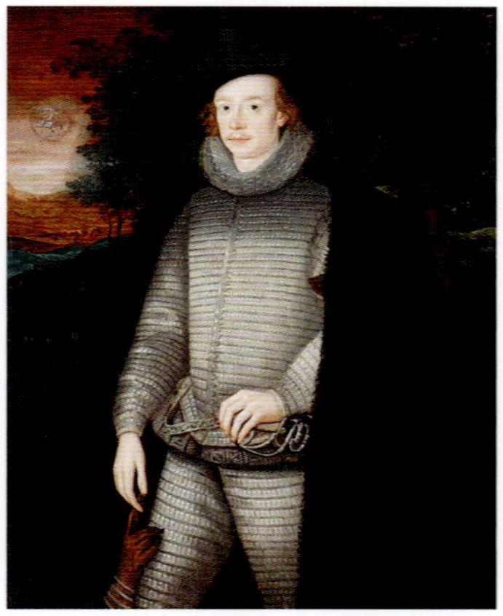

Peake, Robert (attributed to) 1551–1619
John Braddyll of Portfield and Whalley c.1590
oil on panel 97.5 x 74.5 (E)
LANMS.2001.6

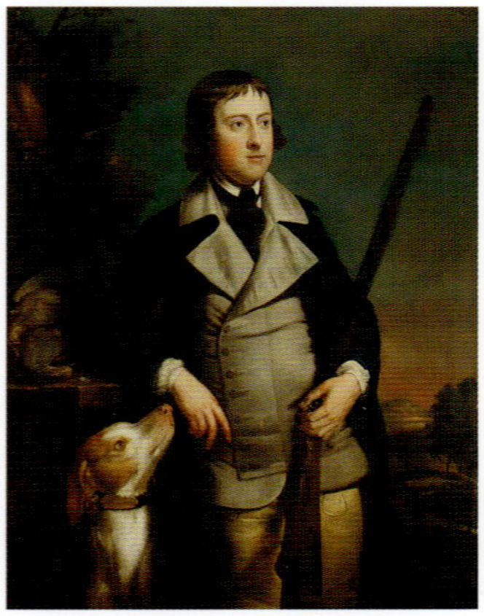

Pickering, Henry 1720–1771
William Hulton with Gun-Dog and Shotgun
1769
oil on canvas 122 x 98 (E)
LOAN.1999.2 (P)

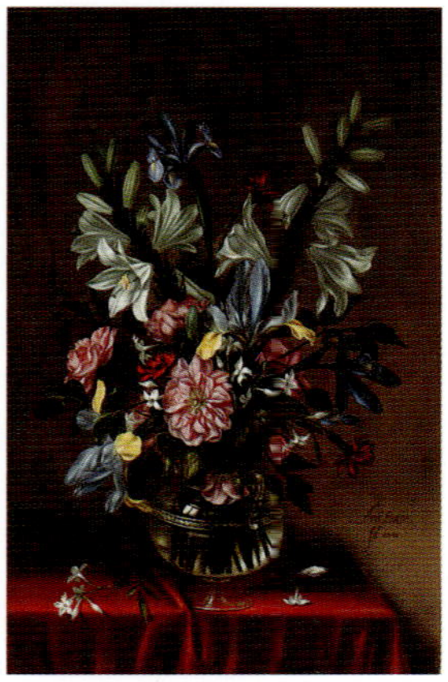

Ponce, Antonio 1608–1677
Still Life with Vase of Flowers 1650
oil on canvas 81 x 59.5 (E)
LANMS.1983.154

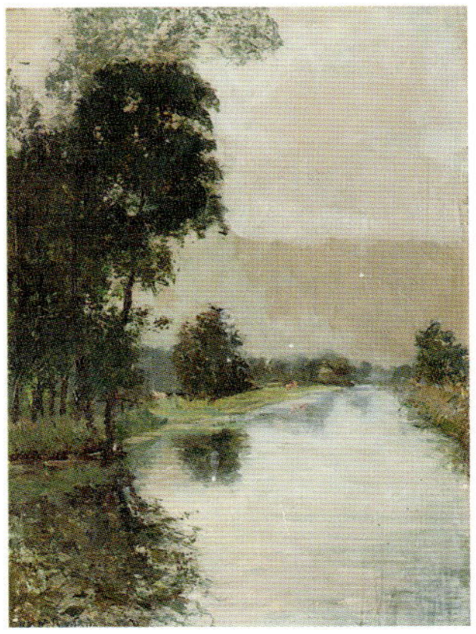

Rankin
River Landscape
oil on board 39 x 31 (E)
ECR.0161.62

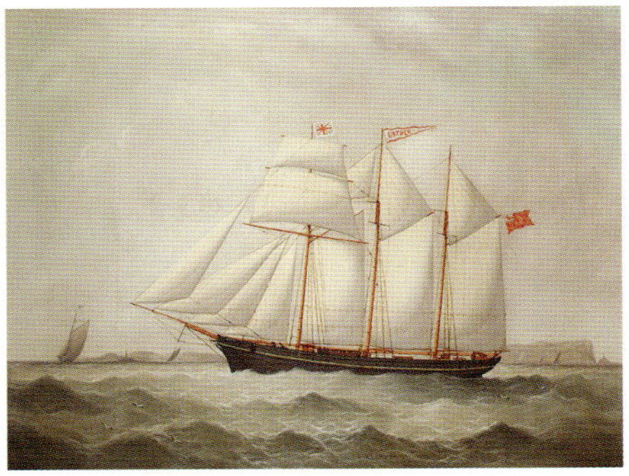

Rawcliffe, John active 1872
'Esther'
oil on canvas 47.5 x 74
LANMS.2011.35

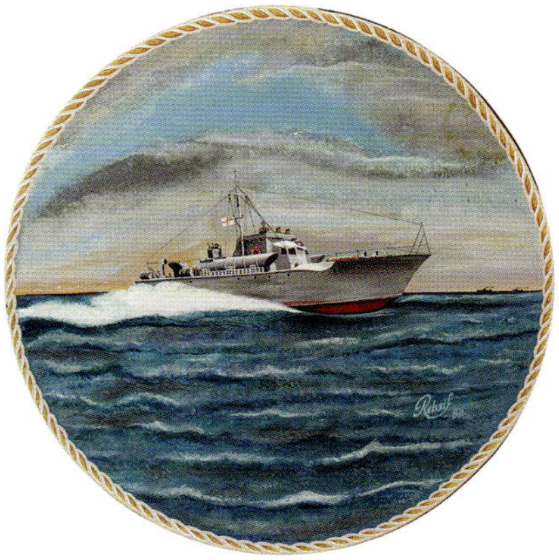

Rehsif
Patrol Boat 1985
oil on board (?) 46 x 46
LANMS.2011.43

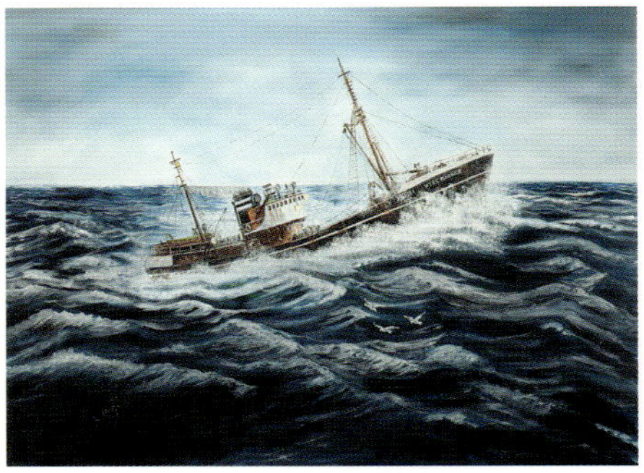

Rogers, Elsie
'Wyre Mariner' 1990
oil on hardboard 50.2 x 75.4
LANMS.2011.54

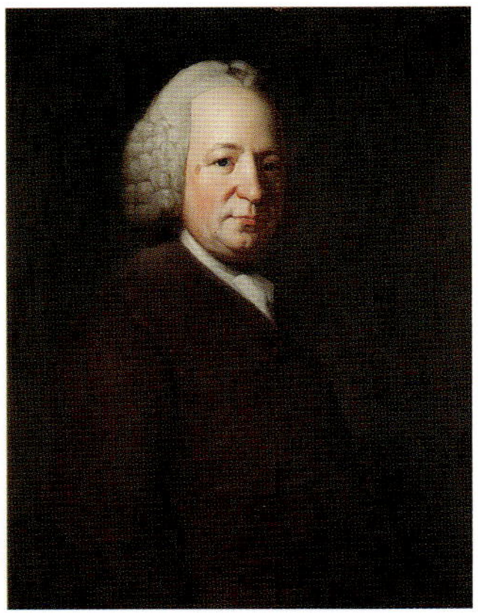

Romney, George 1734–1802
Thomas Hutton Rawlinson (1712–1769) c.1759
oil on canvas 76 x 63.5
LANMS.2006.2.2

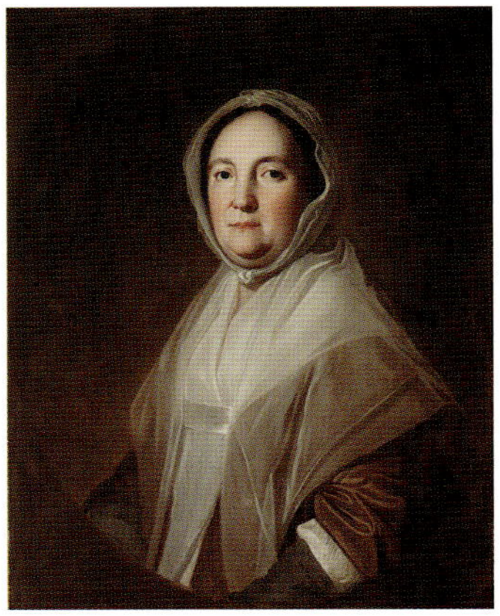

Romney, George 1734–1802
Mary Hutton Rawlinson (1772–1786) c.1765
oil on canvas 76 x 63.5
LANMS.2006.2.3

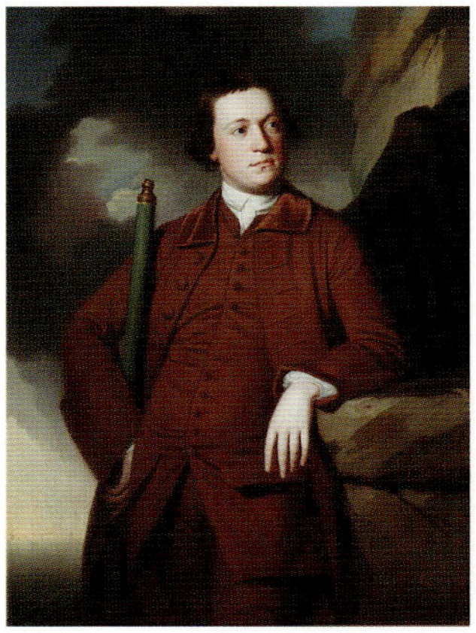

Romney, George 1734–1802
Abraham Rawlinson (1738–1803), MP, of Ellel Hall, near Lancaster c.1765–1767
oil on canvas 127 x 101.5
LANMS.2006.2.1

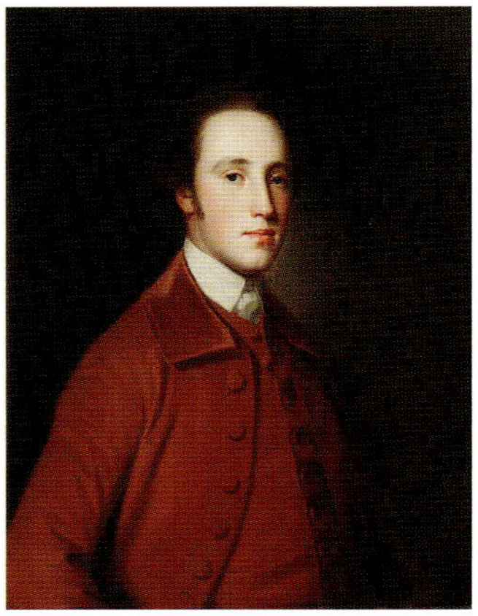

Romney, George 1734–1802
John Satterthwaite c.1780
oil on canvas 70 x 50 (E)
LOAN.1992.1 (P)

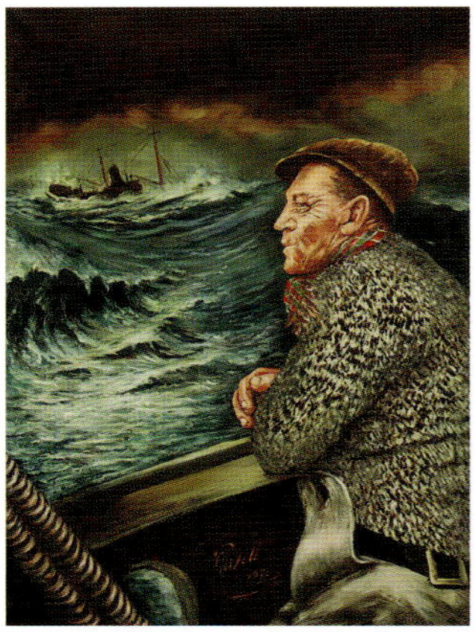

Roskell, Thomas Henry b.1928
Skipper Roskell 1978
oil on canvas 100 x 75
LANMS.2004.22.1

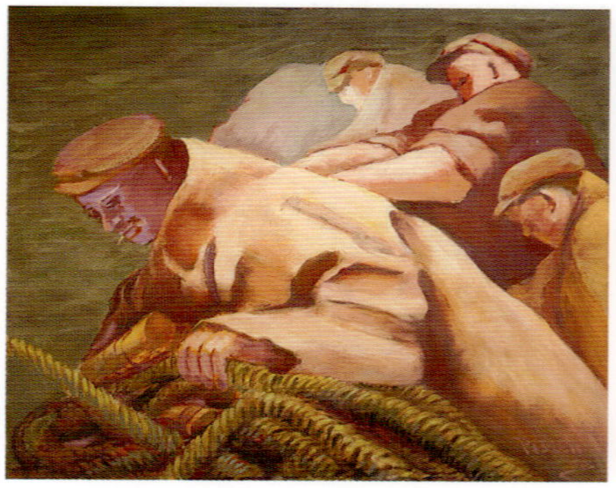

Roskell, Thomas Henry b.1928
Hauling the Nets 2003
oil on canvas 81 x 101.5
LANMS.2004.22.9

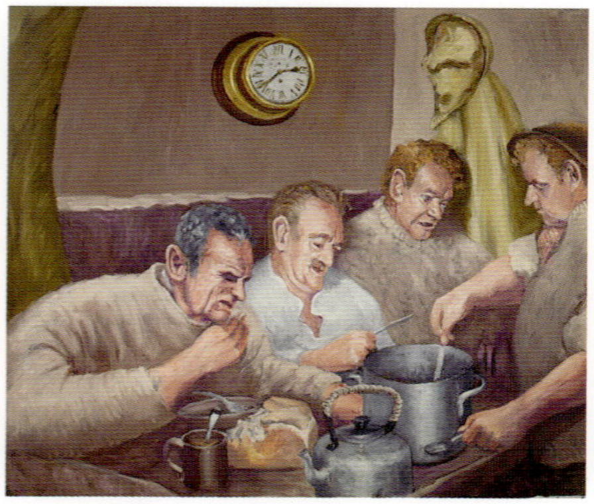

Roskell, Thomas Henry b.1928
Mess Room 2004
oil on canvas 101.5 x 127
LANMS.2004.22.8

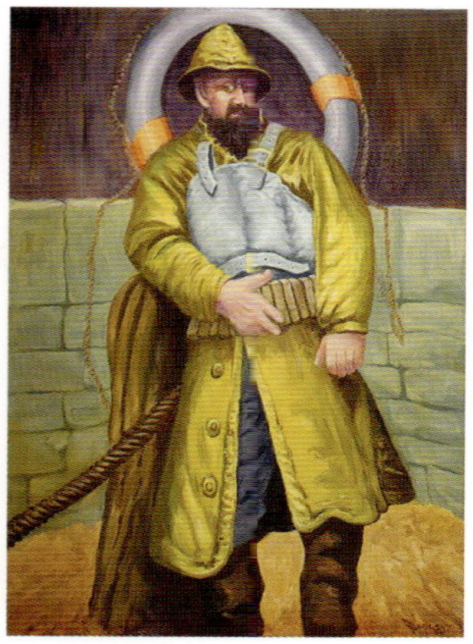

Roskell, Thomas Henry b.1928
Fisherman in Yellow Oilskins
oil on canvas 127 x 101
LANMS.2004.22.7

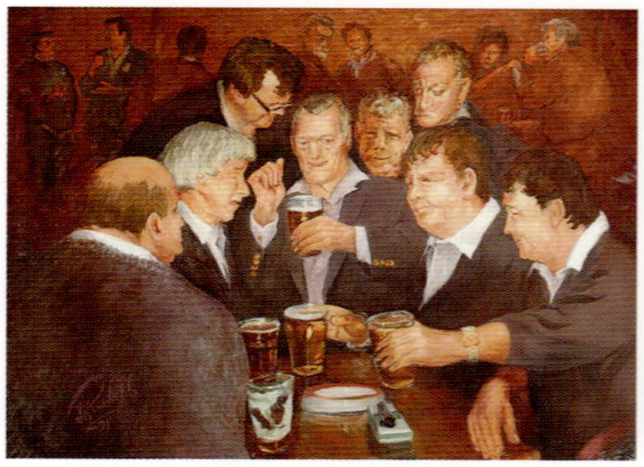

Roskell, Thomas Henry b.1928
George's Birthday
oil on canvas 90 x 121
LANMS.2004.22.3

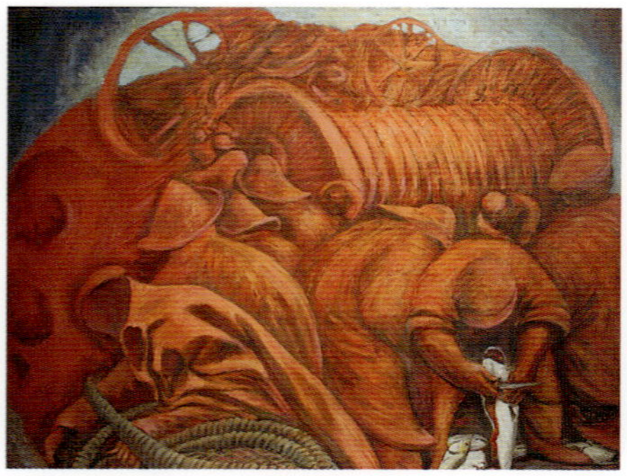

Roskell, Thomas Henry b.1928
Hauling Time
oil on canvas 138 x 184
LANMS.2004.22.2

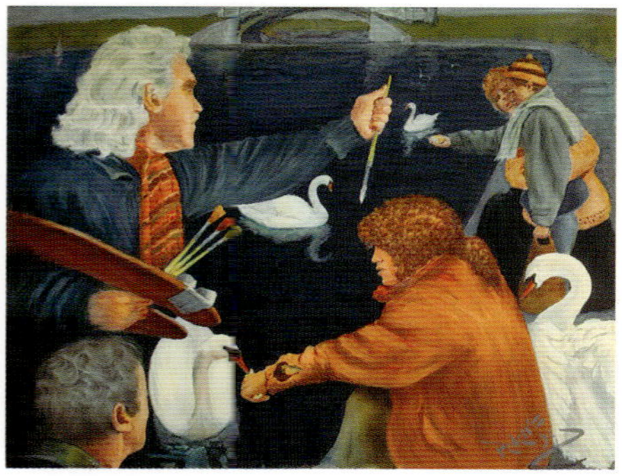

Roskell, Thomas Henry b.1928
Jane Feeding Swans
oil on canvas 99 x 128
LANMS.2004.22.4

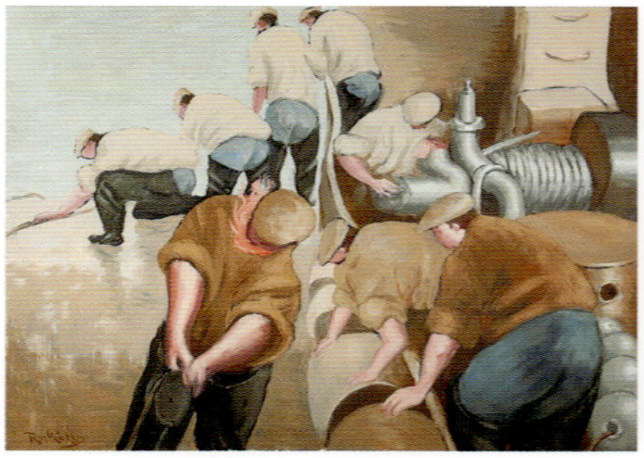

Roskell, Thomas Henry b.1928
On Deck of a Trawler
oil on canvas 101.5 x 127
LANMS.2004.22.6

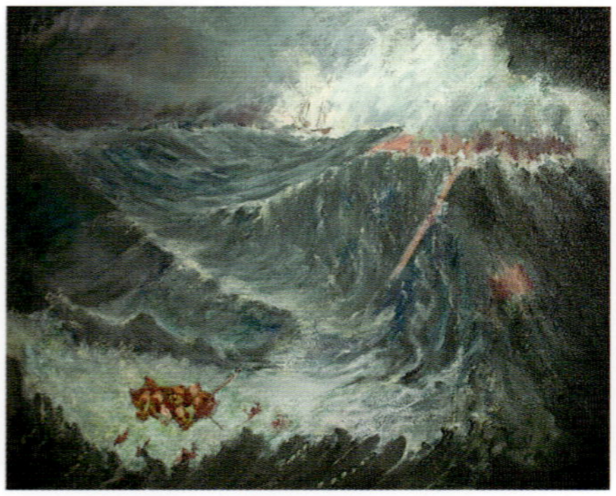

Roskell, Thomas Henry b.1928
Small Boat in Rough Sea
oil on canvas 138 x 184
LANMS.2004.22.5

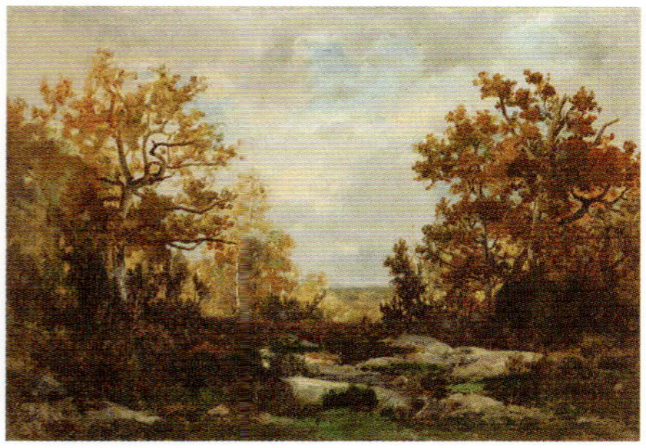

Rousseau, Théodore (studio of) 1812–1867
River in a Wooded Landscape 1850–1910
oil on canvas 36 x 56
LANMS.1995.29.6

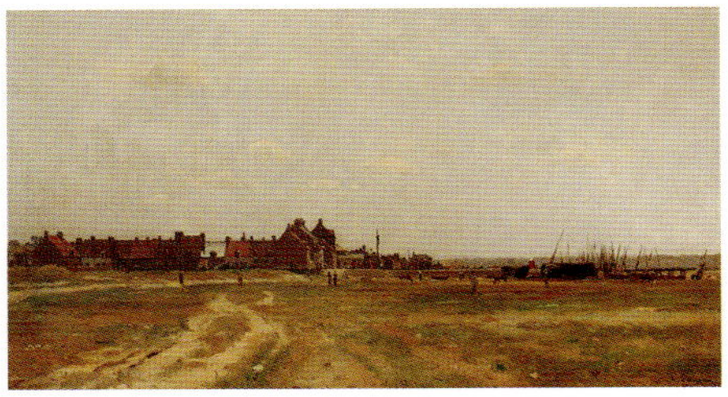

Sauzay, Adrien Jacques 1841–1928
Vue d'Etaples c.1875
oil on panel 32 x 60 (E)
LANMS.1995.29.4

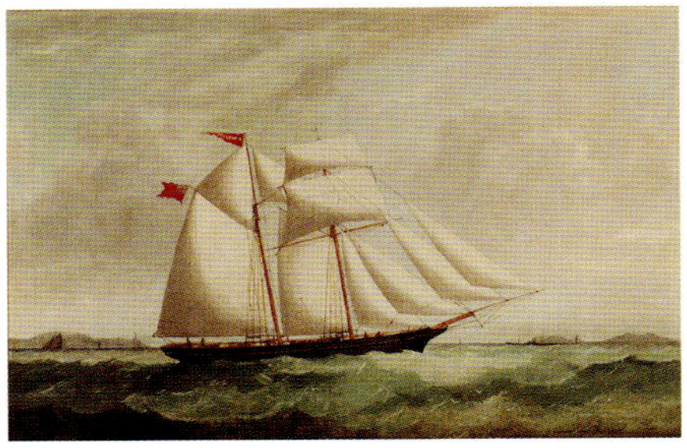

Semple, Joseph 1830–1877
'The Richard Warbrick' 1854
oil on canvas 47.2 x 75.6
LANMS.1974.149.186

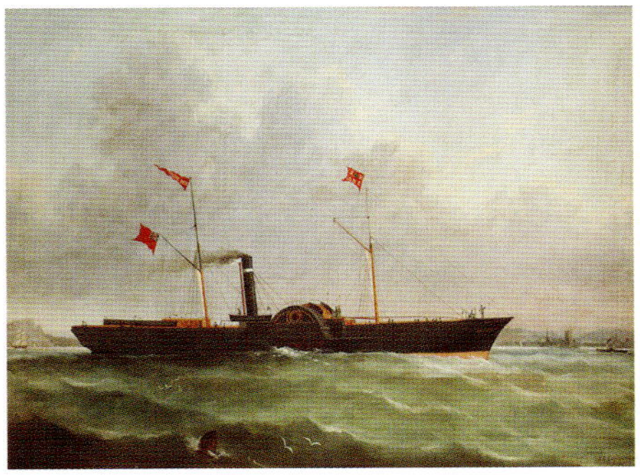

Semple, Joseph 1830–1877
'Royal Consort' Paddle Steamer
oil on canvas 50.5 x 88
LANMS.1974.149.193

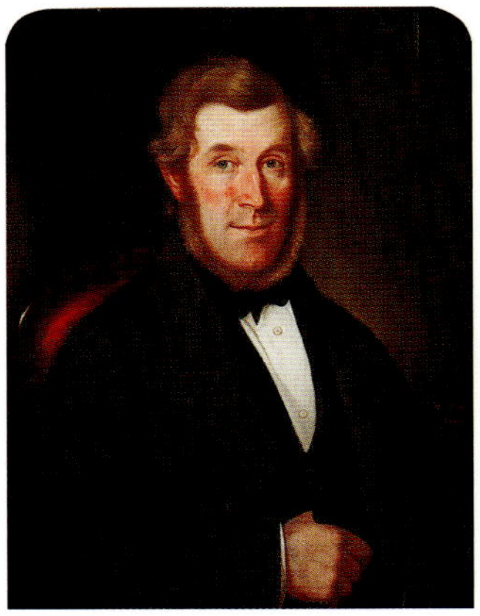

Shaw, John 1819–1876
Thomas Hogg 1860
oil on canvas 75 x 62.5
LANMS.1985.346.220

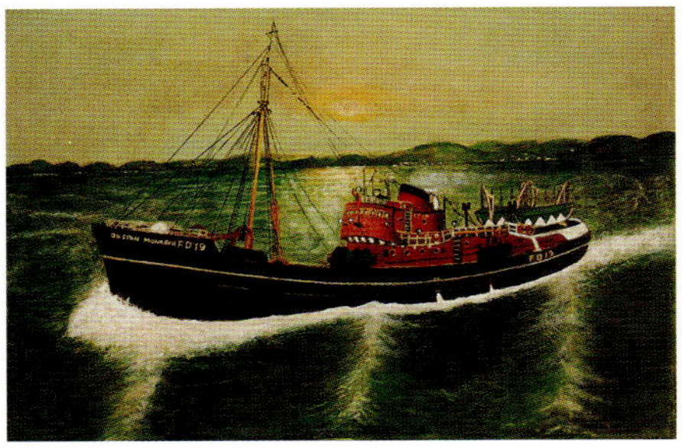

Snape, Raymond active 1983–2001
'Boston Monarch FD19' 1983
oil on paper 39.5 x 71.2
LANMS.2011.29

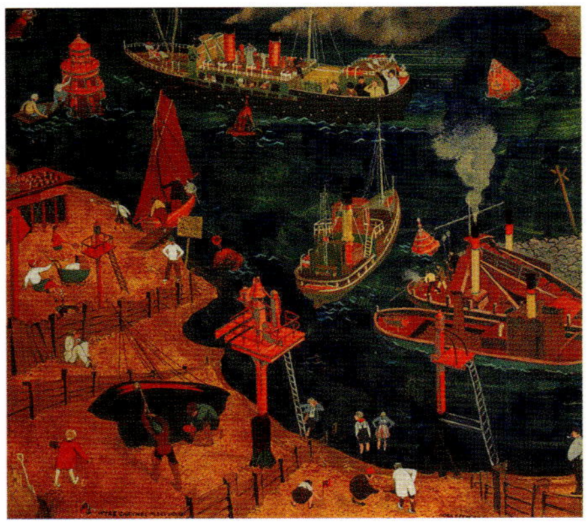

Spencer, Noël 1900–1986
Wyre Channel 1924
tempera on board 54 x 63
LANMS.1975.5

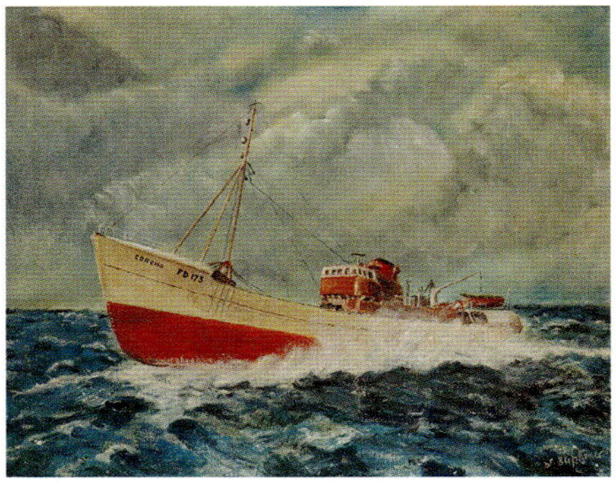

Stephenson, W. active 1960s
'Corena' 1960s
oil on hardboard 40 x 57.5
LANMS.2011.41.1

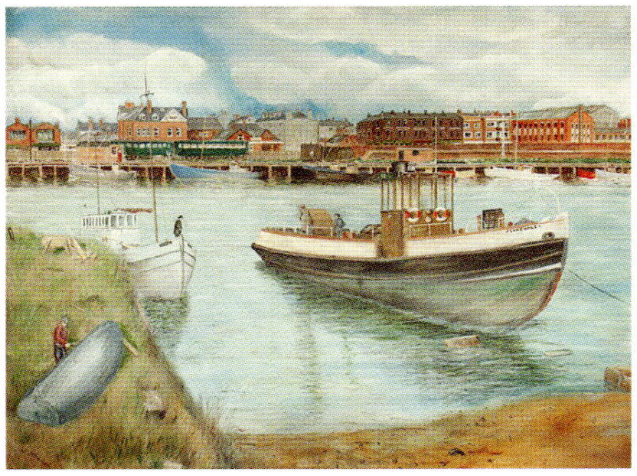

Stephenson, W. active 1960s
Fleetwood Docks 1960s
oil on hardboard 90.5 x 120
LANMS.2011.41.2

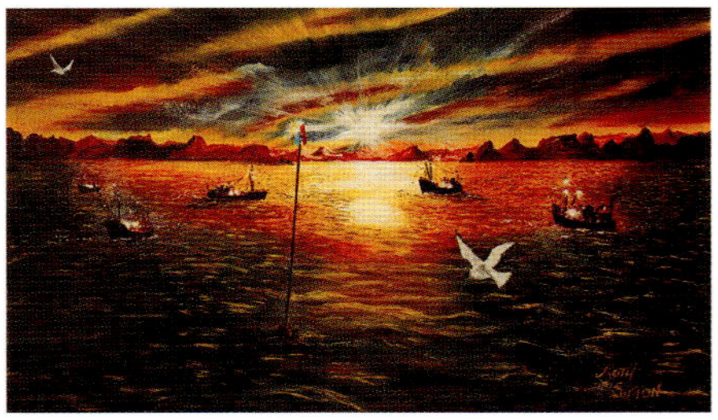

Sutton, Keith
Fishing Boats at Sunset, Iceland 1968
oil on hardboard 60.2 x 121
LANMS.2011.51

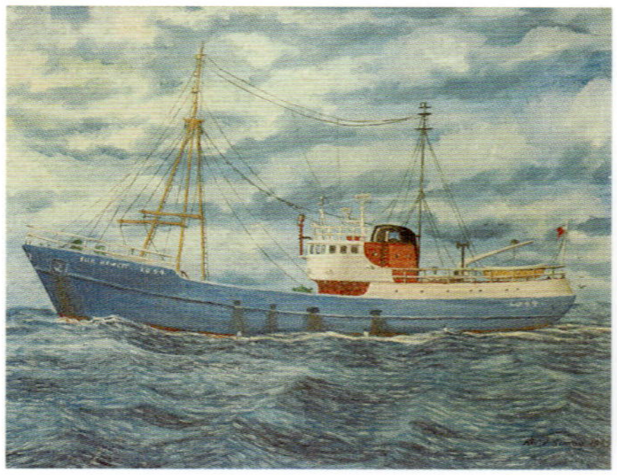

Sutton, Keith
'Ella Hewitt' 1969
oil on board 40.2 x 50
LANMS.2011.55

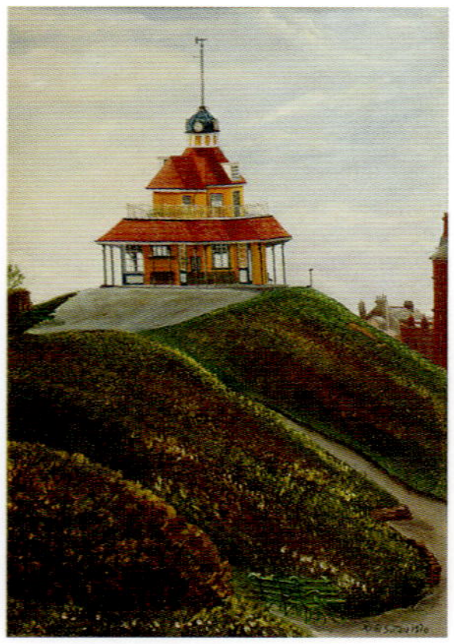

Sutton, Keith
The Mount Pavilion, Fleetwood 1970
oil on canvas 74.5 x 59.5
LANMS.1974.149.114

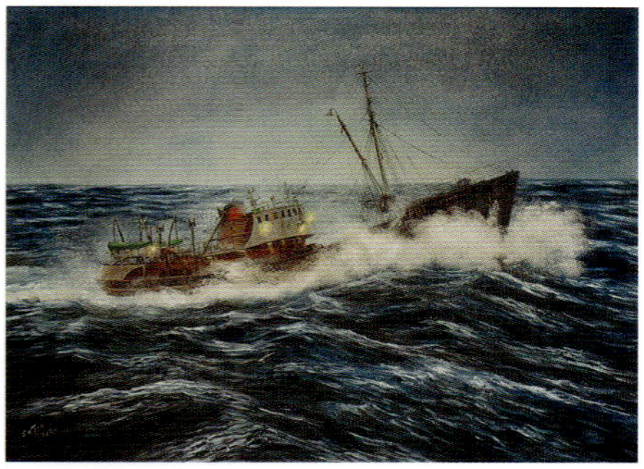

Sutton, Keith
'Fleetwood Lady' 1984
oil on hardboard 50 x 79
LANMS.2010.76.1

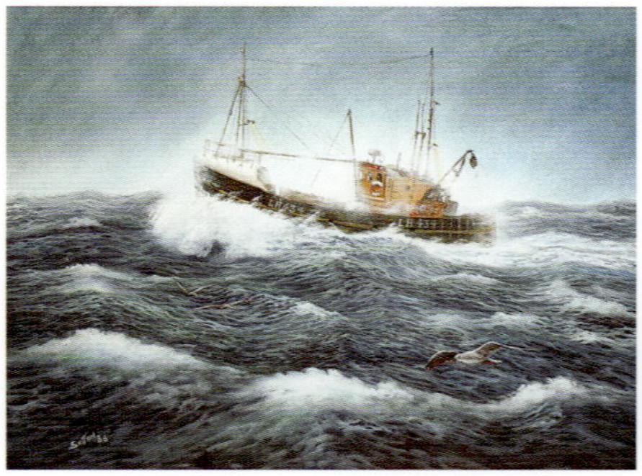

Sutton, Keith
'Antares'
oil on hardboard 50 x 75.2
LANMS.2011.39.1

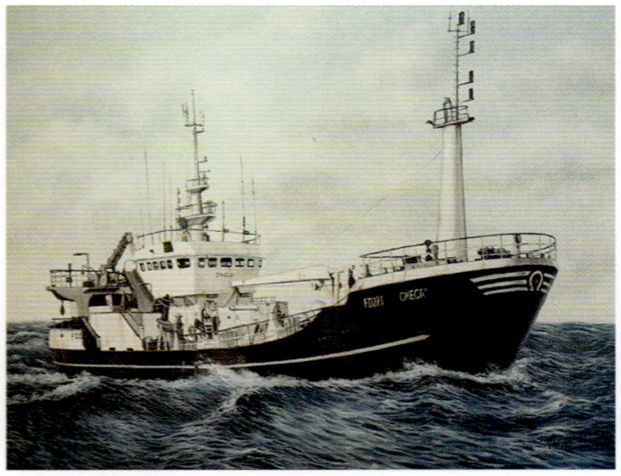

Sutton, Keith
'Omega B'
oil on hardboard 49.5 x 75
LANMS.2010.74

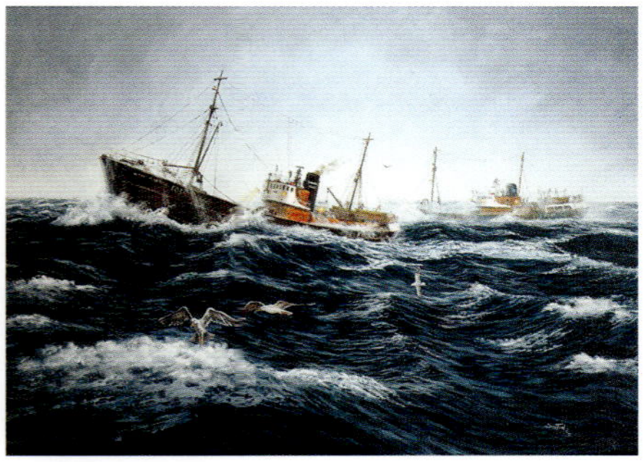

Sutton, Keith
'Wyre Mariner' and 'Ella Hewitt'
oil on hardboard 59 x 90
LANMS.2011.36

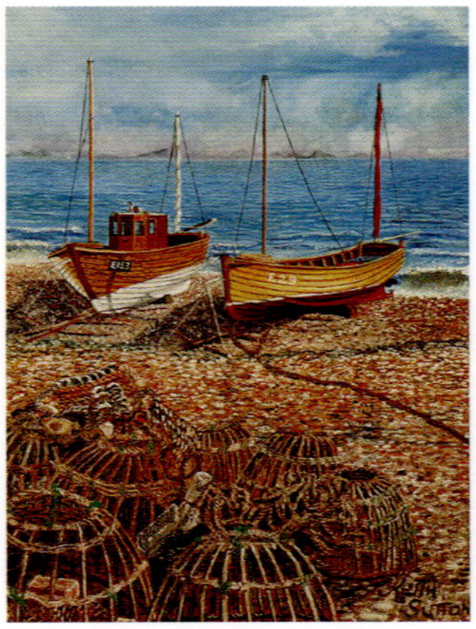

Sutton, Keith
The Lobster Boats
oil on canvas 60.4 x 44.5
LANMS.1974.149.116

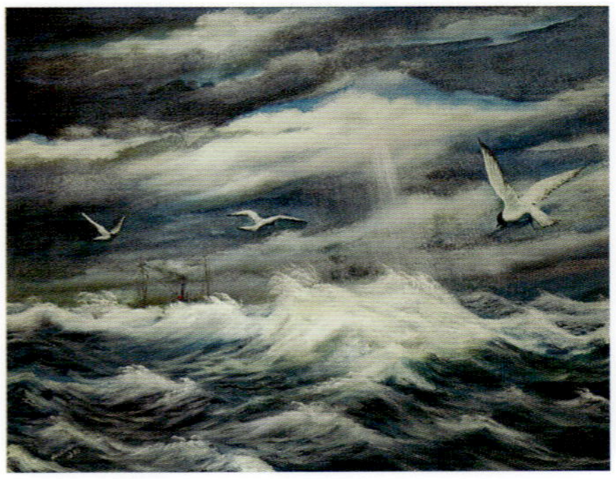

Sutton, Keith
Trawler in Rough Seas
oil on hardboard 57.5 x 70
LANMS.2010.77

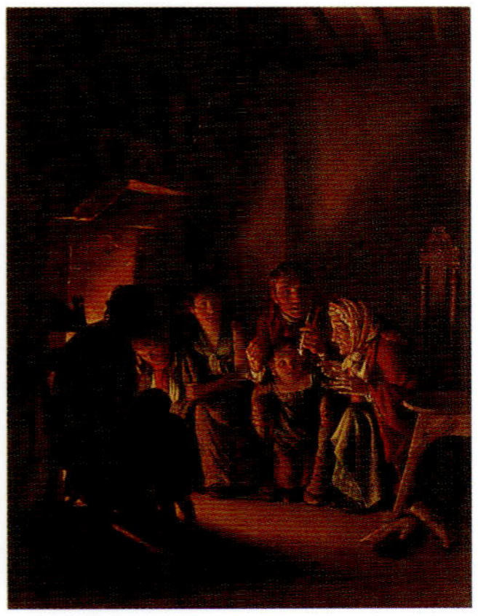

Teniers II, David (after) 1610–1690
Domestic Scene late 18th C
oil on panel 41 x 33.5
LANMS.2002.11.8

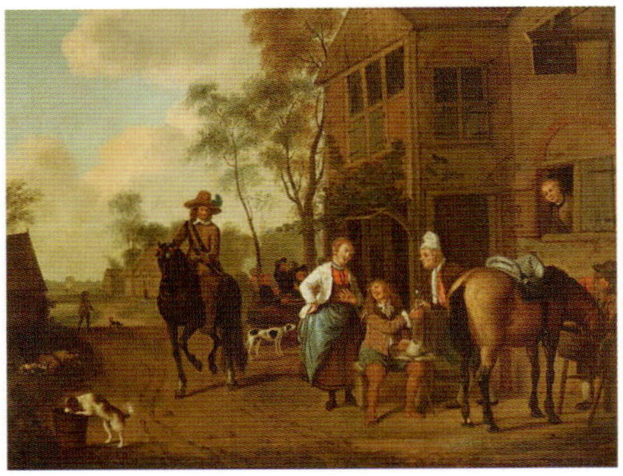

Teniers II, David (after) 1610–1690
Travellers outside an Inn
oil on canvas 47 x 58 (E)
LANMS.2002.11.9

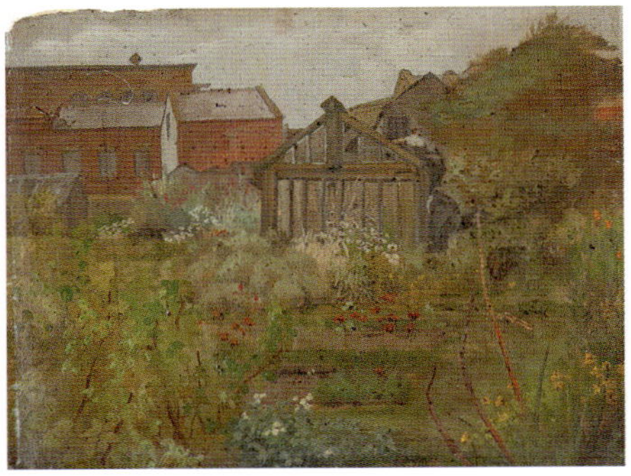

Thornton, Harold 1907–1975
Queen Street Mill from the Allotments c.1929
oil on canvas 17 x 23 (E)
LANMS.2009.1

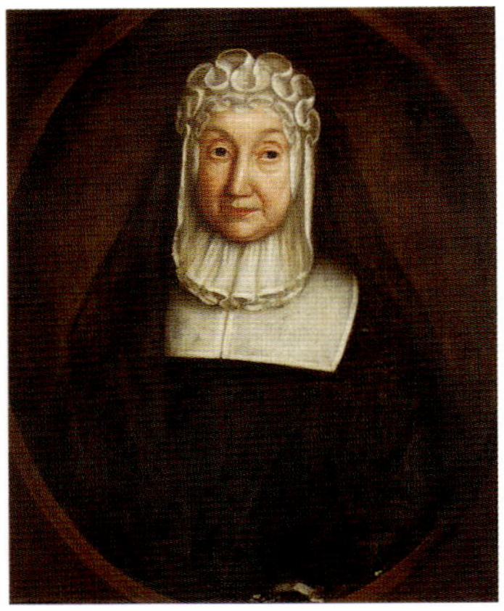

unknown artist
Anne (d.1681), Wife of William Hulton c.1665
oil on canvas 75 x 61 (E)
LOAN.1999.2 (P)

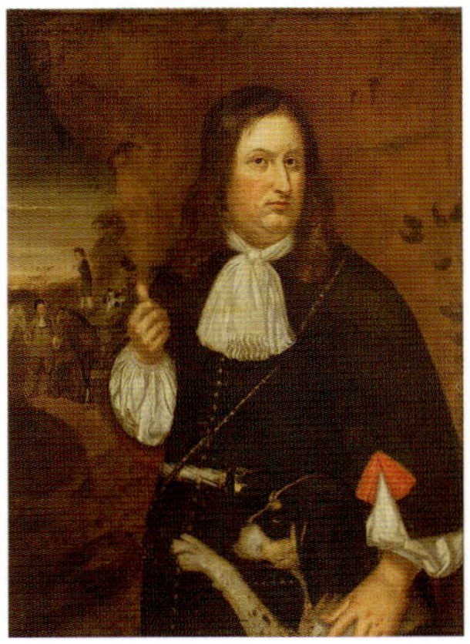

unknown artist
William Hulton (1625–1694), with Grooms and Dogs c.1665
oil on canvas 110 x 86 (E)
LOAN.1999.2 (P)

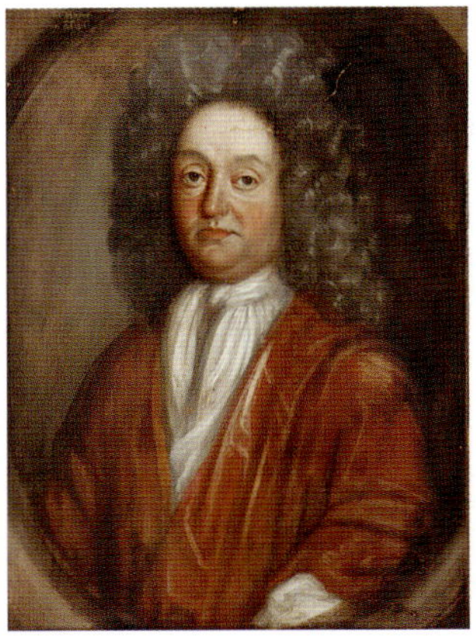

unknown artist
Major Farrington, Esq. c.1715
oil on canvas 76 x 59
LANMS.1984.72

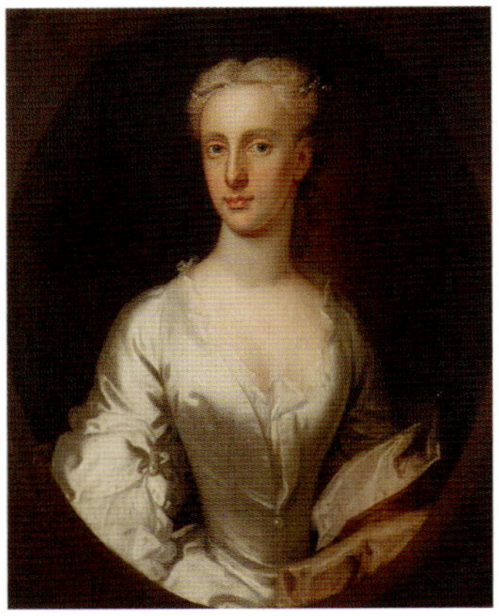

unknown artist
Anne Hulton (1719–1797) c.1740
oil on canvas 75 x 61 (E)
LOAN.1999.2 (P)

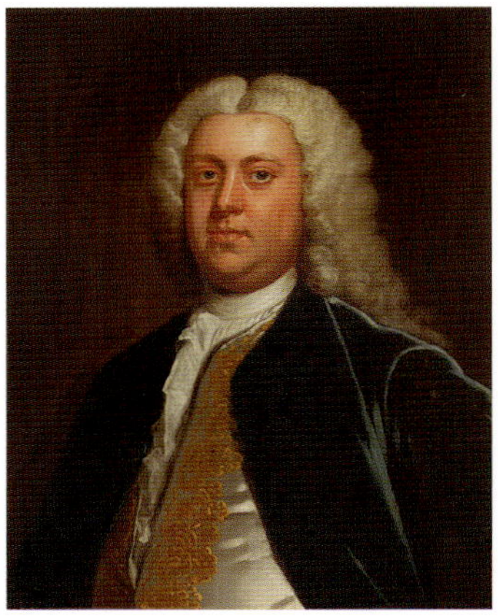

unknown artist
William Hulton (1717–1741) c.1740
oil on canvas 75 x 59 (E)
LOAN.1999.2 (P)

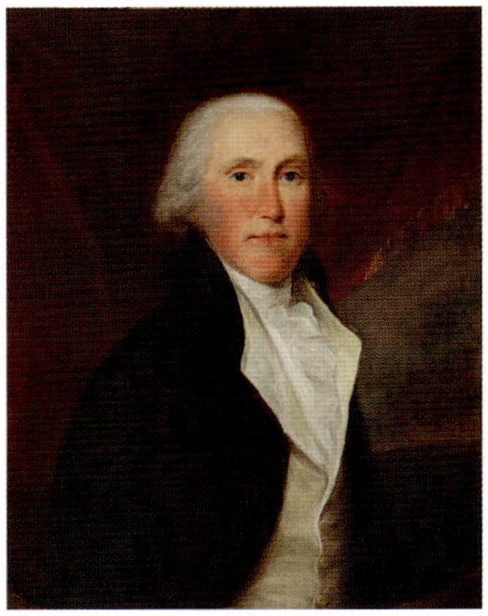

unknown artist
Benjamin Satterthwaite (1718–1792) c.1765
oil on canvas 73 x 61 (E)
LOAN.1992.1 (P)

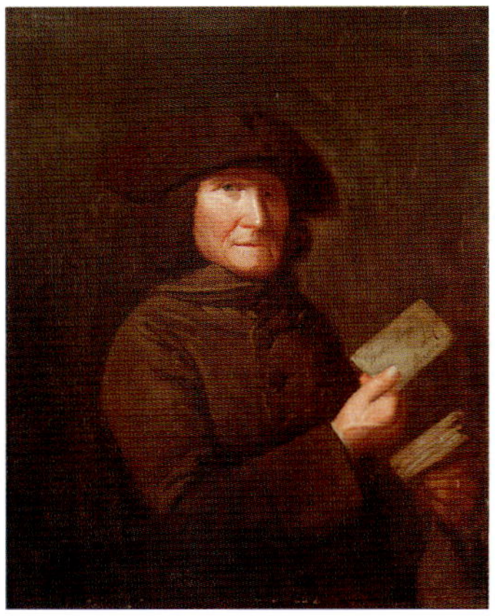

unknown artist
Dr Heys of Preston c.1775
oil on canvas 81 x 68 (E)
LANMS.1987.190

Facing page: Fuseli, Henry, 1741–1825, *The Vision of Catherine of Aragon,* Lytham Art Collection of Fylde Borough Council (p. 263)

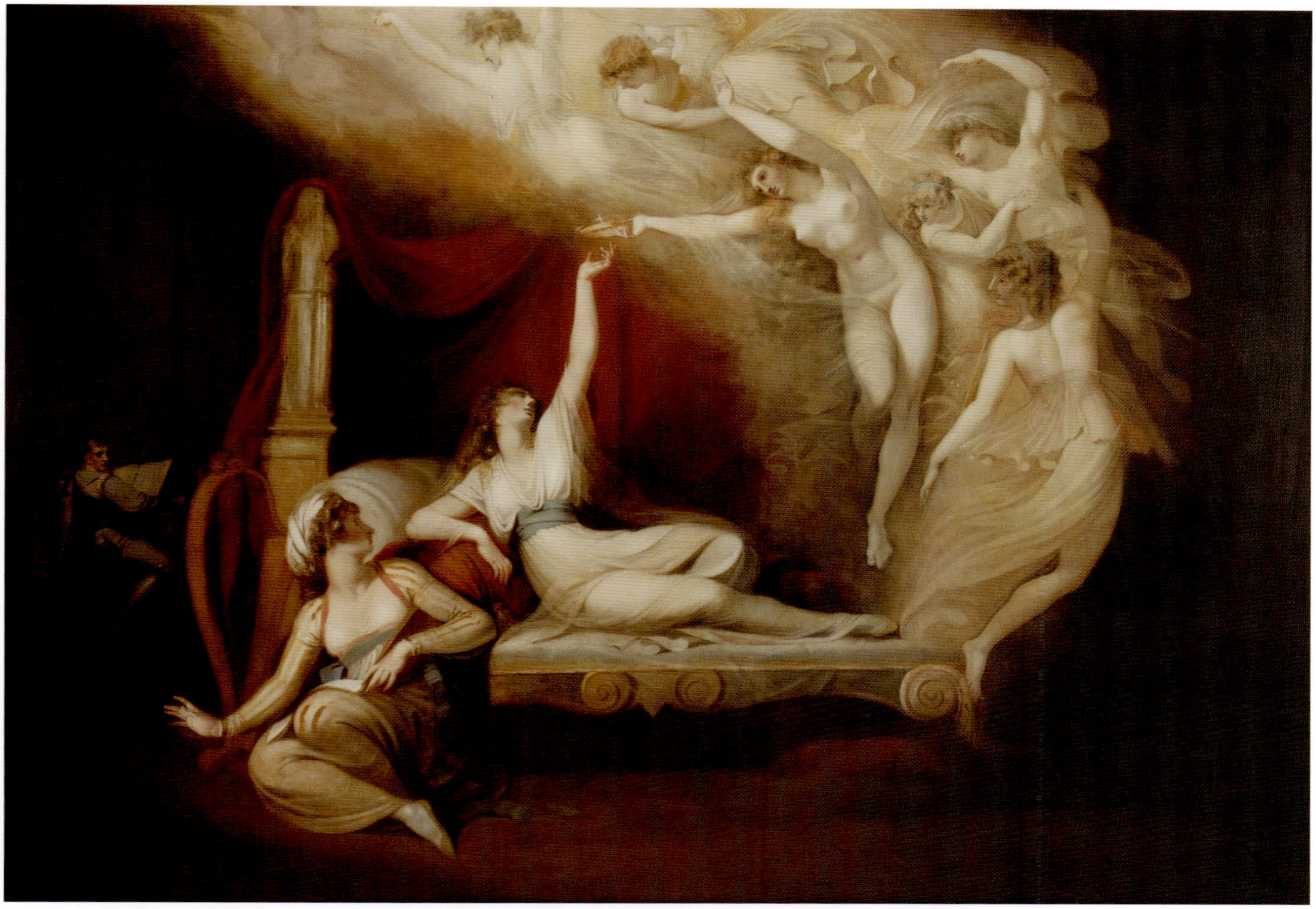

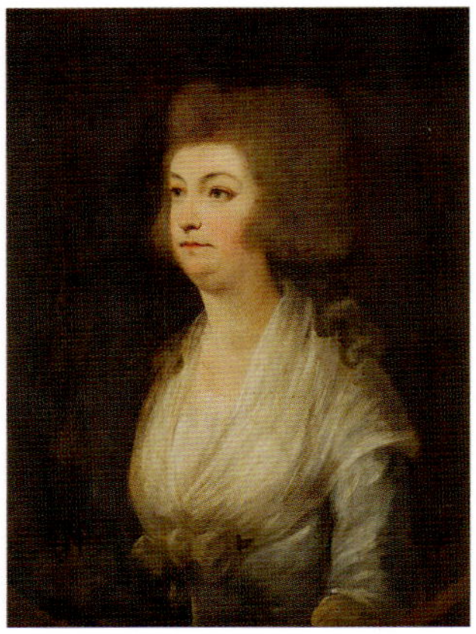

unknown artist
Lydia Rawlinson (1733–1798), Daughter of Thomas Hutton Rawlinson c.1790
oil on canvas 76 x 61
LANMS.2006.2.5

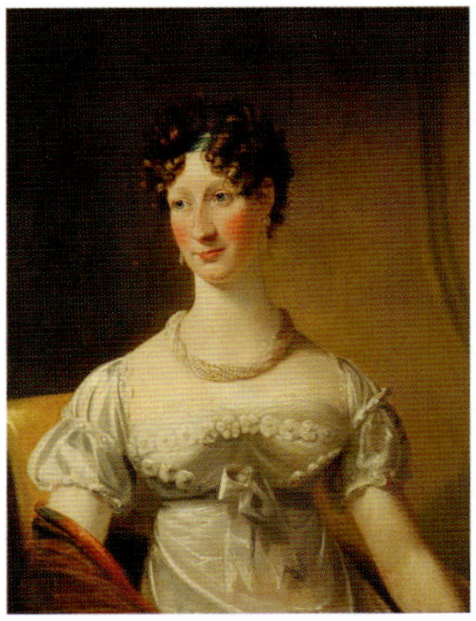

unknown artist
Mrs Ann Mary Hughes c.1800
oil on canvas 72.8 x 60.8
LOAN.1992.1 (P)

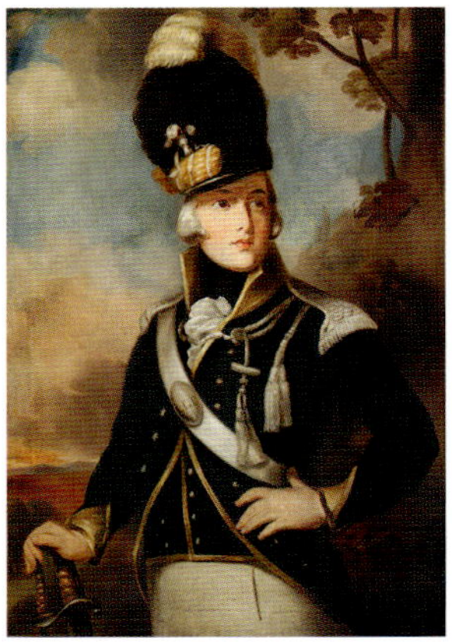

unknown artist
Henry Hulton (1765–1831), in Military Uniform c.1807
oil on canvas 121 x 86.8
LOAN.1999.2 (P)

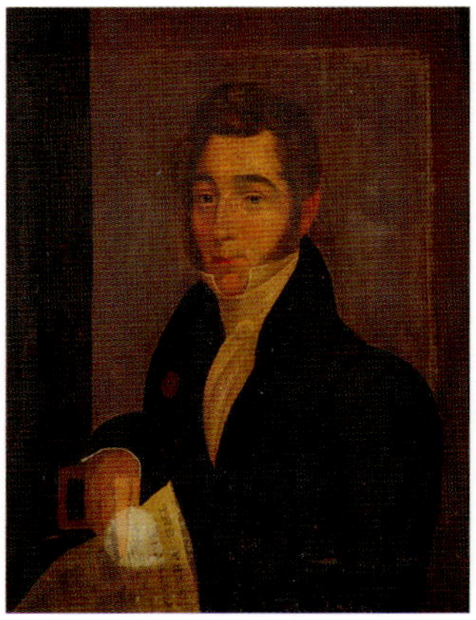

unknown artist
Portrait of 'T. M.' 1830
oil on canvas 75 x 62
LANMS.1996.71

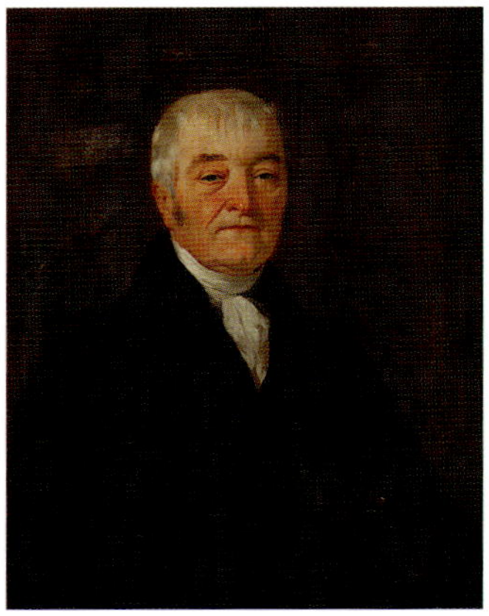

unknown artist
Mr Boardman of Bretherton 1840s
oil on canvas 71 x 62
LANMS.1991.219.2

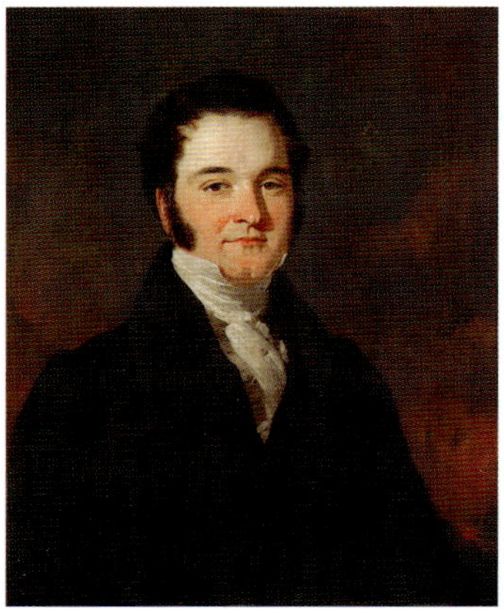

unknown artist
Mr Boardman of Bretherton 1840s
oil on canvas 74 x 60
LANMS.1991.219.3

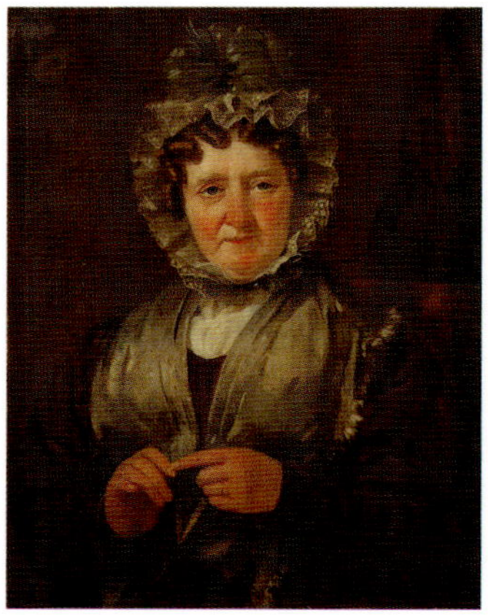

unknown artist
Mrs Boardman of Bretherton 1840s
oil on canvas 73.5 x 61
LANMS.1991.219.1

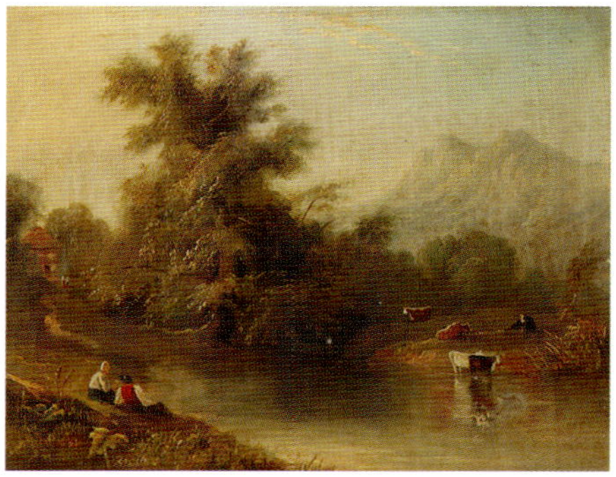

unknown artist
Pastoral Scene by a River c.1850
oil on canvas 31 x 39.2
LANMS.2002.11.7

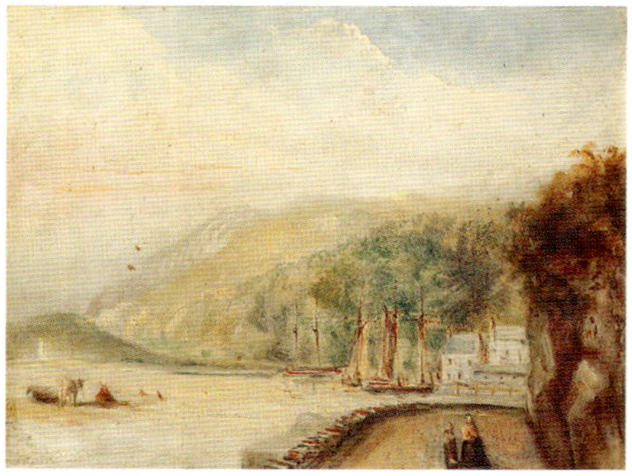

unknown artist
The Rhine Valley at Lorelia c.1870
oil on millboard 21 x 30
1985.294

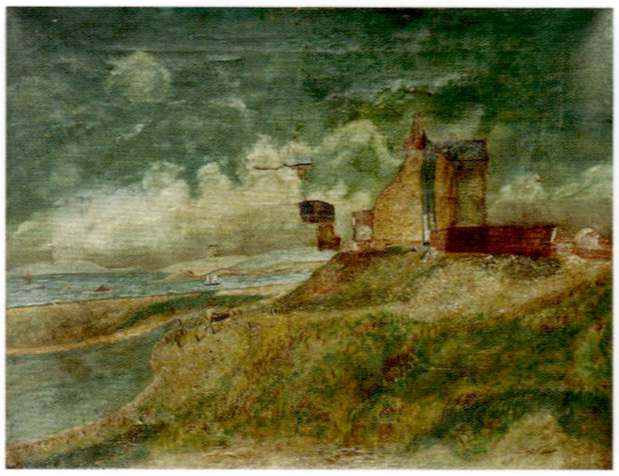

unknown artist
Rossall Point, Fleetwood c.1910
oil on canvas 55 x 67
LANMS.1977.148.4

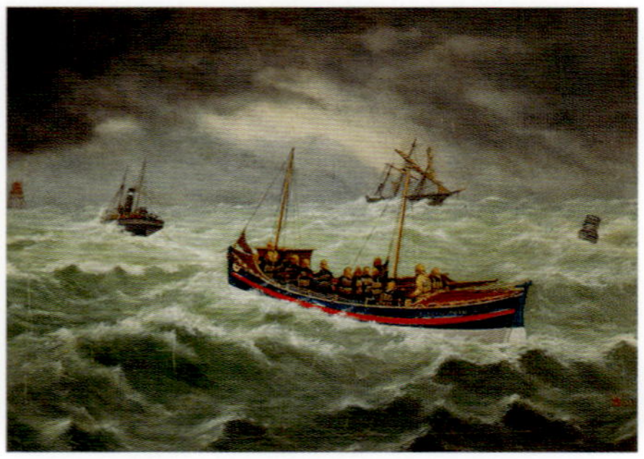

unknown artist
Fleetwood Lifeboat 'Maude Pickup' at Sea
1922
oil on canvas 45 x 70
LANMS.1976.81.2

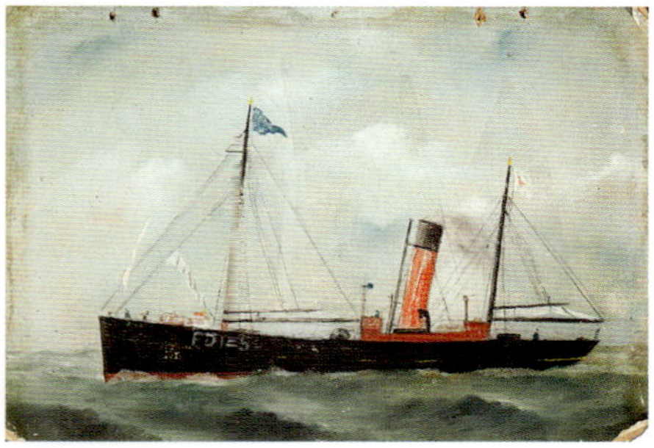

unknown artist
'Ava'
oil on hardboard 15.2 x 23.1
LANMS.2011.49

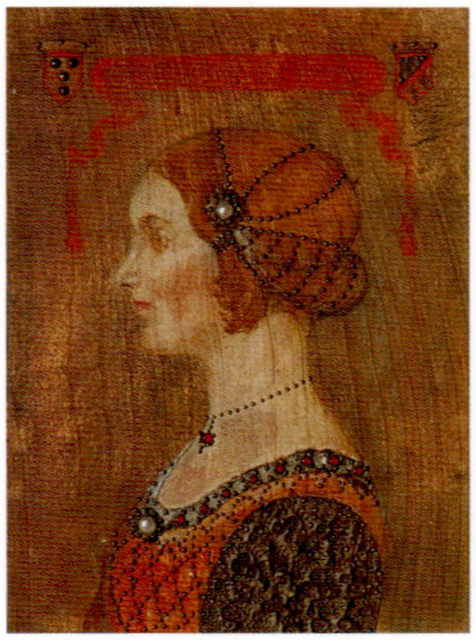

unknown artist
Cecilia
tempera on panel 26 x 19
ECR 0161.60

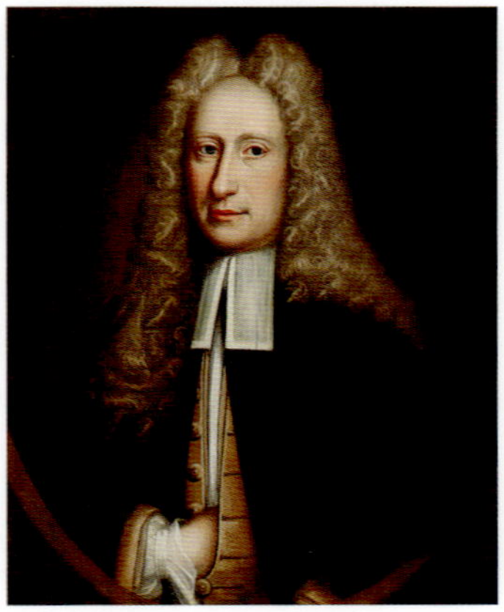

unknown artist
Charles Hulton (?)
oil on canvas 76.5 x 62
LOAN.1999.2 (P)

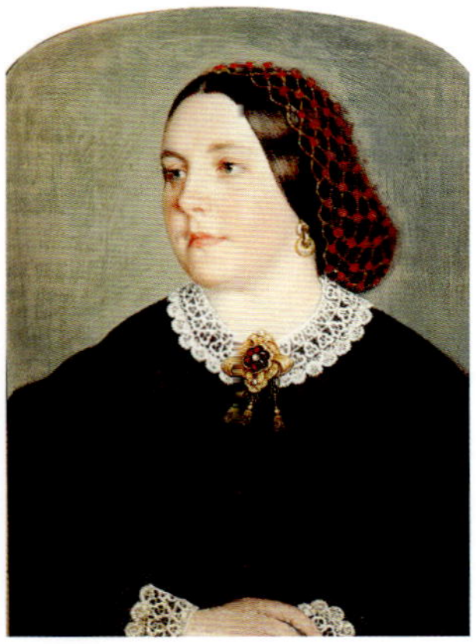

unknown artist
Ellen Turner of Helmshore
oil on canvas 61 x 45
LANMS.1977.83

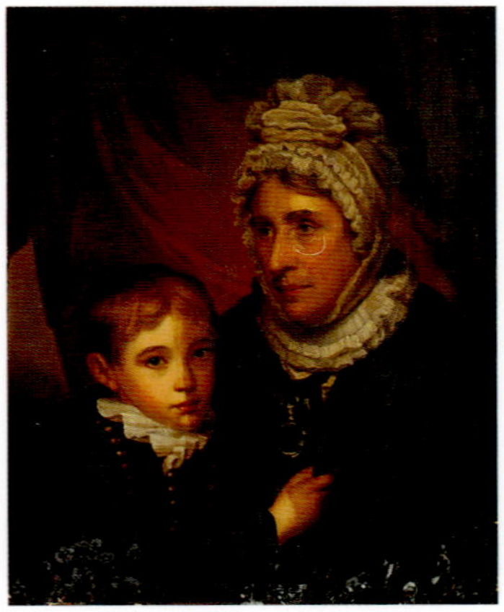

unknown artist
Janet Kerr and Master Nivien Kerr
oil on canvas 77 x 63.5
LANMS.1985.294.110

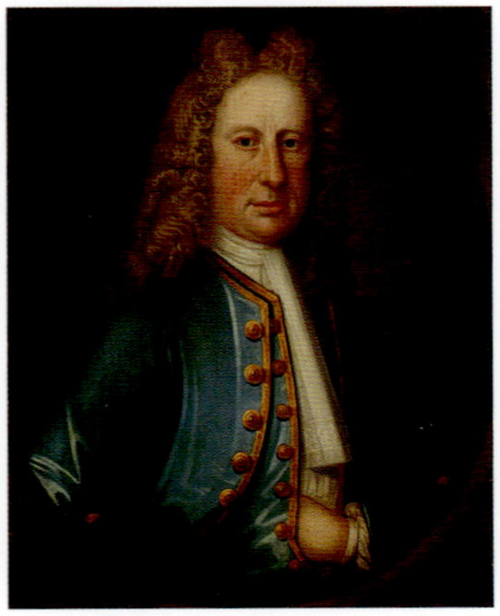

unknown artist
Jessop Hulton (b.1667) (?)
oil on canvas 76.5 x 62
LOAN.1999.2 (P)

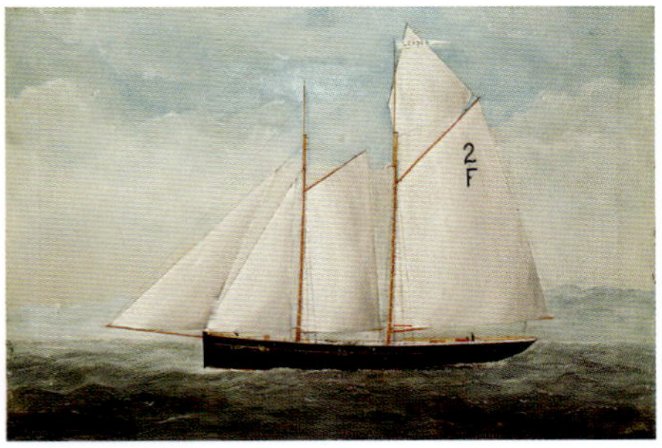

unknown artist
Old Cutter 'Leader F2'
oil on canvas 51 x 76
LANMS.1974.149.56

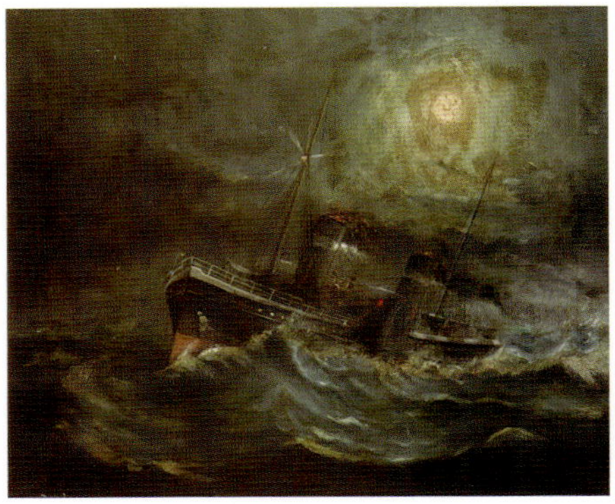

unknown artist
Paddle Steamer in Stormy Sea
oil on canvas 38 x 45
LANMS.1974.149.148

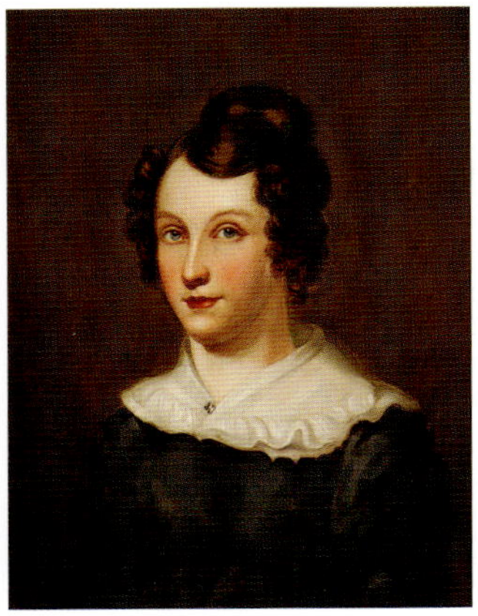

unknown artist
Portrait of a Lady
oil on canvas 61 x 50
LANMS.1985.346.223

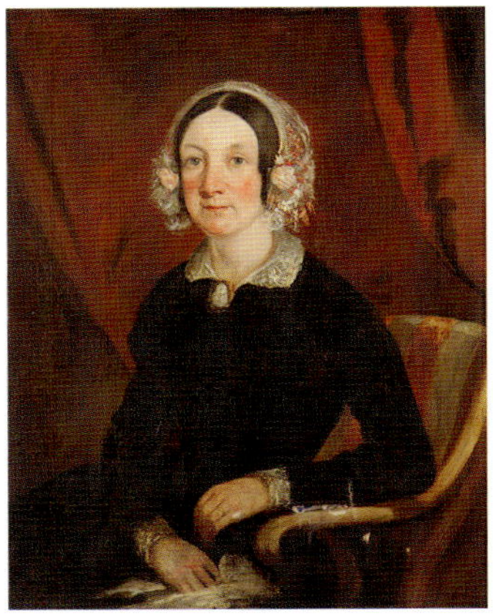

unknown artist
Portrait of a Lady Seated
oil on canvas 77 x 63.5 (E)
LANMS.1985.346.219

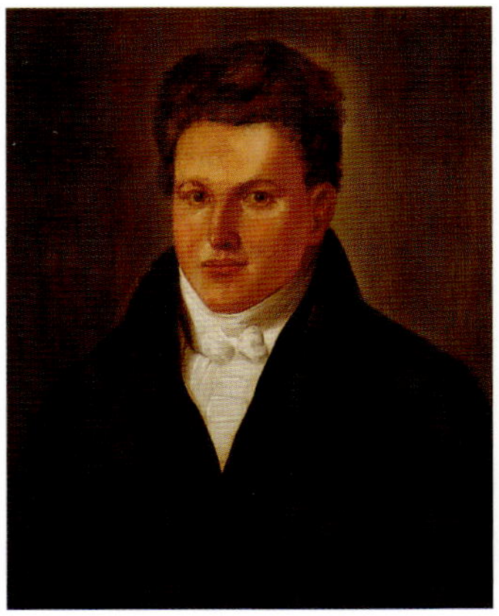

unknown artist
Portrait of a Man Seated
oil on canvas 60 x 50
LANMS.1985.346.222

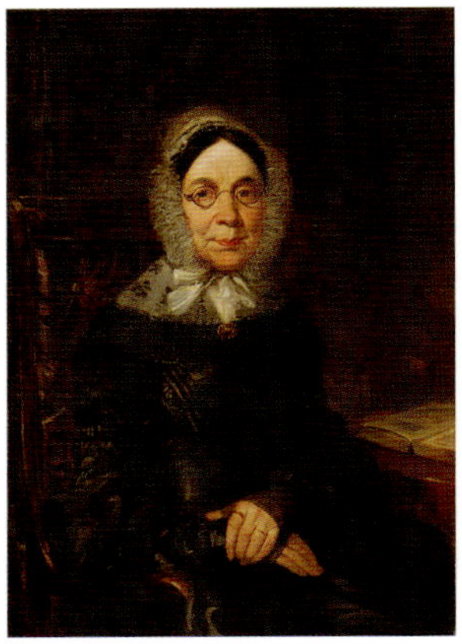

unknown artist
Portrait of a Woman Seated (possibly Dorothy Shaw)
oil on canvas 88 x 61
LANMS.1985.346.221

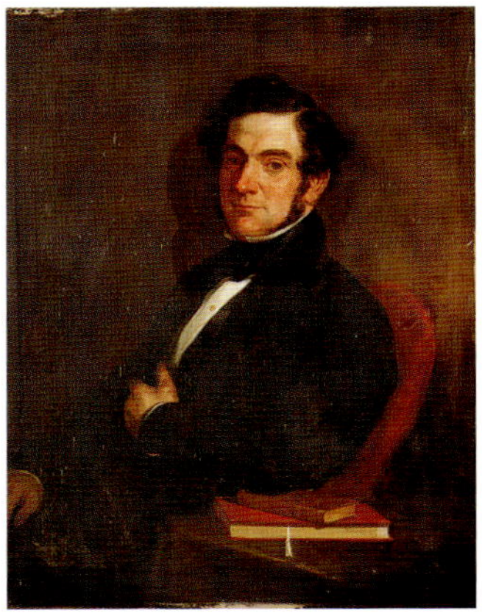

unknown artist
Portrait of an Unknown Gentleman
oil on canvas 92 x 72
LANMS.1985.346.218

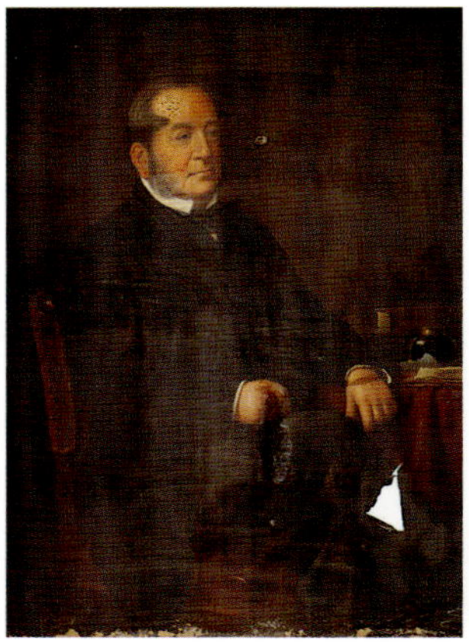

unknown artist
Portrait of an Unknown Gentleman
oil on canvas 127 x 102
LANMS.1991.220

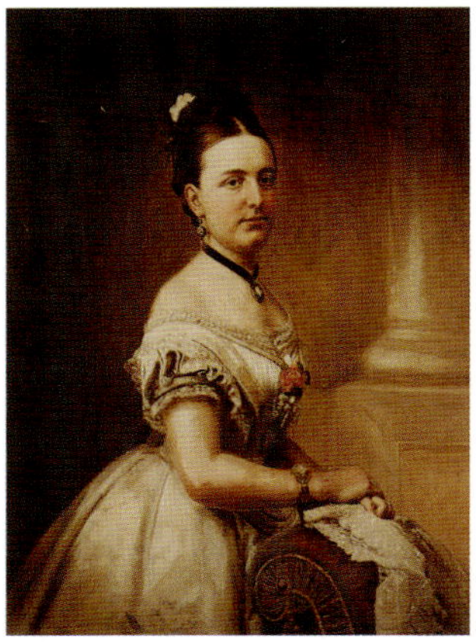

unknown artist
Sarah Hulton
oil on canvas 75 x 62 (E)
LOAN.1999.2 (P)

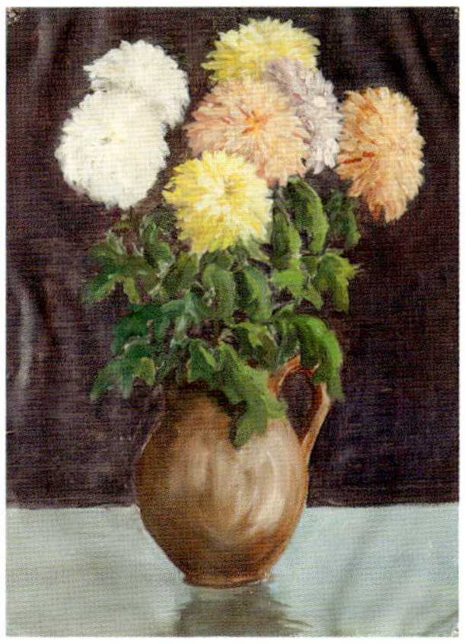

unknown artist
Still Life with Chrysanthemums
oil on paper 52 x 38
MOLSH.2011.60

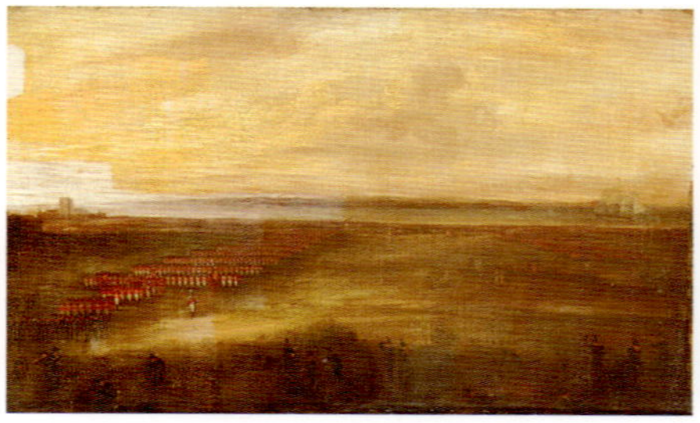

unknown artist
The Lancashire Regiment at Portsmouth
oil on canvas 61 x 92.5
LANMS.1996.70

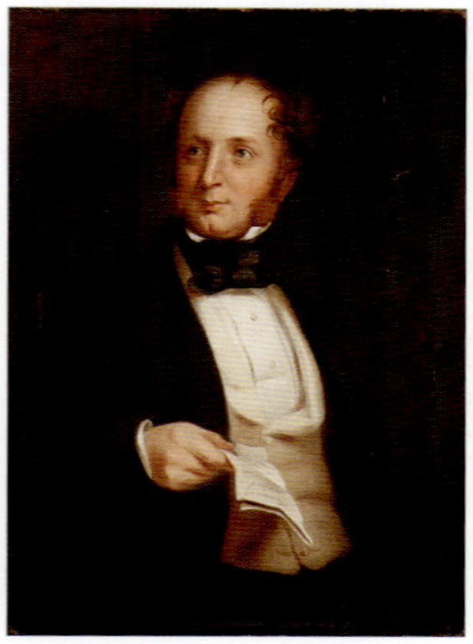

unknown artist
William Ford Hulton (b.1811)
oil on canvas 92 x 71
LOAN.1999.2 (P)

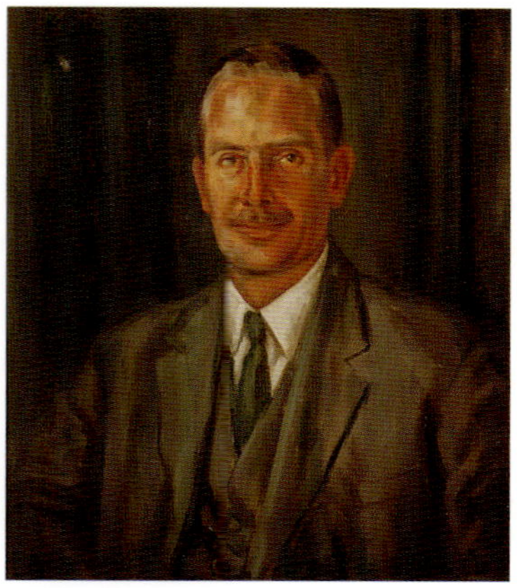

unknown artist
William Hulton (b.1868)
oil on canvas 68 x 59
LOAN.1999.2 (P)

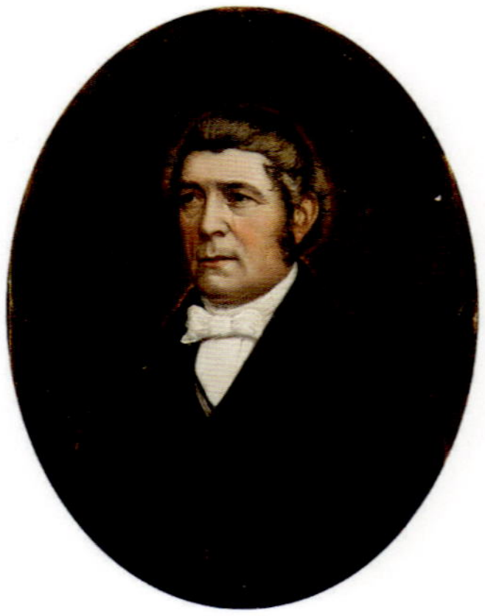

unknown artist
William Turner
oil on hardboard 23 x 18
HMMTC:XXXX14

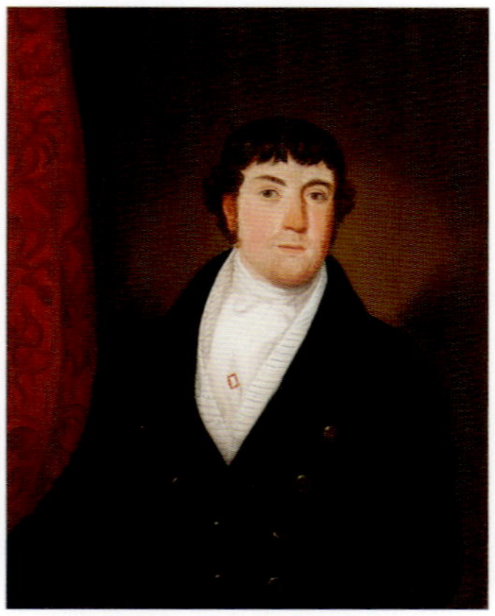

unknown artist
William Turner of Helmshore
oil on canvas 76 x 62
LANMS. 1977.83.2

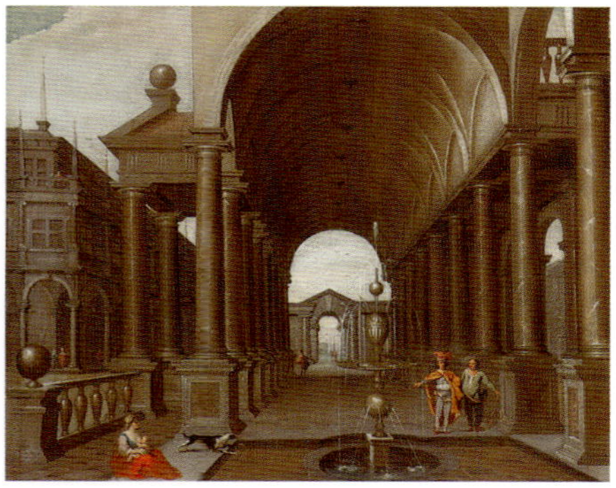

Vries, Hans Vredeman de (school of) 1527–1612
Fountain in the Courtyard of a Palace
oil on canvas 40.6 x 46.1 (E)
LANMS.2002.11.6

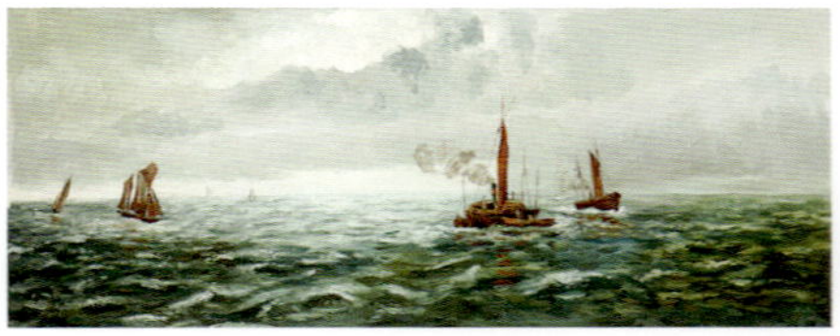

W.
Ships at Sea
oil on canvas 27 x 85.5 (E)
LANTT.001123

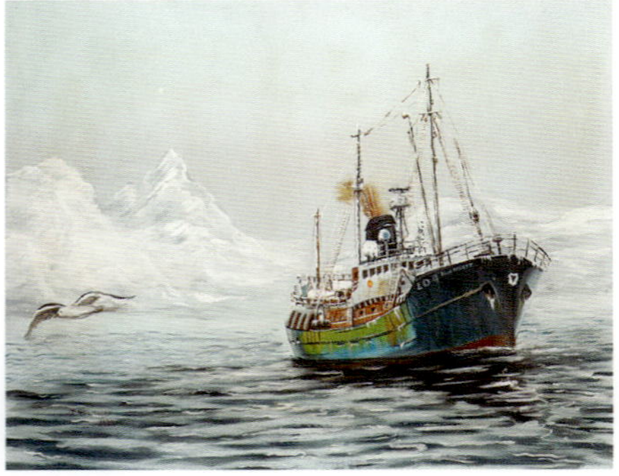

Walmsley, J.
'Ella Hewitt' 1987
oil on hardboard 49 x 75
LANMS.2011.46

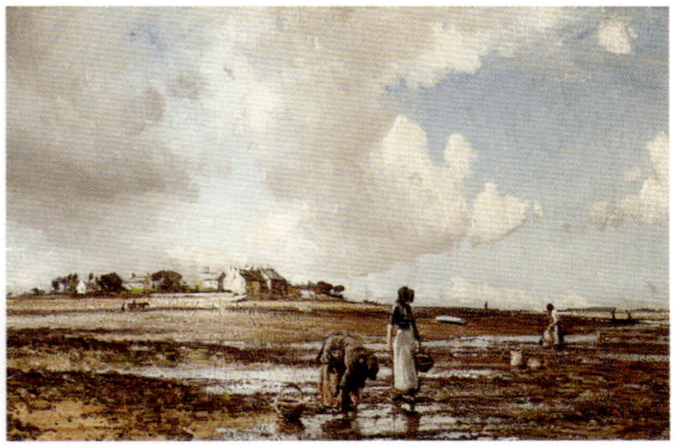

Wells, William Page Atkinson 1872–1923
The Mussel Gatherers at Sunderland Point, Lancashire c.1908
oil on canvas 61 x 102
LANMS.2004.12.1

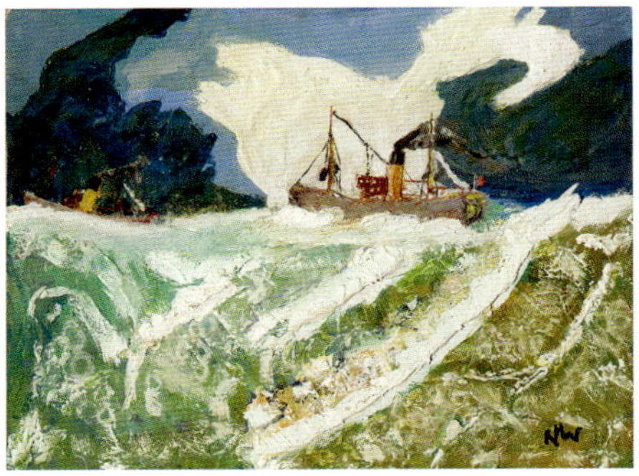

Wilkinson, Neville active 1994
White Sea Fishing Trawlers
oil on hardboard 25.5 x 35.6
LANMS.2011.50

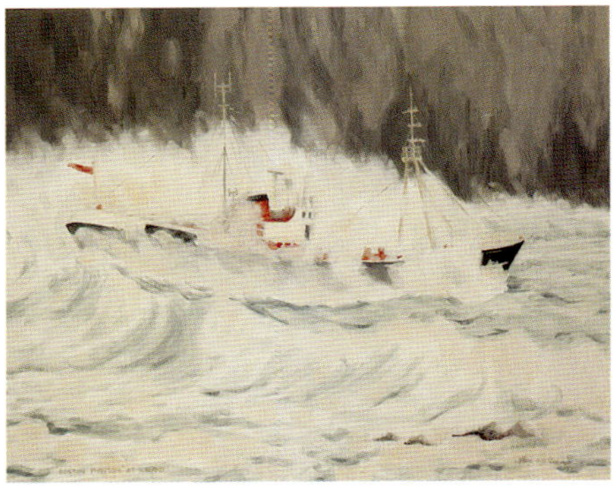

Williams, Alan
'Boston Phantom' at Iceland 1992
oil on hardboard 39.4 x 49.4
LANMS.2010.80.2

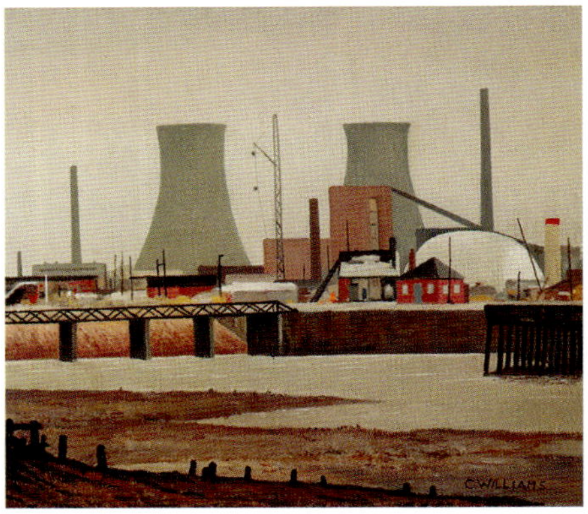

Williams, Charles active 1999–2002
A Grey Day at Fleetwood Power Station 1999
oil on canvas 24.6 x 29.3
LANMS.2010.81.2

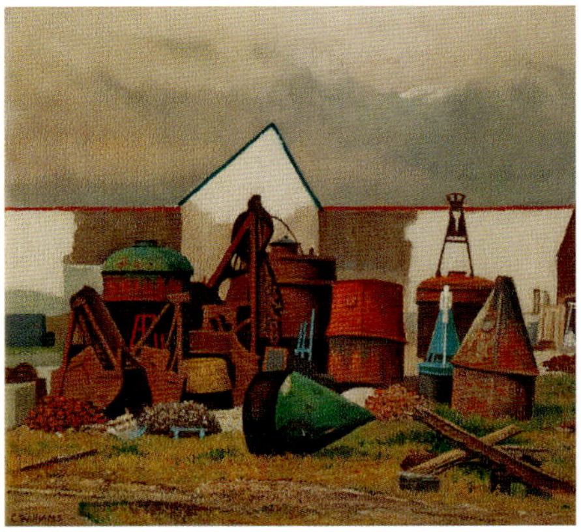

Williams, Charles active 1999–2002
Fleetwood Buoys: Nostalgia 1999
oil on paper 27.3 x 37
LANMS.2010.81.3

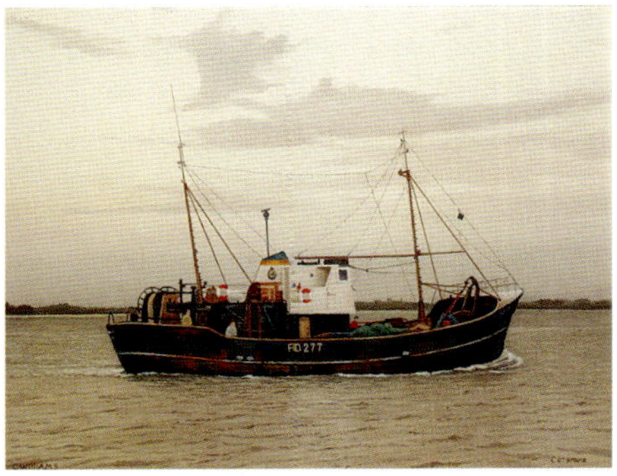

Williams, Charles active 1999–2002
'Cotsmuir'
oil on canvas 29.5 x 44.6
LANMS.2010.81.1

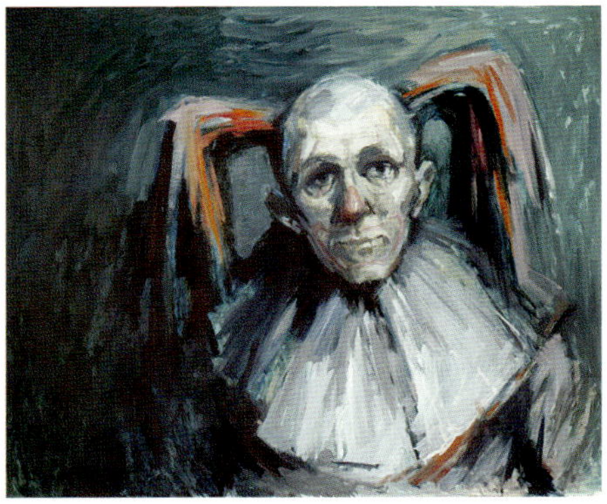

Wood, Elizabeth b.1930
The Entertainer
oil on canvas 89 x 119
LANMS.1974.42.3

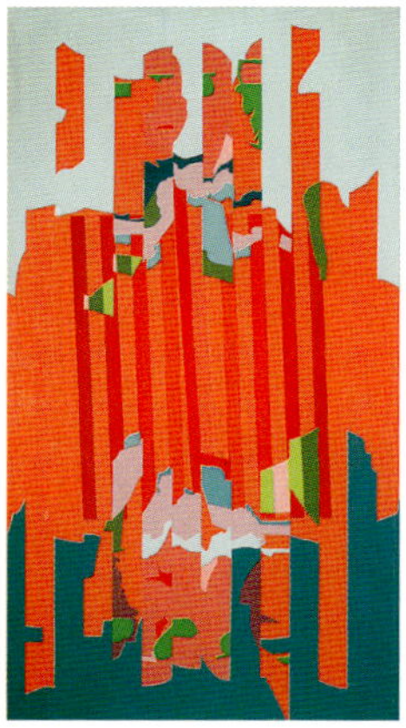

Wood, Keith
Bright Intervals
oil on canvas 116 x 68
LANMS.1974.42.2

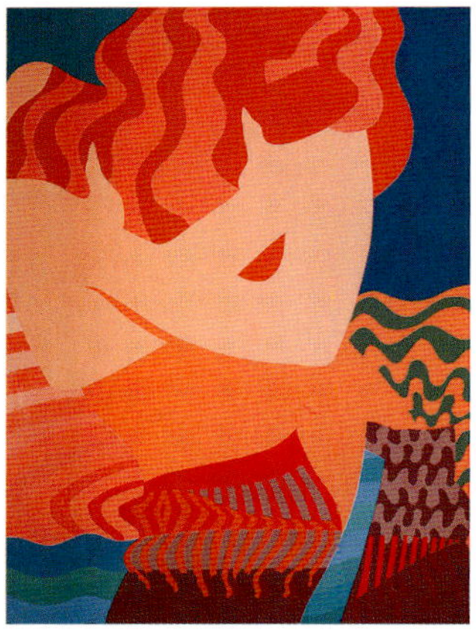

Wood, Keith
Kinky Darling
oil on canvas 119 x 89
LANMS.1974.42.1

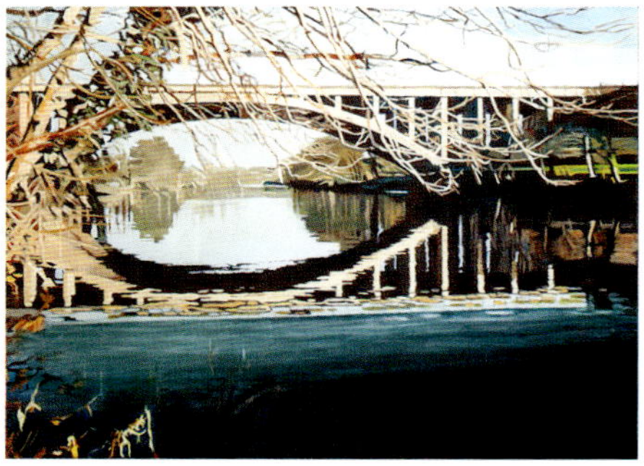

Woodhead, Geoffrey 1941–2007
Motorway Bridge, M6
acrylic on canvas 81 x 98
LANMS.2001.9

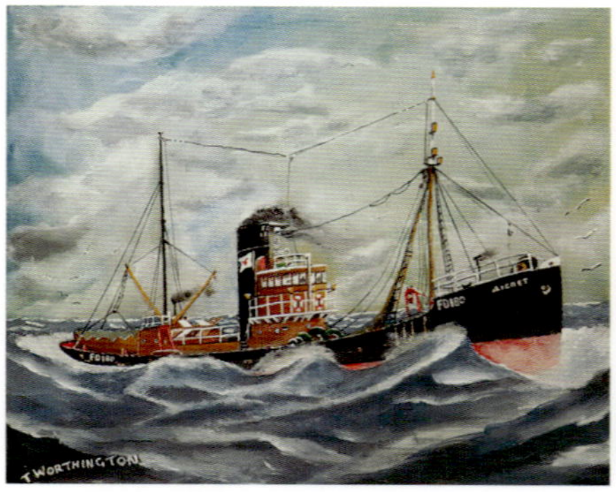

Worthington, T. active 1995
'Aigret'
oil on canvas 38.5 x 54.8
LANMS.2010.78.2

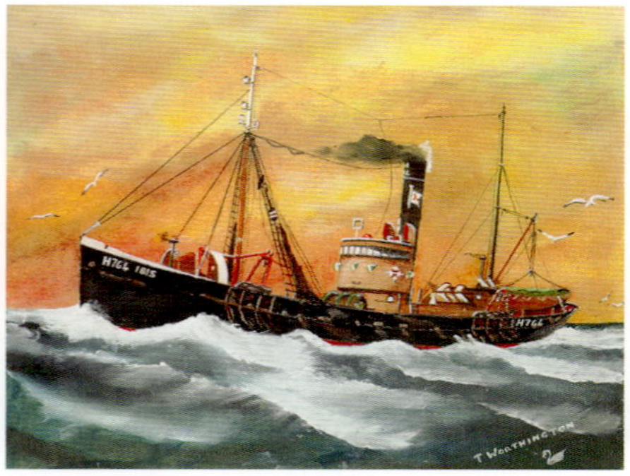

Worthington, T. active 1995
'Ibis'
oil on canvas 38.7 x 54.5
LANMS.2010.78.1

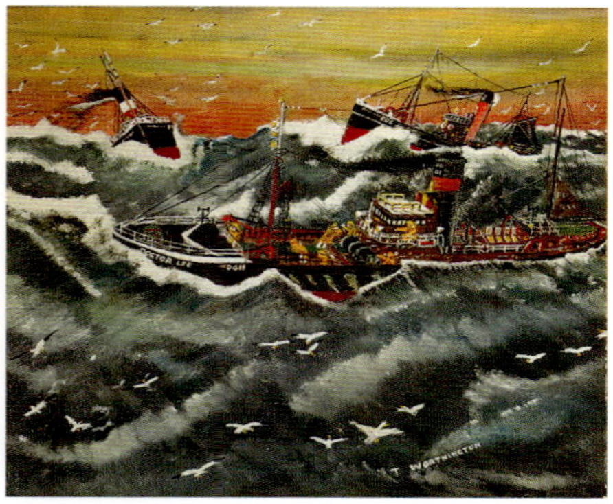

Worthington, T. active 1995
'Nancy Hague', Doctor Lee, Port Jackson
oil on hardboard 55.5 x 60.6
LANMS.2011.33

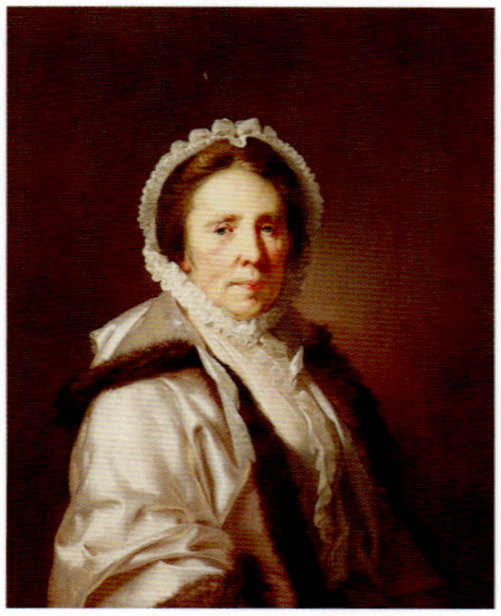

Wright of Derby, Joseph 1734–1797
Mrs James Hardman of Rochdale and Allerton Hall 1769
oil on canvas 76.2 x 63.5
LANMS.1996.74

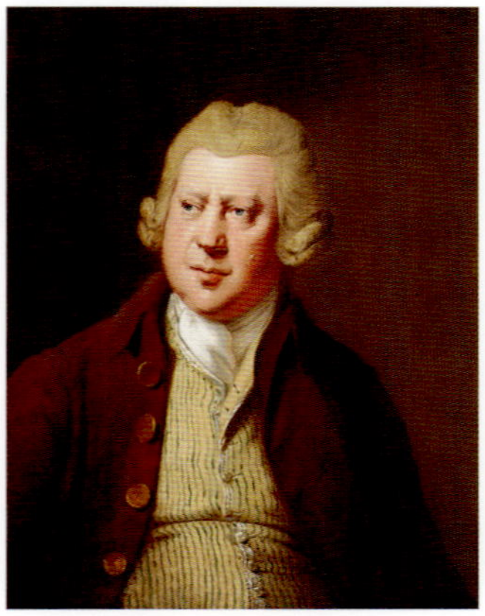

Wright of Derby, Joseph 1734–1797
Sir Richard Arkwright (1732–1792) 1790
oil on canvas 74.5 x 62
LANMS.2004.6

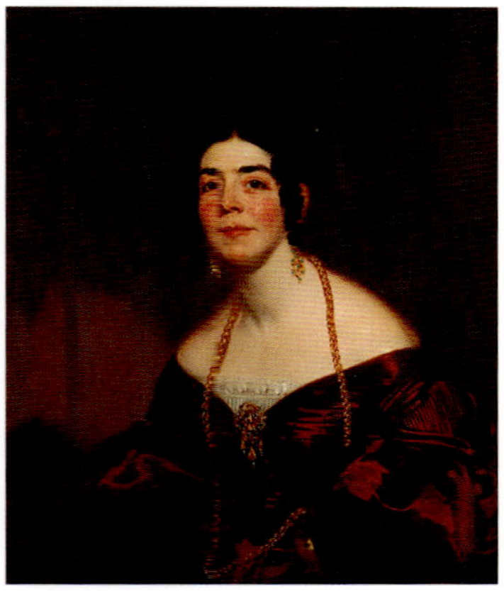

Wyatt, Henry 1794–1840
Ellen Turner of Helmshore (d.1831) 1837
oil on canvas 67.7 x 59 (E)
LANMS.1977.83.6

The Duke of Lancaster's Regiment, Lancashire Infantry Museum

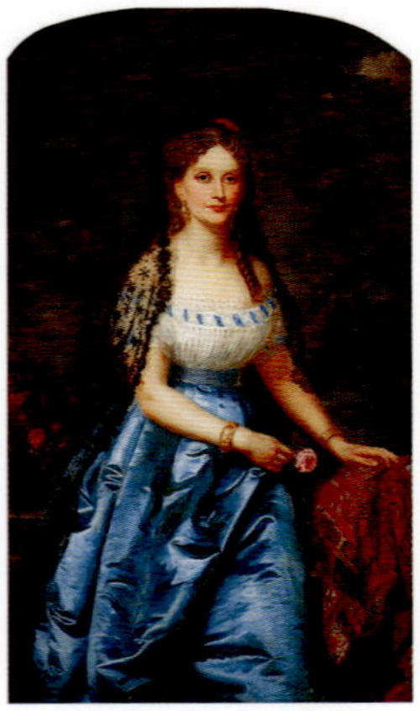

Desanges, Louis William 1822–1906
Lady Farren 1868
oil on canvas 162.5 x 106.7
PRSQL:9046

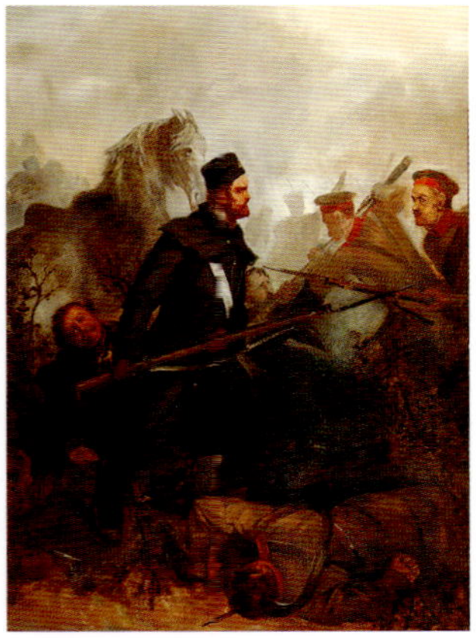

Desanges, Louis William 1822–1906
Private John McDermond, 47th Regiment of Foot, Winning the Victoria Cross, Battle of Inkerman, 5 November 1854 c.1870
oil on canvas 119.3 x 104.1
PRSQL:0015

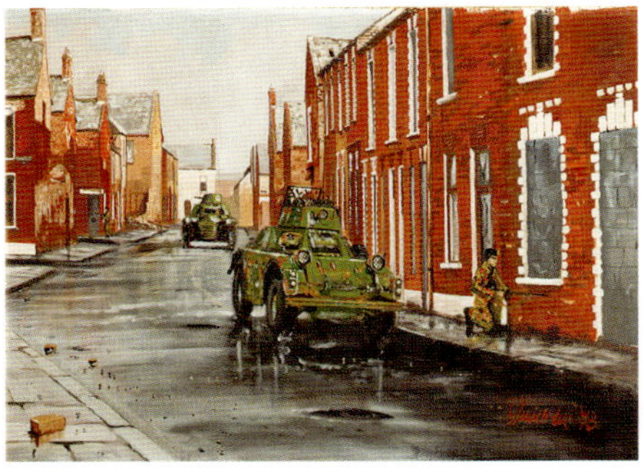

Jowett, G.
Ireland 1973
oil on canvas 48.3 x 76.2
PCF 2

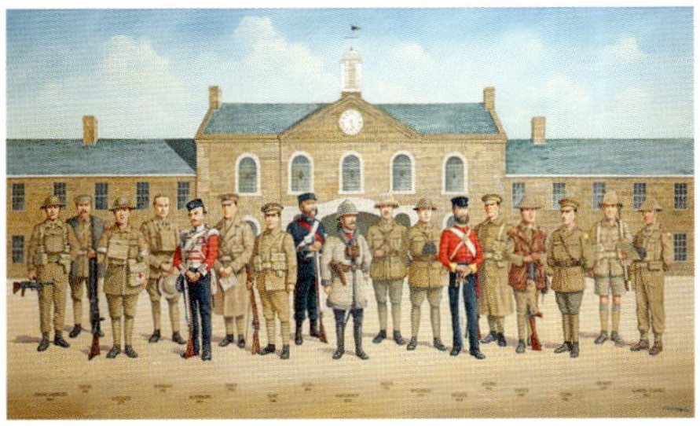

Kompley, P.
Recipients of the Victoria Cross 1994
oil on canvas 104.1 x 162.5
PCF 3

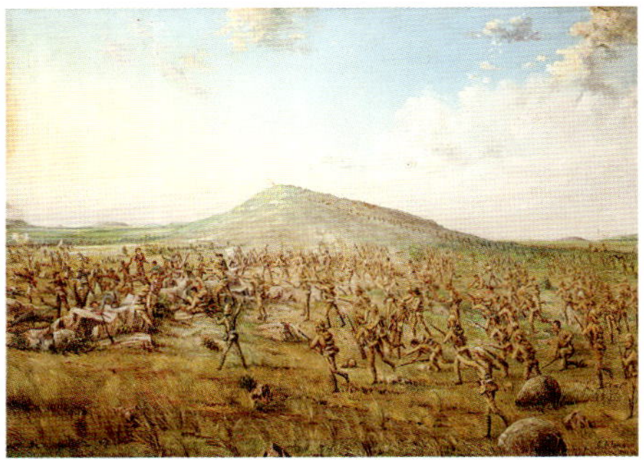

Lamb, J. A.
1st Battalion South Lancashire (Old 40th) Regiment at the Battle of Pieters Hill, 27 February 1900
oil on canvas 99 x 132
QLR A1

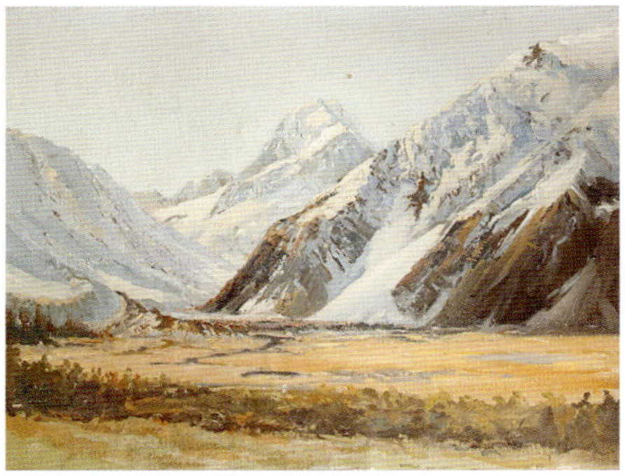

Nielson
Loyals to New Zealand 1964
oil on canvas 63.5 x 71.1
QLR A11

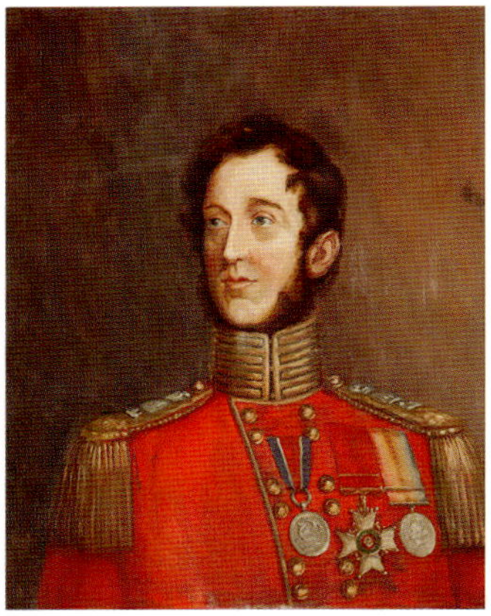

unknown artist
Lieutenant Colonel George Hibbert, CB, 40th Foot, Who Served as an Ensign at Waterloo, and Commanded the Regiment (...) c.1805
oil on canvas 96.5 x 83.8
WAGLR:2409

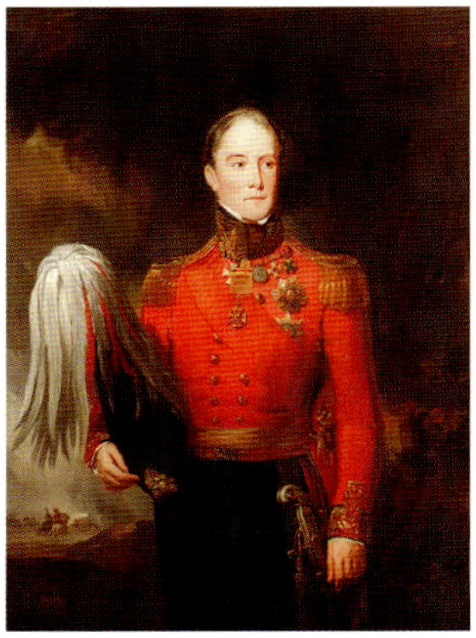

unknown artist
General Sir James Kempt, GCB, GCH 1840
oil on canvas 152.4 x 127
LANCM P1010

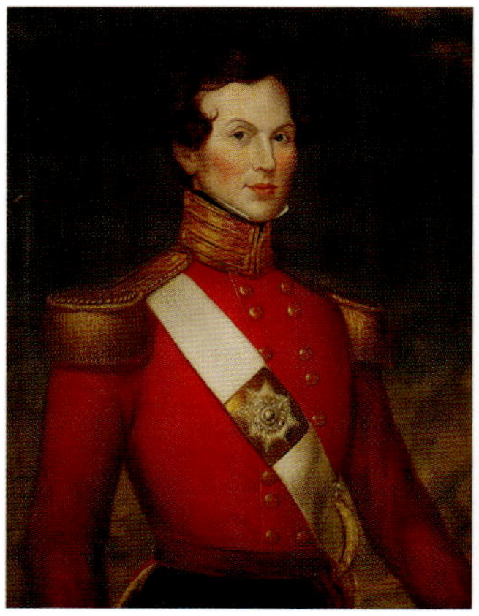

unknown artist
Captain Richard Farren, 47th Regiment of Foot c.1850
oil on canvas 83.8 x 73.6
PRSQL:0911

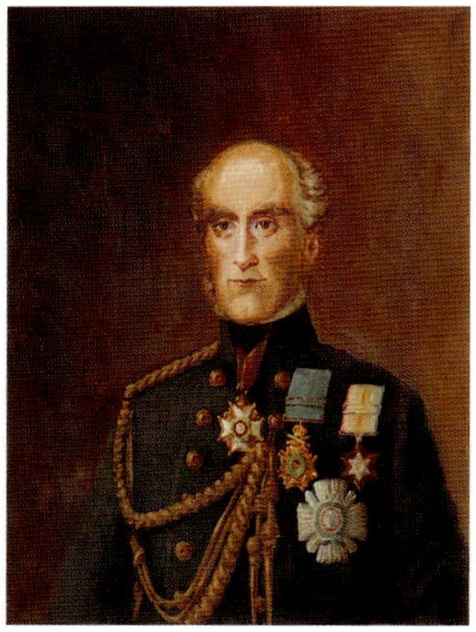

unknown artist
Colonel Sir Thomas Valiant, KCB, KH, Commander of the 82nd Foot (1825–1827) and the 40th Foot (1827–1839) c.1850
oil on canvas 96.5 x 83.8
PCF1

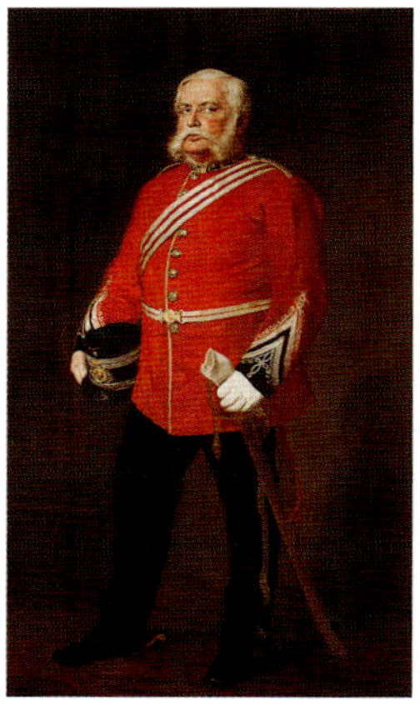

unknown artist
Colonel J. Ireland Blackburne 1875
oil on canvas 292.1 x 147.3
PCF 1

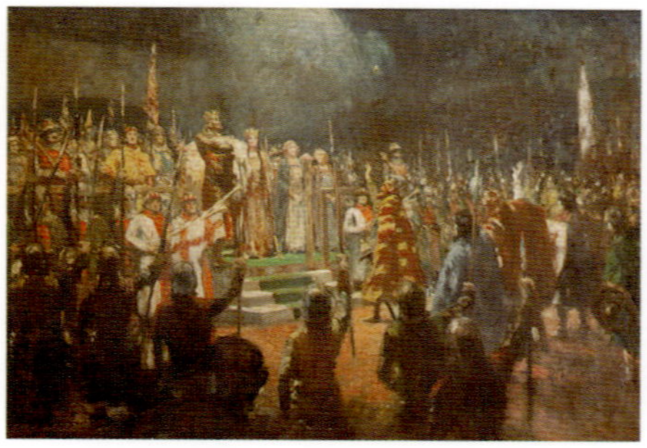

unknown artist
The Royal Tournament, 1932 c.1932
oil on canvas 50 x 70
PCF2

University of Central Lancashire

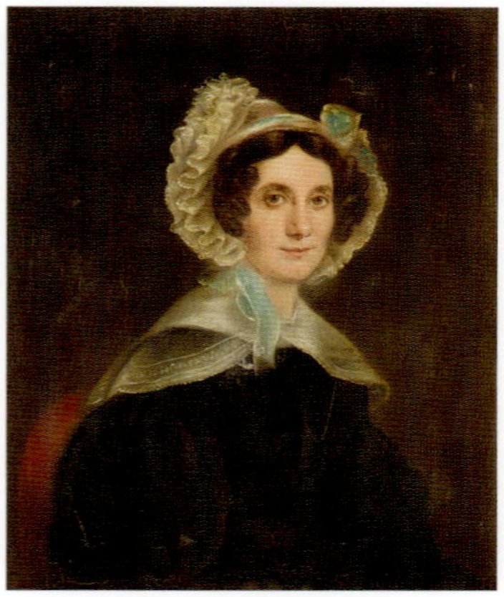

Beattie the elder (attributed to) active 19th C
Jane Livesey
oil on canvas 77 x 64.3
PCF_UCL_6

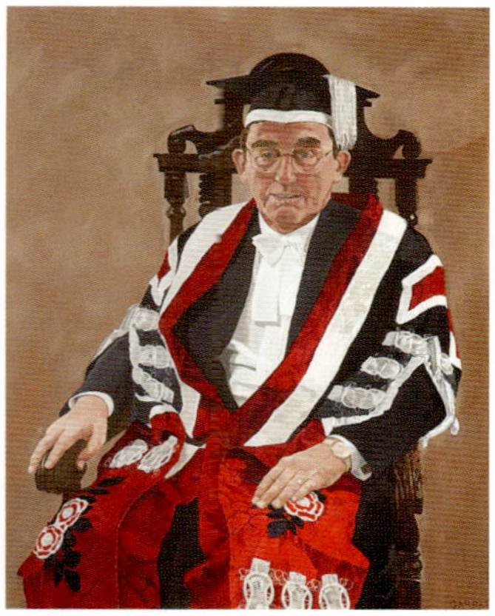

Garrett
Brian Booth, First Vice-Chancellor of the University of Central Lancashire (1989–1998)
1990s
oil on canvas 90 x 63
PCF_UCL_3

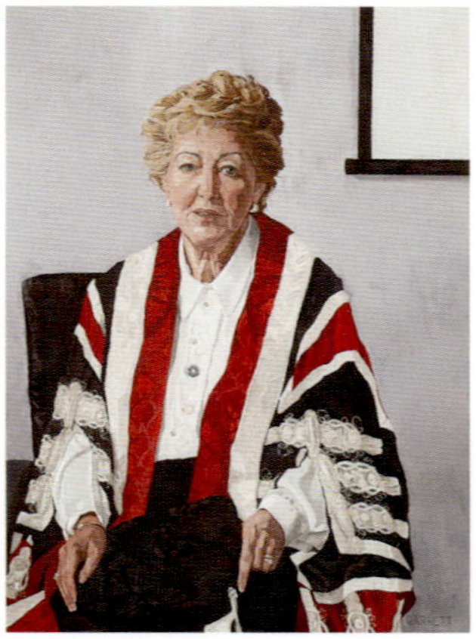

Garrett
Gloria Oates, Chair of the Board at the University of Central Lancashire (1990–2001)
1990s
oil on canvas 93 x 70.5
PCF_UCL_2

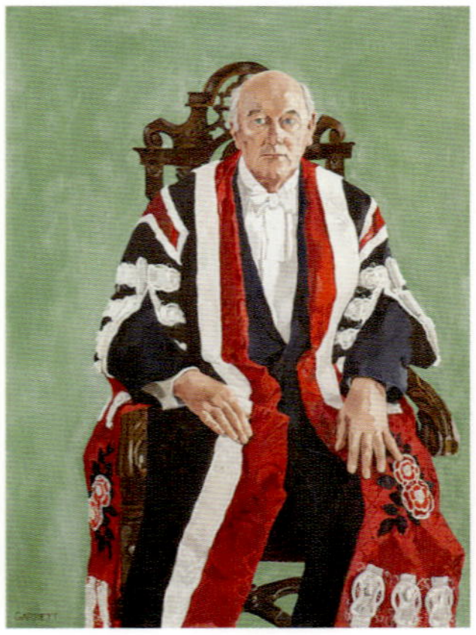

Garrett
Sir Francis Kennedy, First Chancellor of the University of Central Lancashire (1995) 1990s
oil on canvas 90 x 68
PCF_UCL_1

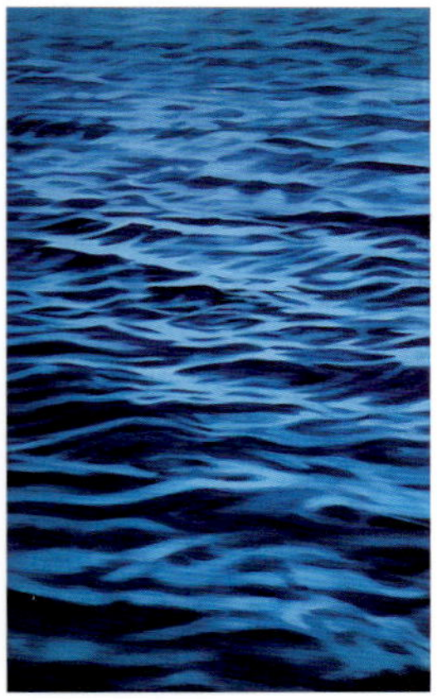

Marshall, Christopher
Waves (Sound of Handa) 1999
acrylic on canvas 183 x 91.5
PCF_UCL_7

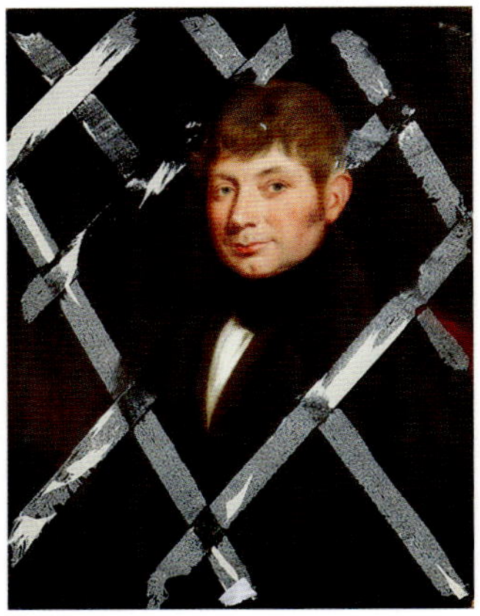

unknown artist
Joseph Livesey
oil on wooden panel 71 x 62
PCF_UCL_5

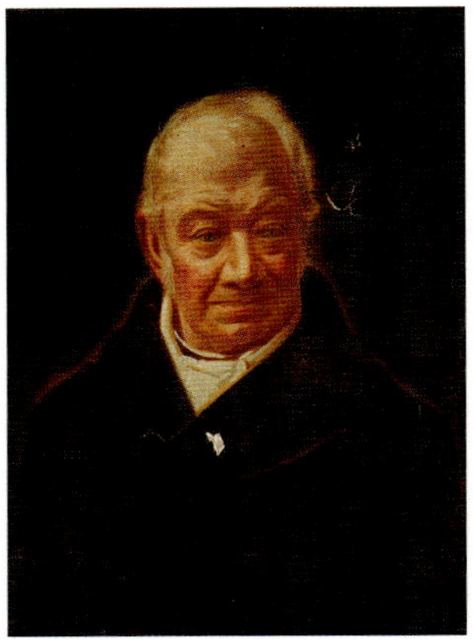

unknown artist
Joseph Livesey, Pioneer of Total Abstinence
oil on canvas 61 x 50.8
PCF_UCL_4

Rossendale Museum

Rossendale Museum has what could be described as a typical municipal art collection, dating from the late nineteenth and early twentieth century. It comprises three main categories of fine art works: portraits of prominent local politicians, civic leaders and members of local families, commissioned from artists in the region; paintings of varied subject matter gifted to the Museum by wealthy local patrons and nationally known artists, and a large group of works, including topographical scenes and more portraits, by local and other artists. The latter constitutes a social historical record of the Rossendale area of East Lancashire.

The fine art collection is housed in the town museum in Whitaker Park, Rawtenstall, which opened in 1904. The current catalogue includes 189 original works in oil. Due to limitations of space the Museum can only show a proportion of its collection on a 'permanent' basis. In the current museum layout there is a total of 50 works on display.

One of the most popular oil paintings in the collection is *The Lifeboat* by Marshall Claxton, a work which toured Australia as part of the National Gallery of Victoria touring exhibition Exiles and Emigrants in 2005 and 2006.

Other works of some note are *Stepping Stones: Pamela* by John Collier, *A Winter Scene* by Alexis de Leeuw, *The Ford* by Auguste-François Bonheur, *Near Southampton* by William Shayer, and *The Devil's Bridge on the St Gothard Pass* by Thomas Creswick.

The acquisition policy states that all future acquisitions will build on the strengths of and enhance existing collections. The focus of collecting is on material with a local relevance and as such work by local artists and of local scenes will be the priority. There is a specific objective within the policy: to complement and enhance existing displays, such as the period drawing room.

The PCF has helped us to fulfil one of the Museum's key objectives of improving access to the fine art collection via an electronic medium. This project gives us the opportunity to make our paintings available to a wider audience, and we are delighted to have had a chance to be involved.

Philip Butler, Museum Manager

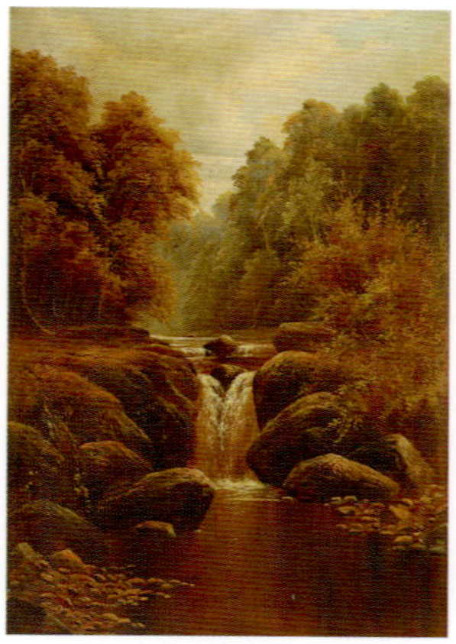

Adam, Joseph Denovan 1879–1931
Waterfall
oil on canvas 99.1 x 78.7
PA-250

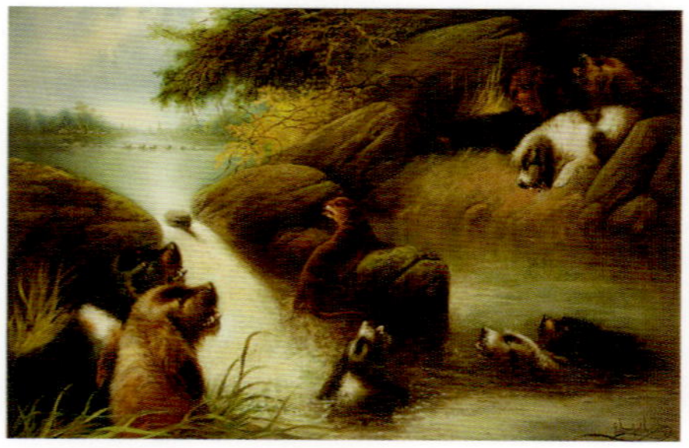

Armfield, Edward 1817–1896
The Otter at Bay
oil on canvas 76.2 x 124.5
PA-130

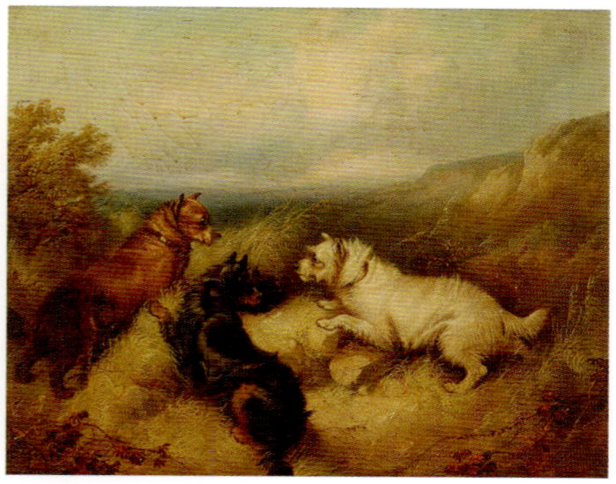

Armfield, George 1810–1893
Three Dogs c.1845–1875
oil on canvas 40.6 x 50.8
PA-217

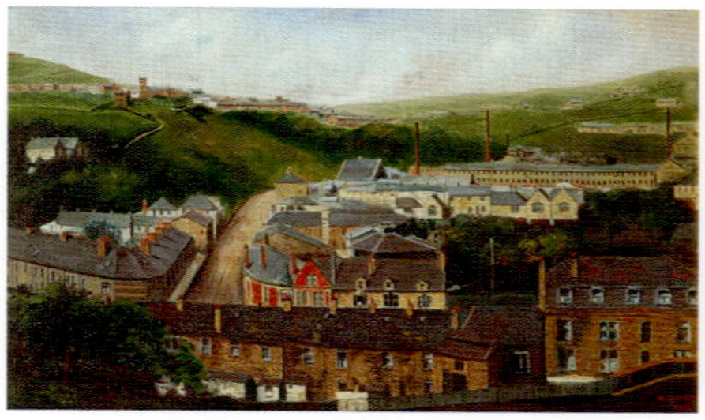

Arnold, W. J.
Centre, Waterfoot
oil on canvas (?) 26.7 x 44.5
PA-165

Aumonier, James 1832–1911
A Lonely Heath c.1852–1911
oil on canvas 119.4 x 180.3
PA-125

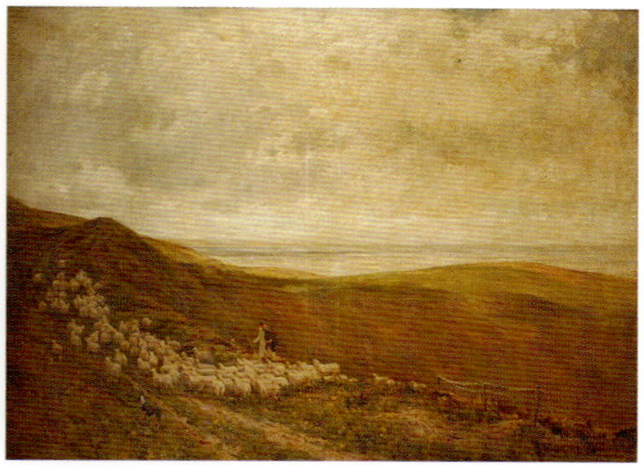

Aumonier, James 1832–1911
On the South Downs c.1852–1911
oil on canvas 124.5 x 190.5
PA-124

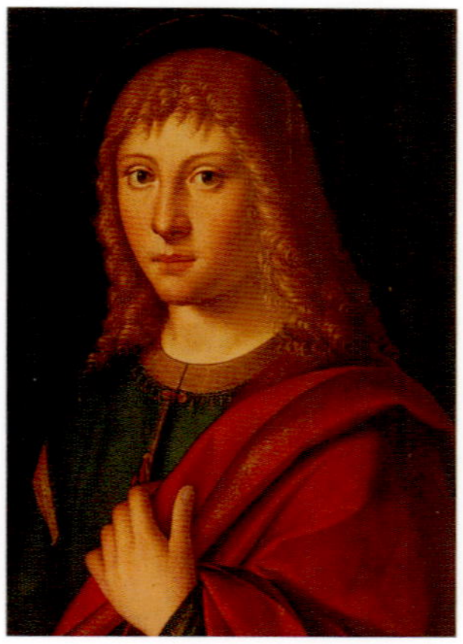

Boccaccino, Boccaccio (style of) 1461–1525
Male Saint (possibly Saint John the Evangelist) 1800–1900
oil on panel 45.7 x 35.6
PA-195

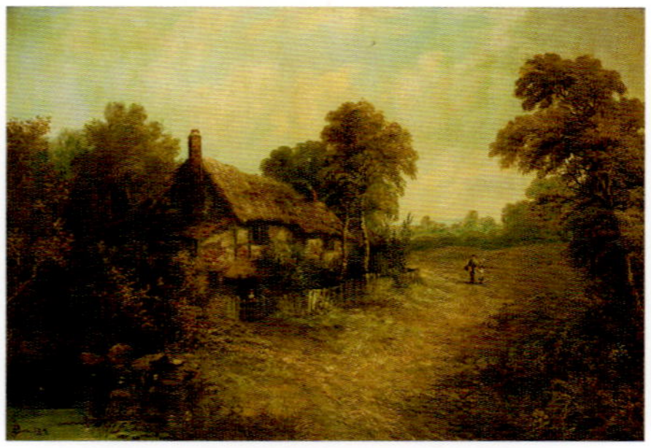

Boel, John Henry active 1875–1922
Cottage in the Wood 1887
oil on canvas 66 x 96.5
PA-141

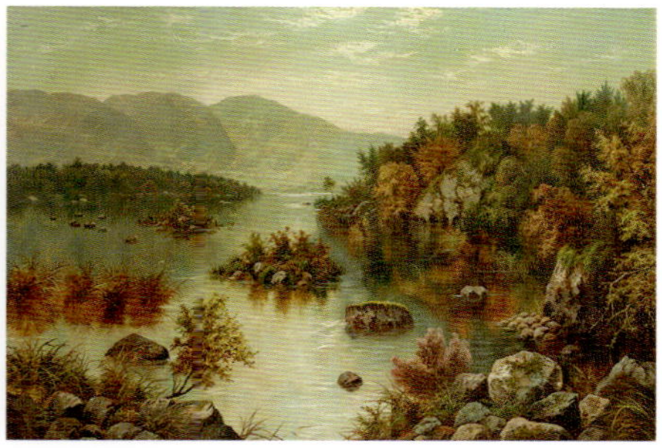

Boel, John Henry active 1875–1922
Loch Lomond 1889
oil on canvas 66 x 96.5
PA-93

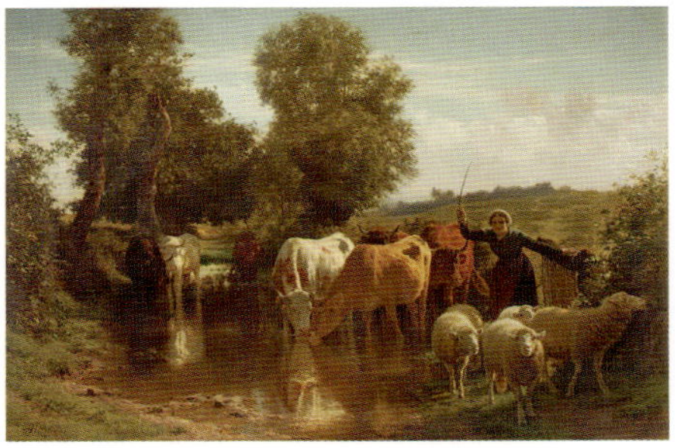

Bonheur, Auguste-François 1824–1884
The Ford
oil on canvas 114.3 x 170.2
PA-158

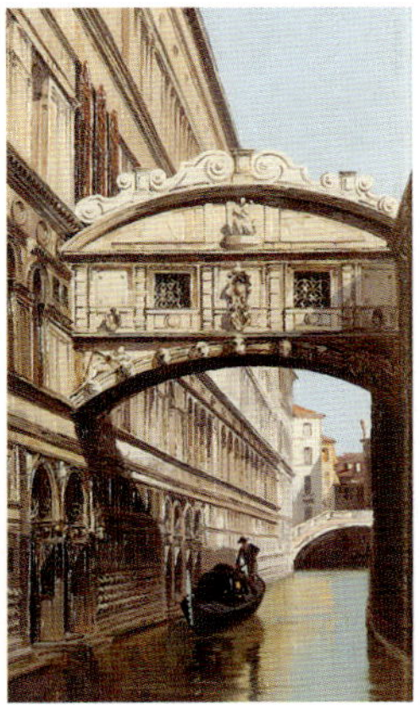

Brandeis, Antonietta 1849–1920
Venetian Waterway
oil on canvas 24.1 x 15.2
PA-225

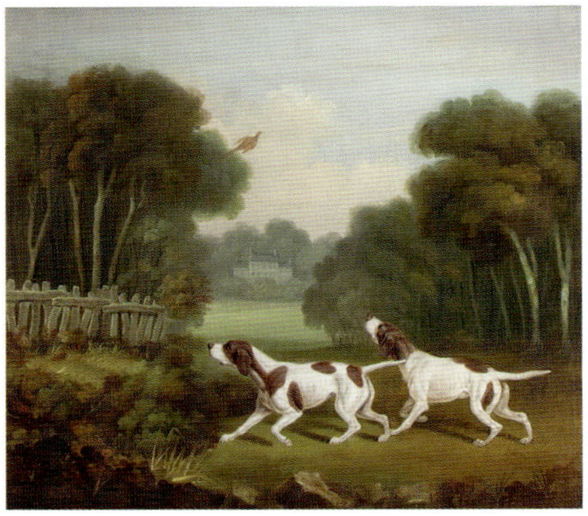

British (English) School
Carter Place c.1790
oil on canvas 64.8 x 77.5
PA-35

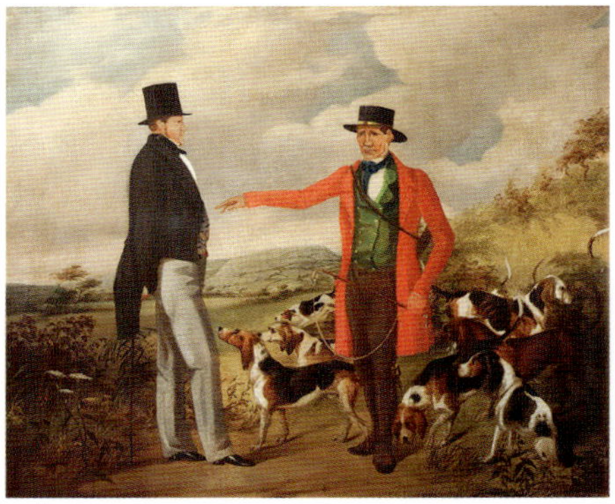

British (English) School
The Rossendale Hunt 1800–1830
oil on canvas 72.4 x 88.9
ZA-193

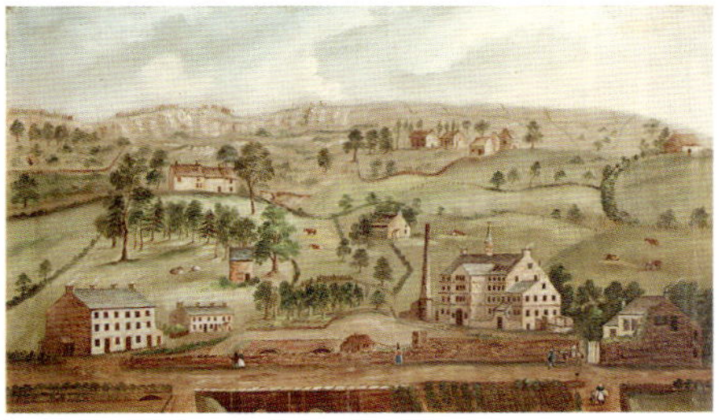

British (English) School
Hareholme Mill c.1800–1830
oil on canvas 50.8 x 83.8
PA-183

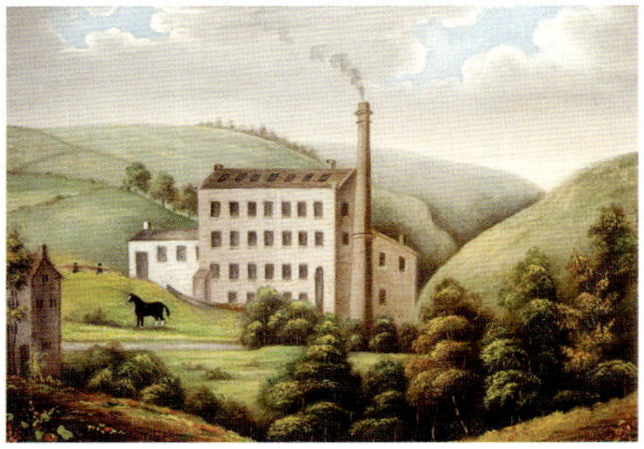

British (English) School
Mill Landscape c.1800–1830
oil on canvas 26.7 x 34.9
PA-39

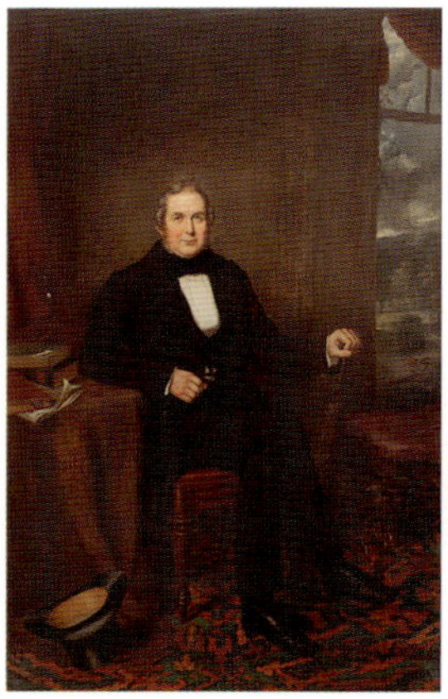

British (English) School
David Whitehead c.1830–1860
oil on canvas 175.3 x 139.7
PA-181

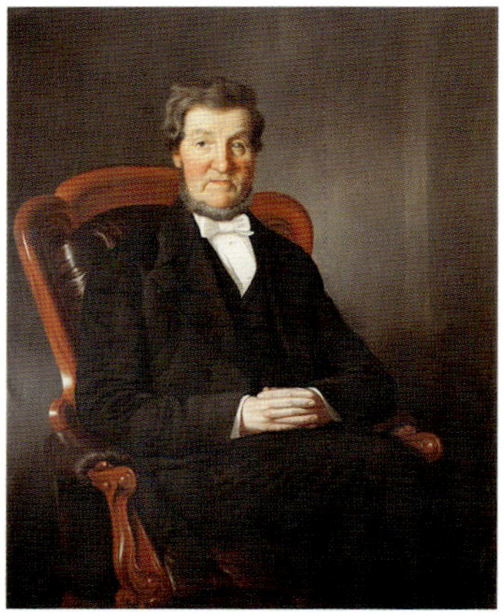

British (English) School
Thomas Whitehead c.1840–1859
oil on canvas 133.4 x 108.6
PA-126

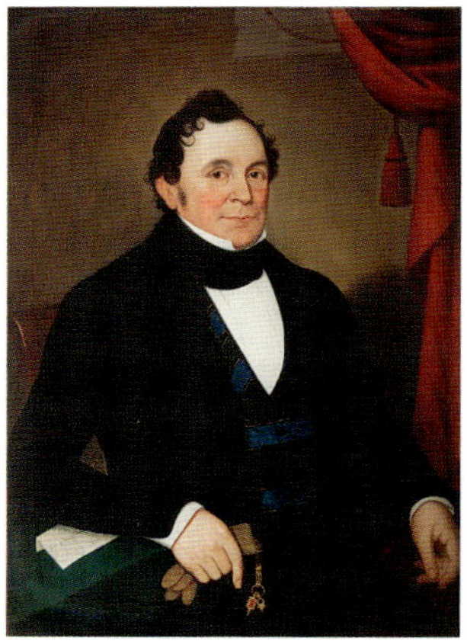

British (English) School
John Ormerod c.1847
oil on canvas 94 x 73.7
PA-73

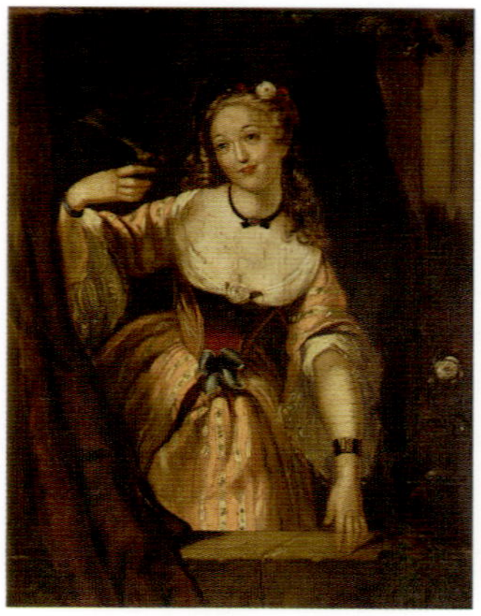

British (English) School
Girl with Blackbird c.1850
oil on canvas (?) 35.6 x 27.9
ZA-180

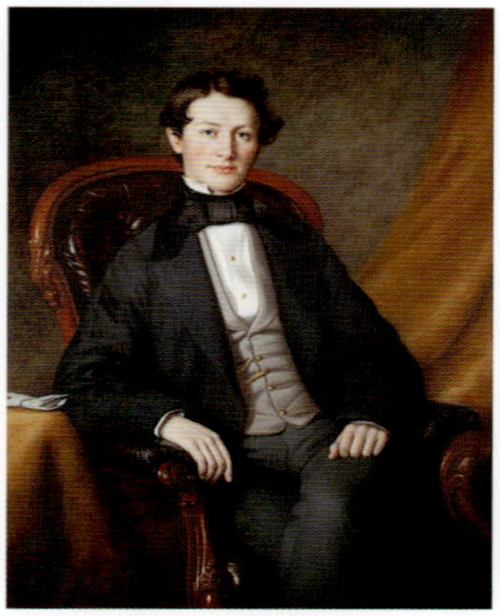

British (English) School
Joseph Wood Whitehead (c.1823–1879) c.1860
oil on canvas 132.1 x 104.1
PA-127

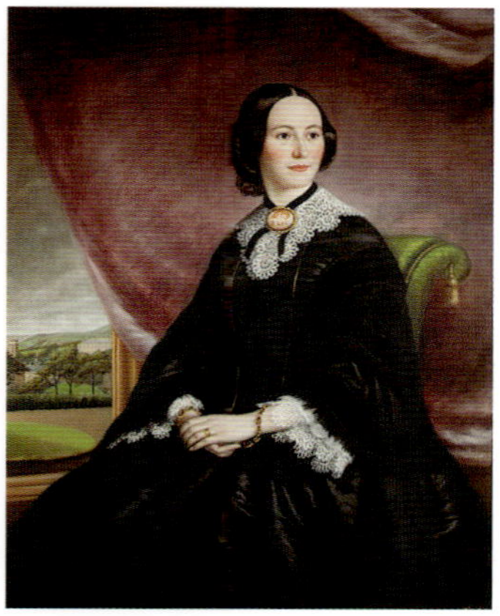

British (English) School
Mrs Joseph Wood Whitehead c.1860
oil on canvas 132.1 x 104.1
PA-132

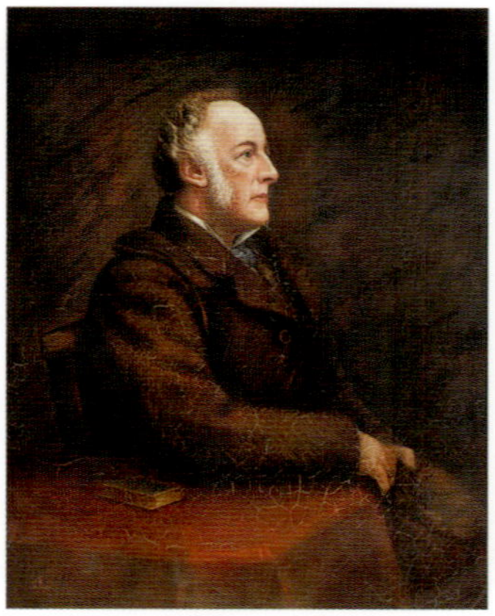

British (English) School
Sir John Everett Millais (1829–1896) c.1860–1896
oil on canvas 115.6 x 101.6
PA-128

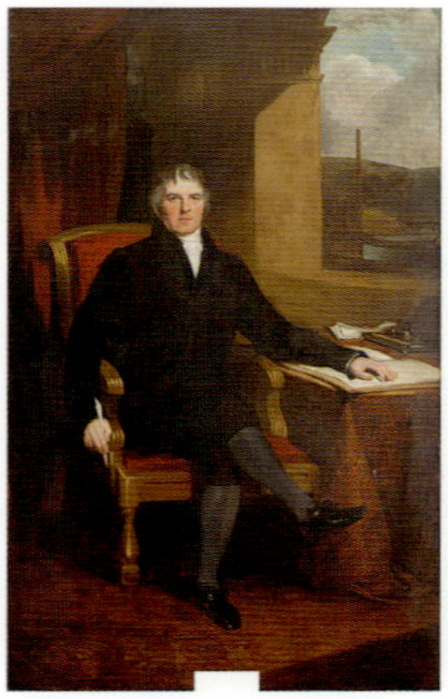

British (English) School
John Hamer
oil on canvas 240 x 150
PA-180

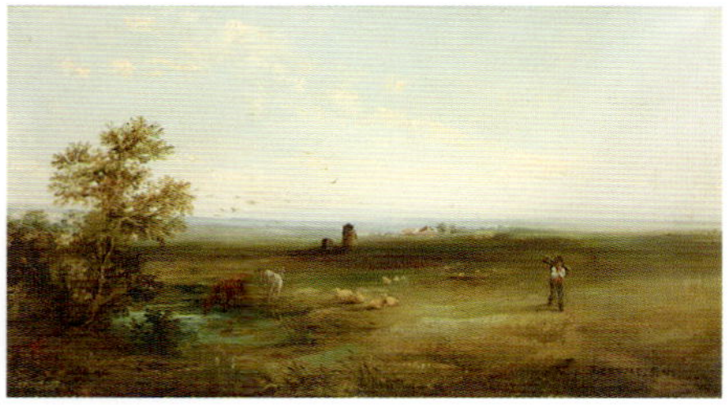

British (English) School
Near Adlington
oil on canvas 17.8 x 43.2
PA-186

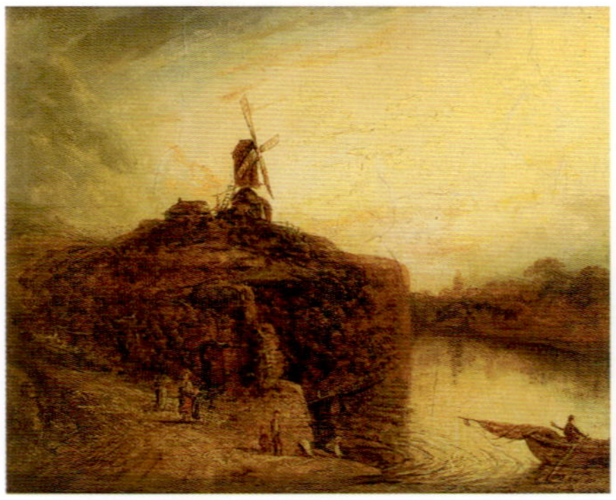

British (English) School
Windmill above a River
oil on canvas 39.4 x 48.9
PA-242

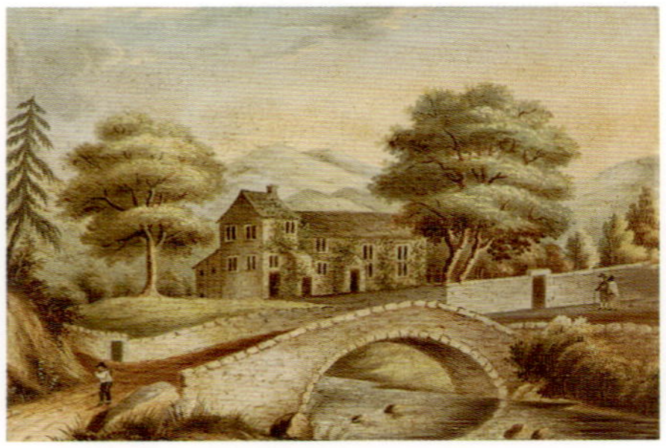

British (English) School (attributed to)
Friends Meeting House, Crawshawbooth
oil on board 22.9 x 33.7
PA-164

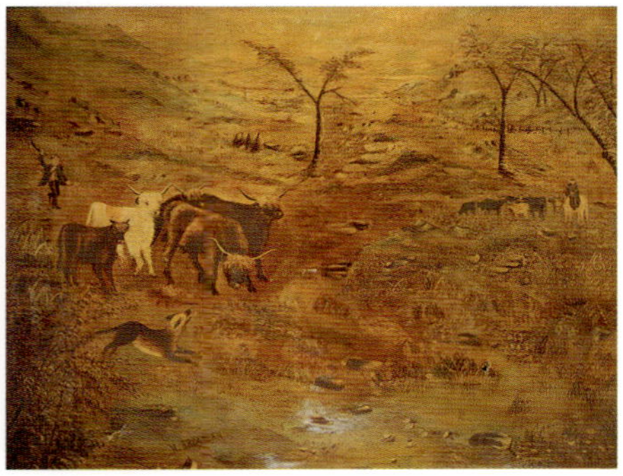

Broadley, W.
Moorland Scene 1903
oil on canvas 91.4 x 127
PA-131

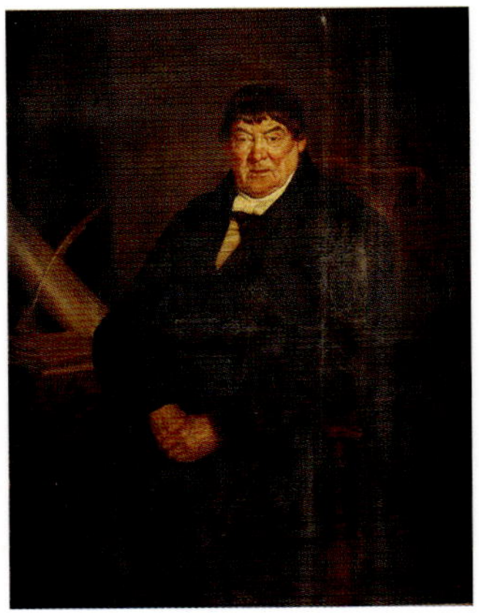

Brodie, Hammond active c.1820–1870
Portrait of a Gentleman
oil on canvas 147.3 x 116.8
PA-122

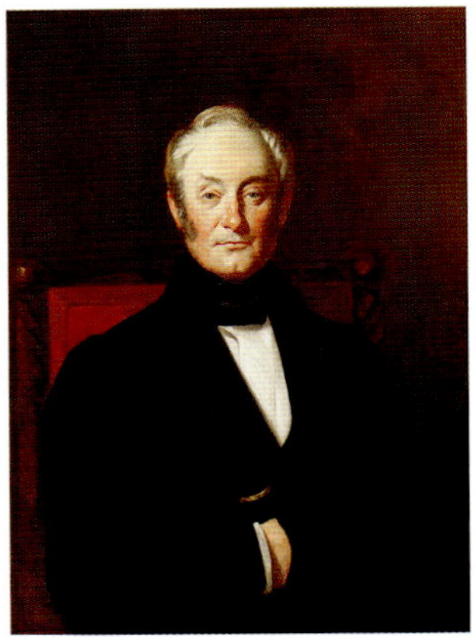

Brodie, John Lamont active c.1834–1881
George Hardman (1794–1852) c.1834–1852
oil on canvas 96.5 x 74.9
PA-149

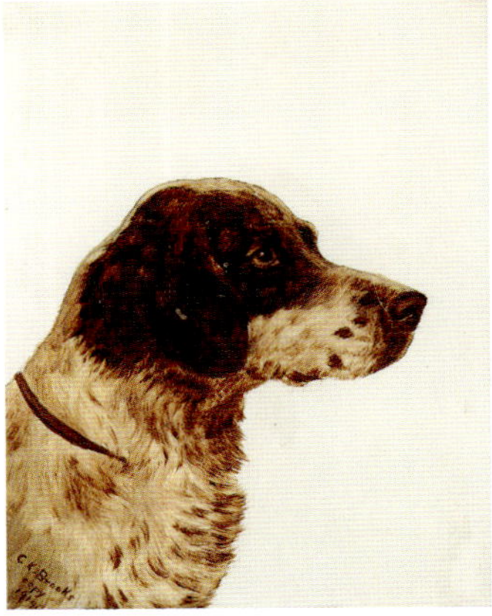

Brooks, Cecily Kate 1887–1975
A Dog 1914
oil on glass 21.6 x 16.5
2001.08.04

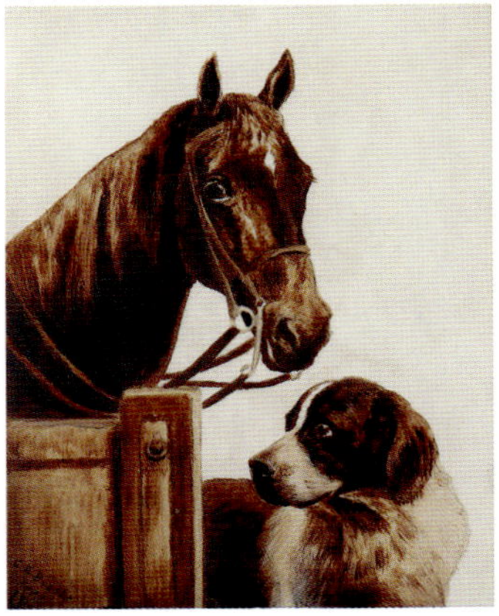

Brooks, Cecily Kate 1887–1975
Horse and Dog 1914
oil on glass 21.6 x 16.5
2001.08.03

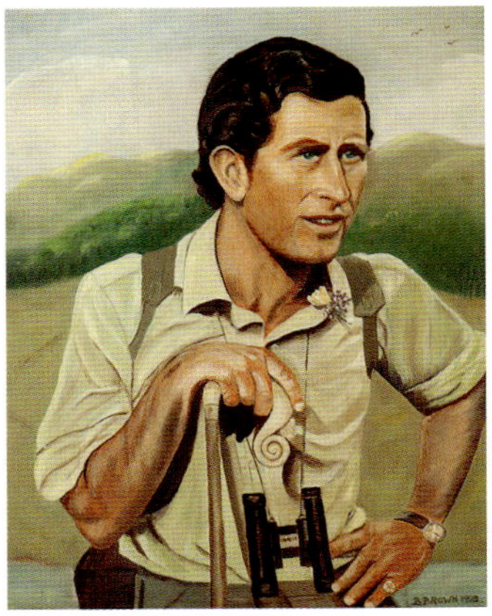

Brown, Barbara
HRH Prince Charles (b.1948) 1982
oil on board 54.6 x 43.8
PA-281

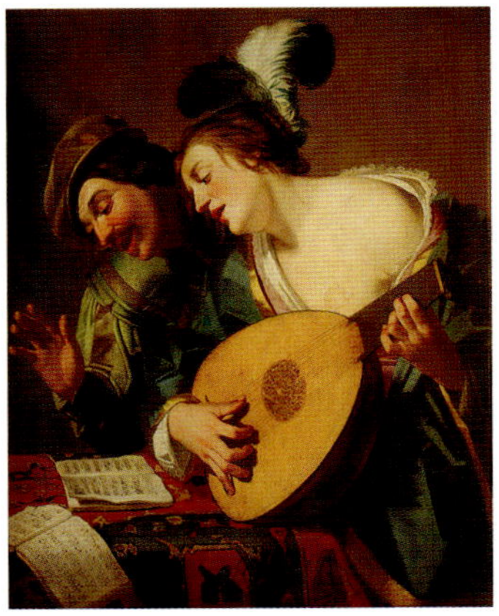

Brugghen, Hendrick ter (style of) 1588–1629
The Music Lesson
oil on canvas 111.8 x 97.8
PA-129

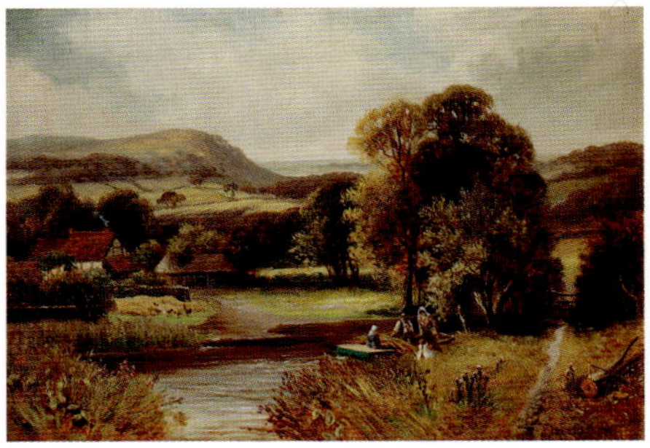

Carlton, Frederick active 1895–1899
Figures on a Boat Gathering Rushes
oil on canvas 49.5 x 74.9
PA-252

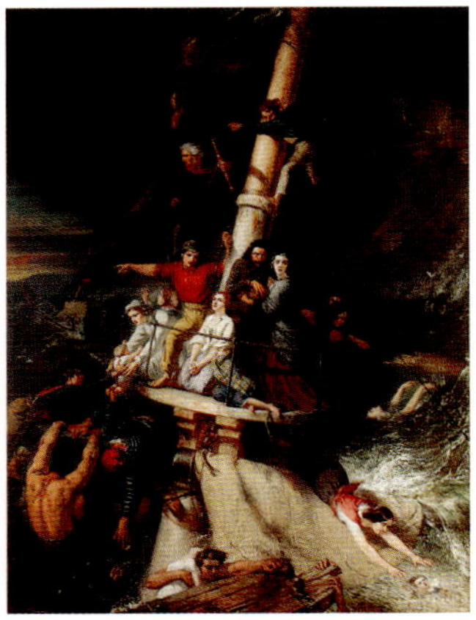

Claxton, Marshall 1813–1881
The Lifeboat
oil on canvas 180.3 x 135.9
PA-255

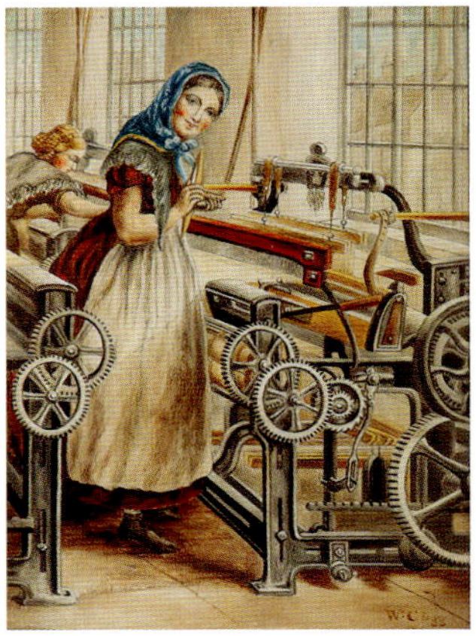

Clegg, William
Girl at Preston Loom 1869
oil on canvas 29.2 x 21.6
PA-238

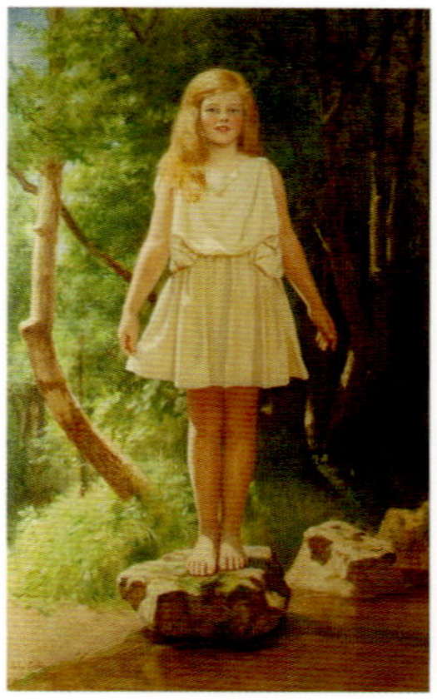

Collier, John 1850–1934
Stepping Stones: Pamela 1929
oil on canvas 188 x 116.8
PA-192

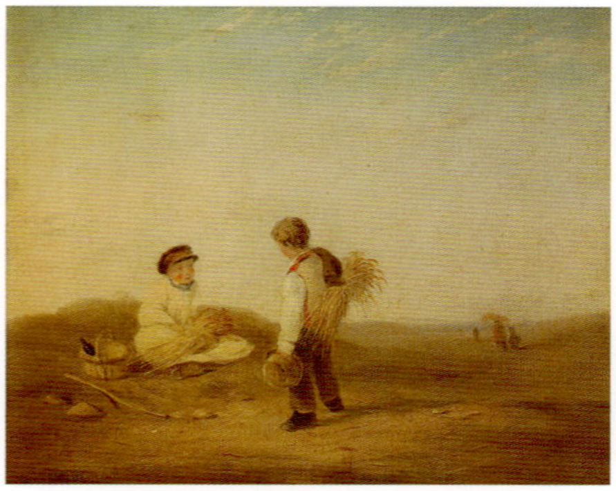

Collins, William (follower of) 1788–1847
Boys Gleaning
oil on canvas 25.4 x 31.8
PA-200

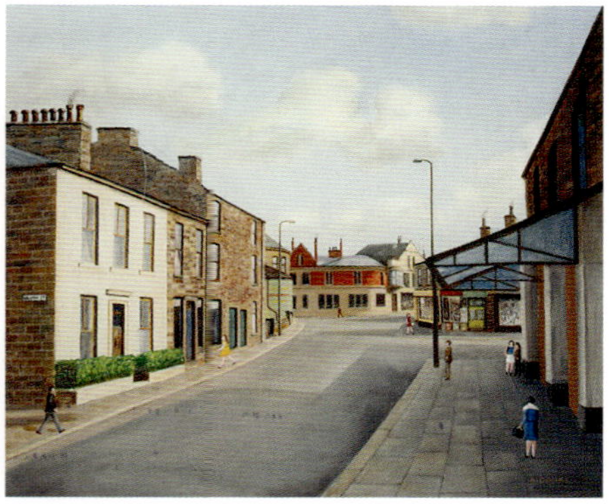

Coupe, A.
Waterfoot Centre
oil on canvas 43.2 x 53.3
2006.1

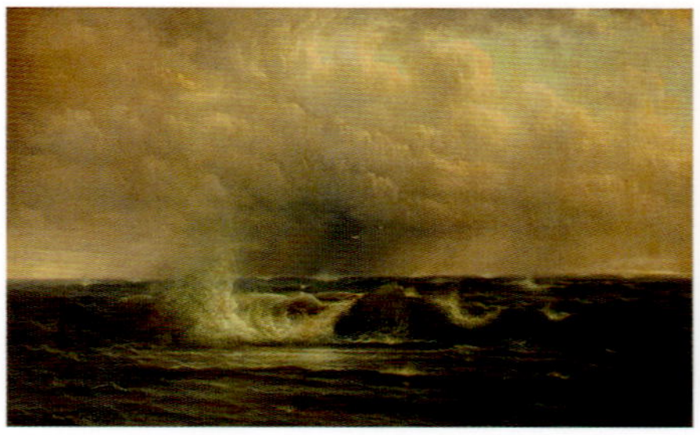

Craig, James B.
Seascape
oil on canvas 76.2 x 124.5
PA-95

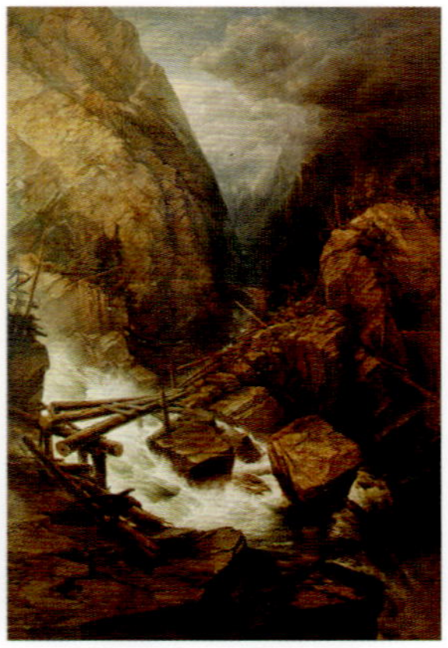

Creswick, Thomas 1811–1869
The Devil's Bridge on the St Gothard Pass c. 1840–1869
oil on canvas 180.3 x 119.4
PA-197

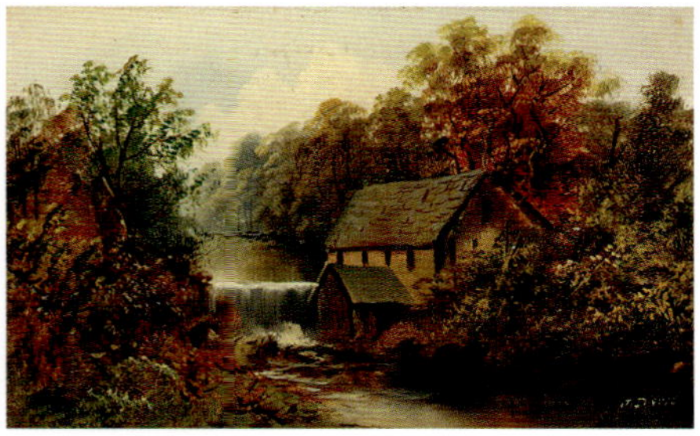

Davis, J. active 19th C
Cottage by Weir
oil on canvas 38.1 x 71.1
PA-59

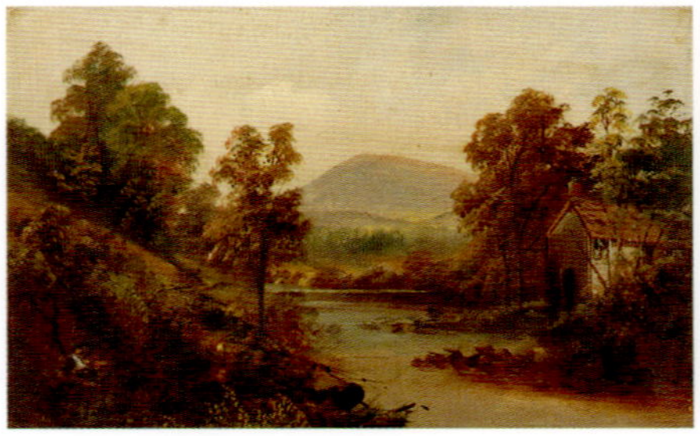

Davis, J. active 19th C
Mountain and Lake with Cottage
oil on canvas 38.1 x 58.4
ZA-171

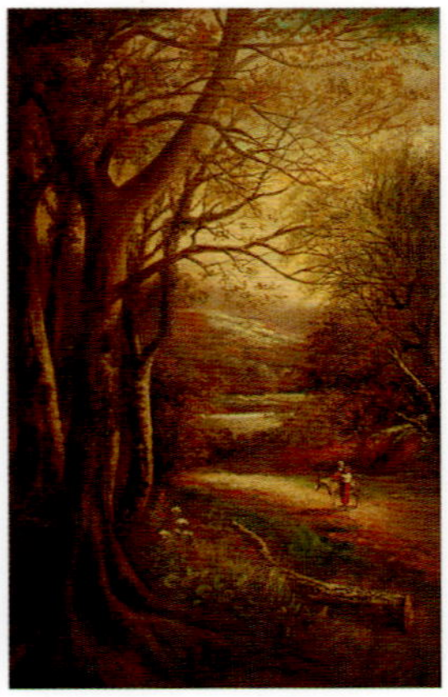

Drake, J.
Spring
oil on canvas 160 x 109.2
PA-111

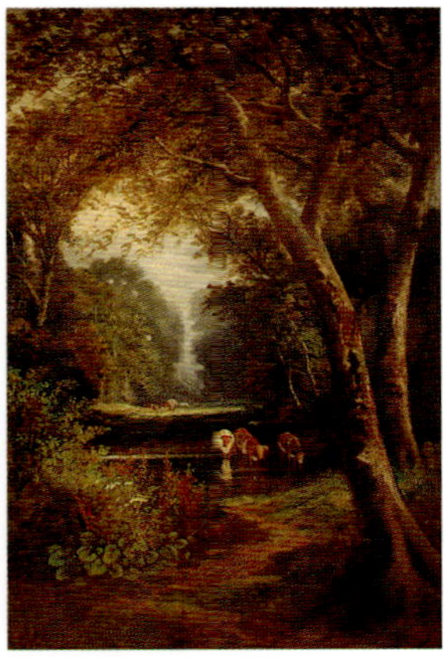

Drake, J.
Summer
oil on canvas 160 x 121.9
PA-133

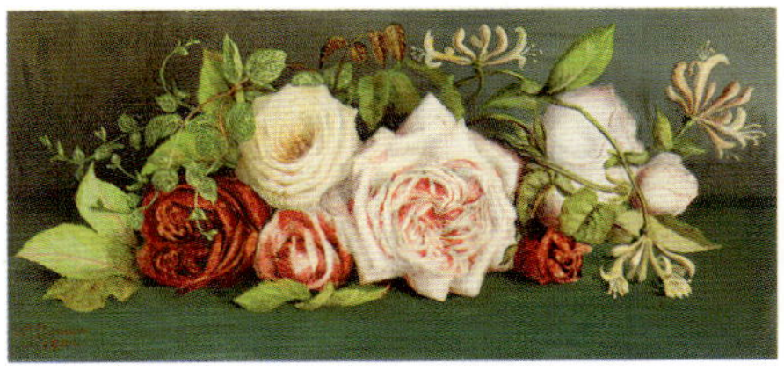

Dunkin, William John 1845–1914
Roses and Honeysuckle 1904
oil on board 19.1 x 44.5
1992.06.29

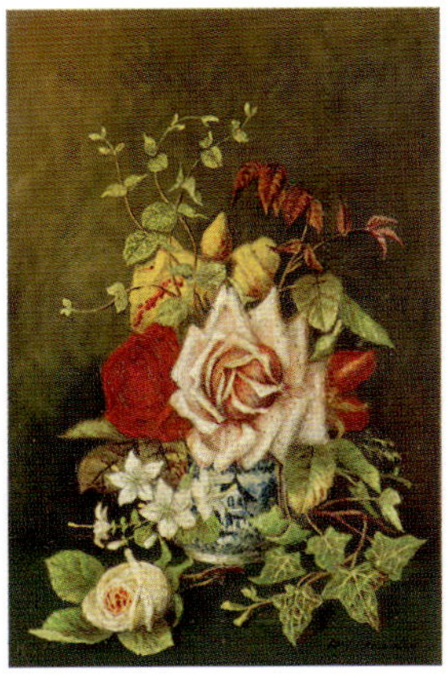

Dunkin, William John 1845–1914
Roses
oil on board 43.8 x 33.7
1992.06.30

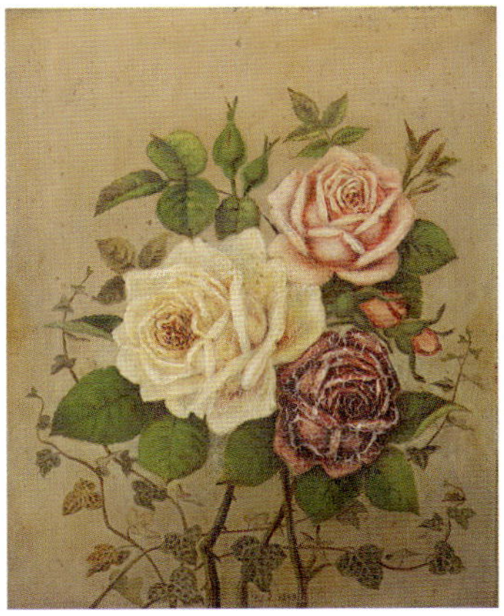

Dunkin, William John 1845–1914
Roses
oil on board (?) 35.6 x 29.2
1992.06.31

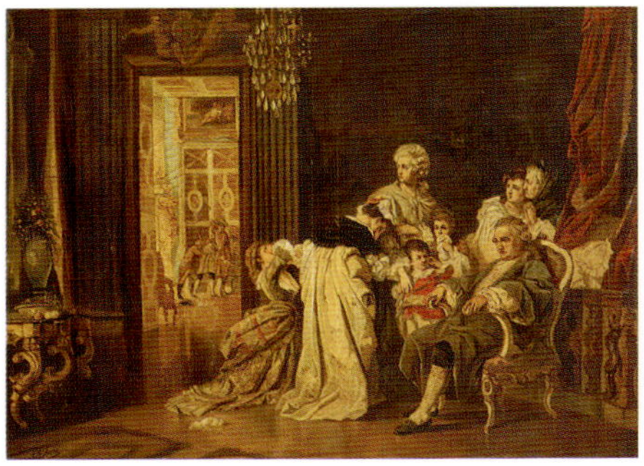

Ebele, J.
Louis XVI and Family
oil on canvas 71.1 x 97.8
PA-103

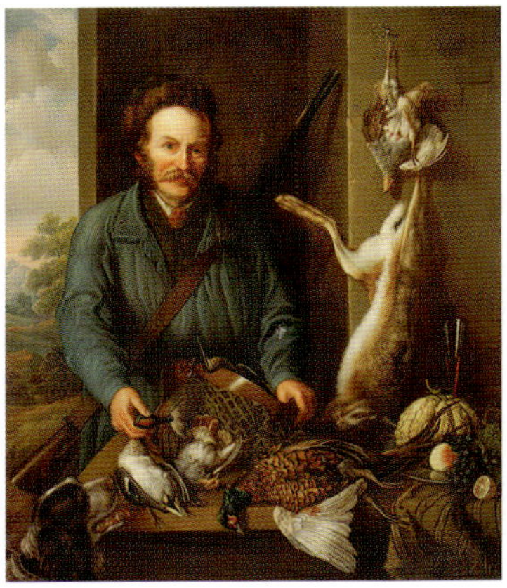

Eikendulf, R.
The Gamekeeper
oil on canvas 134.6 x 119.4
PA-118

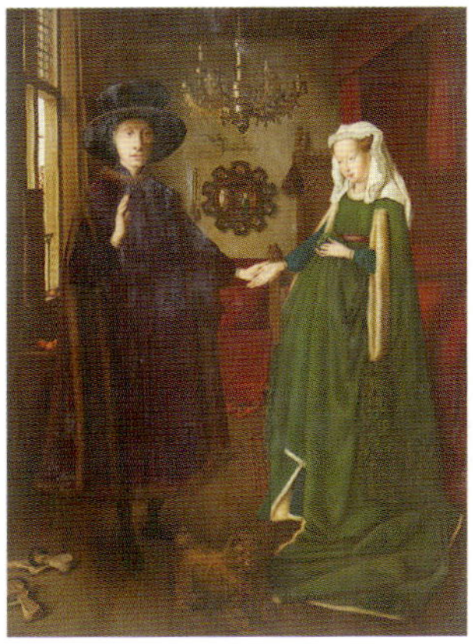

Eyck, Jan van (copy after) 1390–1441
The Arnolfini Betrothal 19th C (?)
oil on canvas 83.8 x 61
PA-231

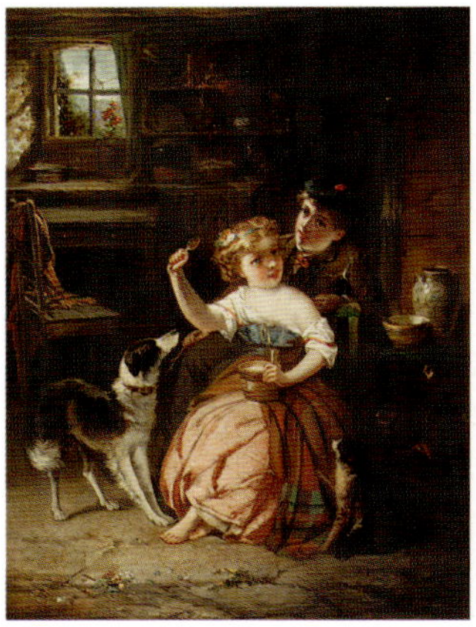

Faed, Thomas (attributed to) 1826–1900
Playmates c.1872
oil on canvas 94 x 74.9
PA-208

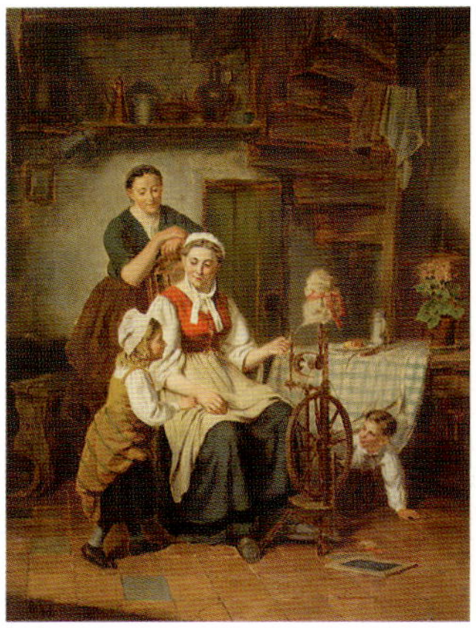

Faed, Thomas (attributed to) 1826–1900
The Spinning Wheel c.1873
oil on canvas 76.2 x 61.0
PA-207

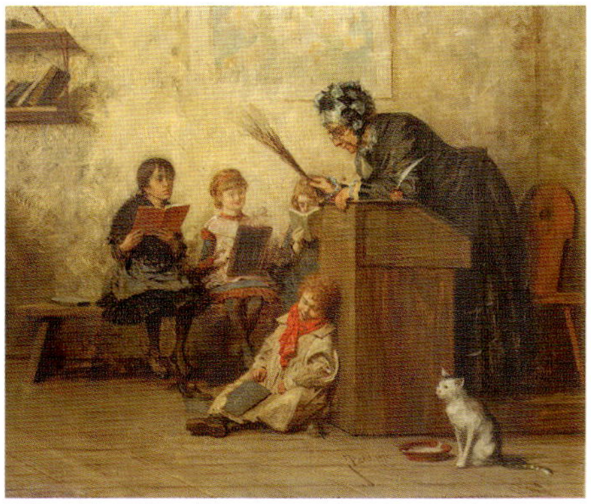

Faed, Thomas (attributed to) 1826–1900
The Dame's School 1879
oil on canvas 44.5 x 54.6
PA-206

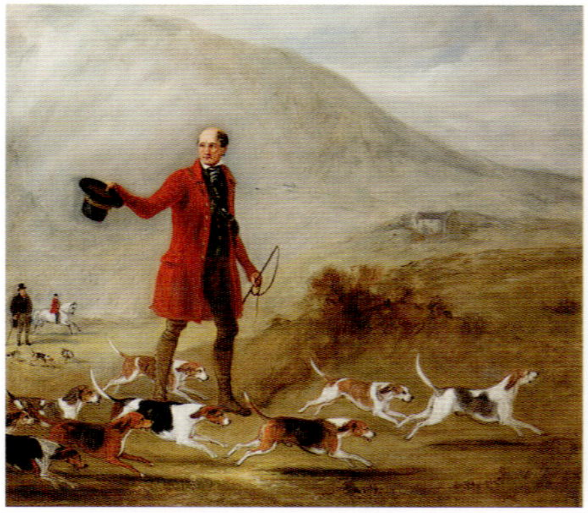

Ferneley II, John 1814–1862
The Rossendale Hunt
oil on canvas 61 x 74.9
ZA-194

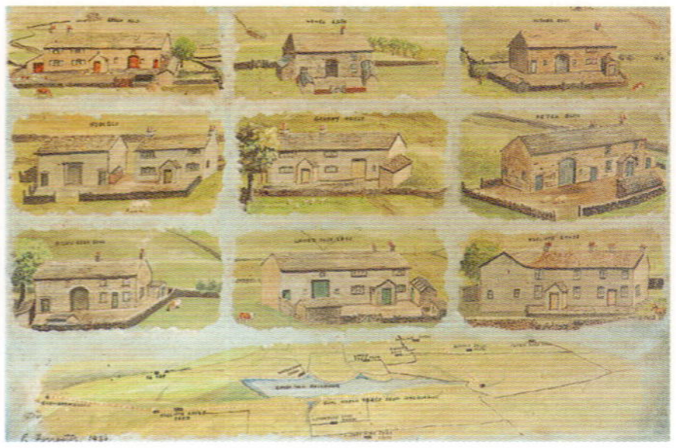

Forrester, Ephraim 1907–1994
Farms in Crawshawbooth / Loveclough 1986
oil on board 43.2 x 59.7
2008.05

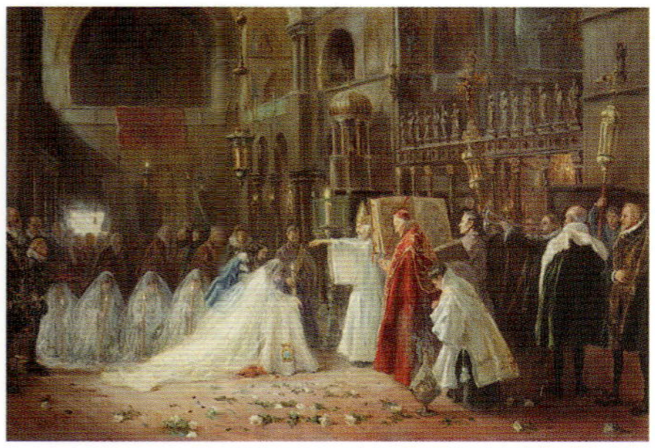

Forti, Giuseppe
The Marriage of Louis XIV
oil on canvas 69.9 x 104.1
PA-105

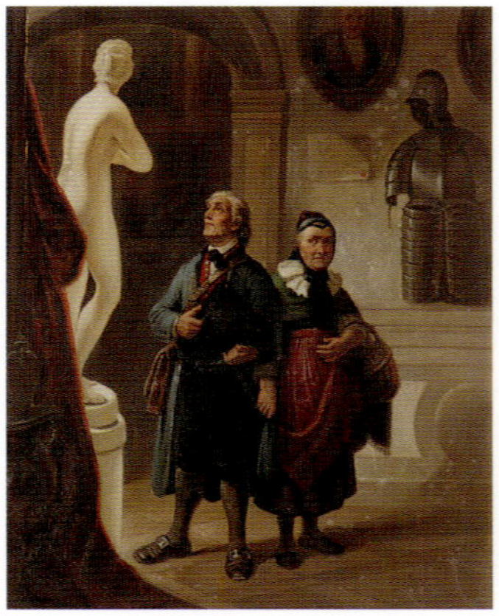

German School
Figures in a Museum c.1880
oil on canvas 55.2 x 47.0
PA-49

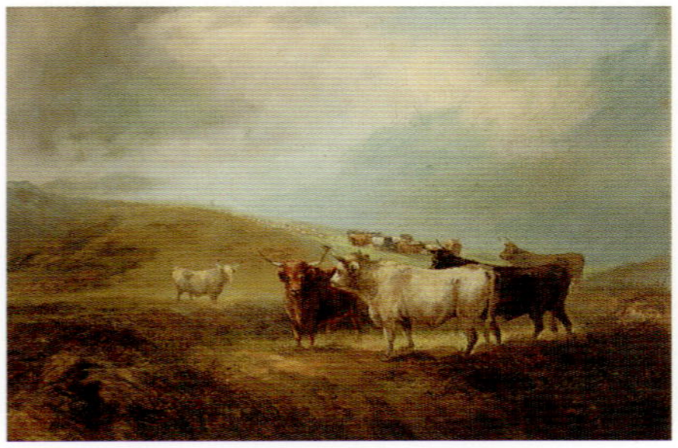

Gibb, Thomas Henry 1833–1893
On the Way to Lowland Pastures 1870
oil on canvas 49.5 x 64.8
PA-279

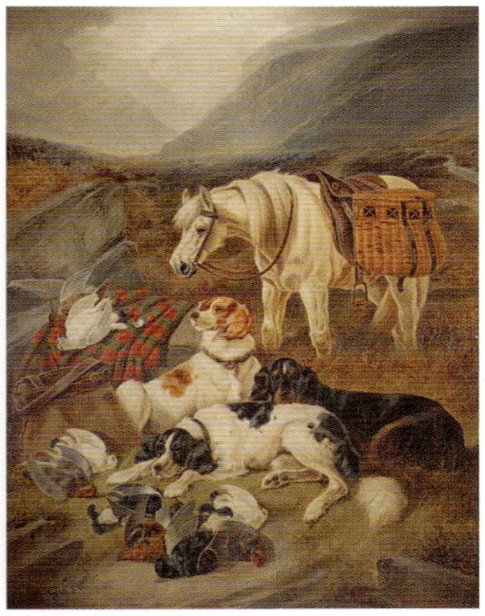

Gifford, John –1900
Pack Horse and Dogs
oil on canvas 134.6 x 109.2
PA-113

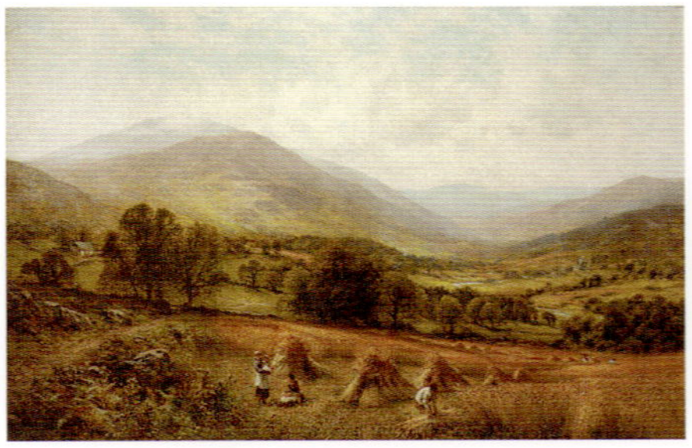

Glendening, Alfred Augustus 1840–1921
Harvesting Scene 1892
oil on canvas 76.2 x 127
PA-104

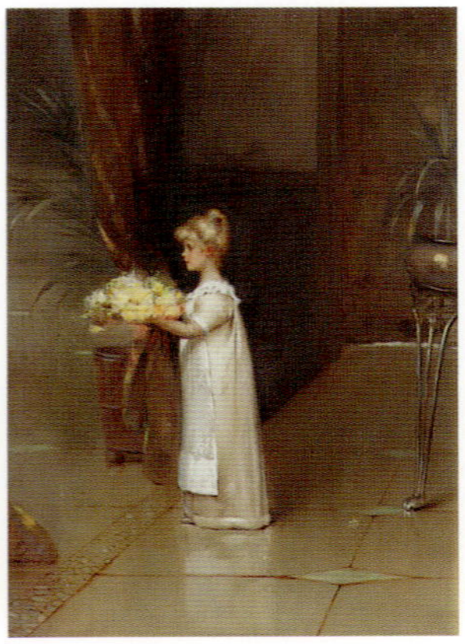

Goodman, Maude 1855–1938
Mother's Birthday c.1908
oil on canvas 43.2 x 33
PA-194

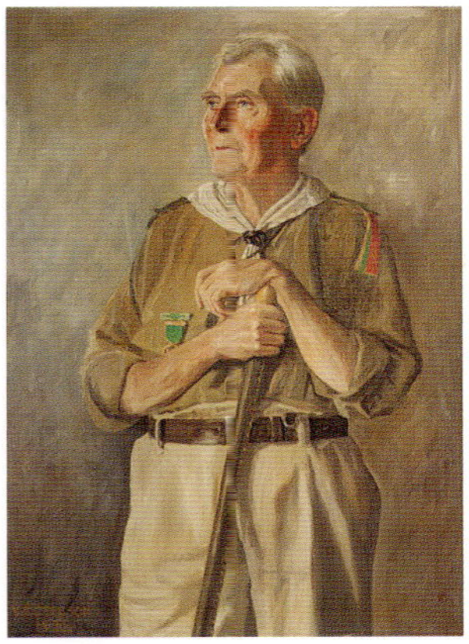

Gregson, V. R. active 1928–1950
Timber Wolf, Rossendale c.1920–1939
oil on cnavas 106.7 x 76.2
PA-262

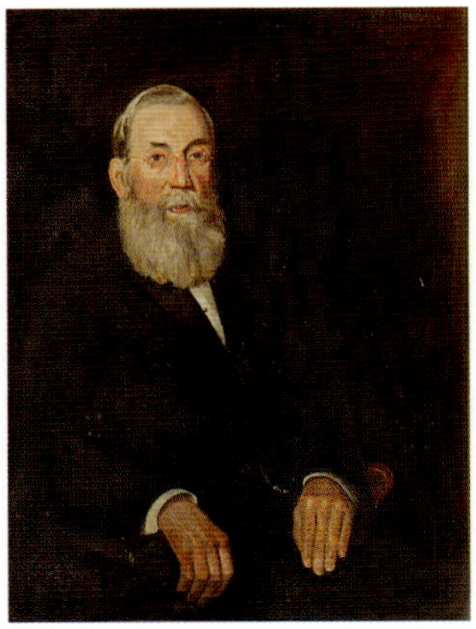

Gregson, V. R. active 1928–1950
Alderman Samuel Compston 1928
oil on canvas 91.4 x 76
PA-151

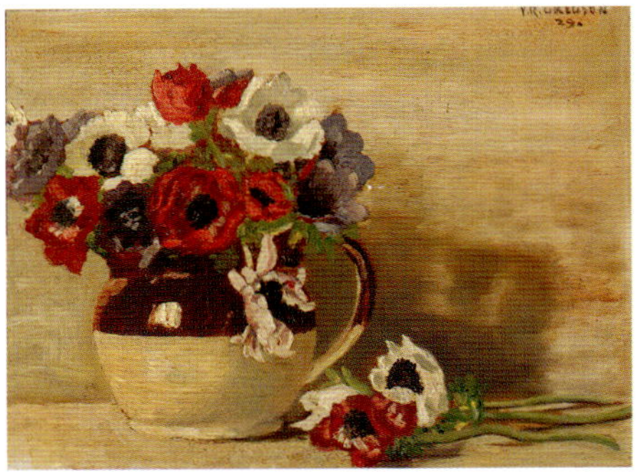

Gregson, V. R. active 1928–1950
Flowers in a Jug 1929
oil on board 24.1 x 34.3
PA-58

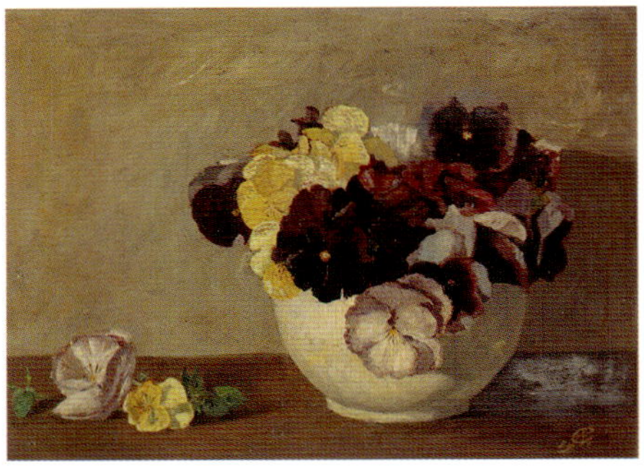

Gregson, V. R. active 1928–1950
Pansies in Bowl 1929
oil on board 24.1 x 34.3
PA-86

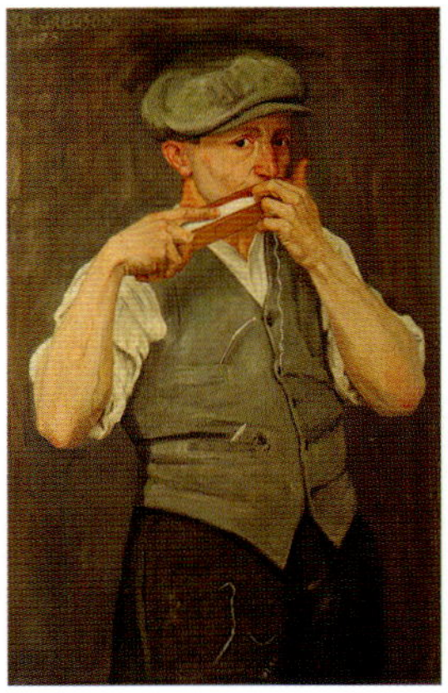

Gregson, V. R. active 1928–1950
Kissing the Shuttle 1931
oil on canvas 90.2 x 59.7
PA-144

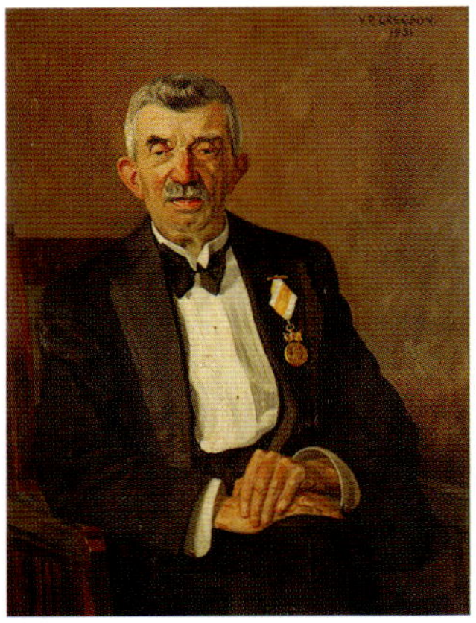

Gregson, V. R. active 1928–1950
Portrait of a Man Wearing a Medal 1931
oil on canvas 86.4 x 68.6
PA-145

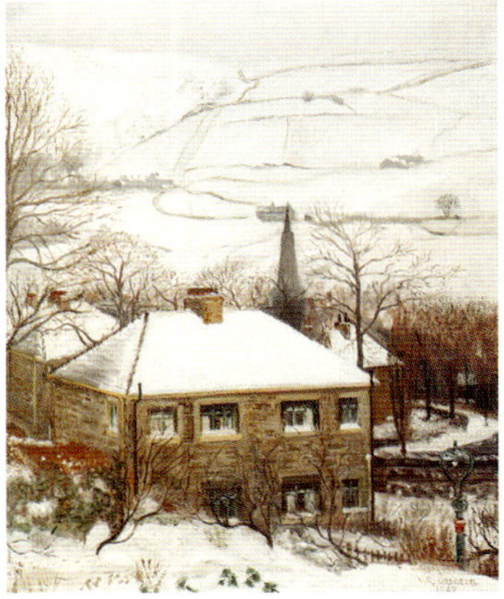

Gregson, V. R. active 1928–1950
Snow in a Pennine Village 1947
oil on canvas 63.5 x 50.8
2007.09.01

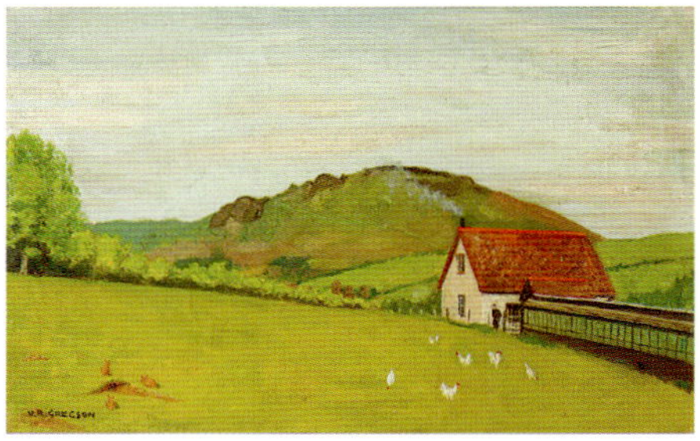

Gregson, V. R. active 1928–1950
The Farm at Cardington 1950
oil on canvas 25.4 x 35.6
2007.12.02

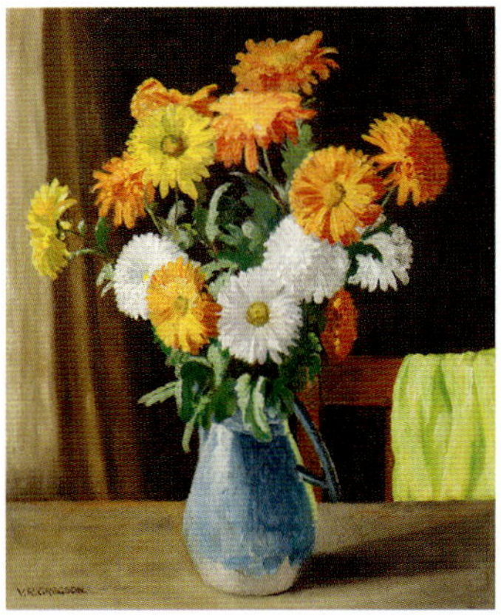

Gregson, V. R. active 1928–1950
Flowers in a Vase
oil on canvas 61 x 50.8
2007.09.03

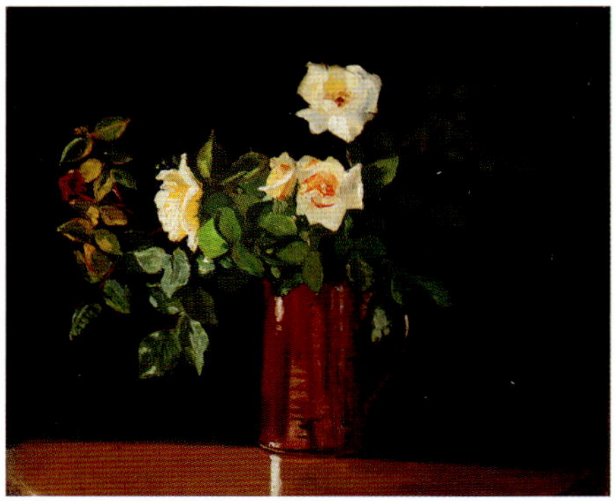

Gregson, V. R. active 1928–1950
Flowers in a Vase
oil on canvas 43.2 x 53.3
2007.09.04

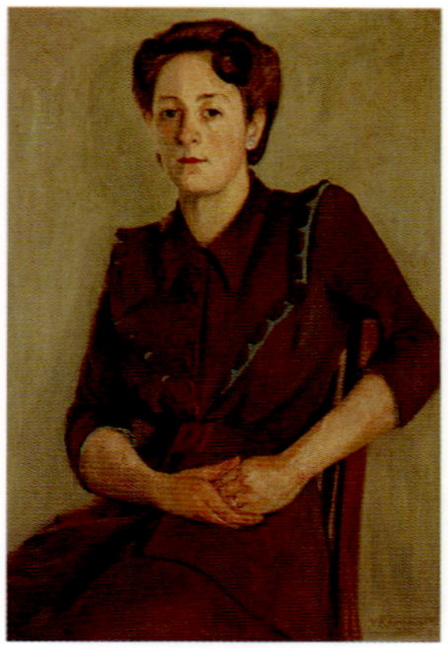

Gregson, V. R. active 1928–1950
Margaret Gregson
oil on canvas 71.1 x 53.3
2007.09.02

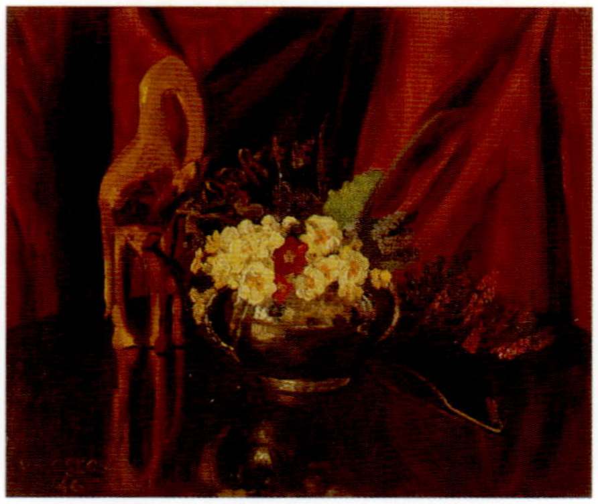

Gregson, V. R. active 1928–1950
Still Life with Flowers
oil on canvas 33 x 43.2
2007.09.05

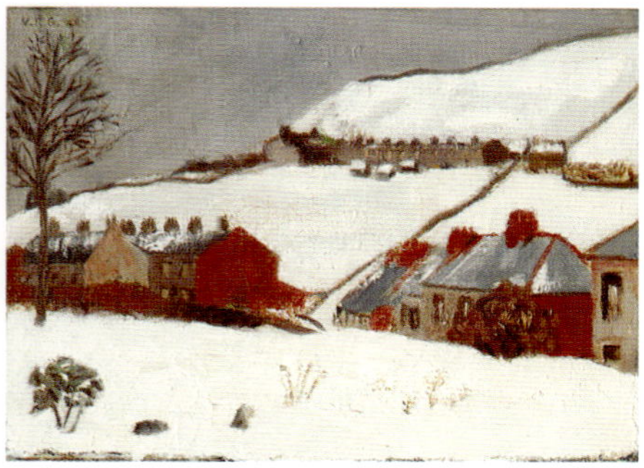

Gregson, V. R. active 1928–1950
Winter
oil on canvas 25.4 x 35.6
2007.12.01

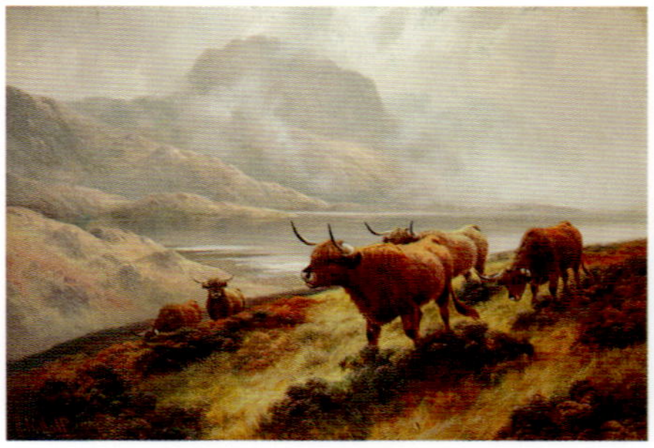

Hall, Henry Robinson 1859–1927
Highland Cattle above Loch Maree
oil on canvas 58.4 x 88.9
PA-109

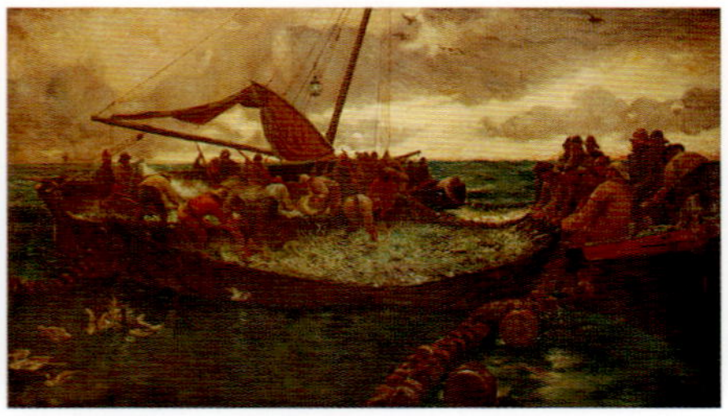

Hall (Mrs), George W.
Pilchards (after Charles Napier Hemy)
oil on canvas 114.3 x 205.7
PA-212

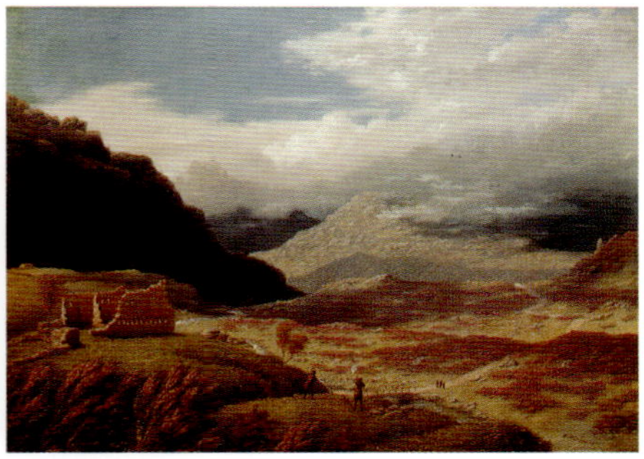

Harvey, George 1806–1876
Rob Roy's Castle, Scotland 1850
oil on canvas 47 x 69.9
PA-213

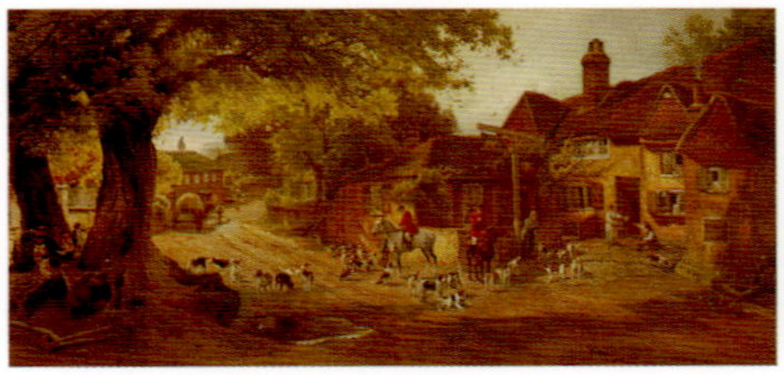

Holder, Edward Henry 1847–1922
Refresher at the Old Inn
oil on canvas 64.8 x 130.8
PA-114

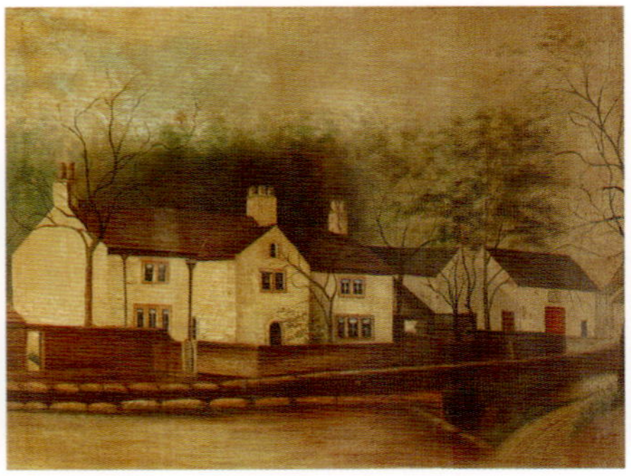

Hollins, Henry active 1902–1914
Loveclough Print Works 1902
oil on canvas 50.8 x 68.6
PA-188

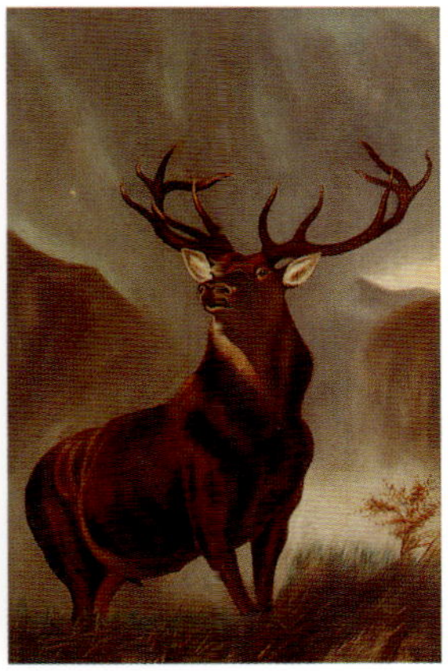

Hollins, Henry active 1902–1914
Stag 1905
oil on canvas 94 x 61
PA-98

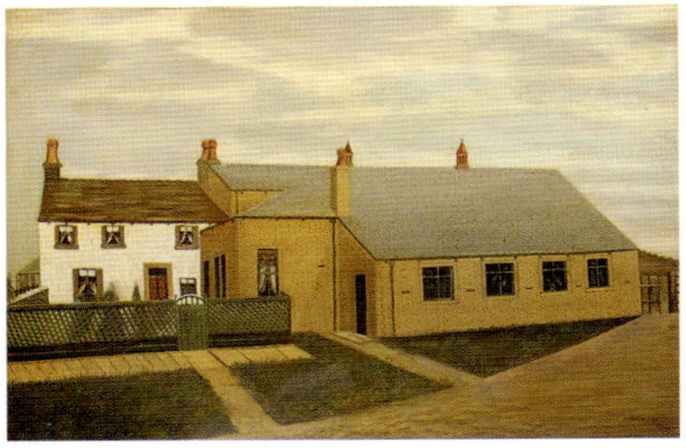

Hollins, Henry active 1902–1914
Spring Hill Farm, Water 1914
oil on canvas 61 x 91.4
PA-269

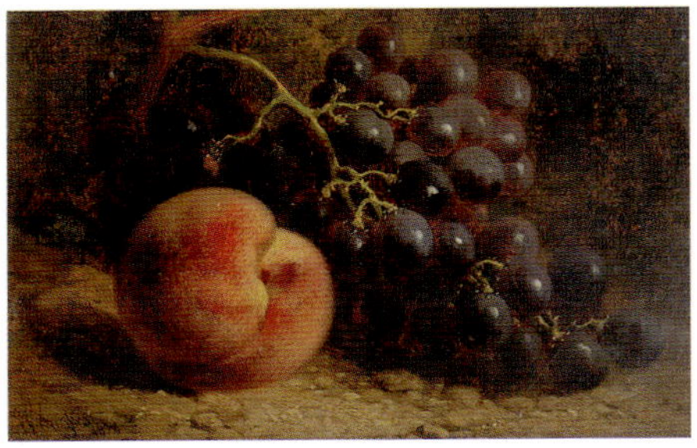

Hughes, William 1842–1901
Still Life of Fruit
oil on canvas 15.2 x 22.9
PA-239

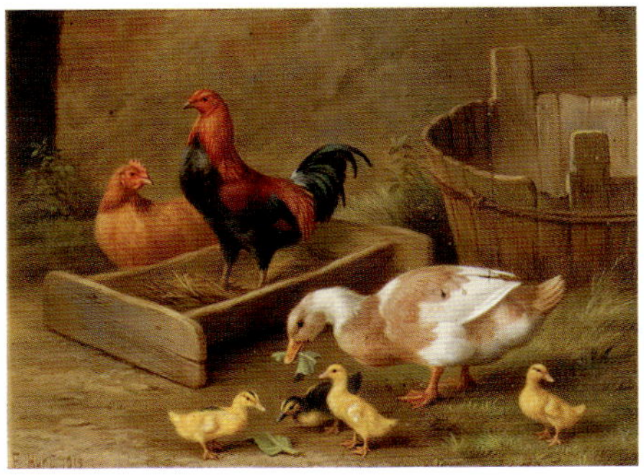

Hunt, Edgar 1876–1953
Poultry 1915
oil on canvas 17.8 x 22.9
PA-214

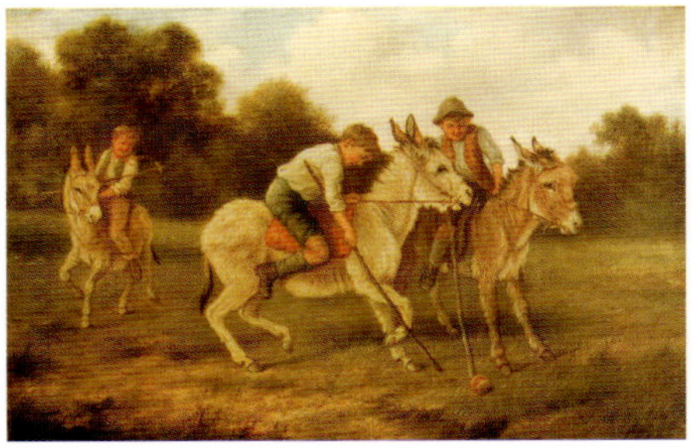

Hunt, Reuben 1879–1962
Rustic Polo
oil on canvas 33 x 45.7
PA-259

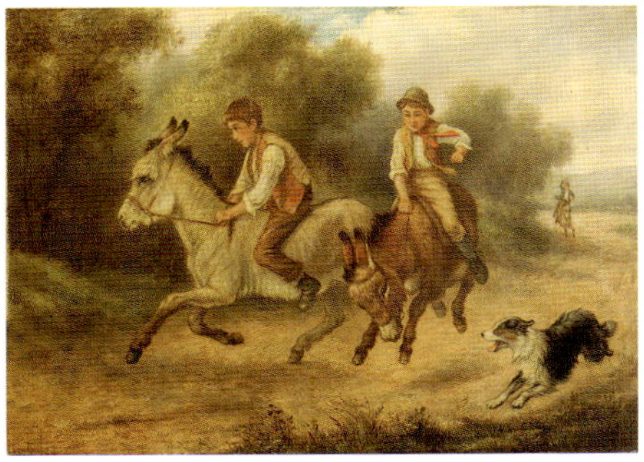

Hunt, Reuben 1879–1962
The Race
oil on canvas 33 x 45.7
PA-237

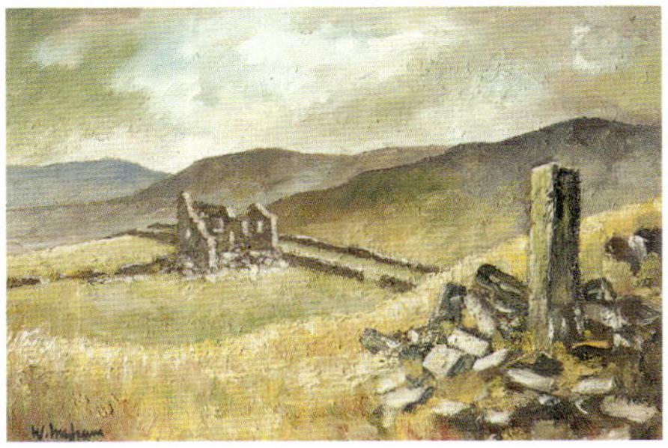

Ingham, William b.1938
Dark Summits
oil on board 24.1 x 34.3
PA-282

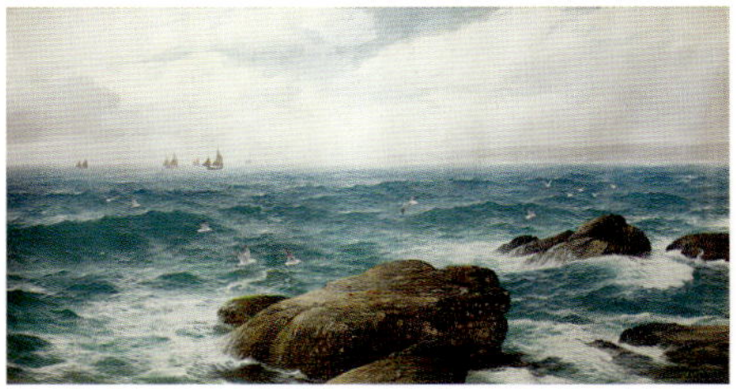

James, David 1853–1904
A Cornish Bay c.1880–1900
oil on canvas 63.5 x 127
PA-136

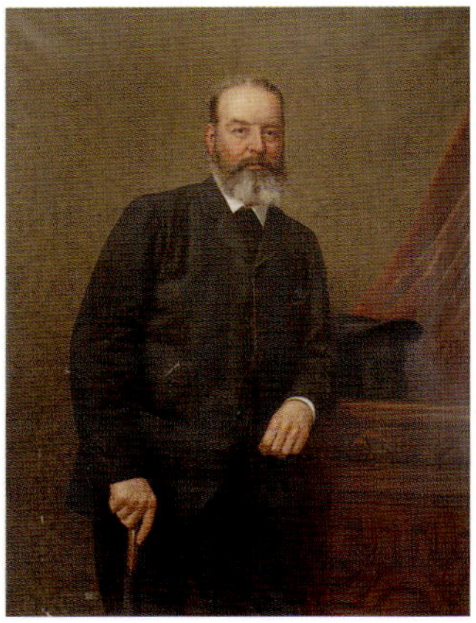

Johnston, William Herbert 1848–1897
George Edward Hardman (1830–1884)
c.1860–1884
oil on canvas 142.2 x 111.8
PA-182

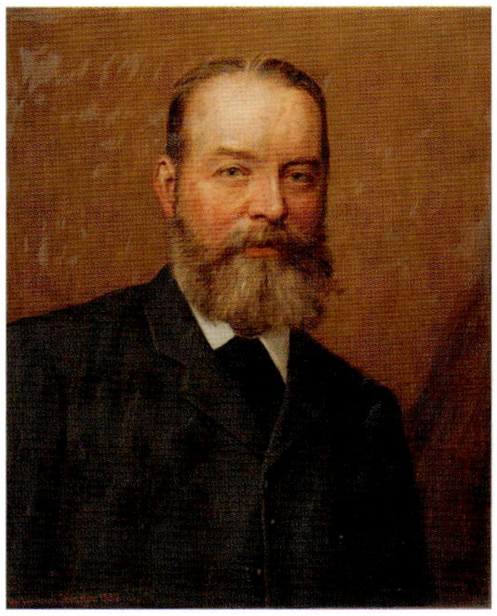

Johnston, William Herbert 1848–1897
George Edward Hardman (1830–1884)
oil on canvas 59.1 x 49.5
PA-79

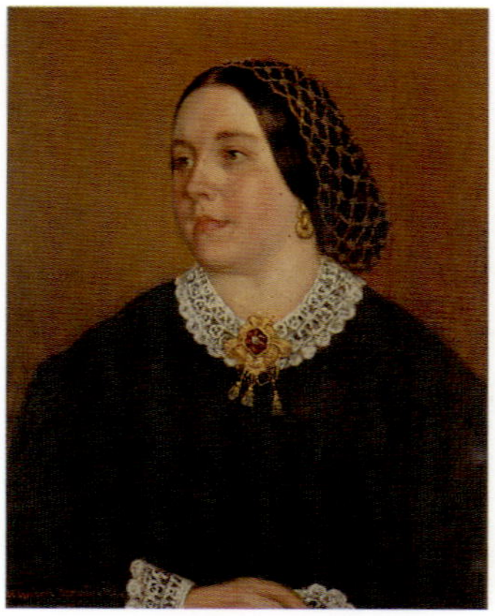

Johnston, William Herbert 1848–1897
Mrs George Edward Hardman
oil on canvas 68.6 x 57.2
PA-78

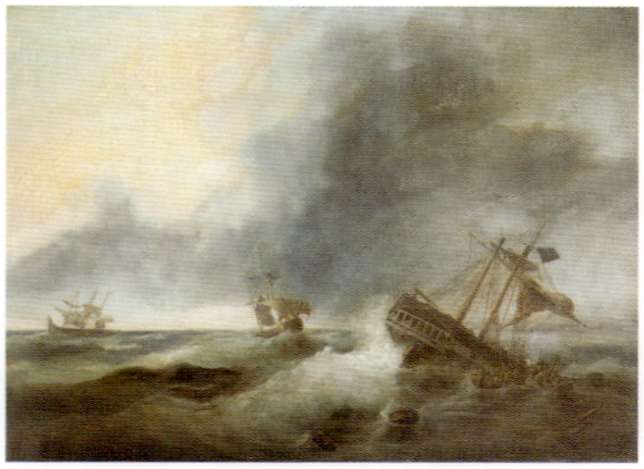

Kannemans, Christiaan Cornelis 1812–1884
The Wreck 1845
oil on canvas 78.7 x 105.4
PA-148

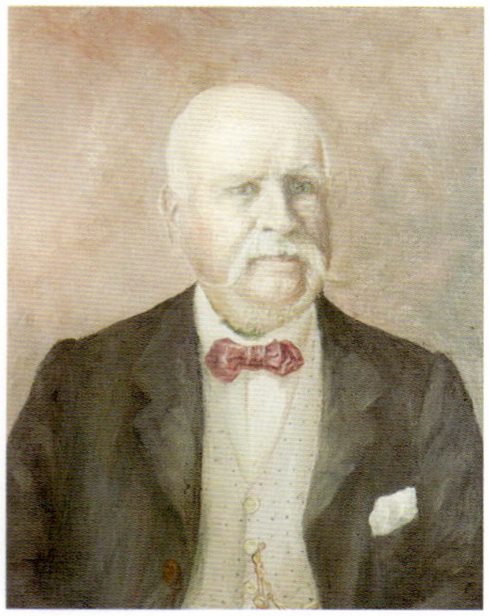

Kelly, David b.1955
Richard Whitaker (1829–1906) 1982
oil on board 61 x 48.3
PA-278

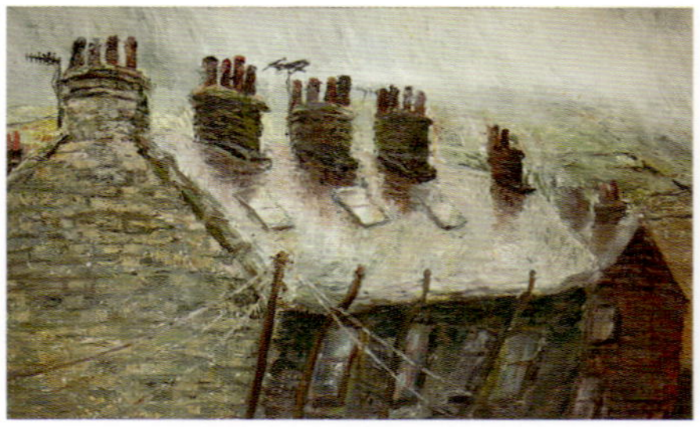

Kelly, David b.1955
Terraced Houses
oil on board 71.1 x 116.8
ZB-26

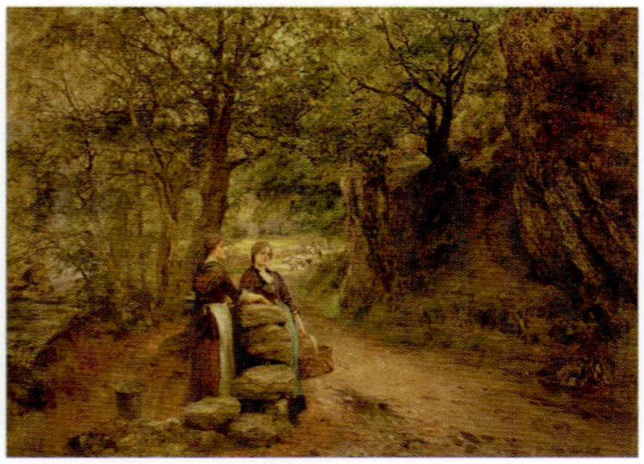

King, Henry John Yeend 1855–1924
Market Morning c.1875–1924
oil on canvas 129.5 x 190.5
PA-161

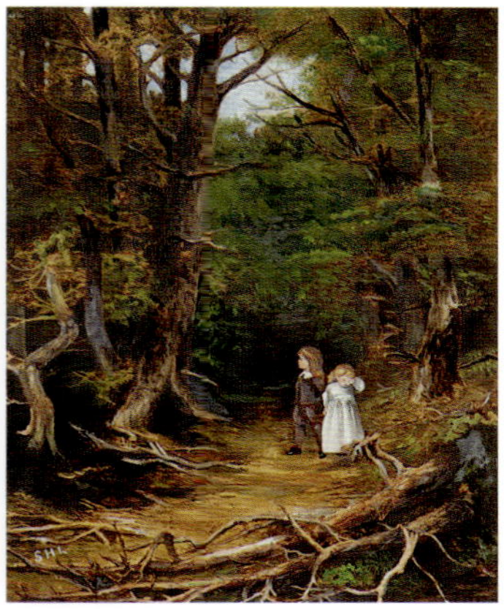

L., S. H.
Babes in the Wood
oil on canvas 30.5 x 25.4
PA-246

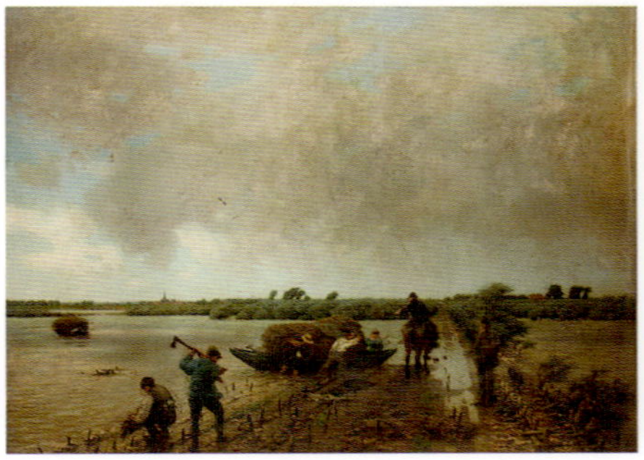

Lamnier, J.
Fenland Scene
oil on canvas 99.1 x 154.9
PA-162

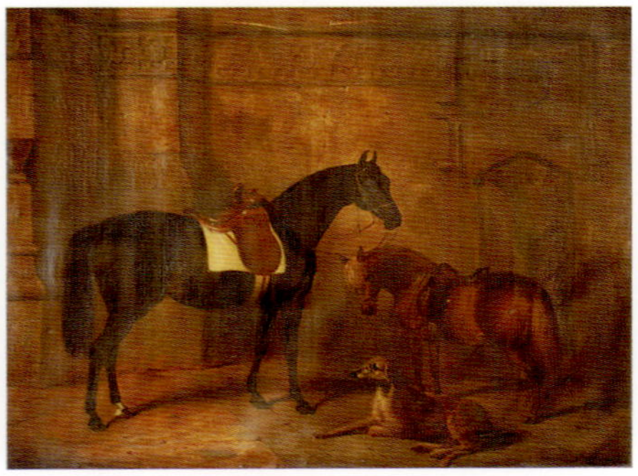

Landseer, Edwin Henry (after) 1802–1873
Horse, Pony and Stag Hound
oil on canvas 119.4 x 158.8
PA-112

Langley, William 1880–1920
The Close of Day
oil on canvas 50.8 x 73.7
PA-43

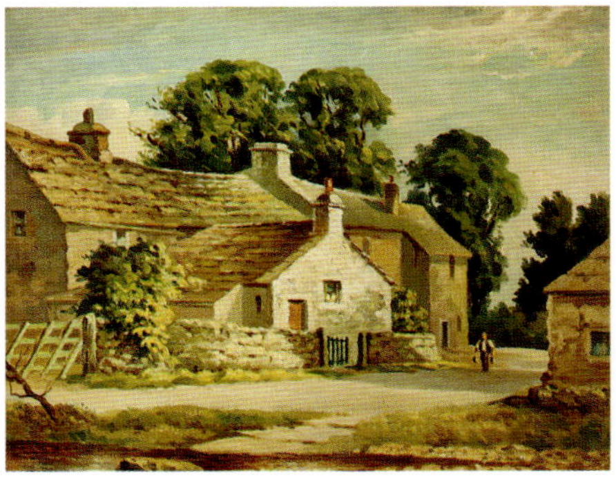

Law, Barry active c.1950–1960
Wycoller
oil on board 43.8 x 54.6
PA-83

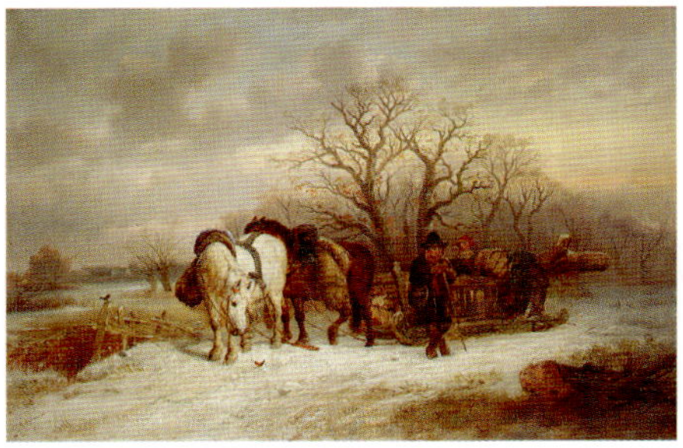

Leeuw, Alexis de 1822–1900
A Winter Scene
oil on canvas (?) 59.7 x 90.2
PA.142

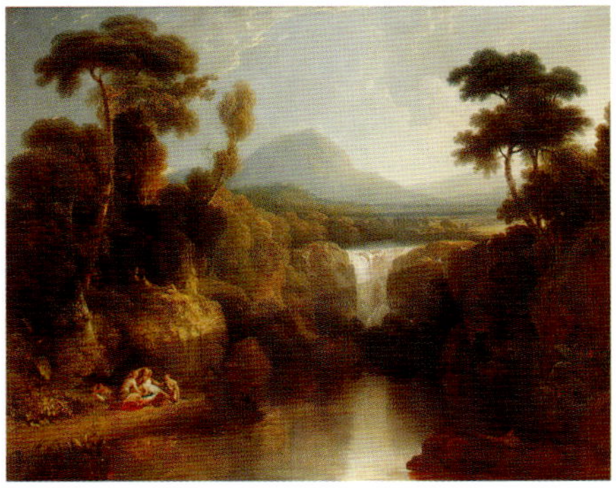

Linton, William (attributed to) 1791–1876
The Bathing Pool c.1815–1876
oil on canvas 109.2 x 142.2
PA-157

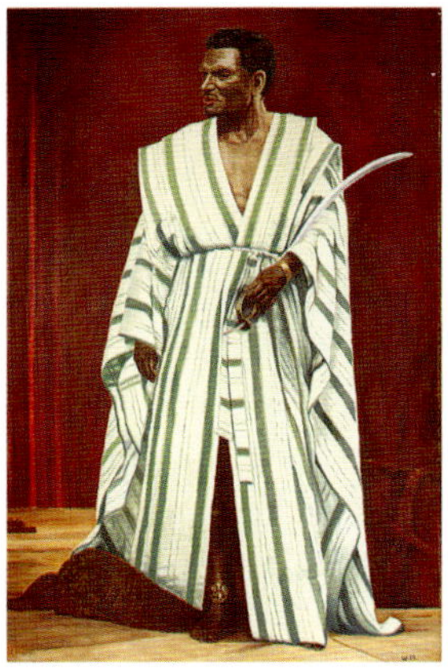

Maden, William
The Moor of Venice
oil on board 193 x 121.9
PA-159

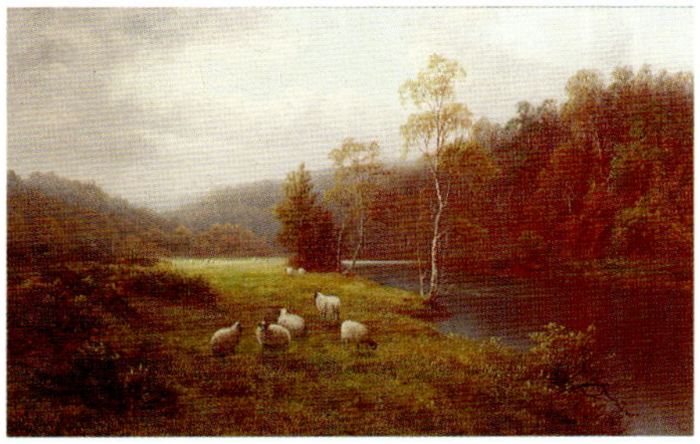

Mellor, William 1851–1931
River Wharfe
oil on canvas 35.6 x 55.9
PA-90

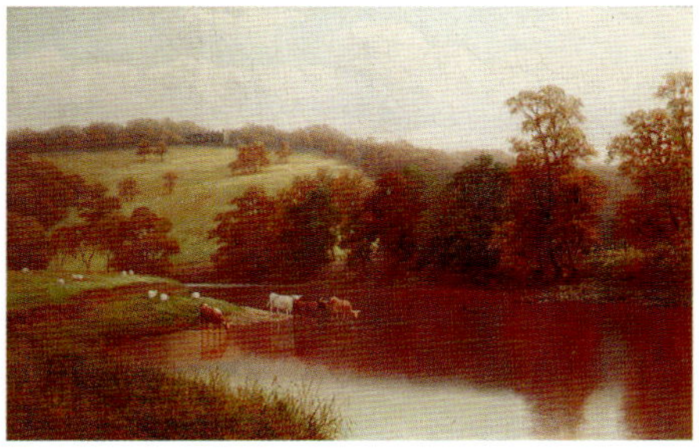

Mellor, William 1851–1931
The Wharfe, near Ilkley
oil on canvas 35.6 x 55.9
PA-264

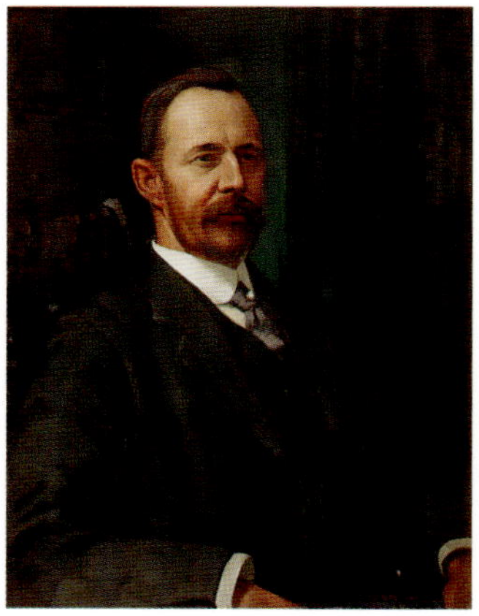

Mooney, Edward Hartley 1878–1938
John Henry Hirst
oil on canvas 76.2 x 64.8
PA-173

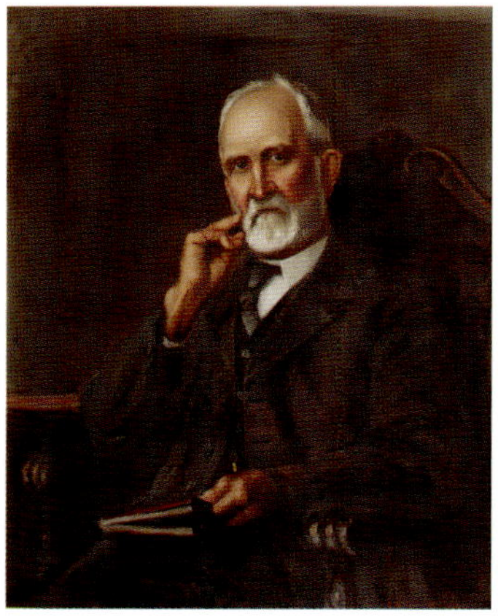

Mooney, Edward Hartley 1878–1938
John William Rothwell
oil on canvas 76.2 x 64.8
PA-171

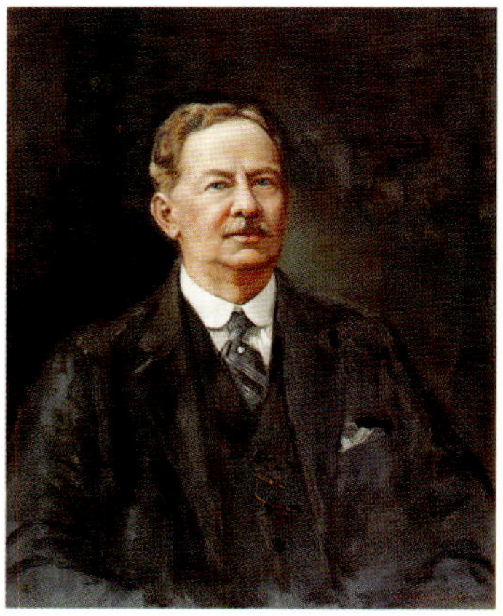

Mooney, Edward Hartley 1878–1938
Joseph Hiram Parker
oil on canvas 76.2 x 64.8
PA-177

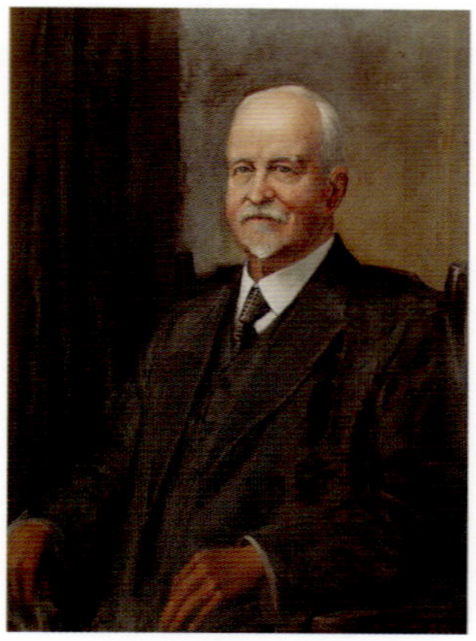

Mooney, Edward Hartley 1878–1938
Joseph Read Brooks
oil on canvas 76.2 x 64.8
PA-172

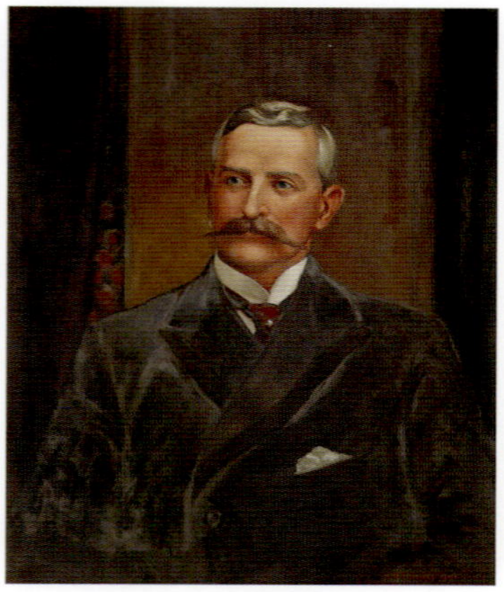

Mooney, Edward Hartley 1878–1938
Richard Ashworth Hoyle
oil on canvas 76.2 x 64.8
PA-166

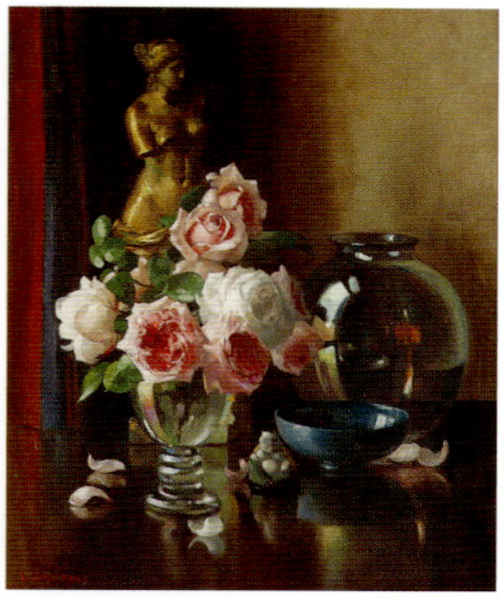

Mooney, Edward Hartley 1878–1938
Roses and Venus
oil on canvas 64.8 x 53.3
PA-41

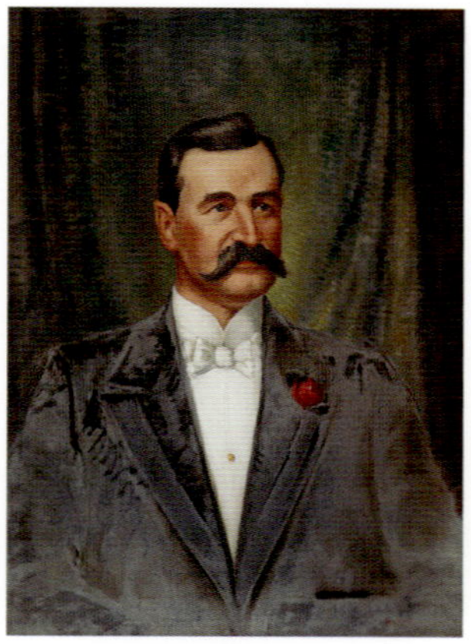

Mooney, Edward Hartley 1878–1938
Samuel McLerie
oil on canvas 76.2 x 64.8
PA-175

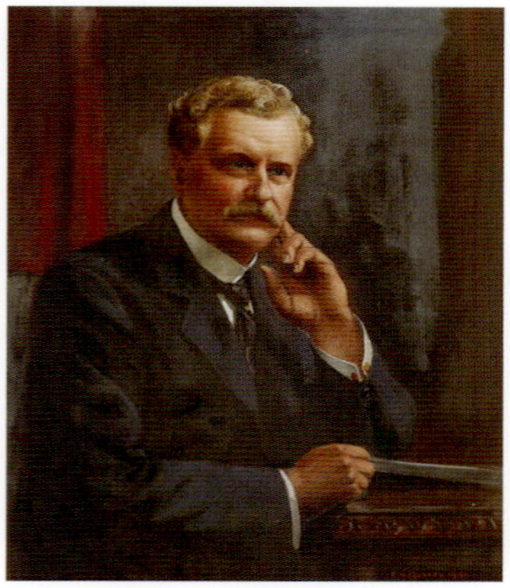

Mooney, Edward Hartley 1878–1938
Sir Henry W. Trickett
oil on canvas 76.2 x 64.8
PA-179

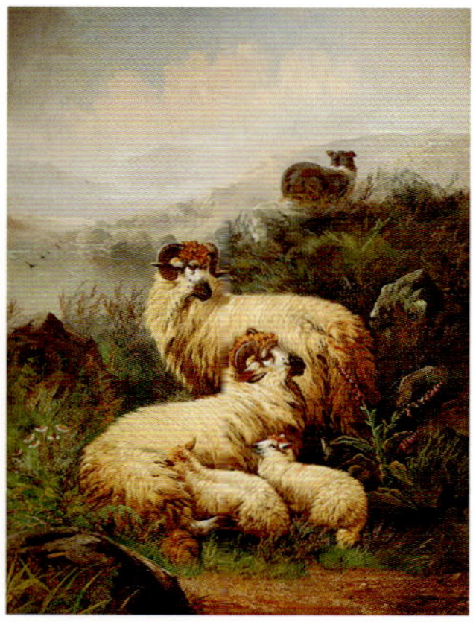

Morris, John W. 1865–1924
Mountain Sheep
oil on canvas 88.9 x 69.9
PA-120

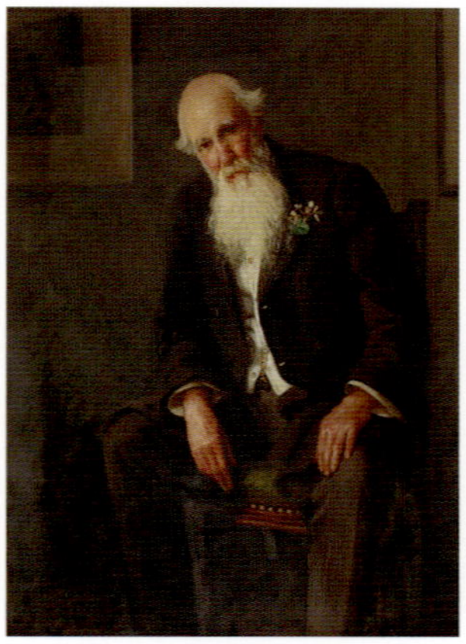

Mostyn, Thomas Edwin 1864–1930
Thomas Newbigging c.1913
oil on canvas 133.4 x 108.6
PA-191

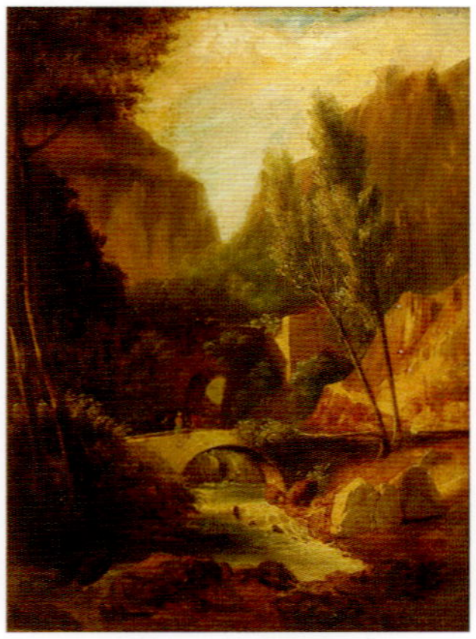

O'Connor, James Arthur 1792–1841
In the Swiss Alps
oil on canvas 39.4 x 30.5
PA-27

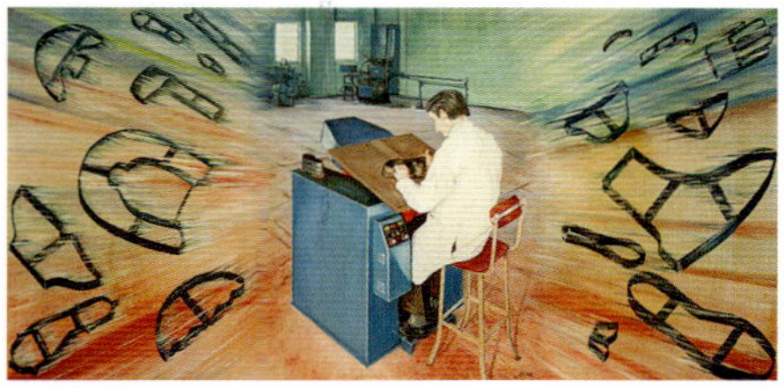

Olesinski, Louis
Mr Thomas Fisher (at Work) 1970
oil on canvas 61 x 121.9
2005.04

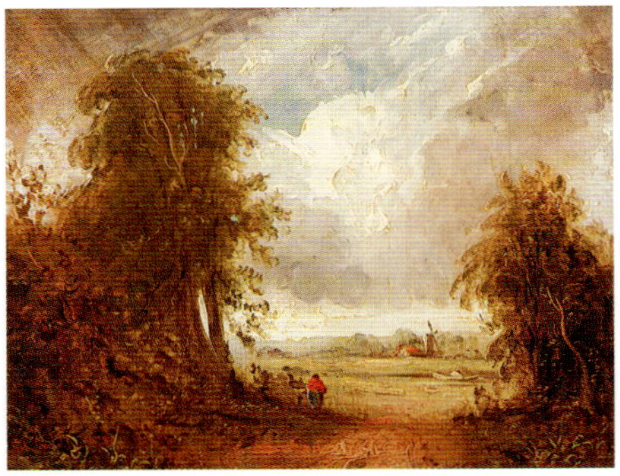

Paul, Joseph 1804–1887
Lane Scene in Suffolk
oil on canvas 25.4 x 31.8
PA-201

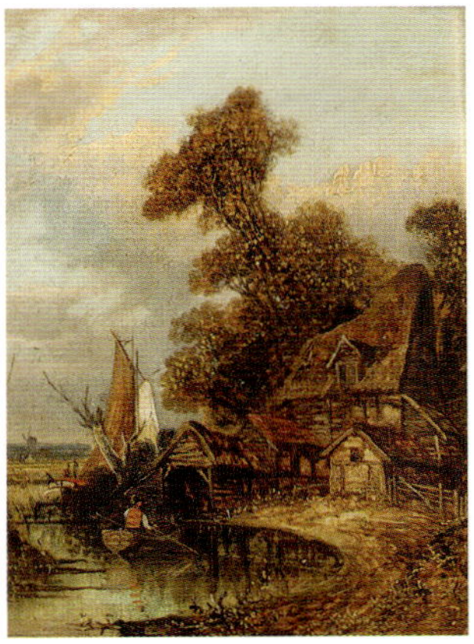

Paul, Joseph 1804–1887
River View near Norwich
oil on canvas 34.3 x 27.9
PA-219

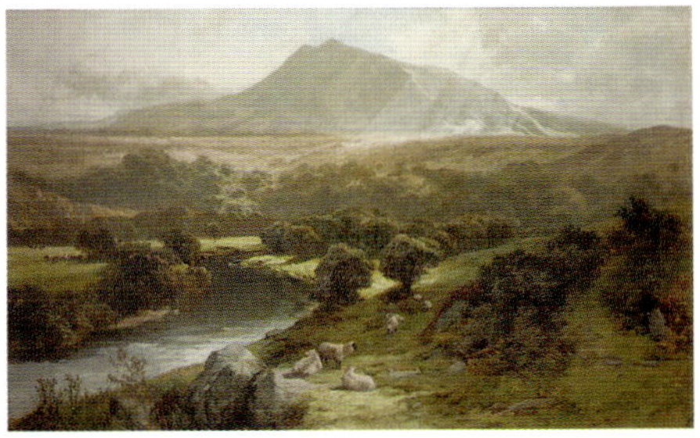

Peel, James 1811–1906
Landscape: River and Mountains 1800–1900
oil on canvas 59.7 x 100.3
PA-96

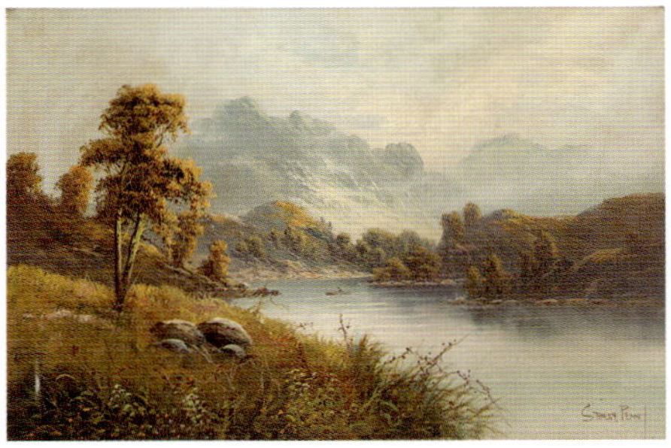

Penn, Stanley active c.1850–1900
Landscape
oil on canvas 53.3 x 78.7
PA-33

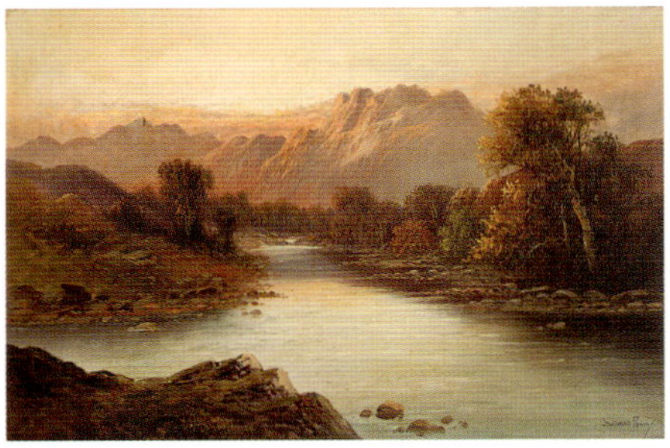

Penn, Stanley active c.1850–1900
Landscape
oil on canvas 49.5 x 74.9
PA-54

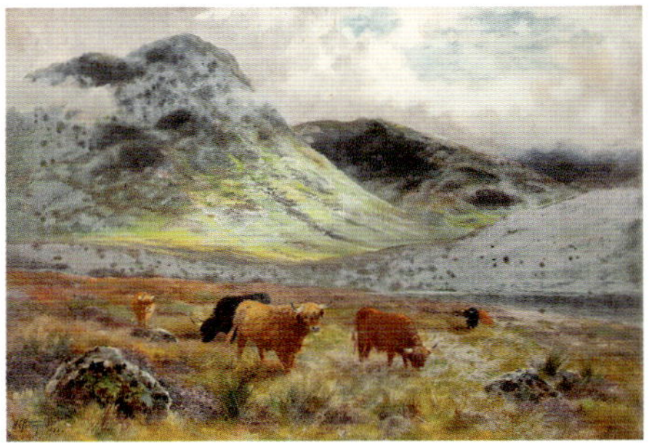

Pettingale, William Edward 1871–1924
Highland Cattle 1923
oil on canvas 55.9 x 81.3
PA-51

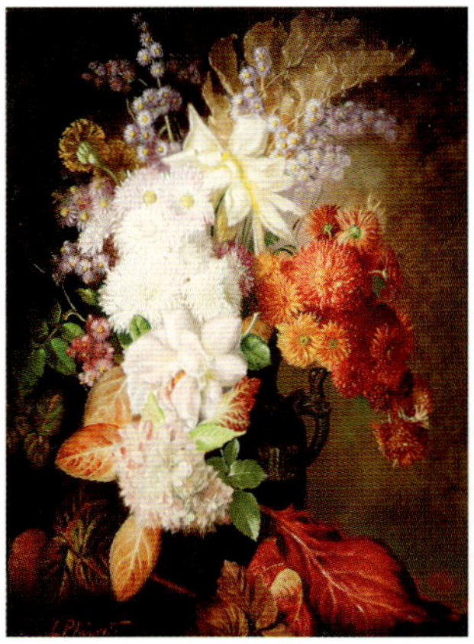

Philpot, Leonard Daniel 1877–1973
Flower Study (Autumn)
oil on canvas 73.7 x 66.0
PA-221

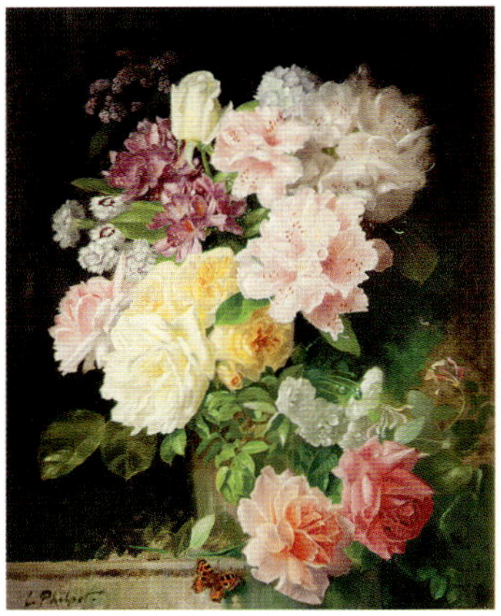

Philpot, Leonard Daniel 1877–1973
Flower Study (Roses and Lilac)
oil on canvas 59.7 x 49.5
PA-222

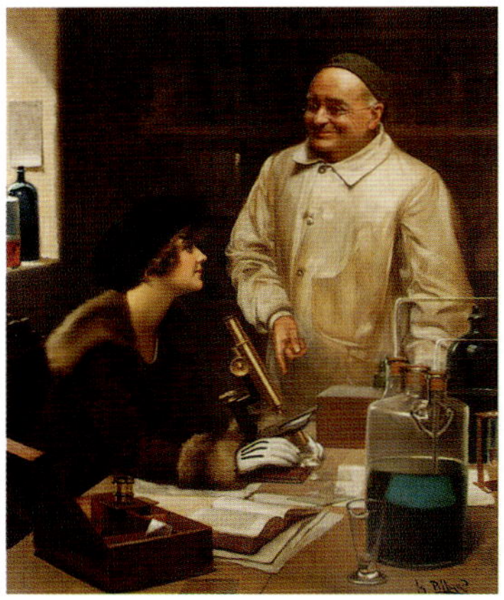

Piffard, Harold Hume 1867–1938
Microscopy 1920s
oil on canvas 88.9 x 68.6
PA-253

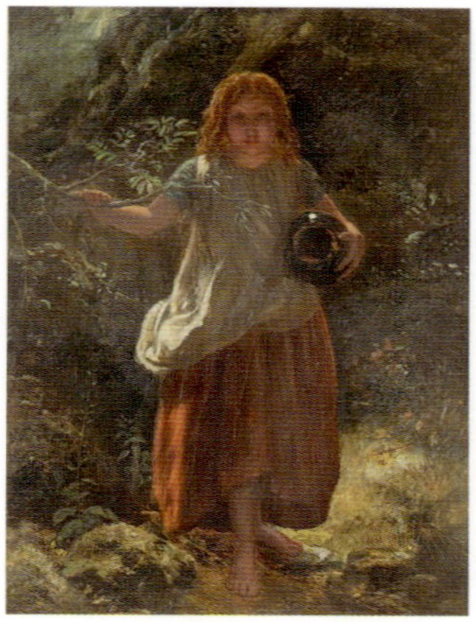

Poole, Paul Falconer 1807–1879
Girl in Wood c.1850
oil on canvas 22.2 x 16.5
PA-223

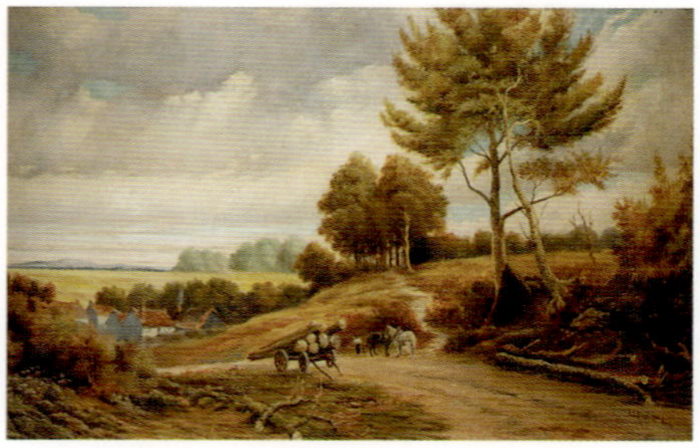

Poskitt, George E.
Carting Timber 1894
oil on canvas 61 x 99.1
PA-140

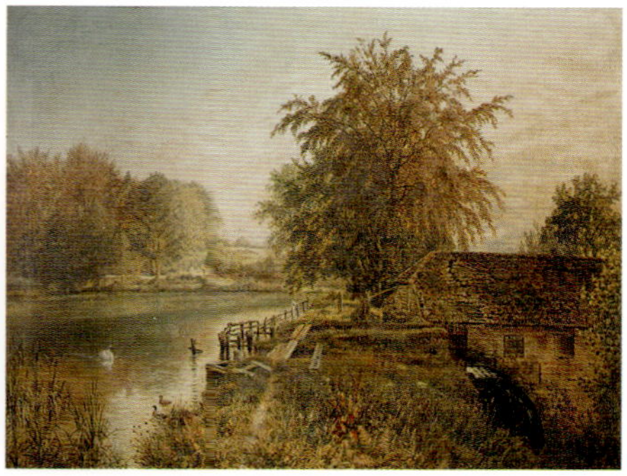

Prote, G. W.
Abinger Mill and Pond
oil on canvas 77.5 x 101.6
PA-94

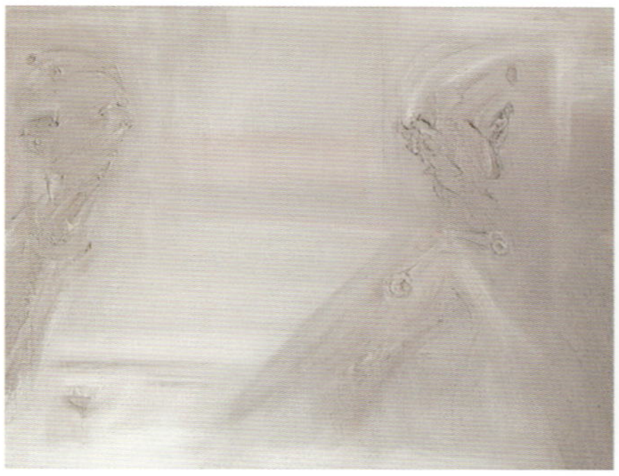

Rawsthorne, Isabel 1912–1992
Alan and Barbara Rawsthorne
oil on board (?) 64 x 85
PA-277

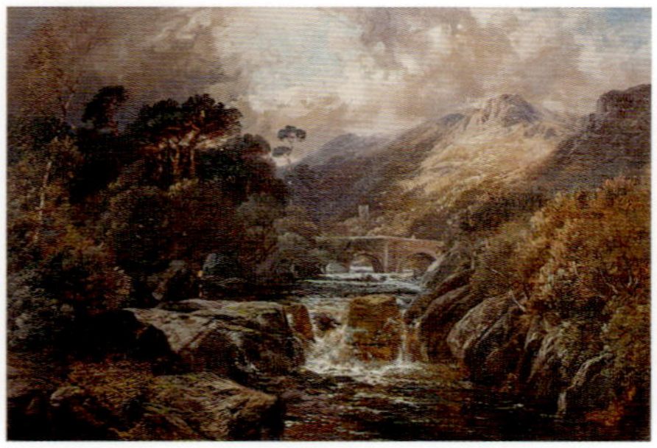

Roe, Clarence 1850–1909
Mountain, River and Bridge
oil on canvas 55.9 x 80
PA-248

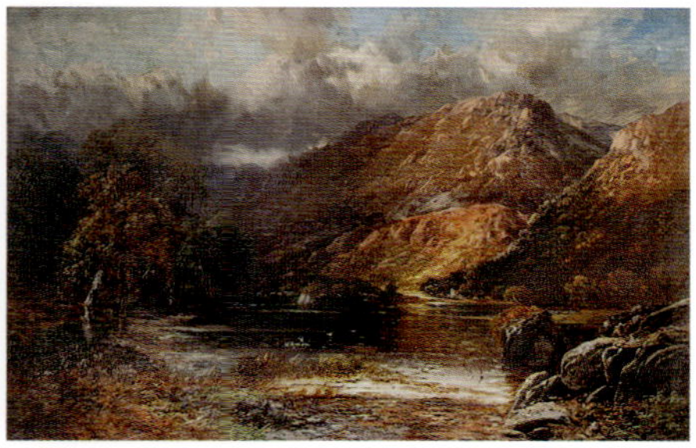

Roe, Clarence 1850–1909
Rydal Water, Westmorland
oil on canvas 48.3 x 73.7
PA-251

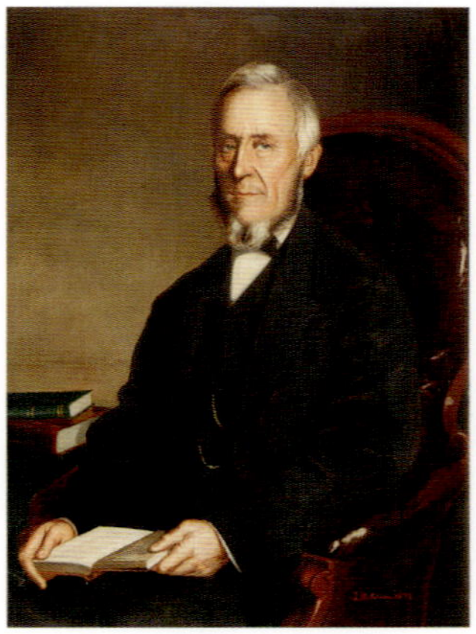

Roscoe, Frederick William 1838–1902
Henry Barlow 1872
oil on canvas 99.1 x 78.7
PA-32

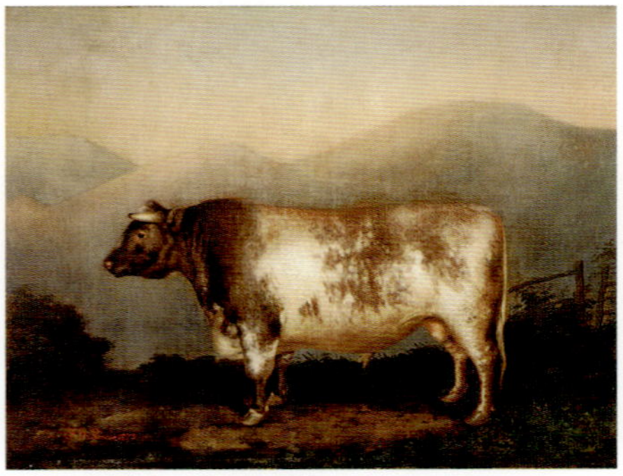

Roscoe, Frederick William 1838–1902
The Horncliffe Bull 1873
oil on canvas 76.2 x 104.1
PA-185

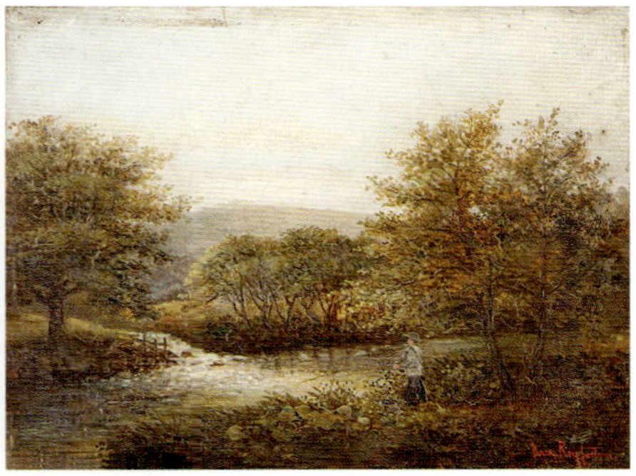

Rowbottom, William Percy 1865–1943
Man Fishing by River 1888
oil on board 15.2 x 19.7
PA-107

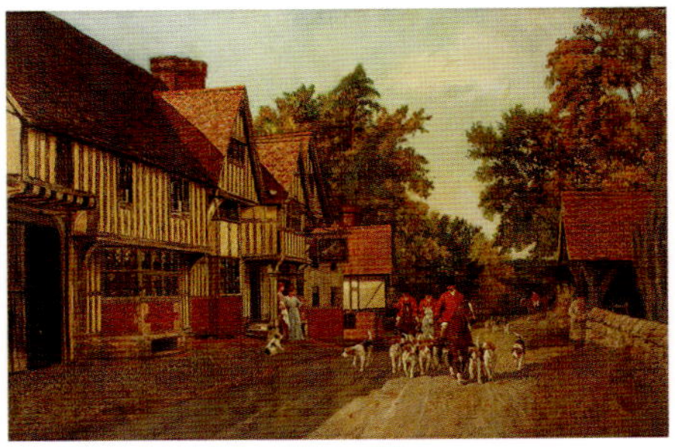

Sanderson-Wells, John 1872–1955
Returning from the Hunt
oil on canvas 91.4 x 137.2
PA-193

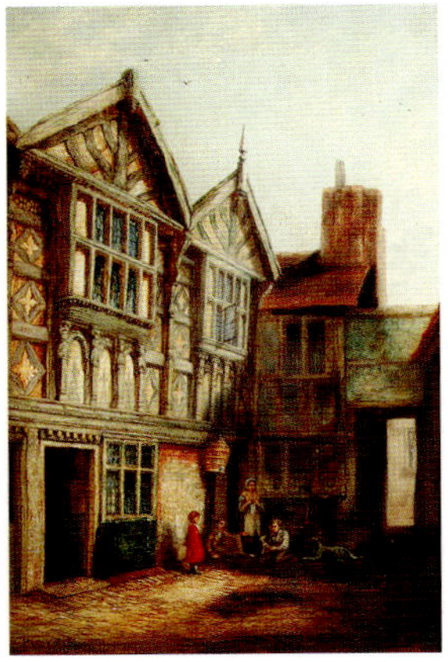

Schäfer, Heinrich 1815–1885
Dutch Street Scene
oil on canvas 38.1 x 27.9
PA-205

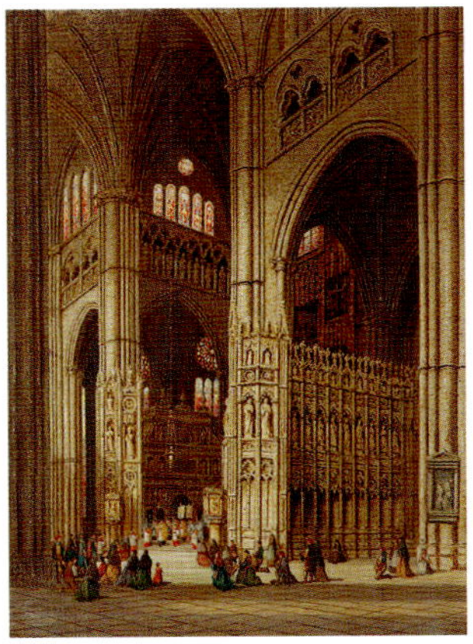

Schäfer, Heinrich 1815–1885
Toledo Cathedral
oil on canvas 73.7 x 55.9
PA-143

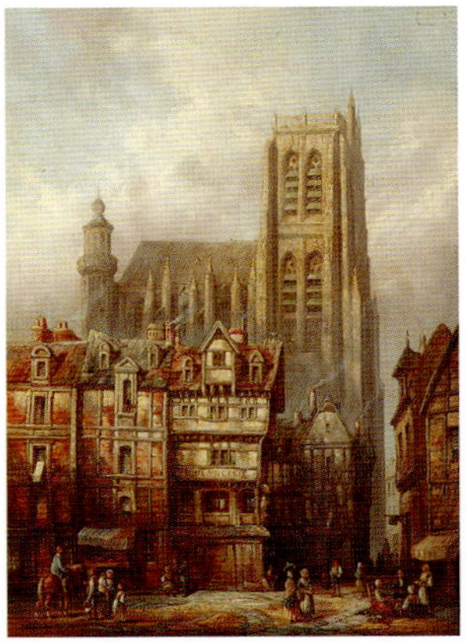

Schäfer, Heinrich (attributed to) 1815–1885
Abbeville, Normandy
oil on canvas 44.5 x 34.3
PA-226

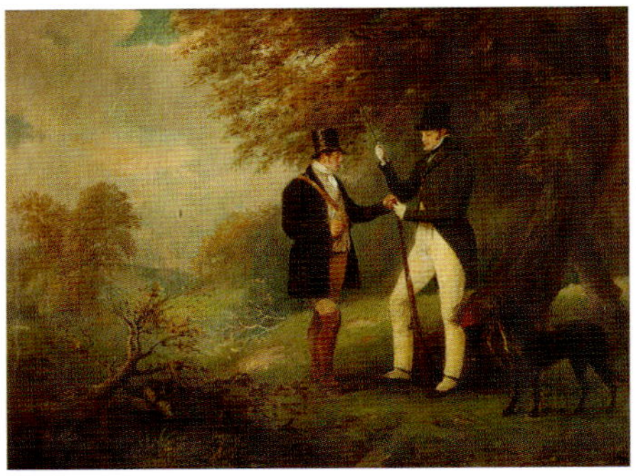

Schwanfelder, Charles Henry 1774–1837
Giles Berry, Esq. 1820
oil on canvas 72.4 x 94.0
PA-146

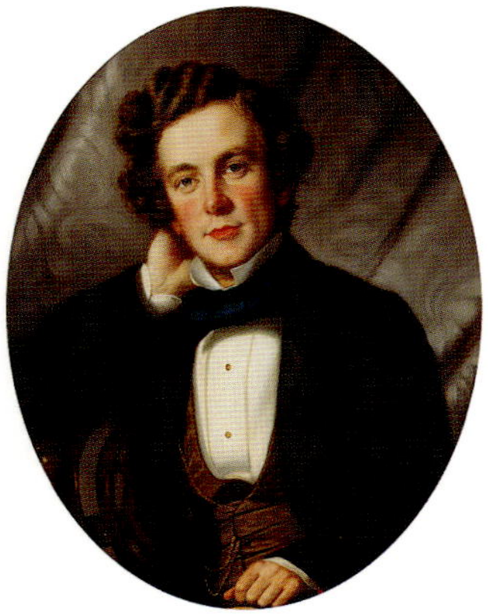

Scott, William Wallace (attributed to) 1820–1905
David Greenwood Whitehead c.1856
oil on canvas 81.3 x 66
PA-72

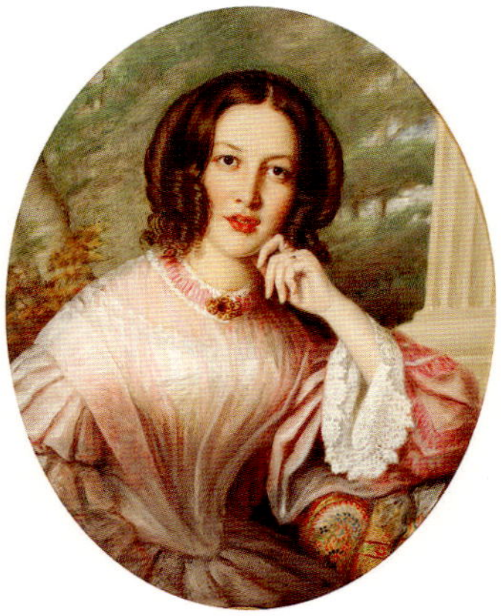

Scott, William Wallace (attributed to) 1820–1905
Jane Whitehead c.1856
oil on canvas 81.3 x 66
PA-71

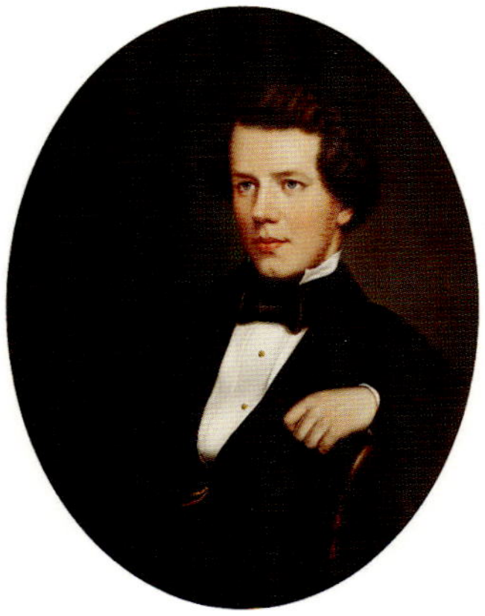

Scott, William Wallace (attributed to) 1820–1905
Peter Halstead Whitehead c.1856
oil on canvas 81.3 x 66
PA-70

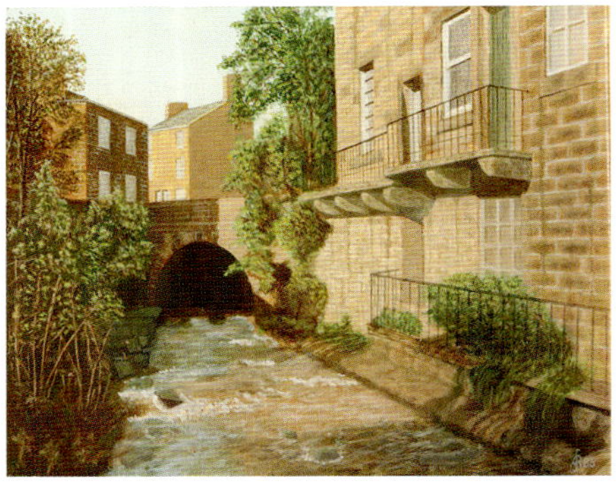

Seville, Ronnie
Little Venice, Waterfoot 1983
oil on canvas 29.2 x 39.4
1996-21-01

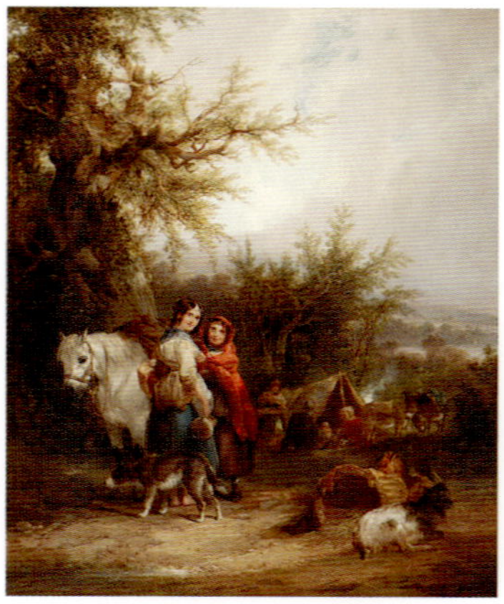

Shayer, William 1788–1879
Near Southampton
oil on canvas 76.2 x 63.5
PA-229

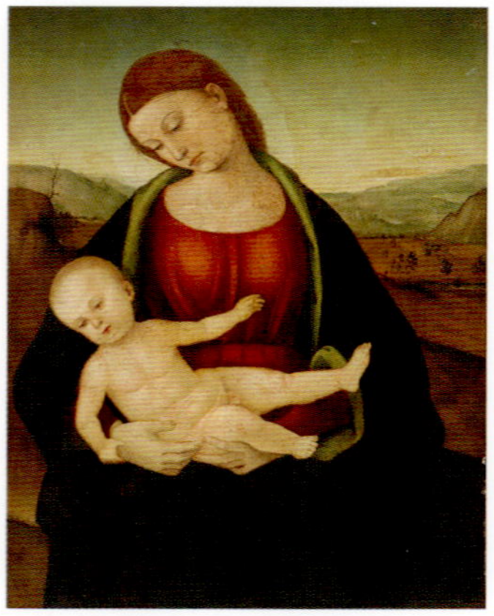

Signorelli, Luca (follower of) 1450–1523
Madonna and Child 1500–1700
oil on panel 49.5 x 40.6
PA-196

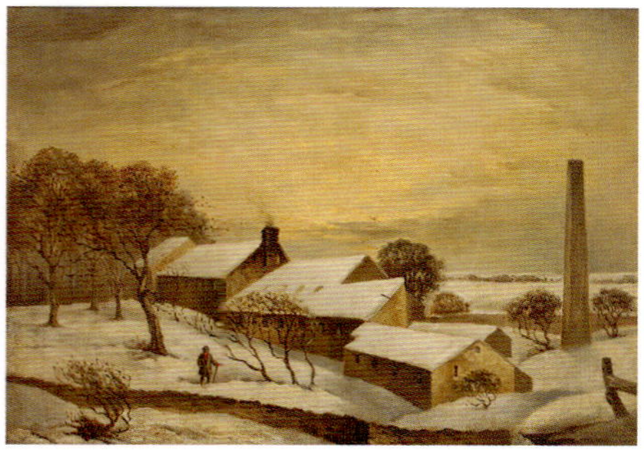

Spencer, James (attributed to) active 1930s
The Story of Whiteheads
oil on board or panel 58.4 x 88.9
ZA-195-1

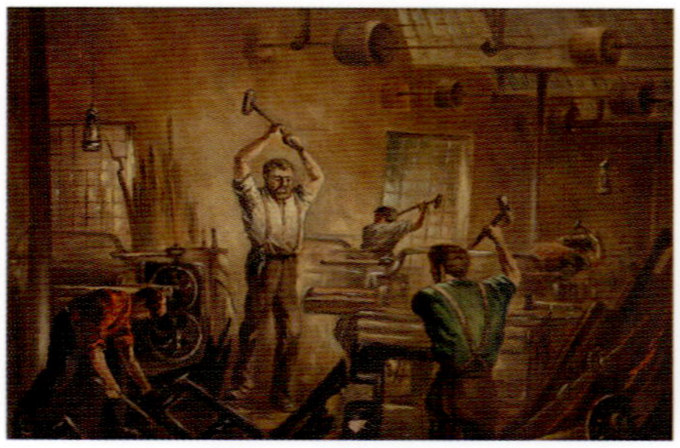

Spencer, James (attributed to) active 1930s
The Story of Whiteheads
oil on board or panel 58.4 x 88.9
ZA-195-2

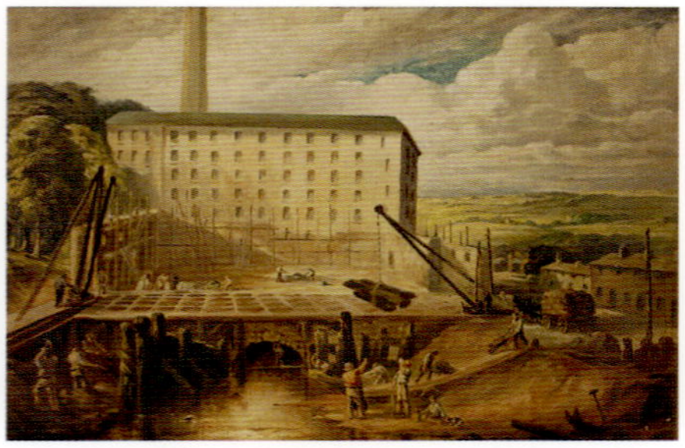

Spencer, James (attributed to) active 1930s
The Story of Whiteheads
oil on board or panel 58.4 x 88.9
ZA-195-3

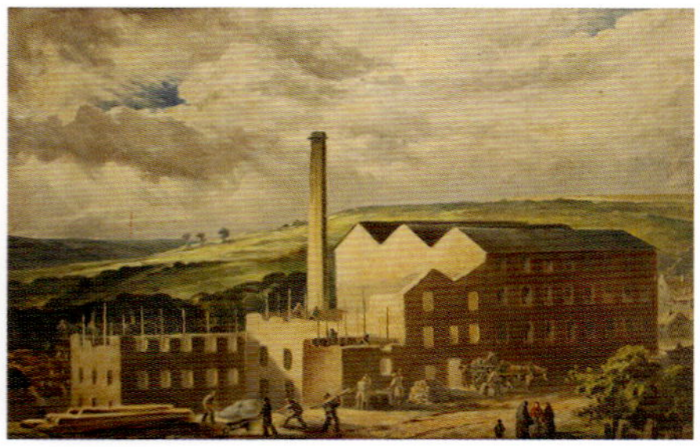

Spencer, James (attributed to) active 1930s
The Story of Whiteheads
oil on board or panel 58.4 x 88.9
ZA-195-4

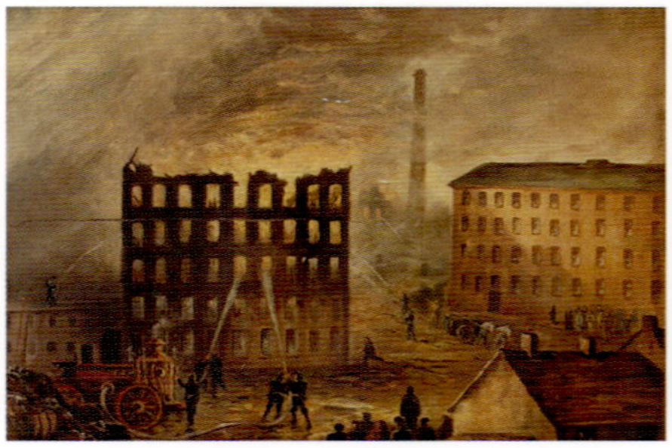

Spencer, James (attributed to) active 1930s
The Story of Whiteheads
oil on board or panel 58 x 88.9
ZA-195-5

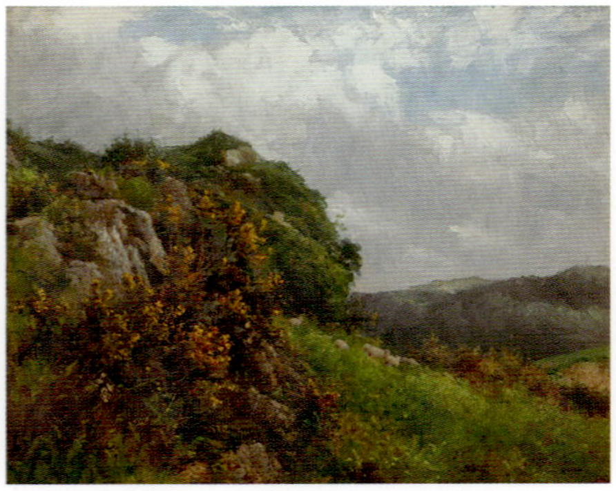

Stamper, James William 1873–1947
Above Deganwy
oil on canvas 38.1 x 53.3
PA-263

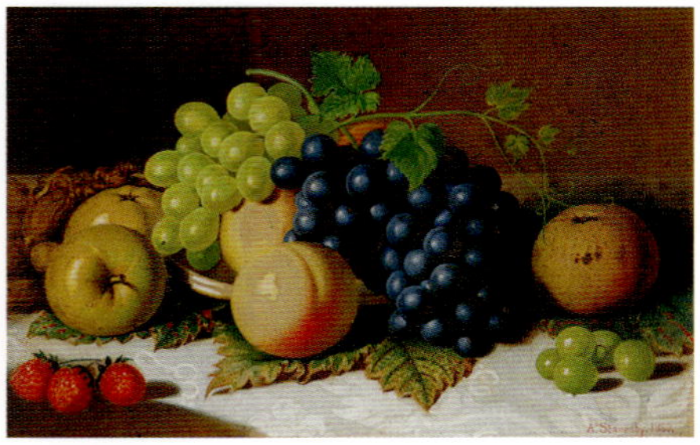

Stanesby, Alexander 1832–1916
Still Life
oil on canvas (?) 22.9 x 38.1
PA-280

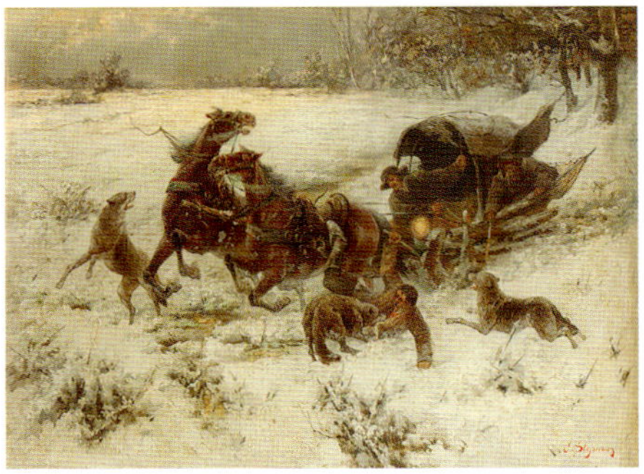

Stojanov, Piotr active 1887–1894
Fighting Off the Wolves
oil on canvas 54.6 x 86.4
PA-91

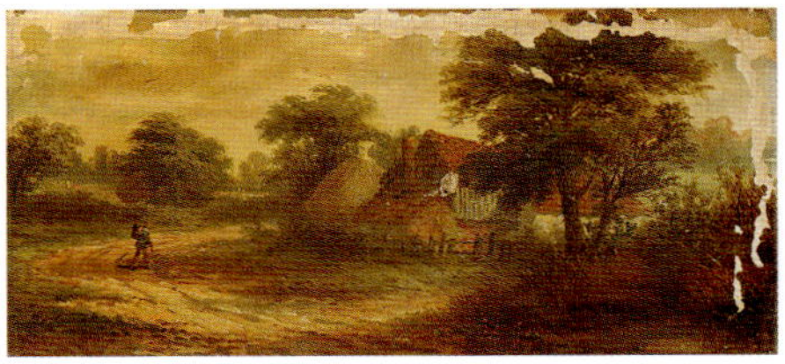

Stonewaid, W. (attributed to) active c.1863–1883
Man by a Cottage c.1863–1883
oil on canvas 31.1 x 61
PA-150

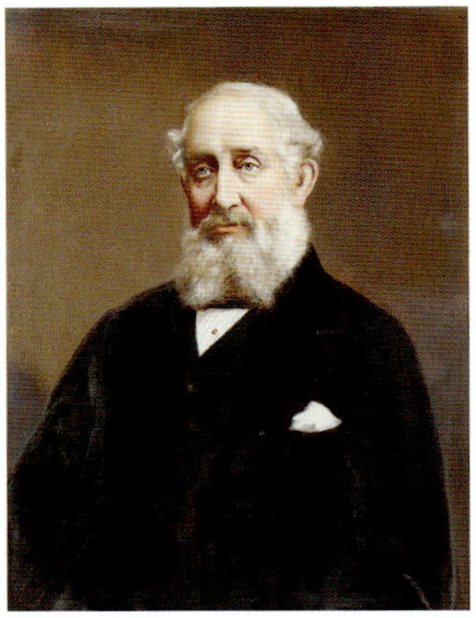

unknown artist
Isaac Bradshaw
oil on canvas (?) 50.8 x 40.6
PA-258

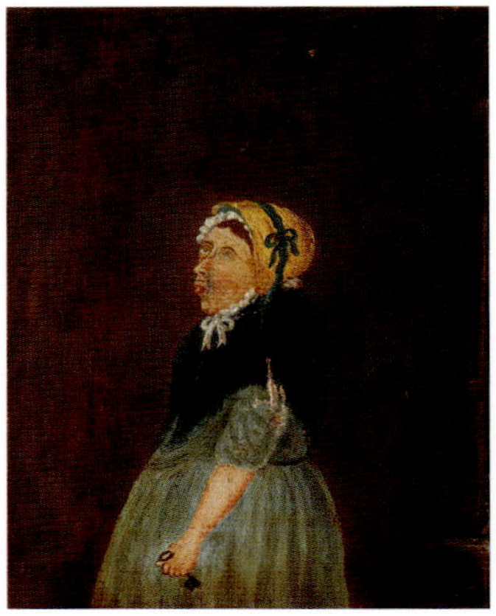

unknown artist
Betty Treacle c.1800–1830
oil on canvas 25.2 x 19.6
PA-187

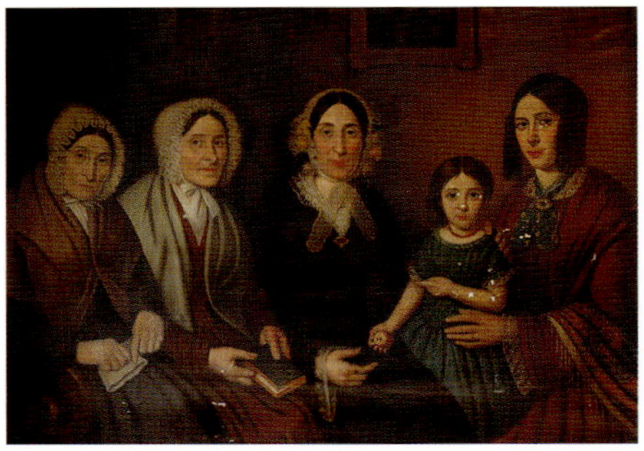

unknown artist
Portrait of Five Females c.1840–1850
oil on canvas 101.6 x 154.9
2007.02.01

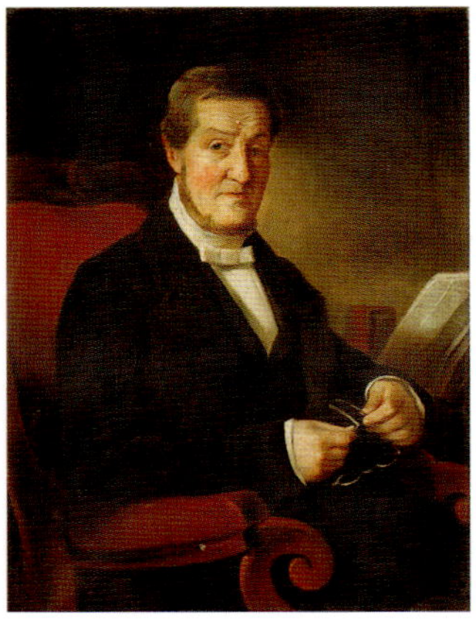

unknown artist
Thomas Whitehead c.1840–1859
oil on canvas 90.2 x 69.9
PA-31

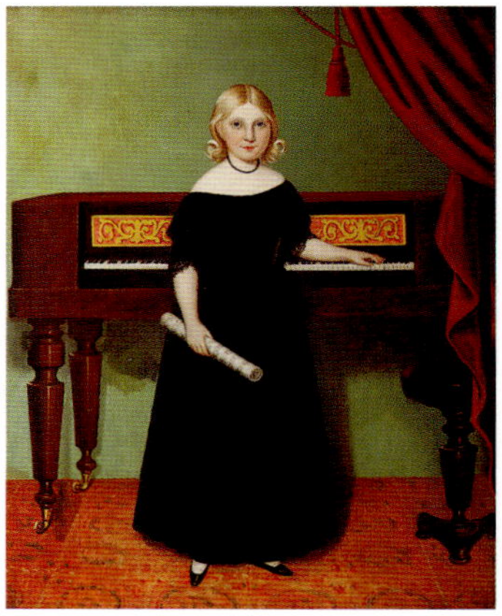

unknown artist
Deborah Rawsthorne (1834–1846) c.1844
oil on board 73.7 x 61.0
PA-275

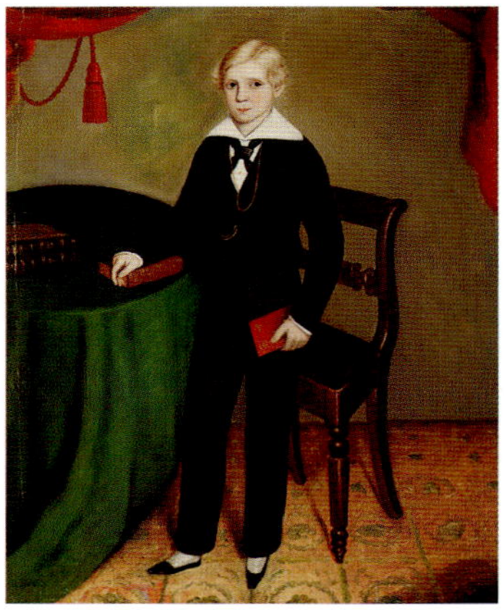

unknown artist
James Rawsthorne (1832–1870) c.1844
oil on board 73.7 x 61
PA-276

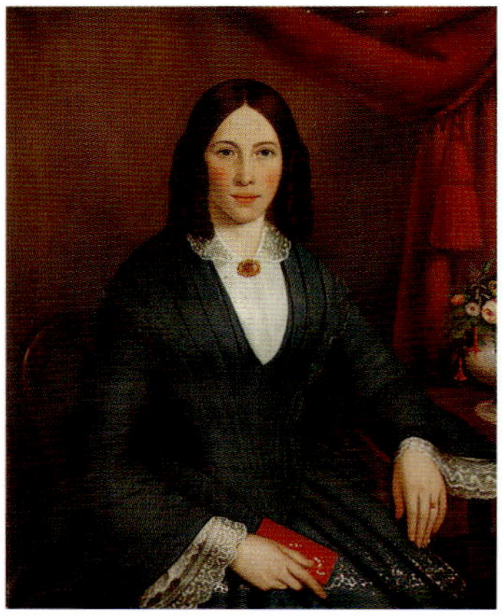

unknown artist
Portrait of a Lady c.1850–1860
oil on canvas 88.9 x 73.7
2007.02.-02

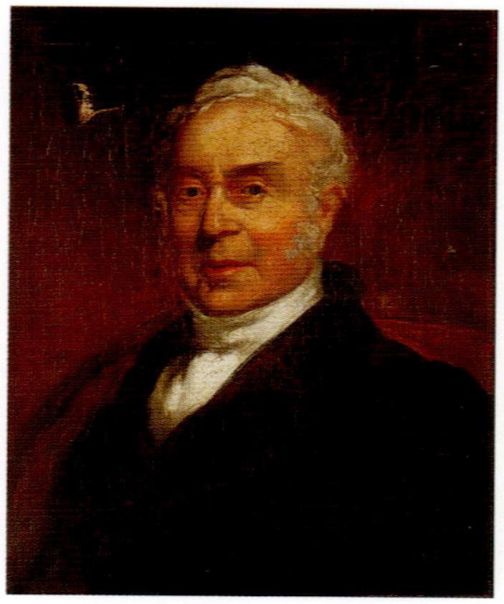

unknown artist
Canon Raines c.1850–1870
oil on canvas 57.2 x 47
PA-26

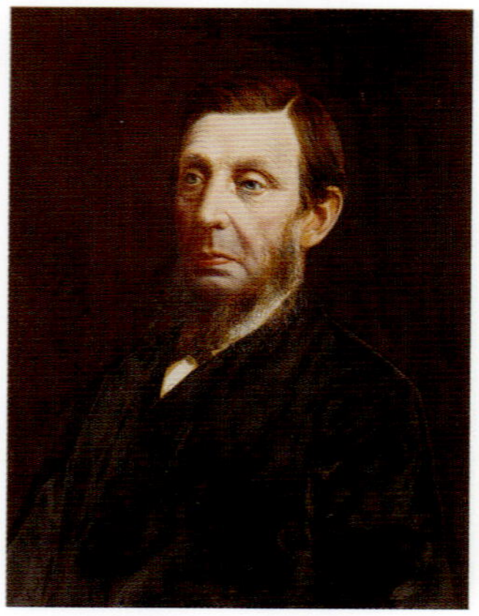

unknown artist
Thomas Aitken of Bacup c.1850–1880
oil on canvas 54.6 x 41.9
2002.01.03

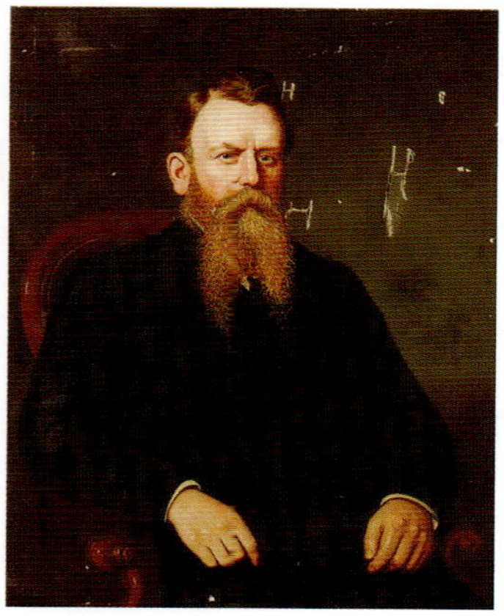

unknown artist
Daniel Ratcliffe c.1850–1900
oil on canvas 91.4 x 71.1
PA-77

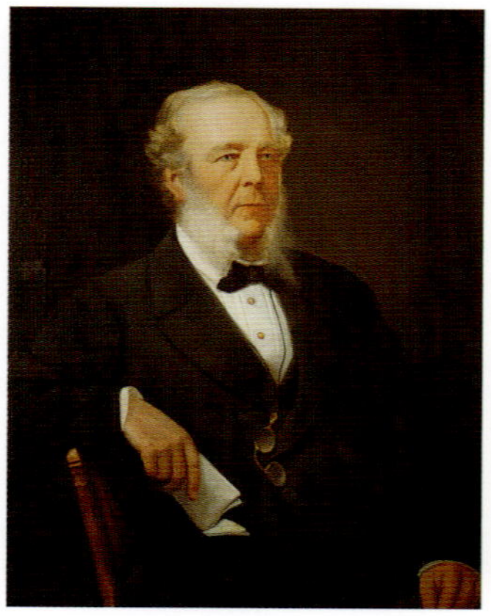

unknown artist
James or Richard Porritt c.1850–1900
oil on canvas 86.4 x 68.6
2005.11.01

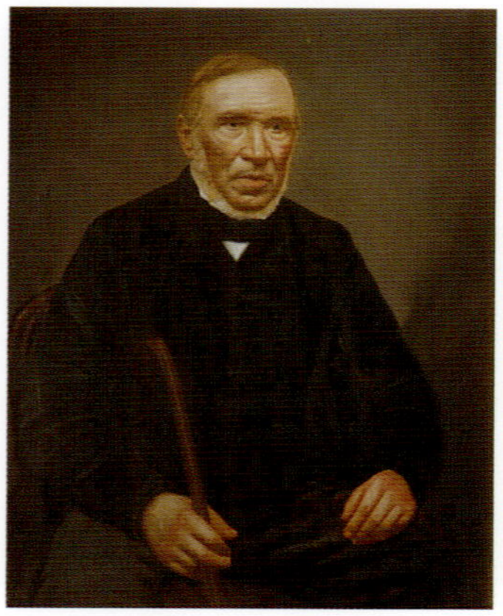

unknown artist
Portrait of a Gentleman c.1850–1900
oil on canvas 48.3 x 38.1
2007.02.04

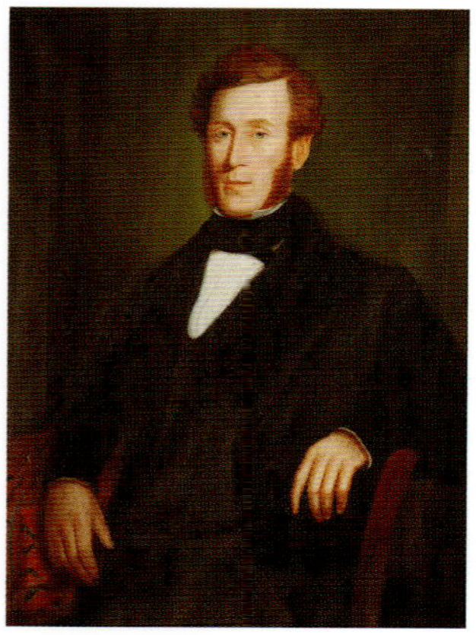

unknown artist
Portrait of a Gentleman c.1855–1860
oil on canvas 88.9 x 71.1
2007.02.03

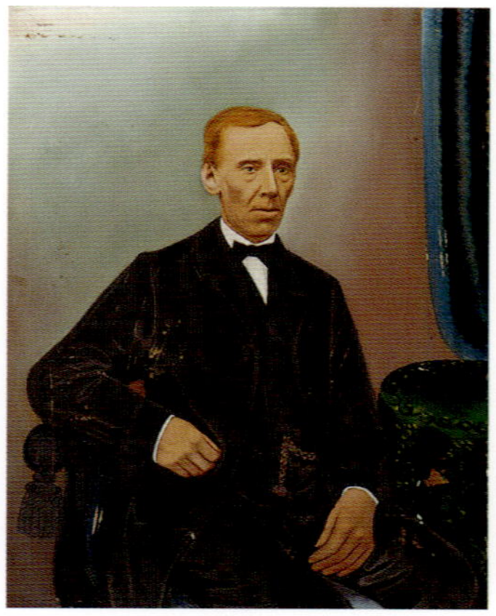

unknown artist
Portrait of an Unknown Gentleman c.1860–1880
oil on cardboard 55.9 x 43.2
PA-74

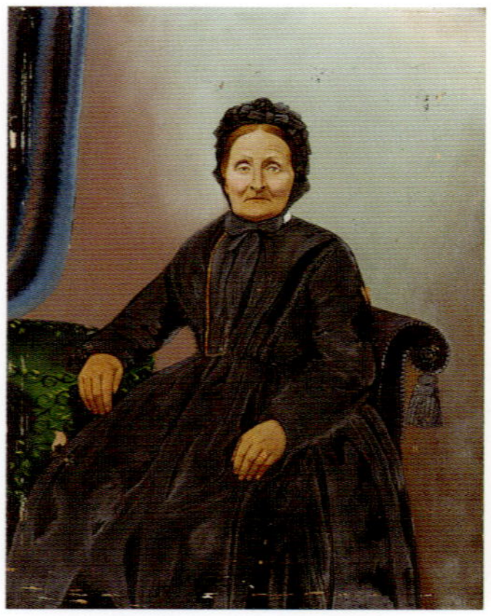

unknown artist
Portrait of an Unknown Lady c.1860–1880
oil on cardboard 55.9 x 43.2
PA-75

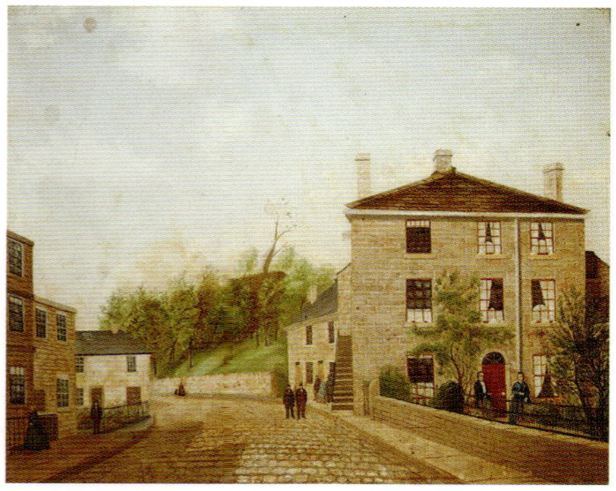

unknown artist
King Street, Rawtenstall c.1860–1920
oil on board 45.7 x 61
PA-156

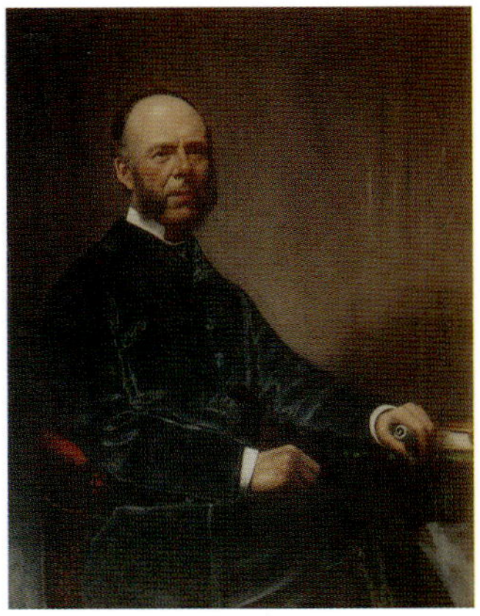

unknown artist
John Ashworth of Cloughfold c.1888
oil on canvas 58.4 x 50.8
2002.01.02

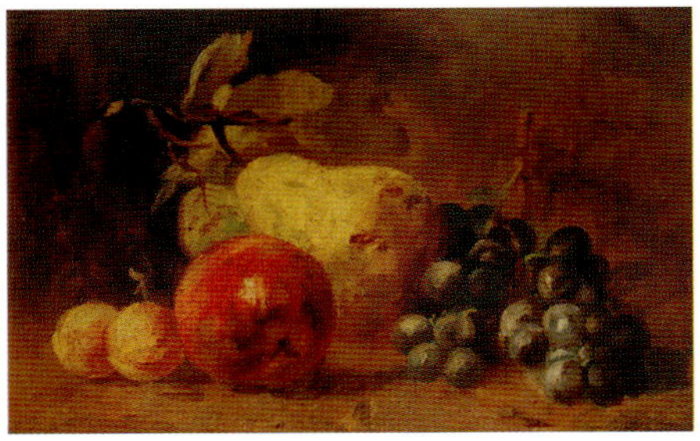

unknown artist
Still Life c.1890
oil on canvas 27.9 x 40.6
PA-123

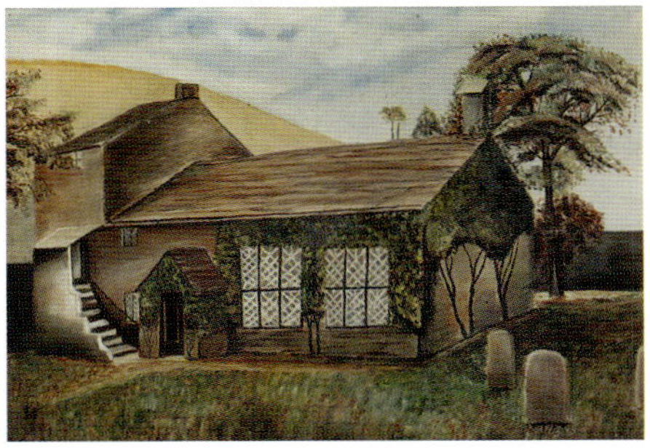

unknown artist
The Friends Meeting House, Crawshawbooth c.1910
oil on canvas 29.2 x 40.6
PA-274

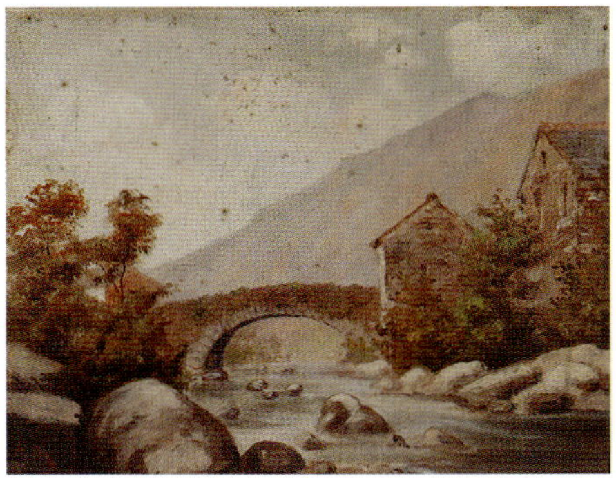

unknown artist
Landscape
oil on board 16.5 x 21.6
PA-268

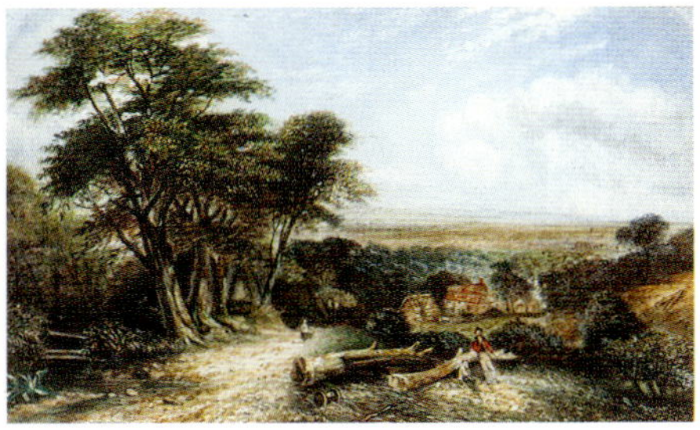

unknown artist
Landscape with Figure
oil on board (?) 14 x 21.6
PA-202

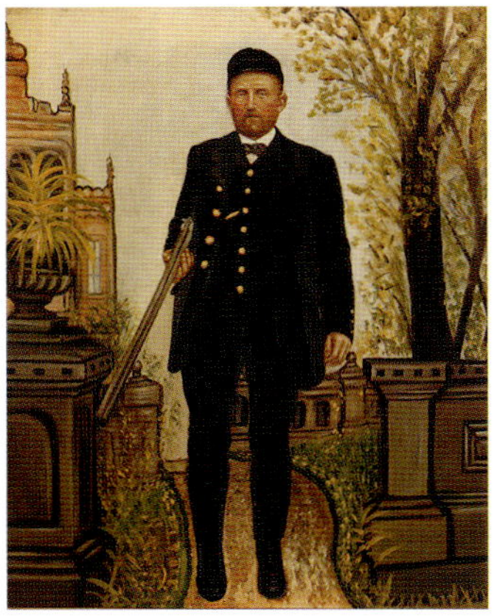

unknown artist
Man with Shotgun
oil on canvas (?) 54.6 x 41.9
PA-63

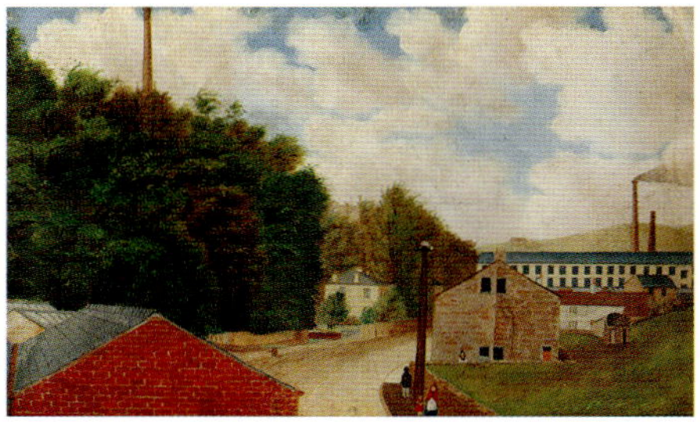

unknown artist
Old View of Reedsholme
oil on board (?) 26 x 43.8
PA-266

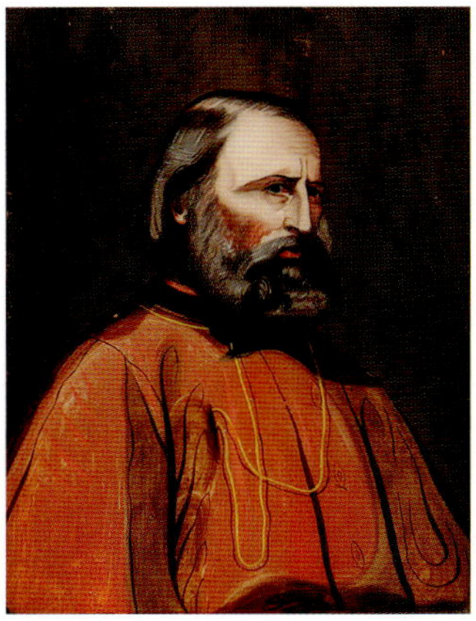

unknown artist
Portrait of a Gentleman
oil on glass 53.3 x 40.6
PA-271

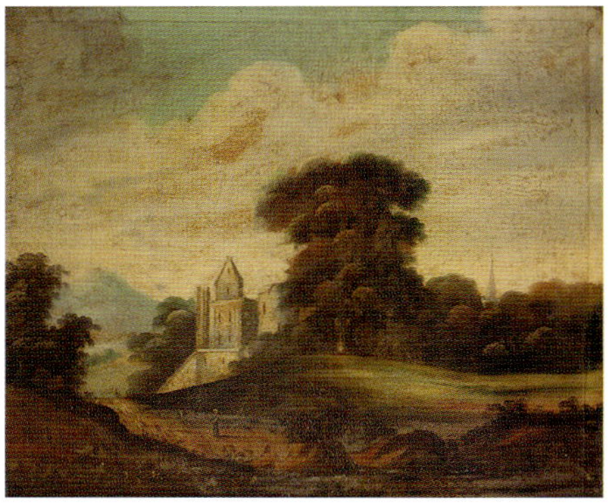

unknown artist
Roslin Castle, near Edinburgh
oil on board 61 x 76.2
PA-47

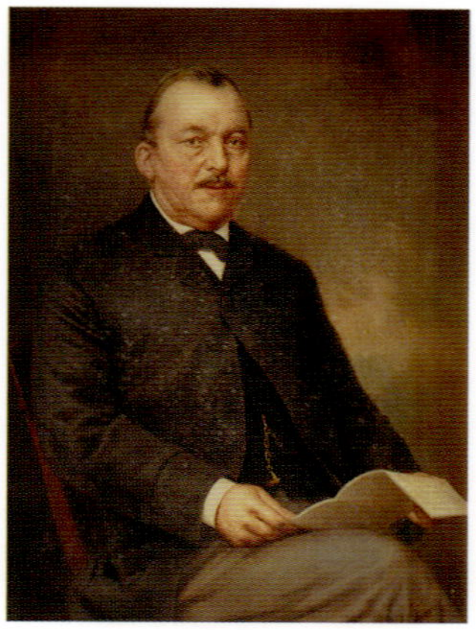

unknown artist
William Henry Shaw, Coal Merchant
oil on canvas 91.4 x 71.1
PA-254

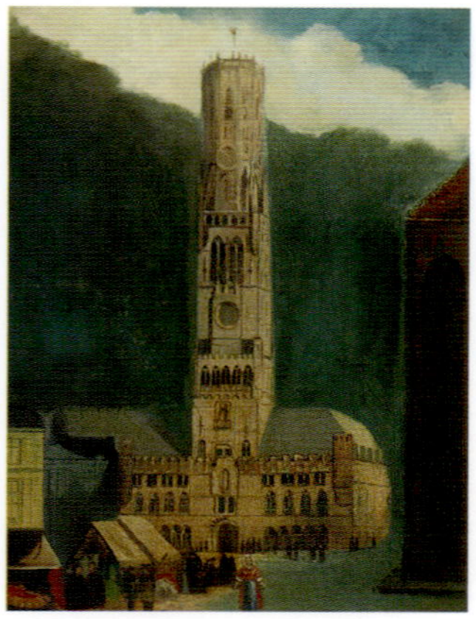

unknown artist
Ypres, the Belfry
oil on paper 45.7 x 35.6
PA-245

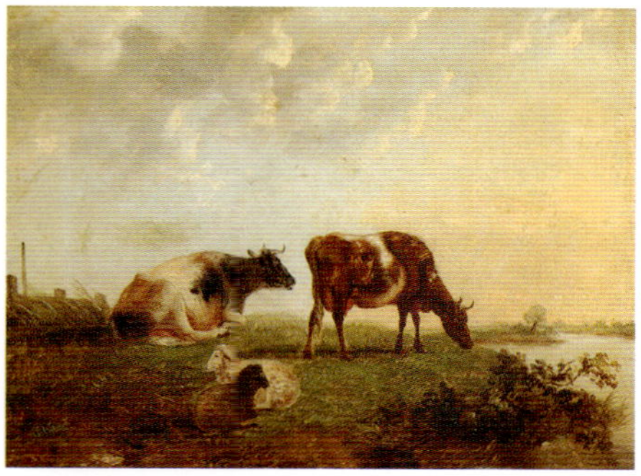

Ward, James 1759–1859
Cattle
oil on canvas 25.4 x 38.1
PA-232

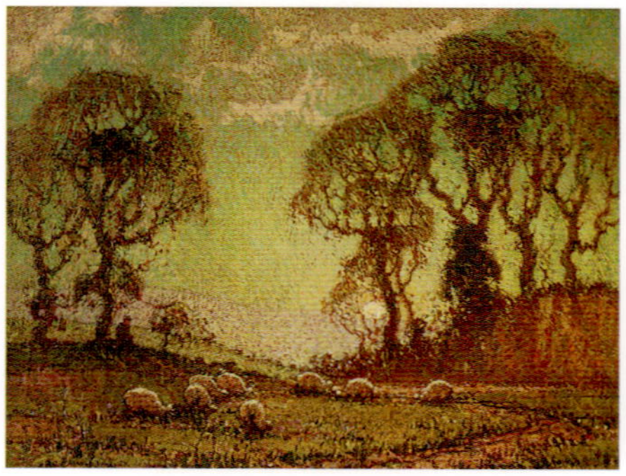

Whaley, Harold 1896–1976
Pastoral Scene c.1900–1930
oil on canvas 52.1 x 58.4
PA-36

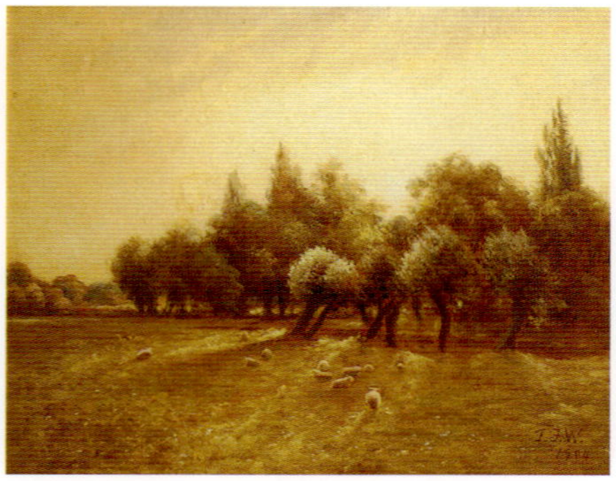

Wilkinson, T. F.
August Afternoon near Dorking 1904
oil on canvas 33 x 43.2
PA-28

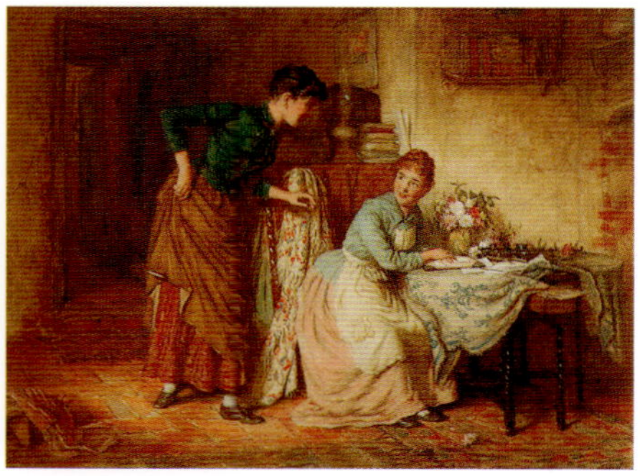

Wright, Robert W. active 1870–1906
Mind Your Own Business
oil on panel 19.1 x 24.1
PA-236

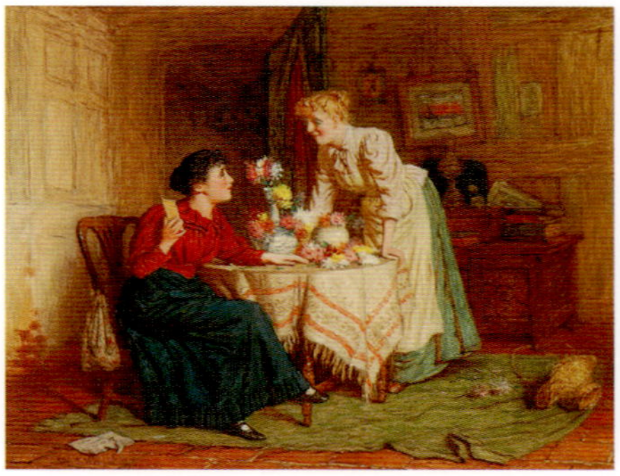

Wright, Robert W. active 1870–1906
The New Photograph
oil on panel 19.1 x 24.1
PA-235

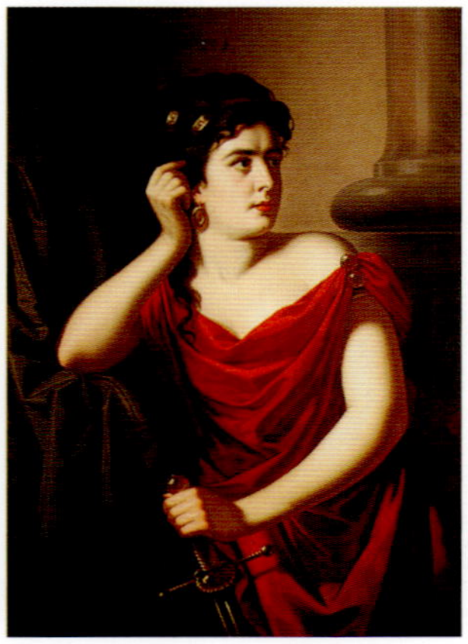

Zadorecki, Marcel Johann active 1872–1939
Portrait of a Classical Heroine 1872
oil on canvas 96.5 x 71.1
PA-135

Paintings Without Reproductions

This section lists all the paintings that have not been included in the main pages of the catalogue. They were excluded as it was not possible to photograph them for this project. Additional information relating to acquisition credit lines or loan details is also included. For this reason the information below is not repeated in the Further Information section.

Haworth Art Gallery

Riley, Percy 1865– 1947, *View from Whalley Nab*, oil on canvas, 47 x 61, HAG126, gift from the artist, not available at the time of photography

Blackburn Museum and Art Gallery

Bouvier, Joseph 1827– 1914, *Figure Subject* (verso), oil on canvas, 19 x 14, 46, bequeathed by Mrs Richard Barton Dodgson, Blackburn, 1884, not available at the time of photography

Burnier, Richard 1826–1884, *Cattle on the Seashore,* oil on canvas, 52 x 86, 101, purchased from J. S. Forbes with the assistance of the Thomas Ainsworth Bequest, 1898, not available at the time of photography

unknown artist, *Deesis*, tempera on panel, 863, purchased from Blackburn Diocesan Board of Finance, 1941, not available at the time of photography

unknown artist, *Prophet Elijah*, tempera on panel, 1076, gift from the Art Fund from the Kathleen Fenwick Bequest, 1982; on loan to Cartwright Hall, not available at the time of photography

Grundy Art Gallery

Balshaw, Fred 1860–1936, *Benjamin Alty*, oil on canvas, G432, gift from T. Thornton, 1948, not available at the time of photography

Mayor, Patti 1872–1962, *Mother and Child*, oil on board, G555, gift from Grundy House Museum, 1985, not available at the time of photography

Miller, P., *Wyre by Wardleys*, oil on canvas, G440, gift from E. A. Robinson, not available at the time of photography

Vivienne, Pauline d.1997, *Françoise on the Spanish Steps*, oil on board, G405, bequeathed by Hilda Stanley, 1975, not available at the time of photography

Turton Tower

unknown artist, *Portrait*, oil on canvas, TTP109, transferred from North Turton Parish Council, 2011, not available at the time of photography

unknown artist, *Portrait of a Lady* (possibly Mrs Ashworth), oil on canvas, PCF15, transferred from North Turton Parish Council, 2011, not available at the time of photography

unknown artist, *Portrait of a Lady* (possibly Mrs Ashworth), oil on canvas, PCF16, transferred from North Turton Parish Council, 2011, not available at the time of photography

Astley Hall Museum and Art Gallery

Cooper, Thomas Sidney (style of) 1803–1902, *Sheep and Goats*, oil on canvas, 1979:114.1, not available at the time of photography

Cooper, Thomas Sidney (style of) 1803–1902, *Sheep and Goats*, oil on canvas, 1979:114.2, not available at the time of photography

Ford, D. G., *Astley Hall*, 1919, oil on canvas, 1967:1, gift from the artist, not available at the time of photography

Northcote, James 1746–1831 (attributed to), *Members of the Anderton Family*, oil on canvas, 1928:1, gift from Mr Francis Anderton, 1928, not available at the time of photography

Short, Frederick Golden 1863–1936, *New Forest*, oil on mill board, 1979:120.2, gift from Violet Caroline Townley-Parker, 1979, not available at the time of photography

Short, Frederick Golden 1863–1936, *New Forest*, oil on mill board, 1979:120.4, gift from Violet Caroline Townley-Parker, 1979, not available at the time of photography

Short, Frederick Golden 1863–1936, *New Forest*, oil on mill board, 1979:120.5, gift from Violet Caroline Townley-Parker, 1979, not available at the time of photography

unknown artist, *Coast Scene*, oil on canvas, 1922:268, gift from Reginald Arthur Tatton, 1922, not available at the time of photography

Clitheroe Castle Museum

unknown artist, *Robert Thompson of Primrose Printworks*, oil on canvas, CL1194, not available at the time of photography

Lancaster City Council

Danks, R., *Williamson Park Lake*, oil on canvas, 40.5 x 61, 15, gift from the artist, not available at the time of photography

Lancaster City Museums

Bell, James 1845–1915, *Christ Church, Lancaster*, 1886, oil on canvas, LANLM.1948.31.1, gift from Mr and Mrs A. E. Wilkinson, 1948, not available at the time of photography

Williamson, William Henry 1820– 1883, *City of Dordt on the Maas, Moonlight, Holland*, 1850–1875, oil on canvas, 75 x 125, LMA 96, not available at the time of photography

Peter Scott Gallery

Barton, Guy 1907–1981, *Begonia*, 1961, oil on canvas, 61 x 76, LANPS.OW206, purchased, not available at the time of photography

Dean, Diana b.1942, *The Red Blind*, 1973, oil on canvas, 160 x 125, LANPS.OW212, purchased, not available at the time of photography

Guppy, James b.1954, *Marat*, oil & acrylic on canvas, LANPS.OW1008, commissioned, not available at the time of photography

Harrington, Anne *Earth, Wind and Fire*, 1986, oil on canvas, 183 x 170, LANPS.OW1013, not available at the time of photography

Johns, Ewart b.1923, *Jill and a Striped Blanket*, oil on canvas, 91 x 91, LANPS.OW239, purchased, not available at the time of photography

Morton, James Hargreaves 1881–1918, *Cattle amongst Trees*, oil on board, 33 x 16, LANPS.WM185, not available at the time of photography

Morton, James Hargreaves 1881–1918, *Grazing Cow*, oil on board, 26.5 x 35, LANPS.WM186, not available at the time of photography

Morton, James Hargreaves 1881–1918, *Line of Trees by Path*, oil on board, 25.5 x 34, LANPS.WM188, not available at the time of photography

Morton, James Hargreaves 1881–1918, *Sunrise/Set over Hills*, oil on board, 22 x 43, LANPS.WM187, not available at the time of photography

Morton, James Hargreaves 1881–1918, *The Farmyard*, oil on board, PSGCT.ZM7, not available at the time of photography

Morton, James Hargreaves 1881–1918, *Trees, Buildings, Path*, oil on board, 24 x 33, LANPS.WM189, not available at the time of photography

Nelson, Ben *House by Water*, oil on board, 27.5 x 35, LANPS.OW1378, gift from Dr Jean Ward, not available at the time of photography

Nicholson, Kate b.1929, *The Seventh Colour*, 1967, oil on paper 79 x 56, LANPS.OW202, purchased, not available at the time of photography

Schmidtmayer, Karel *Eyes of Colour*, oil & collage on canvas, LANPS.OW1354, gift, not available at the time of photography

Schmidtmayer, Karel *The Swoop*, oil & collage on canvas, LANPS.OW1355, gift, not available at the time of photography

Skelton, Mike *Razor*, acrylic on canvas 191 x 152, LANPS.OW185, not available at the time of photography

Stephens, Bev b.1935, *The Rugby Player*, oil on board, LANPS.OW219, purchased, not available at the time of photography

Titherington, Tom 1934–2003, *Untitled*, oil on canvas (?), 94 x 69, LANPS.OW238, not available at the time of photography

The Shire Hall, Lancaster Castle

Northcote, James 1746–1831, *George III on Horseback*, 1806, oil on canvas, 365.8 x 304.8, LC63, commissioned by Thomas Stanley, MP, and John Blackburne, MP, to hang in Lancaster Castle, 1800, not available at the time of photography

Duke of Lancaster's Own Yeomanry Museum

unknown artist, *Staff Sergeant Major F. H. Knowles*, oil on paper, LANOY.395, gift from Mr A. J. Knowles, too fragile to photograph

Harris Museum & Art Gallery

Aikman, William 1682–1731, *Richard Boyle, 3rd Earl of Burlington and 4th Earl of Cork, and His Wife, Dorothy, née Savile*, oil on canvas, 96.5 x 116.8, PRSMG : P306, gift from W. W. Galloway, not available at the time of photography

Clark, James 1858–1943, *Spiritus Adversus Carmen*, oil on canvas, 204.5 x 125, PRSMG : P73, purchased, not available at the time of photography

Clay, John 1796–1858, *Charles Swainson*, oil on canvas, 243 x 150 PRSMG : P76, unknown acquisition method, not available at the time of photography

Collett, Sophie active 1850–1900, *Three Portrait Miniatures*, oil on card, PRSMG : P1877, gift from Miss Barton, not available at the time of photography

Coumont, Charles 1822–1889, *Christ and Saint John the Baptist as Children,* oil on canvas, 104.7 x 138, PRSMG : P1980, unknown acquisition method, not available at the time of photography

Creswick, Thomas 1811–1869, *Scene on the River Cladish,* oil on canvas, 33 x 25.5 PRSMG : P107, bequeathed by Richard Newsham, stolen, 1989, not available at the time of photography

Dessurne, Mark 1825–1885, *Queen Boadicea and Her Warriors,* oil on canvas, 160 x 113.5, PRSMG : P131, purchased, not available at the time of photography

Gill, William Ward 1823–1894, *Landscape,* oil on card, 17 x 29.5, PRSMG : P1879, unknown acquisition method, not available at the time of photography

Hart, Solomon Alexander 1806–1881, *Quarrel Scene between Wolsey and Buckingham (from Shakespeare's 'Henry VIII'),* oil on canvas, 155 x 217.8, PRSMG : P277, bequeathed by Dewhurst, not available at the time of photography

Hodge, Francis Edwin 1883–1949, *'Why have you come?',* oil on card, 40.3 x 30.7, PRSMG : P2008, unknown acquisition method, not available at the time of photography

Keane, John b.1954, *Bee Keeping in the War Zone,* acrylic on paper, 114 x 83, PRSMG : P2240, purchased, not available at the time of photography

Kelly, Gerald Festus 1879–1972, *J. J. Ward, the Guild Mayor of 1952,* oil on canvas, 124.5 x 99, PRSMG : P1468, purchased, not available at the time of photography

Llewellyn, Samuel Henry William 1858–1941, *Lady H. Cartmell,* oil on canvas, 130 x 103, PRSMG : P749, on long-term loan from the sitter's family, not available at the time of photography

Llewellyn, Samuel Henry William 1858–1941, *Sir Harry Cartmell,* oil on canvas, 127 x 101.5, PRSMG : P748, on long-term loan from the sitter's family, not available at the time of photography

Miranda, Alcides da Rocha 1909–2001, *Cabeça,* oil on paper, 44.8 x 35.2, PRSMG : P1360, gift from British Council Fine Art Department, not available at the time of photography

Murillo, Bartolomé Esteban (after) 1617–1682, *Three Boys, Two Throwing Dice,* oil on copper, 50.8 x 43.2, PRSMG : P1548, gift from F. W. Sharples, not available at the time of photography

Mutrie, Annie Feray 1826–1893, *Azaleas,* oil on canvas, 28 x 22.2, PRSMG : P431, unknown acquisition method, stolen 1989, not available at the time of photography

Richardson, Frederick Stuart 1855–1934, *North Sea Crofters,* oil on canvas, 84 x 126, PRSMG : P487, purchased, not available at the time of photography

Roscoe, Frederick William 1838–1902, *Dead Game,* oil on canvas, PRSMG : P1803, gift from F. W. Roscoe, not available at the time of photography

Roscoe, Frederick William 1838–1902, *Still Life – Apples, Grapes and Melon,* oil on panel, 30.7 x 40.3, PRSMG : P1801, gift from the artist, not available at the time of photography

Rosoman, Leonard Henry 1913–2012, *Leaning Figure Touching a Fence,* oil on hardboard, 122 x 155.5, PRSMG : P1737, purchased, not available at the time of photography

Shackleton, William 1872–1933, *The City of the Golden Gates,* oil on paper, 38 x 41.8, PRSMG : P821, gift from M. Shackleton, not available at the time of photography

Shackleton, William 1872–1933, *The City of the Golden Gates,* oil on brown paper, 33 x 35.5, PRSMG : P822, gift from M. Shackleton, not available at the time of photography

Singleton, Rosemary L. active 1958–1959, *November Afternoon,* oil on board, 50.8 x 76.2, PRSMG : P1595, gift from N. Mellalieu, not available at the time of photography

Tarrant, Percy active 1879–1930, *The Sea Between,* oil on cardboard, 23.5 x 15.8, PRSMG : P582, purchased, not available at the time of photography

unknown artist *Mrs Devis on Her Deathbed,* oil on canvas (?), 4.5 x 5.6, PRSMG : P2270, unknown acquisition method, not available at the time of photography

unknown artist *Italian Landscape,* oil on canvas, 58 x 80.5, PRSMG : P621, purchased, not available at the time of photography

unknown artist *Joseph Livesey,* oil on paper, 45.7 x 42, PRSMG : P759, unknown acquisition method, not available at the time of photography

unknown artist *Landscape – near Loch Katherine,* oil on card, 29.2 x 47.4, PRSMG : P1902, unknown acquisition method, not available at the time of photography

unknown artist *Landscape – View of a Valley,* oil on card, 28.6 x 46.3, PRSMG : P1901, unknown acquisition method, not available at the time of photography

unknown artist *Mrs Monk,* oil on canvas, 70 x 45, PRSMG : P769, bequeathed by the sitter, not available at the time of photography

unknown artist *Portrait of a Boy,* oil on canvas, 151.7 x 115, PRSMG : P1969, unknown acquisition method, not available at the time of photography

unknown artist *Portrait of a Lady,* oil on canvas, 141 x 117.5, PRSMG : P1971, unknown acquisition method, not available at the time of photography

unknown artist *Portrait of a Man,* oil on ivory, 11.1 x 9.5, PRSMG : P2201, unknown acquisition method, not available at the time of photography

unknown artist *Portrait of a Woman (or Shepherdess),* oil on canvas, 107.5 x 85.5, PRSMG : P1972, unknown acquisition method, not available at the time of photography

Wasse, Arthur 1854–1930, *Collection of Precious Objects on a Red Cloth,* oil on canvas, 152 x 90 PRSMG : P1970, unknown acquisition method, not available at the time of photography

Wilkinson, Herbert active 1931–1979, *The Visit of HM Queen Elizabeth II to the Harris Museum & Art Gallery,* oil on board, 50.8 x 61, PRSMG : P1825, gift from the artist, not available at the time of photography

Wright, John Michael 1617–1694, *Portrait of a Lady at a Fountain,* oil on canvas, 118 x 86.5, PRSMG : P1822, bequeathed by M. A. L. Williams, not available at the time of photography

Rossendale Museum

unknown artist, *Cavalier and Lady,* c.1880–1920, oil on glass, PA-57, gift from Mrs Taylor, 1949, not available at the time of photography

Collier, John 1850–1934, *Hetty Sorrel,* gift from Arthur C. Bowdler, 1894
Connard, Philip 1875–1958, *Still Life,* purchased from Richard Haworth, Blackburn, 1930 © the copyright holder
Connard, Philip 1875–1958, *Hardy of Chelsea Green,* purchased from Richard Haworth, Blackburn, 1930 © the copyright holder
Cooper, Thomas Sidney 1803–1902, *Cattle,* bequeathed by Miss Annie Thompson, Blackburn, 1949
Cooper, Thomas Sidney 1803–1902, *Cattle and Sheep,* bequeathed by Miss Annie Thompson, Blackburn, 1949
Copnall, Frank Thomas 1870–1949, *George Holden, Mayor of Darwen (1907–1908),* transferred from Darwen Town Hall © the copyright holder
Copnall, Frank Thomas 1870–1949, *Alderman William Thompson, Mayor of Blackburn (1914–1915),* © the copyright holder
Copnall, Frank Thomas 1870–1949, *Joshua Hacking, President of the Blackburn Chamber of Commerce (1917–1925),* gift from the Blackburn Chamber of Commerce, 1987 © the copyright holder
Copnall, Frank Thomas 1870–1949, *Alfred Nuttall, Mayor of Blackburn (1915–1917),* © the copyright holder
Copnall, Frank Thomas 1870–1949, *Thomas Purvis Ritzema (1853–1938),* gift from W. D. Ritzema, Clitheroe, 1958 © the copyright holder
Copnall, Frank Thomas 1870–1949, *Portrait of a Man* (probably an Alderman of Darwen), transferred from Darwen Town Hall © the copyright holder
Copnall, Frank Thomas 1870–1949, *Mrs Charles Costekin or Costello (?),* transferred from Darwen Town Hall © the copyright holder
Copnall, Frank Thomas 1870–1949, *Samuel Crossley, JP, Mayor of Blackburn (1911),* gift to the Borough from friends of the sitter © the copyright holder
Crewdson, Jack *Jubilee Tower, Darwen,* commissioned, 2009 © Blackburn Museum & Art Gallery
Crossland, Henry Symons 1859–1943, *Shackerley Toll Bar, Mellor, Preston New Road,* gift from Mrs Tom Lord, Lytham, 1969
Crossland, James Henry 1852–1939, *Alum Scar,* gift from Miss Annie Aspden, 1934
Cursiter, Stanley 1887–1976, *Roberta,* gift from James Meadowcroft, Blackburn, 1920 estate of Stanley Cursiter 2012. All rights reserved, DACS
Davis, Henry William Banks 1833–1914, *Close of Day,* purchased from Richard Haworth, Blackburn, 1910
de Haas, Johannes Hubertus Leonardus 1832–1908, *Cattle and Landscape,* purchased from Richard Haworth, Blackburn, 1912
Derbyshire, Paul 1936–2007, *Pendle Hill in Winter,* purchased from the artist © the copyright holder
Dimond, Louise 1878–1943, *Floral Decoration,* gift from James Dunn, Blackburn, 1940 © the copyright holder
Dixon, Charles 1872–1934, *The Battle of Jutland,* presented as 1914–1918 war memorial to Darwen Corporation
Dodd, Alan b.1942, *Interior, London N1,* gift from Crown Wallcoverings Ltd, Darwen © the artist
Dolby, James 1909–1975, *Engine Shed* purchased from the artist at Blackburn Artists' Autumn Exhibition, 1966 © the copyright holder
Dolby, James 1909–1975, *Blackburn Bottom Lock,* purchased from the artist at Blackburn Artists' Autumn Exhibition, 1966 © the copyright holder
Du Val active late 19th C, *Alderman T. Farrar Baynes*
Duckworth, Valerie *Graveyard I,* © the copyright holder
Duckworth, Valerie *Two Sisters* purchased © the copyright holder
Dugdale, Thomas Cantrell 1880–1952, *Mr Kersey, Suffolk,* gift from the widow of the artist, 1954 © Joanna Dunham
Duhem, Henri Aimé 1860–1941, *River Scene,* bequeathed by Thomas Ingham, Duckworth Hall, Oswaldtwistle, 1936
Duhem, Marie Geneviève 1871–1918, *A Woodland Scene,* bequeathed by Thomas Ingham, Duckworth Hall, Oswaldtwistle, 1936
Dunstan, Bernard b.1920, *Brushing Hair; Summer Morning,* transferred from the Royal Academy of Arts (Chantrey Bequest), 2000 © the artist/ Bridgeman Art Library
Dyson, A. M. *Last Train from Waterloo Station,* purchased from the artist at exhibition, 1962 © the copyright holder
Eccles, Kenneth *Grane Moorscape,* purchased from the artist © the copyright holder
Edwards, Garth Stuart 1924–2008, *W. A. Henshall, Mayor of Blackburn (1956),* gift from the artist to the sitter; acquired © the artist's estate
Edwards, Garth Stuart 1924–2008, *New Market Construction, Blackburn,* purchased © the artist's estate
Ellis, Edwin 1842–1895, *Welsh Coast,* gift from Richard Thompson, Clayton Le Dale, 1908
Faed, Thomas 1826–1900, *The Silken Gown,* purchased from Richard Haworth, Blackburn, 1898
Ferrier, Kathleen 1912–1953, *Interior,* gift from Winifred Ferrier © the copyright holder
Ferrier, Kathleen 1912–1953, *Still Life (Glass Vase on Sideboard),* gift from Winifred Ferrier © the copyright holder
Ferrier, Winifred 1904–1995, *Still Life (Blue Jug with Yellow Flowers),* gift from Winifred Ferrier © the copyright holder
Fisher, Howard active c.1976–1996, *Ophelia,* purchased from the artist, 1976 © the copyright holder
Fisher, Howard active c.1976–1996, *Sanctuary,* purchased from the artist, 1985 © the copyright holder
Fletcher, Geoffrey Scowcroft 1923–2004, *Wimereux* gift from the artist © Blackburn Museum & Art Gallery
Fletcher, Geoffrey Scowcroft 1923–2004, *Still Life Study,* gift from the artist © Blackburn Museum & Art Gallery
Fletcher, Geoffrey Scowcroft 1923–2004, *St Malo,* gift from the artist © Blackburn Museum & Art Gallery
Fordham, Ethel 1915–1999, *Floral Symphony,* gift from James Dunn, Blackburn, 1942 © the copyright holder
Foster, Barry *Sky Scene,* purchased from the artist © the copyright holder
Fryer, Malcolm b.1937, *Landscape Edge,* purchased at the John Moores Exhibition, Liverpool, 1965 © the copyright holder
Fryer, Malcolm b.1937, *Angus Landscape* © the copyright holder
Fryer, Malcolm b.1937, *Continental Landscape,* purchased from the artist, 1962 © the copyright holder
Gagliardini, Julien Gustave 1846–1927, *A Road at Midday*
Gagliardini, Julien Gustave 1846–1927, *Thomas Ingham (d.c.1936),* bequeathed by the sitter, 1936
Gagliardini, Julien Gustave 1846–1927, *Woman at Spinning Wheel* bequeathed by Thomas Ingham, Duckworth Hall, Oswaldtwistle, 1936
Gagliardini, Julien Gustave 1846–1927, *Fish Market,* bequeathed by Thomas Ingham, Duckworth Hall, Oswaldtwistle, 1936
Gagliardini, Julien Gustave 1846–1927, *French Fisherman,* bequeathed by Thomas Ingham, Duckworth Hall, Oswaldtwistle, 1936
Gagliardini, Julien Gustave 1846–1927, *The Quay,* gift from Thomas Ingham, Duckworth Hall, Oswaldtwistle, 1936
Gagliardini, Julien Gustave 1846–1927, *The Town of Gordes,* bequeathed by Thomas Ingham, Duckworth Hall, Oswaldtwistle, 1936
Gilbert, John 1817–1897, *Keston Common, Kent,* gift from the artist, 1895
Gilbert, John 1817–1897, *Baggage Wagon*gift from the artist, 1895
Gittleson, Albert Abram b.1887, *Portrait of an Unidentified Mayor of Blackburn*
Goodall, Frederick 1822–1904, *Scene on the Nile,* bequeathed by Mrs John Slater, Southport, 1937
Goodall, Frederick 1822–1904, *Rebecca at the Well,* gift from Miss Stock, Blackburn, 1924
Gregson, V. R. active 1928–1950, *Councillor Fred Taylor, Mayor of Darwen (1949–1950),* © the copyright holder
Griffiths, Patricia active 1950–1960s, *Gymkhana,* purchased from the artist, 1962 © the copyright holder
Grimaldi, Giovanni Francesco 1606–1680, *Classical Italian Landscape,* bequeathed by Robert Edward Hart, Blackburn, 1947
Grimbleby, David b.1949, *Drifting Ground,* gift from the artist © the artist
Guarino, Francesco (circle of) 1611–1654, *Isaac Blessing Jacob,* gift from Mrs G. Newman, Blackburn, 1959
H., J. *Church,* © the copyright holder
Hall, Frederick 1860–1948, *Golden Evening,* gift from J. W. Clayton, 1899 © the artist's estate/ Bridgeman Art Library
Hall, Oliver 1869–1957, *Landscape,* gift from an anonymous donor, 1950 © the artist's estate
Hall, Oliver 1869–1957, *Bridge at Toldeo, Spain,* gift from Ward-Thompson, Wilpshire, Blackburn © the artist's estate
Hamilton, Mary active 19th C, *Witton House in Feniscowles,* gift from H. W. Bothamey
Hamnett, Nina 1890–1956, *Still Life,* gift from the Contemporary Art Society, 1963 © the artist's estate/Bridgeman Art Library
Harcourt, George 1868–1947, *John Taylor,* presented to the Borough by the sitter, 1937 © the copyright holder
Harding, James Duffield 1798–1863, *Locarno, Switzerland,* gift from an 'anonymous friend from Wilpshire', 1915
Harrison, George L. 1855–1925, *Innocents Abroad,* gift from Thomas Radcliffe, 1894
Harrison, J. F. *King George V Inspecting the Holcombe Hounds at Houghton Tower,* gift from Miss P. Hardcastle, Godalming, Surrey, 1975 © the copyright holder
Harwood, Frank b.1955, *Open House,* gift from Crown Wallcoverings Ltd, Darwen © the artist
Haslam, Raymond active 1967, *Square Shift,* purchased from the artist, 1967 © the copyright holder
Haworth, Charles Singleton 1884–1917, *La Debutante,* gift from Mr R. Haworth, Haselmere, Surrey, 1969
Haworth, Charles Singleton 1884–1917, *Margaret Haworth,* gift from Mr R. Haworth, Haselmere, Surrey, 1969
Haworth, Charles Singleton 1884–1917, *The Stack Yard, Sydney's Far, Freshfields, near Southport*
Haworth, Charles Singleton 1884–1917, *Self Portrait,* gift from Mr R. Haworth, Haslemere, Surrey, 1969
Hayes, Edwin 1819–1904, *Off Ramsgate,* gift from G. Taylor on behalf of the executors the will of T. Hollins, 1954
Hayes, William active 1850–1882, *James Dickinson (1830–1887),* gift from Miss Dickinson, 1932
Hellawell, Harry 1921–2004, *Landscape Form,* purchased from the artist, 1969 © the copyright holder
Hellawell, Harry 1921–2004, *Release,* purchased from the artist, 1969 © the copyright holder
Hellawell, Harry 1921–2004, *Pram Cover,* purchased from the artist, 1969 © the copyright holder
Herring I, John Frederick 1795–1865, *William Ward on Horseback,* gift from Miss Miriam Eccles Ward, Lytham
Herring I, John Frederick 1795–1865, *Nanny,* purchased from Mr W. H. Cunliffe
Hidalgo y Padilla, Félix Resurreccion 1857–1915, *Still Life (Flowers in a Vase),* bequeathed by Thomas Ingham, Duckworth Hall, Oswaldtwistle, 1936
Hidalgo y Padilla, Félix Resurreccion 1857–1915, *Seascape,* bequeathed by Thomas Ingham, Duckworth Hall, Oswaldtwistle, 1936
Hindle, William 1811–1890, *Landscape,* gift from J. W. Bell, Wilpshire, Blackburn, 1891
Hogarth, William 1697–1764, *The Undertakers Company,* gift from T. B. Lewis as part of the original furnishings of the Lewis Textile Museum
Holmes, Charles John 1868–1936, *Seven Chimneys,* gift from Mr R. B. Lewis, 1969
Hoog, Bernard de 1867–1943, *Dutch Interior,* gift from James Alexander Watson, JP, Blackburn, 1909 © the copyright holder
Hora, H. active 1860–1881, *Thomas Ainsworth (1801–1890), Clerk to the County Magistrates,* bequeathed by the sitter, 1891
Hornel, Edward Atkinson 1864–1933, *End of the Butterfly Chase,* gift from J. Duckworth, Wilpshire, 1912
Hoyoll, Philipp 1818–1876, *Alderman Robert Duckworth, JP,* gift
Hoyoll, Philipp 1818–1876, *Thomas Butterfield,* gift from James Booth, 1900

Hoyoll, Philipp 1818–1876, *Thomas Hart (1799–1859), JP*
Hoyoll, Philipp 1818–1876, *Thomas Thwaites,* bequeathed by Miss Elizabeth Hannah Thwaithes, the daughter of the artist, 1914
Huggins, William 1820–1884, *Head of a Lioness,* purchased from J. J. L. Irving, 1897
Hughes, Norman *Operation Colossus,* unknown acquisition method © the copyright holder
Hughes, Patrick b.1939, *Out into the Interior,* gift from Crown Wallcoverings Ltd, Darwen © DACS 2012
Hughes-Stanton, Herbert Edwin Pelham 1870–1937, *Sunlight across the Sea,* purchased from Richard Haworth, Blackburn, 1913
Hughes-Stanton, Herbert Edwin Pelham 1870–1937, *Villeneuve les Avignon,* purchased from William Whaley Wilkinson, Blackburn, 1928
Hulse, J. W. active late 19th C–early 20th C, *Landscape*
Illidge, Thomas Henry 1799–1851, *James Pickup,* bequeathed by Mrs Richard Barton Dodgson, Blackburn, 1884
Irvin, Albert b.1922, *Rider,* gift from the Contemporary Art Society © Albert Irvin. All rights reserved, DACS 2012
Jacomb-Hood, George Percy 1857–1929, *Sir William Hornby (1841–1928), MP*
Jansen, Willem Georg Frederik 1871–1949, *Hauling Timber*gift from an anonymous donor, 1930 © the copyright holder
Johnson, Llima active late 20th C, *Movement on Staircase,* gift from Crown Wallcoverings Ltd, Darwen © the copyright holder
Johnston, Alexander 1815–1891, *John Bunyan in Bedford Prison,* bequeathed by Miss Tattersall, Low Ibbotsholme, near Windemere, 1969
Johnston, William Herbert 1848–1897, *William Billington (1825–1884), Blackburn Poet and Author,* purchased from donations, 1891
Kerr, Esther Barbara Nicloux 1861–1950, *Freesias,* gift from the artist, 1935 © the copyright holder
Kneller, Godfrey 1646–1723, *Mary II (1662–1694),* gift from William Duckworth, Kirkham, 1928
Knight, Frances active late 20th C, *Untitled,* gift from Crown Wallcoverings Ltd, Darwen © the copyright holder
Knight, Joseph 1837–1909, *Y Garn Mountains,* gift from J. W. Stones, 1984
Knight, Laura 1877–1970, *Ready to Show,* gift from Mrs H. V. Wolstenholme, 1938 © reproduced with permission of the estate of Dame Laura Knight, DBE, RA, 2012. All rights reserved
Kunzel, Prudence 1921–1989, *Railway Bridge* © the copyright holder
La Thangue, Henry Herbert 1859–1929, *A Mountain Frontier,* bequeathed by Mrs K. La Thangue, 1941
La Thangue, Henry Herbert 1859–1929, *A Ligurian Flower Girl,* bequeathed by the widow of © the artist, 1942
La Thangue, Henry Herbert 1859–1929, *Crying Fish in Spain,* bequeathed by Mrs K. La Thangue, 1941
La Thangue, Henry Herbert 1859–1929, *Ligurian Artrobus,* bequeathed by Mrs K. La Thangue, 1941
Lawrence, Thomas (circle of) 1769–1830, *John Fowden Hindle,* bequeathed by Miss M. J. Gregory, 1904
Le Sidaner, Henri Eugène 1862–1939, *Corner of Versailles Park,* bequeathed by Thomas Ingham, Duckworth Hall, Oswaldtwistle, 1936
Leader, Benjamin Williams 1831–1923, *A Fine Autumn Day, North Wales,* purchased from Thomas Agnew & Sons, Manchester, 1893
Leader, Benjamin Williams 1831–1923, *On the Severn below Worcester,* bequeathed by Henry Harrison, Blackburn, 1914
Learoyd, Barbara active 1963–c.1965, *Still Life with Egg,* purchased from the artist, 1965 © the copyright holder
Leighton, Frederic 1830–1896, *Mother and Child,* purchased from Arthur Booth & Son Ltd, London, 1911
Lever, Ruby b.1912, *Darwen*gift from the artist, 2005 © the artist
Linnell, John 1792–1882, *Sheep,* bequeathed by Robert Edward Hart, Blackburn, 1947
Linnell, William 1826–1906, *Hesperus,* bequeathed by Robert Edward Hart, Blackburn, 1947
Long, Edwin 1829–1891, *Diana or Christ?,* gift from John Edmondson, Blackburn, 1919
Lonsdale, James 1777–1839, *John Hornby (1763–1841),* purchased from Gregory Page-Turner, Artware Fine Art, London, 2001
Lund, Ann *The Bronze Figure,* © the copyright holder
MacGregor, William York 1855–1923, *Stirling Bridge,* gift from John Yates, 1966
Magnus, Emma 1856–1936, *Won't You Buy My Pretty Flowers,* gift from a Friend of the Ragged School, 1887
Mali, Christian Friedrich 1832–1906, *The Shepherd's Return,* gift from Miss Stock, Blackburn, 1924
Masson, A. active late 19th C, *Lower Hodder Bridge,* gift from Councillor W. Sharples, 1957
Masson, A. active late 19th C, *Whalley Church,* gift from Councillor W. Sharples, 1957
McEvoy, Ambrose 1878–1927, *Countess of Granard,* purchased from Mrs Mary McEvoy, 1936
Miller, George E. 1913–1983, *Lumb Bank Farm,* purchased at an exhibition in Lewis Art Gallery © the copyright holder
Miller, George E. 1913–1983, *Pleckgate Fold,* purchased from the artist at Blackburn Artists' Exhibition © the copyright holder
Moore, Albert Joseph 1841–1893, *The Loves of the Winds and the Seasons,* purchased from the George Mculloch Collection at Christie's, 1913
Moore, Henry 1831–1895, *Rough Weather in the Mediterranean,* purchased at a sale through Mssrs Brown and Rose, Liverpool, 1908
Morgan, Frederick 1856–1927, *Making Friends,* bequeathed by Arthur Clegg Bowdler, d.1918; received on the death of Miss Bowdler, 1925
Morgan, John 1823–1886, *Playing at Soldiers,* gift from Mrs J. W. Stones, Blackburn, in memory of her mother, 1934
Morris, Philip Richard 1836–1902, *The Good Samaritan,* gift from Arthur C. Bowles, 1902
Morton, James Hargreaves 1881–1918, *Landscape with Bare Trees,* purchased at auction, 1971
Morton, James Hargreaves 1881–1918, *Sheep Shearing,* purchased at auction, 1971
Morton, James Hargreaves 1881–1918, *Washing,* purchased at auction, 1971
Morton, James Hargreaves 1881–1918, *Blue Hills,* purchased at auction, 1971
Morton, James Hargreaves 1881–1918, *Windswept Trees,* purchased at auction, 1971
Munnings, Alfred James 1878–1959, *'Solario',* bequeathed by Colonel Sir John Rutherford Bart, 1932, © Sir Alfred Munnings Art Museum
Murray, David 1849–1933, *St Oswald's Bay, Lulworth,* bequeathed by the executors of the will of the artist Sir Edwin Cooper, London, 1939
Neyt, Bernard 1825–1880, *Church Interior, Amsterdam,* gift from Miss Stock, Blackburn, 1924
Niemann, Edmund John 1813–1876, *Rocky Landscape,* bequeathed by Mrs Richard Barton Dodgson, Blackburn, 1884
O'Neil, Henry Nelson 1817–1880, *The Opera Box,* bequeathed by Mrs Richard Barton Dodgson, Blackburn, 1884
Occonomo active mid-19th C, *Alderman James Thompson, JP, Mayor of Blackburn (1865–1866)*
Ogg, Charles Herbert 1819–1889, *Mrs Richard Barton Dodgson (d.c.1884),* bequeathed by the sitter, 1884
Ogg, Charles Herbert 1819–1889, *Richard James Pickup Dodgson,* bequeathed by Mrs Richard Barton Dodgson, Blackburn, 1884
Ogg, Charles Herbert 1819–1889, *James Boyle,* presented to the Borough by James Boyle Junior, 1883
Ogg, Charles Herbert 1819–1889, *Mr Cross*
Olsson, Albert Julius 1864–1942, *The Reef, St Ives Bay, Cornwall,* purchased from Richard Haworth, Blackburn, 1912 © the copyright holder
Opie, John 1761–1807, *Figure Study,* gift from Mr Henry Whittaker, 1863
Orpen, William 1878–1931, *Sir John Rutherford (1854–1932),* gift from Blackburn Hospital Management Committee, 1953
Parker, Brynhild 1907–1987, *Portrait,* gift from the Contemporary Art Society, 1954 © the copyright holder
Penn, William Charles 1877–1968, *The Victorian Home,* gift from Thomas Barton, JP, Blackpool, 1930 © the artist's estate
Peppercorn, Arthur Douglas 1847–1926, *Landscape,* gift from John Yates, 1966
Platt, Stella 1913–2011, *Queen's Mill, Longridge,* purchased from Prestons of Bolton, 1966 © the artist's estate
Platt, Stella 1913–2011, *Rochdale* (recto), purchased from an exhibition in Manchester, 1971 © the artist's estate
Platt, Stella 1913–2011, *Nude* (verso), purchased from an exhibition in Manchester, 1971 © the artist's estate
Pollitt, J. G. *Sleeping Beauty,* bequeathed by Thomas Ainsworth, 1891
Poole, David b.1931, *Sir George Eddie, Leader of Blackburn Council,* © the artist
Priestman, Bertram 1868–1951, *The Watering Place, Evening,* presented by James A. Watson, JP, 1913 © the copyright holder
Pucz, T. *Russian Moujik,* gift from Lady Thorn, JP, Blackburn, 1940
Pucz, T. *Russian Workman,* gift from Lady Thorn, JP, Blackburn, 1940
Puzier, Robert *Samuel Brooks (1792–1864),* gift from Lloyds Banking Group Archives and Museum
Puzier, Robert *William Brooks (1762–1846),* gift from Lloyds Banking Group Archives and Museum
Quinn, James Peter 1869–1951, *Dr Robert Aitken (1869–1951),* gift from the son of the sitter, Bezza Farm, Salmsbury © the copyright holder
Ranken, William Bruce Ellis 1881–1941, *The Young Polo Player,* gift from the sister of the artist in accordance with his wishes
Rankle, Alan b.1952, *Study for 'Montsegur',* gift from the Tramman Trust through the Art Fund, 2009 © the artist
Redfern, David b.1947, *Look through Any Window,* gift from Crown Wallcoverings Ltd, Darwen © the artist
Reni, Guido (copy after) 1575–1642, *Beatrice Cenci (1577–1599)*
Reynolds, Joshua 1723–1792, *William Fowden,* bequeathed by Miss M. Gregory, London, 1902
Reynolds, Joshua (attributed to) 1723–1792, *Jane Barton,* bequeathed by Mrs Richard Barton Dodgson, Blackburn, 1884
Reynolds, Joshua (style of) 1723–1792, *Study for 'Beggar Man (George White)'*
Riley, Eric C. active 1960s, *Blackburn Market,* purchased from the artist, 1963 © the copyright holder
Riley, Eric C. active 1960s, *New Market Construction,* purchased from the artist © the copyright holder
Roberts, David 1796–1864, *Porch to Roslyn Chapel,* gift from Thomas McLean, London, 1911
Roberts, David 1796–1864, *Toledo Cathedral,* gift from Mr Henry Whittaker, 1863
Romney, George 1734–1802, *Dr Scales,* bequeathed by Mrs Richard Barton Dodgson, Blackburn, 1884
Romney, George (attributed to) 1734–1802, *Mr Barton,* bequeathed by Mrs Richard Barton Dodgson, Blackburn, 1884
Ronner, Henriette 1821–1909, *A Merry Party,* gift from Walter Farnworth, 1894
Roos, Philipp Peter 1657–1706, *Pastoral Landscape,* gift from Dr Alan Smerdon, Blackburn, 1968
Ruith, Horace van 1839–1923, *Water Is Best,* gift from Mrs Lewis, Temperance Movement, Blackburn, 1915
Russell, Edwin Wensley 1830–1915, *Nancy Hargreaves,* gift from Dr and Mrs Davies, Blackburn, 1894
Sartin, Stephen *Martial Cubes,* purchased at Liverpool Walker Art Gallery, John Moores Exhibition, 1969 © the copyright holder
Schaeffer, Johannes Bartholomeus 1927–2000, *Kathleen Ferrier (1912–1953),* gift from Mr Charles Eric Leach, 2010 © Blackburn Museum & Art Gallery
Schuch, H. active 1900, *The Quarrel,* gift from Mrs Harold S. Isherwood, Blackburn, 1939
Scott active late 20th C, *Inside Out,* gift from Crown Wallcoverings Ltd, Darwen © the copyright holder
Scott, Bernard 1918–1990, *Still Life,* purchased from the artist, 1961 © the copyright holder
Sellers, M. *Canal Scene,* purchased from the artist, 1971 © the copyright holder
Shackleton, Peter b.1933, *Boy with White Bird,* purchased from the artist, 1959 © the artist
Shackleton, Peter b.1933, *Fish Boy,* purchased from Anthony Dawson, London, 1972 © the artist

Shackleton, Peter b.1933, *Merry Go Round,* purchased from the artist at an exhibition in Lewis Art Gallery, 1970 © the artist
Shackleton, Peter b.1933, *Circus Horses,* unknown acquisition method © the artist
Shackleton, Peter b.1933, *Summer Landscape,* purchased from Anthony Dawson, London, 1971 © the artist
Shackleton, Peter b.1933, *Winter Stones,* purchased from the artist at an exhibition in Lewis Art Gallery, 1970 © the artist
Shackleton, William 1872–1933, *Mussel Gatherers,* bequeathed by Mary Shackleton, 1938
Sharples, James 1825–1893, *Fruit and Vegetable Still Life,* transferred from Blackburn Technical College
Sharples, James 1825–1893, *The Forge,* on loan from the family of the artist
Sherwood, Vladimir Ossipovitch 1832–1897, *Laying the Foundation Stone to the Cotton Exchange, Blackburn,* purchased, 1875
Sherwood, Vladimir Ossipovitch 1832–1897, *Mr Healey,* gift from Mrs D. Houghton, Preston, 1969
Sherwood, Vladimir Ossipovitch 1832–1897, *Mrs Healey,* gift from Mrs D. Houghton, Preston, 1969
Spencelayh, Charles 1865–1958, *The Scent,* gift from W. G. Gowans, Whalley © the artist's estate/ Bridgeman Art Library
Spencer, Gilbert 1892–1979, *Wooded Landscape,* purchased at auction, Salmesbury Hall, 1980 © the artist's estate/Bridgeman Art Library
Spencer, Rita active 1965, *Market in Antigua,* purchased from the artist, 1965 © the copyright holder
Spencer, Terrance G. active 20th C, *St James' Street, Burnley* © the copyright holder
Stone, Marcus C. 1840–1921, *Two's Company, Three's None,* purchased from Messrs Christie Manson and Woodssale, 1894
Stott, Edward William 1859–1918, *The Watering Place,* purchased from the George Mculloch Collection at Christie's, 1913
Suker, Arthur 1857–1902, *After the Storm, North Cornwall,* gift from James A. Watson, JP
Taylor, J. A. *Darwen Market,* © the copyright holder
Tennant, John F. 1796–1872, *View of Old Llandudno,* gift from Mr and Mrs. J. J. Fielding, Blackburn, 1952
Thompson, Ian active 1960s, *Junction of Saunders Road and Downham Street, Blackburn,* purchased from the artist at West Pennine Artists' Exhibition, 1966 © the copyright holder
Thorburn, Archibald 1860–1935, *Suspense,* gift from Thomas Radcliffe, 1894
Tinker, F. E. *Lock Scavaig, Skye* © the copyright holder
Toynbee, Lawrence 1922–2002, *Square Cut,* purchased from the Leicester Galleries, 1969 © the artist's estate/Bridgeman Art Library
unknown artist *Mrs Fowden Hindle,* bequeathed by Miss M. J. Gregory, 1904
unknown artist *William Fowden Hindle,* bequeathed by Miss M. J. Gregory, 1904
unknown artist *The 1832 Blackburn Election,* on loan from Mr S. B. Pickup, since 1957
unknown artist *Inn Sign with Portrait of Niccolò Paganini,* probably donated after the 'Paganini Inn' was demolished, c.1900
unknown artist *Alderman Richard Martland, MD,* presented to the Borough by friends of the sitter, 1860
unknown artist *Joseph Harrison (1805–1880),* purchased from David Harrison with the assistance of the Victoria and Albert Museum Purchase Grant Fund, 1984
unknown artist *William Rostron, Founder of Scoltabrook (?) Paper Mill, Darwen*
unknown artist *Alderman William Snape, 1st Mayor of Darwen (1878),* transferred from Darwen Town Hall
unknown artist *Alderman William Entwistle, Mayor of Darwen (1883),* transferred from Darwen Town Hall
unknown artist *Corporation Park, Blackburn*
unknown artist *Councillor James Beads, JP,* presented by friends of the sitter, 1889
unknown artist *Charles Philip Huntington (1833–1906), Mayor of Darwen (1897),* transferred from Darwen Town Hall
unknown artist *Councillor Dr James T. Ballantyne, Mayor of Darwen (1898),* transferred from Darwen Town Hall
unknown artist *Henry Harrison (1834–1914), President of the Blackburn Chamber of Commerce (1887–1914),* gift from the Blackburn Chamber of Commerce, 1987
unknown artist *Russian Woman,* gift from Lady Thorn, JP, Blackburn, 1940
unknown artist *Alderman Edwin Hamer, JP* (Blackburn)
unknown artist *Alderman Timothy Lightbrown, Mayor of Blackburn (1884–1886),* transferred from Darwen Town Hall
unknown artist *Blue Abstract with White Horse*
unknown artist *Dr Barlow,* gift from Miss Sturdy, 1886
unknown artist *Dr Barlow,* gift from Mrs MacKinnon, Tir Ucha, Lon Ednfed, Criccieth Gwynedd, 1978
unknown artist *Cottages by River, Malham*
unknown artist *Girl Walking down Stairs,* unknown acquisition method
unknown artist *Hacking Hall*
unknown artist *High Street outside a Public House*
unknown artist *James Hoyle, Mayor of Blackburn (1882–1884)*
unknown artist *John Hargreaves, MP,* gift from A. H. Porter Hargreaves, 1954
unknown artist *Landscape with Bridge*
unknown artist *Man with Clay Pipe* (believed to be Jan Stein)
unknown artist *Portrait of a Man*
unknown artist *Portrait of a Man in Uniform*
unknown artist *Portrait of an Unidentified Mayor* (Blackburn or Darwen)
unknown artist *Portrait of an Unidentified Mayor of Darwen*
unknown artist *Red Abstract*
unknown artist *Robert Raynford Jackson,* gift from Mrs A. W. Lightbourn, 1940
unknown artist *Street Scene, Paris,* bequeathed by Thomas Ingham, Duckworth Hall, Oswaldtwistle, 1936
unknown artist *The Salesbury Centenarian, William Hayhurst,* gift from Mrs J. Hindle, 2005
unknown artist *The Salesbury Centenarian, William Hayhurst*
unknown artist *View of an Unidentified Church*
unknown artist *William Gregson (1820–1890)*
unknown artist *Birth of Saint John the Baptist,* on loan from Colin Strang
unknown artist *Saint Vsevolod, Grand Prince and Wonder Worker,* purchased from the Temple Gallery with the assistance of the Victoria and Albert Museum Purchase Grant Fund, the Art Fund and Friends of Blackburn Museum and Art Gallery, 2000
unknown artist *Old Testament Trinity* (triptych), purchased from Blackburn Diocesan Board of Finance, 1941
unknown artist *Archangel Michael,* on loan from Colin Strang
unknown artist *Scenes from the Life of Saint Nicholas,* gift from the Art Fund from the Kathleen Fenwick Bequest, 1982
unknown artist *The Virgin of God the Sign* (triptych), gift from the Art Fund from the Kathleen Fenwick Bequest, 1982
unknown artist *Virgin and Child* (triptych), purchased from Blackburn Diocesan Board of Finance, 1941
unknown artist *Anastasis,* gift from HM Customs & Excise, 1993
unknown artist *Apparition of the Holy Trinity to Saint Sergei,* gift from HM Customs & Excise, 1993
unknown artist *Archangel Michael,* gift from the Art Fund from the Kathleen Fenwick Bequest, 1982
unknown artist *Bogolubskaya 'The Loved by God',* gift from the Art Fund from the Kathleen Fenwick Bequest, 1982
unknown artist *Christ in Majesty,* gift from the Art Fund from the Kathleen Fenwick Bequest, 1982
unknown artist *Christ Pantocrator,* gift from the Art Fund from the Kathleen Fenwick Bequest, 1982
unknown artist *Christ Vsederzhitel,* gift from HM Customs & Excise, 1993
unknown artist *Christ Vsederzhitel,* gift from HM Customs & Excise, 1993
unknown artist *Christ Vsederzhitel,* gift from HM Customs & Excise, 1993
unknown artist *Christ Vsederzhitel,* gift from HM Customs & Excise, 1993
unknown artist *Constantine and Helen,* gift from the Art Fund from the Kathleen Fenwick Bequest, 1982
unknown artist *Deesis with Saints,* gift from the Art Fund from the Kathleen Fenwick Bequest, 1982
unknown artist *Fedorovskaya, Mother of God,* gift from HM Customs & Excise, 1993
unknown artist *God the All Seeing,* gift from the Art Fund from the Kathleen Fenwick Bequest, 1982
unknown artist *Kazanskaya Mother of God,* gift from HM Customs & Excise, 1993
unknown artist *Mother of God of Unexpected Joy,* gift from HM Customs & Excise, 1993
unknown artist *Mother of God of Unexpected Joy,* gift from HM Customs & Excise, 1993
unknown artist *Mother of God the Sign,* gift from HM Customs & Excise, 1993
unknown artist *Mother of God the Sign (Orans),* gift from HM Customs & Excise, 1993
unknown artist *Mother of God to Those Who Grieve,* gift from HM Customs & Excise, 1993
unknown artist *Our Lady of Kazan*gift from the Art Fund from the Kathleen Fenwick Bequest, 1982
unknown artist *Resurrection and Descent into Hell,* gift from the Art Fund from the Kathleen Fenwick Bequest, 1982
unknown artist *Saint Demetrius Vanquishing a Pagan Saint,* gift from HM Customs & Excise, 1993
unknown artist *Saint Feodor,* gift from the Art Fund from the Kathleen Fenwick Bequest, 1982
unknown artist *Saint George and the Dragon,* on loan from Colin Strang
unknown artist *Saint George and the Dragon,* purchased from Blackburn Diocesan Board of Finance, 1941
unknown artist *Saint John the Baptist,* gift from HM Customs & Excise, 1993
unknown artist *Saint John the Baptist the Foreteller,* gift from the Art Fund from the Kathleen Fenwick Bequest, 1982
unknown artist *Saint Nicholas,* gift from the Art Fund from the Kathleen Fenwick Bequest, 1982
unknown artist *Saint Nicholas,* gift from HM Customs & Excise, 1993
unknown artist *Saint Nicholas,* gift from HM Customs & Excise, 1993
unknown artist *Saint Nicholas,* gift from HM Customs & Excise, 1993
unknown artist *Saint Nicholas of Mira,* purchased from Blackburn Diocesan Board of Finance, 1941
unknown artist *Saint Paraskeva,* gift from HM Customs & Excise, 1993
unknown artist *Saint Paraskeva,* gift from HM Customs & Excise, 1993
unknown artist *Saint Paraskeva Paranitsa,* gift from the Art Fund from the Kathleen Fenwick Bequest, 1982
unknown artist *Saint Serafim of Sarov,* gift from HM Customs & Excise, 1993
unknown artist *Saint Theodosi,* gift from HM Customs & Excise, 1993
unknown artist *Saint Tikhon Zadonsky,* gift from HM Customs & Excise, 1993
unknown artist *Scenes from the Life of Prophet Elijah,* purchased from Blackburn Diocesan Board of Finance, 1941
unknown artist *Slaying Angel*
unknown artist *The Amaryld Vernicle,* purchased from Blackburn Diocesan Board of Finance, 1941
unknown artist *The Burning Bush,* gift from HM Customs & Excise, 1993
unknown artist *The Crowned Virgin and Infant,* purchased from Blackburn Diocesan Board of Finance, 1941
unknown artist *The Forefather Abel,* purchased from the Mark Gallery with the asistance of the Victoria and Albert Museum Purchase Grant Fund and the Art Fund
unknown artist *The Kykko Mother of God or Eleousa,* purchased from Blackburn Diocesan Board of Finance, 1941
unknown artist *The Virgin of Kazan,* purchased from Blackburn Diocesan Board of Finance, 1941
unknown artist *The Virgin of the Unfading Rose,* purchased from Blackburn Diocesan Board of Finance, 1941
unknown artist *The Vladimir Mother of God,* gift from the Art Fund from the Kathleen Fenwick Bequest, 1982
unknown artist *The Vladimir Mother of God,* gift from the Art Fund from the Kathleen Fenwick Bequest, 1982
unknown artist *Tikhvin Mother of God,* gift from HM Customs & Excise, 1993
unknown artist *Tikhvin Mother of*

God, gift from HM Customs & Excise, 1993
unknown artist *Two Men with Globe*
unknown artist *Virgin and Child Enthroned*, purchased from Blackburn Diocesan Board of Finance, 1941
unknown artist *Virgin Hodegetria*, purchased from Blackburn Diocesan Board of Finance, 1941
unknown artist *Vladimir Mother of God*, gift from HM Customs & Excise, 1993
Vastagh, Géza 1866–1919, *A Siesta*, gift from Mrs Herbert Noble, 1922
Verboeckhoven, Eugène Joseph 1798–1881, *Landscape with Sheep*, gift from James Haydock, Whinfield Place, 1963
Verboeckhoven, Eugène Joseph 1798–1881, *Landscape with Sheep*, presented in memory of Alfred Nuttall, Mayor of Blackburn, 1917
Verveer, Elchanon Leonardus 1826–1900, *Sand Dunes at Scheveningen*, gift from Miss Stock, Blackburn, 1924
Veyrassat, Jules Jacques 1828–1893, *Return from Labour*, gift from Miss Stock, Blackburn, 1924
Virtue, John b.1947, *View of Oswaldtwistle*, © John Virtue. All Rights Reserved, DACS 2012
Walker, Ethel 1861–1951, *Seascape*, bequeathed by Sir James Forrest, Manchester Square, London, 1949 © the artist's estate/Bridgeman Art Library
Watkinson, Bob 1914–1992, *Untitled Abstract*, purchased at an exhibition in Lewis Art Gallery, 1973 © the copyright holder
Watkinson, Bob 1914–1992, *Untitled Abstract*, purchased at an exhibition in Lewis Art Gallery © the copyright holder
Weaver, G. R. active 20th C, *Cottages*, © the copyright holder
Webb, James 1825–1895, *Ischia*, bequeathed by Arthur Clegg Bowdler, d.1918; received on the death of Miss Bowdler, 1925
Webb, Ronald William b.1945, *Alto Rhapsody*, gift from the artist, 2008 © the artist
Webster, Thomas George 1800–1886, *The New Sign*, bequeathed by Robert Edward Hart, Blackburn, 1946
Weisbrod, Richard 1906–1991, *Preston Station*, purchased from the artist, 1963 © the copyright holder
Weisbrod, Richard 1906–1991, *Lancashire Snow Scene*, purchased © the copyright holder
Weisbrod, Richard 1906–1991, *At Carro*, purchased from the artist, 1963 © the copyright holder
Weisbrod, Richard 1906–1991, *Railway Yard*, purchased from the artist, 1964 © the copyright holder
Weiss, José 1859–1919, *Arundel Park*, gift from Albert W. Heywood, Alderley Edge, Manchester, 1923
Whaite, Henry Clarence 1828–1912, *The Convent Garden*, purchased from James Kenyon, JP, 1896
Whaite, Henry Clarence 1828–1912, *Thirlmere*, gift from Ms J. W. Stones, Blackburn, 1907
White, Charles F. 1905–1975, *French Village*, purchased from the artist at an exhibition in Lewis Art Gallery, 1970 © the copyright holder
White, Charles F. 1905–1975, *Farm in the Wood*, purchased from the artist at an exhibition in Lewis Art Gallery, 1970 © the copyright holder
Wild, David b.1931, *Winter Landscape, Cliviger* © the artist
Wild, David b.1931, *Nude*, purchased from the artist, 1966 © the artist
Wilkinson, Herbert active 1931–1979, *Alderman Francis John Greeves (d.1945)*, gift to the town from the artist and his wife for George V's Silver Jubilee, 1935 © the copyright holder
Wimperis, Edmund Morison 1835–1900, *A Yorkshire Moor*, gift from Eli Heyworth, JP, 1898
Wimperis, Edmund Morison 1835–1900, *In Wensleydale*, gift from Edwin Leach Hartley, 1904
Wimperis, Edmund Morison 1835–1900, *On a Yorkshire Moor*, gift from Mrs W. Smith, Blackburn, 1962
Wolf, Joseph 1820–1899, *Ptarmigan*, gift from the widow of Alfred Nutall, 1923
Wood, Elizabeth b.1930, *The Bath*, purchased from the artist at Fylde Group Exhibition © the artist
Wood, Elizabeth b.1930, *Clown*, purchased from the artist at an exhibition, 1966 © the artist
Yates, John 1885–1969, *Arley Brook*, gift from the artist © the copyright holder
Yates, John 1885–1969, *Blackburn Fair*, © the copyright holder

East Lancashire Hospitals NHS Trust

Akhtar, Tahira *Fish with Abstract Symbols*, gift from Edge End High School, Nelson © the copyright holder
Bruch, Matthew *It's All about Angles*, © the copyright holder
Collins, Nicola *Travelling Inwards*, © the copyright holder
Corcoran, John b.1940, *Landscape with a Church*, © the copyright holder
Corcoran, John b.1940, *Snowy Scene with a River and a Bridge*, © the copyright holder
Gallagher, Paula *Untitled 1*, © the copyright holder
Gallagher, Paula *Untitled 2*, © the copyright holder
Heath, Eleanor *Painting for the Burger Man* (panel 1 of 3), © the copyright holder
Heath, Eleanor *Painting for the Burger Man* (panel 2 of 3), © the copyright holder
Heath, Eleanor *Painting for the Burger Man* (panel 3 of 3), © the copyright holder
Hughes, Sarah *Red Car in a Jungle with Skyscrapers*, gift from Edge End High School, Nelson © the copyright holder
Jackson, Margaret *Tool Cupboard*, commissioned by Blackburn, Hyndburn and Ribble Valley Health Care NHS Trust © the copyright holder
Maggs, James *Luna Ascendant*, © the copyright holder
Martyn, Channing (possibly) *Floral Window*, © the copyright holder
Millea, Joanne *Amber Lines*, © the copyright holder
Millea, Joanne *Aquamarine Lines*, © the copyright holder
Millea, Joanne *Jade Lines*, © the copyright holder
Millea, Joanne *Magenta Lines*, © the copyright holder
Millea, Joanne *Rose Lines*, © the copyright holder
unknown artist *Abstract Black Figure*, gift from Edge End High School, Nelson
unknown artist *Abstract Tiger*, gift from Edge End High School, Nelson
unknown artist *Bat*, gift from Edge End High School, Nelson
unknown artist *Flowers and Butterflies*, gift from Edge End High School, Nelson
unknown artist *Green Fence with a Butterfly and a Wasp*, gift from Edge End High School, Nelson
unknown artist *Montage with Faces*
unknown artist *Pink and Blue Abstract*, gift from Edge End High School, Nelson
unknown artist *Rainbow with a Plant*, gift from Edge End High School, Nelson
unknown artist *Red Sunset*
unknown artist *The Phoenix*, purchased
unknown artist *Underwater Scene with Octopus, Fish and Sea Horses*, gift from Edge End High School, Nelson
Vivian, Tom Comley 1847–1908, *Caleb Thornber*, gift
Wilkinson, D. A. *Swans* (panel 1 of 3), © the copyright holder
Wilkinson, D. A. *Swans* (panel 2 of 3), © the copyright holder
Wilkinson, D. A. *Swans* (panel 3 of 3), © the copyright holder
Wilkinson, D. A. *Flying Geese* (panel 1 of 3), © the copyright holder
Wilkinson, D. A. *Flying Geese* (panel 2 of 3), © the copyright holder
Wilkinson, D. A. *Flying Geese* (panel 3 of 3), © the copyright holder
Wilkinson, D. A. *Seagulls* (panel 1 of 3), © the copyright holder
Wilkinson, D. A. *Seagulls* (panel 2 of 3), © the copyright holder
Wilkinson, D. A. *Seagulls* (panel 3 of 3), © the copyright holder

Blackpool Town Hall

Brown, J. R. *Surrender of the Rebel Stuart Forces at Preston in 1715*, commissioned from Goodall, Lamb and Heighway Ltd
Brown, J. R. *Final Horse Charge of Richard III at Bosworth Field*, commissioned from Goodall, Lamb and Heighway Ltd
Brown, J. R. *Joining of the Houses of Lancaster and York in 1436*, commissioned from Goodall, Lamb and Heighway Ltd
Marton, W. *Alderman R. B. Mather, JP*
Parrinson, K. *Alderman James Ward*
Townsend, Ernest 1885–1944, *Alderman A. Lindsay Parkinson*, © the copyright holder
unknown artist *Alderman James Heyes*
unknown artist *Alderman James Fish, JP*
unknown artist *Alderman John Bickerstaffe*
unknown artist *Alderman Joseph Heap*
unknown artist *Alderman W. H. Cocker*

Grundy Art Gallery

Adams, Harry William 1868–1947, *Hunt of the Grayling*, purchased, 1926 © the copyright holder
Airy, Anna 1882–1964, *Message of May*, purchased, 1938 © the copyright holder
Aitchison, Craigie Ronald John 1926–2009, *Tree*, gift from the Contemporary Art Society, 1980 © the artist's estate/Bridgeman Art Library
Algie, Jessie 1859–1927, *Pinks*, gift from Mrs R. Bennett
Ansdell, Richard 1815–1885, *Sheep*, gift from Mrs Branwood, 1926
Appleyard, Frederick 1874–1963, *The Nightingale*, purchased, 1924 © the artist's estate
Atherton, John Smith 1877–1943, *Foxfield Estuary*, gift from Mr W. Wilde © the copyright holder
Atherton, John Smith 1877–1943, *Near Bardsea*, gift from Mr W. Wilde, 1956 © the copyright holder
Aumonier, James 1832–1911, *The Thames at Great Marlowe*, gift from Alderman H. Thickett, 1941
Auty, Charles 1858–1936, *Bispham Village in 1880*, gift from A. Ashcroft, 1900
Auty, Charles 1858–1936, *Bispham Village Scene*, gift from Miss D. M. Pearce
Ayrton, Anthony *Alpine Landscape*, gift from W. D. Halstead, 1939 © the copyright holder
Balmford, Hurst 1871–1950, *Lostwithiel, Cornwall*, purchased, 1942 © the copyright holder
Banner, Delmar Harmood 1896–1983, *Great Gable*, gift from the artist © the artist's estate
Bennett, Frank Moss 1874–1952, *Hot Punch*, acquired, 1982 © the artist's estate
Bennett, Frank Moss 1874–1952, *A Good Hand*, acquired, 1982 © the artist's estate
Bennett, Frank Moss 1874–1952, *Un bon mot*, gift from W. Rostron Duckworth © the artist's estate
Berrie, John Archibald Alexander 1887–1962, *Cuthbert Grundy (1846–1946)*, purchased, 1992 © the copyright holder
Birch, Samuel John Lamorna 1869–1955, *The Lonely Pool*, gift from Cuthbert Grundy © the artist's estate
Blakeley, John Harold 1867, *Polperro, Cornwall*, bequeathed
Blaker, Nina *Santa Eulalia, Ibiza*, gift from the artist, 1970 © the copyright holder
Bone, Stephen 1904–1958, *Westminster*, gift from W. D. Halstead, 1939 © estate of Stephen Bone. All rights reserved, DACS 2012
Booth, James William 1867–1953, *Fish Sales, Staithes*, gift from Cuthbert Grundy © the copyright holder
Boulton, Margaret *Moving Dowty Props*, presented to the Mayor and Corporation by the National Coal Board, 1977; transferred © the copyright holder
Brannan, Peter 1926–1994, *The Old Theatre*, unknown acquisition method © the artist's estate
Bray, Phyllis 1911–1991, *Still Life*, gift from the Contemporary Art Society © the artist's estate
Breanski, Alfred de 1852–1928, *The Pass of Leney*, gift from Reverend J. Edwards, 1934
Brundrit, Reginald Grange 1883–1960, *Ribblesdale*, purchased, 1929 © the copyright holder
Bundy, Edgar 1862–1922, *Scandal*, purchased, 1926
Burgess, Arthur James Wetherall 1879–1957, *Abandoned*, gift from Alderman John Bickerstaffe, 1928 © the artist's estate
Burrell, H. *Pavilion Fire, North Pier, 1921*, unknown acquisition method © the copyright holder
Bush, Harry 1883–1957, *The Christmas Tree*, gift from Councillor W. Millington, 1933 © the artist's estate
Camp, Jeffery 1923, *Millbank*, gift from the Contemporary Art Society, 1993 © the artist
Casali, Andrea 1705–1784, *Bacchus and Ariadne*, gift from Mrs R. A. Yerburgh, 1943
Cave, Vera *Roses*, purchased © the copyright holder

Cave, Vera *Spring Flowers,* purchased, 1944 © the copyright holder
Collier, John 1850–1934, *The Amber Necklace,* gift from Mrs J. Collier, 1936
Cooper, Thomas Sidney 1803–1902, *Cattle Grazing,* gift from Alderman John Collins, 1935
Cooper, Thomas Sidney 1803–1902, *Canterbury Meadows,* gift from Councillor J. W. Roberts, 1944
Cooper, Thomas Sidney 1803–1902, *Landscape,* gift from Miss Stansfield, 1955
Crabtree, Jack 1938, *Portrait of the Artist,* gift from Blackpool & Fylde Art Society, 1957 © the artist
Creswick, Thomas 1811–1869, *Bolton Abbey,* gift from R. Holt, 1912
Crome, John 1768–1821, *River Wensum,* gift from Mrs W. R. Brandwood, 1933
Cundall, Charles Ernest 1890–1971, *Rocquebrune-Cap-Martin Station,* purchased from the Royal Academy, 1965 © the artist's estate/Bridgeman Art Library
d'Erlanger, Rodolphe 1872–1932, *Returning from Market,* purchased, 1924
Daubigny, Charles-François 1817–1878, *Cattle and Figures by a River at Dusk,* bequeathed by Lionel Hewlett via the National Art Collections Fund, 1995
de Montfort, Lisa 1906, *Josefina,* purchased, 1950 © the copyright holder
Dignam, Mary Ella Williams 1857–1938, *By the Lake,* unknown acquisition method
Elwell, Frederick William 1870–1958, *Man with a Pint,* purchased, 1933 © the copyright holder
Elwell, Frederick William 1870–1958, *A Boy with a Pig,* purchased from the Royal Academy, 1935 © the copyright holder
Elwell, Mary Dawson 1874–1952, *The Landing in Summer,* purchased, 1930 © the copyright holder
Engelbach, Florence 1872–1951, *White Roses in a Yellow Bowl,* gift from W. R. Duckworth, 1937 © the copyright holder
Eurich, Richard Ernst 1903–1992, *The Window,* purchased from the Royal Academy, 1958 © the artist's estate/Bridgeman Art Library
Faed, Thomas 1826–1900, *Molly's Toilet,* gift from Mrs W. R. Brandwood, 1933
Fidler, Harry 1856–1935, *Going Home,* purchased, 1930
Fidler, Harry 1856–1935, *Timber Wagon,* gift from C. R. Hardman
Fletcher, Geoffrey Scowcroft 1923–2004, *The Smallest Show on Earth,* gift from the artist, 2003 © Grundy Art Gallery, Blackpool
Fletcher, Geoffrey Scowcroft 1923–2004, *Dungeness,* gift from the artist, 2003 © Grundy Art Gallery, Blackpool
Fletcher, Geoffrey Scowcroft 1923–2004, *Notre Dame, Reflections,* gift from the artist, 2003 © Grundy Art Gallery, Blackpool
Fletcher, Geoffrey Scowcroft 1923–2004, *Tarbole,* gift from the artist, 2003 © Grundy Art Gallery, Blackpool
Fletcher, Geoffrey Scowcroft 1923–2004, *Portland,* gift from the artist, 2003 © Grundy Art Gallery, Blackpool
Fletcher, Geoffrey Scowcroft 1923–2004, *Weymouth, June 2000,* gift from the artist, 2003 © Grundy Art Gallery, Blackpool
Fletcher, Geoffrey Scowcroft 1923–2004, *Lytham,* gift from the artist, 2003 © Grundy Art Gallery, Blackpool
Fletcher, Geoffrey Scowcroft 1923–2004, *Wimereux,* gift from the artist, 2003 © Grundy Art Gallery, Blackpool
Fletcher, Geoffrey Scowcroft 1923–2004, *Arco, Lake Garda,* gift from the artist, 2003 © Grundy Art Gallery, Blackpool
Fletcher, Geoffrey Scowcroft 1923–2004, *Café Society,* gift from the artist, 2003 © Grundy Art Gallery, Blackpool
Fletcher, Geoffrey Scowcroft 1923–2004, *Calais, 2002,* gift from the artist, 2003 © Grundy Art Gallery, Blackpool
Fletcher, Geoffrey Scowcroft 1923–2004, *I paglacci Volterra,* gift from the artist, 2003 © Grundy Art Gallery, Blackpool
Fletcher, Geoffrey Scowcroft 1923–2004, *Lake Garda,* gift from the artist, 2003 © Grundy Art Gallery, Blackpool
Fletcher, Geoffrey Scowcroft 1923–2004, *Le Touquet,* gift from the artist, 2003 © Grundy Art Gallery, Blackpool
Fletcher, Geoffrey Scowcroft 1923–2004, *Llandudno, Punch and Judy,* gift from the artist, 2003 © Grundy Art Gallery, Blackpool
Fletcher, Geoffrey Scowcroft 1923–2004, *Old Timers on Prom,* gift from the artist, 2003 © Grundy Art Gallery, Blackpool
Fletcher, Geoffrey Scowcroft 1923–2004, *Ramparts, Montreuil,* gift from the artist, 2003 © Grundy Art Gallery, Blackpool
Fletcher, Geoffrey Scowcroft 1923–2004, *Still Life – Bread, Fruit and Jar,* gift from the artist, 2003 © Grundy Art Gallery, Blackpool
Fletcher, Geoffrey Scowcroft 1923–2004, *Still Life – Fruit,* gift from the artist, 2003 © Grundy Art Gallery, Blackpool
Fletcher, Geoffrey Scowcroft 1923–2004, *Still Life – Fruit,* gift from the artist, 2003 © Grundy Art Gallery, Blackpool
Fletcher, Geoffrey Scowcroft 1923–2004, *Still Life with Sheep Skull,* gift from the artist, 2003 © Grundy Art Gallery, Blackpool
Fletcher, Geoffrey Scowcroft 1923–2004, *Harlequins,* gift from the artist, 2003 © Grundy Art Gallery, Blackpool
Fletcher, Geoffrey Scowcroft 1923–2004, *Lucca,* gift from the artist, 2003 © Grundy Art Gallery, Blackpool
Fletcher, Geoffrey Scowcroft 1923–2004, *Pumpkin Field,* gift from the artist, 2003 © Grundy Art Gallery, Blackpool
Forbes, Stanhope Alexander 1857–1947, *Fading Leaf and Fallen Tree,* purchased from the Royal Academy, 1937 © the artist's estate/Bridgeman Art Library
Fowler, Robert 1853–1926, *Clean Palette,* purchased, 1928
Furini, Francesco 1603–1646, *The Martyrdom of Saint Sebastian,* acquired from G. V. Parker
Glanville, Roy 1911–1965, *The Little Tree,* purchased from the Royal Academy, 1959 © the copyright holder
Glasbury, F. H. *Sunshine and Shadow in Epping Forest,* purchased, 1946 © the copyright holder
Glindoni, Henry Gillard 1852–1913, *Frost Fair 1684,* gift from Mrs C. V. Dowarth
Goodall, Frederick 1822–1904, *Getting in the Sugar Cane, River Nile,* gift from F. W. Millington, 1926
Goodin, Walter 1907–1992, *The River Beverley,* purchased © the copyright holder
Gordon, Jerry 1955, *Batista Beach, Trinidad, 1996,* gift from the artist, 2000 © the artist
Goupil, Jules Adolphe 1839–1883, *Portrait of a Lady,* unknown acquisition method
Greenwood, Orlando 1892–1989, *The Ploughman,* acquired, 1926 © the copyright holder
Grimshaw, John Atkinson (attributed to) 1836–1893, *Liverpool Docks* (panel 1 of 5), gift from R. Bennett
Grimshaw, John Atkinson (attributed to) 1836–1893, *Liverpool Docks* (panel 2 of 5), gift from R. Bennett
Grimshaw, John Atkinson (attributed to) 1836–1893, *Liverpool Docks* (panel 3 of 5), gift from R. Bennett
Grimshaw, John Atkinson (attributed to) 1836–1893, *Liverpool Docks* (panel 4 of 5), gift from R. Bennett
Grimshaw, John Atkinson (attributed to) 1836–1893, *Liverpool Docks* (panel 5 of 5), gift from R. Bennett
Grundy, Cuthbert Cartwright 1846–1946, *Dawn,* gift from Blackpool Sketching Club © the copyright holder
Grundy, Cuthbert Cartwright 1846–1946, *The Old Millhouse, Milnthorpe,* gift from the artist © the copyright holder
Grundy, Cuthbert Cartwright 1846–1946, *View from My Window,* unknown acquisition method © the copyright holder
Grundy, Cuthbert Cartwright 1846–1946, *Throw It Again (Companions),* unknown acquisition method © the copyright holder
Grundy, John Relph Greenhow 1841–1915, *Breakers,* gift from the artist, 1911
Grundy, John Relph Greenhow 1841–1915, *Derwentwater,* gift from the artist
Grundy, John Relph Greenhow 1841–1915, *Coastal Scene with Figures,* unknown acquisition method
Grundy, John Relph Greenhow 1841–1915, *Twilight – Morecambe Bay,* unknown acquisition method
Haines, Wilfred Stanley 1905–1944, *Seventh September 1940,* purchased © the copyright holder
Hall, Frederick 1860–1948, *Homeward,* gift from J. R. G. Grundy, 1913 © the artist's estate/Bridgeman Art Library
Hall, Oliver 1869–1957, *Forest Trees,* unknown acquisition method © the artist's estate
Hargitt, Edward 1835–1895, *Marauders,* gift from Mrs W. R. Branwood, 1933
Harpignies, Henri-Joseph 1819–1916, *Rural Landscape,* bequeathed by Lionel Hewlett via the National Art Collections Fund, 1995
Herkomer, Hubert von 1849–1914, *Haymaking and Lovemaking,* gift from W. G. Bean, 1926
Herring II, John Frederick 1815–1907, *Summer,* gift from Harold Pearson, 1942
Herring II, John Frederick 1815–1907, *Landscape with Horses,* gif from Miss Stansfield, 1955
Hicks, George Elgar 1824–1914, *The Happy Mother,* unknown acquisition method
Hillingford, Robert Alexander 1825–1904, *Much Ado About Nothing,* gift from Mrs Roberts
Hipkins, W. M. *Victoriana,* bequeathed by Hilda Stanley, 1973
Holmes, Charles John 1868–1936, *Penrith Beacon,* acquired, 1949
Hornel, Edward Atkinson 1864–1933, *The Iris Pool,* gift from W. D. Halstead, 1926
Horsnell, Walter Cecil 1911–1997, *Gordale Scar,* purchased, 1945 © the copyright holder
Hossack, G. *Still Life,* gift from John Hossack © the copyright holder
Houston, George 1869–1947, *April in Ayrshire,* gift from R. Beddows, 1926 © the artist's estate
Hoyland, Francis 1930, *Requiem,* gift from the Contemporary Art Society, 1993 © the artist
Hughes, Patrick 1939, *Learning,* unknown acquisition method © DACS 2012
Hughes-Stanton, Herbert Edwin Pelham 1870–1937, *Cagnes,* purchased, 1931
Hughes-Stanton, Herbert Edwin Pelham 1870–1937, *Struggling Light,* gift from R. Harrison, Esq., 1931
Huson, Thomas 1844–1920, *View of North Pier, Blackpool, from the South West,* purchased from The Fulda Gallery, 1993
Hutchinson, Robert Gemmell 1855–1936, *Skipper and His Crew,* purchased
Hutton, Walter Charles Stritch 1871, *They See an Oread,* unknown acquisition method
Isenbart, Marie Victor Émile 1846–1921, *L'été,* gift from Alderman F. W. Millington, 1936
Jack, Richard 1866–1952, *The Quartette,* purchased © the artist's estate
John, Augustus Edwin 1878–1961, *Air Mechanic Shaw (Colonel T. E. Lawrence of Arabia, 1888–1935),* gift from H. T. de Vere-Clifton, 1939 © the artist's estate/Bridgeman Art Library
Johnston, Alexander 1815–1891, *The Pillar Box,* gift from Mrs Percy Honri, 1933
Kemp-Welch, Lucy 1869–1958, *The Waterway,* purchased, 1938 © David Messum
King, Margaret 1932, *Beach Scene, St Annes,* purchased, 1978 © the artist
Kingsley, Harry 1914–1998, *Beswick, Manchester,* gift from the artist, 1983 © the copyright holder
Kingsley, Harry 1914–1998, *Blackpool Weekend,* gift from the artist © the copyright holder
Kingsley, Harry 1914–1998, *The Immigrants, Preston, 1960,* gift from the artist, 1973 © the copyright holder
Kingsley, Harry 1914–1998, *Christmas Day, Manchester, 1971,* gift from the artist © the copyright holder
Kingsley, Harry 1914–1998, *Playmates, Bradford,* gift from the artist, 1974 © the copyright holder
Kingsley, Harry 1914–1998, *The Meeting,* gift from the artist © the copyright holder
Knight, Harold 1874–1961, *Girl Writing,* purchased from the Royal Academy, 1931 © reproduced with permission of the estate of Dame Laura Knight, DBE, RA, 2012. All rights reserved
Knight, Laura 1877–1970, *No.1 Dressing Room,* purchased from the Royal Academy, 1947 © reproduced with permission of the estate of Dame Laura Knight, DBE, RA, 2012. All rights reserved
Kowalski, Nicholas 1956, *Modern Civilisation,* gift from the artist, 1984 © the copyright holder
La Thangue, Henry Herbert 1859–1929, *Ligurian Bridle Path,* purchased, 1942

Lacok *Samuel Lawson Booth,*
Lancaster, Lilian Gardiner 1887–1973, *The Boy and the Cat,* gift from O. N. Roberts, 1933 © the artist's estate
Laugé, Achille 1861–1944, *Vignes en automne,* bequeathed by Lionel Hewlett via the National Art Collections Fund, 1995 © ADAGP, Paris and DACS, London 2012
Leader, Benjamin Williams 1831–1923, *A Summer Evening, Derwentwater,* gift from Dr E. H. Cockroft
Leader, Benjamin Williams 1831–1923, *View near Llanberis, North Wales,* purchased, 1923
Lee, Frederick Richard 1798–1879, *A Highland Stream,* gift from W. C. Turnbull, 1945
Leslie, Charles Robert 1794–1859, *At the Pool,* purchased, 1923
Lindner, Moffat Peter 1852–1949, *A Storm Cloud, Etaples,* purchased from the Royal Academy, 1929 © the artist's estate, Photo credit: Grundy Art Gallery
Linnell, John 1792–1882, *Woods and Forests,* gift from Fred Hipkins, 1958
Llewellyn, Samuel Henry William 1858–1941, *Dubrovnik (Ragusa) Harbour,* purchased from the Royal Academy, 1939
Luce, Maximilien 1858–1941, *Prairie à Eragny,* bequeathed by Lionel Hewlett via the National Art Collections Fund, 1995
Lumb, Levi active 1913–1942, *Cottage at Marton,* © the copyright holder
Lumb, Levi active 1913–1942, *Marton Mere,* unknown acquisition method © the copyright holder
Lumb, Levi active 1913–1942, *Fishing Boats,* purchased, 1945 © the copyright holder
Marshall, George 1815–1860, *Lakeland Scene,* bequeathed, 1982
Mayor, Patti 1872–1962, *Pienso,* bequeathed, 1978 © the copyright holder
Mayor, Patti 1872–1962, *Aunt Sally,* bequeathed, 1985 © the copyright holder
Mayor, Patti 1872–1962, *Black Shawl,* gift from the artist © the copyright holder
Mayor, Patti 1872–1962, *Bush by a River,* bequeathed, 1985 © the copyright holder
Mayor, Patti 1872–1962, *Florrie in a White Blouse,* bequeathed, 1985 © the copyright holder
Mayor, Patti 1872–1962, *Girl in a Green Dress,* bequeathed, 1985 © the copyright holder
Mayor, Patti 1872–1962, *Girl Sewing by a Fireside,* gift from Grundy House Museum, 1985 © the copyright holder
Mayor, Patti 1872–1962, *Girl Thinking,* bequeathed, 1985 © the copyright holder
Mayor, Patti 1872–1962, *Girl Thinking,* bequeathed, 1985 © the copyright holder
Mayor, Patti 1872–1962, *Girl with a Necklace,* gift from Grundy House Museum, 1985 © the copyright holder
Mayor, Patti 1872–1962, *Girl with a Posy,* gift from Grundy House Museum, 1985 © the copyright holder
Mayor, Patti 1872–1962, *Japanese Lady with a Fan,* gift from Grundy House Museum, 1985 © the copyright holder
Mayor, Patti 1872–1962, *Miss Kitty Ferguson,* gift from Grundy House Museum, 1985 © the copyright holder
Mayor, Patti 1872–1962, *Norah,* gift from the artist © the copyright holder
Mayor, Patti 1872–1962, *Portrait of a Gentleman with a Beard,* gift from Grundy House Museum, 1985 © the copyright holder
Mayor, Patti 1872–1962, *Portrait of a Girl,* gift from Grundy House Museum, 1985 © the copyright holder
Mayor, Patti 1872–1962, *Portrait of a Woman,* bequeathed © the copyright holder
Mayor, Patti 1872–1962, *Portrait of an Unknown Woman,* © the copyright holder
Mayor, Patti 1872–1962, *Portrait of Father,* gift from Grundy House Museum, 1985 © the copyright holder
Mayor, Patti 1872–1962, *Self Portrait,* gift from Grundy House Museum, 1985 © the copyright holder
Mayor, Patti 1872–1962, *Self Portrait,* gift from Grundy House Museum, 1985 © the copyright holder
Mayor, Patti 1872–1962, *Self Portrait,* bequeathed © the copyright holder
Mayor, Patti 1872–1962, *Self Portrait in a Sun Hat,* © the copyright holder
Mayor, Patti 1872–1962, *The Hour Glass,* gift from the artist © the copyright holder
Mayor, Patti 1872–1962, *The Red Hat,* gift from the artist © the copyright holder
Mayor, Patti 1872–1962, *Woman Thinking,* bequeathed © the copyright holder
Mayor, Patti 1872–1962, *Young Woman and Seascape,* gift from Grundy House Museum, 1985 © the copyright holder
McCormick, Arthur David 1860–1943, *Mutineers,* purchased, 1925 © the copyright holder
McGinn, Keith 1951, *The Sun Lounge,* purchased, 1982 © the artist
Meadows, James I 1798–1864, *Seascape,* gift from Mary and Marion Wild
Merriott, Jack 1901–1968, *The White Gate,* purchased, 1945 © the artist's estate
Millet, Jean-François (attributed to) 1814–1875, *Farmyard,* gift from Miss S. C. Stansfield
Mills, Reginald 1896–1966, *September Blitz,* purchased, 1942 © the copyright holder
Milne, David *Portrait of a Woman in a Fur Coat,* unknown acquisition method © the copyright holder
Modecia, J. *The Dead Bird,* purchased
Morley, Jospeph Conrad 1866–1934, *The Wreck of the 'Sirene',* gift from W. A. Webb
Mostyn, Thomas Edwin 1864–1930, *The Fleet, Torquay,* purchased, 1924
Mostyn, Thomas Edwin 1864–1930, *In Devonshire,* purchased, 1924
Murray, David 1849–1933, *The Salmon River,* purchased from the Royal Academy, 1934
Murray, David 1849–1933, *Clovelly,* gift from Edwin and Llewelyn William, and A. Cooper Carter, 1939
Neiland, Brendan 1941, *Building Projection,* gift from the Contemporary Art Society, 1988 © the artist
Niemann, W. *Boats at a Quayside,* bequeathed by Ernest Edward Cook through the Art Fund, 1955
Normann, Adelsteen 1848–1918, *Geiranger Fjord, Norway,* purchased, 1944
Okell, A. C. *Shops on Church Street,* unknown acquisition method © the copyright holder
Oliver, Alfred 1871–1947, *Fairy Dell, Capel Curig,* gift from F. Rogers © the copyright holder
Olsson, Albert Julius 1864–1942, *Waterfall in Sweden,* gift from L. H. Franceys, 1941 © the copyright holder
Olsson, Albert Julius 1864–1942, *Silver Sea,* gift from W. D. Halstead © the copyright holder
Oppenheimer, Charles 1875–1961, *Winter Landscape in Galloway,* purchased © the copyright holder
Palmer, Frederick *Variation on Goya's 'Third of May' with Garden Shadow,* purchased, 1979 © the copyright holder
Pierson, J. –2001, *Shop/Kiosk,* gift from the artist © the copyright holder
Pierson, J. –2001, *The Laughing Clown,* gift from the artist © the copyright holder
Poupard, Carol A. *St Annes Pier,* gift from Hilda Stanley, 1971 © the copyright holder
Priestman, Arnold 1854–1925, *The Deer Park, Wharfedale,* gift from W. D. Halstead
Ramsay, Patricia 1886–1974, *Coast of British Columbia,* unknown acquisition method © the artist's estate
Rasmussen, U. 1842–1914, *Hardanger Fjord, Norway,* gift from Sir Lindsay Parkinson & Company Ltd, 1926
Reed, Stanley 1908–1978, *Ingredients,* purchased, 1949 © the copyright holder
Remington, Mary 1910–2003, *The Kitchen Shelf,* purchased © the copyright holder
Ricketts, Charles S. 1866–1931, *Don Juan in Hell,* gift from G. Higgins
Roberts, David 1796–1864, *Rouen Cathedral,* gift from J. L. Walton, 1949
Roberts, David 1796–1864, *Temple Bar,* unknown acquisition method
Roe, Fred 1864–1947, *S. O. S.,* gift from Alderman John Bickerstaffe, 1929 © the artist's estate
Rose, George 1882–1955, *Breaking the Clod,* purchased, 1946 © the copyright holder
Royle, Stanley 1888–1961, *Midwinter,* gift from Councillor W. S. Ashton, 1926 © the artist's estate/Bridgeman Art Library
Sadler, Walter Dendy 1854–1923, *No Enthusiast,* purchased, 1912
Serres, Dominic 1722–1793, *View of Dover,* gift from Alderman Rhodes W. Marshall
Shayer, William 1788–1879, *Cattle,* unknown acquisition method
Shayer, William 1788–1879, *Fisherfolk,* unknown acquisition method
Simpson, Charles Walter 1885–1971, *The Pet Goat,* purchased, 1924 © the artist's estate, Photo Credit: Grundy Art Gallery
Smith, David T. 1920, *The Harbour Entrance,* purchased, 1946 © the copyright holder
Somerville, Howard 1873–1952, *Nigel, a Zulu,* purchased, 1930 © the copyright holder
Somerville, Howard 1873–1952, *Laurita,* gift from Miss M. Adamson, 1953 © the copyright holder
Speed, Harold 1872–1957, *The Labourer's Wife,* purchased, 1937 © the copyright holder
Spencelayh, Charles 1865–1958, *The Laughing Parson,* purchased, 1935 © the artist's estate/Bridgeman Art Library
Spencelayh, Charles 1865–1958 *It's War,* purchased, 1942 © the artist's estate/Bridgeman Art Library
Spooner, Arthur 1873–1962, *Freshwater Bay,* purchased, 1945 © the artist's estate/Bridgeman Art Library
Stanfield, George Clarkson 1828–1878, *Anglers on Lake Maggiore,* unknown acquisition method
Strutt, Alfred William 1856–1924, *A Sporting Offer,* purchased, 1913
Tafani, Emilio C. L. 1885–1963, *Demonstration in Dissection,* purchased, 1945 © the copyright holder
Talmage, Algernon 1871–1939, *The Western Sky,* purchased, 1926
Thors, Joseph 1835–1920, *The Forest of Fontainbleu,* unknown acquisition method
Tol, Dominicus van 1635–1676, *A Philosopher,* gift from Alderman Smith, 1913
Tuke, Henry Scott 1858–1929, *The Green Waterways,* purchased, 1932, Photo Credit: Grundy Art Gallery
unknown artist *Richard Rossall,* gift from Grundy House Museum
unknown artist *Coxswain R. Bickerstaffe*
unknown artist *Dr Cocker,* unknown acquisition method
Verboeckhoven, Eugène Joseph 1798–1881, *Sheep,* gift from W. C. Turnbull, 1946
Vertin, Petrus Gerardus 1819–1893, *Haarlem, Holland,* acquired from R. Bennett
Wadham, Benjamin Brassett 1816–1904, *Child with a Drum,* gift from Grundy House Museum, 1985
Ward, Beryl *Bootskooters,* gift from the artist © the copyright holder
Wasley, Frank 1848–1934, *Near the Port,* unknown acquisition method
Watkinson, Bob 1914–1992, *Ribbon Development,* bequeathed by Hilda Stanley, 1972 © the copyright holder
Watson, Harry 1871–1936, *Saturday,* purchased, 1930
Webb, James 1825–1895, *Moorland Scene,* gift from A. Skinner
Webb, James 1825–1895, *Scene with a Windmill,* gift from A. Skinner
Webster, Walter Ernest 1877–1959, *The Golden Age,* purchased, 1948 © the copyright holder
Welsh, John *Piazza San Marco,* purchased from the Royal Academy, 1963 © the copyright holder
Whaite, Henry Clarence 1828–1912, *Harvest, North Wales,* gift from Cuthbert Grundy
William (senior), Edward Charles 1807–1881, *A View of Norfolk,* unknown acquisition method
Williams, Terrick John 1860–1936, *Morning, Locarno,* gift from James Wood, 1926
Wishart, John Michael 1928–1996, *Lac d'Annecy,* gift from the Contemporary Art Society © the artist's estate
Withers, Alfred 1856–1932, *Old Market Place, Vaison,* purchased, 1929
Wood, Elizabeth 1930, *Patrica Seed (d.1978), MBE,* gift from the artist, 1979 © the artist
Wood, Elizabeth 1930, *Portrait Study,* gift from the artist © the artist
Wood, William Thomas 1877–1958, *April Weather,* purchased, 1944 © the copyright holder
Woods, Albert 1871–1944, *Fylde Mill,* purchased © the copyright holder
Young, Lesley 1942, *Blackpool, November,* purchased, 1989 © the artist

Turton Tower

Clunne-Lees, William 1860–1946, *Samuel Crompton (1753–1827),* transferred from North Turton Parish Council, 2011 © the copyright holder
Duke, Alfred 1836–1915, *Feeding Time at Holcombe Kennels,* transferred from North Turton Parish Council, 2011
Duke, Alfred 1836–1915, *The Holcombe Harriers,* transferred from North Turton Parish Council, 2011
Fisher, Mark 1841–1923, *Sheep Returning from the Fold,* on loan from Blackburn Museum and Art Gallery
Friedenson, Arthur A. 1872–1955, *Clouds of the West,* on loan from Blackburn Museum and Art Gallery © the artist's estate
Griset, Ernest Henri 1844–1907, *Neanderthal Man*
Hayes, Frederick William 1848–1918, *Nant Bridge, Caernarvonshire,* on loan from Towneley Hall Art Gallery and Museums, Burnley
Huson, Thomas 1844–1920, *A Wild Day at the South Stack,* transferred from North Turton Parish Council, 2011
Huson, Thomas 1844–1920, *Coastal Scene,* transferred from North Turton Parish Council, 2011
Huson, Thomas 1844–1920, *Haytime in Anglesey,* transferred from North Turton Parish Council, 2011
Huson, Thomas 1844–1920, *Lake District Scene*
Kneller, Godfrey 1646–1723, *Lady Mary Wortley Montagu (1689–1762),* on loan from Blackburn Museum and Art Gallery
Linton, William 1791–1876, *The Eagley Valley and Birtenshaw Hall,* transferred from North Turton Parish Council, 2011
Richardson the elder, Jonathan 1664–1745, *Portrait of a Gentleman,* (traditionally identified as Samuel Chetham), purchased at Christie's jointly by Blackburn Museum and Art Gallery and Lancashire Museum Service; on loan from Blackburn Museum and Art Gallery
Stark, James 1794–1859, *A View from Norwich,* on loan from Towneley Hall Art Gallery and Museums, Burnley
Topham, Francis Williams 1808–1877, *At the Well,* on loan from Blackburn Museum and Art Gallery
unknown artist *A Bird in a Tree,* transferred from North Turton Parish Council, 2011
unknown artist *A Female Relaxing under a Tree,* transferred from North Turton Parish Council, 2011
unknown artist *Alexander Barlow,* on loan from Blackburn Museum and Art Gallery
unknown artist *Bradshaw Chapel,* transferred from North Turton Parish Council, 2011
unknown artist *Elizabeth Horrocks,* transferred from North Turton Parish Council, 2011
unknown artist *Figures in Sixteenth-Century Costume,* transferred from North Turton Parish Council, 2011
unknown artist *German Heraldic Piece with Three Figures,* transferred from North Turton Parish Council, 2011
unknown artist *James Knowles,* transferred from North Turton Parish Council, 2011
unknown artist *Jane Kay,* transferred from North Turton Parish Council, 2011
unknown artist *Lady Holding a Small Red Book,* transferred from North Turton Parish Council, 2011
unknown artist *Little Red Riding Hood*
unknown artist *Man with a Violin,* transferred from North Turton Parish Council, 2011
unknown artist *Mountain and Lake with Two Figures,* transferred from North Turton Parish Council, 2011
unknown artist *Mrs Knowles,* transferred from North Turton Parish Council, 2011
unknown artist *Portrait of a Gentleman* (thought to be either Edmund Ashworth or James Barlow), transferred from North Turton Parish Council, 2011
unknown artist *Portrait of a Gentleman* (possibly Samuel Crompton (1753–1827) as an Old Man), transferred from North Turton Parish Council, 2011
unknown artist *Portrait of a Gentleman with a Wig,* transferred from North Turton Parish Council, 2011
unknown artist *Portrait of a Lady with a Fancy Bonnet* (possibly Mrs A. Trimble), transferred from North Turton Parish Council, 2011
unknown artist *Stephen Blair,* transferred from North Turton Parish Council, 2011
unknown artist *The Death Mask of Charles I*
unknown artist *The Letter,* on loan from Blackburn Museum and Art Gallery
unknown artist *Thomas Deacon,* transferred from North Turton Parish Council, 2011
unknown artist *View of Turton Tower from the East,* transferred from North Turton Parish Council, 2011
unknown artist *William Horrocks,* transferred from North Turton Parish Council, 2011
Verelst, Maria 1680–1744, *Portrait of a Lady* (traditionally identified as Mary Chetham), purchased at Christie's jointly by Blackburn Museum and Art Gallery and Lancashire Museum Service; on loan from Blackburn Museum and Art Gallery

Towneley Hall Art Gallery & Museum

Adamson, Dorothy 1894–1934, *Going to Pasture,* purchased by Burnley Corporation with the assistance of funds from the Edward Stocks Massey Bequest, 1933
Alma-Tadema, Lawrence 1836–1912, *The Picture Gallery,* purchased by Burnley Corporation with the assistance of the Caleb Thornber Bequest, 1925, Photo Credit: Bridgeman Art Library
Amato, Gennaro d' 1857–1947, *Queen Victoria's Diamond Jubilee,* purchased by Burnley Corporation, 1905 © the copyright holder, Photo Credit: Bridgeman Art Library
Andreotti, Federico 1847–1930, *The Introduction,* purchased by Burnley Corporation with the assistance of funds from the Edward Stocks Massey Bequest, 1949
Ansdell, Richard 1815–1885, *Ferreting,* gift from Mrs Phillips, 1955
Austerberry, Stocks 1842–1899, *Tattersall's Dwellings,* purchased by Burnley Corporation, 1911
Austerberry, Stocks 1842–1899, *Extwistle Hall,* purchased by Burnley Corporation, 1911
Austerberry, Stocks 1842–1899, *Market Cross and Old Sparrow Hawk, Burnley,* purchased by Burnley Corporation, 1911
Balshaw, Fred 1860–1936, *James Holmes,* transferred from Burnley Central Library, 1972
Barker, Thomas 1769–1847, *Landscape with Figures and Cattle,* purchased by Burnley Corporation with the assistance of funds from the Edward Stocks Massey Bequest, 1953
Barma, Hans Smatlak 1903–1978, *The Dolomites Sunset,* purchased by Burnley Corporation with the assistance of funds from the Edward Stocks Massey Bequest, 1952 © the copyright holder
Barmelov, A de. *Lucy Ellen Towneley (c.1818–1900),* gift from Mrs Denham Parker, 1955
Barnes, Archibald George 1887–1972, *Portrait of a Young Lady,* gift from Simon Towneley, 1973 © the copyright holder, Photo Credit: Bridgeman Art Library
Barraud, Henry 1811–1874, *Towneley Pedigrees,* gift from an unknown donor, before 1972, Photo Credit: Bridgeman Art Library
Barret the elder, George 1728–1784, *A Distant View of Towneley Hall,* purchased by Burnley Corporation with the assistance of funds from the Edward Stocks Massey Bequest, 1939
Bassano family active 16th C–17th C, *Moses Striking the Rock,* transferred from Padiham Museum, 1977
Bates, David F. *Old Cruck Building,* purchased by Burnley Borough Council with the assistance of funds from the Edward Stocks Massey Bequest, 1974 © the copyright holder
Beechey, William 1753–1839, *The Honourable Mrs W. Noel,* purchased by Burnley Corporation with the assistance of funds from the Edward Stocks Massey Bequest and the Victoria and Albert Museum Purchase Grant Fund, 1961
Bijlert, Jan van 1597–1671, *Shepherd and Sleeping Girl,* transferred from Padiham Museum, 1977
Bilders, Johannes Wernardus 1811–1890, *A Dutch Landscape,* gift from Mr J. S. Collinge, 1910
Bird, Archibald 1885–1975, *River Scene,* gift from an unknown donor, before 1973 © the copyright holder
Blackburn, Arthur 1853–1925, *Haymaking Scene,* transferred from Padiham Museum, 1977
Boddington, Henry John 1811–1865, *The Calm before the Storm,* purchased by Burnley Corporation with the assistance of funds from the Edward Stocks Massey Bequest, 1949
Bonner, Lonsdale b.1926, *Pilling Marshes,* purchased by Burnley Borough Council with the assistance of funds from the Edward Stocks Massey Bequest, 1974 © the copyright holder
Bownass, Robin Ernest b.1938, *Scrap at the Base of Slag Heap,* purchased by Burnley Borough Council with the assistance of funds from the Edward Stocks Massey Bequest, 1974 © the artist
Bownass, Robin Ernest b.1938, *Scrap at the Base of Slag Heap,* gift from the artist, 1974 © the artist
Brannan, Peter 1926–1994, *Edna Ascroft (d.c.1988),* bequeathed by the sitter, 1988 © the artist's estate
Brannan, Peter 1926–1994, *Frank Ascroft,* bequeathed by Mrs Edna Ascroft, 1988 © the artist's estate
Bratby, John Randall 1928–1992, *Sailboat in the Artist's Studio,* purchased by Burnley Corporation with the assistance of funds from the Edward Stocks Massey Bequest, 1971 © the artist's estate/ Bridgeman Art Library
Bristow, Edmund 1787–1876, *The End of the Chapter,* gift from Mr F. J. Nettlefold, 1948, Photo Credit: Bridgeman Art Library
Bristow, Edmund 1787–1876, *Mischief,* purchased by Burnley Corporation with the assistance of funds from the Edward Stocks Massey Bequest, 1937
British (English) School *The Strachey Family,* on loan from the Strachey Family
Brown, William Beattie 1831–1909, *Landscape with Castle,* transferred from Padiham Museum, 1977
Brundrit, Reginald Grange 1883–1960, *The Wooded Vale,* purchased by Burnley Corporation with the assistance of funds from the Edward Stocks Massey Bequest, 1933 © the copyright holder
Brunery, Francesco 1845–1926, *I Will,* purchased by Burnley Corporation with the assistance of funds from the Edward Stocks Massey Bequest, 1953, Photo Credit: Bridgeman Art Library
Brussel, Paul Theodor van 1754–1795, *Fruit and Flowers on a Marble Table,* purchased by Burnley Corporation with the assistance of funds from the Edward Stocks Massey Bequest, 1938
Bundy, Edgar 1862–1922, *Stradivarius in His Workshop at Cremona,* purchased by Burnley Corporation with the assistance of funds from the Edward Stocks Massey Bequest, 1923, Photo Credit: Bridgeman Art Library
Burgess, John Bagnold 1829–1897, *A Little Spanish Gipsy,* purchased by Burnley Corporation with the assistance of funds from the Edward Stocks Massey Bequest, 1958
Burne-Jones, Edward 1833–1898, *Wood Nymphs,* gift from Viscount Leverhulme, 1922
Buttersworth, James Edward 1817–1894, *Seascape,* gift from Mr F. Tuck, 1938
Callcott, Augustus Wall 1779–1844, *The Temple of Aesculapius,* gift from Maurice, 3rd Lord O'Hagan, and Lady O'Hagan
Carney, W. D. *Centenary Statue, Burnley,* transferred from Burnley Central Library, 1972 © the copyright holder
Carracci, Ludovico (after) 1555–1619, *Christ and the Woman of Canaan,* gift from Lady O'Hagan, 1903
Cawthorne, E. active late 19th C, *Autumn on the Ribble,* gift from Thomas Holt, 1949
Clarke, George Frederick 1823–1906, *Lady Caroline Towneley with Two of Her Daughters, Caroline and Emily* (copy after Francis Grant), gift from Kathleen de Beaumont, 1936
Cobbett, Edward John 1815–1899, *Girl with a Basket of Apples,* gift from H. Sherman, 1951
Cole, George Vicat 1833–1893, *Iffley Mill,* purchased by Burnley Corporation with the assistance of funds from the Edward Stocks Massey Bequest, 1930, Photo Credit: Bridgeman Art Library
Colkett, Samuel David 1806–1863, *A Scene in Norfolk,* purchased by Burnley Corporation with the

assistance of funds from the Edward Stocks Massey Bequest, 1935
Collins II, Charles 1851–1921, *In the Nower, Dorking,* gift from Mr F. J. Nettlefold, 1948
Collinson, Brian *Old Railway Arches, Burnley,* gift from the artist, 1970 © the copyright holder
Constable, John (style of) 1776–1837, *The Gathering Storm,* purchased by Burnley Corporation with the assistance of funds from the Edward Stocks Massey Bequest, 1952
Cooke, Isaac 1846–1922, *2nd Lieutenant Alfred Victor Smith (1891–1915), VC,* purchased by Burnley Corporation with the assistance of funds from public subscription, 1916
Cooke, Isaac 1846–1922, *Private Thomas Whitham (1888–1924), VC,* purchased by Burnley Corporation with the assistance of funds from public subscription, 1919
Cookesley, Margaret Deborah 1844–1927, *The Gambler's Wife,* purchased by Burnley Corporation, 1905
Cooper, Thomas Sidney 1803–1902, *A Summer Afternoon,* purchased by Burnley Corporation, 1909
Cooper, Thomas Sidney 1803–1902, *Evening in the Meadows,* gift from Miss Mosdale, 1970
Cooper, Thomas Sidney 1803–1902, *The Watering Place,* gift from Mrs W. H. Burrows, 1948
Cosway, Richard 1742–1821, *Group of Connoisseurs,* purchased by Burnley Corporation with the assistance of funds from the Edward Stocks Massey Bequest, 1956, Photo Credit: Bridgeman Art Library
Cot, Pierre Auguste (after) 1837–1883, *Le printemps,* transferred from Padiham Museum, 1977
Cox the elder, David 1783–1859, *The Vale of Clwyd,* purchased by Burnley Corporation with the assistance of funds from the Edward Stocks Massey Bequest, 1934, Photo Credit: Bridgeman Art Library
Cox the elder, David 1783–1859, *Haymaking on Snowdon,* bequeathed by Mr Rhoderick MacDonald, 1942, Photo Credit: Bridgeman Art Library
Crabtree, Joseph active 1941–1950, *A View of Towneley Stables,* purchased by Burnley Corporation with the assistance of funds from the Edward Stocks Massey Bequest, 1950 © the copyright holder
Crabtree, Joseph active 1941–1950, *Durham,* purchased by Burnley Corporation with the assistance of funds from the Edward Stocks Massey Bequest, 1950 © the copyright holder
Crabtree, Joseph active 1941–1950, *St Ives,* purchased by Burnley Corporation with the assistance of funds from the Edward Stocks Massey Bequest, 1950 © the copyright holder
Crofts, Ernest 1847–1911, *Cromwell after the Battle of Marston Moor,* purchased by Burnley Corporation, 1912, Photo Credit: Bridgeman Art Library
Cuba, Ivan 1920–2007, *Towneley Hall,* gift from the artist, 1955 © the copyright holder
Cuming, Frederick b.1930, *The Studio,* gift from the S. I. V. Cooke Fund, 1982 the artist/Bridgeman Art Library
D'Oyly-John, Cecil Rochfort 1906–1993, *Café Vins, South of France,* purchased by Burnley Corporation with the assistance of funds from the Edward Stocks Massey Bequest, 1952 © the copyright holder
Daubigny, Charles-François 1817–1878, *River Scene at Sunset,* purchased by Burnley Corporation with the assistance of funds from the Edward Stocks Massey Bequest, 1945
Daubigny, Charles-François 1817–1878, *Sunset on the Sea Coast,* purchased by Burnley Corporation with the assistance of funds from the Edward Stocks Massey Bequest, 1944, Photo Credit: Bridgeman Art Library
Dawson, Ida b.1931, *Market Hall, Burnley,* gift from Burnley and Pendle Hospice, 1999 © the copyright holder
De Lacy, Charles John 1856–1936, *London Bridge,* transferred from Burnley Central Library, 1972, Photo Credit: Bridgeman Art Library
De Wint, Peter 1784–1849, *A Watermill near Egglestone Abbey, Durham,* gift from Mr W. Dean, 1935
De Wint, Peter 1784–1849, *Cilgerran Castle,* purchased by Burnley Corporation with the assistance of funds from the Edward Stocks Massey Bequest, 1937
Diaz de la Peña, Narcisse Virgile 1807–1876, *Four Nymphs in a Wood,* purchased by Burnley Corporation with the assistance of funds from the Edward Stocks Massey Bequest, 1945
Dicksee, Frank 1853–1928, *Harmony,* purchased by Burnley Corporation with the assistance of funds from the Edward Stocks Massey Bequest, 1949
Dods-Withers, Isobelle Ann 1876–1939, *The White House,* gift from Mr John Tattersall, 1925
Duke, Alfred 1836–1915, *Hesitation,* gift from Miss Thompson, 1975, Photo Credit: Bridgeman Art Library
Earp, Henry 1831–1914, *Canterbury Cathedral,* gift from Muriel Barker, 2009
Earp, Henry 1831–1914, *Salisbury Cathedral,* gift from Muriel Barker, 2009
Echtler, Adolf 1843–1914, *St Mark's, Venice,* purchased by Burnley Corporation with the assistance of funds from the Edward Stocks Massey Bequest, 1950, Photo Credit: Bridgeman Art Library
Etty, William 1787–1849, *Standing Female Nude,* purchased by Burnley Corporation with the assistance of funds from the Edward Stocks Massey Bequest, 1945, Photo Credit: Bridgeman Art Library
Etty, William 1787–1849, *Standing Male Nude,* purchased by Burnley Corporation with the assistance of funds from the Edward Stocks Massey Bequest, 1953, Photo Credit: Bridgeman Art Library
Fantin-Latour, Henri (style of) 1836–1904, *Flowers in a Vase,* purchased by Burnley Corporation with the assistance of funds from the Edward Stocks Massey Bequest, 1945
Farquharson, Joseph 1846–1935, *The Sun Had Closed the Winter's Day,* gift from Mr J. Thornber, 1925, Photo Credit: Bridgeman Art Library
Farquharson, Joseph 1846–1935, *Now Came Still Evening On,* gift from Mrs F. Thornber, 1938
Farquharson, Joseph 1846–1935, *The Sun Fast Sinks in the West,* gift from Mr James Lancaster, 1920
Flemish School *The Crucifixion,* gift from Maurice, 3rd Lord O'Hagan, 1926
Flemish School *Saint Matthew, One of the Four Evangelists,* gift from Lady O'Hagan, 1903
Flemish School *Saint John, One of the Four Evangelists,* gift from Lady O'Hagan, 1903
Flemish School *Saint Luke, One of the Four Evangelists,* gift from Lady O'Hagan, 1903
Flemish School *Saint Mark, One of the Four Evangelists,* gift from Lady O'Hagan, 1903
Fryer, William active 19th C, *Seascape,* transferred from Burnley Central Library, 1972
Gheeraerts the younger, Marcus (style of) 1561–1636, *Portrait of a Lady,* purchased by Burnley Corporation with the assistance of funds from the Edward Stocks Massey Bequest, 1953
Gilbert, John 1817–1897, *Rembrandt in His Studio,* gift from Mr Ward Mosedale, 1936, Photo Credit: Bridgeman Art Library
Girard, Paul-Albert 1839–1920, *Moorish Courtyard,* purchased by Burnley Corporation with the assistance of funds from the Edward Stocks Massey Bequest, 1953, Photo Credit: Bridgeman Art Library
Glehn, Wilfrid Gabriel de 1870–1951, *Clare,* purchased by Burnley Corporation with the assistance of funds from the Edward Stocks Massey Bequest, 1933 © Towneley Art Gallery and Museums
Goodall, Frederick 1822–1904, *The Blind Beggar,* purchased by Burnley Corporation, 1904
Graham, Peter 1836–1921, *The Fowlers Crag,* bequeathed by Sir J. O. S. Thursby, 1920, Photo Credit: Bridgeman Art Library
Graham, Peter 1836–1921, *The Head of the Glen,* purchased by Burnley Corporation with the assistance of funds from the William Collinge Bequest, 1911
Graham, Peter 1836–1921, *A Mountain Burn,* gift from an unknown donor, before 1973
Greenwood, Orlando 1892–1989, *The Lady in Black,* purchased by Burnley Corporation with the assistance of funds from the Edward Stocks Massey Bequest, 1945 © the copyright holder
Greenwood, Orlando 1892–1989, *April: Farmer with Bull,* purchased by Burnley Borough Council with the assistance of funds from the Edward Stocks Massey Bequest, 2001 © the copyright holder
Greenwood, Orlando 1892–1989, *Flowers on a Windowsill,* purchased by Burnley Borough Council with the assistance of funds from the Edward Stocks Massey Bequest, 1994 © the copyright holder
Greenwood, Orlando 1892–1989, *Pendle,* purchased by Burnley Borough Council with the assistance of funds from the Edward Stocks Massey Bequest, 1990 © the copyright holder
Greenwood, Orlando 1892–1989, *Portrait of the Artist's Mother,* gift from Mrs Ina Greenwood, 2003 © the copyright holder
Greenwood, Orlando 1892–1989, *Self Portrait,* purchased by Burnley Borough Council with the assistance of funds from the Edward Stocks Massey Bequest, 1990 © the copyright holder
Gresty, Hugh 1899–1958, *Andalusian Village,* purchased by Burnley Borough Council with the assistance of funds from the Edward Stocks Massey Bequest, 1987 © the copyright holder, Photo Credit: Bridgeman Art Library
Gresty, Hugh 1899–1958, *Gothic Suite, Bruges,* gift from Mrs Elizabeth Gresty, 1964 © the copyright holder
Gresty, Hugh 1899–1958, *The Alcántara, Toledo,* gift from Mrs Elizabeth Gresty, 1964 © the copyright holder
Gresty, Hugh 1899–1958, *Woman at a Well,* gift from Mrs Elizabeth Gresty, 1964 © the copyright holder
Grimshaw, Thomas active 1920–1930, *A River Scene,* gift from Miss Browne, 1960 © the copyright holder
Grimshaw, Thomas active 1920–1930, *The Needles, Isle of Wight,* gift from Miss Browne, 1960 © the copyright holder
Hall, Harry 1814–1896, *'Kettledrum',* gift from Lady O'Hagan, 1915, Photo Credit: Bridgeman Art Library
Hallé, Charles Edward 1846–1919, *'Sic transit gloria mundi',* gift from St John's Ambulance, Nelson Branch, 1949
Hamerton, Philip Gilbert 1834–1894, *Sens from the Vineyards,* gift from Mrs Robert Handsley, 1903
Hamerton, Philip Gilbert 1834–1894, *The River Yonne,* gift from Mrs Robert Handsley, 1903
Hardy, Frederick Daniel 1827–1911, *Early Sorrow,* bequeathed by Mr Amos Preston, 1943, Photo Credit: Bridgeman Art Library
Hardy, Heywood 1842–1933, *A Refresher at the 'Dragon',* gift from Miss Mosdale, 1970
Hardy, Heywood 1842–1933, *The Meet, 'Ye Olde Wayside Inn',* gift from Miss Mosdale, 1970
Hardy, Heywood 1842–1933, *The Two Roses,* gift from Miss Mosdale, 1970, Photo Credit: Bridgeman Art Library
Harvey, Harold C. 1874–1941, *The Little Farm,* gift from an unknown donor, before 1973
Hemy, Charles Napier 1841–1917, *Crabbers Bait,* purchased by Burnley Corporation, 1913, Photo Credit: Bridgeman Art Library
Herring I, John Frederick 1795–1865, *Roundheads at an Arundel Church,* purchased by Burnley Corporation with the assistance of funds from the Edward Stocks Massey Bequest, 1949, Photo Credit: Bridgeman Art Library
Herring I, John Frederick 1795–1865, *The Midday Meal,* purchased by Burnley Corporation with the assistance of funds from the Edward Stocks Massey Bequest, 1931
Hickson, Charles C. b.1957, *Urban Intersection (Blue),* purchased by Burnley Borough Council with the assistance of funds from the Edward Stocks Massey Bequest, 1990 © the artist
Hickson, Charles C. b.1957, *Private Pathway,* purchased by Burnley Borough Council with the assistance of funds from the Edward Stocks Massey Bequest, 1990 © the artist
Hilton, Colin Clough 1902–1984, *Whitby Harbour,* purchased by Burnley Corporation with the assistance of funds from the Edward Stocks Massey Bequest, 1964 © the copyright holder
Hilton, Colin Clough 1902–1984, *Woodland Scene, Burnham Beeches,* purchased by Burnley Corporation with the assistance of funds from the Edward Stocks Massey Bequest, 1964 © the copyright holder

Hodges, J. Sidney Willis 1829–1900, *William Thompson in Mayoral Chain,* gift from Miss Thompson, 1975
Hodges, J. Sidney Willis 1829–1900, *Cornelius M. Foden,* transferred from Burnley Central Library, 1972
Hodges, J. Sidney Willis 1829–1900, *Henry Houlding,* gift from The Houlding Testimonial Committee, 1903
Hogley, Stephen Enoch 1842–1927, *Landscape,* gift from Miss C. M. Gill, 1932
Hoog, Bernard de 1867–1943, *A Dutch Interior,* purchased by Burnley Corporation with the assistance of funds from the Edward Stocks Massey Bequest, 1927 © the copyright holder
Hoog, Bernard de 1867–1943, *Morning,* gift from Mr C. M. Foden, 1913 © the copyright holder
Hopley, Edward William John 1816–1869, *Mariamne, Wife of King Herod, and Her Children going to Their Execution,* gift from Mr W. Dean, 1928
Houston, Robert 1891–1940, *The Shores of the Clyde,* purchased by Burnley Corporation with the assistance of funds from the Edward Stocks Massey Bequest, 1933
Hudson, Thomas 1701–1779, *Sir Henry Oxenden (1721–1804),* purchased by Burnley Corporation with the assistance of funds from the Edward Stocks Massey Bequest, 1952
Hulk I, Abraham 1813–1897, *Shipping Becalmed,* gift from G. Eastwood, 1951
Hulk I, Abraham 1813–1897, *Shipping in a Breeze,* gift from G. Eastwood, 1951
Husník, Jakub 1837–1916, *The Holy Family,* (after Peter Paul Rubens), gift from an unknown donor, before 1969
Ibbetson, Julius Caesar 1759–1817, *A Scene in the Lake District,* gift from Mr F. Tuck, 1938
Jacque, Charles Émile 1813–1894, *Breton Lad with Cattle,* purchased by Burnley Corporation with the assistance of funds from the Edward Stocks Massey Bequest, 1945
Japp, Darsie 1883–1973, *In Dentdale,* gift from the Contemporary Art Society, 1924 © the copyright holder
Johnson, George Frederick Waldo 1862–1917, *Shore Scene with Horses,* transferred from Padiham Museum, 1977
Johnston, Alexander 1815–1891, *Scottish Interior,* transferred from Padiham Museum, 1977
Jonghe, Jan Baptiste de 1785–1844, *The Ferry,* purchased by Burnley Corporation with the assistance of funds from the Edward Stocks Massey Bequest, 1951
Kay, James active 19th C, *Ebenezer Chapel, Colne Road, c.1840,* gift from Mrs J. K. Baldwin, 1952
Kernik, W. active 1904, *Entrance to Towneley Holmes, with Cattle,* gift from an unknown donor, before 1973
Kershaw, Walter b.1940, *Nude in a Polythene Interior,* purchased by Burnley Corporation with the assistance of funds from the Edward Stocks Massey Bequest, 1971 © the artist
Knight, Paul active 1883–1904, *Grandmother,* gift from Mrs P. Oldman, 1951, Photo Credit: Bridgeman Art Library
Knight, Paul active 1883–1904, *The Sewing Girl,* gift from Mrs P. Oldman, 1951
Ladbrooke, John Berney 1803–1879, *A Country Lane in Norfolk,* purchased by Burnley Corporation with the assistance of funds from the Edward Stocks Massey Bequest, 1936
Ladbrooke, Robert 1770–1842, *The Old Farmstead,* purchased by Burnley Corporation with the assistance of funds from the Edward Stocks Massey Bequest, 1936
Lancaster, Percy 1878–1951, *The Seashore,* purchased by Burnley Corporation with the assistance of funds from the Edward Stocks Massey Bequest, 1952 © the copyright holder
Landseer, Edwin Henry 1802–1873, *A Saluki Dog,* gift from Mr W. Dean, 1927, Photo Credit: Bridgeman Art Library
Landseer, Edwin Henry (style of) 1802–1873, *Young Girl with a Dog,* purchased by Burnley Corporation with the assistance of funds from the Edward Stocks Massey Bequest, 1951
Lavery, John 1856–1941, *The River Pageant, as Seen from the Home of Sir James Barries, Adelphi Terrace, London, 4 August 1919,* purchased by Burnley Corporation with the assistance of funds from the Edward Stocks Massey Bequest, 1951
Le Jeune, Henry 1819–1904, *Evangeline,* bequeathed by Messrs Lancaster & Parkinson, Photo Credit: Bridgeman Art Library
Leader, Benjamin Williams 1831–1923, *By Mead and Stream,* purchased by Burnley Corporation, 1911, Photo Credit: Bridgeman Art Library
Leighton, Edmund Blair 1852–1922, *How Liza Loved the King,* purchased by Burnley Corporation with the assistance of funds from the Edward Stocks Massey Bequest, 1921, Photo Credit: Bridgeman Art Library
Lely, Peter 1618–1680, *Sir William Ashburnham,* purchased by Burnley Corporation with the assistance of funds from the Edward Stocks Massey Bequest, 1956
Lépine, Stanislas 1835–1892, *River Scene,* purchased by Burnley Corporation with the assistance of funds from the Edward Stocks Massey Bequest, 1944
Levin, Phoebus 1836–1908, *Life in the Hop Garden,* purchased by Burnley Corporation with the assistance of funds from the Edward Stocks Massey Bequest, 1951
Lewin, Stephen Samuel 1848–1909, *The Lost Chord,* gift from Miss Thompson, 1975, Photo Credit: Bridgeman Art Library
Lhermitte, Léon-Augustin 1844–1925, *The Midday Meal,* purchased by Burnley Corporation with the assistance of funds from the Edward Stocks Massey Bequest, 1955, Photo Credit: Bridgeman Art Library
Linnell, John 1792–1882, *The Hastings Coast,* purchased by Burnley Corporation with the assistance of funds from the Edward Stocks Massey Bequest, 1948
Linnell, John 1792–1882, *Pointing Out the Way,* purchased by Burnley Corporation with the assistance of funds from the Edward Stocks Massey Bequest, 1921
Long, Edwin 1829–1891, *The Gods and Their Makers,* purchased by Burnley Corporation with the assistance of funds from the Edward Stocks Massey Bequest, 1952, Photo Credit: Bridgeman Art Library
Lord, Albert 1938–2000, *Bank Hall Colliery, 1962,* gift from Mr E. Tattersall, 2007 © the copyright holder
Lucas, John Seymour 1849–1923, *Vanity,* gift from Mrs P. Oldman, 1951
Lynch, Francis 1866–1932, *Tattersall Wilkinson,* purchased by Burnley Corporation with the assistance of funds from the Edward Stocks Massey Bequest, 1984
Lynch, Francis 1866–1932, *Fred Myers,* purchased by Burnley Corporation with the assistance of funds from public subscription, 1930
Mackenzie, Daniel N. active late 19th C, *Extensive Landscape with Stonemason,* gift from an unknown donor, before 1973
MacWhirter, John 1839–1911, *Autumn, Strathglass, Invernesshire,* gift from Mr N. Parkinson, 1946
MacWhirter, John 1839–1911, *The Waters of Glen Affric,* purchased by Burnley Corporation, 1907
Marston, Edith Floyd 1904–1988, *Vanessa Henderson,* bequeathed by the artist, 1988 © the copyright holder
Meadows, Arthur Joseph 1843–1907, *Carnes,* purchased by Burnley Corporation with the assistance of funds from the Edward Stocks Massey Bequest, 1927, Photo Credit: Bridgeman Art Library
Mellor, William 1851–1931, *A River Scene with Anglers,* gift from Mr Brooks, 1950
Monnoyer, Jean-Baptiste 1636–1699, *Flowers in a Sculptured Vase,* purchased by Burnley Corporation with the assistance of funds from the Edward Stocks Massey Bequest, 1939
Moore, Henry 1831–1895, *A Breezy Day off the Isle of Wight,* purchased by Burnley Corporation, 1913
Morgan, Frederick 1856–1927, *Ring-a-Ring-a-Roses-Oh,* purchased by Burnley Corporation, 1914, Photo Credit: Bridgeman Art Library
Morland, George 1763–1804, *A Rustic Cottage,* purchased by Burnley Corporation with the assistance of funds from the Edward Stocks Massey Bequest, 1943
Moroni, Giovanni Battista (after) 1525–1578, *Locollo Souardi,* purchased by Burnley Corporation with the assistance of funds from the Edward Stocks Massey Bequest, 1952
Morris, Philip Richard 1836–1902, *Portrait of a Lady in a Green Jacket,* gift from Mr W. Dean, 1928
Mostyn, Thomas Edwin 1864–1930, *Garden of Love,* purchased by Burnley Corporation with the assistance of funds from the Edward Stocks Massey Bequest, 1926
Muller, William James 1812–1845, *Wooded Landscape with Children,* purchased by Burnley Corporation with the assistance of funds from the Edward Stocks Massey Bequest, 1945
Murray, David 1849–1933, *River and Rail,* gift from the executors of the will of Sir David Murray, 1939
Naudé, Pieter Hugo 1869–1941, *Dr Brown,* gift from Mrs Naude, 1925
Niemann, Edmund John 1813–1876, *Penmaenmawr,* purchased by Burnley Corporation, 1907
Niemann, Edmund John 1813–1876, *Stapleton,* purchased by Burnley Corporation, 1907
Nisbet, Herkis Hume 1849–1923, *Highland Loch with Ruined Castle,* gift from an unknown donor, before 1973
Noble, John Sargeant 1848–1896, *Death of the Otter,* transferred from Padiham Museum, 1977
Normann, Adelsteen 1848–1918, *Near Gudvangen on the Sogne Fjord,* gift from Mr F. Tuck, 1924
Normann, Adelsteen 1848–1918, *Midsummer Night, Lofoten, Norway,* gift from Lord Crawshaw, 1924
O'Neill, George Bernard 1828–1917, *The Last Day of the Sale,* purchased by Burnley Corporation with the assistance of funds from the Edward Stocks Massey Bequest, 1921
O'Shea *Munn's Corner, 1890,* gift from Mr Cain, 1952
Ogden, Joseph 1862–1925, *The Porch, Spenser's Cottage, Hurstwood,* bequeathed by the artist, 1925
Oliver, Charles William 1911–2004, *Miss Dorothy Howard,* gift from Mr D. Clayton, 1986 © the artist's estate
Parton, Ernest 1845–1933, *In a Fairy Woodland,* purchased by Burnley Corporation with the assistance of funds from the Edward Stocks Massey Bequest, 1948, Photo Credit: Bridgeman Art Library
Partridge, John 1789–1872, *George Glynn and Oswald Petre, Sons of Henry William Petre of Dunkenhalgh,* on loan from the Petre Family
Partridge, John 1789–1872, *Henry Petre, Eldest Son, and Edward Petre, 3rd Son, of Henry William Petre of Dunkenhalgh,* on loan from the Petre Family
Pelham, Thomas Kent 1831–1907, *The Gypsies,* purchased by Burnley Corporation, 1915

Phillip, John 1817–1867, *A Scottish Fair,* purchased by Burnley Corporation with the assistance of funds from the Edward Stocks Massey Bequest, 1933
Philpot, Glyn Warren 1884–1937, *Portrait of a Man,* (possibly Henry Thomas), purchased by Burnley Corporation with the assistance of funds from the Edward Stocks Massey Bequest, 1951, Photo Credit: Bridgeman Art Library
Pothast, Bernard Jean Corneille 1882–1966, *Dutch Interior with Mother and Children,* purchased by Burnley Corporation, 1920 © the copyright holder, Photo Credit: Bridgeman Art Library
Pott, Laslett John 1837–1898, *Waiting for the King's Favourite,* purchased by Burnley Corporation with the assistance of funds from the Edward Stocks Massey Bequest, 1931, Photo Credit: Bridgeman Art Library
Pott, Laslett John 1837–1898, *A Refugee in a Church,* purchased by Burnley Corporation, 1912
Poynter, Edward John 1836–1919, *On the Temple Steps,* purchased by Burnley Corporation with the assistance of funds from the Edward Stocks Massey Bequest, 1952
Preston, Nonnie *Beauty and Temptation,* gift from an unknown donor, before 1973
Procter, Dod 1892–1972, *The Hall Table,* gift from Mrs Elizabeth Gresty, 1964 © the artist's estate/ Bridgeman Art Library, Photo Credit: Bridgeman Art Library
Procter, Ernest 1886–1935, *Flower Study,* gift from Mrs Elizabeth Gresty, 1964

Purdy, James 1900–1972, *Pendle from Bouldsworth*, gift from Mrs Purdy, 1976 © the copyright holder
Raphael (after) 1483–1520, *La Madonna della Sedia*, gift from Mrs P. Oldman, 1951
Read, Matthias 1669–1747, *Distant View of Clitheroe*, purchased by Burnley Borough Council with the assistance of funds from the Edward Stocks Massey Bequest and the Towneley Hall Society, 1989
Reekie, William Maxwell 1869–1948, *An Anglesey Cottage*, gift from the artist, 1926 © the copyright holder, Photo Credit: Bridgeman Art Library
Reinagle, Philip 1749–1833, *The Mountains of Vietri*, gift from Mr W. Dean, 1935
Ripley, R. R. *A Rocky Landscape with Stream*, gift from an unknown donor, before 1973
Roberts, David 1796–1864, *Interior of a Cathedral*, gift from Mr F. Tuck, 1938
Roda, Leonardo 1868–1933, *The Matterhorn*, gift from the Trustees of William Lancaster
Rubens, Peter Paul (after) 1577–1640, *The Descent from the Cross*, gift from Lady O'Hagan, 1903
Rubens, Peter Paul (after) 1577–1640, *Salome with the Head of John the Baptist*, gift from Mrs Wilson, 1955
Ruith, Horace van 1839–1923, *Tattersall Wilkinson of Roggerham*, gift from Mr E. S. Tattersall and Mr F. J. Tattersall, 1913
Sadler, Walter Dendy 1854–1923, *Darby and Joan*, purchased by Burnley Corporation with the assistance of funds from the Edward Stocks Massey Bequest, 1926
Selous, Henry Courtney 1803–1890, *What Does the Sea Say?*, purchased by Burnley Corporation with the assistance of funds from the Edward Stocks Massey Bequest, 1948, Photo Credit: Bridgeman Art Library
Shackleton, William 1872–1933, *Study for 'Japanese Festival'*, gift from Mrs Shackleton, the artist's widow, 1938
Shackleton, William 1872–1933, *The Nymph of Malham Cove*, gift from Mrs Shackleton, the artist's widow, 1938
Shaw, Walter James 1851–1933, *Seascape*, transferred from Padiham Museum, 1977
Shayer, William 1788–1879, *A Woodside Inn*, purchased by Burnley Corporation with the assistance of funds from the Edward Stocks Massey Bequest, 1950, Photo Credit: Bridgeman Art Library
Sidley, Samuel 1829–1896, *Mary, Queen of Scots and John Knox*, purchased by Burnley Corporation with the assistance of funds from the Edward Stocks Massey Bequest, 1954, Photo Credit: Bridgeman Art Library
Smart, Rowley 1887–1934, *Moret-sur-Loing*, purchased by Burnley Corporation with the assistance of funds from the Edward Stocks Massey Bequest, 1953
Smith, John Raphael (attributed to) 1752–1812, *Mr Towneley*, purchased by Burnley Borough Council with the assistance of funds from the Edward Stocks Massey Bequest, 1995
Smythe, Edward Robert 1810–1899, *A Gypsy Scene*, purchased by Burnley Corporation with the assistance of funds from the Edward Stocks Massey Bequest, 1937
Spanish School *Our Saviour*, gift from Lady O'Hagan, 1903
Spanish School *The Madonna*, gift from Lady O'Hagan, 1903
Spencelayh, Charles 1865–1958, *Smile*, purchased from the artist by Burnley Corporation with the assistance of funds from the Edward Stocks Massey Bequest, 1933 © Towneley Art Gallery and Museums, Photo Credit: Bridgeman Art Library
Spencelayh, Charles 1865–1958, *His Favourite*, purchased from the artist by Burnley Corporation with the assistance of funds from the Edward Stocks Massey Bequest, 1933 © Towneley Art Gallery and Museums, Photo Credit: Bridgeman Art Library
Spencelayh, Charles 1865–1958, *Table d'hôte with Music*, bequeathed by Mr Amos Preston, 1943 © the artist's estate/ Bridgeman Art Library, Photo Credit: Bridgeman Art Library
Spencer, Liam David 1964, *Studio Window*, purchased by Burnley Borough Council with the assistance of funds from the Edward Stocks Massey Bequest, 1996 © the artist
Spencer, Liam David 1964, *Town Hall, Burnley*, purchased by Burnley Borough Council with the assistance of funds from the Edward Stocks Massey Bequest, 1996 © the artist
Spencer, Liam David 1964, *Wind Farm, Burnley*, purchased by Burnley Borough Council with the assistance of funds from the Edward Stocks Massey Bequest, 1997 © the artist
Spencer, Liam David 1964, *Towneley Hall*, purchased by Burnley Borough Council with the assistance of funds from the Edward Stocks Massey Bequest, 1997 © the artist
St Clair, Ernest *Highland Cattle in the Snow*, gift from Mr J. S. Collinge, 1920
Stafford, Henry 1830–1873, *'Harlsonia' (Shorthorn Bull)*, gift from an unknown donor, before 1972
Stafford, Henry 1830–1873, *A Shorthorn Cow*, gift from an unknown donor, before 1972
Steadman, Joseph Thomas 1850–1938, *The Disputed Deal*, gift from Miss Thompson, 1975
Stocks, Arthur 1846–1889, *Her Sweetest Flower*, gift from Mr Edward Lord, 1905
Stoskopf, Sebastian 1597–1657, *A Still Life of Wine Glasses and Flagons*, purchased by Burnley Corporation, 1902
Suthers, Leghe 1856–1924, *Breton Girl*, gift from Mr K. Gregson, 1952
Taylor, Joyce B. 1921–2007, *Chrysanths in a Doulton Vase*, gift from James Taylor, 2007 © Towneley Art Gallery and Museums
Taylor, Joyce B. 1921–2007, *In the Market*, gift from James Taylor, 2007 © Towneley Art Gallery and Museums
Taylor, Joyce B. 1921–2007, *The Shell Collector at Home*, gift from James Taylor, 2007 © Towneley Art Gallery and Museums
Thornber, Clara M. *The Valley of Sabden*, purchased by Burnley Corporation with the assistance of funds from the Edward Stocks Massey Bequest, 1961 © the copyright holder
Thornton, Harold 1907–1975, *Anemones*, gift from the artist, 1958 © the artist's estate
Thornton, Harold 1907–1975, *Chrysanthemums*, gift from an unknown donor, before 1978 © the artist's estate
Thornton, Harold 1907–1975, *St Peter's Church, Burnley*, gift from the artist, 1958 © the artist's estate
Thornton, Harold 1907–1975, *Still Life*, gift from the artist, 1958 © the artist's estate
Tosini, Michele (after) 1503–1577, *The Holy Family with the Infant Saint John the Baptist*, purchased by Burnley Corporation with the assistance of funds from the Edward Stocks Massey Bequest, 1952
Towne, Charles 1781–1854, *A Classical Landscape with Figures and Cattle*, purchased by Burnley Corporation with the assistance of funds from the Edward Stocks Massey Bequest, 1937
Towne, Charles 1781–1854, *The Old Watermill*, purchased by Burnley Corporation with the assistance of funds from the Edward Stocks Massey Bequest, 1951, Photo Credit: Bridgeman Art Library
Troyon, Constant 1810–1865, *Landscape, les hauteurs de Suresnes*, purchased by Burnley Corporation with the assistance of funds from the Edward Stocks Massey Bequest, 1944
Underwood, Leon 1890–1975, *Noel Harry Leaver (1889–1951)*, gift from James Taylor, 2003 © the estate of Leon Underwood, courtesy of the Redfern Gallery
unknown artist *John and Mary Towneley and Family*, gift from Maurice, 3rd Lord O'Hagan, 1939
unknown artist *Christopher Towneley (1604–1674)*, gift from Mr John Trappes-Lomax, 1994
unknown artist *Still Life*, purchased by Burnley Corporation, 1902
unknown artist *Cuthbert Kennet of Coxhoe (1652–1689)*, gift from Mr John Trappes-Lomax, 1994
unknown artist *Margaret Towneley (1667–1731), Augustinian Canoness of Paris*, gift from Mr John Trappes-Lomax, 1994
unknown artist *William Towneley of Towneley (1714–1741)*, gift from Mr John Trappes-Lomax, 1994
unknown artist *The Towneley Family at Prayer*, gift from Lady O'Hagan, 1915
unknown artist *Lowerhouse Printworks, Burnley*, purchased by Burnley Borough Council with the assistance of funds from the Edward Stocks Massey Bequest, 1992, Photo Credit: Bridgeman Art Library
unknown artist *Archdeacon Master*, gift from Mr George Baldwin, 1932
unknown artist *Miss L. J. Wood, MBA, MA*, gift from Mr D. Clayton, 1986
unknown artist *A Sculptor in His Studio*, gift from an unknown donor, before 1973
unknown artist *A Seated Female Nude*, gift from an unknown donor, before 1973
unknown artist *A Woman Knitting*, gift from an unknown donor, before 1973
unknown artist *Bank Hall*, gift from Sir J. O. S. Thursby, 1913
unknown artist *Duke Bar, Burnley, around 1850*, gift from Mr J. L. Rawstron, 1971
unknown artist *Entrance to Towneley Park, by Moonlight*, gift from an unknown donor, before 1973
unknown artist *George Towneley of Leighton (1706–1786)*, gift from Mr John Trappes-Lomax, 1994
unknown artist *Henry or William Hargreaves*, gift from Mrs Holt, 1987
unknown artist *Janet Hunter*, bequeathed by Kenneth R. Brown, 1978
unknown artist *Landscape*, transferred from Burnley Central Library, 1972
unknown artist *Survivors from a Shipwreck*, gift from an unknown donor, before 1973
unknown artist *The Skaters*, transferred from Burnley Central Library, 1972
unknown artist *Whins Lane, Simonstone*, transferred from Padiham Museum, 1977
unknown artist *William (c.1631–1676), 2nd Lord Widdrington*, gift from Mr John Trappes-Lomax, 1994
unknown artist *Worsthorne Old Hall*, gift from an unknown donor, before 1973
Valckenborch I, Marten van 1534–1612, *The Building of the Tower of Babel*, purchased by Burnley Corporation with the assistance of funds from the Edward Stocks Massey Bequest, 1950, Photo Credit: Bridgeman Art Library
Verboeckhoven, Eugène Joseph 1798–1881, *Group of Sheep*, purchased by Burnley Corporation with the assistance of funds from the Edward Stocks Massey Bequest, 1931
Vincent, George 1796–1831, *Mouth of the Yare*, purchased by Burnley Corporation with the assistance of funds from the Edward Stocks Massey Bequest, 1935, Photo Credit: Bridgeman Art Library
Virtue, John b.1947, *View of Green Haworth from the North*, purchased by Burnley Borough Council with the assistance of funds from the Edward Stocks Massey Bequest, 1974 © John Virtue. All Rights Reserved, DACS 2012
Ward, Edward Matthew 1816–1879, *King James Receiving News of the Landing of William of Orange*, gift from Mr Edward Lord, 1905, Photo Credit: Bridgeman Art Library
Ward, James 1769–1859, *Interior of a Stable*, gift from Mr W. Dean, 1935
Ward, Vernon 1905–1985, *Wild Geese*, purchased by Burnley Corporation with the assistance of funds from the Edward Stocks Massey Bequest, 1944 © the copyright holder
Waterhouse, John William 1849–1917, *The Unwelcome Companion*, gift from Mrs P. Oldman, 1951, Photo Credit: Bridgeman Art Library
Waterhouse, John William 1849–1917, *Destiny*, purchased by Burnley Corporation, 1905, Photo Credit: Bridgeman Art Library
Watson, Robert 1865–1916, *Highland Cattle*, transferred from Burnley Central Library, 1971
Watson, Robert 1865–1916, *Sheep in a Landscape*, transferred from Burnley Central Library, 1971
Watts, Frederick Waters 1800–1870, *On the Thames*, purchased by Burnley Corporation with the assistance of funds from the Edward Stocks Massey Bequest, 1937
Webb, James 1825–1895, *After a Thunderstorm on the Sussex Coast*, purchased by Burnley Corporation, 1909
Westall, Richard 1765–1836, *The Village Bride*, purchased by Burnley Corporation with the assistance of funds from the Edward Stocks Massey Bequest, 1936

Whaite, Henry Clarence 1828–1912, *The Fairy Glen, Bettws-y-Coed,* gift from Mr James Rowley, 1931
Wild, David b.1931, *Fruhlingstraum, Dream of Spring,* purchased by Burnley Borough Council with the assistance of funds from the Edward Stocks Massey Bequest, 1974 © the artist
Wild, David b.1931, *Towneley Hall,* purchased by Burnley Borough Council with the assistance of funds from the Edward Stocks Massey Bequest, 1993 © the artist
Wild, David b.1931, *Bouldsworth Hill,* bequeathed by Miss Elizabeth Blackburn, 1990 © the artist
Wild, David b.1931, *Hambledon Viewed from the Roof of Burnley College, Twilight,* purchased by Burnley Borough Council with the assistance of funds from the Edward Stocks Massey Bequest, 2000 © the artist
Wilson, Richard (after) 1712–1782, *Italian Landscape (Lake Avernus) with Figures,* gift from Mr Ernest Benn, 1944
Wimperis, Edmund Morison 1835–1900, *A Hampshire Ford,* purchased by Burnley Corporation with the assistance of funds from the Edward Stocks Massey Bequest, 1927
Wimperis, Edmund Morison 1835–1900, *Carting Gravel,* purchased by Burnley Corporation with the assistance of funds from the Edward Stocks Massey Bequest, 1921
Wissing, Willem (after) 1656–1687, *Oliver Cromwell (1599–1658),* purchased by Burnley Corporation with the assistance of funds from the Edward Stocks Massey Bequest, 1967
Wontner, William Clarke 1857–1930, *Jade Necklace for an Eastern Princess,* purchased by Burnley Corporation with the assistance of funds from the Edward Stocks Massey Bequest, 1923, Photo Credit: Bridgeman Art Library
Wood, John 1801–1870, *Two Female Nudes,* transferred from Burnley Central Library, 1983
Woods, Henry 1846–1921, *A Venetian Christening Party,* purchased by Burnley Corporation, 1913
Zoffany, Johann 1733–1810, *Charles Townley and Friends in His Library at Park Street, Westminster,* purchased by Burnley Corporation with the assistance of funds from the Edward Stocks Massey Bequest and the National Art Collections Fund, Photo Credit: Bridgeman Art Library

Astley Hall Museum and Art Gallery

Ansdell, Richard 1815–1885, *Highland Cattle,* gift from Amy Harris, 1930
Banton, T. E. *Amy Hewlett,* gift from L. Hewlett
Booth, Samuel Lawson 1836–1928, *Rivington Lakes,* unknown acquisition method
British (English) School *Captain Robert 'One-Eye' Charnock, Chief Justice,* gift from Reginald Arthur Tatton, 1922
British (English) School *A Gentleman in Clerical Robes,* gift from Reginald Arthur Tatton, 1922
British (English) School *Anne Townley,* gift from Violet Caroline Townley-Parker, 1976
British (English) School *Robert Townley-Parker as Captain of the 53rd Regiment of Foot,* gift from Violet Caroline Townley-Parker, 1979
British (English) School *A Groom with a Chestnut and Palomino Horse in the Grounds of Astley Hall,* gift from Reginald Arthur Tatton, 1922
British (English) School *Charles I (1600–1649) and His Family,* (after Anthony van Dyck), gift from Reginald Arthur Tatton, 1922
British (English) School *Jane Brooke,* gift from Reginald Arthur Tatton, 1922
British (English) School *Richard Brooke (1640–1715),* gift from Reginald Arthur Tatton, 1922
British (English) School *Sir Peter Brooke of Mere,* gift from Reginald Arthur Tatton, 1922
British (English) School *Susannah Townley-Parker, née Brooke (1762–1852),* gift from Reginald Arthur Tatton, 1922
British (English) School *Thomas Townley-Parker (1822–1906),* gift from Reginald Arthur Tatton, 1922
British School *Sir Matthew Hale (1609–1676),* gift from Reginald Arthur Tatton, 1922
British School *Elizabeth Brooke,* gift from Reginald Arthur Tatton, 1922
British School *Peter Brooke,* gift from Reginald Arthur Tatton, 1922
British School *Reginald Arthur Tatton (1857–1926),* gift from Mrs Cull, 1982
British School *Winifred Eva Tatton (c.1867–1939),* gift from Mrs Cull, 1982
British School *A Lady Wearing a Blue Bodice,* (Peter Brooke's Wife), gift from Reginald Arthur Tatton, 1922
British School *Peter Brooke,* gift from Reginald Arthur Tatton, 1922
British School *Portrait of an Unknown Gentleman,* unknown acquisition method
Brockhurst, Gerald Leslie (attributed to) 1890–1978, *Twilight,* purchased from Richard Haworth, 1934 © Richard Woodward
Bure, Paul *Memories,* gift from Councillor A. Gillett, 1922
Clarke, Frederick *Family Horse in Stables,* gift from Violet Caroline Townley-Parker, 1979
Collings, Albert Henry 1858–1947, *Portrait of a Gentleman,* unknown acquisition method © the copyright holder
Dean, Dorothy *Gerald Townley-Parker (1858–1892),* gift from Violet Caroline Townley-Parker, 1979
Eastwood, Walter 1867–1943, *Golden Autumn – Buttermere,* unknown acquisition method © the copyright holder
Eastwood, Walter 1867–1943, *Little Langdale,* unknown acquisition method © the copyright holder
Fisher, Ben active 1890–1908, *Young Girl Asleep,* gift from Mr F. E. F. Burgess, 1934
Fisher, Ralph active 1908–1912, *A Salad,* gift from Mr F. E. F. Burgess, 1934
Flemish School *Venus and Adonis,* gift from Reginald Arthur Tatton, 1922
Frith, William Powell 1819–1909, *Portrait of Two Girls,*
Gibbs, Thomas Binney 1870–1947, *W. W. Burwell, JP, Chairman of Chorley Council,* gift from Connie Monks, MP © the copyright holder
Graham, Peter 1836–1921, *Twilight after Rain,* on loan from Councillor A. Gillett, since 1926
Grant, Francis (circle of) 1803–1878, *Catherine Blackburn,* gift from Violet Caroline Townley-Parker, 1976
Kerseboom, Johann (circle of) 1638–1708, *Thomas Brooke (1684–1734),* gift from Reginald Arthur Tatton, 1922
Kneller, Godfrey (circle of) 1646–1723, *Margaret Wharton,* gift from Reginald Arthur Tatton, 1922
Kneller, Godfrey (circle of) 1646–1723, *Margert Wharton,* gift from Reginald Arthur Tatton, 1922
Lavender, William Richard 1877–1915, *Jeremiah Horrocks (1618–1641),* gift from Miss D. C. Clark, 1962
Lely, Peter (circle of) 1618–1680, *Portrait of an Unknown Lady in a Blue and White Dress Wearing a Pearl Necklace,* unknown acquisition method
Londonio, Francesco (attributed to) 1723–1783, *Goats,* gift from Violet Caroline Townley-Parker, 1979
Londonio, Francesco (attributed to) 1723–1783, *Goats,* gift from Violet Caroline Townley-Parker, 1979
Lonsdale, James 1777–1839, *Anne Townley-Parker,* gift from Reginald Arthur Tatton, 1922
Lonsdale, James 1777–1839, *Susan, Daughter of Thomas Townley-Parker,* gift from Reginald Arthur Tatton, 1922
Lonsdale, James (attributed to) 1777–1839, *Lady Susannah Hoghton,* gift from Reginald Arthur Tatton, 1922
Lorrain, Claude (attributed to) 1604–1682, *Figures Conversing in the Foreground; In the Distance, Bethlehem,* unknown acquisition method
Loudan, William Mouat 1868–1925, *Roman Noble,* gift from Mrs Dickinson, 1935
Lucas, William 1840–1895, *Robert Townley-Parker (1793–1879),* gift from Reginald Arthur Tatton, 1922
Mauzaisse, Jean-Baptiste 1784–1844, *Frank Hall Standish of Duxbury (1799–1840),* (after Gulhierez), gift from Lucy Standish
Millais, John Everett (attributed to) 1829–1896, *William Carr Standish,* gift from Mr W. Cross, 1960
Murillo, Bartolomé Esteban (after) 1617–1682, *The Flower Vendor,* unknown acquisition method
Murillo, Bartolomé Esteban (after) 1617–1682, *The Mystical Marriage of Saint Catherine,* unknown acquisition method
Niemann, Edmund John 1813–1876, *Nottingham Castle,* gift from Councillor A. Gillett, 1922
Rousseau, Théodore 1812–1867, *Paysage au soleil couchant,* unknown acquisition method
Rubens, Peter Paul (after) 1577–1640, *The Adoration of the Magi,* gift from Violet Caroline Townley-Parker, 1979
Short, Frederick Golden 1863–1936, *New Forest,* gift from Violet Caroline Townley-Parker, 1979
Short, Frederick Golden 1863–1936, *New Forest,* gift from Violet Caroline Townley-Parker, 1979
Short, Frederick Golden 1863–1936, *New Forest,* gift from Violet Caroline Townley-Parker, 1979
Short, Frederick Golden 1863–1936, *New Forest,* gift from Violet Caroline Townley-Parker, 1979
Smith, Reginald *Mountain Scene,* gift from J. K. Booth, Esq., 1955
Stanfield, William Clarkson 1793–1867, *A Breezy Day on the Normandy Coast,* unknown acquisition method
Stanfield, William Clarkson (attributed to) 1793–1867, *North Italian Coastal Scene,* unknown acquisition method
Stuart, Sybil *Florence Bennet of Chorley,* unknown acquisition method © the copyright holder
Thomas, C. N. *Church Interior,* gift from Reginald Arthur Tatton, 1922
unknown artist *Thomas Brooke of Houghton,* gift from Reginald Arthur Tatton, 1922
unknown artist *A Tiger Hunt,* gift from Reginald Arthur Tatton, 1922
unknown artist *Church Interior,* gift from Reginald Arthur Tatton, 1922
unknown artist *Count D'Orsey in a Red Jacket on Horseback,* gift from Violet Caroline Townley-Parker, 1979
unknown artist *Cupid,* gift from Reginald Arthur Tatton, 1922
unknown artist *Dead Game and Deerhound,* gift from Reginald Arthur Tatton, 1922
unknown artist *Henry Flemming Hibbert (1850–1927), 1st Bt,* unknown acquisition method
unknown artist *Hunting Scene with Hounds and Tigers,* gift from Reginald Arthur Tatton, 1922
unknown artist *Italian Lake View,* gift from Mrs A. M. Taylor, 1978
unknown artist *Knowsley Hall,* gift from Reginald Arthur Tatton, 1922
unknown artist *Landscape and Figures,* gift from Reginald Arthur Tatton, 1922
unknown artist *Landscape with Astley Hall,* gift from Reginald Arthur Tatton, 1922
unknown artist *The Judgement of Solomon (The Adoration),* gift from Mr Leigh, 1922
unknown artist *Thomas Townley-Parker (1822–1906),* gift from Violet Caroline Townley-Parker, 1976
Verschuring, Hendrik (follower of) 1627–1690, *Battle Scene,* gift from Reginald Arthur Tatton, 1922
Walker, Robert (after) 1599–1658, *Oliver Cromwell (1599–1658),* gift from Reginald Arthur Tatton, 1922
Watson, Robert *Highland Cattle,* gift from Mrs Stansfield, 1946
Webb, Bryon *M. T. H. in a Red Jacket on a Grey Horse with Three Hounds,* (after John Nost Sartorious), gift from Violet Caroline Townley-Parker, 1979
Webb, William Edward 1862–1903, *Ship and Boats,* unknown acquisition method
Westcott, Philip 1815–1878, *Sir Robert Rawlinson (1810–1898),* unknown acquisition method
Wright of Derby, Joseph 1734–1797, *Robert Parker of Cuerden Hall,* gift from Violet Caroline Townley-Parker, 1976

Clitheroe Castle Museum

Cawthorne *Mytton Flatt and River,* gift from J. Moon
Jones, Lily *View of Downham,* original Clitheroe Castle Collections
Satterthwaite, Benjamin 1848–1923, *Downham,* gift from H. Clarke
Satterthwaite, Benjamin 1848–1923, *Whalley Abbey from Whalley Nab,* gift from Mrs M. E. Duckworth
Satterthwaite, Benjamin 1848–1923, *Boating at Brungerley,*

gift from Captain R. C. Musson
unknown artist *A Man Fishing on a River*
unknown artist *Cecilia Thomson,* gift from Mrs Thornton
unknown artist *James Thomson,* gift from Mrs Thornton
unknown artist *The Baptist Chapel, Clitheroe,* gift from Mrs R. Halstead

Clitheroe Library

Danial, H. *Alderman J. T. Whipp*
Espes, E. *John Eastham,*
Luttleson, G. *Alderman A. Roberts, JP*
Quinn, James Peter 1869–1951, *William Self Weeks,* © the copyright holder
Swan, E. active 1938–1944, *Alderman Clement T. Mitchell,* © the copyright holder
unknown artist *James Thomson,*
unknown artist *Reverend Thomas Wilson, BD*
Wilkinson *William Walter Whiteside*

Blackburn with Darwen Borough Council

Carter, Marian b.1925, *Darwen Library,* gift from the artist © the copyright holder
Morton, James Hargreaves 1881–1918, *Swans,* bequeathed by the artist's sister, c.1971
Morton, James Hargreaves 1881–1918, *White Cottage Landscape,* bequeathed by the artist's sister, c.1971
Morton, James Hargreaves (attributed to) 1881–1918, *River Scene,* bequeathed by the artist's sister, c.1971
Riley, James Lewis b.1925, *Co-operative Building, School Street, Darwen,* gift from the artist © the artist
Riley, James Lewis b.1925, *Market Street, Darwen,* gift from the artist © the artist
Riley, James Lewis b.1925, *Self Portrait in a Bellman's Outfit,* gift from the artist © the artist
Riley, James Lewis b.1925, *Sunnyhurst Wood, Darwen,* gift from the artist © the artist
Riley, James Lewis b.1925, *Brigg's Stables, Market, Darwen,* gift from Mike Gerrard, 2010 © the artist
unknown artist *Tower Notches up a Century,* unknown acquisition method

King's Own Royal Regiment Museum

Barnard, Philip Augustus 1812–1897, *Colonel Henry William Breton, 4th Regiment of Foot,* purchased
Devis, Arthur 1712–1787, *Colonel Sir Robert Rich,* gift from Lady Rich
Frye, Thomas 1710–1762, *Lieutenant Colonel George Walsh,* purchased
Gunn, Herbert James 1893–1964, *Richard Leslie Brown, GC,* gift from Mr David Milnes © estate of the artist
Henry Potter & Son *Drum Shell, 1st Volunteer Battalion, King's Own Royal Lancaster Regiment (1883–1901),* gift from H. Potter, Esq.
Howe, R. *10th Lancashire Rifle Volunteers at Camp, Bardsea, 1875,* gift, 1926
Inskipp, E. C. active 1927–1930s, *Lieutenant Colonel Christopher Lefroy Hodgson, King's Own Royal Lancaster Regiment (1901–1927),* gift from Mrs Hodgson, 1966 © the copyright holder
Kearsley, Roy active 1957–1975, *Sir John Salmond (1881–1968), GCB, CMG, CVO, DSO, DCL, LLD, The King's Own Royal Lancaster Regiment (1901–1912), Marshal of the Royal Air Force (1930–1933),* gift from Brigadier John Hardy, 1962 © the copyright holder
Owens, Trevor R. b.1935, *London Midland and Scottish Railway Locomotive Number 6161 'King's Own',* commissioned, 1991 © the copyright holder
Perkins, Frank *The Battle of Culloden, April 1746,* (after David Morier), commissioned, 1997 © the copyright holder, Photo Credit: King's Own Royal Regiment Museum
unknown artist *Colonel John Plumbe-Tempest, 1st Royal Lancashire Militia (1819–1852),* gift from Miss Tempest, 1932
unknown artist *2nd Lieutenant James Mackay, 4th Militia Battalion, King's Own Royal Lancaster Regiment, Killed in Action, 26 September 1901,* purchased, 1983
unknown artist *Captain Thomas Hinde Thompson, 1st Royal Lancashire Militia, 1855,* purchased, 1989

Lancaster City Council

Amriding, Chris 1935–2005, *Abstract Red Brown,* gift from the artist © the copyright holder
Atkinson, Graeme b.1972, *Millennium Bridge,* gift from the artist © the copyright holder
Barker, J. active 1800–1850, *James Giles, Esq., MA (Oxon),* gift from Alderman Charles Herbert Giles, 1917
Barker, J. active 1800–1850, *Mrs Elizabeth Giles,* gift from Alderman Charles Herbert Giles, 1917
Bulfield, Joseph M. active 1894–1912, *Alderman Thomas Preston (d.1894), JP,* gift from Alderman William Smith, 1905
Bulfield, Joseph M. active 1894–1912, *Alderman William Bell,* gift, 1909
Bulfield, Joseph M. active 1894–1912, *Alderman William Smith,* gift, 1909
Bulley, Emma b.1961, *Flower,* gift from the artist © the artist, Photo Credit: Emma Bulley
Cumpsty, David b.1939, *Lookout over Morecambe Bay,* gift from the artist © the artist
Danks, R. *Williamson Park Lake,* gift from the artist © the copyright holder
Danks, R. *Williamson Park Lake,* gift from the artist © the copyright holder
Davy, Isabel *Trees and Cottages,* gift from the artist © the copyright holder
Drzewinski, Kazimierz *Street Scene,* gift from Lublin Twinning Delegation, 1994 © the copyright holder
Elsom, V. *Elizabeth II (b.1926),* unknown acquisition method © the copyright holder
French, David Jonathan b.1963, *Red Blue Landscape with Red Clouds,* gift from the artist © the artist
Gorst, Luke 1849–1929, *Coastal Scene,* gift from the family and the executors of the artist's will
Gray, E. *Castle and Bridge,* © the copyright holder
Grieg, N. *Butterfly,* gift from the artist © the copyright holder
Harrison, R. E. *Mrs Briggs,* unknown acquisition method
Henderson, Cornelius 1799–1852, *George III (1738–1820),* (copy of Thomas Lawrence), gift from the artist, 1840
Henderson, Cornelius 1799–1852, *His Royal Highness the Duke of York (1763–1827),* (copy of Thomas Phillips), gift from the artist, 1840
Hodges, J. Sidney Willis 1829–1900, *Alderman Charles Blades, JP,* gift from Charles Blades Coverdale Storey
Jacobs, Chas b.1957, *Lancaster Montage,* gift from the artist © the artist
Jacobs, Chas b.1957, *Morecambe Sea Front,* gift from Poulton Neighbourhood Management Team © the artist
Keddie, John *Still Life,* gift from the artist © the copyright holder
King, Margaret b.1932, *Sea,* gift from the artist © the artist
Knowles, Arthur 1870–1955, *'Brier' Coming into Harbour,* unknown acquisition method © the copyright holder
Lonsdale, James 1777–1839, *Admiral Lord Nelson (1758–1805),* gift from the artist, 1806
Lonsdale, James 1777–1839, *The Right Honourable William Pitt the Younger (1759–1806),* purchased by the Corporation, 1807
Lonsdale, James 1777–1839, *Alderman Thomas Giles,* gift from Alderman Charles Herbert Giles, 1917
Lonsdale, James 1777–1839, *Samuel Gregson,* gift from Mr B. P. Gregson, 1909
Lonsdale, James 1777–1839, *Samuel Gregson,* gift from the sitter's daughter, 1882
Neale, George Hall 1863–1940, *Alderman George Jackson,* gift from members of the sitter's family
Neale, George Hall 1863–1940, *Sir Thomas Storey, KT,* gift from the sitter's children, 1913
Palin, William Mainwaring 1862–1947, *James Mansergh (1834–1905), FRS,* gift from members of the sitter's family, 1903 © the copyright holder
Somerville, Howard 1873–1952, *James Williamson (1842–1930), Lord Ashton, DL,* gift from Lady Ashton, 1932 © the copyright holder
Somerville, Howard 1873–1952, *Lady Ashton (d.1944), CBE,* gift from the sitter, 1935 © the copyright holder
Spiby, J. *Quaker Meeting House, Lancaster,* gift from the artist © the copyright holder
Stafford, Andrew b.1944, *Trees in a Rocky Wood,* gift from the artist © the artist
Stafford, Andrew b.1944, *Trees in a Rocky Wood,* gift from the artist © the artist
Thaddeus, Henry Jones 1859–1929, *Sir Richard Owen (1804–1892), FRS, KGB,* unknown acquisition method
Threlfall, P. *Abstract Landscape,* gift from the artist © the copyright holder
unknown artist *Misty Blue Hillside,* gift from the artist
unknown artist *Abstract Green Blue,* gift from the artist
unknown artist *Abstract Red Black,* gift from the artist
unknown artist *Abstract Underwater Blue Swirl,* gift from the artist
unknown artist *Abstract with Fluted Side,* gift from the artist
unknown artist *Alcunius Coulthard,* unknown acquisition method
unknown artist *Alderman Greg,* gift from members and ex-members of the Council, 1831
unknown artist *Footpath to Heysham,* unknown acquisition method
unknown artist *Graveyard with Hills,* gift from the artist
unknown artist *James Williamson, Senior (Alderman Williamson),* gift from 'his fellow Townsmen', 1882
unknown artist *Sir Norval Watson Helme (1849–1932), KT,* gift from Mr T. W. Helme, JP, CC
unknown artist *Thomas Swainson,* gift from the sitter's friends, 1884
unknown artist *William Briggs,* unknown acquisition method
unknown artist *William Storey, JP,* gift from the brothers of the sitter, 1883
Walker, John Hanson 1844–1933, *Thomas Greene,* gift from Colonel Greene, 1884
Westcott, Philip 1815–1878, *Alderman Leonard Redmayne,* gift from the Manchester, Liverpool and District Banking Company, 1917
Wiacek, M. *Lublin Street Scene,* gift from Lublin Twinning Delegation (?) © the copyright holder
Willman, J. *Ephraim Barnsbee,* gift from James Caunt, JP

Lancaster City Museums

Adams, Norman 1927–2005, *The Preacher on the Mount,* gift from Mr G. C. Barton, 1973 © the artist's estate
Andre, David *Old Woman*
Ansdell, Richard 1815–1885, *The Water Carriers,* bequeathed by Benjamin Bamber Gardner, 1911
Ashford, G. (attributed to) 1855–1945, *Alderman George Bowness,* transferred from Town Clerk, Lancaster City Council, 1974
Aspinwall, Reginald 1858–1921, *A Dream of the Crook O'Lune,* gift from staff and students, the Storey Institute, 1923
Aspinwall, Reginald 1858–1921, *Caves at Tintagel on the Coast of Cornwall,* bequeathed by Mrs Margaret Bonny, 1951
Aspinwall, Reginald 1858–1921, *Cottage by the Sea,* gift from staff and students, the Storey Institute, 1923
Aspinwall, Reginald 1858–1921, *Falls of Ogwen, Nant Ffrancon,* bequeathed by Harold Wright, 1939
Aspinwall, Reginald 1858–1921, *House by a River and a Bridge by Night,* gift from Mrs E. G. Petty, 1931
Aspinwall, Reginald 1858–1921, *Grassyard Park, Caton,* bequeathed by Harold Wright, 1939
Aspinwall, Reginald 1858–1921, *Heysham Shore,* bequeathed by Harold Wright, 1939
Bale, Charles Thomas 1849–1925, *Fruit and Game,* gift from Mrs B. Brocklebank, 1946
Balmford, Hurst 1871–1950, *Near Wray,* purchased at James Thompson & Sons, 1991 © the copyright holder
Beaumont, A. active 1860–1900, *Paris*
Bell, James 1845–1915, *Lancaster from the Aqueduct Bridge,* gift from Mr and Mrs A. E. Wilkinson, 1948
Bell, James 1845–1915, *St Peter's Cathedral, East Road, Lancaster,* gift from Mr and Mrs A. E. Wilkinson, 1948
Bettany, Desmond b.1919, *The Last Gun Position at Singapore in 1942,* (recto), gift from the artist, 1966 © the copyright holder

Bettany, Desmond b.1919, *Figures with Spear and Goose,* (verso), gift from the artist, 1966 © the copyright holder
Birch, Samuel John Lamorna 1869–1955, *Caton,* bequeathed by Charles E. Barrow, 1975 © the artist's estate
Birch, Samuel John Lamorna 1869–1955, *Lancaster,* gift from Mr W. M. Duncan, 1907 © the artist's estate
Birch, Samuel John Lamorna 1869–1955, *Spring in the Lune Valley,* gift from Frank R. C. Storey, Storey Institute, 1914 © the artist's estate
Birch, Samuel John Lamorna 1869–1955, *Brookhouse,* © the artist's estate
Birch, Samuel John Lamorna 1869–1955, *Trees in the Snow by a River,* bequeathed by Charles E. Barrow, 1975 © the artist's estate
Birch, Samuel John Lamorna 1869–1955, *Landscape with Trees,* bequeathed by Charles E. Barrow, 1975 © the artist's estate
Birch, Samuel John Lamorna 1869–1955, *Trees, Sombre Tones,* bequeathed by Charles E. Barrow, 1975 © the artist's estate
Birch, Samuel John Lamorna 1869–1955, *Moorland, Distant Hills,* bequeathed by Charles E. Barrow, 1975 © the artist's estate
Birch, Samuel John Lamorna 1869–1955, *Trees by a Moorland stream,* bequeathed by Charles E. Barrow, 1975 © the artist's estate
Birch, Samuel John Lamorna 1869–1955, *Stream, Trees, Pastureland,* bequeathed by Charles E. Barrow, 1975 © the artist's estate
Birch, Samuel John Lamorna 1869–1955, *Evensong: the Brook at Halton Green,* gift from staff and students, the Storey Institute, 1923 © the artist's estate
Birch, Samuel John Lamorna 1869–1955, *St Jean Pied de Port, Basse Pyrenees,* bequeathed by Charles E. Barrow, 1975 © the artist's estate
Bonacase, Serge b.1924, *Rythme de la vie, No.18,* transferred from Lancaster Town Hall, 1983 © the copyright holder
Bond, Albert 1905–1998, *Opening and Bagging of Raw Silk Waste at Galgate Silk Mill,* gift from Jerzy Marek, 1983 © the copyright holder
Bond, Albert 1905–1998, *De-Gumming Raw Silk Waste at Galgate Silk Mill,* gift from Jerzy Marek, 1983 © the copyright holder
Bond, Albert 1905–1998, *The Drying Loft at Galgate Silk Mill,* gift from Jerzy Marek, 1983 © the copyright holder
Bond, Albert 1905–1998, *Drawing and Gillroving at Galgate Silk Mill,* gift from Jerzy Marek, 1983 © the copyright holder
Bond, Albert 1905–1998, *Silk Dressing at Galgate Mill,* gift from Jerzy Marek, 1983 © the copyright holder
Bond, Albert 1905–1998, *Spinning, Assembly Winding and Reeling, Galgate Silk Mill,* gift from Jerzy Marek, 1983 © the copyright holder
Bond, Frances 1905–1978, *The Wedding,* gift from Jerzy Marek, 1983 © the copyright holder
Bond, Frances 1905–1978, *The Butterfly Tree,* gift from Mabel Packenham Walsh, 1981 © the copyright holder
Bradshaw, E. 1871–1955, *William Huntington, Esq.,* gift from Mr A. Sutton, 1948 © the copyright holder
Brealey, John *The Old Town Hall, Lancaster,* gift from Mrs P. Spencer, 1986
Brighton, T. *Near Lowgill*
Brown, R. G. 1815–1905, *Two Horses Belonging to John Armstrong,* gift from Mrs Helme, 1935
Brown, R. G. 1815–1905, *Self Portrait,* gift from Miss D. Blacker, 1952
Bull, Michael b.1925, *Ancient Buildings,* gift from Dr Jean Ward, 1986 © the copyright holder
Carter, William 1863–1939, *The Avon, Severn and Welsh Hills,* gift from Mrs John Cliff, 1935
Chesterman, Ross 1909–1999, *Towards Scafell, Cumbria,* gift from Lady Patricia Chesterman, 1999 © the copyright holder
Clarke Marshall, J. *Entertaining the Dons, 1588,* gift from the artist
Craft, Percy Robert 1856–1934, *Walls Have Ears,* gift from H. B. Craft, 1936
Crane, John 1850–1915, *Cattle in a Shallow Stream,* gift from Mr Allen Senior, 1982
Crane, John 1850–1915, *Lancaster from the Canal,* gift from C. Newton, 1965
Crane, John 1850–1915, *Lancaster from the North West,* gift from C. Newton, 1965
Crane, John 1850–1915, *Driving Cattle at Dusk,* bequeathed by Dr P. W. Edmondson, 1991
Crane, John 1850–1915, *Lancaster from Snatchems,* gift from Miss Tomlinson, 1988
Crane, John 1850–1915, *Highland Cow in the Snow,* bequeathed by Dr P. W. Edmondson, 1991
Crane, John 1850–1915, *Distant View of Lancaster from the West,* bequeathed by Charles E. Barrow, 1975
Crane, John 1850–1915, *The Cockler's Return,* gift from Mrs Crane, 1917
Cross, Joseph 1851–1897, *Reginald Aspinwall (1858–1921),* bequeathed by Florence Bessie Hinde, 1956
Cuitt the younger, George 1779–1854, *Vale of Lonsdale,* purchased at James Thompson & Sons, 1989
de Pratere, Edmond Joseph 1826–1888, *Cattle and Drover,* bequeathed by Sir Thomas Storey, 1898
de Vorkavitch, Paul *Coronation of Ivan the Terrible,* gift from Robert Thompson, 1931
Dulla, S. active 1750–1800, *Court Interior,* bequeathed by Bessie Casson, 1960
Eaton, Ernest 1859–1898, *Richard Coupland,* bequeathed by Roger Lay, 2004
Eccles, W. 1875–1955, *Putti Dancing,* gift from Mr Hawkins, 1990 © the copyright holder
Farington, Joseph 1747–1821, *Lancaster from above the Aqueduct Bridge,* purchased from Spink & Son Ltd, 1997
Fell, Sheila Mary 1931–1979, *Gathering Sticks in the Snow,* gift from Mr G. C. Barton, 1973 © the copyright holder
Fildes, Luke 1843–1927, *The Truant Apprentice,* bequeathed by William C. Halliday, 1952
Fraser, A. *Heaton Mersey,* gift from staff and students, the Storey Institute, 1923
Gaisser, Max 1857–1922, *The Conference,* gift from staff and students, the Storey Institute, 1923
Gallon, Robert 1845–1925, *Peak Cavern, Derbyshire,* gift from staff and students, the Storey Institute, 1923
Gallon, Robert 1845–1925, *The Sawmill,* gift from staff and students, the Storey Institute, 1923
Gervaise, Charles Arthur 1821–1891, *Castle and Lake,* gift from Thomas H. Lancaster, 1936
Gervaise, Charles Arthur 1821–1891, *Castle and Lake,* gift from Thomas H. Lancaster, 1936
Gervaise, Charles Arthur 1821–1891, *Castle in Valley,* gift from Thomas H. Lancaster, 1936
Gervaise, Charles Arthur 1821–1891, *Cottages on Cliffs,* gift from Thomas H. Lancaster, 1936
Gervaise, Charles Arthur 1821–1891, *Lancaster Castle Gateway,* gift from Thomas H. Lancaster, 1936
Gervaise, Charles Arthur 1821–1891, *Lancaster Castle Interior,* gift from Thomas H. Lancaster, 1936
Gilbert, William 1832–1896, *Sir Richard Owen (1804–1892),* gift from staff and students, the Storey Institute, 1923
Gilchrist, Philip Thomson 1865–1956, *Bella Villa,* gift from Mrs Dora Taylor © the artist's estate
Gilchrist, Philip Thomson 1865–1956, *Xeres Burning Athens: Flight of the Athenians,* gift from the artist, 1951 © the artist's estate
Goodwin, Albert 1845–1932, *The Tower of London*
Gordon, Jerry b.1955, *Fletcher Christian's Cave on Pitcairn Island,* purchased from the artist, 2000 © the artist
Gorst, Luke 1849–1929, *James Williamson II, Baron (Lord) Ashton,* gift from Mrs Benson, 1939
Gray, Kate active 1864–1931, *The Picture Book,* gift from Mrs B. Brocklebank, 1946
Griffith, Frank 1889–1979, *Rain, Glasson Dock,* purchased from the artist, 1971 © the artist's estate
Guercino (follower of) 1591–1666, *The Sacrifice of Isaac,* gift from Edward Johnson, 1892
Hackworth, T. *Poets' Corner, Westminster Abbey,* gift from Mrs B. Brocklebank, 1946
Harrison, Claude 1922–2009, *Island of Comedians,* purchased from the artist, 1971 © the artist's estate
Haughton, Benjamin 1865–1924, *The Pool, East Downs,* gift from Janet R. M. S. Haughton, 1937
Hayes, E. R. *Llyn Dinas, Beddgelert,* gift from Mrs B. Brocklebank, 1946
Hayter, George 1792–1871, *Joseph Interpreting the Dream of the Chief Baker,* gift from Mr W. Mitchell Barker, 1946
Henderson, John 1765–1853, *Lancaster from the East,* gift from Mrs T. Ellwood, 1931
Henderson, John 1765–1853, *Parson Thomas,* gift from W. G. Welch, 1974
Henderson, John 1765–1853, *St Mary's Church, Lancaster,* gift from staff and students, the Storey Institute, 1923
Henderson, John 1765–1853, *Lancaster from Ladies' Walk,* gift from staff and students, the Storey Institute, 1923
Henderson, John 1765–1853, *Lancaster from the East,* purchased at Sotheby's, 2001
Henderson, John 1765–1853, *Lancaster from the River with Skerton Bridge,* purchased at Dreweatt Neate, Fine Art Auctioneers, 1995
Henderson, John 1765–1853, *Lancaster Old Bridge with Skerton Shipyard Beyond,* gift from Mrs Atkinson, 1928
Henderson, John 1765–1853, *Lancaster with the Aqueduct Bridge*
Henderson, John (attributed to) 1765–1853, *Lancaster Old Bridge*
Henderson, John (attributed to) 1765–1853, *Market Street,* gift from Miss A. R. Longman, 1950
Henderson, John (attributed to) 1765–1853, *Old Loyne Bridge,* gift from Mrs Lancaster, 1936
Henderson, John (attributed to) 1765–1853, *Lancaster from the Ridge,* gift from Mrs Lancaster, 1936
Hitchens, Ivon 1893–1979, *The Red Curtain,* purchased from Crane Kalman Gallery, 1969 © Ivon Hitchens' estate/Jonathan Clark & Co.
Hodgson, Harold 1865–1955, *The Old Mill, Scotforth,* gift from C. H. Hodgson, 1963 © the copyright holder
Hoggatt, William 1879–1961, *Early Spring,* gift from Herbert L. Storey, 1918 © the copyright holder
Hoggatt, William 1879–1961, *Lancaster from Ladies' Walk,* gift from the artist, 1915 © the copyright holder
Hoggatt, William 1879–1961, *The Back Garden at Brookhouse,* gift from Mr W. H. Metcalfe, 1979 © the copyright holder
Hoggatt, William 1879–1961, *Morning Sunlight, Brookhouse,* gift from Harold Wright, 1936 © the copyright holder
Hoggatt, William 1879–1961, *Crook O'Lune,* purchased from Kenneth Parker, 1965 © the copyright holder
Hoggatt, William 1879–1961, *From Green to Gold, the Lune above Caton,* gift from Harold Wright, 1936 © the copyright holder
Hoggatt, William 1879–1961, *St George's Quay, Lancaster,* bequeathed by Mrs E. E. Thompson, 1956 © the copyright holder
Hoggatt, William 1879–1961, *Autumn in a Man Glen,* gift from Herbert L. Storey, 1918 © the copyright holder
Hoggatt, William 1879–1961, *Solitude,* gift from Herbert L. Storey, 1918 © the copyright holder
Hoggatt, William 1879–1961, *The Deemster's Farm, Ballacurry, Port Erin, Isle of Man,* gift from the Misses Cassidy, 1936 © the copyright holder
Holloway, Charles Edward 1838–1897, *Deal Harbour,* gift from Mrs and Miss F. G. Smith, 1950
Hooper, John Horace 1837–1912, *Shiplake from Wargrave Hill,* bequeathed by Sir Thomas Storey, 1898
Hume of Lancaster 1780–1850, *Lancaster Castle Gateway,* purchased from John Lane, 1916
Ibbetson, Julius Caesar 1759–1817, *Lancaster from Cable Street,* gift from William B. Smith, 1930
King, Gunning 1859–1940, *A Sunny Day,* gift from staff and students, the Storey Institute, 1923
King, Margaret b.1932, *The Ashton Memorial, Lancaster,* purchased from the artist, 1992 © the artist
Klíc, Karel 1841–1926, *Sir Thomas Storey (1825–1898),* gift from Messrs Storey Bros & Co., 1892
Knowles, Arthur 1870–1955, *PS 'Man Queen',* purchased from Mrs P. Miller, 1995 © the copyright holder
Knowles, Arthur 1870–1955, *SS 'Brier' and Deep Sea Fishing Boat in a Gale,* gift from Mrs P. B. Long, 1991 © the copyright holder
Knowles, Arthur 1870–1955, *SS 'Manman',* gift from Mrs P. B.

Long, 1991 © the copyright holder

Knowles, Arthur 1870–1955, *Highland Cattle*, bequeathed by Mrs Chapelhow, 1993 © the copyright holder

Lai Fong active c.1870–c.1905, *'Dawpool'*

Lamb, Arthur –2008, *Studio Windowsill*, purchased from the artist, 2000 © the copyright holder

Lambert, W. 1835–1925, *Orchids*, gift from Mr Dodsworth, 1968

Leggat, James (attributed to) 1865–1955, *Fishergirl*, gift from Mrs L. White, 1965 © the copyright holder

Lewis, L. 1775–1845, *Landscape with Figures and Footbridge*, bequeathed by Miss F. H. Slinger, 1945

Linton, William 1791–1876, *Lancaster from the Stone Quarries*, purchased at Christie's, 1988

Linton, William 1791–1876, *Halton Forge on the Lune*, purchased from Mrs Keighley, 1951

Lonsdale, James 1777–1839, *John Dalton, Junior, Son of John and Mary Dalton*, bequeathed by Miss A. E. Dalton, 1983

Lonsdale, James 1777–1839, *Mary Dalton, née Gage*, bequeathed by Miss A. E. Dalton, 1983

Lonsdale, James 1777–1839, *Self Portrait*, gift from Mrs Brooke, 1957

Lonsdale, James 1777–1839, *Bridget Dalton*, bequeathed by Miss A. E. Dalton, 1983

Lonsdale, James 1777–1839, *Elizabeth Dalton*, bequeathed by Miss A. E. Dalton, 1983

Lonsdale, James 1777–1839, *John Dalton of Thurnham*, bequeathed by Miss A. E. Dalton, 1983

Lonsdale, James 1777–1839, *Mary Dalton, Daughter of John Dalton and Mary Dalton, née Gage*, bequeathed by Miss A. E. Dalton, 1983

Lonsdale, Richard T. active c.1836–c.1850, *James John Lonsdale*, gift from an anonymous donor, before 1968

Maartens, Wontern *River Scene with Cattle and Two Men in a Boat*, bequeathed by Sir Thomas Storey, 1898

Marek, Jerzy b.1925, *The Sitting Room*, gift from the artist, 1983 © the artist

Marlow, William (attributed to) 1740–1813, *Bridge End, Lancaster*, purchased from A. Ackerman and Sons, 1935

Mitchell, Sue b.1942, *Chit Chat by the Museum, Lancaster*, purchased from the artist, 2010 © the artist

Montalba, Clara 1842–1929, *The Port of Amsterdam*, gift from F. E. Warburg, 1892

Morris, J. D. *Fairy Glen*, gift from Harold Wright, 1931

Morris, Philip Richard 1836–1902, *The Reaper and the Flowers*, gift from the Right Honourable Lady Ashton, 1930

Morrison, Robert Edward 1851–1924, *Alderman W. N. Briggs, JP, DL*, gift from C. N. Briggs, 1975

Morrison, Robert Edward 1851–1924, *Mrs Briggs, Mayoress*, gift from C. N. Briggs, 1975

Murray, David 1849–1933, *Valley of the Stour, East Bergholt, Suffolk*, bequeathed by the artist, 1939

Murray, George b.1930, *Aspiring Column*, (artist also known as Jerzy Marek), gift from Jerzy Marek, 1983 © the copyright holder

Murray, George b.1930, *Pilot Fish*, (artist also known as Jerzy Marek), gift from Jerzy Marek, 1983 © the copyright holder

Murray, George b.1930, *Sea Column*, (artist also known as Jerzy Marek), gift from Jerzy Marek, 1983 © the copyright holder

Muschamp, Francis Sydney 1851–1929, *Penelope*, gift from staff and students, the Storey Institute, 1923

Neale, George Hall 1863–1940, *Herbert Lushington Storey, JP, DL*, gift from the sitter

Owens, Trevor R. b.1935, *Galgate Station by Night*, gift from the artist, 1990 © the copyright holder

Palin, William Mainwaring 1862–1947, *James Mansergh (1834–1905), Freeman of the Borough*, gift, 1903 © the copyright holder

Pantoja de la Cruz, Juan 1553–1608, *Spanish Noble Woman*, (from the Court of Philip II), gift from staff and students, the Storey Institute, 1923

Paterson, Emily Murray 1855–1934, *Anemones and Wild Flowers*, gift from Mrs A. Steerens, 1935

Pearce, Thirkell 1885–1955, *Eulalie More Dalton*, bequeathed by Miss A. E. Dalton, 1983 © the copyright holder

Pearce, Thirkell 1885–1955, *William Henry Dalton (1832–1902)*, bequeathed by Miss A. E. Dalton, 1983 © the copyright holder

Pearce, Thirkell 1885–1955, *Mrs Dalton*, bequeathed by Miss A. E. Dalton, 1983 © the copyright holder

Pearce, Thirkell 1885–1955, *Lola Maud Dalton*, bequeathed by Miss A. E. Dalton, 1983 © the copyright holder

Phillips, Brian b.1939, *Clock Tower, Morecambe*, found, 1984 © the artist

Pike, Sidney 1846–1907, *The Golf Links*, gift from Mrs Mason, 1963

Pisa, Alberto 1864–1931, *Westminster Bridge*

Platt, Stella 1913–2011, *Road to Bath Mill*, purchased from the artist, 1967 © the artist's estate

Pyne, Thomas 1843–1935, *Trees and River*, bequeathed by Mrs R. A. Docton, 1943

Rampling, Robert 1835–1909, *Bolton-le-Sands from the Canal*, gift from Miss A. R. Longman, 1950

Rhys, Oliver 1853–1928, *Rebecca*, bequeathed by William C. Halliday, 1952

Richmond, William Blake 1842–1921, *Charlotte Elizabeth Fuller-Maitland of Borwick Hall*, gift from staff and students, the Storey Institute, 1923

Roberts, David (attributed to) 1796–1864, *Moorish Church Interior (Eastern Church)*, gift from staff and students, the Storey Institute, 1923

Robinson, Christopher b.1945, *Clare Weze*, purchased from the artist, 1995 © the copyright holder

Romney, George 1734–1802, *Thomas Hutton Rawlinson (1712–1769)*, gift from J. Rawlinson-Ford, 1934

Romney, George 1734–1802, *Abraham Rawlinson (1709–1780)*, purchased from Michael J. Donachie, 2009

Romney, George 1734–1802, *Reverend Oliver Marton, Vicar of Lancaster (1767–1794)*, purchased at Christie's, 1980

Romney, George (attributed to) 1734–1802, *Mary Rawlinson*, gift from J. Rawlinson-Ford, 1934

Romney, George (attributed to) 1734–1802, *Thomas Hutton Rawlinson (1712–1769)*, gift from G. L. Ford, 1932

Romney, George (attributed to) 1734–1802, *Isaac Ford*, gift from J. Rawlinson-Ford, 1934

Salmon, Robert W. (attributed to) 1775–1851, *Lancaster Castle from the River Lune*, purchased at Sotheby's, 1998

Salmon, Robert W. (attributed to) 1775–1851, *View of Lancaster and the Lune Aqueduct*, purchased from Patrick Terenchin, 2010

Salmon, Robert W. (attributed to) 1775–1851, *View of the John O'Gaunt Gateway, Lancaster Castle*, purchased from Patrick Terenchin, 2010

Salomon, Harry Herman 1860–1936, *Portrait of a Man with an Imperial Beard*, gift from staff and students, the Storey Institute, 1923

Sell, Christian 1831–1883, *German Soldiers Surprised in an Inn by the Swedes*, gift from F. E. Warburg, 1892

Serra, Enrique 1859–1918, *Antique Effigy*

Slater, G. F. *Winter Weather*, gift from Harold Wright, 1940

Slinger, Ann 1855–1935, *The Bluecoat Girl*, gift from the artist, 1908

Slinger, Ann 1855–1935, *Stonewell and Pumps*, bequeathed by Miss F. H. Slinger, 1945

Spindler, Louis Pierre 1800–1889, *Jeremiah Wane (1787–1852)*, gift from J. S. Wane, 1970

Spindler, Louis Pierre 1800–1889, *Mrs Ann Rawsthorne*, gift from Miss J. L. Rawsthorne, 1969

Spindler, Louis Pierre 1800–1889, *Reverend John Manby of Lancaster (1806–1844)*, gift from E. B Manby, 1937

Stephenson, G. *Countryside with Hayricks (Morecambe)*, gift from the artist, 1960 © the copyright holder

Stephenson, T. 1865–1945, *Cottage and Boats along the Lune Coast*, (possibly Sunderland Point), gift from Mr G. Stephenson, 1960

Stephenson, T. 1865–1945, *Classical Scene*, gift from Mr G. Stephenson, 1960

Stephenson, T. 1865–1945, *Lakeland Landscape with Country Road*, gift from Mr G. Stephenson, 1960

Stephenson, T. 1865–1945, *Reed Huwe, near Gleaston, Morecambe Bay*, gift from Mr G. Stephenson, 1960

Stephenson, T. 1865–1945, *River Bank with Church Tower and Figures*, gift from Mr G. Stephenson, 1960

Stephenson, T. 1865–1945, *Lloyd George (1863–1945)*, gift from Mr G. Stephenson, 1960

Sugars, Fanny 1856–1933, *Miss Dalton*, bequeathed by Miss A. E. Dalton, 1983

Tate, William (attributed to) 1747–1806, *Mr Dodshon Foster of Lancaster (1730–1793)*, purchased at Sotheby's

Tobin, John b.1924, *Market Square, Lancaster*, gift from the artist, 1967

Turner, Charles E. 1883–1965, *Windsor Castle*, gift from Mrs A. L. Dowling, 1953 © the copyright holder

unknown artist *Tudor Gentleman*, gift from staff and students, the Storey Institute, 1923

unknown artist *Thomas Dalton of Thurnham Hall*, bequeathed by Miss A. E. Dalton, 1983

unknown artist *A Young Lady of the Dalton family*, bequeathed by Miss A. E. Dalton, 1983

unknown artist *An Unidentified Young Lady of the Dalton Family*, bequeathed by Miss A. E. Dalton, 1983

unknown artist *Elizabeth Dalton, First Wife of Robert Dalton of Thurnham*, bequeathed by Miss A. E. Dalton, 1983

unknown artist *Elizabeth Dalton, née Middleton of Leighton*, bequeathed by Miss A. E. Dalton, 1983

unknown artist *Portrait of a Young Lady*, bequeathed by Miss A. E. Dalton, 1983

unknown artist *A Young Gentleman of the Dalton Family of Thurnham*, bequeathed by Miss A. E. Dalton, 1983

unknown artist *An Unidentified Gentleman of the Dalton Family*, (possibly Robert Dalton), bequeathed by Miss A. E. Dalton, 1983

unknown artist *Mary Dalton, née Biddulph*, bequeathed by Miss A. E. Dalton, 1983

unknown artist *Elizabeth Dalton, née Selby*, bequeathed by Miss A. E. Dalton, 1983

unknown artist *William Hoghton*, bequeathed by Miss A. E. Dalton, 1983

unknown artist *A Gentleman of the Belasyse Family*, gift from Miss S. A. Barrow, 1948

unknown artist *Frances Hoghton Dalton*, bequeathed by Miss A. E. Dalton, 1983

unknown artist *Lancaster Old Bridge*, purchased from Mr J. Meadowcroft, 1925

unknown artist *Loyne Bridge, Castle, Parish Church, Old Town Hall and St John's Church*, bequeathed by Mary Thompson, 1937

unknown artist *Mr John Hoghton Dalton*, bequeathed by Miss A. E. Dalton, 1983

unknown artist *A Lady of the Dalton Family*, bequeathed by Miss A. E. Dalton, 1983

unknown artist *Ellenor Godsalve Rawlinson (1716–1766)*, purchased from Michael J. Donachie, 2009

unknown artist *James Booth, Collector of HM Customs, Port of Lancaster*, gift from Miss R. C. Bell, 1930

unknown artist *Lancaster from Skerton with a Sailing Ship*, gift from Mrs E. M. Edington, 1928

unknown artist *Mrs Alice Worswick, née Gillow*, purchased, 1926

unknown artist *Thomas Worswick of Lancaster*, purchased, 1926

unknown artist *A Young Gentleman of the Dalton Family*, bequeathed by Miss A. E. Dalton, 1983

unknown artist *Mrs J. Redmayne*, gift from Miss S. A. Barrow, 1948

unknown artist *The Good Samaritan*, gift from Mr E. C. Birkett, 1948

unknown artist *Lancaster Castle, Church and Old Bridge*, gift from R. Bolton, 1950

unknown artist *John Ford*, gift from R. Charles Ford, 1946

unknown artist *Lancaster from the Ridge*, gift from Mrs E. M. Edington, 1928

unknown artist *Mrs Jane Rawsthorne, née Stout*, gift from Miss J. L. Rawsthorne, 1969

unknown artist *Mrs Mary Ford*, gift from R. Charles Ford, 1946

unknown artist *Hannah Benson-Pease (or Mrs Robert Lawson Ford) as a Child*, gift from J. Rawlinson-Ford, 1934

unknown artist *Last Arch of the Old Loyne Bridge from the North East*, gift from Edward F. Storey, 1892

unknown artist *Coach Crossing Lancaster Sands*, gift from Mr J. D. Hodgson, 1961

unknown artist *Dr David Campbell (1749–1832), MD,* gift from Mrs Atkinson, 1967
unknown artist *John Armstrong,* gift from William Thompson & Co. Ltd, 1971
unknown artist *Heysham Village,* purchased from Fulda Gallery Ltd, 2003
unknown artist *The Judges' Lodgings,* bequeathed by Miss Heald, 1956
unknown artist *Agnes Boyer,* gift from J. A. Seymour Winder, 1937
unknown artist *Castle Gateway,* gift from Herbert Lushington Storey, 1915
unknown artist *Lancaster from the North East,* bequeathed by Miss E. Wearing, 1949
unknown artist *Lancaster with the River, Castle and Church Seen from the North West,* gift from Mrs Atkinson, 1934
unknown artist *St George's Quay - Last Warehouse and Cottages,* purchased from Redman House Antiques, 1983
unknown artist *Thomas Boyer,* gift from J. A. Seymour Winder, 1937
unknown artist *Sir Richard Owen as a Young Man,* gift from staff and students, the Storey Institute, 1923
unknown artist *John Dalton,* bequeathed by Miss A. E. Dalton, 1983
unknown artist *William Constantine,* gift from Bessie R. Constantine, 1933
unknown artist *Dr William Whewhell (1794–1866), DD ,* gift from Councillor H. Warbrick, 1925
unknown artist *Lancaster from Ladies' Walk,* gift from Mrs A. Richardson, 1930
unknown artist *Lancaster from the East,* gift from Mrs E. M. Edington, 1928
unknown artist *Lancaster from the South West,* gift from staff and students, the Storey Institute, 1923
unknown artist *Lancaster Old Town Hall,* purchased from Percy M. Beaven, 1939
unknown artist *Lancaster Old Town Hall,* gift from staff and students, the Storey Institute, 1923
unknown artist *Lancaster from Cable Street,* gift from staff and students, the Storey Institute, 1923
unknown artist *Ingleborough and the Lune Valley,* gift from staff and students, the Storey Institute, 1923
unknown artist *Sir Richard Owen (1804–1892),* gift from Councillor H. Warbrick, 1925
unknown artist *Lancaster Castle from Cable Street,* gift from Herbert Lushington Storey, 1915
unknown artist *Lancaster from the Moor,* gift from staff and students, the Storey Institute, 1923
unknown artist *Edward Storey, Esq. (1820–1913), JP,* gift from Edward F. Storey, 1953
unknown artist *Lancaster from the Old Stone Quarry,* gift from staff and students, the Storey Institute, 1923
unknown artist *Portrait of an Alderman,* gift from staff and students, the Storey Institute, 1923
unknown artist *Sucking on a Black Doctor,* purchased at James Thompson & Sons, 1991
unknown artist *Autumn Trees by a River,* gift from Mrs Mason, 1963
unknown artist *Cottage Interior,* bequeathed by Miss Bessie Casson, 1960
unknown artist *Edward Marton,* gift from O. E. C. Marton, 1946
unknown artist *Joseph Redmayne,* gift from Miss S. A. Barrow, 1948
unknown artist *Joseph Redmayne,*
unknown artist *Kirkby Bridge,*
unknown artist *Lancaster Castle Gateway,* gift from Mr W. J. Sharp, 1929
unknown artist *Lancaster: Last Arch of the Old Bridge from the North West,* bequeathed by John Wilkinson, 1931
unknown artist *Park Field Lodge in Winter*
unknown artist *Portrait of a Gentleman in a Wig and Striped Robe,* bequeathed by Hutton Guy
unknown artist *Portrait of a Lady Holding Drapery in Her Left Hand,* bequeathed by Hutton Guy
unknown artist *Portrait of a Lady in a Frilled Cap and Hood,* bequeathed by Hutton Guy
unknown artist *Portrait of a Man with Mutton Chops,* gift from staff and students, the Storey Institute, 1923
unknown artist *Portrait of an Unknown Woman,* bequeathed by Hutton Guy
unknown artist *Vale of Lonsdale*
unknown artist *View of the Cumberland Hills,* purchased from Fulda Gallery Ltd, 2003
Wane, Harold 1879–1900, *Fishing Boats, Isle of Man,* gift from Miss B. Cann Hughes, 1947
Waterhouse, Alfred 1830–1905, *View of Heysham,* gift from Miss A. R. Longman, 1950
Williamson, William Henry 1820–1883, *Fishing Craft off Dover*
Willman, J. *Moor Place Farm, Golgotha,* gift from William Wadsworth Preston, 1965
Woodhead, Geoffrey 1941–2007, *Carlisle Bridge, Lancaster,* gift from Anthony Yates, 2008 © the copyright holder
Woodhouse, E. active 1880–1940, *Highland Cattle,* bequeathed by Winnie Woodhouse, 1996
Woodhouse, William 1857–1939, *Bison and Wolves,* bequeathed by Winnie Woodhouse, 1996
Woodhouse, William 1857–1939, *Edith Emsley,* bequeathed by Winnie Woodhouse, 1996
Woodhouse, William 1857–1939, *Geraniums,* bequeathed by Winnie Woodhouse, 1996
Woodhouse, William 1857–1939, *Harvesting Balmoral Road, near Kenilcote (the Artist's Home),* bequeathed by Winnie Woodhouse, 1996
Woodhouse, William 1857–1939, *Maria Elizabeth,* bequeathed by Winnie Woodhouse, 1996
Woodhouse, William 1857–1939, *Stocks,* bequeathed by Winnie Woodhouse, 1996
Woodhouse, William 1857–1939, *Marie Elizabeth, the Artist's Wife,* bequeathed by Winnie Woodhouse, 1996
Woodhouse, William 1857–1939, *The Artist's Wife, Maria Elizabeth,* bequeathed by Winnie Woodhouse, 1996
Woodhouse, William 1857–1939, *Roy Woodhouse,* gift from Mr and Mrs Paul Carter, 2004
Woodhouse, William 1857–1939, *Stable Companions,* gift from staff and students, the Storey Institute, 1923
Woodhouse, William 1857–1939, *'Majestic',* gift from Miss D. M. Blacker, 1954
Woodhouse, William 1857–1939, *Marie Winifred (Winnie),* bequeathed by Winnie Woodhouse, 1996
Woodhouse, William 1857–1939, *Roy Woodhouse,* gift from Miss M. W. Woodhouse, 1987
Woodhouse, William 1857–1939, *Still Life, Zetland Ville Roses,* purchased from Studio Arts Gallery, 1994
Woodhouse, William 1857–1939, *The Donkey Boy,* gift from the artist, 1932
Woodhouse, William 1857–1939, *Army Horses in Stables,* bequeathed by Winnie Woodhouse, 1996
Woodhouse, William 1857–1939, *Edith Emsley,* bequeathed by Winnie Woodhouse, 1996
Woodhouse, William 1857–1939, *Egret, Parakeet and Mandarin Duck,* bequeathed by Winnie Woodhouse, 1996
Woodhouse, William 1857–1939, *Grouse Shot in Flight,* on loan to Clitheroe Castle Museum
Woodhouse, William 1857–1939, *Sailing Ships and Steamer,* bequeathed by Winnie Woodhouse, 1996
Woodhouse, William 1857–1939, *Sarah Elmsley,* gift from Mr and Mrs Paul Carter, 2004
Woodhouse, William 1857–1939, *Ship in Full Sail,* bequeathed by Winnie Woodhouse, 1996
Woodhouse, William 1857–1939, *Study of a Head,* bequeathed by Winnie Woodhouse, 1996
Woodhouse, William 1857–1939, *The Artist's Wife, Maria Elizabeth,* gift from Ronald Basil Emsley Woodhouse, 1981
Woodhouse, William 1857–1939, *Vanquished,* bequeathed by Winnie Woodhouse, 1996

Lancaster University Management School

Jacobs, Chas 1957, *Lancaster University Campus,* commissioned, 2008 © the artist
Jacobs, Chas 1957, *Lancaster University City,* commissioned, 2008 © the artist

Peter Scott Gallery

Adams, Norman 1927–2005, *Golgotha 1,* gift © the artist's estate
Adams, Norman 1927–2005, *Seabirds Scarp,* purchased © the artist's estate
Adams, Norman 1927–2005, *Expulsion from the Garden of Eden,* purchased © the artist's estate
Adams, Norman 1927–2005, *Sea, Light, Rocks, Birds,* © the artist's estate
Avrett, Marty b.1945, *Sleeping Cloth Fabric,* © the copyright holder
Bailey, John b.1926, *Apotheosis,* purchased © the copyright holder
Barns-Graham, Wilhelmina 1912–2004, *Contact (Bridge Series),* gift from Irene Manton © by courtesy of the Barns-Graham Charitable Trust
Barns-Graham, Wilhelmina 1912–2004, *Oblongs Cobalt Blue on Violet,* bequeathed by Irene Manton © by courtesy of the Barns-Graham Charitable Trust
Bell, W. G. *The Queen's Head, Workington,* © the copyright holder
Bissier, Julius Heinrich 1893–1965, *4 February 1959, Lake Zurich,* bequeathed by Irene Manton © Archivio Bissier, Ascona / DACS 2012
Britov, Kim Nikolaevich 1925–1996, *Winter Landscape,* gift from Irene Manton © the copyright holder
Brook, Peter 1927–2009, *Galgate Mill,* commissioned © the artist's estate estate
Brook, Peter 1927–2009, *Kendal,* purchased © the artist's estate estate
Cohen, Alfred 1920–2001, *Fairlight No.1,* bequeathed by Irene Manton © estate of Alfred Cohen
Coombs, Charles John Franklin 1908–1989, *Common Cranes in Swedish Lapland,* purchased © the copyright holder
Cooper, Julian b.1947, *Untitled,* purchased from the artist, 1969 © the artist
Dafter, William Robert 1901–1994, *Play Centre,* purchased © the copyright holder
Daniels, Alfred b.1924, *Monreale,* gift © the artist
Day, Bryan *Salmon Nets,* purchased © the copyright holder
Frost, Terry 1915–2003, *Walking down the Quays, St Ives,* bequeathed by Irene Manton © estate of Terry Frost. All rights reserved, DACS 2012
Frost, Terry 1915–2003, *Green and Pink (Border),* gift from Irene Manton © estate of Terry Frost. All rights reserved, DACS 2012
Frost, Terry 1915–2003, *Blue Black Sun,* bequeathed by Irene Manton © estate of Terry Frost. All rights reserved, DACS 2012
Frost, Terry 1915–2003, *Yellow,* bequeathed by Irene Manton © estate of Terry Frost. All rights reserved, DACS 2012
Fryer, Malcolm b.1937, *Abstracted Landscape II,* © the copyright holder
Fryer, Malcolm b.1937, *Copse,* purchased © the copyright holder
Fryer, Malcolm b.1937, *Glenurquhart,* © the copyright holder
Fryer, Malcolm b.1937, *Silverdale,* © the copyright holder
Gentilini, Franco 1909–1981, *Church in Italy,* gift from Irene Manton © DACS 2012
Giovannetti, Luigi Pericle 1916–2001, *Grated Jadegate,* gift from Irene Manton © the copyright holder
Goulding, Arthur 1921–2011, *Whispering,* purchased © the copyright holder
Guthrie, Kathleen 1905–1981, *Waterlow Park,* gift © the artist's estate estate
Haslam, Raymond active 1967, *Spinner,* © the copyright holder
Hayden, Henri 1883–1970, *Extensive Hilly Landscape,* bequeathed by Irene Manton © ADAGP, Paris and DACS, London 2012
Hellawell, Harry 1921–2004, *The Long Night,* purchased © the copyright holder
Hoare, Jeff b.1923, *Open Space,* commissioned © the artist
Hoare, Jeff b.1923, *Open Space,* commissioned © the artist
Hoare, Jeff b.1923, *Open Space,* commissioned © the artist
Hoare, Jeff b.1923, *Open Space,* commissioned © the artist
Hoare, Jeff b.1923, *Open Space,* commissioned © the artist
Hoare, Jeff b.1923, *Open Space,* commissioned © the artist
Hoare, Jeff b.1923, *Ullswater,* © the artist
Hoare, Jeff b.1923, *Untitled,* commissioned © the artist
Jenkins, Paul b.1923, *Philomena Violet Talks,* bequeathed by Irene Manton © Paul Jenkins/ADAGP, Paris and DACS, London 2012
Newcomb, Mary 1922–2008, *Barn and Grasses,* gift from Irene Manton © the artist's estate estate
Nicholson, Winifred 1893–1981, *Harebells near Housesteads Camp,* purchased © trustees of Winifred Nicholson
Nicholson, Winifred 1893–1981, *Snowdrops in Winter, Bankshead,* purchased © trustees of Winifred

Nicholson
Nicholson, Winifred 1893–1981, *Christmas Cacti,* bequeathed by Irene Manton © trustees of Winifred Nicholson
Niemczyc, Adam b.1914, *Woman,* gift from Irene Manton © the copyright holder
Nisbet, Scott 1910–2002, *Phoenix Rising,* purchased from the artist, 1970 © the copyright holder
Nisbet, Scott 1910–2002, *Egyptian Fantasy,* on long-term loan from the artist © the copyright holder
Nisbet, Scott 1910–2002, *Icarus,* on long-term loan from the artist © the copyright holder
Nisbet, Scott 1910–2002, *The Searches,* purchased © the copyright holder
Plummer, Brian b.1934, *Wast Green, Lake District,* purchased © the artist
Poole, David b.1931, *Professor Harry Hanham,* commissioned © the artist
Roeves, A. T. *Untitled,* © the copyright holder
Roeves, A. T. *Untitled,* © the copyright holder
Sedgley, Peter b.1930, *Counterpoint,* gift from Irene Manton © the artist
Sedgley, Peter b.1930, *Untitled,* gift from Irene Manton © the artist
Sedgley, Peter b.1930, *Untitled,* gift from Irene Manton © the artist
Sedgley, Peter b.1930, *Untitled,* gift from Irene Manton © the artist
Sedgley, Peter b.1930, *Untitled,* gift from Irene Manton © the artist
Sedgley, Peter b.1930, *Black Pincer Movement I,* bequeathed by Irene Manton © the artist
Sedgley, Peter b.1930, *Oranges and Lemons I,* gift from Irene Manton © the artist
Sedgley, Peter b.1930, *Glow,* bequeathed by Irene Manton © the artist
Senior, Bryan b.1935, *Pond with Blue Figures,* gift from Irene Manton © the artist
Skelton, Mike *Apples,* gift © the copyright holder
Stephens, Bev b.1935, *The Climber,* purchased © the artist
Stubley, Trevor 1932–2010, *Professor Reynolds,* commissioned © the artist's estate estate
Stubley, Trevor 1932–2010, *Sir Charles Carter (1919–2002),* commissioned © the artist's estate estate
White, Kathleen active 1967–1968, *Suffolk Farm,* gift © the copyright holder
Wood, Elizabeth b.1930, *The Jester,* purchased © the artist
Wood, Tom b.1955, *Professor William Ritchie,* commissioned © the artist

Ruskin Library, Lancaster University

Morton, Concord 1911–1979, *John Howard Whitehouse (1873–1955),* part of the Whitehouse Collection © the copyright holder
Richmond II, Thomas 1802–1874, *John Ruskin (1819–1900),* part of the Whitehouse Collection
Rooke, Thomas Matthews 1842–1942, *Coutances,* part of the Whitehouse Collection © the copyright holder
Rooke, Thomas Matthews 1842–1942, *Rouen,* part of the Whitehouse Collection © the copyright holder
Sands, Henry H. active 1886–1906, *John Ruskin (1819–1900)* (copy after a photograph of 1882 by H. R. Barraud), part of the Whitehouse Collection
Severn, Arthur 1842–1931, *Evening View over Coniston Lake,* part of the Whitehouse Collection
Severn, Arthur (attributed to) 1842–1931, *Brantwood Estate: Beck Leven Running into the Lake,* part of the Whitehouse Collection
Severn, Joseph 1793–1879, *Doge Antonio Grimani Kneeling before Faith* (after Titian), part of the Whitehouse Collection
Severn, Joseph 1793–1879, *Head of the Virgin* (after Titian), part of the Whitehouse Collection
Severn, Joseph 1793–1879, *Saint Agata Martyr* (after Paolo Veronese), part of the Whitehouse Collection
Severn, Joseph 1793–1879, *Saint George and the Dragon* (after Peter Paul Rubens), part of the Whitehouse Collection
Severn, Joseph 1793–1879, *Saint John the Baptist* (after Titian), part of the Whitehouse Collection
Severn, Joseph 1793–1879, *The Mystic Marriage of Saint Catherine* (after Jacopo Tintoretto), part of the Whitehouse Collection

The Shire Hall, Lancaster Castle

Dawson Watson *A Sketch in the Shire Hall (Trial of Edward Gibbon Wakefield, 1826),* Photo credit: by permission of the Chancellor and Council of the Duchy of Lancaster
Harrison, Claude 1922–2009, *Patrick McCall,* © the artist's estate, Photo credit: by permission of the Chancellor and Council of the Duchy of Lancaster
Hayward, Alfred Robert 1875–1971, *P. J. Hibbert,* © the copyright holder, Photo credit: by permission of the Chancellor and Council of the Duchy of Lancaster
Hodges, J. Sidney Willis 1829–1900, *Right Honourable Matthew Talbot Baines, QC, MP,* Photo credit: by permission of the Chancellor and Council of the Duchy of Lancaster
Hodges, J. Sidney Willis 1829–1900, *Right Honourable Richard Assheton Cross (1823–1914),* painted for the Grand Jury Room, Lancaster Castle, Photo credit: by permission of the Chancellor and Council of the Duchy of Lancaster
Hodges, J. Sidney Willis 1829–1900, *Lord Winmarleigh (1802–1892),* Photo credit: by permission of the Chancellor and Council of the Duchy of Lancaster
Letherbarrow junior, John *View of Lancaster Castle,* Photo credit: by permission of the Chancellor and Council of the Duchy of Lancaster
Morrison, Robert Edward 1851–1924, *John Fell, JP, DL,* gift to the sitter by some of his fellow magistrates, 1903; acquired, Photo credit: by permission of the Chancellor and Council of the Duchy of Lancaster
Morrison, Robert Edward 1851–1924, *William Hulton,* commissioned by public subscription, 1907, Photo credit: by permission of the Chancellor and Council of the Duchy of Lancaster
Morrison, Robert Edward 1851–1924, *Edward Bousfield Dawson (d.1916),* gift to the sitter for the Grand Jury Room in Lancaster Castle by his brother magistrates, 1914, Photo credit: by permission of the Chancellor and Council of the Duchy of Lancaster
unknown artist *Gateway to Castle,* Photo credit: by permission of the Chancellor and Council of the Duchy of Lancaster
unknown artist *John Blackburne of Orton Hall (1754–1833),* Photo credit: by permission of the Chancellor and Council of the Duchy of Lancaster
unknown artist *Alexander Butler of Kirkland, High Sheriff (1767),* gift from T. C. Butler-Cole, 1936, Photo credit: by permission of the Chancellor and Council of the Duchy of Lancaster
unknown artist *Hunting Party,* Photo credit: by permission of the Chancellor and Council of the Duchy of Lancaster
unknown artist *Landscape with Church and Mountain,* Photo credit: by permission of the Chancellor and Council of the Duchy of Lancaster
unknown artist *Landscape with House and Church,* Photo credit: by permission of the Chancellor and Council of the Duchy of Lancaster
unknown artist *Thomas Stanley,* Photo credit: by permission of the Chancellor and Council of the Duchy of Lancaster
Walker, Charles John active 1864–1875, *Henry Fletcher Rigge,* Photo credit: by permission of the Chancellor and Council of the Duchy of Lancaster

British Commercial Vehicle Museum

G., R. *Lord Stokes of Leyland (1914–2008),* © the copyright holder
Lambert, Walter *She's a Leyland Lady, 1938,* © the copyright holder
Lambert, Walter *She's a Leyland Lady, 1939,* © the copyright holder
Lambert, Walter *She's a Leyland Lady, 1947,* © the copyright holder
Lambert, Walter *She's a Leyland Lady, 1948,* © the copyright holder
Lambert, Walter *She's a Leyland Lady, 1950,* © the copyright holder
Lambert, Walter *She's a Leyland Lady, 1951,* © the copyright holder
Lambert, Walter *She's a Leyland Lady, 1953,* © the copyright holder
Lambert, Walter *She's a Leyland Lady, 1954,* © the copyright holder
Lambert, Walter *She's a Leyland Lady, 1955,* © the copyright holder
Lambert, Walter *She's a Leyland Lady, 1956,* © the copyright holder
Lambert, Walter *She's a Leyland Lady, 1959,* © the copyright holder
Lambert, Walter *She's a Leyland Lady, 1965,* © the copyright holder
Lambert, Walter *She's a Leyland Lady, 1966,* © the copyright holder
Lambert, Walter *She's a Leyland Lady, 1968,* © the copyright holder
Williams, John *Typical Transport Café Scene, c.1950s,* gift from Gordon Baron © the copyright holder

South Ribble Museum and Exhibition Centre

Anderton, Tom 1894–1956, *Brindle Village: Evening,* gift from the estate of the artist, 1956 © the copyright holder
Anderton, Tom 1894–1956, *Brindle Village: Winter,* gift from the estate of the artist, 1956 © the copyright holder
Anderton, Tom 1894–1956, *Fisherman, Upland Landscape with Bridge* (1), gift from the estate of the artist, 1956 © the copyright holder
Anderton, Tom 1894–1956, *Fisherman, Upland Landscape with Bridge* (2), gift from the estate of the artist, 1956 © the copyright holder
Anderton, Tom 1894–1956, *Girl on a Veranda,* gift from the estate of the artist, 1956 © the copyright holder
Anderton, Tom 1894–1956, *Saint Michael's Mount, Cornwall,* gift from the estate of the artist, 1956 © the copyright holder
Anderton, Tom 1894–1956, *Still Life,* gift from the estate of the artist, 1956 © the copyright holder
Hebeler, F. *Schleswig,* gift from Kreis Schleswig-Flensburg, a representative of Leyland's twin town © the copyright holder
Hill, James Allen 1903–1985, *Panoramic View of Leyland and Farington,* purchased from the artist © the copyright holder
Lambert, Walter *She's a Leyland Lady, 1968,* gift from Leyland Motors Publicity Unit © the copyright holder
unknown artist *Agnes Critchley (1748–1828),* gift from the Trustees of Osbaldeston's Charity, 1988
unknown artist *John Walton,* gift from the Trustees of Osbaldeston's Charity, 1988
unknown artist *Leyland Parish Church,* bequeathed by Mary Wadeson, 2004
unknown artist *Farington Corn Mill,* gift from Miss V. Kite, 1995

Lytham Art Collection of Fylde Borough Council

Andreotti, Federico 1847–1930, *The Proposal,* bequeathed by Miss D. W. Mosedale, 1970
Andrieux, Alfred Louis 1879–1945, *A Lady Seated on a Balcony,* bequeathed by R. E. Eckersley, 1944 © the copyright holder
Ansdell, Richard 1815–1885, *The Red Cow,* gift from James S. Fair, 1937
Ansdell, Richard 1815–1885, *Dog and Mallard: Waiting for Good Bag,* gift from Mr and Mrs J. B. Leaver, 1942, Photo Credit: Fylde Borough Council
Ansdell, Richard 1815–1885, *In the Highlands*
Ansdell, Richard 1815–1885, *Lytham Sandhills,* gift from the artist's grandchildren, 1926
Ansdell, Richard 1815–1885, *The Rescue,* gift from Alderman J. H. Dawson and Mrs Dawson, 1945
Ansdell, Richard 1815–1885, *A Day's Sport,* gift from Alderman J. H. Dawson, 1935
Ansdell, Richard 1815–1885, *Dead Game, Pannier and Plaid,* gift from James S. Fair, 1937
Ansdell, Richard 1815–1885, *Waiting for Master,* gift from Alderman J. H. Dawson, 1944
Ansdell, Richard 1815–1885, *A Brace of Pheasants,* gift from the family of the late Mr B. Bowman
Ansdell, Richard 1815–1885, *On the Road to Seville,* gift from Alderman and Mrs J. H. Dawson, 1947
Ansdell, Richard 1815–1885, *Retriever with Black Capercaillie,* gift from T. Agnew Ansdell and his sister Mrs C. P. Leece, 1959
Ansdell, Richard 1815–1885, *Staghound and Hind,* gift from the family of the late Mr B. Bowman
Ansdell, Richard 1815–1885, *The Herd Lassie,* gift from John Booth, 1925
Ansdell, Richard 1815–1885, *Rabbiting on Lytham Sandhills,* acquired from Talbot De Vere
Ansdell, Richard 1815–1885, *Partridge Shooting,* gift from

Alderman J. H. Dawson
Ansdell, Richard 1815–1885, *A Scottish Landscape with Stalkers,* gift from J. Fair, 1937
Ansdell, Richard 1815–1885, *A Startled Ewe,* gift from James Leslie Schofield, 1952
Ansdell, Richard 1815–1885, *Dog and Game,* gift from Alderman J. H. Dawson
Ansdell, Richard 1815–1885, *Gamekeeper with Spaniels,* gift from Alderman and Mrs J. H. Dawson
Ansdell, Richard 1815–1885, *Gathering Flocks on the Grampian Hills,* gift from Alderman J. H. Dawson, 1950, Photo Credit: Fylde Borough Council
Ansdell, Richard 1815–1885, *Gundogs and Game,* gift from Alderman and Mrs J. H. Dawson, 1953 (?)
Ansdell, Richard 1815–1885, *Hunter and Deer in a Highland Landscape,* gift from Colonel G. G. H. Bolton, 1953
Ansdell, Richard 1815–1885, *Startled Deer,* gift from Alderman and Mrs J. H. Dawson, 1936
Ansdell, Richard 1815–1885, *Startled Deer in a Landscape,* gift from Alderman and Mrs J. H. Dawson, 1938
Ansdell, Richard 1815–1885 & **Frith, William Powell** 1819–1909, *A Boy and a Girl with Hounds,* gift from Mrs Wilson and Mrs Morgan, 1957
Ansdell, Richard 1815–1885 & **Morris, John Charles** active 1851–1889, *Waiting for Master,* gift from Alderman J. H. Dawson, 1944
Baratti, Filippo active 1868–1901, *The Minuet,* bequeathed by Elizabeth Anne Parker, 1938
Barber, Charles Burton 1845–1894, *In Disgrace,* bequeathed by Miss D. W. Mosedale and Elizabeth Mosedale, 1970
Bennet, E. *Easedale, Westmorland,* gift from Mrs S. E. Crompton, 1944
Bennet, E. *On the River Dee, North Wales,* gift from Mrs S. E. Crompton, 1944
Bennett, Alfred 1861–1916, *Landing the Catch,* gift from Mrs S. E. Crompton, 1944
Blaas, Eugen von 1843–1931, *The Italian Flower Girl,* gift from Mrs Percy Bibby, 1941
Bond, William Joseph Julius Caesar 1833–1926, *Shore Scene with Trawlers,* gift from John Ingham, 1954
Bond, William Joseph Julius Caesar 1833–1926, *Returning Home from the Fishing Grounds,* gift from John Ingham, 1954
Bough, Samuel 1822–1878, *Bass Rock, Dumbarton,* gift from William J. Orr and Miss M. l. Orr, 1944
Boyer *Winter in Holland,* bequeathed by Richard Ernest Eckersley, 1944 (?)
Breanski, Alfred de 1852–1928, *Loch Nagar,* gift from Alderman J. H. Dawson
Breanski, Alfred de 1852–1928, *Loch Nagar,* gift from Alderman J. H. Dawson, 1950
Caffieri, Hector 1847–1932, *Portrait of a Lady,* gift from Mrs A. M. Catterall, 1945
Carter, Samuel John 1835–1892, *Fallow Deer with Fawn,* gift from Alderman J. H. Dawson, 1939
Chambers I, George (attributed to) 1803–1840, *On the Thames at Greenwich,* gift from Alderman J. H. Dawson, 1935
Cignani, Carlo (attributed to) 1628–1719, *Esther and Ahasuerus,* gift from Mrs Randolph Smith, 1942 (?)
Clause, M. *Sulby Glen, Isle of Man,* gift from Mrs F. Mather, 1945
Clausen, George (attributed to) 1852–1944, *Shepherd Boy in Wooded Glade,* unknown acquisition method © Clausen estate
Constantine, George Hamilton 1875–1968, *Christ and Mary Magdalene,* unknown acquisition method © the artist's estate
Cooper, Thomas Sidney 1803–1902, *Canterbury Meadows,* bequeathed by Amy Beresford, 1972
Craft, Percy Robert 1856–1934, *The New Curate,* unknown acquisition method
Creswick, Thomas 1811–1869, *The Old Water Mill at Bettws-y-Coed,* unknown acquisition method
Crossley, W. active 1898–1903, *Launching the Lifeboat on the Yorkshire Coast,* gift from Mrs Clegg, 1937
Dyck, Anthony van (copy after) 1599–1641, *Henry Percy, 9th Earl of Northumberland, Wearing the Chancellor's Robes and the Garter Ribbon,* gift from Alderman J. H. Dawson, 1939
Dyson, Louise H. 1892–1942, *One of the Family* (copy after Frederick George Cotman), gift from Alderman J. H. Dawson, 1942 © the copyright holder
Earl, Maud 1863–1943, *A Yorkshire Terrier,* bequeathed by Richard E. Eckersley © the copyright holder
Eastwood, Walter 1867–1943, *The Fell Side, Haweswater,* bequeathed by Isabella Norris King, 1956 © the copyright holder
Elliott, John 1858–1925, *A Bridge near Llangollen,* gift from Charles L. Snelson, 1954
Elliott, John 1858–1925, *Highland Loch*
Elliott, John 1858–1925, *Mountainous Landscape,* unknown acquisition method
Elmore, Alfred 1815–1881, *The Deathbed of Robert, King of Naples,* gift from Major E. H. Booth and Mrs J. K. Booth, 1943
Ensor, Mary Annie 1837–1886, *Bird's Nest and Flowers,* unknown acquisition method
Farnetti, Stefano 1855–1926, *An Italian Fiddler,* gift from William Hindle, 1945
Fuchs, Theodor *Lake Geneva,* gift from the executors of the will of the late H. A. B. Snary through Mrs L W. Kieen, 1941
Fuseli, Henry 1741–1825, *The Vision of Catherine of Aragon,* donated by Alderman J. H. Dawson, 1950
Glendening, Alfred Augustus 1840–1921, *The Village Postman*
Grundy, Cuthbert Cartwright 1846–1946, *Coming Rain,* gift from the artist, 1945 © the copyright holder
Hague, Joshua Anderson 1850–1916, *The Fisherman's Cottage, Deganwy,* gift from Miss B. Moorhouse, 1932
Hague, Joshua Anderson 1850–1916, *The Young Fishwife,* gift from Margaret Nicholson, 1934
Hayes, Edwin 1819–1904, *Dutch Pinks Returning from the Sea, Katwyke, Holland,* gift from Canon C. H. Ellison, 1935 (?)
Heusch, Jacob de 1657–1701, *River Landscape with Figures in a Boat,* unknown acquisition method
Hider, Frank 1861–1933, *Rocky Coast Scene at Sunset, Devon,* gift from Charles L. Snelson, 1954
Hider, Frank 1861–1933, *Shore Scene with Boats in Cornwall,* gift from Charles L. Snelson, 1954
Hoog, Bernard de 1867–1943, *After a Day's Sport,* gift from Alderman J. H. Dawson, 1939 © the copyright holder
Hoog, Bernard de 1867–1943, *Mother and Child (Children),* gift from Richard Shore, 1946 © the copyright holder
Huggins, William 1820–1884, *Children of the Jorden Family,* gift from Margaret Jessie Gourlay, 1955
Kay-Hilton, Jacqueline b.1941, *Happy Days,* gift from Anne Chisholm © the artist
Lamputtier, Com van (attributed to) *Pastoral Scene,* gift from Miss Dent, 1949
Landini, Andrea 1847–1912, *L'impatier,* bequeathed by Miss D. W. Mosedale and Elizabeth Mosedale, 1970
Landini, Andrea 1847–1912, *Mes deux petits amis,* bequeathed by Miss D. W. Mosedale and Elizabeth Mosedale, 1970
Langlois, Mark William 1848–1924, *The Drummer Boy,* gift from Edward G. Sergeant, 1946
Llangl, H. active late 19th C, *A Saint Bernard Dog,* gift from Councillor H. J. Burney, 1942
Lutyens, Charles Augustus Henry 1829–1915, *The Burnley Meet,* gift from Alderman and Mrs J. H. Dawson, 1934
Marshall, Thomas Falcon 1818–1878, *The Village Wedding,* gift from Mrs Crompton
Mennie, J. *Haddon Hall, Derbyshire,* gift from the Misses Riley, 1946
Millington, C. A. active 1882–11913, *W. S. Porritt, the Lifeboat Coxswain,* unknown acquisition method
Morgan, John 1823–1886, *Boys Playing,* unknown acquisition method
Morris, Alfred active 1853–1896, *Sheep and Goat,* bequeathed by Richard Ernest Eckersley, 1944 (?)
Oswald, Charles W. b.1850, *Cattle at Lakeside, Drinking,* gift from Mrs F. M. Mather, 1945
Oswald, Charles W. b.1850, *Cattle Wading in a Lake,* gift from Mrs F. M. Mather, 1945
Parger *Landscape with Horseman*
Rembrandt van Rijn (after) 1606–1669, *A Scene from the Old Testament*
Rigaud, Hyacinthe (attributed to) 1659–1743, *Portrait of an Artist*
Schneider, N. N. active 1753, *Still Life with Dead Game and Fruit,* gift from Mrs Flanagan, 1949
Scott, Hugh Berry 1854–1924, *Dredging on the Ribble,* gift from Alderman J. H. Dawson, 1942
Scott, Hugh Berry 1854–1924, *The Herdsman,* gift from Alderman J. H. Dawson
Shaw, John active 1889–1900, *Town View*
Shayer, William 1788–1879, *The Watering Place,* gift from H. Randell Heys, 1946
Sheffield Junior, George 1839–1892, *A Classical Lake Scene (Carthage),* gift from Alderman J. H. Dawson, 1945
Sonn, Albert H. 1867–1936, *The Dice Throwers,* gift from Agnes Kirby, 1949
Thompson *Pandy Mill, Dolgelly, North Wales,*
unknown artist *Alderman C. F. Critchley*
unknown artist *Portrait of a Lady,* unknown acquisition method
unknown artist *View of a Church*
unknown artist *View of Glencoe*
Verboeckhoven, Eugène Joseph 1798–1881, *Cattle and Sheep in a Landscape,* gift from Mrs Hanson, 1951
Wardleworth, Jack Leigh 1863–1925, *The Thread of Life,* gift from Alderman J. H. Dawson, 1939
Wardleworth, Jack Leigh 1863–1925, *The Thread of Life,* unknown acquisition method
Wasse, Arthur 1854–1930, *Goodbye,* gift from Alderman J. H. Dawson, 1945
West, William (attributed to) 1801–1861, *Christ Blessing the Children,* unknown acquisition method
Williams, Harry (John Henry) (attributed to) 1807–1877, *Village Overlooking an Estuary,* unknown acquisition method
Woodhead, Walter 1861–1946, *A Yorkshire Dale,* © the copyright holder
Woodhead, Walter 1861–1946, *Fylde Landscape,* © the copyright holder
Woodhouse, Susan 1866–1948, *Shore Scene with Beached Boat in Rough Water,* bequeathed by the artist, 1948 © the copyright holder

Duke of Lancaster's Own Yeomanry Museum

Booth, Samuel Lawson 1836–1928, *Colonel W. C. Gerard,* purchased by the Museum Trustees
Craik *T. P. Legh of Lyme Park,* purchased at Sotheby's
Ferneley I, John E. 1782–1860, *Lieutenant Colonel Sir Robert Tolver Gerard, Bt, and His Regiment, the Lancashire Hussars, on Parade,* purchased at Christie's International
unknown artist *Lieutenant Colonel D. H. Bates, MC, TC, Commanding Officer Duke of Lancaster's Own Yeomanry (1930–1934),* gift from Regimental Museum Trustees
Widdas, Ernest Alfred 1879–1960, *Colonel J. Heaton, TD,* gift from J. Heaton © the copyright holder

Harris Museum & Art Gallery

Abbey, Edwin Austin 1852–1911, *Fair Is My Love,* purchased © the copyright holder
Adams, John Clayton 1840–1906, *Surrey Flowers,* purchased
Aldridge, John Arthur Malcolm 1905–1983, *The Dovecote,* gift from the Contemporary Art Society © the copyright holder
Alken, Henry Thomas 1785–1851, *Five Steeplechasers, with a River in the Middle Distance and a Red Flag on the Horizon,* gift from Reginald K. Orlebar
Alken, Henry Thomas 1785–1851, *Steeplechasers Jumping a Fence,* gift from Reginald K. Orlebar
Alken, Henry Thomas 1785–1851, *Three Steeplechasers Clearing a Ditch,* gift from Reginald K. Orlebar
Alken, Henry Thomas 1785–1851, *Two Steeplechasers Clearing a Wall, with Two Steeplechasers in the Middle Distance,* gift from Reginald K. Orlebar
Allen, Harry Epworth 1894–1958, *The Derelict Farm,* purchased © Geraldine Lattey/Harry Epworth Allen Foundation
Allen, Joseph 1769–1839, *Nicholas Grimshaw,* unknown acquisition method
Allen, Joseph 1769–1839, *Mrs Esther Mary Grimshaw,* unknown acquisition method
Alma-Tadema, Lawrence 1836–1912, *Pastime in Ancient Egypt Three Thousand Years Ago,* bequeathed by Dewhurst
Anderton, Tom 1894–1956, *Jedburgh Abbey,* gift from J. H. Barnes © the copyright holder
Anderton, Tom 1894–1956, *Woodland Scene,* gift from Jim

Helliwell © the copyright holder
Ansdell, Richard 1815–1885, *Dull Day, Shooter Returning with Dogs,* bequeathed by Dewhurst
Ansdell, Richard 1815–1885, *The Death of Sir William Lambton at the Battle of Marston Moor,* bequeathed by Dewhurst
Ansdell, Richard 1815–1885, *The Deer Stalker's Return,* bequeathed by Dewhurst ,Bridgeman Art Library
Ansdell, Richard 1815–1885, *Lytham Sand Hills,* bequeathed by Richard Newsham
Ansdell, Richard 1815–1885, *Feeding Goats in the Alhambra,* bequeathed by Richard Newsham
Ansdell, Richard 1815–1885, *A Clear Day, Shooter and Dogs,* bequeathed by Dewhurst
Appelbee, Leonard 1914–2000, *Flower Piece,* purchased © the copyright holder
Armstrong, John 1893–1973, *Burnt Out Aeroplane,* gift from the War Artists' Advisory Committee © the artist's estate/Bridgeman Art Library
Armstrong, John 1893–1973, *A Vision of Saint Teresa,* gift from the Contemporary Art Society © the artist's estate/Bridgeman Art Library, Photo Credit: Bridgeman Art Library
Armstrong, John 1893–1973, *Abstract,* gift from the Contemporary Art Society © the artist's estate/Bridgeman Art Library
Askew, Victor 1909–1974, *The Lea, Sawbridgeworth, Hertfordshire,* purchased © the copyright holder
Aspinwall, Reginald 1858–1921, *Fairy Glen, Betws-y-Coed,* bequeathed by Sumner
Aspinwall, Reginald 1858–1921, *November Eve, Chichester,* purchased
Aspinwall, Reginald 1858–1921, *Cumulus Clouds: Haymaking,* purchased
Aspinwall, Reginald 1858–1921, *Haymaking, Twilight, Caton,* purchased
Aspinwall, Reginald 1858–1921, *Landscape – Rain O'er the Common,* purchased
Aspinwall, Reginald 1858–1921, *Landscape with Bridge,* purchased
Aspinwall, Reginald 1858–1921, *Landscape with Sheep,* gift from the daughters of W. H. Woods
Aspinwall, Reginald 1858–1921, *Springtime on the Wyre, Dolphinholme,* purchased
Aspinwall, Reginald 1858–1921, *The Light of an October Evening, Bolton-le-Sands,* purchased
Aspinwall, Reginald 1858–1921, *Eventide,* unknown acquisition method
Aspinwall, Reginald 1858–1921, *Marshland,* gift from W. W. Galloway
Aspinwall, Reginald 1858–1921, *Morecambe Bay,* gift from F. W. Sharples
Backhuysen I, Ludolf 1630–1708, *Seascape,* bequeathed by Vaughan
Bancroft, David F. active 1900–1950, *Two Good Friends,* unknown acquisition method © the copyright holder
Barker, J. active 1800–1850, *Reverend Robert Harris (1764–1862),* unknown acquisition method
Barnes, Edward Charles 1830–1890, *The Emigrant,* gift from F. W. Sharples
Bateman, James 1893–1959, *Women's Land Army at Work,* gift from the War Artists' Advisory Committee © the copyright holder
Beattie, Robert 1810–1874, *John Horrocks,* gift from Horrocks
Beattie, Robert 1810–1874, *Richard Palmer,* unknown acquisition method
Bedhest *Satterthwaite (?),* gift from J. and S. Ord
Bellany, John b.1942, *Untitled,* bequeathed by Danielle Harrison © the artist/Bridgeman Art Library
Bellany, John b.1942, *Vesperland,* bequeathed by Danielle Harrison © the artist/Bridgeman Art Library
Bellingham-Smith, Elinor 1906–1988, *The Willow Tree,* bequeathed by Dennis Carlton Walmsley © the artist's estate
Bentham, Frances Mary 1871–1941, *Primroses,* purchased
Bentham, Robert H. active 1850–1900, *Lancaster Road, Preston,* unknown acquisition method
Birch, Samuel John Lamorna 1869–1955, *Cattle by a Stream,* bequeathed by E. M. McMath © the artist's estate
Birch, Samuel John Lamorna 1869–1955, *Fallen Acorns,* purchased © the artist's estate
Birley, Oswald Hornby Joseph 1880–1952, *Alderman H. Astley-Bell,* commissioned by the Corporation of Preston © the artist's estate
Bissill, George William 1896–1973, *Shalbourne,* gift from the Contemporary Art Society © the copyright holder
Blamey, Norman Charles 1914–2000, *The New Shoot,* purchased © estate of Norman Blamey. All rights reserved, DACS 2012
Boddington, Henry John 1811–1865, *The Gypsy Encampment,* gift from Reginald K. Orlebar
Bomberg, David 1890–1957, *Composition,* gift from the Contemporary Art Society © the estate of David Bomberg. All rights reserved, DACS 2012
Bomberg, David 1890–1957, *Composition: Stable Interior – Horses with Riders,* gift from the Contemporary Art Society © the estate of David Bomberg. All rights reserved, DACS 2012
Bond, William Joseph Julius Caesar 1833–1926, *Avenham Bridge, Preston, 1857*
Bone, Stephen 1904–1958, *Bringing in a Casualty,* gift from the War Artists' Advisory Committee © estate of Stephen Bone. All rights reserved, DACS 2012
Bone, Stephen 1904–1958, *Destroyer off the Normandy Beaches,* gift from the War Artists' Advisory Committee © estate of Stephen Bone. All rights reserved, DACS 2012
Bone, Stephen 1904–1958, *HM Rescue Tug 'Samsonia', with Water-Boat and HM Yacht 'Martinetta',* gift from the War Artists' Advisory Committee © estate of Stephen Bone. All rights reserved, DACS 2012
Bonheur, Auguste-François 1824–1884, *Oak Tree and Sylvan Glade,* bequeathed by Mr Dewhurst
Booker, H. active 1850–1900, *Come to Me,* bequeathed by Sumner
Booth, H. C. *Market Square, Preston,* gift from W. Alexander
Brangwyn, Frank 1867–1956, *Fishermen's Quarters, Venice,* purchased © the artist's estate/ Bridgeman Art Library
Bridgehouse, Robert 1818–1881, *Waiting for the Tide,* unknown acquisition method
Bright, Henry 1810–1873, *Coast Scene,* purchased
Brindle, James active 1850–1900, *Glasson Dock, Lancaster,* gift from F. W. Sharples
Brindle, James active 1850–1900, *The Mill in the Fylde (Treale Mill),* gift from Garlick
Brindle, James active 1850–1900, *Welsh Coast,* gift from F. W. Sharples
Brockhurst, Gerald Leslie 1890–1978, *Dorette,* purchased © Richard Woodward,Bridgeman Art Library
Brown, John Alfred Arnesby 1866–1955, *Fading Day,* gift from W. H. Woods © the copyright holder
Brown, John Alfred Arnesby 1866–1955, *Homeward,* purchased © the copyright holder
Brown, John Alfred Arnesby 1866–1955, *The Harbour,* purchased © the copyright holder, Photo Credit: Bridgeman Art Library
Burgess, William *Brock,* purchased © the copyright holder
Butler, Charles Ernest 1864–1933, *Rocks at Land's End,* gift from Stephen Simpson
Byars, Hugh Gerard b.1957, *Untitled and Adam and Eve,* bequeathed by Danielle Harrison © the artist
Byars, Hugh Gerard b.1957, *Untitled and Embrace,* bequeathed by Danielle Harrison © the artist
C., W. H. *Landscape, with Crescent Moon, Church and Graveyard,* unknown acquisition method
Calland, G. D. *A Man and a Woman by a Well,* unknown acquisition method
Calvert, Frederick 1785–1845, *Sea View,* purchased
Cameron, David Young 1865–1945, *The Baths of Caracalla,* purchased © the copyright holder
Camp, Jeffery b.1923, *South Coast Walking,* purchased © the artist
Carelli, Consalvo 1818–1900, *Landscape with Figures and Classical Ruins,* gift from F. W. Sharples
Carline, Hilda Anne 1889–1950, *Swans, Cookham Bridge,* purchased © estate of Hilda Carline. All rights reserved, DACS 2012, Photo Credit: Bridgeman Art Library
Carmichael, John Wilson 1799–1868, *Seascape – Boats in Sail,* gift from Reginald K. Orlebar
Carmichael, John Wilson 1799–1868, *Seascape with Boats and Fishermen,* unknown acquisition method
Cassel, F. active 1830–1880, *Playful Dogs,* gift from F. W. Sharples
Castelli active 19th C, *The Three Sisters,* gift from E. M. Troughton
Chambers I, George 1803–1840, *Off Portsmouth, in the Distance Nelson's Flagship, the 'Victory',* bequeathed by Richard Newsham
Charles, E. J. active 1870–1906, *Landscape – Bridge with Cattle,* unknown acquisition method
Chubb, Ralph Nicholas 1892–1960, *A Berkshire Valley,* gift from the artist © the copyright holder
Clark, Octavius T. 1850–1921, *Landscape with Cows,* unknown acquisition method
Clark, Octavius T. 1850–1921, *Landscape with Cows,* unknown acquisition method
Clausen, George 1852–1944, *Bird Scaring – March,* purchased © Clausen estate
Clausen, George 1852–1944, *Sunset,* purchased © Clausen estate
Clay, Alfred Barron 1831–1868, *Phillip Park,* gift from the sitter
Clayton, John active 1800–1850, *Harbour Scene,* unknown acquisition method
Collins, Cecil 1908–1989, *The Priestess,* bequeathed © Tate, London 2012
Collins, William 1788–1847, *The Mariner's Widow,* bequeathed by Richard Newsham
Collins, William 1788–1847, *Welsh Peasants Returning from Market; Scene near Barmouth,* bequeathed by Richard Newsham
Collins, William 1788–1847, *My Favourite Cottage,* gift from F. W. Sharples
Cook, E. active 1850–1900, *Landscape – Lake Scene, Croft with Smoking Chimney,* unknown acquisition method
Cook, E. active 1850–1900, *Landscape – Three Figures by a Riverside,* unknown acquisition method
Cook, E. active 1850–1900, *Windsor Castle,* unknown acquisition method
Cook, E. active 1850–1900, *Landscape – Figures in a Boat,* unknown acquisition method
Cook, E. active 1850–1900, *Landscape – Lane Scene,* unknown acquisition method
Cooke, Anthony R. b.1933, *Shoreham Beach No.18,* purchased © the copyright holder
Cooke, John Percy 1870–1940, *Sir F. W. Tomlinson,* unknown acquisition method
Cooper, Abraham 1787–1868, *Marston Moor,* gift from Lord Ribblesdalex, Photo Credit: Bridgeman Art Library
Cooper, Florence M. active 1886–1935, *Dawn,* gift from B. W. S. Smith
Cope, Charles West 1811–1890, *Prayer Time – Mrs Cope and Her Daughter Florence,* bequeathed by Richard Newsham
Copland *Evening – Old Quay, Preston on Ribble,* unknown acquisition method
Copland *Morning – Old Quay, Preston on Ribble,* unknown acquisition method
Corbet, Matthew Ridley 1850–1902, *Afterglow in Italy – Evening,* purchased
Cotman, John Sell 1782–1842, *Pastoral Landscape,* bequeathed by Richard Newsham
Cox, Elijah Albert 1876–1955, *In the Land Where Time Moves Slowly,* gift from E. A. Cox © London Transport Museum
Cox the elder, David 1783–1859, *Dell Scene near Betws-y-Coed,* bequeathed by Richard Newsham
Cox the elder, David 1783–1859, *Dudley Castle,* bequeathed by Richard Newsham
Cox the elder, David 1783–1859, *Hilly Landscape, North Wales,* bequeathed by Richard Newsham
Cox the elder, David 1783–1859, *The Way to the Hayfield,* bequeathed by Richard Newsham
Cranke, William active 1730–1780, *William Farington,* on loan from Broughton
Cranke, William active 1730–1780, *Henry Farington,* purchased
Cranke the elder, James 1707–1780, *Mrs Winkley and Child,* gift from Lord Ribblesdale
Creffield, Dennis b.1931, *Flowers with Skull,* bequeathed by M. M. Lapsley through the Contemporary Art Society © the artist
Creswick, Thomas 1811–1869, *Summertime, Scene on the Llugwy, North Wales,* bequeathed by Richard Newsham
Creswick, Thomas 1811–1869, *Bolton Abbey,* purchased
Crewdson, J. active 1900–1950, *The 'Lady Alice Kenlis',* gift from John Little © the copyright holder

Crooke, Reginald Hoghton 1864–1929, *Ida,* gift from Ida Crooke
Cross, Joseph 1851–1897, *Flower Piece,* bequeathed by E. M. McMath
Cross, Joseph 1851–1897, *Portrait of an Old Man,* bequeathed by E. M. McMath
Cross, Joseph 1851–1897, *The Stream, Brock,* purchased
Cross, Joseph 1851–1897, *Study of Apples,* gift from H. Woods
Cundall, Charles Ernest 1890–1971, *Albi,* purchased © the artist's estate/Bridgeman Art Library
Cundall, Charles Ernest 1890–1971, *Preston,* gift from Levi Collison © the artist's estate/ Bridgeman Art Library
Czóbel, Béla Adalbert 1883–1976, *Szentendre,* bequeathed by Sarah McLeod © DACS 2012
Dadd, Richard 1817–1886, *Puck,* purchased with the assistance of the Heritage Lottery Fund, the Art Fund, Mrs D. Wade Bequest through the Arts Council and Friends of the Harris Museum & Art Gallery
Danby, Francis 1793–1861, *The Delivery of Israel out of Egypt,* gift from Margaret Gregson, Photo Credit: Bridgeman Art Library
Davies, J. 1828–1891, *The Housekeeper,* purchased
Davies, James H. 1828–1958, *Landscape,* purchased
Day, Walter Percy 1878–1965, *The Eleventh Hour, the Eleventh Day of the Eleventh Month, 1918,* purchased © the copyright holder, Photo Credit: Bridgeman Art Library
de Thame, Gerard b.1958, *Edge of the Night,* gift from the Contemporary Art Society © the artist
Derain, André 1880–1954, *Still Life with Fruit,* bequeathed by Sarah McLeod © ADAGP, Paris and DACS, London 2012
Derain, André 1880–1954, *Jardins a Donnemarie en Montois,* bequeathed by Sarah McLeod © ADAGP, Paris and DACS, London 2012
Devas, Anthony 1911–1958, *Mrs Avice Margaret Pimblett (1880–1963),* purchased © the artist's estate/Bridgeman Art Library
Devas, Anthony 1911–1958, *At the Couturier,* purchased © the artist's estate/Bridgeman Art Library
Devis, Anthony 1729–1816, *The River Ure at Hackfall, near Ripon, West Riding of Yorkshire,* purchased
Devis, Anthony 1729–1816, *The Weeping Rock – A Waterfall at Hackfall near Ripon, West Riding of Yorkshire,* purchased
Devis, Anthony 1729–1816, *Landscape with the Ruins of St Martha's Chapel Beyond,* gift from S. H. Paviere
Devis, Anthony 1729–1816, *St Martha's from Mr Devis's House at Albury, Surrey,* gift from S. H. Paviere
Devis, Anthony 1729–1816, *Albury House, Surrey,* gift from Samuel Courtauld
Devis, Anthony 1729–1816, *Romantic Landscape with Cattle and a Milkmaid,* purchased
Devis, Anthony 1729–1816, *Landscape with St Martha's Chapel,* gift from Harold Parkinson
Devis, Anthony 1729–1816, *Landscape with House on the Edge of a Wood,* purchased
Devis, Anthony 1729–1816, *A River Scene with a Mansion Amongst Trees,* unknown acquisition method
Devis, Anthony 1729–1816, *Dursley, Gloucestershire,* gift from Harold Parkinson
Devis, Anthony 1729–1816, *Landscape – Cottages and Cattle,* purchased
Devis, Anthony 1729–1816, *Landscape – View of Stirling Castle,* unknown acquisition method
Devis, Anthony 1729–1816, *Landscape with a Hut in an Oak Tree and the 'Man in the Moon' Inn,* purchased
Devis, Anthony 1729–1816, *Landscape with Castle,* gift from Harold Parkinson
Devis, Anthony 1729–1816, *Landscape, Church and Village,* purchased
Devis, Anthony 1729–1816, *Oxford,* purchased
Devis, Arthur 1712–1787, *Portrait of the Artist,* purchased
Devis, Arthur 1712–1787, *John Orlebar,* purchased
Devis, Arthur 1712–1787, *The Reverend William Farington,* purchased
Devis, Arthur 1712–1787, *Portrait of the Artist,* purchased, Photo Credit: Bridgeman Art Library
Devis, Arthur 1712–1787, *Elizabeth Faulkner, Wife of Arthur Devis,* purchased
Devis, Arthur 1712–1787, *The Reverend Streynsham Master and His Wife, Margaret of Croston, Lancashire,* gift from HM Government, Photo Credit: Bridgeman Art Library
Devis, Arthur 1712–1787, *Mary du Cane, née Norris,* purchased
Devis, Arthur 1712–1787, *Mr Peter du Cane (1713–1803),* purchased
Devis, Arthur 1712–1787, *Richard, Mary and Peter – The Children of Peter and Mary du Cane,* purchased
Devis, Arthur 1712–1787, *Anthony Devis (1729–1816),* purchased
Devis, Arthur 1712–1787, *Thomas Starkie,* purchased
Devis, Arthur 1712–1787, *The Right Honourable Daniel Pulteney,* transferred from the Corporation of Preston
Devis, Arthur 1712–1787, *Portrait of the Artist,* purchased
Devis, Arthur 1712–1787, *Francis Vincent of Weddington Hall, Warwickshire, with His Wife Mercy and Daughter Ann,* purchased
Devis, Arthur 1712–1787, *Nicholas Fazakerley (d.1767),* transferred from the Corporation of Preston
Devis, Arthur 1712–1787, *Mr and Mrs Richard Bull and Family,* purchased, Photo Credit: Bridgeman Art Library
Devis, Arthur 1712–1787, *Portrait of a Man,* purchased
Devis, Arthur William 1762–1822, *Miss Anderson with Her Dog,* gift from Lady Macleay
Devis, Arthur William 1762–1822, *Miss Ellen Devis,* purchased
Devis, Arthur William 1762–1822, *Portrait of an Actor,* (possibly Charles Dibdin), purchased
Devis, Arthur William 1762–1822, *The Dog Dido,* purchased
Devis, Arthur William 1762–1822, *John Addison,* purchased
Devis, Arthur William 1762–1822, *Ann Debonnaire,* purchased
Devis, Arthur William 1762–1822, *Mrs Anderson and Her Son William,* gift from Lady Macleay
Devis, Arthur William 1762–1822, *William Pitt Amherst (1773–1857), 1st Earl Amherst of Arracan, Viscount Holmesdale and Baron Amherst of Montreal,* purchased
Devis, Arthur William 1762–1822, *Marianna Augusta Cockburn,* purchased
Devis, Arthur William 1762–1822, *William Henry Vane (1766–1842), 3rd Earl of Darlington, Later 1st Duke of Cleveland,* purchased
Devis, Thomas Anthony 1757–1810, *Admiral Michael Clements,* purchased
Devis, Thomas Anthony 1757–1810, *Portrait of a Lady,* purchased
Di Stefano, Arturo b.1955, *Thérèse Lessore Sickert,* purchased © the artist
Dicksee, Frank 1853–1928, *Hesperia,* gift from Henry Eastwood
Dodd, Francis 1874–1949, *Alderman Frederick W. F. Matthew,* commissioned by the Corporation of Preston © the artist's estate
Dollman, John Charles 1851–1934, *During the Time of the Sermonses,* purchased, Photo Credit: Bridgeman Art Library
Downton, John 1906–1991, *Woman at the Window,* gift from The John Downton Trust © Harris Museum and Art Gallery
Draper, Herbert James 1864–1920, *The Ebb,* purchased
Dring, William D. 1904–1990, *Going to Bed,* purchased © the artist's estate/Bridgeman Art Library
Dring, William D. 1904–1990, *Alderman W. Beckett,* purchased © the artist's estate/Bridgeman Art Library
Dugdale, Thomas Cantrell 1880–1952, *Sir Alfred Howarth, JP, Town Clerk of Preston (1907–1933),* commissioned by the Corporation of Preston © Joanna Dunham
Duncan, Joseph b.1920, *Abstract (J'écoute),* gift from the Contemporary Art Society © the copyright holder
Dunlop, Ronald Ossory 1894–1973, *Walberswick,* purchased © the copyright holder
East, Alfred 1844–1913, *An Idyll of Spring,* purchased
East, Alfred 1844–1913, *Kirkstall Abbey,* gift from F. W. Sharples
East, Alfred 1844–1913, *On the Cole near Gardley Woods,* gift from J. T. Swarbrick
Egg, Augustus Leopold 1816–1863, *Girl Making a Bouquet of Flowers,* bequeathed by Richard Newsham, Photo Credit: Bridgeman Art Library
Egg, Augustus Leopold 1816–1863, *The Opera Mantle,* bequeathed by Richard Newsham
Elmore, Alfred 1815–1881, *Supplication,* bequeathed by Richard Newsham, Photo Credit: Bridgeman Art Library
Elwell, Frederick William 1870–1958, *The Curiosity Shop,* purchased © the copyright holder, Photo Credit: Bridgeman Art Library
Elwell, Frederick William 1870–1958, *Girl with a Cigarette,* purchased © the copyright holder, Photo Credit: Bridgeman Art Library
Etty, William 1787–1849, *'By the waters of Babylon we sat down and wept',* bequeathed by Richard Newsham
Etty, William 1787–1849, *Cupid in a Shell,* bequeathed by Richard Newsham
Eurich, Richard Ernst 1903–1992, *D-Day, Reconstruction (Battleships at Sea),* gift from the War Artists' Advisory Committee © the artist's estate/Bridgeman Art Library, Photo Credit: Bridgeman Art Library
Eurich, Richard Ernst 1903–1992, *D-Day, Reconstruction (Beach Landing),* gift from the War Artists' Advisory Committee © the artist's estate/Bridgeman Art Library, Photo Credit: Bridgeman Art Library
Eurich, Richard Ernst 1903–1992, *D-Day, Reconstruction (Bombed Cathedral),* gift from the War Artists' Advisory Committee © the artist's estate/Bridgeman Art Library, Photo Credit: Bridgeman Art Library
Eurich, Richard Ernst 1903–1992, *The Watercourse, Gordale,* purchased © the artist's estate/ Bridgeman Art Library
Eversen, Johannes Hendrik 1906–1995, *Seafood,* purchased © the copyright holder
Farquharson, David 1839–1907, *Sunrise,* unknown acquisition method
Ferguson, James active 1830–1860, *Avenham Park,* unknown acquisition method
Ferguson, James active 1830–1860, *The Ribble from Stanley Terrace,* purchased
Fildes, Luke 1843–1927, *Adoration,* purchased
Fisher, Percy Harland 1867–1944, *Dog With His Master's Dinner - La Fontaine's Fables,* gift from W. W. Galloway © the copyright holder, Photo Credit: Bridgeman Art Library
Fisk, William Henry 1827–1884, *Awaiting Publication of 'Le Moniteur' for News of the Arrest of Robespierre,* gift from the Harris Institute, Photo Credit: Bridgeman Art Library
Fitton, James 1899–1982, *The Long Green,* purchased © the artist's estate
Fitton, James 1899–1982, *Fresco,* purchased © the artist's estate
Fletcher, Edwin Henry Eugene 1857–1945, *The Pool of London,* gift from W. J. Mansley © the copyright holder
Fletcher, Geoffrey Scowcroft 1923–2004, *Le Portel,* gift from the artist © the artist's estate
Flint, William Russell 1880–1969, *Artemis and Chione,* purchased © the artist's estate
Flint, William Russell 1880–1969, *Matinee entr'acte – An Essay in Portraiture,* purchased © the artist's estate
Forbes, Stanhope Alexander 1857–1947, *Fishing Boats – Sketch,* gift from F. W. Sharples © the artist's estate/Bridgeman Art Library
Forbes, Stanhope Alexander 1857–1947, *On the Bridge,* purchased © the artist's estate/ Bridgeman Art Library, Photo Credit: Bridgeman Art Library
Forrester, Denzil b.1956, *Dub Scratchers,* purchased © the artist
Foster, Myles Birket 1825–1899, *The Wreck, Morning after the Storm, Scene at Dunstanbora,* gift from J. R. Smith
Fowler, F. *River Landscape,* unknown acquisition method
Freud, Lucian 1922–2011, *Still Life with Squid and Sea Urchin,* gift from the Contemporary Art Society © estate of Lucian Freud, Photo Credit: Bridgeman Art Library
Frith, William Powell 1819–1909, *Nora Creina,* bequeathed by Richard Newsham
Frith, William Powell 1819–1909, *A Scene from 'Le Bourgeois Gentilhomme',* bequeathed by Richard Newsham
Frith, William Powell 1819–1909, *At the Opera,* bequeathed by Richard Newsham
Fry, Roger Eliot 1866–1934, *A Game of Bowls,* gift from the Contemporary Art Society

Gabrysch, Leonard 1921–1993, *Window Gazers,* gift from Barton Townley © the copyright holder
Gandy, Herbert 1857–1934, *Companions,* gift from William Houghton Ainsworth
Gerrard, Charles 1892–1964, *The Young Dancer,* purchased © the copyright holder
Gilbert, John 1817–1897, *Sancho Panza,* gift from Nettleford Trustees
Gill, William Ward 1823–1894, *Swansea Bay,* unknown acquisition method
Ginner, Charles 1878–1952, *Rooftops,* purchased © the copyright holder
Glover, John 1767–1849, *Landscape,* gift from Clay
Goodall, Frederick 1822–1904, *The Tired Gleaners,* bequeathed by Richard Newsham
Goodall, Frederick 1822–1904, *The Sudden Rising of the Nile,* gift from William Smith
Goodwin, Albert 1845–1932, *Florence, Evening,* purchased, Photo Credit: Bridgeman Art Library
Gore, Spencer 1878–1914, *Garden at Hertingfordbury,* gift from the Contemporary Art Society, Photo Credit: Bridgeman Art Library
Gotch, Thomas Cooper 1854–1931, *A Golden Dream,* purchased, Photo Credit: Bridgeman Art Library
Green, H. Vaughan active 1880–1900, *A Sunny Evening, Lochranza,* gift from J. T. Swarbrick
Green, H. Vaughan active 1880–1900, *Landscape,* gift from H. Woods
Greenwood, Orlando 1892–1989, *Anemones,* purchased © the copyright holder
Greenwood, Orlando 1892–1989, *I Will Give You a Castle,* purchased © the copyright holder
Greenwood, Orlando 1892–1989, *June,* purchased © the copyright holder
Gribble, Bernard Finnigan 1872–1962, *Scapa Flow, 21 June 1919,* purchased © the artist's estate, Photo Credit: Bridgeman Art Library
Grimshaw, John Atkinson 1836–1893, *In the Golden Olden Times,* gift from W. W. Galloway, Photo Credit: Bridgeman Art Library
Grimshaw, John Atkinson 1836–1893, *Golden Visions,* gift from W. W. Galloway
Grimshaw, John Atkinson 1836–1893, *The Rector's Garden, Queen of the Lilies,* bequeathed by Dewhurst
Grundy, Cuthbert Cartwright 1846–1946, *Autumn,* gift from the artist © the copyright holder
Gunn, Herbert James 1893–1964, *Pauline in the Yellow Dress,* purchased © estate of the artist
Gunn, Herbert James 1893–1964, *James Harrison,* gift from Thomas Harrison © estate of the artist
Gunn, Herbert James 1893–1964, *Richard Durham,* purchased © estate of the artist
H., J. *The Chorley Family of Preston,* purchased, Photo Credit: Bridgeman Art Library
Hambling, Maggi b.1945, *July Sunrise, Orwell Estuary, No.2,* purchased © the artist/Bridgeman Art Library
Hambling, Maggi b.1945, *Harold Parker, Preston's Guild Mayor (1992),* purchased © the artist/ Bridgeman Art Library
Harrison, Claude 1922–2009, *Frank Jamieson,* commissioned by the Corporation of Preston © the artist's estate
Harrison, Frederick Clifford 1901–1984, *Still Life – Plates,* purchased © the copyright holder
Harvey, James *Girl Feeding a Goat,* unknown acquisition method
Hawthorne, Elwin 1905–1954, *Street Scene,* gift from the Contemporary Art Society © the artist's estate
Hayes, Claude 1852–1922, *Evensong,* purchased
Haythorn, Mabel active 1900–1950, *Pas des fleurs,* unknown acquisition method © the copyright holder
Hedley, Ralph 1848–1913, *'Go, and God's will be done!',* unknown acquisition method
Henderson, Keith 1883–1982, *The Word,* purchased © the copyright holder
Herbert, John Rogers 1810–1890, *Cordelia Disinherited,* bequeathed by Vaughan
Herbert, John Rogers 1810–1890, *The Judgement of Daniel,* bequeathed by Richard Newsham, Photo Credit: Bridgeman Art Library
Herbert, Sydney 1854–1914, *San Giorgio Maggiore, Venice,* unknown acquisition method
Herring I, John Frederick (school of) 1795–1865, *Two Racehorses – 'Grey Momus' and 'Caravan' – Racing,* bequeathed by M. A. L. Williams
Herring I, John Frederick (school of) 1795–1865, *Two Racehorses – 'Charles XII' and 'Buella' – with Jockeys,* bequeathed by M. A. L. Williams
Heyworth, Alfred 1926–1976, *Ann with Indoor Plants,* purchased © the copyright holder
Hicks, Philip b.1928, *Mirror on the Balcony Overlooking the Bay,* gift from the Contemporary Art Society © the artist
Highmore, Joseph 1692–1780, *Portrait of a Gentleman,* unknown acquisition method
Hillier, Tristram Paul 1905–1983, *The Argument,* gift from the Contemporary Art Society © the artist's estate/Bridgeman Art Library, Photo Credit: Bridgeman Art Library
Hillier, Tristram Paul 1905–1983, *January Landscape, Somerset,* purchased © the artist's estate/ Bridgeman Art Library
Himid, Lubaina b.1954, *Hannibal's Sister,* purchased © the artist
Himid, Lubaina b.1954, *Tuesday,* purchased © the artist
Himid, Lubaina b.1954, *Weave,* purchased © the artist
Hitchens, Ivon 1893–1979, *Two Ways through a Wood,* purchased © Ivon Hitchens' estate/Jonathan Clark & Co.
Hodkinson, W. E. *Clifton Windmill,* purchased © the copyright holder
Hogarth, William 1697–1764, *Lord Lovat,* unknown acquisition method
Holland, James 1799–1870, *Rotterdam,* bequeathed by Richard Newsham
Holland, James 1799–1870, *The Chancel,* gift from F. W. Sharples
Hollis, Gerald b.1908, *A Welsh Cottage,* purchased © the copyright holder
Holman, W. H. *Landscape with Cattle,* unknown acquisition method
Holmes, Charles John 1868–1936, *Langdale Pikes,* gift from Dickson, Joseph and Healy
Holmes, Charles John 1868–1936, *Scholar Gipsy,* gift from Joseph Dickson
Holmes, Charles John 1868–1936, *Watendlath Tarn, near Keswick,* purchased
Holmes, Charles John 1868–1936, *Farmyard, Winter,* purchased
Holmes, Richard 1868–1938, *Blacksmith at Work,* unknown acquisition method
Holmes, Richard 1868–1938, *Jacobite Troops Surrendering Their Arms to General Wills in Preston Market Place, 1715,* unknown acquisition method
Hook, James Clarke 1819–1907, *The Rescue of the Brides of Venice,* bequeathed by Richard Newsham
Hook, James Clarke 1819–1907, *Welcome, Bonny Boat! The Fisherman's Return (Scene at Clovelly, North Devon),* bequeathed by Richard Newsham
Hooper, John Horace 1852–1906, *Cookham on Thames,* gift from F. W. Sharples
Hope, Robert 1869–1936, *Portrait of a Lady with a Motoring Veil,* purchased
Horsley, John Callcott 1817–1903, *Forfeits,* bequeathed by R. Orlebar
Houston, George 1869–1947, *Seed Time in Ayrshire,* purchased © the artist's estate
Houston, John Adam 1812–1884, *View near Trarbach on the Moselle,* gift from John Billington Booth
Houston, John Adam 1812–1884, *The Secreting of the Regalia of Scotland in Kineff Church, 1652,* gift from John Billington Booth
Howson, Peter b.1958, *Untitled and Two Figures in a Wood,* bequeathed by Danielle Harrison © the artist/courtesy Flowers Gallery, London
Hoyoll, Philipp 1818–1876, *Isaac Simpson,* purchased
Hoyoll, Philipp 1818–1876, *Mary Simpson,* purchased
Hoyoll, Philipp 1818–1876, *Stephen Simpson,* gift from Wendy Stuart
Hughes, Arthur 1832–1915, *Bedtime,* gift from S. H. Pavière
Hughes, William 1842–1901, *Lemons and Flowers,* bequeathed by Fearnside
Hughes, William 1842–1901, *Pomegranates and Flowers,* bequeathed by Fearnside
Hughes, William 1842–1901 *Still Life – Fruit,* bequeathed by Fearnside
Hughes-Stanton, Herbert Edwin Pelham 1870–1937, *Early Morning – Les beaux Provence,* purchased
Hulbert, Thelma 1913–1995, *Window on the Terrace,* gift from the Contemporary Art Society © the copyright holder
Hunt, Alfred William 1830–1896, *Styhead Pass, Borrowdale,* bequeathed by R. S. Lewty
Hunt, Charles 1803–1877, *The Masquerade,* gift from the Fine Art Society
Hunter, Colin 1841–1904, *Signs of Herring,* purchased
Jackowski, Andrzej b.1947, *The Fir Tree,* purchased © the artist
Jackson, G. active 1798–1816, *Edward Robert Travers,* unknown acquisition method
Jackson, Joseph 1858–1922, *Anderton's Wood, near Preston,* gift from E. Kay
Jackson, Joseph 1858–1922, *In Summer Time,* purchased
Jacomb-Hood, George Percy 1857–1929, *State Room, Governor's House, Royal Hospital, Chelsea,* purchased
Jamieson, Alexander 1873–1937, *The Old Moat, Weston Turville,* purchased
Jenkinson, John P. active 1790–1821, *View of Preston from Penwortham Hill,* purchased
Jérôme, Ambrosini 1810–1883, *Rubens Presenting His Picture 'Peace and War' to Charles I,* gift from J. R. Smith
John, Augustus Edwin 1878–1961, *Dorelia,* purchased © the artist's estate/Bridgeman Art Library
Jones, Charles 1836–1902, *Seaside Landscape with Sheep,* bequeathed by Dewhurst
Jonzen, Basil 1913–1967, *Coast at Puerto de la Cruz,* gift from the Contemporary Art Society, image unavailable due to copyright restrictions
Jowett, Percy Hague 1882–1955, *Window in Cornwall,* purchased © the artist's estate
Joy, Thomas Musgrave 1812–1866, *Fredrica Horne,* gift from the Contemporary Art Society
Jutsum, Henry 1816–1869, *Landscape,* gift from Robert Ashcroft
Kay, Bernard b.1927, *Deserted Hill Village,* gift from Ewart Bradshaw © the artist
Keane, John b.1954, *Controlling Interest,* purchased © the artist/ courtesy Flowers Gallery, London
Kemm, Robert 1830–1895, *A Muleteer of Granada,* gift from William Houghton Ainsworth
Kemm, Robert 1830–1895, *The Spanish Fruit Seller,* gift from R. Hack, Photo Credit: Bridgeman Art Library
Kerr, Charles Henry Malcolm 1858–1907, *Chrysanthemums,* gift from G. Kerr, Photo Credit: Bridgeman Art Library
King, Gunning 1859–1940, *Hampshire Meads,* purchased
King, Henry John Yeend 1855–1924, *Girl at a Well,* gift from Mrs Morris
Kitchen, R. *Hoghton Bottoms, near Preston,* unknown acquisition method © the copyright holder
Knell, William Calcott 1830–1880, *Fishing Boats off Harwich,* gift from F. W. Sharples
Knell, William Calcott 1830–1880, *Summer Morning off Yarmouth,* gift from F. W. Sharples
Knight, Harold 1874–1961, *The Girl and the Letter,* purchased © reproduced with permission of the estate of Dame Laura Knight, DBE, RA, 2012. All rights reserved
Knight, Harold 1874–1961, *Girl Reading,* purchased © reproduced with permission of the estate of Dame Laura Knight, DBE, RA, 2012. All rights reserved, Photo Credit: Bridgeman Art Library
Knight, Laura 1877–1970, *Susie and the Wash Basin,* purchased © reproduced with permission of the estate of Dame Laura Knight, DBE, RA, 2012. All rights reserved, Photo Credit: Bridgeman Art Library
Knight, Laura 1877–1970, *A Musical Clown,* purchased © reproduced with permission of the estate of Dame Laura Knight, DBE, RA, 2012. All rights reserved
Knight, Laura 1877–1970, *In for Repairs,* gift from the War Artists' Advisory Committee © reproduced with permission of the estate of Dame Laura Knight, DBE, RA, 2012. All rights reserved, Photo Credit: Bridgeman Art Library
Krut, Ansel b.1959, *The Ventriloquist's Convention,* gift © the artist
Lai Ming-Hoi, Victor b.1961, *After Talking with Michael,* bequeathed by Danielle Harrison © the copyright holder
Landseer, Edwin Henry 1802–1873, *A Puppy Teasing a Frog,* bequeathed by Richard Newsham, Photo Credit: Bridgeman Art Library

Landseer, Edwin Henry (attributed to) 1802–1873, *Catherine Seyton Looking from the Battlements at Loch Leven Castle,* bequeathed by Richard Newsham
Le Bas, Edward 1904–1966, *By the Window,* purchased © the copyright holder
Le Brun, Christopher b.1951, *Grove,* purchased © the artist/ Bridgeman Art Library
Leader, Benjamin Williams 1831–1923, *Cambria's Coast,* purchased
Lee, Frederick Richard 1798–1879, *Study of a Woman,* purchased
Leese, Spencer 1843–1894, *Lancashire Coast Scene,* gift from W. G. Mankinson
Leighton, Frederic 1830–1896, *Interior of the Grand Mosque, Damascus,* purchased, Photo Credit: Bridgeman Art Library
Leslie, Charles Robert 1794–1859, *Olivia Raising her Veil,* bequeathed by Richard Newsham, Photo Credit: Bridgeman Art Library
Leslie, Charles Robert 1794–1859, *The Present,* bequeathed by Richard Newsham, Photo Credit: Bridgeman Art Library
Leslie, Charles Robert 1794–1859, *Consultation,* bequeathed by Richard Newsham
Leslie, Charles Robert 1794–1859, *Perdita,* bequeathed by Richard Newsham
Leslie, Charles Robert 1794–1859, *Sir John Falstaff,* bequeathed by Richard Newsham, Photo Credit: Bridgeman Art Library
Levy, Emmanuel 1900–1986, *The Red Shawl,* purchased © the copyright holder
Lewis, John Frederick 1804–1876, *A Bashi-Bazouk,* bequeathed by Richard Newsham
Lewis, John Frederick 1804–1876, *The Attendant on the Bath,* bequeathed by Richard Newsham
Lewis, John Frederick 1804–1876, *In the Bey's Garden,* bequeathed by Richard Newsham, Photo Credit: Bridgeman Art Library
Linnell, John 1792–1882, *An Overshot Mill,* bequeathed by Vaughan
Linnell, John 1792–1882, *Kensington Gravel Pits,* bequeathed by Richard Newsham
Linnell, John 1792–1882, *L'allegro, 'Many a youth and many a maid, dancing in the chequered shade',* bequeathed by Richard Newsham
Linnell, John 1792–1882, *Summer Evening, Boys Bathing,* bequeathed by Richard Newsham
Linnell, John 1792–1882, *The Fallen Monarch of the Forest,* bequeathed by Richard Newsham
Linnell, John 1792–1882, *The Disobedient Prophet (1 Kings, Chapter 13),* bequeathed by Richard Newsham
Linnell, John 1792–1882, *The Woodcutter's Return,* bequeathed by Richard Newsham
Linnell, John 1792–1882, *The Vale of Dolwyddelan, as it was in 1814,* bequeathed by Richard Newsham
Linnell, John 1792–1882, *The Traveller's Rest,* bequeathed by Richard Newsham
Linnell, John 1792–1882, *Haying and Playing,* gift from J. R. Smith
Linnell, John 1792–1882, *Scene on the Thames with Boats,* bequeathed by Richard Newsham
Liverseege, Henry 1803–1832, *Friar Tuck,* gift from Reginald K. Orlebar, Photo Credit: Bridgeman Art Library
Lockwood, Enid *The Guild, 1328,* © the copyright holder
Logsdail, William 1859–1944, *Mary Logsdail,* purchased © the artist's estate/Bridgeman Art Library
Logsdail, William 1859–1944, *Master Coleridge Hills,* on loan from Mrs B. Applegate © the artist's estate/Bridgeman Art Library
Logsdail, William 1859–1944, *The Children of James Todd,* bequeathed by Mrs Todd © the artist's estate/ Bridgeman Art Library, Photo Credit: Bridgeman Art Library
Lonsdale, James 1777–1839, *Samuel Horrocks (1767–1842),* gift from Helen Mills
Lonsdale, James 1777–1839, *Dr William St Clair,* gift from Helen Mills
Lonsdale, James 1777–1839, *Robert Holden,* gift from Mrs Allen
Lonsdale, James 1777–1839, *William Farington of Shawe Hall,* unknown acquisition method
Lowry, Laurence Stephen 1887–1976, *Millworkers,* purchased © the estate of L. S. Lowry. All rights reserved, DACS 2012
Lucas, George 1840–1912, *Landscape,* unknown acquisition method
Lynch, Thomas active 1830–1880, *View of Avenham Park with Tram Bridge,* gift from S. Wager
Maclise, Daniel 1806–1870, *Rosalind and Celia,* bequeathed by Richard Newsham, Photo Credit: Bridgeman Art Library
Markiewicz, Herbert Otto b.1900, *Alderman R. C. Pye,* purchased © the copyright holder
Marriott, Frederick 1860–1941, *Saint Cecilia,* unknown acquisition method
Mayor, Patti 1872–1962, *The Half-Timer,* purchased © the copyright holder
Mayor, Patti 1872–1962, *The Sewing Maid,* gift from the artist © the copyright holder
Mayor, Patti 1872–1962, *Portrait of a Girl with an Apple,* gift from the artist © the copyright holder
Mayor, Patti 1872–1962, *Self Portrait,* gift from the artist © the copyright holder
Mayor, Patti 1872–1962, *Portrait of a Girl in a Cap,* purchased © the copyright holder
Mayor, Patti 1872–1962, *Portrait of a Young Girl,* gift from Jane Hewitson © the copyright holder
Mayor, Patti 1872–1962, *Miss Mary Martin,* gift from the sitter © the copyright holder
Mayor, Patti 1872–1962, *Head of a Boy,* gift from Jane Hewitson © the copyright holder
Mayor, Patti 1872–1962, *A Bowl Filled with Red Flowers,* unknown acquisition method © the copyright holder
McCulloch, Horatio 1805–1867, *Dunbar Castle,* gift from F. W. Sharples
McCulloch, Ian b.1935, *Near Quang Tri, Vietnam,* gift from the Contemporary Art Society © the artist
McGregor, Robert 1847–1922, *Three Generations,* purchased
McKeever, Ian b.1946, *Traditional Landscape: Beside the Brambled Ditch,* gift from the Contemporary Art Society © Ian McKeever. All rights reserved, DACS 2012
McKeever, Ian b.1946, *Old Trees – Blue,* purchased © Ian McKeever. All rights reserved, DACS 2012
McLean, Bruce b.1944, *Untitled,* purchased © the artist
Meade, Arthur 1863–1948, *A Wind-Swept Shore,* purchased © the artist's estate
Mellor, William 1851–1931, *On the Lledr, North Wales,* unknown acquisition method
Melville, Arthur 1855–1904, *The White Piano,* gift from A. Margerison
Menzies, John active 1871–1939, *September Morning in the Hebrides,* purchased
Merchant, Henry active 1883–1940, *Glories of Summer,* purchased
Mieris the younger, Frans van (attributed to) 1689–1763, *Interior with Two Figures,* bequeathed by Fearnside
Milner, Frederick 1855–1939, *Near Ludlow,* gift from S. Milner
Milner, Frederick 1855–1939, *Marshland,* purchased
Mohalyi, Yolanda 1909–1978, *Painting No.7,* gift © the copyright holder
Monamy, Peter 1681–1749, *A Gentleman Taking Leave of His Family,* bequeathed by John Frederick Tillotson
Moody, Victor Hume 1896–1990, *Crossing the Brook,* purchased © the artist's estate
Moore, Pandora active 1954–1958, *Chloe,* purchased © the copyright holder
Morland, George 1763–1804, *Huntsman Asking the Way,* gift from F. W. Sharples
Morland, George 1763–1804, *Portrait of a Man,* bequeathed by Jukes
Morris, Cedric Lockwood 1889–1982, *The Farmyard, Dorset,* gift from the Contemporary Art Society © trustees of the Cedric Lockwood Morris Estate/ Foundation
Morris, Philip Richard 1836–1902, *The First Born,* gift from J. R. Smith, Photo Credit: Bridgeman Art Library
Morris, William 1834–1896, *Landscape,* gift from M. Foster
Morrison, Robert Edward 1851–1924, *Sir William Ascroft,* gift from Ashcroft
Moynihan, Rodrigo 1910–1990, *Gabriele Annan,* purchased © the artist's estate
Moynihan, Rodrigo 1910–1990, *Dennis Carlton Walmsley,* bequeathed by the sitter © the artist's estate
Muller, F. 1812–1882, *Madonna and Child* (copy of Raphael), bequeathed by Fearnside
Muller, William James 1812–1845, *Scene near Whitchurch,* bequeathed by Richard Newsham
Muller, William James 1812–1845, *Whitchurch,* bequeathed by Richard Newsham
Muller, William James 1812–1845, *Classical Landscape,* gift from F. W. Sharples
Muller, William James 1812–1845, *Elizabethan Interior: The Court Messenger,* bequeathed by Dewhurst
Muller, William James 1812–1845, *Salmon Trap, near Pont-y-Pridd, South Wales,* bequeathed by Richard Newsham
Muller, William James 1812–1845, *Scene in Wales,* bequeathed by Richard Newsham
Munnings, Alfred James 1878–1959, *Whitsuntide – A Gala Day,* gift from H. Woods © Sir Alfred Munnings Art Museum, Photo Credit: Bridgeman Art Library
Munnings, Alfred James 1878–1959, *The Last of the Fair,* purchased, © Sir Alfred Munnings Art Museum
Munnings, Alfred James 1878–1959, *The Inn Yard,* gift from E. E. Ord, © Sir Alfred Munnings Art Museum
Munnings, Alfred James 1878–1959, *The Full River,* purchased, © Sir Alfred Munnings Art Museum, Photo Credit: Bridgeman Art Library
Munnings, Alfred James 1878–1959, *Old John, the Coachman,* bequeathed by E. M. McMath, © Sir Alfred Munnings Art Museum
Murillo, Bartolomé Esteban (after) 1617–1682, *The Children of the Shell,* unknown acquisition method
Murray, David 1849–1933, *The Water Cart,* unknown acquisition method
Nasmyth, Patrick 1787–1831, *Landscape with Sportsmen,* gift from F. W. Sharples
Naviasky, Philip 1894–1982, *Connemara,* purchased © the artist's estate
Naziere, David active 19th C, *Hungarian Gipsy,* unknown acquisition method
Netscher, Caspar 1639–1684, *Diana,* bequeathed by Jukes
Netscher, Caspar 1639–1684, *Isaac Newton (1642–1727),* bequeathed by Jukes
Newton, Algernon Cecil 1880–1968, *The House by the Canal,* purchased © the copyright holder, Photo Credit: Bridgeman Art Library
Newton, Kenneth 1933–1984, *Water Barrel and Carrier,* purchased © the artist's estate
Nicholls, Bertram 1883–1974, *By a Sussex Stream,* purchased © the copyright holder
Nicholls, Bertram 1883–1974, *Ragusa,* purchased © the copyright holder
Nickson, Robert Peter *Study for 'Ward's End',* gift from J. K. Booth © the copyright holder
O'Neill, George Bernard 1828–1917, *The Message,* bequeathed by Richard Newsham
Oakes, John Wright 1820–1887, *Slate Quarries, Llanberis,* gift from Reginald K. Orlebar
Olsson, Albert Julius 1864–1942, *Sunset at Land's End,* purchased © the copyright holder
Osborne, Walter Frederick 1859–1903, *Summertime,* purchased
Oulton, Thérèse b.1953, *Spoils,* purchased © the artist
Park, John Anthony 1880–1962, *Port Gavern at Low Tide,* purchased © the artist's estate
Park, John Anthony 1880–1962, *Morning Tide,* purchased © the artist's estate, Photo Credit: Bridgeman Art Library
Park, John Anthony 1880–1962, *Aloysius Smith (Trader Horn),* purchased © the artist's estate
Park, John Anthony 1880–1962, *Roman Bridge, Pollensa, Mallorca,* purchased © the artist's estate
Park, John Anthony 1880–1962, *Portrait of the Artist,* gift from Mrs Dolphin © the artist's estate
Park, John Anthony 1880–1962, *Harbour Scene with Yachts,* gift from Agnes Holden © the artist's estate
Park, John Anthony 1880–1962, *Preston Market in the Olden Days,* gift from W. J. Mansley © the artist's estate
Peel, James 1811–1906, *Totteridge, near Hampstead,* gift from F. W. Sharples
Pejo, John active 1900–1950, *Horses and Jockeys,* gift from Dunne, J © the copyright holder
Pether, Henry 1801–1880, *Westminster in the Moonlight,* gift from M. Foster
Pether, Henry 1801–1880, *Scene on the Thames,* gift from M. Foster
Phillip, John 1817–1867, *Spanish Industry,* bequeathed by Richard Newsham, Photo Credit: Bridgeman Art Library

Phillip, John 1817–1867, *Church Interior with Figures,* gift from F. W. Sharples

Philpot, Leonard Daniel 1877–1973, *June's Largesse,* purchased © the copyright holder

Phizackerley, Patrick Terence 1931–2002, *Tiger,* gift from an anonymous donor © the copyright holder

Pigott, William Henry 1810–1901, *Yorkshire Coast,* gift from F. W. Sharples

Pilbro, Anthony b.1954, *Adam and Eve,* bequeathed by Danielle Harrison © the artist

Pilbro, Anthony b.1954, *A Portrait,* bequeathed by Danielle Harrison © the artist

Pissarro, Lucien 1863–1944, *Eden Valley,* gift from the Contemporary Art Society © the artist's estate

Poole, Paul Falconer 1807–1879, *Crossing the Heath, Windy Day,* bequeathed by Richard Newsham, Photo Credit: Bridgeman Art Library

Poole, Paul Falconer 1807–1879, *Autumn: Welsh Girl at a Mountain Stream,* bequeathed by Richard Newsham

Poole, Paul Falconer 1807–1879, *Shepherd Boys and the Scarecrow,* bequeathed by Richard Newsham

Porter, Frederick James 1883–1944, *Hanover Square,* gift from the Contemporary Art Society © the copyright holder

Pott, Laslett John 1837–1898, *Priscilla, the Courtship of Miles Standish,* purchased, Photo Credit: Bridgeman Art Library

Powell, Charles Martin 1775–1824, *Seascape,* gift from F. W. Sharples

Pritt, William 1870–1944, *August Moonlight,* purchased © the copyright holder

Pritt, William 1870–1944, *Impression of the 1922 Guild,* unknown acquisition method © the copyright holder

Pritt, William 1870–1944, *Michaelmas Flowers,* purchased © the copyright holder

Pritt, William 1870–1944, *Hodder Bridge,* gift from A. M. MacFarlane © the copyright holder

Pritt, William 1870–1944, *Old Walton Bridge,* unknown acquisition method © the copyright holder

Proctor, Adam Edwin 1864–1913, *The Carpenter's Shop,* gift from H. Woods

Provis, Alfred 1818–1890, *Harvest Ale,* gift from A. M. Pimblett

Pyne, James Baker 1800–1870, *Mount Etna from the Theatre, Taormina,* bequeathed by Dewhurst

Ralphs, D. *Park School, Preston,* gift © the copyright holder

Raven, John Samuel 1829–1877, *'Let the hills be joyful together',* gift from W. Holiday

Raven, John Samuel 1829–1877, *Seascape: Hastings Coast Scene,* gift from Miss Allen

Redpath, Anne 1895–1965, *Flower Stall at Lisbon,* purchased © the artist's estate/Bridgeman Art Library

Reinagle, Ramsay Richard 1775–1862, *Landscape,* gift from Lord Ribblesdale

Reinagle, Ramsay Richard 1775–1862, *Windermere,* gift from Lord Ribblesdale

Richards, Albert 1919–1945, *Inglesham Church and Rectory,* purchased with the assistance of the Art Fund © the copyright holder

Richards, Albert 1919–1945, *The Minute Halt,* purchased with the assistance of the Art Fund © the copyright holder

Richards, William Trost 1833–1905, *After a Gale,* purchased

Richmond, W. active 19th C, *Profiles of Two Heads,* unknown acquisition method

Richmond, William Blake 1842–1921, *A Sibyl,* unknown acquisition method

Ridgewell, John 1937–2004, *Reflections,* purchased © the artist's estate

Roberts, David 1796–1864, *Antwerp Cathedral,* bequeathed by Richard Newsham

Roberts, David 1796–1864, *Shrine of Saint Gomar at Lierre, Belgium,* bequeathed by Richard Newsham, Photo Credit: Bridgeman Art Library

Roberts, David 1796–1864, *The Tombs of the Scaligeri at Verona,* bequeathed by Richard Newsham

Roberts, William Patrick 1895–1980, *The Common Market,* purchased © estate of John David Roberts. By courtesy of The William Roberts Society, Photo Credit: Bridgeman Art Library

Robertson, George 1724–1788, *Jamaican Landscape,* bequeathed by Jukes, Photo Credit: Bridgeman Art Library

Robin, Jean Baptiste Claude 1734–1818, *Portrait of a Man,* bequeathed by Jukes

Robinson, Edward 1896–1975, *Tom Finney (b.1922),* purchased © the copyright holder

Romney, George 1734–1802, *Serena Reading,* purchased with the assistance of the Heritage Lottery Fund, the Art Fund, the Victoria and Albert Purchase Grant Fund, and the Friends of the Harris Museum & Art Gallery, Photo Credit: Bridgeman Art Library

Romney, George (attributed to) 1734–1802, *John Flaxman (1755–1826),* purchased

Romney, George (attributed to) 1734–1802, *Mr Threlfall and Mrs Ann Threlfall,* gift from E. Garside

Roscoe, Frederick William 1838–1902, *Entrance to the Willows, Ashton-on-Ribble,* unknown acquisition method

Roscoe, Frederick William 1838–1902, *Still Life – Grapes, Orange and Hazelnuts,* gift from the artist

Rosenvinge, Olaf 1913–2004, *Bavarian Idyll,* purchased © the artist's estate

Rosenvinge, Olaf 1913–2004, *Portrait of a Boy,* unknown acquisition method © the artist's estate

Royle, Herbert F. 1870–1958, *Morning in the Hay Meadows,* purchased © the artist's estate

Salisbury, Frank O. 1874–1962, *Sir Frank Hollins,* loan © estate of Frank O. Salisbury. All rights reserved, DACS 2012

Sanderson, William *The Ayr Harbour,* purchased © the copyright holder

Sant, James 1820–1916, *The Novice,* bequeathed by Richard Newsham

Sant, James 1820–1916, *Julie, Daughter of Spencer H. Gollan, Esq.,* gift from the sitter

Schafer, Henry Thomas 1854–1915, *Ratisbon, Bavaria,* gift from F. W. Sharples

Schafer, Henry Thomas 1854–1915, *Mayence,* bequeathed by Sumner

Scheibitz, Thomas b.1968, *Low Sweetie,* gift © DACS 2012

Scott, Hugh Berry 1854–1924, *Harvesting, a Field of Yellow Plenty,* purchased

Seabrooke, Elliott 1886–1950, *Bank of Trees,* gift from the Contemporary Art Society © the copyright holder

Seabrooke, Elliott 1886–1950, *Joseph Livesey,* unknown acquisition method © the copyright holder

Seed, T. active 1838–1850, *Portrait of an Unknown Man with a Gun,* unknown acquisition method

Sewell, Robert *The Prizewinner,* purchased © the copyright holder

Shackleton, William 1872–1933, *The City of the Golden Gates,* gift from M. Shackleton

Shalders, George 1826–1873, *Scene in Wales,* gift from William Houghton Ainsworth

Shaw, Charles Edward 1870–1959, *General View of Preston,* gift from G. Brown ©the copyright holder

Shaw, Charles Edward 1870–1959, *Portrait of a Gentleman,* gift from Mrs Bagnall ©the copyright holder

Shaw, Charles Edward 1870–1959, *Sporting,* gift from Robert Gardner ©the copyright holder

Sherwood, Vladimir Ossipovitch 1832–1897, *The Preston By-Election of 1862,* purchased, Photo Credit: Bridgeman Art Library

Sickert, Walter Richard 1860–1942, *Two Women,* gift from the Contemporary Art Society © estate of Walter R. Sickert. All rights reserved, DACS 2012

Simm, William Norris 1885–1948, *Sir Richard Arkwright (1732–1792),* commissioned ©the copyright holder

Simm, William Norris 1885–1948, *Alderman John Crook Hamilton,* commissioned ©the copyright holder

Simm, William Norris 1885–1948, *Dr Sir Charles Brown,* commissioned ©the copyright holder

Simm, William Norris 1885–1948, *John Forshaw,* commissioned ©the copyright holder

Simm, William Norris 1885–1948, *Alderman Edmund Birley,* commissioned ©the copyright holder

Simm, William Norris 1885–1948, *Frederick Stanley (1841–1908), 16th Earl of Derby, Guild Mayor (1902),* commissioned ©the copyright holder

Singleton, Rosemary L. active 1958–1959, *Typical,* gift from an anonymous donor ©the copyright holder

Smith, Charles active 1857–1908, *Dartford Heath, Kent,* gift from F. W. Sharples

Smith, James Burrell 1822–1897, *Landscape,* unknown acquisition method

Smith, John Brandon 1848–1884, *Killarney,* bequeathed by Vaughan

Smith, Matthew Arnold Bracy 1879–1959, *Pont Aven Landscape,* bequeathed by Sarah McLeod © by permission of the copyright holder

Smith, Matthew Arnold Bracy 1879–1959, *Reflections,* gift from the Contemporary Art Society © by permission of the copyright holder

Smith, Matthew Arnold Bracy 1879–1959, *Roses in a Vase,* bequeathed © by permission of the copyright holder

Snyders, Frans (studio of) 1579–1657, *The Fruit Stall,* gift from W. H. Harris, Photo Credit: Bridgeman Art Library

Soest, Gerard 1600–1681, *Lady and Attendant with Fruit,* purchased

Solbach, K. *Landscape with a Pond,* gift from Paul Lampkin

Solomon, Solomon Joseph 1860–1927, *An Allegory,* purchased

Somerscales, John 1846–1945, *The Temple of Isis at Philae,* commissioned © the copyright holder

Somerscales, John 1846–1945, *Pyramids at Giza,* commissioned © the copyright holder

Somerscales, John 1846–1945, *The Colossi of Memnon at Thebes,* commissioned © the copyright holder

Somerscales, John 1846–1945, *The Great Temple of Amun-Ra at Karnak,* commissioned © the copyright holder

Somerscales, John 1846–1945, *The Nile at Aswan,* commissioned © the copyright holder

Somerscales, John 1846–1945, *The Sphin, Gizeh,* commissioned © the copyright holder

Somerscales, John 1846–1945, *The Temple of Kom Ombo,* commissioned © the copyright holder

Somerscales, John 1846–1945, *The Temple of Kom Ombo,* commissioned © the copyright holder

Somerscales, Thomas Jacques 1842–1927, *Hove to for a Pilot,* purchased

Somerscales, Thomas Jacques 1842–1927, *A Strong Breeze in the Channel,* gift from Mrs Morris

Spear, Ruskin 1911–1990, *Alf and the Canary,* purchased © the artist's estate/Bridgeman Art Library

Spear, Ruskin 1911–1990, *Alderman Gray,* commissioned © the artist's estate/Bridgeman Art Library

Spencelayh, Charles 1865–1958, *Why War?,* purchased © the artist's estate/Bridgeman Art Library

Spencer, Stanley 1891–1959, *Wisteria,* purchased © the estate of Stanley Spencer 2012. All rights reserved DACS

Spencer, Stanley 1891–1959, *Resurrection: The Hill of Zion,* purchased © the estate of Stanley Spencer 2012. All rights reserved DACS, Photo Credit: Bridgeman Art Library

Spender active 19th C, *Peter Haydock,* unknown acquisition method

Stead, Frederick 1863–1940, *Will-o'-the-wisp,* purchased

Stevens, Norman 1937–1988, *Barn,* purchased © the artist's estate

Stokes, Adrian Scott 1854–1935, *Islands of the Adriatic,* purchased

Stokes, Adrian Scott 1854–1935, *The Setting Sun,* purchased

Stott, Edward William 1859–1918, *A Cottage Madonna,* purchased

Strevens, John Lloyd 1902–1990, *Dressing Up,* purchased © the copyright holder

Stuart, Charles active 1854–1904, *Disputed Rights,* gift from Frank Calvert

Symons, Mark Lancelot 1887–1935, *Molly in the Garden,* purchased, Photo Credit: Bridgeman Art Library

T., E. *John Best,* unknown acquisition method

Talmage, Algernon 1871–1939, *The Chalk Pit,* purchased

Tayler, Albert Chevallier 1862–1925, *The Anniversary,* purchased, Photo Credit: Bridgeman Art Library

Tennant, John F. 1796–1872, *Landscape with Figures, near St Omer,* purchased

Thomas, Glynne *Kitchen Study,* purchased © the copyright holder

Thompson, Charles Herbert 1870–1946, *Portrait of a Woman Holding Roses,* unknown acquisition method © the copyright holder

Thompson, G. active 19th C, *Landscape,* unknown acquisition method
Thompson, G. active 19th C, *Landscape,* unknown acquisition method
Thornley, Georges William 1857–1935, *Seascape – Fishing Boats,* gift from F. W. Sharples
Thornley, Georges William 1857–1935, *Racing Yachts,* unknown acquisition method
Thornley, Georges William 1857–1935, *Racing Yachts in Rough Seas,* unknown acquisition method
Thornton, Alfred Henry Robinson 1863–1939, *November,* gift from the Contemporary Art Society
Tillemans, Peter (attributed to) 1684–1734, *Figures in a Landscape,* gift from F. W. Sharples
Tilson, Joe b.1928, *Road to Eleusis 2,* purchased © Joe Tilson 2012. All rights reserved, DACS
Tomson, Clifton circle of 1775–1828, *Horse and Greyhound,* gift from Lord Ribblesdale
Turner *Joseph Swarbrick,* unknown acquisition method
unknown artist *Summer Flowers,* bequeathed by Jukes
unknown artist *John Atherton,* unknown acquisition method
unknown artist *Portrait of a Lady in Blue and White Dress,* gift from W. W. Galloway
unknown artist *Portrait of a Man,* gift from W. W. Galloway
unknown artist *William Cross of Red Scar (1771–1827),* gift from A. Margerison
unknown artist *The Reverend Roger Carus Wilson,* bequeathed by Mrs Wilson
unknown artist *Samuel Horrocks, Guild Mayor (1842),* gift from Helen Mills
unknown artist *Hugh Foster,* gift from Miss Foster
unknown artist *Mrs Buxton of Royal Lodge, Preston,* unknown acquisition method
unknown artist *George Jacson, JP,* gift from Maria M. Horrocks
unknown artist *John Horrocks,* gift from Maria M. Horrocks
unknown artist *Mr Thomas Swindlehurst,* gift from Mrs Lamartine-Yates
unknown artist *Mrs Thomas Swindlehurst,* gift from Mrs Lamartine-Yates
unknown artist *Portrait of a Lady in Highland Costume,* unknown acquisition method
unknown artist *Grace Ascroft,* gift from E. M. Hedley
unknown artist *William Ascroft,* gift from E. M. Hedley
unknown artist *Alderman John Goodier, Mayor of Preston (1860–1861),* unknown acquisition method
unknown artist *Salome with the Head of John the Baptist,* unknown acquisition method
unknown artist *Margaret Pedder,* unknown acquisition method
unknown artist *Portrait of an Elderly Couple,* bequeathed by Andreas Buckley Begg
unknown artist *Landscape with a Swan on a Lake,* unknown acquisition method
unknown artist *Landscape with a Waterfall,* unknown acquisition method
unknown artist *Portrait of a Man Reading a Letter,* unknown acquisition method
unknown artist *A Magdalene,* unknown acquisition method
unknown artist *Bay Horse*
unknown artist *Benjamin Sykes,* gift from the sitter
unknown artist *Boy on a Stone Bench with a Capful of Cherries,* unknown acquisition method
unknown artist *Boy Watching a Cat Steal Fish,* unknown acquisition method
unknown artist *Boys Blowing Bubbles,* unknown acquisition method
unknown artist *Caritas,* unknown acquisition method
unknown artist *Charles Robert Brown,* gift from I. and U. Brown
unknown artist *Coastal Scene,* unknown acquisition method
unknown artist *Coastal Scene with Castle,* unknown acquisition method
unknown artist *Colonel T. Birchall of Ribbleton,* unknown acquisition method
unknown artist *Edmund Grimshaw*
unknown artist *Father Joseph Dunn*
unknown artist *Figure with a Book and a Quill Pen,* unknown acquisition method
unknown artist *Frightened People on a Hillside,* unknown acquisition method
unknown artist *Gipsy Girl,* unknown acquisition method
unknown artist *Henry Hunt, MP for Preston,* gift from Margaret Ellen Sisson
unknown artist *Hunting Scene: Dog with Game,* unknown acquisition method
unknown artist *Interior – Chambermaid and Man with Books,* unknown acquisition method
unknown artist *J. Arrowsmith, DD,* unknown acquisition method
unknown artist *Landscape,* unknown acquisition method
unknown artist *Landscape,* unknown acquisition method
unknown artist *Landscape,* unknown acquisition method
unknown artist *Landscape,* unknown acquisition method
unknown artist *Landscape,* unknown acquisition method
unknown artist *Landscape – Man Driving Cattle and Sheep,* unknown acquisition method
unknown artist *Landscape – Panoramic View of a River Valley,* unknown acquisition method
unknown artist *Landscape with a Lake in the Foreground and Mountains in the Middle Distance,* unknown acquisition method
unknown artist *Landscape with a Mountain Lake, a Small Castle and Fishermen,* unknown acquisition method
unknown artist *Landscape with a Tree, Water and Hills,* unknown acquisition method
unknown artist *Landscape with Mountains*
unknown artist *Lord Ribblesdale*
unknown artist *Man Fishing*
unknown artist *Mary, Queen of Scots (1542–1587),* gift from F. W. Sharples
unknown artist *Miles Myres,* unknown acquisition method
unknown artist *Moonlight,* unknown acquisition method
unknown artist *Mother and Child,* unknown acquisition method
unknown artist *Mythological Scenes,* (possibly 'The Judgment of Paris'), unknown acquisition method
unknown artist *Portrait of a Girl Holding a Cat,* unknown acquisition method
unknown artist *Portrait of a Girl Holding Flowers,* unknown acquisition method
unknown artist *Portrait of a Lady,* unknown acquisition method
unknown artist *Portrait of a Lady with a Black Dress and Brooch,* unknown acquisition method
unknown artist *Portrait of a Man,* unknown acquisition method
unknown artist *Portrait of a Man,* unknown acquisition method
unknown artist *Portrait of a Man,* unknown acquisition method
unknown artist *Portrait of a Man,* unknown acquisition method
unknown artist *Portrait of a Man,* unknown acquisition method
unknown artist *Portrait of a Man,* unknown acquisition method
unknown artist *Portrait of a Man,* gift from F. E. Myres
unknown artist *Portrait of a Man,* unknown acquisition method
unknown artist *Portrait of a Man,* unknown acquisition method
unknown artist *Portrait of a Man,* unknown acquisition method
unknown artist *Portrait of a Man Holding a Gardening Magazine,* unknown acquisition method
unknown artist *Portrait of a Man in Black with Sidewhiskers and a Newspaper,* unknown acquisition method
unknown artist *Portrait of a Man with a Gold Embroidered Lace Cravatte,* unknown acquisition method
unknown artist *Portrait of a Woman,* unknown acquisition method
unknown artist *Portrait of a Woman,* unknown acquisition method
unknown artist *Portrait of a Woman Holding a Rose,* unknown acquisition method
unknown artist *Portrait of a Woman in a Flowered Bonnet,* unknown acquisition method
unknown artist *Portrait of a Young Man,* unknown acquisition method
unknown artist *Portrait of an Elderly Man,* (possibly Joseph Livesey), unknown acquisition method
unknown artist *Preston from the Old Quay,* unknown acquisition method
unknown artist *Preston Market Place, 1820,* unknown acquisition method
unknown artist *Reverend John Clay,* unknown acquisition method
unknown artist *River Landscape,* unknown acquisition method
unknown artist *Samuel G. Crane,* gift from Miss Bell
unknown artist *Seated Figure with Three Dogs,* unknown acquisition method
unknown artist *Sir Edward Stanley, Mayor of Preston (1731–1732),* unknown acquisition method
unknown artist *Sir Robert Ascroft,* gift from W. Ashcroft
unknown artist *Still Life – Grapes, Apple and Pear,* unknown acquisition method
unknown artist *The Alchemist,* purchased
unknown artist *Three Dutch People in National Costume,* unknown acquisition method
unknown artist *Walton le Dale from Frenchwood,* purchased
unknown artist *Woman with Three Children and a Dog,* unknown acquisition method
Vaughan, Michael b.1938, *Blue Cross and Grey Block,* gift from the Contemporary Art Society © the artist
Verboeckhoven, Charles Louis 1802–1889, *Coast Scene,* gift from F. W. Sharples
Verboeckhoven, Eugène Joseph 1798–1881, *Sheep,* bequeathed by E. Turner
Verelst, Herman 1642–1702, *Portrait of a Lady with a Dog,* bequeathed by M. A. L. Williams
Verelst, Willem (attributed to) 1700–1756, *Prince Charles Edward Stuart (1720–1788), Son of the Old Pretender,* purchased
W., T. *Edmund Robert Harris (c.1804–1877),* on loan from the Harris Free Library, Museum and Art Gallery Endowment Trust
Wade, Thomas 1828–1891, *'Come whoam to thi childer an' me',* purchased
Wade, Thomas 1828–1891, *The First Night at Sea,* bequeathed by William H. Fell
Wade, Thomas 1828–1891, *William Edmondson Fell,* bequeathed by William H. Fell
Wade, Thomas 1828–1891, *'Where's the boy that minds the sheep?',* purchased
Wade, Thomas 1828–1891, *Interior with a Boy Drawing,* purchased
Wade, Thomas 1828–1891, *Carting Turf from Farington Moss,* purchased
Wade, Thomas 1828–1891, *A Stitch in Time,* purchased
Wade, Thomas 1828–1891, *The Poacher's Home,* purchased
Wade, Thomas 1828–1891, *Sailing Feathers,* purchased
Wade, Thomas 1828–1891, *A Girl Knitting,* purchased
Wade, Thomas 1828–1891, *Waiting,* purchased
Wade, Thomas 1828–1891, *'Can you see any green in my eye?',* purchased
Wade, Thomas 1828–1891, *'Come whoam to thi childer an' me',* purchased
Wade, Thomas 1828–1891, *'Come whoam to thi childer an' me',* purchased
Wade, Thomas 1828–1891, *Cottage Interior,* purchased
Wade, Thomas 1828–1891, *Falstaff,* gift from Mrs Fell
Wade, Thomas 1828–1891, *Fiddler and Dancing Peasants,* purchased
Wade, Thomas 1828–1891, *Man on a White Horse in Mountain Scenery,* purchased
Wade, Thomas 1828–1891, *Man Tickling a Woman's Nose with a Feather,* unknown acquisition method, Photo Credit: Bridgeman Art Library
Wade, Thomas 1828–1891, *Rustic Lovers on the Outskirts of a Town,* purchased
Wade, Thomas 1828–1891, *The Old Mill, Kirkham,* purchased
Waite, Edward Wilkins 1854–1924, *'The mellow year is hastening to its close',* purchased, Photo Credit: Bridgeman Art Library
Walbourne, Ernest 1872–1927, *Children's Delight,* gift from J. R. Smith
Walbourne, Ernest 1872–1927, *One for Baby,* gift from J. R. Smith, Photo Credit: Bridgeman Art Library
Walker, Ethel 1861–1951, *Iris and Kathleen,* gift from the Contemporary Art Society © the artist's estate/Bridgeman Art Library
Wallace, Robin 1879–1952, *Lancaster Quay,* purchased © the copyright holder
Waller, Samuel Edmund 1850–1903, *One and Twenty,* gift from Sir Meyrick Hollins
Ward *Lake with Canoists,* unknown acquisition method
Ward, Edward Matthew 1816–1879, *The Royal Family of France in the Prison of the Temple,* bequeathed by Richard Newsham, Photo Credit: Bridgeman Art Library

Ward, John Stanton 1917–2007, *Linda,* purchased © the artist's estate/Bridgeman Art Library
Ward, Martin Theodore 1799–1874, *Dog and Game Bird,* gift from F. W. Sharples
Ware, William 1915–1997, *Landscape on the Loire,* gift from J. Dunne © the artist's estate
Waterhouse, John William 1849–1917, *Psyche Entering Cupid's Garden,* purchased, Photo Credit: Bridgeman Art Library
Waterlow, Ernest Albert 1850–1919, *La Cote d'Azur,* purchased
Watson, Charles John 1846–1927, *Sheep,* gift from Miss Greenwood
Watson, George Spencer 1869–1934, *Nude,* purchased, Photo Credit: Bridgeman Art Library
Watson, Sydney Robert 1892–1971, *Highland Cattle – Loch Long, Argyllshire,* gift from E. M. Troughton © the copyright holder
Watson, Sydney Robert 1892–1971, *Highland Sheep,* gift from E. M. Troughton © the copyright holder
Watts, George Frederick 1817–1904, *The Genius of Greek Poetry,* purchased, Photo Credit: Bridgeman Art Library
Watts, James Thomas 1853–1930, *Autumn Evening on the Wharfe,* gift from F. W. Sharples
Webb, William Edward 1862–1903, *The Jetty at Deal,* unknown acquisition method
Webster, Thomas George 1800–1886, *A Tea Party,* bequeathed by Richard Newsham, Photo Credit: Bridgeman Art Library
Weight, Carel Victor Morlais 1908–1997, *Crucifixion,* purchased © the artist's estate/Bridgeman Art Library, Photo Credit: Bridgeman Art Library
Weight, Carel Victor Morlais 1908–1997, *Hamlet,* gift from the artist © the artist's estate/ Bridgeman Art Library
Wells, William Page Atkinson 1872–1923, *Landscape with a White House,* gift from B. S. Smith
Wells, William Page Atkinson 1872–1923, *Landscape – Girl in a Meadow,* gift from Miss Sudell
Wells, William Page Atkinson 1872–1923, *The Lune at Sunderland Point,* gift from J. R. Charnley
Wells, William Page Atkinson 1872–1923, *Beneath the Haldon Hills, Devon,* purchased
Westcott, Philip 1815–1878, *Robert Towneley Parker (1793–1879), MP for Preston,* commissioned
Wetherbee, George Faulkner 1851–1920, *'Forever wilt thou love and she be fair',* purchased
Whaite, Henry Clarence 1828–1912, *The Coming Storm,* gift from Robert Holt Edmondson
Wheelwright, Rowland 1870–1955, *'Trust her not, she is fooling thee',* purchased © the copyright holder
Whiteford, Kate b.1952, *Lustra,* purchased © the artist, Photo Credit: Bridgeman Art Library
Williams, Terrick John 1860–1936, *Ribbons and Laces,* purchased
Williams, Walter Heath 1835–1906, *The Pass of Llanberis,* gift from Miss Troughton
Wilson, Richard 1712–1782, *Landscape,* gift from Benjamin and Ford Booth
Winstanley, Hamlet 1694–1756, *George II (1683–1760),* gift from Edward Stanley
Winstanley, Hamlet 1694–1756, *Richard Shepherd,* unknown acquisition method
Witherington, William Frederick 1785–1865, *Llanberis Pass,* gift from Walter Smirk
Wontner, William Clarke 1857–1930, *Portrait of a Young Woman,* gift from R. T. Easterby
Wood, Harold b.1918, *St Peter's Church, Preston, from Fylde Road,* gift from Geoffrey Parrish © the copyright holder
Wood, Harold b.1918, *A View of Preston,* purchased © the copyright holder
Woodhouse, William 1857–1939, *Pit Pony,* purchased
Woods, Albert 1871–1944, *Twilight, St Ives Harbour,* purchased © the copyright holder
Woods, Albert 1871–1944, *Lancaster Road in Snowy Weather,* purchased © the copyright holder
Woods, Albert 1871–1944, *Preston Corporation Chrysanthemum House,* purchased © the copyright holder
Woods, Albert 1871–1944, *A Peaceful Valley, Whitewell,* gift from J. Tod © the copyright holder
Woods, Albert 1871–1944, *Autumn in the Woods,* © the copyright holder
Woods, Albert 1871–1944, *Snowballing,* unknown acquisition method © the copyright holder,Bridgeman Art Library
Woods, Albert 1871–1944, *Sunderland Point,* purchased © the copyright holder
Woods, Albert 1871–1944, *William Allan Lambert,* gift from A. Lambert © the copyright holder
Woods, Henry 1846–1921, *A Venetian Vintage,* purchased
Wouwerman, Philips 1619–1668, *Landscape,* purchased
Wouwerman, Philips 1619–1668, *Landscape,* purchased
Wright of Derby, Joseph 1734–1797, *Richard Arkwright (1732–1792),* purchased jointly by the Harris Museum & Art Gallery and the National Portrait Gallery, London with the assistance of the National Heritage Memorial Fund, the Art Fund, The Trustees of the Harris Free Library, Museum and Art Gallery Trust, the Friends of the Harris Museum amd Art Gallery, the Portrait Fund, PRISM, the Headley Trust, the Bowland Charitable Trust, the Halecat charitable Trust, Nicholas & Judith Godison through the Art Fund, Hutton Historical Society, Soroptimist International of Preston, pupils of Fulwood High School and over 130 individual donations, 2008
Wynfield, David Wilkie 1837–1887, *Ruth and Boaz,* gift
Yeats, Jack Butler 1871–1957, *The Coast of Clare from Dun Aengus,* bequeathed by Sarah McLeod © estate of Jack B. Yeats. All rights reserved, DACS 2012

Her Majesty's Court Service, Preston Crown Court

Berrie, John Archibald Alexander 1887–1962, *Sir James Openshaw,* © the copyright holder
British School *Thomas Clayton, Esq. (1777–1854), High Sheriff*
British School *Thomas Batty Addison, Esq. (1788–1874)*
British School *His Honour Judge Openshaw*
Llewellyn, Samuel Henry William 1858–1941, *Sir Harcourt Everard Clare (1854–1922)*
Macnee, Daniel 1806–1882, *Reverend John Shepherd Birley (1805–1883)*
Riviere, Hugh Goldwin 1869–1956, *Henry Wilson Worsley-Taylor* © the artist's estate

14th/20th King's Hussars Museum

Matthews, J. *Officers of the 14th King's Hussars,* gift from Mrs P. Fleming
unknown artist *Major John Woolmer Smith, 14th Light Dragoons,* purchased by the Museum Trustees with the assistance of the Army Museums Ogilby Trust
unknown artist *Major James Leith Winning the Victoria Cross,* gift from the National Army Museum
unknown artist *Indian Servant with Boots,* gift from Miss E. G. Brooks
unknown artist *Indian Servant with Horse,* gift from Miss E. G. Brooks

Lancashire County Council

Berrie, John Archibald Alexander 1887–1962, *Sir James Travis-Clegg (1874–1942),* © the copyright holder
Berrie, John Archibald Alexander 1887–1962, *Sir William Hodgson,* © the copyright holder
Holt, John *May Grane,* © the copyright holder
Slattery, Edward 1892–1974, *Ross Mill,* gift to the town of Bacup © the copyright holder
unknown artist *Sir Henry Hibbert (1850–1927), Bt*
unknown artist *Sir Henry Wade Deacon*
unknown artist *Sir William Scott Barrett, Kt*
unknown artist *The Right Honorable Sir John Hibbert*

Lancashire County Museum Service

Aspinwall, Reginald 1858–1921, *Sunderland Point,* purchased from Mr Michael Fulda, Fulda Gallery Ltd, Salford
Austrian School (possibly) *Picture Clock,* gift from Mrs Olive Shallcross, 1998
Baxter, Ron *Liners at Quayside,* transferred from 'Old' Fleetwood Library © the copyright holder
Berry, R. *Milton Street Primary School, Fleetwood,* © the copyright holder
Bigg, William Redmore 1755–1828, *A Bottle of Wine,* bequeathed by George Palmer Holt through the Art Fund, 1992
Bigg, William Redmore 1755–1828, *A Glass of Milk,* bequeathed by George Palmer Holt through the Art Fund, 1992
Birkett, Mary *Fleetwood Lower Lighthouse,* purchased from Mrs E. Penny, 1986 © the copyright holder
British (English) School *Georgiana Hulton, Wife of William Ford,* on loan from a private collection
British (English) School *Sally (Sarah) Chorley (1774–1852),* purchased from Mr Edward Walker
Brodie, John Lamont active c.1834–1881, *Portrait of a Boy in Highland Dress,* bequeathed by Irene Ackroyd Hardman, 1977
Brown, R. G. 1815–1905, *Horse and Dog in Stable,* gift from Miss M. R. Clarke, 1985
Caille, Léon Émile 1836–1907, *Mother and Daughter in Domestic Interior,* presented anonymously to the Judges' Lodgings through the Art Fund, 2001
Calvert, Frederick 1785–1845, *Shipping Scene with Lighthouse,* presented anonymously to the Judges' Lodgings through the Art Fund, 2001
Canaletto (school of) 1697–1768, *Piazza Navona, Rome,* bequeathed by George Palmer Holt through the Art Fund, 1992
Cartmell, John Thomas 1905–1975, *Beach with Blue Boat and Rocks,* gift from Mrs M. Cartmell, 1987 © the copyright holder
Cartmell, John Thomas 1905–1975, *Boat with Portholes,* gift from Mrs M. Cartmell, 1987 © the copyright holder
Cartmell, John Thomas 1905–1975, *Sailing Ship with Light Brown Sails,* gift from Mrs M. Cartmell, 1987 © the copyright holder
Cartmell, John Thomas 1905–1975, *Ship with Red Sails by Black Rocks,* gift from Mrs M. Cartmell, 1987 © the copyright holder
Cartmell, John Thomas 1905–1975, *Shipping Scene,* gift from Mrs M. Cartmell, 1987 © the copyright holder
Cartmell, John Thomas 1905–1975, *Shipping Scene,* gift from Mrs M. Cartmell, 1987 © the copyright holder
Cartmell, John Thomas 1905–1975, *Shipping Scene,* gift from Mrs M. Cartmell, 1987 © the copyright holder
Cartmell, John Thomas 1905–1975, *Tall Ship in Full Sail,* gift from Mrs M. Cartmell, 1987 © the copyright holder
Cartmell, John Thomas 1905–1975, *Trawler on Rough Grey Sea,* gift from Mrs M. Cartmell, 1987 © the copyright holder
Cartmell, John Thomas 1905–1975, *Two Boats,* gift from Mrs M. Cartmell, 1987 © the copyright holder
Cartmell, John Thomas 1905–1975, *Two Boats with Red Sails,* gift from Mrs M. Cartmell, 1987 © the copyright holder
Cartmell, John Thomas 1905–1975, *Two Trawlers,* gift from Mrs M. Cartmell, 1987 © the copyright holder
Charlton, John 1849–1917, *George P. Holt,* bequeathed by the sitter through the Art Fund, 1992
Collins, J. A. active 1994–2002, *Beached Trawler,* gift from the artist, 2002 © the copyright holder
Cowell, T. F. *Old Cottages and Old House in Warren Street,* transferred from 'Old' Fleetwood Library © the copyright holder
Dahl I, Michael (follower of) 1656–1743, *Beatrix Hulton (1722–1774), Wife of Thomas Lister of Gisburne Park,* on loan from a private collection
Delpy, Hippolyte-Camille 1842–1910, *A River at Dusk,* bequeathed by Lionel Hewlett through the Art Fund, 1995
Devis, Arthur 1712–1787, *Hornby Hall and Castle,* purchased by private treaty at Christie's with the assistance of the Victoria and Albert Museum Purchase Grant Fund, 1992
Devis, Arthur 1712–1787, *Squire John ffrance (1727–1817) of Rawcliffe Hall, Lancashire,* purchased at Sotheby's with the assistance of the Victoria and Albert Museum Purchase Grant Fund
Draper, Herbert James 1864–1920, *The Mother of George P. Holt,* bequeathed by George Palmer Holt through the Art Fund, 1992
Duckett, J. *The 'Wyre Victory' in Fleetwood Dock,* gift from Mr J.

Duckett, 1990 © the copyright holder
English, Francis *View of Fleetwood,* purchased from Mr Michael Fulda, Fulda Gallery Ltd, Salford, with the assistance of the Victoria and Albert Museum Purchase Grant Fund
English, J. W. *M7 in the Centre of a Life Buoy,* gift from Mr Cliff Beech, 2009 © the copyright holder
French School *Figures in a Landscape,* presented anonymously to the Judges' Lodgings through the Art Fund, 2001
Frith, William Powell 1819–1909, *Hugh and Dolly Varden,* (from the novel 'Barnaby Rudge' by Charles Dickens), bequeathed by George Palmer Holt through the Art Fund, 1992
Gheeraerts the younger, Marcus 1561–1636, *Sir William ffaryngton of Worden Hall (1537–1610), Leyland, Lancashire,* purchased from Fulda Gallery Ltd, Salford, with the assistance of the Victoria and Albert Museum Purchase Grant Fund
Goyen, Jan van (attributed to) 1596–1656, *Landscape with Travellers outside an Inn,* presented anonymously to the Judges' Lodgings through the Art Fund, 2001
Green, J. W. *The 'Falcon',* transferred from 'Old' Fleetwood Library
Green, J. W. *Pilot Cutter 'Leader F2' in Full Sail,* transferred from 'Old' Fleetwood Library
Griff, B. *'Wyre Mariner',* gift from Mr W. C. Griffiths, 1995 © the copyright holder
Guest, A. Vera *'Royalist FD24',* gift from Mrs Beatrice Vernon, 2009 © the copyright holder
Guillaumin, Armand 1841–1927, *La Creuse a Genetin,* bequeathed by Lionel Hewlett through the Art Fund, 1995
Guillaumin, Armand 1841–1927, *Les Dunes de la Covarde, Ile de Re,* bequeathed by Lionel Hewlett through the Art Fund, 1995
H., M. E. *'Majestic GY682',* gift from Mr Hudson, 2003
Haslam, Raymond active 1967, *Cleanway,* purchased from Anne Haslam, 1974 © the copyright holder
Haslam, Raymond active 1967, *Crashed Cortina,* purchased from the artist © the copyright holder
Henderson, Ian b.1939, *Contemporary Treatment of Windswept Skelmersdale Landscape,* gift from the Office of Commissions for New Towns © Dr Ian Henderson DCA
Henderson, Ian b.1939, *Digmore Area from Back Lane, Showing Earth-Moving and Beginning of Pimbo Industrial Area,* gift from the Office of Commissions for New Towns © Dr Ian Henderson DCA
Henderson, Ian b.1939, *Future View from Ashursts Ridge Looking Out over the Designated Area,* gift from the Office of Commissions for New Towns © Dr Ian Henderson DCA
Henderson, Ian b.1939, *Landscape in Green, Beige and Black,* gift from the Office of Commissions for New Towns © Dr Ian Henderson DCA
Henderson, Ian b.1939, *Laying Sewage Pipe Sections at Tawd Bridge,* gift from the Office of Commissions for New Towns © Dr Ian Henderson DCA
Henderson, Ian b.1939, *Skelmersdale New Town,* gift from the Office of Commissions for New Towns © Dr Ian Henderson DCA
Henderson, Ian b.1939, *Snowscape from Spencer's Lane Looking towards Gillibrands and New Church Farm along Wigan Road,* gift from the Office of Commissions for New Towns © Dr Ian Henderson DCA
Henderson, Ian b.1939, *View of Beacon and Designated Area from Ormskirk Approach,* gift from Office of Commissions for New Towns © Dr Ian Henderson DCA
Henderson, Ian b.1939, *View of Digmore Redevelopment Area,* gift from the Office of Commissions for New Towns © Dr Ian Henderson DCA
Henderson, Ian b.1939, *View of New Church Farm from Gillibrands Industrial Area,* gift from the Office of Commissions for New Towns © Dr Ian Henderson DCA
Henderson, Ian b.1939, *View of Skelmersdale New Town Designated Area from behind Ravenhead Brick Works,* gift from the Office of Commissions for New Towns © Dr Ian Henderson DCA
Horne, B. J. *'Boston Phantom',* gift from B. Thorne, 1991 © the copyright holder
Jinks, Len *The Fisherman,* acquired from the artist © the copyright holder
Johnston, T. *'Duke of Albany',* transferred from 'Old' Fleetwood Library
Johnston, T. *'Duke of Connaught',* transferred from 'Old' Fleetwood Library
Kershaw, Walter b.1940, *Fiddlers Ferry,* purchased from the artist © the artist
Knowles, Arthur 1870–1955, *Fleetwood Deep Sea Trawlers Hove To in a Gale of Wind in the Channel,* gift from Fleetwood Museum Trust, 2010 © the copyright holder
Lander, John Saint-Helier (after) 1869–1944, *Baron Hewart of Bury (1840–1943),* purchased from Mr Greg Page-Turner, 2000 © the copyright holder
Lawrence, Thomas 1769–1830, *Joseph Farington (1747–1821), RA,* purchased from P. & D. Colnaghi & Co. Ltd with the assistance of the Art Fund and the Victoria and Albert Museum Purchase Grant Fund, 1992
Linton, William 1791–1876, *Broad Oak Printworks, near Accrington,* purchased at Christie's with the assistance of the Art Fund and the Victoria and Albert Museum Purchase Grant Fund, 2003
Linton, William 1791–1876, *Bury from Blackford Bridge,* purchased from Fulda Gallery Ltd, Salford, with the assistance of the Victoria and Albert Museum Purchase Grant Fund
Livingstone, John active 1840–1846, *'Her Majesty' Paddle Steamer,* transferred from 'Old' Fleetwood Library
Livingstone, John (possibly) active 1840–1846, *'Prince of Wales'*
Long, E. *HMT 'Northern Sun',* gift from Patricia Woolley, 2004 © the copyright holder
Lonsdale, Richard T. active c.1836–c.1850, *The Drawing Room at Whittington Hall,* purchased from Gurr-Johns Ltd, Fine Art Dealers, with the assistance of the Art Fund and the Victoria and Albert Museum Purchase Grant Fund, 1997
Lumb, Levi active 1913–1942, *Docked Trawlers, Fleetwood,* purchased from John Sellick Fine Art, 1999 © the copyright holder
Lumb, Levi active 1913–1942, *Ferry at Knott End,* purchased from John Sellick Fine Art, 1999 © the copyright holder
Lumb, Levi active 1913–1942, *Trawlers, Fleetwood Dock,* purchased from John Sellick Fine Art, 1999 © the copyright holder
Lurçat, Jean 1892–1966, *Baigneuses,* bequeathed by George Palmer Holt through the Art Fund, 1992 ADAGP, Paris and DACS, London 2012
Martin, Daniel (follower of) *William Hulton of Hulton Park (1739–1773),* on loan from a private collection
Maufra, Maxime 1861–1918, *Soleil Couchant en Mer, Quiberon,* bequeathed by Lionel Hewlett through the Art Fund, 1995
Morland, George 1763–1804, *Landscape with Ruined Castle,* bequeathed by Lionel Hewlett through the Art Fund, 1995
Morland, George (after) 1763–1804, *Feeding Time in the Farmyard,* bequeathed by Lionel Hewlett through the Art Fund, 1995
Mortel, Jan 1650–1719, *Still Life with Fish, Bread and Fruit,* presented anonymously to the Judges' Lodgings through the Art Fund, 2001
North Sergeant, M. *Portrait of a Lady in a Pink Dress,* gift from Grundy House Museum © the copyright holder
O'Moore, A. S. *'Wyre Vanguard',* gift from Mrs D. M. Rothwell, 1995
Os, Jan van 1744–1808, *Still Life with Dead Bird, Fruit and Flowers,* bequeathed by George Palmer Holt through the Art Fund, 1992
Peake, Robert (attributed to) 1551–1619, *John Braddyll of Portfield and Whalley,* purchased from Historical Portraits with the assistance of the Heritage Lottery Fund, the Art Fund and the Victoria and Albert Museum Purchase Grant Fund, 2000
Pickering, Henry 1720–1771, *William Hulton with Gun-Dog and Shotgun,* on loan from a private collection
Ponce, Antonio 1608–1677, *Still Life with Vase of Flowers,* transferred from Broughton Tower School
Rankin *River Landscape,* transferred from Broughton Tower School
Rawcliffe, John active 1872, *'Esther'*
Rehsif *Patrol Boat,* gift from Mrs S. Whitworth, 2009 © the copyright holder
Rogers, Elsie *'Wyre Mariner',* gift from Mrs S. Lunn, 2000 © the copyright holder
Romney, George 1734–1802, *Thomas Hutton Rawlinson (1712–1769),* purchased from Mr Edward Walker with the assistance of the Heritage Lottery Fund and the Victoria and Albert Museum Purchase Grant Fund
Romney, George 1734–1802, *Mary Hutton Rawlinson (1772–1786),* purchased from Mr Edward Walker with the assistance of the Heritage Lottery Fund and the Victoria and Albert Museum Purchase Grant Fund
Romney, George 1734–1802, *Abraham Rawlinson (1738–1803), MP, of Ellel Hall, near Lancaster,* purchased from Mr Edward Walker with the assistance of the Heritage Lottery Fund, the Art Fund and the Victoria and Albert Museum Purchase Grant Fund, 2006
Romney, George 1734–1802, *John Satterthwaite,* on loan from a private collection
Roskell, Thomas Henry b.1928, *Skipper Roskell,* gift from the artist, 2001 © the artist
Roskell, Thomas Henry b.1928, *Hauling the Nets,* gift from the artist, 2004 © the artist
Roskell, Thomas Henry b.1928, *Mess Room,* gift from the artist, 2004 © the artist
Roskell, Thomas Henry b.1928, *Fisherman in Yellow Oilskins,* gift from the artist, 2004 © the artist
Roskell, Thomas Henry b.1928, *George's Birthday,* gift from the artist, 2001 © the artist
Roskell, Thomas Henry b.1928, *Hauling Time,* gift from the artist, 2001 © the artist
Roskell, Thomas Henry b.1928, *Jane Feeding Swans,* gift from the artist, 2001 © the artist
Roskell, Thomas Henry b.1928, *On Deck of a Trawler,* gift from the artist, 2004 © the artist
Roskell, Thomas Henry b.1928, *Small Boat in Rough Sea,* gift from the artist, 2004 © the artist
Rousseau, Théodore (studio of) 1812–1867, *River in a Wooded Landscape,* bequeathed by Lionel Hewlett through the Art Fund, 1995
Sauzay, Adrien Jacques 1841–1928, *Vue d'Etaples,* bequeathed by Lionel Hewlett through the Art Fund, 1995
Semple, Joseph 1830–1877, *'The Richard Warbrick',* transferred from 'Old' Fleetwood Library
Semple, Joseph 1830–1877, *'Royal Consort' Paddle Steamer,* transferred from 'Old' Fleetwood Library
Shaw, John 1819–1876, *Thomas Hogg,* transferred from Grundy House Museum
Snape, Raymond active 1983–2001, *'Boston Monarch FD19',* gift from the artist, 2001 © the copyright holder
Spencer, Noël 1900–1986, *Wyre Channel,* gift from the artist, 1975 © the copyright holder
Stephenson, W. active 1960s, *'Corena',* gift from Mr George Bollenberg, 2010 © the copyright holder
Stephenson, W. active 1960s, *Fleetwood Docks,* gift from Mr George Bollenberg, 2010 © the copyright holder
Sutton, Keith *Fishing Boats at Sunset, Iceland,* gift from Mr R. A. Lee, 1996 © the copyright holder
Sutton, Keith *'Ella Hewitt',* gift from Mr Baines, 1997 © the copyright holder
Sutton, Keith *The Mount Pavilion, Fleetwood,* transferred from 'Old' Fleetwood Library © the copyright holder
Sutton, Keith *'Fleetwood Lady',* gift from Mr Robert Wright, 2008 © the copyright holder
Sutton, Keith *'Antares',* gift from Mrs Chard, 2002 © the copyright holder
Sutton, Keith *'Omega B',* gift from Mr John Laird, 2005 © the copyright holder
Sutton, Keith *'Wyre Mariner' and 'Ella Hewitt',* gift from Mr Richard Watson, 1995 © the copyright holder
Sutton, Keith *The Lobster Boats,* transferred from 'Old' Fleetwood Library © the copyright holder
Sutton, Keith *Trawler in Rough Seas,* gift from Mr Peter Horsley, Maritime, Commercial & Industrial Photographer, 2005 © the copyright holder
Teniers II, David (after) 1610–1690, *Domestic Scene,* gift from an anonymous donor
Teniers II, David (after) 1610–1690, *Travellers outside an*

Inn, gift from an anonymous donor
Thornton, Harold 1907–1975, *Queen Street Mill from the Allotments,* gift from Mr K. Thornton © the artist's estate
unknown artist *Anne (d.1681), Wife of William Hulton,* on loan from a private collection
unknown artist *William Hulton (1625–1694), with Grooms and Dogs,* on loan from a private collection
unknown artist *Major Farrington, Esq.,* gift from Reginald Sharpe, France
unknown artist *Anne Hulton (1719–1797),* on loan from a private collection
unknown artist *William Hulton (1717–1741),* on loan from a private collection
unknown artist *Benjamin Satterthwaite (1718–1792),* on loan from a private collection
unknown artist *Dr Heys of Preston,* purchased from Mr R. J. Wilkinson, 1991
unknown artist *Lydia Rawlinson (1733–1798), Daughter of Thomas Hutton Rawlinson,* purchased from Mr Edward Walker
unknown artist *Mrs Ann Mary Hughes,* on loan from a private collection
unknown artist *Henry Hulton (1765–1831), in Military Uniform,* on loan from a private collection
unknown artist *Portrait of 'T. M.',* purchased from Fulda Gallery Ltd, Salford
unknown artist *Mr Boardman of Bretherton,* purchased from Warren & Wignall Ltd, 1991
unknown artist *Mr Boardman of Bretherton,* purchased from Warren & Wignall Ltd, 1991
unknown artist *Mrs Boardman of Bretherton,* purchased from Warren & Wignall Ltd, 1991
unknown artist *Pastoral Scene by a River,* presented anonymously to the Judges' Lodgings through the Art Fund, 2001
unknown artist *The Rhine Valley at Lorelia,* bequeathed by Miss M. R. M. Clarke
unknown artist *Rossall Point, Fleetwood*
unknown artist *Fleetwood Lifeboat 'Maude Pickup' at Sea,* gift from Mr Richard Willoughby, Fleetwood Lifeboat Station, 1976
unknown artist *'Ava',* purchased from Old Talbot Gallery, 2002
unknown artist *Cecilia,* transferred from Broughton Tower School
unknown artist *Charles Hulton (?),* on loan from a private collection
unknown artist *Ellen Turner of Helmshore,* bequeathed by Irene Ackroyd Hardman, 1977
unknown artist *Janet Kerr and Master Nivien Kerr,* bequeathed by Miss M. R. M. Clarke
unknown artist *Jessop Hulton (b.1667) (?),* on loan from a private collection
unknown artist *Old Cutter 'Leader F2',* transferred from 'Old' Fleetwood Library
unknown artist *Paddle Steamer in Stormy Sea,* transferred from 'Old' Fleetwood Library
unknown artist *Portrait of a Lady,* transferred from Grundy House Museum
unknown artist *Portrait of a Lady Seated,* gift from Grundy House Museum
unknown artist *Portrait of a Man Seated,* transferred from Grundy House Museum
unknown artist *Portrait of a Woman Seated,* (possibly Dorothy Shaw), transferred from Grundy House Museum
unknown artist *Portrait of an Unknown Gentleman,* transferred from Grundy House Museum
unknown artist *Portrait of an Unknown Gentleman,* gift from Colne Town Hall
unknown artist *Sarah Hulton,* on loan from a private collection
unknown artist *Still Life with Chrysanthemums,* unknown acquisition method
unknown artist *The Lancashire Regiment at Portsmouth,* purchased from Fulda Gallery Ltd, Salford
unknown artist *William Ford Hulton (b.1811),* on loan from a private collection
unknown artist *William Hulton (b.1868),* on loan from a private collection
unknown artist *William Turner,* on loan from Higher Mill Trust
unknown artist *William Turner of Helmshore,* bequeathed by Irene Ackroyd Hardman, 1977
Vries, Hans Vredeman de (school of) 1527–1612, *Fountain in the Courtyard of a Palace,* gift from an anonymous donor
W. *Ships at Sea,* found blocking up a fireplace, Clitheroe
Walmsley, J. *'Ella Hewitt',* gift from Mr P. and Mrs J. Burras, 2010 © the copyright holder
Wells, William Page Atkinson 1872–1923, *The Mussel Gatherers at Sunderland Point, Lancashire,* purchased from Mr Michael Fulda, Fulda Gallery Ltd, Salford, with the assistance of the Art Fund and the Victoria and Albert Museum Purchase Grant Fund, 2004
Wilkinson, Neville active 1994, *White Sea Fishing Trawlers,* gift from the artist, 1994 © the copyright holder
Williams, Alan *'Boston Phantom' at Iceland,* gift from Mr Jim Brooks, 2005 © the copyright holder
Williams, Charles active 1999–2002, *A Grey Day at Fleetwood Power Station,* gift from the artist, 2002 © the copyright holder
Williams, Charles active 1999–2002, *Fleetwood Buoys: Nostalgia,* gift from the artist, 2002 © the copyright holder
Williams, Charles active 1999–2002, *'Cotsmuir',* gift from the artist, 2002 © the copyright holder
Wood, Elizabeth b.1930, *The Entertainer,* purchased from Mr and Mrs Wood, 1974 © the artist
Wood, Keith *Bright Intervals,* purchased from Mr and Mrs Wood, 1974 © the copyright holder
Wood, Keith *Kinky Darling,* purchased from Mr and Mrs Wood, 1974 © the copyright holder
Woodhead, Geoffrey 1941–2007, *Motorway Bridge, M6,* purchased from the artist © the copyright holder
Worthington, T. active 1995, *'Aigret',* gift from Reverend Keith Sillis, 2002 © the copyright holder
Worthington, T. active 1995, *'Ibis',* gift from Reverend Keith Sillis, 2002 © the copyright holder
Worthington, T. active 1995, *'Nancy Hague', Doctor Lee, Port Jackson,* gift from the artist, 1995 © the copyright holder
Wright of Derby, Joseph 1734–1797, *Mrs James Hardman of Rochdale and Allerton Hall,* purchased from The Leger Galleries Ltd with the assistance of the Victoria and Albert Museum Purchase Grant Fund and the Art Fund, 1996
Wright of Derby, Joseph 1734–1797, *Sir Richard Arkwright (1732–1792),* purchased from Historical Portraits with the assistance of the Victoria and Albert Museum Purchase Grant Fund and The Pilgrim Trust
Wyatt, Henry 1794–1840, *Ellen Turner of Helmshore (d.1831),* bequeathed by Irene Ackroyd Hardman, 1977

The Duke of Lancaster's Regiment, Lancashire Infantry Museum

Desanges, Louis William 1822–1906, *Lady Farren*
Desanges, Louis William 1822–1906, *Private John McDermond, 47th Regiment of Foot, Winning the Victoria Cross, Battle of Inkerman, 5 November 1854*
Jowett, G. *Ireland,* © the copyright holder
Kompley, P. *Recipients of the Victoria Cross,* © the copyright holder
Lamb, J. A. *1st Battalion South Lancashire (Old 40th) Regiment at the Battle of Pieters Hill, 27 February 1900,* presented to the officers of the South Lancashire Regiment by Lieutenant Colonel R. H. Hall, DSO, on the expiration of his command from the Battalion, 1934
Nielson *Loyals to New Zealand,* presented by the New Zealand Army in commemoration of the visit of 1 Loyals to New Zealand in 1964
unknown artist *Lieutenant Colonel George Hibbert, CB, 40th Foot, Who Served as an Ensign at Waterloo, and Commanded the Regiment (1845–1847),* gift
unknown artist *General Sir James Kempt, GCB, GCH*
unknown artist *Captain Richard Farren, 47th Regiment of Foot,* gift from Lady Farren
unknown artist *Colonel Sir Thomas Valiant, KCB, KH, Commander of the 82nd Foot (1825–1827) and the 40th Foot (1827–1839)*
unknown artist *Colonel J. Ireland Blackburne,* presented to the sitter by the Officers of the 4th Royal Lancashire Militia on his being appointed Honorary Colonel of the Regiment, 1875; gift from Major G. Ireland Blackburne, 1932
unknown artist *The Royal Tournament, 1932*

University of Central Lancashire

Beattie the elder (attributed to) active 19th C, *Jane Livesey,* on indefinite loan from the British National Temperance League
Garrett *Brian Booth, First Vice-Chancellor of the University of Central Lancashire (1989–1998),* commissioned © the copyright holder
Garrett *Gloria Oates, Chair of the Board at the University of Central Lancashire (1990–2001),* commissioned © the copyright holder
Garrett *Sir Francis Kennedy, First Chancellor of the University of Central Lancashire (1995),* commissioned © the copyright holder
Marshall, Christopher *Waves (Sound of Handa),* purchased from the artist © the copyright holder
unknown artist *Joseph Livesey,* on indefinite loan from the British National Temperance League
unknown artist *Joseph Livesey, Pioneer of Total Abstinence,* on indefinite loan from the British National Temperance League

Rossendale Museum

Adam, Joseph Denovan 1879–1931, *Waterfall,* gift from Harold Hoyle, 1951–1952; transferred from the Borough of Bacup, 1979
Armfield, Edward 1817–1896, *The Otter at Bay,* gift from Mrs J. McLerie, 1931
Armfield, George 1810–1893, *Three Dogs,* bequeathed by Mrs Louisa Hamer, 1969
Arnold, W. J. *Centre, Waterfoot,* unknown acquisition method
Aumonier, James 1832–1911, *A Lonely Heath,* gift from J. S. Aumonier, 1939
Aumonier, James 1832–1911, *On the South Downs,* gift from J. S. Aumonier, 1939
Boccaccino, Boccaccio style of 1461–1525, *Male Saint,* (possibly Saint John the Evangelist), purchased (?)
Boel, John Henry active 1875–1922, *Cottage in the Wood,* unknown acquisition method
Boel, John Henry active 1875–1922, *Loch Lomond,* unknown acquisition method
Bonheur, Auguste-François 1824–1884, *The Ford,* gift from Mrs E. A. Parker, 1938
Brandeis, Antonietta 1849–1920, *Venetian Waterway,* bequeathed by Mrs Louisa Hamer, 1969
British (English) School *Carter Place,* gift from Mrs G. Hardman, 1934 (?)
British (English) School *The Rossendale Hunt,* gift from Miss Irene Hardman, 1976
British (English) School *Hareholme Mill,* gift from Mrs Law, 1962
British (English) School *Mill Landscape,* unknown acquisition method
British (English) School *David Whitehead,* gift from Mrs Howarth Massey Caton and Mrs Trevor Law, 1929
British (English) School *Thomas Whitehead,* gift from J. Ashworth, 1902
British (English) School *John Ormerod,* unknown acquisition method
British (English) School *Girl with Blackbird,* unknown acquisition method
British (English) School *Joseph Wood Whitehead (c.1823–1879),* gift from Mrs J. Hardman, 1910
British (English) School *Mrs Joseph Wood Whitehead,* gift from Mrs J. Hardman, 1910
British (English) School *Sir John Everett Millais (1829–1896),* gift from J. W. Stansfield, H. H. King, J. T. Lord, W. Gornall, W. Hardman and S. O. Ashworth, 1917
British (English) School *John Hamer,* gift, 1936–1938
British (English) School *Near Adlington,* bequeathed by Mrs Louisa Hamer, 1969
British (English) School *Windmill above a River,* bequeathed by Mrs Louisa Hamer, 1969
British (English) School attributed to *Friends Meeting House, Crawshawbooth,* gift from Mrs H. Spencer through Councillor A. Peel, 1952
Broadley, W. *Moorland Scene,* unknown acquisition method

Brodie, Hammond active c.1820–1870, *Portrait of a Gentleman,* unknown acquisition method
Brodie, John Lamont active c.1834–1881, *George Hardman (1794–1852),* gift from the executors of Hardman Bros, 1952
Brooks, Cecily Kate 1887–1975, *A Dog,* bequeathed by Miss Marian Haworth through Valerie Haworth, 2001 © the copyright holder
Brooks, Cecily Kate 1887–1975, *Horse and Dog,* bequeathed by Miss Marian Haworth through Valerie Haworth, 2001 © the copyright holder
Brown, Barbara *HRH Prince Charles (b.1948),* purchased © the copyright holder
Brugghen, Hendrick ter style of 1588–1629, *The Music Lesson,* gift from Miss Hickman, 1933
Carlton, Frederick active 1895–1899, *Figures on a Boat Gathering Rushes,* gift from Harold Hoyle, 1951–1952; transferred from the Borough of Bacup, 1979
Claxton, Marshall 1813–1881, *The Lifeboat,* gift from Mrs Rowland Rawlinson, 1927
Clegg, William *Girl at Preston Loom,* bequeathed by Mrs Louisa Hamer, 1969
Collier, John 1850–1934, *Stepping Stones: Pamela,* gift from Mrs J. Collier, 1936
Collins, William follower of 1788–1847, *Boys Gleaning,* bequeathed by Mrs Louisa Hamer, 1969
Coupe, A. *Waterfoot Centre,* gift from Inghams Solicitors, 2006 © the copyright holder
Craig, James B. *Seascape,* gift from Mr H. Lord, 1947
Creswick, Thomas 1811–1869, *The Devil's Bridge on the St Gothard Pass,* gift from Mrs Rowland Rawlinson, 1938
Davis, J. active 19th C, *Cottage by Weir,* unknown acquisition method
Davis, J. active 19th C, *Mountain and Lake with Cottage,* unknown acquisition method
Drake, J. *Spring,* gift from Thomas Hill, 1931
Drake, J. *Summer,* gift from Thomas Hill, 1931
Dunkin, William John 1845–1914, *Roses and Honeysuckle,* gift from Mr J. S. Dearden, 1992
Dunkin, William John 1845–1914, *Roses,* gift from Mr J. S. Dearden, 1992
Dunkin, William John 1845–1914, *Roses,* gift from Mr J. S. Dearden, 1992
Ebele, J. *Louis XVI and Family,* gift from Mr J. McGregor, 1946
Eikendulf, R. *The Gamekeeper,* gift from J. R. Haworth, 1931
Eyck, Jan van (copy after) 1390–1441, *The Arnolfini Betrothal,* bequeathed by Mrs Louisa Hamer, 1969
Faed, Thomas (attributed to) 1826–1900, *Playmates,* bequeathed by Mrs Louisa Hamer, 1969
Faed, Thomas (attributed to) 1826–1900, *The Spinning Wheel,* bequeathed by Mrs Louisa Hamer, 1969
Faed, Thomas attributed to 1826–1900, *The Dame's School,* bequeathed by Mrs Louisa Hamer, 1969
Ferneley II, John 1814–1862, *The Rossendale Hunt,* gift from Miss Irene Hardman, 1976
Forrester, Ephraim 1907–1994, *Farms in Crawshawbooth / Loveclough,* gift from Pamela Whitehead, 2008 © the copyright holder
Forti, Giuseppe *The Marriage of Louis XIV,* gift from Mrs J. McLerie, 1931
German School *Figures in a Museum,* unknown acquisition method
Gibb, Thomas Henry 1833–1893, *On the Way to Lowland Pastures,* unknown acquisition method
Gifford, John –1900, *Pack Horse and Dogs,* unknown acquisition method
Glendening, Alfred Augustus 1840–1921, *Harvesting Scene,* gift from Mrs Rowland Rawlinson, 1938
Goodman, Maude 1855–1938, *Mother's Birthday,* unknown acquisition method
Gregson, V. R. active 1928–1950, *Timber Wolf, Rossendale,* unknown acquisition method © the copyright holder
Gregson, V. R. active 1928–1950, *Alderman Samuel Compston,* unknown acquisition method © the copyright holder
Gregson, V. R. active 1928–1950, *Flowers in a Jug,* unknown acquisition method © the copyright holder
Gregson, V. R. active 1928–1950, *Pansies in Bowl,* unknown acquisition method © the copyright holder
Gregson, V. R. active 1928–1950, *Kissing the Shuttle,* gift from Mrs Read, 1953 © the copyright holder
Gregson, V. R. active 1928–1950, *Portrait of a Man Wearing a Medal,* gift from Mrs Read, 1953 © the copyright holder
Gregson, V. R. active 1928–1950, *Snow in a Pennine Village,* gift from Yvonne Clegg, 2007 © the copyright holder
Gregson, V. R. active 1928–1950, *The Farm at Cardington,* gift from Yvonne Clegg, 2007 © the copyright holder
Gregson, V. R. active 1928–1950, *Flowers in a Vase,* gift from Yvonne Clegg, 2007 © the copyright holder
Gregson, V. R. active 1928–1950, *Flowers in a Vase,* gift from Yvonne Clegg, 2007 © the copyright holder
Gregson, V. R. active 1928–1950, *Margaret Gregson,* gift from Yvonne Clegg, 2007 © the copyright holder
Gregson, V. R. active 1928–1950, *Still Life with Flowers,* gift from Yvonne Clegg, 2007 © the copyright holder
Gregson, V. R. active 1928–1950, *Winter,* gift from Yvonne Clegg, 2007 © the copyright holder
Hall, Henry Robinson 1859–1927, *Highland Cattle above Loch Maree,* gift from Mr A. W. Arning, 1934
Hall (Mrs), George W. *Pilchards,* (after Charles Napier Hemy), bequeathed by Mrs Louisa Hamer, 1969
Harvey, George 1806–1876, *Rob Roy's Castle, Scotland,* bequeathed by Mrs Louisa Hamer, 1969
Holder, Edward Henry 1847–1922, *Refresher at the Old Inn,* gift from Mrs J. H. Parker, 1931
Hollins, Henry active 1902–1914, *Loveclough Print Works,* unknown acquisition method
Hollins, Henry active 1902–1914, *Stag,* unknown acquisition method
Hollins, Henry active 1902–1914, *Spring Hill Farm, Water,* gift from Mr Howarth, 1949
Hughes, William 1842–1901, *Still Life of Fruit,* bequeathed by Mrs Louisa Hamer, 1969
Hunt, Edgar 1876–1953, *Poultry,* bequeathed by Mrs Louisa Hamer, 1969 © the copyright holder
Hunt, Reuben 1879–1962, *Rustic Polo,* bequeathed by Mrs Louisa Hamer, 1969 © the copyright holder
Hunt, Reuben 1879–1962, *The Race,* bequeathed by Mrs Louisa Hamer, 1969 © the copyright holder
Ingham, William 1938, *Dark Summits,* purchased the artist
James, David 1853–1904, *A Cornish Bay,* unknown acquisition method
Johnston, William Herbert 1848–1897, *George Edward Hardman (1830–1884),* gift from St Mary's School, 1969
Johnston, William Herbert 1848–1897, *George Edward Hardman (1830–1884),* unknown acquisition method
Johnston, William Herbert 1848–1897, *Mrs George Edward Hardman,* unknown acquisition method
Kannemans, Christiaan Cornelis 1812–1884, *The Wreck,* gift from Mrs G. Hardman, 1935
Kelly, David 1955, *Richard Whitaker (1829–1906),* purchased (?) © the copyright holder
Kelly, David 1955, *Terraced Houses,* unknown acquisition method © the copyright holder
King, Henry John Yeend 1855–1924, *Market Morning,* gift from Mrs R. Ashworth, 1929
L., S. H. *Babes in the Wood,* bequeathed by Mrs Louisa Hamer, 1969
Lamnier, J. *Fenland Scene,* unknown acquisition method
Landseer, Edwin Henry after 1802–1873, *Horse, Pony and Stag Hound,* unknown acquisition method
Langley, William 1880–1920, *The Close of Day,* unknown acquisition method
Law, Barry active c.1950–1960, *Wycoller,* purchased © the copyright holder
Leeuw, Alexis de 1822–1900, *A Winter Scene,* unknown acquisition method
Linton, William attributed to 1791–1876, *The Bathing Pool,* gift from Miss Hickman, 1933
Maden, William *The Moor of Venice,* unknown acquisition method © the copyright holder
Mellor, William 1851–1931, *River Wharfe,* gift from Mrs Teasdale, 1971
Mellor, William 1851–1931, *The Wharfe, near Ilkley,* gift from Mrs Teasdale, 1971
Mooney, Edward Hartley 1878–1938, *John Henry Hirst,* gift from Mrs J. H. Hirst and W. Hirst, Esq., 1931
Mooney, Edward Hartley 1878–1938, *John William Rothwell,* gift from Rossendale Valley Boot, Shoe and Slipper Manufacturers Association, 1931
Mooney, Edward Hartley 1878–1938, *Joseph Hiram Parker,* gift from Mrs J. H. Parker, 1931
Mooney, Edward Hartley 1878–1938, *Joseph Read Brooks,* gift from the Brooks family, 1931
Mooney, Edward Hartley 1878–1938, *Richard Ashworth Hoyle,* gift from Mrs R. A. Hoyle, 1931
Mooney, Edward Hartley 1878–1938, *Roses and Venus,* gift from Mooney, 1931
Mooney, Edward Hartley 1878–1938, *Samuel McLerie,* gift from D. McLerie, Esq. and Mrs J. McLerie, 1931
Mooney, Edward Hartley 1878–1938, *Sir Henry W. Trickett,* gift from Lady Trickett, 1931
Morris, John W. 1865–1924, *Mountain Sheep,* unknown acquisition method
Mostyn, Thomas Edwin 1864–1930, *Thomas Newbigging,* unknown acquisition method
O'Connor, James Arthur 1792–1841, *In the Swiss Alps,* unknown acquisition method
Olesinski, Louis *Mr Thomas Fisher (at Work),* gift from Mr Griffiths, 2005 © the copyright holder
Paul, Joseph 1804–1887, *Lane Scene in Suffolk,* bequeathed by Mrs Louisa Hamer, 1969
Paul, Joseph 1804–1887, *River View near Norwich,* bequeathed by Mrs Louisa Hamer, 1969
Peel, James 1811–1906, *Landscape: River and Mountains,* unknown acquisition method
Penn, Stanley active c.1850–1900, *Landscape,* unknown acquisition method
Penn, Stanley active c.1850–1900, *Landscape,* unknown acquisition method
Pettingale, William Edward 1871–1924, *Highland Cattle,* unknown acquisition method
Philpot, Leonard Daniel 1877–1973, *Flower Study (Autumn),* bequeathed by Mrs Louisa Hamer, 1969 © the copyright holder
Philpot, Leonard Daniel 1877–1973, *Flower Study (Roses and Lilac),* bequeathed by Mrs Louisa Hamer, 1969 © the copyright holder
Piffard, Harold Hume 1867–1938, *Microscopy,* gift from Harold Hoyle, 1951–1952; transferred from the Borough of Bacup, 1979
Poole, Paul Falconer 1807–1879, *Girl in Wood,* bequeathed by Mrs Louisa Hamer, 1969
Poskitt, George E. *Carting Timber,* gift from Mr G. R. Holt, 1938
Prote, G. W. *Abinger Mill and Pond,* unknown acquisition method
Rawsthorne, Isabel 1912–1992, *Alan and Barbara Rawsthorne,* gift from Miss Barbara Rawsthorne, 1983 © the copyright holder
Roe, Clarence 1850–1909, *Mountain, River and Bridge,* gift from Harold Hoyle, 1951–1952; transferred from the Borough of Bacup, 1979
Roe, Clarence 1850–1909, *Rydal Water, Westmorland,* gift from Harold Hoyle, 1951–1952; transferred from the Borough of Bacup, 1979
Roscoe, Frederick William 1838–1902, *Henry Barlow,* bequeathed by H. B. Worswick, 1949
Roscoe, Frederick William 1838–1902, *The Horncliffe Bull,* gift from John Whitworth (?), 1933 (?)
Rowbottom, William Percy 1865–1943, *Man Fishing by River,* unknown acquisition method © the copyright holder
Sanderson-Wells, John 1872–1955, *Returning from the Hunt,* gift from Oliver Eatough, 1915 © the copyright holder
Schäfer, Heinrich 1815–1885, *Dutch Street Scene,* bequeathed by Mrs Louisa Hamer, 1969
Schäfer, Heinrich 1815–1885, *Toledo Cathedral,* gift from Herbert Worswick, 1931
Schäfer, Heinrich attributed to 1815–1885, *Abbeville, Normandy,* bequeathed by Mrs Louisa Hamer, 1969
Schwanfelder, Charles Henry 1774–1837, *Giles Berry, Esq.,* gift from Councillor J. R. Sellers, 1917
Scott, William Wallace (attributed to) 1820–1905, *David Greenwood Whitehead,* bequeathed by Reverend D. G. B. Macrae, 1942

Scott, William Wallace (attributed to) 1820–1905, *Jane Whitehead,* bequeathed by Reverend D. G. B. Macrae, 1942
Scott, William Wallace (attributed to) 1820–1905, *Peter Halstead Whitehead,* bequeathed by Reverend D. G. B. Macrae, 1942
Seville, Ronnie *Little Venice, Waterfoot,* purchased © the copyright holder
Shayer, William 1788–1879, *Near Southampton,* bequeathed by Mrs Louisa Hamer, 1969
Signorelli, Luca follower of 1450–1523, *Madonna and Child,* purchased (?)
Spencer, James (attributed to) active 1930s, *The Story of Whiteheads,* unknown acquisition method © the copyright holder
Spencer, James (attributed to) active 1930s, *The Story of Whiteheads,* unknown acquisition method © the copyright holder
Spencer, James (attributed to) active 1930s, *The Story of Whiteheads,* unknown acquisition method © the copyright holder
Spencer, James (attributed to) active 1930s, *The Story of Whiteheads,* unknown acquisition method © the copyright holder
Spencer, James (attributed to) active 1930s, *The Story of Whiteheads,* unknown acquisition method © the copyright holder
Stamper, James William 1873–1947, *Above Deganwy,* unknown acquisition method © the copyright holder
Stanesby, Alexander 1832–1916, *Still Life,* unknown acquisition method
Stojanov, Piotr active 1887–1894, *Fighting Off the Wolves,* gift from Mr T. Hallsworth, 1947
Stonewaid, W. attributed to active c.1863–1883, *Man by a Cottage,* unknown acquisition method
unknown artist *Isaac Bradshaw,* gift from Mrs Hamer (?), 1953 (?)
unknown artist *Betty Treacle,* gift from Mrs H. W. Spencer, 1961
unknown artist *Portrait of Five Females,* gift from Mrs D. Ferguson, 2007
unknown artist *Thomas Whitehead,* bequeathed by Reverend D. G. B. Macrae, 1942
unknown artist *Deborah Rawsthorne (1834–1846),* gift from Miss Barbara Rawsthorne, 1983
unknown artist *James Rawsthorne (1832–1870),* gift from Miss Barbara Rawsthorne, 1983
unknown artist *Portrait of a Lady,* gift from Mrs D. Ferguson, 2007
unknown artist *Canon Raines,* unknown acquisition method
unknown artist *Thomas Aitken of Bacup,* gift from Bethlehem Unitarian Church through Miss M. Whitaker, 2002
unknown artist *Daniel Ratcliffe,* gift from Mrs H. H. Ratcliffe, 1949
unknown artist *James or Richard Porritt,* gift from Ramsbottom Heritage Society, 2005
unknown artist *Portrait of a Gentleman,* gift from Mrs D. Ferguson, 2007
unknown artist *Portrait of a Gentleman,* gift from Mrs D. Ferguson, 2007
unknown artist *Portrait of an Unknown Gentleman,* unknown acquisition method
unknown artist *Portrait of an Unknown Lady,* unknown acquisition method
unknown artist *King Street, Rawtenstall,* unknown acquisition method
unknown artist *John Ashworth of Cloughfold,* gift from Bethlehem Unitarian Church through Miss M. Whitaker, 2002
unknown artist *Still Life,* unknown acquisition method
unknown artist *The Friends Meeting House, Crawshawbooth,* gift from Mrs H. Hoyle (?), 1952
unknown artist *Landscape,* unknown acquisition method
unknown artist *Landscape with Figure,* bequeathed by Mrs Louisa Hamer, 1969
unknown artist *Man with Shotgun,* unknown acquisition method
unknown artist *Old View of Reedsholme,* gift from Mr R. Heap, 1917
unknown artist *Portrait of a Gentleman,* unknown acquisition method
unknown artist *Roslin Castle, near Edinburgh,* gift from Mr R. H. Waddington, 1936
unknown artist *William Henry Shaw, Coal Merchant,* gift from Haslingden Library, 1978
unknown artist *Ypres, the Belfry,* bequeathed by Mrs Louisa Hamer, 1969
Ward, James 1769–1859, *Cattle,* bequeathed by Mrs Louisa Hamer, 1969
Whaley, Harold 1896–1976, *Pastoral Scene,* gift from Ralph Green, 1933 © the copyright holder
Wilkinson, T. F. *August Afternoon near Dorking,* gift from Miss C. Whitehead, 1929
Wright, Robert W. active 1870–1906, *Mind Your Own Business,* bequeathed by Mrs Louisa Hamer, 1969
Wright, Robert W. active 1870–1906, *The New Photograph,* bequeathed by Mrs Louisa Hamer, 1969
Zadorecki, Marcel Johann active 1872–1939, *Portrait of a Classical Heroine,* bequeathed by Dr and Mrs Wilson (?), 1946

Lancashire County Council County Hall
Fishergate, Preston PR1 8XJ
Telephone 01772 533254

Haslingden Library
Deardengate, Haslingden BB4 5QL
Telephone 01706 215690

Lancashire County Museum Service:

Lancashire County Museums HQ
Stanley Street, Preston PR1 4YP
Telephone 01772 534061

Fleetwood Museum
Queens Terrace, Fleetwood FY7 6BT
Telephone 01253 876621

Helmshore Mills Textile Museum
Holcombe Road, Helmshore BB4 4NP
Telephone 01706 226459/218838

Judges' Lodgings, Lancaster
Church Street, Lancaster LA1 1YS
Telephone 01524 32808

Museum of Lancashire
Stanley Street, Preston PR1 4YP
Telephone 01772 534075

Queen Street Mill Textile Museum
Harle Syke, Burnley BB10 2HX
Telephone 01282 412555

The Duke of Lancaster's Regiment, Lancashire
Infantry Museum
Fulwood Barracks, Preston PR2 8AA
Telephone 01772 260362

University of Central Lancashire
Preston, PR1 2HE
Telephone 01772 201201

Rossendale

Rossendale Museum
Whitaker Park, Haslingden Road, Rawtenstall,
Rossendale BB4 6RE
Telephone 01706 260785

Index of Artists

In this catalogue, artists' names and the spelling of their names follow the preferred presentation of the name in the Getty Union List of Artist Names (ULAN) as of February 2004, if the artist is listed in ULAN.

The page numbers next to each artist's name below direct readers to paintings that are by the artist; are attributed to the artist; or, in a few cases, are more loosely related to the artist being, for example, 'after', 'the circle of' or copies of a painting by the artist. The precise relationship between the artist and the painting is listed in the catalogue.

Acknowledgements

The Public Catalogue Foundation would like to thank the individual artists and copyright holders for their permission to reproduce for free the paintings in this catalogue. Exhaustive efforts have been made to locate the copyright owners of all the images included within this catalogue and to meet their requirements. Copyright credit lines for copyright owners who have been traced are listed in the Further Information section.

The Public Catalogue Foundation would like to express its great appreciation to the following organisations and individuals for their kind assistance in the preparation of this catalogue:

Bridgeman Art Library
Flowers East
Marlborough Fine Art
National Association of Decorative & Fine Arts Societies (NADFAS)
National Gallery, London
National Portrait Gallery, London
Royal Academy of Arts, London
Tate

Lynne Asghar
Susan Ashworth
Lisa Ayres
Stephen Barnes
Phillip Bourne
Chris Bryan
Stephen Bull
Philip Butler
Carl Carrington
Emily Cooke
Helen Cooper
Michelle Cooper
Ken Cross
Andrew Curtis
Jane Davies
Heather Davis
Peter Donnelly
Amanda Draper
Georgina Gates
Will Griffith
Amy Grundy
Sheila Hall
Joanna Hayward
Sheila Higson
Alison Hughes
David Hunt
Tom Ireland
Rachel Jackson
Louise Jacobsson
Fiona Jenkins
Tony Kitto
Alex Leese
Lindsey McCormick
Veronica McDonnell
Kevin McLaughlin
Ros McMenamin
Vanessa Mitchell
Libby Packham
Mary Painter
Mary Palmer
Colin Penny
Margaret Race
Jennifer Rennie
Yvonne Robins
Stephen Sartin
Richard Smith
Mike Townend
Stuart Tulloch
Stephen Wildman
Caroline Wilkinson
Geoff Willetts

The Public Catalogue Foundation

The Public Catalogue Foundation is a registered charity. It was launched in 2003 to create a photographic record of the entire national collection of oil, tempera and acrylic paintings in public ownership in the United Kingdom.

Whilst our public galleries and civic buildings hold arguably the greatest collection of oil paintings in the world, over 80 per cent of these are not on view. Few collections have a complete photographic record of their paintings let alone a comprehensive illustrated catalogue. What is publicly owned is not publicly accessible.

The Foundation is publishing a series of fully illustrated, county-by-county catalogues that will cover, eventually, the entire national UK collection. To date, it has published over 30 volumes, presenting over 72,000 paintings.

In partnership with the BBC, the Foundation will make its database of the entire UK collection of 200,000 oil paintings available online through a new website called *Your Paintings*. The website was launched in the summer of 2011.

Your Paintings (*www.bbc.co.uk/arts/yourpaintings*) offers a variety of ways of searching for paintings as well as further information about the paintings and artists, including links to the participating collections' websites. For those interested in paintings and the subjects they portray *Your Paintings* is an unparalleled learning resource.

Collections benefit substantially from the work of the Foundation, not least from the digital images that are given to them for free following photography, and from the increased recognition that the project brings. These substantial benefits come at no financial cost to the collections.

The Foundation is funded by a combination of support from individuals, charitable trusts, companies and the public sector although the latter provides less than 20 per cent of the Foundation's financial support.

Supporters

Master Patrons

The Public Catalogue Foundation is greatly indebted to the following Master Patrons who have helped it in the past or are currently working with it to raise funds for the publication of their county catalogues. All of them have given freely of their time and have made an enormous contribution to the work of the Foundation.

Peter Andreae *(Hampshire)*
Sir Henry Aubrey-Fletcher, Bt, Lord Lieutenant of Buckinghamshire *(Buckinghamshire)*
Sir Nicholas Bacon, DL, High Sheriff of Norfolk *(Norfolk)*
Sir John Bather, Lord Lieutenant of Derbyshire *(Derbyshire)*
The Hon. Mrs Bayliss, JP, Lord Lieutenant of Berkshire *(Berkshire)*
Ian Bonas *(County Durham)*
Peter Bretherton *(West Yorkshire: Leeds)*
Michael Brinton, Lord Lieutenant of Worcestershire *(Worcestershire)*
Sir Hugo Brunner, KCVO, JP *(Oxfordshire)*
Mr John Bush, OBE, Lord-Lieutenant of Wiltshire *(Wiltshire)*
Lady Butler *(Warwickshire)*
Richard Compton *(North Yorkshire)*
George Courtauld, DL, Vice Lord Lieutenant of Essex *(Essex)*

The Countess of Darnley, Lord Lieutenant of Herefordshire *(Herefordshire)*
The Marquess of Downshire *(North Yorkshire)*
Martin Dunne, Lord Lieutenant of Warwickshire *(Warwickshire)*
Sir Henry Elwes, KCVO, Lord-Lieutenant of Gloucestershire *(Gloucestershire)*
Jenny Farr, MBE, DL *(Nottinghamshire)*
John Fenwick *(Tyne & Wear Museums)*
Mark Fisher, MP *(Staffordshire)*
Patricia Grayburn, MBE, DL *(Surrey)*
The Earl of Halifax, KStJ, JP, DL *(East Riding of Yorkshire)*
Lord Roy Hattersley, PC *(South Yorkshire: Sheffield*
Algy Heber-Percy, Lord Lieutenant of Shropshire *(Shropshire)*
The Lady Mary Holborow, Lord Lieutenant of Cornwall *(Cornwall)*
Sarah Holman *(Warwickshire)*
Tommy Jowitt *(West Yorkshire)*
Alderman Sir David Lewis, The Rt Hon. The Lord Mayor of London, 2007–2008 *(The City of London)*
Sir Michael Lickiss *(Cornwall)*
Magnus Linklater *(Scotland)*
Lord Marlesford, DL *(Suffolk)*
Dr Bridget McConnell *(Glasgow)*
Lady Sarah Nicholson *(County Durham)*
Malcolm V. L. Pearce, MP *(Somerset)*
Sir John Riddell, Lord Lieutenant of Northumberland *(Northumberland)*
Venetia Ross Skinner *(Dorset)*
The Most Hon. The Marquess of Salisbury, PC, DL *(Hertfordshire)*
Julia Somerville *(Government Art Collection)*
Tim Stevenson, OBE, Lord Lieutenant of Oxfordshire *(Oxfordshire)*
Phyllida Stewart-Roberts, OBE *(East Sussex)*
Lady Juliet Townsend, Lord Lieutenant of Northamptonshire *(Northamptonshire)*
Leslie Weller, DL *(West Sussex)*
Sir Samuel C. Whitbread, KCVO, Lord Lieutenant of Bedfordshire *(Bedfordshire)*

Financial support

The Public Catalogue Foundation is particularly grateful to the following organisations and individuals who have given it generous financial support since the project started in 2003.

National Sponsor

Christie's

Benefactors (£10,000–£50,000)

The 29th May 1961 Charitable Trust
Arts Council England
The Barbour Trust
Binks Trust
City of Bradford Metropolitan District Council
Deborah Loeb Brice Foundation
The Bulldog Trust
A. & S. Burton 1960 Charitable Trust
Christie's
City of London Corporation
The John S. Cohen Foundation
Covent Garden London
Creative Scotland
Department for Culture, Media and Sport
Sir Harry Djanogly, CBE
Mr Lloyd Dorfman
Dunard Fund
The Elmley Foundation
Fenwick Ltd
Fidelity UK Foundation
Marc Fitch Fund
The Foyle Foundation
J. Paul Getty Jr Trust
Hampshire County Council
The Charles Hayward Foundation
Peter Harrison Foundation
Mr Robert Hiscox
Hiscox plc
David Hockney, CH, RA
ICAP plc

The Jordan Charitable Foundation
Kent County Council
The Linbury Trust
The Manifold Trust
Paul Mellon Centre for Studies in British Art
The Mercers' Company
Robert Warren Miller
Mr & Mrs A. Mittal
The Monument Trust
Miles Morland
Allan and Carol Murray
National Gallery Trust
Stavros Niarchos Foundation
Norfolk County Council
Northern Rock Foundation
Nottingham City Council
Malcolm V. L. Pearce, MP
P. F. Charitable Trust
The Pilgrim Trust
Provident Financial
RAB Capital plc
The Radcliffe Trust
Renaissance East Midlands
Renaissance West Midlands
Renaissance Yorkshire
Saga Group Ltd
Scottish Government
The Bernard Sunley Charitable Foundation
Townsend Family Trust
University College, London
University of Leeds
The Walker Trust
The Wolfson Foundation
Sir Siegmund Warburg's Voluntary Settlement
Garfield Weston Foundation
Mr & Mrs A. H. Wilkinson
The Wixamtree Trust

Series Patrons
(Minimum donation of £2,500)

James & Lindsay Adam
Sir John Bather
Harry Bott
Janey Buchan
Mrs Rhona Callander
Dr Peter Cannon-Brookes
The John S. Cohen Foundation
Bushey Museum in memory of Lavender Watson
Mr Lloyd Dorfman
Lord Douro
Jenny Farr, MBE, DL
Mrs Greta Fenston
The FIRS Trust
Glasgow Museums
Patricia Grayburn, MBE, DL
G. Laurence Harbottle
R. K. Harrison Insurance Services Limited
Paul & Fiona Hart
Paul & Kathrine Haworth
Lord & Lady Heseltine
Patrik Holden & Lin Hinds
Neil Honebon
Michael Jacobson
Grace Jenkins
Dr David Johnson, DL
The Keatley Trust
John Kendall, Esq.
Michael A. Lambert, CBE
David & Amanda Leathers
Miles Morland
Allan & Carol Murray
North East Regional Museums Hub
The University of Northampton
Nottingham Civic Society
Richard & Amika Oldfield
The Roper Family Charitable Trust
Adam Sedgwick
Sir Harry & Lady Soloman
Stuart M. Southall
Simon Still
Chloe Teacher
University of Surrey
David & Cissy Walker
Tony Wilkinson
Mr & Mrs Jo Windsor
Mr & Mrs Charles Wyvill

Catalogue Patrons
(£1,000–£10,000)

The 29th May 1961 Charitable Trust
ACE Study Tours
Adams & Remers
Marcus & Kate Agius
The AIM Foundation
D. C. R. Allen
John Alston, CBE
Amberley Castle
The Astor Foundation
The Aylesford Family Charitable Trust
Chairman of Cornwall County Council, Mrs Doris Anson, OBE, JP
Archant Ltd

G. F. Armitage Family Charitable Trust
Mr Ian Askew
Aurelius Charitable Trust
The Bacon Charitable Trust
Lawrence Banks, CBE, DL
Barlow Robbins LLP
Mr James & Lady Emma Barnard
Basingstoke and Deane Borough Council
Bath & North East Somerset District Council Heritage Services
Robert Baxter, DL
Birmingham Common Good Trust
Sir Christopher Bland
Johnnie Boden
The Charlotte Bonham-Carter Charitable Trust
H. R. Pratt Boorman Family Foundation
A. J. H. du Boulay Charitable Trust
The Bowerman Charitable Trust
Viscountess Boyd Charitable Trust
Lord & Lady Bradbury
Bramdean Asset Management LLP
Peter Bretherton
Brewin Dolphin
J. & M. Britton Charitable Trust
Mrs T. Brotherton-Ratcliffe
Janey Buchan
Mr & Mrs Patrick Burgess
Mr & Mrs Mark Burrell
Arnold J. Burton Charitable Trust
Bushey Museum in Memory of Lavender Watson
Mrs Anne Cadbury, OBE, JP, DL
Roger Cadbury
C. J. R. & Mrs C. L. Calderwood
Sir Ralph Carr-Ellison
Mr & Mrs J. Chambers
Chichester District Council
His Honour Richard Cole, DL & Mrs Sheila Cole
The Timothy Colman Charitable Trust
Mr & Mrs Derek Coombs
The Helen Jean Cope Trust
Mr & Mrs Ian Copesteak
Cornwall County Council
Mr S. J. D. Corsan
Graeme Cottam & Gloriana Marks de Chabris
Coutts Charitable Trust
David Crane Trust
Elaine Craven, Earl Street Employment Consultants Ltd
Harriett Cullen
Culture North East
Rt Hon. Viscount Daventry
N. Davie-Thornhill
Brigadier Mike Dauncey, DSO, DL
De La Rue Charitable Trust
Mr Robert Dean
Deborah Gage (Works of Art) Ltd
Derek Johns Ltd, London
Derby City Council
Derby High School Trust Ltd
Derbyshire Building Society
Derbyshire Community Foundation (The Ashby Fund)
J. N. Derbyshire Trust
The Duke of Devonshire's Charitable Trust
S. Dewhirst Charitable Trust
Sir Harry Djanogly, CBE
Dorset County Council
Lord Douro
Professor Patrick & Dr Grace Dowling
Dunn Family Charitable Trust
East Sussex County Council
Eastbourne Borough Council
EEMLAC, through the Association for Suffolk Museums
Lord & Lady Egremont
Sir John & Lady Elliott
Andrew & Lucy Ellis
Peter & Judy Ellwood
Essex County Council
John & Felicity Fairbairn
Fairfield Charitable Trust
Jenny Farr, MBE, DL
John Feeney Charitable Trust
The Trustees of the Finnis Scott Foundation
The Fishmongers' Company
David & Ann FitzWilliam-Lay
Elizabeth & Val Fleming
The Follett Trust
Richard & Elizabeth Fothergill

Christopher & Catherine Foyle
Freemasons of Derbyshire
The Friends of Historic Essex
The Friends of the Laing Art Gallery
The Friends of the Royal Pavilion, Art Gallery & Museums, Brighton
The Friends of Southampton's Museums, Archives and Galleries
The Friends of Sunderland Museums
The Friends of York Art Gallery (E. J. Swift Bequest)
Philip Gibbs
The Hon. H. M. T. Gibson's Charity Trust
Lewis & Jacqueline Golden
The Goldsmiths' Company
Gorringes
Charles Gregson
The Grocers' Company
The Gulland Family
David Gurney
Philip Gwyn
Sir Ernest Hall
The Earl of Halifax, KStJ, JP, DL
The W. A. Handley Charity Trust
The Hartnett Charitable Trust
Hazlitt, Gooden & Fox Ltd
Heartwood Wealth Management Ltd
The Trustees of the King Henry VIII Endowed Trust, Warwick
The Rt Hon. the Lord Heseltine, CH, PC & Lady Heseltine
The Lady Hind Trust
Hobart Charitable Trust
Edward and Anna Hocknell
David Hockney CH, RA
Patrick Holden & Lin Hinds
Mrs Michael Hollingbery
The Holman Family
Mr & Mrs A. Holman-West
The Honourable Company of Gloucestershire
The Hope Scott Trust
David & Prue Hopkinson
Major & Mrs Bill Hutchinson
His Honour Gabriel Hutton
Isle of Wight Council
The J. and S. B. Charitable Trust
Alan & Penny Jerome
James & Lucilla Joll Charitable Trust
Mr & Mrs Peter Jones
Tommy Jowitt
The Keatley Trust
Kent Messenger Group
Garrett Kirk, Jr
Mr John Kirkland, OBE & Mrs Sheila Kirkland
Robert Kirkland
Kirklees Council
The David Laing Foundation
Landau Foundation
Lord Lea of Crondall, OBE
The Leche Trust
Leeds Art Collections Fund
Leeds City Council
Leeds Philosophical and Literary Society
The Hon. David Legh, DL
Lord Leverhulme's Charitable Trust
Mr & Mrs John Lewis
Mark & Sophie Lewisohn
Tom Lugg & the Lane Family
The Orr Mackintosh Foundation
The MacRobert Trust
Maidstone Borough Council
John Manser
Mr & Mrs Derek Mapp
Walter & Barbara Marais
The Marlay Group
Marshall Charitable Trust
Stephen & Carolyn Martin
Tom & Anne Martin
The Medlock Charitable Trust
The Piet Mendels Foundation
MLA East of England
MLA North East of England
Museums Galleries Scotland
Mr Paul Myners
Rupert Nabarro
Nancie Massey Charitable Trust
Newcastle City Council
Bryan Norman
Lord & Lady Northampton
The University of Northampton
NP Aerospace Ltd
Oakmoor Trust
Jasper & Virginia Olivier
The Orr Mackintosh Foundation
Mr Christopher Oughtred
The Owen Family Trust

Sir Idris Pearce
Roger Neville Russ Peers
The Pennycress Trust
Perkins Family
The Lord & Lady Phillimore
Mrs Margaret Pollett
Simon & Ursula Pomeroy
The Portland Family
Portsmouth City Council
George Pragnell Ltd
The Prince Philip Trust Fund for the Royal Borough of Windsor and Maidenhead
Provident Financial plc
Mr John Rank
Rathbone Investment Management Ltd
The Hans and Märit Rausing Charitable Trust
Roger & Jane Reed
Renaissance North East
Renaissance South East
Renaissance South West
Michael Renshall, CBE, MA, FCA
Sir John Riddell
Sir Miles & Lady Rivett-Carnac
Rockley Charitable Trust
Rolls-Royce plc
The Roper Family Charitable Trust
Rothschild Foundation
Royal Cornwall Museum
Graham & Ann Rudd
Sir Nigel Rudd
Russell New
The J. S. & E. C. Rymer Charitable Trust
The Earl St Aldwyn
The Sammermar Trust
Scarfe Charitable Trust
Andrew & Belinda Scott
The Trustees of the Finnis Scott Foundation
Shaftesbury PLC
Mr W. Sharpe
The Shears Foundation
Robert Shields, DL
Smith & Williamson
South West of England Regional Development Agency
Caroline M. Southall
Stuart M. Southall
Southampton City Council
The Jessie Spencer Trust
Hugh & Catherine Stevenson
Mrs Andrew Stewart-Roberts, OBE
Mr Michael Stone
Mr Peter Stormonth Darling
The Stratford-upon-Avon Town Trust
Strutt and Parker
Suffolk County Council, through the Association for Suffolk Museums
Surrey County Council
The John Swire 1989 Charitable Trust
The Tanner Trust
Tennants Auctioneers
Tesco Charity Trust
The Thistle Trust
Prof. Caroline Tisdall
Trusthouse Charitable Foundation
Gladwyn Turbutt
TWM Business Partners
Tyne & Wear Museums
University College Falmouth
University of Derby
University of Essex
David & Grizelda Vermont
Wakefield Metropolitan District Council
Robert & Felicity Waley-Cohen
The Peggy Walker Charitable Trust
The Walland Trust Fund
John Wates Charitable Trust
Leslie Weller, DL
The Welton Foundation
West Sussex County Council
Mr & Mrs David Wigglesworth
Wilkin & Sons Ltd
Mr & Mrs Jo Windsor
Peter Wolton Charitable Trust
Michael J. Woodhall, FRICS
Sir Philip Wroughton
Mrs Angela Yeoman

First published in 2012 by The Public Catalogue Foundation, Printed Catalogue Division, 8 Frederick's Place, London, EC2R 8AB

ISBN 978-1-904931-92-8

Designed by Sally Jeffery

Printed in Hong Kong by Paramount Printing Company Limited